# INTERNATIONAL HISTORICAL STATISTICS

## THE AMERICAS 1750-1988

# INTERNATIONAL HISTORICAL STATISTICS

## THE AMERICAS
## 1750-1988

### SECOND EDITION

# B. R. Mitchell

M

stockton
press

Published in the United States and Canada by
STOCKTON PRESS, 1993
257 Park Avenue South, New York, N.Y. 10010, USA

ISBN 1-56159-062-2


Second edition first published in the United Kingdom
by MACMILLAN PUBLISHERS LTD, 1993
Distributed by Globe Book Services Ltd
Brunel Road, Houndmills,
Basingstoke, Hants RG21 2XS, England

ISBN 0-333-58515-1

A catalogue record for this book
is available from The British Library

Typeset in Great Britain and printed in Hong Kong

# CONTENTS

# INTRODUCTION

Historical statistics are now recognized, as never before, as a major raw material of much economic history, especially of that concerned with economic growth and development. In response to this, national collections of historical statistics began to make their appearance from the late 1940s onwards. Towards the end of the 1960s, it seemed that the time was ripe for gathering together the main statistical series for all the major countries of the world, and a beginning was made with those of Europe, for which there was more material available than for most others.[1] This was followed by *International Historical Statistics: Africa and Asia*, and the first edition of the present work[2] which then included Australasia. This will be included with Africa and Asia in the forth coming new edition. The objective of these books has been to provide economists and historians with a wide range of statistical data without the difficulty of identifying sources, of obtaining access to them, and the often considerable labour of extracting the figures from many different places and, one hopes, ensuring that they form part of comparable series.

In all these continent-wide compilations, the sources relied on have been, for the most part, official national and international abstracts of statistics, rather than detailed publications. As a result, there are more breaks in continuity than are strictly necessary, since compilers of abstracts are continually trying to improve coverage and presentation; and whilst older, long-running series may often still be put together from detailed sources, the process is time-consuming and sometimes requires access to publications which are not readily available outside their country of origin. However, I am assured by many who have used the earlier volumes that these breaks are not often of as much importance as they seem to the compiler.

Even more irritating, to the compiler at any rate, are the gaps which sometimes appear in series, especially when he knows that they are not the result of a failure on the part of officials to collect and publish the data, but of his own failure to find them. As I pointed out in introducing the original Africa and Asia volume, such gaps could eventually be filled; but there are sharply diminishing returns to search effort when one has collected perhaps 99 per cent of available material, and publication of a not wholly complete collection continues to seem better than a paralysing perfectionism. I shall, of course, be as grateful for any help which users of this work can give me in improving the coverage for the future as I am for that which has improved this present edition.

All the countries covered in this volume were at one time colonies of European powers. The quality and availability of their statistics seems to bear a fairly close relationship to that of their original mother country, at any rate until fairly recently. The former British colonies published a fairly large amount of data at a comparatively early date in the 19th century, or even earlier; and the few, and small, French colonies in these continents were rather similar in some respects. The former Spanish colonies, on the other hand, tended to produce statistical material about as irregularly as did Spain itself throughout much of the 19th century. Brazil, in contrast, has a better record in this respect than Portugal, and it has some of the earliest series for any South American country where the subject covered is one involving a high degree of government involvement.

It should not need to be said that there are pitfalls for the unwary user of statistics, and this is scarcely the place to attempt to summarize those traps of which any introductory textbook will warn. However, there are certain problems which are of particular prominence in historical statistics, to which attention may properly be drawn. It is glaringly obvious that the biggest single problem is lack of availability of the data we should like to have, even, in some cases, for quite recent periods. But there is a comparably important problem in the existence of data which *seem* to relate to the same things in different countries or at different times, but which do not in fact do so. Some sort of data are available in these cases, but not the precise sort which we want. Basically these problems are ones of definition—in some times and places exports include bullion, in others they do not; pig iron can include or exclude ferro-alloys; bank deposits may include inter-bank deposits, or they may not; and so on. Often there is nothing one can do about this lack of uniformity except indicate its existence and warn against glib comparisons. (One can find little comfort, however, in the fact that failure to observe such warnings is one of the main reasons why statistics have sometimes been held to be worse than 'damned lies'!) Kindred definitional difficulties are provided by changes in boundaries, though these are less important than for Europe. A list of them is given below.

Two other problems are peculiar to historical statistics. The first is, in a sense, a mechanical one. That is the variable and unknown efficiency of past collectors and compilers of statistics, and of their printers, and the impossibility of even being able to check on these qualities. This is something one simply has to live with, keeping a vigilant eye on one's own credulity, and endeavouring to estimate margins of error so far as that is possible. Too often, users of historical statistics simply take best-estimate figures for their calculations, without working out the effects on their analysis of compounding margins of error.

The second peculiar problem concerns the purposes for which statistics were usually collected up to around the end of the 19th century, and, indeed, for which they often are still. William Robson rightly said that 'the most important methodological development of the present century' is 'the introduction of measurement in varying degrees in virtually every one of the social sciences',[3] and it is only with this development that there has come much collection and publication of statistical material for its own sake, as it were. Actually, it began to develop a little before the end of the 19th century in some countries; but still, it is generally true to say that most statistics prior to 1900 were by-products of taxation or military preparedness, or at any rate of desire for honesty in administration. Some early series, therefore, have to be viewed with a measure of scepticism, because there was a premium on avoiding inclusion in the data. Registration of one's true age, if one was a young man liable to military service, and the smuggling of dutiable imports are but two of the most obvious examples. But understatement is not the only error to which statistics have been liable. Population and wealth have sometimes been inflated to impress potential enemies, or for prestige, or to enhance the power of a ruling group. To all these difficulties there is no ready solution. All one can do is be careful, and keep a firm rein on credulity, without going to the other extreme of a stultifying total scepticism.

These few generalities are not intended as a critique of the usefulness of statistics in historical studies, but simply as a warning against their careless and casual use in comparisons over time and between different countries. It has been rightly said that 'numbers are useful when they attain a level of subtlety and precision beyond that of words'.[4] Let the user of this volume be in no doubt of the need to seek for subtlety and of the difficulties in the way of precision.

Some of the problems peculiar to each topic are mentioned briefly in the introduction to each of the separate sections; but it must be pointed out that these are not intended to be comprehensive critiques of the statistics presented. To do this properly would require at least another volume, and it is the intention here only to draw the user's attention to the main types of difficulty in using the statistics. The problems for each individual country are not generally dealt with, unless they are outstandingly important. However, most of them are readily apparent from a careful use of the notes and footnotes to the tables.

Whilst the general plan of the first edition has been followed in this one, there are various changes. Possibly the most obvious is the omission of the section on climate. This was done to save space, and in the light of the general opinion expressed by those who could be consulted that these were amongst the least useful tables. No other table has been omitted, though two or three have been compressed. Newly available material has been included in several tables, and two completely new ones have been added: One giving estimates of annual population and the other providing money supply data for the last four decades. Another considerable change has been the expansion of the detail provided in the balance of payments table.

[1] B.R. Mitchell, *European Historical Statistics, 1750–1970* (London, 1975; second edition (extended to 1975), 1980; and third edition (extended to 1988), 1992).
[2] London, 1982 and 1984.
[3] W.A. Robson (ed.), *Man and the Social Sciences* (London, 1972).
[4] W. Paul Strassman, *Risk and Technological Innovation* (Ithaca, NY, 1959), p. 5.

## Boundary Changes

Boundary changes of the kind following wars in Europe have not been unknown in both North and South America, though the extension of the frontier of settlement has been of greater importance in changing the area of most of the national units covered in this volume. These are less easy to identify with precision, and no attempt to do so is made here, since for most purposes such extensions are best conceived of as economic expansions rather than shifts in the locus of units of statistical record. The list that follows is therefore confined to changes of status or in borders:

### NORTH AMERICA

Canada:      The Dominion of Canada was established in 1867 from the former British colonies of Upper and Lower Canada (i.e. Ontario and Quebec), New Brunswick, Nova Scotia, Prince Edward Island, and British Columbia.

Costa Rica:      Declared independent of Spain in 1821. Part of the Confederation of Central America 1824–38.

Cuba:      Declared independent of Spain in 1898.

Dominican Republic:      Declared independent of Spain in 1821, but held by Haiti from 1822 to 1844.

El Salvador:      Part of the Confederation of Central America to 1838, when it became independent.

Guatemala:      Declared independent of Spain in 1821. Part of the Confederation of Central America 1823–38.

Haiti:      Declared independent of France 1804 (having been Spanish to 1697). Occupied by the United States 1915–34.

Honduras:      Part of the Confederation of Central America to 1838, when it became independent.

Jamaica:      A Spanish colony, occupied by Britain in 1655 and formally ceded in 1670. Independent from 1962.

Mexico:      Declared independent of Spain in 1810 and acknowledged so in 1821. Texas became independent of it *de facto* in 1836, and, along with the northern provinces which now form Arizona, California, New Mexico, and parts of Colorado, Nevada and Utah, was ceded to the USA in 1845. Another small area, the Gadsden Purchase, was transferred in 1853.

Nicaragua:      Part of the Confederation of Central America to 1838, when it became independent.

Panama:      A province of Colombia to 1903, when it became independent.

Puerto Rico:      Acquired by the United States from Spain in 1899.

Trinidad and Tobago:      Trinidad was a Spanish colony until ceded to Britain in 1802. Tobago was joined to it administratively in 1899.

United States of America:      Declared independent from Britain in 1776, and acknowledged in 1783. Enlarged in 1803 by the Louisiana Purchase, in 1819 by Spain's cession of Florida and neighbouring areas, in 1845 by the Mexican cession, and in 1853 by the Gadsden Purchase. Alaska was acquired from Russia in 1867, and Hawaii from its native rulers in 1898. Both became States in 1960.

## SOUTH AMERICA

Argentina:      The Spanish Viceroyalty of the River Plate formed an autonomous government in 1810 and became formally independent in 1816. No stable central government existed in the area which later became Argentina until 1862. Adjustments of boundaries with Bolivia, Chile, and Paraguay have taken place subsequently, but they have been more in the nature of initial demarcations in unsettled territory than of transfers of territory, with the exception of the transfer of Misiones from Paraguay in 1876.

Bolivia:        Part of the Viceroyalty of the River Plate (see Argentina), to 1825, when it became independent. It has since suffered three major losses of territory—its coastal region (essentially the present province of Antofagasta) to Chile in 1884, part of its Amazonian northern region (the present Acre territory) to Brazil in 1903, and a large part of the Gran Chaco to Paraguay in the early 1930s (formally ceded in 1938).

Brazil:         A Portuguese colony, declared a separate kingdom under a king of the Portuguese royal house in 1815, and an independent empire in 1822. (It became a republic in 1889.) Boundary changes have been more in the nature of initial delineations than of transfers of territory, though Acre was acquired from Bolivia in 1903, and there were some transfers from Paraguay in 1872.

Chile:          Declared independent of Spain in 1810, and acknowledged so in 1818. It gained Antofagasta from Bolivia and Tarapaca from Peru in 1883–4 following the War of the Pacific. Africa and Tacna were also taken, the latter being returned in 1929 and the former being confirmed as Chilean.

Colombia:       Became independent of Spain in 1819 as part of Gran Colombia—the former New Granada, including Ecuador, Venezuela, and present-day Panama. Ecuador and Venezuela became separate in 1830, whereafter Colombia was known as New Granada to 1863. The province of Panama became independent in 1903. Minor boundary adjustments have occurred with Peru and Venezuela.

Ecuador:        Seceded from Gran Colombia and became independent in 1830. Small parts of its former eastern province were ceded to Brazil in 1904 and to Colombia in 1916, but they were more in the nature of initial boundary delineation than of territorial transfers. A large part of the remainder of the province was ceded to Peru in 1942.

Guyana:         The Dutch Colonies of Demerara, Essequibo, and Berbice were captured by Britain in 1796 and formally ceded in 1814, whereafter they were known as British Guiana until independence in 1966. The designation Guyana is used throughout this book.

Paraguay:       Part of the Spanish Viceroyalty of the River Plate (see Argentina) which established its independence in 1814. Following the war of 1865–70, some territory north of the Apa river was transferred to Brazil (in 1872) and Misiones and some of the southern Chaco was transferred to Argentina in 1876. A large part of Gran Chaco was acquired from Bolivia in the early 1930s (formally in 1938).

Peru:           Declared independent of Spain in 1821, and acknowledged in 1824. Lost Tarapaca province and Africa and Tacna to Chile in 1883, though the last was returned in 1929. A large part of Ecuador's eastern province was gained in 1942.

Surinam:        Alternatively known as Dutch Guiana prior to its independence in 1975.

Uruguay:        Part of the Spanish Viceroyalty of the River Plate, it became independent in 1825 after a confused period when Brazil had occupied it.

Venezuela:      Seceded from Gran Colombia and became independent in 1830.

## Currency Changes

A major source of difficulty in comparing some statistics over time is changes in currency units. To some extent this has been finessed in this volume by presenting older series in terms of more recent units. However, this is not always either possible or desirable. The following list of changes may be useful:

### NORTH AMERICA

Costa Rica: The colón replaced the peso in 1900 at the official rate of 1 colón = 1 silver peso.

El Salvador: The colón replaced the peso in 1920 at the official rate of 1 colón = 1 peso.

Guatemala: The quetzal replaced the peso in 1924 at the rate of 1 quetzal = 60 paper pesos.

Honduras: The name 'peso' was changed to 'lempira' in the early 1930s.

Jamaica: The Jamaican dollar replaced the pound in 1969 at the rate of 2 dollars = 1 pound.

Nicaragua: The cordoba replaced the peso in 1912 at the rate of 1 cordoba = 12.5 pesos.

### SOUTH AMERICA

Argentina: A new peso worth 100 old pesos was issued in 1970. In 1983 this was replaced by the peso argentino, worth 10,000 of the previous currency. This was replaced in turn in 1985 by the australe, at the rate of 1 australe = 1,000 pesos argentinos.

Bolivia: The peso replaced the boliviano in 1963 at the rate of 1 peso = 1,000 bolivianos, but was in turn replaced by the (new) boliviano at the rate of 1 boliviano = 1 million pesos.

Brazil: The name 'milreis' was replaced by 'cruzeiro' in 1942. A new cruzeiro, worth 1,000 old cruzeiros, was issued in 1966. This was replaced by the cruzado in 1986 at the rate of 1 cruzado = 1,000 cruzeiros. This has in turn been replaced recently by a further new cruzeiro, equal to 1,000 cruzados, and this currency has been used for a few revised statistics.

Chile: The escudo replaced the peso in 1959 at the rate of 1 escudo = 1,000 pesos. In 1975 a new peso was issued at the rate of 1 peso = 1,000 escudos.

Paraguay: The guaranie replaced the peso in 1943 at the rate of 1 guaranie = 100 paper or 1.75 gold pesos.

Peru: The inti replaced the sol in 1985 at the rate of 1 inti = 1,000 soles.

Uruguay: A new peso worth 1,000 old pesos was issued in 1975.

# SOURCES

The main national sources used have been the official publications of the various governments. In order to avoid excessive repetition of these in the notes to the tables, there follows a list of those used in more than a very few of the tables in this book.

Argentina:    *Anuario del Dirección General de estadística* (1892–1914)
*Anuario estadístico: comercio exterior* (1915–47)
*Anuario estadístico de la República Argentina* (1946 ongoing)
*Anuario geográfico Argentino* (1941)
*Boletín de estadística*
*Censo de Poblacion* (1869, 1895, 1914, 1947, 1960, 1970)
*Estadística agrícola* (1902/4–1917/18)
*Digesto de Hacienda* (1900–1949)
*Resumenes estadísticos retrospéctives, 1900–1959*
In addition, the following unofficial publication was used extensively: Ernesto Tornquist & Co. Ltd., *The Economic Development of the Argentine Republic in the Last Fifty Years* (Buenos Aires, 1919)

Barbados:    *Abstract of Statistics* (1956 ongoing)
*Quarterly Digest of Statistics* (1956 ongoing)

Bolivia:    *Boletín estadístico* (1901 ongoing)
*Censo de Poblacion* (1900, 1950, 1976)
*Comercio exterior* (1920 ongoing)
*Extracto estadístico de Bolivia* (1936)
*Bolivia en cifras* (1973 ongoing)

Brazil:    *Anuário estatístico do Brasil* (1908/12, 1936 ongoing)
*Censo de população* (1872, 1890, 1900, 1920, 1940, 1950, 1960, 1970)
In addition, the following unofficial publication was used: Armin K. Ludwig, *Brazil: A Handbook of Historical Statistics* (Boston, 1985)

British Colonies in general:    Blue Books for individual colonies and *Colonial Reports* (in Parliamentary Papers to 1921)
*Tables of Revenue, Population and Commerce, etc. of the United Kingdom and its Dependencies* (1820–52, in Parliamentary Papers)
*Statistical Abstract for the Colonies* (1850–1965 with slight variations in title. In Parliamentary Papers to 1947)
*Statistical Tables relating to the Colonies* (1854–1914 in Parliamentary Papers)

Canada:    *The Canada Year Book* (1905 ongoing)
*Statistical Year-book of Canada* (1886–1904)
In addition, the following unofficial publication was used extensively: M.C. Urquhart and K.A. Buckley (eds.), *Historical Statistics of Canada* (1st edition, Cambridge, 1965, and Second edition, Ottawa, 1983)

Chile:    *Anuario estadístico* (1848/58–1925; in sub-series by subject from 1911)
*Censo de poblacion* (1895, 1907, 1920, 1930, 1940, 1952, 1960, 1970)
*Síntesis estadística* (1928 ongoing)
*Estadística Chilena* (1928 ongoing)

Colombia:    *Anales de economía y estadística* (1938 ongoing)
*Anuario estadístico* (1905, 1915 ongoing)

*Boletín mensual de estadística* (1951 ongoing)
*Censo de poblacion* (1905, 1912, 1918, 1951, 1964, 1973)
*Sintesis estadística de Colombia* (1941)

Costa Rica:     *Anuario estadístico* (1883–93, 1907–45, 1948 ongoing)
                *Informe* (of the Direccion General de Estadística) (1897–1908, 1920–47)
                *Censo de poblacion* (1927, 1950, 1963, 1973)

Cuba:           *Anuario Azucarero de Cuba*
                Anuario estadístico (1914, 1952–57)
                *Census of Cuba* (US Department of War, 1899)
                In addition, the following unofficial publications were used: The Cuban Economic
                Research Project of the University of Miami, *A Study on Cuba* (Miami, 1965) and
                Susan B. Schroeder, *Cuba: A Handbook of Historical Statistics* (Boston, 1982)

Dominican       *Anuario estadístico* (1936–54)
Republic:       *21 Años de Estadísticas, 1936–1956* (1956)

Ecuador:        *Anuario de comercio exterior* (1957 ongoing)
                *Ecuador en cifras, 1938 a 1942* (1943)
                *El trimestre estadístico* (1945–47)
                *Síntesis estadística* (1955–62)

El Salvador:    *Anuario estadístico* (1911–23, 1927 ongoing)

Guatemala:      *Annales estadísticos* (1882–83)
                *Anuario* or *Informe* (of the Dirección General de Estadística) (1882–9, 1891,
                1893–4, 1898 & 1928).
                *Anuario estadístico* (1975)
                *Censo de Poblacion* (1921, 1940, 1950, 1964, 1973)
                *Guatemala en cifras* (1955 ongoing)

Guyana:         *Quarterly Statistical Digest* (1965 ongoing)

Haiti:          *Bulletin Trimestriel de Statistique* (1951 ongoing)

Honduras:       *Anuario estadístico* (1889, 1950 ongoing)
                *Censo de poblacion* (1910, 1930, 1940, 1950, 1961, 1974)

Jamaica:        *Digest* or *Abstract of Statistics* (1947 ongoing)

Mexico:         *Anuario estadístico* (1893 ongoing)
                *Censo de poblacion* (1895, 1910, 1921, 1930, 1940, 1950, 1960, 1970)
                *Statistics on the Mexican Economy* (1977)

Nicaragua:      *Anuario estadístico* (1930–47, 1964 ongoing)
                *Boletin Mensuel de estadístico* (1930 ongoing)

Panama:         *Extracto estadístico* (1941/3 ongoing)

Paraguay:       *Anuario estadístico* (1886–7, 1914–17, 1940 ongoing)
                *Boletín estadístico* (1957 ongoing)
                *Mensaje del Presidente* (1882 ongoing)

Peru:           *Anuario estadístico* (1944 ongoing)
                *Censo de poblacion* (1940, 1961, 1972)
                *Extracto estadístico* (1919–43)

Puerto Rico:        *Monthly Statistical Report* (1943 ongoing)
                    *Statistical Abstract* (1949 ongoing)

Surinam:            *Jaarcijfers* (1887–1922)

Trinidad            *Statistical Digest* (1951 ongoing)
and Tobago:

United States:      *Commerce and Navigation of the United States* (1822–1965)
                    *Historical Statistics of the United States* (Bicentennial edition, 1975)
                    *Statistical Abstract* (1887 ongoing)

Uruguay:            *Anuario estadístico* (1884 ongoing)
                    *Censo de poblacion* (1963)
                    *Síntesis estadística* (1919–36)

Venezuela:          *Anuario estadístico* (1872–1912, 1938 ongoing)
                    *Censo de poblacion* (1926, 1936, 1941, 1950, 1961, 1971)
                    In addition, the following unofficial publication was used: Miguel Izard, *Series
                    estadísticas para la história de Venezuela* (Mérida, 1970)

In addition, certain gaps have been filled from the British *Statistical Abstract for Foreign Countries*
(1872–1912, in Parliamentary Papers, where certain other foreign statistics were published occasionally from 1844 onwards), from British *Consular Reports* (in Parliamentary Papers), and from publications of the German Statistical Office, *Die Wirtschaft des Auslandes, 1900–1927* and *Statistisches
Handbuch der Weltwirtschaft.*

The phrase 'ongoing' should not be taken to imply that publication has always been continuous.

# ACKNOWLEDGEMENTS

In compiling a volume of this kind I have, inevitably, contracted a large number of debts for the help which I have been given by a great variety of people. It is impossible to mention every single one of them here, and I hope that those who are not named below will accept this general expression of my gratitude.

My major obligation must be to those librarians and their staffs who have put up with the persistent demands which I have made upon them. I would particularly like to thank Mr Finkell and Mr. Ross of the Marshall Library, Cambridge; Mrs Peppercorn of the Department of Applied Economics Library, Cambridge; Mr Vickery and Mr Noblett and their staff in the Official Publications Department of the Cambridge University Library; Mrs Hulass and her staff at the Woolwich Repository of the British Library; and the staff of the Benson Latin American Collection at the University of Texas at Austin.

The Central Statistical Offices of the Republics of Guatemala and Panama very kindly filled certain gaps in the data for their countries.

I have received advice and help in identifying sources, and in other aspects of my work, from several of my colleagues and others scattered around the world. In this connection, I would particularly like to thank Professor W.W. Rostow, Dr Gabriel Palma, Dr Brian Pollitt, Mrs Marie Ruiz, and Mr C. Short, together with my wife, Ann, who has helped me with the compilation in numerous ways. I would also like to take this opportunity to thank Mrs. Penelope Allport and all others at Macmillan who have been helpful and understanding in seeing the book through to publication.

The publishers have made every effort to contact copyright-holders, but if they have inadvertently overlooked any, they will be pleased to make the necessary arrangement at the first opportunity.

# WEIGHTS AND MEASURES: CONVERSION RATIOS

The following is not a complete guide to all weights and measures used during the period covered by this volume. It is simply a list of those conversion ratios used in compiling the tables given here.

1 long (or imperial) ton = 1.016047 metric tons
1 short ton = 0.9072 metric tons

1 acre = 0.404686 hectares

1 mile = 1.609344 kilometres

1 Imperial gallon = 0.0454596 hectolitres
1 US gallon = 0.037854 hectolitres
1 US barrel (oil) = 158.95 litres
1 Imperial bushel = 0.363677 hectolitres

# SYMBOLS

… = not available
- - = less than half the smallest digit used in the table
— = nil

# A.   POPULATION AND VITAL STATISTICS

The principal sources of population data are official censuses, administrative enumerations, and registration records. The earliest of these in the Americas, at other than a very local level, date from around the beginning of the period covered in the work, and cover Spanish colonial territories which later became independent nations. Individual British colonies in North America also organized enumerations at such a comparatively early date, though the first census covering the United States was not taken until after independence. Such of this early material as has seemed at all reliable, even in a very approximate way, has been included in table 1. Similar material has also been included for the cities shown in table 4.

Apart from the United States, which began in 1790, reasonably regular censuses started around the middle of the nineteenth century in most of the countries covered here. There are many exceptions to this statement, however, particularly with regard to regularity. Indeed, Latin America generally has never come anywhere near the former British colonies in this respect, although Mexico and, with one exception, Brazil have had a decennial census in the twentieth century. Chile, Colombia, Cuba, Honduras, Panama and (from 1920) Venezuela have also been reasonably regular in this period. At the other extreme, Haiti had no census until 1950, Peru had none between 1876 and 1940, and Uruguay none between 1908 and 1963. Bolivia, Ecuador, Paraguay, and various Central American countries also had long periods without a full enumeration.

It is generally agreed by demographers that the almost universal tendency of censuses is to under-enumerate,[1] and the probability is that, as in the United States, this was usually more pronounced in earlier than later censuses. This should be borne in mind in using the statistics shown here, but, unfortunately, it is only in a few recent cases that one can estimate the likely margin of error even approximately. Perhaps it can be regarded as reasonable to assume that regular censuses, other than the first one or two of a series, are accurate to within less than ten per cent overall, and probably a good deal less than that in most cases. Isolated censuses are likely to have a higher margin of error, most especially in large countries.

Some kinds of information elicited in censuses are likely to be less accurate than others. Data about occupations present special difficulties, which are considered in the next chapter. But the age-distribution data, shown in table 2, probably contain the largest margins of error of all. For in addition to accidental errors, this information is peculiarly liable to deliberate falsification by respondents. Moreover, the sort of ignorance of their precise age which appears to have been common amongst older Balkan peoples up to the 1920s is also likely to have affected the largely illiterate Indian population of many Latin American countries until fairly recently.

Regional population statistics are shown here in table 3 only for the larger countries, for which such data are likely to have fairly general interest. They are subject to all the general problems pertaining to censuses and there are, in addition, changes in boundaries which sometimes impair their comparability over time. Similar changes affect the cities, whose populations are shown in table 4, for as cities grow in population, so they tend to grow in space, taking in areas which, whilst not previously uninhabited, are clearly not part of a city. This presents no conceptual problem, and the general rule adopted here has been to show the statistics which apply to the city limits of the year to which they refer. A problem does arise, however, when suburban areas which became functionally part of a central city remain administratively separate from it, a very common situation in recent times in the United States. The solution normally adopted here has been to show two figures in such cases, one for the city proper and the other of the urban agglomeration, for all periods since 1930.

Demographers may find the vital statistics here among the least sophisticated that are nowadays available; but they have the merit, from the historical point of view, of being extant for much longer periods than the more refined series. But just as censuses tend to underestimate, so a proportion of vital events escapes the registrars' nets. This is particularly true of most Latin American countries where, in any case, civil registration usually began late and has continued to be incomplete. However, even in the United States, national vital statistics were not collected until well into the twentieth century, and as late as 1940 birth registration was estimated to be only 92.5 per cent complete. Generally speaking, the smaller a country and the more homogeneous its population the earlier it acquired useful vital statistics. Thus Chile and Uruguay were the leaders in Latin American registration, and Brazil had still not got an effective system in the 1980s. The principle adopted here in tables 5 and 6 has been to show such rates as are available which are believed to have reasonable continuity, even if they are understatements. Estimates of the *actual* rates for quinquennial periods, made by O. Andrew Collver, are given in an appendix (A6a) to table 6.

A variety of statistics on overseas migration is available for different countries, though it is of an extremely heterogeneous nature, making comparisons between countries often hazardous. A selection of this material is given in table 8, though much more is available in the sources noted there.

[1] See the discussion in the introduction to Chapter A of *Historical Statistics of the United States*, p. 1 (cited on p. xiii above) and the sources mentioned there.

**A1    NORTH AMERICA: POPULATION OF COUNTRIES** (in thousands)

### ALASKA

| Date | Total | M | F |
|---|---|---|---|
| 1880 | 33 | … | … |
| 1890 | 32 | 19 | 13 |
| 1900 | 64 | 46 | 18 |
| 1910 | 64 | 46 | 18 |
| 1920 | 55 | 35 | 20 |
| 1929 | 59 | 36 | 24 |
| 1939 | 73 | 43 | 30 |
| 1950 | 129 | 79 | 49 |

Incorporated in U.S.A.

### ANTIGUA

| Date | Total | M | F |
|---|---|---|---|
| 1851 | 37 | 18 | 20 |
| 1861 | 37 | 17 | 20 |
| 1871 | 35 | 16 | 19 |
| 1881 | 35 | 16 | 19 |
| 1891 | 37 | 17 | 20 |
| 1901 | 35 | 16 | 19 |
| 1911 | 32 | 14 | 18 |
| 1921 | 30 | 13 | 17 |
| 1946 | 42 | 19 | 23 |
| 1960 | 54 | 25 | 29 |
| 1970 | 66 | 31 | 34 |

### BAHAMAS

| Date | Total | M | F |
|---|---|---|---|
| 1851 | 28 | 13 | 14 |
| 1861 | 35 | 17 | 18 |
| 1871 | 39 | 19 | 20 |
| 1881 | 44 | 21 | 23 |
| 1891 | 48 | 23 | 25 |
| 1901 | 54 | 25 | 29 |
| 1911 | 56 | 25 | 31 |
| 1921 | 53 | 24 | 29 |
| 1931 | 60 | 28 | 32 |
| 1943 | 69 | 32 | 37 |
| 1953 | 85 | 39 | 46 |
| 1963 | 130 | 63 | 67 |
| 1970 | 175 | 87 | 88 |
| 1980 | 223 | 109 | 114 |

### BARBADOS

| Date | Total | M | F |
|---|---|---|---|
| 1851 | 136 | 62 | 74 |
| 1861 | 153 | 71 | 82 |
| 1871 | 162 | 73 | 89 |
| 1881 | 172 | 77 | 95 |
| 1891 | 183 | 82 | 101 |
| 1901 | 196 | 88 | 107 |
| 1911 | 172 | 71 | 102 |
| 1921 | 157 | 63 | 93 |
| 1946 | 194 | 86 | 107 |
| 1960 | 233 | 106 | 127 |
| 1970 | 235 | 110 | 125 |
| 1980 | 252 | 120 | 132 |

### BELIZE/BRITISH HONDURAS

| Date | Total | M | F |
|---|---|---|---|
| 1861 | 26 | 14 | 12 |
| 1871 | 25 | 13 | 12 |
| 1881 | 27 | 14 | 13 |
| 1891 | 31 | 16 | 15 |
| 1901 | 37 | 19 | 18 |
| 1911 | 40 | 20 | 20 |
| 1921 | 45 | 23 | 23 |
| 1931 | 51 | 26 | 26 |
| 1946 | 59 | 29 | 30 |
| 1960 | 90 | 44 | 46 |
| 1970 | 120 | 60 | 60 |
| 1980 | 143 | 72 | 71 |

### BERMUDA

| Date | Total | M | F |
|---|---|---|---|
| 1843 | 10 | 4 | 6 |
| 1851 | 11 | 5 | 6 |
| 1861 | 12 | 5 | 7 |
| 1871 | 12 | 5 | 7 |
| 1881 | 14 | 6 | 8 |
| 1891 | 15 | 7 | 8 |
| 1901 | 18 | 9 | 9 |
| 1911 | 19 | 9 | 10 |
| 1921 | 20 | 10 | 10 |
| 1931 | 28 | 14 | 14 |
| 1939 | 31 | 15 | 16 |
| 1950 | 37 | 18 | 19 |
| 1960 | 43[1] | 21 | 21 |
| 1970 | 52 | 26 | 26 |
| 1980 | 68 | 34 | 34 |

### BRITISH VIRGIN ISLANDS

| Date | Total | M | F |
|---|---|---|---|
| 1841 | 6.7 | 3.1 | 3.6 |
| 1871 | 6.7 | 3.4 | 3.3 |
| 1881 | 5.3 | 2.6 | 2.7 |
| 1891 | 4.6 | 2.1 | 2.5 |
| 1901 | 4.9 | 2.3 | 2.7 |
| 1911 | 5.6 | 2.6 | 2.9 |
| 1921 | 5.1 | 2.3 | 2.7 |
| 1946 | 6.5 | 3.1 | 3.4 |
| 1960 | 7.3 | 3.6 | 3.8 |
| 1970 | 9.7 | 5.1 | 4.5 |
| 1980 | 11.0 | 5.6 | 5.4 |

### CANADA[2]

| Date | Total | M | F |
|---|---|---|---|
| 1851 | 2,436 | 1,250 | 1,186 |
| 1861 | 3,230 | 1,660 | 1,570 |
| 1871 | 3,689 | 1,869 | 1,820 |
| 1881 | 4,325 | 2,189 | 2,136 |
| 1891 | 4,833 | 2,460 | 2,373 |
| 1901 | 5,371 | 2,752 | 2,620 |
| 1911 | 7,207 | 3,822 | 3,385 |
| 1921 | 8,788 | 4,530 | 4,258 |
| 1931 | 10,377 | 5,373 | 5,002 |
| 1941 | 11,507[2] | 5,901[2] | 5,606[2] |
| 1951 | 14,009 | 7,089 | 6,921 |
| 1956 | 16,081 | 8,152 | 7,929 |
| 1961 | 18,238 | 9,219 | 9,019 |
| 1966 | 20,015 | 10,054 | 9,961 |
| 1971 | 21,568 | 10,795 | 10,773 |
| 1981 | 24,343 | 12,068 | 12,275 |
| 1986 | 25,309 | 12,486 | 12,824 |

### CAYMAN ISLANDS

| Date | Total | M | F |
|---|---|---|---|
| 1891 | 4.3 | … | … |
| 1911 | 5.6 | 2.4 | 3.1 |
| 1921 | 5.3 | 2.2 | 3.0 |
| 1943 | 6.7 | 3.0 | 3.7 |
| 1960 | 7.6 | 3.1 | 4.5 |
| 1970 | 10.5 | 5.0 | 5.5 |
| 1979 | 16.7 | 8.1 | 8.6 |

Abbreviations used throughout this table: **M** males; **F** females

**A1     NORTH AMERICA: Population of Countries** (in thousands)

### COSTA RICA[3]

| Date | Total | M | F |
|------|-------|---|---|
| 1824 | 65 | ... | ... |
| 1836 | 78 | ... | ... |
| 1844 | 94[4] | ... | ... |
| 1864 | 120 | 58 | 62 |
| 1875 | 153 | ... | ... |
| 1883 | 182 | 90 | 92 |
| 1892 | 243 | 122 | 121 |
| 1927 | 472 | 238 | 233 |
| 1950 | 801 | 400 | 401 |
| 1963 | 1,336 | 669 | 667 |
| 1973 | 1,872 | 939 | 933 |
| 1981 | 2,417 | 1,208 | 1,209 |

### CUBA[5]

| Date | Total | M | F |
|------|-------|---|---|
| 1774 | 172 | 101 | 71 |
| 1792 | 272 | 155 | 117 |
| 1817 | 572 | ... | ... |
| 1827 | 704 | 404 | 301 |
| 1841 | 1,008 | 584 | 424 |
| 1861 | 1,397 | 801 | 596 |
| 1877 | 1,522 | 846 | 664 |
| 1887 | 1,632 | 866 | 743 |
| 1899 | 1,573 | 758 | 815 |
| 1907 | 2,049 | 1,075 | 974 |
| 1919 | 2,889 | 1,531 | 1,358 |
| 1931 | 3,962 | 2,103 | 1,860 |
| 1943 | 4,779 | 2,499 | 2,280 |
| 1953 | 5,829 | 2,985 | 2,844 |
| 1970 | 8,569 | 4,393 | 4,176 |
| 1981 | 9,724 | 4,915 | 4,809 |

### DOMINICA

| Date | Total | M | F |
|------|-------|---|---|
| 1844 | 22 | 11 | 12 |
| 1861 | 25 | 12 | 13 |
| 1871 | 27 | 13 | 14 |
| 1881 | 28 | 13 | 15 |
| 1891 | 27 | 12 | 15 |
| 1901 | 29 | 13 | 16 |
| 1911 | 34 | 15 | 19 |
| 1921 | 37 | 17 | 20 |
| 1946 | 48 | 22 | 25 |
| 1960 | 60 | 28 | 32 |
| 1970 | 71 | 34 | 37 |
| 1981 | 74 | 37 | 37 |

### DOMINICAN REPUBLIC

| Date | Total | M | F |
|------|-------|---|---|
| 1920 | 895 | 446 | 448 |
| 1935 | 1,479 | 751 | 729 |
| 1950 | 2,136 | 1,071 | 1,065 |
| 1960 | 3,047 | 1,536 | 1,511 |
| 1970 | 4,006 | 1,999 | 2,007 |
| 1981 | 5,648 | 2,832 | 2,816 |

### EL SALVADOR[6]

| Date | Total | M | F |
|------|-------|---|---|
| 1901 | 1,007 | 494 | 513 |
| 1930 | 1,434 | 717 | 718 |
| 1950 | 1,856 | 918 | 937 |
| 1961 | 2,511 | 1,237 | 1,274 |
| 1971 | 3,555 | 1,763 | 1,791 |

### GRENADA

| Date | Total | M | F |
|------|-------|---|---|
| 1851 | 33 | 16 | 17 |
| 1861 | 32 | 15 | 16 |
| 1871 | 38 | 18 | 20 |
| 1881 | 42 | 20 | 22 |
| 1891 | 53 | 26 | 28 |
| 1901 | 63 | 30 | 33 |
| 1911 | 67 | 30 | 36 |
| 1921 | 66 | 29 | 37 |
| 1946 | 72 | 32 | 41 |
| 1960 | 89 | 41 | 48 |
| 1970 | 94 | 44 | 50 |
| 1981 | 89 | 43 | 46 |

### GUADELOUPE[7]

| Date | Total | M | F |
|------|-------|---|---|
| 1852 | 125 | ... | ... |
| 1861 | 138 | ... | ... |
| 1876 | 176 | ... | ... |
| 1901 | 182 | ... | ... |
| 1906 | 190 | ... | ... |
| 1911 | 212 | ... | ... |
| 1921 | 230 | ... | ... |
| 1926 | 243 | ... | ... |
| 1931 | 267 | ... | ... |
| 1936 | 304 | ... | ... |
| 1954 | 229 | 112 | 118 |
| 1961 | 283 | 138 | 145 |
| 1967 | 313 | 153 | 159 |
| 1974 | 324 | ... | ... |
| 1982 | 327 | 160 | 167 |

### GUATEMALA

| Date | Total | M | F |
|------|-------|---|---|
| 1771 | 315 | ... | ... |
| 1848 | 706 | ... | ... |
| 1880 | 1,225 | 605 | 620 |
| 1893 | 1,364 | 677 | 687 |
| 1921 | 2,005 | 992 | 1,013 |
| 1940 | 3,283[8] | 1,660 | 1,623 |
| 1950 | 2,791 | 1,411 | 1,380 |
| 1964 | 4,288 | 2,172 | 2,116 |
| 1973 | 5,160 | 2,589 | 2,571 |
| 1981 | 6,054 | 3,016 | 3,038 |

### HAITI

| Date | Total | M | F |
|------|-------|---|---|
| 1950[9] | 3,097 | 1,505 | 1,592 |
| 1971 | 4,330 | 2,090 | 2,240 |
| 1982 | 5,054 | 2,448 | 2,605 |

### HONDURAS

| Date | Total | M | F |
|------|-------|---|---|
| 1791 | 96 | ... | ... |
| 1801 | 130 | ... | ... |
| 1881 | 307 | 151 | 157 |
| 1887 | 332 | 163 | 169 |
| 1895 | 399 | 196 | 203 |
| 1901 | 544 | 267 | 276 |
| 1905 | 500 | 244 | 256 |
| 1910 | 553 | 271 | 283 |
| 1916 | 606 | 300 | 306 |
| 1926 | 701 | 348 | 352 |
| 1930 | 854 | 424 | 430 |
| 1935 | 962 | 480 | 482 |
| 1940 | 1,108 | 556 | 552 |
| 1945 | 1,200 | 602 | 599 |
| 1950[10] | 1,369 | 686 | 683 |
| 1961[10] | 1,885 | 939 | 948 |
| 1974 | 2,657 | 1,317 | 1,340 |

*See p. 7 for footnotes*

**A1    NORTH AMERICA: Population of Countries** (in thousands)

### JAMAICA

| Date | Total | M | F |
|------|-------|---|---|
| 1844 | 377 | 182 | 196 |
| 1861 | 441 | 214 | 228 |
| 1871 | 506 | 247 | 260 |
| 1881 | 581 | 283 | 298 |
| 1891 | 639 | 306 | 334 |
| 1901 | 756 | 366 | 390 |
| 1911 | 831 | 397 | 434 |
| 1921 | 858 | 402 | 456 |
| 1943 | 1,246 | 603 | 643 |
| 1953 | 1,487 | 727 | 760 |
| 1960 | 1,624 | 781 | 843 |
| 1970 | 1,849 | 901 | 948 |
| 1982 | 2,206 | 1,080 | 1,126 |

### MARTINIQUE[7]

| Date | Total | M | F |
|------|-------|---|---|
| 1867 | 153 | ... | ... |
| 1876 | 164 | ... | ... |
| 1886 | 175 | ... | ... |
| 1894 | 189 | ... | ... |
| 1901 | 208 | ... | ... |
| 1905 | 182 | ... | ... |
| 1910 | 184 | ... | ... |
| 1921 | 244 | ... | ... |
| 1927 | 228 | ... | ... |
| 1931 | 235 | ... | ... |
| 1936 | 247 | ... | ... |
| 1954 | 239 | 115 | 124 |
| 1961 | 291 | 140 | 151 |
| 1967 | 320 | 155 | 165 |
| 1974 | 324 | ... | ... |
| 1982 | 327 | 158 | 168 |

### MEXICO[11]

| Date | Total | M | F |
|------|-------|---|---|
| 1831 | 6,382 | ... | ... |
| 1873 | 9,210 | ... | ... |
| 1895 | 12,632 | 6,281 | 6,352 |
| 1900 | 13,607 | 6,752 | 6,855 |
| 1910 | 13,607 | 7,504 | 7,656 |
| 1921 | 14,335 | 7,004 | 7,331 |
| 1930 | 16,553 | 8,119 | 8,434 |
| 1940 | 19,654 | 9,696 | 9,958 |
| 1950 | 25,791 | 12,697 | 13,094 |
| 1960 | 34,923 | 17,415 | 17,508 |
| 1970 | 48,225 | 24,066 | 24,160 |
| 1980 | 66,847 | 33,039 | 33,808 |

### MONTSERRAT

| Date | Total | M | F |
|------|-------|---|---|
| 1851 | 7.1 | 3.1 | 3.9 |
| 1861 | 7.6 | 3.4 | 4.2 |
| 1871 | 8.7 | 4.0 | 4.7 |
| 1881 | 10.0 | 5.0 | 5.0 |
| 1891 | 12.0 | 5.0 | 6.0 |
| 1901 | 12.0 | 6.0 | 7.0 |
| 1911 | 12.0 | 5.0 | 7.0 |
| 1921 | 12.0 | 5.0 | 7.0 |
| 1946 | 14.0 | 6.0 | 8.0 |
| 1960 | 12.0 | 5.0 | 7.0 |
| 1970 | 11.0 | 5.0 | 6.0 |
| 1980 | 12.0 | 6.0 | 6.0 |

### NETHERLANDS ANTILLES

| Date | Total | M | F |
|------|-------|---|---|
| 1930 | 76 | 38 | 39 |
| 1960 | 189 | 93 | 96 |
| 1971 | 218 | 107 | 112 |
| 1981 Aruba | 60 | 29 | 31 |
| 1981 rest | 172 | 83 | 89 |

### NEWFOUNDLAND

| Date | Total | M | F |
|------|-------|---|---|
| 1836 | 75 | ... | ... |
| 1845 | 97 | 53 | 44 |
| 1857 | 124 | 64 | 58 |
| 1869 | 147 | ... | ... |
| 1874 | 161 | 83 | 78 |
| 1884[12] | 193 | 99 | 94 |
| 1891[12] | 198 | 101 | 97 |
| 1901[12] | 217 | 111 | 106 |
| 1911[12] | 239 | 122 | 116 |
| 1921 | 263 | 134 | 129 |
| 1935 | 290 | 149 | 141 |
| 1945 | 322 | 165 | 157 |

incorporated in Canada

### NICARAGUA

| Date | Total | M | F |
|------|-------|---|---|
| 1906 | 505 | ... | ... |
| 1920 | 638 | 312 | 327 |
| 1940[13] | 983 | 477 | 506 |
| 1950 | 1,057 | 520 | 537 |
| 1963 | 1,536 | 758 | 778 |
| 1971 | 1,878 | 922 | 956 |

### PANAMA[14]

| Date | Total | M | F |
|------|-------|---|---|
| 1911[15] | 291 | 150 | 141 |
| 1920[15] | 446 | 228 | 218 |
| 1930 | 467 | 239 | 228 |
| 1940[15] | 567 | 291 | 276 |
| 1950 | 805 | 410 | 396 |
| 1960 | 1,076 | 546 | 530 |
| 1970 | 1,428 | 724 | 704 |
| 1980[14] | 1,831 | 928 | 903 |

### PANAMA CANAL ZONE

| Date | Total | M | F |
|------|-------|---|---|
| 1912 | 63 | 45 | 18 |
| 1920 | 22 | 15 | 8 |
| 1930 | 39 | 26 | 13 |
| 1940 | 52 | 38 | 14 |
| 1950 | 53 | 31 | 22 |
| 1960 | 42 | 23 | 19 |
| 1970 | 44 | 24 | 20 |

included in Panama

### PUERTO RICO

| Date | Total | M | F |
|------|-------|---|---|
| 1765 | 45 | ... | ... |
| 1775 | 70 | ... | ... |
| 1800 | 155 | ... | ... |
| 1815 | 221 | ... | ... |
| 1832 | 330 | ... | ... |
| 1846 | 448 | ... | ... |
| 1860 | 583 | 296 | 287 |
| 1877 | 732 | 375 | 358 |
| 1887 | 799 | 399 | 400 |
| 1899 | 953 | 468 | 482 |
| 1910 | 1,118 | 557 | 561 |
| 1920 | 1,300 | 648 | 652 |
| 1930 | 1,544 | 772 | 772 |
| 1935 | 1,724 | 862 | 862 |
| 1940 | 1,869 | 938 | 931 |
| 1950 | 2,211 | 1,111 | 1,100 |
| 1960 | 2,350 | 1,163 | 1,187 |
| 1970 | 2,712 | 1,330 | 1,382 |
| 1980 | 3,197 | 1,557 | 1,640 |

*See p. 7 for footnotes*

## A1   NORTH AMERICA: Population of Countries (in thousands)

### ST KITTS, NEVIS & ANGUILLA[39]

| Date | Total | M | F |
|---|---|---|---|
| 1861 | 34 | 16 | 18 |
| 1871 | 40 | 19 | 21 |
| 1881 | 44 | 21 | 24 |
| 1891 | 48 | 22 | 26 |
| 1901 | 46 | 20 | 26 |
| 1911 | 43 | 18 | 25 |
| 1921 | 38 | 15 | 23 |
| 1946 | 46 | 21 | 25 |
| 1960 | 57 | 26 | 31 |
| 1980[39] | 43 | 21 | 22 |

### ST LUCIA

| Date | Total | M | F |
|---|---|---|---|
| 1851 | 24 | 12 | 13 |
| 1861 | 27 | 13 | 14 |
| 1871 | 32 | 16 | 16 |
| 1881 | 39 | 19 | 20 |
| 1891 | 42 | 20 | 24 |
| 1901 | 50 | 24 | 26 |
| 1911 | 49 | 22 | 26 |
| 1921 | 52 | 24 | 28 |
| 1946 | 70 | 33 | 37 |
| 1960 | 86 | 41 | 45 |
| 1970 | 101 | 48 | 53 |
| 1980 | 113 | 55 | 59 |

### ST VINCENT

| Date | Total | M | F |
|---|---|---|---|
| 1851 | 30 | 14 | 16 |
| 1861 | 32 | 15 | 17 |
| 1871 | 36 | 17 | 19 |
| 1881 | 41 | 19 | 22 |
| 1891 | 41 | 19 | 22 |
| 1901 | 48 | ... | ... |
| 1911 | 42 | 18 | 24 |
| 1921 | 44 | 19 | 25 |
| 1931 | 48 | 21 | 27 |
| 1946 | 62 | 28 | 34 |
| 1960 | 80 | 38 | 42 |
| 1970 | 87 | 41 | 46 |
| 1980 | 98 | 47 | 50 |

### TRINIDAD & TOBAGO

| Date | Total | M | F |
|---|---|---|---|
| 1851* | 69 | 35 | 33 |
| 1851† | 14 | 7 | 7 |
| 1861* | 84 | 46 | 38 |
| 1861† | 15 | 7 | 8 |
| 1871* | 110 | 60 | 49 |
| 1871† | 17 | 8 | 8 |
| 1881* | 153 | 84 | 69 |
| 1881† | 18 | 9 | 9 |
| 1891 | 218 | 117 | 101 |
| 1901 | 274 | 144 | 129 |
| 1911 | 334 | 174 | 159 |
| 1921 | 366 | 187 | 179 |
| 1931 | 413 | 207 | 206 |
| 1946 | 558 | 280 | 278 |
| 1960 | 828 | 412 | 416 |
| 1970 | 941 | 466 | 475 |
| 1980 | 1,080 | 540 | 540 |

*Trinidad;   †Tobago

### TURKS & CAICOS ISLANDS

| Date | Total | M | F |
|---|---|---|---|
| 1871 | 4.7 | 2.3 | 2.4 |
| 1881 | 4.7 | 2.2 | 2.5 |
| 1891 | 4.7 | 2.2 | 2.5 |
| 1901 | 5.3 | 2.4 | 2.9 |
| 1911 | 5.6 | 2.5 | 3.1 |
| 1921 | 5.5 | 2.5 | 3.1 |
| 1943 | 6.1 | 2.8 | 3.3 |
| 1954 | 5.1 | 2.1 | 3.0 |
| 1960 | 5.7 | 2.7 | 3.1 |
| 1970 | 5.6 | 2.7 | 2.9 |
| 1980 | 7.4 | 3.6 | 3.8 |

### USA[16]

| Date | Total | M | F |
|---|---|---|---|
| 1790 | 3,929 | [1,615][17] | [1,557][17] |
| 1800 | 5,308 | [2,195][17] | [2,111][17] |
| 1810 | 7,240 | [2,988][17] | [2,874][17] |
| 1820 | 9,638 | 4,897 | 4,742 |
| 1830 | 12,866 | 6,530 | 6,336 |
| 1840 | 17,069 | 8,689 | 8,381 |
| 1850 | 23,192 | 11,838 | 11,354 |
| 1860 | 31,443 | 16,085 | 15,358 |
| 1870 | 39,818[18] | 19,494 | 19,065 |
| 1880 | 50,156 | 25,519 | 24,637 |
| 1890 | 62,948 | 32,237 | 30,711 |
| 1900 | 75,995 | 38,816 | 37,178 |
| 1910 | 91,972 | 47,332 | 44,640 |
| 1920 | 105,711 | 53,900 | 51,810 |
| 1930 | 122,775 | 62,137 | 60,638 |
| 1940 | 131,669 | 66,062 | 65,608 |
| 1950 | 150,697[16] | 74,833[16] | 75,864[16] |
| 1960 | 179,323 | 88,331 | 90,992 |
| 1970 | 203,212 | 98,912 | 104,300 |
| 1980 | 226,546 | 110,053 | 116,493 |

### US/Danish VIRGIN ISLANDS

| Date | Total | M | F |
|---|---|---|---|
| 1850 | 40 | ... | ... |
| 1855 | 37 | 16 | 21 |
| 1860 | 38 | ... | ... |
| 1870 | 38 | ... | ... |
| 1880 | 34 | 15 | 19 |
| 1890 | 33 | 15 | 17 |
| 1901 | 31 | 14 | 16 |
| 1911 | 27 | 13 | 15 |
| 1917 | 26 | 12 | 14 |
| 1930 | 22 | 10 | 12 |
| 1940 | 25 | 12 | 13 |
| 1950 | 27 | 13 | 14 |
| 1960 | 32 | 16 | 16 |
| 1970 | 62 | 31 | 31 |
| 1980 | 97 | 46 | 50 |

*See p. 7 for footnotes*

## A1    SOUTH AMERICA: POPULATION OF COUNTRIES (in thousands)

### ARGENTINA[19]

| Date | Total | M | F |
|---|---|---|---|
| 1869 | 1,737 | 892 | 845 |
| 1895 | 3,955 | 2,089 | 1,866 |
| 1914 | 7,885[20] | 4,227 | 3,658 |
| 1947 | 15,894[20] | 8,145 | 7,749 |
| 1960 | 20,759[21] | 10,032 | 9,973 |
| 1970 | 23,390 | 11,617 | 11,773 |
| 1980 | 27,947 | 13,756 | 14,191 |

### BOLIVIA

| Date | Total | M | F |
|---|---|---|---|
| 1854 | 2,326[22] / 1,544 | ... | ... |
| 1882 | 1,172[22] / 1,098 | ... | ... |
| 1900 | 1,696[23] | 819 | 814 |
| 1950 | 3,019[23] | 1,326 | 1,378 |
| 1976 | 4,648 | 2,280 | 2,368 |

### BRAZIL[24]

| Date | Total | M | F |
|---|---|---|---|
| 1854 | 7,678 | ... | ... |
| 1872 | 9,930 | 5,124 | 4,807 |
| 1890 | 14,334 | 7,238 | 7,096 |
| 1900 | 17,438 | 8,901 | 8,538 |
| 1920 | 30,636 | 15,444 | 15,192 |
| 1940 | 41,165 | 20,614 | 20,622 |
| 1950 | 51,976 | 25,885 | 26,059 |
| 1960 | 70,119 | 35,011 | 35,108 |
| 1970 | 92,342 | 45,755 | 46,587 |
| 1980 | 121,149 | 60,299 | 60,850 |

### CHILE

| Date | Total | M | F |
|---|---|---|---|
| 1835 | 1,111[25] | ... | ... |
| 1843 | 1,192[25] | ... | ... |
| 1854 | 1,516[25] | 713 | 726 |
| 1865 | 1,819 | 906 | 913 |
| 1875 | 2,076 | 1,034 | 1,042 |
| 1885 | 2,507 | 1,249 | 1,250 |
| 1895 | 2,804[25] | 1,333 | 1,355 |
| 1907 | 3,229[25] | 1,609 | 1,611 |
| 1920 | 3,824[25] | 1,843 | 1,872 |
| 1930 | 4,391[25] | 2,123 | 2,165 |
| 1940 | 5,094[25] | 2,490 | 2,554 |
| 1952 | 6,207[25] | 2,913 | 3,020 |
| 1960 | 7,374[26] | 3,613 | 3,761 |
| 1970 | 8,885[26] | 4,344 | 4,541 |
| 1982 | 11,330 | 5,553 | 5,776 |

### COLOMBIA

| Date | Total | M | F |
|---|---|---|---|
| 1770 | 807 | ... | ... |
| 1778 | 829 | ... | ... |
| 1782 | 1,047 | ... | ... |
| 1825 | 1,229 | 601 | 629 |
| 1835 | 1,686 | 810 | 876 |
| 1843 | 1,932 | 925 | 1,007 |
| 1851 | 2,244 | 1,089 | 1,155 |
| 1864 | 2,694 | ... | ... |
| 1870 | 2,392 | ... | ... |
| 1905 | 4,355 | 2,020 | 2,124 |
| 1912 | 5,072[27] | 2,392 | 2,585 |
| 1918 | 5,855[27] | 2,749 | 2,947 |
| 1938 | 8,702 | 4,313 | 4,389 |
| 1951[28] | 11,548 | 5,742 | 5,806 |
| 1964 | 17,485 | 8,615 | 8,870 |
| 1973 | 22,552 | 11,004 | 11,548 |
| 1985 | 27,838 | 13,778 | 14,060 |

### ECUADOR

| Date | Total | M | F |
|---|---|---|---|
| 1950 | 3,203 | 1,595 | 1,608 |
| 1962 | 4,476 | 2,236 | 2,240 |
| 1974 | 6,522 | 3,258 | 3,263 |
| 1982 | 8,061 | 4,021 | 4,040 |

### FALKLAND ISLANDS/MALVINAS

| Date | Total | M | F |
|---|---|---|---|
| 1850 | 0.4 | 0.3 | 0.1 |
| 1861 | 0.6 | 0.4 | 0.2 |
| 1871 | 0.8 | 0.5 | 0.2 |
| 1881 | 1.6 | 1.0 | 0.6 |
| 1891 | 1.8 | 1.1 | 0.7 |
| 1901 | 2.0 | 1.2 | 0.8 |
| 1911 | 3.3 | 2.4 | 0.9 |
| 1921 | 3.3 | 2.5 | 0.9 |
| 1931 | 3.1 | 2.1 | 1.0 |
| 1946 | 2.2 | 1.2 | 1.0 |
| 1953 | 2.2 | 1.2 | 1.0 |
| 1962 | 2.2 | 1.2 | 1.0 |
| 1972 | 2.0 | 1.1 | 0.9 |
| 1980 | 1.9 | 1.0 | 0.8 |

### FRENCH GUIANA[29]

| Date | Total | M | F |
|---|---|---|---|
| 1901 | 22 | ... | ... |
| 1907 | 24 | ... | ... |
| 1911 | 26 | ... | ... |
| 1915 | 26 | ... | ... |
| 1922 | 26 | ... | ... |
| 1926 | 28 | ... | ... |
| 1931 | 22 | ... | ... |
| 1936 | 24 | ... | ... |
| 1946 | 22 | ... | ... |
| 1954 | 28 | 11 | 12 |
| 1961 | 34 | 17 | 16 |
| 1967 | 44 | 24 | 20 |
| 1974 | 55 | ... | ... |
| 1982 | 73 | 38 | 35 |

*See p. 7 for footnotes*

**A1     SOUTH AMERICA: Population of Countries** (in thousands)

### GUYANA/BRITISH GUIANA

| Date | Total | M | F |
|------|-------|-----|-----|
| 1841 | 98 | 50 | 48 |
| 1851 | 128 | 67 | 60 |
| 1861 | 148 | 80 | 68 |
| 1871 | 193 | 109 | 85 |
| 1881 | 252 | 140 | 112 |
| 1891 | 278 | 152 | 127 |
| 1911 | 296 | 154 | 142 |
| 1921 | 298 | 151 | 146 |
| 1931 | 311 | 155 | 156 |
| 1946[30] | 376 | 183 | 187 |
| 1960 | 560 | 279 | 281 |
| 1970 | 700 | 348 | 352 |
| 1980 | 759 | 376 | 383 |

### PARAGUAY

| Date | Total | M | F |
|------|-------|-----|-----|
| 1886 | 264 | ... | ... |
| 1899 | 644 | ... | ... |
| 1936[31] | 932 | ... | ... |
| 1950 | 1,408[32] | 649 | 679 |
| 1962[31] | 1,817 | 896 | 921 |
| 1972 | 2,358 | 1,169 | 1,189 |
| 1982 | 3,030 | 1,521 | 1,508 |

### PERU[33]

| Date | Total | M | F |
|------|-------|-----|-----|
| 1795 | 1,232 | ... | ... |
| 1836 | 1,374 | ... | ... |
| 1850 | 2,001 | ... | ... |
| 1862 | 2,488 | ... | ... |
| 1876 | 2,699 | ... | ... |
| 1940 | 7,023[34] | 3,068 | 3,140 |
| 1961 | 10,420[34] | 4,926 | 4,981 |
| 1972 | 14,122[34] | 6,785 | 6,754 |
| 1981 | 17,005 | 8,490 | 8,515 |

### SURINAM/DUTCH GUIANA

| Date | Total | M | F |
|------|-------|-----|-----|
| 1921 | 119[35] | 56 | 52 |
| 1950 | 184 | 92 | 92 |
| 1971 | 385 | 193 | 192 |
| 1980 | 352 | 173 | 179 |

### URUGUAY

| Date | Total | M | F |
|------|-------|-----|-----|
| 1852 | 132 | ... | ... |
| 1860 | 223 | 121 | 96 |
| 1900 | 916 | 475 | 441 |
| 1908 | 1,043 | 531 | 512 |
| 1963 | 2,596 | 1,290 | 1,305 |
| 1975 | 2,782 | 1,363 | 1,419 |
| 1985 | 2,955 | 1,439 | 1,516 |

### VENEZUELA

| Date | Total | M | F |
|------|-------|-----|-----|
| 1810 | 802 | ... | ... |
| 1825 | 707 | ... | ... |
| 1838 | 887 | ... | ... |
| 1844 | 1,219 | ... | ... |
| 1855 | 1,564 | ... | ... |
| 1873 | 1,784 | [736][36] | [805][36] |
| 1881 | 2,075 | 1,006 | 1,070 |
| 1891 | 2,324 | 1,137 | 1,186 |
| 1920 | 2,412[37] | 1,136 | 1,229 |
| 1926 | 3,027[37] | 1,415 | 1,476 |
| 1936 | 3,468[37] | 1,652 | 1,712 |
| 1941 | 3,951[37] | 1,909 | 1,942 |
| 1950 | 5,092[37] | 2,552 | 2,482 |
| 1961[38] | 7,524 | 3,824 | 3,700 |
| 1971 | 10,722 | 5,350 | 5,372 |
| 1981 | 14,517 | 7,259 | 7,258 |

*See p. 7 for footnotes*

**Population of Countries** (in thousands)

NOTES

1.      SOURCES: UN, *Demographic Yearbooks*, national censuses, and the national publications on p. xiv–xvi. Statistics for Colombia 1825–51 come from Miguel Urrutia and Mario Arrubla (eds.), *Compendio de Estadisticas Historicas de Colombia* (Bogota, 1970).
2.      A few of the figures given are official estimates rather than the results of complete censuses, but all were published as being comparable to the latter.
3.      Totals are sometimes larger than the sums of males and females, because of the inclusion of people whose sex was not distinguished.
4.      For boundary changes see pp.xi–xii
5.      It is not always clear exactly which definition of population the statistics refer to. So far as possible, the data for population actually present are given, with known exceptions referred to in footnotes.

FOOTNOTES

[1] *Dejure* population. A further 2 thousand should be added for under-enumeration and for residents temporarily abroad.
[2] In vol. 1 of the 1941 Census of Canada the following figures were given of total white population, based on earlier censuses:
**mean population (in thousands) of the decade centred on:**

| | | | | | |
|---|---|---|---|---|---|
| 1701 | 17 | 1751 | 71 | 1801 | 362 |
| 1711 | 22 | 1761 | 90 | 1811 | 517 |
| 1721 | 32 | 1771 | 105 | 1821 | 750 |
| 1731 | 45 | 1781 | 150 | 1831 | 1,085 |
| 1741 | 59 | 1791 | 233 | 1841 | 1,654 |

Newfoundland is shown separately prior to its incorporation in Canada in 1949.
[3] Authoritative estimates of total population at earlier dates are as follows (in thousands): 1700–19; 1751–24; 1778–34; 1801–53.
[4] This figure has been adjusted for under-enumeration, the reported total being 80.
[5] Statistics to 1943 are of *de facto* population. Subsequently they are of *de jure* population.
[6] R. Barón Castro, *La Población de El Salvador* (Madrid, 1942) bases the following estimates (in thousands) on earlier defective censuses:

| | Total | Males | Females |
|---|---|---|---|
| 1807 | 165 | 80 | 85 |
| 1882 | 613 | 291 | 322 |
| 1892 | 704 | 350 | 354 |

[7] Data to 1936 are believed to be grossly over-enumerated.
[8] This figure is believed to be about one million too high.
[9] Excluding any adjustment for under-enumeration, which is believed to require an addition of 8.3%.
[10] Excluding any adjustment for under-enumeration, which is believed to require additions of 10% in 1950 and 5.3% in 1961.
[11] Authoritative estimates of total population at other dates are as follows:

| | | | | | |
|---|---|---|---|---|---|
| 1803 | 5,765 | 1831 | 6,382 | 1854 | 7,853 |
| 1820 | 6,204 | 1838 | 7,044 | 1862 | 8,816 |

[12] Excluding Labrador, the total population of which was as follows (in thousands):

| | | | |
|---|---|---|---|
| 1881 | 4 | 1901 | 4 |
| 1891 | 4 | 1911 | 4 |

[13] These figures are believed to be too high.
[14] Excluding the Canal Zone (q.v.) except in 1980. Statistics to 1930 are of *de jure* population. Subsequently they are of *de facto* population.
[15] Excluding tribal populations, which were enumerated as follows: 1911–47; 1940–56.
[16] Alaska and Hawaii are shown separately prior to their admission as states. The following estimates of total population are given in *Historical Statistics of the United States*:

| | | | | | | | |
|---|---|---|---|---|---|---|---|
| 1610 | 0.35 | 1660 | 75 | 1710 | 332 | 1760 | 1,594 |
| 1620 | 2.2 | 1670 | 112 | 1720 | 466 | 1770 | 2,148 |
| 1630 | 4.6 | 1680 | 152 | 1730 | 629 | 1780 | 2,780 |
| 1640 | 27.0 | 1690 | 210 | 1740 | 906 | | |
| 1650 | 50.0 | 1700 | 251 | 1750 | 1,171 | | |

[17] The sex breakdown is for the white population only in these years.
[18] The total includes adjustment for under-enumeration in Southern states.
[19] The 1869 census gave the following earlier estimates of total population:

| | | | | | |
|---|---|---|---|---|---|
| 1809 | 406 | 1829 | 634 | 1849 | 935 |
| 1819 | 527 | 1839 | 768 | 1859 | 1,304 |

[20] Excluding any adjustment for under-enumeration, which is believed to require additions of 1.5% in 1914 and 1% in 1947.

[21] This figure has been adjusted for under-enumeration, the reported total being 20,006.
[22] The first figure relates to the territory at the time of the census, the second to the reduced area at the time of the next census.
[23] These figures have been adjusted for under-enumeration, the reported totals being 1,634 in 1900 and 2,704 in 1950.
[24] Earlier estimates accepted by the compilers of the 1920 census are as follows (in thousands): 1808–2,419; 1823–3,961.
[25] These figures have been adjusted for under-enumeration and, in 1907 and 1920, for Arica department, which was not tabulated by sex. The reported totals were as follows:

| 1835 | 1,010 | 1843 | 1,084 | 1854 | 1,439 |
|------|-------|------|-------|------|-------|
| 1895 | 2,696 | 1907 | 3,221 | 1920 | 3,715 |
| 1930 | 4,287 | 1940 | 5,044 | 1950 | 5,933 |

[26] Excluding adjustments for under-enumeration, which are believed to require additions of 5.4% in 1960 and 8.5% in 1970.
[27] Including tribal population which was not tabulated by sex, and numbered 94 in 1912 and 158 in 1918.
[28] Including an adjustment of 192 for under-enumeration.
[29] Statistics to 1946 are believed to be substantially over-enumerated. They exclude Inini, which had a population of 5,000 in 1946.
[30] Excluding 6,000 Amerindians of unknown sex.
[31] These figures are known to be incomplete.
[32] This figure has been adjusted for under-enumeration, the reported total being 1,341 (including 13 not tabulated by sex).
[33] Official estimates of total population for 1896 and 1927 were 3,462 thousand and 5,157 thousand respectively.
[34] These figures have been adjusted for under-enumeration, the reported totals being 6,208 in 1940; 9,907 in 1961 and 13,538 in 1972.
[35] Including 11,000 Indian and negro population of the interior who were not tabulated by sex.
[36] Excluding Amazonas, Mérida and Trujillo.
[37] Including jungle population who were not tabulated by sex.
[38] Excluding any adjustment for under-enumeration, which is believed to require an addition of 5.8%.
[39] Excluding Anguilla in 1980.

**A2    NORTH AMERICA: POPULATION OF MAJOR COUNTRIES BY SEX AND AGE GROUPS** (in thousands)

# CANADA

| | 1851 | | 1861 | | 1871 | | 1881 | | 1891 | | 1901 | | 1911 | |
|---|---|---|---|---|---|---|---|---|---|---|---|---|---|---|
| | M | F | M | F | M | F | M | F | M | F | M | F | M | F |
| 0–4 | 233 | 218 | 277 | 266 | 276 | 265 | 304 | 295 | 309 | 302 | 326 | 320 | 450 | 440 |
| 5–9 | 173 | 173 | 218 | 211 | 264 | 255 | 284 | 278 | 300 | 292 | 313 | 306 | 396 | 389 |
| 10–14 | 152 | 146 | 203 | 196 | 243 | 233 | 262 | 251 | 282 | 272 | 297 | 285 | 356 | 346 |
| 15–19 | 136 | 141 | 187 | 187 | 202 | 206 | 240 | 243 | 262 | 259 | 283 | 275 | 355 | 331 |
| 20–24 | 112 | 111 | 154 | 150 | 172 | 179 | 215 | 221 | 242 | 240 | 260 | 255 | 390 | 322 |
| 25–29 | 93 | 91 | 129 | 125 | 138 | 144 | 168 | 169 | 199 | 196 | 220 | 209 | 374 | 289 |
| 30–34 | 75 | 70 | 103 | 97 | 111 | 112 | 134 | 132 | 167 | 158 | 192 | 177 | 313 | 246 |
| 35–39 | 62 | 56 | 84 | 77 | 94 | 94 | 117 | 115 | 142 | 132 | 176 | 160 | 260 | 211 |
| 40–44 | 54 | 47 | 72 | 64 | 81 | 77 | 100 | 97 | 121 | 114 | 155 | 139 | 215 | 177 |
| 45–49 | 43 | 38 | 59 | 51 | 72 | 67 | 83 | 83 | 102 | 96 | 127 | 115 | 180 | 153 |
| 50–54 | 35 | 29 | 48 | 41 | 60 | 53 | 73 | 70 | 89 | 84 | 107 | 99 | 154 | 133 |
| 55–59 | 27 | 22 | 38 | 33 | 48 | 42 | 58 | 54 | 68 | 64 | 83 | 79 | 114 | 100 |
| 60–64 | 19 | 16 | 32 | 26 | 38 | 31 | 53 | 46 | 63 | 58 | 74 | 69 | 95 | 84 |
| 65–69 | 13 | 10 | 24 | 18 | 31 | 25 | 37 | 32 | 45 | 40 | 55 | 52 | 68 | 64 |
| 70–74 | | | | | | | 26 | 23 | 33 | 30 | 39 | 37 | 48 | 46 |
| 75–79 | 22 | 20 | 30 | 26 | 43 | 36 | 16 | 15 | 20 | 18 | 25 | 23 | 30 | 29 |
| 80 and over | | | | | | | 14 | 13 | 17 | 16 | 20 | 20 | 24 | 25 |
| Unknown | — | — | — | — | — | — | — | — | — | — | — | — | — | — |

| | 1921 | | 1931 | | 1941 | | 1951 | | 1961 | | 1971 | | 1981 | |
|---|---|---|---|---|---|---|---|---|---|---|---|---|---|---|
| | M | F | M | F | M | F | M | F | M | F | M | F | M | F |
| 0–4 | 534 | 525 | 543 | 531 | 535 | 518 | 879 | 843 | 1,154 | 1,102 | 930 | 887 | 914 | 869 |
| 5–9 | 529 | 521 | 573 | 560 | 529 | 517 | 714 | 684 | 1,064 | 1,016 | 1,152 | 1,102 | 912 | 865 |
| 10–14 | 462 | 452 | 543 | 531 | 556 | 545 | 575 | 556 | 948 | 908 | 1,181 | 1,129 | 985 | 936 |
| 15–19 | 405 | 400 | 526 | 514 | 565 | 555 | 532 | 526 | 729 | 704 | 1,074 | 1,040 | 1,182 | 1,133 |
| 20–24 | 352 | 361 | 464 | 448 | 518 | 514 | 538 | 551 | 587 | 597 | 942 | 948 | 1,174 | 1,170 |
| 25–29 | 349 | 340 | 410 | 376 | 488 | 479 | 553 | 578 | 614 | 595 | 801 | 783 | 1,084 | 1,093 |
| 30–34 | 344 | 310 | 368 | 341 | 432 | 412 | 513 | 530 | 644 | 627 | 661 | 645 | 1,021 | 1,017 |
| 35–39 | 343 | 291 | 359 | 329 | 396 | 363 | 504 | 496 | 631 | 640 | 645 | 619 | 822 | 808 |
| 40–44 | 287 | 241 | 348 | 298 | 349 | 328 | 446 | 423 | 560 | 559 | 641 | 622 | 675 | 663 |
| 45–49 | 238 | 199 | 322 | 264 | 333 | 303 | 388 | 356 | 516 | 500 | 613 | 626 | 635 | 621 |
| 50–54 | 196 | 167 | 268 | 221 | 316 | 276 | 340 | 322 | 443 | 420 | 519 | 534 | 622 | 622 |
| 55–59 | 149 | 133 | 199 | 168 | 275 | 232 | 293 | 278 | 362 | 244 | 472 | 482 | 568 | 612 |
| 60–64 | 127 | 113 | 157 | 138 | 219 | 189 | 264 | 242 | 293 | 291 | 382 | 395 | 462 | 517 |
| 65–69 | 91 | 82 | 121 | 110 | 163 | 145 | 228 | 205 | 240 | 247 | 296 | 324 | 391 | 454 |
| 70–74 | 61 | 57 | 89 | 83 | 111 | 106 | 160 | 155 | 196 | 206 | 206 | 252 | 281 | 352 |
| 75–79 | 36 | 36 | 50 | 49 | 67 | 68 | 94 | 94 | 134 | 140 | 140 | 186 | 180 | 252 |
| 80 and over | 28 | 31 | 35 | 39 | 50 | 57 | 69 | 81 | 104 | 123 | 140 | 201 | 159 | 292 |
| Unknown | — | — | — | — | — | — | — | — | — | — | — | — | — | — |

Abbreviations used throughout this table: **M** males **F** females

**A2     NORTH AMERICA: Population of Major Countries by Sex and Age Groups** (in thousands)

## COSTA RICA

| | 1864 M | 1864 F | 1883 M | 1883 F | 1892 M | 1892 F | 1927 M | 1927 F | 1950 M | 1950 F | 1963 M | 1963 F | 1973 M | 1973 F |
|---|---|---|---|---|---|---|---|---|---|---|---|---|---|---|
| 0–4 | 10 | 10 | 15 | 14 | 20 | 19 | 37 | 37 | 67 | 65 | 126 | 123 | 131 | 128 |
| 5–9 | 9 | 9 | 13 | 13 | 17 | 17 | 32 | 31 | 57 | 55 | 110 | 107 | 147 | 142 |
| 10–14 | 8 | 7 | 12 | 10 | 15 | 14 | 29 | 29 | 50 | 49 | 86 | 84 | 141 | 136 |
| 15–19 | 6 | 7 | 9 | 9 | 12 | 12 | 25 | 27 | 40 | 44 | 64 | 66 | 111 | 111 |
| 20–24 | 5 | 6 | 8 | 9 | 11 | 12 | 22 | 22 | 38 | 39 | 51 | 53 | 82 | 85 |
| 25–29 | 5 | 6 | 8 | 8 | 11 | 11 | 18 | 19 | 29 | 30 | 41 | 44 | 61 | 63 |
| 30–34 | 4 | 5 | 7 | 7 | 10 | 10 | 15 | 14 | 24 | 24 | 38 | 39 | 50 | 50 |
| 35–39 | 3 | 3 | 5 | 5 | 7 | 6 | 14 | 13 | 23 | 24 | 33 | 34 | 44 | 47 |
| 40–44 | 2 | 3 | 4 | 5 | 6 | 6 | 13 | 11 | 18 | 18 | 27 | 27 | 40 | 40 |
| 45–49 | 2 | 2 | 3 | 3 | 4 | 4 | 10 | 8 | 14 | 14 | 23 | 22 | 32 | 32 |
| 50–54 | 2 | 2 | 3 | 3 | 4 | 4 | 8 | 7 | 12 | 12 | 21 | 20 | 27 | 27 |
| 55–59 | 1 | 1 | 1 | 2 | 2 | 2 | 5 | 4 | 8 | 8 | 13 | 13 | 20 | 20 |
| 60–64 | 1 | 1 | 2 | 2 | 2 | 2 | 4 | 4 | 8 | 7 | 13 | 13 | 19 | 19 |
| 65–69 | - - | - - | 1 | 1 | 1 | 1 | 2 | 2 | 5 | 4 | 7 | 8 | 12 | 12 |
| 70–74 | - - | - - | - - | 1 | 1 | 1 | 2 | 2 | 3 | 3 | 6 | 6 | 10 | 10 |
| 75–79 | - - | - - | - - | - - | - - | - - | } 2 | 2 { | 2 | 2 | } 7 | 8 { | 5 | 5 |
| 80 and over | - - | - - | - - | - - | 1 | 1 | | | 2 | 2 | | | 6 | 6 |
| Unknown | - - | - - | - - | - - | - - | - - | - - | - - | - - | - - | 1 | 1 | — | — |

## CUBA

| | 1899 M | 1899 F | 1907 M | 1907 F | 1919 M | 1919 F | 1943 M | 1943 F | 1953 M | 1953 F | 1970 M | 1970 F | 1981 M | 1981 F |
|---|---|---|---|---|---|---|---|---|---|---|---|---|---|---|
| 0–4 | | | 173 | 169 | 208 | 202 | 323 | 305 | 376 | 361 | 606 | 579 | 366 | 348 |
| 5–9 | } 293 | 284 { | 114 | 111 | 222 | 215 | 294 | 280 | 364 | 349 | 598 | 571 | 535 | 511 |
| 10–14 | | | 93 | 88 | 191 | 186 | 276 | 261 | 340 | 328 | 417 | 396 | 610 | 579 |
| 15–19 | 84 | 94 | 117 | 119 | 150 | 147 | 227 | 228 | 269 | 289 | 390 | 378 | 589 | 573 |
| 20–24 | 79 | 74 | 125 | 109 | 110 | 89 | 240 | 244 | 264 | 257 | 365 | 356 | 404 | 402 |
| 25–29 | 73 | 64 | 100 | 85 | 128 | 111 | 208 | 202 | 223 | 230 | 332 | 320 | 357 | 362 |
| 30–34 | 64 | 55 | } 139 | 114 { | 122 | 94 | 181 | 173 | 203 | 201 | 287 | 275 | 345 | 348 |
| 35–39 | } 101 | 84 { | | | 105 | 80 | 189 | 150 | 190 | 193 | 234 | 230 | 310 | 312 |
| 40–44 | | | 105 | 83 | 76 | 56 | 139 | 97 | 183 | 164 | 216 | 212 | 270 | 267 |
| 45–49 | 64 | 53 | | | 61 | 44 | 91 | 75 | 160 | 133 | 191 | 183 | 220 | 222 |
| 50–54 | | | } 60 | 50 { | 51 | 42 | 106 | 79 | 121 | 89 | 179 | 167 | 199 | 196 |
| 55–59 | } 37 | 31 { | | | 35 | 27 | 80 | 62 | 76 | 63 | 162 | 153 | 173 | 171 |
| 60–64 | | | | | | | 60 | 46 | 83 | 69 | 142 | 122 | 159 | 154 |
| 65–69 | | | | | | | 33 | 27 | 57 | 48 | 127 | 101 | 136 | 133 |
| 70–74 | } 19 | 19 | 48 | 46 | 72 | 66 { | 22 | 20 | 36 | 31 | 52 | 40 | 108 | 104 |
| 75–79 | | | | | | | 13 | 13 | 19 | 17 | 43 | 40 | 80 | 73 |
| 80 and over | | | | | | | 15 | 17 | 18 | 21 | 50 | 52 | 55 | 54 |
| Unknown | - - | - - | 1 | 1 | 1 | 1 | — | — | 2 | 1 | — | — | — | — |

A2    **NORTH AMERICA: Population of Major Countries by Sex and Age Groups** (in thousands)

## DOMINICAN REPUBLIC

| | 1920 M | 1920 F | | 1935 M | 1935 F | 1950 M | 1950 F | 1960 M | 1960 F | 1970 M | 1970 F |
|---|---|---|---|---|---|---|---|---|---|---|---|
| 0–6 | 109 | 105 | 0–4 | 124 | 121 | 189 | 186 | 283 | 277 | 344 | 337 |
| 7–14 | 104 | 97 | 5–9 | 124 | 120 | 151 | 147 | 247 | 241 | 330 | 326 |
| 15–20 | 58 | 65 | 10–14 | 102 | 94 | 142 | 135 | 203 | 190 | 285 | 282 |
| 21–60 | 161 | 167 | 15–19 | 74 | 79 | 102 | 124 | 133 | 153 | 212 | 236 |
| 61 and over | 15 | 14 | 20–24 | 64 | 70 | 105 | 109 | 121 | 135 | 156 | 173 |
| Unknown | — | — | | | | | | | | | |
| | | | 25–29 | 59 | 58 | 78 | 79 | 104 | 109 | 117 | 128 |
| | | | 30–34 | 45 | 41 | 60 | 60 | 95 | 93 | 104 | 106 |
| | | | 35–39 | 42 | 37 | 60 | 55 | 78 | 74 | 102 | 104 |
| | | | 40–44 | 33 | 29 | 48 | 43 | 66 | 58 | 91 | 82 |
| | | | 45–49 | 23 | 20 | 37 | 31 | 52 | 45 | 63 | 58 |
| | | | 50–54 | 18 | 18 | 31 | 29 | 47 | 42 | 58 | 50 |
| | | | 55–59 | 10 | 9 | 21 | 15 | 29 | 22 | 35 | 29 |
| | | | 60–64 | 13 | 12 | 20 | 19 | 32 | 29 | 38 | 34 |
| | | | 65–69 | 6 | 5 | 10 | 9 | 14 | 12 | 20 | 18 |
| | | | 70–74 | 6 | 7 | 8 | 10 | 14 | 13 | 20 | 20 |
| | | | 75–79 | 3 | 3 | 4 | 4 | } 18 | 19 { | 8 | 8 |
| | | | 80 and over | 5 | 6 | 7 | 10 | | | 14 | 17 |
| | | | Unknown | — | — | - - | - - | — | — | — | — |

## EL SALVADOR

| | 1930 M | 1930 F | | 1950 M | 1950 F | 1961 M | 1961 F | 1971 M | 1971 F |
|---|---|---|---|---|---|---|---|---|---|
| 0–4 | 104 | 103 | 0–4 | 146 | 143 | 218 | 214 | 301 | 297 |
| 5–7 | 62 | 60 | 5–9 | 127 | 124 | 193 | 190 | 296 | 285 |
| 8–14 | 130 | 118 | 10–14 | 116 | 108 | 160 | 150 | 242 | 230 |
| 15–17 | 40 | 45 | 15–19 | 97 | 102 | 117 | 125 | 175 | 184 |
| 18–22 | 78 | 85 | 20–24 | 84 | 93 | 101 | 113 | 143 | 153 |
| 23–29 | 81 | 86 | 25–29 | 66 | 74 | 81 | 92 | 109 | 121 |
| 30–39 | 96 | 94 | 30–34 | 55 | 57 | 73 | 78 | 99 | 101 |
| 40–49 | 58 | 57 | 35–39 | 54 | 58 | 66 | 73 | 91 | 95 |
| 50–59 | 37 | 39 | 40–44 | 44 | 45 | 55 | 57 | 74 | 77 |
| 60–69 | 21 | 20 | 45–49 | 34 | 35 | 44 | 46 | 59 | 63 |
| 70–79 | 6 | 8 | 50–54 | 31 | 32 | 37 | 39 | 48 | 51 |
| 80 and over | 3 | 5 | 55–59 | 17 | 19 | 25 | 26 | 34 | 36 |
| Unknown | — | — | 60–64 | 19 | 19 | 29 | 29 | 34 | 34 |
| | | | 65–69 | 10 | 10 | 14 | 15 | 21 | 23 |
| | | | 70–74 | 7 | 8 | 10 | 11 | 18 | 19 |
| | | | 75–79 | 4 | 4 | 6 | 7 | 9 | 10 |
| | | | 80 and over | 5 | 7 | 7 | 9 | 9 | 13 |
| | | | Unknown | 1 | 1 | 1 | - - | - - | - - |

**A2      NORTH AMERICA: Population of Major Countries by Sex and Age Groups** (in thousands)

## GUATEMALA

|            | 1893 | | 1921 | |
|------------|------|------|------|------|
|            | M | F | M | F |
| 0–4        | [271][1] | | 153 | 150 |
| 6–7        | [233][1] | | 59 | 57 |
| 8–14       | | | 175 | 163 |
| 15–18      | 124 | | 81 | 83 |
| 19–30      | 324 | | 226 | 253 |
| 31–40      | 167 | | 126 | 129 |
| 41–50      | 165 | | 78 | 83 |
| 51–60      | | | 49 | 50 |
| 61 and over | 100 | | 45 | 45 |
| Unknown    | — | | — | — |

|            | 1940 | | 1950 | | 1964 | | 1973 | | 1981 | |
|------------|------|------|------|------|------|------|------|------|------|------|
|            | M | F | M | F | M | F | M | F | M | F |
| 0–4        | 260 | 253 | 240 | 230 | 379 | 370 | 440 | 431 | 535 | 522 |
| 5–9        | 250 | 237 | 195 | 185 | 335 | 323 | 395 | 383 | 456 | 445 |
| 10–14      | 227 | 204 | 173 | 156 | 281 | 262 | 348 | 330 | 386 | 371 |
| 15–19      | 168 | 174 | 150 | 156 | 219 | 219 | 275 | 286 | 314 | 335 |
| 20–24      | 142 | 135 | 135 | 142 | 175 | 177 | 231 | 239 | 262 | 286 |
| 25–29      | 120 | 127 | 110 | 110 | 148 | 150 | 169 | 178 | 205 | 222 |
| 30–34      | 102 | 104 | 85 | 78 | 137 | 133 | 141 | 141 | 175 | 176 |
| 35–39      | 94 | 95 | 78 | 78 | 121 | 120 | 131 | 137 | 145 | 153 |
| 40–44      | 79 | 77 | 57 | 61 | 96 | 90 | 116 | 113 | 124 | 122 |
| 45–49      | 63 | 60 | 53 | 51 | 75 | 68 | 93 | 91 | 102 | 104 |
| 50–54      | 44 | 46 | 42 | 43 | 59 | 60 | 75 | 72 | 92 | 91 |
| 55–59      | 33 | 33 | 31 | 28 | 43 | 41 | 52 | 48 | 65 | 63 |
| 60–64      | 34 | 34 | 28 | 26 | 45 | 42 | 49 | 46 | 61 | 55 |
| 65–69      | 19 | 17 | 15 | 13 | 25 | 23 | 28 | 28 | 36 | 35 |
| 70–74      | 9 | 11 | 8 | 9 | 16 | 16 | 22 | 22 | 25 | 25 |
| 75–79      | 5 | 6 | 5 | 5 | 10 | 9 | 12 | 12 | 16 | 16 |
| 80 and over | 8 | 11 | 6 | 8 | 9 | 10 | 12 | 13 | 17 | 18 |
| Unknown    | 1 | 2 | — | — | - - | - - | — | — | — | — |

*See p. 29 for footnotes*

**A2    NORTH AMERICA: Population of Major Countries by Sex and Age Groups** (in thousands)

## HAITI

| | 1950 | | 1971 | | 1982 | |
|---|---|---|---|---|---|---|
| | M | F | M | F | M | F |
| 0–4 | 186 | 189 | 301 | 303 | 357 | 373 |
| 5–9 | 199 | 201 | 295 | 300 | 329 | 343 |
| 10–14 | 203 | 194 | 295 | 290 | 289 | 289 |
| 15–19 | 154 | 154 | 230 | 245 | 252 | 260 |
| 20–24 | 121 | 146 | 159 | 188 | 213 | 244 |
| 25–29 | 125 | 152 | 135 | 168 | 173 | 220 |
| 30–34 | 85 | 104 | 106 | 132 | 137 | 149 |
| 35–39 | 108 | 122 | 120 | 146 | 128 | 141 |
| 40–44 | 81 | 77 | 106 | 107 | 110 | 122 |
| 45–49 | 68 | 65 | 95 | 91 | 107 | 104 |
| 50–54 | 51 | 48 | 70 | 65 | 93 | 84 |
| 55–59 | 28 | 29 | 48 | 46 | 59 | 56 |
| 60–64 | 34 | 37 | 45 | 49 | 62 | 62 |
| 65–69 | 19 | 22 | 31 | 37 | 38 | 40 |
| 70–74 | 18 | 22 | 25 | 31 | 36 | 38 |
| 75–79 | 8 | 10 | 12 | 17 | 21 | 26 |
| 80 and over | 10 | 15 | 16 | 27 | 45 | 54 |
| Unknown | 6 | 5 | - - | - - | — | — |

## HONDURAS

| | 1930 | | 1940 | | 1950 | | 1961 | | 1974 | |
|---|---|---|---|---|---|---|---|---|---|---|
| | M | F | M | F | M | F | M | F | M | F |
| 0–4 | 71 | 69 | 95 | 94 | 110 | 106 | 181 | 176 | 246 | 240 |
| 5–9 | 62 | 61 | 76 | 73 | 91 | 87 | 157 | 151 | 216 | 209 |
| 10–14 | 51 | 48 | 69 | 64 | 84 | 78 | 121 | 114 | 187 | 180 |
| 15–19 | 47 | 47 | 60 | 69 | 70 | 69 | 89 | 95 | 140 | 149 |
| 20–24 | 40 | 43 | 50 | 52 | 61 | 63 | 76 | 82 | 108 | 120 |
| 25–29 | 31 | 35 | 40 | 44 | 50 | 51 | 62 | 68 | 79 | 88 |
| 30–34 | 27 | 30 | 35 | 35 | 41 | 42 | 55 | 56 | 68 | 70 |
| 35–39 | 23 | 23 | 30 | 30 | 38 | 39 | 47 | 49 | 62 | 66 |
| 40–44 | 20 | 20 | 27 | 26 | 32 | 32 | 37 | 37 | 51 | 53 |
| 45–49 | 15 | 14 | 20 | 19 | 27 | 27 | 31 | 31 | 43 | 44 |
| 50–54 | 11 | 13 | 16 | 16 | 23 | 25 | 25 | 26 | 34 | 35 |
| 55–59 | 9 | 9 | 12 | 12 | 17 | 18 | 18 | 18 | 24 | 25 |
| 60–64 | { | | 11 | 11 | 16 | 16 | 18 | 18 | 23 | 22 |
| 65–69 | | | 6 | 6 | 10 | 10 | 10 | 9 | 14 | 14 |
| 70–74 | 17 | 18 | 4 | 4 | 6 | 7 | 6 | 6 | 11 | 11 |
| 75–79 | | | } 5 | 5 { | 5 | 5 | 4 | 4 | 6 | 6 |
| 80 and over | | | | | 5 | 6 | 3 | 4 | 5 | 6 |
| Unknown | 2 | 2 | 1 | 1 | — | — | 1 | - - | — | — |

A2      **NORTH AMERICA: Population of Major Countries by Sex and Age Groups** (in thousands)

## JAMAICA

|             | 1881 |    | 1891 |    | 1911 |    | 1921 |    |
|             | M    | F  | M    | F  | M    | F  | M    | F  |
|-------------|------|----|------|----|------|----|------|----|
| 0–4         | 38   | 38 | 41   | 42 | 57   | 58 | 56   | 56 |
| 5–9         | 37   | 38 | 39   | 40 | 59   | 59 | 60   | 60 |
| 10–14       | 36   | 36 | 44   | 42 | 50   | 48 | 53   | 53 |
| 15–19       | 27   | 29 | 32   | 35 | 39   | 41 | 41   | 47 |
| 20–24       | 28   | 30 | 29   | 35 | 37   | 45 | 36   | 49 |
| 25–34       | 44   | 47 | 42   | 53 | 57   | 69 | 50   | 67 |
| 35–44       | 29   | 30 | 32   | 36 | 41   | 45 | 42   | 51 |
| 45–54       | 18   | 19 | 24   | 24 | 28   | 32 | 32   | 34 |
| 55–64       | 11   | 13 | 11   | 13 | 17   | 20 | 18   | 21 |
| 65–74       | 6    | 7  | 5    | 7  | 9    | 11 | 9    | 11 |
| 75 and over | 5    | 6  | 5    | 7  | 4    | 6  | 5    | 7  |
| Unknown     | 4    | 4  | 1    | -- | --   | -- | --   | -- |

|             | 1943 |    | 1953 |    | 1960 |    | 1970 |    | 1982 |    |
|             | M    | F  | M    | F  | M    | F  | M    | F  | M    | F  |
|-------------|------|----|------|----|------|----|------|----|------|----|
| 0–4         | 78   | 78 | 108  | 109| 135  | 133| 145  | 142| 135  | 133|
| 5–9         | 78   | 78 | 102  | 83 | 111  | 110| 151  | 150| 143  | 142|
| 10–14       | 70   | 70 | 88   | 70 | 87   | 87 | 123  | 121| 146  | 143|
| 15–19       | 55   | 61 | 63   | 71 | 68   | 76 | 81   | 85 | 131  | 132|
| 20–24       | 53   | 62 | 59   | 73 | 57   | 68 | 59   | 67 | 102  | 111|
| 25–29       | 50   | 57 | 51   | 66 | 50   | 61 | 49   | 53 | 74   | 81 |
| 30–34       | 46   | 48 | 46   | 52 | 43   | 51 | 39   | 42 | 59   | 62 |
| 35–39       | 39   | 41 | 43   | 51 | 41   | 49 | 37   | 43 | 47   | 50 |
| 40–44       | 35   | 35 | 44   | 42 | 40   | 42 | 37   | 40 | 42   | 43 |
| 45–49       | 25   | 25 | 33   | 35 | 39   | 39 | 33   | 36 | 35   | 37 |
| 50–54       | 20   | 22 | 29   | 31 | 33   | 34 | 32   | 35 | 36   | 39 |
| 55–59       | 14   | 16 | 17   | 19 | 24   | 25 | 29   | 30 | 29   | 30 |
| 60–64       | 13   | 16 | 15   | 18 | 18   | 20 | 25   | 27 | 27   | 31 |
| 65–69       | 8    | 10 | 8    | 11 | 10   | 13 | 19   | 20 | 25   | 26 |
| 70–74       | 7    | 9  | 7    | 11 | 8    | 11 | 12   | 14 | 21   | 23 |
| 75–79       | 3    | 5  | 4    | 6  | 5    | 8  | 7    | 9  | 13   | 15 |
| 80 and over | 4    | 7  | 4    | 8  | 5    | 10 | 7    | 13 | 11   | 19 |
| Unknown     | --   | -- | --   | 1  | —    | —  | —    | —  | —    | —  |

**A2    NORTH AMERICA: Population of Major Countries by Sex and Age Groups** (in thousands)

## MEXICO

| | 1895 M | 1895 F | 1900 M | 1900 F | 1910 M | 1910 F | 1921 M | 1921 F | 1930[1] M | 1930[1] F |
|---|---|---|---|---|---|---|---|---|---|---|
| 0–4 | 1,094 | 1,060 | 1,190 | 1,157 | 1,366 | 1,297 | 946 | 928 | [1,527] | [1,483] |
| 5–9 | 896 | 840 | 928 | 870 | 1,102 | 1,046 | 940 | 899 | [911] | [883] |
| 10–14 | 692 | 661 | 739 | 705 | 816 | 779 | 935 | 858 | [882] | [804] |
| 15–19 | 605 | 732 | 670 | 795 | 718 | 852 | 728 | 822 | [792] | [892] |
| 20–24 | } 1,119 | 1,243 | 1,179 | 1,325 { | 627 | 712 | 610 | 704 | [735] | [842] |
| 25–29 | | | | | 699 | 787 | 547 | 655 | [687] | [773] |
| 30–34 | } 820 | 802 | 877 | 874 { | 420 | 397 | 468 | 526 | [543] | [581] |
| 35–39 | | | | | 534 | 555 | 445 | 469 | [501] | [529] |
| 40–44 | } 820 | 816 | 909 | 897 { | 270 | 249 | 343 | 388 | [380] | [427] |
| 45–49 | | | | | 335 | 354 | 268 | 270 | [314] | [321] |
| 50–54 | | | | | 148 | 136 | 219 | 249 | [255] | [289] |
| 55–59 | | | | | 226 | 236 | 141 | 138 | [163] | [162] |
| 60–64 | } 227 | 190 | 250 | 219 { | 89 | 78 | } 346 | 354 | [427] | [455] |
| 65–69 | | | | | 89 | 84 | | | | |
| 70–74 | | | | | 31 | 28 | | | | |
| 75–79 | | | | | 35 | 35 | | | | |
| 80 and over | | | | | 21 | 21 | | | | |
| Unknown | 8 | 8 | 11 | 13 | 9 | 10 | 70 | 69 | 3 | — |

| | 1940 M | 1940 F | 1950 M | 1950 F | 1960 M | 1960 F | 1970 M | 1970 F | 1980 M | 1980 F |
|---|---|---|---|---|---|---|---|---|---|---|
| 0–4 | 1,448 | 1,416 | 2,000 | 1,970 | 2,936 | 2,840 | 4,152 | 4,016 | 4,699 | 4,649 |
| 5–9 | 1,441 | 1,387 | 1,865 | 1,809 | 2,706 | 2,611 | 3,935 | 3,788 | 5,173 | 5,111 |
| 10–14 | 1,247 | 1,156 | 1,600 | 1,510 | 2,234 | 2,124 | 3,271 | 3,125 | 4,575 | 4,520 |
| 15–19 | 970 | 1,027 | 1,249 | 1,384 | 1,739 | 1,796 | 2,491 | 2,563 | 3,767 | 3,890 |
| 20–24 | 740 | 808 | 1,067 | 1,233 | 1,405 | 1,542 | 1,930 | 2,102 | 2,972 | 3,182 |
| 25–29 | 752 | 839 | 982 | 1,038 | 1,196 | 1,309 | 1,575 | 1,685 | 2,325 | 2,479 |
| 30–34 | 634 | 684 | 699 | 733 | 1,009 | 1,043 | 1,285 | 1,311 | 1,886 | 1,952 |
| 35–39 | 671 | 701 | 748 | 798 | 959 | 962 | 1,235 | 1,276 | 1,665 | 1,742 |
| 40–44 | 450 | 488 | 587 | 622 | 674 | 687 | 959 | 974 | 1,360 | 1,385 |
| 45–49 | 363 | 395 | 535 | 539 | 610 | 623 | 830 | 807 | 1,135 | 1,181 |
| 50–54 | 284 | 317 | 405 | 423 | 527 | 536 | 590 | 602 | 913 | 951 |
| 55–59 | 206 | 220 | 261 | 267 | 405 | 395 | 502 | 510 | 733 | 733 |
| 60–64 | 205 | 215 | 265 | 289 | 372 | 373 | 451 | 467 | 542 | 573 |
| 65–69 | 111 | 115 | 165 | 169 | 203 | 211 | 345 | 357 | 417 | 458 |
| 70–74 | 79 | 84 | 114 | 127 | 161 | 172 | 242 | 246 | 339 | 366 |
| 75–79 | 44 | 45 | 63 | 66 | 91 | 97 | 120 | 133 | 229 | 252 |
| 80 and over | 50 | 60 | 72 | 90 | 121 | 139 | 152 | 196 | 220 | 281 |
| Unknown | 3 | 2 | 21 | 26 | 65 | 49 | — | — | 93 | 100 |

*See p. 29 for footnotes*

**A2　　NORTH AMERICA: Population of Major Countries by Sex and Age Groups** (in thousands)

## NICARAGUA

| | 1920 | | 1940 | | 1950 | | 1963 | | 1971 | |
|---|---|---|---|---|---|---|---|---|---|---|
| | M | F | M | F | M | F | M | F | M | F |
| 0–4 | | | 79 | 81 | 86 | 83 | 141 | 137 | 163 | 159 |
| 5–9 | | 202 | 69 | 70 | 79 | 75 | 135 | 130 | 158 | 156 |
| 10–14 | | | 61 | 62 | 70 | 64 | 101 | 96 | 135 | 131 |
| 15–19 | | 151 | 53 | 54 | 53 | 58 | 71 | 77 | 98 | 106 |
| 20–24 | | | 42 | 44 | 47 | 52 | 58 | 64 | 73 | 82 |
| 25–29 | | 117 | 36 | 39 | 40 | 44 | 51 | 57 | 57 | 65 |
| 30–34 | | | 30 | 31 | 29 | 31 | 40 | 42 | 45 | 49 |
| 35–39 | | 74 | 27 | 30 | 30 | 32 | 40 | 43 | 46 | 51 |
| 40–44 | | | 22 | 25 | 21 | 23 | 29 | 30 | 36 | 37 |
| 45–49 | | 46 | 16 | 18 | 18 | 19 | 24 | 25 | 29 | 31 |
| 50–54 | | | 12 | 15 | 16 | 17 | 20 | 21 | 23 | 25 |
| 55–59 | | 29 | 9 | 11 | 9 | 10 | 13 | 14 | 16 | 17 |
| 60–64 | | | 8 | 11 | 10 | 11 | 15 | 16 | 15 | 17 |
| 65–69 | | | 5 | 5 | 5 | 5 | | 13 | 8 | 9 |
| 70–74 | | 17 | 3 | 4 | 5 | | 13 | 15 | 8 | 9 |
| 75–79 | | | 2 | 2 | 2 | 3 | | | 4 | 5 |
| 80 and over | | | 2 | 3 | 3 | 4 | 7 | 10 | 5 | 6 |
| Unknown | | 2 | - - | - - | — | — | — | — | — | — |

## PANAMA

| | 1920 | | | 1940 | | 1950 | | 1960 | | 1970 | | 1980 | |
|---|---|---|---|---|---|---|---|---|---|---|---|---|---|
| | M | F | | M | F | M | F | M | F | M | F | M | F |
| 0–5 | 39 | 39 | 0–4 | 42 | 41 | 62 | 61 | 92 | 90 | 117 | 114 | 118 | 115 |
| 6–21 | 71 | 75 | 5–9 | 38 | 37 | 54 | 53 | 79 | 77 | 109 | 107 | 122 | 121 |
| 22–60 | 112 | 97 | 10–14 | 33 | 31 | 43 | 42 | 66 | 64 | 88 | 85 | 118 | 111 |
| 61 and over | 6 | 6 | 15–19 | 27 | 30 | 36 | 37 | 53 | 54 | 72 | 73 | 100 | 100 |
| | | | 20–24 | 29 | 28 | 33 | 33 | 45 | 46 | 62 | 63 | 79 | 82 |
| | 1930 | | 25–29 | 26 | 25 | 31 | 30 | 38 | 38 | 51 | 51 | 67 | 68 |
| | M | F | 30–34 | 19 | 16 | 27 | 25 | 33 | 32 | 42 | 41 | 59 | 59 |
| | | | 35–39 | 17 | 16 | 25 | 23 | 30 | 29 | 37 | 36 | 48 | 48 |
| 0–6 | 46 | 45 | 40–44 | 28 | 23 | 18 | 15 | 27 | 24 | 32 | 29 | 40 | 41 |
| 7–15 | 53 | 49 | 45–49 | | | 14 | 13 | 23 | 21 | 28 | 25 | 34 | 32 |
| 16–20 | 23 | 26 | | | | | | | | | | | |
| 21–30 | 39 | 40 | 50–54 | 18 | 14 | 12 | 11 | 17 | 15 | 25 | 22 | 29 | 29 |
| 31–40 | 32 | 29 | 55–59 | | | 9 | 8 | 13 | 12 | 20 | 18 | 24 | 23 |
| | | | 60–64 | 9} | 8 | 9 | 8 | 11 | 10 | 15 | 13 | 22 | 20 |
| 41–50 | 22 | 18 | 65–69 | | | 5 | 5 | 7 | 7 | 10 | 10 | 16 | 15 |
| 51–60 | 11 | 9 | 70–74 | | | 3 | 3 | 6 | 5 | 7 | 7 | 11 | 10 |
| 61–70 | 5 | 4 | | 3 | 3 | | | | | | | | |
| 71–80 | 2 | 2 | 75–79 | | | 2 | 2 | 3 | 3 | 9 | 10 | 7 | 7 |
| 81 and over | - - | 1 | 80 and over | 1 | 2 | 2 | 2 | 3 | 4 | | | 6 | 8 |
| | | | Unknown | — | — | 1 | - - | — | — | — | — | 3 | 3 |
| Unknown | 7 | 4 | | | | | | | | | | | |

**A2    NORTH AMERICA: Population of Major Countries by Sex and Age Groups** (in thousands)

## PUERTO RICO

| | 1899 M | 1899 F | 1940 M | 1940 F | 1950 M | 1950 F | 1960 M | 1960 F | 1970 M | 1970 F | 1980 M | 1980 F |
|---|---|---|---|---|---|---|---|---|---|---|---|---|
| 0–4 | 77 | 74 | 142 | 138 | 185 | 181 | 180 | 175 | 161 | 157 | 173 | 167 |
| 5–9 | 73 | 71 | 128 | 124 | 161 | 157 | 166 | 162 | 171 | 167 | 168 | 162 |
| 10–14 | 65 | 59 | 114 | 113 | 139 | 132 | 162 | 159 | 170 | 165 | 172 | 166 |
| 15–19 | 43 | 50 | 99 | 107 | 109 | 111 | 123 | 124 | 144 | 148 | 168 | 169 |
| 20–24 | 42 | 47 | 102 | 104 | 91 | 102 | 80 | 92 | 108 | 126 | 129 | 143 |
| 25–29 | 39 | 45 | 72 | 76 | 76 | 82 | 62 | 74 | 85 | 98 | 111 | 125 |
| 30–34 | 31 | 33 | 52 | 51 | 67 | 65 | 59 | 68 | 73 | 83 | 107 | 122 |
| 35–39 | 24 | 23 | 51 | 51 | 67 | 66 | 62 | 69 | 68 | 77 | 91 | 103 |
| 40–44 | 22 | 22 | 44 | 42 | 48 | 43 | 53 | 54 | 62 | 67 | 78 | 88 |
| 45–49 | 13 | 13 | 36 | 33 | 40 | 36 | 54 | 52 | 59 | 63 | 68 | 77 |
| 50–54 | 16 | 17 | 31 | 26 | 37 | 35 | 40 | 35 | 53 | 53 | 61 | 69 |
| 55–59 | 8 | 7 | 19 | 16 | 25 | 22 | 34 | 31 | 49 | 47 | 57 | 62 |
| 60–64 | 8 | 10 | 18 | 18 | 26 | 23 | 29 | 29 | 41 | 41 | 51 | 54 |
| 65–69 | 4 | 3 | 12 | 13 | 16 | 17 | 25 | 24 | 33 | 33 | 46 | 49 |
| 70–74 | 3 | 4 | 8 | 9 | 11 | 11 | 16 | 15 | 22 | 22 | 32 | 34 |
| 75–79 | 1 | 1 | 9 | 12 | 14 | 17 | 10 | 11 | 14 | 15 | 22 | 24 |
| 80 and over | 2 | 3 | | | | | 9 | 12 | 17 | 22 | 21 | 26 |
| Unknown | - - | - - | - - | 1 | — | — | — | — | — | — | — | — |

## TRINIDAD AND TOBAGO

| | 1891 M | 1891 F | 1901 M | 1901 F | 1911 M | 1911 F | 1921 M | 1921 F |
|---|---|---|---|---|---|---|---|---|
| 0–4 | 13 | 13 | 16 | 17 | 21 | 20 | 21 | 21 |
| 5–9 | 12 | 12 | 16 | 15 | 19 | 19 | 22 | 22 |
| 10–14 | 11 | 10 | 14 | 13 | 17 | 16 | 20 | 19 |
| 15–19 | 8 | 9 | 12 | 12 | 14 | 15 | 16 | 18 |
| 20–24 | 11 | 11 | 15 | 14 | 17 | 18 | 17 | 19 |
| 25–29 | 13 | 10 | 15 | 13 | 18 | 16 | 15 | 16 |
| 30–34 | 11 | 8 | 13 | 10 | 15 | 12 | 14 | 14 |
| 35–39 | 10 | 7 | 12 | 9 | 13 | 11 | 14 | 12 |
| 40–44 | 9 | 6 | 10 | 7 | 12 | 9 | 14 | 10 |
| 45–49 | 6 | 4 | 7 | 5 | 9 | 6 | 10 | 8 |
| 50–54 | 5 | 4 | 6 | 4 | 7 | 5 | 8 | 6 |
| 55–59 | 2 | 2 | 3 | 2 | 4 | 3 | 4 | 4 |
| 60–64 | 3 | 2 | 3 | 3 | 4 | 3 | 4 | 4 |
| 65–69 | 1 | 1 | 1 | 1 | 2 | 2 | 2 | 2 |
| 70–74 | 1 | 1 | 1 | 1 | 1 | 1 | 2 | 2 |
| 75–79 | - - | - - | 1 | 1 | 1 | 1 | 1 | 1 |
| 80 and over | 1 | 1 | 1 | 1 | 1 | 1 | 1 | 1 |
| Unknown | - - | - - | - - | - - | — | — | — | — |

**A2**    **NORTH AMERICA: Population of Major Countries by Sex and Age Groups** (in thousands)

## TRINIDAD AND TOBAGO

| | 1931 | | 1946 | | 1960 | | 1970 | | 1980 | |
|---|---|---|---|---|---|---|---|---|---|---|
| | M | F | M | F | M | F | M | F | M | F |
| 0–4 | 23 | 24 | 44 | 44 | 66 | 65 | 61 | 65 | 63 | 62 |
| 5–9 | 25 | 25 | 34 | 34 | 59 | 59 | 73 | 59 | 61 | 57 |
| 10–14 | 22 | 21 | 27 | 27 | 51 | 51 | 63 | 51 | 60 | 60 |
| 15–19 | 19 | 22 | 23 | 26 | 39 | 41 | 51 | 41 | 65 | 66 |
| 20–24 | 20 | 22 | 25 | 26 | 32 | 33 | 40 | 33 | 55 | 55 |
| 25–29 | 17 | 18 | 23 | 23 | 25 | 27 | 28 | 27 | 44 | 44 |
| 30–34 | 15 | 15 | 21 | 20 | 24 | 25 | 24 | 25 | 35 | 35 |
| 35–39 | 13 | 14 | 19 | 19 | 23 | 24 | 21 | 24 | 28 | 28 |
| 40–44 | 13 | 12 | 16 | 15 | 22 | 20 | 20 | 20 | 23 | 23 |
| 45–49 | 12 | 10 | 13 | 12 | 19 | 18 | 20 | 18 | 18 | 19 |
| 50–54 | 9 | 8 | 9 | 9 | 16 | 14 | 18 | 14 | 17 | 19 |
| 55–59 | 6 | 5 | 8 | 7 | 12 | 11 | 14 | 11 | 16 | 15 |
| 60–64 | 5 | 5 | 6 | 6 | 8 | 8 | 11 | 8 | 14 | 13 |
| 65–69 | 3 | 3 | 5 | 6 | 6 | 8 | 8 | 8 | 11 | 13 |
| 70–74 | 2 | 2 | 3 | 4 | 4 | 5 | 5 | 5 | 7 | 9 |
| 75–79 | 1 | 1 | 1 | 2 | 2 | 3 | 2 | 3 | 4 | 6 |
| 80 and over | 1 | 2 | 1 | 2 | 2 | 3 | 2 | 3 | 3 | 5 |
| Unknown | — | — | — | — | — | — | — | — | 4 | 3 |

## USA (whites)[2]

| | 1790 | | 1800 | | 1810 | | 1820 | |
|---|---|---|---|---|---|---|---|---|
| | M | F | M | F | M | F | M | F |
| 0–9 | 802 | ... | 764 | 715 | 1,035 | 981 | 1,345 | 1,281 |
| 10–15 | | ... | 353 | 324 | 468 | 448 | 613 | 605 |
| 16–25 | | ... | 393 | 401 | 548 | 562 | 776 | 781 |
| 26–44 | 813 | ... | 432 | 412 | 572 | 544 | 766 | 737 |
| 45 and over | | ... | 262 | 248 | 365 | 338 | 495 | 463 |

| | 1830 | | 1840 | | 1850 | | 1860 | | 1870 | |
|---|---|---|---|---|---|---|---|---|---|---|
| | M | F | M | F | M | F | M | F | M | F |
| 0–4 | 973 | 922 | 1,271 | 1,203 | 1,472 | 1,424 | 2,091 | 2,026 | 2,399 | 2,321 |
| 5–9 | 782 | 751 | 1,024 | 987 | 1,372 | 1,332 | 1,789 | 1,739 | 2,104 | 2,048 |
| 10–14 | 670 | 639 | 880 | 837 | 1,226 | 1,177 | 1,590 | 1,523 | 2,103 | 2,033 |
| 15–19 | 573 | 596 | 756 | 792 | 1,041 | 1,088 | 1,401 | 1,452 | 1,731 | 1,780 |
| 20–24 | 956 | 918 | 1,322 | 1,253 | 1,869 | 1,758 | 2,497 | 2,420 | 1,592 | 1,643 |
| 25–29 | | | | | | | | | 1,328 | 1,353 |
| 30–34 | 593 | 556 | 866 | 779 | 1,289 | 1,128 | 1,867 | 1,636 | 1,132 | 1,133 |
| 35–39 | | | | | | | | | 1,048 | 999 |
| 40–44 | 368 | 356 | 537 | 502 | 840 | 749 | 1,224 | 1,058 | 882 | 834 |
| 45–49 | | | | | | | | | 752 | 655 |
| 50–54 | 229 | 224 | 315 | 305 | 499 | 460 | 740 | 659 | 655 | 550 |
| 55–59 | | | | | | | | | 425 | 370 |
| 60–64 | | | | | | | | | 359 | 328 |
| 65–69 | | | | | | | | | 227 | 213 |
| 70–74 | 211 | 210 | 279 | 281 | 411 | 408 | 597 | 586 | 155 | 153 |
| 75–79 | | | | | | | | | 78 | 81 |
| 80 and over | | | | | | | | | 58 | 67 |
| Unknown | | 5 | — | 6 | — | 7 | 3 | 14 | 11 | 751 |

**A2   NORTH AMERICA: Population of Major Countries by Sex and Age Groups** (in thousands)

## USA (whites)[2] (contd)

| | 1880 M | 1880 F | 1890 M | 1890 F | 1900 M | 1900 F | 1910 M | 1910 F | 1920 M | 1920 F |
|---|---|---|---|---|---|---|---|---|---|---|
| 0–4 | 2,949 | 2,851 | 3,351 | 3,229 | 4,011 | 3,908 | 4,729 | 4,594 | 5,261 | 5,113 |
| 5–9 | 2,756 | 2,686 | 3,277 | 3,196 | 3,862 | 3,776 | 4,285 | 4,190 | 5,099 | 4,988 |
| 10–14 | 2,483 | 2,398 | 3,044 | 2,948 | 3,519 | 3,440 | 4,006 | 3,912 | 4,735 | 4,634 |
| 15–19 | 2,150 | 2,202 | 2,819 | 2,856 | 3,258 | 3,258 | 3,999 | 3,969 | 4,142 | 4,172 |
| 20–24 | 2,219 | 2,183 | 2,741 | 2,708 | 3,145 | 3,190 | 4,071 | 3,915 | 4,019 | 4,167 |
| 25–29 | 1,838 | 1,704 | 2,407 | 2,240 | 2,943 | 2,820 | 3,792 | 3,465 | 4,094 | 4,047 |
| 30–34 | 1,548 | 1,431 | 2,201 | 1,944 | 2,619 | 2,385 | 3,297 | 2,970 | 3,776 | 3,563 |
| 35–39 | 1,353 | 1,295 | 1,831 | 1,608 | 2,360 | 2,100 | 3,024 | 2,708 | 3,665 | 3,300 |
| 40–44 | 1,112 | 1,079 | 1,496 | 1,370 | 2,055 | 1,797 | 2,537 | 2,243 | 2,987 | 2,768 |
| 45–49 | 962 | 900 | 1,271 | 1,178 | 1,652 | 1,454 | 2,162 | 1,899 | 2,779 | 2,409 |
| 50–54 | 856 | 772 | 1,083 | 1,008 | 1,396 | 1,238 | 1,916 | 1,639 | 2,294 | 2,024 |
| 55–59 | 610 | 545 | 793 | 738 | 1,040 | 981 | 1,364 | 1,200 | 1,741 | 1,565 |
| 60–64 | 516 | 461 | 686 | 637 | 826 | 795 | 1,077 | 993 | 1,462 | 1,310 |
| 65–69 | 342 | 316 | 479 | 446 | 610 | 587 | 792 | 758 | 999 | 926 |
| 70–74 | 225 | 219 | 333 | 308 | 412 | 397 | 519 | 512 | 656 | 643 |
| 75–79 | 126 | 129 | 183 | 178 | 240 | 238 | 307 | 314 | 391 | 410 |
| 80 and over | 85 | 102 | 129 | 145 | 155 | 170 | 206 | 232 | 252 | 306 |
| Unknown | — | — | 145 | 94 | 98 | 47 | 94 | 40 | 78 | 45 |

| | 1930 M | 1930 F | 1940 M | 1940 F | 1950 M | 1950 F | 1960[3] M | 1960[3] F | 1970 M | 1970 F | 1980[3] M | 1980[3] F |
|---|---|---|---|---|---|---|---|---|---|---|---|---|
| 0–4 | 5,158 | 4,984 | 4,701 | 4,528 | 7,244 | 6,940 | 8,849 | 8,509 | 7,374 | 7,049 | 6,484 | 6,150 |
| 5–9 | 5,662 | 5,500 | 4,745 | 4,584 | 5,915 | 5,681 | 8,202 | 7,885 | 8,633 | 8,264 | 6,685 | 6,348 |
| 10–14 | 5,415 | 5,279 | 5,259 | 5,094 | 4,945 | 4,750 | 7,457 | 7,182 | 9,034 | 8,647 | 7,408 | 7,052 |
| 15–19 | 5,132 | 5,116 | 5,616 | 5,448 | 4,686 | 4,645 | 5,837 | 5,771 | 8,291 | 8,079 | 8,634 | 8,328 |
| 20–24 | 4,747 | 4,866 | 5,114 | 5,227 | 5,003 | 5,176 | 4,646 | 4,825 | 6,941 | 7,341 | 8,683 | 8,605 |
| 25–29 | 4,324 | 4,385 | 4,892 | 5,012 | 5,350 | 5,575 | 4,722 | 4,834 | 5,850 | 5,962 | 8,005 | 7,980 |
| 30–34 | 4,117 | 4,094 | 4,573 | 4,633 | 5,081 | 5,276 | 5,218 | 5,371 | 4,925 | 5,042 | 7,300 | 7,345 |
| 35–39 | 4,225 | 4,053 | 4,254 | 4,262 | 4,956 | 5,103 | 5,447 | 5,694 | 4,784 | 4,936 | 5,831 | 5,930 |
| 40–44 | 3,773 | 3,494 | 3,995 | 3,941 | 4,574 | 4,617 | 5,117 | 5,306 | 5,194 | 5,412 | 4,850 | 4,976 |
| 45–49 | 3,327 | 3,054 | 3,843 | 3,690 | 4,080 | 4,089 | 4,828 | 4,957 | 5,258 | 5,587 | 4,639 | 4,818 |
| 50–54 | 2,836 | 2,610 | 3,452 | 3,229 | 3,756 | 3,779 | 4,286 | 4,408 | 4,833 | 5,169 | 4,918 | 5,240 |
| 55–59 | 2,240 | 2,080 | 2,790 | 2,637 | 3,351 | 3,345 | 3,729 | 3,898 | 4,311 | 4,696 | 4,853 | 5,385 |
| 60–64 | 1,800 | 1,697 | 2,232 | 2,184 | 2,829 | 2,823 | 3,122 | 3,429 | 3,647 | 4,157 | 4,173 | 4,803 |
| 65–69 | 1,330 | 1,278 | 1,737 | 1,762 | 2,225 | 2,364 | 2,684 | 3,055 | 2,808 | 3,491 | 3,482 | 4,331 |
| 70–74 | 937 | 908 | 1,183 | 1,031 | 1,514 | 1,669 | 2,018 | 2,373 | 2,108 | 2,875 | 2,552 | 3,543 |
| 75–79 | 516 | 528 | 681 | 737 | } 1,625 | } 1,983 | 1,255 | 1,580 | 1,438 | 2,115 | 1,650 | 2,660 |
| 80 and over | 340 | 404 | 481 | 581 | | | 950 | 1,388 | 1,292 | 2,204 | 1,538 | 3,193 |
| Unknown | 43 | 35 | — | — | — | — | — | — | 23[11] | | | |

**A2    NORTH AMERICA: Population of Major Countries by Sex and Age Groups** (in thousands)

## USA (negroes)

| Age | 1820 M | 1820 F | 1830 M | 1830 F | 1840 M | 1840 F | 1850 M | 1850 F |
|---|---|---|---|---|---|---|---|---|
| 0–4 | | | | | 479 | 477 | 297 | 304 |
| 5–9 | 392[4] | 370[4] | 402 | 395 | | | 268 | 269 |
| 10–14 | | | | | | | 248 | 241 |
| 15–19 | 227[5] | 231[5] | 356[7] | 357[7] | 444[7] | 447[7] | 197 | 205 |
| 20–24 | | | | | | | 326 | 324 |
| 25–29 | | | 213[8] | 218[8] | 271[8] | 282[8] | | |
| 30–34 | 187[6] | 180[6] | | | | | 201 | 207 |
| 35–39 | | | | | | | | |
| 40–44 | | | | | | | | |
| 45–49 | | | 141[9] | 136[9] | 174[9] | 170[9] | 127 | 131 |
| 50–54 | | | | | | | | |
| 55–59 | | | | | | | 77 | 74 |
| 60–64 | | | | | | | | |
| 65–69 | 95 | 89 | 54 | 56 | 66 | 66 | | |
| 70–74 | | | | | | | 69 | 70 |
| 75–79 | | | | | | | | |
| 80 and over | | | | | | | | |
| Unknown | — | — | — | — | — | — | 2 | 2 |

| Age | 1860 M | 1860 F | 1870 M | 1870 F | 1880 M | 1880 F | 1890 M | 1890 F |
|---|---|---|---|---|---|---|---|---|
| 0–4 | 355 | 364 | 397 | 395 | … | … | 530[10] | 518[10] |
| 5–9 | 318 | 320 | 332 | 328 | … | … | 549[10] | 544[10] |
| 10–14 | 307 | 294 | 329 | 316 | … | … | 526[10] | 507[10] |
| 15–19 | 245 | 256 | 252 | 269 | … | … | 422 | 449 |
| 20–24 | 394 | 389 | 232 | 266 | … | … | 350 | 381 |
| 25–29 | | | 175 | 204 | … | … | 272 | 288 |
| 30–34 | 247 | 253 | 131 | 154 | … | … | 203 | 207 |
| 35–39 | | | 123 | 136 | … | … | | |
| 40–44 | 162 | 162 | 102 | 115 | … | … | 344 | 364 |
| 45–49 | | | 85 | 84 | … | … | | 242 |
| 50–54 | 93 | 91 | 84 | 77 | … | … | 257 | |
| 55–59 | | | 44 | 37 | … | … | | |
| 60–64 | | | 48 | 44 | … | … | 145 | 124 |
| 65–69 | | | 24 | 21 | … | … | 46 | 38 |
| 70–74 | 81 | 82 | 18 | 19 | … | … | 30 | 29 |
| 75–79 | | | 8 | 9 | … | … | 16 | 16 |
| 80 and over | | | 10 | 12 | … | … | 17 | 22 |
| Unknown | 14 | 12 | 512 | | | | 28 | 26 |

**A2**     **NORTH AMERICA: Population of Major Countries by Sex and Age Groups** (in thousands)

## USA (negroes) (contd)

| | 1900 | | 1910 | | 1920 | | 1930 | |
|---|---|---|---|---|---|---|---|---|
| | M | F | M | F | M | F | M | F |
| 0–4 | 604 | 611 | 629 | 634 | 569 | 575 | 611 | 619 |
| 5–9 | 600 | 602 | 619 | 627 | 631 | 635 | 680 | 689 |
| 10–14 | 549 | 543 | 578 | 577 | 616 | 621 | 623 | 628 |
| 15–19 | 474 | 508 | 508 | 552 | 513 | 570 | 596 | 655 |
| 20–24 | 459 | 510 | 482 | 549 | 487 | 568 | 554 | 650 |
| 25–29 | 361 | 377 | 422 | 459 | 424 | 485 | 501 | 571 |
| 30–34 | 262 | 262 | 332 | 336 | 332 | 366 | 417 | 448 |
| 35–39 | 233 | 241 | 320 | 313 | 384 | 390 | 430 | 460 |
| 40–44 | 179 | 188 | 230 | 226 | 276 | 284 | 339 | 348 |
| 45–49 | 168 | 158 | 200 | 186 | 321 | 231 | 323 | 307 |
| 50–54 | 155 | 136 | 179 | 147 | 228 | 171 | 278 | 227 |
| 55–59 | 97 | 82 | 115 | 95 | 129 | 101 | 174 | 135 |
| 60–64 | 86 | 76 | 101 | 85 | 112 | 88 | 133 | 109 |
| 65–69 | 56 | 47 | 68 | 56 | 76 | 61 | 83 | 72 |
| 70–74 | 36 | 36 | 41 | 38 | 47 | 44 | 51 | 48 |
| 75–79 | 20 | 20 | 23 | 21 | 27 | 25 | 29 | 30 |
| 80 and over | 20 | 25 | 21 | 26 | 23 | 28 | 27 | 32 |
| Unknown | 25 | 24 | 17 | 14 | 14 | 10 | 7 | 7 |

| | 1940 | | 1950 | | 1960[3] | | 1970 | | 1980 | |
|---|---|---|---|---|---|---|---|---|---|---|
| | M | F | M | F | M | F | M | F | M | F |
| 0–4 | 622 | 627 | 948 | 943 | 1,363 | 1,360 | 1,220 | 1,213 | 1,228 | 1,208 |
| 5–9 | 644 | 651 | 761 | 768 | 1,195 | 1,196 | 1,377 | 1,370 | 1,255 | 1,235 |
| 10–14 | 661 | 669 | 674 | 678 | 989 | 984 | 1,407 | 1,403 | 1,344 | 1,329 |
| 15–19 | 630 | 675 | 592 | 635 | 741 | 756 | 1,202 | 1,221 | 1,489 | 1,496 |
| 20–24 | 550 | 645 | 564 | 668 | 569 | 642 | 840 | 974 | 1,300 | 1,425 |
| 25–29 | 530 | 616 | 580 | 669 | 548 | 631 | 658 | 771 | 1,084 | 1,237 |
| 30–34 | 468 | 525 | 511 | 593 | 564 | 663 | 568 | 685 | 871 | 1,018 |
| 35–39 | 463 | 523 | 530 | 609 | 569 | 652 | 541 | 655 | 662 | 795 |
| 40–44 | 400 | 415 | 469 | 504 | 508 | 578 | 544 | 654 | 567 | 685 |
| 45–49 | 348 | 345 | 419 | 444 | 480 | 534 | 520 | 603 | 515 | 628 |
| 50–54 | 283 | 267 | 350 | 352 | 407 | 445 | 459 | 531 | 505 | 624 |
| 55–59 | 207 | 190 | 264 | 251 | 365 | 393 | 405 | 469 | 467 | 570 |
| 60–64 | 154 | 142 | 195 | 190 | 259 | 290 | 334 | 399 | 385 | 486 |
| 65–69 | 152 | 145 | 189 | 213 | 229 | 258 | 277 | 350 | 332 | 445 |
| 70–74 | 84 | 79 | 109 | 114 | 151 | 173 | 184 | 232 | 234 | 329 |
| 75–79 | 41 | 42 | } 113 | 127 { | 94 | 109 | 110 | 145 | 153 | 235 |
| 80 and over | 32 | 41 | | | 66 | 87 | 105 | 157 | 128 | 231 |
| Unknown | — | — | — | — | — | — | [11] | [11] | — | — |

**A2**     **SOUTH AMERICA: POPULATION OF MAJOR COUNTRIES BY SEX AND AGE GROUPS** (in thousands)

# ARGENTINA

| | 1869[2] | | 1895 | | 1914 | | 1947 | | 1960 | | 1970 | | 1980 | |
|---|---|---|---|---|---|---|---|---|---|---|---|---|---|---|
| | **M** | **F** | **M** | **F** | **M** | **F** | **M** | **F** | **M** | **F** | **M** | **F** | **M** | **F** |
| 0–4 | [159] | [157] | 299 | 291 | 582 | 567 | 902 | 881 | 1,079 | 1,052 | 1,197 | 1,158 | 1,640 | 1,601 |
| 5–9 | [137] | [128] | 282 | 270 | 517 | 504 | 798 | 779 | 1,050 | 1,026 | 1,163 | 1,134 | 1,407 | 1,377 |
| 10–14 | [106] | [98] | 233 | 211 | 438 | 421 | 772 | 753 | 976 | 963 | 1,114 | 1,087 | 1,240 | 1,216 |
| 15–19 | [90] | [101] | 190 | 202 | 434 | 406 | 789 | 781 | 834 | 852 | 1,059 | 1,040 | 1,170 | 1,165 |
| 20–24 | }[170] | [155]{ | 173 | 174 | 458 | 383 | 749 | 741 | 755 | 776 | 970 | 981 | 1,096 | 1,121 |
| 25–29 | | | 190 | 158 | 420 | 323 | 642 | 644 | 766 | 774 | 843 | 860 | 1,058 | 1,076 |
| 30–34 | }[111] | [96]{ | 165 | 129 | 332 | 235 | 618 | 610 | 773 | 788 | 785 | 796 | 980 | 991 |
| 35–39 | | | 154 | 115 | 264 | 207 | 598 | 561 | 721 | 722 | 779 | 767 | 860 | 871 |
| 40–44 | }[67] | [58]{ | 115 | 90 | 212 | 155 | 553 | 473 | 607 | 609 | 770 | 770 | 772 | 779 |
| 45–49 | | | 95 | 63 | 166 | 125 | 468 | 403 | 591 | 589 | 684 | 699 | 744 | 751 |
| 50–54 | }[35] | [31]{ | 68 | 52 | 140 | 106 | 386 | 312 | 521 | 498 | 562 | 585 | 710 | 748 |
| 55–59 | | | 42 | 30 | 94 | 71 | 316 | 262 | 443 | 413 | 518 | 549 | 618 | 658 |
| 60–64 | }[15] | [14]{ | 33 | 30 | 73 | 62 | 225 | 194 | 330 | 326 | 436 | 455 | 468 | 534 |
| 65–69 | | | 15 | 14 | 39 | 34 | 142 | 136 | 237 | 236 | 322 | 350 | 398 | 477 |
| 70–74 | }[3] | [3]{ | 11 | 13 | 27 | 26 | 84 | 85 | 160 | 172 | 202 | 244 | 282 | 356 |
| 75–79 | | | 5 | 5 | }25 | 30{ | 44 | 51 | 85 | 100 | 123 | 157 | 181 | 247 |
| 80 and over | | | 6 | 10 | | | 32 | 47 | 56 | 82 | 91 | 142 | 131 | 224 |
| Unknown | - - | - - | 12 | 10 | 4 | 2 | 27 | 38 | 21 | 28 | – | – | – | – |

# BOLIVIA

| | 1900 | | | 1950 | | 1976 | |
|---|---|---|---|---|---|---|---|
| | **M** | **F** | | **M** | **F** | **M** | **F** |
| 0–6 | 108 | 106 | 0–4 | 216 | 210 | 371 | 371 |
| 7–13 | 104 | 101 | 5–9 | 194 | 185 | 323 | 320 |
| 14–17 | 61 | 63 | 10–14 | 141 | 125 | 279 | 273 |
| 18–25 | 106 | 107 | 15–19 | 135 | 133 | 241 | 248 |
| 26–30 | 91 | 91 | 20–24 | 116 | 130 | 195 | 217 |
| 31–40 | 124 | 125 | 25–29 | 104 | 118 | 171 | 172 |
| 41 and over | 169 | 169 | 30–34 | 78 | 89 | 136 | 141 |
| Unknown | 55 | 54 | 35–39 | 77 | 87 | 122 | 130 |
| | | | 40–44 | 55 | 65 | 92 | 103 |
| | | | 45–49 | 49 | 55 | 94 | 101 |
| | | | 50–54 | 39 | 47 | 64 | 74 |
| | | | 55–59 | 30 | 33 | 54 | 59 |
| | | | 60–64 | 38 | 39 | 49 | 53 |
| | | | 65–69 | 19 | 19 | 35 | 36 |
| | | | 70–74 | 15 | 18 | 20 | 28 |
| | | | 75–79 | 7 | 8 | 15 | 17 |
| | | | 80 and over | 14 | 16 | 21 | 24 |
| | | | Unknown | - - | - - | – | – |

*See p. 29 for footnotes*

**A2    SOUTH AMERICA: Population of Major Countries by Sex and Age Groups** (in thousands)

# BRAZIL

| | 1872 M | 1872 F | 1890 M | 1890 F | 1900 M | 1900 F | 1920 M | 1920 F |
|---|---|---|---|---|---|---|---|---|
| 0–4 | 560 | 499 | 2,122 | | 1,522 | 1,453 | 2,318 | 2,275 |
| 5–9 | 604 | 576 | 2,069 | | 1,344 | 1,257 | 2,326 | 2,249 |
| 10–14 | 540 | 551 | 1,710 | | 1,048 | 998 | 1,989 | 1,920 |
| 15–19 | 540 | 527 | 1,400 | | 900 | 954 | 1,997 | 2,221 |
| 20–24 | 555 | 520 | 1,352 | | 773 | 785 | 1,069 | 1,070 |
| 25–29 | 556 | 523 | 2,182 | | 714 | 733 | 1,231 | 1,258 |
| 30–34 | 667 | 597 | 1,802 | | 1,047 | 988 | 1,847 | 1,713 |
| 35–39 | | | | | | | | |
| 40–44 | 465 | 436 | 1,233 | | 710 | 637 | 1,263 | 1,138 |
| 45–49 | | | | | | | | |
| 50–54 | 324 | 289 | 733 | | 412 | 359 | 753 | 698 |
| 55–59 | | | | | | | | |
| 60–64 | 202 | 184 | 430 | | 187 | 168 | 408 | 393 |
| 65–69 | | | | | | | | |
| 70–74 | 107 | 95 | 160 | | 69 | 69 | 148 | 160 |
| 75–79 | | | | | | | | |
| 80 and over | 97 | 86 | 84 | | 31 | 33 | 54 | 71 |
| Unknown | 6 | 5 | 59 | | 75 | 55 | 39 | 27 |

| | 1940 M | 1940 F | 1950 M | 1950 F | 1960 M | 1960 F | 1970 M | 1970 F | 1980 M | 1980 F |
|---|---|---|---|---|---|---|---|---|---|---|
| 0–4 | 3,256 | 3,184 | 4,236 | 4,135 | 5,712 | 5,484 | 6,970 | 6,842 | 8,461 | 8,188 |
| 5–9 | 2,924 | 2,835 | 3,561 | 3,455 | 5,159 | 5,002 | 6,800 | 6,660 | 7,230 | 7,042 |
| 10–14 | 2,682 | 2,646 | 3,165 | 3,144 | 4,287 | 4,287 | 5,934 | 5,925 | 6,807 | 6,743 |
| 15–19 | 2,158 | 2,286 | 2,645 | 2,858 | 3,446 | 3,697 | 4,995 | 5,258 | 6,488 | 6,789 |
| 20–24 | 1,836 | 1,978 | 2,384 | 2,607 | 2,964 | 3,197 | 4,037 | 4,249 | 5,656 | 5,970 |
| 25–29 | 1,649 | 1,707 | 2,030 | 2,102 | 2,522 | 2,687 | 3,173 | 3,331 | 4,806 | 4,948 |
| 30–34 | 1,300 | 1,281 | 1,622 | 1,623 | 2,254 | 2,261 | 2,801 | 2,864 | 3,955 | 3,915 |
| 35–39 | 1,166 | 1,154 | 1,524 | 1,517 | 1,956 | 2,034 | 2,502 | 2,587 | 3,181 | 3,231 |
| 40–44 | 1,004 | 946 | 1,228 | 1,161 | 1,653 | 1,580 | 2,288 | 2,247 | 2,884 | 2,843 |
| 45–49 | 786 | 706 | 1,019 | 958 | 1,400 | 1,327 | 1,795 | 1,752 | 2,295 | 2,406 |
| 50–54 | 641 | 606 | 811 | 774 | 1,124 | 1,065 | 1,486 | 1,454 | 2,043 | 2,113 |
| 55–59 | 413 | 386 | 550 | 516 | 828 | 770 | 1,160 | 1,128 | 1,637 | 1,673 |
| 60–64 | 338 | 352 | 473 | 463 | 728 | 685 | 903 | 888 | 1,230 | 1,333 |
| 65–69 | 187 | 199 | 255 | 260 | 396 | 376 | 605 | 612 | 1,064 | 1,131 |
| 70–74 | 128 | 156 | 165 | 196 | 267 | 280 | 389 | 417 | | |
| 75–79 | 65 | 79 | 83 | 102 | 139 | 151 | 195 | 223 | 1,372 | 1,568 |
| 80 and over | 68 | 104 | 81 | 127 | 123 | 167 | 204 | 281 | | |
| Unknown | 15 | 18 | 54 | 63 | 53 | 57 | 93 | 91 | 36 | 33 |

**A2    SOUTH AMERICA: Population of Major Countries by Sex and Age Groups** (in thousands)

# CHILE

|  | 1895 | | 1907 | | 1920 | | 1930 | |
|---|---|---|---|---|---|---|---|---|
|  | M | F | M | F | M | F | M | F |
| 0–4 | 222 | 215 | [256][12] | [249][12] | 239 | 235 | 296 | 294 |
| 5–9 | 182 | 172 | [171][12] | [164][12] | 257 | 250 | 270 | 266 |
| 10–14 | 154 | 150 | 196 | 183 | 226 | 216 | 238 | 231 |
| 15–19 | 134 | 148 | [204][12] | [218][12] | 194 | 204 | 229 | 240 |
| 20–24 | 122 | 128 | [104][12] | [104][12] | 174 | 180 | 206 | 211 |
| 25–29 | 121 | 133 | 146 | 149 | 155 | 164 | 172 | 190 |
| 30–34 | 78 | 79 | } 200 | } 203 | 125 | 127 | 145 | 143 |
| 35–39 | 89 | 95 | | | 118 | 118 | 132 | 137 |
| 40–44 | 52 | 50 | } 148 | } 147 | 102 | 100 | 110 | 108 |
| 45–49 | 56 | 59 | | | 72 | 68 | 90 | 88 |
| 50–54 | 28 | 28 | } 100 | } 98 | 65 | 69 | 74 | 76 |
| 55–59 | 41 | 41 | | | 39 | 37 | 49 | 50 |
| 60–64 | 17 | 17 | } 61 | } 62 | 43 | 50 | 44 | 52 |
| 65–69 | 16 | 17 | | | 17 | 20 | 26 | 27 |
| 70–74 | 7 | 7 | } 26 | } 29 | 20 | 22 | 20 | 24 |
| 75–79 | 7 | 8 | | | 8 | 8 | 10 | 11 |
| 80 and over | 6 | 8 | 13 | 17 | 12 | 17 | 12 | 18 |
| Unknown | — | — | — | — | — | — | — | — |

|  | 1940 | | 1952 | | 1960 | | 1970 | | 1982 | |
|---|---|---|---|---|---|---|---|---|---|---|
|  | M | F | M | F | M | F | M | F | M | F |
| 0–4 | 314 | 308 | 392 | 387 | 555 | 550 | 567 | 556 | 662 | 642 |
| 5–9 | 322 | 313 | 392 | 387 | 492 | 489 | 624 | 620 | 605 | 587 |
| 10–14 | 307 | 302 | 327 | 323 | 421 | 415 | 560 | 555 | 592 | 575 |
| 15–19 | 256 | 256 | 281 | 291 | 355 | 370 | 447 | 467 | 613 | 600 |
| 20–24 | 219 | 238 | 274 | 299 | 288 | 311 | 371 | 398 | 585 | 576 |
| 25–29 | 204 | 223 | 212 | 234 | 252 | 275 | 302 | 324 | 488 | 483 |
| 30–34 | 177 | 175 | 185 | 195 | 247 | 260 | 249 | 267 | 416 | 420 |
| 35–39 | 155 | 166 | 179 | 197 | 200 | 215 | 247 | 267 | 367 | 376 |
| 40–44 | 137 | 132 | 163 | 159 | 178 | 185 | 223 | 233 | 302 | 312 |
| 45–49 | 109 | 107 | 127 | 133 | 157 | 167 | 172 | 185 | 247 | 259 |
| 50–54 | 86 | 88 | 114 | 116 | 138 | 141 | 149 | 163 | 222 | 237 |
| 55–59 | 68 | 66 | 79 | 82 | 103 | 109 | 127 | 141 | 180 | 199 |
| 60–64 | 55 | 63 | 69 | 78 | 86 | 97 | 106 | 117 | 140 | 162 |
| 65–69 | 33 | 34 | 44 | 49 | 61 | 68 | 80 | 92 | 109 | 135 |
| 70–74 | 23 | 29 | 31 | 38 | 38 | 46 | 54 | 64 | 78 | 104 |
| 75–79 | 12 | 14 | 15 | 19 | 23 | 29 | 31 | 39 | 47 | 69 |
| 80 and over | 12 | 20 | 15 | 25 | 20 | 33 | 35 | 53 | 35 | 63 |
| Unknown | — | — | 13 | 8 | — | — | — | — | — | — |

*See p. 29 for footnotes*

**A2    SOUTH AMERICA: Population of Major Countries by Sex and Age Groups** (in thousands)

## COLOMBIA

| | 1918 M | 1918 F | 1938 M | 1938 F | 1951 M | 1951 F | 1964 M | 1964 F | 1973 M | 1973 F | 1985 M | 1985 F |
|---|---|---|---|---|---|---|---|---|---|---|---|---|
| 0–4 | 412 | 418 | 672 | 666 | 951 | 922 | 1,562 | 1,523 | 1,796 | 1,736 | 1,717 | 1,653 |
| 5–9 | 356 | 351 | 630 | 617 | 794 | 769 | 1,419 | 1,382 | 1,748 | 1,704 | 1,751 | 1,694 |
| 10–14 | 319 | 312 | 547 | 522 | 684 | 658 | 1,148 | 1,121 | 1,598 | 1,596 | 1,639 | 1,587 |
| 15–19 | 242 | 282 | 421 | 472 | 545 | 605 | 836 | 930 | 1,283 | 1,370 | 1,582 | 1,673 |
| 20–24 | 234 | 257 | 406 | 415 | 532 | 551 | 671 | 746 | 987 | 1,074 | 1,440 | 1,560 |
| 25–29 | 219 | 242 | 334 | 358 | 409 | 447 | 550 | 616 | 743 | 815 | 1,152 | 1,265 |
| 30–34 | 179 | 203 | 265 | 266 | 342 | 337 | 500 | 530 | 604 | 659 | 938 | 969 |
| 35–39 | 159 | 172 | 266 | 264 | 318 | 334 | 443 | 481 | 539 | 594 | 813 | 852 |
| 40–44 | 131 | 150 | 199 | 205 | 248 | 240 | 360 | 359 | 470 | 502 | 619 | 605 |
| 45–49 | 92 | 100 | 154 | 150 | 194 | 197 | 291 | 301 | 387 | 407 | 515 | 529 |
| 50–54 | 81 | 98 | 137 | 142 | 183 | 176 | 262 | 256 | 319 | 332 | 456 | 464 |
| 55–59 | 50 | 54 | 79 | 77 | 110 | 106 | 167 | 164 | 247 | 253 | 346 | 348 |
| 60–64 | 58 | 66 | 88 | 98 | 107 | 117 | 164 | 176 | 192 | 199 | 288 | 291 |
| 65–69 | 28 | 30 | 40 | 41 | 62 | 63 | 92 | 97 | 138 | 144 | 195 | 205 |
| 70–74 | 23 | 28 | 34 | 43 | 46 | 57 | 68 | 81 | 92 | 101 | 150 | 155 |
| 75–79 | 13 | 14 | 16 | 17 | 24 | 27 | 39 | 44 | 54 | 61 | 89 | 95 |
| 80 and over | 23 | 29 | 23 | 36 | 29 | 43 | 41 | 62 | 44 | 61 | 87 | 114 |
| Unknown | 133 | 143 | 3 | 2 | — | — | — | — | — | — | — | — |

## ECUADOR

| | 1950 M | 1950 F | 1962 M | 1962 F | 1974 M | 1974 F | 1982 M | 1982 F |
|---|---|---|---|---|---|---|---|---|
| 0–4 | 271 | 263 | 386 | 376 | 517 | 516 | 613 | 596 |
| 5–9 | 231 | 224 | 355 | 344 | 496 | 485 | 560 | 548 |
| 10–14 | 193 | 178 | 285 | 269 | 445 | 430 | 519 | 510 |
| 15–19 | 158 | 160 | 214 | 221 | 349 | 354 | 441 | 440 |
| 20–24 | 140 | 148 | 183 | 195 | 285 | 296 | 385 | 395 |
| 25–29 | 119 | 126 | 157 | 168 | 218 | 226 | 302 | 317 |
| 30–34 | 94 | 96 | 136 | 134 | 180 | 180 | 250 | 253 |
| 35–39 | 91 | 95 | 116 | 122 | 157 | 164 | 198 | 204 |
| 40–44 | 68 | 73 | 97 | 95 | 140 | 139 | 172 | 169 |
| 45–49 | 55 | 59 | 77 | 78 | 110 | 110 | 131 | 138 |
| 50–54 | 56 | 53 | 69 | 68 | 96 | 94 | 125 | 123 |
| 55–59 | 34 | 34 | 45 | 44 | 68 | 67 | 87 | 87 |
| 60–64 | 33 | 37 | 48 | 49 | 68 | 71 | 83 | 84 |
| 65–69 | 18 | 19 | 24 | 24 | 41 | 42 | 53 | 54 |
| 70–74 | 15 | 19 | 20 | 23 | 38 | 40 | 46 | 47 |
| 75–79 | 7 | 9 | } 24 | } 29 | 17 | 19 | } 56 | } 66 |
| 80 and over | 11 | 16 | | | 22 | 31 | | |
| Unknown | - - | - - | — | — | — | — | — | — |

**A2      SOUTH AMERICA: Population of Major Countries by Sex and Age Groups** (in thousands)

## GUYANA*

|         | 1911 | | 1921 | | 1931 | | 1946 | | 1960 | | 1970 | | 1980 | |
|---------|----|----|----|----|----|----|----|----|----|----|----|----|----|----|
|         | M  | F  | M  | F  | M  | F  | M  | F  | M  | F  | M  | F  | M  | F  |
| 0–4     | 14 | 15 | 15 | 15 | 23 | 22 | 26 | 26 | 49 | 49 | 56 | 55 | 49 | 49 |
| 5–9     | 17 | 17 | 18 | 18 | 19 | 19 | 24 | 23 | 46 | 45 | 60 | 59 | 53 | 53 |
| 10–14   | 15 | 15 | 15 | 14 | 15 | 14 | 20 | 20 | 35 | 35 | 50 | 50 | 53 | 52 |
| 15–19   | 11 | 12 | 13 | 15 | 14 | 17 | 18 | 19 | 25 | 26 | 40 | 40 | 48 | 49 |
| 20–24   | 15 | 16 | 15 | 15 | 13 | 14 | 16 | 17 | 21 | 21 | 28 | 29 | 37 | 40 |
| 25–29   | 15 | 14 | 12 | 13 | 14 | 14 | 13 | 14 | 17 | 19 | 19 | 20 | 28 | 29 |
| 30–34   | 14 | 11 | 12 | 11 | 10 | 10 | 13 | 13 | 16 | 16 | 16 | 17 | 22 | 22 |
| 35–39   | 13 | 10 | 12 | 11 | 11 | 11 | 11 | 11 | 14 | 15 | 15 | 16 | 16 | 17 |
| 40–44   | 12 | 8  | 11 | 9  | 9  | 8  | 11 | 10 | 12 | 12 | 14 | 14 | 14 | 14 |
| 45–49   | 8  | 6  | 9  | 7  | 9  | 8  | 9  | 9  | 12 | 11 | 13 | 12 | 13 | 13 |
| 50–54   | 6  | 5  | 7  | 6  | 6  | 5  | 6  | 6  | 9  | 9  | 10 | 10 | 11 | 11 |
| 55–59   | 4  | 3  | 4  | 3  | 5  | 5  | 6  | 6  | 8  | 7  | 10 | 9  | 9  | 9  |
| 60–64   | 3  | 3  | 3  | 3  | 3  | 3  | 4  | 5  | 6  | 6  | 6  | 6  | 7  | 7  |
| 65–69   | 2  | 2  | 2  | 2  | 2  | 2  | 3  | 4  | 4  | 4  | 5  | 6  | 6  | 6  |
| 70–74   | 1  | 1  | 1  | 1  | 1  | 1  | 2  | 2  | 2  | 3  | 2  | 3  | 4  | 4  |
| 75–79   | -- | 1  | 1  | 1  | 1  | 1  | 1  | 1  | 1  | 2  | 1  | 2  | 2  | 2  |
| 80 and over | 1 | 1 | 1 | 1 | -- | 1 | 1 | 1 | 1 | 2 | 1 | 2 | 3 | 3 |
| Unknown | 1  | 1  | 1  | 1  | -- | -- | -- | -- | —  | —  | —  | —  | 1  | 1  |

* Formerly British Guiana

## PARAGUAY

|         | 1950 | | 1962 | | 1972 | | 1982 | |
|---------|-----|-----|-----|-----|-----|-----|-----|-----|
|         | M   | F   | M   | F   | M   | F   | M   | F   |
| 0–4     | 111 | 107 | 159 | 153 | 187 | 181 | 236 | 228 |
| 5–9     | 100 | 96  | 148 | 142 | 183 | 177 | 202 | 194 |
| 10–14   | 86  | 81  | 119 | 114 | 168 | 159 | 192 | 184 |
| 15–19   | 63  | 66  | 91  | 94  | 131 | 132 | 168 | 167 |
| 20–24   | 58  | 64  | 69  | 76  | 93  | 98  | 146 | 146 |
| 25–29   | 47  | 52  | 52  | 58  | 72  | 77  | 118 | 116 |
| 30–34   | 37  | 40  | 53  | 56  | 63  | 65  | 93  | 89  |
| 35–39   | 32  | 39  | 44  | 48  | 51  | 56  | 75  | 76  |
| 40–44   | 25  | 29  | 38  | 41  | 52  | 53  | 67  | 65  |
| 45–49   | 21  | 24  | 29  | 34  | 41  | 44  | 48  | 51  |
| 50–54   | 18  | 21  | 27  | 29  | 37  | 38  | 51  | 51  |
| 55–59   | 15  | 17  | 18  | 21  | 27  | 29  | 37  | 37  |
| 60–64   | 15  | 16  | 17  | 20  | 23  | 26  | 30  | 33  |
| 65–69   | 10  | 11  | 11  | 12  | 15  | 19  | 22  | 25  |
| 70–74   | 6   | 8   | 9   | 11  | 12  | 14  | 17  | 19  |
| 75–79   | 3   | 4   | 6   | 8   | 7   | 8   | 10  | 13  |
| 80 and over | 3 | 5 | 5 | 9 | 8 | 13 | 11 | 14 |
| Unknown | —   | —   | --  | --  | —   | —   | —   | —   |

**A2**     **SOUTH AMERICA: Population of Major Countries by Sex and Age Groups** (in thousands)

## PERU

| | 1940 M | 1940 F | 1961 M | 1961 F | 1972 M | 1972 F | 1981 M | 1981 F |
|---|---|---|---|---|---|---|---|---|
| 0–4 | 486 | 475 | 840 | 831 | 1,108 | 1,093 | 1,490 | 1,464 |
| 5–9 | 468 | 455 | 739 | 728 | 1,023 | 1,000 | 1,281 | 1,266 |
| 10–14 | 383 | 345 | 595 | 557 | 884 | 829 | 1,150 | 1,152 |
| 15–19 | 296 | 293 | 494 | 480 | 715 | 698 | 1,002 | 984 |
| 20–24 | 264 | 267 | 421 | 428 | 572 | 579 | 845 | 836 |
| 25–29 | 227 | 255 | 360 | 381 | 458 | 472 | 694 | 690 |
| 30–34 | 191 | 194 | 312 | 308 | 390 | 381 | 566 | 565 |
| 35–39 | 179 | 194 | 261 | 279 | 356 | 373 | 458 | 459 |
| 40–44 | 137 | 141 | 209 | 211 | 307 | 298 | 387 | 388 |
| 45–49 | 118 | 124 | 177 | 187 | 242 | 246 | 328 | 330 |
| 50–54 | 85 | 94 | 143 | 149 | 195 | 193 | 273 | 276 |
| 55–59 | 65 | 74 | 110 | 115 | 149 | 151 | 219 | 224 |
| 60–64 | 57 | 73 | 99 | 112 | 133 | 141 | 167 | 173 |
| 65–69 | 36 | 46 | 60 | 70 | 89 | 98 | 123 | 130 |
| 70–74 | 28 | 40 | 42 | 55 | 66 | 77 | 86 | 94 |
| 75–79 | 17 | 24 | } 63 | 86 { | 35 | 43 | } 90 | 106 |
| 80 and over | 30 | 43 | | | 48 | 66 | | |
| Unknown | 1 | 1 | 2 | 3 | 13 | 15 | — | — |

## SURINAM

| | 1950 M | 1950 F | 1964 M | 1964 F |
|---|---|---|---|---|
| 0–4 | 14 | 14 | 27 | 26 |
| 5–9 | 11 | 12 | 27 | 27 |
| 10–14 | 10 | 10 | 21 | 20 |
| 15–19 | 9 | 9 | 15 | 15 |
| 20–24 | 7 | 7 | 11 | 12 |
| 25–29 | 6 | 6 | 10 | 11 |
| 30–34 | 4 | 5 | 9 | 10 |
| 35–39 | 4 | 4 | 8 | 8 |
| 40–44 | 4 | 4 | 7 | 7 |
| 45–49 | 3 | 4 | 5 | 5 |
| 50–54 | 4 | 3 | 5 | 4 |
| 55–59 | 3 | 3 | 4 | 4 |
| 60–64 | 3 | 2 | 3 | 3 |
| 65–69 | 2 | 2 | 3 | 3 |
| 70–74 | 1 | 1 | 2 | 2 |
| 75–79 | - - | 1 | 1 | 1 |
| 80 and over | - - | - - | 1 | 1 |
| Unknown | 6 | 6 | 4 | 3 |

**A2     SOUTH AMERICA: Population of Major Countries by Sex and Age Groups** (in thousands)

## URUGUAY

| | 1900 M | 1900 F | 1908 M | 1908 F | 1963 M | 1963 F | 1975 M | 1975 F | 1985 M | 1985 F |
|---|---|---|---|---|---|---|---|---|---|---|
| 0–4 | 68 | 67 | 85 | 83 | 131 | 123 | 129 | 126 | 131 | 126 |
| 5–9 | 66 | 65 | 68 | 66 | 124 | 120 | 121 | 120 | 140 | 135 |
| 10–14 | 61 | 59 | 63 | 63 | 114 | 109 | 129 | 124 | 131 | 126 |
| 15–19 | 52 | 56 | 57 | 62 | 103 | 104 | 117 | 119 | 116 | 114 |
| 20–24 | 45 | 44 | 52 | 53 | 97 | 96 | 100 | 104 | 113 | 114 |
| 25–29 | 38 | 35 | 44 | 46 | 91 | 95 | 92 | 96 | 106 | 110 |
| 30–34 | } 56 | } 48 | 33 | 29 | 100 | 101 | 87 | 89 | 95 | 99 |
| 35–39 | | | 31 | 30 | 93 | 95 | 85 | 90 | 87 | 92 |
| 40–44 | } 44 | } 33 | 22 | 18 | 85 | 84 | 90 | 92 | 82 | 86 |
| 45–49 | | | 22 | 20 | 73 | 76 | 88 | 90 | 78 | 83 |
| 50–54 | } 25 | } 18 | 16 | 12 | 73 | 69 | 79 | 81 | 80 | 85 |
| 55–59 | | | 15 | 12 | 61 | 56 | 66 | 67 | 77 | 83 |
| 60–64 | } 13 | } 10 | 8 | 6 | 50 | 52 | 60 | 66 | 65 | 72 |
| 65–69 | | | 6 | 6 | 37 | 41 | 47 | 52 | 50 | 60 |
| 70–74 | } 5 | } 4 | 3 | 3 | 27 | 30 | 35 | 41 | 40 | 52 |
| 75–79 | | | 2 | 3 | 15 | 20 | 21 | 30 | 26 | 38 |
| 80 and over | 2 | 2 | 1 | 2 | 12 | 20 | 17 | 30 | 23 | 42 |
| Unknown | 1 | - - | 1 | 1 | 6 | 16 | — | — | — | — |

## VENEZUELA

| | 1920 M | 1920 F | | 1920 M | 1920 F |
|---|---|---|---|---|---|
| 0–7 | 231 | 240 | 29–35 | 127 | 104 |
| 7–14 | 227 | 245 | 36–42 | 104 | 83 |
| 15–21 | 193 | 160 | 43–45 | 31 | 29 |
| 22–28 | 177 | 147 | 46 and over | 139 | 125 |

| | 1963 M | 1963 F | 1941 M | 1941 F | 1950 M | 1950 F | 1961 M | 1961 F | 1971 M | 1971 F | 1981 M | 1981 F |
|---|---|---|---|---|---|---|---|---|---|---|---|---|
| 0–4 | 240 | 234 | 292 | 286 | 433 | 415 | 698 | 676 | 879 | 857 | 1,089 | 1,052 |
| 5–9 | 241 | 230 | 267 | 256 | 353 | 335 | 591 | 572 | 825 | 809 | 975 | 948 |
| 10–14 | 215 | 197 | 246 | 227 | 299 | 276 | 458 | 444 | 733 | 721 | 911 | 899 |
| 15–19 | 164 | 185 | 191 | 212 | 244 | 252 | 340 | 339 | 602 | 618 | 829 | 826 |
| 20–24 | 159 | 174 | 183 | 191 | 236 | 238 | 312 | 307 | 468 | 494 | 715 | 731 |
| 25–29 | 136 | 149 | 154 | 167 | 202 | 198 | 283 | 268 | 339 | 360 | 609 | 625 |
| 30–34 | 104 | 114 | 124 | 127 | 170 | 157 | 265 | 238 | 293 | 295 | 488 | 492 |
| 35–39 | 98 | 102 | 106 | 109 | 156 | 145 | 211 | 195 | 269 | 270 | 359 | 363 |
| 40–44 | 80 | 88 | 94 | 97 | 125 | 115 | 174 | 157 | 242 | 227 | 300 | 295 |
| 45–49 | 65 | 60 | 80 | 72 | 98 | 87 | 146 | 135 | 193 | 181 | 252 | 249 |
| 50–54 | 52 | 59 | 58 | 61 | 83 | 82 | 113 | 106 | 155 | 149 | 221 | 216 |
| 55–59 | 33 | 32 | 38 | 38 | 52 | 50 | 84 | 83 | 116 | 117 | 166 | 166 |
| 60–64 | 29 | 38 | 32 | 41 | 42 | 51 | 62 | 69 | 94 | 97 | 126 | 131 |
| 65–69 | } 33 | } 49 | 16 | 19 | 22 | 26 | 36 | 42 | 58 | 63 | 90 | 100 |
| 70–74 | | | 10 | 16 | 15 | 23 | 22 | 29 | 41 | 48 | 62 | 73 |
| 75–79 | | | 6 | 8 | 8 | 11 | 13 | 18 | 20 | } 26 | } 66 | } 93 |
| 80 and over | | | 7 | 13 | 10 | 18 | 13 | 25 | 23 | 39 | | |
| Unknown | 2 | 2 | 4 | 3 | 5 | 3 | — | — | — | — | — | — |

**Population of Major Countries by Sex and Age Groups** (in thousands)

NOTES

1.   SOURCES: UN, *Demographic Yearbooks,* national censuses, and the national publications on p. xiv–xvi.
2.   Notes 4 and 5 to table B1 also apply to this table.

FOOTNOTES

[1] Age groups are 0–6 and 7–14.
[2] Prior to 1980 this includes some Asians and other non-negroes.
[3] Including Alaska and Hawaii for the first time.
[4] Under 14 years old.
[5] 14–25.
[6] 26–44.
[7] 10–23.
[8] 24–35.
[9] 36–54.
[10] Estimates based on population under 15 and age distribution of negro and other races.
[11] All races are included with whites.
[12] Age groups are 0–5, 6–10, 11–15, etc.
[13] Age groups are 0–5, 6–9, 15–20, and 21–24.

**A3      NORTH AMERICA: POPULATION OF MAJOR ADMINISTRATIVE DIVISIONS** (in thousands)

## CANADA (provinces)

|  | 1851 | 1861 | 1871 | 1881 | 1891 | 1901 | 1911 |
|---|---|---|---|---|---|---|---|
| Alberta | ... | ... | ... | ... | ...[1] | 73 | 374 |
| British Columbia | 55[2] | 52[2] | 36 | 49 | 98 | 179 | 392 |
| Manitoba | ... | ...[1] | 25 | 62 | 153 | 255 | 461 |
| New Brunswick | 194 | 252 | 286 | 321 | 331 | 352 | |
| Newfoundland[3] | ... | ... | ... | ... | ... | ... | ... |
| North west Territories | 6[2] | 7[2] | 48 | 56 | 99 | 20 | 7 |
| Nova Scotia | 277 | 331 | 388 | 441 | 450 | 460 | 492 |
| Ontario | 952 | 1,396 | 1,621 | 1,927 | 2,114 | 2,183 | 2,527 |
| Prince Edward Island | 63[4] | 81 | 94 | 109 | 109 | 103 | 94 |
| Quebec | 890 | 1,112 | 1,192 | 1,359 | 1,489 | 1,649 | 2,006 |
| Saskatchewan | ... | ... | ... | ... | ...[1] | 91 | 492 |
| Yukon | ... | ... | ... | ... | ... | 27 | 9 |

|  | 1921 | 1931 | 1941 | 1951 | 1961 | 1971 | 1981 |
|---|---|---|---|---|---|---|---|
| Alberta | 588 | 732 | 796 | 940 | 1,332 | 1,628 | 2,238 |
| British Columbia | 525 | 694 | 818 | 1,165 | 1,629 | 2,185 | 2,744 |
| Manitoba | 610 | 700 | 730 | 777 | 922 | 988 | 1,026 |
| New Brunswick | 388 | 408 | 457 | 516 | 598 | 635 | 696 |
| Newfoundland[3] | ... | ... | ... | 361 | 458 | 522 | 568 |
| North west Territories | 8 | 9 | 12 | 16 | 23 | 35 | 46 |
| Nova Scotia | 524 | 513 | 578 | 643 | 737 | 789 | 847 |
| Ontario | 2,924 | 3,432 | 3,788 | 4,598 | 6,236 | 7,703 | 8,625 |
| Prince Edward Island | 89 | 88 | 95 | 98 | 105 | 112 | 123 |
| Quebec | 2,361 | 2,875 | 3,332 | 4,056 | 5,259 | 6,028 | 6,438 |
| Saskatchewan | 758 | 922 | 896 | 832 | 925 | 926 | 968 |
| Yukon | 4 | 4 | 5 | 9 | 15 | 18 | 23 |

*See p. 29 for footnotes*

**A3     NORTH AMERICA: Population of Major Administrative Divisions** (in thousands)

## MEXICO (states)

| | 1895 | 1900 | 1910 | 1921 | 1930 | 1940 | 1950 | 1960 | 1970 | 1980 |
|---|---|---|---|---|---|---|---|---|---|---|
| Aguascalientes | 104 | 102 | 120 | 108 | 133 | 162 | 188 | 243 | 338 | 519 |
| Baja California | } 42 { | 8 | 10 | 24 | 48 | 79 | 227 | 520 | 870 | 1,178 |
| Baja California Sur | | 40 | 42 | 39 | 47 | 51 | 61 | 82 | 128 | 215 |
| Campeche | 88 | 87 | 87 | 76 | 85 | 90 | 122 | 168 | 252 | 421 |
| Coahuila | 236 | 297 | 362 | 394 | 436 | 551 | 721 | 908 | 1,115 | 1,557 |
| Colima | 56 | 65 | 78 | 92 | 62 | 79 | 112 | 164 | 241 | 346 |
| Chiapas | 315 | 361 | 439 | 422 | 530 | 680 | 907 | 1,211 | 1,569 | 2,085 |
| Chihuahua | 267 | 328 | 406 | 402 | 492 | 624 | 846 | 1,227 | 1,613 | 2,005 |
| Federal District | 485 | 541 | 721 | 906 | 1,230 | 1,757 | 3,050 | 4,871 | 6,874 | 8,831 |
| Durango | 294 | 370 | 483 | 337 | 404 | 484 | 630 | 761 | 939 | 1,182 |
| Guanajuato | 1,047 | 1,062 | 1,082 | 860 | 988 | 1,046 | 1,329 | 1,736 | 2,270 | 3,006 |
| Guerrero | 418 | 479 | 594 | 567 | 642 | 733 | 919 | 1,187 | 1,597 | 2,110 |
| Hidalgo | 548 | 605 | 646 | 622 | 678 | 772 | 850 | 995 | 1,194 | 1,547 |
| Jalisco | 1,108 | 1,154 | 1,209 | 1,192 | 1,255 | 1,418 | 1,747 | 2,443 | 3,297 | 4,372 |
| Mexico | 837 | 934 | 989 | 885 | 990 | 1,146 | 1,393 | 1,898 | 3,833 | 7,564 |
| Michoacán | 890 | 936 | 992 | 940 | 1,048 | 1,182 | 1,423 | 1,852 | 2,324 | 2,869 |
| Morelos | 160 | 160 | 180 | 103 | 132 | 183 | 273 | 386 | 616 | 947 |
| Nayarit | 149 | 150 | 171 | 163 | 168 | 217 | 290 | 390 | 544 | 726 |
| Nuevo León | 309 | 328 | 365 | 336 | 418 | 541 | 740 | 1,079 | 1,695 | 2,513 |
| Oaxaca | 883 | 949 | 1,040 | 976 | 1,085 | 1,193 | 1,421 | 1,727 | 2,015 | 2,369 |
| Puebla | 980 | 1,021 | 1,102 | 1,025 | 1,150 | 1,295 | 1,626 | 1,974 | 2,508 | 3,348 |
| Querétaro | 227 | 232 | 245 | 220 | 234 | 245 | 286 | 355 | 486 | 740 |
| Quintana Roo | — | — | 9 | 11 | 11 | 19 | 27 | 50 | 88 | 226 |
| San Luis Potosi | 588 | 575 | 628 | 446 | 580 | 679 | 856 | 1,048 | 1,282 | 1,674 |
| Sinaloa | 259 | 297 | 324 | 341 | 396 | 493 | 636 | 838 | 1,267 | 1,850 |
| Sonora | 191 | 222 | 265 | 275 | 316 | 364 | 511 | 783 | 1,099 | 1,514 |
| Tabasco | 135 | 160 | 187 | 210 | 224 | 286 | 363 | 496 | 768 | 1,063 |
| Tamaulipas | 208 | 219 | 250 | 287 | 344 | 459 | 718 | 1,024 | 1,457 | 1,924 |
| Tlaxcala | 167 | 172 | 184 | 179 | 205 | 224 | 285 | 347 | 421 | 557 |
| Veracruz | 856 | 981 | 1,133 | 1,160 | 1,377 | 1,619 | 2,040 | 2,728 | 3,815 | 5,388 |
| Yucatán | 298 | 310 | 340 | 358 | 386 | 418 | 517 | 614 | 758 | 1,064 |
| Zacatecas | 453 | 462 | 477 | 379 | 459 | 565 | 665 | 818 | 952 | 1,137 |

*See p. 43 for footnotes*

**A3    NORTH AMERICA: Population of Major Administrative Divisions** (in thousands)

## USA (states)

| | 1790 | 1800 | 1810 | 1820 | 1830 | 1840 | 1850 | 1860 | 1870 | 1880 |
|---|---|---|---|---|---|---|---|---|---|---|
| *New England* | 1,009 | 1,233 | 1,472 | 1,660 | 1,955 | 2,235 | 2,728 | 3,135 | 3,488 | 4,011 |
| Connecticut[5] | 238 | 251 | 262 | 275 | 298 | 310 | 371 | 460 | 537 | 623 |
| Maine[6] | 97 | 152 | 229 | 298 | 399 | 502 | 583 | 628 | 627 | 649 |
| Massachusetts[7] | 379 | 423 | 472 | 523 | 610 | 738 | 995 | 1,231 | 1,457 | 1,783 |
| New Hampshire[8] | 142 | 184 | 214 | 244 | 269 | 285 | 318 | 326 | 318 | 347 |
| Rhode Island[9] | 69 | 69 | 77 | 83 | 97 | 109 | 148 | 175 | 217 | 277 |
| Vermont[10] | 85 | 154 | 218 | 236 | 281 | 292 | 314 | 315 | 331 | 332 |
| *Middle Atlantic* | 959 | 1,403 | 2,015 | 2,700 | 3,588 | 4,526 | 5,899 | 7,459 | 8,811 | 10,497 |
| New Jersey[11] | 184 | 211 | 246 | 278 | 321 | 373 | 490 | 672 | 906 | 1,131 |
| New York[12] | 340 | 589 | 959 | 1,373 | 1,919 | 2,429 | 3,097 | 3,881 | 4,383 | 5,083 |
| Pennsylvania | 434 | 602 | 810 | 1,049 | 1,348 | 1,724 | 2,312 | 2,906 | 3,522 | 4,283 |
| *East North Central* | ... | 51 | 272 | 793 | 1,470 | 2,925 | 4,523 | 6,927 | 9,125 | 11,207 |
| Illinois | ... | ... | 12[17] | 55 | 157 | 476 | 851 | 1,712 | 2,540 | 3,078 |
| Indiana | ... | 6[15] | 24[15] | 147 | 343 | 686 | 988 | 1,350 | 1,681 | 1,978 |
| Michigan | ... | ... | 5[18] | 9[18] | 32[18] | 212 | 398 | 749 | 1,184 | 1,637 |
| Ohio | ... | 45[16] | 231 | 581 | 938 | 1,519 | 1,980 | 2,340 | 2,665 | 3,198 |
| Wisconsin | ... | ... | ... | ... | ... | 31[19] | 305 | 776 | 1,055 | 1,315 |
| | | | | | | ... | | | | |
| *West North Central* | ... | ... | 20 | 67 | 140 | 427 | 880 | 2,170 | 3,857 | 6,157 |
| Iowa | ... | ... | ... | ... | ... | 43[20] | 192 | 675 | 1,194 | 1,625 |
| Kansas | ... | ... | ... | ... | ... | ... | ... | 107 | 364 | 996 |
| Minnesota | ... | ... | ... | ... | ... | ... | 6 | 172 | 440 | 781 |
| Missouri | ... | ... | 20 | 67 | 140 | 384 | 682 | 1,182 | 1,721 | 2,168 |
| Nebraska | ... | ... | ... | ... | ... | ... | ... | 29 | 123 | 452 |
| North Dakota | ... | ... | ... | ... | ... | ... | ... | } 5[21] { | 2 | 37 |
| South Dakota | ... | ... | ... | ... | ... | ... | ... | | 12 | 98 |
| *South Atlantic* | 1,852 | 2,286 | 2,675 | 3,061 | 3,646 | 3,925 | 4,679 | 5,365 | 5,854 | 7,597 |
| Delaware | 59 | 64 | 73 | 73 | 77 | 78 | 92 | 112 | 125 | 147 |
| District of Columbia | ... | 8 | 15 | 23 | 30 | 34 | 52 | 75 | 132 | 178 |
| Florida | ... | ... | ... | ... | 35 | 54 | 87 | 140 | 188 | 269 |
| Georgia | 83 | 163 | 252 | 341 | 517 | 691 | 906 | 1,057 | 1,184 | 1,542 |
| Maryland[13] | 320 | 342 | 381 | 407 | 447 | 470 | 583 | 687 | 781 | 935 |
| North Carolina | 394 | 478 | 556 | 639 | 738 | 753 | 869 | 993 | 1,071 | 1,400 |
| South Carolina | 249 | 346 | 415 | 503 | 581 | 594 | 669 | 704 | 706 | 996 |
| Virginia[14] | 692 | 808 | 878 | 938 | 1,044 | 1,025 | 1,119 | 1,220 | 1,225 | 1,513 |
| West Virginia | 56 | 79 | 105 | 137 | 177 | 225 | 302 | 377 | 442 | 618 |

*See p. 43 for footnotes*

**A3    NORTH AMERICA: Population of Major Administrative Divisions** (in thousands)

## USA (states) (contd)

| | 1790 | 1800 | 1810 | 1820 | 1830 | 1840 | 1850 | 1860 | 1870 | 1880 |
|---|---|---|---|---|---|---|---|---|---|---|
| *East South Central* | 109 | 335 | 709 | 1,190 | 1,816 | 2,575 | 3,363 | 4,021 | 4,404 | 5,585 |
| Alabama | ... | 1[22] | 9[22] | 128 | 310 | 591 | 772 | 964 | 997 | 1,263 |
| Kentucky | 74 | 221 | 407 | 564 | 688 | 780 | 982 | 1,156 | 1,321 | 1,649 |
| Mississippi | ... | 8[22] | 31[22] | 75 | 137 | 376 | 607 | 791 | 828 | 1,132 |
| Tennessee | 36 | 106 | 262 | 423 | 682 | 829 | 1,002 | 1,110 | 1,259 | 1,542 |
| *West South Central* | ... | ... | 78 | 168 | 246 | 450 | 940 | 1,748 | 2,030 | 3,334 |
| Arkansas | ... | ... | 1 | 14 | 30 | 98 | 210 | 435 | 484 | 803 |
| Louisiana | ... | ... | 77 | 153 | 216 | 352 | 518 | 708 | 727 | 940 |
| Oklahoma | ... | ... | ... | ... | ... | ... | ... | ... | ... | ... |
| Texas | ... | ... | ... | ... | ... | ... | 213 | 604 | 819 | 1,592 |
| *Mountain* | ... | ... | ... | ... | ... | ... | 73 | 175 | 315 | 653 |
| Arizona | ... | ... | ... | ... | ... | ... | ... | ... | 10 | 40 |
| Colorado | ... | ... | ... | ... | ... | ... | ... | 34 | 40 | 194 |
| Idaho | ... | ... | ... | ... | ... | ... | ... | ... | 15 | 33 |
| Montana | ... | ... | ... | ... | ... | ... | ... | ... | 21 | 39 |
| Nevada | ... | ... | ... | ... | ... | ... | ... | 7[23] | 42 | 62 |
| New Mexico | ... | ... | ... | ... | ... | ... | 62 | 94[24] | 92 | 120 |
| Utah | ... | ... | ... | ... | ... | ... | 11 | 40[25] | 87 | 144 |
| Wyoming | ... | ... | ... | ... | ... | ... | ... | ... | 9 | 21 |
| *Pacific*[26] | ... | ... | ... | ... | ... | ... | 106 | 444 | 675 | 1,115 |
| Alaska[26] | ... | ... | ... | ... | ... | ... | ... | ... | ... | [33] |
| California | ... | ... | ... | ... | ... | ... | 93 | 380 | 560 | 865 |
| Hawaii[26] | ... | ... | ... | ... | ... | ... | ... | ... | ... | ... |
| Oregon | ... | ... | ... | ... | ... | ... | 12 | 52 | 91 | 175 |
| Washington | ... | ... | ... | ... | ... | ... | 1[27] | 12[28] | 24 | 75 |

*See p. 43 for footnotes*

*See p. 43 for footnotes*

**A3      NORTH AMERICA: Population of Major Administrative Divisions** (in thousands)

## USA (states) (contd)

|  | 1890 | 1900 | 1910 | 1920 | 1930 | 1940 | 1950 | 1960 | 1970 | 1980 |
|---|---|---|---|---|---|---|---|---|---|---|
| *New England* | 4,701 | 5,592 | 6,553 | 7,401 | 8,166 | 8,437 | 9,314 | 10,509 | 11,848 | 12,348 |
| Connecticut[5] | 746 | 908 | 1,115 | 1,381 | 1,607 | 1,709 | 2,007 | 2,535 | 3,032 | 3,108 |
| Maine[6] | 661 | 694 | 742 | 768 | 797 | 847 | 914 | 969 | 994 | 1,125 |
| Massachusetts[7] | 2,239 | 2,805 | 3,366 | 3,852 | 4,250 | 4,317 | 4,691 | 5,149 | 5,689 | 5,737 |
| New Hampshire[8] | 377 | 412 | 431 | 443 | 465 | 492 | 533 | 607 | 738 | 921 |
| Rhode Island[9] | 346 | 429 | 543 | 604 | 687 | 713 | 792 | 859 | 950 | 947 |
| Vermont[10] | 332 | 344 | 356 | 352 | 360 | 359 | 378 | 390 | 445 | 511 |
| *Middle Atlantic* | 12,706 | 15,455 | 19,316 | 22,261 | 26,261 | 27,539 | 30,164 | 34,168 | 37,263 | 36,787 |
| New Jersey[11] | 1,445 | 1,884 | 2,537 | 3,156 | 4,041 | 4,160 | 4,835 | 6,067 | 7,168 | 7,365 |
| New York[12] | 6,003 | 7,269 | 9,114 | 10,385 | 12,588 | 13,479 | 14,830 | 16,782 | 18,241 | 17,558 |
| Pennsylvania | 5,258 | 6,302 | 7,665 | 8,720 | 9,631 | 9,900 | 10,498 | 11,319 | 11,794 | 11,864 |
| *East North Central* | 13,478 | 15,986 | 18,251 | 21,476 | 25,297 | 26,626 | 30,399 | 36,225 | 40,262 | 41,682 |
| Illinois | 3,826 | 4,822 | 5,639 | 6,485 | 7,631 | 7,897 | 8,712 | 10,081 | 11,114 | 11,427 |
| Indiana | 2,192 | 2,516 | 2,701 | 2,930 | 3,239 | 3,428 | 3,934 | 4,662 | 5,194 | 5,490 |
| Michigan | 2,094 | 2,421 | 2,810 | 3,668 | 4,842 | 5,256 | 6,372 | 7,823 | 8,875 | 9,262 |
| Ohio | 3,672 | 4,158 | 4,767 | 5,759 | 6,647 | 6,908 | 7,947 | 9,706 | 10,652 | 10,798 |
| Wisconsin | 1,693 | 2,069 | 2,334 | 2,632 | 2,939 | 3,138 | 3,435 | 3,952 | 4,418 | 4,706 |
| *West North Central* | 8,932 | 10,347 | 11,638 | 12,544 | 13,297 | 13,517 | 14,061 | 15,394 | 16,327 | 17,183 |
| Iowa | 1,912 | 2,232 | 2,225 | 2,404 | 2,471 | 2,538 | 2,621 | 2,758 | 2,825 | 2,914 |
| Kansas | 1,428 | 1,470 | 1,691 | 1,769 | 1,881 | 1,801 | 1,905 | 2,179 | 2,249 | 2,364 |
| Minnesota | 1,310 | 1,751 | 2,076 | 2,387 | 2,564 | 2,792 | 2,982 | 3,414 | 3,805 | 4,076 |
| Missouri | 2,679 | 3,107 | 3,293 | 3,404 | 3,629 | 3,785 | 3,955 | 4,320 | 4,677 | 4,917 |
| Nebraska | 1,063 | 1,066 | 1,192 | 1,296 | 1,378 | 1,316 | 1,326 | 1,411 | 1,484 | 1,570 |
| North Dakota | 191 | 319 | 577 | 647 | 681 | 642 | 620 | 632 | 618 | 653 |
| South Dakota | 349 | 402 | 584 | 637 | 693 | 643 | 653 | 681 | 666 | 691 |
| *South Atlantic* | 8,858 | 10,443 | 12,195 | 13,990 | 15,794 | 17,823 | 21,182 | 25,972 | 30,678 | 36,959 |
| Delaware | 168 | 185 | 202 | 223 | 238 | 267 | 318 | 446 | 548 | 594 |
| District of Columbia | 230 | 279 | 331 | 438 | 487 | 663 | 802 | 764 | 757 | 638 |
| Florida | 391 | 529 | 753 | 968 | 1,468 | 1,897 | 2,771 | 4,952 | 6,789 | 9,746 |
| Georgia | 1,837 | 2,216 | 2,609 | 2,896 | 2,909 | 3,124 | 3,445 | 3,943 | 4,590 | 5,463 |
| Maryland[13] | 1,042 | 1,188 | 1,295 | 1,450 | 1,632 | 1,821 | 2,343 | 3,101 | 3,922 | 4,217 |
| North Carolina | 1,618 | 1,894 | 2,206 | 2,559 | 3,170 | 3,572 | 4,062 | 4,556 | 5,082 | 5,882 |
| South Carolina | 1,151 | 1,340 | 1,515 | 1,684 | 1,739 | 1,900 | 2,117 | 2,383 | 2,591 | 3,122 |
| Virginia[14] | 1,656 | 1,854 | 2,062 | 2,309 | 2,422 | 2,678 | 3,319 | 3,967 | 4,648 | 5,347 |
| West Virginia | 763 | 959 | 1,221 | 1,464 | 1,729 | 1,902 | 2,006 | 1,860 | 1,744 | 1,950 |

*See p. 43 for footnotes*

**A3    NORTH AMERICA: Population of Major Administrative Divisions** (in thousands)

## USA (states) (contd)

| | 1890 | 1900 | 1910 | 1920 | 1930 | 1940 | 1950 | 1960 | 1970 | 1980 |
|---|---|---|---|---|---|---|---|---|---|---|
| *East South Central* | 6,429 | 7,548 | 8,410 | 8,893 | 9,887 | 10,778 | 10,477 | 12,050 | 12,808 | 14,666 |
| Alabama | 1,513 | 1,829 | 2,138 | 2,348 | 2,646 | 2,833 | 3,062 | 3,567 | 3,444 | 3,894 |
| Kentucky | 1,859 | 2,147 | 2,290 | 2,417 | 2,615 | 2,846 | 2,945 | 3,038 | 3,219 | 3,661 |
| Mississippi | 1,290 | 1,551 | 1,797 | 1,791 | 2,010 | 2,184 | 2,179 | 2,178 | 2,217 | 2,521 |
| Tennessee | 1,768 | 2,021 | 2,185 | 2,338 | 2,617 | 2,916 | 3,292 | 3,567 | 3,924 | 4,591 |
| *West South Central* | 4,741 | 6,532 | 8,785 | 10,242 | 12,177 | 13,065 | 14,538 | 16,951 | 19,326 | 23,747 |
| Arkansas | 1,128 | 1,312 | 1,574 | 1,752 | 1,854 | 1,949 | 1,910 | 1,786 | 1,923 | 2,286 |
| Louisiana | 1,119 | 1,382 | 1,656 | 1,799 | 2,102 | 2,364 | 2,684 | 3,257 | 3,643 | 4,206 |
| Oklahoma | 259 | 790 | 1,657 | 2,028 | 2,396 | 2,336 | 2,233 | 2,328 | 2,559 | 3,025 |
| Texas | 2,236 | 3,049 | 3,897 | 4,663 | 5,825 | 6,415 | 7,711 | 9,580 | 11,197 | 14,229 |
| *Mountain* | 1,214 | 1,675 | 2,634 | 3,336 | 3,702 | 4,150 | 5,075 | 6,855 | 8,289 | 11,373 |
| Arizona | 88 | 123 | 204 | 334 | 436 | 499 | 750 | 1,302 | 1,772 | 2,718 |
| Colorado | 413 | 540 | 799 | 940 | 1,036 | 1,123 | 1,325 | 1,754 | 2,207 | 2,890 |
| Idaho | 89 | 162 | 326 | 432 | 445 | 525 | 589 | 667 | 713 | 944 |
| Montana | 143 | 243 | 376 | 549 | 538 | 559 | 591 | 675 | 694 | 787 |
| Nevada | 47 | 42 | 82 | 77 | 91 | 110 | 160 | 285 | 489 | 800 |
| New Mexico | 160 | 195 | 327 | 360 | 423 | 532 | 681 | 951 | 1,016 | 1,303 |
| Utah | 211 | 277 | 373 | 449 | 508 | 550 | 689 | 891 | 1,059 | 1,461 |
| Wyoming | 63 | 93 | 146 | 194 | 226 | 251 | 291 | 330 | 332 | 470 |
| *Pacific*[26] | 1,888 | 2,417 | 4,192 | 5,567 | 8,194 | 9,733 | 14,487 | 21,198 | 26,549 | 31,800 |
| Alaska[26] | [32] | [64] | [64] | [55] | [59][29] | [73][30] | [129] | 226 | 302 | 402 |
| California | 1,213 | 1,485 | 2,378 | 3,427 | 5,677 | 6,907 | 10,586 | 15,717 | 19,953 | 23,668 |
| Hawaii[26] | ... | [154] | [192] | [256] | [368] | [423] | [500] | 633 | 770 | 965 |
| Oregon | 318 | 414 | 673 | 783 | 954 | 1,090 | 1,521 | 1,769 | 2,091 | 2,633 |
| Washington | 357 | 518 | 1,142 | 1,357 | 1,563 | 1,736 | 2,379 | 2,853 | 3,409 | 4,132 |

*See p. 43 for footnotes*

**A3    SOUTH AMERICA: POPULATION OF MAJOR ADMINISTRATIVE DIVISIONS** (in thousands)

## ARGENTINA (provinces)

|  | 1869 | 1895 | 1914 | 1947 | 1960 | 1970 | 1980 |
|---|---|---|---|---|---|---|---|
| Federal Capital | 187 | 664 | 1,576 | 2,983 | 2,967 | 2,972 | 2,923 |
| Buenos Aires | 308 | 921 | 2,066 | 4,272 | 6,735 | 8,775 | 10,865 |
| Catamarca | 80 | 90 | 100 | 147 | 172 | 172 | 208 |
| Chaco | 45 | 10 | 46 | 431 | 535 | 567 | 701 |
| Chubut | ...[31] | 4 | 23 | 59 | 142 | 190 | 263 |
| Comodoro Rivadavia | ... | ... | ... | 52 | ... | ... | ... |
| Córdoba | 211 | 351 | 735 | 1,498 | 1,760 | 2,060 | 2,408 |
| Corrientes | 129 | 240 | 347 | 525 | 543 | 564 | 661 |
| Entre Ríos | 134 | 292 | 425 | 787 | 804 | 812 | 908 |
| Formosa | ...[31] | 5 | 19 | 114 | 178 | 234 | 296 |
| Jujuy | 40 | 50 | 77 | 167 | 240 | 302 | 410 |
| La Pampa | 21 | 26 | 101 | 169 | 158 | 172 | 208 |
| La Rioja | 49 | 70 | 80 | 111 | 128 | 136 | 164 |
| Mendoza | 65 | 116 | 278 | 588 | 826 | 973 | 1,196 |
| Misiones | 3 | 33 | 54 | 246 | 391 | 443 | 589 |
| Neuquén | ... | 15 | 29 | 87 | 111 | 155 | 244 |
| Río Negro | ...[31] | 9 | 42 | 134 | 193 | 263 | 383 |
| Salta | 89 | 118 | 141 | 291 | 413 | 510 | 663 |
| San Juan | 60 | 84 | 119 | 261 | 352 | 384 | 466 |
| San Luis | 53 | 81 | 116 | 166 | 174 | 183 | 214 |
| Santa Cruz | ...[31] | 1 | 10 | 25 | 53 | 84 | 115 |
| Santa Fé | 89 | 397 | 900 | 1,703 | 1,865 | 2,136 | 2,466 |
| Santiago del Estero | 133 | 162 | 262 | 479 | 477 | 495 | 595 |
| Tierra del Fuego | ...[31] | - - | 3 | 5 | 7 | 13 | 27 |
| Tucumán | 109 | 216 | 333 | 593 | 780 | 766 | 973 |

## BOLIVIA (provinces)

|  | 1900 | 1950 | 1976 |
|---|---|---|---|
| Beni | 32 | 120 | 168 |
| Chuquisaca | 204 | 283 | 359 |
| Cochabamba | 328 | 490 | 721 |
| El Litoral | 41 | ... | ... |
| La Paz | 446 | 948 | 1,465 |
| Oruro | 86 | 210 | 310 |
| Pando | 32 | 20 | 34 |
| Potosi | 326 | 534 | 658 |
| Santa Cruz | 210 | 286 | 711 |
| Tarija | 103 | 127 | 187 |

*See p. 43 for footnotes*

**A3    SOUTH AMERICA: Population of Major Administrative Divisions** (in thousands)

## BRAZIL (states)

| | 1872 | 1890 | 1900 | 1920 | 1940 | 1950 | 1960 | 1970 | 1980 |
|---|---|---|---|---|---|---|---|---|---|
| *North* | 323 | 476 | 695 | 1,439 | 1,462 | 1,845 | 2,562 | 3,604 | 5,880 |
| Rondônia | ... | ... | ... | ... | ... | 37 | 70 | 111 | 491 |
| Acre | ... | ... | ... | 92 | 80 | 115 | 158 | 215 | 301 |
| Amazonas | 58 | 148 | 250 | 363 | 438 | 514 | 708 | 955 | 1,430 |
| Roraima | ... | ... | ... | ... | ... | 18 | 28 | 41 | 79 |
| Pará | 275 | 328 | 445 | 984 | 945 | 1,123 | 1,529 | 2,167 | 3,403 |
| Amapá | ... | ... | ... | ... | ... | 37 | 68 | 114 | 175 |
| *North-East* | 4,639 | 6,002 | 6,750 | 11,246 | 14,434 | 17,973 | 22,182 | 28,112 | 34,812 |
| Maranhão | 359 | 431 | 499 | 874 | 1,235 | 1,583 | 2,469 | 2,993 | 3,996 |
| Piauí | 202 | 268 | 334 | 609 | 817 | 1,046 | 1,242 | 1,681 | 2,139 |
| Ceará | 722 | 806 | 849 | 1,319 | 2,091 | 2,695 | 3,296 | 4,362 | 5,288 |
| Rio Grande do Norte | 234 | 268 | 274 | 537 | 768 | 968 | 1,146 | 1,550 | 1,898 |
| Paraíba | 376 | 457 | 491 | 961 | 1,422 | 1,713 | 2,001 | 2,383 | 2,770 |
| Pernambuco | 842 | 1,030 | 1,178 | 2,155 | 2,688 | 3,395 | 4,096 | 5,161 | 6,142 |
| Alagoas | 348 | 511 | 649 | 979 | 951 | 1,093 | 1,258 | 1,588 | 1,983 |
| Fernando de Noronha | ... | ... | ... | ... | ... | 1 | 1 | 1 | 1 |
| Sergipe | 176 | 311 | 356 | 477 | 542 | 644 | 752 | 901 | 1,140 |
| Bahia | 1,380 | 1,920 | 2,118 | 3,334 | 3,918 | 4,835 | 5,920 | 7,493 | 9,454 |
| *South East* | 4,017 | 6,104 | 7,824 | 13,655 | 18,346 | 22,548 | 30,631 | 39,853 | 51,734 |
| Minas Gerais | 2,040 | 3,184 | 3,594 | 5,888 | 6,763 | 7,782 | 9,658 | 11,487 | 13,379 |
| Espírito Santo | 82 | 136 | 210 | 457 | 790 | 957 | 1,171 | 1,599 | 2,023 |
| Rio de Janeiro | 783 | 877 | 926 | 1,559 | 1,848 | 2,297 | 3,363 | 4,743 | } 11,292 |
| Guanabara | 275 | 523 | 811 | 1,158 | 1,764 | 2,377 | 3,248 | 4,252 | |
| São Paulo | 837 | 1,385 | 2,282 | 4,592 | 7,180 | 9,134 | 12,809 | 17,772 | 25,041 |
| *South* | 721 | 1,431 | 1,796 | 3,537 | 5,735 | 7,841 | 11,753 | 16,496 | 19,031 |
| Parana | 127 | 249 | 327 | 686 | 1,236 | 2,116 | 4,268 | 6,930 | 7,629 |
| Santa Catarina | 160 | 284 | 320 | 669 | 1,178 | 1,561 | 2,118 | 2,902 | 3,628 |
| Rio Grande do Sul | 435 | 897 | 1,149 | 2,183 | 3,321 | 4,165 | 5,367 | 6,665 | 7,774 |
| *Centre West* | 221 | 320 | 373 | 759 | 1,259 | 1,737 | 2,943 | 5,073 | 7,545 |
| Mato Grosso | 60 | 93 | 118 | 247 | 432 | 522 | 890 | 1,597[32] | 1,139 |
| Mato Grosso do Sul | ... | ... | ... | ... | ... | ... | ... | ... | 1,370 |
| Goiás | 160 | 228 | 255 | 512 | 826 | 1,215 | 1,913 | 2,939 | 3,860 |
| Federal District | ... | ... | ... | ... | ... | ... | 140 | 537 | 1,177 |

**A3      SOUTH AMERICA: Population of Major Administrative Divisions** (in thousands)

## CHILE (provinces)

| | 1835 | 1843 | 1854 | 1865 | 1875 | 1885 | 1895 | 1907 |
|---|---|---|---|---|---|---|---|---|
| Aconcagua | 82 | 92 | 112 | 146 | 133 | 176 | 113 | 175 |
| Antofagasta | — | — | — | 2 | 2 | 34 | 44 | 113 |
| Arauco | ... | ... | 10 | 17 | 40 | 69 | 59 | 62 |
| Atacama | 28 | 25 | 51 | 77 | 69 | 64 | 60 | 64 |
| Aysén | — | — | — | — | — | — | — | — |
| Bío-Bío | 7 | 19 | 40 | 59 | 76 | 102 | 89 | 98 |
| Cautín | — | — | — | — | 6 | 38 | 78 | 140 |
| Chiloé | 44 | 49 | 50 | 59 | 65 | 73 | 78 | 89 |
| Colchagua | 102 | 91 | 116 | 142 | 148 | 156 | 158 | 159 |
| Concepción | 67 | 92 | 104 | 139 | 151 | 182 | 188 | 217 |
| Coquimbo | 72 | 78 | 111 | 146 | 158 | 176 | 161 | 175 |
| Curicó | 65 | 60 | 77 | 91 | 93 | 100 | 103 | 107 |
| Linares | 38 | 43 | 64 | 85 | 119 | 111 | 102 | 109 |
| Llanquihue | 9 | 19 | 26 | 38 | 48 | 63 | 78 | 105 |
| Magallanes | — | — | - - | - - | 1 | 1 | 5 | 17 |
| Malleco | — | — | — | 3 | 20 | 59 | 98 | 110 |
| Maule | 53 | 76 | 93 | 103 | 118 | 124 | 120 | 110 |
| Ñuble | 73 | 81 | 101 | 125 | 137 | 150 | 153 | 166 |
| O'Higgins | ... | ... | 65 | 80 | 77 | 89 | 85 | 93 |
| Osorno | ... | ... | ... | ... | ... | ... | ... | ... |
| Santiago | 218 | 208[32] | 208 | 261 | 289 | 329 | 416 | 516 |
| Tacna | — | — | — | — | — | 30 | 24 | 29 |
| Talca | 61 | 71 | 79 | 101 | 110 | 133 | 129 | 132 |
| Tarapacá | — | — | — | — | — | 45 | 90 | 110 |
| Valdivia | 7 | 14 | 18 | 23 | 35 | 51 | 61 | 118 |
| Valparaíso | 80 | 76 | 116 | 143 | 179 | 203 | 221 | 281 |

| | 1920[33] | 1930[33] | 1940 | 1952 | 1960 | 1970 |
|---|---|---|---|---|---|---|
| Aconcagua | 160/422 | 464/103 | 118 | 128 | 140 | 161 |
| Antofagasta | 172 | 171/145 | 145 | 184 | 214 | 251 |
| Arauco | 60/— | —/ 61 | 66 | 72 | 89 | 99 |
| Atacama | 48 | 61 | 84 | 80 | 114 | 152 |
| Aysén | —/ 2 | 10/ 9 | 17 | 25 | 37 | 51 |
| Bío-Bío | 107/166 | 181/114 | 127 | 138 | 167 | 193 |
| Cautín | 194/313 | 384/315 | 375 | 362 | 393 | 421 |
| Chiloé | 110/178 | 183/ 93 | 102 | 99 | 99 | 111 |
| Colchagua | 166/282 | 296/126 | 131 | 138 | 158 | 168 |
| Concepción | 247/291 | 329/268 | 308 | 410 | 538 | 638 |
| Coquimbo | 160/176 | 198 | 246 | 256 | 306 | 337 |
| Curicó | 108/— | —/ 75 | 81 | 89 | 107 | 114 |
| Linares | 119/— | —/123 | 135 | 147 | 170 | 189 |
| Llanquíhue | 137/— | —/ 92 | 117 | 130 | 166 | 198 |
| Magallanes | 29 | 38 | 49 | 55 | 73 | 89 |
| Malleco | 121/— | —/136 | 154 | 157 | 174 | 176 |
| Maule | 113/204 | 197/ 74 | 70 | 72 | 79 | 82 |
| Ñuble | 170/224 | 232 | 243 | 250 | 285 | 315 |
| O'Higgins | 119/— | —/171 | 200 | 223 | 259 | 307 |
| Osorno | ... | —/ 87 | 107 | 122 | 144 | 159 |
| Santiago | 685/718 | 968 | 1,269 | 1,749 | 2,430 | 3,218 |
| Tacna | 39/— | ... | ... | ... | ... | ... |
| Talca | 134/202 | 218/142 | 157 | 174 | 205 | 231 |
| Tarapacá | 101 | 113 | 104 | 103 | 123 | 175 |
| Valdivia | 175/187 | 236/149 | 192 | 231 | 255 | 275 |
| Valparaíso | 320/— | —/360 | 425 | 492 | 613 | 727 |

*See p. 43 for footnotes*

**A3    SOUTH AMERICA: Population of Major Administrative Divisions** (in thousands)

### CHILE (contd) (regions)

|  | 1970 | 1980 |  | 1970 | 1980 |  | 1970 | 1980 |
|---|---|---|---|---|---|---|---|---|
| Antofagasta | 251 | 342 | Coquimbo | 337 | 420 | O'Higgins | 475 | 587 |
| Araucania | 597 | 698 | Los Lagos | 743 | 849 | Santiago | 3,218 | 4,318 |
| Atacarma | 152 | 183 | Magellanes | 89 | 132 | Tarapaca | 175 | 275 |
| Aysen | 51 | 66 | Maulé | 616 | 731 | Valparaiso | 888 | 1,210 |
| Bio Bio | 1,146 | 1,519 |  |  |  |  |  |  |

### COLOMBIA

|  | 1835 | 1843 | 1851 | 1864 | 1871 | 1881 |
|---|---|---|---|---|---|---|
| *Departments* |  |  |  |  |  |  |
| Antioquia | 158 | 190 | 243 | 303 | 366 | 470 |
| Bolivar | 178 | 192 | 206 | 217 | 247 | 280 |
| Boyacá | 289 | 332 | 380 | 456 | 483 | 702 |
| Caucá | 210 | 269 | 324 | 386 | 435 | 621 |
| Cundinamarca | 256 | 279 | 317 | 393 | 410 | 569 |
| Magdalera | 61 | 62 | 68 | 89 | 85 | 90 |
| Panama | 115 | 119 | 138 | 221 | 221 | 285 |
| Santander | 262 | 306 | 360 | 378 | 425 | 556 |
| Tolima | 157 | 183 | 208 | 220 | 231 | 306 |

### COLOMBIA (contd)

|  | 1905 | 1912 | 1918 | 1928 | 1938 | 1951 | 1964 |
|---|---|---|---|---|---|---|---|
| *Departments* |  |  |  |  |  |  |  |
| Antioquia | 651 | 741 | 823 | 1,011 | 1,189 | 1,570 | 2,477 |
| Atlántico | 112 | 115 | 136 | 243 | 268 | 428 | 717 |
| Bolívar | 198 | 416 | 457 | 643 | 765 | 991 | 1,006 |
| Boyacá | 503 | 585 | 655 | 950 | 737 | 779 | 1,058 |
| Caldas | 246 | 341 | 428 | 624 | 770 | 1,068 | 1,456 |
| Caucá | 223 | 212 | 239 | 318 | 356 | 443 | 607 |
| Chocó | 48 | 83 | 91 | 85 | 111 | 131 | 182 |
| Córdoba | — | — | — | — | — | — | 586 |
| Cundinamarca | 631 | 718 | 812 | 1,057 | 1,175 | 1,624 | 2,820 |
| Huila | 154 | 158 | 183 | 207 | 217 | 294 | 416 |
| La Guajira | 1 | 53 | 23 | 33 | 53 | 52 | 147 |
| Magdalena | 125 | 150 | 211 | 302 | 342 | 457 | 789 |
| Meta | 6 | 28 | 34 | 19 | 52 | 67 | 166 |
| Nariño | 248 | 292 | 341 | 412 | 466 | 547 | 706 |
| Norte de Santander | 164 | 204 | 239 | 329 | 346 | 387 | 534 |
| Santander | 386 | 403 | 439 | 595 | 616 | 748 | 1,001 |
| Tolima | 218 | 282 | 329 | 445 | 548 | 712 | 841 |
| Valle del Cauca | 215 | 217 | 272 | 506 | 613 | 1,107 | 1,733 |
| *Comisarias and Intendencias* |  |  |  |  |  |  |  |
| Amazonas | — | — | ... | 2 | 6 | 8 | 13 |
| Arauca | 7 | 7 | 10 | 13 | 11 | 13 | 24 |
| Caquetá | — | 24 | 74 | 14 | 21 | 47 | 104 |
| Casanare | — | — | — | — | — | 22 | — |
| Guianía | — | — | — | — | — | — | 4 |
| Putumayo | 1 | 31 | 41 | 17 | 16 | 22 | 56 |
| San Andrés & Providencia | 4 | 5 | 6 | 6 | 7 | 6 | 17 |
| Vaupes | — | 6 | 6 | 9 | 8 | 9 | 13 |
| Vichada | — | — | 6 | 11 | 9 | 12 | 10 |

**A3      SOUTH AMERICA: Population of Major Administrative Divisions** (in thousands)

## COLOMBIA (contd)

| Departments | 1973 | 1985 | Departments (contd) | 1973 | 1985 |
|---|---|---|---|---|---|
| Antioquia | 3,133 | 3,888 | Quindio | 337 | 378 |
| Atlántico | 1,017 | 1,429 | Risaralda | 475 | 625 |
| Bogota | 2,880 | 3,983 | Santander | 1,191 | 1,438 |
| Bolivar | 908 | 1,198 | Sucre | 411 | 529 |
| Boyaca | 1,135 | 1,098 | Tolima | 956 | 1,052 |
| Caldas | 740 | 838 | Valle de Cauca | 2,353 | 2,847 |
| Caquetá | 64 | 214 | | | |
| Cauca | 735 | 796 | *Comisarias and Intendencias* | | |
| Cesar | 394 | 585 | Amazonas | 16 | 30 |
| Choco | 226 | 243 | Arauca | 46 | 70 |
| | | | Casanare | 35 | 110 |
| Córdoba | 771 | 914 | Guaviare | 14 | 35 |
| Cundinamarca | 1,184 | 1,382 | Guianía | 6 | 9 |
| Huila | 496 | 648 | | | |
| La Guajira | 214 | 255 | Putumayo | 67 | 120 |
| Magdalena | 625 | 769 | San Andrés & Providencia | 23 | 36 |
| | | | Vaupés | 9 | 19 |
| Meta | 258 | 412 | Vichada | 12 | 14 |
| Nariño | 856 | 1,019 | | | |
| Norte de Santander | 730 | 884 | | | |

**A3**      **SOUTH AMERICA: Population of Major Administrative Divisions** (in thousands)

## PERU (departments)

| | 1862 | 1876 | 1896[34] | 1927[34] | 1940 | 1961 | 1972 | 1981 |
|---|---|---|---|---|---|---|---|---|
| Amazonas | 33 | 34 | 71 | 80 | 90 | 118 | 196 | 268 |
| Ancash | 264 | 285 | 429 | 480 | 465 | 589 | 727 | 854 |
| Apurimac | 117 | 119 | 177 | 280 | 281 | 338 | 308 | 343 |
| Arequipa | 136 | 157 | 229 | 360 | 271 | 411 | 531 | 738 |
| Ayacucho | 183 | 142 | 302 | 320 | 414 | 448 | 460 | 524 |
| Cajamarca | 177 | 213 | 442 | 450 | 568 | 749 | 916 | 1,083 |
| Callao | 19 | 34 | 48 | 75 | 84 | 214 | 316 | 454 |
| Cuszco | 234 | 243 | 439 | 700 | 565 | 614 | 713 | 874 |
| Huancavelica | 107 | 103 | 224 | 230 | 266 | 299 | 331 | 362 |
| Huánuco | 75 | 79 | 145 | 200 | 277 | 362 | 421 | 506 |
| Ica | 61 | 60 | 91 | 120 | 145 | 244 | 358 | 447 |
| Junín | 203 | 210 | 394 | 450 | 500 | 506 | 691 | 897 |
| La Libertad | 133 | 147 | 251 | 381 | 404 | 588 | 806 | 992 |
| Lambayeque | 52 | 87 | 124 | 140 | 200 | 347 | 515 | 709 |
| Lima | 207 | 226 | 298 | 550 | 849 | 2,319 | 3,485 | 4,993 |
| Loreto | 52 | 62 | 101 | 150 | 321 | 331 | 246 | 475 |
| Madre de Dios | — | — | — | 5 | 25 | 15 | 22 | 36 |
| Moqueguce | 27 | 29 | 42 | 40 | 36 | 58 | 75 | 103 |
| Pasco | ... | ... | ... | ... | ... | 126 | 177 | 231 |
| Piura | 130 | 136 | 214 | 300 | 431 | 717 | 855 | 1,156 |
| Puno | } 225 | 259 | 537 { | 700 | 646 | 687 | 780 | 910 |
| San Martin | | | | 65 | 121 | 163 | 224 | 332 |
| Tacna | 34 | 36 | 50 | 60 | 38 | 69 | 96 | 148 |
| Tumbes | — | — | — | 12 | 26 | 52 | 75 | 108 |
| Ucayali... | ... | ... | ... | ... | ... | ... | [156] | 220 |

*See p. 56 for footnotes*

**A3    SOUTH AMERICA: Population of Major Administrative Divisions** (in thousands)

## VENEZUELA (states)

|  | 1873 | 1881 | 1891 | 1920 | 1926 | 1936 | 1941 | 1950 | 1961 | 1971 | 1981 |
|---|---|---|---|---|---|---|---|---|---|---|---|
| Federal District | 60 | 69 | 113 | 140 | 195 | 283 | 380 | 700 | 1,258 | 1,861 | 2,071 |
| Amzoátegui | 101 | 124 | 134 | 104 | 114 | 130 | 156 | 238 | 382 | 506 | 684 |
| Apure | 19 | 21 | 23 | 39 | 43 | 58 | 71 | 85 | 118 | 165 | 188 |
| Aragua | 94 | 105 | 95 | 96 | 106 | 130 | 138 | 193 | 313 | 543 | 892 |
| Barinas | 59 | 57 | 63 | 55 | 57 | 56 | 63 | 81 | 139 | 231 | 326 |
| Bolívar | 34 | 51 | 56 | 66 | 75 | 83 | 95 | 122 | 214 | 392 | 668 |
| Carabobo | 118 | 136 | 169 | 126 | 147 | 172 | 191 | 243 | 382 | 659 | 1,062 |
| Cojedes | 86 | 84 | 88 | 82 | 82 | 48 | 50 | 52 | 73 | 94 | 134 |
| Falcón | 100 | 114 | 139 | 128 | 179 | 215 | 33 | 258 | 340 | 408 | 504 |
| Guárico | 191 | 203 | 184 | 122 | 125 | 120 | 135 | 164 | 245 | 319 | 393 |
| Lara | 144 | 176 | 190 | 220 | 271 | 291 | 333 | 370 | 489 | 671 | 945 |
| Mérida | 68 | 78 | 89 | 123 | 150 | 179 | 193 | 210 | 271 | 347 | 459 |
| Miranda | 129 | 136 | 141 | 174 | 190 | 217 | 228 | 278 | 492 | 856 | 1,421 |
| Monagas | 48 | 56 | 75 | 62 | 68 | 93 | 123 | 176 | 246 | 298 | 389 |
| Nueva Esparta | 31 | 38 | 40 | 56 | 69 | 73 | 69 | 76 | 89 | 119 | 197 |
| Portuguesa | 80 | 96 | 96 | 53 | 59 | 72 | 87 | 121 | 204 | 297 | 425 |
| Sucre | 55 | 78 | 92 | 150 | 216 | 262 | 291 | 333 | 402 | 469 | 586 |
| Táchira | 69 | 84 | 102 | 147 | 173 | 216 | 246 | 308 | 399 | 511 | 660 |
| Trujillo | 109 | 131 | 147 | 179 | 219 | 243 | 264 | 285 | 327 | 381 | 434 |
| Yaracuy | 72 | 82 | 86 | 108 | 123 | 124 | 127 | 133 | 175 | 224 | 301 |
| Zulia | 59 | 107 | 151 | 119 | 223 | 291 | 346 | 524 | 920 | 1,299 | 1,674 |
| Amazonas Territory | 23 | 18 | 45 | 49 | 60 | 41 | 4 | 7 | 12 | 22 | 46 |
| Delta Amacuro Territory | 6 | 18 | 7 | 13 | 27 | 20 | 28 | 31 | 34 | 48 | 57 |
| Federal Dependencies | — | — | — | — | — | - - | 1 | 1 | 1 | - - | 1 |

## A3 Population of Major Administrative Divisions (in thousands)

NOTES

1. SOURCES: As for table A1.
2. Notes 4 and 5 for table A1 also apply to this table.

FOOTNOTES

[1] Included in Northwest Territories.
[2] Kenneth Buckley, in M.C. Urquhart and K.A.H. Buckley, *Historical Statistics of Canada* (Cambridge, 1965), estimated that the Indian population in the western provinces and territories was under-enumerated by about 30,000 in 1851 and 40,000 in 1861.
[3] Newfoundland was incorporated in Canada in 1949.
[4] In 1848.
[5] Earlier censuses showed total population as follows: 1756—131; 1774—198; 1782—209.
[6] Earlier censuses showed total population as follows: 1764/5—22; 1776—48; 1784—50.
[7] Earlier censuses showed total population as follows: 1764/5—224; 1776—291; 1784—307.
[8] Earlier censuses showed total population as follows: 1767—53; 1773—73; 1775—81; 1786—96.
[9] Earlier censuses showed total population as follows: 1708—7; 1730—18; 1748—34; 1755—41; 1774—60; 1783—52.
[10] A census in 1771 showed total population as 5 thousand.
[11] Earlier censuses showed total population as follows: 1726—32; 1738—47; 1745—61; 1772—122; 1784—149.
[12] Earlier censuses showed total population as follows: 1698—18; 1703—21; 1723—41; 1731—50; 1737—60; 1746—62; 1749—73; 1756—97; 1771—163; 1786—239.
[13] Earlier censuses showed total population as follows: 1704—35; 1710—43; 1712—46; 1755—154; 1782—254.
[14] Data relate to the territory of the state after the separation of West Virginia in 1862. Earlier censuses of the whole colony showed the following total populations: 1624/5—1; 1634—5; 1699—58; 1701—58.
[15] Including portions later incorporated in other territories.
[16] Territory north-west of the Ohio River.
[17] Illinois Territory.
[18] Michigan Territory as constituted at the time. Boundaries were changed in 1816, 1818, 1834 and 1836.
[19] Including that part of Minnesota north-east of the Mississippi River.
[20] Including that part of Minnesota lying west of the Mississippi River and a line drawn from its source northwards to the Canadian border.
[21] Dakota Territory.
[22] Data relate to those parts of the Mississippi territory which constitute the present state.
[23] Nevada Territory as organized in 1861.
[24] Including the area taken to form part of Arizona Territory in 1863.
[25] Excluding that part taken to form Colorado Territory in 1861.
[26] Alaska and Hawaii are not included in the regional population until 1960.
[27] Those parts of Oregon Territory later taken to form part of Washington Territory.
[28] Includes the population of Idaho and parts of Montana and Wyoming.
[29] 1929.
[30] 1939.
[31] The combined population of these Patagonian territories in 1869 was 24 thousand.
[32] This province was subsequently divided.
[33] The first figure is for the province as defined at the time of the census, the second is for its territory at the next census.
[34] Estimates rather than census figures.
[35] Included in Boyaca.

## A4   NORTH AMERICA: POPULATION OF MAJOR CITIES (in thousands)

| | c1750 | 1790 | 1800 | 1810 | 1820 | 1830 | 1840 | 1850 | 1860 | 1870 | 1880 | 1890 |
|---|---|---|---|---|---|---|---|---|---|---|---|---|
| Akron (USA) | — | — | — | — | — | — | — | 3 | 3 | 10 | 17 | 28 |
| Albany (USA) | … | 3 | 5 | 11 | 13 | 24 | 34 | 51 | 62 | 69 | 91 | 95 |
| Albuquerque (USA) | — | — | — | — | — | — | — | — | — | — | — | 4 |
| Allentown (USA) | — | 4 | 4 | 4 | 5 | 6 | 8 | 10 | 8 | 14 | 18 | 25 |
| Anaheim (USA) | … | … | … | … | … | … | … | … | … | … | 1 | 1 |
| Atlanta (USA) | — | — | — | — | — | — | … | 3 | 10 | 22 | 37 | 66 |
| Austin (USA) | — | — | — | — | — | — | — | 1 | 2 | 4 | 11 | 15 |
| Baltimore (USA) | … | 14 | 26 | 36 | 63 | 81 | 102 | 169 | 212 | 267 | 332 | 434 |
| Birmingham (USA) | — | — | — | — | — | — | — | — | — | — | 3 | 26 |
| Boston (USA) | 16 [1765] | 18 | 25 | 33 | 43 | 61 | 93 | 137 | 178 | 251 | 363 | 448 |
| Buffalo (USA) | — | — | — | — | 2 | 9 | 18 | 42 | 81 | 118 | 155 | 256 |
| Calgary (Canada) | — | — | — | — | — | — | — | — | — | — | — | 4 |
| Charleston, SC (USA) | … | 16 | 19 | 25 | 25 | 30 | 29 | 43 | 41 | 49 | 50 | 55 |
| Charlotte (USA) | — | — | — | — | — | — | … | 1 | 1 | 4 | 7 | 12 |
| Chicago (USA) | — | — | — | — | — | — | 4 | 30 | 109 | 299 | 503 | 1,100 |
| Chihuahua (Mexico) | … | … | 12 [1803] | … | … | 11 | … | … | 14 | 12 | 16 [1882] | 18 [1895] |
| Cincinnati (USA) | … | — | — | 3 | 10 | 25 | 46 | 115 | 161 | 216 | 255 | 297 |
| Ciudad Juarez (Mexico) | … | … | … | … | … | … | … | 2 | … | … | — | 7 [1893] |
| Cleveland (USA) | — | — | — | — | — | — | 6 | 17 | 43 | 93 | 160 | 261 |
| Columbus, Ohio (USA) | — | — | — | — | — | 2 | 6 | 18 | 19 | 31 | 52 | 88 |
| Corpus Christi (USA) | — | — | — | — | — | — | — | — | - - | 3 | 4 | 4 |
| Dallas (USA) | — | — | — | — | — | — | — | — | — | 3 | 10 | 38 |
| Dayton (USA) | — | — | — | … | 1 | 3 | 6 | 11 | 20 | 30 | 39 | 61 |
| Denver (USA) | — | — | — | — | — | — | — | — | — | 5 | 36 | 107 |
| Des Moines (USA) | — | — | — | — | — | — | — | 1 | 4 | 12 | 22 | 50 |
| Detroit (USA) | — | — | — | … | 1 | 2 | 9 | 21 | 46 | 80 | 116 | 206 |
| El Paso (USA) | — | — | — | — | — | — | — | — | — | — | 1 | 10 |
| Fall River (USA) | — | — | — | 1 | 2 | 4 | 7 | 12 | 14 | 27 | 49 | 74 |

**A4  NORTH AMERICA: Population of Major Cities** (in thousands)

| | c1750 | 1790 | 1800 | 1810 | 1820 | 1830 | 1840 | 1850 | 1860 | 1870 | 1880 | 1890 |
|---|---|---|---|---|---|---|---|---|---|---|---|---|
| Fort Worth (USA) | — | — | — | — | — | — | — | — | — | — | 7 | 23 |
| Grand Rapids (USA) | — | — | — | — | — | — | — | 3 | 8 | 17 | 32 | 60 |
| Greensboro (USA) | — | — | — | — | — | ... | ... | ... | ... | ... | 2 | 3 |
| Guadalajara (Mexico) | ... | ... | 20[03] | ... | 47[23] | ... | ... | 63[52] | 71[62] | 65 | 75[78] | 95[93] |
| Guatemala City | ... | ... | ... | ... | ... | ... | ... | 37 | ... | 45 | 51 | 72[93] |
| Hamilton (Canada) | — | — | — | — | ... | ... | 3[136] | 14 | 27 | 29 | 36 | 49 |
| Hartford, Conn. (USA) | — | 4 | 5 | 4 | 5 | 7 | 9 | 18 | 29 | 37 | 42 | 53 |
| Havana (Cuba) | ... | 44 | ... | 96 | ... | 94[27] | 135 | ... | ... | ... | ... | 198[87] |
| Houston (USA) | — | — | — | — | — | — | — | 2 | 5 | 9 | 17 | 28 |
| Indianapolis (USA) | — | — | — | — | — | — | 3 | 8 | 19 | 48 | 75 | 105 |
| Jacksonville (USA) | — | — | — | — | — | — | — | 1 | 2 | 7 | 8 | 17 |
| Jersey City (USA) | — | ... | ... | ... | ... | ... | 3 | 7 | 29 | 83 | 121 | 163 |
| Kansas City, Mo. (USA) | — | — | — | — | — | — | — | — | 4 | 32 | 56 | 133 |
| Kingston (Jamaica) | ... | ... | ... | ... | ... | ... | ... | ... | 27 | 34 | 39 | 49 |
| León (Mexico) | ... | 6 | ... | ... | ... | ... | ... | 17 | ... | ... | ... | 48[93] |
| London (Canada) | — | — | — | — | — | — | — | 7 | 12 | 18 | 28 | 32 |
| Long Beach (USA) | — | — | — | — | — | — | — | — | — | — | — | 1 |
| Los Angeles (USA) | — | — | — | — | — | — | — | 2 | 4 | 6 | 11 | 50 |
| Louisville (USA) | ... | — | ... | 1 | 4 | 10 | 21 | 43 | 68 | 101 | 124 | 161 |
| Managua (Nicaragua) | ... | — | ... | ... | ... | — | ... | ... | ... | 8 | 12 | 18 |
| Memphis (USA) | — | — | — | — | — | — | ... | 9 | 23 | 40 | 34 | 64 |
| Mérida (Mexico) | ... | ... | 10[03] | ... | ... | ... | ... | ... | 24[62] | 30 | 35[78] | 37[95] |
| Mexico City | ... | 131[93] | 137[03] | 168 | 180 | ... | 205[38] | 170[52] | 200[62] | 225 | 250 | 327[93] |
| Milwaukee (USA) | — | — | — | — | — | — | 2 | 20 | 45 | 71 | 116 | 204 |
| Minneapolis (USA) | — | — | — | — | — | — | — | — | 3 | 13 | 47 | 165 |
| Monterrey (Mexico) | ... | ... | 11 | ... | ... | ... | ... | 14[52] | 15[62] | 14 | 40 | 43[93] |
| Montreal (Canada) | 6[65] | 18 | ... | ... | 32[25] | 44 | ... | 58 | 90 | 107 | 155 | 220 |

**A4    NORTH AMERICA: Population of Major Cities** (in thousands)

| | c1750 | 1790 | 1800 | 1810 | 1820 | 1830 | 1840 | 1850 | 1860 | 1870 | 1880 | 1890 |
|---|---|---|---|---|---|---|---|---|---|---|---|---|
| Nashville (USA) | — | ... | ... | ... | ... | 6 | 7 | 10 | 17 | 26 | 43 | 76 |
| Newark, NJ (USA) | — | ... | ... | ... | 7 | 11 | 17 | 39 | 72 | 115 | 137 | 182 |
| New Orleans (USA) | 3[69] | 5[88] | 8[97] | 17 | 27 | 46 | 102 | 116 | 169 | 191 | 216 | 242 |
| New York (USA)[1] | 22[73] | 33 | 60 | 96 | 131 | 218 | 349 | 696 | 1,175 | 1,478 | 1,912 | 2,507 |
| Norfolk (USA) | ... | ... | 7 | ... | 8 | 10 | 11 | 14 | 15 | 19 | 22 | 35 |
| Oakland (USA) | — | — | — | — | — | — | — | ... | 2 | 11 | 35 | 49 |
| Oklahoma City (USA) | — | — | — | — | — | — | — | — | — | — | — | 4 |
| Omaha (USA) | — | — | — | — | — | — | — | — | 2 | 16 | 30 | 140 |
| Ottawa (Canada) | — | — | — | — | — | ... | ... | 8 | 15 | 24 | 31 | 44 |
| Panama City | ... | ... | ... | ... | 17 | ... | ... | ... | 18 | ... | 20 | ... |
| Paterson, NJ (USA) | ... | ... | ... | ... | 1 | ... | 8 | 11 | 20 | 34 | 51 | 78 |
| Philadelphia (USA) | 12[31] | 43 | 69 | 95 | 119 | 161 | 206 | 340 | 566 | 674 | 847 | 1,047 |
| Phoenix (USA) | — | — | — | — | — | — | — | — | — | — | — | 3 |
| Pittsburgh (USA)[2] | — | - - | 2 | 5 | 7 | 18 | 31 | 68 | 78 | 139 | 235 | 344 |
| Portland, Oreg. (USA) | — | — | — | — | — | — | — | 1 | 3 | 8 | 18 | 46 |
| Providence, RI (USA) | 3 | 6 | 8 | 10 | 12 | 17 | 23 | 42 | 51 | 69 | 105 | 132 |
| Puebla (Mexico) | ... | 57[93] | 68[103] | ... | 60 | ... | ... | 72[52] | 75 | 65 | 73[82] | 91[93] |
| Quebec (Canada) | 9[65] | 14 | ... | ... | 22[25] | 36 | ... | 42 | 60 | 60 | 62 | 63 |
| Richmond, Va. (USA) | — | 4 | 6 | 10 | 12 | 16 | 20 | 28 | 38 | 51 | 64 | 81 |
| Rochester (USA) | — | 2 | 2 | 2 | 2 | 9 | 20 | 36 | 48 | 62 | 89 | 134 |
| Sacramento (USA) | — | — | — | — | — | — | — | 7 | 14 | 16 | 21 | 26 |
| St Louis (USA) | — | ... | ... | ... | 4 | 7 | 16 | 78 | 161 | 311 | 351 | 452 |
| St Paul, Minn. (USA) | — | — | — | — | — | — | — | 1 | 10 | 20 | 41 | 133 |
| St Petersburg (USA) | — | — | — | — | — | — | — | — | — | — | — | - - |
| Salt Lake City (USA) | — | — | — | — | — | — | — | 10 | 8 | 13 | 21 | 45 |
| San Antonio (USA) | ... | — | — | — | — | — | — | 3 | 8 | 12 | 21 | 38 |
| San Bernardino (USA) | — | — | — | — | — | — | — | — | 1 | 3 | 2 | 4 |
| San Diego (USA) | — | — | — | — | — | — | — | — | 1 | 2 | 3 | 16 |
| San Francisco (USA) | ... | ... | ... | ... | ... | ... | ... | 35[52] | 57 | 149 | 234 | 299 |

*See p. 56 for footnotes*

**A4 NORTH AMERICA: Population of Major Cities** (in thousands)

| | c1750 | 1790 | 1800 | 1810 | 1820 | 1830 | 1840 | 1850 | 1860 | 1870 | 1880 | 1890 |
|---|---|---|---|---|---|---|---|---|---|---|---|---|
| San José (Costa Rica) | ... | ... | 11 | ... | 15[24] | ... | 20[44] | ... | ... | ... | ... | 19[92] |
| San José (USA) | — | — | ... | ... | ... | ... | ... | 4 | ... | 9 | 13 | 18 |
| San Luis Potosí (Mexico) | ... | ... | ... | ... | ... | ... | ... | ... | 11[57] | ... | 35 | 63[93] |
| San Salvador (El Salvador) | ... | ... | ... | 7[07] | 13 | ... | ... | 17[55] | ... | 25[74] | ... | 31[87] |
| Santo Domingo (Dominican Rep.) | ... | ... | 12 | ... | ... | ... | ... | 12 | ... | ... | ... | 25 |
| Seattle (USA) | — | — | — | — | — | — | — | — | — | — | 4 | 43 |
| Springfield, Mass. (USA) | — | 2 | 2 | 3 | 4 | 7 | 11 | 12 | 15 | 27 | 33 | 44 |
| Syracuse (USA) | ... | ... | ... | ... | ... | ... | 7 | 22 | 28 | 43 | 52 | 88 |
| Tampa (USA) | — | — | — | — | — | — | — | 1 | ... | 1 | 1 | 6 |
| Tegucigalpa (Honduras) | ... | ... | ... | ... | ... | ... | ... | 8 | ... | ... | 12 | 13 |
| Toledo (USA) | — | — | — | — | — | — | 1 | 4 | 14 | 32 | 50 | 81 |
| Toronto (Canada) | — | — | — | — | 2[24] | 4 | 13 | 31 | 45 | 59 | 96 | 181 |
| Tucson (USA) | — | — | — | — | — | — | — | — | — | ... | ... | 5 |
| Vancouver (Canada) | — | — | — | — | — | — | — | — | — | ... | ... | 14 |
| Veracruz (Mexico) | ... | ... | 16[03] | ... | 11 | ... | 7[42] | 8[52] | 11[62] | 10 | 15 | 19[93] |
| Washington, DC (USA) | — | — | 3 | 8 | 13 | 18 | 23 | 40 | 61 | 109 | 178 | 230 |
| Wichita (USA) | — | — | — | — | — | — | — | — | — | — | 5 | 24 |
| Windsor (Canada) | — | — | — | — | — | — | — | ... | ... | 4 | 7 | 10 |
| Winnipeg (Canada) | — | — | — | — | — | — | — | — | — | – | 8 | 26 |
| Worcester, Mass. (USA) | ... | 2 | 2 | 3 | 3 | 4 | 7 | 17 | 25 | 41 | 58 | 85 |
| Yonkers (USA) | — | — | — | — | — | — | — | — | — | — | 19 | 32 |
| Youngstown (USA) | — | — | — | — | — | — | — | 3 | 3 | 8 | 15 | 33 |

**A4   NORTH AMERICA: Population of Major Cities** (in thousands)

| | 1900 | 1910 | 1920 | 1930 | 1940 | 1940 | 1950 | 1950 | 1960 | 1960 | 1970 | 1970 | 1980 | 1980 |
|---|---|---|---|---|---|---|---|---|---|---|---|---|---|---|
| Akron (USA) | 43 | 69 | 208 | 255 | 245 | 339 | 275 | 410 | 290 | 605 | 275 | 679 | 237 | 660 |
| Albany (USA) | 94 | 100 | 113 | 127 | 131 | 466[3] | 135 | 514[3] | 130 | 715[3] | 116 | 778[3] | 102 | 836[3] |
| Albuquerque (USA) | 6 | 11 | 15 | 27 | 35 | 69 | 97 | 146 | 201 | 276 | 245 | 316 | 333 | 420 |
| Allentown (USA) | 35 | 52 | 74 | 93 | 97 | 397[4] | 107 | 438[4] | 108 | 545[4] | 110 | 594[4] | 104 | 635[4] |
| Anaheim (USA) | 1 | 3 | 6 | 11 | 11 | … | 15 | … | 104 | 704[5] | 166 | 1,421[5] | 219 | 1,933[5] |
| Atlanta (USA) | 90 | 155 | 201 | 270 | 302 | 518 | 331 | 672 | 487 | 1,169 | 495 | 1,596 | 425 | 2,138 |
| Austin (USA) | 22 | 30 | 35 | 53 | 88 | 111 | 132 | 161 | 187 | 232 | 254 | 323 | 346 | 537 |
| Baltimore (USA) | 509 | 558 | 734 | 805 | 859 | 1,083 | 950 | 1,337 | 939 | 1,804 | 905 | 2,071 | 787 | 2,200 |
| Birmingham (USA) | 38 | 133 | 179 | 260 | 268 | 460 | 326 | 559 | 341 | 747 | 301 | 767 | 284 | 884 |
| Boston (USA) | 561 | 671 | 748 | 781 | 771 | 2,178 | 801 | 2,370 | 697 | 2,688 | 641 | 2,899 | 563 | 2,806 |
| Buffalo (USA) | 352 | 424 | 507 | 573 | 576 | 958 | 580 | 1,089 | 533 | 1,307 | 463 | 1,349 | 358 | 1,243 |
| Calgary (Canada) | 4 | 44 | 63 | 84 | 89 | … | 129 | 139 | 250 | 279 | 403 | 417 | 593 | … |
| Charleston, SC (USA) | 56 | 59 | 68 | 62 | 71 | 121 | 70 | 165 | … | 279 | … | 336 | … | 430 |
| Charlotte (USA) | 18 | 34 | 46 | 83 | 101 | 152 | 134 | 197[4] | 202 | 444[6] | 241 | 558[6] | 315 | 971[6] |
| Chicago (USA) | 1,699 | 2,185 | 2,702 | 3,376 | 3,397 | 4,826 | 3,621 | 5,495 | 3,550 | 6,221 | 3,367 | 6,978 | 3,005 | 6,060 |
| Chihuahua (Mexico) | 30 | 40 | 48 | 62 | 57 | … | 87 | … | 150 | … | 257 | … | 386 | … |
| Cincinnati (USA) | 326 | 364 | 401 | 451 | 456 | 787 | 504 | 904 | 503 | 1,268 | 453 | 1,385 | 385 | 1,401 |
| Ciudad Juarez (Mexico) | 8 | 11 | 19 | 43 | 49 | … | 123 | … | 262 | … | 407 | … | 544 | … |
| Cleveland (USA) | 382 | 561 | 797 | 900 | 878 | 1,267 | 915 | 1,466 | 876 | 1,909 | 751 | 2,064 | 574 | 1,899 |
| Columbus, Ohio (USA) | 126 | 182 | 237 | 291 | 306 | 389 | 376 | 503 | 471 | 845 | 540 | 1,018 | 565 | 1,244 |
| Corpus Christi (USA) | 5 | 8 | 11 | 28 | 57 | 93 | 108 | 165 | 168 | 267 | 205 | 285 | 232 | 326 |
| Dallas (USA) | 43 | 92 | 159 | 260 | 295 | 399 | 434 | 615 | 680 | 1,738[7] | 844 | 2,378[7] | 905 | 2,931[7] |
| Dayton (USA) | 85 | 117 | 153 | 201 | 211 | 331 | 244 | 457 | 262 | 727 | 244 | 853 | 194 | 942 |
| Denver (USA) | 134 | 213 | 256 | 288 | 322 | 408 | 416 | 564 | 494 | 935[8] | 515 | 1,239[8] | 493 | 1,618[8] |
| Des Moines (USA) | 62 | 86 | 126 | 143 | 160 | 196 | 178 | 226 | 209 | 287 | 201 | 314 | 191 | 368 |
| Detroit (USA) | 286 | 466 | 994 | 1,569 | 1,623 | 2,377 | 1,850 | 3,016 | 1,670 | 3,950 | 1,511 | 4,435 | 1,203 | 4,488 |
| Edmonton (Canada) | 4 | 31 | 59 | 79 | 94 | 98 | 160 | 173 | 281 | 338 | 438 | 496 | 532 | 657 |
| El Paso (USA) | 16 | 39 | 78 | 102 | 97 | 131 | 130 | 195 | 277 | 314 | 322 | 359 | 425 | 480 |
| Fall River (USA) | 105 | 119 | 120 | 115 | 115 | 135 | 112 | 137 | 100 | … | 97 | … | 93 | … |
| Fort Lauderdale (USA) | … | … | … | 9 | 18 | … | 36 | … | 84 | 334[9] | 140 | 620[9] | 153 | 1,018[9] |

**A 4  NORTH AMERICA: Population of Major Cities** (in thousands)

| | 1900 | 1910 | 1920 | 1930 | 1940 | 1940 | 1950 | 1950 | 1960 | 1960[5] | 1970 | 1970[5] | 1980 | 1980[5] |
|---|---|---|---|---|---|---|---|---|---|---|---|---|---|---|
| Fort Worth (USA) | 27 | 73 | 106 | 163 | 178 | 226 | 279 | 361 | 396 | ... | 393 | ... | 385 | ... |
| Gary (USA) | ... | 17 | 55 | 100 | 112 | ... | 134 | ... | 178 | 574[10] | 175 | 633[10] | 152 | 643[10] |
| Grand Rapids (USA) | 88 | 113 | 138 | 169 | 164 | 246 | 177 | 288 | 177 | 462 | 198 | 539 | 182 | 602 |
| Greensboro (USA) | 10 | 16 | 20 | 54 | 59 | 280[11] | 74 | 337[11] | 120 | 622[11] | 144 | 724[11] | 156 | 852[11] |
| Guadalajara (Mexico) | 101 | 119 | 143 | 185 | 229 | ... | 377 | ... | 737 | ... | 1,194 | 1,456 | 1,626 | 2,245 |
| Guatemala City | 74[98] | 90 | 116 | 121[28] | 186 | ... | 284 | ... | 439 | ... | 769 | ... | 754 | ... |
| Hamilton (Canada) | 53 | 82 | 114 | 156 | 166 | 176 | 208 | 260 | 274 | 395 | 309 | 499 | 306 | 542 |
| Hartford, Conn. (USA) | 80 | 99 | 138 | 164 | 166 | 296 | 177 | 358 | 162 | 588 | 158 | 721 | 136 | 716 |
| Havana (Cuba) | 236 | 312 | 364[22] | 581 | 660[43] | 785[53] | 785[43] | 1,218[53] | 978 | 1,463 | 1,001[67] | 1,557[67] | ... | 1,929 |
| Houston (USA) | 45 | 79 | 138 | 292 | 385 | 529 | 596 | 807 | 938 | 1,430 | 1,233 | 1,999 | 1,595 | 2,736 |
| Indianapolis (USA) | 169 | 234 | 314 | 364 | 387 | 461 | 427 | 552 | 476[12] | 944 | 745[12] | 1,111 | 701 | 1,167 |
| Jacksonville (USA) | 28 | 58 | 92 | 130 | 173 | 210 | 205 | 304 | 201[13] | 530 | 529[13] | 622 | 541 | 722 |
| Jersey City (USA) | 206 | 268 | 298 | 317 | 301 | ... | 299 | ... | 276 | 611 | 261 | 608 | 224 | 557 |
| Kansas City, Mo. (USA) | 164 | 248 | 324 | 400 | 399 | 687 | 457 | 814 | 476 | 1,109 | 507 | 1,274 | 448 | 1,433 |
| Kingston (Jamaica) | ... | 60 | 64 | ... | 110 | 289[43] | 142[55] | 338[55] | 123 | 377 | 112 | 475 | 104 | 525 |
| León (Mexico) | 59 | 58 | 54 | 99 | 86 | ... | 123 | ... | 210 | ... | 365 | ... | 593 | ... |
| London (Canada) | 38 | 46 | 61 | 71 | 78 | 87 | 95 | 122 | 170 | 181 | 223 | 286 | 254 | 284 |
| Long Beach (USA) | 2 | 18 | 56 | 142 | 164 | | 251 | | 344 | | 359 | | 361 | |
| Los Angeles (USA) | 102 | 319 | 577 | 1,238 | 1,504 | 2,916[14] | 1,970 | 4,368[14] | 2,479 | 6,039[12] | 2,816 | 7,042[14] | 2,969 | 7,478 |
| Louisville (USA) | 205 | 224 | 235 | 308 | 319 | 451 | 369 | 577 | 391 | 754 | 361 | 867 | 299 | 957 |
| Managua (Nicaragua) | 30 | 39[06] | 59 | 33[26] | 63 | ... | 109 | ... | 235 | ... | 399 | ... | 615 | ... |
| Memphis (USA) | 102 | 131 | 162 | 253 | 293 | 358 | 396 | 482 | 498 | 727 | 624 | 834 | 646 | 913 |
| Mérida (Mexico) | 44 | 62 | 79 | 91 | 115 | ... | 159 | ... | 191 | ... | 242 | ... | 400 | ... |
| Mexicali (Mexico) | — | — | — | ... | 19 | ... | 65 | ... | 175 | ... | 263 | ... | 342 | ... |
| Mexico City | 345 | 471 | 615 | 1,029 | 1,448 | ... | 2,234 | 3,050 | 2,832 | 4,871 | 6,874 | 8,590 | 8,831 | 12,932 |
| Miami (USA) | 2 | 5 | 30 | 111 | 172 | 268 | 249 | 495 | 292 | 935 | 335 | 1,268 | 347 | 1,626 |
| Milwaukee (USA) | 285 | 374 | 457 | 578 | 587 | 767 | 637 | 871 | 741 | 1,279 | 717 | 1,404 | 636 | 1,397 |
| Minneapolis (USA) | 203 | 301 | 381 | 464 | 492 | 941[15] | 522 | 1,117[15] | 483 | 1,598[15] | 434 | 1,965[15] | 371 | 2,137[15] |
| Monterrey (Mexico) | 62 | 79 | 88 | 133 | 186 | ... | 333 | ... | 597 | ... | 858 | ... | 1,085 | 1,916 |
| Montreal (Canada) | 268 | 470 | 619 | 819 | 903 | 1,145 | 1,022 | 1,395 | 1,191 | 2,110 | 1,214 | 2,743 | 980 | 2,828 |

Note: For Long Beach and Los Angeles (USA), the figures in the second 1940, 1950, 1960, 1970 and 1980 columns are braced together (combined): 2,916[14], 4,368[14], 6,039[12], 7,042[14] and 7,478 respectively.

*See p. 56 for footnotes*

**A4    NORTH AMERICA: Population of Major Cities** (in thousands)

| | 1900 | 1910 | 1920 | 1930 | 1940 | 1950 | 1950 | 1960 | 1960 | 1970 | 1970 | 1980 | 1980 |
|---|---|---|---|---|---|---|---|---|---|---|---|---|---|
| Nashville (USA) | 81 | 110 | 118 | 154 | 167 | 174 | 322 | 171[16] | 597 | 448[16] | 699 | 456 | 851 |
| Newark, NJ (USA) | 246 | 347 | 415 | 442 | 430 | 439 | ... | 405 | 1,833 | 382 | 2,057 | 329 | 1,879 |
| New Orleans (USA) | 287 | 339 | 387 | 459 | 495 | 570 | 685 | 628 | 907 | 593 | 1,046 | 558 | 1,256 |
| New York (USA) | 3,437 | 4,767 | 5,620 | 6,930 | 7,455 | 7,892 | 9,556 | 7,782 | 9,540 | 7,895 | 9,974 | 7,072 | 8,275 |
| Norfolk (USA) | 47 | 67 | 116 | 130 | 144 | 214 | 446[17] | 305 | 629[17] | 308 | 733[17] | 267 | 1,160[17] |
| Oakland (USA) | 67 | 150 | 216 | 284 | 302 | 385 | [18] | 368 | [18] | 362 | [18] | 339 | [18] |
| Oklahoma City (USA) | 10 | 64 | 91 | 185 | 204 | 244 | 325 | 324 | 566 | 366 | 699 | 404 | 861 |
| Omaha (USA) | 103 | 124[19] | 192[19] | 214 | 224 | 251 | 366 | 302 | 458 | 347 | 543 | 313 | 585 |
| Ottawa (Canada) | 60 | 87 | 108 | 127 | 155 | 202 | 292 | 268 | 430 | 302 | 603 | 295 | 718 |
| Panama City | ... | 38 | 67 | 74 | 112 | 128 | ... | 273 | ... | 349 | ... | 386 | ... |
| Paterson, NJ (USA) | 105 | 126 | 136 | 139 | 140 | 139 | ... | 144 | 407[20] | 145 | 461[20] | 138 | [29] |
| Philadelphia (USA) | 1,294 | 1,549 | 1,824 | 1,951 | 1,931 | 2,072 | 3,671 | 2,003 | 4,343 | 1,949 | 4,824 | 1,688 | 4,717 |
| Phoenix (USA) | 6 | 11 | 29 | 48 | 65 | 107 | 332 | 439 | 664 | 582 | 969 | 790 | 1,509 |
| Pittsburgh (USA)2 | 452 | 534 | 588 | 670 | 672 | 677 | 2,213 | 604 | 2,405 | 520 | 2,401 | 424 | 2,219 |
| Port-au-Prince (Haiti) | 70 | 105 | ... | 100 | 115 | 134 | ... | 240 | ... | 459 | 494 | 450 | 763 |
| Portland, Oreg. (USA) | 90 | 207 | 258 | 302 | 305 | 374 | 705 | 373 | 822 | 383 | 1,007 | 368 | 1,298 |
| Providence, RI (USA) | 176 | 224 | 238 | 253 | 254 | 249 | 737[21] | 207 | 821[21] | 179 | 909[21] | 157 | 926[21] |
| Puebla (Mexico) | 94 | 96 | 96 | 123 | 138 | 211 | ... | 289 | ... | 402 | ... | 773 | ... |
| Quebec (Canada) | 69 | 78 | 95 | 131 | 151 | 164 | 275 | 172 | 358 | 186 | 481 | 166 | 576 |
| Richmond, Va. (USA) | 85 | 128 | 172 | 183 | 193 | 230 | 328 | 220 | 457 | 250 | 542 | 219 | 761 |
| Rochester (USA) | 163 | 218 | 296 | 328 | 325 | 332 | 488 | 319 | 801 | 296 | 962 | 242 | 971 |
| Sacramento (USA) | 29 | 45 | 66 | 86 | 85 | 138 | 277 | 192 | 626 | 254 | 804 | 276 | 1,100 |
| St Louis (USA) | 575 | 687 | 773 | 822 | 816 | 857 | 1,681 | 750 | 2,144 | 622 | 2,411 | 453 | 2,377 |
| St Paul, Minn. (USA) | 163 | 215 | 235 | 272 | 288 | 311 | [15] | 313 | [15] | 310 | [15] | 270 | [15] |
| St Petersburg (USA) | 2 | 4 | 14 | 40 | 61 | 97 | [22] | 181 | [22] | 216 | [22] | 239 | [22] |
| Salt Lake City (USA) | 54 | 93 | 118 | 140 | 150 | 182 | 275 | 189 | 576 | 176 | 705 | 163 | 960 |
| San Antonio (USA) | 53 | 97 | 161 | 232 | 254 | 408 | 500 | 588 | 736 | 654 | 888 | 786 | 1,072 |
| San Bernardino (USA) | 6 | 13 | 19 | 37 | 44 | 63 | 282[23] | 92 | 810[23] | 104 | 1,141[23] | 119 | 1,558[23] |
| San Diego (USA) | 18 | 40 | 74 | 148 | 203 | 334 | 557 | 573 | 1,033 | 697 | 1,358 | 876 | 1,862 |
| San Francisco (USA) | 343 | 417 | 507 | 634 | 635 | 775 | 2,241[18] | 740 | 2,649[18] | 716 | 3,107[18] | 679 | 3,251[18] |

*See p. 56 for footnotes*

**A4    NORTH AMERICA: Population of Major Cities** (in thousands)

| | 1900 | 1910 | 1920 | 1930 | 1940 | 1940 | 1950 | 1950 | 1960 | 1960 | 1970 | 1970 | 1980 | 1980 |
|---|---|---|---|---|---|---|---|---|---|---|---|---|---|---|
| San José (Costa Rica) | 24 | 32 | 39 | 51[27] | 68 | ... | 87 | 140 | 174 | 331 | 215 | 395 | 275 | 451 |
| San José (USA) | 22 | 29 | 40 | 58 | 68 | 175 | 95 | 291 | 204 | 642 | 446 | 1,065 | 629 | 1,295 |
| San Juan (Puerto Rico) | 32 | 49 | 71 | 115 | 169 | 303 | 225 | 466 | 432 | 542 | 453 | 695 | 425 | 1,086 |
| San Luis Potosí (Mexico) | 61 | 68 | 83 | ... | 104 | ... | 155 | ... | 194 | ... | 268 | ... | 342 | ... |
| San Salvador (El Salvador) | 59 | ... | 80 | 96 | 110 | ... | 162 | ... | 248 | ... | 337 | ... | 425 | ... |
| Santiago de Cuba | 43 | 45[07] | 70[22] | 102 | 118[43] | ... | 163[53] | ... | 213 | ... | 278 | ... | 347 | ... |
| Santo Domingo (Dominican Rep.) | 20 | 22 | 31 | 71[35] | 117[45] | ... | 182 | ... | 367 | ... | 671 | ... | 1,313 | ... |
| Seattle (USA) | 81 | 237 | 315 | 366 | 368 | 505 | 468 | 733 | 557 | 1,107[24] | 531 | 1,425[24] | 494 | 1,607[24] |
| Springfield, Mass. (USA) | 62 | 89 | 130 | 150 | 150 | 365[25] | 162 | 407[25] | 174 | 504[25] | 164 | 542[25] | 152 | 515[25] |
| Syracuse (USA) | 108 | 137 | 172 | 209 | 206 | 295 | 221 | 342 | 216 | 564 | 197 | 637 | 170 | 643 |
| Tampa (USA) | 16 | 38 | 52 | 101 | 108 | 272[22] | 125 | 409[22] | 275 | 809[22] | 278 | 1,089[22] | 272 | 1,614[22] |
| Tegucigalpa (Honduras) | 13 | 22 | 26 | 40 | 47 | ... | 72 | 100 | 134 | ... | 275[73] | 302[73] | 444 | 485 |
| Tijuana (Mexico) | ... | ... | ... | ... | 16 | ... | 60 | ... | 152 | ... | 277 | ... | 429 | ... |
| Toledo (USA) | 132 | 168 | 243 | 291 | 282 | 344 | 304 | 396 | 318 | 695 | 384 | 763 | 355 | 617 |
| Toronto (Canada) | 219 | 382 | 522 | 631 | 667 | 910 | 676 | 1,117 | 672 | 1,824 | 713 | 2,628 | 599 | 2,999 |
| Torreón (Mexico) | 14 | 34 | 51 | 66 | 88 | ... | 147 | ... | 203 | ... | 251 | ... | 328 | ... |
| Tucson (USA) | 8 | 13 | 20 | 33 | 36 | 73 | 45 | ... | 213 | 266 | 263 | 352 | 331 | 531 |
| Tulsa (USA) | 1 | 18 | 72 | 141 | 142 | 193 | 183 | 252 | 262 | 475 | 332 | 549 | 361 | 657 |
| Vancouver (Canada) | 27 | 100 | 163 | 247 | 275 | 377 | 345 | 562 | 385 | 790 | 426 | 1,082 | 414 | 1,268 |
| Veracruz (Mexico) | 29 | 49 | 54 | 72 | 76 | ... | 107 | ... | 154 | ... | 230 | ... | 285 | ... |
| Virginia Beach (USA) | ... | ... | ... | ... | ... | ... | 5 | [17] | 8 | [17] | 172 | [17] | 262 | [17] |
| Washington, DC (USA) | 279 | 331 | 438 | 487 | 663 | 968 | 802 | 1,464 | 764 | 2,097 | 757 | 2,910 | 638 | 3,251 |
| Wichita (USA) | 25 | 52 | 72 | 111 | 115 | 143 | 168 | 222 | 255 | 382 | 277 | 389 | 280 | 442 |
| Windsor (Canada) | 12 | 18 | 39 | 63 | 105 | 124 | 120 | 158 | 114 | 193 | 203 | 259 | 192 | 246 |
| Winnipeg (Canada) | 42 | 136 | 179 | 219 | 222 | 300 | 236 | 354 | 265 | 476 | 246 | 540 | 564 | 585 |
| Worcester, Mass. (USA) | 118 | 146 | 180 | 195 | 194 | 253 | 203 | 276 | 187 | 354 | 177 | 372 | 162 | 403 |
| Yonkers (USA) | 48 | 80 | 100 | 135 | 143 | [26] | 153 | [26] | 191 | [26] | 204 | [26] | 195 | [26] |
| Youngstown (USA) | 45 | 79 | 132 | 170 | 168 | 474[27] | 168 | 528[27] | 167 | 509[27] | 140 | 537[27] | 116 | 531[27] |

See p. 56 for footnotes

**A4    SOUTH AMERICA: POPULATION OF MAJOR CITIES** (in thousands)

| | c1750 | 1790 | 1800 | 1810 | 1820 | 1830 | 1840 | 1850 | 1860 | 1870 | 1880 | 1890 |
|---|---|---|---|---|---|---|---|---|---|---|---|---|
| Arequipa (Peru) | ... | 24[95] | 28[04] | ... | 25 | ... | ... | 25[48] | 26[62] | ... | 29[76] | 35 |
| Asunción (Paraguay) | ... | 7 | ... | ... | ... | ... | ... | 10 | ... | ... | ... | 25[86] |
| Barquisimeto (Venezuela) | ... | ... | ... | ... | ... | ... | ... | ... | ... | 7[73] | 29 | 31[88] |
| Barranquilla (Colombia) | ... | ... | ... | ... | ... | ... | ... | 6 | ... | 12 | ... | ... |
| Belém (Brazil) | ... | ... | 12 | ... | 12 | 12 | ... | ... | ... | 62[72] | ... | 50 |
| Bogotá (Colombia) | ... | 18[93] | 24 | ... | ... | ... | 40[43] | 30 | ... | 41 | 96[84] | ... |
| Bucaramanga (Colombia) | ... | ... | ... | ... | ... | ... | 6[43] | 10 | 11[64] | 11 | ... | ... |
| Buenos Aires (Argentina) | 11[44] | 22[70] | 40 | 46 | 55[22] | ... | 65[38] | 99[55] | 140[64] | 187 | ... | 433[87] |
| Cali (Colombia) | ... | ... | ... | ... | ... | ... | ... | 11 | ... | 13 | ... | 35 |
| Callao (Peru) | ... | 7[93] | ... | ... | ... | ... | 3 | 8 | 18[62] | 15[66] | 34[76] | 35 |
| Campinas (Brazil) | — | 1 | 2 | ... | 6 | 8 | ... | ... | ... | ... | ... | 34 |
| Caracas (Venezuela) | 19 | ... | 31 | ... | ... | ... | ... | ... | ... | 49[73] | 56 | 72 |
| Cartagena (Colombia) | ... | ... | 24 | ... | ... | ... | ... | 10 | ... | 9 | ... | ... |
| Córdoba (Argentina) | ... | 6 | 12 | 11[13] | 10[25] | ... | 14 | ... | 18[57] | 29 | ... | 48[95] |
| Cúcuta (Colombia) | ... | ... | ... | ... | ... | ... | ... | 6 | ... | 9 | ... | ... |
| Curitiba (Brazil) | ... | 3[80] | ... | ... | ... | 13 | 12[45] | ... | ... | 13[72] | ... | 25 |
| Duque de Caxias (Brazil) | ... | ... | ... | ... | ... | ... | ... | ... | ... | ... | ... | ... |
| Fortaleza (Brazil) | ... | ... | ... | ... | ... | ... | ... | ... | ... | 42[72] | ... | 41 |
| Guyaquil (Equador) | ... | ... | 14 | ... | 13 | ... | ... | ... | 20[57] | ... | 36 | 45 |
| La Paz (Bolivia) | ... | ... | ... | ... | ... | ... | ... | ... | ... | ... | ... | 40 |
| La Plata (Argentina) | — | — | ... | — | ... | ... | — | — | — | 1 | 2 | ... |
| Lima (Peru) | — | 53[92] | ... | ... | 65 | 60[27] | 56[36] | 70 | 94[57] | ... | 101[76] | ... |
| Maceió (Brazil) | ... | ... | ... | ... | ... | ... | ... | ... | ... | 28[72] | ... | 31 |
| Manaus (Brazil) | ... | ... | ... | ... | ... | ... | ... | ... | ... | 29[72] | ... | 39 |
| Manizales (Colombia) | ... | ... | ... | ... | ... | ... | ... | 3 | ... | 11 | 15[84] | ... |
| Maracaibo (Venezuela) | ... | ... | 22 | ... | ... | ... | ... | ... | ... | 22[73] | 25 | 29 |
| Maracay (Venezuela) | ... | ... | 8 | ... | ... | ... | ... | ... | ... | 3[73] | 4 | 4 |

## A4  SOUTH AMERICA: Population of Major Cities (in thousands)

| | c1750 | 1790 | 1800 | 1810 | 1820 | 1830 | 1840 | 1850 | 1860 | 1870 | 1880 | 1890 |
|---|---|---|---|---|---|---|---|---|---|---|---|---|
| Mar del Plata (Argentina) | ... | ... | ... | ... | ... | ... | ... | ... | ... | ... | ... | ... |
| Medellín (Colombia) | ... | 9[85] | 5 | ... | 5[25] | ... | 9[43] | 14 | 12 | 30 | 37[84] | 29[95] |
| Mendoza (Argentina) | ... | ... | 10 | ... | ... | 12[26] | ... | ... | ... | 8 | 12 | ... |
| Montevideo (Uruguay) | ... | ... | 14 | ... | ... | 15 | 31[43] | 34 | 58 | 105[72] | 164 | 215 |
| Natal (Brazil) | ... | ... | ... | ... | ... | ... | ... | ... | ... | 20[72] | ... | 14 |
| Niterói (Brazil) | ... | ... | ... | ... | ... | ... | ... | ... | ... | 48[72] | ... | 34 |
| Pôrto Alegre (Brazil) | ... | ... | 4 | ... | ... | ... | ... | ... | ... | 44[72] | ... | 52 |
| Quito (Ecuador) | ... | 28[80] | ... | ... | ... | ... | ... | ... | 36[57] | ... | ... | 50 |
| Recife (Brazil) | ... | ... | 15 | 25 | ... | 41[28] | 72 | ... | 90[62] | 97[72] | ... | 112 |
| Rio de Janeiro (Brazil) | 29 | ... | 43 | 50[07] | 113 | 125 | 141 | 166 | 198 | 275[72] | 360 | 523 |
| Rosario (Argentina) | ... | ... | 0.4 | ... | ... | ... | 2 | 3 | 10[58] | 23 | ... | 51[87] |
| Salvador (Brazil) | 34 | ... | 46 | 100 | 115 | 130[35] | 140 | 150[52] | ... | 129[72] | ... | 174 |
| San Juan (Argentina) | ... | 6[77] | ... | 4[12] | ... | 8[26] | ... | ... | 9 | 8 | ... | 10[95] |
| Santiago (Chile) | ... | ... | 45 | ... | ... | ... | ... | ... | ... | 115[65] | 130[75] | 189[85] |
| Santa Fé (Argentina) | ... | ... | 4[97] | 5 | 7[17] | ... | ... | ... | 6[58] | 11 | ... | 14[87] |
| Santos (Brazil) | ... | ... | 6 | ... | ... | 5[28] | 6[36] | ... | 6[58] | 10[72] | ... | 13 |
| São Paolo (Brazil) | ... | 8 | ... | ... | 20 | ... | 12[36] | 15[55] | 8[62] | 31[72] | ... | 65 |
| Trujillo (Peru) | 9[63] | ... | 4 | 4[12] | 5[18] | 10[26] | ... | ... | ... | ... | 8[76] | 8 |
| Tucumán (Argentina) | ... | ... | ... | ... | ... | ... | ... | 17[45] | ... | 17 | ... | ... |
| Valencia (Venezuela) | ... | ... | 7 | ... | ... | ... | ... | ... | ... | 16[73] | ... | 28 |
| Valparaíso (Chile) | ... | ... | 6 | ... | ... | ... | ... | 52[54] | ... | 70[65] | 98[75] | 105[85] |

## A4   SOUTH AMERICA: Population of Major Cities (in thousands)

| | 1900 | 1910 | 1920 | 1930 | 1940 | 1950 | 1950 | 1960 | 1960 | 1970 | 1970 | 1980 | 1980 |
|---|---|---|---|---|---|---|---|---|---|---|---|---|---|
| Arequipa (Peru) | 35 | 40 | 44[17] | 46 | 61 | 97 | … | 135 | … | 302[72] | … | 498 | … |
| Asunción (Paraguay) | … | 80 | … | 90 | 120 | 207 | 219 | 305 | … | 399 | 473 | 457[82] | 708[82] |
| Barquisimeto (Venezuela) | … | … | 24 | 23[26] | 54 | 105 | … | 200 | … | 331 | … | 497 | … |
| Barranquilla (Colombia) | 40[05] | 49[12] | 65[18] | 140[28] | 152[38] | 280 | … | 521[64] | … | 662[73] | 727[73] | … | 917[85] |
| Belém (Brazil) | 97 | 271 | 236 | 279[29] | 206 | 255 | … | 402 | … | 633 | … | 933 | … |
| Belo Horizonte (Brazil) | 13 | 35 | 55 | 109[29] | 211 | 353 | … | 693 | … | 1,235 | … | 1,781 | 2,279 |
| Bogotá (Colombia) | 100[05] | 121[12] | 144[18] | 235[28] | 330[38] | 648 | … | 813[64] | … | 2,855[73] | … | 4,177 | … |
| Brasília (Brazil) | — | — | — | … | — | — | — | 142 | … | 537 | … | 1,177 | … |
| Bucaramanga (Colombia) | 20[05] | 20[12] | 25[18] | 44[28] | 51[38] | 112 | … | 251 | … | 292[73] | 341[73] | … | 352[85] |
| Buenos Aires (Argentina) | 664[95] | 1,576[14] | 1,663 | 2,149 | 2,705 | 2,981[47] | 4,722[47] | 2,967 | 6,739 | 2,972 | 8,353 | 2,923 | 9,948 |
| Cali (Colombia) | 31[05] | 28[12] | 46[18] | 123[28] | 102[38] | 284 | … | 251[64] | … | 898[73] | 923[73] | … | 1,369[85] |
| Callao (Peru) | 29[98] | … | 53 | 64 | 69 | 88 | … | 156 | … | 297 | … | 443 | … |
| Campinas (Brazil) | 45[02] | … | 116 | … | 130 | 102 | … | 180 | … | 329 | … | 665 | … |
| Caracas (Venezuela) | … | 87[15] | 92 | 135[26] | 269 | 495 | 694 | 788 | 1,336 | 1,663 | 2,175 | 1,817 | 2,944 |
| Cartagena (Colombia) | 10[05] | 37[12] | 51[18] | 92[28] | 85[38] | 129 | … | 198[64] | … | 293[73] | … | … | 531[85] |
| Córdoba (Argentina) | 48[95] | 135[14] | 140 | 253 | 274 | 370[47] | … | 586 | … | 782 | 799 | 971 | 983 |
| Cúcuta (Colombia) | 15[05] | 20[12] | 29[18] | 49[28] | 57[38] | 70 | 95 | 147[64] | 175[64] | 220[73] | 228[73] | … | 384[85] |
| Curitiba (Brazil) | 50 | 61 | 79 | 100[29] | 141 | 181 | … | 361 | … | 609 | … | 1,025 | 1,093 |
| Duque de Caxias (Brazil) | … | … | … | … | … | 74 | … | 176 | … | 257 | … | 576 | … |
| Fortaleza (Brazil) | 48 | 66 | 79 | 99[29] | 180 | 270 | … | 515 | … | 858 | … | 1,308 | 1,340 |
| Goiânia (Brazil) | — | — | — | 27 | 48 | 53 | … | 151 | … | 381 | … | 718 | 723 |
| Guayaquil (Equador) | 60 | 85 | 94 | 120 | 147[38] | 259 | … | 511 | … | 861[72] | … | 1,199[82] | … |
| La Paz (Bolivia) | 53 | 80 | 107[18] | 147[29] | 301[42] | 321 | … | 353[62] | … | 538 | … | 813 | … |
| La Plata (Argentina) | 45[95] | 90[14] | 151[22] | 166[28] | 200 | 207[47] | … | 337 | … | 391 | 506 | 459 | 566 |
| Lima (Peru) | 130[03] | 141[08] | 176 | 281 | 521 | 835 | … | 1,262 | 1,436 | 2,834 | 3,303 | 4,165 | 4,669 |
| Maceió (Brazil) | 36 | 61 | 74 | 104[29] | 90 | 121 | … | 168 | … | 264 | … | 399 | … |
| Manaus (Brazil) | 50 | 77 | 76 | 84[29] | 106 | 140 | … | 175 | … | 312 | … | 633 | … |
| Manizales (Colombia) | 25[05] | 35[12] | 43[18] | 81[28] | 86[38] | 89 | 126 | 187[64] | 222[64] | 200[73] | 207[73] | … | 283[85] |
| Maracaibo (Venezuela) | … | … | 47 | 75[26] | 122 | 236 | … | 421 | … | 652 | … | 889 | … |
| Maracay (Venezuela) | … | … | 7 | 11[26] | 33 | 65 | … | 135 | … | 255 | … | 440 | … |

**A4    SOUTH AMERICA: Population of Major Cities** (in thousands)

| | 1900 | 1910 | 1920 | 1930 | 1940 | 1940 | 1950 | 1950 | 1960 | 1960 | 1970 | 1970 | 1980 | 1980 |
|---|---|---|---|---|---|---|---|---|---|---|---|---|---|---|
| Mar del Plata (Argentina) | 5[95] | 28[14] | ... | 50 | 55[38] | ... | 115[47] | ... | 211 | ... | 302 | ... | 415 | ... |
| Medellín (Colombia) | 55[05] | 71[12] | 79[18] | 120[28] | 168[38] | ... | 358 | ... | 777[64] | ... | 1,071[73] | 1,417[73] | ... | 1,452[85] |
| Mendoza (Argentina) | 28[95] | 59[14] | ... | 59 | 102[42] | ... | 97[47] | 212[47] | 109 | ... | 124 | 471 | 119 | 606 |
| Montevideo (Uruguay) | 268 | 328 | 385 | 482 | 770 | ... | 784 | ... | 1,159[63] | ... | 1,230[75] | ... | 1,252[85] | ... |
| Natal (Brazil) | 16 | 27 | 31 | 51 | 55 | ... | 103 | ... | 160 | ... | 264 | ... | 417 | ... |
| Niterói (Brazil) | 53 | 80 | 85 | 108[29] | 142 | ... | 186 | ... | 243 | ... | 324 | ... | 397 | ... |
| Nova Iguaçu (Brazil) | ... | ... | ... | ... | 21 | ... | 59 | ... | 135 | ... | 331 | 728 | 1,095 | ... |
| Osasco (Brazil) | ... | ... | ... | ... | ... | ... | 43 | ... | 116 | ... | 283 | ... | 475 | ... |
| Pôrto Alegre (Brazil) | 73 | 130 | 180 | 273[29] | 272 | ... | 394 | ... | 641 | ... | 886 | ... | 1,125 | 2,133 |
| Quito (Ecuador) | 40 | 70 | 81 | 92 | 128[38] | ... | 210 | – | 355 | ... | 565[72] | ... | 866[82] | ... |
| Recife (Brazil) | 113 | 193 | 239 | 341[29] | 348 | ... | 525 | ... | 797 | ... | 1,061 | ... | 1,204 | 2,307 |
| Rio de Janeiro (Brazil) | 811 | 870 | 1,158 | 1,469[29] | 1,764 | ... | 2,377 | ... | 3,307 | ... | 4,252 | ... | 5,091 | 9,619 |
| Rosario (Argentina) | 92[95] | 223[14] | 250 | 481 | 517 | ... | 468[47] | ... | 591 | 672 | 699 | 811 | 794 | 957 |
| Salvador (Brazil) | 206 | 319 | 283 | 330[29] | 290 | ... | 417 | ... | 656 | ... | 1,007 | ... | 1,502 | 1,563 |
| San Juan (Argentina) | 10[95] | 21[14] | ... | 17 | 80 | ... | 82[47] | ... | 107 | ... | 113 | 223 | 118 | 292 |
| Santiago (Chile) | 256[95] | 333[07] | 507 | 696 | 640 | 952 | 665 | 1,348 | 1,169 | 1,900 | 3,274 | 3,351 | 3,853 | 3,899 |
| Santa André (Brazil) | ... | ... | ... | ... | 62 | ... | 98 | ... | 232 | ... | 419 | ... | 553 | ... |
| Santa Fé (Argentina) | 22[95] | 60[14] | 84 | 121 | 149 | ... | 169[47] | ... | 209 | ... | 252 | ... | 292 | ... |
| Santos (Brazil) | 30 | 86 | 103 | ... | 156 | ... | 198 | ... | 262 | ... | 341 | ... | 417 | 848 |
| São Goncales (Brazil) | ... | ... | ... | ... | 8 | ... | 21 | ... | 64 | ... | 430 | ... | 615 | ... |
| São Paolo (Brazil) | 240 | 346 | 579 | 880[29] | 1,326 | ... | 2,198 | ... | 3,825 | ... | 5,929 | ... | 8,493 | 12,273 |
| Trujillo (Peru) | 8[96] | ... | 20 | 30[28] | 39 | ... | 48 | ... | 100 | ... | 242[72] | ... | 539 | ... |
| Tucumán (Argentina) | 34[95] | 94[14] | ... | 91 | 149 | ... | 194[47] | ... | 272 | 288 | 361 | 366 | 394 | 499 |
| Valencia (Venezuela) | ... | ... | 29 | 37[26] | 55 | ... | 89 | ... | 164 | ... | 367 | ... | 616 | ... |
| Valparaíso (Chile) | 122[95] | 162[07] | 182 | 193 | 210 | ... | 219 | ... | 259 | ... | 293 | ... | 266 | ... |

**A4** **Population of Major Cities** (in thousands)

NOTES

1. SOURCES: UN and League of Nations, *Statistical Yearbooks,* and the national publications on p. xiv–xvi. Official estimates as well as census figures have been used. Where none is available for years ending in 9, 0, or 1, that for the nearest available date has been used, and this has been indicated.
2. With a few exceptions, the cities in this table had a population of 200,000 or more in or about 1970, or the urban agglomeration of which they were the nucleus had a population of at least 500,000. There are a few additions which seem to be of particular historical interest.
3. Statistics to 1930 all relate to the cities proper except as indicated in footnotes. Subsequently two figures are given where available, the first for the cities proper, the second for their urban agglomeration.

FOOTNOTES

[1] The population was said to be 9 thousand in 1731. Including Brooklyn and, from 1850, other places later incorporated in the city.
[2] Including Allegheny, which was consolidated with Pittsburgh between 1900 and 1910, from 1850.
[3] Albany-Schenectady-Troy.
[4] Allentown-Bethlehem-Easton.
[5] Anaheim-Santa Ana-Garden Grove.
[6] Charlotte-Gastonia.
[7] Dallas-Forth Worth (see under Dallas).
[8] Denver-Boulder.
[9] Fort Lauderdale-Hollywood.
[10] Gary-Hammond-East Chicago.
[11] Greensboro-Winston Salem-High Point.
[12] Indianapolis and Marion County were consolidated between 1960 and 1970.
[13] Jacksonville and Duval County were consolidated between 1960 and 1970.
[14] Los Angeles-Long Beach.
[15] Minneapolis-St Paul (see under Minneapolis).
[16] Nashville and Davidson County were consolidated between 1960 and 1970.
[17] Norfolk-Virginia Beach-Portsmouth.
[18] San Francisco-Oakland (see under San Francisco).
[19] Omaha and South Omaha were consolidated between 1910 and 1920. Combined population: 1890–149; 1900–129; 1910–150.
[20] Paterson-Clifton-Passaic.
[21] Providence-Warwick-Pawtucket.
[22] Tampa-St Petersburg (see under Tampa).
[23] Riverside-San Bernardino-Ontario.
[24] Seattle-Everett.
[25] Springfield-Chicopee-Holyoke.
[26] Part of New York metropolitan area.
[27] Youngstown-Warren.
[28] Including suburbs.

**A5    NORTH AMERICA: MID-YEAR POPULATION ESTIMATES** (in thousands)

| | USA[1] | | USA | | Canada[2] | Costa Rica | Jamaica | Trinidad | USA |
|---|---|---|---|---|---|---|---|---|---|
| 1790 | 3,929 | 1825 | 11,252 | 1860 | ... | ... | ... | ... | 31,513 |
| 1791 | 4,050 | 1826 | 11,580 | 1861 | ... | ... | ... | ... | |
| 1792 | 4,194 | 1827 | 11,909 | 1862 | ... | ... | ... | ... | 33,188 |
| 1793 | 4,332 | 1828 | 12,237 | 1863 | ... | ... | ... | ... | 34,026 |
| 1794 | 4,469 | 1829 | 12,565 | 1864 | ... | ... | ... | ... | 34,863 |
| 1795 | 4,607 | 1830 | 12,901 | 1865 | ... | ... | ... | ... | 35,701 |
| 1796 | 4,745 | 1831 | 13,321 | 1866 | ... | ... | ... | ... | 36,538 |
| 1797 | 4,883 | 1832 | 13,742 | 1867 | 3,463 | ... | ... | ... | 37,376 |
| 1798 | 5,021 | 1833 | 14,162 | 1868 | 3,511 | ... | ... | ... | 38,213 |
| 1799 | 5,159 | 1834 | 14,582 | 1869 | 3,565 | ... | ... | ... | 39,051 |
| 1800 | 5,297 | 1835 | 15,003 | 1870 | 3,625 | ... | ... | ... | 39,905 |
| 1801 | 5,486 | 1836 | 15,423 | 1871 | 3,689 | ... | ... | ... | 40,938 |
| 1802 | 5,679 | 1837 | 15,843 | 1872 | 3,754 | ... | ... | ... | 41,972 |
| 1803 | 5,872 | 1838 | 16,264 | 1873 | 3,826 | ... | ... | ... | 43,006 |
| 1884 | 6,065 | 1839 | 16,684 | 1874 | 3,895 | ... | ... | ... | 44,040 |
| 1805 | 6,258 | 1840 | 17,120 | 1875 | 3,954 | ... | ... | ... | 45,073 |
| 1806 | 6,451 | 1841 | 17,733 | 1876 | 4,009 | ... | ... | ... | 46,107 |
| 1807 | 6,644 | 1842 | 18,345 | 1877 | 4,064 | ... | ... | ... | 47,141 |
| 1808 | 6,838 | 1843 | 18,957 | 1878 | 4,120 | ... | ... | ... | 48,174 |
| 1809 | 7,031 | 1844 | 19,569 | 1879 | 4,185 | ... | ... | ... | 49,208 |
| 1810 | 7,224 | 1845 | 20,182 | 1880 | 4,255 | ... | 558 | ... | 50,262 |
| 1811 | 7,460 | 1846 | 20,794 | 1881 | 4,325 | ... | 575 | ... | 51,542 |
| 1812 | 7,700 | 1847 | 21,406 | 1882 | 4,375 | ... | 586 | ... | 52,821 |
| 1813 | 7,939 | 1848 | 22,018 | 1883 | 4,430 | ... | 590 | 160 | 54,100 |
| 1814 | 8,179 | 1849 | 22,631 | 1884 | 4,487 | ... | 591 | 164 | 55,379 |
| 1815 | 8,419 | 1850 | 23,261 | 1885 | 4,537 | 201 | 592 | 169 | 56,658 |
| 1816 | 8,659 | 1851 | 24,086 | 1886 | 4,580 | 206 | 597 | 175 | 57,938 |
| 1817 | 8,899 | 1852 | 24,911 | 1887 | 4,626 | 211 | 600 | 181 | 59,217 |
| 1818 | 9,139 | 1853 | 25,736 | 1888 | 4,678 | 216 | 606 | 187 | 60,496 |
| 1819 | 9,379 | 1854 | 26,561 | 1889 | 4,729 | 225 | 617 | 193 | 61,775 |
| 1820 | 9,618 | 1855 | 27,386 | | | | | | |
| 1821 | 9,939 | 1856 | 28,212 | | | | | | |
| 1822 | 10,268 | 1857 | 29,037 | | | | | | |
| 1823 | 10,596 | 1858 | 29,862 | | | | | | |
| 1824 | 10,924 | 1859 | 30,687 | | | | | | |

**A5     NORTH AMERICA: Mid-Year Population Estimates** (in thousands)

| | Barbados | Canada[2] | Costa Rica | Cuba | Dominican Republic | El Salvador | Guatemala | Haiti |
|------|------|------|------|------|------|------|------|------|
| 1890 | ... | 4,779 | 235 | ... | ... | ... | ... | ... |
| 1891 | ... | 4,833 | 245 | ... | ... | ... | ... | ... |
| 1892 | ... | 4,883 | 255 | ... | ... | ... | ... | ... |
| 1893 | ... | 4,931 | 262 | ... | ... | ... | ... | ... |
| 1894 | ... | 4,979 | 269 | ... | ... | ... | ... | ... |
| 1895 | ... | 5,026 | 276 | ... | ... | ... | ... | ... |
| 1896 | ... | 5,074 | 282 | ... | ... | ... | ... | ... |
| 1897 | ... | 5,122 | 287 | ... | ... | ... | ... | ... |
| 1898 | ... | 5,175 | 294 | ... | ... | ... | ... | ... |
| 1899 | ... | 5,235 | 297 | 1,573 | ... | ... | ... | ... |
| 1900 | ... | 5,301 | 307 | 1,600 | 600 | 801 | 885 | 1,250 |
| 1901 | ... | 5,371 [2] | 313 | 1,679 | 614 | 819 | 910 | 1,294 |
| 1902 | ... | 5,494 | 318 | 1,758 | 628 | 838 | 936 | 1,338 |
| 1903 | ... | 5,651 | 323 | 1,837 | 642 | 856 | 961 | 1,381 |
| 1904 | ... | 5,827 | 330 | 1,879 | 656 | 874 | 987 | 1,425 |
| 1905 | ... | 6,002 | 336 | 1,927 | 670 | 893 | 1,013 | 1,468 |
| 1906 | ... | 6,097 | 341 | 1,979 | 684 | 911 | 1,029 | 1,512 |
| 1907 | ... | 6,411 | 347 | 2,034 | 698 | 929 | 1,046 | 1,555 |
| 1908 | ... | 6,625 | 353 | 2,092 | 712 | 948 | 1,062 | 1,559 |
| 1909 | ... | 6,800 | 358 | 2,154 | 726 | 966 | 1,079 | 1,643 |
| 1910 | 172 | 6,988 | 364 | 2,219 | 740 | 985 | 1,096 | 1,687 |
| 1911 | 173 | 7,207 | 370 | 2,287 | 753 | 1,003 | 1,119 | 1,730 |
| 1912 | 172 | 7,389 | 375 | 2,358 | 767 | 1,021 | 1,142 | 1,774 |
| 1913 | 173 | 7,632 | 381 | 2,413 | 781 | 1,040 | 1,165 | 1,818 |
| 1914 | 173 | 7,879 | 387 | 2,507 | 795 | 1,058 | 1,180 | 1,862 |
| 1915 | 177 | 7,981 | 393 | 2,585 | 809 | 1,076 | 1,196 | 1,907 |
| 1916 | 182 | 8,001 | 398 | 2,664 | 823 | 1,095 | 1,211 | 1,949 |
| 1917 | 185 | 8,060 | 404 | 2,746 | 837 | 1,113 | 1,226 | 1,993 |
| 1918 | 190 | 8,148 | 410 | 2,828 | 851 | 1,131 | 1,241 | 2,037 |
| 1919 | 197 | 8,311 | 415 | 2,912 | 865 | 1,150 | 1,257 | 2,080 |
| 1920 | ...—[7] | 8,556 | 421 | 2,997 | 879 | 1,168 | 1,272 | 2,124 |
| 1921 | 155 | 8,788 | 425 | 3,083 | 912 | 1,193 | 1,319 | 2,151 |
| 1922 | 155 | 8,919 | 431 | 3,170 | 946 | 1,217 | 1,367 | 2,178 |
| 1923 | 155 | 9,010 | 439 | 3,257 | 981 | 1,244 | 1,416 | 2,206 |
| 1924 | 155 | 9,143 | 447 | 3,345 | 1,017 | 1,274 | 1,471 | 2,232 |
| 1925 | 156 | 9,294 | 456 | 3,432 | 1,054 | 1,301 | 1,514 | 2,260 |
| 1926 | 157 | 9,451 | 466 | 3,519 | 1,092 | 1,325 | 1,557 | 2,292 |
| 1927 | 158 | 9,637 | 472 | 3,606 | 1,131 | 1,351 | 1,602 | 2,325 |
| 1928 | 159 | 9,835 | 479 | 3,507 | 1,172 | 1,385 | 1,660 | 2,357 |
| 1929 | 158 | 10,029 | 489 | 3,577 | 1,213 | 1,412 | 1,706 | 2,390 |
| 1930 | 159 | 10,208 | 499 | 3,647 | 1,256 | 1,443 | 1,755 | 2,422 |
| 1931 | 159 | 10,376 | 508 | 3,962 | 1,300 | 1,456 | 1,813 | 2,460 |
| 1932 | 161 | 10,510 | 518 | 3,962 | 1,345 | 1,474 | 1,864 | 2,498 |
| 1933 | 164 | 10,633 | 528 | 3,962 | 1,391 | 1,493 | 1,909 | 2,535 |
| 1934 | 166 | 10,741 | 540 | 4,039 | 1,438 | 1,512 | 1,943 | 2,573 |
| 1935 | 168 | 10,845 | 551 | 4,071 | 1,484 | 1,531 | 1,975 | 2,611 |
| 1936 | 170 | 10,950 | 563 | 4,109 | 1,520 | 1,551 | 2,023 | 2,654 |
| 1937 | 173 | 11,045 | 576 | 4,165 | 1,558 | 1,571 | 2,066 | 2,697 |
| 1938 | 175 | 11,152 | 590 | 4,228 | 1,595 | 1,591 | 2,113 | 2,741 |
| 1939 | 177 | 11,267 | 605 | 4,253 | 1,634 | 1,612 | 2,150 | 2,784 |

**A5    NORTH AMERICA: Mid-Year Population Estimates** (in thousands)

| | Honduras | Jamaica | Martinique | Mexico | Nicaragua | Panama | Puerto Rico | Trinidad & Tobago[3] | USA[4] |
|---|---|---|---|---|---|---|---|---|---|
| 1890 | ... | 630 | ... | ... | ... | ... | ... | 197 | 63,056 |
| 1891 | ... | 637 | ... | ... | ... | ... | ... | 208 | 64,361 |
| 1892 | ... | 648 | ... | ... | ... | ... | ... | 217 | 65,666 |
| 1893 | ... | 661 | ... | 12,257 | ... | ... | | ...[3] | 66,970 |
| 1894 | ... | 673 | ... | 12,443 | ... | ... | ... | 224 | 68,275 |
| 1895 | ... | 684 | ... | 12,632 | ... | ... | ... | 234 | 69,580 |
| 1896 | ... | 695 | ... | 12,822 | ... | ... | ... | 242 | 70,885 |
| 1897 | ... | 706 | ... | 13,014 | ... | ... | ... | 249 | 72,129 |
| 1898 | ... | 718 | ... | 13,209 | ... | ... | ... | 257 | 73,494 |
| 1899 | ... | 731 | ... | 13,406 | ... | ... | ... | 265 | 74,799 |
| 1900 | 420 | 745 | ... | 13,607 | 420 | 263 | ... | 273 | 76,094 |
| 1901 | 436 | 748 | ... | 13,755 | 434 | 270 | | 276 | 77,584 |
| 1902 | 452 | 747 | ... | 13,905 | 448 | 276 | | 277 | 79,163 |
| 1903 | 468 | 781 | ... | 14,056 | 462 | 283 | | 290 | 80,632 |
| 1904 | 484 | 792 | ... | 14,209 | 477 | 290 | | 299 | 82,166 |
| 1905 | 500 | 798 | ... | 14,363 | 491 | 297 | | 308 | 83,822 |
| 1906 | 511 | 805 | ... | 14,519 | 505 | 304 | | 315 | 85,450 |
| 1907 | 521 | 810 | ... | 14,677 | 515 | 311 | | 320 | 87,008 |
| 1908 | 532 | 813 | ... | 14,837 | 524 | 318 | | 340 | 88,710 |
| 1909 | 542 | 820 | ... | 14,998 | 534 | 325 | | 342 | 90,490 |
| 1910 | 553 | 824 | ... | 15,160 | 543 | 332 | | 353 | 92,407 |
| 1911 | 562 | 831 | ... | 15,083 | 553 | 339 | | 354 | 93,863 |
| 1912 | 571 | 839 | ... | 15,007 | 562 | 352 | | 342 | 95,335 |
| 1913 | 579 | 846 | ... | 14,931 | 572 | 364 | | 348 | 97,225 |
| 1914 | 588 | 851 | ... | 14,855 | 581 | 378 | | 354 | 99,111 |
| 1915 | 597 | 861 | ... | 14,780 | 591 | 389 | | 361 | 100,546 |
| 1916 | 606 | 874 | ... | 14,705 | 600 | 401 | | 368 | 101,961 |
| 1917 | 633 | 869 | ... | 14,630 | 610 | 413 | | 374 | 103,268[5] |
| 1918 | 660 | 864 | ... | 14,556 | 619 | 426 | | 379 | 103,208[5] |
| 1919 | 688 | 857 | ... | 14,482 | 629 | 437 | | 384 | 104,514[5] |
| 1920 | 715 | 855 | ... | 14,409 | 638 | 447 | 1,312 | 389 | 106,461 |
| 1921 | 742 | 860 | 244 | 14,335 | 643 | 449 | 1,336 | 367 | 108,538 |
| 1922 | 769 | 879 | ... | 14,566 | 647 | 451 | 1,359 | 371 | 110,049 |
| 1923 | 796 | 891 | ... | 14,801 | 652 | 453 | 1,383 | 376 | 111,947 |
| 1924 | 824 | 900 | ... | 15,040 | 656 | 455 | 1,407 | 379 | 114,109 |
| 1925 | 851 | 910 | | 15,282 | 660 | 457 | 1,431 | 382 | 115,829 |
| 1926 | 878 | 930 | ... | 15,528 | 665 | 459 | 1,455 | 385 | 117,397 |
| 1927 | 893 | 946 | 228 | 15,778 | 670 | 462 | 1,478 | 388 | 119,035 |
| 1928 | 911 | 966 | ... | 16,032 | 674 | 464 | 1,502 | 392 | 120,509 |
| 1929 | 928 | 985 | ... | 16,290 | 679 | 466 | 1,526 | 398 | 121,770[4] |
| 1930 | 948 | 1,009 | ... | 16,553 | 683 | 471 | 1,552 | 405 | 123,188 |
| 1931 | 968 | 1,039 | 235 | 16,840 | 687 | 486 | 1,584 | 412 | 124,149 |
| 1932 | 989 | 1,061 | ... | 17,132 | 692 | 501 | 1,615 | 417 | 124,949 |
| 1933 | 1,007 | 1,082 | ... | 17,429 | 697 | 516 | 1,647 | 422 | 125,690 |
| 1934 | 1,023 | 1,098 | ... | 17,731 | 711 | 531 | 1,679 | 428 | 126,485 |
| 1935 | 1,042 | 1,113 | ... | 18,038 | 728 | 546 | 1,710 | 435 | 127,362 |
| 1936 | 1,058 | 1,130 | 247 | 18,350 | 746 | 561 | 1,743 | 442 | 128,181 |
| 1937 | 1,076 | 1,142 | ... | 18,668 | 765 | 575 | 1,777 | 450 | 128,961 |
| 1938 | 1,098 | 1,163 | ... | 18,991 | 785 | 590 | 1,810 | 458 | 129,969 |
| 1939 | 1,122 | 1,191 | 252 | 19,320 | 806 | 605 | 1,844 | 466 | 131,028 |

**A5 NORTH AMERICA: Mid-Year Population Estimates** (in thousands)

| | Barbados | Canada[6] | Costa Rica | Cuba | Dominican Republic | El Salvador | Guadeloupe | Guatemala | Haiti |
|---|---|---|---|---|---|---|---|---|---|
| 1940 | 179 | 11,381 | 619 | 4,291 | 1,674 | 1,633 | ... | 2,201 | 2,827 |
| 1941 | 179 | 11,507 | 633 | 4,326 | 1,715 | 1,654 | ... | 2,252 | 2,876 |
| 1942 | 180 | 11,654 | 647 | 4,372 | 1,757 | 1,675 | ... | 2,300 | 2,936 |
| 1943 | 182 | 11,795 | 661 | 4,779 | 1,800 | 1,697 | ... | 2,339 | 2,979 |
| 1944 | 183 | 11,946 | 677 | 4,849 | 1,844 | 1,719 | ... | 2,384 | 3,032 |
| 1945 | 187 | 12,072 | 695 | 4,932 | 1,889 | 1,742 | ... | 2,438 | 3,087 |
| 1946 | 193 | 12,292 | 709 | 5,039 | 1,935 | 1,764 | 190 | 2,498 | 3,143 |
| 1947 | 199 | 12,551 | 726 | 5,152 | 1,982 | 1,788 | 193 | 2,567 | 3,200 |
| 1948 | 202 | 12,823[6] 13,167 | 746[7] 808 | 5,287 | 1,997 | 1,811 | 197 | 2,642 | 3,258[7] 3233 |
| 1949 | 206 | 13,475 | 832 | 5,399 | 2,061 | 1,835 | 201 | 2,724 | 3,293 |
| 1950 | 211 | 13,737 | 859 | 5,516 | 2,129 | 1,859 | 210 | 2,805 | 3,097 |
| 1951 | 215 | 14,050 | 888 | 5,638 | 2,216 | 1,912 | 214 | 2,892 | 3,149 |
| 1952 | 218 | 14,496 | 920 | 5,759 | 2,297 | 1,965 | 219 | 2,981 | 3,200 |
| 1953 | 221 | 14,886 | 954 | 6,129 | 2,379 | 2,020 | 224 | 3,075 | 3,251 |
| 1954 | 225 | 15,330 | 989 | 6,254 | 2,464 | 2,077 | 230 | 3,171 | 3,302 |
| 1955 | 227 | 15,736 | 1,028 | 6,381 | 2,554 | 2,135 | 237 | 3,269 | 3,354 |
| 1956 | 226 | 16,123 | 1,069 | 6,513 | 2,644 | 2,195 | 244 | 3,371 | 3,407 |
| 1957 | 226 | 16,677 | 1,110 | 6,641 | 2,740 | 2,257 | 251 | 3,476 | 3,460 |
| 1958 | 228 | 17,120 | 1,153 | 6,763 | 2,839 | 2,321 | 258 | 3,584 | 3,514 |
| 1959 | 231 | 17,522 | 1,200 | 6,901 | 2,941 | 2,386 | 265 | 3,695 | 3,568 |
| 1960 | 233 | 17,909 | 1,254 | 7,027 | 3,038 | 2,454 | 275 | 3,966 | 3,623 |
| 1961 | 233 | 18,271 | 1,298 | 7,134 | 3,126 | 2,527 | 281 | 4,088 | 3,679 |
| 1962 | 234 | 18,614 | 1,343 | 7,254 | 3,220 | 2,627 | 289 | 4,214 | 3,736 |
| 1963 | 237 | 18,964 | 1,391 | 7,415 | 3,315 | 2,721 | 297 | 4,345[7] | 3,793 |
| 1964 | 241 | 19,325 | 1,439 | 7,612 | 3,412 | 2,824 | 308 | 4,312 | 3,852 |
| 1965 | 244 | 19,678 | 1,490 | 7,810 | 3,513 | 2,928 | 315 | 4,437 | 3,912 |
| 1966 | 247 | 20,048 | 1,541 | 7,985 | 3,616 | 3,037 | 319 | 4,565 | 3,972 |
| 1967 | 249 | 20,412 | 1,590 | 8,139 | 3,723 | 3,151 | 320 | 4,698 | 4,035 |
| 1968 | 252 | 20,744 | 1,634 | 8,284 | 3,833 | 3,266 | 318 | 4,837 | 4,098 |
| 1969 | 253 | 21,028 | 1,685 | 8,421 | 3,946 | 3,390 | 323 | 4,966 | 4,163 |
| 1970 | 238 | 21,324 | 1,727 | 8,551 | 4,062 | 3,534 | 327 | 5,272 | 4,235 |
| 1971 | 240 | 21,592 | 1,798 | 8,692 | 4,182 | 3,647[7] | 332[7] | 5,425 | 4,315 |
| 1972 | 241 | 21,822 | 1,842 | 8,862 | 4,305 | 3,668 | 320 | 5,582 | 4,368 |
| 1973 | 239 | 22,072 | 1,873 | 9,036 | 4,476 | 3,771 | 325 | 5,744 | 4,440 |
| 1974 | 244 | 22,360 | 1,922 | 9,194 | 4,614 | 3,887 | 325 | 6,050 | 4,514 |
| 1975 | 246 | 22,697 | 1,968 | 9,299 | 4,752 | 4,005 | 328 | 6,243 | 4,584 |
| 1976 | 246 | 22,993 | 2,009 | 9,430 | 4,890 | 4,122 | 329 | 6,434[7] 6,191 | 4,668 |
| 1977 | 247 | 23,273 | 2,066 | 9,547 | 5,028 | 4,255 | 328 | 6,364 | 4,749 |
| 1978 | 248 | 23,517 | 2,115 | 9,644 | 5,166 | 4,353 | 327 | 6,543 | 4,833 |
| 1979 | 249 | 23,747 | 2,166 | 9,720 | 5,305 | 4,435 | 327 | 6,726 | 4,919 |
| 1980 | 249 | 24,043 | 2,245 | 9,724 | 5,443 | 4,508 | 327 | 6,917 | 5,009 |
| 1981 | 250 | 24,342 | 2,271 | 9,724 | 5,581 | 4,587 | 328 | 7,113 | 5,100 |
| 1982 | 250 | 24,583 | 2,324 | 9,801 | 5,744 | 4,662 | 328 | 7,315 | 5,054 |
| 1983 | 251 | 24,787 | [2,435][8] | 9,897 | 6,123 | 4,724 | 329 | 7,524 | 5,130 |
| 1984 | 252 | 24,978 | 2,417 | 9,994 | 6,269 | 4,780 | 330 | 7,740 | 5,207 |
| 1985 | 253 | 25,165 | 2,489[8] | 10,098 | 6,416 | 4,819 | 333 | 7,963 | 5,285 |
| 1986 | 253 | 25,353 | 2,717 | 10,199 | 6,565 | 4,913 | 335 | 8,195 | 5,364 |
| 1987 | 254 | 25,617 | 2,781 | 10,301 | 6,716 | 5,009 | 337 | 8,434 | 5,444 |
| 1988 | 254 | 25,911 | 2,851 | 10,412 | 6,867 | 5,107 | 340 | 8,681 | 5,526 |

**A5    NORTH AMERICA: Mid-Year Population Estimates** (in thousands)

| | Honduras | Jamaica | Martinique | Mexico | Nicaragua | Panama | Puerto Rico | Trinidad & Tobago | USA[9] |
|---|---|---|---|---|---|---|---|---|---|
| 1940 | 1,146 | 1,212 | ... | 19,815 | 825 | 620 | 1,880 | 476 | 132,122 |
| 1941 | 1,171 | 1,230 | ... | 20,332 | 844 | 636 | 1,935 | 492 | 133,402 |
| 1942 | 1,195 | 1,254 | ... | 20,866 | 863 | 651 | 1,987 | 510 | 134,860 |
| 1943 | 1,213 | 1,249 | ... | 21,418 | 880 | 669 | 2,033 | 525 | 136,739 |
| 1944 | 1,237 | 1,259 | ... | 21,988 | 900 | 685 | 2,062 | 536 | 138,397 |
| 1945 | 1,261 | 1,266 | ... | 22,576 | 923 | 703[7] | 2,099 | 547 | 139,928 |
| 1946 | 1,287 | 1,298 | 209 | 23,183 | 947 | 727 | 2,141 | 561 | 141,389 |
| 1947 | 1,320 | 1,327 | 212 | 23,811 | 977 | 746 | 2,162 | 583 | 144,126 |
| 1948 | 1,353 | 1,343 | 215 | 24,461 | 1,001 | 767 | 2,187 | 600 | 146,631 |
| 1949 | 1,389 | 1,365 | 218 | 25,132 | 1,028 | 788 | 2,197 | 616 | 149,188 |
| 1950 | 1,445 | 1,403 | 222 | 26,282 | 1,052 | 795 | 2,218 | 632 | 151,684 |
| 1951 | 1,485 | 1,430 | 226 | 27,039 | 1,083 | 818 | 2,235 | 649 | 154,287 |
| 1952 | 1,528 | 1,457 | 230 | 27,846 | 1,116 | 842 | 2,227 | 663 | 156,954 |
| 1953 | 1,572 | 1,486 | 234 | 28,701 | 1,149 | 867 | 2,204 | 678 | 159,565 |
| 1954 | 1,617 | 1,518 | 239 | 29,605 | 1,183 | 893 | 2,214 | 698 | 162,391 |
| 1955 | 1,665 | 1,542 | 247 | 30,557 | 1,218 | 919 | 2,250 | 721 | 165,275 |
| 1956 | 1,715 | 1,564 | 253 | 31,557 | 1,255 | 946 | 2,249 | 743 | 168,221 |
| 1957 | 1,768 | 1,595 | 258 | 32,607 | 1,292 | 973 | 2,260 | 765 | 171,274 |
| 1958 | 1,823 | 1,630 | 271 | 33,704 | 1,330 | 1,002 | 2,299 | 789 | 174,141 |
| 1959 | 1,880 | 1,598 | 279 | 34,851 | 1,370 | 1,031 | 2,321 | 817 | 177,073[9] |
| | | | | | | | | | 177,830 |
| 1960 | 1,943 | 1,628 | 285 | 34,994 | 1,411 | 1,062 | 2,358 | 841 | 180,671 |
| 1961 | 2,020 | 1,646 | 289 | 36,158 | 1,453 | 1,094 | 2,402 | 867 | 183,691 |
| 1962 | 2,096 | 1,660 | 294 | 37,367 | 1,496 | 1,130 | 2,447 | 900 | 186,538 |
| 1963 | 2,169 | 1,696 | 294 | 38,623 | 1,541 | 1,162 | 2,495 | 924 | 189,242 |
| 1964 | 2,238 | 1,740 | 301 | 39,928 | 1,579 | 1,197 | 2,550 | 951 | 191,889 |
| 1965 | 2,304 | 1,760 | 307 | 41,284 | 1,619 | 1,234 | 2,594 | 974 | 194,303 |
| 1966 | 2,384 | 1,784 | 314 | 42,694 | 1,660 | 1,272 | 2,624 | 995 | 196,560 |
| 1967 | 2,466 | 1,802 | 321 | 44,161 | 1,701 | 1,310 | 2,645 | 1,010 | 198,712 |
| 1968 | 2,552 | 1,821 | 326 | 45,686 | 1,744 | 1,351 | 2,669 | 1,021 | 200,706 |
| 1969 | 2,638 | 1,844 | 332 | 47,274[8] | 1,788 | 1,392 | 2,717 | 1,028 | 202,677 |
| 1970 | 2,639 | 1,869 | 338 | 50,695 | 1,833 | 1,434 | 2,718 | 1,027 | 205,052 |
| 1971 | 2,720 | 1,901 | 341 | 52,452 | 1,889 | 1,478[8] | 2,775 | 1,033 | 207,661 |
| 1972 | 2,805 | 1,932 | 334 | 54,273 | 1,954 | 1,546 | 2,868 | 1,045 | 209,896 |
| 1973 | 2,895 | 1,972 | 332 | 56,161 | 2,015 | 1,592 | 2,870 | 1,058[8] | 211,909 |
| 1974 | 2,991 | 2,008 | 330 | 58,118 | 2,089 | 1,634 | 2,890 | 1,000 | 213,854 |
| 1975 | 3,093 | 2,047 | 328 | 60,145[10] | 2,162 | 1,704 | 2,933 | 1,009 | 215,973 |
| 1976 | 3,202 | 2,083 | 328 | 61,979 | 2,244 | 1,748 | 3,024 | 1,023 | 218,035 |
| 1977 | 3,318 | 2,097 | 327 | 63,813 | 2,325 | 1,792 | 3,061 | 1,035 | 220,239 |
| 1978 | 3,439 | 2,088 | 326 | 65,658 | 2,410 | 1,835 | 3,113 | 1,049 | 222,585 |
| 1979 | 3,564 | 2,112 | 326 | 67,517 | 2,644 | 1,878 | 3,149 | 1,064 | 225,055 |
| 1980 | 3,691 | 2,133 | 326 | 69,655 | 2,733 | 1,956 | 3,206 | 1,082 | 227,757 |
| 1981 | 3,821 | 2,162 | 326 | 71,305 | 2,860 | 1,999 | 3,247 | 1,094 | 230,138 |
| 1982 | 3,955 | 2,200 | 327 | 72,968 | 2,955 | 2,044 | 3,263 | 1,116 | 232,520 |
| 1983 | 4,092 | 2,241 | 327 | 74,633 | 3,058 | 2,089 | 3,265 | 1,139 | 234,799 |
| 1984 | 4,232 | 2,280 | 327 | 76,293 | 3,163 | 2,134 | 3,270 | 1,170 | 237,001 |
| 1985 | 4,372 | 2,311 | 331 | 77,938 | 3,273 | 2,180 | 3,283 | 1,178 | 239,279 |
| 1986 | 4,514 | 2,336 | 332 | 79,563 | 3,384 | 2,227 | 3,273 | 1,196 | 241,625 |
| 1987 | 4,656 | 2,351 | 334 | 81,163 | 3,502 | 2,274 | 3,294 | 1,212 | 243,942 |
| 1988 | 4,802 | 2,356 | 336 | 82,734 | 3,622 | 2,322 | 3,293 | 1,212 | 246,307 |

**A5        SOUTH AMERICA: MID-YEAR POPULATION ESTIMATES** (in thousands)

|      | Argentina | Brazil | Chile | Guyana | Peru |
|------|-----------|--------|-------|--------|------|
| 1850 | ... | ... | 1,294 | ... | ... |
| 1851 | ... | 7,344 | 1,326 | ... | ... |
| 1852 | ... | 7,456 | 1,358 | ... | ... |
| 1853 | ... | 7,570 | 1,391 | ... | ... |
| 1854 | ... | 7,686 | 1,423 | ... | ... |
| 1855 | ... | 7,803 | 1,454 | ... | ... |
| 1856 | ... | 7,923 | 1,501 | ... | ... |
| 1857 | ... | 8,044 | 1,517 | ... | ... |
| 1858 | ... | 8,167 | 1,551 | ... | ... |
| 1859 | ... | 8,291 | 1,584 | ... | ... |
| 1860 | ... | 8,418 | 1,618 | ... | |
| 1861 | ... | 8,547 | 1,653 | ... | ... |
| 1862 | ... | 8,678 | 1,688 | ... | ... |
| 1863 | ... | 8,810 | 1,725 | ... | ... |
| 1864 | ... | 8,945 | 1,757 | ... | ... |
| 1865 | 1,559 | 9,082 | 1,795 | ... | ... |
| 1866 | 1,616 | 9,221 | 1,832 | ... | ... |
| 1867 | 1,675 | 9,362 | 1,856 | ... | ... |
| 1868 | 1,737 | 9,505 | 1,880 | ... | ... |
| 1869 | 1,802 | 9,650 | 1,905 | ... | ... |
| 1870 | 1,859 | 9,797 | 1,931 | ... | ... |
| 1871 | 1,910 | 9,947 | 1,956 | ... | ... |
| 1872 | 1,963 | 10,099 | 1,982 | ... | ... |
| 1873 | 2,017 | 10,289 | 2,009 | ... | ... |
| 1874 | 2,073 | 10,486 | 2,035 | ... | ... |
| 1875 | 2,132 | 10,687 | 2,062 | ... | ... |
| 1876 | 2,192 | 10,891 | 2,097 | ... | ... |
| 1877 | 2,255 | 11,099 | 2,138 | ... | [440][11] |
| 1878 | 2,320 | 11,311 | 2,181 | ... | ... |
| 1879 | 2,387 | 11,528 | 2,224 | ... | [438][11] |
| 1880 | 2,457 | 11,748 | 2,269 | 248 | ... |
| 1881 | 2,529 | 11,973 | 2,314 | 250 | ... |
| 1882 | 2,602 | 12,202 | 2,360 | 255 | [505][11] |
| 1883 | 2,678 | 12,435 | 2,408 | 259 | 513 |
| 1884 | 2,757 | 12,673 | 2,456 | 262 | 540 |
| 1885 | 2,839 | 12,916 | 2,503 | 267 | 571 |
| 1886 | 2,923 | 13,163 | 2,536 | 272 | 590 |
| 1887 | 3,011 | 13,414 | 2,555 | 276 | 605 |
| 1888 | 3,108 | 13,671 | 2,572 | 278 | 631 |
| 1889 | 3,212 | 13,932 | 2,591 | 280 | 666 |
| 1890 | 3,323 | 14,199 | 2,609 | 280 | 695 |
| 1891 | 3,434 | 14,506 | 2,627 | 275 | 707 |
| 1892 | 3,548 | 14,857 | 2,646 | 271 | 718 |
| 1893 | 3,668 | 15,216 | 2,655 | 275 | 738 |
| 1894 | 3,793 | 15,583 | 2,674 | 280 | 762 |
| 1895 | 3,906 | 15,960 | 2,698 | 279 | 785 |
| 1896 | 4,013 | 16,346 | 2,733 | 277 | 806 |
| 1897 | 4,152 | 16,741 | 2,774 | 279 | 830 |
| 1898 | 4,296 | 17,145 | 2,816 | 279 | 852 |
| 1899 | 4,418 | 17,560 | 2,859[10] | 282 | 879[10] |

**A5    SOUTH AMERICA: Mid-Year Population Estimates** (in thousands)

|  | Argentina | Bolivia | Brazil | Chile | Colombia | Ecuador | Guyana | Paraguay | Peru | Uraguay | Venezuela |
|---|---|---|---|---|---|---|---|---|---|---|---|
| 1900 | 4,542 | 1,766 | 17,984 | 2,959 | 3,894 | 1,300 | 287 | 490 | 3,000 | 943 | 2,445 |
| 1901 | 4,674 | 1,785 | 18,392 | 2,994 | 3,944 | 1,312 | 291 | 506 | 3,100 | 965 | 2,451 |
| 1902 | 4,806 | 1,803 | 18,782 | 3,030 | 3,994 | 1,324 | 298 | 522 | 3,200 | 990 | 2,458 |
| 1903 | 4,924 | 1,822 | 19,180 | 3,066 | 4,044 | 1,336 | 299 | 539 | 3,300 | 1,019 | 2,465 |
| 1904 | 5,040 | 1,840 | 19,587 | 3,102 | 4,094 | 1,348 | 295 | 555 | 3,400 | 1,033 | 2,471 |
| 1905 | 5,197 | 1,859 | 20,003 | 3,139 | 4,144 | 1,360 | 296 | 571 | 3,500 | 1,071 | 2,492 |
| 1906 | 5,407 | 1,877 | 20,427 | 3,176 | 4,277 | 1,372 | 298 | 580 | 3,600 | 1,103 | 2,512 |
| 1907 | 5,673 | 1,896 | 20,860 | 3,213 | 4,409 | 1,384 | 299 | 590 | 3,700 | 1,141 | 2,532 |
| 1908 | 5,988 | 1,914 | 21,303 | 3,253 | 4,542 | 1,396 | 297 | 600 | 3,800 | 1,054 | 2,554 |
| 1909 | 6,288 | 1,933 | 21,754 | 3,294 | 4,674 | 1,408 | 298 | 610 | 3,900 | 1,095 | 2,575 |
| 1910 | 6,615 | 1,951 | 22,216 | 3,336 | 4,807 | 1,421 | 301 | 620 | 4,000 | 1,132 | 2,596 |
| 1911 | 6,934 | 1,970 | 22,687 | 3,378 | 4,940 | 1,433 | 301 | 630 | 4,100 | 1,178 | 2,612 |
| 1912 | 7,268 | 1,988 | 23,168 | 3,425 | 5,072 | 1,445 | 297 | 640 | 4,187 | 1,226 | 2,639 |
| 1913 | 7,652 | 2,007 | 23,660 | 3,465 | 5,193 | 1,457 | 302 | 650 | 4,267 | 1,279 | 2,661 |
| 1914 | 7,917 | 2,025 | 24,161 | 3,509 | 5,318 | 1,469 | 307 | 657 | 4,347 | 1,316 | 2,633 |
| 1915 | 8,072 | 2,044 | 24,674 | 3,553 | 5,447 | 1,481 | 311 | 664 | 4,427 | 1,346 | 2,705 |
| 1916 | 8,225 | 2,062 | 25,197 | 3,598 | 5,579 | 1,493 | 314 | 671 | 4,508 | 1,379 | 2,727 |
| 1917 | 8,374 | 2,081 | 25,732 | 3,644 | 5,715 | 1,505 | 318 | 678 | 4,588 | 1,407 | 2,750 |
| 1918 | 8,517 | 2,099 | 26,277 | 3,690 | 5,855 | 1,517 | 315 | 685 | 4,668 | 1,439 | 2,772 |
| 1919 | 8,672 | 2,118 | 26,835 | 3,737 | 6,029 | 1,529 | 309 | 692 | 4,748 | 1,463 | 2,795 |
| 1920 | 8,861 | 2,136 | 27,404 | 3,785 | 6,089 | 1,541 | 303 | 679 | 4,828 | 1,481 | 2,818 |
| 1921 | 9,092 | 2,161 | 27,969 | 3,853 | 6,211 | 1,570 | ... | 715 | 4,908 | 1,499 | 2,843 |
| 1922 | 9,368 | 2,186 | 28,542 | 3,907 | 6,336 | 1,610 | 298 | 732 | 4,989 | 1,517 | 2,870 |
| 1923 | 9,706 | 2,212 | 29,126 | 3,961 | 6,463 | 1,646 | 298 | 749 | 5,069 | 1,535 | 2,898 |
| 1924 | 10,054 | 2,237 | 29,723 | 4,017 | 6,512 | 1,685 | 298 | 767 | 5,148 | 1,553 | 2,925 |
| 1925 | 10,398 | 2,263 | 30,332 | 4,073 | 6,724 | 1,724 | 300 | 785 | 5,229 | 1,571 | 2,953 |
| 1926 | 10,692 | 2,289 | 30,953 | 4,130 | 6,859 | 1,762 | 302 | 803 | 5,313 | 1,604 | 2,981 |
| 1927 | 10,965 | 2,316 | 31,587 | 4,188 | 6,996 | 1,800 | 306 | 822 | 5,399 | 1,636 | 3,012 |
| 1928 | 11,282 | 2,343 | 32,234 | 4,246 | 7,136 | 1,944 | 307 | 841 | 5,482 | 1,669 | 3,047 |
| 1929 | 11,592 | 2,370 | 32,894 | 4,305 | 7,279 | 1,891 | 307 | 860 | 5,567 | 1,701 | 3,082 |
| 1930 | 11,896 | 2,397 | 33,568 | 4,365 | 7,425 | 1,944 | 309 | 880 | 5,651 | 1,734 | 3,118 |
| 1931 | 12,016 | 2,425 | 34,256 | 4,429 | 7,574 | 1,995 | 312 | 901 | 5,748 | 1,761 | 3,154 |
| 1932 | 12,402 | 2,453 | 34,957 | 4,495 | 7,726 | 2,050 | 315 | 922 | 5,844 | 1,788 | 3,191 |
| 1933 | 12,623 | 2,482 | 35,673 | 4,563 | 7,880 | 2,095 | 319 | 944 | 5,941 | 1,815 | 3,227 |
| 1934 | 12,834 | 2,511 | 36,404 | 4,631 | 8,068 | 2,140 | 322 | 966 | 6,037 | 1,842 | 3,264 |
| 1935 | 13,044 | 2,540 | 37,150 | 4,700 | 8,199 | 2,196 | 325 | 988 | 6,134 | 1,869 | 3,300 |
| 1936 | 13,620 | 2,569 | 37,911 | 4,771 | 8,363 | 2,249 | 330 | 1,012 | 6,243 | 1,890 | 3,382 |
| 1937 | 13,490 | 2,599 | 38,687 | 4,842 | 8,531 | 2,298 | 334 | 1,036 | 6,353 | 1,911 | 3,464 |
| 1938 | 13,725 | 2,629 | 39,480 | 4,914 | 8,702 | 2,355 | 337 | 1,061 | 6,462 | 1,932 | 3,546 |
| 1939 | 13,948 | 2,659 | 40,289 | 4,988 | 8,896 | 2,412 | 339 [12] | 1,086 | 6,572 | 1,953 | 3,628 |
| 1940 | 14,169 | 2,690 | 41,114 | 5,063 | 9,094 | 2,466 | 344 | 1,111 | 6,681 | 1,974 | 3,710 |
| 1941 | 14,401 | 2,721 | 42,069 | 5,149 | 9,296 | 2,521 | 351 | 1,137 | 6,979 | 1,994 | 3,803 |
| 1942 | 14,631 | 2,785 | 43,069 | 5,244 | 9,503 | 2,575 | 358 | 1,164 | 6,915 | 2,014 | 3,914 |
| 1943 | 14,877 | 2,817 | 44,093 | 5,341 | 9,719 | 2,641 | 363 | 1,191 | 7,035 | 2,034 | 4,028 |
| 1944 | 15,130 | 1,850 | 45,141 | 5,440 | 9,931 | 2,712 | 366 | 1,219 | 7,159 | 2,055 | 4,146 |

**A5      SOUTH AMERICA: Mid-Year Population Estimates** (in thousands)

|  | Argentina | Bolivia | Brazil | Chile | Colombia | Ecuador | Guyana | Paraguay | Peru | Uruguay | Venezuela |
|---|---|---|---|---|---|---|---|---|---|---|---|
| 1945 | 15,390 | 2,850 | 46,215 | 5,541 | 10,152 | 2,781 | 370 | 1,247 | 7,285 | 2,076 | 4,267 |
| 1946 | 15,654 | 2,883 | 47,313 | 5,643 | 10,378 | 2,853 | 377 | 1,275 | 7,415 | 2,098 | 4,391 |
| 1947 | 15,929 | 2,916 | 48,438 | 5,748 | 10,609 | 2,953 | 390 | 1,305 | 7,547 | 2,121 | 4,548 |
| 1948 | 16,284 | 2,950 | 49,590 | 5,854 | 10,845 | 3,043 | 400 | 1,335 | 7,682 | 2,144 | 4,686 |
| 1949 | 16,671 | 2,984 | 50,769 | 5,962 | 11,087 | 3,135 | 412 | 1,366 | 7,822 | 2,169 | 4,828 |
| 1950 | 17,150 | 3,019 | 51,944 | 6,091 | 11,334 | 3,225 | 423 | 1,371 | 7,969 | 2,195 | 4,962 |
| 1951 | 17,468 | 3,065 | 53,888 | 6,221 | 11,615 | 3,317 | 434 | 1,410 | 8,118 | 2,224 | 5,166 |
| 1952 | 17,824 | 3,125 | 55,502 | 6,352 | 11,986 | 3,412 | 446 | 1,449 | 8,267 | 2,255 | 5,391 |
| 1953 | 18,194 | 3,189 | 57,164 | 6,482 | 12,369 | 3,511 | 459 | 1,487 | 8,425 | 2,288 | 5,619 |
| 1954 | 18,564 | 3,256 | 58,876 | 6,613 | 12,765 | 3,615 | 472 | 1,530 | 8,597 | 2,319 | 5,852 |
| 1955 | 18,928 | 3,322 | 60,640 | 6,743 | 13,172 | 3,722 | 486 | 1,564 | 8,790 | 2,348 | 6,089 |
| 1956 | 19,281 | 3,392 | 62,456 | 6,912 | 13,593 | 3,833 | 500 | 1,604 | 9,004 | 2,375 | 6,331 |
| 1957 | 19,625 | 3,464 | 64,326 | 7,080 | 14,028 | 3,949 | 515 | 1,645 | 9,235 | 2,400 | 6,578 |
| 1958 | 19,961 | 3,539 | 66,253 | 7,248 | 14,476 | 4,070 | 532 | 1,688 | 9,483 | 2,429 | 6,830 |
| 1959 | 20,289 | 3,729 | 68,237 | 7,417 | 14,938 | 4,195 | 550 | 1,730 | 9,746 | 2,459 | 7,086 |
| 1960 | 20,611 | 3,825 | 70,281 | 7,585 | 15,416 | 4,325 | 568 | 1,774 | 10,022 | 2,491 | 7,349 |
| 1961 | 20,930 | 3,920 | 72,262 | 7,770 | 15,908 | 4,461 | 585 | 1,820 | 10,320 | 2,523 | 7,612 |
| 1962 | 21,245 | 4,019 | 74,279 | 7,955 | 16,417 | 4,602 | 601 | 1,867 | 10,630 | 2,555 | 7,870 |
| 1963 | 21,558 | 4,121 | 76,352 | 8,140 | 16,941 | 4,749 | 618 | 1,915 | 10,947 | 2,586 | 8,413[8] |
| 1964 | 21,868 | 4,226 | 78,483 | 8,325 | 17,484 | 4,902 | 631 | 1,965 | 11,272 | 2,617 | 8,423 |
| 1965 | 22,179 | 4,334 | 80,674 | 8,510 | 17,996 | 5,061 | 645 | 2,016 | 11,607 | 2,647 | 8,711 |
| 1966 | 22,488 | 4,445 | 82,926 | 8,682 | 18,468 | 5,227 | 661 | 2,070 | 11,952 | 2,677 | 9,006 |
| 1967 | 22,800 | 4,561 | 85,240 | 8,853 | 18,956 | 5,399 | 677 | 2,124 | 12,307 | 2,709 | 9,310 |
| 1968 | 23,113 | 4,680 | 87,620 | 9,025 | 19,462 | 5,792[8] | 690 | 2,183 | 12,675 | 2,740 | 9,623 |
| 1969 | 23,428 | 4,774 | 90,065 | 9,197 | 19,984 | 5,766 | 699 | 2,240 | 13,055 | 2,771 | 9,944 |
| 1970 | 23,748 | 4,931 | 92,520 | 9,369 | 20,527 | 5,962 | 709 | 2,301 | 13,447 | 2,802 | 10,275 |
| 1971 | 24,068 | 5,063 | 95,171 | 9,545 | 21,088 | 6,165 | 724 | 2,365 | 13,830 | 2,833 | 10,612 |
| 1972 | 24,392 | 5,195 | 97,845 | 9,704 | 21,668 | 6,378 | 741 | 2,431 | 14,224 | 2,865[8] | 10,939 |
| 1973 | 24,820 | 5,331 | 99,917 | 9,861 | 22,343 | 6,599 | 758 | 2,510 | 14,628 | 2,840 | 11,280[8] |
| 1974 | 25,620 | 5,470[8] | 102,396 | 10,026 | 22,981 | 6,830 | 769 | 2,600 | 14,746 | 2,840 | 12,220 |
| 1975 | 26,052 | 4,894 | 104,936 | 10,196 | 23,644 | 7,035 | 781 | 2,686 | 15,161 | 2,829 | 12,665 |
| 1976 | 26,480 | 5,027 | 107,539 | 10,372 | 23,968 | 7,243 | 794 | 2,779 | 15,573 | 2,847 | 13,119 |
| 1977 | 26,912 | 5,163 | 110,207 | 10,663 | 24,434 | 7,455 | 806 | 2,854 | 15,990 | 2,862 | 13,590 |
| 1978 | 27,348 | 5,304 | 112,941 | 10,816 | 24,906 | 7,671 | 820 | 2,948 | 16,414 | 2,877 | 14,071 |
| 1979 | 27,789 | 5,449 | 118,553 | 10,975 | 25,376 | 7,893 | 848 | 3,046 | 16,849 | 2,896 | 14,552 |
| 1980 | 28,237 | 5,600 | 121,286 | 11,145 | 25,892 | 8,123 | 865 | 3,147 | 17,295 | 2,914 | 15,024 |
| 1981 | 28,694 | 5,755 | 124,068 | 11,327 | 26,426 | 8,361 | 883 | 3,250 | 17,755 | 2,932 | 15,485 |
| 1982 | 29,158 | 5,919 | 126,898 | 11,519 | 26,965 | 8,606 | 901 | 3,358 | 18,226 | 2,951 | 15,940 |
| 1983 | 29,627 | 6,082 | 129,766 | 11,717 | 27,502 | 8,857 | 918 | 3,468 | 18,707 | 2,970 | 16,394 |
| 1984 | 30,097 | 6,253 | 132,659 | 11,919 | 28,056 | 9,115 | 936 | 3,580 | 19,198 | 2,989 | 16,851 |
| 1985 | 30,564 | 6,429 | 135,564 | 12,122 | 28,624 | 9,378 | ... | 3,693 | 19,698 | 3,008 | 17,317 |
| 1986 | 31,030 | 6,611 | 138,493 | 12,327 | 29,188 | 9,647 | 972 | 3,807 | 20,207 | 3,026 | 17,792 |
| 1987 | 31,497 | 6,799 | 141,452 | 12,536 | 29,729 | 9,923 | 989 | 3,922 | 20,727 | 3,043 | 18,272 |
| 1988 | 31,534 | 6,973 | 144,428 | 12,748 | 30,241 | 10,204 | 1,007 | 4,039 | 21,256 | 3,060 | 18,757 |

**A4     Mid-Year Population Estimates**

NOTES

1.  SOURCES:- The national publications listed on pp. xiv–xvi; UN, *Demographic Yearbook;* and, for Latin American countries (except Argentina, Brazil, Chile, Costa Rica, and Mexico) from 1900 to about 1950, James W. Wilkie (ed.), *Statistical Abstract of Latin America* vol. 20 (Los Angeles, 1982).
2.  Where necessary and possible, and except as indicated in footnotes, statistics for dates other than mid-year have been converted by straight-line interpolation between adjacent estimates.
3.  In principle, except as indicated in footnotes, the estimates relate to population actually present.

FOOTNOTES

[1] Earlier estimates are available for the British colonies which later constituted the USA as follows (in thousands):-

| 1700 | 251 | 1730 | 629 | 1760 | 1,594 |
| 1710 | 332 | 1740 | 906 | 1770 | 2,148 |
| 1720 | 466 | 1750 | 1,171 | 1780 | 2,780 |

[2] Estimates to 1901 are at 1 April.
[3] Trinidad only to 1892.
[4] Armed forces overseas are included from 1930. They numbered 111 thousand in that year.
[5] The following figures are available including armed forces overseas for these years (in thousands):-

| 1917 | 103,414 | 1918 | 104,550 | 1919 | 105,063 |

[6] Newfoundland is included from 1948 (2nd line).
[7] Later revisions were not carried back further than this. In the case of Barbados the figures for 1914–19 are unreliable and are included here only because they provide the basis for the vital rates in table A6.
[8] The reason for this break is not given in the source.
[9] Alaska and Hawaii are included from 1959 (2nd line).
[10] This break occurs on a change of source (see note 1 above).
[11] Estimates at 31 December.
[12] Subsequently including estimates for remote tribes.

## A6      NORTH AMERICA: VITAL STATISTICS: RATES PER 1,000 POPULATION

Key: B = births; D = deaths; M = marriages

**1879–1929**

| | Barbados | | | Canada[3] | | | Costa Rica | | | El Salvador | | |
|---|---|---|---|---|---|---|---|---|---|---|---|---|
| | B | D | M | B | D | M | B | D | M | B | D | M |
| 1879 | ... | ... | ... | ... | ... | ... | ... | ... | ... | ... | ... | ... |
| 1880 | ... | ... | ... | ... | ... | ... | ... | ... | ... | ... | ... | ... |
| 1881 | ... | ... | ... | ... | ... | ... | ... | ... | ... | ... | ... | ... |
| 1882 | ... | ... | ... | ... | ... | ... | ... | ... | ... | ... | ... | ... |
| 1883 | ... | ... | ... | ... | ... | ... | ... | ... | ... | ... | ... | ... |
| 1884 | ... | ... | ... | ... | ... | ... | ... | ... | ... | ... | ... | ... |
| 1885 | ... | ... | ... | ... | ... | ... | ... | ... | ... | ... | ... | ... |
| 1886 | ... | ... | ... | ... | ... | ... | ... | ... | ... | ... | ... | ... |
| 1887 | ... | ... | ... | ... | ... | ... | ... | ... | ... | ... | ... | ... |
| 1888 | ... | ... | ... | ... | ... | ... | ... | ... | ... | ... | ... | ... |
| 1889 | ... | ... | ... | ... | ... | ... | ... | ... | ... | ... | ... | ... |
| 1890 | ... | ... | ... | ... | ... | ... | ... | ... | ... | ... | ... | ... |
| 1891 | ... | ... | ... | ... | ... | ... | ... | ... | ... | ... | ... | ... |
| 1892 | ... | ... | ... | ... | ... | ... | ... | ... | ... | ... | ... | ... |
| 1893 | ... | ... | ... | ... | ... | ... | ... | ... | ... | ... | ... | ... |
| 1894 | ... | ... | ... | ... | ... | ... | ... | ... | ... | ... | ... | ... |
| 1895 | ... | ... | ... | ... | ... | ... | ... | ... | ... | ... | ... | ... |
| 1896 | ... | ... | ... | ... | ... | ... | ... | ... | ... | ... | ... | ... |
| 1897 | ... | ... | ... | ... | ... | ... | ... | ... | ... | ... | ... | ... |
| 1898 | ... | ... | ... | ... | ... | ... | ... | ... | ... | ... | ... | ... |
| 1899 | ... | ... | ... | ... | ... | ... | ... | ... | ... | ... | ... | ... |
| 1900 | ... | ... | ... | 27.2 | 16.2 | 6.9 | 41.5 | 23.0 | ... | ... | ... | ... |
| 1901 | ... | ... | ... | 31.2 | 14.1 | 7.0 | 36.7 | 26.3 | ... | ... | ... | ... |
| 1902 | ... | ... | ... | 31.3 | 13.4 | 6.8 | 35.2 | 25.3 | ... | ... | ... | ... |
| 1903 | ... | ... | ... | 31.3 | 13.2 | 7.3 | 36.3 | 22.8 | ... | ... | ... | ... |
| 1904 | ... | ... | ... | 31.4 | 13.5 | 7.3 | 38.4 | 22.6 | ... | ... | ... | ... |
| 1905 | ... | ... | ... | 31.0 | 13.0 | 7.4 | 37.8 | 27.7 | ... | ... | ... | ... |
| 1906 | ... | ... | ... | 29.9 | 13.2 | 7.5 | 39.3 | 24.6 | ... | ... | ... | ... |
| 1907 | ... | ... | ... | 29.5 | 12.8 | 7.5 | 42.0 | 25.2 | ... | ... | ... | ... |
| 1908 | ... | ... | ... | 30.3 | 12.6 | 7.3 | 42.3 | 25.2 | ... | ... | ... | ... |
| 1909 | ... | ... | ... | 30.2 | 12.8 | 7.7 | 42.3 | 24.8 | ... | ... | ... | ... |
| 1910 | 37.2 | 25.5 | 5.1 | 30.4 | 13.1 | 8.2 | 41.7 | 25.6 | ... | ... | ... | ... |
| 1911 | 35.2 | 26.3 | 4.7 | 30.1 | 13.4 | 8.6 | 43.3 | 24.4 | ... | ... | ... | ... |
| 1912 | 36.8 | 41.0 | 4.1 | 31.3 | 13.0 | 9.4 | 42.8 | 23.4 | ... | ... | ... | ... |
| 1913 | 31.9 | 21.3 | 3.4 | 31.7 | 13.1 | 9.1 | 43.1 | 22.8 | ... | ... | ... | ... |
| 1914 | 37.4 | 36.5 | 3.3 | 31.9 | 12.6 | 8.4 | 44.3 | 22.5 | ... | ... | ... | ... |
| 1915 | 29.5 | 19.2 | 3.1 | 31.9 | 12.5 | 7.9 | 43.4 | 21.9 | ... | ... | ... | ... |
| 1916 | 32.2 | 22.7 | 3.9 | 30.7 | 13.0 | 8.0 | 41.2 | 23.0 | ... | ... | ... | ... |
| 1917 | 28.8 | 24.9 | 3.8 | 29.1 | 12.7 | 7.5 | 41.7 | 22.5 | ... | ... | ... | ... |
| 1918 | 30.2 | 20.6 | 5.4 | 28.8 | 15.9 | 6.8 | 40.0 | 30.5 | ... | ... | ... | ... |
| 1919 | 34.9 | 39.3 | 4.9 | 27.7 | 13.7 | 8.3 | 36.2 | 27.6 | ... | ... | ... | ... |
| 1920 | 37.5 | 33.4 | 5.4 | 29.2[3] | 13.3[3] | 9.2[3] | 38.5 | 28.6 | ... | 36.5 | 20.9 | 2.6 |
| 1921 | 32.6 | 43.3 | 4.3 | 29.3 | 11.6 | 7.9 | 38.2 | 21.0 | ... | ... | ... | 2.4 |
| 1922 | 34.3 | 22.4 | 4.7 | 28.3 | 11.6 | 7.2 | 38.5 | 20.9 | ... | ... | ... | 2.9 |
| 1923 | 37.4 | 37.1 | 4.8 | 26.7[3] | 11.8[3] | 7.3[3] | 38.1 | 20.1 | ... | ... | ... | 3.4 |
| 1924 | 32.9 | 29.5 | 4.8 | 26.7 | 10.9 | 7.1 | 38.7 | 22.3 | ... | ... | ... | 3.1 |
| 1925 | 34.9 | 29.5 | 5.3 | 26.1 | 10.7 | 6.9 | 38.3[4] | 24.0[4] | ... | 35.6 | 20.4 | 3.4 |
| 1926 | 31.3 | 29.6 | 5.8 | 24.7 | 11.4 | 7.0 | 46.9 | 23.1 | ... | 36.7 | 22.7 | 3.9 |
| 1927 | 31.6 | 20.2 | 6.7 | 24.3 | 11.0 | 7.2 | 47.9 | 22.6 | 7.8 | 36.4 | 17.9 | 3.5 |
| 1928 | 33.8 | 30.1 | 7.3 | 24.1 | 11.2 | 7.5 | 48.2 | 23.6 | 7.2 | 38.4 | 19.3 | 3.3 |
| 1929 | 32.0 | 23.7 | 6.6 | 23.5 | 11.4 | 7.7 | 46.3 | 24.2 | 6.3 | 35.2 | 14.2 | 3.4 |

*See p. 80 for footnotes*

**A6     NORTH AMERICA: Vital Statistics: Rates per 1,000 Population**

**1879–1929**

| | Jamaica[1] | | | Mexico | | | Newfoundland | | | Puerto Rico | | |
|---|---|---|---|---|---|---|---|---|---|---|---|---|
| | **B** | **D** | **M** | **B** | **D** | **M** | **B** | **D** | **M** | **B** | **D** | **M** |
| 1879 | 33.6 | 23.3 | ... | ... | ... | ... | ... | ... | ... | ... | ... | ... |
| 1880 | 38.3 | 27.0 | ... | ... | ... | ... | ... | ... | ... | ... | ... | ... |
| 1881 | 36.7 | 26.0 | 3.7 | ... | ... | ... | ... | ... | ... | ... | ... | ... |
| 1882 | 35.3 | 20.2 | 4.0 | ... | ... | ... | ... | ... | ... | ... | ... | ... |
| 1883 | 40.7 | 22.6 | 4.8 | ... | ... | ... | ... | ... | ... | ... | ... | ... |
| 1884 | 36.3 | 22.8 | 5.0 | ... | ... | ... | ... | ... | ... | ... | ... | ... |
| 1885 | 38.1 | 22.8 | 5.1 | ... | ... | ... | ... | ... | ... | ... | ... | ... |
| 1886 | 36.4 | 23.5 | 4.0 | ... | ... | ... | ... | ... | ... | ... | ... | ... |
| 1887 | 34.9 | 24.4 | 4.4 | ... | ... | ... | ... | ... | ... | ... | ... | ... |
| 1888 | 39.5 | 22.5 | 5.5 | ... | ... | ... | ... | ... | ... | ... | ... | ... |
| 1889 | <u>35.6</u> | <u>22.4</u>₁ | <u>5.2</u>₁ | ... | ... | ... | ... | ... | ... | ... | ... | ... |
| 1890 | 38.6 | 25.3 | 5.6 | ... | ... | ... | ... | ... | ... | ... | ... | ... |
| 1891 | 38.3 | 22.8 | 5.3 | ... | ... | ... | ... | ... | ... | ... | ... | ... |
| 1892 | 37.2 | 20.8 | 5.1 | ... | ... | ... | ... | ... | ... | ... | ... | ... |
| 1893 | 40.9 | 22.2 | 5.6 | ... | ... | ... | ... | ... | ... | ... | ... | ... |
| 1894 | 37.1 | 21.0 | 5.3 | ... | ... | ... | ... | ... | ... | ... | ... | ... |
| 1895 | 38.8 | 22.7 | 4.7 | ... | ... | ... | ... | ... | ... | ... | ... | ... |
| 1896 | 38.5 | 22.1 | 4.3 | ... | ... | ... | ... | ... | ... | ... | ... | ... |
| 1897 | 39.8 | 23.0 | 3.7 | ... | ... | ... | ... | ... | ... | ... | ... | ... |
| 1898 | 38.0 | 21.0 | 4.6 | ... | ... | ... | ... | ... | ... | ... | ... | ... |
| 1899 | 42.1 | 22.7 | 5.1 | ... | ... | ... | ... | ... | ... | ... | ... | ... |
| 1900 | 35.7 | 21.6 | 4.3 | 34.0 | 32.7 | ... | ... | ... | ... | ... | ... | ... |
| 1901 | 42.5 | 22.8 | 4.4 | 34.2 | 32.3 | ... | ... | ... | ... | ... | ... | ... |
| 1902 | 39.3 | 19.8 | 4.6 | 33.7 | 34.4 | ... | ... | ... | ... | ... | ... | ... |
| 1903 | 40.1 | 24.8 | 4.5 | 33.4 | 32.6 | ... | ... | ... | ... | ... | ... | ... |
| 1904 | 36.5 | 24.9 | 3.6 | 34.8 | 31.4 | ... | ... | ... | ... | ... | ... | ... |
| 1905 | 39.4 | 22.2 | 3.9 | 34.1 | 32.9 | ... | ... | ... | ... | ... | ... | ... |
| 1906 | 38.9 | 26.8 | 6.8 | 32.2 | 33.1 | ... | ... | ... | ... | ... | ... | ... |
| 1907 | 36.0 | 29.2 | 7.7 | 32.8 | 33.0 | ... | 29.5 | 17.6 | 7.8 | ... | ... | ... |
| 1908 | 38.7 | 23.1 | 4.3 | 34.3 | 31.8 | ... | 28.2 | 17.4 | 7.4 | ... | ... | ... |
| 1909 | 39.4 | 22.7 | 4.3 | 34.0 | 32.3 | ... | 30.0 | 15.4 | 7.2 | ... | ... | ... |
| 1910 | 38.5 | 23.1 | 4.0 | 32.0 | 33.3 | ... | 29.7 | 15.2 | 7.5 | 33.6 | 23.8 | ... |
| 1911 | 39.1 | 22.3 | 4.3 | ... | ... | ... | 28.4 | 16.0 | 7.3 | 34.3 | 23.3 | ... |
| 1912 | 39.2 | 25.4 | 3.8 | ... | ... | ... | 31.1 | 16.7 | 7.5 | 35.1 | 23.4 | ... |
| 1913 | 36.0 | 22.1 | 3.2 | ... | ... | ... | 29.9 | 17.8 | 7.5 | 36.5 | 19.8 | ... |
| 1914 | 39.8 | 21.9 | 3.2 | ... | ... | ... | 30.4 | 15.6 | 6.3 | 39.8 | 18.7 | ... |
| 1915 | <u>35.5</u>₁ | <u>22.1</u>₁ | <u>3.1</u>₁ | ... | ... | ... | 30.0 | 14.0 | 6.1 | 37.2 | 20.7 | ... |
| 1916 | 34.2 | 23.1 | 3.4 | ... | ... | ... | 26.5 | 17.8 | 6.4 | 35.1 | 23.9 | ... |
| 1917 | 35.2 | 27.8 | 3.4 | ... | ... | ... | 26.2 | 17.1 | 6.9 | 35.4 | 30.9 | ... |
| 1918 | 35.4 | 34.2 | 3.2 | ... | ... | ... | 28.4 | 19.6 | 7.1 | 40.9 | 30.9 | ... |
| 1919 | 34.9 | 22.9 | 3.9 | ... | ... | ... | 27.0 | 16.0 | 8.2 | 35.9 | 23.7 | ... |
| 1920 | 42.1 | 26.2 | 5.0 | ... | ... | ... | 29.0 | 15.6 | 6.9 | 38.4 | 22.8 | ... |
| 1921 | 34.9 | 28.3 | 3.5 | ... | ... | ... | 27.2 | 12.8 | 5.7 | 38.3 | 22.5 | ... |
| 1922 | 37.4 | 23.0 | 3.8 | 31.4 | 25.3 | 3.8 | 27.8 | 13.7 | 5.5 | 37.4 | 21.8 | ... |
| 1923 | 38.7 | 23.0 | 3.8 | 32.0 | 24.4 | 3.8 | 27.8 | 13.7 | 5.2 | 37.0 | 19.6 | ... |
| 1924 | 37.0 | 21.9 | 3.5 | 30.8 | 25.6 | 4.1 | 25.6 | 15.9 | 5.3 | 38.3 | 19.4 | ... |
| 1925 | 34.9 | 21.6 | 4.1 | 33.1 | 26.5 | 4.5 | 26.0 | 13.8 | 6.3 | 37.1 | 23.4 | ... |
| 1926 | 38.4 | 20.5 | 4.3 | 31.2 | 24.9 | 4.9 | 27.0 | 13.0 | 6.4 | 38.3 | 22.3 | ... |
| 1927 | 34.7 | 21.1 | 4.6 | 30.5 | 24.0 | 5.1 | 26.5 | 13.7 | 5.6 | 39.6 | 22.8 | 6.6 |
| 1928 | 35.8 | 19.7 | 4.5 | 32.3 | 25.3 | 5.2 | 24.6 | 13.8 | 6.1 | 35.3 | 19.8 | 6.9 |
| 1929 | 34.2 | 18.4 | 4.3 | 39.3 | 26.8 | 5.4 | 24.2 | 14.4 | 6.0 | 34.4 | 26.8 | 5.4 |

*See p. 80 for footnotes*

**A6       NORTH AMERICA: Vital Statistics: Rates per 1,000 Population**

1879–1929

| | Trinidad and Tobago[2] | | | USA[5] | | | | |
|---|---|---|---|---|---|---|---|---|
| | B | D | M | B | | D | | M |
| | | | | whites | negroes[6] | whites | negroes[6] | |
| 1879 | ... | ... | ... | ... | ... | ... | ... | ... |
| 1880 | ... | ... | ... | ... | ... | ... | ... | ... |
| 1881 | ... | ... | ... | ... | ... | ... | ... | ... |
| 1882 | ... | ... | ... | ... | ... | ... | ... | ... |
| 1883 | 37.0 | 29.2 | 4.6 | ... | ... | ... | ... | ... |
| 1884 | 34.7 | 27.9 | 4.2 | ... | ... | ... | ... | ... |
| 1885 | 36.0 | 28.7 | 3.4 | ... | ... | ... | ... | ... |
| 1886 | 36.6 | 27.9 | 3.2 | ... | ... | ... | ... | ... |
| 1887 | 34.1 | 27.3 | 3.5 | ... | ... | ... | ... | ... |
| 1888 | 36.2 | 31.0 | 4.1 | ... | ... | ... | ... | ... |
| 1889 | 35.3 | 30.1 | 4.0 | ... | ... | ... | ... | ... |
| 1890 | 32.0 | 28.5 | 5.0[2] | ... | ... | ... | ... | ... |
| 1891 | 32.2 | 27.0 | 4.9 | ... | ... | ... | ... | ... |
| 1892 | 33.4[2] | 24.8[2] | 4.0 | ... | ... | ... | ... | ... |
| 1893 | 33.8 | 27.5 | 4.6 | ... | ... | ... | ... | ... |
| 1894 | 33.9 | 24.9 | 4.3 | ... | ... | ... | ... | ... |
| 1895 | 34.6 | 25.3 | 4.3 | ... | ... | ... | ... | ... |
| 1896 | 33.8 | 26.6 | 4.6 | ... | ... | ... | ... | ... |
| 1897 | 31.8 | 28.4 | 4.1 | ... | ... | ... | ... | ... |
| 1898 | 31.0 | 26.3 | 4.4 | ... | ... | ... | ... | ... |
| 1899 | 36.5 | 24.4 | 5.0 | ... | ... | ... | ... | ... |
| 1900 | 36.6[2] | 25.0[2] | 4.4[2] | ... | ... | 17.0 | 25.0 | ... |
| 1901 | 34.7 | 25.2 | 4.2 | ... | ... | 16.2 | 24.3 | ... |
| 1902 | 35.1 | 23.5 | 4.0 | ... | ... | 15.3 | 23.6 | ... |
| 1903 | 34.3 | 24.5 | 4.1 | ... | ... | 15.4 | 24.5 | ... |
| 1904 | 37.1 | 21.3 | 4.8 | ... | ... | 16.2 | 26.1 | ... |
| 1905 | 36.8 | 26.3 | 3.7 | ... | ... | 15.7 | 25.5 | ... |
| 1906 | 34.7 | 25.3 | 3.5 | ... | ... | 15.5 | 24.2 | ... |
| 1907 | 32.8 | 25.4 | 4.4 | ... | ... | 15.7 | 24.3 | ... |
| 1908 | 33.8 | 23.1 | 4.0 | ... | ... | 14.5 | 22.4 | ... |
| 1909 | 33.2 | 21.8 | 3.9 | 29.2 | ... | 14.0 | 21.8 | ... |
| 1910 | 32.3 | 20.8 | 4.2 | 29.2 | ... | 14.5 | 21.7 | ... |
| 1911 | 34.3 | 23.2 | 4.2 | 29.1 | ... | 13.7 | 21.3 | ... |
| 1912 | 33.8 | 29.7 | 3.7 | 29.0 | ... | 13.4 | 20.6 | ... |
| 1913 | 33.6 | 23.1 | 3.7 | 28.8 | ... | 13.5 | 20.3 | ... |
| 1914 | 33.0 | 23.2 | 3.6 | 29.3 | ... | 13.0 | 20.2 | ... |
| 1915 | [31.5][2] | [21.3][2] | [3.7][2] | 28.9 | ... | 12.9 | 20.2 | ... |
| 1916 | 32.4 | 20.4 | 3.9 | 28.5 | ... | 13.4 | 19.1 | ... |
| 1917 | 33.6 | 21.3 | 3.8 | 27.9 | 32.9 | 13.5 | 20.4 | ... |
| 1918 | 31.0 | 21.7 | 3.8 | 27.6 | 33.0 | 17.5 | 25.6 | ... |
| 1919 | 30.1 | 24.5 | 3.6 | 25.3 | 32.4 | 12.4 | 17.9 | ... |
| 1920 | 30.1 | 23.8 | 3.5 | 26.9 | 35.0 | 12.6 | 17.7 | 12.0 |
| 1921 | 30.6 | 23.2 | 3.7 | 27.3 | 35.8 | 11.1 | 15.5 | 10.7 |
| 1922 | 32.1 | 22.7 | 3.9 | 25.4 | 33.2 | 11.3 | 15.2 | 10.3 |
| 1923 | 34.7 | 20.9 | 3.5 | 25.2 | 33.2 | 11.7 | 16.5 | 11.0 |
| 1924 | 33.7 | 20.0 | 5.3 | 25.1 | 34.6 | 11.0 | 17.1 | 10.4 |
| 1925 | 33.1 | 20.6 | 6.3 | 24.1 | 34.2 | 11.1 | 17.4 | 10.3 |
| 1926 | 32.0 | 22.0 | 6.4 | 23.1 | 33.4 | 11.6 | 17.8 | 10.2 |
| 1927 | 30.4 | 18.7 | 5.7 | 22.7 | 31.1 | 10.8 | 16.4 | 10.1 |
| 1928 | 29.6 | 19.9 | 5.5 | 21.5 | 28.5 | 11.4 | 17.1 | 9.8 |
| 1929 | 31.7 | 19.4 | 5.0 | 20.5 | 27.3 | 11.3 | 16.9 | 10.1 |

See p. 80 for footnotes

**A6     NORTH AMERICA: Vital Statistics: Rates per 1,000 Population**

**1930–1979**

|      | Barbados | | | Canada[3] | | | Costa Rica | | |
|------|------|------|------|------|------|------|------|------|------|
|      | B | D | M | B | D | M | B | D | M |
| 1930 | 32.7 | 23.1 | 6.3 | 23.9 | 10.8 | 7.0 | 47.4 | 22.5 | 6.0 |
| 1931 | 30.4 | 28.2 | 6.0 | 23.2 | 10.2 | 6.4 | 46.9 | 24.7 | 5.8 |
| 1932 | 33.5 | 20.6 | 6.3 | 22.5 | 10.0 | 5.9 | 45.7 | 21.9 | 6.3 |
| 1933 | 32.5 | 21.9 | 6.5 | 21.0 | 9.7 | 6.0 | 44.6 | 21.7 | 5.9 |
| 1934 | 32.4 | 25.1 | 6.1 | 20.7 | 9.5 | 6.8 | 44.2 | 18.6 | 6.5 |
| 1935 | 31.6 | 22.0 | 4.9 | 20.5 | 9.9 | 7.1 | 45.2 | 22.9 | 6.3 |
| 1936 | 34.8 | 20.3 | 5.8 | 20.3 | 9.9 | 7.4 | 45.2 | 21.0 | 6.3 |
| 1937 | 32.8 | 20.3 | 5.5 | 20.1 | 10.4 | 7.9 | 44.5 | 19.2 | 7.2 |
| 1938 | 30.5 | 21.4 | 5.0 | 20.7 | 9.7 | 7.9 | 45.5 | 17.7 | 6.6 |
| 1939 | 31.1 | 19.1 | 6.6 | 20.6 | 9.7 | 9.2 | 44.7 | 19.3 | 6.7 |
| 1940 | 32.4 | 18.5 | 6.3 | 21.6 | 9.8 | 10.8 | 45.3 | 18.1 | 6.0 |
| 1941 | 32.3 | 21.8 | 5.4 | 22.4 | 10.1 | 10.6 | 45.5 | 18.1 | 6.3 |
| 1942 | 31.0 | 18.2 | 6.6 | 23.5 | 9.8 | 10.9 | 43.7 | 21.0 | 6.0 |
| 1943 | 32.3 | 17.1 | 8.0 | 24.2 | 10.1 | 9.4 | 46.1 | 17.7 | 5.8 |
| 1944 | 32.4 | 18.3 | 7.8 | 24.0 | 9.8 | 8.5 | 44.2 | 16.7 | 6.9 |
| 1945 | 32.3 | 16.9 | 7.7 | 24.3 | 9.5 | 9.0 | 46.8 | 15.5 | 6.9 |
| 1946 | 31.9 | 17.0 | 7.1 | 27.2 | 9.4 | 10.9 | 45.0 | 13.9 | 6.0 |
| 1947 | 32.7 | 16.3 | 5.3 | 28.9 | 9.4 | 10.1 | 44.7 | 14.9 | 7.6 |
| 1948 | 32.5 | 15.7 | 4.4 | 27.3 | 9.3 | 9.6 | 44.5 | 13.2 | 4.7 |
| 1949 | 32.0 | 14.6 | 4.6 | 27.3 | 9.3 | 9.2 | 44.2 | 12.7 | 7.3 |
| 1950 | 30.5 | 12.8 | 4.8 | 27.1 | 9.1 | 9.1 | 46.5 | 12.2 | 7.8 |
| 1951 | 31.6 | 14.0 | 5.1 | 27.2 | 9.0 | 9.2 | 48.5 | 11.7 | 8.2 |
| 1952 | 33.5 | 14.6 | 4.7 | 27.9 | 8.7 | 8.9 | 49.8 | 11.6 | 7.6 |
| 1953 | 33.0 | 13.5 | 4.6 | 28.1 | 8.6 | 8.8 | 47.9 | 11.9 | 7.3 |
| 1954 | 33.6 | 11.3 | 5.1 | 28.5 | 8.2 | 8.4 | 49.4 | 10.8 | 7.0 |
| 1955 | 33.4 | 12.7 | 4.7 | 28.2 | 8.2 | 48.9 | 10.7 | 6.8 | |
| 1956 | 31.3 | 10.8 | 4.9 | 28.0 | 8.2 | 8.3 | 48.5 | 9.8 | 6.5 |
| 1957 | 32.4 | 10.9 | 5.3 | 28.2 | 8.2 | 8.0 | 47.9 | 10.4 | 6.4 |
| 1958 | 31.2 | 10.1 | 4.5 | 27.5 | 7.9 | 7.7 | 47.2 | 9.2 | 6.8 |
| 1959 | 30.8 | 9.0 | 4.4 | 27.4 | 8.0 | 7.6 | 48.3 | 9.3 | 6.8 |
| 1960 | 33.6 | 9.1 | 4.7 | 26.7 | 7.8 | 7.3 | 47.5 | 8.8 | 7.2 |
| 1961 | 29.0 | 10.4 | 4.3 | 26.0 | 7.7 | 7.0 | 46.9 | 8.2 | 6.7 |
| 1962 | 29.4 | 9.0 | 4.1 | 25.2 | 7.7 | 7.0 | 45.4 | 8.9 | 5.9 |
| 1963 | 28.5 | 8.8 | 4.2 | 24.6 | 7.8 | 6.9 | 45.3 | 9.0 | 5.9 |
| 1964 | 27.0 | 8.8 | 3.7 | 23.4 | 7.6 | 7.2 | 43.0 | 9.4 | 5.6 |
| 1965 | 26.1 | 7.8 | 3.9 | 21.3 | 7.6 | 7.4 | 42.3 | 8.6 | 5.7 |
| 1966 | 25.6 | 8.2 | ... | 19.3 | 7.5 | 7.8 | 40.7 | 7.4 | 5.6 |
| 1967 | 21.9 | 8.2 | 3.9 | 18.2 | 7.4 | 8.1 | 39.0 | 7.1 | 5.6 |
| 1968 | 21.7 | 8.1 | 3.8 | 17.6 | 7.4 | 8.3 | 36.2 | 6.5 | 5.8 |
| 1969 | 20.5 | 7.8 | 4.0 | 17.6 | 7.3 | 8.7 | 34.4 | 6.9 | 5.8 |
| 1970 | 20.4 | 8.7 | 4.6 | 17.5 | 7.3 | 8.8 | 33.2 | 6.6 | 6.3 |
| 1971 | 21.5 | 8.6 | 4.5 | 16.8 | 7.3 | 8.9 | 31.3 | 5.9 | 6.4 |
| 1972 | 21.9 | 8.5 | 3.9 | 15.9 | 7.4 | 9.2 | 31.2 | 5.9 | 7.0 |
| 1973 | 20.9 | 9.4 | 4.0 | 15.6 | 7.4 | 9.0 | 28.5 | 5.2 | 7.0 |
| 1974 | 19.8 | 8.8 | 3.8 | 15.5 | 7.4 | 8.9 | 29.5 | 4.9 | 7.4 |
| 1975 | 19.1 | 8.8 | 4.1 | 15.8 | 7.4 | 8.7 | 29.5 | 4.9 | 7.5 |
| 1976 | 18.6 | 9.5 | 2.9 | 15.7 | 7.3 | 8.4 | 29.8 | 4.7 | 7.3 |
| 1977 | 17.5 | 8.7 | 2.8 | 15.5 | 7.2 | 8.1 | 31.1 | 4.3 | 7.5 |
| 1978 | 17.4 | 8.4 | 2.8 | 15.3 | 7.2 | 7.9 | 29.9 | 4.1 | 7.8 |
| 1979 | 17.2 | 8.6 | 3.8 | 15.4 | 7.1 | 7.9 | 30.2 | 4.2 | ... |

**A6      NORTH AMERICA: Vital Statistics: Rates per 1,000 Population**

**1930–1979**

| | Cuba | | | El Salvador | | | Guadeloupe | | |
|------|------|------|------|------|------|------|------|------|------|
| | B | D | M | B | D | M | B | D | M |
| 1930 | ... | ... | ... | 45.9 | 21.8 | 3.8 | ... | ... | ... |
| 1931 | 25.2 | 10.2 | 3.3 | 46.0 | 22.7 | 3.3 | ... | ... | ... |
| 1932 | 16.7 | 10.9 | 3.0 | 41.2 | 22.1 | 3.1 | ... | ... | ... |
| 1933 | 17.0 | 12.4 | 2.7 | 42.3 | 23.8 | 3.3 | ... | ... | ... |
| 1934 | 19.2 | 11.6 | 4.2 | 41.6 | 25.5 | 3.7 | ... | ... | ... |
| 1935 | 19.5 | 12.0 | 4.6 | 40.2 | 25.2 | 3.8 | ... | ... | ... |
| 1936 | 19.5 | 10.7 | 4.7 | 43.5 | 21.4 | 3.7 | ... | ... | ... |
| 1937 | 23.1 | 10.2 | 5.0 | 41.8 | 20.7 | 4.0 | ... | ... | ... |
| 1938 | 25.3 | 11.1 | 4.4 | 43.5 | 19.0 | 3.8 | ... | ... | ... |
| 1939 | 15.5 | 9.8 | 3.7 | 44.2 | 19.5 | 3.8 | ... | ... | ... |
| 1940 | 18.1 | 9.7 | ... | 45.4 | 19.0 | 3.7 | ... | ... | ... |
| 1941 | 16.9 | 9.3 | ... | 43.5 | 18.3 | 4.0 | ... | ... | ... |
| 1942 | ... | 9.4 | ... | 42.4 | 22.7 | 3.9 | ... | ... | ... |
| 1943 | ... | 10.4 | ... | 41.9 | 22.5 | 3.6 | ... | ... | ... |
| 1944 | 36.0 | 10.0 | ... | 42.0 | 19.6 | 4.0 | ... | ... | ... |
| 1945 | 20.8 | 10.6 | ... | 42.6 | 18.1 | 3.5 | ... | ... | ... |
| 1946 | 23.9 | 8.0 | ... | 40.6 | 17.5 | 4.1 | ... | 16.9 | 6.9 |
| 1947 | 30.1 | 7.9 | ... | 46.9 | 17.1 | 4.0 | ... | 17.4 | 7.5 |
| 1948 | 29.9 | 7.6 | ... | 44.3 | 16.7 | 3.6 | 37.4 | 16.9 | 8.0 |
| 1949 | 29.8 | 7.5 | ... | 45.9 | 15.3 | 4.0 | 39.9 | 14.3 | 7.5 |
| 1950 | 29.6 | 7.1 | ... | 48.5 | 14.7 | 5.4 | 37.3 | 14.1 | 5.6 |
| 1951 | 25.4 | 7.3 | ... | 49.0 | 15.2 | 4.5 | 39.3 | 13.7 | 5.2 |
| 1952 | 25.1 | 6.5 | ... | 49.3 | 16.5 | 4.1 | 38.6 | 14.7 | 5.8 |
| 1953 | 29.6 | 6.3 | ... | 48.7 | 15.0 | 4.4 | 38.8 | 12.8 | 5.3 |
| 1954 | ... | 5.9 | ... | 49.1 | 15.3 | 4.0 | 39.0 | 11.6 | 6.5 |
| 1955 | ... | 6.1 | 4.6 | 49.2 | 14.6 | 3.8 | 40.3 | 11.7 | 5.2 |
| 1956 | ... | 5.8 | 4.7 | 48.5 | 12.8 | 4.0 | 39.7 | 10.1 | 5.2 |
| 1957 | 29.3 | 6.3 | 4.8 | 50.9 | 14.6 | 4.2 | 37.6 | 11.4 | 5.4 |
| 1958 | 27.3 | 6.5 | 4.5 | 49.6 | 14.1 | 3.8 | 38.2 | 9.6 | 5.0 |
| 1959 | 30.5 | 6.6 | 4.6 | 48.5 | 12.6 | 7.2 | 37.0 | 8.9 | 5.4 |
| 1960 | 31.5 | 6.3 | 9.2 | 49.5 | 11.4 | 3.8 | 38.4 | 9.7 | 5.8 |
| 1961 | 33.8 | 6.6 | 10.4 | 49.4 | 11.3 | 3.5 | 35.7 | 8.4 | 5.5 |
| 1962 | 36.9 | 7.3 | 8.4 | 48.4 | 11.5 | 3.6 | 37.7 | 8.1 | 5.1 |
| 1963 | 35.2 | 6.9 | 7.6 | 49.0 | 10.9 | 3.7 | 36.1 | 8.1 | 5.5 |
| 1964 | 35.2 | 6.4 | 6.2 | 47.1 | 10.4 | 3.9 | 33.9 | 7.6 | 5.4 |
| 1965 | 34.2 | 6.5 | 8.9 | 46.9 | 10.6 | 3.5 | 33.7 | 8.1 | 5.3 |
| 1966 | 32.8 | 6.5 | 6.1 | 45.4 | 10.0 | 3.3 | 34.1 | 7.8 | 5.1 |
| 1967 | 31.4 | 6.3 | 6.4 | 44.4 | 9.2 | 3.3 | 32.5 | 8.1 | 5.6 |
| 1968 | 29.8 | 6.6 | 10.3 | 43.2 | 9.1 | 3.3 | 33.2 | 8.1 | 5.6 |
| 1969 | 28.3 | 6.7 | 10.2 | 42.1 | 9.9 | 3.3 | 30.5 | 7.6 | 5.5 |
| 1970 | 27.7 | 6.3 | 13.4 | 40.0 | 9.9 | 3.3 | 29.3 | 7.7 | 6.0 |
| 1971 | 29.5 | 6.0 | 13.0 | 42.3 | 7.9 | 3.7 | 31.2 | 7.0 | 5.3 |
| 1972 | 30.8 | 5.5 | 8.9 | 40.8 | 8.8 | 3.8 | 30.5 | 7.3 | 5.3 |
| 1973 | 25.1 | 5.7 | 7.0 | 40.3 | 8.4 | 4.0 | 29.3 | 7.3 | 5.2 |
| 1974 | 22.2 | 5.6 | 7.3 | 43.2 | 7.8 | 4.2 | 27.0 | 7.5 | 4.6 |
| 1975 | 20.7 | 5.4 | 7.0 | 39.9 | 7.9 | 4.2 | 25.1 | 7.1 | ... |
| 1976 | 19.9 | 5.6 | 6.5 | 40.2 | 7.5 | 4.4 | 21.1 | 7.2 | ... |
| 1977 | 17.7 | 5.9 | 6.5 | 41.7 | 7.8 | 4.2 | 19.3 | 6.9 | 4.4 |
| 1978 | 15.4 | 5.7 | 6.1 | 39.7 | 6.9 | 4.1 | 17.2 | 6.6 | 4.4 |
| 1979 | 14.8 | 5.6 | 6.5 | 39.3 | 7.4 | 4.3 | 17.8 | 6.6 | 4.4 |

**A6     NORTH AMERICA: Vital Statistics: Rates per 1,000 Population**

**1930–1979**

| | Guatemala | | | Honduras[7] | | | Jamaica | | |
|---|---|---|---|---|---|---|---|---|---|
| | B | D | M | B | D | M | B | D | M |
| 1930 | 56.8 | 24.7 | 2.8 | 37.4 | 16.1 | 3.3 | 37.5 | 17.3 | 4.2 |
| 1931 | 54.7 | 24.3 | 2.4 | 38.6 | 15.4 | 2.7 | 35.3 | 18.9 | 3.5 |
| 1932 | 50.3 | 23.6 | 2.1 | ... | 14.9 | ... | 32.7 | 17.4 | 3.7 |
| 1933 | 47.5 | 27.3 | 2.1 | 31.8 | 14.5 | 3.9 | 33.4 | 19.7 | 3.3 |
| 1934 | 47.0 | 30.6 | 2.2 | 32.7 | 13.8 | 2.3 | 31.7 | 17.3 | 3.9 |
| 1935 | 48.1 | 27.4 | 2.3 | 34.5 | 13.9 | 2.9 | 34.1 | 18.0 | 4.2 |
| 1936 | 47.8 | 24.7 | 2.0 | 31.5 | 16.6 | 2.6 | 32.9 | 17.7 | 3.9 |
| 1937 | 46.5 | 24.4 | 2.2 | 36.2[7] | 18.0[7] | 3.0[7] | 31.5 | 15.6 | 4.6 |
| 1938 | 46.4 | 26.3 | 2.5 | ... | 16.3 | ... | 33.3 | 16.8 | 4.7 |
| 1939 | 47.4 | 29.6 | 2.8 | 37.5 | 15.9 | 2.8 | 32.3 | 15.1 | 4.6 |
| 1940 | 48.2 | 25.0 | 2.2 | 37.1 | 15.9 | 3.0 | 30.8 | 15.4 | 3.9 |
| 1941 | 43.8 | 25.1 | 2.1 | 37.3 | 16.7 | 2.6 | 31.4 | 14.4 | 4.6 |
| 1942 | 42.6 | 31.5 | 2.1 | 36.7 | 18.5 | 2.5 | 32.7 | 14.3 | 4.8 |
| 1943 | 42.2 | 31.1 | 2.4 | 36.3 | 18.5 | 2.6 | 31.5 | 14.1 | 4.4 |
| 1944 | 42.2 | 26.5 | 2.8 | 36.3 | 16.9 | 3.3 | 33.2 | 15.1 | 5.1 |
| 1945 | 42.9 | 24.5 | 2.9 | 36.5 | 16.0 | 3.0 | 30.0 | 14.9 | 5.0 |
| 1946 | 48.2 | 24.7 | 3.2 | 37.9 | 14.5 | 3.1 | 30.8 | 13.3 | 5.8 |
| 1947 | 52.2 | 24.7 | 2.9 | 38.8 | 13.7 | 3.4 | 31.9 | 14.1 | 4.5 |
| 1948 | 51.9 | 23.5 | 3.0 | 39.5 | 14.0 | 3.4 | 30.7 | 13.2 | 4.1 |
| 1949 | 51.6 | 21.8 | 3.4 | 40.0[7] | 13.3[7] | 3.5[7] | 32.3 | 12.3 | 4.3 |
| 1950 | 50.9 | 21.8 | 3.7 | 39.9 | 11.8 | 3.7 | 33.5 | 11.9 | 4.6 |
| 1951 | 52.3 | 19.6 | 3.7 | 41.0 | 11.1 | 4.0 | 34.6 | 12.3 | 4.5 |
| 1952 | 50.9 | 24.2 | 3.8 | 39.7 | 12.5 | 4.2 | 34.3 | 11.7 | 4.6 |
| 1953 | 50.9 | 23.0 | 3.8 | 41.7 | 11.6 | 32.3 | 10.6 | 4.9 | |
| 1954 | 51.3 | 18.3 | 4.1 | 41.7 | 11.1 | 4.3 | 36.4 | 11.1 | 5.2 |
| 1955 | 48.6 | 20.5 | 3.7 | 43.0 | 11.3 | 3.4 | 37.5 | 10.3 | 5.9 |
| 1956 | 48.4 | 19.7 | 4.8 | 40.7 | 10.1 | 4.1 | 37.2 | 9.7 | 6.3 |
| 1957 | 49.0 | 20.4 | 4.9 | 43.2 | 10.4 | 3.8 | 37.9 | 9.2 | 6.3 |
| 1958 | 48.2 | 21.1 | 4.7 | 43.1 | 11.1 | 3.7 | 39.0 | 9.5 | 5.2 |
| 1959 | 49.2 | 17.1 | 5.2 | 42.0 | 9.5 | 9.6 | 40.0 | 10.3 | 5.3 |
| 1960 | 48.9 | 17.3 | 4.4 | 42.3 | 9.3 | 3.9 | 42.0 | 8.8 | 6.0 |
| 1961 | 49.3 | 16.1 | 4.0 | 42.5 | 8.9 | 3.1 | 40.2 | 8.6 | 5.4 |
| 1962 | 47.3 | 17.1 | 3.6 | 44.0 | 8.9 | 3.3 | 39.1 | 8.5 | 5.0 |
| 1963 | 47.2 | 17.1 | 3.7 | 43.2 | 9.0 | 3.0 | 39.0 | 8.9 | 4.8 |
| 1964 | 45.5 | 15.9 | 3.6 | 44.9 | 9.2 | 3.4 | 39.3 | 7.6 | 4.8 |
| 1965 | 45.3 | 16.9 | 3.4 | 43.3 | 8.5 | 3.5 | 39.6 | 8.0 | 4.6 |
| 1966 | 45.2 | 16.6 | 3.6 | 42.1 | 8.6 | 3.3 | 40.0 | 8.0 | 4.2 |
| 1967 | 41.8 | 15.2 | 3.6 | 41.6 | 8.0 | 3.2 | 37.3 | 7.4 | 4.3 |
| 1968 | 42.6 | 16.4 | 3.4 | 42.1 | 8.1 | 3.5 | 35.7 | 7.9 | 4.5 |
| 1969 | 42.2 | 17.2 | 3.6 | 41.1 | 8.5 | 3.0 | 35.1 | 7.6 | 4.8 |
| 1970 | 40.4 | 14.7 | 3.6 | 40.6 | 7.7 | 3.7 | 34.4 | 7.7 | 4.8 |
| 1971 | 42.0 | 13.9 | 3.7 | 43.2 | 7.5 | 3.1 | 34.9 | 7.6 | 4.4 |
| 1972 | 43.6 | 12.2 | 3.9 | 43.6 | 7.7 | 3.3 | 34.3 | 7.2 | 4.6 |
| 1973 | 41.8 | 12.1 | 4.0 | 41.9 | 7.2 | 3.8 | 31.4 | 7.2 | 4.5 |
| 1974 | 43.1 | 11.5 | 4.2 | 42.2 | 6.5 | 3.8 | 30.6 | 7.2 | 4.3 |
| 1975 | 41.4 | 12.6 | 3.9 | 41.9 | 6.2 | 3.6 | 30.0 | 6.9 | 5.0 |
| 1976 | 43.1 | 13.2 | 4.3 | 43.2 | 5.7 | 4.3 | 29.6 | 7.0 | 4.4 |
| 1977 | 44.7 | 11.3 | 4.4 | 43.9 | 5.6 | 4.2 | 28.6 | 6.8 | 4.1 |
| 1978 | 43.8 | 10.2 | 4.3 | ... | ... | 4.1 | 27.7 | 5.9 | 4.5 |
| 1979 | 44.0 | 10.7 | 4.2 | ... | ... | 4.0 | 27.7 | 6.2 | 4.2 |

**A6      NORTH AMERICA: Vital Statistics: Rates per 1,000 Population**

**1930–1979**

| | Martinique | | | Mexico | | | Newfoundland | | | Panama[8] | | |
|---|---|---|---|---|---|---|---|---|---|---|---|---|
| | B | D | M | B | D | M | B | D | M | B | D | M |
| 1930 | ... | ... | ... | 39.4 | 26.6 | 6.1 | 23.8 | 14.0 | 5.9 | 31.6 | 13.1 | 2.9 |
| 1931 | ... | ... | ... | 43.8 | 25.9 | 5.9 | 23.3 | 13.4 | 5.6 | 41.5 | 16.4 | 2.3 |
| 1932 | ... | ... | ... | 43.3 | 26.1 | 5.6 | 24.0 | 12.7 | 5.5 | 38.6 | 15.8 | 2.2 |
| 1933 | ... | ... | ... | 42.2 | 25.7 | 5.8 | 23.4 | 12.1 | 5.6 | 33.6 | 15.6 | 3.1 |
| 1934 | ... | ... | ... | 44.3 | 23.8 | 6.7 | 23.5 | 12.1 | 6.5 | 37.1 | 15.7 | 3.4 |
| 1935 | ... | ... | ... | 42.3 | 22.6 | 6.6 | 23.0 | 13.5 | 6.6 | 32.0 | 11.9 | 3.6 |
| 1936 | ... | ... | ... | 43.0 | 23.5 | 6.5 | 25.2 | 13.0 | 6.7 | 38.5 | 12.7 | 3.7 |
| 1937 | ... | ... | ... | 44.1 | 24.4 | 6.9 | 25.0 | 13.5 | 7.1 | 38.0 | 13.1 | 5.0 |
| 1938 | ... | ... | ... | 43.5 | 22.9 | 6.9 | 24.8 | 12.1 | 7.3 | 45.5 | 14.2 | 3.6 |
| 1939 | ... | ... | ... | 44.6 | 23.0 | 6.9 | 27.5 | 11.7 | 8.4 | 27.9 | 11.4 | 3.5 |
| 1940 | ... | ... | ... | 44.3 | 23.2 | 7.9 | 26.3 | 11.8 | 7.7 | ... | ... | ... |
| 1941 | ... | ... | ... | 43.5 | 22.1 | 6.2 | 27.3 | 12.5 | 8.8 | 37.4 | 13.3 | 5.6 |
| 1942 | ... | ... | ... | 45.5 | 22.8 | 8.5 | 28.6 | 12.3 | 10.6 | 37.0 | 12.8 | 4.5 |
| 1943 | ... | ... | ... | 45.5 | 22.4 | 7.5 | 28.3 | 11.4 | 8.7 | 37.7 | 13.0 | 3.5 |
| 1944 | ... | ... | ... | 44.2 | 20.6 | 6.8 | 29.4 | 12.3 | 9.5 | 37.8 | 12.3 | 4.0 |
| 1945 | ... | ... | ... | 44.9 | 19.5 | 6.7 | 34.9 | 10.4 | 9.8 | 37.7 | 11.8 | 4.6 |
| 1946 | ... | 20.5 | ... | 43.7 | 19.4 | 5.9 | 36.5 | 10.4 | 9.3 | 37.0 | 11.2 | 4.1 |
| 1947 | ... | 21.3 | ... | 46.1 | 16.6 | 5.8 | 37.5 | 9.9 | 8.7 | 37.2[8] | 11.7[8] | 3.5 |
| 1948 | 35.6 | 18.9 | ... | 45.2 | 16.9 | 6.4 | 33.8 | 9.0 | 7.6 | 32.8 | 9.4 | 3.3 |
| 1949 | 36.9 | 17.0 | ... | 45.2 | 17.9 | 6.6 | 35.6 | 8.3 | 7.1 | 30.2 | 9.0 | 3.3 |
| 1950 | 38.0 | 13.5 | 6.0 | 45.5 | 16.2 | 6.9 | incorporated | | | 31.3 | 9.0 | 3.4 |
| 1951 | 38.7 | 14.8 | 5.8 | 44.6 | 17.3 | 6.7 | in | | | 30.5 | 8.1 | 3.5 |
| 1952 | 37.9 | 13.9 | 5.6 | 43.8 | 15.0 | 6.9 | Canada | | | 34.5 | 8.1 | 3.3 |
| 1953 | 40.2 | 10.5 | 7.7 | 45.0 | 15.9 | 6.4 | | | | 36.2 | 8.8 | 3.5 |
| 1954 | 40.0 | 10.5 | 5.3 | 46.4 | 13.1 | 7.0 | | | | 37.3 | 8.4 | 3.9 |
| 1955 | 39.6 | 10.8 | 5.5 | 45.1 | 13.3 | 6.9 | | | | 37.6 | 8.8 | 3.4 |
| 1956 | 40.1 | 10.0 | 5.4 | 45.2 | 11.7 | 7.1 | | | | 37.6 | 8.8 | 3.4 |
| 1957 | 40.7 | 9.8 | 5.4 | 45.5 | 12.7 | 6.5 | | | | 38.8 | 8.9 | 3.3 |
| 1958 | 38.7 | 10.4 | 4.9 | 42.9 | 12.0 | 6.6 | | | | 37.7 | 8.3 | 5.5 |
| 1959 | 38.2 | 8.6 | 5.5 | 45.6 | 11.4 | 6.8 | | | | 39.1 | 8.7 | 14.4 |
| 1960 | 37.4 | 9.4 | 5.6 | 44.6 | 11.2 | 6.9 | | | | 39.1 | 8.7 | 3.4 |
| 1961 | 36.6 | 7.9 | 5.4 | 43.8 | 10.3 | 6.3 | | | | 39.5 | 8.0 | 3.4 |
| 1962 | 36.2 | 8.6 | 5.2 | 43.9 | 10.4 | 6.4 | | | | 40.0 | 7.8 | 3.3 |
| 1963 | 34.7 | 8.3 | 5.4 | 43.8 | 10.3 | 6.5 | | | | 39.5 | 7.0 | 3.7 |
| 1964 | 34.4 | 8.0 | 5.3 | 44.6 | 9.8 | 6.8 | | | | 38.9 | 7.3 | 3.7 |
| 1965 | 35.0 | 7.8 | 5.1 | 44.1 | 9.4 | 6.9 | | | | 38.4 | 7.1 | 3.8 |
| 1966 | 32.1 | 7.7 | 5.0 | 44.1 | 9.6 | 7.0 | | | | 38.8 | 7.2 | 3.9 |
| 1967 | 30.9 | 7.4 | 5.2 | 43.2 | 9.2 | 6.9 | | | | 37.3 | 6.8 | 4.0 |
| 1968 | 30.6 | 7.0 | 5.2 | 44.3 | 9.6 | 7.0 | | | | 37.4 | 7.1 | 4.1 |
| 1969 | 27.4 | 7.5 | 5.2 | 42.6 | 9.4 | 7.1 | | | | 36.5 | 7.0 | 4.9 |
| 1970 | 28.5 | 7.6 | 5.4 | 42.1 | 9.6 | 7.0 | | | | 35.8 | 7.1 | 5.0 |
| 1971 | 28.2 | 6.8 | 5.1 | 42.5 | 8.7 | 7.2 | | | | 35.9 | 6.7 | 5.0 |
| 1972 | 26.4 | 7.0 | 4.6 | 43.2 | 8.8 | 7.8 | | | | 34.9 | 6.0 | 4.8 |
| 1973 | 23.4 | 7.2 | 4.9 | 45.8 | 8.2 | 8.1 | | | | 32.2 | 5.8 | 4.6 |
| 1974 | 21.3 | 7.4 | 4.3 | 43.4 | 7.5 | 8.0 | | | | 31.8 | 5.6 | 4.7 |
| 1975 | 20.5 | 6.8 | 4.5 | 37.5 | 7.2 | 7.8 | | | | 31.6 | 5.2 | 4.9 |
| 1976 | 17.9 | ... | 3.9 | 34.6 | 7.4 | 7.7 | | | | 30.3 | 5.2 | 4.7 |
| 1977 | 16.5 | 6.6 | 3.8 | 37.6 | 7.1 | 7.3 | | | | 29.4 | 4.8 | 5.0 |
| 1978 | 15.5 | 6.7 | 4.0 | 35.7 | 6.4 | 7.0 | | | | 28.9 | 3.9 | 5.0 |
| 1979 | 16.7 | 6.5 | 4.0 | 36.3 | 6.3 | 6.8 | | | | 28.2 | ... | 5.4 |

**A6  NORTH AMERICA: Vital Statistics: Rates per 1,000 Population**

1930–1971

| | Puerto Rico | | | Trinidad & Tobago | | | USA | | | | |
|---|---|---|---|---|---|---|---|---|---|---|---|
| | B | D | M | B | D | M | B | | D | | M |
| | | | | | | | whites | negroes[6] | whites | negroes[6] | |
| 1930 | 35.2 | 20.4 | 6.4 | 31.4 | 19.1 | 4.5 | 20.6 | 27.5 | 10.8 | 16.3 | 9.2 |
| 1931 | 45.3 | 22.3 | 6.1 | 30.0 | 20.1 | 4.0 | 19.5 | 26.6 | 10.6 | 15.5 | 8.6 |
| 1932 | 41.1 | 22.0 | 5.5 | 29.0 | 17.1 | 4.3 | 18.7 | 26.9 | 10.5 | 14.5 | 7.9 |
| 1933 | 37.4 | 22.3 | 5.8 | 31.1 | 19.6 | 4.6 | 17.6 | 25.5 | 10.3 | 14.1 | 8.7 |
| 1934 | 39.1 | 18.9 | 7.3 | 29.8 | 18.6 | 4.5 | 18.1 | 26.3 | 10.6 | 14.8 | 10.3 |
| 1935 | 39.5 | 18.0 | 6.6 | 33.0 | 17.5 | 4.7 | 17.9 | 25.8 | 10.6 | 14.3 | 10.4 |
| 1936 | 39.6 | 20.0 | 7.9 | 33.1 | 16.3 | 4.7 | 17.6 | 25.1 | 11.1 | 15.4 | 10.7 |
| 1937 | 38.2 | 20.9 | 7.9 | 31.6 | 17.4 | 5.8 | 17.9 | 26.0 | 10.8 | 14.9 | 11.3 |
| 1938 | 38.6 | 18.7 | 5.1 | 33.0 | 15.9 | 6.1 | 18.4 | 26.3 | 10.3 | 14.0 | 10.3 |
| 1939 | 39.6 | 17.7 | 5.8 | 31.1 | 16.1 | 6.5 | 18.0 | 26.1 | 10.3 | 13.5 | 10.7 |
| 1940 | 38.6 | 18.3 | 10.3 | 34.7 | 15.8 | 6.6 | 18.6 | 26.7 | 10.4 | 13.8 | 12.1 |
| 1941 | 39.8 | 18.3 | 7.8 | 33.5 | 16.1 | 7.2 | 19.5 | 27.3 | 10.2 | 13.5 | 12.7 |
| 1942 | 40.2 | 16.2 | 8.1 | 34.7 | 17.7 | 10.0 | 21.5 | 27.7 | 10.1 | 12.7 | 13.2 |
| 1943 | 38.7 | 14.3 | 7.1 | 38.5 | 16.6 | 8.0 | 22.1 | 28.3 | 10.7 | 12.8 | 11.7 |
| 1944 | 40.6 | 14.4 | 7.9 | 39.0 | 15.0 | 7.2 | 20.5 | 27.4 | 10.4 | 12.4 | 10.9 |
| 1945 | 41.9 | 13.7 | 8.3 | 39.5 | 14.5 | 6.2 | 19.7 | 26.5 | 10.4 | 11.9 | 12.2 |
| 1946 | 41.6 | 12.9 | 9.5 | 38.8 | 13.8 | 5.8 | 23.6 | 38.4 | 9.8 | 11.1 | 16.4 |
| 1947 | 42.2 | 11.8 | 7.8 | 38.3 | 13.4 | 5.6 | 26.1 | 31.2 | 9.9 | 11.4 | 13.9 |
| 1948 | 40.2 | 12.0 | 7.0 | 39.9 | 12.2 | 5.8 | 24.0 | 32.4 | 9.7 | 11.4 | 12.4 |
| 1949 | 39.0 | 10.6 | 7.4 | 37.2 | 12.2 | 6.1 | 23.6 | 33.0 | 9.5 | 11.2 | 10.6 |
| 1950 | 38.8 | 9.9 | 9.3 | 37.5 | 12.1 | 6.0 | 23.0 | 33.3 | 9.5 | 11.2 | 11.1 |
| 1951 | 37.6 | 10.0 | 8.1 | 36.7 | 12.0 | 6.5 | 23.9 | 33.8 | 9.5 | 11.1 | 10.4 |
| 1952 | 36.1 | 9.2 | 8.2 | 34.6 | 12.1 | 6.5 | 24.1 | 33.6 | 9.4 | 11.0 | 9.9 |
| 1953 | 35.3 | 8.2 | 9.0 | 37.7 | 10.7 | 7.0 | 24.0 | 34.1 | 9.4 | 10.8 | 9.8 |
| 1954 | 35.2 | 7.6 | 8.8 | 41.9 | 9.8 | 6.7 | 24.2 | 34.9 | 9.1 | 10.1 | 9.2 |
| 1955 | 34.6 | 7.2 | 8.4 | 41.9 | 10.4 | 6.5 | 23.8 | 34.7 | 9.2 | 10.0 | 9.3 |
| 1956 | 34.8 | 7.4 | 8.4 | 37.0 | 9.6 | 7.0 | 24.0 | 35.4 | 9.3 | 10.1 | 9.5 |
| 1957 | 33.7 | 7.1 | 8.5 | 37.7 | 9.5 | 6.1 | 24.0 | 35.3 | 9.5 | 10.5 | 8.9 |
| 1958 | 33.2 | 7.0 | 8.7 | 37.6 | 9.2 | 7.5 | 23.3₉ | 34.3₉ | 9.4₉ | 10.3₉ | 8.4₉ |
| 1959 | 32.4 | 6.8 | 8.7 | 37.4 | 9.2 | 6.8 | 22.9₁₀ | 32.9₁₀ | 9.3₁₀ | 9.9₁₀ | 8.5₁₀ |
| 1960 | 32.4 | 6.7 | 8.6 | 39.5 | 7.9 | 7.1 | 22.7 | 32.1 | 9.5 | 10.1 | 8.5 |
| 1961 | 31.4 | 6.8 | 8.9 | 37.9 | 8.1 | 6.8 | 22.2 | 31.6 | 9.3 | 9.6 | 8.5 |
| 1962 | 31.3 | 6.7 | 9.0 | 37.9 | 7.2 | 6.3 | 21.4 | 30.5 | 9.4 | 9.8 | 8.5 |
| 1963 | 31.0 | 6.9 | 9.2 | 35.6 | 7.2 | 6.0 | 20.7 | 29.7 | 9.5 | 10.1 | 8.8 |
| 1964 | 31.0 | 7.2 | 9.2 | 34.6 | 7.0 | 6.6 | 20.0 | 29.1 | 9.4 | 9.7 | 9.0 |
| 1965 | 30.7 | 6.8 | 10.4 | 32.8 | 6.9 | 6.0 | 18.3 | 27.6 | 9.4 | 9.6 | 9.3 |
| 1966 | 28.9 | 6.7 | 9.7 | 30.2 | 7.1 | 5.6 | 17.4 | 26.1 | 9.5 | 9.7 | 9.5 |
| 1967 | 26.9 | 6.3 | 10.0 | 28.2 | 6.7 | 5.4 | 16.8 | 25.0 | 9.4 | 9.4 | 9.7 |
| 1968 | 25.6 | 6.5 | 10.1 | 27.5 | 7.0 | 5.6 | 16.6 | 24.2 | 9.6 | 9.9 | 10.4 |
| 1969 | 25.0 | 6.5 | 11.0 | 24.4 | 6.9 | 6.1 | 16.9 | 24.4 | 9.5 | 9.6 | 10.6 |
| 1970 | 24.9 | 6.7 | 10.7 | 26.2 | 6.8 | 6.3 | 17.4 | 25.1 | 9.5 | 9.4 | 10.6 |
| 1971 | 25.8 | 6.5 | 11.7 | 26.5 | 6.8 | 6.5 | 16.2 | 24.7 | 9.3 | 9.2 | 11.0 |
| 1972 | 24.1 | 6.6 | 11.7 | 28.2 | 7.0 | 7.0 | 14.6 | 22.9 | 9.5 | 9.2 | 10.9 |
| 1973 | 24.0 | 6.5 | 11.9 | 26.6 | 7.1 | 6.6 | 13.9 | 21.9 | 9.4 | 9.1 | 10.8 |
| 1974 | 24.3 | 6.4 | 11.6 | 26.2 | 6.3 | 6.6 | 14.0 | 21.4 | 9.2 | 8.7 | 10.5 |
| 1975 | 23.9 | 6.1 | 11.2 | 25.4 | 6.4 | 7.0 | 13.6 | 20.7 | 8.9 | 8.8 | 10.0 |
| 1976 | 24.3 | 6.6 | 11.2 | 26.5 | 7.2 | 7.4 | 13.8 | 21.1 | 9.0 | 8.2 | 9.9 |
| 1977 | 24.5 | 6.5 | 11.3 | 26.9 | 7.1 | 7.3 | 14.1 | 21.4 | 8.7 | 8.6 | 9.9 |
| 1978 | 24.1 | 6.4 | 10.7 | 27.0 | 6.5 | 7.4 | 14.0 | 21.3 | 8.8 | 8.6 | 10.3 |
| 1979 | 23.4 | 6.4 | 10.7 | 27.9 | 6.6 | 8.0 | 14.5 | 22.0 | 8.7 | 8.4 | 10.4 |

**A6  NORTH AMERICA: Vital Statistics: Rates per 1,000 Population**

| | Barbados | | | Canada | | | Costa Rica | | | Cuba | | |
|---|---|---|---|---|---|---|---|---|---|---|---|---|
| | B | D | M | B | D | M | B | D | M | B | D | M |
| 1980 | 16.7 | 8.1 | 4.2 | 15.4 | 7.1 | 7.9 | 29.4 | 4.1 | 7.8 | 14.1 | 5.7 | 7.1 |
| 1981 | 17.7 | 7.5 | 4.8 | 15.3 | 7.0 | 7.8 | 29.8 | 4.0 | 7.3 | 14.0 | 5.9 | 7.5 |
| 1982 | 18.0 | 8.0 | 4.9 | 15.1 | 7.1 | 7.6 | 30.7 | 3.9 | 8.0 | 16.3 | 5.8 | 8.2 |
| 1983 | 17.9 | 8.2 | 5.0 | 15.0 | 7.0 | 7.4 | 30.0 | 3.9 | 7.9 | 16.7 | 5.9 | 7.7 |
| 1984 | 16.7 | 7.8 | 4.6 | 15.1 | 7.0 | 7.4 | 31.4 | 4.1 | 8.5 | 16.6 | 6.0 | 7.6 |
| 1985 | 16.9 | 8.4 | 4.7 | 14.9 | 7.2 | 7.3 | 33.9 | 4.2 | ... | 18.0 | 6.4 | 8.0 |
| 1986 | 15.9 | 8.5 | 5.8 | 14.7 | 7.3 | 6.9 | ... | 3.8 | ... | 16.3 | 6.2 | 8.3 |
| 1987 | 15.1 | 8.7 | 6.0 | 14.4 | 7.2 | 7.1 | 28.9 | 3.8 | 7.8 | 17.4 | 6.3 | 7.7 |
| 1988 | 14.8 | 8.8 | 8.1 | 14.5 | 7.3 | 7.2 | 28.5 | 3.8 | 8.0 | 18.0 | 6.5 | 7.9 |

| | El Salvador | | | Guadeloupe | | | Guatemala | | | Jamaica | | |
|---|---|---|---|---|---|---|---|---|---|---|---|---|
| | B | D | M | B | D | M | B | D | M | B | D | M |
| 1980 | 37.7 | 8.6 | 5.3 | 19.7 | 6.5 | 4.9 | 43.9 | 10.3 | 4.5 | 26.9 | 5.8 | 3.6 |
| 1981 | 35.6 | 8.2 | 4.6 | 19.8 | 6.5 | 4.8 | 43.4 | 10.6 | 4.5 | 26.8 | 6.1 | 3.2 |
| 1982 | 33.6 | 7.1 | 4.4 | 20.2 | 6.4 | 4.8 | 42.7 | 10.4 | 4.3 | 26.9 | 4.9 | 4.0 |
| 1983 | 30.5 | 6.9 | 4.1 | 20.4 | 6.7 | 4.8 | 40.8 | 9.9 | 3.8 | 27.1 | 5.5 | 3.7 |
| 1984 | 29.8 | 6.0 | 3.5 | 20.2 | 6.8 | 5.0 | 40.3 | 8.5 | 4.3 | 25.2 | 5.9 | 4.6 |
| 1985 | ... | ... | 3.8 | 20.3 | 6.9 | 4.8 | 41.0 | 8.7 | 4.8 | 24.3 | 6.0 | 5.1 |
| 1986 | ... | ... | 3.9 | 19.2 | 6.7 | 5.1 | 39.0 | 8.5 | ... | 23.1 | 5.7 | 4.6 |
| 1987 | ... | ... | ... | 19.5 | 7.3 | ... | 38.5 | 7.9 | 5.3 | 22.2 | 5.3 | 4.6 |
| 1988 | ... | ... | ... | ... | ... | ... | 39.3 | 7.5 | 5.3 | 22.8 | 5.2 | 4.4 |

| | Martinique | | | Mexico | | | Panama | | | Puerto Rico | | |
|---|---|---|---|---|---|---|---|---|---|---|---|---|
| | B | D | M | B | D | M | B | D | M | B | D | M |
| 1980 | 16.4 | 6.6 | 3.6 | 34.9 | 6.3 | 7.2 | 26.9 | ... | 5.2 | 22.8 | 6.4 | 10.3 |
| 1981 | 16.6 | 6.3 | 3.7 | 35.5 | 6.0 | 6.7 | 26.9 | ... | 5.2 | 22.0 | 6.5 | 9.8 |
| 1982 | 16.5 | 6.5 | 4.0 | 32.8 | 5.7 | 7.2 | 26.7 | ... | 5.5 | 21.3 | 6.6 | 9.3 |
| 1983 | 17.3 | 6.8 | 4.1 | 35.0 | 5.5 | 6.8 | 26.4 | ... | 5.4 | 20.1 | 6.6 | 9.1 |
| 1984 | 17.5 | 6.3 | 4.0 | 32.9 | 5.4 | 6.7 | 26.5 | ... | 5.7 | 19.4 | 6.6 | 9.1 |
| 1985 | 17.3 | 6.5 | 4.0 | 34.1 | 5.3 | 7.3 | 26.6 | ... | 5.7 | 19.4 | 7.0 | 9.2 |
| 1986 | 17.9 | 6.3 | 4.6 | ... | ... | 7.3 | 25.9 | ... | 5.4 | 19.4 | 7.1 | ... |
| 1987 | 18.9 | 6.4 | 4.6 | ... | 5.8 | 7.4 | 25.3 | ... | 4.9 | 19.5 | 7.3 | 10.1 |
| 1988 | 19.0 | 6.2 | 4.6 | ... | ... | 7.6 | 24.8 | ... | 5.2 | 19.5 | 7.6 | 9.8 |

| | Trinidad & Tobago | | | U.S.A. | | | | |
|---|---|---|---|---|---|---|---|---|
| | B | D | M | B | | D | | M |
| | | | | whites | negroes | whites | negroes | |
| 1980 | 27.6 | 6.9 | 8.2 | 14.9 | 22.1 | 8.9 | 8.8 | 10.6 |
| 1981 | 28.9 | 6.6 | 7.4 | 14.8 | 21.6 | 8.8 | 8.4 | 10.6 |
| 1982 | 28.8 | 6.8 | 8.4 | 14.9 | 21.4 | 8.7 | 8.2 | 10.6 |
| 1983 | 29.2 | 6.6 | 7.5 | 14.6 | 20.9 | 8.8 | 8.3 | 10.5 |
| 1984 | 27.0 | 6.7 | 7.2 | 14.5 | 20.8 | 8.9 | 8.3 | 10.5 |
| 1985 | 28.6 | 6.8 | 6.7 | 14.8 | 21.1 | 9.0 | 8.5 | 10.1 |
| 1986 | 26.6 | 6.4 | 7.6 | 14.5 | 21.2 | 9.0 | 8.5 | 10.0 |
| 1987 | 24.1 | 6.6 | 6.3 | 14.5 | 21.6 | 9.0 | 8.6 | 9.9 |
| 1988 | 22.5 | 6.6 | 6.0 | 14.7 | 22.2 | 9.1 | 8.7 | 9.7 |

**SOUTH AMERICA: VITAL STATISTICS: RATES PER 1,000 POPULATION**

**1848–1889**

| | Chile | | | Uruguay | | |
|---|---|---|---|---|---|---|
| | **B** | **D** | **M** | **B** | **D** | **M** |
| 1848 | 36.8 | ... | 6.9 | ... | ... | ... |
| 1849 | 37.4 | ... | 6.8 | ... | ... | ... |
| 1850 | 41.3 | 18.8 | 7.2 | ... | ... | ... |
| 1851 | 38.5 | 20.5 | 6.8 | ... | ... | ... |
| 1852 | 40.9 | 19.5 | 7.8 | ... | ... | ... |
| 1853 | 44.7 | 22.9 | 7.8 | ... | ... | ... |
| 1854 | 43.3 | 21.7 | 7.4 | ... | ... | ... |
| 1855 | 44.7 | 21.1 | 7.5 | ... | ... | ... |
| 1856 | 45.5 | 22.7 | 8.3 | ... | ... | ... |
| 1857 | 44.8 | 24.5 | 7.5 | ... | ... | ... |
| 1858 | 41.6 | 22.3 | 6.8 | ... | ... | ... |
| 1859 | 41.6 | 25.0 | 6.6 | ... | ... | ... |
| 1860 | 47.6 | 28.9 | 6.9 | ... | ... | ... |
| 1861 | 39.6 | 27.0 | 6.5 | ... | ... | ... |
| 1862 | 40.8 | 24.4 | 6.2 | ... | ... | ... |
| 1863 | 40.8 | 26.8 | 6.2 | ... | ... | ... |
| 1864 | 42.3 | 34.6 | 6.1 | ... | ... | ... |
| 1865 | 36.0 | 29.4 | 5.9 | ... | ... | ... |
| 1866 | 38.4 | 25.5 | 5.7 | ... | ... | ... |
| 1867 | 39.5 | 25.7 | 6.2 | ... | ... | ... |
| 1868 | 41.3 | 23.4 | 6.8 | ... | ... | ... |
| 1869 | 42.1 | 26.1 | 7.1 | ... | ... | ... |
| 1870 | 42.3 | 24.7 | 7.0 | ... | ... | ... |
| 1871 | 41.5 | 25.4 | 7.2 | ... | ... | ... |
| 1872 | 44.1 | 29.2 | 8.0 | ... | ... | ... |
| 1873 | 44.9 | 28.2 | 8.7 | ... | ... | ... |
| 1874 | 44.7 | 27.6 | 8.2 | ... | ... | ... |
| 1875 | 42.6 | 28.3 | 8.2 | ... | ... | ... |
| 1876 | 40.6 | 30.2 | 7.2 | ... | ... | ... |
| 1877 | 38.9 | 29.4 | 6.4 | ... | ... | ... |
| 1878 | 36.5 | 28.0 | 6.1 | ... | ... | ... |
| 1879 | 40.6 | 27.7 | 6.6 | ... | ... | ... |
| 1880 | 38.2 | 31.2 | 6.3 | ... | ... | ... |
| 1881 | 44.4 | 27.4 | 7.0 | ... | ... | ... |
| 1882 | 40.2 | 28.0 | 7.2 | 43.0 | 18.1 | 6.7 |
| 1883 | 40.6 | 25.7 | 7.2 | 42.6 | 16.3 | 6.6 |
| 1884 | 41.1 | 24.2 | 7.3 | 38.9 | 17.3 | 6.3 |
| 1885 | 25.0 | 27.0 | 2.1 | 40.7 | 16.7 | 6.2 |
| 1886 | 29.0 | 26.7 | 2.4 | 41.5 | 18.3 | 5.2 |
| 1887 | 29.4 | 31.6 | 2.7 | 42.1 | 20.2 | 5.9 |
| 1888 | 32.1 | 3.3 | 42.0 | 18.8 | 6.4 | |
| 1889 | 38.0 | 34.7 | 4.4 | 41.6 | 19.1 | 6.4 |

**A6      SOUTH AMERICA: Vital Statistics: Rates per 1,000  Population**

| | Argentina | | | Chile | | | Colombia | | |
|---|---|---|---|---|---|---|---|---|---|
| | B | D | M | B | D | M | B | D | M |
| 1890 | ... | ... | ... | 37.9 | 36.7 | 4.2 | ... | ... | ... |
| 1891 | ... | ... | ... | 30.3 | 34.1 | 2.6 | ... | ... | ... |
| 1892 | ... | ... | ... | 39.3 | 37.6 | 4.8 | ... | ... | ... |
| 1893 | ... | ... | ... | 39.2 | 34.3 | 5.2 | ... | ... | ... |
| 1894 | ... | ... | ... | 41.1 | 33.7 | 5.7 | ... | ... | ... |
| 1895 | ... | ... | ... | 39.1 | 31.4 | 5.1 | ... | ... | ... |
| 1896 | ... | ... | ... | 37.6 | 30.5 | 5.8 | ... | ... | ... |
| 1897 | ... | ... | ... | 39.6 | 31.2 | 4.9 | ... | ... | ... |
| 1898 | ... | ... | ... | 37.4 | 29.1 | 5.0 | ... | ... | ... |
| 1899 | ... | ... | ... | 37.6 | 29.5 | 4.7 | ... | ... | ... |
| 1900 | ... | ... | ... | 38.4 | 36.0 | 4.6 | ... | ... | ... |
| 1901 | ... | ... | ... | 39.3 | 36.7 | 6.0 | ... | ... | ... |
| 1902 | ... | ... | ... | 38.7 | 28.8 | 5.6 | ... | ... | ... |
| 1903 | ... | ... | ... | 38.0 | 28.4 | 5.2 | ... | ... | ... |
| 1904 | ... | ... | ... | 37.9 | 28.1 | 5.3 | ... | ... | ... |
| 1905 | ... | ... | ... | 38.2 | 35.2 | 5.5 | ... | ... | ... |
| 1906 | ... | ... | ... | 36.9 | 33.0 | 5.8 | ... | ... | ... |
| 1907 | ... | ... | ... | 38.8 | 29.7 | 6.5 | ... | ... | ... |
| 1908 | ... | ... | ... | 39.7 | 31.9 | 6.6 | ... | ... | ... |
| 1909 | ... | ... | ... | 39.1 | 31.7 | 5.9 | ... | ... | ... |
| 1910 | 38.3 | 18.9 | 7.3 | 38.9 | 31.7 | 5.8 | ... | ... | ... |
| 1911 | 37.9 | 18.2 | 7.1 | 39.4 | 31.9 | 5.9 | ... | ... | ... |
| 1912 | 38.6 | 17.0 | 7.4 | 39.5 | 30.4 | 6.2 | ... | ... | ... |
| 1913 | 38.0 | 16.2 | 7.2 | 40.6 | 31.0 | 6.2 | ... | ... | ... |
| 1914 | 36.7 | 15.4 | 6.0 | 39.0 | 28.6 | 5.4 | ... | ... | ... |
| 1915 | 35.3 | 15.8 | 5.8 | 38.6 | 27.3 | 5.4 | 28.3 | 18.6 | 4.4 |
| 1916 | 35.3 | 17.1 | 5.9 | 40.3 | 27.9 | 5.6 | ... | ... | ... |
| 1917 | 33.6 | 16.1 | 5.5 | 41.2 | 29.6 | 5.9 | ... | ... | ... |
| 1918 | 32.9 | 18.2 | 5.9 | 36.9 | 27.5 | 5.5 | ... | ... | ... |
| 1919 | 32.7 | 18.4 | 6.3 | 35.9 | 34.1 | 5.3 | ... | ... | ... |
| 1920 | 32.3 | 15.5 | 7.1 | 39.1 | 30.7 | 6.6 | ... | ... | 4.8 |
| 1921 | 32.8 | 15.8 | 6.9 | 39.0 | 32.7 | 6.6 | ... | ... | 4.1 |
| 1922 | 33.1 | 14.0 | 7.1 | 38.4 | 28.4 | 6.5 | 27.5 | 15.0 | 4.1 |
| 1923 | 34.0 | 14.8 | 7.2 | 39.2 | 32.8 | 6.7 | 26.6 | 13.6 | 4.2 |
| 1924 | 32.8 | 14.3 | 7.4 | 39.7 | 29.2 | 8.4 | 25.5 | 12.9 | 4.3 |
| 1925 | 31.8 | 14.1 | ... | 40.0 | 27.8 | 7.3 | 26.4 | 13.0 | 5.0 |
| 1926 | 31.2 | 13.6 | ... | 40.0 | 27.2 | 7.6 | 27.7 | 14.4 | 5.3 |
| 1927 | 30.7 | 14.1 | 7.5 | 41.5 | 26.3 | 7.8 | 27.5 | 14.5 | 4.9 |
| 1928 | 30.8 | 13.2 | 7.6 | 52.2 | 23.7 | 11.1 | 29.5 | 13.7 | 5.1 |
| 1929 | 30.2 | 13.8 | 7.7 | 41.2 | 25.8 | 9.8 | 30.4 | 13.1 | 5.1 |
| 1930 | 29.5 | 12.7 | 6.9 | 39.8 | 24.7 | 9.2 | 28.1 | 13.3 | 3.9 |
| 1931 | 28.5 | 12.7 | 6.4 | 34.6 | 22.0 | 6.7 | 27.1 | 12.1 | 3.8 |
| 1932 | 28.1 | 11.1 | 6.0 | 34.0 | 22.8 | 6.6 | 22.2 | 9.8 | 3.9 |
| 1933 | 26.1 | 11.8 | 5.9 | 33.1 | 26.8 | 6.7 | 28.4 | 15.5 | 4.1 |
| 1934 | 25.5 | 11.7 | 6.3 | 33.2 | 26.8 | 7.0 | 29.9 | 15.6 | 4.6 |
| 1935 | 25.2 | 13.1 | 6.6 | 33.3 | 25.0 | 7.3 | 30.1 | 15.3 | 4.6 |
| 1936 | 24.5 | 11.9 | 6.6 | 33.5 | 25.3 | 7.5 | 29.5 | 15.5 | 4.6 |
| 1937 | 24.1 | 12.0 | 6.8 | 32.3 | 24.0 | 8.3 | 30.8 | 15.4 | 5.0 |
| 1938 | 24.3 | 12.4 | 6.5 | 32.1 | 24.5 | 8.1 | 32.2 | 17.3 | 4.9 |
| 1939 | 24.1 | 11.3 | 6.8 | 33.3 | 24.6 | 9.6 | 31.5 | 17.6 | 5.0 |

**A6    SOUTH AMERICA: Vital Statistics: Rates per 1,000 Population**

**1890–1939**

| | Guyana | | | Uruguay | | | Venezuela | | |
|---|---|---|---|---|---|---|---|---|---|
| | B | D | M | B | D | M | B | D | M |
| 1890 | ... | ... | ... | 40.7 | 21.2 | 5.9 | ... | ... | ... |
| 1891 | 26.6 | 37.4 | ... | 40.6 | 17.1 | 4.9 | 36.6 | 23.2 | 2.8 |
| 1892 | 28.0 | 39.8 | ... | 39.6 | 17.0 | 4.7 | 36.3 | 23.1 | 2.8 |
| 1893 | 27.3 | 35.5 | ... | 37.6 | 17.2 | 4.6 | 35.6 | 22.7 | 2.5 |
| 1894 | 24.8 | 33.4 | ... | 38.1 | 18.5 | 4.9 | 35.5 | 20.4 | 1.8 |
| 1895 | 28.9 | 29.5 | ... | 39.2 | 15.6 | 5.8 | ... | ... | ... |
| 1896 | 32.5 | 26.3 | ... | 37.8 | 15.6 | 5.0 | ... | ... | ... |
| 1897 | 33.6 | 27.9 | ... | 32.1 | 14.5 | 3.3 | ... | ... | ... |
| 1898 | 29.7 | 33.9 | ... | 33.6 | 14.4 | 5.0 | ... | ... | ... |
| 1899 | 28.8 | 29.1 | ... | 34.3 | 12.8 | 5.0 | ... | ... | ... |
| 1900 | 36.7 | 25.1 | ... | 32.6 | 13.7 | 4.8 | ... | ... | ... |
| 1901 | 35.9 | 23.6 | ... | 32.8 | 12.9 | 4.6 | ... | ... | ... |
| 1902 | 33.4 | 28.1 | ... | 31.8 | 13.6 | 4.6 | ... | ... | ... |
| 1903 | 29.0 | 28.9 | ... | 32.0 | 13.4 | 4.7 | ... | ... | ... |
| 1904 | 30.3 | 28.8 | ... | 26.0 | 11.1 | 2.6 | 28.4 | 19.8 | 2.6 |
| 1905 | 33.6 | 27.4 | ... | 31.5 | 12.7 | 5.6 | 27.7 | 23.4 | 2.2 |
| 1906 | 32.9 | 28.8 | ... | 29.5 | 13.7 | 5.7 | 28.1 | 21.3 | 2.5 |
| 1907 | 28.3 | 36.9 | ... | 30.5 | 14.1 | 5.7 | 29.3 | 20.6 | 2.4 |
| 1908 | 27.3 | 30.8 | ... | 33.6 | 13.6 | 5.8 | 27.8 | 22.3 | 2.4 |
| 1909 | 29.3 | 30.0 | ... | 32.5 | 13.9 | 6.2 | 28.1 | 20.7 | 2.3 |
| 1910 | 27.5 | 34.4 | ... | 31.7 | 14.5 | 6.1 | 31.8 | 21.3 | 2.4 |
| 1911 | 28.8 | 31.7 | ... | 31.8 | 14.0 | 6.0 | 32.0 | 21.2 | 3.1 |
| 1912 | 33.1 | 29.2 | ... | 31.9 | 13.6 | 6.3 | 28.7 | 24.9 | 3.5 |
| 1913 | 34.6 | 24.2 | ... | 32.2 | 12.3 | 5.8 | 28.8 | 19.9 | 3.7 |
| 1914 | 34.4 | 27.4 | ... | 29.7 | 11.8 | 4.7 | 28.3 | 19.3 | 2.8 |
| 1915 | 31.3 | 27.7 | ... | 28.6 | 12.8 | 4.3 | 27.7 | 23.3 | 2.5 |
| 1916 | 26.5 | 27.1 | ... | 27.1 | 14.9 | 4.3 | 27.4 | 24.3 | 2.5 |
| 1917 | 28.4 | 30.4 | ... | 26.4 | 12.5 | 4.5 | 28.2 | 21.0 | 3.1 |
| 1918 | 25.1 | 40.6 | ... | 27.4 | 14.1 | 4.8 | 27.4 | 24.5 | 4.6 |
| 1919 | 26.0 | 40.4 | ... | 27.2 | 13.1 | 5.2 | 29.7 | 22.2 | 6.1 |
| 1920 | 32.9 | 26.5 | ... | 26.6 | 12.9 | 5.6 | 26.3 | 19.4 | 5.3 |
| 1921 | 34.5 | 30.9 | ... | 26.2 | 12.2 | 5.2 | 25.2 | 21.1 | 2.7 |
| 1922 | 27.8 | 29.1 | 3.6 | 26.0 | 10.6 | 4.9 | 26.6 | 19.7 | 2.9 |
| 1923 | 30.4 | 28.3 | 3.9 | 25.4 | 11.4 | 5.3 | 28.3 | 18.8 | 3.7 |
| 1924 | 32.4 | 25.6 | 3.4 | 25.8 | 11.8 | 5.7 | 27.9 | 18.5 | 3.2 |
| 1925 | 33.5 | 24.2 | 3.9 | 25.1 | 11.5 | 5.6 | 32.4 | 17.5 | 3.9 |
| 1926 | 34.7 | 25.5 | 3.6 | 25.4 | 10.5 | 5.6 | 30.7 | 22.2 | 5.7 |
| 1927 | 32.6 | 26.0 | 3.6 | 24.6 | 11.5 | 5.9 | 30.1 | 19.5 | 4.6 |
| 1928 | 28.3 | 27.9 | 3.5 | 25.0 | 10.7 | 6.2 | 30.2 | 18.8 | 4.0 |
| 1929 | 31.7 | 23.5 | 3.3 | 24.2 | 10.8 | 6.4 | 30.2 | 17.2 | 3.8 |
| 1930 | 33.8 | 23.2 | 3.3 | 24.4 | 10.7 | 6.3 | 29.7 | 17.2 | 3.2 |
| 1931 | 31.6 | 22.0 | 3.2 | 23.3 | 11.0 | 5.8 | 28.1 | 18.4 | 2.8 |
| 1932 | 34.3 | 21.2 | 3.7 | 22.5 | 10.1 | 5.1 | 28.4 | 17.1 | 3.1 |
| 1933 | 32.8 | 24.6 | 4.1 | 21.0 | 10.3 | 4.8 | 27.9 | 18.5 | 2.6 |
| 1934 | 29.0 | 24.8 | 3.8 | 20.6 | 10.0 | 5.3 | 27.0 | 18.1 | 3.0 |
| 1935 | 34.7 | 20.8 | 4.3 | 20.4 | 10.6 | 5.6 | 27.8 | 16.6 | 2.7 |
| 1936 | 35.7 | 20.6 | 4.4 | 19.8 | 9.7 | 5.9 | 31.9 | 17.4 | 3.1 |
| 1937 | 33.8 | 22.1 | 4.3 | 19.9 | 10.4 | 6.7 | 33.7 | 18.1 | 4.0 |
| 1938 | 29.9 | 25.8 | 4.2 | 19.8 | 10.3 | 7.0 | 33.7 | 18.3 | 4.0 |
| 1939 | 28.3 | 19.8 | 4.7 | 20.1 | 9.1 | 7.0 | 35.9 | 18.7 | 4.4 |

**A6    SOUTH AMERICA: Vital Statistics: Rates per 1,000 Population**

**1940–1988**

| | Argentina | | | Chile | | | Colombia | | |
|---|---|---|---|---|---|---|---|---|---|
| | **B** | **D** | **M** | **B** | **D** | **M** | **B** | **D** | **M** |
| 1940 | 24.0 | 10.7 | 6.5 | 33.4 | 22.9 | 9.0 | 32.2 | 15.2 | 4.8 |
| 1941 | 23.7 | 10.4 | 6.8 | 32.6 | 19.6 | 8.3 | 32.7 | 15.5 | 5.3 |
| 1942 | 23.3 | 10.3 | 7.1 | 33.1 | 19.9 | 8.3 | 33.1 | 16.0 | 5.4 |
| 1943 | 24.2 | 10.1 | 7.4 | 33.1 | 19.3 | 8.1 | 32.1 | 17.1 | 5.3 |
| 1944 | 25.2 | 10.2 | 7.9 | 33.2 | 18.9 | 8.0 | 32.2 | 16.4 | 5.4 |
| 1945 | 25.2 | 10.3 | 8.0 | 33.3 | 19.3 | 7.7 | 31.7 | 15.7 | 5.2 |
| 1946 | 24.7 | 9.6 | 8.0 | 36.2 | 16.6 | 7.5 | 32.8 | 15.5 | 5.3 |
| 1947 | 25.0 | 9.9 | 8.7 | 36.0 | 16.1 | 7.9 | 33.8 | 14.4 | 5.2 |
| 1948 | 25.3 | 9.4 | 8.6 | 35.3 | 16.7 | 7.9 | 34.9 | 14.2 | 5.3 |
| 1949 | 25.1 | 9.0 | 8.4 | 34.7 | 17.3 | 7.8 | 35.1 | 14.0 | 5.0 |
| 1950 | 25.5 | 9.0 | 8.3 | 34.0 | 15.0 | 7.5 | 36.5 | 14.2 | 5.6 |
| 1951 | 25.2 | 8.9 | 8.1 | 33.9 | 15.0 | 7.3 | 36.1 | 14.2 | 5.3 |
| 1952 | 24.7 | 8.6 | 7.6 | 32.6 | 13.0 | 8.1 | 36.4 | 12.8 | 5.6 |
| 1953 | 25.0 | 8.9 | 7.9 | 34.5 | 12.4 | 8.4 | 38.1 | 13.2 | 5.7 |
| 1954 | 24.7 | 8.4 | 7.7 | 33.4 | 12.8 | 8.2 | 37.2 | 11.8 | 6.0 |
| 1955 | 24.4 | 8.9 | 7.5 | 34.9 | 12.9 | 8.8 | 38.8 | 12.3 | 5.9 |
| 1956 | 24.6 | 8.4 | 7.5 | 34.3 | 12.1 | 8.4 | 39.6 | 12.7 | 5.9 |
| 1957 | 24.4 | 9.2 | 7.5 | 37.1 | 12.8 | 7.6 | 40.1 | 12.4 | 5.9 |
| 1958 | 23.7 | 8.3 | 7.4 | 36.3 | 12.2 | 7.3 | 40.5 | 12.0 | 5.8 |
| 1959 | 23.5 | 8.5 | 7.3 | 36.1 | 12.6 | 7.5 | 40.7 | 11.8 | 5.9 |
| 1960 | 22.9 | 8.7 | 7.0 | 34.4 | 12.4 | 7.4 | 38.8 | 11.9 | 6.0 |
| 1961 | 22.8 | 8.4 | 6.8 | 34.7 | 11.6 | 7.4 | 39.4 | 11.0 | 6.1 |
| 1962 | 23.1 | 8.6 | 6.5 | 36.3 | 11.8 | 6.9 | 39.6 | 10.8 | 5.9 |
| 1963 | 22.8 | 8.6 | 6.2 | 34.0 | 12.0 | 7.0 | 39.3 | 10.4 | 5.4 |
| 1964 | 22.7 | 8.7 | 6.9 | 33.1 | 11.2 | 7.3 | 38.6 | 10.0 | ... |
| 1965 | 21.7 | 8.9 | 6.9 | 32.3 | 10.5 | 7.6 | 36.9 | 9.9 | ... |
| 1966 | 21.3 | 8.6 | 6.7 | 30.9 | 10.2 | 7.6 | 35.9 | 9.5 | ... |
| 1967 | 21.1 | 8.6 | 6.6 | 31.6 | 9.5 | 7.4 | 35.3 | 9.5 | ... |
| 1968 | 21.3 | 9.2 | 6.7 | 27.2 | 9.0 | 7.2 | 32.0 | 8.7 | ... |
| 1969 | 24.8 | 9.5 | ... | 25.7 | 8.8 | 7.3 | 34.6 | 7.7 | ... |
| 1970 | 22.7 | 9.4 | 7.7 | 27.6 | 8.5 | 7.6 | ... | 6.6 | 5.4 |
| 1971 | 22.8 | 9.3 | 7.8 | 28.1 | 8.8 | 8.9 | 37.8 | 6.9 | 5.0 |
| 1972 | 22.4 | 9.0 | 7.5 | 27.4 | 9.0 | 8.8 | 34.4 | 7.5 | 4.8 |
| 1973 | 22.6 | 9.1 | 7.6 | 26.8 | 8.2 | 8.5 | 33.2 | 9.1 | 5.6 |
| 1974 | 23.5 | 9.0 | 8.0 | 25.9 | 7.8 | 8.0 | 32.2 | 9.0 | 5.8 |
| 1975 | 23.8 | 8.8 | 7.7 | 24.2 | 7.3 | 7.5 | 31.1 | 9.0 | 6.2 |
| 1976 | 23.9 | 9.1 | 7.5 | 23.0 | 7.4 | 7.1 | 30.0 | 9.0 | ... |
| 1977 | 24.7 | 8.7 | 6.9 | 21.4 | 7.0 | 7.0 | 30.4 | ... | 7.0 |
| 1978 | 24.3 | 8.4 | 6.6 | 21.3 | 6.7 | 7.2 | 30.2 | ... | ... |
| 1979 | 24.8 | 8.5 | 6.3 | 21.4 | 6.8 | 7.3 | 29.9 | ... | ... |
| 1980 | 24.7 | 8.5 | 5.9 | 22.2 | 6.7 | 7.7 | 29.7 | ... | ... |
| 1981 | 23.7 | 8.4 | 5.6 | 23.4 | 6.2 | 8.0 | 28.8 | ... | ... |
| 1982 | 22.8 | 8.0 | ... | 23.8 | 6.1 | 7.0 | 27.9 | ... | ... |
| 1983 | 22.5 | 8.2 | 6.0 | 22.2 | 8.4 | 7.0 | 27.7 | ... | ... |
| 1984 | 22.0 | 8.5 | ... | 22.2 | 6.3 | 7.3 | 27.6 | ... | ... |
| 1985 | 22.6 | 8.0 | ... | 21.6 | 6.1 | 7.5 | 27.4 | ... | ... |
| 1986 | 22.1 | 7.9 | ... | 22.1 | 5.9 | 7.6 | ... | ... | ... |
| 1987 | 21.3 | 8.0 | ... | 22.3 | 5.6 | 7.6 | ... | ... | ... |
| 1988 | 20.7 | 8.4 | ... | 23.3 | 5.8 | 8.1 | ... | ... | ... |

**A6     SOUTH AMERICA: Vital Statistics: Rates per 1,000 Population**

**1940–1988**

| | Guyana* | | | Uruguay | | | Venezuela | | |
|---|---|---|---|---|---|---|---|---|---|
| | B | D | M | B | D | M | B | D | M |
| 1940 | 35.0 | 18.6 | 4.3 | 19.9 | 9.6 | 6.7 | 36.0 | 16.6 | 4.6 |
| 1941 | 35.8 | 15.7 | 5.2 | 20.4 | 9.4 | 7.4 | 35.3 | 16.4 | 4.2 |
| 1942 | 38.8 | 17.4 | 6.1 | 19.4 | 9.4 | 7.2 | 35.6 | 16.2 | 4.1 |
| 1943 | 33.6 | 24.8 | 6.0 | 19.6 | 9.4 | 7.2 | 36.1 | 15.9 | 4.2 |
| 1944 | 28.8 | 22.0 | 5.4 | 20.7 | 9.0 | 7.6 | 35.5 | 17.0 | 3.9 |
| 1945 | 36.6 | 17.9 | 5.0 | [21.6][11] | 8.7 | 8.0 | 36.2 | 15.0 | 4.1 |
| 1946 | 35.6 | 15.5 | 4.9 | [23.5][11] | 8.8 | 8.1 | 37.6 | 14.7 | 4.5 |
| 1947 | 39.4 | 14.6 | 4.6 | 20.1 | 9.0 | 8.2 | 38.2 | 13.4 | 4.4 |
| 1948 | 41.4 | 14.5 | 4.4 | 18.7 | 8.9 | 7.8 | 39.2 | 12.8 | 4.6 |
| 1949 | 41.6 | 13.5 | 4.9 | 18.7 | 8.6 | 8.2 | 41.2 | 11.9 | 4.9 |
| 1950 | 40.2 | 14.8 | 4.7 | 18.6 | 8.0 | 7.9 | 42.6 | 10.9 | 5.0 |
| 1951 | 42.3 | 13.5 | 4.5 | 18.5 | 8.6 | 8.2 | 43.4 | 11.0 | 4.9 |
| 1952 | 43.8 | 13.5 | 4.4 | 18.8 | 8.4 | 7.5 | 42.5 | 10.6 | 4.9 |
| 1953 | 43.9 | 13.3 | 4.1 | 18.8 | 8.5 | 8.8 | 44.3 | 9.6 | 5.2 |
| 1954 | 42.9 | 12.4 | 4.1 | 19.4 | 8.2 | 8.9 | 44.8 | 9.7 | 5.3 |
| 1955 | 43.4 | 11.9 | 4.3 | 21.4 | 8.7 | 8.7 | 44.3 | 9.7 | 5.0 |
| 1956 | 43.3 | 11.2 | 4.2 | 23.5 | 8.3 | 8.5 | 43.9 | 9.4 | 5.7 |
| 1957 | 44.6 | 11.6 | 4.1 | 23.1 | 8.9 | 8.6 | 43.2 | 9.4 | 5.3 |
| 1958 | 44.5 | 10.3 | 3.7 | 23.1 | 8.5 | 8.5 | 42.7 | 8.6 | 5.1 |
| 1959 | 44.5 | 10.1 | 3.7 | 22.6 | 9.4 | 8.3 | 45.8 | 8.3 | 5.6 |
| 1960 | 41.7 | 9.5 | 4.0 | 23.9 | 8.5 | 7.8 | 46.0 | 7.1 | 5.3 |
| 1961 | 41.6 | 9.0 | 4.0 | 25.0 | 8.8 | 8.4 | 45.3 | 7.3 | 5.1 |
| 1962 | 42.1 | 8.1 | 3.8 | 25.3 | 8.7 | 7.8 | 43.4 | 7.0 | 5.2 |
| 1963 | 41.8 | 8.9 | 3.3 | 23.8 | 8.9 | 7.6 | 43.4 | 7.2 | 5.2 |
| 1964 | 40.5 | 8.2 | 3.7 | 23.4 | 9.0 | 7.5 | 43.4 | 7.2 | 5.6 |
| 1965 | 40.0 | 8.2 | 4.1 | 22.2 | 9.1 | 7.7 | 43.6 | 7.1 | 5.7 |
| 1966 | 39.9 | 8.2 | 4.2 | 21.4 | 9.0 | 7.6 | 41.8 | 6.8 | 5.8 |
| 1967 | 35.9 | 7.5 | 4.0 | 22.0 | 9.5 | 8.0 | 42.5 | 6.6 | 5.7 |
| 1968 | 35.5 | 7.8 | 4.0 | 22.1 | 9.2 | 7.9 | 38.8 | 6.7 | 5.8 |
| 1969 | 31.9 | 7.4 | ... | 20.1 | 9.7 | 8.6 | 38.7 | 6.8 | 5.9 |
| 1970 | 33.4 | 6.8 | ... | 19.5 | 9.2 | 8.4 | 37.0 | 6.6 | 5.9 |
| 1971 | 31.7 | 7.2 | ... | 19.8 | 10.3 | 8.4 | 37.0 | 6.6 | 6.2 |
| 1972 | 33.9 | 8.1 | ... | 19.9 | 10.6 | 7.9 | 35.7 | 6.7 | 5.6 |
| 1973 | 31.9 | 7.4 | ... | 20.0 | 10.2 | 8.0 | 34.4 | 6.8 | 6.3 |
| 1974 | 30.0 | 8.0 | ... | 20.5 | 10.1 | 8.9 | 35.4 | 6.0 | 7.1 |
| 1975 | 29.7 | 7.6 | ... | 20.9 | 9.7 | 8.6 | 35.2 | 5.9 | 7.1 |
| 1976 | 30.5 | 7.9 | ... | 20.8 | 10.1 | 8.0 | 35.2 | 5.7 | 7.2 |
| 1977 | ... | 7.3 | ... | 20.3 | 10.1 | 7.8 | 34.2 | 5.5 | 7.1 |
| 1978 | ... | 7.3 | ... | 19.9 | 9.7 | 7.9 | 33.8 | 5.2 | 7.1 |
| 1979 | ... | ... | ... | 19.3 | 9.8 | 7.9 | 33.1 | 5.1 | 7.0 |
| 1980 | ... | ... | ... | 18.5 | 10.3 | 7.7 | 32.8 | 5.1 | 6.2 |
| 1981 | ... | ... | ... | 18.4 | 9.4 | 7.7 | 32.1 | 5.2 | 5.9 |
| 1982 | ... | ... | ... | 18.5 | 9.2 | 6.8 | 32.0 | 4.8 | 5.7 |
| 1983 | ... | ... | ... | 18.0 | 9.6 | 6.5 | 31.4 | 4.6 | 5.7 |
| 1984 | ... | ... | ... | 17.8 | 10.0 | 6.8 | 29.9 | 4.6 | 5.5 |
| 1985 | ... | ... | ... | 17.9 | 9.5 | 7.4 | 29.0 | 4.6 | 5.4 |
| 1986 | ... | ... | ... | 17.8 | 9.5 | 7.2 | 28.3 | 4.4 | 5.6 |
| 1987 | ... | ... | ... | 17.6 | 9.6 | 7.2 | 28.3 | 4.4 | 5.7 |
| 1988 | ... | ... | ... | | | | 27.8 | 4.4 | 6.0 |

## A6    Vital Statistics: Rates per 1,000 Population

NOTES

1. SOURCES: The national publications on p. xiv–xvi; UN, *Demographic Yearbook;* and League of Nations, *Statistical Year-Book.* Canadian statistics to 1920 come from O. J. Firestone, *Canada's Economic Development, 1867–1953* (London, Bowes & Bowes, 1958).
2. In principle, birth rates relate to live births and death rates exclude stillbirths.

FOOTNOTES

[1] Data to 1889 are for years ending 30 September. From 1890 to 1915 they are for years ending 31 March in the year following that shown. Birth, death, and marriage rates for the six months from 1 October 1889 to 31 March 1890 were at annual rates of 35.8, 28.2, and 5.9 respectively.

[2] Data to 1892 (1890 for marriage rate) are for Trinidad alone. For the period 1901 to 1914 they relate to years beginning 1 April. The 1915 figures are for the last three quarters of the year.

[3] The figures to 1920 are estimates, the derivation of which is described in the source cited in Note 1 above. Earlier figures for the Province of Quebec are given in the same source and are as follows:

| | B | | B | D | M | | B | D | M |
|---|---|---|---|---|---|---|---|---|---|
| 1867 | 43.5 | 1879 | 42.8 | ... | ... | 1890 | 37.8 | 22.3 | 6.3 |
| 1868 | 42.8 | 1880 | 42.4 | ... | ... | 1891 | 38.9 | 22.2 | 6.2 |
| 1869 | 42.3 | 1881 | 40.7 | ... | ... | 1892 | 37.1 | 21.4 | 6.5 |
| 1870 | 41.6 | 1882 | 41.7 | ... | ... | 1893 | 37.5 | 21.6 | 6.5 |
| 1871 | 41.6 | 1883 | 41.7 | ... | ... | 1894 | 34.9 | 21.0 | 6.1 |
| 1872 | 42.7 | 1884 | 38.5 | 19.4 | 6.6 | 1895 | 37.9 | 20.5 | 6.6 |
| 1873 | 42.9 | 1885 | 37.4 | 25.2 | 6.6 | 1896 | 38.2 | 19.9 | 6.4 |
| 1874 | 44.0 | 1886 | 40.2 | 23.1 | 6.8 | 1897 | 37.1 | 21.8 | 6.5 |
| 1875 | 46.0 | 1887 | 39.7 | 20.7 | 6.9 | 1898 | 37.9 | 20.0 | 6.8 |
| 1876 | 45.2 | 1888 | 39.1 | 21.6 | 7.0 | 1899 | 35.2 | 20.4 | 6.9 |
| 1877 | 44.1 | 1889 | 38.5 | 21.9 | 6.5 | 1900 | 33.0 | 20.1 | 6.2 |
| 1878 | 44.4 | | | | | | | | |

M. C. Urquhart and K. A. H. Buckley (eds.), *Historical Statistics of Canada* (Cambridge and Toronto, 1965) give the following decennial estimates for the Roman Catholic population of the Province of Quebec:

| | B | D | M | | B | D | M | | B | D | M |
|---|---|---|---|---|---|---|---|---|---|---|---|
| 1661–70 | 59.6 | 20.3 | 14.0 | 1761–70 | 64.5 | 11.2 | 33.5 | 1861–70 | 45.0 | 7.3 | 21.0 |
| 1671–80 | 55.3 | 7.5 | 9.4 | 1771–80 | 61.7 | 9.8 | 33.0 | 1871–80 | 47.0 | 7.8 | 24.8 |
| 1681–90 | 42.9 | 8.1 | 16.2 | 1781–90 | 57.4 | 9.2 | 29.9 | 1881–90 | 42.6 | ... | ... |
| 1691–1700 | 49.9 | 9.8 | 16.0 | 1791–1800 | 57.5 | 9.6 | 27.8 | | | | |
| 1701–10 | 57.1 | 9.0 | 23.9 | 1801–10 | 56.7 | 9.4 | 29.1 | | | | |
| 1711–20 | 56.9 | 10.1 | 22.1 | 1811–20 | 55.1 | 9.5 | 27.1 | | | | |
| 1721–30 | 55.5 | 10.2 | 24.4 | 1821–30 | 56.9 | 9.4 | 27.5 | | | | |
| 1731–40 | 56.9 | 9.5 | 25.8 | 1831–40 | 55.1 | 9.1 | 27.9 | | | | |
| 1741–50 | 55.9 | 10.4 | 28.7 | 1841–50 | 52.1 | 8.7 | 23.4 | | | | |
| 1751–60 | 59.6 | 11.3 | 38.2 | 1851–60 | 45.2 | 7.3 | 19.4 | | | | |

Yukon and Northwest Territories are excluded to 1923, but Newfoundland is included from 1921, though it is also shown separately to 1949.

[4] Subsequent statistics are later revisions which are more complete.

[5] The following estimates of earlier total and white birth rates are given in Henry D. Sheldon, *The Older Population of the United States* (New York, John Wiley & Sons, 1958), and in Warren S. Thompson and P. K. Whelpton, *Population Trends in the United States* (New York, McGraw-Hill, 1933 respectively:

| | Total | Whites | | Total | Whites | | Total | Whites |
|---|---|---|---|---|---|---|---|---|
| 1800 | ... | 55.0 | 1840 | 51.8 | 48.3 | 1880 | 39.8 | 35.2 |
| 1810 | ... | 54.3 | 1850 | ... | 43.3 | 1890 | ... | 31.5 |
| 1820 | 55.2 | 52.8 | 1860 | 44.3 | 41.4 | 1900 | 32.3 | 30.1 |
| 1830 | ... | 51.4 | 1870 | ... | 38.3 | | | |

[6] i.e. non-whites.

[7] Data to 1937 are for years ending 31 July. From 1938 to 1949 they are for years ending 30 June.

[8] Excluding the Canal Zone. Revised figures back to 1948 are lower for both birth and death rates than the original series for the first few years after 1948, and it may be presumed that earlier statistics are overstated.

[9] Subsequently including Alaska.

[10] Subsequently including Hawaii.

[11] Late registrations are included.

**A6a    NORTH AMERICA: COLLVER'S ESTIMATES OF AVERAGE VITAL RATES FOR QUINQUENNIA, 1895–1959**

Key:     BR = birth rate; DR = death rate; IMR = infant mortality rate

| | Cuba | | | El Salvador | | | Guatemala | | |
|---|---|---|---|---|---|---|---|---|---|
| | BR | DR | IMR | BR | DR | IMR | BR | DR | IMR |
| 1895–99 | … | … | … | … | … | … | … | … | … |
| 1900–04 | 44.6 | 23.7 | 136 | 43.8 | 29.7 | 176 | 45.8 | 35.4 | 155 |
| 1905–09 | 47.4 | 23.3 | 146 | 43.5 | 31.4 | 188 | 43.6 | 34.0 | 155 |
| 1910–14 | 44.7 | 21.4 | 140 | 44.7 | 31.1 | 169 | 46.6 | 33.0 | 142 |
| 1915–19 | 40.7 | 22.2 | 136 | 42.9 | 41.2 | 214 | 43.2 | 40.8 | 147 |
| 1920–24 | 36.7 | 19.3 | 135 | 46.6 | 32.8 | 185 | 48.3 | 33.7 | 142 |
| 1925–29 | 32.9 | 15.2 | 110 | 47.1 | 34.1 | 191 | 49.2 | 32.6 | 123 |
| 1930–34 | 31.3 | 13.3 | 76 | 46.5 | 32.7 | 185 | 46.2 | 31.7 | 125 |
| 1935–39 | 30.9 | 12.7 | 78 | 45.4 | 29.6 | 164 | 44.2 | 30.7 | 128 |
| 1940–44 | 31.9 | 10.9 | 61 | 45.2 | 28.5 | 152 | 45.2 | 28.5 | 127 |
| 1945–49 | 30.0 | 8.7 | 52 | 44.8 | 22.8 | 135 | 49.1 | 26.5 | 124 |
| 1950–54 | … | … | … | 47.9 | 20.0 | 109 | 50.9 | 23.4 | 116 |
| 1955–59 | … | … | … | 47.9 | 17.7 | 107 | 49.0 | 20.0 | 98 |

| | Honduras | | | Mexico | | | Panama | | |
|---|---|---|---|---|---|---|---|---|---|
| | BR | DR | IMR | BR | DR | IMR | BR | DR | IMR |
| 1895–99 | … | … | … | 47.3 | 34.4 | 226 | … | … | … |
| 1900–04 | … | … | … | 46.5 | 33.4 | 220 | 40.3 | 21.0 | 130 |
| 1905–09 | … | … | … | 46.0 | 32.9 | 220 | 40.2 | 19.7 | 130 |
| 1910–14 | 43.7 | 24.5 | 126 | 43.2 | 46.6 | 228 | 42.0 | 19.0 | 122 |
| 1915–19 | 41.7 | 27.4 | 140 | 40.6 | 48.3 | 215 | 37.3 | 17.3 | 121 |
| 1920–24 | 44.3 | 23.1 | 111 | 45.3 | 28.4 | 178 | 40.0 | 17.3 | 110 |
| 1925–29 | 44.1 | 23.1 | 112 | 44.3 | 26.7 | 153 | 39.0 | 16.6 | 110 |
| 1930–34 | 42.0 | 21.7 | 106 | 44.1 | 26.7 | 142 | 37.4 | 15.1 | 101 |
| 1935–39 | 41.9 | 22.1 | 118 | 43.5 | 23.5 | 129 | 37.8 | 12.6 | 80 |
| 1940–44 | 43.8 | 23.9 | 126 | 43.8 | 21.8 | 120 | 39.5 | 12.7 | 81 |
| 1945–49 | 44.5 | 19.0 | 106 | 44.5 | 17.8 | 105 | 38.3 | 10.8 | 70 |
| 1950–54 | 46.0 | 14.9 | 74 | 45.0 | 15.4 | 92 | 38.5 | 9.1 | 60 |
| 1955–59 | 46.0 | 12.5 | 64 | 45.8 | 12.5 | 78 | 40.5 | 9.1 | 71 |

**A6a    SOUTH AMERICA: COLLVER'S ESTIMATES OF AVERAGE VITAL RATES FOR QUINQUENNIA, 1850–1959**

| | Argentina | | | Bolivia | | Chile | | | Colombia | | |
|---|---|---|---|---|---|---|---|---|---|---|---|
| | BR | DR | IMR | BR | DR | BR | DR | IMR | BR | DR | IMR |
| 1850–54 | ... | ... | ... | ... | ... | 44.6 | 35.0 | ... | ... | ... | ... |
| 1855–59 | ... | ... | ... | ... | ... | 47.5 | 34.7 | ... | ... | ... | ... |
| 1860–64 | 46.8 | 31.7 | 188 | ... | ... | 46.9 | 34.3 | ... | ... | ... | ... |
| 1865–69 | 46.7 | 31.4 | 186 | ... | ... | 46.2 | 34.5 | ... | ... | ... | ... |
| 1870–74 | 46.2 | 30.7 | 185 | ... | ... | 47.5 | 34.0 | ... | ... | ... | ... |
| 1875–79 | 45.6 | 30.0 | 181 | ... | ... | 44.9 | 33.7 | ... | ... | ... | ... |
| 1880–84 | 45.0 | 29.1 | 179 | ... | ... | 48.0 | 33.9 | ... | ... | ... | ... |
| 1885–89 | 44.6 | 27.6 | 171 | ... | ... | 46.6 | 33.3 | ... | ... | ... | ... |
| 1890–94 | 42.9 | 25.1 | 162 | ... | ... | 45.9 | 32.7 | ... | ... | ... | ... |
| 1895–99 | 42.4 | 23.8 | 155 | ... | ... | 45.0 | 30.3 | ... | ... | ... | ... |
| 1900–04 | 41.0 | 21.6 | 146 | ... | ... | 44.7 | 31.6 | 261 | 43.0 | 26.6 | 186 |
| 1905–09 | 40.0 | 20.1 | 138 | ... | ... | 44.6 | 33.2 | 269 | 44.0 | 26.8 | 183 |
| 1910–14 | 40.3 | 17.7 | 121 | ... | ... | 44.4 | 31.5 | 261 | 44.1 | 26.0 | 177 |
| 1915–19 | 36.1 | 16.5 | 113 | ... | ... | 43.3 | 31.0 | 248 | 44.1 | 25.1 | 171 |
| 1920–24 | 34.3 | 14.0 | 100 | ... | ... | 42.2 | 31.3 | 250 | 44.6 | 23.7 | 159 |
| 1925–29 | 32.4 | 13.1 | 96 | ... | ... | 43.8 | 26.4 | 223 | 44.9 | 22.4 | 150 |
| 1930–34 | 28.9 | 11.6 | 82 | ... | ... | 40.2 | 24.5 | 212 | 43.3 | 22.5 | 155 |
| 1935–39 | 25.7 | 11.6 | 89 | ... | ... | 38.4 | 23.8 | 207 | 42.6 | 21.6 | 152 |
| 1940–44 | 25.7 | 10.4 | 74 | 45.1 | 20.5 | 38.3 | 20.1 | 170 | 42.4 | 20.3 | 143 |
| 1945–49 | 25.2 | 9.6 | 74 | 47.0 | 19.1 | 37.0 | 17.5 | 146 | 43.4 | 20.8 | 143 |
| 1950–54 | ... | ... | ... | 42.4 | 16.2 | 37.0 | 13.7 | 119 | 44.0 | 18.4 | 125 |
| 1955–59 | ... | ... | ... | ... | ... | 37.6 | 12.5 | 112 | 45.1 | 16.0 | 106 |

| | Ecuador | | | Peru | | Venezuela | | |
|---|---|---|---|---|---|---|---|---|
| | BR | DR | IMR | BR | DR | BR | DR | IMR |
| 1850–54 | ... | ... | ... | ... | ... | ... | ... | ... |
| 1855–59 | ... | ... | ... | ... | ... | ... | ... | ... |
| 1860–64 | ... | ... | ... | ... | ... | ... | ... | ... |
| 1865–69 | ... | ... | ... | ... | ... | ... | ... | ... |
| 1870–74 | ... | ... | ... | ... | ... | ... | ... | ... |
| 1875–79 | ... | ... | ... | ... | ... | ... | ... | ... |
| 1880–84 | ... | ... | ... | ... | ... | ... | ... | ... |
| 1885–89 | ... | ... | ... | ... | ... | 44.4 | 32.3 | 176 |
| 1890–94 | ... | ... | ... | ... | ... | 45.5 | 28.2 | 150 |
| 1895–99 | ... | ... | ... | ... | ... | 43.1 | 29.4 | 165 |
| 1900–04 | ... | ... | ... | ... | ... | 41.8 | 29.1 | 169 |
| 1905–09 | ... | ... | ... | ... | ... | 43.6 | 29.8 | 166 |
| 1910–14 | ... | ... | ... | ... | ... | 44.5 | 28.3 | 154 |
| 1915–19 | 46.5 | 30.2 | 188 | ... | ... | 41.4 | 29.7 | 165 |
| 1920–24 | 47.7 | 28.9 | 176 | ... | ... | 41.2 | 26.0 | 153 |
| 1925–29 | 49.1 | 28.2 | 167 | ... | ... | 43.1 | 24.6 | 138 |
| 1930–34 | 48.5 | 25.7 | 154 | ... | ... | 39.9 | 21.9 | 130 |
| 1935–39 | 47.7 | 25.6 | 157 | ... | ... | 40.2 | 21.1 | 130 |
| 1940–44 | 46.0 | 24.0 | 149 | 44.5 | 28.8 | 41.5 | 19.8 | 120 |
| 1945–49 | 45.9 | 20.0 | 134 | 44.9 | 24.7 | 43.6 | 16.1 | 102 |
| 1950–54 | 46.4 | 17.6 | 120 | 45.5 | 22.4 | 44.2 | 12.3 | 88 |
| 1955–59 | 46.5 | 15.7 | 112 | 46.2 | 18.6 | 44.3 | 10.9 | 76 |

NOTE

This table has been included because of the generally acknowledged incompleteness of most Latin American vital statistics, at least until recent times. It is compiled from O. Andrew Collver, *Birth Rates in Latin America: New Estimates of Historical Trends and Fluctuations* (Berkeley Institute of International Studies, University of California, 1965).

**A7      NORTH AMERICA: INFANT MORTALITY RATES**

**1879–1889**

| | Jamaica[1] |
|---|---|
| 1879 | 163 |
| 1880 | 197 |
| 1881 | 173 |
| 1882 | 141 |
| 1883 | 153 |
| 1884 | 166 |
| 1885 | 159 |
| 1886 | 154 |
| 1887 | 170 |
| 1888 | 162 |
| 1889 | 175[1] |
| 1890 | 188 |
| 1891 | 175 |
| 1892 | 164 |
| 1893 | 169 |
| 1894 | 168 |
| 1895 | 178 |
| 1896 | 176 |
| 1897 | 177 |
| 1898 | 175 |
| 1899 | 170 |

| | Barbados | Canada[2] | Costa Rica | Cuba | El Salvador |
|---|---|---|---|---|---|
| 1900 | ... | 187 | ... | ... | ... |
| 1901 | ... | 167 | ... | ... | ... |
| 1902 | ... | 136 | ... | ... | ... |
| 1903 | ... | 134 | ... | ... | ... |
| 1904 | ... | 110 | ... | ... | ... |
| 1905 | ... | ... | ... | ... | ... |
| 1906 | 420 | 130 | ... | ... | ... |
| 1907 | 302 | ... | ... | ... | ... |
| 1908 | 319 | 209 | ... | ... | ... |
| 1909 | 252 | 139 | 199 | ... | ... |
| 1910 | 268 | 174 | 197 | ... | ... |
| 1911 | 263 | 185 | 188 | ... | ... |
| 1912 | 416 | 161 | 187 | ... | ... |
| 1913 | 243 | 168 | 200 | ... | ... |
| 1914 | 403 | 161 | 185 | ... | ... |
| 1915 | 193 | 153 | 178 | ... | ... |
| 1916 | 242 | 165 | 184 | ... | ... |
| 1917 | 289 | 136 | 171 | ... | ... |
| 1918 | 205 | 138 | 218 | ... | ... |
| 1919 | 352 | 142 | 196 | ... | ... |
| 1920 | 270 | 163[2] | 248 | ... | ... |
| 1921 | 401 | 102 | 210 | ... | ... |
| 1922 | 187 | 102 | 225 | ... | ... |
| 1923 | 368 | 103[2] | 216 | ... | ... |
| 1924 | 298 | 94 | 228 | ... | ... |
| 1925 | 312 | 93 | 257 | ... | ... |
| 1926 | 314 | 102 | 178 | ... | ... |
| 1927 | 201 | 95 | 172 | ... | 129 |
| 1928 | 331 | 90 | 169 | ... | 142 |
| 1929 | 239 | 93 | 182 | ... | 156 |
| 1930 | 231 | 91 | 155 | ... | 130 |
| 1931 | 298 | 86 | 179 | ... | 154 |
| 1932 | 198 | 75 | 149 | 113 | 134 |
| 1933 | 235 | 74 | 164 | 132 | 141 |
| 1934 | 256 | 73 | 136 | 100 | 136 |
| 1935 | 220 | 72 | 157 | 127 | 140 |
| 1936 | 198 | 68 | 153 | 106 | 120 |
| 1937 | 217 | 77 | 142 | 87 | 133 |
| 1938 | 221 | 64 | 122 | 83 | 117 |
| 1939 | 194 | 61 | 140 | ... | 116 |

**A7    NORTH AMERICA: Infant Mortality Rates**

| | Guatemala[6] | Honduras[7] | Jamaica[1] | Mexico | Puerto Rico[3] | Trinidad & Tobago | USA | |
|---|---|---|---|---|---|---|---|---|
| | | | | | | | whites | negroes[4] |
| 1900 | ... | ... | 174 | 287 | ... | ... | ... | ... |
| 1901 | ... | ... | 163 | 266 | ... | ... | ... | ... |
| 1902 | ... | ... | 162 | 332 | ... | ... | ... | ... |
| 1903 | ... | ... | 187 | 310 | ... | ... | ... | ... |
| 1904 | ... | ... | 193 | 267 | ... | ... | ... | ... |
| 1905 | ... | ... | 165 | 287 | ... | ... | ... | ... |
| 1906 | ... | ... | 198 | 319 | ... | ... | ... | ... |
| 1907 | ... | ... | 224 | 311 | ... | ... | ... | ... |
| 1908 | ... | ... | 172 | 288 | ... | ... | ... | ... |
| 1909 | ... | ... | 175 | 294 | ... | ... | ... | ... |
| 1910 | ... | ... | 178 | 323 | ... | ... | ... | ... |
| 1911 | ... | ... | 188 | ... | 168 | ... | ... | ... |
| 1912 | ... | ... | 194 | ... | 164 | ... | ... | ... |
| 1913 | ... | ... | 172 | ... | 157 | ... | ... | ... |
| 1914 | ... | ... | 167 | ... | 125 | ... | ... | ... |
| 1915 | ... | ... | $176_1$ | ... | 141 | ... | 99 | 181 |
| 1916 | ... | ... | [176] | ... | 152 | ... | 99 | 185 |
| 1917 | ... | ... | 185 | ... | 199 | ... | 90 | 151 |
| 1918 | ... | ... | 176 | ... | 173 | 138 | 97 | 161 |
| 1919 | ... | ... | 162 | ... | 142 | 155 | 83 | 130 |
| 1920 | ... | ... | 173 | ... | 146 | 175 | 82 | 132 |
| 1921 | ... | ... | 197 | ... | 162 | 140 | 72 | 108 |
| 1922 | ... | ... | 177 | 223 | 152 | 139 | 73 | 110 |
| 1923 | ... | ... | 171 | 222 | 143 | 130 | 73 | 117 |
| 1924 | ... | ... | 161 | 232 | 128 | 124 | 67 | 113 |
| 1925 | ... | ... | 173 | 216 | 148 | 134 | 68 | 111 |
| 1926 | ... | ... | 168 | 209 | 150 | 143 | 70 | 112 |
| 1927 | ... | ... | 173 | 193 | 167 | 121 | 61 | 100 |
| 1928 | ... | ... | 157 | 193 | 146 | 129 | 64 | 106 |
| 1929 | ... | ... | 160 | 168 | 179 | 128 | 63 | 102 |
| 1930 | 84 | 106 | 141 | 132 | 133 | 127 | 60 | 100 |
| 1931 | 84 | 95 | 154 | 138 | $133_3$ | 144 | 57 | 93 |
| 1932 | 84 | ... | 141 | 138 | 132 | 109 | $53^8$ | $86^8$ |
| 1933 | 107 | ... | 150 | 139 | 140 | 131 | $53^8$ | $91^8$ |
| 1934 | 108 | 106 | 132 | 130 | 114 | 127 | $54^8$ | $94^8$ |
| 1935 | 100 | 87 | 138 | 126 | 115 | 99 | 52 | 83 |
| 1936 | 91 | 109 | 131 | 131 | 128 | 97 | 53 | 88 |
| 1937 | 99 | 102 | 118 | 131 | 138 | 120 | 50 | 83 |
| 1938 | $101_6$ | $..._7$ | 129 | 128 | 121 | 98 | 47 | 79 |
| 1939 | 128 | 106 | 121 | 123 | 113 | 104 | 44 | 74 |

**A7      NORTH AMERICA: Infant Mortality Rates**

|      | Barbados | Canada[2] | Costa Rica | Cuba | El Salvador | Guatemala[6] |
|------|----------|-----------|------------|------|-------------|--------------|
| 1940 | 180 | 58 | 132 | ... | 121 | 109 |
| 1941 | 224 | 61 | 123 | ... | 105 | 108 |
| 1942 | 175 | 55 | 157 | ... | 117 | 144 |
| 1943 | 164 | 55 | 117 | 71 | 110 | 120 |
| 1944 | 171 | 56 | 125 | [58][5] | 118 | 115 |
| 1945 | 149 | 52 | 110 | [69][5] | 108 | 97 |
| 1946 | 160 | 48 | 111 | [41][5] | 113 | 114 |
| 1947 | 166 | 46 | 108 | [42][5] | 96 | 110 |
| 1948 | 154 | 44 | 93 | [39][5] | 100 | 117 |
| 1949 | 129 | 43 | 100 | [38][5] | 93 | 102 |
| 1950 | 125 | 42 | 90 | [35][5] | 81 | 107 |
| 1951 | 136 | 39 | 86 | [39][5] | 77 | 92 |
| 1952 | 145 | 38 | 89 | 38 | 85 | 112 |
| 1953 | 139 | 36 | 90 | 38 | 83 | 103 |
| 1954 | 109 | 32 | 81 | 33 | 82 | 88 |
| 1955 | 135 | 31 | 83 | 36 | 77 | 101 |
| 1956 | 97 | 32 | 74 | 34 | 70 | 89 |
| 1957 | 87 | 31 | 82 | 37 | 87 | 100 |
| 1958 | 82 | 30 | 72 | ... | 89 | 104 |
| 1959 | 71 | 28 | 70 | 32 | 78 | 90 |
| 1960 | 60 | 27 | 71 | 35 | 76 | 92 |
| 1961 | 84 | 27 | 65 | 37 | 70 | 85 |
| 1962 | 54 | 28 | 71 | 40 | 71 | 91 |
| 1963 | 62 | 26 | 74 | 36 | 68 | 93 |
| 1964 | 52 | 25 | 82 | 38 | 65 | 88 |
| 1965 | 39 | 24 | 72 | 38 | 71 | 93 |
| 1966 | 48 | 23 | 63 | 38 | 62 | 90 |
| 1967 | 54 | 22 | 60 | 37 | 63 | 89 |
| 1968 | 46 | 21 | 60 | 39 | 59 | 92 |
| 1969 | 42 | 19 | 67 | 47 | 63 | 91 |
| 1970 | 46 | 19 | 61 | 36 | 67 | 87 |
| 1971 | 29 | 18 | 56 | 34 | 52 | 82 |
| 1972 | 31 | 17 | 54 | 27 | 58 | 79 |
| 1973 | 38 | 16 | 45 | 29 | 59 | 80 |
| 1974 | 31 | 15 | 38 | 29 | 53 | 75 |
| 1975 | 33 | 14 | 38 | 27 | 58 | 81 |
| 1976 | 28 | 13 | 33 | 23 | 55 | 76 |
| 1977 | 25 | 12 | 28 | 25 | 59 | 70 |
| 1978 | 30 | 12 | 24 | 22 | 51 | 68 |
| 1979 | 25 | 11 | 23 | 19 | 53 | 70 |
| 1980 | 23 | 10 | 20 | 20 | 42 | 65 |
| 1981 | 17 | 10 | 19 | 18 | 44 | 64 |
| 1982 | 24 | 9 | 19 | 17 | 42 | 64 |
| 1983 | 14 | 8 | 19 | 17 | 44 | 66 |
| 1984 | 13 | 8 | 19 | 15 | 35 | 55 |
| 1985 | 8 | 8 | 19 | 16 | ... | 56 |
| 1986 | 10 | 8 | 18 | 14 | ... | 57 |
| 1987 | 16 | 7 | 17 | 13 | ... | 52 |
| 1988 | 15 | 7 | 15 | 12 | ... | 47 |

**A7    NORTH AMERICA: Infant Mortality Rates**

| | Honduras[7] | Jamaica | Mexico | Puerto Rico[3] | Trinidad & Tobago | USA | |
|---|---|---|---|---|---|---|---|
| | | | | | | whites | negroes[4] |
| 1940 | 109 | 112 | 126 | 114 | 106 | 43 | 74 |
| 1941 | 106 | 104 | 123 | 116 | 109 | 41 | 75 |
| 1942 | 110 | 98 | 118 | 103 | 119 | 37 | 65 |
| 1943 | 127 | 93 | 117 | 96 | 93 | 37 | 62 |
| 1944 | 109[7] | 99 | 114 | 99 | 80 | 37 | 60 |
| 1945 | ... | 102 | 108 | 93 | 84 | 36 | 57 |
| 1946 | 90 | 89 | 111 | 84 | 79 | 32 | 49 |
| 1947 | 89 | 92 | 96 | 71 | 81 | 30 | 48 |
| 1948 | 94 | 87 | 102 | 78 | 75 | 30 | 46 |
| 1949 | 93 | 81 | 106 | 68 | 80 | 29 | 47 |
| 1950 | 86 | 78 | 96 | 67 | 80 | 27 | 44 |
| 1951 | 55 | 81 | 99 | 67 | 78 | 26 | 45 |
| 1952 | 64 | 75 | 90 | 66 | 89 | 25 | 47 |
| 1953 | 64 | 64 | 95 | 63 | 70 | 25 | 45 |
| 1954 | 60 | 67 | 81 | 58 | 60 | 24 | 43 |
| 1955 | 55 | 63 | 83 | 56 | 68 | 24 | 43 |
| 1956 | 53 | 55 | 71 | 55 | 64 | 23 | 42 |
| 1957 | 59 | 55 | 80 | 50 | 56 | 23 | 44 |
| 1958 | 65 | 62 | 80 | 53 | 63 | 24 | 46 |
| 1959 | 54 | 70 | 74 | 48 | 62 | 23 | 44 |
| 1960 | 52 | 51 | 74 | 43 | 45 | 23 | 43 |
| 1961 | 50 | 49 | 70 | 41 | 45 | 22 | 41 |
| 1962 | 44 | 50 | 70 | 42 | 38 | 22 | 41 |
| 1963 | 47 | 50 | 69 | 45 | 41 | 22 | 41 |
| 1964 | 45 | 40 | 65 | 52 | 35 | 22 | 41 |
| 1965 | 41 | 39 | 61 | 39 | 38 | 21 | 40 |
| 1966 | 38 | 35 | 63 | 39 | 42 | 21 | 39 |
| 1967 | 35 | 30 | 63 | 37 | 36 | 20 | 36 |
| 1968 | 34 | 35 | 64 | 33 | 37 | 19 | 34 |
| 1969 | 36 | 33 | 68 | 39 | 40 | 18 | 33 |
| 1970 | 33 | 32 | 69 | 34 | 34 | 18 | 31 |
| 1971 | 39 | 27 | 63 | 27 | 31 | 17 | 28 |
| 1972 | 43 | 31 | 61 | 27 | 25 | 16 | 28 |
| 1973 | 40 | 26 | 52 | 24 | 26 | 16 | 26 |
| 1974 | 34 | 26 | 47 | 23 | 26 | 15 | 25 |
| 1975 | 34 | 23 | 53 | 21 | 26 | 14 | 24 |
| 1976 | 31 | 20 | 52 | 20 | 25 | 13 | 23 |
| 1977 | 29 | 15 | 49 | 20 | 21 | 12 | 22 |
| 1978 | 27 | ... | 40 | 18 | 20 | 12 | 21 |
| 1979 | ... | ... | 39 | 20 | 18 | 11 | 20 |
| 1980 | ... | ... | 39 | 19 | 22 | 11 | 19 |
| 1981 | ... | ... | 33 | 19 | 16 | 10 | 18 |
| 1982 | ... | ... | 33 | 17 | 16 | 10 | 17 |
| 1983 | ... | 12 | 30 | 17 | 13 | 10 | 17 |
| 1984 | ... | 13 | 29 | 16 | 14 | 9 | 16 |
| 1985 | ... | ... | 25 | 15 | 12 | 9 | 16 |
| 1986 | ... | ... | ... | 14 | 11 | 9 | 16 |
| 1987 | ... | ... | ... | 14 | 11 | 9 | 15 |
| 1988 | ... | ... | ... | 13 | ... | 8 | 15 |

**A7   SOUTH AMERICA: INFANT MORTALITY RATES** (in thousands)

|      | Argentina | Chile | Colombia | Guyana* | Peru | Uruguay | Venezuela |
|------|-----------|-------|----------|---------|------|---------|-----------|
| 1901 | ... | 340 | ... | ... | ... | ... | ... |
| 1902 | ... | 270 | ... | ... | ... | ... | ... |
| 1903 | ... | 264 | ... | 205 | ... | ... | ... |
| 1904 | ... | 286 | ... | 201 | ... | ... | ... |
| 1905 | ... | 249 | ... | 187 | ... | ... | ... |
| 1906 | ... | 327 | ... | 201 | ... | ... | ... |
| 1907 | ... | 298 | ... | 256 | ... | ... | ... |
| 1908 | ... | 318 | ... | 198 | ... | ... | ... |
| 1909 | ... | 315 | ... | 209 | ... | ... | ... |
| 1910 | ... | 267 | ... | 235 | ... | ... | ... |
| 1911 | 148 | 333 | ... | 229 | ... | ... | ... |
| 1912 | 143 | 287 | ... | 190 | ... | ... | ... |
| 1913 | 130 | 286 | ... | 179 | ... | ... | ... |
| 1914 | 125 | 255 | ... | 170 | ... | ... | ... |
| 1915 | 124 | 254 | ... | 184 | ... | ... | ... |
| 1916 | 124 | 241 | ... | 190 | ... | ... | ... |
| 1917 | 128 | 269 | ... | 199 | ... | ... | ... |
| 1918 | 138 | 255 | ... | 223 | ... | ... | ... |
| 1919 | 134 | 306 | ... | 185 | ... | ... | ... |
| 1920 | 127 | 263 | ... | 148 | ... | ... | ... |
| 1921 | 116 | 278 | ... | 195 | ... | 107 | ... |
| 1922 | 112 | 240 | ... | 186 | ... | 94 | ... |
| 1923 | 112 | 283 | ... | 177 | ... | 104 | ... |
| 1924 | 116 | 266 | 142 | 165 | ... | 108 | ... |
| 1925 | 121 | 258 | 122 | 155 | ... | 115 | ... |
| 1926 | 119 | 251 | 148 | 159 | ... | 93 | ... |
| 1927 | 126 | 226 | 144 | 158 | ... | 106 | ... |
| 1928 | 113 | 212 | 129 | 185 | ... | 100 | ... |
| 1929 | 107 | 224 | 123 | 146 | ... | 93 | ... |
| 1930 | 100 | 234 | 106 | 146 | ... | 100 | 150 |
| 1931 | 100 | 232 | 125 | 139 | ... | 110 | 156 |
| 1932 | 95 | 235 | ... | 139 | ... | 99 | ... |
| 1933 | 87 | 258 | 143 | 154 | ... | 93 | 162 |
| 1934 | 97 | 262 | 117 | 168 | ... | 96 | 158 |
| 1935 | 106 | 251 | 156 | 122 | ... | 102 | 137 |
| 1936 | 97 | 252 | 153 | 120 | ... | 92 | 134 |
| 1937 | 95 | 241 | 150 | 121 | ... | 96 | 135 |
| 1938 | 103 | 236 | 156 | 166 | ... | 99 | 139 |
| 1939 | 90 | 225 | 162 | 120 | ... | 82 | 132 |

**A7      SOUTH AMERICA: Infant Mortality Rates** (in thousands)

| | Argentina | Chile | Colombia | Guyana* | Peru | Uruguay | Venezuela |
|---|---|---|---|---|---|---|---|
| 1940 | 90 | 217 | 142 | 104 | 128 | 86 | 122 |
| 1941 | 85 | 200 | 150 | 84 | 131 | 83 | 121 |
| 1942 | 86 | 195 | 154 | 97 | 115 | 93 | 115 |
| 1943 | 80 | 194 | 157 | 141 | 126 | 78 | 109 |
| 1944 | 81 | 181 | 155 | 136 | 115 | 66 | 117 |
| 1945 | 82 | 184 | 151 | 101 | 109 | ... | 99 |
| 1946 | 74 | 160 | 150 | 87 | 113 | 62 | 102 |
| 1947 | 78 | 161 | 140 | 85 | 107 | 71 | 100 |
| 1948 | 69 | 147 | 136 | 78 | 109 | 61 | 98 |
| 1949 | 67 | 155 | 134 | 77 | 105 | 52 | 91 |
| 1950 | 68 | 139 | 124 | 86 | 104 | 64 | 81 |
| 1951 | 67 | 135 | 120 | 77 | 105 | 55 | 80 |
| 1952 | 65 | 129 | 111 | 82 | 100 | 51 | 79 |
| 1953 | 63 | 112 | 120 | 81 | 105 | 51 | 74 |
| 1954 | 60 | 125 | 103 | 73 | 95 | 49 | 69 |
| 1955 | 62 | 120 | 104 | 70 | 95 | 47 | 70 |
| 1956 | 57 | 110 | 104 | 68 | 96 | 44 | 67 |
| 1957 | 68 | 114 | 100 | 68 | 108 | 53 | 66 |
| 1958 | 61 | 121 | 104 | 62 | 103 | 49 | 58 |
| 1959 | 59 | 117 | 97 | 57 | 97 | 57 | 61 |
| 1960 | 62 | 125 | 100 | 63 | 92 | 47 | 54 |
| 1961 | 59 | 111 | 90 | 51 | 89 | 42 | 53 |
| 1962 | 59 | 115 | 90 | 49 | 80 | 42 | 47 |
| 1963 | 62 | 105 | 90 | 54 | 85 | 44 | 48 |
| 1964 | 59 | 108 | 83 | 41 | 54 | 45 | 49 |
| 1965 | 57 | 107 | 82 | 52 | 74 | 50 | 48 |
| 1966 | 57 | 108 | 80 | 45 | 64 | 43 | 47 |
| 1967 | 56 | 100 | 78 | 47 | 72 | 59 | 41 |
| 1968 | 55 | 92 | 70 | 42 | 74 | 54 | 43 |
| 1969 | 53 | 87 | 61 | 41 | 75 | 49 | 43 |
| 1970 | 52 | 79 | 50 | 38 | 65 | 43 | 49 |
| 1971 | 50 | 78 | 45 | 42 | 54 | 48 | 50 |
| 1972 | 49 | 77 | 53 | 50 | 58 | 50 | 53 |
| 1973 | 47 | 66 | 89 | 46 | ... | 50 | 54 |
| 1974 | 46 | 65 | 50 | ... | ...9 | 48 | 46 |
| 1975 | 44 | 58 | 47 | ... | 107 | 49 | 44 |
| 1976 | 43 | 57 | 47 | ... | 106 | 46 | 43 |
| 1977 | 41 | 50 | 39 | ... | 105 | 48 | 39 |
| 1978 | 38 | 40 | ... | ... | 104 | 44 | 35 |
| 1979 | 33 | 38 | ... | ... | 103 | 40 | 33 |
| 1980 | 33 | 33 | ... | ... | 101 | 38 | 32 |
| 1981 | 34 | 27 | ... | ... | 100 | 33 | |
| 1982 | 30 | 24 | ... | ... | 99 | 29 | 28 |
| 1983 | 30 | 22 | ... | ... | 97 | 28 | 26 |
| 1984 | 30 | 20 | ... | ... | 95 | 30 | 27 |
| 1985 | 25 | 19 | ... | ... | 93 | 29 | 26 |
| 1986 | 26 | 19 | ... | ... | 90 | 28 | 25 |
| 1987 | 26 | 18 | ... | ... | 95 | 24 | 24 |
| 1988 | 26 | 19 | ... | ... | 95 | ... | 21 |

**A7      Infant Mortality Rates**

NOTES

1.   SOURCES: As for table B5.
2.   The data relate to deaths of infants under one year old per 1,000 live births.

FOOTNOTES

[1] Data to 1889 are for years ending 30 September. From 1890 to 1915 they are for years ending 31 March in the year following that shown. The rate for the six months from 1 October 1889 to 31 March 1890 was on an annual basis. The 1916 figure is for the last three quarters of the year.
[2] Province of Quebec only to 1920. Subsequently the present territory (including Newfoundland), but excluding Yukon and Northwest Territories in 1921–23.
[3] Data to 1931 are for years ending 30 June.
[4] i.e. non-whites.
[5] Excluding infants dying within 24 hours of birth.
[6] Data to 1938 exclude the live-born who died immediately.
[7] Data to 1937 are for years ending 31 July, and from 1939 to 1944 they are for years ending 30 June.
[8] Mexicans are included with negroes.
[9] Subsequent figures are from national sources. The U.N. *Demographic Yearbooks* give a different series for 1982 onwards, *viz.*

| 1982 | 95 | 1984 | 136 | 1986 | ... | 1988 | 95 |
| 1983 | 141 | 1985 | 91 | 1987 | 122 | | |

**A8      NORTH AMERICA: INTERNATIONAL MIGRATIONS** (in thousands)

Key:      a = Immigrants (cabin and other passengers) through Montreal and Quebec
          b = Immigrant arrivals
          c = East Indian immigrants less those repatriated
          d = Immigrants less those repatriated
          e = Emigrant departures
          f = Arrivals by sea less departures
          g = Polynesian and Indian immigrants less those repatriated
          h = Total arrivals less departures i = Total arrivals
          j = Total departures

## 1815–1859

|      | Canada | Guadeloupe | | Jamaica[1] | Trinidad & Tobago[3] | USA[4] |
|------|--------|------|------|------|------|------|
|      | a | b | c | d | d | b |
| 1815 | 1.2 | ... | ... | ... | ... | ... |
| 1816 | ... | ... | ... | ... | ... | ... |
| 1817 | ... | ... | ... | ... | ... | ... |
| 1818 | ... | ... | ... | ... | ... | ... |
| 1819 | ... | ... | ... | ... | ... | ... |
| 1820 | ... | ... | ... | ... | ... | 8.4 |
| 1821 | ... | ... | ... | ... | ... | 9.1 |
| 1822 | ... | ... | ... | ... | ... | 6.9 |
| 1823 | ... | ... | ... | ... | ... | 6.4 |
| 1824 | ... | ... | ... | ... | ... | 7.9 |
| 1825 | ... | ... | ... | ... | ... | 10 |
| 1826 | ... | ... | ... | ... | ... | 11 |
| 1827 | 16 | ... | ... | ... | ... | 19 |
| 1828 | 13 | ... | ... | ... | ... | 27 |
| 1829 | 16 | ... | ... | ... | ... | 23 |
| 1830 | 28 | ... | ... | ... | ... | 23 |
| 1831 | 50 | ... | ... | ... | ... | 23 |
| 1832 | 52 | ... | ... | ... | ... | [60][4] |
| 1833 | 22 | ... | ... | ... | ... | 59 |
| 1834 | 31 | ... | ... | - - | ... | 65 |
| 1835 | 13 | ... | ... | 0.9 | ... | 45 |
| 1836 | 28 | ... | ... | 1.2 | ... | 76 |
| 1837 | 22 | ... | ... | 0.4 | ... | 79 |
| 1838 | 3.3 | ... | ... | − | ... | 39 |
| 1839 | 7.4 | ... | ... | − | 1.0 | 68 |
| 1840 | 22 | ... | ... | 0.1 | 2.0 | 84 |
| 1841 | 28 | ... | ... | 2.2 | 2.0 | 80 |
| 1842 | 44 | ... | ... | 1.0 | 2.9 | 105 |
| 1843 | 22 | ... | ... | 0.4 | 2.8 | [52][4] |
| 1844 | 20 | ... | ... | 0.5 | 2.5 | 79 |
| 1845 | 25 | ... | ... | 0.6 | 1.6 | 114 |
| 1846 | 33 | ... | ... | 2.4 | 2.9 | 154 |
| 1847 | 74 | ... | ... | 2.5 | 3.1 | 235 |
| 1848 | 28 | ... | ... | 1.9 | 0.9 | 227 |
| 1849 | 38 | ... | ... | 1.1 | 1.9 | 297 |
| 1850 | 32 | ... | ... | 0.5 | 0.8 | 310₄ |
| 1851 | 41 | ... | ... | 0.8 | −0.2 | 379 |
| 1852 | 39 | 29 | ... | - - | 1.1 | 372 |
| 1853 | 37 | 29 | ... | −1.1 | 2.5 | 369 |
| 1854 | 53 | 37 | 0.3 | - - | 0.7 | 428 |
| 1855 | 21 | 25 | 0.4 | 0.2 | 0.1 | 201 |
| 1856 | 22 | 23 | 1.1 | − | 0.3 | 200 |
| 1857 | 32 | 34 | 1.4 | 0.4 | 1.2 | 251 |
| 1858 | 13 | 12 | 1.4 | −0.1 | 1.8 | 123 |
| 1859 | 8.8 | 6.3 | 1.7 | − | 3.4 | 121 |

**A8    NORTH AMERICA: International Migrations** (in thousands)

| | Canada | | Guadeloupe | Jamaica[1] | Trinidad & Tobago[3] | USA[4] |
|---|---|---|---|---|---|---|
| | a | b | c | d | d | b |
| 1860 | 10 | 6.3 | 0.8 | 0.6 | 2.9 | 154 |
| 1861 | 20 | 14 | 1.9 | 2.1 | 2.2 | 92 |
| 1862 | 22 | 18 | 0.9 | 2.6 | 2.1 | 92 |
| 1863 | 19 | 21 | 1.5 | 1.1 | 1.8 | 176 |
| 1864 | 19 | 25 | 0.6 | — | 0.9 | 193 |
| 1865 | 21 | 19 | 0.2 | — | 2.8 | 248 |
| 1866 | 29 | 11 | 1.2 | — | 2.4 | 319 |
| 1867 | 31 | 11 | 3.1 | 1.6 | 3.3 | 316 |
| 1868 | 34 | 13 | 1.0 | — | 1.4 | [139][4] |
| 1869 | 43 | 19 | 0.9 | 1.4 | 3.0 | 353 |
| 1870 | 44 | 25 | 0.9 | 0.9 | 1.5 | 387 |
| 1871 | 37 | 28 | 0.6 | 0.4 | 1.3 | 321 |
| 1872 | 35 | 37 | 0.5 | 1.1 | 3.2$_3$ | 405 |
| 1873 | 37 | 50 | 1.4 | [1.6][2] | 2.9 | 460 |
| 1874 | 24 | 39 | 1.3 | [1.4][2] | 2.1 | 313 |
| 1875 | 16 | 27 | 0.8 | [1.2][2] | 3.3 | 227 |
| 1876 | 11 | 26 | 1.3 | ... | 1.0 | 170 |
| 1877 | 7.7 | 27 | 0.9 | ... | 1.2 | 142 |
| 1878 | 10 | 30 | 2.2 | ... | 2.6 | 138 |
| 1879 | 17 | 40 | 2.1 | ... | 2.1 | 178 |
| 1880 | 25 | 39 | 2.7 | ... | 2.7 | 457 |
| 1881 | ... | 48 | 2.8 | ... | 2.2 | 669 |
| 1882 | ... | 112 | 0.5 | ... | 2.6 | 789 |
| 1883 | ... | 134 | 1.3 | ... | 1.5 | 603 |
| 1884 | ... | 104 | ... | ... | 2.5 | 519 |
| 1885 | ... | 79 | ... | ... | 1.1 | 395 |
| 1886 | ... | 69 | ... | ... | 1.6 | 334 |
| 1887 | ... | 85 | ... | ... | 1.5 | 490 |
| 1888 | ... | 89 | ... | ... | 1.4 | 547 |
| 1889 | ... | 92 | ... | ... | 2.6 | 444 |
| 1890 | ... | 75 | ... | ... | 2.3 | 455 |
| 1891 | ... | 82 | ... | ... | 2.9 | 560 |
| 1892 | ... | 31 | ... | ... | 2.6 | 580 |
| 1893 | ... | 30 | ... | ... | 1.2 | 440 |
| 1894 | ... | 21 | ... | ... | 1.8 | 286 |
| 1895 | ... | 19 | ... | ... | 1.8 | 259 |
| 1896 | ... | 17 | ... | ... | 2.4 | 343 |
| 1897 | ... | 22 | ... | ... | 1.1 | 231 |
| 1898 | ... | 32 | ... | ... | 0.5 | 229 |
| 1899 | ... | 45 | ... | ... | 0.5$_3$ | 312 |

**A8     NORTH AMERICA: International Migrations** (in thousands)

| | Canada | Cuba | Dominican Rep. | El Salvador | Guatemala | Jamaica[1] | Mexico[8] | | Trinidad & Tobago[3] | USA[4] |
|---|---|---|---|---|---|---|---|---|---|---|
| | b | b | h | h | h | h | b | e | d | b |
| 1900 | 42 | ... | ... | ... | ... | ... | ... | ... | −0.1 | 449 |
| 1901 | 56 | 23 | ... | ... | ... | ... | ... | ... | 1.8 | 488 |
| 1902 | 89 | 12 | ... | ... | ... | 0.8 | ... | ... | 1.6 | 649 |
| 1903 | 139 | 18 | ... | ... | ... | -- - | ... | ... | 1.7 | 857 |
| 1904 | 131 | 29 | ... | ... | ... | −3.1 | ... | ... | 0.5 | 813 |
| 1905 | 141 | 54 | ... | ... | ... | −3.9 | ... | ... | 2.9 | 1,026 |
| 1906 | 212 | 35 | ... | ... | ... | ... | ... | ... | 1.7 | 1,101 |
| 1907 | 272 | 32 | ... | ... | ... | ... | ... | ... | 1.1 | 1,285 |
| 1908 | 143 | 28 | ... | ... | ... | −0.8 | ... | ... | 1.7 | 783 |
| 1909 | 174 | 31 | ... | ... | ... | −3.0 | 42 | ... | 1.9 | 752 |
| 1910 | 287 | 38 | ... | ... | ... | −4.9 | 50 | ... | 2.6 | 1,042 |
| 1911 | 331 | 38 | ... | ... | ... | 0.2 | 38 | 36 | 2.7 | 879 |
| 1912 | 376 | 38 | ... | ... | ... | −1.8 | 41 | 38 | 1.8 | 838 |
| 1913 | 401 | 44 | ... | ... | ... | −2.6 | 27 | 26 | 0.4 | 1,198 |
| 1914 | 150 | 26 | ... | ... | ... | 2.9 | 9.2 | 7.1 | 0.4 | 1,218 |
| 1915 | 37 | 33 | ... | ... | ... | [−2.3][1] | 7.2 | 6.8 | [- -][3] | 327 |
| 1916 | 56 | 55 | ... | ... | ... | −2.5 | 13 | 11 | 0.5 | 299 |
| 1917 | 73 | 57 | ... | ... | ... | −8.7₁ | 18 | 9.7 | 0.7₃ | 295 |
| | | | | | | | | | h | |
| 1918 | 42 | 37 | ... | ... | ... | −4.1 | 9.7 | 8.5 | 0.8 | 111 |
| 1919 | 108 | 80 | ... | ... | ... | −14 | 16 | 13 | 3.2 | 141 |
| 1920 | 139 | 174 | ... | ... | ... | 2.2 | 21 | 13 | 2.1 | 430 |
| 1921 | 92 | 59 | ... | ... | ... | 2.6 | 37 | 22 | 3.1 | 805 |
| 1922 | 64 | 26 | ... | ... | ... | 1.9 | 36 | 25 | 2.2 | 310 |
| 1923 | 134 | 75 | ... | ... | ... | −5.1 | 41 | 32 | −1.7 | 523 |
| 1924 | 124 | 85 | ... | ... | ... | −3.5 | 41 | 30 | −1.6 | 707 |
| 1925 | 85 | 56 | ... | ... | 0.5 | 0.2 | 44 | 30 | −1.5 | 294 |
| 1926 | 136 | 32 | ... | ... | 0.8 | 3.6 | 35 | 30 | −1.5 | 304 |
| 1927 | 159 | 31 | ... | ... | 0.3 | 3.9 | 26 | 19 | −0.3 | 335 |
| 1928 | 167 | 27 | ... | ... | 0.6 | 5.4 | 30₈ | 17₈ | 1.6 | 307 |
| 1929 | 165 | 17 | ... | ... | −0.2 | 4.1 | 85 | 43 | 1.3 | 280 |
| 1930 | 105 | 12 | ... | ... | −0.2 | 7.6 | 85 | 32 | 4.9 | 242 |
| 1931 | 28 | 3 | ... | ... | 0.3 | 12 | 135 | 22 | 1.6 | 97 |
| 1932 | 21 | 2 | ... | ... | −0.3 | 6.8 | 82 | 10 | − | 36 |
| 1933 | 14 | 3 | ... | ... | −0.8 | 2.1 | 37 | 7.6 | 1.1 | 23 |
| 1934 | 12 | 3 | ... | 0.8 | −0.9 | −1.0 | 28 | 8.1 | 1.3 | 29 |
| 1935 | 11 | 4 | ... | 1.9 | −1.0 | −0.6 | 19 | 9.2 | 1.2 | 35 |
| 1936 | 12 | 4 | −0.1 | 3.2 | 0.2 | −3.2 | 16 | 8.0 | 0.9 | 36 |
| 1937 | 15 | ... | −6.2 | 1.3 | -- - | −3.9 | 12 | 6.5 | 1.4 | 50 |
| 1938 | 17 | ... | 0.1 | −1.1 | 0.3 | 2.3 | 13 | 5.9 | 1.0 | 68 |
| 1939 | 17 | ... | 1.2 | 2.6 | ... | 1.9 | 2.3 | 4.7 | 1.5 | 83 |
| 1940 | 11 | ... | 1.5 | 1.0 | ... | 4.7 | 15 | 5.4 | 2.4 | 71 |
| 1941 | 9 | ... | −0.7 | 0.2 | 1.6 | 2.5 | 9.0 | 7.0 | 13 | 52 |
| 1942 | 8 | ... | −0.6 | 0.7 | 0.6 | - - | 9.8 | 6.1 | 7.2 | 29 |
| 1943 | 9 | ... | −0.4 | −5.7 | −0.7 | −2.5 | 6.5 | 7.3 | 1.8 | 24 |
| 1944 | 13 | ... | −1.3 | ... | −0.3 | 14 | 9.7 | 6.9 | −2.3 | 29 |

**A8**    **NORTH AMERICA: International Migrations** (in thousands)

| | Canada | Cuba | Dominican Republic | El Salvador | Guatemala | Jamaica[1] | Mexico | | Trinidad & Tobago[3] | USA[4] |
|---|---|---|---|---|---|---|---|---|---|---|
| | b | b | h | h | h | h | b | e | d | b |
| 1945 | 23 | ... | −1.5 | −1.4 | 0.9 | −4.6 | 9.4 | 9.2 | −1.7 | 38 |
| 1946 | 72 | ... | 1.2 | 0.8 | 2.1 | −2.3 | 10 | 13 | 1.5 | 109 |
| 1947 | 64 | ... | 1.6 | −0.6 | 0.7 | −1.8 | 9.1 | 11 | 3.6 | 147 |
| | | h | | | | | | | | |
| 1948 | 125 | −4 | −0.3 | 2.3 | ... | −2.0 | 8.9 | 11 | −0.5 | 171 |
| 1949 | 95 | −3 | 0.2 | 1.1 | ... | −0.3 | 11 | 14 | 0.4 | 188 |
| 1950 | 74 | 3 | −1.0 | 0.8 | | −11.0 | 13 | 13 | 1.2 | 249 |
| 1951 | 194 | 1 | −1.1 | 1.1 | −-- | −4.5 | 23 | 15 | −0.8 | 206 |
| 1952 | 164 | 1 | −1.5 | 9.5 | 0.6 | −3.9 | 24 | 17 | −1.6 | 266 |
| 1953 | 169 | ... | −1.5 | −0.1 | −0.3 | −4.3 | 28 | 13 | - - | 170 |
| 1954 | 154 | ... | −0.5 | ... | 1.4 | −8.4 | 29 | 16 | −0.4 | 208 |
| 1955 | 110 | ... | 4.7 | ... | 2.4 | −19.0 | 27 | 20 | −0.2 | 238 |
| 1956 | 171 | ... | −1.9 | −2.4 | −-- | −18.0 | 29 | 23 | 6.1 | 322 |
| 1957 | 289 | ... | −2.6 | 2.2 | 2.2 | −1.4 | 35 | 20 | 0.9 | 327 |
| 1958 | 132 | ... | 8.6 | 1.4 | −5.0 | −11.0 | 36 | 20 | 3.7 | 253 |
| 1959 | 107 | ... | ... | ... | −1.6 | −21.0 | 40 | 20 | 4.8 | 261 |
| 1960 | 104 | −38 | −1.7 | 4.2 | −8.4 | −34.0 | 43 | 22 | −0.1 | 265 |
| 1961 | 72 | −68 | 2.5 | 1.7 | −0.1 | −39.0 | 43 | 22 | 0.4 | 271 |
| 1962 | 75 | −66 | −6.7 | −3.4 | 0.9 | −32.0 | 46 | 28 | 2.5 | 284 |
| 1963 | 93 | −12 | −0.9 | 0.3 | 4.7 | −1.5 | 49 | 34 | 3.1 | 306 |
| 1964 | 113 | −12 | −11 | 1.0 | −4.4 | −14.0 | 56 | 36 | −0.4 | 292 |
| 1965 | 147 | −17 | −2.3 | −1.8 | 6.9 | 5.1 | 58 | 55 | −3.0 | 297 |
| 1966 | 195 | ... | −9.7 | 4.5 | 47.0 | −2.9 | 61 | 60 | −5.1 | 323 |
| 1967 | 223 | ... | −13 | 4.0 | −3.9 | −16.0 | 73 | 60 | −9.0 | 362 |
| 1968 | 184 | ... | −15 | 3.1 | 9.3 | ... | 116 | 66 | −9.1 | 454 |
| 1969 | 162 | ... | −16 | 4.7 | −11.0 | −29.0 | 111 | 65 | −16 | 359 |
| 1970 | 148 | ... | −9.4 | −2.0 | 12.0 | −23 | 165 | 65 | −17 | 373 |
| 1971 | 122 | ... | ... | −0.9 | 18.0 | −32 | 184 | 61 | −7.5 | 370 |
| 1972 | 122 | ... | −6.0 | −24.1 | 7.6 | −10 | 220 | 66 | −7.0 | 385 |
| 1973 | 184 | ... | −2.5 | −10.0 | 47.0 | −10 | 317 | 74 | −9.6 | 400 |
| 1974 | 218 | ... | −15.6 | −2.5 | 94.0 | −13 | 101 | 79 | −6.7 | 395 |
| 1975 | 188 | ... | −9.9 | −19.4 | 183 | −12 | 96 | 79 | −7.8 | 386 |
| 1976 | 149 | ... | ... | −2.5 | 65 | −22 | 158 | 74 | −2.2 | 399 |
| 1977 | 115 | ... | ... | −26.6 | ... | −21 | 111 | 66 | −2.6 | 462 |
| 1978 | 86 | ... | ... | −54.2 | ... | −18 | 275 | 80 | −10.5 | 601 |
| 1979 | 112 | ... | ... | −59.6 | ... | −21 | 145 | 76 | −9.3 | 460 |
| 1980 | 143 | ... | ... | −80.6 | ... | −24.0 | 213 | 87 | −4.0 | 531 |
| 1981 | 129 | ... | ... | −23.6 | ... | −5.9 | 248 | 94 | −3.2 | 597 |
| 1982 | 121 | ... | ... | −124.9 | ... | −9.8 | 148 | 75 | +2.2 | 594 |
| 1983 | 189 | ... | ... | −60.7 | ... | −4.3 | ... | 70 | +1.1 | 560 |
| 1984 | 88 | ... | ... | −40.1 | ... | −10.0 | ... | 87 | −11.8 | 544 |
| 1985 | 84 | ... | −113 | −27.4 | ... | −13 | ... | 73 | −7.4 | 570 |
| 1986 | 99 | ... | −158 | ... | ... | −20 | ... | ... | −15.4 | 602 |
| 1987 | 152 | ... | ... | ... | ... | −31 | ... | ... | −10.7 | 602 |
| 1988 | 162 | ... | ... | ... | ... | −39 | ... | ... | ... | 643 |

**A8    SOUTH AMERICA: INTERNATIONAL MIGRATIONS** (in thousands)

**1815–1834**

| | Brazil[5] |
| --- | --- |
| | b |
| 1815 | ... |
| 1816 | ... |
| 1817 | ... |
| 1818 | ... |
| 1819 | ... |
| 1820 | 1.7 |
| 1821 | ... |
| 1822 | ... |
| 1823 | ... |
| 1824 | 0.1 |
| 1825 | 0.9 |
| 1826 | 0.8 |
| 1827 | 1.1 |
| 1828 | 2.1 |
| 1829 | 2.4 |
| 1830 | ... |
| 1831 | ... |
| 1832 | ... |
| 1833 | ... |
| 1834 | ... |

**1835–1884**

| | Argentina[6] | | Brazil[5] | Guyana*[7] | Paraguay | Uruguay | |
| --- | --- | --- | --- | --- | --- | --- | --- |
| | b | e | b | d | b | b | e |
| 1835 | ... | ... | ... | 0.6 | ... | 0.6 | ... |
| 1836 | ... | ... | 1.2 | 1.1 | ... | 3.1 | ... |
| 1837 | ... | ... | 0.6 | 1.8 | ... | 2.6 | ... |
| 1838 | ... | ... | 0.4 | 1.9 | ... | 5.4 | ... |
| 1839 | ... | ... | 0.4 | 0.2 | ... | 1.2 | ... |
| 1840 | ... | ... | 0.3 | 0.9 | ... | 2.5 | ... |
| 1841 | ... | ... | 0.6 | 8.1 | ... | 7.9 | ... |
| 1842 | ... | ... | 0.6 | 2.7 | ... | 9.9 | ... |
| 1843 | ... | ... | 0.7 | 0.6 | ... | ... | ... |
| 1844 | ... | ... | ... | 0.9 | ... | ... | ... |
| 1845 | ... | ... | 0.1 | 3.6 | ... | ... | ... |
| 1846 | ... | ... | 0.4 | 12.0 | ... | ... | ... |
| 1847 | ... | ... | 2.4 | 7.8 | ... | ... | ... |
| 1848 | ... | ... | - - | 5.5 | ... | ... | ... |
| 1849 | ... | ... | - - | 0.2 | ... | ... | ... |
| | | | | d | | | |
| 1850 | ... | ... | 2.1 | 2.0 | ... | ... | ... |
| 1851 | ... | ... | 4.4 | 1.3 | ... | ... | ... |
| 1852 | ... | ... | 2.7 | 3.6 | ... | ... | ... |
| 1853 | ... | ... | 11.0 | 5.3 | ... | ... | ... |
| 1854 | ... | ... | 9.2 | 2.3 | ... | ... | ... |
| 1855 | ... | ... | 12 | 3.4 | ... | ... | ... |
| 1856 | ... | ... | 14 | 2.0 | ... | ... | ... |
| 1857 | 5.0 | ... | 14 | 2.3 | ... | ... | ... |
| 1858 | 4.7 | ... | 19 | 2.9 | ... | ... | ... |
| 1859 | 4.7 | ... | 20 | 4.0 | ... | ... | ... |
| 1860 | 5.7 | ... | 16.0 | 8.2 | ... | ... | ... |
| 1861 | 6.3 | ... | 13.0 | 7.2 | ... | ... | ... |
| 1862 | 6.7 | ... | 14.0 | 8.4 | ... | ... | ... |
| 1863 | 10.0 | ... | 7.6 | 3.1 | ... | ... | ... |
| 1864 | 12.0 | ... | 9.6 | 7.9 | ... | ... | ... |
| 1865 | 12 | ... | 6.5 | 7.0 | ... | ... | ... |
| 1866 | 14 | ... | 7.7 | 4.2 | ... | 9.3 | ... |
| 1867 | 13 | ... | 11.0 | 4.6 | ... | 17.0 | ... |
| 1868 | 26 | ... | 11.0 | 3.3 | ... | 17.0 | ... |
| 1869 | 29 | ... | 12.0 | 7.9 | ... | 20.0 | ... |
| 1870 | 31 | ... | 5.2 | 5.6 | ... | 21 | ... |
| 1871 | 15 | 11.0 | 12.0 | 3.1 | ... | 18 | ... |
| 1872 | 26 | 9.2 | 19.0 | 5.5 | ... | 12 | ... |
| 1873 | 48 | 18.0 | 15.0 | 11 | ... | 24 | ... |
| 1874 | 41 | 21.0 | 20.0 | 7.2 | ... | 14 | ... |
| 1875 | 18 | 26 | 15 | 4.1 | ... | 5.3 | ... |
| 1876 | 15 | 13 | 31 | 3.0 | ... | 5.6 | ... |
| 1877 | 15 | 18 | 29 | 4.5 | ... | 6.2 | ... |
| 1878 | 24 | 15 | 24 | 10.0 | ... | 9.5 | ... |
| 1879 | 33 | 24 | 23 | 7.4 | ... | 11.0 | 7.0 |
| 1880 | 27 | 20.0 | 30 | 3.6 | ... | 9.3 | 6.8 |
| 1881 | 31 | 22.0 | 12 | 2.9[7] | 0.1 | 8.3 | 6.3 |
| 1882 | 41 | 8.7 | 30 | 3.1 | 0.2 | 10.0 | 6.2 |
| 1883 | 52 | 9.5 | 34 | 1.0 | 0.2 | 11.0 | 6.1 |
| 1884 | 50 | 14.0 | 25 | 3.3 | 0.3 | 12.0 | 6.0 |

**A8**     **SOUTH AMERICA: International Migrations** (in thousands)

1885–1929

| | Argentina[6] | | Brazil[5] | Colombia[7] | Guyana*[7] | Paraguay | Uruguay | | Venezuela |
|---|---|---|---|---|---|---|---|---|---|
| | b | e | b | h | d | b | b | e | d |
| 1885 | 81 | 15 | 35 | ... | 5.5 | - - | 16 | 6.7 | ... |
| 1886 | 66 | 14 | 33 | ... | 1.6 | 0.1 | 12 | 6.5 | ... |
| 1887 | 95 | 14 | 56 | ... | 2.9 | 0.8 | 13 | 6.3 | ... |
| 1888 | 129 | 17 | 133 | ... | 1.0 | 1.1 | 17 | 7.6 | ... |
| 1889 | 219 | 41 | 65 | ... | 1.5 | 1.9 | 27 | 11.0 | ... |
| 1890 | 78 | 49 | 107 | ... | 2.5 | 0.8 | 24.0 | 20 | ... |
| 1891 | 28 | 72 | 217 | ... | 2.8 | 0.4 | 12.0 | 20 | ... |
| 1892 | 40 | 30 | 86 | ... | 2.7 | 0.5 | 12.0 | 88 | ... |
| 1893 | 52 | 26 | 135 | ... | 3.4 | 0.5 | 9.5 | 6.3 | ... |
| 1894 | 55 | 21 | 61 | ... | 7.2 | 0.2 | 12.0 | 6.0 | ... |
| 1895 | 61 | 20 | 168 | ... | 0.4 | 0.3 | 9.2 | 6.4 | ... |
| 1896 | 103 | 20 | 158 | ... | 0.3 | 0.2 | 11.0 | 5.9 | ... |
| 1897 | 73 | 31 | 146 | ... | −0.3 | 0.2 | 9.1 | 6.8 | ... |
| 1898 | 67 | 31 | 78 | ... | 1.2 | 0.4 | 9.5 | 6.4 | ... |
| 1899 | 84 | 38 | 55 | ... | 3.2 | 0.3 | 9.0 | 5.8 | ... |
| 1900 | 85 | 38 | 40 | ... | 3.4 | 0.1 | 8.9 | 6.7 | ... |
| 1901 | 90 | 49 | 85 | ... | 3.1 | 0.5 | 9.6 | 6.7 | ... |
| 1902 | 58 | 45 | 52 | ... | 0.3 | 0.6 | 6.9 | 6.9 | ... |
| 1903 | 75 | 41 | 34 | ... | 1.2 | 0.3 | 7.3 | 6.2 | ... |
| 1904 | 126 | 39 | 46 | ... | −0.3 | 0.4 | 7.0 | 5.9 | ... |
| 1905 | 177 | 43 | 70 | ... | −0.1 | 0.6 | 7.9 | 6.1 | ... |
| 1906 | 253 | 60 | 74 | ... | 0.3 | 1.2 | 8.7 | 5.8 | ... |
| 1907 | 209 | 90 | 68 | ... | - - | ... | 8.6 | 6.5 | 0.9 |
| 1908 | 256 | 85 | 95 —[5] | ... | 0.4 | ... | 8.9 | 5.9 | 3.2 |
| | | | 91 | ... | | | | | |
| 1909 | 231 | 95 | 84 | | 1.1 | ... | 9.3 | 7.8 | 2.2 |
| 1910 | 290 | 98 | 87 | ... | 0.5 | ... | 11 | 8.4 | 1.0 |
| 1911 | 226 | 121 | 134 | ... | 0.7 | ... | 14 | 8.8 | 3.0 |
| 1912 | 323 | 120 | 178 | ... | 1.4 | ... | 18 | 9.5 | 1.6 |
| 1913 | 302 | 157 | 190 | ... | 0.7 —[7] | ... | 17 | 12.0 | 0.9 |
| | | | | | 2.0 | | | | |
| 1914 | 115 | 179 | 79 | ... | 2.7 | ... | 10 | 12 | 0.9 |
| 1915 | 45 | 111 | 30 | ... | 1.3 | ... | 5.6 | 6.9 | 1.0 |
| 1916 | 33 | 73 | 31 | ... | 1.6 | ... | 4.7 | 5.0 | 1.0 |
| 1917 | 18 | 51 | 30 | ... | 0.8 | ... | 4.4 | 4.0 | 0.7 |
| 1918 | 14 | 24 | 20 | ... | 1.8 | 0.3 | 5.2 | 4.3 | 0.3 |
| 1919 | 41 | 42 | 36 | ... | −0.5 | 0.4 | 11.0 | 6.0 | −0.4 |
| 1920 | 87 | 57 | 69 | ... | −0.6 | 0.3 | 10.0 | 7.1 | −0.7 |
| 1921 | 98 | 45 | 58 | ... | −0.4 | 0.6 | 9.2 | 5.3 | 0.9 |
| 1922 | 129 | 46 | 65 | ... | - - | 0.2 | 11.0 | 6.2 | 0.8 |
| 1923 | 195 | 47 | 85 | ... | 0.7 | 0.1 | 17.0 | 6.6 | −0.3 |
| | | | | | | | h | | |
| 1924 | 160 | 46 | 96 | ... | - - - | 0.5 | 15 | | 1.9 |
| 1925 | 125 | 50 | 83 | ... | 0.4 | 0.3 | 15 | | 1.2 |
| 1926 | 135 | 56 | 119 | 3.0 | −0.4 | 0.3 | 18 | | 5.1 |
| 1927 | 162 | 58 | 98 | 4.5 | −0.4 | 0.4 | 19 | | 3.5 |
| 1928 | 129 | 54 | 78 | 2.8 | −0.8 | 0.4 | 20 | | 0.4 |
| 1929 | 140 | 58 | 96 | 2.4 | −0.7 | 0.3 | 17 | | 1.9 |

**A8      SOUTH AMERICA: International Migrations** (in thousands)

**1930–1975**

| | Argentina | | Brazil[5] | Colombia | Guyana*[7] | Paraguay | Uruguay | Venezuela |
|---|---|---|---|---|---|---|---|---|
| | b | e | b | h | d | b | h | d |
| 1930 | 124.0 | 60.0 | 63.0 | −5.2 | −0.4 | 1.8 | 27.0 | 1.6 |
| 1931 | 56.0 | 53.0 | 127.0 | −2.6 | 0.3 | 0.5 | 15.0 | 0.6 |
| 1932 | 31.0 | 43.0 | 31.0 | 0.9 | 0.1 | 0.9 | 4.6 | −1.2 |
| 1933 | 24.0 | 35.0[6] | 46.0 | 2.8 | 0.8 | 0.4 | 1.7 | −0.6 |
| | | 50.0 | | | | | | |
| 1934 | 28.0 | 42.0 | 46.0 | 4.0 | 0.6 | 0.6 | 5.5 | −1.0 |
| 1935 | 35.0 | 37.0 | 30.0 | 1.2 | 0.6 | 1.1 | 0.4 | 0.5 |
| 1936 | 36.0 | 37.0 | 13.0 | 1.1 | −0.3 | 2.5 | 4.7 | 3.0 |
| 1937 | 41.0 | 37.0 | 35.0 | 0.9 | 0.2 | 4.8 | 7.6 | 2.8 |
| 1938 | 38.0 | 33.0 | 19.0 | 3.3 | ... | 4.5 | 9.3 | 2.8 |
| 1939 | 15.0 | 29.0 | 23.0 | 1.4 | ... | 2.1 | 0.4 | 2.6 |
| 1940 | 6.2 | 14.0 | 18.0 | 0.4 | ... | 0.2 | −5.2 | 0.6 |
| 1941 | 4.7 | 13.0 | 9.9 | −3.4 | ... | 0.3 | −1.8 | −2.2 |
| 1942 | 1.8 | 4.2 | 2.4 | −- - | ... | 0.1 | −4.7 | −3.7 |
| 1943 | 0.8 | 2.9 | 1.3 | 0.1 | ... | ... | −6.7 | −4.2 |
| 1944 | 0.8 | ...[6] | 1.6 | 0.7 | ... | ... | −2.0 | 0.7 |
| 1945 | 1.0 | 1.3 | 3.2 | 2.2 | ... | - - | ... | 5.3 |
| 1946 | 4.4 | 4.6 | 13.0 | 3.3 | ... | - - | ... | 2.7 |
| 1947 | 39.0 | 8.9 | 19.0 | 1.4 | ... | 2.6 | ... | 9.2 |
| 1948 | 119.0 | 13.0 | 22 | ... | ... | ... | ... | 35.0 |
| 1949 | 152.0 | 17.0 | 24.0 | 0.4 | ... | ... | ... | 24.0 |
| 1950 | 128.0 | 25.0 | 35.0 | −1.6 | −0.5 | ... | ... | 27.0 |
| 1951 | 98.0 | 27.0 | 63.0 | 0.5 | −0.6 | ... | ... | 23.0 |
| 1952 | 64.0 | 45.0 | 85.0 | −3.1 | 2.2 | ... | ... | 30.0 |
| 1953 | 35.0 | 32.0 | 80.0 | −- - | ... | ... | 9.8 | 41.0 |
| 1954 | 44.0 | 19.0 | 72.0 | −1.3 | ... | ... | ... | 44.0 |
| 1955 | 30.0 | 18.0 | 55.0 | ... | −1.3 | ... | 18.0 | 54.0 |
| 1956 | 18.0 | 18.0 | 45.0 | 2.1 | −1.7 | 0.7 | 25.0 | 41.0 |
| 1957 | 27.0[6] | 24.0 | 54.0 | −1.1 | −1.0 | 2.3 | ... | 44.0 |
| 1958 | 20.0 | ... | 50.0 | −1.4 | −1.1 | 1.5 | ... | 10.0 |
| 1959 | 16.0 | ... | 45.0 | −3.7 | −9.2 | ... | ... | 9.8 |
| 1960 | 8.8 | ... | 41.0 | −1.9 | 7.7 | 1.0 | 37.0 | −10.0 |
| 1961 | 9.1 | ... | 44.0 | −2.7 | 8.6 | 1.7 | 21.0 | −5.0 |
| 1962 | 9.5 | ... | 31.0 | −4.6 | −0.9 | 1.3 | −11.0 | −8.2 |
| 1963 | 5.7 | ... | 24.0 | 11.0 | −3.0 | 2.7 | ... | −7.2 |
| 1964 | 3.7 | ... | ... | 10.0 | −3.7 | 1.7 | ... | 12.0 |
| 1965 | 3.9 | ... | ... | 15.0 | −2.8 | 1.3 | ... | 7.4 |
| 1966 | 3.2 | ... | ... | −5.2 | −0.7 | 1.7 | ... | −5.3 |
| 1967 | 3.8 | ... | 11 | −5.0 | −2.4 | 1.1 | −11.0 | −25.0 |
| 1968 | 4.9 | ... | 13.0 | −15 | −4.8 | 0.9 | ... | −59.0 |
| 1969 | 6.3 | ... | 6.6 | 0.9 | −4.6 | 1.3 | ... | −36.0 |
| 1970 | 7.4 | ... | 6.9 | ... | −12.0 | 1.3 | −1.1 | −63.0 |
| 1971 | 4.6 | ... | 6.4 | ... | −2.1 | 1.5 | 12.0 | 39.0 |
| 1972 | 3.5 | ... | 8.8 | ... | −8.0 | 2.6 | 50.0 | 3.4 |
| 1973 | ... | ... | 5.9 | ... | −7.0 | 4.5 | ... | 9.7 |
| 1974 | ... | ... | 6.8 | 7.4 | −9.3 | 6.3 | ... | 71.0 |

**A8    SOUTH AMERICA: International Migrations** (in thousands)

|      | Brazil | Colombia | Guyana | Paraguay | Venezuela |
|------|--------|----------|--------|----------|-----------|
|      | **b**  | **h**    | **d**  | **b**    | **d**     |
| 1975 | 12.0   | 18.0     | −7.7   | 5.5      | 28        |
| 1976 | …      | …        | …      | …        | 61        |
| 1977 | …      | …        | …      | …        | −12       |
| 1978 | …      | …        | …      | …        | 180       |
| 1979 | 6.8    | …        | …      | …        | 52        |
| 1980 | …      | −4.4     | …      | 5.1      | −6        |
| 1981 | …      | −16.0    | …      | 10.0     | −95       |
| 1982 | …      | 13.0     | …      | 5.9      | −21       |
| 1983 | 3.7    | 32.0     | …      | …        | …         |
| 1984 | 3.5    | 5.3      | …      | …        | …         |
| 1985 | …      | 1.8      | …      | …        | −13       |
| 1986 | 4..2   | 2.5      | …      | …        | −12       |
| 1987 | …      | 1.0      | …      | …        | −19       |
| 1988 | …      | −28.0    | …      | …        | −5        |

NOTES

1.  SOURCES: The main sources used have been Imre Ferenczi and Walter F. Willcox, *International Migrations*, vol. 1 (New York, 1929); UN, *Sex and Age of International Migrants: Statistics for 1918–1947* (1953); UN, *Economic Characteristics of International Migrants: Statistics for Selected Countries, 1918–1954* (no date); and the annual UN, *Demographic Yearbook*. In addition, the following data came from the national publications on p. xiv–xvi: Canada to 1959; Trinidad and Tobago 1923–47; USA 1869–75; Brazil; British Guiana 1924–38; Venezuela to 1978.

2.  Definitions of migrants vary very greatly from time to time and from place to place. So far as possible the changes are indicated in the column headings and in footnotes.

3.  Net movements of foreigners 1908–75 are given in Markos J. Mamalakis, *Historical Statistics of Chile*, vol. 2. (Westport, Conn., 1980).

FOOTNOTES

[1] Data for 1873–1917 apply to 'coolies' (i.e. indentured East Indians). For 1902–14 they are for years beginning 1 April. The 1915 figure is for the 9 months ending 31 December.

[2] Exclusive of those repatriated.

[3] Data to 1899 apply to 'coolies', covering only those moving at the public expense from 1873. From 1900 to 1918 only indentured East Indian 'coolies' are covered. From 1900 to 1914 data are for years beginning 1 April. The 1915 figure is for the 9 months ending 31 December.

[4] Alien arrivals at Gulf and Atlantic ports to 1849, with Pacific ports included from 1850 to 1868 (though ports in the control of the Confederacy were excluded during 1861–65. From 1868 data refer, in principle, to aliens arriving with intent to reside, and from 1906 to aliens arriving with intent to settle. Arrivals in Alaska are included irregularly from 1871 to 1903, but regularly thereafter. Arrivals in Hawaii are included from 1901, in Puerto Rico from 1902, and in the US Virgin Islands from 1942. Arrivals at land frontiers were included in a very incomplete fashion in the early years, and not fully until 1908. There were changes in the categories of people included in the statistics at various times. The main ones were the exclusion of immigrants who came as first- or second-class passengers from 1892 to 1903, and the exclusion of aliens in transit from 1904, and of resident aliens returning from visits abroad from 1907. There were changes in the treatment of aliens entering via land frontiers in 1930, 1946 and 1953. Data are for years ending 30 June except for 1820–31 and 1844–50 (which are for years ending 30 September), and 1851–67 (which are for calendar years). The figure for 1832 is for the 15 months ending 31 December, that for 1843 is for the 9 months ending 30 September, and that for 1868 is for the first half-year.

[5] Immigrants were defined as third-class passengers arriving at Brazilian ports to 1907 (1st line). From 1907 (2nd line) to 1964 only aliens were included.

[6] Immigrants and emigrants were defined as alien second- and third-class passengers, except that all classes were counted as emigrants from 1933 (2nd line) to 1943. Only movements by sea are covered to 1957.

[7] Data from 1882 to 1913 (1st line) relate to immigrants from and emigrants to India only.

[8] Aliens only to 1928.

# B    LABOUR FORCE

The Statistics in this section cover a wide range of topics and come from a variety of sources. The occupation data up to 1966 were largely derived by Professor Bairoch and his colleagues from national censuses of population. The problems of accuracy referred to in the last section appear here also. But a still more significant difficulty is the very considerable variations which have occurred in classification, both between countries and over time. Professor Bairoch's group refer to 'the frequent changes in criteria and methods used in census taking', and say that 'it is practically impossible to come up with statistics that are perfectly comparable in time and space'.[1] The best we can hope for, therefore, is that the figures in table 1 are usable as a guide to structural changes within countries, and for rough international comparisons.

An even greater degree of heterogeneity is to be found in the unemployment statistics, some of which come from trade union records (of varying character and reliability), some from insurance statistics (which can be just as variable), and some from either total registration or sample surveys. In addition to variations in the definition of the unemployed, where percentages are shown there are also likely to be variations in the definition of the total workforce. It will be readily understood, therefore, that comparisons between countries must be made with due regard to changes in the nature of the series, and that comparisons between countries must not be made without taking differences of definition into account. The same applies to the statistics of industrial disputes, shown in table 3, though there is more homogeneity within each country's data. It is noticeable that dictatorships, both of the Right and of the Left, have tended to suppress statistics of both unemployment and industrial disputes, and this accounts for some of the gaps in these series.

Information on wages is often plentiful but of extreme heterogeneity and complexity, and statistics are notoriously intractable. Because of this, it is perhaps best to treat the indices shown in tables 4 and 5 as little more than impressions of the general course of money wages. Apart from the well-known technical problems of index numbers, dealt with in any textbook of statistics, there are problems in each country of availability and selection of data; of weighting different occupations; and of the appropriateness (which often takes the form of assessing obsolescence) of the chosen weights; of the differences between hourly, daily or weekly wage rates, and between rates and actual earnings. Moreover, it must be stressed that these tables are concerned with money wages, not real wages, for which very rough estimates may be made by using the data in section 1. In general, comparisons between countries are extremely difficult, and require a degree of original research which it has not been possible to afford here. In fact, the whole subject, despite its obvious interest to politicians and others with axes to grind, has received very little scholarly attention, though there is a number of studies of individual countries.

[1] P. Bairoch et al, La Population Active et sa Structure (Brussels, 1968).

**B1 NORTH AMERICA: ECONOMICALLY ACTIVE POPULATION BY MAJOR INDUSTRIAL GROUPS**
(in thousands)[1]

**BARBADOS** 1946–1981

| | Agriculture, Forestry & Fishing | Extractive Industry | Manufacturing Industry[2] | Construction | Commerce, Finance, etc | Transport & Communications | Services[3] | Others Occupied |
|---|---|---|---|---|---|---|---|---|
| *Males* | | | | | | | | |
| 1946 | 15 | 0.4 | 11 | 8.0 | 5 | 4.0 | 7 | 0.3 |
| 1960 | 13 | 0.4 | 10 | 9.0 | 7 | 4.0 | 7 | 0.1 |
| 1970 | 9 | 0.3 | 9 | 10.0 | 6[4] | 4.0 | 11[4] | 2 |
| 1981 | 6 | - - | 8 | 6.0 | 14 | 4.0 | 20 | — |
| *Females* | | | | | | | | |
| 1946 | 11 | — | 7 | 0.3 | 7 | 0.1 | 15 | — |
| 1960 | 9 | 0.1 | 4 | 0.3 | 8 | 0.3 | 13 | — |
| 1970 | 5 | - - | 5 | 0.3 | 6[4] | 0.6 | 15[4] | 1 |
| 1981 | 4 | - - | 8 | 0.2 | 13 | 1 | 17 | — |

**CANADA[5]** 1891–1981

| | Agriculture, Forestry & Fishing | Extractive Industry | Manufacturing Industry[2] | Construction | Commerce, Finance, etc | Transport & Communications | Services[3] | Others Occupied |
|---|---|---|---|---|---|---|---|---|
| *Males* | | | | | | | | |
| 1891[6] | 766 | 15 | 176 | 87 | 81 | 60 | 88 | 137 |
| 1901[6] | 751 | 28 | 229 | 89 | 92 | 81 | 101 | 173 |
| 1911 | 995 | 63 | 639 | | 241 | 211 | 210 | — |
| 1921 | 1,093 | 51 | 748 | | 314 | 226 | 250 | — |
| 1931 | 1,199 | 59 | 593 | | 323 | 249 | 288 | 551[8] |
| 1941[7] | 1,207 | 93 | 808 | 219 | 414 | 245 | 651 | 41 |
| 1951[7] | 970 | 102 | 1,142 | 345 | 578 | 354 | 577 | 55 |
| 1961 | 704 | 117 | 1,243 | 456 | 750 | 423 | 896 | 117 |
| 1971 | 465 | 112 | 1,372 | 530 | 1,193 | 466 | 1,147 | 381 |
| 1981 | 487 | 145 | 1,696 | 718 | 1,799 | 585 | 1,431 | 228 |
| *Females* | | | | | | | | |
| 1891[6] | 12.0 | — | 62 | - - | 7 | 1 | 116 | 4 |
| 1901[6] | 9.0 | - - | 71 | - - | 8 | 1 | 136 | 14 |
| 1911 | 16 | - - | 99 | | 42 | 7 | 201 | — |
| 1921 | 18 | - - | 106 | | 97 | 21 | 247 | — |
| 1931 | 25 | — | 85 | | 63 | 17 | 348 | 129[8] |
| 1941[7] | 20 | 1 | 183 | 2 | 141 | 19 | 463 | 5 |
| 1951[7] | 38 | 2 | 280 | 6 | 276 | 49 | 501 | 13 |
| 1961 | 81 | 5 | 317 | 12 | 404 | 74 | 832 | 42 |
| 1971 | 116 | 8 | 416 | 28 | 912 | 97 | 1,084 | 92 |
| 1981 | 132 | 24 | 441 | 76 | 1,832 | 186 | 1,779 | 176 |

**COSTA RICA** 1950–1984

| | Agriculture, Forestry & Fishing | Extractive Industry | Manufacturing Industry[2] | Construction | Commerce, Finance, etc | Transport & Communications | Services[3] | Others Occupied |
|---|---|---|---|---|---|---|---|---|
| *Males* | | | | | | | | |
| 1950 | 144 | 1 | 25 | 12 | 17 | 9 | 15 | 8 |
| 1963 | 191 | 1 | 39 | 23 | 32 | 14 | 27 | 5 |
| 1973 | 209 | 1 | 57 | 39 | 61 | 24 | 54 | 9 |
| 1984 | 242 | 2 | 83 | 41 | 77 | 19 | 92 | 64 |
| *Females* | | | | | | | | |
| 1950 | 5 | — | 7 | - - | 4 | 1 | 26 | - - |
| 1963 | 4 | — | 11 | - - | 7 | 1 | 41 | 1 |
| 1973 | 5 | - - | 19 | - - | 20 | 1 | 65 | 1 |
| 1984 | 8 | - - | 32 | - - | 31 | 2 | 84 | 19 |

**B1    NORTH AMERICA: Economically Active Population by Major Industrial Groups** (in thousands)

## CUBA                                                                                          1919–1981

| | Agriculture, Forestry & Fishing | Extractive Industry | Manufacturing Industry[2] | Construction | Commerce, Finance, etc | Transport & Communications | Services[3] | Others Occupied |
|---|---|---|---|---|---|---|---|---|
| *Males* | | | | | | | | |
| 1919 | 454 | 1 | 161 | | 145 | | 98 | — |
| 1943 | 620 | 6 | 154 | 26 | 140 | 33 | 103 | 284 |
| 1953 | 804 | 9 | 286 | 64 | 212 | 100 | 230 | 10 |
| 1970 | 751 | 15 | 416 | 154 | 634 | 150 | 438 | 30 |
| 1981 | 678 | 21 | 452 | 279 | 712[9] | 205 | [9] | 88 |
| *Females* | | | | | | | | |
| 1919 | 8 | — | 29 | | 3 | | 50 | — |
| 1943 | 11 | — | 36 | - - | 9 | 1 | 69 | 31 |
| 1953 | 15 | - - | 50 | 1 | 20 | 4 | 166 | 1 |
| 1970 | 39 | 1 | 101 | 3 | 320 | 11 | 209 | 7 |
| 1981 | 113 | 4 | 192 | 34 | 680[9] | 43 | [9] | 40 |

## DOMINICAN REPUBLIC                                                                            1920–1981

| | Agriculture, Forestry & Fishing | Extractive Industry | Manufacturing Industry[2] | Construction | Commerce, Finance, etc | Transport & Communications | Services[3] | Others Occupied |
|---|---|---|---|---|---|---|---|---|
| *Total* | | | | | | | | |
| 1920 | 138 | | 23 | | 12 | 2 | 15 | 14 |
| *Males* | | | | | | | | |
| 1950 | 436 | - - | 43 | 20 | 33 | 12 | 32 | 94 |
| 1960 | 495 | 2 | 58 | 21 | 43 | 21 | 38 | 54 |
| 1970 | 458 | 1 | 83 | 25 | 77 | 39 | 87 | 127 |
| 1981 | 378 | 4 | 179 | 78 | 147 | 37 | 157 | 285 |
| *Females* | | | | | | | | |
| 1950 | 13 | — | 16 | — | 9 | - - | 36 | 56 |
| 1960 | 9 | — | 12 | - - | 12 | - - | 54 | 2 |
| 1970 | 9 | - - | 20 | 4 | 20 | 4 | 67 | 109 |
| 1981 | 42 | - - | 59 | 3 | 68 | 4 | 206 | 131 |

## EL SALVADOR                                                                                   1950–1971

| | Agriculture, Forestry & Fishing | Extractive Industry | Manufacturing Industry[2] | Construction | Commerce, Finance, etc | Transport & Communications | Services[3] | Others Occupied |
|---|---|---|---|---|---|---|---|---|
| *Males* | | | | | | | | |
| 1950 | 399 | 2 | 51 | 19 | 19 | 10 | 30 | 17 |
| 1961 | 472 | 1 | 71 | 33 | 27 | 17 | 38 | 6 |
| 1971 | 609 | 1 | 78 | 32 | 48 | 24 | 83 | 39 |
| *Females* | | | | | | | | |
| 1950 | 13 | — | 25 | - - | 17 | - - | 48 | 5 |
| 1961 | 15 | — | 34 | - - | 25 | - - | 67 | 2 |
| 1971 | 23 | - - | 40 | - - | 46 | 1 | 125 | 17 |

## GUATEMALA                                                                                     1950–1981

| | Agriculture, Forestry & Fishing | Extractive Industry | Manufacturing Industry[2] | Construction | Commerce, Finance, etc | Transport & Communications | Services[3] | Others Occupied |
|---|---|---|---|---|---|---|---|---|
| *Males* | | | | | | | | |
| 1950 | 642 | 1 | 78 | 26 | 36 | 15 | 42 | 4 |
| 1964 | 841 | 2 | 114 | 34 | 59 | 28 | 65 | 9 |
| 1973 | 866 | 2 | 170 | 62 | 80 | 37 | 86 | 31[10] |
| 1981 | 887 | 2 | 142 | 85 | 113 | 41 | 113 | 65 |
| *Females* | | | | | | | | |
| 1950 | 18 | — | 35 | - - | 17 | - - | 53 | - - |
| 1964 | 20 | - - | 37 | - - | 24 | 1 | 84 | 1 |
| 1973 | 15 | - - | 47 | - - | 34 | 1 | 108 | 7[10] |
| 1981 | 22 | - - | 43 | 1 | 55 | 2 | 102 | 23 |

## HAITI

| | Agriculture, Forestry & Fishing | Extractive Industry | Manufacturing Industry[2] | Construction | Commerce, Finance, etc | Transport & Communications | Services[3] | Others Occupied |
|---|---|---|---|---|---|---|---|---|
| *Males* | | | | | | | | |
| 1950 | 771 | - - | 38 | 10 | 7 | 6 | 26 | 3 |
| 1971 | 880 | 1 | 53 | 18 | 21 | 11 | 64 | 178 |
| 1982 | 849 | 9 | 67 | 19 | 67 | 14 | 65 | 27 |
| *Females* | | | | | | | | |
| 1950 | 683 | - - | 48 | - - | 54 | - - | 45 | 2 |
| 1971 | 549 | - - | 68 | - - | 176 | 1 | 94 | 213 |
| 1982 | 374 | 10 | 56 | 4 | 223 | 2 | 60 | 25 |

## B1 NORTH AMERICA: Economically Active Population by Major Industrial Groups (in thousands)[1]

### HONDURAS — 1950–1974

| | Agriculture, Forestry & Fishing | Extractive Industry | Manufacturing Industry[2] | Construction | Commerce, Finance, etc | Transport & Communications | Services[3] | Others Occupied |
|---|---|---|---|---|---|---|---|---|
| *Total* | | | | | | | | |
| 1950 | 538 | 3 | 39 | 7 | 8 | 7 | 29 | 17 |
| *Males* | | | | | | | | |
| 1961 | 376 | 2 | 32 | 11 | 18 | 8 | 27 | 22 |
| 1974 | 452 | 2 | 54 | 24 | 40 | 20 | 38 | 7 |
| *Females* | | | | | | | | |
| 1961 | 4 | — | 13 | - - | 9 | 1 | 43 | 5 |
| 1974 | 9 | - - | 32 | - - | 25 | 1 | 50 | 1 |

### JAMAICA — 1943–1982

| | Agriculture, Forestry & Fishing | Extractive Industry | Manufacturing Industry[2] | Construction | Commerce, Finance, etc | Transport & Communications | Services[3] | Others Occupied |
|---|---|---|---|---|---|---|---|---|
| *Males* | | | | | | | | |
| 1943 | 183 | - - | 34 | 31 | 16 | | 58 | |
| 1953 | 226 | 8 | 43 | 19 | 19 | 13 | 27[11] | 27 |
| 1960 | 197 | 4 | 49 | 49 | 26 | 17 | 37 | 4 |
| 1973 | 174 | | 65 | 53 | 32 | 23 | 77 | 5 |
| 1982 | 113 | 5 | 47 | 21 | 29 | 16 | 63 | 30 |
| *Females* | | | | | | | | |
| 1943 | 45 | - - | 25 | 4 | 22 | | 87 | |
| 1953 | 74 | - - | 35 | 2 | 33 | 2 | 79[11] | 8 |
| 1960 | 39 | 1 | 44 | 1 | 35 | 2 | 96 | 7 |
| 1973 | 47 | | 30 | 2 | 68 | 7 | 165 | 3 |
| 1982 | 14 | 1 | 14 | 1 | 42 | 5 | 85 | 19 |

### MARTINIQUE — 1961–1982

| | Agriculture, Forestry & Fishing | Extractive Industry | Manufacturing Industry[2] | Construction | Commerce, Finance, etc | Transport & Communications | Services[3] | Others Occupied |
|---|---|---|---|---|---|---|---|---|
| *Males* | | | | | | | | |
| 1961 | 24 | - - | 8 | 8 | 3 | 4 | 8 | 1 |
| 1967 | 18 | - - | 8 | 10 | 4 | 5 | 11 | 1 |
| 1974 | 12 | - - | 5 | 8 | 7 | 4 | 13 | 5 |
| 1982 | 7 | 2 | 3 | 8 | 12 | 4 | 12 | 6 |
| *Females* | | | | | | | | |
| 1961 | 11 | — | 4 | - - | 6 | - - | 14 | 1 |
| 1967 | 8 | - - | 2 | - - | 7 | - - | 14 | - - |
| 1974 | 4 | - - | 2 | - - | 7 | - - | 20 | 4 |
| 1982 | 3 | — | 2 | - - | 16 | 1 | 17 | 2 |

### MEXICO — 1900–1980

| | Agriculture, Forestry & Fishing | Extractive Industry | Manufacturing Industry[2] | Construction | Commerce, Finance, etc | Transport & Communications | Services[3] | Others Occupied |
|---|---|---|---|---|---|---|---|---|
| *Males* | | | | | | | | |
| 1900[12] | 3,130 | 97 | 496 | | 189 | 58 | 208[13] | 174 |
| 1910[12] | 3,519 | 95 | 422 | | 221 | 54 | 316 | 43 |
| 1921 | 3,459 | 26 | 439 | | 222 | 74 | 155 | 439 |
| 1930 | 3,601 | 51 | 526 | 61 | 234 | 106 | 231 | 170 |
| 1940 | 3,791 | 105 | 462 | 105 | 456 | 147 | 216 | 144 |
| 1960 | 5,480 | 132 | 1,344 | 394 | 785 | 338 | 760 | 64 |
| 1970 | 4,837 | 167 | 1,771[14] | 553 | 863 | 351 | 1,438[14] | 509 |
| 1980 | 4,958 | 354 | 1,991 | 1,094 | 1,464 | 606 | 1,177 | 4,194 |
| *Females* | | | | | | | | |
| 1900[12] | 27 | 1 | 262 | | 49 | - - | 3,799[13] | 186 |
| 1910[12] | 62 | 1 | 228 | | 56 | - - | 566 | 35 |
| 1921 | 31 | 2 | 194 | | 49 | 1 | 234 | 212 |
| 1930 | 26 | - - | 105 | — | 40 | 1 | 161 | 372 |
| 1940 | 40 | 1 | 72 | 1 | 97 | 3 | 199 | 433 |
| 1960 | 664 | 10 | 254 | 14 | 290 | 19 | 767 | 18 |
| 1970 | 267 | 14 | 453 | 18 | 334 | 17 | 1,127[14] | 238 |
| 1980 | 743 | 159 | 706 | 214 | 698 | 78 | 1,274 | 2,232 |
| *Total* | | | | | | | | |
| 1950 | 4,824 | 97 | 998[14] | 225 | 684 | 211 | 879 | 355 |

**B1      NORTH AMERICA: Economically Active Population by Major Industrial Groups** (in thousands)[1]

## NICARAGUA                                                                                  1940–1971

|  | Agriculture, Forestry & Fishing | Extractive Industry | Manufactur- ing Industry[2] | Construction | Commerce, Finance, etc | Transport & Communica- tions | Services[3] | Others Occu- pied |
|---|---|---|---|---|---|---|---|---|
| *Males* | | | | | | | | |
| 1940 | 248 | 5 | 18[15] | 4 | ...[15] | 2 | 4 | 17 |
| 1950 | 218 | 3 | 28 | 9 | 10 | 6 | 10 | — |
| 1963 | 269 | 4 | 39 | 16 | 17 | 12 | 22 | 1 |
| 1971 | 228 | 3 | 47 | 20 | 30 | 17 | 43 | 7 |
| *Females* | | | | | | | | |
| 1940 | 10 | — | 19[15] | — | ...[15] | - - | 6 | 22 |
| 1950 | 5 | — | 11 | - - | 5 | - - | 25 | — |
| 1963 | 14 | - - | 18 | — | 17 | - - | 46 | 1 |
| 1971 | 9 | - - | 18 | - - | 24 | 1 | 56 | 2 |

## PANAMA[16]                                                                                  1940–1980

|  | Agriculture, Forestry & Fishing | Extractive Industry | Manufactur- ing Industry[2] | Construction | Commerce, Finance, etc | Transport & Communica- tions | Services[3] | Others Occu- pied |
|---|---|---|---|---|---|---|---|---|
| *Males* | | | | | | | | |
| 1940 | 103 | - - | 9 | 8 | 9 | 4 | 12 | 26[17] |
| 1950 | 124 | - - | 14 | 7 | 15 | 6 | 15 | 15[17] |
| 1960 | 151 | - - | 21 | 14 | 21 | 9 | 27 | 19[17] |
| 1970 | 179 | 1 | 30 | 27 | 44 | 14 | 40 | 19[17] |
| 1980 | 137 | 1 | 48 | 29 | 54 | 24 | 55 | 19 |
| *Females* | | | | | | | | |
| 1940 | 6 | — | 5 | - - | 2 | - - | 18 | 4[17] |
| 1950 | 7 | — | 6 | - - | 5 | 1 | 23 | 4[17] |
| 1960 | 5 | — | 7 | - - | 10 | 1 | 41 | 5[17] |
| 1970 | 9 | - - | 13 | 1 | 23 | 2 | 62 | 5[17] |
| 1980 | 6 | - - | 13 | 1 | 31 | 5 | 73 | 5 |

## PUERTO RICO                                                                                  1940–1990

|  | Agriculture, Forestry & Fishing | Extractive Industry | Manufactur- ing Industry[2] | Construction | Commerce, Finance, etc | Transport & Communica- tions | Services[3] | Others Occu- pied |
|---|---|---|---|---|---|---|---|---|
| *Males* | | | | | | | | |
| 1940 | 224 | 1 | 43 | 16 | 45 | 18 | 35 | 3 |
| 1950 | 216 | 2 | 56 | 31 | 56 | 26 | 61 | 9 |
| 1960 | 134 | 2 | 72 | 51 | 73 | 27 | 78 | 12 |
| 1973 | 63 | 1 | 111 | 112 | 140 | 39 | 169 | 4 |
| 1980 | 29 | 1 | 109 | 64 | 149 | 43 | 135 | 8 |
| *Females* | | | | | | | | |
| 1940 | 6 | — | 64 | - - | 6 | 1 | 51 | 1 |
| 1950 | 4 | — | 54 | - - | 9 | 1 | 64 | 4 |
| 1960 | 2 | — | 43 | 1 | 19 | 2 | 71 | 7 |
| 1973 | 3 | — | 87 | 1 | 52 | 5 | 135 | 5 |
| 1980 | 1 | - - | 74 | 3 | 56 | 16 | 154 | 7 |

**B1    NORTH AMERICA: Economically Active Population by Major Industrial Groups** (in thousands)[1]

## TRINIDAD & TOBAGO                                                   1946–1980

| | Agriculture, Forestry & Fishing | Extractive Industry | Manufactur- ing Industry[2] | Construction | Commerce, Finance, etc | Transport & Communica- tions | Services[3] | Others Occu- pied |
|---|---|---|---|---|---|---|---|---|
| *Males* | | | | | | | | |
| 1946 | 48 | 7 | 48 | | 13 | 12 | 26 | 6 |
| 1956 | 48 | 15 | 61 | | 19 | 19 | 22 | — |
| 1960 | 44 | 13 | 36 | 29 | 23 | 15 | 33 | - - |
| 1971 | 55 | | 109 | | 29 | 22 | 38 | — |
| 1980 | 29 | 18 | 34 | 58 | 33 | 23 | 44 | 8 |
| *Females* | | | | | | | | |
| 1946 | 11 | - - | 11 | | 6 | 1 | 23 | 1 |
| 1956 | 19 | - - | 15 | | 12 | 1 | 34 | — |
| 1960 | 11 | - - | 10 | 1 | 12 | 1 | 34 | - - |
| 1971 | 20 | | 19 | | 18 | 2 | 39 | — |
| 1980 | 5 | 1 | 12 | 6 | 28 | 4 | 40 | 3 |

## USA                                                                1820–1980

| | Agriculture, Forestry & Fishing | Extractive Industry | Manufactur- ing Industry[2] | Construction | Commerce, Finance, etc | Transport & Communica- tions | Services[3] | Others Occu- pied |
|---|---|---|---|---|---|---|---|---|
| *Total* | | | | | | | | |
| 1820 | 2,070[18] | ... | 350 | | ... | | ... | 460 |
| 1830 | 2,770[18] | ... | ... | | ... | | ... | 1,160 |
| 1840 | 3,720[18] | 15 | 790 | | ... | | ... | 895 |
| 1850 | 4,925 | 90 | 1,260[20] | | 420[20] | | 940 | 65 |
| 1860 | 6,260 | 170 | 1,930[20] | | 780[20] | | 1,310 | 80 |
| 1870 | 6,910[19] | 180[19] | 2,750[20][19] | | 1,350[20][19] | | 1,700[19] | 30[19] |
| | 6,490 | 200 | 2,250[20] | 750 | 830 | 640[20] | 1,620 | 140 |
| 1880 | 8,705 | 310 | 3,170[20] | 830 | 1,220 | 860[20] | 2,100 | 195 |
| 1890 | 10,170 | 480 | 4,750[20] | 1,440 | 1,990 | 1,530[20] | 3,210 | 170 |
| 1900 | 10,920 | 760 | 6,340[20] | 1,660 | 2,760 | 2,100[20] | 4,160 | 370 |
| 1910 | 11,590 | 1,050 | 8,230[20] | 2,300 | 3,890 | 3,190[20] | 5,880 | 600 |
| 1920 | 11,400 | 1,230 | 10,880[20] | 2,170 | 4,860 | 4,190[20] | 6,500 | 380 |
| 1930 | 10,750[19] | 1,150[19] | 10,990[20][19] | 3,030[19] | 7,450[19] | 4,850[20][19] | 9,280[19] | 1,340[19] |
| *Males* | | | | | | | | |
| 1940 | 8,628 | 1,098 | 9,652 | 3,463 | 6,333 | 2,540 | 6,318 | 1,418 |
| 1950 | 6,568 | 947 | 12,192 | 3,661 | 8,350 | 3,186 | 7,801 | 1,015 |
| 1960 | 4,069 | 681 | 14,557 | 4,141 | 9,117 | 3,031 | 9,985 | 1,732 |
| 1970 | 3,040 | 494 | 16,750 | 4,972 | 11,097 | 3,262 | 14,503 | — |
| 1980 | 2,936 | 870 | 17,130 | 6,326 | 15,135 | 3,863 | 15,434 | — |
| *Females* | | | | | | | | |
| 1940 | 513 | 12 | 2,674 | 46 | 2,154 | 300 | 6,232 | 634 |
| 1950 | 612 | 24 | 3,915 | 103 | 4,497 | 616 | 6,240 | 528 |
| 1960 | 450 | 33 | 4,898 | 162 | 5,915 | 684 | 9,075 | 1,115 |
| 1970 | 633 | 38 | 6,393 | 251 | 8,702 | 1,013 | 14,251 | — |
| 1980 | 729 | 133 | 7,843 | 527 | 14,589 | 1,427 | 19,027 | — |

**B1      SOUTH AMERICA: ECONOMICALLY ACTIVE POPULATION BY MAJOR INDUSTRIAL GROUPS** (in thousands)[1]

## ARGENTINA                                                                    1895–1980

| | Agriculture, Forestry & Fishing | Extractive Industry | Manufacturing Industry[2] | Construction | Commerce, Finance, etc | Transport & Communications | Services[3] | Others Occupied |
|---|---|---|---|---|---|---|---|---|
| *Males* | | | | | | | | |
| 1895 | 326 | | 185 | | 133 | 63 | 288 | 524 |
| 1914 | 488 | 1 | 487 | | 272 | 109 | 229 | 891 |
| 1947[21] | 1,534 | 32 | 1,053 | 334 | 748 | 375 | 779 | 179 |
| 1960 | 1,345 | 42 | 1,577 | 416 | 734 | 450 | 719 | 601 |
| 1970 | 1,243 | 43 | 1,448 | 699 | 1,192 | 541 | 974 | 582 |
| 1980 | 1,123 | 44 | 1,651 | 981 | 1,487 | 425 | 1,044 | 495 |
| *Females* | | | | | | | | |
| 1895 | 67 | | 181 | | 10 | - - | 211 | 664 |
| 1914 | 42 | — | 353 | | 21 | 2 | 241 | 26 |
| 1947[21] | 88 | 1 | 404 | 4 | 107 | 12 | 596 | 22 |
| 1960 | 116 | 2 | 424 | 7 | 171 | 28 | 800 | 168 |
| 1970 | 88 | 2 | 420 | 12 | 385 | 52 | 1,125 | 205 |
| 1980 | 78 | 3 | 438 | 22 | 611 | 36 | 1,355 | 197 |

## BOLIVIA                                                                       1950–1976

| | Agriculture, Forestry & Fishing | Extractive Industry | Manufacturing Industry[2] | Construction | Commerce, Finance, etc | Transport & Communications | Services[3] | Others Occupied |
|---|---|---|---|---|---|---|---|---|
| *Males* | | | | | | | | |
| 1950 | 275 | 39 | 96 | 25 | 33 | 21 | 18 | 7 |
| 1976 | 604 | 57 | 91 | 82 | 60 | 54 | 166 | 45 |
| *Females* | | | | | | | | |
| 1950 | 397 | 4 | 55 | 1 | 24 | 1 | 52 | 2 |
| 1976 | 89 | 3 | 57 | 1 | 60 | 2 | 116 | 9 |

## BRAZIL                                                                        1872–1980

| | Agriculture, Forestry & Fishing | Extractive Industry | Manufacturing Industry[2] | Construction | Commerce, Finance, etc | Transport & Communications | Services[3] | Others Occupied |
|---|---|---|---|---|---|---|---|---|
| *Total* | | | | | | | | |
| 1872 | 3,261 | | 789 | | 102 | 22 | 1,143 | — |
| 1900 | | 5,251 | | | 323 | 72 | 2,478 | — |
| 1920 | 6,452 | | 1,189 | | 498 | 254 | 758 | — |
| *Males* | | | | | | | | |
| 1940[22] | 8,183 | 345 | 1,107 | | 746 | 460 | 939 | — |
| 1950[16] | 9,609 | | 1,842 | | 972 | 668 | 1,480 | 38[23] |
| 1960 | 10,523 | 523 | 1,513[24] | 776 | 1,345 | 1,044 | 1,291 | 1,580[24] |
| 1970 | 11,833 | 172 | 2,813 | 1,705 | 2,249 | 1,183 | 2,916 | 551 |
| 1980 | 11,376 | 5,790 | | 3,096 | 6,055 | 1,671 | 2,317 | 861 |
| *Females* | | | | | | | | |
| 1940[22] | 1,270 | 45 | 293 | | 55 | 14 | 563 | — |
| 1950[16] | 761 | | 389 | | 102 | 29 | 1,218 | 9[23] |
| 1960 | 1,175 | 50 | 493[24] | 8 | 175 | 45 | 1,442 | 669[24] |
| 1970 | 1,258 | 3 | 618 | 15 | 448 | 62 | 3,600 | 162 |
| 1980 | 1,733 | 1,734 | | 55 | 5,146 | 145 | 2,540 | 394 |

**B1    SOUTH AMERICA: Economically Active Population by Major Industrial Groups** (in thousands)[1]

## CHILE                                                                                    1920–1992

| | Agriculture, Forestry & Fishing | Extractive Industry | Manufactur- ing Industry[2] | Construction | Commerce, Finance, etc | Transport & Communica- tions | Services[3] | Others Occu- pied |
|---|---|---|---|---|---|---|---|---|
| *Males* | | | | | | | | |
| 1920 | 442 | 56 | 177 | | 96 | 62 | 89 | 71 |
| 1930 | 481 | 77 | 205 | | 120 | 67 | 91 | 29 |
| 1940 | 581 | 94 | 205 | 58 | 124 | 71 | 185 | 2 |
| 1952 | 606 | 99 | 277 | 101 | 167 | 90 | 193 | 64 |
| 1960 | 639 | 90 | 327 | 135 | 182 | 112 | 232 | 120 |
| 1970 | 552 | 79 | 356 | 172 | 245 | 154 | 336 | 186 |
| 1982 | 625 | 76 | 408 | 228 | 192 | 423 | 496 | 205 |
| *Females* | | | | | | | | |
| 1920 | 50 | - - | 149 | | 23 | 3 | 119 | 6 |
| 1930 | 25 | 1 | 91 | | 28 | 3 | 109 | 12 |
| 1940 | 40 | 2 | 93 | 1 | 39 | 4 | 245 | 2 |
| 1952 | 42 | 2 | 133 | 1 | 56 | 6 | 286 | 13 |
| 1960 | 24 | 2 | 103 | 1 | 59 | 6 | 312 | 28 |
| 1970 | 19 | 2 | 111 | 3 | 102 | 12 | 313 | 55 |
| 1982 | 21 | 2 | 105 | 4 | | | 517 | 64 |

## COLOMBIA                                                                                1938–1973

| | Agriculture, Forestry & Fishing | Extractive Industry | Manufactur- ing Industry[2] | Construction | Commerce, Finance, etc | Transport & Communica- tions | Services[3] | Others Occu- pied |
|---|---|---|---|---|---|---|---|---|
| *Males* | | | | | | | | |
| 1938[25] | 1,758 | 52 | 180[27] | 84 | 130 | 59 | 133[27] | 25 |
| 1951[26] | 1,930 | 45 | 304 | 131 | 158 | 124 | 236 | 116 |
| 1964 | 2,311 | 61 | 489 | 217 | 332 | 179 | 374 | 138 |
| 1973 | 1,493 | 27 | 506 | 195 | 469 | 153 | 352 | 725 |
| *Females* | | | | | | | | |
| 1938[25] | 52 | 23 | 261[27] | 2 | 31 | 3 | 178[27] | 5 |
| 1951[26] | 93 | 16 | 157 | 2 | 45 | 6 | 362 | 19 |
| 1964 | 116 | 20 | 180 | 3 | 109 | 12 | 552 | 39 |
| 1973 | 53 | 9 | 193 | 5 | 199 | 14 | 486 | 238 |

## ECUADOR                                                                                 1950–1982

| | Agriculture, Forestry & Fishing | Extractive Industry | Manufactur- ing Industry[2] | Construction | Commerce, Finance, etc | Transport & Communica- tions | Services[3] | Others Occu- pied |
|---|---|---|---|---|---|---|---|---|
| *Males* | | | | | | | | |
| 1950 | 552 | 5 | 126 | 26 | 50 | 26 | 66 | 37 |
| 1962[16] | 762 | 3 | 149 | 47 | 74 | 42 | 92 | 39 |
| 1974 | 857 | 6 | 167 | 84 | 153 | 52 | 192 | 75 |
| 1982 | 728 | 7 | 226 | 155 | 215 | 96 | 344 | 29 |
| *Females* | | | | | | | | |
| 1950 | 89 | - - | 108 | 1 | 26 | 1 | 76 | 17 |
| 1962[16] | 40 | - - | 66 | 1 | 23 | 1 | 99 | 5 |
| 1974 | 40 | - - | 67 | 2 | 56 | 3 | 138 | 18 |
| 1982 | 59 | - - | 74 | 3 | 101 | 5 | 211 | 10 |

**B1     SOUTH AMERICA: Economically Active Population by Major Industrial Groups** (in thousands)[1]

## GUYANA*                                                                                          1946–1980

| | Agriculture, Forestry & Fishing | Extractive Industry | Manufacturing Industry[2] | Construction | Commerce, Finance, etc | Transport & Communications | Services[3] | Others Occupied |
|---|---|---|---|---|---|---|---|---|
| *Males* | | | | | | | | |
| 1946[16] | 51 | 4 | 17 | 7 | 8 | 6 | 11 | 1 |
| 1960 | 50 | 6 | 22 | 13 | 13 | 7 | 13 | - - |
| 1980 | 44 | 9 | 25 | 6 | 11 | 8 | 36 | 15 |
| *Females* | | | | | | | | |
| 1946[16] | 16 | — | 6 | - - | 4 | - - | 14 | - - |
| 1960 | 10 | - - | 15 | - - | 6 | - - | 16 | — |
| 1980 | 5 | 1 | 5 | - - | 7 | 1 | 22 | - - |

## PARAGUAY                                                                                          1950–1982

| | Agriculture, Forestry & Fishing | Extractive Industry | Manufacturing Industry[2] | Construction | Commerce, Finance, etc | Transport & Communications | Services[3] | Others Occupied |
|---|---|---|---|---|---|---|---|---|
| *Males* | | | | | | | | |
| 1950[16] | 212 | - - | 40 | 13 | 18 | 9 | 34 | —[28] |
| 1962[16] | 291 | - - | 50 | 18 | 25 | 15 | 58 | 17 |
| 1972 | 347 | 1 | 63 | 27 | 40 | 20 | 59 | 15 |
| 1982 | 423 | 1 | 83 | 70 | 66 | 28 | 92 | 65 |
| *Females* | | | | | | | | |
| 1950[16] | 23 | — | 29 | - - | 12 | - - | 34 | —[28] |
| 1962[16] | 31 | — | 45 | - - | 17 | 1 | 45 | 4 |
| 1972 | 21 | — | 45 | - - | 25 | 1 | 62 | 3 |
| 1982 | 23 | - - | 44 | - - | 38 | 2 | 82 | 15 |

## PERU                                                                                          1940–1981

| | Agriculture, Forestry & Fishing | Extractive Industry | Manufacturing Industry[2] | Construction | Commerce, Finance, etc | Transport & Communications | Services[3] | Others Occupied |
|---|---|---|---|---|---|---|---|---|
| *Males* | | | | | | | | |
| 1940[16] | 1,061 | 44 | 166 | 45 | 76 | 49 | 126 | 33 |
| 1961[16] | 1,341 | 65 | 307 | 104 | 203 | 89 | 242 | 99 |
| 1972 | 1,403 | 52 | 361 | 169 | 311 | 158 | 378 | 148 |
| 1981 | 1,597 | 92 | 436 | 194 | 504 | 196 | 658 | 162 |
| *Females* | | | | | | | | |
| 1940[16] | 486 | 1 | 215 | 1 | 36 | 2 | 128 | 8 |
| 1961[16] | 215 | 2 | 116 | 1 | 79 | 5 | 234 | 27 |
| 1972 | 133 | 1 | 127 | 2 | 134 | 7 | 286 | 48 |
| 1981 | 267 | 5 | 138 | 4 | 250 | 14 | 410 | 110 |

## URUGUAY                                                                                          1963–1985

| | Agriculture, Forestry & Fishing | Extractive Industry | Manufacturing Industry[2] | Construction | Commerce, Finance, etc | Transport & Communications | Services[3] | Others Occupied |
|---|---|---|---|---|---|---|---|---|
| *Males* | | | | | | | | |
| 1963 | 177 | 2 | 175 | 55 | 103 | 55 | 134 | 45 |
| 1975 | 165 | 2 | 156 | 59 | 121 | 49 | 162 | 61 |
| 1985 | 156 | 2 | 157 | 64 | 121 | 51 | 170 | 56 |
| *Females* | | | | | | | | |
| 1963 | 7 | - - | 70 | - - | 26 | 3 | 135 | 14 |
| 1975 | 10 | - - | 66 | 1 | 43 | 5 | 154 | 24 |
| 1985 | 14 | - - | 76 | 1 | 61 | 8 | 200 | 24 |

## VENEZUELA                                                                                          1941–1981

| | Agriculture, Forestry & Fishing | Extractive Industry | Manufacturing Industry[2] | Construction | Commerce, Finance, etc | Transport & Communications | Services[3] | Others Occupied |
|---|---|---|---|---|---|---|---|---|
| *Males* | | | | | | | | |
| 1941 | 595 | 22 | 69 | 39 | 93 | 42 | 102 | — |
| 1950[16] | 669 | 42 | 129 | 90 | 133 | 51 | 171 | 30 |
| 1961[16] | 745 | 44 | 242 | 126 | 265 | 102 | 308 | 110 |
| 1971 | 593 | 36 | 353 | 155 | 312 | 115 | 401 | 344 |
| 1981 | 515 | 49 | 539 | 378 | 644 | 245 | 578 | 365 |
| *Females* | | | | | | | | |
| 1941 | 41 | 1 | 98 | 1 | 8 | - - | 130 | — |
| 1950[16] | 36 | 3 | 49 | 1 | 17 | 2 | 171 | 7 |
| 1961[16] | 29 | 3 | 79 | 2 | 40 | 4 | 264 | 25 |
| 1971 | 18 | 2 | 84 | 4 | 66 | 9 | 376 | 109 |
| 1981 | 19 | 6 | 154 | 22 | 283 | 32 | 613 | 107 |

**B1     Economically Active Population by Major Industrial Groups** (in thousands)


NOTES

1.  SOURCES: The immediate source of most statistics up to 1961 is P. Bairoch *et al, The Working Population and its Structure* (Institut de Sociologie, Université Libre de Bruxelles, 1968). The original sources are described in detail there. Later statistics are taken from ILO, *Yearbook of Labour Statistics.* Canadian statistics for 1891 and 1901 are taken from M. C. Urquhart and K. A. H. Buckley (eds.), *Historical Statistics of Canada* (Cambridge and Toronto, 1965); American statistics to 1930 are taken from *Historical Statistics of the United States;* Argentinian statistics for 1895 are taken from Ernesto Tornquist & Co. Ltd, *The Economic Development of the Argentine Republic in the last Fifty Years* (Buenos Aires, 1919).

2.  Professor Bairoch and his colleagues 'tried to as great an extent as possible to unify the statistics in different countries during different periods', but were unable to achieve anything like perfect comparability. Comparisons between countries must be made with especially great caution owing to differences in classification, including differences in the definition of 'economically active'

3.  Where the original data were for an occupational rather than an industrial classification, this was usually transposed, with, of course, some degree of estimation involved.


FOOTNOTES

[1] Unless otherwise indicated, all statistics relate to the boundaries of the year concerned.
[2] Unless otherwise indicated, gas, water, electricity and sanitary service workers are included under this heading.
[3] Unless otherwise indicated, armed forces are included under this heading.
[4] Banks, insurance, etc are included with 'Services'.
[5] In 1881 total numbers engaged in agricultural pursuits were 662 thousand, with 715 thousand in non-agricultural pursuits.
[6] Labourers and clerical workers are not included in the sector in which they worked but in 'Others Occupied'.
[7] Excluding Yukon and Northwest Territories.
[8] Including the armed forces.
[9] Services are included with Commerce etc.
[10] Including those seeking employment for the first time.
[11] Excluding the armed forces.
[12] A small number of females was probably included with males.
[13] Including domestics in agriculture and housewives.
[14] Gas, water, etc, but not electricity, are included in 'Services' rather than in 'Manufacturing Industry'.
[15] Commerce, finance, etc, are included in 'Manufacturing Industry'.
[16] Excluding tribal Indians.
[17] Including those working in the Canal Zone.
[18] Agriculture only.
[19] There were changes in classification.
[20] Public utility employees are included with 'Transport & Communications' rather than 'Manufacturing Industry'.
[21] Unemployed people are excluded.
[22] Excluding domestic activities.
[23] A further 32 thousand were unclassified by either sex or occupation.
[24] Public utility employees are included with 'Others Occupied' rather than 'Manufacturing Industry'.
[25] Excluding certain localities and all the indigenous population.
[26] Excluding the indigenous population of Norte de Santander department.
[27] Sanitation services are included under 'Services' rather than 'Manufacturing Industry'.
[28] 13 thousand were unclassified either by sex or by occupation.

**B2** **NORTH AMERICA: UNEMPLOYMENT** (numbers in thousands; percentage of appropriate workforce)

| | Canada[1] | | Mexico[10] | USA[2] | |
|---|---|---|---|---|---|
| | No. | % | No. | No. | % |
| 1890 | ... | ... | ... | 904 | 4.0 |
| 1891 | ... | ... | ... | 1,265 | 5.4 |
| 1892 | ... | ... | ... | 728 | 3.0 |
| 1893 | ... | ... | ... | 2,860 | 11.7 |
| 1894 | ... | ... | ... | 4,612 | 18.4 |
| 1895 | ... | ... | ... | 3,510 | 13.7 |
| 1896 | ... | ... | ... | 3,782 | 14.4 |
| 1897 | ... | ... | ... | 3,890 | 14.5 |
| 1898 | ... | ... | ... | 3,351 | 12.4 |
| 1899 | ... | ... | ... | 1,819 | 6.5 |
| 1900 | ... | ... | ... | 1,420 | 5.0 |
| 1901 | ... | ... | ... | 1,205 | 4.0 |
| 1902 | ... | ... | ... | 1,097 | 3.7 |
| 1903 | ... | ... | ... | 1,204 | 3.9 |
| 1904 | ... | ... | ... | 1,691 | 5.4 |
| 1905 | ... | ... | ... | 1,381 | 4.3 |
| 1906 | ... | ... | ... | 574 | 1.7 |
| 1907 | ... | ... | ... | 945 | 2.8 |
| 1908 | ... | ... | ... | 2,780 | 8.0 |
| 1909 | ... | ... | ... | 1,824 | 5.1 |
| 1910 | ... | ... | ... | 2,150 | 5.9 |
| 1911 | ... | ... | ... | 2,518 | 6.7 |
| 1912 | ... | ... | ... | 1,759 | 4.6 |
| 1913 | ... | ... | ... | 1,671 | 4.3 |
| 1914 | ... | ... | ... | 3,120 | 7.9 |
| 1915 | ... | ... | ... | 3,377 | 8.5 |
| 1916 | ... | ... | ... | 2,043 | 5.1 |
| 1917 | ... | ... | ... | 1,848 | 4.6 |
| 1918 | ... | ... | ... | 536 | 1.4 |
| 1919 | ... | ... | ... | 546 | 1.4 |
| 1920 | ... | ... | ... | 2,132 | 5.2 |
| 1921 | 192 | 5.8 | ... | 4,918 | 11.7 |
| 1921 | 150 | 4.4 | ... | 2,859 | 6.7 |
| 1923 | 110 | 3.2 | ... | 1,049 | 2.4 |
| 1924 | 158 | 4.5 | ... | 2,190 | 5.0 |
| 1925 | 157 | 4.4 | ... | 1,453 | 3.2 |
| 1926 | 108 | 3.0 | ... | 801 | 1.8 |
| 1927 | 67 | 1.8 | ... | 1,519 | 3.3 |
| 1928 | 65 | 1.7 | ... | 1,982 | 4.2 |
| 1929 | 116 | 2.9 | ... | 1,550 | 3.2 |
| 1930 | 371 | 9.1 | 90 | 4,340 | 8.7 |
| 1931 | 481 | 11.6 | 287 | 8,020 | 15.9 |
| 1932 | 741 | 17.6 | 339 | 12,060 | 23.6 |
| 1933 | 826 | 19.3 | 276 | 12,830 | 24.9 |
| 1934 | 631 | 14.5 | 235 | 11,340 | 21.7 |
| 1935 | 625 | 14.2 | 191 | 10,610 | 20.1 |
| 1936 | 571 | 12.8 | 187 | 9,030 | 16.9 |
| 1937 | 411 | 9.1 | 180 | 7,700 | 14.3 |
| 1938 | 522 | 11.4 | 209 | 10,390 | 19.0 |
| 1939 | 529 | 11.4 | 199 | 9,480 | 17.2 |

**B2** **NORTH AMERICA: Unemployment** (numbers in thousands; percentage of appropriate workforce)

| | Barbados | | Canada[1] | | Costa Rica[6] | | Guatemala[8] | Honduras | Jamaica | |
|---|---|---|---|---|---|---|---|---|---|---|
| | No. | % | No. | % | No. | % | No. | No. | No. | % |
| 1940 | ... | ... | 423 | 9.2 | ... | ... | ... | ... | ... | ... |
| 1941 | ... | ... | 195 | 4.4 | ... | ... | ... | ... | ... | ... |
| 1942 | ... | ... | 135 | 3.0 | ... | ... | ... | ... | ... | ... |
| 1943 | ... | ... | 76 | 1.7 | ... | ... | ... | ... | ... | ... |
| 1944 | ... | ... | 63 | 1.4 | ... | ... | ... | ... | ... | ... |
| 1945 | ... | ... | 73 | 1.6 | ... | ... | ... | ... | ... | ... |
| 1946 | ... | ... | 124 | 2.6 | ... | ... | ... | ... | ... | ... |
| 1947 | ... | ... | 92 | 1.9 | ... | ... | ... | ... | ... | ... |
| 1948 | ... | ... | 81 | 1.6 | ... | ... | ... | ... | ... | ... |
| 1949 | ... | ... | 101[4] | 2.0[4] | ... | ... | ... | ... | ... | ... |
| 1950 | ... | ... | 142 | 2.7 | ... | ... | ... | ... | ... | ... |
| 1951 | ... | ... | 81 | 1.5 | ... | ... | ... | ... | ... | ... |
| 1952 | ... | ... | 105 | 2.0 | ... | ... | ... | ... | ... | ... |
| 1953 | ... | ... | 115 | 2.1 | ... | ... | ... | ... | ... | ... |
| 1954 | ... | ... | 221 | 4.0 | ... | ... | ... | ... | ... | ... |
| 1955 | ... | ... | 214[1] | 3.8[1] | ... | ... | | | ... | ... |
| | | | 245 | | 4.4 | | | | | |
| 1956 | ... | ... | 197 | 3.4 | ... | ... | ... | ... | ... | ... |
| 1957 | ... | ... | 278 | 4.6 | ... | ... | ... | ... | ... | ... |
| 1958 | ... | ... | 432 | 7.0 | ... | ... | ... | ... | ... | ... |
| 1959 | 3.05 | ... | 372 | 6.0 | ... | ... | 0.63 | ... | ... | ... |
| 1960 | 4.56 | ... | 446 | 7.0 | ... | ... | 0.22 | ... | ... | ... |
| 1961 | 4.32 | ... | 466 | 7.1 | ... | ... | 0.15 | ... | ... | ... |
| 1962 | 5.22 | ... | 390 | 5.9 | ... | ... | 0.11 | ... | ... | ... |
| 1963 | 2.06 | ... | 374 | 5.5 | ... | ... | 0.13 | ... | ... | ... |
| 1964 | 1.70 | ... | 324 | 4.7 | ... | ... | 0.10 | ... | ... | ... |
| 1965 | 1.16 | ... | 280 | 3.9 | ... | ... | 0.08 | ... | ... | ... |
| 1966 | 1.61 | ... | 267 | 3.6 | ... | ... | 0.19 | ... | ... | ... |
| 1967 | 1.42 | ... | 315 | 4.1 | ... | ... | 0.33 | ... | ... | ... |
| 1968 | 0.82 | ... | 382 | 4.8 | ... | ... | 0.65 | 47 | [145][9] | [19.9][9] |
| 1969 | 0.69 | ... | 376 | 4.7 | ... | ... | 0.74 | 47 | 132 | 17.6 |
| 1970 | 0.23 | ... | 487 | 5.9 | ... | ... | 0.66 | 49 | ... | ... |
| 1971 | 0.13 | ... | 543 | 6.4 | ... | ... | 0.66 | 51 | ... | ... |
| 1972 | 0.21 | ... | 552 | 6.3 | ... | ... | 0.62[8] | 52 | 185 | 23.2 |
| 1973 | 0.42 | ... | 509 | 5.6 | ... | ... | 0.57 | 53 | 176 | 21.9 |
| 1974 | 0.19 | ... | 570[1] | 5.4[1] | ... | ... | 0.44 | 52 | 174 | 21.2 |
| 1975 | ... | ... | 690 | 6.9 | ... | ... | 0.93 | 79 | 175 | 20.5 |
| 1976 | 0.16 | 15.6 | 726 | 7.1 | 42 | 6.3 | 0.36 | 81[5] | 211 | 22.4 |
| | | | | | | | | 101 | | |
| 1977 | 0.16 | 15.7 | 849 | 8.1 | 32 | 4.6 | 0.22 | 105 | 215 | 24.1 |
| 1978 | 0.14 | 13.7 | 908 | 8.3 | 33 | 4.5 | 0.24 | 109 | 223 | 24.3 |
| 1979 | [0.12][3] | [11.3][3] | 836 | 7.4 | 37 | 4.9 | 0.22 | 113 | 259 | 27.5 |
| 1980 | [0.13][3] | [11.4][3] | 865[5] | 7.5[5] | 46 | 5.9 | 0.23 | 117 | 262 | 27.3 |
| 1981 | 0.12 | 10.8 | 898 | 7.5 | 70 | 8.7 | 0.26 | 113 | 256 | 25.9 |
| 1982 | 0.16 | 13.7 | 1,308 | 11.0 | 79 | 9.4 | 0.58 | 128 | 278 | 27.6 |
| 1983 | 0.17 | 15.0 | 1,434 | 11.8 | 76 | 9.0 | 0.31 | 254 | 266 | 26.4 |
| 1984 | 0.19 | 17.1 | 1,384 | 11.2 | [44][7] | [5.0][7] | 0.40 | ... | 267 | 25.5 |
| 1985 | 0.21 | 18.7 | 1,311 | 10.5 | 61 | 6.8 | 0.22 | ... | 261 | 25.0 |
| 1986 | 0.21 | 17.7 | 1,215 | 9.5 | 57 | 6.2 | 0.27 | ... | 250 | 23.6 |
| 1987 | 0.21 | 17.4 | 1,150 | 8.8 | 54 | 5.9 | 0.22 | ... | 224 | 21.0 |
| 1988 | 0.21 | 17.4 | 1,031 | 7.8 | 55 | 5.5 | 0.21 | ... | 203 | 18.4 |

**B2    NORTH AMERICA: Unemployment** (numbers in thousands; percentage of appropriate workforce)

| | Mexico[10] | | Panama[11] | | Puerto Rico | | Trinidad & Tobago | | USA[2] | |
|------|------|------|------|------|------|------|------|------|------|------|
| | No | % | No. | % | No. | % | No. | % | No. | % |
| 1940 | 185 | ... | ... | ... | ... | ... | ... | ... | 8,120 | 14.6 |
| 1941 | 181 | ... | ... | ... | ... | ... | ... | ... | 5,560 | 9.9 |
| 1942 | 158 | ... | ... | ... | ... | ... | ... | ... | 2,660 | 4.7 |
| 1943 | ... | ... | ... | ... | ... | ... | ... | ... | 1,070 | 1.9 |
| 1944 | ... | ... | ... | ... | ... | ... | ... | ... | 670 | 1.2 |
| 1945 | ... | ... | ... | ... | ... | ... | ... | ... | 1,040 | 1.9 |
| 1946 | ... | ... | ... | ... | [80][12] | [12.0][12] | ... | ... | 2,270 | 3.9 |
| 1947 | ... | ... | ... | ... | 76 | 11.1 | /... | ... | 2,311 | 3.9 |
| 1948 | ... | ... | ... | ... | 71 | 10.4 | ... | ... | 2,276 | 3.8 |
| 1949 | ... | ... | ... | ... | 79 | 11.2 | ... | ... | 3,637 | 5.9 |
| 1950 | ... | ... | ... | ... | [98][13] | [13.7][13] | ... | ... | 3,288 | 5.3 |
| 1951 | ... | ... | ... | ... | 114 | 16.2 | ... | ... | 2,055 | 3.3 |
| 1952 | ... | ... | ... | ... | 100 | 15.2 | ... | ... | 1,883[2] | 3.0[2] |
| 1953 | ... | ... | ... | ... | 91 | 14.4 | ... | ... | 1,834 | 2.9 |
| 1954 | ... | ... | ... | ... | 97 | 15.4 | ... | ... | 3,532 | 5.5 |
| 1955 | ... | ... | ... | ... | 92 | 14.3 | ... | ... | 2,852 | 4.4 |
| 1956 | ... | ... | ... | ... | 83 | 13.0 | ... | ... | 2,750 | 4.1 |
| 1957 | ... | ... | ... | ... | 82 | 13.0 | ... | ... | 2,859 | 4.3 |
| 1958 | ... | ... | ... | ... | 89 | 13.9 | ... | ... | 4,602 | 6.8 |
| 1959 | ... | ... | ... | ... | 87 | 13.8 | ... | ... | 3,740 | 5.5 |
| 1960 | ... | ... | ... | ... | 77 | 12.1 | ... | ... | 3,852 | 5.5 |
| 1961 | ... | ... | ... | ... | 85 | 12.6 | ... | ... | 4,714 | 6.7 |
| 1962 | ... | ... | ... | ... | 86 | 12.6 | ... | ... | 3,911 | 5.5 |
| 1963 | ... | ... | 21 | 5.8 | 83 | 11.8 | ... | ... | 4,070 | 5.7 |
| 1964 | ... | ... | 27 | 7.4 | 81 | 11.1 | ... | ... | 3,786 | 5.2 |
| 1965 | ... | ... | 29 | 7.6 | 91 | 12.0 | 48 | 14.0 | 3,366 | 4.5 |
| 1966 | ... | ... | 20 | 5.1 | 86 | 11.8 | 49 | 14.0 | 2,875 | 3.8 |
| 1967 | ... | ... | 25 | 6.2 | 87 | 11.7 | 54 | 15.0 | 2,975 | 3.8 |
| 1968 | ... | ... | 31 | 7.0 | 83 | 11.1 | 54 | 15.0 | 2,817 | 3.6 |
| 1969 | ... | ... | 30 | 6.6 | 76 | 10.0 | 48 | 13.5 | 2,831 | 3.5 |
| 1970 | ... | ... | 33 | 7.1 | 83 | 10.8 | 46 | 12.5 | 4,088 | 4.9 |
| 1971 | ... | ... | 36 | 7.6 | 93 | 11.6 | [46][14] | [12.6][14] | 4,993 | 5.9 |
| 1972 | ... | ... | 33 | 6.8 | 100 | 11.9 | ... | ... | 4,882 | 5.6 |
| 1973 | ... | ... | 35 | 7.0 | 98 | 11.6 | 59 | 15.4 | 4,365 | 4.9 |
| 1974 | ... | ... | 30[11] | 5.8[11] | 110 | 13.2 | 60 | 15.3 | 5,156 | 5.6 |
| 1975 | 382 | 7.2 | 32[11] | 6.4[11] | 149 | 18.1 | 59 | 15.0 | 7,929 | 8.3 |
| 1976 | 375 | 6.7 | 34 | 6.7 | 167 | 19.5 | ... | ... | 7,406 | 7.6 |
| 1977 | 472 | 8.0 | 45[11] | 8.7[11] | 174 | 19.9 | 57 | 13.4 | 6,991 | 6.9 |
| 1978 | 424 | 6.9 | 44 | 8.1 | 161 | 18.1 | 53 | 12.0 | 6,202 | 6.0 |
| 1979 | ... | 5.7 | 51 | 8.8 | 153 | 17.0 | 49[5] | 11.0[5] | 6,137 | 5.8 |
| | | 4.5 | | | | | | | | |
| 1980 | ... | 4.2 | ... | ... | 156 | 17.1 | 42 | 10.0 | 7,637 | 7.0 |
| 1981 | ... | 4.2 | ... | ... | 184 | 19.9 | 45 | 10.2 | 8,273 | 7.3 |
| 1982 | ... | 6.8 | 51 | 8.4 | 208 | 22.8 | 44 | 10.0 | 10,678 | 9.5 |
| 1983 | ... | 6.0 | 64 | 9.7 | 220 | 23.4 | 50 | 11.0 | 10,717 | 9.5 |
| 1984 | ... | 4.8 | 69 | 10.1 | 198 | 20.7 | 63 | 13.5 | 8,539 | 7.5 |
| 1985 | ... | 4.9 | 88 | 12.3 | 211 | 21.8 | 73 | 15.5 | 8,312 | 7.2 |
| 1986 | ... | | 76 | 10.5 | 188 | 18.9 | 81 | 17.2 | 8,237 | 7.0 |
| 1987 | ... | | 91 | 11.8 | 171 | 16.8 | 107 | 22.3 | 7,425 | 6.2 |
| 1988 | ... | | 128 | 16.3 | 158 | 15.0 | 105 | 22.0 | 6,701 | 5.5 |

**B2    SOUTH AMERICA: UNEMPLOYMENT** (numbers in thousands; percentages of appropriate workforce)

### 1931–1959

| | Chile[15] No | Guyana No | Surinam[16] No |
|---|---|---|---|
| 1931 | 29.0 | ... | ... |
| 1932 | 107.0 | ... | ... |
| 1933 | 72.0 | ... | ... |
| 1934 | 30.0 | ... | ... |
| 1935 | 11.0 | ... | ... |
| 1936 | 6.5 | ... | ... |
| 1937 | 3.2 | ... | ... |
| 1938 | 4.6 | ... | ... |
| 1939 | 9.4 | ... | ... |
| 1940 | 8.6 | ... | ... |
| 1941 | 4.1 | ... | ... |
| 1942 | 2.5 | ... | ... |
| 1943 | 3.6[15] / 2.8 | ... | ... |
| 1944 | 3.3 | ... | ... |
| 1945 | 3.5 | ... | ... |
| 1946 | 3.4 | ... | ... |
| 1947 | 3.7 | ... | ... |
| 1948 | 3.2 | ... | ... |
| 1949 | 3.4 | ... | ... |
| 1950 | 2.9 | 1.6 | ... |
| 1951 | 2.6 | ... | ... |
| 1952 | 3.3 | 3.2 | ... |
| 1953 | 2.8 | 3.4 | ... |
| 1954 | 3.8 | 3.5 | ... |
| 1955 | 3.8 | 3.2 | [3.3][13] |
| 1956 | 6.2 | 3.9 | 3.0 |
| 1957 | 7.4 | 4.3 | 2.4 |
| 1958 | 9.4 | 53 | 3.7 |
| 1959 | 9.0 | 4.8 | 5.2 |

### 1960–1988

| | Argentina[17] No | % | Bolivia No | % | Brazil[19] No | % |
|---|---|---|---|---|---|---|
| 1960 | ... | ... | ... | ... | ... | ... |
| 1961 | ... | ... | ... | ... | ... | ... |
| 1962 | ... | ... | ... | ... | ... | ... |
| 1963 | ... | ... | ... | ... | ... | ... |
| 1964 | [178][18] | [5.7][18] | ... | ... | ... | ... |
| 1965 | 167 | 5.3 | ... | ... | ... | ... |
| 1966 | 173 | 5.6 | ... | ... | ... | ... |
| 1967 | 199 | 6.4 | ... | ... | ... | ... |
| 1968 | 153 | 5.0 | ... | ... | 710 | ... |
| 1969 | 140 | 4.3 | ... | ... | 698 | ... |
| 1970 | 158 | 4.8 | ... | ... | 725 | ... |
| 1971 | 196 | 6.0 | 123 | 9.0 | 723 | ... |
| 1972 | 221 | 6.6 | 112 | 8.1 | 1,034 | ... |
| 1973 | 173 | 5.6 | 101 | 7.1 | 968 | ... |
| 1974 | 121 | 3.4 | 89 | 6.1 | ... | ... |
| 1975 | 97 | 2.3 | 77 | 5.2 | ... | ... |
| 1976 | 159 | 4.5 | 87 | 5.5 | 713 | 1.8 |
| 1977 | 103 | 2.8 | 89 | 5.3 | 953 | 2.3 |
| 1978 | 102 | 2.8 | 95 | 5.5 | 1,003[19] | 2.4[19] |
| 1979 | 69 | 2.0 | 99 | 5.6 | 1,210 | 2.8 |
| 1980 | 82 | 2.3 | 106 | 5.8 | ... | ... |
| 1981 | 175 | 4.5 | 180 | 9.7 | 2,023 | 4.3 |
| 1982 | 184 | 4.8 | 201 | 10.5 | 2,533 | ... |
| 1983 | 159 | 4.2 | 278 | 14.2 | 2,474 | 4.9 |
| 1984 | 152 | 3.8 | 303 | 15.1 | 2,234 | 4.3 |
| 1985 | 216 | 5.3 | 371 | 18.0 | [1,862][20] | [3.4][20] |
| 1986 | [178][18] | [4.4][18] | 415 | 20.0 | 1,380 | 2.4 |
| 1987 | 230 | 5.3 | 431 | 20.5 | 2,133 | 3.7 |
| 1988 | 251 | 5.9 | 388 | 18.0 | 2,319 | 3.9 |

**B2**     **SOUTH AMERICA: Unemployment** (numbers in thousands; percentages of appropriate workforce)

| | Chile[15] | | Colombia[25] | | Guyana[26] | Peru | | Surinam[16] | Uruguay[27] | | Venezuela[29] | |
|---|---|---|---|---|---|---|---|---|---|---|---|---|
| | No | % | No | % | No | No | % | No | No | % | No | % |
| 1960 | 12 | ... | ... | ... | 4.2 | ... | ... | 4.0 | ... | ... | ... | ... |
| 1961 | 13 | ... | ... | ... | 4.6 | ... | ... | 3.6 | ... | ... | ... | ... |
| 1962 | 12 | ... | ... | ... | 5.5 | ... | ... | 3.6 | ... | ... | ... | ... |
| 1963 | 11 | ... | ... | ... | 4.6 | ... | ... | 3.9 | ... | ... | ... | ... |
| 1964 | ... | ... | ... | ... | 5.1 | ... | ... | 3.3 | ... | ... | ... | ... |
| 1965 | ...[15] | ...[15] | ... | ... | 12.3 | ... | ... | 3.0 | ... | ... | ... | ... |
| 1966 | [159][21] | [5.7][21] | ... | ... | 12.1 | ... | ... | 2.6 | ... | ... | ... | ... |
| 1967 | [132][22] | [4.7][22] | ... | ... | 8.9 | ... | ... | 2.5 | ... | ... | 217 | 7.7 |
| 1968 | 137 | 4.8 | ... | ... | 7.6 | ... | ... | 2.5 | 43 | 8.4 | 182 | 6.3 |
| 1969 | 128 | 4.7 | ... | ... | 6.4 | 243 | 5.9 | 2.1 | 45 | 8.7 | 192 | 6.5 |
| 1970 | 101 | 3.4 | ... | ... | 5.2 | 201 | 4.7 | 2.2 | 39 | 7.5 | 199 | 6.3 |
| 1971 | 113 | 3.8 | ... | ... | 4.4 | 196 | 4.4 | 1.0 | 41 | 7.6 | 195 | 6.0 |
| 1972 | [93][23] | [3.1][23] | ... | ... | 3.4 | 194 | 4.2 | 0.9 | [42][14] | [7.7][14] | ... | ... |
| 1973 | ... | ... | ... | ... | 2.9 | 191 | 4.2 | 2.0 | [49][14] | [8.9][14] | ... | ... |
| 1974 | ...[15] | ...[15] | ... | ... | 2.3 | 187 | 4.0 | 2.2 | [38][28] | [3.1][28] | 220 | ... |
| 1975 | 468 | 14.7 | 251 | 10.5 | 3.2 | 237 | 4.9 | 2.4 | ... | ... | 269 | 7.6 |
| 1976 | 406 | 13.0 | 269 | 10.4 | 3.0 | 258 | 5.2 | 1.9 | 68 | 12.8 | 234 | 6.0 |
| 1977 | 378 | 11.6 | 261 | 9.4 | 2.5 | 298 | 5.8 | 1.6 | 64 | 11.8 | 193 | 4.8 |
| 1978 | 495 | 14.2 | 244 | 8.2 | 2.0 | 341 | 6.5 | 2.7 | 53 | 10.2 | 193 | 4.6 |
| 1979 | 474 | 13.6 | 293 | 8.9 | 2.6 | 388 | 7.1 | 2.5 | 43 | 8.4 | 231 | 5.4 |
| 1980 | 378 | 10.4 | 321 | 9.1 | 15.6 | 391 | 7.0 | 2.4 | 40₅ | 7.3₅ | 272₅ | 6.2₅ |
| 1981 | 417 | 11.3 | 266 | 8.1 | 20.3 | 392 | 6.8 | 3.8[16] | 37 | 6.6 | 325 | 6.4 |
| 1982 | 718 | 19.6 | 312 | 9.1 | 27.0 | 417 | 7.0 | 7.4 | [61][14] | [11.7][14] | 374 | 7.1 |
| 1983 | 552 | 14.6 | 407 | 11.1 | 7.2 | 566 | 9.2 | 10.7 | 90 | 15.4 | 536 | 9.8 |
| 1984 | 541₅ | 13.9₅ | 503 | 13.1 | 11.7 | 667 | 10.5 | 12.9 | 84 | 13.9 | 706 | 13.4 |
| 1985 | 517[24] | 12.1[24] | 500 | 14.0 | 13.3 | 773 | 11.8 | 17.0 | 78 | 13.0 | 767 | 11.6 |
| 1986 | 374 | 8.8 | 483 | 13.0 | 10.6 | 554 | 8.2 | 13.4[16] | [64][14] | [11.4][14] | 668 | 9.9 |
| 1987 | 343 | 7.9 | 429 | 11.1 | 9.2 | ... | ... | 2.8 | 48 | 9.3 | 573 | 7.2 |
| 1988 | 286 | 6.3 | 403 | 10.1 | ... | ... | ... | 3.0 | 57 | 9.1 | 498 | 6.4 |

**B2      Unemployment** (numbers in thousands; percentage of appropriate workforce)

NOTES

1. SOURCES: ILO, *Yearbook of Labour Statistics* (1935–), and the national publications on
   p. xiv–xvi. The US figures to 1928 were derived by *Historical Statistics of the United States* from
   Stanley Lebergott, *Manpower in Economic Growth* (McGraw-Hill, New York, 1964).
2. Generally speaking, the statistics are averages of monthly or quarterly figures unless otherwise indicated,
   and relate to persons over the normal age for the end of compulsory schooling.
3. The variety of different indicators of unemployment used is clear from the footnotes. This should serve as
   a warning against incautious comparisons.

FOOTNOTES

[1] Persons without a job and seeking work to 1955 (1st line); all unemployed persons aged 14 and over (or 15 and over from 1975) subsequently.

[2] Unemployed persons aged 14 and over to 1946 or 16 and over subsequently. There are slight breaks in comparability in 1953 and 1962.

[3] Average of first three quarters only.

[4] Newfoundland is included from 1950.

[5] Series subsequently revised.

[6] In July (except as noted in other footnotes).

[7] In November.

[8] Guatemala City only to 1972, with Quezaltenango, Escuintila, and Puerto Barrios added subsequently.

[9] Average of July and October.

[10] Statistics are for the major metropolitan cities only.

[11] In one month in each year, generally in summer, but in October in 1974 and 1977 and in November in 1975.

[12] Average of March—December.

[13] Average of April—December.

[14] First half-year only.

[15] Applicants for work to 1943 (1st line), registered unemployed subsequently. New series introduced in 1966 and 1975 greatly improved the coverage. From the latter date, statistics relate to the last quarter of each year except as noted in footnote 24. Percentage figures for Greater Santiago covering the gaps in the national statistics are as follows:

| 1963 | 5.1 | 1972 | 3.3 |
|------|-----|------|-----|
| 1964 | 5.3 | 1973 | 4.8 |
| 1965 | 5.4 | 1974 | 8.3 |
| 1966 | 5.4 | 1975 | 15.0 |

[16] Paramaribo only to 1981. A new system, requiring frequent re-registration, was instituted in 1987.

[17] Greater Buenos Aires only.

[18] In October.

[19] Data relate to Rio de Janeiro, Guanabara, São Paulo, and other areas ranging according to the survey. The coverage is improved in 1979, and probably again in 1981.

[20] In September.

[21] Average of August and December.

[22] Average of April, August, and December.

[23] In March.

[24] Average of November 1985 to January 1986.

[25] Six main cities only.

[26] Main urban districts only.

[27] Montevideo only, excluding domestic servants.

[28] Average of August 1974 to February 1975.

[29] Most figures relate to only part of the year.

## B3    NORTH AMERICA: INDUSTRIAL DISPUTES

Key:-  a = number of strikes and lockouts; b = number of workers involved (in thousands ; c = number of man-days' work lost (in thousands)

| | U.S.A. | | | Canada | | | U.S.A. | |
|---|---|---|---|---|---|---|---|---|
| | a | b | | a | b | c | a | b |
| 1880 | ... | ... | 1900 | ... | ... | ... | 1,839 | 568 |
| 1881 | 477 | 130 | 1901 | 99 | 24 | 738 | 3,012 | 564 |
| 1882 | 476 | 159 | 1902 | 125 | 13 | 203 | 3,240 | 692 |
| 1883 | 506 | 170 | 1903 | 175 | 38 | 859 | 3,648 | 788 |
| 1884 | 485 | 165 | 1904 | 103 | 11 | 193 | 2,419 | 574 |
| 1885 | 695 | 258 | 1905 | 96 | 13 | 246 | 2,186 | 302 |
| 1886 | 1,572 | 610 | 1906 | 150 | 23 | 378 | ... | ... |
| 1887 | 1,503 | 439 | 1907 | 188 | 34 | 520 | ... | ... |
| 1888 | 946 | 163 | 1908 | 76 | 26 | 704 | ... | ... |
| 1889 | 1,111 | 260 | 1909 | 90 | 18 | 881 | ... | ... |
| 1890 | 1,897 | 373 | 1910 | 101 | 22 | 731 | ... | ... |
| 1891 | 1,786 | 330 | 1911 | 100 | 29 | 1,821 | ... | ... |
| 1892 | 1,359 | 239 | 1912 | 181 | 43 | 1,136 | ... | ... |
| 1893 | 1,375 | 288 | 1913 | 152 | 41 | 1,036 | ... | ... |
| 1894 | 1,404 | 690 | 1914 | 63 | 10 | 491 | 1,204 | ... |
| 1895 | 1,255 | 407 | 1915 | 63 | 11 | 95 | 1,593 | ... |
| 1896 | 1,066 | 249 | 1916 | 120 | 27 | 237 | 3,789 | ... |
| 1897 | 1,110 | 416 | 1917 | 160 | 50 | 1,124 | 4,450 | ... |
| 1898 | 1,098 | 263 | 1918 | 230 | 80 | 648 | 3,353 | ... |
| 1899 | 1,838 | 432 | 1919 | 336 | 149 | 3,401 | 3,630 | ... |

| | Canada | | | Mexico[6] | | U.S.A. | | |
|---|---|---|---|---|---|---|---|---|
| | a | b | c | a | b | a | b | c |
| 1920 | 322 | 60 | 800 | ... | ... | 3,411 | ... | ... |
| 1921 | 168 | 28 | 1,049 | ... | ... | 2,385 | ... | ... |
| 1922 | 104 | 44 | 1,529 | ... | ... | 1,112 | ... | ... |
| 1923 | 86 | 34 | 672 | ... | ... | 1,553 | ... | ... |
| 1924 | 70 | 34 | 1,295 | ... | ... | 1,249 | ... | ... |
| 1925 | 87 | 29 | 1,193 | ... | ... | 1,301 | ... | ... |
| 1926 | 77 | 24 | 267 | ... | ... | 1,035 | ... | ... |
| 1927 | 74 | 22 | 153 | ... | ... | 707 | 330 | 26,200 |
| 1928 | 98 | 18 | 224 | ... | ... | 604 | 314 | 12,600 |
| 1929 | 90 | 13 | 152 | 14 | 3,473 | 921 | 289 | 5,350 |
| 1930 | 67 | 14 | 92 | 15 | 3,718 | 637 | 183 | 3,320 |
| 1931 | 88 | 11 | 204 | 11 | 227 | 810 | 342 | 6,890 |
| 1932 | 116 | 23 | 255 | [56][7] | [3,574][7] | 841 | 324 | 10,500 |
| 1933 | 125 | 27 | 318 | [13][7] | [11,084][7] | 1,695 | 1,170 | 16,900 |
| 1934 | 191 | 46 | 575 | 202 | 14,685 | 1,856 | 1,470 | 19,600 |
| 1935 | 120 | 33 | 289 | 642 | 145,212 | 2,014 | 1,120 | 15,500 |
| 1936 | 156 | 35 | 277 | 674 | 113,885 | 2,172 | 789 | 13,900 |
| 1937 | 278 | 72 | 886 | 576[6] | 61,732[6] | 4,740 | 1,861 | 28,425 |
| 1938 | 147 | 20 | 149 | 319 | 13,435 | 2,772 | 688 | 9,148 |
| 1939 | 122 | 41 | 225 | 303 | 14,486 | 2,613 | 1,171 | 17,812 |

**B3     NORTH AMERICA: Industrial Disputes**

| | Barbados | | | Canada | | | Costa Rica | | | El Salvador | | |
|---|---|---|---|---|---|---|---|---|---|---|---|---|
| | a | b | c | a | b | c | a | b | c | a | b | c |
| 1940 | ... | ... | ... | 168 | 61 | 266 | ... | ... | ... | ... | ... | ... |
| 1941 | ... | ... | ... | 231 | 87 | 434 | ... | ... | ... | ... | ... | ... |
| 1942 | ... | ... | ... | 354 | 114 | 450 | ... | ... | ... | ... | ... | ... |
| 1943 | ... | ... | ... | 402 | 218 | 1,041 | ... | ... | ... | ... | ... | ... |
| 1944 | ... | ... | ... | 199 | 75 | 490 | ... | ... | ... | ... | ... | ... |
| 1945 | ... | ... | ... | 197 | 96 | 1,457 | ... | ... | ... | ... | ... | ... |
| 1946 | ... | ... | ... | 228 | 139 | 4,516 | ... | ... | ... | ... | ... | ... |
| 1947 | ... | ... | ... | 236 | 104 | 2,397 | ... | ... | ... | ... | ... | ... |
| 1948 | ... | ... | ... | 154 | 43 | 886 | ... | ... | ... | ... | ... | ... |
| 1949 | ... | ... | ... | 137 | 51 | 1,064 | ... | ... | ... | ... | ... | ... |
| 1950 | ... | ... | ... | 161 | 192 | 1,389 | ... | ... | ... | ... | ... | ... |
| 1951 | ... | ... | ... | 259 | 103 | 902 | ... | ... | ... | ... | ... | ... |
| 1952 | ... | ... | ... | 222 | 121 | 2,880 | ... | ... | ... | ... | ... | ... |
| 1953 | 2 | 121 | ... | 174 | 56 | 1,325 | ... | ... | ... | ... | ... | ... |
| 1954 | 3 | 331 | 1.3 | 174 | 62 | 1,475 | ... | ... | ... | ... | ... | ... |
| 1955 | 3 | 1,257 | 14.0 | 159 | 60 | 1,875 | ... | ... | ... | ... | ... | ... |
| 1956 | 9 | 1,467 | 31.0 | 229 | 89 | 1,246 | ... | ... | ... | ... | ... | ... |
| 1957 | 24 | 2,207 | 6.0 | 249 | 91 | 1,635 | ... | ... | ... | ... | ... | ... |
| 1958 | [1 | 18,763 | 169.0][1] | 262 | 112 | 2,872 | ... | ... | ... | ... | ... | ... |
| 1959 | 4 | 255 | 1.0 | 218 | 100 | 2,287 | ... | ... | ... | ... | ... | ... |
| 1960 | — | — | — | 274 | 49 | 739 | ... | ... | ... | ... | ... | ... |
| 1961 | — | — | — | 287 | 98 | 1,335 | ... | ... | ... | ... | ... | ... |
| 1962 | 10 | 512 | 1.3 | 311 | 74 | 1,418 | ... | ... | ... | ... | ... | ... |
| 1963 | 5 | 289 | 0.6 | 332 | 83 | 917 | ... | ... | ... | ... | ... | ... |
| 1964 | 4 | 293 | 1.0 | 343 | 101 | 1,581 | ... | ... | ... | ... | ... | ... |
| 1965 | 3 | 366 | 1.3 | 501 | 172 | 2,350 | ... | ... | ... | ... | ... | ... |
| 1966 | 6 | 1,969 | 4.3 | 617 | 411 | 5,178 | ... | ... | ... | ... | ... | ... |
| 1967 | 5 | 411 | 2.2 | 522 | 252 | 3,975 | ... | ... | ... | ... | ... | ... |
| 1968 | — | — | — | 582 | 224 | 5,083 | ... | ... | ... | ... | ... | ... |
| 1969 | 3 | 489 | 2.8 | 595 | 307 | 7,752 | ... | ... | ... | ... | ... | ... |
| 1970 | — | — | — | 542 | 262 | 6,540 | ... | ... | ... | ... | ... | ... |
| 1971 | 3[2] | 415 | 54.0 | 569 | 240 | 2,867 | ... | ... | ... | 12 | 11.0 | 197.0 |
| 1972 | 7 | 1,353 | 1.5 | 598 | 706 | 7,754 | ... | ... | ... | 23 | 3.9 | 42.0 |
| 1973 | 71 | 2,549 | 4.1 | 724 | 348 | 5,776 | 14 | 8.3 | 18.0 | 6 | 0.6 | 7.1 |
| 1974 | 2 | 550 | 2.4 | 1,218 | 581 | 9,222 | 8 | 15.0 | 329.0 | 6 | 37.0 | ... |
| 1975 | 3 | 823 | 3.4 | 1,171 | 506 | 10,909 | 18 | 11.0 | 47.0 | 14 | 2.9 | 39.0 |
| 1976 | 2 | 282 | 0.1 | 1,039 | 1,571 | 11,610 | 14 | ... | ... | 2 | 25.0 | 602.0 |
| 1977 | — | — | — | 803 | 218 | 3,308 | 10 | 11.0 | 74.0 | 19 | 33.0 | 155.0 |
| 1978 | — | — | — | 1,058 | 402 | 7,393 | 14 | 20.0 | 177.0 | 29 | 7.2 | 73.0 |
| 1979 | 1 | 45 | 0.3 | 1,050 | 462 | 7,834 | 20 | 26.0 | 275.0 | 103 | 29.0 | 292.0 |
| 1980 | 7 | 2,166 | 14.3 | 1,028 | 441 | 8,975 | 61 | 25.0 | 427.0 | [42][3] | [12.0][3] | [44.0][3] |
| 1981 | 8 | 2,219 | 7.0 | 1,048 | 339 | 8,878 | 6 | 7.4 | 167.0 | 15 | 5.3 | 138.0 |
| 1982 | 17 | 6,084 | 8.0 | 677 | 444 | 5,795 | 14 | 13.0 | 286.0 | 4 | 0.4 | 5.0 |
| 1983 | 5 | 1,031 | 8.9 | 645 | 329 | 4,444 | 16 | 8.3 | 309.0 | 15 | 2.7 | 93.0 |
| 1984 | 3 | 582 | 0.9 | 717 | 187 | 3,872 | 12 | 13.0 | 254 | 36 | 26.0 | 233.0 |
| 1985 | 5 | 886 | 5.3 | 829 | 162 | 3,125 | 10 | 11.0 | 44.0 | 54 | 30.0 | 351.0 |
| 1986 | 2 | 85 | 0.1 | 735 | 484 | 7,106 | 23 | 38.0 | 40.0 | 54 | 18.0 | 2,233.0 |
| 1987 | 7 | 988 | 2.3 | 658[2] | 583[2] | 3,984[2] | 7 | 5.2 | 0.9 | 25 | 4.0 | 778.0 |
| | | | | 64 | 533 | 2,400 | | | | | | |
| 1988 | 10 | 862 | 0.7 | 53 | 161 | 3,405 | 16 | 3.0 | 36.0 | | | |

**B3    NORTH AMERICA: Industrial Disputes**

| | Guadeloupe | | | Guatemala | | | Haiti | | | Jamaica | | |
|---|---|---|---|---|---|---|---|---|---|---|---|---|
| | a | b | c | a | b | c | a | b | c | a | b | c |
| 1940 | ... | ... | ... | ... | ... | ... | ... | ... | ... | ... | ... | ... |
| 1941 | ... | ... | ... | ... | ... | ... | ... | ... | ... | ... | ... | ... |
| 1942 | ... | ... | ... | ... | ... | ... | ... | ... | ... | ... | ... | ... |
| 1943 | ... | ... | ... | ... | ... | ... | ... | ... | ... | ... | ... | ... |
| 1944 | ... | ... | ... | ... | ... | ... | ... | ... | ... | ... | ... | ... |
| 1945 | ... | ... | ... | ... | ... | ... | ... | ... | ... | 154 | 12.0 | 92.0 |
| 1946 | ... | ... | ... | ... | ... | ... | ... | ... | ... | 110 | 16.0 | 239.0 |
| 1947 | ... | ... | ... | ... | ... | ... | ... | ... | ... | 27 | 13.0 | 259.0 |
| 1948 | ... | ... | ... | ... | ... | ... | ... | ... | ... | 23 | 3.2 | 10.0 |
| 1949 | ... | ... | ... | ... | ... | ... | ... | ... | ... | 7 | 0.4 | 2.7 |
| 1950 | ... | ... | ... | ... | ... | ... | ... | ... | ... | 58 | 13.0 | 75.0 |
| 1951 | ... | ... | ... | ... | ... | ... | ... | ... | ... | 53 | 13.0 | 166.0 |
| 1952 | ... | ... | ... | ... | ... | ... | ... | ... | ... | 42 | 6.3 | 79.0 |
| 1953 | ... | ... | ... | ... | ... | ... | ... | ... | ... | 18 | 4.6 | 71.0 |
| 1954 | ... | ... | ... | ... | ... | ... | ... | ... | ... | 25 | 3.2 | 40.0 |
| 1955 | ... | ... | ... | ... | ... | ... | ... | ... | ... | 28 | 8.2 | 132.0 |
| 1956 | ... | ... | ... | ... | ... | ... | ... | ... | ... | 15 | 5.7 | 50.0 |
| 1957 | ... | ... | ... | ... | ... | ... | ... | ... | ... | 105 | [20.0][5] | [612.0][5] |
| 1958 | ... | ... | ... | ... | ... | ... | ... | ... | ... | 61 | [20.0][5] | [182.0][5] |
| 1959 | ... | ... | ... | ... | ... | ... | ... | ... | ... | 59 | 39.0 | 443.0 |
| 1960 | 2 | 450 | 1.4 | ... | ... | ... | ... | ... | ... | 69 | 12.0 | 65.0 |
| 1961 | 2 | 520 | 0.9 | ... | ... | ... | ... | ... | ... | 53 | 13.0 | 99.0 |
| 1962 | 3 | 1,450 | 5.8 | ... | ... | ... | ... | ... | ... | 83 | 16.0 | 124.0 |
| 1963 | 4 | 165 | 0.3 | ... | ... | ... | ... | ... | ... | 45 | 11.0 | 203.0 |
| 1964 | 5 | 32,000 | 96.0 | ... | ... | ... | ... | ... | ... | 41 | 8.6 | 68.0 |
| 1965 | 5 | 310 | 1.3 | ... | ... | ... | ... | ... | ... | 37 | 25.0 | 290.0 |
| 1966 | 2 | 89 | 0.1 | ... | ... | ... | ... | ... | ... | 69 | 30.0 | 181.0 |
| 1967 | 18 | 4,900 | 39.0 | 8 | 4.0 | 51.0 | ... | ... | ... | 95 | 18.0 | 174.0 |
| 1968 | 3 | 3,127 | 30.0 | 4 | 7.5 | 324.0 | ... | ... | ... | 94 | 23.0 | 225.0 |
| 1969 | 3 | 236 | 0.8 | 2 | 3.1 | 16.0 | ... | ... | ... | 46 | 8.6 | 91.0 |
| 1970 | 4 | 121 | 0.9 | 36 | 27.0 | 51.0 | ... | ... | ... | 70 | 23.0 | 335.0 |
| 1971 | 6 | 12,818 | [146.0][4] | 1 | 0.1 | 0.5 | ... | ... | ... | 77 | 19.0 | 76.0 |
| 1972 | 8 | 1,485 | 67.0 | 4 | 4.9 | 33.0 | ... | ... | ... | 55 | 30.0 | 266.0 |
| 1973 | 8 | 4,277 | 17.0 | 16 | 23.0 | 257.0 | ... | ... | ... | 90 | 19.0 | 237.0 |
| 1974 | 3 | 249 | 0.5 | 53 | 44.0 | 563.0 | ... | ... | ... | 137 | 21.0 | 769.0 |
| 1975 | 4 | 267 | 1.8 | 7 | 8.3 | 53.0 | ... | ... | ... | 205 | 11.0 | 113.0 |
| 1976 | 4 | 267 | 20.0 | 16 | 5.8 | 168.0 | ... | ... | ... | 142 | 12.0 | 140.0 |
| 1977 | 51 | 5,021 | 19.0 | 9 | 8.7 | 61.0 | 2,647 | 0.8 | ... | 163[8] | 13.0 | 82.0 |
| 1978 | 48 | 5,847 | 17.0 | 229 | 145.0 | 1,479.0 | 1,337 | 1.6 | 9.1 | 678 | ... | ... |
| 1979 | 35 | ... | 22.0 | 7 | 42.0 | 41.0 | 751 | 2.1 | 20 | 608 | ... | ... |
| 1980 | ... | 2,746 | 11.0 | 51 | 69.0 | 817.0 | 2,946 | 3.7 | 22 | 557 | ... | ... |
| 1981 | ... | ... | ... | 3 | 1.3 | 37.0 | 2,728 | 3.7 | 22 | 625 | ... | ... |
| 1982 | ... | ... | ... | — | — | — | 2,642 | 3.5 | 24 | 129 | ... | ... |
| 1983 | 41 | 1,976 | 11.0 | — | — | — | 2,161 | 2.8 | ... | 86 | ... | ... |
| 1984 | 30 | 1,066 | 9.7 | ... | ... | ... | 1,845 | 2.6 | ... | 62 | ... | ... |
| 1985 | 31 | 1,396 | 27.0 | ... | ... | ... | 1,653 | 3.0 | 2,094 | 83 | ... | ... |
| 1986 | 14 | 858 | 9.3 | 33 | ... | ... | 1,767 | 3.8 | 645 | 391 | ... | ... |
| 1987 | 17 | 515 | 6.4 | ... | ... | ... | ... | ... | ... | 370 | ... | ... |
| 1988 | 27 | 1,555 | 15.0 | ... | ... | ... | ... | ... | ... | 66 | 18.0 | 46.0 |

**B3     NORTH AMERICA: Industrial Disputes**

| | Martinique | | | Mexico[6] | | | Panama | | |
|---|---|---|---|---|---|---|---|---|---|
| | a | b | c | a | b | c | a | b | c |
| 1940 | ... | ... | ... | 357 | 19,784 | ... | ... | ... | ... |
| 1941 | ... | ... | ... | 142 | 12,892 | ... | ... | ... | ... |
| 1942 | ... | ... | ... | 98 | 13,643 | ... | ... | ... | ... |
| 1943 | ... | ... | ... | 766 | 81,557 | ... | ... | ... | ... |
| 1944 | ... | ... | ... | 887 | 44,166 | ... | ... | ... | ... |
| 1945 | ... | ... | ... | 220 | 48,055 | ... | ... | ... | ... |
| 1946 | ... | ... | ... | ... | ... | ... | ... | ... | ... |
| 1947 | ... | ... | ... | ... | ... | ... | ... | ... | ... |
| 1948 | ... | ... | ... | ... | ... | ... | ... | ... | ... |
| 1949 | ... | ... | ... | ... | ... | ... | ... | ... | ... |
| 1950 | ... | ... | ... | ... | ... | ... | ... | ... | ... |
| 1951 | ... | ... | ... | ... | ... | ... | ... | ... | ... |
| 1952 | ... | ... | ... | ... | ... | ... | ... | ... | ... |
| 1953 | ... | ... | ... | 167 | 38,552 | ... | ... | ... | ... |
| 1954 | ... | ... | ... | 93 | 25,759 | ... | ... | ... | ... |
| 1955 | ... | ... | ... | 135 | 10,710 | ... | ... | ... | ... |
| 1956 | ... | ... | ... | 159 | 7,573 | ... | ... | ... | ... |
| 1957 | ... | ... | ... | 193 | 7,134 | ... | ... | ... | ... |
| 1958 | ... | ... | ... | 740 | 60,611 | ... | ... | ... | ... |
| 1959 | ... | ... | ... | 379 | 62,770 | ... | ... | ... | ... |
| 1960 | 2 | 2,900 | 29.0 | 377 | 63,567 | ... | ... | ... | ... |
| 1961 | 3 | 21,700 | 505.0 | 373 | 33,184 | ... | ... | ... | ... |
| 1962 | — | — | — | 725 | 80,989 | ... | ... | ... | ... |
| 1963 | 6 | 24,800 | 216.0 | 504 | 26,035 | ... | ... | ... | ... |
| 1964 | 5 | 7,440 | 23.0 | 568 | 16,508 | ... | ... | ... | ... |
| 1965 | 6 | 12,530 | 37.0 | 67 | ... | ... | ... | ... | ... |
| 1966 | 7 | 1,983 | 8.2 | 91 | ... | ... | ... | ... | ... |
| 1967 | 8 | 5,563 | 55.0 | 78 | 8,457 | ... | ... | ... | ... |
| 1968 | 5 | 3,106 | 12.0 | 156 | ... | ... | 3 | 1.1 | 0.6 |
| 1969 | 4 | 2,369 | 18.0 | 144 | ... | ... | 9 | 1.8 | 1.0 |
| 1970 | 4 | 2,332 | 16.0 | 206 | 14,329 | ... | 6 | 7.5 | 13.0 |
| 1971 | 9 | 3,968 | 32.0 | 204 | 9,299 | ... | 280 | 16.0 | ... |
| 1972 | 8 | 7,710 | 268.0 | 207 | 2,684 | ... | ... | ... | ... |
| 1973 | 5 | 656 | 10.0 | 211 | 8,395 | ... | 11 | 1.4 | ... |
| 1974 | 2 | 6,150 | 48.0 | 742 | 17,863 | ... | 3 | 0.2 | 1.1 |
| 1975 | 5 | 5,725 | 131.0 | 236 | 9,680 | ... | 8 | ... | ... |
| 1976 | 15 | 7,664 | 25.0 | 547 | 23,684 | ... | 15 | 2.1 | 19.0 |
| 1977 | ... | ... | ... | 476 | 13,411 | ... | 4 | 0.2 | 0.9 |
| 1978 | ... | ... | ... | 758 | 14,976 | ... | 3 | 0.9 | 3.0 |
| 1979 | ... | ... | ... | 795 | 17,264 | ... | 10 | 1.2 | 44.0 |
| 1980 | 23 | 1,862 | 6.4 | 1,339 | ... | ... | 18 | 2.4 | 159.0 |
| 1981 | ... | ... | ... | 1,066 | ... | ... | 16 | 7.8 | 248.0 |
| 1982 | ... | ... | ... | 1,925 | ... | 1,363 | 7 | 1.3 | 546.0 |
| 1983 | ... | ... | ... | 216 | ... | 775 | 9 | 6.7 | 87.0 |
| 1984 | ... | ... | ... | 427 | ... | 238 | 12 | 0.8 | 16.0 |
| 1985 | ... | ... | ... | 159 | ... | 334 | 7 | 0.8 | 20.0 |
| 1986 | ... | ... | ... | 312 | ... | 121 | 13 | 8.1 | 316.0 |
| 1987 | ... | ... | ... | 174 | ... | 82 | 7 | 1.7 | 450.0 |
| 1988 | ... | ... | ... | 132 | ... | 8 | 3 | 0.5 | 25.0 |

**B3    NORTH AMERICA: Industrial Disputes***

| | Puerto Rico | | | Trinidad & Tobago | | | USA | | |
|---|---|---|---|---|---|---|---|---|---|
| | a | b | c | a | b | c | a | b | c |
| 1940 | ... | ... | ... | ... | ... | ... | 2,508 | 577 | 6,701 |
| 1941 | ... | ... | ... | ... | ... | ... | 4,288 | 2,363 | 23,048 |
| 1942 | ... | ... | ... | ... | ... | ... | 2,968 | 840 | 4,183 |
| 1943 | ... | ... | ... | ... | ... | ... | 3,752 | 1,981 | 13,501 |
| 1944 | 64 | 34.0 | ... | ... | ... | ... | 4,956 | 2,116 | 8,721 |
| 1945 | 56 | 145.0 | ... | ... | ... | ... | 4,750 | 3,467 | 38,025 |
| 1946 | 81 | 25.0 | ... | ... | ... | ... | 4,985 | 4,600 | 116,000 |
| 1947 | 81 | 11.0 | 81 | ... | ... | ... | 3,693 | 2,170 | 34,600 |
| 1948 | 52 | 6.8 | 61 | ... | ... | ... | 3,419 | 1,960 | 34,100 |
| 1949 | 60 | 153.0 | 1,014 | ... | ... | ... | 3,606 | 3,030 | 50,500 |
| 1950 | 24 | 4.2 | 20 | ... | 3.1 | 16.0 | 4,843 | 2,410 | 38,800 |
| 1951 | 55 | 20.0 | 118 | 13 | 0.9 | 6.9 | 4,737 | 2,220 | 22,900 |
| 1952 | 49 | 27.0 | 224 | 5 | ... | ... | 5,117 | 3,540 | 59,100 |
| 1953 | 43 | 26.0 | 94 | 7 | 1.2 | 49.0 | 5,091 | 2,400 | 28,300 |
| 1954 | 49 | 23.0 | 64 | 5 | 2.7 | 13.0 | 3,468 | 1,530 | 22,600 |
| 1955 | 33 | 18.0 | 347 | 3 | 0.4 | 21.0 | 4,320 | 2,650 | 28,200 |
| 1956 | 26 | 4.6 | 48 | 6 | 11.0 | 244.0 | 3,825 | 1,900 | 33,100 |
| 1957 | 39 | 4.8 | 50 | 6 | 0.8 | 0.8 | 3,673 | 1,390 | 16,500 |
| 1958 | 39 | 12.0 | 94 | 13 | 1.8 | 13.0 | 3,694 | 2,060 | 23,900 |
| 1959 | 39 | 6.1 | 94 | 69 | 13.0 | 24.0 | 3,708 | 1,880 | 69,000 |
| 1960 | 47 | 6.7 | 105 | 31 | 21.0 | 181.0 | 3,333 | 1,320 | 19,100 |
| 1961 | 52 | 10.0 | 125 | 35 | 12.0 | 145.0 | 3,367 | 1,450 | 16,300 |
| 1962 | 50 | 8.5 | 65 | 75 | 16.0 | 165.0 | 3,614 | 1,230 | 18,600 |
| 1963 | 47 | 14.0 | 85 | 48 | 18.0 | 205.0 | 3,362 | 941 | 16,100 |
| 1964 | 54 | 7.9 | 59 | 44 | 8.1 | 96.0 | 3,655 | 1,640 | 22,900 |
| 1965 | 40 | 9.6 | 98 | 4 | 7.2 | 88.0 | 3,963 | 1,550 | 23,300 |
| 1966 | 64 | 13.0 | 137 | — | — | — | 4,405 | 1,960 | 25,400 |
| 1967 | 52 | 7.0 | 48 | 5 | 0.6 | 3.1 | 4,595 | 2,870 | 42,100 |
| 1968 | 49 | 9.0 | 55 | 9 | 0.7 | 18.0 | 5,045 | 2,649 | 49,018 |
| 1969 | 73 | 12.0 | 114 | 9 | 2.8 | 20.0 | 5,700 | 2,481 | 42,869 |
| 1970 | 93 | 19.0 | 191 | 64 | 11.0 | 100.0 | 5,716 | 3,305 | 66,414 |
| 1971 | 77 | 14.0 | 232 | 75 | 18.0 | 136.0 | 5,138 | 3,280 | 47,589 |
| 1972 | 107 | 24.0 | 223 | 34 | 8.7 | 24.0 | 5,010 | 1,714 | 27,066 |
| 1973 | 76 | 18.0 | 141 | 74 | 16.0 | 95.0 | 5,353 | 2,251 | 27,948 |
| 1974 | 95 | 22.0 | 289 | 78 | 56.0 | 253.0 | 6,074 | 2,778 | 47,991 |
| 1975 | 65 | 20.0 | 165 | 88 | 36.0 | 777.0 | 5,031[9] | 1,746[9] | 31,237[9] |
| | | | | | | | 235 | 965 | 17,563 |
| 1976 | 37 | 8.6 | 332 | 44 | 27.0 | 141.0 | 231 | 1,518 | 23,962 |
| 1977 | 35 | 15.0 | 326 | 16 | 54.0 | 104.0 | 298 | 1,212 | 21,258 |
| 1978 | 33 | 11.0 | 699 | 38 | 11.0 | 113.0 | 219 | 1,006 | 23,774 |
| 1979 | 27 | 3.6 | 49 | 42 | 10.0 | 216.0 | 235 | 1,021 | 20,409 |
| 1980 | 27 | 5.8 | 118 | 27 | 7.5 | 118.0 | 187 | 795 | 20,844 |
| 1981 | 31 | 7.4 | 82 | 14 | 2.6 | 51.0 | 145 | 729 | 16,908 |
| 1982 | 13 | 7.9 | 383 | 11 | 2.5 | 21.0 | 96 | 656 | 9,061 |
| 1983 | 9 | 1.4 | 10 | 38 | 4.7 | 55.0 | 81 | 909 | 17,461 |
| 1984 | 12 | 1.9 | 37 | 38 | 12.0 | 260.0 | 62 | 376 | 8,499 |
| 1985 | 11 | 0.7 | 27 | 45 | 6.9 | 77.0 | 54 | 324 | 7,079 |
| 1986 | 14 | 2.8 | 39 | 16 | 1.2 | 81.0 | 69 | 533 | 11,861 |
| 1987 | 7 | 1.2 | 4 | 10 | 2.7 | 31.0 | 46 | 174 | 4,469 |
| 1988 | 6 | 0.5 | 18 | 11 | 1.0 | 7.1 | 40 | 118 | 4,381 |

**B3    SOUTH AMERICA: INDUSTRIAL DISPUTES**

| | Argentina[10] | | | Chile[11] | | | Uruguay | | |
|---|---|---|---|---|---|---|---|---|---|
| | a | b | c | a | b | c | a | b | c |
| 1924 | 71 | 279.0 | ... | ... | ... | ... | 22 | 0.9 | 22.0 |
| 1925 | 86 | 14.0 | ... | ... | ... | ... | 11 | 0.3 | 11.0 |
| 1926 | 62 | 15.0 | ... | ... | ... | ... | 5 | 0.6 | 12.0 |
| 1927 | 56 | 27.0 | 363 | ... | ... | ... | 13 | 4.7 | 53.0 |
| 1928 | 137 | 74.0 | 251 | ... | ... | ... | 3 | 0.3 | 421.0 |
| 1929 | 116 | 53.0 | 543 | ... | ... | ... | 31 | 2.0 | 91.0 |
| 1930 | 127 | 38.0 | 853 | ... | ... | ... | 8 | 1.4 | 11.0 |
| 1931 | 42 | 8.4 | 58 | ... | ... | ... | 56 | 1.8 | 103.0 |
| 1932 | 122 | 165.0 | 136 | 6 | 0.6 | ... | 6 | 2.1 | ... |
| 1933 | 52 | 3.3 | 40 | 10 | 0.7 | ... | 2 | 0.4 | 87.0 |
| 1934 | 42 | 26.0 | 742 | 13 | 3.1 | ... | 17 | 0.9 | 71.0 |
| 1935 | 69 | 52.0 | 2,643 | 30 | 5.4 | ... | 2 | 8.7 | 3.5 |
| 1936 | 109 | 85.0 | 1,344 | 20 | 7.8 | ... | ... | ... | ... |
| 1937 | 82 | 50.0 | 518 | 21 | 3.0 | ... | 23 | 2.0 | 12.0 |
| 1938 | 44 | 8.9 | 229 | 15 | 11.0 | ... | ... | 4.9 | 20.0 |
| 1939 | 49 | 9.7 | 241 | 26 | 11.0 | ... | 20 | 17.0 | 539.0 |
| 1940 | 53 | 13.0 | 225 | 45 | 19.0 | ... | 13 | 0.8 | 16.0 |
| 1941 | 54 | 6.6 | 248 | 31 | 2.9 | ... | 17 | 1.1 | 24.0 |
| 1942 | 113 | 40.0 | 634 | 19 | 2.7 | 33 | 17 | 1.3 | 6.7 |
| 1943 | 85 | 6.8 | 87 | 127 | 49.0 | 40 | 14 | 1.2 | 52.0 |
| 1944 | 27 | 9.1 | 41 | 91 | ... | ... | 6 | 9.5 | 40.0 |
| 1945 | 47 | 44.0 | 509 | ... | ... | ... | ... | ... | ... |
| 1946 | 142 | 334.0 | 2,048 | 196 | 95.0 | ... | ... | ... | ... |
| 1947 | 64 | 54.0 | 3,467 | 176 | 68.0 | 1,116 | ... | ... | ... |
| 1948 | 103 | 278.0 | 3,159 | 40 | 11.0 | 647 | ... | ... | ... |
| 1949 | 36 | 29.0 | 510 | 50 | 21.0 | 739 | ... | ... | ... |

## B3     SOUTH AMERICA: Industrial Disputes*

| | Argentina[10] | | | Bolivia | | Brazil | Chile | | | Colombia | | |
|---|---|---|---|---|---|---|---|---|---|---|---|---|
| | a | b | c | a | c | a | a | b | c | a | b | c |
| 1950 | 30 | 97.0 | 2,032.0 | ... | ... | ... | 218 | 79.0 | 2,278 | ... | ... | ... |
| 1951 | 23 | 16.0 | 152.0 | ... | ... | ... | 193 | 89.0 | 1,565 | ... | ... | ... |
| 1952 | 14 | 16.0 | 313.0 | ... | ... | ... | 215 | 152.0 | 1,767 | ... | ... | ... |
| 1953 | 40 | 5.5 | 59.0 | ... | ... | ... | 208 | 123.0 | 1,453 | ... | ... | ... |
| 1954 | 18 | 120.0 | 1,449.0 | ... | ... | ... | 364 | 99.0 | 1,795 | ... | ... | ... |
| 1955 | 21 | 12.0 | 144.0 | ... | ... | ... | 274 | 128.0 | 1,099 | ... | ... | ... |
| 1956 | 50 | 854.0 | 5,167.0 | ... | ... | ... | 147 | 105.0 | 1,657 | ... | ... | ... |
| 1957 | 56 | 304.0 | 3,391.0 | ... | ... | ... | 80 | 30.0 | 228 | ... | ... | ... |
| 1958 | 84 | 277.0 | 6,245.0 | ... | ... | ... | 120 | 48.0 | 196 | ... | ... | ... |
| 1959 | 45 | 1,411.0 | 10,078.0 | ... | ... | ... | 204 | 82.0 | 870 | ... | ... | ... |
| 1960 | 26 | 130.0 | 1,662.0 | ... | ... | ... | 257 | 89.0 | ... | ... | ... | ... |
| 1961 | 43 | 236.0 | 1,755.0 | ... | ... | ... | 262 | 112.0 | ... | ... | ... | ... |
| 1962 | 15 | 42.0 | 269.0 | ... | ... | ... | 401 | 84.0 | ... | ... | ... | ... |
| 1963 | 20 | 207.0 | 812.0 | ... | ... | ... | 416 | 117.0 | ... | ... | ... | ... |
| 1964 | 27 | 144.0 | 636.0 | ... | ... | ... | 564 | 138.0 | ... | ... | ... | ... |
| 1965 | 32 | 204.0 | 591.0 | ... | ... | ... | 723 | 182.0 | ... | ... | ... | ... |
| 1966 | 27 | 236.0 | 1,004.0 | ... | ... | ... | 1,073 | 195.0 | 2,015 | ... | ... | ... |
| 1967 | 6 | 0.5 | 2.7 | ... | ... | ... | 1,114 | 225.0 | 1,990 | ... | ... | ... |
| 1968 | 7 | 1.6 | 16.0 | ... | ... | ... | 1,124 | 293.0 | 3,652 | ... | ... | ... |
| 1969 | 8 | 6.7 | 150.0 | ... | ... | ... | 1,277 | 362.0 | 1,179 | ... | ... | ... |
| 1970 | 5 | 2.9 | 33.0 | ... | ... | ... | 1,819 | 656.0 | 2,805 | ... | ... | ... |
| 1971 | 16 | 69.0 | 159.0 | ... | ... | ... | 2,696 | 299.0 | 1,388 | ... | ... | ... |
| 1972 | 12 | 61.0 | 153.0 | ... | ... | ... | 3,325 | 394.0 | 1,678 | ... | ... | ... |
| 1973 | ...[10] | ...[10] | ...[10] | ... | ... | ... | 2,050 | 711.0 | 2,503 | ... | ... | ... |
| 1974 | 543 | 272.0 | 652.0 | ... | ... | ... | ... | ... | ... | ... | ... | ... |
| 1975 | 1,266 | ... | ... | ... | ... | ... | ... | ... | ... | ... | ... | ... |
| 1976 | ... | ... | ... | ... | ... | ... | ... | ... | ... | ... | ... | ... |
| 1977 | ... | ... | ... | ... | ... | ... | ... | ... | ... | ... | ... | ... |
| 1978 | ... | ... | ... | ... | ... | ... | ... | ... | ... | 266 | 23.0 | ... |
| 1979 | ... | ... | ... | ... | ... | ... | ... | ... | ... | 137 | 30.0 | ... |
| 1980 | ... | ... | ... | ... | 0.16 | 81 | 89 | 30.0 | 428 | 261 | 31.0 | ... |
| 1981 | ... | ... | ... | 31 | 0.04 | 79 | ... | 25.0 | 676 | 219 | 23.0 | ... |
| 1982 | ... | ... | ... | 301 | ... | 126 | ... | 2.4 | 52 | 149 | 60.0 | ... |
| 1983 | ... | ... | ... | 261 | 0.74 | 312 | 41 | 4.4 | 58 | 146 | 54.0 | 2.305 |
| 1984 | ... | ... | ... | 500 | 2.57 | 534 | 38 | 3.6 | 42 | 147 | 31.0 | 0.925 |
| 1985 | ... | ... | ... | 319 | 1.62 | 843 | 42 | 8.5 | 132 | 87 | 10.0 | 0.461 |
| 1986 | ... | ... | ... | 188 | 0.90 | 1,493 | 41 | 3.9 | 61 | 15 | 3.8 | 0.728 |
| 1987 | ... | ... | ... | 207 | 1.25 | ... | ... | ... | ... | 17[13] | 6.7[13] | 0.432[13] |
| 1988 | ... | ... | ... | 164 | 0.98 | ... | ... | ... | ... | 243 | 25.0 | 0.185 |

**B3    SOUTH AMERICA: Industrial Disputes**

| | Guyana | | | Peru | | | Surinam | | | Venezuela | | |
|---|---|---|---|---|---|---|---|---|---|---|---|---|
| | a | b | c | a | b | c | a | b | c | a | b | c |
| 1950 | ... | ... | ... | ... | ... | ... | ... | ... | ... | ... | ... | ... |
| 1951 | ... | ... | ... | ... | ... | ... | ... | ... | ... | ... | ... | ... |
| 1952 | ... | ... | ... | ... | ... | ... | ... | ... | ... | ... | ... | ... |
| 1953 | 30 | 36.0 | 584.0 | ... | ... | ... | ... | ... | ... | ... | ... | ... |
| 1954 | 26 | 5.5 | 69.0 | ... | ... | ... | 3 | 131 | 0.3 | ... | ... | ... |
| 1955 | 21 | 8.4 | 33.0 | ... | ... | ... | 1 | 107 | 0.1 | ... | ... | ... |
| 1956 | 56 | 7.2 | 23.0 | ... | ... | ... | 4 | 1,666 | 16.0 | ... | ... | ... |
| 1957 | 41 | 13.0 | 65.0 | 161 | 45 | 192 | 2 | 43 | 0.1 | ... | ... | ... |
| 1958 | 51 | 8.1 | 16.0 | 213 | 48 | 1,263 | 1 | 1,218 | 56.0 | 15 | ... | 39.0 |
| 1959 | 35 | 5.2 | 16.0 | 233 | ... | ... | ... | ... | ... | 15 | 6.8 | 105.0 |
| 1960 | 43 | 6.3 | 17.0 | 285 | ... | ... | 1 | 80 | 0.1 | 36 | 9.6 | 41.0 |
| 1961 | 55 | 11.0 | 29.0 | 341 | ... | ... | 5 | 245 | 1.6 | 14 | 12.0 | 49.0 |
| 1962 | 53 | 13.0 | 55.0 | 380 | ... | ... | 5 | 1,782 | 10.0 | 19 | 4.8 | 48.0 |
| 1963 | 56 | 36.0 | 459.0 | 422 | ... | ... | – | – | – | 9 | 2.0 | 28.0 |
| 1964 | 45 | 11.0 | 42.0 | 398 | ... | ... | – | – | – | 27 | 3.5 | 13.0 |
| 1965 | 146 | 48.0 | 137.0 | 397 | 136 | 803 | 4 | 578 | 1.1 | 24 | 4.7 | 18.0 |
| 1966 | 172 | 38.0 | 109.0 | 394 | 127 | 1,461 | 2 | 196 | 0.7 | 12 | 3.2 | 8.0 |
| 1967 | 170 | 31.0 | 152.0 | 414 | 142 | 1,047 | 4 | 727 | 3.2 | 29 | 3.0 | 5.6 |
| 1968 | 136 | 56.0 | 306.0 | 364 | 108 | 422 | 4 | 1,919 | 25.0 | 14 | 6.5 | 11.0 |
| 1969 | 126 | 18.0 | 39.0 | 372 | 92 | 486 | 26 | 5,063 | 62.0 | 83 | 21.0 | ... |
| 1970 | 159 | 84.0 | 454.0 | 345 | 111 | 723 | 7 | 420 | 1.5 | 64 | 24.0 | 234.0 |
| 1971 | 198 | 41.0 | 142.0 | 377 | 161 | 1,360 | 49 | 6,641 | 22.0 | 106 | 39.0 | |
| 1972 | 175 | 45.0 | 135.0 | 409 | 131 | 791 | 15 | 2,826 | 44.0 | 172[12] | [25.0][7] | [146.0][7] |
| 1973 | 186 | 35.0 | 93.0 | 788 | 416 | 1,961 | 30 | 5,073 | 32.0 | 250 | 46.0 | 145.0 |
| 1974 | 151 | 62.0 | 155.0 | 570 | 363 | 1,677 | 12 | 3,438 | 27.0 | 116 | 17.0 | 130.0 |
| 1975 | 129 | 69.0 | 551.0 | 779 | 617 | 2,534 | 8 | 1,999 | 17.0 | 100 | 26.0 | 101.0 |
| 1976 | 400 | 82.0 | 229.0 | 440 | 258 | 853 | 24 | 2,044 | 9.1 | 171 | 34.0 | 91.0 |
| 1977 | 383 | 90.0 | 964.0 | 234 | 1,315 | 1,726 | 12 | 2,845 | 6.5 | 214 | 64.0 | 86.0 |
| 1978 | 300 | 52.0 | 76.0 | 364 | 1,398 | 4,518 | 11 | 772 | 3.2 | 140 | 25.0 | 40.0 |
| 1979 | 219 | 106.0 | 324.0 | 653 | 841 | 1,676 | 8 | 2,186 | 11.0 | 145 | 23.0 | 50.0 |
| 1980 | 333 | 41.0 | 68.0 | 739 | 481 | 2,240 | 17 | 3,439 | 15.0 | 195 | 68.0 | 315.0 |
| 1981 | 621 | 88.0 | 126.0 | 871 | 857 | 2,497 | 13 | 6,250 | 7.2 | 129 | 30.0 | 256.0 |
| 1982 | 653 | 82.0 | 141.0 | 809 | 572 | 2,844 | 53 | 8,421 | 27.0 | 102 | 15.0 | 330.0 |
| 1983 | 731 | 104.0 | 290.0 | 643 | 786 | 2,537 | 6 | 2,613 | 6.5 | 67 | 17.0 | 418.0 |
| 1984 | 493 | 60.0 | 152.0 | 509 | 697 | 1,712 | 51 | 11,847 | 120.0 | 73 | 12.0 | 108.0 |
| 1985 | 718 | 94.0 | 1.4 | 566 | 235 | 1,528 | 9 | 3,772 | 19.0 | 99 | 13.0 | 96.0 |
| 1986 | 453 | 48.0 | 0.8 | 648 | 249 | 2,108 | 10 | 2,538 | 17.0 | ... | ... | ... |
| 1987 | 497 | 58.0 | 0.9 | 726 | 312 | 1,147 | 3 | 460 | 9.8 | ... | ... | ... |
| 1988 | ... | ... | ... | 815 | 691 | 4,740 | 8 | 663 | 5.6 | ... | ... | ... |

## B3    Industrial Disputes

NOTES

1. SOURCES: ILO, *Yearbook of Labour Statistics,* and the national publications on p. xiv–xvi.
2. Except as indicated in footnotes, the number of workers involved and the days' work lost by them relate to all those clearly affected by a particular dispute, not just to those directly involved.
3. The reporting systems of countries differ considerably, and comparisons should not be made without taking these differences into account.

FOOTNOTES

[1] This relates to a dispute on the sugar estates only.
[2] Subsequent statistics relate only to disputes involving 500 workers or more.
[3] First half-year only.
[4] Excluding agriculture.
[5] These figures relate to a smaller number of disputes than the total.
[6] Excluding lockouts from 1938 and workers indirectly involved throughout.
[7] Incomplete statistics.
[8] Subsequent statistics are from national sources and clearly have a more comprehensive coverage.
[9] Subsequent statistics relate only to disputes involving 1,000 workers or more and lasting at least one full shift.
[10] Buenos Aires City to 1972 and Greater Buenos Aires thereafter. Lockouts, general strikes, and strikes less than one day are excluded, as are workers indirectly involved.
[11] Excluding lockouts and workers indirectly involved.
[12] Including 57 for which no data are available.
[13] Subsequently including "paros" (suspensions of work activities). The numbers of days lost are as given by the I.L.O., although they seems to be improbably small.

**B4    NORTH AMERICA: MONEY WAGES IN INDUSTRY**

Key:- a = average daily wages of artisans in the Philadelphia area; b = daily wage rates on the Erie Canal; c = average daily wage rates of 5 skilled grades in manufacturing establishments; d = average annual earnings of non-farm employees; e = average hourly earnings in manufacturing; f = daily wage rates of carpenters, masons, labourers, and painters in the Toronto area for year ending 30 June to 1901 (1st line); average daily wages in non-agricultural occupations from 1901 (2nd line) to 1958 (1st line); and weekly earnings in manufacturing subsequently; g = weekly earnings in manufacturing; h = average daily earnings in manufacturing; i = average monthly earnings in manufacturing; j average daily earnings to 1949, and monthly earnings (including salaries) subsequently k = minimum hourly rates to 1956; weekly earnings 1956–64; and minimum daily rates from 1974; l = monthly earnings in manufacturing and mining to 1945 and in manufacturing alone from 1946 to 1956; minimum hourly earnings of unskilled workers in manufacturing subsequently; m = average daily earnings in non-agricultural sectors in East Central Colombia to 1953; average hourly earnings in manufacturing from 1955 to 1979, and average monthly earnings subsequently.

| | U.S.A. | | U.S.A | | | Canada | USA | | |
|---|---|---|---|---|---|---|---|---|---|
| | a | | a | b | | f | b | c | d |
| | 1830=100 | | 1830=100 | 1830=100 | | | 1830=100 | 1865=100 | 1865=100 |
| 1785 | 77 | 1825 | 101 | ... | 1860 | ... | 140 | 65 | 71 |
| 1786 | 58 | 1826 | 98 | ... | 1861 | ... | 130 | 67 | 72 |
| 1787 | 58 | 1827 | 100 | ... | 1862 | ... | 120 | 71 | 75 |
| 1788 | 56 | 1828 | 101 | 80 | 1863 | ... | 160 | 80 | 90 |
| 1789 | 58 | 1829 | 104 | 100 | 1864 | ... | 180 | 93 | 99 |
| 1790 | 58 | 1830 | 100 | 100 | 1865 | ... | 200 | 100 | 100 |
| 1791 | 61 | 1831 | ... | 100 | 1866 | ... | 240 | 105 | 96 |
| 1792 | 58 | 1832 | ... | 80 | 1867 | ... | 220 | 104 | 94 |
| 1793 | 72 | 1833 | ... | 100 | 1868 | ... | 200 | 103 | 97 |
| 1794 | 80 | 1834 | ... | 100 | 1869 | ... | 240 | 104 | 97 |
| 1795 | 96 | 1835 | ... | 100 | 1870 | ... | 200 | 104 | 96 |
| 1796 | 101 | 1836 | ... | 100 | 1871 | ... | 200 | 103 | 94 |
| 1797 | 106 | 1837 | ... | 100 | 1872 | ... | 200 | 106 | 95 |
| 1798 | 91 | 1838 | ... | 100 | 1873 | ... | 200 | 105 | 91 |
| 1799 | 94 | 1839 | ... | 120 | 1874 | ... | 200 | 99 | 86 |
| 1800 | 95 | 1840 | ... | 120 | 1875 | ... | 200 | 96 | 83 |
| 1801 | 90 | 1841 | ... | 120 | 1876 | ... | 200 | 90 | 79 |
| 1802 | 76 | 1842 | ... | 120 | 1877 | ... | 160 | 87 | 76 |
| 1803 | 83 | 1843 | ... | 100 | 1878 | ... | 160 | 86 | 74 |
| 1804 | 92 | 1844 | ... | 100 | 1879 | ... | 200 | 86 | 73 |
| 1805 | 91 | 1845 | ... | 80 | 1880 | ... | 200 | 90 | 75 |
| 1806 | 96 | 1846 | ... | 80 | 1881 | ... | 200 | ... | 80 |
| 1807 | 97 | 1847 | ... | 100 | 1882 | ... | ... | ... | 84 |
| 1808 | 85 | 1848 | ... | 110 | 1883 | ... | ... | ... | 86 |
| 1809 | 90 | 1849 | ... | 130 | 1884 | ... | ... | ... | 86 |
| 1810 | 99 | 1850 | ... | 120 | 1885 | ... | ... | ... | 87 |
| 1811 | 102 | 1851 | ... | 120 | 1886 | ... | ... | ... | 88 |
| 1812 | 91 | 1852 | ... | 120 | 1887 | ... | ... | ... | 90 |
| 1813 | 88 | 1853 | ... | 120 | 1888 | ... | ... | ... | 91 |
| | | | | | | 1891=100 | | | |
| 1814 | 94 | 1854 | ... | 140 | 1889 | 101 | ... | ... | 92 |
| 1815 | 110 | 1855 | ... | 140 | | | | | |
| 1816 | 109 | 1856 | ... | 140 | | | | | |
| 1817 | 99 | 1857 | ... | 140 | | | | | |
| 1818 | 108 | 1858 | ... | 120 | | | | | |
| 1819 | 94 | 1859 | ... | 120 | | | | | |
| 1820 | 90 | | | | | | | | |
| 1821 | 79 | | | | | | | | |
| 1822 | 95 | | | | | | | | |
| 1823 | 85 | | | | | | | | |
| 1824 | 90 | | | | | | | | |

**B4      NORTH AMERICA: Money Wages in Industry**

|      | Canada | Mexico |  | USA |  |
|------|--------|--------|--------|--------|--------|
|      | f | g | d | e | g |
|      | *1891=100* | *1955=100* | *1865=100* | *1955=100* | *1955=100* |
| 1890 | 99.0 | ... | 93 | 9.5 | ... |
| 1891 | 100.0 | ... | 94 | 9.6 | ... |
| 1892 | 101.0 | ... | 94 | 9.7 | ... |
| 1893 | 101.0 | ... | 89 | 9.8 | ... |
| 1894 | 96.0 | ... | 82 | 9.6 | ... |
| 1895 | 95.0 | ... | 86 | 9.6 | ... |
| 1896 | 97.0 | ... | 86 | 9.8 | ... |
| 1897 | 94.0 | ... | 86 | 9.7 | ... |
| 1898 | 98.0 | ... | 86 | 9.7 | ... |
| 1899 | 93.0 | ... | 92 | 10.0 | ... |
| 1900 | 94.0 | ... | 94 | 10.3 | ... |
| 1901 | 98.0[1] | ... | ... | 10.5 | ... |
|      | *1955=100* |  |  |  |  |
|      | 13.1 |  |  |  |  |
| 1902 | 13.8 | ... | ... | 10.8 | ... |
| 1903 | 14.3 | ... | ... | 11.3 | ... |
| 1904 | 14.6 | ... | ... | 11.3 | ... |
| 1905 | 14.9 | ... | ... | 11.4 | ... |
| 1906 | 15.5 | ... | ... | 11.8 | ... |
| 1907 | 15.9 | ... | ... | 12.3 | ... |
| 1908 | 16.4 | ... | ... | 11.9 | ... |
| 1909 | 16.7 | ... | ... | 12.0 | 12.9 |
| 1910 | 17.2 | ... | ... | 12.4 | ... |
| 1911 | 16.9 | ... | ... | 12.6 | ... |
| 1912 | 17.5 | ... | ... | 13.1 | ... |
| 1913 | 18.0 | ... | ... | 13.6 | ... |
| 1914 | 18.2 | ... | ... | 13.7 | 14.4 |
| 1915 | 18.3 | ... | ... | 13.7 | 14.8 |
| 1916 | 19.6 | ... | ... | 15.3 | 16.7 |
| 1917 | 22.5 | ... | ... | 17.4 | 19.8 |
| 1918 | 26.4 | ... | ... | 21.4 | 25.3 |
| 1919 | 31.1 | ... | ... | 25.3 | 28.9 |
| 1920 | 36.9 | ... | ... | 29.6 | 34.4 |
| 1921 | 33.7 | ... | ... | 27.4 | 29.0 |
| 1922 | 31.4 | ... | ... | 25.8 | 28.1 |
| 1923 | 32.3 | ... | ... | 28.0 | 31.1 |
| 1924 | 32.7 | ... | ... | 29.0 | 31.3 |
| 1925 | 32.3 | ... | ... | 29.0 | 31.8 |
| 1926 | 32.5 | ... | ... | 29.0 | 32.2 |
| 1927 | 33.2 | ... | ... | 29.0 | 32.3 |
| 1928 | 33.7 | ... | ... | 30.1 | 32.6 |
| 1929 | 34.2 | ... | ... | 30.1 | 32.7 |
| 1930 | 34.4 | ... | ... | 29.6 | 30.4 |
| 1931 | 33.3 | ... | ... | 27.4 | 27.3 |
| 1932 | 30.9 | ... | ... | 23.7 | 22.3 |
| 1933 | 29.4 | ... | ... | 23.7 | 22.0 |
| 1934 | 29.6 | ... | ... | 28.5 | 24.0 |
| 1935 | 30.5 | ... | ... | 29.0 | 26.3 |
| 1936 | 31.1 | ... | ... | 29.6 | 28.5 |
| 1937 | 33.4 | ... | ... | 33.3 | 31.5 |
|      |  | *1955=100* |  |  |  |
| 1938 | 34.4 | 20.9 | ... | 33.3 | 29.2 |
| 1939 | 34.5 | 22.1 | ... | 33.9 | 31.2 |

**B4      NORTH AMERICA: Money Wages in Industry**

| | *Barbados* | Canada | Costa Rica | Dominican Republic | El Salvador[6] | Guatemala[7] | Honduras |
|---|---|---|---|---|---|---|---|
| | g[2] | f | i[5] | j[5] | g[2] | e | h |
| | *1959=100* | *1955=100* | *1973=100* | *1955=100* | *1959=100* | *1955=100* | *1955=100* |
| 1940 | ... | 35.9 | ... | ... | ... | ... | ... |
| 1941 | ... | 39.0 | ... | ... | ... | ... | ... |
| 1942 | ... | 42.3 | ... | ... | ... | ... | ... |
| 1943 | ... | 46.1 | ... | ... | ... | ... | ... |
| 1944 | ... | 47.6 | ... | ... | ... | ... | ... |
| 1945 | ... | 48.9 | ... | ... | ... | ... | ... |
| 1946 | ... | 53.6 | ... | ... | ... | ... | ... |
| 1947 | ... | 59.9 | ... | 78.5 | ... | ... | ... |
| 1948 | ... | 67.5 | ... | 86.3 | ... | ... | ... |
| 1949 | ... | 70.6 | ... | 83.5 | ... | ... | ... |
| 1950 | ... | 74.5 | ... | 84.9₁ | ... | ... | ... |
| 1951 | ... | 84.1 | ... | 93.3 | ... | ... | ... |
| 1952 | ... | 90.1 | ... | 109.5 | ... | [85.6][8] | ... |
| 1953 | ... | 94.3 | ... | 105.9 | ... | 85.9 | 78.4 |
| 1954 | ... | 97.3 | ... | 100.6 | ... | 96.4 | 88.6 |
| 1955 | ... | 100.0 | ... | 100.0 | ... | 100.0 | 100.0 |
| 1956 | ... | 104.9 | ... | 100.6 | ... | 100.7 | 99.6 |
| 1957 | ... | 110.4 | ... | 100.8 | 95.3 | 101.3 | 87.3 |
| 1958 | ... | 114.7₁ | ... | 104.2 | 98.0 | 106.2 | 76.6 |
| 1959 | 100.0 | 120.6 | ... | 108.7 | 100.0 | 109.5 | 83.6 |
| 1960 | 108 | 123.7 | ... | 101.4₅ | ...₄ 94.5 | 109.5 | 100.7 |
| 1961 | 101 | 127.7 | ... | 104.7 | 105.8 | 111.8 | ... |
| 1962 | 133 | 131.6 | ... | 182.9 | 107.2 | 115.4 | 114.5 |
| 1963 | 122 | 136.4 | ... | 166.6 | 107.5 | 118.3 | 113.5 |
| 1964 | 123 | 142.3 | ... | 228.5 | 110.2 | 116.7 | 129.5 |
| 1965 | 140 | 149.0 | ... | 213.9 | 115.5 | 121.9 | 123.1 |
| 1966 | 147 | 157.2 | ... | 200.4 | 123.1 | 126.8 | 142.0 |
| 1967 | [139][3] | 166.1 | ... | 161.6 | 127.4 | 131.0 | ... |
| 1968 | 159 | 178.4 | ... | 180.1 | 134.5 | 135.3 | ... |
| 1969 | 174 | 191.6 | ... | 207.8 | 136.2 | 141.5 | ... |
| 1970 | 206 | 205.3 | ... | 201.3 | 140.6 | 141.5 | ... |
| 1971 | 223 | 223.2 | ... | 204.3 | 142.6 | 142.2 | ... |
| 1972 | [231][3] | 242.6 | ... | 218.3 | 142.5 | 142.5 | ... |
| 1973 | 283 | 261.5 | 100.0 | 207.9 | 151.7 | 142.5₇ | ... |
| 1974 | 355 | 291.6 | 119.0 | 238.2 | 170.4 | 144.4 | ... |
| 1975 | 411 | 335.2 | 141.4 | 335.9 | 157.2 | 150.3 | ... |
| 1976 | 459 | 378.9 | 162.4 | 380.7 | 200.7 | 161.4 | ... |
| 1977 | 544 | 417.9 | 181.9 | 371.3 | 216.0 | 173.2 | ... |
| 1978 | ... | 448.7 | 206.7 | 407.1 | 234.9 | 196.7 | ... |
| 1979 | ... | 488.8 | 237.4 | 414.7 | 264.5 | 205.2 | ... |
| 1980 | ... | 537.5 | 281.1 | 434.7 | 363.3 | 297.1 | ... |
| 1981 | ... | 602.8 | 341.0 | 465.9 | 384.2 | 333.7 | ... |
| 1982 | ... | 666.5₄ | 519.1 | 519.1 | 391.2 | 350.0 | ... |
| 1983 | ... | 692.2 | 836.1 | 532.8 | 455.2 | 382.7 | ... |
| 1984 | ... | 731.4 | [1,077] | 597.1 | 460.8 | 284.3 | ... |
| 1985 | ... | 766.8 | 1,314 | 705.6 | 497.0 | 290.8 | ... |
| 1986 | ... | 791.7₄ | 1,452 | ... | ... | ... | ... |
| 1987 | ... | 816.1 | 2,001 | ... | ... | ... | ... |
| 1988 | ... | 855.6 | 2,220 | ... | ... | ... | ... |

**B4      NORTH AMERICA: Money Wages in Industry**

| | Mexico | Nicaragua | Panama | Puerto Rico | Trinidad & Tobago | USA | |
|---|---|---|---|---|---|---|---|
| | g | e | e | e | k | e | g |
| | *1955=100* | *1959=100* | *1955=100* | *1955=100* | *1955=100* | *1955=100* | *1955=100* |
| 1940 | 23.6 | ... | ... | ... | ... | 35.5 | 33.0 |
| 1941 | 24.1 | ... | ... | ... | ... | 39.2 | 39.0 |
| 1942 | 30.0 | ... | ... | ... | ... | 45.7 | 48.5 |
| 1943 | 33.2 | ... | ... | ... | ... | 51.6 | 56.9 |
| 1944 | 36.5 | ... | ... | ... | ... | 54.3 | 60.4 |
| 1945 | 41.6 | ... | ... | ... | ... | 54.8 | 58.4 |
| 1946 | 45.6 i | ... | ... | [62.7][11] | ... | 58.1 | 57.2 |
| 1947 | 49.4 | ... | ... | 72.7 | ... | 65.6 | 65.0 |
| 1948 | 54.4 | ... | ... | 75.5 | ... | 71.5 | 70.2 |
| 1949 | 59.0 | ... | ... | 75.4 | ... | 74.2 | 71.2 |
| 1950 | 64.2 | ... | ... | 74.8 | ... | 77.4 | 77.0 |
| 1951 | 71.4 | ... | ... | 79.8 | 75.0 | 83.9 | 83.7 |
| 1952 | 74.6 | ... | ... | 84.3 | 80.6 | 88.7 | 88.7 |
| 1953 | 79.2 | ... | ... | 88.0 | 92.6 | 93.5 | 93.1 |
| 1954 | 87.3 | ... | ... | 91.4 | 95.4 | 95.7 | 93.1 |
| 1955 | 100. | ... | 100. | 100. | 100. | 100. | 100. |
| 1956 | 108.8 | ... | 84.1 | 112.5 | 105.6₁ | 104.8 | 104.1 |
| 1957 | 113.2 | ... | 88.6 | 133.5 | 121.7 | 110.2 | 107.8 |
| 1958 | 124.5 | 99.4 | 93.2 | 145.4 | 140.9 | 113.4 | 109.3 |
| 1959 | 138.3 | 100. | 100.0 | 152.5 | 137.5 | 117.7 | 116.6 |
| 1960 | 151.9 | 99.4 | 118.2₄ | 162.3 | 141.9 | 121.5 | 118.5 |
| 1961 | 158.9 | 105.6 | 113.6 | 173.9 | 194.8 | 124.7 | 122.0 |
| 1962 | 172.5 | 118.8 | 122.7 | 186.6 | 202.2 | 128.5 | 127.6 |
| 1963 | 203.0 | 125.0 | 136.4 | 198.2 | 202.7 | 132.3 | 131.6 |
| 1964 | 221.6 | 118.8 | 143.2 | 208.1 | 219.4 | 136.0 | 136.0 |
| 1965 | 236.9 | 130.0 | 147.7 | 217.4 | ... | 140.3 | 142.0 |
| 1966 | 247.8 | ... | 152.3 | 228.0 | ... | 146.2 | 148.4 |
| 1967 | 262.6 | 179.4 | 159.1 | 245.4 | ... | 152.2 | 151.8 |
| 1968 | 276.2 | 190.0 | 165.9 | 272.4 | ... | 161.8 | 161.8 |
| 1969 | 290.0 | 204.4 | 168.2 | 291.2 | ... | 171.5 | 171.1 |
| 1970 | 204.7 | 202.5 | 181.8 | 309.9 | ... | 180.1 | 176.7 |
| 1971 | 331.1 | 204.4 | 184.1 | 329.2 | ... | 191.9 | 188.2 |
| 1972 | 349.9 | 214.6 | 186.4 | 352.1 | ... | 205.4 | 204.4 |
| 1973 | 393.9 | 230.1 | 197.7 | 375.0 | 1974=100¹ 100 | 219.9 | 217.3 |
| 1974 | 501.6 | 267.1 | 222.7 | 408.5 | | 237.6 | 233.6 |
| 1975 | 610.4 | 297.2 | 243.2 | 450.7 | 126.2 | 259.7 | 252.0 |
| 1976 | 763.3 | 319.7 | 254.5 | 489.4 | 156.4 | 280.6 | 276.5 |
| 1977 | 1,001 | 338.5 | 270.5 | 531.7 | 182.8 | 305.4 | 302.4 |
| 1978 | 1,152 | 356.7 | 270.5 | 591.5 | 216.7 | 331.7 | 329.3 |
| 1979 | 1,346 | 462.4 | 284.1 | 649.6 | 271.4 | 360.2 | 355.7 |
| 1980 | 1,636 | 584.7 | ... | 707.7 | 340.7 | 390.9 | 381.2 |
| 1981 | 2,145 | ... | 340.9 | 772.9 | 443.4 | 429.6 | 420.1 |
| 1982 | 3,362 | ... | 347.7 | 816.9 | 532.0 | 456.5 | 436.3 |
| 1983 | 4,983 | ... | 384.1 | 850.4 | 621.6 | 474.7 | 467.8 |
| 1984 | 7,921 | ... | 411.4 | 883.8 | 679.0 | 494.1 | 494.1 |
| 1985 | 12,568₄ | ... | 413.6 | 913.7 | 715.6 | 512.9 | 510.4 |
| 1986 | 20,770 | ... | ... | 934.9 | 742.3 | 523.1 | 523.1 |
| 1987 | 45,407 | ... | ... | 957.7 | 727.8 | 532.8 | 536.7 |
| 1988 | 92,046 | ... | ... | 961.3 | 729.9 | 547.3 | 552.2 |

## B4 SOUTH AMERICA: MONEY WAGES IN INDUSTRY

| | Argentina[9] | Brazil | Chile | Colombia | Ecuador | Peru[12] | Uruguay[13] | Venezuela |
|------|------|------|------|------|------|------|------|------|
| | e | e | h | m | g | h | i | i |
| | *1955=100* | *1955=100* | *1955=100* | *1948=100* | *1959=100* | *1955=100* | *1970=100* | *1964=100* |
| 1937 | 8.1 | ... | 2.7 | ... | ... | ... | ... | ... |
| 1938 | 8.1 | ... | 3.1 | 42.1 | ... | ... | ... | ... |
| 1939 | 8.2 | ... | 3.6 | 44.2 | ... | ... | ... | ... |
| 1940 | 8.2 | ... | 4.4 | 45.4 | ... | ... | ... | ... |
| 1941 | 8.5 | ... | 5.4 | 45.1 | ... | ... | ... | ... |
| 1942 | 9.0 | ... | 7.1 | 46.9 | ... | ... | ... | ... |
| 1943 | 9.6 | ... | 7.9 | 49.9 | ... | ... | ... | ... |
| 1944 | 10.4 | ... | 9.4 | 61.5 | ... | ... | ... | ... |
| 1945 | 11.4[1] | ... | 10.6 | 68.7 | ... | ... | ... | ... |
| 1946 | 14.2 | 24.9 | 12.3 | 76.4 | ... | 21.2 | ... | ... |
| 1947 | ... | 29.1 | 16.6 | 91.9 | ... | 32.6 | ... | ... |
| 1948 | 27.4 | 32.9 | 20.4 | 100.0 | ... | 41.8 | ... | ... |
| 1949 | 37.1 | 36.9 | 24.3 | 123.0 | ... | 54.0 | ... | ... |
| 1950 | 45.2 | 40.8 | 28.2 | 167.8 | ... | 66.8 | ... | ... |
| 1951 | 57.2 | 43.5 | 31.0 | 162.7 | ... | 73.5 | ... | ... |
| 1952 | 70.4 | 50.3 | 40.0 | 149.0 | ... | 81.5 | ... | ... |
| 1953 | 76.8 | 51.6 | 45.3 | 154.0 | ... | 89.6 | ... | ... |
| 1954 | 89.4 | 75.6 | 58.0 | ... *1955=100* | ... | 93.9 | ... | ... |
| 1955 | 100 | 100 | 100 | 100 | ... | 100 | ... | ... |
| 1956 | 113.6[1] | 125.1 | 158.9 | 110.6 | ... | 111.8[4] | ... | ... |
| 1957 | 149.9 | 151.9 | 212.0 | 147.0 | [99.7][11] | 117.8 | ... | ... |
| 1958 | 207.3 | 175.4 | 453.9 | 166.7 | 98.5 | 130.8 | ... | ... |
| 1959 | 354.7 | 238.5[1] | 554.5 | 181.8[4] | 100 | 153.3 | ... | ... |
| | | *i[5]* | | | | | | |
| 1960 | 464.0 | ... | 638.1 | 237.9 | 100.1 | 172.8 | ... | ... |
| 1961 | 572.4 | ... | 733.2 | 274.2 | 102.4 | 187.5 | ... | ... |
| 1962 | 714.9 | 662.8 | 867.2 | 315.2 | 107.5 | 203.4 | ... | ... |
| 1963 | 872.0 | 1,337.1 | 1,153.6 | 437.9 | 111.7 | 214.6 | ... | ... |
| 1964 | 1,128.4 | 2,480.9 *1964=100* | 1,754.7 | 498.5 | 121.8 | 253.3 | ... | 100 |
| 1965 | 1,496.8 | 155.5[4] | 2,446.0 | 553.0 | 125.5 | 295.2 | ... | 105.0 |
| 1966 | 2,040.5 | 273.7 | 3,541.8 | 628.8 | 131.3 | 320.3 | ... | 106.8 |
| 1967 | 2,642.3 | 358.7 | 4,514.0 | 693.9 | 140.1 | ... | 33.8 | 111.9 |
| 1968 | 2,745.1 | 468.7 | 6,055.0 | 765.2 | 153.6 | 393.1 | 70.3 | 121.0 |
| 1969 | 3,018.5 *1969=100* | 593.5 | 8,329.1 *1969=100* | 837.8 | 186.2 | 439.8 | 90.4 | 117.7 |
| 1970 | 118.0 | 741.9 | 143.1 | 980.3[4] | 199.1 | 471.0 | 100 | 127.1 |
| 1971 | 162.4 | 929.1 | 206.1 | 1,100.0 | 224.9 | 502.8 | 128.3 | 135.2 |
| 1972 | 236.8 | 1,177.3 | 328.4 | 1,198.5 | 265.7 | 622.9 | 191.0 | 144.8 |
| 1973 | 416.4 | 1,454.6 | 985.0 | 1,363.6 | 299.0 | 764.1 | 363.0 | 144.6 |
| 1974 | 535.9 | 1,899.7 | 6,332.8 *1974=100* | 1,621.2 | 370.4 *e* | 946.1 | 638.7 | 170.6 |
| 1975 | 1,454.5 | 2,687.4 | 451.1 | 1,993.9 | 452.6 | 998.3 | 1,051.8 | 195.0 |
| 1976 | 4,458.7 | 3,943.6 | 1,789.3 | 2,474.2 | 559.0 | 1,270.3 | 1,431.7 | 200.4 |
| 1977 | 9,944.9 | ... | 5,104.6 | 3,107.6 | 624.1 | 1,540.0 | 1,944.2 | 218.8 |
| 1978 | 16,959 | ... | 8,759.0 | 4,021.2 | 682.4 | 2,106.7 | 2,670.3 | 247.5 |
| 1979 | 43,220 *1979=100* | ... | 13,013 *1979=100* | 5,397.0[1] *1979=100* | 867.8 | 3,072.2[4] *1979=100* | 4,007.6 *1979=100* | 441.3 |
| 1980 | 244.4 | ... | 153.3 | 132.5 | 1,227.7 | 189.2 | 155.6 | 553.8 |
| 1981 | 571.2 | ... | 207.3 | 172.3 | 1,368.3 | 314.2 | 222.6 | 643.8 |
| 1982 | 1,668.9 | ... | 231.3 | 222.4 | 1,478.1 | 523.5 | 256.9 | ... |
| 1983 | 10,464 | ... | 264.1 | 281.3 | 1,899.9 | 903.2 | 304.1 | ... |
| 1984 | 84,603 *1984=100* | ... | 313.1 | 348.0 | 2,469.1 | 1,597.5 | 460.9 | ... |
| 1985 | 645.2 | ... | 388.4 | 421.1 | ... | 3,399.5[4] | 782.6 | ... |
| 1986 | 1,369.9 | ... | 477.8 | 521.3 | ... | 11,529 | 1,485.1 | 672.1 |
| 1987 | 2,757.3 | ... | 577.7 | 639.8 | ... | 20,478 | 2,638.7 | 983.5 |
| 1988 | ... | ... | 700.6 | 813.0 | ... | 96,457 | 4,375.5 | ... |

**B4     Money Wages in Industry**

NOTES

1.   SOURCES: The main sources used were ILO, *Year Book* (1931–34); ILO, *Yearbook of Labour
     Statistics* (1935–); and the national publications on p. xiv–xvi. In addition the following were used:
     Canada to 1958– M.C. Urquhart and K.A.H. Buckley, *Historical Statistics of Canada* (Cambridge
     and Toronto, 1965);
2.   In principle, the indices relate to annual averages, but it is clear that in practice most are based on a lim-
     ited number of observations in each year. Where an individual figure is known to deviate from the norm
     for a series this is indicated.
3.   The currency unit applicable to the base-year of each index is employed throughout the currency of that
     index, irrespective of the date when the unit may have been changed.

FOOTNOTES

[1] See key to this table.
[2] Adult males only.
[3] March and September only.
[4] A new series has been spliced on to the old without, in principle, changing the scope.
[5] Including extractive industries and services to 1960 (1st line).
[6] Department of San Salvador only.
[7] Guatemala City only to 1973
[8] Last quarter-year only.
[9] An earlier index of monthly earnings of workers in Buenos Aires is available as follows (1939=100):-

| 1930 | 93 | 1933 | 87 | 1936 | 93 |
| 1931 | 87 | 1934 | 83 | 1937 | 96 |
| 1932 | 84 | 1935 | 90 | 1938 | 95 |

[10] Including salaries.
[11] April—December only.
[12] Lima and Callao only.
[13] Montevideo only.

# B5    NORTH AMERICA: WAGES IN AGRICULTURE

| | USA[1] |
|---|---|
| | *1909=100* |
| 1818 | 44.4 |
| 1826 | 41.5 |
| 1830 | 41.5 |
| 1850 | 50.9 |
| 1860 | 64.1 |
| 1870 | 77.8 |
| 1880 | 54.9 |
| 1890 | 65.4 |
| 1899 | 68.4 |
| 1909 | 100.0 |

| | Canada[2] | Mexico[3] | USA[1] |
|---|---|---|---|
| | *1955=100* | *1955=100* | *1909=100* |
| 1914 | 17.7 | ... | ... |
| 1915 | 18.8 | ... | ... |
| 1916 | 22.2 | ... | ... |
| 1917 | 39.0 | ... | ... |
| 1918 | 43.4 | ... | ... |
| 1919 | 49.2 | ... | 194.9 |
| 1920 | 54.3 | ... | ... |
| 1921 | 41.9 | ... | ... |
| 1922 | 36.6 | ... | ... |
| 1923 | 37.9 | ... | ... |
| 1924 | 36.6 | ... | ... |
| 1925 | 36.3 | ... | ... |
| 1926 | 37.4 | ... | ... |
| 1927 | 38.5 | 18.8 | ... |
| 1928 | 38.3 | 19.6 | ... |
| 1929 | 37.3 | 17.7 | 189.7 |
| 1930 | 33.1 | 16.0 | ... |
| 1931 | 25.2 | 15.4 | ... |
| 1932 | 19.0 | 13.1 | ... |
| 1933 | 17.7 | 12.5[3] | ... |
| 1934 | 18.7 | 20.7 | ... |
| 1935 | 19.9 | 20.7 | ... |
| 1936 | 21.5 | 23.0 | ... |
| 1937 | 23.3 | 23.0 | 134 |
| 1938 | 23.9 | 24.9 | 130 |
| 1939 | 25.1 | 24.9 | 130 |
| 1940 | 30.0[2] | 24.7 | 131.7 |
| | 29.2 | | |
| 1941 | 34.7 | 24.7 | 160.0 |
| 1942 | 43.1 | 25.7 | 206.0 |
| 1943 | 55.5 | 25.7 | 271.0 |
| 1944 | 60.3 | 31.4 | 322.0 |
| 1945 | 64.5 | 31.4 | 356.0 |
| 1946 | 69.5 | 39.0 | 386.0 |
| 1947 | 74.5 | 39.0 | 407.0 |
| 1948 | 80.5 | 45.6 | 427.2[1] |
| | | | *1955=100* |
| | | | 85.9 |
| 1949 | 82.3 | 45.6 | 82.8 |

**B5      NORTH AMERICA: Wages in Agriculture**

|  | Barbados[4] | Canada[2] | Costa Rica[6] | Mexico | USA[1] |
|---|---|---|---|---|---|
|  | *1955=100* | *1955=100* | *1955=100* | *1955=100* | *1955=100* |
| 1950 | ... | 79.0 | ... | 50.6 | 83.1 |
| 1951 | ... | 90.3 |  | 50.6 | 92.6 |
| 1952 | ... | 98.4 | 69.1 | 86.5 | 97.9 |
| 1953 | 100.0 | 101.6 | 100.0 | 86.5 | 99.6 |
| 1954 | 100.0 | 98.4 | 100.0 | 92.0 | 97.9 |
| 1955 | 100.0 | 100.0 | 100.0 | 100.0 | 100.0 |
| 1956 | 104.0 | 106.5 | 100.0 | 113.9 | 104.4 |
| 1957 | 116.0 | 112.9 | 106.3 | 113.9 | 107.9 |
| 1958 | 130.0 | 114.5 | 112.8 | 130.4 | 112.1 |
| 1959 | 130.0 | 116.1 | 112.8 | 159.1 | 118.2 |
| 1960 | 130.0 | 119.4 | 112.8 | 178.3 | 121.2 |
| 1961 | 144.0 | 124.2 | 112.8 | 178.3 | 123.6 |
| 1962 | 172.0 | 124.2 | [120.2][7] | 207.6 | 126.8 |
| 1963 | 172.0 | 129.0 | 120.2 | 207.6 | 130.4 |
| 1964 | 186.0 | 135.5 | 120.2 | 256.1 | 133.9 |
| 1965 | 186.0[4] | 143.5 | 136.2 | 256.1 | 140.9 |
| 1966 | 113.5 | 154.8 | 136.2 | 298.9 | 152.6 |
| 1967 | 102.3 | 166.1 | 136.2 | 298.9 | 165.9 |
| 1968 | 118.0 | 177.4 | 136.2 | 348.3 | 179.3 |
| 1969 | 133.0 | 193.5 | 142.6 | 348.3 | 197.0 |
| 1970 | 138.6 | 201.6 | 142.6 | 403.0 | 210.4 |
| 1971 | 164.7 | 211.3[5] | 159.6 | 446.4 | 219.3 |
| 1972 | 209.9 | 229.3 | 171.3 | 527.2 | 234.1 |
| 1973 | 211.5 | 264.1 | 171.3 | ... | 256.3 |
| 1974 | 270.2 | 312.0 | 242.6 | ... | 284.4[5] |
| 1975 | 321.9 | 372.9 | 268.1 | 876.4 | 304.3 |
| 1976 | 403.3 | 431.4 | 319.1 | 1,322.2 | 328.9 |
| 1977 | 403.6 | 487.5 | 360.6 | 1,454.0 | 358.2 |
| 1978 | ... | 518.6 | 425.5 | 1,682.5 | 376.9 |
| 1979 | ... | 555.6 | 476.6 | 2,030.6 | 419.1 |
| 1980 | ... | 584.6 | 560.6 | 2,550.6 | 447.2 |
| 1981 | ... | 614.9 | 696.8 | 3,400.6 | ... |
| 1982 | ... | 646.8 | 1,276.6 | 4,783.8 | ... |
| 1983 | ... | 675.7 | 1,959.6[6] | 8,004.8 | ... |
| 1984 | ... | 697.8 | [2,508.5][6] | 12,360.0 | ... |
| 1985 | ... | ... | 2,915.4 | 19,703.0 | ... |
| 1986 | ... | ... | 3,324.5 | 33,633.0 | ... |
| 1987 | ... | ... | 4,277.6 | 73,289.0 | ... |
| 1988 | ... | ... | 5,088.1 | 137,224.0 | ... |

## B5    SOUTH AMERICA: WAGES IN AGRICULTURE

| | Chile[8] | Peru[9] | | Chile[8] | Peru[9] | | Chile[8] | Peru[9] | | Chile[8] | Peru[9] |
|---|---|---|---|---|---|---|---|---|---|---|---|
| *1938=100* | *1955=100* | | *1938=100* | *1955=100* | | *1938=100* | *1955=100* | | *1938=100* | *1955=100* | |
| 1929 | 67.1 | ... | 1934 | ...[8] | 9.8 | 1939 | 121.2 | 7.9 | 1944 | 257.9 | 18.1 |
| 1930 | 69.7 | ... | 1935 | 74.6 | 10.1 | 1940 | 140.3 | 8.1 | 1945 | 259.6 | 21.7 |
| 1931 | 73.6 | 8.7 | 1936 | 80.3 | 11.3 | 1941 | 161.3 | 10.2 | 1946 | 406.4 | 21.7 |
| 1932 | 78.8 | 7.3 | 1937 | 80.3 | 8.9 | 1942 | 182.6 | 14.5 | 1947 | 484.2 | ... |
| 1933 | 84.1 | 9.3 | 1938 | 100 | 8.2 | 1943 | 229.7 | 15.7 | | | |

| | Argentina[10] | Chile[8] | Colombia[11] | Guyana[12] | Peru[9] | Uruguay[13] |
|---|---|---|---|---|---|---|
| | *1969=100* | *1938=100* | *1955=100* | *1955=100* | *1955=100* | *1969=100* |
| 1948 | ... | 661.2 | 58.7 | ... | ... | ... |
| 1949 | ... | 838.2 | 61.3 | ... | ... | ... |
| 1950 | ... | 1,015.2 | 72.0 | ... | ... | ... |
| 1951 | ... | 1,057.3 | 77.3 | ... | ... | ... |
| 1952 | ... | 1,380.4 | 77.3 | ... | 73.4 | ... |
| 1953 | ... | 1,825.9[8] | 83.5 | 94.7 | 98.8 | ... |
| | | *1955=100* | | | | |
| | | 49.0 | | | | |
| 1954 | ... | 62.9 | 93.3 | 96.0 | 99.9 | ... |
| 1955 | ... | 100.0 | 100.0 | 100.0 | 100.0 | ... |
| 1956 | ... | 144.9 | 102.7 | 102.5 | 122.1 | ... |
| 1957 | ... | 190.4 | 116.8 | 101.2 | 142.3 | ... |
| 1958 | ... | 229.2 | 126.7 | 101.6 | 180.3 | ... |
| 1959 | ... | 316.9 | 139.5 | 103.4 | 191.0 | ... |
| 1960 | 12.2 | 348.3 | 155.2 | 114.3 | 199.5 | ... |
| 1961 | 13.3 | 398.9 | 176.0 | 141.0 | 224.3 | ... |
| 1962 | 18.1 | 466.3 | 197.1 | 142.2 | 254.8 | 4.6 |
| 1963 | 20.9 | 719.1 | 256.0 | 160.9 | ... | 4.6 |
| 1964 | 33.2 | 1,078.7 | 306.7 | 171.1 | ... | 6.6 |
| 1965 | 48.4 | 1,831.5 | 318.7 | 173.6 | ... | 6.6 |
| 1966 | 64.1 | 2,303.3 | 380.3 | 180.7 | ... | 15.5 |
| 1967 | 84.2 | 2,696.6 | 393.3 | 184.5 | ... | 32.5 |
| 1968 | 89.7 | 3,134.8 | 414.7 | 183.9[12] | ... | 84.7 |
| 1969 | 100.0 | 4,202.2 | 506.7 | 212.6 | ... | 100.0 |
| | | *1969=100* | | | | |
| 1970 | 125.4 | 160.4 | 514.7 | 227.7 | ... | 125.0 |
| 1971 | 192.5 | 267.4 | ... | 235.1 | ... | 159.0 |
| 1972 | 275.0 | [401.1][9] | ... | 249.2 | ... | 229.0 |
| 1973 | 493.8 | [846.7][10] | ... | 246.2 | ... | 408.4 |
| 1974 | 705.0 | 11,000.0 | ... | 283.7 | ... | 866.4 |
| | | *1974=100* | | | | |
| 1975 | 1,851.1 | 528.7 | ... | 330.7 | ... | 1,487.4 |
| 1976 | 5,531.2 | 2,164.6 | 1,646.7 | 394.0 | ... | 1,891.7 |
| 1977 | 11,694 | 5,036.6 | 2,456.8 | 387.0 | ... | 3,321.3 |
| 1978 | 20,933 | 7,347.1 | 3,176.8 | 514.7 | ... | 4,779.8 |
| 1979 | 53,858 | 9,719.6 | 3,936.8 | 491.0 | ... | 7,574.0 |
| | *1979=100* | *1979=100* | | | | *1979=100* |
| 1980 | 243.8 | 135.4 | 4,840 | 620.1 | ... | 143.0 |
| 1981 | 567.7 | 160.7 | ... | 746.2 | ... | 174.6 |
| 1982 | 1,663.5 | 259.4 | ... | ... | ... | 192.1 |
| 1983 | 10,774 | 265.9 | ... | ... | ... | 265.7 |
| 1984 | 82,353 | 272.4 | ... | ... | ... | 517.2 |
| | *1984=100* | | | | *1986=100* | |
| 1985 | 550.9 | 337.6 | ... | ... | ... | 913.8 |
| 1986 | 1,156.4 | 389.9 | ... | ... | 100.0 | 1,542.1 |
| 1987 | 2,456.8 | ... | ... | ... | 239.7 | 2,438.4 |
| 1988 | ... | ... | ... | ... | 1,117.6 | 4,142.6 |

**B5      Wages in Agriculture**

NOTE

All the notes to table B4 also apply to this table.

FOOTNOTES

[1] Average monthly earnings with board to 1948 (1st line), subsequently average hourly rates. The figures for 1940 and 1948 are based on Lebergott's series reproduced in *Historical Statistics of the United States,* with statistics for 1937–39 and 1941–47 interpolated on the basis of data derived from the ILO.

[2] The general index of farm wage rates to 1940 (1st line); subsequently day rates of general male farm hands paid wholly in cash.

[3] Minimum rates for regular day workers. The series from 1934 is completely new and cannot be compared with earlier figures.

[4] Middle rate per hour to 1965 and average weekly earnings subsequently. The index is for male sugar cane day labour.

[5] A new series has been spliced on to the old without, in principle, changing the scope.

[6] Minimum hourly rates of general farm hands on coffee plantations to 1983, and earnings of similar workers in July subsequently (November in 1984).

[7] Beginning December.

[8] Minimum daily rates for adult male permanent workers to 1953 (1st line), and for all adult male workers subsequently. The series from 1935 onwards cannot be compared with earlier figures.

[9] Average daily earnings of males to 1962 and of all workers in 1986–88.

[10] October 1972 to December 1973.

[11] Average daily rates of adult males.

[12] Day rates of sugar cane workers to 1968 and average weekly earnings subsequently.

[13] Average monthly earnings of workers paid wholly in cash.

# C.    AGRICULTURE

Apart from figures for sugar in Europe's West Indian colonies, there are few agricultural statistics until around 1840, and few on a regular annual basis until the 1890s or later, though they begin for the USA in the 1860s. The main exceptions to this statement are foreign trade data, which are generally available for the countries for which trade in agricultural commodities became of major importance by the time such importance had been attained, if not earlier: by the 1850s, at least, and considerably earlier for sugar, cotton, and tobacco.

There is no reason to suppose that the agricultural statistics proper, once they were collected, are in any way grossly or systematically unreliable. However, in many countries, and for many of the major subsistence crops, 'collection' has not always been an appropriate word to apply to the process by which the statistics have been engendered. All crop statistics are a matter of estimation, whether by local crop reporters or by officials sitting at desks in the Ministry of Agriculture or in the FAO; and some of the estimation, particularly for crops like cassava, or for areas with little or no official presence in rural areas distant from major cities, can only be described as guesswork. Judging by some of the revisions which have been made to previously-published figures, the guesswork has not always been well-informed. The principle employed here in all of the first 14 tables has been to include estimates, from whatever source, provided they seem reasonable in the light of later recorded figures.

Tables 1 to 9 and 11 to 13 present a selection of statistics of crop areas and outputs and of the output of major livestock products. Data, where available, are shown for commodities which are of some significance in each particular country. The same applies to fish landings in table 14 and to the livestock species whose numbers are given in table 10. In interpreting these latter, it should be remembered that changes in the time of year at which a livestock count is taken can have a considerable effect on numbers, and that changes in the average age of flocks and herds have had a major effect, over time, on the productivity of a given stock of animals.

The export statistics, which occupy tables 15 to 19 are a small selection of those available. The intention is to show the major international movements of agricultural and forest products for the period for which they have been significant. With the exception of sugar, tobacco, and cotton, this period began at the earliest when trans-oceanic freight rates became low enough for commodities with relatively high bulk-to-value ratios to be shipped to Western Europe. By their nature these commodities were not much susceptible to illegal trade, and whilst the same cannot be said of tobacco (and, perhaps, sugar), it is the import statistics of Europe which are likely to have been affected, rather than those of the exporters. In any case, such trade was mainly a phenomenon of the colonial period in American history.

**C1**  **NORTH AMERICA: AREA OF MAIN ARABLE CROPS** (in thousands of hectares)

:Key:-  Bwt = buckwheat; P = potatoes; SP= sweet potatoes; SB = sugar beat; SC = sugar cane

|  | Canada | | | |
|---|---|---|---|---|
|  | **Wheat** | **Barley** | **Oats** | **Rye** |
| 1851 | 489 | 30 | 406 | 37 |
| 1861 | 661 | 104 | 661 | 62 |
| 1871 | 667 | … | … | … |
| 1881 | 948 | … | … | … |

| | Guadeloupe | | Jamaica | Trinidad & Tobago[2] |
|---|---|---|---|---|
| | Sugar Cane | | SC | SC |
| 1848 | 17 | 1876 | 19 | … |
| 1849 | 15 | 1877 | 19 | … |
| | | 1878 | 19 | … |
| | | 1879 | 18 | … |
| 1850 | 15 | 1880 | 17 | … |
| 1851 | 15 | 1881 | 16 | … |
| 1852 | 16 | 1882 | 16 | … |
| 1853 | 18 | 1883 | 17 | … |
| 1854 | 20 | 1884 | 17 | … |
| 1855 | 14 | 1885 | 16 | … |
| 1856 | 14 | 1886 | 15 | … |
| 1857 | 15 | 1887 | 14 | 24 |
| 1858 | 16 | 1888 | 14 | 24 |
| 1859 | 18 | 1889 | 13 | 24 |
| 1860 | 18 | 1890 | 13 | 24 |
| 1861 | 18 | 1891 | 13 | 24 |
| 1862 | 19 | 1892 | 13 | 24 |
| 1863 | 18 | 1893 | 13 | 24 |
| 1864 | 18 | 1894 | 13 | 24 |
| 1865 | … | 1895 | 13 | 24 |
| 1866 | 16 | 1896 | 12 | 24 |
| 1867 | 16 | 1897 | 12 | 23 |
| 1874 | 19 | 1898 | 11 | 23_2 |
| 1879 | 22 | 1899 | 11 | 22 |
| 1884 | 26 | 1900 | 10 | 21 |
| | | 1901 | 11 | 21 |
| 1889 | 23 | 1902 | 11 | 21 |
| | | 1903 | 10 | 24 |
| 1894 | 24 | 1904 | 10 | 24 |
| 1899 | 23 | 1905 | 11 | 25 |
| | | 1906 | 12 | 26 |
| 1902 | 27 | 1907 | 12 | 24 |
| | | 1908 | 11 | 27 |
| 1906 | 25 | 1909 | 12 | 26 |

**C1      NORTH AMERICA: Area of Main Arable Crops** (in thousands of hectares)

| | Barbados | Canada[1] | | | | | | |
|---|---|---|---|---|---|---|---|---|
| | SC | Wheat | Barley | Oats | Rye | Mixed Grain | P's | SB |
| 1882 | ... | [802] | ... | ... | ... | ... | [75] | ... |
| 1883 | ... | [719] | [343] | [561] | ... | ... | [65] | ... |
| 1884 | ... | [795] | [331] | [661] | ... | ... | [72] | ... |
| 1885 | ... | [766] | [300] | [653] | ... | ... | [73] | ... |
| 1886 | ... | [822] | [263] | [688] | ... | ... | [70] | ... |
| 1887 | ... | [740] | [317] | [716] | ... | ... | [60] | ... |
| 1888 | ... | [734] | [333] | [744] | ... | ... | [61] | ... |
| 1889 | ... | [693] | [391] | [818] | ... | ... | [62] | ... |
| 1890 | ... | [746] | [387] | [867] | ... | ... | [64] | ... |
| 1891 | ... | 1,094[942] | 351[298] | 1,603[935] | ... | ... | [77] | — |
| 1892 | ... | [922] | [260] | [869] | ... | ... | [70] | ... |
| 1893 | ... | [1,009] | [242] | [888] | ... | ... | [63] | ... |
| 1894 | ... | [920] | [236] | [941] | ... | ... | [63] | ... |
| 1895 | ... | [817] | [245] | [1,115] | ... | ... | [73] | ... |
| 1896 | ... | [853] | [256] | [1,156] | ... | ... | [81] | ... |
| 1897 | ... | [863] | [239] | [1,160] | ... | ... | [77][1] | ... |
| 1898 | ... | [1,034][1] | [245][1] | [1,174][1] | ... | ... | [74] | ... |
| 1899 | ... | [1,320] | [251] | [1,288] | ... | ... | [94] | ... |
| 1900 | ... | [1,404] | [280] | [1,317] | ... | ... | [92] | — |
| 1901 | ... | 1,209 | 353 | 2,172 | 47 | 110 | [178][1] | ... |
| 1902 | 12 | [1,543] | [347] | [1,400] | ... | ... | [97] | ... |
| 1903 | ... | [1,514] | [418] | [1,501] | ... | ... | [92] | ... |
| 1904 | ... | [1,707] | [490] | [1,665] | ... | ... | [91] | ... |
| 1905 | ... | [1,711] | [495] | [1,742] | ... | ... | [78] | ... |
| 1906 | ... | [1,978] | [529] | [1,853] | ... | ... | [75] | ... |
| 1907 | ... | [2,440][1] | [551][1] | [2,041][1] | ... | ... | [80][1] | ... |
| 1908 | 14 | [2,449] | [681] | [2,928] | ... | ... | [202] | ... |
| 1909 | 12 | 2,657 | 706 | 3,201 | 40 | 236 | ... | ... |

**C1** **NORTH AMERICA: Area of Main Arable Crops** (in thousands of hectares)

| | | | | | | USA[3] | | | | | | |
|---|---|---|---|---|---|---|---|---|---|---|---|---|
| | Wheat | Barley | Oats | Rye | Maize | Bwt | Rice | P | SP | SB | SC |
| 1866 | 6,235 | 305 | 3,211 | 611 | 12,147 | 312 | ... | 496 | ... | ... | ... |
| 1867 | 6,774 | 428 | 3,309 | 667 | 12,997 | 328 | ... | 522 | ... | ... | ... |
| 1868 | 7,746 | 431 | 3,601 | 656 | 14,211 | 316 | ... | 567 | 132 | ... | ... |
| 1869 | 8,577 | 501 | 3,867 | 660 | 14,501 | 308 | ... | 599 | 142 | ... | ... |
| 1870 | 8,476 | 539 | 4,188 | 631 | 15,535 | 299 | ... | 584 | 142 | ... | ... |
| 1871 | 8,996 | 546 | 4,476 | 643 | 16,998 | 293 | ... | 605 | 152 | ... | ... |
| 1872 | 9,292 | 575 | 4,771 | 633 | 17,638 | 311 | ... | 631 | 153 | ... | ... |
| 1873 | 10,063 | 596 | 4,860 | 628 | 17,840 | 304 | ... | 624 | 159 | ... | ... |
| 1874 | 11,052 | 659 | 5,170 | 635 | 19,279 | 302 | ... | 669 | 164 | ... | ... |
| 1875 | 11,486 | 689 | 5,510 | 626 | 21,224 | 321 | ... | 724 | 172 | ... | ... |
| 1876 | 11,446 | 798 | 5,904 | 716 | 22,370 | 330 | ... | 722 | 186 | ... | ... |
| 1877 | 11,316 | 794 | 5,996 | 746 | 23,795 | 340 | ... | 760 | 184 | ... | ... |
| 1878 | 13,508 | 748 | 6,406 | 771 | 24,143 | 339 | ... | 760 | 194 | ... | ... |
| 1879 | 14,304 | 779 | 6,457 | 739 | 25,183 | 341 | ... | 794 | 183 | ... | ... |
| 1880 | 15,417 | 805 | 6,643 | 709 | 25,311 | 331 | ... | 796 | 190 | ... | ... |
| 1881 | 14,890 | 891 | 6,846 | 708 | 25,506 | 324 | ... | 824 | 178 | ... | ... |
| 1882 | 14,769 | 985 | 7,719 | 842 | 26,773 | 324 | ... | 897 | 190 | ... | ... |
| 1883 | 14,402 | 1,001 | 8,345 | 859 | 27,587 | 325 | ... | 960 | 190 | ... | ... |
| 1884 | 15,574 | 1,090 | 8,893 | 850 | 27,856 | 316 | ... | 934 | 193 | ... | ... |
| 1885 | 14,202 | 1,158 | 9,450 | 768 | 29,078 | 334 | ... | 945 | 192 | ... | ... |
| 1886 | 14,695 | 1,225 | 9,885 | 788 | 29,911 | 325 | ... | 968 | 195 | ... | ... |
| 1887 | 14,922 | 1,319 | 10,632 | 803 | 29,662 | 323 | ... | 998 | 200 | ... | ... |
| 1888 | 14,151 | 1,329 | 11,253 | 883 | 31,353 | 329 | ... | 1,054 | 208 | ... | ... |
| 1889 | 14,608 | 1,357 | 11,613 | 910 | 31,426 | 327 | ... | 1,053 | 211 | ... | ... |
| 1890 | 14,846 | 1,315 | 11,442 | 856 | 30,264 | 332 | ... | 1,035 | 215 | ... | ... |
| 1891 | 16,629 | 1,453 | 11,232 | 882 | 31,912 | 335 | ... | 1,066 | 217 | ... | ... |
| 1892 | 17,393 | 1,561 | 11,399 | 906 | 31,126 | 340 | ... | 1,019 | 220 | ... | ... |
| 1893 | 16,507 | 1,493 | 11,844 | 875 | 32,307 | 326 | ... | 1,058 | 221 | ... | ... |
| 1894 | 16,255 | 1,473 | 11,961 | 877 | 32,403 | 326 | ... | 1,161 | 222 | ... | ... |
| 1895 | 15,782 | 1,694 | 12,507 | 971 | 36,616 | 324 | 118 | 1,250 | 221 | ... | ... |
| 1896 | 16,523 | 1,672 | 12,241 | 1,052 | 36,047 | 346 | 109 | 1,201 | 225 | ... | ... |
| 1897 | 17,569 | 1,667 | 11,667 | 940 | 36,408 | 335 | 117 | 1,137 | 215 | ... | ... |
| 1898 | 20,439 | 1,665 | 11,868 | 892 | 35,525 | 321 | 127 | 1,164 | 221 | ... | ... |
| 1899 | 21,182 | 1,810 | 11,839 | 833 | 38,280 | 325 | 137 | 1,189 | 215 | ... | ... |
| 1900 | 19,912 | 1,903 | 12,565 | 861 | 38,385 | 320 | 146 | 1,213 | 219 | ... | ... |
| 1901 | 20,577 | 2,008 | 12,501 | 975 | 38,211 | 327 | 171 | 1,194 | 226 | ... | ... |
| 1902 | 18,714 | 2,215 | 12,690 | 989 | 39,326 | 328 | 221 | 1,245 | 226 | ... | ... |
| 1903 | 19,609 | 2,522 | 13,026 | 915 | 37,860 | 333 | 221 | 1,246 | 229 | ... | ... |
| 1904 | 17,464 | 2,662 | 13,253 | 892 | 38,537 | 336 | 232 | 1,298 | 231 | ... | ... |
| 1905 | 18,739 | 2,694 | 13,527 | 930 | 38,747 | 334 | 185 | 1,320 | 232 | ... | ... |
| 1906 | 18,709 | 2,729 | 13,633 | 872 | 38,698 | 332 | 204 | 1,317 | 237 | ... | ... |
| 1907 | 17,862 | 2,774 | 13,937 | 839 | 38,888 | 337 | 228 | 1,349 | 241 | ... | ... |
| 1908 | 18,252 | 2,998 | 13,885 | 862 | 38,561 | 341 | 241 | 1,383 | 251 | ... | ... |
| 1909 | 17,912 | 3,115 | 14,189 | 895 | 40,550 | 352 | 268 | 1,487 | 259 | 170 | 118 |

**C1      NORTH AMERICA: Area of Main Arable Crops** (in thousands of hectares)

| | Barbados | Canada[1] | | | | | | | Costa Rica | | |
|---|---|---|---|---|---|---|---|---|---|---|---|
| | SC | Wheat | Barley | Oats | Rye | Mixed Grain | P's | SB | Maize | Rice | SC |
| 1910 | 12 | 3,136 | 755 | 3,765 | 37 | 236 | 184 | ... | 27 | 3 | 13 |
| 1911 | 12 | 3,587 | 519 | 3,503 | 47 | 173 | 209 | 8 | ... | ... | ... |
| 1912 | 12 | 4,490 | 616 | 3,902 | 53 | 213 | 208 | 8 | ... | ... | 10 |
| 1913 | 12 | 4,450 | 640 | 4,033 | 51 | 201 | 214 | 7 | ... | ... | ... |
| 1914 | 13 | 4,458 | 653 | 4,222 | 48 | 192 | 217 | 5 | 31 | 3 | 12 |
| 1915 | 14 | 4,166 | 605 | 4,072 | 45 | 187 | 224 | 7 | ... | ... | ... |
| 1916 | 14 | 6,114 | 695 | 4,677 | 49 | 189 | 191 | 6 | ... | ... | ... |
| 1917 | 14 | 6,220 | 730 | 4,450 | 60 | 167 | 266 | 6 | ... | ... | ... |
| 1918 | 14 | 5,972 | 968 | 5,388 | 86 | 201 | 298 | 7 | ... | ... | ... |
| 1919 | 14 | 7,023 | 1,276 | 5,985 | 225 | 373 | 331 | 10 | ... | ... | ... |
| 1920 | 14 | 7,740 | 1,071 | 6,051 | 305 | 365 | 317 | 15 | ... | ... | ... |
| 1921 | 14 | 7,378 | 1,033 | 6,414 | 263 | 329 | 284 | 11 | ... | ... | ... |
| 1922 | 14 | 9,413 | 1,132 | 6,859 | 745 | 348 | 277 | 6 | 29 | 6 | 17 |
| 1923 | 14 | 9,074 | 1,052 | 5,885 | 852 | 316 | 227 | 7 | 26 | 7 | 17 |
| 1924 | 14 | 8,857 | 1,127 | 5,823 | 586 | 342 | 227 | 13 | 20 | 7 | 18 |
| 1925 | 14 | 8,926 | 1,379 | 5,864 | 361 | 343 | 221 | 14 | 20 | 7 | 16 |
| 1926 | 14 | 8,413 | 1,426 | 5,081 | 260 | 348 | 212 | 12 | 24 | 8 | 18 |
| 1927 | 14 | 9,266 | 1,476 | 5,156 | 305 | 387 | 232 | 11 | 32 | 7 | 18 |
| 1928 | 14 | 9,089 | 1,419 | 5,358 | 301 | 406 | 242 | 14 | 32 | 6 | 15 |
| 1929 | 14 | 9,761 | 1,975 | 5,316 | 340 | 448 | 220 | 13 | 34 | 6 | 12 |
| 1930 | 14 | 10,180 | 2,398 | 5,050 | 401 | 453 | 231 | 17 | ... | ... | ... |
| 1931 | 14 | 10,076 | 2,250 | 5,366 | 586 | 486 | 236 | 17 | ... | ... | ... |
| 1932 | 15 | 10,666 | 1,534 | 5,195 | 323 | 484 | 211 | 18 | ... | ... | ... |
| 1933 | 15 | 11,000 | 1,521 | 5,321 | 313 | 479 | 214 | 18 | ... | ... | ... |
| 1934 | 15 | 10,518 | 1,480 | 5,475 | 236 | 472 | 230 | 15 | ... | ... | ... |
| 1935 | 16 | 9,706 | 1,462 | 5,557 | 277 | 469 | 205 | 21 | 29 | 9 | 13 |
| 1936 | 16 | 9,759 | 1,573 | 5,704 | 291 | 466 | 203 | 21 | ... | ... | ... |
| 1937 | 16 | 10,362 | 1,796 | 5,377 | 253 | 474 | 215 | 19 | 19 | 11 | 11 |
| 1938 | 16 | 10,348 | 1,753 | 5,280 | 362 | 456 | 211 | 18 | ... | ... | ... |
| 1939 | 16 | 10,494 | 1,802 | 5,265 | 300 | 469 | 210 | 24 | 27 | ... | ... |
| 1940 | 17 | 10,828 | 1,759 | 5,176 | 446 | 493 | 221 | 33 | 28 | 11 | 12 |
| 1941 | 16 | 11,625 | 1,757 | 4,977 | 419 | 494 | 205 | 29 | 29 | 11 | 13 |
| 1942 | 15 | 8,882 | 2,150 | 4,969 | 376 | 581 | 205 | 26 | 29 | 13 | 13 |
| 1943 | 15 | 8,725 | 2,784 | 5,476 | 529 | 599 | 216 | 21 | 28 | 11 | 13 |
| 1944 | 15 | 6,772 | 3,293 | 5,963 | 208 | 507 | 216 | 23 | 30 | 9 | 10 |
| 1945 | 15 | 9,177 | 2,836 | 5,428 | 263 | 516 | 205 | 24 | 31 | 12 | ... |
| 1946 | 17 | 9,388 | 2,810 | 5,346 | 199 | 489 | 211 | 27 | ... | 13 | ... |
| 1947 | 16 | 9,865 | 2,503 | 4,768 | 288 | 471 | 201[1] | 24 | ... | 12 | 5 |
| 1948 | 16 | 9,762 | 2,991 | 4,343 | 486 | 397 | 206 | 24 | ... | 10 | 13 |
| 1949 | 17 | 9,593 | 2,590 | 4,392 | 952 | 537 | 207 | 34 | 51 | 22 | 15 |

**C1   NORTH AMERICA: Area of Main Arable Crops** (in thousands of hectares)

|      | Cuba | | | Dominican Republic | | | El Salvador | | | |
|------|------|------|------|------|------|------|------|------|---------|------|
|      | Maize | Rice | SC | Maize | Rice | SC | Maize | Rice | Sorghum | SC |
| 1910 | ... | ... | ... | ... | ... | ... | ... | ... | ... | ... |
| 1911 | ... | ... | ... | ... | ... | ... | ... | ... | ... | ... |
| 1912 | ... | ... | 542 | ... | ... | ... | ... | ... | ... | ... |
| 1913 | ... | ... | 540 | ... | ... | ... | ... | ... | ... | ... |
| 1914 | ... | ... | ... | ... | ... | 24 | ... | ... | ... | ... |
| 1915 | ... | ... | ... | ... | ... | 25 | 89 | ... | ... | ... |
| 1916 | ... | ... | ... | ... | ... | ... | 127 | ... | ... | ... |
| 1917 | ... | ... | ... | ... | ... | 21 | ... | ... | ... | 9 |
| 1918 | ... | ... | ... | ... | ... | 36 | 91 | 11 | ... | 7 |
| 1919 | ... | ... | ... | ... | ... | 40 | 180 | 6 | ... | ... |
| 1920 | ... | ... | ... | ... | ... | ... | 252 | ... | ... | ... |
| 1921 | ... | ... | ... | ... | ... | ... | ... | ... | ... | 12 |
| 1922 | ... | ... | ... | ... | ... | ... | ... | ... | ... | ... |
| 1923 | ... | ... | ... | ... | ... | ... | ... | ... | ... | ... |
| 1924 | ... | ... | ... | ... | ... | ... | 258 | 5 | ... | 11 |
| 1925 | ... | ... | ... | ... | ... | ... | ... | ... | ... | ... |
| 1926 | ... | ... | ... | ... | ... | ... | ... | ... | ... | ... |
| 1927 | ... | ... | ... | ... | ... | ... | ... | ... | ... | ... |
| 1928 | ... | ... | ... | ... | ... | ... | ... | ... | ... | ... |
| 1929 | ... | ... | 1,192 | ... | ... | ... | 133 | ... | ... | ... |
| 1930 | ... | ... | ... | ... | ... | ... | 140 | 8 | ... | 10 |
| 1931 | ... | 13 | ... | ... | ... | ... | 140 | 8 | ... | 9 |
| 1932 | ... | ... | 582 | ... | ... | ... | 136 | 8 | ... | 10 |
| 1933 | ... | 18 | 581 | ... | ... | ... | 139 | 10 | ... | 11 |
| 1934 | 25 | ... | 559 | ... | ... | ... | 133 | 11 | ... | 8 |
|      |    |    | 574 |    |    |    |    |    |    |    |
| 1935 | ... | ... | ... | 36 | ... | ... | 159 | 13 | ... | 10 |
| 1936 | ... | ... | ... | ... | ... | ... | 156 | 9 | ... | 10 |
| 1937 | ... | 7 | 582 | ... | ... | ... | 158 | 12 | ... | 9 |
| 1938 | 21 | 8 | 581 | ... | ... | ... | 84 | 9 | ... | 8 |
| 1939 | 38 | 11 | 637 | ... | 52 | 97 | 106 | 13 | ... | 10 |
| 1940 | 29 | 11 | 747 | ... | ... | ... | 117 | 13 | ... | 12 |
| 1941 | ... | 11 | 847 | ... | ... | ... | 158 | 14 | ... | 14 |
| 1942 | ... | 13 | 646 | ... | 39 | ... | 160 | 22 | ... | 15 |
| 1943 | ... | 11 | 968 | ... | 33 | ... | 142 | 19 | ... | 15 |
| 1944 | ... | 9 | 948 | ... | 47 | ... | 154 | 23 | ... | 16 |
| 1945 | ...[4] | 54 | 1,019 | 61 | 45 | ... | 154 | 23 | ... | ... |
| 1946 | 244 | ... | 1,151 | 73 | 36 | ... | 124 | 14 | ... | 5 |
| 1947 | 250 | 60 | 1,220 | 82 | 32 | 92 | 157 | 21 | 73 | 5 |
| 1948 | 280 | 60 | 1,150 | 77 | 47 | 97 | 198 | 29 | 114 | ... |
| 1949 | 270 | 50 | 1,193 | 62 | 44 | 97 | ... | 13 | ... | 12 |

**C1    NORTH AMERICA: Area of Main Arable Crops** (in thousands of hectares)

| | Guadeloupe | Guatemala | | | | Haiti | | | Honduras | |
|---|---|---|---|---|---|---|---|---|---|---|
| | SC | Wheat | Maize | Rice | SC | Maize | Rice | SC | Maize | SC |
| 1910 | ... | ... | ... | ... | ... | ... | ... | ... | ... | ... |
| 1911 | 28 | ... | ... | ... | ... | ... | ... | ... | ... | ... |
| 1912 | ... | ... | ... | ... | ... | ... | ... | ... | ... | ... |
| 1913 | ... | ... | ... | ... | ... | ... | ... | ... | ... | ... |
| 1914 | ... | ... | 201 | 8 | ... | ... | ... | ... | ... | ... |
| 1915 | 37 | ... | 230 | 6 | ... | ... | ... | ... | ... | ... |
| 1916 | 38 | ... | 267 | 6 | ... | ... | ... | ... | ... | ... |
| 1917 | 40 | 18 | 250 | 12 | ... | ... | ... | ... | ... | ... |
| 1918 | ... | 4 | 263 | 18 | ... | ... | ... | ... | ... | ... |
| 1919 | ... | 9 | 273 | 6 | ... | ... | ... | ... | ... | ... |
| 1920 | ... | 10 | 224 | 3 | ... | ... | ... | ... | ... | ... |
| 1921 | ... | 8 | 125 | 3 | 13 | ... | ... | ... | ... | ... |
| 1922 | 35 | 11 | 185 | 3 | 23 | ... | ... | ... | ... | ... |
| 1923 | 35 | 6 | 151 | 3 | 13 | ... | ... | ... | ... | ... |
| 1924 | 35 | 14 | 172 | 2 | 11 | ... | ... | ... | ... | ... |
| 1925 | 35 | 9 | 155 | 1 | 13 | ... | ... | ... | 176 | 14 |
| 1926 | 35 | 10 | 102 | 1 | 12 | ... | ... | ... | 178 | 17 |
| 1927 | 28 | 9 | 117 | 2 | 11 | ... | ... | ... | 177 | 24 |
| 1928 | 28 | 8 | 121 | 1 | 12 | ... | ... | 18 | 185 | 26 |
| 1929 | 28 | 7 | 141 | 2 | 12 | ... | ... | 18 | 184 | 20 |
| 1930 | 28 | 9 | 169 | 2 | 12 | ... | ... | 18 | 192 | 21 |
| 1931 | 28 | 6 | 147 | 2 | 13 | ... | 81 | 16 | 182 | 20 |
| 1932 | 28 | 6 | 147 | 2 | 11 | ... | 91 | 16 | 200 | 18 |
| 1933 | 28 | 7 | 135 | 3 | 9 | ... | 91 | 16 | 206 | 16 |
| 1934 | 20 | 7 | 139 | 2 | 8 | ... | 92 | 16 | 203 | 14 |
| 1935 | 21 | 9 | 137 | 5 | 8 | ... | 92 | 16 | 196 | 14 |
| 1936 | 22 | 20 | 280 | 8 | 14 | ... | ... | ... | 214 | 15 |
| 1937 | 22 | 17 | 311 | 9 | 16 | ... | ... | ... | 208 | 14 |
| 1938 | ... | 17 | 333 | ... | ... | ... | ... | ... | 222 | 15 |
| 1939 | 30 | 19 | 385 | 10 | 15 | ... | ... | ... | 228 | 16 |
| 1940 | 31 | 21 | 505 | 11 | 19 | ... | ... | ... | 232 | 15 |
| 1941 | 37 | 25 | 523 | 12 | 19 | ... | ... | ... | 239 | 15 |
| 1942 | 32 | 26 | 584 | 13 | 18 | ... | ... | ... | 242 | 16 |
| 1943 | 24 | 22 | 358 | 8 | 18 | ... | ... | ... | 239 | 18 |
| 1944 | 24 | 22 | 328 | 5 | 15 | ... | ... | ... | 245 | 18 |
| 1945 | 25 | 21 | 221 | 5 | ... | ... | ... | ... | 256 | 19 |
| 1946 | 13 | 21 | 208 | ... | ... | ... | 10 | ... | 255 | 20 |
| 1947 | 15 | 16 | 197 | 3 | 15 | 120 | 10 | 18 | 262 | 21 |
| 1948 | 15 | ... | ... | ... | ... | 120 | 23 | ... | 274 | 21 |
| 1949 | 15 | 31 | 540 | 8 | 18 | ... | 33 | ... | 279 | 22 |

**C1    NORTH AMERICA: Area of Main Arable Crops** (in thousands of hectares)

| | Jamaica | Martinique | Mexico | | | | | | | Nicaragua | | Panama | Puerto Rico | Trinidad & Tobago |
|---|---|---|---|---|---|---|---|---|---|---|---|---|---|---|
| | SC | SC | Wheat | Barley | Oats | Maize | Rice | P | SC | Maize | Rice | Rice | SC | SC |
| 1910 | 13 | ... | 1,063 | 555 | ... | ... | 84 | ... | ... | ... | ... | ... | 74 | 25 |
| 1911 | 14 | ... | 696 | 577 | ... | ... | 86 | ... | ... | ... | ... | ... | ... | 21 |
| 1912 | 13 | ... | ... | ... | ... | 2,466 | ... | ... | ... | ... | ... | ... | 85 | 18 |
| 1913 | 13 | ... | 600 | 610 | ... | ... | ... | ... | ... | ... | ... | ... | ... | 21 |
| 1914 | 13 | ... | ... | ... | ... | 1,922 | ... | ... | ... | ... | ... | ... | 82 | 20 |
| 1915 | 14 | ... | ... | ... | ... | ... | ... | ... | ... | ... | ... | ... | 82 | 22 |
| 1916 | 14 | ... | ... | ... | ... | ... | ... | ... | ... | ... | ... | ... | 83 | 21 |
| 1917 | 15 | ... | ... | ... | ... | ... | ... | ... | ... | ... | ... | ... | 104 | 24 |
| 1918 | 17 | ... | 950 | 1,928 | ... | 1,608 | ... | ... | ... | ... | ... | ... | 97 | 30 |
| 1919 | 19 | ... | ... | ... | ... | ... | ... | ... | ... | ... | ... | ... | 92 | 18 |
| 1920 | 23 | ... | ... | ... | ... | ... | ... | ... | ... | ... | ... | ... | 97 | 24 |
| 1921 | 18 | ... | 923 | 283 | ... | 2,946 | 20 | ... | ... | ... | ... | ... | 98 | 23 |
| 1922 | 19 | ... | 1,060 | 282 | ... | 2,856 | 22 | ... | ... | ... | ... | ... | 99 | 25 |
| 1923 | 19 | ... | 1,236 | 282 | ... | 3,209 | 22 | ... | ... | ... | ... | ... | 96 | 24 |
| 1924 | 18 | ... | 568 | 288 | ... | 3,267 | 43 | ... | ... | ... | ... | ... | 96 | 14 |
| 1925 | 21 | ... | 455 | 175 | ... | 2,936 | 50 | ... | 65 | ... | ... | ... | 98 | 13 |
| 1926 | 18 | ... | 518 | 181 | ... | 3,137 | 53 | ... | 70 | ... | ... | ... | 96 | 13 |
| 1927 | ... | ... | 528 | 176 | ... | 3,181 | 50 | ... | 67 | ... | ... | ... | 96 | 13 |
| 1928 | 17 | ... | 516 | 178 | ... | 3,122 | 45 | ... | 65 | ... | ... | ... | 102 | 18 |
| 1929 | 18 | ... | 521 | 161 | ... | 2,865 | 35 | ... | 70 | ... | ... | ... | 103 | 18 |
| 1930 | 17 | ... | 490 | 146 | ... | 3,075 | 37 | ... | 77 | 25 | ... | ... | 113 | ... |
| 1931 | 17 | ... | 604 | 150 | ... | 3,378 | 36 | ... | 78 | 28 | ... | ... | 119 | 24 |
| 1932 | 16 | ... | 445 | 160 | 3 | 3,243 | 34 | ... | 75 | 36 | ... | ... | 121 | 25 |
| 1933 | ... | ... | 472 | 159 | 4 | 3,198 | 34 | ... | 64 | 50 | ... | ... | 121 | 25 |
| 1934 | ... | ... | 493 | 157 | 3 | 2,970 | 32 | ... | 63 | ... | ... | ... | 121 | 27 |
| 1935 | 16 | ... | 460 | 148 | 4 | 2,966 | 31 | ... | 76 | ... | ... | ... | 121 | 29 |
| 1936 | 16 | ... | 508 | 145 | 3 | 2,852 | 40 | ... | 92 | ... | ... | ... | 121 | 33 |
| 1937 | 17 | ... | 484 | 144 | ... | 3,000 | 40 | ... | 87 | 42 | ... | ... | 121 | 33 |
| 1938 | 18 | ... | 501 | 149 | ... | 3,094 | 39 | ... | 87 | 27 | ... | ... | 127 | 33 |
| 1939 | 18 | 16 | 563 | 146 | 19 | 3,267 | 45 | ... | 94 | ... | ... | ... | 123 | 33 |
| 1940 | ... | ... | 601 | 142 | 35 | 3,342 | 62 | 18 | 98 | ... | ... | ... | 136 | 33 |
| 1941 | ... | ... | 583 | 168 | 34 | 3,392 | 53 | 23 | 116 | ... | ... | 30 | 137 | 33 |
| 1942 | 26 | ... | 600 | 156 | 34 | 3,758 | 65 | 27 | 127 | ... | ... | 30 | 129 | 33 |
| 1943 | 26 | ... | 510 | 161 | 36 | 3,083 | 66 | 27 | 139 | ... | ... | 33 | 127 | 33 |
| 1944 | 25 | ... | 527 | 162 | 36 | 3,355 | 68 | 27 | 140 | 89 | 16 | 35 | 136 | 33 |
| 1945 | 25 | 14 | 468 | 165 | 33 | 3,451 | 59 | 27 | 141 | 77 | 15 | 40 | 142 | 24 |
| 1946 | ... | 13 | 415 | 171 | 31 | 3,313 | 64 | 27 | 148 | 50 | 9 | 46 | 148 | 26 |
| 1947 | 32 | 14 | 499 | 171 | 44 | 3,512 | 72 | 28 | 157 | 86 | 10 | 52 | 149 | 26 |
| 1948 | 32 | 11 | 577 | 202 | 33 | 3,722 | 82 | 28 | 173 | 76 | 15 | 54 | 152 | 33 |
| 1949 | 42 | 13 | 535 | 215 | 79 | 3,792 | 108 | 29 | 201 | 98 | 15 | 60 | 150 | 34 |

**C1     NORTH AMERICA: Area of Main Arable Crops** (in thousands of hectares)

| | | | | | | | | | | | | |
|---|---|---|---|---|---|---|---|---|---|---|---|---|
| | | | | | **U.S.A.**[3] | | | | | | | |
| | **Wheat** | **Barley** | **Oats** | **Rye** | **Maize** | **Bwt** | **Rice** | **Sorghum** | **P** | **SP** | **SB** | **SC** |
| 1910 | 18,532 | 3,054 | 14,910 | 915 | 41,386 | 340 | 270 | ... | 1,475 | 257 | 161 | 126 |
| 1911 | 19,823 | 3,081 | 15,034 | 992 | 41,032 | 326 | 257 | ... | 1,429 | 244 | 192 | 128 |
| 1912 | 19,592 | 3,052 | 15,072 | 1,102 | 41,056 | 315 | 260 | ... | 1,418 | 237 | 225 | 83 |
| 1913 | 21,049 | 3,105 | 15,073 | 1,250 | 40,552 | 313 | 292 | ... | 1,407 | 241 | 235 | 103 |
| 1914 | 22,506 | 3,097 | 15,060 | 1,272 | 39,577 | 304 | 261 | ... | 1,383 | 231 | 195 | 88 |
| 1915 | 24,404 | 2,946 | 15,703 | 1,383 | 40,721 | 305 | 299 | ... | 1,389 | 254 | 247 | 74 |
| 1916 | 21,655 | 3,085 | 15,822 | 1,428 | 40,696 | 318 | 341 | ... | 1,325 | 266 | 269 | 92 |
| 1917 | 18,934 | 3,421 | 16,837 | 2,049 | 44,877 | 375 | 386 | ... | 1,538 | 293 | 269 | 100 |
| 1918 | 24,713 | 3,722 | 17,185 | 2,715 | 41,357 | 412 | 446 | ... | 1,456 | 299 | 240 | 95 |
| 1919 | 29,825 | 2,662 | 16,026 | 2,908 | 39,718 | 297 | 438 | 1,465 | 1,335 | 320 | 280 | 73 |
| 1920 | 25,235 | 3,010 | 17,293 | 1,960 | 41,019 | 295 | 526 | 1,630 | 1,336 | 310 | 353 | 77 |
| 1921 | 26,129 | 2,863 | 18,429 | 1,969 | 41,745 | 259 | 401 | 1,497 | 1,456 | 331 | 330 | 93 |
| 1922 | 24,847 | 2,671 | 16,319 | 2,740 | 40,608 | 295 | 426 | 1,363 | 1,579 | 331 | 214 | 98 |
| 1923 | 23,035 | 2,894 | 16,287 | 2,002 | 40,923 | 279 | 354 | 1,701 | 1,367 | 273 | 266 | 88 |
| 1924 | 21,231 | 2,848 | 16,939 | 1,596 | 40,639 | 298 | 339 | 1,427 | 1,257 | 228 | 330 | 66 |
| 1925 | 21,223 | 3,313 | 17,903 | 1,541 | 41,007 | 300 | 345 | 1,585 | 1,137 | 257 | 262 | 77 |
| 1926 | 22,912 | 3,204 | 17,342 | 1,387 | 40,247 | 275 | 411 | 1,704 | 1,138 | 261 | 274 | 52 |
| 1927 | 24,131 | 3,830 | 16,329 | 1,403 | 39,804 | 309 | 416 | 1,724 | 1,288 | 293 | 292 | 30 |
| 1928 | 23,968 | 5,154 | 16,239 | 1,344 | 40,605 | 275 | 393 | 1,665 | 1,416 | 257 | 261 | 53 |
| 1929 | 25,654 | 5,489 | 15,440 | 1,270 | 39,580 | 255 | 348 | 1,426 | 1,226 | 262 | 278 | 78 |
| 1930 | 25,348 | 5,111 | 16,126 | 1,475 | 41,061 | 232 | 391 | 1,407 | 1,270 | 271 | 314 | 76 |
| 1931 | 23,352 | 4,525 | 16,266 | 1,278 | 43,247 | 205 | 391 | 1,798 | 1,412 | 346 | 289 | 74 |
| 1932 | 23,411 | 5,344 | 16,875 | 1,356 | 44,749 | 184 | 354 | 1,781 | 1,444 | 429 | 309 | 89 |
| 1933 | 20,001 | 3,902 | 14,782 | 973 | 42,864 | 186 | 323 | 1,762 | 1,385 | 367 | 398 | 86 |
| 1934 | 17,542 | 2,662 | 11,920 | 777 | 37,309 | 192 | 329 | 959 | 1,456 | 388 | 312 | 95 |
| 1935 | 20,762 | 5,033 | 16,232 | 1,645 | 38,839 | 204 | 331 | 1,860 | 1,404 | 382 | 309 | 102 |
| 1936 | 19,880 | 3,371 | 13,619 | 1,090 | 37,698 | 153 | 397 | 1,130 | 1,198 | 311 | 314 | 99 |
| 1937 | 25,968 | 4,034 | 14,383 | 1,548 | 38,012 | 170 | 445 | 1,989 | 1,236 | 311 | 305 | 115 |
| 1938 | 28,003 | 4,294 | 14,586 | 1,654 | 37,296 | 181 | 435 | 1,902 | 1,161 | 321 | 374 | 120 |
| 1939 | 21,314 | 5,155 | 13,541 | 1,547 | 35,725 | 150 | 423 | 1,899 | 1,138 | 295 | 372 | 103 |
| 1940 | 21,559 | 5,473 | 14,338 | 1,297 | 34,977 | 157 | 433 | 2,579 | 1,146 | 262 | 369 | 97 |
| 1941 | 22,636 | 5,777 | 15,443 | 1,446 | 34,543 | 136 | 491 | 2,434 | 1,090 | 296 | 306 | 103 |
| 1942 | 20,142 | 6,863 | 15,458 | 1,535 | 35,356 | 152 | 590 | 2,424 | 1,081 | 278 | 386 | 117 |
| 1943 | 20,783 | 6,030 | 15,748 | 1,073 | 37,255 | 204 | 596 | 2,788 | 1,311 | 347 | 223 | 115 |
| 1944 | 24,180 | 4,978 | 16,083 | 863 | 38,046 | 206 | 599 | 3,667 | 1,125 | 294 | 225 | 111 |
| 1945 | 26,372 | 4,231 | 16,891 | 749 | 35,461 | 162 | 607 | 2,559 | 1,078 | 261 | 289 | 107 |
| 1946 | 27,156 | 4,201 | 17,325 | 646 | 35,444 | 155 | 640 | 2,699 | 1,023 | 258 | 325 | 116 |
| 1947 | 30,157 | 4,450 | 15,332 | 806 | 33,544 | 204 | 691 | 2,218 | 810 | 221 | 356 | 119 |
| 1948 | 29,307 | 4,818 | 15,896 | 833 | 34,308 | 134 | 730 | 2,961 | 802 | 184 | 281 | 125 |
| 1949 | 30,720 | 3,995 | 15,295 | 629 | 34,639 | 109 | 752 | 2,560 | 710 | 191 | 278 | 172 |

**C1 NORTH AMERICA: Area of Main Arable Crops** (in thousands of hectares)

| | Barbados | Canada[1] | | | | | | | | Costa Rica | | |
|---|---|---|---|---|---|---|---|---|---|---|---|---|
| | SC | Wheat | Barley | Oats | Rye | Maize | Mixed Grain | P's | SB | Maize | Rice | SC |
| 1950 | 17 | 11,083 | 2,397 | 4,447 | 488 | 124 | 586 | 204 | 41 | 49 | 34 | 23 |
| 1951 | 18 | 11,052 | 2,635 | 4,526 | 461 | 127 | 575 | 115 | 38 | 62 | 36 | 22 |
| 1952 | 19 | 10,220 | 3,173 | 4,815 | 456 | 137 | 617 | 124 | 37 | 52 | 29 | 24 |
| 1953 | 19 | 10,588 | 3,431 | 4,475 | 500 | 146 | 636 | 134 | 33 | 75 | 37 | 17 |
| 1954 | 19 | 10,677 | 3,605 | 3,995 | 609 | 169 | 627 | 125 | 37 | 66 | 33 | 20 |
| 1955 | 19 | 10,335 | 3,174 | 4,068 | 318 | 205 | 676 | 129 | 33 | 50 | 36 | 22 |
| 1956 | 19 | 9,146 | 4,001 | 4,435 | 302 | 206 | 688 | 130 | 32 | ... | 37 | ... |
| 1957 | 19 | 9,219 | 3,395 | 4,237 | 221 | 208 | 631 | 130 | 34 | ... | 37 | ... |
| 1958 | 19 | 8,725 | 3,806 | 3,573 | 220 | 202 | 583 | 126 | 40 | ... | 45 | ... |
| 1959 | 20 | 8,963 | 3,758 | 3,737 | 208 | 198 | 566 | 119 | 37 | ... | 58 | ... |
| 1960 | 19 | 9,915 | 3,192 | 3,678 | 216 | 184 | 594 | 119 | 35 | ... | 53 | ... |
| 1961 | 20 | 10,245 | 2,237 | 3,457 | 227 | 162 | 634 | 125 | 34 | 50 | 54 | 30 |
| 1962 | 19 | 10,853 | 2,139 | 4,277 | 258 | 178 | 616 | 118 | 34 | 54 | 54 | 35 |
| 1963 | 21 | 11,156 | 2,500 | 3,779 | 284 | 224 | 593 | 116 | 39 | 59 | 51 | 35 |
| 1964 | 21 | 12,018 | 2,224 | 3,231 | 282 | 265 | 621 | 113 | 41 | 65 | 50 | 35 |
| 1965 | 22 | 11,453 | 2,477 | 3,384 | 323 | 302 | 663 | 121 | 34 | 80 | 54 | 36 |
| 1966 | 22 | 12,016 | 3,019 | 3,207 | 294 | 326 | 715 | 130 | 33 | 78 | 56 | 31 |
| 1967 | 20 | 12,189 | 3,284 | 3,009 | 277 | 354 | 675 | 124 | 34 | 81 | 38 | 32 |
| 1968 | 20 | 11,907 | 3,576 | 3,058 | 275 | 387 | 675 | 125 | 32 | 82 | 40 | 33 |
| 1969 | 20 | 10,104 | 3,859 | 3,098 | 375 | 396 | 704 | 126 | 32 | 70 | 38 | 38 |
| 1970 | 20 | 5,052 | 4,064 | 2,893 | 411 | 484 | 785 | 129 | 28 | 42 | 47 | 38 |
| 1971 | 20 | 7,854 | 5,658 | 2,764 | 387 | 571 | 832 | 110 | 33 | 52 | 36 | 41 |
| 1972 | 20 | 8,640 | 5,062 | 2,470 | 257 | 537 | 836 | 100 | 31 | 55 | 32 | 45 |
| 1973 | 19 | 9,575 | 4,839 | 2,711 | 256 | 530 | 810 | 106 | 28 | 52 | 65 | 43 |
| 1974 | 17 | 8,934 | 4,775 | 2,471 | 341 | 591 | 728 | 115 | 27 | 41 | 80 | 37 |
| 1975 | 16 | 9,487 | 4,468 | 2,411 | 320 | 635 | 736 | 106 | 32 | 65 | 87 | 37 |
| 1975 | 16 | 11,252 | 4,353 | 2,409 | 250 | 709 | 645 | 107 | 32 | 60 | 80 | 38 |
| 1977 | 16 | 10,114 | 4,751 | 2,131 | 250 | 724 | 624 | 113 | 26 | 44 | 71 | 30 |
| 1978 | 16 | 10,579 | 4,259 | 1,829 | 318 | 783 | 606 | 111 | 25 | 37 | 76 | 43 |
| 1979 | 16 | 10,489 | 3,724 | 1,541 | 330 | 893 | 593 | 113 | 24 | 50 | 80 | 45 |
| 1980 | 16 | 11,098 | 4,634 | 1,515 | 310 | 958 | 569 | 107 | 27 | 39 | 60 | 49 |
| 1981 | 16 | 12,427 | 5,476 | 1,561 | 445 | 1,139 | 545 | 111 | 29 | 47 | 80 | 51 |
| 1982 | 16 | 12,554 | 5,189 | 1,633 | 447 | 1,107 | 531 | 113 | 29 | 54 | 77 | 44 |
| 1983 | 14 | 13,697 | 4,333 | 1,400 | 428 | 1,075 | 511 | 113 | 31 | 62 | 88 | 36 |
| 1984 | 14 | 13,158 | 4,566 | 1,406 | 370 | 1,192 | 462 | 118 | 27 | 61 | 72 | 52 |
| 1985 | 14 | 13,729 | 4,750 | 1,263 | 353 | 1,123 | 439 | 115 | 12 | 74 | 74 | 49 |
| 1986 | 14 | 14,239 | 4,829 | 1,287 | 315 | 994 | 383 | 109 | 23 | 76 | 60 | 50 |
| 1987 | 13 | 13,486 | 5,005 | 1,263 | 313 | 999 | 391 | 114 | 22 | 75 | 56 | 48 |
| 1988 | 12 | 12,987 | 5,152 | 1,371 | 257 | 981 | 386 | 111 | 21 | 61 | 64 | 48 |

C1     **NORTH AMERICA: Area of Main Arable Crops** (in thousands of hectares)

| | Cuba | | | Dominican Republic | | | El Salvador | | | |
|---|---|---|---|---|---|---|---|---|---|---|
| | Maize[4] | Rice | SC | Maize | Rice | SC | Maize | Rice | Sorghum | SC |
| 1950 | 166 | 50 | 1,257 | 72 | 47 | 102 | 177 | 14 | 82 | 13 |
| 1951 | 180 | 69 | 1,425 | 71 | 46 | 104 | ... | 16 | ... | 11 |
| 1952 | 150 | ... | 1.040 | 65 | 51 | 103 | 203 | 16 | 93 | ... |
| 1953 | ... | 85 | 1,070 | 65 | 51 | 108 | 185 | 14 | 102 | ... |
| 1954 | 176 | 93 | 1,072 | ... | ... | ... | 177 | 12 | 107 | 6 |
| 1955 | 176 | 134 | ... | ... | ... | ... | 173 | 10 | 122 | 6 |
| 1956 | 183 | 162 | ... | ... | 49 | ... | 187 | 12 | 124 | 7 |
| 1957 | 175 | 109 | ... | ... | 49 | 158 | 171 | 16 | 86 | 8 |
| 1958 | 155 | 110 | 1,068 | ... | ... | 147 | 179 | 13 | 89 | 14 |
| 1959 | 185 | 168 | 1,156 | ... | ... | 183 | 178 | 9 | 84 | 15 |
| 1960 | 191 | 160 | 1,261 | ... | ... | 146 | 178 | 11 | 87 | 12 |
| 1961 | 160 | 150 | 1,132 | 35 | 58 | 147 | 190 | 9 | 98 | 13 |
| 1962 | 153 | 164 | 1,074 | 32 | 58 | 130 | 199 | 11 | 93 | 15 |
| 1963 | 141 | 85 | 1,002 | 30 | 60 | 135 | 172 | 9 | 96 | 15 |
| 1964 | 132 | 71 | 1,055 | 30 | 65 | 116 | 165 | 15 | 87 | 24 |
| 1965 | 120 | 38 | 979 | 25 | 76 | 120 | 193 | 13 | 111 | 24 |
| 1966 | 127 | 32 | 1,039 | 25 | 76 | 142 | 208 | 20 | 107 | 24 |
| 1967 | 121 | 44 | 1,013 | 25 | 81 | 120 | 192 | 28 | 104 | 24 |
| 1968 | 120 | 88 | 944 | 28 | 88 | 138 | 200 | 27 | 114 | 19 |
| 1969 | 120 | 146 | 1,460 | 27 | 84 | 146 | 194 | 11 | 114 | 20 |
| 1970 | 120 | 195 | 1,251 | 26 | 83 | 151 | 206 | 12 | 124 | 20 |
| 1971 | 130 | 168 | 1,181 | 26 | 74 | 150 | 210 | 15 | 126 | 28 |
| 1972 | 130 | 170 | 1,073 | 27 | 67 | 150 | 204 | 11 | 130 | 30 |
| 1973 | 130 | 225 | 1,103 | 26 | 66 | 145 | 202 | 10 | 119 | 33 |
| 1974 | 130 | 204 | 1,180 | 29 | 67 | 152 | 211 | 11 | 127 | 36 |
| 1975 | ... | 178 | 1,224 | 25 | 66 | 154 | 246 | 17 | 132 | 42 |
| 1976 | ... | 163 | 1,137 | 33 | 114 | 164 | 234 | 14 | 125 | 42 |
| 1977 | ... | 152 | 1,237 | 24 | 113 | 172 | 245 | 12 | 132 | 41 |
| 1978 | ... | 152 | 1,313 | 24 | 103 | 174 | 264 | 14 | 137 | 41 |
| 1979 | ... | 147 | 1,392 | 19 | 109 | 178 | 276 | 15 | 143 | 37 |
| 1980 | ... | 147 | 1,209 | 24 | 111 | 180 | 292 | 17 | 119 | 34 |
| 1981 | ... | 144 | 1,327 | 29 | 111 | 185 | 276 | 14 | 115 | 27 |
| 1982 | ... | 151 | 1,200 | 21 | 93 | 188 | 239 | 11 | 119 | 32 |
| 1983 | ... | 149 | 1,350 | 27 | 119 | 188 | 242 | 13 | 111 | 41 |
| 1984 | ... | 161 | 1,348 | 58 | 118 | 188 | 243 | 15 | 116 | 39 |
| 1985 | ... | 159 | 1,329 | 38 | 110 | 175 | 253 | 17 | 114 | 40 |
| 1986 | ... | 171 | 1,358 | 32 | 112 | 180 | 257 | 12 | 120 | 42 |
| 1987 | ... | 169 | 1,297 | 36 | 112 | 180 | 279 | 12 | 125 | 41 |
| 1988 | ... | 172 | 1,351 | 34 | 98 | 170 | 282 | 14 | 122 | 34 |

**C1    NORTH AMERICA: Area of Main Arable Crops** (in thousands of hectares)

| | Guadeloupe | Guatemala | | | | Haiti | | | Honduras | |
|---|---|---|---|---|---|---|---|---|---|---|
| | SC | Wheat | Maize | Rice | SC | Maize | Rice | SC | Maize | SC |
| 1950 | 16 | ... | ... | ... | ... | ... | 30 | 10 | 291 | 22 |
| 1951 | 16 | 42 | 534 | 9 | 22 | ... | ... | ... | 299 | 23 |
| 1952 | ... | 36 | 478 | 8 | ... | ... | ... | ... | 307 | 25 |
| 1953 | 25 | 38 | 483 | 10 | ... | ... | ... | ... | 304 | 26 |
| 1954 | 18 | 33 | 520 | 8 | 25 | ... | ... | ... | 254 | 28 |
| 1955 | 19 | 34 | 551 | 8 | 24 | ... | ... | ... | 291 | 23 |
| 1956 | 19 | 35 | 615 | 8 | 25 | ... | ... | ... | 325 | 23 |
| 1957 | 20 | 33 | 620 | 9 | 24 | ... | ... | ... | 339 | 23 |
| 1958 | 21 | 33 | 624 | 10 | 25 | 335 | 65 | ... | 360 | 23 |
| 1959 | 23 | 34 | 682 | 11 | 26 | ... | ... | ... | 376 | 24 |
| 1960 | 27 | 31 | 652 | 10 | 13 | ... | ... | ... | 374 | 25 |
| 1961 | 27 | 34 | 625 | 9 | 26 | 300 | 48 | ... | 252 | 25 |
| 1962 | 28 | 39 | 639 | 10 | 28 | ... | 54 | ... | 266 | 25 |
| 1963 | 28 | 38 | 688 | 13 | 28 | ... | 55 | 90 | 263 | 26 |
| 1964 | 28 | 39 | 698 | 11 | 34 | ... | 60 | ... | 294 | 26 |
| 1965 | 32 | 27 | 676 | 8 | 38 | ... | 65 | ... | 279 | 27 |
| 1966 | 30 | 31 | 659 | 8 | 45 | 305 | 70 | ... | 280 | 28 |
| 1967 | 30 | 36 | 697 | 12 | 42 | 320 | 70 | ... | 280 | 28 |
| 1968 | 29 | 30 | 691 | 14 | 45 | 300 | 72 | ... | 281 | 28 |
| 1969 | 32 | 29 | 735 | 14 | 45 | 305 | 75 | ... | 282 | 31 |
| 1970 | 32 | 30 | 695 | 9 | 36 | 310 | 75 | 75 | 283 | 30 |
| 1971 | 28 | 31 | 660 | 20 | 40 | 320 | 75 | ... | 283 | 27 |
| 1972 | 27 | 37 | 832 | 16 | 42 | 330 | 50 | ... | 284 | 27 |
| 1973 | 27 | 28 | 844 | 22 | 53 | 238 | 43 | ... | 287 | 26 |
| 1974 | 27 | 43 | 562 | 15 | 58 | ... | 45 | ... | 286 | 26 |
| 1975 | 27 | 39 | 514 | 19 | 63 | ... | 48 | ... | 331 | 26 |
| 1976 | 23 | 37 | 514 | 19 | 91 | 239 | 50 | ... | 381 | 28 |
| 1977 | 22 | 45 | 641 | 12 | 82 | 248 | 40 | ... | 431 | 28 |
| 1978 | 21 | 52 | 591 | 11 | 77 | ... | 52 | ... | 418 | 27 |
| 1979 | 21 | 59 | 622 | 13 | 74 | 234 | 54 | ... | 352 | 30 |
| 1980 | 21 | 50 | 655 | 13 | 79 | 225 | 50 | 80 | 339 | 24 |
| 1981 | 19 | 41 | 681 | 11 | 83 | 200 | ... | ... | 339 | 35 |
| 1982 | | 37 | 669 | 8 | 78 | 185 | ... | ... | 287 | 52 |
| 1983 | 16 | 41 | 800 | 12 | 90 | 171 | ... | ... | 308 | 52 |
| 1984 | 13 | 30 | 599 | 16 | 89 | 200 | 55 | ... | 367 | 39 |
| 1985 | 12 | 33 | 660 | 15 | 94 | ... | 35 | 85 | 289 | 45 |
| 1986 | 14 | 27 | 675 | 15 | 90 | 175 | ... | ... | 345 | 42 |
| 1987 | 14 | 28 | 749 | 18 | 84 | ... | 50 | ... | 284 | 41 |
| 1988 | 14 | 28 | 644 | 27 | 96 | ... | 46 | ... | 518 | 41 |

**C1    NORTH AMERICA: Area of Main Arable Crops** (in thousands of hectares)

| | Jamaica | Martinique | Mexico | | | | | | | |
|---|---|---|---|---|---|---|---|---|---|---|
| | SC | SC | Wheat | Barley | Oats | Maize | Rice | Sorghum | P's | SC |
| 1950 | 46 | 13 | 644 | 230 | 80 | 4,328 | 106 | ... | 30 | 183 |
| 1951 | 47 | 13 | 673 | 231 | 82 | 4,428 | 104 | ... | 31 | 198 |
| 1952 | 45 | 13 | 593 | 231 | 82 | 4,236 | 82 | ... | 31 | 210 |
| 1953 | 62 | 13 | 657 | 222 | 86 | 4,857 | 94 | ... | 31 | 222 |
| 1954 | 62 | ... | 765 | 231 | 87 | 5,253 | 90 | ... | 32 | 247 |
| 1955 | 62 | 14 | 800 | 241 | 88 | 5,371 | 96 | ... | 35 | 258 |
| 1956 | | 14 | 937 | 246 | 89 | 5,460 | 115 | ... | 37 | 199 |
| 1957 | 61 | 14 | 958 | 237 | 96 | 5,392 | 117 | ... | 41 | 258 |
| 1958 | 68 | 13 | 840 | 239 | 98 | 6,372 | 121 | 120 | 45 | 282 |
| 1959 | 76 | 13 | 937 | 243 | 96 | 6,324 | 127 | 107 | 48 | 315 |
| 1960 | 82 | 13 | 840 | 240 | 80 | 5,558 | 143 | 116 | 44 | 346 |
| 1961 | 77 | 13 | 837 | 233 | 85 | 6,288 | 146 | 117 | 46 | 348 |
| 1962 | 77 | 12 | 748 | 193 | 86 | 6,372 | 134 | 118 | 46 | 362 |
| 1963 | 61 | 13 | 819 | 232 | 91 | 6,793 | 135 | 198 | 50 | 378 |
| 1964 | 60 | 9 | 818 | 212 | 91 | 7,461 | 133 | 276 | 48 | 446 |
| 1965 | 60 | 9 | 858 | 226 | 92 | 7,718 | 138 | 314 | 39 | 461 |
| 1966 | 60 | 7 | 731 | 241 | 78 | 8,287 | 153 | 576 | 41 | 488 |
| 1967 | 60 | 7 | 778 | 237 | 53 | 7,611 | 168 | 673 | 38 | 489 |
| 1968 | 55 | 8 | 791 | 251 | 42 | 7,676 | 139 | 830 | 47 | 505 |
| 1969 | 55 | 8 | 841 | 238 | 40 | 7,104 | 153 | 883 | 32 | 526 |
| 1970 | 58 | 8 | 886 | 250 | 60 | 7,440 | 150 | 971 | 38 | 547 |
| 1971 | 59 | 8 | 614 | 255 | 40 | 7,692 | 154 | 937 | 40 | 481 |
| 1972 | 59 | 9 | 687 | 385 | 39 | 7,292 | 156 | 1,110 | 39 | 465 |
| 1973 | 58 | 9 | 640 | 262 | 47 | 7,606 | 150 | 1,185 | 55 | 505 |
| 1974 | 63 | 8 | 774 | 173 | 60 | 6,717 | 173 | 1,153 | 54 | 491 |
| 1975 | 62 | 6 | 778 | 286 | 59 | 6,694 | 257 | 1,116 | 57 | 479 |
| 1976 | 65 | 7 | 894 | 364 | 66 | 6,783 | 159 | 1,251 | 56 | 496 |
| 1977 | 51 | 7 | 709 | 248 | 64 | 7,470 | 180 | 1,413 | 54 | 488 |
| 1978 | 44 | 6 | 760 | 296 | 65 | 7,191 | 121 | 1,399 | 61 | 537 |
| 1979 | 47 | 5 | 599 | 222 | 54 | 5,502 | 149 | 1,456 | 56 | 538 |
| 1980 | 49 | 5 | 739 | 329 | 48 | 6,955 | 132 | 1,579 | 71 | 546 |
| 1981 | 43 | 5 | 861 | 274 | 70 | 8,150 | 180 | 1,767 | 68 | 522 |
| 1982 | 44 | 5 | 1,013 | 225 | 69 | 5,643 | 175 | 1,275 | 68 | 526 |
| 1983 | 44 | 4 | 857 | 303 | 70 | 7,421 | 133 | 1,518 | 74 | 505 |
| 1984 | 40 | 4 | 1,033 | 283 | 117 | 6,972 | 153 | 1,622 | 71 | 517 |
| 1985 | 47 | 4 | 1,224 | 282 | 99 | 7,498 | 220 | 1,236 | 72 | 540 |
| 1986 | 37 | 4 | 1,201 | 264 | ... | 6,417 | 158 | 1,533 | ... | 469 |
| 1987 | 36 | 3 | 988 | 286 | ... | 6,801 | 155 | 1,853 | ... | 519 |
| 1988 | 36 | ... | 912 | 247 | ... | 6,506 | 126 | 1,800 | ... | 415 |

**C1** **NORTH AMERICA: Area of Main Arable Crops** (in thousands of hectares)

| | Nicaragua | | | Panama | | | Puerto Rico | Trinidad & Tobago |
|---|---|---|---|---|---|---|---|---|
| | Maize | Rice | SC | Maize | Rice | SC | SC | SC |
| 1950 | 112 | 16 | 14 | 69 | 68 | ... | 154 | 34 |
| 1951 | 97 | 13 | ... | 71 | 66 | 15 | 170 | 34 |
| 1952 | 122 | 24 | ... | 73 | 67 | 20 | 170 | 34 |
| 1953 | 136 | 34 | 16 | 86 | 79 | 14 | 162 | ... |
| 1954 | 119 | 14 | 17 | 86 | 83 | ... | 152 | 34 |
| 1955 | 160 | 19 | ... | 83 | 87 | 14 | 151 | 35 |
| 1956 | 179 | 25 | 18 | 83 | 85 | ... | 142 | 32 |
| 1957 | 147 | 24 | 19 | 86 | 89 | 17 | 129 | 32 |
| 1958 | 133 | 23 | 20 | 90 | 95 | 14 | 135 | 32 |
| 1959 | 130 | 21 | 20 | 86 | 97 | 16 | 135 | 33 |
| 1960 | 132 | 21 | 22 | 79 | 89 | 17 | 129 | 33 |
| 1961 | 165 | 24 | 28 | 92 | 100 | 22 | 121 | 34 |
| 1962 | 173 | 23 | 17 | 82 | 100 | 14 | 144 | 34 |
| 1963 | 161 | 22 | 21 | 94 | 103 | 26 | 119 | 23 |
| 1964 | 175 | 23 | 21 | 99 | 121 | 18 | 113 | 33 |
| 1965 | 195 | 25 | 25 | 105 | 133 | 17 | 107 | 33 |
| 1966 | 198 | 26 | 25 | 108 | 132 | 18 | 103 | 36 |
| 1967 | 228 | 26 | 27 | 113 | 130 | 17 | 93 | 36 |
| 1968 | 215 | 32 | 28 | 100 | 129 | 17 | 71 | 35 |
| 1969 | 257 | 40 | 30 | 103 | 126 | 17 | 74 | 35 |
| 1970 | 250 | 40 | 34 | 69 | 96 | 18 | 74 | 35 |
| 1971 | 266 | 26 | 34 | 63 | 96 | 20 | 60 | 38 |
| 1972 | 211 | 26 | 35 | 66 | 105 | 22 | 60 | 37 |
| 1973 | 221 | 29 | 35 | 68 | 105 | 25 | 53 | 39 |
| 1974 | 263 | 30 | 36 | 76 | 112 | 26 | 49 | 38 |
| 1975 | 210 | 30 | 38 | 74 | 115 | 30 | 52 | 32 |
| 1976 | 228 | 21 | 39 | 66 | 97 | 30 | 50 | 34 |
| 1977 | 212 | 25 | 42 | 76 | 105 | 37 | 47 | 32 |
| 1978 | 228 | 28 | 45 | 65 | 99 | 41 | 41 | 34 |
| 1979 | 140 | 19 | 42 | 66 | 99 | 44 | 39 | 39 |
| 1980 | 197 | 42 | 32 | 66 | 98 | 48 | 34 | 34 |
| 1981 | 200 | 42 | 39 | 56 | 100 | 53 | 31 | 28 |
| 1982 | 164 | 45 | 44 | 59 | 95 | 50 | 24 | 25 |
| 1983 | 183 | 44 | 46 | 71 | 107 | 38 | 24 | 20 |
| 1984 | 189 | 41 | 43 | 63 | 93 | 38 | 23 | 27 |
| 1985 | 161 | 41 | 46 | 79 | 91 | 35 | 21 | 14 |
| 1986 | 156 | 37 | 46 | 84 | 86 | 34 | 21 | 14 |
| 1987 | 191 | 40 | 41 | 78 | 86 | 31 | 22 | 18 |
| 1988 | 200 | 38 | 36 | 77 | 87 | 31 | 22 | 17 |

**C1　NORTH AMERICA: Area of Main Arable Crops** (in thousands of hectares)

| | Wheat | Barley | Oats | Rye | Maize | B'wheat | Rice | Sorghum | P's | SP's | SB | SC |
|---|---|---|---|---|---|---|---|---|---|---|---|---|
| | | | | | | | **USA**[3] | | | | | |
| 1950 | 24,931 | 4,514 | 15,907 | 709 | 33,111 | 102 | 662 | 4,187 | 687 | 198 | 374 | 170 |
| 1951 | 25,039 | 3,814 | 14,258 | 697 | 32,670 | 81 | 808 | 3,458 | 546 | 126 | 280 | 164 |
| 1952 | 28,785 | 3,333 | 14,978 | 564 | 32,755 | 66 | 808 | 2,155 | 565 | 130 | 269 | 172 |
| 1953 | 27,454 | 3,513 | 15,190 | 579 | 32,561 | 72 | 874 | 2,547 | 622 | 139 | 301 | 175 |
| 1954 | 21,997 | 5,411 | 16,410 | 726 | 32,450 | 61 | 1,032 | 4,575 | 572 | 134 | 355 | 159 |
| 1955 | 19,138 | 5,877 | 15,974 | 829 | 32,119 | 43 | 739 | 5,217 | 569 | 138 | 299 | 151 |
| 1956 | 20,140 | 5,201 | 13,489 | 657 | 30,451 | 40 | 635 | 3,727 | 555 | 112 | 318 | 138 |
| 1957 | 17,707 | 6,018 | 13,786 | 695 | 29,082 | 40 | 542 | 7,965 | 550 | 111 | 355 | 148 |
| 1958 | 21,467 | 5,986 | 12,645 | 727 | 29,228 | 35 | 573 | 6,687 | 578 | 104 | 361 | 137[8] |
| 1959 | 20,929 | 6,017 | 11,233 | 590 | 33,145 | 24 | 642 | 5,893 | 539 | 104 | 367 | 165 |
| 1960 | 20,995 | 5,607 | 10,760 | 683 | 32,649 | 19 | 645 | 6,314 | 561 | 77 | 387 | 165 |
| 1961 | 20,870 | 5,183 | 9,666 | 624 | 26,469 | 19 | 643 | 4,445 | 599 | 74 | 436 | 179 |
| 1962 | 17,680 | 4,944 | 9,056 | 802 | 26,092 | 17 | 718 | 4,683 | 545 | 82 | 446 | 193 |
| 1963 | 18,415 | 4,547 | 8,623 | 643 | 27,647 | 18 | 717 | 5,393 | 535 | 69 | 500 | 220 |
| 1964 | 20,138 | 4,564 | 7,996 | 686 | 26,462 | 20 | 723 | 4,520 | 515 | 61 | 565 | 265 |
| 1965 | 20,056 | 3,700 | 7,478 | 596 | 26,129 | … | 726 | 5,273 | 560 | 68 | 505 | 236 |
| 1966 | 20,077 | 4,130 | 7,228 | 516 | 26,640 | … | 796 | 5,185 | 592 | 63 | 470 | 239 |
| 1967 | 23,614 | 3,714 | 6,482 | 430 | 28,319 | … | 797 | 6,065 | 590 | 56 | 454 | 241 |
| 1968 | 22,162 | 3,929 | 7,095 | 403 | 26,144 | … | 952 | 5,621 | 557 | 55 | 571 | 234 |
| 1969 | 19,079 | 3,857 | 7,256 | 522 | 25,641 | … | 861 | … | 572 | 55 | 624 | 217 |
| 1970 | 17,630 | 3,896[5] | 7,543 | 577 | 26,799[6] | … | 735 | 5,491 | 575 | 52 | 574 | 236 |
| | | 3,936 | | | 23,212 | | | | | | | |
| 1971 | 19,293 | 4,109 | 6,383 | 710 | 25,919 | … | 736 | 6,597 | 563 | 46 | 543 | 262 |
| 1972 | 19,135 | 3,929 | 5,473 | 439 | 23,237 | … | 736 | 5,410 | 507 | 46 | 538 | 284 |
| 1973 | 21,800 | 4,231 | 5,692 | 418 | 25,047 | … | 878 | 6,415 | 528 | 46 | 493 | 300 |
| 1974 | 26,552 | 3,306 | 5,344 | 363 | 26,449 | … | 1,026 | 5,615 | 563 | 49 | 491 | 297 |
| 1975 | 28,081 | 3,453 | 5,298 | 295 | 27,318 | … | 1,140 | 6,214 | 512 | 47 | 614 | 313 |
| 1976 | 28,640 | 3,358 | 4,834 | 292 | 28,854 | … | 1,004 | 5,958 | 556 | 48 | 598 | 302 |
| 1977 | 26,895 | 3,871 | 5,442 | 285 | 28,680 | … | 910 | 5,703 | 550 | 46 | 492 | 307 |
| 1978 | 22,863 | 3,743 | 4,503 | 375 | 29,109 | … | 1,202 | 5,427 | 556 | 45 | 514 | 301 |
| 1979 | 25,275 | 3,044 | 3,917 | 352 | 29,300 | … | 1,161 | 5,221 | 514 | 46 | 453 | 297 |
| 1980 | 28,727 | 2,944 | 3,501 | 273 | 29,555 | … | 1,340 | 5,068 | 467 | 41 | 481 | 297 |
| 1981 | 32,784 | 3,706 | 3,810 | 286 | 30,230 | … | 1,535 | 5,551 | 501 | 44 | 497 | 306 |
| 1982 | 31,963 | 3,688 | 4,297 | 292 | 29,554 | … | 1,320 | 5,766 | 515 | 45 | 416 | 307 |
| 1983 | 24,843 | 3,938 | 3,671 | 363 | 20,834 | … | 878 | 4,047 | 503 | 41 | 427 | 311 |
| 1984 | 27,085 | 4,545 | 3,304 | 397 | 29,103 | … | 1,134 | 6,214 | 527 | 42 | 444 | 302 |
| 1985 | 26,197 | 4,696 | 3,309 | 290 | 30,442 | … | 1,009 | 6,792 | 551 | 43 | 446 | 312 |
| 1986 | 24,574 | 4,859 | 2,776 | 274 | 27,988 | … | 955 | 5,609 | 494 | 38 | 482 | 322 |
| 1987 | 22,646 | 4,070 | 2,802 | 272 | 23,960 | … | 944 | 4,291 | 578 | 38 | 507 | 333 |
| 1988 | 21,524 | 3,090 | 2,239 | 241 | 23,593 | … | 1,174 | 3,659 | 503 | 36 | 526 | 342 |

**C1     SOUTH AMERICA: AREA OF MAIN ARABLE CROPS** (in thousands of hectares)

| | Argentina | | | Guyana |
|---|---|---|---|---|
| | Wheat | Maize | SC | SC |
| 1872 | 73 | 130 | 2.5 | ... |
| 1882 | ... | ... | ... | 31 |
| 1883 | ... | ... | ... | 32 |
| 1884 | 243 | ... | ... | 32 |
| 1885 | ... | ... | ... | 31 |
| 1886 | ... | ... | ... | 31 |
| 1887 | ... | ... | ... | 31 |
| 1888 | 815 | 802 | 23.0 | 31 |
| 1889 | ... | ... | ... | 31 |

| | Argentina | | | | | | | Chile | | | |
|---|---|---|---|---|---|---|---|---|---|---|---|
| | Wheat | Barley | Oats | Rye | Maize | P | SC | Wheat | Barley | Maize | P |
| 1890 | 1,202 | ... | ... | ... | ... | ... | ... | ... | ... | ... | ... |
| 1891 | 1,320 | ... | ... | ... | ... | ... | ... | ... | ... | ... | ... |
| 1892 | 1,600 | ... | ... | ... | ... | ... | ... | ... | ... | ... | ... |
| 1893 | 1,840 | ... | ... | ... | ... | ... | ... | ... | ... | ... | ... |
| 1894 | 2,050 | ... | ... | ... | ... | ... | ... | ... | ... | ... | ... |
| 1895 | 2,260 | ... | ... | ... | 1,244 | 21 | 48 | ... | ... | ... | ... |
| 1896 | 2,500 | ... | ... | ... | ... | ... | ... | ... | ... | ... | ... |
| 1897 | 2,600 | ... | 22 | ... | ... | ... | ... | ... | ... | ... | ... |
| 1898 | 3,200 | ... | 22 | ... | 850 | ... | ... | ... | ... | ... | ... |
| 1899 | 3,250 | 49 | 23 | ... | 1,009 | 32 | ... | ... | ... | ... | ... |
| 1900 | 3,380 | 52 | 32 | 1 | 1,255 | ... | 50 | ... | ... | ... | ... |
| 1901 | 3,296 | 52 | 33 | 2 | 1,406 | 35 | 54 | ... | ... | ... | ... |
| 1902 | 3,695 | 13 | 56 | 1 | 1,802 | 44 | 60 | 350 | 41 | 20 | 47 |
| 1903 | 4,320 | 31 | 48 | 3 | 2,100 | 38 | 60 | 268 | 50 | 22 | 48 |
| 1904 | 4,903 | 48 | 51 | 4 | 2,287 | 39 | 63 | 422 | 76 | 29 | 36 |

| | Guyana | Uruguay | | | |
|---|---|---|---|---|---|
| | SC | Wheat | Barley | Oats | Maize |
| 1890 | 32 | ... | ... | ... | ... |
| 1891 | 32 | ... | ... | ... | ... |
| 1892 | 32 | 159 | 2 | - - | ... |
| 1893 | 31 | 207 | 4 | - - | ... |
| 1894 | 31 | 204 | 3 | - - | ... |
| 1895 | 28 | ... | ... | ... | ... |
| 1896 | 28 | ... | ... | ... | ... |
| 1897 | 27 | ... | ... | ... | ... |
| 1898 | 26 | 274 | 2 | - - | ... |
| 1899 | 26 | 328 | 1 | - - | 146 |
| 1900 | 27 | 277 | 1 | - - | 182 |
| 1901 | 29 | 293 | 1 | - - | 178 |
| 1902 | 31 | 266 | 1 | - - | 162 |
| 1903 | 32 | ... | 1 | - - | ... |
| 1904 | 30 | 261 | 1 | - - | 177 |

**C1      SOUTH AMERICA: Area of Main Arable Crops** (in thousands of hectares)

| | | | | | Argentina | | | | |
|---|---|---|---|---|---|---|---|---|---|
| | Wheat | Barley | Oats | Rye | Maize | Millet | Rice | P's | SC |
| 1905 | 5,675 | 50 | 72 | 4 | 2,717 | ... | ... | 40 | 66 |
| 1906 | 5,692 | 50 | 146 | 5 | 2,851 | ... | ... | 44 | 71 |
| 1907 | 5,759 | 94 | 386 | 9 | 2,719 | ... | ... | 48 | 71 |
| 1908 | 6,063 | 61 | 633 | 10 | 2,974 | ... | ... | 48 | 71 |
| 1909 | 5,837 | 60 | 575 | 11 | 3,005 | ... | 8 | 49 | 79 |
| 1910 | 6,253 | 60 | 801 | 13 | 3,215 | ... | 8 | 52 | 94 |
| 1911 | 6,897 | 68 | 1,031 | 15 | 3,422 | ... | 3 | 108 | 97 |
| 1912 | 6,918 | 108 | 1,192 | 40 | 3,830 | ... | 4 | 112 | 99 |
| 1913 | 6,574 | 169 | 1,249 | 92 | 4,152 | ... | 4 | 119 | 106 |
| 1914 | 6,261 | 161 | 1,161 | 93 | 4,203 | ... | 3 | 124 | 125 |
| 1915 | 6,645 | 175 | 1,038 | 86 | 4,018 | ... | 7 | 130 | 134 |
| 1916 | 6,511 | 157 | 1,022 | 73 | 3,630 | ... | 5 | 134 | 86 |
| 1917 | 7,234 | 244 | 1,295 | 10 | 3,527 | ... | 7 | 135 | 112 |
| 1918 | 6,870 | 249 | 1,206 | ... | 3,340 | ... | 7 | 134 | 91 |
| 1919 | 7,045 | 271 | 931 | 83 | 3,312 | ... | 7 | 150 | 93 |
| 1920 | 6,076 | 250 | 834 | 88 | 3,274 | ... | 11 | 158 | 95 |
| 1921 | 5,763 | 251 | 852 | 98 | 2,972 | ... | 11 | 136 | 85 |
| 1922 | 6,578 | 242 | 1,059 | 148 | 3,177 | ... | 6 | 146 | 100 |
| 1923 | 6,897 | 227 | 864 | 155 | 3,435 | ... | 4 | 163 | 104 |
| 1924 | 6,465 | 165 | 692 | 65 | 2,912 | ... | 5 | 118 | 109 |
| 1925 | 7,130 | 291 | 906 | 144 | 3,899 | ... | 5 | 106 | 122 |
| 1926 | 7,670 | 328 | 898 | 170 | 3,667 | ... | 4 | 113 | 131 |
| 1927 | 8,173 | 317 | 705 | 216 | 3,562 | ... | 4 | 126 | 122 |
| 1928 | 9,076 | 369 | 890 | 351 | 3,518 | ... | 3 | 123 | 122 |
| 1929 | 6,436 | 325 | 874 | 220 | 4,220 | ... | 4 | 133 | 141 |
| 1930 | 7,902 | 321 | 908 | 202 | 4,685 | ... | 4 | 176 | 142 |
| 1931 | 6,486 | 409 | 826 | 388 | 3,852 | ... | 6 | 141 | 143 |
| 1932 | 7,200 | 519 | 894 | 480 | 3,764 | ... | 13 | 140 | 144 |
| 1933 | 7,301 | 558 | 668 | 290 | 4,112 | ... | 19 | 138 | 145 |
| 1934 | 6,942 | 633 | 855 | 533 | 5,702 | ... | 15 | 148 | 145 |
| 1935 | 4,730 | 507 | 553 | 232 | 5,135 | | 15 | 122 | 147 |
| 1936 | 7,115 | 538 | 776 | 273 | 4,361 | ... | 16 | 79 | 148 |
| 1937 | 6,979 | 455 | 716 | 204 | 2,957 | 118 | 16 | 113 | 188 |
| 1938 | 7,897 | 499 | 722 | 433 | 3,502 | 105 | 31 | 125 | 189 |
| 1939 | 5,065 | 621 | 880 | 541 | 5,695 | 132 | 31 | 189 | 188 |
| 1940 | 6,718 | 605 | 570 | 300 | 4,932 | 66 | 21 | 183 | 190 |
| 1941 | 5,933 | 338 | 470 | 214 | 4,089 | 69 | 33 | 215 | 187 |
| 1942 | 4,875 | 320 | 626 | 253 | 1,767 | 37 | 34 | 180 | 213 |
| 1943 | 5,989 | 530 | 1,067 | 803 | 3,700 | 49 | 52 | 189 | 230 |
| 1944 | 4,361 | 411 | 1,021 | 328 | 2,054 | 57 | 39 | 186 | 239 |

**C1    SOUTH AMERICA: Area of Main Arable Crops** (in thousands of hectares)

| | Bolivia | | | | | Brazil | | | | | |
|---|---|---|---|---|---|---|---|---|---|---|---|
| | Wheat | Barley | Maize | Rice | P's | Wheat | Maize | Rice | P's | Cassava | SC |
| 1905 | ... | ... | ... | ... | ... | ... | ... | ... | ... | ... | ... |
| 1906 | ... | ... | ... | ... | ... | ... | ... | ... | ... | ... | ... |
| 1907 | ... | ... | ... | ... | ... | ... | ... | ... | ... | ... | ... |
| 1908 | ... | ... | ... | ... | ... | ... | ... | ... | ... | ... | ... |
| 1909 | ... | ... | ... | ... | ... | ... | ... | ... | ... | ... | ... |
| 1910 | ... | ... | ... | ... | ... | ... | ... | ... | ... | ... | ... |
| 1911 | ... | ... | ... | ... | ... | ... | ... | ... | ... | ... | ... |
| 1912 | ... | ... | ... | ... | ... | ... | ... | ... | ... | ... | ... |
| 1913 | ... | ... | ... | ... | ... | ... | ... | ... | ... | ... | ... |
| 1914 | ... | ... | ... | ... | ... | ... | ... | ... | ... | ... | ... |
| 1915 | ... | ... | ... | ... | ... | ... | ... | ... | ... | ... | ... |
| 1916 | ... | ... | ... | ... | ... | ... | 3,058 | ... | ... | ... | ... |
| 1917 | ... | ... | ... | ... | ... | ... | ... | ... | ... | ... | ... |
| 1918 | ... | ... | ... | ... | ... | ... | ... | ... | ... | ... | ... |
| 1919 | ... | ... | ... | ... | ... | ... | ... | ... | ... | ... | ... |
| 1920 | ... | ... | ... | ... | ... | 100 | 2,252 | 366 | ... | ... | ... |
| 1921 | ... | ... | ... | ... | ... | ... | 2,592 | 567 | 50 | ... | 551 |
| 1922 | ... | ... | ... | ... | ... | 107 | 3,058 | 243 | 32 | ... | ... |
| 1923 | 90 | 160 | 260 | 21 | 204 | 62 | 3,424 | 344 | 30 | ... | 300 |
| 1924 | 93 | 170 | 274 | 19 | 220 | 98 | 2,500 | 544 | 45 | ... | ... |
| 1925 | 98 | 185 | 280 | 22 | 231 | 97 | 2,550 | ... | 50 | ... | 320 |
| 1926 | 102 | 187 | 265 | 24 | 264 | 97 | 2,514 | 389 | 50 | ... | 305 |
| 1927 | ... | ... | ... | ... | ... | 133 | 2,204 | ... | 31 | ... | 273 |
| 1928 | 15 | 93 | 345 | 12 | 260 | 145 | 4,934 | 1,100 | 38 | ... | 485 |
| 1929 | 26 | 95 | 350 | 11 | 248 | ... | ... | ... | ... | ... | ... |
| 1930 | 43 | 98 | 348 | 10 | 260 | ... | ... | ... | ... | ... | ... |
| 1931 | 50 | 98 | 350 | ... | 300 | 142 | 3,170 | 719 | 24 | ... | 348 |
| 1932 | ... | ... | ... | ... | ... | 164 | 3,722 | 856 | 44 | ... | 328 |
| 1933 | ... | ... | ... | ... | ... | 168 | 4,352 | 865 | 42 | ... | 430 |
| 1934 | ... | ... | ... | ... | ... | 172 | 3,988 | 807 | 34 | ... | 474 |
| 1935 | ... | ... | ... | ... | ... | 145 | 4,076 | 949 | 54 | ... | 438 |
| 1936 | ... | ... | ... | ... | ... | 154 | 3,872 | 888 | 46 | ... | 461 |
| 1937 | ... | ... | ... | ... | ... | 162 | 3,877 | 888 | 62 | 388 | 454 |
| 1938 | ... | ... | ... | ... | ... | 174 | 4,254 | 979 | 78 | 473 | 474 |
| 1939 | 34 | 37 | 27 | 6 | 26 | 212 | 4,379 | 1,076 | 80 | 538 | 496 |
| 1940 | ... | ... | ... | ... | ... | 201 | 3,904 | 872 | 66 | | |
| 1941 | ... | ... | ... | ... | ... | 272 | 4,112 | 1,001 | 70 | | |
| 1942 | ... | ... | ... | ... | ... | 277 | 4,059 | 1,059 | 72 | | |
| 1943 | ... | ... | ... | ... | ... | 290 | 4,290 | 1,170 | 102 | | |
| 1944 | ... | 50 | 100 | 12 | 70 | | 4,101 | 1,428 | 84 | | |

**C1    SOUTH AMERICA: Area af Main Arable Crops** (in thousands of hectares)

| | Chile | | | | | Colombia | | | | | |
|---|---|---|---|---|---|---|---|---|---|---|---|
| | Wheat | Barley | Oats | Maize | P's | Wheat | Barley | Maize | Rice | P's | SC |
| 1905 | 390 | 102 | ... | 33 | ... | ... . | ... | ... | ... | ... | ... |
| 1906 | 365 | 73 | ... | 21 | 27 | ... | ... | ... | ... | ... | ... |
| 1907 | 460 | 56 | ... | 26 | ... | ... | ... | ... | ... | ... | ... |
| 1908 | 445 | 52 | ... | 25 | ... | ... | ... | ... | ... | ... | ... |
| 1909 | 442 | 44 | 25 | 27 | 28 | ... | ... | ... | ... | ... | ... |
| 1910 | 392 | 34 | 24 | 19 | 27 | ... | ... | ... | ... | ... | ... |
| 1911 | 442 | 42 | 28 | 23 | 27 | ... | ... | ... | ... | ... | ... |
| 1912 | 446 | 53 | 38 | 26 | 32 | ... | ... | ... | ... | ... | ... |
| 1913 | 412 | 62 | 49 | 24 | 33 | ... | ... | ... | ... | ... | ... |
| 1914 | 435 | 57 | 61 | 32 | 32 | ... | ... | ... | ... | ... | ... |
| 1915 | 462 | 49 | 65 | 27 | 32 | 57 | 13 | 168 | 6 | 21 | 83 |
| 1916 | 515 | 51 | 51 | 20 | 29 | ... | ... | ... | ... | ... | ... |
| 1917 | 527 | 40 | 32 | 26 | 33 | ... | ... | ... | ... | ... | ... |
| 1918 | 494 | 44 | 20 | 23 | 29 | ... | ... | ... | ... | ... | ... |
| 1919 | 484 | 51 | 26 | 25 | 31 | ... | ... | ... | ... | ... | ... |
| 1920 | 509 | 58 | 32 | 28 | 34 | ... | ... | ... | ... | ... | ... |
| 1921 | 544 | 57 | 28 | 32 | 33 | ... | ... | ... | ... | ... | ... |
| 1922 | 596 | 62 | 33 | 28 | 32 | ... | ... | ... | ... | ... | ... |
| 1923 | 621 | 63 | 41 | 28 | 29 | ... | ... | ... | ... | ... | ... |
| 1924 | 578 | 71 | 54 | 17 | 29 | ... | ... | 148 | 17 | 57 | 106 |
| 1925 | 585 | 80 | 58 | 22 | 26 | ... | ... | 149 | 17 | 57 | 111 |
| 1926 | 600 | 63 | 55 | 25 | 31 | ... | ... | 156 | 18 | 60 | 117 |
| 1927 | 665 | 68 | 68 | 47 | 45 | ... | ... | 200 | 17 | 102 | 98 |
| 1928 | 694 | 78 | 89 | 47 | 45 | 60 | ... | 114 | 19 | 67 | ... |
| 1929 | 699 | 62 | 120 | 38 | 43 | ... | ... | ... | ... | ... | ... |
| 1930 | 651 | 67 | 78 | 37 | 45 | ... | ... | ... | ... | ... | ... |
| 1931 | 614 | 43 | 67 | 54 | 51 | 110 | ... | ... | ... | ... | ... |
| 1932 | 593 | 63 | 69 | 66 | 56 | 109 | ... | 596 | 45 | 32 | ... |
| 1933 | 851 | 95 | 107 | 48 | 54 | 109 | ... | ... | ... | ... | ... |
| 1934 | 858 | 60 | 76 | 46 | 56 | 148 | ... | 555 | 47 | 27 | ... |
| 1935 | 776 | 66 | 87 | 42 | 43 | 150 | ... | ... | ... | ... | ... |
| 1936 | 776 | 72 | 113 | 50 | 51 | 206 | ... | ... | ... | ... | ... |
| 1937 | 765 | 98 | 121 | 43 | 51 | 200 | ... | 556 | 67 | 68 | 272 |
| 1938 | 828 | 82 | 137 | 43 | 54 | ... | ... | ... | ... | ... | ... |
| 1939 | 828 | 53 | 107 | 45 | 46 | ... | ... | ... | ... | ... | ... |
| 1940 | 780 | 52 | 80 | 52 | 54 | ... | ... | ... | ... | ... | ... |
| 1941 | 730 | 49 | 68 | 48 | 52 | ... | ... | ... | ... | ... | ... |
| 1942 | 751 | 47 | 88 | 55 | 55 | ... | ... | ... | ... | ... | ... |
| 1943 | 797 | 44 | 102 | 53 | 53 | ... | ... | ... | ... | ... | ... |
| 1944 | 805 | 53 | 120 | 45 | 49 | ... | ... | ... | ... | ... | ... |

**C1** **SOUTH AMERICA: Area of Main Arable Crops** (in thousands of hectares)

| | Ecuador | | | Guyana | | Peru | | | | | |
|------|-------|------|---------|------|-----|-------|--------|-------|------|------|-----|
| | Maize | Rice | Cassava | Rice | SC | Wheat | Barley | Maize | Rice | P's | SC |
| 1905 | ... | ... | ... | ... | 31 | ... | ... | ... | ... | ... | ... |
| 1906 | ... | ... | ... | 10 | 32 | ... | ... | ... | ... | ... | ... |
| 1907 | ... | ... | ... | 10 | 30 | ... | ... | ... | ... | ... | ... |
| 1908 | ... | ... | ... | 12 | 29 | ... | ... | ... | ... | ... | ... |
| 1909 | ... | ... | ... | 15 | 30 | 80 | 65 | 52 | 50 | ... | ... |
| 1910 | ... | ... | ... | 13 | 30 | 75 | 67 | 53 | 56 | ... | ... |
| 1911 | ... | ... | ... | 15 | 29 | ... | ... | ... | ... | ... | 37 |
| 1912 | ... | ... | ... | 17 | 29 | ... | ... | ... | ... | ... | 40 |
| 1913 | ... | ... | ... | ... | 29 | ... | ... | ... | ... | ... | 41 |
| 1914 | ... | ... | ... | ... | 30 | ... | ... | ... | ... | ... | 43 |
| 1915 | ... | ... | ... | ... | 31 | ... | ... | ... | 25 | ... | 41 |
| 1916 | ... | ... | ... | ... | 32 | ... | ... | ... | 25 | ... | 45 |
| 1917 | ... | ... | ... | ... | 31 | 70 | 40 | 74 | 28 | 36 | 50 |
| 1918 | ... | ... | ... | ... | 30 | 98 | ... | ... | 31 | ... | |
| 1919 | ... | ... | ... | 30 | 29 | 83 | ... | ... | 29 | ... | 40 |
| 1920 | ... | ... | ... | 27 | 27 | 83 | ... | ... | 27 | ... | 49 |
| 1921 | ... | ... | ... | 23 | 26 | 94 | ... | ... | 27 | ... | 50 |
| 1922 | ... | ... | ... | 20 | 25 | 113 | ... | ... | 29 | ... | 51 |
| 1923 | ... | ... | ... | 16 | 22 | 123 | ... | ... | 36 | ... | 53 |
| 1924 | ... | ... | ... | 16 | 23 | 90 | ... | ... | 35 | ... | 56 |
| 1925 | ... | ... | ... | 16 | 23 | 93 | ... | ... | 31 | ... | 53 |
| 1926 | ... | ... | ... | 20 | 24 | 88 | ... | ... | 27 | ... | 53 |
| 1927 | ... | ... | ... | 20 | 23 | 115 | ... | ... | 26 | ... | $\frac{57_{11}}{32}$ |
| 1928 | ... | ... | ... | 22 | 23 | 105 | 125 | 280 | 35 | 285 | 29 |
| 1929 | ... | ... | ... | 26 | 22 | 142 | ... | ... | 30 | ... | 41 |
| 1930 | ... | 15 | ... | 26 | 22 | 143 | ... | ... | 47 | ... | 30 |
| 1931 | ... | 12 | ... | 34 | 22 | 117 | ... | ... | 48 | ... | 36 |
| 1932 | ... | ... | ... | 36 | 23 | 118 | ... | ... | 54 | ... | 31 |
| 1933 | ... | ... | ... | 35 | 22 | 121 | ... | ... | 60 | ... | 31 |
| 1934 | ... | ... | ... | 29 | 24 | 106 | ... | ... | 46 | ... | 33 |
| 1935 | ... | ... | ... | 34 | 26 | 97 | ... | ... | 47 | ... | 32 |
| 1936 | ... | ... | ... | 25 | 26 | 108 | ... | ... | 47 | ... | 31 |
| 1937 | ... | ... | ... | 29 | 25 | 114 | | ... | 37 | ... | 31 |
| 1938 | ... | ... | ... | 25 | 28 | 122 | | ... | 42 | ... | ... |
| 1939 | 130 | 40 | 10 | 29 | 26 | 136 | ... | ... | 42 | ... | 32 |
| 1940 | ... | ... | ... | 25 | 26 | 135 | ... | ... | 49 | ... | 30 |
| 1941 | ... | ... | ... | 42 | 25 | 120 | ... | ... | 62 | ... | 34 |
| 1942 | ... | ... | ... | 39 | 25 | 117 | ... | ... | 47 | ... | 30 |
| 1943 | ... | ... | ... | 35 | 25 | 106 | ... | ... | 51 | ... | 29 |
| 1944 | ... | ... | ... | 37 | 24 | 102 | ... | ... | 58 | ... | 32 |

**C1     SOUTH AMERICA: Area of Main Arable Crops** (in thousands of hectares)

| | Surinam | Uruguay | | | | | |
|---|---|---|---|---|---|---|---|
| | Rice | Wheat | Barley | Oats | Maize | Sorghum | P's |
| 1905 | ... | 288 | 2 | 1 | 166 | ... | ... |
| 1906 | ... | 252 | 2 | 2 | 212 | ... | ... |
| 1907 | ... | 248 | 2 | 2 | 174 | ... | ... |
| 1908 | ... | 277 | 2 | 4 | 204 | ... | ... |
| 1909 | ... | ... | 3 | 7 | 216 | ... | ... |
| 1910 | ... | 258 | 1 | 12 | 202 | ... | ... |
| 1911 | ... | 323 | 3 | 35 | 239 | ... | ... |
| 1912 | ... | 330 | 1 | 20 | 255 | ... | ... |
| 1913 | ... | 369 | 6 | 39 | 280 | ... | ... |
| 1914 | ... | 317 | 2 | 33 | 319 | ... | ... |
| 1915 | ... | 384 | 4 | 43 | 282 | ... | ... |
| 1916 | ... | 316 | 5 | 57 | 254 | ... | ... |
| 1917 | ... | 395 | 2 | 67 | 239 | ... | ... |
| 1918 | ... | 340 | 2 | 34 | 224 | - - | 2.0 |
| 1919 | ... | 275 | 2 | 33 | 200 | - - | 2.0 |
| 1920 | 5 | 283 | 2 | 52 | 231 | - - | 4.0 |
| 1921 | 9 | 329 | 1 | 43 | 194 | - - | 4.0 |
| 1922 | ... | 268 | 1 | 35 | 230 | - - | 3.0 |
| 1923 | ... | 427 | 2 | 49 | 186 | - - | 5.0 |
| 1924 | ... | 344 | 3 | 56 | 164 | - - | 5.0 |
| 1925 | ... | 387 | 3 | 60 | 164 | - - | 4.0 |
| 1926 | ... | 400 | 2 | 41 | 176 | - - | 3.0 |
| 1927 | ... | 466 | 3 | 65 | 231 | - - | 4.0 |
| 1928 | ... | 439 | 3 | 54 | 177 | - - | 5.0 |
| 1929 | ... | 444 | 6 | 83 | 215 | - - | 4.0 |
| 1930 | ... | 388 | 4 | 42 | 195 | - - | 6.0 |
| 1931 | 11 | 437 | 4 | 60 | 210 | - - | 6.0 |
| 1932 | 11 | 383 | 4 | 59 | 205 | - - | 7.0 |
| 1933 | 13 | 481 | 6 | 86 | 230 | - - | 7.0 |
| 1934 | 11 | 445 | 9 | 78 | 243 | - - | 8.0 |
| 1935 | 12 | 513 | 14 | 83 | 215 | - - | 8.0 |
| 1936 | 15 | 399 | 11 | 73 | 218 | 1 | 7.0 |
| 1937 | 14 | 556 | 16 | 90 | 214 | 1 | 4.7 |
| 1938 | 16 | 508 | 21 | 99 | 219 | 1 | 7.9 |
| 1939 | 18 | 471 | 18 | 87 | 209 | 1 | 8.9 |
| 1940 | 17 | 375 | 23 | 91 | 232 | 1 | 8.6 |
| 1941 | 17 | 454 | 22 | 62 | 213 | 1 | 9.0 |
| 1942 | 14 | 399 | 20 | 78 | 186 | 1 | 10.0 |
| 1943 | 12 | 331 | 25 | 163 | 237 | - - | 13.0 |
| 1944 | 11 | 351 | 22 | 60 | 186 | 1 | 11.0 |

**C1**   **SOUTH AMERICA: Area of Main Arable Crops** (in thousands of hectares)

| | | | | | | Argentina | | | | | | |
|------|-------|--------|------|-------|-------|--------|------|--------------------|------|------|------|-----|
| | Wheat | Barley | Oats | Rye | Maize | Millet | Rice | Sorghum[7] | P's | SP's | SC |
| 1945 | 4,044 | 704 | 741 | 570 | 2,749 | 145 | 43 | ... | 180 | ... | 240 |
| 1946 | 5,619 | 982 | 805 | 923 | 2,615 | 298 | 44 | ... | 180 | ... | 218 |
| 1947 | 4,717 | 660 | 667 | 701 | 2,602 | 350 | 41 | ... | 157 | 34 | ... |
| 1948 | 4,343 | 538 | 642 | 567 | 2,667 | 167 | 49 | ... | 170 | 37 | 236 |
| 1949 | 4,534 | 393 | 516 | 467 | 2,036 | 149 | 43 | ... | 171 | 36 | 210 |
| 1950 | 5,241 | 580 | 631 | 985 | 942 | 84 | 42 | ... | 199 | 32 | 250 |
| 1951 | 2,740 | 351 | 418 | 152 | 1,714 | 161 | 47 | ... | 227 | 31 | 250 |
| 1952 | 5,579 | 840 | 963 | 1,414 | 1,431 | 274 | 56 | 73 | 154 | 30 | 256 |
| 1953 | 4,996 | 653 | 729 | 836 | 2,356 | 329 | 61 | 86 | 191 | 33 | 272 |
| 1954 | 5,462 | 786 | 695 | 1,110 | 2,414 | 126 | 63 | 84 | 223 | 33 | 284 |
| 1955 | 4,062 | 828 | 654 | 890 | 1,863 | 141 | 55 | 99 | 217 | 29 | 287 |
| 1956 | 5,392 | 1,012 | 956 | 1,220 | 2,240 | 194 | 54 | 63 | 205 | 31 | 303 |
| 1957 | 4,394 | 833 | 876 | 893 | 1,958 | 166 | 57 | 57 | 203 | 36 | 286 |
| 1958 | 5,242 | 897 | 796 | 1,064 | 2,448 | 155 | 60 | 69 | 183 | 32 | 281 |
| 1959 | 4,378 | 907 | 798 | 1,317 | 2,361 | 208 | 52 | 91[7] 645 | 189 | 29 | 275 |
| 1960 | 3,599 | 719 | 768 | 733 | 2,415 | 207 | 56 | 610 | 215 | 35 | 242 |
| 1961 | 4,421 | 742 | 597 | 695 | 2,744 | 201 | 46 | 787 | 203 | 38 | 223 |
| 1962 | 3,745 | 361 | 412 | 287 | 2,757 | 159 | 53 | 861 | 143 | 36 | 207 |
| 1963 | 5,676 | 695 | 693 | 655 | 2,645 | 145 | 52 | 828 | 166 | 36 | 224 |
| 1964 | 6,135 | 553 | 570 | 773 | 2,971 | 168 | 54 | 984 | 179 | 35 | 231 |
| 1965 | 4,601 | 384 | 421 | 331 | 3,062 | 115 | 68 | 820 | 204 | 36 | 250 |
| 1966 | 5,214 | 411 | 412 | 420 | 3,275 | 163 | 47 | 1,123 | 165 | 36 | 242 |
| 1967 | 5,812 | 496 | 519 | 565 | 3,451 | 188 | 62 | 1,033 | 163 | 42 | 191 |
| 1968 | 5,837 | 539 | 443 | 604 | 3,378 | 210 | 71 | 1,266 | 200 | 41 | 185 |
| 1969 | 5,191 | 457 | 327 | 528 | 3,556 | 197 | 88 | 1,456 | 203 | 46 | 195 |
| 1970 | 3,701 | 356 | 300 | 360 | 4,017 | 132 | 102 | 2,111 | 190 | 44 | 192 |
| 1971 | 4,315 | 479 | 357 | 433 | 4,066 | 151 | 77 | 2,369 | 179 | 42 | 211 |
| 1972 | 4,965 | 602 | 399 | 747 | 3,147 | 116 | 83 | 1,564 | 147 | 35 | 243 |
| 1973 | 3,958 | 502 | 395 | 656 | 3,662 | 198 | 77 | 2,282 | 117 | 42 | 272 |
| 1974 | 4,233 | 369 | 282 | 375 | 3,486 | 208 | 83 | 2,324 | 105 | 33 | 298 |
| 1975 | 5,271 | 439 | 338 | 300 | 3,070 | 194 | 93 | 2,010 | 111 | 41 | 293 |
| 1976 | 6,428 | 476 | 383 | 340 | 2,766 | 231 | 87 | 1,903 | 108 | 38 | 339 |
| 1977 | 3,910 | 310 | 430 | 240 | 2,532 | 255 | 91 | 2,461 | 111 | 36 | 350 |
| 1978 | 4,685 | 355 | 500 | 260 | 2,630 | 244 | 95 | 2,254 | 115 | 34 | 343 |
| 1979 | 4,787 | 246 | 410 | 225 | 2,800 | 238 | 102 | 2,044 | 110 | 34 | 306 |
| 1980 | 5,023 | 173 | 350 | 210 | 2,490 | 182 | 82 | 1,279 | 112 | 34 | 314 |
| 1981 | 6,400 | 115 | 299 | 162 | 3,394 | 187 | 82 | 2,135 | 117 | 24 | 320 |
| 1982 | 7,320 | 119 | 408 | 174 | 3,170 | 132 | 114 | 2,510 | 102 | 32 | 309 |
| 1983 | 6,880 | 96 | 414 | 153 | 2,970 | 160 | 81 | 2,551 | 108 | 28 | 313 |
| 1984 | 5,900 | 107 | 384 | 157 | 3,014 | 114 | 129 | 2,392 | 114 | 31 | 319 |
| 1985 | 5,382 | 76 | 333 | 115 | 3,340 | 125 | 105 | 2,002 | ... | 32 | 288 |
| 1986 | 4,893 | 94 | 312 | 65 | 3,231 | 94 | 113 | 1,322 | 107 | 32 | 296 |
| 1987 | 4,789 | 131 | 476 | 96 | 2,900 | 62 | 95 | 1,005 | 105 | 29 | 290 |
| 1988 | 4,468 | 125 | 446 | 55 | 2,438 | 55 | 92 | 956 | 113 | 30 | 297 |

**C1    SOUTH AMERICA: Area of Main Arable Crops** (in thousands of hectares)

| | Bolivia | | | | | |
|---|---|---|---|---|---|---|
| | **Wheat** | **Barley** | **Maize** | **Rice** | **Potatoes** | **Sugar Cane** |
| 1945 | 18 | … | … | … | 24 | … |
| 1946 | … | 50 | … | … | 60 | … |
| 1947 | 19 | 54 | 118 | 11 | 59 | … |
| 1948 | 35 | 54 | 117 | 12 | 59 | … |
| 1949 | 37 | 52 | … | … | 62 | … |
| 1950 | … | … | … | … | … | … |
| 1951 | … | … | … | … | 69 | … |
| 1952 | … | … | … | … | 71 | … |
| 1953 | … | … | … | … | … | … |
| 1954 | 84 | 62 | 116 | 17 | 113 | 10 |
| 1955 | … | … | … | 18 | … | … |
| 1956 | … | … | … | 19 | … | 13 |
| 1957 | … | … | … | 17 | … | 16 |
| 1958 | 22 | 76 | 98 | 7 | 62 | … |
| 1959 | 20 | 83 | 89 | 13 | 53 | … |
| 1960 | … | 50 | … | 16 | … | 40 |
| 1961 | 70 | 91 | 207 | 24 | … | 27 |
| 1962 | 80 | 92 | 214 | 27 | 109 | 30 |
| 1963 | 106 | 92 | 218 | 29 | 112 | 30 |
| 1964 | 109 | 93 | 220 | 31 | 110 | 30 |
| 1965 | 63 | 98 | 214 | 33 | 115 | 22 |
| 1966 | 74 | 93 | 203 | 34 | 110 | 24 |
| 1967 | 45 | 86 | 210 | 31 | 103 | 33 |
| 1968 | 75 | 91 | 217 | 34 | 88 | 37 |
| 1969 | 76 | 92 | 218 | 49 | 92 | 40 |
| 1970 | 78 | 78 | 219 | 53 | 95 | 40 |
| 1971 | 81 | 98 | 225 | 48 | 97 | 27 |
| 1972 | 63 | 101 | 215 | 46 | 112 | 40 |
| 1973 | 69 | 104 | 215 | 41 | 116 | 44 |
| 1974 | 74 | 108 | 219 | 53 | 118 | 46 |
| 1975 | 77 | 112 | 230 | 74 | 128 | 52 |
| 1976 | 81 | 116 | 235 | 72 | 128 | 72 |
| 1977 | 73 | 112 | 244 | 65 | 126 | 75 |
| 1978 | 87 | 90 | 262 | 66 | 157 | 70 |
| 1979 | 98 | 82 | 278 | 51 | 130 | 67 |
| 1980 | 100 | 76 | 293 | 66 | 169 | 66 |
| 1981 | 96 | 83 | 313 | 63 | 177 | 70 |
| 1982 | 104 | 84 | 286 | 54 | 174 | 68 |
| 1983 | 71 | 46 | 261 | 44 | 108 | 71 |
| 1984 | 89 | 90 | 322 | 115 | 143 | 70 |
| 1985 | 100 | 94 | 349 | 113 | 198 | 78 |
| 1986 | 106 | 95 | 249 | 92 | 144 | 70 |
| 1987 | 95 | 93 | 302 | 93 | 142 | 66 |
| 1988 | 82 | 89 | 293 | 96 | 144 | 58 |

**C1**   **SOUTH AMERICA: Area of Main Arable Crops** (in thousands of hectares)

| | Brazil | | | | | | | Chile | | | | |
|---|---|---|---|---|---|---|---|---|---|---|---|---|
| | Wheat | Maize | Rice | P's | SP's | Cassava | SC | Wheat | Barley | Oats | Maize | P's |
| 1945 | 316 | 4,092 | 1,498 | 87 | 108 | 898 | 657 | 728 | 44 | 70 | 46 | 60 |
| 1946 | 301 | 4,323 | 1,681 | 117 | 114 | 908 | 758 | 745 | 53 | 75 | 47 | 57 |
| 1947 | 392 | 4,323 | 1,650 | 128 | 121 | 911 | 773 | 819 | 62 | 90 | 48 | 49 |
| 1948 | 536 | 4,347 | 1,662 | 128 | 121 | 913 | 819 | 867 | 55 | 99 | 47 | 52 |
| 1949 | 630 | 4,517 | 1,758 | 155 | 114 | 941 | 797 | 833 | 45 | 91 | 46 | 53 |
| 1950 | 652 | 4,678 | 1,964 | 148 | 102 | 957 | 828 | 816 | 51 | 99 | 55 | 50 |
| 1951 | 725 | 4,682 | 1,967 | 152 | 101 | 964 | 874 | 762 | 53 | 107 | 50 | 53 |
| 1952 | 810 | 4,864 | 1,873 | 152 | 103 | 1,015 | 920 | 779 | 67 | 99 | 48 | 53 |
| 1953 | 910 | 5,120 | 2,072 | 163 | 103 | 1,062 | 991 | 761 | 47 | 89 | 52 | 54 |
| 1954 | 1,081 | 5,528 | 2,425 | 165 | 107 | 1,103 | 1,027 | 805 | 61 | 95 | 54 | 57 |
| 1955 | 1,196 | 5,651 | 2,511 | 179 | 113 | 1,149 | 1,073 | 779 | 61 | 98 | 57 | 58 |
| 1956 | 886 | 5,998 | 2,555 | 185 | 116 | 1,178 | 1,124 | 766 | 60 | 103 | 57 | 65 |
| 1957 | 1,154 | 6,095 | 2,525 | 190 | 120 | 1,193 | 1,172 | 807 | 60 | 106 | 64 | 69 |
| 1958 | 1,446 | 5,790 | 2,515 | 192 | 112 | 1,227 | 1,208 | 886 | 66 | 112 | 76 | 80 |
| 1959 | 1,186 | 6,189 | 2,683 | 188 | 126 | 1,239 | 1,291 | 885 | 65 | 111 | 75 | 83 |
| 1960 | 1,141 | 6,681 | 2,966 | 199 | 133 | 1,342 | 1,340 | 838 | 65[9] | 108 | 74[9] | 85 |
| 1961 | 1,022 | 6,886 | 3,174 | 191 | 137 | 1,381 | 1,367 | 849[9] / 769 | 45 | 113[9] / 83 | 83 | 93 |
| 1962 | 743 | 7,348 | 3,350 | 196 | 145 | 1,476 | 1,467 | 769 | 43 | 83 | 85 | 91 |
| 1963 | 793 | 7,958 | 3,722 | 200 | 152 | 1,618 | 1,509 | 751 | 39 | 80 | 84 | 89 |
| 1964 | 734 | 8,106 | 4,182 | 209 | 158 | 1,716 | 1,519 | 748 | 42 | 70 | 88 | 85 |
| 1965 | 767 | 8,771 | 4,619 | 202 | 168 | 1,750 | 1,705 | 727 | 38 | 70 | 88 | 91 |
| 1966 | 717 | 8,703 | 4,005 | 199 | 175 | 1,780 | 1,636 | 780 | 39 | 66 | 81 | 76 |
| 1967 | 831 | 9,274 | 4,291 | 217 | 185 | 1,914 | 1,681 | 719 | 50 | 68 | 92 | 77 |
| 1968 | 970 | 9,584 | 4,459 | 227 | 182 | 1,998 | 1,687 | 700 | 72 | 109 | 89 | 80 |
| 1969 | 1,407 | 9,654 | 4,621 | 221 | 185 | 2,029 | 1,672 | 743 | 44 | 81 | 58 | 76 |
| 1970 | 1,895 | 9,858 | 4,979 | 214 | 181 | 2,025 | 1,725 | 740 | 47 | 73 | 74 | 72 |
| 1971 | 2,269 | 10,550 | 4,764 | 250 | 184 | 2,050 | 1,692 | 727 | 53 | 75 | 77 | 80 |
| 1972 | 2,320 | 10,539 | 4,533 | 202 | 185 | 2,100 | 2,000 | 712 | 67 | 84 | 84 | 79 |
| 1973 | 1,839 | 9,908 | 4,795 | 206 | 159 | 2,104 | 1,959 | 534 | 64 | 76 | 86 | 67 |
| 1974 | 2,471 | 10,294 | 4,164 | 181 | ... | 2,008 | 2,159 | 571 | 80 | 97 | 107 | 93 |
| 1975 | 2,931 | 10,473 | 5,279 | 193 | 153 | 2,098 | 2,022 | 686 | 66 | 94 | 92 | 72 |
| 1976 | 3,539 | 11,176 | 6,583 | 202 | 138 | 2,105 | 2,095 | 698 | 58 | 79 | 96 | 68 |
| 1977 | 3,153 | 11,797 | 5,992 | 196 | 117 | 2,176 | 2,270 | 628 | 63 | 75 | 116 | 86 |
| 1978 | 2,811 | 11,125 | 5,624 | 211 | 98 | 2,149 | 2,391 | 580 | 64 | 75 | 94 | 91 |
| 1979 | 3,831 | 11,319 | 5,452 | 204 | 92 | 2,111 | 2,537 | 560 | 60 | 79 | 130 | 81 |
| 1980 | 3,122 | 11,451 | 6,243 | 181 | 84 | 2,016 | 2,608 | 546 | 49 | 92 | 116 | 89 |
| 1981 | 1,920 | 11,502 | 6,102 | 171 | 84 | 2,067 | 2,826 | 432 | 46 | 80 | 126 | 90 |
| 1982 | 2,829 | 12,601 | 6,016 | 182 | 82 | 2,133 | 3,086 | 374 | 57 | 68 | 115 | 77 |
| 1983 | 1,879 | 10,706 | 5,108 | 169 | 77 | 2,061 | 3,479 | 359 | 38 | 85 | 118 | 67 |
| 1984 | 1,742 | 12,018 | 5,351 | 173 | 81 | 1,816 | 3,656 | 471 | 33 | 96 | 138 | 81 |
| 1985 | 2,677 | 11,798 | 4,755 | 155 | 80 | 1,868 | 3,912 | 506 | 35 | 85 | 131 | 63 |
| 1986 | 3,864 | 12,466 | 5,585 | 161 | 79 | 2,052 | 3,952 | 569 | 23 | 64 | 105 | 53 |
| 1987 | 3,456 | 13,503 | 5,980 | 177 | 76 | 1,936 | 4,314 | 677 | 16 | 56 | 87 | 58 |
| 1988 | 3,480 | 13,182 | 5,961 | 173 | 68 | 1,757 | 4,117 | 577 | 24 | 61 | 90 | 62 |

**C1      SOUTH AMERICA: Area of Main Arable Crops** (in thousands of hectares)

| | Colombia | | | | | | | |
|------|-------|--------|-------|------|---------|----------|---------|------------|
| | **Wheat** | **Barley** | **Maize** | **Rice** | **Sorghum** | **Potatoes** | **Cassava** | **Sugar Cane** |
| 1945 | ... | ... | ... | ... | ... | ... | ... | ... |
| 1946 | 180 | 32 | 668 | 124 | — | 96 | ... | 180 |
| 1947 | 95 | 23 | 460 | 91 | — | 126 | ... | ... |
| 1948 | 177 | 24 | 685 | 149 | — | 102 | ... | ... |
| 1949 | 181 | 45 | 707 | 112 | — | 115 | 85 | 168 |
| 1950 | 145 | 44 | 652 | 133 | — | 39 | 141 | 259 |
| 1951 | 174 | 47 | 768 | 145 | — | 50 | 160 | 269 |
| 1952 | 188 | 51 | 844 | 150 | — | 61 | 160 | 269 |
| 1953 | 175 | 63 | 700 | 153 | — | 58 | 154 | 264 |
| 1954 | 195 | 53 | 680 | 175 | — | 62 | 148 | 270 |
| 1955 | 182 | 43 | 830 | 188 | — | 56 | 144 | 273 |
| 1956 | 170 | 50 | 828 | 190 | — | 55 | 140 | 273 |
| 1957 | 178 | 48 | 624 | 190 | — | 61 | 140 | 273 |
| 1958 | 160 | 43 | 693 | 197 | — | 43 | 133 | 279 |
| 1959 | 166 | 60 | 721 | 206 | — | 62 | 125 | 276 |
| 1960 | 160 | 56 | 730 | 227 | 3 | 54 | 120 | 290 |
| 1961 | 160 | 48 | 711 | 237 | 3 | 48 | 115 | 294 |
| 1962 | 150 | 49 | 697 | 280 | 3 | 75 | 138 | 293 |
| 1963 | 113 | 58 | 689 | 254 | 5 | 68 | 142 | 317 |
| 1964 | 100 | 58 | 772 | 302 | 24 | 76 | 125 | 325 |
| 1965 | 120 | 46 | 869 | 375 | 30 | 66 | 142 | 326 |
| 1966 | 110 | 55 | 846 | 350 | 30 | 67 | 142 | 327 |
| 1967 | 68 | 61 | 790 | 291 | 40 | 79 | 144 | 361 |
| 1968 | 108 | 47 | 788 | 266 | 40 | 81 | 152 | 368 |
| 1969 | 58 | 49 | 681 | 280 | 44 | 84 | 155 | 379 |
| 1970 | 45 | 51 | 661 | 257 | 54 | 89 | 244 | 247 |
| 1971 | 47 | 56 | 666 | 242 | 92 | 88 | 249 | 247 |
| 1972 | 61 | 63 | 624 | 258 | 84 | 89 | 251 | 261 |
| 1973 | 56 | 52 | 580 | 291 | 135 | 99 | 250 | 273 |
| 1974 | 45 | 59 | 570 | 355 | 151 | 92 | 250 | 272 |
| 1975 | 30 | 76 | 573 | 372 | 134 | 110 | 257 | 249 |
| 1976 | 33 | 68 | 648 | 366 | 174 | 125 | 223 | 254 |
| 1977 | 34 | 47 | 581 | 324 | 190 | 130 | 210 | 255 |
| 1978 | 30 | 68 | 671 | 406 | 225 | 137 | 217 | 278 |
| 1979 | 31 | 74 | 616 | 442 | 221 | 151 | 222 | 286 |
| 1980 | 38 | 63 | 614 | 416 | 206 | 142 | 208 | 292 |
| 1981 | 44 | 36 | 629 | 421 | 231 | 160 | 207 | 279 |
| 1982 | 45 | 35 | 636 | 446 | 291 | 165 | 171 | 270 |
| 1983 | 46 | 18 | 582 | 397 | 272 | 161 | 173 | 275 |
| 1984 | 43 | 17 | 593 | 364 | 238 | 160 | 153 | 291 |
| 1985 | 45 | 31 | 541 | 386 | 192 | 139 | 154 | 346 |
| 1986 | 46 | 38 | 592 | 325 | 227 | 160 | 153 | 347 |
| 1987 | 41 | 47 | 623 | 345 | 259 | 157 | 159 | 347 |
| 1988 | 38 | 53 | 664 | 383 | 266 | 170 | 149 | 337 |

**C1     SOUTH AMERICA: Area of Main Arable Crops** (in thousands of hectares)

| | Ecuador | | | | | | | Guyana | |
| | Wheat | Barley | Maize | Rice | P's | Cassava | SC | Rice | SC |
|---|---|---|---|---|---|---|---|---|---|
| 1945 | ... | ... | ... | ... | ... | ... | ... | 43 | 24 |
| 1946 | ... | ... | ... | ... | 26 | ... | ... | 41 | 26 |
| 1947 | 71 | 75 | ... | ... | 25 | ... | 33 | 41 | 28 |
| 1948 | 76 | 90 | 99 | 84 | 21 | ... | 20 | 37 | 27 |
| 1949 | 60 | 100 | 70 | 100 | 22 | ... | 25 | 42 | 28 |
| 1950 | 38 | 59 | 73 | 67 | 25 | ... | 20 | 39 | 29 |
| 1951 | ... | 108 | ... | 81 | 16 | ... | ... | 47 | 33 |
| 1952 | 44 | 108 | 109 | 59 | 17 | ... | 36 | 62 | 32 |
| 1953 | 43 | 103 | 110 | 81 | 25 | ... | 47 | 55 | 32 |
| 1954 | 50 | 107 | 115 | 78 | 27 | ... | 44 | 65 | 31 |
| 1955 | 65 | 110 | ... | 63 | 32 | 16 | 45 | 70 | 31 |
| 1956 | 65 | 112 | 146 | 59 | ... | ... | 48 | 55 | 34 |
| 1957 | 69 | 120 | 151 | 50 | 33 | 19 | 59 | 55 | 35 |
| 1958 | 59 | 128 | 191 | 70 | 31 | 19 | 59 | 74 | ... |
| 1959 | 55 | 128 | 203 | 84 | 34 | 22 | 61 | 79 | 40 |
| 1960 | ... | ... | 209 | 88 | 33 | 27 | | 89 | 44 |
| 1961 | 79 | 93 | 228 | 95 | 32 | 25 | 63 | 91 | 41 |
| 1962 | 85 | 151 | 212 | 112 | 33 | 23 | 65 | 105 | 39 |
| 1963 | 67 | 165 | 247 | 113 | 32 | 27 | 72 | 81 | 39 |
| 1964 | 71 | 164 | 300 | 109 | 39 | 24 | 93 | 126 | 43 |
| 1965 | 69 | 157 | 307 | 103 | 44 | 25 | 97 | 136 | 42 |
| 1966 | 65 | 143 | 267 | 101 | 44 | 28 | 113 | 125 | 47 |
| 1967 | 80 | 144 | 364 | 114 | 48 | 34 | 108 | 103 | 43 |
| 1968 | 79 | 123 | 383 | 107 | 44 | 39 | 86 | 127 | 51 |
| 1969 | 99 | 125 | 300 | 109 | 47 | 40 | 108 | 113 | 43 |
| 1970 | 76 | 134 | 292 | 71 | 47 | 35 | 95 | 111 | 43 |
| 1971 | 67 | 135 | 352 | 92 | 53 | 37 | 100 | 102 | 54 |
| 1972 | 56 | 102 | 352 | 80 | 38 | 41 | 100 | 80 | 53 |
| 1973 | 47 | 93 | 265 | 85 | 44 | 54 | 89 | 93 | 56 |
| 1974 | 56 | 61 | 272 | 103 | 39 | 49 | 101 | 116 | 56 |
| 1975 | 70 | 72 | 277 | 132 | 39 | 43 | 115 | 134 | 41 |
| 1976 | 76 | 72 | 239 | 130 | 41 | 33 | 85 | 83 | 54 |
| 1977 | 41 | 60 | 247 | 107 | 36 | 31 | 109 | 136 | 51 |
| 1978 | 27 | 32 | 185 | 77 | 30 | 24 | 104 | 115 | 56 |
| 1979 | 30 | 31 | 219 | 111 | 27 | 20 | 103 | 88 | 57 |
| 1980 | 32 | 26 | 226 | 127 | 30 | 25 | 108 | 95 | 52 |
| 1981 | 31 | 29 | 244 | 131 | 32 | 26 | 104 | 88 | 57 |
| 1982 | 33 | 34 | 217 | 132 | 35 | 20 | 92 | 93 | 52 |
| 1983 | 26 | 30 | 206 | 93 | 27 | 20 | 80 | 78 | 51 |
| 1984 | 24 | 31 | 245 | 139 | 33 | 24 | 89 | 97 | 48 |
| 1985 | 18 | 29 | 255 | 136 | 37 | 22 | 87 | 78 | 39 |
| 1986 | 41 | 64 | 480 | 228 | 54 | 20 | 97 | 74 | 47 |
| 1987 | 39 | 61 | 476 | 276 | 56 | 22 | 97 | 99 | 44 |
| 1988 | 39 | 61 | 454 | 288 | 48 | 21 | 108 | 99 | 43 |

**C1    SOUTH AMERICA: Area of Main Arable Crops** (in thousands of hectares)

| | Paraguay | | | | Peru | | | | | | | |
|------|-------|-------|---------|-----|-------|--------|-------|------|------|------|---------|-----|
| | Wheat | Maize | Cassava | SC | Wheat | Barley | Maize | Rice | P's | SP's | Cassava | SC |
| 1945 | 4 | 72 | ... | 19 | 99 | ... | ... | 60 | 129 | ... | ... | 29 |
| 1946 | 3 | ... | ... | ... | 97 | ... | ... | 51 | 150 | ... | ... | 31 |
| 1947 | 2 | 98 | ... | 11 | 142 | 179 | 380 | 57 | 207 | 25 | 20 | 30 |
| 1948 | 2 | 79 | 51 | 12 | 147 | 165 | 345 | 56 | 176 | 40 | 28 | 32 |
| 1949 | 1 | ... | 85 | 8 | 146 | 186 | ... | 48 | 199 | 42 | 29 | 32 |
| 1950 | 1 | ... | ... | 7 | 162 | 185 | ... | 42 | 228 | 35 | 32 | 32 |
| 1951 | 1 | 101 | ... | ... | 162 | 182 | 252 | 51 | 242 | 36 | 33 | 29 |
| 1952 | 1 | 82 | ... | 11 | 170 | 185 | 283 | 59 | 242 | 12 | 20 | 36 |
| 1953 | 2 | 84 | 62 | 13 | 172 | 191 | 226 | 66 | 238 | 29 | 15 | 36 |
| 1954 | 2 | 84 | ... | 14 | 166 | 194 | 232 | 65 | 246 | 10 | 15 | 36 |
| 1955 | 2 | 92 | 61 | 13 | 159 | 185 | 236 | 62 | 235 | 12 | 17 | 38 |
| 1956 | ... | ... | 68 | 20 | 139 | 169 | 234 | 67 | 224 | 10 | 20 | 39 |
| 1957 | 15 | 105 | ... | 19 | 146 | 170 | 238 | 60 | 219 | 12 | 19 | ... |
| 1958 | 20 | 98 | 66 | 21 | 138 | 190 | 262 | 71 | 218 | 13 | 22 | 41 |
| 1959 | 15 | 110 | 67 | 21 | 158 | 202 | 253 | 70 | 221 | 16 | 24 | 47 |
| 1960 | 12 | ... | 68 | 22 | 154 | 198 | 253 | 87 | 238 | 15 | 24 | 47 |
| 1961 | 8 | 92 | 70 | 22 | 153 | 183 | 327 | 81 | 258 | 12 | 41 | 52 |
| 1962 | 10 | 95 | 71 | 22 | 154 | 180 | 331 | 87 | 253 | 12 | 39 | 55 |
| 1963 | 10 | 96 | 71 | 23 | 153 | 180 | 339 | 73 | 254 | 13 | 44 | 54 |
| 1964 | 11 | 159 | 103 | 27 | 149 | 179 | 347 | 82 | 262 | 13 | 50 | 51 |
| 1965 | 7 | 162 | 108 | 27 | 153 | 176 | 342 | 75 | 251 | 12 | 41 | 64 |
| 1966 | 8 | 151 | 102 | 26 | 148 | 178 | 350 | 96 | 255 | 12 | 40 | 59 |
| 1967 | 21 | 173 | 97 | 26 | 151 | 185 | 357 | 107 | 272 | 12 | 42 | 61 |
| 1968 | 32 | 180 | 101 | 21 | 136 | 173 | 311 | 76 | 262 | 12 | 37 | 54 |
| 1969 | 34 | 128 | 103 | 21 | 139 | 182 | 364 | 110 | 304 | 13 | 38 | 57 |
| 1970 | 45 | 187 | 127 | 26 | 136 | 186 | 382 | 140 | 289 | 14 | 39 | 57 |
| 1971 | 42 | 190 | 121 | 40 | 139 | 183 | 374 | 147 | 286 | 14 | 36 | 56 |
| 1972 | 32 | 184 | 97 | 31 | 138 | 182 | 301 | 105 | 263 | 13 | 37 | 56 |
| 1973 | 20 | 186 | 80 | 28 | 164 | 185 | 430 | 110 | 277 | 12 | 37 | 51 |
| 1974 | 30 | 243 | 80 | 42 | 154 | 187 | 320 | 89 | 280 | 13 | 37 | 54 |
| 1975 | 25 | 223 | 107 | 41 | 134 | 163 | 363 | 122 | 251 | 14 | 38 | 57 |
| 1976 | 29 | 257 | 106 | 42 | 134 | 163 | 385 | 133 | 253 | 14 | 36 | 63 |
| 1977 | 28 | 288 | 116 | 48 | 135 | 180 | 415 | 138 | 250 | 16 | 38 | 56 |
| 1978 | 32 | 276 | 120 | 35 | 107 | 160 | 383 | 110 | 255 | 16 | 38 | 54 |
| 1979 | 52 | 353 | 126 | 35 | 96 | 153 | 361 | 131 | 242 | 14 | 35 | 54 |
| 1980 | 47 | 377 | 136 | 37 | 69 | 165 | 258 | 96 | 194 | 15 | 38 | 49 |
| 1981 | 49 | 400 | 178 | 41 | 102 | 170 | 316 | 151 | 202 | 6 | 32 | 39 |
| 1982 | 70 | 420 | 180 | 36 | 84 | 168 | 347 | 169 | 217 | 5 | 27 | 46 |
| 1983 | 75 | 370 | 145 | 40 | 81 | 81 | 340 | 195 | 156 | 11 | 33 | 45 |
| 1984 | 106 | 447 | 184 | 40 | 79 | 91 | 380 | 249 | 172 | 10 | 33 | 53 |
| 1985 | 170 | 470 | 186 | 55 | 81 | 95 | 371 | 193 | 188 | 7 | 32 | 53 |
| 1986 | 162 | 376 | 200 | 59 | 98 | 98 | 429 | 161 | 192 | 14 | 35 | 50 |
| 1987 | 198 | 567 | 205 | 64 | 102 | 107 | 454 | 229 | 212 | 8 | 45 | 47 |
| 1988 | 235 | 622 | 230 | 56 | 115 | 119 | 478 | 219 | 236 | 7 | 37 | 46 |

**C1    SOUTH AMERICA: Area of Main Arable Crops** (in thousands of hectares)

| | Surinam | Uruguay | | | | | | Venezuela[10] | | | |
| | Rice | Wheat | Barley | Oats | Maize | Sorghum | P's | Maize | Rice | Cassava | SC |
|---|---|---|---|---|---|---|---|---|---|---|---|
| 1945 | 13 | 354 | 24 | 71 | 201 | 2 | 8 | ... | ... | ... | ... |
| 1946 | 17 | 267 | 19 | 43 | 153 | 2 | 8 | ... | ... | ... | ... |
| 1947 | 16 | 505 | 18 | 55 | 158 | 3 | 8 | 230 | 14 | ... | ... |
| 1948 | 18 | 502 | 30 | 79 | 161 | 2 | 8 | 376 | 8 | 12 | 68 |
| 1949 | 18 | 501 | 30 | 99 | 137 | 2 | 9 | 351 | ... | 54 | 71 |
| 1950 | 18 | 496 | 27 | 59 | 160 | 2 | 11 | 342 | 31 | ... | ... |
| 1951 | 19 | 545 | 22 | 58 | 332 | 2 | 19 | ... | ... | ... | ... |
| 1952 | 20 | 514 | 26 | 58 | 259 | 3 | 15 | 270 | 40 | 53 | ... |
| 1953 | 20 | 737 | 42 | 67 | 301 | 5 | 14 | 277 | 46 | 54 | ... |
| 1954 | 22 | 732 | 44 | 41 | 263 | 3 | 16 | 259 | 63 | 49 | 56 |
| 1955 | 22 | 780 | 33 | 50 | 247 | ... | 19 | 257 | 55 | 40 | 56 |
| 1956 | 25 | 561 | 62 | 65 | 308 | ... | 17 | 474 | 40 | 40 | 53 |
| 1957 | 28 | 778 | 28 | 121 | 299 | ... | 18 | 283 | 30 | 45 | 41 |
| 1958 | 31 | 691 | 67 | 90 | 357 | ... | ... | 297 | 12 | ... | 41 |
| 1959 | 29 | 293 | 44 | 39 | 310 | ... | 30 | 280 | 28 | 43 | 47 |
| 1960 | 30 | 520 | 67 | 80 | 259 | | 31 | 398 | 42 | 61 | 51 |
| 1961 | 26 | 436 | 46 | 86 | 284 | 33 | 16 | 389 | 58 | 33 | 55 |
| 1962 | 27 | 400 | 40 | 81 | 267 | 33 | 20 | 483 | 69 | 26 | 61 |
| 1963 | 28 | 354 | 47 | 85 | 236 | 33 | 23 | 427 | 74 | 25 | 63 |
| 1964 | 30 | 527 | 39 | 81 | 167 | 31 | 25 | 443 | 91 | 25 | 64 |
| 1965 | 34 | 547 | 32 | 126 | 192 | 32 | 26 | 462 | 105 | 25 | 62 |
| 1966 | 29 | 380 | 46 | 92 | 231 | 37 | 26 | 467 | 110 | 26 | 62 |
| 1967 | 34 | 222 | 30 | 54 | 226 | 32 | 22 | 616 | 114 | 35 | 57 |
| 1968 | 35 | 532 | 40 | 88 | 162 | 38 | 15 | 626 | 115 | 41 | 57 |
| 1969 | 36 | 336 | 39 | 75 | 175 | 41 | 22 | 641 | 119 | 39 | 59 |
| 1970 | 36 | 337 | 41 | 83 | 183 | 44 | 21 | 588 | 130 | 39 | 59 |
| 1971 | 39 | 340 | 52 | 69 | 180 | 54 | 24 | 588 | 113 | 40 | 66 |
| 1972 | 37 | 185 | 31 | 65 | 181 | 42 | 23 | 465 | 65 | 41 | 70 |
| 1973 | 45 | 283 | 35 | 78 | 226 | 113 | 25 | 439 | 113 | 34 | 70 |
| 1974 | 44 | 430 | 22 | 61 | 193 | 100 | 26 | 462 | 117 | 40 | 77 |
| 1975 | 48 | 456 | 44 | 84 | 153 | 54 | 26 | 506 | 114 | 37 | 78 |
| 1976 | 48 | 508 | 38 | 58 | 172 | 54 | 26 | 489 | 93 | 40 | 75 |
| 1977 | 50 | 297 | 43 | 30 | 138 | 95 | 23 | 496 | 166 | 38 | 84 |
| 1978 | 55 | 192 | 53 | 34 | 163 | 89 | 19 | 506 | 166 | 41 | 76 |
| 1979 | 59 | 313 | 40 | 66 | 94 | 39 | 21 | 519 | 218 | 38 | 77 |
| 1980 | 65 | 227 | 36 | 36 | 132 | 50 | 13 | 366 | 226 | 41 | 77 |
| 1981 | 66 | 296 | 63 | 25 | 146 | 74 | 21 | 312 | 243 | 43 | 74 |
| 1982 | 70 | 234 | 32 | 48 | 95 | 57 | 21 | 305 | 223 | 30 | 77 |
| 1983 | 73 | 255 | 52 | 53 | 93 | 56 | 19 | 310 | 164 | 41 | 79 |
| 1984 | 75 | 226 | 68 | 50 | 83 | 47 | 19 | 313 | 151 | 41 | 82 |
| 1985 | 75 | 212 | 64 | 33 | 89 | 63 | 22 | 467 | 181 | 40 | 87 |
| 1986 | 75 | 186 | 51 | 42 | 76 | 40 | 17 | 650 | 124 | 40 | 105 |
| 1987 | 71 | 157 | 61 | 58 | 88 | 31 | 15 | 685 | 136 | 40 | 117 |
| 1988 | 70 | 177 | 83 | 52 | 74 | 45 | 19 | 640 | 135 | 41 | 117 |

**C1** **Area of Main Arable Crops** (in thousands of hectares)

NOTES

1. SOURCES: The national publications on p. xiv–xvi; International Institute of Agriculture, *Yearbook of Agricultural Statistics;* and FAO, *Yearbook of Food and Agricultural Statistics.*
2. Most statistics are of areas sown, or, to be more precise, of areas under crops on a particular date during the summer. Some statistics are of areas harvested and where this is known it is indicated in footnotes.
3. For some countries and crops data may be reported for either of the calendar years in which the crop-year lies, and practice in this respect has not always been consistent. So far as possible, the series shown here *are* consistent, and the year of harvest has been preferred where a choice is available.

FOOTNOTES

[1] Statistics in square brackets relate to Ontario and Manitoba only to 1898 (except that 1883 is for Ontario only, as is the potato figure in 1888). From 1899 to 1907 they relate to Ontario, Manitoba, Alberta, New Brunswick and Saskatchewan, and the potato statistics are for Ontario, Manitoba and New Brunswick. The 1908 figures, and the 1901 figure for potatoes, are exclusive of British Columbia.

[2] Trinidad only to 1898.

[3] Statistics are of area harvested, for grain in the case of small grains and for all purposes in the case of maize.

[4] Subsequent statistics are estimates derived from the F.A.O. A series with much lower figures is available in national sources from 1970, said to cover both state and private sectors, as follows:—

| | | | | | | | |
|------|----|------|----|------|----|------|----|
| 1970 | 36 | 1974 | 31 | 1978 | 47 | 1982 | 54 |
| 1971 | 50 | 1975 | 29 | 1979 | 48 | 1983 | 62 |
| 1972 | 31 | 1976 | 26 | 1980 | 51 | 1984 | 58 |
| 1973 | 29 | 1977 | 53 | 1981 | 53 | 1985 | 63 |

[5] All barley from 1970 (2nd line), barley for grain previously.

[6] Maize for grain only from 1970 (2nd line).

[7] The definition of sorghum was widened from 1959 (2nd line).

[8] Subsequently including Hawaii.

[9] Subsequently area harvested rather than area sown.

[10] The following earlier estimates are available for maize and sugar cane in Rafael Cartay, *Historia Economica de Venezuela 1830–1900* (Valencia, 1988):—

| | Maize | Cane | | Maize | Cane |
|--------|-------|------|------|-------|------|
| 1872–3 | 15 | ... | 1888 | ... | 40 |
| 1875 | 15 | 35 | 1924 | 97 | ... |
| 1884 | 27 | 39 | 1937 | 229 | 59 |

**C2     NORTH AMERICA: OUTPUT OF MAIN ARABLE CROPS** (in thousands of metric tons)*

Key:     Bwt = buckwheat; P = potatoes; SP = sweet potatoes

| | Canada | | | | | | |
|---|---|---|---|---|---|---|---|
| | Wheat | Barley | Oats | Rye | Maize | Bwt | P |
| 1827 | [80][1] | [8][1] | [38][1] | ... | ... | [19][1] | [185][1] |
| 1831 | [93][1] | ... | [49][1] | ... | ... | [23][1] | [200][1] |
| 1842 | [88][2] | [22][2] | [74][2] | [7][2] | [18][2] | [8][2] | [220][2] |
| 1844 | [26][1] | [26][1] | [112][1] | [8][1] | [3][1] | [8][1] | [270][1] |
| 1848 | [206][2] | [11][2] | [109][2] | [11][2] | [29][2] | [9][2] | [129][2] |
| 1851 | 429 | 24 | 314 | 16 | [56][3] | [45][3] | [386][3] |
| 1861 | 742 | 101 | 598 | 46 | ... | ... | ... |
| 1871 | 455 | 250 | 655 | 27 | [97][4] | 81 | 1,288 |
| 1881 | 880 | 367 | 1,087 | 53 | ... | 107 | 1,507 |
| 1891 | 1,149 | 375 | 1,287 | 34 | ... | 109 | 1,456 |
| 1900 | 1,512 | 484[5] | 2,336[5] | ... | ... | ... | 1,507[6] |
| 1901 | 2,404 | 527 | 1,864 | 59 | ... | 99 | 735 |
| 1902 | 2,642 | 754 | 2,421 | ... | ... | ... | 559 |
| 1903 | 2,229 | 761 | 2,515 | ... | ... | ... | 711 |
| 1904 | 1,955 | 828 | 2,467 | ... | ... | ... | 671 |

| | Guatemala | Mexico | | | |
|---|---|---|---|---|---|
| | Maize | Wheat | Barley | Maize | Rice |
| 1894 | 159 | 226 | 535 | 1,902 | 14 |
| 1895 | ... | 265 | 100 | 1,770 | 12 |
| 1899 | 297 | ... | ... | ... | ... |
| 1901 | ... | 327 | 163 | 2,305 | ... |
| 1902 | ... | 230 | 128 | 1,927 | ... |
| 1903 | ... | 286 | ... | 2,402 | ... |
| 1904 | ... | 256 | 156 | 2,174 | ... |

*For sugar see table C3, p. 185.

**C2　　NORTH AMERICA: Output of Main Arable Crops** (in thousands of metric tons)

| | USA | | | | | | | | |
|---|---|---|---|---|---|---|---|---|---|
| | Wheat | Barley | Oats | Rye | Maize[7] | B'wheat | Rice | P | SP |
| 1839 | 2,313 | 87 | 1,785 | 474 | 9,602 | 159 | ... | ... | ... |
| 1849 | 2,722 | 109 | 2,134 | 360 | 15,037 | 195 | ... | 1,791 | 955 |
| 1859 | 4,708 | 348 | 2,511 | 536 | 21,311[7] | 383 | ... | 3,024 | 1,050 |
| 1866 | 4,627 | 392 | 3,367 | 448 | 18,568 | 258 | ... | 3,038 | ... |
| 1867 | 5,742 | 523 | 3,237 | 498 | 20,168 | 243 | ... | 2,712 | ... |
| 1868 | 6,695 | 501 | 3,338 | 437 | 23,369 | 229 | ... | 3,274 | 712 |
| 1869 | 7,892 | 631 | 4,122 | 455 | 19,864 | 227 | ... | 3,935 | 567 |
| 1870 | 6,913 | 631 | 3,890 | 397 | 28,576 | 201 | ... | 2,936 | 771 |
| 1871 | 7,402 | 610 | 4,442 | 431 | 29,008 | 202 | ... | 3,667 | 701 |
| 1872 | 7,375 | 697 | 4,746 | 426 | 32,488 | 225 | ... | 3,635 | 677 |
| 1873 | 8,763 | 675 | 4,456 | 410 | 25,604 | 226 | ... | 3,524 | 830 |
| 1874 | 9,689 | 784 | 3,963 | 440 | 26,900 | 218 | ... | 3,568 | 752 |
| 1875 | 8,546 | 718 | 5,298 | 430 | 36,831 | 239 | ... | 4,894 | 811 |
| 1876 | 8,409 | 893 | 4,746 | 489 | 37,543 | 209 | ... | 3,337 | 953 |
| 1877 | 10,777 | 849 | 6,314 | 555 | 38,508 | 258 | ... | 4,727 | 878 |
| 1878 | 12,220 | 806 | 6,430 | 553 | 39,753 | 261 | ... | 3,902 | 966 |
| 1879 | 12,492 | 914 | 6,024 | 503 | 44,503 | 256 | ... | 4,611 | 844 |
| 1880 | 13,662 | 980 | 6,067 | 490 | 43,360 | 240 | ... | 4,495 | 1,001 |
| 1881 | 11,049 | 1,067 | 6,474 | 487 | 31,624 | 189 | ... | 3,472 | 619 |
| 1882 | 15,023 | 1,306 | 7,838 | 679 | 44,579 | 232 | ... | 5,370 | 1,041 |
| 1883 | 11,947 | 1,241 | 8,796 | 645 | 41,962 | 156 | ... | 6,180 | 776 |
| 1884 | 15,540 | 1,480 | 9,304 | 676 | 49,481 | 221 | ... | 5,660 | 808 |
| 1885 | 10,886 | 1,393 | 9,783 | 552 | 52,275 | 252 | ... | 5,365 | 1,001 |
| 1886 | 13,989 | 1,611 | 19,899 | 606 | 45,290 | 235 | ... | 5,309 | 974 |
| 1887 | 13,363 | 1,568 | 10,102 | 572 | 40,769 | 210 | ... | 4,344 | 961 |
| 1888 | 11,539 | 1,655 | 11,220 | 722 | 57,178 | 212 | ... | 6,522 | 1,119 |
| 1889 | 13,716 | 1,764 | 12,062 | 750 | 58,270 | 254 | ... | 5,931 | 1,117 |
| 1890 | 12,220 | 1,524 | 8,840 | 670 | 41,912 | 261 | ... | 4,630 | 1,122 |
| 1891 | 18,452 | 2,047 | 12,149 | 751 | 59,337 | 280 | ... | 7,174 | 1,142 |
| 1892 | 16,656 | 2,068 | 10,480 | 729 | 48,186 | 264 | ... | 5,176 | 1,157 |
| 1893 | 13,771 | 1,894 | 10,262 | 678 | 48,262 | 225 | ... | 5,558 | 1,138 |
| 1894 | 14,751 | 1,611 | 10,886 | 680 | 41,023 | 240 | ... | 5,380 | 1,239 |
| 1895 | 14,751 | 2,264 | 13,426 | 752 | 64,392 | 271 | 152 | 8,222 | 1,120 |
| 1896 | 14,233 | 2,112 | 11,249 | 809 | 67,846 | 300 | 106 | 7,150 | 1,048 |
| 1897 | 16,492 | 2,243 | 12,047 | 791 | 58,117 | 312 | 140 | 5,393 | 1,037 |
| 1898 | 20,901 | 2,134 | 12,222 | 738 | 59,718 | 265 | 170 | 6,541 | 1,266 |
| 1899 | 17,826 | 2,569 | 13,601 | 660 | 67,211 | 244 | 183 | 7,418 | 1,054 |
| 1900 | 16,302 | 2,112 | 13,717 | 696 | 67,617 | 255 | 200 | 7,068 | 1,140 |
| 1901 | 20,765 | 2,700 | 11,612 | 782 | 43,588 | 330 | 259 | 5,645 | 1,201 |
| 1902 | 18,697 | 3,179 | 15,633 | 860 | 70,462 | 295 | 297 | 8,071 | 1,222 |
| 1903 | 18,044 | 3,244 | 12,846 | 735 | 63,884 | 311 | 390 | 7,519 | 1,319 |
| 1904 | 15,132 | 3,614 | 14,689 | 723 | 68,252 | 337 | 392 | 9,512 | 1,385 |

**C2      NORTH AMERICA: Output of Main Arable Crops** (in thousands of metric tons)

| | Canada | | | | | | | | Costa Rica | |
|---|---|---|---|---|---|---|---|---|---|---|
| | Wheat | Barley | Oats | Rye | Maize | B'wheat | Mixed Grain | P's | Maize | Rice |
| 1905 | 2,913 | 895 | 2,857 | ... | ... | ... | ... | 618 | ... | ... |
| 1906 | 3,690 | 1,009 | 3,109 | ... | ... | ... | ... | 667 | ... | ... |
| 1907 | 2,535 | 881₅ 967 | 2,529₅ 3,353 | | | | | 825 | ... | ... |
| 1908 | 3,060 | 1,018 | 3,861 | ... | ... | ... | ... | 857₆ 2,249 | ... | ... |
| 1909 | 4,538 | 1,206 | 5,451 | 43 | 581 | 156 | 346 | 3,020 | ... | ... |
| 1910 | 4,538 | 1,206 | 5,451 | 44 | 489 | 170 | 352 | 2,697 | ... | ... |
| 1911 | 3,595 | 628 | 3,784 | 39 | 364 | 157 | 237 | 1,509 | ... | ... |
| 1912 | 6,293 | 968 | 5,640 | 64 | 487 | 184 | 285 | 1,944 | ... | ... |
| 1913 | 6,100 | 1,075 | 6,040 | 65 | 430 | 229 | 312 | 2,310 | ... | ... |
| 1914 | 6,306 | 1,052 | 6,241 | 58 | 426 | 182 | 287 | 2,138 | ... | ... |
| 1915 | 4,389 | 788 | 4,828 | 51 | 354 | 188 | 297 | 2,332 | ... | ... |
| 1916 | 10,710 | 1,176 | 7,171 | 63 | 365 | 171 | 318 | 1,643 | ... | ... |
| 1917 | 7,152 | 931 | 6,326 | 73 | 160 | 130 | 192 | 1,723 | ... | ... |
| 1918 | 6,361 | 1,199 | 6,215 | 98 | 197 | 156 | 293 | 2,174 | ... | ... |
| 1919 | 5,146 | 1,683 | 6,575 | 216 | 361 | 248 | 647 | 2,840 | ... | ... |
| 1920 | 5,260 | 1,228 | 6,082 | 259 | 430 | 230 | 505 | 3,418 | ... | ... |
| 1921 | 7,163 | 1,378 | 8,185 | 287 | 364 | 196 | 588 | 3,642 | ... | ... |
| 1922 | 8,188 | 1,300 | 6,573 | 545 | 379 | 179 | 404 | 2,921 | ... | ... |
| 1923 | 10,880 | 1,565 | 7,576 | 822 | 350 | 211 | 503 | 2,529 | ... | ... |
| 1924 | 12,905 | 1,676 | 8,698 | 590 | 346 | 212 | 540 | 2,517 | 6 | 4 |
| 1925 | 7,133 | 1,934 | 6,261 | 349 | 305 | 248 | 581 | 2,570 | 6 | 4 |
| 1926 | 10,763 | 1,897 | 6,204 | 233 | 268 | 230 | 601 | 1,824 | 7 | 5 |
| 1927 | 11,080 | 2,177 | 5,913 | 309 | 198 | 215 | 615 | 2,129 | 8 | 4 |
| 1928 | 13,054 | 2,111 | 6,781 | 396 | 108 | 237 | 683 | 2,107 | 8 | 2 |
| 1929 | 15,423 | 2,970 | 6,973 | 371 | 133 | 237 | 710 | 2,277 | ... | ... |
| 1930 | 8,224 | 2,228 | 4,362 | 334 | 132 | 228 | 649 | 1,811 | ... | ... |
| 1931 | 11,449 | 2,943 | 6,526 | 559 | 148 | 237 | 803 | 2,188 | ... | ... |
| 1932 | 8,745 | 1,467 | 5,063 | 135 | 138 | 151 | 715 | 2,373 | ... | ... |
| 1933 | 12,058 | 1,759 | 6,039 | 215 | 128 | 183 | 708 | 1,788 | ... | ... |
| 1934 | 7,672 | 1,379 | 4,742 | 106 | 128 | 185 | 599 | 1,939 | ... | ... |
| 1935 | 7,507 | 1,388 | 4,952 | 120 | 173 | 188 | 688 | 2,182 | ... | ... |
| 1936 | 7,673 | 1,828 | 6,082 | 244 | 197 | 173 | 717 | 1,754 | ... | ... |
| 1937 | 5,966 | 1,566 | 4,191 | 109 | 155 | 187 | 610 | 1,797 | 19 | 10 |
| 1938 | 4,904 | 1,810 | 4,140 | 147 | 138 | 169 | 656 | 1,930 | ... | ... |
| 1939 | 9,798 | 2,226 | 5,727 | 279 | 195 | 154 | 711 | 1,630 | 24 | 12 |
| 1940 | 14,169 | 2,246 | 5,928 | 389 | 206 | 149 | 800 | 1,651 | 26 | 12 |
| 1941 | 14,701 | 2,270 | 5,868 | 355 | 177 | 146 | 783 | 1,919 | 25 | 12 |
| 1942 | 8,565 | 2,404 | 4,720 | 283 | 347 | 90 | 828 | 1,680 | 25 | 14 |
| 1943 | 15,133 | 5,574 | 9,893 | 614 | 373 | 97 | 1,117 | 1,801 | 25 | 11 |
| 1944 | 7,685 | 4,537 | 7,118 | 163 | 203 | 116 | 546 | 1,812 | 26 | 9 |

**C2    NORTH AMERICA: Output of Main Arable Crops** (in thousands of metric tons)

| | Cuba | | Dominican Republic | | El Salvador | | Guatemala | | | Honduras |
| --- | --- | --- | --- | --- | --- | --- | --- | --- | --- | --- |
| | Maize | Rice | Maize | Rice | Maize | Rice | Wheat | Maize | Rice | Maize |
| 1911 | ... | ... | 8 | ... | ... | ... | ... | ... | ... | ... |
| 1912 | ... | ... | 8 | ... | ... | ... | ... | 300 | ... | ... |
| 1913 | ... | ... | 8 | ... | ... | ... | 10 | ... | 2 | ... |
| 1914 | ... | ... | 8 | ... | ... | 7 | 11 | 461 | 8 | ... |
| 1915 | ... | ... | 8 | ... | ... | 18 | 17 | 500 | 11 | ... |
| 1916 | ... | ... | 8 | ... | ... | ... | 16 | ... | 6 | ... |
| 1917 | ... | ... | ... | ... | ... | ... | 19 | 512 | 15 | ... |
| 1918 | ... | ... | ... | ... | 106 | 6 | 3 | 377 | 13 | ... |
| 1919 | ... | ... | 9 | ... | 127 | 10 | 7 | 243 | 4 | ... |
| 1920 | ... | ... | 9 | ... | 271 | ... | 9 | 200 | 2 | ... |
| 1921 | ... | ... | ... | ... | ... | ... | 10 | 312 | 2 | ... |
| 1922 | ... | ... | ... | ... | ... | ... | 6 | 297 | 3 | ... |
| 1923 | ... | ... | ... | ... | 250 | 10 | 4 | 249 | ... | ... |
| 1924 | ... | ... | ... | ... | 270 | 10 | 6 | 243 | 2 | ... |
| 1925 | ... | ... | ... | ... | ... | ... | 4 | 215 | 1 | ... |
| 1926 | ... | ... | ... | ... | ... | ... | 7 | 176 | 1 | 134 |
| 1927 | ... | ... | ... | ... | ... | ... | 6 | 213 | 2 | 123 |
| 1928 | ... | ... | ... | ... | ... | ... | 5 | 207 | 1 | 141 |
| 1929 | ... | 28 | ... | ... | 228 | 11 | 5 | 280 | 2 | 130 |
| 1930 | ... | ... | ... | ... | 280 | ... | 5 | 302 | 2 | 145 |
| 1931 | ... | 18 | ... | ... | 120 | 5 | 4 | 292 | 2 | 111 |
| 1932 | ... | ... | ... | ... | 107 | 5 | 5 | 316 | 2 | 150 |
| 1933 | ... | 26 | ... | ... | 136 | 7 | 5 | 305 | 3 | 157 |
| 1934 | 89 | ... | ... | ... | 136 | 9 | 5 | 285 | 2 | 141 |
| 1935 | ... | ... | ... | ... | 188 | 17 | 6 | 307 | 7 | 118 |
| 1936 | ... | ... | 64 | 38 | 152 | 11 | 16 | 284 | 7 | 171 |
| 1937 | ... | 7 | 51 | 39 | 161 | 14 | 11 | 286 | ... | 133 |
| 1938 | 22 | 10 | 49 | 42 | 345 | 13 | 13 | 323 | ... | 164 |
| 1939 | 45 | 15 | 76 | 46 | 131 | 16 | 15 | 461 | 19 | 175 |
| 1940 | 41 | 22 | 71 | 39 | 158 | 17 | 18 | 624 | 19 | 170 |
| 1941 | ... | 30 | 74 | 45 | 217 | 20 | 22 | 687 | 21 | 198 |
| 1942 | ... | 29 | 70 | 42 | 211 | 25 | 23 | 692 | 27 | 195 |
| 1943 | ... | 45 | 61 | 42 | 192 | 16 | 12 | 315 | 12 | 159 |
| 1944 | ... | 36 | 75 | 55 | 157 | 19 | 13 | 264 | 9 | 167 |

**C2    NORTH AMERICA: Output of Main Arable Crops** (in thousands of metric tons)

| | Mexico | | | | | | Nicaragua | | Panama |
| | Wheat | Barley | Oats | Maize | Rice | P | Maize | Rice | Rice |
|---|---|---|---|---|---|---|---|---|---|
| 1905 | 303 | 140 | ... | 2,135 | ... | ... | ... | ... | ... |
| 1906 | 350 | 161 | ... | 2,715 | ... | ... | ... | ... | ... |
| 1907 | 312 | 229 | - - | 1,572 | 33 | 17 | ... | ... | ... |
| 1908 | 257 | ... | ... | 2,679 | ... | ... | ... | ... | ... |
| 1909 | 272 | 152 | ... | ... | ... | ... | ... | ... | ... |
| 1910 | 326 | 134 | ... | 2,059 | 28 | ... | ... | ... | ... |
| 1911 | 326 | 142 | ... | 1,720 | ... | ... | ... | ... | ... |
| 1912 | 326 | 122 | ... | 2,096 | ... | ... | ... | ... | ... |
| 1913 | 291 | 215 | - - | 3,374 | 25 | 15 | ... | ... | ... |
| 1914 | 218 | 236 | ... | 1,993 | 25 | ... | ... | ... | ... |
| 1915 | 109 | 218 | ... | 2,683 | ... | ... | ... | ... | ... |
| 1916 | 291 | 215 | - - | 3,374 | 25 | 15 | ... | ... | ... |
| 1917 | ... | ... | ... | ... | ... | ... | ... | ... | ... |
| 1918 | ... | 386 | ... | 1,930 | 18 | 12 | ... | ... | ... |
| 1919 | 285 | ... | ... | 2,857 | ... | ... | ... | ... | ... |
| 1920 | 280 | ... | ... | 2,349 | ... | ... | ... | ... | ... |
| 1921 | 139 | 86 | ... | 1,804 | 30 | ... | ... | ... | ... |
| 1922 | 371 | 85 | ... | 1,734 | 33 | 25 | ... | ... | ... |
| 1923 | 372 | 85 | ... | 2,574 | 32 | 22 | ... | ... | ... |
| 1924 | 282 | 108 | ... | 2,701 | 53 | 40 | ... | ... | ... |
| 1925 | 298 | 83 | ... | 1,969 | 86 | 38 | ... | ... | ... |
| 1926 | 334 | 94 | ... | 2,135 | 91 | 43 | ... | ... | ... |
| 1927 | 385 | 98 | ... | 2,059 | 83 | 53 | ... | ... | ... |
| 1928 | 357 | 86 | ... | 2,173 | 83 | 54 | ... | ... | ... |
| 1929 | 367 | 55 | ... | 1,469 | 67 | 39 | ... | ... | ... |
| 1930 | 370 | 59 | ... | 1,377 | 75 | 46 | 31 | ... | ... |
| 1931 | 525 | 69 | ... | 2,139 | 72 | 50 | 35 | 1 | ... |
| 1932 | 313 | 66 | 2 | 1,974 | 72 | 52 | 45 | 1 | ... |
| 1933 | 392 | 71 | 4 | 1,924 | 67 | 52 | 63 | 2 | ... |
| 1934 | 354 | 73 | 2 | 1,724 | 69 | 59 | ... | ... | ... |
| 1935 | 397 | 82 | 3 | 1,656 | 71 | 60 | ... | ... | ... |
| 1936 | 439 | 80 | 3 | 1,597 | 86 | 76 | ... | ... | ... |
| 1937 | 342 | 78 | ... | 1,635 | 75 | 69 | 15 | 2 | ... |
| 1938 | 386 | 75 | ... | 1,693 | 80 | 71 | 19 | 3 | ... |
| 1939 | 429 | 97 | 11 | 1,977 | 103 | 71 | ... | ... | ... |
| 1940 | 464 | 112 | 19 | 1,640 | 108 | 71 | ... | ... | ... |
| 1941 | 434 | 114 | 31 | 2,124 | 109 | 92 | ... | 16 | 43 |
| 1942 | 489 | 108 | 28 | 2,363 | 108 | 118 | ... | 16 | 44 |
| 1943 | 364 | 93 | 25 | 1,808 | 115 | 124 | ... | 15 | 48 |
| 1944 | 374 | 101 | 21 | 2,316 | 104 | 125 | ... | 10 | 51 |

**C2     NORTH AMERICA: Output of Main Arable Crops** (in thousands of metric tons)

| | USA | | | | | | | | | |
|---|---|---|---|---|---|---|---|---|---|---|
| | Wheat | Barley | Oats | Rye | Maize | Bwt | Rice | Sorghum | P | SP |
| 1905 | 19,214 | 3,745 | 16,025 | 792 | 75,035 | 348 | 327 | ... | 8,184 | 1,461 |
| 1906 | 20,166 | 3,897 | 14,849 | 752 | 77,041 | 322 | 363 | ... | 9,293 | 1,441 |
| 1907 | 17,118 | 3,288 | 11,627 | 718 | 66,398 | 310 | 424 | ... | 9,066 | 1,430 |
| 1908 | 17,499 | 3,723 | 12,033 | 728 | 65,204 | 321 | 457 | ... | 8,307 | 1,554 |
| 1909 | 18,615 | 3,767 | 14,718 | 764 | 66,322 | 322 | 481 | ... | 10,619 | 1,472 |
| 1910 | 17,009 | 3,092 | 16,054 | 739 | 72,469 | 316 | 505 | ... | 9,309 | 1,505 |
| 1911 | 16,819 | 3,157 | 12,860 | 797 | 62,867 | 302 | 463 | ... | 8,238 | 1,379 |
| 1912 | 19,867 | 4,289 | 19,639 | 963 | 74,882 | 329 | 484 | ... | 11,055 | 1,413 |
| 1913 | 20,438 | 3,462 | 15,081 | 1,026 | 57,736 | 222 | 494 | ... | 9,048 | 1,397 |
| 1914 | 24,412 | 3,875 | 15,473 | 1,070 | 64,112 | 281 | 479 | ... | 10,022 | 1,351 |
| 1915 | 27,460 | 4,507 | 20,829 | 1,188 | 71,859 | 273 | 533 | ... | 9,165 | 1,578 |
| 1916 | 17,282 | 3,462 | 16,533 | 1,095 | 61,597 | 224 | 807 | ... | 7,359 | 1,535 |
| 1917 | 16,873 | 3,963 | 20,945 | 1,534 | 73,866 | 296 | 709 | ... | 10,850 | 1,815 |
| 1918 | 24,602 | 4,899 | 20,742 | 2,123 | 62,004 | 314 | 816 | ... | 9,420 | 1,711 |
| 1919 | 25,909 | 2,852 | 16,068 | 2,003 | 68,049 | 277 | 876 | 1,829 | 8,092 | 1,953 |
| 1920 | 22,942 | 3,723 | 20,960 | 1,578 | 78,006 | 265 | 1,054 | 2,235 | 10,040 | 1,921 |
| 1921 | 22,289 | 2,896 | 15,168 | 1,555 | 74,374 | 257 | 802 | 1,803 | 8,854 | 1,839 |
| 1922 | 23,051 | 3,331 | 16,663 | 2,569 | 68,761 | 256 | 850 | 1,270 | 11,305 | 1,955 |
| 1923 | 20,656 | 3,462 | 17,810 | 1,425 | 73,028 | 252 | 678 | 1,575 | 9,971 | 1,593 |
| 1924 | 22,915 | 3,592 | 20,553 | 1,485 | 56,466 | 272 | 666 | 1,499 | 10,455 | 1,120 |
| 1925 | 18,207 | 4,180 | 20,394 | 1,077 | 71,072 | 273 | 674 | 1,448 | 8,068 | 1,251 |
| 1926 | 22,643 | 3,614 | 16,721 | 888 | 64,696 | 239 | 858 | 1,803 | 8,753 | 1,579 |
| 1927 | 23,813 | 5,204 | 15,865 | 1,300 | 66,449 | 279 | 908 | 2,057 | 10,060 | 1,769 |
| 1928 | 24,875 | 7,141 | 19,044 | 967 | 67,719 | 220 | 895 | 1,956 | 11,628 | 1,476 |
| 1929 | 22,425 | 6,118 | 16,141 | 899 | 63,909 | 190 | 807 | 1,270 | 9,073 | 1,622 |
| 1930 | 24,140 | 6,575 | 18,492 | 1,153 | 52,834 | 152 | 917 | 965 | 9,357 | 1,362 |
| 1931 | 25,637 | 4,354 | 16,315 | 833 | 65,433 | 194 | 911 | 1,829 | 10,459 | 1,679 |
| 1932 | 20,493 | 6,510 | 18,202 | 993 | 74,425 | 146 | 850 | 1,676 | 10,197 | 2,160 |
| 1933 | 15,023 | 3,331 | 10,683 | 523 | 60,912 | 170 | 769 | 1,372 | 9,340 | 1,862 |
| 1934 | 14,315 | 2,547 | 7,896 | 414 | 36,806 | 196 | 797 | 483 | 11,063 | 1,938 |
| 1935 | 17,091 | 6,292 | 17,563 | 1,446 | 58,397 | 185 | 805 | 1,473 | 10,312 | 2,027 |
| 1936 | 17,145 | 3,222 | 11,510 | 616 | 38,254 | 140 | 1,017 | 762 | 8,817 | 1,491 |
| 1937 | 23,786 | 4,833 | 17,084 | 1,241 | 67,135 | 148 | 1,090 | 1,778 | 10,245 | 1,700 |
| 1938 | 25,038 | 5,595 | 15,807 | 1,422 | 64,747 | 147 | 1,072 | 1,702 | 9,685 | 1,711 |
| 1939 | 20,166 | 6,053 | 13,905 | 980 | 65,560 | 125 | 1,103 | 1,321 | 9,318 | 1,540 |
| 1940 | 22,180 | 6,771 | 18,086 | 1,009 | 62,410 | 141 | 1,119 | 2,184 | 10,258 | 1,290 |
| 1941 | 25,637 | 7,903 | 17,171 | 1,145 | 67,363 | 131 | 1,048 | 2,896 | 9,680 | 1,560 |
| 1942 | 26,371 | 9,340 | 19,494 | 1,344 | 77,956 | 144 | 1,319 | 2,794 | 10,040 | 1,633 |
| 1943 | 22,969 | 7,032 | 16,547 | 729 | 75,339 | 192 | 1,327 | 2,794 | 12,489 | 1,775 |
| 1944 | 28,848 | 6,009 | 16,678 | 572 | 78,438 | 195 | 1,405 | 4,521 | 10,449 | 1,703 |

**C2** **NORTH AMERICA: Output of Main Arable Crops** (in thousands of metric tons)

| | Canada | | | | | | | | Costa Rica | |
|---|---|---|---|---|---|---|---|---|---|---|
| | Wheat | Barley | Oats | Rye | Maize | Bwt | Mixed Grain | P | Maize | Rice |
| 1945 | 11,290 | 4,078 | 7,311 | 215 | 304 | 103 | 888 | 2,004 | 28 | 13 |
| 1946 | 8,609 | 3,240 | 5,417 | 149 | 270 | 94 | 733 | 1,446 | ... | 23 |
| 1947 | 11,202 | 3,197 | 5,565 | 221 | 280 | 86 | 864 | 1,894 | 21 | 14 |
| 1948 | 9,212 | 3,046 | 4,167 | 346 | 175 | 91 | 548 | 1,724 | 21 | 13 |
| 1949 | 10,380 | 3,315 | 5,325 | 699 | 323 | 68 | 974 | 2,014 | 22 | 18 |
| 1950 | 9,961 | 2,570 | 4,697 | 259 | 355 | 58 | 877 | 1,927 | 100 | 33 |
| 1951 | 12,696 | 3,647 | 6,196 | 330 | 358 | 64 | 1,140 | 1,988 | 87 | 33 |
| 1952 | 15,068 | 5,344 | 7,617 | 447 | 404 | 66 | 1,260 | 1,358 | 69 | 41 |
| 1953 | 19,104 | 6,348 | 7,266 | 610 | 538 | 62 | 1,162 | 1,676 | 80 | 48 |
| 1954 | 17,255 | 5,707 | 6,384 | 733 | 586 | 78 | 1,229 | 1,896 | 62 | 34 |
| 1955 | 9,035 | 3,814 | 4,725 | 325 | 632 | 54 | 1,155 | 1,459 | 47 | 34 |
| 1956 | 14,129 | 5,467 | 6,160 | 352 | 903 | 53 | 1,202 | 1,823 | 42 | 50 |
| 1957 | 15,595 | 5,858 | 7,210 | 214 | 707 | 69 | 1,209 | 1,920 | 60 | 34 |
| 1958 | 10,688 | 4,703 | 4,887 | 213 | 750 | 48 | 1,139 | 1,984 | ... | 57 |
| 1959 | 10,834 | 5,178 | 5,332 | 196 | 757 | 44 | 1,158 | 1,797 | ... | 55 |
| 1960 | 14,108 | 4,695 | 5,308 | 214 | 785 | 31 | 1,136 | 1,615 | ... | 56 |
| 1961 | 7,713 | 2,452 | 4,379 | 166 | 742 | 26 | 1,112 | 2,012 | 53 | 57 |
| 1962 | 15,393 | 3,611 | 7,597 | 311 | 848 | 24 | 1,310 | 2,127 | 59 | 60 |
| 1963 | 19,691 | 4,817 | 6,876 | 350 | 919 | 26 | 1,283 | 2,099 | 63 | 65 |
| 1964 | 16,349 | 3,668 | 5,352 | 314 | 1,342 | 28 | 1,291 | 2,157 | 70 | 68 |
| 1965 | 17,674 | 4,753 | 6,169 | 453 | 1,511 | 19 | 1,466 | 2,087 | 84 | 72 |
| 1966 | 22,516 | 6,558 | 5,778 | 437 | 1,685 | 25 | 1,478 | 2,490 | 82 | 77 |
| 1967 | 16,137 | 5,414 | 4,691 | 304 | 1,882 | 28 | 1,560 | 2,130 | 85 | 81 |
| 1968 | 17,686 | 7,084 | 5,591 | 331 | 2,062 | 30 | 1,747 | 2,409 | 86 | 84 |
| 1969 | 18,623 | 8,238 | 5,728 | 419 | 1,865 | 37 | 1,783 | 2,362 | 73 | 104 |
| 1970 | 9,023 | 9,051 | 5,673 | 570 | 2,564 | 62 | 2,012 | 2,511 | 47 | 79 |
| 1971 | 14,412 | 13,099 | 5,606 | 557 | 2,946 | 52 | 2,186 | 2,066 | 61 | 92 |
| 1972 | 14,514 | 11,285 | 4,630 | 344 | 2,528 | 37 | 2,129 | 1,869 | 64 | 89 |
| 1973 | 16,159 | 10,223 | 5,041 | 363 | 2,803 | 30 | 1,980 | 2,056 | 87 | 104 |
| 1974 | 13,304 | 8,790 | 3,929 | 480 | 2,620 | 26 | 1,648 | 2,511 | 61 | 127 |
| 1975 | 17,081 | 9,510 | 4,480 | 523 | 3,645 | 20 | 1,833 | 2,205 | 68 | 196 |
| 1976 | 23,587 | 10,513 | 4,831 | 440 | 3,771 | 20 | 1,569 | 2,350 | 92 | 150 |
| 1977 | 19,858 | 11,802 | 4,283 | 407 | 4,249 | 44 | 1,607 | 2,525 | 85 | 169 |
| 1978 | 21,137 | 10,397 | 3,568 | 605 | 4,480 | 73 | 1,639 | 2,513 | 62 | 196 |
| 1979 | 17,196 | 8,478 | 2,879 | 525 | 5,276 | 36 | 1,559 | 2,752 | 73 | 220 |
| 1980 | 19,292 | 11,394 | 2,911 | 455 | 5,753 | 25 | 1,511 | 2,478 | 75 | 231 |
| 1981 | 24,802 | 13,724 | 3,188 | 927 | 6,683 | 53 | 1,459 | 2,647 | 83 | 222 |
| 1982 | 26,736 | 13,966 | 3,637 | 913 | 6,522 | 29 | 1,484 | 2,781 | 82 | 146 |
| 1983 | 26,465 | 10,209 | 2,773 | 828 | 5,931 | 36 | 1,162 | 2,556 | 94 | 247 |
| 1984 | 21,188 | 10,279 | 2,576 | 664 | 6,778 | 23 | 1,238 | 2,793 | 103 | 223 |
| 1985 | 24,252 | 12,387 | 2,736 | 569 | 6,970 | 22 | 1,265 | 2,994 | 119 | 224 |
| 1986 | 31,378 | 14,569 | 3,251 | 609 | 5,912 | 39 | 1,083 | 2,761 | 120 | 185 |
| 1987 | 25,992 | 13,957 | 2,995 | 493 | 7,015 | 44 | 1,087 | 3,033 | 127 | 163 |
| 1988 | 15,996 | 10,212 | 2,993 | 268 | 5,369 | 31 | 864 | 2,778 | 98 | 196 |

**C2     NORTH AMERICA: Output of Main Arable Crops** (in thousands of metric tons)

| | Cuba | | Dominican Republic | | El Salvador | | | Guatemala | | | Haiti | |
|---|---|---|---|---|---|---|---|---|---|---|---|---|
| | Maize | Rice | Maize | Rice | Maize | Rice | Sorghum | Wheat | Maize | Rice | Maize | Rice |
| 1945 | ... | 64 | 82 | 59 | 157 | 19 | ... | 14 | 191 | 6 | ... | ... |
| 1946 | 216 | 81 | 77 | 52 | 118 | 16 | ... | 13 | 294 | 9 | ... | 12 |
| 1947 | 223 | 70 | 77 | 49 | 171 | 23 | 121 | 8 | 166 | 6 | 60 | 22 |
| 1948 | 252 | 70 | 79 | 62 | 255 | 34 | 166 | ... | ... | ... | 95 | 24 |
| 1949 | 278 | 60 | 69 | 59 | ... | 20 | ... | 16 | 378 | 8 | 102 | 31 |
| 1950 | 165 | 75 | 83 | 60 | 203 | 20 | 95 | ... | ... | ... | ... | 31 |
| 1951 | 180 | 117 | 98 | 70 | ... | 26 | ... | 26 | 428 | 11 | ... | ... |
| 1952 | 210 | 164 | 88 | 73 | 181 | 27 | 91 | 22 | 433 | 10 | ... | ... |
| 1953 | 251 | 192 | 82 | 74 | 181 | 24 | 108 | 20 | 413 | 11 | ... | ... |
| 1954 | 178 | 181 | 92 | 78 | 175 | 16 | 119 | 18 | 368 | 10 | ... | ... |
| 1955 | 170 | 215 | 90 | 74 | 158 | 13 | 124 | 15 | 365 | 9 | ... | ... |
| 1956 | 180 | 279 | 97 | 79 | 186 | 16 | 134 | 20 | 450 | 10 | ... | ... |
| 1957 | 178 | 261 | 94 | 99 | 178 | 27 | 98 | 18 | 429 | 11 | ... | ... |
| 1958 | 147 | 253 | 98 | 116 | 142 | 20 | 82 | 22 | 469 | 12 | 230 | 42 |
| 1959 | 196 | 326 | 99 | 113 | 151 | 19 | 75 | 22 | 500 | 15 | ... | ... |
| 1960 | 212 | 323 | 101 | 120 | 178 | 20 | 82 | 21 | 506 | 14 | ... | ... |
| 1961 | 160 | 213 | 50 | 113 | 176 | 18 | 84 | 25 | 518 | 13 | 228 | 55 |
| 1962 | 152 | 230 | 48 | 111 | 214 | 26 | 88 | 32 | 559 | 16 | 229 | 60 |
| 1963 | 140 | 140 | 46 | 118 | 207 | 21 | 91 | 36 | 589 | 18 | 230 | 64 |
| 1964 | 129 | 123 | 43 | 143 | 192 | 33 | 88 | 36 | 643 | 20 | 232 | 68 |
| 1965 | 117 | 55 | 38 | 167 | 203 | 35 | 106 | 27 | 646 | 13 | 234 | 72 |
| 1966 | 127 | 68 | 43 | 178 | 266 | 50 | 115 | 30 | 594 | 15 | 234 | 76 |
| 1967 | 120 | 93 | 39 | 147 | 209 | 78 | 108 | 32 | 607 | 21 | 246 | 77 |
| 1968 | 115 | 100 | 40 | 181 | 258 | 83 | 124 | 33 | 689 | 25 | 220 | 77 |
| 1969 | 115 | 205 | 43 | 195 | 279 | 38 | 128 | 33 | 709 | 27 | 242 | 83 |
| 1970 | 115 | 366 | 45 | 210 | 363 | 44 | 147 | 31 | 786 | 15 | 240 | 80 |
| 1971 | 125 | 355 | 49 | 212 | 377 | 55 | 156 | 33 | 747 | 59 | 252 | 81 |
| 1972 | 89 | 316 | 50 | 214 | 238 | 36 | 146 | 38 | 802 | 44 | 257 | 92 |
| 1973 | 87 | 322 | 47 | 226 | 406 | 37 | 156 | 47 | 813 | 25 | 204 | 118 |
| 1974 | 95 | 437 | 49 | 252 | 353 | 32 | 131 | 51 | 799 | 20 | 204 | 119 |
| 1975 | 94$_8$ 20 | 447 | 46 | 219 | 439 | 61 | 175 | 45 | 934 | 28 | 180 | 108 |
| 1976 | ... | 451 | 67 | 312 | 342 | 36 | 156 | 48 | 846 | 24 | 180 | 131 |
| 1977 | ... | 456 | 65 | 308 | 380 | 33 | 151 | 56 | 842 | 25 | 168 | 90 |
| 1978 | ... | 457 | 66 | 351 | 507 | 51 | 162 | 60 | 906 | 26 | 161 | 114 |
| 1979 | 17 | 425 | 38 | 377 | 523 | 58 | 160 | 57 | 941 | 37 | 183 | 122 |
| 1980 | 23 | 478 | 35 | 398 | 529 | 61 | 140 | 58 | 902 | 42 | 179 | 120 |
| 1981 | 23 | 461 | 41 | 400 | 500 | 50 | 136 | 55 | 997 | 33 | 176 | 116 |
| 1982 | 22 | 520 | 31 | 447 | 414 | 35 | 124 | 49 | 1,100 | 49 | 171 | 113 |
| 1983 | 30 | 518 | 42 | 501 | 443 | 43 | 123 | 70 | 1,046 | 46 | 186 | 124 |
| 1984 | 29 | 555 | 84 | 507 | 527 | 63 | 140 | 61 | 922 | 44 | 186 | 124 |
| 1985 | 33 | 524 | 91 | 494 | 495 | 69 | 133 | 54 | 1,073 | 38 | 196 | 129 |
| 1986 | 35 | 576 | 47 | 468 | 432 | 47 | 148 | 56 | 1,196 | 48 | 206 | 135 |
| 1987 | 42 | 466 | 47 | 515 | 578 | 42 | 26 | 57 | 1,172 | 44 | 205 | 120 |
| 1988 | 40 | 489 | 56 | 499 | 587 | 57 | 138 | 45 | 1,324 | 69 | 202 | 115 |

**C2　NORTH AMERICA: Output of Main Arable Crops** (in thousands of metric tons)

| | Honduras | Mexico | | | | | | | Nicaragua | | Panama | |
|---|---|---|---|---|---|---|---|---|---|---|---|---|
| | Maize | Wheat | Barley | Oats | Maize | Rice | Sorghum | P | Maize | Rice | Maize | Rice |
| 1945 | 187 | 347 | 112 | 22 | 2,186 | 121 | ... | 127 | 26 | 19 | 31 | 52 |
| 1946 | 180 | 340 | 119 | 25 | 2,383 | 139 | ... | 124 | 34 | 6 | ... | 54 |
| 1947 | 177 | 422 | 117 | 33 | 2,518 | 138 | ... | 129 | 54 | 10 | ... | 61 |
| 1948 | 207 | 477 | 149 | 18 | 2,832 | 163 | ... | 128 | 48 | 14 | 46 | 75 |
| 1949 | 196 | 503 | 160 | 59 | 2,871 | 185 | ... | 130 | 81 | 20 | ... | 80 |
| 1950 | 210 | 587 | 162 | 59 | 3,122 | 187 | ... | 135 | 104 | 23 | 62 | 84 |
| 1951 | 223 | 590 | 164 | 50 | 3,424 | 180 | ... | 138 | 91 | 13 | 68 | 83 |
| 1952 | 222 | 512 | 165 | 51 | 3,202 | 151 | ... | 139 | 123 | 37 | 72 | 92 |
| 1953 | 219 | 671 | 165 | 50 | 3,720 | 152 | ... | 149 | 139 | 50 | 77 | 111 |
| 1954 | 184 | 839 | 167 | 61 | 4,488 | 170 | ... | 150 | 96 | 25 | 76 | 99 |
| 1955 | 210 | 850 | 192 | 70 | 4,490 | 210 | ... | 167 | 142 | 22 | 81 | 98 |
| 1956 | 235 | 1,243 | 197 | 71 | 4,382 | 235 | ... | 180 | 138 | 30 | 74 | 96 |
| 1957 | 246 | 1,377 | 174 | 79 | 4,500 | 240 | ... | 197 | 105 | 33 | 78 | 86 |
| 1958 | 265 | 1,337 | 178 | 84 | 5,277 | 252 | 156 | 224 | 108 | 33 | 78 | 114 |
| 1959 | 285 | 1,266 | 180 | 80 | 5,563 | 261 | 179 | 250 | 99 | 32 | 79 | 117 |
| 1960 | 293 | 1,190 | 180 | 68 | 5,420 | 328 | 209 | 294 | 119 | 34 | 63 | 96 |
| 1961 | 258 | 1,402 | 174 | 68 | 6,246 | 333 | 291 | 303 | 140 | 39 | 74 | 109 |
| 1962 | 280 | 1,455 | 151 | 74 | 6,337 | 289 | 296 | 380 | 150 | 37 | 72 | 110 |
| 1963 | 284 | 1,703 | 186 | 79 | 6,870 | 296 | 402 | 414 | 142 | 47 | 76 | 111 |
| 1964 | 333 | 2,203 | 171 | 80 | 8,454 | 274 | 526 | 413 | 158 | 48 | 82 | 128 |
| 1965 | 236 | 2,150 | 193 | 81 | 8,936 | 378 | 747 | 319 | 171 | 54 | 84 | 151 |
| 1966 | 335 | 1,647 | 220 | 63 | 9,721 | 372 | 1,411 | 348 | 176 | 63 | 84 | 140 |
| 1967 | 336 | 2,122 | 200 | 48 | 8,603 | 418 | 1,605 | 377 | 202 | 68 | 89 | 151 |
| 1968 | 337 | 2,081 | 251 | 41 | 9,062 | 347 | 2,128 | 472 | 216 | 87 | 84 | 163 |
| 1969 | 338 | 2,326 | 201 | 41 | 8,411 | 395 | 2,453 | 488 | 231 | 110 | 88 | 165 |
| 1970 | 339 | 2,676 | 213 | 63 | 8,879 | 405 | 2,565 | 422 | 236 | 81 | 56 | 127 |
| 1971 | 340 | 1,831 | 306 | 34 | 9,786 | 369 | 2,335 | 442 | 243 | 82 | 54 | 136 |
| 1972 | 341 | 1,809 | 294 | 28 | 9,223 | 375 | 2,441 | 461 | 131 | 74 | 44 | 125 |
| 1973 | 343 | 2,091 | 392 | 39 | 8,609 | 451 | 3,270 | 640 | 191 | 78 | 55 | 162 |
| 1974 | 344 | 2,789 | 250 | 51 | 7,848 | 469 | 3,499 | 603 | 203 | 80 | 59 | 178 |
| 1975 | 358 | 2,798 | 440 | 87 | 8,449 | 717 | 4,126 | 693 | 192 | 89 | 65 | 185 |
| 1976 | 389 | 3,363 | 549 | 48 | 8,017 | 463 | 4,027 | 687 | 201 | 57 | 64 | 144 |
| 1977 | 439 | 2,456 | 418 | 49 | 10,138 | 567 | 4,325 | 631 | 181 | 76 | 80 | 186 |
| 1978 | 455 | 2,785 | 505 | 60 | 10,930 | 402 | 4,193 | 923 | 254 | 85 | 64 | 162 |
| 1979 | 354 | 2,287 | 368 | 50 | 8,458 | 494 | 3,917 | 1,053 | 173 | 115 | 64 | 170 |
| 1980 | 387 | 2,785 | 530 | 60 | 12,374 | 445 | 4,812 | 1,065 | 182 | 116 | 55 | 170 |
| 1981 | 481 | 3,189 | 559 | 77 | 14,766 | 644 | 6,296 | 861 | 193 | 164 | 57 | 195 |
| 1982 | 366 | 4,462 | 396 | 71 | 10,030 | 521 | 4,717 | 941 | 109 | 176 | 66 | 176 |
| 1983 | 458 | 3,460 | 557 | 251 | 13,061 | 441 | 4,846 | 835 | 99 | 171 | 74 | 199 |
| 1984 | 507 | 4,506 | 619 | 180 | 12,932 | 484 | 5,009 | 1,017 | 124 | 162 | 71 | 175 |
| 1985 | 424 | 5,214 | 544 | 138 | 14,103 | 809 | 6,550 | 989 | 234 | 156 | 96 | 186 |
| 1986 | 484 | 4,770 | 515 | ... | 11,721 | 545 | 4,833 | ... | 234 | 144 | 96 | 180 |
| 1987 | 443 | 4,415 | 617 | ... | 11,607 | 591 | 6,298 | ... | 277 | 149 | 98 | 180 |
| 1988 | 500 | 3,665 | 350 | ... | 10,600 | 456 | 5,895 | ... | 280 | 111 | 92 | 183 |

**C2**    **NORTH AMERICA: Output of Main Arable Crops** (in thousands of metric tons)

| | USA | | | | | | | | | |
|---|---|---|---|---|---|---|---|---|---|---|
| | Wheat | Barley | Oats | Rye | Maize[7] | Bwt | Rice | Sorghum | P | SP |
| 1945 | 30,154 | 5,813 | 22,121 | 602 | 72,875 | 141 | 1,391 | 2,438 | 11,414 | 1,528 |
| 1946 | 31,352 | 5,770 | 21,453 | 470 | 81,715 | 148 | 1,474 | 2,693 | 13,263 | 1,517 |
| 1947 | 36,985 | 6,140 | 17,070 | 648 | 59,819 | 156 | 1,597 | 2,362 | 10,586 | 1,238 |
| 1948 | 35,243 | 6,880 | 21,047 | 658 | 91,571 | 132 | 1,736 | 3,328 | 12,244 | 1,075 |
| 1949 | 29,882 | 5,160 | 17,708 | 460 | 82,248 | 108 | 1,849 | 3,582 | 10,929 | 1,125 |
| 1950 | 27,732 | 6,619 | 19,871 | 544 | 78,108 | 96 | 1,761 | 5,944 | 11,753 | 1,237 |
| 1951 | 26,888 | 5,595 | 18,550 | 547 | 74,323 | 72 | 2,091 | 4,140 | 8,880 | 726 |
| 1952 | 35,543 | 4,964 | 17,665 | 410 | 83,620 | 70 | 2,186 | 2,311 | 9,575 | 728 |
| 1953 | 31,923 | 5,378 | 16,736 | 480 | 81,537 | 70 | 2,397 | 2,947 | 10,509 | 862 |
| 1954 | 26,780 | 8,252 | 20,466 | 659 | 77,676 | 59 | 2,912 | 5,690 | 9,958 | 780 |
| 1955 | 25,446 | 8,774 | 21,714 | 739 | 81,791 | 40 | 2,536 | 6,172 | 10,328 | 980 |
| 1956 | 27,351 | 8,208 | 16,707 | 541 | 87,506 | 40 | 2,243 | 5,207 | 11,149 | 788 |
| 1957 | 26,018 | 9,645 | 18,724 | 724 | 86,363 | 36 | 1,947 | 14,428 | 11,001 | 819 |
| 1958 | 39,652 | 10,385 | 20,336 | 843 | 94,619 | 33 | 2,030 | 14,758 | 12,106 | 797 |
| 1959 | 30,426 | 9,144 | 15,241 | 586 | 106,608 | 22 | 2,433 | 12,904 | 11,125 | 856 |
| 1960 | 36,876 | 9,340 | 16,736 | 841 | 109,580[7] | 18 | 2,476 | 15,749 | 11,662 | 674 |
| 1961 | 33,529 | 8,540 | 14,665 | 694 | 91,388 | 19 | 2,458 | 12,192 | 13,298 | 654 |
| 1962 | 29,718 | 9,314 | 14,693 | 1,034 | 91,604 | 18 | 2,996 | 12,955 | 12,018 | 777 |
| 1963 | 31,212 | 8,554 | 14,015 | 741 | 102,093 | 21 | 3,187 | 14,860 | 12,306 | 652 |
| 1964 | 34,928 | 8,407 | 12,371 | 825 | 88,504 | 22 | 3,319 | 11,761 | 10,941 | 589 |
| 1965 | 35,805 | 8,559 | 13,493 | 846 | 104,217 | ... | 3,460 | 17,095 | 13,211 | 702 |
| 1966 | 35,514 | 8,539 | 11,661 | 706 | 105,861 | ... | 3,856 | 18,162 | 13,941 | 620 |
| 1967 | 41,031 | 8,139 | 11,523 | 608 | 123,458 | ... | 4,054 | 19,186 | 13,870 | 612 |
| 1968 | 42,365 | 9,279 | 13,800 | 583 | 113,023 | ... | 4,724 | 18,568 | 13,405 | 607 |
| 1969 | 39,264 | 9,298 | 14,020 | 767 | 119,056 | ... | 4,169 | 18,541 | 14,174 | 652 |
| 1970 | 36,784 | 9,060 | 13,285 | 936 | 105,471 | ... | 3,801 | 17,363 | 14,779 | 609 |
| 1971 | 44,053 | 10,069 | 12,745 | 1,252 | 143,421 | ... | 3,890 | 22,245 | 14,489 | 532 |
| 1972 | 42,082 | 9,193 | 10,025 | 741 | 141,733 | ... | 3,875 | 20,550 | 13,447 | 565 |
| 1973 | 46,561 | 9,091 | 9,568 | 667 | 144,042 | ... | 4,208 | 23,623 | 13,613 | 569 |
| 1974 | 48,497 | 6,503 | 8,719 | 490 | 119,420 | ... | 5,098 | 15,983 | 15,531 | 631 |
| 1975 | 57,886 | 8,255 | 9,275 | 405 | 148,361 | ... | 5,826 | 19,128 | 14,605 | 600 |
| 1976 | 58,481 | 8,339 | 7,845 | 380 | 159,751 | ... | 5,246 | 18,284 | 16,223 | 610 |
| 1977 | 55,671 | 9,314 | 10,927 | 440 | 165,235 | ... | 4,501 | 20,143 | 16,118 | 617 |
| 1978 | 48,323 | 9,901 | 8,443 | 611 | 184,613 | ... | 6,040 | 18,575 | 16,616 | 596 |
| 1979 | 58,081 | 8,343 | 7,646 | 569 | 201,383 | ... | 5,985 | 20,546 | 15,533 | 606 |
| 1980 | 64,800 | 7,863 | 6,659 | 419 | 168,647 | ... | 6,629 | 14,712 | 13,737 | 497 |
| 1981 | 75,806 | 10,309 | 7,396 | 478 | 206,222 | ... | 8,289 | 22,333 | 15,358 | 578 |
| 1982 | 75,251 | 11,233 | 8,602 | 532 | 209,180 | ... | 6,969 | 21,372 | 16,109 | 648 |
| 1983 | 65,858 | 11,080 | 6,923 | 689 | 106,041 | ... | 4,523 | 12,384 | 15,146 | 548 |
| 1984 | 70,618 | 13,046 | 6,875 | 825 | 194,928 | ... | 6,296 | 22,004 | 16,448 | 589 |
| 1985 | 65,999 | 12,876 | 7,559 | 524 | 225,478 | ... | 6,120 | 28,456 | 18,466 | 674 |
| 1986 | 56,926 | 13,292 | 5,608 | 496 | 209,555 | ... | 6,049 | 23,829 | 16,398 | 575 |
| 1987 | 57,363 | 11,529 | 5,429 | 495 | 181,142 | ... | 5,879 | 18,778 | 17,484 | 547 |
| 1988 | 49,303 | 6,314 | 3,158 | 373 | 125,193 | ... | 7,253 | 14,648 | 15,875 | 537 |

**C2     SOUTH AMERICA: OUTPUT OF MAIN ARABLE CROPS** (in thousands of metric tons)

| | | | | | Argentina | | | |
|---|---|---|---|---|---|---|---|---|
| | Wheat | Barley | Oats | Rye | Maize | Millet | Rice | P |
| 1890 | 845 | ... | ... | ... | ... | ... | ... | ... |
| 1891 | 980 | ... | ... | ... | ... | ... | ... | ... |
| 1892 | 1,593 | ... | ... | ... | ... | ... | ... | ... |
| 1893 | 2,238 | ... | ... | ... | ... | ... | ... | ... |
| 1894 | 1,670 | ... | ... | ... | ... | ... | ... | ... |
| 1895 | 1,263 | ... | ... | ... | 2,240 | ... | ... | ... |
| 1896 | 860 | ... | ... | ... | ... | ... | ... | ... |
| 1897 | 1,453 | ... | ... | ... | ... | ... | ... | ... |
| 1898 | 2,857 | ... | ... | ... | 1,700 | ... | ... | ... |
| 1899 | 2,767 | ... | 22 | ... | 1,413 | ... | ... | ... |
| 1900 | 2,034 | ... | 25 | ... | 2,511 | ... | ... | ... |
| 1901 | 1,534 | ... | 33 | ... | 2,134 | ... | ... | ... |
| 1902 | 2,824 | ... | 57 | ... | 3,783 | ... | ... | ... |
| 1903 | 3,529 | ... | 48 | ... | 4,450 | ... | ... | ... |
| 1904 | 4,103 | ... | 51 | ... | 3,574 | ... | ... | ... |
| 1905 | 3,672 | ... | 80 | ... | 4,951 | ... | ... | ... |
| 1906 | 4,245 | ... | 180 | ... | 1,823 | ... | ... | ... |
| 1907 | 5,239 | 36 | 493 | ... | 3,456 | ... | ... | ... |
| 1908 | 4,250 | 36 | 464 | ... | 4,500 | ... | ... | ... |
| 1909 | 3,566 | 28 | 530 | ... | 4,450 | ... | ... | 303 |
| 1910 | 3,973 | 20 | 685 | 10 | 7,030 | ... | ... | 304 |
| 1911 | 4,523 | 22 | 1,004 | 11 | 7,515 | ... | ... | 660 |
| 1912 | 5,100 | 25 | 1,100 | 36 | 4,995 | ... | 8 | 719 |
| 1913 | 2,850 | 86 | 618 | 85 | 6,684 | ... | 9 | 725 |
| 1914 | 4,604 | 84 | 717 | 46 | 8,260 | ... | 8 | 682 |
| 1915 | 4,600 | 72 | 1,093 | 51 | 4,093 | ... | 17 | 861 |
| 1916 | 2,180 | 13 | 461 | 22 | 1,495 | ... | 12 | 863 |
| 1917 | 5,973 | 42 | 996 | ... | 4,335 | ... | 17 | 848 |
| 1918 | 4,670 | 49 | 490 | ... | 5,696 | ... | 17 | 862 |
| 1919 | 5,905 | 56 | 829 | 22 | 6,571 | ... | 16 | 974 |
| 1920 | 4,249 | 80 | 736 | 21 | 5,853 | ... | 26 | 1,018 |
| 1921 | 5,199 | 130 | 444 | 43 | 4,475 | ... | 26 | 864 |
| 1922 | 5,330 | 169 | 807 | 90 | 4,473 | ... | 15 | 905 |
| 1923 | 6,744 | 259 | 1,108 | 99 | 7,030 | ... | 9 | 960 |
| 1924 | 5,202 | 152 | 776 | 37 | 4,732 | ... | 12 | 690 |
| 1925 | 5,202 | 371 | 1,168 | 120 | 8,170 | ... | 10 | 645 |
| 1926 | 6,262 | 400 | 962 | 132 | 8,150 | ... | 9 | 1,045 |
| 1927 | 7,683 | 317 | 759 | 168 | 7,765 | ... | 7 | 688 |
| 1928 | 9,500 | 366 | 946 | 228 | 5,886 | ... | 6 | 694 |
| 1929 | 4,427 | 351 | 991 | 112 | 7,128 | ... | 6 | 879 |
| 1930 | 6,322 | 305 | 885 | 105 | 10,660 | ... | 5 | 1,251 |
| 1931 | 5,979 | 431 | 1,059 | 248 | 7,603 | ... | 10 | 920 |
| 1932 | 6,556 | 700 | 1,010 | 320 | 6,802 | ... | 24 | 786 |
| 1933 | 7,787 | 735 | 833 | 184 | 6,526 | ... | 34 | 919 |
| 1934 | 6,550 | 781 | 901 | 397 | 11,480 | ... | 35 | 776 |
| 1935 | 3,850 | 442 | 521 | 153 | 10,051 | ... | 34 | 516 |
| 1936 | 6,802 | 442 | 804 | 216 | 8,640 | ... | 38 | 322 |
| 1937 | 5,650 | 394 | 757 | 131 | 4,424 | 55 | 48 | 952 |
| 1938 | 10,319 | 440 | 732 | 275 | 4,864 | 90 | 104 | 849 |
| 1939 | 3,558 | 726 | 803 | 370 | 10,375 | 98 | 97 | 1,071 |

**C2     SOUTH AMERICA: Output of Main Arable Crops** (in thousands of metric tons)

| | Bolivia | | | | | Brazil | | | | | |
|---|---|---|---|---|---|---|---|---|---|---|---|
| | Wheat | Barley | Maize | Rice | P | Wheat | Maize | Rice | P | SP | Cassava |
| 1909 | ... | ... | ... | ... | ... | ... | ... | 45 | ... | ... | ... |
| 1910 | ... | ... | ... | ... | ... | ... | ... | ... | ... | ... | ... |
| 1911 | ... | ... | ... | ... | ... | ... | ... | ... | ... | ... | ... |
| 1912 | ... | ... | ... | ... | ... | ... | ... | ... | ... | ... | ... |
| 1913 | ... | ... | ... | ... | ... | ... | ... | ... | ... | ... | ... |
| 1914 | ... | ... | ... | ... | ... | ... | ... | ... | ... | ... | ... |
| 1915 | ... | ... | ... | ... | ... | ... | ... | [224] | ... | ... | ... |
| 1916 | ... | ... | ... | ... | ... | ... | 5,175 | 296 | 180 | ... | ... |
| 1917 | ... | ... | ... | ... | ... | ... | 2,421 | 372 | ... | ... | ... |
| 1918 | ... | ... | ... | ... | ... | ... | ... | [309] | 141 | ... | ... |
| 1919 | ... | ... | ... | ... | ... | 87 | 5,000 | 832 | 146 | ... | 2,899 |
| 1920 | ... | ... | ... | ... | ... | 136 | 5,388 | 693 | 191 | ... | ... |
| 1921 | ... | ... | ... | ... | ... | 139 | 5,514 | 767 | 286 | ... | ... |
| 1922 | ... | ... | ... | ... | ... | 80 | 5,603 | 918 | 208 | ... | ... |
| 1923 | 48 | 230 | 280 | 24 | 286 | 118 | 4,940 | 666 | 241 | ... | ... |
| 1924 | 45 | 242 | 291 | 23 | 306 | 106 | 4,481 | 709 | 232 | ... | ... |
| 1925 | 50 | 255 | 298 | 25 | 315 | 154 | 4,369 | 779 | 278 | ... | ... |
| 1926 | 51 | 251 | 270 | 25 | 309 | 135 | 5,097 | 910 | 246 | ... | ... |
| 1927 | ... | ... | ... | ... | ... | 126 | 4,691 | 1,013 | 228 | ... | ... |
| 1928 | 12 | 76 | 690 | 37 | 338 | 126 | 5,271 | 967 | 257 | ... | ... |
| 1929 | 21 | 80 | 630 | 32 | 372 | 171 | 5,027 | 913 | 309 | ... | ... |
| 1930 | 36 | 90 | 710 | 31 | 364 | 134 | 4,750 | 1,078 | 361 | ... | 5,210 |
| 1931 | 40 | 98 | 660 | ... | 510 | 164 | 5,770 | 1,202 | 400 | ... | 4,848 |
| 1932 | ... | ... | ... | ... | ... | 156 | 5,608 | 1,186 | 380 | ... | 4,983 |
| 1933 | ... | ... | ... | 11 | ... | 145 | 5,292 | 1,185 | 315 | ... | 5,293 |
| 1934 | ... | ... | ... | ... | ... | 146 | 5,933 | 1,367 | 359 | ... | 4,541 |
| 1935 | ... | ... | ... | ... | ... | 144 | 5,721 | 1,214 | 335 | ... | 4,947 |
| 1936 | ... | ... | ... | ... | ... | 149 | 5,776 | 1,232 | 323 | ... | 5,013 |
| 1937 | ... | ... | ... | ... | ... | 161 | 5,560 | 1,529 | 382 | ... | 6,021 |
| 1938 | ... | ... | ... | ... | ... | 150 | 5,394 | 1,485 | 457 | ... | 7,122 |
| 1939 | ... | ... | ... | ... | ... | 102 | 4,876 | 1,320 | 444 | ... | 7,332 |
| 1940 | 33 | ... | ... | ... | ... | 232 | 5,438 | 1,688 | 453 | ... | 7,763 |
| 1941 | 54 | ... | ... | ... | ... | 217 | 5,276 | 1,881 | 417 | ... | 7,916 |
| 1942 | ... | ... | ... | 10 | ... | 223 | 5,210 | 1,894 | 518 | ... | 8,936 |
| 1943 | ... | ... | ... | ... | ... | ... | 5,575 | 2,110 | ... | ... | 10,333 |
| 1944 | 14 | 60 | 150 | 15 | 403 | ... | 4,847 | 2,147 | 596 | 968 | 11,415 |

**C2 SOUTH AMERICA: Output of Main Arable Crops** (in thousands of metric tons)

| | Chile | | | | | Colombia | | | | |
|------|-------|--------|------|-------|-----|-------|--------|-------|------|-----|
| | Wheat | Barley | Oats | Maize | P | Wheat | Barley | Maize | Rice | P |
| 1900 | ... | ... | ... | ... | ... | ... | ... | ... | ... | ... |
| 1901 | ... | ... | ... | ... | ... | ... | ... | ... | ... | ... |
| 1902 | 375 | 73 | ... | 31 | 409 | ... | ... | ... | ... | ... |
| 1903 | 273 | 76 | ... | 29 | 282 | ... | ... | ... | ... | ... |
| 1904 | 489 | 145 | ... | 38 | 167 | ... | ... | ... | ... | ... |
| 1905 | 329 | 104 | ... | 32 | 178 | ... | ... | ... | ... | ... |
| 1906 | 331 | 81 | ... | 22 | 85 | ... | ... | ... | ... | ... |
| 1907 | ... | ... | ... | ... | ... | ... | ... | ... | ... | ... |
| 1908 | 575 | 82 | 20 | 34 | 219 | ... | ... | ... | ... | ... |
| 1909 | 481 | 86 | 34 | 30 | 174 | ... | ... | ... | ... | ... |
| 1910 | 536 | 80 | 37 | 35 | 214 | ... | ... | ... | ... | ... |
| 1911 | 612 | 71 | 49 | 39 | 263 | ... | ... | ... | ... | ... |
| 1912 | 642 | 100 | 65 | 42 | 238 | ... | ... | ... | ... | ... |
| 1913 | 446 | 121 | 64 | 38 | 250 | ... | ... | ... | ... | ... |
| 1914 | 517 | 83 | 103 | 47 | 260 | ... | ... | ... | ... | ... |
| 1915 | 550 | 95 | 99 | 40 | 316 | 28 | 4 | 166 | 13 | 33 |
| 1916 | 612 | 105 | 81 | 34 | 247 | ... | ... | ... | ... | ... |
| 1917 | 629 | 72 | 46 | 37 | 262 | ... | ... | ... | ... | ... |
| 1918 | 552 | 80 | 29 | 33 | 242 | ... | ... | ... | ... | ... |
| 1919 | 542 | 80 | 38 | 37 | 282 | ... | ... | ... | ... | ... |
| 1920 | 631 | 110 | 46 | 43 | 326 | ... | ... | ... | ... | ... |
| 1921 | 643 | 99 | 42 | 45 | 315 | ... | ... | ... | ... | ... |
| 1922 | 706 | 110 | 41 | 43 | 308 | ... | ... | ... | ... | ... |
| 1923 | 765 | 115 | 58 | 35 | 266 | ... | ... | ... | ... | ... |
| 1924 | 666 | 108 | 66 | 27 | 283 | ... | ... | ... | 15 | 146 |
| 1925 | 726 | 150 | 80 | 36 | 273 | ... | ... | 125 | 16 | 154 |
| 1926 | 634 | 99 | 71 | 40 | 306 | ... | ... | 129 | 16 | 155 |
| 1927 | 833 | 126 | 93 | 72 | 430 | 52 | ... | 200 | 15 | 226 |
| 1928 | 808 | 133 | 103 | 71 | 434 | 42 | ... | 100 | 16 | 238 |
| 1929 | 913 | 100 | 151 | 60 | 402 | ... | ... | ... | ... | ... |
| 1930 | 577 | 84 | 74 | 69 | 447 | 47 | ... | ... | ... | ... |
| 1931 | 577 | 67 | 72 | 75 | 410 | 77 | ... | ... | ... | ... |
| 1932 | 782 | 144 | 103 | 82 | 478 | 68 | ... | 475 | 59 | 161 |
| 1933 | 961 | 146 | 104 | 67 | 611 | 77 | ... | ... | ... | ... |
| 1934 | 820 | 83 | 69 | 69 | 463 | 99 | ... | 500 | 55 | 225 |
| 1935 | 866 | 107 | 99 | 52 | 344 | 102 | ... | ... | 107 | ... |
| 1936 | 779 | 97 | 100 | 69 | 445 | 124 | ... | ... | 75 | ... |
| 1937 | 824 | 163 | 120 | 56 | 437 | 91 | ... | 491 | 100 | 236 |
| 1938 | 967 | 109 | 153 | 63 | 487 | ... | ... | ... | 100 | ... |
| 1939 | 860 | 73 | 85 | 77 | 417 | ... | ... | ... | 95 | ... |
| 1940 | 783 | 75 | 68 | 65 | 428 | 57 | ... | ... | 127 | ... |
| 1941 | 783 | 69 | 67 | 68 | 522 | 64 | ... | ... | 111 | 458 |
| 1942 | 856 | 73 | 78 | 69 | 512 | 60 | ... | ... | 119 | 628 |
| 1943 | 994 | 75 | 114 | 71 | 414 | 65 | ... | ... | 120 | 131 |
| 1944 | 921 | 84 | 101 | 57 | 444 | 51 | ... | ... | 121 | 345 |

**C2      SOUTH AMERICA: Output of Main Arable Crops** (in thousands of metric tons)

| | Ecuador | | | Guyana | Paraguay | | Peru | | | | |
|---|---|---|---|---|---|---|---|---|---|---|---|
| | **Wheat** | **Maize** | **Rice** | **Rice** | **Maize** | **Cassava** | **Wheat** | **Barley** | **Maize** | **Rice** | **P** |
| 1909 | ... | ... | ... | 6 | ... | ... | 78 | 60 | 80 | 102 | ... |
| 1910 | ... | ... | ... | 6 | 16 | ... | ... | ... | 160 | 84 | ... |
| 1911 | ... | ... | ... | 5 | 13 | ... | ... | ... | ... | ... | ... |
| 1912 | ... | ... | ... | 7 | 16 | ... | ... | ... | ... | ... | ... |
| 1913 | ... | ... | ... | 4 | 20 | ... | ... | ... | ... | ... | ... |
| 1914 | ... | ... | ... | 7 | 21 | ... | ... | ... | ... | 44 | ... |
| 1915 | ... | ... | ... | 8 | 23 | ... | 78 | 41 | 121 | 42 | 224 |
| 1916 | ... | ... | ... | 12 | ... | ... | 71 | 37 | 117 | 60 | 201 |
| 1917 | ... | ... | ... | 11 | 20 | ... | 71 | 37 | 106 | 65 | 175 |
| 1918 | ... | ... | ... | 11 | ... | ... | 62 | ... | ... | 64 | ... |
| 1919 | ... | ... | ... | 10 | ... | ... | 72 | ... | ... | 55 | ... |
| 1920 | ... | ... | ... | 12 | 52 | ... | 64 | ... | ... | 55 | ... |
| 1921 | ... | ... | ... | 13 | 47 | ... | 82 | ... | ... | 55 | ... |
| 1922 | ... | ... | ... | 17 | 58 | ... | 82 | ... | ... | 66 | ... |
| 1923 | ... | ... | ... | 20 | 34 | ... | 76 | ... | ... | 65 | ... |
| 1924 | ... | ... | ... | 21 | 36 | ... | 78 | ... | ... | 37 | ... |
| 1925 | ... | ... | ... | 26 | 58 | ... | 87 | ... | ... | 44 | ... |
| 1926 | ... | ... | ... | 21 | 39 | ... | 73 | ... | ... | 40 | ... |
| 1927 | ... | ... | ... | 23 | ... | ... | 86 | ... | ... | 54 | ... |
| 1928 | ... | ... | ... | 19 | 65 | ... | 84 | 119 | 452 | 59 | 820 |
| 1929 | ... | ... | 42 | 19 | 63 | ... | 121 | ... | ... | 104 | ... |
| 1930 | ... | ... | 15 | 21 | 62 | ... | 123 | ... | ... | 102 | ... |
| 1931 | ... | ... | 26 | 25 | 63 | ... | 95 | ... | ... | 136 | ... |
| 1932 | ... | ... | 24 | 15 | ... | ... | 85 | ... | ... | 88 | ... |
| 1933 | ... | ... | 30 | 21 | ... | ... | 73 | ... | ... | 85 | ... |
| 1934 | ... | ... | 39 | 19 | ... | ... | 48 | ... | ... | 77 | ... |
| 1935 | ... | ... | 41 | 19 | 45 | ... | 58 | ... | ... | 104 | ... |
| 1936 | ... | ... | 39 | 18 | 66 | ... | 82 | ... | ... | 66 | ... |
| 1937 | ... | ... | 52 | 17 | 69 | ... | 90 | ... | ... | 91 | ... |
| 1938 | ... | ... | 42 | 22 | 77 | ... | 103 | ... | ... | 93 | ... |
| 1939 | 23 | 74 | 65 | 27 | ... | ... | 112 | ... | ... | 123 | ... |
| 1940 | 28 | ... | 92 | 52 | ... | ... | 102 | ... | ... | 151 | ... |
| 1941 | 25 | ... | 123 | 87 | 119 | 1,024 | 100 | ... | ... | 100 | ... |
| 1942 | 24 | ... | 164 | 83 | 115 | 1,019 | 101 | ... | ... | 117 | ... |
| 1943 | 21 | ... | 131 | 89 | ... | ... | 90 | ... | ... | 158 | ... |
| 1944 | 26 | ... | 99 | 100 | ... | ... | 84 | ... | ... | 131 | ... |

**C2**    **SOUTH AMERICA: Output of Main Arable Crops** (in thousands of metric tons)

| | Surinam | Uruguay | | | | | | Venezuela | | |
|---|---|---|---|---|---|---|---|---|---|---|
| | Rice | Wheat | Barley | Oats | Maize | P | | Maize | Rice | P |
| 1875 | ... | ... | ... | ... | ... | ... | | 102 | ... | ... |
| 1884 | ... | ... | ... | ... | ... | ... | | 252 | - - | 18 |
| 1892 | ... | 91 | 1 | - - | ... | ... | | ... | ... | ... |
| 1893 | ... | 157 | 3 | - - | ... | ... | | ... | ... | ... |
| 1894 | ... | 245 | 1 | - - | ... | ... | | 102 | 4 | 5 |
| 1898 | ... | 195 | 1 | - - | ... | ... | | ... | ... | ... |
| 1899 | ... | 188 | 4 | - - | 77 | ... | | ... | ... | ... |
| 1900 | ... | 100 | 4 | 1 | 142 | ... | | ... | ... | ... |
| 1901 | ... | 207 | 10 | 1 | 129 | ... | | ... | ... | ... |
| 1902 | ... | 143 | 7 | 2 | 134 | ... | | ... | ... | ... |
| 1903 | ... | ... | ... | ... | ... | ... | | ... | ... | ... |
| 1904 | ... | 206 | 6 | 4 | 112 | ... | | ... | ... | ... |
| 1905 | ... | 125 | 8 | 5 | 82 | ... | | ... | ... | ... |
| 1906 | ... | 187 | 16 | 18 | 136 | ... | | ... | ... | ... |
| 1907 | ... | 202 | 19 | 35 | 102 | ... | | ... | ... | ... |
| 1908 | ... | 233 | 31 | 67 | 169 | ... | | ... | ... | ... |
| 1909 | 2 | ... | ... | ... | 166 | ... | | ... | ... | ... |
| 1910 | 2 | 163 | 1 | 9 | 92 | ... | | ... | ... | ... |
| 1911 | 2 | 284 | 2 | 27 | 202 | ... | | ... | ... | ... |
| 1912 | 2 | 149 | 1 | 13 | 136 | ... | | ... | ... | ... |
| 1913 | 2 | 160 | 4 | 27 | 181 | ... | | ... | ... | ... |
| 1914 | 2 | 98 | 1 | 14 | 289 | ... | | ... | ... | ... |
| 1915 | 4 | 269 | 3 | 33 | 117 | ... | | ... | ... | ... |
| 1916 | 6 | 147 | 2 | 28 | 173 | ... | | ... | ... | ... |
| 1917 | 4 | 355 | 2 | 54 | 191 | ... | | ... | ... | ... |
| 1918 | 3 | 188 | 2 | 19 | 167 | 4 | | ... | ... | ... |
| 1919 | 9 | 162 | 2 | 22 | 117 | 4 | | ... | ... | ... |
| 1920 | 7 | 211 | 2 | 36 | 200 | 4 | | ... | ... | ... |
| 1921 | 9 | 271 | 1 | 30 | 122 | 8 | | ... | ... | ... |
| 1922 | 10 | 140 | 1 | 15 | 165 | 5 | | ... | ... | ... |
| 1923 | 11 | 363 | 2 | 31 | 117 | 9 | | ... | ... | ... |
| 1924 | 14 | 270 | 2 | 46 | 136 | 13 | | 154 | 5 | 5 |
| 1925 | 10 | 273 | 2 | 35 | 136 | 9 | | ... | ... | ... |
| 1926 | 16 | 279 | 2 | 21 | 85 | 9 | | ... | ... | ... |
| 1927 | 15 | 419 | 3 | 48 | 225 | 11 | | ... | ... | ... |
| 1928 | 18 | 335 | 2 | 37 | 53 | 15 | | ... | ... | ... |
| 1929 | 24 | 358 | 6 | 56 | 182 | 9 | | ... | ... | ... |
| 1930 | 21 | 201 | 3 | 20 | 146 | 15 | | ... | ... | ... |
| 1931 | 24 | 306 | 3 | 45 | 161 | 24 | | ... | ... | ... |
| 1932 | 25 | 147 | 1 | 11 | 106 | 30 | | ... | ... | ... |
| 1933 | 27 | 399 | 5 | 47 | 132 | 30 | | ... | ... | ... |
| 1934 | 13 | 290 | 7 | 32 | 162 | 28 | | ... | ... | ... |
| 1935 | 26 | 411 | 13 | 56 | 124 | 22 | | ... | ... | ... |
| 1936 | 34 | 252 | 7 | 29 | 116 | 30 | | 164 | 4 | 11 |
| 1937 | 35 | 451 | 15 | 48 | 133 | 18 | | 361 | 13 | 6 |
| 1938 | 36 | 421 | 17 | 52 | 159 | 38 | | ... | ... | ... |
| 1939 | 41 | 270 | 14 | 40 | 127 | 38 | | ... | ... | ... |

**C2**     **SOUTH AMERICA: Output of Main Arable Crops** (in thousands of metric tons)

| | Argentina | | | | | | | | | |
|---|---|---|---|---|---|---|---|---|---|---|
| | Wheat | Barley | Oats | Rye | Maize | Millet | Rice | Sorghum | P | SP |
| 1940 | 8,150 | 689 | 540 | 240 | 10,238 | 41 | 56 | ... | 1,053 | ... |
| 1941 | 6,487 | 370 | 450 | 140 | 9,034 | 39 | 108 | ... | 1,442 | ... |
| 1942 | 6,400 | 350 | 580 | 151 | 1,943 | 39 | 99 | ... | 1,032 | ... |
| 1943 | 6,800 | 719 | 925 | 557 | 8,730 | 28 | 175 | ... | 1,400 | ... |
| 1944 | 4,085 | 573 | 1,099 | 189 | 2,966 | 43 | 139 | ... | 1,027 | ... |
| 1945 | 3,907 | 836 | 797 | 293 | 3,574 | 67 | 158 | ... | 1,182 | 355 |
| 1946 | 5,615 | 1,171 | 685 | 552 | 5,815 | ... | 140 | ... | 814 | 398 |
| 1947 | 6,664 | 834 | 801 | 521 | 6,500 | ... | 112 | ... | 1,063 | 384 |
| 1948 | 5,200 | 613 | 733 | 305 | 3,450 | 57 | 121 | 57 | 1,013 | 358 |
| 1949 | 5,144 | 395 | 540 | 277 | 836 | 62 | 130 | 62 | 1,167 | 344 |
| 1950 | 5,796 | 762 | 733 | 631 | 2,670 | 136 | 141 | 136 | 1,559 | 314 |
| 1951 | 2,100 | 336 | 438 | 81 | 2,040 | 208 | 174 | 50 | 960 | 256 |
| 1952 | 7,634 | 1,175 | 1,269 | 1,335 | 3,500 | 290 | 194 | 68 | 1,376 | 321 |
| 1953 | 6,200 | 894 | 991 | 607 | 4,450 | 104 | 212 | 62 | 1,671 | 358 |
| 1954 | 7,690 | 1,112 | 890 | 844 | 2,546 | 123 | 172 | 74 | 1,375 | 284 |
| 1955 | 5,250 | 951 | 723 | 654 | 3,870 | 229 | 164 | 53 | 1,548 | 303 |
| 1956 | 7,100 | 1,364 | 1,140 | 880 | 2,698 | 157 | 193 | 46 | 1,311 | 375 |
| 1957 | 5,810 | 1,010 | 995 | 630 | 4,806 | 163 | 217 | 64 | 1,374 | 316 |
| 1958 | 6,720 | 1,050 | 850 | 817 | 4,932 | 216 | 162 | 951 | 1,398 | 241 |
| 1959 | 5,837 | 1,116 | 983 | 1,060 | 4,108 | 247 | 190 | 831 | 1,860 | 356 |
| 1960 | 3,960 | 773 | 843 | 505 | 4,850 | 261 | 149 | 1,477 | 2,072 | 388 |
| 1961 | 5,725 | 800 | 700 | 510 | 5,220 | 215 | 182 | 1,598 | 1,184 | 365 |
| 1962 | 5,700 | 345 | 487 | 163 | 4,360 | 155 | 178 | 1,176 | 1,453 | 366 |
| 1963 | 8,940 | 1,020 | 906 | 538 | 5,350 | 189 | 190 | 1,487 | 1,492 | 342 |
| 1964 | 11,260 | 826 | 805 | 652 | 5,140 | 113 | 268 | 1,059 | 2,489 | 341 |
| 1965 | 6,079 | 404 | 480 | 245 | 7,040 | 186 | 165 | 2,386 | 1,484 | 362 |
| 1966 | 6,247 | 438 | 540 | 270 | 8,510 | 224 | 217 | 1,618 | 1,797 | 444 |
| 1967 | 7,320 | 588 | 690 | 352 | 6,560 | 229 | 283 | 2,033 | 1,967 | 379 |
| 1968 | 5,740 | 556 | 490 | 360 | 6,860 | 196 | 345 | 2,616 | 2,340 | 480 |
| 1969 | 7,020 | 570 | 425 | 377 | 9,360 | 125 | 407 | 4,068 | 2,336 | 438 |
| 1970 | 4,920 | 367 | 360 | 181 | 9,930 | 183 | 288 | 4,784 | 1,958 | 454 |
| 1971 | 5,680 | 553 | 475 | 256 | 5,860 | 105 | 294 | 2,502 | 1,340 | 328 |
| 1972 | 7,900 | 880 | 566 | 690 | 9,700 | 227 | 260 | 5,159 | 1,535 | 474 |
| 1973 | 6,560 | 732 | 561 | 613 | 9,900 | 229 | 316 | 6,074 | 2,173 | 295 |
| 1974 | 5,970 | 430 | 327 | 306 | 7,700 | 200 | 351 | 5,000 | 1,349 | 419 |
| 1975 | 8,570 | 523 | 433 | 273 | 5,855 | 200 | 309 | 4,938 | 1,528 | 348 |
| 1976 | 11,000 | 760 | 530 | 330 | 8,300 | 294 | 320 | 5,167 | 1,769 | 348 |
| 1977 | 5,300 | 353 | 570 | 170 | 9,700 | 340 | 310 | 6,730 | 1,593 | 330 |
| 1978 | 8,100 | 554 | 676 | 210 | 8,700 | 330 | 312 | 7,200 | 1,694 | 320 |
| 1979 | 8,100 | 339 | 522 | 202 | 6,400 | 310 | 266 | 6,200 | 1,568 | 322 |
| 1980 | 7,780 | 217 | 433 | 155 | 12,900 | 188 | 286 | 2,960 | 2,247 | 302 |
| 1981 | 8,300 | 132 | 339 | 149 | 9,600 | 238 | 437 | 7,603 | 1,817 | 247 |
| 1982 | 15,000 | 211 | 637 | 148 | 9,000 | 154 | 277 | 8,060 | 2,013 | 368 |
| 1983 | 13,000 | 166 | 593 | 130 | 9,500 | 179 | 480 | 8,156 | 2,118 | 310 |
| 1984 | 13,600 | 238 | 610 | 140 | 11,900 | 136 | 379 | 6,930 | 2,244 | 325 |
| 1985 | 8,700 | 118 | 400 | 105 | 12,100 | 158 | 439 | 6,256 | 2,022 | 377 |
| 1986 | 8,700 | 133 | 495 | 60 | 9,250 | 107 | 371 | 4,061 | 1,836 | 409 |
| 1987 | 9,000 | 282 | 718 | 88 | 9,200 | 77 | 415 | 3,040 | 1,915 | 462 |
| 1988 | 7,800 | 317 | 620 | 41 | 4,260 | 91 | 469 | 3,200 | 2,867 | ... |

**C2** **SOUTH AMERICA: Output of Main Arable Crops** (in thousands of metric tons)

| | Bolivia | | | | | Brazil | | | | | |
|---|---|---|---|---|---|---|---|---|---|---|---|
| | Wheat | Barley | Maize | Rice | P's | Wheat | Maize | Rice | P | SP | Cassava |
| 1945 | 14 | ... | ... | ... | 82 | 233 | 5,721 | 2,759 | 432 | 924 | 11,556 |
| 1946 | ... | 54 | ... | ... | 380 | 248 | 5,503 | 2,596 | 575 | 871 | 12,223 |
| 1947 | 14 | 36 | 190 | 15 | 400 | 359 | 5,607 | 2,554 | 585 | 934 | 11,845 |
| 1948 | 24 | 36 | 188 | 18 | 406 | 405 | 5,449 | 2,720 | 585 | 934 | 12,455 |
| 1949 | 28 | ... | ... | ... | ... | 438 | 6,162 | 3,218 | 748 | 923 | 12,616 |
| 1950 | ... | ... | ... | ... | ... | 532 | 6,024 | 3,182 | 707 | 833 | 12,532 |
| 1951 | ... | ... | ... | ... | 270 | 424 | 5,907 | 2,931 | 735 | 823 | 11,918 |
| 1952 | ... | ... | ... | ... | ... | 690 | 5,984 | 3,072 | 735 | 831 | 12,809 |
| 1953 | ... | ... | ... | 28 | ... | 772 | 6,789 | 3,367 | 815 | 895 | 13,441 |
| 1954 | 46 | 44 | 138 | 29 | 189 | 871 | 6,690 | 3,737 | 815 | 958 | 14,493 |
| 1955 | ... | ... | ... | 32 | ... | 1,101 | 6,999 | 3,489 | 898 | 1,042 | 14,863 |
| 1956 | 16 | 35 | 94 | 27 | ... | 885 | 7,763 | 4,151 | 1,003 | 1,043 | 15,316 |
| 1957 | 12 | 55 | 110 | 11 | 155 | 781 | 7,370 | 3,829 | 999 | 1,086 | 15,443 |
| 1958 | 11 | 60 | 100 | 21 | 160 | 589 | 7,787 | 4,101 | 1,017 | 1,053 | 15,380 |
| 1959 | 40 | 50 | 200 | 23 | 189 | 611 | 8,672 | 4,795 | 1,025 | 1,188 | 16,575 |
| 1960 | 40 | 52 | 205 | 23 | 500 | 713 | 9,036 | 5,392 | 1,113 | 1,283 | 17,613 |
| 1961 | 35 | 60 | 259 | 34 | 617 | 545 | 9,587 | 5,557 | 1,080 | 1,356 | 18,058 |
| 1962 | 40 | 61 | 265 | 39 | 531 | 706 | 10,418 | 5,740 | 1,134 | 1,448 | 19,843 |
| 1963 | 55 | 63 | 271 | 43 | 546 | 392 | 9,408 | 6,345 | 1,168 | 1,546 | 22,249 |
| 1964 | 57 | 62 | 200 | 47 | 561 | 643 | 12,112 | 7,580 | 1,264 | 1,598 | 24,356 |
| 1965 | 55 | 60 | 277 | 51 | 575 | 585 | 11,371 | 5,802 | 1,246 | 1,721 | 24,993 |
| 1966 | 41 | 60 | 269 | 52 | 549 | 615 | 12,824 | 6,792 | 1,329 | 1,913 | 24,710 |
| 1967 | 27 | 56 | 278 | 57 | 520 | 629 | 12,814 | 6,652 | 1,467 | 2,226 | 27,268 |
| 1968 | 45 | 60 | 288 | 66 | 598 | 856 | 12,693 | 6,394 | 1,606 | 2,120 | 29,203 |
| 1969 | 53 | 61 | 289 | 83 | 627 | 1,374 | 14,216 | 7,553 | 1,507 | 2,175 | 30,074 |
| 1970 | 62 | 62 | 280 | 73 | 655 | 1,844 | 14,130 | 6,593 | 1,583 | 2,134 | 29,464 |
| 1971 | 69 | 66 | 293 | 85 | 698 | 2,132 | 14,891 | 6,761 | 1,580 | 2,210 | 30,258 |
| 1972 | 51 | 70 | 269 | 75 | 704 | 983 | 14,186 | 7,160 | 1,589 | 2,249 | 31,000 |
| 1973 | 57 | 72 | 276 | 67 | 730 | 2,031 | 16,273 | 6,764 | 1,337 | 1,814 | 26,559 |
| 1974 | 62 | 75 | 277 | 85 | 749 | 2,859 | 16,335 | 7,782 | 1,672 | 1,673 | 24,715 |
| 1975 | 62 | 80 | 305 | 127 | 834 | 1,788 | 17,751 | 9,757 | 1,655 | 1,600 | 25,812 |
| 1976 | 70 | 92 | 338 | 113 | 824 | 3,216 | 19,256 | 8,994 | 1,898 | 1,378 | 24,839 |
| 1977 | 57 | 60 | 305 | 121 | 679 | 2,066 | 13,569 | 7,296 | 1,896 | 1,074 | 25,929 |
| 1978 | 57 | 59 | 337 | 91 | 738 | 2,691 | 16,306 | 7,595 | 2,014 | 882 | 25,459 |
| 1979 | 68 | 52 | 378 | 76 | 730 | 2,927 | 20,372 | 9,776 | 2,154 | 819 | 24,962 |
| 1980 | 60 | 49 | 383 | 95 | 787 | 2,702 | 21,117 | 8,228 | 1,940 | 726 | 23,466 |
| 1981 | 67 | 57 | 504 | 101 | 867 | 2,210 | 21,842 | 9,735 | 1,912 | 762 | 24,516 |
| 1982 | 66 | 61 | 450 | 86 | 900 | 1,827 | 18,731 | 7,742 | 2,155 | 747 | 24,009 |
| 1983 | 40 | 30 | 337 | 62 | 316 | 2,237 | 21,164 | 9,027 | 1,827 | 682 | 21,848 |
| 1984 | 75 | 72 | 489 | 166 | 675 | 1,983 | 22,018 | 9,025 | 2,171 | 763 | 21,466 |
| 1985 | 74 | 75 | 554 | 173 | 768 | 4,320 | 20,531 | 10,374 | 1,947 | 756 | 23,125 |
| 1986 | 81 | 78 | 457 | 137 | 697 | 5,690 | 26,803 | 10,419 | 1,836 | 769 | 25,621 |
| 1987 | 77 | 79 | 481 | 164 | 815 | 6,035 | 24,750 | 11,806 | 2,331 | 757 | 23,464 |
| 1988 | 63 | 69 | 456 | 171 | 826 | 5,751 | 26,508 | 11,107 | 2,299 | 677 | 21,612 |

**C2**    **SOUTH AMERICA: Output of Main Arable Crops** (in thousands of metric tons)

| | Chile | | | | | Colombia | | | | | | |
|---|---|---|---|---|---|---|---|---|---|---|---|---|
| | Wheat | Barley | Oats | Maize | P | Wheat | Barley | Maize | Rice | Sorghum | P | Cassava |
| 1945 | 905 | 69 | 64 | 61 | 635 | 60 | ... | 615 | 123 | — | 418 | ... |
| 1946 | 899 | 92 | 70 | 68 | 569 | 120 | 24 | 620 | 197 | — | 460 | ... |
| 1947 | 1,071 | 107 | 72 | 74 | 524 | 78 | 26 | 570 | 219 | — | 499 | ... |
| 1948 | 1,113 | 94 | 85 | 71 | 533 | 118 | 29 | 636 | 303 | — | 486 | ... |
| 1949 | 821 | 64 | 64 | 61 | 461 | 128 | 51 | 738 | 319 | — | 538 | 841 |
| 1950 | 975 | 83 | 82 | 71 | 424 | 102 | 50 | 620 | 241 | — | 360 | 768 |
| 1951 | 916 | 82 | 88 | 69 | 452 | 127 | 49 | 585 | 318 | — | 550 | 870 |
| 1952 | 989 | 140 | 91 | 66 | 537 | 140 | 61 | 928 | 330 | — | 600 | 870 |
| 1953 | 955 | 56 | 97 | 97 | 606 | 140 | | 800 | 289 | — | 610 | 870 |
| 1954 | 1,078 | 89 | 108 | 102 | 610 | 146 | 48 | 943 | 278 | — | 650 | 871 |
| 1955 | 1,048 | 101 | 107 | 97 | 646 | 166 | 52 | 940 | 324 | — | 580 | 674 |
| 1956 | 988 | 98 | 112 | 100 | 636 | 110 | 59 | 741 | 300 | — | 623 | 700 |
| 1957 | 1,214 | 102 | 131 | 132 | 782 | 100 | 60 | 746 | 378 | — | 682 | 700 |
| 1958 | 1,205 | 115 | 119 | 156 | 614 | 155 | 75 | 851 | 410 | — | 565 | 700 |
| 1959 | 1,114 | 117 | 111 | 146 | 668 | 140 | 101 | 701 | 422 | — | 785 | 720 |
| 1960 | 1,123 | 105 | 132 | 145 | 815 | 145 | 106 | 864 | 450 | 6 | 653 | 680 |
| 1961 | 1,031 | 72 | 101 | 163 | 765 | 142 | 99 | 758 | 474 | 7 | 551 | 650 |
| 1962 | 970 | 73 | 82 | 181 | 848 | 162 | 108 | 754 | 585 | 8 | 871 | 780 |
| 1963 | 1,136 | 70 | 94 | 176 | 808 | 90 | 118 | 782 | 550 | 12 | 572 | 800 |
| 1964 | 1,159 | 80 | 86 | 242 | 703 | 85 | 114 | 968 | 600 | 60 | 867 | 700 |
| 1965 | 1,116 | 74 | 82 | 270 | 803 | 110 | 90 | 871 | 672 | 70 | 762 | 800 |
| 1966 | 1,346 | 88 | 107 | 285 | 717 | 125 | 95 | 850 | 680 | 60 | 760 | 840 |
| 1967 | 1,204 | 118 | 115 | 362 | 725 | 80 | 95 | 850 | 662 | 90 | 800 | 850 |
| 1968 | 1,220 | 157 | 163 | 321 | 603 | 105 | 75 | 886 | 786 | 110 | 850 | 886 |
| 1969 | 1,214 | 80 | 95 | 154 | 684 | 75 | 76 | 920 | 689 | 100 | 900 | 950 |
| 1970 | 1,307 | 97 | 111 | 239 | 836 | 54 | 87 | 877 | 737 | 118 | 962 | 1,956 |
| 1971 | 1,368 | 114 | 112 | 258 | 733 | 53 | 107 | 819 | 864 | 240 | 869 | 1,990 |
| 1972 | 1,195 | 139 | 111 | 283 | 624 | 69 | 98 | 806 | 1,000 | 210 | 823 | 2,010 |
| 1973 | 747 | 107 | 109 | 294 | 1,012 | 72 | 81 | 739 | 1,151 | 280 | 1,031 | 1,998 |
| 1974 | 939 | 150 | 150 | 366 | 738 | 59 | 97 | 792 | 1,540 | 337 | 1,012 | 2,026 |
| 1975 | 1,003 | 121 | 131 | 329 | 539 | 39 | 122 | 723 | 1,614 | 335 | 1,320 | 2,021 |
| 1976 | 866 | 89 | 96 | 248 | 928 | 45 | 71 | 884 | 1,560 | 428 | 1,516 | 1,846 |
| 1977 | 1,219 | 143 | 124 | 355 | 981 | 39 | 81 | 753 | 1,307 | 406 | 1,609 | 1,960 |
| 1978 | 893 | 126 | 93 | 257 | 770 | 38 | 119 | 862 | 1,715 | 517 | 1,996 | 2,044 |
| 1979 | 995 | 112 | 150 | 489 | 903 | 42 | 137 | 870 | 1,830 | 501 | 2,066 | 1,909 |
| 1980 | 966 | 105 | 173 | 405 | 1,007 | 46 | 109 | 854 | 1,784 | 431 | 1,727 | 2,150 |
| 1981 | 686 | 91 | 131 | 518 | 842 | 62 | 56 | 880 | 1,878 | 532 | 2,105 | 2,150 |
| 1982 | 650 | 118 | 118 | 425 | 684 | 71 | 56 | 899 | 2,023 | 568 | 2,149 | 1,552 |
| 1983 | 586 | 73 | 146 | 512 | 1,036 | 78 | 28 | 864 | 1,814 | 595 | 2,187 | 1,555 |
| 1984 | 988 | 74 | 163 | 721 | 909 | 59 | 28 | 864 | 1,715 | 590 | 2,463 | 1,386 |
| 1985 | 1,165 | 85 | 170 | 772 | 792 | 76 | 60 | 763 | 1,742 | 499 | 1,910 | 1,367 |
| 1986 | 1,626 | 68 | 124 | 721 | 727 | 82 | 73 | 788 | 1,521 | 600 | 2,281 | 1,335 |
| 1987 | 1,874 | 48 | 128 | 617 | 928 | 74 | 92 | 860 | 1,473 | 704 | 2,243 | 1,260 |
| 1988 | 1,734 | 82 | 157 | 661 | 882 | 63 | 97 | 908 | 1,777 | 707 | 2,520 | 1,282 |

**C2** **SOUTH AMERICA: Output of Main Arable Crops** (in thousands of metric tons)

| | Ecuador | | | | | Guyana | Paraguay | | |
|------|-------|--------|-------|------|------|--------|-------|-------|---------|
| | Wheat | Barley | Maize | Rice | P | Rice | Wheat | Maize | Cassava |
| 1945 | ... | ... | ... | 158 | ... | 108 | 2 | ... | ... |
| 1946 | ... | 35 | ... | 157 | 122 | 109 | 1 | 168 | 810 |
| 1947 | 25 | ... | ... | 173 | 90 | 95 | 2 | 106 | 739 |
| 1948 | 28 | 62 | 69 | 135 | 58 | 109 | 2 | 105 | 1,239 |
| 1949 | 28 | 69 | 64 | 169 | 59 | 63 | 1 | 84 | ... |
| 1950 | 20 | 42 | 68 | 94 | 82 | 89 | ... | ... | ... |
| 1951 | 26 | ... | 79 | 95 | 47 | 111 | 1 | 100 | 991 |
| 1952 | 26 | 77 | 99 | 116 | 82 | 125 | 7 | 95 | 900 |
| 1953 | 26 | 83 | 80 | 160 | 127 | 134 | 1 | 107 | ... |
| 1954 | 34 | 93 | 145 | 113 | ... | 152 | 2 | 116 | 940 |
| 1955 | 42 | 83 | ... | 153 | 268 | 151 | 3 | 100 | ... |
| 1956 | 40 | 85 | 147 | 131 | ... | 133 | ... | ... | ... |
| 1957 | 42 | 82 | 138 | 120 | 281 | 97 | 12 | 120 | |
| 1958 | 39 | 92 | 155 | 176 | 246 | 170 | 14 | 130 | 995 |
| 1959 | 47 | 92 | 157 | 175 | 260 | 176 | 10 | 125 | 1,005 |
| 1960 | 58 | 78 | 160 | 186 | 302 | 214 | 9 | 143 | 979 |
| 1961 | 78 | 70 | 153 | 163 | 271 | 238 | 7 | 110 | 994 |
| 1962 | 67 | 106 | 138 | 187 | 305 | 242 | 7 | 124 | 997 |
| 1963 | 53 | 130 | 192 | 191 | 275 | 174 | 9 | 120 | 1,000 |
| 1964 | 47 | 81 | 129 | 167 | 324 | 264 | 7 | 206 | 1,449 |
| 1965 | 61 | 93 | 191 | 157 | 396 | 279 | 7 | 210 | 1,512 |
| 1966 | 64 | 78 | 177 | 185 | 352 | 249 | 9 | 166 | 1,437 |
| 1967 | 73 | 82 | 231 | 173 | 403 | 198 | 25 | 225 | 1,460 |
| 1968 | 80 | 62 | 177 | 288 | 367 | 210 | 32 | 180 | 1,504 |
| 1969 | 94 | 62 | 210 | 233 | 457 | 191 | 31 | 153 | 1,549 |
| 1970 | 81 | 110 | 256 | 232 | 542 | 210 | 33 | 259 | 1,580 |
| 1971 | 63 | 102 | 250 | 243 | 681 | 185 | 46 | 230 | 1,690 |
| 1972 | 51 | 106 | 258 | 189 | 473 | 159 | 17 | 210 | 1,197 |
| 1973 | 45 | 79 | 246 | 235 | 539 | 169 | 13 | 273 | 1,108 |
| 1974 | 55 | 56 | 256 | 266 | 503 | 281 | 35 | 282 | 1,109 |
| 1975 | 65 | 63 | 273 | 364 | 499 | 292 | 18 | 301 | 1,428 |
| 1976 | 65 | 63 | 275 | 356 | 499 | 173 | 29 | 351 | 1,573 |
| 1977 | 40 | 41 | 218 | 328 | 417 | 355 | 28 | 401 | 1,719 |
| 1978 | 29 | 22 | 176 | 225 | 343 | 305 | 38 | 335 | 1,838 |
| 1979 | 31 | 21 | 218 | 318 | 255 | 240 | 58 | 550 | 1,888 |
| 1980 | 31 | 24 | 242 | 381 | 323 | 256 | 62 | 585 | 2,031 |
| 1981 | 41 | 27 | 281 | 434 | 392 | 251 | 84 | 521 | 2,012 |
| 1982 | 39 | 35 | 324 | 384 | 416 | 276 | 99 | 619 | 2,511 |
| 1983 | 27 | 30 | 229 | 270 | 314 | 224 | 139 | 730 | 2,610 |
| 1984 | 25 | 25 | 326 | 437 | 390 | 283 | 140 | 730 | 2,775 |
| 1985 | 18 | 27 | 371 | 372 | 423 | 236 | 187 | 801 | 2,861 |
| 1986 | 33 | 44 | 415 | 576 | 389 | 259 | 240 | 469 | 2,875 |
| 1987 | 31 | 43 | 397 | 781 | 354 | 226 | 318 | 1,001 | 3,468 |
| 1988 | 34 | 50 | 408 | 955 | 338 | 200 | 432 | 1,200 | 3,891 |

**C2    SOUTH AMERICA: Output of Main Arable Crops** (in thousands of metric tons)

| | | | | Peru | | | |
|---|---|---|---|---|---|---|---|
| | Wheat | Barley | Maize | Rice | P | SP | Cassava |
| 1945 | 87 | ... | ... | 153 | 599 | ... | – ... |
| 1946 | 90 | ... | 544 | 192 | 657 | ... | ... |
| 1947 | 127 | 208 | 612 | 179 | 1,265 | ... | 200 |
| 1948 | 137 | 190 | 621 | 207 | 1,077 | ... | 277 |
| 1949 | 129 | 213 | | 162 | 1,115 | ... | 300 |
| 1950 | 144 | 218 | ... | 213 | 1,364 | ... | 313 |
| 1951 | 157 | 202 | 436 | 207 | 1,325 | ... | 330 |
| 1952 | 162 | 217 | 458 | 265 | 1,315 | 85 | 218 |
| 1953 | 169 | 226 | 418 | 277 | 1,385 | 92 | 215 |
| 1954 | 163 | 226 | 304 | 251 | 1,453 | 73 | 201 |
| 1955 | 152 | 208 | 304 | 249 | 1,309 | 83 | 228 |
| 1956 | 123 | 159 | 265 | 243 | 1,013 | 77 | 278 |
| 1957 | 138 | 166 | 294 | 246 | 1,046 | 86 | 275 |
| 1958 | 127 | 202 | 333 | 285 | 1,222 | 108 | 298 |
| 1959 | 161 | 195 | 339 | 249 | 1,217 | 152 | 319 |
| 1960 | 154 | 217 | 340 | 358 | 1,145 | 129 | 350 |
| 1961 | 154 | 198 | 451 | 332 | 1,492 | 145 | 407 |
| 1962 | 153 | 185 | 460 | 374 | 1,416 | 146 | 390 |
| 1963 | 153 | 182 | 480 | 270 | 1,427 | 159 | 438 |
| 1964 | 143 | 183 | 503 | 351 | 1,531 | 166 | 497 |
| 1965 | 147 | 179 | 557 | 291 | 1,568 | 124 | 449 |
| 1966 | 135 | 154 | 574 | 374 | 1,499 | 133 | 487 |
| 1967 | 141 | 172 | 584 | 461 | 1,712 | 150 | 507 |
| 1968 | 113 | 146 | 526 | 286 | 1,592 | 145 | 399 |
| 1969 | 127 | 164 | 585 | 444 | 1,856 | 156 | 450 |
| 1970 | 125 | 170 | 615 | 587 | 1,929 | 178 | 498 |
| 1971 | 122 | 159 | 615 | 591 | 1,968 | 168 | 482 |
| 1972 | 120 | 163 | 628 | 482 | 1,713 | 154 | 446 |
| 1973 | 123 | 155 | 599 | 483 | 1,713 | 156 | 460 |
| 1974 | 127 | 151 | 606 | 494 | 1,722 | 146 | 469 |
| 1975 | 126 | 149 | 634 | 537 | 1,640 | 162 | 400 |
| 1976 | 127 | 150 | 726 | 570 | 1,667 | 163 | 402 |
| 1977 | 115 | 146 | 734 | 594 | 1,616 | 158 | 414 |
| 1978 | 104 | 130 | 590 | 468 | 1,695 | 153 | 410 |
| 1979 | 102 | 131 | 621 | 560 | 1,695 | 149 | 403 |
| 1980 | 77 | 116 | 453 | 420 | 1,380 | 142 | 555 |
| 1981 | 119 | 127 | 587 | 712 | 1,705 | 155 | 486 |
| 1982 | 101 | 127 | 631 | 775 | 1,800 | 151 | 513 |
| 1983 | 76 | 87 | 585 | 798 | 1,200 | 157 | 510 |
| 1984 | 84 | 108 | 776 | 1,156 | 1,463 | 166 | 535 |
| 1985 | 92 | 109 | 702 | 878 | 1,557 | 100 | 341 |
| 1986 | 121 | 116 | 876 | 726 | 1,658 | 143 | 344 |
| 1987 | 131 | 114 | 909 | 1,169 | 1,707 | 123 | 466 |
| 1988 | 153 | 134 | 908 | 1,129 | 2,108 | 156 | 392 |

**C2**  **SOUTH AMERICA: Output of Main Arable Crops** (in thousands of metric tons)

| | Surinam* | Uruguay | | | | | | | Venezuela | | | |
|---|---|---|---|---|---|---|---|---|---|---|---|---|
| | Rice | Wheat | Barley | Oats | Maize | Rice | Sorghum | P | Maize | Rice | P | Cassava |
| 1940 | 32 | 192 | 10 | 19 | 119 | 11 | - - | 30 | ... | ... | ... | ... |
| 1941 | 51 | 372 | 14 | 36 | 117 | 20 | - - | 28 | ... | 6 | ... | ... |
| 1942 | 41 | 337 | 13 | 39 | 47 | 15 | - - | 35 | ... | 15 | ... | ... |
| 1943 | 33 | 301 | 24 | 78 | 232 | 17 | - - | 30 | ... | 18 | ... | ... |
| 1944 | 34 | 181 | 15 | 31 | 66 | 21 | - - | 58 | 315 | 26 | 7.0 | ... |
| 1945 | 37 | 217 | 16 | 38 | 140 | 31 | - - | 34 | ... | 19 | ... | ... |
| 1946 | 51 | 182 | 11 | 20 | 82 | 35 | - - | 30 | ... | 15 | ... | ... |
| 1947 | 39 | 424 | 11 | 38 | 115 | 37 | - - | 30 | 300 | 10 | 15 | ... |
| 1948 | 58 | 518 | 26 | 51 | 137 | 45 | - - | 38 | 300 | 10 | 17 | 74 |
| 1949 | 50 | 452 | 27 | 59 | 85 | 40 | - - | 31 | 323 | ... | 27 | 149 |
| 1950 | 50 | 435 | 25 | 34 | 89 | 37 | - - | 40 | 361 | 32 | 22 | ... |
| 1951 | 58 | 478 | 18 | 38 | 278 | 47 | - - | 88 | 313 | 36 | 32 | 188 |
| 1952 | 54 | 427 | 22 | 38 | 117 | 53 | - - | 51 | 343 | 49 | 24 | 209 |
| 1953 | 58 | 819 | 40 | 60 | 208 | 62 | - - | 57 | 355 | 57 | 34 | 253 |
| 1954 | 67 | 854 | 41 | 33 | 156 | 68 | - - | 83 | 326 | 98 | 36 | 194 |
| 1955 | 65 | 829 | 30 | 41 | 192 | 66 | ... | 74 | 317 | 75 | 45 | 157 |
| 1956 | 71 | 589 | 43 | 56 | 218 | 64 | ... | 60 | 350 | 50 | 65 | 204 |
| 1957 | 55 | 598 | 22 | 52 | 209 | 57 | ... | 68 | 340 | 22 | 106 | 190 |
| 1958 | 85 | 360 | 25 | 33 | 276 | 58 | ... | ... | 358 | 19 | 70 | 189 |
| 1959 | 79 | 183 | 29 | 21 | 133 | 49 | ... | 114 | 336 | 39 | 93 | 218 |
| 1960 | 81 | 420 | 49 | 62 | 78 | 53 | ... | 115 | 439 | 72 | 134 | 340 |
| 1961 | 72 | 372 | 28 | 64 | 224 | 61 | 15 | 88 | 420 | 81 | 74 | 300 |
| 1962 | 79 | 452 | 35 | 57 | 155 | 61 | 15 | 87 | 540 | 103 | 121 | 323 |
| 1963 | 75 | 237 | 18 | 56 | 206 | 77 | 16 | 115 | 430 | 131 | 111 | 342 |
| 1964 | 88 | 646 | 40 | 86 | 91 | 47 | 17 | 100 | 475 | 166 | 124 | 312 |
| 1965 | 101 | 620 | 28 | 97 | 63 | 90 | 16 | 125 | 521 | 200 | 136 | 301 |
| 1966 | 112 | 329 | 31 | 72 | 182 | 84 | 15 | 142 | 557 | 195 | 126 | 320 |
| 1967 | 120 | 144 | 14 | 33 | 117 | 110 | 28 | 105 | 633 | 223 | 133 | 316 |
| 1968 | 116 | 470 | 48 | 73 | 69 | 104 | 30 | 52 | 661 | 245 | 143 | 341 |
| 1969 | 113 | 403 | 41 | 60 | 129 | 134 | 51 | 138 | 670 | 244 | 124 | 310 |
| 1970 | 145 | 388 | 45 | 78 | 139 | 139 | 35 | 118 | 710 | 226 | 125 | 317 |
| 1971 | 145 | 302 | 32 | 60 | 166 | 122 | 72 | 150 | 713 | 153 | 115 | 323 |
| 1972 | 123 | 187 | 29 | 59 | 141 | 128 | 57 | 106 | 506 | 165 | 109 | 318 |
| 1973 | 164 | 297 | 31 | 55 | 229 | 137 | 225 | 133 | 454 | 302 | 124 | 272 |
| 1974 | 162 | 526 | 28 | 47 | 225 | 158 | 193 | 129 | 554 | 297 | 152 | 293 |
| 1975 | 175 | 456 | 34 | 61 | 157 | 186 | 77 | 121 | 653 | 363 | 152 | 317 |
| 1976 | 173 | 505 | 47 | 48 | 210 | 217 | 118 | 166 | 417 | 206 | 132 | 353 |
| 1977 | 203 | 173 | 38 | 17 | 121 | 228 | 162 | 120 | 774 | 496 | 179 | 322 |
| 1978 | 224 | 174 | 57 | 23 | 172 | 226 | 184 | 102 | 591 | 502 | 171 | 304 |
| 1979 | 236 | 435 | 71 | 59 | 71 | 248 | 54 | 135 | 612 | 614 | 191 | 350 |
| 1980 | 258 | 307 | 55 | 32 | 126 | 288 | 84 | 99 | 575 | 619 | 199 | 325 |
| 1981 | 281 | 388 | 85 | 21 | 181 | 330 | 192 | 177 | 452 | 681 | 171 | 327 |
| 1982 | 301 | 363 | 45 | 27 | 97 | 419 | 123 | 149 | 501 | 609 | 217 | 342 |
| 1983 | 268 | 419 | 81 | 50 | 104 | 323 | 107 | 109 | 488 | 449 | 225 | 325 |
| 1984 | 302 | 349 | 113 | 48 | 112 | 340 | 119 | 144 | 547 | 408 | 245 | 331 |
| 1985 | 299 | 246 | 80 | 20 | 108 | 423 | 152 | 163 | 868 | 472 | 191 | 310 |
| 1986 | 300 | 232 | 77 | 28 | 92 | 394 | 105 | 111 | 1,173 | 322 | 196 | 322 |
| 1987 | 272 | 308 | 124 | 58 | 104 | 335 | 90 | 126 | 1,267 | 373 | 216 | 318 |
| 1988 | 265 | 414 | 204 | 64 | 118 | 381 | 121 | 143 | 1,281 | 383 | 221 | 328 |

**C2    Output of Main Arable Crops** (in thousands of metric tons)


NOTES

1.   SOURCES: As for table C1, with Venezulan data to 1924 and in 1937 from Rafael Cartay, *Historia Economica de Venezuela 1830–1890* (Valencia, 1988).
2.   Where statistics were given in units of volume in the source, they have been converted to units of weight by applying the ratios used by the FAO.
3.   For some countries and crops data may be reported for either of the calendar years in which the crop-year lies, and practice in this respect has not always been consistent. So far as possible, the series shown there *are* consistent for each country, and the year of harvest has been preferred if a choice is available.


FOOTNOTES

[1] Lower Canada only. Figures under the buckwheat heading are of all grains not separately specified.
[2] Upper Canada only.
[3] Upper & Lower Canada, New Brunswick, and Nova Scotia.
[4] All grains not separately specified.
[5] From 1901 to 1907 (1st line) Alberta, Manitoba, New Brunswick, Ontario, and Saskatchewan only.
[6] From 1901 to 1908 (1st line) Manitoba, New Brunswick, and Ontario only.
[7] Corn harvested for grain only prior to 1866 and from 1961.
[8] Later figures are from national sources. No explanation of the discrepancy is available.
[9] Rio Grande do Sul and São Paulo only.

**C3** **NORTH AMERICA: OUTPUT OF SUGAR** (in thousands of metric tons)

Key:  SB = Sugar Beet Output

## 1750–1784

| | Barbados[1] | Guadeloupe[1] | Jamaica[1] | Martinique[1] |
|---|---|---|---|---|
| 1750 | 7 | ... | 21 | 20 |
| 1751 | 4 | ... | 20 | ... |
| 1752 | 7 | ... | 19 | 18 |
| 1753 | 9 | ... | 22 | 21 |
| 1754 | 6 | ... | 24 | ... |
| 1755 | 9 | ... | 22 | ... |
| 1756 | 7 | ... | 22 | ... |
| 1757 | 7 | ... | 25 | ... |
| 1758 | 7 | ... | 24 | ... |
| 1759 | 6 | ... | 36 | ... |
| 1760 | 8 | ... | 40 | ... |
| 1761 | 9 | ... | 29 | ... |
| 1762 | 10 | ... | 25 | ... |
| 1763 | 9 | ... | 34 | ... |
| 1764 | 10 | ... | 33 | ... |
| 1765 | 10 | ... | 27 | 11 |
| 1766 | 9 | ... | 33 | 9 |
| 1767 | 6 | 8 | 36 | 7 |
| 1768 | 8 | ... | 41 | 8 |
| 1769 | 8 | ... | 37 | 9 |
| 1770 | 9 | ... | 37 | 12 |
| 1771 | 5 | ... | 35 | 10 |
| 1772 | 7 | ... | 42 | 10 |
| 1773 | 6 | ... | 52 | 11 |
| 1774 | 7 | ... | 46 | 13 |
| 1775 | 4 | ... | 48 | 12 |
| 1776 | 6 | ... | 37 | 13 |
| 1777 | 4 | ... | 26 | 13 |
| 1778 | 2 | ... | 33 | ... |
| 1779 | 4 | ... | 41 | ... |
| 1780 | 3 | ... | 45 | ... |
| 1781 | ... | ... | ... | 4 |
| 1782 | ... | ... | ... | 9 |
| 1783 | ... | ... | ... | 11 |
| 1784 | ... | ... | ... | 11 |

## 1785–1829

| | Barbados[1] | Cuba[1] | Guadeloupe[1] | Jamaica[1] | Martinique[1] | Puerto Rico | Trinidad[1] |
|---|---|---|---|---|---|---|---|
| 1785 | ... | ... | ... | ... | ... | ... | ... |
| 1786 | ... | 13 | ... | ... | 12 | ... | ... |
| 1787 | ... | 12 | ... | ... | 12 | ... | ... |
| 1788 | ... | 14 | ... | 60 | 13 | ... | ... |
| 1789 | ... | 14 | ... | 60 | 5 | ... | ... |
| 1790 | ... | 16 | 9 | 56 | ... | ... | ... |
| 1791 | ... | 17 | ... | 61 | ... | ... | ... |
| 1792 | 9 | 19 | ... | 56 | ... | ... | ... |
| 1793 | ... | 18 | ... | 52 | ... | ... | ... |
| 1794 | ... | 21 | ... | 65 | ... | ... | ... |
| 1795 | ... | 14 | ... | 64 | ... | ... | ... |
| 1796 | ... | 24 | ... | 65 | ... | ... | ... |
| 1797 | ... | 24 | ... | 52 | ... | ... | ... |
| 1798 | ... | 27 | ... | 64 | ... | ... | ... |
| 1799 | ... | 34 | ... | 74 | ... | ... | 3 |
| 1800 | 6 | 29 | ... | 71 | ... | ... | 3 |
| 1801 | ... | 32 | ... | 92 | ... | ... | 6 |
| 1802 | ... | 42 | ... | 94 | ... | ... | 5 |
| 1803 | ... | 32 | ... | 77 | ... | ... | 5 |
| 1804 | ... | 39 | ... | 76 | ... | ... | 6 |
| 1805 | ... | 35 | ... | 101 | ... | ... | 10 |
| 1806 | ... | 32 | ... | 99 | ... | ... | 10 |
| 1807 | 8 | 37 | ... | 91 | ... | ... | 10 |
| 1808 | ... | 26 | ... | 79 | ... | ... | 9 |
| 1809 | 6 | 59 | ... | 77 | ... | ... | 8 |
| 1810 | 9 | 38 | ... | 75 | ... | ... | 7 |
| 1811 | ... | ... | ... | 89 | ... | ... | 6 |
| 1812 | ... | ... | ... | 63 | ... | ... | 7 |
| 1813 | ... | ... | ... | 68 | ... | ... | 7 |
| 1814 | 11 | ... | ... | 74 | ... | ... | 7 |
| 1815 | 10 | 44 | ... | 81 | ... | ... | 8 |
| 1816 | 15 | 41 | 5 | 71 | ... | ... | 7 |
| 1817 | 12 | 44 | 18 | 87 | ... | ... | 7 |
| 1818 | 13 | 42 | 21 | 84 | 16 | ... | 7 |
| 1819 | 14 | 39 | 19 | 82 | 18 | ... | 8 |
| 1820 | 9 | 44 | 22 | 90 | 21 | ... | 8 |
| 1821 | 11 | 48 | 23 | 85 | 22 | ... | 8 |
| 1822 | 8 | 53 | 23 | 72 | 20 | ... | 9 |
| 1823 | 16 | 61 | 24 | 72 | 21 | ... | 8 |
| 1824 | 12 | 50 | 31 | 74 | 20 | ... | 8 |
| 1825 | 13 | ... | 24 | 57 | 26 | ... | 9 |
| 1826 | 12 | ... | 34 | 76 | 28 | ... | 10 |
| 1827 | 10 | ... | 28 | 67 | 24 | ... | 12 |
| 1828 | 17 | ... | 36 | 69 | 33 | 9 | 13 |
| 1829 | 13 | 74 | 39 | 70 | 29 | 13 | 14 |

**C3   NORTH AMERICA: Output of Sugar** (in thousands of metric tons)

| | Barbados[1] | Cuba[1] | Guadeloupe[1] | Jamaica[1] | Martinique[1] | Puerto Rico | Trinidad[1] |
|---|---|---|---|---|---|---|---|
| 1830 | 17 | ... | 23 | 70 | 28 | 15 | 10 |
| 1831 | 16 | ... | 35 | 71 | 28 | 14 | 17 |
| 1832 | 14 | ... | 33 | 73 | 22 | 16 | 16 |
| 1833 | 20 | ... | 31 | 69 | 20 | 16 | 15 |
| 1834 | 20 | ... | 38 | 64 | 26 | 16 | 17 |
| 1835 | 18 | ... | 32 | 58 | 24 | 20 | 15 |
| 1836 | 19 | 168 | 35 | 53 | 22 | 23 | 16 |
| 1837 | 23 | ... | 25 | 46 | 20 | 21 | 15 |
| 1838 | 24 | 149 | 35 | 54 | 26 | 31 | 15 |
| 1839 | 20 | 132 | 37 | 40 | 29 | 31 | 14 |
| 1840 | 11 | 163 | 30 | 27 | 22 | 37 | 12 |
| 1841 | 13 | 165 | 29 | 28 | 25 | 38 | 14 |
| 1842 | 16 | ... | 35 | 41 | 28 | 42 | 15 |
| 1843 | 18 | ... | 27 | 34 | 25 | 32 | 16 |
| 1844 | 17 | ... | 35 | 28 | 33 | 37 | 14 |
| 1845 | 18 | ... | 34 | 38 | 30 | 42 | 18 |
| 1846 | 15 | ... | 26 | 29 | 26 | 40 | 18 |
| 1847 | 24 | ... | 38 | 38 | 31 | 47 | 20 |
| 1848 | 20 | ...[1] | 20 | 32 | 18 | 46 | 20 |
| 1849 | 25 | 227 | 18 | 32 | 20 | 46 | 22 |
| 1850 | 27 | 268 | 13 | 29 | 15 | 51 | 19 |
| 1851 | 30 | 256 | 20 | 32 | 23 | 54 | 22 |
| 1852 | 38 | 327 | 17 | 26 | 26 | 42 | 25 |
| 1853 | 29 | 380 | 17 | 22 | 22 | 50 | 24 |
| 1854 | 34 | 398 | 24 | 26 | 25 | 49 | 27 |
| 1855 | 30 | 354 | 22 | 23 | 21 | 46 | 21 |
| 1856 | 32 | 361 | 23 | 19 | 28 | 53 | 25 |
| 1857 | 30 | 391 | 22 | 21 | 26 | 39 | 22 |
| 1858 | 38 | 545 | 28 | 27 | 28 | 56 | 28 |
| 1859 | 30[1] | 454 | 28 | 23 | 30 | 40 | 27 |
| 1860 | 38 | 473 | 29 | 26 | 38 | 53 | 27 |
| 1861 | 44 | 533 | 17 | 27 | 32 | 59 | 27 |
| 1862 | 41 | 515 | 31 | 28 | 32 | 58 | 25 |
| 1863 | 38 | 584 | 30 | 26 | 30 | 53 | 31 |
| 1864 | 32 | 630 | 16 | 24 | 24 | 42 | 34 |
| 1865 | 42 | 622 | ... | 25 | 30 | 55 | 28 |
| 1866 | 51 | 607 | 27 | 27 | 35 | 51 | 41 |
| 1867 | 47 | 761 | 28 | 25 | 29 | 55 | 43 |
| 1868 | 52 | 738 | ... | 29 | 38 | 56 | 42 |
| 1869 | 30 | 738 | ... | 23 | 37 | 66 | 47 |

**C3    NORTH AMERICA: Output of Sugar** (in thousands of metric tons)

| | Barbados | Canada SB | Costa Rica | Cuba | Dominican Republic | El Salvador | Guadeloupe[1] | Guatemala |
|---|---|---|---|---|---|---|---|---|
| 1870 | 35 | ... | ... | 556 | ... | — | 40 | ... |
| 1871 | 48 | ... | ... | 701 | ... | — | 41 | ... |
| 1872 | 35 | ... | ... | 787 | ... | — | 40 | ... |
| 1873 | 33 | ... | ... | 692 | ... | — | 38 | ... |
| 1874 | 42 | ... | ... | 730 | ... | — | 41 | ... |
| 1875 | 58 | ... | ... | 599 | ... | — | 53 | ... |
| 1876 | 33 | ... | ... | 528 | ... | — | 43 | ... |
| 1877 | 44 | ... | ... | 542 | ... | — | 43 | ... |
| 1878 | 39 | ... | ... | 681 | ... | — | 56 | ... |
| 1879 | 51 | ... | ... | 539 | ... | — | 54 | ... |
| | | | | | | | —[1] | |
| 1880 | 48 | ... | ... | 502 | ... | — | 47 | ... |
| 1881 | 46 | ... | ... | 605 | ... | — | 37 | ... |
| 1882 | 49 | ... | ... | 468 | ... | — | 58 | ... |
| 1883 | 47 | ... | ... | 563 | ... | — | 60 | ... |
| 1884 | 55 | ... | ... | 662 | ... | — | 57 | ... |
| 1885 | 54 | ... | ... | 743 | ... | — | 45 | ... |
| 1886 | 41 | ... | ... | 657 | ... | — | 58 | ... |
| 1887 | 61 | ... | ... | 667 | ... | — | 49 | ... |
| 1888 | 65 | ... | ... | 569 | ... | — | ... | ... |
| 1889 | 58 | ... | ... | 643 | ... | — | 67 | ... |
| 1890 | 76 | ... | ... | 829 | ... | — | 40 | ... |
| 1891 | 45 | ... | ... | 993 | ... | — | 30 | ... |
| 1892 | 53 | ... | ... | 829 | ... | — | 46 | ... |
| 1893 | 60 | ... | ... | 1,071 | ... | — | 47 | ... |
| 1894 | 59 | ... | ... | 1,020 | ... | 1 | 44 | |
| 1895 | 34 | ... | ... | 229 | ... | 1 | 42 | ... |
| 1896 | 46 | ... | ... | 215 | ... | 3 | 51 | ... |
| 1897 | 52 | ... | ... | 310 | ... | 4 | 45 | ... |
| 1898 | 48 | ... | ... | 341 | ... | 4 | 45 | ... |
| 1899 | 47 | ... | ... | 305 | ... | 5 | 47 | |
| 1900 | 50 | ... | ... | 646 | ... | 5 | 28 | ... |
| 1901 | 64 | ... | ... | 864 | ... | 6 | 41 | 10 |
| 1902 | 59 | ... | ... | 1,015 | ... | 7 | 39 | 9 |
| 1903 | 65 | ... | ... | 1,057 | ... | 6 | 37 | 8 |
| 1904 | 58 | ... | ... | 1,182 | 48 | 6 | 29 | 8 |
| 1905 | 53 | ... | ... | 1,198 | 55 | 6 | 44 | 7 |
| 1906 | 57 | ... | ... | 1,451 | 56 | 6 | 41 | 7 |
| 1907 | 39 | ... | ... | 977 | 64 | 5 | 37 | 8 |
| 1908 | 37 | ... | ... | 1,538 | 77 | 6 | 26 | 7 |
| 1909 | 46 | 99 | 3 | 1,833 | 95 | 6 | 43 | 7 |

**C3     NORTH AMERICA: Output of Sugar** (in thousands of metric tons)

| | Jamaica[1] | Martinique[1] | Mexico | Nicaragua | Puerto Rico | Trinidad & Tobago[12] | U.S.A[1] | |
|---|---|---|---|---|---|---|---|---|
| | | | | | | | SB | Sugar from cane |
| 1870 | 25 | 38 | ... | — | 89 | 42 | ... | ... |
| 1871 | 30 | 42 | ... | — | 94 | 54 | ... | ... |
| 1872 | 29 | 30 | ... | — | 81 | 47 | ... | ... |
| 1873 | 24 | 38 | ... | — | 86 | 61 | ... | ... |
| 1874 | 23 | 43 | ... | — | 71 | 45 | ... | ... |
| 1875 | 23 | 51 | ... | — | 74 | 28 | ... | ... |
| 1876 | 24 | 39 | ... | — | 66 | 43 | ... | ... |
| 1877 | 22 | 41 | ... | — | 51 | 55 | ... | ... |
| 1878 | 21 | 44 | ... | — | 76 | 58 | ... | ... |
| 1879 | 26[1] | 47[1] | ... | — | 155 | 54[1] | ... | ... |
| 1880 | 28 | 39 | ... | — | 101 | 58 | ... | ... |
| 1881 | 18 | 42 | ... | — | 57 | 48 | ... | ... |
| 1882 | 33 | 48 | ... | — | 84 | 59 | ... | ... |
| 1883 | 31 | 47 | ... | — | 80 | 58 | ... | ... |
| 1884 | 30 | 49 | ... | — | 99 | 66 | ... | ... |
| 1885 | 25 | 39 | ... | — | 89 | 67 | ... | 146 |
| 1886 | 17 | 30 | ... | — | 64 | 50 | ... | 92 |
| 1887 | 23 | 40 | ... | — | 81 | 71 | ... | 180 |
| 1888 | 25 | 30 | ... | — | 62 | 63 | ... | 165 |
| 1889 | 16 | 36 | ... | — | 64 | 60 | ... | 146 |
| 1890 | 19 | 34 | ... | — | 58 | 60 | ... | 246 |
| 1891 | 24 | 32 | ... | — | 48 | 54 | ... | 183 |
| 1892 | 22 | 20 | 55 | — | 67 | 56 | ... | 248 |
| 1893 | 25 | 33 | 49 | 1 | 43 | 50 | ... | 303 |
| 1894 | 24 | 37 | 54 | 1 | 48 | 53 | ... | 361 |
| 1895 | 23 | 29 | 144 | 1 | 60 | 57 | ... | 271 |
| 1896 | 21 | 34 | 71 | 2 | 56 | 60 | ... | 321 |
| 1897 | 20 | 35 | 66 | 4 | 58 | 56 | ... | 353 |
| 1898 | 25 | 32 | 68 | 4 | 55 | 59[2] | ... | 283 |
| 1899 | 28 | 32 | 69 | 4 | 36 | 60 | ... | 162 |
| 1900 | 24 | 30 | 75 | 4 | 74 | 47 | ... | 314 |
| 1901 | 25 | 35 | 68 | 4 | 94 | 62 | ... | 366 |
| 1902 | 30 | 29 | 82 | 4 | 91 | 60 | ... | 375 |
| 1903 | 23 | 24 | 100 | 5 | 126 | 49 | ... | 260 |
| 1904 | 19 | 30 | 102 | 4 | 137 | 52 | ... | 314 |
| 1905 | 21 | 42 | 95 | 4 | 195 | 39 | ... | 383 |
| 1906 | 32 | 37 | 93 | 4 | 188 | 64 | ... | 262 |
| 1907 | 29 | 36 | 115 | 4 | 209 | 51 | ... | 387 |
| 1908 | 24 | 38 | 99 | 4 | 252 | 50 | ... | 404 |
| 1909 | 19 | 40 | 125 | 4 | 315 | 54 | 3,846 | 326[1] |
| | | | | | | | | 307 |

**C3   NORTH AMERICA: Output of Sugar** (in thousands of metric tons)

| | Barbados | Canada | Costa Rica | Cuba | Dominican Republic | El Salvador | Guadeloupe | Guatemala | Haiti | Honduras |
|---|---|---|---|---|---|---|---|---|---|---|
| | | SB | | | | | | | | |
| 1910 | 32 | 78 | 3 | 1,873 | 88 | 7 | 38 | 7 | ... | ... |
| 1911 | 34 | 171 | 3 | 1,926 | 91 | 7 | 39 | 8 | ... | ... |
| 1912 | 15 | 159 | 3 | 2,468 | 84 | 11 | 27 | 11 | ... | ... |
| 1913 | 35 | 182 | 3 | 2,639 | 116 | 5 | 40 | 11 | ... | ... |
| 1914 | 35 | 134 | 5 | 2,650 | 118 | 9 | 34 | 13 | ... | ... |
| 1915 | 61 | 99 | 6 | 3,082 | 137 | 12 | 34 | 16 | ... | ... |
| 1916 | 58 | 128 | 5 | 3,103 | 132 | 12 | 31 | 15 | ... | ... |
| 1917 | 39 | 64 | 4 | 3,528 | 126 | 9 | 27 | 23 | ... | ... |
| 1918 | 57 | 107 | 5 | 4,073 | 168 | 17 | 19 | 13 | 5 | ... |
| 1919 | 43 | 163 | 5 | 3,794 | 179 | 14 | 24 | 15 | 5 | ... |
| 1920 | 35 | 218 | 5 | 3,996 | 168 | 18 | 27 | 10 | 5 | ... |
| 1921 | 32 | 374 | 5 | 4,097 | 187 | 19 | 21 | 25 | 12 | ... |
| 1922 | 58 | 243 | 5 | 3,705 | 187 | 20 | 25 | 25 | 10 | ... |
| 1923 | 50 | 172 | ... | 4,177 | 216 | 19 | 28 | 13 | 6 | ... |
| 1924 | 56 | 196 | ... | 5,273 | 316 | 19 | 39 | 26 | 7 | ... |
| 1925 | 55 | 303 | ... | 5,011 | 360 | 19 | 35 | 17 | 11 | 2 |
| 1926 | 62 | 416 | 28 | 4,581 | 308 | 18 | 36 | 25 | 13 | 10 |
| 1927 | 72 | 461 | 32 | 4,107 | 353 | 17 | 33 | 39 | 13 | 21 |
| 1928 | 72 | 336 | 50 | 5,239 | 360 | 16 | 23 | 56 | 13 | 24 |
| 1929 | 57 | 379 | ... | 4,746 | 366 | 15 | 27 | 57 | 19 | 18 |
| 1930 | 43 | 332 | ... | 3,172 | 358 | 12 | 19 | 41 | 19 | 15 |
| 1931 | 84 | 424 | ... | 2,490 | 405 | ... | 37 | 36 | 21 | 12 |
| 1932 | 98 | 396 | ... | 1,935 | 341 | 22 | 46 | 31 | 25 | 8 |
| 1933 | 84 | 459 | ... | 2,210 | 362 | 20 | 42 | 30 | 23 | 5 |
| 1934 | 47 | 401 | ... | 2,460 | 402 | 19 | 30 | 33 | 33 | 1 |
| 1935 | 107 | 375 | ... | 2,477 | 426 | 27 | 40 | 35 | 38 | — |
| 1936 | 110 | 416 | ... | 2,883 | 458 | 30 | 47 | 33 | 37 | — |
| 1937 | 91 | 504 | ... | 2,887 | 454 | 32 | 59 | 35 | 41 | — |
| 1938 | 138 | 383 | ... | 2,888 | 428 | 29 | 58 | 35 | 41 | — |
| 1939 | 71 | 452 | 28 | 2,698 | 431 | 31 | 60 | 35 | 40 | — |
| 1940 | 76 | 532 | 35 | 2,336 | 456 | 41 | 61 | 41 | 32 | - - |
| 1941 | 91 | 748 | 32 | 3,247 | 400 | 46 | 62 | 44 | 35 | - - |
| 1942 | 135 | 646 | 32 | 2,760 | 483 | 47 | 70 | 43 | 44 | 1 |
| 1943 | 86 | 650 | 17 | 4,051 | 428 | 48 | 47 | 44 | 58 | 1 |
| 1944 | 101 | 430 | ... | 3,354 | 509 | 46 | 29 | 40 | 46 | 1 |
| 1945 | 110 | 513 | ... | 3,728 | 369 | ...[3] | 28 | ... | ... | 1 |
| 1946 | 132 | 562 | 8 | 4,061 | 463 | 22 | 28 | 58 | 40 | 1 |
| 1947 | 123 | 668 | 15 | 5,850 | 464 | 27 | 35 | 62 | 45 | 1 |
| 1948 | 79 | 550 | 21 | 6,057 | 428 | 27 | 28 | 58 | 41 | 1 |
| 1949 | 155 | 571 | 25 | 5,228 | 477 | 24 | 43 | 64 | 43 | 2 |

*Agriculture*

**C3**   **NORTH AMERICA: Output of Sugar** (in thousands of metric tons)

| | Jamaica | Martinique | Mexico | Nicaragua | Panama | Puerto Rico | Trinidad & Tobago | U.S.A. | | |
|---|---|---|---|---|---|---|---|---|---|---|
| | | | | | | | | | Sugar | |
| | | | | | | | | SB | from beet | from cane |
| 1910 | 29 | 36 | 122 | 3 | — | 317 | 53 | 3,754 | ... | 328 |
| 1911 | 29 | 40 | 136 | 3 | — | 337 | 48 | 4,592 | ... | 334 |
| 1912 | 18 | 40 | 146 | 2 | — | 361 | 42 | 5,124 | ... | 151 |
| 1913 | 13 | 39 | 157 | 4 | — | 319 | 43 | 5,340 | ... | 279 |
| 1914 | 22 | 39 | 145 | 5 | — | 314 | 56 | 5,067 | ... | 229 |
| 1915 | 19 | 34 | 104 | 2 | — | 439 | 60 | 5,907 | ... | 128 |
| 1916 | 32 | 21 | 102 | 3 | — | 456 | 65 | 5,650 | ... | 288 |
| 1917 | 37 | 21 | 103 | 3 | — | 412 | 72 | 5,425 | ... | 228 |
| 1918 | 36 | 8 | 108 | 3 | — | 368 | 46 | 5,397 | ... | 263 |
| 1919 | 39 | 17 | 115 | 4 | — | 444 | 49 | 5,825 | ... | 113 |
| 1920 | 33 | 27 | 118 | 4 | — | 446 | 59 | 7,746 | ... | 163 |
| 1921 | 23 | 39 | 111 | 4 | 3 | 370 | 56 | 7,060 | ... | 303 |
| 1922 | 40 | 26 | 128 | 4 | 4 | 269 | 48 | 4,702 | ... | 274 |
| 1923 | 35 | 33 | 137 | 5 | 6 | 369 | 42 | 6,356 | ... | 152 |
| 1924 | 49 | 48 | 165 | 5 | 5 | 600 | 53 | 6,811 | ... | 82 |
| 1925 | 57 | 45 | 163 | 5 | 6 | 547 | 71 | 6,696 | ... | 129 |
| 1926 | 63 | 40 | 192 | 5 | 4 | 571 | 75 | 6,553 | ... | 44 |
| 1927 | 54 | 45 | 184 | 6 | 3 | 682 | 53 | 7,033 | ... | 65 |
| 1928 | 59 | 38 | 167 | 6 | 4 | 532 | 83 | 6,442 | 1,030 | 123 |
| 1929 | 68 | 38 | 181 | 6 | 4 | 786 | 91 | 6,636 | 988 | 198 |
| 1930 | 51 | 40 | 216 | 6 | 4 | 711 | 81 | 8,345 | 1,173 | 195 |
| 1931 | 59 | 43 | 263 | 7 | 4 | 900 | 100 | 7,169 | 1,122 | 167 |
| 1932 | 56 | 51 | 229 | 7 | 4 | 757 | 99 | 8,228 | 1,317 | 240 |
| 1933 | 74 | 51 | 187 | 7 | 4 | 1,010 | 123 | 10,006 | 1,594 | 227 |
| 1934 | 78 | 47 | 190 | 7 | 4 | 708 | 107 | 6,821 | 1,126 | 238 |
| 1935 | 93 | 50 | 268 | 8 | 4 | 840 | 120 | 7,174 | 1,150 | 347 |
| 1936 | 108 | 51 | 305 | 8 | 3 | 904 | 157 | 8,190 | 1,266 | 397 |
| 1937 | 120 | 52 | 279 | 8 | 5 | 977 | 157 | 7,946 | 1,250 | 416 |
| 1938 | 120 | 65 | 307 | 8 | 5 | 773 | 136 | 10,430 | 1,636 | 530 |
| 1939 | 101 | 60 | 330 | 8 | 4 | 924 | 131 | 9,780 | 1,595 | 459 |
| 1940 | 159 | 64 | 294 | 9 | 4 | 845 | 94 | 11,062 | 1,721 | 301 |
| 1941 | 158 | 49 | 330 | 11 | 4 | 1,041 | 134 | 9,382 | 1,441 | 377 |
| 1942 | 168 | 21 | 420 | 14 | 4 | 943 | 106 | 10,600 | 1,566 | 415 |
| 1943 | 154 | 3 | 412 | 14 | 5 | 656 | 72 | 5,939 | 905 | 451 |
| 1944 | 155 | 8 | 390 | 17 | 6 | 874 | 76 | 6,094 | 958 | 396 |
| 1945 | 167 | 35 | 373 | 12 | 5 | 825 | 78 | 7,816 | 1,159 | 431 |
| 1946 | 181 | 16 | 376 | 17 | 7 | 987 | 111 | 9,600 | 1,382 | 386 |
| 1947 | 173 | 25 | 490 | 16 | 9 | 1,005 | 112 | 11,343 | 1,665 | 342 |
| 1948 | 196 | 23 | 612 | 18 | 11 | 1,158 | 118 | 8,549 | 1,243 | 433 |
| 1949 | 242 | 23 | 645 | 19 | 11 | 1,178 | 162 | 9,250 | 1,424 | 473 |

**C3    NORTH AMERICA: Output of Sugar** (in thousands of metric tons)

| | Barbados | Canada SB | Costa Rica | Cuba | Dominican Republic | El Salvador | Guadeloupe | Guatemala | Haiti | Honduras |
|---|---|---|---|---|---|---|---|---|---|---|
| 1950 | 159 | 779 | 21 | 5,558 | 474 | 24 | 65 | 71 | 50 | 3 |
| 1951 | 191 | 1,012 | 21 | 5,759 | 533 | 28 | 75 | 52 | 58 | 5 |
| 1952 | 171 | 875 | 30₄ 60 | 7,225 | 577 | 27₃ 36 | 96 | 58 | 58 | 6₄ 27 |
| 1953 | 163 | 928 | 61 | 5,159 | 602 | 36 | 87 | 82 | 55 | 30 |
| 1954 | 182 | 816 | 64 | 4,890 | 655 | 42 | 104 | 88 | 46 | 31 |
| 1955 | 174 | 911 | 64 | 4,528 | 626 | 59 | 117 | 98 | 53 | 26 |
| 1956 | 154 | 890 | 48 | 4,740 | 754 | 59 | 130 | 109 | 58 | 27 |
| 1957 | 208 | 810 | 65 | 5,673 | 806 | 73 | 118 | 135 | 57 | 30 |
| 1958 | 155 | 956 | 66 | 5,784 | 808 | 70 | 117 | 142 | 46 | 32 |
| 1959 | 187 | 1,202 | 78 | 5,964 | 809 | 74 | 142 | 129 | 49 | 32 |
| 1960 | 156 | 1,124 | 84 | 5,862 | 1,112 | 80 | 152 | 141 | 60 | 36 |
| 1961 | 162 | 997 | 102 | 6,767 | 873 | 71 | 168 | 127 | 73 | ... |
| 1962 | 161 | 1,003 | 104 | 4,815 | 865 | 82 | 170 | 157 | 70 | 41 |
| 1963 | 194 | 1,003 | 123 | 3,821 | 806 | 88 | 167 | 167 | 69 | 48 |
| 1964 | 164 | 1,166 | 177 | 4,398 | 825 | 88 | 167 | 161 | 61 | 48 |
| 1965 | 199 | 1,177 | 142 | 6,051 | 580 | 135 | 190 | 155 | 65 | 51 |
| 1966 | 175 | 1,036 | 170 | 4,455 | 691 | 142 | 167 | 187 | 59 | 59 |
| 1967 | 204 | 1,057 | 177 | 6,236 | 819 | 148 | 137 | 225 | 61 | 68 |
| 1968 | 162 | 992 | 158 | 5,315 | 668 | 163 | 141 | 200 | 63 | 86 |
| 1969 | 142 | 870 | 161 | 4,724 | 864 | 138 | 162 | 222 | 59 | 98 |
| 1970 | 157 | 978 | 153 | 8,538 | 1,015 | 122 | 160 | 171 | 64 | 81 |
| 1971 | 137 | 1,103 | 157 | 5,950 | 1,131 | 158 | 151 | 204 | 69 | 92 |
| 1972 | 113 | 970 | 176 | 4,688 | 1,201 | 187 | 82 | 239 | 70 | 71 |
| 1973 | 118 | 902 | 198 | 5,350 | 1,153 | 190 | 121 | 271 | 66 | 97 |
| 1974 | 113 | 753 | 219 | 6,044 | 1,230 | 232 | 96 | 314 | 69 | 155 |
| 1975 | 101 | 943 | 196 | 6,432 | 1,234 | 257 | 87 | 386 | 58 | 85 |
| 1976 | 106 | 1,172 | 188 | 6,279 | 1,287 | 262 | 96 | 545 | 54 | 86 |
| 1977 | 124 | 1,011 | 191 | 6,607 | 1,258 | 286 | 91 | 519 | 48 | 107 |
| 1978 | 101 | 947 | 208 | 7,457 | 1,199 | 288 | 81 | 410 | 52 | 125 |
| 1979 | 114 | 855 | 212 | 8,048 | 1,200 | 277 | 105 | 377 | 61 | 165 |
| 1980 | 132 | 901 | 191 | 6,787 | 1,039 | 179 | 92 | 397 | 54 | 191 |
| 1981 | 94 | 1,216 | 195 | 7,926 | 1,108 | 174 | 59 | 444 | 52 | 198 |
| 1982 | 89 | 1,018 | 182 | 8,279 | 1,255 | 194 | 72 | ... | 66 | 218 |
| 1983 | 85 | 1,167 | 193 | 7,460 | 1,219 | 234 | 57 | 532 | 49 | 210 |
| 1984 | 100 | 926 | 241 | 8,331 | 1,156 | 245 | 41 | 464 | 50 | 218 |
| 1985 | 100 | 400 | 218 | 8,101 | 921 | 270 | 53 | 576 | 57 | 219 |
| 1986 | 111 | 945 | 220 | 7,467 | 895 | 270 | 66 | 589 | 41 | 230 |
| 1987 | 83 | 989 | 217 | 7,232 | 866 | 247 | 63 | 629 | 33 | 190 |
| 1988 | 86 | 768 | 206 | 8,119 | 777 | 174 | 76 | 679 | 35 | 172 |

**C3     NORTH AMERICA: Output of Sugar** (in thousands of metric tons)

| | Jamaica | Martinique | Mexico | Nicaragua | Panama | Puerto Rico | Trinidad & Tobago | U.S.A. SB | sugar from beet | sugar from cane |
|---|---|---|---|---|---|---|---|---|---|---|
| 1950 | 276 | 37 | 740 | 2 | 14 | 1,123 | 149 | 12,279 | 1,823 | 512 |
| 1951 | 272 | 50 | 816 | 2 | 16 | 1,234 | 143 | 9,509 | 1,405 | 380 |
| 1952 | 270 | 21 | 868 | 31 [4] / 54 | 19 [4] / 29 | 1,061 | 140 | 9,225 | 1,365 | 549 |
| 1953 | 336 | 54 | 894 | 57 | 28 | 1,092 | 155 | 10,962 | 1,647 | 572 |
| 1954 | 369 | 71 | 979 | 57 | 29 | 1,058 | 176 | 12,775 | 1,853 | 553 |
| 1955 | 403 | 82 | 1,021 | 61 | 24 | 1,047 | 196 | 11,096 | 1,578 | 521 |
| 1956 | 368 | 86 | 926 | 55 | 25 | 898 | 163 | 11,789 | 1,784 | 509 |
| 1957 | 377 | 70 | 1,198 | 67 | 32 | 847 | 170 | 14,066 | 1,985 | 483 |
| 1958 | 351 | 67 | 1,303 | 82 | 34 | 986 | 191 | 13,744 | 1,996 | 525 |
| 1959 | 382 | 77 | 1,414 | 91 | 33 | 925 | 184 | 15,436 | 2,123 | 559 |
| 1960 | 431 | 79 | 1,648 | 84 | 30 | 1,007 | 221 | 14,897 | 2,223 | 572 |
| 1961 | 447 | 90 | 1,528 | 83 | 32 | 915 | 252 | 16,061 | 2,181 | 778 |
| 1962 | 441 | 84 | 1,547 | 108 | 32 | 987 | 206 | 16,557 | 2,357 | 774 |
| 1963 | 492 | 92 | 1,943 | 116 | 42 | 898 | 233 | 21,163 | 2,812 | 1,075 |
| 1964 | 482 | 62 | 2,178 | 125 | 56 | 814 | 233 | 21,218 | 3,023 | 1,041 |
| 1965 | 497 | 70 | 2,333 | 139 | 55 | 801 | 257 | 18,976 | 2,625 | 1,002 |
| 1966 | 508 | 53 | 2,361 | 80 | 47 | 742 | 214 | 18,454 | 2,566 | 1,101 |
| 1967 | 456 | 47 | 2,677 | 119 | 69 | 586 | 204 | 17,415 | 2,435 | 1,322 |
| 1968 | 452 | 37 | 2,496 | 124 | 75 | 439 | 247 | 23,009 | 3,145 | 1,101 |
| 1969 | 389 | 31 | 2,744 | 135 | 79 | 417 | 244 | 25,162 | 3,021 | 973 |
| 1970 | 376 | 27 | 2,365 | 140 | 75 | 291 | 221 | 23,930 | 3,014 | 1,136 |
| 1971 | 385 | 29 | 2,562 | 170 | 85 | 268 | 221 | 24,581 | 3,222 | 1,094 |
| 1972 | 379 | 22 | 2,526 | 166 | 80 | 229 | 235 | 25,773 | 3,294 | 1,466 |
| 1973 | 331 | 23 | 2,821 | 149 | 81 | 261 | 184 | 22,225 | 2,917 | 1,288 |
| 1974 | 372 | 14 | 2,834 | 168 | 104 | 271 | 186 | 20,070 | 2,645 | 1,325 |
| 1975 | 361 | 16 | 2,727 | 199 | 133 | 274 | 167 | 26,947 | 3,645 | 1,560 |
| 1976 | 369 | 14 | 2,720 | 246 | 143 | 279 | 207 | 26,658 | 3,533 | 1,583 |
| 1977 | 295 | 15 | 2,728 | 225 | 184 | 239 | 179 | 22,686 | 2,819 | 1,480 |
| 1978 | 292 | 17 | 3,072 | 219 | 180 | 185 | 148 | 23,394 | 2,983 | 1,366 |
| 1979 | 283 | 12 | 3,078 | 223 | 226 | 174 | 144 | 19,954 | 2,611 | 1,512 |
| 1980 | 232 | 6 | 2,765 | 171 | 200 | 158 | 114 | 21,321 | 2,856 | 1,507 |
| 1981 | 205 | 3 | 2,586 | 196 | 155 | 137 | 94 | 24,982 | 3,073 | 1,809 |
| 1982 | 202 | 2 | 2,873 | 228 | 162 | 102 | 79 | 18,955 | 2,482 | 1,626 |
| 1983 | 198 | 4 | 3,108 | ... | 181 | 90 | 77 | 19,044 | 2,448 | 1,859 |
| 1984 | 193 | 5 | 3,297 | 249 | 174 | 87 | 70 | 20,080 | 2,632 | 1,604 |
| 1985 | 225 | 9 | 3,489 | 248 | 158 | 98 | 81 | 20,438 | 2,721 | 1,892 |
| 1986 | 206 | 8 | 4,031 | 262 | 131 | 87 | 92 | 22,826 | 3,098 | 1,836 |
| 1987 | 189 | 6 | 4,061 | 198 | 120 | 87 | 85 | 25,466 | 3,626 | 2,205 |
| 1988 | 222 | 7 | 3,806 | 209 | 105 | 93 | 91 | 22,507 | 3,221 | [7] |

**C3    SOUTH AMERICA: OUTPUT OF SUGAR** (in thousands of metric tons)

**1827–1869**

| | Guyana |
|---|---|
| 1827 | 44 |
| 1828 | 63 |
| 1829 | 57 |
| 1830 | 60 |
| 1831 | 61 |
| 1832 | 59 |
| 1833 | 56 |
| 1834 | 55 |
| 1835 | 48 |
| 1836 | 59 |
| 1837 | 50 |
| 1838 | 56 |
| 1839 | 49 |
| 1840 | 34 |
| 1841 | 36 |
| 1842 | 30 |
| 1843 | 32 |
| 1844 | 33 |
| 1845 | 35 |
| 1846 | 35 |
| 1847 | 23 |
| 1848 | 42 |
| 1849 | 41 |
| 1850 | 30 |
| 1851 | 33 |
| 1852 | 38 |
| 1853 | 50 |
| 1854 | 39 |
| 1855 | 49 |
| 1856 | 49 |
| 1857 | 46 |
| 1858 | 52 |
| 1859 | 52 |
| 1860 | 49 |
| 1861 | 55 |
| 1862 | 64 |
| 1863 | 58 |
| 1864 | 69 |
| 1865 | 65 |
| 1866 | 77 |
| 1867 | 81 |
| 1868 | 74 |
| 1869 | 80 |

| | Argentina | Brazil | Ecuador | Guyana | Peru | Venezuela |
|---|---|---|---|---|---|---|
| 1870 | 1 | … | — | 68 | … | … |
| 1871 | … | … | — | 76 | … | … |
| 1872 | … | … | — | 94 | … | … |
| 1873 | … | … | — | 78 | 16 | … |
| 1874 | … | … | — | 85 | 34 | … |
| 1875 | … | … | — | 88 | 50 | … |
| 1876 | 3 | … | — | 84 | 71 | … |
| 1877 | … | … | — | 106 | 78 | … |
| 1878 | … | … | — | 99 | 85 [1] | … |
| 1879 | 7 | 246 | — | 77 | 80 | … |
| 1880 | 9 | 161 | — | 94 | 50 | … |
| 1881 | 9 | 247 | — | 97 | 30 | … |
| 1882 | 15 | 224 | — | 91 | 24 | … |
| 1883 | 20 | 329 | — | 123 | 6 | … |
| 1884 | 24 | 274 | — | 115 | 32 | … |
| 1885 | 25 | 112 | — | 124 | 35 | … |
| 1886 | 25 | 226 | — | 95 | 52 | … |
| 1887 | 25 | 270 | — | 110 | 54 | … |
| 1888 | 35 | 230 | — | 133 | 64 | … |
| 1889 | 49 | 120 | — | 107 | 41 | … |
| 1890 | 41 | 175 | — | 114 | 41 | … |
| 1891 | 46 | 185 | — | 104 | 52 | … |
| 1892 | 58 | 200 | — | 116 | 60 | … |
| 1893 | 62 | 275 | — | 115 | 75 | … |
| 1894 | 85 | 275 | — | 110 | 79 | … |
| 1895 | 130 | 229 | — | 104 | 76 | … |
| 1896 | 163 | 214 | — | 103 | 111 | … |
| 1897 | 112 | 205 | — | 109 | 110 | … |
| 1898 | 76 | 151 | — | 102 | 109 | … |
| 1899 | 90 | 180 | 6 | 98 | 118 | 2 |
| 1900 | 117 | 307 | 6 | 86 | 120 | 3 |
| 1901 | 158 | 354 | 7 | 96 | 124 | 3 |
| 1902 | 123 | 190 | 6 | 107 | 147 | 3 |
| 1903 | 143 | 199 | 6 | 122 | 157 | 3 |
| 1904 | 128 | 198 | 7 | 128 | 160 | 3 |
| 1905 | 136 | 279 | 8 | 108 | 161 | 3 |
| 1906 | 117 | 272 | 5 | 127 | 145 | 3 |
| 1907 | 109 | 217 | 5 | 122 | 157 | 3 |
| 1908 | 161 | 276 | 5 | 101 | 155 | 3 |
| 1909 | 124 | 294 | 6 | 119 | 150 | 3 |

**C3     SOUTH AMERICA: Output of Sugar** (in thousands of metric tons)

|      | Argentina | Brazil | Colombia | Ecuador | Guyana | Peru | Venezuela |
|------|-----------|--------|----------|---------|--------|------|-----------|
| 1910 | 146 | 332 | ... | 6 | 118 | 179 | 3 |
| 1911 | 175 | 302 | ... | 5 | 110 | 188 | 3 |
| 1912 | 147 | [147][5] | ... | 7 | 88 | 179 | 3 |
| 1913 | 274 | [158][5] | ... | 4 | 108 | 223 | 4 |
| 1914 | 333 | 312 | ... | 7 | 119 | 258 | 4 |
| 1915 | 148 | [190][5] | 13 | 8 | 121 | 276 | 9 |
| 1916 | 84 | [244][5] | ... | 12 | 116 | 253 | 19 |
| 1917 | 87 | 441 | ... | 11 | 110 | 288 | 11 |
| 1918 | 127 | 400 | ... | 11 | 109 | 295 | 17 |
| 1919 | 295 | ... | ... | 10 | 88 | 330 | 19 |
| 1920 | 207 | 646 | ... | 12 | 89 | 314 | 23 |
| 1921 | 199 | 710 | ... | 13 | 113 | 269 | 16 |
| 1922 | 210 | 761 | ... | 17 | 92 | 319 | 16 |
| 1923 | 258 | 813 | ... | 20 | 93 | 321 | 18 |
| 1924 | 250 | 832 | 38 | 21 | 109 | 317 | 21 |
| 1925 | 395 | 883 | 39 | 26 | 100 | 276 | 22 |
| 1926 | 477 | 693 | 41 | 21 | 116 | 376 | 21 |
| 1927 | 424 | 847 | 35 | 23 | 118 | 375 | 20 |
| 1928 | 375 | 967 | 30 | 19 | 119 | 362 | 20 |
| 1929 | 341 | 1,020 | ... | 19 | 130 | 428 | 23 |
| 1930 | 383 | 1,050 | 21 | 21 | 128 | 400 | 20 |
| 1931 | 348 | 982 | 26 | 25 | 151 | 390 | 21 |
| 1932 | 350 | 1,027 | 40 | 15 | 144 | 388 | 24 |
| 1933 | 320 | 1,085 | 37 | 21 | 134 | 390 | 20 |
| 1934 | 346 | 1,155 | 36 | 19 | 181 | 399 | 19 |
| 1935 | 391 | 1,019 | 33 | 19 | 199 | 410 | 23 |
| 1936 | 437 | 940 | 31 | 18 | 190 | 389 | 21 |
| 1937 | 371 | 956 | 42 | 17 | 200 | 356 | 23 |
| 1938 | 466 | 1,100 | 41 | 22 | 192 | 368 | 26 |
| 1939 | 522 | 1,258 | 41 | 27 | 170 | 471 | 18 |
| 1940 | 540 | 1,281 | 48 | 28 | 191 | 462 | 19 |
| 1941 | 408 | 1,234 | 62 | 31 | 195 | 468 | 19 |
| 1942 | 361 | 1,272 | 67 | 28 | 136 | 390 | 30 |
| 1943 | 410 | 1,255 | 73 | 27 | 141 | 418 | 35 |
| 1944 | 459 | 1,250 | 81 | 23 | 160 | 423 | 33 |
| 1945 | 455 | 1,265 | 81 | 31 | 164 | ... | 27 |
| 1946 | 635 | 1,460 | 81 | 34 | 160 | 391 | 27 |
| 1947 | 606 | 1,582 | 76 | 35 | 174 | 420 | 29 |
| 1948 | 565 | 1,751 | 83 | 44 | 166 | 412 | 27 |
| 1949 | 549 | 1,646 | 109 | 41 | 188 | 472 | 41 [4] |
|      |           |        |          |         |        |      | 149 |

**C3**    **SOUTH AMERICA: Output of Sugar** (in thousands of metric tons)

|      | Argentina | Brazil | Colombia | Ecuador | Guyana | Peru | Venezuela |
|------|-----------|--------|----------|---------|--------|------|-----------|
| 1950 | 615   | 1,845 | 157   | 46 [4] / 68 | 194 | 451 | 174 |
| 1951 | 651   | 1,862 | 198   | 76   | 193 | 490 | 168 |
| 1952 | 560   | 2,114 | 197   | 81   | 247 | 494 | 164 |
| 1953 | 710   | 2,296 | 190   | 89   | 244 | 626 | 173 |
| 1954 | 778   | 2,395 | 241   | 85   | 243 | 638 | 179 |
| 1955 | 584   | 2,383 | 253   | 80   | 254 | 677 | 217 |
| 1956 | 728   | 2,518 | 261   | 81   | 268 | 718 | 282 |
| 1957 | 714   | 3,108 | 234   | 105  | 290 | 703 | 275 |
| 1958 | 1,102 | 3,715 | 264   | 107  | 311 | 708 | 233 |
| 1959 | 969   | 3,533 | 277   | 119  | 289 | 733 | 243 |
| 1960 | 850   | 3,724 | 329   | [109][6] | 340 | 827 | 256 |
| 1961 | 694   | 3,890 | 363   | [125][6] | 330 | 823 | 279 |
| 1962 | 798   | 3,574 | 402   | 171  | 331 | 805 | 294 |
| 1963 | 1,055 | 3,616 | 368   | 171  | 322 | 852 | 317 |
| 1964 | 998   | 4,008 | 428   | 183  | 263 | 791 | 358 |
| 1965 | 1,310 | 5,016 | 485   | 221  | 314 | 783 | 410 |
| 1966 | 1,040 | 4,567 | 537   | 249  | 294 | 830 | 410 |
| 1967 | 785   | 4,646 | 597   | 232  | 349 | 821 | 351 |
| 1968 | 936   | 4,623 | 683   | 248  | 322 | 768 | 392 |
| 1969 | 978   | 4,713 | 709   | 277  | 370 | 650 | 424 |
| 1970 | 979   | 5,762 | 672   | 310  | 316 | 771 | 460 |
| 1971 | 996   | 6,045 | 744   | 317  | 375 | 882 | 526 |
| 1972 | 1,303 | 6,639 | 824   | 310  | 320 | 899 | 551 |
| 1973 | 1,638 | 7,293 | 810   | 329  | 270 | 897 | 506 |
| 1974 | 1,530 | 9,641 | 895   | 373  | 345 | 992 | 590 |
| 1975 | 1,353 | 6,186 | 970   | 287  | 311 | 964 | 535 |
| 1976 | 1,559 | 7,598 | 935   | 301  | 343 | 930 | 482 |
| 1977 | 1,666 | 8,760 | 854   | 295  | 246 | 900 | 450 |
| 1978 | 1,397 | 7,767 | 963   | 353  | 330 | 856 | 402 |
| 1979 | 1,411 | 7,027 | 1,114 | 357  | 303 | 695 | 351 |
| 1980 | 1,716 | 8,547 | 1,189 | 370  | 273 | 542 | 374 |
| 1981 | 1,624 | 8,393 | 1,148 | 321  | 306 | 478 | 304 |
| 1982 | 1,623 | 9,314 | 1,303 | 254  | 288 | 613 | 333 |
| 1983 | 1,625 | 9,576 | 1,379 | 220  | 248 | 442 | 385 |
| 1984 | 1,545 | 9,332 | 1,178 | 329  | 238 | 603 | 372 |
| 1985 | 1,174 | 8,274 | 1,367 | 273  | 265 | 727 | 504 |
| 1986 | 1,120 | 8,649 | 1,297 | 286  | 249 | 599 | 542 |
| 1987 | 1,063 | 8,458 | 1,390 | 341  | 225 | 560 | 584 |
| 1988 | 1,132 | 8,582 | 1,364 | 292  | 169 | 592 | 583 |

## C3      Output of Sugar

NOTES

1.  SOURCES:- As for table C1, with output for Barbados to 1859, Cuba to 1841, Guadeloupe, Jamaica, Martinique, and Trinidad to 1879, and Peru to 1878 from Noel Deerr, *The History of Sugar* (London, 1949), where some data are available for years before 1750. There may be some slight break in continuity between these and later figures. Data for U.S.A. to 1909 (1st line) are from *Anuario Azucarero de Cuba*.
2.  Data may be reported for either calendar year in which the crop-year lies, and practice in this respect may not always have been consistent, though most statistics appear to relate to the second year.

FOOTNOTES

[1] See note 1 above.
[2] Trinidad only to 1898.
[3] Centrifugal sugar only from 1946 to 1952 (1st line).
[4] Previously centrifugal sugar only.
[5] Data are for 148 factories out of 215.
[6] Centrifugal sugar only.
[7] Output including Hawaii was 3,023 in 1987 and 2,988 in 1988.

**C4**     **AREA OF FLAX, GROUNDNUTS AND SOYA BEANS** (in thousands of hectares)[1]

**1888–1934**

| | NORTH AMERICA | | | | SOUTH AMERICA | | |
| | Canada | USA | | | Argentina | | Uruguay |
| | Flax | Flax | Groundnuts | Soya Beans | Flax | Groundnuts | Flax |
|---|---|---|---|---|---|---|---|
| 1888 | ... | ... | ... | ... | 121 | ... | ... |
| 1889 | ... | 544 | ... | ... | ... | ... | 0.1 |
| 1890 | ... | 924 | ... | ... | ... | ... | ... |
| 1891 | ... | 826 | ... | ... | ... | ... | ... |
| 1892 | ... | 576 | ... | ... | ... | ... | 0.1 |
| 1893 | ... | 521 | ... | ... | ... | ... | 0.1 |
| 1894 | ... | 590 | ... | ... | ... | ... | 0.9 |
| 1895 | ... | 825 | ... | ... | 387 | ... | ... |
| 1896 | ... | 748 | ... | ... | ... | ... | ... |
| 1897 | ... | 552 | ... | ... | ... | ... | ... |
| 1898 | ... | 764 | ... | ... | 333 | ... | 1.4 |
| 1899 | ... | 851 | ... | ... | 355 | ... | 1.3 |
| 1900 | ... | 1,118 | ... | ... | 607 | ... | 4.0 |
| 1901 | 9 | 1,284 | ... | ... | 783 | ... | 11.0 |
| 1902 | ... | 1,569 | ... | ... | 1,307 | ... | 34.0 |
| 1903 | ... | 847 | ... | ... | 1,488 | ... | ... |
| 1904 | ... | | ... | ... | 1,083 | ... | 19.0 |
| 1905 | ... | 987 | ... | ... | 1,023 | ... | 18.0 |
| 1906 | ... | 1,039 | ... | ... | 1,191 | ... | 30.0 |
| 1907 | ... | 1,092 | ... | ... | 1,391 | ... | 26.0 |
| 1908 | ... | 951 | ... | ... | 1,534 | ... | 18.0 |
| 1909 | 56 | 842 | 217 | 1 | 1,456 | ... | ... |
| 1910 | 56 | 899 | 188 | ... | 1,504 | ... | 38.0 |
| 1911 | 236 | 1,065 | 191 | ... | 1,630 | ... | 58.0 |
| 1912 | 547 | 1,190 | 194 | ... | 1,733 | ... | 57.0 |
| 1913 | 818 | 791 | 188 | ... | 1,779 | ... | 52.0 |
| 1914 | 628 | 632 | 213 | ... | 1,723 | ... | 41.0 |
| 1915 | 439 | 452 | 250 | ... | 1,619 | ... | 18.0 |
| 1916 | 187 | 525 | 355 | ... | 1,298 | ... | 15.0 |
| 1917 | 266 | 761 | 532 | ... | 1,309 | ... | 15.0 |
| 1918 | 372 | 722 | 537 | ... | 1,384 | ... | 21.0 |
| 1919 | 432 | 523 | 387 | 46 | 1,766 | ... | 33.0 |
| 1920 | 442 | 667 | 403 | ... | 1,930 | ... | 32.0 |
| 1921 | 578 | 463 | 397 | ... | 1,575 | ... | 25.0 |
| 1922 | 216 | 450 | 332 | ... | 1,747 | ... | 34.0 |
| 1923 | 229 | 815 | 323 | ... | 2,169 | 33 | 42.0 |
| 1924 | 255 | 1,431 | 439 | 181 | 2,177 | 37 | 59.0 |
| 1925 | 517 | 1,223 | 403 | 168 | 2,453 | 53 | 75.0 |
| 1926 | 341 | 1,107 | 348 | 180 | 2,520 | 60 | 71.0 |
| 1927 | 299 | 1,118 | 439 | 230 | 2,741 | 53 | 71.0 |
| 1928 | 193 | 1,057 | 491 | 234 | 2,808 | 56 | 78.0 |
| 1929 | 153 | 1,234 | 511 | 287 | 2,117 | 53 | 118.0 |
| 1930 | 155 | 1,530 | 434 | 435 | 2,731 | 45 | 210.0 |
| 1931 | 236 | 984 | 583 | 462 | 3,344 | 50 | 179.0 |
| 1932 | 262 | 805 | 607 | 405 | 2,588 | 47 | 136.0 |
| 1933 | 187 | 543 | 493 | 422 | 1,974 | 78 | 106.0 |
| 1934 | 99 | 405 | 613 | 630 | 2,875 | 83 | 162.0 |

**C4      Area of Flax, Groundnuts and Soya Beans** (in thousands of hectares)[1]

**1935–19**

| | NORTH AMERICA | | | | | |
| | Canada | | Mexico | USA | | |
| | Flax | Soya Beans | Soya Beans | Flax | Groundnuts | Soya Beans |
|---|---|---|---|---|---|---|
| 1935 | 92 | ... | ... | 860 | 606 | 1,180 |
| 1936 | 124 | ... | ... | 455 | 672 | 955 |
| 1937 | 193 | 4 | ... | 375 | 622 | 1,047 |
| 1938 | 98 | 4 | ... | 366 | 685 | 1,228 |
| 1939 | 85 | 4 | ... | 879 | 772 | 1,746 |
| 1940 | 121 | 4 | ... | 1,288 | 830 | 1,945 |
| 1941 | 155 | 4 | ... | 1,322 | 769 | 2,383 |
| 1942 | 422 | 18 | ... | 1,784 | 1,358 | 4,004 |
| 1943 | 622 | 14 | ... | 2,303 | 1,428 | 4,208 |
| 1944 | 1,208 | 15 | ... | 1,056 | 1,242 | 4,146 |
| 1945 | 493 | 19 | ... | 1,532 | 1,279 | 4,346 |
| 1946 | 353 | 24 | ... | 984 | 1,271 | 4,019 |
| 1947 | 359 | 25 | ... | 1,671 | 1,367 | 4,618 |
| 1948 | 725 | 38 | ... | 2,013 | 1,334 | 4,323 |
| 1949 | 792 | 42 | ... | 2,043 | 934 | 4,242 |
| 1950 | 126 | 57 | ... | 1,655 | 915 | 5,587 |
| 1951 | 236 | 63 | ... | 1,580 | 802 | 5,510 |
| 1952 | 469 | 70 | ... | 1,337 | 584 | 5,842 |
| 1953 | 449 | 87 | ... | 1,849 | 613 | 6,001 |
| 1954 | 387 | 103 | ... | 2,292 | 561 | 6,899 |
| 1955 | 477 | 87 | ... | 1,989 | 675 | 7,535 |
| 1956 | 743 | 98 | ... | 2,215 | 560 | 8,345 |
| 1957 | 1,231 | 104 | ... | 1,940 | 599 | 8,441 |
| 1958 | 1,411 | 106 | ... | 1,489 | 614 | 9,710 |
| 1959 | 1,032 | 102 | ... | 1,187 | 581 | 9,158 |
| 1960 | 830 | 104 | ... | 1,352 | 565 | 9,573 |
| 1961 | 844 | 86 | 10 | 1,017 | 480 | 10,928 |
| 1962 | 585 | 89 | 11 | 1,136 | 567 | 11,173 |
| 1963 | 681 | 92 | 27 | 1,284 | 565 | 11,580 |
| 1964 | 800 | 93 | 31 | 1,143 | 565 | 12,461 |
| 1965 | 937 | 107 | 27 | 1,123 | 582 | 13,941 |
| 1966 | 716 | 113 | 54 | 1,042 | 575 | 14,789 |
| 1967 | 414 | 117 | 70 | 799 | 568 | 16,108 |
| 1968 | 617 | 119 | 133 | 847 | 582 | 16,750 |
| 1969 | 947 | 130 | 163 | 1,054 | 589 | 16,728 |
| 1970 | 1,363 | 136 | 112 | 1,153 | 594 | 17,097 |
| 1971 | 715 | 149 | 123 | 625 | 589 | 17,280 |
| 1972 | 535 | 164 | 229 | 466 | 602 | 18,453 |
| 1973 | 587 | 190 | 312 | 685 | 605 | 22,580 |
| 1974 | 587 | 168 | 315 | 677 | 596 | 21,192 |

**C4** **Area of Flax, Groundnuts and Soya Beans** (in thousands of hectares)[1]

**1935–1974**

| | SOUTH AMERICA | | | | | |
|---|---|---|---|---|---|---|
| | Argentina | | | Brazil | | Uruguay |
| | Flax | Groundnuts | Soya Beans | Groundnuts | Soya Beans | Flax |
| 1935 | 2,268 | 73 | ... | ... | ... | 126 |
| 1936 | 3,086 | 89 | ... | ... | ... | 144 |
| 1937 | 2,303 | 103 | ... | ... | ... | 134 |
| 1938 | 2,342 | 93 | ... | ... | ... | 183 |
| 1939 | 2,180 | 49 | ... | ... | ... | 236 |
| 1940 | 2,409 | 77 | ... | ... | ... | 171 |
| 1941 | 2,322 | 62 | ... | ... | ... | 85 |
| 1942 | 2,271 | 108 | ... | ... | ... | 137 |
| 1943 | 2,018 | 109 | ... | ... | ... | 103 |
| 1944 | 1,254 | 145 | ... | 41 | ... | 163 |
| 1945 | 1,392 | 142 | ... | 33 | ... | 240 |
| 1946 | 1,537 | 154 | ... | 46 | ... | 167 |
| 1947 | 1,351 | 114 | ... | 49 | ... | 121 |
| 1948 | 869 | 119 | ... | 142 | ... | 189 |
| 1949 | 960 | 73 | ... | 136 | ... | 233 |
| 1950 | 847 | 76 | 1 | 137 | ... | 140 |
| 1951 | 448 | 105 | 1 | 141 | 34 | 149 |
| 1952 | 869 | 142 | 1 | 137 | 60 | 184 |
| 1953 | 552 | 175 | ... | 139 | 63 | 221 |
| 1954 | 633 | 182 | 1 | 166 | 68 | 92 |
| 1955 | 444 | 149 | — | 163 | 74 | 89 |
| 1956 | 1,077 | 196 | 1 | 170 | 81 | 105 |
| 1957 | 1,075 | 222 | 1 | 228 | 97 | 116 |
| 1958 | 995 | 240 | 1 | 249 | 107 | 168 |
| 1959 | 1,117 | 260 | 1 | 255 | 114 | 118 |
| 1960 | 957 | 190 | 1 | 291 | 171 | 98 |
| 1961 | 1,172 | 189 | 1 | 436 | 241 | 118 |
| 1962 | 1,315 | 280 | 10 | 476 | 314 | 144 |
| 1963 | 1,217 | 266 | 19 | 423 | 340 | 160 |
| 1964 | 1,084 | 344 | 12 | 430 | 360 | 132 |
| 1965 | 1,004 | 378 | 16 | 541 | 432 | 113 |
| 1966 | 801 | 333 | 16 | 644 | 491 | 69 |
| 1967 | 616 | 328 | 17 | 694 | 612 | 66 |
| 1968 | 810 | 287 | 20 | 606 | 722 | 51 |
| 1969 | 791 | 244 | 28 | 613 | 906 | 82 |
| 1970 | 834 | 211 | 26 | 670 | 1,319 | 144 |
| 1971 | 440 | 310 | 36 | 662 | 1,589 | 92 |
| 1972 | 441 | 294 | 68 | 670 | 2,274 | 74 |
| 1973 | 390 | 379 | 157 | 506 | 3,615 | 48 |
| 1974 | 501 | 345 | 334 | 362 | 5,143 | 42 |

**C4**      **Area of Flax, Groundnuts and Soya Beans** (in thousands of hectares)[1]

| | SOUTH AMERICA | | | | | |
|---|---|---|---|---|---|---|
| | Argentina | | | Brazil | | Uruguay |
| | Flax | Groundnuts | Soya Beans | Groundnuts | Soya Beans | Flax |
| 1975 | 446 | 357 | 356 | 348 | 5,824 | 70 |
| 1976 | 833 | 309 | 434 | 375 | 6,416 | 98 |
| 1977 | 884 | 367 | 660 | 229 | 7,070 | 69 |
| 1978 | 817 | 428 | 1,150 | 254 | 7,782 | 79 |
| 1979 | 978 | 393 | 1,600 | 289 | 8,256 | 61 |
| 1980 | 726 | 279 | 2,030 | 313 | 8,774 | 98 |
| 1981 | 818 | 197 | 1,880 | 245 | 8,501 | 37 |
| 1982 | 939 | 179 | 1,986 | 237 | 8,202 | 18 |
| 1983 | 804 | 125 | 2,281 | 212 | 8,137 | 7 |
| 1984 | 643 | 146 | 2,910 | 151 | 9,421 | 13 |
| 1985 | 688 | 145 | 3,269 | 193 | 10,153 | 13 |
| 1986 | 745 | 173 | 3,316 | 162 | 9,182 | 11 |
| 1987 | 655 | 238 | 3,510 | 144 | 9,134 | 8 |
| 1988 | 557 | 190 | 4,373 | 102 | 10,524 | 4 |

NOTES

1.   SOURCES: As for table C1
2.   Note 2 of table C3 also applies to this table.

FOOTNOTE

[1] For areas of cotton see table C6

## C5    NORTH AMERICA: OUTPUT OF MAJOR OIL CROPS (in thousands of metric tons)

Key: C= cottonseed; G= groundnuts; L= linseed; OO= olive oil SB= soya beans

### 1865–1899                                                                    1900–1939

| | USA | | | | Canada | Mexico | USA | | | |
|---|---|---|---|---|---|---|---|---|---|---|
| | C | L | | | L | C | C | G | L | SB |
| 1865 | ... | ... | | 1900 | ... | ... | 4,082 | ... | 406 | ... |
| 1866 | 784 | ... | | 1901 | 5 | ... | 3,834 | ... | 701 | ... |
| 1867 | 945 | ... | | 1902 | ... | ... | 4,290 | ... | 917 | ... |
| 1868 | 884 | ... | | 1903 | ... | ... | 3,973 | ... | 645 | ... |
| 1869 | 1,014 | ... | | 1904 | ... | ... | 5,413 | ... | 574 | ... |
| 1870 | 1,620 | ... | | 1905 | ... | ... | 4,264 | ... | 729 | ... |
| 1871 | 1,109 | ... | | 1906 | ... | ... | 5,351 | ... | 701 | ... |
| 1872 | 1,471 | ... | | 1907 | ... | ... | 4,473 | ... | 605 | ... |
| 1873 | 1,559 | ... | | 1908 | ... | ... | 5,337 | ... | 523 | ... |
| 1874 | 1,422 | ... | | 1909 | 41 | ... | 4,030 | 161 | 495 | ... |
| 1875 | 1,732 | ... | | 1910 | 60 | ... | 4,677 | 174 | 290 | ... |
| 1876 | 1,657 | ... | | 1911 | 116 | ... | 6,323 | 166 | 470 | ... |
| 1877 | 1,809 | ... | | 1912 | 420 | ... | 5,477 | 164 | 714 | ... |
| 1878 | 1,911 | ... | | 1913 | 711 | ... | 5,703 | 174 | 384 | ... |
| 1879 | 2,200 | 183 | | 1914 | 477 | ... | 6,491 | 191 | 328 | ... |
| 1880 | 2,560 | 191 | | 1915 | 195 | ... | 4,502 | 218 | 287 | ... |
| 1881 | 2,068 | 198 | | 1916 | 166 | ... | 4,613 | 302 | 300 | ... |
| 1882 | 2,751 | 218 | | 1917 | 225 | ... | 4,547 | 449 | 213 | ... |
| 1883 | 2,223 | 218 | | 1918 | 162 | ... | 4,845 | 429 | 325 | ... |
| 1884 | 2,202 | 241 | | 1919 | 165 | ... | 4,599 | 312 | 173 | 30 |
| 1885 | 2,566 | 236 | | 1920 | 149 | ... | 5,412 | 316 | 277 | ... |
| 1886 | 2,542 | 254 | | 1921 | 218 | ... | 3,201 | 308 | 206 | ... |
| 1887 | 2,772 | 249 | | 1922 | 112 | ... | 3,928 | 237 | 267 | ... |
| 1888 | 2,789 | 254 | | 1923 | 136 | ... | 4,085 | 258 | 422 | ... |
| 1889 | 3,010 | 269 | | 1924 | 194 | ... | 5,488 | 323 | 793 | 133 |
| 1890 | 3,449 | 488 | | 1925 | 264 | 86 | 6,486 | 327 | 566 | 133 |
| 1891 | 3,599 | 424 | | 1926 | 170 | 149 | 7,247 | 300 | 470 | 142 |
| 1892 | 2,682 | 300 | | 1927 | 163 | 75 | 5,224 | 383 | 640 | 188 |
| 1893 | 2,991 | 264 | | 1928 | 133 | 117 | 5,733 | 383 | 485 | 215 |
| 1894 | 4,035 | 267 | | 1929 | 98 | 106 | 5,811 | 407 | 404 | 256 |
| 1895 | 2,879 | 544 | | 1930 | 56 | 74 | 5,469 | 316 | 551 | 378 |
| 1896 | 3,427 | 450 | | 1931 | 138 | 88 | 6,632 | 479 | 300 | 471 |
| 1897 | 4,425 | 335 | | 1932 | 67 | 41 | 5,275 | 427 | 292 | 414 |
| 1898 | 4,645 | 470 | | 1933 | 74 | 106 | 4,999 | 372 | 175 | 367 |
| 1899 | 3,767 | 508 | | 1934 | 17 | 96 | 3,861 | 460 | 145 | 631 |
| | | | | 1935 | 25 | 126 | 4,204 | 523 | 378 | 1,931 |
| | | | | 1936 | 45 | 161 | 4,964 | 572 | 135 | 917 |
| | | | | 1937 | 49 | 135 | 7,116 | 559 | 180 | 1,257 |
| | | | | 1938 | 21 | 118 | 4,491 | 585 | 203 | 1,685 |
| | | | | 1939 | 34 | 119 | 4,417 | 550 | 498 | 2,452 |

**C5**    **NORTH AMERICA: Output of Major Oil Crops** (in thousands of metric tons)

**1940–1988**

| | Canada | | El Salvador[1] | Guatemala[1] | Mexico | | Nicaragua | USA | | | |
|------|------|------|------|------|------|------|------|------|------|------|------|
| | L | SB | C | C | C | SB | C | C | G | L | SB |
| 1940 | 56 | — | 4 | 2 | 110 | ... | 3 | 4,795 | 801 | 785 | 2,123 |
| 1941 | 83 | — | 4 | 2 | 137 | ... | 4 | 4,130 | 669 | 815 | 2,917 |
| 1942 | 185 | 6 | 5 | 2 | 170 | ... | 2 | 4,719 | 995 | 1,041 | 5,103 |
| 1943 | 421 | 24 | 6 | - - | 193 | ... | 2 | 4,253 | 987 | 1,270 | 5,174 |
| 1944 | 502 | 16 | 6 | 1 | 174 | ... | 2 | 4,447 | 944 | 551 | 5,228 |
| 1945 | 242 | 19 | 5 | - - | 161 | ... | 1 | 3,324 | 926 | 879 | 5,258 |
| 1946 | 169 | 23 | 8 | 2 | 149 | ... | - - | 3,188 | 924 | 574 | 5,536 |
| 1947 | 184 | 29 | 7 | 2 | | ... | - - | 4,247 | 990 | 1,031 | 5,076 |
| 1948 | 376 | 30 | 8 | 2 | 199 | ... | 1 | 5,393 | 1,060 | 1,392 | 6,183 |
| 1949 | 502 | 50 | 10 | 2 | 346 | ... | 9 | 5,950 | 846 | 1,092 | 6,374 |
| 1950 | 61 | 71 | 11 | 2 | 443 | ... | 11 | 3,724 | 923 | 1,021 | 8,143 |
| 1951 | 135 | 90 | 17 | 5 | 485 | ... | 35 | 5,703 | 753 | 881 | 7,724 |
| 1952 | 258 | 105 | 16 | 7 | 447 | ... | 25 | 5,615 | 615 | 767 | 8,132 |
| 1953 | 317 | 112 | 20 | 10 | 469 | ... | 46 | 6,122 | 714 | 958 | 7,326 |
| 1954 | 265 | 136 | 33 | 13 | 661 | ... | 95 | 5,179 | 457 | 1,049 | 9,283 |
| 1955 | 299 | 130 | 50 | 15 | 871 | ... | 70 | 5,482 | 702 | 1,026 | 10,170 |
| 1956 | 517 | 163 | 55 | 16 | 681 | ... | 84 | 4,905 | 729 | 1,194 | 12,228 |
| 1957 | 952 | 143 | 63 | 22 | 753 | ... | 95 | 4,181 | 651 | 638 | 13,156 |
| 1958 | 523 | 176 | 72 | 26 | 917 | ... | 92 | 4,353 | 823 | 950 | 15,793 |
| 1959 | 608 | 179 | 57 | 24 | 636 | ... | 53 | 5,435 | 691 | 539 | 14,503 |
| 1960 | 468 | 185 | 81 | 33 | 787 | ... | 59 | 5,340 | 779 | 772 | 15,107 |
| 1961 | 368 | 180 | 110 | 43 | 767 | 20 | 99 | 5,423 | 752 | 564 | 18,468 |
| 1962 | 407 | 180 | 138 | 86 | 825 | 22 | 126 | 5,569 | 780 | 819 | 18,212 |
| 1963 | 536 | 136 | 121 | 107 | 908 | 56 | 159 | 5,617 | 881 | 788 | 19,029 |
| 1964 | 516 | 190 | 155 | 115 | 932 | 60 | 207 | 5,658 | 952 | 620 | 19,074 |
| 1965 | 741 | 219 | 86 | 131 | 953 | 58 | 189 | 5,522 | 1,084 | 899 | 23,014 |
| 1966 | 559 | 245 | 65 | 103 | 858 | 95 | 195 | 3,592 | 1,096 | 594 | 25,270 |
| 1967 | 238 | 220 | 59 | 124 | 811 | 131 | 171 | 2,912 | 1,124 | 509 | 26,575 |
| 1968 | 500 | 246 | 73 | 124 | 966 | 275 | 158 | 4,209 | 1,155 | 685 | 30,127 |
| 1969 | 700 | 209 | 78 | 94 | 637 | 287 | 116 | 3,690 | 1,150 | 887 | 30,839 |
| 1970 | 1,243 | 283 | 76 | 92 | 550 | 215 | 111 | 3,690 | 1,351 | 751 | 30,675 |
| 1971 | 567 | 280 | 91 | 92 | 655 | 232 | 125 | 3,846 | 1,363 | 462 | 32,009 |
| 1972 | 447 | 375 | 110 | 134 | 679 | 366 | 163 | 4,892 | 1,485 | 353 | 34,581 |
| 1973 | 493 | 397 | 121 | 155 | 572 | 585 | 178 | 4,550 | 1,576 | 409 | 42,118 |
| 1974 | 351 | 280 | 124 | 193 | 846 | 491 | 234 | 4,091 | 1,664 | 344 | 33,102 |
| 1975 | 445 | 367 | 125 | 193 | 345 | 599 | 197 | 2,919 | 1,745 | 395 / | 42,140 |
| 1976 | 277 | 250 | 98 | 187 | 349 | 302 | 184 | 3,739 | 1,696 | 199 | 35,043 |
| 1977 | 653 | 580 | 119 | 230 | 659 | 516 | 191 | 5,009 | 1,685 | 384 | 48,098 |
| 1978 | 572 | 516 | 134 | 249 | 576 | 334 | 201 | 3,873 | 1,793 | 219 | 50,860 |
| 1979 | 815 | 657 | 119 | 268 | 605 | 707 | 186 | 5,242 | 1,800 | 305 | 61,526 |
| 1980 | 465 | 690 | 109 | 251 | 538 | 322 | 37 | 4,056 | 1,044 | 201 | 48,922 |
| 1981 | 467 | 607 | 68 | 189 | 530 | 712 | 120 | 5,803 | 1,806 | 198 | 54,136 |
| 1982 | 734 | 857 | 63 | 115 | 289 | 648 | 102 | 4,304 | 1,560 | 296 | 59,611 |
| 1983 | 444 | 735 | 60 | 76 | 355 | 686 | 119 | 2,791 | 1,495 | 175 | 44,518 |
| 1984 | 694 | 944 | 45 | 92 | 436 | 685 | 126 | 4,671 | 1,998 | 178 | 50,644 |
| 1985 | 897 | 1,048 | 44 | 91 | 314 | 928 | 98 | 4,789 | 1,870 | 211 | 57,113 |
| 1986 | 1,026 | 988 | 26 | 66 | 226 | 710 | 77 | 3,448 | 1,679 | 293 | 54,622 |
| 1987 | 729 | 1,270 | 15 | 42 | 414 | 828 | 93 | 5,234 | 1,640 | 189 | 52,737 |
| 1988 | 373 | 1,153 | 14 | 71 | 491 | 226 | 50 | 5,499 | 1,806 | 41 | 42,153 |

## C5    SOUTH AMERICA: OUTPUT OF MAJOR OIL CROPS (in thousands of metric tons)

### 1890–1934

| | Argentina | | | Brazil | Colombia | Peru | Uruguay |
|---|---|---|---|---|---|---|---|
| | C | G | L | C | C | C | L |
| 1890 | ... | ... | ... | ... | ... | ... | ... |
| 1891 | ... | ... | ... | ... | ... | ... | ... |
| 1892 | ... | ... | 50 | ... | ... | ... | ... |
| 1893 | ... | ... | 120 | ... | ... | ... | ... |
| 1894 | ... | ... | 270 | ... | ... | ... | 1 |
| 1895 | ... | ... | 232 | ... | ... | ... | ... |
| 1896 | ... | ... | 185 | ... | ... | ... | ... |
| 1897 | ... | ... | 160 | ... | ... | ... | ... |
| 1898 | ... | ... | 219 | ... | ... | ... | ... |
| 1899 | ... | ... | 225 | ... | ... | ... | 1 |
| 1900 | ... | ... | 390 | ... | ... | ... | 2 |
| 1901 | ... | ... | 365 | ... | ... | ... | 9 |
| 1902 | ... | ... | 711 | ... | ... | ... | 21 |
| 1903 | ... | ... | 938 | ... | ... | ... | ... |
| 1904 | ... | ... | 740 | ... | ... | ... | 14 |
| 1905 | ... | ... | 592 | ... | ... | ... | 11 |
| 1906 | ... | ... | 826 | ... | ... | ... | 22 |
| 1907 | ... | ... | 1,101 | ... | ... | ... | 18 |
| 1908 | ... | ... | 1,049 | ... | ... | ... | 13 |
| 1909 | ... | ... | 717 | ... | ... | ... | ... |
| 1910 | ... | ... | 595 | ... | ... | ... | 17 |
| 1911 | ... | ... | 572 | ... | ... | ... | 22 |
| 1912 | ... | ... | 1,130 | ... | ... | ... | 33 |
| 1913 | ... | ... | 938 | ... | ... | ... | 25 |
| 1914 | ... | ... | 1,143 | ... | ... | ... | 15 |
| 1915 | ... | ... | 895 | ... | ... | ... | 10 |
| 1916 | ... | ... | 102 | ... | ... | ... | 3 |
| 1917 | ... | ... | 498 | ... | ... | ... | 9 |
| 1918 | ... | ... | 782 | ... | ... | ... | 13 |
| 1919 | ... | ... | 1,267 | ... | ... | ... | 24 |
| 1920 | ... | ... | 1,524 | 233 | ... | ... | 25 |
| 1921 | ... | ... | 916 | 251 | ... | 68 | 13 |
| 1922 | ... | ... | 1,209 | 245 | ... | 84 | 18 |
| 1923 | 14 | 40 | 1,473 | 253 | ... | 75 | 30 |
| 1924 | 31 | 37 | 1,145 | 362 | ... | 78 | 39 |
| 1925 | 36 | 48 | 1,908 | 332 | 6 | 78 | 52 |
| 1926 | 68 | 69 | 1,755 | 275 | 8 | 71 | 50 |
| 1927 | 31 | 59 | 2,100 | 251 | 13 | 87 | 50 |
| 1928 | 51 | 65 | 1,991 | 240 | 6 | 95 | 52 |
| 1929 | 67 | ... | 1,270 | 291 | 5 | 82 | 82 |
| 1930 | 79 | 66 | 1,990 | 223 | ... | 104 | 128 |
| 1931 | 74 | 66 | 2,262 | 263 | ... | 94 | 123 |
| 1932 | 84 | 59 | 1,575 | 177 | 5 | 91 | 38 |
| 1933 | 78 | 78 | 1,590 | 353 | 6 | 91 | 73 |
| 1934 | 107 | 104 | 2,025 | 664 | 6 | 101 | 86 |
| 1935 | 164 | 93 | 1,519 | 694 | 5 | 129 | 76 |
| 1936 | 200 | 114 | 1,978 | 820 | 5 | 146 | 77 |
| 1937 | 77 | 72 | 1,539 | 945 | 8 | 142 | 95 |
| 1938 | 128 | 69 | 1,410 | 1,019 | 11 | 135 | 112 |
| 1939 | 161 | 45 | 1,080 | 1,000 | 11 | 142 | 135 |

## C5    SOUTH AMERICA: Output of Major Oil Crops (in thousands of metric tons)

1935–1988

| | Argentina | | | | | Brazil | | | Colombia | Peru | Uruguay |
|------|------|------|------|------|------|------|------|------|------|------|------|
| | C | G | L | OO | SB | C | G | SB | C | C | L |
| 1940 | 160 | 84 | 1,720 | ... | ... | 1,094 | 14 | ... | 7 | 122 | 55 |
| 1941 | 93 | 61 | 1,600 | ... | ... | 1,174 | 12 | ... | 10 | 114 | 47 |
| 1942 | 155 | 83 | 1,348 | ... | ... | 880 | 12 | ... | 8 | 96 | 46 |
| 1943 | 205 | 96 | 1,573 | ... | ... | 1,158 | 25 | ... | 10 | 114 | 73 |
| 1944 | 232 | 199 | 787 | ... | ... | 1,167 | 29 | ... | 5 | 118 | 103 |
| 1945 | 135 | 158 | 964 | ... | ... | 746 | 31 | ... | 10 | 119 | 131 |
| 1946 | 118 | 139 | 1,034 | ... | ... | 744 | 41 | ... | 9 | 118 | |
| 1947 | 128 | 107 | 942 | ... | ... | 683 | 50 | 12 | 12 | 107 | 72 |
| 1948 | 170 | 120 | 433 | 1 | ... | 629 | 139 | 18 | 13 | 100 | 98 |
| 1949 | 190 | 85 | 676 | 2 | ... | 780 | 139 | ... | 16 | 113 | 117 |
| 1950 | 249 | 61 | 559 | 3 | ... | 774 | 136 | 35 | 21 | 119 | 75 |
| 1951 | 187 | 93 | 313 | 2 | 1 | 620 | 118 | 61 | 19 | 127 | 90 |
| 1952 | 239 | 155 | 584 | 2 | 1 | 942 | 151 | 78 | 32 | 147 | 142 |
| 1953 | 238 | 204 | 410 | 3 | ... | 695 | 146 | 88 | 51 | 146 | 109 |
| 1954 | 258 | 170 | 405 | 2 | 1 | 742 | 168 | 117 | 80 | 185 | 65 |
| 1955 | 221 | 118 | 238 | 7 | — | 814 | 186 | 107 | 70 | 174 | 63 |
| 1956 | 222 | 216 | 620 | 4 | 1 | 762 | 181 | 115 | 64 | 181 | 50 |
| 1957 | 201 | 318 | 630 | 8 | 1 | 744 | 192 | 122 | 58 | 170 | 72 |
| 1958 | 330 | 240 | 620 | 4 | 1 | 751 | 228 | 131 | 73 | 192 | 73 |
| 1959 | 181 | 241 | 825 | 7 | 1 | 886 | 357 | 152 | 157 | 199 | 72 |
| 1960 | 165 | 209 | 562 | 8 | 1 | 1,019 | 408 | 206 | 194 | 220 | 50 |
| 1961 | 229 | 266 | 818 | 4 | 1 | 1,158 | 584 | 271 | 197 | 221 | 67 |
| 1962 | 200 | 433 | 839 | 8 | 11 | 1,205 | 648 | 342 | 218 | 247 | 96 |
| 1963 | 257 | 312 | 771 | 7 | 19 | 1,239 | 604 | 323 | 177 | 247 | 84 |
| 1964 | 198 | 333 | 815 | 10 | 14 | 1,121 | 470 | 305 | 176 | 231 | 62 |
| 1965 | 267 | 439 | 570 | 12 | 17 | 1,258 | 743 | 523 | 162 | 218 | 71 |
| 1966 | 213 | 411 | 577 | 11 | 18 | 1,181 | 895 | 595 | 208 | 204 | 38 |
| 1967 | 158 | 354 | 385 | 13 | 21 | 1,072 | 751 | 716 | 265 | 161 | 40 |
| 1968 | 138 | 283 | 510 | 12 | 22 | 1,266 | 754 | 654 | 334 | 174 | 27 |
| 1969 | 218 | 217 | 640 | 20 | 32 | 1,372 | 754 | 1,057 | 357 | 158 | 56 |
| 1970 | 272 | 235 | 680 | 10 | 27 | 1,271 | 928 | 1,509 | 376 | 156 | 90 |
| 1971 | 167 | 388 | 316 | 21 | 59 | 947 | 945 | 1,977 | 322 | 143 | 42 |
| 1972 | 173 | 252 | 330 | 9 | 78 | 1,277 | 956 | 3,666 | 412 | 108 | 43 |
| 1973 | 244 | 440 | 297 | 24 | 272 | 1,215 | 590 | 5,012 | 335 | 148 | 29 |
| 1974 | 238 | 290 | 381 | 19 | 496 | 1,070 | 453 | 7,877 | 420 | 155 | 26 |
| 1975 | 314 | 375 | 377 | 17 | 485 | 1,138 | 442 | 9,893 | 401 | 120 | 39 |
| 1976 | 267 | 338 | 750 | 12 | 695 | 806 | 510 | 11,227 | 409 | 99 | 62 |
| 1977 | 324 | 600 | 810 | 12 | 1,400 | 1,008 | 321 | 12,513 | 480 | 122 | 46 |
| 1978 | 414 | 371 | 600 | 15 | 2,500 | 975 | 325 | 9,541 | 330 | 166 | 40 |
| 1979 | 330 | 671 | 743 | 22 | 3,700 | 1,085 | 455 | 10,240 | 282 | 191 | 31 |
| 1980 | 272 | 293 | 585 | 12 | 3,500 | 1,072 | 483 | 15,156 | 353 | 172 | 65 |
| 1981 | 153 | 289 | 600 | 15 | 3,770 | 1,107 | 355 | 15,007 | 366 | 163 | 21 |
| 1982 | 270 | 293 | 795 | 13 | 4,150 | 1,238 | 317 | 12,836 | 154 | 124 | 11 |
| 1983 | 202 | 236 | 660 | 16 | 4,000 | 995 | 284 | 14,582 | 130 | 140 | 5 |
| 1984 | 326 | 329 | 550 | 11 | 7,000 | 1,380 | 249 | 15,541 | 243 | 178 | 8 |
| 1985 | 293 | 343 | 460 | 11 | 6,500 | 1,810 | 339 | 18,278 | 185 | ... | 8 |
| 1986 | 207 | 379 | 622 | 12 | 7,100 | 1,466 | 217 | 13,335 | 184 | 167 | 7 |
| 1987 | 174 | 500 | 535 | 9 | 7,000 | 1,070 | 196 | 16,969 | 241 | 130 | 6 |
| 1988 | 467 | 443 | 430 | 10 | 9,900 | 1,620 | 170 | 18,021 | 243 | 180 | 3 |

NOTES

1. SOURCES: As for table C1
2. Note 2 of table C3 also applies to this table.

FOOTNOTE

[1] Earlier figures are available but the amounts are negligible.

**C6** **NORTH AMERICA: AREA AND OUTPUT OF COTTON AND TOBACCO** (in thousands of hectares and thousands of metric tons)

| | USA Cotton Output | | USA Cotton Output | | Mexico Cotton Output | Mexico Tobacco Output | USA Cotton Area | USA Cotton Output | USA Tobacco Area | USA Tobacco Output |
|---|---|---|---|---|---|---|---|---|---|---|
| 1790 | 0.7 | 1825 | 121 | 1865 | ... | ... | ... | 475 | ... | ... |
| 1791 | 0.9 | 1826 | 166 | 1866 | ... | ... | 3,102 | 476 | 159 | 143 |
| 1792 | 1.4 | 1827 | 128 | 1867 | ... | ... | 3,182 | 572 | 150 | 118 |
| 1793 | 2.3 | 1828 | 154 | 1868 | ... | ... | 2,822 | 537 | 149 | 130 |
| 1794 | 3.9 | 1829 | 173 | 1869 | ... | ... | 3,137 | 683 | 160 | 120 |
| 1795 | 3.9 | 1830 | 166 | 1870 | ... | ... | 3,738 | 987 | 172 | 156 |
| 1796 | 4.8 | 1831 | 183 | 1871 | ... | ... | 3,353 | 674 | 170 | 148 |
| 1797 | 5.2 | 1832 | 185 | 1872 | ... | ... | 3,877 | 892 | 199 | 175 |
| 1798 | 7.0 | 1833 | 211 | 1873 | ... | ... | 4,451 | 945 | 208 | 173 |
| 1799 | 9.5 | 1834 | 218 | 1874 | ... | ... | 4,352 | 870 | 153 | 98 |
| 1800 | 17.0 | 1835 | 241 | 1875 | ... | ... | 4,592 | 1,050 | 302 | 276 |
| 1801 | 23.0 | 1836 | 256 | 1876 | ... | ... | 4,754 | 1,015 | 253 | 211 |
| 1802 | 26.0 | 1837 | 324 | 1877 | ... | ... | 5,101 | 1,082 | 319 | 282 |
| 1803 | 29.0 | 1838 | 248 | 1878 | ... | ... | 5,479 | 1,151 | 263 | 206 |
| 1804 | 31.0 | 1839 | 375 | 1879 | ... | ... | 5,857 | 1,305 | 256 | 214 |
| 1805 | 33.0 | 1840 | 306 | 1880 | ... | ... | 6,443 | 1,498 | 263 | 213 |
| 1806 | 38.0 | 1841 | 317 | 1881 | ... | ... | 6,670 | 1,237 | 282 | 193 |
| 1807 | 38.0 | 1842 | 462 | 1882 | ... | ... | 6,328 | 1,576 | 301 | 263 |
| 1808 | 36.0 | 1843 | 397 | 1883 | ... | ... | 6,594 | 1,296 | 304 | 231 |
| 1809 | 39.0 | 1844 | 472 | 1884 | ... | ... | 6,819 | 1,289 | 305 | 263 |
| 1810 | 40.0 | 1845 | 410 | 1885 | ... | ... | 7,253 | 1,491 | 330 | 277 |
| 1811 | 38.0 | 1846 | 364 | 1886 | ... | ... | 7,434 | 1,475 | 343 | 276 |
| 1812 | 36.0 | 1847 | 483 | 1887 | ... | ... | 7,605 | 1,598 | 292 | 213 |
| 1813 | 36.0 | 1848 | 593 | 1888 | ... | 4 | 7,899 | 1,574 | 361 | 300 |
| 1814 | 33.0 | 1849 | 469 | 1889 | ... | 5 | 8,171 | 1,695 | 307 | 238 |
| 1815 | 47.0 | 1850 | 484 | 1890 | ... | 6 | 8,473 | 1,962 | 344 | 294 |
| 1816 | 59.0 | 1851 | 635 | 1891 | ... | 7 | 8,702 | 2,049 | 386 | 339 |
| 1817 | 62.0 | 1852 | 710 | 1892 | 16 | 10 | 7,636 | 1,520 | 420 | 343 |
| 1818 | 59.0 | 1853 | 627 | 1893 | 9 | 3 | 8,197 | 1,699 | 444 | 348 |
| 1819 | 79.0 | 1854 | 614 | 1894 | 17 | 9 | 8,857 | 2,062 | 402 | 348 |
| 1820 | 76.0 | 1855 | 731 | 1895 | 37 | 57 | 8,029 | 1,624 | 407 | 338 |
| 1821 | 86.0 | 1856 | 652 | 1896 | 39 | 15 | 9,401 | 1,935 | 420 | 345 |
| 1822 | 100.0 | 1857 | 683 | 1897 | 33 | 9 | 10,170 | 2,472 | 396 | 319 |
| 1823 | 88.0 | 1858 | 852 | 1898 | 46 | 45 | 10,002 | 2,558 | 452 | 412 |
| 1824 | 102.0 | 1859 | 1,022 | 1899 | 23 | 10 | 9,778 | 2,120 | 446 | 395 |
| | | 1860 | 871 | | | | | | | |
| | | 1861 | 1,019 | | | | | | | |
| | | 1862 | 362 | | | | | | | |
| | | 1863 | 102 | | | | | | | |
| | | 1864 | 68 | | | | | | | |

**C6    NORTH AMERICA: Area and Output of Cotton and Tobacco** (in thousands of hectares and thousands of metric tons)

| | Canada | | Cuba | | Dominican Republic | | El Salvador | |
|---|---|---|---|---|---|---|---|---|
| | Tobacco | | Tobacco | | Tobacco | | Cotton | |
| | Area | Output[1] | Area | Output | Area | Output | Area | Output |
| 1900 | ... | ... | ... | ... | ... | ... | ... | ... |
| 1901 | ... | 5.1 | ... | ... | ... | ... | ... | ... |
| 1902 | ... | ... | ... | 21 | ... | ... | ... | ... |
| 1903 | ... | ... | ... | 26 | ... | ... | ... | ... |
| 1904 | ... | ... | ... | 26 | ... | ... | ... | ... |
| 1905 | ... | ... | ... | 30 | ... | 10 | ... | ... |
| 1906 | ... | ... | ... | 24 | ... | 14 | ... | ... |
| 1907 | ... | ... | ... | 50 | ... | 12 | ... | ... |
| 1908 | ... | ... | ... | 13 | ... | 15 | ... | ... |
| 1909 | ... | ... | ... | 47 | ... | 14 | ... | ... |
| 1910 | ... | ... | ... | 38 | ... | 19 | ... | ... |
| 1911 | ... | 8.0 | ... | 30 | ... | 16 | ... | ... |
| 1912 | ... | ... | ... | 19 | ... | 8 | ... | ... |
| 1913 | 4 | 2.9 | ... | 33 | ... | 11 | ... | ... |
| 1914 | 4 | 5.7 | ... | 37 | ... | 4 | ... | ... |
| 1915 | 4 | 4.5 | ... | 23 | ... | 9 | ... | ... |
| 1916 | 2 | 4.1 | ... | 19 | ... | 9 | ... | ... |
| 1917 | 3 | 2.7 | ... | 28 | ... | ... | ... | ... |
| 1918 | 5 | 3.9 | ... | 37 | ... | ... | ... | ... |
| 1919 | 13 | 6.5 | ... | ... | ... | 14 | ... | ... |
| 1920 | 21 | 15.0 | ... | 57 | ... | 23 | ... | ... |
| 1921 | 5 | 22.0 | ... | 20 | ... | 7 | ... | ... |
| 1922 | 10 | 6.0 | ... | 24 | ... | 7 | ... | ... |
| 1923 | 10 | 12.0 | ... | 18 | ... | 16 | ... | ... |
| 1924 | 9 | 9.7 | ... | 27 | ... | 16 | ... | ... |
| 1925 | 11 | 8.5 | ... | 27 | ... | 20 | ... | ... |
| 1926 | 14 | 13.0 | ... | 26 | 16 | 8 | ... | ... |
| 1927 | 18 | 13.0 | ... | 28 | ... | 18 | ... | ... |
| 1928 | 17 | 20.0 | 61 | 27 | ... | 14 | ... | ... |
| 1929 | 15 | 19.0 | ... | 31 | ... | 20 | ... | ... |
| 1930 | 17 | 13.0 | ... | 37 | ... | 11 | ... | ... |
| 1931 | 22 | 17.0 | 69 | 37 | ... | ... | ... | ... |
| 1932 | 22 | 23.0 | 38 | 16 | ... | 6 | ... | ... |
| 1933 | 19 | 24.0 | 45 | 17 | ... | 6 | ... | ... |
| 1934 | 17 | 20.0 | 42 | 21 | ... | 10 | ... | ... |
| 1935 | 19 | 18.0 | 47 | 19 | ... | 7 | ... | ... |
| 1936 | 22 | 25.0 | 44 | 19 | ... | 9 | ... | ... |
| 1937 | 28 | 21.0 | 49 | 25 | ... | 9 | ... | ... |
| 1938 | 34 | 33.0 | 45 | 25 | ... | 14 | ... | ... |
| 1939 | 37 | 46.0 | 41 | 21 | ... | 11 | ... | ... |
| 1940 | 27 | 49.0 | 44 | 26 | ... | 6 | 3 | 2 |
| 1941 | 29 | 29.0 | 36 | 19 | ... | 6 | 3 | 2 |
| 1942 | 32 | 43.0 | 40 | 23 | ... | 6 | 4 | 2 |
| 1943 | 29 | 41.0 | 32 | 19 | ... | 12 | 5 | 3 |
| 1944 | 36 | 31.0 | 51 | 30 | ... | 5 | 5 | 3 |

**C6**  **NORTH AMERICA: Area and Output of Cotton and Tobacco** (in thousands of hectares and thousands of metric tons)

| | Mexico | | | | USA | | | |
|---|---|---|---|---|---|---|---|---|
| | Cotton | | Tobacco | | Cotton | | Tobacco | |
| | Area | Output | Area | Output | Area | Output | Area | Output |
| 1900 | ... | 22 | ... | 9 | 10,071 | 2,296 | 439 | 386 |
| 1901 | ... | 22 | ... | 12 | 10,947 | 2,156 | 444 | 402 |
| 1902 | ... | 23 | ... | 4 | 11,154 | 2,411 | 481 | 435 |
| 1903 | ... | 37 | ... | 13 | 11,235 | 2,234 | 490 | 443 |
| 1904 | ... | 55 | ... | 13 | 12,172 | 3,048 | 415 | 389 |
| 1905 | ... | 148 | ... | 18 | 11,231 | 2,399 | 446 | 426 |
| 1906 | ... | 59 | ... | 16 | 12,709 | 3,010 | 454 | 441 |
| 1907 | ... | 34 | ... | 9 | 12,436 | 2,519 | 422 | 402 |
| 1908 | ... | 25 | ... | 7 | 12,582 | 3,003 | 408 | 379 |
| 1909 | ... | ... | ... | ... | 12,365 | 2,269 | 523 | 478 |
| 1910 | ... | 44 | ... | ... | 12,751 | 2,633 | 566 | 518 |
| 1911 | ... | 35 | ... | ... | 14,130 | 3,559 | 459 | 427 |
| 1912 | ... | 52 | ... | ... | 13,175 | 3,108 | 540 | 507 |
| 1913 | ... | 45 | ... | 12 | 14,247 | 3,210 | 524 | 450 |
| 1914 | ... | ... | ... | ... | 14,413 | 3,654 | 509 | 470 |
| 1915 | ... | 21 | ... | ... | 12,121 | 2,534 | 574 | 525 |
| 1916 | ... | 18 | ... | 12 | 13,383 | 2,596 | 600 | 547 |
| 1917 | ... | 14 | ... | ... | 13,049 | 2,559 | 654 | 601 |
| 1918 | ... | 79 | ... | 13 | 14,179 | 2,726 | 696 | 655 |
| 1919 | ... | ... | ... | 19 | 13,317 | 2,527 | 793 | 655 |
| 1920 | ... | ... | ... | ... | 13,924 | 3,046 | 783 | 684 |
| 1921 | ... | 32 | ... | 7 | 11,606 | 1,802 | 542 | 456 |
| 1922 | ... | 44 | 5 | 11 | 12,691 | 2,212 | 654 | 569 |
| 1923 | ... | 38 | 10 | 11 | 14,387 | 2,300 | 751 | 689 |
| 1924 | ... | 43 | 12 | 13 | 15,986 | 3,091 | 689 | 565 |
| 1925 | 172 | 44 | 16 | 9 | 17,962 | 3,653 | 709 | 624 |
| 1926 | 248 | 78 | 16 | 9 | 18,052 | 4,077 | 659 | 585 |
| 1927 | 132 | 39 | 17 | 10 | 15,516 | 2,938 | 630 | 549 |
| 1928 | 203 | 60 | 18 | 13 | 17,172 | 3,283 | 754 | 623 |
| 1929 | 199 | 53 | 17 | 13 | 17,495 | 3,362 | 801 | 695 |
| 1930 | 158 | 39 | 13 | 11 | 17,176 | 3,160 | 860 | 748 |
| 1931 | 129 | 46 | 14 | 11 | 15,663 | 3,878 | 805 | 710 |
| 1932 | 78 | 22 | 13 | 11 | 14,525 | 2,949 | 569 | 462 |
| 1933 | 172 | 57 | 13 | 10 | 11,891 | 2,959 | 704 | 622 |
| 1934 | 169 | 48 | 14 | 12 | 10,872 | 2,185 | 515 | 492 |
| 1935 | 266 | 68 | 16 | 14 | 11,133 | 2,413 | 582 | 591 |
| 1936 | 343 | 86 | 15 | 13 | 12,033 | 2,812 | 583 | 528 |
| 1937 | 336 | 74 | 22 | 20 | 13,607 | 4,297 | 709 | 712 |
| 1938 | 260 | 66 | 21 | 19 | 9,813 | 2,709 | 648 | 629 |
| 1939 | 262 | 68 | 19 | 21 | 9,634 | 2,680 | 809 | 853 |
| 1940 | 254 | 65 | 21 | 24 | 9,656 | 2,850 | 571 | 662 |
| 1941 | 316 | 81 | 20 | 20 | 8,999 | 2,437 | 529 | 572 |
| 1942 | 362 | 103 | 22 | 19 | 9,147 | 2,907 | 557 | 639 |
| 1943 | 409 | 116 | 17 | 14 | 8,745 | 2,592 | 590 | 638 |
| 1944 | 390 | 106 | 20 | 20 | 7,939 | 2,774 | 708 | 885 |

**C6    NORTH AMERICA: Area and Output of Cotton and Tobacco** (in thousands of hectares and thousands of metric tons)

| | Canada | | Cuba | | Dominican Republic | | El Salvador | | Guatemala | |
|---|---|---|---|---|---|---|---|---|---|---|
| | Tobacco | | Tobacco | | Tobacco | | Cotton | | Cotton | |
| | Area | Output | Area | Output | Area | Output | Area | Output | Area | Output |
| 1945 | 38 | 48 | 53 | 32 | ... | 16 | 10 | 2 | ... | ... |
| 1946 | 45 | 42 | 57 | 36 | 26 | 32 | 11 | 4 | 3 | ... |
| 1947 | 51 | 64 | 58 | 36 | 15 | 21 | 15 | 4 | 3 | ... |
| 1948 | 45 | 48 | 43 | 26 | 20 | 20 | 13 | 7 | 4 | 1 |
| 1949 | 44 | 57 | 60 | ... | 15 | 26 | 17 | 5 | 3 | 2 |
| 1950 | 41 | 63 | 58 | ... | 20 | 22 | 19 | 7 | 2 | 2 |
| 1951 | 48 | 55 | 54 | 36 | 18 | 18 | 30 | 10 | 8 | 2 |
| 1952 | 37 | 70 | 56 | 35 | 18 | 17 | 28 | 11 | 9 | 3 |
| 1953 | 41 | 63 | 62 | 50 | 19 | 17 | 21 | 13 | 11 | 6 |
| 1954 | 53 | 63 | 62 | 50 | 21 | 19 | 30 | 20 | 16 | 8 |
| 1955 | 44 | 84 | 62 | 50 | 20 | 18 | 46 | 31 | 21 | 10 |
| 1956 | 52 | 61 | 58 | 46 | 20 | 19 | 38 | 32 | 13 | 10 |
| 1957 | 55 | 73 | 60 | 52 | 22 | 21 | 40 | 36 | 18 | 14 |
| 1958 | 54 | 75 | 60 | 53 | 24 | 21 | 54 | 40 | 28 | 16 |
| 1959 | 52 | 89 | 56 | 41 | 20 | 18 | 39 | 31 | 18 | 15 |
| 1960 | 55 | 77 | 59 | 52 | 22 | 23 | 43 | 41 | 26 | 21 |
| 1961 | 56 | 95 | 55 | 47 | 19 | 26 | 77 | 61 | 46 | 26 |
| 1962 | 53 | 92 | 53 | 45 | 22 | 27 | 94 | 72 | 72 | 53 |
| 1963 | 46 | 91 | 58 | 48 | 25 | 25 | 88 | 75 | 90 | 66 |
| 1964 | 35 | 70 | 55 | 44 | 19 | 28 | 114 | 82 | 98 | 72 |
| 1965 | 38 | 77 | 65 | 44 | 19 | 19 | 111 | 52 | 100 | 82 |
| 1966 | 53 | 106 | 60 | 51 | 20 | 21 | 82 | 39 | 84 | 59 |
| 1967 | 57 | 97 | 54 | 45 | 19 | 19 | 49 | 35 | 90 | 78 |
| 1968 | 55 | 99 | 54 | 46 | 18 | 16 | 41 | 43 | 96 | 74 |
| 1969 | 54 | 112 | 45 | 36 | 18 | 21 | 51 | 46 | 85 | 56 |
| 1970 | 44 | 101 | 60 | 46 | 20 | 23 | 56 | 55 | 74 | 57 |
| 1971 | 39 | 102 | 59 | 40 | 21 | 26 | 62 | 55 | 71 | 56 |
| 1972 | 42 | 85 | 64 | 44 | 25 | 28 | 73 | 68 | 70 | 81 |
| 1973 | 49 | 117 | 66 | 45 | 31 | 44 | 85 | 69 | 89 | 96 |
| 1974 | 50 | 116 | 69 | 50 | 31 | 34 | 95 | 75 | 104 | 121 |
| 1975 | 42 | 106 | 66 | 42 | 16 | 35 | 88 | 74 | 111 | 107 |
| 1976 | 37 | 81 | 69 | 52 | 25 | 45 | 74 | 60 | 84 | 99 |
| 1977 | 44 | 104 | 60 | 46 | 28 | 35 | 79 | 70 | 122 | 136 |
| 1978 | 49 | 116 | 61 | 40 | 40 | 54 | 99 | 79 | 123 | 149 |
| 1979 | 47 | 79 | 57 | 33 | 37 | 45 | 102 | 65 | 122 | 161 |
| 1980 | 46 | 108 | 20 | 7 | 27 | 37 | 85 | 62 | 123 | 151 |
| 1981 | 47 | 112 | 68 | 54 | 33 | 40 | 58 | 43 | 100 | 114 |
| 1982 | 31 | 70 | 65 | 42 | 35 | 34 | 53 | 40 | 66 | 71 |
| 1983 | 47 | 112 | 51 | 30 | 30 | 34 | 49 | 41 | 56 | 55 |
| 1984 | 41 | 89 | 54 | 45 | 29 | 28 | 37 | 30 | 58 | 59 |
| 1985 | 40 | 97 | 63 | 45 | 21 | 27 | 37 | 25 | 63 | 59 |
| 1986 | 31 | 67 | 58 | 46 | 27 | 29 | 27 | 14 | 66 | 44 |
| 1987 | 30 | 61 | 56 | 39 | 23 | 29 | 13 | 12 | 31 | 28 |
| 1988 | 29 | 70 | 50 | 39 | 23 | 30 | 13 | 10 | 40 | 42 |

**C6** **NORTH AMERICA: Area and Output of Cotton and Tobacco** (in thousands of hectares and thousands of metric tons)

| | Mexico | | | | Nicaragua | | U.S.A. | | | |
| | Cotton | | Tobacco | | Cotton | | Cotton | | Tobacco | |
| | Area | Output | Area | Output | Area | Output | Area | Output | Area | Output |
|---|---|---|---|---|---|---|---|---|---|---|
| 1945 | 366 | 98 | 19 | 19 | ... | ... | 6,891 | 2,045 | 737 | 903 |
| 1946 | 327 | 91 | 37 | 36 | ... | ... | 7,116 | 1,960 | 793 | 596 |
| 1947 | 333 | 96 | 35 | 38 | ... | ... | 8,632 | 2,690 | 749 | 956 |
| 1948 | 405 | 120 | 36 | 36 | 3 | 4 | 9,272 | 3,374 | 629 | 898 |
| 1949 | 549 | 208 | 35 | 34 | 15 | 1 | 11,104 | 3,658 | 657 | 893 |
| 1950 | 761 | 260 | 35 | 35 | 17 | 4 | 7,221 | 2,271 | 647 | 921 |
| 1951 | 884 | 288 | 35 | 36 | 35 | 9 | 10,906 | 3,436 | 720 | 1,058 |
| 1952 | 784 | 265 | 35 | 36 | 30 | 12 | 10,490 | 3,433 | 717 | 1,023 |
| 1953 | 753 | 274 | 36 | 37 | 42 | 19 | 9,850 | 3,734 | 661 | 934 |
| 1954 | 922 | 391 | 37 | 38 | 86 | 47 | 7,791 | 3,106 | 675 | 1,018 |
| 1955 | 1,059 | 508 | 43 | 53 | 87 | 35 | 6,851 | 3,339 | 605 | 995 |
| 1956 | 873 | 426 | 45 | 54 | 70 | 42 | 6,319 | 3,019 | 552 | 987 |
| 1957 | 916 | 478 | 51 | 70 | 61 | 48 | 5,487 | 2,487 | 454 | 757 |
| 1958 | 1,028 | 526 | 52 | 71 | 74 | 49 | 4,795 | 2,611 | 436 | 787 |
| 1959 | 751 | 380 | 53 | 72 | 67 | 28 | 6,118 | 3,302 | 467 | 815 |
| 1960 | 899 | 470 | 54 | 72 | 61 | 33 | 6,195 | 3,238 | 462 | 882 |
| 1961 | 794 | 450 | 52 | 67 | 78 | 57 | 6,327 | 3,247 | 475 | 935 |
| 1962 | 787 | 486 | 43 | 53 | 95 | 74 | 6,301 | 3,228 | 495 | 1,050 |
| 1963 | 847 | 535 | 52 | 68 | 119 | 94 | 5,751 | 3,330 | 476 | 1,063 |
| 1964 | 809 | 565 | 52 | 68 | 135 | 125 | 5,688 | 3,297 | 436 | 1,011 |
| 1965 | 813 | 577 | 52 | 69 | 162 | 111 | 5,509 | 3,255 | 395 | 841 |
| 1966 | 695 | 521 | 40 | 57 | 151 | 115 | 3,866 | 2,080 | 394 | 856 |
| 1967 | 662 | 495 | 40 | 61 | 147 | 102 | 3,236 | 1,621 | 388 | 893 |
| 1968 | 705 | 552 | 35 | 47 | 126 | 93 | 4,111 | 2,379 | 356 | 776 |
| 1969 | 513 | 397 | 40 | 72 | 109 | 69 | 4,472 | 2,175 | 372 | 818 |
| 1970 | 411 | 334 | 43 | 80 | 96 | 73 | 4,514 | 2,219 | 364 | 865 |
| 1971 | 458 | 397 | 41 | 65 | 110 | 79 | 4,642 | 2,281 | 339 | 773 |
| 1972 | 523 | 417 | 43 | 82 | 143 | 103 | 5,254 | 2,984 | 341 | 793 |
| 1973 | 421 | 392 | 39 | 61 | 143 | 106 | 4,844 | 2,825 | 359 | 790 |
| 1974 | 567 | 513 | 40 | 72 | 182 | 146 | 5,086 | 2,513 | 390 | 902 |
| 1975 | 227 | 206 | 40 | 68 | 179 | 123 | 3,560 | 1,807 | 440 | 990 |
| 1976 | 235 | 224 | 40 | 67 | 144 | 110 | 4,416 | 2,304 | 423 | 969 |
| 1977 | 420 | 418 | 40 | 55 | 198 | 118 | 5,372 | 3,133 | 387 | 868 |
| 1978 | 350 | 366 | 45 | 70 | 212 | 123 | 5,018 | 2,364 | 390 | 918 |
| 1979 | 405 | 349 | 47 | 72 | 174 | 113 | 5,192 | 3,185 | 335 | 692 |
| 1980 | 372 | 373 | 49 | 94 | 45 | 22 | 5,348 | 2,422 | 373 | 810 |
| 1981 | 355 | 335 | 35 | 56 | 94 | 76 | 5,601 | 3,406 | 395 | 936 |
| 1982 | 200 | 196 | 40 | 67 | 93 | 64 | 3,937 | 2,605 | 367 | 905 |
| 1983 | 232 | 229 | 37 | 53 | 116 | 81 | 2,973 | 1,692 | 319 | 648 |
| 1984 | 316 | 280 | 37 | 41 | 115 | 87 | 4,200 | 2,827 | 320 | 784 |
| 1985 | 193 | 220 | 35 | 48 | 115 | 69 | 4,140 | 2,924 | 278 | 686 |
| 1986 | 157 | 144 | 44 | 64 | 59 | 49 | 3,427 | 2,119 | 235 | 527 |
| 1987 | 222 | 220 | 44 | 53 | 60 | 49 | 4,059 | 3,214 | 238 | 540 |
| 1988 | 298 | 300 | 45 | 67 | 41 | 33 | 4,835 | 3,355 | 257 | 622 |

**C6      SOUTH AMERICA: AREA AND OUTPUT OF COTTON AND TOBACCO** (in thousands of hectares and thousands of metric tons)

| | Argentina | | | | Brazil | | | |
| | Cotton | | Tobacco | | Cotton | | Tobacco | |
| | Area | Output | Area | Output | Area | Output | Area | Output |
|------|------|--------|------|--------|-------|--------|------|--------|
| 1900 | ... | 0.2 | 13 | ... | ... | 34 | ... | ... |
| 1901 | ... | 0.3 | 11 | ... | ... | 55 | ... | ... |
| 1902 | ... | 0.1 | 10 | ... | ... | 51 | ... | ... |
| 1903 | ... | 0.5 | 10 | ... | ... | 48 | ... | ... |
| 1904 | ... | 0.7 | 18 | ... | ... | 59 | ... | ... |
| 1905 | ... | 0.5 | 17 | 4 | ... | 80 | ... | ... |
| 1906 | ... | 0.5 | 14 | 5 | ... | 76 | ... | ... |
| 1907 | ... | 0.4 | 10 | 6 | ... | 50 | ... | ... |
| 1908 | ... | 0.4 | 10 | 10 | ... | 58 | ... | ... |
| 1909 | 2 | 0.4 | 10 | 7 | ... | 59 | ... | ... |
| 1910 | 2 | 0.4 | 10 | 6 | ... | 78 | ... | ... |
| 1911 | 2 | 0.4 | 10 | 6 | ... | 91 | ... | ... |
| 1912 | 3 | 0.7 | 10 | 5 | ... | 103 | ... | ... |
| 1913 | 2 | 0.5 | 15 | 5 | ... | 101 | ... | ... |
| 1914 | 3 | 0.8 | 15 | 4 | ... | 73 | ... | ... |
| 1915 | 4 | 0.9 | 8 | 11 | 204 | 74 | ... | 45 |
| 1916 | 3 | 0.7 | 10 | 6 | 203 | 87 | ... | ... |
| 1917 | 12 | 3.0 | 11 | 4 | 294 | 118 | ... | ... |
| 1918 | 13 | 3.0 | 6 | ... | 245 | 97 | ... | ... |
| 1919 | 13 | 3.0 | 8 | 10 | 277 | 108 | ... | 74 |
| 1920 | 24 | 6.0 | 13 | 15 | 326 | 100 | ... | 87 |
| 1921 | 16 | 4.0 | 14 | 17 | 575 | 108 | ... | 80 |
| 1922 | 23 | 6.0 | 7 | 8 | 612 | 105 | 63 | 71 |
| 1923 | 63 | 13.0 | 9 | 11 | 628 | 108 | 79 | 62 |
| 1924 | 105 | 15.0 | 8 | 10 | 637 | 155 | 67 | 59 |
| 1925 | 110 | 29.0 | 9 | 10 | 534 | 142 | 65 | 57 |
| 1926 | 72 | 13.0 | 5 | 11 | 399 | 118 | 82 | 65 |
| 1927 | 85 | 25.0 | 9 | 14 | 525 | 108 | ... | 87 |
| 1928 | 104 | 26.0 | 11 | 11 | 519 | 103 | 110 | 110 |
| 1929 | 122 | 33.0 | 13 | 13 | 581 | 125 | 90 | 88 |
| 1930 | 127 | 30.0 | 13 | 11 | | 95 | ... | 98 |
| 1931 | 136 | 37.0 | 15 | 13 | 738 | 113 | ... | 100 |
| 1932 | 138 | 33.0 | 14 | 15 | 634 | 76 | ... | 92 |
| 1933 | 195 | 43.0 | 12 | 10 | 889 | 151 | 9 | 100 |
| 1934 | 286 | 64.0 | 22 | 24 | 1,589 | 284 | 124 | 102 |
| 1935 | 309 | 81.0 | 16 | 15 | 1,765 | 297 | 96 | 91 |
| 1936 | 289 | 31.0 | 12 | 11 | 1,968 | 352 | 102 | 84 |
| 1937 | 330 | 51.0 | 12 | 8 | 2,236 | 405 | 105 | 91 |
| 1938 | 340 | 71.0 | 19 | 20 | 2,350 | 437 | 107 | 93 |
| 1939 | 295 | 79.0 | 20 | 19 | 2,273 | 429 | 96 | 95 |
| 1940 | 298 | 50.0 | 22 | 18 | 2,412 | 469 | 96 | 95 |
| 1941 | 308 | 81.0 | 17 | 15 | 2,493 | 503 | 96 | 93 |
| 1942 | 336 | 108.0 | 19 | 18 | 1,931 | 377 | 102 | 92 |
| 1943 | 370 | 120.0 | 20 | 19 | 2,424 | 496 | ... | ... |
| 1944 | 359 | 72.0 | 22 | 22 | 2,808 | 592 | ... | ... |

**C6    SOUTH AMERICA: Area and Output of Cotton and Tobacco** (in thousands of hectares and thousands of metric tons)

| | Colombia | | Paraguay | | Peru | |
| | Tobacco | | Tobacco | | Cotton | |
| | Area | Output | Area | Output | Area | Output |
|---|---|---|---|---|---|---|
| 1900 | ... | ... | ... | ... | ... | 7 |
| 1901 | ... | ... | ... | ... | ... | 8 |
| 1902 | ... | ... | ... | ... | ... | 7 |
| 1903 | ... | ... | ... | ... | ... | 8 |
| 1904 | ... | ... | ... | ... | ... | 8 |
| 1905 | ... | ... | ... | ... | ... | 9 |
| 1906 | ... | ... | ... | ... | ... | 10 |
| 1907 | ... | ... | ... | ... | ... | 12 |
| 1908 | ... | ... | ... | ... | ... | 16 |
| 1909 | ... | ... | ... | ... | ... | 21 |
| 1910 | ... | ... | 8 | 9 | ... | 14 |
| 1911 | ... | ... | 6 | 7 | ... | 16 |
| 1912 | ... | ... | 7 | 8 | ... | 19 |
| 1913 | ... | ... | 7 | 8 | ... | 24 |
| 1914 | ... | ... | 9 | 10 | 56 | 23 |
| 1915 | 7 | 6 | 8 | 10 | 56 | 21 |
| 1916 | ... | ... | ... | ... | 65 | 28 |
| 1917 | ... | ... | 14 | 14 | 64 | 27 |
| 1918 | ... | ... | ... | ... | 90 | 31 |
| 1919 | ... | ... | ... | ... | 90 | 34 |
| 1920 | ... | ... | 10 | 12 | 109 | 38 |
| 1921 | ... | ... | 9 | 10 | 108 | 40 |
| 1922 | ... | ... | 13 | 11 | 114 | 43 |
| 1923 | ... | ... | 11 | 10 | 114 | 46 |
| 1924 | 16 | 12 | 12 | 12 | 118 | 47 |
| 1925 | 16 | 13 | ... | 12 | 120 | 46 |
| 1926 | 17 | 13 | 9 | 9 | 128 | 53 |
| 1927 | 13 | 10 | ... | 9 | 128 | 53 |
| 1928 | 7 | 9 | 8 | 13 | 115 | 49 |
| 1929 | ... | ... | 8 | 13 | 127 | 66 |
| 1930 | ... | ... | 9 | 14 | 134 | 59 |
| 1931 | ... | ... | 9 | 14 | 127 | 51 |
| 1932 | ... | 8 | ... | ... | 123 | 53 |
| 1933 | ... | 8 | ... | 1 | 130 | 60 |
| 1934 | ... | 11 | ... | 5 | 149 | 74 |
| 1935 | ... | 10 | 18 | 16 | 162 | 85 |
| 1936 | ... | 11 | 6 | 6 | 166 | 84 |
| 1937 | 7 | 15 | 4 | 4 | 157 | 82 |
| 1938 | 6 | ... | 9 | 8 | 191 | 86 |
| 1939 | 9 | ... | ... | ... | 177 | 82 |
| 1940 | 8 | 19 | 7 | 4 | 180 | 83 |
| 1941 | | ... | 5 | 4 | 170 | 71 |
| 1942 | | ... | 6 | 4 | 156 | 70 |
| 1943 | 15 | ... | 6 | 6 | 125 | 57 |
| 1944 | | ... | 6 | ... | 132 | 67 |

**C6**  **SOUTH AMERICA: Area and Output of Cotton and Tobacco** (in thousands of hectares and thousands of metric tons)

| | Argentina | | | | Brazil | | | |
|---|---|---|---|---|---|---|---|---|
| | Cotton | | Tobacco | | Cotton | | Tobacco | |
| | Area | Output | Area | Output | Area | Output | Area | Output |
| 1945 | 332 | 62 | 28 | 27 | 2,722 | 378 | 114 | 109 |
| 1946 | 361 | 69 | 30 | 29 | 2,480 | 378 | 136 | 119 |
| 1947 | 420 | 78 | 26 | 27 | 2,470 | 347 | 134 | 111 |
| 1948 | 465 | | 17 | 22 | 2,308 | 320 | 144 | 118 |
| 1949 | 517 | 130 | 24 | 26 | 2,497 | 396 | 145 | 115 |
| 1950 | 458 | 99 | 24 | 27 | 2,689 | 393 | 142 | 108 |
| 1951 | 461 | 142 | 36 | 26 | 2,487 | 349 | 160 | 106 |
| 1952 | 561 | 125 | 37 | 39 | 3,035 | 515 | 154 | 118 |
| 1953 | 533 | 123 | 38 | 36 | 2,587 | 375 | 168 | 132 |
| 1954 | 551 | 137 | 33 | 33 | 2,487 | 395 | 184 | 147 |
| 1955 | 550 | 114 | 31 | 32 | 2,617 | 428 | 196 | 148 |
| 1956 | 533 | 122 | 35 | 41 | 2,663 | 400 | 180 | 144 |
| 1957 | 545 | 105 | 40 | 45 | 2,771 | 397 | 179 | 140 |
| 1958 | 641 | 171 | 28 | 25 | 2,707 | 381 | 181 | 144 |
| 1959 | 496 | 100 | 30 | 28 | 2,746 | 466 | 191 | 151 |
| 1960 | 461 | 89 | 36 | 41 | 2,930 | 536 | 213 | 161 |
| 1961 | 499 | 124 | 46 | 48 | 3,234 | 609 | 228 | 168 |
| 1962 | 537 | 108 | 38 | 47 | 3,458₂ | 634 | 232 | 187 |
| | | | | | 2,226 | | | |
| 1963 | 519 | 133 | 42 | 55 | 2,226 | 652 | 250 | 207 |
| 1964 | 520 | 99 | 44 | 49 | 2,327 | 590 | 251 | 210 |
| 1965 | 534 | 138 | 48 | 53 | 2,327 | 662 | 274 | 248 |
| 1966 | 441 | 116 | 48 | 45 | 2,226 | 622 | 265 | 228 |
| 1967 | 330 | 87 | 59 | 63 | 2,023 | 564 | 261 | 243 |
| 1968 | 282 | 72 | 59 | 62 | 2,266 | 666 | 276 | 258 |
| 1969 | 406 | 112 | 54 | 54 | 2,631 | 697 | 258 | 250 |
| 1970 | 452 | 145 | 69 | 66 | 2,873 | 673 | 245 | 244 |
| 1971 | 367 | 84 | 65 | 62 | 2,428 | 499 | 255 | 254 |
| 1972 | 398 | 85 | 68 | 74 | 2,631 | 672 | 260 | 263 |
| 1973 | 457 | 125 | 74 | 71 | 2,428 | 640 | 234 | 234 |
| 1974 | 474 | 127 | 83 | 98 | 2,307 | 646 | 226 | 296 |
| 1975 | 505 | 172 | 88 | 98 | 2,226 | 577 | 239 | 286 |
| 1976 | 414 | 140 | 79 | 95 | 1,902 | 417 | 286 | 299 |
| 1977 | 518 | 160 | 75 | 90 | 2,145 | 627 | 311 | 357 |
| 1978 | 607 | 220 | 62 | 63 | 2,023 | 518 | 328 | 405 |
| 1979 | 669 | 174 | 75 | 70 | 2,023 | 540 | 326 | 422 |
| 1980 | 568 | 145 | 58 | 62 | 3,699 | 553 | 316 | 405 |
| 1981 | 282 | 84 | 47 | 52 | 3,511 | 571 | 298 | 366 |
| 1982 | 399 | 152 | 55 | 69 | 3,644 | 639 | 319 | 420 |
| 1983 | 343 | 112 | 60 | 74 | 2,926 | 540 | 312 | 393 |
| 1984 | 470 | 180 | 61 | 75 | 3,114 | 723 | 282 | 414 |
| 1985 | 447 | 171 | 58 | 60 | 3,590 | 926 | 269 | 411 |
| 1986 | 339 | 120 | 49 | 66 | 3,160 | 735 | 279 | 387 |
| 1987 | 273 | 100 | 51 | 70 | 1,968 | 552 | 298 | 397 |
| 1988 | 492 | 282 | 55 | 72 | 2,558 | 837 | 283 | 430 |

**C6    SOUTH AMERICA: Area and Output of Cotton and Tobacco** (in thousands of hectares and thousands of metric tons)

| | Colombia | | | | Paraguay | | Peru | |
|---|---|---|---|---|---|---|---|---|
| | Cotton | | Tobacco | | Tobacco | | Cotton | |
| | Area | Output | Area | Output | Area | Output | Area | Output |
| 1945 | ... | ... | 16 | 16 | 7 | 6 | 150 | 71 |
| 1946 | ... | ... | 16 | 19 | 9 | 11 | 125 | 70 |
| 1947 | 63 | 5 | 18 | 18 | 11 | 13 | 130 | 67 |
| 1948 | 87 | 6 | 20 | 20 | 7 | 9 | 150 | 67 |
| 1949 | 36 | 6 | 18 | 20 | 4 | 5 | 134 | 74 |
| 1950 | 37 | 8 | 19 | 20 | 5 | 5 | 160 | 84 |
| 1951 | 40 | 7 | 20 | 22 | 7 | 7 | 190 | 96 |
| 1952 | 55 | 11 | 20 | 22 | 7 | 7 | 190 | 96 |
| 1953 | 67 | 17 | 20 | 26 | 7 | 7 | 205 | 97 |
| 1954 | 82 | 28 | 26 | 26 | 10 | 10 | 209 | 114 |
| 1955 | 84 | 25 | 22 | 39 | 6 | 6 | 217 | 109 |
| 1956 | 69 | 22 | 21 | 36 | 5 | 6 | 227 | 114 |
| 1957 | 63 | 21 | 22 | 37 | 5 | 5 | 231 | 104 |
| 1958 | 77 | 26 | 23 | 38 | 7 | 7 | 238 | 116 |
| 1959 | 131 | 66 | 23 | 39 | 10 | 10 | 236 | 120 |
| 1960 | 150 | 67 | 15 | 25 | 8 | 9 | 252 | 133 |
| 1961 | 150 | 76 | 14 | 28 | 12 | 15 | 244 | 134 |
| 1962 | 169 | 62 | 19 | 39 | 20 | 25 | 253 | 149 |
| 1963 | 141 | 73 | 22 | 42 | 10 | 12 | 257 | 149 |
| 1964 | 150 | 66 | 22 | 41 | 14 | 18 | 246 | 139 |
| 1965 | 148 | 65 | 26 | 40 | 7 | 9 | 238 | 131 |
| 1966 | 164 | 88 | 27 | 44 | 11 | 14 | 204 | 121 |
| 1967 | 175 | 97 | 23 | 43 | 18 | 22 | 181 | 97 |
| 1968 | 199 | 120 | 23 | 43 | 20 | 24 | 166 | 105 |
| 1969 | 236 | 125 | 24 | 45 | 13 | 18 | 169 | 95 |
| 1970 | 267 | 128 | 23 | 42 | 14 | 18 | 144 | 92 |
| 1971 | 219 | 112 | 23 | 39 | 16 | 18 | 136 | 86 |
| 1972 | 242 | 145 | 24 | 36 | 17 | 23 | 129 | 68 |
| 1973 | 251 | 116 | 26 | 40 | 20 | 27 | 152 | 89 |
| 1974 | 258 | 146 | 25 | 41 | 24 | 33 | 142 | 81 |
| 1975 | 281 | 139 | 34 | 58 | 28 | 39 | 97 | 63 |
| 1976 | 286 | 142 | 30 | 39 | 30 | 41 | 98 | 65 |
| 1977 | 377 | 162 | 33 | 58 | 22 | 27 | 118 | 72 |
| 1978 | 328 | 111 | 18 | 47 | 21 | 26 | 123 | 87 |
| 1979 | 186 | 97 | 19 | 60 | 15 | 20 | 135 | 100 |
| 1980 | 217 | 122 | 18 | 47 | 8 | 11 | 149 | 102 |
| 1981 | 221 | 129 | 30 | 50 | 10 | 19 | 157 | 94 |
| 1982 | 99 | 57 | 31 | 49 | 12 | 22 | 134 | 36 |
| 1983 | 119 | 77 | 29 | 48 | 15 | 20 | 84 | 76 |
| 1984 | 223 | 92 | 21 | 35 | 16 | 25 | 99 | 99 |
| 1985 | 196 | 118 | 18 | 27 | 14 | 17 | 150 | 99 |
| 1986 | 190 | 119 | 18 | 29 | 9 | 15 | 162 | 89 |
| 1987 | 229 | 134 | 21 | 35 | 9 | 14 | 120 | 67 |
| 1988 | 215 | 125 | 21 | 36 | 6 | 14 | 133 | 93 |

NOTES

1.  SOURCES: As for table C1.
2.  Note 2 of table C3 also applies to this table.

FOOTNOTES.

[1] Earlier figures are available as follows:- 1871 0.7, 1891 1.9.
[2] Figures from 1962 (2nd line) are derived from the International Cotton Advisory Committee, which the FAO has preferred to the earlier official series.

C7     **NORTH AMERICA: OUTPUT OF COCOA, COFFEE AND TEA** (in thousands of metric tons)

**1875–19**

| | Costa Rica | Cuba | Dominican Republic | | El Salvador | Guatemala | Mexico | | Puerto Rico | Trinidad & Tobago |
|---|---|---|---|---|---|---|---|---|---|---|
| | Coffee | Coffee | Cocoa | Coffee | Coffee | Coffee | Cocoa | Coffee | Coffee | Cocoa |
| 1875 | ... | ... | ... | ... | ... | ... | ... | ... | ... | ... |
| 1876 | ... | ... | ... | ... | ... | ... | ... | ... | ... | ... |
| 1877 | ... | ... | ... | ... | ... | ... | ... | 8 | ... | ... |
| 1878 | ... | ... | ... | ... | ... | ... | ... | ... | ... | ... |
| 1879 | ... | ... | ... | ... | ... | ... | ... | ... | ... | ... |
| 1880 | ... | ... | ... | ... | ... | ... | ... | ... | ... | ... |
| 1881 | ... | ... | ... | ... | ... | ... | ... | ... | ... | ... |
| 1882 | ... | ... | ... | ... | ... | ... | ... | ... | ... | ... |
| 1883 | ... | ... | ... | ... | ... | ... | ... | ... | ... | ... |
| 1884 | 19 | ... | ... | ... | ... | 23 | ... | ... | ... | ... |
| 1885 | ... | ... | ... | ... | ... | 24 | ... | ... | ... | ... |
| 1886 | ... | ... | ... | ... | ... | ... | ... | ... | ... | ... |
| 1887 | ... | ... | ... | ... | ... | ... | ... | ... | ... | ... |
| 1888 | 14 | ... | ... | ... | ... | 27 | ... | ... | ... | ... |
| 1889 | 16 | ... | ... | ... | ... | ... | ... | ... | ... | ... |
| 1890 | 15 | ... | ... | ... | ... | ... | ... | ... | ... | ... |
| 1891 | 17 | ... | ... | ... | ... | 27 | ... | ... | ... | ... |
| 1892 | 17 | ... | ... | ... | ... | 34 | ... | 11 | ... | ... |
| 1893 | 15 | ... | ... | ... | ... | 35 | ... | 3 | ... | ... |
| 1894 | ... | ... | ... | ... | ... | 36 | ... | 17 | ... | 9.8 |
| 1895 | ... | ... | ... | ... | ... | 36 | ... | 19 | ... | 12.0 |
| 1896 | ... | ... | ... | ... | ... | 38 | ... | 13 | ... | 11.0 |
| 1897 | ... | ... | ... | ... | ... | 30 | ... | 26 | 23 | 11.0 |
| 1898 | ... | ... | ... | ... | ... | 44 | ... | 16 | ... | 11.0 |
| 1899 | 16 | ... | ... | ... | ... | 45 | ... | 38 | ... | 13.0 |
| 1900 | 17 | ... | ... | ... | ... | 36 | ... | 21 | ... | 14.0 |
| 1901 | 14 | ... | 7 | ... | ... | 42 | 1 | 27 | ... | 12.0 |
| 1902 | 17 | ... | 9 | ... | ... | 47 | 1 | 10 | ... | 17.0 |
| 1903 | 13 | ... | 8 | ... | ... | 36 | 1 | 29 | ... | 15.0 |
| 1904 | 18 | ... | 13 | ... | ... | ... | 1 | 34 | ... | 22.0 |
| 1905 | 14 | ... | 12 | ... | ... | ... | 1 | 40 | ... | 22.0 |
| 1906 | 17 | 3 | 14 | ... | ... | ... | 1 | 39 | ... | 13.0 |
| 1907 | 9 | ... | 10 | ... | ... | ... | 1 | 50 | ... | 18.0 |
| 1908 | 12 | ... | 19 | ... | ... | ... | 1 | 40 | ... | 21.0 |
| 1909 | 13 | ... | 15 | ... | ... | ... | 1 | ... | ... | 23.0 |
| 1910 | 13 | ... | 16 | ... | ... | ... | 2 | 32 | ... | 26.0 |
| 1911 | 12 | ... | 19 | ... | ... | ... | 2 | ... | ... | 22.0 |
| 1912 | 13 | ... | 20 | ... | ... | 54 | 2 | 32 | ... | 19.0 |
| 1913 | 17 | ... | 19 | ... | ... | 42 | 2 | 37 | ... | 21.0 |
| 1914 | 12 | ... | 20 | ... | ... | 47 | 2 | ... | ... | 28.0 |
| 1915 | 17 | ... | 20 | ... | ... | 49 | 2 | 37 | ... | 24.0 |
| 1916 | 12 | ... | 21 | ... | ... | 45 | 2 | 9 | ... | 24.0 |
| 1917 | 12 | ... | 23 | ... | ... | 24 | 2 | 37 | ... | 31.0 |
| 1918 | 14 | ... | 19 | ... | ... | 49 | 2 | 48 | ... | 26.0 |
| 1919 | 14 | ... | 22 | ... | ... | 45 | 2 | 58 | 24 | 27.0 |

**C7    NORTH AMERICA: Output of Cocoa, Coffee and Tea** (in thousands of metric tons)

| | Costa Rica | Cuba | Dominican Republic | | El Salvador | Guatemala | Haiti |
|---|---|---|---|---|---|---|---|
| | Coffee | Coffee | Cocoa | Coffee | Coffee | Coffee | Coffee |
| 1920 | 13 | ... | 23 | ... | ... | 24 | ... |
| 1921 | 19 | ... | 26 | ... | ... | 48 | ... |
| 1922 | 11 | ... | 19 | ... | 48 | 48 | ... |
| 1923 | 18 | ... | 19 | ... | 54 | 33 | ... |
| 1924 | 15 | ... | 23 | ... | 43 | 38 | ... |
| 1925 | 18 | 20 | 23 | ... | 46 | 44 | ... |
| 1926 | 16 | 16 | 20 | ... | 30 | 61 | ... |
| 1927 | 19 | 21 | 26 | ... | 68 | 62 | ... |
| 1928 | 20 | 20 | 19 | ... | 61 | 41 | ... |
| 1929 | 23 | 21 | 21 | ... | 65 | 44 | ... |
| 1930 | 23 | 24 | 20 | ... | 75 | 41 | ... |
| 1931 | 19 | 27 | 26 | 16 | 48 | 54 | ... |
| 1932 | 28 | 27 | 21 | 22 | 64 | 50 | ... |
| 1933 | 19 | 26 | 19 | 20 | 58 | 36₂ | ... |
| 1934 | 24 | 28 | 21 | 19 | 59 | 52 | ... |
| 1935 | 21 | 37 | 26 | 24 | 57 | 56 | ... |
| 1936 | 26 | 31 | 22 | 29 | 72 | 58 | ... |
| 1937 | 24 | 32 | 21 | 19 | 64 | 57 | 37 |
| 1938 | 22 | 31 | 29 | 19 | 68 | 54 | 37 |
| 1939 | 18 | 32 | 30 | 21 | 67 | 52 | 41 |
| 1940 | 22 | 30 | 24 | 20 | 58 | 50 | 28 |
| 1941 | 24 | 31 | 20 | 22 | 65 | 50 | 35 |
| 1942 | 24 | 36 | 21 | 20 | 67 | 52 | 26 |
| 1943 | 19 | 35 | 25 | 18 | 62 | 59 | 23 |
| 1944 | 22 | 26 | 25 | 19 | 58 | 60 | 30 |
| 1945 | 27 | 21 | 24 | 20 | 50 | 53 | 42 |
| 1946 | 16 | 35 | 25 | 17 | 62 | 56 | 36 |
| 1947 | 18 | 35 | 31 | 21 | 68 | 51 | 35 |
| 1948 | 18 | 28 | 28 | 22 | 90 | 57 | 35 |
| 1949 | 22 | 40 | 26 | 28 | 78 | 56 | 40 |
| 1950 | 24 | 33 | 33 | 25 | 72 | 54 | 33 |
| 1951 | 21 | 29 | 31 | 31 | 59 | 63 | 29 |
| 1952 | 33 | 27 | 32 | 34 | 78 | 58 | 27 |
| 1953 | 23 | 36 | 31 | 32 | 60 | 61 | 36 |
| 1954 | 35 | 39 | 33 | 33 | 77 | 65 | 24 |
| 1955 | 25 | 56 | 36 | 33 | 73 | 69 | 41 |
| 1956 | 34 | 37 | 28 | 32 | 91 | 74₁ | 27 |
| 1957 | 46 | 44 | 35 | 36 | 84 | 86 | 45 |
| 1958 | 51 | 30 | 36 | 32 | 93 | 84 | 27 |
| 1959 | 50 | 48 | 33 | 35 | 103 | 105 | 39 |
| 1960 | 54 | 42 | 40 | 35 | 99 | 99 | 26 |
| 1961 | 62 | 37 | 35 | 36 | 123 | 101 | 44 |
| 1962 | 58 | 58 | 33 | 34 | 98 | 108 | 35 |
| 1963 | 64 | 35 | 38 | 41 | 123 | 105 | 35 |
| 1964 | 50 | 32 | 41 | 41 | 123 | 108 | 33 |
| 1965 | 61 | 24 | 25 | 47 | 109 | 126 | 37 |
| 1966 | 73 | 33 | 28 | 45 | 123 | 106 | 31 |
| 1967 | 76 | 34 | 26 | 42 | 145 | 109 | 32 |
| 1968 | 69 | 30 | 27 | 45 | 124 | 108 | 30 |
| 1969 | 85 | 30 | 26 | 44 | 144 | 114 | 27 |

**C7    NORTH AMERICA: Output of Cocoa, Coffee and Tea** (in thousands of metric tons)

| | Honduras | Mexico | | Nicaragua | Puerto Rico | Trinidad & Tobago |
|---|---|---|---|---|---|---|
| | Coffee | Cocoa | Coffee | Coffee | Coffee | Cocoa |
| 1920 | ... | 2 | 45 | ... | 23 | 28 |
| 1921 | ... | 2 | 34 | ... | 20 | 35 |
| 1922 | ... | 2 | 40 | ... | 20 | 23 |
| 1923 | ... | 2 | 41 | ... | 10 | 30 |
| 1924 | ... | 2 | 28 | ... | 12 | 25 |
| 1925 | 4 | 2 | 48 | ... | 11 | 22 |
| 1926 | 5 | 1 | 50 | ... | 13 | 22 |
| 1927 | 5 | 1 | 52 | ... | 11 | 23 |
| 1928 | 6 | 1 | 53 | ... | 7 | 26 |
| 1929 | 5 | 1 | 52 | ... | 2 | 28 |
| 1930 | 5 | 1 | 49 | ... | 6 | 24 |
| 1931 | 5 | 1 | 47 | ... | 5 | 27 |
| 1932 | 6 | 1 | 41 | ... | 5 | 18 |
| 1933 | 6 | 1 | 55 | ... | 4 | 22 |
| 1934 | 6 | 1 | 46 | ... | 4 | 13 |
| 1935 | 6 | 1 | 52 | ... | 9 | 16 |
| 1936 | 6 | 1 | 63 | ... | 9 | 16 |
| 1937 | 6 | 1 | 60 | ... | 8 | 12 |
| 1938 | 6 | 1 | 57 | ... | 9 | 16 |
| 1939 | 6 | 2 | 55 | ... | 11 | 7 |
| 1940 | 6 | 1 | 52 | ... | 7 | 11 |
| 1941 | 6 | 1 | 52 | ... | 13 | 8 |
| 1942 | 8 | 2 | 52 | ... | 8 | 5 |
| 1943 | 8 | 2 | 52 | ... | 10 | 4 |
| 1944 | 9 | 2 | 60 | ... | 14 | 5 |
| 1945 | 10 | 2 | 55 | ... | 7 | 4 |
| 1946 | 10 | 3 | 57 | 14 | 13 | 4 |
| 1947 | 9 | 7 | 55 | 15 | 11 | 4 |
| 1948 | 11 | 7 | 53 | 14 | 10 | 8 |
| 1949 | 13 | 7 | 59 | 20 | 11 | 6 |
| 1950 | 14 | 9 | 66 | 24 | 8 | |
| 1951 | 14 | 9 | 68 | 20 | 14 | 7 |
| 1952 | 15 | 9 | 71 | 22 | 8 | 10 |
| 1953 | 18 | 8 | 88 | 20 | 14 | 7 |
| 1954 | 18 | 13 | 85 | 24 | 9 | 8 |
| 1955 | 18 | 14 | 93 | 20 | 16 | 9 |
| 1956 | 18 | 14 | 88 | 23 | 7 | 8 |
| 1957 | 20 | 15 | 97 | 22 | 16 | 8 |
| 1058 | 22 | 15 | 122 | 22 | 11 | 8 |
| 1959 | 22 | 13 | 98 | 24 | 16 | 7 |
| 1960 | 23 | 17 | 124 | 24 | 12 | 6 |
| 1961 | 21 | 27 | 127 | 23 | 16 | 6 |
| 1962 | 28 | 30 | 140 | 28 | 18 | 6 |
| 1963 | 29 | 17 | 137 | 30 | 14 | 5 |
| 1964 | 29 | 21 | 156 | 31 | 17 | 5 |
| 1965 | 32 | 24 | 162 | 40 | 14 | 5 |
| 1966 | 30 | 25 | 183 | 32 | 13 | 4 |
| 1967 | 40 | 24 | 225 | 37 | 15 | 6 |
| 1968 | 31 | 26 | 213 | 30 | 12 | 5 |
| 1969 | 40 | 20 | 173 | 34 | 9 | 5 |

**C7    NORTH AMERICA: Output of Cocoa, Coffee and Tea** (in thousands of metric tons)

| | Costa Rica | Cuba | Dominican Republic | | El Salvador | Guatemala | Haiti |
|---|---|---|---|---|---|---|---|
| | Coffee | Coffee | Cocoa | Coffee | Coffee | Coffee | Coffee |
| 1970 | 73 | 29 | 38 | 43 | 130 | 127 | 33 |
| 1971 | 89 | 28 | 33 | 45 | 145 | 128 | 32 |
| 1972 | 79 | 29 | 36 | 45 | 148 | 143 | 32 |
| 1973 | 96 | 30 | 36 | 59 | 127 | 149 | 33 |
| 1974 | 84 | 29 | 38 | 54 | 159 | 157 | 31 |
| 1975 | 80 | 20 | 31 | 52 | 165 | 139 | 39 |
| 1976 | 82 | 27 | 33 | 57 | 148 | 158 | 32 |
| 1977 | 87 | 17 | 34 | 60 | 147 | 168 | 31 |
| 1978 | 98 | 15 | 37 | 43 | 158 | 170 | 27 |
| 1979 | 99 | 23 | 36 | 60 | 186 | 161 | 40 |
| 1980 | 106 | 19 | 28 | 60 | 184 | 163 | 28 |
| 1981 | 113 | 22 | 33 | 52 | 156 | 177 | 33 |
| 1982 | 115 | 29 | 43 | 63 | 146 | 194 | 32 |
| 1983 | 124 | 18 | 45 | 68 | 155 | 171 | 36 |
| 1984 | 137 | 22 | 35 | 72 | 164 | 143 | 36 |
| 1985 | 124 | 24 | 41 | 52 | 134 | 169 | 37 |
| 1986 | 128 | 25 | 44 | 62 | 143 | 158 | 38 |
| 1987 | 138 | 26 | 39 | 67 | 148 | 182 | 30 |
| 1988 | 145 | 29 | 41 | 68 | 120 | 190 | 32 |

| | Honduras | Mexico | | Nicaragua | Puerto Rico | Trinidad & Tobago |
|---|---|---|---|---|---|---|
| | Coffee | Cocoa | Coffee | Coffee | Coffee | Cocoa |
| 1970 | 36 | 29 | 185 | 39 | 15 | 6 |
| 1971 | 42 | 26 | 187 | 42 | 11 | 4 |
| 1972 | 47 | 38 | 203 | 35 | 12 | 5 |
| 1973 | 42 | 33 | 222 | 37 | 14 | 3 |
| 1974 | 45 | 35 | 221 | 41 | 10 | 4 |
| 1975 | 47 | 34 | 228 | 49 | 11 | 5 |
| 1976 | 48 | 31 | 212 | 57 | 11 | 3 |
| 1977 | 50 | 25 | 182 | 55 | 9 | 3 |
| 1978 | 60 | 42 | 242 | 65 | 12 | 3 |
| 1979 | 72 | 38 | 220 | 56 | 9 | 3 |
| 1980 | 64 | 38 | 220 | 59 | 12 | 2 |
| 1981 | 75 | 30 | 244 | 61 | 14 | 3 |
| 1982 | 72 | 41 | 313 | 71 | 13 | 2 |
| 1983 | 79 | 33 | 313 | 44 | 16 | 2 |
| 1984 | 72 | 36 | 240 | 51 | 12 | 2 |
| 1985 | 75 | 49 | 270 | 50 | 14 | 1 |
| 1986 | 76 | 47 | 375 | 43 | 11 | 1 |
| 1987 | 80 | 41 | 318 | 37 | 16 | 2 |
| 1988 | 91 | 57 | 283 | 43 | 13 | 2 |

**C7     SOUTH AMERICA: OUTPUT OF COCOA, COFFEE AND TEA** (in thousands of metric tons)

### 1840–1879

| | Ecuador[4] |
|---|---|
| | Cocoa |
| 1840 | 6 |
| 1841 | 5 |
| 1842 | 3 |
| 1843 | 7 |
| 1844 | 4 |
| 1845 | 4 |
| 1846 | 5 |
| 1847 | 5 |
| 1848 | 10 |
| 1849 | 6 |
| 1850 | 5 |
| 1851 | 4 |
| 1852 | 6 |
| 1853 | 6 |
| 1854 | 5 |
| 1855 | 7 |
| 1856 | 6 |
| 1857 | 7 |
| 1858 | 9 |
| 1859 | 6 |
| 1860 | 8 |
| 1861 | 8 |
| 1862 | 7 |
| 1863 | 7 |
| 1864 | 5 |
| 1865 | 6 |
| 1866 | 10 |
| 1867 | 9 |
| 1868 | 5 |
| 1869 | 8 |
| 1870 | 11 |
| 1871 | 8 |
| 1872 | 8 |
| 1873 | 11 |
| 1874 | 11 |
| 1875 | 8 |
| 1876 | 10 |
| 1877 | 9 |
| 1878 | 5 |
| 1879 | 14 |

### 1880–1924

| | Brazil | | Colombia | Ecuador[4] | Venezuela[6] |
|---|---|---|---|---|---|
| | Cocoa | Coffee | Cocoa | Cocoa | Cocoa |
| 1880 | ... | ... | ... | 15 | ... |
| 1881 | ... | ... | ... | 10 | ... |
| 1882 | ... | ... | ... | 9 | ... |
| 1883 | ... | ... | ... | 9 | ... |
| 1884 | ... | ... | ... | 8 | ... |
| 1885 | ... | ... | ... | 10[5] | ... |
| | | | | 12 | |
| 1886 | ... | ... | ... | 19 | ... |
| 1887 | ... | ... | ... | 16 | ... |
| 1888 | ... | ... | ... | 13 | ... |
| 1889 | ... | ... | ... | 27 | |
| 1890 | ... | ... | ... | 18 | ... |
| 1891 | ... | ... | ... | 10 | ... |
| 1892 | ... | ... | ... | 16 | ... |
| 1893 | ... | ... | ... | 20 | ... |
| 1894 | ... | ... | ... | 19 | ... |
| 1895 | ... | ... | ... | 18 | ... |
| 1896 | ... | ... | ... | 17 | ... |
| 1897 | ... | ... | ... | 16 | ... |
| 1898 | ... | ... | ... | 21 | ... |
| 1899 | ... | ... | ... | 27 | ... |
| 1900 | ... | 690 | ... | 19 | ... |
| 1901 | 18 | 975 | 3 | 23 | 9 |
| 1902 | 20 | 778 | 3 | 24 | 8 |
| 1903 | 21 | 699 | 3 | 23 | 8 |
| 1904 | 23 | 635 | 3 | 28 | 14 |
| 1905 | 21 | 662 | 3 | 21 | 12 |
| 1906 | 25 | 1,224 | 3 | 22 | 14 |
| 1907 | 24 | 680 | 3 | 19 | 12 |
| 1908 | 32 | 782 | 3 | 31 | 16 |
| 1909 | 33 | 927 | 3 | 31 | 16 |
| 1910 | 29 | 660 | 3 | 36 | 16 |
| 1911 | 35 | 794 | 3 | 39 | 18 |
| 1912 | 30[2] | 727 | 3 | 36 | 14 |
| 1913 | 29 | 868 | 3 | 42 | 18 |
| 1914 | 41 | 810 | 3 | 44 | 17 |
| 1915 | 44 | 958 | 4 | 35 | 18 |
| 1916 | 43 | 766 | 3 | 49 | 15 |
| 1917 | 55 | 951 | 3 | 46 | 20 |
| 1918 | 41 | 584 | 3 | 37 | 19 |
| 1919 | 62 | 789 | 4 | 37 | 19 |
| 1920 | 67 | 788 | 4 | 39 | 17 |
| 1921 | 35 | 1,027 | 4 | 40 | 22 |
| 1922 | 59 | 857 | 4 | 40 | 21 |
| 1923 | 57 | 857 | 4 | 29 | 22 |
| 1924 | 68 | 952 | 5 | 30 | 17 |

**C7** **SOUTH AMERICA: Output of Cocoa, Coffee and Tea** (in thousands of metric tons)

**1925–1969**

| | Argentina | Brazil | | Colombia | | Ecuador | | Venezuela | |
|---|---|---|---|---|---|---|---|---|---|
| | Tea | Cocoa | Coffee | Cocoa | Coffee | Cocoa | Coffee | Cocoa | Coffee |
| 1925 | ... | 60 | 888 | 5 | ... | 30 | ... | 23 | ... |
| 1926 | ... | 72 | 960 | 5 | ... | 18 | ... | 15 | ... |
| 1927 | ... | 71 | 1,102 | 5 | ... | 20 | ... | 17 | ... |
| 1928 | ... | 73 | 1,671 | 6 | ... | 20 | ... | 20 | ... |
| 1929 | ... | 64 | 1,577 | 5 | ... | 15 | ... | 21 | ... |
| 1930 | ... | 69 | 1,634 | 5 | 195 | 17 | ... | 16 | 67 |
| 1931 | ... | 77 | 1,302 | 6 | 204 | 14 | ... | 16 | 58 |
| 1932 | ... | 104 | 1,536 | 11 | 203 | 15 | ... | 16 | 49 |
| 1933 | ... | 100 | 1,777 | 9 | 217 | 10 | ... | 17 | 48 |
| 1934 | ... | 108 | 1,653 | 11 | 230 | 19 | ... | 14 | 57 |
| 1935 | ... | 127 | 1,136 | 10 | 210 | 20 | ... | 15 | 64 |
| 1936 | ... | 127 | 1,577 | 9 | 252 | 19 | ... | 17 | 72 |
| 1937 | ... | 119 | 1,462 | 11 | 262 | 21 | 17 | 18 | 60 |
| 1938 | ... | 142 | 1,404 | 11 | 268 | 19 | 17 | 20 | 39 |
| 1939 | ... | 135 | 1,157 | 12 | 265 | 15 | 17 | 15 | 65 |
| 1940 | ... | 128 | 1,002 | 14 | 267 | 11 | 15 | 15 | 48 |
| 1941 | ... | 132 | 962 | 12 | 286 | 14 | 18 | 17 | 39 |
| 1942 | ... | 109 | 830 | 12 | 329 | 14 | 15 | 17 | 33 |
| 1943 | ... | 178 | 922 | 9 | 317 | 18 | ... | 18 | 33 |
| 1944 | ... | 117 | ... | 8 | 332 | 14 | 25 | 16 | 45 |
| 1945 | ... | 120 | 835 | 10 | 329 | 17 | 14 | 15 | 45 |
| 1946 | ... | 122 | 917 | 11 | 346 | 17 | 17 | 17 | 44 |
| 1947 | ... | 119 | 948 | 8 | 365 | 16 | 18 | 20 | 47 |
| 1948 | ... | 129 | 1,037 | 11 | 368 | 16 | 20 | 17 | 47 |
| 1949 | ... | 162 | 1,068 | 14 | 368 | 20 | 13 | 23 | 51 |
| 1950 | 1 | 136 | 1,071 | 15 | 338 | 21 | 23 | 17 | 34 |
| 1951 | 1 | 105 | 1,080 | 15 | 302 | 32 | 22 | 18 | 43 |
| 1952 | 1 | 97 | 1,125 | 15 | 403 | 24 | 24 | 16 | 54 |
| 1953 | 1 | 123 | 1,111 | 15 | 384 | 29 | [23][5] | 18 | 45 |
| 1954 | 2 | 172 | 1,037 | 15 | 403 | 26 | [35][5] | 17 | 53 |
| 1955 | 2 | 158 | 1,370 | 14 | 377 | 34 | [23][5] | 19 | 53 |
| 1956 | 3 | 168 | 979 | 12 | 335 | 31 | 40 | 16 | 46 |
| 1957 | 2 | 147 | 1,409 | 12 | 365 | 27 | 51 | 15 | 57 |
| 1958 | 10 | 164 | 1,696 | 12 | 469 | 33 | 46 | 18 | 60 |
| 1959 | 3 | 178 | 2,629 | 13 | 462 | 41 | 39 | 19 | 61 |
| 1960 | 5 | 163 | 1,797 | 14 | 480 | 44 | 33 | 17 | 59 |
| 1961 | 7 | 156 | 2,110[3] / 2,229 | 17 | 450 | 44 | 54 | 19 | 57 |
| 1962 | 8 | 140 | 2,190 | 17 | 482 | 45 | 56 | 21 | 54 |
| 1963 | 10 | 144 | 1,651 | 16 | 450 | 36 | 43 | 21 | 61 |
| 1964 | 13 | 154 | 1,042 | 18 | 468 | 48 | 50 | 20 | 56 |
| 1965 | 11 | 161 | 2,294 | 17 | 492 | 50 | 66 | 20 | 54 |
| 1966 | 19 | 170 | 1,203 | 18 | 456 | 43 | 74 | 20 | 61 |
| 1967 | 15 | 195 | 1,508 | 17 | 477 | 60 | 66 | 21 | 62 |
| 1968 | 15 | 149 | 1,058 | 18 | 480 | 85 | 63 | 19 | 46 |
| 1969 | 20 | 211 | 1,284 | 19 | 480 | 48 | 56 | 18 | 61 |

**C7     SOUTH AMERICA: Output of Coffee, Cocoa and Tea** (in thousands of metric tons)[1]

| | Argentina | Brazil | | Colombia | | Ecuador | | Venezuala | |
|---|---|---|---|---|---|---|---|---|---|
| | Tea | Cocoa | Coffee | Cocoa | Coffee | Cocoa | Coffee | Cocoa | Coffee |
| 1970 | 17 | 201 | 755 | 19 | 501 | 54 | 72 | 19 | 61 |
| 1971 | 21 | 182 | 1,550 | 21 | 485 | 71 | 62 | 19 | 58 |
| 1972 | 29 | 164 | 1,475 | 22 | 480 | 68 | 71 | 17 | 40 |
| 1973 | 29 | 159 | 873 | 23 | 468 | 63 | 75 | 20 | 66 |
| 1974 | 25 | 242 | 1,615 | 25 | 540 | 91 | 70 | 18 | 46 |
| 1975 | 28 | 265 | 1,272 | 26 | 480 | 75 | 76 | 20 | 65 |
| 1976 | 35 | 251 | 376 | 29 | 558 | 65 | 87 | 15 | 40 |
| 1977 | 22 | 226 | 975 | 27 | 648 | 72 | 83 | 16 | 58 |
| 1978 | 26 | 279 | 1,268 | 31 | 720 | 72 | 75 | 15 | 59 |
| 1979 | 29 | 309 | 1,333 | 32 | 762 | 77 | 90 | 15 | 54 |
| 1980 | 36 | 296 | 1,061 | 34 | 756 | 91 | 69 | 13 | 58 |
| 1981 | 23 | 336 | 2,032 | 38 | 808 | 80 | 86 | 15 | 60 |
| 1982 | 33 | 364 | 958 | 43 | 728 | 85 | 84 | 14 | 58 |
| 1983 | 41 | 380 | 1,672 | 37 | 824 | 45 | 81 | 14 | 59 |
| 1984 | 41 | 330 | 1,420 | 39 | 694 | 49 | 97 | 12 | 62 |
| 1985 | 47 | 431 | 1,911 | 43 | 678 | 131 | 121 | 11 | 64 |
| 1986 | 41 | 459 | 1,041 | 47 | 713 | 90 | 118 | 12 | 66 |
| 1987 | 45 | 329 | 2,203 | 54 | 652 | 58 | 112 | 13 | 70 |
| 1988 | 32 | 375 | 1,352 | 54 | 780 | 85 | 144 | 14 | 71 |

NOTES

1. SOURCES: As for table C1, with cocoa statistics for the Dominican Republic and Colombia to 1949, Ecuador and Venezuela to 1954 and Brazil to 1919, taken from *Cocoa Statistics,* published annually by Gill & Duffus.
2. Statistics are not always for calendar years, but so far as possible they have been shown against the year in which the bulk of the production was harvested. (Most cocoa statistics, for example, are for years ended 30 September.)

FOOTNOTES

[1] Registered production only to 1956, estimated to be about 90% of the total.
[2] Subsequent figures are revised and not strictly comparable with earlier ones.
[3] Data to 1961 (1st line) are derived from the Brazil Coffee Institute. Official data are preferred subsequently.
[4] Data to 1885 (1st line) are of cocoa received for shipment at Guyaquil.
[5] Exportable crop only.
[6] Rafael Cartay, *Historia Economica de Venezuela 1830–1900* gives the following earlier figures:-

| | Cocoa | Coffee |
|---|---|---|
| 1875 | 5 | 40 |
| 1884 | 8 | 55 |
| 1894 | 11 | 106 |

**C8 NORTH AMERICA: OUTPUT OF FRUIT** (in thousands of metric tons)

**1880–1929**

| | Canada | Costa Rica[1] | Guatemala[2] | Honduras[4] | Jamaica | Mexico | Nicaragua[6] | USA | |
|---|---|---|---|---|---|---|---|---|---|
| | Apples | Bananas | Bananas | Bananas | Bananas[5] | Oranges | Bananas | Apples | Citrus Fruit[8] |
| 1883 | ... | 2.8 | ... | ... | ... | ... | ... | ... | ... |
| 1884 | ... | 11.0 | ... | ... | ... | ... | ... | ... | ... |
| 1885 | ... | 10.0 | ... | ... | ... | ... | ... | ... | ... |
| 1886 | ... | 15.0 | ... | ... | ... | ... | ... | ... | ... |
| 1887 | ... | 23.0 | ... | ... | 21 | ... | ... | ... | ... |
| 1888 | ... | 22.0 | ... | ... | 45 | ... | ... | ... | ... |
| 1889 | ... | 25.0 | ... | ... | 42[5] | ... | ... | 2,921 | ... |
| 1890 | ... | 26.0 | ... | ... | ... | ... | ... | ... | ... |
| 1891 | ... | 29.0 | ... | ... | 70 | ... | ... | ... | ... |
| 1892 | ... | 30.0 | ... | ... | 44 | ... | ... | ... | ... |
| 1893 | ... | 32.0 | ... | ... | 60 | ... | ... | ... | ... |
| 1894 | ... | 35.0 | ... | ... | 75 | ... | ... | ... | ... |
| 1895 | ... | 40.0 | ... | ... | 68 | ... | ... | ... | ... |
| 1896 | ... | 43.0 | ... | ... | 61 | ... | ... | ... | ... |
| 1897 | ... | 50.0 | ... | ... | 70 | ... | ... | ... | ... |
| 1898 | ... | 59.0 | ... | ... | 101 | ... | ... | ... | ... |
| 1899 | ... | 75.0 | ... | ... | 116 | ... | ... | 3,580 | 250 |
| 1900 | ... | 87.0 | ... | ... | 119 | ... | ... | ... | ... |
| 1901 | ... | 98.0 | ... | ... | 159 | ... | ... | ... | ... |
| 1902 | ... | 106.0 | ... | ... | 205 | ... | ... | ... | ... |
| 1903 | ... | 131.0 | ... | ... | 113 | ... | ... | ... | ... |
| 1904 | ... | 154.0 | ... | ... | 129 | ... | ... | ... | ... |
| 1905 | ... | 185.0 | ... | ... | 217 | ... | ... | ... | ... |
| 1906 | ... | 275.0 | ... | ... | 232 | ... | ... | ... | ... |
| 1907 | ... | 258.0 | ... | ... | 202 | 38 | ... | ... | ... |
| 1908 | ... | 256.0 | ... | ... | 211[5] | ... | ... | | |
| 1909 | ... | 238.0 | ... | ... | 242 | ... | ... | 2,968 | 827 |
| 1910 | ... | 231.0 | ... | ... | 204 | ... | ... | ... | ... |
| 1911 | ... | 236.0 | ... | ... | 239 | ... | ... | ... | ... |
| 1912 | ... | 270.0 | ... | ... | 194 | ... | ... | ... | ... |
| 1913 | ... | 284.0 | ... | ... | 168 | ... | ... | ... | ... |
| 1914 | ... | 258.0 | ... | ... | 234 | ... | ... | ... | ...[8] |
| 1915 | ... | 242.0 | ... | ... | 118 | ... | ... | ... | 786 |
| 1916 | ... | 256.0 | ... | ... | 50 | ... | ... | 1,376 | 905 |
| 1917 | ... | 200.0 | ... | ... | 35 | ... | ... | | 393 |
| 1918 | ... | ... | ... | ... | 46 | ... | ... | | 897 |
| 1919 | ... | 185.0 | 69 | ... | 140 | ... | 17 | 2,787[7] | 840 |
| 1920 | ... | 220.0 | 100 | ... | 131 | ... | 25 | 4,566 | 1,104 |
| 1921 | ... | 211.0 | 121 | ... | 144 | ... | 40 | 2,021 | 754 |
| 1922 | 236 | 182.0 | 138 | ... | 184 | ... | 55 | 4,137 | 1,123 |
| 1923 | 235 | 189.0 | 153 | ... | 180 | ... | 71 | 4,140 | 1,372 |
| 1924 | 207 | 205.0 | 199 | ... | 173 | ... | 59 | 3,505[1] | 1,100 |
| 1925 | 178 | 212.0 | 132 | 632 | 217 | ... | 63 | 3,519 | 1,234 |
| 1926 | 181 | 217.0 | 122 | 670 | 265 | ... | 46 | 5,032 | 1,440 |
| 1927 | 172 | 200.0 | 120 | 784 | 306 | 100 | 50 | 2,520 | 1,156 |
| 1928 | 198 | 186.0 | 127 | 954 | 247 | 101 | 65 | 3,815 | 1,990 |
| 1929 | 237 | 155.0 | 146 | 946 | 319 | 101 | 86 | 2,721 | 1,230[8] |
| | | | | | | | | | 1,829 |

**C8    NORTH AMERICA: Output of Fruit** (in thousands of metric tons)

1930–1969

| | Canada | Costa Rica[1] | Dominican Republic | Guadeloupe | Guatemala[2] | Honduras[4] | Jamaica | |
|---|---|---|---|---|---|---|---|---|
| | Apples | Bananas | Bananas | Bananas | Bananas | Bananas | Bananas[5] | Citrus Fruit |
| 1930 | ... | 148 | ... | ... | ... | 1,003 | 356 | ... |
| 1931 | 232 | 129 | ... | ... | 138 | 1,159 | 323 | ... |
| 1932 | 171 | 110 | ... | ... | 123 | 1,027 | 295 | ... |
| 1933 | 335 | 109 | ... | ... | 130 | 893 | 153 | ... |
| 1934 | 267 | 82 | ... | ... | 121 | 843 | 231 | ... |
| 1935 | 276 | 74 | ... | ... | 129 | 690 | 295 | ... |
| 1936 | 252 | 99 | ... | ... | 173 | 675 | 272 | ... |
| 1937 | 310 | 140 | ... | ... | 198 | 589 | 390 | ... |
| 1938 | 320 | 140 | ... | ... | 218 | 618 | 345 | ... |
| 1939 | 335 | ... | ... | ... | 236 | 656 | 272 | ... |
| 1940 | 263 | 80 | ... | ... | 169 | 746 | 100 | ... |
| 1941 | 219 | 123 | ... | ... | 141 | 699 | 81 | ... |
| 1942 | 265 | 58 | ... | ... | 102 | 509 | 19 | ... |
| 1943 | 262 | 61 | ... | ... | 52 | 499 | 4 | ... |
| 1944 | 364 | 48 | ... | ... | 100 | 650 | 16 | ... |
| 1945 | 156 | 56 | ... | ... | 174 | 742 | 26 | ... |
| 1946 | 394 | 112 | 342 | 48 | 222 | 787 | 84 | ... |
| 1947 | 319 | 140 | 366 | ... | 290 | 867 | 80 | 78 |
| 1948 | 274 | 190 | 250 | 72 | 273 | 847 | 88[5] / 147 | 78 |
| 1949 | 370 | 223 | 380 | 72 | 120 | 789 | 155 | 78 |
| 1950 | 330 | 222 | 389 | 75 | ... | 845 | 122 | 99 |
| 1951 | 278 | 217[1] / 413 | 375 | 90 | 120 | 872 | 80 | 72 |
| 1952 | 246 | 531 | 376 | 105 | 87 | 850 | 103 | 71 |
| 1953 | 239 | ... | ... | 108 | 174 | 863 | 240 | 94 |
| 1954 | 296 | 429 | 393 | 115 | 144[2] / 154 | 747 | 264 | 102 |
| 1955 | 391 | 456 | 277 | 110 | 134 | 700 | 266 | 103 |
| 1956 | 254 | 342 | 326 | 125 | 125 | 899 | 279 | 79 |
| 1957 | 319 | ... | 343 | 125 | 130 | 869[4] / 705 | 254 | 74 |
| 1958 | 347 | ... | 364 | 140 | 152 | 735 | 245 | 73 |
| 1959 | 317 | ... | 457 | 165 | 178 | 900 | 254 | 90 |
| 1960 | 304 | ... | 488 | 170 | 244 | 832 | 254 | 86 |
| 1961 | 337 | 410 | 424 | 165 | 197[3] | 881 | 263 | 111 |
| 1962 | 410 | 521 | 400 | 163 | 139 | 840 | 272 | 119 |
| 1963 | 469 | 466 | 290 | 168 | 185 | 801 | 281 | 102 |
| 1964 | 409 | 486 | 252 | 162 | 138 | 831 | 290 | 108 |
| 1965 | 455 | 567 | 270 | 162 | 52 | 1,090 | 327 | 110 |
| 1966 | 430 | 399 | 238 | 180 | 96 | 1,002[4] / 1,151 | 320 | 116 |
| 1967 | 446 | 512 | 238 | 180 | 76 | 1,011 | 275 | 105 |
| 1968 | 410 | 703 | 343 | 140 | 76 | 1,002 | 210 | 93 |
| 1969 | 444 | 967 | 267 | 145 | 80[3] | 994 | 155 | 116 |

**C8     NORTH AMERICA: Output of Fruit** (in thousands of metric tons)

**1930–1969**

| | Martinique | Mexico | | Nicaragua[6] | Panama[1] | USA | |
|---|---|---|---|---|---|---|---|
| | Bananas | Bananas | Oranges | Bananas | Bananas | Apples | Citrus Fruit[8] |
| 1930 | ... | ... | 111 | 82 | ... | 3,197 | 2,920 |
| 1931 | ... | ... | 125 | 63 | ... | 4,193 | 2,621 |
| 1932 | ... | ... | 113 | 71 | ... | 2,997 | 2,624 |
| 1933 | ... | ... | 92 | 78 | ... | 3,034 | 2,466 |
| 1934 | ... | ... | 113 | 57 | ... | 2,167 | 3,390 |
| 1935 | ... | ... | 113 | 63 | ... | 2,870 | 2,758 |
| 1936 | ... | ... | 146 | 40 | ... | 2,003 | 3,314 |
| 1937 | ... | ... | 147 | 53 | ... | 3,129 | 4,065 |
| 1938 | ... | ... | 167 | 38 | 152 | 2,161 | 4,723[8] |
| 1939 | ... | ... | 183 | ... | ... | 2,845 | 4,093 |
| 1940 | ... | ... | 208 | 23 | 119 | 2,277 | 5,134 |
| 1941 | ... | ... | 229 | 15 | 115 | 2,505 | 5,004 |
| 1942 | ... | ... | 240 | 2 | 48 | 2,618 | 5,711 |
| 1943 | ... | ... | 264 | — | 19 | 1,818 | 6,432 |
| 1944 | ... | ... | 284 | — | 23 | 2,546 | 7,463 |
| 1945 | ... | ... | 295 | 2 | 52 | 1,363 | 6,673 |
| 1946 | 8 | 302 | 342 | 6[6] | 159 | 2,437 | 7,135 |
| 1947 | 25 | 298 | 345 | 7 | 106 | 2,307 | 7,069 |
| 1948 | 45 | 300 | 400 | 14 | 130 | 1,945 | 6,020 |
| 1949 | 55 | 308 | 411 | 15 | 218 | 2,917 | 5,866 |
| 1950 | 85 | 257 | 555 | 13 | 189 | 2,710 | 6,832 |
| 1951 | 95 | 187 | 502 | 9 | 136[1] 356 | 2,425 | 6,682 |
| 1952 | 82 | 204 | 534 | 8 | 298 | 2,056 | 6,635 |
| 1953 | ... | 203 | 557 | 9 | 335 | 2,076 | 7,458 |
| 1954 | 62 | 205 | 598 | 12 | 345 | 2,436 | 7,316 |
| 1955 | 65 | 207 | 595 | 9 | 430 | 2,314 | 7,466 |
| 1956 | 98 | 246 | 625 | 4 | 390 | 2,206 | 7,567 |
| 1957 | 115 | 270 | 656 | 2 | 465 | 2,596 | 6,441 |
| 1958 | 115 | 274 | 662 | 2 | 445 | 2,776 | 7,357 |
| 1959 | 155 | 276 | 674 | 2 | 486 | 2,762 | 7,202 |
| 1960 | 146 | 317 | 766 | 4 | 439 | 2,363 | 6,847 |
| 1961 | 185 | 341 | 772 | 1 | 452 | 2,756 | 7,802 |
| 1962 | 170 | 367 | 883 | 7 | 417 | 2,739 | 5,946 |
| 1963 | 130 | 940 | 855 | 19 | 422 | 2,609 | 5,656 |
| 1964 | 120 | 949 | 845 | 27 | 485 | 2,866 | 6,930 |
| 1965 | 220 | 960 | 1,401 | 8 | 579 | 2,781 | 7,874 |
| 1966 | 260 | 978 | 1,537 | 14 | 586 | 2,612 | 10,375 |
| 1967 | 240 | 986 | 1,805 | 42 | 592 | 2,447 | 7,555 |
| 1968 | 245 | 1,040 | 1,721 | 42 | 949 | 2,468 | 10,175 |
| 1969 | 220 | 1,025 | 1,626 | 22 | 1,019 | 3,063 | 10,313 |

**C8     NORTH AMERICA: Output of Fruit** (in thousands of metric tons)

Key:     CF = Citrus fruit

| | Canada | Costa Rica | Dominican Republic | Guadeloupe | Guatemala | Honduras | Jamaica | |
|---|---|---|---|---|---|---|---|---|
| | Apples | Bananas | Bananas | Bananas | Bananas | Bananas | Bananas | CF |
| 1970 | 406 | 1,146 | 275 | 126 | 487 | 985 | 185 | 130 |
| 1971 | 398 | 1,250 | 286 | 148 | 495 | 977 | 194 | 150 |
| 1972 | 393 | 1,250 | 290 | 174 | 510 | 969 | 199 | 149 |
| 1973 | 375 | 1,198 | 310 | 175 | 520 | 961 | 160 | 77 |
| 1974 | 406 | 1,151 | 302 | 162 | 500 | 871 | 132 | 95 |
| 1975 | 460 | 1,121 | 318 | 165 | 520 | 907 | 127 | 95 |
| 1976 | 409 | 1,187 | 318 | 148 | 550 | 944 | 144 | 95 |
| 1977 | 411 | 1,125 | 314 | 142 | ... | 982 | 148 | 93 |
| 1978 | 452 | 1,183 | 315 | 170 | ... | 1,022 | 160 | 101 |
| 1979 | 435 | 1,154 | 275 | 116 | 556 | 1,068 | 130 | ... |
| 1980 | 553 | 1,107 | 301 | 83 | 527 | 1,058 | 165 | 102 |
| 1981 | 422 | 1,141 | 320 | 150 | 536 | 1,022 | 174 | 84 |
| 1982 | 478 | 1,153 | 320 | ... | 601 | 948 | 188 | 89 |
| 1983 | 485 | 1,155 | 320 | 142 | ... | 939 | 160 | 89 |
| 1984 | 434 | 1,169 | ... | 163 | 483 | ... | 181 | 82 |
| 1985 | 479 | 1,008 | 314 | 127 | 538 | 1,263 | 190 | 89 |
| 1986 | 388 | 1,096 | 422 | 144 | 551 | 1,167 | 191 | 100 |
| 1987 | 506 | 1,139 | 373 | 148 | 525 | 1,392 | 208 | 121 |
| 1988 | 486 | 1,156 | 391 | 150 | 406 | 1,408 | 146 | 147 |

| | Martinique | Mexico | | Nicaragua | Panama | U.S.A. | |
|---|---|---|---|---|---|---|---|
| | Bananas | Bananas | Oranges | Bananas | Bananas | Apples | CF |
| 1970 | 158 | 1,136 | 1,555 | 217 | 947 | 2,838 | 10,307 |
| 1971 | 165 | 1,116 | 1,999 | 219 | 1,013 | 2,758 | 10,837 |
| 1972 | 240 | 1,149 | 1,318 | 230 | 988 | 2,663 | 11,044 |
| 1973 | 170 | 1,070 | 1,466 | 260 | 964 | 2,824 | 12,604 |
| 1974 | 220 | 1,070 | 1,778 | 305 | 977 | 2,941 | 12,168 |
| 1975 | 180 | 1,194 | 2,322 | 234 | 989 | 3,416 | 13,237 |
| 1976 | 275 | 1,199 | 1,787 | 236 | 999 | 2,939 | 13,415 |
| 1977 | 290 | 1,276 | 1,857 | 237 | 1,028 | 3,026 | 13,828 |
| 1978 | 305 | 1,384 | 1,902 | 240 | 1,056 | 3,446 | 12,932 |
| 1979 | 184 | 1,553 | 1,717 | 240 | 1,000 | 3,694 | 12,092 |
| 1980 | 94 | 1,501 | 1,950 | 231 | 1,050 | 4,004 | 14,955 |
| 1981 | 187 | 1,591 | 1,789 | 239 | 1,045 | 3,517 | 13,703 |
| 1982 | ... | 1,572 | 1,995 | 237 | 1,057 | 3,681 | 10,934 |
| 1983 | 178 | 1,640 | 2,069 | 212 | 1,045 | 3,798 | 12,344 |
| 1984 | 181 | 2,093 | 1,720 | 200 | 1,056 | 3,779 | 9,793 |
| 1985 | 181 | 1,151 | 1,745 | 212 | 1,067 | 3,594 | 9,559 |
| 1986 | 212 | 1,473 | 1,909 | 186 | 907 | 3,598 | 10,026 |
| 1987 | 212 | 1,770 | 1,934 | 204 | 1,251 | 4,875 | 10,874 |
| 1988 | 209 | 1,566 | 2,099 | 229 | 1,081 | 4,154 | 11,565 |

C8    **SOUTH AMERICA: OUTPUT OF FRUIT** (in thousands of metric tons)

## 1933–1969

| | Argentina | | | Brazil | | Ecuador | | Paraguay | | Peru | Venezuala | |
|---|---|---|---|---|---|---|---|---|---|---|---|---|
| | Apples | Bananas | CF | Bananas | CF[9] | Bananas[10] | CF[11] | Bananas | CF | CF | Bananas | CF |
| 1933 | ... | ... | ... | ... | 1,037 | ... | ... | ... | ... | ... | ... | ... |
| 1934 | ... | ... | ... | ... | 1,152 | ... | ... | ... | ... | ... | ... | ... |
| 1935 | ... | ... | ... | ... | 1,146 | ... | ... | ... | ... | ... | ... | ... |
| 1936 | ... | ... | ... | ... | 1,221 | ... | ... | ... | ... | ... | ... | ... |
| 1937 | ... | ... | ... | ... | 1,136 | ... | ... | ... | ... | ... | ... | ... |
| 1938 | ... | ... | ... | ... | 1,242 | 55 | ... | ... | ... | ... | ... | ... |
| 1939 | ... | ... | ... | 1,755 | 1,189 | ... | ... | ... | ... | ... | ... | ... |
| 1940 | ... | ... | 487 | 1,503 | 1,273 | 47 | 48 | ... | ... | ... | ... | ... |
| 1941 | ... | ... | 482 | 1,620 | 1,263 | 34 | 58 | ... | ... | ... | ... | ... |
| 1942 | ... | ... | 639 | 1,600 | 1,240 | 22 | 26 | ... | ... | ... | ... | ... |
| 1943 | ... | ... | 401 | 1,698 | 1,246 | 15 | 61[11] | ... | ... | ... | ... | ... |
| 1944 | ... | ... | 392 | 1,854 | 973 | 14 | ... | ... | ... | ... | ... | ... |
| 1945 | ... | ... | 320 | 2,146 | 1,001 | 17 | ... | ... | ... | ... | ... | ... |
| 1946 | ... | ... | 391 | 2,344 | 1,048 | 36 | ... | ... | ... | ... | ... | ... |
| 1947 | ... | ... | 382 | 2,549 | 1,035 | 69 | 10 | ... | 206 | 113 | ... | ... |
| 1948 | 173 | ... | 407 | 2,726 | 1,062 | 174 | 7 | ... | 207 | 302 | 59 | ... |
| 1949 | 229 | ... | 448 | 2,854 | 1,226 | 199 | 6 | ... | 244 | 356 | 42 | ... |
| 1950 | 196 | ... | 407 | 3,257 | 1,246 | ... | 5 | ... | 180 | 363 | 60 | ... |
| 1951 | 284 | ... | 437 | 3,393 | 1,203 | 246 | 4[11] | ... | 130 | 399 | ... | ... |
| 1952 | 224 | ... | 419 | 3,703 | 1,236[9] | 430 | ... | ... | ... | 415 | ... | ... |
| | | ... | | | 1,262 | | | | | | | |
| 1953 | 268 | ... | 442 | 3,257 | 1,364 | 406 | 176 | ... | 203 | ... | 49 | ... |
| 1954 | 242 | | 475 | 3,964 | 1,409 | 492 | ... | ... | ... | ... | 52 | ... |
| 1955 | 361 | ... | 516 | 4,086 | 1,436 | 613 | 184 | ... | ... | ... | ... | ... |
| 1956 | 256 | 11 | 536 | 4,481 | 1,516 | 579 | ... | ... | 148 | ... | 700 | ... |
| 1957 | 442 | 5 | 719 | 4,665 | 1,598 | 669[10] | 156 | ... | 143 | ... | 1,074 | ... |
| | | | | | | 1,160 | | | | | | |
| 1958 | 283 | 3 | 755 | 4,595 | 1,648 | 1,340 | 155 | ... | 135 | ... | 924 | 37 |
| 1959 | 464 | 3 | 791 | 4,885 | 1,759 | 2,024 | 166 | 161 | 135 | ... | ... | 37 |
| 1960 | 431 | 9 | 732 | 5,127 | 1,853 | 2,304 | 161 | 141 | 134 | ... | 1,332 | 40 |
| 1961 | 415 | 12 | 844 | 3,529 | 1,951 | 2,204 | 171 | 145 | 150 | 170 | 1,004 | ... |
| 1962 | 397 | 47 | 813 | 3,909 | 2,053 | 2,109 | 182 | 141 | 202 | 180 | 874 | ... |
| 1963 | 474 | 36 | 821 | 4,070 | 2,321 | 2,098 | 173 | 196 | 209 | 191 | 1,456 | 127 |
| 1964 | 371 | 66 | 854 | 4,397 | 2,263 | 3,300 | 170 | 195 | 215 | 205 | 742 | 138 |
| 1965 | 544 | 37 | 663 | 4,531 | 2,529 | 3,304 | 217 | 232 | 229 | 213 | 825 | 151 |
| 1966 | ... | 104 | 962 | 4,626 | 2,588 | 2,956 | 230 | 251 | 235 | 248 | 840 | 142 |
| 1967 | ... | 130 | 823 | 5,236 | 2,748 | 3,163 | 230 | 259 | 243 | 270 | 859 | 146 |
| 1968 | ... | 53 | 1,079 | 5,484 | 2,983 | 2,693 | 232 | 250 | 240 | 297 | 949 | 158 |
| 1969 | ... | 141 | 1,344 | 6,023 | 3,179 | 2,800 | 231 | 250 | 259 | 357 | 948 | 170 |

**C8      SOUTH AMERICA: Output of Fruit** (in thousands of metric tons)

|      | Argentina | | | Brazil | | Ecuador | | Paraguay | | Peru | Venezuela | |
|------|--------|---------|-------|---------|--------|---------|------|---------|------|------|---------|------|
|      | Apples | Bananas | CF    | Bananas | CF     | Bananas | CF   | Bananas | CF   | CF   | Bananas | CF   |
| 1970 | 445    | 223     | 1,425 | 6,408   | 3,537  | 2,700   | 221  | 249     | 259  | 357  | 968     | 184  |
| 1971 | 424    | 225     | 1,598 | 6,806   | 3,500  | 3,512   | 219  | 250     | 263  | 334  | 989     | 194  |
| 1972 | 512    | 311     | 1,302 | 7,000   | 4,228  | 3,296   | 201  | 250     | 250  | 337  | 997     | 206  |
| 1973 | 233    | 352     | 1,444 | 7,128   | 5,276  | 3,203   | 208  | 255     | 182  | 284  | 902     | 217  |
| 1974 | 786    | 399     | 1,546 | 6,974   | 6,625  | 3,397   | 377  | 258     | 250  | 312  | 937     | 231  |
| 1975 | 608    | 374     | 1,483 | 5,311   | 6,743  | 2,544   | 401  | 259     | 192  | 322  | 860     | 245  |
| 1976 | 577    | 278     | 1,399 | 5,761   | 7,871  | 2,571   | 393  | 254     | 199  | 275  | 900     | 250  |
| 1977 | 820    | 220     | 1,480 | 6,415   | 7,592  | 2,451   | 586  | 252     | 298  | 245  | 875     | 320  |
| 1978 | 810    | 129     | 1,450 | 6,240   | 6,810  | 2,152   | 613  | 254     | 293  | 273  | 900     | 314  |
| 1979 | 972    | 144     | 1,365 | 6,133   | 7,370  | 2,032   | 618  | 306     | 336  | 258  | 961     | 369  |
| 1980 | 958    | 146     | 1,478 | 6,721   | 9,363  | 2,269   | 648  | 300     | 343  | 238  | 890     | 351  |
| 1981 | 908    | 77      | 1,465 | 6,710   | 10,008 | 2,010   | 636  | 305     | 345  | 217  | 915     | 368  |
| 1982 | 804    | 89      | 1,394 | 6,821   | 10,181 | 1,999   | 618  | 314     | 347  | 237  | 921     | 372  |
| 1983 | 817    | 126     | 1,394 | 6,566   | 10,179 | 1,642   | 307  | 315     | 360  | 233  | 934     | 434  |
| 1984 | 922    | 161     | 1,371 | 7,062   | 14,035 | 1,678   | 370  | 325     | 360  | 237  | 965     | 362  |
| 1985 | 982    | 163     | 1,431 | 4,815   | 15,049 | 1,970   | 337  | 311     | 492  | 246  | 989     | 370  |
| 1986 | 594    | 190     | 1,525 | 5,052   | 14,422 | 2,316   | 283  | 325     | 478  | 277  | 1,007   | 384  |
| 1987 | 1,074  | 243     | 1,776 | 5,131   | 15,830 | 2,387   | 308  | 423     | 524  | 276  | 1,038   | 388  |
| 1988 | 925    | 250     | 1,562 | 5,156   | 16,168 | 2,576   | 199  | 449     | 552  | 340  | 1,100   | 424  |

NOTES

1.   SOURCES: The national publications on p. xiv–xvi ; International Institute of Agriculture, Year-
     book of Agricultural Statistics; and FAO, Yearbook of Food and Agricultural Statistics.
2.   Statistics refer to commercial production.
3.   Note 2 of table C3 also applies to this table.

FOOTNOTES

[1] Exports to 1951 (1st line).
[2] Exports to 1954 (1st line).
[3] The FAO Yearbooks do not indicate any breaks, but the markedly lower figures between 1962 and 1969 are FAO estimates, whereas the others are from official national sources, and it seems probable that the latter covered plantains as well as bananas.
[4] Except from 1957 (2nd line) to 1966 (1st line), data relate to plantains as well as bananas.
[5] Exports to 1948 (1st line). Data are for years ending 30 September to 1889 and years beginning 1 April from 1891 to 1908.
[6] Exports to 1946.
[7] Statistics to 1919 (except for citrus fruit in 1915–19) are derived from censuses. In 1924 the census figure for apples was 3,122.
[8] Data to 1929 (1st line) relate to orange output in California and Florida only. From 1929 (2nd line) to 1938 they are for the citrus fruit output of the seven main producing states. The census figure for total citrus fruit output in 1919 was 1,400 thousand tons.
[9] Oranges only to 1952 (1st line).
[10] Exports to 1957 (1st line).
[11] Oranges only to 1943. Exports from 1947 to 1951.

**C9** **SOUTH AMERICA: AREA OF VINEYARDS AND OUTPUT OF WINE** (in thousands of hectares and thousands of hectolitres)

| | Argentina | | Brazil | | Chile | | Uruguay | |
|---|---|---|---|---|---|---|---|---|
| | Area[1] | Output | Area | Output | Area | Output | Area[2] | Output |
| 1896 | 28 | 574 | ... | ... | ... | ... | ... | ... |
| 1897 | ... | ... | ... | ... | ... | ... | ... | ... |
| 1898 | ... | ... | ... | ... | ... | ... | 4 | 34 |
| 1899 | ... | ... | ... | ... | ... | ... | ... | ... |
| 1900 | ... | 1,151 | ... | ... | ... | ... | ... | ... |
| 1901 | ... | 1,844 | ... | ... | 30 | 1,062 | ... | ... |
| 1902 | 48 | 1,360 | ... | ... | 30 | | 4 | 70 |
| 1903 | 50 | 1,892 | ... | ... | 30 | 597 | ... | ... |
| 1904 | 54 | 1,741 | ... | ... | 38 | 756 | 4 | 105 |
| 1905 | 54 | 1,838 | ... | ... | 38 | 728 | 4 | 116 |
| 1906 | 61 | 2,426 | ... | ... | 32 | 553 | 5 | 95 |
| 1907 | 74 | 2,621 | ... | ... | ... | ... | 5 | 115 |
| 1908 | 122 | 2,843 | ... | ... | 59 | 1,900 | 5 | 186 |
| 1909 | 122 | 2,338 | ... | ... | 66 | 2,300 | 6 | 162 |
| 1910 | 122 | 3,396 | ... | ... | 66 | 2,227 | 6 | 170 |
| 1911 | 105 | 3,781 | ... | ... | 52 | 1,332 | 6 | 147 |
| 1912 | 100 | 4,260 | ... | ... | 57 | 1,964 | 6 | 106 |
| 1913 | 102 | 4,989 | ... | ... | 61 | 2,263 | 6 | 194 |
| 1914 | 106 | 5,151 | ... | ... | 66 | 2,952 | 6 | 165 |
| 1915 | 132 | 3,940 | ... | ... | 71 | 3,081 | 6 | 114 |
| 1916 | 124 | 4,406 | ... | ... | 57 | 1,614 | 6 | 206 |
| 1917 | 115 | 5,133 | ... | ... | 64 | 2,243 | 6 | 192 |
| 1918 | 116 | 4,529 | ... | ... | 89 | 2,066 | 7 | 256 |
| 1919 | 113 | 4,575 | ... | ... | 67 | 1,658 | 7 | 194 |
| 1920 | 113 | 5,134 | ... | 480 | 66 | 1,789 | 7 | 194 |
| 1921 | 120 | 6,155 | ... | 473 | 67 | 1,861 | 7 | 361 |
| 1922 | 121 | 5,155 | ... | 750 | 67 | 2,137 | 7 | 230 |
| 1923 | 126 | 5,435 | ... | 442 | 68 | 2,353 | 8 | 320 |
| 1924 | 146 | 5,463 | ... | 707 | 68 | 2,124 | 8 | 343 |
| 1925 | 137 | 6,635 | ... | 717 | 69 | 1,590 | 9 | 362 |
| 1926 | 123 | 5,282 | ... | 819 | 71 | 1,966 | 10 | 293 |
| 1927 | 128 | 4,649 | ... | 861 | 71 | 3,085 | 10 | 399 |
| 1928 | 133 | 7,656 | ... | 841 | 81 | 3,451 | 11 | 359 |
| 1929 | ... | 8,368 | ... | 753 | 82 | 3,278 | 12 | 409 |
| 1930 | 141 | 5,734 | ... | 1,367 | 85 | 3,202 | 12 | 495 |
| 1931 | 143 | 5,585 | ... | 1,248 | 86 | 2,425 | 13 | 379 |
| 1932 | 157 | 2,187 | ... | 933 | 84 | 2,315 | 14 | 533 |
| 1933 | 157 | 7,347 | ... | 686 | 84 | 3,078 | 14 | 473 |
| 1934 | 169 | 7,548 | ... | 526 | 86 | 2,925 | 15 | 583 |
| 1935 | 169 | 4,365 | ... | 762 | 89 | 2,220 | 15 | 357 |
| 1936 | 169 | 5,812 | ... | 858 | 101 | 3,438 | 15 | 561 |
| 1937 | ... | 7,948 | ... | 772 | 102 | 3,547 | 16 | 725 |
| 1938 | ... | 9,262 | 24 | 828 | 104 | 3,595 | 16 | 684 |
| 1939 | 143 | 6,631 | 24 | 802 | 102 | 2,818 | 16 | 599 |
| 1940 | 138 | 6,707 | 32 | 750 | 102 | 2,656 | 17 | 446 |
| 1941 | 139 | 7,615 | 34 | 629 | 101 | 2,784 | ... | 616 |
| 1942 | 139 | 6,916 | 35 | 626 | 100 | 2,710 | ... | 689 |
| 1943 | 120 | 10,662 | 34 | 709 | 99 | 2,849 | ... | 773 |
| 1944 | 135 | 8,489 | 31 | ... | 99 | 3,808 | ... | 718 |

**C9    SOUTH AMERICA: Area of Vineyards and Output of Wine** (in thousands of hectares and thousands of hectolitres)

| | Argentina | | Brazil | | Chile | | Uruguay | |
|---|---|---|---|---|---|---|---|---|
| | Area[1] | Output | Area | Output | Area | Output | Area | Output |
| 1945 | 117 | 7,101 | 32 | 782 | ... | 2,881 | ... | 531 |
| 1946 | 159 | 8,940 | 32 | 850 | 87 | 2,627 | ... | ... |
| 1947 | 159 | 10,344 | 33 | 970 | 87 | 2,615 | 18 | 658 |
| 1948 | 157 | 11,624 | 37 | 900 | 89 | 2,366 | 18 | 720 |
| 1949 | 157 | 10,397 | 35 | 621 | 91 | 3,140 | 18 | 807 |
| 1950 | 157 , 170 | 12,509 | 36 | 977 | 90 | 3,603 | 17 | 731 |
| 1951 | 170 | 11,503 | 37 | 821 | 88 | 3,395 | 17 | 961 |
| 1952 | 177 | 10,794 | 41 | 852 | 98 | 2,200 | ... | 719 |
| 1953 | 198 | 13,001 | 42 | 1,020 | ... | 3,646 | 18 | 971 |
| 1954 | 207 | 10,686 | 45 | 743 | ... | 3,526 | 20 | 901 |
| 1955 | 213 | 17,672 | 48 | 743 | 108 | 3,045 | 19 | 769 |
| 1956 | 216 | 13,422 | 50 | 1,376 | 108 | 3,654 | ... | 874 |
| 1957 | 224 | 8,616 | 54 | 1,698 | ... | 3,579 | ... | ... |
| 1958 | 229 | 14,098 | 56 | 1,670 | 108 | 3,720 | ... | 680 |
| 1959 | 230 | 17,767 | 59 | 1,560 | 108 | 3,638 | ... | 967 |
| 1960 | 234 | 15,826 | 61 | 1,500 | 100 | 3,688 | ... | 810 |
| 1961 | 239 | 16,750 | 65 | 1,580 | 101 | 4,853 | 20 | 800 |
| 1962 | 245 | 19,172 | 70 | 1,390 | 108 | 5,529 | 20 | 703 |
| 1963 | 253 | 20,744 | 71 | 1,180 | 108 | 4,563 | 20 | 842 |
| 1964 | 261 | 19,533 | 68 | 999 | 108 | 4,837 | 20 | 782 |
| 1965 | 267 | 18,271 | 69 | 1,928 | 103 | 3,648 | 20 | 867 |
| 1966 | 271 | 21,917 | 67 | 1,830 | 113 | 4,736 | 19 | 1,061 |
| 1967 | 276 | 28,171 | 65 | 1,750 | 109 | 4,885 | 20 | 934 |
| 1968 | 291 | 19,513 | 73 | 1,988 | 114 | 5,360 | 20 | 837 |
| 1969 | 298 | 17,916 | 60 | 1,580 | 112 | 4,024 | 20 | 760 |
| 1970 | 295 | 18,360 | 66 | 1,900 | 125 | 4,006 | 20 | 910 |
| 1971 | 322 | 21,783 | 67 | 1,900 | 130 | 5,251 | 20 | 910 |
| 1972 | 319 | 19,986 | 60 | 2,300 | 125 | 6,400 | 22 | 900 |
| 1973 | 313 | 22,567 | 56 | 2,362 | ... | 5,690 | ... | 900 |
| 1974 | 325 | 27,183 | 53 | 2,036 | ... | 4,665 | ... | 900 |
| 1975 | 331 | 22,103 | 58 | 2,036 | ... | 4,649 | ... | 900 |
| 1976 | 339 | 28,197 | 62 | 2,195 | ... | 5,143 | ... | 820 |
| 1977 | 341 | 23,319 | 60 | 2,641 | ... | 5,786 | ... | 470 |
| 1978 | 346 | 29,267 | 58 | 2,850 | 101 | 5,612 | ... | 470 |
| 1979 | 366 | 25,975 | 60 | 2,850 | 106 | 5,925 | 16 | 550 |
| 1980 | 312 | 23,302 | 57 | 2,000 | 108 | 5,860 | 12 | 571 |
| 1981 | 320 | 21,633 | 58 | 2,900 | 110 | 5,943 | 12 | 971 |
| 1982 | 318 | 24,984 | 58 | 2,750 | 112 | 6,100 | 18 | 836 |
| 1983 | 319 | 24,719 | 58 | 2,750 | 121 | 5,200 | 18 | 751 |
| 1984 | 317 | 18,808 | 57 | 2,730 | 112 | 4,000 | 17 | 666 |
| 1985 | 265 | 17,180 | 58 | 2,800 | 112 | 4,500 | ... | 710 |
| 1986 | 262 | 18,520 | 59 | 2,800 | ... | 4,500 | ... | 710 |
| 1987 | 282 | 24,440 | 59 | 2,820 | 115 | 3,000 | ... | 740 |
| 1988 | 274 | 19,100 | 58 | 3,760 | 118 | 3,800 | ... | 740 |

NOTES

1. SOURCES: As for table C1, with Argentinian output for 1900–39 taken from *Anuario Geografico Argentino* (Buenos Aires, 1941).
2. It is only recently that data on wine output in the U.S.A. have been published. Statistics since 1970 are as follows:-

| | | | | | | | |
|------|--------|------|--------|------|--------|------|--------|
| 1970 | 9,688  | 1975 | 14,535 | 1980 | 18,400 | 1985 | 18,100 |
| 1971 | 13,699 | 1976 | 14,366 | 1981 | 16,300 | 1986 | 17,700 |
| 1972 | 12,040 | 1977 | 14,179 | 1982 | 19,500 | 1987 | 17,000 |
| 1973 | 15,813 | 1978 | 16,160 | 1983 | 14,760 | 1988 | 18,450 |
| 1974 | 14,241 | 1979 | 16,050 | 1984 | 16,656 | | |

FOOTNOTES

[1] Data to 1950 (1st line) are of vines in bearing only.
[2] In 1892–94 the area was given as 3 thousand hectares.

**C10    NORTH AMERICA: NUMBERS OF LIVESTOCK** (in thousands, poultry in millions)

| | Canada[1] | | | | |
|---|---|---|---|---|---|
| | Horses | Cattle | Pigs | Sheep | Poultry[3] |
| 1851 | [401][2] | [1,707][2] | [828][2] | [2,066][2] | ... |
| 1861 | 722 | 2,316 | 1,228 | 2,506 | ... |
| 1871 | 837 | 2,624 | 1,366 | 3,156 | ... |
| 1881 | 1,059 | 3,515 | 1,208 | 3,049 | ... |
| 1891 | 1,471 | 4,121 | 1,734 | 2,564 | ... |
| 1901 | 1,578 | 5,576 | 2,354 | 2,510 | 16.7 |
| 1906 | 1,963 | 7,202 | 3,379 | 2,543 | ... |
| 1907 | 2,106 | 7,153 | 3,701 | 2,350 | ... |
| 1908 | 2,248 | 6,995 | 3,546 | 2,380 | ... |
| 1909 | 2,327 | 6,651 | 3,287 | 2,327 | ... |
| 1910 | 2,478 | 6,515 | 3,304 | 2,246 | ... |
| 1911 | 2,599 | 6,526 | 3,635 | 2,174 | 29.8 |
| 1912 | 2,694 | 6,686 | 3,684 | 2,172 | ... |
| 1913 | 2,827 | 6,855 | 3,683 | 2,333 | ... |
| 1914 | 2,992 | 6,911 | 3,640 | 2,310 | ... |
| 1915 | 3,115 | 7,221 | 3,464 | 2,359 | ... |
| 1916 | 3,167 | 7,499 | 3,562 | 2,334 | 34.1 |
| 1917 | 3,210 | 7,789 | 3,292 | 2,422 | 34.9 |
| 1918 | 3,346 | 8,251 | 3,677 | 2,636 | 35.8 |
| 1919 | 3,445 | 8,485 | 3,623 | 2,949 | 37.6 |
| 1920 | 3,404 | 8,153 | 3,152 | 3,179 | 35.6 |
| 1921 | 3,452 | 8,370 | 3,324 | 3,200 | 41.1 |
| 1922 | 3,401 | 8,267 | 3,493 | 3,045 | 45.5 |
| 1923 | 3,341 | 7,975 | 3,986 | 2,601 | 47.1 |
| 1924 | 3,384 | 8,135 | 4,594 | 2,499 | 48.3 |
| 1925 | 3,348 | 7,976 | 4,009 | 2,628 | 48.7 |
| 1926 | 3,361 | 7,818 | 4,037 | 2,830 | 49.7 |
| 1927 | 3,297 | 7,604 | 4,302 | 2,968 | 50.9 |
| 1928 | 3,265 | 7,458 | 4,217 | 3,128 | 54.2 |
| 1929 | 3,264 | 7,518 | 4,048 | 3,350 | 59.8 |
| 1930 | 3,191 | 7,686 | 3,735 | 3,438 | 60.5 |
| 1931 | 3,114 | 7,973 | 4,700 | 3,627 | 61.3 |
| 1932 | 3,084 | 8,548 | 4,670 | 3,604 | 59.7 |
| 1933 | 2,973 | 8,954 | 3,854 | 3,307 | 54.7 |
| 1934 | 2,918 | 9,070 | 3,736 | 3,291 | 55.0 |
| 1935 | 2,911 | 8,973 | 3,651 | 3,224 | 52.5 |
| 1936 | 2,878 | 8,829 | 4,136 | 3,159 | 54.4 |
| 1937 | 2,845 | 8,915 | 4,016 | 3,071 | 52.2 |
| 1938 | 2,770 | 8,491 | 3,527 | 3,047 | 51.7 |
| 1939 | 2,761 | 8,374 | 4,364 | 2,911 | 55.7 |
| 1940 | 2,780 | 8,380 | 6,002 | 2,887 | 57.0 |
| 1941 | 2,789 | 8,517 | 6,081 | 2,840 | 59.0 |
| 1942 | 2,759 | 8,712 | 6,808 | 2,972 | 66.3 |
| 1943 | 2,667 | 9,122 | 7,413 | 3,107 | 68.8 |
| 1944 | 2,568 | 9,544 | 6,790 | 3,213 | 77.2 |

| | Costa Rica | | | |
|---|---|---|---|---|
| | Horses | Cattle | Pigs | Poultry[4] |
| 1910 | 60 | 333 | 70 | ... |
| 1914 | 52 | 336 | 64 | ... |
| 1915 | 65 | 347 | 76 | ... |
| 1922 | 95 | 477 | 114 | ... |
| 1923 | 105 | 426 | 92 | ... |
| 1924 | 116 | 404 | 76 | ... |
| 1925 | 104 | 433 | 71 | ... |
| 1926 | 127 | 423 | 76 | ... |
| 1927 | 126 | 478 | 129 | ... |
| 1928 | 102 | 443 | 104 | ... |
| 1929 | 85 | 399 | 83 | 1.0 |

For Cuba see next page

| | Dominican Republic | | | | | |
|---|---|---|---|---|---|---|
| | Horses | Mules | Asses | Cattle | Pigs | Goats |
| 1920 | 156 | 49 | ... | 609 | 557 | 656 |
| 1921 | 163 | 65 | ... | 647 | 674 | 706 |
| 1922 | 115 | 34 | 76 | 577 | 843 | 360 |
| 1923 | 126 | 37 | 85 | 635 | 927 | 381 |
| 1924 | 139 | 41 | 93 | 701 | 1,020 | 419 |
| 1930 | 150 | 45 | 105 | 900 | 1,100 | 650 |
| 1935 | 266 | 45 | 93 | 913 | 880 | 373 |
| 1939 | 245 | 48 | 68 | 819 | 783 | 447 |

**C10  NORTH AMERICA: Numbers of Livestock** (in thousands, poultry in millions)

| | Cuba | | | | | |
| | Horses | Mules | Cattle | Pigs | Sheep | Goats |
|---|---|---|---|---|---|---|
| 1846 | 240[5] | | 1,027 | 929 | 83 | |
| 1862 | 330[5] | | 1,241 | 723 | 79 | |
| 1881 | 205[5] | | 916 | 325 | 60 | |
| 1892 | 647 | | 2,585 | 535 | 95 | |
| 1894 | 585 | | 2,486 | 570 | 78 | |
| 1899 | 108 | | 377 | 359 | 29 | |
| 1902 | 168 | 31 | 1,000 | ... | ... | ... |
| 1903 | 208 | 33 | 1,304 | ... | ... | ... |
| 1904 | 269 | 44 | 1,700 | ... | ... | ... |
| 1905 | 343 | 46 | 2,176 | ... | ... | ... |
| 1906 | 402 | 51 | 2,579 | ... | ... | ... |
| 1907 | 453 | 55 | 2,754 | ... | ... | ... |
| 1908 | 500 | 57 | 2,969 | ... | ... | ... |
| 1909 | 555 | 59 | 3,076 | ... | ... | ... |
| 1910 | 613 | 61 | 3,212 | ... | ... | ... |
| 1911 | 457 | 31 | 2,329 | ... | ... | ... |
| 1912 | 561 | 41 | 2,830 | ... | ... | ... |
| 1913 | 625 | 46 | 3,141 | ... | ... | ... |
| 1914 | 673 | 50 | 3,395 | ... | ... | ... |
| 1915 | 720 | 54 | 3,704 | ... | ... | ... |
| 1916 | 750 | 58 | 3,962 | ... | ... | ... |
| 1917 | ... | ... | ... | ... | ... | ... |
| 1918 | 779 | 65 | 3,966 | ... | ... | ... |
| 1919 | ... | ... | ... | ... | ... | ... |
| 1920 | 841 | 71 | 4,593 | ... | ... | ... |
| 1921 | 859 | 72 | 4,771 | ... | ... | ... |
| 1922 | 889 | 78 | 4,877 | ... | ... | ... |
| 1923 | 844 | 77 | 5,085 | ... | ... | ... |
| 1924 | 785 | 71 | 4,600 | ... | ... | ... |
| 1925 | 685 | 72 | 4,512 | ... | ... | ... |
| 1926 | 747 | 72 | 4,704 | ... | ... | ... |
| 1927 | 759 | 73 | 4,786 | ... | ... | ... |
| 1928 | 634 | 68 | 4,421 | ... | ... | ... |
| 1929 | 758 | 92 | 4,865 | 591 | 102 | 33 |
| 1930 | 635 | 85 | 4,991 | 650 | 112 | 37 |
| 1931 | 623 | 73 | 4,349 | 715 | ... | 41 |
| 1932 | 599 | 80 | 4,462 | 787 | 135 | 45 |
| 1933 | 552 | 62 | 4,123 | 865 | 149 | 49 |
| 1934 | 569 | 64 | 4,515 | 952 | 164 | 54 |
| 1935 | 599 | 80 | 4,651 | 952 | 164 | 54 |
| 1936 | ... | ... | ... | ... | ... | ... |
| 1937 | 588 | 84 | 5,074 | ... | ... | ... |
| 1938 | 636 | 86 | 5,559 | ... | ... | ... |
| 1939 | 572 | 77 | 4,900 | ... | ... | ... |
| 1940 | 391 | 33 | 5,334 | 857 | 141 | ... |

**C10**  **NORTH AMERICA: Numbers of Livestock** (in thousands, poultry in millions)

### El Salvador

| | Horses[6] | Cattle | Pigs | Poultry[3] |
|---|---|---|---|---|
| 1905 | 74 | 284 | 423 | ... |
| 1929 | 66 | 338 | 335 | ... |
| 1930 | 83 | 374 | 360 | ... |
| 1931 | 103 | 438 | 367 | ... |
| 1932 | 123 | 454 | 230 | ... |
| 1933 | 150 | 523 | 336 | ... |
| 1934 | 165 | 577 | 396 | ... |
| 1935 | 181 | 609 | 425 | ... |
| 1936 | 187 | 646 | 473 | ... |
| 1937 | 201 | 670 | 543 | ... |
| 1938 | 221 | 680 | 577 | ... |
| 1939 | 114 | 451 | 598 | 1.2 |
| 1940 | 143 | 542 | 328 | 1.5 |
| 1941 | 192 | 716 | 481 | 2.4 |
| 1942 | 207 | 743 | 518 | 2.4 |
| 1943 | 183 | 673 | 417 | 1.9 |
| 1944 | 222 | 779 | 503 | 2.2 |

### Haiti

| | Horses | Asses | Cattle | Pigs | Sheep | Goats |
|---|---|---|---|---|---|---|
| 1926 | 110 | 270 | 57 | 170 | 2 | 189 |
| 1927 | 115 | 310 | 67 | 185 | 5 | 216 |
| 1928 | 250 | 340 | 75 | 200 | 5 | 220 |
| 1929 | 280 | 340 | 80 | 220 | 8 | 240 |
| 1930 | 310 | 380 | 90 | 240 | 10 | 260 |
| 1931 | 350 | 400 | 92 | 260 | 12 | 280 |
| 1932 | 400 | 600 | 100 | 250 | 15 | 300 |
| 1933 | 400 | 650 | 105 | 350 | 15 | 310 |
| 1934 | 400 | ... | 110 | 360 | 16 | 320 |
| 1935 | 400 | ... | 125 | 375 | 16 | 330 |

### Honduras

| | Horses | Cattle | Pigs | Goats | Poultry |
|---|---|---|---|---|---|
| 1910 | 64 | 466 | ... | [24][9] | ... |
| 1914 | 68 | 489 | 150 | [23][9] | ... |
| 1930 | 167 | 517 | 298 | 9 | 2.0 |

*For Jamaica see next page*

### Guatemala

| | Horses | Mules | Cattle | Pigs | Sheep | Goats | Poultry |
|---|---|---|---|---|---|---|---|
| 1913 | 64 | ... | 557 | 188 | 514 | 11 | ... |
| 1914 | 114 | | 655 | 177 | 402 | 59 | ... |
| 1915 | 116 | | 620 | 103 | 383 | ... | ... |
| 1920 | 63 | ... | 297 | 41 | 105 | ... | ... |
| 1921 | 86 | ... | 319 | 96 | 185 | 17 | ... |
| 1922 | 55 | ... | 246 | 33 | 113 | 9 | ... |
| 1923 | 69 | ... | 233 | 57 | 248 | 10 | ... |
| 1924 | 72 | ... | 245 | 53 | 114 | 18 | ... |
| 1925 | 94 | ... | 564 | 93 | 148 | 24 | ... |
| 1926 | 55 | ... | 260 | 51 | 98 | 16 | ... |
| 1927 | 75 | ... | 310 | 70 | 216 | 20 | ... |
| 1928 | 53 | ... | 298 | 89 | 241 | 24 | ... |
| 1929 | 59 | ... | 396 | 72 | 189 | 19 | ... |
| 1930 | 63[7] | ... | 416[7] | 79[7] | 184[7] | 21[7] | ... |
| 1931 | 57 | ... | 387 | 87 | 147 | 16 | ... |
| 1932 | 65 | ... | 369 | 89 | 166 | 18 | ... |
| 1933 | 79 | ... | 451 | 103 | 179 | 22 | ... |
| 1934 | 77 | ... | 469 | 112 | 181 | 15 | ... |
| 1935 | 81 | ... | 445 | 120 | 196 | 17 | ... |
| 1936 | 85 | ... | 489 | 125 | 234 | 20 | 0.8[8] |
| 1937 | 96 | ... | 548 | 163 | 246 | 20 | ... |
| 1938 | 127 | ... | 523 | 155 | 241 | 22 | ... |
| 1939 | 168 | ... | 605 | ... | 378 | 51 | ... |
| 1940 | 117 | ... | 612 | 276 | 383 | 44 | ... |
| 1941 | 106 | ... | 630 | 290 | 435 | 42 | ... |
| 1942 | 107 | ... | 729 | 290 | 438 | 44 | ... |
| 1943 | 96 | ... | 657 | 240 | 368 | 38 | ... |

### Mexico

| | Horses | Mules | Asses | Cattle |
|---|---|---|---|---|
| 1900 | 859 | 334 | 288 | 5,142 |
| 1920 | [929][10] | [354][10] | [288][10] | [2,163][10] |
| 1926 | 1,036 | 686 | 850 | 5,585 |
| 1930 | 1,887 | 751 | 2,160 | 10,082 |
| 1940 | 1,757 | 933 | 2,342 | 11,622 |

| | Pigs | Sheep | Goats | Poultry |
|---|---|---|---|---|
| 1900 | 616 | 3,424 | ... | ... |
| 1920 | [1,654][10] | [1,090][10] | [1,988][10] | ... |
| 1926 | 2,903 | 2,698 | 5,244 | ... |
| 1930 | 3,698 | 3,674 | 6,544 | 20.7 |
| 1940 | 5,068 | 4,401 | 6,850 | 36.4 |

**C10    NORTH AMERICA: Numbers of Livestock** (in thousands, poultry in millions)

| | Jamaica | | | |
|---|---|---|---|---|
| | Horses & Mules | Cattle | Pigs | Sheep |
| 1869 | 74 | 122 | ... | ... |
| 1881 | 43 | 82 | ... | ... |
| 1882 | 48 | 85 | ... | ... |
| 1883 | 46 | 84 | ... | ... |
| 1884 | 62 | 133 | ... | ... |
| 1885 | 63 | 131 | ... | ... |
| 1886 | 66 | 118 | ... | ... |
| 1887 | 66 | 116 | ... | ... |
| 1888 | 68 | 114 | ... | ... |
| 1889 | 68 | 113 | ... | ... |
| 1890 | 68 | 113 | ... | 14 |
| 1891 | 70 | 108 | ... | 14 |
| 1892 | 69 | 98 | ... | 16 |
| 1893 | 71 | 101 | ... | 17 |
| 1894 | 69 | 104 | ... | 15 |
| 1895 | 46 | 100 | ... | 13 |
| 1896 | 47 | 120 | ... | 14 |
| 1897 | 49 | 121 | ... | 15 |
| 1898 | 49 | 122 | ... | 15 |
| 1899 | 50 | 122 | 17 | 15 |
| 1900 | 55 | 119 | 18 | 16 |
| 1901 | 58 | 120 | 20 | 17 |
| 1902 | 58 | 120 | 20 | 17 |
| 1903 | 52 | 119 | 25 | 18 |
| 1904 | 74 | 108 | 27 | 20 |
| 1905 | 73 | 112 | 28 | 17 |
| 1906 | 68 | 110 | 29 | 16 |
| 1907 | 50 | 105 | 29 | 15 |
| 1908 | 52 | 102 | 30 | 14 |
| 1909 | 53 | 110 | 31 | 13 |
| 1910 | 52 | 111 | 32 | 12 |
| 1911 | 59 | 108 | 31 | 12 |
| 1912 | 54 | 116 | 31 | 12 |
| 1913 | 53 | 116 | 31 | 10 |
| 1914 | 55 | 115 | 31 | 11 |

| | Jamaica | | | | |
|---|---|---|---|---|---|
| | Horses & Mules | Asses | Cattle | Pigs | Sheep |
| 1915 | 51 | ... | 114 | 31 | 9 |
| 1916 | 47 | ... | 114 | 32 | 12 |
| 1917 | 50 | ... | 167 | ... | 12 |
| 1918 | ... | ... | ... | ... | ... |
| 1919 | ... | 17 | 170 | ... | ... |
| 1920 | 29 | 17 | 158 | ... | 8 |
| 1921 | ... | 17 | 141 | ... | 8 |
| 1922 | ... | 17 | 141 | ... | 8 |
| 1923 | ... | 16 | 112 | ... | 5 |
| 1924 | ... | 15 | 133 | ... | 4 |
| 1925 | ... | 15 | 133 | ... | 5 |
| 1926 | ... | 15 | 114 | ... | 8 |
| 1927 | ... | 14 | 116 | ... | 5 |
| 1928 | ... | 14 | 114 | ... | 7 |
| 1929 | ... | 13 | 106 | ... | 7 |
| 1930 | ... | 11 | 109 | ... | 7 |
| 1931 | ... | 10 | 110 | ... | 8 |
| 1932 | ... | 10 | 123 | ... | 8 |
| 1933 | ... | 8 | 124 | ... | 8 |
| 1934 | ... | 9 | 126 | ... | 8 |
| 1935 | ... | 9 | 122 | ... | 8 |
| 1936 | ... | 8 | 102 | ... | 10 |
| 1937 | ... | 10 | 126 | ... | 9 |
| 1938 | ... | 10 | 124 | ... | 11 |
| 1943 | 38 | 51 | 226 | 218 | 13[12] |

| | Nicaragua | | | |
|---|---|---|---|---|
| | Horses | Cattle | Pigs | Poultry |
| 1908 | 28 | ... | 12 | ... |
| 1930 | 150 | 800 | 400 | 1.5 |

| | Panama | | | |
|---|---|---|---|---|
| | Horses | Cattle | Pigs | Poultry[3] |
| 1916 | 15 | 200 | 30 | ... |
| 1928 | ... | ... | 60 | ... |
| 1929 | ... | ... | 67 | ... |
| 1930 | ... | ... | 90 | ... |
| 1931 | ... | ... | 105 | ... |
| 1934 | ... | 370 | ... | ... |
| 1935 | ... | ... | ... | 0.3 |
| 1942 | ... | 334 | 138 | 1.1 |
| 1943 | ... | 382 | 150 | 1.2 |
| 1944 | ... | 445 | 165 | 1.3 |

**C10    NORTH AMERICA: Numbers of Livestock** (in thousands, poultry in millions)

### Puerto Rico

| | Horses | Cattle | Pigs | Goats | Poultry[10] |
|---|---|---|---|---|---|
| 1910 | 58 | 316 | 106 | 49 | ... |
| 1920 | 57 | 279 | 137 | 58 | ... |
| 1930 | 50 | 311 | 104 | 56 | ... |
| 1935 | 43 | 285 | 113 | 57 | ... |
| 1940 | ... | 343 | ... | 111 | 0.9 |

### U.S.A.

| | Horses | Mules | Cattle | Pigs | Sheep |
|---|---|---|---|---|---|
| 1867 | 6,820 | 1,000 | 28,636 | 34,389 | 44,997 |
| 1868 | 7,051 | 1,057 | 29,238 | 33,304 | 43,808 |
| 1869 | 7,304 | 1,130 | 30,060 | 32,570 | 39,802 |
| 1870 | 7,633 | 1,245 | 31,082 | 33,781 | 36,449 |
| 1871 | 8,054 | 1,305 | 32,107 | 36,688 | 34,063 |
| 1872 | 8,441 | 1,360 | 33,078 | 39,296 | 34,312 |
| 1873 | 8,767 | 1,419 | 33,830 | 39,794 | 35,782 |
| 1874 | 9,055 | 1,485 | 34,821 | 38,377 | 36,234 |
| 1875 | 9,333 | 1,548 | 35,361 | 35,834 | 37,237 |
| 1876 | 9,606 | 1,608 | 36,140 | 35,715 | 37,477 |
| 1877 | 9,910 | 1,674 | 37,333 | 39,333 | 38,147 |
| 1878 | 10,230 | 1,746 | 39,396 | 43,375 | 38,942 |
| 1879 | 10,574 | 1,816 | 41,420 | 43,767 | 41,678 |
| 1880 | 10,903 | 1,878 | 43,347 | 44,327 | 44,867 |
| 1881 | 11,187 | 1,912 | 44,501 | 43,076 | 47,371 |
| 1882 | 11,444 | 1,928 | 45,738 | 42,566 | 48,883 |
| 1883 | 11,794 | 1,975 | 47,387 | 43,440 | 50,935 |
| 1884 | 12,215 | 2,047 | 49,804 | 45,961 | 51,101 |
| 1885 | 12,700 | 2,102 | 52,463 | 47,330 | 49,620 |
| 1886 | 13,276 | 2,162 | 54,868 | 45,457 | 46,654 |
| 1887 | 13,821 | 2,213 | 56,602 | 42,563 | 44,217 |
| 1888 | 14,490 | 2,260 | 58,599 | 42,134 | 43,011 |
| 1889 | 15,064 | 2,295 | 59,178 | 44,508 | 42,365 |
| 1890 | 15,732 | 2,322 | 60,014 | 48,130 | 42,693 |
| 1891 | 16,329 | 2,377 | 59,968 | 47,435 | 43,882 |
| 1892 | 16,846 | 2,459 | 58,126 | 45,165 | 44,628 |
| 1893 | 17,289 | 2,550 | 55,119 | 43,652 | 44,567 |
| 1894 | 17,709 | 2,632 | 51,713 | 46,522 | 43,414 |
| 1895 | 17,849 | 2,708 | 49,510 | 47,628 | 41,827 |
| 1896 | 17,876 | 2,782 | 49,205 | 49,154 | 39,609 |
| 1897 | 17,803 | 2,836 | 50,447 | 51,232 | 38,891 |
| 1898 | 17,698 | 2,918 | 52,868 | 53,282 | 40,097 |
| 1899 | 17,728 | 3,012 | 55,927 | 51,558 | 42,688 |
| 1900 | 17,856 | 3,139 | 59,739 | 51,055 | 45,065 |
| 1901 | 17,955 | 3,190 | 62,576 | 50,681 | 46,126 |
| 1902 | 17,968 | 3,264 | 64,418 | 47,858 | 46,196 |
| 1903 | 18,121 | 3,353 | 66,004 | 48,100 | 44,436 |
| 1904 | 18,331 | 3,465 | 66,442 | 51,623 | 41,908 |

| | Horses | Mules | Cattle | Pigs | Sheep | Poultry[11] |
|---|---|---|---|---|---|---|
| 1905 | 18,491 | 3,586 | 66,111 | 53,176 | 40,410 | ... |
| 1906 | 18,806 | 3,680 | 65,009 | 53,633 | 41,965 | ... |
| 1907 | 19,090 | 3,814 | 63,754 | 56,543 | 43,460 | ... |
| 1908 | 19,444 | 3,949 | 61,989 | 58,388 | 45,095 | ... |
| 1909 | 19,731 | 4,085 | 60,774 | 52,508 | 47,098 | 340 |
| 1910 | 19,972 | 4,239 | 58,993 | 48,072 | 46,939 | 356 |
| 1911 | 20,418 | 4,429 | 57,225 | 55,366 | 46,055 | 382 |
| 1912 | 20,726 | 4,551 | 55,675 | 55,394 | 42,972 | 367 |
| 1913 | 21,008 | 4,683 | 56,592 | 53,747 | 40,544 | 365 |
| 1914 | 21,308 | 4,870 | 59,461 | 52,853 | 38,059 | 367 |
| 1915 | 21,431 | 5,062 | 63,849 | 56,600 | 36,263 | 379 |
| 1916 | 21,334 | 5,200 | 67,438 | 60,596 | 36,260 | 369 |
| 1917 | 21,306 | 5,353 | 70,979 | 57,578 | 35,246 | 359 |
| 1918 | 21,238 | 5,485 | 73,040 | 62,931 | 36,704 | 363 |
| 1919 | 20,922 | 5,568 | 72,094 | 64,326 | 38,360 | 391 |
| 1920 | 20,091 | 5,651 | 70,400 | 60,159 | 37,328 | 381 |
| 1921 | 19,369 | 5,768 | 68,714 | 58,942 | 35,426 | 370 |
| 1922 | 18,764 | 5,824 | 68,795 | 59,849 | 33,565 | 395 |
| 1923 | 18,125 | 5,893 | 67,546 | 69,304 | 32,597 | 415 |
| 1924 | 17,378 | 5,907 | 65,996 | 66,576 | 32,859 | 435 |
| 1925 | 16,651 | 5,918 | 63,373 | 55,770 | 34,469 | 435 |
| 1926 | 16,083 | 5,903 | 60,576 | 52,105 | 35,719 | 438 |
| 1927 | 15,388 | 5,804 | 58,178 | 55,496 | 38,067 | 461 |
| 1928 | 14,792 | 5,656 | 57,322 | 61,873 | 40,689 | 475 |
| 1929 | 14,234 | 5,510 | 58,877 | 59,042 | 43,481 | 449 |
| 1930 | 13,742 | 5,382 | 61,003 | 55,705 | 45,577 | 468 |
| 1931 | 13,195 | 5,273 | 63,030 | 54,835 | 47,720 | 450 |
| 1932 | 12,664 | 5,148 | 65,801 | 59,301 | 47,682 | 437 |
| 1933 | 12,291 | 5,046 | 70,280 | 62,127 | 47,303 | 445 |
| 1934 | 12,052 | 4,945 | 74,369 | 58,621 | 48,244 | 434 |
| | 11,861 | 4,822 | 68,846 | 39,066 | 46,139 | 390 |
| | 11,598 | 4,628 | 67,847 | 42,975 | 44,435 | 403 |
| | 11,342 | 4,460 | 66,098 | 43,083 | 45,251 | 424 |
| | 10,995 | 4,250 | 65,249 | 44,525 | 44,972 | 390 |
| | 10,629 | 4,163 | 66,029 | 50,012 | 45,463 | 419 |
| | 10,444 | 4,034 | 68,309 | 61,165 | 46,266 | 438 |
| | 10,193 | 3,911 | 71,755 | 54,353 | 47,441 | 423 |
| | 9,873 | 3,782 | 76,025 | 60,607 | 49,346 | 477 |
| | 9,605 | 3,626 | 81,204 | 73,881 | 48,196 | 542 |
| | 9,192 | 3,421 | 85,334 | 83,741 | 44,270 | 582 |

**C10    NORTH AMERICA: Numbers of Livestock** (in thousands, poultry in millions)

| | Canada | | | | | Costa Rica | | | |
|---|---|---|---|---|---|---|---|---|---|
| | Horses | Cattle | Pigs | Sheep | Poultry[3] | Horses | Cattle | Pigs | Poultry[4] |
| 1945 | 2,374 | 9,632 | 4,964 | 3,032 | 74.5 | ... | ... | ... | ... |
| 1946 | 2,136 | 9,174 | 4,277 | 2,792 | 73.2 | ... | ... | ... | ... |
| 1947 | 1,937 | 9,085 | 4,957 | 2,465 | 78.1 | ... | 506 | ... | ... |
| 1948 | 1,789 | 8,984 | 3,946 | 2,050 | 62.6 | ... | 515 | ... | ... |
| 1949 | 1,642 | 8,641 | 4,452 | 1,773 | 63.6 | 77 | 641 | 112 | 1.28 |
| 1950 | 1,496 | 8,343 | 4,372 | 1,579 | 55.8 | 80 | 685 | 112 | 1.32 |
| 1951 | 1,304 | 8,363 | 4,914 | 1,461 | 64.5 | 71 | 657 | 120 | ... |
| 1952 | 1,179 | 9,153 | 5,428 | 1,534 | 59.0 | 80 | 696 | 103 | 1.39 |
| 1953 | 1,055 | 9,806 | 3,970 | 1,592 | 64.9 | 90 | 762 | 115 | ... |
| 1954 | 917 | 10,170 | 4,440 | 1,636 | 69.4 | 80 | 705 | 115 | ... |
| 1955 | 832 | 10,603 | 4,800 | 1,634 | 65.0 | ... | 954 | 95 | 1.28 |
| 1956 | 782 | 11,011 | 4,731 | 1,620 | 67.5 | ... | ... | ... | ... |
| 1957 | 722 | 11,265 | 4,758 | 1,628 | 71.6 | ... | ... | ... | ... |
| 1958 | 661 | 10,990 | 5,931 | 1,630 | 72.3 | ... | 1,002 | ... | ... |
| 1959 | 601 | 11,058 | 6,519 | 1,608 | 71.6 | ... | 1,057 | ... | ... |
| 1960 | 555 | 11,337 $_{12}$ | 5,070 $_{12}$ | 1,607 $_{12}$ | 67.3 $_{12}$ | 94 | 1,097 | 130 | 1.60 |
| | | 10,704 | 5,003 | 1,069 | 68.8 | | | | |
| 1961 | 514 | 10,940 | 5,138 | 984 | 69.4 | 96 | 1,126 | 135 | 1.75 |
| 1962 | 480 | 11,214 | 4,995 | 904 | 64.9 | 100 | 1,122 | 135 | 1.81 |
| 1963 | 457 | 11,560 | 5,350 | 878 | 66.5 | 100 | 1,051 | 145 | 2.05 |
| 1964 | 427 | 11,908 | 5,577 | 852 | 68.6 | 101 | 1,117 | 171 | 2.20 |
| 1965 | 401 | 11,651 | 5,108 | 783 | 67.4 | 101 | 1,106 | 196 | 2.40 |
| 1966 | 389 | 11,757 | 5,785 | 700 | 71.7 | 103 | 1,294 | 221 | 2.78 $_4$ |
| | | | | | | | | | 3.25 |
| 1967 | 373 | 11,783 | 6,060 | 671 | 80.1 | 105 | 1,288 | 165 | 3.46 |
| 1968 | 363 | 11,409 | 5,697 | 620 | 76.9 | 107 | 1,350 | 170 | 3.68 |
| 1969 | 344 | 11,634 | 6,460 | 616 | 83.3 | 108 | 1,414 | 175 | 3.92 |
| 1970 | 328 | 11,992 | 7,735 | 670 | 92.5 | 109 | 1,496 | 198 | 3.98 |
| 1971 | 357 | 12,275 | 7,402 | 617 | 90.2 | 111 | 1,574 | 210 | 4.33 |
| 1972 | 353 | 12,615 | 6,960 | 597 | 91.0 | 113 | 1,655 | 225 | 4.45 |
| 1973 | 345 | 13,218 | 6,455 | 580 | 96.2 | 101 | 1,766 | 216 | 4.60 |
| 1974 | 345 | 14,016 | 5,913 | 559 | 87.0 | 110 | 1,741 | 220 | 4.80 |
| 1975 | 345 | 14,055 | 5,708 | 467 | 83.3 | 112 | 1,790 | 225 | 5.0 |
| 1976 | 350 | 13,710 | 6,170 | 418 | 70.6 | 107 | 1,841 | 215 | 5.0 |
| 1977 | 350 | 12,870 | 6,653 | 389 | 76.4 | 109 | 1,920 | 215 | 5.0 |
| 1978 | 350 | 12,328 | 8,074 | 430 | 78.5 | 111 | 2,002 | 215 | 5.0 |
| 1979 | 350 | 12,403 | 9,688 | 481 | 78.5 | 112 | 2,093 | 207 | 6.0 |
| 1980 | 370 | 12,166 | 10,190 | 530 | 80.4 | 113 | 2,181 | 223 | 5.0 |
| 1981 | 370 | 12,088 | 10,035 | 564 | 82.5 | 113 | 2,275 | 240 | 5.0 |
| 1982 | 370 | 12,638 | 10,286 | 809 | 77.0 | 113 | 2,276 | 243 | 5.0 |
| 1983 | 380 | 12,284 | 10,795 | 791 | 94.0 | 113 | 2,365 | 236 | 6.0 |
| 1984 | 380 | 12,160 | 10,154 | 748 | 93.0 | 113 | 2,429 | 223 | 6.0 |
| 1985 | 385 | 11,788 | 9,885 | 694 | 96.0 | 113 | 2,509 | 220 | 6.0 |
| 1986 | 340 | 11,750 | 10,493 | 701 | 98.0 | 114 | 2,329 | 222 | 5.0 |
| 1987 | 340 | 12,060 | 10,890 | 697 | 108.0 | 114 | 2,345 | 238 | 5.0 |
| 1988 | 340 | 12,195 | 10,635 | 728 | 107.0 | 114 | 2,190 | 223 | 5.0 |

**C10     NORTH AMERICA: Numbers of Livestock** (in thousands, poultry in millions)

|  | | | | Cuba | | | |
|------|--------|-------|-------|-------|-------|-------|----------|
|  | **Horses** | **Mules** | **Cattle** | **Pigs** | **Sheep** | **Goats** | **Poultry**[3] |
| 1945 | 311 | 25 | 3,884 | 669 | 114 | 85 | ... |
| 1946 | 409 | 34 | 4,115 | 1,338 | 154 | 139 | 7.2 |
| 1947 | ... | ... | 4,100 | ... | ... | ... | ... |
| 1948 | ... | ... | 4,000 | ... | ... | ... | ... |
| 1949 | ... | ... | 4,100 | ... | ... | ... | ... |
| 1950 | ... | ... | ... | 1,344 | ... | ... | ... |
| 1951 | ... | ... | 4,116 | 1,286 | ... | ... | 6.9 |
| 1952 | 412 | 31 | 4,042 | 1,285 | 193 | 161 | 7.4 |
| 1953 | ... | ... | ... | 1,340 | ... | ... | ... |
| 1954 | ... | ... | 4,150 | 1,365 | ... | ... | ... |
| 1955 | 400 | 32 | 4,500 | 1,395 | 210 | 180 | 7.7 |
| 1956 | ... | ... | ... | 1,440 | ... | ... | ... |
| 1957 | ... | ... | ... | 1,500 | ... | ... | ... |
| 1958 | ... | ... | 5,840 | ... | ... | ... | ... |
| 1959 | ... | ... | 5,760 | ... | ... | ... | ... |
| 1960 | 470 | 30 | 5,025 | 1,700 | 222 | 190 | ... |
| 1961 | 480 | 30 | 5,776 | 1,750 | 215 | 170 | ... |
| 1962 | 490 | 30 | 6,200 | 1,750 | 219 | 180 | ... |
| 1963 | 500 | 30 | 6,378 | 1,540 | 148 | 190[13] | ... |
|  |  |  |  |  |  | 65 |  |
| 1964 | 500 | 24 | 6,611 | 1,746 | 170 | 71 | ... |
| 1965 | 536 | 27 | 6,700 | 1,810 | 240 | 80 | ... |
| 1966 | 550 | 31 | 6,774 | 1,670 | 245 | 81 | ... |
| 1967 | 711 | 37 | 7,172 | 1,531 | 260 | 82 | ... |
| 1968 | 695 | 37 | 7,250 | 1,500 | 270 | 82 | ...[14] |
| 1969 | 696 | 38[13] | 7,100[13] | 1,490 | 280 | 84 | 12.4 |
|  |  | 32 | 6,100 |  |  |  |  |
| 1970 | 747 | 29 | 5,738 | 1,460 | 290 | 83 | 13.6 |
| 1971 | 765 | 27 | 5,487 | 1,450 | 300 | 83 | 13.3 |
| 1972 | 783 | 27 | 5,354 | 1,450 | 310 | 86 | 16.4 |
| 1973 | 799 | 26 | 5,486 | 1,450 | 320 | 88 | 15.9 |
| 1974 | 804 | 29 | 5,450 | 1,450 | 330 | 90 | 18.3 |
| 1975 | 811 | 27 | 5,622 | 1,460 | 340 | 92 | 18.1 |
| 1976 | 815 | 27 | 5,644 | 1,506 | 346[14] | 94[14] | 19.9 |
|  |  |  |  |  | 112 | 23 |  |
| 1977 | 819 | 27 | ... | ... | 123 | 22 | 19.7 |
| 1978 | 807 | 23 | 5,274 | ...[14] | 134 | 20 | 22.4 |
| 1979 | 814 | 24 | ... | 691 | 163 | 20 | 24.9 |
| 1980 | 812 | 25 | 5,057 | 765 | 209 | 21 | 24.6 |
| 1981 | 810 | 26 | ... | 840 | 259 | 22 | 24.0 |
| 1982 | 790 | 26 | ... | 853 | 318 | 25 | 23.1 |
| 1983 | 781 | 28 | ... | 911 | 352 | 24 | 25.7 |
| 1984 | 759 | 29 | 5,115 | 1,009 | 441 | 30 | 26.7 |
| 1985 | 740 | 30 | 5,020 | 1,038 | 495 | 30 | 25.9 |
| 1986 | 740 | 30 | 5,007 | 1,101 | ... | ... | 25.0 |
| 1987 | 718 | 31 | 4,984 | 1,093 | ... | ... | 26.0 |
| 1988 | 703 | 32 | 4,927 | 1,169 | ... | ... | 27.0 |

**C10    NORTH AMERICA: Numbers of Livestock** (in thousands, poultry in millions)

| | Dominican Republic | | | | | | | El Salvador | | | | |
|---|---|---|---|---|---|---|---|---|---|---|---|---|
| | Horses | Mules | Asses | Cattle | Pigs | Goats | Poultry[3] | Horses[5] | Mules | Cattle | Pigs | Poultry[3] |
| 1945 | 143 | 43 | 83 | ... | ... | 346 | 2.07 | 156 | ... | 650 | 342 | 1.77 |
| 1946 | 136 | 42 | 77 | 597 | 547 | 304 | 1.99 | 157 | ... | 686 | 284 | 1.76 |
| 1947 | 139 | 45 | 79 | 602 | 537 | 333 | 1.82 | 183₅ | ... | 765 | 348 | 1.89 |
| 1948 | 139 | 46 | 79 | ... | 546 | 331 | 2.04 | ... | ... | ... | ... | ... |
| 1949 | 142₁₃ | 47 | 80 | 885 | 533 | 334₁₃ | 2.17 | ... | ... | ... | ... | ... |
| 1950 | 243 | 43 | 81 | 694 | 1,158 | 596 | 2.16 | 122 | 37 | 825 | 419 | 2.76 |
| 1951 | ... | 45 | 79 | 769 | 641 | ... | 1.53 | ... | ... | ... | ... | ... |
| 1952 | ... | 46₁₃ | 75 | 857 | 833 | ... | 1.73 | ... | ... | 615 | 265 | ... |
| 1953 | 250 | 71 | 78₁₃ | 933 | 888 | ... | 2.69 | 87 | 29 | 827 | 261 | 1.77 |
| 1954 | 242 | 70 | 135 | 917 | 947 | 503 | 1.35 | 90 | 34 | 968 | 339 | 2.08 |
| 1955 | 242 | 70 | 136 | 923 | 1,408 | 700 | 1.05 | 90 | 37 | 1,304 | 291 | 1.83 |
| 1956 | 242 | 79 | 137 | 930 | 1,414 | 724 | 3.63 | 90 | 37 | 1,371 | 301 | 2.01 |
| 1957 | 242 | 81 | 139 | 936 | 1,523 | 749 | 3.50 | 91 | 37 | 917 | 267 | 1.77 |
| 1958 | 242 | 83 | 140 | 943 | 1,584 | 774 | 3.75 | 75 | 27 | ... | ... | 1.46 |
| 1959 | 241 | 84 | 142 | 949 | 1,648 | 801 | 4.79 | ... | ... | 827 | 221 | ... |
| 1960 | 253 | 85 | 145 | 1,005 | 1,713 | 828 | ... | ... | ... | 916 | 324 | ... |
| 1961 | 255 | 85 | 145 | 1,005 | 1,171 | 852 | 4.9 | 74 | 27 | ... | 323 | 1.85 |
| 1962 | 255 | 85 | 145 | 972 | 1,036 | 878 | 5.0 | 74 | 27 | 918 | 323 | 1.88 |
| 1963 | 255 | 85 | 145 | 981 | 900 | 902 | 5.2 | 74 | 27 | 919 | 323 | 1.90 |
| 1964 | 255 | 85 | 145 | 990 | 1,000 | 928 | 5.25 | 74 | 27 | 920 | 322 | 1.92 |
| 1965 | 203 | 89 | 149 | 1,000 | 1,175 | 954 | 5.3 | 74 | 27 | 925 | 322 | 1.98 |
| 1966 | 200 | 90 | 150 | 1,050 | 1,200 | 790 | 5.3₁₃ / 6.3 | 70 | 27 | 1,340 | 408 | 2.00 |
| 1967 | 200 | 90 | 153 | 1,082 | 1,250 | 780 | 6.5 | 69 | 25 | 1,371 | 416 | 2.05 |
| 1968 | 190 | 91 | 154 | 1,090 | 1,275 | 780 | 6.7 | 68 | 24 | 1,410 | 417 | 2.10 |
| 1969 | 180 | 92 | 158₁₃ / 129 | 1,100 | 1,300 | 775 | 7.0 | 67 | 23 | 1,241 | 421 | 2.14 |
| 1970 | 183 | 93 | 126 | 1,399 | 1,050 | 760 | 7.2 | 79 | 23 | 993 | 408 | ... |
| 1971 | 180 | 94 | 125 | 1,423 | 1,100 | 750 | 7.3 | 81 | 22 | 1,000 | 415 | ... |
| 1972 | 178 | 94 | 123 | 1,500 | 760 | 328 | 7.4 | 81 | 22 | 1,008 | 465 | ... |
| 1973 | 200 | 94 | 121 | 1,837 | 750 | 335 | 7.1 | 81 | 22 | 1,038 | 480 | ... |
| 1974 | 201 | 94 | 119 | 1,900 | 700 | 340 | 7.2 | 81 | 22 | 1,031 | 420 | 2.60 |
| 1975 | 202 | 95 | 119 | 1,950 | 705 | 350 | 7.3 | 81 | 21 | 1,109 | 425 | 2.76 |
| 1976 | 202 | 95 | 119 | 2,000 | 753 | 355 | 7.4 | 86 | 21 | 1,283 | 430 | 3.36 |
| 1977 | 203 | 96 | 119 | 2,050 | 718 | 360 | 7.6 | 87 | 21 | 1,350 | 515 | 4.41 |
| 1978 | 203 | 97 | 119 | 2,150 | 600 | 370 | 7.8 | 88 | 21 | 1,387 | 503 | 5.14 |
| 1979 | 204 | 97 | 119 | 2,153 | 250 | 380 | 8.0 | 89 | 22 | 1,440 | 560 | 5.30 |
| 1980 | 204 | 98 | 120 | 1,810 | ... | 385 | 8.2 | 88 | 22 | 1,211 | 421 | 5.06 |
| 1981 | 204 | 99 | 120 | 1,949 | ... | 385 | 8.3 | 88 | 22 | 1,106 | 386 | 5.0 |
| 1982 | 204 | 99 | 120 | 2,154 | 375 | 463 | 8.0 | 89 | 23 | 954 | 400 | 6.0 |
| 1983 | 204 | 99 | 120 | 2,020 | ... | 465 | 9.0 | 90 | 23 | 937 | 400 | 4.0 |
| 1984 | 300 | 130 | 120 | 1,922 | ... | 465 | 14.0 | 90 | 23 | 980 | 375 | 5.0 |
| 1985 | 300 | 130 | 140 | 2,055 | 368 | 480 | 17.0 | 92 | 23 | 1,050 | 397 | 5.0 |
| 1986 | 300 | 130 | 140 | 2,092 | 389 | 521 | 17.0 | 92 | 23 | 1,088 | 411 | 5.0 |
| 1987 | 310 | 132 | 142 | 2,129 | 409 | 534 | 19.0 | 93 | 23 | 1,144 | 418 | 5.0 |
| 1988 | 310 | 132 | 142 | 2,245 | 429 | 543 | 22.0 | 93 | 23 | 1,162 | 442 | 5.0 |

**C10    NORTH AMERICA: Numbers of Livestock** (in thousands, poultry in millions)

| | Horses | Mules | Cattle | Pigs | Sheep | Goats | Poultry[15] |
|---|---|---|---|---|---|---|---|
| | | | | **Guatemala** | | | |
| 1945 | ... | ... | ... | ... | ... | ... | ... |
| 1946 | ... | ... | ... | ... | ... | ... | ... |
| 1947 | 155 | 56 | 911 | 374 | 618 | 64 | ... |
| 1948 | 157 | 60 | 893 . | 415 | 718 | 79 | ... |
| 1949 | 183 | 58 | 903 | 415 | 712 | 79 | ... |
| 1950 | ... | ... | ... | ... | ... | ... | 4.5 |
| 1951 | ... | ... | 1,194 | 415 | 889 | 77 | ... |
| 1952 | ... | 62 | 1,270 | 462 | 813 | 134 | ... |
| 1953 | 189 | 59 | 1,218 | 435 | 865 | 91 | ... |
| 1954 | 171 | 57 | 993 | 390 | 739 | 86 | ... |
| 1955 | 169 | 59 | 1,033 | 362 | 756 | 78 | ... |
| 1956 | 177 | 57 | 1,049 | 401 | 826 | 84 | ... |
| 1957 | 171 | 57 | 1,113 | 403 | 840 | 88 | ... |
| 1958 | 174 | 55 | 1,142 | 406 | 792 | 89 | ... |
| 1959 | 161 | 54 | 1,062 | 431 | 841 | 93 | ... |
| 1960 | 166 | 54 | 1,134 | 409 | 677 | 89 | ...[15] |
| 1961 | 156 | 53 | 1,122 | 388 | 792 | 86 | 4.8 |
| 1962 | 164 | 55 | 1,263 | 381 | 702 | 89 | 4.5 |
| 1963 | 156 | 53 | 1,324 | 438 | 748 | 89 | 5.4 |
| 1964 | 155 | 53 | 1,384 | 495 | 794 | 89 | 5.5 |
| 1965 | 154 | 53 | 1,328 | 543 | 818 | 90 | 5.7 |
| 1966 | 153 | 52 | 1,242 | 594 | 632 | 91 | 5.9 |
| 1967 | 152 | 51 | 1,371 | 662 | 565 | 92 | 6.1 |
| 1968 | 151 | 50 | 1,395 | 728 | 550 | 92 | 6.3 |
| 1969 | 150 | 50 | 1,443 | 806 | 631 | 66 | 6.6[15] |
| | | | | | | | 9.3 |
| 1970 | 145 | 48 | 1,585 | 896 | 521 | 82 | 9.6 |
| 1971 | 140 | 45 | 1,740 | 881 | 528 | 80 | 9.7 |
| 1972 | 130 | 45 | 1,808 | 881 | 572 | 77 | 9.9 |
| 1973 | 130 | 40 | 1,562 | 646 | 414 | 76 | 10.1 |
| 1974 | 125 | 40 | 1,713 | 659 | 540 | 76 | 11.0 |
| 1975 | 102 | 43 | 2,270 | 522 | 470 | 76 | 12.2 |
| 1976 | 100 | 43 | 1,431 | 667 | 612 | 76 | 9.2 |
| 1977 | 100 | 43 | 1,500 | 704 | 600 | 76 | 11.2 |
| 1978 | 100 | 43 | 1,575 | 747 | 685 | 76 | 13.5 |
| 1979 | 100 | 43 | 1,653 | 792 | 679 | 76 | 13.8 |
| 1980 | 100 | 43 | 1,730 | 835 | 734 | 76 | 14.0 |
| 1981 | 100 | 43 | 2,280 | ... | ... | 76 | 14.2 |
| 1982 | 100 | 37 | 2,185 | 806 | 613 | 73 | 15.0 |
| 1983 | 100 | 37 | 2,224 | 806 | 657 | 76 | 15.0 |
| 1984 | 100 | 37 | 2,254 | 834 | 680 | 76 | 15.0 |
| 1985 | 100 | 38 | 2,160 | 862 | 660 | 75 | 15.0 |
| 1986 | 110 | 38 | 2,004 | 850 | 666 | 76 | 14.0 |
| 1987 | 112 | 38 | 2,010 | 820 | 667 | 76 | 15.0 |
| 1988 | 112 | 38 | 2,023 | 800 | 660 | 76 | 15.0 |

**C10** **NORTH AMERICA: Numbers of Livestock** (in thousands, poultry in millions)

| | Haiti | | | | | | | |
|---|---|---|---|---|---|---|---|---|
| | Horses | Mules | Asses | Cattle | Pigs | Sheep | Goats | Poultry |
| 1950 | ... | ... | ... | ... | ... | ... | ... | 3.9 |
| 1951 | ... | ... | ... | ... | ... | ... | ... | ... |
| 1952 | ... | ... | ... | ... | ... | ... | ... | ... |
| 1953 | ... | ... | ... | ... | ... | ... | ... | 4.7 |
| 1954 | ... | ... | ... | ... | ... | ... | ... | 4.3 |
| 1955 | ... | ... | ... | ... | ... | ... | ... | 4.1 |
| 1956 | ... | ... | ... | ... | ... | ... | ... | 4.3 |
| 1957 | ... | ... | ... | ... | ... | ... | ... | 4.7 |
| 1958 | 255 | 56 | 163 | 669 | 1,136 | 52 | 891 | 4.7 |
| 1959 | ... | ... | ... | ... | ... | ... | ... | 4.8 |
| 1960 | 255 | 56 | 163 | 672 | 1,138 | 53 | 890 | 4.8 |
| 1961 | 255 | 60 | 163 | 675 | 1,235 | 54 | 967 | 4.4 |
| 1962 | 283 | 62 | 163 | 685 | 1,268 | 58 | 993 | 4.6 [13] 3.3 |
| 1963 | 290 | 64 | 163 | 690 | 1,301 | 59 | 1,019 | 3.3 |
| 1964 | 297 | 65 | 163 | 694 | 1,334 | 61 | 1,045 | 3.2 |
| 1965 | 303 | 67 | 150 | 699 | 1,367 | 62 | 1,070 | 3.0 |
| 1966 | 334 | 74 | 145 | 769 | 1,504 | 69 | 1,177 | 3.3 |
| 1967 | 367 | 81 | 141 | 845 | 1,654 | 76 | 1,295 | 3.6 |
| 1968 | 319 | 83 | 140 [13] | 900 | 1,700 | 78 | 1,300 | 3.6 |
| 1969 | 327 | 73 | 209 | 713 | 1,480 | 73 | 1,189 | 3.6 |
| 1970 | 335 | 74 | 214 | 718 | 1,520 | 74 [13] 69 | 1,221 | 3.6 [13] 3.2 |
| 1971 | 344 | 76 | 219 | 722 | 1,560 | 71 | 1,245 | 3.2 |
| 1972 | 352 | 78 | 225 | 727 | 1,602 | 73 | 1,287 | 3.3 |
| 1973 | 361 | 80 | 230 | 732 | 1,645 | 75 | 1,321 | 3.4 |
| 1974 | 370 | 81 | 235 | 737 | 1,690 | 77 | 1,356 | 3.4 |
| 1975 | 379 | 83 | 240 | 742 | 1,735 | 79 | 1,380 | 3.5 |
| 1976 | 385 | 84 | 242 | 850 | 1,800 | 81 | 1,100 | 3.9 |
| 1977 | 392 | 85 | 245 | 900 | 1,900 | 83 | 945 | 4.0 |
| 1978 | 400 | 79 | 202 | 900 | 2,000 | 85 | 997 | 4.6 |
| 1979 | 407 | 80 | 204 | 1,000 | 1,500 | 87 | 995 | 4.7 |
| 1980 | 410 | 80 | 206 | 1,000 | 1,500 | 89 | 1,000 | 4.8 |
| 1981 | 415 | 81 | 208 | 1,100 | 1,100 | 90 | 1,000 | 4.9 |
| 1982 | 420 | 82 | 210 | 1,200 | 600 | 91 | 1,000 | 5.0 |
| 1983 | 425 | 83 | 212 | 1,300 | 500 | 92 | 1,100 | 7.0 |
| 1984 | 425 | 83 | 212 | 1,350 | 500 | 92 | 1,100 | 8.0 |
| 1985 | 425 | 83 | 212 | 1,350 | 500 | 92 | 1,100 | 8.0 |
| 1986 | 425 | 84 | 215 | 1,400 | 700 | 92 | 1,100 | 10.0 |
| 1987 | 430 | 84 | 216 | 1,474 | 750 | 93 | 1,150 | 12.0 |
| 1988 | 430 | 85 | 216 | 1,545 | 900 | 94 | 1,200 | 13.0 |

**C10     NORTH AMERICA: Numbers of Livestock** (in thousands, poultry in millions)

| | | | | Honduras | | | |
|---|---|---|---|---|---|---|---|
| | Horses | Mules | Asses | Cattle | Pigs | Goats | Poultry |
| 1945 | 147 | 66 | 20 | 849 | 318 | 24 | ... |
| 1946 | 156 | 67 | 21 | 918 | 323 | 22 | ... |
| 1947 | 155 | 75 | 21 | 945 | 399 | 24 | ... |
| 1948 | 209 | 72 | 20 | 823 | 376 | 21 | ... |
| 1949 | 198 | 69 | 22 | 856 | 407 | 33 | ... |
| 1950 | 140 | 81 | 23 | 889 | 523 | 36 | ... |
| 1951 | 188 | 77 | 28 | 907 | 521 | 39 | 2.0 |
| 1952 | ... | 90 | 23 | 1,168 | 530 | 53 | 3.5 |
| 1953 | ... | 93 | 23 | 1,124 | ... | ... | 6.6 |
| 1954 | ... | 85 | 21 | 1,120 | 592 | 46 | 5.6 |
| 1955 | 192 | 86 | 22 | 1,121 | 615 | 46 | 5.6 |
| 1956 | ... | ... | ... | ... | ... | ... | ... |
| 1957 | ... | ... | ... | ... | ... | ... | ... |
| 1958 | ... | ... | ... | ... | ... | ... | ... |
| 1959 | ... | ... | ... | ... | ... | ... | ... |
| 1960 | 238 | 95 | 32 | 1,387 | 695 | 41 | 5.7 |
| 1961 | 252 | 99 | 35 | 1,454 | 711 | 43 | 5.2 |
| 1962 | 266 | 103 | 39 | 1,587 | 727 | 46 | 5.0 |
| 1963 | 274 | 106 | 40 | 1,635 | 749 | 47 | 4.6 |
| 1964 | 281 | 110 | 40 | 1,700 | 785 | 48 | 5.2 |
| 1965 | 282 | 110 | 40 | 1,720 | 901 | 50 | 5.8 |
| 1966 | 285 | 110 | 41 | 1,510 | 775 | 52 | 5.9 |
| 1967 | 288 | 115 | 42 | 1,540 | 787 | 53 | 6.1 |
| 1968 | 290 | 117 | 43 | 1,559 | 795 | 54 | 6.5 |
| 1969 | 285 | 118 | 44 | 1,578 | 803 | 55 | 6.8 |
| 1970 | 280 | 118 | 46 | 1,598 | 811 | 56 | 7.0 |
| 1971 | 275 | 118 | 48 | 1,618 | 824 | 57 | 7.3 |
| 1972 | 277 | 118 | 49 | 1,641 | 837 | 58 | 7.6 |
| 1973 | 280 | 118 | 50 | 1,795 | 511 | 59 | 7.7 |
| 1974 | 278 | 117 | 48 | 1,817 | 511 | 57 | 7.6 |
| 1975 | 280 | 118 | 49 | 1,839 | 520 | 58 | 7.6 |
| 1976 | 280 [13] | 118 [13] | 49 [13] | 1,862 | 525 | 16 | 7.8 [13] |
| 1977 | 152 | 68 | 22 | 1,900 | 530 | 15 | 4.2 |
| 1978 | 150 | 68 | 22 | 2,234 | 531 | 22 | 4.3 |
| 1979 | 149 | 68 | 21 | 2,262 | 534 | 22 | 4.4 |
| 1980 | 150 | 68 | 21 | 2,358 | 406 | 22 | 4.8 |
| 1981 | 151 | 68 | 21 | 2,499 | 409 | 22 | 4.9 |
| 1982 | 152 | 68 | 21 | 2,086 | 410 | 24 | 5.0 |
| 1983 | 167 | 68 | 22 | 2,695 | 491 | 26 | 5.0 |
| 1984 | 168 | 68 | 22 | 2,770 | 558 | 27 | 5.0 |
| 1985 | 169 | 68 | 22 | 2,803 | 563 | 28 | 5.0 |
| 1986 | 170 | 68 | 22 | 2,859 | 567 | 29 | 7.0 |
| 1987 | 170 | 69 | 22 | 2,824 | 600 | 25 | 8.0 |
| 1988 | 170 | 69 | 22 | 2,759 | ... | ... | 8.0 |

**C10**    **NORTH AMERICA: Numbers of Livestock** (in thousands, poultry in millions)

|  | Jamaica | | | | | | |
|---|---|---|---|---|---|---|---|
|  | Horses & Mules | Asses | Cattle | Pigs | Sheep | Goats | Poultry |
| 1945 | ... | ... | ... | ... | ... | ... | ... |
| 1946 | ... | ... | ... | ... | ... | ... | ... |
| 1947 | ... | ... | ... | ... | ... | ... | ... |
| 1948 | ... | ... | ... | ... | ... | ... | ... |
| 1949 | ... | ... | ... | ... | ... | ... | ... |
| 1950 | 38 | 51 | 248 | 142 | 17 | 350 | ... |
| 1951 | 38 | 51 | 248 | 142 | 17 | 350 | ... |
| 1952 | 38 | 51 | 248 | 142 | 17 | 350 | ... |
| 1953 | 38 | 51 | 248 | 142 | 17 | 350 | ... |
| 1954 | 38 | 51 | 248 | 151 | 17 | 350 | ... |
| 1955 | 38 | 51 | 248 | 152 | 17 | 350 | ... |
| 1956 | 38 | 51 | 248 | ... | ... | ... | ... |
| 1957 | 24 | 64 | 276 | 212 | 12 | 224 | 1.3 |
| 1958 | 23 | 66 | 300 | 196 | 13 | 269 | 1.3 |
| 1959 | 22 | 66 | 300 | 196 | 13 | 269 | 1.4 |
| 1960 | 24 | 66 | 295 | 196 | 13 | 269 | ... |
| 1961 | 17 | 39 | 240 | 128 | 10 | 270 | 1.6 |
| 1962 | 17 | 39 | 240 | 128 | 10 | 269 | 1.9 |
| 1963 | 17 | 39 | 240 | 128 | 10 | 270 | 2.0 |
| 1964 | 17 | 39 | 240 | 128 | 10 | 267 | 2.1 |
| 1965 | 17 | 39 | 240 | 150 | 10 | 312 | 2.1 |
| 1966 | 17 | 38 | 240 | 150 | 10 | 321 | 2.1 |
| 1967 | 17 | 37 | 240 | 160 | 11 | 330 | 2.2 |
| 1968 | 17 | 36 | 248 | 170 | 12 | 340 | 2.2 |
| 1969 | 17 | 34 | 270 | 180 | 13 | 358 | 2.2 [13] |
| 1970 | 16 | 32 | 270 | 190 | 7 | 360 | 2.2 |
|  |  |  |  |  |  |  | 3.1 |
| 1971 | 15 | 30 | 270 | 200 | 5 | 360 | 4.2 |
| 1972 | 15 | 30 | 272 | 210 | 5 | 300 | 3.5 |
| 1973 | 15 | 30 | 274 | 222 | 5 | 300 | 3.6 |
| 1974 | 15 | 30 | 276 | 230 | 5 | 320 | 3.6 |
| 1975 | 15 | 28 | 280 | 235 | 5 | 330 | 3.7 |
| 1976 | 15 | 27 | 282 | 240 | 6 | 340 | 3.8 |
| 1977 | 14 | 26 | 285 | 245 | 6 | 350 | 3.9 |
| 1978 | 14 | 26 | 290 | 250 | 6 | 370 | 4.0 |
| 1979 | 14 | 25 | 300 | 255 | 6 | 380 | 4.1 |
| 1980 | 13 | 25 | 305 | 260 | 6 | 390 | 4.2 |
| 1981 | 13 | 24 | 310 | 265 | 6 | 400 | 4.3 |
| 1982 | 14 | 24 | 310 | 230 | 3 | 410 | 4.0 |
| 1983 | 14 | 24 | 290 | 240 | 3 | 420 | 5.0 |
| 1984 | 14 | 23 | 280 | 245 | 3 | 430 | 5.0 |
| 1985 | 14 | 23 | 290 | 245 | 3 | 430 | 5.0 |
| 1986 | 14 | 23 | 290 | 246 | 3 | 440 | 5.0 |
| 1987 | 14 | 23 | 290 | 250 | 3 | 440 | 6.0 |
| 1988 | 14 | 23 | 290 | 250 | 3 | 440 | 6.0 |

**C10　NORTH AMERICA: Numbers of Livestock** (in thousands, poultry in millions)

| | Mexico | | | | | | | |
|---|---|---|---|---|---|---|---|---|
| | Horses | Mules | Asses | Cattle | Pigs | Sheep | Goats | Poultry[16] |
| 1945 | 2,641 | 1,001 | 2,471 | 12,783 | ... | 4,742 | 6,885 | ... |
| 1946 | ... | ... | ... | ... | ... | ... | ... | ... |
| 1947 | 2,685 | 1,120 | 2,505 | 12,743 | 5,622 | 4,897 | 6,894 | 38.0 |
| 1948 | 2,722 | 1,225 | 2,636 | 13,217 | 5,704 | 4,965 | 6,946 | 39.5 |
| 1949 | ... | ... | ... | ... | ... | ... | ... | ... |
| 1950 | 3,581 | 1,539 | 2,768 | 15,713 | 6,896 | 5,086 | 8,522 | 34.3 |
| 1951 | ... | ... | ... | ... | ... | ... | ... | ... |
| 1952 | ... | ... | ... | ... | ... | ... | ... | ... |
| 1953 | 4,235 | 1,975 | 2,990 | 18,078 | 7,919 | 5,385 | 9,394 | 81.4 |
| 1954 | 4,417 | 2,102 | 3,049 | 18,725 | 8,199 | 5,463 | 9,626 | 88.9 |
| 1955 | 4,607 | 2,237 | 3,109 | 19,397 | 8,489 | 5,542 | 9,865 | 97.2 |
| 1956 | 4,806 | 2,381 | 3,170 | 20,093 | 8,789 | 5,623 | 10,110 | 106.3 |
| 1957 | 5,013 | 2,535 | 3,233 | 20,814 | 9,101 | 5,705 | 10,362 | 116.2 |
| 1958 | 5,228 | 2,698 | 3,297 | 21,561 | 9,423 | 5,788 | 10,620 | 127.1 |
| 1959 | ...[13] | ...[13] | ...[13] | ...[13] | ... | ... | ... | ...[16] |
| 1960 | 4,047 | 1,579 | 2,861 | 31,385 | 10,689 | 5,853 | 8,928 | 100.0 |
| 1961 | 4,169 | 2,141 | 2,946 | 30,800 | 11,231 | 5,994 | 9,197 | 96.0 |
| 1962 | 4,377 | 1,660 | 2,849 | 30,184 | 12,079 | 5,724 | 10,446 | 80.0 |
| 1963 | 4,600 | 1,731 | 3,087 | 28,914 | 12,507 | 5,783 | 11,367 | 63.4 |
| 1964 | 4,800 | 1,817 | 3,241 | 31,516 | 13,132 | 6,073 | 11,936 | 85.1 |
| 1965 | 4,750 | 1,908 | 3,403 | 22,395 | 13,751[13] 9,650 | 6,376 | 12,582[13] 9,300 | 89.3 |
| 1966 | 4,890 | 2,003 | 3,573 | 22,800 | 9,730 | 6,695 | 9,350 | 94.0 |
| 1967 | 5,038 | 2,775 | 3,353 | 23,294 | 9,756 | 6,639 | 9,392 | 99.0 |
| 1968 | 5,048 | 2,745 | 3,330 | 23,628 | 9,979 | 6,706 | 9,416 | 104.4 |
| 1969 | 5,743 | 3,173 | 3,519 | 24,876 | 10,298 | 6,113 | 9,127 | 132.6 |
| 1970 | 5,026 | 2,603 | 3,199 | 25,124 | 9,970 | 5,320 | 8,488 | 140.3 |
| 1971 | 4,423 | 2,655 | 3,039 | 25,827 | 10,983 | 5,480 | 8,063 | 142.6 |
| 1972 | 6,066 | 3,259 | 3,392 | 27,042 | 10,753 | 5,644 | 8,996 | 144.9 |
| 1973 | 6,127 | 2,719 | 3,289 | 27,585 | 10,860 | 5,380 | 9,871 | 147.2 |
| 1974 | 6,376 | 3,295 | 2,891 | 27,863 | 11,466 | 5,280 | 8,556 | ... |
| 1975 | 6,490 | 3,302 | 3,318 | 28,376 | 11,694 | 5,300 | 8,627 | 133.6 |
| 1976 | 6,551 | 3,270 | 3,282 | 28,935 | 11,986 | 7,860 | 8,343 | 143.6 |
| 1977 | 6,479 | 3,239 | 3,245 | 29,333 | 12,321 | 7,856 | 8,193 | 150.2 |
| 1978 | 6,447 | 3,207 | 3,233 | 29,920 | 12,578 | 7,850 | 8,103 | 161.5 |
| 1979 | 6,300 | 3,109 | 3,233 | 34,590 | 13,222 | 7,318 | 7,185 | 169.8 |
| 1980 | 5,625 | 3,283 | 2,807 | 35,689 | 17,562 | 6,567 | 10,004 | 187.8 |
| 1981 | 5,635 | 3,447 | 2,812 | 36,839 | 18,373 | 6,657 | 10,320 | 204.8 |
| 1982 | 6,134 | 3,130 | 3,182 | 37,522 | 19,364 | 6,270 | 9,809 | 201.3 |
| 1983 | 6,134 | 3,130 | 3,182 | 30,374 | 19,393 | 6,120 | 9,553 | 203.7 |
| 1984 | 6,135 | 3,130 | 3,183 | 31,489 | 18,579 | 6,373 | 9,981 | 213.6 |
| 1985 | 6,140 | 3,130 | 3,183 | 31,123 | 18,397 | 5,699 | 10,079 | 219.0 |
| 1986 | 6,150 | 3,150 | 3,184 | 31,156 | 18,722 | 5,926 | 10,442 | 246.0 |
| 1987 | 6,160 | 3,160 | 3,185 | 31,200 | 14,240 | 5,761 | 10,086 | 224.0 |
| 1988 | 6,170 | 3,170 | 3,186 | 34,999 | 14,080 | ... | ... | 202.0 |

**C10    NORTH AMERICA: Numbers of Livestock** (in thousands, poultry in millions)

| | Nicaragua | | | | | Panama | | | |
|---|---|---|---|---|---|---|---|---|---|
| | Horses | Mules | Cattle | Pigs | Poultry | Horses | Cattle | Pigs | Poultry[3] |
| 1945 | ... | ... | ... | ... | ... | ... | 534 | 184 | 1.4 |
| 1946 | ... | ... | 939 | ... | ... | ... | ... | ... | ... |
| 1947 | 185 | 57 | 978 | 664 | ... | 119 | 576 | 209 | 1.5 |
| 1948 | ... | ... | 1,018 | ... | ... | ... | ... | ... | ... |
| 1949 | ... | ... | 1,060 | ... | ... | ... | ... | ... | ... |
| 1950 | ... | ... | 1,103 | ... | ... | 158 | 570 | 182 | 1.6 |
| 1951 | 114 | ... | 1,182 | 234 | 1.2 | ... | ... | ... | ... |
| 1952 | ... | ... | ... | ... | ... | ... | 568 | 241 | ... |
| 1953 | ... | ... | ... | ... | ... | 171 | 579 | 226 | 1.7 |
| 1954 | ... | ... | ... | ... | ... | ... | 578[17] | 215[17] | 2.1[17] |
| 1955 | ... | ... | ... | ... | ... | ... | 587 | 182 | 1.9 |
| 1956 | ... | ... | ... | ... | ... | ... | 614 | 182 | 1.9 |
| 1957 | ... | ... | 1,331 | ... | ... | ... | 638 | 218 | 1.8 |
| 1958 | ... | ... | ... | ... | ... | ... | 661 | 246 | 2.1 |
| 1959 | ... | ... | 1,425 | ... | ... | ... | 666 | 248 | 2.2 |
| 1960 | 164 | 40 | 1,496 | 388 | 1.8 | 160 | 773 | ... | 2.4 |
| 1961 | 169 | 42 | 1,374 | 405 | 2.0 | 160 | 761 | 222 | 2.5 |
| 1962 | 175 | 44 | 1,651 | 423 | 2.2 | 160 | 835 | 204 | 2.4 |
| 1963 | 175 | 44 | 1,734 | 423 | 2.2 | 160 | 842 | 213 | 2.4 |
| 1964 | 175 | 44 | 1,821 | 424 | 2.3 | 160 | 891 | 189 | 2.2 |
| 1965 | 174 | 44 | 1,540 | 450 | 2.4 | 162 | 969 | 176 | 2.5 |
| 1966 | 173 | 44 | 2,020 | 524 | 2.7 | 161 | 1,011 | 167 | 2.7 |
| 1967 | 172 | 44 | 2,155 | 552 | 2.8 | 160 | 1,037 | 169 | 2.6 |
| 1968 | 171 | 44 | 2,293 | 583 | 2.8 | 159 | 1,119 | 174 | 2.6 |
| 1969 | 210 | 43 | 2,431 | 615 | 3.0 | 158 | 1,157 | 196 | 2.9 |
| 1970 | ... | 42 | ... | 624 | 3.1 | 163 | 1,188 | 195 | 2.9 |
| 1971 | ... | 41 | ... | 630 | 3.2 | 164 | 1,260 | 152 | 3.8 |
| 1972 | 230 | 41 | 2,295 | 590 | 3.3 | 164 | 1,289 | 159 | 3.7 |
| 1973 | 240 | 40 | 2,462 | 600 | 3.4 | 164 | 1,312 | 188 | 3.7 |
| 1974 | 250 | 44 | 2,558 | 650 | 3.9 | 164 | 1,333 | 175 | 3.8 |
| 1975 | 260 | 44 | 2,660 | 670 | 4.1 | 164 | 1,348 | 166 | 3.7 |
| 1976 | 270 | 44 | 2,768 | 690 | 4.3 | 164 | 1,361 | 179 | 4.3 |
| 1977 | 275 | 44 | 2,782 | 710 | 4.5 | 164 | 1,374 | 202 | 4.4 |
| 1978 | 280 | 44 | 2,737 | 725 | 4.1 | 164 | 1,395 | 204 | 4.9 |
| 1979 | 275 | 45 | 2,401 | 500 | 4.7 | 165 | 1,437 | 190 | 4.9 |
| 1980 | 270 | 45 | 2,324 | 510 | 4.8 | 165 | 1,405 | 195 | 4.8 |
| 1981 | 275 | 45 | 2,379 | 520 | 5.0 | 166 | 1,426 | 209 | 5.1 |
| 1982 | 270 | 45 | 2,116 | 540 | 5.0 | 166 | 1,456 | 206 | 5.0 |
| 1983 | 270 | 45 | 2,344 | 744 | 5.0 | 167 | 1,459 | 197 | 6.0 |
| 1984 | 270 | 45 | 2,369 | 745 | 5.0 | 168 | 1,452 | 195 | 6.0 |
| 1985 | 270 | 45 | 2,100 | 750 | 5.0 | 169 | 1,447 | 208 | 6.0 |
| 1986 | 255 | 45 | 1,850 | 749 | 7.0 | 170 | 1,430 | 250 | 7.0 |
| 1987 | 250 | 45 | 1,700 | 700 | 7.0 | 170 | 1,410 | 229 | 7.0 |
| 1988 | 250 | 45 | 1,650 | 680 | 7.0 | 171 | 1,423 | 211 | 6.0 |

**C10    NORTH AMERICA: Numbers of Livestock** (in thousands, poultry in millions)

| | Puerto Rico | | | | | USA[19] | | | | | |
|------|--------|--------|------|-------|-----------|--------|-------|--------|--------|--------|-----------|
| | Horses | Cattle | Pigs | Goats | Poultry[18] | Horses | Mules | Cattle | Pigs | Sheep | Poultry[11] |
| 1945 | ... | ... | ... | ... | ... | 8,715 | 3,235 | 85,573 | 59,373 | 39,609 | 516 |
| 1946 | ... | ... | ... | ... | ... | 8,081 | 3,027 | 82,235 | 61,306 | 35,525 | 523 |
| 1947 | 50 | 384 | 220 | 103 | ... | 7,340 | 2,789 | 80,554 | 56,810 | 31,805 | 467 |
| 1948 | 39 | 388 | ... | ... | ... | 6,704 | 2,575 | 77,171 | 54,590 | 29,486 | 500 |
| 1949 | 36 | 400 | ... | ... | ... | 6,096 | 2,402 | 76,830 | 56,257 | 26,940 | 431 |
| 1950 | 33 | 422[13] | 227[13] | 106[13] | ... | 5,548 | 2,233 | 77,963 | 58,937 | 26,182 | 457 |
| 1951 | 39 | 375 | 96 | 32 | ... | 7,036 | | 82,083 | 62,269 | 27,251 | 431 |
| 1952 | 31 | 386 | 91 | 31 | 0.8 | 6,150 | | 88,072 | 62,117 | 27,944 | 427 |
| 1953 | 36 | 405 | 86 | 27 | 1.0 | 5,403 | | 94,241 | 51,755 | 27,593 | 398 |
| 1954 | 40 | 408 | 97 | 24 | 0.8 | 4,791 | | 95,679 | 45,114 | 27,079 | 397 |
| 1955 | ... | 404 | 75 | 23 | 0.8 | 4,309 | | 96,592 | 50,474 | 27,137 | 391 |
| 1956 | ... | 408 | 97 | 24 | 0.7 | 3,958 | | 95,900 | 55,354 | 26,890 | 384 |
| 1957 | 30 | 403 | 97 | 31 | 0.8 | 3,632 | | 92,860 | 51,897 | 26,348 | 391 |
| 1958 | 31 | 412 | 102 | 26 | 1.1 | 3,415 | | 91,176 | 51,517 | 27,167 | 374 |
| 1959 | 31 | 433 | 104 | 26 | 1.1 | 3,189 | | 93,322 | 58,045 | 28,108 | 387 |
| 1960 | 31 | 473 | 163 | 26 | 1.2 | 3,089 | | 96,236[19] | 59,026[19] | 28,849[19] | 369[19] |
| 1961 | 28 | 476 | 164 | 25 | 1.3[18] / 3.2 | ... | | 97,700 | 55,560 | 28,320 | 366 |
| 1962 | 23 | 495 | 163 | 25 | 3.5 | ... | | 100,369 | 56,619 | 26,719 | 377 |
| 1963 | 22 | 515 | 154 | 25 | 3.8 | ... | | 104,488 | 57,993 | 25,122 | 376 |
| 1964 | 21 | 498 | 162 | 25 | 3.6 | ... | | 107,903 | 56,757 | 23,455 | 382 |
| 1965 | 21 | 495 | 176 | 24 | 3.4 | ... | | 109,000 | 50,792 | 21,843 | 394 |
| 1966 | 19 | 490 | 180 | 24 | 3.6 | ... | | 108,862 | 47,414 | 21,456 | 393 |
| 1967 | 20 | 497 | 184 | 24 | 3.5 | ... | | 108,645 | 53,249 | 20,661 | 429 |
| 1968 | 19 | 507 | 194 | 23 | 3.6 | ... | | 109,152[20] | 58,777 | 19,105 | 425 |
| 1969 | 18 | 518 | 191 | 21 | 3.9 | ... | | 109,885 | 60,632 | 18,332 | 424 |
| 1970 | 17 | 530 | 198 | 20 | 4.0 | ... | | 112,303 | 57,046 | 17,411 | 433 |
| 1971 | 18 | 538 | 210 | 20 | 4.4 | ... | | 114,578 | 67,433 | 16,898 | 406 |
| 1972 | 18 | 548 | 224 | 20 | 4.6 | ... | | 117,862 | 62,507 | 15,767[21] / 18,710 | 404 |
| 1973 | 19 | 541 | 233 | 20 | 4.5 | ... | | 121,534 | 59,180 | 17,724 | 409 |
| 1974 | 19 | 546 | 244 | 21 | 4.8 | ... | | 127,670 | 61,106 | 16,394 | 384 |
| 1975 | 19 | 561 | 269 | 21 | 5.0 | ... | | 132,028 | 54,693 | 14,515 | 380[11] / 2,950 |
| 1976 | 20 | 571 | 332 | 21 | 5.5 | ... | | 127,976 | 49,267 | 13,376 | 3,273 |
| 1977 | 20 | 562 | 279 | 21 | 5.5 | ... | | 122,810 | 54,934 | 12,766 | 3,394 |
| 1978 | 20 | 524 | 232 | 21 | 5.8 | ... | | 116,375 | 56,539 | 12,421 | 3,614 |
| 1979 | 20 | 479 | 212 | 21 | 6.8 | ... | | 110,864 | 60,356 | 12,365 | 3,951 |
| 1980 | 20 | 489 | 230 | 21 | 7.1 | ... | | 111,192 | 67,353 | 12,687 | 3,963 |
| 1981 | 20 | 536 | 216 | 21 | 7.5 | ... | | 114,321 | 64,512 | 12,936 | 4,148 |
| 1982 | 21 | 576 | 205 | ... | 6.0 | ... | | 115,604 | 58,688 | 12,966 | 4,149 |
| 1983 | 21 | 593 | 203 | ... | 6.0 | ... | | 115,001 | 54,534 | 12,140 | 4,184 |
| 1984 | 21 | 580 | 210 | ... | 6.0 | ... | | 113,700 | 56,694 | 11,487 | 4,282 |
| 1985 | 21 | 600 | 206 | 15 | 7.0 | ... | | 109,749 | 54,073 | 10,443 | 4,479 |
| 1986 | 22 | 580 | 199 | 14 | 8.0 | ... | | 105,468 | 52,313 | 9,983 | 4,646 |
| 1987 | 22 | 579 | 195 | 14 | 9.0 | ... | | 102,118 | 50,920 | 10,334 | 5,003 |
| 1988 | 22 | 592 | 195 | 14 | 11.0 | ... | | 99,622 | 54,620 | 10,572 | 5,186 |

**C10    SOUTH AMERICA: NUMBERS OF LIVESTOCK** (in thousands, poultry in millions)

### Argentina

| | Horses | Mules | Asses | Cattle | Pigs | Sheep | Goats | Poultry |
|---|---|---|---|---|---|---|---|---|
| 1875 | 3,916 | 124 | 267 | 13,338 | 257 | 57,501 | 2,863 | ... |
| 1888 | 4,263 | ... | ... | 21,964 | 403 | 66,701 | ... | ... |
| 1895 | 4,467 | 483 | ... | 21,702 | 653 | 74,380 | 2,749 | ... |
| 1908 | 7,531 | 465 | ... | 29,117 | 1,404 | 67,212 | ... | 18.1 |
| 1909 | ... | ... | ... | ... | ... | ... | ... | ... |
| 1910 | 8,435 | ... | ... | 28,828 | ... | 73,013 | ... | ... |
| 1911 | 8,894 | 535 | 319 | 28,786 | 2,900 | 80,402 | 4,302 | ... |
| 1912 | 9,239 | 556 | 328 | 29,123 | 3,045 | 83,546 | 4,431 | ... |
| 1913 | 9,366[22] | 584[22] | 345[22] | 30,796[22] | 3,197[22] | 81,485[22] | 4,564[22] | ...[22] |
| 1914 | 8,324 | 565 | 260 | 25,867 | 2,901 | 43,225 | 4,325 | 28.9 |
| 1915 | ... | ... | ... | 26,388 | ... | 43,677 | ... | ... |
| 1916 | ... | ... | ... | ... | ... | ... | ... | ... |
| 1917 | 8,823 | 595 | 276 | 27,053 | 3,260 | 44,855 | 4,583 | ... |
| 1918 | ... | ... | ... | ... | ... | ... | ... | ... |
| 1919 | 9,293 | 611 | 284 | 27,721 | 3,199 | 45,767 | 4,763 | ... |
| 1920 | 9,367 | 618 | 287 | 27,943 | 3,237 | 45,996 | 4,796 | ... |
| 1921 | ... | ... | ... | 28,138 | 3,221 | 46,134 | 4,820 | ... |
| 1922 | 9,432 | 623 | 289 | 37,065 | 1,437 | 36,209 | 4,820 | ... |
| 1930 | 9,858 | 660 | 377 | 32,212 | 3,769 | 44,413 | 5,647 | 47.1 |
| 1934 | ... | ... | ... | 38,868 | ... | 39,330 | ... | ... |
| 1937 | 8,319 | 517 | 264 | 33,207 | 3,966 | 43,883 | 4,649 | 52.9 |
| 1938 | 8,262 | ... | ... | 34,318 | 3,382 | 45,917 | 4,761 | ... |
| 1942 | 6,757 | 509 | ... | 31,460 | 5,707 | 50,904 | 2,838 | ... |

### Bolivia

| | Horses | Mules | Asses | Cattle | Pigs | Sheep | Goats | Poultry |
|---|---|---|---|---|---|---|---|---|
| 1910 | 97 | 45 | 173 | 734 | 114 | 1,449 | 468 | ... |
| 1925 | 198 | 155 | 189 | 2,145 | 362 | 3,436 | 348 | ... |
| 1926 | 204 | 175 | 190 | 2,320 | 498 | 4,220 | 442 | ... |
| 1927 | 320 | ... | ... | 1,404 | 268 | 4,151 | 416 | ... |
| 1928 | 373 | 246 | 140 | 1,855 | 336 | 5,552 | 748 | ... |
| 1929 | 384 | 256 | 156 | 1,960 | 384 | 4,786 | 978 | ... |
| 1930 | 386 | 260 | 158 | 2,050 | 390 | 5,020 | 979 | ... |
| 1931 | 390 | 264 | 160 | 2,064 | 398 | 5,232 | 987 | 5.1 |
| 1938 | ... | ... | ... | 1,842 | 523 | 2,608 | ... | ... |

**C10    SOUTH AMERICA: Numbers of Livestock** (in thousands, poultry in millions)

| | | Brazil | | | | | |
|---|---|---|---|---|---|---|---|
| | **Horses** | **Mules & Asses** | **Cattle** | **Pigs** | **Sheep** | **Goats** | **Poultry[28]** |
| 1912 | 7,290 | 3,208 | 30,705 | 18,401 | 10,550 | 10,049 | ... |
| 1916 | 6,065 | 3,222 | 28,962 | 17,329 | 7,205 | 6,920 | ... |
| 1920 | 5,254 | 1,865 | 34,271 | 16,169 | 7,933 | 5,087 | ... |
| 1931 | 6,836 | 2,813 | 47,530 | 22,147 | 10,709 | 5,273 | ... |
| 1935 | 6,052 | 3,233 | 40,514 | 23,183 | 12,645 | 5,871 | ... |
| 1937 | 6,202 | 3,387 | 40,860 | 25,398 | 13,560 | 6,019 | ... |
| 1938 | 6,713 | 4,119 | 41,883 | 23,543 | 14,167 | 5,906 | ... |
| 1939 | 6,583 | 3,948 | 40,745 | 21,763 | 10,745 | 6,006 | ... |
| 1940 | 6,462 | 3,712 | 41,546 | 21,687 | 10,855 | 6,221 | 59.3 |

| | | Chile | | | | |
|---|---|---|---|---|---|---|
| | **Horses** | **Cattle** | **Pigs** | **Sheep** | **Goats** | **Poultry[23]** |
| 1900 | ... | 830 | ... | 1,335 | ... | ... |
| 1902 | ... | 969 | ... | 1,009 | ... | ... |
| 1906 | ... | 2,675 | 339 | 4,528 | ... | ... |
| 1907 | ... | ... | ... | ... | ... | ... |
| 1908 | 517 | 2,304 | 216 | 4,224 | ... | ... |
| 1909 | ... | ... | ... | ... | ... | ... |
| 1910 | 347 | 1,635 | 178 | 1,636 | 205 | ... |
| 1911 | 352 | 1,640 | 160 | 3,538 | 210 | ... |
| 1912 | 421 | 1,760 | 166 | 4,169 | 273 | ... |
| 1913 | 489 | 2,084 | 184 | 4,567 | 288 | ... |
| 1914 | 458 | 1,969 | 221 | 4,602 | 299 | ... |
| 1915 | 458 | 1,944 | 229 | 4,545 | 394 | ... |
| 1916 | 443 | 1,869 | 260 | 4,568 | 386 | ... |
| 1917 | 403 | 2,030 | 301 | 4,183 | 376 | ... |
| 1918 | 411 | 2,225 | 326 | 4,434 | 451 | ... |
| 1919 | 392 | 2,163 | 292 | 4,500 | 460 | ... |
| 1922 | 329 | 1,996 | 263 | 4,569 | 525 | ... |
| 1925 | 324 | 1,918 | 247 | 4,094 | 357 | ... |
| 1930 | 441 | 2,388 | 331 | 6,263 | 789 | ... |
| 1935 | ... | 2,463 | ... | ... | ... | ... |
| 1936 | 528 | 2,573 | 572 | 5,749 | 810 | ... |
| 1937 | ... | 2,460 | ... | ... | ... | ... |
| 1938 | ... | 2,635 | ... | ... | ... | ... |
| 1938 | ... | 2,356 | ... | ... | ... | 1.1 |
| 1940 | ... | 2,421 | ... | ... | ... | 0.9 |
| 1941 | ... | 2,418 | ... | ... | ... | 1.2 |
| 1942 | ... | 2,346 | ... | ... | ... | 1.2 |
| 1943 | ... | 2,391 | ... | ... | ... | 1.3 |
| 1944 | ... | 2,311 | ... | ... | ... | 1.6 |

**C10    SOUTH AMERICA: Numbers of Livestock** (in thousands, poultry in millions)

| | | Colombia | | | | | |
|---|---|---|---|---|---|---|---|
| | Horses | Mules | Asses | Cattle | Pigs | Sheep | Goats |
| 1915 | 526 | 340 | | 3005 | 711 | ... | 164 |
| 1924 | 964 | 354 | 160 | 6,500 | 1,338 | 771 | 405 |
| 1925 | 978 | 354 | 138 | 6,476 | 1,366 | 780 | 407 |
| 1926 | 980 | 360 | 140 | 6,500 | 1,400 | 800 | 410 |
| 1927 | 978 | 346 | 157 | 6,727 | 1,366 | 771 | 407 |
| 1928 | ... | ... | ... | ... | ... | ... | ... |
| 1929 | 929 | 329 | 149 | 7,343 | 1,434 | 810 | 427 |
| 1932 | 926 | 453 | 288 | 7,592 | 1,545 | 831 | 518 |
| 1934 | 972 | 476 | 303 | 7,972 | 1,622 | 872 | 544 |
| 1935 | ... | ... | ... | 8,337 | ... | ... | ... |
| 1938 | ... | ... | ... | 9,018 | ... | ... | ... |

| | Ecuador | | |
|---|---|---|---|
| | Horses | Pigs | Goats |
| 1934 | 85 | ... | 300 |
| 1935 | 80 | ... | 350 |
| 1938 | 103 | ... | ... |
| 1939 | 104 | 350 | ... |
| 1941 | 117 | 820 | ... |
| 1943 | 117 | 836 | ... |

| | | | Falkland Islands | | | | | | |
|---|---|---|---|---|---|---|---|---|---|
| | Sheep | | Sheep | | Sheep | | Sheep | | Sheep |
| 1850 | 0.6 | 1870 | 65 | 1890 | 667 | 1910 | 725 | 1930 | 607 |
| 1851 | 0.5 | 1871 | 78 | 1891 | 643 | 1911 | 706 | 1931 | 609 |
| 1852 | 1.0 | 1872 | 125 | 1892 | 771 | 1912 | 711 | 1932 | 616 |
| 1853 | 2.0 | 1873 | 149 | 1893 | 763 | 1913 | 698 | 1933 | 615 |
| 1854 | 2.5 | 1874 | 179 | 1894 | 791 | 1914 | 701 | 1934 | 607 |
| 1855 | 3.0 | 1875 | 185 | 1895 | 762 | 1915 | 891 | 1935 | 616 |
| 1856 | 3.0 | 1876 | 271 | 1896 | 732 | 1916 | 690 | 1936 | 609 |
| 1857 | 4.5 | 1877 | 283 | 1897 | 786 | 1917 | 697 | 1937 | 604 |
| 1858 | 7.7 | 1878 | 351 | 1898 | 780 | 1918 | 670 | 1938 | 602 |
| 1859 | 7.9 | 1879 | 411 | 1899 | 762 | 1919 | 670 | 1939 | 601 |
| 1860 | 11 | 1880 | ... | 1900 | 778 | 1920 | 646 | 1940 | 605 |
| 1861 | 12 | 1881 | ... | 1901 | 762 | 1921 | 668 | 1941 | 624 |
| 1862 | 15 | 1882 | 429 | 1902 | 714 | 1922 | 667 | 1942 | 634 |
| 1863 | 19 | 1883 | 473 | 1903 | 681 | 1923 | 647 | 1943 | 633 |
| 1864 | 26 | 1884 | 517 | 1904 | 702 | 1924 | 635 | 1944 | 628 |
| 1865 | 27 | 1885 | 486 | 1905 | 701 | 1925 | 631 | | |
| 1866 | 31 | 1886 | 563 | 1906 | 703 | 1926 | 606 | | |
| 1867 | 35 | 1887 | 582 | 1907 | 696 | 1927 | 607 | | |
| 1868 | 58 | 1888 | 590 | 1908 | 689 | 1928 | 631 | | |
| 1861 | 60 | 1889 | 676 | 1809 | 716 | 1929 | 613 | | |

**C10    SOUTH AMERICA: Numbers of Livestock** (in thousands, poultry in millions)

| | Guyana | | | | Guyana | | |
|---|---|---|---|---|---|---|---|
| | **Cattle** | **Pigs** | **Sheep** | | **Cattle** | **Pigs** | **Sheep** |
| 1903 | 70 | 12 | 12 | | | | |
| 1904 | 86 | 12 | 17 | | | | |
| 1905 | 77 | 13 | 18 | 1925 | 135 | 16 | 24 |
| 1906 | 85 | 16 | 24 | 1926 | 138 | 16 | 29 |
| 1907 | 72 | 13 | 17 | 1927 | 141 | 18 | 24 |
| 1908 | 70 | 13 | 18 | 1928 | 154 | 24 | 26 |
| 1909 | 72 | 13 | 17 | 1929 | 154 | 23 | 27 |
| 1910 | 72 | 17 | 18 | 1930 | 155 | 24 | 29 |
| 1911 | 81 | 17 | 19 | 1931 | 181 | 21 | 22 |
| 1912 | 72 | 17 | 18 | 1932 | 186 | 18 | 33 |
| 1913 | 81 | 14 | 19 | 1933 | 160 | 19 | 35 |
| 1914 | 90 | 11 | 20 | 1934 | 150 | 14 | 18 |
| 1915 | 98 | 14 | 22 | 1935 | 128 | 23 | 28 |
| 1916 | 93 | 12 | 23 | 1936 | 131 | 23 | 26 |
| 1917 | 99 | 12 | 22 | 1937 | 130 | 27 | 33 |
| 1918 | 77 | 13 | 21 | 1938 | 135 | 26 | 33 |
| 1919 | 79 | 15 | 19 | 1939 | 133 | 27 | 32 |
| 1920 | 112 | 17 | 21 | 1940 | 135 | 24 | 33 |
| 1921 | 123 | 12 | 20 | 1941 | 141 | 23 | 34 |
| 1922 | 112 | 13 | 17 | 1942 | 158 | 25 | 48 |
| 1923 | 102 | 12 | 15 | 1943 | 160 | 42 | 36 |
| 1924 | 113 | 13 | 16 | 1944 | 171 | 46 | 37 |

| | Paraguay | | | | |
|---|---|---|---|---|---|
| | **Horses** | **Cattle** | **Pigs** | **Sheep**[30] | **Goats** |
| 1915 | 478 | 5,249 | 61 | 600 | 87 |
| 1918 | 490 | 5,500 | 87 | 600 | 93 |
| 1926 | 210 | 2,973 | 45 | 195 | … |
| 1932 | 372 | 3,984 | 52 | 229 | … |
| 1933 | 296 | 3,244 | 49 | 203 | … |
| 1934 | 237 | 2,920 | 29 | 142 | … |
| 1935 | 186 | 3,052 | 33 | 136 | … |
| 1936 | 198 | 3,219 | 35 | 146 | … |
| 1940 | … | … | … | | |
| 1941 | … | … | … | 220 | |
| 1942 | 214 | 4,030 | 50 | … | |
| 1943 | … | … | … | 250 | |
| 1944 | 135 | 3,187 | 59 | 255 | |

| | Peru | | | | | | |
|---|---|---|---|---|---|---|---|
| | **Horses** | **Mules** | **Asses** | **Cattle** | **Pigs** | **Sheep & Goats** | **Poultry** |
| 1917 | … | … | … | 1,000 | 400 | 6,900 | … |
| 1921 | … | … | … | 1,302 | … | 11,056 | … |
| 1922 | … | … | … | 1,293 | 429 | 11,334 | … |
| 1924 | 193 | … | … | … | … | … | … |
| 1929 | 432 | 130 | 265 | 1,806 | 689 | 11,209 | 3.2 |

**C10    SOUTH AMERICA: Numbers of Livestock** (in thousands, poultry in millions)

| | Uruguay | | | | | |
|---|---|---|---|---|---|---|
| | Horses[24] | Mules & Asses[24] | Cattle | Pigs[24] | Sheep[24] | Poultry[3] |
| 1860 | 518 | 813 | 3,632 | 6 | 1,990 | ... |
| 1897 | 357 | ... | 4,963 | 30 | 14,452 | ... |
| 1898 | 364 | ... | 4,927 | 35 | 15,538 | ... |
| 1899 | 395 | ... | 5,219 | 34 | 15,122 | ... |
| 1900 | 561 | ... | 6,827 | 94 | 18,609[24] | ... |
| 1901 | 575 | ... | 6,327 | 48 | 17,625 | ... |
| 1902 | 660 | ... | 7,029 | 52 | 17,927 | ... |
| 1903 | 578 | ... | 6,948 | 49 | 18,559 | ... |
| 1904 | 479 | ... | 7,305 | 41 | 14,416 | ... |
| 1905 | 450[24] | ... | 6,029 | 36[24] | 13,916[24] | ... |
| 1908 | 556 | ... | 8,193 | 180 | 26,286 | ... |
| 1916 | 555 | ... | 7,802 | 304 | 11,473 | ... |
| 1924 | 513 | ... | 8,432 | 251 | 14,443 | ... |
| 1927 | ... | ... | ... | ... | 22,500 | ... |
| 1930 | 623 | ... | 7,128 | 308 | 20,558 | ... |
| 1932 | ... | ... | 7,372 | ... | 15,406 | ... |
| 1937 | 644 | ... | 8,297 | 346 | 17,931 | 4.8 |

| | Venezuela | | | | | | |
|---|---|---|---|---|---|---|---|
| | Horses | Mules | Asses | Cattle | Pigs | Sheep | Goats |
| 1804 | 180 | 90 | ... | 1,200 | ... | ... | ... |
| 1839 | 78 | 39 | 141 | 2,086 | 363 | 1,910 | |
| 1873 | 94 | 47 | 281 | 1,390 | 363 | 1,128 | |
| 1876 | 385 | | 520 | 2,158 | 660 | 2,309 | |
| 1883 | 292 | 248 | 659 | 2,927 | 976 | 3,491 | |
| 1886 | 622 | | 770 | 5,275 | 1,439 | 4,646 | |
| 1887 | 365 | 289 | 813 | 6,687 | 1,666 | 5,158 | |
| 1888 | 388 | 301 | 859 | 8,476 | 1,930 | 5,728 | |
| 1894 | 209 | 89 | 383 | 2,352 | 1,618 | 134 | 1,561 |
| 1899 | 191 | – | – | 2,004 | ... | 1,844 | |
| 1910 | 111 | 28 | 141 | 1,750 | 195 | 1,026 | |
| 1918 | 157 | 53 | 195 | 1,516 | 501 | 113 | 2,155 |
| 1920 | ... | ... | ... | 2,078 | ... | ... | ... |
| 1921 | 168 | 55 | 200 | 2,600 | 512 | ... | ... |
| 1922 | ... | ... | ... | 2,278 | ... | ... | ... |
| 1924 | 115 | 49 | 121 | 2,327 | 295 | 1,079 | |
| 1929 | ... | ... | ... | 2,750 | 500 | 125 | 2,250 |
| 1936 | 194 | 43 | 191 | 3,091 | ... | ... | ... |
| 1937 | 209 | 47 | 248 | 4,300 | 296 | 108 | 1,365 |

**C10**     **SOUTH AMERICA: Numbers of Livestock** (in thousands, poultry in millions)

| | Argentina | | | | | | | |
|---|---|---|---|---|---|---|---|---|
| | Horses | Mules | Asses | Cattle | Pigs | Sheep | Goats | Poultry |
| 1945 | 7,473 | ... | ... | ... | 8,010 | 56,182 | ... | ... |
| 1946 | ... | ... | ... | ... | ... | ... | ... | ... |
| 1947 | 7,238 | 330 | 170 | 41,268 | 2,981 | 50,857 | 4,934 | ... |
| 1948 | ... | ... | ... | ... | 3,500 | ... | ... | ... |
| 1949 | ... | ... | ... | ... | ... | ... | ... | ... |
| 1950 | ... | ... | ... | ... | ... | ... | ... | ... |
| 1951 | 7,265 | ... | ... | ... | ... | ... | ... | ... |
| 1952 | ... | ... | ... | ... | ... | ... | ... | ... |
| 1953 | 7,181 | 402 | ... | 45,750 | 4,020 | 56,216 | ... | 43.8 |
| 1954 | ... | ... | ... | 43,596 | 3,512 | 46,772 | ... | ... |
| 1955 | ... | ... | ... | ... | ... | 43,785 | ... | 44.5 |
| 1956 | 5,872 | ... | ... | 46,940 | 4,011 | 45,166 | 1,476 | ... |
| 1957 | 5,428 | ... | ... | 43,980 | 3,489 | 45,931 | ... | ... |
| 1958 | 4,846 | ... | ... | 40,736 | 3,142 | 47,010 | ... | ... |
| 1959 | 4,701 | ... | ... | 41,206 | 3,501 | 48,847 | ... | ... |
| 1960 | 4,800 | ... | ... | 44,550 | 3,800 | 50,200 | ... | 45.0 |
| 1961 | 4,184 | 300 | 100 | 43,165 | 3,787 | 50,150 | 5,000 | 47.5 |
| 1962 | 3,930 | 300 | 100 | 43,300 | 3,075 | 47,305 | 4,970 | 41.8 |
| 1963 | 3,761 | 300 | 100 | 40,009 | 3,417 | 46,158 | 4,980 | 41.0 |
| 1964 | 3,763 | 300 | 100 | 42,300 | 3,400 | 47,500 | 4,998 | 31.5 |
| 1965 | 3,760 | 300 | 100 | 46,709 | 3,700 | 49,000 | 5,098 | 35.0 |
| 1966 | 3,780 | 300 | 100 | 48,800 | 3,100 | 48,500 | 5,200 | 34.0 |
| 1967 | 3,800 | 280 | 98 | 51,227 | 3,000 | 48,000 | 5,280 | 38.5 |
| 1968 | 3,700 | 270 | 97 | 51,465 | 3,400 | 47,800 | 5,300 | 42.1 |
| 1969 | 3,650 | 270 | 95 | 48,298 | 4,098 | 44,320 | 5,330 | 44.7 |
| 1970 | 3,620 | $\frac{260}{200}$ 13 | 94 | 48,440 | 4,400 | 43,000 | 5,380 | 50.8 |
| 1971 | 3,600 | ... | 94 | 49,786 | 4,900 | 41,000 | 5,300 | 34.5 |
| 1972 | 3,540 | ... | 90 | 52,300 | 4,500 | 40,000 | 5,250 | 35.2 |
| 1973 | 3,500 | 170 | 85 | 54,771 | 5,000 | 40,000 | 5,500 | 34.0 |
| 1974 | 3,500 | 167 | 88 | 55,355 | 4,127 | 34,691 | 5,400 | 36.0 |
| 1975 | 3,400 | 165 | 90 | 58,700 | 4,200 | 34,000 | 4,000 | 34.7 |
| 1976 | 3,500 | 165 | 90 | 58,174 | 4,127 | 34,485 | 4,000 | 32.4 |
| 1977 | 3,073 | 165 | 90 | 61,054 | 3,332 | 35,220 | 3,500 | 31.3 |
| 1978 | 3,050 | 165 | 90 | 57,791 | 3,600 | 34,200 | 3,200 | 32.0 |
| 1979 | 3,000 | 165 | 90 | 56,864 | 3,552 | 35,220 | 3,000 | 35.4 |
| 1980 | 3,000 | 165 | 90 | 55,760 | 3,800 | 32,000 | 3,000 | 38.8 |
| 1981 | 3,073 | 165 | 90 | 54,235 | 3,900 | 31,418 | 3,000 | 40.0 |
| 1982 | 3,000 | 165 | 90 | 52,717 | 3,900 | 30,401 | 3,000 | 42.0 |
| 1983 | 3,050 | 165 | 90 | 53,937 | 3,800 | 30,000 | 2,900 | 43.0 |
| 1984 | 2,970 | 165 | 90 | 54,594 | 3,800 | 33,800 | 3,098 | 42.0 |
| 1985 | 3,000 | 165 | 90 | 54,000 | 4,000 | 29,441 | 3,100 | 42.0 |
| 1986 | 3,000 | 165 | 90 | 53,480 | 4,100 | 29,243 | 3,100 | 47.0 |
| 1987 | 3,000 | 165 | 90 | 51,683 | 4,100 | 28,750 | 3,100 | 42.0 |
| 1988 | 2,900 | 165 | 90 | 50,782 | 4,100 | 29,167 | 3,200 | 47.0 |

**C10 SOUTH AMERICA: Numbers of Livestock** (in thousands, poultry in millions)

| | Horses | Mules | Asses | Cattle | Pigs | Sheep | Goats | Poultry[3] |
|---|---|---|---|---|---|---|---|---|
| | | | | **Bolivia** | | | | |
| 1947 | 256 | 102 | 301 | 3,041 | 1,020 | 4,289 | 1,089 | ... |
| 1948 | 442 | 109 | 519 | 3,499 | 1,465 | 4,195 | 1,910 | ... |
| 1949 | ... | ... | ... | ... | 1,200 | ... | ... | |
| 1950 | ... | ... | ... | 3,849 | ... | ... | ... | 1.6 |
| 1951 | ... | ... | ... | 2,227 | ... | ... | ... | ... |
| 1952 | ... | ... | ... | ... | ... | ... | ... | ... |
| 1953 | ... | ... | 207 | ... | ... | ... | ... | ... |
| 1954 | ... | ... | ... | 2,260 | ... | 6,464 | ... | ... |
| 1955 | ... | ... | ... | ... | ... | ... | ... | ... |
| 1956 | ... | ... | ... | ... | ... | ... | ... | ... |
| 1957 | ... | ... | ... | ... | ... | ... | ... | ... |
| 1958 | ... | ... | ... | ... | ... | ... | ... | ... |
| 1959 | 189 | 49 | 399 | 2,449 | 596 | 5,549 | 1,176 | 2.0 |
| 1960 | ... | ... | ... | ... | ... | ... | ... | ... |
| 1961 | 191 | 56 | 445 | ... | 619 | 5,965 | 1,700 | ... |
| 1962 | 193 | 59 | 468 | 2,490 | 631 | 6,174 | 1,764 | 2.1 |
| 1963 | 194 | 62 | 490 | 2,739 | 642 | 6,300 | 1,940 | 2.2 |
| 1964 | 195 | 66 | 513 | 2,672 | 654 | 6,097 | 1,250 | 2.2 |
| 1965 | 214 | 72 | 550 | 2,693 | 704 | 6,144 | 1,259 | 2.2 |
| 1966 | 223 | 73 | 560 | 2,700 | 710 | 6,150 | 2,000 | 2.9 |
| 1967 | 244 | 75 | 590 | 2,132 | 719 | 6,378 | 2,100 | 3.0 |
| 1968 | 264 | 81 | 620 | 2,184 | 777 | 6,460 | 2,150 | 3.0 |
| 1969 | 284 | 85 | 640 | 2,238 | 837 | 6,723 | 2,300 | 3.1 |
| 1970 | 290 | 86 | 650 | 2,291 | 900 | 6,787 | 2,400 | 3.1 |
| 1971 | 300 | 88 | 670 | 2,132 | 953 | 6,965 | 2,300 | 3.2 |
| 1972 | 300 | 90 | 660 | 2,200 | 1,000 | 7,144 | 2,543 | 3.3[13] / 4.8 |
| 1973 | 310 | 90 | 660 | 2,277 | 1,050 | 7,323 | 2,645 | 5.0 |
| 1974 | 320 | 92 | 683 | 2,366[13] / 2,755 | 1,103 | 7,506 | 2,748 | 5.0 |
| 1975 | 340 | 92 | 701 | 2,877 | 1,158 | 7,694 | 2,793 | 5.2 |
| 1976 | 360 | 94 | 720 | 3,398 | 1,232 | 7,988 | 2,893 | 7.1 |
| 1977 | 370 | 96 | 740 | 3,578 | 1,292 | 8,229 | 2,914 | 8.0 |
| 1978 | 380 | 98 | 760 | 3,772 | 1,351 | 8,462 | 2,946 | 8.2 |
| 1979 | 390 | 100 | 770 | 3,990[13] | 1,412 | 8,722 | 2,978 | 8.3 |
| 1980 | 400 | 102[25] | 770[25] | 4,699 | 1,601 | 9,057 | 2,007 | 8.5 |
| 1981 | 410 | 104 | 780 | 4,488 | 1,647 | 9,308 | 2,013 | 8.8 |
| 1982 | 410[13] | 105[13] | 790[13] | 4,602 | 1,706 | 9,677 | 2,045 | 9 |
| 1983 | 300 | 82 | 600 | 4,878 | 1,910 | 10,632 | 1,757 | 10 |
| 1984 | 293 | 80 | 600 | 4,149 | ... | 5,152 | 1,296 | 6 |
| 1985 | 311 | 80 | 600 | 4,333 | 1,725 | 5,553 | 1,298 | 7 |
| 1986 | 310 | 80 | 600 | 4,584 | 1,650 | 5,995 | 1,383 | 9 |
| 1987 | 315 | 80 | 610 | 4,898 | 1,902 | 6,478 | 1,507 | 11 |
| 1988 | 315 | 80 | 620 | 5,202 | 2,019 | 7,005 | ... | 12 |

**C10    SOUTH AMERICA: Numbers of Livestock** (in thousands, poultry in millions)

| | | | | Brazil | | | | |
|---|---|---|---|---|---|---|---|---|
| | Horses | Mules | Asses | Cattle | Pigs | Sheep | Goats | Poultry[28] |
| 1946 | 6,522 | 2,717 | 1,344 | 44,613 | 24,344 | 13,283 | 6,768 | ... |
| 1947 | 6,768 | 2,952 | 1,374 | 46,358 | 23,815 | 15,542 | 7,363 | ... |
| 1948 | 6,907 | 2,908 | 1,464 | 47,927 | 22,503 | 14,640 | 7,869 | ... |
| 1949 | 6,928 | 3,097 | 1,536 | 50,178 | 23,881 | 13,804 | 8,309 | 57.3 |
| 1950 | ... | ... | ... | ... | ... | ... | ... | 59.1 |
| 1951 | 6,937 | 3,101 | 1,572 | 52,655 | 26,059 | 14,251 | 8,526 | 61.0 |
| 1952 | 6,994 | 3,181 | 1,593 | 53,513 | 27,801 | 15,891 | 8,840 | 65.8 [28] |
| | | | | | | | | 116.3 |
| 1953 | 7,111 | 3,215 | 1,611 | 55,854 | 30,916 | 16,264 | 8,822 | 127.3 |
| 1954 | 7,059 | 3,133 | 1,612 | 57,626 | 32,721 | 16,800 | 8,915 | ... |
| 1955 | 7,286 | 3,241 | 1,674 | 61,442 | 35,555 | 17,503 | 9,481 | 146.7 |
| 1956 | 7,564 | 3,390 | 1,774 | 63,608 | 38,606 | 18,484 | 9,879 | 146.7 |
| 1957 | 7,935 | 3,576 | 1,876 | 66,695 | 41,416 | 18,867 | 10,339 | 157.8 |
| 1958 | 8,128 | 3,760 | 1,967 | 69,548 | 44,190 | 20,164 | 10,640 | 161.0 |
| 1959 | 8,185 | 3,917 | 1,946 | 71,420 | 45,262 | 19,921 | 10,194 | 166.9 |
| 1960 | 8,333 | 4,047 | 2,031 | 72,829 | 46,823 | 18,995 | 10,644 | 175.4 |
| 1961 | 8,273 | 4,081 | 2,175 | 73,962 | 47,944 | 18,162 | 11,195 | 185.8 |
| 1962 | 8,374 | 4,205 | 2,256 | 76,176 | 50,051 | 19,162 | 11,560 | 197.5 |
| 1963 | 8,692 | 4,421 | 2,393 | 79,076 | 52,941 | 19,718 | 12,397 | 208.2 |
| 1964 | 8,903 | 4,586 | 2,552 | 79,855 | 55,990 | 21,033 | 13,210 | 238.2 |
| 1965 | 9,222 | 4,749 | 2,727 | 84,167 | 58,705 | 21,906 | 13,826 | 254.4 |
| 1966 | 9,344 | 4,856 | 2,851 | 90,505 | 62,534 | 22,312 | 14,253 | 255.6 |
| 1967 | 9,155 | 4,745 | 2,858 | 89,969 | 62,080 | 22,170 | 13,927 | 263.0 |
| 1968 | 9,238 | 4,804 | 2,971 | 89,896 | 63,406 | 23,065 | 14,332 | 270.6 |
| 1969 | 9,146 | 4,830 | 2,996 | 92,739 [13] | 64,924 | 24,606 | 14,815 | 275.9 |
| | | | | 72,966 | | | | |
| 1970 | 9,100 | 4,796 | 2,958 | 75,447 | 65,867 [13] | 24,449 | 14,637 | 281.1 |
| | | | | | 30,846 | | | |
| 1971 | 9,114 | 4,793 | 2,952 | 78,452 | 31,541 | 24,270 | 14,609 | 224.1 |
| 1972 | 8,992 | 4,710 | 2,800 | 81,000 | 32,100 | 25,000 | 14,440 | 235.3 |
| 1973 | 9,350 [13] | 4,700 [13] | 2,800 [13] | 85,000 | 33,000 | 25,500 [13] | 16,000 [13] | 255.0 |
| 1974 | 6,889 | 1,702 | 1,984 | 90,437 | 37,587 | 18,356 | 6,394 | 271.7 |
| 1975 | 5,217 | 1,755 | 1,568 | 92,495 | 34,192 | 18,877 | 7,171 | 274.3 |
| 1976 | 5,507 | 1,822 | 1,691 | 102,532 | 37,640 | 17,828 | 7,101 | 311.9 |
| 1977 | 5,157 | 1,631 | 1,464 | 107,349 | 38,742 | 18,002 | 7,485 | 339.0 |
| 1978 | 4,934 | 1,514 | 1,423 | 107,297 | 34,532 | 18,009 | 7,424 | 331.6 |
| 1979 | 4,853 | 1,488 | 1,363 | 106,943 | 33,699 | 17,418 | 7,665 | 345.7 |
| 1980 | 4,928 | 1,586 | 1,340 | 109,177 | 35,695 | 17,806 | 8,070 | 387.7 |
| 1981 | 5,055 | 1,605 | 1,330 | 118,971 | 34,183 | 18,381 | 8,326 | 441.3 |
| 1982 | 5,227 | 1,750 | 1,331 | 121,785 | 32,429 | 19,054 | 8,865 | 450.0 |
| 1983 | 5,260 | 1,829 | 1,316 | 123,488 | 33,176 | 18,588 | 9,037 | 469.9 |
| 1984 | 5,289 | 1,836 | 1,237 | 124,186 | 31,678 | 18,121 | 8,936 | 450.8 |
| 1985 | 5,442 | 1,946 | 1,246 | 127,655 | 32,327 | 18,447 | 9,675 | 462.8 |
| 1986 | 5,550 | 1,943 | 1,274 | 128,423 | 32,248 | 18,659 | 10,020 | 470.1 |
| 1987 | 5,735 | 1,921 | 1,286 | 132,222 | 32,539 | 19,660 | 10,595 | 495.6 |
| 1988 | 5,855 | 1,952 | 1,295 | 135,726 | 32,480 | 19,860 | 10,792 | 514.5 |

**C10    SOUTH AMERICA: Numbers of Livestock** (in thousands, poultry in millions)

| | Chile | | | | | |
| | Horses | Cattle | Pigs | Sheep | Goats | Poultry[23] |
|---|---|---|---|---|---|---|
| 1945 | ... | 2,348 | ... | 5,900 | ... | 1.7 |
| 1946 | ... | 2,397 | ... | 5,700 | ... | 2.2 |
| 1947 | 523 | 2,338 | 585 | 6,432 | 636 | 2.2 |
| 1948 | 523 | 2,324 | 585 | 6,435 | 636 | 2.2[23] |
| 1949 | ... | 2,344 | 600 | 6,435 | 636 | ... |
| 1950 | ... | 2,331 | 660 | ... | ... | ... |
| 1951 | ... | 2,186 | 875 | 5,794 | ... | ... |
| 1952 | 500 | 2,592 | 894 | 5,797 | ... | ... |
| 1953 | 451 | 2,594 | 913 | 5,800 | ... | ... |
| 1954 | 605 | 2,595 | 978 | 5,933 | 1,099 | ... |
| 1955 | 500 | 2,856 | 741 | 6,540 | 1,300 | ... |
| 1956 | 571 | 2,560 | 1,032 | 5,947 | 1,300 | ... |
| 1957 | 573 | 2,900 | 986 | 6,067 | ... | ... |
| 1958 | 555 | 2,912 | 931 | 6,136 | ... | ... |
| 1959 | 554 | 2,809 | 964 | 6,298 | ... | ... |
| 1960 | 558 | 2,913 | 958 | 6,343 | 1,380 | ... |
| 1961 | 555 | 2,990 | 950 | 6,436 | 1,400 | 9.6 |
| 1962 | 547 | 3,046 | 950 | 6,422 | 1,421 | 10.3 |
| 1963 | 494 | 3,017 | 959 | 6,552 | 1,030 | 11.0 |
| 1964 | 478 | 2,845 | 1,022 | 6,690 | 980 | 11.7 |
| 1965 | 475 | 2,870 | 1,007 | 6,596 | 933 | 12.0 |
| 1966 | 470 | 2,900 | 1,022 | 6,502 | 930 | 13.0 |
| 1967 | 465 | 3,097 | 1,085 | 6,675 | 925 | 14.0 |
| 1968 | 460 | 2,876 | 1,090 | 6,600 | 920 | 15.5 |
| 1969 | 480 | 2,911 | 1,120 | 6,500 | 910 | 16.5 |
| 1970 | 478 | 2,999 | 1,140 | 6,400 | 900 | 17.0 |
| 1971 | 475 | 2,860 | 1,040 | 5,907 | 870 | 18.0 |
| 1972 | 480 | 3,188 | 966 | 5,529 | 850 | 19.0 |
| 1973 | 470 | 3,165 | 968 | 5,353 | 830 | 19.5 |
| 1974 | 450 | 3,457 | 866 | 5,544 | 830 | 18.0 |
| 1975 | 450 | 3,606 | 701 | 5,644 | 800 | 18.5 |
| 1976 | 443 | 3,389 | 895 | 5,674 | 584 | 19.5 |
| 1977 | 450 | 3,427 | 924 | 5,699 | 600 | 20 |
| 1978 | 450 | 3,487 | 979 | 5,692 | 600 | 22 |
| 1979 | 450 | 3,575 | 1,036 | 5,928 | 600 | 24 |
| 1980 | 450 | 3,664 | 1,068 | 6,064 | 600 | 25 |
| 1981 | 450 | 3,750 | 1,100 | 6,185 | 600 | 26 |
| 1982 | 430 | 3,800 | 1,150 | 6,000 | 600 | 21 |
| 1983 | 450 | 3,865 | 1,100 | 6,200 | 600 | 20 |
| 1984 | 480 | 3,650 | 1,070 | 6,000 | 600 | 18 |
| 1985 | 490 | 3,400 | 1,100 | 5,800 | 600 | 19 |
| 1986 | 490 | 3,217 | 1,150 | 5,980 | 600 | 19 |
| 1987 | 490 | 3,371 | 1,300 | 6,470 | 600 | 23 |
| 1988 | 490 | 3,468 | 1,360 | 6,429 | 600 | 26 |

**C10**    **SOUTH AMERICA: Numbers of Livestock** (in thousands, poultry in millions)

| | Colombia | | | | | | | |
|---|---|---|---|---|---|---|---|---|
| | Horses | Mules | Asses | Cattle | Pigs | Sheep | Goats | Poultry |
| 1945 | ... | ... | ... | 12,570 | ... | ... | ... | ... |
| 1946 | 1,077 | 476 | 252 | 13,169 | 1,679 | 1,168 | 653 | ... |
| 1947 | 1,183 | 528 | 260 | 14,542 | 2,162 | 1,022 | 470 | ... |
| 1948 | ... | ... | ... | ... | 2,470 | 1,062 | 531 | ... |
| 1949 | ... | ... | ... | ... | ... | 1,198 | ... | 18.6 |
| 1950 | 1,298 | 542 | 461 | 15,512 | 2,782 | 1,339 | 638 | 21.1 |
| 1951 | ... | ... | ... | ... | ... | 1,350 | ... | ... |
| 1952 | ... | ... | ... | ... | ... | 1,341 | ... | ... |
| 1953 | ... | ... | ... | ... | ... | ... | ... | ... |
| 1954 | [1,159] $^{26}_{27}$ | [410] $^{26}_{27}$ | [282] $^{26}_{27}$ | [10,994] $^{26}_{27}$ | [1,824] $^{26}_{27}$ | [1,114] $^{26}_{27}$ | [294] $^{26}_{27}$ | [14.4] [26] |
| 1955 | [1,285] [26] | [459] [26] | [325] [26] | [12,500] [26] | [1,727] [26] | [1,128] [26] | [342] [26] | [15.0] [26] |
| 1956 | 1,331 | 492 | 353 | [13,390] [26] | [1,455] [26] | [1,126] [26] | [215] [26] | [14.0] [26] |
| 1957 | ... | ... | ... | ... | ... | ... | ... | ... |
| 1958 | ... | ... | ... | 14,840 | ... | ... | ... | ... |
| 1959 | ... | ... | ... | 15,100 | ... | ... | ... | ... |
| 1960 | 1,155 | 440 | 359 | 15,400 | 1,994 | 1,260 | [350] [26] | 18.0 |
| 1961 | 1,100 | 420 | 361 | 15,627 | 2,000 | 1,100 | [357] [26] | 19.7 |
| 1962 | 937 | 360 | 297 | 15,861 | 2,700 | 1,400 | [360] [26] | 22.0 |
| 1963 | 960 | 370 | 298 | 16,099 | 2,400 | 1,500 | [370] [26] | 25.0 |
| 1964 | 983 | 380 | 298 | 14,116 | 2,326 | 1,630 | [374] [26] | 25.5 |
| 1965 | 951 | 356 | 368 | 15,020 | 2,400 | 1,702 | 688 | 21.5 |
| 1966 | 975 | 375 | 400 | 18,082 | 2,300 | 1,720 | 765 | 25.3 |
| 1967 | 1,086 | 400 | 436 | 18,883 | 2,058 | 1,966 | 865 | 30.3 |
| 1968 | 1,098 | 400 [13] / 350 | 438 [13] / 330 | 19,576 | 3,708 | 1,500 | 886 | 32.7 |
| 1969 | 778 | 353 | 315 | 20,200 | 1,420 | 1,818 | 630 | 35.4 |
| 1970 | 839 | 367 | 327 | 20,800 | 1,470 | 1,962 | 654 | 32.0 |
| 1971 | 866 | 381 | 340 | 21,400 | 1,520 | 2,025 | 660 | 33.2 |
| 1972 | 859 | 385 | 356 | 22,100 | 1,540 | 2,036 | 660 | 33.5 |
| 1973 | 860 [13] / 1,331 | 420 | 450 | 23,032 | 1,729 | 1,619 | 637 | 35.0 |
| 1974 | 1,379 | 484 | 526 | 22,501 | 1,805 | 1,888 | 675 | 40.0 |
| 1975 | 1,435 | 499 | 543 | 23,222 | 1,877 | 1,921 | 626 | 42.7 |
| 1976 | 1,485 | 515 | 560 | 23,859 | 1,876 | 2,026 | 623 | 47.1 [13] |
| 1977 | 1,535 | 531 | 578 | 24,335 | 1,876 | 2,138 | 626 | 28.9 |
| 1978 | 1,588 | 548 | 597 | 24,342 | 1,884 | 2,255 | 632 | 30.8 |
| 1979 | 1,644 | 552 | 616 | 24,132 | 1,916 | 2,357 | 639 | 27.1 |
| 1980 | 1,696 | 587 | 640 | 23,945 | 2,078 | 2,413 | 645 | 30 |
| 1981 | 1,710 | 590 | 645 | 24,251 | 2,094 | 2,427 | 652 | 31 |
| 1982 | 1,744 | 595 | 650 | 24,499 | 2,179 | 2,749 | 657 | 33 |
| 1983 | 1,779 | 600 | 650 | 24,000 | 2,244 | 2,660 | 729 | 34 |
| 1984 | 1,815 | 600 | 650 | 22,441 | 2,312 | 2,689 | 797 | 35 |
| 1985 | 1,906 | 600 | 650 | 23,271 | 2,381 | 2,500 | 879 | 35 |
| 1986 | 1,950 | 600 | 650 | 23,593 | 2,440 | 2,568 | 905 | 35 |
| 1987 | 1,950 | 600 | 650 | 23,971 | 2,511 | 2,652 | 932 | 36 |
| 1988 | 1,950 | 600 | 650 | 24,307 | 2,586 | 2,652 | 932 | 39 |

**C10    SOUTH AMERICA: Numbers of Livestock** (in thousands, poultry in millions)

| | | | | Ecuador | | | | | Falkland Islands |
|---|---|---|---|---|---|---|---|---|---|
| | Horses | Mules | Asses | Cattle | Pigs | Sheep | Goats | Poultry[3] | Sheep |
| 1945 | ... | ... | ... | ... | ... | ... | ... | ... | 619 |
| 1946 | 117 | 31 | 65 | 1,185 | 819 | 1,447 | ... | ... | 612 |
| 1947 | 111 | 54 | 100 | 1,520 | ... | 1,802 | 1,382 | ... | 604 |
| 1948 | 111 | 54 | 100 | 1,600 | 547 | 1,800 | ... | ... | 619 |
| 1949 | ... | ... | ... | ... | ... | ... | ... | ... | 619 |
| 1950 | ... | ... | ... | ... | ... | ... | ... | ... | 611 |
| 1951 | 98 | 30 | 41 | 1,200 | 259 | 1,559 | 349 | ... | 597 |
| 1952 | ... | ... | ... | ... | ... | ... | ... | ... | 584 |
| 1953 | ... | ... | ... | ... | ... | ... | ... | ... | 594 |
| 1954 | ... | ... | ... | 1,169 | ... | ... | ... | ... | 600 |
| 1955 | ... | ... | ... | 1,274 | 994 | 1,242 | 137 | 3.7 | 611 |
| 1956 | ... | ... | ... | 1,363 | ... | ... | ... | ... | 598 |
| 1957 | ... | ... | ... | 1,363 | 1,081 | 1,502 | 137 | 3.8 | 600 |
| 1958 | ... | ... | ... | ... | ... | ... | ... | ... | 611 |
| 1959 | ... | ... | ... | 1,530 | ... | ... | ... | ... | 621 |
| 1960 | 186 | 86 | 150 | 1,550 | 1,340 | 1,667 | ... | ... | 610 |
| 1961 | 199 | 92 | 150 | 1,720 | 1,410 | 1,703 | 152 | 4.2 | 617 |
| 1962 | 212 | 98 | 150 | 1,909 | 1,117 | 1,749 | 158 | 4.4 | 619 |
| 1963 | 225 | 104 | 166 | 2,000 | 1,182 | 1,644 | 164 | 4.7 | 637 |
| 1964 | 226 | 105 | 167 | 2,100 | 1,246 | 1,681 | 164 | 5.0 | 627 |
| 1965 | 227 | 106 | 167 | 2,200 | 1,260 | 1,718 | 165 | 5.3 | 627 |
| 1966 | 227 | 106 | 170 | 2,300 | 1,270 | 1,749 | 171 | 5.3 | 621 |
| 1967 | 230 | 108 | 172 | 2,393 | 1,294 | 1,780 | 178 | 5.4 | 628 |
| 1968 | 233 | 110 | 173 | 2,400 | 1,300 | 1,811 | 184 | 5.4 | 621 |
| 1969 | 237 | 112 | 175 | 2,434 | 1,330 [10] | 1,830 | 185 | 5.4 | 623 |
| 1970 | 240 | 113 [10] / 92 | 180 | 2,500 | 1,920 | 1,895 | 187 | 5.4 | 629 |
| 1971 | 250 | ... | 183 | 2,518 | 1,980 | 1,900 | 189 | 5.4 [13] / 7.1 | 637 |
| 1972 | 255 | ... | 185 | 2,580 | 2,047 | 1,980 | 192 | 7.7 | 634 |
| 1973 | 270 | 89 | 187 | 2,700 | 2,200 | 2,020 | 194 | 9.8 | 613 |
| 1974 | 285 | 90 | 190 | 2,800 | 2,366 | 2,060 | 196 | 10.0 | 628 |
| 1975 | 285 | 90 | 192 | 2,800 | 2,543 | 2,105 | 201 | 12.9 | 644 |
| 1976 | 289 | 92 | 194 | 2,793 | 2,734 | 2,147 | 230 | 15.1 | 645 |
| 1977 | 291 | 90 | 190 | 2,860 | 2,935 | 2,174 | 240 | 21.1 | 638 |
| 1978 | 297 | 92 | 196 | 2,767 | 3,150 | 2,198 | 246 | 23.3 | 648 |
| 1979 | 309 | 97 | 204 | 2,846 | 3,385 | 2,318 | 251 | 23.0 | 659 |
| 1980 | 314 | 98 | 207 | 2,916 | 3,549 | 2,318 | 257 | 22.5 [13] | 663 |
| 1981 | 318 | 99 | 210 | 3,135 | 3,318 | 2,335 | 263 | 38 | 650 |
| 1982 | 322 | 101 | 212 | 3,200 | 3,520 | 2,341 | 269 | 39. | ... |
| 1983 | 327 | 102 | 215 | 3,270 | 3,735 | 2,303 | 275 | 42 | 669 |
| 1984 | 331 | 104 | 218 | 3,456 | 3,792 | 2,311 | 280 | 43 | 679 |
| 1985 | 337 | 112 | 189 | 3,578 | 4,049 | 2,086 | 287 | 41 | 692 |
| 1986 | 372 | 105 | 162 | 3,765 | 4,181 | 1,959 | 228 | 50 | 699 |
| 1987 | 404 | 113 | 215 | 3,884 | 4,160 | 1,293 | 262 | 49 | 692 |
| 1988 | 438 | 116 | 279 | 3,997 | 4,160 | 1,296 | 301 | 48 | ... |

C10    **SOUTH AMERICA: Numbers of Livestock** (in thousands; poultry in millions)

| | Guyana | | | | Paraguay | | | | | |
|---|---|---|---|---|---|---|---|---|---|---|
| | Cattle | Pigs | Sheep | Poultry[3,29] | Horses | Cattle | Pigs | Sheep[30] | Goats[30] | Poultry[31] |
| 1945 | 185 | 43 | 44 | 0.5 | ... | ... | ... | 306 | | ... |
| 1946 | 189 | 35 | 48 | 0.5 | 333 | 3,453 | 65 | 337 | | ... |
| 1947 | 193 | 30 | 51 | 0.4 | 404 | 3,365 | ... | 222 | | 2.8 |
| 1948 | 186 | 28 | 44 | 0.4 | 354 | ... | ... | 195 | | 4.0 |
| 1949 | 166 | 28 | 37 | 0.4 | 294 | 3,865 | ... | 206 | | ... |
| 1950 | 166 | 28 | 37 | ... | ... | 3,857 | ... | 210 | | ... |
| 1951 | 174 | 25 | 43 | 0.4 | 361 | 4,132 | 250 | 217 | | ... |
| 1952 | 170 | 22 | 41 | 0.4 | 354 | 4,163 | ... | 223 | | 2.9 |
| 1953 | 167 | 22 | 39 | 0.5 | 337 | 4,336 | ... | 218 | | 3.8 |
| 1954 | 172 | 37 | 36 | 0.6[29] | 354 | 4,008 | ... | 222[30] | | 3.8 |
| 1955 | 172 | ... | ... | ... | 517[20] | 4,426 | 439 | 351 | 57 | ... |
| 1956 | 172 | 37 | 37 | ... | 329 | 3,929 | 456 | 370 | 60 | ... |
| 1957 | 172 | 37 | 36 | ... | 307 | 3,703 | 461 | 386 | 62 | ... |
| 1958 | 175 | ... | 40 | ... | 292 | 3,666 | 476 | 402 | 64 | ... |
| 1959 | 175 | ... | ... | ... | 321 | 4,004 | 523 | 442 | 71 | ... |
| 1960 | 180 | 37 | 40 | 1.1 | 342 | 4,695 | 575 | 486 | 78 | 5.3 |
| 1961 | 220 | 40 | 52 | 1.2 | 563 | 5,300 | 512 | 361 | 59 | 5.4 |
| 1962 | 225 | 45 | 45 | 1.3 | 570 | 5,353 | 525 | 360 | 59 | 5.5 |
| 1963 | 270 | 50 | 54 | 1.4 | 629 | 5,407 | 752 | 420 | 50 | 5.7 |
| 1964 | 332 | 66 | 87 | 2.6 | 673 | 5,461 | 810 | 438 | 48 | 6.3 |
| 1965 | 350 | 65 | 87 | 3.0 | 691 | 5,461 | 861 | 442 | 48 | 6.1 |
| 1966 | 315 | 68 | 83 | 3.5 | 710 | 5,516 | 786 | 441 | 47 | 6.4 |
| 1967 | 306 | 83 | 100 | 4.6 | 720 | 5,485 | 710 | 402 | 50 | 6.4 |
| 1968 | 250 | 79 | 98 | 5.9 | 730 | 5,529 | 636 | 363 | 54 | 6.4 |
| 1969 | 257 | 81 | 99 | 6.4 | 694 | 4,340 | 589 | 325 | 59 | 6.2 |
| 1970 | 258 | 82 | 99 | 7.0 | 326 | 4,459 | 579 | 333 | 59 | 6.3 |
| 1971 | 260 | 90 | 100 | 8.0 | 316 | 4,548 | 617 | 340 | 87 | 6.4 |
| 1972 | 265 | 100 | 102 | 8.8 | 331 | 4,756 | 725 | 335 | 100 | 6.6[31] |
| | | | | | | | | | | 8.2 |
| 1973 | 270 | 110 | 104 | 9.0 | 326 | 4,845 | 841 | 354 | ... | 8.3 |
| 1974 | 275 | 120 | 106 | 9.5 | 325 | 5,043 | 975 | 366 | 108 | 9.0 |
| 1975 | 280 | 125 | 108 | 10.0 | 325 | 5,568 | 1,102 | 370 | 108 | 9.3 |
| 1976 | 260 | 130 | 110 | 10.8 | 326 | 5,800 | 1,174 | 374 | 113 | 10.1 |
| 1977 | 270 | 130 | 112 | 11.5 | 328 | 5,810 | 1,201 | 403 | 120 | 11.4 |
| 1978 | 290 | 134 | 113 | 12.0 | 329 | 5,203 | 1,273 | 423 | 126 | 12.5 |
| 1979 | 295 | 135 | 114 | ... | 330 | 5,300 | 1,300 | 430 | 130 | 13 |
| 1980 | 300 | 137 | 115 | 13 | 330 | 5,400 | 1,310 | 430 | 135 | 13 |
| 1981 | 305 | 140 | 116 | 14 | 330 | 5,500[13] | 1,330 | 435 | 140 | 14 |
| 1982 | 170 | 142 | 117 | 14 | 330 | 6,400 | 1,350 | 440 | 145 | 14 |
| 1983 | 180 | 170 | 118 | 15 | 313 | 6,795 | 1,109 | 372 | 113 | 13 |
| 1984 | 199 | 160 | 118 | 15 | 314 | 6,956 | 1,278 | 378 | 118 | 13 |
| 1985 | 200 | 180 | 120 | 15 | 317 | 7,151 | 1,508 | 388 | 123 | 15 |
| 1986 | 210 | 185 | 120 | 15 | 323 | 7,374 | 1,809 | 411 | 129 | 15 |
| 1987 | 210 | 185 | 120 | 15 | 328 | 7,780 | 2,108 | 430 | 138 | 16 |
| 1988 | 210 | 185 | 120 | 15 | 330 | 8,074 | 2,305 | 449 | 146 | 17 |

**C10    SOUTH AMERICA: Numbers of Livestock** (in thousands, poultry in millions)

| | | | | Peru | | | | |
|---|---|---|---|---|---|---|---|---|
| | **Horses** | **Mules** | **Asses** | **Cattle** | **Pigs** | **Sheep** | **Goats** | **Poultry**[32] |
| 1945 | 453 | 120 | 349 | 2,662 | 770 | 15,000 | 950 | ... |
| 1946 | 453 | 123 | 350 | ... | 775 | 16,000 | 962 | 8.0 |
| 1947 | 453 | 123 | 349 | 2,662 | 777 | 17,288 | 962 | 9.5 |
| 1948 | 518 | 150 | 433 | 2,639 | 864 | 17,748 | 924 | ... |
| 1949 | 550 | 159 | 432 | 2,883 | 960 | 18,518 | 1,093 | 9.1 |
| 1950 | 432 | 156 | 415 | 2,824 | 995 | 17,752 | 2,207 | ... |
| 1951 | 529 | 178 | 404 | 3,140 | 1,203 | 16,268 | 1,917 | ... |
| 1952 | 533 | 181 | 407 | 3,188 | 1,270 | 15,905 | 2,038 | 10.8 |
| 1953 | 533 | 181 | 407 | 3,413 | 1,346 | 16,190 | 2,285 | 12.1 |
| 1954 | 533 | 181 | 407 | 3,477 | 1,352 | 16,822 | 2,456 | 11.2 |
| 1955 | 529 | 177 | 397 | 3,439 | 1,341 | 16,505 | 2,254 | 11.3 |
| 1956 | 518 | 173 | 388 | 3,380 | 1,281 | 15,204 | 3,464 | 11.0 |
| 1957 | 512 | 171 | 384 | 3,224 | 1,364 | 14,130 | 3,555 | 11.8 |
| 1958 | 560 | 183 | 420 | 3,372 | 1,432 | 14,760 | 5,196 | 12.4 |
| 1959 | 567 | 189 | 426 | 3,590 | 1,464 | 15,136 | 5,075 | 12.4 |
| 1960 | 580 | 193 | 435 | 3,820 | 1,625 | 16,009 | 3,769 | 15.5 |
| 1961 | 589 | 197 | 442 | 3,824 | 1,540 | 15,937 | 3,831 | 17.6 |
| 1962 | 616 | 197 | 442 | 3,927[13] | 1,620[13] | 16,340[13] | 3,950 | 21.6[13] |
| | | | | 3,326 | 1,807 | 14,087 | | 23.2 |
| 1963 | 615 | 200 | 445 | 3,466 | 1,897 | 14,115 | 4,099 | 24.6 |
| 1964 | 494 | 165 | 370 | 3,625 | 1,997 | 14,548 | 3,950 | 26.4 |
| 1965 | 532 | 177 | 399 | 3,644 | 1,843 | 15,218 | 3,959 | 13.9 |
| 1966 | 595 | 199 | 447 | 3,686 | 1,782 | 15,233 | 3,916 | 15.9 |
| 1967 | 600 | 200 | 450 | 3,711 | 1,829 | 16,041 | 1,866 | 18.0 |
| 1968 | 620 | 210 | 460 | 3,810 | 1,813 | 16,220 | 1,821 | 20.0 |
| 1969 | 640 | 220 | 485 | 4,060 | 1,939 | 16,811 | 1,855 | 21.0 |
| 1970 | 667 | 230 | 505 | 4,127 | 1,930 | 17,063 | 1,860 | 21.5[32] |
| | | | | | | | | 19.3 |
| 1971 | 700 | 228 | 530 | 4,310 | 2,071 | 16,918 | 1,946 | 24.4 |
| 1972 | 685 | 211 | 514[13] | 4,145 | 2,075 | 15,033 | 1,950 | 24.7 |
| 1973 | 634 | 212 | 476 | 4,103 | 2,083 | 15,105 | 1,950 | 26.1 |
| 1974 | 636 | 212 | 478 | 4,144 | 2,132 | 15,400 | 2,012 | 29.4 |
| 1975 | 637 | 211 | 479 | 4,150 | 2,136 | 15,280 | 2,050 | 34.8 |
| 1976 | ... | ... | ... | 4,189 | 2,141 | 15,294 | 2,060 | 37.7 |
| 1977 | 643 | 214 | 483 | 4,184 | 2,052 | 15,150 | 2,070 | 39.6 |
| 1978 | 645 | 215 | 485 | 4,229 | 2,043 | 15,000 | 2,000 | 37.5 |
| 1979 | 648 | 216 | 486 | 4,310 | 2,071 | 14,800 | 2,000 | 36.2 |
| 1980 | 650 | 217 | 488 | 4,207 | 2,058 | 14,700 | 2,000 | 42.0 |
| 1981 | 653 | 218 | 489 | 4,265 | 2,116 | 14,099 | 1,950 | 45.2 |
| 1982 | 653 | 218 | 489 | 4,318 | 2,211 | 14,277 | 1,900 | 47.9 |
| 1983 | 653 | 218 | 489 | 4,050 | 2,145 | 12,928 | 1,786 | 45.1 |
| 1984 | 655 | 220 | 490 | 4,051 | 2,214 | 12,701 | 1,700 | 42.7 |
| 1985 | 655 | 220 | 490 | 4,000 | 2,046 | 12,929 | 1,700 | 41 |
| 1986 | 655 | 220 | 490 | 3,980 | 2,174 | 13,060 | 1,720 | 48 |
| 1987 | 655 | 220 | 490 | 4,029 | 2,224 | 13,118 | 1,740 | 50 |
| 1988 | 655 | 220 | 490 | 4,037 | 2,301 | 13,037 | 1,720 | 53 |

**C10    SOUTH AMERICA: Numbers of Livestock** (in thousands, poultry in millions)

| | Uruguay | | | | | Venezuela | | | | | | | |
|---|---|---|---|---|---|---|---|---|---|---|---|---|---|
| | Horses | Cattle | Pigs | Sheep | Poultry[3] | Horses | Mules | Asses | Cattle | Pigs | Sheep | Goats | Poultry[3] |
| 1945 | ... | ... | ... | 19,559 | ... | ... | ... | ... | ... | ... | ... | ... | ... |
| 1946 | 575 | 6,821 | 274 | 19,800 | ... | ... | ... | ... | ... | ... | ... | ... | ... |
| 1947 | ... | ... | ... | 22,000 | ... | ... | ... | ... | ... | ... | ... | ... | ... |
| 1948 | 546 | ... | ... | ... | ... | ... | ... | ... | ... | ... | ... | ... | ... |
| 1949 | ... | ... | ... | 22,646 | ... | ... | ... | ... | ... | ... | ... | ... | ... |
| 1950 | ... | ... | 259 | 23,409 | ... | 335 | 62 | 387 | 5,674 | 1,451 | 101 | 1,273 | 9.3 |
| 1951 | 667 | 8,154 | 259 | 24,543 | 5.1 | ... | ... | ... | ... | ... | ... | ... | ... |
| 1952 | ... | | 275 | 25,677 | ... | ... | ... | ... | ... | ... | ... | ... | ... |
| 1953 | ... | 8,013 | 260 | 25,699 | ... | ... | ... | ... | ... | ... | ... | ... | ... |
| 1954 | ... | 7,819 | 235 | 24,492 | ... | ... | ... | ... | 6,230 | ... | ... | ... | ... |
| 1955 | ... | 7,433 | 381 | 23,303 | 5.7 | ... | ... | ... | 6,380 | ... | ... | ... | ... |
| 1956 | ... | ... | ... | ... | ... | 533 | 130 | 427 | 7,162 | 2,362 | 176 | 921 | 11.7 |
| 1957 | 557 | ... | ... | ... | ... | ... | ... | ... | ... | ... | ... | ... | ... |
| 1958 | ... | ... | ... | ... | ... | ... | ... | ... | ... | ... | ... | ... | ... |
| 1959 | ... | 6,902 | ... | 21,293 | ... | ... | ... | ... | ... | ... | ... | ... | ... |
| 1960 | ... | 7,505 | ... | ... | ... | 388 | 65 | 402 | 6,441 | 1,781 | 83 | 1,251 | 12.5 |
| 1961 | 498 | 8,792 | 383 | 21,738 | 6.5 | 390 | 65 | 410 | 6,459 | 1,820 | 85 | 1,250 | 12.7 |
| 1962 | 480 | 8,835 | 400 | 22,300 | 6.8 | 397 | 67 | 420 | 6,502 | 1,814 | 99 | 1,250 | 17.7 |
| 1963 | 475 | 8,866 | 413 | 21,829 | 7.0 | 397 | 68 | 435 | 6,572 | 1,847 | 99 | 1,249 | 13.4 |
| 1964 | 463 | 9,145 | 431 | 21,905 | 7.3 | 401 | 70 | 453 | 6,650 | 1,882 | 98 | 1,247 | 13.6 |
| 1965 | 451 | 8,142 | 438 | 21,874 | 7.5 | 406 | 71 | 471 | 7,380 | 1,977 | 89 | 1,626 | 13.9 |
| 1966 | 450 | 8,188 | 383 | 21,800 | 7.5 | 410 | 73 | 475 | 7,612 | 1,552 | 93 | 1,495 | 14.2 |
| 1967 | 450 | 8,300 | 375 | 21,900 | 7.8[13] <br> 4.7 | 414 | 74 | 480 | 7,852 | 1,548 | 94 | 1,556 | 14.4[13] <br> 16.0 |
| 1968 | 440 | 8,600 | 380 | 22,100 | 4.7 | 419 | 75 | 485 | 8,102 | 1,480 | 99 | 1,598 | 16.6 |
| 1969 | 440 | 8,900 | 380 | 22,606 | 4.6 | 423 | 76 | 495 | 8,289 | 1,601 | 101 | 1,424 | 17.3 |
| 1970 | 421 | 8,564 | 419 | 19,893 | 5.3 | 428 | 77 | 500 | 8,485 | 1,609 | 96 | 1,383 | 18.7 |
| 1971 | 420 | 8,727 | 400 | 17,220 | 6.3 | 432 | 78 | 510 | 8,549 | 1,761 | 99 | 1,397 | 20.5 |
| 1972 | 410 | 9,273 | 420 | 15,452 | 6.5 | 445 | 79 | 522 | 8,730 | 1,767 | 99 | 1,413 | 19.8 |
| 1973 | 430 | 9,860 | 430 | 15,902 | 7.0 | 450 | 80 | 533 | 8,843 | 1,570 | 100 | 1,419 | 22.8 |
| 1974 | 450 | 10,790 | 415 | 15,373 | 7.2 | 454 | 81 | 545 | 9,089 | 1,795 | 101 | 1,427 | 24.6 |
| 1975 | 470 | 11,536 | 418 | 15,062 | 7.3 | 458 | 77 | 480 | 9,404 | 1,880 | 103 | 1,285 | 29.4 |
| 1976 | 509 | 10,385 | 445 | 15,546 | 7.5 | 463 | 76 | 470 | 9,546 | 1,916 | 275 | 1,286 | 35.7 |
| 1977 | 491 | 10,128 | 461 | 16,030 | 7.6 | 470 | 75 | 460 | 9,919 | 2,040 | 298 | 1,339 | 32.4 |
| 1978 | 520 | 10,007 | 398 | 16,161 | 7.6 | 474 | 75 | 455 | 10,249 | 2,046 | 320 | 1,354 | 37.0 |
| 1979 | 525 | 10,301 | 412 | 17,234 | 7.7 | 478 | 74 | 450 | 10,625 | 2,141 | 344 | 1,338 | 40.9 |
| 1980 | 530 | 11,173 | 450 | 20,034 | 8 | 482 | 74 | 450 | 11,052 | 2,280 | 336 | 1,381 | 44 |
| 1981 | 506 | 11,421 | 450 | 20,391 | 6 | 481 | 74 | 448 | 11,500 | 2,303 | 382 | 1,312 | 41 |
| 1982 | 495 | 11,237 | 430 | 20,307 | 6 | 412 | 73 | 445 | 11,575 | 2,459 | 356 | 1,322 | 42 |
| 1983 | 453 | 9,704 | 440 | 20,447 | 6 | 491 | 72 | 445 | 12,286 | 2,699 | 365 | 1,335 | 48 |
| 1984 | 469 | 9,062 | 235 | 20,738 | 6 | 495 | 72 | 440 | 11,844 | 2,935 | 422 | 1,340 | 51 |
| 1985 | 464 | 9,629 | 200 | 21,195 | 6 | 495 | 72 | 440 | 12,083 | 3,011 | ... | ... | 54 |
| 1986 | 469 | 9,300 | 195 | 24,372 | 7 | 495 | 72 | 440 | 12,331 | 3,187 | 425 | 1,400 | 56 |
| 1987 | 437 | 9,945 | 220 | 24,006 | 7 | 495 | 72 | 440 | 12,641 | 3,349 | 425 | 1,450 | 59 |
| 1988 | 466 | 10,331 | 215 | 24,689 | 8 | 495 | 72 | 440 | 12,856 | 2,856 | 425 | 1,450 | 61 |

## C10 Numbers of Livestock (in thousands; poultry in millions)

NOTES

1. SOURCES: As for table C1 with most Venezuelan statistics to 1937 from Rafael Cartay, *Historia Economica de Venezuela 1830–1900* (Valencia, 1988). Valencia
2. Statistics in this table relate to a count taking place at some point during the year shown, or, in the case of FAO estimates, to a 12-month period ending in September. The exact date is not always given in the sources, and in some cases there were changes which affected the comparability of the figures. Where this is known it has been indicated in footnotes, but a number of unexplained discrepancies probably arise from this.
3. Where estimates are continued unchanged over several years, it is probably wise to regard them with some caution. Where a later count has rendered estimates previously made for the years preceding such a count unbelievable, they have been ignored here, and 'not available' symbols substituted.

FOOTNOTES

[1] Statistics for some part of Canada are available for various dates before 1851. The following are those for the 18th and 19th centuries (in thousands):

| Lower Canada | Horses | Cattle | Pigs | Sheep | | Upper Canada | Horses | Cattle | Pigs | Sheep |
|---|---|---|---|---|---|---|---|---|---|---|
| 1706 | 2 | 14 | ... | 2 | | 1826 | 24 | 112 | ... | ... |
| 1719 | 4 | 18 | 14 | 8 | | 1827 | 25 | 124 | ... | ... |
| 1720 | 5 | 25 | 18 | 12 | | 1828 | 26 | 134 | ... | ... |
| 1721 | 6 | 23 | 16 | 14 | | 1829 | 28 | 143 | ... | ... |
| 1734 | 5 | 33 | 24 | 20 | | 1830 | 31 | 147 | ... | ... |
| 1765 | 13 | 50 | 29 | 28 | | 1831 | 33 | 156 | ... | ... |
| 1784 | 30 | 99 | 70 | 85 | | 1832 | 37 | 167 | ... | ... |
| 1827 | 142 | 389 | 242 | 829 | | 1833 | 40 | 173 | ... | ... |
| 1831 | 117 | 470 | 295 | 543 | | 1834 | 43 | 179 | ... | ... |
| 1844 | 147 | 592 | 198 | 603 | | 1835 | 48 | 196 | ... | ... |
| **New Brunswick** | | | | | | 1836 | 55 | 215 | ... | ... |
| 1840 | 18 | 90 | 72 | 141 | | 1837 | 57 | 218 | ... | ... |
| | | | | | | 1837 | 57 | 218 | ... | ... |
| | | | | | | 1838 | 57 | 218 | ... | ... |
| **Nova Scotia** | | | | | | 1839 | 66 | 221 | ... | ... |
| 1827 | 13 | 111 | 71 | 174 | | 1840 | 73 | 247 | ... | ... |
| | | | | | | 1841 | 75 | 264 | ... | ... |
| | | | | | | 1842 | 114 | 505 | 394 | 576 |
| | | | | | | 1848 | 151 | 566 | 484 | 835 |

[2] Excluding Prince Edward Island.
[3] Chickens only.
[4] Chickens only to 1966 (1st line).
[5] Including asses.
[6] Most, and perhaps all statistics up to 1947 include mules and asses. These numbered 28 thousand in 1939.
[7] The count was in April instead of the usual June.
[8] Excluding geese.
[9] Including sheep.
[10] Incomplete figures.
[11] Chickens only (but excluding broilers) to 1975 (1st line). All chickens and turkeys subsequently.
[12] Earlier statistics are for 1 June, later for 1 December.
[13] The reason for this break is not given in the source.
[14] Later figures relate to animals on state-operated farms only.
[15] Chickens only from 1961 to 1969 (1st line).
[16] Chickens only from 1960.
[17] Earlier statistics are for June, later for September.
[18] Chickens on agricultural holdings only to 1961 (1st line).
[19] Alaska and Hawaii are included from 1961.
[20] Subsequently at 1 December in the year before that indicated.
[21] Stock sheep only to 1972 (1st line), lambs included subsequently. Earlier figures which include lambs are available in the FAO, *Yearbook of Agricultural Statistics.*
[22] The date of the count was changed from summer to winter.
[23] Chickens only to 1948.
[24] Excluding Montevideo is 1905, except for sheep in 1900.
[25] National sources give a figure of 2,318 for mules and asses together in this year.
[26] These statistics exclude the *Intendencias* and *Comisarias.*
[27] Earlier statistics are for May or June, later for October.
[28] Chickens only to 1952 (1st line).
[29] Excluding chickens on sugar plantations to 1954.
[30] Statistics to 1954 are incomplete. For 1940–54 they are said, in official sources, to cover sheep and goats. It is probable that the earlier figures of sheep, from 1926 on, given by the FAO also include goats.
[31] Chickens only to 1972 (1st line)
[32] Chickens only from 1970 (2nd line).

**C11    NORTH AMERICA: OUTPUT OF COW'S MILK** (in thousands of metric tons)

| | Canada | Costa Rica | Guatemala | Honduras | U.S.A. |
|---|---|---|---|---|---|
| 1889 | ... | ... | ... | ... | 20,324 |
| 1899 | ... | ... | ... | ... | 28,343 |
| 1909 | ... | ... | ... | ... | 29,126 |
| 1919 | ... | ... | ... | ... | 30,447 |
| 1920 | 4,979 | ... | ... | ... | ... |
| 1921 | 5,397 | ... | ... | ... | ... |
| 1922 | 5,492 | ... | ... | ... | ... |
| 1923 | 5,809 | ... | ... | ... | ... |
| 1924 | 5,980 | ... | ... | ... | 40,479 |
| 1925 | 6,088 | ... | ... | ... | 41,140 |
| 1926 | 6,112 | ... | ... | 57 | 42,332 |
| 1927 | 5,858 | ... | ... | 58 | 43,169 |
| 1928 | 5,764 | ... | ... | 58 | 43,474 |
| 1929 | 5,629 | ... | ... | 61 | 44,900 |
| 1930 | 6,088 | ... | 121 | 62 | 45,431 |
| 1931 | 6,504 | ... | 92 | 63 | 46,733 |
| 1932 | 6,349 | ... | 186 | 65 | 47,087 |
| 1933 | 6,388 | ... | 193 | 67 | 47,519 |
| 1934 | 6,555 | ... | 142 | 68 | 46,095 |
| 1935 | 6,610 | ... | 143 | 70 | 45,906 |
| 1936 | 6,859 | ... | 182 | 71 | 46,452 |
| 1937 | 6,861 | ... | 608 | 73 | 46,225 |
| 1938 | 7,176 | ... | 468 | 75 | 47,993 |
| 1939 | 7,158 | ... | 415 | 77 | 48,440 |
| 1940 | 7,007 | 363 | 418 | 78 | 49,628 |
| 1941 | 7,288 | 356 | 435 | 80 | 52,203 |
| 1942 | 7,592 | 345 | 497 | 83 | 53,766 |
| 1943 | 7,590 | 337 | ... | 84 | 53,078 |
| 1944 | 7,642 | ... | ... | 86 | 53,081 |

| | Canada | Costa Rica | Cuba | Dominican Republic |
|---|---|---|---|---|
| 1945 | 7,640 | ... | ... | 55 |
| 1946 | 7,317 | ... | ... | 53 |
| 1947 | 7,413 | ... | 499 | 52 |
| 1948 | 7,158 | ... | 499 | 54 |
| 1949 | 7,220 | ... | 421 | 55 |
| 1950 | 6,950 | ... | ... | 57 |
| 1951 | 6,944 | 179 | ... | 60 |
| 1952 | 6,944 | 124 [1] / 108 | ... | 61 |
| 1953 | 7,274 | 119 | 624 | ... |
| 1954 | 7,497 | 144 | 750 | ... |
| 1955 | 7,687 | 95 | 735 | ... |
| 1956 | 7,696 | 123 | 760 | ... |
| 1957 | 7,727 | 76 | 806 | ... |
| 1958 | 8,016 | ... | 828 | ... |
| 1959 | 7,998 | ... | 979 | ... |
| 1960 | 8,057 | ... | 1,130 [1] / 767 | ... |
| 1961 | 8,325 | ... [1] | 700 / 350 | ... |
| 1962 | 8,346 | 127 | 370 | 181 |
| 1963 | 8,369 | 149 | 390 | 182 |
| 1964 | 8,402 | 163 | 420 | 186 |
| 1965 | 8,336 | 160 | 440 | 200 |
| 1966 | 8,345 | 150 | 462 | 210 |
| 1967 | 8,267 | 157 | 566 | 231 |
| 1968 | 8,337 | 178 | 530 | 240 |
| 1969 | 8,495 | 186 | 520 | 260 |
| 1970 | 8,314 | 194 | 500 [1] / 690 | 283 |
| 1971 | 7,932 | 202 | 675 | 304 |
| 1972 | 8,026 | 219 | 758 | 315 |
| 1973 | 7,667 | 210 | 781 | 330 |
| 1974 | 7,633 | 248 | 799 | 340 |
| 1975 | 7,751 | 259 | 860 | 320 |
| 1976 | 7,693 | 261 | 1,000 | 340 |
| 1977 | 7,742 | 279 | 1,066 | 325 |
| 1978 | 7,615 | 294 | 1,150 | 340 |
| 1979 | 7,095 | 316 | 1,180 | 409 |
| 1980 | 7,855 | 318 | 1,080 | 431 |
| 1981 | 8,025 | 308 | 1,180 | 440 |
| 1982 | 8,258 | 302 | 1,091 | 450 |
| 1983 | 8,019 | 325 | 1,109 | 460 |
| 1984 | 8,096 | 347 | ... | 495 |
| 1985 | 7,891 | 376 | 1,100 | 379 |
| 1986 | 7,925 | 414 | 1,111 | 337 |
| 1987 | 7,986 | 410 | 1,128 | 289 |
| 1988 | 8,229 | 415 | 1,122 | 290 |

**C11** **NORTH AMERICA: Output of Cow's Milk** (in thousands of metric tons)

| | El Salvador | Guatemala | Honduras | Jamaica | Mexico[2] | Nicaragua | Panama | Puerto Rico[3] | USA[4] |
|---|---|---|---|---|---|---|---|---|---|
| 1945 | ... | ... | 88 | ... | ... | ... | ... | ... | 54,353 |
| 1946 | ... | ... | 91 | ... | ... | ... | ... | 105 | 53,386 |
| 1947 | 102 | ... | 94 | ... | ... | 147 | ... | ... | 52,986 |
| 1948 | 107 | ... | 96 | ... | ... | 153 | ... | 134 | 51,107 |
| 1949 | ... | ... | 99 | 30 | ... | 183 | ... | ... | 52,663 |
| 1950 | ... | 206 | 102 | 38 | 1,539 | 190 | ... | 160 | 52,890 |
| 1951 | ... | ... | 105 | 38 | ... | ... | ... | 147 | 52,018 |
| 1952 | 138 | 175 | 108 | 40 | ... | 169 | 33 | 148 | 52,014 |
| 1953 | 164 | 175 | 113 | 40 | 1,730 | ... | 51 | 153 | 54,531 |
| 1954 | 193 | 89 | 116 | 40 | 1,895 | ... | 37 | 182 | 55,381 |
| 1955 | ... | 92 | 105 | ... | 1,985 | ... | 36 | 194 | 55,767 |
| 1956 | ... | 92 | 105 | ... | | ... | 44 | 220 | 56,636 |
| 1957 | ... | 93 | 108 | 37 | 2,750 | ... | 54 | 262 | 56,530 |
| 1958 | ... | 128 | 111 | 37 | | ... | 51 | 269 | 55,892 |
| 1959 | ... | 127 | 115 | 35 | 2,489 | ... | 51 | 301 | 55,333[4] |
| 1960 | ... | 144 | 119 | 35 | 2,370 | ... | 45 | 324 | 55,841 |
| 1961 | ... | 126 | 125 | 33[1] 40 | 2,327 | 190 | 48 | 339 | 57,020 |
| 1962 | ... | 183 | 123 | 38 | 2,284 | 192 | 53 | 313 | 57,266 |
| 1963 | ... | 209 | 128 | 39 | 2,237 | 175 | 56 | 325 | 56,791 |
| 1964 | ... | 199 | 131 | 40 | 2,304 | 181 | 60 | 333 | 57,591 |
| 1965 | ... | 213 | 135 | 40 | 2,373 | 182 | 63 | 350 | 56,324 |
| 1966 | ... | 208 | 137 | 41[1] 30 | 2,444 | 183 | 71 | 354 | 54,382 |
| 1967 | ... | 231 | 156 | 33 | 2,591 | 185 | 73 | 356 | 53,856 |
| 1968 | 159 | 234 | 167 | 39 | 2,671 | 176 | 72 | 367 | 53,172 |
| 1969 | 167 | 253 | 167 | 43 | 3,023 | 191 | 79 | 371 | 52,665 |
| 1970 | 169 | 262 | 162 | 46 | 3,053[1] 3,919 | 201 | 73 | 370 | 53,073 |
| 1971 | 170 | 270 | 169 | 47 | 4,068 | 210 | 76 | 374 | 53,780 |
| 1972 | 172 | 280 | 176 | 49 | 4,190 | 218[1] | 72 | 383 | 54,442 |
| 1973 | 187 | 290 | 182 | 48 | 4,227 | 385 | 66 | 384 | 52,386 |
| 1974 | 200 | 300 | 175 | 47 | 4,523 | 415 | 64 | 374 | 52,429 |
| 1975 | 235 | 310 | 180 | 46 | 4,980 | 446 | 73 | 380 | 52,343 |
| 1976 | 294 | 320 | 190 | 47 | 5,344 | 462 | 75 | 407 | 54,512 |
| 1977 | 244 | 314 | 192 | 48 | 5,731 | 462 | 86 | 436 | 55,635 |
| 1978 | 253 | 310 | 202 | 48 | 6,426 | 465 | 98 | 440 | 55,093 |
| 1978 | 264 | 315 | 202 | 48 | 6,848 | 386 | 95 | 438 | 55,978 |
| 1980 | 291 | 320 | 277 | 48 | 6,951 | 165 | 94 | 407 | 58,244 |
| 1981 | 293 | 325 | 209 | 51 | 6,885 | 124 | 98 | 416 | 60,161 |
| 1982 | 268 | 319 | 279 | 48 | 7,138 | 124 | 93 | 399 | 61,599 |
| 1983 | 249 | 320 | 281 | 48 | 7,171 | 125 | 88 | 384 | 63,354 |
| 1984 | 213 | 360 | 244 | 49 | 7,101 | 125 | 96 | 351 | 61,439 |
| 1985 | 234 | 370 | 247 | ... | 7,173 | 167 | 98 | 363 | 65,166 |
| 1986 | 232 | 364 | 269 | 48 | 6,373 | 191 | 111 | 340 | 65,036 |
| 1987 | 240 | 366 | 283 | 49 | 7,499 | 181 | 119 | 353 | 64,731 |
| 1988 | 295 | ... | 299 | 49 | 8,830 | 197 | 112 | 346 | 65,840 |

**C11**     **SOUTH AMERICA: OUTPUT OF COW'S MILK** (in thousands of metric tons)

| | Argentina[4] | Brazil[5] | Chile | Colombia | Ecuador | Paraguay | Peru | Uruguay | Venezuela |
|---|---|---|---|---|---|---|---|---|---|
| 1925 | 1,158 | 1,856 | 170 | ... | ... | ... | ... | ... | ... |
| 1926 | 1,212 | 1,901 | 187 | ... | ... | ... | ... | ... | ... |
| 1927 | 1,056 | 1,957 | 202 | ... | ... | ... | ... | ... | ... |
| 1928 | 1,067 | 2,016 | 283[2] | ... | ... | ... | ... | ... | ... |
| 1929 | 973 | 2,076 | ... | ... | ... | ... | 191 | ... | ... |
| 1930 | 1,159 | 2,138 | ... | ... | ... | ... | ... | ... | ... |
| 1931 | 1,343 | 2,321 | ... | ... | ... | ... | ... | ... | ... |
| 1932 | 1,345 | 2,371 | ... | ... | ... | ... | ... | ... | ... |
| 1933 | 1,218 | 2,459 | ... | ... | ... | ... | ... | ... | ... |
| 1934 | 1,155 | 2,514 | ... | ... | ... | ... | ... | ... | ... |
| 1935 | 1,143 | 2,521[5] | 230 | ... | ... | ... | ... | ... | ... |
| 1936 | 1,283 | 3,828 | 235 | ... | ... | ... | ... | ... | ... |
| 1937 | 1,288 | 3,862 | ... | ... | ... | ... | 191 | 368 | ... |
| 1938 | 1,399 | 3,934 | ... | ... | ... | ... | ... | ... | ... |
| 1939 | 1,568 | 4,305[5] | ... | ... | ... | ... | ... | ... | ... |
| 1940 | 1,687 | ... | ... | ... | ... | ... | ... | ... | ... |
| 1941 | 2,006 | ... | ... | ... | ... | ... | ... | ... | ... |
| 1942 | 1,903 | ... | ... | ... | ... | ... | ... | ... | ... |
| 1943 | 2,178 | ... | 436 | ... | ... | ... | ... | 406 | ... |
| 1944 | 2,245 | ... | 524 | ... | ... | ... | ... | ... | ... |
| 1945 | 2,083 | ... | 516 | ... | ... | ... | 263 | 356 | ... |
| 1946 | 2,403[4] | ... | 588 | ... | ... | ... | 273 | ... | ... |
| 1947 | 4,169 | ... | 598 | ... | ... | ... | 300 | ... | ... |
| 1948 | 4,214 | ... | 575 | 1,740 | ... | ... | 318 | 361 | ... |
| 1949 | 4,002 | 2,377 | 663 | ... | 168 | ... | 332 | 395 | 361 |
| 1950 | 4,032 | 2,495 | 698 | 2,007 | ... | ... | 315 | 446 | ... |
| 1951 | 4,061 | 2,562 | 704 | 1,949 | ... | ... | 321 | 498 | ... |
| 1952 | 4,478 | 2,833 | 634 | ... | 169 | 124 | 345 | 546 | ... |
| 1953 | 4,891 | 3,215 | 701 | 1,801 | ... | 126 | 387 | 566 | ... |
| 1954 | 4,801 | 3,441 | 771 | 1,780 | 270 | 126 | 389 | 586 | 289 |
| 1955 | 4,999 | 3,673 | 825 | 2,095 | ... | ... | 390 | 600 | 327 |
| 1956 | 5,126 | 4,238 | ... | 2,085 | 330 | 129 | 392 | 630 | 374 |
| 1957 | 4,662 | 4,407 | ... | 2,085 | 360 | 130 | 390 | 702 | 377 |
| 1958 | 4,481 | 4,603 | 764 | ... | 375 | 132[1] / 75 | 372 | 627 | ... |
| 1959 | 4,478 | 4,792 | 754 | 1,965 | 386 | 75 | 397 | 619 | 387 |
| 1960 | 4,511 | 5,052 | 784 | 1,905[1] / 1,753 | 414 | 76 | 419 | 773 | 434 |
| 1961 | 4,486[1] / 4,151 | 5,227 | 799 | 1,753 | 405 | 78 | 437 | 746 | 458 |
| 1962 | 4,143 | 5,460 | 762 | 1,785 | 397 | 79 | 453 | 765 | 496 |
| 1963 | 4,367 | 5,550 | 821 | 1,833 | 386 | 80 | 475 | 781 | 538 |
| 1964 | 4,534 | 6,340 | 856 | 1,860 | 400 | 82 | 499 | 763 | 604 |
| 1965 | 4,276 | 6,775 | 835 | 1,973 | 400 | 84 | 714 | 736 | 645 |
| 1966 | 4,732 | 6,889 | 856 | 2,020 | 440[1] / 500 | 86 | 725 | 742 | 683 |
| 1967 | 4,366 | 6,905 | 873 | 2,080 | 600 | 87 | 726 | 619 | 717 |
| 1968 | 4,683 | 7,235 | 939 | 2,070 | 677 | 86 | 730 | 680 | 771 |
| 1969 | 4,556 | 7,253 | 1,012 | 2,160 | 685 | 87 | 762 | 762 | 889 |
| 1970 | 4,190 | 7,353 | 1,104 | 2,250 | 705 | 88 | 825 | 763 | 952 |
| 1971 | 4,825 | 7,346 | 969 | 2,340 | 717 | 89 | 897 | 706 | 1,000 |
| 1972 | 5,385 | 7,323 | 907 | 2,450 | 730 | 92 | 816 | 727 | 1,081 |
| 1973 | 5,221 | 7,763 | 882 | 2,300 | 763 | 95 | 804 | 675 | 1,055 |
| 1974 | 5,292 | 9,022 | 933 | 2,027 | 766 | 110 | 813 | 711 | 1,134 |

**C11    SOUTH AMERICA: Output of Cow's Milk** (in thousands of metric tons)

|      | Argentina | Brazil | Chile | Colombia | Ecuador | Paraguay | Peru | Uruguay | Venezuela |
|------|-----------|--------|-------|----------|---------|----------|------|---------|-----------|
| 1975 | 5,650 | 9,971 | 986 | 2,096 | 784 | 121 | 813 | 745 | 1,224 |
| 1976 | 5,799 | 10,667 | 1,054 | 2,276 | 809 | 128 | 821 | 765 | 1,198 |
| 1977 | 5,309 | 9,862 | 1,035 | 2,303 | 849 | 136 | 820 | 730 | 1,244 |
| 1978 | 5,213 | 10,500 | 1,008 | 2,360 | 866 | 149 | 822 | 753 | 1,270 |
| 1979 | 5,349 | 10,503 | 983 | 2,395 | 754 | 162 | 824 | 784 | 1,302 |
| 1980 | 5,307 | 11,956 | 1,080 | 2,165 | 924 | 163 | 780 | 820 | 1,311 |
| 1981 | 5,155 | ... | 1,163 | 2,623 | 916 | 168 | 785 | 830 | 1,352 |
| 1982 | 5,781 | 11,817 | 1,056 | 2,570 | 967 | 124 | 805 | 843 | 1,472 |
| 1983 | 5,300 | 11,818 | 900 | 2,647 | 981 | 160 | 752 | 896 | 1,511 |
| 1984 | 5,200 | 12,303 | 880 | 2,858 | 1,020 | 175 | 780 | 851 | 1,570 |
| 1985 | 5,742 | 12,452 | 1,012 | 2,816 | 988 | 182 | 809 | 922 | 1,532 |
| 1986 | 6,118 | 12,879 | 1,092 | 3,017 | 1,260 | 188 | 819 | 959 | 1,580 |
| 1987 | 6,444 | 13,399 | 1,128 | 3,142 | 1,270 | 194 | 830 | 988 | 1,598 |
| 1988 | 6,168 | 13,941 | 1,149 | 3,155 | 1,406 | 200 | 850 | 990 | 1,715 |

NOTES

1.  SOURCES: As for table C1.
2.  The basis on which the statistics have been collected has varied from country to country and over time, so that comparisons must be made with caution.
3.  Where necessary, conversions from liquid measures have been made on the assumption that the specific gravity of milk is 1.031.

FOOTNOTES

[1] This break is not explained in the source.
[2] One earlier figure is available, *viz.* 1940–1,368.
[3] One earlier figure is available, *viz.* 1939–63.
[4] Including Alaska and Hawaii from 1960.
[5] Statistics to 1946 are of deliveries to dairies.
[6] Statistics to 1935 exclude milk for butter and cheese manufacture. Those for 1936–39 include goat's milk.

**C12    NORTH AMERICA: OUTPUT OF BUTTER** (in thousands of metric tons)

| | Canada | USA | | Canada | USA | | Canada | Mexico | USA |
|---|---|---|---|---|---|---|---|---|---|
| 1849 | ... | 142 | 1910 | 91 [1] [26] | 774 | 1950 | 131 | ... | 748 |
| 1850 | 15 | ... | 1911 | ... | 799 | 1951 | 129 | ... | 655 |
| 1859 | ... | 209 | 1912 | ... | 722 | 1952 | 138 | ... | 636 |
| 1860 | 23 | ... | 1913 | ... | 729 | 1953 | 146 | ... | 729 |
| | | | 1914 | ... | 764 | 1954 | 150 | ... | 738 |
| 1869 | ... | 233 | | | | 1955 | 151 | ... | 701 |
| 1870 | 34 | 187 | 1915 | [38] | 794 | 1956 | 144 | ... | 704 |
| | | | 1916 | [37] | 813 | 1957 | 143 | ... | 696 |
| 1871 | ... | 213 | 1917 | [40] | 746 | 1958 | 158 | ... | 674 |
| 1872 | ... | 197 | 1918 | [42] | 682 | 1959 | 153 | ... | 640 |
| 1873 | ... | 257 | 1919 | [47] | 747 | 1960 | 150 | ... | 651 [3] 670 |
| 1874 | ... | 265 | 1920 | [51] [1] 98 | 714 | 1961 | 165 | ... | 697 |
| 1875 | ... | 252 | 1921 | 107 | 793 | 1962 | 169 | ... | 716 |
| 1876 | ... | 307 | 1922 | 118 | 848 | 1963 | 164 | ... | 659 |
| 1877 | ... | 316 | 1923 | 124 | 904 | 1964 | 164 | 13 | 666 |
| 1878 | ... | 329 | 1924 | 130 | 937 | | | | |
| 1879 | ... | 366 | | | | 1965 | 157 | 14 | 611 |
| 1880 | 47 | 370 | 1925 | 125 | 944 | 1966 | 155 | 14 | 512 |
| 1881 | ... | 264 | 1926 | 127 | 967 | 1967 | 153 | 15 | 562 |
| 1882 | ... | 337 | 1927 | 126 | 992 | 1968 | 156 | 16 | 533 |
| 1883 | ... | 383 | 1928 | 121 | 962 | 1969 | 162 | 17 | 511 |
| 1884 | ... | 394 | 1929 | 122 | 991 | | | | |
| | | | | | | 1970 | 153 | 18 | 518 |
| 1885 | ... | 423 | 1930 | 128 | 975 | 1971 | 134 | 19 | 520 |
| 1886 | ... | 449 | 1931 | 146 | 1,016 | 1972 | 136 | 20 | 500 |
| 1887 | ... | 444 | 1932 | 142 | 1,046 | 1973 | 118 | 21 | 417 |
| 1888 | ... | 444 | 1933 | 144 | 1,077 | 1974 | 109 | 22 | 436 |
| 1889 | ... | 586 | 1934 | 151 | 1,037 | | | | |
| | | | | | | 1975 | 133 | 23 | 446 |
| 1890 | 51 | 531 | 1935 | 153 | 1,003 | 1976 | 118 | 23 | 444 |
| 1891 | ... | 495 | 1936 | 157 | 983 | 1977 | 117 | 24 | 493 |
| 1892 | ... | 480 | 1937 | 155 | 968 | 1978 | 105 | 25 | 451 |
| 1893 | ... | 475 | 1938 | 163 | 1,021 | 1979 | 101 | 24 | 447 |
| 1894 | ... | 482 | 1939 | 161 | 1,002 | | | | |
| | | | | | | 1980 | 107 | 21 | 519 |
| 1895 | ... | 588 | 1940 | 156 | 1,016 | 1981 | 117 | 21 | 557 |
| 1896 | ... | 728 | 1941 | 163 | 1,029 | 1982 | 126 | 23 | 570 |
| 1897 | ... | 695 | 1942 | 157 | 966 | 1983 | 108 | 24 | 589 |
| 1898 | ... | 668 | 1943 | 158 | 914 | 1984 | 112 | 25 | 500 |
| 1899 | ... | 677 | 1944 | 151 | 825 | | | | |
| | | | | | | 1985 | 100 | 25 | 566 |
| 1900 | 64 | 699 | 1945 | 150 | 771 | 1986 | 103 | 21 | 545 |
| 1901 | ... | 714 | 1946 | 138 | 681 | 1987 | 98 | 26 | 508 |
| 1902 | ... | 635 | 1947 | 147 | 744 | 1988 | 109 | 32 | 548 |
| 1903 | ... | 674 | 1948 | 145 | 682 | | | | |
| 1904 | ... | 699 | 1949 | 141 | 766 | | | | |
| 1905 | ... | 756 | | | | | | | |
| 1906 | ... | 701 | | | | | | | |
| 1907 | [21] [1] | 697 | | | | | | | |
| 1908 | ... | 800 | | | | | | | |
| 1909 | ... | 736 | | | | | | | |

**C12    SOUTH AMERICA: OUTPUT OF BUTTER** (in thousands of metric tons)

| | Argentina | Brazil[2] | | Argentina | Brazil[2] | | | Argentina | Brazil[2] |
|---|---|---|---|---|---|---|---|---|---|
| 1904 | 8.8 | ... | | | | | | | |
| 1905 | 8.8 | ... | 1935 | 28 | 21 | | 1965 | 42 | 25 |
| 1906 | 8.0 | ... | 1936 | 32 | 21 | | 1966 | 46 | 25 |
| 1907 | 6.7 | ... | 1937 | 32 | 21 | | 1967 | 41 | 36 |
| 1908 | 7.2 | ... | 1938 | 29 | 27 | | 1968 | 39 | 32 |
| 1909 | 7.2 | ... | 1939 | 34 | 34 | | 1969 | 35 | 43 |
| 1910 | 7.5 | ... | 1940 | 37 | 35 | | 1970 | 28 | 45 |
| 1911 | 7.9 | ... | 1941 | 44 | ... | | 1971 | 36 | 50 |
| 1912 | 9.5 | ... | 1942 | 41 | ... | | 1972 | 49 | 52 |
| 1913 | 10 | ... | 1943 | 47 | 14 | | 1973 | 37 | 60 |
| 1914 | 9.3 | ... | 1944 | 47 | 15 | | 1974 | 35 | 60 |
| 1915 | 10 | ... | 1945 | 43 | 18 | | 1975 | 40 | 63 |
| 1916 | 11 | ... | 1946 | 51 | 21 | | 1976 | 40 | 66 |
| 1917 | 15 | 6.4 | 1947 | 51 | 20 | | 1977 | 30 | 69 |
| 1918 | 25 | 6.6 | 1948 | 42 | 20 | | 1978 | 29 | 90 |
| 1919 | 26 | 6.6 | 1949 | 39 | 22 | | 1979 | 33 | 92 |
| 1920 | 29 | 8.6 | 1950 | 45 | 25 | | 1980 | 29 | 94 |
| 1921 | 33 | 6.9 | 1951 | 43 | 20 | | 1981 | 32 | 95 |
| 1922 | 33 | 8.9 | 1952 | 46 | 26 | | 1982 | 37 | 70 |
| 1923 | 41 | 9.2 | 1953 | 58 | 25 | | 1983 | 34 | 70 |
| 1924 | 39 | 9 | 1954 | 61 | 24 | | 1984 | 28 | 73 |
| 1925 | 33 | 9.6 | 1955 | 57 | 28 | | 1985 | 33 | 74 |
| 1926 | 35 | 10 | 1956 | 66 | 28 | | 1986 | 32 | 72 |
| 1927 | 29 | 12 | 1957 | 56 | 27 | | 1987 | 34 | 77 |
| 1928 | 31 | 13 | 1958 | 52 | 30 | | 1988 | 34 | 79 |
| 1929 | 28 | 13 | 1959 | 61 | 29 | | | | |
| 1930 | 34 | 12 | 1960 | 60 | 25 | | | | |
| 1931 | 36 | 12 | 1961 | 55 | 26 | | | | |
| 1932 | 27 | 19 | 1962 | 49 | 30 | | | | |
| 1933 | 33 | 20 | 1963 | 51 | 22 | | | | |
| 1934 | 29 | 24 | 1964 | 51 | 25 | | | | |

NOTE

SOURCES: As for table C1.

FOOTNOTES

[1] Creamery butter only in 1907 and from 1910 (2nd line) to 1920 (1st line).
[2] Government-inspected butter only.
[3] Subsequently including Alaska and Hawaii.

**C13    NORTH AMERICA: OUTPUT OF MEAT** (in thousands of metric tons)

| | Canada | Cuba | Dominican Republic | El Salvador | Guatemala | Honduras | Mexico | USA |
|---|---|---|---|---|---|---|---|---|
| 1899 | ... | ... | ... | ... | ... | ... | ... | 5,763 |
| 1900 | ... | ... | ... | ... | ... | ... | ... | 5,827 |
| 1901 | ... | ... | ... | ... | ... | ... | ... | 5,961 |
| 1902 | ... | ... | ... | ... | ... | ... | ... | 5,727 |
| 1903 | ... | ... | ... | ... | ... | ... | ... | 6,061 |
| 1904 | ... | ... | ... | ... | ... | ... | ... | 6,165 |
| 1905 | ... | ... | ... | ... | ... | ... | ... | 6,450 |
| 1906 | ... | ... | ... | ... | ... | ... | ... | 6,564 |
| 1907 | ... | ... | ... | ... | ... | ... | ... | 6,705 |
| 1908 | ... | ... | ... | ... | ... | ... | ... | 6,982 |
| 1909 | ... | ... | ... | ... | ... | ... | ... | 6,686 |
| 1910 | ... | ... | ... | ... | ... | ... | ... | 6,349 |
| 1911 | ... | ... | ... | ... | ... | ... | ... | 6,744 |
| 1912 | ... | ... | ... | ... | ... | ... | ... | 6,556 |
| 1913 | ... | ... | ... | ... | ... | ... | ... | 6,566 |
| 1914 | ... | ... | ... | ... | ... | ... | ... | 6,397 |
| 1915 | ... | ... | ... | ... | ... | ... | ... | 6,752 |
| 1916 | ... | ... | ... | ... | ... | ... | ... | 7,215 |
| 1917 | ... | ... | ... | ... | ... | ... | ... | 7,031 |
| 1918 | ... | ... | ... | ... | ... | ... | ... | 7,866 |
| 1919 | ... | ... | ... | ... | ... | ... | ... | 7,412 |
| 1920 | 488 | ... | ... | ... | ... | ... | ... | 6,955 |
| 1921 | 458 | ... | ... | ... | ... | ... | ... | 6,885 |
| 1922 | 522 | ... | ... | ... | ... | ... | ... | 7,320 |
| 1923 | 534 | ... | ... | ... | ... | ... | ... | 8,032 |
| 1924 | 566 | ... | ... | ... | ... | ... | ... | 7,981 |
| 1925 | 570 | ... | ... | ... | ... | ... | ... | 7,529 |
| 1926 | 582 | ... | ... | ... | ... | 8 | ... | 7,552 |
| 1927 | 591 | ... | ... | ... | ... | 8 | ... | 7,448 |
| 1928 | 579 | 63 | ... | ... | ... | 8 | ... | 7,370 |
| 1929 | 576 | 84 | ... | ... | ... | 8 | ... | 7,324 |
| 1930 | 532 | 87 | ... | ... | ... | 8 | ... | 7,265 |
| 1931 | 548 | 79 | ... | ... | ... | 9 | 169 | 7,464 |
| 1932 | 567 | 65 | ... | ... | ... | 9 | 167 | 7,447 |
| 1933 | 583 | 60 | ... | ... | ... | 10 | 180 | 7,900 |
| 1934 | 624 | 70 | ... | ... | 26 | 10 | 199 | 8,544 |
| 1935 | 603 | 65 | ... | ... | 38 | 11 | 204 | 6,544 |
| 1936 | 655 | 68 | 17 | ... | 28 | 11 | 214 | 7,603 |
| 1937 | 677 | 86 | 17 | ... | 26 | 11 | 220 | 7,125 |
| 1938 | 636 | 77 | 15 | 24 | 26 | 11 | 217 | 7,475 |
| 1939 | 643 | 81 | 14 | 24 | 27 | 11 | 219 | 7,958 |
| 1940 | 763 | 87 | 14 | 26 | 34 | 11 | 222 | 8,653 |
| 1941 | 913 | 97 | 15 | 26 | ... | 12 | 228 | 8,876 |
| 1942 | 991 | 109 | 15 | 28 | ... | 12 | 169 | 9,939 |
| 1943 | 1,079 | ... | 19 | 28[2] | ... | 13 | 161 | 11,105 |
| 1944 | 1,187 | ... | ... | ... | ... | 13 | 155 | 11,421 |

**C13    NORTH AMERICA: Output of Meat** (in thousands of metric tons)

| | Canada | Cuba | Dominican Republic | El Salvador[2] | Guatemala | Honduras | Jamaica | Mexico | Nicaragua | Panama | Puerto Rico | USA |
|---|---|---|---|---|---|---|---|---|---|---|---|---|
| 1945 | 1,127 | ... | ... | ... | ... | 13 | ... | 181 | ... | ... | ... | 10,746 |
| 1946 | 975 | ... | ... | ... | ... | 13 | ... | ... | ... | ... | ... | 10,396 |
| 1947 | 949 | ... | 23 | ... | ... | 13 | 10 | 203 | ... | ... | ... | 10,586 |
| 1948 | 887 | 77 | 22 | ... | ... | 14 | 11 | 203 | 15 | ... | ... | 9,662 |
| 1949 | 853 | 84 | 21 | ... | ... | 15 | 12 | 201 | 18 | ... | ... | 9,826 |
| 1950 | 827 | ... | ... | ... | 36 | 14 | 13 | 221 | ... | ... | ... | 10,013 |
| 1951 | 815 | 84 | ... | ... | 35 | 14 | 13 | 213 | ... | ... | ... | 9,933 |
| 1952 | 923 | 63 | ... | 21 | 35 | 15 | 13 | 219 | ... | 16 | ... | 10,430 |
| 1953 | 882 | ... | ... | 20 | 35 | 15 | 16 | ... | ... | ... | ... | 11,198 |
| 1954 | 924 | ... | ... | 19 | 39 | ... | 17 | 317 | ... | ... | ... | 11,437 |
| 1955 | 979 | ... | 20 | 20 | 41 | ... | 16 | 324 | ... | 19 | 17 | 12,199 |
| 1956 | 1,017 | ... | 22 | 20 | 35 | ... | ... | ... | ... | 20 | 18 | 12,716 |
| 1957 | 1,052 | ... | 22 | ... | 36 | ... | 15 | 396 | ... | 22 | 19 | 12,183 |
| 1958 | 1,069 | ... | 25 | ... | 38 | 15 | 15 | 415 | ... | 23 | 20 | 11,638 |
| 1959 | 1,161 | ... | 31 | ... | 38 | 16 | 16 | 411 | ... | 24 | 21 | 12,392 |
| 1960 | 1,114 | ... | 29 | ... | 41 | ... | 15 | 423 | ... | 23 | 20 | 12,795 |
| 1961 | 1,101 | ... | 29 | ... | 40 | 18 | 17 | 430 | 22 | 27 | 25 | 12,981 |
| 1962 | 1,102 | ... | 21 | 22 | 40 | 18 | 16 | 462 | 22 | 31 | 19 | 13,135 |
| 1963 | 1,155 | 229 | 26 | 24 | 43 | 21 | 16 | 485 | 22 | 32 | 26 | 13,861 |
| 1964 | 1,273 | 236 | 25 | 23 | 40 | 19 | 17 | 505 | 43 | 32 | 30 | 14,820 |
| 1965 | 1,335 | 242 | 26 | 23 | 42[1] / 52 | 21[1] / 28 | 17 | 532 | 39 | 32 | 32 | 14,288 |
| 1966 | 1,331 | 217 | 27 | 23 | 52 | 30 | 17 | 538 | 44 | 35 | 32 | 14,779 |
| 1967 | 1,401 | 217 | 34 | 38 | 62 | 32 | 17 | 583[6] / 788 | 48 | 34 | 32 | 15,510 |
| 1968 | 1,435 | 224 | 40 | 25 | 63 | 35 | 17 | 798 | 55 | 35 | 32 | 15,984 |
| 1969 | 1,363 | 225 | 42 | 26 | 70 | 39 | 19 | 816 | 62 | 37 | 32 | 16,009 |
| 1970 | 1,476 | 212 | 43 | 30 | 72 | 40 | 19 | 839 | 72 | 39 | 31 | 16,448 |
| 1971 | 1,578 | 200 | 45 | ... | 78 | 48 | 15 | 904 | 75 | 42 | 33 | 17,144 |
| 1972 | 1,558 | 191 | 53 | 36 | 79 | 50 | 17 | 879 | 74 | 45 | 35 | 16,810 |
| 1973 | 1,547 | 169 | 56 | 39 | 76 | 52 | 21 | 825 | 77 | 44 | 37 | 15,830 |
| 1974 | 1,595 | 152 | 57 | 45 | 70 | 44 | 21 | 920 | 64 | 46 | 37 | 17,188 |
| 1975 | 1,638 | 157 | 57 | 40 | 75 | 48 | 21 | 923 | 82 | 50 | 36 | 16,675 |
| 1976 | 1,706 | 169 | 63 | 45 | 91 | 51 | 20 | 944 | 92 | 54 | 40 | 17,965 |
| 1977 | 1,685 | 190 | 63 | 42 | 83 | 50 | 21 | 1,028 | 100 | 54 | 45 | 18,013 |
| 1978 | 1,682 | 204 | 69 | 47 | 86 | 63 | 21 | 1,058 | 100 | 47 | 51 | 17,497 |
| 1979 | 1,689 | 208 | 70 | 45 | 83 | 69 | 19 | 1,870[8] | 98 | 45 | 51 | 17,066 |
| 1980 | 1,832 | 206 | 62 | 44 | 72 | 73 | 21 | 2,044 | 66 | 48 | 38 | 17,680 |
| 1981 | 1,861 | 213 | 53 | 35 | 79 | 72 | 22 | 2,199 | 56 | 54 | 36 | 17,707 |
| 1982 | 1,866 | 214 | 55 | 35 | 72 | 57 | 21 | 2,284 | 68 | 60 | 37 | 17,045 |
| 1983 | 1,893 | 220 | 59 | 35 | 75 | 44 | 23 | 2,485 | 59 | 61 | 38 | 17,815 |
| 1984 | 1,865 | 229 | 61 | 36 | 74 | 46 | 24 | 2,432 | 59 | 64 | 39 | 17,819 |
| 1985 | 1,939 | 233 | 72 | 35 | 74 | 45 | 23 | 2,279 | 57 | 71 | 42 | 17,872 |
| 1986 | 1,953 | 243 | 74 | 36 | 57 | 38 | 23 | 2,269 | 59 | 73 | 50 | 17,824 |
| 1987 | 1,922 | 237 | 79 | 34 | 66 | 56 | 22 | 2,139 | 55 | 71 | 52 | 17,717 |
| 1988 | ... | 237 | 82 | 34 | 74 | 57 | 22 | 2,256 | 46 | 61 | 44 | 18,115 |

**C13** **SOUTH AMERICA: OUTPUT OF MEAT** (in thousands of metric tons)

| | Argentina[3] | Brazil | Chile[5] | Colombia | Uruguay[3] | Venezuela |
|---|---|---|---|---|---|---|
| 1910 | ... | ... | ... | ... | ... | ... |
| 1911 | ... | ... | ... | ... | ... | ... |
| 1912 | ... | ... | ... | ... | ... | ... |
| 1913 | ... | ... | ... | ... | ... | ... |
| 1914 | 1,118 | ... | ... | ... | ... | ... |
| 1915 | 1,104 | ... | ... | ... | ... | ... |
| 1916 | 1,226 | ... | ... | ... | ... | ... |
| 1917 | 1,291 | ... | ... | ... | ... | ... |
| 1918 | 1,519 | ... | ... | ... | ... | ... |
| 1919 | 1,233 | ... | ... | ... | ... | ... |
| 1920 | 1,113 | ... | ... | ... | ... | ... |
| 1921 | 1,186 | ... | ... | ... | ... | ... |
| 1922 | 1,571 | ... | ... | ... | ... | ... |
| 1923 | 1,884 | ... | ... | ... | ... | ... |
| 1924 | 2,117 | ... | ... | ... | ... | ... |
| 1925 | 2,034 | 724 | ... | ... | ... | ... |
| 1926 | 1,868 | 634 | ... | ... | ... | ... |
| 1927 | 1,944 | 740 | ... | ... | ... | ... |
| 1928 | 1,775 | 712 | ... | ... | ... | ... |
| 1929 | 1,747 | 677 | ... | ... | ... | ... |
| 1930 | 1,788 | 757 | ... | ... | ... | ... |
| 1931 | 1,638 | 745 | 135 | ... | 252 | ... |
| 1932 | 1,653 | 674 | 135 | ... | 198 | ... |
| 1933 | 1,741 | 864 | 135 | ... | 218 | ... |
| 1934 | 1,812 | 934 | 130 | 232 | 236 | ... |
| 1935 | 1,839 | 1,076 | 128 | 232 | 262 | ... |
| 1936 | 1,909 | 1,072 | 147 | 230 | 222 | ... |
| 1937 | 2,068 | 1,123 | 137 | 226 | 242 | ... |
| 1938 | 2,022 | 1,081 | 135 | 227 | 233 | ... |
| 1939 | 2,135 | 1,085 | 145 | 222 | 248 | 53 |
| 1940 | 2,011 | 979 | 157 | 221 | 230 | 64 |
| 1941 | 2,247 | 1,016 | 167 | 224 | 252 | 61 |
| 1942 | 2,234 | 1,019 | 167 | 248 | 252 | 63 |
| 1943 | 2,248 | 947 | 169[5] / 202 | ... | 285 | 60 |
| 1944 | 2,371 | 903 | 202 | ... | ... | 64 |
| 1945 | 2,113 | 901 | 216 | ... | 303 | 70 |
| 1946 | 2,207 | 1,011 | 219 | ... | ... | 77 |
| 1947 | 2,459 | 1,053 | 194 | ... | 293 | 73 |
| 1948 | 2,345 | 1,165 | 196 | ... | 313 | 74 |
| 1949 | 2,387 | 1,218 | 155 | 328 | 376 | 81 |

C13     **SOUTH AMERICA: Output of Meat** (in thousands of metric tons)

| | Argentina[3] | Bolivia[4] | Brazil | Chile[5] | Colombia | Ecuador | Paraguay | Peru | Uruguay[3] | Venezuela |
|---|---|---|---|---|---|---|---|---|---|---|
| 1950 | 2,372 | ... | 1,226[1] 1,461 | 152 | 335 | ... | ... | ... | 381 | 88 |
| 1951 | 2,171 | ... | 1,577 | 141 | ... | . . | ... | ... | 386 | 86 |
| 1952 | 2,117 | ... | 1,494 | 153 | ... | ... | 70 | ... | 382 | 88 |
| 1953 | 2,113 | ... | 1,555 | 160 | ... | ... | ... | ... | 409 | 96 |
| 1954 | 2,176 | ... | 1,611 | 188 | ... | ... | ... | ... | 349 | 98 |
| 1955 | 2,501 | ... | 1,576 | 153 | ... | ... | ... | ... | 342 | 101 |
| 1956 | 2,856 | ... | 1,752 | ... | ... | ... | ... | ... | 355 | 105 |
| 1957 | 2,827 | ... | 1,843 | 182 | ... | ... | ... | ... | ... | 113 |
| 1958 | 2,893 | 29 | 2,011 | 198 | ... | ... | ... | ... | 298 | 120 |
| 1959 | 2,281 | 18 | 1,964 | 202 | ... | 58 | ... | 148 | 297 | 135 |
| 1960 | 2,250 | 27 | 1,872 | 183 | ... | 59 | ... | 151 | 324 | 142 |
| 1961 | 2,509 | 28 | 1,945 | 199 | 427 | 61 | ... | 151 | ... | 164 |
| 1962 | 2,704 | 20 | 1,989 | 217 | 429 | 61 | ... | 148 | 341 | 167 |
| 1963 | 2,913 | 35 | 1,983 | 237 | 418 | 71 | 127 | 153 | 392 | 177 |
| 1964 | 2,308 | 37 | 2,065 | 208 | 468 | 72 | 141 | 164 | 442 | 190 |
| 1965 | 2,371 | 42 | 2,148 | 210 | 448 | 73 | 138 | 153 | 403 | 196 |
| 1966 | 2,742 | 42 | 2,173 | 225 | 480 | 70 | 151 | 170 | 334 | 212 |
| 1967 | 2,953 | 42[4] 74 | 2,226 | 223 | 483 | 83 | 153 | 174 | 323 | 223 |
| 1968 | 2,963 | 79 | 2,469 | 247 | 485 | 84 | 141 | 173 | 428 | 228 |
| 1969 | 3,292 | 82 | 2,619 | 242 | 500 | 86 | 136 | 186 | 451 | 259 |
| 1970 | 3,021 | 90 | 2,669 | 249 | 489 | 89 | 162 | 190 | 466 | 253 |
| 1971 | 2,448 | 91 | 2,657 | 228 | 531 | 92 | 164 | 191 | 356 | 267 |
| 1972 | 2,550 | 99 | 2,925 | 181 | 495 | 97 | 166 | 192 | 362 | 275 |
| 1973 | 2,545 | 106 | 2,961 | 161 | 499 | 98 | 164 | 189 | 368 | 309 |
| 1974 | 2,524 | 109 | 2,902 | 251 | 515 | 108 | 167 | 190 | 408 | 297 |
| 1975 | 2,825 | 113 | 2,981 | 269 | 577 | 114 | 156 | 188 | 412 | 357 |
| 1976 | 3,204 | 120 | 3,035 | 244 | 654 | 119 | 162 | 189 | 466 | 371 |
| 1977 | 3,192 | 128 | 3,337 | 223 | 650 | 128 | 186 | 189 | 405 | 363 |
| 1978 | 3,265 | 133 | 3,218 | 219 | 685 | 145 | 184 | 190 | 377 | 400 |
| 1979 | 3,415 | 142 | 3,066 | 232 | 703 | 154 | 190 | 187 | 318 | 421 |
| 1980 | 3,210 | 143 | 3,115 | 232 | 698 | 146 | 195 | 185 | 388 | 455 |
| 1981 | 3,313 | 150 | 3,119 | 261 | 747 | 139 | 204 | 195 | 454 | 434 |
| 1982 | 2,898 | 158 | 3,292 | 305 | 709 | 145 | 206 | 197 | 462 | 430 |
| 1983 | 2,708 | 172 | 3,302 | 319 | 689 | 150 | 210 | 216 | 493 | 442 |
| 1984 | 2,888 | 181 | 2,905 | 308 | 725 | 155 | 219 | 201 | 360 | 426 |
| 1985 | 3,077 | 194 | 3,061 | 259 | 740 | 157 | 225 | 195 | 393 | 454 |
| 1986 | 3,085 | 187 | 2,835 | 270 | 736 | 166 | 228 | 191 | 392 | 462 |
| 1987 | 3,041 | 198 | 3,311 | 282 | 720 | 168 | 212 | 216 | 381 | 425 |
| 1988 | 2,990 | 222 | 2,868 | 316 | 733 | 172 | 253 | 236 | 379 | 470 |

NOTES

1. SOURCES: As for table C1.
2. Except as indicated in footnotes, the statistics in this table generally relate to the carcass weight of beef and veal, lamb and mutton, and pork (excluding offal and edible fat) from indigenous animals. In some cases where it was a significant amount, goat meat is also included.

FOOTNOTES

[1] The reason for this break is not given in the source.
[2] Including meat from imported animals.
[3] Excluding production on farms.
[4] Commercial production only to 1967 (1st line).
[5] Excluding cold storage production and production on farms to 1943 (1st line).
[6] This break probably occurs through the inclusion of slaughterings on farms and in most small towns, which were previously excluded.
[7] Beef and pork only.
[8] There was a large unexplained increase in pork production in this year.

**C14    NORTH AMERICA: LANDINGS OF FISH** (in thousands of metric tons)

| Year | Newfound-land[2] |
|---|---|
| 1805 | ... |
| 1806 | 39 |
| 1807 | 34 |
| 1808 | 29 |
| 1809 | 41 |
| 1810 | 45 |
| 1811 | 47 |
| 1812 | 36 |
| 1813 | 45 |
| 1814 | 48 |
| 1815 | 55 |
| 1816 | 53 |
| 1817 | 52 |
| 1818 | 51 |
| 1819 | 47 |
| 1820 | 46 |
| 1821 | 46 |
| 1822 | 45 |
| 1823 | 44 |
| 1824 | 44 |
| 1825 | 49 |
| 1826 | 49 |
| 1827 | 46 |
| 1828 | 46 |
| 1829 | 47 |
| 1830 | 48 |
| 1831 | 38 |
| 1832 | 31 |
| 1833 | 35 |
| 1834 | 41 |
| 1835 | 36 |
| 1836 | 43 |
| 1837 | 40 |
| 1838 | 37 |
| 1839 | 44 |
| 1840 | 47 |
| 1841 | 51 |
| 1842 | 51 |
| 1843 | 48 |
| 1844 | 43 |
| 1845 | 51 |
| 1846 | 45 |
| 1847 | 43 |
| 1848 | 47 |
| 1849 | 60 |

| Year | Canada[1] | Newfound-land[2] | USA[3] |
|---|---|---|---|
| 1850 | ... | 55 | ... |
| 1851 | ... | 52 | ... |
| 1852 | ... | 49 | ... |
| 1853 | ... | 47 | ... |
| 1854 | ... | 39 | ... |
| 1855 | ... | 56 | ... |
| 1856 | ... | 64 | ... |
| 1857 | ... | 71 | ... |
| 1858 | ... | 53 | ... |
| 1859 | ... | 62 | ... |
| 1860 | ... | 68 | ... |
| 1861 | ... | 63 | ... |
| 1862 | ... | 65 | ... |
| 1863 | ... | 51 | ... |
| 1864 | ... | 52 | ... |
| 1865 | ... | 49 | ... |
| 1866 | ... | 45 | ... |
| 1867 | ... | 51 | ... |
| 1868 | ... | 45 | ... |
| 1869 | 70 | 56 | ... |
| 1870 | 79 | 59 | ... |
| 1871 | 92 | 59 | ... |
| 1872 | 112 | 57 | ... |
| 1873 | 120 | 67 | ... |
| 1874 | 109 | 81 | ... |
| 1875 | 102 | 58 | ... |
| 1876 | 113 | 54 | ... |
| 1877 | 111 | 53 | ... |
| 1878 | 123 | 53 | ... |
| 1879 | 145 | 71 | ... |
| 1880 | 149 | 70 | 774 |
| 1881 | 146 | 78 | ... |
| 1882 | 123 | 71 | ... |
| 1883 | 146 | 78 | ... |
| 1884 | 139 | 74 | ... |
| 1885 | 147 | 65 | ... |
| 1886 | 147 | 68 | ... |
| 1887 | 147 | 55 | ... |
| 1888 | 143 | 60 | ... |
| 1889 | 123[1] / 146 | 55 | 764 |
| 1890 | 141[1] | 53 | 797 |
| 1891 | 143 | 63 | 775 |
| 1892 | 153 | 53 | 749 |
| 1893 | 146 | 54 | ... |
| 1894 | 153 | 56 | ... |

| Year | Canada[1] | Cuba | Mexico | Newfound-land[2] | USA[3] |
|---|---|---|---|---|---|
| 1895 | 133 | ... | ... | 67[2] | ... |
| 1896 | 132 | ... | ... | 58 | ... |
| 1897 | 131[1] | ... | ... | 58 | ... |
| 1898 | 123 | ... | ... | 62 | ... |
| 1899 | 155 | ... | ... | 66 | ... |
| 1900 | 144 | ... | ... | 63 | ... |
| 1901 | 163 | ... | ... | 65 | ... |
| 1902 | 156 | ... | ... | 73 | ... |
| 1903 | 131 | ... | ... | 69 | ... |
| 1904 | 129 | ... | ... | 61 | ... |
| 1905 | 127 | ... | ... | 75 | 908 |
| 1906 | 114 | ... | ... | 72 | 928 |
| 1907 | ... | ... | ... | 77 | 875 |
| 1908 | 121 | ... | ... | 88 | 931 |
| 1909 | 140[1] | ... | ... | 76 | ... |
| 1910 | 162[1] / 350 | ... | ... | 60 | ... |
| 1911 | 338 | ... | ... | 71 | ... |
| 1912 | 322 | ... | ... | 72 | ... |
| 1913 | 326 | ... | ... | 63 | ... |
| 1914 | 316 | ... | ... | 56 | ... |
| 1915 | 325 | ... | ... | 72 | ... |
| 1916 | 300 | ... | ... | 80 | ... |
| 1917 | 302 | ... | ... | 93 | 1,214 |
| 1918 | 313 | ... | ... | 85 | ... |
| 1919 | 322[1] / 335 | ... | ... | 91 | ... |
| 1920 | 306 | ... | ... | 69 | ... |
| 1921 | 264 | ... | ... | 81 | 1,023 |
| 1922 | 325 | ... | 4 | 75 | 1,188 |
| 1923 | 289 | ... | 10 | 64 | 1,236 |
| 1924 | 334 | ... | 7 | 59[2] | 1,116 |
| 1925 | 358 | ... | 13 | 63 | 1,311 |
| 1926 | 400 | ... | 12 | 73[2] | 1,302 |
| 1927 | 349 | ... | 16 | 80 | 1,273 |
| 1928 | 390 | ... | 15 | 66 | 1,388 |
| 1929 | 346 | ... | 12 | 64[2] | 1,583 |
| 1930 | 347 | ... | 11 | 59 | 1,462 |
| 1931 | 294 | ... | 8 | 52 | 1,193 |
| 1932 | 266 | ... | 8 | 53 | 1,185 |
| 1933 | 286 | ... | 6 | 57 | 1,359 |
| 1934 | 315 | ... | 12 | 52 | 1,862 |
| 1935 | 311 | 7 | 11 | 53 | 1,876 |
| 1936 | 371 | 7 | 11 | 56 | 2,189 |
| 1937 | 353 | 8 | 12 | 47 | 1,974 |
| 1938 | 339 | 8 | 19 | 53 | 1,930 |
| 1939 | 374 | 7 | 57 | 46 | 2,016 |

**C14    NORTH AMERICA: Landings of Fish** (in thousands of metric tons)

|      | Canada[1] | Cuba | Mexico | Newfoundland[2] | Panama | USA[3] |
|------|-----------|------|--------|-----------------|--------|--------|
| 1940 | 431       | 7    | 63     | 58              | ...    | 1,842  |
| 1941 | 385       | 6    | 52     | 35              | ...    | 2,223  |
| 1942 | 399       | 4    | 54     | 39              | ...    | 1,758  |
| 1943 | 386       | 4    | 61     | 39              | ...    | 1,888  |
| 1944 | 390       | 5    | ...    | 39              | ...    | 2,056  |
| 1945 | 474       | 5    | ...    | 51              | ...    | 2,086  |
| 1946 | 492       | 5    | ...    | 52[2] 377       | ...    | 2,026  |
| 1947 | 454       | 9    | 54     | 363             | ...    | 1,973  |
| 1948 | 545       | 8    | 68     | 335             | ...    | 2,047  |
| 1949 | 489[1] 1,000 | 8 | 68     | ...             | ...    | 2,179  |
| 1950 | 1,048     | 8    | 74     | ...             | ...    | 2,223  |
| 1951 | 1,013     | 6    | 75     | ...             | ...    | 2,011  |
| 1952 | 940       | 9    | 58     | ...             | ...    | 2,010  |
| 1953 | 924       | 10   | 67     | ...             | 1      | 2,035  |
| 1954 | 1,027     | 12   | 91     | ...             | ...    | 2,155  |
| 1955 | 965       | 13   | 106    | ...             | ...    | 2,181  |
| 1956 | 1,106     | 16   | 145    | ...             | ...    | 2,390  |
| 1957 | 997       | 22   | 118    | ...             | ...    | 2,172  |
| 1958 | 1,008     | 22   | 164    | ...             | ...    | 2,153[3] |
| 1959 | 1,054     | 28   | 192    | ...             | 15     | 2,323  |
| 1960 | 935       | 31   | 198    | ...             | 11     | 2,242  |
| 1961 | 1,020     | 31   | 225    | ...             | 11     | 2,353  |
| 1962 | 1,124     | 35   | 219    | ...             | 14     | 2,429  |
| 1963 | 1,198     | 37   | 243    | ...             | 13     | 2,199  |
| 1964 | 1,211     | 37   | 249    | ...             | 26     | 2,060  |
| 1965 | 1,262     | 41   | 256    | ...             | 39     | 2,167  |
| 1966 | 1,346     | 44   | 287    | ...             | 72     | 1,980  |
| 1967 | 1,296     | 66   | 350    | ...             | 72     | 1,839  |
| 1968 | 1,499     | 66   | 364    | ...             | 72     | 1,887  |
| 1969 | 1,405     | 80   | 353    | ...             | 32     | 1,967  |
| 1970 | 1,389     | 106  | 387    | ...             | 52     | 2,230  |
| 1971 | 1,290     | 126  | 425    | ...             | 72     | 2,276  |
| 1972 | 1,132     | 140  | 426    | ...             | 63     | 2,760  |
| 1973 | 1,121     | 150  | 448    | ...             | 92     | 2,796  |
| 1974 | 974       | 165  | 402    | ...             | 69     | 2,847  |
| 1975 | 993       | 143  | 467    | ...             | 117    | 2,842  |
| 1976 | 1,102     | 194  | 479    | ...             | 184    | 3,050  |
| 1977 | 1,235     | 185  | 517    | ...             | 239    | 2,980  |
| 1978 | 1,367     | 213  | 782    | ...             | 139    | 3,416  |
| 1979 | 1,415     | 153  | 955    | ...             | 165    | 3,528  |
| 1980 | 1,347     | 186  | 1,222  | ...             | 216    | 3,654  |
| 1981 | 1,417     | 165  | 1,536  | ...             | 149    | 3,794  |
| 1982 | 1,403     | 195  | 1,321  | ...             | 117    | 4,033  |
| 1983 | 1,349     | 198  | 1,064  | ...             | 169    | 4,319  |
| 1984 | 1,284     | 200  | 1,104  | ...             | 142    | 4,991  |
| 1985 | 1,453     | 220  | 1,226  | ...             | 291    | 4,949  |
| 1986 | 1,510     | 245  | 1,305  | ...             | 144    | 5,167  |
| 1987 | 1,562     | 215  | 1,419  | ...             | 180    | 5,986  |
| 1988 | 1,597     | 231  | 1,363  | ...             | 112    | 5,966  |

**C14** **SOUTH AMERICA: LANDINGS OF FISH** (in thousands of metric tons)

| | Argentina | Brazil[3] | Chile | Colombia | Ecuador | Peru | Venezuela |
|---|---|---|---|---|---|---|---|
| 1930 | 44 | ... | ... | ... | ... | ... | ... |
| 1931 | 34 | ... | 17 | ... | ... | ... | ... |
| 1932 | 33 | ... | 23 | ... | ... | ... | ... |
| 1933 | 29 | ... | 27 | ... | ... | ... | ... |
| 1934 | 34 | ... | 26 | ... | ... | ... | ... |
| 1935 | 45 | ... | 29 | ... | ... | ... | ... |
| 1936 | 47 | ... | 35 | ... | ... | ... | ... |
| 1937 | 50 | ... | 37 | ... | ... | ... | ... |
| 1938 | 55 | ... | 32 | ... | 2 | 5 | ... |
| 1939 | 55 | 103 | 37 | ... | 2 | 5 | 22 |
| 1940 | 55 | 111 | 38 | ... | ... | 6 | 33 |
| 1941 | 60 | 116 | 37 | ... | ... | 12 | 43 |
| 1942 | 58 | 120 | 32 | ... | ... | 21 | 37 |
| 1943 | 62 | 123 | 41 | ... | ... | 27 | 59 |
| 1944 | 57 | 115 | 40 | ... | ... | 30 | 65 |
| 1945 | 54 | 122 | 47 | ... | ... | 32 | 68 |
| 1946 | 57 | 122 | 61 | ... | ... | 28 | 77 |
| 1947 | 65 | 140 | 61 | ... | 3 | 37 | 76 |
| 1948 | 71 | 144 | 65 | 15 | 3 | 48 | 92 |
| 1949 | 65 | 153 | 77 | ... | 5 | 45 | 75 |
| 1950 | 58 | 153 | 88 | ... | 15 | 74 | 78 |
| 1951 | 78 | 158 | 94 | 16 | 10 | 127 | 75 |
| 1952 | 79 | 175 | 119 | 16 | 9 | 137 | 63 |
| 1953 | 77 | 161 | 107 | 16 | 9 | 148 | 63 |
| 1954 | 78 | 172 | 144 | 16 | 13 | 176 | 52 |
| 1955 | 79 | 190 | 214 | 18 | 15 | 213 | 70 |
| 1956 | 75 | 208 | 188 | 21 | 22 | 322 | 61 |
| 1957 | 83 | 212 | 213 | 30 | 26 | 511 | 84 |
| 1958 | 84 | 212<u> </u>$_3$ | 226 | 25 | 31 | 961 | 78 |
| 1959 | 90 | 239 | 273 | 21 | 36 | 2,187 | 83 |
| 1960 | 105 | 251 | 340 | 30 | 44 | 3,569 | 85 |
| 1961 | 102 | 275 | 430 | 43 | 39 | 5,291 | 85 |
| 1962 | 101 | 379 | 643 | 48 | 43 | 7,164 | 95 |
| 1963 | 131 | 346 | 762 | 45 | 50 | 7,091 | 97 |
| 1964 | 169 | 369 | 1,161 | 50 | 46 | 9,322 | 111 |
| 1965 | 205 | 389 | 709 | 54 | 54 | 7,632 | 117 |
| 1966 | 251 | 393 | 1,383 | 59 | 48 | 8,845 | 114 |
| 1967 | 241 | 420 | 1,053 | 93 | 58 | 10,199 | 109 |
| 1968 | 224 | 495 | 1,393 | ... | 69 | 10,556 | 126 |
| 1969 | 181 | 492 | 1,095 | 58 | 87 | 9,244 | 134 |
| 1970 | 216 | 526 | 1,181 | 55 | 91 | 12,535 | 126 |
| 1971 | 218 | 582 | 1,487 | 38 | 107 | 10,529 | 139 |
| 1972 | 278 | 602 | 792 | 111 | 108 | 4,724 | 152 |
| 1973 | 276 | 699 | 664 | 105 | 154 | 2,329 | 162 |
| 1974 | 214 | 726 | 1,128 | 62 | 174 | 4,145 | 145 |

**C14    SOUTH AMERICA: Landing of Fish** (in thousands of metric tons)

|      | Argentina | Brazil | Chile | Colombia | Ecuador | Peru  | Venezuela |
|------|-----------|--------|-------|----------|---------|-------|-----------|
| 1975 | 214       | 753    | 899   | 67       | 224     | 3,446 | 153       |
| 1976 | 266       | 653    | 1,379 | 75       | 298     | 4,343 | 146       |
| 1977 | 380       | 748    | 1,319 | 64       | 433     | 2,549 | 146       |
| 1978 | 519       | 752    | 1,959 | 80       | 617     | 3,443 | 166       |
| 1979 | 568       | 779    | 2,630 | 63       | 605     | 3,652 | 169       |
| 1980 | 385       | 735    | 2,817 | 76       | 639     | 2,709 | 185       |
| 1981 | 361       | 755    | 3,394 | 95       | 539     | 2,717 | 185       |
| 1982 | 475       | 733    | 3,673 | 71       | 607     | 3,513 | 221       |
| 1983 | 416       | 754    | 3,978 | 58       | 372     | 1,569 | 231       |
| 1984 | 315       | 835    | 4,499 | 79       | 883     | 3,317 | 259       |
| 1985 | 406       | 838    | 4,804 | 72       | 1,087   | 4,136 | 265       |
| 1986 | 420       | 794    | 5,572 | 83       | 1,003   | 5,614 | 284       |
| 1987 | 559       | 733    | 4,815 | 86       | 680     | 4,584 | 309       |
| 1988 | 491       | 750    | 5,210 | 85       | 769     | 6,637 | 294       |

NOTES

1.    SOURCES: The national publications on p. xiv–xvi; League of Nations and UN, *Statistical Year-books;* and FAO, *Yearbook of Fisheries Statistics.*
2.    The definitions of fish landings vary from country to country, but except as indicated in footnotes they are generally consistent for each country.
3.    In general the statistics relate to fresh round weight.

FOOTNOTES

[1] Statistics to 1909 relate to cod, with haddock included from 1889 (1st line). The cod statistics are derived from O.E. Sette, *Statistics of the Catch of Cod off the East Coast of North America to 1926* (Ottawa, 1927), who converted marketings to fresh round weight. The haddock statistics are derived from A. W. H. Needler, *Statistics of the Haddock Fishery in North American Waters* (Ottawa, 1929), who converted marketings to fresh gutted weight. Haddock landings data are available for 1880–88 also, but were regarded as of doubtful accuracy by Needler. For what they are worth they are as follows:

| 1880 | 20 | 1883 | 31 | 1886 | 39 |
| 1881 | 21 | 1884 | 39 | 1887 | 39 |
| 1882 | 32 | 1885 | 34 | 1888 | 43 |

Statistics from 1910 (2nd line) onwards relate to the main species landed on both the Atlantic and Pacific Coasts, with inland fisheries included from 1919 (2nd line). The statistics are based on the records of the Dominion Bureau of Statistics, except that figures of West Coast halibut landings derived from Bell, Dunlop and Fremen, *Pacific Coast Halibut Landings 1888 to 1950 and Catch according to Area of Origin* have been preferred for the period 1915–50. (See *Historical Statistics of Canada,* pp. 389 and 392 for the reasons for this choice.) Data for 1909–16 are for years beginning 1 April. There is an adjustment to the recorded figure for 1897. Newfoundland is included from 1949.

[2] Data to 1946 (1st line) relate to exports of dried cod only. From 1896 to 1924 and from 1927 to 1929 the statistics are for years beginning 1 July. Newfoundland is included in Canada from 1949.

[3] Including whales to 1958.

**C15** **EXPORTS OF WHEAT BY MAIN TRADING COUNTRIES** (in thousands of metric tons)

| | NORTH AMERICA | | SOUTH AMERICA | | NORTH AMERICA | | SOUTH AMERICA |
|---|---|---|---|---|---|---|---|
| | Canada[1] | USA[2] | Argentina | | Canada[1] | USA[2] | Argentina |
| 1852 | ... | 73 | ... | 1900 | 265 | 2,775 | 1,930 |
| 1853 | ... | 92 | ... | 1901 | 711 | 3,594 | 904 |
| 1854 | ... | 219 | ... | 1902 | 898 | 4,215 | 645 |
| | | | | 1903 | 457 | 3,108 | 1,681 |
| 1855 | ... | 22 | ... | 1904 | 400 | 1,204 | 2,305 |
| 1856 | ... | 222 | ... | | | | |
| 1857 | ... | 397 | ... | 1905 | 1,099 | 120 | 2,868 |
| 1858 | ... | 243 | ... | 1906 | 1,073[1] | 962 | 2,248 |
| 1859 | ... | 82 | ... | 1907 | 1,188 | 2,084 | 2,681 |
| | | | | 1908 | 1,337 | 2,732 | 1,636 |
| 1860 | ... | 113 | ... | 1909 | 1,354 | 1,821 | 2,514 |
| 1861 | ... | 850 | ... | | | | |
| | | | | 1910 | 1,247 | 1,270 | 1,884 |
| 1862 | ... | 1,015 | ... | 1911 | 1,755 | 646[2] | 2,286 |
| 1863 | ... | 984 | ... | 1912 | 2,536 | 1,760 | 2,629 |
| 1864 | ... | 645 | ... | 1913 | 3,277 | 2,708 | 2,812 |
| | | | | 1914 | 1,957 | 4,732 | 981 |
| 1865 | ... | 270 | ... | | | | |
| 1866 | ... | 152 | ... | 1915 | 4,293 | 5,605 | 2,512 |
| | | | | 1916 | 5,161 | 4,193 | 2,295 |
| 1867 | ... | 167 | ... | 1917 | 4,093 | 2,890 | 936 |
| 1868 | 76 | 434 | ... | 1918 | 1,138 | 3,026 | 2,996 |
| 1869 | 97 | 478 | ... | 1919 | 2,122 | 4,030 | 3,286 |
| | | | | | | | |
| 1870 | 48 | 996 | — | 1920 | 3,517 | 5,941 | 5,008 |
| 1871 | 81 | 934 | - - | 1921 | 3,715 | 7,622 | 1,704 |
| 1872 | 119 | 719 | - - | 1922 | 5,853 | 4,482 | 3,802 |
| 1873 | 179 | 1,067 | - - | 1923 | 6,991 | 2,682 | 3,706 |
| 1874 | 119 | 1,933 | 0.4 | 1924 | 5,219 | 4,526 | 4,384 |
| | | | | | | | |
| 1875 | 165 | 1,444 | — | 1925 | 6,795 | 2,355 | 2,993 |
| 1876 | 65 | 1,499 | - - | 1926 | 6,763 | 3,764 | 2,035 |
| 1877 | 120 | 1,097 | 0.2 | 1927 | 7,264 | 4,580 | 4,226 |
| 1878 | 180 | 1,971 | 2.5 | 1928 | 10,082 | 2,621 | 5,296 |
| 1879 | 139 | 3,330 | 26 | 1929 | 4,817 | 2,452 | 6,613 |
| | | | | | | | |
| 1880 | 69 | 4,170 | 1.2 | 1930 | 5,912 | 2,390 | 2,213 |
| 1881 | 105 | 1,376 | 0.2 | 1931 | 5,207[1] | 2,185 | 3,639 |
| 1882 | 160 | 2,593 | 1.7 | 1932 | 6,211 | 1,494 | 3,442 |
| 1883 | 20 | 2,895 | 61 | 1933 | 5,234 | 242 | 3,929 |
| 1884 | 64 | 1,915 | 108 | 1934 | 4,570 | 463 | 4,794 |
| | | | | | | | |
| 1885 | 93 | 2,304 | 78 | 1935 | 4,509 | 6 | 3,860 |
| 1886 | 153 | 1,572 | 38 | 1936 | 6,614 | 51 | 1,610 |
| | | | | 1937 | 2,613 | 948 | 3,887 |
| 1887 | 59 | 2,775 | 238 | 1938 | 3,108 | 2,365 | 1,940 |
| 1888 | 13 | 1,790 | 179 | 1939 | 4,434 | 1,720 | 4,746 |
| 1889 | 11 | 1,263 | 23 | | | | |
| | | | | 1940 | 3,788 | 391 | 3,640 |
| 1890 | 57 | 1,480 | 328 | 1941 | 5,352 | 357 | 2,390 |
| 1891 | 237 | 1,500 | 396 | 1942 | 5,892 | 180 | 2,176 |
| 1892 | 252 | 4,280 | 470 | 1943 | 5,967 | 322 | 1,955 |
| 1893 | 252 | 3,188 | 1,008 | 1944 | 7,938 | 273 | 2,326 |
| 1894 | 240 | 2,406 | 1,608 | | | | |
| | | | | | | | |
| 1895 | 270 | 2,071 | 1,010 | | | | |
| 1896 | 214 | 1,651 | 532 | | | | |
| 1897 | 516 | 2,165 | 102 | | | | |
| 1898 | 280 | 4,034 | 645 | | | | |
| 1899 | 458 | 3,783 | 1,713 | | | | |

**C15    Exports of Wheat by Main Trading Countries** (in thousands of metric tons)

| | NORTH AMERICA | | SOUTH AMERICA | | NORTH AMERICA | | SOUTH AMERICA |
|---|---|---|---|---|---|---|---|
| | Canada[1] | USA[2] | Argentina | | Canada | USA | Argentina |
| 1945 | 8,973 | 3,504 | 2,358 | 1970 | 10,746 | 17,443 | 2,302 |
| 1946 | 4,288 | 5,093 | 1,387 | 1971 | 12,869 | 16,221 | 811 |
| 1947 | 4,366 | 4,552 | 2,284 | 1972 | 13,832 | 21,317 | 1,640 |
| 1948 | 3,692 | 8,913 | 2,174 | 1973 | 12,305 | 37,444 | 2,971 |
| 1949 | 5,726 | 9,261 | 1,847 | 1974 | 10,122 | 25,733 | 1,726 |
| 1950 | 4,436 | 5,605 | 2,767 | 1975 | 11,039 | 30,966 | 1,758 |
| 1951 | 6,452 | 11,497 | 2,455 | 1976 | 10,553 | 26,527 | 3,155 |
| 1952 | 9,140 | 10,056 | 63 | 1977 | 14,272 | 23,826 | 5,635 |
| 1953 | 7,890 | 6,408 | 2,527 | 1978 | 14,423 | 32,395 | 1,608 |
| 1954 | 5,667 | 5,226 | 2,943 | 1979 | 11,696 | 31,719 | 4,279 |
| 1955 | 5,167 | 6,025 | 3,617 | 1980 | 16,760 | 33,972 | 4,495 |
| 1956 | 8,227 | 11,131 | 2,526 | 1981 | 15,472 | 41,717 | 3,766 |
| 1957 | 6,323 | 11,276 | 2,660 | 1982 | 19,205 | 38,745 | 3,801 |
| 1958 | 7,393 | 8,994 | 2,113 | 1983 | 21,808 | 36,570 | 10,181 |
| 1959 | 7,173 | 9,731 | 2,399 | 1984 | 21,091 | 40,135 | 7,245 |
| 1960 | 6,606 | 13,745 | 2,486 | 1985 | 16,983 | 23,571 | 9,583 |
| 1961 | 9,964 | 17,158 | 1,066 | 1986 | 15,957 | 23,280 | 4,021 |
| 1962 | 8,047 | 14,139 | 2,832 | 1987 | 22,140 | 29,100 | 4,192 |
| 1963 | 10,731 | 17,473 | 1,831 | 1988 | 20,087 | 38,490 | 3,643 |
| 1964 | 13,615 | 20,575 | 3,710 | | | | |
| 1965 | 11,882 | 17,700 | 6,661 | | | | |
| 1966 | 14,577 | 22,483 | 5,055 | | | | |
| 1967 | 9,535 | 17,474 | 2,060 | | | | |
| 1968 | 9,246 | 16,118 | 2,423 | | | | |
| 1969 | 6,686 | 12,086 | 2,345 | | | | |
| 1970 | 10,746 | 17,443 | 2,302 | | | | |
| 1971 | 12,869 | 16,221 | 811 | | | | |
| 1972 | 13,832 | 21,317 | 1,640 | | | | |
| 1973 | 12,305 | 37,444 | 2,971 | | | | |
| 1974 | 10,122 | 25,733 | 1,726 | | | | |

NOTES

1.    SOURCES: The national publications on p. xiv–xvi, and F.A.O. *Yearbook of Food and Agricultural Statistics.*
2.    Earlier figures are available for the USA, and for some individual Canadian colonies, but the amounts involved are small.

FOOTNOTES

[1] Data to 1906 are for years beginning 1 July, and from 1907 to 1931 they are for years beginning 1 April.
[2] Years ending 30 June to 1911.

**C16** **NORTH AMERICA: EXPORTS OF SUGAR BY MAIN TRADING COUNTRIES** (in thousands of metric tons)

| | Barbados[1] | Guadeloupe | Jamaica | Martinique | Puerto Rico[2] | Trinidad & Tobago |
|---|---|---|---|---|---|---|
| 1816 | ... | 5.3 | ... | ... | ... | ... |
| 1817 | ... | 18 | ... | ... | ... | ... |
| 1818 | ... | 21 | ... | ... | ... | ... |
| 1819 | ... | 19 | ... | 16 | ... | ... |
| 1820 | ... | 22 | ... | 21 | ... | ... |
| 1821 | ... | 23 | ... | 22 | ... | ... |
| 1822 | ... | 23 | ... | 20 | ... | ... |
| 1823 | ... | 24 | ... | 21 | ... | ... |
| 1824 | ... | 31 | ... | 20 | ... | ... |
| 1825 | ... | 24 | ... | 26 | ... | ... |
| 1826 | ... | 34 | ... | 28 | ... | ... |
| 1827 | ... | 28 | ... | 25 | ... | ... |
| 1828 | ... | 36 | ... | 33 | ... | ... |
| 1829 | ... | 39 | ... | 29 | ... | ... |
| 1830 | ... | 23 | ... | 28 | ... | ... |
| 1831 | ... | 35 | 73 | 28 | ... | ... |
| 1832 | ... | 33 | 73 | 22 | ... | ... |
| 1833 | 19 | 31 | 62 | 20 | ... | 17 |
| 1834 | 20 | 38 | 71 | 26 | ... | 19 |
| 1835 | 18 | 32 | 69 | 24 | ... | 16 |
| 1836 | 19 | 35 | 61 | 22 | ... | 18 |
| 1837 | 23 | 25 | 55 | 20 | ... | 14 |
| 1838 | 23 | 35 | 64 | 26 | ... | 15 |
| 1839 | 20 | 37 | 43 | 29 | ... | 15 |
| 1840 | 10 | 30 | 29 | 22 | ... | 13 |
| 1841 | 13 | 29 | 30 | 25 | ... | 14 |
| 1842 | 14 | 35 | 45 | 28 | ... | 15 |
| 1843 | 18 | 27 | 35 | 25 | ... | 17 |
| 1844 | 16 | 35 | 31 | 33 | ... | 16 |
| 1845 | 19 | 34 | 42 | 30 | ... | 18 |
| 1846 | 15 | 26 | 31 | 26 | ... | 18 |
| 1847 | 25 | 38 | 45 | 31 | ... | 21 |
| 1848 | 20 | 20 | 34 | 18 | ... | 19 |
| 1849 | 25 | 18 | 35 | 20 | ... | 21 |
| 1850 | 32 | 13 | 30 | 15 | ... | 17 |
| 1851 | 35 | 20 | 25 | 23 | ... | 20 |
| 1852 | 44 | 17 | 27 | 26 | ... | 17 |
| 1853 | 33 | 17 | 21 | 22 | 114 | 22 |
| 1854 | 40 | 24 | 28 | 25 | 71 | 23 |
| 1855 | 36 | 22 | 26 | 21 | ... | 20 |
| 1856 | 39 | 23 | 23 | 28 | ... | 25 |
| 1857 | 34 | 22 | 28 | 26 | ... | 26 |
| 1858 | 47 | 28 | 32 | 28 | ... | 31 |
| 1859 | 39 | 29 | 28 | 30 | ... | 26 |

C16    **NORTH AMERICA: Exports of Sugar by Main Trading Countries** (in thousands of metric tons)

| | Barbados[1] | Cuba[4] | Dominican Republic[3] | Guadeloupe | Jamaica[5] | Martinique | Puerto Rico[2] | Trinidad & Tobago[6] |
|---|---|---|---|---|---|---|---|---|
| 1860 | 42 | ... | ... | 29 | 30 | 33 | ... | 27 |
| 1861 | 48 | ... | ... | 17 | 33 | 32 | ... | 28 |
| 1862 | 43 | ... | ... | 31 | 31 | 32 | ... | 37 |
| 1863 | 41 | ... | ... | 30 | 28 | 30 | ... | 34 |
| 1864 | 36 | ... | ... | 16 | 27 | 24 | ... | 36 |
| 1865 | 45 | ... | ... | 24 | 25 | 30 | ... | 28 |
| 1866 | 54 | ... | ... | 34 | 31 | 35 | ... | 41 |
| 1867 | 52 | ... | ... | 23 | 26 | 29 | ... | 42 |
| 1868 | 55 | ... | ... | 31 | 32 | 38 | ... | 42 |
| 1869 | 31 | ... | ... | 29 | 25 | 37 | ... | 47 |
| 1870 | 38 | ... | ... | 34 | 30 | 38 | 107 | 42 |
| 1871 | 52 | ... | ... | 38 | 36 | 42 | ... | 54 |
| 1872 | 38 | ... | ... | 32 | 34 | 40 | ... | 47 |
| 1873 | 36 | ... | ... | 36 | 27 | 38 | ... | 61 |
| 1874 | 46 | ... | ... | 35 | 27 | 43 | ... | 45 |
| 1875 | 63 | ... | ... | 48 | 27 | 51 | ... | 59 |
| 1876 | 37 | ... | ... | 35 | 28 | 39 | ... | 52 |
| 1877 | 46 | ... | ... | 43 | 29 | 41 | ... | 47 |
| 1878 | 42 | ... | ... | 48 | 25 | 44 | ... | 53 |
| 1879 | 55 | ... | ... | 48 | 28 | 47 | ... | 68 |
| 1880 | 52 | ... | 4.5 | 41 | 31 | 39 | ... | 54 |
| 1881 | 50 | ... | 4.2 | 42 | 20 | 42 | ... | 44 |
| 1882 | 52 | ... | 8.5 | 58 | 37 | 48 | ... | 56 |
| 1883 | 48 | ... | 8.4 | 52 | 30 | 47 | ... | 55 |
| 1884 | 56 | ... | 16 | 55 | 30 | 49 | ... | 62 |
| 1885 | 41 | ... | 19 | 41 | 25 | 39 | 90 | 65 |
| 1886 | 42 | ... | 10 | 37 | 17 | 30 | 66 | 49 |
| 1887 | 63 | ... | 9.4 | 55 | 23 | 40 | 81 | 68 |
| 1888 | 67 | ... | ... | 48 | 25 | 30 | 62 | 56 |
| 1889 | 60 | ... | ... | 45 | 16[5] | 36 | 62 | 51 |
| 1890 | 78 | 472 | ... | 47 | 19 | 34 | 58 | 53 |
| 1891 | 46 | 649 | ... | 30 | 22 | 32 | 51 | 47 |
| 1892 | 54 | 900 | ... | 46 | 19 | 20 | 42 | 51 |
| 1893 | 61 | 836 | ... | 41 | 21 | 33 | 43 | 47 |
| 1894 | 60 | 965 | ... | 44 | 20 | 37 | 48 | 48 |
| 1895 | 33 | 837 | ... | 30 | 20 | 29 | 60 | 56 |
| 1896 | 45 | 496 | ... | 43 | 16 | 34 | 56 | 56 |
| 1897 | 54 | 261 | 49 | 40 | 14 | 35 | 58 | 50 |
| 1898 | 49 | 200 | 51 | 37 | 18 | 32 | 56 | 52 |
| 1899 | 42 | 301 | 56 | 40 | 20 | 32 | 36 | 53 |
| 1900 | 46 | 320[4] | 54 | 28 | 15 | 34 | 74 | 41[6] |
| 1901 | 59 | 499 | 46 | 39 | 16 | 40 | 94 | 46 |
| 1902 | 48 | 808 | 46 | 41 | 21 | 40 | 83 | 48 |
| 1903 | 35 | 974 | 49 | 39 | 14 | 29 | 103 | 41 |
| 1904 | 57 | 1,131 | 48[3] | 36 | 10 | 24 | 118 | 48 |

**C16    NORTH AMERICA: Exports of Sugar by Main Trading Countries** (in thousands of metric tons)

| | Barbados[1] | Cuba[4] | Dominican Republic[3] | Guadeloupe | Jamaica[5] | Martinique | Puerto Rico[2] | Trinidad & Tobago[6] |
|---|---|---|---|---|---|---|---|---|
| 1905 | 42 | 1,103 | 48 | 27 | 12 | 30 | 123 | 37 |
| 1906 | 52 | 1,205 | 55 | 43 | 14 | 42 | 186 | 46 |
| 1907 | 35 | 1,326 | 49 | 39 | 11 | 37 | 185 | 47 |
| 1908 | 36 | 905 | 63 | 36 | [6.3][5] | 36 | 213 | 40 [6] |
| 1909 | 31 | 1,425 | 71 | 25 | 10 | 38 | 222 | 46 |
| 1910 | 46 | 1,778 | 93 | 43 | 20 | 40 | 258 | 47 |
| 1911 | 45 | 1,442 | ... | 37 | 20 | 35 | 293 | 39 |
| 1912 | 48 | 1,950 | ... | 38 | 10 | 40 | 330 | 34 |
| 1913 | 32 | 2,485 | 79 | 27 | 5 | 32 | 347 | 33 |
| 1914 | 55 | 2,529 | 101 | 40 | 16 | 39 | 291 | 49 |
| 1915 | 41 | 2,600 | 103 | 34 | 15 | 39 | 267 | 51 |
| 1916 | 75 | 2,978 | 123 | 34 | 29 | 34 | 385 | 59 |
| 1917 | 71 | 2,922 | 132 | 31 | 33 | 21 | 443 | 64 |
| 1918 | 58 | 2,309 | 120 | 27 | 27 | 21 | 364 | 36 |
| 1919 | 71 | 4,081 | 162 | 19 | 38 | 22 | 330 | 38 |
| 1920 | 49 | 3,169 | 159 | 24 | 37 | 20 | 401 | 49 |
| 1921 | 37 | 2,908 | 184 | 25 | 27 | 24 | 447 | 47 |
| 1922 | 52 | 5,064 | 172 | 20 | 52 | 19 | 364 | 53 |
| 1923 | 64 | 3,513 | 170 | 23 | 26 | 23 | 325 | 36 |
| 1924 | 55 | 4,029 | 221 | 27 | 24 | 31 | 382 | 44 |
| 1925 | 67 | 5,060 | 301 | 38 | 38 | 46 | 564 | 62 |
| 1926 | 65 | 4,809 | 338 | 34 | 49 | 43 | 521 | 67 |
| 1927 | 74 | 4,273 | 296 | 25 | 51 | 36 | 534 | 43 |
| 1928 | 83 | 4,038 | 348 | 31 | 50 | 38 | 614 | 75 |
| 1929 | 86 | 5,029 | 323 | 1 | 38 | 35 | 463 | 83 |
| 1930 | 76 | 3,311 | 351 | 25 | 60 | 37 | 736 | 70 |
| 1931 | 57 | 2,763 | 321 | 17 | 45 | 20 | 687 | 87 |
| 1932 | 98 | 2,659 | 440 | 45 | 39 | 48 | 813 | 87 |
| 1933 | 104 | 2,321 | 294 | 41 | 46 | 48 | 692 | 110 |
| 1934 | 118 | 2,341 | 334 | 29 | 55 | 45 | 753 | 95 |
| 1935 | 71 | 2,466 | 498 | 38 | 70 | 50 | 744 | 107 |
| 1936 | 122 | 2,640 | 435 | 43 | 79 | 51 | 785 | 145 |
| 1937 | 127 | 2,710 | 430 | 61 | 97 | 46 | 826 | 145 |
| 1938 | 103 | 2,641 | 406 | 45 | 107 | 51 | 775 | 122 |
| 1939 | 154 | 2,784 | 409 | 59 | 105 | 66 | 833 | 116 |
| 1940 | 87 | 2,099 | 418 | 60 | 83 | 58 | 763 | 79 |
| 1941 | 91 | 3,230 | 389 | 32 | 140 | 29 | 823 | 110 |
| 1942 | 66 | 1,799 | 193 | 17 | 130 | 16 | 814 | 86 |
| 1943 | 130 | 3,752 | 395 | 0.4 | 143 | 9.7 | 819 | 55 |
| 1944 | 119 | 3,935 | 755 | 43 | 134 | 34 | 649 | 56 |

**C16　　NORTH AMERICA: Exports of Sugar by Main Trading Countries** (in thousands of metric tons)

| | Barbados[1] | Cuba[4] | Dominican Republic[3] | Guadeloupe | Jamaica[5] | Martinique | Puerto Rico[2] | Trinidad & Tobago |
|---|---|---|---|---|---|---|---|---|
| 1945 | 123 | 3,752 | 330 | 113 | 120 | 48 | 806 | 60 |
| 1946 | 118 | 3,710 | 416 | 36 | 151 | 17 | 778 | 88 |
| 1947 | 106 | 5,486 | 469 | 29 | 130 | 14 | 841 | 91 |
| 1948 | 70 | 5,820 | 384 | 30 | 153 | 14 | 886 | 97 |
| 1949 | 142 | 4,883 | 442 | 42 | 196 | 18 | 1,042 | 141 |
| 1950 | 152 | 5,079 | 438 | 54 | 226 | 33 | 854 | 128 |
| 1951 | 175 | 5,389 | 482 | 72 | 216 | 46 | 945 | 119 |
| 1952 | 163 | 4,968 | 548 | 93 | 203 | 33 | 1,022 | 116 |
| 1953 | 154 | 5,391 | 555 | 84 | 279 | 50 | 1,025 | 132 |
| 1954 | 167 | 4,149 | 508 | 103 | 327 | 66 | 896 | 152 |
| 1955 | 159 | 4,613 | 575 | 126 | 294 | 78 | 972 | 172 |
| 1956 | 143 | 5,331 | 694 | 123 | 379 | 72 | 1,022 | 140 |
| 1957 | 196 | 5,366 | 766 | 113 | 308 | 59 | 820 | 144 |
| 1958 | 147 , 132 | 5,451 | 669 | 114 | 283 | 61 | 740 | 161 |
| 1959 | 159 | 4,876 | 668 | 136 | 317 | 69 | 861 | 154 |
| 1960 | 132 | 5,513 | 1,099 | 148 | 358 | 71 | ... | 191 |
| 1961 | 143 | 6,500 | 769 | 159 | 386 | 74 | ... | 219 |
| 1962 | 138 | 5,100 | 813 | 173 | 385 | 79 | ... | 171 |
| 1963 | 174 | 3,477 | 652 | 165 | 401 | 84 | ... | 196 |
| 1964 | 143 | 4,051 | 650 | 162 | 424 | 53 | ... | 196 |
| 1965 | 162 | 5,167 | 521 | 168 | 431 | 74 | ... | 216 |
| 1966 | 157 | 4,315 | 548 | 158 | 414 | 33 | ... | 173 |
| 1967 | 178 | 5,476 | 647 | 123 | 358 | 38 | ... | 163 |
| 1968 | 161 | 5,410 | 605 | 162 | 390 | 28 | ... | 205 |
| 1969 | 121 | 5,535 | 618 | 120 | 299 | 24 | ... | 204 |
| 1970 | 132 | 7,498 | 764 | ... | 298 | 16 | ... | 177 |
| 1971 | 118 | 5,511 | 994 | ... | 202 | 17 | ... | 174 |
| 1972 | 94 | 4,140 | 1,099 | 77 | 280 | 9.5 | ... | 191 |
| 1973 | 111 | 4,797 | 1,065 | 114 | 265 | 17 | ... | 148 |
| 1974 | 90 | 5,491 | 1,040 | 71 | 274 | 2.6 | ... | 176 |
| 1975 | 73 | 5,744 | 939 | 71 | 258 | 4.4 | ... | 110 |
| 1976 | 84 | 5,764 | 963 | 86 | 233 | 2.9 | ... | 158 |
| 1977 | 101 | 6,238 | 1,101 | 82 | 217 | 1.7 | ... | 140 |
| 1978 | 79 | 7,197 | 901 | 66 | 199 | 2.3 | ... | 103 |
| 1979 | 83 | 7,199 | 986 | 93 | 191 | 0.2 | ... | 88 |
| 1980 | 109 | 6,170 | 794 | 86 | 132 | — | ... | 64 |
| 1981 | 54 | 7,055 | 855 | 56 | 121 | 0.1 | ... | 67 |
| 1982 | 59 | 7,727 | 827 | 54 | 135 | - - | ... | 50 |
| 1983 | 48 | 7,011 | 916 | 41 | 137 | - - | ... | 63 |
| 1984 | 80 | 7,007 | 828 | 45 | 157 | — | ... | 64 |
| 1985 | 55 | 7,206 | 655 | 30 | 152 | — | ... | 66 |
| 1986 | 81 | 6,697 | 449 | 64 | 143 | — | ... | 57 |
| 1987 | 74 | 6,479 | 553 | 5.8 | 136 | — | ... | 47 |
| 1988 | 56 | 6,967 | 514 | 90 | 153 | — | ... | 54 |

**C16 SOUTH AMERICA: EXPORTS OF SUGAR BY MAIN TRADING COUNTRIES** (in thousands of metric tons)

| | 1821–1859 | | | | 1860–1899 | | |
|---|---|---|---|---|---|---|---|
| | Brazil[7] | Guyana*[3] | | | Brazil[7] | Guyana*[8] | Peru |
| | | | | 1860 | 90 | 60 | ... |
| 1821 | 35 | ... | | 1861 | 65 | 69 | ... |
| 1822 | 37 | ... | | 1862 | 155 | 62 | ... |
| 1823 | 54 | ... | | 1863 | 145 | 74 | ... |
| 1824 | 45 | ... | | 1864 | 95 | 71 | ... |
| 1825 | 35 | ... | | 1865 | 108 | 83 | ... |
| 1826 | 35 | 44 | | 1866 | 131 | 88 | ... |
| 1827 | 50 | 63 | | 1867 | 87 | 80 | ... |
| 1828 | 68 | 57 | | 1868 | 124 | 87 | ... |
| 1829 | 55 | 60 | | 1869 | 65 | 73 | ... |
| 1830 | 65 | 61 | | 1870 | 138 | 92 | ... |
| 1831 | 63 | 59 | | 1871 | 116 | 101 | ... |
| 1832 | 76 | 56 | | 1872 | 173 | 86 | ... |
| 1833 | [45][7] | 55<sub>3</sub> / 46 | | 1873 | 196 | 92 | ... |
| 1834 | 56 | 40 | | 1874 | 155 | 95 | ... |
| 1835 | 72 | 53 | | 1875 | 207 | 90 | ... |
| 1836 | 83 | 57 | | 1876 | 122 | 115 | ... |
| 1837 | 73 | 49 | | 1877 | 183 | 108 | ... |
| 1838 | 90 | 43 | | 1878 | 171 | 84 | ... |
| 1839 | 68 | 30 | | 1879 | 147 | 103 | ... |
| 1840 | 81 | 32 | | 1880 | 216 | 107 | 58 |
| 1841 | 98 | 27 | | 1881 | 161 | 101 | 44 |
| 1842 | 72 | 29 | | 1882 | 247 | 134 | 45 |
| 1843 | 77 | 29 | | 1883 | 179 | 125 | 35 |
| 1844 | 83 | 31 | | 1884 | 329 | 134 | 34 |
| 1845 | 110 | 28 | | 1885 | 274 | 103 | 46 |
| 1846 | 104 | 20 | | 1886 | 112 | 120 | 44 |
| 1847 | 104 | 35 | | 1887 | 226<sub>7</sub> | 145 | 36 |
| 1848 | 114 | 34 | | 1888 | 158 | 110 | 41 |
| 1849 | 125 | 30 | | 1889 | 106 | 117 | 53 |
| 1850 | 116 | 36 | | 1890 | 134 | 107 | 39 |
| 1851 | 132 | 42 | | 1891 | 185 | 119<sub>8</sub> | 38 |
| 1852 | 111 | 53 | | 1892 | 162 | 115 | 48 |
| 1853 | 158 | 52 | | 1893 | 104 | 110 | 44 |
| 1854 | 119 | 55 | | 1894 | 152 | 104 | 34 |
| 1855 | 120 | 53 | | 1895 | 164 | 103 | 59 |
| 1856 | 109 | 50 | | 1896 | 173 | 119 | 72 |
| 1857 | 113 | 56 | | 1897 | 128 | 103 | 105 |
| 1858 | 107 | 57 | | 1898 | 126 | 98 | 106 |
| 1859 | 156 | 54 | | 1899 | 50 | 86 | 104 |

**C16     SOUTH AMERICA: Exports of Sugar by Main Trading Countries** (in thousands of metric tons)

| | 1900–44 | | | | 1945–1988 | | |
|---|---|---|---|---|---|---|---|
| | Brazil | Guyana*[8] | Peru | | Brazil | Guyana* | Peru |
| 1900 | 92 | 96 | 112 | 1945 | 27 | 135 | 322 |
| 1901 | 187 | 107 | 115 | 1946 | 22 | 150 | 260 |
| 1902 | 137 | 122 | 117 | 1947 | 17 | 188 | 276 |
| 1903 | 22 | 128 | 128 | 1948 | 342 | 139 | 352 |
| 1904 | 7.9 | 108 | 132 | 1949 | 57 | 177 | 285 |
| 1905 | 38 | 118 | 134 | 1950 | 24 | 176 | 291 |
| 1906 | 85 | 117 | 137 | 1951 | 18 | 183 | 264 |
| 1907 | 13 | 102[8] | 111 | 1952 | 43 | 238 | 285 |
| 1908 | 32 | 117 | 125 | 1953 | 256 | 215 | 408 |
| 1909 | 68 | 110 | 125 | 1954 | 162 | 248 | 423 |
| 1910 | 58 | 103 | 123 | 1955 | 573 | 246 | 483 |
| 1911 | 36 | 101 | 124 | 1956 | 19 | 250 | 428 |
| 1912 | 4.8 | 79 | 148 | 1957 | 424 | 260 | 496 |
| 1913 | 5.4 | 89 | 143 | 1958 | 759 | 305 | 411 |
| 1914 | 32 | 109 | 176 | 1959 | 617 | 259 | 480 |
| 1915 | 59 | 120 | 220 | 1960 | 771 | 314 | ... |
| 1916 | 54 | 104 | 239 | 1961 | 783 | 318 | 557 |
| 1917 | 138 | 116 | ... | 1962 | 445 | 315 | 479 |
| 1918 | 116 | 96 | ... | 1963 | 524 | 278 | 496 |
| 1919 | 69 | 85 | 272 | 1964 | 253 | 238 | 425 |
| 1920 | 109 | 85 | 250 | 1965 | 760 | 317 | 366 |
| 1921 | 172 | 110 | 239 | 1966 | 1,005 | 283 | 430 |
| 1922 | 252 | 92 | 274 | 1967 | 1,001 | 298 | 475 |
| 1923 | 153 | 85 | 293 | 1968 | 1,026 | 298 | 467 |
| 1924 | 35 | 87 | 266 | 1969 | 1,099 | 332 | 270 |
| 1925 | 3.2 | 99 | 208 | 1970 | 1,126 | 283 | 435 |
| 1926 | 17 | 86 | 330 | 1971 | 1,261 | 342 | 432 |
| 1927 | 49 | 113 | 300 | 1972 | 2,535 | 305 | 430 |
| 1928 | 30 | 117 | 306 | 1973 | 2,798 | 229 | 452 |
| 1929 | 15 | 102 | 363 | 1974 | 2,254 | 307 | 429 |
| 1930 | 85 | 116 | 339 | 1975 | 1,515 | 289 | 420 |
| 1931 | 11 | 121 | 330 | 1976 | 807 | 300 | 299 |
| 1932 | 41 | 139 | 325 | 1977 | 1,830 | 230 | 434 |
| 1933 | 25 | 129 | 369 | 1978 | 1,347 | 285 | 249 |
| 1934 | 24 | 132 | 418 | 1979 | 1,394 | 268 | 283 |
| 1935 | 85 | 177 | 326 | 1980 | 1,961 | 252 | 54 |
| 1936 | 90 | 182 | 326 | 1981 | 1,785 | 269 | – |
| 1937 | 0.3 | 185 | 313 | 1982 | 1,550 | 255 | 140 |
| 1938 | 8.1 | 185 | 250 | 1983 | 1,721 | 211 | 17 |
| 1939 | 50 | 182 | 272 | 1984 | 1,848 | 215 | 40 |
| 1940 | 67 | 145 | 302 | 1985 | 1,356 | 230 | 60 |
| 1941 | 25 | 157 | 378 | 1986 | 1,234 | 219 | 52 |
| 1942 | 46 | 137 | 309 | 1987 | 1,101 | 195 | 30 |
| 1943 | 12 | 133 | 181 | 1988 | 984 | 143 | 36 |
| 1944 | 70 | 181 | 223 | | | | |

**C16     Exports of Sugar by Main Trading Countries** (in thousands of metric tons)

NOTES

1.  SOURCES: The main sources have been the national publications on p. xiv–xvi; League of Nations, *International Trade Statistics;* UN, *Yearbook of International Trade Statistics;* and FAO, *The World Sugar Economy in Figures, 1880–1959* (Rome, 1961). The Peru statistics to 1910 are from Rosemary Thorp and Geoffrey Bertram, *Peru, 1890–1977* (London, 1978). Dominican Republic statistics to 1904 are from Noel Deerr, *The History of Sugar* (London, 1949), who has a somewhat different series for the years that follow. His data apparently apply to crop-years beginning in the year shown, and they are probably incomplete prior to 1897. Deerr is also the source of British Guiana figures to 1832 (1st line), and this series is also different for later years than that shown here, which comes from the Sessional Papers of the UK Parliament. He gives earlier figures for British Guiana as follows (in thousands of metric tons):

| | | | | | | | | | |
|---|---|---|---|---|---|---|---|---|---|
| 1745 | 0.7 | 1755 | ... | 1765 | 2.3 | 1775 | ... | 1785 | 3.0 |
| 1746 | 0.8 | 1756 | 1.2 | 1766 | 2.5 | 1776 | 2.4 | | |
| 1747 | 0.3 | 1757 | 1.0 | 1767 | 2.5 | 1777 | 1.9 | 1804 | 1.4 |
| 1748 | 1.3 | 1758 | 0.5 | 1768 | 1.8 | 1778 | 4.2 | | |
| 1749 | 2.2 | 1759 | ... | 1769 | 2.1 | 1779 | 3.6 | | |
| 1750 | 1.5 | 1760 | 0.5 | 1770 | 3.5 | 1780 | 2.4 | | |
| 1751 | 0.9 | 1761 | 0.7 | 1771 | 1.9 | 1781 | 1.0 | | |
| 1752 | 1.6 | 1762 | 1.8 | 1772 | 2.0 | 1782 | ... | | |
| 1753 | 0.3 | 1763 | 1.8 | 1773 | 2.3 | 1783 | ... | | |
| 1754 | 0.2 | 1764 | 1.8 | 1774 | 3.2 | 1784 | 2.4 | | |

2.  Most statistics are of raw and refined sugar aggregates, but it is possible that in some the refined sugar component has been converted to raw equivalent.

FOOTNOTES

[1] Including the sugar equivalent of fancy molasses to 1958 (1st line).
[2] Years ending 30 June. Small amounts of exports other than to the USA may be excluded in 1910–19.
[3] See Note 1 above.
[4] Exports to the USA only to 1900.
[5] Years beginning 1 April from 1890 to 1907. The 1908 figure is for the last three quarters of the year.
[6] Years beginning 1 April from 1901 to 1908.
[7] Years ending 30 June from 1834 to 1887. The 1833 figure is for the first half-year. Exports in the second half of 1887 were 95 thousand tons.

**C17    EXPORTS OF PRINCIPAL LIVESTOCK PRODUCTS BY MAIN TRADING COUNTRIES** (in thousands of metric tons)

| | NORTH AMERICA | | | SOUTH AMERICA | | | |
| | Canada[1] | | USA[2] | Argentina | | Uruguay | |
| | Butter | Cheese | Meat | Meat[3] | Wool[4] | Meat[5] | Wool |
|---|---|---|---|---|---|---|---|
| 1850 | ... | ... | ... | ... | 7.7 | ... | ... |
| 1851 | ... | ... | ... | ... | ... | ... | ... |
| 1852 | ... | ... | 2.6 | ... | ... | ... | ... |
| 1853 | ... | ... | 8.3 | ... | 7.4 | ... | ... |
| 1854 | ... | ... | 21 | ... | 8.1 | ... | ... |
| 1855 | ... | ... | 17 | ... | 9.4 | ... | ... |
| 1856 | ... | ... | 19 | ... | 12 | ... | ... |
| 1857 | ... | ... | 20 | ... | 14 | ... | ... |
| 1858 | ... | ... | 9.5 | ... | 14 | ... | ... |
| 1859 | ... | ... | 5.4 | ... | 18 | ... | ... |
| 1860 | ... | ... | 12 | ... | 18 | ... | ... |
| 1861 | ... | ... | 23 | ... | 22 | ... | ... |
| 1862 | ... | ... | 64 | ... | 24 | ... | ... |
| 1863 | ... | ... | 99 | ... | 32 | ... | ... |
| 1864 | ... | ... | 50 | ... | 35 | ... | ... |
| 1865 | ... | ... | 21 | ... | 47 | ... | ... |
| 1866 | ... | ... | 17 [2] / 39 | ... | 55 | ... | ... |
| 1867 | ... | ... | 30 | ... | 56 | ... | ... |
| 1868 | 4.8 | 2.8 | 43 | ... | 65 | ... | ... |
| 1869 | 4.9 | 2.0 | 46 | ... | 58 | 32 | 19 |
| 1870 | 5.6 | 2.6 | 41 | ... | 58 | 26 | 13 |
| 1871 | 7.0 | 3.8 | 70 | ... | 57 | 26 | 16 |
| 1872 | 8.6 | 7.4 | 150 | ... | 67 | 34 | 16 |
| 1873 | 6.9 | 8.8 | 223 | ... | 72 | 37 | 16 |
| 1874 | 5.5 | 11 | 206 | ... | 69 | 36 | 17 |
| 1875 | 4.2 | 15 | 161 | ... | 66 | 23 | 10 |
| 1876 | 5.6 | 16 | 190 | ... | 79 | ... | ... |
| 1877 | 6.7 | 16 | 281 | ... | 84 | 23 | 17 |
| 1878 | 5.9 | 17 | 344 | ... | 91 [4] | 33 | 17 |
| 1879 | 6.5 | 21 | 412 | ... | 92 | 23 | 18 |
| 1880 | 8.4 | 18 | 448 | ... | 98 | 37 | 19 |
| 1881 | 8.0 | 18 | 456 | ... | 104 | 26 | 15 |
| 1882 | 6.9 | 23 | 302 | ... | 111 | 26 | 21 |
| 1883 | 3.7 | 26 | 239 | ... | 118 | 37 | 31 |
| 1884 | 3.7 | 32 | 279 | ... | 114 | 49 | 27 |
| 1885 | 3.3 | 36 | 290 | ... | 128 | 36 | 29 |
| 1886 | 2.1 | 35 | 302 | ... | 132 | 47 | 32 |
| 1887 | 2.5 | 33 | 284 / 303 | 12 | 109 | 29 | 26 |
| 1888 | 2.0 | 38 | 280 | 18 | 132 | 39 | 38 |
| 1889 | 0.8 | 40 | 321 | 17 | 142 | 39 | 45 |
| 1890 | 0.9 | 43 | 473 | 20 | 118 | 39 | 22 |
| 1891 | 1.7 | 48 | 487 | 23 | 139 | ... | 26 |
| 1892 | 2.6 | 54 | 473 | 25 | 155 | 40 | 28 |
| 1893 | 3.2 | 61 | 395 | 25 | 123 | 44 | 29 |
| 1894 | 2.5 | 70 | 400 | 36 [3] | 162 | 56 | 39 |

**C17 Exports of Principal Livestock Products by Main Trading Countries** (in thousands of metric tons)

1895–1934

| | NORTH AMERICA | | | SOUTH AMERICA | | | |
| | Canada[1] | | USA[2] | Argentina | | Uruguay | |
| | Butter | Cheese | Meat | Meat[3] | Wool[4] | Meat[5] | Wool |
|---|---|---|---|---|---|---|---|
| 1895 | 1.7 | 66 | 424 | 43 | 206 | 56 | 51 |
| 1896 | 2.7 | 75 | 446 | 48 | 192 | 56 | 43 |
| 1897 | 5.2 | 74 | 519 | 55 | 211 | 57 | 52 |
| 1898 | 5.1 | 89 | 587 | 66 | 228 | 52 | 41 |
| 1899 | 9.1 | 86 | 602 | $66_3$ | 244 | 60 | 39 |
| 1900 | 11 | 84 | 564 | 82 | 106 | 58 | 27 |
| 1901 | 7.4 | 89 | 577 | 109 | 235 | 47 | 46 |
| 1902 | 13 | 91 | 519 | 152 | 203 | 44 | 43 |
| 1903 | 15 | 104 | 411 | 164 | 200 | 58 | 45 |
| 1904 | 11 | 106 | 441 | 189 | 176 | 63 | 45 |
| 1905 | 14 | 98 | 428 | 233 | 199 | 50 | 33 |
| 1906 | $15_1$ | $98_1$ | 506 | 222 | 157 | 53 | 41 |
| 1907 | [8.2] | [81] | $448_2$ 620 | 210 | 162 | 56 | 45 |
| 1908 | 2.2 | 86 | 385 | 263 | 183 | 59 | 53 |
| 1909 | 2.9 | 75 | 289 | 282 | 185 | 63 | 58 |
| 1910 | 2.1 | 82 | 187 | 340 | 159 | 67 | 47 |
| 1911 | 1.4 | 83 | 242 | 414 | 141 | 69 | 61 |
| 1912 | 4 | 74 | 220 | 431 | 174 | 63 | 81 |
| 1913 | 0.4 | 70 | 230 | 425 | 131 | 81 | 68 |
| 1914 | 0.6 | 66 | 215 | 441 | 125 | 88 | 45 |
| 1915 | 1.2 | 62 | 594 | 430 | 137 | 122 | 38 |
| 1916 | 1.6 | 77 | 591 | 524 | 141 | 100 | 31 |
| 1917 | 3.6 | 82 | 600 | 536 | 161 | 122 | 40 |
| 1918 | 2.2 | 77 | 1,113 | 737 | 125 | 130 | 34 |
| 1919 | 6.2 | 69 | 1,004 | 581 | 167 | 155 | 66 |
| 1920 | 8 | 57 | 496 | 487 | 106 | 118 | 33 |
| 1921 | 4.4 | 61 | 361 | 471 | 170 | 96 | 57 |
| 1922 | 3.8 | 61 | 337 | 524 | 200 | 124 | 48 |
| 1923 | 10 | 52 | 456 | 703 | 153 | 157 | 44 |
| 1924 | 6.2 | 53 | 352 | 897 | 128 | 159 | 45 |
| 1925 | 11 | 58 | 269 | $828_3$ 886 | 144 | $179_5$ 155 | 41 |
| 1926 | ... | 69 | 211 | 837 | 146 | 150 | 54 |
| 1927 | ... | 48 | 160 | 902 | 158 | 132 | 69 |
| 1928 | ... | 51 | 163 | 707 | 127 | 88 | 53 |
| 1929 | 0.6 | 42 | 185 | 688 | 130 | 99 | 51 |
| 1930 | 0.5 | 36 | 181 | 639 | 136 | 140 | 75 |
| 1931 | 4.8 | 38 | 128 | 629 | 141 | 100 | 66 |
| 1932 | 1.6 | 39 | 94 | 574 | 131 | 72 | 43 |
| 1933 | 2 | 34 | 109 | 561 | 159 | 68 | 52 |
| 1934 | 0.2 | 28 | 120 | 560 | 111 | 59 | 24 |

**C17     Exports of Principal Livestock Products by Main Trading Countries** (in thousands of metric tons)

1935–1974

| | NORTH AMERICA | | | SOUTH AMERICA | | | |
| | Canada[1] | | USA[2] | Argentina | | Uruguay | |
| | Butter | Cheese | Meat | Meat[3] | Wool | Meat[4] | Wool |
|------|------|------|------|------|------|------|------|
| 1935 | 3.5 | 25 | 85 | 560 | 137 | 59 | 50 |
| 1936 | 2.3 | 37 | 78 | 586 | 140 | 48 | 46 |
| 1937 | 1.9 | 40 | 76 | 648 | 116 | 71 | 41 |
| 1938 | 1.8 | 37 | 94 | 639 | 152 | 75 | 54 |
| 1939 | 5.6 | 41 | 112 | 661 | 149 | 67 | 49 |
| 1940 | 0.6 | 48 | 100 | 537 | 136 | 62 | 55 |
| 1941 | 0.7 | 42 | 78 | 637 | 169 | 95 | 44 |
| 1942 | 0.7 | 64 | 47 | 697 | 100 | 70 | 19 |
| 1943 | 4.3 | 59 | 32 | 658 | 89 | 75 | 56 |
| 1944 | 2.1 | 60 | 44 | 789 | 90 | … | 60 |
| 1945 | 2.5 | 61 | 34 | 514 | 159 | 36 | 73 |
| 1946 | 2.0 | 48 | 53 | 548 | 206 | 41 | 57 |
| 1947 | 1.4 | 25 | 142 | 687 | 172 | 13 | 68 |
| 1948 | 0.4 | 18 | 63 | 509 | 182 | 40 | 56 |
| 1949 | 0.5 | 24 | 62 | 497 | 96 | 72 | 48 |
| 1950 | 0.7 | 29 | 61 | 346 | 142 | 76 | 90 |
| 1951 | 0.2 | 14 | 71 | 294 | 60 | 67 | 34 |
| 1952 | 0.4 | 1.0 | 84 | 236 | 106 | 54 | 46 |
| 1953 | 0.1 | 7.5 | 89 | 269 | 155 | 49 | 80 |
| 1954 | 0.1 | 2.3 | 78 | 284 | 98 | 52 | 54 |
| 1955 | 3.3 | 6.2 | 86 | 392 | 109 | 4.1 | 50 |
| 1956 | 1.0 | 5.5 | 115 | 574 | 109 | 35 | 64 |
| 1957 | - - | 3.8 | 122 | 601 | 88 | 38 | 28 |
| 1958 | - - | 7.1 | 77 | 655 | 105 | 21 | 59 |
| 1959 | 4.8 | 9.1 | 90 | 538 | 141 | 24 | 35 |
| 1960 | 1.4 | 8.6 | 89 | 438 | 140 | 52 | 35 |
| 1961 | - - | 8.9 | 88 | 436 | 140 | 43 | 72 |
| 1962 | - - | 12 | 84 | 570 | 159 | 55 | 46 |
| 1963 | 2.5 | 12 | 119 | 670 | 147 | 66 | 41 |
| 1964 | 17 | 14 | 143 | 544 | 102 | 125 | 22 |
| 1965 | 1.3 | 15 | 105 | 469 | 130 | 80 | 56 |
| 1966 | 0.1 | 16 | 106 | 560 | 151 | 65 | 41 |
| 1967 | - - | 13 | 112 | 546 | 122 | 65 | 45 |
| 1968 | - - | 20 | 131 | 407 | 139 | 110 | 52 |
| 1969 | - - | 16 | 149 | 578 | 109 | 126 | 38 |
| 1970 | - - | 18 | 131 | 513 | 102 | 160 | 45 |
| 1971 | 2.0 | 16 | 142 | 346 | 92 | 104 | 47 |
| 1972 | - - | 9.9 | 161 | 517 | 85 | 122 | 27 |
| 1973 | … | 5.5 | 193 | 425 | 81 | 106 | 21 |
| 1974 | … | 5.1 | | 182 | 46 | 109 | 29 |

**C17    Exports of Principal Livestock Products by Main Trading Countries** (in thousands of metric tons)

| | NORTH AMERICA | | SOUTH AMERICA | | | |
| | Canada | USA | Argentina | | Uruguay | |
| | Cheese | Meat | Meat | Wool | Meat | Wool |
|------|------|------|------|------|------|------|
| 1975 | 3.6 | 197 | 166 | 84 | 92 | 36 |
| 1976 | 2.4 | 263 | 364 | 92 | 155 | 24 |
| 1977 | 1.9 | 257 | 389 | 110 | 116 | 29 |
| 1978 | 2.2 | 284 | 435 | 107 | 103 | 32 |
| 1979 | 3.2 | 296 | 449 | 86 | 69 | 16 |
| 1980 | 3.1 | 282 | 293 | 91 | 111 | 41 |
| 1981 | 4.8 | 314 | 317 | 113 | 167 | 47 |
| 1982 | 5.1 | 299 | 345 | 84 | 141 | 45 |
| 1983 | 4.8 | 300 | 266 | 81 | 172 | 37 |
| 1984 | 5.4 | 307 | 163 | 74 | 106 | 28 |
| 1985 | 11.0 | 284 | 155 | 66 | 103 | 26 |
| 1986 | 12.0 | 352 | 158 | 69 | 156 | 40 |
| 1987 | 11.0 | 399 | 147 | 63 | 71 | 41 |
| 1988 | 10.0 | 474 | 170 | 53 | 92 | 34 |

NOTES

1.  SOURCES: The national publications on p. xii–xiv; League of Nations, *International Trade Statistics;* and UN, *Yearbook of International Trade Statistics.*
2.  The definition of meat is very variable, but it is believed that all changes have been noted in footnotes. Lard, tallow, etc, are probably not included in any case.

FOOTNOTES

[1] Data to 1906 are for years ending 30 June, and those for 1908 to 1931 are for years beginning 1 April. The 1907 figures are for the nine months from 1 July 1907 to 31 March 1908.

[2] Data to 1866 (1st line) are of bacon and hams only. From 1866 (2nd line) salt and fresh beef and pickled and fresh pork are also included. Mutton is included from 1877, but the effect of this on the continuity of the series is negligible, as is the exclusion of fresh pork and pickled beef from 1883. Canned beef is included from 1887 (2nd line). From 1907 (2nd line) the statistics relate to all meat and meat products except lard and tallow.

[3] Frozen mutton to 1894, frozen and chilled beef and mutton from 1895 to 1899, with preserved meat included from 1900. In both cases the break is negligible. From 1925 (2nd line) all kinds of meat are included.

[4] Exports from Buenos Aires for years ending 31 October to 1878.

[5] All kinds of meat to 1925 (1st line). Fresh, frozen, and chilled beef, mutton, and pork subsequently.

**C18   NORTH AMERICA: EXPORTS OF VARIOUS AGRICULTURAL COMMODITIES BY MAIN TRADING COUNTRIES** (in thousands of metric tons, except as otherwise indicated)

| | 1790–1834 | | | | 1835–1874 | | | | | |
|---|---|---|---|---|---|---|---|---|---|---|
| | Trinidad[1] | USA[2] | | | | Costa Rica | Guatemala | Trinidad[1] | USA[2] | |
| | Cocoa | Cotton[3] | Tobacco | | | Coffee | Coffee | Cocoa | Cotton[3] | Tobacco |
| | | | (million hogsheads) | | | | | | | (million hogsheads) |
| 1790 | ... | ... | 118 | | 1835 | ... | ... | 1.6 | 176 | 94 |
| 1791 | ... | - - | 101 | | 1836 | ... | ... | 1.4 | 192 | 109 |
| 1792 | ... | - - | 112 | | 1837 | ... | ... | 1.0 | 201 | 100 |
| 1793 | ... | - - | 60 | | 1838 | ... | ... | 1.2 | 270 | 111 |
| 1794 | ... | 1 | 77 | | 1839 | ... | ... | 1.2 | 188 | 79 |
| 1795 | ... | 3 | 61 | | 1840 | ... | ... | 1.0 | 337 | 119 |
| 1796 | ... | 3 | 69 | | 1841 | ... | ... | 1.1 | 240 | 148 |
| 1797 | ... | 2 | 58 | | 1842 | ... | ... | 1.3 | 265 | 159 |
| 1798 | ... | 4 | 69 | | 1843 | ... | ... | 0.9 | [359][2] | [94][2] |
| 1799 | ... | 5 | 96 | | 1844 | ... | ... | 1.0 | 301 | 163 |
| 1800 | ... | 8 | 79 | | 1845 | ... | ... | 1.4 | 396 | 147 |
| 1801 | ... | 10 | 104 | | 1846 | ... | ... | 1.1 | 249 | 150 |
| 1802 | ... | 13 | 78 | | 1847 | ... | ... | 1.6 | 239 | 136 |
| 1803 | ... | 19 | 86 | | 1848 | ... | ... | 1.0 | 369 | 131 |
| 1804 | ... | 17 | 83 | | 1849 | ... | ... | 2.1 | 464 | 102 |
| 1805 | ... | 17 | 71 | | 1850 | ... | ... | 1.6 | 288 | 146 |
| 1806 | ... | 16 | 83 | | 1851 | ... | ... | 2.5 | 421 | 96 |
| 1807 | ... | 29 | 62 | | 1852 | ... | ... | 3.1 | 496 | 137 |
| 1808 | ... | 5 | 10 | | 1853 | ... | ... | 2.2 | 504 | 160 |
| 1809 | ... | 23 | 54 | | 1854 | ... | ... | 1.5 | 448 | 126 |
| 1810 | ... | 42 | 84 | | 1885 | ... | ... | 2.1 | 457 | 150 |
| 1811 | ... | 28 | 36 | | 1856 | 7.6 | ... | 2.1 | 613 | 117 |
| 1812 | ... | 13 | 26 | | 1857 | 11 | ... | 2.2 | 475 | 157 |
| 1813 | ... | 9 | 5 | | 1858 | 6.1 | ... | 2.5 | 507 | 128 |
| 1814 | ... | 8 | 3 | | 1859 | 11 | ... | 2.7 | 629 | 199 |
| 1815 | ... | 38 | 85 | | 1860 | 9.1 | ... | 1.9 | 802 | 167 |
| 1816 | ... | 37 | 69 | | 1861 | 5.1 | ... | 3.0 | 139 | 161 |
| 1817 | ... | 39 | 62 | | 1862 | 4.9 | ... | 1.7 | [2.3][5] | 107 |
| 1818 | ... | 43 | 84 | | 1863 | 3.9 | ... | 3.4 | [5.2][5] | 112 |
| 1819 | ... | 40 | 69 | | 1864 | 5.1 | ... | 2.3 | [5.4][5] | 110 |
| | | | | | | | | | | (thousand metric tons) |
| 1820 | ... | 58 | 84 | | 1865 | 5.1 | ... | 3.1 | [3.9][5] | 68 |
| 1821 | ... | 57 | 67 | | 1866 | 6.1 | ... | 2.7 | 295 | 87 |
| 1822 | ... | 66 | 83 | | 1867 | 8.2 | ... | 3.6 | 300 | 84 |
| 1823 | ... | 79 | 99 | | 1868 | 9.1 | ... | 3.5 | 356 | 93 |
| 1824 | ... | 64 | 78 | | 1869 | 7.9 | ... | 2.9 | 292 | 83 |
| 1825 | ... | 80 | 76 | | 1870 | 9.4 | ... | 3.4 | 435 | 84 |
| 1826 | ... | 93 | 64 | | 1871 | 11 | 6.0 | 3.1 | 664 | 98 |
| 1827 | ... | 133 | 100 | | 1872 | 7.0 | 6.4 | 3.3 | 423 | 107 |
| 1828 | ... | 96 | 96 | | 1873 | 11 | 6.9 | 4.2 | 544 | 97 |
| 1829 | ... | 120 | 77 | | 1874 | 9.1 | 7.4 | 5.1 | 616 | 144 |
| 1830 | ... | 135 | 84 | | | | | | | |
| 1831 | ... | 126 | 87 | | | | | | | |
| 1832 | ... | 146 | 107 | | | | | | | |
| 1833 | 1.3 | 147 | 83 | | | | | | | |
| 1834 | 1.3 | 175 | 88 | | | | | | | |

**C18    NORTH AMERICA: Exports of Various Agricultural Commodities by Main Trading Countries** (in thousands of metric tons, except as otherwise indicated)

### 1875–1924

| | Costa Rica | Cuba | Dominican Republic | | El Salvador | | Guatemala |
|---|---|---|---|---|---|---|---|
| | Coffee | Tobacco | Cocoa | Tobacco | Coffee | Cotton | Coffee |
| 1875 | 11 | ... | ... | ... | ... | — | 7.5 |
| 1876 | 4.8 | ... | ... | ... | ... | — | 9.5 |
| 1877 | 11 | ... | ... | ... | ... | — | 9.6 |
| 1878 | 8.2 | ... | ... | ... | ... | — | 9.5 |
| 1879 | 11 | ... | ... | ... | ... | — | 11 |
| 1880 | 11 | ... | ... | ... | ... | — | 13 |
| 1881 | 7.8 | ... | ... | ... | ... | — | 12 |
| 1882 | 4 | ... | ... | ... | ... | — | 14 |
| 1883 | 9.2 | ... | ... | ... | 10 | — | 18 |
| 1884 | 17 | ... | ... | ... | 10 | — | 17 |
| 1885 | 9.2 | ... | ... | ... | ... | — | 24 |
| 1886 | 9.1 | ... | ... | ... | ... | — | 24 |
| 1887 | 13 | ... | ... | ... | ... | — | 22 |
| 1888 | 10 | ... | ... | ... | ... | — | 17 |
| 1889 | 13 | ... | ... | ... | ... | — | 25 |
| 1890 | 15 | ... | ... | ... | ... | — | 23 |
| 1891 | 14 | ... | ... | ... | ... | — | 24 |
| 1892 | 11 | ... | ... | ... | ... | — | 22 |
| 1893 | 11 | ... | ... | ... | ... | — | 27 |
| 1894 | 11 | ... | ... | ... | ... | — | 28 |
| 1895 | 11 | 14 | ... | ... | 15 | — | 32 |
| 1896 | 12 | 7.6 | ... | ... | ... | — | 32 |
| 1897 | 14 | ... | ... | ... | ... | — | 35 |
| 1898 | 20 | ... | ... | ... | ... | — | 38 |
| 1899 | 15 | ... | ... | ... | ... | — | 39 |
| 1900 | 16 | ... | ... | ... | ... | — | 34 |
| 1901 | 17 | 5.7 | ... | ... | 20 | — | 31 |
| 1902 | 14 | 7.5 | ... | ... | 19 | — | 36 |
| 1903 | 17 | 19 | 7.8 | ... | 27 | — | 27 |
| 1904 | 13 | 13 | 14 | ... | 35 | — | 30 |
| 1905 | 18 | 15 | 13 | ... | 28 | — | 37 |
| 1906 | 14 | 13 | 15 | ... | 29 | — | 32 |
| 1907 | 17 | 8.7 | 10 | ... | 26 | — | 51 |
| 1908 | 9.0 | 18 | 19 | ... | 25 | — | 26 |
| 1909 | 12 | 22 | 15 | ... | 29 | — | 41 |
| 1910 | 12 | 16 | 17 | 10 | 28 | — | 31 |
| 1911 | 13 | 14 | 20 | 14 | 30 | — | 36 |
| 1912 | 12 | 19 | 21 | 5.8 | 27 | — | 33 |
| 1913 | 13 | 14 | 15 | 10 | 29 | — | 40 |
| 1914 | 18 | 16 | 21 | 3.7 | 35 | — | 38 |
| 1915 | 12 | 17 | 20 | ... | 30 | — | 36 |
| 1916 | 17 | 18 | 22 | ... | 36 | — | 40 |
| 1917 | 12 | 13 | 23 | ... | 36 | — | 42 |
| 1918 | 11 | 12 | 19 | ... | 36 | — | 36 |
| 1919 | 14 | 16 | 22 | ... | 33 | — | 41 |
| 1920 | 14 | 13 | 23 | 16 | 38 | — | 43 |
| 1921 | 13 | 12 | 27 | 9 | 28 | — | 43 |
| 1922 | 19 | 16 | 19 | 8 | 43 | — | 43 |
| 1923 | 11 | 13 | 20 | 16 | 42 | - - | 44 |
| 1924 | 18 | 14 | 23 | 16 | 49 | 0.4 | 41 |

**C18**    **NORTH AMERICA: Exports of Various Agricultural Commodities by Main Trading Countries** (in thousands of metric tons, except as otherwise indicated)

**1875–1924**

| | Haiti[5] | Mexico | | Nicaragua | Trinidad | USA[2] | |
|---|---|---|---|---|---|---|---|
| | Coffee | Coffee | Cotton | Coffee | Cocoa | Cotton[3] | Tobacco |
| 1875 | ... | ... | ... | ... | 3.5 | 572 | 102 |
| 1876 | ... | ... | ... | ... | 4.9 | 676 | 99 |
| 1877 | ... | ... | ... | ... | 5.0 | 656 | 128 |
| 1878 | ... | 4.4 | - - | ... | 4.9 | 729 | 129 |
| 1879 | ... | 7.1 | - - | ... | 6.1 | 739 | 146 |
| 1880 | ... | 6.8 | ... | ... | 5.3 | 826 | 98 |
| 1881 | ... | 8.7 | ... | ... | 5.2 | 994 | 103 |
| 1882 | ... | 10 | ... | ... | 5.6 | 789 | 102 |
| 1883 | ... | 8.6 | — | ... | 5.8 | 1,038 | 107 |
| 1884 | ... | 6.9 | - - | ... | 6.7 | 845 | 94 |
| 1885 | ... | 5.8 | - - | ... | 6.8 | 858 | 99 |
| 1886 | ... | 8.4 | ... | ... | 9.0 | 934 | 128 |
| 1887 | ... | 8.3 | - - | ... | 6.2 | 984 | 133 |
| 1888 | ... | 6.5 | - - | ... | 11 | 1,027 | 113 |
| 1889 | ... | 9.2 | — | ... | 7 | 1,082 | 96 |
| 1890 | ... | 10 | — | ... | 11 | 1,121 | 111 |
| 1891 | ... | 15 | — | ... | 8.4 | 1,319 | 108 |
| 1892 | ... | 11 | — | ... | 13 | 1,331 | 109 |
| 1893 | ... | 15 | - - | ... | 9.9 | 1,003 | 112 |
| 1894 | ... | 19 | - - | ... | 11,[1] / 9.8 | 1,217 | 122 |
| 1895 | ... | 17 | - - | 9.0 | 12 | 1,595 | ... |
| 1896 | ... | 11 | - - | ... | 11 | 1,059 | ... |
| 1897 | ... | 15 | - - | ... | 11 | 1,408 | ... |
| 1898 | ... | 20 | - - | ... | 11 | 1,746 | 114 |
| | | | | | **Trinidad & Tobago** | | |
| 1899 | ... | 18 | - - | ... | 13 | 1,712 | 123 |
| 1900 | ... | 23 | 0.3 | ... | 14,[1] | 1,406 | 152 |
| 1901 | ... | 15 | 0.1 | ... | 14 | 1,511 | 139 |
| 1902 | 29 | 22 | 0.2 | 8.9 | 17 | 1,588 | 132 |
| 1903 | 22 | 19 | - - | 8.4 | 16 | 1,607 | 162 |
| 1904 | 22 | 18 | - - | 9.8 | 18 | 1,389 | 138 |
| 1905 | 28 | 19 | - - | 8.3 | 22 | 1,953 | 149 |
| 1906 | 29 | 19 | - - | 8.8 | 13 | 1,648 | 137 |
| 1907 | 27 | 14 | 8.0 | 9.1 | 23 | 2,049 | 151 |
| 1908 | 29 | 21 | 3.5 | 9.3 | 22,[1] | 1,731 | 147 |
| 1909 | 19 | 27 | 0.2 | 8.4 | 23 | 2,018 | 128 |
| 1910 | 36 | 19 | 0.3 | 12 | 26 | 1,455 | 160 |
| 1911 | 24 | 19 | 0.2 | 7.6 | 23 | 1,830 | 160 |
| 1912 | 36 | 21 | 0.4 | 6.2 | 19 | 2,511 | 170 |
| 1913 | 26 | ... | ... | 12 | 22 | 2,069 | 188 |
| 1914 | ... | ... | ... | 10 | 29 | 2,160 | 203 |
| 1915 | 16 | ... | ... | 9.1 | 25 | 1,998 | 158 |
| 1916 | 20 | ... | ... | 10 | 24 | 1,653 | 216 |
| 1917 | 24 | ... | ... | 8.4 | 32 | 1,123 | 114 |
| 1918 | 20 | ... | ... | 12 | 27 | 961 | 183 |
| 1919 | 49 | ... | ... | 15 | 28 | 1,528 | 347 |
| 1920 | 31 | 11 | 24 | 7.0 | 22 | 1,442 | 212 |
| 1921 | 21 | 15 | 36 | 14 | 34 | 1,515 | 234 |
| 1922 | 27 | 25 | 16 | 8.9 | 23 | 1,430 | 195 |
| 1923 | 36 | 18 | 2.9 | 14 | 31 | 1,244 | 215 |
| 1924 | 29 | 18 | 16 | 18 | 26 | 1,580 | 248 |

**C18    NORTH AMERICA: Exports of Various Agricultural Commodities by Main Trading Countries** (in thousands of metric tons, except as otherwise indicated)

### 1925–1969

| | Costa Rica | Cuba | Dominican Republic | | El Salvador | | Guatemala | |
|---|---|---|---|---|---|---|---|---|
| | Coffee | Tobacco | Cocoa | Tobacco | Coffee | Cotton | Coffee | Cotton |
| 1925 | 15 | 15 | 23 | 22 | 32 | 2.2 | 45 | — |
| 1926 | 18 | 18 | 20 | 10 | 51 | 0.3 | 43 | — |
| 1927 | 16 | 18 | 27 | 20 | 36 | - - | 53 | — |
| 1928 | 19 | 21 | 19 | 14 | 53 | - - | 44 | — |
| 1929 | 20 | 21 | 21 | 17 | 47 | - - | 44 | — |
| 1930 | 24 | 26 | 21 | 13 | 59 | 0.1 | 57 | — |
| 1931 | 23 | 18 | 26 | 6.8 | 55 | - - | 36 | — |
| 1932 | 19 | 16 | 17 | 4.4 | 40 | - - | 46 | — |
| 1933 | 28 | 13 | 20 | 5.7 | 56 | - - | 35 | — |
| 1934 | 19 | 12 | 22 | 9.7 | 50 | - - | 49 | — |
| 1935 | 24 | 14 | 28 | 6.9 | 50 | — | 40 | — |
| 1936 | 21 | 10 | 18 | 4.8 | 49 | — | 50 | — |
| 1937 | 23 | 12 | 20 | 3.2 | 67 | - - | 47 | — |
| 1938 | 22 | 13 | 28 | 7.4 | 53 | — | 49 | — |
| 1939 | 18 | 13 | 28 | 8.6 | 55 | — | 44 | — |
| 1940 | 18 | 12 | 23 | 3.6 | 56 | - - | 42 | — |
| 1941 | 21 | 13 | 19 | ... | 41 | 0.6 | 43 | — |
| 1942 | 20 | 12 | 18 | 3.4 | 52 | 0.9 | 56 | — |
| 1943 | 24 | 15 | 28 | 7.5 | 56 | 1 | 50 | — |
| 1944 | 19 | 15 | 26 | 0.9 | 63 | 0.9 | 51 | — |
| 1945 | 22 | 14 | 19 | 9.1 | 57 | 0.6 | 51 | — |
| 1946 | 16 | 21 | 25 | 29 | 48 | 1.0 | 50 | — |
| 1947 | 18 | 12 | 30 | 15 | 63 | 0.9 | 56 | — |
| 1948 | 24 | 13 | 26 | 14 | 60 | 3.3 | 49 | — |
| 1949 | 17 | 12 | 20 | 21 | 75 | 1.7 | 55 | — |
| 1950 | 17 | 62 | 26 | 14 | 69 | 3.0 | 55 | — |
| 1951 | 19 | 17 | 23 | 16 | 66 | 3.4 | 50 | — |
| 1952 | 21 | 18 | 22 | 15 | 67 | 6.5 | 61 | — |
| 1953 | 28 | 16 | 25 | 9.5 | 66 | 9.5 | 57 | — |
| 1954 | 23 | 19 | 21 | 12 | 62 | 9.1 | 52 | 5.2 |
| 1955 | 28 | 22 | 23 | 13 | 72 | 14 | 58 | 6.6 |
| 1956 | 23 | 21 | 18 | 13 | 65 | 30 | 63 | 8.2 |
| 1957 | 29 | 25 | 24 | 12 | 83 | 27 | 62 | 7.2 |
| 1958 | 46 | 26 | 21 | 12 | 81 | 33 | 71 | 10 |
| 1959 | 43 | 26 | 22 | 12 | 83 | 47 | 83 | 11 |
| 1960 | 47 | 26 | 27 | 15 | 90 | 30 | 80 | 13 |
| 1961 | 52 | ... | 15 | 22 | 87 | 40 | 79 | 22 |
| 1962 | 57 | ... | 21 | 18 | 105 | 60 | 84 | 32 |
| 1963 | 55 | 13 | 26 | 17 | 101 | 64 | 98 | 46 |
| 1964 | 51 | 17 | 28 | 25 | 109 | 65 | 76 | 64 |
| 1965 | 48 | 18 | 23 | 15 | 100 | 68 | 95 | 64 |
| 1966 | 55 | 11 | 26 | 13 | 97 | 44 | 109 | 82 |
| 1967 | 66 | 11 | 24 | 20 | 121 | 29 | 81 | 57 |
| 1968 | 69 | 16 | 25 | 16 | 118 | 22 | 94 | 65 |
| 1969 | 68 | 15 | 25 | 18 | 113 | 34 | 101 | 73 |

**C18    NORTH AMERICA: Exports of Various Agricultural Commodities by Main Trading Countries** (thousands of metric tons)

1925–1969

| | Haiti[5] | Mexico | | Nicaragua | | Trinidad & Tobago | USA[2] | |
|---|---|---|---|---|---|---|---|---|
| | Coffee | Coffee | Cotton | Coffee | Cotton | Cocoa | Cotton[3] | Tobacco |
| 1925 | 31 | 24 | 12 | 11 | — | 22 | 1,989 | 212 |
| 1926 | 36 | 21 | 28 | 18 | — | 23 | 2,128 | 217 |
| 1927 | 29 | 26 | 26 | 10 | — | 24 | 2,221 | 230 |
| 1928 | 41 | 32 | 23 | 18 | — | 26 | 2,028 | 261 |
| 1929 | 29 | 30 | 21 | 13 | — | 28 | 1,806 | 252 |
| 1930 | 34 | 31 | 3.0 | 15 | — | 24 | 1,584 | 254 |
| 1931 | 26 | 27 | 11 | 16 | — | 26 | 1,663 | 229 |
| 1932 | 23 | 20 | 5.5 | 8.1 | — | 19 | 2,180 | 176 |
| 1933 | 42 | 41 | 1.4 | 14 | — | 23 | 2,052 | 191 |
| 1934 | 34 | 38 | 3.5 | 15 | — | 12 | 1,428 | 190 |
| 1935 | 19 | 32 | 27 | 19 | — | 20 | 1,467 | 173 |
| 1936 | 36 | 43 | 52 | 13 | — | 13 | 1,349 | 185 |
| 1937 | 25 | 35 | 9.4 | 16 | — | 12 | 1,462 | 190 |
| 1938 | 25 | 35 | 22 | 14 | — | 19 | 1,108 | 215 |
| 1939 | 29 | 35 | 7.7 | 17 | — | 7.6 | 1,162 | 148 |
| 1940 | 16 | 26 | 5.4 | 15 | — | 11 | 928 | 98 |
| 1941 | 23 | 28 | 13 | 13 | — | 8.5 | 283 | 119 |
| 1942 | 18 | 22 | 0.5 | 13 | — | 4.6 | 244 | 108 |
| 1943 | 26 | 34 | 5.4 | 12 | — | 3.6 | 382 | 178 |
| 1944 | 23 | 36 | 29 | 13 | — | 4.8 | 241 | 127 |
| 1945 | 30 | 36 | 29 | 12 | — | 3.5 | 582 | 213 |
| 1946 | 24 | 33 | 46 | 12 | 0.1 | 3.0 | 907 | 291 |
| 1947 | 25 | 33 | 85 | 10 | 0.1 | 4.1 | 626 | 224 |
| 1948 | 23 | 31 | 49 | 15 | 0.1 | 8.3 | 669 | 188 |
| 1949 | 33 | 49 | 123 | 6.8 | 0.4 | 5.8 | 1,228 | 224 |
| 1950 | 23 | 46 | 163 | 21 | 0.3 | 7.4 | 1,344 | 214 |
| 1951 | 25 | 52 | 178 | 16 | 4.4 | 8.8 | 1,188 | 235 |
| 1952 | 31 | 52 | 230 | 19 | 9.5 | 6.4 | 971 | 177 |
| 1953 | 23 | 74 | 235 | 19 | 13 | 9.9 | 679[3] 642 | 233 |
| 1954 | 32 | 70 | 259 | 17 | 23 | 8.0 | 944 | 204 |
| 1955 | 20 | 84 | 352 | 23 | 44 | 7.5 | 564 | 243 |
| 1956 | 31 | 74 | 422 | 17 | 36 | 9.9 | 1,033 | 230 |
| 1957 | 18 | 89 | 284 | 22 | 36 | 7.3 | 1,574 | 223 |
| 1958 | 35 | 79 | 341 | 23 | 43 | 8.3 | 1,044 | 173 |
| 1959 | 22 | 74 | 407 | 16 | 62 | 7.3 | 834 | 208 |
| 1960 | 24 | 83 | 316 | 22 | 27 | 7.2 | 1,708 | 224 |
| 1961 | 20 | 93 | 305 | 21 | 33 | 5.7 | 1,450 | 227 |
| 1962 | 31 | 95 | 425 | 21 | 56 | 5.9 | 873 | 213 |
| 1963 | 23 | 68 | 370 | 24 | 73 | 6.6 | 989 | 229 |
| 1964 | 23 | 104 | 322 | 23 | 93 | 4.6 | 1,189 | 232 |
| 1965 | 23 | 81 | 409 | 28 | 125 | 4.9 | 807 | 212 |
| 1966 | 24 | 95 | 429 | 23 | 111 | 4.8 | 816 | 250 |
| 1967 | 17 | 78 | 271 | 26 | 110 | 4.7 | 901 | 259 |
| 1968 | 19 | 99 | 316 | 28 | 105 | 5.9 | 878 | 272 |
| 1969 | 19 | 97 | 370 | 27 | 91 | 3.9 | 544 | 262 |

**C18**  **NORTH AMERICA: Exports of Various Agricultural Commodities by Main Trading Countries** (in thousands of metric tons)

| | Costa Rica | Cuba | Dominican Republic | | El Salvador | | Guatemala | |
|---|---|---|---|---|---|---|---|---|
| | Coffee | Tobacco | Cocoa | Tobacco | Coffee | Cotton | Coffee | Cotton |
| 1970 | 69 | 14 | 34 | 20 | 112 | 42 | 96 | 50 |
| 1971 | 64 | 11 | 29 | 26 | 99 | 49 | 101 | 48 |
| 1972 | 86 | 12 | 33 | 33 | 104 | 59 | 115 | 75 |
| 1973 | 73 | 15 | 26 | 31 | 120 | 63 | 115 | 85 |
| 1974 | 90 | 16 | 28 | 42 | 145 | 44 | 122 | 107 |
| 1975 | 77 | 14 | 23 | 37 | 144 | 79 | 136 | 98 |
| 1976 | 64 | 15 | 25 | 33 | 154 | 52 | 119 | 93 |
| 1977 | 67 | 19 | 26 | 20 | 135 | 51 | 133 | 124 |
| 1978 | 86 | 14 | 28 | 27 | 65 | 77 | 132 | 128 |
| 1979 | 97 | 13 | 26 | 42 | 186 | 56 | 144 | 147 |
| 1980 | 72 | 2.7 | 24 | 21 | 147 | 53 | 129 | 137 |
| 1981 | 96 | 7.9 | 28 | 40 | 132 | 30 | 103 | 77 |
| 1982 | 94 | 18 | 40 | 12 | 141 | 32 | 141 | 67 |
| 1983 | 108 | 14 | 35 | 14 | 159 | 37 | 143 | 39 |
| 1984 | 113 | 9.8 | 32 | 16 | 161 | 5.5 | 127 | 52 |
| 1985 | 124 | 18 | 31 | 14 | 148 | 24 | 173 | 51 |
| 1986 | 94 | 15 | 36 | 18 | 123 | 5.9 | 155 | 37 |
| 1987 | 139 | 19 | 39 | 13 | 146 | 2.6 | 146 | 16 |
| 1988 | 120 | 19 | 47 | 17 | 123 | 3.5 | 141 | 32 |

| | Haiti | Mexico | | Nicaragua | | Trinidad & Tobago | U.S.A. | |
|---|---|---|---|---|---|---|---|---|
| | Coffee | Coffee | Cotton | Coffee | Cotton | Cocoa | Cotton | Tobacco |
| 1970 | 16 | 85 | 214 | 30 | 68 | 6.1 | 677 | 234 |
| 1971 | 22 | 97 | 166 | 33 | 78 | 3.6 | 936 | 217 |
| 1972 | 19 | 101 | 204 | 33 | 102 | 5.0 | 701 | 278 |
| 1973 | 19 | 137 | 179 | 38 | 100 | 3.5 | 1,246 | 284 |
| 1974 | 19 | 120 | 166 | 32 | 132 | 3.8 | 1,173 | 301 |
| 1975 | 18 | 143 | 157 | 41 | 133 | 4.8 | 871 | 265 |
| 1976 | 27 | 168 | 143 | 53 | 113 | 3.0 | 779 | 266 |
| 1977 | 16 | 103 | 131 | 50 | 116 | 3.2 | 1,013 | 291 |
| 1978 | 19 | 107 | 191 | 55 | 129 | 3.2 | 1,333 | 321 |
| 1979 | 14 | 115 | 212 | 56 | 114 | 2.7 | 1,508 | 260 |
| 1980 | 25 | 175 | 172 | 47 | 20 | 2.2 | 1,809 | 274 |
| 1981 | 14 | 122 | 183 | 53 | 75 | 3.0 | 1,269 | 267 |
| 1982 | 15 | 160 | 126 | 48 | 60 | 2.4 | 1,393 | 261 |
| 1983 | 24 | 220 | 70 | 56 | 79 | 1.7 | 1,204 | 240 |
| 1984 | 19 | 174 | 122 | 42 | 82 | 1.5 | 1,500 | 249 |
| 1985 | 18 | 227 | 77 | 40 | 67 | 1.3 | 1,095 | 251 |
| 1986 | 17 | 208 | 56 | 39 | 49 | 1.3 | 657 | 218 |
| 1987 | 13 | 223 | 52 | 38 | 47 | 1.5 | 1,195 | 199 |
| 1988 | 14 | 170 | 89 | 33 | 35 | 1.7 | 1,173 | 220 |

**C18 SOUTH AMERICA: EXPORTS OF VARIOUS AGRICULTURAL COMMODITIES BY MAIN TRADING COUNTRIES** (in thousands of metric tons)

| | Brazil[4] | | | | Colombia | Ecuador |
|---|---|---|---|---|---|---|
| | Cocoa | Coffee | Cotton | Rubber | Coffee | Cocoa |
| 1821 | 1.0 | 7.7 | 11 | ... | ... | ... |
| 1822 | 0.7 | 11 | 13 | ... | ... | ... |
| 1823 | 0.7 | 14 | 13 | ... | ... | ... |
| 1824 | 1.3 | 16 | 12 | ... | ... | ... |
| 1825 | 1.5 | 13 | 15 | ... | ... | ... |
| 1826 | 1.6 | 19 | 5.1 | ... | ... | ... |
| 1827 | 2.0 | 26 | 10 | - - | ... | ... |
| 1828 | 0.7 | 27 | 14 | 0.1 | ... | ... |
| 1829 | 1.2 | 28 | 14 | 0.1 | ... | ... |
| 1830 | 0.7 | 29 | 16 | 0.2 | ... | ... |
| 1831 | 0.9 | 33 | 16 | 0.1 | ... | ... |
| 1832 | 1.8 | 43 | 10 | 0.2 | ... | ... |
| 1833 | [0.8][4] | [34][4] | [7.3][4] | [0.1][4] | ... | ... |
| 1834 | 1.2 | 67 | 12 | 0.2 | ... | ... |
| 1835 | 0.8 | 58 | 11 | 0.2 | ... | ... |
| 1836 | 1.3 | 63 | 13 | 0.2 | ... | ... |
| 1837 | 1.2 | 55 | 13 | 0.3 | ... | ... |
| 1838 | 2.8 | 69 | 11 | 0.2 | ... | ... |
| 1839 | 3.0 | 80 | 9.4 | 0.4 | ... | ... |
| 1840 | 3.0 | 83 | 10 | 0.4 | ... | ... |
| 1841 | 2.9 | 74 | 10 | 0.4 | ... | ... |
| 1842 | 2.7 | 82 | 9.4 | 0.2 | 0.7 | ... |
| 1843 | 2.2 | 87 | 10 | 0.2 | 1.1 | ... |
| 1844 | 2.8 | 92 | 12 | 0.2 | 1.2 | ... |
| 1845 | 2.0 | 92 | 12 | 0.4 | 1.4 | ... |
| 1846 | 2.9 | 103 | 9.5 | 0.4 | ... | ... |
| 1847 | 3.0 | 143 | 8.9 | 0.6 | ... | ... |
| 1848 | 2.4 | 140 | 9.4 | 0.7 | ... | ... |
| 1849 | 3.7 | 126 | 13 | 0.8 | ... | ... |
| 1850 | 4.1 | 87 | 17 | 0.9 | ... | ... |
| 1851 | 3.9 | 149 | 13 | 1.4 | ... | ... |
| 1852 | 4.3 | 140 | 13 | 1.6 | ... | ... |
| 1853 | 3.4 | 146 | 15 | 1.6 | ... | ... |
| 1854 | 4.6 | 128 | 13 | 2.3 | ... | ... |
| 1855 | 2.2 | 191 | 13 | 2.9 | 2.1 | ... |
| 1856 | 2.4 | 171 | 15 | 2.1 | 2.1 | ... |
| 1857 | 3.5 | 191 | 16 | 1.6 | 2.5 | ... |
| 1858 | 3.6 | 143 | 15 | 1.6 | 2.9 | ... |
| 1859 | 4.1 | 164 | 17 | 1.7 | 3.3 | 6.8 |
| 1860 | 3.2 | 151 | 11 | 2.5 | 3.9 | 7.7 |
| 1861 | 3.5 | 214 | 9.0 | 2.5 | ... | 10.0 |
| 1862 | 3.0 | 145 | 13 | 2.3 | ... | 7.2 |
| 1863 | 3.9 | 128 | 16 | 3.1 | ... | 7.1 |
| 1864 | 3.4 | 120 | 20 | 3.4 | ... | 5.9 |

**C18  SOUTH AMERICA: Exports of Various Agricultural Commodities by Main Trading Countries** (in thousands of metric tons)

| | Argentina | | Brazil[4] | | | | Colombia | Ecuador | | Peru |
|---|---|---|---|---|---|---|---|---|---|---|
| | Linseed | Maize | Cocoa | Coffee | Cotton | Rubber | Coffee | Cocoa | Coffee | Cotton |
| 1865 | — | ... | 3.2 | 159 | 25 | 3.3 | 0.4 | 5.2 | ... | ... |
| 1866 | — | ... | 2.6 | 146 | 43 | 3.5 | 4.7 | 10 | ... | ... |
| 1867 | — | ... | 2.9 | 189 | 39 | 4.7 | 4.1 | 9.2 | ... | ... |
| 1868 | — | ... | 3.9 | 214 | 42 | 5.0 | 6.2 | 9.8 | ... | ... |
| 1869 | — | ... | 2.8 | 228 | 39 | 4.7 | 3.8 | 8.0 | 0.1 | ... |
| 1870 | — | ... | 4.6 | 187 | 43 | 4.8 | 4.0 | 11 | 0.1 | ... |
| 1871 | — | 0.1 | 4.5 | 230 | 45 | 5.0 | 6.4 | 8.5 | 0.2 | ... |
| 1872 | — | 0.1 | 5.5 | 244 | 79 | 5.7 | 8.0 | 8.4 | 0.3 | ... |
| 1873 | — | 1.5 | 4.3 | 210 | 46 | 5.1 | 7.4 | 12 | 0.3 | ... |
| 1874 | — | 3.5 | 4.6 | 166 | 56 | 6.7 | 10 | 11 | 0.5 | ... |
| 1875 | — | 0.2 | 5.3 | 231 | 44 | 5.8 | 4.6 | 8.1 | 0.5 | ... |
| 1876 | — | 8.1 | 5.2 | 204 | 28 | 5.7 | 3.4 | 10 | 0.4 | ... |
| 1877 | — | 9.8 | 5.8 | 213 | 31 | 6.2 | 2.2 | 9.3 | 0.5 | ... |
| 1878 | 0.1 | 17 | 4.6 | 231 | 18 | 6.6 | 4.6 | 4.6 | ... | ... |
| 1879 | 0.2 | 30 | 5.1 | 294 | 25 | 6.5 | 4.7 | 14 | 0.3 | ... |
| 1880 | 1 | 15 | 5.0 | 157 | 11 | 6.9 | 6.5 | 17 | 0.8 | 2.3 |
| 1881 | 6.4 | 25 | 6.8 | 220 | 13 | 6.7 | ... | 10 | 0.6 | 2.0 |
| 1882 | 23 | 107 | 7.5 | 245 | 22 | 6.8 | ... | 9.3 | 0.6 | 2.2 |
| 1883 | 23 | 19 | 6.8 | 401 | 34 | 7.5 | ... | 7.7 | 0.8 | 2.1 |
| 1884 | 34 | 114 | 7 | 319 | 33 | 9.2 | ... | 8.5 | 0.6 | 1.6 |
| 1885 | 69 | 198 | 6.2 | 374 | 24 | 7.9 | ... | 11 | 0.9 | 2.2 |
| 1886 | 38 | 232 | 4.2 | 326 | 15 | 8.2 | ... | 17 | 1.4 | 3.6 |
| 1887 | 81 | 362 | 6.9[4] | 365[4] | 23[4] | 8.6[4] | 6.7 | 16 | 1.1 | 2.5 |
| 1888 | 40 | 162 | 10 | 207 | 22 | 17 | ... | 11 | 1.4 | 3.7 |
| 1889 | 28 | 433 | 9.0 | 335 | 14 | 16 | ... | 12 | 1 | 3.4 |
| 1890 | 31 | 707 | 6.2 | 307 | 13 | 15 | ... | 16 | 1.2 | 4.2 |
| 1891 | 12 | 66 | 10 | 322 | 20 | 17 | ... | 9.7 | 1.3 | 4.8 |
| 1892 | 43 | 446 | 6.5 | 427 | 12 | 18 | ... | 15 | 1.7 | 9.8 |
| 1893 | 72 | 85 | 10 | 318 | 39 | 19 | ... | 19 | 1.9 | 8.0 |
| 1894 | 104 | 55 | 8.5 | 335 | 27 | 20 | 28 | 18 | 2.7 | 4.5 |
| 1895 | 276 | 772 | 11 | 403 | 9.5 | 28 | 29 | 17 | 2.6 | 5 |
| 1896 | 230 | 1,571 | 9.0 | 405 | 7.2 | 24 | 38 | 16 | 1.6 | 4.7 |
| 1897 | 162 | 375 | 10 | 568 | 12 | 22 | 34 | 15 | 1.2 | 5.6 |
| 1898 | 158 | 717 | 11 | 556 | 8.1 | 21 | 38 | 20 | 1.7 | 6.7 |
| 1899 | 218 | 1,116 | 13 | 586 | 3.7 | 21 | 23 | 24 | 1.2 | 5.9 |
| 1900 | 223 | 713 | 15 | 549 | 21 | 24 | ... | 18 | 1.5 | 7.2 |
| 1901 | 338 | 1,112 | 16 | 886 | 12 | 30 | ... | 22 | 1.3 | 8.0 |
| 1902 | 341 | 1,193 | 21 | 789 | 32 | 29 | ... | 22 | 2.2 | 6.7 |
| 1903 | 594 | 2,104 | 21 | 776 | 28 | 32 | ... | 23 | 1.8 | 7.7 |
| 1904 | 881 | 2,470 | 23 | 602 | 13 | 32 | ... | 29 | 3.5 | 7.5 |
| 1905 | 655 | 2,222 | 21 | 649 | 24 | 35 | 31 | 21 | 2.2 | 8.6 |
| 1906 | 538 | 2,694 | 25 | 838 | 32 | 35 | 38 | 23 | 2.7 | 10 |
| 1907 | 764 | 1,277 | 24 | 941 | 28 | 36 | 34 | 20 | 1.1 | 12 |
| 1908 | 1,056 | 1,712 | 33 | 759 | 3.6 | 38 | 36 | 32 | 3.7 | 16 |
| 1909 | 887 | 2,273 | 34 | 1,013 | 10 | 39 | 42 | 32 | 3.3 | 21 |

**C18** **SOUTH AMERICA: Exports of Various Agricultural Commodities by Main Trading Countries** (in thousands of metric tons)

| | Argentina | | Brazil | | | | Colombia | Ecuador | | Peru |
|---|---|---|---|---|---|---|---|---|---|---|
| | Linseed[6] | Maize | Cocoa | Coffee | Cotton | Rubber | Coffee | Cocoa | Coffee | Cotton |
| 1910 | 605 | 2,660 | 29 | 583 | 11 | 39 | 34 | 36 | 3.9 | 14 |
| 1911 | 416 | 125 | 35 | 675 | 15 | 37 | 38 | 39 | 4.6 | 16 |
| 1912 | 515 | 4,835 | 30 | 725 | 17 | 42 | 56 | 38 | 2.8 | 19 |
| 1913 | 1,017 | 4,807 | 30 | 796 | 37 | 36 | 61 | 39 | 3.7 | 24 |
| 1914 | 842 | 3,542 | 41 | 576 | 30 | 33 | 62 | 45 | 3 | 23 |
| 1915 | 981 | 4,331 | 45 | 1,024 | 5.2 | 35 | 68 | 35 | 2.3 | 21 |
| 1916 | 640 | 2,874 | 44 | 782 | 1.1 | 31 | 73 | 44 | 3.2 | 24 |
| 1917 | 141 | 894 | 56 | 636 | 5.9 | 34 | 63 | 42 | 2.7 | 17 |
| 1918 | 391 | 665 | 42 | 446 | 2.6 | 23 | 69 | 37 | 1.6 | 22 |
| 1919 | 855 | 2,485 | 63 | 778 | 12 | 33 | 101 | 42 | 1.7 | 38 |
| 1920 | 1,063 | 4,475 | 55 | 691 | 25 | 24 | 87 | 43 | 1.6 | 34 |
| 1921 | 1,357 | 2,830 | 43 | 742 | 20 | 17 | 141 | 41 | 6.1 | 36 |
| 1922 | 938 | 2,833 | 46 | 760 | 34 | 20 | 106 | 44 | 4.1 | 40 |
| 1923 | 1,036 | 2,839 | 65 | 868 | 19 | 18 | 124 | 31 | 5.6 | 43 |
| 1924 | 1,358 | 4,527 | 69 | 854 | 6.5 | 22 | 133 | 33 | 5.8 | 40 |
| 1925 | 961 | 2,936 | 64 | 809 | 31 | 24 | 117 | 33 | 4.1 | 42 |
| 1926 | 1,673 | 4,907 | 63 | 825 | 17 | 23 | 147 | 22 | 6.1 | 50 |
| 1927 | 1,895 | 8,344 | 75 | 907 | ... | 26 | 141 | 24 | 5.9 | 57 |
| 1928 | 1,944 | 6,372 | 72 | 833 | 10 | 19 | 160 | 23 | 9.2 | 47 |
| 1929 | 1,617 | 5,048 | 66 | 857 | 4.8 | 20 | 170 | 18 | 7.3 | 46 |
| 1930 | 1,170 | 4,670 | 67 | 917 | 30 | 14 | 190 | 20 | 9.5 | 55 |
| 1931 | 1,880 | 9,767 | 76 | 1,071 | 21 | 13 | 182 | 15 | 8.3 | 47 |
| 1932 | 2,028 | 7,055 | 98 | 716 | 0.5 | 6.2 | 191 | 15 | 8.0 | 46 |
| 1933 | 1,392 | 5,019 | 99 | 928 | 12 | 9.5 | 200 | 11 | 7.0 | 55 |
| 1934 | 1,374 | 5,471 | 102 | 849 | 127 | 11 | 185 | 19 | 14 | 68 |
| 1935 | 1,778 | 7,052 | 112 | 920 | 139 | 12 | 226 | 20 | 13 | 78 |
| 1936 | 1,488 | 8,382 | 122 | 851 | 200 | 13 | 236 | 20 | 14 | 81 |
| 1937 | 1,802 | 9,087 | 105 | 727 | 236 | 15 | 248 | 21 | 15 | 81 |
| 1938 | 1,265 | 2,642 | 128 | 1,027 | 269 | 12 | 254 | 18 | 14 | 69 |
| 1939 | 1,183 | 3,196 | 132 | 890 | 324 | 12 | 222 | 14 | 13 | 77 |
| 1940 | 752 | 1,875 | 107 | 723 | 224 | 12 | 267 | 11 | 15 | 51 |
| 1941 | 665 | 553 | 133 | 663 | 288 | 11 | 175 | 14 | 12 | 83 |
| 1942 | 315 | 220 | 72 | 437 | 154 | 12 | 259 | 14 | 6.1 | 34 |
| 1943 | 646 | 190 | 115 | 607 | 78 | 15 | 315 | 18 | 12 | 36 |
| 1944 | 275[6] | 550 | 102 | 813 | 108 | 21 | 294 | 14 | 14 | 26 |
| 1945 | 46 | 572 | 83 | 850 | 164 | 19 | 309 | 17 | 11 | 60 |
| 1946 | 148 | 2,200 | 130 | 930 | 353 | 18 | 340 | 17 | 7.6 | 120 |
| 1947 | 214 | 2,366 | 99 | 890 | 285 | 14 | 320 | 20 | 10 | 56 |
| 1948 | 46 | 2,534 | 72 | 1,050 | 259 | 5.4 | 335 | 17 | 20 | 52 |
| 1949 | 69 | 1,063 | 132 | 1,162 | 140 | 3.2 | 325 | 20 | 10 | 42 |
| 1950 | 206 | 794 | 132 | 890 | 129 | 4.5 | 269 | 26 | 20 | 66 |
| 1951 | 258 | 298 | 96 | 982 | 143 | 5.4 | 288 | 24 | 17 | 62 |
| 1952 | 28 | 652 | 58 | 949 | 28 | 3.2 | 302 | 24 | 20 | 83 |
| 1953 | 113 | 1,083 | 109 | 933 | 140 | 3.7 | 398 | 22 | 18 | 90 |
| 1954 | 245 | 2,185 | 121 | 655 | 309 | 4.3 | 345 | 31 | 21 | 84 |

**C18** **SOUTH AMERICA: Exports of Various Agricultural Commodities by Main Trading Countries** (in thousands of metric tons)

| | Argentina | | Brazil | | | | Colombia | Ecuador | | Peru |
|---|---|---|---|---|---|---|---|---|---|---|
| | Linseed[6] | Maize | Cocoa | Coffee | Cotton | Rubber | Coffee | Cocoa | Coffee | Cotton |
| 1955 | 156 | 362 | 122 | 822 | 176 | 3.4 | 352 | 25 | 23 | 85 |
| 1956 | 61 | 1,065 | 126 | 1,008 | 143 | 2.6 | 304 | 30 | 26 | 109 |
| 1957 | 141 | 789 | 110 | 859 | 66 | 3.0 | 289 | 27 | 29 | 82 |
| 1958 | 162 | 1,679 | 103 | 773 | 40 | 2.4 | 326 | 22 | 30 | 108 |
| 1959 | 218 | 2,686 | 80 | 1,046 | 78 | 3.0 | 385 | 29 | 24 | 115 |
| 1960 | 169 | 2,570 | 125 | 1,009 | 95 | 3.5 | 356 | 36 | 32 | 100 |
| 1961 | 204 | 1,730 | 120 | 1,018 | 206 | 8.1 | 339 | 33 | 23 | 114 |
| 1962 | 264 | 2,931 | 73 | 983 | 216 | 5.8 | 394 | 32 | 33 | 140 |
| 1963 | 213 | 2,447 | 83 | 1,171 | 222 | 2.7 | 368 | 35 | 30 | 125 |
| 1964 | 205 | 3,339 | 86 | 987 | 217 | 4.2 | 385 | 27 | 25 | 116 |
| 1965 | 239 | 2,804 | 110 | 810 | 196 | 7.9 | 338 | 39 | 48 | 116 |
| 1966 | 121 | 3,752 | 135 | 1,114 | 236 | 4.7 | 334 | 32 | 43 | 115 |
| 1967 | 211 | 4,318 | 136 | 1,116 | 189 | 5.7 | 366 | 45 | 58 | 70 |
| 1968 | 79 | 2,893 | 96 | 1,119 | 248 | 4.6 | 395 | 70 | 49 | 68 —[7] 67 |
| 1969 | 147 | 4,024 | 137 | 1,140 | 439 | 4.8 | ... | 35 | 38 | 88 |
| 1970 | — | 5,232 | 141 | 983 | 396 | 5.3 | 394 | 40 | 52 | 69 |
| 1971 | 183 | 6,128 | 163 | 1,058 | 261 | 5.0 | 390 | ... | ... | 52 |
| 1972 | 106 | 3,005 | 157 | 1,084 | 305 | 4.1 | 391 | 54 | 61 | 50 |
| 1973 | 97 | 4,033 | 134 | 1,111 | 283 | 4.0 | 405 | 39 | 76 | 48 |
| 1974 | 80 | 5,525 | 186 | 721 | 83 | 1.8 | 412 | 80 | 60 | 46 |
| 1975 | 84 | 3,887 | 223 | 813 | 107 | 1.7 | 490 | 53 | 61 | 37 |
| 1976 | 113 | 3,080 | 177 | 849 | 6 | 1.0 | 373 | 50 | 87 | 39 |
| 1977 | 199 | 5,431 | 146 | 544 | 35 | 1.0 | 310 | 60 | 54 | 21 |
| 1978 | 240 | 5,895 | 226 | 665 | 45 | 0.9 | 536 | 71 | 99 | 18 |
| 1979 | 184 | 5,960 | 270 | 615 | 0.3 | 0.3 | 659 | 75 | 84 | 16 |
| 1980 | 223 | 3,481 | 245 | 826 | 9 | 0.1 | 663 | 72 | 56 | 30 |
| 1981 | 175 | 9,164 | 254 | 874 | 30 | 0.1 | 544 | 66 | 59 | 31 |
| 1982 | 176 | 5,226 | 240 | 938 | 56 | - - | 532 | 61 | 79 | 53 |
| 1983 | 203 | 6,525 | 271 | 986 | 180 | - - | 553 | 13 | 80 | 20 |
| 1984 | 212 | 5,518 | 248 | 1,032 | 32 | 0.1 | 599 | 54[8] 47 | 72 | 8 |
| 1985 | 142 | 7,069 | 323 | 1,034 | 87 | - - | 585 | 69 | 75 | 25 |
| 1986 | 126 | 7,411 | 272 | 478 | 37 | - - | 667 | 38 | 109 | 21 |
| 1987 | 183 | 3,987 | 275 | 988 | 174 | — | 662 | 44 | 102 | 9 |
| 1988 | 152 | 4,217 | 278 | 904 | 35 | - - | 568 | 45 | 76 | 10 |

**C18** **Exports of Various Agricultural Commodities by Main Trading Countries** (in thousands of metric tons, except as otherwise indicated)

NOTE

SOURCES: The national publications on p. xiv–xvi; League of Nations, *International Trade Statistics;* and UN, *Yearbook of International Trade Statistics.* Colombian statistics to 1887 are taken from Robert C. Beyer, *The Colombian Coffee Industry: Origins and Major Trends, 1740–1940* (PhD thesis, University of Minnesota, 1947).

FOOTNOTES

[1] Data to 1894 (1st line) include re-exports. Data for 1901 to 1908 are for years beginning 1 April.
[2] Data to 1842 are for years ending 30 September. From 1844 to 1915 they are for years ending 30 June. The 1843 figures are for the nine months from 1 October 1842 to 30 June 1843.
[3] Data to 1953 (1st line) are of unmanufactured cotton. Subsequently they are of raw cotton excluding linters.
[4] Data from 1834 to 1887 are for years ending 30 June. The 1833 figures are for the first half-year only. Figures for the second half of 1887 are as follows: cocoa—2.9; coffee—102; cotton—16; rubber—6.7.
[5] Years ending 30 September.
[6] Linseed to 1944, linseed oil subsequently. Linseed exports in 1945 and 1946 were 135 and 38 thousand tons respectively, and were negligible subsequently. Linseed oil exports prior to 1945 were as follows: 1939—2; 1940—6; 1941—10; 1942—34; 1943—35; 1944—25.
[7] Subsequently excluding linters.
[8] Subsequently only beans.

## C19 EXPORTS OF TIMBER PRODUCTS BY MAIN TRADING COUNTRIES

| | 1900–1939 | | | | | 1940–1988 | | | |
|---|---|---|---|---|---|---|---|---|---|
| | Canada[1] | | | USA | | Canada[1] | | | USA |
| | Lumber | Newsprint | Wood pulp | Lumber | | Lumber | Newsprint | Wood pulp | Lumber |
| | (thousand million feet) | (thousand tons) | (thousand tons) | (thousand million feet) | | (thousand million feet) | (thousand tons) | (thousand tons) | (thousand million feet) |
| 1900 | ... | ... | ... | 1.7 | 1945 | 2.0 | 2,775 | 1,302 | 0.4 |
| 1901 | ... | ... | ... | 1.5 | 1946 | 2.1 | 3,500 | 1,287 | 0.6 |
| 1902 | ... | ... | ... | 1.4 | 1947 | 2.7 | 3,829 | 1,541 | 1.4 |
| 1903 | ... | ... | ... | 1.9 | 1948 | 2.5[1] | 3,926[1] | 1,631[1] | 0.6 |
| 1904 | ... | ... | ... | 2.0 | 1949 | 2.2 | 4,345 | 1,412 | 0.7 |
| 1905 | ... | ... | ... | 1.8 | 1950 | 3.6 | 4,480 | 1,675 | 0.5 |
| 1906 | ... | ... | ... | 2.1 | 1951 | 3.4 | 4,638 | 2,035 | 1.0 |
| 1907 | ... | ... | ... | 2.3 | 1952 | 3.3 | 4,833 | 1,761 | 0.7 |
| 1908 | ... | ... | 218 | 1.8 | 1953 | 3.4 | 4,876 | 1,769 | 0.6 |
| 1909 | ... | ... | 255 | 2.0 | 1954 | 4.0 | 5,009 | 1,978 | 0.7 |
| 1910 | ... | ... | 298 | 2.3 | 1955 | 4.6 | 5,228 | 2,146 | 0.8 |
| 1911 | ... | ... | 236 | 2.7 | 1956 | 4.0 | 5,413 | 2,154 | 0.8 |
| 1912 | ... | ... | 316 | 2.9 | 1957 | 3.6 | 5,435 | 2,071 | 0.8 |
| 1913 | ... | ... | 270 | 3.0 | 1958 | 3.9 | 5,156 | 2,013 | 0.7 |
| 1914 | ... | ... | 386 | 2.1 | 1959 | 4.2 | 5,369 | 2,238 | 0.8 |
| | | | | | | (million cubic metres[2]) | | | |
| 1915 | ... | ... | 330 | 1.3 | 1960 | 12 | 5,621 | 2,423 | 0.9 |
| 1916 | ... | 477 | 507 | 1.3 | 1961 | 13 | 5,673 | 2,660 | 0.8 |
| 1917 | ... | 541 | 464 | 1.1 | 1962 | 13 | 5,578 | 2,840 | 0.8 |
| 1918 | ... | 577 | 530 | 1.1 | 1963 | 14 | 5,635 | 3,122 | 0.9 |
| 1919 | ... | 642 | 643 | 1.5 | 1964 | 16 | 6,183 | 3,402 | 1.0 |
| 1920 | 1.9 | 691 | 744 | 1.7 | 1965 | 17 | 6,522 | 3,606 | 0.9 |
| 1921 | 1.0 | 643 | 478 | 1.3 | 1966 | 16 | 7,095 | 3,850 | 1.0 |
| 1922 | 2.0 | 870 | 742 | 2.0 | 1967 | 17 | 6,771 | 3,978 | 1.1 |
| 1923 | 2.4 | 1,032 | 794 | 2.5 | 1968 | 18 | 6,785 | 4,619 | 1.2 |
| 1924 | 2.1 | 1,098 | 709 | 2.7 | 1969 | 17 | 7,471 | 5,360 | 1.1 |
| 1925 | 2.2 | 1,272 | 872 | 2.6 | 1970 | 19 | 7,339 | 5,153 | 1.3 |
| 1926 | 2.2 | 1,571 | 913 | 2.8 | 1971 | 21 | 7,075 | 5,270 | 1.1 |
| 1927 | 2.2 | 1,707 | 797 | 3.1 | 1972 | 24 | 7,350 | 5,663 | 1.4 |
| 1928 | 1.9 | 2,002 | 784 | 3.2 | 1973 | 24 | 7,617 | 6,017 | 2.0 |
| 1929 | 2.0 | 2,282 | 754 | 3.2 | 1974 | 21 | 7,892 | 6,534 | 1.7 |
| 1930 | 1.6 | 2,116 | 689 | 2.4 | 1975 | 16 | 6,350 | 5,043 | 1.6 |
| 1931 | 1.1 | 1,822 | 565 | 1.7 | 1976 | 26 | 6,997 | 6,269 | 1.8 |
| 1932 | 0.8 | 1,612 | 410 | 1.2 | 1977 | 33 | 7,266 | 6,243 | 1.7 |
| 1933 | 1.1 | 1,667 | 552 | 1.3 | 1978 | 35 | 7,868 | 6,751 | 1.7 |
| 1934 | 1.5 | 2,190 | 550 | 1.3 | 1979 | 35 | 7,778 | 7,196 | 2.1 |
| 1935 | 1.4 | 2,336 | 601 | 1.3 | 1980 | 34 | 7,707 | 7,354 | 2.3 |
| 1936 | 1.9 | 2,715 | 684 | 1.3 | 1981 | 32 | 7,987 | 6,869 | 2.3 |
| 1937 | 2.0 | 3,134 | 790 | 1.4 | 1982 | 31 | 7,078 | 6,342 | 2.0 |
| 1938 | 1.8 | 2,200 | 503 | 1.0 | 1983 | 39 | 7,475 | 11,550 | 2.2 |
| 1939 | 2.2 | 2,412 | 640 | 1.1 | 1984 | 43 | 8,127 | 7,193 | 2.1 |
| 1940 | 2.5 | 2,942 | 970 | 1.0 | 1985 | 44 | 8,285 | 7,263 | 1.9 |
| 1941 | 2.3 | 2,959 | 1,281 | 0.7 | 1986 | 43 | 8,563 | 7,856 | 2.4 |
| 1942 | 2.2 | 2,726 | 1,371 | 0.5 | 1987 | 48 | 8,772 | 8,504 | 3.2 |
| 1943 | 1.7 | 2,549 | 1,412 | 0.3 | 1988 | 49 | 8,567 | 8,643 | 4.5 |
| 1944 | 1.9 | 2,546 | 1,277 | 0.4 | | | | | |

NOTE

SOURCES: The national publications on p. xii–xiv, except for Canadian lumber exports 1960–75, which come from FAO, *Yearbook of Forestry Statistics.*

FOOTNOTES

[1] Newfoundland became part of Canada from 1 April 1949.
[2] The figure for 1959 in million cubic metres is 11.

# D    INDUSTRY

Apart from table 1, which gives indices of industrial production, and table 13, showing the number of cotton spindles, all the tables in this section consist of physical output and external trade volume statistics for major commodities which possess an adequate degree of homogeneity to allow aggregation and meaningful comparisons between countries. Inevitably, these are mostly basic commodities rather than finished goods; yarn and cloth rather than clothing, metals rather than machinery. The picture they give of industrial development is necessarily biased and partial. However, until very recent times there is little that could be added to them in the way of continuous statistical series for industries making finished products.

Probably enough has been written about the problems of constructing indices of industrial production for most users to be aware of their pitfalls. Even given all the desired basic information, an index which accurately reflects the composition of industrial output in any one year will not, in a changing world, have precisely the right weighting of activities for another year. Where the components of an index are expressed in terms of values rather than volume, changes in relative prices will be an added source of possible misrepresentation. Changing the weights and linking indices is one solution to this problem and often the best one; but it takes away exact precision of comparability. Such precision, however, can easily become unreal and meaningless where new commodities and activities are added to, and sometimes displace, old ones. All worthwhile indices of industrial production, then, are compromises between relevance and exact comparability over time. The skill of the constructor is in picking the base-years and linking points which produce least distortion and appear to represent best the reality of industrial activity and change. Judgement on these matters inevitably contains subjective elements, and it is safe to say that there is no objectively perfect index.

Technical problems have been compounded in many cases by lack of sufficient basic information.

As was mentioned above, statistics on the more complex products of industry have not been collected until quite recently, with rare exceptions in the most industrialized countries. Moreover, some of the statistics have been concerned with taxation in one form or another, and clearly such data are not unbiased. On the whole, it seems wise to treat nineteenth-century indices of production, and all of those for less-developed countries, with a measure of caution.

The remaining tables in this section are reasonably straightforward, though not always so much so as they seem at first glance. Most of the commodities covered are fairly homogeneous, though hardly one is perfectly so. The main reasons for such variations as are not obvious are referred to in the notes following each table and in the footnotes.

## D1    NORTH AMERICA: INDICES OF INDUSTRIAL PRODUCTION

Key: MF = manufacturing

| | 1860–1899 | | | | | | | | |
|---|---|---|---|---|---|---|---|---|---|
| | USA | | | Canada | | Mexico | | USA | |
| | Mf | Mining | | Mf | Mining | Mf | Mining | Mf | Mining |
| | *1899=100* | *1899=100* | | | | *1900=100* | | *1899=100* | *1899=100* |
| 1860 | 16 | ... | 1900 | ... | ... | 100 | ... | 101 | 105 |
| 1861 | 16 | ... | 1901 | ... | ... | 102 | ... | 112 | 111 |
| 1862 | 15 | ... | 1902 | ... | ... | 106 | ... | 129 | 114 |
| 1863 | 17 | ... | 1903 | ... | ... | 113 | ... | 129 | 130 |
| 1864 | 18 | ... | 1904 | ... | ... | 120 | ... | 124 | 131 |
| 1865 | 17 | ... | 1905 | ... | ... | 127 | ... | 142 | 148 |
| 1866 | 21 | ... | 1906 | ... | ... | 130 | ... | 151 | 154 |
| 1867 | 22 | ... | 1907 | ... | ... | 135 | ... | 153 | 189 |
| 1868 | 23 | ... | 1908 | ... | ... | 139 | ... | 123 | 157 |
| 1869 | 25 | ... | 1909 | ... | ... | 145 | ... | 158 | 177 |
| 1870 | 25 | ... | 1910 | ... | ... | 147 | ... | 164 | 188 |
| 1871 | 26 | ... | 1911 | ... | ... | 139 | ... | 155 | 186 |
| 1872 | 31 | ... | 1912 | ... | ... | 113 | ... | 187 | 200 |
| 1873 | 30 | ... | 1913 | ... | ... | 130 | ... | 196 | 212 |
| 1874 | 29 | ... | 1914 | ... | ... | 98 | ... | 186 | 197 |
| 1875 | 28 | ... | | | | *1938=100* | | *1938=100* | *1938=100* |
| 1876 | 28 | ... | | | | 30 | | 63 | 61 |
| 1877 | 30 | ... | 1915 | ... | ... | 36 | ... | 74 | 66 |
| 1878 | 32 | ... | 1916 | ... | ... | 33 | ... | 88 | 74 |
| 1879 | 36 | ... | 1917 | ... | ... | 30 | ... | 87 | 78 |
| | | | 1918 | ... | ... | 29 | ... | 86 | 79 |
| 1880 | 42 | 35 | 1919 | ... | ... | 37 | ... | 75 | 69 |
| 1881 | 46 | 39 | | | | | | | |
| 1882 | 49 | 44 | 1920 | ... | ... | 35 | ... | 82 | 80 |
| 1883 | 50 | 46 | 1921 | ... | ... | 35 | ... | 66 | 67 |
| 1884 | 47 | 47 | 1922 | ... | ... | 47 | ... | 84 | 71 |
| | | | | *1938=100* | *1938=100* | | | | |
| 1885 | 47 | 48 | 1923 | 66 | | 54 | ... | 95 | 97 |
| 1886 | 57 | 54 | 1924 | 65 | 61 | 56 | ... | 91 | 92 |
| 1887 | 60 | 59 | | | | | | | |
| 1888 | 62 | 62 | 1925 | 71 | 67 | 58 | ... | 101 | 95 |
| | | | 1926 | 81 | 72 | 66 | ... | 107 | 103 |
| 1889 | 67 | 67 | 1927 | 86 | 73 | 58 | ... | 108 | 105 |
| 1890 | 72 | 72 | 1928 | 94 | 82 | 62 | ... | 111 | 104 |
| 1891 | 73 | 74 | | | | | *1938=100* | | |
| 1892 | 79 | 78 | 1929 | 100 | 85 | 66 | 118 | 124 | 114 |
| 1893 | 70 | 74 | | | | | | | |
| 1894 | 68 | 71 | 1930 | 90 | 71 | 69 | ... | 106 | 101 |
| | | | 1931 | 79 | 61 | 83 | ... | 89 | 85 |
| 1895 | 81 | 79 | 1932 | 66 | 54 | 60 | ... | 67 | 69 |
| 1896 | 74 | 82 | 1933 | 67 | 55 | 55 | ... | 78 | 75 |
| 1897 | 80 | 85 | 1934 | 78 | 66 | 83 | ... | 85 | 82 |
| 1898 | 91 | 90 | | | | | | | |
| 1899 | 100 | 100 | 1935 | 86 | 73 | 81 | 88 | 102 | 87 |
| | | | 1936 | 95 | 81 | 93 | 92 | 120 | 104 |
| | | | 1937 | 109 | 95 | 97 | 104 | 128 | 116 |
| | | | 1938 | 100 | 100 | 100 | 100 | 100 | 100 |
| | | | 1939 | 108 | 108 | 98 | 96 | 127 | 111 |
| | | | 1940 | 133 | 115 | 104 | 94 | 147 | 123 |
| | | | 1941 | 174 | 120 | 111 | 96 | 195 | 135 |
| | | | 1942 | 212 | 119 | 121 | 105 | 244 | 142 |
| | | | 1943 | 230 | 105 | 127 | 106 | 294 | 145 |
| | | | 1944 | 234 | 95 | 138 | 97 | 287 | 150 |

**D1    NORTH AMERICA: Indices of Industrial Production** 1958=100

### 1988

| | Canada | | Dominican Republic[1] | El Salvador[1] | Guatemala[1] | Mexico | | Nicaragua[1] | Panama[1] | USA | |
|---|---|---|---|---|---|---|---|---|---|---|---|
| | Mf | Mining | | | | Mf | Mining | | | Mf | Mining |
| 1944 | 75 | 34 | ... | ... | ... | 43 | 89 | ... | ... | 91 | 83 |
| 1945 | 66 | 33 | ... | ... | ... | 46 | 90 | ... | ... | 77 | 80 |
| 1946 | 60 | 31 | ... | ... | 60 | 47 | 70 | ... | ... | 63 | 79 |
| 1947 | 66 | 35 | ... | ... | 63 | 48 | 88 | ... | ... | 69 | 89 |
| 1948 | 69 | 40 | ... | ... | 65 | 50 | 81 | ... | ... | 72 | 92 |
| 1949 | 71 | 45 | ... | ... | 66 | 52 | 82 | ... | ... | 68 | 80 |
| 1950 | 75 | 49 | ... | ... | 69 | 56 | 90 | ... | ... | 79 | 89 |
| 1951 | 82 | 55 | ... | ... | 68 | 60 | 87 | ... | ... | 86 | 97 |
| 1952 | 84 | 58 | ... | ... | 72 | 59 | 93 | ... | ... | 89 | 95 |
| 1953 | 90 | 62 | ... | ... | 71 | 60 | 89 | 63 | ... | 96 | 97 |
| 1954 | 87 | 71 | ... | 82 | 72 | 71 | 86 | 72 | ... | 91 | 93 |
| 1955 | 96 | 82 | ... | 81 | 76 | 80 | 93 | 82 | ... | 102 | 103 |
| 1956 | 103 | 94 | ... | 88 | 82 | 88 | 99 | 82 | ... | 107 | 108 |
| 1957 | 102 | 100 | ... | 102 | 92 | 95 | 97 | 89 | ... | 107 | 108 |
| 1958 | 100 | 100 | 100 | 100 | 100 | 100 | 100 | 100 | 100 | 100 | 100 |
| 1959 | 107 | 113 | 96 | 95 | 106 | 104 | 109 | ... | 109 | 112 | 105 |
| 1960 | 109 | 114 | 112 | 106 | 106 | 119 | 107 | 133 | 133 | 114 | 108 |
| 1961 | 113 | 117 | 101 | 108 | 113 | 123 | 108 | 145 | 149 | 116 | 109 |
| 1962 | 123 | 125 | 123 | 120 | 111 | 131 | 110 | 152 | 193 | 125 | 112 |
| 1963 | 131 | 132 | 127 | 141 | 126 | 143 | 115 | 159 | 237 | 133 | 117 |
| 1964 | 143 | 149 | 135 | 183 | 133 | 163 | 121 | 178 | 237 | 142 | 122 |
| 1965 | 158 | 155 | 109 | 224 | 147 | 179 | 117 | 202 | 271 | 156 | 127 |
| 1966 | 168 | 158 | 132 | 228 | 154 | 196 | 122 | 213 | 300 | 172 | 134 |
| 1967 | 172 | 167 | 141 | 263 | 159 | 209 | 125 | 235 | 321 | 175 | 136 |
| 1968 | 184 | 179 | 136 | 252 | 158 | 227 | 132 | 260 | 358 | 186 | 142 |
| 1969 | 195 | 182 | 161 | 263 | 176 | 248 | 138 | 283 | 387 | 195 | 150 |
| 1970 | 193 | 206 | 183 | 289 | 183 | 264 | 142 | 317 | 417 | 186 | 153 |
| 1971 | 205 | 215 | 204 | 301 | 196 | 272 | 137 | 362 | 471 | 189 | 150 |
| 1972 | 213 | 229 | 235 | 310 | 207 | 297 | 144 | 400 | 492 | 209 | 153 |
| 1973 | 238 | 256 | 244 | 344 | 225 | 325 | 153 | 438 | 517 | 228 | 156 |
| 1974 | 245 | 256 | 262 | 321 | 236 | 347 | 169 | 416 | 512 | 226 | 156 |
| 1975 | 234 | 235 | 273 | 370 | 234 | 362 | 160 | 463 | 504 | 203 | 154 |
| 1976 | 248 | 240 | 295 | 411 | 257 | 372 | 170 | 486 | 494 | 227 | 155 |
| 1977 | 256 | 249 | 326 | 427 | 290 | 385 | 171 | 486 | 530 | 241 | 160 |
| 1978 | 267 | 222 | 335 | 449 | 307 | 420 | 175 | 467 | 556 | 257 | 169 |
| 1979 | 284 | 244 | 363 | 438 | 328 | 458 | 183 | 332 | 620 | 270 | 171 |
| 1980 | 275 | 249 | 390 | 378 | 349 | 494 | 223 | 386 | 620 | 241 | 180 |
| 1981 | 278 | 234 | 374 | 344 | 335 | 531 | 258 | 397 | 664 | 268 | 189 |
| 1982 | 242 | 229 | 406 | 317 | 321 | 510 | 285 | 394 | 682 | 249 | 175 |
| 1983 | 259 | 247 | 406 | 325 | 314 | 472 | 273 | ... | 676 | 263 | 165 |
| 1984 | 297 | 281 | 437 | 328 | 318 | 495 | 277 | ... | 651 | 292 | 178 |
| 1985 | 314 | 289 | 452 | 344 | 318 | 528 | 280 | ... | 664 | 299 | 175 |
| 1986 | 322 | 291 | ... | ... | ... | 503 | 268 | ... | 682 | 302 | 160 |
| 1987 | 333 | 311 | ... | ... | ... | 522 | 278 | ... | 707 | 324 | 162 |
| 1988 | 356 | 343 | ... | ... | ... | 538 | 279 | ... | | 331 | 165 |

**D1    SOUTH AMERICA: INDICES OF INDUSTRIAL PRODUCTION**

## 1938=100

| | Brazil | | | Brazil | Chile | | | Brazil | Chile | |
|---|---|---|---|---|---|---|---|---|---|---|
| | MF | | | MF | MF | Mining | | MF | MF | Mining |
| 1914 | 8 | | 1925 | 36 | ... | ... | 1935 | 70 | 89 | 81 |
| 1915 | 10 | | 1926 | 40 | ... | ... | 1936 | 80 | 91 | 83 |
| 1916 | 13 | | 1927 | 46 | 58 | 82 | 1937 | 94 | 98 | 114 |
| 1917 | 20 | | 1928 | 60 | 64 | 123 | 1938 | 100 | 100 | 100 |
| 1918 | 20 | | 1929 | 56 | 77 | 132 | 1939 | 120 | 100 | 99 |
| 1919 | 25 | | | | | | | | | |
| 1920 | 25 | | 1930 | 49 | 78 | 94 | 1940 | 151 | 111 | 107 |
| 1921 | 25 | | 1931 | 48 | 58 | 64 | 1941 | 166 | 123 | 123 |
| 1922 | 32 | | 1932 | 46 | 66 | 35 | 1942 | 171 | 121 | 119 |
| 1923 | 49 | | 1933 | 50 | 72 | 43 | 1943 | 183 | 123 | 118 |
| 1924 | 37 | | 1934 | 57 | 79 | 70 | 1944 | 204 | 117 | 118 |

## 1958=100

| | Argentina | | Brazil | | Chile | | Colombia | | Ecuador[1] | Peru[1] | Uruguay[1] | Venezuela | |
|---|---|---|---|---|---|---|---|---|---|---|---|---|---|
| | MF | Mining | MF | Mining | MF | Mining | MF | Mining | | | | MF | Mining |
| 1935 | 38 | 28 | 12 | ... | 39 | 68 | ... | ... | ... | ... | ... | ... | ... |
| 1936 | 40 | 33 | 13 | ... | 40 | 70 | ... | ... | ... | ... | ... | ... | ... |
| 1937 | 42 | 39 | 16 | ... | 43 | 96 | ... | ... | ... | ... | ... | ... | ... |
| 1938 | 45 | 44 | 17 | 42 | 44 | 85 | ... | ... | ... | ... | ... | ... | ... |
| 1939 | 47 | 50 | 20 | ... | 44 | 84 | ... | ... | ... | ... | ... | ... | ... |
| 1940 | 46 | 56 | 25 | ... | 49 | 90 | ... | ... | ... | ... | ... | ... | ... |
| 1941 | 48 | 58 | 28 | ... | 54 | 104 | ... | ... | ... | ... | ... | ... | ... |
| 1942 | 54 | 61 | 29 | ... | 54 | 101 | ... | ... | ... | ... | ... | ... | ... |
| 1943 | 56 | 59 | 31 | ... | 54 | 100 | ... | ... | ... | ... | ... | ... | ... |
| 1944 | 62 | 61 | 34 | 51 | 52 | 100 | ... | ... | ... | ... | ... | ... | ... |
| 1945 | 59 | 58 | 37 | 52 | 58 | 98 | ... | ... | ... | 48 | ... | ... | ... |
| 1946 | 64 | 53 | 37 | 49 | 62 | 87 | ... | ... | ... | 47 | ... | ... | ... |
| 1947 | 74 | 56 | 43 | 51 | 63 | 98 | ... | ... | ... | 49 | ... | ... | ... |
| 1948 | 72 | 56 | 41 | 56 | 66 | 104 | 48 | ... | ... | 50 | ... | 25 | 44 |
| 1949 | 67 | 58 | 46 | 59 | 69 | 90 | ... | ... | ... | 57 | ... | 29 | 43 |
| 1950 | 68 | 58 | 52 | 59 | 66 | 89 | 56 | 70 | ... | 58 | ... | 34 | 49 |
| 1951 | 70 | 67 | 57 | 67 | 79 | 94 | 58 | 78 | ... | 65 | ... | 39 | 57 |
| 1952 | 68 | 72 | 60 | 68 | 87 | 94 | 63 | 78 | ... | 68 | ... | 47 | 61 |
| 1953 | 68 | 77 | 63 | 70 | 94 | 83 | 70 | 82 | 71 | 76 | 94 | 55 | 60 |
| 1954 | 73 | 81 | 68 | 69 | 98 | 88 | 78 | 84 | ... | 82 | 86 | 65 | 67 |
| 1955 | 81 | 84 | 76 | 74 | 94 | 97 | 84 | 86 | 81 | 87 | 84 | 75 | 79 |
| 1956 | 85 | 88 | 81 | 82 | 100 | 100 | 92 | 94 | 86 | 92 | 89 | 81 | 91 |
| 1957 | 91 | 92 | 86 | 85 | 97 | 101 | 96 | 98 | 94 | 101 | 96 | 92 | 106 |
| 1958 | 100 | 100 | 100 | 100 | 100 | 100 | 100 | 100 | 100 | 100 | 100 | 100 | 100 |
| 1959 | 92 | 114 | 108 | 125 | 114 | 115 | 108 | 116 | 109 | 109 | 96 | 117 | 107 |

**D1 SOUTH AMERICA: Indices of Industrial Production**

**1958=100**

| | Argentina | | Brazil | | Chile | | Colombia | | Ecuador[1] | Peru[1] | Uruguay[1] | Venezuela | |
|---|---|---|---|---|---|---|---|---|---|---|---|---|---|
| | Mf | Mining | Mf | Mining | Mf | Mining | Mf | Mining | | | | Mf | Mining |
| 1960 | 101 | 156 | 124 | 142 | 112 | 112 | 115 | 120 | 125 | 125 | 99 | 121 | 112 |
| 1961 | 111 | 203 | 138 | 168 | 120 | 120 | 122 | 113 | 139 | 132 | 97 | 125 | 108 |
| 1962 | 106 | 228 | 149 | 166 | 131 | 131 | 130 | 113 | 144 | 146 | 97 | 137 | 116 |
| 1963 | 101 | 228 | 149 | 197 | 139 | 135 | 137 | 127 | 152 | 157 | 96 | 147 | 116 |
| 1964 | 116 | 236 | 155 | 201 | 147 | 143 | 145 | 137 | 188 | 172 | 104 | 162 | 126 |
| 1965 | 136 | 245 | 149 | 268 | 154 | 140 | 152 | 147 | 208 | 188 | 103 | 174 | 129 |
| 1966 | 137 | 259 | 166 | 288 | 164 | 152 | 162 | 142 | 227 | 202 | 105 | 178 | 126 |
| 1967 | 139 | 291 | 171 | 300 | 163 | 144 | 167 | 144 | 255 | 216 | 100 | 185 | 130 |
| 1968 | 148 | 326 | 198 | 334 | 163 | 147 | 178 | 138 | 279 | 227 | 105 | 194 | 133 |
| 1969 | 164 | 360 | 220 | 355 | 169 | 153 | 190 | 163 | 307 | 232 | 110 | 200 | 137 |
| 1970 | 174 | 383 | 244 | 345 | 169 | 152 | 207 | 160 | 345 | 270 | 115 | 213 | 143 |
| 1971 | 186 | 399 | 271 | 359 | 195 | 156 | 225 | 162 | 379 | 297 | 113 | 228 | 137 |
| 1972 | 196 | 406 | 310 | 359 | 200 | 150 | 244 | 151 | 414 | 322 | 113 | 238 | 124 |
| 1973 | 203 | 395 | 361 | 359 | 192 | 152 | 267 | 159 | 452 | 346 | 113 | 260 | 131 |
| 1974 | 213 | 403 | 390 | 379 | 185 | 180 | 281 | 149 | 514 | 386 | 116 | 268 | 119 |
| 1975 | 202 | 383 | 405 | 376 | 133 | 168 | 283 | 141 | 559 | 405 | 124 | 272 | 94 |
| 1976 | 200 | 391 | 458 | 380 | 139 | 192 | 303 | 138 | 615 | 425 | 126 | 321 | ... |
| 1977 | 211 | 433 | 469 | 381 | 153 | 194 | 316 | 134 | 690 | 405 | 134 | 380 | ... |
| 1978 | 188 | 443 | 491 | 401 | 165 | 190 | 345 | 140 | 751 | 392 | 141 | 408 | ... |
| 1979 | 218 | 473 | 525 | 452 | 178 | 198 | 360 | 138 | 821 | 405 | 150 | 465 | ... |
| 1980 | 213 | 497 | 570 | 508 | 189 | 207 | 368 | 148 | 873 | 426 | 155 | 567 | ... |
| 1981 | 179 | 502 | 513 | 498 | 191 | 223 | 357 | 159 | 891 | 414 | 147 | 606 | ... |
| 1982 | 177 | 502 | 513 | 528 | 160 | 247 | 345 | 171 | 917 | 345 | 122 | 663 | ... |
| 1983 | 193 | 502 | 485 | 615 | 168 | 246 | 345 | 193 | 882 | 362 | 109 | 674 | ... |
| 1984 | 197 | 502 | 519 | 798 | 184 | 259 | 379 | 239 | 935 | 375 | 118 | 861 | ... |
| 1985 | 179 | 487 | 565 | 889 | 185 | 268 | 390 | ... | 987 | 398 | 122 | 997 | ... |
| 1986 | 200 | 487 | 627 | 925 | 199 | 270 | 415 | ... | 1,022 | 469 | 130 | 1,235 | ... |
| 1987 | 198 | 468 | 633 | 915 | 209 | 268 | 437 | ... | 1,048 | 529 | 144 | 1,762 | ... |
| 1988 | 185 | 518 | 602 | 942 | 225 | 278 | 446 | ... | 1,100 | ... | 141 | ... | ... |

NOTES

1. SOURCES: Based on the national publications listed on p.xiv–xvi, the League of Nations and UN, *Statistical Yearbooks* and *Yearbook of Industrial Statistics* (under various names). The US manufacturing production series is based on the index in Edwin Frickey, *Production in the United States, 1860–1914* (Cambridge, Mass., 1947) to 1888, on the index in John W. Kendrick, *Productivity Trends in the United States* (Princeton, 1961) from 1889 to 1950, and on the Federal Reserve Board index subsequently. The US mining production series is based on the Bureau of Mines index.
2. All indices have been converted, where necessary, to a base year in 1899, 1938, or 1958, and different indices have been crudely spliced together.
3. Except as indicated in the footnote or headings, indices relate to manufacturing production alone, excluding mining, construction, and usually utilities also.

FOOTNOTES

[1] This is a general index of industrial production, not just manufacturing.

**D2** **NORTH AMERICA: OUTPUT OF COAL** (in thousands of metric tons)

| | 1800–1849 | | | | | | 1850–1899 | |
|---|---|---|---|---|---|---|---|---|
| | USA | | | | Canada[1] | Mexico | USA | |
| | Bituminous | Anthracite | | | | | Bituminous | Anthracite |
| 1800 | 98 | - - | | 1850 | ... | ... | 3,655 | 3,925 |
| 1801 | 103 | - - | | 1851 | ... | ... | 4,164 | 5,274 |
| 1802 | 11 | - - | | 1852 | ... | ... | 4,453 | 5,817 |
| 1803 | 115 | - - | | 1853 | ... | ... | 5,534 | 6,036 |
| 1804 | 128 | - - | | 1854 | ... | ... | 6,676 | 6,956 |
| 1805 | 132 | - - | | 1855 | ... | ... | 6,843 | 7,808 |
| 1806 | 138 | - - | | 1856 | ... | ... | 7,250 | 8,128 |
| 1807 | 144 | - - | | 1857 | ... | ... | 7,961 | 7,818 |
| 1808 | 150 | 1 | | 1858 | 228 | ... | 8,025 | 7,990 |
| 1809 | 154 | 1 | | 1859 | 266 | ... | 8,280 | 9,155 |
| 1810 | 160 | 2 | | 1860 | 314 | ... | 8,216 | 9,965 |
| 1811 | 171 | 2 | | 1861 | 328, 332 | ... | 7,943 | 9,294 |
| 1812 | 184 | 2 | | 1862 | 404 | ... | 8,513 | 9,241 |
| 1813 | 198 | 2 | | 1863 | 436 | ... | 9,507 | 11,128 |
| 1814 | 213 | 2 | | 1864 | [401][2] | ... | 10,356 | 11,818 |
| 1815 | 230 | 2 | | 1865 | 785, | ... | 11,203 | 10,956 |
| 1816 | 252 | 2 | | 1866 | ... | ... | 11,807 | 14,319 |
| 1817 | 275 | 2 | | 1867 | 572 | ... | 12,553 | 14,576 |
| 1818 | 299 | 3 | | 1868 | 565 | ... | 14,736 | 16,064 |
| 1819 | 290 | 3 | | 1869 | 624 | ... | 18,056 | 16,639 |
| 1820 | 299 | 4 | | 1870 | 683 | ... | 18,571 | 18,106 |
| 1821 | 317 | 4 | | 1871 | } 2,751 { | ... | 20,736 | 17,658 |
| 1822 | 327 | 5 | | 1872 | | ... | 24,776 | 22,438 |
| 1823 | 336 | 9 | | 1873 | | ... | 28,668 | 23,248 |
| 1824 | 376 | 14 | | 1874 | 965 | ... | 27,881 | 22,015 |
| 1825 | 396 | | | 1875 | 934 | ... | 29,626 | 20,975 |
| 1826 | 447 | 55 | | 1876 | 903 | ... | 28,868 | 20,677 |
| 1827 | 483 | 73 | | 1877 | 941 | ... | 31,194 | 23,278 |
| 1828 | 516 | 93 | | 1878 | 989 | ... | 33,038 | 19,677 |
| 1829 | 551 | 135 | | 1879 | 1,021 | ... | 36,673 | 27,404 |
| 1830 | 586 | 213 | | 1880 | 1,345 | ... | 46,046 | 25,991 |
| 1831 | 630 | 234 | | 1881 | 1,394 | ... | 47,124 | 28,957 |
| 1832 | 699 | 455 | | 1882 | 1,676 | ... | 53,449 | 31,861 |
| 1833 | 747 | 601 | | 1883 | 1,650 | ... | 58,840 | 34,888 |
| 1834 | 827 | 464 | | 1884 | 1,801 | ... | 65,079 | 33,708 |
| 1835 | 961 | 689 | | 1885 | 1,743 | ... | 65,111 | 34,778 |
| 1836 | 968 | 839 | | 1886 | 1,921 | ... | 67,717 | 35,412 |
| 1837 | 971 | 1,056 | | 1887 | 2,204 | ... | 80,342 | 38,182 |
| 1838 | 1,035 | 887 | | 1888 | 2,361 | ... | 92,569 | 42,293 |
| 1839 | 1,135 | 1,024 | | 1889 | 2,411 | ... | 86,804 | 41,320 |
| 1840 | 1,220 | 1,024 | | 1890 | 2,799 | ... | 100,972 | 42,156 |
| 1841 | 1,229 | 1,145 | | 1891 | 3,246 | 200 | 106,958 | 45,963 |
| 1842 | 1,336 | 1,307 | | 1892 | 2,983 | 350 | 115,083 | 47,603 |
| 1843 | 1,465 | 1,502 | | 1893 | 3,432 | 260 | 116,469 | 48,959 |
| 1844 | 1,627 | 1,930 | | 1894 | 3,490 | 300 | 107,792 | 47,102 |
| 1845 | 1,902 | 32,382 | | 1895 | 3,155 | 270 | 122,577 | 52,616 |
| 1846 | 2,112 | 2,751 | | 1896 | 3,398 | 253 | 124,865 | 49,302 |
| 1847 | 2,387 | 3,380 | | 1897 | 3,435 | 359 | 133,917 | 47,729 |
| 1848 | 2,794 | 3,630 | | 1898 | 3,786 | 367 | 151,132 | 48,428 |
| 1849 | 3,191 | 3,785 | | 1899 | 4,468 | 409 | 175,380 | 54,810 |

**D2   NORTH AMERICA: Output of Coal** (in thousands of metric tons)

| | Canada[1] | | Mexico | USA | |
|---|---|---|---|---|---|
| | Hard Coal | Brown Coal | | Bituminous[4] | Anthracite |
| 1900 | 5,241 | | 388 | 192,610 | 52,043 |
| 1901 | 5,884 | | 670 | 204,868 | 61,210 |
| 1902 | 6,774 | | 710 | 236,065 | 37,534 |
| 1903 | 7,221 | | 780 | 256,506 | 67,682 |
| 1904 | 7,489 | | 832 | 252,796 | 66,367 |
| 1905 | 7,863 | | 920 | 285,820 | 70,452 |
| 1906 | 8,857 | | 768 | 311,051 | 64,666 |
| 1907 | 9,535 | | 1,025 | 358,119 | 77,659 |
| 1908 | 9,876 | | 866 | 301,706 | 75,540 |
| 1909 | 9,526 | | 1,300 | 344,498 | 73,545 |
| 1910 | 11,711 | | 1,304 | 378,397 | 76,644 |
| 1911 | 10,272 | | 1,400 | 368,233 | 82,068 |
| 1912 | 13,166 | | 982 | 408,329 | 76,532 |
| 1913 | 13,619 | | 600 | 434,029 | 83,030 |
| 1914 | 12,372 | | 780 | 383,471 | 82,392 |
| 1915 | 12,036 | | 450 | 401,542 | 80,735 |
| 1916 | 13,139 | | 300 | 455,879 | 79,449 |
| 1917 | 12,743 | | 431 | 500,577 | 90,367 |
| 1918 | 13,588[1] | | 782 | 525,610 | 89,653 |
| 1919 | 12,627 | | 728 | 422,621 | 79,916 |
| 1920 | 12,021 | 3,353 | 716 | 515,886 | 80,282 |
| 1921 | 10,684 | 2,976 | 735 | 377,318 | 82,076 |
| 1922 | 10,588 | 3,163 | 933 | 383,075 | 49,608 |
| 1923 | 12,164 | 3,250 | 1,262 | 512,165 | 84,676 |
| 1924 | 9,139 | 3,233 | 1,227 | 438,794 | 79,766 |
| 1925 | 8,628 | 3,288 | 1,444 | 471,784 | 56,079 |
| 1926 | 11,637 | 3,262 | 1,309 | 520,150 | 76,600 |
| 1927 | 12,341 | 3,469 | 1,031 | 469,707 | 72,662 |
| 1928 | 12,440[2] | 3,495[2] | 1,022 | 454,268 | 68,355 |
| | 15,504 | 428 | | | |
| 1929 | 15,345 | 526 | 1,054 | 485,334 | 66,976 |
| 1930 | 12,973 | 526 | 1,294 | 424,133 | 62,945 |
| 1931 | 10,504 | 603 | 922 | 346,625 | 54,110 |
| 1932 | 9,843 | 806 | 691 | 280,964 | 45,228 |
| 1933 | 9,954 | 845 | 647 | 302,665 | 44,943 |
| 1934 | 11,700 | 829 | 782 | 326,013 | 51,862 |

| | Canada[1] | | Mexico | USA | | |
|---|---|---|---|---|---|---|
| | Hard Coal | Brown Coal | | Hard Coal | Brown Coal | Anthracite |
| 1935 | 11,760 | 839 | 1,255 | 335,316 | 2,495 | 47,318 |
| 1936 | 12,886 | 930 | 1,308 | 395,513 | 2,821 | 49,514 |
| 1937 | 13,411 | 955 | 1,242 | 401,259 | 2,920 | 47,043 |
| 1938 | 12,039 | 929 | 1,093 | 313,475 | 2,720 | 41,820 |
| 1939 | 13,364 | 872 | 877 | 355,446 | 2,760 | 46,708 |
| 1940 | 14,939 | 997 | 816 | 415,339 | 2,666 | 46,706 |
| 1941 | 15,333 | 1,201 | 856 | 463,910 | 2,518 | 51,136 |
| 1942 | 15,933 | 1,182 | 914 | 525,951 | 2,659 | 54,729 |
| 1943 | 14,689 | 1,512 | 1,053 | 532,906 | 2,494 | 55,015 |
| 1944 | 14,201 | 1,245 | 904 | 559,953 | 2,317 | 57,789 |

**D2    NORTH AMERICA: Output of Coal** (in thousands of metric tons except as indicated)

| | Canada[1] | | Mexico | USA | | |
|---|---|---|---|---|---|---|
| | | | | Bituminous[4] | | Anthracite |
| | Hard Coal | Brown Coal | | Hard Coal | Brown Coal | |
| 1945 | 13,584 | 1,391 | 915 | 521,584 | 2,421 | 49,835 |
| 1946 | 14,776 | 1,382 | 978 | 481,946 | 2,420 | 54,891 |
| 1947 | 12,971 | 1,425 | 1,040 | 569,486 | 2,607 | 51,882 |
| 1948 | 15,296 | 1,442 | 1,057 | 541,075 | 2,799 | 51,837 |
| 1949 | 15,649 | 1,697 | 1,075 | 394,422 | 2,805 | 38,739 |
| 1950 | 15,364 | 1,999 | 912 | 465,332 | 3,057 | 39,986 |
| 1951 | 14,845 | 2,017 | 1,119 | 481,147 | 2,986 | 38,710 |
| 1952 | 14,058 | 1,890 | 1,317 | 420,774 | 2,737 | 36,816 |
| 1953 | 12,591 | 1,834 | 1,432 | 412,261 | 2,586 | 28,076 |
| 1954 | 11,609 | 1,921 | 1,314 | 352,771 | 2,579 | 26,384 |
| 1955 | 11,362 | 2,081 | 1,342 | 418,636 | 2,872 | 23,773 |
| 1956 | 11,407 | 2,125 | 1,548 | 451,774 | 2,611 | 26,218 |
| 1957 | 9,925 | 2,041 | 1,548 | 444,609 | 2,365 | 22,986 |
| 1958 | 8,558 | 2,044 | 1,476[3] | 370,148 | 2,202 | 19,206 |
| 1959 | 7,874 | 1,767 | 961 | 371,402 | 2,384 | 18,732 |
| 1960 | 8,020 | 1,969 | 1,074 | 374,455 | 2,491 | 17,071 |
| 1961 | 7,429 | 2,004 | 1,063 | 362,833 | 2,738 | 15,827 |
| 1962 | 7,283 | 2,047 | 1,106 | 380,196 | 2,771 | 15,326 |
| 1963 | 7,894 | 1,700 | 1,225 | 413,879 | 2,454 | 16,572 |
| 1964 | 8,460 | 1,809 | 1,277 | 439,121 | 2,676 | 15,589 |
| 1965 | 8,641 | 1,872 | 943 | 461,797 | 2,761 | 13,466 |
| 1966 | 8,449 | 1,885 | 1,261 | 480,808 | 3,521 | 11,740 |
| 1967 | 8,296 | 1,812 | 1,424 | 497,261 | 4,073 | 11,118 |
| 1968 | 7,928 | 2,041 | 1,558 | 490,268 | 4,370 | 10,397 |
| 1969 | 7,849 | 1,832 | 2,458 | 503,935 | 4,547 | 9,501 |
| 1970 | 11,598 | 3,465 | 2,959 | 541,562 | 5,409 | 8,826 |
| 1971 | 13,728 | 2,994 | 3,513 | 495,132 | 5,808[4] | 7,917 |
| 1972 | 15,810 | 2,978 | 3,614 | 530,147 | 9,978 | 6,447 |
| 1973 | 16,618 | | 4,263 | 523,966 | 12,848 | 6,196 |
| 1974 | 17,784 | | 5,166 | 531,160 | 14,041 | 6,003 |
| | | | | (million metric tons) | | |
| 1975 | 15,751 | 9,507 | 5,193 | 570.3 | 18.0 | 5.6 |
| 1976 | 14,389 | 11,086 | 5,650 | 592.4 | 23.1 | 5.6 |
| 1977 | 15,317 | 13,203 | 6,610 | 601.6 | 26.5 | 5.3 |
| 1978 | 17,141 | 13,343 | 6,756 | 571.1 | 32.3 | 4.6 |
| 1979 | 18,610 | 14,587 | 7,357 | 666.2 | 38.0 | 4.4 |
| 1980 | 20,173 | 16,514 | 7,010 | 704.9 | 42.3 | 5.5 |
| 1981 | 21,739 | 18,349 | 8,086 | 695.9 | 46.5 | 4.9 |
| 1982 | 22,379 | 20,528 | 7,634 | 708.2 | 47.9 | 4.2 |
| 1983 | 22,563 | 22,224 | 8,996 | 652.9 | 52.9 | 3.7 |
| 1984 | 32,063 | 25,339 | 9,522 | 751.7 | 57.3 | 3.8 |
| 1985 | 34,310 | 26,544 | 9,790 | 731.6 | 65.7 | 4.3 |
| 1986 | 30,542 | 26,506 | 10,157 | 747.0 | 66.8 | 3.9 |
| 1987 | 32,651 | 28,556 | 11,137 | 759.6 | 70.7 | 3.3 |
| 1988 | 38,585 | 32,059 | 10,586 | 780.7 | 78.1 | 3.3 |

**D2**  **SOUTH AMERICA: OUTPUT OF COAL** (in thousands of metric tons)

| | Argentina | Brazil | Chile | Colombia | Peru | Venezuela[6] |
|---|---|---|---|---|---|---|
| 1895 | ... | ... | 200 | ... | ... | ... |
| 1896 | ... | ... | 205 | ... | ... | ... |
| 1897 | ... | ... | 244 | ... | ... | ... |
| 1898 | ... | ... | 283 | ... | 10 | ... |
| 1899 | ... | ... | 242 | ... | ... | ... |
| 1900 | ... | ... | 325 | ... | 48 | ... |
| 1901 | ... | ... | 600 | ... | 45 | ... |
| 1902 | ... | ... | 750 | ... | ... | ... |
| 1903 | ... | ... | 827 | ... | ... | ... |
| 1904 | ... | ... | 752 | ... | 60 | ... |
| 1905 | ... | ... | 794 | ... | 75 | ... |
| 1906 | ... | ... | 932 | ... | 77 | ... |
| 1907 | ... | ... | 833 | ... | 186 | ... |
| 1908 | ... | ... | 940 | ... | 311 | ... |
| 1909 | ... | ... | 899 | ... | 311 | ... |
| 1910 | ... | ... | 1,074 | ... | 307 | ... |
| 1911 | ... | ... | 1,188 | ... | 324 | ... |
| 1912 | ... | ... | 1,334 | ... | 268 | ... |
| 1913 | ... | 26 | 1,283 | ... | 274 | 7 |
| 1914 | ... | ... | 1,807 | ... | 284 | 9 |
| 1915 | ... | ... | 1,172 | ... | 291 | 13 |
| 1916 | ... | ... | 1,418 | ... | 319 | 18 |
| 1917 | ... | ... | 1,539 | ... | 354 | 20 |
| 1918 | ... | ... | 1,516 | ... | 346 | ... |
| 1919 | ... | ... | 1,485 | ... | 344 | 30 |
| 1920 | ... | 302 | 1,063 | ... | 378 | ... |
| 1921 | ... | 260 | 1,275 | ... | 357 | 28 |
| 1922 | ... | 400 | 1,053 | .... | 303 | 29 |
| 1923 | ... | 324 | 1,164 | ... | 253 | 26 |
| 1924 | ... | 298 | 1,539 | ... | 155 | 25 |
| 1925 | ... | 378 | 1,453 | ... | 102 | 25 |
| 1926 | ... | 361 | 1,491 | ... | 170 | 16 |
| 1927 | ... | 347 | 1,482 | ... | 162 | 16 |
| 1928 | ... | 330 | 1,376 | ... | 178 | 16[6] |
| | | | | ... | | 18 |
| 1929 | ... | 373 | 1,508 | | 221 | 19 |
| 1930 | ... | 385 | 1,442 | ... | 201 | 9 |
| 1931 | ... | ... | 1,100 | ... | 141 | 1 |
| 1932 | ... | 541 | 1,080 | ... | 26 | 1 |
| 1933 | ... | 641 | 1,538 | 90 | 30 | 5 |
| 1934 | ... | 719 | 1,808 | 251 | 35 | 6 |
| 1935 | ... | 826 | 1,900 | 378 | 85 | 1 |
| 1936 | ... | 649 | 1,875 | 392 | 90 | 6 |
| 1937 | ... | 763 | 1,988 | 341 | 99 | 7 |
| 1938 | ... | 907 | 2,044 | 331 | 75 | 6 |
| 1939 | 1 | 1,047 | 1,850 | 349 | 108 | 3 |
| 1940 | 1 | 1,336 | 1,938 | 521 | 113 | 5 |
| 1941 | 1 | 1,408 | 2,060 | 403 | 117 | 6 |
| 1942 | 4 | 1,775 | 2,151 | 578 | 149 | 9 |
| 1943 | 9 | 2,078 | 2,265 | 483 | 187 | 11 |
| 1944 | 5 | 1,908 | 2,279 | 499 | 173 | 9 |

**D2      SOUTH AMERICA: Output of Coal** (in thousands of metric tons)

| | Argentina | Brazil | Chile | | Colombia | Peru | Venezuela[6] |
|---|---|---|---|---|---|---|---|
| | | | Hard Coal | Brown Coal | | | |
| 1945 | 3 | 2,073 | 2,079 | | 534 | 201 | 7 |
| 1946 | 3 | 1,897 | 1,966 | | 551 | 230 | 4 |
| 1947 | 14 | 1,999 | 2,067 | | 506 | 215 | 3 |
| 1948 | 17 | 2,025 | 1,994 | | 514 | 189 | 3 |
| 1949 | 18 | 2,129 | 2,141 | | 521[5] | 170 | 2 |
| 1950 | 26 | 1,959 | 2,217 | | 1,011 | 196 | 1[6] |
| 1951 | 40 | 1,962 | 1,956 | 257 | 1,115 | 186 | 28 |
| 1952 | 112 | 1,960 | 2,174 | 273 | 966 | 225 | 25 |
| 1953 | 37 | 2,025 | 2,038 | 267 | 1,230 | 210 | 29 |
| 1954 | 33 | 2,055 | 1,879 | 238 | 1,500 | 206 | 32 |
| 1955 | 75 | 2,268[7] 1,676 | 1,889 | 229 | 1,850 | 136 | 31 |
| 1956 | 97 | 1,550 | 1,887 | 210 | 2,000 | 145 | 31 |
| 1957 | 123 | 1,466 | 1,748[8] | 173[8] | 2,000 | 141 | 35 |
| 1958 | 136 | 1,312 | 1,670 | 75 | 2,440 | 223 | 36 |
| 1959 | 184 | 1,284 | 1,655 | 79 | 2,480 | 173 | 34 |
| 1960 | 175 | 1,277 | 1,297 | 68 | 2,600 | 162 | 35 |
| 1961 | 236 | 1,256 | 1,531 | 91 | 2,800 | 167 | 31 |
| 1962 | 211 | 1,583 | 1,638 | 84 | 3,000 | 162 | 27 |
| 1963 | 207 | 1,542 | 1,515 | 89 | 3,200 | 131 | 42 |
| 1964 | 335 | 1,782 | 1,592 | 85 | 3,000 | 147 | 36 |
| 1965 | 374 | 2,186 | 1,544 | 85 | 3,072 | 129 | 31 |
| 1966 | 357 | 2,144 | 1,462 | 80 | 2,500 | 150 | 34 |
| 1967 | 411 | 2,295 | 1,357 | 40 | 3,100 | 167 | 34 |
| 1968 | 472 | 2,364 | 1,417 | 57 | 3,100 | 161 | 31 |
| 1969 | 522 | 2,437 | 1,491 | 68 | 3,300 | 162 | 32 |
| 1970 | 616 | 2,361 | 1,351 | 63 | 2,268 | 156 | 40 |
| 1971 | 632 | 2,498 | 1,492 | 65 | 2,540 | 103 | 43 |
| 1972 | 675 | 2,497 | 1,310 | 63 | 2,631 | 104 | 40 |
| 1973 | 451 | 2,427 | 1,374 | 61 | 3,048 | 10 | 50 |
| 1974 | 626 | 3,181 | 1,444 | 41 | 3,266 | — | 57 |
| 1975 | 502 | 2,817 | 1,461 | 46 | 3,447 | 23 | 60 |
| 1976 | 615 | 3,391 | 1,261 | 28 | 3,629 | 20 | 87 |
| 1977 | 533 | 4,009 | 1,306 | 30 | 3,814 | 25 | 121 |
| 1978 | 434 | 4,582 | 1,129 | 30 | 4,019 | 26 | 81 |
| 1979 | 727 | 5,028 | 926 | 35 | 4,618 | 28 | 55 |
| 1980 | 390 | 5,241 | 968 | 40 | 4,112 | 44 | 44 |
| 1981 | 498 | 5,689 | 1,099 | 36 | 4,325 | 94 | 46 |
| 1982 | 515 | 6,346 | 985 | 40 | 4,422 | 73 | 47 |
| 1983 | 486 | 6,737 | 990 | 40 | 5,192 | 92 | 39 |
| 1984 | 509 | 7,519 | 1,184 | 40 | 6,637 | 105 | 51 |
| 1985 | 400 | 7,712 | 1,291 | 35 | 8,974 | 125 | 41 |
| 1986 | 365 | 7,391 | 1,633 | 35 | 10,800 | 135 | 57 |
| 1987 | 373 | 6,884 | 1,567 | 36 | 14,594 | 130 | 238 |
| 1988 | 511 | 7,331 | 1,926 | 37 | 15,101 | 120 | 1,072 |

**D2     Output of Coal** (in thousands of metric tons)


NOTES

1.   SOURCES: The national publications listed on p. xiv–xvi; League of Nations and UN, *Statistical Yearbooks;* and UN, *Yearbook of Industrial Statistics* (under various names). US figures to 1885 were derived by *Historical Statistics of the United States,* from H. N. Eavenson, *The First Century and a Quarter of American Coal Industry* (Pittsburgh, 1942).
2.   Lignite is normally included with brown coal. Where there is no indication, output was usually of hard coal only, except where hard and brown coal are later distinguished separately.


FOOTNOTES

[1] Nova Scotia only to 1865, the figures to 1861 (1st line) being of shipments from mines. Dominion statistics to 1918 are of sales plus colliery consumption.
[2] Lignite is included with hard coal from 1928 (2nd line).
[3] Waste coal is excluded subsequently. In the year of the change it was calculated as 38% of production.
[4] Texas lignite is not included until 1972.
[5] Coal shipped by rail to 1949.
[6] Excluding state mines to 1928 (1st line) and mines outside Guárico State until 1951.
[7] The reason for this break is not given in the source. A revised figure for 1948, comparable with the later statistics was given, viz. 1,424.
[8] A small amount of production was transferred between categories.
[9] Sub-bituminous coal is counted as brown coal from 1975.

**D3    NORTH AMERICA: OUTPUT OF CRUDE PETROLEUM** (in thousands of metric tons)

### 1859–1942

|      | Canada[1] | USA   |      | Canada[1] | Mexico[3] | Trinidad & Tobago[4] | USA     |
|------|-----------|-------|------|-----------|-----------|----------------------|---------|
| 1859 | ...       | - -   | 1900 | 93        | —         | —                    | 8,483   |
| 1860 | ...       | 67    | 1901 | 81        | 1         | —                    | 9,252   |
| 1861 | ...       | 282   | 1902 | 69        | 6         | —                    | 11,836  |
| 1862 | ...       | 408   | 1903 | 64        | 11        | —                    | 13,395  |
| 1863 | ...       | 348   | 1904 | 66        | 19        | —                    | 15,611  |
| 1864 | ...       | 282   |      |           |           |                      |         |
| 1865 | ...       | 333   | 1905 | 83        | 38        | —                    | 17,962  |
| 1866 | ...       | 480   | 1906 | 74        | 75        | —                    | 16,866  |
| 1867 | 25        | 446   | 1907 | 102       | 151       | —                    | 22,146  |
| 1868 | 26        | 486   | 1908 | 69        | 589       | —                    | 23,804  |
| 1869 | 29        | 562   | 1909 | 55        | 407       | ...                  | 24,423  |
| 1870 | 33        | 701   | 1910 | 41        | 545       | 17                   | 27,941  |
| 1871 | 35        | 694   | 1911 | 38        | 1,881     | 40                   | 29,393  |
| 1872 | 40        | 839   | 1912 | 32        | 2,481     | 70                   | 29,725  |
| 1873 | 48        | 1,319 | 1913 | 30        | 3,851     | 90                   | 33,126  |
| 1874 | 22        | 1,457 | 1914 | 28        | 3,931     | 146                  | 35,435  |
| 1875 | 29        | 1,172 | 1915 | 28        | 4,901     | [93][7]              | 37,481  |
| 1876 | 41        | 1,218 | 1916 | 26        | 6,079     | 129                  | 40,102  |
| 1877 | 41        | 1,780 | 1917 | 28        | 8,290     | 223                  | 44,709  |
| 1878 | 41        | 2,053 | 1918 | 40        | 9,569     | 308                  | 47,457  |
| 1879 | 75        | 2,655 | 1919 | 31        | 13,054    | 256                  | 52,099  |
| 1880 | 46        | 3,505 | 1920 | 26        | 23,549    | 290                  | 62,122  |
| 1881 | 48        | 3,688 | 1921 | 26        | 27,707    | 342                  | 64,718  |
| 1882 | 51        | 4,047 | 1922 | 25        | 26,114    | 340                  | 76,415  |
| 1883 | 62        | 3,127 | 1923 | 23        | 21,431    | 424                  | 100,371 |
| 1884 | 75        | 3,229 | 1924 | 22        | 20,011    | 564                  | 98,024  |
| 1885 | 77        | 2,915 | 1925 | 43        | 16,549    | 610                  | 104,622 |
| 1886 | 76        | 3,742 | 1926 | 47        | 12,954    | 737                  | 106,474 |
| 1887 | 93        | 3,771 | 1927 | 61        | 9,186     | 797                  | 123,486 |
| 1888 | 91        | 3,682 | 1928 | 80        | 7,184     | 1,139                | 123,592 |
| 1889 | 92        | 4,689 | 1929 | 144       | 6,401     | 1,217                | 138,104 |
| 1890 | 104       | 6,110 | 1930 | 196       | 5,662     | 1,315                | 123,117 |
| 1891 | 99        | 7,239 | 1931 | 198       | 4,733     | 1,371                | 116,683 |
| 1892 | 102       | 6,735 | 1932 | 134       | 4,699     | 1,425                | 107,645 |
| 1893 | 104       | 6,457 | 1933 | 142       | 4,870     | 1,345                | 122,536 |
| 1894 | 108       | 6,579 | 1934 | 135       | 5,462     | 1,576                | 122,715 |
| 1895 | 95        | 7,052 | 1935 | 128       | 5,758     | 1,688                | 134,679 |
| 1896 | 95        | 8,128 | 1936 | 122       | 5,871     | 1,915                | 148,611 |
| 1897 | 93        | 8,063 | 1937 | 309       | 6,711     | 2,243                | 172,865 |
| 1898 | 99        | 7,382 | 1938 | 873       | 5,510     | 2,566                | 164,107 |
| 1899 | 106       | 7,609 | 1939 | 1,017     | 6,138     | 2,865                | 170,946 |
|      |           |       | 1940 | 1,128     | 6,301     | 3,226                | 182,873 |
|      |           |       | 1941 | 1,330     | 6,160     | 2,976                | 189,496 |
|      |           |       | 1942 | 1,360     | 4,982     | 3,204                | 187,390 |

**D3    NORTH AMERICA: Output of Crude Petroleum** (in thousands of metric tons)

| | Canada[1] | Cuba | Mexico | Trinidad & Tobago | USA |
|---|---|---|---|---|---|
| 1943 | 1,295 | - - | 5,031 | 3,104 | 203,468 |
| 1944 | 1,304 | 2 | 5,467 | 3,141 | 226,751 |
| 1945 | 1,091 | 10 | 6,231 | 3,061 | 231,582 |
| 1946 | 966 | 11 | 7,045 | 2,936 | 234,323 |
| 1947 | 982 | 17 | 8,053 | 2,988 | 250,952 |
| 1948 | 1,660 | 13 | 8,372 | 2,846 | 273,007 |
| 1949 | 2,815 | 9 | 7,818 | 3,011 | 248,919 |
| 1950 | 3,925 | 2 | 10,363 | 3,015 | 266,708 |
| 1951 | 6,435 | 2 | 11,062 | 3,026 | 303,754 |
| 1952 | 8,276 | 1 | 11,059 | 3,086 | 309,447 |
| 1953 | 10,941 | 1 | 10,362 | 3,162 | 318,535 |
| 1954 | 12,984 | 3 | 11,967 | 3,343 | 312,846 |
| 1955 | 17,492 | 48 | 12,786 | 3,523 | 335,744 |
| 1956 | 23,260 | 71 | 12,970 | 4,093 | 353,698 |
| 1957 | 24,594 | 52 | 12,627 | 4,820 | 353,646 |
| 1958 | 22,383 | 45 | 13,380 | 5,286 | 330,955 |
| 1959 | 24,832 | 25 | 13,969 | 5,790 | 347,929 |
| 1960 | 25,630 | 14 | 14,171 | 5,994 | 347,975 |
| 1961 | 29,863 | 10 | 15,278 | 6,476 | 354,303 |
| 1962 | 33,020 | 12 | 16,000 | 6,916 | 361,658 |
| 1963 | 34,845 | 31 | 16,483 | 6,888 | 372,001 |
| 1964 | 37,147 | 37 | 16,535 | 7,036 | 376,609 |
| 1965 | 39,457 | 57 | 16,874 | 6,913 | 384,946 |
| 1966 | 43,248 | 69 | 17,317 | 7,727 | 409,170 |
| 1967 | 47,333 | 116 | 18,702 | 9,197 | 434,573 |
| 1968 | 50,433 | 198 | 20,015 | 9,467 | 449,885 |
| 1969 | 53,767 | 206 | 21,058 | 8,126 | 455,602 |
| 1970 | 62,000 | 159 | 21,508 | 7,223 | 475,289 |
| 1971 | 66,193 | 120 | 21,416 | 6,671 | 466,704 |
| 1972 | 75,421 | 112 | 22,166 | 7,246 | 466,956 |
| 1973 | 88,028 | 138 | 23,257 | 8,804 | 654,190 |
| 1974 | 82,529 | 168 | 29,593 | 9,641 | 432,794 |
| 1975 | 70,166 | 226 | 36,889 | 11,216 | 413,090 |
| 1976 | 64,523 | 234 | 41,336 | 10,990 | 401,252 |
| 1977 | 64,668 | 256 | 49,303 | 11,832 | 405,712 |
| 1978 | 64,333 | 288 | 62,346 | 11,854 | 428,490 |
| 1979 | 73,279 | 288 | 75,461 | 11,072 | 420,818 |
| 1980 | 70,405 | 274 | 99,938 | 10,983 | 424,196 |
| 1981 | 62,928 | 259 | 120,203 | 9,780 | 421,804 |
| 1982 | 62,163 | 541 | 142,783 | 9,144 | 425,591 |
| 1983 | 66,408 | 742 | 139,758 | 8,255 | 427,515 |
| 1984 | 70,668 | 770 | 139,946 | 8,758 | 438,127 |
| 1985 | 72,004 | 868 | 135,755 | 9,097 | 441,479 |
| 1986 | 72,302 | 938 | 126,211 | 8,722 | 428,154 |
| 1987 | 75,411 | 895 | 132,086 | 8,061 | 419,442 |
| 1988 | 79,248 | 717 | 130,675 | 7,858 | 410,079 |

**D3    SOUTH AMERICA: OUTPUT OF CRUDE PETROLEUM** (in thousands of metric tons)

| | Argentina | Bolivia | Brazil | Chile | Colombia | Ecuador | Peru | Venezuela |
|---|---|---|---|---|---|---|---|---|
| 1915 | 76 | — | — | — | — | — | 344 | 5 |
| 1916 | 130 | — | — | — | — | — | 346 | 10 |
| 1917 | 180 | — | — | — | — | — | 347 | 18 |
| 1918 | 199 | — | — | — | — | — | 335 | 48 |
| 1919 | 172 | — | — | — | — | — | 349 | 63 |
| 1920 | 243 | — | — | — | — | — | 373 | 70 |
| 1921 | 323 | — | — | — | — | — | 489 | 218 |
| 1922 | 439 | — | — | — | 46 | — | 701 | 335 |
| 1923 | 497 | — | — | — | 61 | — | 752 | 639 |
| 1924 | 677 | — | — | — | 64 | — | 1,046 | 1,335 |
| 1925 | 924 | — | — | — | 144 | 23 | 1,220 | 2,864 |
| 1926 | 1,143 | — | — | — | 920 | 30 | 1,427 | 5,207 |
| 1927 | 1,263 | — | — | — | 2,144 | 76 | 1,341 | 8,969 |
| 1928 | 1,318 | 1 | — | — | 2,841 | 154 | 1,592 | 15,349 |
| 1929 | 1,362 | 3 | — | — | 2,911 | 196 | 1,777 | 19,891 |
| 1930 | 1,305 | 4 | — | — | 2,782 | 221 | 1,656 | 20,109 |
| 1931 | 1,652 | 2 | — | — | 2,484 | 250 | 1,340 | 17,221 |
| 1932 | 1,875 | 5 | — | — | 2,237 | 227 | 1,313 | 17,120 |
| 1933 | 1,951 | 14 | — | — | 1,792 | 230 | 1,762 | 17,334 |
| 1934 | 1,998 | 20 | — | — | 2,399 | 232 | 2,162 | 19,935 |
| 1935 | 2,037 | 21 | — | — | 2,434 | 245 | 2,253 | 21,723 |
| 1936 | 2,212 | 13 | — | — | 2,594 | 272 | 2,324 | 22,619 |
| 1937 | 2,340 | 16 | — | — | 2,807 | 285 | 2,300 | 27,204 |
| 1938 | 2,444 | 18 | — | — | 2,984 | 297 | 2,097 | 27,485 |
| 1939 | 2,663 | 28 | — | — | 3,300 | 305 | 1,794 | 29,967 |
| 1940 | 2,948 | 38 | - - | — | 3,535 | 310 | 1,609 | 26,896 |
| 1941 | 3,150 | 31 | - - | — | 3,408 | 205 | 1,583 | 33,184 |
| 1942 | 3,392 | 40 | 4 | — | 1,465 | 301 | 1,810 | 21,650 |
| 1943 | 3,553 | 43 | 6 | — | 1,853 | 305 | 1,948 | 26,238 |
| 1944 | 3,467 | 41 | 8 | — | 3,133 | 382 | 1,914 | 37,597 |
| 1945 | 3,274 | 50 | 10 | — | 3,157 | 345 | 1,827 | 47,304 |
| 1946 | 2,976 | 47 | 9 | — | 3,102 | 307 | 1,639 | 56,822 |
| 1947 | 3,126 | 49 | 13 | — | 3,455 | 311 | 1,699 | 63,611 |
| 1948 | 3,323 | 60 | 19 | — | 3,284 | 338 | 1,879 | 70,215 |
| 1949 | 3,232 | 88 | 14 | 7 | 4,111 | 338 | 1,968 | |
| 1950 | 3,357 | 80 | 38 | 8 | 4,711 | 347 | 2,007 | ... |
| 1951 | 3,501 | 68 | 90 | 99 | 5,311 | 357 | 2,151 | ... |
| 1952 | 3,552 | 67 | 98 | 119 | 6,351 | 375 | 2,191 | ... |
| 1953 | 4,078 | 78 | 120 | 164 | 5,454 | 391 | 2,137 | 92,140 |
| 1954 | 4,231 | 221 | 130 | 226 | 5,530 | 415 | 2,292 | 98,998 |
| 1955 | 4,365 | 351 | 265 | 336 | 5,493 | 466 | 2,303 | 113,041 |
| 1956 | 4,437 | 417 | 530 | 462 | 6,104 | 451 | 2,455 | 129,178 |
| 1957 | 4,858 | 466 | 1,321 | 565 | 6,327 [3] | 421 | 2,567 | 145,830 |
| 1958 | 5,102 | 448 | 2,473 | 726 | 6,342 | 410 | 2,502 | 135,636 |
| 1959 | 6,206 | 413 | 3,083 | 838 | 7,261 | 364 | 2,368 | 144,850 |

**D3      SOUTH AMERICA: Output of Crude Petroleum** (in thousands of metric tons)

| | Argentina | Bolivia | Brazil | Chile | Colombia | Ecuador | Peru[5] | Venezuela[6] |
|---|---|---|---|---|---|---|---|---|
| 1960 | 8,898 | 466 | 3,870 | 943 | 7,584 | 360 | 2,572 | 149,372 |
| 1961 | 11,752 | 390 | 4,549 | 1,208 | 7,238 | 386 | 2,587 | 152,616 |
| 1962 | 13,661 | 364 | 4,367 | 1,524 | 7,059 | 340 | 2,822 | 167,147 |
| 1963 | 13,514 | 443 | 4,669 | 1,722 | 8,228 | 325 | 2,867 | 169,671 |
| 1964 | 13,961 | 428 | 4,353 | 1,784 | 8,597 | 369 | 3,181 | 178,230 |
| 1965 | 13,672 | 438 | 4,488 | 1,656 | 10,123 | 376 | 3,081 | 182,409 |
| 1966 | 14,559 | 779 | 5,548 | 1,620 | 9,938 | 342 | 3,075 | 176,418 |
| 1967 | 15,953 | 1,838 | 7,079 | 1,620 | 9,603 | 290 | 3,453 | 185,489 |
| 1968 | 17,525 | 1,897 | 7,823 | 1,785 | 9,010 | 233 | 3,613 | 189,231 |
| 1969 | 18,166 | 1,876 | 8,360 | 1,711 | 10,934 | 209 | 3,519 | 187,916 |
| 1970 | 20,026 | 1,122 | 7,980 | 1,468 | 11,327 | 193 | 3,550 | 194,306 |
| 1971 | 21,578 | 1,710 | 8,303 | 1,402 | 11,127 | 179 | 3,053 | 185,280 |
| 1972 | 22,130 | 2,031 | 8,138 | 1,417 | 10,142 | 4,016 | 3,204 | 168,342 |
| 1973 | 21,476 | 2,196 | 8,276 | 1,276 | 9,493 | 10,615 | 3,482 | 175,774 |
| 1974 | 21,139 | 2,112 | 8,617 | 1,110 | 8,686 | 8,989 | 3,815 | 156,167 |
| 1975 | 20,773 | 1,874 | 8,352 | 994 | 8,102 | 8,155 | 3,553 | 122,400 |
| 1976 | 20,810 | 1,890 | 8,344 | 938 | 7,553 | 9,488 | 3,779 | 120,170 |
| 1977 | 22,167 | 1,612 | 8,025 | 928 | 7,106 | 9,283 | 4,571 | 117,189 |
| 1978 | 23,236 | 1,506 | 8,002 | 780 | 6,755 | 10,223 | 7,528 | 113,628 |
| 1979 | 24,279 | 1,294 | 8,262 | 1,010 | 6,410 | 10,874 | 9,413 | 124,106 |
| 1980 | 25,281 | 1,107 | 9,083 | 1,604 | 6,501 | 10,417 | 9,664 | 114,788 |
| 1981 | 25,534 | 1,029 | 10,675 | 1,950 | 6,912 | 10,745 | 9,538 | 111,688 |
| 1982 | 25,196 | 1,134 | 12,984 | 2,003 | 7,320 | 10,746 | 9,729 | 100,391 |
| 1983 | 25,200 | 1,030 | 16,595 | 1,919 | 7,851 | 12,088 | 8,589 | 94,470 |
| 1984 | 24,637 | 969 | 23,216 | 1,879 | 8,653 | 13,088 | 9,358 | 94,850 |
| 1985 | 23,607 | 917 | 27,493 | 1,591 | 8,887 | 14,243 | 9,296 | 88,186 |
| 1986 | 22,283 | 816 | 28,784 | 1,485 | 15,289 | 14,551 | 9,027 | 93,933 |
| 1987 | 21,999 | 836 | 28,463 | 1,319 | 19,415 | 8,856 | 8,754 | 95,449 |
| 1988 | 23,119 | 842 | 27,853 | 1,057 | 18,939 | 15,806 | 7,579 | 101,987 |

NOTES

1.    SOURCES: As for table D2
2.    Output from oil shale is not included in this table.
3.    Data for many countries is given originally in measures of capacity (i.e. the barrel of 42 US gallons). The conversion ratios used by UN and League of Nations statisticians have been followed generally here, when they are available. For periods prior to 1921, the ratios used in the early 1920s have been employed.

FOOTNOTES

[1] The conversion ratio used to 1920 is 7.66 barrels=1 ton. Crude petroleum from tar sands is not included. Since the beginning of extraction in 1967 production has been as follows (in thousands of tons):

| | | | | | |
|---|---|---|---|---|---|
| 1967 | 61 | 1970 | 1,625 | 1973 | 2,481 |
| 1968 | 774 | 1971 | 2,020 | 1974 | 2,270 |
| 1969 | 1,357 | 1972 | 2,531 | 1975 | 2,120 |

[2] The conversion ratio used to 1917 is 7.50 barrels = 1 ton.
[3] The conversion ratio used to 1927 is 6.98 barrels = 1 ton.
[4] The conversion ratio used to 1920 is 7.18 barrels = 1 ton. Data to 1914 are for years beginning 1 April, the 1915 figure being for the period April–December.
[5] Production began in 1907 and statistics to 1914 are available as follows:—1908 2; 1909 2; 1910 3; 1911 2; 1912 9; 1913 18; 1914 41.
[6] Earlier statistics are available as follows:—

| | | | | | | | | | | | |
|---|---|---|---|---|---|---|---|---|---|---|---|
| 1884 | 1 | 1890 | 4 | 1895 | 13 | 1900 | 38 | 1905 | 50 | 1910 | 168 |
| 1885 | 1 | 1891 | 15 | 1896 | 13 | 1901 | 39 | 1906 | 71 | 1911 | 195 |
| 1886 | 1 | 1892 | 22 | 1897 | 13 | 1902 | 32 | 1907 | 100 | 1912 | 234 |
| 1887 | 2 | 1893 | 15 | 1898 | 20 | 1903 | 37 | 1908 | 126 | 1913 | 273 |
| 1888 | 2 | 1894 | 13 | 1899 | 27 | 1904 | 39 | 1909 | 188 | 1914 | 245 |
| 1889 | 2 | | | | | | | | | | |

The conversion ratio used to 1920 is 7.57 barrels = 1 ton.
[7] Production in 1914 was 2 thousand tons. The conversion ratio used to 1920 is 6.70 barrels = 1 ton.

**D4    NORTH AMERICA: OUTPUT OF NATURAL GAS** (in millions of cubic metres to 1966, and Petajoules subsequently)

| | Canada | Mexico | Trinidad & Tobago | USA[3] | | Canada | Mexico | Trinidad & Tobago | USA[3] |
|---|---|---|---|---|---|---|---|---|---|
| 1900 | ... | ... | ... | 3,625 | 1945 | 1,371 | 976 | 393 | 114,457 |
| 1901 | ... | ... | ... | 5,097 | 1946 | 1,356 | 974 | 402 | 117,600 |
| 1902 | ... | ... | ... | 5,833 | 1947 | 1,491 | 1,189 | 407 | 129,748 |
| 1903 | ... | ... | ... | 6,768 | 1948 | 1,659 | 1,248 | 465 | 145,775 |
| 1904 | ... | ... | ... | 7,277 | 1949 | 1,712 | 1,293 | 489 | 153,477 |
| 1905 | ... | ... | ... | 9,061 | 1950 | 1,921 [1] / 1,870 | 1,793 [1,2] / 920 | 475 | 177,886 |
| 1906 | ... | ... | ... | 11,015 | 1951 | 2,130 | 1,310 | 471 | 211,159 |
| 1907 | ... | ... | ... | 11,525 | 1952 | 2,450 | 1,440 | 478 | 226,903 |
| 1908 | ... | ... | ... | 11,383 | 1953 | 2,785 | 1,440 | 501 | 237,777 |
| 1909 | ... | ... | ... | 13,620 | 1954 | 3,330 | 1,440 | 515 | 247,574 |
| 1910 | ... | ... | ... | 14,413 | 1955 | 4,130 | 1,850 | 498 | 266,320 |
| 1911 | 330 | ... | ... | 14,527 | 1956 | 4,630 | 1,800 | 547 | 285,490 |
| 1912 | 433 | ... | ... | 15,914 | 1957 | 6,025 | 2,380 | 600 | 302,424 |
| 1913 | 580 | ... | ... | 16,480 | 1958 | 9,320 | 3,810 | 663 | 312,335 |
| 1914 | 614 | ... | ... | 16,764 | 1959 | 11,390 | 4,730 | 714 | 341,105 |
| 1915 | 570 | ... | ... | 17,811 | 1960 | 14,270 | 4,900 | 766 | 361,634 |
| 1916 | 721 | ... | ... | 21,323 | 1961 | 17,730 | 5,260 | 832 | 373,273 |
| 1917 | 776 | ... | ... | 22,512 | 1962 | 25,270 | 5,410 | 850 | 390,800 |
| 1918 | 570 | ... | ... | 20,416 | 1963 | 25,705 | 6,100 | 832 | 415,323 |
| 1919 | 565 | ... | ... | 21,124 | 1964 | 34,575 | 7,000 | 1,089 | 437,835 |
| 1920 | 477 | ... | ... | 22,993 | 1965 | 37,389 | 7,440 | 1,174 | 454,202 |
| 1921 | 399 | ... | ... | 19,086 | 1966 | 34,119 / 1,290 | 7,580 / 387 | 1,379 / 54 | 487,268 / 17,932 |
| 1922 | 416 | ... | ... | 21,974 | 1967 | 1,406 | 443 | 59 | 18,932 |
| 1923 | 452 | ... | ... | 29,025 | 1968 | 1,600 | 442 | 62 | 20,156 |
| 1924 | 421 | ... | ... | 32,904 | 1969 | 1,863 | 436 | 62 | 21,571 |
| 1925 | 479 | ... | ... | 34,263 | 1970 | 2,113 | 451 | 73 | 22,860 |
| 1926 | 544 | ... | ... | 37,831 | 1971 | 2,314 | 420 | 71 | 23,517 |
| 1927 | 605 | ... | ... | 41,654 | 1972 | 2,612 | 461 | 73 | 23,524 |
| 1928 | 639 | ... | ... | 45,194 | 1973 | 2,794 | 502 | 71 | 23,410 |
| 1929 | 804 | ... | ... | 55,274 | 1974 | 2,735 | 522 | 65 | 22,080 |
| 1930 | 832 | ... | ... | 56,039 | 1975 | 2,795 | 523 | 59 | 20,724 |
| 1931 | 733 | ... | ... | 48,762 | 1976 | 2,820 | 520 | 77 | 20,552 |
| 1932 | 663 | 257 | ... | 45,137 | 1977 | 2,962 | 573 | 92 | 18,921 |
| 1933 | 655 | 313 | ... | 45,222 | 1978 | 2,856 | 701 | 114 | 18,846 |
| 1934 | 656 | 347 | ... | 51,423 | 1979 | 3,041 | 832 | 128 | 19,415 |
| 1935 | 705 | ... | ... | 55,756 | 1980 | 2,790 | 1,036 | 146 | 19,256 |
| 1936 | 796 | ... | ... | 63,005 | 1981 | 2,748 | 1,033 | 134 | 19,057 |
| 1937 | 917 | 118 | ... | 70,028 | 1982 | 2,825 | 1,638 | 148 | 17,655 |
| 1938 | 947 | ... | ... | 66,771 | 1983 | 2,740 | 1,452 | 157 | 15,986 |
| 1939 | 996 | 1,165 | 325 | 71,868 | 1984 | 2,972 | 1,112 | 158 | 17,341 |
| 1940 | 1,168 | 1,163 | 391 | 77,418 | 1985 | 3,189 | 1,068 | 192 | 16,365 |
| 1941 | 1,232 | 1,126 | 391 | 81,949 | 1986 | 2,988 | 1,005 | 151 | 15,974 |
| 1942 | 1,294 | 1,055 | 419 | 89,085 | 1987 | 3,254 | 1,011 | 158 | 16,488 |
| 1943 | 1,254 | 879 | 393 | 99,562 | 1988 | 3,758 | 968 | 146 | 16,583 |
| 1944 | 1,276 | 934 | 358 | 108,029 | | | | | |

**D4**  **SOUTH AMERICA: OUTPUT OF NATURAL GAS** (in millions of cubic metres to 1966, and Petajoules subsequently)

|  | Argentina | Bolivia | Brazil | Chile | Colombia | Ecuador | Peru | Venezuela |
|---|---|---|---|---|---|---|---|---|
| 1929 | 260 | ... | — | ... | ... | ... | ... | ... |
| 1930 | 265 | ... | — | ... | ... | ... | ... | ... |
| 1931 | 330 | ... | — | ... | ... | ... | ... | ... |
| 1932 | 450 | ... | — | ... | ... | 6 | ... | 534 |
| 1933 | 605 | ... | — | ... | ... | 9 | ... | 532 |
| 1934 | 732 | ... | — | ... | ... | 10 | ... | 584 |
| 1935 | 618 | ... | — | ... | 493 | 10 | ... | 617 |
| 1936 | 534 | ... | — | ... | 508 | 19 | ... | 642 |
| 1937 | 505 | ... | — | ... | 512 | 46 | ... | 668 |
| 1938 | 491 | ... | — | ... | 512 | 55 | ... | 810 |
| 1939 | 519 | ... | — | ... | 496 | 58 | ... | ... |
| 1940 | 536 | ... | — | ... | 599 | 59 | ... |  |
| 1941 | 593 | ... | — | ... | 678 | 42 | ... | 518 |
| 1942 | 676 | ... | 1 | ... | 553 | 54 | ... | 424 |
| 1943 | 677 | ... | 6 | ... | 533 | 49 | ... | 346 |
| 1944 | 662 | ... | 4 | ... | 682 | 64 | ... | 568 |
| 1945 | 609 | ... | 1 | ... | 678 | 70 | ... | 654 |
| 1946 | 566 | ... | 9 | ... | 620 | 66 | ... | 803 |
| 1947 | 583 | ... | 1 | ... | 563 | 87 | ... | 1,128 |
| 1948 | 606 | ... | 3 | ... | 349 | 106 | ... | 1,177 |
| 1949 | 664 | ... | 2 | ... | 494 | 109 | ... | 1,089 |
| 1950 | 755 | ... | 5 | ... | 510 | 132 | 405 | 1,117 |
| 1951 | 830 | ... | 8 | ... | 489 | 152 | 410 | 1,440 |
| 1952 | 898 | ... | 7 | 59 | 204 | ... | 410 | 1,752 |
| 1953 | 698 | ... | 27 | 70 | 484 | ... | 410 | 2,172 |
| 1954 | 707 | ... | 63 | 90 | 545 | ... | 410 | 2,448 |
| 1955 | 719 | 6 | 62 | 112 | 539 | ... | 410 | 2,748 |
| 1956 | 764 | 7 | 84 | 150 | 621 | ... | 415 | 2,994 |
| 1957 | 852 | 8 | 158 | 250 | 633 | ... | 500 | 3,624 |
| 1958 | 866 | 6 | 300 | 450 | 794 | ... | 425 | 3,929 |
| 1959 | 861 | 7 | 429 | 600 | 908 [2] | ... | 420 | 4,192 |
|  |  |  |  |  | 388 |  |  |  |
| 1960 | 1,383 | 6 | 535 | 823 | 404 | ... | 415 | 4,606 |
| 1961 | 2,357 | 50 | 527 | 1,201 | 417 | ... | 420 | 4,891 |
| 1962 | 2,978 | 57 | 511 | 1,570 | 592 | ... | 430 | 5,189 |
| 1963 | 3,406 | 59 | 503 | 1,532 | 702 | ... | 440 | 5,610 |
| 1964 | 3,751 | 85 | 532 | 1,300 | 762 | ... | 448 | 6,103 |
| 1965 | 4,222 | 80 | 684 | 1,284 | 906 | ... | 437 | 6,538 |
| 1966 | 4,577 | 93 | 789 | 1,134 | 1,099 | ... | 457 | 6,856 |
|  | 159 | 3 | 5 | 41 | ... |  | 13 | 291 |
| 1967 | 167 | 3 | 5 | 43 | ... | ... | 12 | 319 |
| 1968 | 186 | 3 | 5 | 44 | ... | 1 | 14 | 329 |
| 1969 | 185 | 4 | 5 | 43 | 49 | 1 | 14 | 339 |

**D4      SOUTH AMERICA: Output of Natural Gas** (in Petajoules)

|      | Argentina | Bolivia | Brazil | Chile | Colombia | Ecuador | Peru | Venezuela |
|------|-----------|---------|--------|-------|----------|---------|------|-----------|
| 1970 | 209 | 1 | 3 | 48 | 55 | 1 | 16 | 382 |
| 1971 | 224 | 1 | 5 | 51 | 61 | 1 | 15 | 398 |
| 1972 | 219 | 37 | 9 | 52 | 72 | 1 | 16 | 402 |
| 1973 | 234 | 57 | 10 | 46 | 75 | 1 | 15 | 480 |
| 1974 | 252 | 60 | 21 | 46 | 73 | 1 | 16 | 494 |
| 1975 | 265 | 59 | 25 | 46 | 73 | 2 | 24 | 480 |
| 1976 | 268 | 61 | 20 | 46 | 75 | 2 | 21 | 453 |
| 1977 | 270 | 64 | 40 | 54 | 85 | 2 | 19 | 510 |
| 1978 | 255 | 68 | 32 | 59 | 113 | 2 | 20 | 528 |
| 1979 | 303 | 74 | 35 | 41 | 121 | 2 | 19 | 611 |
| 1980 | 327 | 84 | 41 | 27 | 140 | 2 | 21 | 643 |
| 1981 | 340 | 90 | 37 | 33 | 150 | 3 | 25 | 647 |
| 1982 | 393 | 93 | 43 | 34 | 157 | 4 | 26 | 682 |
| 1983 | 457 | 90 | 63 | 37 | 172 | 4 | 19 | 668 |
| 1984 | 478 | 86 | 77 | 37 | 173 | 4 | 24 | 741 |
| 1985 | 509 | 85 | 97 | 38 | 172 | 4 | 24 | 727 |
| 1986 | 553 | 92 | 110 | 34 | 169 | 4 | 25 | 805 |
| 1987 | 657 | 91 | 114 | 34 | 171 | 2 | 25 | 799 |
| 1988 | 775 | 101 | 111 | 45 | 173 | 4 | 24 | 809 |

NOTES

1.   SOURCES: As for table D2.
2.   The statistics normally relate to natural gas from gasfields only (exclusive of waste), and exclude methane from coalfields.

FOOTNOTES

[1] Subsequent figures exclude shrinkage.
[2] Subsequent figures exclude repressured and wasted gas.
[3] Marketed production.

**D5**  **NORTH AMERICA: OUTPUT OF IRON ORE** (in thousands of metric tons)

Key:   A = crude weight, B = weight of Fe content

| | Canada | Cuba[1] | Mexico | Newfoundland | USA |
|---|---|---|---|---|---|
| | A | A | B | A | A |
| 1860 | ... | ... | ... | ... | 2,919 |
| 1870 | ... | ... | ... | ... | 3,893 |
| 1875 | ... | ... | ... | ... | 4,082 |
| 1880 | ... | ... | ... | ... | 7,234 |
| 1881 | ... | ... | ... | ... | 7,234 |
| 1882 | ... | ... | ... | ... | 9,144 |
| 1883 | ... | ... | ... | ... | 8,534 |
| 1884 | ... | ... | ... | ... | 8,332 |
| 1885 | ... | ... | ... | ... | 7,722 |
| 1886 | 58 | ... | ... | ... | 10,160 |
| 1887 | 69 | ... | ... | ... | 11,481 |
| 1888 | 72 | ... | ... | ... | 12,257 |
| 1889 | 76 | ... | ... | ... | 14,751 |
| 1890 | 70 | 370 | ... | ... | 16,293 |
| 1891 | 63 | 268 | ... | 19 | 14,825 |
| 1892 | 93 | 348 | ... | ... | 16,559 |
| 1893 | 114 | 357 | ... | 38 | 11,774 |
| 1894 | 100 | 160 | ... | 41 | 12,071 |
| 1895 | 93 | 388 | ... | ... | 16,214 |
| 1896 | 83 | 420 | ... | 67 | 16,262 |
| 1897 | 46 | 461 | ... | 93 | 17,799 |
| 1898 | 53 | 171 | ... | 136 | 19,746 |
| 1899 | 68 | 383 | ... | 338 | 24,994 |
| 1900 | 111 | 454 | 3 | 323 | 27,738 |
| 1901 | 285 | 561 | 3 | 758 | 29,058 |
| 1902 | 367 | 711 | 2 | 767 | 35,866 |
| 1903 | 239 | 634 | 10 | 641 | 35,358 |
| 1904 | 199 | 393 | 23 | 660 | 27,941 |
| 1905 | 264 | 554 | 20 | 753 | 43,080 |
| 1906 | 226 | 664 | 31 | 928 | 48,516 |
| 1907 | 284 | 658[1] | 23 | 898 | 52,551 |
| 1908 | 216 | 833 | 24 | 950 | 36,560 |
| 1909 | 243 | 945 | 49 | 1,020 | 52,117 |
| 1910 | 235 | 1,441 | 55 | 1,127 | 57,930 |
| 1911 | 190 | 1,183 | 64 | 1,191 | 44,581 |
| 1912 | 196 | 1,422 | 58 | 1,272 | 56,035 |
| 1913 | 279 | 1,608 | 13 | 1,456 | 62,975 |
| 1914 | 222 | 834 | — | 575 | 42,105 |
| 1915 | 361 | 841 | 2 | 788 | 56,417 |
| 1916 | 249 | 724 | 20 | 918 | 76,374 |
| 1917 | 195 | 562 | 19 | 801 | 76,497 |
| 1918 | 192 | 654 | 26 | 770 | 70,776 |
| 1919 | 179 | 203 | 31 | 453 | 61,943 |
| 1920 | 117 | 84 | 26 | 600 | 68,689 |
| 1921 | 54 | 132 | 34 | 348 | 29,964 |
| 1922 | 16 | 452 | 42 | 1,018 | 47,885 |
| 1923 | 28 | 374 | 51 | 733 | 70,464 |
| 1924 | — | 481 | 52 | 993 | 55,138 |

**D5**     **NORTH AMERICA: Output of Iron Ore** (in thousands of metric tons)

| | Canada | | Cuba | | Mexico | Newfoundland[2] | | U.S.A. | |
|---|---|---|---|---|---|---|---|---|---|
| | A | B | A | B | B | A | B | A | B |
| 1925 | — | — | 567 | ... | 76 | 1,150 | 598 | 62,902 | |
| 1926 | — | — | 587 | ... | 49 | 877 | 456 | 68,708 | |
| 1927 | — | — | 422 | ... | 41 | 1,229 | 639 | 62,732 | |
| 1928 | — | — | 401 | 225 | 48 | 1,509 | 785 | 63,195 | 31,649 |
| 1929 | — | — | 682 | 383 | 76 | 1,518 | 789 | 74,200 | 37,226 |
| 1930 | — | — | 249 | 109 | 62 | 1,473 | 766 | 59,346 | 29,681 |
| 1931 | — | — | 227 | 104 | 39 | 546 | 283 | 31,632 | 15,876 |
| 1932 | — | — | 188 | 87 | 16 | 323 | 168 | 10,005 | 5,028 |
| 1933 | — | — | 229 | 129 | 50 | 326 | 170 | 17,835 | 8,918 |
| 1934 | — | — | 80 | 45 | 68 | 514 | 267 | 24,983 | 12,584 |
| 1935 | — | — | 182 | 102 | 67 | 673 | 350 | 31,030 | 15,608 |
| 1936 | — | — | 362 | 203 | 79 | 908 | 471 | 49,572 | 25,078 |
| 1937 | — | — | 400 | 224 | 90 | 1,635 | 850 | 73,251 | 36,991 |
| 1938 | — | — | 125[1] 145 | 70[1] 81 | 99 | 1,707 | 887 | 28,903 | 14,322 |
| 1939 | 112 | 60 | 46 | 26 | 111 | 1,680 | 874 | 52,562 | 26,423 |
| 1940 | 376 | 201 | 96 | 54 | 70 | 1,533 | 798 | 74,879 | 37,918 |
| 1941 | 468 | 250 | 57 | 32 | 72 | 983 | 508 | 93,893 | 47,819 |
| 1942 | 494 | 264 | 100 | 56 | 103 | 1,212 | 630 | 107,219 | 54,767 |
| 1943 | 582 | 293 | 51 | 29 | 138 | 551 | 284 | 102,873 | 52,127 |
| 1944 | 502 | 276 | 13 | 8 | 187 | 472 | 244 | 95,628 | 48,653 |
| 1945 | 1,030 | 567 | — | — | 175 | 983 | 511 | 89,794 | 45,822 |
| 1946 | 1,406 | 773 | — | — | 171 | 1,237 | 648 | 71,980 | 36,154 |
| 1947 | 1,741 | 958 | 39 | 22 | 226 | 1,467 | 763 | 94,586 | 47,709 |
| 1948 | 1,213 | 667 | 23 | 13 | 227 | 1,492 | 789 | 102,624 | 50,891 |
| 1949 | 3,334[2] | 1,834[2] | 7 | 4 | 247 | ... | ... | 86,300 | 43,288 |
| 1950 | 3,270 | 1,799 | 7 | 4 | 286 | ... | ... | 99,618 | 49,306 |
| 1951 | 4,247 | 2,335 | 10 | 6 | 313 | ... | ... | 118,375 | 60,123 |
| 1952 | 4,783 | 2,630 | 52 | 30 | 340 | ... | ... | 99,489 | 50,013 |
| 1953 | 5,906 | 3,248 | 164 | 92 | 331 | ... | ... | 119,888 | 60,376 |
| 1954 | 6,679 | 3,673 | 16 | 9 | 314 | ... | ... | 79,383 | 39,952 |
| 1955 | 14,772 | 8,125 | 141 | 79 | 429 | ... | ... | 104,656 | 53,635 |
| 1956 | 20,274 | 11,151 | ... | 4 | 489 | ... | ... | 99,448 | 51,185 |
| 1957 | 20,205 | 11,113 | ... | 8 | 569 | ... | ... | 107,851 | 55,424 |
| 1958 | 14,266 | 7,847 | ... | 6 | 581 | ... | ... | 68,796 | 36,701 |
| 1959 | 22,215 | 12,218[3] 12,663 | ... | 5 | 535 | ... | ... | 61,243 | 32,129 |
| 1960 | 19,551 | 11,140 | ... | 1 | 521 | ... | ... | 90,209 | 47,867 |
| 1961 | 18,470 | 10,528 | ... | 1 | 687 | ... | ... | 72,474 | 39,103 |
| 1962 | 24,820 | 14,148 | ... | 1 | 1,354 | ... | ... | 72,982 | 39,671 |
| 1963 | 27,346 | 16,150 | ... | 1 | 1,397 | ... | ... | 74,780 | 41,542 |
| 1964 | 34,769 | 20,766 | ... | 1 | 1,392 | ... | ... | 86,197 | 47,681 |
| 1965 | 34,208 | 21,822 | ... | 1 | 1,593 | ... | ... | 88,842 | 50,175 |
| 1966 | 36,914 | 22,702 | ... | ... | 1,481 | ... | ... | 91,594 | 51,750 |
| 1967 | 38,390 | 23,610 | ... | ... | 1,617 | ... | ... | 85,530 | 49,152 |
| 1968 | 43,040 | 26,469 | ... | ... | 1,921 | ... | ... | 87,243 | 50,172 |
| 1969 | 36,336 | 22,347 | ... | ... | 2,097 | ... | ... | 89,745 | 52,512 |
| 1970 | 47,458 | 29,187 | ... | ... | 2,612 | ... | ... | 91,200 | 53,308 |
| 1971 | 42,957 | 26,418 | ... | ... | 2,819 | ... | ... | 82,058 | 49,235 |
| 1972 | 38,735 | 23,822 | ... | ... | 3,053 | ... | ... | 76,644 | 46,754 |
| 1973 | 47,498 | 29,211 | ... | ... | 3,113 | ... | ... | 89,076 | 54,336 |
| 1974 | 46,785 | 28,772 | ... | ... | 3,338 | ... | ... | 85,709 | 52,283 |

## D5 OUTPUT OF IRON ORE (in thousands of metric tons)

### NORTH AMERICA

|      | Canada | | Mexico | U.S.A. | |
|------|--------|--------|--------|--------|--------|
|      | A | B | B | A | B |
| 1975 | 44,893 | 27,609 | 3,369 | 80,132 | 49,041 |
| 1976 | 55,416 | 34,081 | 3,644 | 81,277 | 50,154 |
| 1977 | 53,621 | 32,977 | 3,587 | 56,645 | 35,043 |
| 1978 | 42,931 | 26,403 | 3,556 | 82,892 | 51,579 |
| 1979 | 59,617 | 36,664 | 4,041 | 87,091 | 54,500 |
| 1980 | 49,068 | 30,177 | 5,087 | 70,730 | 44,592 |
| 1981 | 49,551 | 30,654 | 5,749 | 74,348 | 47,286 |
| 1982 | 33,198 | 20,501 | 5,382 | 36,002 | 23,005 |
| 1983 | 32,959 | 20,105 | 5,306 | 38,165 | 24,554 |
| 1984 | 39,930 | 24,357 | 5,489 | 52,092 | 33,640 |
| 1985 | 39,502 | 24,096 | 5,161 | 49,533 | 31,797 |
| 1986 | 36,167 | 22,062 | 4,817 | 39,486 | 25,293 |
| 1987 | 37,702 | 23,060 | 4,965 | 47,648 | 30,525 |
| 1988 | 39,934 | 24,302 | 5,564 | 57,515 | 36,468 |

### SOUTH AMERICA

|      | Chile | |      | Argentina | Brazil | | Chile | |
|------|-------|--|------|-----------|--------|--|-------|--|
|      | A | |      | A | A[4] | B | A | B |
| 1911 | 29 | | 1925 | ... | ... | ... | 1,234 | 814 |
| 1912 | 7 | | 1926 | ... | ... | ... | 1,396 | 921 |
| 1913 | 14 | | 1927 | ... | ... | ... | 1,508 | 995 |
| 1914 | 64 | | 1928 | ... | ... | ... | 1,525 | 1,006 |
|      |    | | 1929 | ... | ... | ... | 1,812 | 1,196 |
| 1915 | 147 | | 1930 | ... | ... | ... | 1,689 | 1,118 |
| 1916 | 56 | | 1931 | ... | ... | ... | 742 | 440 |
| 1917 | 5 | | 1932 | ... | ... | ... | 172 | 167 |
| 1918 | — | | 1933 | ... | ... | ... | 565 | 350 |
| 1919 | 1 | | 1934 | ... | ... | ... | 973 | 584 |
| 1920 | 3 | | 1935 | ... | ... | ... | 862 | 517 |
| 1921 | 8 | | 1936 | ... | 110 | 75 | 1,462 | 815 |
| 1922 | 290 | | 1937 | 3 | 242 | 164 | 1,558 | 916 |
| 1923 | 673 | | 1938 | 2 | 486 | 330 | 1,615 | 950 |
| 1924 | 1,050 | | 1939 | 4 | 363 | 246 | 1,691 | 995 |
|      |    | | 1940 | 3 | 404 | 274 | 1,804 | 1,061 |
|      |    | | 1941 | 4 | 828 | 561 | 1,697 | 1,011 |
|      |    | | 1942 | 1 | 704 | 477 | 409 | 245 |
|      |    | | 1943 | - - | 811 | 550 | 5 | 3 |
|      |    | | 1944 | 2 | 770 | 522 | 18 | 11 |

**D5  SOUTH AMERICA: OUTPUT OF IRON ORE** (in thousands of metric tons)

| | Argentina | | Brazil | | Chile | | Colombia | | Peru | | Venezuela | |
|---|---|---|---|---|---|---|---|---|---|---|---|---|
| | A | B | A | B | A | B | A | B | A | B | A | B |
| 1945 | 1 | - - | 650 | 442 | 277 | 173 | — | — | — | — | — | — |
| 1946 | 52 | 27 | 583 | 396 | 1,177 | 738 | — | — | — | — | — | — |
| 1947 | ... | ... | 611 | 415 | 1,738 | 1,084 | — | — | — | — | — | — |
| 1948 | 33 | 17 | 1,572 | 1,069 | 2,711 | 1,681 | — | — | — | — | — | — |
| 1949 | 38 | 19 | 1,888 | 1,284 | 2,743 | 1,662 | — | — | — | — | — | — |
| 1950 | 40 | 20 | 1,987 | 1,351 | 2,950 | 1,770 | — | — | — | — | 199 | 127 |
| 1951 | 55 | 27 | 2,407 | 1,637 | 3,160 | 1,960 | — | — | — | — | 1,270 | 813 |
| 1952 | 67 | 34 | 3,162 | 2,150 | 2,362 | 1,426 | — | — | — | — | 1,970 | 1,261 |
| 1953 | 77 | 36 | 3,617 | 2,460 | 2,939 | 1,747 | — | — | ... | 577 | 2,296 | 1,470 |
| 1954 | 77 | 30 | 3,071 | 2,088 | 2,285 | 1,310 | ... | 35 | ... | 1,157 | 5,389 | 3,469 |
| 1955 | 76 | 38 | 3,382 | 2,300 | 1,720 | 940 | ... | 149 | ... | 1,059 | 8,439 | 5,401 |
| 1956 | 65 | 33 | 4,075 | 2,771 | 3,002 | 1,563 | ... | 168 | ... | 1,614 | 11,105 | 7,107 |
| 1957 | 67 | 32 | 4,977 | 3,384 | 3,081 | 1,706 | ... | 253 | ... | 2,148 | 15,296 | 9,024 |
| 1958 | 66 | 29 | 5,185 | 3,526 | 3,759 | 2,296 | ... | 238 | ... | 2,017 | 15,485 | 9,136 |
| 1959 | 105 | 48 | 8,841 | 6,057 | 4,649 | 2,936 | ... | 172 | ... | 2,145 | 17,201 | 10,149 |
| 1960 | 135 | 58 | 9,345 | 6,355 | 6,041 | 3,804 | 655 | 178 | 5,232 | 3,947 | 19,490 | 12,474 |
| 1961 | 139 | 60 | 10,221 | 6,950 | 6,990 | 4,426 | 673 | ... | 5,376 | 4,723 | 14,565 | 9,322 |
| 1962 | 123 | 54 | 10,778 | 7,301 | 8,092 | 5,160 | 643 | ... | 5,917 | 3,445 | 13,266 | 8,490 |
| 1963 | 100 | 46 | 11,218 | 7,629 | 8,510 | 5,481 | 690 | ... | 6,624 | 4,975 | 11,747 | 7,518 |
| 1964 | 65 | 45 | 16,960 | 11,452 | 9,910 | 6,361 | 731 | ... | 6,528 | 4,187 | 15,645 | 10,013 |
| 1965 | 116 | 54 | 18,159 | 13,725 | 12,721 | 7,756 | 706 | ... | 9,000 | 4,459 | 17,650 | 11,296 |
| 1966 | 156 | 69 | 24,818 | 15,763 | 12,212 | 7,788 | 660 | ... | 11,683 | 4,554 | 17,841 | 11,418 |
| 1967 | 226 | 100 | 22,661 | 14,772 | 10,789 | 6,853 | 856 | ... | 11,484 | 5,314 | 17,124 | 10,959 |
| 1968 | 277 | 121 | 24,776 | 16,682 | 11,916 | 7,428 | 578 | ... | 11,931 | 5,421 | 12,665 | 9,922 |
| 1969 | 299 | 133 | 27,959 | 18,748 | 11,534 | 7,161 | 352 | ... | 11,960 | 5,853 | 19,745 | 12,410 |
| 1970 | 239 | 107 | 36,381 | 24,739 | 11,265 | 6,940 | 453 | ... | 12,585 | 6,249 | 22,070 | 14,080 |
| 1971 | 282 | 125 | 37,486 | 25,490 | 11,228 | 6,854 | 442 | 170 | 11,603 | 5,617 | 20,240 | 12,522 |
| 1972 | 259 | 115 | 46,471 | 31,600 | 8,640 | 5,303 | 416 | 180 | 9,414 | 6,086 | 17,327 | 11,267 |
| 1973 | 237 | 105 | 55,019 | 37,413 | 9,416 | 5,797 | 480 | 202 | 8,964 | 5,852 | 22,155 | 14,096 |
| 1974 | 415 | 212 | 91,488 | 62,212 | 10,297 | 6,299 | 510 | 209 | 9,525 | 6,220 | 25,983 | 16,384 |
| 1975 | 286 | 139 | 108,162 | 73,550 | 11,007 | 6,772 | 595 | 247 | 7,753 | 5,067 | 24,772 | 15,359 |
| 1976 | 506 | 273 | 107,395 | 73,027 | 10,055 | 6,186 | 542 | 229 | 4,776 | 2,199 | 18,685 | 11,958 |
| 1977 | 1,030 | 544 | 100,817 | 68,556 | 8,021 | 4,941 | 505 | 212 | 6,185 | 4,107 | 13,683 | 8,757 |
| 1978 | 909 | 483 | 103,896 | 70,649 | 7,813 | 4,769 | 497 | 209 | 4,923 | 3,275 | 13,515 | 8,650 |
| 1979 | 611 | 396 | 117,502 | 79,901 | 8,225 | 4,978 | 397 | 174 | 5,444 | 3,629 | 15,261 | 9,766 |
| 1980 | 437 | 275 | 139,697 | 94,993 | 8,835 | 5,344 | 506 | 226 | 5,704 | 3,844 | 16,102 | 10,304 |
| 1981 | 398 | 249 | 122,709 | 83,442 | 8,514 | 5,190 | 433 | 189 | 6,069 | 4,073 | 15,722 | 9,935 |
| 1982 | 587 | 389 | 119,939 | 81,559 | 6,470 | 3,874 | 470 | 205 | 5,774 | 3,904 | 11,680 | 6,605 |
| 1983 | 609 | 390 | 114,190 | 77,649 | 5,974 | 3,602 | 456 | 210 | 4,287 | 2,949 | 9,297 | 5,949 |
| 1984 | 571 | 346 | 143,842 | 97,813 | 7,116 | 4,250 | 441 | 203 | 3,979 | 2,784 | 13,055 | 8,355 |
| 1985 | 639 | 389 | 168,120 | 113,718 | 6,510 | 3,945 | 455 | 209 | 4,881 | 3,476 | 14,753 | 9,442 |
| 1986 | 810 | 514 | 175,725 | 119,493 | 7,009 | 4,311 | 523 | 209 | 5,026 | 3,343 | 16,753 | 10,722 |
| 1987 | 567 | 360 | 182,745 | 134,106 | 6,690 | 4,078 | 611 | 283 | 5,100 | 3,358 | 17,111 | 11,380 |
| 1988 | 1,119 | 379 | 200,617 | 146,002 | 7,866 | 4,801 | 614 | 287 | 4,189 | 2,839 | 18,321 | 12,116 |

**D5**     **Output of Iron Ore**

NOTES

1.   SOURCES: The national publications listed on p. xiv–xvi League of Nations and UN, *Statistical Yearbooks,* and British Iron and Steel Federation, *Statistical Year Books.*

FOOTNOTES

[1] Data to 1907 are of exports, and from 1908 to 1938 (1st line) they are of
[2] Newfoundland production is included in Canada from April 1949.
[3] The reason for this break is not given in the source.
[4] Production for several years prior to 1936 was estimated at 30,000 tons.

## D6 OUTPUT OF MAIN NON FERROUS METAL ORES

**ANTIMONY** (Sb content) (in metric tons)

| | NORTH AMERICA | | | SOUTH AMERICA | | | NORTH AMERICA | | | | SOUTH AMERICA | |
|---|---|---|---|---|---|---|---|---|---|---|---|---|
| | Canada | Mexico | USA[1] | Bolivia[2] | Peru[3] | | Canada | Guatemala | Mexico | USA | Bolivia | Peru |
| 1893 | ... | - - | ... | ... | ... | 1945 | 707 | ... | 8,754 | 1,751 | 5,535 | 2,301 |
| 1894 | ... | 80 | ... | ... | ... | 1946 | 291 | ... | 6,572 | 2,272 | 6,964 | 1,213 |
| | | | | | | 1947 | 522 | ... | 6,926 | 4,823 | 10,857 | 1,292 |
| 1895 | ... | 600 | ... | ... | ... | 1948 | 141 | ... | 7,380 | 5,887 | 12,260 | 1,636 |
| 1896 | ... | 3,200 | ... | ... | ... | 1949 | 72 | ... | 5,753 | 1,484 | 10,275 | 739 |
| 1897 | ... | 5,900 | ... | ... | ... | | | | | | | |
| 1898 | ... | 10,000 | ... | ... | ... | 1950 | 292 | ... | 5,878 | 2,265 | 8,781 | 2,274 |
| 1899 | ... | 3,010 | ... | ... | ... | 1951 | 3,040 | ... | 6,825 | 3,150 | 11,816 | 1,115 |
| | | | | | | 1952 | 1,057 | ... | 5,532 | 1,960 | 9,806 | 715 |
| 1900 | ... | 2,313 | ... | ... | ... | 1953 | 675 | ... | 3,687 | 337 | 5,784 | 963 |
| 1901 | ... | 5,103 | ... | ... | ... | 1954 | 591 | ... | 4,182 | 695 | 5,218 | 846 |
| 1902 | ... | 1,218 | ... | ... | ... | | | | | | | |
| 1903 | ... | 2,304 | ... | ... | ... | 1955 | 917 | ... | 3,818 | 574 | 5,359 | 871 |
| 1904 | ... | 1,694 | ... | ... | ... | 1956 | 971 | ... | 4,556 | 535 | 5,112 | 969 |
| | | | | | | 1957 | 617 | ... | 5,202 | 643 | 6,374 | 835 |
| 1905 | ... | 1,978 | ... | ... | ... | 1958 | 389 | ... | 2,747 | 640 | 5,278 | 874 |
| 1906 | ... | 2,418 | ... | ... | ... | 1959 | 752 | ... | 3,286 | 615 | 5,502 | 719 |
| 1907 | ... | 4,615 | ... | ... | ... | | | | | | | |
| 1908 | ... | 4,046 | ... | ... | ... | 1960 | 749 | ... | 4,231 | 576 | 5,327 | 817 |
| 1909 | ... | 3,730 | ... | ... | ... | 1961 | 604 | ... | 3,609 | 625 | 6,740 | 789 |
| | | | | | | 1962 | 876 | ... | 4,769 | 572 | 6,651 | 522 |
| 1910 | ... | 3,730 | 2,022 | 298 | ... | 1963 | 726 | ... | 4,826 | 585 | 7,563 | 611 |
| 1911 | ... | 4,131 | 2,045 | 175 | ... | 1964 | 722 | ... | 4,788 | 573 | 9,640 | 682 |
| 1912 | ... | 1,698 | 1,768 | 51 | ... | | | | | | | |
| 1913 | ... | 937 | — | 35 | — | 1965 | 590 | ... | 4,467 | 767 | 8,760 | 647 |
| 1914 | ... | 1,047 | — | 104 | — | 1966 | 638 | 14 | 4,478 | 841[2] | 10,667 | 848 |
| | | | | | | | | | | 8,076 | | |
| 1915 | ... | 739 | 4,535 | 10,037 | 522 | 1967 | 575 | 50 | 3,738 | 809 | 8,387 | 742 |
| 1916 | ... | 829 | 4,082 | 12,739 | 1,876 | 1968 | 526 | 9 | 3,464 | 777 | 8,283 | 786 |
| | | | | | | 1969 | 372 | 100 | 3,225 | 851 | 9,025 | 613 |
| 1917 | ... | 2,647 | 961 | 10,288 | 901 | 1970 | 329 | 1,297 | 4,468 | 1,025 | 11,766 | 1,050 |
| 1918 | ... | 3,269 | 173 | 3,010 | 323 | 1971 | 147 | 885 | 3,361 | 930 | 11,878 | 796 |
| 1919 | ... | 471 | — | 105 | 60 | | | | | | | |
| | | | | | | 1972 | 213 | 900 | 2,976 | 444 | 13,338 | 791 |
| 1920 | ... | 623 | — | 484 | 10 | 1973 | 2,400 | 873 | 2,388 | 494 | 14,933 | 417 |
| 1921 | ... | 45 | —[1] | 282 | 9 | 1974 | 2,500 | 435 | 2,407 | 600 | 13,060 | 851 |
| 1922 | ... | 464 | 4 | 185 | ... | | | | | | | |
| 1923 | ... | 490 | 9 | 312 | ... | 1975 | 2,654 | 856 | 3,137 | 804 | 16,089 | 277 |
| 1924 | ... | 775 | 29 | 621 | ... | | | | | | | |
| 1925 | ... | 1,398 | 30 | 1,384 | 28 | 1976 | 3,324 | 1,120 | 2,546 | 257 | 17,015 | 603 |
| | | | | | —[3] | 1977 | 3,165 | 916 | 2,698 | 553 | 16,341 | 819 |
| | | | | | 17 | 1978 | 3,005 | 230 | 2,457 | 724 | 13,336 | 745 |
| 1926 | ... | 2,614 | 39 | 3,440 | 99 | 1979 | 2,954 | 660 | 2,872 | 655 | 14,420 | 546 |
| 1927 | ... | 1,924 | — | 4,005 | — | | | | | | | |
| 1928 | ... | 3,342 | 78 | 3,543 | 140 | 1980 | 2,361 | 556 | 2,176 | 311 | 15,465 | 394 |
| 1929 | ... | 2,925 | — | 3,779 | 108 | 1981 | 1,670 | 510 | 1,800 | 586 | 15,296 | 433 |
| | | | | | | 1982 | 455 | — | 1,565 | 456 | 13,978 | 394 |
| 1930 | ... | 3,032 | — | 1,160 | 59 | 1983 | 385 | — | 2,518 | 760 | 9,950 | 323 |
| 1931 | ... | 5,443 | — | 1,348 | 30 | 1984 | 554 | 74 | 3,064 | 505 | 9,281 | 372 |
| 1932 | ... | 1,735 | 380 | 1,470 | 31 | | | | | | | |
| 1933 | ... | 1,950 | 533 | 1,896 | 40 | 1985 | 1,075 | 1,638 | 4,266 | ...[4] | 8,925 | 377 |
| 1934 | ... | 2,668 | 367 | 2,024 | 168 | 1986 | 3,805 | 1,530 | 3,337 | ...[4] | 10,243 | 356 |
| | | | | | | 1987 | 3,706 | 1,575 | 2,839 | ...[4] | 10,635 | 29 |
| 1935 | ... | 4,570 | 507 | 3,402 | 343 | 1988 | 2,977 | 1,335 | 2,185 | ...[4] | 9,943 | 12 |
| 1936 | — | 7,303 | 685 | 6,524 | 1,244 | | | | | | | |
| 1937 | 22 | 10,639 | 1,148 | 7,128 | 1,419 | | | | | | | |
| 1938 | 11 | 8,069 | 590 | 9,437 | 1,688 | | | | | | | |
| 1939 | 556 | 7,873 | 357 | 10,060 | 1,549 | | | | | | | |
| 1940 | 1,177 | 12,267 | 448 | 11,753 | 881 | | | | | | | |
| 1941 | 1,445 | 11,138 | 1,101 | 14,872 | 1,564 | | | | | | | |
| 1942 | 1,379 | 11,695 | 2,671 | 17,643 | 1,584 | | | | | | | |
| 1943 | 505 | 13,682 | 5,040 | 17,973 | 2,681 | | | | | | | |
| 1944 | 879 | 10,930 | 4,296 | 7,448 | 1,258 | | | | | | | |

## D6    Output of Main Non-ferrous Metal Ores

**BAUXITE** (in thousands of metric tons)

| | NORTH AMERICA | SOUTH AMERICA | |
| --- | --- | --- | --- |
| | USA[7] | Guyana[8] | Surinam |
| 1885 | — | ... | — |
| 1886 | — | ... | — |
| 1887 | — | ... | — |
| 1888 | — | ... | — |
| 1889 | 1 | ... | — |
| 1890 | 2 | ... | — |
| 1891 | 4 | ... | — |
| 1892 | 11 | ... | — |
| 1893 | 9 | ... | — |
| 1894 | 11 | ... | — |
| 1895 | 17 | ... | — |
| 1896 | 18 | ... | — |
| 1897 | 21 | ... | — |
| 1898 | 25 | ... | — |
| 1899 | 34 | ... | — |
| 1900 | 23 | ... | — |
| 1901 | 20 | ... | — |
| 1902 | 27 | ... | — |
| 1903 | 46 | ... | — |
| 1904 | 52 | ... | — |
| 1905 | 58 | ... | — |
| 1906 | 72 | ... | — |
| 1907 | 96 | ... | — |
| 1908 | 51 | ... | — |
| 1909 | 134 | ... | — |
| 1910 | 153 | ... | — |
| 1911 | 160 | ... | — |
| 1912 | 164 | ... | — |
| 1913 | 214 | ... | — |
| 1914 | 222 | ... | — |
| 1915 | 305 | ... | — |
| 1916 | 432 | ... | — |
| 1917 | 578 | 2.1 | — |
| 1918 | 616 | 4.3 | — |
| 1919 | 383 | 2.0 | — |
| 1920 | 529 | 32.0 | — |
| 1921 | 142 | 20.0 | — |
| 1922 | 315 | ... | 13 |
| 1923 | 531 | 136.0 | 13 |
| 1924 | 353 | 188.0 | 60 |
| 1925 | 322 | 197.0 | 87 |
| 1926 | 398 | 222.0 | 46 |
| 1927 | 326 | 193.0 | 176 |
| 1928 | 381 | 201.0 | 214 |
| 1929 | 372 | 220.0 | 210 |
| 1930 | 336 | 149.0 | 265 |
| 1931 | 199 | 160.0 | 173 |
| 1932 | 98 | 85.0 | 126 |
| 1933 | 157 | 42.0 | 104 |
| 1934 | 160 | 66.0 | 103 |
| 1935 | 238[7] / 249 | 140.0 | 113 |
| 1936 | 386 | 213.0 | 235 |
| 1937 | 432 | 367.0 | 392 |
| 1938 | 316 | 455.0 | 377 |
| 1939 | 381 | 478.0 | 512 |

| | NORTH AMERICA | | | | SOUTH AMERICA | | |
| --- | --- | --- | --- | --- | --- | --- | --- |
| | Dominican Republic[4] | Haiti[5] | Jamaica[6] | USA[7] | Brazil | Guyana[8] | Surinam |
| 1940 | — | — | — | 446 | 6 | 614 | 614 |
| 1941 | — | — | — | 952 | 13 | 1,112 | 1,116 |
| 1942 | — | — | — | 2,644 | 30 | 1,178 | 1,250 |
| 1943 | — | — | — | 6,333 | 69 | 1,973 | 1,694 |
| 1944 | — | — | — | 2,869 | 15 | 928 | 762 |
| 1945 | — | — | — | 997 | 20 | 680 | 747 |
| 1946 | — | — | — | 1,122 | 4 | 1,134 | 1,020 |
| 1947 | — | — | — | 1,221 | 7 | 1,381 | 1,742 |
| 1948 | — | — | — | 1,480 | 15 | 1,996 | 1,983 |
| 1949 | — | — | — | 1,167 | 16 | 1,827 | 2,162 |
| 1950 | — | — | — | 1,356 | 19 | 1,679 | 2,045 |
| 1951 | — | — | — | 1,878 | 19 | 2,107 | 2,700 |
| 1952 | — | — | 420 | 1,694 | 14 | 2,426 | 3,168 |
| 1953 | — | — | 1,240 | 1,605 | 19 | 2,311 / 3,359 | 3,273 |
| 1954 | — | — | 2,098 | 2,027 | 28 | 3,373 | 3,362 |
| 1955 | — | — | 2,709 | 1,817 | 45 | 3,523 | 3,123 |
| 1956 | — | — | 3,256 | 1,772 | 70 | 3,369 | 3,485 |
| 1957 | — | 318 | 4,708 | 1,439 | 64 | 2,989 | 3,377 |
| 1958 | — | 329 | 5,874 | 1,332 | 70 | 2,185 | 2,988 |
| 1959 | 771 | 298 | 5,304 | 1,727 | 97 | 2,325 | 3,430 |
| 1960 | 689 | 346 | 5,841 | 2,030 | 121 | 3,422 | 3,455 |
| 1961 | 749 | 306 | 6,566 | 1,248 | 111 | 3,253 | 3,453 |
| 1962 | 675 | 506 | 7,705 | 1,391 | 191 | 3,592 | 3,297 |
| 1963 | 723 | 442 | 7,078 | 1,549 | 170 | 2,861 | 3,508 |
| 1964 | 820 | 411 | 7,828 | 1,627 | 188 | 3,483 | 3,993 |
| 1965 | 893 | 428 | 8,722[6] | 1,681 | 169 | 4,302 | 4,360 |
| 1966 | 818 | 412 | 9,226 | 1,825 | 268 | 3,348 | 5,563 |
| 1967 | 1,091 | 370 | 9,396 | 1,681 | 261 | 3,475 | 5,466 |
| 1968 | 1,008 | 430 | 8,415 | 1,692 | 285 | 3,545 | 5,660 |
| 1969 | 1,103 | 748 | 10,624 | 1,873 | 351 | 4,306 | 6,236 |
| 1970 | 1,086 | 673 | 12,106 | 2,562 | 510 | 4,418 | 6,011 |
| 1971 | 1,032 | 715 | 12,543 | 2,458 | 566 | 4,234 | 6,717 |
| 1972 | 1,087 | 725 | 12,989 | 2,235 | 765 | 3,727 | 6,777 |
| 1973 | 1,086 | 779 | 13,489 | 2,324 | 849 | 3,622 | 6,718 |
| 1974 | 1,196 | 793 | 15,086 | 2,408 | 858 | 3,606 | 6,863 |
| 1975 | 785 | 522 | 11,157 | 2,199 | 969 | 3,830 | 4,751 |
| 1976 | 621 | 733 | 10,473 | 2,420 | 998 | 3,203 | 4,587 |
| 1977 | 576 | 685 | 11,417 | 2,436 | 1,352 | 3,344 | 4,856 |
| 1978 | 558 | 639 | 11,732 | 2,066 | 1,401 | 3,014 | 5,025 |
| 1979 | 524 | 518 | 11,502 | 2,186 | 2,884 | 1,994 | 4,769 |
| 1980 | 510 | 477 | 12,049 | 1,869 | 6,688 | 1,629 | 4,893 |
| 1981 | 406 | 488 | 11,683 | 1,847 | 6,969 | 1,511 | 4,125 |
| 1982 | 152 | 431 | 8,158 | 896 | 6,290 | 1,172 | 3,060 |
| 1983 | — | — | 7,725 | 679 | 7,199 | 1,088 | 2,793 |
| 1984 | — | — | 8,605 | 856 | 10,355 | 1,349 | 3,375 |
| 1985 | — | — | 6,219 | 674 | 9,963 | 1,601 | 3,738 |
| 1986 | — | — | 6,953 | 510 | 6,463 | 1,467 | 3,731 |
| 1987 | 187 | — | 7,702 | 576 | 8,750 | 1,362 | 2,522 |
| 1988 | 168 | — | 7,315 | 588 | 8,083 | 1,339 | 3,434 |

**D6    Output of Main Non-ferrous Metal Ores**

**CHROMIUM** ($Cr_2O_3$ content) (in thousands of metric tons)

| | NORTH AMERICA | | SOUTH AMERICA | | | NORTH AMERICA | | SOUTH AMERICA |
|---|---|---|---|---|---|---|---|---|
| | Cuba | USA[10] | Brazil | | | Cuba | USA[10] | Brazil |
| 1915 | ... | 2 | ... | | 1950 | 15 | - - | 2 |
| 1916 | ... | 25 | ... | | 1951 | ... | 3 | 2 |
| 1917 | ... | 24 | ... | | 1952 | 6 | 9 | 1 |
| 1918 | ... | 45 | ... | | 1953 | 22 | 22 | 2 |
| 1919 | ... | 28 | ... | | 1954 | 25 | 57 | 1 |
| 1920 | 1 | 1 | 4 | | 1955 | 27 | 54 | 2 |
| 1921 | 1 | - - | ... | | 1956 | 19 | 78 | 2 |
| 1922 | - - | - - | ... | | 1957 | 42 | 59 | 4 |
| 1923 | 11 | - - | ... | | 1958 | 27 | 52 | 3 |
| 1924 | 8 | - - | ... | | 1959 | 17 | [37][10] | 4 |
| 1925 | 12 | - - | ... | | 1960 | 10 | [37][10] | 4 |
| 1926 | 36 | - - | 2 | | 1961 | 9 | [29][10] | 10 |
| 1927 | 16 | - - | 2 | | 1962 | 10 | — | 16 |
| 1928 | 15 | - - | - - | | 1963 | 19 | — | 17 |
| 1929 | 23 | - - | — | | 1964 | 11 | — | 8 |
| 1930 | 18 | - - | — | | 1965 | 14 | — | 3 |
| 1931 | 7 | - - | — | | 1966 | 13 | — | 10 |
| 1932 | - - | - - | — | | 1967 | 15 | — | 9 |
| 1933 | 8 | - - | — | | 1968 | 17 | — | 12 |
| 1934 | 16 | - - | — | | 1969 | 16 | — | 15 |
| 1935 | 16 | - - | — | | 1970 | 8 | — | 28 |
| 1936 | 23 | - - | 2 | | 1971 | 5 | — | 83 |
| 1937 | 31 | 1 | - - | | 1972 | 13 | — | 146 |
| 1938 | 12 | - - | - - | | 1973 | 13 | — | 124 |
| 1939 | 17 | 2 | 2 | | 1974 | 9 | — | 110 |
| 1940 | 16 | 1 | 2 | | 1975 | 9 | — | 183 |
| 1941 | 74 | 5 | 2 | | 1976 | 5 | — | 231 |
| 1942 | 86 | 40 | 3 | | 1977 | 5 | — | 178 |
| 1943 | 100 | 60 | 4 | | 1978 | 7 | — | 249 |
| 1944 | 68 | 18 | 2 | | 1979 | 7 | — | 232 |
| 1945 | 62 | 6 | 1 | | 1980 | 7 | — | 217 |
| 1946 | 53 | 2 | — | | 1981 | 5 | — | 241 |
| 1947 | 44 | - - | — | | 1982 | 7 | — | 159 |
| 1948 | 17 | 2 | 1 | | 1983 | 8 | — | 111 |
| 1949 | 11 | - - | 2 | | 1984 | 9 | — | 129 |
| | | | | | 1985 | 9 | — | 131 |
| | | | | | 1986 | 12 | — | 90 |
| | | | | | 1987 | 13 | — | 94 |
| | | | | | 1988 | 13 | — | 109 |

## D6 Output of Main Non-ferrous Metal Ores

**COPPER** (Cu content) (in thousands of metric tons)

| | NORTH AMERICA | SOUTH AMERICA | | | NORTH AMERICA | | | | SOUTH AMERICA | | |
|---|---|---|---|---|---|---|---|---|---|---|---|
| | U.S.A. | Chile | | Canada[11] | Cuba | Mexico | U.S.A.[12] | Bolivia[2] | Chile | Peru |
| 1844 | ... | 8 | | | | | | | | | |
| 1845 | - - | 8 | 1880 | ... | ... | ... | 27 | ... | 40 | ... |
| 1846 | - - | 10 | 1881 | ... | ... | ... | 33 | 3 | 40 | 1 |
| 1847 | - - | 9 | 1882 | ... | ... | - - | 41 | 3 | 45 | - - |
| 1848 | 1 | 9 | 1883 | ... | ... | - - | 52 | 2 | 32 | - - |
| 1849 | 1 | 10 | 1884 | ... | ... | 1.0 | 66 | 2 | 45 | - - |
| 1850 | 1 | 12 | 1885 | ... | ... | - - | 75 | 2 | 40 | - - |
| 1851 | 1 | 8 | 1886 | 2 | ... | - - | 72 | 1 | 38 | - - |
| 1852 | 1 | 15 | 1887 | 2 | ... | 2.0 | 82 | 1 | 30 | - - |
| 1853 | 2 | 13 | 1888 | 3 | ... | 3.0 | 103 | 2 | 34 | - - |
| 1854 | 2 | 15 | 1889 | 3 | ... | 4.0 | 103 | 1 | 25 | - - |
| 1855 | 3 | 19 | 1890 | 3 | ... | 4.0 | 117 | 2 | 27 | - - |
| 1856 | 4 | 21 | 1891 | 4 | ... | 5.7 | 129 | 2 | 21 | - - |
| 1857 | 5 | 24 | 1892 | 3 | ... | 7.9 | 156 | ... | 21 | - - |
| 1858 | 6 | 25 | 1893 | 4 | ... | 9.6 | 149 | 2 | 23 | - - |
| 1859 | 6 | 23 | 1894 | 3 | ... | 12.0 | 161 | 2 | 23 | - - |
| 1860 | 7 | 34 | 1895 | 4 | ... | 12.0 | 173 | 2 | 22 | 1 |
| 1861 | 8 | 33 | 1896 | 4 | ... | 11.0 | 209 | 2 | 24 | 1 |
| 1862 | 10 | 37 | 1897 | 6 | ... | 12.0 | 224 | 2 | 21 | 1 |
| 1863 | 9 | 32 | 1898 | 8 | ... | 16.0 | 239 | 2 | 26 | 3 |
| 1864 | 8 | 42 | 1899 | 7 | ... | 19.0 | 259 | 2 | 26 | 5 |
| 1865 | 9 | 41 | 1900 | 9 | ... | 22.0 | 275 | 2 | 28 | 8 |
| 1866 | 9 | 33 | 1901 | 17 | ... | 34.0 | 273 | 2 | 30 | 10 |
| 1867 | 10 | 43 | 1902 | 16 | ... | 36.0 | 299 | 2 | 27 | 9 |
| 1868 | 12 | 41 | 1903 | 19 | ... | 46.0 | 317 | 2 | 30 | 10 |
| 1869 | 13 | 51 | 1904 | 19 | 1 | 52.0 | 369 | 2 | 31 | 10 |
| 1870 | 13 | 44 | 1905 | 22 | 1 | 65.0 | 409 | 2 | 29 | 12 |
| 1871 | 13 | 39 | 1906 | 25 | - - | 62.0 | 416[12] / 417 | 2 | 26 | 13 |
| 1872 | 13 | 49 | 1907 | 26 | - - | 57.0 | 384 | 2 | 29 | 21 |
| 1873 | 16 | 42 | 1908 | 29 | 3 | 38.0 | 434 | 3 | 42 | 20 |
| 1874 | 18 | 48 | 1909 | 24 | 3 | 57.0 | 511 | 3 | 43 | 20 |
| 1875 | 18 | 48 | 1910 | 25 | 4 | 48.0 | 494 | 3 | 38 | 27 |
| 1876 | 19 | 52 | 1911 | 25 | 4 | 56.0 | 506 | 2 | 36 | 28 |
| 1877 | 21 | 44 | 1912 | 35 | 4 | 57.0 | 567 | 2 | 42 | 27 |
| 1878 | 22 | 48 | 1913 | 35 | 3 | 53.0 | 560 | 4 | 42 | 28 |
| 1879 | 23 | 46 | 1914 | 34 | 6 | 27.0 | 521 | 3 | 45 | 27 |
| | | | 1915 | 46 | 9 | - - | 675 | 8 | 52 | 35 |
| | | | 1916 | 53 | 10 | 28.0 | 910 | 8 | 71 | 43 |
| | | | 1917 | 50 | 11 | 51.0 | 860 | 10 | 102 | 45 |
| | | | 1918 | 54 | 13 | 70.0 | 866 | 8 | 107 | 44 |
| | | | 1919 | 34 | 8 | 52.0 | 550 | 7 | 80 | 39 |
| | | | 1920 | 37 | 8 | 49.0 | 555 | 10 | 100 | 33 |
| | | | 1921 | 22 | 8 | 15.0 | 211 | 10 | 59 | 33 |
| | | | 1922 | 19 | 11 | 27.0 | 438 | 11 | 130 | 36 |
| | | | 1923 | 39 | 11 | 53.0 | 670 | 11 | 182 | 44 |
| | | | 1924 | 47 | 12 | 49.0 | 729 | 7 | 190 | 38 |

**D6     Output of Main Non-ferrous Metal Ores**

**COPPER** (Cu content) (in thousands of metric tons)

| | NORTH AMERICA | | | | | | | SOUTH AMERICA | | |
|---|---|---|---|---|---|---|---|---|---|---|
| | Canada[11] | Cuba | Haiti | Mexico | Newfound-land | Nicaragua | USA | Bolivia | Chile | Peru |
| 1925 | 51 —[13] | 12 | — | 51 | ... | — | 761 | 7 | 192 | 38 |
| 1926 | 60 | 12 | — | 54 | ... | — | 783 | 8 | 203 | 41 |
| 1927 | 64 | 14 | — | 59 | — | — | 748 | 9 | 243 | 48 |
| 1928 | 92 | 17 | — | 65 | - - | — | 821 | 9 | 287 | 53 |
| 1929 | 112 | 14 | — | 81 | 1 | — | 905 | 7 | 321 | 54 |
| 1930 | 138 | 16 | — | 73 | 1 | — | 640 | 4 | 220 | 48 |
| 1931 | 133 | 13 | — | 54 | 2 | — | 480 | 2 | 223 | 46 |
| 1932 | 112 | 5 | — | 35 | 2 | — | 216 | 2 | 103 | 22 |
| 1933 | 136 | 7 | — | 40 | 3 | — | 173 | 2 | 163 | 25 |
| 1934 | 165 | 6 | — | 44 | 4 | — | 215 | 2 | 257 | 28 |
| 1935 | 190 | 6 | — | 39 | 3 | — | 345 | 2 | 267 | 30 |
| 1936 | 191 | 12 | — | 30 | 5 | — | 557 | 3 | 256 | 33 |
| 1937 | 240 | 13 | — | 46 | 9 | — | 764 | 4 | 413 | 36 |
| 1938 | 259 | 14 | — | 42 | 8 | — | 506 | 3 | 351 | 38 |
| 1939 | 276 | 11 | — | 44 | 10 | — | 661 | 4 | 341 | 36 |
| 1940 | 297 | 10 | — | 38 | 9 | — | 797 | 7 | 365 | 44 |
| 1941 | 292 | 10 | — | 49 | 7 | — | 869 | 7 | 469 | 37 |
| 1942 | 274 | 10 | — | 51 | 6 | — | 980 | 6 | 484 | 35 |
| 1943 | 261 | 7 | — | 50 | 6 | — | 990 | 6 | 497 | 33 |
| 1944 | 248 | 7 | — | 41 | 5 | — | 882 | 6 | 498 | 32 |
| 1945 | 216 | 9 | — | 62 | 5 | — | 701 | 6 | 470 | 32 |
| 1946 | 167 | 12 | — | 61 | 5 | — | 552 | 6 | 361 | 25 |
| 1947 | 205 | 13 | — | 64 | 4 | — | 769 | 6 | 427 | 23 |
| 1948 | 218[11] | 16 | — | 59 | 4 | — | 757 | 7 | 445 | 18 |
| 1949 | 239 | 17 | — | 57 | ... | — | 683 | 5 | 371 | 28 |
| 1950 | 240 | 21 | — | 62 | ... | — | 825 | 5 | 363 | 30 |
| 1951 | 245 | 20 | — | 67 | ... | — | 842 | 5 | 381 | 32 |
| 1952 | 234 | 18 | — | 59 | ... | — | 839 | 5 | 409 | 30 |
| 1953 | 230 | 15 | — | 60 | ... | — | 840 | 5 | 361 | 34 |
| 1954 | 275 | 15 | — | 55 | ... | — | 758 | 4 | 364 | 38 |
| 1955 | 296 | 18 | — | 55 | ... | — | 906 | 4 | 434 | 43 |
| 1956 | 322 | 15 | — | 55 | ... | — | 1,002 | 4 | 490 | 48 |
| 1957 | 326 | 14 | — | 61 | ... | — | 986 | 4 | 486 | 54 |
| 1958 | 313 | 13 | — | 65 | ... | — | 888 | 3 | 467 | 56 |
| 1959 | 359 | 9 | — | 57 | ... | 1 | 748 | 2 | 546 | 54 |

## D6    Output of Main Non-ferrous Metal Ores

**COPPER** (Cu content) (in thousands of metric tons)

|  | NORTH AMERICA | | | | | | SOUTH AMERICA | | |
|---|---|---|---|---|---|---|---|---|---|
|  | Canada | Cuba | Haiti | Mexico | Nicaragua | U.S.A. | Bolivia[2] | Chile | Peru |
| 1960 | 399 | 12 | 1 | 60 | 5 | 980 | 2 | 536 | 209 |
| 1961 | 398 | 5 | 3 | 49 | 6 | 1,057 | 2 | 553 | 223 |
| 1962 | 415 | 6 | 4 | 47 | 7 | 1,114 | 2 | 592 | 176 |
| 1963 | 411 | 6 | 6 | 56 | 7 | 1,101 | 3 | 602 | 180 |
| 1964 | 442 | 6 | 6 | 53 | 9 | 1,131 | 5 | 634 | 176 |
| 1965 | 461 | 6 | 10 | 69 | 10 | 1,226 | 5 | 590 | 199 |
| 1966 | 459 | 5 | 8 | 74 | 10 | 1,297 | 6 / 5 | 661 | 200 |
| 1967 | 556 | 5 | 4 | 56 | 9 | 866 | 6 | 664 | 193 |
| 1968 | 575 | 5 | 6 | 61 | 12 | 1,093 | 6 | 667 | 213 |
| 1969 | 520 | 4 | 6 | 66 | 4 | 1,401 | 8 | 699 | 210 |
| 1970 | 610 | - - | 5 | 61 | 3 | 1,560 | 8 | 711 | 218 |
| 1971 | 655 | — | 7 | 63 | 4 | 1,381 | 7 | 717 | 213 |
| 1972 | 720 | 2 | — | 79 | 2 | 1,510 | 8 | 726 | 226 |
| 1973 | 824 | 2 | — | 81 | 2 | 1,559 | 8 | 743 | 215 |
| 1974 | 821 | 3 | — | 83 | 2 | 1,449 | 7 | 905 | 222 |
| 1975 | 734 | 3 | — | 78 | 2 | 1,282 | 6 | 831 | 166 |
| 1976 | 731 | 3 | — | 89 | 2 | 1,457 | 5 | 1,013 | 228 |
| 1977 | 759 | 3 | — | 90 | 2 | 1,364 | 3 | 1,053 | 327 |
| 1978 | 659 | 3 | — | 87 | 2 | 1,358 | 3 | 1,029 | 376 |
| 1979 | 636 | 3 | — | 107 | 2 | 1,447 | 2 | 1,068 | 397 |
| 1980 | 716 | 3 | — | 175 | 2 | 1,181 | 2 | 1,063 | 336 |
| 1981 | 718 | 3 | — | 230 | 2 | 1,538 | 3 | 1,105 | 323 |
| 1982 | 612 | 3 | — | 239 | 2 | 1,147 | 2 | 1,255 | 354 |
| 1983 | 653 | 3 | — | 206 | 1 | 1,038 | 2 | 1,255 | 319 |
| 1984 | 722 | 3 | — | 189 | 1 | 1,103 | 2 | 1,307 | 354 |
| 1985 | 739 | 3 | — | 168 | 1 | 1,105 | 2 | 1,360 | 401 |
| 1986 | 699 | 3 | — | 175 | 1 | 1,144 | - - | 1,399 | 397 |
| 1987 | 794 | 3 | — | 231 | 1 | 1,244 | — | 1,413 | 406 |
| 1988 | 756 | 3 | — | 268 | 1 | 1,420 | - - | 1,472 | 298 |

**D6    Output of Main Non-ferrous Metal Ores**

**GOLD** (in metric tons)

| | NORTH AMERICA | | | NORTH AMERICA | | | SOUTH AMERICA | | |
|---|---|---|---|---|---|---|---|---|---|
| | Mexico[14] | USA[15] | | Canada[16] | Mexico[14] | USA[15] | Brazil | Chile | Colombia |
| 1835 | ... | 1.2 | 1880 | ... | 1.4 | 54 | ... | ... | ... |
| 1836 | ... | 0.8 | 1881 | ... | 1.4 | 52 | ... | ... | ... |
| 1837 | ... | 0.5 | 1882 | ... | 1.6 | 49 | ... | ... | ... |
| 1838 | ... | 0.7 | 1883 | ... | 1.4 | 45 | ... | 0.1 | ... |
| 1839 | ... | 0.7 | 1884 | 1.4 | 1.0 | 46 | ... | 0.1 | 5.8 |
| 1840 | ... | 0.7 | 1885 | 1.7 | 1.0 | 48 | ... | 0.1 | 3.8 |
| 1841 | ... | 0.9 | 1886 | 2.2 | 1.0 | 52 | ... | 0.2 | 3.8 |
| 1842 | ... | 1.3 | 1887 | 1.8 | 1.0 | 50 | ... | 0.5 | 4.5 |
| 1843 | ... | 1.8 | 1888 | 1.6 | 1.0 | 50 | ... | 0.9 | 4.5 |
| 1844 | ... | 1.7 | 1889 | 2 | 1.4 | 50 | ... | 0.4 | 5.2 |
| 1845 | ... | 1.5 | 1890 | 1.7 | 1.6 | 49 | ... | 0.7 | 5.4 |
| 1846 | ... | 1.7 | 1891 | 1.4 | 1.9 | 50 | ... | 0.6 | 5.2 |
| 1847 | ... | 1.3 | 1892 | 1.4 | 1.8 | 50 | ... | 1.0 | 5.2 |
| 1848 | ... | 15 | 1893 | 1.5 | 7.0 | 54 | ... | 0.8 | 4.4 |
| 1849 | ... | 60 | 1894 | 1.7 | 9.0 | 59 | 3.2 | 1.5 | 4.4 |
| 1850 | ... | 75 | 1895 | 3.1 | 10 | 70 | 3.3 | 2.1 | 4.4 |
| 1851 | ... | 83 | 1896 | 4.1 | 11 | 80 | 1.5 | 1.1 | 3.3 |
| 1852 | ... | 90 | 1897 | 9.1 | 14 | 86 | 1.8 | 0.5 | 3.4 |
| 1853 | ... | 98 | 1898 | 21 | 12 | 97 | 2.4 | 1.3 | 3.2 |
| 1854 | ... | 90 | 1899 | 32 | 14 | 107 | 3.2 | 2.0 | 2.8 |
| 1855 | ... | 83 | 1900 | 42 | 15[14] | 119 | 4.2 | 2.4 | 1.8 |
| 1856 | ... | 83 | 1901 | 36 | 14 | 118 | 4.2 | 1.6 | 4.2 |
| 1857 | ... | 83 | 1902 | 32 | 15 | 120 | 3.1 | 1.0 | 3.8 |
| 1858 | ... | 75 | 1903 | 28 | 16 | 111 | 3.4 | 1.0 | 4.1 |
| 1859 | ... | 75 | 1904 | 25 | 19 | 121[15] / 122 | 3.0 | 1.0 | 2.9 |
| 1860 | ... | 69 | 1905 | 21 | 24 | 133 | 3.0 | 1.4 | 3.9 |
| 1861 | ... | 65 | 1906 | 17 | 27 | 146 | 3.6 | 1.4 | 3.3 |
| 1862 | ... | 59 | 1907 | 13 | 29 | 131 | 3.0 | 1.9 | 4.9 |
| 1863 | ... | 60 | 1908 | 15 | 32 | 138 | 3.3 | 0.5 | 5.1 |
| 1864 | ... | 69 | 1909 | 14 | 34 | 149 | 3.4 | 0.7 | 4.8 |
| 1865 | ... | 80 | 1910 | 15 | 41 | 143 | 2.9 | 0.7 | 5.0 |
| 1866 | ... | 80 | 1911 | 15 | 37 | 146 | 5.7 | 0.5 | 4.8 |
| 1867 | ... | 78 | 1912 | 19 | 32 | 139 | 5.4 | 2.6 | 4.4 |
| 1868 | ... | 72 | 1913 | 25 | 26 | 134 | 3.4 | 0.2 | 4.4 |
| 1869 | ... | 74 | 1914 | 24 | 8.6 | 137 | 3.2 | 0.3 | 7.0 |
| 1870 | 3.4 | 75 | 1915 | 29 | 7.4 | 148 | 3.6 | 1.2 | 8.2 |
| 1871 | 1.5 | 65 | 1916 | 29 | 12 | 137 | 4.3 | 1.9 | 9.3 |
| 1872 | 2.0 | 54 | 1917 | 23 | 24 | 121 | 4.5 | 1.9 | 7.5 |
| 1873 | 1.6 | 54 | 1918 | 22 | 25 | 100 | 4.2 | 1.9 | 7.3 |
| 1874 | 1.6 | 50 | 1919 | 24 | 24 | 86 | 3.0 | 2.0 | 9.0 |
| 1875 | 1.5 | 50 | 1920 | 24 | 23 | 74 | 3.9 | 1.7 | 8.7 |
| 1876 | 1.1 | 60 | 1921 | 29 | 21 | 73 | 4.2 | 1.4 | 9.0 |
| 1877 | 1.3 | 71 | 1922 | 39 | 23 | 71 | 4.6 | 2.5 | 7.5 |
| 1878 | 1.4 | 77 | 1923 | 38 | 24 | 75 | 4.5 | 2.0 | 5.9 |
| 1879 | 1.5 | 59 | 1924 | 47 | 25 | 76 | 4.5 | 2.1 | 8.9 |

**D6    Output of Main Non-ferrous Metal Ores**

**GOLD** (in metric tons)

| | NORTH AMERICA | | | SOUTH AMERICA | | |
|---|---|---|---|---|---|---|
| | Canada[16] | Mexico | U.S.A. | Brazil | Chile | Colombia |
| 1925 | 54 | 25 | 72 | 3.4 | 1.9 | 7.9 |
| 1926 | 55 | 24 | 69 | 3.2 | 1.8 | 5.6 |
| 1927 | 58 | 22 | 66 | 3.2 | 1.9 | 5.1 |
| 1928 | 59 | 22 | 67 | 3.3 | 1.1 | 4.5 |
| 1929 | 60 | 20 | 64 | 3.7 | 1.0 | 4.2 |
| 1930 | 65 | 21 | 67 | 4.2 | 0.6 | 4.9 |
| 1931 | 84 | 19 | 69 | 3.9 | 0.7 | 6.0 |
| 1932 | 95 | 18 | 71 | 3.7 | 1.2 | 7.7 |
| 1933 | 92 | 20 | 71 | 3.7 | 4.6 | 9.3 |
| 1934 | 92 | 21 | 86 | 3.5 | 7.4 | 11 |
| 1935 | 102 | 21 | 101 | 3.7 | 8.3 | 10 |
| 1936 | 117 | 23 | 118 | 3.9 | 7.7 | 12 |
| 1937 | 127 | 26 | 128 | 4.5 | 8.5 | 14 |
| 1938 | 147 | 29 | 133 | 4.4 | 9.1 | 16 |
| 1939 | 158 | 26 | 145 | 4.6 | 10.2 | 18 |
| 1940 | 165 | 27 | 151 | 4.7 | 10.4 | 20 |
| 1941 | 166 | 25 | 148 | 4.6 | 8.2 | 20 |
| 1942 | 151 | 25 | 108 | 4.9 | 5.8 | 19 |
| 1943 | 114 | 20 | 42 | 5.0 | 5.4 | 18 |
| 1944 | 91 | 16 | 31 | 5.2 | 6.3 | 17 |
| 1945 | 84 | 16 | 30 | 5.1 | 5.6 | 16 |
| 1946 | 88 | 13 | 49 | 4.4 | 7.2 | 14 |
| 1947 | 95 | 14 | 66 | 4.2 | 5.3 | 12 |
| 1948 | 110[16] | 11 | 63 | 4.1 | 5.1 | 10 |
| 1949 | 128 | 13 | 62 | 3.7 | 5.6 | 11 |
| 1950 | 138 | 13 | 74 | 4.0 | 5.8 | 12 |
| 1951 | 137 | 12 | 62 | 4.1 | 5.4 | 13 |
| 1952 | 139 | 14 | 59 | 4.4 | 5.2 | 13 |
| 1953 | 126 | 15 | 61 | 3.6 | 4.1 | 14 |
| 1954 | 136 | 12 | 57 | 3.7 | 3.9 | 12 |
| 1955 | 141 | 12 | 56 | 3.4 | 3.8 | 12 |
| 1956 | 136 | 11 | 57 | 3.8 | 2.9 | 14 |
| 1957 | 137 | 11 | 56 | 3.8 | 3.2 | 10 |
| 1958 | 142 | 10 | 54 | 3.6 | 3.5 | 12 |
| 1959 | 139 | 9.8 | 50 | 3.5 | 2.4 | 12 |
| 1960 | 144 | 9.1 | 52 | 3.7 | 3.4 | 13 |
| 1961 | 139 | 8.4 | 48 | 3.8 | 1.5 | 12 |
| 1962 | 130 | 7.4 | 48 | 4.0 | 1.8 | 12 |
| 1963 | 125 | 7.4 | 45 | 4.1 | 2.4 | 10 |
| 1964 | 119 | 6.5 | 45 | 4.4 | 2.0 | 11 |

**D6     Output of Main Non-ferrous Metal Ores**

**GOLD** (in metric tons)

| | NORTH AMERICA | | | SOUTH AMERICA | | |
|---|---|---|---|---|---|---|
| | Canada | Mexico | U.S.A. | Brazil | Chile | Colombia |
| 1965 | 112 | 6.7 | 53 | 5.6 | 1.6 | 9.9 |
| 1966 | 102 | 6.6 | 56 | 6.1 | 1.6 | 8.7 |
| 1967 | 92 | 5.7 | 49 | 6.1 | 1.8 | 8.0 |
| 1968 | 85 | 4.6 | 46 | 6.1 | 1.8 | 7.5 |
| 1969 | 79 | 5.6 | 54 | 6.1 | 1.8 | 6.8 |
| 1970 | 75 | 6.2 | 54 | 5.8 | 1.6 | 6.3 |
| 1971 | 70 | 4.7 | 47 | 5.1 | 2.0 | 5.9 |
| 1972 | 65 | 4.5 | 50 | 7.2 | 2.9 | 5.9 |
| 1973 | 61 | 4.1 | 37 | 6.9 | 3.2 | 6.7 |
| 1974 | 53 | 4.2 | 35 | 5.9 | 3.7 | 8.2 |
| 1975 | 51 | 4.5 | 33 | 5.4 | 4.0 | 9.6 |
| 1976 | 53 | 5.1 | 33 | 4.9 | 4.0 | 9.5 |
| 1977 | 54 | 6.6 | 34 | 5.4 | 3.6 | 8.0 |
| 1978 | 54 | 6.3 | 31 | 9.4 | 3.2 | 7.6 |
| 1979 | 51 | 5.9 | 30 | 4.5 | 3.5 | 8.4 |
| 1980 | 51 | 6.1 | 30 | 14 | 6.8 | 16 |
| 1981 | 49 | 6.3 | 43 | 17 | 12 | 16 |
| 1982 | 65 | 6.1 | 46 | 26 | 17 | 15 |
| 1983 | 74 | 6.9 | 62 | 54 | 18 | 14 |
| 1984 | 83 | 7.1 | 65 | 37 | 17 | 25 |
| 1985 | 88 | 7.5 | 75 | 30 | 17 | 36 |
| 1986 | 103 | 7.8 | 116 | 23 | 18 | 40 |
| 1987 | 116 | 8.0 | 154 | 36 | 17 | 27 |
| 1988 | 130 | 9.1 | 201 | 56 | 21 | 29 |

# Output of Main Non-ferrous Metal Ores

**LEAD (Pb content)** (in thousands of metric tons)

| | NORTH AMERICA | | |
|---|---|---|---|
| | Canada[11] | Mexico[14] | USA[17] |
| 1883 | — | 15 | ... |
| 1884 | — | 15 | ... |
| 1885 | — | 18 | ... |
| 1886 | — | 16 | ... |
| 1887 | 0.1 | 18 | ... |
| 1888 | 0.3 | 30 | ... |
| 1889 | 0.1 | 28 | ... |
| 1890 | - - | 22 | ... |
| 1891 | - - | 30 | ... |
| 1892 | 0.4 | 48 | ... |
| 1893 | 1.0 | 64 | ... |
| 1894 | 2.6 | 57 | ... |
| 1895 | 7.5 | 68 | ... |
| 1896 | 11 | 63 | ... |
| 1897 | 18 | 70 | ... |
| 1898 | 14 | 71 | ... |
| 1899 | 10 | 85 | ... |
| 1900 | 29 | 64[14] | ... |
| 1901 | 24 | 94 | ... |
| 1902 | 10 | 107 | ... |
| 1903 | 8.2 | 101 | ... |
| 1904 | 17 | 95 | ... |
| 1905 | 25 | 101 | ... |
| 1906 | 25 | 74 | ... |
| 1907 | 22 | 76 | 331 |
| 1908 | 20 | 127 | 300 |
| 1909 | 21 | 118 | 349 |
| 1910 | 15 | 124 | 347 |
| 1911 | 11 | 117 | 387 |
| 1912 | 16 | 105 | 401 |
| 1913 | 17 | 68 | 438 |
| 1914 | 16 | 21 | 458 |
| 1915 | 21 | 57 | 492 |
| 1916 | 19 | 20 | 546 |
| 1917 | 15 | 64 | 570 |
| 1918 | 23 | 99 | 510 |
| 1919 | 20 | 71 | 390 |

| | NORTH AMERICA | | | | SOUTH AMERICA | | | |
|---|---|---|---|---|---|---|---|---|
| | Canada[11] | Mexico | New-foundland | USA[17] | Argentina | Bolivia[2] | Brazil | Peru |
| 1920 | 16 | 83 | ... | 451 | ... | 1.0 | ... | 0.6 |
| 1921 | 30 | 61 | ... | 376 | ... | 2.9 | ... | 0.5 |
| 1922 | 42 | 110 | ... | 433 | ... | 4.1 | ... | 0.7 |
| 1923 | 50 | 156 | ... | 496 | ... | 5.5 | ... | 0.7 |
| 1924 | 80 | 165 | - - | 541 | 1.2 | 20.0 | ... | 0.8 |
| 1925 | 115 | 172 | — | 621 | 2.6 | 22.0 | ... | 3.5 |
| 1926 | 129 | 211 | — | 620 | 5.4 | 18.0 | ... | 10 |
| 1927 | 141 | 244 | — | 604 | 4.0 | 15.0 | ... | 5.2 |
| 1928 | 153 | 235 | — | 569 | 1.9 | 13.0 | ... | 17 |
| 1929 | 148 | 247 | 11 | 588 | 3.1 | 15.0 | ... | 21 |
| 1930 | 151 | 233 | 18 | 506 | 3.0 | 12.0 | ... | 20 |
| 1931 | 121 | 227 | 25 | 367 | 3.9 | 6.7 | ... | 2.6 |
| 1932 | 116 | 137 | 36 | 266 | 2.8 | 5.5 | ... | 4.6 |
| 1933 | 121 | 119 | 35 | 247 | 4.3 | 7.8 | ... | 2 |
| 1934 | 157 | 166 | 38 | 261 | 2.8 | 11 | ... | 9.1 |
| 1935 | 154 | 184 | 36 | 300 | 2.5 | 10 | ... | 28 |
| 1936 | 174 | 216 | 31 | 338 | 6.8 | 14 | ... | 30 |
| 1937 | 187 | 218 | 29 | 422 | 15.0 | 18 | ... | 42 |
| 1938 | 190 | 282 | 32 | 335 | 22.0 | 13 | ... | 58 |
| 1939 | 176 | 220 | 27 | 376 | 28.0 | 14 | ... | 46 |
| 1940 | 214 | 196 | 30 | 415 | 29.0 | 12 | ... | 50 |
| 1941 | 209 | 155 | 30 | 419 | 23.0 | 16 | ... | 50 |
| 1942 | 232 | 198 | 25 | 450 | 26.0 | 12 | ... | 45 |
| 1943 | 201 | 218 | 33 | 411 | 18.0 | 11 | ... | 48 |
| 1944 | 138 | 185 | 30 | 378 | 19.0 | 9 | ... | 52 |
| 1945 | 157 | 205 | 25 | 354 | 16.0 | 9.5 | ... | 54 |
| 1946 | 161 | 140 | 25 | 304 | 20.0 | 8.4 | ... | 44 |
| 1947 | 147 | 223 | 21 | 348 | 19.0 | 11 | ... | 55 |
| 1948 | 152 | 193 | 20 | 354 | 18.0 | 26 | ... | 48 |
| 1949 | 145 | 221 | ... | 372 | 15.0 | 26 | ... | 65 |
| 1950 | 150 | 238 | ... | 391 | 17.0 | 31 | ... | 65 |
| 1951 | 143 | 225 | ... | 352 | 20.0 | 31 | ... | 82 |
| 1952 | 153 | 246 | ... | 354 | 17.0 | 30 | ... | 96 |
| 1953 | 176 | 221 | ... | 311 | 18.0 | 24 | 2.9 | 115 |
| 1954 | 198 | 217 | ... | 295 | 19.0 | 18 | 2.7 | 110 |
| 1955 | 184 | 211 | ... | 307 | 22.0 | 19 | 3.7 | 119[13] |
| 1956 | 171 | 200 | ... | 320 | 28.0 | 22 | 3.5 | 132 |
| 1957 | 165 | 215 | ... | 307 | 30.0 | 26 | 3.5 | 151 |
| 1958 | 169 | 202 | ... | 243 | 29.0 | 23 | 5.8 | 137 |
| 1959 | 169 | 191 | ... | 232 | 30.0 | 22 | 5.5 | 150 |

**Output of Main Non-ferrous Metal Ores**

**LEAD** (Pb content) (in thousands of metric tons)

| | NORTH AMERICA | | | SOUTH AMERICA | | | |
|---|---|---|---|---|---|---|---|
| | Canada[11] | Mexico | USA[17] | Argentina | Bolivia[2] | Brazil[18] | Peru |
| 1960 | 187[11] / 192 | 191 | 224 | 27 | 21 | 10 | 166 |
| 1961 | 166 | 181 | 238 | 28 | 20 | 4.9 | 176 |
| 1962 | 192 | 193 | 215 | 30 | 19 | 14 | 167 |
| 1963 | 180 | 190 | 230 | 26 | 20 | 10 | 149 |
| 1964 | 187 | 175 | 259 | 26 | 18 | 13[18] / 22 | 151 |
| 1965 | 275 | 170 | 273 | 32 | 17 | 24 | 154 |
| 1966 | 293 | 182 | 297 | 29 | 21[2] / 20 | 23 | 161 |
| 1967 | 308 | 164 | 287 | 32 | 21 | 24 | 160 |
| 1968 | 328 | 174 | 326 | 27 | 21 | 27 | 154 |
| 1969 | 300 | 171 | 462 | 39 | 22 | 28 | 162 |
| 1970 | 358 | 177 | 519 | 36 | 22 | 28 | 164 |
| 1971 | 368 | 157 | 525 | 40 | 21 | 28 | 172 |
| 1972 | 335 | 161 | 562 | 38 | 22 | 30 | 190 |
| 1973 | 342 | 167 | 547 | 35 | 21 | 26 | 198 |
| 1974 | 294 | 193 | 602 | 38 | 18 | 26 | 179 |
| 1975 | 349 | 163 | 564 | 30 | 18 | 22 | 154 |
| 1976 | 256 | 165 | 553 | 33 | 19 | 23 | 175 |
| 1977 | 281 | 163 | 537 | 34 | 19 | 24 | 176 |
| 1978 | 320 | 170 | 530 | 30 | 18 | 31 | 183 |
| 1979 | 311 | 173 | 526 | 32 | 16 | 22 | 184 |
| 1980 | 252 | 145 | 550 | 33 | 17 | 22 | 174 |
| 1981 | 273 | 157 | 445 | 33 | 17 | 22 | 205 |
| 1982 | 272 | 146 | 512 | 33 | 12 | 19 | 198 |
| 1983 | 272 | 167 | 449 | 32 | 12 | 19 | 207 |
| 1984 | 264 | 183 | 323 | 28 | 7 | 19 | 194 |
| 1985 | 268 | 207 | 414 | 29 | 6 | 17 | 211 |
| 1986 | 334 | 183 | 340 | 27 | 3 | 14 | 194 |
| 1987 | 373 | 177 | 311 | 26 | 9 | 15 | 204 |
| 1988 | 367 | 171 | 385 | 28 | 12 | 13 | 149 |

## D6 Output of Main Non-ferrous Metal Ores

**MERCURY** (Hg content) (in metric tons)

### 1850–1879

| | NORTH AMERICA | | NORTH AMERICA | | NORTH AMERICA |
|---|---|---|---|---|---|
| | USA | | USA | | USA |
| 1850 | 268 | 1860 | 347 | 1870 | 1,044 |
| 1851 | 964 | 1861 | 1,246 | 1871 | 1,099 |
| 1852 | 694 | 1862 | 1,459 | 1872 | 1,097 |
| 1853 | 773 | 1863 | 1,408 | 1873 | 959 |
| 1854 | 1,041 | 1864 | 1,648 | 1874 | 963 |
| 1855 | 1,145 | 1865 | 1,839 | 1875 | 1,744 |
| 1856 | 1,145 | 1866 | 1,615 | 1876 | 2,523 |
| 1857 | 979 | 1867 | 1,631 | 1877 | 2,755 |
| 1858 | 1,076 | 1868 | 1,656 | 1878 | 2,216 |
| 1859 | 451 | 1869 | 1,173 | 1879 | 2,556 |

**MANGANESE** (Mn content) (in thousands of metric tons)   **MERCURY** (Hg content) (in metric tons)

| | NORTH AMERICA | | SOUTH AMERICA | | NORTH AMERICA | |
|---|---|---|---|---|---|---|
| | Cuba | USA[20] | Brazil[21] | Chile | Mexico | U.S.A |
| 1880 | ... | 5.8 | ... | ... | ... | 2,040 |
| 1881 | ... | 4.9 | ... | ... | ... | 2,072 |
| 1882 | ... | 4.6 | ... | ... | ... | 1,780 |
| 1883 | ... | 6.2 | ... | ... | ... | 1,590 |
| 1884 | ... | 10 | ... | ... | ... | 1,087 |
| 1885 | ... | 23 | ... | ... | ... | 1,092 |
| 1886 | ... | 31 | ... | ... | ... | 1,021 |
| 1887 | ... | 35 | ... | ... | ... | 1,152 |
| 1888 | ... | 30 | ... | ... | ... | 1,132 |
| 1889 | ... | 25 | ... | ... | ... | 902 |
| 1890 | 22 | 20 | ... | 49 | ... | 780 |
| 1891 | 22 | 23 | ... | 35 | 250 | 780 |
| 1892 | 15 | 14 | ... | 50 | 240 | 954 |
| 1893 | 14 | 8 | ... | 50 | 286 | 1,027 |
| 1894 | 15 | 6 | ... | 48 | 300 | 1,036 |
| 1895 | 16 | 10 | 5 | 24 | 213 | 1,230 |
| 1896 | 12 | 10 | 14 | 26 | 218 | 1,047 |
| 1897 | — | 11 | 16 | 24 | 294 | 907 |
| 1898 | — | 16 | 26 | 21 | 253 | 1,058 |
| 1899 | — | 10 | 65 | 41 | 324 | 1,037 |

**D6    Output of Main Non-ferrous Metal Ores**

| | MANGANESE (Mn content) (in thousands of metric tons) | | | | | MERCURY (Hg content) (in metric tons) | |
|---|---|---|---|---|---|---|---|
| | | | | | | **1895–1934** | |
| | NORTH AMERICA | | | SOUTH AMERICA | | NORTH AMERICA | |
| | Cuba[19] | Mexico | USA[20] | Brazil[21] | Chile | Mexico | USA |
| 1900 | 22 | — | 12 | 108 | 26.0 | 124 | 964 |
| 1901 | 25 | — | 12 | 100 | 19.0 | 128 | 1,012 |
| 1902 | 40 | — | 8 | 157 | 13.0 | 191 | 1,168 |
| 1903 | 21 | — | 3 | 162 | 17.0 | 188 | 1,213 |
| 1904 | 18 | — | 3 | 208 | 2.3 | 190 | 1,177 |
| 1905 | 8 | — | 4 | 224 | 1.3 | 190 | 1,036 |
| 1906 | 14 | — | 7 | 121 | — | 200 | 893 |
| 1907 | 35 | — | 6 | 237 | — | 200 | 734 |
| 1908 | 1 | — | 6 | 166 | — | 200 | 672 |
| 1909 | 3 | — | 2[20] | 240 | — | 200 | 717 |
| 1910 | 6 | — | 2 | 254 | — | 251 | 701 |
| 1911 | 10 | — | 2 | 174 | — | 165 | 723 |
| 1912 | 11 | — | 2 | 155 | — | 165 | 853 |
| 1913 | 12[19] | — | 4 | 122 | — | 166 | 688 |
| 1914 | 2 | — | 3 | 184 | — | 162 | 563 |
| 1915 | 60 | — | 10 | 289 | — | 94 | 716 |
| 1916 | 37 | — | 32 | 502 | — | 52 | 1,019 |
| 1917 | 43 | 0.1 | 131 | 533 | — | 33 | 1,223 |
| 1918 | 76 | 2.9 | 311 | 395 | — | 164 | 1,118 |
| 1919 | 32 | 2.8 | 56 | 206 | — | 119 | 728 |
| 1920 | 23 | 1.1 | 96 | 459 | — | 76 | 456 |
| 1921 | 0.6 | 0.6 | 14 | 276 | — | 46 | 216 |
| 1922 | 9.2 | 0.7 | 14 | 341 | 0.4 | 42 | 217 |
| 1923 | 20 | 2.2 | 32 | 236 | 2.1 | 45 | 270 |
| 1924 | 29 | 1.8 | 57 | 159 | 2.0 | 37 | 342 |
| 1925 | 24 | 3.3 | 100 | 312 | 5.3 | 39 | 312 |
| 1926 | 25 | 3.3 | 47 | 320 | 5.3 | 45 | 260 |
| 1927 | 130 | 1.0 | 45 | 242 | 3.7 | 81 | 384 |
| 1928 | 87 | 0.7 | 48[20] / 20 | 362[21] / 174 | 4.4 | 87 | 616 |
| 1929 | 84 | 0.7 | 27 | 141 | 1.5 | 83 | 816 |
| 1930 | 2.1 | 0.7 | 30 | 92 | 2.9 | 166 | 743 |
| 1931 | 1.2 | 0.3 | 16 | 46 | 0.2 | 251 | 860 |
| 1932 | 3.5 | 0.3 | 8 | 10 | 0.2 | 253 | 435 |
| 1933 | 15 | 0.6 | 8 | 12 | 10.0 | 154 | 333 |
| 1934 | 32 | 0.9 | 12 | 1 | 1.9 | 158 | 532 |
| 1935 | 23 | 1.4 | 13 | 22 | 2.0 | 216 | 604 |
| 1936 | 18 | 1.3 | 17 | 56[21] | 2.3 | 183 | 571 |
| 1937 | 57 | 1.5 | 23 | 126 | 5.7 | 170 | 569 |
| 1938 | 63[19] / 148 | 0.8 | 12 | 147 | 4.4 | 294 | 620 |
| 1939 | 145 | 0.5 | 13 | 124 | 5.3 | 254 | 642 |

**D6    Output of Main Non-ferrous Metal Ores**

MANGANESE (Mn content) (in thousands of metric tons)       MERCURY (Hg content) (in metric tons)

**1935–1975**

| | NORTH AMERICA | | | SOUTH AMERICA | | NORTH AMERICA | | | SOUTH AMERICA |
|---|---|---|---|---|---|---|---|---|---|
| | Cuba | Mexico | USA[20] | Brazil | Chile | Canada | Mexico | USA | Peru |
| 1940 | 161 | 0.3 | 18 | 150 | 9.7 | 140 | 402 | 1,302 | … |
| 1941 | 318 | 1.0 | 40 | 217 | 9.9 | 243 | 797 | 1,549 | … |
| 1942 | 231 | 11 | 92 | 170 | 15 | 470 | 1,118 | 1,753 | … |
| 1943 | 123 | 23 | 99 | 123 | 24 | 767 | 976 | 1,790 | 11[9] |
| 1944 | 184 | 29 | 119 | 114 | 9.6 | 334 | 795 | 1,299 | 5.3[9] |
| 1945 | 242 | 19 | 94 | 119 | 3.5 | — | 567 | 1,060 | 7.2[9] |
| 1946 | 227 | 11 | 76 | 83 | 4.2 | — | 402 | 874 | 0.2[9] |
| 1947 | 2.1 | 14 | 70 | 81 | 4.4 | — | 334 | 801 | — |
| 1948 | 4.7 | 24 | 69 | 72 | 11 | — | 165 | 496 | — |
| 1949 | 6.0 | 24 | 64 | 102 | 14 | — | 181 | 342 | — |
| 1950 | 12 | 14 | 69 | 86 | 17 | — | 130 | 156 | — |
| 1951 | 42 | 28 | 48 | 90 | 19 | — | 278 | 251 | — |
| 1952 | 116 | 41 | 57 | 110 | 24 | — | 301 | 433 | — |
| 1953 | 163 | 76 | 75 / 108 | 102 | 25 | — | 401 | 494 | — |
| 1954 | 123 | 83 | 100 | 71 | 17 | — | 509 | 639 | 2 |
| 1955 | 111 | 36 | 151 | 93 | 20 | — | 1,030 | 653 | 5 |
| 1956 | 105 | 62 | 165 | 137 | 22 | — | 673 | 833 | 12 |
| 1957 | 60 | 80 | 181 | 404 | 25 | — | 726 | 1,194 | 14 |
| 1958 | 29 | 79 | 145 | 388 | 17 | — | 777 | 1,312 | 68 |
| 1959 | 25 | 77 | 109 | 454 | 18 | — | 566 | 1,077 | 87 |
| 1960 | 18 | 72 | 47 | 438 | 20 | — | 693 | 1,145 | 105 |
| 1961 | 19 | 69 | 33 | 447 | 15 | — | 624 | 1,091 | 103 |
| 1962 | 33 | 63 | 34 | 515 | 19 | — | 650 | 906 | 120 |
| 1963 | 15 | 54 | 48 | 552 | 21 | — | 562 | 658 | 107 |
| 1964 | 28 | 64 | 35 | 649 | 9.2 | 252 | 433 | 488 | 113 |
| 1965 | 34 | 59 | 47 | 659 | 7.8 | 69 | 662 | 675 | 107 |
| 1966 | 35 | 31 | 45 | 634 | 8.4 | … | 761 | 759 | 142 |
| 1967 | 29 | 31 | 42 | 572 | 6.6 | 172 | 497 | 820 | 104 |
| 1968 | 28 | 27 | 35 | 842 | 11 | 196 | 593 | 995 | 104 |
| 1969 | 11 | 60 | 57 | 1,045 | 11 | 731 | 777 | 1,022 | 124 |
| 1970 | 11 | 99 | 47 | 1,202 | 11 | 827 | 1,043 | 941 | 110 |
| 1971 | 10 | 96 | 24 | 1,264 | 10 | 638 | 1,220 | 616 | 119 |
| 1972 | 7 | 106 | 17 | 1,057 | 7 | 505 | 776 | 253 | 125 |
| 1973 | 6 | 131 | 23 | 1,142 | 6 | 475 | 700 | 75 | 123 |
| 1974 | 11 | 145 | 32 | 1,232 | 11 | 532 | 894 | 75 | 112 |
| 1975 | 8 | 154 | 17 | 1,245 | 8 | 456 | 490 | 254 | 53 |
| 1976 | … | 163 | 28 | 1,268 | 7 | — | 518 | 797 | — |
| 1977 | … | 175 | 25 | 1,204 | 7 | — | 333 | 974 | — |
| 1978 | … | 188 | 35 | 1,207 | 8 | — | 76 | 833 | — |
| 1979 | … | 177 | 28 | 1,236 | 9 | — | 68 | 1,018 | — |
| 1980 | … | 161 | 21 | 1,339 | 9 | — | 145 | 1,057 | — |
| 1981 | … | 208 | 22 | 1,393 | 9 | — | 240 | 962 | — |
| 1982 | … | 183 | 4 | 2,225 | 5 | — | 295 | 888 | — |
| 1983 | … | 133 | 3 | 1,141 | 8 | — | 221 | 864 | — |
| 1984 | … | 181 | 8 | 1,537 | 8 | — | 384 | 657 | — |
| 1985 | … | 151 | 4 | 1,105 | 12 | — | 264 | 570 | — |
| 1986 | … | 174 | 2 | 1,134 | 11 | — | 345 | 483 | — |
| 1987 | … | 146 | … | 979 | 11 | — | 344 | … | — |
| 1988 | … | 169 | … | 994 | 14 | — | 345 | … | — |

## D6     Output of Main Non-ferrous Metal Ores

**MOLYBDENUM** (Mo content) (in metric tons)

**1910–1939**

| | NORTH AMERICA | | | SOUTH AMERICA | | | NORTH AMERICA | | | SOUTH AMERICA | |
|---|---|---|---|---|---|---|---|---|---|---|---|
| | Canada | Mexico | USA | Chile | Peru | | Canada | Mexico | USA | Chile | Peru |
| 1910 | ... | ... | — | — | ... | 1950 | 28 | — | 20,205 | 992 | 1 |
| 1911 | ... | ... | — | — | ... | 1951 | 104 | — | 17,217 | 1,725 | 3 |
| 1912 | ... | ... | — | — | ... | 1952 | 138 | — | 19,376 | 1,644 | 3 |
| 1913 | ... | ... | — | — | ... | 1953 | 88 | — | 24,414 | 1,364 | 5 |
| 1914 | ... | ... | 1 | — | ... | 1954 | 205 | 71 | 29,039 | 1,204 | 1 |
| 1915 | ... | ... | 83 | — | ... | 1955 | 378 | 25 | 29,352 | 1,273 | — |
| 1916 | ... | ... | 93 | — | ... | 1956 | 382 | 14 | 25,912 | 1,408 | — |
| 1917 | ... | ... | 159 | — | ... | 1957 | 355 | 13 | 25,920 | 1,338 | — |
| 1918 | ... | ... | 391 | — | ... | 1958 | 403 | 26 | 19,200 | 1,285 | 1 |
| 1919 | ... | ... | 135 | — | ... | 1959 | 340 | 26 | 23,487 | 2,299 | — |
| 1920 | ... | ... | 15 | — | ... | 1960 | 348 | 60 | 31,725 | 1,852 | — |
| 1921 | ... | ... | ... | — | ... | 1961 | 350 | 2 | 30,279 | 1,831 | — |
| 1922 | ... | ... | ... | — | ... | 1962 | 371 | 58 | 22,909 | 2,440 | 5 |
| 1923 | ... | ... | 10 | — | ... | 1963 | 378 | 41 | 29,865 | 2,906 | 538 |
| 1924 | ... | ... | 135 | — | ... | 1964 | 556 | 53 | 29,528 | 3,852 | 639 |
| 1925 | 6 | 1 | 523 | — | ... | 1965 | 4,335 | 49 | 35,067 | 3,752 | 680 |
| 1926 | 6 | — | 650 | — | ... | 1966 | 9,342 | 90 | 41,581 | 4,668 | 672 |
| 1927 | — | — | 1,037 | — | ... | 1967 | 9,696 | 38 | 37,011 | 4,740 | 924 |
| 1928 | — | — | 1,510 | — | ... | 1968 | 10,190 | 48 | 42,296 | 3,853 | 810 |
| 1929 | 4 | — | 1,771 | — | ... | 1969 | 13,450 | 202 | 46,725 | 4,841 | 224 |
| 1930 | — | — | 1,706 | — | — | 1970 | 15,319 | 141 | 50,068 / 50,508 | 5,701 | 1,012 |
| 1931 | — | 4 | 1,413 | — | 1 | 1971 | 10,279 | 79 | 49,710 | 6,321 | 1,337 |
| 1932 | — | 3 | 1,076 | — | 4 | 1972 | 12,925 | 78 | 50,865 | 5,885 | 1,278 |
| 1933 | — | 40 | 2,613 | — | 5 | 1973 | 13,786 | 41 | 52,553 | 4,940 | 1,056 |
| 1934 | — | 466 | 4,253 | — | 9 | 1974 | 13,942 | 43 | 50,808 | 9,757 | 1,085 |
| 1935 | — | 686 | 4,941 | — | 8 | 1975 | 13,026 | 17 | 48,072 | 9,091 | 739 |
| 1936 | — | 534 | 8,147 | — | 10 | 1976 | 14,618 | 16 | 51,362 | 10,899 | 850 |
| 1937 | 4 | 629 | 13,663 | — | 58 | 1977 | 16,568 | 1 | 55,524 | 10,938 | 456 |
| 1938 | 3 | 483 | 11,670 | — | 111 | 1978 | 13,943 | 11 | 59,803 | 13,196 | 730 |
| 1939 | 1 | 523 | 14,704 | 30 | 205 | 1979 | 11,175 | 48 | 65,303 | 13,560 | 1,196 |
| 1940 | 5 | 309 | 11,489 | 267 | 166 | 1980 | 11,889 | 74 | 68,351 | 13,668 | 2,688 |
| 1941 | 47 | 522 | 17,407 | 229 | 146 | 1981 | 14,134 | 451 | 63,458 | 15,360 | 2,488 |
| 1942 | 43 | 855 | 30,135 | 580 | 153 | 1982 | 16,460 | 5,190 | 38,274 | 20,048 | 2,893 |
| 1943 | 178 | 1,137 | 24,474 | 680 | 85 | 1983 | 10,194 | 5,866 | 15,237 | 15,264 | 2,628 |
| 1944 | 509 | 716 | 17,882 | 1,051 | 62 | 1984 | 11,557 | 4,054 | 47,021 | 16,861 | 3,085 |
| 1945 | 228 | 468 | 15,279 | 841 | 29 | 1985 | 7,852 | 3,761 | 49,173 | 18,389 | 3,833 |
| 1946 | 184 | 818 | 7,315 | 560 | 4 | 1986 | 11,251 | 3,350 | 42,627 | 16,581 | 3,491 |
| 1947 | 207 | 136 | 10,065 | 402 | 2 | 1987 | 11,829 | 4,400 | 34,072 | 16,941 | 3,352 |
| 1948 | 83 | — | 13,457 | 532 | 2 | 1988 | 13,100 | 4,456 | 43,063 | 15,527 | 2,370 |
| 1949 | — | — | 10,560 | 558 | 2 | | | | | | |

**D6       Output of Main Non-ferrous Metal Ores**

**NICKEL** (Ni content) (in metric tons)

### 1885–1929

| | NORTH AMERICA | | | NORTH AMERICA | | | | NORTH AMERICA | | |
|---|---|---|---|---|---|---|---|---|---|---|
| | Canada[11] | | | Canada[11] | Cuba | USA | | Canada[11] | Cuba | U.S.A. |
| 1885 | ... | 1920 | 28.0 | | | | 1955 | 159 | 14 | 4.0 |
| 1886 | ... | 1921 | 8.8 | | | | 1956 | 162 | 15 | 6.7 |
| 1887 | ... | 1922 | 8.0 | | | | 1957 | 171 | 20 | 12 |
| 1888 | ... | 1923 | 28 | | | | 1958 | 127 | 18 | 12 |
| 1889 | 0.4 | 1924 | 31 | | | | 1959 | 169 | 18 | 12 |
| 1890 | 0.6 | 1925 | 33 | | | | 1960 | 195 | 13 | 13 |
| 1891 | 1.8 | 1926 | 30 | | | | 1961 | 211 | 15 | 12 |
| 1892 | 1.1 | 1927 | 30 | | | | 1962 | 211 | 17 | 12 |
| 1893 | 1.8 | 1928 | 44 | | | | 1963 | 197 | 20 | 12 |
| 1894 | 2.2 | 1929 | 50 | | | | 1964 | 207 | 23 | 14 |
| 1895 | 1.8 | 1930 | 47 | — | ... | | 1965 | 235 | 28 | 15 |
| 1896 | 1.5 | 1931 | 30 | — | ... | | 1966 | 203 | 28 | 14 |
| 1897 | 1.8 | 1932 | 14 | — | ... | | 1967 | 226 | 33 | 14 |
| 1898 | 2.5 | 1933 | 38 | — | ... | | 1968 | 240 | 38 | 16 |
| 1899 | 2.6 | 1934 | 58 | — | ... | | 1969 | 194 | 35 | 15 |
| 1900 | 3.2 | 1935 | 63 | — | ... | | 1970 | 277 | 37 | 14 |
| 1901 | 4.2 | 1936 | 77 | — | ... | | 1971 | 267 | 36 | 15 |
| 1902 | 4.9 | 1937 | 102 | — | ... | | 1972 | 235 | 37 | 15 |
| 1903 | 5.7 | 1938 | 96 | — | ... | | 1973 | 249 | 35 | 17 |
| 1904 | 4.8 | 1939 | 103 | — | ... | | 1974 | 269 | 34 | 15 |
| 1905 | 8.6 | 1940 | 111 | — | ... | | 1975 | 242 | 37 | 15 |
| 1906 | 9.7 | 1941 | 128 | — | ... | | 1976 | 241 | 37 | 15 |
| 1907 | 9.6 | 1942 | 129 | — | ... | | 1977 | 233 | 37 | 13 |
| 1908 | 8.7 | 1943 | 131 | 2.4 | ... | | 1978 | 128 | 35 | 12 |
| 1909 | 12 | 1944 | 125 | 4.7 | ... | | 1979 | 126 | 32 | 14 |
| 1910 | 17 | 1945 | 111 | 11 | ... | | 1980 | 185 | 38 | 13 |
| 1911 | 15 | 1946 | 87 | 11 | ... | | 1981 | 155 | 40 | 11 |
| 1912 | 20 | 1947 | 108 | 2.0 | ... | | 1982 | 89 | 38 | 3 |
| 1913 | 23 | 1948 | 120 | — | ... | | 1983 | 125 | 39 | — |
| 1914 | 20 | 1949 | 117 | — | ... | | 1984 | 174 | 33 | 13 |
| 1915 | 31 | 1950 | 112 | — | ... | | 1985 | 170 | 36 | 6 |
| 1916 | 38 | 1951 | 125 | — | ... | | 1986 | 164 | 35 | 1 |
| 1917 | 38 | 1952 | 128 | 8.1 | ... | | 1987 | 189 | 37 | — |
| 1918 | 42 | 1953 | 130 | 13 | ... | | 1988 | 199 | 44 | — |
| 1919 | 20 | 1954 | 151 | 13 | 1.8 | | | | | |

**D6      Output of Main Non-ferrous Metal Ores**

**SILVER** (metal content) (in metric tons)

| | NORTH AMERICA | SOUTH AMERICA |
|---|---|---|
| | USA | Chile |
| 1834 | 0.2 | ... |
| 1835 | 0.6 | ... |
| 1836 | 0.6 | ... |
| 1837 | 0.6 | ... |
| 1838 | 0.6 | ... |
| 1839 | 0.6 | ... |
| 1840 | 0.6 | ... |
| 1841 | 0.6 | ... |
| 1842 | 0.6 | ... |
| 1843 | 0.6 | ... |
| 1844 | 0.6 | 28 |
| 1845 | 1.2 | 36 |
| 1846 | 1.2 | 41 |
| 1847 | 1.2 | 41 |
| 1848 | 1.2 | 50 |
| 1849 | 1.2 | 71 |
| 1850 | 1.2 | 92 |
| 1851 | 1.2 | 80 |
| 1852 | 1.2 | 86 |
| 1853 | 1.2 | 57 |
| 1854 | 1.2 | 69 |
| 1855 | 1.2 | 62 |
| 1856 | 1.2 | 57 |
| 1857 | 1.2 | 35 |
| 1858 | 1.2 | 27 |
| 1859 | 2.4 | 16 |
| 1860 | 3.6 | 34 |
| 1861 | 48 | 28 |
| 1862 | 108 | 48 |
| 1863 | 204 | 49 |
| 1864 | 265 | 36 |

| | NORTH AMERICA | | | SOUTH AMERICA | | | | |
|---|---|---|---|---|---|---|---|---|
| | Canada | Mexico[14] | USA[15] | Argentina | Bolivia[23] | Chile | Colombia | Peru |
| 1865 | ... | ... | 271 | ... | ... | 22 | ... | ... |
| 1866 | ... | ... | 241 | ... | ... | 38 | ... | ... |
| 1867 | ... | ... | 325 | ... | ... | 65 | ... | ... |
| 1868 | ... | ... | 289 | ... | ... | 70 | ... | ... |
| 1869 | ... | ... | 289 | ... | ... | 83 | ... | ... |
| 1870 | ... | 967 | 385 | ... | ... | 46 | ... | ... |
| 1871 | ... | 516 | 553 | ... | ... | 54 | ... | ... |
| 1872 | ... | 489 | 692 | ... | ... | 37 | ... | ... |
| 1873 | ... | 514 | 860 | ... | ... | 65 | ... | ... |
| 1874 | ... | 523 | 898 | ... | ... | 75 | ... | ... |
| 1875 | ... | 570 | 763 | ... | ... | 74 | ... | ... |
| 1876 | 5.6 | 607 | 933 | | 82 | 35 | ... | 58 |
| 1877 | 3.7 | 614 | 997 | ... | 67 | 43 | ... | 58 |
| 1878 | 5.5 | 673 | 1,089 | ... | 88 | 41 | ... | 58 |
| 1879 | 1.6 | 715 | 982 | 10 | 265 | 60 | ... | 58 |
| 1880 | 1.6 | 715 | 943 | ... | 265 | 84 | ... | 58 |
| 1881 | 1.6 | 723 | 1,034 | ... | 265 | 38 | ... | 47 |
| 1882 | 1.6 | 775 | 1,126 | ... | 265 | 97 | 18 | 46 |
| 1883 | 5.0 | 812 | 1,111 | ... | 385 | 77 | ... | 46 |
| 1884 | 5.0 | 836 | 1,174 | 10 | 241 | 67 | 18 | 46 |
| 1885 | 5.0 | 917 | 1,241 | 12 | 241 | 156 | 9.6 | 48 |
| 1886 | 5.0 | 962 | 1,235 | 1.4 | 241 | 155 | 9.6 | 96 |
| 1887 | 11 | 1,011 | 1,298 | 0.7 | 199 | 194 | 24 | 75 |
| 1888 | 14 | 957 | 1,424 | 10 | 230 | 183 | 24 | 75 |
| 1889 | 12 | 1,023 | 1,558 | 15 | 263 | 124 | 15 | 69 |
| 1890 | 12 | 1,151 | 1,696 | 15 | 301 | 74 | 20 | 66 |
| 1891 | 13 | 1,350 | 1,814 | 15 | 373 | 34 | 41 | 70 |
| 1892 | 10 | 1,423 | 1,975 | 15 | 393 | 101 | 41 | 59 |
| 1893 | 13 | 1,423 | 1,866 | 22 | 424 | 97 | 53 | 59 |
| 1894 | 26 | 1,491 | 1,540 | 37 | 684 | 145 | 53 | 108 |
| 1895 | 49 | 1,557 | 1,733 | 10 | 684 | 137 | 53 | 98 |
| 1896 | 100 | 1,715 | 1,830 | 10 | 198 | 150 | 106 | 120 |
| 1897 | 173 | 1,772 | 1,675 | 12 | 255 | 141 | 157 | 102 |
| 1898 | 138 | 1,716 | 1,693 | 12 | 342 | 132 | 171 | 165 |
| 1899 | 106 | 1,817 | 1,703 | 12 | 337 | 129 | 110 | 203 |
| 1900 | 139 | 1,773[14] | 1,793 | 1.2 | 341 | 73 | 58 | 227 |
| 1901 | 172 | 1,795 | 1,717 | 1.4 | 404 | 68 | 59 | 111 |
| 1902 | 133 | 1,898 | 1,726 | 1.2 | 279 | 51 | 55 | 133 |
| 1903 | 100 | 2,019 | 1,689 | 2.9 | 189 | 51 | 35 | 171 |
| 1904 | 111 | 1,973 | 1,794[15] 1,742 | 2.0 | 117 | 27 | 29 | 145 |
| 1905 | 187 | 1,891 | 1,750 | 4.7 | 96 | 26 | 21 | 191 |
| 1906 | 264 | 1,803 | 1,784 | 0.4 | 110 | 26 | 24 | 230 |
| 1907 | 398 | 1,954 | 1,633 | 0.7 | 149 | 28 | 33 | 208 |
| 1908 | 688 | 2,221 | 1,582 | 3.9 | 157 | 30 | 43 | 199 |
| 1909 | 856 | 2,213 | 1,783 | 8.2 | 157 | 44 | 13 | 208 |

## D6    Output of Main Non-ferrous Metal Ores

**SILVER** (metal content) (in metric tons)

| | NORTH AMERICA | | | | | SOUTH AMERICA | | | | |
| | Canada[22] | Honduras | Mexico | Newfound-land | USA | Argentina | Bolivia[23] | Chile | Colombia | Peru |
|---|---|---|---|---|---|---|---|---|---|---|
| 1910 | 1,022 | ... | 2,417 | — | 1,791 | 8.1 | 144 | 42 | 27.0 | 253 |
| 1911 | 1,013 | ... | 2,518 | — | 1,901 | 6.3 | 128 | 35 | 25.0 | 289 |
| 1912 | 994 | ... | 2,527 | — | 2,054 | 2.5 | 124 | 40 | 18.0 | 324 |
| 1913 | 991 | ... | 2,199 | — | 2,214 | 1.1 | 124 | 40 | 18.0 | 299 |
| 1914 | 885 | ... | 857 | — | 2,166 | ... | 71 | 37 | 11.0 | 287 |
| 1915 | 828 | ... | 1,231 | — | 2,250 | ... | 77 | 40 | 11.0 | 293 |
| 1916 | 792 | ... | 926 | — | 2,453 | 0.7 | 78 | 47 | 10.0 | 335 |
| 1917 | 691 | ... | 1,307 | — | 2,198 | 0.9 | 76 | 53 | 10.0 | 338 |
| 1918 | 665 | ... | 1,945 | — | 2,117 | 0.8 | 76 | 47 | ... | 304 |
| 1919 | 498 | ... | 2,050 | — | 1,614 | 0.8 | 76 | 41 | 15.0 | 305 |
| 1920 | 415 | ... | 2,069 | — | 1,758 | 0.9 | 68[24] / 192 | 81 | 15.0 | 286 |
| 1921 | 421 | ... | 2,005 | — | 1,436 | 0.8 | 187 | 80 | 16.0 | 307 |
| 1922 | 579 | ... | 2,522 | — | 1,904 | 0.8 | 167 | 84 | 0.1 | 410 |
| 1923 | 579 | ... | 2,825 | — | 2,188 | 0.9 | 162 | 104 | 0.1 | 580 |
| 1924 | 614 | ... | 2,844 | — | 1,993 | 0.6 | 151 | 94 | 0.1 | 582 |
| 1925 | 629 | ... | 2,889 | — | 2,075 | 0.6 | 135 | 101 | 0.1 | 645 |
| 1926 | 696 | ... | 3,044 | — | 1,944 | 0.5 | 181 | 101 | 0.1 | 701 |
| 1927 | 707 | ... | 3,248 | — | 1,855 | 0.5 | 168 | 47 | 4.1 | 572 |
| 1928 | 682 | ... | 3,374 | — | 1,800 | 0.5 | 175 | 45 | 1.5 | 679 |
| 1929 | 720 | ... | 3,386 | 17 | 1,893 | 0.5 | 150 | 49 | 1.7 | 660 |
| 1930 | 823 | ... | 3,272 | 17 | 1,484 | 0.5 | 221 | 24 | 2.1 | 479 |
| 1931 | 640 | ... | 2,677 | 30 | 929 | ... | 179 | 9.0 | 2.7 | 273 |
| 1932 | 571 | ... | 2,156 | 42 | 708 | 1.6 | 128 | 3.1 | 2.8 | 211 |
| 1933 | 472 | 122 | 2,118 | 38 | 719 | 1.6 | 170 | 8.0 | 3.4 | 232 |
| 1934 | 511 | 96 | 2,306 | 34 | 1,020 | 1.9 | 166 | 33 | 4.0 | 322 |
| 1935 | 517 | 83 | 2,351 | 35 | 1,509 | 1.6 | 193 | 40 | 4.1 | 548 |
| 1936 | 570 | 99 | 2,409 | 39 | 1,902 | 16 | 318 | 47 | 4.7 | 619 |
| 1937 | 715 | 106 | 2,634 | 45 | 2,221 | 66 | 294 | 58 | 5.2 | 543 |
| 1938 | 691 | 112 | 2,520 | 51 | 1,919 | 82 | 198 | 43 | 6.0 | 639 |
| 1939 | 720 | 139 | 2,360 | 44 | 2,002 | 148 | 225 | 37 | 7.5 | 585 |
| 1940 | 741 | 133 | 2,570 | 47 | 2,191 | 116 | 175 | 47 | 8.1 | 602 |
| 1941 | 677 | 118 | 2,437 | 62 | 2,085 | 91 | 229 | 39 | 8.4 | 470 |
| 1942 | 644 | 120 | 2,640 | 34 | 1,682 | 89 | 253 | 28 | 7.7 | 499 |
| 1943 | 539 | 111 | 2,686 | 39 | 1,290 | 72 | 227 | 31 | 6.5 | 456 |
| 1944 | 424 | 112 | 2,286 | 36 | 1,072 | 53 | 211 | 31 | 6.2 | 492 |
| 1945 | 403 | 110 | 1,900 | 34 | 903 | 90 | 208 | 25 | 5.2 | 404 |
| 1946 | 390 | 102 | 1,346 | 35 | 713 | 96 | 190 | 17 | 4.7 | 384 |
| 1947 | 389 | 94 | 1,830 | 30 | 1,114 | 76[13] | 194 | 23 | 3.4 | 335 |
| 1948 | 501[22] | 97 | 1,789 | 27 | 1,185 | 212 | 235 | 27 | 3.4 | 289 |
| 1949 | 549 | 127 | 1,538 | ... | 1,079 | 240 | 206 | 24 | 3.3 | 330 |
| 1950 | 722 | 136 | 1,528 | ... | 1,321 | 235 | 204 | 29 | 3.6 | 416 |
| 1951 | 719 | 125 | 1,362 | ... | 1,237 | 240 | 223 | 37 | 4.0 | 541 |
| 1952 | 784 | [111][5] | 1,566 | ... | 1,227 | 340 | 220 | 44 | 3.8 | 597 |
| 1953 | 880 | [173][5] | 1,463 | ... | 1,169 | 223 | 190 | 47 | 3.7 | 611 |
| 1954 | 968 | [107][5] | 1,241 | ... | 1,149 | 155 | 157 | 46 | 3.5 | 635 |

## D6    Output of Main Non-ferrous Metal Ores

**SILVER** (metal content) (in metric tons)

| | NORTH AMERICA | | | | SOUTH AMERICA | | | | |
| --- | --- | --- | --- | --- | --- | --- | --- | --- | --- |
| | Canada | Honduras | Mexico | U.S.A. | Argentina | Bolivia[23] | Chile | Colombia | Peru |
| 1955 | 870 | 56 | 1,492 | 1,157 | 100 | 184 | 53 | 3.5 | 714 |
| 1956 | 884 | 63 | 1,340 | 1,204 | 50 | 235 | 57 | 3.4 | 746 |
| 1957 | 896 | 70 | 1,466 | 1,187 | 69 | 167 | 48 | 3.3 | 773 |
| 1958 | 969 | 86 | 1,462 | 1,061 | 48 | 188 | 47 | 3.3 | 806 |
| 1959 | 993 | 98 | 1,371 | 970 | 67 | 139 | 55 | 3.2 | 847 |
| 1960 | 1,058 | 92 | 1,385 | 957 | 70 | 152 | 45 | 4.2 | 953 [13] 1,016 |
| 1961 | 976 | 110 | 1,255 | 1,082 | 64 | 121 | 68 | 4.0 | 1,055 |
| 1962 | 947 | 99 | 1,282 | 1,145 | 65 | 117 | 58 | 4.1 | 1,031 |
| 1963 | 931 | 98 | 1,330 | 1,096 | 60 | 151 | 79 | 3.3 | 1,095 |
| 1964 | 930 | 100 | 1,298 | 1,130 | 60 | 150 | 87 | 4.1 | 1,070 |
| 1965 | 1,004 | 114 | 1,254 | 1,238 | 71 | 128 | 86 | 3.6 | 1,134 |
| 1966 | 1,039 | 120 | 1,306 | 1,358 | 69 | 103 | 100 | 3.4 | 1,149 |
| 1967 | 1,130 | 120 | 1,190 | 1,006 | 53 | 110 | 98 | 3.4 | 999 |
| 1968 | 1,400 | 168 | 1,245 | 1,018 | 77 | 113 | 116 | 3.1 | 1,127 |
| 1969 | 1,354 | 116 | 1,334 | 1,303 | 97 | 150 | 96 | 2.4 | 1,175 |
| 1970 | 1,423 | 117 | 1,332 | 1,400 | 88 | 148 | 76 | 2.4 | 1,217 |
| 1971 | 1,431 | 76 | 1,140 | 1,293 | 99 | 145 | 85 | 2 | 1,264 |
| 1972 | 1,393 | 108 | 1,166 | 1,158 | 102 | 143 | 146 | 2 | 1,269 |
| 1973 | 1,477 | 104 | 1,206 | 1,166 | 76 | 165 | 157 | 2 | 1,287 |
| 1974 | 1,332 | 118 | 1,168 | 1,050 | 96 | 179 | 208 | 2 | 1,215 |
| 1975 | 1,234 | 89 | 1,183 | 1,087 | 72 | 204 | 194 | 3 | 1,201 |
| 1976 | 1,281 | 114 | 1,326 | 1,068 | 70 | 177 | 228 | 3 | 1,202 |
| 1977 | 1,314 | 88 | 1,463 | 1,187 | 76 | 209 [23] 181 | 263 | 3 | 1,132 |
| 1978 | 1,267 | 87 | 1,579 | 1,225 | 64 | 196 | 255 | 3 | 1,337 |
| 1979 | 1,147 | 76 | 1,537 | 1,179 | 69 | 179 | 272 | 3 | 1,364 |
| 1980 | 1,070 | 54 | 1,473 | 1,006 | 73 | 190 | 299 | 5 | 1,337 |
| 1981 | 1,203 | 56 | 1,655 | 1,265 | 78 | 205 | 361 | 4 | 1,470 |
| 1982 | 1,291 | 53 | 1,550 | 1,252 | 84 | 170 | 382 | 4 | 1,663 |
| 1983 | 1,197 | 83 | 1,911 | 1,351 | 78 | 187 | 468 | 3 | 1,739 |
| 1984 | 1,327 | 89 | 1,987 | 1,387 | 62 | 142 | 490 | 4 | 1,651 |
| 1985 | 1,197 | 86 | 2,153 | 1,227 | 68 | 111 | 517 | 5 | 1,915 |
| 1986 | 1,088 | 41 | 2,303 | 1,074 | 66 | 100 | 500 | 5 | 1,926 |
| 1987 | 1,375 | 23 | 2,415 | 1,241 | 60 | 140 | 500 | 5 | 2,054 |
| 1988 | 1,371 | 49 | 2,359 | 1,661 | 79 | 232 | 507 | 7 | 1,552 |

**D6    Output of Main Non-ferrous Metal Ores**

**TIN** (Sn content) (in metric tons)

| | SOUTH AMERICA | | NORTH AMERICA | SOUTH AMERICA | | | NORTH AMERICA | SOUTH AMERICA | | |
|---|---|---|---|---|---|---|---|---|---|---|
| | Bolivia | | Canada | Argentina | Bolivia | | Canada | Argentina | Bolivia | Brazil |
| 1870 | 102 | 1910 | — | ... | 23,129 | 1945 | 385 | 1,101 | 43,168 | ... |
| 1871 | ... | 1911 | — | ... | 22,434 | 1946 | 396 | 795 | 38,222 | ... |
| 1872 | ... | 1912 | — | ... | 23,027 | 1947 | 324 | 558 | 33,800 | ... |
| 1873 | ... | 1913 | — | ... | 26,355 | 1948 | 314 | 284 | 37,935 | 187 |
| 1874 | ... | 1914 | — | ... | 22,355 | 1949 | 280 | 224 | 34,662 | ... |
| 1875 | 305 | 1915 | — | ... | 21,794 | 1950 | 362 | 261 | 31,714 | 183 |
| 1876 | 315 | 1916 | — | ... | 21,145 | 1951 | 157 | 241 | 33,664 | 200 |
| 1877 | 315 | 1917 | — | ... | 27,858 | 1952 | 97 | 265 | 32,472 | 233 |
| 1878 | 325 | 1918 | — | ... | 29,280 | 1953 | [292][25] | 156 | 35,384 | 212 |
| 1879 | 335 | 1919 | — | ... | 27,389 | 1954 | [151][25] | 97 | 29,287 | 170 |
| 1880 | 366 | 1920 | — | ... | 29,542 | 1955 | [224][25] | 86 | 28,369 | 148 |
| 1881 | 305 | 1921 | — | ... | 28,957 | 1956 | [343][25] | 86 | 27,273 | 178 |
| 1882 | 356 | 1922 | — | ... | 28,129 | 1957 | [322][25] | 185[13] | 28,242 | 298 |
| 1883 | 501 | 1923 | — | ... | 31,128 | 1958 | [361][25] | 90 | 18,013 | 416 |
| 1884 | 207 | 1924 | — | ... | 32,059 | 1959 | 339 | 107 | 24,193 | 468[13] |
| 1885 | 228 | 1925 | — | ... | 32,741 | 1960 | 282 | 140 | 20,543 | 1,581 |
| 1886 | 360 | 1926 | — | ... | 30,543 | 1961 | 508 | 261 | 20,996 | 590 |
| 1887 | 998 | 1927 | — | ... | 36,383 | 1962 | 296 | 235 | 22,150 | 743 |
| 1888 | 1,385 | 1928 | — | 22 | 42,074 | 1963 | 421 | 229 | 22,603 | 1,172 |
| 1889 | 1,411 | 1929 | — | 2 | 47,081 | 1964 | 160 | 348 | 24,587 | 802 |
| 1890 | 1,691 | 1930 | — | — | 38,756 | 1965 | 171 | 505 | 23,407 | 1,842 |
| 1891 | 1,584 | 1931 | — | — | 31,234 | 1966 | 322 | 465 | 25,932 | 1,624 |
| 1892 | 2,864 | 1932 | — | 6 | 20,919 | 1967 | 198 | 815 | 27,721 | 1,761 |
| 1893 | 2,956 | 1933 | — | 51 | 14,961 | 1968 | 162 | 712 | 29,568 | 1,865 |
| 1894 | 3,538 | 1934 | — | 234 | 23,224 | 1969 | 131 | 869 | 30,045[13] | 2,033 |
| 1895 | 4,166 | 1935 | — | 640 | 25,408 | 1970 | 120 | 1,172 | 30,100 | 3,610 |
| 1896 | 4,104 | 1936 | — | 904 | 24,438 | 1971 | 145 | 711 | 20,290 | 2,098 |
| 1897 | 5,594 | 1937 | — | 1,356 | 25,531 | 1972 | 159 | 559 | 32,405 | 2,813 |
| 1898 | 4,536 | 1938 | — | 1,747 | 25,894 | 1973 | 132 | 432 | 28,568 | 3,742 |
| 1899 | 5,588 | 1939 | — | 1,729 | 27,916 | 1974 | 324 | 556 | 29,151 | 4,400 |
| 1900 | 9,198 | 1940 | — | 1,480 | 38,531 | 1975 | 319 | 538 | 31,952 | 4,512 |
| 1901 | 13,124 | 1941 | 29 | 1,189 | 42,740 | 1976 | 275 | 358 | 30,315 | 5,482 |
| 1902 | 10,604 | 1942 | 562 | 872 | 38,907 | 1977 | 328 | 537 | 33,740 | 5,761 |
| 1903 | 12,533 | 1943 | 353 | 785 | 40,960 | 1978 | 360 | 362 | 30,881 | 6,320 |
| 1904 | 12,902 | 1944 | 235 | 1,002 | 39,341 | 1979 | 337 | 386 | 27,791 | 6,645 |
| 1905 | 16,582 | | | | | 1980 | 243 | 351 | 27,271 | 6,930 |
| 1906 | 17,624 | | | | | 1981 | 248 | 413 | 29,801 | 8,297 |
| 1907 | 16,607 | | | | | 1982 | 135 | 342 | 24,343 | 8,218 |
| 1908 | 17,692 | | | | | 1983 | 140 | 291 | 25,278 | 13,275 |
| 1909 | 21,340 | | | | | 1984 | 209 | 274 | 19,911 | 19,957 |
| | | | | | | 1985 | 119 | 451 | 16,136 | 26,514 |
| | | | | | | 1986 | 2,356 | 379 | 10,479 | 26,405 |
| | | | | | | 1987 | 3,397 | 186 | 8,128 | 28,523 |
| | | | | | | 1988 | 3,840 | 446 | 10,504 | 44,102 |

**D6     Output of Main Non-ferrous Metal Ores**

**TUNGSTEN** (WO3 content) (in metric tons)

| | NORTH AMERICA | | | SOUTH AMERICA | | | |
|---|---|---|---|---|---|---|---|
| | Canada[11] | Mexico | USA | Argentina | Bolivia[26] | Brazil | Peru[27] |
| 1900 | — | ... | 20 | — | ... | — | ... |
| 1901 | — | ... | 77 | — | ... | — | ... |
| 1902 | — | ... | 80 | — | ... | — | ... |
| 1903 | — | ... | 126 | — | ... | — | ... |
| 1904 | — | ... | 319 | — | ... | — | ... |
| 1905 | — | ... | 347 | — | ... | — | ... |
| 1906 | — | ... | 401 | — | ... | — | ... |
| 1907 | — | ... | 708 | — | ... | — | ... |
| 1908 | — | ... | 289 | — | ... | — | ... |
| 1909 | — | ... | 699 | — | ... | — | ... |
| 1910 | — | ... | 786 | — | ... | — | ... |
| 1911 | — | ... | 492 | — | ... | — | ... |
| 1912 | 13 | ... | 574 | — | ... | — | ... |
| 1913 | — | ... | 664 | — | 282 | — | ... |
| 1914 | — | ... | 427 | — | 276 | — | ... |
| 1915 | — | ... | 1,007 | — | 793 | — | ... |
| 1916 | — | ... | 2,556 | — | 3,035 | — | ... |
| 1917 | - - | ... | 2,653 | — | 3,888 | — | ... |
| 1918 | 12 | ... | 2,185 | — | 3,417 | — | ... |
| 1919 | — | ... | 142 | — | 1,995 | — | ... |
| 1920 | — | ... | 93 | — | 708 | — | ... |
| 1921 | — | ... | ... | — | 161 | — | ... |
| 1922 | — | ... | ... | — | 7 | — | ... |
| 1923 | — | ... | 103 | — | — | — | ... |
| 1924 | — | ... | 244 | — | - - | — | ... |
| 1925 | — | ... | 513 | — | 73[26] / 50 | — | 4 |
| 1926 | — | ... | 597 | — | 65 | — | — |
| 1927 | — | ... | 503 | 5 | 52 | — | — |
| 1928 | — | — | 522 | 15 | 17 | — | — |
| 1929 | — | 6 | 358 | 38 | 977 | — | 1 |
| 1930 | — | 17 | 303 | 59 | 532 | — | — |
| 1931 | — | — | 606 | 12 | 246 | — | — |
| 1932 | — | — | 171 | 4 | 411 | — | — |
| 1933 | — | — | 386 | — | 143 | — | — |
| 1934 | — | 74 | 885 | 238 | 530 | — | 11 |
| 1935 | — | 50 | 1,034 | 351 | 817 | — | 54 |
| 1936 | — | 52 | 1,128 | 426 | 1,044 | — | 55 |
| 1937 | — | 31 | 1,511 | 453 | 1,081 | 5 | 18 |
| 1938 | — | 70 | 1,315 | 685 | 1,518 | 2 | 102 |
| 1939 | 4 | 109 | 1,851 | 518 | 2,002 | 6 | 160 |
| 1940 | 5 | 103 | 2,296 | 812 | 2,510 | 8 | 183 |
| 1941 | 38 | 91 | 2,835 | 660 | 2,613 | 24 | 202 |
| 1942 | 236 | 92 | 4,029 | 913 | 3,363 | — | 222 |
| 1943 | 684 | 245 | 5,156 | 926 | 4,141 | 875 | 433 |
| 1944 | 402 | 160 | 4,439 | 1,245 | 4,761 | 1,492 | 381 |

**D6**     **Output of Main Non-ferrous Metal Ores**

**TUNGSTEN** (WO3 content) (in metric tons)

| | NORTH AMERICA | | | SOUTH AMERICA | | | |
|---|---|---|---|---|---|---|---|
| | Canada[11] | Mexico | USA | Argentina | Bolivia[26] | Brazil[27] | Peru[28] |
| 1945 | - - | 64 | 2,389 | 628 | 2,311 | 1,529 | 314 |
| 1946 | — | 45 | 2,242 | 44 | 1,273 | 1,107 | 305 |
| 1947 | 225 | 46 | 1,335 | 54 | 1,581 | 920 | 347 |
| 1948 | 474 | 80 | 1,741 | 101 | 1,491 | 792 | 212 |
| 1949 | 114 | 39 | 1,194 | 103 | 1,526 | 352 | 272 |
| 1950 | 129 | 40 | 2,081 | 14 | 1,476 | 434 | 309 |
| 1951 | 1 | 195 | 2,709 | 79 | 1,631 | 952 | 281 |
| 1952 | 677 | 267 | 3,286 | 331 | 2,224 | 788 | 350 |
| 1953 | 1,109 | 409 | 4,140 | 417 | 2,295 | 940 | 545 |
| 1954 | 985 | 327 | 5,910 | 599 | 2,667 | 791 | 462 |
| 1955 | 881 | 341 | 7,085 | 595 | 3,231 | 583 | 486 |
| 1956 | 1,030 | 342 | 6,363 | 663 | 2,860 | 783 | 676 |
| 1957 | 872 | 160 | 2,383 | 739 | 2,618 | 614 | 661 |
| 1958 | 313 | 4 | 1,636 | 601 | 1,337 | 1,276 | 540 |
| 1959 | — | 75 | 1,576 | 473 | 1,454 | 1,044 | 295 |
| 1960 | — | 110 | 3,162 | 487 | 1,290 | 847 | 293 |
| 1961 | — | 105 | 3,560 | 486 | 1,694 | 617 | 233 |
| 1962 | 2 | 47 | 3,639 | 351 | 1,523 | 620 | 237 [28] |
| 1963 | 555 | 20 | 2,442 | 100 | 1,368 | 278 | 175 |
| 1964 | 485 | 5 | 3,991 | 37 | 1,244 | 212 | 587 |
| 1965 | 1,734 | 110 | 3,432 | 87 | 1,112 [26] / 1,038 | 252 | 430 |
| 1966 | 1,934 | 86 | 3,250 | 87 | 1,344 | 349 | 514 |
| 1967 | 122 | 188 | 2,980 | 135 | 1,740 | 378 | 495 |
| 1968 | 1,626 | 266 | 3,568 | 233 | 1,770 | 460 | 677 |
| 1969 | 1,843 | 289 | 3,177 | 184 | 1,848 | 526 | 869 |
| 1970 | 1,690 | 288 | 4,224 | 181 | 1,990 | 597 | 1,014 |
| 1971 | 2,097 | 408 | ... | 173 | 2,238 | 866 | 958 |
| 1972 | 2,018 | 362 | ... | 199 | 2,537 | 905 | 1,203 |
| 1973 | 2,105 | 348 | 3,202 | 105 | 2,376 | 1,001 | 1,077 |
| 1974 | 1,280 | 309 | 3,554 | 94 | 1,776 | 985 [27] / 1,641 | 703 |
| 1975 | 1,280 | 277 | 2,490 | 58 | 2,311 | 1,644 | 625 |
| 1976 | 1,172 | 235 | 2,662 | 62 | 3,132 | 1,685 | 838 |
| 1977 | 1,719 | 191 | 2,732 | 70 | 3,063 | 2,026 | 526 |
| 1978 | 1,811 | 234 | 3,130 | 97 | 3,073 | 1,937 | 582 |
| 1979 | 2,289 | 252 | 3,014 | 59 | 3,114 [13] / 2,384 | 1,934 | 564 |
| 1980 | 2,580 | 266 | 2,738 | 35 | 2,661 | 1,897 | 331 |
| 1981 | 3,178 | 199 | 3,545 | 11 | 2,778 | 2,550 | 334 |
| 1982 | 2,052 | 99 | 1,575 | 17 | 2,534 | 2,602 | 682 |
| 1983 | 2,938 | 90 | 980 | 41 | 2,490 | 1,842 | 762 |
| 1984 | 328 | 274 | 1,203 | 38 | 1,893 | 1,892 | 699 |
| 1985 | 3,715 | 282 | 996 | 17 | 1,643 | 2,050 | 723 |
| 1986 | 3,005 | 294 | 780 | 20 | 1,094 | 1,502 | 742 |
| 1987 | 1,273 | 213 | 34 | 15 | 638 | 1,364 | 259 |
| 1988 | — | 206 | 230 | 14 | 900 | 1,212 | 545 |

**D6      Output of Main Non-ferrous Metal Ores**

**VANADIUM** (V content) (in metric tons)

| | NORTH AMERICA | | | | SOUTH AMERICA | | | |
|---|---|---|---|---|---|---|---|---|
| | USA | | | USA | Peru[29] | | | Peru |
| 1905 | ... | | 1950 | 2,085 | 1905 | — | 1950 | 432 |
| 1906 | ... | | 1951 | 2,758 | 1906 | — | 1951 | 655 |
| 1907 | ... | | 1952 | 3,255 | 1907 | 25 | 1952 | 437 |
| 1908 | ... | | 1953 | 4,212 | 1908 | 252 | 1953 | 331 |
| 1909 | ... | | 1954 | 4,472 | 1909 | 392 | 1954 | 190 |
| 1910 | ... | | 1955 | 4,521 | 1910 | 802 | 1955 | 71 |
| 1911 | 249 | | 1956 | 5,113 | 1911 | 504 | 1956–1988 | — |
| 1912 | 272 | | 1957 | 6,617 | 1912 | 683 | | |
| 1913 | 392 | | 1958 | 6,592 | 1913 | ... | | |
| 1914 | 410 | | 1959 | 6,706 | 1914 | 14 | | |
| 1915 | 569 | | 1960 | 7,300 | 1915 | 803 | | |
| 1916 | 417 | | 1961 | 5,769 | 1916 | 773 | | |
| 1917 | 439 | | 1962 | 6,937 | 1917 | 819 | | |
| 1918 | 250 | | 1963 | 5,486 | 1918 | 375 | | |
| 1919 | 258 | | 1964 | 4,703 | 1919 | 502 | | |
| 1920 | 478 | | 1965 | 5,117 | 1920 | 1,111 | | |
| 1921 | 183 | | 1966 | 5,157 | 1921 | 199 | | |
| 1922 | 24 | | 1967 | 4,616 | 1922 | ... | | |
| 1923 | 58 | | 1968 | 6,446 | 1923 | 354 | | |
| 1924 | ... | | 1969 | 5,205[13] | 1924 | 614 | | |
| | | | | 5,059 | | | | |
| 1925 | 196 | | 1970 | 4,825 | 1925 | 246 | | |
| 1926 | 300 | | 1971 | 4,765 | 1926 | 857 | | |
| 1927 | ... | | 1972 | 4,433 | 1927 | 717 | | |
| 1928 | ... | | 1973 | 3,971 | 1928 | 73 | | |
| 1929 | ... | | 1974 | 4,418 | 1929 | 902[29] | | |
| | | | | | | 510 | | |
| 1930 | | ... | 1975 | 4,303 | 1930 | 268 | | |
| 1931 | ... | | 1976 | 6,691 | 1931 | — | | |
| 1932 | 245 | | 1977 | 5,900 | 1932 | — | | |
| 1933 | 2 | | 1978 | 3,875 | 1933 | — | | |
| 1934 | 6 | | 1979 | 5,008 | 1934 | 74 | | |
| 1935 | 23 | | 1980 | 4,360 | 1935 | 67 | | |
| 1936 | 64 | | 1981 | 4,650 | 1936 | 161 | | |
| 1937 | 493 | | 1982 | 3,718 | 1937 | 583 | | |
| 1938 | 732 | | 1983 | 1,969 | 1938 | 826 | | |
| 1939 | 900 | | 1984 | 1,467 | 1939 | 569 | | |
| 1940 | 981 | | 1985 | ... | 1940 | 1,150 | | |
| 1941 | 1,140 | | 1986 | ... | 1941 | 991 | | |
| 1942 | 2,014 | | 1987 | ... | 1942 | 1,015 | | |
| 1943 | 2,534 | | 1988 | ... | 1943 | 881 | | |
| 1944 | 1,600 | | | | 1944 | 518 | | |
| 1945 | 1,344 | | | | 1945 | 688 | | |
| 1946 | 577 | | | | 1946 | 322 | | |
| 1947 | 961 | | | | 1947 | 435 | | |
| 1948 | 811 | | | | 1948 | 511 | | |
| 1949 | 1,434 | | | | 1949 | 456 | | |

**D6** **Output of Main Non-ferrous Metal Ores**

**ZINC** (Zn content) (in thousands of metric tons)

| | NORTH AMERICA | | | | SOUTH AMERICA |
|---|---|---|---|---|---|
| | Canada | Mexico | Newfoundland | USA[17] | Peru |
| 1893 | ... | 0.4 | — | ... | — |
| 1894 | ... | 0.3 | — | ... | — |
| 1895 | ... | 0.5 | — | ... | — |
| 1896 | ... | 0.5 | — | ... | — |
| 1897 | ... | 0.6 | — | ... | — |
| 1898 | 0.4 | 1.2 | — | ... | — |
| 1899 | 0.4 | 0.7 | — | ... | — |
| 1900 | 0.1 | 1.1 | — | ... | — |
| 1901 | — | 0.9 | — | ... | — |
| 1902 | 0.1 | 0.7 | — | ... | — |
| 1903 | 0.4 | 1 | — | ... | — |
| 1904 | 0.2 | 0.8 | — | ... | — |
| 1905 | 8.1 | 2.0 | — | ... | — |
| 1906 | 0.9 | 23 | — | ... | — |
| 1907 | 1.8 | 23 | — | 230 | — |
| 1908 | — | 16 | — | 212 | — |
| 1909 | 16 | 3.0 | — | 274 | — |
| 1910 | 4.5 | 1.8 | — | 294 | — |
| 1911 | 2.7 | 1.6 | — | 301 | — |
| 1912 | 5.4 | 1.3 | — | 350 | — |
| 1913 | 7.2 | 1 | — | 375 | — |
| 1914 | 9.9 | 0.8 | — | 377 | — |
| 1915 | 14 | 5.8 | — | 533 | — |
| 1916 | 11 | 37 | — | 638 | — |
| 1917 | 13 | 45 | — | 647 | — |
| 1918 | 16 | 21 | — | 577 | — |
| 1919 | 15 | 12 | — | 498 | — |
| 1920 | 18 | 16 | — | 533 | — |
| 1921 | 24 | 1.3 | — | 233 | — |
| 1922 | 26 | 6.1 | — | 428 | — |
| 1923 | 27 | 18 | — | 554 | — |
| 1924 | 45 | 25 | — | 579 | 0.1 |
| 1925 | 50 | 46 | — | 645 | 1.9 |
| 1926 | 68 | 105 | — | 703 | 15 |
| 1927 | 75 | 138 | — | 652 | 11 |
| 1928 | 84 | 162 | — | 631 | 5.5 |
| 1929 | 89 | 174 | 23 | 657 | 12 |
| 1930 | 121 | 124 | 30 | 540 | 11 |
| 1931 | 108 | 120 | 44 | 372 | — |
| 1932 | 78 | 57 | 66 | 259 | 0.2 |
| 1933 | 90 | 89 | 75 | 349 | 0.2 |
| 1934 | 135 | 125 | 88 | 398 | 5.6 |
| 1935 | 145 | 136 | 72 | 470 | 4.7 |
| 1936 | 151 | 150 | 64 | 522 | 11 |
| 1937 | 168 | 155 | 64 | 568 | 29 |
| 1938 | 173 | 172 | 67 | 469 | 25 |
| 1939 | 179 | 134 | 60 | 530 | 36 |

## D6 Output of Main Non-ferrous Metal Ores

**ZINC** (Zn content) (in thousands of metric tons)

| | NORTH AMERICA | | | | SOUTH AMERICA |
|---|---|---|---|---|---|
| | Canada[11] | Mexico | Newfoundland | USA[17] | Peru |
| 1940 | 192 | 115 | 65 | 603 | 18 |
| 1941 | 232 | 155 | 63 | 680 | 23 |
| 1942 | 263 | 189 | 51 | 697 | 24 |
| 1943 | 277 | 197 | 60 | 675 | 33 |
| 1944 | 250 | 219 | 64 | 652 | 49 |
| 1945 | 235 | 210 | 51 | 557 | 61 |
| 1946 | 214 | 139 | 49 | 521 | 53 |
| 1947 | 189 | 196 | 40 | 578 | 58 |
| 1948 | 212[11] | 179 | 39 | 571 | 59 |
| 1949 | 261 | 178 | ... | 538 | 72 |
| 1950 | 284 | 223 | ... | 565 | 88 |
| 1951 | 309 | 180 | ... | 618 | 101 |
| 1952 | 337 | 227 | ... | 604 | 128 |
| 1953 | 364 | 226 | ... | 497 | 139 |
| 1954 | 341 | 224 | ... | 430 | 159 |
| 1955 | 393 | 269 | ... | 467 | 166 |
| 1956 | 383 | 249 | ... | 492 | 178 |
| 1957 | 375 | 243 | ... | 482 | 178 |
| 1958 | 386 | 224 | ... | 374 | 160[15] |
| | | | | | 123 |
| 1959 | 359 | 264 | ... | 386 | 133 |
| 1960 | 390 | 262 | ... | 395 | 157 |
| 1961 | 402 | 269 | ... | 421 | 171 |
| 1962 | 455 | 251 | ... | 459 | 184 |
| 1963 | 451 | 240 | ... | 480 | 195 |
| 1964 | 662 | 236 | ... | 521 | 237 |
| 1965 | 826 | 225 | ... | 554 | 254 |
| 1966 | 950 | 219 | ... | 519 | 258 |
| 1967 | 1,135 | 241 | ... | 498 | 305 |
| 1968 | 1,155 | 240 | ... | 480 | 291 |
| 1969 | 1,194 | 253 | ... | 502 | 313 |
| 1970 | 1,239 | 266 | ... | 485 | 361 |
| 1971 | 1,134 | 265 | ... | 456 | 386 |
| 1972 | 1,129 | 272 | ... | 434 | 448 |
| 1973 | 1,227 | 271 | ... | 434 | 459 |
| 1974 | 1,127 | 263 | ... | 454 | 440 |
| 1975 | 1,055 | 229 | ... | 426 | 365 |
| 1976 | 982 | 259 | ... | 439 | 456 |
| 1977 | 1,070 | 265 | ... | 408 | 403 |
| 1978 | 1,067 | 245 | ... | 303 | 457 |
| 1979 | 1,100 | 245 | ... | 267 | 491 |
| 1980 | 884 | 238 | ... | 317 | 419 |
| 1981 | 995 | 212 | ... | 312 | 410 |
| 1982 | 966 | 232 | ... | 300 | 460 |
| 1983 | 988 | 257 | ... | 275 | 492 |
| 1984 | 1,063 | 290 | ... | 253 | 466 |
| 1985 | 1,049 | 275 | ... | 226 | 608 |
| 1986 | 988 | 271 | ... | 203 | 598 |
| 1987 | 1,158 | 271 | ... | 216 | 612 |
| 1988 | 1,347 | 262 | ... | 244 | 485 |

## D6    Output of Main Non-ferrous Metal Ores

### NOTES

1.  SOURCES: The national publications listed on p. xiv–xvi; League of Nations and UN, *Statistical Yearbooks;* Imperial Institute, *Statistical Summary of the Mineral Industry of the British Empire and Foreign Countries;* and R.P. Rothwell, *The Mineral Industry: its Statistics, Technology and Trade in the United States and other Countries* (New York, 1892–).
2.  So far as possible, and except as indicated in footnotes, the data in this table relate to the recoverable metallic content of ores (including concentrates).

### FOOTNOTES

1 Excluding antimony recovered as a by-product by primary lead refineries. Data to 1921 relate to the weight of ore.
[2] Statistics to 1966 (1st line) are of exports.
[3] Statistics to 1925 (1st line) are of the gross weight of output.
[4] Dried equivalent of crude ore.
[5] Exports
[6] Dried equivalent of crude ore from 1966.
[7] Statistics are of production for 1919–28 and 1940–75, production or shipments (the terms were used interchangeably) for 1929–34, and of shipments for all other years. From 1935 (2nd line) they are of dried bauxite equivalent.
[8] Dried equivalent of crude ore to 1953 (1st line).
[9] Output in 1939 was 9 thousand tons. Earlier figures of exports are 1936 7, 1937 9, and 1938 13.
[10] Statistics are of shipments (for government only in 1959–61). Content up to 1927 has been estimated on the assumption that it was 54% of gross weight. Small amounts were produced from 1880 onwards, but the amounts involved are insignificant.
[11] Statistics are of shipments from mines. Newfoundland is included from 1949. (There is no break in the case of nickel or tungsten.
[12] Statistics to 1906 (1st line) are of smelter production from domestic ores. Subsequently they are of estimated recoverable content of domestically-mined ores.
[13] There was a change in the method of calculating output.
[14] Years beginning 1 July to 1900.
[15] Production at refinery stage to 1904 (1st line), content of mined ores subsequently. Total gold production for the period 1792 to 1834 was 21 tons.
[16] Including Newfoundland from 1949, its output in 1948 being 0.3 tons.
[17] Estimated recoverable content of domestically-mined ores.
[18] Primary production only to 1964 (1st line).
[19] Statistics from 1914 to 1938 (1st line) are of exports.
[20] Shipments from mines of ores of 40% or more Mn content to 1910, of 35% or more Mn content from then to 1953 (1st line), and of 10% or more Mn content subsequently. Gross weight to 1928 (1st line).
[21] Statistics to 1936 are of exports. Gross weight to 1928 (1st line).
[22] Including Newfoundland from 1949.
[23] Statistics to 1977 (1st line) are of exports.
[24] This break occurs on a change of source.
[25] Tin content of exports and of tin-lead alloys.
[26] Gross weight of exports to 1925 (1st line), and content of exports from then to 1965 (1st line).
[27] Concentrated tungsten from 1974 (2nd line)
[28] Exports to 1962.
[29] Gross weight to 1929 (1st line).

**D7      OUTPUT OF MAIN NON-METALLIC MINERALS** (in thousands of metric tons)

### 1880–1924

| | ASBESTOS | | PHOSPHATE ROCK | POTASH (K2O content) | NATIVE SULPHUR (unrefined) | |
| | NORTH AMERICA | | NORTH AMERICA | NORTH AMERICA | NORTH AMERICA | SOUTH AMERICA |
| | Canada[1] | USA | USA | USA | USA[2] | Chile |
|---|---|---|---|---|---|---|
| 1880 | ... | ... | 214 | ... | 1 | ... |
| 1881 | ... | ... | 271 | ... | 1 | ... |
| 1882 | ... | ... | 337 | ... | 1 | ... |
| 1883 | ... | ... | 384 | ... | 1 | ... |
| 1884 | ... | ... | 439 | ... | - - | ... |
| 1885 | ... | ... | 684 | ... | 1 | ... |
| 1886 | 2.7 | ... | 438 | ... | 2 | ... |
| 1887 | 4.5 | ... | 489 | ... | 3 | ... |
| 1888 | 3.6 | ... | 459 | ... | — | ... |
| 1889 | 5.4 | ... | 555 | ... | - - | ... |
| 1890 | 9.1 | ... | 518 | ... | — | ... |
| 1891 | 8.2 | ... | 597 | ... | 1 | ... |
| 1892 | 5.4 | ... | 693 | ... | 2 | ... |
| 1893 | 5.4 | ... | 956 | ... | 1 | ... |
| 1894 | 7.3 | ... | 1,013 | ... | - - | 1 |
| 1895 | 8.2 | ... | 1,056 | ... | 2 | 1 |
| 1896 | 11.0 | ... | 946 | ... | 5 | 1 |
| 1897 | 27.0 | ... | 1,056 | ... | 2 | 1 |
| 1898 | 22.0 | ... | 1,330 | ... | 1 | 1 |
| 1899 | 24.0 | ... | 1,540 | ... | 4 | 1 |
| 1900 | 26.0 | ... | 1,515 | ... | 3 | 3 |
| 1901 | 36.0 | ... | 1,508 | ... | 7 | 3 |
| 1902 | 36.0 | ... | 1,514 | ... | 7 | 3 |
| 1903 | 38.0 | ... | 1,607 | ... | 7 | ... |
| 1904 | 44.0 | ... | 1,904 | ... | 86 | 4 |
| 1905 | 62.0 | ... | 1,978 | ... | 224 | 4 |
| 1906 | 74.0 | ... | 2,114 | ... | 300 | 5 |
| 1907 | 82.0 | ... | 2,301 | ... | 192 | 3 |
| 1908 | 83.0 | ... | 2,424 | ... | 370 | 3 |
| 1909 | 79.0 | ... | 2,376 | ... | 278 | 5 |
| 1910 | 93.0 | ... | 2,698 | ... | 251 | 4 |
| 1911 | 115.0 | ... | 3,102 | ... | 208 | 5 |
| 1912 | 123.0 | ... | 3,021 | ... | 801 | 4 |
| 1913 | 146.0 | ... | 3,161 | ... | 499 | 7 |
| 1914 | 107.0 | ... | 2,778 | ... | 425 | 10 |
| 1915 | 124.0 | ... | 1,865 | 1 | 529 | 10 |
| 1916 | 140.0 | ... | 2,014 | 9 | 660 | 15 |
| 1917 | 140.0 | ... | 2,625 | 30 | 1,152 | 19 |
| 1918 | 143.0 | ... | 2,531 | 35 | 1,376 | 20 |
| 1919 | 144.0 | ... | 2,308 | 42 | 1,210 | 19 |
| 1920 | 181.0 | ... | 4,170 | 37 | 1,275 | 13 |
| 1921 | 84.0 | ... | 2,098 | 4 | 1,909 | 10 |
| 1922 | 149.0 | 0.1 | 2,457 | 10 | 1,860 | 12 |
| 1923 | 210.0 | 0.2 | 3,055 | 17 | 2,069 | 11 |
| 1924 | 205.0 | 0.3 | 2,914 | 20 | 1,240 | 10 |

**D7** **Output of Main Non-metallic Minerals** (in thousands of metric tons)

## 1925–1964

| | ASBESTOS | | PHOSPHATE ROCK | POTASH (K2O content) | | NATIVE SULPHUR (unrefined) | | |
| | NORTH AMERICA | | NORTH AMERICA | NORTH AMERICA | | NORTH AMERICA | | SOUTH AMERICA |
| | Canada[1] | USA | USA | Canada | USA[3] | Mexico | USA[2] | Chile |
|---|---|---|---|---|---|---|---|---|
| 1925 | 249 | 1.1 | 3,538 | ... | 24 | ... | 1,432 | 9 |
| 1926 | 253 | 1.2 | 3,262 | ... | 23 | ... | 1,920 | 10 |
| 1927 | 249 | 2.7 | 3,222 | ... | 45 | ... | 2,146 | 12 |
| 1928 | 248 | 2.0 | 3,557 | ... | 54 | ... | 2,014 | 16 |
| 1929 | 278 | 2.9 | 3,821 | ... | 53 | ... | 2,400 | 16 |
| 1930 | 220 | 3.8 | 3,989 | ... | 52 | ... | 2,600 | 13 |
| 1931 | 149 | 2.9 | 2,576 | ... | 58 | ... | 2,163 | 11 |
| 1932 | 112 | 3.2 | 1,734 | ... | 51 | ... | 904 | 9 |
| 1933 | 143 | 4.3 | 2,530 | ... | 126 | ... | 1,429 | 13 |
| 1934 | 142 | 4.6 | 2,880 | ... | 103 | ... | 1,444 | 21 |
| 1935 | 191 | 8.1 | 3,091 | ... | 204 | ... | 1,659 | 20 |
| 1936 | 273 | 10 | 3,406 | ... | 202 | ... | 2,049 | 26 |
| 1937 | 372 | 11 | 4,019 | ... | 242 | ... | 2,786 | 23 |
| 1938 | 263 | 9 | 3,799 | ... | 259 | ... | 2,432 | 28 |
| 1939 | 330 | 14 | 3,817 | ... | 332 | ... | 2,125 | 32 |
| 1940 | 315 | 18 | 4,067 | ... | 357 | ... | 2,776 | 35 |
| 1941 | 433 | 22 | 4,765 | ... | 482 | ... | 3,190 | 25 |
| 1942 | 399 | 14 | 4,719 | ... | 618 | ... | 3,516 | 24 |
| 1943 | 432 | 5 | 5,208 | ... | 664 | ... | 2,580 | 26 |
| 1944 | 380 | 6 | 5,463 | ... | 742 | ... | 3,270 | 26 |
| 1945 | 424 | 11 | 5,900 | ... | 789 | 10 | 3,813 | 21 |
| 1946 | 506 | 13 | 6,971 | ... | 842 | 6 | 3,922 | 9 |
| 1947 | 600 | 22 | 9,172 | ... | 955 | 3 | 4,512 | 12 |
| 1948 | 650 | 34 | 8,808 | ... | 1,037 | 3 | 4,947 | 13 |
| 1949 | 521 | 39 | 9,131 | ... | 1,017 | 5 | 4,821 | 8 |
| 1950 | 794 | 38 | 11,292 | ... | 1,158₂ / 1,168 | 11 | 5,276 | ... 15 |
| 1951 | 883 | 47 | ... 10,948 | ... | 1,288 | 10 | 5,363 | ... 30 |
| 1952 | 843 | 49 | ... 12,259 | ... | 1,511 | 12 | 5,378 | ... 49 |
| 1953 | 827 | 49 | ... 12,704 | ... | 1,734 | 12 | 5,238 | ... 33 |
| 1954 | 838 | 43 | ... 14,043 | ... | 1,768 | 63 | 5,669 | ... 44 |
| 1955 | 965 | 40 | ... 12,462 | ... | 1,875 | 492 | 5,893 | ... 57 |
| 1956 | 920 | 37 | ... 16,000 | ... | 1,970 | 771 | 6,588 | ... 38 |
| 1957 | 949 | 40 | ... 14,200 | ... | 2,056 | 1,040 | 5,668 | ... 19 |
| 1958 | 839 | 40 | ... 15,118 | ... | 1,948 | 1,243 | 4,720 | ... 24 |
| 1959 | 953 | 41 | ... 16,124 | ... | 2,162 | 1,314 | 4,714 | ... 21 |
| 1960 | 1,015 | 41 | ... 17,797 | ... | 2,394 | 1,302 | 5,118 | ... 31 |
| 1961 | 1,065 | 48 | ... 18,857 | ... | 2,479 | 1,191 | 5,565 | ... 39 |
| 1962 | 1,103 | 48 | ... 19,693 | 135 | 2,225 | 1,395 | 5,106 | ... 54 |
| 1963 | 1,157 | 60 | ... 20,174 | 569 | 2,598 | 1,553 | 4,960 | ... 42 |
| 1964 | 1,288 | 92 | ... 23,328 | 779 | 2,628 | 1,734 | 5,312 | ... 44 |

**D7**    **Output of Main Non-metallic Minerals** (in thousands of metric tons)

1965–1988

| | ASBESTOS | | | PHOSPHATE ROCK | POTASH (K2O content) | | NATIVE SULPHUR (unrefined) | | | |
| | NORTH AMERICA | | SOUTH AMERICA | NORTH AMERICA | NORTH AMERICA | | NORTH AMERICA | | SOUTH AMERICA | |
| | Canada | USA | Brazil[4] | USA | Canada | USA[2] | Mexico | USA | Brazil | Chile |
|---|---|---|---|---|---|---|---|---|---|---|
| 1965 | 1,259 | 107 | ... | 26,704 | 1,353 | 2,849 | 1,581 | 6,214 | ... | 46 |
| 1966 | 1,351 | 114 | ... | 35,420 | 1,806 | 3,012 | 1,701 | 7,114 | ... | 53 |
| 1967 | 1,318 | 112 | 2 | 36,079 | 2,163 | 2,993 | 1,891 | 7,127 | ... | 56 |
| 1968 | 1,448 | 109 | 5 | 37,422 | 2,647 | 2,469 | 1,685 | 7,580 | ... | 62 |
| 1969 | 1,462 | 114 | 10 | 34,224 | 3,168 | 2,544 | 1,716 | 7,261 | ... | 99 |
| 1970 | 1,508 | 114 | 18 | 35,143 | 3,103 | 2,476 | 1,381 | 7,196 | ... | 109 |
| 1971 | 1,483 | 119 | 20 | 35,277 | 3,629 | 2,347 | 1,178 | 7,138 | ... | 106 |
| 1972 | 1,530 | 119 | 33 | 37,041 | 3,494 | 2,412 | 944 | 7,407 | ... | 78 |
| 1973 | 1,690 | 136 | 45 | 38,226 | 4,453 | 2,361 | 1,608 | 7,727 | 1 | 31 |
| 1974 | 1,644 | 99 | 62 | 41,446 | 5,776 | 2,315 | 2,322 | 8,028 | 9 | 32 |
| 1975 | 1,056 | 89 | 74 | 44,276 | 4,676 | 2,269 | 2,164 | 7,327 | 20 | 21 |
| 1976 | 1,536 | 105 | 93 | 44,662 | 5,215 | 2,177 | 2,150 | 6,365 | 30 | |
| 1977 | 1,517 | 92 | 93 | 47,256 | 5,764 | 2,229 | 1,856 | 5,915 | 44 | 32 |
| 1978 | 1,422 | 93 | 123 | 50,037 | 6,344 | 2,253 | 1,818 | 5,648 | 57 | 32 |
| 1979 | 1,493 | 93 | 138 | 51,611 | 7,074 | 2,225 | 2,025 | 6,357 | 92 | 77 |
| 1980 | 1,323 | 80 | 170 | 54,415 | 7,201 | 2,239 | 2,102 | 6,391 | 131 | 87 |
| 1981 | 1,133 | 76 | 138 | 53,624 | 6,549 | 2,156 | 2,077 | 6,348 | 102 | 115 |
| 1982 | 837 | 64 | 146 | 37,414 | 5,295 | 1,784 | 1,815 | 4,210 | 146 | 105 |
| 1983 | 829 | 70 | 159 | 42,573 | 6,294 | 1,429 | 1,602 | 3,202 | 193 | 99 |
| 1984 | 837 | 58 | 135 | 49,197 | 7,527 | 1,564 | 1,826 | 4,193 | 216 | 54 |
| 1985 | 750 | 58 | 165 | 50,835 | 6,661 | 1,296 | 2,020 | 5,011 | 229 | 79 |
| 1986 | 662 | 51 | 204 | 40,320 | 6,753 | 1,202 | 2,051 | 4,043 | 271 | 57 |
| 1987 | 665 | 51 | 213 | 40,954 | 7,668 | 1,262 | 2,304 | 3,202 | 313 | 37 |
| 1988 | 705 | 18 | 208 | 45,389 | 8,190 | 1,521 | 2,138 | 3,174 | 322 | 38 |

NOTE

SOURCES: The national publications listed on p. xiv–xvi; League of Nations and U.N., *Statistical Yearbooks.*

FOOTNOTES

[1] Shipments from mines.
[2] Production of Frasch-process mines. Sulphur from coal, gases, pyrites, etc.
[3] Sales by producers to 1950 (1st line).
[4] Asbestos fibres only.

**D8**   **OUTPUT OF PIG IRON** (in thousands of metric tons)

| | NORTH AMERICA |  | NORTH AMERICA | | | | NORTH AMERICA | | | SOUTH AMERICA |
|---|---|---|---|---|---|---|---|---|---|---|
| | USA | | Canada[1] | Mexico[2] | USA | | Canada[1] | Mexico[2] | USA | Brazil |
| 1810 | 54 | 1855 | — | ... | 711 | 1900 | 90 | ... | 14,011 | ... |
| 1811 | ... | 1856 | — | ... | 801 | 1901 | 249 | ... | 16,133 | ... |
| 1812 | ... | 1857 | — | ... | 724 | 1902 | 325 | ... | 18,107 | ... |
| 1813 | ... | 1858 | — | ... | 640 | 1903 | 270 | ... | 18,298 | ... |
| 1814 | ... | 1859 | — | ... | 763 | 1904 | 275 | ... | 16,762 | ... |
| 1815 | ... | 1860 | — | ... | 835 | 1905 | 477 | ... | 23,361 | ... |
| 1816 | ... | 1861 | — | ... | 664 | 1906 | 543 | 25 | 25,713 | ... |
| 1817 | ... | 1862 | — | ... | 715 | 1907 | 591 | 16 | 26,195 | ... |
| 1818 | ... | 1863 | — | ... | 860 | 1908 | 572 | 17 | 16,192 | ... |
| 1819 | ... | 1864 | — | ... | 1,031 | 1909 | 687 | 59 | 26,209 | ... |
| 1820 | 20 | 1865 | — | ... | 845 | 1910 | 726 | 45 | 27,742 | ... |
| 1821 | ... | 1866 | — | ... | 1,225 | 1911 | 832 | ... | 24,029 | ... |
| 1822 | ... | 1867 | — | ... | 1,326 | 1912 | 920 | ... | 30,204 | ... |
| 1823 | ... | 1868 | — | ... | 1,454 | 1913 | 1,024 | ... | 31,463 | ... |
| 1824 | ... | 1869 | — | ... | 1,739 | 1914 | 710 | ... | 23,707 | ... |
| 1825 | ... | 1870 | — | ... | 1,692 | 1915 | 829 | ... | 30,396 | ... |
| 1826 | ... | 1871 | — | ... | 1,735 | 1916 | 1,061 | ... | 40,068 | ... |
| 1827 | ... | 1872 | — | ... | 2,590 | 1917 | 1,062[1] / 1,103 | ... | 39,241 | ... |
| 1828 | 132 | 1873 | — | ... | 2,602 | 1918 | 1,124 | ... | 39,681 | ... |
| 1829 | 144 | 1874 | — | ... | 2,439 | 1919 | 877 | ... | 31,513 | ... |
| 1830 | 168 | 1875 | — | ... | 2,057 | 1920 | 1,015 | ... | 37,519 | ... |
| 1831 | 194 | 1876 | — | ... | 1,899 | 1921 | 627 | 42 | 16,956 | ... |
| 1832 | 203 | 1877 | — | ... | 2,100 | 1922 | 411 | 24 | 27,657 | ... |
| 1833 | ... | 1878 | — | ... | 2,338 | 1923 | 937 | 44 | 41,009 | 25 |
| 1834 | ... | 1879 | — | ... | 2,786 | 1924 | 638 | 19 | 31,910 | 25 |
| 1835 | ... | 1880 | — | ... | 3,896 | 1925 | 606 | 49 | 37,289 | 30 |
| 1836 | ... | 1881 | — | ... | 4,211 | 1926 | 827 | 62 | 40,045 | 21 |
| 1837 | ... | 1882 | — | ... | 4,697 | 1927 | 778 | 41 | 37,152 | 15 |
| 1838 | ... | 1883 | — | ... | 4,669 | 1928 | 1,100 | 49 | 38,769 | 26 |
| 1839 | ... | 1884 | — | ... | 4,164 | 1929 | 1,188 | 60 | 43,298 | 36 |
| 1840 | 291 | 1885 | — | ... | 4,110 | 1930 | 825 | 58 | 32,261 | 35 |
| 1841 | ... | 1886 | — | ... | 5,774 | 1931 | 474 | 53 | 18,715 | 28 |
| 1842 | 219 | 1887 | 23 | ... | 6,520 | 1932 | 163 | 20 | 8,921 | 29 |
| 1843 | ... | 1888 | 20 | ... | 6,594 | 1933 | 262 | 54 | 13,590 | 47 |
| 1844 | ... | 1889 | 24 | ... | 7,726 | 1934 | 444 | 65 | 16,398 | 59 |
| 1845 | ... | 1890 | 20 | ... | 9,350 | 1935 | 667 | 63 | 21,715 | 64 |
| 1846 | 777 | 1891 | 22 | ... | 8,412 | 1936 | 767 | 86 | 31,571 | 78 |
| 1847 | 813 | 1892 | 39 | ... | 9,304 | 1937 | 997 | 58 | 37,758 | 98 |
| 1848 | 813 | 1893 | 51 | ... | 7,238 | 1938 | 774 | 98 | 19,474 | 122 |
| 1849 | 660 | 1894 | 45 | ... | 6,764 | 1939 | 845 | 99 | 32,321 | 160 |
| 1850 | 572 | 1895 | 39 | ... | 9,598 | | | | | |
| 1851 | ... | 1896 | 61 | ... | 8,762 | | | | | |
| 1852 | 508 | 1897 | 53 | ... | 9,808 | | | | | |
| 1853 | ... | 1898 | 70 | ... | 11,963 | | | | | |
| 1854 | 668 | 1899 | 93 | ... | 13,839 | | | | | |

**D8    Output of Pig Iron** (in thousands of metric tons)

| | NORTH AMERICA | | | SOUTH AMERICA | | | | | |
|---|---|---|---|---|---|---|---|---|---|
| | Canada[1] | Mexico[2] | USA | Argentina[3] | Brazil[4] | Chile[3] | Colombia | Peru[3] | Venezuela |
| 1940 | 1,323 | 92 | 43,027 | ... | 186 | 7 | — | ... | — |
| 1941 | 1,572 | 95 | 51,456 | - - | 209 | 17 | — | ... | — |
| 1942 | 1,981 | 122 | 55,317 | — | 214 | 13 | — | ... | — |
| 1943 | 1,774 | 160 | 56,969 | 1 | 248 | 18 | — | ... | — |
| 1944 | 1,836 | 159 | 57,060 | 3 | 292 | 13 | — | ... | — |
| 1945 | 1,769 | 210 | 49,855 | 3 | 260 | 14 | — | ... | — |
| 1946 | 1,402 | 240 | 42,024 | 12 | 371 | 14 | — | ... | — |
| 1947 | 1,987 | 236 | 54,559 | 16 | 481 | 11 | — | ... | — |
| 1948 | 2,140 | 176 | 56,166 | 17 | 552 | 14 | — | ... | — |
| 1949 | 2,146 | 206 | 49,820 | 19 | 512 | 19 | — | ... | — |
| 1950 | 2,266 | 227 | 60,211 | 18 | 729 | 110 | — | ... | — |
| 1951 | 2,557 | 254 | 65,746 | 19 | 776 | 240 | — | ... | — |
| 1952 | 2,643 | 305 | 57,507 | 32 | 812[4] | 270 | — | ... | — |
| 1953 | 2,872 | 242 | 70,035 | 36 | 894 | 286 | — | ... | — |
| 1954 | 2,111 | 237 | 54,206 | 40 | 1,109 | 305 | 88 | ... | — |
| 1955 | 3,089 | 312 | 71,906 | 35 | 1,087 | 256 | 99 | ... | — |
| 1956 | 3,455 | 409 | 70,461 | 29 | 1,188 | 368 | 128 | ... | — |
| 1957 | 3,559 | 414 | 73,409 | 34 | 1,289 | 382 | 142 | ... | — |
| 1958 | 2,878 | 478 | 53,402 | 29 | 1,407 | 304 | 149 | 18 | — |
| 1959 | 3,917 | 556 | 56,367 | 32 | 1,588 | 290 | 145 | 40 | — |
| 1960 | 4,025 | 683 | 62,250 | 181 | 1,783 | 266 | 280 | 39 | — |
| 1961 | 4,594 | 867 | 60,524 | 399 | 1,976 | 285 | 327 | 51 | 5 |
| 1962 | 4,912 | 912 | 61,358 | 396 | 2,009 | 383 | 294 | 39 | 123 |
| 1963 | 5,519 | 832[2] 858 | 66,873 | 424 | 2,415 | 418 | 204 | 29 | 302 |
| 1964 | 6,090 | 959 | 78,772 | 589 | 2,488 | 437 | 198 | 27 | 323 |
| 1965 | 6,582 | 985 | 82,480 | 663 | 2,590 | 309 | 199 | 20 | 334 |
| 1966 | 6,696 | 1,464 | 85,279 | 520 | 2,950 | 433 | 167 | 12 | 351 |
| 1967 | 6,450 | 1,699 | 81,168 | 601 | 3,016 | 498 | 203 | 31 | 422 |
| 1968 | 7,747 | 2,040 | 82,883 | 574 | 3,173 | 442 | 198 | 111 | 539 |
| 1969 | 6,954 | 2,222 | 88,536 | 589 | 3,792 | 485 | 201 | 167 | 520 |
| 1970 | 8,424 | 2,353 | 85,141 | 815 | 4,296 | 481 | 229 | 77 | 510 |
| 1971 | 8,010 | 2,428 | 75,722 | 861 | 4,812 | 500 | 243 | 136 | 515 |
| 1972 | 8,722 | 2,778 | 82,861 | 849 | 5,511 | 487 | 288 | 163 | 536 |
| 1973 | 9,737 | 2,885 | 94,102 | 804 | 5,781 | 458 | 271 | 253 | 534 |
| 1974 | 9,670 | 3,307 | 89,423 | 1,066 | 7,704 | 516 | 269 | 303 | 562 |
| 1975 | 9,309 | 3,082 | 74,253 | 1,088 | 7,393 | 439 | 294 | 308 | 538 |
| 1976 | 10,026 | 3,548 | 80,541 | 1,321 | 8,477 | 445 | 287 | 231 | 425 |
| 1977 | 9,854 | 4,206 | 75,371 | 1,143 | 9,746 | 475 | 224 | 245 | 508 |
| 1978 | 10,578 | 5,058 | 81,053 | 1,470 | 10,447 | 587 | 298 | 246 | 429 |
| 1979 | 11,081 | 5,026 | 80,629 | 1,183 | 12,073 | 663 | 241 | 258 | 534 |
| 1980 | 11,182 | 5,330 | 63,748 | 1,080 | 13,116 | 708 | 280 | 263 | 559 |
| 1981 | 10,025 | 5,555 | 68,121 | 952 | 11,151 | 618 | 234 | 187 | 474 |
| 1982 | 8,218 | 5,223 | 40,033 | 1,057 | 11,175 | 459 | 208 | 161 | 255 |
| 1983 | 8,806 | 5,161 | 44,898[5] | 962 | 13,286 | 552 | 243 | 140 | 226 |
| 1984 | 9,864 | 5,588 | 48,232 | 894 | 17,628 | 607 | 253 | 66 | 383 |
| 1985 | 9,887 | 5,331 | 46,789 | 1,351 | 19,420 | 587 | 235 | 207 | 528 |
| 1986 | 9,486 | 5,312 | 41,022 | 1,668 | 20,881 | 603 | 318 | 273 | 575 |
| 1987 | 9,968 | 5,377 | 44,669 | 1,798 | 21,867 | 628 | 327 | 252 | 551 |
| 1988 | 9,739 | 5,564 | 50,676 | 1,640 | 24,172 | 794 | 352 | 253 | 588 |

**D8 Output of Pig Iron**

NOTES

1. SOURCES: The national publications listed on p. xiv–xvi UN, *Statistical Yearbook;* and British Iron and Steel Federation, *Statistics of the Iron and Steel Industries.*
2. Output of ferro-alloys is normally included in these statistics.

FOOTNOTES

[1] Excluding ferro-alloys to 1917 (2nd line).
[2] Excluding ferro-alloys to 1963 (2nd line).
[3] Excluding ferro-alloys.
[4] Excluding ferro-alloys to 1953.
[5] Subsequently including silico-manganese.

**D9 NORTH AMERICA: OUTPUT OF CRUDE STEEL** (in thousands of metric tons)

| | Canada | Mexico[3] | USA[1] | | Canada | Mexico | USA[1] | | Canada | Cuba[2] | Mexico[3] | USA[1] |
|---|---|---|---|---|---|---|---|---|---|---|---|---|
| 1867 | ... | ... | 20 | 1910 | 746 | 68 | 26,514 | 1950 | 3,070 | ... | 390 | 87,848 |
| 1868 | ... | ... | 27 | 1911 | 800 | ... | 24,056 | 1951 | 3,237 | ... | 467 | 95,435 |
| 1869 | ... | ... | 32 | 1912 | 869 | ... | 31,753 | 1952 | 3,359 | | 537 | 84,520 |
| 1870 | ... | ... | 70 | 1913 | 1,061 | ... | 31,803 | 1953 | 3,734 | | 462 | 101,250 |
| 1871 | ... | ... | 74 | 1914 | 752 | ... | 23,890 | 1954 | 2,898 | ... | 454 | 80,115 |
| 1872 | ... | ... | 145 | 1915 | 926 | ... | 32,667 | 1955 | 4,114 | ... | 510 | 106,173 |
| 1873 | ... | ... | 202 | 1916 | 1,296 | ... | 43,460 | 1956 | 4,809 | ... | 591 | 104,522 |
| 1874 | ... | ... | 219 | 1917 | 1,584 | ... | 45,784 | 1957 | 4,598 | ... | 687 | 102,253 |
| 1875 | ... | ... | 396 | 1918 | 1,700 | ... | 45,176 | 1958 | 3,955 | ... | 988[3] | 77,342 |
| 1876 | ... | ... | 542 | 1919 | 935 | ... | 35,228 | 1959 | 5,354 | ... | 1,213 | 84,773 |
| 1877 | ... | ... | 579 | 1920 | 1,118 | 32 | 42,809 | 1960 | 5,270 | ... | 1,500 | 90,067 |
| 1878 | ... | ... | 744 | 1921 | 678 | 43 | 20,101 | 1961 | 5,886 | ... | 1,725 | 88,917 |
| 1879 | ... | ... | 950 | 1922 | 494 | 53 | 36,173 | 1962 | 6,507 | ... | 1,851 | 89,202 |
| 1880 | ... | ... | 1,267 | 1923 | 899 | 60 | 45,665 | 1963 | 7,436 | 63 | 1,974 | 99,120 |
| 1881 | ... | ... | 1,614 | 1924 | 661 | 38 | 38,540 | 1964 | 8,282 | 52 | 2,284 | 115,281 |
| 1882 | ... | ... | 1,765 | 1925 | 765 | 76 | 46,122 | 1965 | 9,132 | 36 | 2,394 | 119,260 |
| 1883 | ... | ... | 1,700 | 1926 | 789 | 79 | 49,069 | 1966 | 9,093 | 67 | 2,780 | 121,655 |
| 1884 | ... | ... | 1,576 | 1927 | 922 | 66 | 45,656 | 1967 | 8,797 | 120 | 3,059 | 115,406 |
| 1885 | ... | ... | 1,739 | 1928 | 1,255 | 81 | 52,371 | 1968 | 10,161 | 120 | 3,270 | 119,262 |
| 1886 | ... | ... | 2,604 | 1929 | 1,400 | 102 | 57,339 | 1969 | 9,350 | 119 | 3,470 | 128,152 |
| 1887 | ... | ... | 3,393 | 1930 | 1,026 | 103 | 41,352 | 1970 | 11,198 | 140 | 3,846 | 119,309 |
| 1888 | ... | ... | 2,946 | 1931 | 683 | 76 | 26,363 | 1971 | 11,040 | 111 | 3,784 | 109,265 |
| 1889 | ... | ... | 3,440 | 1932 | 345 | 58 | 13,901 | 1972 | 11,859 | 187 | 4,396 | 120,875 |
| 1890 | ... | ... | 4,346 | 1933 | 417 | 76 | 23,605 | 1973 | 13,386 | 221 | 4,652 | 136,804 |
| 1891 | ... | ... | 3,967 | 1934 | 770 | 103 | 26,474 | 1974 | 13,623 | 250 | 5,046 | 132,196 |
| 1892 | ... | ... | 5,007 | 1935 | 957 | 111 | 34,640 | 1975 | 13,025 | 298 | 5,196 | 105,897 |
| 1893 | ... | ... | 4,085 | 1936 | 1,134 | 113 | 48,534 | 1976 | 13,290 | 250 | 5,243 | 116,121 |
| 1894 | 26 | ... | 4,483 | 1937 | 1,425 | 106 | 51,380 | 1977 | 13,581 | 330 | 5,529 | 113,701 |
| 1895 | 17 | ... | 6,213 | 1938 | 1,174 | 142 | 28,805 | 1978 | 14,898 | 324 | 6,712 | 124,314 |
| 1896 | 16 | ... | 5,366 | 1939 | 1,407 | 142 | 47,898 | 1979 | 16,078 | 313 | 7,023 | 123,688 |
| 1897 | 19 | ... | 7,272 | 1940 | 2,045 | 147 | 60,765 | 1980 | 15,901 | 292 | 7,003 | 101,456 |
| 1898 | 22 | ... | 9,076 | 1941 | 2,460 | 142 | 75,150 | 1981 | 14,811 | 317 | 7,448 | 109,614 |
| 1899 | 22 | ... | 10,811 | 1942 | 2,821 | 174 | 78,047 | 1982 | 11,871 | 290 | 6,926 | 67,656 |
| 1900 | 24 | ... | 10,352 | 1943 | 2,725 | 167 | 80,592 | 1983 | 12,832 | 352 | 6,747 | 76,762 |
| 1901 | 27 | ... | 13,690 | 1944 | 2,736 | 175 | 81,322 | 1984 | 14,699 | 325 | 7,293 | 83,940 |
| 1902 | 185 | ... | 15,187 | 1945 | 2,611 | 230 | 72,304 | 1985 | 13,459 | 401 | 7,174 | 80,067 |
| 1903 | 184 | ... | 14,768 | 1946 | 2,111 | 258 | 60,421 | 1986 | 14,081 | 412 | 6,960 | 74,032 |
| 1904 | 151 | ... | 14,082 | 1947 | 2,672 | 290 | 77,015 | 1987 | 14,737 | 402 | 7,210 | 80,876 |
| 1905 | 410 | ... | 20,345 | 1948 | 2,903 | 292 | 80,413 | 1988 | 15,193 | 321 | 7,311 | 91,765 |
| 1906 | 580 | 33 | 23,774 | 1949 | 2,892 | 373 | 70,740 | | | | | |
| 1907 | 641 | 32 | 23,737 | | | | | | | | | |
| 1908 | 534 | 29 | 14,248 | | | | | | | | | |
| 1909 | 685 | 60 | 24,339 | | | | | | | | | |

**D9    SOUTH AMERICA: OUTPUT OF CRUDE STEEL** (in thousands of metric tons)

| | Argentina[6] | Brazil[4] | Chile[5] | Colombia[5] | Peru | Uruguay | Venezuela |
|---|---|---|---|---|---|---|---|
| 1940 | 24 | 141 | ... | — | — | ... | ... |
| 1941 | 45 | 155 | ... | — | — | ... | ... |
| 1942 | 53 | 160 | ... | — | — | ... | ... |
| 1943 | 73 | 186 | ... | — | — | ... | ... |
| 1944 | 150 | 221 | ... | — | — | ... | ... |
| 1945 | ... | 206 | ... | — | — | ... | ... |
| 1946 | 133 | 343 | 21 | — | — | ... | ... |
| 1947 | 125 | 387 | 31 | — | — | ... | ... |
| 1948 | 122 | 483 | 30 | — | — | ... | ... |
| 1949 | 125 | 615 | 32 | — | — | ... | ... |
| 1950 | 130 | 789 | 56 | — | — | ... | ... |
| 1951 | 132 | 843 | 178 | — | — | ... | ... |
| 1952 | 126 | 893 | 243 | — | — | ... | ... |
| 1953 | 174 | 1,016 | 313 | — | — | ... | ... |
| 1954 | 186 | 1,148 | 321 | — | — | ... | ... |
| 1955 | 218 | 1,162 | 290 | 77 | — | ... | ... |
| 1956 | 202 | 1,375 | 381 | 90 | — | ... | ... |
| 1957 | 221 | 1,299 | 388 | 114 | 7 | ... | ... |
| 1958 | 244 | 1,362 | 348 | 121 | 20 | ... | ... |
| 1959 | 214 | 1,608 | 415 | 109 | 51 | ... | 50 |
| 1960 | 277 | 2,260 | 422 | 157 | 60 | 10 | 47 |
| 1961 | 442 | 2,443 | 363 | 181 | 76 | 9 | 75 |
| 1962 | 644 | 2,396 | 495 | 194 | 71 | 9 | 225 |
| 1963 | 913 | 2,737 | 489 | 200 | 76 | 7 | 364 |
| 1964 | 1,267 | 2,938 | 544 | 200 | 82 | 14 | 441 |
| 1965 | 1,371 | 2,983 | 441 | 204 | 94 | 13 | 625 |
| 1966 | 1,286 | 3,782 | 540 | 174 | 80 | 10 | 537 |
| 1967 | 1,348 | 3,734 | 596 | 207 | 80 | 14 | 690 |
| 1968 | 1,579 | 4,453 | 526 | 199 | 106 | 8 | 860 |
| 1969 | 1,720 | 4,925 | 601 | 206 | 194 | 14 | 840 |
| 1970 | 1,859 | 5,390 | 547 | 239 | 94 | 16 | 927 |
| 1971 | 1,743 | 6,011 | 610 | 248 | 179 | 15 | 924 |
| 1972 | 1,929 | 6,518 | 581 | 275 | 181 | 13 | 964 |
| 1973 | 1,995 | 7,149 | 508 | 263 | 356 | 12 | 907 |
| 1974 | 2,196 | 7,507 | 596 | 244 | 450 | 14 | 895 |
| 1975 | 2,043 | 8,308 | 458 | 266 | 432 | 16 | 919 |
| 1976 | 2,244 | 9,169 | 448 | 252 | 349 | 14 | 937 |
| 1977 | 2,671 | 11,164 | 509 | 209 | 379 | 18 | 855 |
| 1978 | 2,651 | 12,107 | 574 | 265 | 374 | 7 | 860 |
| 1979 | 3,090 | 13,891 | 657 | $\underline{234}$[5] <br> 400 | 436 | 16 | 1,473 |
| 1980 | 2,556 | 15,337 | 704 | 420 | 447 | 18 | 1,784 |
| 1981 | 2,389 | 13,226 | 644 | 420 | 364 | 14 | 1,818 |
| 1982 | 2,752 | 12,995 | 492 | 422 | 273 | 28 | 2,215 |
| 1983 | 2,828 | 14,671 | 618 | 482 | 299 | 46 | 2,320 |
| 1984 | 2,508 | 18,386 | 692 | 507 | 337 | 41 | 2,770 |
| 1985 | 2,775 | 20,456 | 689 | 525 | 414 | 39 | 3,061 |
| 1986 | 3,116 | 21,233 | 706 | 632 | 486 | 31 | 3,402 |
| 1987 | 3,463 | 22,227 | 726 | 691 | 503 | 30 | 3,721 |
| 1988 | 3,527 | 24,657 | 899 | 777 | 496 | 29 | 3,650 |

**D9      Output of Crude Steel**

NOTES

1.   SOURCES: As for table D8.
2.   Except as indicated in footnotes, the statistics in this table relate to ingots and castings produced by the Bessemer, Siemens-Martin, and later-invented processes.

FOOTNOTES

[1] Excluding steel for castings made in foundries by companies not producing ingots.
[2] Crude steel for casting only.
[3] Ingots only to 1958.
[4] Excluding alloy steels. Earlier figures are available as follows:—

| 1925 | 8  | 1930 | 21 | 1935 | 64  |
|------|----|------|----|------|-----|
| 1926 | 10 | 1931 | 23 | 1936 | 74  |
| 1927 | 8  | 1932 | 34 | 1937 | 76  |
| 1928 | 21 | 1933 | 54 | 1938 | 98  |
| 1929 | 27 | 1934 | 62 | 1939 | 114 |

[5] Ingots only (to 1979 (1st line) in the case of Colombia).
[6] Production began in 1939, when output was 18 thousand tons.

## D10 OUTPUT OF ALUMINIUM (in thousands of metric tons)

| | NORTH AMERICA | | | | NORTH AMERICA | | | | SOUTH AMERICA | |
|---|---|---|---|---|---|---|---|---|---|---|
| | Canada | USA | | | Canada | Mexico | USA | | Brazil[1] | Venezuela |
| | | primary | secondary | | | | primary | secondary | | |
| 1895 | — | - - | ... | 1940 | | — | 187 | 73 | — | — |
| 1896 | — | 1 | ... | 1941 | | — | 280 | 97 | — | — |
| 1897 | — | 1 | ... | 1942 | | — | 473 | 178 | — | — |
| 1898 | — | 1 | ... | 1943 | | — | 835 | 285 | — | — |
| 1899 | — | 2 | ... | 1944 | | — | 695 | 295 | — | — |
| 1900 | — | 3 | ... | 1945 | | — | 449 | 271 | — | — |
| 1901 | 0.1 | 3 | ... | 1946 | | — | 372 | 252 | — | — |
| 1902 | 0.9 | 3 | ... | 1947 | | — | 519 | 313 | — | — |
| 1903 | 0.8 | 3 | ... | 1948 | | — | 566 | 260 | — | — |
| 1904 | 1.0 | 4 | ... | 1949 | | — | 547 | 164 | — | — |
| 1905 | 1.2 | 5 | ... | 1950 | 360 | — | 652 | 221 | — | — |
| 1906 | 2.1 | 6 | ... | 1951 | 406 | — | 759 | 265 | — | — |
| 1907 | 2.7 | 6 | ... | 1952 | 453 | — | 850 | 276 | — | — |
| 1908 | 0.4 | 7 | ... | 1953 | 497 | — | 1,136 | 334 | 1.2 | — |
| 1909 | 2.8 | 5 | ... | 1954 | 506 | — | 1,325 | 265 | 1.5 | — |
| 1910 | 4.4 | 14 | ... | 1955 | 556 | — | 1,420 | 305 | 1.7 | — |
| 1911 | 4.4 | 16 | ... | 1956 | 563 | — | 1,523 | 308 | 6.3 | — |
| 1912 | 5.5 | 17 | ... | 1957 | 505 | — | 1,495 | 328 | 8.9 | — |
| 1913 | 6.4 | 22 | 5 | 1958 | 575 | — | 1,420 | 263 | 12 | — |
| 1914 | 6.6 | 26 | 5 | 1959 | 538 | — | 1,773 | 326 | 18 | — |
| 1915 | 8.3 | 41 | 7 | 1960 | 691 | — | 1,827 | 299 | 18 | — |
| 1916 | 9.6 | 53 | 17 | 1961 | 602 | — | 1,727 | 309 | 20 | — |
| 1917 | 10 | 59 | 15 | 1962 | 626 | — | 1,921 | 419 | 20 | — |
| 1918 | 11 | 56 | 14 | 1963 | 653 | 4.8 | 2,098 | 459 | 18 | — |
| 1919 | 9.8 | 58 | 17 | 1964 | 764 | 15 | 2,316 | 500 | 27 | — |
| 1920 | 10 | 63 | 15 | 1965 | 753 | 19 | 2,499 | 581 | 30 | — |
| 1921 | 2.9 | 24 | 8 | 1966 | 807 | 20 | 2,693 | 629 | 33 | — |
| 1922 | 5.8 | 34 | 15 | 1967 | 874 | 21 | 2,966 | 633 | 37 | 3 |
| 1923 | 11 | 58 | 19 | 1968 | 888 | 22 | 2,953 | 741 | 51 | 10 |
| 1924 | 12 | 68 | 24 | 1969 | 979 | 32 | 3,441 | 817 | 56 | 14 |
| 1925 | 14 | 64 | 40 | 1970 | 962 | 34 | 3,607 | 709 | 48 | 23 |
| 1926 | 18 | 67 | 40 | 1971 | 1,002 | 40 | 3,561 | 741 | 49 | 22 |
| 1927 | 38 | 74 | 42 | 1972 | 907 | 40 | 3,740 | 948 | 61 | 23 |
| 1928 | 38 | 95 | 44 | 1973 | 930 | 39 | 4,109 | 1,040 | 97 | 24 |
| 1929 | 29 | 103 | 44 | 1974 | 1,007 | 41 | 4,448 | 1,079 | 98 | 43 |
| 1930 | 35 | 104 | 35 | 1975 | 878 | 40 | 3,519 | 1,049 | 118 | 49 |
| 1931 | 31 | 80 | 38 | 1976 | 631 | 42 | 3,857 | 1,244 | 139 | 45 |
| 1932 | 18 | 48 | 22 | 1977 | 973 | 43 | 4,117 | 1,355 | 167 | 43 |
| 1933 | 16 | 39 | 30 | 1978 | 1,048 | 43 | 4,358 | 1,410 | 186 | 66 |
| 1934 | 16 | 34 | 42 | 1979 | 860 | 43 | 4,557 | 1,500 | 238 | 193 |
| 1935 | 21 | 54 | 47 | 1980 | 1,068 | 43 | 4,654 | 1,469 | 291 | 328 |
| 1936 | 27 | 102 | 47 | 1981 | 1,116 | 43 | 4,489 | 1,667 | 256 | 313 |
| 1937 | 43 | 133 | 57 | 1982 | 1,065 | 42 | 3,274 | 1,549 | 299 | 274 |
| 1938 | 65 | 130 | 35 | 1983 | 1,091 | 40 | 3,353 | 1,648 | 401 | 335 |
| 1939 | 75 | 149 | 49 | 1984 | 1,222 | 44 | 4,099 | 1,606 | 455 | 385 |
| | | | | 1985 | 1,282 | 43 | 3,500 | 1,762 | 549 | 403 |
| | | | | 1986 | 1,355 | 46 | 3,037 | 1,773 | 757 | 421 |
| | | | | 1987 | 1,540 | 79 | 3,343 | 1,986 | 843 | 430 |
| | | | | 1988 | 1,535 | 75 | 3,944 | 2,122 | 871 | 443 |

NOTES

SOURCES: The national publications listed on pp.xii–xiv, League of Nations and UN, *Statistical Yearbooks*.

FOOTNOTES

[1] Output of main establishments only

**D11    NORTH AMERICA: OUTPUT OF REFINED COPPER, LEAD, TIN, AND ZINC** (in thousands of metric tons)

| | USA | | | Canada | | USA | |
| | Lead[1,2] | Zinc[3] | | Copper | Lead | Lead[2] | Zinc[3] |
|---|---|---|---|---|---|---|---|
| 1821 | 1.7 | ... | 1860 | ... | ... | 14 | 0.7 |
| 1822 | 1.7 | ... | 1861 | ... | ... | 13 | 1.4 |
| 1823 | 1.9 | ... | 1862 | ... | ... | 13 | 1.4 |
| 1824 | 1.8 | ... | 1863 | ... | ... | 13 | 1.5 |
| | | | 1864 | ... | ... | 14 | 1.6 |
| 1825 | 2.0 | ... | | | | | |
| 1826 | 2.2 | ... | 1865 | ... | ... | 13 | 1.9 |
| 1827 | 4.1 | ... | 1866 | ... | ... | 15 | 1.8 |
| 1828 | 6.8 | ... | 1867 | ... | ... | 14 | 2.9 |
| 1829 | 7.8 | ... | 1868 | ... | ... | 15 | 3.4 |
| | | | 1869 | ... | ... | 16 | 3.9 |
| 1830 | 7.3 | ... | | | | | |
| 1831 | 6.8 | ... | 1870 | ... | ... | 16 | 4.9 |
| 1832 | 9.1 | ... | 1871 | ... | ... | 18 | 6.3 |
| 1833 | 10 | ... | 1872 | ... | ... | 23 | 7.1 |
| 1834 | 11 | ... | 1873 | ... | ... | 38 | 8.7 |
| | | | 1874 | ... | ... | 46 | 12 |
| 1835 | 12 | ... | | | | | |
| 1836 | 14 | ... | 1875 | ... | ... | 53 | 15 |
| 1837 | 12 | ... | 1876 | ... | ... | 57 | 15 |
| 1838 | 14 | ... | 1877 | ... | ... | 73 | 14 |
| 1839 | 16 | ... | 1878 | ... | ... | 81 | 18 |
| | | | 1879 | ... | ... | 82 | 19 |
| 1840 | 15 | ... | | | | | |
| 1841 | 19 | ... | 1880 | ... | ... | 87 | 23 |
| 1842 | 22 | ... | 1881 | ... | ... | 104 | 27 |
| 1843 | 23 | ... | 1882 | ... | ... | 118 | 31 |
| 1844 | 24 | ... | 1883 | ... | ... | 127 | 33 |
| | | | 1884 | ... | ... | 124 | 35 |
| 1845 | 27 | ... | | | | | |
| | | | 1885 | ... | ... | 114[2] | 37 |
| 1846 | 25 | ... | 1886 | ... | ... | 120 | 39 |
| 1847 | 25 | ... | 1887 | ... | ... | 142 | 46 |
| 1848 | 23 | ... | 1888 | ... | ... | 142 | 51 |
| 1849 | 21 | ... | 1889 | ... | ... | 162 | 53 |
| 1850 | 20 | ... | 1890 | ... | ... | 143[2] | 58 |
| | | | 1891 | ... | ... | 180 | 73 |
| 1851 | 17 | ... | 1892 | ... | ... | 189 | 79 |
| 1852 | 14 | ... | 1893 | ... | ... | 203 | 72 |
| 1853 | 15 | ... | 1894 | ... | ... | 194 | 68 |
| 1854 | 15 | ... | | | | | |
| | | | 1895 | ... | ... | 214 | 81 |
| 1855 | 14 | ... | 1896 | ... | ... | 234 | 74 |
| 1856 | 15 | ... | 1897 | 0.1 | ... | 256 | 91 |
| 1857 | 14 | ... | 1898 | 0.6 | ... | 274 | 105 |
| 1858 | 14 | - - | 1899 | 0.9 | ... | 270 | 117 |
| 1859 | 15 | - - | | | | | |
| | | | 1900 | 0.5 | ... | 334 | 112 |
| | | | 1901 | 0.4 | ... | 337 | 128 |
| | | | 1902 | 0.3 | ... | 334 | 142 |
| | | | 1903 | 7.2 | ... | 335 | 144[3] |
| | | | 1904 | 8.0 | 3.4 | 357 | 169 |

**D11    NORTH AMERICA: Output of Refined Copper, Lead, Tin, and Zinc** (in thousands of metric tons)

| | Canada | | | Mexico | | |
|---|---|---|---|---|---|---|
| | Copper[4] | Lead[13] | Zinc | Copper[5] | Lead | Zinc |
| 1905 | 11 | 7.2 | — | ... | ... | — |
| 1906 | 14 | 9.3 | — | ... | ... | — |
| 1907 | 14 | 12 | — | ... | ... | — |
| 1908 | 14 | 17 | — | ... | ... | — |
| 1909 | 13 | 19 | — | ... | ... | — |
| 1910 | 13 | 15 | — | ... | ... | — |
| 1911 | 9.7 | 11 | 0.9 | ... | ... | — |
| 1912 | 16 | 16 | 1.9 | ... | ... | — |
| 1913 | 15 | 17 | 2.5 | 44 | 55 | — |
| 1914 | 14 | 17 | 3.3 | ... | ... | — |
| 1915 | ... | 20 | 4.5 | ... | ... | — |
| 1916 | ... | 15 | 11 | ... | ... | — |
| 1917 | ... | 15 | 14 | ... | ... | — |
| 1918 | ... | 14 | 16 | ... | ... | — |
| 1919 | ... | 16 | 15 | ... | 79 | — |
| 1920 | ... | 13 | 18 | 33 | 82 | — |
| 1921 | 15 | 28 | 24 | 7.5 | 60 | — |
| 1922 | 13 | 37 | 25 | 21 | 114 | — |
| 1923 | 14 | 46 | 27 | 38 | 150 | — |
| 1924 | 16 | 59 | 25 | 32 | 134 | — |
| 1925 | 24 | 97 | 35 | 33 | 143 | 1.3 |
| 1926 | 31 | 117 | 56 | 38 | 174 | 5.9 |
| 1927 | 33 | 134 | 66 | 40 | 214 | 6.4 |
| 1928 | 57 | 137 | 74 | 46 | 215 | 11 |
| 1929 | 73 | 138 | 78 | 58 | 230 | 15 |
| 1930 | 102 | 138 | 110 | 53 | 231 | 29 |
| 1931 | 111 | 126 | 108 | 43 | 208 | 36 |
| 1932 | 96 | 115 | 78 | 34 | 137 | 30 |
| 1933 | 118 | 115 | 83 | 40 | 117 | 27 |
| 1934 | 152 | 143 | 122 | 47 | 162 | 29 |
| 1935 | 176 | 149 | 136 | 41 | 174 | 32 |
| 1936 | 173 | 165 | 137 | 33 | 203 | 31 |
| 1937 | 210 | 181 | 144 | 46 | 201 | 34 |
| 1938 | 216 | 182 | 156 | 37 | 231 | 37 |
| 1939 | 229 | 173 | 159 | 39 | 214 | 36 |
| 1940 | 256 | 200 | 168 | 31 | 192 | 34 |
| 1941 | 255 | 207 | 194 | 41 | 151 | 32 |
| 1942 | 244 | 221 | 196 | 45 | 193 | 52 |
| 1943 | 233 | 203 | 187 | 43 | 212 | 54 |
| 1944 | 224 | 129 | 153 | 33 | 178 | 49 |
| 1945 | 198 | 148 | 165 | 53 | 201 | 49 |
| 1946 | 151[4] / 152 | 150 | 168 | 52 | 138 | 42 |
| 1947 | 184 | 147 | 162 | 58 | 218 | 57 |
| 1948 | 201 | 145 | 178 | 49 | 187 | 48 |
| 1949 | 205 | 133 | 187 | 49 | 212 | 54 |

**D11    NORTH AMERICA: Output of Refined Copper, Lead, Tin, and Zinc** (in thousands of metric tons)

| | USA | | | | | | | |
|---|---|---|---|---|---|---|---|---|
| | Copper | | Lead | | Tin | | Zinc | |
| | Primary | Secondary | Primary | Secondary[7] | Primary | Secondary | Primary | Secondary[7] |
| 1905 | ... | ... | 352 | ... | — | — | 185 | ... |
| 1906 | 489 | ... | 367 | ... | — | — | 204 | ... |
| 1907 | 468 | ... | 375 | 23 | — | — | 227 | 23 |
| 1908 | 516 | ... | 360 | 17 | — | — | 191 | 21 |
| 1909 | 631 | ... | 405 | 38 | — | — | 232 | 44 |
| 1910 | 645 | 59 | 427 | 50 | — | — | 244 | 63 |
| 1911 | 650 | 69 | 442 | 49 | — | — | 260 | 68 |
| 1912 | 711 | 97 | 436 | 61 | — | — | 307 | 85 |
| 1913 | 733 | 83 | 420 | 66 | — | — | 314 | 81 |
| 1914 | 696 | 80 | 492 | 55 | — | 11 | 320 | 77 |
| 1915 | 741 | 110 | 499 | 72 | — | 12 | 444 | 99 |
| 1916 | 1,025 | 159 | 518 | 87 | 2.1 | 17 | 606 | 117 |
| 1917 | [1,099][6] | 177 | 554 | 85 | 5.5 | 18 | 607 | 120 |
| 1918 | 1,086 | 160 | 581 | 88 | 9.3 | 22 | 470 | 124 |
| 1919 | 803 | 138 | 437 | 111 | 11 | 22 | 423 | 118 |
| 1920 | 692 | 153 | 480 | 113 | 16 | 21 | 420 | 128 |
| 1921 | 431 | 120 | 407 | 94 | 11 | 15 | 182 | 84 |
| 1922 | 569 | 184 | 483 | 145 | 8.3 | 18 | 321 | 146 |
| 1923 | 898 | 246 | 561 | 176 | 6.8 | 27 | 463 | 149 |
| 1924 | 1,025 | 241 | 626 | 186 | 0.4 | 28 | 469 | 142 |
| 1925 | 1,000 | 264 | 696 | 206 | — | 28 | 520 | 142 |
| 1926 | 1,053 | 306 | 725 | 252 | 0.3 | 30 | 561 | 152 |
| 1927 | 1,055 | 308 | 723 | 250 | ... | 34 | 537 | 153 |
| 1928 | 1,128 | 332 | 709 | 280 | 0.1 | 33 | 547 | 165 |
| 1929 | 1,243 | 421 | 703 | 282 | 0.1 | 31 | 567 | 160 |
| 1930 | 978 | 310 | 583 | 232 | 0.3 | 24 | 452 | 116 |
| 1931 | 681 | 237 | 402 | 213 | - - | 18 | 265 | 93 |
| 1932 | 309 | 164 | 256 | 180 | - - | 13 | 188 | 64 |
| 1933 | 336 | 236 | 239 | 204 | - - | 20 | 279 | 109 |
| 1934 | 404 | 282 | 282 | 189 | - - | 23 | 330 | 86 |
| 1935 | 534 | 328 | 294 | 245 | 0.2 | 25 | 382 | 117 |
| 1936 | 746 | 347 | 362 | 238 | 0.2 | 25 | 446 | 146 |
| 1937 | 968 | 371 | 424 | 250 | 0.2 | 27 | 505 | 151 |
| 1938 | 719 | 242 | 348 | 204 | ... | ... | 405 | 108 |
| 1939 | 916 | 260 | 439 | 219 | ... | ... | 460 | 172 |
| 1940 | 1,192 | 303 | 484 | 236 | 1.4 | 30 | 613 | 201 |
| 1941 | 1,266 | 374 | 518 | 361 | 1.8 | 38 | 746 | 258 |
| 1942 | 1,283 | 387 | 514 | 293 | 16 | 34 | 809 | 300 |
| 1943 | 1,251 | 388 | 426 | 310 | 22 | 34 | 855 | 334 |
| 1944 | 1,108 | 414 | 422 | 301 | 31 | 30 | 789 | 313 |
| 1945 | 1,006 | 451 | 402 | 329 | 41 | 32 | 694 | 327 |
| 1946 | 797 | 369 | 307 | 356 | 44 | 25 | 661 | 273 |
| 1947 | 1,052 | 457 | 400 | 464 | 34 | 27 | 728 | 282 |
| 1948 | 1,005 | 459 | 369 | 454 | 37 | 27 | 715 | 295 |
| 1949 | 842 | 348 | 433 | 374 | 36 | 23 | 739 | 216 |

**D11** **NORTH AMERICA: Output of Refined Copper, Lead, Tin, and Zinc** (in thousands of metric tons)

| | Canada | | | | Mexico | | |
|---|---|---|---|---|---|---|---|
| | Copper | | Lead[13] | Zinc | Copper[5] | Lead | Zinc |
| | Primary | Secondary | | | | | |
| 1950 | 216 | ... | 155 | 185 | 48 | 231 | 54 |
| 1951 | 223 | ... | 147 | 188 | 59 | 214 | 60 |
| 1952 | 178 | ... | 166 | 202 | 51 | 237 | 50 |
| 1953 | 215 | ... | 150 | 228 | 52 | 214 | 53 |
| 1954 | 230 | ... | 151 | 194 | 43[5] / 32 | 209 | 55 |
| 1955 | 262 | ... | 135 | 233 | 35 | 202 | 56 |
| 1956 | 298 | ... | 134 | 232 | 32 | 191 | 56 |
| 1957 | 293 | ... | 130 | 224 | 28 | 207 | 57 |
| 1958 | 299 | ... | 121 | 229 | 28 | 197 | 58 |
| 1959 | 331 | ... | 123 | 232 | 29 | 186 | 56 |
| 1960 | 378 | ... | 144 | 237 | 28 | 185 | 53 |
| 1961 | 369 | ... | 156 | 243 | 27 | 175 | 52 |
| 1962 | 347 | ... | 138 | 254 | 31 | 189 | 57 |
| 1963 | 344 | ... | 141 | 258 | 31 | 185 | 57 |
| 1964 | 370 | ... | 137 | 306 | 35 | 171 | 59 |
| 1965 | 394[4] | ... | 169 | 325 | 46 | 165 | 59 |
| 1966 | 379 | 23 | 168 | 347 | 48 | 179 | 59 |
| 1967 | 421 | 33 | 177 | 367 | 48 | 161 | 71 |
| 1968 | 447 | 29 | 183 | 387 | 52 | 147 | 80 |
| 1969 | 380 | 28 | 170 | 423 | 57 | 144 | 80 |
| 1970 | 460 | 33 | 186 | 413 | 54 | 151 | 81 |
| 1971 | 449 | 29 | 168 | 373 | 53 | 151 | 78 |
| 1972 | 470 | 26 | 187 | 476 | 60 | 154 | 84 |
| 1973 | 469 | 29 | 187 | 533 | 57 | 142 | 71 |
| 1974 | 533 | 26 | 126 | 438 | 68 | 158 | 137 |
| 1975 | 501 | 28 | 171 | 427 | 63 | 138 | 154 |
| 1976 | 485 | 25 | 176 | 472 | 75 | 128 | 175 |
| 1977 | 476 | 32 | 187[13] / 241 | 495 | 73 | 137 | 174 |
| 1978 | 418 | 28 | 246 | 495 | 75 | 150 | 173 |
| 1979 | 365 | 32 | 252 | 580 | 82 | 158 | 162 |
| 1980 | 475 | 30 | 235 | 592 | 86 | 131 | 144 |
| 1981 | 477 | 29 | 238 | 619 | 61 | 138 | 126 |
| 1982 | 338 | 24 | 242 | 512 | 61 | 129 | 127 |
| 1983 | 464 | 35 | 242 | 617 | 81 | 153 | 174 |
| 1984 | 504 | 32 | 252 | 683 | 61 | 154 | 166 |
| 1985 | 500 | 25 | 240 | 692 | 65 | 185 | 175 |
| 1986 | 493 | 24 | 258 | 571 | 65 | 173 | 174 |
| 1987 | 491 | 24 | 226 | 610 | 130 | 175 | 188 |
| 1988 | 529 | 38 | 268 | 703 | 130 | 175 | 108 |

**D11    NORTH AMERICA: Output of Refined Copper, Lead, Tin, and Zinc** (in thousands of metric tons)

| | USA | | | | | | | |
|---|---|---|---|---|---|---|---|---|
| | Copper | | Lead | | Tin | | Zinc | |
| | Primary | Secondary | Primary | Secondary | Primary | Secondary | Primary | Secondary[7] |
| 1950 | 1,125 | 440 | 461 | 438 | 33 | 32 | 765 | 296 |
| 1951 | 1,095 | 416 | 379 | 470 | 31 | 31 | 800 | 285 |
| 1952 | 1,068 | 376 | 429 | 428 | 23 | 29 | 820 | 282 |
| 1953 | 1,173 | 390 | 424 | 442 | 38 | 28 | 831 | 267 |
| 1954 | 1,099 | 369 | 442 | 430 | 27 | 27 | 728 | 247 |
| 1955 | 1,218 | 467 | 435 | 455 | 23 | 29 | 874 | 276 |
| 1956 | 1,309 | 425 | 492 | 460 | 18 | 30 | 892 | 255 |
| 1957 | 1,319 | 403 | 484 | 444 | 1.6 | 25 | 894[8] | 240 |
| 1958 | 1,227 | 373 | 427 | 364 | 5.4 | 23 | 709 | 209 |
| 1959 | 996 | 427 | 309 | 409 | 11 | 24 | 724 | 251 |
| 1960 | 1,378 | 390 | 347 | 426 | 14 | 22 | 725 | 241 |
| 1961 | 1,406 | 373 | 408 | 411 | 8.7 | 23 | 768 | 216 |
| 1962 | 1,462 | 377 | 341 | 403 | 5.6 | 22 | 798[8] | 238 |
| 1963 | 1,448 | 383 | 358 | 448 | 1.5 | 23 | 810 | 243 |
| 1964 | 1,503 | 430 | 408 | 491 | 4.0 | 24 | 865 | 271 |
| 1965 | 1,553 | 466 | 379 | 522 | 3.1 | 25 | 902 | 321 |
| 1966 | 1,552 | 485 | 400 | 520 | 3.9 | 26 | 930 | 327 |
| 1967 | 1,028 | 438 | 345 | 502 | 3.1 | 23 | 852 | 290 |
| 1968 | 1,304 | 472 | 424 | 500 | 3.6 | 23 | 926 | 322 |
| 1969 | 1,581 | 522 | 579 | 548 | 0.4 | 23 | 944 | 341 |
| 1970 | 1,601 | 457 | 605 | 542 | 4.5 | 20 | 796 | 308 |
| 1971 | 1,444 | 404 | 590 | 542 | 4.1 | 20 | 695 | 326 |
| 1972 | 1,699 | 415 | 617 | 560 | 4.4 | 21 | 574 | 352 |
| 1973 | 1,695 | 422 | 612 | 593 | 4.9 | 21 | 629 | 348 |
| 1974 | 1,501 | 451 | 611 | 634 | 6.1 | 19[11] 2.0 | 504 | 307[7] 71 |
| 1975 | 1,309 | 312 | 577 | 597 | 6.5 | 1.9 | 397 | 52 |
| 1976 | 1,396 | 340 | 592 | 659 | 5.7 | 1.5 | 453 | 62 |
| 1977 | 1,357 | 350 | 549 | 758 | 6.7 | 1.7 | 408 | 46 |
| 1978 | 1,449 | 420 | 566 | 769 | 5.9 | 1.6 | 407 | 35 |
| 1979 | 1,517 | 498 | 578 | 743 | 4.6 | 1.8 | 472 | 53 |
| 1980 | 1,215 | 515 | 550 | 675 | 3.0 | 1.7 | 340 | 29 |
| 1981 | 1,544 | 494 | 495 | 658 | 2.0 | 1.6 | 347 | 50 |
| 1982 | 1,227 | 467 | 517 | 581 | 3.5 | 1.1 | 228 | 74 |
| 1983 | 1,182 | 402 | 519 | 515 | 2.5 | 1.2 | 236 | 69 |
| 1984 | 1,174 | 306 | 389 | 591 | 4..0 | 1.1 | 253 | 78 |
| 1985 | 1,057 | 372 | 494 | 573 | 3.0 | 1.3 | 261 | 73 |
| 1986 | 1,074 | 406 | 370 | 581 | 3.2 | 1.1 | 253 | 63 |
| 1987 | 1,127 | 415 | 374 | 668 | 3.9 | 1.4 | 261 | 83 |
| 1988 | 1,406 | 451 | 392 | 698 | 1.5 | 0.6 | 241 | 88 |

**D11   SOUTH AMERICA: OUTPUT OF REFINED COPPER, LEAD, TIN, AND ZINC** (in thousands of metric tons)

| | Chile |
|---|---|
| | Copper[9] |
| 1847 | 9.8 |
| 1848 | 10 |
| 1849 | 11 |
| 1850 | 12 |
| 1851 | 8.4 |
| 1852 | 17 |
| 1853 | 15 |
| 1854 | 17 |
| 1855 | 22 |
| 1856 | 24 |
| 1857 | 25 |
| 1858 | 25 |
| 1859 | 23 |
| 1860 | 34 |
| 1861 | 34 |
| 1862 | 37 |
| 1863 | 32 |
| 1864 | 43 |
| 1865 | 41 |
| 1866 | 33 |
| 1867 | 43 |
| 1868 | 42 |
| 1869 | 52 |
| 1870 | 34 |
| 1871 | 39 |
| 1872 | 49 |
| 1873 | 42 |
| 1874 | 48 |
| 1875 | 48 |
| 1876 | 52 |
| 1877 | 44 |
| 1878 | 49 |
| 1879 | 46 |
| 1880 | 40 |
| 1881 | 40 |
| 1882 | 45 |
| 1883 | 40 |
| 1884 | 45 |
| 1885 | 40 |
| 1886 | 38 |
| 1887 | 30 |
| 1888 | 34 |
| 1889 | 25 |
| 1890 | 27 |
| 1891 | 21 |
| 1892 | 21 |
| 1893 | 23 |
| 1894 | 23 |

| | Argentina | Chile | Peru | |
|---|---|---|---|---|
| | Lead | Copper[9] | Copper | Lead |
| 1895 | ... | 23 | — | ... |
| 1896 | ... | 24 | — | ... |
| 1897 | ... | 21 | — | ... |
| 1898 | ... | 26 | — | ... |
| 1899 | ... | 26 | — | ... |
| 1900 | ... | 28 | — | ... |
| 1901 | ... | 30 | — | ... |
| 1902 | ... | 27 | — | ... |
| 1903 | ... | 30 | — | ... |
| 1904 | ... | 31 | — | ... |
| 1905 | ... | 29[9] / 23 | — | ... |
| 1906 | ... | 19 | 1.5 | ... |
| 1907 | ... | 17 | 8.8 | ... |
| 1908 | ... | 20 | 13 | ... |
| 1909 | ... | 19 | 16 | ... |
| 1910 | ... | 18 | 19 | ... |
| 1911 | ... | 16 | 21 | ... |
| 1912 | ... | 17 | 20 | ... |
| 1913 | 1.0 | 20 | 20 | ... |
| 1914 | ... | 25 | 25 | ... |
| 1915 | ... | 35 | 33 | ... |
| 1916 | ... | 57 | 40 | ... |
| 1917 | ... | 85 | 43 | ... |
| 1918 | ... | 102 | 44 | ... |
| 1919 | ... | 73 | 38 | ... |
| 1920 | 3.5 | 93 | 32 | ... |
| 1921 | 2.5 | 47 | 31 | ... |
| 1922 | 3.6 | 113 | 36 | ... |
| 1923 | 3.6 | 162 | 43 | ... |
| 1924 | 4.5 | 174 | 34 | ... |
| 1925 | 7.7 | 175 | 37 | ... |
| 1926 | 8.5 | 190 | 38 | ... |
| 1927 | 7.8 | 226 | 46 | ... |
| 1928 | 8.4 | 274 | 52 | ... |
| 1929 | 9.0 | 302 | 53 | ... |
| 1930 | 9.0 | 208 | 47 | ... |
| 1931 | 7.6 | 215 | 44 | ... |
| 1932 | 7.1 | 97 | 21 | ... |
| 1933 | 9.6 | 157 | 25 | ... |
| 1934 | 5.0 | 247 | 27 | 1.2 |
| 1935 | 4.1 | 259 | 29 | 6.4 |
| 1936 | 11 | 245 | 33 | 8.9 |
| 1937 | 9.1 | 396 | 34 | 19 |
| 1938 | 11 | 337 | 36 | 26 |
| 1939 | 15 | 326 | 34 | 24 |

**D11    SOUTH AMERICA: Output of Refined Copper, Lead, Tin, and Zinc** (in thousands of metric tons)

| | Argentina | | Bolivia | Brazil | | | Chile | Peru | | |
|---|---|---|---|---|---|---|---|---|---|---|
| | Lead[12] | Zinc | Tin | Lead[12] | Tin[10] | Zinc | Copper[9] | Copper[9] | Lead | Zinc |
| 1940 | 13 | — | — | — | — | — | 347 | 34 | 31 | 0.2 |
| 1941 | 20 | — | — | — | — | — | 456 | 28 | 33 | 0.7 |
| 1942 | 24 | 0.4 | — | — | — | — | 477 | 29 | 38 | 0.9 |
| 1943 | 29 | 0.7 | — | — | 0.1 | — | 488 | 28 | 43 | 1.5 |
| 1944 | 22 | 1.0 | — | — | 0.2 | — | 490 | 26 | 39 | 1.5 |
| 1945 | 21 | 1.0 | — | 0.1 | 0.2 | — | 462 | 25 | 42 | 1.6 |
| 1946 | 22 | 1.8 | — | 0.4 | 0.2 | — | 359 | 19 | 38 | 0.9 |
| 1947 | 21 | 2.6 | - - | 0.4 | 0.2 | — | 408 | 18 | 33 | 1 |
| 1948 | 24 | 1.6 | 0.1 | ... | 0.2 | — | 425 | 13 | 35 | 0.7 |
| 1949 | 18 | 2.7 | — | 1.1 | 0.2 | — | 351 | 21 | 37 | 0.6 |
| 1950 | 19 | 3.7 | 0.4 | 4.2 | 0.1 | — | 345 | 20 | 32 | 1.3 |
| 1951 | 24 | 8.6 | - - | 3.0 | 0.1 | — | 360 | 23 | 44 | 0.9 |
| 1952 | 20 | 12 | 0.3 | 1.3 | 0.1 | — | 383 | 20 | 50 | 5 |
| 1953 | 13 | 13 | 2 | 2.9 | 0.6 | — | 336[9] 216 | 24[9] 23 | 59 | 8.9 |
| 1954 | 26 | 11 | 0.2 | 2.7 | 1.9 | — | 191 | 25 | 58 | 15 |
| 1955 | 18 | 14 | 0.1 | 3.7 | 1.2 | — | 241 | 28 | 61 | 17 |
| 1956 | 24 | 14 | 0.5 | 3.5 | 1.6 | — | 240 | 18 | 60 | 9.5 |
| 1957 | 26 | 14 | 0.3 | 3.5 | 1.4 | — | 222 | 28 | 69 | 30 |
| 1958 | 33 | 15 | 0.7 | 5.8 | 0.6 | — | 186 | 28 | 64 | 29 |
| 1959 | 31 | 13 | 0.9 | 5.5 | 1.2 | — | 260 | 28 | 57 | 27 |
| 1960 | 26 | 17 | 1.0 | 10 | 1.3 | — | 225 | 30 | 74 | 32 |
| 1961 | 28 | 15 | 2.0 | 4.9 | 1.5 | — | 226 | 34 | 78 | 32 |
| 1962 | 24 | 18 | 2.1 | 14 | 2.4 | — | 263 | 34 | 68 | 32 |
| 1963 | 24 | 18 | 2.5 | 16 | 2.1 | — | 259 | 37 | 81 | 54 |
| 1964 | 23 | 21 | 3.7 | 13 | 1.2 | — | 278 | 38 | 90 | 60 |
| 1965 | 32 | 23 | 3.5 | 9.2 | 1.4 | 0.4 | 289 | 40 | 87 | 61 |
| 1966 | 22 | 22 | 1.1 | 14 | 1.8 | 0.5 | 357 | 37 | 89 | 63 |
| 1967 | 22 | 22 | 1.1 | 14 | 1.9 | 1.9 | 386 | 36 | 82 | 62 |
| 1968 | 25 | 22 | 0.1 | 19 | 1.7 | 5.0 | 399 | 38 | 86 | 66 |
| 1969 | 22 | 25 | 0.1 | 21 | 2.7 | 4.2 | 453 | 35 | 78 | 65 |
| 1970 | 38 | 29 | 0.3 | 20 | 3.3 | 13 | 461 | 36 | 73 | 71 |
| 1971 | 44 | 30 | 6.8 | 26 | 4.4 | 16 | 399 | 33 | 68 | 59 |
| 1972 | 40 | 40 | 6.5 | 25 | 4.6 | 16 | 461 | 39 | 86 | 70 |
| 1973 | 32 | 37 | 7.0 | 38 | 4.5 | 23 | 415 | 39 | 83 | 70 |
| 1974 | 37 | 35 | 6.1 | 42[12] 63 | 6.6 | 10 | 538 | 39 | 81 | 71 |
| 1975 | 36 | 37 | 7.6 | 63 | 6.8 | 31 | 535 | 54 | 71 | 66 |
| 1976 | 40[12] 50 | 31 | 9.8 | 69 | 6.7 | 43 | 632 | 132 | 74 | 67 |
| 1977 | 45 | 29 | 13 | 77 | 7.7 | 47 | 676 | 188 | 84 | 67 |
| 1978 | 30 | 24 | 16 | 80 | 9.3 | 56 | 749 | 185 | 80 | 63 |
| 1979 | 50 | 35 | 16 | 99 | 10 | 63 | 782 | 230 | 91 | 68 |
| 1980 | 42 | 28 | 18 | 90 | 8.8 | 78 | 811 | 231 | 87 | 64 |
| 1981 | 35 | 29 | 20 | 71 | 7.8 | 92 | 775 | 200 | 84 | 126 |
| 1982 | 31 | 31 | 17 | 53 | 9.3 | 96 | 729 | 224 | 82 | 160 |
| 1983 | 31 | 32 | 14 | 63 | 13 | 100 | 693 | 195 | 65 | 154 |
| 1984 | 28 | 30 | 16 | 64 | 19 | 107 | 753 | 219 | 71 | 148 |
| 1985 | 29 | 33 | 14 | 70 | 25 | 116 | 725 | 227 | 83 | 163 |
| 1986 | 31 | 31 | 10 | 72 | 25 | 131 | 784 | 226 | 67 | 156 |
| 1987 | 32 | 34 | 8.1 | 74 | 29 | 139 | 795 | 225 | 71 | 147 |
| 1988 | 35 | 31 | 11 | 85 | 42 | 140 | 853 | 179 | 54 | 123 |

**D11    Output of Refined Copper, Lead, Tin, and Zinc** (in thousands of metric tons)

NOTES

1.  SOURCES: As for table D10.
2.  Secondary production (i.e. remelted from scrap) is shown separately if it is significant, where possible, but is generally included with primary production in earlier years. Secondary production normally does not include production from 'new' scrap (i.e. the recycled waste of primary production).

FOOTNOTES

[1] Average annual production for 1801–10 was 1 thousand short tons, and for 1811–20 it was 1,500 short tons (=0.9 and 1.4 thousand metric tons respectively).
[2] Including lead from imported ores from 1886 and from imported base bullion from 1891.
[3] Production from domestic ores only to 1903.
[4] Smelter production to 1946 (1st line). Secondary production is included with primary to 1965.
[5] Smelter production to 1954 (1st line).
[6] Includes some refined copper imports.
[7] Including production from 'new' scrap and zinc recovered in alloys to 1974 (1st line).
[8] Including zinc in concentrates used directly in alloying operations in 1958–62.
[9] Smelter production to 1953 (1st line) (from 1905 (2nd line) in the case of Chile), refined copper output subsequently. Earlier data for Chile are of the metal content of ore.
[10] Smelter production.
[11] This break probably arises from the exclusion of tin recovered in alloys.
[12] Primary soft lead only to 1977 (1st line) for Canada, 1976 (1st line) for Argentina, and 1974 (1st line) for Brazil.

**D12    RAW COTTON CONSUMPTION** (in thousands of metric tons)

| | NORTH AMERICA | | | NORTH AMERICA | | | SOUTH AMERICA | |
|---|---|---|---|---|---|---|---|---|
| | Canada[1] | USA | | Canada[1] | Mexico | USA | Brazil | Peru |
| 1860 | ... | 184 | 1900 | 27 | ... | 803 | ... | ... |
| 1861 | ... | 183 | 1901 | 25 | 43 | 785 | ... | ... |
| 1862 | ... | 80 | 1902 | | 28 | 888 | ... | ... |
| 1863 | ... | 62 | 1903 | 27[1] | 29 | 912 | ... | ... |
| 1864 | ... | 48 | 1904 | 25 | 31 | 867 | ... | ... |
| 1865 | ... | 75 | 1905 | 28 | 36 | 985 | ... | ... |
| 1866 | ... | 134 | 1906 | 31 | 37 | 1,062 | ... | ... |
| 1867 | ... | 156 | 1907 | 29 | 36 | 1,083 | ... | ... |
| 1868 | ... | 184 | 1908 | 27 | 35 | 978 | ... | ... |
| 1869 | ... | 187 | 1909 | 34 | 35 | 1,141 | ... | ... |
| 1870 | ... | 174 | 1910 | 30 | 35 | 1,045 | ... | ... |
| 1871 | ... | 224 | 1911 | 34 | ... | 1,024 | ... | ... |
| 1872 | ... | 250 | 1912 | 36 | ... | 1,169 | ... | ... |
| 1873 | ... | 243 | 1913 | 36 | ... | 1,260 | ... | ... |
| 1874 | ... | 264 | 1914 | 33 | ... | 1,281 | ... | ... |
| 1875 | ... | 239 | 1915 | 44 | ... | 1,308 | ... | ... |
| 1876 | ... | 273 | 1916 | 44 | ... | 1,585 | ... | 3.2 |
| 1877 | ... | 286 | 1917 | 39 | ... | 1,667 | ... | 3.4 |
| 1878 | ... | 318 | 1918 | 49 | ... | 1,673 | ... | 3.6 |
| 1879 | ... | 317 | 1919 | 39 | ... | 1,355 | ... | 3.4 |
| 1880 | ... | 327 | 1920 | 52 | ... | 1,472 | 84 | 3.1 |
| 1881 | 5.3 | 406 | 1921 | 40 | 36 | 1,178 | 76 | 2.9 |
| 1882 | 8.8 | 403 | 1922 | 50 | 35 | 1,426 | 86 | 2.9 |
| 1883 | 13 | 444 | 1923 | 51 | 32 | 1,592 | 83 | 3.1 |
| 1884 | 9.4 | 395 | 1924 | 42 | 31 | 1,354 | 88 | 3.2 |
| 1885 | 11 | 367 | 1925 | 57 | 41 | 1,492 | 106 | 3.3 |
| 1886 | 14 | 456 | 1926 | 61 | 42 | 1,581 | 97 | 3.6 |
| 1887 | 15 | 446 | 1927 | 62 | 41 | 1,741 | 92 | 3.9 |
| 1888 | 15 | 480 | 1928 | 61 | 39 | 1,658 | 102 | 3.9 |
| 1889 | 18 | 503 | 1929 | 62 | 39 | 1,735 | 79 | 3.7 |
| 1890 | 17 | 548 | 1930 | 46 | 41 | 1,505 | 68 | 4.1 |
| 1891 | 18 | 567 | 1931 | 42 | 35 | 1,301 | 73 | 3.8 |
| 1892 | 21 | 620 | 1932 | 44 | 34 | 1,198 | 90 | 4.3 |
| 1893 | 19 | 526 | 1933 | 55 | 41 | 1,502 | 94 | 5.1 |
| 1894 | 16 | 501 | 1934 | 65 | 50 | 1,408 | ... | 6.2 |
| 1895 | 26 | 650 | 1935 | 55 | 50 | 1,324 | ... | 6.7 |
| 1896 | 18 | 544 | 1936 | 68 | 54 | 1,543 | ... | 6.7 |
| 1897 | 19 | 619 | 1937 | 72 | 56 | 1,909 | ... | 6.5 |
| 1898 | 29 | 756 | 1938 | 84 | 51 | 1,407 | ... | 6.8 |
| 1899 | 25 | 799 | 1939 | ... | 49 | 1,678 | 139 | 7.4 |
| | | | 1940 | 115 | 52 | 1,926 | ... | 7.8 |
| | | | 1941 | 109 | 57 | 2,413 | ... | 10 |
| | | | 1942 | 112 | 65 | 2,756 | ... | 12 |
| | | | 1943 | 92 | 68 | 2,700 | ... | 11 |
| | | | 1944 | 83 | 69 | 2,462 | ... | ... |
| | | | 1945 | 82 | 69 | 2,406 | ... | ... |
| | | | 1946 | 82 | ... | 2,225 | ... | ... |
| | | | 1947 | 82 | ... | 2,397 | ... | ... |

**D12     Raw Cotton Consumption** (in thousands of metric tons)

| | NORTH AMERICA | | | | SOUTH AMERICA | | | | | | |
|---|---|---|---|---|---|---|---|---|---|---|---|
| | Canada[1] | Cuba | Mexico | USA | Argentina[3] | Brazil | Chile[3] | Colombia[3] | Peru | Uruguay[3] | Venezuela[3] |
| 1948 | 80 | … | 75 | 2,288[2] 2,077 | 81 | 182 | 11 | 22 | 13 | 6.1 | 5.4 |
| 1949 | 83 | … | 68 | 1,735 | 81 | 179 | 15 | 25 | 14 | 4.1 | 4.8 |
| 1950 | 91 | 5.9 | 67 | 1,957 | 85 | 179 | 18 | 24 | 13 | 4.6 | 2.8 |
| 1951 | 104 | 6.7 | 73 | 2,313 | 100 | 182 | 14 | 24 | 13 | 5.6 | 3.3 |
| 1952 | 74 | 5.6 | 68 | 2,014 | 108 | 179 | 14 | 23 | 12 | 5.2 | 3.5 |
| 1953 | 77 | 4.3 | 72 | 2,074 | 81 | 174 | 20 | 27 | 12 | 4.8 | 4.6 |
| 1954 | 63 | 6.7 | 72 | 1,884 | 92 | 195 | 20 | 29 | 15 | 6.9 | 4.1 |
| 1955 | 73 | 6.1 | 84 | 1,936 | 107 | 217 | 20 | 33 | 16 | 8.7 | 5.2 |
| 1956 | 79 | 6.5 | 97 | 2,020 | 114 | 228 | 21 | 35 | 15 | 6.5 | 6.3 |
| 1957 | 77 | 8 | 102 | 1,894 | 118 | 223 | 20 | 37 | 15 | 7.8 | 8 |
| 1958 | 71 | 8.2 | 104 | 1,756 | 113 | 228 | 17 | 40 | 14 | 8.7 | 7.4 |
| 1959 | 72 | 6.9 | 104 | 1,906 | 119 | 249 | 13 | 42 | 15 | 7.2 | 8 |
| 1960 | 69 | 9.1 | 105 | 1,971 | 105 | 257 | 18 | 47 | 17 | 9.8 | 9.3 |
| 1961 | 73 | 12 | 108 | 1,802 | 108 | 271 | 23 | 51 | 17 | 7.6 | 9.1 |
| 1962 | 84 | 14 | 111 | 1,945 | 105 | 282 | 24 | 53 | 18 | 5.6 | 11 |
| 1963 | 81 | 16 | 111 | 1,833 | 76 | 282 | 25 | 56 | 18 | 5 | 12 |
| 1964 | 91 | 17 | 121 | 1,877 | 101 | 271 | 26 | 58 | 18 | 6.9 | 15 |
| 1965 | 93 | 18 | 130 | 2,002 | 112 | 266 | 28 | 63 | 20 | 7.6 | 17 |
| 1966 | 91 | 20 | 141 | 2,059 | 113 | 260 | 28 | 63 | 20 | 8.7 | 18 |
| 1967 | 92 | 18 | 145 | 2,057 | 107 | 271 | 28 | 65 | 18 | 6.3 | 18 |
| 1968 | 85 | 20 | 154 | 1,947 | 94 | 271 | 28 | 65 | 17 | 7.4 | 17 |
| 1969 | 85 | 20 | 149 | 1,787 | 103 | 288 | 28 | 67 | 17 | 5.9 | 21 |
| 1970 | 78 | 20 | 149 | 1,733 | 103 | 293 | 29 | 71 | 20 | 5.6 | 21 |
| 1971 | 76 | 20 | 146 | 1,749 | 107 | 299 | 28 | 75 | 26 | 6.7 | 22 |
| 1972 | 79 | 20 | 163 | 1,743 | 108 | 325 | 29 | 78 | 30 | 5.2 | 25 |
| 1973 | 74 | 20 | 174 | 1,691 | 101 | 369 | 24 | 84 | 31 | 4.8 | 27 |
| 1974 | 71 | 19 | 146 | 1,749 | 113 | 299 | 29 | 75 | 26 | 6.7 | 22 |
| 1975 | 51 | 23 | 178 | 1,276 | 112 | 412 | 29 | 65 | 30 | 6.1 | 28 |
| 1976 | 56 | 26 | 181 | 1,583 | 117 | 444 | 27 | 61 | 32 | 4.1 | 34 |
| 1977 | 48 | 28 | 165 | 1,453 | 117 | 455 | 23 | 79 | 41 | 4.8 | 30 |
| 1978 | 52 | 30 | 160 | 1,417 | 104 | 488 | 22 | 88 | 55 | 6 | 26 |
| 1979 | 56 | 33 | 165 | 1,383 | 109 | 531 | 24 | 70 | 55 | 6 | 24 |
| 1980 | 59 | 35 | 165 | 1,416 | 102 | 564 | 16 | 82 | 52 | 6 | 20 |
| 1981 | 48 | 37 | 159 | 1,232 | 76 | 570 | 12 | 59 | 50 | 5 | 16 |
| 1982 | 49 | 39 | 144 | 1,128 | 85 | 569 | 11 | 47 | 42 | 5 | 17 |
| 1983 | 55 | 42 | 124 | 1,274 | 96 | 560 | 11 | 47 | 41 | 5 | 21 |
| 1984 | 51 | 44 | 119 | 1,232 | 110 | 581 | 11 | 58 | 49 | 5 | 33 |
| 1985 | 52 | 44 | 131 | 1,276 | 118 | 654 | 11 | 67 | 63 | 5 | 39 |
| 1986 | 48 | 47 | 127 | 1,477 | 132 | 731 | 12 | 77 | 76 | 4 | 34 |
| 1987 | 45 | 46 | 133 | 1,706 | 133 | 735 | 15 | 86 | 82 | 2 | 30 |
| 1988 | 45 | 45 | 151 | 1,567 | 124 | 706 | 16 | 79 | 73 | 2 | 30 |

NOTES

1.  SOURCES: The national publications listed on p. xiv–xvi for Canada, USA to 1948 (1st line), and all other countries to 1947 (except 1939). Other data are from the publications of the International Federation of Cotton and Allied Textile Industries (under various names).
2.  Data from the last-mentioned source are for years ending 31 July.

FOOTNOTES

[1] Imports of raw cotton and waste for years ending 30 June to 1902. Subsequently, to 1937, imports of raw cotton.
[2] Note the change of year indicated in Note 2 above.
[3] Figures for the year ended 31 July 1939 are available as follows:—Argentina 33, Chile 4.3, Colombia 12, Uruguay 0.4, Venezuela 2.4.

**D13    COTTON SPINDLES** (in thousands)

| | NORTH AMERICA | | | | |
|---|---|---|---|---|---|
| | Canada | Cuba | El Salvador | Mexico | USA |
| 1900 | 774 | ... | ... | 491 | 20,318 |
| 1914 | 860 | ... | ... | 750 | 31,520 |
| 1920 | 1,200 | ... | ... | 720 | 35,834 |
| 1930 | 1,277 | ... | ... | 767 | 34,031 |
| 1939 | 1,159 | ... | 14 | 884 | 25,911 |
| 1950 | 1,121 | ... | 32 | 986 | 23,007 |
| 1960 | 817 | ... | 73 | 1,350 | 19,916 |
| 1970 | 755 | 237 | 127 | 2,704 | 19,559 |

| | SOUTH AMERICA | | | | | | | |
|---|---|---|---|---|---|---|---|---|
| | Argentina | Brazil | Chile | Colombia | Ecuador | Peru | | Venezuela |
| 1853 | ... | 4 | ... | ... | ... | ... | ... | ... |
| 1866 | ... | 14 | ... | ... | ... | ... | ... | ... |
| 1885 | ... | 66 | ... | ... | ... | ... | ... | ... |
| 1900 | ... | 288 | ... | ... | ... | ... | ... | ... |
| 1914 | ... | 1,400 | ... | ... | ... | ... | ... | ... |
| 1920 | ... | 1,600 | ... | ... | ... | ... | ... | ... |
| 1930 | ... | 2,775 | ... | ... | ... | ... | ... | ... |
| 1939 | 329 | 2,765 | 33 | 105 | 42 | 118 | ... | 42 |
| 1950 | 531 | 3,291 | 175 | 358 | 49 | 148 | ... | 60 |
| 1960 | 1,038 | 3,840 | 219 | 485 | 88 | 210 | 135 | 132 |
| 1970 | 1,070 | 3,588 | 403 | 649 | 116 | 265 | 180 | 287 |

NOTES

1.  SOURCES: The main source used has been the publications of the International Federation of Cotton and Allied Textile Industries (IFCATI) (under various names). Data for Brazil 1853–85, 1905, 1910, and 1915, are from Stanley J. Stein, *The Brazilian Cotton Manufacture* (Cambridge, Mass., 1957).
2.  In principle, the statistics in this table relate to spinning spindles in place. Rayon spinning spindles are included.
3.  IFCATI data refer to 1 March to 1912, 31 July from then to 1958, and 31 December subsequently.
4.  Annual figures, where available, are given in earlier editions of this work, up to 1974.

**D14    OUTPUT OF COTTON YARN** (in thousands of metric tons)

| | NORTH AMERICA | | | SOUTH AMERICA | | | |
|---|---|---|---|---|---|---|---|
| | Canada[1] | Mexico[2] | USA | Argentina | Brazil[5] | Chile[6] | Paraguay |
| 1928 | ... | 3.8 | ... | ... | ... | ... | |
| 1929 | ... | 4.1 | ... | ... | ... | ... | |
| 1930 | ... | 3.8 | ... | ... | ... | ... | |
| 1931 | ... | 3.5 | ... | ... | ... | ... | |
| 1932 | ... | 3.9 | ... | ... | ... | ... | |
| 1933 | ... | 4.7 | ... | ... | ... | ... | |
| 1934 | ... | 7.0 | ... | ... | ... | ... | |
| 1935 | ... | 7.1 | ... | 16 | ... | ... | |
| 1936 | 59 | 7.6 | ... | 21 | ... | ... | |
| 1937 | 62 | 7.3 | 1,410 | 26 | ... | 2.3 | |
| 1938 | 54 | 7.7 | ... | 24 | ... | 3.5 | |
| 1939 | 65 | 7.8 | 1,424 | 29 | ... | 3.6 | |
| 1940 | 89 | 8.5 | ... | 33 | ... | 3.4 | |
| 1941 | 96 | 9.3 | ... | 38 | ... | 3.4 | |
| 1942 | 97 | 12 | ... | 50 | ... | 3.9 | |
| 1943 | 85 | 12 | ... | 55 | 125 | $\underline{6.2}_6$ | |
| 1944 | 76 | 11 | ... | 63 | 149 | 2.1 | |
| 1945 | 74 | 8.0 | ... | 64 | 159 | 2.0 | |
| 1946 | 74 | 7.6 | ... | 65 | 168 | 1.5 | |
| 1947 | 76 | 4.9 | 1,715 | 66 | ... | 2.8 | |
| 1948 | 82 | 5.9 | ... | 70 | 196 | 3.3 | |
| 1949 | 81 | 5.2 | ... | 70 | 210 | 4.1 | |
| 1950 | 93 | 6.5 | ... | 77 | ... | 4.4 | |
| 1951 | 90 | 4.9 | ... | 91 | 76 | 1.6 | |
| 1952 | 71 | 5.2 | ... | 82 | 74 | 2.9 | |
| 1953 | 67 | 4.5 | ... | 76 | 71 | 3.9 | |
| 1954 | 62 | 4.9 | 1,695 | 85 | 87 | 11 | |
| 1955 | 67 | $\underline{5.7}_2$ | ... | 95 | 91 | 16 | |
| 1956 | 71 | 44 | ... | 101 | 96 | 13 | |
| 1957 | 68 | 49 | ... | 99 | 91 | ... | |
| 1958 | 60 | 50 | 1,645 | 99 | 95 | ... | |
| 1959 | 68 | 51 | 1,839 | 86 | 101 | ... | |
| 1960 | 65 | 50 | 1,655 | 95 | 106 | ... | |
| 1961 | 70 | 51 | 1,763 | 95 | 112 | ... | |
| 1962 | 77 | $\underline{50}_3$ | 1,805 | 77 | 114 | 21 | 11 |
| 1963 | 79 | 104 | 1,761 | 73 | 111 | 23 | 13 |
| 1964 | 87 | 117 | 1,871 | 89 | 110 | 25 | 11 |
| 1965 | 89 | 120 | 1,958 | 98 | 100 | 26 | 14 |
| 1966 | 77 | 136 | 2,006 | 94 | 109 | 26 | 9 |
| 1967 | 81 | 139 | 1,877 | 84 | 98 | 26 | 9 |
| 1968 | $\underline{79}_1$ | 106 | 1,694 | 85 | 111 | 26 | 10 |
| 1969 | 85 | 145 | 1,594 | 89 | 118 | 26 | 13 |
| 1970 | 77 | 132 | 1,525 | 90 | $118_5$ | 27 | 12 |
| 1971 | 78 | 130 | 1,567 | 94 | ... | 27 | 5 |
| 1972 | 86 | 131 | 1,517 | 89 | 275 | 29 | 13 |
| 1973 | 77 | 163 | 1,388 | 85 | 322 | 23 | 22 |
| 1974 | 78 | 179 | 1,261 | 89 | 335 | ... | 24 |

**D14** **Output of Cotton Yarn** (in thousands of metric tons)

| | NORTH AMERICA | | | SOUTH AMERICA | | | |
|---|---|---|---|---|---|---|---|
| | Canada | Mexico | USA | Argentina | Brazil | Chile | Paraguay |
| 1975 | 62 | 157 | 1,101 | 89 | 360 | ... | 32 |
| 1976 | 63 | 153 | 1,221 | 98 | 380 | ... | 34 |
| 1977 | 61 | 143 | 1,141 | 105 | 390 | ... | 73 |
| 1978 | 66₈ | 146 | 1,096 | 86 | 460 | ... | 91 |
| 1979 | 26 | 154 | 1,112 | 90 | 500 | 3.8 | 73 |
| 1980 | 24 | ... | 1,114 | 75 | 510 | 4.8 | 75 |
| 1981 | 41 | ... | 987 | 79 | 483 | 4.0 | 106 |
| 1982 | 45 | ... | 932 | 80 | 493 | 4.6 | 91 |
| 1983 | 45 | 126 | 1,055 | 93 | 473 | 3.6 | 77 |
| 1984 | 45 | ... | 956 | 105 | 674 | 7.5 | 105 |
| 1985 | 43 | ... | 977 | 91 | 963 | 8.3 | 160 |
| 1986 | 40 | ... | 1,127 | 114 | 793 | 9.4 | 100 |
| 1987 | 37 | ... | 1,288 | 100 | 633 | 9.9 | 84 |
| 1988 | 36 | ... | 1,227 | 100 | 691 | 4.3 | ... |

NOTES

1.  SOURCES: The national publications listed on p. xiv–xvi, UN, *Statistical Yearbooks,* and *Cotton-World Statistics.*
2.  Except as indicated in footnotes, tyre cord yarns are excluded and yarns made from waste and from mixed fibres of more than 50% cotton are included.

FOOTNOTES

[1] Excluding yarn made in carpet mills to 1968. Including tyre cord yarn.
[2] Production for sale only to 1955. The reason for the break between 1962 and 1963 is not given in the source. Mixed yarns are not included.
[3] Including tyre cord yarns.
[4] Mixed yarns are not included.
[5] São Paulo state only to 1970.
[6] Yarns for sale only from 1944.
[7] Yarns for sale only from 1951 (2nd line), including tyre cord yarns from 1962. Data relate to years ended 30 June.
[8] Shipments from factories subsequently.

## D15 OUTPUT OF COTTON TISSUES

| | NORTH AMERICA | | | SOUTH AMERICA | | | | | |
|---|---|---|---|---|---|---|---|---|---|
| | Canada | Mexico | USA | Argentina | Brazil | Chile | Colombia | Peru | Venezuela |
| | (millions metres) | (thousand tons) | (million square metres) | (thousand tons) | (million metres) | (million metres) | (million metres) | (millions metres) | (million metres) |
| 1853 | ... | ... | ... | ... | 1.2 | ... | ... | ... | ... |
| 1866 | ... | ... | ... | ... | 3.6 | ... | ... | ... | ... |
| 1882 | ... | ... | ... | ... | 22 | ... | ... | ... | ... |
| 1885 | ... | ... | ... | ... | 21 | ... | ... | ... | ... |
| 1899 | ... | ... | 3,312 | ... | ... | ... | ... | ... | ... |
| 1904 | ... | ... | 3,657 | ... | 242 | ... | ... | ... | ... |
| 1909 | ... | ... | 4,757 | ... | ... | ... | ... | ... | ... |
| 1911 | ... | ... | ... | ... | 379 | ... | ... | ... | ... |
| 1912 | ... | ... | ... | ... | 400 | ... | ... | ... | ... |
| 1913 | ... | ... | ... | ... | 385 | ... | ... | ... | ... |
| 1914 | ... | ... | 5,059 | ... | 314 | ... | ... | ... | ... |
| 1915 | ... | ... | ... | ... | 471 | ... | ... | ... | ... |
| 1916 | ... | ... | ... | ... | 474 | ... | ... | ... | ... |
| 1917 | ... | ... | ... | ... | 548 | ... | ... | ... | ... |
| 1918 | ... | ... | ... | ... | 494 | ... | ... | ... | ... |
| 1919 | ... | ... | 5,673 | ... | 584 | ... | ... | ... | ... |
| 1920 | ... | ... | ... | ... | 587 | ... | ... | ... | ... |
| 1921 | ... | ... | 5,135 | ... | 552 | ... | ... | ... | ... |
| 1922 | ... | ... | ... | ... | 627 | ... | ... | ... | ... |
| 1923 | ... | ... | 6,228 | ... | 940 | ... | ... | ... | ... |
| 1924 | ... | ... | ... | ... | 580 | ... | ... | ... | ... |
| 1925 | 121 | ... | 5,782 | ... | 536 | ... | ... | ... | ... |
| 1926 | 98 | ... | ... | ... | 539 | ... | ... | ... | ... |
| 1927 | 144 | ... | 6,844 | ... | 594 | ... | ... | ... | ... |
| 1928 | 103[1] 208 | ... | ... | ... | 582 | ... | ... | ... | ... |
| 1929 | 196 | ... | 6,432[3] 6,805 | ... | 478 | ... | ... | ... | ... |
| 1930 | 176 | ... | ... | ... | 476 | ... | ... | ... | ... |
| 1931 | 173 | ... | 5,840 | ... | 634 | ... | ... | ... | ... |
| 1932 | 177 | ... | ... | ... | 631 | ... | ... | ... | ... |
| 1933 | 208 | ... | 6,455 | ... | 639 | ... | ... | ... | ... |
| 1934 | 214 | ... | ... | ... | 716 | ... | ... | ... | ... |
| 1935 | 204 | ... | 5,843 | ... | 753 | ... | ... | ... | ... |
| 1936 | 218 | ... | ... | ... | 915 | ... | ... | ... | ... |
| 1937 | 236 | 38 | 7,728 (million metres) 7,921 | ... | 964 | 13 | ... | ... | ... |
| 1938 | 195 | 38 | ... | ... | 846 | 13 | ... | ... | 3.0 |
| 1939 | 241 | 36 | 7,578 | ... | 894 | 13 | ... | ... | 4.2 |
| 1940 | 283 | 38 | ... | ... | 840 | 15 | 73 | ... | 5.1 |
| 1941 | 321 | 44 | 9,539 | ... | 990 | 17 | 65 | ... | 6.8 |
| 1942 | 306 | 46 | 10,157 | ... | 1,069 | 17 | 111 | ... | 20 |
| 1943 | 254 | 47 | 9,668 | ... | 1,414 | 20 | ... | ... | 24 |
| 1944 | 241 | 48 | 8,730 | ... | 1,383 | 23 | ... | ... | 22 |
| 1945 | 224 | 48 | 7,974 | ... | 1,085 | 24 | 142 | ... | 21 |
| 1946 | 217 | 47 | 8,361 | ... | 1,142 | 23[6] 47 | ... | ... | 22 |
| 1947 | 233 | 46 | 8,977 | ... | 1,063 | 45 | 157 | 67 | 23 |
| 1948 | 229 | 47 | 8,815 | 66 | 1,120 | 45 | 166 | 71 | 21 |
| 1949 | 205 | 42 | 7,686 | ... | 1,137 | 52 | 164 | ... | 14 |

## D15    Output of Cotton Tissues

| | Canada[1] | Cuba | Mexico | USA | Argentina | Brazil | Chile[6] | Colombia | Peru[7] | Venezuela[7] |
|---|---|---|---|---|---|---|---|---|---|---|
| | (million metres) | (million sq. metres) | (thousand tons) | (million metres) | (thousand tons) | (million metres) | (million metres) | (million metres) | (million metres) | (million metres) |
| 1950 | 297 | ... | 44 | 9,156[4] | ... | 1,189 | 70 | 160 | ... | 9.2 |
| 1951 | 277 | ... | 37 | 9,268 | ... | 1,112 | 73 | 157 | ... | 11 |
| 1952 | 238[1] | ... | 35 | 8,701 | 78 | 997 | 75 | 180 | ... | 13 |
| 1953 | 229 | ... | 37 | 9,330 | 72 | ... | 81 | 181 | ... | 14 |
| 1954 | 242 | ... | 29 | 9,044 | 74 | ... | 86 | 173 | ... | 14 |
| 1955 | 287 | ... | 36 | 9,304 | 80 | 1,240 | 86 | 166 | ... | 16 |
| 1956 | 286 | ... | 43 | 9,434 | 86 | 1,252 | 88 | 211 | ... | 16 |
| 1957 | 276 | ... | 46 | 8,718 | 84 | 1,106 | ...[5] | 203 | ... | 21 |
| 1958 | 259 | ... | 44 | 8,206 | 84 | 1,273 | 68 | 219 | ... | 23 |
| 1959 | 250 | ... | 49 | 8,781 | 73 | ... | 72 | 249 | 85 | 32 |
| 1960 | 240 | ... | 49 | 8,564 | 82 | ... | 83 | 277 | 91 | 36 |
| 1961 | 278 | ... | 46 | 8,383 | 81 | ... | 84 | 281 | 87 | 40 |
| 1962 | 281 | 94 | 47[2] | 8,456 | 65 | ... | 77 | 307 | 91 | 50 |
| 1963 | 290 | 90 | 99 | 8,009 | 63 | ... | 89 | 299 | 85 | 59 |
| 1964 | 302 | 105 | 113 | 8,199 | 77 | ... | 89 | 309 | 94 | 69 |
| 1965 | 271 (million square metres) 292 | 96 | 115 | 8,447 | 83 | 1,262 | 92 | 298 | 83 | 72 |
| 1966 | 259 | 108 | 115 | 8,083 | 73 | 1,343 | 95 | 295 | 93 | 72 |
| 1967 | 270 | 112 | 125 | 7,569 | 71 | 1,230 | 99 | ... | 76 | 71 |
| 1968 | 250 | 105 | 95 | 6,837 | 73 | 1,409 | 102 | 298 | 84 | 72 |
| 1969 | 227 | 91 | 128 | 6,369 | 77 | 1,426[5] | 101 | 300 | ... | 81 |
| 1970 | 181 | 76 | 119 | 5,711 | 76 | 784 | 97 | ... | ... | 80 |
| 1971 | 175 | 87 | 116 | 5,613 | 78 | 774 | 94 | ... | ... | 78 |
| 1972 | 202 | 98 | 115 | 5,174 | 75 | 777 | 82 | ... | ... | 94 |
| 1973 | 169 | 117 | 138 | 4,650 | 74 | 846 | 82 | ... | 95 | |
| 1974 | 269 | 127 | 150 | 4,242 | 72 | 818 | 86 | ... | 112 | ... |
| | | | | | | | | | (million tons) | |
| 1975 | ... | 138 | 123 | 3,744 | 70 | 864[5] | 53 | ... | 34 | ... |
| 1976 | ... | 134 | 73 | 4,314 | 93 | 1,075 | 50 | ... | 25 | ... |
| 1977 | ... | 145 | 69 | 3,983 | 98 | 1,011 | 59 | ... | 30 | ... |
| 1978 | ... | 147 | 67 | 3,664 | 87 | 1,123 | 68 | ... | ... | ... |
| 1979 | ... | 143 | 68 | 3,225 | 101 | 1,207 | 67 | ... | ... | ... |
| | | | | (million square metres) 4,069 | | | | (million tons) | | |
| 1980 | ... | 148 | 67 | 3,726 | 85 | 1,252 | 53 | ... | ... | ... |
| 1981 | ... | 149 | 71 | 3,272 | 74 | 1,018 | 36 | 38 | ... | ... |
| 1982 | ... | 138 | 66 | 3,173 | 75 | ...[2] | 27 | 30 | ... | ... |
| 1983 | ... | 156 | 66 | 3,505 | 88 | 1,643 | 28 | 27 | ... | ... |
| 1984 | ... | 156 | 64 | 3,346 | 98 | 1,490 | 41 | 29 | 21 | ... |
| 1985 | ... | 177 | 71 | 3,278 | 81 | 1,816 | 45 | 34 | 22 | ... |
| 1986 | ... | 183 | 71 | 3,648 | 106 | 1,968 | 52 | 27 | 33 | ... |
| 1987 | ... | 202 | 87 | 3,990 | 87 | 1,974 | 51 | 29 | 31 | ... |
| 1988 | ... | 203 | ... | 3,781 | 88 | 1,805 | 32 | 34 | 27 | ... |

NOTES

1. SOURCES: The national publications listed on p.xiv–xvi, UN, *Statistical Yearbooks,* and *Cotton-World Statistics.*
2. Fabrics of mixed fibres with cotton predominating are included in this table.

FOOTNOTES

[1] Broad-woven fabrics only to 1928 (1st line). Data from 1953 are of factory shipments.
[2] Subsequently including finished fabrics.
[3] A more inclusive classification was employed subsequently.
[4] The reason for this break is not given in the source.
[5] Production by main establishments only in 1970–75.
[6] Incomplete data to 1946 (1st line).
[7] Including finished fabrics.

## D16    WOOL INDUSTRY INDICATORS

| | NORTH AMERICA | | | | | SOUTH AMERICA | |
|---|---|---|---|---|---|---|---|
| | Canada | | | USA | | Argentina[6] | Uruguay[6] |
| | Yarn[1] Output | Tissues[3] Output | Wool Consumption | Yarn Output | Tissues Output | Wool Consumption | Wool Consumption |
| | (thousand tons) | (million metres) | (thousand tons) | (thousand tons) | (million square metres) | (thousand tons) | (thousand tons) |
| 1899 | ... | ... | ... | [27] | 357 | ... | ... |
| 1904 | ... | ... | ... | 50 | 423 | ... | ... |
| 1909 | ... | ... | ... | 59 | 477 | ... | ... |
| 1914 | ... | ... | ... | 56 | 472 | ... | ... |
| 1918 | ... | ... | 181 | ... | ... | ... | ... |
| 1919 | ... | ... | 149 | 53 | 428 | ... | ... |
| 1920 | ... | ... | 143 | ... | ... | ... | ... |
| 1921 | ... | ... | 156 | 55 | 413 | ... | ... |
| 1922 | ... | ... | 184 | ... | ... | ... | ... |
| 1923 | ... | ... | 192 | 78 | 525 | ... | ... |
| 1924 | ... | ... | 155 | ... | ... | ... | ... |
| 1925 | ... | ... | 159 | 66 | 485 | ... | ... |
| 1926 | ... | ... | 155 | ... | ... | ... | ... |
| 1927 | ... | ... | 161 | 61 | 467 | ... | ... |
| 1928 | ... | 8.5 | 151 | ... | ... | ... | ... |
| 1929 | ... | 8.5 | 167 | 67 | 430[5] / 348 | ... | ... |
| 1930 | ... | 6.3 | 119 | ... | ... | ... | ... |
| 1931 | ... | 8.4 | 141 | 57 | 271 | ... | ... |
| 1932 | ... | 10 | 104 | ... | ... | ... | ... |
| 1933 | 4.0 | 13 | 144 | 55 | 304 | ... | ... |
| 1934 | 4.0 | 13 | 104 | ...[4] | ... | ... | ... |
| 1935 | 4.7 | 15 | 189 | 44 | 400 | ... | ... |
| 1936 | 5.2 | 16 | 184 | ... | 393 | ... | ... |
| 1937 | 5.2 | 17 | 173 | 34[4] / 262 | 394 | ... | ... |
| 1938 | 4.1[1] / 11 | 13 | 129 | ... | 301[5] (million metres) | ... | ... |
| 1939 | 18 | 16 | 180 | 270 | 340 | ... | ... |
| 1940 | 31 | 25 | 185 | ... | ... | ... | ... |
| 1941 | 31 | 25 | 294 | ... | ... | ... | ... |
| 1942 | 32 | 27 | 274 | ... | 483 | ... | ... |
| 1943 | 30 | 26 | 289 | ... | 491 | ... | ... |
| 1944 | 28 | 24 | 282 | 388 | 483 | ... | ... |
| 1945 | 29 | 25 | 293 | 375[2] | 451 | ... | ... |
| 1946 | 31 | 27 | 335 | 417 | 552 | ... | ... |
| 1947 | 32 | 27 | 317 | 350 | 458 | 23 | 3.6 |
| 1948 | 31 | 26 | 314 | 362 | 455 | 27 | 3.6 |
| 1949 | 27 | 25 | 227 | 312 | 379[5] | 32 | 3.5 |
| 1950 | 28 | 23 | 288 | 367[2] | 383 | 34 | 6 |
| 1951 | 28 | 24 | 220 | 358 | 343 | 32 | 7.5 |
| 1952 | 25 | 24 | 212 | 341 | 321 | 30 | 13 |
| 1953 | 22 | 22[3] | 224 | 343 | 307 | 25 | 19 |
| 1954 | 19 | 15 | 173 | 279 | 260 | 28 | 16 |

## D16    Wool Industry Indicators

| | NORTH AMERICA | | | | | SOUTH AMERICA | |
| | Canada | | | USA | | Argentina[6] | Uruguay[6] |
| | Yarn[1] Output | Tissues Output | Wool Consumption | Yarn Output | Tissues Output[6] | Wool Consumption | Wool Consumption |
| | (thousand tons) | (million metres) | (thousand tons) | (thousand tons) | (million metres) | (thousand tons) | (thousand tons) |
|---|---|---|---|---|---|---|---|
| 1955 | 21 | 21 | 188 | 317 | 290 | 31 | 18 |
| 1956 | 24 | 21 | 200 | 346 | 297 | 27 | 21 |
| 1957 | 21 | 18 | 167 | 308 | 269 | 32 | 12 |
| 1958 | 18 | 15 | 150 | 294 | 248 | 28 | 15 |
| 1959 | 19 | 17 | 197 | 250 | 284 | 26 | 20 |
| 1960 | 16 | 14[3] 25 | 186 | 238 | 262 | 20 | 17 |
| 1961 | 13 | 27 | 187 | 230 | 262 | 25 | 20 |
| 1962 | 18 | 28 | 195 | 238 | 284 | 16 | 19 |
| 1963 | 16 | 30 | 187 | 244 | 260 | 16 | 21 |
| 1964 | 19 | 32 | 162 | 217 | 233 | 24 | 22 |
| 1965 | 19 | 30 | 176 | 248 | 244 | 24 | 18 |
| 1966 | 17 | 32 | 139 | 226 | 241 | 21 | 22 |
| 1967 | 14 | 28 | 143 | 281 | 218 | 21 | 22 |
| 1968 | 14[1] | 30 | 150 | 286 | 222 | 22 | 23 |
| | | (million square metres) | | | | | |
| | 15 | 31 | | | | | |
| 1969 | | 31 | 142 | 173 | 203 | 25 | 21 |
| 1970 | 15 | 28 | 109 | 141 | 163 | 27 | 22 |
| 1971 | 16 | 23 | 87 | 116 | 104 | 34 | 20 |
| 1972 | 16 | 27 | 99 | 116 | 93 | 36 | 19 |
| 1973 | 17 | 31 | 67 | 89 | 97 | 31 | 18 |
| 1974 | 12 | 29 | 41 | 64 | 73 | 32 | 12 |
| 1975 | 2.7 | 31 | 48 | 59 | 72 | 32 | 18 |
| 1976 | 3.2 | 29 | 53 | 61 | 89 | 32 | 23 |
| 1977 | 3.8 | 28 | 47 | 64 | 93 | 37 | 21 |
| 1978 | 4.0 | 28 | 50 | 63 | 107 | 35 | 23 |
| 1979 | 4.2 | … | 54[7] 65 | 64 | 106 | 26[7] 26 | 21 |
| 1980 | 3.5 | … | 62 | 57 | 105 | 22 | 26 |
| 1981 | … | … | 70 | 62 | 96 | 13 | 30 |
| 1982 | … | … | 58 | 54 | 59 | 20 | 27 |
| 1983 | … | … | 72 | 59 | 61 | 25 | 29 |
| 1984 | … | … | 77 | 57 | 86 | 27 | 32 |
| | | | | | (m. square metres) | | |
| | | | | | 133 | | |
| 1985 | … | … | 61 | 50 | 116 | 26 | 33 |
| 1986 | … | … | 70 | 62 | 167 | 28 | … |
| 1987 | … | … | 68 | 61 | 154 | 28 | … |
| 1988 | … | … | 60 | 55 | 160 | … | … |

NOTE

1. SOURCES: The national publications listed on p.xiv–xvi and League of Nations and UN, Statistical Yearbooks.
2. In principle, the output of mixed yarn and tissues in which wool predominates is included in this table.

FOOTNOTES

[1] Worsted yarn only to 1938 (1st line). Excluding yarn made in carpet mills to 1968.
[2] A proportion of worsted yarn is excluded from 1946 to 1950.
[3] Factory shipments form 1954 and deliveries from 1960 (2nd line).
[4] Yarns for sale only to 1937 (1st line). The reason for the break between 1933 and 1935 is not given in the source.
[5] Apparel fabrics only from 1929 (2nd line) to 1938, but excluding upholstery to 1921. The reason for the break between 1949 and 1950 is not given in the source, but it is not of major significance.
[6] Years ended 30 September.
[7] Consumption at the spinning stage subsequently.

**D17** **OUTPUT OF ARTIFICIAL AND SYNTHETIC FIBRES** (in thousands of metric tons)

Key:    a= rayon and acetate filaments; b= non-cellulosic filaments

| | NORTH AMERICA | | | | | SOUTH AMERICA | | |
| | Canada | | Mexico | USA | | Argentina | Brazil | Colombia |
| | a | b | a[2] | a[3] | b | a | a | a |
|------|------|-----|------|-------|-----|------|------|------|
| 1910 | — | — | — | ... | — | — | — | ... |
| 1911 | — | — | — | 1.0 | — | — | — | ... |
| 1912 | — | — | — | 1.3 | — | — | — | ... |
| 1913 | — | — | — | 1.8 | — | — | — | ... |
| 1914 | — | — | — | 2.3 | — | — | — | ... |
| 1915 | — | — | — | 3.0 | — | — | — | ... |
| 1916 | — | — | — | 3.0 | — | — | — | ... |
| 1917 | — | — | — | 3.1 | — | — | — | ... |
| 1918 | — | — | — | 2.7 | — | — | — | ... |
| 1919 | — | — | — | 4.2 | — | — | — | ... |
| 1920 | — | — | — | 3.9 | — | — | — | ... |
| 1921 | — | — | — | 9.0[3] | — | — | — | ... |
| 1922 | — | — | — | 11 | — | — | — | ... |
| 1923 | — | — | — | 17 | — | — | — | ... |
| 1924 | — | — | — | 17 | — | — | — | ... |
| 1925 | 0.2 | — | — | 24 | — | — | — | ... |
| 1926 | 0.9 | — | — | 28 | — | — | 0.1 | ... |
| 1927 | 1.1 | — | — | 34 | — | — | 0.3 | ... |
| 1928 | 1.5 | — | — | 44 | — | — | 0.3 | ... |
| 1929 | 1.7 | — | — | 55 | — | — | 0.2 | ... |
| 1930 | 2.1 | — | — | 58 | — | — | 0.3 | ... |
| 1931 | 2.7 | — | — | 69 | — | — | 0.5 | ... |
| 1932 | 3.3 | — | — | 62 | — | — | 0.7 | ... |
| 1933 | 3.8 | — | — | 98 | — | — | 0.9 | ... |
| 1934 | 4.8 | — | — | 96 | — | — | 1.2 | ... |
| 1935 | 6.0 | — | — | 119 | — | — | 1.6 | ... |
| 1936 | 6.2 | — | — | 131 | — | 0.2 | 2.2 | ... |
| 1937 | 7.5 | — | — | 155 | — | 0.8 | 3.3 | ... |
| 1938 | 6.2 | — | — | 130 | — | 1.2 | 5.5 | ... |
| 1939 | 6.4 | — | — | 172 | — | 2.4 | 7.2 | 0.1 |
| 1940 | 8.9 | — | — | 214 | 1.2 | 2.7 | 7.8 | 0.3 |
| 1941 | 9.5 | — | — | 260 | 3.4 | 3.5 | 8.5 | 0.5 |
| 1942 | 8.6 | — | - - | 287 | 5.5 | 3.8 | 8.7 | 0.6 |
| 1943 | 8.0 | — | 0.2 | 301 | 8.0 | 3.5 | 7.7 | 0.6 |
| 1944 | 9.4 | — | 0.2 | 328 | 11 | 3.8 | 9.8 | 0.7 |
| 1945 | 10 | — | 0.2 | 359 | 13 | 4.4 | 10 | 1.0 |
| 1946 | 9.8 | — | 0.2 | 387 | ... | 5.1 | 11 | 1.4 |
| 1947 | 13 | — | 1.3 | 442 | ... | 4.8 | 13 | ... |
| 1948 | 15 | 1.2 | 4.6 | 510 | 30 | 4.7 | 12 | 1.5 |
| 1949 | 17 | — | 9.8 | 452 | ... | 7.1 | 16 | 1.4 |

**D17**    **Output of Artificial and Synthetic Fibres** (in thousands of metric tons)

| | NORTH AMERICA | | | | | | SOUTH AMERICA | | | | | |
|---|---|---|---|---|---|---|---|---|---|---|---|---|
| | Canada | | Mexico | | USA | | Argentina | | Brazil | | Colombia | |
| | a | b | a[2] | b | a | b | a | b | a | b | a | b |
| 1950 | 24 | 2.3 | 9.1 | — | 571 | 56 | 7.4 | 0.1 | 20 | — | 1.7 | — |
| 1951 | 26 | 2.9 | 11 | — | 587 | 77 | 7.4 | 0.2 | 25 | — | 1.8 | — |
| 1952 | 28 | 3.7 | 11 | — | 515 | 96 | 7.4 | 0.2 | 26 | — | 3.7 | — |
| 1953 | 29 | 4.5 | 11 | — | 543 | 112 | 8.6 | 0.1 | 27 | — | 5.4 | — |
| 1954 | 32 | 5.5 | 14 | 0.1 | 493 | 129 | 9.9 | 0.2 | 30 | — | 5.2 | — |
| 1955 | 36 | 5.6 | 17 | 0.1 | 572 | 172 | 11 | 0.3 | 32 | 0.2 | 6.8 | — |
| 1956 | 35 | 6.3 | 19 | 0.1 | 521 | 182 | 12 | 0.3 | 34 | 0.4 | 6.3 | — |
| 1957 | 34 | 9.3 | 16 | 0.2 | 517 | 234 | 13 | 0.4 | 35 | 1.3 | 8.1 | — |
| 1958 | 30 | 11 | 18 | 0.3 | 469 | 222 | 14 | 0.4 | 34 | 1.9 | 7.8 | — |
| 1959 | 39 | 13 | 20 | 0.4 | 529 | 293 | 11 | 0.6 | 36 | 2.9 | 7.8 | - - |
| 1960 | 34 | 17 | 21 | 0.7 | 467 | 307 | 11 | 1.1 | 41 | 4.5 | 7.7 | - - |
| 1961 | 34 | 19 | 21 | 1.3 | 497 | 341 | 16 | 1.8 | 42 | 5.7 | 6.9 | 0.1 |
| 1962 | 40 | 23 | 23[2] | 2.9 | 577 | 405 | 12 | 2.2 | 42 | 8.7 | 11 | 0.9 |
| 1963 | 44 | 26 | 22 | 4.6 | 612 | 524 | 10 | 4.6 | 40 | 10 | 13 | 0.9 |
| 1964 | 49 | 30 | 25 | 6.0 | 650 | 638 | 18 | 9.7 | 41 | 13 | 13 | 0.9 |
| 1965 | 52 | 38 | 26 | 8.8 | 693 | 807 | 20 | 13 | 42 | 15 | 10 | 3.0 |
| 1966 | 46 | 45 | 27 | 12 | 689 | 945 | 16 | 15 | 46 | 19 | 8.7 | 3.2 |
| 1967 | 44 | 51 | 29 | 15 | 620 | 1,067 | 13 | 17 | 46 | 18 | 9.0 | 5.3 |
| 1968 | 46 | 69 | 30 | 22 | 723 | 1,465 | 11 | 18 | 53 | 27 | 9.7 | 8.0 |
| 1969 | 43 | 76 | 33 | 26 | 715 | 1,600 | 11 | 23 | 48 | 30 | 9.0 | 11 |
| 1970 | 35 | 73 | 34 | 39 | 623 | 1,627 | 9.8 | 25 | 48 | 44 | 8.8 | 13 |
| 1971 | 38 | 86[1] | 35 | 62 | 631 | 1,946 | 14 | 33 | 53 | 52 | 11 | 15 |
| 1972 | 41 | 80 | 34 | 85 | 632 | 2,430 | 16 | 39 | 55 | 73 | 9 | 20 |
| 1973 | 43 | 94 | 37 | 99 | 616 | 2,862 | 18 | 46 | 59 | 103 | 7.4 | 24 |
| 1974 | 41 | 92 | 34 | 126 | 544 | 2,823 | 18 | 47 | 54 | 116 | 7.0 | 23 |
| 1975 | 28 | 96 | 33 | 148 | 340 | 2,670 | 14 | 47 | 49 | 126 | 5.6 | 27 |
| 1976 | 27 | 98 | 34 | 133 | 381 | 3,007 | 10 | 41 | 54 | 157 | 3.4 | 34 |
| 1977 | 37 | 115 | 25 | 158 | 403 | 3,324 | 11 | 43 | 50 | 160 | 3.3 | 39 |
| 1978 | 39 | 123 | 25 | 171 | 410 | 3,522 | 8 | 39 | 46 | 180 | 3.4 | 41 |
| 1979 | 45 | 122 | 24 | 183 | 422 | 3,828 | 10 | 52 | 50 | 214 | 3.4 | 37 |
| 1980 | 44 | 122 | 26 | 194 | 366 | 3,242 | 3.6 | 35 | 51 | 231 | 2.4 | 39 |
| 1981 | 42 | 110 | 26 | 213 | 349 | 3,275 | 1.1 | 25 | 46 | 202 | 1.8 | 44 |
| 1982 | 37 | 97 | 28 | 201 | 265 | 2,603 | 1.6 | 31 | 44 | 198 | 1.8 | 40 |
| 1983 | 40 | 112 | 20 | 219 | 299 | 3,008 | 1.7 | 43 | 40 | 185 | 1.8 | 40 |
| 1984 | 44 | 129 | 18 | 222 | 285 | 2,937 | 3.6 | 52 | 47 | 216 | 1.8 | 47 |
| 1985 | 35 | 133 | 19 | 235 | 253 | 2,864 | 2.9 | 37 | 47 | 217 | 1.8 | 48 |
| 1986 | 38 | 140 | 19 | 221 | 281 | 2,919 | 8.5 | 58 | 50 | 237 | 1.8 | 47 |
| 1987 | 37 | 130 | 20 | 237 | 275 | 3,094 | 5.8 | 57 | 49 | 248 | 2.3 | 49 |
| 1988 | 42 | 134 | 20 | … | 279 | 3,147 | 3.5 | 51 | 51 | 240 | 2.4 | 50 |

NOTE

SOURCES: The national publications listed on p. xiv–xvi and League of Nations and UN, *Statistical Yearbooks.*

FOOTNOTES

[1] Subsequently excluding olefin.
[2] Excluding high tenacity yarn to 1962.
[3] Statistics to 1921 may contain a very small amount of imports.

**D18 OUTPUT OF SULPHURIC ACID, HYDROCHLORIC ACID, NITRIC ACID, AND CAUSTIC SODA** (in thousands of metric tons)

Key: CS = caustic soda; HA = hydrochloric acid; NA = nitric acid; SA = sulphuric acid

| | NORTH AMERICA | | | | | SOUTH AMERICA | | | |
| | Canada | USA | | | | Argentina | | Chile | Peru |
| | SA | SA[1] | HA | NA[1] | CS | SA | CS | SA | SA |
|------|------|-------|-----|------|--------|-----|-----|------|------|
| 1899 | ... | 1,068 | ... | ... | 151[3] | ... | ... | ... | ... |
| 1904 | ... | 1,289 | ... | ... | 79[3] | ... | ... | ... | ... |
| 1909 | ... | 2,045 | ... | ... | 120[3] | ... | ... | ... | ... |
| 1914 | ... | 2,809 | ... | ... | 265[3] | ... | ... | ... | ... |
| 1919 | 41 | 3,830 | ... | ... | 284 | ... | ... | ... | ... |
| 1920 | 62 | ... | ... | ... | ... | ... | ... | ... | ... |
| 1921 | 40 | 3,015 | ... | ... | 217 | ... | ... | ... | ... |
| 1922 | 52 | ... | ... | ... | ... | ... | ... | ... | ... |
| 1923 | 74 | 4,521 | ... | ... | 396 | ... | ... | ... | ... |
| 1924 | 61 | ... | ... | ... | ... | ... | ... | ... | ... |
| 1925 | 70 | 4,831 | ... | ... | 451 | ... | ... | ... | ... |
| 1926 | 91 | ... | ... | ... | ... | ... | ... | ... | ... |
| 1927 | 83 | 5,059 | ... | ... | 520 | ... | ... | ... | ... |
| 1928 | 81 | ... | ... | ... | ... | ... | ... | ... | ... |
| 1929 | 94 | 5,857 | 74 | 130 | 691 | ... | ... | ... | ... |
| 1930 | 91 | ... | ... | ... | ... | ... | ... | ... | ... |
| 1931 | 101 | 4,198 | 50 | 106 | 598 | ... | ... | ... | ... |
| 1932 | 116 | ... | ... | ... | ... | ... | ... | ... | ... |
| 1933 | 125 | ... | 57 | 87 | 623 | ... | ... | ... | ... |
| 1934 | 174 | ... | ... | ... | ... | ... | ... | ... | ... |
| 1935 | 190 | 4,436 | 79 | 87 | 689 | ... | ... | ... | ... |
| 1936 | 204 | ... | ... | ... | ... | ... | ... | ... | ... |
| 1937 | 239 | 5,469 | 110 | 160 | 879 | ... | ... | ... | ... |
| 1938 | 227 | 3,799 | ... | ... | ... | ... | ... | ... | ... |
| 1939 | 216 | 4,350 | 112 | 152 | 948 | 41 | 15 | 3 | ... |
| 1940 | 273 | 5,208[1] | ... | ... | ...[8] | ... | ... | 2 | ... |
| 1941 | 304 | 6,142 | 207 | 315 | 1,297 | 53 | 20 | 5 | ... |
| 1942 | 421 | 7,034 | 269 | 388 | 1,428 | 57 | 23 | 4 | 1.7 |
| 1943 | 474 | 7,658 | 311 | 438 | 1,614 | 61 | 22 | 4 | 5.9 |
| 1944 | 580 | 8,384 | 346 | 428 | 1,698 | 71 | 23 | 4 | 5.9 |

D18    **NORTH AMERICA: Output of Sulphuric Acid, Hydrochloric Acid, Nitric Acid, and Caustic Soda** (in thousands of metric tons)

| | Canada | | | | Cuba | Mexico | | USA | | | |
|---|---|---|---|---|---|---|---|---|---|---|---|
| | SA | HA | NA | CS | SA | SA | CS | SA[1] | HA | NA[1] | CS |
| 1945 | 603 | ... | ... | ... | ... | ... | ... | 8,638 | 370 | 406 | 1,691 |
| 1946 | 538 | ... | ... | ... | ... | ... | ... | 8,349 | 310 | 521 | 1,699 |
| 1947 | 607 | ... | ... | ... | ... | ... | ... | 9,779 | 402 | 1,079 | 1,908 |
| 1948 | 616 | ... | ... | ... | ... | ... | ... | 10,393 | 416 | 1,028 | 2,156 |
| 1949 | 642 | ... | ... | 101 | ... | ... | ... | 10,371 | 448 | 1,025 | 2,017 |
| 1950 | 686 | ... | ... | 138 | 25 | 43 | ... | 11,820 | 561 | 1,212 | 2,278 |
| 1951 | 745 | ... | ... | 150 | 27 | 57 | ... | 12,131 | 631 | 1,372 | 2,818 |
| 1952 | 741 | ... | ... | 172 | 24 | 92 | 9.1 | 12,075 | 620 | 1,487 | 2,750 |
| 1953 | 746 | ... | ... | 174 | 26 | 103 | 13 | 12,703[1] | 702 | 1,602[1] | 2,960 |
| 1954 | 838 | 6.1 | 211 | 181 | 28 | 110 | 18 | 13,042 | 693 | 2,077 | 3,093 |
| 1955 | 862 | 6.2 | 215 | 205 | 28 | 125 | 23 | 14,746 | 760 | 2,352 | 3,552 |
| 1956 | 954 | 7.3 | 209 | 232 | 32 | 157 | 26 | 14,964 | 822 | 2,352 | 3,835 |
| 1957 | 1,170 | 7.8 | 182 | 239 | 32 | 186 | 34 | 14,932 | 860 | 2,580 | 3,934 |
| 1958 | 1,439 | 16 | 208 | 285 | ... | 200 | 40 | 14,470 | 749 | 2,453 | 3,623 |
| 1959 | 1,578 | 19 | 255 | 309 | ... | 243 | 52 | 15,974 | 867 | 2,789 | 4,308 |
| 1960 | 1,518 | 19 | 243 | 338 | 44 | 269 | 66 | 16,223 | 880 | 3,007 | 4,510 |
| 1961 | 1,464 | 17 | 248 | 376 | 58 | 276 | 65 | 16,191 | 826 | 3,066 | 4,458 |
| 1962 | 1,559 | 22 | 289 | 392 | 136 | 339 | 73 | 17,873 | 954 | 3,329 | 4,976 |
| 1963 | 1,625 | 24 | 310 | 440 | 135 | 387 | 88 | 18,993 | 956 | 3,849 | 5,275 |
| 1964 | 1,761 | 26 | 353 | 498 | 189 | 433 | 80 | 20,796 | 1,122 | 4,293 | 5,796 |
| 1965 | 1,964 | 31 | 344 | 583 | 192 | 508 | 102 | 22,540 | 1,243 | 4,444 | 6,197 |
| 1966 | 2,268 | 41 | 392 | 650 | 226 | 579 | 110 | 25,750 | 1,380 | 5,002 | 6,891 |
| 1967 | 2,495 | 42 | 384 | 731 | 265 | 640 | 118 | 26,141 | 1,479 | 5,863 | 7,618 |
| 1968 | 2,587 | 47 | 358 | 766 | 316 | 780 | 140 | 25,895 | 1,585 | 5,772[2] | 8,045 |
| | | | | | | | | | | 6,343 | |
| 1969 | 2,175 | 60 | 475 | 856 | 319 | 1,067 | 154 | 26,795 | 1,733 | 6,553 | 8,997 |
| 1970 | 2,475 | 64 | 503 | 860 | 315 | 1,235 | 166 | 26,784 | 1,827 | 6,897 | 9,200 |
| 1971 | 2,661 | 70 | 543 | 869 | 361 | 1,433 | 171 | 26,340 | 1,905 | 6,929 | 8,769 |
| 1972 | 2,749 | 75 | 610 | 921 | 392 | 1,518 | 174 | 28,290 | 2,089 | 7,241 | 9,269 |
| 1973 | 2,980 | 81 | 715 | 1,029 | 377 | 1,966 | 188 | 28,613 | 2,282 | 7,658 | 9,694 |
| 1974 | 2,821 | 91 | 436 | 1,030 | 376 | 2,091 | 222 | 29,982 | 2,181 | 7,425 | 10,341 |
| 1975 | 2,723 | 88 | 365 | 845 | 410 | 2,047 | 209 | 28,290 | 1,790 | 6,418 | 8,410 |
| 1976 | 2,842 | 109 | ... | 1,000 | 392 | 2,178 | 228 | 30,460 | 2,203 | 6,813 | 9,202 |
| 1977 | 3,140 | 136 | ... | 1,014 | 375 | 2,295 | 263 | 34,771 | 2,420 | 7,244 | 9,977 |
| 1978 | 3,261 | 155 | ... | 1,036 | 347 | 2,372 | 247 | 37,472 | 2,533 | 7,196 | 10,258 |
| 1979 | 3,666 | 154 | ... | 1,138 | 296 | 2,041 | 231 | 39,186 | 2,803 | 8,087 | 11,572 |
| 1980 | 4,295 | 177 | 713 | 1,459 | 401 | 2,359 | 224 | 40,050 | 2,619 | 8,373 | 10,544 |
| 1981 | 4,117 | 186 | 861 | 1,458 | 413 | 2,619 | 296 | 36,953 | 2,335 | 8,247 | 9,633 |
| 1982 | 3,085 | 143 | 977 | 1,367 | 332 | 2,732 | 365 | 30,143 | 2,222 | 6,703 | 8,512 |
| 1983 | 3,679 | 170 | 855 | 1,528 | 356 | 2,996 | 363 | 33,975 | 2,238 | 6,320 | 9,106 |
| 1984 | 4,043 | 161 | 1,101 | 1,575 | 336 | 3,196 | 350 | 37,914 | 2,442 | 7,073 | 9,899 |
| 1985 | 3,890 | 158 | 1,128 | 1,589 | 373 | 2,222 | 363 | 35,964 | 2,546 | 6,924 | 9,805 |
| 1986 | 3,536 | 153 | 1,024 | 1,697 | 395 | 2,149 | 382 | 32,650 | 2,170 | 6,110 | 9,643 |
| 1987 | 3,437 | 164 | 1,000 | 1,770 | 370 | ... | 331 | 35,612 | 2,718 | 6,554 | 10,716 |
| 1988 | 3,805 | 179 | 907 | 1,720 | 391 | ... | 326 | 38,229 | 2,395 | 7,249 | 9,769 |

**D18 SOUTH AMERICA: OUTPUT OF SULPHURIC ACID, HYDROCHLORIC ACID, NITRIC ACID, AND CAUSTIC SODA** (in thousands of metric tons)

| | Argentina | | Brazil | | Chile[7] | Colombia | Peru | | Venezuela |
|---|---|---|---|---|---|---|---|---|---|
| | SA[4] | CS | SA[6] | CS[5] | SA | SA | SA[9] | NA | SA |
| 1945 | 71 | 23 | ... | ... | 5 | ... | 5.9 | ... | ... |
| 1946 | 68 | 23 | ... | ... | 5 | ... | 2.6 | ... | ... |
| 1947 | 81 | 28 | ... | ... | 5 | ... | 2.8 | ... | ... |
| 1948 | 75 | 30 | ... | ... | 5 | ... | 6.1 | ... | ... |
| 1949 | 77 | 26 | ... | ... | 4 | ... | 3.6 | ... | ... |
| 1950 | 77 | 28 | 122 | ... | 9 | ... | 8.4 | ... | ... |
| 1951 | 64 | 31 | 108 | ... | 12 | ... | 10 | ... | ... |
| 1952 | 60 | 31 | 150 | ... | 16 | ... | 10 | ... | ... |
| 1953 | 56 | 30 | 97 | 20 | 13 | 8 | 10 | ... | ... |
| 1954 | 57 | 35 | ... | 15 | 19 | ... | 12 | ... | ... |
| 1955 | 68 | 37 | 88 | 31 | 18 | ... | 12 | ... | ... |
| 1956 | 78 | 37 | 134 | 50 | 45 | 2 | 10 | ... | ... |
| 1957 | 72 | 40 | 122 | 50 | 45 | 12 | 13 | ... | ... |
| 1958 | 64 | 51 | 175 | 60[5] | 45 | 9 | 16 | ... | ... |
| 1959 | 63 | 54 | 202 | 63 | 60 | 15 | 18 | ... | 7 |
| 1960 | 60[4] 132 | 47 | 215 | 68 | 84 | 19 | 30 | 14 | 7 |
| 1961 | 127 | 54 | 231 | 77 | 117 | 23 | 29 | 23 | 12 |
| 1962 | 118 | 55 | 259 | 84 | 129 | 25 | 29 | 28 | 15 |
| 1963 | 109 | 58 | 288 | 85 | 136 | 18 | 33 | 28 | 36 |
| 1964 | 151 | 61 | 300 | 89 | 178 | 16 | 37 | 35 | 51 |
| 1965 | 162 | 76 | 252 | 89 | 193 | 24 | 38 | 36 | 58 |
| 1966 | 149 | 75 | 300 | 99 | 180 | 34 | 39 | 32 | 52 |
| 1967 | 154 | 69 | 365 | 112 | 220 | 18 | 37 | 35 | 49 |
| 1968 | 163 | 79 | 367 | 138 | 249 | 47 | 46 | 36 | 99 |
| 1969 | 184 | 88 | 421 | 115 | 327 | 41 | 56 | 40 | 80 |
| 1970 | 180 | 95 | ... | 137 | 373 | 41 | 60 | 32 | 68 |
| 1971 | 188 | 113 | ... | 136 | 425 | ... | 19 | ... | 30 |
| 1972 | 242 | 123 | ... | 197 | 530[2] | 48 | 61 | ... | 79 |
| 1973 | 233 | 120 | 835 | 210 | 195 | 52 | 67 | ... | 68 |
| 1974 | 243 | 117 | 925[2] | 214 | 155 | 51 | 54 | ... | 93 |
| 1975 | 225 | 113 | ... | 241 | 110 | 47 | 54 | ... | 117 |
| 1976 | 234 | 110 | 1,439 | 259 | 130 | 49 | 57 | ... | 82 |
| 1977 | 251 | 121 | 1,556 | 317 | 132 | 42 | 63 | ... | 42 |
| 1978 | 244 | 101 | 1,596 | 577 | 127 | 45 | 58 | ... | 92 |
| 1979 | 279 | 110 | 1,910 | 645 | 100 | 54 | 68 | ... | 128 |
| 1980 | 250 | 104 | 2,408 | 691 | ... | 59 | 62 | ... | 114 |
| 1981 | 232 | 105 | 2,516 | 759 | ... | 49 | 184 | ... | 79 |
| 1982 | 250 | 115 | 2,681 | 760 | ... | 40 | 227 | ... | 113 |
| 1983 | 262 | 128 | 2,983 | 746 | ... | 53 | 210 | ... | 139 |
| 1984 | 254 | 125 | 3,484 | 857 | ... | ... | 205 | ... | 158 |
| 1985 | 235 | 121 | 3,660 | 886 | ... | 62 | 213 | ... | 156 |
| 1986 | 251 | 129 | 3,820 | 988 | ... | 68 | 209 | ... | 164 |
| 1987 | 253 | 119 | 4,004 | 954 | ... | 68 | 212 | ... | 197 |
| 1988 | 258 | 117 | 4,049 | 1,007 | ... | 75 | 174 | ... | 172 |

**D18    Output of Sulphuric Acid, Hydrochloric Acid, Nitric Acid and Caustic Soda** (in thousands of metric tons)

NOTES

1.   SOURCES: The national publications listed on p. xiv–xvi, and League of Nations and UN, *Statistical Yearbooks.*
2.   So far as possible, output is given in terms of 100% $H_2SO_4$, HCl, $HNO_3$, and NaOH.

FOOTNOTES

[1] Government plants are excluded to 1954. Coverage of sulphuric acid is not complete to 1939.
[2] The reason for this break is not given in the source.
[3] Amount for sale.
[4] Data to 1960 (1st line) are based on sample surveys.
[5] Data to 1958 are in terms of less than 100% NaOH.
[6] Statistics represent about 90% of total output.
[7] Strength not reported.
[8] Production in the soap, paper, and pulp industries is excluded to 1939.
[9] Excluding weak acid.

**D19    NORTH AMERICA: TIMBER INDUSTRY INDICATORS** (output in units shown)

Key:     a = million board feet; b = thousand metric tons; c = million cubic metres; d = thousand cubic metres

| | Canada[1] | | | USA | | | |
|---|---|---|---|---|---|---|---|
| | Lumber | Wood Pulp | Paper[2] | Industrial Roundwood | Lumber | Wood Pulp | Paper[2] |
| | a | b | b | c | a | b | b |
| 1799 | ... | ... | ... | ... | | ... | ... |
| 1809 | ... | ... | ... | ... | | ... | 3 |
| 1819 | ... | ... | ... | ... | | ... | 11 |
| 1829 | ... | ... | ... | ... | | ... | ... |
| 1839 | ... | ... | ... | ... | | ... | 34 |
| 1849 | ... | ... | ... | ... | | ... | 71 |
| 1859 | ... | ... | ... | ... | | ... | 115 |
| 1869 | ... | ... | ... | ... | 12,756 | 1 | 350 |
| 1879 | ... | ... | ... | ... | 18,125 | 21 | 410 |
| 1889 | ... | ... | ... | ... | 27,039 | 278 | 848 |
| 1899 | ... | ... | ... | ... | 35,078 | 1,070 | 1,967 |
| 1900 | ... | ... | ... | 206 | ... | ... | ... |
| 1901 | ... | ... | ... | 215 | ... | ... | ... |
| 1902 | ... | ... | ... | 223 | ... | ... | ... |
| 1903 | ... | ... | ... | 233 | ... | ... | ... |
| 1904 | ... | ... | ... | 240 | 34,127 | 1,744 | 2,819 |
| 1905 | ... | ... | ... | 244 | 30,503 | ... | ... |
| 1906 | ... | ... | ... | 261 | 37,551 | ... | ... |
| 1907 | ... | ... | ... | 271 | 40,256 | 2,312 | ... |
| 1908 | 3,348 | 329 | ... | 247 | 33,224 | 1,922 | ... |
| 1909 | 3,815 | 404 | ... | 263 | 44,510 | 2,264 | 3,739 |
| 1910 | 4,452 | 431 | ... | 263 | 40,018 | 2,299 | ... |
| 1911 | 4,918 | 451 | ... | 255 | 37,003 | 2,437 | ... |
| 1912 | 4,390 | 620 | ... | 264 | 39,158 | ... | ... |
| 1913 | 3,817 | 776 | ... | 260 | 38,387 | ... | ... |
| 1914 | 3,946 | 848 | ... | 243 | 37,348 | 2,624 | 4,675 |
| 1915 | 3,843 | 975 | ... | 227 | 31,242 | ... | ... |
| 1916 | 3,491 | 1,176 | ... | 242 | 34,791 | 3,116 | ... |
| 1917 | 4,152 | 1,328 | 777 | 225 | 33,193 | 3,184 | 5,265 |
| 1918 | 3,887 | 1,412 | 878 | 207 | 29,362 | 3,006 | 5,387 |
| 1919 | 3,820 | 1,557 | 989 | 219 | 34,552 | 3,191 | 5,412 |

**D19    NORTH AMERICA: Timber Industry Indicators** (output in units shown)

| | Canada[1] | | | Mexico | Newfoundland | USA | | | |
|---|---|---|---|---|---|---|---|---|---|
| | Lumber | Wood pulp | Paper[2] | Sawn wood | Wood pulp | Industrial Roundwood | Lumber | Wood pulp | Paper[2] |
| | a | b | b | e | b | c | a | b | b |
| 1920 | 4,299 | 1,778 | 1,102 | ... | ... | 220 | 29,878 | 3,467 | 6,518 |
| 1921 | 2,869 | 1,405 | 924 | ... | ... | 186 | 26,961 | 2,609 | 4,838 |
| 1922 | 3,139 | 1,950 | 1,240 | ... | ... | 215 | 31,569 | 3,195 | 6,237 |
| 1923 | 3,728 | 2,246 | 1,442 | ... | 125 | 242 | 37,166 | 3,437 | 7,140 |
| 1924 | 3,879 | 2,236 | 1,559 | ... | 138 | 234 | 35,931 | 3,377 | 7,194 |
| 1925 | 3,889 | 2,516 | 1,710 | ... | 145 | 236 | 38,339 | 3,594 | 8,166 |
| 1926 | 4,185 | 2,930 | 2,056 | ... | 188 | 233 | 36,936 | 3,987 | 8,885 |
| 1927 | 4,098 | 2,975 | 2,240 | ... | 214 | 220 | 34,532 | 3,913 | 9,074 |
| 1928 | 4,337 | 3,273 | 2,585 | ... | 210 | 217 | 34,142 | 4,092 | 9,437 |
| 1929 | 4,742 | 3,648 | 2,900 | ... | 210 | 228 | 36,886 | 4,412 | 10,106 |
| 1930 | 3,989 | 3,283 | 2,655 | ... | 261 | 179 | 26,051 | 4,200 | 9,225 |
| 1931 | 2,498 | 2,874 | 2,369 | ... | 255 | 130 | 16,523 | 4,000 | 8,511 |
| 1932 | 1,810 | 2,416 | 2,078 | ... | 239 | 96 | 10,151 | 3,411 | 7,256 |
| 1933 | 1,958 | 2,703 | 2,194 | ... | 241 | 114 | 13,961 | 3,879 | 8,337 |
| 1934 | 2,578 | 3,299 | 2,785 | ... | 278 | 123 | 15,494 | 4,024 | 8,334 |
| 1935 | 2,973 | 3,509 | 2,976 | ... | 296 | 144 | 19,539 | 4,469 | 9,506 |
| 1936 | 3,412 | 4,069 | 3,454 | ... | 287 | 170 | 24,355 | 5,166 | 10,864 |
| 1937 | 4,006 | 4,665 | 3,942 | ... | 320 | 180 | 25,997 | 5,963 | 11,646 |
| 1938 | 3,768 | 3,328 | 2,947 | ... | 242 | 158 | 21,646 | 5,383 | 10,325 |
| 1939 | 3,977 | 3,779 | 3,267 | ... | ... | 180 | 25,148 | 6,344 | 12,256 |
| 1940 | 4,629 | 4,800 | 3,918 | ... | 357 | 198 | 28,934 | 8,128 | 13,140 |
| 1941 | 4,941 | 5,190 | 4,105 | ... | 374 | 228 | 33,613 | 9,412 | 16,113 |
| 1942 | 4,935 | 5,086 | 3,839 | ... | 348 | 229 | 36,332 | 9,782 | 15,498 |
| 1943 | 4,364 | 4,784 | 3,598 | ... | 288 | 214 | 34,289 | 8,782 | 15,455 |
| 1944 | 4,512 | 4,782 | 3,669 | ... | 325 | 211 | 32,938 | 9,170 | 15,588 |
| 1945 | 4,514 | 5,081 | 3,955 | ... | 356 | 187 | 28,122 | 9,223 | 15,759 |
| 1946 | 5,083 | 6,001 | 4,851 | ... | 366 | 218 | 34,112 | 9,623 | 17,489 |
| 1947 | 5,878 | 6,581 | 5,239 | ... | 399 | 229 | 35,404 | 10,837 | 19,143 |
| 1948 | 5,909 [1] | 6,963 [1] | 5,501 [1] | ... | 424 | 237 | 37,000 | 11,677 | 19,865 |
| 1949 | 5,915 | 7,124 | 5,933 | ... | ... | 208 | 32,178 | 11,074 | 18,429 |
| 1950 | 6,554 | 7,687 | 6,180 | ... | ... | 241 | 38,007 | 13,471 | 22,113 |
| 1951 | 6,949 | 8,450 | 6,554 | ... | ... | 247 | 37,204 | 14,990 | 23,629 |
| 1952 | 6,808 | 8,136 | 6,534 | 926 | ... | 248 | 37,462 | 14,944 | 22,152 |
| 1953 | 7,306 | 8,235 | 6,692 | 887 | ... | 249 | 36,742 | 15,909 | 24,136 |
| 1954 | 7,244 | 8,775 | 6,940 | 890 | ... | 248 | 36,356 | 16,603 | 24,381 |
| 1955 | 7,920 | 9,209 | 7,257 | 923 | ... | 261 | 37,380 | 18,812 | 27,377 |
| 1956 | 7,740 | 9,738 | 7,681 | 936 | ... | 272 | 38,199 | 20,008 | 28,523 |
| 1957 | 7,100 | 9,458 | 7,530 | 815 | ... | 244 | 32,901 | 19,777 | 27,870 |
| 1958 | 7,179 | 9,197 | 7,331 | ... | ... | 242 | 33,385 | 19,773 | 27,962 |
| 1959 | 7,591 [4] | 9,827 | 7,756 [2] | 896 | ... | 266 | 37,166 | 22,120 | 30,858 |
| | 18 | | 7,554 | | | | | | |

**D19**     **NORTH AMERICA: Timber Industry Indicators** (output in units shown)

| | Canada[1] | | | Mexico | USA | | | |
|---|---|---|---|---|---|---|---|---|
| | Sawn wood[6] | Wood pulp | Paper[2] | Sawn wood | Industrial Roundwood | Lumber | Wood pulp | Paper[2] |
| | c | b | b | d | c | a | b | b |
| 1960 | 19 | 10,398 | 7,934 | 926 | 253 | 32,926[7] | 22,966 | 31,247 |
| 1961 | 20 | 10,574 | 7,975 | 801 | 248 | 32,019 | 24,061 | 32,431 |
| 1962 | 21 | 11,007 | 8,055 | 879 | 256 | 33,178 | 25,318 | 34,057 |
| 1963 | 23 | 11,316 | 8,218 | 1,043 | 271 | 34,706 | 27,325 | 35,589 |
| 1964 | 23 | 12,467 | 8,961 | 1,268 | 288 | 36,559 | 29,406 | 37,832 |
| 1965 | 26 | 12,861 | 9,758 | 1,259 | 298 | 36,762 | 30,838 | 39,989 |
| 1966 | 25 | 14,517 | 10,563 | 1,384 | 301 | 36,584 | 33,206 | 42,740 |
| 1967 | 25 | 14,435 | 10,316 | 1,466 | 295 | 34,741 | 33,273 | 42,571 |
| 1968 | 27 | 15,261 | 10,398 | 1,479 | 312 | 36,475 | 37,097 | 46,489 |
| 1969 | 27 | 16,864 | 11,354 | 1,422 | 311 | 35,824 | 38,839 | 49,158 |
| 1970 | 27 | 16,609 | 11,251 | 1,572 | 315 | 34,668 | 39,504 | 48,549 |
| 1971 | 31 | 16,508 | 11,161 | 1,534 | 320 | 36,988 | 39,855 | 49,986 |
| 1972 | 33 | 17,455 | 12,038 | 1,803 | 324 | 37,745 | 42,427 | 53,796 |
| 1973 | 36 | 18,561 | 12,578 | 1,938 | 333 | 38,595 | 41,221 | 55,973 |
| 1974 | 32 | 19,656 | 13,218 | 2,055 | 320 | 34,608 | 41,379 | 54,340 |
| 1975 | 27 | 14,831 | 10,067 | 1,986 | 291 | 32,619 | 36,808 | 47,537 |
| 1976 | 37 | 17,688 | 11,791 | 2,147 | 325 | 36,967 | 40,307 | 51,757 |
| 1977 | 42 | 17,773 | 12,152 | 2,259 | 352 | 39,362 | 41,618 | 53,347 |
| 1978 | 45 | 19,216 | 13,286 | 2,299 | 394 | 40,498 | 43,145 | 55,154 |
| 1979 | 45 | 19,516 | 13,486 | 2,109 | 422 | 40,569 | 45,318 | 57,410 |
| 1980 | 44 | 19,945 | 13,390 | 1,991 | 418 | 35,354 | 46,187 | 56,839 |
| 1981 | 40 | 19,578 | 13,835 | 1,928 | 419 | 31,672 | 47,200 | 57,667 |
| 1982 | 37 | 17,007 | 12,408 | 1,669 | 397 | 30,010 | 44,786 | 54,899 |
| 1983 | 42 | 19,221 | 13,353 | 1,827 | 438 | 34,572 | 47,660 | 58,804 |
| 1984 | 50 | 20,451 | 14,222 | 1,975 | 475 | 37,065 | 50,398 | 62,366 |
| 1985 | 55 | 20,250 | 14,448 | 2,205 | 476 | 36,445 | 49,061 | 60,959 |
| 1986 | 55 | 21,512 | 15,259 | 2,143 | 511 | 41,999 | 51,927 | 64,444 |
| 1987 | 62 | 22,645 | 16,044 | 2,410 | 530 | 44,886 | 54,058 | 67,532 |
| 1988 | 61 | 23,282 | 16,639 | … | 533 | 44,730 | 55,530 | 69,587 |

**D19    SOUTH AMERICA: TIMBER INDUSTRY INDICATORS** (output in units shown)

| | Brazil | Chile | Colombia | | Brazil | Chile | Colombia |
|---|---|---|---|---|---|---|---|
| | Sawn wood | Sawn wood | Sawn wood | | Sawn wood | Sawn wood | Sawn wood |
| 1937 | 3,500 | 467 | ... | 1970 | 8,035 | 1,075 | 1,100 |
| 1946 | ... | 853 | ... | 1971 | 8,100 | 1,093 | 1,180 |
| 1947 | 4,011 | 755 | ... | 1972 | 7,550 | 1,134 | 1,258 |
| 1948 | 3,907 | 669 | ... | 1973 | 7,109 | 1,059 | 1,261 |
| 1949 | 4,225 | 536 | ... | 1974 | 7,642 | 1,478 | 934 |
| 1950 | 2,970 | 425 | ... | 1975 | 10,128 | 1,320 | 954 |
| 1951 | 4,227 | 520 | ... | 1976 | 11,243 | 1,223 | ... |
| 1952 | 4,021 | 537 | ... | 1977 | 12,643 | 1,267 | ... |
| 1953 | 4,025 | 509 | 730 | 1978 | 13,337 | 1,478 | ... |
| 1954 | 4,076 | 698 | ... | 1979 | 14,070 | 2,199 | 983 |
| 1955 | 4,426 | 584 | ... | 1980 | 14,881 | 2,186 | 970 |
| 1956 | 4,387 [3] | 741 | ... | 1981 | 15,852 | 1,735 | 1,006 |
|      | 7,254 | | | 1982 | 16,470 | 1,176 | 721 |
| 1957 | 6,226 | 786 | ... | 1983 | 17,199 | 1,610 | ... |
| 1958 | 6,534 | ... | ... | 1984 | 17,781 | 2,001 | ... |
| 1959 | 6,092 | 721 | ... | 1985 | 17,781 | 2,057 | ... |
| 1960 | 5,700 | 876 | ... | 1986 | 18,063 | 2,287 | ... |
| 1961 | 6,100 | 746 | 990 | 1987 | ... | 2,680 | ... |
| 1962 | 6,300 | 1,031 | ... | 1988 | 18,179 | 2,170 | ... |
| 1963 | 5,363 | 785 | ... | | | | |
| 1964 | 5,531 | 1,015 | 910 | | | | |
| 1965 | 5,661 | 1,019 | 910 | | | | |
| 1966 | 6,072 | 1,063 | 920 | | | | |
| 1967 | 6,618 | 851 | 930 | | | | |
| 1968 | 6,965 | 1,055 | 950 | | | | |
| 1969 | 7,467 | 1,013 | 1,052 | | | | |

NOTES

1.   SOURCES: The national publications listed on p. xiv–xvi and League of Nations and UN, *Statistical Yearbooks.*
2.   The board foot is a measure of lumber 1 foot long × 1 foot deep × 1 inch wide

FOOTNOTES

[1] Including Newfoundland from 1949.
[2] All paper and products. Data for Canada from 1959 (2nd line) are of paper and paperboard.
[3] A wider definition was employed subsequently.
[4] Sawn wood and sleepers subsequently.
[5] Subsequently excluding some paper products.
[6] Including sleepers.
[7] Including Alaska and Hawaii subsequently.

**D20**  **NORTH AMERICA: OUTPUT AND ASSEMBLY OF MOTOR VEHICLES** (in thousands)

Key:  PC = passenger cars; CV = commercial vehicles

| | Canada | | USA[1] | |
| --- | --- | --- | --- | --- |
| | PC | CV | PC | CV |
| 1900 | ... | ... | 4.1 | ... |
| 1901 | ... | ... | 7.0 | ... |
| 1902 | ... | ... | 9.0 | ... |
| 1903 | ... | ... | 11 | ... |
| 1904 | ... | ... | 22 | 0.7 |
| 1905 | ... | ... | 24 | 0.7 |
| 1906 | ... | ... | 33 | 0.8 |
| 1907 | ... | ... | 43 | 1.0 |
| 1908 | ... | ... | 64 | 1.5 |
| 1909 | ... | ... | 124 | 3.3 |
| 1910 | ... | ... | 181 | 6.0 |
| 1911 | ... | ... | 199 | 11 |
| 1912 | ... | ... | 356 | 22 |
| 1913 | ... | ... | 461 | 24 |
| 1914 | ... | ... | 548 | 25 |
| 1915 | ... | ... | 896 | 74 |
| 1916 | ... | ... | 1,526 | 92 |
| 1917 | ... | ... | 1,746 | 128 |
| 1918 | 70 | 7.3 | 943 | 227 |
| 1919 | 68 | 7.9 | 1,652 | 225 |
| 1920 | 79 | 10 | 1,906 | 322 |
| 1921 | 57 | 5.1 | 1,468 | 148 |
| 1922 | 79 | 8.2 | 2,274 | 270 |
| 1923 | 106 | 19 | 3,625 | 409 |
| 1924 | 98 | 18 | 3,186 | 417 |
| 1925 | 120 | 26 | 3,735 | 531 |
| 1926 | 154 | 30 | 3,692 | 609 |
| 1927 | 137 | 30 | 2,937 | 465 |
| 1928 | 176 | 18 | 3,775 | 583 |
| 1929 | 189 | 50 | 4,455 | 882 |
| 1930 | 116 | 17 | 2,787 | 575 |
| 1931 | 65 | 17 | 1,948 | 432 |
| 1932 | 48 | 10 | 1,104 | 228 |
| 1933 | 48 | 12 | 1,561 | 329 |
| 1934 | 80 | 24 | 2,161 | 576 |
| 1935 | 112 | 37 | 3,274 | 697 |
| 1936 | 108 | 34 | 3,679 | 782 |
| 1937 | 133 | 54 | 3,929 | 891 |
| 1938 | 105 | 42 | 2,020 | 489 |
| 1939 | 90 | 47 | 2,889 | 700 |
| 1940 | 103 | 113 | 3,717 | 755 |
| 1941 | 91 | 174 | 3,780 | 1,061 |
| 1942 | 12 | 216 | 223 | 819 |
| 1943 | — | 178 | 0.1 | 700 |
| 1944 | — | 158 | 0.6 | 737 |
| 1945 | 1.9 | 131 | 70 | 656 |
| 1946 | 92 | 80 | 2,149 | 941 |
| 1947 | 167 | 91 | 3,558 | 1,239 |
| 1948 | 167 | 97 | 3,909 | 1,376 |
| 1949 | 194 | 99 | 5,119 | 1,134 |

**D20     NORTH AMERICA: Output and Assembly of Motor Vehicles** (in thousands)

| | Canada | | Mexico | | USA[1] | |
|---|---|---|---|---|---|---|
| | PC | CV | PC | CV | PC | CV |
| 1950 | 284 | 106 | ... | ... | 6,666 | 1,337 |
| 1951 | 283 | 133 | ... | ... | 5,338 | 1,427 |
| 1952 | 283 | 150 | 21 | 27 | 4,321 | 1,218 |
| 1953 | 360 | 121 | 14 | 22 | 6,117 | 1,206 |
| 1954 | 287 | 70 | 13 | 20 | 5,559 | 1,042 |
| 1955 | 375 | 79 | 12 | 20 | 7,920 | 1,249 |
| 1956 | 374 | 94 | 13 | 26 | 5,816 | 1,104 |
| 1957 | 340 | 73 | 18 | 23 | 6,113 | 1,107 |
| 1958 | 297 | 59 | 20 | 19 | 4,258 | 877 |
| 1959 | 301 | 67 | 27 | 21 | 5,591 | 1,137 |
| 1960 | 326 | 72 | 25 | 20 | 6,675 | 1,194 |
| 1961 | 324 | 63 | 33 | 20 | 5,543 | 1,134 |
| 1962 | 425 | 80 | 41 | 22 | 6,933 | 1,240 |
| 1963 | 532 | 99 | 50 | 26 | 7,638 | 1,463 |
| 1964 | 560 | 111 | 66 | 33 | 7,752 | 1,540 |
| 1965 | 707 | 140 | 67 | 28 | 9,306 | 1,752 |
| 1966 | 684 | 188 | 85 | 33 | 8,598 | 1,731 |
| 1967 | 712 | 211 | 86 | 39 | 7,437 | 1,539 |
| 1968 | 886 | 261 | 103 | 44 | 8,822 | 1,896 |
| 1969 | 1,033 | 300 | 114 | 51 | 8,224 | 1,919 |
| 1970 | 923 | 236 | 137 | 53 | 6,547 | 1,692 |
| 1971 | 1,097 | 280 | 160 | 54 | 8,585 | 2,053 |
| 1972 | 1,155 | 320 | 170 | 63 | 8,824 | 2,447 |
| 1973 | 1,228 | 347 | 208 | 74 | 9,658 | 2,980 |
| 1974 | 1,166 | 359 | 260 | 90 | 7,331 | 2,727 |
| 1975 | 1,045 | 379 | 262 | 98 | 6,713 | 2,272 |
| 1976 | 1,137 | 503 | 229 | 92 | 8,498 | 2,979 |
| 1977 | 1,163 | 583 | 196 | 84 | 9,201 | 3,441 |
| 1978 | 1,140 | 634 | 249 | 131 | 9,165 | 3,706 |
| 1979 | 961 | 626 | 290 | 148 | 8,419 | 3,037 |
| 1980 | 847 | 528 | 316 | 169 | 6,400 | 1,667 |
| 1981 | 803 | 520 | 369 | 218 | 6,255 | 1,701 |
| 1982 | 808 | 468 | 324 | 152 | 5,049 | 1,906 |
| 1983 | 971 | 554 | 214 | 70 | 6,739 | 2,414 |
| 1984 | 1,022 | 808 | 247 | 100 | 7,621 | 3,075 |
| 1985 | 1,075 | 856 | 285 | 139 | 8,002 | 3,357 |
| 1986 | 1,061 | 785 | 198 | 120 | 7,516 | 3,393 |
| 1987 | 810 | 825 | 278 | 113 | 7,085 | 3,821 |
| 1988 | 1,008 | 1,018 | 345 | 148 | 7,105 | 4,121 |

**D20    SOUTH AMERICA: OUTPUT AND ASSEMBLY OF MOTOR VEHICLES** (in thousands)

| | Argentina[2] | | Brazil | | Chile[3] | | Colombia[3] | | Peru[3] | | Venezuela | |
|---|---|---|---|---|---|---|---|---|---|---|---|---|
| | PC | CV | PC | CV | PC | CV | PC | CV | PC | CV | PC | CV |
| 1949 | — | — | — | — | — | — | — | — | — | — | — | 1.2 |
| 1950 | — | — | — | — | — | — | — | — | — | — | 0.1 | 2.9 |
| 1951 | — | — | — | — | — | — | — | — | — | — | 1.9 | 4.6 |
| 1952 | — | 2.9 | — | — | — | — | — | — | — | — | 3.9 | 4.7 |
| 1953 | — | 4.4 | — | — | — | — | — | — | — | — | 5.9 | 4.5 |
| 1954 | 1.5 | 5.1 | — | — | — | — | — | — | — | — | 7.9 | 6.3 |
| 1955 | 1.6 | 7.5 | — | — | — | — | — | — | — | — | 12 | 6.1 |
| 1956 | 2.3 | 5.5 | — | 6.1 | — | — | — | — | — | — | 9.2 | 4.6 |
| 1957 | 9.8 | 21 | 9.3 | 21 | — | — | — | — | — | — | 8.9 | 5.9 |
| 1958 | 21 | 11 | 17 | 45 | — | — | — | — | — | — | 7.5 | 5.9 |
| 1959 | 21 | 9.6 | 30 | 66 | — | — | — | — | — | — | 8.7 | 6.2 |
| 1960 | 50 | 39 | 57 | 76 | — | — | — | — | — | 0.2 | 6.5 | 3.9 |
| 1961 | 85 | 50 | 73 | 73 | — | — | 0.6 | — | — | 0.1 | 8.8 | 2.9 |
| 1962 | 94 | 35 | 97 | 94 | 5.2 | 1.3 | 2.0 | 0.5 | — | 0.6 | 8.8 | 2.9 |
| 1963 | 80 | 26 | 100 | 74 | 6.6 | 1.3 | 0.7 | 0.8 | — | 0.6 | 17 | 5.7 |
| 1964 | 119 | 47 | 111 | 73 | 6.6 | 1.2 | 0.9 | 1.0 | — | 1.0 | 30 | 11 |
| 1965 | 141 | 56 | 113 | 72 | 6.7 | 1.9 | 0.4 | 1.1 | 1.7 | 1.1 | 41 | 15 |
| 1966 | 137 | 42 | 135 | 90 | 5.1 | 2.0 | 0.7 | 0.6 | 7.7 | 5.3 | 45 | 13 |
| 1967 | 134 | 41₆ 23 | 141 | 85 | 10 | 3.2 | 1.5 | 1.1 | 12 | 5.7 | 42 | 11 |
| 1968 | 132 | 3 | 169 | 109 | 14 | 4.4 | 1.2 | 1.5 | 7.7 | 2.4 | 43 | 15 |
| 1969 | 156 | 38 | 243 | 109 | 19 | 3.6 | 4.2 | 3.9 | 13 | 4.3 | 56 | 15 |
| 1970 | 169 | 30 | 255 | 161 | 21 | 3.9 | 7.7 | 9.8 | 10 | 4.2 | 48 | 13 |
| 1971 | 196 | 34 | 363 | 152 | 21 | 2.2 | 14 | 10 | 11 | 5.6 | 56 | ... |
| 1972 | 202 | 36 | 437 | 177 | 23 | 2.9 | 18 | 7.6 | 16 | 7.7 | 64 | 25 |
| 1973 | 220 | 37 | 492 | 251 | 16 | 3 | 21 | 5.2 | 20 | 12 | 66 | 31 |
| 1974 | 214 | 54 | 562 | 337 | 9 | 4.9 | 30 | 6.6 | 19 | 11 | 79 | 39 |
| 1975 | 185 | 42 | 525 | 374 | 5 | 2.5 | 21 | 8.6 | 21 | 13 | 92 | 52 |
| 1976 | 141 | 38 | 527 | 453 | 5 | 2.0 | 25 | 11 | 22 | 12 | 97 | 66 |
| 1977 | 168 | 51 | 482 | 424 | 9 | 2.9 | 28 | 8.9 | 18 | 7.7 | 99 | 64 |
| 1978 | 135 | 33 | 559 | 495 | 17 | 3.5 | 32 | 13 | 7 | 4.2 | 104 | 79 |
| 1979 | 190 | 46 | 568 | 543₆ 219 | 18 | 2.6 | 33 | 16 | 6 | 4.9 | 92 | 66 |
| 1980 | 218 | 44 | 652 | 232 | 25 | 4.1 | 32 | 11 | 11 | 8.0 | 94 | 61 |
| 1981 | 138 | 23 | 605 | 195 | 22 | 5.3 | 25 | 11 | 13 | 8.9 | 82 | 72 |
| 1982 | 110 | 19 | 686 | 187 | 8 | 2.3 | 27 | 9.1 | 16 | 5.8 | 94 | 61 |
| 1983 | 132 | 25 | 746 | 148 | 3 | 1.5 | 21 | 6.8 | 8 | 1.7 | 72 | 40 |
| 1984 | 143 | 23 | 673 | 185 | 4 | 2.6 | 34 | 11 | 6 | 2.7 | 70 | 40 |
| 1985 | 120 | 17 | 754 | 208 | 5 | 3.5 | 33 | 5.9 | 6 | 3.2 | 72 | 44 |
| 1986 | 147 | 20 | 815 | 241 | 2 | 3.0 | 36 | 8.1 | 7 | 5.6 | 85 | 52 |
| 1987 | 158 | 19 | 683 | 237 | 3 | 4.5 | 43 | 8.9 | 5 | 8.4 | 65 | 47 |
| 1988 | 125 | 13 | 780 | 263 | 4 | 6.2 | 47 | 14 | 2 | 4.6 | 60 | 49 |

NOTES

1.  SOURCES: The national publications listed on p. xiv–xvi and League of Nations and UN, *Statistical Yearbooks.*
2.  Except as indicated in footnotes, the statistics relate to the production and assembly of complete vehicles, other than motor cycles.

FOOTNOTES

¹ Factory sales.
² Production and assembly.
³ Assembly only.
⁴ Years ended 30 June.
⁵ Subsequently including part-finished vehicles.
⁶ The reason for this break is not given in the source. It may result from the exclusion of agricultural tractors.

**D21    NORTH AMERICA: OUTPUT OF BEER** (in thousands of hectolitres)

| | Canada[1] | USA[2] |
|---|---|---|
| 1870 | ... | 7,744 |
| 1871 | ... | 9,035 |
| 1872 | ... | 10,208 |
| 1873 | ... | 11,264 |
| 1874 | ... | 11,264 |
| 1875 | ... | 11,147 |
| 1876 | ... | 11,616 |
| 1877 | ... | 11,499 |
| 1878 | ... | 11,968 |
| 1879 | ... | 13,024 |
| 1880 | ... | 15,606 |
| 1881 | ... | 16,779 |
| 1882 | ... | 19,947 |
| 1883 | ... | 20,886 |
| 1884 | ... | 22,294 |
| 1885 | ... | 22,528 |
| 1886 | ... | 24,288 |
| 1887 | ... | 27,104 |
| 1888 | 744 | 28,982 |
| 1889 | 782 | 29,451 |
| 1890 | 821 | 32,384 |
| 1891 | 770 | 35,787 |
| 1892 | 781 | 37,430 |
| 1893 | 832 | 40,598 |
| 1894 | 801 | 39,190 |
| 1895 | 819 | 39,424 |
| 1896 | 813 | 42,123 |
| 1897 | 903 | 40,481 |
| 1898 | 959 | 44,001 |
| 1899 | 1,059 | 43,062 |
| 1900 | 1,141 | 46,347 |
| 1901 | 1,256 | 47,638 |
| 1902 | 1,171 | 52,331 |
| 1903 | 1,242 | 54,795 |
| 1904 | 1,379 | 56,673 |
| 1905 | 1,511 | 58,081 |
| 1906 | ... | 64,182 |
| 1907 | 1,764 | 68,758 |
| 1908 | 1,696 | 68,993 |
| 1909 | 1,753 | 66,059 |
| 1910 | ... | 69,814 |
| 1911 | 2,190 | 74,273 |
| 1912 | 2,360 | 72,982 |
| 1913 | ... | 76,620 |
| 1914 | ... | 77,676 |

| | Canada[1] | Costa Rica[3] | Cuba | Dominican Republic | El Salvador |
|---|---|---|---|---|---|
| 1915 | ... | ... | ... | ... | ... |
| 1916 | ... | ... | ... | ... | ... |
| 1917 | ... | ... | ... | ... | ... |
| 1918 | 1,183 | ... | ... | ... | ... |
| 1919 | 1,676 | ... | ... | ... | ... |
| 1920 | 1,614 | ... | ... | ... | ... |
| 1921 | 1,746 | ... | 313 | ... | ... |
| 1922 | 1,672 | ... | 286 | ... | ... |
| 1923 | 2,004 | ... | 407 | ... | ... |
| 1924 | 2,198 | ... | 473 | ... | ... |
| 1925 | 2,384 | ... | 452 | ... | ... |
| 1926 | 2,353 | ... | 468 | ... | ... |
| 1927 | 2,655 | ... | 516 | ... | ... |
| 1928 | 2,993 | ... | 422 | ... | ... |
| 1929 | 2,884 | ... | 431 | ... | ... |
| 1930 | 2,686 | ... | 362 | ... | ... |
| 1931 | 2,377 | ... | 221 | ... | ... |
| 1932 | 1,849 | ... | 161 | ... | 7.1 |
| 1933 | 1,860 | ... | 186 | ... | 20 |
| 1934 | 2,368 | ... | 229 | ... | 21 |
| 1935 | 2,598 | ... | 303 | ... | 17 |
| 1936 | 2,742 | ... | 357 | 10 | 16 |
| 1937 | 3,062 | ... | 437 | 9.3 | 15 |
| 1938 | 2,879 | ... | 406 | 8.0 | 14 |
| 1939 | 3,023 | ... | 385 | 10 | 19 |
| 1940 | 3,592 | ... | 403 | 11 | 8.9 |
| 1941 | 4,595 | ... | 454 | 12 | 11 |
| 1942 | 4,954 | ... | 433 | 17 | 14 |
| 1943 | 4,731 | ... | 436 | 12 | 16 |
| 1944 | 5,570 | ... | 597 | 20 | 22 |
| 1945 | 6,316 | ... | 780 | 35 | 24 |
| 1946 | 7,083 | ... | 814 | 35 | 32 |
| 1947 | 7,874 | ... | 844 | 51 | 38 |
| 1948 | 8,218 | ... | 998 | 50 | 42 |
| 1949 | 8,204 | ... | 965 | 67 | ... |
| 1950 | 8,094 | ... | 1,043 | 66 | 94 |
| 1951 | 8,665 | 25 | 1,255 | 71 | 141 |
| 1952 | 9,455 | 27 | 1,437 | 92 | 194 |
| 1953 | 9,672 | 29 | 1,188 | 85 | 217 |
| 1954 | 9,606 | 38 | 1,202 | 76 | 183 |
| 1955 | 10,098 | 54 | 1,179 | 71 | 158 |
| 1956 | 10,293 | 60 | 1,205 | 83 | 158 |
| 1957 | 10,894 | 67 | 1,292 | 105 | 200 |
| 1958 | 10,649 | 74 | 1,232 | 132 | 169 |
| 1959 | 11,202 | 79 | 1,557 | 125 | 131 |
| 1960 | 11,489 | 89 | ... | 94 | 145 |
| 1961 | 11,688 | 91 | 1,394 | 87 | 139 |
| 1962 | 12,276 | 86 | 927 | 225 | 142 |
| 1963 | 12,732 | 86 | 891 | 286 | 139 |
| 1964 | 13,056 | 89 | 1,036 | 302 | 128 |

**D21** **NORTH AMERICA: Output of Beer** (in thousands of hectolitres)

| | Guatemala | Honduras | Jamaica[4] | Mexico | Nicaragua | Panama | Puerto Rico[5] | USA[2] |
|---|---|---|---|---|---|---|---|---|
| 1915 | ... | ... | ... | ... | | | | 70,166 |
| 1916 | ... | ... | ... | ... | | | | 68,758 |
| 1917 | ... | ... | ... | ... | | | | 71,340 |
| 1918 | ... | ... | ... | ... | | | | 59,019 |
| 1919 | ... | ... | ... | ... | | | | 32,502 |
| 1920 | ... | ... | ... | ... | | | | 10,795 |
| 1921 | ... | ... | ... | ... | | | | 10,795 |
| 1922 | ... | ... | ... | ... | | | | 7,392 |
| 1923 | ... | ... | ... | ... | | | | 6,219 |
| 1924 | ... | ... | ... | ... | | | | 5,749 |
| 1925 | ... | ... | ... | 540 | | | | 5,884 |
| 1926 | ... | ... | ... | 680 | | | | 5,749 |
| 1927 | ... | ... | ... | 720 | | | | 5,163 |
| 1928 | ... | ... | ... | 679 | | | | 4,928 |
| 1929 | ... | ... | ... | 720 | | | | 4,576 |
| 1930 | ... | ... | ... | 720 | ... | ... | ... | 4,319 |
| 1931 | 16 | ... | ... | 547 | ... | ... | ... | 3,681 |
| 1932 | 11 | ... | ... | 425 | ... | ... | ... | 3,245 |
| 1933 | 12 | ... | ... | 530 | ... | 73 | ... | 11,496[2] |
| 1934 | 8.3 | ... | ... | 674 | ... | 68 | ... | 44,209 |
| 1935 | 8.2 | ... | ... | 825 | ... | 75 | ... | 53,069 |
| 1936 | 11 | ... | ... | 989 | ... | 84 | ... | 60,794 |
| 1937 | 22 | ... | 11 | 1,208 | ... | 90 | ... | 68,932 |
| 1938 | 25 | ... | 12 | 1,298 | 4.9 | 102 | ... | 66,107 |
| 1939 | 26 | ... | 11 | 1,605 | 7.9 | 105 | ... | 63,210 |
| 1940 | 27 | ... | 7.7 | 1,792 | 12 | 129 | ... | 64,408 |
| 1941 | ... | ... | 13 | 1,836 | 13 | 170 | ... | 64,785 |
| 1942 | ... | ... | 12 | 2,198 | 15 | 232 | ... | 74,762 |
| 1943 | 44 | ... | 12₄ | 2,593 | 17 | 275 | [104][6] | 83,225 |
| 1944 | 59 | ... | 20 | 3,161 | 15 | 246 | 131 | 95,762 |
| 1945 | 79 | ... | 25 | 3,687 | 18 | 262 | 159 | 101,458 |
| 1946 | 82 | ... | 34 | 4,205 | 18 | 233 | 158 | 99,551 |
| 1947 | 104 | ... | 41 | 3,222 | 16 | 218 | 175 | 102,912 |
| 1948 | 102 | ... | 54 | 3,360 | 18 | 172 | 120 | 106,996 |
| 1949 | 97 | ... | 32 | 4,045 | 17 | 145 | 98 | 105,292 |
| 1950 | 96 | ... | 37 | 4,949 | 17 | 131 | 110 | 104,202 |
| 1951 | 95 | ... | 49 | 6,015 | 19 | 147 | 132 | 104,400 |
| 1952 | 96 | ... | 63 | 5,721 | 26 | 169 | 363 | 105,133 |
| 1953 | 113 | 94 | 71 | 5,657 | 30 | 164 | 515 | 106,111 |
| 1954 | 112 | 101 | 82 | 6,559 | 34 | 154 | 548 | 108,606 |
| 1955 | 111 | 131 | 91 | 6,589 | 43 | 149 | 552 | 105,356 |
| 1956 | 130 | 161 | 100 | 7,292 | 47 | 153 | 501 | 106,420 |
| 1957 | 155 | 178 | 106 | 7,525 | 40 | 182 | 536 | 105,463 |
| 1958 | 187 | 161 | 120 | 7,308 | 47 | 184 | 581 | 104,441 |
| 1959 | 202 | 147 | 138 | 7,908 | 42 | 189 | 642 | 106,744 |
| 1960 | 166 | 139 | 153 | 8,525 | 41 | 209 | 688 | 110,938 |
| 1961 | 161 | 139 | 178 | 8,403 | 45 | 233 | 732 | 109,704 |
| 1962 | 154 | 150 | 204 | 8,500 | 57 | 246 | 793 | 113,132 |
| 1963 | 179 | 144 | 183 | 8,550 | 76 | 272 | 802 | 114,943 |
| 1964 | 203 | 175 | 225 | 10,280 | 97 | 276 | 870 | 120,876 |

**D21    NORTH AMERICA: Output of Beer** (in thousands of hectolitres)

| | Canada[1] | Costa Rica[3] | Cuba | Dominican Republic | El Salvador |
|---|---|---|---|---|---|
| 1965 | 13,584 | 92 | 993 | 200 | 133 |
| 1966 | 14,344 | 95 | 1,089 | 201 | 131 |
| 1967 | 14,786 | 99 | 1,360 | 176 | 129 |
| 1968 | 15,057 | 102 | 784 | 252 | 135 |
| 1969 | 15,921 | 105 | 659 | 314 | 153 |
| 1970 | 16,864 | 109 | 1,002 | 374 | 184 |
| 1971 | 18,404 | 112 | 1,309 | 427 | 204 |
| 1972 | 19,224 | 140 | 1,666 | 488 | 229 |
| 1973 | 20,347 | 200 | 1,851 | 484 | 237 |
| 1974 | 20,902 | 220 | 1,808 | 486 | 329 |
| 1975 | 21,500 | 270 | 2,111 | 445 | 386 |
| 1976 | 21,712 | 139 | 2,169 | 475 | 484 |
| 1977 | 21,898 | 168 | 2,199 | 648 | 578 |
| 1978 | 22,032 | 170 | 2,338 | 804 | 581 |
| 1979 | 24,106 | … | 2,307 | 991 | 414 |
| 1980 | 22,655 | … | 2,365 | 1,173 | 351 |
| 1981 | 23,085 | … | 2,243 | 1,101 | 427 |
| 1982 | 22,658 | … | 2,421 | 1,119 | 420 |
| 1983 | 23,332 | … | 2,582 | 999 | 344 |
| 1984 | 23,558 | … | 2,607 | 945 | … |
| 1985 | 23,237 | … | 2,736 | 1,038 | … |
| 1986 | 23,547 | … | 2,931 | 1,099 | … |
| 1987 | | … | 3,288 | 1,269 | … |
| 1988 | | … | 3,324 | … | … |

| | Guatemala | Honduras | Jamaica | Mexico | Nicaragua | Panama | Puerto Rico[5] | USA |
|---|---|---|---|---|---|---|---|---|
| 1965 | 226 | 190 | 266 | 11,080 | 111 | 292 | 894 | 126,739 |
| 1966 | 241 | 186 | 294 | 11,660 | 125 | 307 | 942 | 128,759 |
| 1967 | 244 | 185 | 311 | 12,254 | 140 | 321 | 759 | 136,770 |
| 1968 | 247 | 201 | 335 | 12,519 | 180 | 308 | 824 | 137,897 |
| 1969 | 272 | 226 | 401 | 13,649 | 128 | 353 | 934 | 143,920 |
| 1970 | 299 | 258 | 432 | 14,321 | 137 | 366 | 937 | 157,996 |
| 1971 | 328 | 283 | 430 | 12,656 | 144 | 378 | 593 | 157,354 |
| 1972 | 356 | 287 | 506 | 15,137 | … | 284 | 708 | 164,671 |
| 1973 | 421 | 323 | 567 | 17,325 | … | 349 | 814 | 167,789 |
| 1974 | 480 | 298 | 578 | 19,732 | … | 393 | 454 | 179,523 |
| 1975 | 526 | 302 | 663 | 19,684 | 150 | 423 | 493 | 185,389 |
| 1976 | 572 | 233 | 606 | 19,358 | 160 | 433 | 601 | 179,523[2] |
| 1977 | 598 | 309 | 558 | 21,642 | 160 | 355 | 463 | 167,789 |
| 1978 | 700 | 374 | 612 | 22,568 | 165 | 433 | 509 | 195,434 |
| 1979 | 700 | 380 | 515 | 25,461 | 357 | 559 | 736 | 216,155 |
| 1980 | 789 | 433 | 636 | 26,876 | 477 | 670 | 721 | 227,772 |
| 1981 | 718 | 471 | 563 | 28,635 | 480 | 694 | 692 | 227,303 |
| 1982 | 645 | 397 | 581 | 28,028 | 470 | 713 | 546 | 228,007 |
| 1983 | 672 | 469 | 604 | 24,139 | 503 | 708 | 377 | 228,945 |
| 1984 | 715 | 511 | 517 | 25,616 | 522 | 734 | 347 | 228,955 |
| 1985 | 613 | 500 | 568 | 27,215 | … | 797 | 260 | 228,960 |
| 1986 | 795 | 548 | 632 | 27,353 | … | 925 | 261 | 230,588 |
| 1987 | 869 | 580 | 700 | 31,482 | … | 1,014 | 266 | 229,321 |
| 1988 | … | 656 | 745 | 33,261 | … | 871 | 350 | 231,985 |

**D21    SOUTH AMERICA: OUTPUT OF BEER** (in thousands of hectolitres)

| | Argentina | Bolivia | Brazil[7] | Chile | Colombia | Ecuador | Paraguay | Peru[9] | Uruguay[10] | Venezuela |
|---|---|---|---|---|---|---|---|---|---|---|
| 1891 | ... | ... | ... | ... | ... | ... | ... | ... | [7.5][10] | ... |
| 1892 | ... | ... | ... | ... | ... | ... | ... | ... | 22 | ... |
| 1893 | ... | ... | ... | ... | ... | ... | ... | ... | 16 | ... |
| 1894 | ... | ... | ... | ... | ... | ... | ... | ... | 19 | ... |
| 1895 | 156 | ... | ... | ... | ... | ... | ... | ... | 15 | ... |
| 1896 | ... | ... | ... | ... | ... | ... | ... | ... | 13 | ... |
| 1897 | ... | ... | ... | ... | ... | ... | ... | ... | 12 | ... |
| 1898 | ... | ... | ... | ... | ... | ... | ... | ... | 11 | ... |
| 1899 | ... | ... | ... | ... | ... | ... | ... | ... | 1 | ... |
| 1900 | ... | ... | ... | ... | ... | ... | ... | ... | 15 | ... |
| 1901 | ... | ... | ... | ... | ... | ... | ... | ... | 16 | ... |
| 1902 | ... | ... | ... | ... | ... | ... | ... | ... | 17 | ... |
| 1903 | ... | ... | ... | ... | ... | ... | ... | ... | 19 | ... |
| 1904 | ... | ... | ... | ... | ... | ... | ... | ... | 18 | ... |
| 1905 | ... | ... | ... | ... | ... | ... | ... | ... | 22 | ... |
| 1906 | 648 | ... | ... | ... | ... | ... | ... | ... | 30 | ... |
| 1907 | 701 | ... | ... | ... | ... | ... | ... | ... | 31 | ... |
| 1908 | 816 | ... | ... | ... | ... | ... | ... | ... | 35 | ... |
| 1909 | 863 | ... | ... | ... | ... | ... | ... | ... | 39 | ... |
| 1910 | 981 | ... | ... | ... | ... | ... | ... | ... | 44 | ... |
| 1911 | 1,003 | ... | 681 | ... | ... | ... | ... | ... | 52 | ... |
| 1912 | 1,094 | ... | 863 | ... | ... | ... | ... | ... | 66 | ... |
| 1913 | 1,255 | ... | 976 | ... | ... | ... | ... | ... | 79 | ... |
| 1914 | 751 | ... | 879 | ... | ... | ... | ... | ... | 68 | ... |
| 1915 | 733 | ... | 765 | ... | ... | ... | ... | ... | 47 | ... |
| 1916 | 772 | ... | 726 | ... | ... | ... | ... | ... | 50 | ... |
| 1917 | 788 | ... | 586 | 430 | ... | ... | ... | ... | 53 | ... |
| 1918 | 962 | ... | 600 | 430 | ... | ... | ... | ... | 60 | ... |
| 1919 | ... | ... | 799 | ... | ... | ... | ... | ... | 68 | ... |
| 1920 | ... | ... | 819 | 450 | ... | ... | ... | ... | 89 | ... |
| 1921 | ... | ... | 898 | 394 | ... | ... | ... | ... | 87 | ... |
| 1922 | ... | ... | 1,108 | 355 | ... | ... | ... | ... | 91 | ... |
| 1923 | ... | ... | 1,243 | 531 | ... | ... | ... | ... | 97 | ... |
| 1924 | ... | ... | 1,277 | 613 | ... | ... | ... | ... | 95 | ... |
| 1925 | 2,002 | ... | 1,423 | 515 | ... | ... | ... | ... | 109 | ... |
| 1926 | 2,030 | ... | 1,426 | ... | ... | ... | ... | ... | 117 | ... |
| 1927 | 2,127 | ... | 1,580 | 412 | ... | ... | ... | 20 | 143 | ... |
| 1928 | 1,981 | ... | 1,742 | 418 | ... | ... | ... | 17 | 135 | ... |
| 1929 | 2,132 | ... | 1,766 | 508 | ... | ... | ... | 18 | 159 | ... |
| 1930 | 1,828 | ... | 1,456 | 552 | ... | ... | 17 | 112 | 152 | ... |
| 1931 | 1,347 | ... | 1,063 | 371 | ... | ... | ... | 88 | 147 | ... |
| 1932 | 1,158 | ... | 1,076 | 367 | ... | ... | 4.6 | 71 | 121[10] | ... |
| 1933 | 983 | ... | 1,141 | 392 | ... | ... | 4.6 | 70 | 102 | ... |
| 1934 | 1,344 | ... | 1,181 | 444 | ... | ... | 7.1 | 88 | 116 | ... |
| 1935 | 1,330 | ... | 1,792 | 578 | ... | ... | 13 | 104 | 112 | ... |
| 1936 | 1,237 | ... | 1,905 | 623 | 648 | ... | 11 | 122 | 123 | ... |
| 1937 | 1,436 | 129 | 1,953 | 699 | 581 | ... | 7.7 | 142 | 142 | 115 |
| 1938 | 1,412 | 155 | 1,857 | 619 | ... | 125 | 7.2 | 149 | 149 | 141 |
| 1939 | 1,539 | 155 | 2,077 | 675 | ... | 118 | 7.7 | 186 | 156 | 192 |

**D21**    **SOUTH AMERICA: Output of Beer** (in thousands of hectolitres)

| | Argentina | Bolivia | Brazil[7] | Chile | Colombia | Ecuador | Paraguay | Peru[9] | Uraguay | Venezuela |
|---|---|---|---|---|---|---|---|---|---|---|
| 1940 | 1,478 | 149 | 2,061 | 781 | 783 | 127 | 7.8 | 194 | 178 | 219 |
| 1941 | 1,476 | 175 | 2,013 | 726 | 881 | 147 | 7.8 | 209 | 166 | 216 |
| 1942 | 1,848 | 193 | 1,982 | 635 | 914 | 209 | 10 | 239 | 187 | 217 |
| 1943 | 2,161 | 224 | 2,257 | 664 | 913 | 262 | 16 | 262 | 189 | 241 |
| 1944 | 2,298 | 215 | 3,139 | 642 | ... | 274 | 23 | 311 | 193 | 316 |
| 1945 | 2,575 | 214 | ... | 684 | 1,226 | 257 | 31 | 345 | 210 | 401 |
| 1946 | 2,467 | 215 | ... | 790 | ... | 257 | 35 | 368 | 239 | 437 |
| 1947 | 3,151 | 221 | ... | 852 | 1,842 | 269 | 28 | 351 | 276 | 502 |
| 1948 | 3,446 | 267 | ... | 880 | 2,334 | 234 | 39 | 316 | 213 | 578 |
| 1949 | 3,738 | 278 | ... | 920 | 2,514 | 222 | 40 | 334 | 368 | 683 |
| 1950 | 3,894 | 274 | ... | 915 | 3,327 | 262 | 32 | 444 | 411 | 806 |
| 1951 | 4,009 | 305 | ... | 914 | 3,380 | 356 | 41 | 556 | 459 | 1,007 |
| 1952 | 3,881 | 299 | ... | 1,072 | 3,856 | 437 | 53 | 663 | 561 | 1,187 |
| 1953 | 3,447 | 290 | ... | 1,240 | 4,423 | 492 | 57 | 811 | ... | 1,244 |
| 1954 | 3,732 | 285 | ... | 1,203 | 4,657 | 582 | 55 | 923 | ... | 1,280 |
| 1955 | 3,689 | 219 | 7,131 | 1,332 | 4,512 | 570 | 52 | 963[9] | ... | 1,348 |
| 1956 | 3,522 | 220 | 6,553 | 1,421 | 4,727 | 553[8] / 332 | 45 | 984 | ... | 1,395 |
| 1957 | 3,568 | 194 | 6,242 | 1,416 | 5,182 | 370 | 52 | 1,219 | 621 | 1,539 |
| 1958 | 3,875 | 196 | 7,502 | 1,199 | 5,990 | 399 | 53 | 1,171 | 626 | 1,891 |
| 1959 | 2,323 | 168 | ... | 1,118 | 5,923[8] / 6,155 | 402 | 55 | 1,203 | 629 | 2,162 |
| 1960 | 2,430 | 176 | ... | 1,307 | 6,425 | 406 | 51 | 1,461 | 525 | 2,411 |
| 1961 | 2,436 | 199 | ... | 1,199 | 6,471 | 390 | 64 | 1,429 | 1,038 | 2,407 |
| 1962 | 1,987 | 216 | 7,360 | 1,309 | 6,514 | 378 | 62 | 1,541 | 638 | 2,477 |
| 1963 | 1,239 | 235 | 7,167 | 1,253 | 6,529 | 345 | 82 | 1,637 | 956 | 2,488 |
| 1964 | 1,722 | 257 | 6,605 | 1,093 | 6,632 | 417 | 86 | 1,646 | 689 | 2,626 |
| 1965 | 2,492 | 249 | 7,576 | 1,649 | 6,854 | 441 | 85 | 1,726 | 646 | 2,779 |
| 1966 | 2,256 | 287 | 8,441 | 1,774 | 6,837 | 446 | 97 | 2,098 | 517 | 2,971 |
| 1967 | 2,496 | 302 | 7,845 | 1,761 | 5,847 | 442 | 103 | 2,121 | 494 | 3,324 |
| 1968 | 3,012 | 306 | 7,969 | 1,727 | 5,671 | 502 | 114 | 2,188 | 660 | 3,559 |
| 1969 | 3,172 | 341 | 9,087 | 1,563 | 6,395 | 516 | 157 | 2,320 | ... | 4,844 |
| 1970 | 3,565 | 381 | 9,132 | 1,776 | 7,058 | 647 | 175 | 2,344 | 810 | 4,954 |
| 1971 | 2,970 | 412 | 10,450 | 2,192 | ... | 643 | 164 | 2,940 | 860 | 4,367 |
| 1972 | 2,970 | 426 | 9,723 | 2,293 | 7,720 | 740 | 181 | 3,000 | 865 | 4,504 |
| 1973 | 3,033 | 442 | 11,298 | 2,058 | 7,649 | 822 | 208 | 3,426 | 745 | 4,600 |
| 1974 | 4,456 | 563 | 12,157 | 1,054 | 8,194 | 889 | 253 | 3,826 | 620 | 4,580 |
| 1975 | 3,955 | 752 | 12,518[7] | 1,833 | 8,406 | 1,060 | 301 | 4,296 | 670 | 4,261 |
| 1976 | 2,839 | 957 | 40,825 | 1,083 | 9,577 | 1,370 | 332 | 5,096 | 600 | 4,400 |
| 1977 | 2,710 | 1,058 | 21,519 | 1,361 | 10,578 | 1,677 | 451 | 4,691 | 650 | 4,600 |
| 1978 | 2,048 | 1,113 | 31,897 | 1,404 | 11,317 | 1,957 | 514 | 3,964 | 660 | 4,750 |
| 1979 | 2,148 | 814 | [30,089][7] | 1,591 | 11,467 | 2,010 | 591 | 4,600 | 670 | 4,900 |
| 1980 | 2,280 | 1,162 | 27,824 | 1,808 | 12,871 | 632 | 621 | 5,325 | ... | ... |
| 1981 | 2,102 | 1,141 | 28,928 | 1,904 | 13,536 | 728 | 632 | 5,141 | ... | ... |
| 1982 | 2,225 | 901 | ... | 1,797 | 13,383 | 769 | 696 | 5,556 | ... | ... |
| 1983 | 3,157 | 717 | 25,861 | 1,760 | 14,494 | 626 | 717 | 5,230 | ... | ... |
| 1984 | 4,079 | 701 | 25,980 | 1,781 | ... | ... | 753 | 5,388 | ... | ... |
| 1985 | 3,827 | 606 | 27,092 | 1,892 | 15,509 | ... | 768 | 5,724 | 468 | ... |
| 1986 | 5,548 | 803 | 34,002 | 2,050 | 16,915 | ... | 887 | 7,473 | 678 | ... |
| 1987 | 5,861 | ... | 33,893 | 2,548 | 15,355 | ... | 918 | 8,564 | 709 | ... |
| 1988 | 5,232 | ... | 36,445 | 2,650 | 11,973 | ... | 903 | 7,047 | 603 | ... |

**D21**    **Output of Beer** (in thousands of hectolitres)

NOTES

1.  SOURCES: The national publications listed on p. xiv–xvi and League of Nations and UN, *Statistical Yearbooks.*
2.  All types of beer have been aggregated in this table, including virtually non-alcoholic malt liquor, though home-brewed beer is not covered.

FOOTNOTES

[1] Years beginning 1 April.
[2] Years ending 30 June to 1976 and years ending 30 September thereafter. Alaska and Hawaii are included throughout except for the period 7 April to 30 June 1933.
[3] Years ending 30 September.
[4] Years beginning 1 April to 1943.
[5] Years ending 30 June.
[6] 11 months.
[7] Production by main establishments only to 1975 and in 1979.
[8] The reason for this break is not given in the source.
[9] Consumption of domestically produced beer to 1955.
[10] Years ending 30 June from 1892 to 1932. The 1891 figure is for the first half-year only.

**D22**    **NORTH AMERICA: OUTPUT OF ELECTRIC ENERGY** (in gigaWalt hours)

| | Bahamas[1] | Barbados[2] | Canada[3] | Cuba[4] | Dominican Republic[5] | Guatemala[6] | Jamaica[7] |
|---|---|---|---|---|---|---|---|
| 1919 | ... | ... | 5,497 | ... | ... | ... | ... |
| 1920 | ... | ... | 5,895 | ... | ... | ... | ... |
| 1921 | ... | ... | 5,614 | ... | ... | ... | ... |
| 1922 | ... | ... | 6,741 | ... | ... | ... | ... |
| 1923 | ... | ... | 8,099 | ... | ... | ... | ... |
| 1924 | ... | ... | 9,315 | ... | ... | ... | ... |
| 1925 | ... | ... | 10,110 | ... | ... | ... | ... |
| 1926 | ... | ... | 12,093 | ... | ... | ... | ... |
| 1927 | ... | ... | 14,549[3] | ... | ... | ... | ... |
| | | | 15,377 | | | | |
| 1928 | ... | ... | 17,509 | 236 | ... | ... | ... |
| 1929 | 2.9 | ... | 19,306 | 263 | ... | ... | ... |
| 1930 | ... | ... | 19,468 | 265 | ... | ... | ... |
| 1931 | ... | ... | 17,620 | 235 | ... | ... | ... |
| 1932 | ... | ... | 17,453 | 213 | ... | ... | ... |
| 1933 | ... | ... | 18,697 | 208 | ... | ... | ... |
| 1934 | ... | ... | 22,749 | 235 | ... | ... | ... |
| 1935 | ... | ... | 24,927 | 252 | ... | ... | ... |
| 1936 | ... | ... | 27,099 | 274 | 13 | ... | ... |
| 1937 | 4.9 | ... | 30,225 | 307 | 15 | 25 | 16 |
| 1938 | 5.3 | 3.1 | 28,603 | 324 | 24 | 27 | 18 |
| 1939 | ... | ... | 30,979 | 343 | 23 | 28 | 20 |
| 1940 | ... | ... | 33,062 | 356 | 28 | 29 | 27 |
| 1941 | ... | ... | 36,479 | 370 | 28 | 30 | 30 |
| 1942 | ... | ... | 41,007 | 379 | 28 | 32 | 31 |
| 1943 | ... | ... | 43,950 | 397 | 25 | 35 | 29 |
| 1944 | ... | ... | 43,571 | 430 | 29 | 32 | 35 |

**D22    NORTH AMERICA: Output of Electric Energy** (in gigaWatt hours)

| | Martinique | Mexico[5] | Panama[8] | Puerto Rico | Trinidad & Tobago[10] | USA[5] |
|---|---|---|---|---|---|---|
| 1902 | ... | ... | ... | ... | ... | 5,969 |
| 1907 | ... | ... | ... | ... | ... | 14,121 |
| 1912 | ... | ... | ... | ... | ... | 24,752 |
| 1917 | ... | ... | ... | ... | ... | 43,429 |
| 1920 | ... | ... | ... | ... | ... | 56,559 |
| 1921 | ... | ... | ... | ... | ... | 53,125 |
| 1922 | ... | ... | ... | ... | ... | 61,204 |
| 1923 | ... | ... | ... | ... | ... | 71,399 |
| 1924 | ... | ... | ... | ... | ... | 75,892 |
| 1925 | ... | ... | ... | ... | ... | 84,666 |
| 1926 | ... | 1,262 | ... | ... | ... | 94,222 |
| 1927 | ... | 1,381 | ... | ... | ... | 101,390 |
| 1928 | ... | ... | ... | ... | ... | 108,069 |
| 1929 | ... | ... | ... | ... | ... | 116,747 |
| 1930 | ... | 1,464 | ... | ... | ... | 114,637 |
| 1931 | ... | 1,490 | ... | ... | ... | 109,373 |
| 1932 | ... | 1,425 | ... | ... | ... | 99,359 |
| 1933 | ... | 1,529 | ... | ... | 3.5 | 102,655 |
| 1934 | ... | 1,834 | ... | ... | 3.7 | 110,404 |
| 1935 | 2.0 | 2,064 | ... | ... | 4.1 | 118,935 |
| 1936 | 2.7 | 2,245 | ... | ... | 4.3 | 136,006 |
| 1937 | 2.7 | 2,480 | 27 | 120 | 4.7 | 146,476 |
| 1938 | 3.3 | 2,512 | 29 | 134 | 5.4 | 141,955 |
| 1939 | 3.8 | 2,462 | 31 | 155 | 7.4 | 161,308 |
| 1940 | 4.8 | 2,529 | 37 | 173 | 8.5 | 179,907 |
| 1941 | 6.0 | 2,524 | 44 | 214 | 14.0 | 208,306 |
| 1942 | 6.1 | 2,625 | 45 | 235 | 18.0 | 233,146 |
| 1943 | 4.9 | 2,739 | 50 | 265 | 23.0 | 267,540 |
| 1944 | 5.4 | 2,750 | 54 | 283 | 25.0 | 279,525 |

**D22    NORTH AMERICA: Output of Electric Energy** (in gigaWatt hours)

| | Bahamas[1] | Barbados[2] | Belize | Bermuda | Canada[3] | Costa Rica | Cuba[4] | Dominican Republic[5] |
|---|---|---|---|---|---|---|---|---|
| 1945 | ... | ... | ... | ... | 42,720 | ... | 488 | 34 |
| 1946 | ... | ... | ... | ... | 44,663 | ... | 532 | 40 |
| 1947 | ... | ... | ... | ... | 47,174 | ... | 571 | 49 |
| 1948 | 13 | 10 | ... | ... | 47,262 | ... | 639 | 58 |
| 1949 | 15 | ... | ... | ... | 50,890 [3] | ... | 690 | 72 |
| 1950 | 16 | 11 | ... | 38 | 55,382 | 180 | 758 | 79 |
| 1951 | 19 | 11 | ... | 41 | 61,776 | 190 | 836 | 96 |
| 1952 | 22 | 12 | ... | 44 | 66,497 | 200 | 918 | 112 |
| 1953 | 24 | 17 | ... | 48 | 70,301 | 219 | 1,006 | 167 |
| 1954 | 28 | 18 | ... | 51 | 74,540 | 241 | 1,088 | 185 |
| 1955 | 32 | 20 | ... | 57 | 82,221 | 271 | 1,200 [4] 1,842 | 195 |
| 1956 | 37 | 22 | ... | 60 | 88,455 | 328 | 2,063 | 232 |
| 1957 | 45 | 25 | ... | 69 | 91,115 | 347 | 2,358 | 258 |
| 1958 | 51 | 28 | 4.4 | 76 | 97,526 | 365 | 2,589 | 284 |
| 1959 | 65 | 33 | 5.2 | 80 | 104,671 | 387 | 2,806 | 316 |
| 1960 | 76 | 38 | 5.8 | 92 | 114,457 | 438 | 2,981 | 349 |
| 1961 | 89 | 43 | 6.2 | 103 | 113,713 | 461 | 3,030 | 372 |
| 1962 | 101 | 47 | 6.8 | 118 | 117,469 | 491 | 2,998 | 439 |
| 1963 | 113 | 53 [2] | 9.2 | 124 | 122,325 | 518 | 3,057 | 452 |
| 1964 | 123 | 66 | 11.0 | 133 | 143,987 | 573 | 3,250 | 532 |
| 1965 | 137 [1] | 75 | 12.0 | 146 | 144,274 | 660 | 3,423 | 500 |
| 1966 | 250 | 78 | 14.0 | 163 | 158,135 | 697 | 4,074 | 623 |
| 1967 | 300 | 95 | 15.0 | 174 | 165,625 | 757 | 4,486 | 697 |
| 1968 | 370 | 110 | 18.0 | 190 | 176,378 | 833 | 4,700 | 761 |
| 1969 | 422 | 131 | 22.0 | 208 | 191,102 | 901 | 4,266 | 864 |
| 1970 | 489 | 146 | 23.0 | 226 | 204,723 | 1,028 | 4,888 | 1,003 |
| 1971 | 543 | 160 | 26.0 | 251 | 216,472 | 1,148 | 5,021 | 1,068 |
| 1972 | 631 | 188 | 28.0 | 278 | 240,213 | 1,266 | 5,265 | 1,687 |
| 1973 | 645 | 212 | 32.0 | 300 | 263,335 | 1,346 | 5,703 | 2,254 |
| 1974 | 662 | 203 | 35.0 | 299 | 280,256 | 1,467 | 6,018 | 2,406 |
| 1975 | 684 | 214 | 39.0 | 299 | 273,392 | 1,531 | 6,583 | 2,556 |
| 1976 | 649 | 228 | 43.0 | 311 | 294,043 | 1,701 | 7,191 | 2,580 |
| 1977 | 687 | 264 | 45.0 | 327 | 326,184 | 1,828 | 7,706 | 2,243 |
| 1978 | 743 | 287 | 48.0 | 333 | 345,165 | 1,998 | 8,481 | 2,395 |
| 1979 | 829 | 315 | 53.0 | 333 | 363,176 | 2,000 | 9,403 | 3,268 |
| 1980 | 853 | 332 | 54.0 | 332 | 377,518 | 2,202 | 9,990 | 3,317 |
| 1981 | 762 | 349 | 55.0 | 342 | 390,937 | 2,349 | 10,576 | 3,582 |
| 1982 | 814 | 355 | 57.0 | 353 | 387,460 | 2,457 | 11,071 | 3,206 |
| 1983 | 871 | 375 | 58.0 | 368 | 408,443 | 2,918 | 11,551 | 3,400 |
| 1984 | 866 | 383 | 67.0 | 382 | 437,990 | 3,069 | 12,292 | 4,009 |
| 1985 | 854 | 390 | 71.0 | 395 | 459,045 | 2,826 | 12,199 | 4,229 |
| 1986 | 910 | 390 | 74.0 | 400 | 468,593 | 2,949 | 13,176 | 4,614 |
| 1987 | 965 | 425 | 75.0 | 435 | 496,335 | 3,133 | 13,594 | 5,296 |
| 1988 | 975 | 449 | 77.0 | 458 | 504,285 | 3,193 | 14,543 | 5,300 |

**D22    NORTH AMERICA: Output of Electric Energy** (in gigaWatt hours)

| | El Salvador | Guadeloupe | Guatemala[6] | Haiti | Honduras | Jamaica[7] | Martinique | Mexico[5] |
|---|---|---|---|---|---|---|---|---|
| 1945 | ... | ... | 35 | ... | ... | 37 | 5.9 | 3,069 |
| 1946 | ... | ... | 39 | ... | ... | 46 | 7.4 | 3,317 |
| 1947 | ... | ... | 41 | ... | ... | 52 | 8.8 | 3,599 |
| 1948 | ... | 2.4 | 45[6] | ... | ... | 56 | 9.8 | 3,969 |
| | | | 55 | | | | | |
| 1949 | ... | 3.0 | 62 | ... | ... | 67 | 11 | 4,328 |
| 1950 | 65 | 4.0 | 70[6] | [9.6][13] | 46 | 76[6] | 12 | 4,423 |
| | | | 80 | | | 166 | | |
| 1951 | 70 | 6.0 | 95 | 18.0 | 55 | 188 | 12 | 4,908 |
| 1952 | 93 | ... | 105 | 16.0 | 60 | 209 | 13 | 5,337 |
| 1953 | 125 | 7.1 | 115 | 19 | 62 | 228 | 14 | 5,703 |
| 1954 | 133 | 7.3 | 125 | 21 | 54 | 257 | 15 | 6,282 |
| 1955 | 144 | 8.5 | 140 | 23 | 59 | 285 | 16 | 7,002 |
| 1956 | 165 | 9.4 | 171 | 27 | 66 | 328 | 17 | 8,173 |
| 1957 | 185 | 11 | 193 | 34 | 75 | 373 | 18 | 8,463 |
| 1958 | 213 | 14 | 219 | 47 | 80 | 390 | 20 | 9,057 |
| 1959 | 235 | 17 | 243 | 53 | 86 | 453 | 21 | 9,693 |
| 1960 | 256 | 21 | 281 | 60 | 97 | 508 | 23 | 10,813 |
| 1961 | 273 | 24 | 291 | 65[14] | 102 | 580 | 25 | 11,754 |
| | | | | 90 | | | | |
| 1962 | 300 | 29 | 324 | 95 | 108 | 610 | 28 | 12,608 |
| 1963 | 340 | 34 | 364 | 95 | 115 | 649 | 32 | 13,645 |
| 1964 | 379 | 40 | 434 | 95 | 128 | 712 | 37 | 15,736 |
| 1965 | 418 | 46 | 449 | 96 | 175 | 798 | 45 | 17,245 |
| 1966 | 477 | 52 | 492 | 100 | 204 | 867 | 54 | 18,843 |
| 1967 | 524 | 62 | 531 | 105 | 232 | 977 | 63 | 20,658 |
| 1968 | 569 | 75 | 589 | 110 | 268[14] | 1,069 | 74 | 22,781 |
| 1969 | 617 | 88 | 720 | 115 | 282 | 1,275 | 87 | 25,554 |
| 1970 | 671 | 99 | 759 | 118 | 315 | 1,541 | 103 | 28,707 |
| 1971 | 743 | 110 | 847 | 120 | 347 | 1,676 | 128 | 31,313 |
| 1972 | 836 | 123 | 936 | 133 | 389 | 2,022 | 143 | 34,457 |
| 1973 | 912 | 140 | 1,020 | 141 | 436 | 2,187 | 161 | 37,084 |
| 1974 | 986 | 155 | 1,104 | 145 | 490 | 2,283 | 171 | 40,766 |
| 1975 | 1,059 | 167 | 1,167 | 158 | 545 | 2,331 | 179 | 43,329 |
| 1976 | 1,161 | 190 | 1,245 | 209 | 606 | 2,378 | 194 | 48,387 |
| 1977 | 1,303 | 220 | 1,443 | 215 | 682 | 2,375 | 220 | 52,704 |
| 1978 | 1,451 | 255 | 1,554 | 246 | 756 | 2,279 | 242 | 57,257 |
| 1979 | 1,578 | 265 | 1,618 | 280 | 847 | 2,218 | 253 | 62,860 |
| 1980 | 1,543 | 310 | 1,671 | 315 | 928 | 2,195 | 275 | 66,954 |
| 1981 | 1,474 | 345 | 1,668 | 325 | 1,014 | 2,213 | 298 | 73,559 |
| 1982 | 1,489 | 395 | 1,623 | 360 | 1,090 | 2,252 | 340 | 80,589 |
| 1983 | 1,600 | 410 | 1,617 | 373 | 1,150 | 2,399 | 392 | 82,243 |
| 1984 | 1,684 | 461 | 1,690 | 385 | 1,060 | 2,288 | 409 | 86,971 |
| 1985 | 1,785 | 491 | 1,755 | 411 | 1,065 | 2,286 | 442 | 93,405 |
| 1986 | 1,757 | 546 | 1,760 | 438 | 1,075 | 2,452 | 477 | 97,117 |
| 1987 | 1,971 | 622 | 1,770 | 445 | 1,085 | 2,606 | 536 | 104,791 |
| 1988 | 1,870 | 681 | 1,785 | 445 | 1,090 | 2,585 | 585 | 109,861 |

**D22    NORTH AMERICA: Output of Electric Energy** (in gigaWatt hours)

| | Netherlands Antilles | Nicaragua | Panama[8] | Panama Canal Zone[9] | Puerto Rico[9] | Trinidad & Tobago[10] | USA[5,11] | US Virgin Islands[5] |
|---|---|---|---|---|---|---|---|---|
| 1945 | ... | ... | 53 | ... | 306 | 30 | 271,255 | ... |
| 1946 | ... | ... | 61 | ... | 344 | 32 | 269,361 | ... |
| 1947 | ... | ... | 69 | ... | 419 | 35 | 307,310 | ... |
| 1948 | ... | 77 | 70 | 266 | 476 | 40 | 336,808 | ... |
| 1949 | ... | 79 | 74 | 270 | 517 | 45 | 345,066 | ... |
| 1950 | 660 | 80 | $\underline{85}_8$ 103 | 252 | 580 | $\underline{48}_{10}$ 168 | 388,674 | 4.9 |
| 1951 | 660 | 84 | 108 | 235 | 660 | 192 | 433,358 | 6.8 |
| 1952 | 660 | 90 | 116 | 254 | 735 | 211 | 463,055 | 7.7 |
| 1953 | 660 | 96 | 124 | 267 | 837 | 236 | 514,169 | 10 |
| 1954 | 665 | 105 | 132 | 254 | 895 | 260 | 544,645 | 12 |
| 1955 | 670 | 110 | 142 | 253 | 1,050 | 279 | 629,010 | 16 |
| 1956 | 686 | 119 | 157 | 258 | 1,225 | 311 | 684,804 | 19 |
| 1957 | 719 | 128 | 175 | 255 | 1,494 | 330 | 716,356 | 22 |
| 1958 | 784 | 143 | 197 | 250 | 1,641 | 383 | $724,752_{11}$ | 25 |
| 1959 | 813 | 166 | 217 | 246 | 1,875 | 449 | 797,567 | 29 |
| 1960 | 825 | 183 | 230 | 269 | 2,151 | 470 | 844,188 | 34 |
| 1961 | 824 | 195 | 263 | 301 | 2,438 | 504 | 881,496 | 44 |
| 1962 | 859 | 212 | 325 | 330 | 2,742 | 570 | 946,526 | 52 |
| 1963 | 869 | 251 | 348 | 368 | 3,164 | 626 | 1,011,418 | 69 |
| 1964 | 1,022 | 281 | 420 | 418 | 3,638 | 817 | 1,083,741 | 76 |
| 1965 | 1,080 | 311 | 510 | 444 | 4,100 | 908 | 1,157,583 | 97 |
| 1966 | 1,168 | 366 | 524 | 489 | 4,730 | 1,007 | 1,249,444 | 125 |
| 1967 | 1,144 | 411 | 582 | 585 | 5,409 | 1,035 | 1,317,301 | 172 |
| 1968 | 1,178 | 484 | 670 | 614 | 6,182 | 1,119 | 1,436,028 | 258 |
| 1969 | 1,267 | 551 | 859 | 638 | $7,110_9$ | 1,213 | 1,552,757 | 388 |
| 1970 | 1,289 | 627 | 956 | 570 | 7,308 | 1,202 | 1,639,771 | 578 |
| 1971 | 1,419 | 657 | 1,037 | 634 | 8,818 | 1,226 | 1,717,521 | 621 |
| 1972 | 1,500 | 754 | 1,151 | 713 | 10,299 | 1,307 | 1,853,390 | 670 |
| 1973 | 1,550 | 714 | 1,359 | 678 | 11,642 | 1,210 | 1,964,830 | 705 |
| 1974 | 1,600 | 874 | 1,434 | 735 | 11,781 | 1,314 | 1,967,289 | 720 |
| 1975 | 1,690 | 932 | 1,447 | 708 | 10,974 | 1,207 | 2,003,002 | 720 |
| 1976 | 1,660 | 1,038 | 1,546 | 674 | 12,839 | 1,412 | 2,123,406 | 720 |
| 1977 | 1,650 | 1,142 | 1,630 | 543 | 13,554 | 1,576 | 2,211,031 | 740 |
| 1978 | 1,834 | 1,136 | 1,564 | 634 | 13,850 | 1,675 | 2,285,880 | 760 |
| 1979 | $\underline{2,060}_{14}$ 1,675 | 951 | 1,893 | 552 | 13,340 | 1,818 | 2,318,783 | 790 |
| 1980 | 1,090 | 1,068 | 1,813 | | 13,206 | 2,056 | 2,354,384 | 800 |
| 1981 | 1,100 | 1,106 | 1,905 | | 12,866 | 2,301 | 2,359,258 | 845 |
| 1982 | 1,250 | 1,054 | 2,092 | | 11,863 | 2,683 | 2,302,287 | 855 |
| 1983 | 1,275 | 941 | 2,262 | | 12,066 | 2,905 | 2,367,634 | 875 |
| 1984 | 1,175 | 973 | 2,272 | | 12,557 | 2,998 | 2,479,297 | 880 |
| 1985 | 1,125 | 1,059 | 2,450 | | 12,316 | 3,018 | 2,567,276 | 900 |
| 1986 | ... | 1,063 | 2,689 | | 12,870 | 3,297 | 2,597,518 | 920 |
| 1987 | ... | 1,063 | 2,902 | | 13,757 | 3,479 | 2,716,004 | 963 |
| 1988 | ... | 1,068 | 2,778 | | 14,403 | 3,470 | 2,853,740 | 970 |

**D22    SOUTH AMERICA: OUTPUT OF ELECTRIC ENERGY** (in gigaWatt hours)

| | Argentina[14] | Bolivia[14] | Brazil[15] | Chile[16] | Colombia[17] | Paraguay[18] | Peru[19] | Uruguay[20] | Venezuela[21] |
|---|---|---|---|---|---|---|---|---|---|
| 1909 | ... | ... | ... | ... | ... | ... | ... | 7 | ... |
| 1910 | ... | ... | ... | ... | ... | ... | ... | 10 | ... |
| 1911 | ... | ... | ... | ... | ... | ... | ... | 14 | ... |
| 1912 | ... | ... | ... | ... | ... | ... | ... | 20 | ... |
| 1913 | ... | ... | ... | ... | ... | ... | ... | 23 | ... |
| 1914 | ... | ... | ... | ... | ... | ... | ... | 23 | ... |
| 1915 | ... | ... | ... | ... | ... | ... | ... | 24 | ... |
| 1916 | ... | ... | ... | ... | ... | ... | ... | 30 | ... |
| 1917 | ... | ... | ... | ... | ... | ... | ... | 34 | ... |
| 1918 | ... | ... | ... | ... | ... | ... | ... | 37 | ... |
| 1919 | ... | ... | ... | ... | ... | ... | ... | 45 | ... |
| 1920 | ... | ... | ... | ... | ... | ... | ... | 51 | ... |
| 1921 | ... | ... | ... | ... | ... | ... | .. | 54 | ... |
| 1922 | ... | ... | ... | ... | ... | ... | ... | 56 | ... |
| 1923 | ... | ... | ... | 113 | ... | ... | ... | 61 | ... |
| 1924 | ... | ... | ... | 165 | ... | ... | ... | 65[20] | ... |
| | | | | | | | | 76 | |
| 1925 | ... | ... | ... | 214 | ... | ... | ... | 84 | ... |
| 1926 | ... | ... | ... | 239 | ... | ... | ... | 87 | ... |
| 1927 | 1,045 | ... | ... | 255 | ... | ... | ... | 97 | ... |
| 1928 | 1,130 | ... | 520 | 257 | ... | ... | ... | 109 | ... |
| 1929 | 1,292 | ... | 540 | 285 | ... | ... | ... | 125 | ... |
| 1930 | 1,433 | ... | 535 | 312 | ... | ... | ... | 142 | ... |
| 1931 | 1,474 | ... | 541 | 312 | ... | ... | 41 | 158 | ... |
| 1932 | 1,550 | ... | 555 | 293 | ... | ... | 36 | 151 | ... |
| 1933 | 1,615 | ... | 610 | 320 | 92 | ... | 38 | 148 | ... |
| 1934 | 1,735 | ... | 687 | 365 | 110 | ... | 45 | 162 | ... |
| 1935 | 1,861 | ... | 768 | 391 | 131 | ... | 53 | 166 | ... |
| 1936 | 2,051 | ... | 849 | 422 | 165 | ... | 60 | 201 | ... |
| 1937 | 2,199 | 48 | 1,025 | 477 | 186 | ... | 69 | 203 | ... |
| 1938 | 2,328 | 67 | 1,122 | 502 | 213 | ... | 76 | 229 | 106 |
| 1939 | 2,461 | 71 | 1,210 | 509 | 251 | ... | 87 | 245 | 112 |
| 1940 | 2,550 | 85 | 1,276 | 570 | 254 | ... | 98 | 282 | 137 |
| 1941 | 2,644 | 93 | 1,391 | 614 | 270 | 13 | 110 | ... | 160 |
| 1942 | 2,773 | 98 | 1,498 | 640 | 280 | 14 | 122 | ... | 170 |
| 1943 | 2,927 | 118 | 1,621 | 697 | 302 | 15 | 129 | ... | 175 |
| 1944 | 3,064 | 118 | 1,778 | 730 | 340 | 17 | 138 | ... | 189 |

**D22    SOUTH AMERICA: Output of Electric Energy** (in giga Watt hours)

|  | Argentina[4] | Bolivia[4] | Brazil[15] | Chile[16] | Colombia[17] | Ecuador |
|---|---|---|---|---|---|---|
| 1945 | 2,976 | 131 | 1,899 | 893 | 396 | … |
| 1946 | 3,263 | 138 | 2,032 | 987 | 463 | … |
| 1947 | 3,576 | 145 | 2,204 | 1,083 | 517 | … |
| 1948 | 4,034 | 171 | 2,452[15] | 1,166[16] | 545 | 105 |
|  |  |  | 6,797 | 2,906 |  |  |
| 1949 | 4,121 | 172 | 7,610 | 2,844 | 625 | 125 |
| 1950 | 4,430[4] | 174[4] | 8,208 | 2,943 | 705[17] | 118 |
|  | 5,155 | 226 |  |  | 1,147 |  |
| 1951 | 5,468 | 225 | 8,758 | 3,224 | 1,254 | 141 |
| 1952 | 5,551 | 230 | 10,029 | 3,361 | 1,440 | 153 |
| 1953 | 5,963 | 370 | 10,341 | 3,337 | 1,663 | 167 |
| 1954 | 6,466 | 390 | 11,871 | 3,590 | 1,950 | 188 |
| 1955 | 7,035 | 387 | 13,655 | 3,866 | 2,250 | 259 |
| 1956 | 7,665 | 400 | 15,447 | 4,046 | 2,403 | 281 |
| 1957 | 8,191 | 421 | 16,963 | 4,190 | 2,850 | 299 |
| 1958 | 9,418 | 444 | 19,766 | 4,146 | 3,034 | 324 |
| 1959 | 9,544 | 433 | 21,108 | 4,605 | 3,413 | 349 |
| 1960 | 10,459 | 447 | 22,865 | 4,592 | 3,750 | 387 |
| 1961 | 11,547 | 463 | 24,405 | 4,880 | 3,776 | 411 |
| 1962 | 11,887 | 495 | 27,158 | 5,286 | 4,280 | 451 |
| 1963 | 12,449 | 531 | 27,869 | 5,623 | 5,268 | 495 |
| 1964 | 13,928 | 534 | 29,094 | 5,932 | 5,916 | 551 |
| 1965 | 15,383 | 566 | 30,128 | 6,131 | 5,824 | 572 |
| 1966 | 15,927 | 619 | 32,654 | 6,662 | 6,319 | 609 |
| 1967 | 16,687 | 640 | 34,238 | 6,892 | 7,055 | 672 |
| 1968 | 17,952 | 702 | 38,181 | 6,918 | 7,197 | 749 |
| 1969 | 20,014 | 739 | 41,648 | 7,214 | 8,157 | 850 |
| 1970 | 21,727 | 787 | 45,460 | 7,550 | 8,750 | 949 |
| 1971 | 23,624 | 832 | 50,988 | 8,524 | 9,500 | 1,050 |
| 1972 | 25,306 | 872 | 56,995 | 8,934 | 10,999 | 1,117 |
| 1973 | 26,660 | 918 | 64,727 | 8,766 | 11,881 | 1,256 |
| 1974 | 27,951 | 993 | 71,698 | 9,297 | 12,613 | 1,430 |
| 1975 | 29,468 | 1,057 | 78,936 | 8,732 | 13,345 | 1,650 |
| 1976 | 30,216 | 1,132 | 89,979 | 9,276 | 14,757 | 1,885 |
| 1977 | 32,413 | 1,260 | 100,822 | 9,776 | 15,369 | 2,260 |
| 1978 | 33,434 | 1,354 | 112,575 | 10,360 | 17,358 | 2,565 |
| 1979 | 37,640 | 1,432 | 124,673 | 11,133 | 19,139 | 2,954 |
| 1980 | 39,676 | 1,564 | 139,485 | 11,751 | 20,624 | 3,352 |
| 1981 | 38,838 | 1,677 | 142,198 | 11,979 | 20,704 | 3,730 |
| 1982 | 39,804 | 1,677 | 151,999 | 11,872 | 26,183 | 4,118 |
| 1983 | 42,998 | 1,668 | 161,969 | 12,624 | 27,334 | 4,289 |
| 1984 | 44,914 | 1,511 | 178,532 | 13,498 | 29,888 | 4,207 |
| 1985 | 45,265 | 1,510 | 192,731 | 14,040 | 30,268 | 4,806 |
| 1986 | 48,984 | 1,515 | 201,353 | 14,820 | 33,564 | 5,301 |
| 1987 | 52,165 | 1,520 | 202,349 | 15,636 | 35,368 | 5,353 |
| 1988 | 53,062 | 1,883 | 214,117 | 16,914 | 38,338 | 5,603 |

**D22    SOUTH AMERICA: Output of Electric Energy** (in gigaWatt hours)

| | French Guiana | Guyana | Paraguay[18] | Peru[19] | Surinam | Uruguay[20] | Venezuela |
|------|------|------|------|------|------|------|------|
| 1945 | ... | ... | 19 | 150 | ... | ... | 212 |
| 1946 | ... | ... | 21 | 164 | ... | 350 | 239 |
| 1947 | ... | ... | 21 | 182 | ... | ... | 282 |
| 1948 | ... | ... | 28[18] / 37 | 204 | ... | 532 | 344 |
| 1949 | 0.2 | ... | 40 | 232 | ... | 574 | 409 |
| 1950 | 0.4 | ... | 44 | 237[19] / 322 | 35 | 616 | 520[21] / 1,220 |
| 1951 | 0.7 | 38 | 48 | 344 | 35 | 682 | 1,460 |
| 1952 | 1.0 | 43 | 52 | 461[19] / 1,051 | 38 | 753 | 1,670 |
| 1953 | ... | 44 | 55 | 1,219 | 40 | 845 | 1,988 |
| 1954 | 1.7 | 50 | 60 | 1,384 | 42 | 927 | 2,190 |
| 1955 | 2.3 | 55 | 64 | 1,524 | 43 | 1,024 | 2,385 |
| 1956 | 2.6 | 59 | 65 | 1,594 | 55 | 1,065 | 2,650 |
| 1957 | 2.9 | 67 | 75 | 1,792 | 66 | 1,155 | 3,103 |
| 1958 | 3.2 | 70 | 82 | 1,990 | 66 | 1,237 | 3,791 |
| 1959 | 3.8 | 72 | 87 | 2,219 | 72 | 1,176 | 4,497 |
| 1960 | 4.4 | 92 | 96 | 2,656 | 79 | 1,244 | 4,651 |
| 1961 | 4.7 | 124 | 107 | 2,945 | 87 | 1,327 | 5,217 |
| 1962 | 5.8 | 147 | 107 | 3,067 | 112 | 1,559 | 5,922 |
| 1963 | 7.4 | 143 | 125 | 3,419 | 119 | 1,578[20] / 1,639 | 6,771 |
| 1964 | 8.7 | 212 | 129 | 3,689 | 128 | 1,819 | 7,597 |
| 1965 | 11 | 220 | 135 | 3,839 | 244 | 1,744 | 8,197 |
| 1966 | 13 | 240 | 151 | 4,336 | 681 | 1,918 | 8,593 |
| 1967 | 20 | 260 | 165 | 4,770 | 843 | 1,944 | 9,277 |
| 1968 | 29 | 287 | 179 | 5,008 | 1,076 | 1,940 | 10,646 |
| 1969 | 42 | 312 | 203 | 5,288 | 1,242 | 2,090 | 11,494 |
| 1970 | 55 | 323 | 218 | 5,529 | 1,322 | 2,200 | 12,708 |
| 1971 | 60 | 329 | 246 | 5,949 | 1,362 | 2,360 | 13,386 |
| 1972 | 62 | 340 | 273 | 6,289 | 1,465 | 2,405 | 14,829 |
| 1973 | 67 | 361 | 379 | 6,655 | 1,528 | 2,520 | 16,077 |
| 1974 | 63 | 370 | 504 | 7,275 | 1,588 | 2,358 | 18,222 |
| 1975 | 66 | 383 | 599 | 7,486 | 1,201 | 2,444 | 19,591 |
| 1976 | 65 | 392 | 604 | 7,911 | 1,335 | 2,665 | 20,539 |
| 1977 | 71 | 431 | 532 | 8,627 | 1,421 | 2,876 | 23,452 |
| 1978 | 89 | 409 | 516 | 8,765 | 1,511 | 3,046 | 25,955 |
| 1979 | 102 | 407 | 644 | 9,265 | 1,530 | 2,960 | 32,033 |
| 1980 | 113 | 414 | 725 | 10,039 | 1,577 | 3,355 | 35,932 |
| 1981 | 124 | 429 | 747 | 10,757 | 1,367 | 3,603 | 37,542 |
| 1982 | 138 | 354 | 681 | 11,350 | 1,332 | 3,593 | 39,964 |
| 1983 | 164 | 400 | 818 | 10,675 | 1,107 | 7,343 | 43,493 |
| 1984 | 181 | 400 | 920 | 11,717 | 1,250 | 7,244 | 44,330 |
| 1985 | 207 | 390 | 1,260 | 12,115 | 1,300 | 6,602 | 47,997 |
| 1986 | 223 | 390 | 1,643 | 12,985 | 1,325 | 7,429 | 51,093 |
| 1987 | 249 | 385 | 2,290 | 14,195 | 1,330 | 7,578 | 54,706 |
| 1988 | 282 | 385 | 2,900 | 14,135 | 1,350 | 6,998 | 57,773 |

**D22** **Output of Electric Energy** (in giga Watt hours)

NOTES

1. SOURCES: The national publications listed on p. xiv–xvi; League of Nations and UN, *Statistical Yearbooks;* UN, *World Energy Supplies.*
2. Except as indicated in footnotes, the statistics are of gross output (i.e inclusive of electricity consumed in the power stations and of transmission losses).

FOOTNOTES

[1] Excluding Out islands to 1965.
[2] Years ended 30 June to 1963.
[3] Net output, excluding output of industrial and railway establishments to 1927 (1st line). Newfoundland is included from 1950. Its output in 1930 was 795.
[4] Public supply only to 1955 (1st line).
[5] Net output.
[6] Consumption in Guatemala City and neighbourhood to 1948 (1st line). Public supply only in 1949 and 1950 (1st line).
[7] Public supply only to 1950 (1st line).
[8] Public supply of Panama City and Colón only to 1950 (1st line).
[9] Years ended 30 June, beginning 1970 in the case of Puerto Rico.
[10] Public supply only, excluding San Fernando to 1950 (1st line).
[11] Including Alaska and Hawaii from 1959.
[12] Belize town only to 1962.
[13] January–September.
[14] The reason for this break is not given in the source.
[15] Rio de Janeiro and São Paulo cities only to 1948 (1st line). Total production to 1939 was 2,987.
[16] Public supply only to 1948 (1st line). Total supply in 1938 was 1,634.
[17] Three main enterprises only to 1950 (1st line).
[18] Ascension only to 1948 (1st line).
[19] Lima and Callao only to 1950 (1st line). Public supply only in 1949 and 1950 (1st line).
[20] Public supply only to 1963 (1st line). Data to 1924 (1st line) are for Montevideo only and are for years beginning 1 July.
[21] Public supply in the state of Miranda plus 24 enterprises in the rest of the country to 1950 (1st line). Total public supply in 1950 was 552.

**D23    IMPORTS AND EXPORTS OF COAL BY MAIN TRADING COUNTRIES** (in thousands of metric tons)

| | NORTH AMERICA | | | | SOUTH AMERICA |
| | Canada[1] | | USA | | Argentina[2] |
| | Imports | Exports | Imports | Exports | Imports |
|---|---|---|---|---|---|
| 1867 | ... | ... | 518 | 289 | ... |
| 1868 | ... | 240 | 400 | 283 | ... |
| 1869 | ... | 399 | 445 | ... | ... |
| 1870 | ... | 260 | 423 | 232 | ... |
| 1871 | ... | 288 | 438 | 272 | ... |
| 1872 | ... | 269 | 493 | 407 | ... |
| 1873 | ... | 367 | 469 | 594 | ... |
| 1874 | ... | 379 | 501 | 776 | ... |
| 1875 | ... | 261 | 444 | 528 | ... |
| 1976 | ... | 252 | 409 | 577 | ... |
| 1877 | ... | 227 | 504 | 752 | ... |
| 1878 | ... | 308 | 582 | 671 | ... |
| 1879 | ... | 287 | 495 | 673 | ... |
| 1880 | 886 | 313 | 479 | 625 | ... |
| 1881 | 1,051 | 381 | 664 | 664 | ... |
| 1882 | 1,157 | 382 | 808 | 882 | ... |
| 1883 | 1,520 | 403 | 657 | 1,038 | ... |
| 1884 | 1,813 | 410 | 763 | 1,316 | ... |
| 1885 | 1,762 | 435, [1] | 787 | 1,292 | ... |
| 1886 | 1,781 | 473 | 826 | 1,231 | ... |
| 1887 | 2,069 | 527 | 847 | 1,557 | 409 |
| 1888 | 3,084 | 534 | 1,128 | 1,860 | 336 |
| 1889 | 2,341 | 603 | 1,039 | 1,822 | 661 |
| 1890 | 2,417 | 657 | 965 | 1,961 | 516 |
| 1891 | 2,774 | 881 | 1,110 | 2,374 | 354 |
| 1892 | 2,881 | 748 | 1,420 | 2,594 | 522 |
| 1893 | 2,915 | 871 | 1,174 | 3,156 | 586 |
| 1894 | 2,729 | 1,002 | 1,258 | 3,678 | 751 |
| 1895 | 2,750 | 917 | 1,423 | 3,907 | 854 |
| 1896 | 3,015 | 1,004 | 1,367 | 3,654 | 869 |
| 1897 | 2,927 | 894 | 1,334 | 3,742 | 784 |
| 1898 | 3,061 | 1,043 | 1,297 | 4,098 | 885 |
| 1899 | 3,804 | 1,173 | 1,279 | 5,272 | 1,101 |

**D23**    **Imports and Exports of Coal by Main Trading Countries** (in thousands of metric tons)

| | NORTH AMERICA | | | | SOUTH AMERICA | |
| | Canada[1] | | USA | | Argentina[2] | Brazil |
| | Imports | Exports | Imports | Exports | Imports | Imports |
|------|------|------|------|------|------|------|
| 1900 | 4,013 | 1,622 | 1,735 | 7,179 | 780 | ... |
| 1901 | 4,413 | 1,428 | 2,009 | 7,882 | 939 | 793 |
| 1902 | 4,707 | 1,898 | 2,145 | 6,410 | 1,060 | 944 |
| 1903 | 5,007 | 1,774 | 3,847 | 7,335 | 1,079 | 920 |
| 1904 | 6,293 | 1,412 | 2,051 | 8,802 | 1,431 | 988 |
| 1905 | 6,741 | 1,483 | 1,581 | 9,082 | 1,501 | 1,055 |
| 1906 | 6,753[1] | 1,665 | 1,882 | 9,523 | 2,358 | 1,208 |
| 1907 | 9,662 | 1,718 | 1,727 | 11,695 | 2,357 | 1,301 |
| 1908 | 9,341 | 1,569 | 2,029 | 12,840 | 2,869 | 1,355 |
| 1909 | 8,957 | 1,441 | 1,251 | 12,052 | 2,234 | 1,348 |
| 1910 | 9,614 | 2,156 | 1,659 | 13,650 | 3,354 | 1,582 |
| 1911 | 13,208 | 1,362 | 1,793 | 15,640 | 3,746 | 1,736 |
| 1912 | 13,241 | 1,930 | 1,323 | 18,693 | 3,739[2] | 2,099 |
| | | | | | 3,532 | |
| 1913 | 16,513 | 1,417 | 1,605 | 20,562 | 3,801 | 2,262 |
| 1914 | 13,355 | 1,291 | 1,396 | 19,849 | 3,221 | 1,540 |
| 1915 | 11,309 | 1,603 | 1,547 | 20,631 | 2,525 | 1,164 |
| 1916 | 15,949 | 1,937 | 1,560 | 23,515 | 1,728 | 1,024 |
| 1917 | 18,921 | 1,572 | 1,325 | 27,077 | 627 | 818 |
| 1918 | 19,667 | 1,648 | 952 | 24,783 | 712 | 637 |
| 1919 | 15,688 | 1,878 | 993 | 22,762 | 1,170 | 927 |
| 1920 | 17,095 | 2,321 | 1,158 | 39,844 | 1,909[2] | 1,121 |
| | | | | | 2,046 | |
| 1921 | 16,603 | 1,803 | 1,149 | 25,227 | 1,721 | 843 |
| 1922 | 11,815 | 1,650 | 4,803 | 13,664 | 2,220 | 1,176 |
| 1923 | 19,042 | 1,500 | 1,979 | 24,080 | 2,579 | 1,470 |
| 1924 | 15,173 | 701 | 485 | 19,158 | 3,299 | 1,620 |
| 1925 | 14,832 | 713 | 894 | 18,725 | 3,148 | 1,703 |
| 1926 | 15,040 | 933 | 1,179 | 35,654 | 2,808 | 1,772 |
| 1927 | 16,408 | 1,010 | 607 | 19,358 | 3,489 | 2,008 |
| 1928 | 15,609 | 784 | 845 | 17,690 | 3,122 | 1,950 |
| 1929 | 16,514 | 765 | 891 | 18,901 | 3,136 | 2,067 |
| 1930 | 17,031 | 567 | 831 | 16,719 | 3,061 | 1,746 |
| 1931 | 11,903 | 327 | 766 | 12,613 | 2,619 | 1,134 |
| 1932 | 10,849 | 259 | 720 | 9,178 | 2,387 | 1,099 |
| 1933 | 10,164 | 235 | 592 | 9,137 | 2,246 | 1,207 |
| 1934 | 11,771 | 278 | 597 | 11,038 | 2,480 | 1,080 |
| 1935 | 10,958 | 379 | 701 | 10,297 | 2,388 | 1,315 |
| 1936 | 11,905 | 374 | 805 | 11,188 | 2,633 | 1,290 |
| 1937 | 13,309 | 322 | 578 | 13,661 | 3,075 | 1,516 |
| 1938 | 11,804 | 320 | 548 | 11,248 | 2,787 | 1,382 |
| 1939 | 13,507 | 341 | 608 | 12,864 | 2,925 | 1,201 |
| 1940 | 15,810 | 458 | 460 | 17,358 | 2,023 | 1,150 |
| 1941 | 18,496 | 482 | 422 | 21,881 | 1,012 | 1,013 |
| 1942 | 22,622 | 740 | 579 | 24,841 | 519 | 593 |
| 1943 | 25,500 | 1,007 | 726 | 27,193 | 576 | 538 |
| 1944 | 26,058[1] | 916 | 435 | 27,413 | 617 | 468 |

**D23    Imports and Exports of Coal by Main Trading Countries** (in thousands of metric tons)

| | NORTH AMERICA | | | | SOUTH AMERICA | |
| | Canada[1] | | USA | | Argentina[2] | Brazil |
| | Imports | Exports | Imports | Exports | Imports | Imports |
|------|---------|---------|---------|---------|---------|---------|
| 1945 | 22,736 | 763 | 424 | 28,710 | 768 | 698 |
| 1946 | 23,684 | 782 | 404 | 43,267 | 1,144 | 1,038 |
| 1947 | 26,210 | 649 | 272 | 70,014 | 1,215 | 1,531 |
| 1948 | 28,008 | 1,155 | 265 | 47,723 | 2,177 | 1,060 |
| 1949 | [20,135][1] | 392 | 286 | 29,742 | 1,341 | 767 |
| 1950 | 24,453 | 358 | 331 | 26,635 | 1,447 | 1,083 |
| 1951 | 24,313 | 395 | 289 | 56,861 | 2,168 | 1,005 |
| 1952 | 22,619 | 353 | 264 | 47,387 | 1,740 | 885 |
| 1953 | 21,102 | 231 | 234 | 33,098 | 1,184 | 742 |
| 1954 | 16,852 | 199 | 186 | 30,746 | 1,506 | 408 |
| 1955 | 17,907 | 538 | 306 | 49,377 | 1,177 | 564 |
| 1956 | 20,510 | 539 | 323 | 66,948 | 1,352 | 446 |
| 1957 | 17,669 | 359 | 334 | 73,281 | 1,156 | 894 |
| 1958 | 13,144 | 307 | 344 | 47,693 | 1,354 | 567 |
| 1959 | 12,912 | 430 | 343 | 35,417 | 1,321 | 634 |
| 1960 | 12,303 | 774 | 237 | 34,456 | 1,402 | 1,035 |
| 1961 | 11,164 | 852 | 150 | 33,026 | 1,216 | 858 |
| 1962 | 11,443 | 811 | 218 | 36,482 | 620 | 892 |
| 1963 | 12,130 | 957 | 247 | 45,754 | 769 | 866 |
| 1964 | 13,597 | 1,258 | 266 | 44,946 | 691 | 1,352 |
| 1965 | 15,054 | 1,398 | 167 | 46,295 | 657 | 1,048 |
| 1966 | 14,910 | 1,449 | 161 | 45,421 | 698 | 1,744 |
| 1967 | 14,618 | 1,522 | 206 | 45,455 | 806 | 1,537 |
| 1968 | 15,429 | 1,699 | 203 | 46,408 | 520 | 1,408 |
| 1969 | 15,678 | 1,771 | 99 | 51,584 | 431 | 1,921 |
| 1970 | 17,033 | 4,512 | 33 | 65,096 | 746 | 1,989 |
| 1971 | 16,462 | 7,626 | 101 | 51,986 | 717 | 1,717 |
| 1972 | 17,484 | 8,264 | 43 | 51,474 | 428 | 1,856 |
| 1973 | 14,951 | 11,645 | 115 | 48,627 | 781 | 1,696 |
| 1974 | 12,389 | 11,407 | 1,887 | 55,043 | 821 | 1,596 |
| 1975 | 15,258 | 12,060 | 853 | 60,172 | 1,027 | 2,761 |
| 1976 | 14,553 | 12,241 | 1,092 | 54,466 | 802 | 3,174 |
| 1977 | 15,266 | 12,573 | 1,495 | 49,285 | 1,246 | 3,563 |
| 1978 | 13,226 | 14,188 | 2,680 | 36,946 | 952 | 3,640 |
| 1979 | 17,541 | 14,440 | 1,868 | 59,929 | 405 | 4,479 |
| 1980 | 15,618 | 14,701 | 1,033 | 83,250 | 788 | 4,526 |
| 1981 | 14,620 | 16,612 | 946 | 102,124 | 878 | 4,353 |
| 1982 | 15,432 | 15,885 | 673 | 96,440 | 739 | 4,236 |
| 1983 | 14,451 | 17,376 | 1,153 | 70,574 | 492 | 6,295 |
| 1984 | 18,767 | 24,816 | 1,167 | 73,940 | 537 | 8,104 |
| 1985 | 14,727 | 28,019 | 1,771 | 84,102 | 764 | 8,260 |
| 1986 | 12,981 | 26,435 | 2,007 | 77,603 | 1,157 | 8,946 |
| 1987 | 13,815 | 25,944 | 1,585 | 72,239 | 1,254 | 10,591 |
| 1988 | 15,214 | 30,158 | 1,936 | 86,228 | 1,383 | 10,712 |

**D23    Imports and Exports of Coal by Main Trading Countries** (in thousands of metric tons)

NOTES

1.  SOURCES: The national publications listed on p. xiv–xvi; League of Nations, *International Trade Statistics*; and UN, *Yearbook of International Trade Statistics.*
2.  All kinds of coal are aggregated, but, except as indicated, coke is not included.
3.  Coal used for ships' bunkers is not normally included.

FOOTNOTES

[1] Data to 1885 for exports and to 1906 for imports are for years ending 30 June. Newfoundland is included as part of Canada from 1 April 1949. Briquettes are included to 1944.
[2] Data to 1912 (1st line) include coke. From 1912 (2nd line) to 1920 (1st line) they are of net imports.

**D24 NORTH AMERICA: IMPORTS AND EXPORTS OF PETROLEUM BY MAIN TRADING COUNTRIES** (in thousands of metric tons, except as otherwise indicated)

Key:     CP = crude petroleum, PP = petroleum products

| | Canada[1] | | Mexico | Trinidad & Tobago | USA[3] | |
| | CP | | CP & PP | CP & PP | CP | |
| | Imports[2] | Exports | Exports | Exports | Imports | Exports[4] |
| | (thousand barrels) | | | (million gallons) | (thousand barrels) | |
| 1870 | ... | — | — | — | ... | 248 |
| 1871 | ... | — | — | — | ... | 269 |
| 1872 | ... | — | — | — | ... | 390 |
| 1873 | ... | — | — | — | ... | 468 |
| 1874 | ... | — | — | — | ... | 344 |
| 1875 | ... | — | — | — | ... | 394 |
| 1876 | ... | — | — | — | ... | 603 |
| 1877 | ... | — | — | — | ... | 685 |
| 1878 | ... | — | — | — | ... | 573 |
| 1879 | ... | — | — | — | ... | 681 |
| 1880 | 20 | — | — | — | ... | 875 |
| 1881 | 41 | — | — | — | ... | 963 |
| 1882 | 86 | — | — | — | ... | 1,072 |
| 1883 | 88 | 31 | — | — | ... | 1,405 |
| 1884 | 90 | 10 | — | — | ... | 1,897 |
| 1885 | 108 | 7 | — | — | ... | 1,939 |
| 1886 | 109 | 14 | — | — | ... | 1,818 |
| 1887 | 123 | 6 | — | — | ... | 1,920 |
| 1888 | 129 | 7 | — | — | ... | 1,846 |
| 1889 | 133 | 12 | — | — | ... | 2,028 |
| 1890 | 145 | 13 | — | — | ... | 2,299 |
| 1891 | 145 | 9 | — | — | ... | 2,303 |
| 1892 | 161 | 3 | — | — | ... | 2,486[3] |
| 1893 | 171 | 2 | — | — | ... | 2,660 |
| 1894 | 188 | 1 | — | — | ... | 2,903 |
| 1895 | 217 | — | — | — | ... | 2,650 |
| 1896 | 229 | — | — | — | ... | 2,641[3] |
| 1897 | 240 | — | — | — | ... | 2,893 |
| 1898 | 259[2] | — | — | — | ... | 2,736 |
| 1899 | 8 | — | — | — | ... | 2,802 |
| 1900 | 10 | — | — | — | ... | 3,290 |
| 1901 | 10 | — | — | — | ... | 3,024 |
| 1902 | 17 | — | — | — | ... | 3,458 |
| 1903 | 61 | — | — | — | ... | 3,012 |
| 1904 | 123 | — | — | — | ... | 2,647 |
| 1905 | 643 | — | — | — | ... | 3,004 |
| 1906 | [379][1] | — | — | — | ... | 3,525 |
| 1907 | 712 | — | — | — | ... | 3,007 |
| 1908 | 903 | — | — | — | ... | 3,552 |
| 1909 | ... | — | — | -- | ... | 4,056 |
| 1910 | 1,532 | — | — | — | ... | 4,288 |
| 1911 | 2,047 | — | 100 | 8 | ... | 4,806 |
| 1912 | 3,431 | 1 | 1,220 | 4 | ... | 4,493 |
| 1913 | 4,630 | — | 3,250 | 14 | 17,809 | 4,633 |
| 1914 | 5,577 | — | 3,560 | 12 | 17,247 | 2,970 |

**D24 NORTH AMERICA: Imports and Exports of Petroleum by Main Trading Countries** (in thousands of metric tons, except as otherwise indicated)

| | Canada | | Mexico | Trinidad & Tobago | | | USA | | | |
|---|---|---|---|---|---|---|---|---|---|---|
| | CP | | CP & PP | CP | | PP | CP | | PP | |
| | Imports[2] | Exports | Exports | Imports | Exports | Exports | Imports | Exports | Imports | Exports |
| | (thousand barrels) | | | (million gallons) | | | (thousand barrels) | | (million barrels) | |
| 1915 | 5,503 | 1 | 3,760 | — | 14 | | 18,140 | 3,768 | ... | ... |
| 1916 | 7,231 | 4 | 4,060 | — | 34 | | 30,570 | 4,096 | ... | ... |
| 1917 | 9,328 | — | 7,000 | — | 15 | 23 | 30,127 | 4,098 | ... | ... |
| 1918 | 10,789 | 8 | 7,820 | — | 13 | 33 | 37,736 | 4,901 | ... | ... |
| 1919 | 11,585 | 17 | 11,380 | — | 14 | 35 | 52,822 | 6,019 | ... | ... |
| | | | | | | | (million barrels) | | | |
| 1920 | 8,312 | 77 | 21,687 | — | 5 | 32 | 106 | 9.3 / 8.8 | 2.6 | 70 |
| 1921 | 10,158 | 154 | 25,656 | — | 4 | 39 | 125 | 9.6 | 3.4 | 62 |
| 1922 | 12,014 | 201 | 26,951 | — | 9 | 47 | 127 | 11 | 8.7 | 64 |
| 1923 | 11,219 | 68 | 20,564 | — | 12 | 74 | 82 | 18 | 18 | 84 |
| 1924 | 13,317 | 522 | 19,371 | — | 12 | 90 | 78 | 18 | 17 | 99 |
| 1925 | 12,584 | 211 | 14,443 | — | 11 | 100 | 62 | 13 | 16 | 100 |
| 1926 | 16,298 | 601 | 10,261 | — | 13 | 113 | 60 | 15 | 21 | 117 |
| 1927 | 19,562 | 537 | 6,324 | — | 16 | 108 | 58 | 16 | 13 | 126 |
| 1928 | 24,404 | 615 | 4,327 | 5 | 26 | 143 | 80 | 19 | 12 | 136 |
| 1929 | 30,291 | 805 | 3,909 | — | 32 | 179 | 79 | 26 | 30 | 137 |
| 1930 | 28,931 | 550 | 4,047 | 6 | 37 | 154 | 62 | 24 | 43 | 133 |
| 1931 | 29,070 | 465 | 3,367 | 2 | 93 | 115 | 47 | 26 | 39 | 99 |
| 1932 | 25,432 | 208 | 3,394 | 2 | 92 | 132 | 45 | 27 | 30 | 74 |
| 1933 | 27,270 | 305 | 3,302 | 14 | 41 | 136 | 32 | 37 | 14 | 68 |
| 1934 | 30,643 | — | 3,792 | 24 | 17 | 200 | 36 | 41 | 15 | 72 |
| 1935 | 33,052 | — | 3,535 | 15 | 10 | 255 | 32 | 51 | 20 | 74 |
| 1936 | 35,833 | — | 3,701 | 18 | 15 | 308 | 32 | 50 | 25 | 79 |
| 1937 | 38,915 | — | 3,605 | 14 | 22 | 333 | 27 | 67 | 30 | 102 |
| 1938 | 34,245 | — | 1,223 | 18 | 23 | 418 | 26 | 77 | 28 | 116 |
| 1939 | 37,095 | — | 1,977 | 12 | 8 | 351 | 33 | 72 | 26 | 117 |
| 1940 | 42,623 | — | 1,744 | 14 | 6 | 192 | 43 | 51 | 41 | 79 |
| 1941 | 46,791 | — | 2,097 | 8 | 6 | 42 | 51 | 33 | 47 | 76 |
| 1942 | 44,120 | 1 | 828 | 3 | — | 14 | 12 | 34 | 24 | 83 |
| 1943 | 49,754 | — | 779 | — | — | 12 | 14 | 41 | 50 | 109 |
| 1944 | 57,048 | — | 664 | 38 | — | 13 | 45 | 34 | 48 | 173 |
| 1945 | 56,806 | — | 1,105 | 74 | — | 118 | 74 | 33 | 39 | 150 |
| 1946 | 63,407 | — | 1,255 | 101 | 3 | 421 | 86 | 42 | 52 | 111 |
| 1947 | 68,447 | — | 1,892 | 206 | 31 | 498 | 98 | 46 | 62 | 118 |
| 1948 | 75,559 | 1 | 1,784 | 310 | 73 | 652 | 129 | 40 | 59 | 95 |
| 1949 | 73,947 | — | 1,921 | 395 | 89 | 732 | 154 | 33 | 82 | 86 |

**D24  NORTH AMERICA: Imports and Exports of Petroleum by Main Trading Countries** (in thousands of metric tons, except as otherwise indicated)

**1950–1988**

| | Canada | | Mexico | | Trinidad & Tobago | | | USA | | | |
|---|---|---|---|---|---|---|---|---|---|---|---|
| | CP | | CP | PP | CP | | PP | CP | | PP | |
| | Imports[2] | Exports | Exports | Exports | Imports | Exports | Exports | Imports | Exports | Imports | Exports |
| 1950 | 11,351 | — | 1,836 | | 1,587 | 310 | 2,594 | 24,880 | 4,705 | 18,598 | 6,121 |
| 1951 | 12,018 | 46 | 1,138 | | 2,302 | 278 | 2,909 | 25,070 | 3,865 | 18,449 | 11,711 |
| 1952 | 11,717 | 192 | 2,184 | | 2,425 | 267 | 2,932 | 29,340 | 3,610 | 20,203 | 12,537 |
| 1953 | 11,469 | 337 | 2,354 | | 2,447 | 289 | 3,034 | 33,105 | 2,695 | 21,340 | 12,245 |
| 1954 | 11,367 | 315 | 3,514 | | 2,361 | 430 | 3,185 | 34,111 | 1,838 | 20,242 | 10,659 |
| 1955 | 12,500 | 1,995 | 4,190 | | 2,522 | 406 | 3,721 | 39,942 | 1,564 | 24,225 | 11,040 |
| 1956 | 15,370 | 5,771 | 3,791 | | 2,803 | 550 | 4,573 | 47,922 | 3,868 | 26,780 | 11,536 |
| 1957 | 16,087 | 7,488 | 2,326 | | 2,616 | 488 | 5,045 | 52,632 | 6,790 | 29,181 | 15,392 |
| 1958 | 15,133 | 4,261 | 1,736 | | 3,660 | 407 | 5,944 | 48,906 | 587 | 34,093 | 7,656 |
| 1959 | 16,210 | 4,487 | 1,913 | | 4,465 | 465 | 7,057 | 49,279 | 341 | 39,420 | 7,211 |
| 1960 | 17,749 | 5,681 | 1,202 | | 5,733 | 698 | 7,761 | 51,874 | 418 | 39,874 | 6,106 |
| 1961 | 18,664 | 8,772 | 2,119 | | 8,749 | 803 | 10,136 | 53,098 | 436 | 42,225 | 4,481 |
| 1962 | 18,850 | 12,318 | 2,735 | | 8,966 | 967 | 11,019 | 57,094 | 242 | 45,603 | 4,240 |
| 1963 | 20,645 | 12,223 | 2,706 | | 9,728 | 1,052 | 13,774 | 57,361 | 230 | 47,604 | 5,712 |
| 1964 | 20,216 | 13,619 | 2,560 | | 11,805 | 1,501 | 15,153 | 60,829 | 184 | 50,873 | 4,828 |
| 1965 | 20,192 | 14,527 | 2,603 | | 13,082 | 1,559 | 15,546 | 62,404 | 136 | 59,556 | 4,149 |
| 1966 | 20,271 | 16,636 | 2,071 | | 13,048 | 1,473 | 16,370 | 61,573 | 201 | 65,841 | 3,960 |
| 1967 | 23,909 | 20,221 | 2,003 | | 11,382 | 1,962 | 16,073 | 56,676 | 3,586 | 69,159 | 5,552 |
| 1968 | 25,042 | 22,527 | 2,124 | | 12,948 | 2,178 | 17,592 | 64,915 | 244 | 77,083 | 4,740 |
| 1969 | 25,107 | 26,542 | 2,600 | | 14,561 | 2,469 | 18,322 | 70,497 | 194 | 86,488 | 4,336 |
| 1970 | 29,293 | 32,096 | — | 2,629 | 15,713 | 2,849 | 17,556 | 66,239 | 674 | 103,087 | 4,428 |
| 1971 | 34,221 | 34,848 | — | 1,872 | 14,634 | 2,594 | 16,488 | 83,837 | 68 | 108,210 | 3,597 |
| 1972 | 40,519 | 42,615 | — | 755 | 14,841 | 2,042 | 16,492 | 111,114 | 26 | 120,400 | 3,185 |
| 1973 | 43,359 | 50 | — | 816 | 14,096 | 3,329 | 15,315 | 161,269 | 94 | 141,883 | 2,996 |
| 1974 | 41,723 | 40,111 | 818 | 825 | 12,999 | 4,506 | 15,188 | 172,573 | 145 | 122,567 | 1,894 |
| 1975 | 41,424 | 30,833 | 4,848 | 354 | 7,895 | 6,835 | 9,646 | 203,124 | 290 | 93,079 | 1,845 |
| 1976 | 36,585 | 19,960 | 4,861 | 152 | 11,532 | 6,284 | 13,138 | 261,670 | 397 | 98,405 | 1,722 |
| 1977 | 33,613 | 14,074 | 10,147 | 206 | 8,922 | 6,993 | 11,311 | 325,976 | 2,461 | 106,353 | 1,144 |
| 1978 | 31,158 | 12,265 | 18,760 | 80 | 7,946 | 7,161 | 9,026 | 313,076 | 7,783 | 100,047 | 1,613 |
| 1979 | 30,928 | 13,517 | 26,586 | 426 | 7,225 | 6,267 | 8,097 | 321,695 | 11,555 | 91,896 | 1,152 |
| 1980 | 28,095 | 9,591 | 34,669 | 2,189 | 7,346 | 6,251 | 9,344 | 261,440 | 14,148 | 77,404 | 4,021 |
| 1981 | 25,779 | 8,041 | 56,518 | 3,454 | 6,928 | 5,817 | 6,148 | 218,244 | 11,213 | 70,115 | 9,350 |
| 1982 | 17,206 | 10,291 | 77,573 | 2,158 | 3,669 | 4,375 | 5,595 | 174,626 | 11,632 | 66,457 | 19,480 |
| 1983 | 12,564 | 14,016 | 79,907 | 4,039 | — | 4,841 | 710 | 166,934 | 8,082 | 66,921 | 17,314 |
| 1984 | 12,451 | 17,560 | 80,206 | 5,273 | — | 4,378 | 3,538 | 171,943 | 8,930 | 76,952 | 16,262 |
| 1985 | 14,249 | 23,942 | 74,340 | 6,148 | 189 | 4,806 | 3,466 | 160,861 | 10,046 | 65,396 | 18,168 |
| 1986 | 17,799 | 28,762 | 66,746 | 4,943 | 217 | 4,498 | 3,520 | 209,471 | 7,595 | 78,337 | 17,680 |
| 1987 | 20,053 | 30,512 | 69,854 | 4,039 | 249 | 3,882 | 3,795 | 233,923 | 7,550 | 74,155 | 18,361 |
| 1988 | 22,152 | 34,968 | 67,845 | 4,375 | 648 | 3,638 | 3,953 | 256,123 | 7,807 | 86,469 | 19,405 |

**D24    SOUTH AMERICA: IMPORTS AND EXPORTS OF PETROLEUM BY MAIN TRADING COUNTRIES** (in thousands of metric tons)

1900–1944

| | Brazil | | Colombia | Netherlands Antilles | | | Peru | Venezuela | |
|---|---|---|---|---|---|---|---|---|---|
| | CP | PP | CP | CP | | PP | CP & PP | CP | PP |
| | Imports | Imports | Exports | Imports | Exports | Exports | Exports | Exports | Exports |
| 1900 | ... | ... | ... | ... | ... | ... | — | ... | — |
| 1901 | ... | ... | ... | ... | ... | ... | — | ... | — |
| 1902 | ... | 68 | ... | ... | ... | ... | 1.6 | ... | — |
| 1903 | ... | 65 | ... | ... | ... | ... | 14 | ... | — |
| 1904 | ... | 68 | ... | ... | ... | ... | 11 | ... | — |
| 1905 | ... | 77 | ... | ... | ... | ... | 7.9 | ... | — |
| 1906 | ... | 77 | ... | ... | ... | ... | 17 | ... | — |
| 1907 | ... | 85 | ... | ... | ... | ... | 32 | ... | — |
| 1908 | ... | 86 | ... | ... | ... | ... | 49 | ... | — |
| 1909 | ... | 92 | ... | ... | ... | ... | 100 | ... | — |
| 1910 | ... | 113 | ... | ... | ... | ... | 74 | ... | — |
| 1911 | ... | 103 | ... | ... | ... | ... | 100 | ... | — |
| 1912 | ... | 141 | ... | ... | ... | ... | 161 | ... | — |
| 1913 | ... | 162 | ... | ... | ... | ... | 180 | ... | — |
| 1914 | ... | 143 | ... | ... | ... | ... | 137 | ... | — |
| 1915 | ... | 193 | ... | ... | ... | ... | 220 | ... | — |
| 1916 | ... | 241 | ... | ... | ... | ... | 280 | ... | — |
| 1917 | ... | 172 | ... | ... | ... | ... | 217 | 9 | — |
| 1918 | ... | 80 | ... | ... | ... | ... | 182 | 22 | — |
| 1919 | ... | 327 | ... | ... | ... | ... | 256 | 2 | — |
| 1920 | ... | 339 | ... | ... | ... | ... | 178 | 41 | — |
| 1921 | ... | 401 | ... | ... | ... | ... | 321 | 184 | — |
| 1922 | ... | 298 | ... | ... | ... | ... | 529 | 286 | — |
| 1923 | ... | 332 | ... | ... | ... | ... | 572 | 546 | — |
| 1924 | ... | 452 | - - | ... | ... | ... | 786 | 1,253 | — |
| 1925 | ... | 542 | — | ... | ... | ... | 951 | 2,720 | — |
| 1926 | ... | 500 | 644 | 3,982 | 333 | 2,743 | 1,199 | 4,893 | - - |
| 1927 | ... | 706 | 1,875 | 4,264 | 670 | 4,022 | 1,171 | 8,420 | 8 |
| 1928 | ... | 735 | 2,488 | 9,867 | 449 | 10,603 | 1,271 | 14,715 | 43 |
| 1929 | ... | 793 | 2,577 | 12,331 | 516 | 11,032 | 1,542 | 19,220 | 40 |
| 1930 | ... | 769 | 2,656 | 16,047 | 1,589 | 13,033 | 1,448 | 20,458 | 53 |
| 1931 | ... | 728 | 2,376 | 13,329 | 1,014 | 14,122 | 1,200 | 17,280 | ... |
| 1932 | ... | 615 | 2,211 | 13,040 | 1,086 | 11,640 | 1,126 | 16,192 | 713 |
| 1933 | ... | 787 | 1,695 | 13,954 | 1,203 | 12,456 | 1,588 | 16,718 | 837 |
| 1934 | ... | 832 | 2,351 | 15,431 | 1,223 | 13,552 | 1,976 | 18,780 | 902 |
| 1935 | 2.4 | 843 | 2,279 | 17,289 | 885 | 15,310 | 2,026 | 20,446 | 1,033 |
| 1936 | 13 | 978 | 2,356 | 18,790 | 1,272 | 17,110 | 2,063 | 22,343 | 973 |
| 1937 | 38 | 1,068 | 2,546 | 21,941 | 762 | 19,907 | 2,058 | 25,112 | 853 |
| 1938 | 48 | 1,132 | 2,648 | 23,789 | 1,083 | 22,290 | 1,708 | 26,611 | 930 |
| 1939 | 42 | 1,233 | 2,441 | 22,200 | 828 | 19,486 | 1,447 | 28,269 | 985 |
| 1940 | 49 | 1,209 | 3,050 | 17,940 | 247 | 16,700 | 1,157 | 23,438 | 1,318 |
| 1941 | 46 | 1,061 | 3,015 | 21,863 | — | 21,903 | 1,240 | 28,796 | 3,287 |
| 1942 | 11 | 736 | 1,002 | 12,739 | — | 13,098 | 1,461 | 18,082 | 3,375 |
| 1943 | 37 | 748 | 1,444 | 20,575 | — | 18,751 | 1,543 | 22,853 | 1,968 |
| 1944 | 18 | 736 | 2,524 | 25,796 | — | 24,812 | 1,311 | 32,461 | 1,907 |

**D24  SOUTH AMERICA: Imports and Exports of Petroleum by Main Trading Countries** (in thousands of metric tons)

| | Brazil | | Colombia | Netherlands Antilles | | | | Peru | | | Venezuela |
|---|---|---|---|---|---|---|---|---|---|---|---|
| | CP | PP | CP | CP | | PP | CP | PP | CP | PP |
| | Imports | Imports | Exports | Imports | Exports | Exports | Exports | Exports | Exports | Exports |
| 1945 | 10 | 936 | 2,650 | 29,973 | 47 | 28,545 | 1,223 | | 41,653 | 3,473 |
| 1946 | 37 | 1,594 | 2,422 | 33,600 | 703 | 30,585 | 1,056 | | 30,150 | 3,962 |
| 1947 | 8.7 | 2,471 | 2,665 | 38,079 | 1,869 | 32,987 | 926 | | 56,391 | 4,091 |
| 1948 | — | 3,149 | 2,561 | 38,998 | 2,102 | 38,238 | 1,033 | | 62,682 | 4,775 |
| 1949 | — | 3,516 | 3,287 | ... | ... | 46,276 | 1,079 | | 60,020 | 5,388 |
| 1950 | 11 | 4,339 | 3,910 | 42,180 | 1,237 | 39,687 | 848 | | 64,460 | 8,741 |
| 1951 | 20 | 5,008 | 3,932 | 45,473 | 757 | 42,713 | 869 | | 72,010 | 10,883 |
| 1952 | 18 | 5,941 | 3,752 | 43,995 | 949 | 43,587 | 854 | | 76,115 | 12,044 |
| 1953 | 30 | 6,315 | 3,559 | 40,549 | 1,139 | 39,704 | 649 | | 69,920 | 15,184 |
| 1954 | 142 | 7,427 | 4,339 | 43,741 | 2,069 | 34,470 | 698 | | 75,650 | 16,630 |
| 1955 | 3,513 | 5,003 | 3,510 | 45,117 | 2,946 | 35,740 | 841 | | 84,820 | 19,630 |
| 1956 | 4,889 | 4,386 | 4,056 | 45,071 | 2,336 | 37,443 | 982 | | 97,010 | 22,814 |
| 1957 | 4,846 | 3,592 | 3,729 | 41,281 | 926 | 34,512 | 1,007 | | 109,080 | 23,468 |
| 1958 | 5,652 | 4,137 | 3,298 | 36,699 | 1,243 | 33,030 | 668 | | 100,619 | 26,600 |
| 1959 | 5,742 | 3,528 | 3,981 | 39,107 | 1,563 | 31,734 | 641 | | 103,200 | 29,759 |
| 1960 | 5,684 | 4,097 | 4,353 | 38,833 | 945 | 31,539 | 762 | | 104,628 | 34,629 |
| 1961 | 7,549 | 2,973 | 3,861 | 40,846 | 1,436 | 32,367 | 648 | | 106,280 | 36,362 |
| 1962 | 9,961 | 1,069 | 3,402 | 41,342 | 1,430 | 34,106 | 586 | | 115,583 | 39,150 |
| 1963 | 10,375 | 1,093 | 4,364 | 40,210 | 940 | 34,751 | 493 | | 115,720 | 41,817 |
| 1964 | 10,803 | 818 | 4,248 | 40,834 | 486 | 35,575 | 431 | | 122,385 | 44,165 |
| 1965 | 10,247 | 803 | 5,610 | 40,811 | 375 | 34,674 | 435 | | 121,390 | 46,684 |
| 1966 | 11,322 | 858 | 4,920 | 39,761 | 344 | 33,333 | 330 | | 117,920 | 46,171 |
| 1967 | 10,559 | 959 | 4,308 | 41,436 | 597 | 34,487 | 431 | | 126,462 | 46,888 |
| 1968 | 12,525 | 1,744 | 2,551 | 40,325 | 318 | 34,228 | 587 | | 129,050 | 45,338 |
| 1969 | 14,910 | 716 | 4,002 | 42,469 | 356 | 36,352 | 290 | | 129,451 | 46,879 |
| 1970 | 15,797 | 558 | 4,203 | 47,413 | 660 | 39,449 | 235 | — | 127,591 | 51,502 |
| 1971 | 18,731 | 1,114 | 3,512 | 39,967 | 305 | 32,042 | 150 | 33 | 120,798 | 48,161 |
| 1972 | 25,257 | 640 | 2,016 | 39,054 | 566 | 31,745 | 145 | 142 | 111,478 | 46,248 |
| 1973 | 34,879 | 800 | 1,340 | 45,293 | 1,855 | 40,192 | 160 | 200 | 110,907 | 51,565 |
| 1974 | 34,831 | 809 | 68 | 41,334 | 784 | 36,893 | — | 402 | 92,450 | 47,829 |
| 1975 | 35,730 | 198 | — | 25,522 | 549 | 24,802 | 195 | 317 | 76,718 | 28,948 |
| 1976 | 40,996 | 1,109 | — | 35,060 | 908 | 23,366 | 364 | 295 | 71,565 | 38,001 |
| 1977 | 40,592 | 964 | — | 28,979 | 1,874 | 21,119 | 85 | 496 | 69,069 | 31,225 |
| 1978 | 44,750 | 372 | — | 28,548 | 1,023 | 22,396 | 1,445 | 506 | 65,216 | 35,049 |
| 1979 | 50,158 | 552 | — | 26,500 | 998 | 22,100 | 2,568 | 821 | 74,455 | 33,928 |
| 1980 | 43,333 | 1,902 | — | 31,177 | 1,001 | 22,765 | 2,390 | 806 | 68,369 | 28,008 |
| 1981 | 42,211 | 1,165 | — | 25,700 | 500 | 21,153 | 2,000 | 875 | 66,923 | 23,402 |
| 1982 | 39,810 | 2,907 | — | 24,500 | 600 | 18,516 | 1,500 | 1,222 | 56,115 | 23,323 |
| 1983 | 36,438 | 1,173 | — | 24,000 | 653 | 18,925 | 1,132 | 1,901 | 51,235 | 22,954 |
| 1984 | 32,425 | 439 | — | 20,000 | 200 | 16,694 | 1,000 | 2,503 | 52,546 | 22,667 |
| 1985 | 26,980 | 1,257 | — | 8,450 | 100 | 6,414 | 1,190 | 2,567 | 43,327 | 23,715 |
| 1986 | 29,871 | 1,779 | 4,425 | 8,150 | 100 | 5,950 | 656 | 2,361 | 49,766 | 25,100 |
| 1987 | 30,643 | 2,113 | 7,336 | 9,867 | 552 | 7,649 | 166 | 2,565 | 53,866 | 19,539 |
| 1988 | 31,739 | 3,456 | 7,314 | 10,200 | 300 | 7,549 | 300 | 2,205 | 52,156 | 24,405 |

**D24     Imports and Exports of Petroleum by Main Trading Countries** (in thousands of metric tons, except a otherwise indicated)

NOTES

1.   SOURCES: Data to 1949 are from the national publications listed on p. xiv–xvi supplemented by League of Nations and UN, *International Trade Statistics.* Data from 1950 are from UN, *World Energy Supplies.*
2.   Definitions of both crude petroleum and petroleum products have varied from time to time in most countries. So far as possible changes are indicated in footnotes.
3.   Data on products from 1950 relate only to energy products.

FOOTNOTES

[1] Data to 1885 for exports and 1905 for imports are for years beginning 1 July. The 1906 import figures are for the nine months from 1 July 1906 to 31 March 1907; the 1907 and 1908 figures are for years beginning 1 April.
[2] Including refined products to 1898.
[3] Data for 1893–96 are for years ending 30 June.
[4] All crude mineral oils to 1916 and including re-exports to 1928. Shipments to Puerto Rico are included to 1920 (1st line).

**D25** **IMPORTS AND EXPORTS OF IRON ORE BY MAIN TRADING COUNTRIES** (in thousands of metric tons)

**1870–1914**

| | NORTH AMERICA | | | | SOUTH AMERICA |
|---|---|---|---|---|---|
| | Canada[2] | | USA | | Chile |
| | Imports | Exports | Imports | Exports | Exports |
| 1870 | ... | ... | ... | ... | ... |
| 1871 | ... | ... | 24 | ... | ... |
| 1872 | ... | ... | 24 | ... | ... |
| 1873 | ... | ... | 47 | ... | ... |
| 1874 | ... | ... | 59 | ... | ... |
| 1875 | ... | ... | 58 | ... | ... |
| 1876 | ... | ... | 17 | ... | ... |
| 1877 | ... | ... | 31 | ... | ... |
| 1878 | ... | ... | 28 | ... | ... |
| 1879 | ... | ... | 289 | ... | ... |
| 1880 | ... | ... | 501 | ... | ... |
| 1881 | ... | ... | 796 | ... | ... |
| 1882 | ... | ... | 599 | ... | ... |
| 1883 | ... | ... | 499 | ... | ... |
| 1884 | ... | ... | 496 | ... | ... |
| 1885 | ... | ... | 397 | ... | ... |
| 1886 | ... | ... | 1,056 | ... | ... |
| 1887 | ... | ... | 1,213 | ... | ... |
| 1888 | ... | ... | 596 | ... | ... |
| 1889 | ... | ... | 868 | ... | ... |
| 1890 | ... | ... | 1,267 | ... | — |
| 1891 | ... | ... | 928 | ... | 1.7 |
| 1892 | ... | ... | 820 | ... | — |
| 1893 | ... | ... | 535 | ... | — |
| 1894 | ... | ... | 170 | ... | — |
| 1895 | ... | ... | 532 | ... | 0.3 |
| 1896 | ... | ... | 694 | ... | — |
| 1897 | ... | ... | 498 | ... | — |
| 1898 | ... | ... | 190 | ... | — |
| 1899 | ... | ... | 685 | 42 | — |
| 1900 | ... | 5 | 912 | 52 | — |
| 1901 | ... | — | 983 | 66 | — |
| 1902 | ... | — | 1,184 | 89 | - - |
| 1903 | ... | — | 996 | 82 | — |
| 1904 | ... | — | 496 | 217 | — |
| 1905 | ... | — | 860 | 211 | - - |
| 1906 | ... | 68 | 1,077 | 269 | — |
| 1907 | ... | 24 | 1,249 | 283 | — |
| 1908 | ... | 4 | 789 | 314 | — |
| 1909 | ... | 20 | 1,722 | 463 | — |
| 1910 | ... | 103 | 2,633 | 761 | — |
| 1911 | ... | 34 | 1,841 | 780 | 29 |
| 1912 | [1,858][1] | 107 | 2,139 | 1,215 | 6.5 |
| 1913 | 1,762 | 114 | 2,637 | 1,059 | 14 |
| 1914 | 1,041 | 122 | 1,373 | 561 | 64 |

**D25    Imports and Exports of Iron Ore by Main Trading Countries** (in thousands of metric tons)

1915–19

| | NORTH AMERICA | | | | SOUTH AMERICA | | | |
| | Canada[2] | | USA | | Brazil | Chile | Peru | Venezuela |
| | Imports | Exports | Imports | Exports | Exports | Exports | Exports | Exports |
|---|---|---|---|---|---|---|---|---|
| 1915 | 1,364 | 73 | 1,363 | 719 | ... | 147 | ... | — |
| 1916 | 2,123 | 146 | 1,347 | 1,203 | ... | — | ... | — |
| 1917 | 2,042 | 149 | 988 | 1,150 | ... | — | ... | — |
| 1918 | 1,997 | 118 | 800 | 1,276 | ... | — | ... | — |
| 1919 | 1,527 | 13 | 484 | 1,013 | ... | — | ... | — |
| 1920 | 1,800 | 18 | 1,293 | 1,163 | ... | — | ... | — |
| 1921 | 600 | 4 | 321 | 447 | ... | 8.0 | ... | — |
| 1922 | 805 | 2 | 1,153 | 612 | ... | 290 | ... | — |
| 1923 | 1,762 | 7 | 2,812 | 1,135 | ... | 673 | ... | — |
| 1924 | 828 | 5 | 2,080 | 605 | ... | 1,050 | ... | — |
| 1925 | 941 | 4 | 2,226 | 641 | ... | 1,234 | ... | — |
| 1926 | 1,330 | 1 | 2,596 | 883 | ... | 1,396 | ... | — |
| 1927 | 1,349 | 2 | 2,663 | 913 | ... | 1,508 | ... | — |
| 1928 | 2,017 | 3 | 2,492 | 1,303 | ... | 1,525 | ... | — |
| 1929 | 2,221 | 4 | 3,189 | 1,325 | ... | 1,816 | ... | — |
| 1930 | 1,348 | 1 | 2,820 | 764 | ... | 1,558 | ... | — |
| 1931 | 733 | 2 | 1,490 | 443 | ... | 712 | ... | — |
| 1932 | 62 | 1 | 591 | 84 | ... | 199 | ... | — |
| 1933 | 187 | 2 | 875 | 157 | ... | 510 | ... | — |
| 1934 | 886 | 3 | 1,451 | 619 | ... | 953 | ... | — |
| 1935 | 1,370 | 3 | 1,516 | 672 | ... | 845 | ... | — |
| 1936 | 1,195 | 3 | 2,268 | 655 | ... | 1,350 | ... | — |
| 1937 | 1,928 | 5 | 2,481 | 1,284 | 186 | 1,473 | ... | — |
| 1938 | 1,182 | — | 2,156 | 601 | 369 | 1,571 | ... | — |
| 1939 | 1,601 | 10 | 2,452 | 1,074 | 397 | 1,592 | ... | — |
| 1940 | 2,194 | 228 | 2,519 | 1,408 | 256 | 1,713 | ... | — |
| 1941 | 2,953 | 256 | 2,382 | 1,939 | 421 | 1,622 | ... | — |
| 1942 | 2,451 | 269 | 743 | 2,555 | 316 | 418 | ... | — |
| 1943 | 3,544 | 340 | 405 | 2,464 | 323 | — | ... | — |
| 1944 | 2,836 | 280 | 471 | 2,193 | 206 | — | ... | — |
| 1945 | 3,393 | 700 | 1,217 | 2,096 | 300 | 218 | ... | — |
| 1946 | 200 | 1,039 | 2,798 | 1,530 | 64 | 1,814 | ... | — |
| 1947 | 3,578 | 1,588 | 4,975 | 2,856 | 197 | 1,747 | ... | — |
| 1948 | 3,901 | 971 | 6,190 | 3,130 | 599 | 2,625 | ... | — |
| 1949 | [2,225][2] | [2,315][2] | 7,510 | 2,464 | 676 | 2,675 | ... | — |
| 1950 | 2,786 | 2,021 | 8,414 | 2,592 | 890 | 2,596 | ... | — |
| 1951 | 3,475 | 2,264 | 10,303 | 4,398 | 1,320 | 2,687 | ... | — |
| 1952 | 3,872 | 3,490 | 9,918 | 5,205 | 1,561 | 1,828 | ... | — |
| 1953 | 3,781 | 4,373 | 11,252 | 4,320 | 1,547 | 2,442 | 890 | 1,973 |
| 1954 | 2,753 | 4,909 | 16,045 | 3,196 | 1,678 | 1,720 | 1,927 | 5,449 |
| 1955 | 4,118 | 13,217 | 23,849 | 4,589 | 2,565 | 1,237 | 1,697 | 7,791 |
| 1956 | 4,599 | 18,384 | 30,899 | 5,596 | 2,745 | 2,071 | 2,674 | 10,905 |
| 1957 | 4,118 | 18,261 | 34,191 | 5,082 | 3,550 | 3,074 | 3,677 | 15,587 |
| 1958 | 3,096 | 12,590 | 27,986 | 3,630 | 2,831 | 3,638 | 2,510 | 16,068 |
| 1959 | 2,541 | 18,850 | 36,189 | 3,015 | 3,988 | 4,261 | 3,320 | 17,379 |

**D25** **Imports and Exports of Iron Ore by Main Trading Countries** (in thousands of metric tons)

| | NORTH AMERICA | | | | SOUTH AMERICA | | | | |
| | Canada[2] | | USA | | Argentina | Brazil | Chile | Peru | Venezuela |
| | Imports | Exports | Imports | Exports | Imports | Exports | Exports | Exports | Exports |
|---|---|---|---|---|---|---|---|---|---|
| 1960 | 4,587 | 16,837 | 35,133 | 5,358 | — | 5,240 | 5,191 | 5,171 | 19,320 |
| 1961 | 4,199 | 15,107 | 26,219 | 5,038 | 317 | 6,282 | 6,197 | 5,573 | 14,565 |
| 1962 | 4,679 | 21,993 | 33,945 | 5,993 | 515 | 7,650 | 7,246 | 5,149 | 13,285 |
| 1963 | 5,411 | 24,238 | 33,797 | 6,921 | 757 | 8,268 | 7,092 | 5,749 | 12,319 |
| 1964 | 5,317 | 30,963 | 43,089 | 7,075 | 1,019 | 9,730 | 9,114 | 5,824 | 14,893 |
| 1965 | 4,840 | 31,294 | 45,827 | 7,199 | 1,033 | 12,731 | 10,729 | 7,246 | 17,006 |
| 1966 | 4,393 | 31,186 | 47,001 | 7,904 | 707 | 12,910 | 11,095 | 7,680 | 17,037 |
| 1967 | 2,439 | 31,911 | 45,386 | 6,001 | 880 | 14,279 | 9,894 | 8,497 | 16,487 |
| 1968 | 2,794 | 40,332 | 44,646 | 5,978 | 616 | 15,050 | 10,497 | 8,710 | 15,053 |
| 1969 | 2,297 | 31,256 | 36,975 | 5,243 | 467 | 21,478 | 9,655 | 9,503 | 18,992 |
| 1970 | 2,160 | 39,348 | 45,612 | 5,580 | 1,448 | 28,061 | 9,908 | 9,644 | 21,089 |
| 1971 | 1,384 | 34,164 | 40,768 | 3,110 | 1,592 | 31,020 | 10,304 | 9,468 | 19,162 |
| 1972 | 1,753 | 29,275 | 36,335 | 2,129 | 1,029 | 30,512 | 5,454 | 8,941 | 16,509 |
| 1973 | 2,689 | 37,668 | 43,991 | 2,791 | 1,235 | 44,963 | 8,122 | 9,002 | 21,659 |
| 1974 | 2,333 | 37,448 | 48,800 | 2,360 | 1,003 | 59,439 | 9,390 | 8,398 | 26,277 |
| 1975 | 4,842 | 36,034 | 47,493 | 2,578 | 1,520 | 72,522 | 9,066 | 5,620 | 19,405 |
| 1976 | 3,020 | 44,685 | 45,102 | 2,960 | 1,745 | 67,086 | 8,965 | 4,515 | 15,671 |
| 1977 | 2,505 | 45,060 | 38,513 | 2,177 | 2,377 | 56,762 | 6,705 | 6,433 | 11,835 |
| 1978 | 4,686 | 31,929 | 34,156 | 4,282 | 2,395 | 66,370 | 3,129 | 4,869 | 12,828 |
| 1979 | 5,913 | 48,849 | 34,312 | 5,348 | 2,919 | 75,588 | 6,980 | 5,529 | 12,976 |
| 1980 | 5,875 | 38,994 | 25,460 | 5,780 | 2,391 | 78,958 | 7,600 | 5,500 | 11,752 |
| 1981 | 5,792 | 41,452 | 28,789 | 5,635 | 2,559 | 85,798 | 6,640 | 5,156 | 12,423 |
| 1982 | 3,357 | 27,281 | 14,951 | 3,229 | 2,106 | 80,927 | 5,767 | 5,596 | 6,616 |
| 1983 | 4,013 | 25,528 | 13,542 | 3,842 | 1,904 | 74,200 | 4,594 | 4,194 | 6,245 |
| 1984 | 4,947 | 30,737 | 17,435 | 5,073 | 2,213 | 90,294 | 5,230 | 4,089 | 8,456 |
| 1985 | 5,800 | 32,259 | 16,221 | 5,114 | 2,455 | 94,218 | 4,824 | 5,224 | 9,032 |
| 1986 | 5,367 | 31,030 | 17,018 | 4,553 | 3,183 | 91,135 | 4,650 | 4,209 | 10,027 |
| 1987 | 5,213 | 29,679 | 16,849 | 5,094 | 3,342 | 95,332 | 5,384 | 4,429 | 11,700 |
| 1988 | 4,856 | 30,523 | 20,183 | 5,289 | 3,300 | 112,839 | 6,682 | 4,520 | 12,128 |

NOTES

1.  SOURCES: The national publications listed on p. xiv–xvi League of Nations, *International Trade Statistics;* and UN, *Yearbook of International Trade Statistics.*
2.  Statistics refer to crude weight of ore.

FOOTNOTES

[1] Nine months ending 31 December.
[2] Including Newfoundland and Labrador as part of Canada from April 1949.

# E.     EXTERNAL TRADE

Because it has long been an important source of revenue to governments, external trade provides more statistical material at an earlier date for most countries than does any other economic activity. It was always one of the first things to be recorded by colonial administrations, though the Spanish and Portuguese were less diligent in this respect than other colonizers. However, as independent regimes established their authority they began to follow West European practice in this field. Unfortunately, it was standard practice in most Latin American countries until around the middle of the nineteenth-century, or later, to record the values of imports and exports in terms of officially fixed 'prices' for each commodity. Since these were not normally kept up-to-date, the recorded values, both for individual goods and in the aggregate, tended to become increasingly misleading as a representation of the actual values of imports and exports. The size of the gap which could develop is well illustrated by the Uruguayan figures in table 1 for 1913, when the system was changed.

Most Latin American countries have followed the practice of continental Europe in recording their external trade in two forms—'general' and 'special' trade. The former includes all commodities entering or leaving a country; the latter relates only to commodities intended for internal use or to commodities which have been, in some sense, produced within the country. It is the latter, the 'special' trade, or its equivalent in Anglo-Saxon countries, which has been shown in this section wherever possible. It must be noted, however, that the exact definition of 'special' trade has not been rigidly fixed, though the scope for major variations is obviously lacking. Moreover, statements of origin or intention to sell can be both honestly and dishonestly mistaken. However, these sources of unreliability or lack of comparability in the figures are not likely to be of very great significance. Nor, for the period and countries covered here, is smuggling, since most of the goods exported were of relatively low bulk-to-value ratios and tariffs on both imports and exports were not usually very high except where the means of enforcement were reasonably well developed. For practical purposes, therefore, it seems possible to take most of the statistics in this section as reasonably, though not perfectly, accurate. The main exceptions are probably some of the small countries of Central America, where the bureaucracies were incapable of policing and recording foreign trade effectively until well into the twentieth century.[1]

It is clear that one major influence on the course of these statistics has been the changes which have taken place in price levels, above all since 1914. It has not been found practicable to include a list showing variations in exchange rates, though these obviously have a bearing on any analysis of external trade. Information on these for the period since World War II is to be found in the UN, *Yearbook of International Trade;* and an idea of changing price levels in those countries and periods for which data are available can be got from section I below. Alterations in the internal value of currency units are listed on p. xi above.

Table 2, showing the trade of each country with others which have at various times been its chief trading partners, presents its own peculiar problems. The main one of these is that the records of no two countries tell precisely the same story about their trade with each other. The main cause of this is confusion between countries of shipment, of consignment, and of origin. Different systems have been used at various times in most countries, and even when allowance is made for this, it is clear that the system supposedly in use has not always been followed with precise accuracy in every case. This table does not cover all the countries for which data are available, though it is only smaller ones, and colonial and ex-colonial territories where trade has been overwhelmingly with the colonizing country, which have been omitted.

It would be extremely useful to have statistics showing a breakdown of the trade of the various countries by major commodity groups. Unfortunately, changes in definition occur in the published statistics of every country with very great frequency, and to produce reasonably consistent and comparable series for even one country is a considerable enterprise. Reluctantly, therefore, such commodity group statistics have been omitted. However, it has been possible to include, in table 3, series show-ing the value of the major individual commodities exported by a number of countries, since most of these commodities have been either fairly homogeneous basic ones, or else the exports of industrial countries with unusually well-presented national data.

[1] The British Department of Overseas Trade, *Report on the Financial and Commercial Conditions in the Republic of Honduras* (London, 1921), said that 'there exists a large clandestine export of goods which fails to appear in the records of the Custom Houses.' It seems unlikely that this was true of only one country in the area.

## E1 NORTH AMERICA: EXTERNAL TRADE AGGREGATES IN CURRENT VALUES

**1790–1839**

| | Barbados[1] | | Cuba | | Guadeloupe[2] | | Jamaica[1,3] | | Martinique[2] | |
|---|---|---|---|---|---|---|---|---|---|---|
| | Imports | Exports | Imports | Exports | Imports | Exports | Imports | Exports | Imports | Exports |
| | (thousand pounds) | | (million pesos fuertes) | | (million francs) | | (thousand pounds) | | (million francs) | |
| 1790 | ... | ... | 5.9 | 11 | ... | ... | ... | ... | ... | ... |
| 1791 | ... | ... | 12 | 13 | ... | ... | ... | ... | ... | ... |
| 1792 | ... | ... | 11 | 7.3 | ... | ... | ... | ... | ... | ... |
| 1793 | ... | ... | 6.9 | 12 | ... | ... | ... | ... | ... | ... |
| 1794 | ... | ... | 5.5 | 18 | ... | ... | ... | ... | ... | ... |
| 1795 | ... | ... | 19 | 17 | ... | ... | ... | ... | ... | ... |
| 1796 | ... | ... | ... | ... | ... | ... | ... | ... | ... | ... |
| 1797 | ... | ... | ... | ... | ... | ... | ... | ... | ... | ... |
| 1798 | ... | ... | ... | ... | ... | ... | ... | ... | ... | ... |
| 1799 | ... | ... | ... | ... | ... | ... | ... | ... | ... | ... |
| 1800 | ... | ... | ... | ... | ... | ... | ... | ... | ... | ... |
| 1801 | ... | ... | ... | ... | ... | ... | ... | ... | ... | ... |
| 1802 | ... | ... | ... | ... | ... | ... | ... | ... | ... | ... |
| 1803 | ... | ... | 12 | 8.1 | ... | ... | ... | ... | ... | ... |
| 1804 | ... | ... | 10 | 8.2 | ... | ... | ... | ... | ... | ... |
| 1805 | ... | ... | 12 | 5.8 | ... | ... | ... | ... | ... | ... |
| 1806 | ... | ... | 11 | 6.4 | ... | ... | ... | ... | ... | ... |
| 1807 | ... | ... | 7.8 | 5.5 | ... | ... | ... | ... | ... | ... |
| 1808 | ... | ... | 9.1 | 3.8 | ... | ... | ... | ... | ... | ... |
| 1809 | ... | ... | 13 | 9.2 | ... | ... | ... | ... | ... | ... |
| 1810 | ... | ... | 16 | 7.9 | ... | ... | ... | ... | ... | ... |
| 1811 | ... | ... | 12 | 7.3 | ... | ... | ... | ... | ... | ... |
| 1812 | ... | ... | 5.9 | 4.0 | ... | ... | ... | ... | ... | ... |
| 1813 | ... | ... | 9.3 | 6.1 | ... | ... | ... | ... | ... | ... |
| 1814 | ... | ... | 11 | 11 | ... | ... | ... | ... | ... | ... |
| 1815 | ... | ... | ... | ... | ... | ... | ... | ... | ... | ... |
| 1816 | ... | ... | 13 | 84 | ... | ... | ... | ... | ... | ... |
| 1817 | ... | ... | ... | ... | ... | ... | ... | ... | ... | ... |
| 1818 | ... | ... | ... | ... | ... | ... | ... | ... | ... | ... |
| 1819 | ... | ... | ... | ... | ... | ... | ... | ... | ... | ... |
| 1820 | ... | ... | ... | ... | ... | ... | ... | ... | ... | ... |
| 1821 | ... | ... | ... | ... | 11 | 16 | ... | ... | 16 | 16 |
| 1822 | ... | ... | ... | ... | 10 | 20 | ... | ... | 14 | 19 |
| 1823 | ... | ... | ... | ... | 13 | 14 | ... | ... | 16 | 14 |
| 1824 | ... | ... | ... | ... | 18 | 25 | ... | ... | 16 | 16 |
| 1825 | ... | ... | ... | ... | 15 | 17 | ... | ... | 20 | 17 |
| 1826 | ... | ... | 15 | 14 | 20 | 20 | ... | ... | 27 | 21 |
| 1827 | ... | ... | 17 | 14 | 19 | 18 | ... | ... | 23 | 18 |
| 1828 | ... | ... | 20 | 13 | 20 | 22 | ... | ... | 21 | 19 |
| 1829 | ... | ... | 19 | 4 | 22 | 23 | ... | ... | 21 | 18 |
| 1830 | ... | ... | 16 | 16 | 11 | 18 | ... | ... | 12 | 17 |
| 1831 | ... | ... | 16 | 13 | 13 | 24 | ... | ... | 14 | 17 |
| 1832 | 461 | 286 | 15 | 14 | 22 | 24 | 1,593 | 2,814 | 19 | 17 |
| 1833 | 439 | 418 | 19 | 14 | 12 | 19 | 1,519 | 2,490 | 12 | 13 |
| 1834 | 454 | 625 | 19 | 14 | 14 | 18 | 1,590 | 3,149 | 14 | 13 |
| 1835 | 505 | 579 | 21 | 14 | 16 | 19 | 2,019 | 3,095 | 17 | 14 |
| 1836 | 616 | 637 | 23 | 15 | 20 | 19 | 2,109 | 3,316 | 15 | 13 |
| 1837 | 627 | 787 | 23 | 20 | 16 | 18 | 1,957 | 2,828 | 17 | 13 |
| 1838 | 718 | 848 | 25 | 20 | 15[2] | 17[2] | 1,877 | 3,299 | 15[2] | 12[2] |
| | | | | | 19 | 24 | | | 19 | 20 |
| 1839 | 784 | 687 | 25 | 21 | 19 | 29 | 2,244 | 2,485 | 21 | 22 |

**E1    NORTH AMERICA: External Trade Aggregates in Current Values**

**1790–1839**

| | Mexico[4] | | Newfoundland[1,5] | | Trinidad[1] | | USA[1,6] | |
|---|---|---|---|---|---|---|---|---|
| | **Imports** | **Exports** | **Imports** | **Exports** | **Imports** | **Exports** | **Imports** | **Exports** |
| | (thousand pounds) | | (thousand pounds) | | (thousand pounds) | | (million US dollars) | |
| 1790 | ... | ... | ... | ... | ... | ... | 23 | 20 |
| 1791 | ... | ... | ... | ... | ... | ... | 29 | 19 |
| 1792 | ... | ... | ... | ... | ... | ... | 32 | 21 |
| 1793 | ... | ... | ... | ... | ... | ... | 31 | 26 |
| 1794 | ... | ... | ... | ... | ... | ... | 35 | 33 |
| 1795 | ... | ... | ... | ... | ... | ... | 70 | 48 |
| 1796 | 7,969 | 8,308 | ... | ... | ... | ... | 81 | 59 |
| 1797 | 2,234 | 1,423 | ... | ... | ... | ... | 75 | 51 |
| 1798 | 3,247 | 3,371 | ... | ... | ... | ... | 69 | 61 |
| 1799 | 6,722 | 8,716 | ... | ... | ... | ... | 79 | 79 |
| 1800 | 4,709 | 6,058 | ... | ... | ... | ... | 91 | 71 |
| 1801 | 3,487 | 1,971 | ... | ... | ... | ... | 111 | 93 |
| 1802 | 21,999 | 38,447 | ... | ... | ... | ... | 76 | 72 |
| 1803 | 19,867 | 14,483 | ... | ... | ... | ... | 65 | 56 |
| 1804 | 16,526 | 21,458 | ... | ... | ... | ... | 85 | 78 |
| 1805 | 3,914 | 341 | ... | ... | ... | ... | 121 | 96 |
| 1806 | 7,138 | 5,479 | ... | ... | ... | ... | 129 | 102 |
| 1807 | 16,737 | 22,507 | ... | ... | ... | ... | 139 | 108 |
| 1808 | 10,413 | 13,599 | ... | ... | ... | ... | 57 | 22 |
| 1809 | 20,431 | 28,278 | ... | ... | ... | ... | 59 | 52 |
| 1810 | 20,431 | 15,917 | ... | ... | ... | ... | 85 | 67 |
| 1811 | 11,347 | 9,867 | ... | ... | ... | ... | 53 | 61 |
| 1812 | 5,241 | 5,118 | ... | ... | ... | ... | 77 | 39 |
| 1813 | 7,932 | 12,100 | ... | ... | ... | ... | 22 | 28 |
| 1814 | 9,670 | 10,393 | ... | ... | ... | ... | 13 | 7 |
| 1815 | 10,986 | 9,181 | ... | ... | ... | ... | 113 | 53 |
| 1816 | 10,006 | 6,675 | ... | ... | ... | ... | 147 | 82 |
| 1817 | 8,686 | 8,520 | ... | ... | ... | ... | 99 | 88 |
| 1818 | 5,765 | 4,731 | ... | ... | ... | ... | 122 | 93 |
| 1819 | 10,999 | 8,675 | ... | ... | ... | ... | 87 | 70 |
| 1820 | 3,552 | 10,894 | ... | ... | ... | ... | 74 | 70 |
| 1821 | ... | ... | ... | ... | ... | ... | 63 | 65 |
| 1822 | ... | ... | ... | ... | ... | ... | 83 | 72 |
| 1823 | 3,919 | 2,346 | ... | ... | ... | ... | 77 | 74 |
| 1824 | 12,082 | 4,099 | ... | ... | ... | ... | 80 | 76 |
| 1825 | 19,094 | 5,503 | ... | ... | ... | ... | 96[6] | 100[6] |
| | | | | | | | 96 | 99 |
| 1826 | 15,451 | 9,006 | ... | ... | ... | ... | 84 | 77 |
| 1827 | 15,882 | 18,672 | ... | ... | ... | ... | 78 | 80 |
| 1828 | 10,508 | 14,489 | ... | ... | ... | ... | 88 | 71 |
| 1829 | ... | ... | ... | ... | ... | ... | 74 | 70 |
| 1830 | ... | ... | ... | ... | ... | ... | 70 | 73 |
| 1831 | ... | ... | ... | ... | ... | ... | 102 | 78 |
| 1832 | ... | ... | 574 | 594 | 230 | 236 | 100 | 86 |
| 1833 | ... | ... | 596 | 715 | 287 | 268 | 107 | 90 |
| 1834 | ... | ... | 556 | 663 | 253 | 381 | 123 | 103 |
| 1835 | ... | ... | 577 | 737 | 316 | 370 | 148 | 120 |
| 1836 | ... | ... | 580 | 787 | 469 | 488 | 183 | 128 |
| 1837 | ... | ... | 711 | 864 | 444 | 469 | 138 | 114 |
| 1838 | ... | ... | 580 | 728 | 409 | 494 | 102 | 107 |
| 1839 | ... | ... | 624 | 818 | 466 | 359 | 160 | 116 |

**E1    NORTH AMERICA: External Trade Aggregates in Current Values**

**1840–1884**

| | Barbados[1] | | Canada[7] | | Costa Rica[8] | | Cuba | | Dominican Republic | |
|---|---|---|---|---|---|---|---|---|---|---|
| | Imports | Exports | Imports | Exports | Imports | Exports | Imports | Exports | Imports | Exports |
| | (thousand pounds) | | (million Canadian dollars) | | (million pesos) | | (million pesos fuertes) | | (million pesos) | |
| 1840 | 599 | 344 | ... | ... | ... | ... | 25 | 26 | ... | ... |
| 1841 | 578 | 410 | ... | ... | ... | ... | 25 | 27 | ... | ... |
| 1842 | 578 | 557 | ... | ... | ... | ... | 25 | 27 | ... | ... |
| 1843 | 617 | 547 | ... | ... | ... | ... | 23 | 25 | ... | ... |
| 1844 | 594 | 562 | ... | ... | ... | ... | 25 | 25 | ... | ... |
| 1845 | 654 | 562 | ... | ... | ... | ... | 28 | 19 | ... | ... |
| 1846 | 679 | 513 | ... | ... | ... | ... | 23 | 22 | ... | ... |
| 1847 | 546 | 738 | ... | ... | ... | ... | 32 | 28 | ... | ... |
| 1848 | 426 | 560 | ... | ... | ... | ... | 25 | 26 | ... | ... |
| 1849 | 572 | 659 | ... | ... | ... | ... | 26 | 22 | ... | ... |
| 1850 | 734 | 832 | ... | ... | ... | ... | 29 | 26 | ... | ... |
| 1851 | 788 | 888 | ... | ... | ... | ... | 32 | 31 | ... | ... |
| 1852 | 768 | 952 | ... | ... | ... | ... | 30 | 27 | ... | ... |
| 1853 | 571 | 775 | ... | ... | ... | ... | 28 | 31 | ... | ... |
| 1854 | 597 | 946 | ... | ... | 1.0 | 0.8 | 31 | 33 | ... | ... |
| 1855 | 645 | 790 | ... | ... | 0.7 | 0.8 | 31 | 35 | ... | ... |
| 1856 | 841 | 971 | ... | ... | 0.9 | 0.8 | 32 | 32 | ... | ... |
| 1857 | 976 | 1,345 | ... | ... | - - | 1.3 | 35 | 33 | ... | ... |
| 1858 | 1,335 | 1,468 | ... | ... | 1.0 | 1.0 | 39 | 34 | ... | ... |
| 1859 | 1,049 | 1,226 | ... | ... | 0.9 | 1.4 | 43 | 57 | ... | ... |
| 1860 | 942 | 984 | ... | ... | 1.1 | 1.3 | 34 | 42 | ... | ... |
| 1861 | 924 | 1,075 | ... | ... | 0.8 | 1.8 | ... | ... | ... | ... |
| 1862 | 913 | 1,068 | ... | ... | 0.9 | 1.7 | 41 | 55 | ... | ... |
| 1863 | 878 | 981 | ... | ... | 1.1 | 1.4 | ... | ... | ... | ... |
| 1864 | 910 | 926 | ... | ... | 1.6 | 1.6 | ... | ... | ... | ... |
| 1865 | 953 | 1,161 | ... | ... | 1.5 | 1.6 | ... | ... | ... | ... |
| 1866 | 988 | 1,247 | ... | ... | 1.4 | 1.8 | ... | ... | ... | ... |
| 1867 | 990 | 1,245 | 67 | 53 | 1.3 | 2.2 | ... | ... | ... | ... |
| 1868 | 1,134 | 1,270 | 63 | 56 | 0.9 | 2.2 | ... | ... | 1.1 | ... |
| 1869 | 1,026 | 935 | 67 | 66 | 1.2 | 2.4 | ... | ... | 1.4 | ... |
| 1870 | 1,070 | 973 | 84 | 67 | 1.4 | 2.7 | ... | ... | 1.3 | ... |
| 1871 | 1,192 | 1,299 | 105 | 79 | 1.7 | 3.6 | ... | ... | 1.3 | ... |
| 1872 | 1,125 | 1,021 | 125 | 86 | 2.8 | 2.8 | ... | ... | 1.1 | 1.2 |
| 1873 | 1,194 | 1,024 | 123 | 87 | 3.8 | 6.0 | ... | ... | ... | ... |
| 1874 | 1,031 | 1,141 | 117 | 77 | 2.9 | 4.6 | ... | ... | ... | ... |
| 1875 | 1,187 | 1,475 | 93 | 80 | 2.9 | 4.6 | ... | ... | ... | ... |
| 1876 | 1,028 | 964 | 94 | 75 | 3.3 | 2.3 | ... | ... | ... | ... |
| 1877 | 1,144 | 1,098 | 90 | 79 | ... | 5.0 | 59 | 67 | ... | ... |
| 1878 | 1,103 | 1,078 | 79 | 71 | 2.5 | 3.4 | ... | ... | ... | ... |
| 1879 | 1,023 | 1,259 | 70 | 86 | 3.4 | 4.2 | ... | ... | ... | ... |
| 1880 | 1,171 | 1,166 | 90 | 97 | 2.4 | 3.5 | ... | ... | 1.7 | 1.3 |
| 1881 | 1,119 | 1,140 | 111 | 102 | 2.2 | 2.4 | ... | ... | 1.6 | 1.5 |
| 1882 | 1,163 | 1,193 | 122 | 97 | ...[8] | 3.7[8] | ... | ... | 2.0 | 1.9 |
| | | | | | (million colones) | | | | | |
| 1883 | 1,155 | 1,141 | 106 | 89 | 5 | 4 | ... | ... | 3.1 | 2.1 |
| 1884 | 1,156 | 1,319 | 100 | 87 | 8 | 8 | ... | ... | 2.5 | 2.6 |

**E1      NORTH AMERICA: External Trade Aggregates in Current Values**

**1840–1884**

| | El Salvador | | Guadeloupe[2] | | Guatemala[10] | | Jamaica[1,3] | | Martinique[2] | |
|---|---|---|---|---|---|---|---|---|---|---|
| | Imports | Exports | Imports | Exports | Imports | Exports | Imports | Exports | Imports | Exports |
| | (thousand gold pesos) | (thousand silver pesos) | (million francs) | | (thousand gold pesos) | (thousand silver pesos) | (thousand pounds) | | million francs | |
| 1840 | ... | ... | 22 | 23 | ... | ... | 2,184 | 2,209 | 26 | 19 |
| 1841 | ... | ... | 22 | 23 | ... | ... | 1,335 | 1,910 | 24 | 20 |
| 1842 | ... | ... | 20 | 23 | ... | ... | 1,877 | 2,231 | 21 | 21 |
| 1843 | ... | ... | 27 | 19 | ... | ... | 1,696 | 1,847 | 29 | 20 |
| 1844 | ... | ... | 32 | 22 | ... | ... | 1,476 | 1,609 | 26 | 22 |
| 1845 | ... | ... | 29 | 26 | ... | ... | 1,559 | 1,851 | 26 | 24 |
| 1846 | ... | ... | 27₂ | 19 | ... | ... | 1,420 | 1,479 | 29₂ | 19₂ |
| 1847 | ... | ... | 27 | 27 | ... | ... | 1,322 | 1,938 | 28 | 24 |
| 1848 | ... | ... | 12 | 14 | ... | ... | 1,023 | 1,341 | 14 | 15 |
| 1849 | ... | ... | 17 | 13 | ... | ... | 1,118 | 1,068 | 26 | 14 |
| 1850 | ... | ... | 18 | 9.2 | ... | ... | 1,218 | 1,217 | 22 | 12 |
| 1851 | ... | ... | 26 | 12 | 1,404 | 1,404 | 1,129 | 980 | 36 | 15 |
| 1852 | ... | ... | 25 | 12 | 1,581 | 869 | 838 | 927 | 30 | 19 |
| 1853 | ... | ... | 21 | 10 | 971 | 599 | 864 | 837 | 27 | 16 |
| 1854 | ... | ... | 23 | 16 | 874 | 2,033 | 985 | 660 | 29 | 19 |
| 1855 | ... | 787 | 24 | 16 | 826 | 1,283 | 900 | 1,003 | 26 | 16 |
| 1856 | ... | 765 | 24 | 16 | 1,206 | 1,707 | 962 | 935 | 32 | 21 |
| 1857 | ... | 1,285 | 28 | 14 | 1,066 | 1,605 | 765 | 1,235 | 29 | 19 |
| 1858 | ... | 1,304 | 28 | 20 | 1,136 | 2,025 | 1,040 | 1,170 | 33 | 21 |
| 1859 | 1,336 | 1,761 | 25 | 19 | 1,224 | 1,767 | 853 | 961 | 28 | 22 |
| 1860 | 950 | 1,391 | 30 | 20 | 1,520 | 1,871 | 1,203 | 1,226 | 28 | 23 |
| 1861 | 1,349 | 2,291 | 27 | 18 | 1,495 | 1,107 | 1,089 | 1,215 | 31 | 22 |
| 1862 | 1,304 | 2,686 | 25 | 23 | 1,093 | 1,368 | 1,142 | 1,113 | 30 | 22 |
| 1863 | ... | 1,673 | 23 | 21 | 745 | 1,498 | 1,088 | 1,008 | 26 | 25 |
| 1864 | 1,234 | 1,665 | 19 | 14 | 1,415 | 1,563 | 1,143 | 947 | 27 | 19 |
| 1865 | 1,689 | 2,848 | 19 | 18 | 1,650 | 1,833 | 1,051₃ | 912 | 29 | 20 |
| 1866 | 1,664 | 2,135 | 21 | 21 | 1,699 | 1,680 | 1,031 | 1,153 | 30 | 22 |
| 1867 | 1,876 | 2,896 | 19 | 16 | 1,575 | 1,920 | 859 | 1,045 | 30 | 21 |
| 1868 | 1,949 | 3,448 | 19 | 22 | 1,665 | 2,188 | 1,025 | 1,139 | 30 | 29 |
| 1869 | 3,729 | 3,769 | 21 | 25 | 1,753 | 2,291 | 1,224 | 1,163 | 31 | 32 |
| 1870 | 4,199 | 3,894 | 19 | 27 | 1,375 | 2,045 | 1,300 | 1,283 | 27 | 30 |
| 1871 | 2,580 | 3,810 | 24 | 29 | 2,403 | 2,658 | 1,331 | 1,249 | 33 | 35 |
| 1872 | 2,951 | 3,881 | 28 | 26 | 2,269 | 2,704 | 1,560 | 1,418 | 35 | 32 |
| 1873 | 2,103 | 3,477 | 28 | 25 | 1,192 | 2,364 | 1,733 | 1,226 | 32 | 28 |
| 1874 | 2,835 | 3,841 | 25 | 22 | 3,054 | 2,301 | 1,763 | 1,442 | 28 | 33 |
| 1875 | 2,690 | 3,180 | 25 | 31 | 2,586 | 3,217 | 1,760 | 1,410 | 30 | 36 |
| 1876 | 2,102 | 3,605 | 22 | 23 | 2,717 | 3,767 | 1,700 | 1,517 | 26 | 28 |
| 1877 | 2,586 | 3,961 | 27 | 35 | 3,134 | 3,773 | 1,552 | 1,459 | 29 | 34 |
| 1878 | 2,501 | 3,626 | 25 | 35 | 3,238 | 3,919 | 1,493 | 1,211 | 30 | 30 |
| 1879 | 2,549 | 4,128 | 29 | 28 | 2,929 | 4,606 | 1,347 | 1,358 | 30 | 34 |
| 1880 | 2,295 | 4,073 | 27 | 31 | 3,036 | 4,425 | 1,475 | 1,513 | 32 | 34 |
| 1881 | 2,705 | 4,902 | 26 | 32 | 3,665 | 4,084 | 1,393₃ | 1,179 | 27 | 32 |
| 1882 | 3,170 | 5,227 | 27 | 42 | 2,652 | 3,719 | 1,318 | 1,549 | 28 | 39 |
| 1883 | 2,401 | 5,861 | 28 | 32 | 2,031 | 5,718 | 1,625 | 1,469 | 33 | 36 |
| 1884 | 2,647 | 6,066 | 25 | 27 | 3,830 | 4,938 | 1,569 | 1,484 | 28 | 26 |

## E1 NORTH AMERICA: External Trade Aggregates in Current Values

**1840–1884**

| | Mexico[4] | | Newfoundland[1,5] | | Nicaragua[11] | | Trinidad[1] | | USA[1,6] | |
|---|---|---|---|---|---|---|---|---|---|---|
| | Imports | Exports | Imports | Exports | Imports | Exports | Imports | Exports | Imports | Exports |
| | (thousand pounds) | | (thousand pounds) | | (thousand gold pesos or cordobas) | | (thousand pounds) | | (million US dollars) | |
| 1840 | ... | ... | 671 | 896 | ... | ... | 537 | 362 | 104 | 129 |
| 1841 | ... | ... | 666 | 908 | ... | ... | 533 | 474 | 127 | 118 |
| 1842 | ... | ... | 650 | 787 | ... | ... | 386 | 458 | 99 | 103 |
| 1843 | ... | ... | 667 | 913 | ... | ... | 430 | 407 | [47][6] | [84][6] |
| 1844 | ... | ... | 709 | 853 | ... | ... | 437 | 404 | 107 | 110 |
| 1845 | ... | ... | 655 | 875 | ... | ... | 450 | 430 | 116 | 112 |
| 1846 | ... | ... | 727 | 689 | ... | ... | 494 | 497 | 121 | 112 |
| 1847 | ... | ... | 760 | 807 | ... | ... | 394 | 512 | 125 | 158 |
| 1848 | ... | ... | 634 | 860 | ... | ... | 284 | 268 | 152 | 143 |
| 1849 | ... | ... | 725[5] | 891[5] | ... | ... | 416 | 388 | 144 | 143 |
| 1850 | ... | ... | 867 | 976 | ... | ... | 477 | 319 | 177 | 147 |
| 1851 | ... | ... | 943 | 960 | ... | ... | 548 | 390 | 213 | 196 |
| 1852 | ... | ... | 796 | 966 | ... | ... | 493 | 459 | 209 | 170 |
| 1853 | ... | ... | 912 | 1,171 | ... | ... | 504 | 446 | 266 | 205 |
| 1854 | ... | ... | 965 | 1,020 | ... | ... | 559 | 381 | 302 | 238 |
| 1855 | ... | ... | 1,153 | 1,142 | ... | ... | 555 | 388 | 261 | 220 |
| 1856 | ... | ... | 1,272 | 1,339 | ... | ... | 666 | 575 | 313 | 282 |
| 1857 | ... | 44,000 | 1,413 | 1,651 | ... | ... | 801 | 1,074 | 354 | 298 |
| 1858 | ... | ... | 1,173 | 1,319 | ... | ... | 826 | 786 | 271 | 275 |
| 1859 | ... | ... | 1,324 | 1,357 | ... | ... | 735 | 821 | 336 | 296 |
| 1860 | ... | ... | 1,254 | 1,272 | ... | ... | 829 | 715 | 360 | 342 |
| 1861 | | | 1,153 | 1,093 | ... | ... | 857 | 645 | 293 | 222 |
| 1862 | | | 1,1007 | 1,172 | ... | ... | 734 | 740 | 192 | 192 |
| 1863 | | | 1,077 | 1,233 | ... | ... | 711 | 796 | 247 | 206 |
| 1864 | 25,842 | 1,165 | 1,067 | 1,111 | ... | ... | 884 | 1,102 | 318 | 164[6] |
| 1865 | | | 1,104 | 1,144 | ... | ... | 810 | 820 | 242 | 175 |
| 1866 | | | 1,205 | 1,186 | ... | ... | 930 | 1,032 | 438 | 364 |
| 1867 | | | 1,156 | 1,056 | ... | ... | 859 | 1,087 | 401 | 317 |
| 1868 | ... | ... | 897 | 888 | ... | ... | 928 | 1,116 | 362 | 303 |
| 1869 | ... | ... | 1,095 | 1,270 | ... | ... | 1,027 | 1,381 | 424 | 307 |
| 1870 | ... | ... | 1,387 | 1,298 | ... | ... | 1,043 | 1,278 | 450 | 418 |
| 1871 | ... | ... | 1,258 | 1,311 | ... | ... | 1,218 | 1,497 | 534 | 475 |
| | (million pesos) | | | | | | | | | |
| 1872 | 20 | 32 | 1,399 | 1,189 | ... | ... | 1,234 | 1,440 | 632 | 474 |
| 1873 | 23 | 28 | 1,410 | 1,361 | ... | ... | 1,324 | 1,734 | 655 | 562 |
| 1874 | 22 | 27 | 1,532 | 1,528 | ... | ... | 1,343 | 1,412 | 576 | 619 |
| 1875 | ... | ... | 1,533 | 1,340 | ... | ... | 1,508 | 1,625 | 540 | 538 |
| 1876 | ... | ... | 1,501 | 1,367 | ... | ... | 1,666 | 1,637 | 469 | 565 |
| 1877 | 28 | 28 | 1,534 | 1,425 | ... | ... | 1,708 | 2,094 | 466 | 632 |
| 1878 | ... | 30 | 1,431 | 1,173 | ... | ... | 1,901 | 1,839 | 453 | 720 |
| 1879 | ... | 33 | 1,513 | 1,233 | ... | ... | 2,223 | 2,265 | 461 | 730 |
| 1880 | ... | 30 | 1,451 | 1,174 | ... | ... | 2,382 | 2,186 | 680 | 850 |
| 1881 | ... | 29 | 1,430 | 1,629 | 1,284 | 1,433 | 2,226 | 2,099 | 654 | 919 |
| 1882 | ... | 42 | 1,740 | 1,459 | 1,182 | 1,517 | 2,400 | 2,452 | 733 | 768 |
| 1883 | 34 | 47 | 1,902 | 1,471 | ... | ... | 2,663 | 2,687 | 734 | 841 |
| 1884 | 36 | 47 | 1,682 | 1,368 | ... | ... | 3,084 | 2,770 | 683 | 767 |

## E1 NORTH AMERICA: External Trade Aggregates in Current Values

### 1885–1929

| | Barbados[1] | | Canada[7] | | Costa Rica[8] | | Cuba[9] | | Dominican Republic | | El Salvador | |
|---|---|---|---|---|---|---|---|---|---|---|---|---|
| | Imports | Exports | Imports | Exports | Imports | Exports | Imports | Exports | Imports | Exports | Imports | Exports |
| | | | | | | | | | | | (thousand gold pesos) | (thousand silver pesos) |
| | (thousand pounds) | | (million Canadian dollars) | | (million colones) | | (million pesos fuertes) | | (million pesos) | | | |
| 1885 | 891 | 1,004 | 96 | 85 | 8 | 5 | ... | ... | 2.1 | 2.5 | 2,134 | 5,716 |
| 1886 | 863 | 740 | 105 | 90 | 8 | 5 | ... | ... | ... | ... | 4,428 | 4,755 |
| 1887 | 983 | 1,063 | 101 | 90 | 12 | 10 | ... | ... | 2.1 | 2.7 | 3,275 | 5,230 |
| 1888 | 1,058 | 1,075 | 109 | 87 | 11 | 9 | ... | ... | ... | ... | 4,082 | 6,758 |
| 1889 | 1,211 | 1,030 | 112 | 94 | 14 | 10 | ... | ... | 2.4 | 2.9 | 2,886 | 5,674 |
| 1890 | 1,194 | 1,204 | 112 | 97 | 14 | 14 | ... | ... | 2.4 | 3.9 | 2,401 | 7,579 |
| 1891 | 1,068 | 814 | 115 | 112 | 18 | 13 | ... | ... | 2.7 | 2.9 | 3,200 | 7,073 |
| 1892 | 1,082 | 927 | 115 | 114 | 12 | 10 | 56 | 90 | 2.4 | 3.6 | 5,758 | 6,838 |
| 1893 | 1,373 | 1,243 | 109 | 116 | 13 | 9 | ... | ... | 2.8 | 5.7 | 1,854 | 7,492 |
| 1894 | 1,279 | 985 | 101 | 109 | 9 | 11 | ... | ... | 2.9 | 5.4 | 2,171 | 6,611 |
| 1895 | 957 | 587 | 105 | 116 | 8 | 11 | ... | ... | ... | ... | ... | ... |
| 1896 | 1,049 | 758 | 107 | 134 | 10 | 12 | ... | ... | 3.4 | 4.4 | ... | ... |
| 1897 | 1,009 | 736 | 126 | 160 | 12 | 12 | ... | ... | 3.4 | 9.3 | ... | ... |
| 1898 | 1,059 | 769 | 149 | 155 | 9 | 12 | ... | ... | 3.4 | 11.6 | ... | ... |
| 1899 | 998 | 846 | 173 | 183 | 10 | 11 | ... | ... | ... | ... | ... | ... |
| | | | | | | | (million US dollars) | | | | | |
| 1900 | 1,045 | 919 | 178 | 195 | 14 | 14 | 71 | 45 | ... | ... | ... | ... |
| | | | | | | | | | | | (million colones) | |
| 1901 | 1,022 | 950 | 197 | 210 | 9 | 12 | 65 | 63 | ... | ... | 6.5 | 11 |
| 1902 | 873 | 592 | 225 | 225 | 10 | 12 | 65 | 51 | ... | ... | 6.9 | 10 |
| 1903 | 822 | 553 | 244 | 211 | 12 | 16 | 59 | 78 | ... | ... | 7.7 | 14 |
| 1904 | 1,069 | 861 | 252 | 201 | 13 | 15 | 70 | 93 | ... | ... | 9.0 | 17 |
| 1905 | 1,043 | 936 | 284 | 247 | 11 | 17 | 84 | 99 | 2.7 | 6.9 | 11 | 14 |
| 1906 | 1,192 | 875 | [250][7] | [192][7] | 16 | 19 | 104 | 105 | 4.0 | 6.6 | 10 | 16 |
| 1907 | 1,272 | 847 | 352 | 263 | 17 | 20 | 96 | 111 | 4.9 | 7.9 | 8.6 | 15 |
| 1908 | 1,226 | 880 | 289 | 260 | 12 | 17 | 97 | 97 | 4.9 | 9.6 | 11 | 15 |
| 1909 | 1,119 | 822 | 370 | 299 | 13 | 18 | 84 | 116 | 4.4 | 8.6 | 11 | 17 |
| 1910 | 1,345 | 1,004 | 453 | 290 | 17 | 18 | 98 | 144 | 6.3 | 10.8 | 11 | 18 |
| | | | | | | | (million pesos) | | | | | |
| | | | | | | | 103 | 150 | | | | |
| 1911 | 1,540 | 931 | 522 | 308 | 19 | 19 | 113 | 123 | 6.9 | 11.0 | 13 | 22 |
| 1912 | 1,465 | 996 | 671 | 377 | 22 | 21 | 123 | 172 | 8.2 | 12.4 | 16 | 22 |
| 1913 | 1,353 | 761 | 619 | 455 | 19 | 22 | 140 | 164 | 9.3 | 10.5 | 15 | 23 |
| 1914 | 1,300 | 846 | 456 | 461 | 16 | 23 | 118 | 173 | 6.7 | 10.6 | 14 | 27 |
| 1915 | 1,270 | 1,053 | 508 | 779 | 10 | 21 | 140 | 235 | 9.1 | 15.2 | 11 | 26 |
| 1916 | 1,851 | 2,002 | 846 | 1,179 | 14 | 24 | 215 | 321 | 10.7 | 21.5 | 17 | 29 |
| 1917 | 2,285 | 1,939 | 964 | 1,586 | 12 | 24 | 256 | 356 | 17.4 | 22.4 | 18 | 27 |
| 1918 | 2,986 | 2,223 | 920[7] | 1,269[7] | 8 | 21 | 293 | 407 | 19.7 | 22.4 | 15 | 25 |
| 1919 | 3,876 | 2,754 | 941 | 1,290 | 16 | 38 | 355 | 573 | 22.0 | 39.6 | 21 | 34 |
| 1920 | 5,135 | 4,371 | 1,337 | 1,298 | 48 | 27 | 556 | 794 | 46.5 | 58.7 | 26 | 36 |
| 1921 | 2,642 | 1,425 | 799 | 814 | 20 | 26 | 353 | 278 | 24.6 | 20.6 | 18 | 18 |
| 1922 | 2,484 | 1,245 | 762 | 894 | 18 | 31 | 178 | 325 | 14.3 | 15.2 | 15 | 33 |
| 1923 | 2,522 | 2,130 | 903 | 1,016 | 21 | 28 | 267 | 421 | 18.2 | 26.0 | 18 | 35 |
| 1924 | 2,556 | 1,820 | 808 | 1,042 | 48 | 66 | 288 | 435 | 21.6 | 30.3 | 28 | 49 |
| 1925 | 2,296 | 1,375 | 890 | 1,252 | 55 | 66 | 296 | 354 | 25.3 | 26.8 | 39 | 34 |
| 1926 | 2,155 | 1,205 | 1,008 | 1,277 | 55 | 76 | 259 | 302 | 23.8 | 24.9 | 52 | 49 |
| 1927 | 2,300 | 1,537 | 1,087 | 1,231 | 65 | 72 | 258 | 324 | 27.8 | 31.2 | 30 | 28 |
| 1928 | 2,349 | 1,470 | 1,222 | 1,364 | 72 | 79 | 213 | 278 | 26.8 | 28.8 | 38 | 49 |
| 1929 | 2,040 | 1,247 | 1,299 | 1,178 | 81 | 73 | 216 | 272 | 22.7 | 23.7 | 36 | 37 |

**E1    NORTH AMERICA: External Trade Aggregates in Current Values**

| | Guadeloupe | | Guatemala[10] | | Haiti[1,13] | | Honduras[14] | | Jamaica[3] | | Martinique | |
|---|---|---|---|---|---|---|---|---|---|---|---|---|
| | Imports | Exports | Imports | Exports | Imports | Exports | Imports | Exports | Imports | Exports | Imports | Exports |
| | | | (thousand gold pesos) | (thousand silver pesos) | | | | | | | | |
| | (million francs) | | | | (million gourdes) | | (thousand gold pesos) | | (thousand pounds) | | (million francs) | |
| 1885 | 20 | 18 | 3,103 | 6,070 | ... | ... | ... | ... | 1,488 | 1,409 | 22 | 21 |
| 1886 | 17 | 16 | 3,236 | 6,720 | ... | ... | ... | ... | 1,326 | 1,280 | 24 | 20 |
| 1887 | 20 | 22 | 3,743 | 9,039 | ... | ... | ... | ... | 1,322 | 1,509 | 23 | 21 |
| 1888 | 24 | 26 | 5,344 | 7,087 | ... | ... | ... | ... | 1,696 | 1,829 | 23 | 23 |
| 1889 | 24 | 26 | 7,587 | 13,248 | ... | ... | ... | ... | 1,598[3] | 1,615[3] | 23 | 23 |
| 1890 | 23 | 21 | 7,640 | 14,402 | ... | ... | ... | ... | 2,189 | 1,903 | 30 | 23 |
| 1891 | 20 | 15 | 7,807 | 14,175 | ... | ... | ... | ... | 1,760 | 1,722 | 34 | 23 |
| 1892 | 21 | 22 | 6,010 | 14,869 | ... | ... | ... | ... | 1,941 | 1,760 | 33 | 18 |
| 1893 | 20 | 23 | 6,383 | 14,087 | ... | ... | ... | ... | 2,158 | 2,076 | 26 | 24 |
| 1894 | 23 | 21 | 6,180 | 20,325 | ... | ... | ... | ... | 2,192 | 1,921 | 29 | 23 |
| | | | | (thousand gold pesos) | | | | | | | | |
| 1895 | 16 | 12 | 8,689 | ... | 6.2 | 14 | ... | ... | 2,289 | 1,873 | 21 | 20 |
| 1896 | 20 | 18 | 11,429 | 9,973 | 6.1 | 9.4 | 1,325 | 3,131 | 1,856 | 1,470 | 23 | 21 |
| 1897 | 18 | 15 | 8,585 | 7,910 | 6.4 | 13 | 3,263 | 2,649 | 1,661 | 1,441 | 21 | 19 |
| 1898 | 18 | 17 | 4,851 | 4,882 | 5.5 | 13 | ... | ... | 1,815 | 1,663 | 24 | 22 |
| 1899 | 18 | 18 | 4,118 | 8,371 | 3.9 | 13 | 1,410 | 2,657 | 1,844 | 1,868 | 25 | 26 |
| 1900 | 20 | 15 | 3,127 | 7,393 | 7.2 | 14 | 1,074 | 2,636 | 1,722 | 1,797 | 25 | 27 |
| 1901 | 20 | 17 | 4,259 | 7,519 | 5.5 | 13 | 1,737 | 2,576 | 1,756 | 1,939 | 26 | 23 |
| 1902 | 16 | 17 | 4,017 | 9,032 | ... | ... | 1,294 | 1,763 | 2,029 | 2,292 | 19 | 16 |
| 1903 | 16 | 18 | 2,972 | 6,719 | ... | ... | 1,434 | 1,715 | 2,014 | 1,543 | 20 | 15 |
| 1904 | 13 | 13 | 5,041 | 7,552 | ... | ... | 2,223 | 2,173 | 1,682 | 1,437 | 15 | 13 |
| 1905 | 13 | 16 | 6,844 | 8,238 | ... | ... | 2,363 | 2,419 | 1,942 | 1,843 | 15 | 18 |
| 1906 | 13 | 15 | 7,221 | 7,136 | ... | ... | 2,512 | 2,880 | 2,261 | 1,992 | 15 | 19 |
| 1907 | 13 | 16 | 7,317 | 10,174 | ... | ... | 2,332 | 2,080 | 2,914 | 2,376 | 16 | 19 |
| 1908 | 15 | 17 | 5,812 | 6,756 | ... | ... | 2,830 | 1,834 | 2,420[3] | 2,268[3] | 15 | 21 |
| 1909 | 14 | 12 | 5,251 | 10,079 | 5.9 | ... | 2,592 | 1,991 | 2,562 | 2,628 | 16 | 22 |
| 1910 | 17 | 24 | 6,514 | 10,982 | 7.7 | ... | 2,696 | 2,296 | 2,615 | 2,568 | 20 | 28 |
| 1911 | 19 | 20 | 8,167 | 11,006 | 7.9 | ... | 3,561 | 2,908 | 2,866 | 2,948 | 20 | 23 |
| 1912 | 20 | 26 | 9,822 | 13,157 | 9.9 | 17 | 4,238 | 2,049 | 3,050 | 2,709 | 22 | 31 |
| 1913 | 20 | 18 | 10,062 | 14,450 | 8.7 | ... | 5,133 | 3,048 | 2,837 | 2,430[3] 2,249 | 22 | 29 |
| 1914 | 18 | 26 | 9,331 | 12,742 | 7.6 | ... | 6,625 | 3,397 | 2,553 | 2,831 | 22 | 30 |
| 1915 | 20 | 27 | 5,072 | 11,551 | 4.3 | ... | 5,875 | 3,458 | 2,327 | 2,227 | 23 | 43 |
| 1916 | 25 | 42 | 8,539 | 10,634 | 1.9 | 1.8 | 4,452 | 4,191 | 3,032 | 2,803 | 34 | 61 |
| 1917 | 40 | 51 | 8,700 | 7,828 | 1.7 | 1.7 | 6,293 | 5,353 | 3,298 | 2,479 | 57 | 81 |
| 1918 | 40 | 51 | 8,412 | 11,312 | ... | ... | 4,784 | 4,587 | 3,376 | 2,686 | 55 | 51 |
| 1919 | 64 | 104 | 14,216 | 22,408 | 17 | 21 | 6,931 | 5,998 | 4,872 | 5,626 | 75 | 173 |
| | | | (million quetzales) | | | | | | | | | |
| 1920 | 118 | 146 | 18 | 18 | 27 | 19 | 12,861 | 5,867 | 10,309 | 6,830 | 132 | 129 |
| 1921 | 79 | 75 | 13 | 12 | 12[13] | 5[13] | 16,723 | 5,429 | 5,460 | 3,053 | 85 | 89 |
| 1922 | 72 | 85 | 10 | 12 | 62 | 54 | 12,467 | 4,650 | 4,834 | 4,170 | 67 | 95 |
| 1923 | 86 | 105 | 13 | 15 | 71 | 73 | 14,342 | 8,681 | 5,556 | 4,278 | 95 | 118 |
| 1924 | 108 | 185 | 17 | 24 | 74 | 71 | 9,618 | 6,985 | 5,085 | 3,134 | 142 | 180 |
| 1925 | 133 | 155 | 23 | 29 | 101 | 97 | 12,003 | 10,030 | 5,631 | 3,934 | 162 | 179 |
| 1926 | 145 | 168 | 27 | 29 | 94 | 101 | 9,475 | 11,635 | 5,633 | 4,248 | 223 | 222 |
| 1927 | 158 | 183 | 26 | 34 | 79 | 76 | 10,330 | 16,118 | 5,997 | 4,857 | 213 | 229 |
| 1928 | 153 | 178 | 31 | 28 | 101 | 113 | 12,567 | 21,870 | 6,374 | 4,181 | 228 | 252 |
| 1929 | 231 | 135 | 30 | 25 | 86 | 84 | 14,861 | 23,075 | 7,023 | 4,656 | 266 | 310 |

**E1    NORTH AMERICA: External Trade Aggregates in Current Values**

**1885–1929**

| | Mexico[4] | | Newfoundland[1,5] | | Nicaragua[11] | | Panama[15] | | Trinidad[1,12] | | USA[1,6] | |
|---|---|---|---|---|---|---|---|---|---|---|---|---|
| | Imports | Exports | Imports | Exports | Imports | Exports | Imports | Exports | Imports | Exports | Imports | Exports |
| | | | | | (thousand gold pesos or cordobas) | | | | | | | |
| | (million pesos) | | (thousand pounds) | | | | (million balboas) | | (thousand pounds) | | (million US dollars) | |
| 1885 | 39 | 44 | 1,396 | 985 | ... | ... | ... | ... | 2,241 | 2,247 | 595 | 776 |
| 1886 | 41 | 49 | 1,254 | 1,013 | ... | ... | ... | ... | 2,504 | 2,509 | 653 | 710 |
| 1887 | 43 | 49 | 1,124 | 1,078 | ... | ... | ... | ... | 1,919 | 1,871 | 709 | 742 |
| 1888 | 40 | 60 | 1,546 | 1,371 | ... | ... | ... | ... | 1,944[12] | 2,133[12] | 739 | 724 |
| 1889 | 52 | 62 | 1,376 | 1,276 | ... | ... | ... | ... | 2,127 | 2,348 | 763 | 779 |
| 1890 | ... | 63 | 1,326 | 1,271 | ... | ... | ... | ... | 2,272 | 2,199 | 810 | 893 |
| 1891 | ... | 75 | 1,431 | 1,549 | ... | ... | ... | ... | 2,121 | 2,083 | 863 | 907 |
| 1892 | 43 | 88 | ... | ... | ... | ... | ... | ... | 2,105 | 2,272 | 847 | 1,063 |
| 1893 | 30 | 79 | 1,578 | 1,309 | ... | ... | ... | ... | 2,289 | 2,336 | 889 | 889 |
| 1894 | 34 | 91 | 1,493 | 1,211 | ... | ... | ... | ... | 2,168 | 2,017 | 668 | 942 |
| 1895 | 42 | 105 | 1,233[5] | 1,278[5] | 4,235 | 5,138 | ... | ... | 2,291 | 2,076 | 752 | 855 |
| 1896 | 42 | 111 | 1,230 | 1,364 | ... | ... | ... | ... | 2,477 | 2,177 | 809 | 944 |
| 1897 | 44 | 129 | 1,220 | 1,012 | 2,642 | 3,058 | ... | ... | 2,173 | 2,000 | 796 | 1,113 |
| 1898 | 51 | 138 | 1,066 | 1,074 | 2,866 | 3,184 | ... | ... | 2,294 | 2,332 | 647 | 1,286 |
| 1899 | 61[4] / 120 | 150 | 1,297 | 1,425 | ... | ... | ... | ... | 2,536 | 2,573 | 728 | 1,283 |
| 1900 | 133 | 158 | 1,541 | 1,773 | 3,517 | 3,961 | ... | ... | 2,500 | 2,585 | 885 | 1,451 |
| 1901 | 151 | 172 | 1,536 | 1,718 | 2,302 | 3,478 | ... | ... | 2,652 | 2,446 | 859 | 1,552 |
| 1902 | 191 | 207 | 1,611 | 1,964 | 1,273 | 3,047 | ... | ... | 2,672 | 2,472 | 931 | 1,432 |
| 1903 | 178 | 210 | 1,743 | 2,051 | 2,461 | 3,652 | ... | ... | 2,526 | 2,275 | 1,050 | 1,464 |
| 1904 | 178 | 209 | 1,942 | 2,134 | 3,202 | 3,926 | ... | ... | 2,629 | 2,479 | 1,019 | 1,510 |
| 1905 | 220 | 271 | 2,113 | 2,193 | 3,407 | 3,542 | ... | ... | 3,304 | 3,169 | 1,145 | 1,568 |
| 1906 | 232 | 248 | 2,141 | 2,484 | 3,409 | 4,231 | 7.4 | 1.1 | 3,121 | 2,872 | 1,271 | 1,810 |
| 1907 | 222 | 243 | 2,143 | 2,487 | 3,224 | 3,364 | 9.6 | 2.0 | 3,375 | 2,500 | 1,458 | 1,938 |
| 1908 | 157 | 231 | 2,367 | 2,429 | 2,959 | 3,648 | 7.8 | 1.8 | 2,683[12] | 3,908[12] | 1,228 | 1,919 |
| 1909 | 195 | 260 | 2,349 | 2,230 | 2,583 | 3,989 | 8.8 | 1.5 | 3,289 | 3,218 | 1,326 | 1,719 |
| 1910 | 206 | 294 | 2,631 | 2,431 | 2,856 | 4,545 | 10.0 | 1.8 | 3,343 | 3,468 | 1,592 | 1,800 |
| 1911 | 183 | 298 | 2,751 | 2,462 | 5,724 | 6,579 | 9.9 | 2.9 | 5,019 | 4,769 | 1,573 | 2,114 |
| 1912 | 192 | 300 | 3,029 | 2,852 | 4,967 | 2,932 | 9.9 | 2.1 | 4,682 | 4,473 | 1,700 | 2,269 |
| 1913 | 171 | 319 | 3,291 | 3,016 | 5,770 | 6,609 | 11.2 | 5.4 | 4,968 | 5,206 | 1,854 | 2,538 |
| 1914 | [86][4] | [160][4] | 3,123 | 3,111 | 4,134 | 3,968 | 9.9 | 3.8 | 4,183 | 4,201 | 1,924 | 2,420 |
| 1915 | [53][4] | 251 | 2,539 | 2,700 | 3,159 | 3,572 | 9.0 | 3.4 | 4,430[12] / 3,013 | 5,379[12] / 4,027 | 1,703[6] | 2,820[6] |
| 1916 | [85][4] | 487 | 3,377 | 3,899 | 4,778 | 4,243 | 9.2 | 5.7 | 3,565 | 4,188 | 2,424 | 5,554 |
| 1917 | 190[4] | 307 | 4,382 | 4,601 | 6,393 | 4,808 | 9.2 | 5.6 | 4,157 | 4,702 | 3,005 | 6,318 |
| 1918 | 276 | 376 | 5,528 | 6,198 | 5,930 | 6,016 | 7.8 | 2.9 | 4,476 | 4,516 | 3,102 | 6,402 |
| 1919 | 237 | 394 | 6,844 | 7,561 | 7,912 | 10,153 | 11.4 | 3.8 | 5,159 | 6,187 | 3,993 | 8,159 |
| 1920 | 397 | 855 | 8,332 | 7,167 | 13,864 | 8,910 | 17.6 | 3.6 | 8,487 | 8,025 | 5,366 | 8,342 |
| 1921 | 493 | 757 | 5,943 | 4,613 | 5,310 | 6,629 | 11.4 | 2.5 | 6,846 | 4,402 | 2,572 | 4,537 |
| 1922 | 309 | 644 | 3,743 | 4,004 | 5,123 | 6,345 | 10.3 | 2.5 | 4,576 | 3,990 | 3,184 | 3,895 |
| 1923 | 315 | 568 | 3,972 | 4,308 | 7,268 | 9,604 | 12.7 | 2.4 | 4,285 | 4,612 | 3,866 | 4,239 |
| 1924 | 321 | 615 | 5,687 | 4,712 | 8,807 | 12,001 | 13.8 | 3.0 | 4,273 | 4,700 | 3,684 | 4,701 |
| | | | | | (million gold cordobas) | | | | | | | |
| 1925 | 391 | 682 | 7,480 | 5,051 | 10.4 | 11.7 | 16.1 | 3.7 | 4,346 | 4,895 | 4,292 | 5,009 |
| 1926 | 381 | 692 | 5,661 | 5,665 | 10.3 | 12.2 | 15.7 | 3.5 | 4,349 | 5,285 | 4,501 | 4,901 |
| 1927 | 346 | 634 | 5,305 | 6,339 | 10.2 | 8.4 | 14.7 | 3.9 | 5,072 | 5,573 | 4,240 | 4,941 |
| 1928 | 358 | 592 | 5,678 | 6,916 | 13.4 | 11.3 | 16.2 | 4.1 | 5,252 | 6,139 | 4,159 | 5,215 |
| 1929 | 382 | 591 | 6,008 | 7,564 | 11.8 | 10.4 | 19.3 | 4.1 | 5,932 | 6,392 | 4,463 | 5,324 |

**E1　　NORTH AMERICA: External Trade Aggregates in Current Values**

| | Barbados[1] | | Canada[7] | | Costa Rica | | Cuba | | Dominican Republic | | El Salvador | |
|---|---|---|---|---|---|---|---|---|---|---|---|---|
| | Imports | Exports | Imports | Exports | Imports | Exports | Imports | Exports | Imports | Exports | Imports | Exports |
| | (thousand pounds) | | (million Canadian dollars) | | (million colones) | | (million pesos) | | (million pesos) | | (million colones) | |
| 1930 | 1,732 | 1,038 | 1,008 | 883 | 43 | 65 | 163 | 167 | 15.2 | 18.6 | 24 | 27 |
| 1931 | 1,492 | 1,043 | 628 | 600 | 35 | 57 | 80 | 119 | 10.2 | 13.1 | 15 | 23 |
| 1932 | 1,657 | 1,369 | 453 | 498 | 24 | 38 | 51 | 81 | 7.8 | 11.0 | 13 | 14 |
| 1933 | 1,740 | 1,370 | 401 | 535 | 29 | 49 | 42 | 84 | 9.3 | 9.4 | 16 | 20 |
| 1934 | 1,915 | 1,470 | 513 | 656 | 37 | 37 | 73 | 107 | 10.6 | 12.6 | 21 | 24 |
| 1935 | 1,841 | 1,123 | 550 | 738 | 47 | 49 | 96 | 128 | 9.8 | 15.2 | 22 | 26 |
| 1936 | 2,004 | 1,483 | 635 | 951 | 58 | 54 | 103 | 155 | 9.9 | 14.8 | 21 | 24 |
| 1937 | 2,220 | 1,632 | 809 | 1,012 | 67 | 65 | 130 | 186 | 11.7 | 17.9 | 26 | 37 |
| 1938 | 2,086 | 1,340 | 677 | 849 | 71 | 57 | 106 | 142 | 11.3 | 14.7 | 23 | 26 |
| | | | | | (million US dollars) | | | | | | | |
| | | | | | 12.6 | 9.3 | | | | | | |
| 1939 | 2,378 | 2,028 | 751 | 936 | 16.9 | 8.6 | 106 | 148 | 11.6 | 18.4 | 22 | 30 |
| | (million local dollars) | | | | | | | | | | | |
| 1940 | 11.1 | 8.1 | 1,082 | 1,193 | 16.8 | 7.0 | 104 | 127 | 10.5 | 18.0 | 20 | 26 |
| 1941 | 11.1 | 9.1 | 1,449 | 1,640 | 17.8 | 9.8 | 134 | 211 | 11.7 | 16.6 | 21 | 25 |
| 1942 | 9.7 | 6.5 | 1,644 | 2,385 | 12.3 | 10.2 | 147 | 182 | 11.5 | 19.8 | 21 | 43 |
| 1943 | 14.1 | 11.2 | 1,735 | 3,001 | 20.4 | 12.2 | 177 | 351 | 14.4 | 36 | 29 | 54 |
| 1944 | 16.4 | 12.1 | 1,759 | 3,483 | 21.5 | 10.4 | 208 | 433 | 18.5 | 60 | 31 | 55 |
| 1945 | 16.7 | 13.8 | 1,556 | 3,267 | 26.9 | 11.5 | 238 | 410 | 18.1 | 43 | 34 | 52 |
| 1946 | 24.0 | 15.1 | 1,865 | 2,339 | 33.0 | 14.3 | 299 | 476 | 28 | 65 | 52 | 63 |
| 1947 | 34.2 | 17.8 | 2,574 | 2,812 | 48.1 | 31.0 | 520 | 747 | 53 | 83 | 92 | 99 |
| 1948 | 30.5 | 14.6 | 2,637[7] | 3,110[7] | 42.3 | 45.9 | 527 | 710 | 65 | 83 | 104 | 112 |
| 1949 | 33.9 | 22.5 | 2,761[7] | 3,022[7] | 43.4 | 48.2 | 451 | 578 | 46 | 74 | 101 | 135 |
| 1950 | 38.7 | 27.6 | 3,174 | 3,157 | 46.0 | 55.6 | 515 | 642 | 44 | 87 | 121 | 171 |
| 1951 | 51.9 | 35.5 | 4,085 | 3,963 | 55.7 | 63.4 | 640 | 766 | 59 | 119 | 157 | 212 |
| 1952 | 54.2 | 40.0 | 4,030 | 4,356 | 67.9 | 73.3 | 618 | 675 | 97 | 115 | 173 | 218 |
| 1953 | 45.5 | 41.0 | 4,383 | 4,173 | 73.7 | 80.1 | 490 | 640 | 86 | 105 | 181 | 222 |
| 1954 | 48.8 | 40.4 | 4,093 | 3,947 | 80.0 | 84.7 | 488 | 539 | 83 | 120 | 217 | 263 |
| 1955 | 55.2 | 38.8 | 4,712 | 4,351 | 87.5 | 80.9 | 575 | 594 | 98 | 115 | 230 | 267 |
| 1956 | 61.3 | 36.2 | 5,705 | 4,863 | 91.2 | 67.4 | 649 | 666 | 108 | 121 | 262 | 282 |
| 1957 | 68.3 | 49.0 | 5,623 | 4,920 | 103 | 83.4 | 773 | 808 | 116 | 147 | 288 | 346 |
| 1958 | 73.4 | 40.1 | 5,192 | 4,926 | 99 | 91.9 | 777 | 733 | 129 | 128 | 270 | 290 |
| 1959 | 74.9 | 46.7 | 5,654[16] | 5,179[16] | 103 | 76.7 | 673 | 637 | 117 | 130 | 249 | 283 |
| | | | 5,509 | 5,140 | | | | | | | | |
| 1960 | 83.3 | 40.9 | 5,483 | 5,387 | 110 | 85.8 | 580 | 618 | 87 | 174 | 306 | 292 |
| 1961 | 80.3 | 43.3 | 5,781 | 5,902 | 107 | 84.1 | 639[9] | 625 | 69 | 143 | 272 | 298 |
| 1962 | 89.1 | 50.3 | 6,294 | 6,357 | 113 | 93.0 | 759 | 521 | 129 | 172 | 312 | 341 |
| 1963 | 98.9 | 69.8 | 6,578 | 6,990 | 124 | 95.0 | 867 | 544 | 160 | 174 | 379 | 385 |
| 1964 | 109 | 60.3 | 7,488 | 8,303 | 139 | 114 | 1,019 | 714 | 192 | 179 | 478 | 445 |
| 1965 | 116 | 64.3 | 8,633 | 8,767 | 178 | 112 | 866 | 691 | 87 | 125 | 501 | 472 |
| 1966 | 131 | 70.0 | 10,072 | 10,325 | 178 | 136 | 925 | 598 | 161 | 137 | 550 | 472 |
| 1967 | 134 | 71.6 | 10,872 | 11,420 | 191 | 144 | 999 | 705 | 175 | 156 | 560 | 518 |
| 1968 | 168 | 80.2 | 12,358 | 13,624 | 214 | 171 | 1,102 | 651 | 197 | 163 | 534 | 530 |
| 1969 | 195 | 74.3 | 14,130 | 14,890 | 245 | 190 | 1,222 | 671 | 217 | 183 | 523 | 505 |
| 1970 | 235 | 79.1 | 13,952 | 16,820 | 317 | 231 | 1,311 | 1,050 | 278 | 214 | 534 | 571 |
| 1971 | 244 | 80.3 | 15,617 | 17,820 | 350 | 225 | 1,387 | 861 | 310 | 241 | 619 | 608 |
| 1972 | 270 | 84.5 | 18,669 | 20,150 | 343 | 279 | 1,190 | 771 | 338 | 348 | 695 | 754 |
| 1973 | 329 | 104 | 23,324 | 25,420 | 455 | 345 | 1,467 | 1,153 | 422 | 442 | 934 | 896 |
| 1974 | 418 | 172 | 31,692 | 32,441 | 720 | 440 | 2,226 | 2,236 | 673 | 637 | 1,409 | 1,156 |

**E1    NORTH AMERICA: External Trade Aggregates in Current Values**

## 1930–1974

| | Guadeloupe | | Guatemala[10] | | Haiti[1] | | Honduras[14] | | Jamaica | | Martinique | |
|---|---|---|---|---|---|---|---|---|---|---|---|---|
| | Imports | Exports | Imports | Exports | Imports | Exports | Imports | Exports | Imports | Exports | Imports | Exports |
| | (million francs) | | (million quetzales) | | (million gourdes) | | (thousand gold pesos) | | (thousand pounds) | | (million francs) | |
| 1930 | 229 | 193 | 16 | 23 | 64 | 71 | 15,946 | 25,096 | 6,099 | 4,080 | 237 | 282 |
| 1931 | 189 | 137 | 13 | 15 | 48 | 45 | 10,193 | 18,558 | 4,943 | 3,334 | 220 | 180 |
| 1932 | 167 | 190 | 7.4 | 11 | 37 | 36 | 7,497 | 14,839 | 4,751 | 3,240 | 191 | 201 |
| 1933 | 153 | 191 | 7.5 | 9.2 | 38 | 47 | 6,114 | 12,313 | 4,365 | 2,499 | 192 | 200 |
| 1934 | 150 | 152 | 9.9 | 15 | 46 | 52 | 8,330 | 10,477 | 4,765 | 3,174 | 187 | 184 |
| 1935 | 112 | 160 | 12 | 12 | 41 | 36 | 9,465 | 8,621 | 5,009 | 3,813 | 140 | 166 |
| 1936 | 125 | 171 | 14 | 17 | 38 | 47 | 8,213 | 6,993 | 5,072 | 3,803 | 156 | 191 |
| 1937 | 195 | 294 | 21 | 18 | 46 | 45 | 9,887 | 7,476 | 6,135 | 4,962 | 214 | 231 |
| 1938 | 251 | 296 | 21 | 18 | 38 | 35 | 9,468 | 5,443 | 6,423 | 5,028 | 235 | 310 |
| | | | | | | | (million lempiras) | | | | | |
| | | | | | | | [18.8][14] | [31.8][14] | | | | |
| 1939 | 241 | 278 | 19 | 19 | 41 | 36 | 19.4 | 45 | 6,501 | 4,753 | 234 | 319 |
| 1940 | 184 | 282 | 16 | 12 | 40 | 27 | 20 | 44 | 6,152 | 3,204 | 225 | 330 |
| 1941 | 201 | 137 | 16[10] | 14 | 37 | 33 | 20 | 42 | 6,442 | 3,959 | 215 | 183 |
| 1942 | 168 | 82 | 14 | 20 | 42 | 43 | 22 | 41 | 5,460 | 4,050 | 207 | 90 |
| 1943 | 158 | 30 | 18 | 20 | 49 | 53 | 19 | 18 | 7,209 | 4,236 | 136 | 81 |
| 1944 | 385 | 286 | 21 | 24 | 80 | 81 | 24 | 39 | 8,968 | 4,478 | 526 | 248 |
| 1945 | 451 | 986 | 23 | 30 | 66 | 86 | 26 | 55 | 9,586 | 4,959 | 602 | 580 |
| 1946 | 1,116 | 1,495 | 36 | 37[17] 53 | 80 | 114 | 37 | 60 | 12,450 | 8,750 | 1,583 | 1,563 |
| 1947 | 2,803 | 3,589 | 57 | 66 | 136 | 157 | 56 | 85 | 18,941 | 10,168 | 3,667 | 4,117 |
| 1948 | 5,415 | 3,835 | 68 | 67 | 161 | 154 | 71 | 98 | 19,678 | 11,387 | 6,406 | 4,696 |
| 1949 | 6,987 | 6,842 | 68 | 63 | 157 | 155 | 67 | 114 | 19,225 | 12,134 | 8,638 | 5,185 |
| | | | | | | | (million local dollars) | | | | | |
| 1950 | 7,422 | 6,008 | 71 | 79 | 181 | 192 | 67 | 131 | 45 | 32 | 7,432 | 5,306 |
| 1951 | 9,147 | 8,102 | 81 | 84 | 223 | 248 | 79[14] | 128[14] | 61 | 36 | 10,912 | 7,498 |
| 1952 | 12,440 | 9,966 | 76 | 95 | 253 | 265 | 115 | 124 | 73 | 37 | 13,405 | 6,932 |
| 1953 | 11,744 | 8,785 | 80 | 100 | 226 | 189 | 108 | 135 | 71 | 52 | 12,198 | 6,883 |
| 1954 | 12,684 | 11,709 | 86 | 105 | 238 | 278 | 103 | 112 | 75 | 63 | 12,637 | 8,857 |
| 1955 | 13,056 | 11,881 | 104[10] | 107[10] | 196 | 174 | 108 | 98 | 91 | 69 | 13,754 | 8,972 |
| 1956 | 12,695 | 10,181 | 138 | 123 | 232 | 233 | 117 | 146 | 117 | 80 | 13,079 | 9,893 |
| 1957 | 16,842 | 12,380 | 147 | 116 | 191 | 165 | 137 | 130 | 133 | 103 | 17,455 | 12,915 |
| | (million new francs) | | | | | | | | | | (million new francs) | |
| 1958 | 201 | 142 | 150 | 107 | 227 | 211 | 131 | 139 | 129 | 96 | 174 | 122 |
| 1959 | 207 | 172 | 134 | 108 | 169 | 130 | 124[14] | 137 | 137 | 96 | 211 | 155 |
| 1960 | 238 | 171 | 138 | 117 | 202 | 191 | 143 | 126 | 155 | 113 | 233 | 159 |
| 1961 | 259 | 178 | 134 | 113 | 164 | 152 | 144 | 146 | 151 | 127 | 251 | 166 |
| 1962 | 284 | 174 | 136 | 118 | 186 | 204 | 160 | 163 | 159 | 130 | 281 | 166 |
| 1963 | 342 | 188 | 171 | 154 | 180 | 216 | 190 | 167 | 161 | 144 | 364 | 176 |
| 1964 | 392 | 172 | 202 | 164 | 180 | 190 | 203 | 188 | 207 | 154 | 389 | 145 |
| 1965 | 421 | 187 | 228 | 188 | 186 | 189 | 244 | 253 | 206 | 153 | 449 | 186 |
| 1966 | 448 | 183 | 208 | 229 | 180 | 192 | 298 | 291 | 234 | 163 | 457 | 221 |
| 1967 | 492 | 160 | 247 | 202 | 182 | 168 | 329 | 316 | 253 | 163 | 520 | 212 |
| 1968 | 504 | 180 | 249 | 227 | 188 | 178 | 369 | 358 | 320 | 183 | 537 | 197 |
| 1969 | 546 | 176 | 250 | 255 | 194 | 186 | 368 | 342 | 363 | 212 | 651 | 182 |
| 1970 | 709 | 209 | 284 | 290 | 275 | 202 | 441 | 363 | 438 | 289 | 810 | 167 |
| 1971 | 692 | 231 | 303 | 283 | 302 | 237 | 387 | 388 | 460 | 283 | 860 | 189 |
| 1972 | 747 | 201 | 324 | 328 | 345 | 220 | 386 | 419 | 489 | 300 | 872 | 228 |
| 1973 | 896 | 285 | 431 | 436 | 416 | 264 | 524 | 523 | 615 | 355 | 1,083 | 244 |
| 1974 | 1,104 | 278 | 701 | 572 | 626 | 358 | 760 | 588 | 851 | 549 | 1,405 | 347 |

**E1 NORTH AMERICA: External Trade Aggregates in Current Values**

**1930–1974**

| | Mexico | | Newfoundland[1,5] | | Nicaragua[11] | | Panama[15] | | Trinidad & Tobago | | USA | |
|---|---|---|---|---|---|---|---|---|---|---|---|---|
| | Imports | Exports | Imports | Exports | Imports | Exports | Imports | Exports | Imports | Exports | Imports | Exports |
| | (million pesos) | | (thousand pounds) | | (million gold cordobas) | | (million balboas) | | (thousand pounds) | | (million US dollars) | |
| 1930 | 350 | 459 | 6,549 | 8,232 | 8.2 | 7.9 | 18.3 | 3.3 | 5,334 | 5,150 | 3,104 | 3,897 |
| 1931 | 217 | 400 | 5,190 | 6,895 | 6.0 | 6.2 | 13.5 | 2.6 | 3,911 | 4,045 | 2,119 | 2,451 |
| 1932 | 181 | 305 | 3,727 | 6,612 | 3.5 | 4.2 | 8.9 | 2.0 | 3,692 | 3,937 | 1,342 | 1,625 |
| 1933 | 244 | 365 | 3,117 | 6,044 | 3.8 | 4.5 | 9.3 | 2.3 | 4,002 | 3,777 | 1,510 | 1,694 |
| 1934 | 334 | 644 | 3,350 | 5,355 | 4.6 | 4.6 | 13.6 | 2.7 | 4,486 | 4,350 | 1,758 | 2,149 |
| 1935 | 406 | 750 | 3,954 | 5,567 | 5.1 | 5.1 | 15.6 | 3.6 | 4,372 | 4,336 | 2,402 | 2,302 |
| 1936 | 464 | 775 | 4,251 | 5,794 | 5.6 | 3.8 | 19.0 | 3.7 | 5,664 | 5,607 | 2,605 | 2,468 |
| 1937 | 614 | 892 | 4,846 | 5,684 | 5.6 | 6.2 | 21.8 | 8.4 | 7,466 | 6,176 | 3,176 | 3,361 |
| 1938 | 494 | 838 | 5,593 | 7,001 | 5.1 | 4.3 | 17.7 | 7.5 | 7,395 | 6,483 | 2,191 | 3,102 |
| 1939 | 630 | 914 | 5,134 | 6,714 | 6.4 | 4.8 | 20 | 6.7 | 7,242 | 5,836 | 2,403 | 3,192 |
| 1940 | 669 | 960 | 6,341 | 7,450 | 7.1 | 3.7 | 23 | 6.9 | 9,394 | 5,180 | 2,684 | 4,025 |
| 1941 | 915 | 730 | 7,974 | 8,388 | 10.4 | 4.6 | 33 | 6.2 | 11,976 | 3,393 | 3,392 | 5,153 |
| 1942 | 753 | 990 | 14,513 | 8,854 | 6.8 | 5.9 | 38 | 3.8 | 11,478 | 2,477 | 2,797 | 8,081 |
| 1943 | 910 | 1,130 | 11,770 | 6,950 | 14 | 7.7 | 40 | 3.7 | 12,456 | 2,353 | 3,409 | 12,996 |
| 1944 | 1,895 | 1,047 | 14,042 | 9,988 | 10 | 7.8 | 38 | 3.9 | 14,373 | 2,614 | 3,952 | 14,386 |
| | | | | | | | | | (million local dollars) | | | |
| 1945 | 1,604 | 1,272 | 14,792 | 10,946 | 12 | 6.9 | 46 | 6 | 65 | 58 | 4,186 | 9,897 |
| 1946 | 2,637 | 1,975 | … | … | 15 | 11 | 56 | 7.9[17] | 75 | 61 | 5,000 | 9,775 |
| | | | | | | | | 13 | | | | |
| 1947 | 3,230 | 2,162 | … | … | 21 | 13 | 76 | 15[15] | 118 | 86 | 5,824 | 15,369 |
| 1948 | 2,950 | 2,595 | … | … | 24 | 19 | 64 | 24 | 131 | 132 | 7,195 | 12,665 |
| 1949 | 3,524 | 3,389 | … | … | 21 | 16 | 60 | 24 | 154 | 138 | 6,696 | 12,074 |
| 1950 | 4,402 | 4,339 | included with Canada | | 25 | 27 | 61 | 23 | 168 | 176 | 8,962 | 10,282 |
| 1951 | 7,112 | 5,447 | | | 30 | 37 | 66 | 25 | 219 | 214 | 11,070 | 15,041 |
| 1952 | 6,984 | 5,126 | | | 40 | 42 | 73 | 23 | 244 | 230 | 10,820 | 15,206 |
| 1953 | 6,985 | 4,836 | | | 44 | 46 | 71 | 26 | 236 | 256 | 11,010 | 15,782 |
| 1954 | 8,926 | 6,936 | | | 58[11] | 55 | 72 | 31 | 249 | 262 | 10,372 | 15,114 |
| 1955 | 11,046 | 9,484 | | | 70 | 72 | 75 | 36 | 294 | 285 | 11,568 | 15,556 |
| 1956 | 13,396 | 10,671 | | | 69 | 58 | 83 | 31 | 301 | 330 | 12,906 | 19,102 |
| 1957 | 14,440 | 8,729 | | | 81 | 64 | 99 | 35 | 356 | 393 | 13,418 | 20,873 |
| 1958 | 14,108 | 8,846 | | | 78 | 64 | 94 | 33 | 412 | 425 | 13,351 | 17,920 |
| 1959 | 12,583 | 9,007 | | | 67 | 65 | 93 | 35 | 448 | 449 | 15,692 | 17,655 |
| 1960 | 14,831 | 9,247 | | | 72 | 63 | 109 | 21 | 504 | 491 | 15,075 | 20,612 |
| 1961 | 14,233 | 9,997 | | | 74 | 68 | 124 | 24 | 584 | 593 | 14,761 | 21,036 |
| 1962 | 14,287 | 11,029 | | | 98 | 90 | 145 | 40 | 606 | 592 | 16,457 | 21,715 |
| 1963 | 15,496 | 11,504 | | | 111 | 107 | 181 | 60 | 646 | 641 | 17,211 | 23,389 |
| 1964 | 18,657 | 12,492 | | | 136 | 125 | 181 | 70 | 731 | 699 | 18,750 | 26,652 |
| 1965 | 19,496 | 13,610 | | | 160 | 144 | 208 | 79 | 817 | 690 | 21,431 | 27,532 |
| 1966 | 20,064 | 14,535 | | | 182 | 142 | 235 | 89 | 778 | 735 | 25,620 | 30,434 |
| 1967 | 21,824 | 13,798 | | | 202 | 152 | 251 | 94 | 724 | 763 | 26,892 | 31,627 |
| 1968 | 24,527 | 14,759 | | | 183 | 162 | 266 | 99 | 854 | 943 | 33,226 | 34,636 |
| 1969 | 25,974 | 17,312 | | | 176 | 159 | 294 | 113 | 966 | 948 | 36,043 | 38,006 |
| 1970 | 28,994 | 16,025 | | | 198 | 179 | 357 | 110 | 1,085 | 961 | 39,756 | 42,590 |
| 1971 | 28,130 | 17,070 | | | 210 | 187 | 396 | 117 | 1,327 | 1,039 | 45,516 | 43,498 |
| 1972 | 33,981 | 20,926 | | | 218 | 249 | 440 | 123 | 1,468 | 1,068 | 55,282 | 48,959 |
| 1973 | 47,668 | 25,881 | | | 326 | 278 | 502 | 138 | 1,553 | 1,372 | 68,658 | 70,246 |
| | | | | | (million paper cordobas) | | | | | | | |
| 1974 | 75,709 | 37,021 | | | 3,939 | 2,671 | 822 | 211 | 3,778 | 4,166 | 107,112 | 97,144 |

**E1    NORTH AMERICA: External Trade Aggregates in Current Values**

| | Barbados[1] | | Canada | | Costa Rica | | Cuba | | Dominican Republic | | El Salvador | |
|---|---|---|---|---|---|---|---|---|---|---|---|---|
| | Imports | Exports | Imports | Exports | Imports | Exports | Imports | Exports | Imports | Exports | Imports | Exports |
| | (million local dollars) | | (million local dollars) | | (million US dollars) | | (million pesos) | | (million pesos) | | (million colones) | |
| 1975 | 437 | 217 | 34,691 | 32,246 | 694 | 493 | 3,113 | 2,952 | 773 | 894 | 1,495 | 1,329 |
| 1976 | 475 | 173 | 37,444 | 38,397 | 770 | 593 | 3,180 | 2,692 | 764 | 716 | 1,837 | 1,858 |
| 1977 | 549 | 191 | 42,332 | 44,554 | 1,021 | 828 | 3,462 | 2,918 | 848 | 780 | 2,323 | 2,431 |
| 1978 | 629 | 261 | 50,102 | 53,183 | 1,166 | 865 | 3,574 | 3,440 | 861 | 675 | 2,568 | 2,002 |
| 1979 | 848 | 304 | 62,871 | 65,641 | 1,397 | 934 | 3,687 | 3,499 | 1,080 | 869 | 2,598 | 2,828 |
| 1980 | 1,055 | 455 | 69,274 | 76,159 | 1,540 | 1,002 | 4,627 | 3,967 | 1,498 | 962 | 2,404 | 2,684 |
| 1981 | 1,148 | 393 | 79,482 | 83,812 | 1,208 | 1,008 | 5,114 | 4,224 | 1,450 | 1,188 | 2,461 | 1,992 |
| 1982 | 1,107 | 518 | 67,856 | 84,530 | 889 | 870 | 5,531 | 4,933 | 1,256 | 768 | 2,142 | 1,749 |
| 1983 | 1,238 | 646 | 75,608 | 90,612 | 988 | 873 | 6,222 | 5,535 | 1,279 | 785 | 2,229 | 1,838 |
| 1984 | 1,321 | 784 | 95,460 | 112,384 | 1,094 | 1,006 | 7,227 | 5,476 | 1,257 | 868 | 2,444 | 1,813 |
| 1985 | 1,222 | 708 | 104,355 | 119,475 | 1,098 | 976 | 8,035 | 5,991 | 3,875 | 2,347 | 2,403 | 1,697 |
| 1986 | 1,181 | 553 | 112,678 | 120,490 | 1,147 | 1,120 | 7,569 | 5,325 | 4,165 | 2,086 | 4,284 | 3,563 |
| 1987 | 1,036 | 311 | 116,076 | 125,087 | 1,383 | 1,158 | 7,611 | 5,401 | 6,885 | 2,710 | 4,970 | 2,955 |
| 1988 | 1,170 | 349 | 131,554 | 137,695 | 1,410 | 1,246 | 7,579 | 5,518 | 11,362 | 5,518 | 5,244 | 2,829 |

| | Guadeloupe | | Guatemala | | Haiti | | Honduras | | Jamaica | | Martinique | |
|---|---|---|---|---|---|---|---|---|---|---|---|---|
| | Imports | Exports | Imports | Exports | Imports | Exports | Imports | Exports | Imports | Exports | Imports | Exports |
| | (million francs) | | (million quetzales) | | (million gourdes) | | (million lempiras) | | (million local dollars) | | (million Francs) | |
| 1975 | 1,315 | 353 | 724 | 623 | 745 | 399 | 809 | 606 | 1,021 | 690 | 1,453 | 408 |
| 1976 | 1,515 | 429 | 839 | 760 | 1,034 | 622 | 906 | 794 | 830 | 573 | 1,965 | 594 |
| 1977 | 1,844 | 387 | 1,052 | 1,160 | 1,063 | 743 | 1,159 | 1,037 | 782 | 699 | 2,099 | 630 |
| 1978 | 1,910 | 499 | 1,286 | 1,090 | 1,166 | 777 | 1,398 | 1,225 | 1,260 | 1,142 | 2,241 | 567 |
| 1979 | 2,540 | 648 | 1,504 | 1,241 | 1,360 | 927 | 1,652 | 1,467 | 1,755 | 1,446 | 2,870 | 567 |
| 1980 | 3,074 | 446 | 1,598 | 1,520 | 1,771 | 1,131 | 2,017 | 1,659 | 2,087 | 1,715 | 3,564 | 492 |
| 1981 | 3,334 | 509 | 1,673 | 1,226 | 2,240 | 757 | 1,891 | 1,458 | 2,623 | 1,735 | 4,188 | 895 |
| 1982 | 4,117 | 548 | 1,388 | 1,120 | 1,936 | 813 | 1,384 | 1,336 | 2,460 | 1,367 | 4,835 | 764 |
| 1983 | 5,039 | 627 | 1,126 | 1,159 | 2,203 | 769 | 1,605 | 1,344 | 2,841 | 1,392 | 5,578 | 867 |
| 1984 | 5,231 | 751 | 1,278 | 1,128 | 2,361 | 893 | 1,787 | 1,451 | 4,509 | 2,897 | 5,648 | 924 |
| 1985 | 5,745 | 669 | 1,175 | 1,057 | 2,208 | 871 | 1,776 | 1,529 | 6,147 | 3,128 | 6,050 | 1,300 |
| 1986 | 5,457 | 748 | 960 | 1,044 | 1,774 | 930 | 1,750 | 1,708 | 5,322 | 3,226 | 6,065 | 1,445 |
| 1987 | 6,229 | 564 | 1,479 | 981 | 1,872 | 1,101 | 1,797 | 1,616 | 6,790 | 3,874 | 6,708 | 1,163 |
| 1988 | 7,237 | 973 | 1,557 | 1,034 | 1,721 | 913 | 1,866 | 1,737 | 7,901 | 4,559 | 7,723 | 1,172 |

| | Mexico | | Nicaragua | | Panama | | Trinidad & Tobago | | USA | |
|---|---|---|---|---|---|---|---|---|---|---|
| | Imports | Exports | Imports | Exports | Imports | Exports | Imports | Exports | Imports | Exports |
| | (million pesos) | | (million cordobas) | | (million galboas) | | (million local dollars) | | (million US dollars) | |
| 1975 | 82,131 | 37,405 | 3,632 | 2,636 | 816 | 286 | 3,239 | 3,875 | 105,880 | 108,113 |
| 1976 | 90,900 | 53,675 | 3,739 | 3,808 | 780 | 238 | 4,904 | 5,392 | 132,498 | 115,413 |
| 1977 | 126,352 | 96,779 | 5,353 | 4,474 | 778 | 251 | 4,365 | 5,231 | 160,411 | 121,293 |
| 1978 | 177,278 | 134,313 | 4,173 | 4,539 | 845 | 256 | 4,721 | 4,895 | 186,044 | 143,766 |
| 1979 | 287,135 | 201,109 | 3,334 | 5,244 | 1,063 | 303 | 5,051 | 6,265 | 222,228 | 182,025 |
| | (thousand million pesos) | | | | | | | | | |
| 1980 | 446 | 351 | 8,916 | 4,526 | 1,289 | 358 | 7,626 | 9,785 | 256,984 | 220,786 |
| 1981 | 614 | 476 | 10,044 | 5,023 | 1,393 | 328 | 7,499 | 9,026 | 273,352 | 233,739 |
| 1982 | 743 | 1,230 | 7,794 | 4,078 | 1,407 | 375 | 8,873 | 7,372 | 254,885 | 212,275 |
| 1983 | 1,096 | 2,692 | 8,109 | 4,309 | 1,412 | 321 | 6,197 | 5,646 | 269,878 | 200,538 |
| 1984 | 2,006 | 4,054 | 8,303 | 3,873 | 1,423 | 276 | 4,606 | 5,216 | 341,177 | 217,888 |
| 1985 | 3,536 | 5,588 | 25,558 | 7,991 | 1,392 | 333 | 3,739 | 5,247 | 361,626 | 213,146 |
| 1986 | 6,730 | 9,299 | 57,915 | 16,187 | 1,229 | 341 | 4,860 | 4,989 | 387,054 | 217,336 |
| 1987 | 17,314 | 27,505 | 64,581 | 20,993 | 1,306 | 348 | 4,387 | 5,265 | 424,082 | 252,866 |
| 1988 | 43,078 | 46,949 | ... | ... | 751 | 280 | 4,310 | 5,424 | 459,565 | 322,225 |

**E1    SOUTH AMERICA: EXTERNAL TRADE AGGREGATES IN CURRENT VALUES**

1821–1854

| | Brazil[19] | | Colombia | | Guyana[1,21] | | Peru[27] | | Surinam | | Venezuela[23] | |
|---|---|---|---|---|---|---|---|---|---|---|---|---|
| | Imports | Exports | Imports | Exports | Imports | Exports | Imports | Exports | Imports | Exports | Imports | Exports |
| | (million paper milreis) | | (million gold pesos) | | (thousand pounds) | | (million pesos) | | (million guilders) | | (million bolivares) | |
| 1821 | 21 | 20 | ... | ... | ... | ... | 4.6 | 5.9 | ... | ... | ... | ... |
| 1822 | 22 | 20 | ... | ... | ... | ... | 3.3 | 3.2 | ... | ... | ... | ... |
| 1823 | 19 | 21 | ... | ... | ... | ... | ... | ... | ... | ... | ... | ... |
| 1824 | 24 | 19 | ... | ... | ... | ... | ... | ... | ... | ... | ... | ... |
| 1825 | 23 | 21 | ... | ... | ... | ... | ... | ... | ... | ... | ... | ... |
| 1826 | 19 | 17 | ... | ... | ... | ... | 4.5 | 4.0 | ... | ... | ... | ... |
| 1827 | 27 | 25 | ... | ... | | | ... | ... | ... | ... | ... | ... |
| 1828 | 32 | 32 | ... | ... | | | ... | ... | ... | ... | ... | ... |
| 1829 | 36 | 33 | ... | ... | | | ... | ... | ... | ... | ... | ... |
| 1830 | 42 | 35 | ... | ... | | | ... | ... | ... | ... | 8.2 | 8.7 |
| 1831 | 33 | 32 | ... | ... | ... | ... | 8.0 | 5.0 | ... | ... | 13 | 11 |
| 1832 | 32[19] | 32[19] | ... | ... | 573 | 1,719 | 5.5 | 5.1 | ... | ... | 13 | 12 |
| 1833 | 36 | 33 | ... | ... | 558 | 1,837 | ... | ... | ... | ... | 13 | 14 |
| 1834 | 37 | 33 | ... | ... | 653 | 1,529 | ... | ... | ... | ... | 17 | 17 |
| 1835 | 41 | 41 | 3.8 | 1.7 | 711 | 1,771 | ... | ... | ... | ... | 15 | 20 |
| 1836 | 45 | 34 | 4.8 | 2.8 | 912 | 2,094 | ... | ... | ... | ... | 23 | 25 |
| 1837 | 41 | 34 | 3.1 | 3.1 | 957 | 1,698 | ... | ... | ... | ... | 15 | 21 |
| 1838 | 49 | 42 | 3.7 | 1.5 | 1,059 | 1,680 | ... | ... | ... | ... | 22 | 27 |
| 1839 | 52 | 43 | 3.7 | 3.8 | 1,209 | 1,348 | 4.6 | 5.3 | ... | ... | 31 | 30 |
| 1840 | 58 | 42 | 4.0 | ... | 988 | 1,888 | ... | ... | ... | ... | 37 | 31 |
| 1841 | 56 | 39 | 1.6 | 0.7 | 886 | 1,166 | ... | ... | ... | ... | 32 | 38 |
| 1842 | 51 | 41 | 2.7 | 1.3 | 672 | 1,136 | ... | ... | ... | ... | 26 | 34 |
| 1843 | 55 | 44 | 5.0 | ... | 715 | 991 | ... | ... | ... | ... | 22 | 30 |
| 1844 | 55 | 47 | 4.8 | 2.9 | 664 | 1,119 | ... | ... | ... | ... | 25 | 28 |
| 1845 | 52 | 54 | 3.5 | 2.6 | 831 | 992 | 5.1 | 4.8 | ... | ... | 27 | 36 |
| 1846 | 56 | 52 | 2.0 | 2.0 | 884 | 776 | 4.3 | 5.1 | ... | ... | 25 | 32 |
| 1847 | 47 | 58 | 1.4 | 2.0 | 771 | 1,109 | 4.9 | 6.2 | ... | ... | 19 | 28 |
| 1848 | 52 | 56 | 2.3 | 1.4 | 601 | 887 | 5.8 | 7.7 | ... | ... | 14 | 28 |
| 1849 | 59 | 55 | 3.3 | 1.0 | 570 | 673 | ... | ... | ... | ... | 21 | 25 |
| 1850 | 77 | 68 | 5.0 | 3.9 | 785 | 815 | ... | ... | 2.1 | 3.9 | 28 | 32 |
| 1851 | 93 | 67 | 8.0 | 4.6 | 855 | 865 | 6.1 | 7.5 | ... | ... | 30 | 33 |
| 1852 | 87 | 74 | 7.0 | 5.0 | 965 | 978 | ... | ... | 1.9 | 2.8 | 23 | 30 |
| 1853 | 86 | 77 | 5.4 | 3.7 | 847 | 1,015 | 7.2 | 8.6 | 2.0 | 3.0 | 29 | 36 |
| 1854 | 85 | 91 | 4.0 | 5.5 | 916 | 1,405 | 7.6 | 8.9 | 2.2 | 3.1 | 31 | 34 |

**E1　SOUTH AMERICA: External Trade Aggregates in Current Values**

**1855–1894**

| | Argentina[18] | | Brazil[19] | | Chile[20] | | Colombia | | Ecuador[25] | | Guyana[1,21] | |
|---|---|---|---|---|---|---|---|---|---|---|---|---|
| | Imports | Exports | Imports | Exports | Imports | Exports | Imports | Exports | Imports | Exports | Imports | Exports |
| | (million gold pesos) | | (million paper milreis) | | (million gold pesos) | | (million gold pesos) | | (million sucres) | | (thousand pounds) | |
| 1855 | ... | ... | 93 | 94 | ... | ... | 5.9 | 5.1 | ... | ... | 886 | 1,331 |
| 1856 | ... | ... | 125 | 115 | ... | ... | 9.4 | 5.6 | ... | ... | ... | ... |
| 1857 | ... | ... | 130 | 96 | 51 | 50 | 8.0 | 7.1 | ... | ... | ... | ... |
| 1858 | ... | ... | 127 | 107 | 46 | 46 | 7.2 | 9.1 | ... | ... | ... | ... |
| 1859 | ... | ... | 113 | 113 | 47 | 50 | 8.3 | 9.2 | ... | ... | 1,180 | 1,229 |
| 1860 | ... | ... | 124 | 123 | 54 | 62 | 10.2 | 10.8 | ... | ... | 1,146 | 1,513 |
| 1861 | ... | ... | 111 | 121 | 41 | 50 | 9.9 | 10.9 | ... | ... | 1,340 | 1,584 |
| 1862 | ... | ... | 99 | 122 | 43 | 56 | 10.2 | 10.5 | ... | ... | 1,107 | 1,365 |
| 1863 | ... | ... | 126 | 131 | 50 | 49 | 17.9 | 9.5 | ... | ... | 1,122 | 1,679 |
| 1864 | 23 | 22 | 132 | 141 | 46 | 67 | 25.5 | 22.6 | ... | ... | 1,509 | 1,845 |
| 1865 | 30 | 26 | 138 | 157 | 54 | 65 | 23.6 | 16.9 | ... | ... | 1,359 | 2,090 |
| 1866 | 37 | 27 | 143 | 156 | 49 | 69 | 27.8 | 15.1 | ... | ... | 1,531 | 2,171 |
| 1867 | 39 | 33 | 141 | 185 | 65 | 80 | 23.2 | 12.0 | ... | ... | 1,499 | 2,366 |
| 1868 | 42 | 30 | 167 | 203 | 66 | 76 | 24.6 | 14.7 | ... | ... | 1,618 | 2,232 |
| 1869 | 41 | 32 | 168 | 197 | 70 | 71 | 24.1 | 17.6 | ... | ... | 1,572 | 2,164 |
| 1870 | 49 | 30 | 162 | 168 | 72 | 68 | 23.8 | 15.4 | ... | ... | 1,897 | 2,383 |
| 1871 | 46 | 27 | 150 | 191 | 68 | 82 | 24.8 | 15.8 | ... | ... | 1,897 | 2,749 |
| 1872 | 62 | 47 | 159 | 215 | 89 | 96 | 30.0 | 19.8 | ... | ... | 2,014 | 2,463 |
| 1873 | 73 | 47 | 153 | 190 | 94 | 95 | 39.0 | 15.3 | ... | ... | 1,765 | 2,217 |
| 1874 | 58 | 45 | 168 | 208 | 97 | 93 | 33.6 | 20.4 | ... | ... | 1,873 | 2,762 |
| 1875 | 58 | 52 | 172 | 184 | 95 | 87 | 17.8 | 28.9 | ... | ... | 1,837 | 2,337 |
| 1876 | 36 | 48 | 157 | 196 | 88 | 85 | 21.9 | 14.5 | ... | ... | 1,983 | 3,031 |
| 1877 | 40 | 45 | 164 | 186 | 73 | 69 | 19.9 | 12.7 | ... | ... | 2,230 | 3,049 |
| 1878 | 44 | 37 | 164 | 204 | 63 | 70 | 22.5 | 16.2 | ... | ... | 2,151 | 2,508 |
| 1879 | 46 | 49 | 174 | 222 | 57 | 78 | 26.0 | 18.3 | ... | ... | 2,065 | 2,716 |
| 1880 | 46 | 58 | 180 | 231 | 64 | 88 | 23.5 | 19.4 | ... | ... | 2,003 | 2,618 |
| 1881 | 56 | 58 | 182 | 210 | 84 | 104 | 26.5 | 20.7 | ... | ... | 1,784 | 2,597 |
| 1882 | 61 | 60 | 190 | 197 | 108 | 140 | 26.9 | 17.8 | ... | 5.5 | 2,100 | 3,209 |
| 1883 | 80 | 60 | 203 | 217 | 115 | 149 | 27.0 | 14.6 | ... | 4.9 | 2,225 | 3,172 |
| 1884 | 94 | 68 | 178 | 226 | 112 | 122 | 25.3 | 10.6 | 7.6 | 10 | 1,999 | 2,322 |
| 1885 | 92 | 84 | 198 | 195 | 85 | 108 | 16.1 | 7.3 | ... | 4.9 | 1,467 | 1,801 |
| 1886 | 95 | 70 | 207 | 264 | 93 | 108 | 20.9 | 8.9 | ... | 6.6 | 1,436 | 1,843 |
| 1887 | 117 | 84 | [104][19] | [125][19] | 103 | 127 | 25.8 | 11.7 | ... | 10 | 1,603 | 2,191 |
| 1888 | 128 | 100 | 216 | 237 | 129 | 154 | 26.1 | 10.2 | ... | 9.1 | 1,586 | 2,025 |
| 1889 | 165 | 123 | 218 | 256 | 137 | 139 | 21.7 | 9.2 | 9.7 | 7.9 | 1,804 | 2,471 |
| 1890 | 142 | 101 | 295 | 326 | 144 | 144 | 25.1 | 12.2 | 10 | 9.7 | 1,887 | 2,162 |
| 1891 | 67 | 103 | 512 | 574 | 135 | 139 | 24.1 | 18.2 | 7.2 | 7.4 | 1,708[21] | 2,533[21] |
| 1892 | 91 | 113 | 590 | 784 | 165 | 135 | 19.8 | 9.7 | 8.4 | 12 | 1,780 | 2,433 |
| 1893 | 96 | 94 | 652 | 706 | 144 | 152 | 20.6 | 11.0 | 11 | 15 | 1,921 | 2,359 |
| 1894 | 93 | 102 | 782 | 767 | 114 | 152 | 16.3 | 10.3 | ... | ... | 1,669 | 2,040 |

## E1    SOUTH AMERICA: External Trade Aggregates in Current Values

### 1855–1894

| | Netherlands Antilles[28] | | Paraguay[26] | | Peru[27] | | Surinam | | Uruguay[22] | | Venezuela[23] | |
|---|---|---|---|---|---|---|---|---|---|---|---|---|
| | Imports | Exports | Imports | Exports | Imports | Exports | Imports | Exports | Imports | Exports | Imports | Exports |
| | (million guilders) | | (thousand gold pesos) | | (million pesos) | | (million guilders) | | (million pesos fuertes) | | (million bolivares) | |
| 1855 | ... | ... | ... | ... | ... | ... | 2.4 | 3.4 | ... | ... | 28 | 36 |
| 1856 | ... | ... | ... | ... | ... | ... | 2.6 | 4.3 | ... | ... | 37 | 39 |
| 1857 | ... | ... | ... | ... | ... | ... | 3.0 | 5.6 | ... | ... | 37 | 29 |
| 1858 | ... | ... | ... | ... | 15 | 16 | 3.5 | 3.4 | ... | ... | 40 | 44 |
| 1859 | ... | ... | ... | ... | 15 | 17 | 2.9 | 3.3 | ... | ... | 34 | 43 |
| 1860 | ... | ... | ... | ... | 15 | 35 | 3.1 | 4.5 | ... | ... | 24 | 30 |
| 1861 | ... | ... | ... | ... | 15 | 37 | 3.3 | 3.5 | ... | ... | 22 | 38 |
| 1862 | ... | ... | ... | ... | ... | ... | 2.9 | 3.6 | 8.2 | 8.8 | 17 | 31 |
| | | | | | (million soles) | | | | | | | |
| 1863 | ... | ... | ... | ... | 15 | 35 | 3.7 | 3.1 | ... | ... | 14 | 25 |
| 1864 | ... | ... | ... | ... | ... | ... | 4.8 | 3.1 | 8.4 | 6.3 | 48 | 42 |
| 1865 | ... | ... | ... | ... | ... | ... | 4.5 | 2.2 | ... | ... | 41 | 46 |
| 1866 | ... | ... | ... | ... | 15 | 22 | ... | ... | 14.6 | 10.7 | 31 | 38 |
| 1867 | ... | ... | ... | ... | 11 | 23 | ... | ... | 17.7 | 12.1 | 22 | 17 |
| 1868 | ... | ... | ... | ... | 12 | 20 | 4.0 | 3.1 | 16.1 | 12.1 | 32 | 27 |
| 1869 | ... | ... | ... | ... | 11 | 20 | 3.6 | 2.6 | 16.8 | 13.9 | 15 | 35 |
| 1870 | ... | ... | ... | ... | 12 | 21 | 4.0 | 2.7 | 15.0 | 12.8 | 23 | 55 |
| 1871 | ... | ... | ... | ... | 12 | 21 | 4.0 | 2.9 | 14.9 | 13.3 | 40 | 60 |
| 1872 | ... | ... | ... | ... | 13 | 19 | 3.7 | 3.2 | 18.8 | 15.5 | 46 | 70 |
| 1873 | ... | ... | ... | ... | 15 | 21 | 3.6 | 2.6 | 21.1 | 16.3 | 27 | 74 |
| 1874 | ... | ... | ... | ... | 14 | 20 | 4.0 | 3.2 | 17.2 | 15.2 | 53 | 87 |
| 1875 | ... | ... | ... | ... | 16 | 19 | 3.1 | 2.4 | 12.4 | 12.7 | 75 | 81 |
| 1876 | ... | ... | ... | ... | 20 | 21 | 3.2 | 2.8 | 12.8 | 13.7 | 73 | 71 |
| 1877 | ... | ... | ... | ... | 24 | 32 | 3.5 | 3.8 | 15.0 | 15.9 | 65 | 75 |
| 1878 | ... | ... | ... | ... | 23 | 25 | 3.6 | 2.0 | 15.9 | 17.5 | 42 | 58 |
| 1879 | ... | ... | 956 | 1,582 | ... | ... | 3.6 | 3.1 | 15.9 | 16.6 | 49 | 52 |
| 1880 | ... | ... | 1,030 | 1,613 | ... | ... | 3.9 | 3.6 | 19.5 | 19.8 | 45 | 69 |
| 1881 | ... | ... | 1,293 | 1,929 | ... | ... | 4.8 | 3.9 | 17.9 | 20.2 | 58 | 70 |
| 1882 | ... | ... | 1,417 | 1,651 | ... | ... | 4.3 | 3.7 | 18.2 | 22.1 | 86 | 99 |
| 1883 | ... | ... | 1,040 | 1,766 | 5.3 | 2.0 | 5.2 | 3.7 | 20.3 | 25.2 | 70 | 74 |
| 1884 | ... | ... | 1,448 | 1,573 | 8.2 | 2.0 | 5.3 | 4.1 | 24.6 | 24.8 | 59 | 77 |
| 1885 | ... | ... | 1,477 | 1,601 | 8.2 | 2.4 | 4.8 | 3.1 | 25.3 | 25.3 | 62 | 82 |
| 1886 | ... | ... | 1,918 | 2,103 | 9.9 | 2.4 | 4.6 | 3.0 | 20.2 | 23.8 | 73 | 91 |
| 1887 | 3.2 | 0.5 | ... | ... | 11 | 10 | 5.1 | 3.5 | 24.6 | 18.7 | 79 | 90 |
| 1888 | 2.8 | 0.6 | 3,320 | 2,589 | 9.6 | 11 | 4.3 | 3.3 | 29.5 | 28.0 | 81 | 97 |
| 1889 | 3.4 | 0.7 | 3,222 | 2,301 | 10 | 11 | 4.9 | 3.5 | 36.8 | 26.0 | 84 | 101 |
| 1890 | 3.7 | 0.8 | 2,726 | 3,504 | 12 | 12 | 5.3 | 4.3 | 32.4 | 29.1 | 67 | 120 |
| 1891 | 4.1 | 0.5 | 1,845 | 3,166 | 15 | 12 | 5.9 | 4.0 | 19.0 | 27.0 | 71 | 105 |
| 1892 | 3.4 | 0.3 | 2,190 | 1,687 | 15 | 18 | 5.2 | 3.9 | 18.4 | 26.0 | 53 | 89 |
| 1893 | 4.1 | 0.3 | 2,533 | 1,302 | 11 | 17 | 5.7 | 5.5 | 19.7 | 27.7 | 73 | 108 |
| 1894 | 3.2 | 0.3 | 2,222 | 1,808 | 12 | 12 | 6.2 | 5.1 | 23.8 | 33.5 | 62 | 99 |

**E1    SOUTH AMERICA: External Trade Aggregates in Current Values**

**1895–1934**

| | Argentina[18] | | Bolivia | | Brazil[19] | | Chile[20] | | Colombia | |
|---|---|---|---|---|---|---|---|---|---|---|
| | Imports | Exports | Imports[24] | Exports | Imports | Exports | Imports | Exports | Imports | Exports |
| | | | | | (million paper milreis or | | | | | |
| | (million gold pesos) | | (million bolivianos) | | cruzeiros) | | (million gold pesos) | | (million gold pesos) | |
| 1895 | 95 | 120 | ... | ... | 844 | 883 | 146 | 154 | 17.8 | 10.5 |
| 1896 | 112 | 117 | ... | ... | 864 | 864 | 156 | 156 | 22.9 | 13.0 |
| 1897 | 98 | 101 | ... | ... | 846 | 1,011 | 139 | 137 | 22.3 | 12.0 |
| 1898 | 107 | 134 | ... | ... | 933 | 1,011 | 102 | 168 | 16.2 | 13.1 |
| 1899 | 117 | 185 | 13 | 27 | 865 | 955 | 106 | 163 | 13.7 | 12.8 |
| 1900 | 113 | 155 | 13 | 36 | 645 | 850 | 129 | 168 | 9.0 | 9.1 |
| 1901 | 114 | 168 | 17 | 37 | 448 | 861 | 139 | 174 | 15.7 | 9.3 |
| 1902 | 103 | 179 | 14 | 28 | 471 | 736 | 133 | 187 | 12.5 | 8.1 |
| 1903 | 131 | 221 | 16 | 25 | 486 | 743 | 142 | 196 | 18.3 | 10.5 |
| 1904 | 187 | 264 | 21 | 31 | 513 | 770 | 157 | 218 | 22.4 | 16.6 |
| 1905 | 205 | 323 | 28 | 42 | 455 | 685 | 189 | 273 | 15.0 | 12.9 |
| 1906 | 270 | 292 | 35 | 56 | 499 | 800 | 238 | 287 | 16.7 | 13.7 |
| 1907 | 286 | 296 | 38 | 50 | 645 | 861 | 294 | 280 | 17.8 | 13.2 |
| 1908 | 273 | 366 | 41 | 47 | 567 | 706 | 267 | 319 | 17.4 | 12.0 |
| 1909 | 303 | 397 | 37 | 64 | 593 | 1,017 | 262 | 298 | 16.9 | 14.4 |
| 1910 | 352[18] | 373[18] | 49 | 75 | 714 | 939 | 297 | 371 | 17.4 | 14.4 |
| | (million paper pesos) | | | | | | | | | |
| | 862 | 884 | | | | | | | | |
| 1911 | 920 | 778 | 58 | 83 | 794 | 1,004 | 349 | 383 | 18.1 | 18.5 |
| 1912 | 1,016 | 1,140 | 50 | 90 | 951 | 1,120 | 334 | 397 | 24.0 | 25.6 |
| 1913 | 1,128 | 1,180 | 55 | 94 | 1,007 | 982 | 326 | 442 | 28.5 | 29.9 |
| 1914 | 733 | 916 | 40 | 66 | 562 | 756 | 270 | 309 | 21.0 | 26.4 |
| 1915 | 694 | 1,323 | 23 | 95 | 583 | 1,042 | 152 | 335 | 17.8 | 25.6 |
| 1916 | 832 | 1,302 | 31 | 101 | 811 | 1,137 | 222 | 523 | 29.7 | 30.6 |
| 1917 | 864 | 1,250 | 50 | 158 | 838 | 1,192 | 339 | 723 | 24.8 | 31.9 |
| 1918 | 1,138 | 1,822 | 70 | 183 | 989 | 1,137 | 395 | 811 | 21.8 | 34.9 |
| 1919 | 1,490 | 2,343 | 62 | 144 | 1,334 | 2,179 | 387 | 331 | 47.5 | 78.1 |
| 1920 | 2,125 | 2,373 | 65 | 156 | 2,091 | 1,752 | 441 | 804 | 113.6 | 64.4 |
| 1921 | 1,703 | 1,525 | 71 | 67 | 1,690 | 1,710 | 368 | 456 | 37.0 | 53.2 |
| 1922 | 1,567 | 1,536 | 50 | 95 | 1,653 | 2,332 | 237 | 350 | 47.0 | 46.8 |
| 1923 | 1,974 | 1,753 | 63 | 108 | 2,267 | 3,297 | 329 | 562 | 67.2 | 56.0 |
| 1924 | 1,883 | 2,299 | 63 | 115 | 2,780 | 3,864 | 363 | 636 | 62.3 | 84.2 |
| 1925 | 1,993 | 1,973 | 68 | 111 | 3,377 | 4,022 | 403 | 635 | 97.2 | 83.2 |
| 1926 | 1,869 | 1,800 | 70 | 114 | 2,706 | 3,191 | 430 | 496 | 124.0 | 110.2 |
| 1927 | 1,947 | 2,294 | 66 | 121 | 3,273 | 3,644 | 358 | 559 | 139.2 | 107.6 |
| 1928 | 1,902 | 2,396 | 64 | 109 | 3,695 | 3,970 | 399 | 655 | 162.4 | 132.5 |
| 1929 | 1,959 | 2,168 | 71 | 123 | 3,528 | 3,860 | 539 | 775 | 141.5 | 121.7 |
| 1930 | 1,680 | 1,396 | 58 | 88 | 2,344[19] | 2,888[19] | 467 | 449 | 70 | 104 |
| 1931 | 1,174 | 1,456 | 30 | 57 | 1,881 | 3,358 | 235 | 280 | 46 | 80 |
| 1932 | 836 | 1,288 | 22 | 46 | 1,519 | 2,501 | 71 | 94 | 34 | 67 |
| 1933 | 897 | 1,121 | 41 | 67 | 2,165 | 2,780 | 61 | 112 | 56 | 68 |
| 1934 | 1,110 | 1,438 | 67 | 116 | 2,503 | 3,459 | 71 | 154 | 98 | 124 |

**E1    SOUTH AMERICA: External Trade Aggregates in Current Values**

1895–1934

| | Ecuador[25] | | Guyana[1,21] | | Netherlands Antilles[28] | | Paraguay[26] | |
|---|---|---|---|---|---|---|---|---|
| | Imports | Exports | Imports | Exports | Imports | Exports | Imports | Exports |
| | (million sucres) | | (thousand pounds) | | (million guilders) | | (thousand gold pesos) | |
| 1895 | ... | ... | 1,444 | 1,769 | 2.6 | 0.3 | 2,460 | 2,121 |
| 1896 | ... | 22 | 1,342 | 1,899 | 3.0 | 0.4 | 2,786 | 2,049 |
| 1897 | 18 | 31 | 1,283 | 1,784 | 2.7 | 0.3 | 2,211[26] | 2,555[26] |
| 1898 | 9.9 | 14 | 1,371 | 1,776 | 2.0 | 0.3 | 2,608 | 2,463 |
| 1899 | ... | 17 | 1,319 | 1,928[21] | 1.9 | 0.3 | 2,511 | 2,291 |
| 1900 | 13 | 15 | 1,307 | 1,982 | 2.7 | 0.3 | 2,556 | 2,652 |
| 1901 | 15 | 16 | 1,297 | 1,716 | 2.2 | 0.3 | 3,023 | 2,565 |
| 1902 | 14 | 18 | 1,371 | 1,757 | 2.4 | 0.3 | 2,426 | 3,073 |
| 1903 | 11 | 19 | 1,600 | 1,754 | 3.0 | 0.3 | 3,506 | 4,047 |
| 1904 | 15 | 23 | 1,479 | 1,932 | 2.7 | 0.5[28] | 3,566 | 3,196 |
| 1905 | 16 | 19 | 1,584 | 1,916 | 3.2 | 1.0 | 4,679 | 2,833 |
| 1906 | 17 | 22 | 1,634 | 1,786 | 3.2 | 1.0 | 6,324 | 2,695 |
| 1907 | 20 | 23 | 1,698 | 1,644 | 3.8 | 1.3 | 7,513 | 3,236 |
| 1908 | 21 | 27 | 1,778 | 2,044 | 2.8 | 0.9 | 4,073 | 3,867 |
| 1909 | 19 | 25 | 1,710 | 1,921 | 3.2 | 0.9 | 3,788 | 5,137 |
| | | | | | | | (million gold pesos) | |
| 1910 | 16 | 28 | 1,652 | 1,722 | 3.2 | 1.7 | 6.4 | 4.9 |
| 1911 | ... | 26 | 1,665[21] | 2,084[21] | 4.2[28] | 2.0 | 6.7 | 4.7 |
| 1912 | 21 | 25 | 1,632 | 1,727 | ... | ... | 5.4 | 4.2 |
| 1913 | 18 | 32 | 1,611 | 2,110 | 4.8 | 2.3 | 8.1 | 5.6 |
| 1914 | 17 | 26 | 1,597 | 2,454 | 4.7 | 2.2 | 5.1 | 5.6 |
| 1915 | 15 | 25 | 1,833 | 3,201 | 4.7 | 2.3 | 3.1 | 8.9 |
| 1916 | 19 | 35 | 2,190 | 3,476 | 6.2 | 2.4 | 7.0 | 8.9 |
| 1917 | 21 | 32 | 2,906 | 3,951 | 6.9 | 2.8 | 9.2 | 11.7 |
| 1918 | 17 | 27 | 3,394 | 3,083 | 7.3 | 2.7 | 11.1 | 11.4 |
| 1919 | 25 | 43 | 3,275 | 3,925 | 8.7 | 2.8 | 15.8 | 19.0 |
| 1920 | 44 | 50 | 4,723 | 5,686 | 7.3 | 11 | 13.1 | 15.0 |
| 1921 | 24 | 34 | 3,273 | 3,424 | 19 | 13 | 8.4 | 9.3 |
| 1922 | 34 | 46 | 2,293 | 2,925 | 20 | 14 | 5.7 | 9.9 |
| 1923 | 37 | 38 | 2,669 | 3,758 | 30 | 19 | 8.6 | 12.5 |
| 1924 | 52 | 61 | 2,744 | 3,394 | 51 | 32 | 15.7 | 12.4 |
| 1925 | 55 | 73 | 2,908 | 3,131 | 71 | 60 | 17.7 | 15.7 |
| 1926 | 47 | 64 | 2,599 | 2,733 | 107 | 95 | 12.2 | 15.5 |
| 1927 | 57 | 82 | 2,471 | 3,339 | 142 | 135 | 12.0 | 14.3 |
| 1928 | 81 | 93 | 2,471 | 3,110 | 268 | 260 | 14.3 | 15.9 |
| 1929 | 84 | 86 | 2,216 | 2,557 | 361 | 309 | 13.8 | 13.5 |
| 1930 | 64 | 81 | 1,971 | 2,222 | 407 | 417 | 15.1 | 14.2 |
| 1931 | 44 | 57 | 1,595 | 2,011 | 248 | 343 | 10.1 | 12.9 |
| 1932 | 25 | 49 | 1,690 | 2,205 | 140 | 182 | 6.4 | 12.9 |
| 1933 | 32 | 44 | 1,801 | 2,075 | 150 | 195 | 7.2 | 9.5 |
| 1934 | 62 | 102 | 1,749 | 1,892 | 155 | 161 | 11.3 | 12.4 |

**E1    SOUTH AMERICA: External Trade Aggregates in Current Values**

**1895–1934**

| | Peru[27] | | Surinam | | Uruguay[22] | | Venezuela[23] | |
|---|---|---|---|---|---|---|---|---|
| | **Imports** | **Exports** | **Imports** | **Exports** | **Imports** | **Exports** | **Imports** | **Exports** |
| | (million soles) | | (million guilders) | | (million pesos fuertes) | | (million bolivares) | |
| 1895 | 11 | 15 | 5.2 | 5.5 | 25.4 | 32.5 | 61 | 111 |
| 1896 | 18 | 25 | 5.3 | 4.4 | 25.5 | 30.4 | 69 | 93 |
| 1897 | 16 | 28 | 5.3 | 5.2 | 19.5 | 29.3 | 44 | 74 |
| 1898 | 19 | 30 | 5.7 | 5.2 | 24.8 | 30.3 | 72 | 93 |
| 1899 | 21 | 33 | 6.1 | 5.5 | 25.7 | 36.6 | 54 | 78 |
| 1900 | 23 | 45 | 6.2 | 5.5 | 24.0 | 29.4 | ...[23] | ...[23] |
| 1901 | 27 | 43 | 7.1 | 5.4 | 23.7 | 27.7 | 56 | 80 |
| 1902 | 34 | 37 | 6.2 | 4.1 | 23.5 | 33.6 | 64 | 76 |
| 1903 | 38 | 39 | 6.3 | 4.3 | 25.1 | 37.3 | 28 | 40 |
| 1904 | 44 | 41 | 7.4 | 3.7 | 21.2 | 38.5 | 59 | 81 |
| 1905 | 44 | 58 | 6.6 | 4.4 | 30.8 | 30.8 | 48 | 73 |
| 1906 | 50 | 58 | 6.3 | 4.8 | 34.5 | 33.4 | 45 | 81 |
| 1907 | 55 | 57 | 6.9 | 5.9 | 37.5 | 34.9 | 52 | 81 |
| 1908 | 53 | 55 | 7.0 | 6.0 | 37.5 | 40.3 | 54 | 78 |
| 1909 | 43 | 65 | 7.2 | 6.6 | 36.9 | 45.1 | 49 | 83 |
| 1910 | $\frac{50}{45}$[27] | 71 | 7.4 | 8.3 | 40.8 | 40.9 | 64 | 91 |
| 1911 | 52 | 74 | 8.3 | 9.2 | 44.8 | 42.5 | 95 | 114 |
| 1912 | 50 | 93 | 7.5 | 8.4 | 49.8 | 48.8 | 107[23] | 124 |
| 1913 | 60 | 91 | 7.1 | 9.5 | 50.4 | $\frac{45.1}{68.5}$[22] | 85 | 151 |
| 1914 | 46 | 87 | 6.4 | 6.5 | 37.2[22] | 58.2 | 68 | 108 |
| 1915 | 30 | 115 | 5.4 | 6.9 | 40.6 | 73.3 | 69 | 114 |
| 1916 | 75 | 165 | 5.9 | 8.1 | 52.9 | 73.9 | 101 | 108 |
| 1917 | 107 | 186 | 7.6 | 8.9 | 66.6 | 103 | 101 | 115 |
| 1918 | 96 | 200 | 6.2 | 7.1 | 101 | 116 | 73 | 100 |
| 1919 | 119 | 269 | 9.0 | 9.0 | 113 | 147 | 140 | 256 |
| 1920 | 177 | 351 | 14 | 7.5 | 133 | 81 | 306 | 168 |
| 1921 | 167 | 165 | 13 | 6.6 | 94 | 70 | 96 | 127 |
| 1922 | 106 | 186 | 11 | 5.7 | 82 | 77 | 100 | 133 |
| 1923 | 139 | 238 | 7.9 | 8.4 | [102][22] | 101 | 153 | 153 |
| 1924 | 178 | 247 | 7.5 | 7.4 | 82 | 107 | 193 | 212 |
| 1925 | 182 | 214 | 9.5 | 9.9 | 95 | 99 | 274 | 327 |
| 1926 | 194 | 237 | 10.0 | 7.7 | ... | 94 | 402 | 391 |
| 1927 | 194 | 310 | 9.3 | 11.8 | ... | 96 | 359 | 440 |
| 1928 | 176 | 314 | 9.2 | 11.5 | ... | 101 | 384 | 604 |
| 1929 | 190 | 334 | 8.6 | 7.8 | ... | 93 | 443 | 774 |
| 1930 | 137 | 224 | 9.1 | 8.2 | 94 | 101 | 359 | $\frac{735}{960}$[29] |
| | | | | | (million US dollars) | | | |
| | | | | | 137 | 149 | | |
| 1931 | 102 | 175 | 6.6 | 5.8 | 109 | 76 | 207 | 639 |
| 1932 | 76 | 169 | 5.6 | 4.2 | 44 | 46 | 153 | 666 |
| 1933 | 107 | 245 | 4.9 | 3.3 | 51 | 53 | 143 | 326 |
| 1934 | 171 | 300 | 5.3 | 3.8 | 50 | 56 | 131 | 414 |

**E1    SOUTH AMERICA: External Trade Aggregates in Current Values**

**1935–1974**

| | Argentina | | Bolivia | | Brazil[19] | | Chile[20] | | Colombia | |
|---|---|---|---|---|---|---|---|---|---|---|
| | Imports | Exports | Imports[24] | Exports | Imports | Exports | Imports | Exports | Imports | Exports |
| | (million paper pesos) | | (million bolivianos) | | (million paper cruzeiros) | | (million gold pesos) | | (million gold pesos) | |
| 1935 | 1,175 | 1,569 | 71 | 149 | 3,856 | 4,104 | 98 | 155 | 120 | 124 |
| | | | (million US dollars) | | | | | | | |
| 1936 | 1,117 | 1,656 | 15 | 29 | 4,268 | 4,895 | 116 | 183 | 134 | 137 |
| 1937 | 1,558 | 2,311 | 16 | 35 | 5,314 | 5,092 | 143 | 311 | 170 | 152 |
| 1938 | 1,461 | 1,400 | 19 | 27 | 5,195 | 5,097 | 166 | 225 | 159 | 144 |
| 1939 | 1,338 | 1,573 | 17 | 34 | 4,994 | 5,610 | 137 | 220 | 183 | 136 |
| 1940 | 1,499 | 1,428 | 20 | 49 | 4,960 | 4,961 | 169 | 226 | 148 | 125 |
| 1941 | 1,277 | 1,465 | 28 | 60 | 5,503 | 6,726 | 175 | 256 | 170 | 134 |
| 1942 | 1,274 | 1,789 | 33 | 65 | 4,678 | 7,500 | 208 | 288 | 105 | 171 |
| 1943 | 942 | 2,192 | 39 | 81 | 6,220 | 8,729 | 212 | 287 | 147 | 219 |
| 1944 | 1,007 | 2,360 | 38 | 77 | 8,121 | 10,727 | 233 | 315 | 175 | 227 |
| 1945 | 1,154 | 2,498 | 40 | 80 | 8,743 | 12,198 | 252 | 330 | 281 | 246 |
| 1946 | 2,332 | 3,973 | 51 | 74 | 13,028 | 18,230 | 318 | 350 | 403 | 352 |
| 1947 | 5,349 | 5,505 | 60 | 81 | 22,789 | 21,179 | 429 | 451 | 639 | 446 |
| 1948 | 6,190 | 5,542 | 69 | 113 | 20,984 | 21,697 | 435 | 532 | 589 | 505 |
| | (million US dollars) | | | | (million US dollars) | | | | (million US dollars) | |
| | 1,562 | 1,629 | | | 1,121 | 1,180 | | | 324 | 277 |
| 1949 | 1,180 | 1,044 | 78 | 101 | 1,103 | 1,096 | 492 | 479 | 265 | 321 |
| 1950 | 964 | 1,178 | 56 | 94 | 1,085 | 1,355 | 400 | 458 | 365 | 396 |
| 1951 | 1,480 | 1,169 | 86 | 151 | 1,987 | 1,769 | 532 | 601 | 419 | 463 |
| 1952 | 1,179 | 688 | 93 | 141 | 1,986 | 1,418 | 599 | 736 | 415 | 473 |
| 1953 | 795 | 1,125 | 68 | 113 | 1,318 | 1,539 | 542 | 663 | 547 | 596 |
| 1954 | 979 | 1,027 | 66[24] | 92 | 1,629 | 1,562 | 555 | 652 | 672 | 657 |
| 1955 | 1,173 | 929 | 81 | 100 | 1,306 | 1,423 | 609 | 768 | 669 | 580 |
| 1956 | 1,128 | 944 | 84 | 107 | 1,234 | 1,482 | 572 | 881 | 657 | 599 |
| 1957 | 1,310 | 975 | 90 | 95 | 1,488 | 1,392 | 714 | 741 | 483 | 511 |
| 1958 | 1,233 | 994 | 80 | 63 | 1,353 | 1,243 | 671 | 629 | 400 | 461 |
| 1959 | 993 | 1,009 | 65 | 76 | 1,374 | 1,282 | 668 | 804 | 416 | 473 |
| 1960 | 1,249 | 1,079 | 72 | 66 | 1,462 | 1,269 | 808 | 793 | 519 | 465 |
| 1961 | 1,460 | 964 | 78 | 73 | 1,460 | 1,403 | 956 | 822 | 557 | 434 |
| 1962 | 1,357 | 1,216 | 97 | 75 | 1,475 | 1,214 | 828 | 861 | 540 | 463 |
| 1963 | 981 | 1,365 | 103 | 81 | 1,487 | 1,406 | 1,031 | 877 | 506 | 447 |
| 1964 | 1,077 | 1,410 | 103 | 112 | 1,263 | 1,430 | 983 | 1,013 | 586 | 548 |
| 1965 | 1,199 | 1,493 | 134 | 129 | 1,096 | 1,595 | 977 | 1,113 | 453 | 539 |
| 1966 | 1,124 | 1,593 | 138 | 127 | 1,496 | 1,741 | 1,225 | 1,425 | 674 | 508 |
| 1967 | 1,096 | 1,465 | 151 | 150 | 1,667 | 1,654 | 1,176 | 1,477 | 497 | 510 |
| | | | | | | | (million US dollars) | | | |
| | | | | | | | 722 | 908 | | |
| 1968 | 1,169 | 1,368 | 153 | 152 | 2,129 | 1,881 | 744 | 936 | 643 | 558 |
| 1969 | 1,576 | 1,612 | 165 | 172 | 2,265 | 2,311 | 908 | 1,068 | 685 | 607 |
| 1970 | 1,694 | 1,773 | 159 | 190 | 2,849 | 2,739 | 930 | 1,234 | 843 | 727 |
| 1971 | 1,868 | 1,740 | 170 | 181 | 3,701 | 2,904 | 980 | 961 | 929 | 689 |
| 1972 | 1,905 | 1,941 | 185 | 201 | 4,783 | 3,990 | 941 | 855 | 859 | 969 |
| 1973 | 2,230 | 3,266 | 230 | 260 | 6,999 | 6,199 | 1,098 | 1,231 | 1,062 | 1,177 |
| 1974 | 3,635 | 3,931 | 366 | 556 | 14,168 | 7,951 | 1,681 | 1,247 | 1,597 | 1,417 |

**E1    SOUTH AMERICA: External Trade Aggregates in Current Values**

**1935–1974**

| | Ecuador[25] | | Guyana[1,21] | | Netherlands Antilles[28] | | Paraguay | |
|---|---|---|---|---|---|---|---|---|
| | Imports | Exports | Imports | Exports | Imports | Exports | Imports | Exports |
| | (million sucres) | | (thousand pounds) | | (million guilders) | | (million gold pesos) | |
| 1935 | 97 [25] | 103 | 1,834 | 2,269 | 174 | 167 | 11.6 | 11.4 |
| 1936 | 118 | 108 | 2,003 | 2,490 | 197 | 202 | 9.8 | 9.4 |
| 1937 | 132 | 145 | 2,443 | 2,830 | 296 | 270 | 12.4 | 12.1 |
| 1938 | 148 | 133 | 2,252 | 2,772 | 389 | 341 | 13.1 | 12.0 |
| 1939 | 147 | 126 | 2,290 | 3,065 | 322 | 344 | 12.6 | 13.2 |
| 1940 | 171 | 137 | 2,991 | 3,166 | 256 | 251 | 14.9 | 11.4 |
| 1941 | 149 | 170 | 3,632 | 4,075 | 300 | 345 | 12.2 | 15.2 |
| 1942 | 198 | 267 | 3,825 | 4,016 | 262 | 214 | 17.2 | 16.5 |
| 1943 | 218 | 366 | 5,200 | 4,905 | 345 | 298 | 22.0 | 20.2 |
| 1944 | 331 | 440 | 4,708 | 5,097 | 385 | 397 | 22.9 | 24.2 |
| | | | | | | | (million guaranies) | |
| 1945 | 323 | 362 | 4,426 [21] | 4,496 [21] | 473 | 443 | 55 | 69 |
| | | | (million local dollars) | | | | | |
| | | | 21 | 21 | | | | |
| 1946 | 414 | 512 | 26 | 27 | 504 | 512 | 66 | 83 |
| 1947 | 604 | 594 | 42 | 34 | 633 | 566 | 68 | 66 |
| 1948 | 671 | 623 | 48 | 37 | 869 | 767 | 75 | 87 |
| 1949 | 622 | 438 | 51 | 46 | 975 | 814 | 88 | 102 |
| | (million US dollars) | | | | | | (million US dollars) | |
| 1950 | 41.2 | 74.0 | 56 | 51 | 1,130 | 1,037 | 18.8 | 33.1 |
| 1951 | 52.5 | 70.5 | 67 | 58 | 1,449 | 1,325 | 25.4 | 37.7 |
| 1952 | 58.0 | 102 | 83 [21] | 81 [21] | 1,523 | 1,377 | 30.7 | 31.3 |
| 1953 | 62.8 | 92.3 | 72 | 83 | 1,389 | 1,349 | 24.3 | 30.7 |
| 1954 | 100 | 125 | 80 | 85 | 1,544 | 1,458 | 32.9 | 34.0 |
| 1955 | 95.0 | 114 | 95 | 90 | 1,567 | 1,516 | 29.0 | 35.1 |
| 1956 | 89.9 | 116 | 100 | 95 | 1,657 | 1,588 | 24.6 | 36.7 |
| 1957 | 97.8 | 133 | 119 | 108 | 1,813 | 1,645 | 27.4 | 32.9 |
| 1958 | 104 | 133 | 116 | 97 | 1,694 | 1,525 | 32.6 | 34.1 |
| 1959 | 97.3 | 141 | 111 | 103 | 1,465 | 1,342 | 26.2 | 31.2 |
| 1960 | 115 | 145 | 147 | 125 | 1,286 | 1,241 | 32.4 | 27.0 |
| 1961 | 106 | 127 | 147 | 147 | 1,353 | 1,337 | 34.7 | 30.7 |
| 1962 | 97.1 | 143 | 126 | 161 | 1,360 | 1,297 | 34.7 | 33.5 |
| 1963 | 128 | 148 | 118 | 173 | 1,313 | 1,242 | 32.6 | 40.2 |
| 1964 | 152 | 159 | 150 | 167 | 1,225 | 1,188 | 33.8 | 49.8 |
| 1965 | 169 | 170 | 179 | 166 | 1,164 | 1,136 | 47.4 | 57.3 |
| 1966 | 172 | 184 | 202 | 183 | 1,165 | 1,116 | 50.2 | 49.4 |
| 1967 | 214 | 190 | 225 | 192 | 1,261 | 1,146 | 60.7 | 48.3 |
| 1968 | 255 | 226 | 219 | 229 | 1,267 | 1,130 | 61.5 | 47.6 |
| 1969 | 242 | 153 | 236 | 234 | 1,307 | 1,178 | 70.3 | 51.0 |
| 1970 | 274 | 190 | 268 | 266 | 1,504 | 1,275 | 63.8 | 64.1 |
| 1971 | 340 | 199 | 268 | 288 | 1,660 | 1,366 | 70.3 | 65.2 |
| 1972 | 319 | 326 | 298 | 300 | 1,565 | 1,364 | 69.9 | 86.2 |
| 1973 | 537 | 487 | 373 | 288 | 2,868 | 2,465 | 105 | 127 |
| 1974 | 962 | 926 | 567 | 602 | 6,536 | 5,815 | 171 | 170 |

E1      **SOUTH AMERICA: External Trade Aggregates in Current Values**

**1935–1974**

| | Peru[27] | | Surinam | | Uruguay | | Venezuela[23] | |
|---|---|---|---|---|---|---|---|---|
| | **Imports** | **Exports** | **Imports** | **Exports** | **Imports** | **Exports** | **Imports** | **Exports** |
| | (million soles) | | (million guilders) | | (million US dollars) | | (million bolivares) | |
| 1935 | 181 | 309 | 5.4 | 3.4 | 48 | 77 | [165][23] | 447 |
| 1936 | 200 | 332 | 5.7 | 4.5 | 53 | 72 | [212][23] | 582 |
| 1937 | 235 | 365 | 6.8 | 5.2 | 65 | 78 | [304][23] | 599 |
| 1938 | 260 | 336 | 6.8 | 5.8 | 62 | 62 | 311 | 559 |
| 1939 | 256 | 377 | 7.8 | 7.3 | 52 | 63 | 328 | 510 |
| 1940 | 319 | 398 | 8.5 | 7.3 | 55 | 66 | 311 | 487 |
| 1941 | 358 | 484 | 9.4 | 11 | 63 | 71 | 288 | 718 |
| 1942 | 333 | 489 | 15 | 13 | 64 | 58 | 216 | 501 |
| 1943 | 449 | 459 | 22 | 14 | 64 | 100 | 222 | 620 |
| 1944 | 514 | 547 | 16 | 6.9 | 72 | 98 | 372 | 867 |
| 1945 | 550 | 673 | 12 | 7.4 | 94 | 122 | 602 | 1,112 |
| 1946 | 802 | 974 | 16 | 12 | 147 | 153 | 983 | 1,614 |
| 1947 | 1,092 | 957 | 31 | 25 | 215 | 162 | 1,857 | 2,324 |
| 1948 | 1,091 | 1,021 | 36 | 26 | 200 | 179 | 2,431 | 3,360 |
| 1949 | 2,692 | 2,031 | 38 | 34 | 182 | 192 | 2,376 | 3,483 |
| 1950 | 2,704 | 2,887 | 39 | 31 | 201 | 254 | 1,991 | 3,889 |
| 1951 | 3,972 | 3,744 | 46 | 40 | 309 | 236 | 2,271 | 4,533 |
| 1952 | 5,453 | 4,423 | 56 | 46 | 237 | 209 | 2,528 | 4,858 |
| | (million US dollars) | | | | | | | |
| | 287 | 234 | | | | | | |
| 1953 | 293 | 219 | 54 | 50 | 193 | 270 | 2,733 | 4,841 |
| 1954 | 250 | 245 | 52 | 55 | 274 | 249 | 3,063 | 5,661 |
| 1955 | 299 | 271 | 52 | 50 | 228 | 184 | 3,155 | 6,275 |
| 1956 | 384 | 311 | 62 | 59 | 213 | 211 | 3,438 | 7,090 |
| 1957 | 448 | 330 | 73 | 65 | 255 | 128 | 5,587 | 7,921 |
| 1958 | 334 | 291 | 71 | 62 | 151 | 139 | 4,783 | 7,720 |
| 1959 | 317 | 314 | 85 | 77 | 160 | 98 | 4,717 | 7,937 |
| 1960 | 373 | 434 | 102 | 82 | 244 | 129 | 3,553 | 8,147 |
| 1961 | 468 | 496 | 101 | 78 | 206 | 175 | 3,522 | 8,092 |
| 1962 | 539 | 543 | 103 | 80 | 230 | 153 | 3,871 | 8,689 |
| 1963 | 553 | 540 | 110 | 87 | 177 | 165 | 3,655 | 8,807 |
| 1964 | 571 | 666 | 152 | 90 | 198 | 179 | 4,886 | 9,241 |
| 1965 | 719 | 666 | 179 | 110 | 150 | 191 | 5,590 | 12,076 |
| 1966 | 816 | 763 | 169 | 171 | 164 | 186 | 5,120 | 11,941 |
| 1967 | 820 | 755 | 193 | 198 | 171 | 159 | 5,632 | 11,238 |
| 1968 | 630 | 866 | 188 | 217 | 157 | 179 | 6,532 | 11,175 |
| 1969 | 600 | 865 | 208 | 246 | 197 | 200 | 6,748 | 11,104 |
| 1970 | 622 | 1,044 | 217 | 255 | 231 | 233 | 7,382 | 11,691 |
| 1971 | 750 | 893 | 237 | 295 | 229 | 206 | 8,252 | 13,996 |
| 1972 | 796 | 944 | 259 | 306 | 212 | 214 | 9,471 | 12,993 |
| 1973 | 1,024 | 1,049 | 281 | 316 | 285 | 32 | 10,856 | 20,431 |
| 1974 | 1,595 | 1,517 | 411 | 481 | 487 | 382 | 16,249 | 47,435 |

**E1    SOUTH AMERICA: External Trade Aggregates in Current Values**

| | Argentina | | Bolivia | | Brazil | | Chile | | Colombia | |
|---|---|---|---|---|---|---|---|---|---|---|
| | Imports | Exports | Imports | Exports | Imports | Exports | Imports | Exports | Imports | Exports |
| | (million US dollars) | | (million US dollars) | | (million US dollars) | | (million US dollars) | | (million US dollars) | |
| 1975 | 3,947 | 2,961 | 575 | 444 | 12,210 | 8,670 | 1,338 | 1,552 | 1,495 | 1,465 |
| 1976 | 3,033 | 3,916 | 594 | 568 | 13,532 | 10,128 | 1,684 | 2,083 | 1,708 | 1,745 |
| 1977 | 4,162 | 5,652 | 591 | 632 | 13,069 | 12,120 | 2,414 | 2,190 | 2,028 | 2,443 |
| 1978 | 3,834 | 6,400 | 769 | 629 | 14,538 | 12,659 | 3,002 | 2,478 | 2,836 | 3,003 |
| 1979 | 6,700 | 7,810 | 980 | 760 | 19,372 | 15,244 | 4,218 | 3,894 | 3,233 | 3,300 |
| 1980 | 10,541 | 8,021 | 678 | 942 | 24,961 | 20,132 | 5,124 | 4,671 | 4,663 | 3,945 |
| 1981 | 9,430 | 9,143 | 975 | 912 | 24,079 | 23,293 | 6,364 | 3,906 | 5,199 | 2,956 |
| 1982 | 5,337 | 7,625 | 577 | 828 | 21,069 | 20,175 | 3,831 | 3,709 | 5,478 | 3,095 |
| 1983 | 4,504 | 7,836 | 589 | 755 | 16,801 | 21,899 | 2,969 | 3,835 | 4,968 | 3,081 |
| 1984 | 4,585 | 8,107 | 492 | 724 | 15,210 | 27,005 | 3,480 | 3,657 | 4,497 | 3,462 |
| 1985 | 3,814 | 8,396 | 552 | 623 | 14,332 | 25,639 | 3,007 | 3,823 | 4,141 | 3,552 |
| 1986 | 4,724 | 6,852 | 716 | 564 | 15,557 | 22,349 | 3,157 | 4,222 | 3,861 | 5,102 |
| 1987 | 5,818 | 6,360 | 776 | 566 | 16,581 | 26,225 | 4,023 | 5,102 | 4,322 | 4,642 |
| 1988 | 5,322 | 9,135 | 604 | 601 | 16,055 | 33,783 | 4,924 | 7,048 | 5,002 | 5,037 |

| | Ecuador[25] | | Guyana | | Netherlands Antilles[28] | | Paraguay | |
|---|---|---|---|---|---|---|---|---|
| | Imports | Exports | Imports | Exports | Imports | Exports | Imports | Exports |
| | (million US dollars) | | (million local dollars) | | (million guilders) | | (million US dollars) | |
| 1975 | 943 | 897 | 811 | 858 | 5,088 | 4,315 | 179 | 176 |
| 1976 | 959 | 1,258 | 927 | 711 | 6,601 | 4,544 | 180 | 181 |
| 1977 | 1,189 | 1,436 | 804 | 662 | 5,631 | 4,764 | 255 | 279 |
| 1978 | 1,627 | 1,494 | 711 | 750 | 5,682 | 4,754 | 318 | 257 |
| 1979 | 1,986 | 2,067 | 810 | 746 | 7,911 | 7,138 | 438 | 305 |
| 1980 | 2,253 | 2,481 | 1,010 | 992 | 10,216 | 9,292 | 517 | 310 |
| 1981 | 2,246 | 2,542 | 1,236 | 974 | 10,551 | 9,750 | 506 | 295 |
| 1982 | 2,189 | 2,341 | 841 | 724 | 9,157 | 8,803 | 561 | 330 |
| 1983 | 1,465 | 2,203 | 691 | 567 | 8,148 | 7,937 | 506 | 284 |
| 1984 | 1,716 | 2,581 | 945 | 808 | 7,258 | 6,719 | 563 | 386 |
| 1985 | 1,674 | 2,780 | 1,082 | 875 | 4,061[28] | 3,023[28] | 719 | 403 |
| 1986 | 1,867 | 2,171 | 1,036 | 991 | 2,002 | 1,664 | 733 | 275 |
| 1987 | 2,052 | 1,989 | 2,450 | 2,367 | 2,703 | 2,354 | 590 | 379 |
| 1988 | 1,714 | 2,165 | 2,410 | 2,300 | 2,527 | 2,040 | 555 | 607 |

| | Peru | | Surinam | | Uruguay | | Venezuela | |
|---|---|---|---|---|---|---|---|---|
| | Imports | Exports | Imports | Exports | Imports | Exports | Imports | Exports |
| | (million US dollars) | | (million guilders) | | (million US dollars) | | (thousand million bolivares) | |
| 1975 | 2,380 | 1,315 | 450 | 495 | 556 | 384 | 22.8 | 39.9 |
| 1976 | 1,798 | 1,296 | 525 | 492 | 587 | 547 | 25.8 | 41.1 |
| 1977 | 1,598 | 1,647 | 710 | 553 | 730 | 607 | 42.0 | 43.5 |
| 1978 | 1,356 | 1,805 | 724 | 734 | 774 | 686 | 45.6 | 42.0 |
| 1979 | 1,475 | 3,380 | 734 | 793 | 1,206 | 788 | 41.3 | 64.0 |
| 1980 | 2,573 | 3,265 | 900 | 918 | 1,680 | 1,059 | 45.8 | 85.5 |
| 1981 | 3,803 | 3,249 | 1,014 | 846 | 1,641 | 1,215 | 50.7 | 86.4 |
| 1982 | 3,080 | 3,227 | 913 | 765 | 1,110 | 1,023 | 50.1 | 70.6 |
| 1983 | 2,147 | 3,027 | 808 | 655 | 787 | 1,045 | 33.7 | 64.5 |
| 1984 | 1,869 | 3,130 | 617 | 635 | 777 | 934 | 47.6 | 99.9 |
| 1985 | 1,588 | 2,705 | 533 | 587 | 708 | 909 | 55.6 | 116 |
| 1986 | 2,163 | 2,467 | 435 | 430 | 870 | 1,088 | 67.4 | 78.6 |
| 1987 | 2,825 | 2,626 | 525 | 537 | 1,142 | 1,189 | 115 | 122 |
| 1988 | 2,556 | 2,672 | 348 | 413 | 1,157 | 1,404 | 166 | 147 |

**E1    APPENDIX: Trade of Canadian Colonies before Confederation** (in thousand pounds)

**1830–1867**

| | Ontario & Quebec[30] | | New Brunswick | | Nova Scotia | | Prince Edward Island | | British Columbia | |
|---|---|---|---|---|---|---|---|---|---|---|
| | Imports | Exports | Imports | Exports | Imports[32] | Exports | Imports[37] | Exports | Imports | Exports |
| 1830 | ... | ... | ... | ... | ... | ... | ... | ... | — | — |
| 1831 | ... | ... | ... | ... | ... | ... | ... | ... | — | — |
| 1832 | 1,568 | 952 | 532 | 472 | 766 | 392 | ... | 8 | — | — |
| 1833 | 1,665 | 965 | 549 | 469 | 769 | 460 | ... | 4 | — | — |
| 1834 | 1,064 | 1,019 | 568 | 491 | 713 | 427 | ... | 11 | — | — |
| 1835 | 1,496 | 897 | 622 | 577 | 625 | 487 | ... | 9 | — | — |
| 1836 | 1,941 | 1,035 | 864 | 548 | 745 | 481 | ... | 12 | — | — |
| 1837 | 1,602 | 909 | 731 | 588 | 800 | 520 | ... | 7 | — | — |
| 1838 | 1,413 | 969 | 720 | 656 | 933 | 558 | ... | 12 | — | — |
| 1839 | 2,137 | 1,099 | 1,012 | 690 | 1,223 | 686 | ... | 14 | — | — |
| 1840 | 1,903 | 1,626 | 846 | 637 | 1,290 | 782 | ... | 15 | — | — |
| 1841 | 1,936 | 1,884 | 843 | 667 | 1,426 | 917 | ... | 12 | — | — |
| 1842 | 1,923 | 1,327 | 329 | 368 | 1,009 | 669 | ... | 9 | — | — |
| 1843 | 1,127 | 1,381 | 428 | 482 | 816 | 442 | ... | 11 | — | — |
| 1844 | 2,384 | 1,758 | 672 | 546 | 912 | 422 | ... | 15 | — | — |
| 1845 | 2,600 | 2,185 | 893 | 721 | 876[32] | 447 | ... | 26 | — | — |
| 1846 | 2,363 | 1,953 | 861 | 796 | 837 | 476 | 51 | 29 | — | — |
| 1847 | 2,162 | 2,079 | 926 | 618 | 1,045 | 597 | 75 | 30 | — | — |
| 1848 | 1,426 | 1,329 | 517 | 562 | 768 | 459 | 36 | 15 | — | — |
| 1849 | 1,570[31] | 1,333[31] | 596[31] | 547[31] | 796[31] | 473[31] | 61[31] | 21[31] | — | — |
| 1850 | 3,489 | 2,660 | 816 | 658 | 1,056 | 671 | 123 | 60 | — | — |
| 1851 | 4,404 | 2,838 | 980 | 772 | 1,125 | 494 | 134 | 69 | — | — |
| 1852 | 4,168 | 3,146 | 1,111 | 796 | 1,062 | 785 | 172 | 106 | — | — |
| 1853 | 6,572 | 4,891 | 1,716 | 1,072 | 1,417 | 1,079 | 211 | 127 | — | — |
| 1854 | 8,327 | 4,730 | 2,069 | 1,104 | 1,791 | 1,248 | 274 | 151 | — | — |
| 1855 | 7,415 | 5,792 | 1,431 | 826 | 1,883 | 1,472 | 268 | 147 | — | — |
| 1856 | 8,956 | 6,585 | 1,521 | 1,073 | 1,870 | 1,373 | 238 | 112 | — | — |
| 1857 | 8,102 | 5,549 | 1,419 | 918 | 1,936 | 1,394 | 259 | 134 | — | — |
| 1858 | 5,975 | 4,823 | 1,163 | 811 | 1,615 | 1,264 | 186 | 135 | — | — |
| 1859 | 6,895 | 5,089 | 1,416 | 1,073 | 1,620 | 1,378 | 235 | 179 | — | — |
| 1860 | 7,078 | 7,116 | 1,447 | 916 | 1,702 | 1,324 | 230 | 201 | 257 | 611 |
| 1861 | 8,847 | 7,523 | 1,238 | 947 | 1,523 | 1,155 | 210 | 163 | 699 | 13 |
| 1862 | 9,986 | 6,903 | 1,292 | 803 | 1,689 | 1,129 | 211 | 151 | 1,305 | 12 |
| 1863 | 9,445[30] | 8,596[30] | 1,596 | 1,029 | 2,040 | 1,309 | 293 | 209 | 1,232 | 58 |
| 1864 | 10,365 | 9,108 | 1,864 | 1,053 | 2,521 | 1,435 | 338 | 203 | 1,242 | 1,856 |
| 1865 | 9,296 | 8,850 | 1,476 | 1,153 | 2,876 | 1,766 | 381 | 292 | 1,092 | 1,159 |
| 1866 | 11,209 | 11,342 | 2,083 | 1,328 | 2,876 | 1,609 | 445 | 247 | ... | ... |
| 1867 | 12,302 | 9,752 | ... | ... | ... | ... | 294 | 260 | 332 | 777 |

## E1 External Trade Aggregates in Current Values

### NOTES

1. SOURCES: The national publications listed on p. xiv–xvi; League of Nations, *International Trade Statistics;* UN, *Yearbook of International Trade Statistics.* Colombian data for 1835–44 are from Jorge E. Rodriguez and William P. McGreavey in Miguel Urrutia and Mario Arrubla (eds.), *Compendio de Estadisticas Historicas de Colombia* (Bogotà, 1970), and those for 1845–1929 are from William P. McGreavey, *An Economic History of Colombia, 1845–1930* (Cambridge, 1971). Peruvian data to 1896 are based on Laura Randall, *A Comparative Economic History of Latin America 1500–1914, vol 4 Peru* (New York, 1977).

2. Except as indicated in footnotes, statistics are, in principle, of merchandise trade only, and are of 'special' rather than 'general trade—i.e. imports for domestic consumption and exports of domestic origin plus re-exports of commodities originally entered for domestic consumption. In some cases, however, it is impossible to discover the exact composition of the statistics.

3. Imports are normally valued c.i.f. and exports f.o.b.

### FOOTNOTES

[1] 'General' trade including bullion and specie until or unless otherwise indicated.

[2] Trade with France only to 1838 (1st line). These statistics are at official (i.e. fixed) values, as is the French component of the subsequent statistics to 1846.

[3] Years ending 30 September to 1889 and years beginning 1 April from 1890 to 1908. Bullion and specie are included to 1913 (1st line), there being no break in that year in the import series. Import data for 1866–81 are of 'special' rather than 'general' trade.

[4] 'General' trade. Data are for years beginning 1 July from 1861 to 1913. The 1914 figures are for the second half-year only. Total exports from 1519 to 1776 were valued at 155,161 million pesos and from 1779 to 1791 at 244,052 million pesos. Up to 1899 (1st line) the gold peso was used to value imports. The import figures for 1915 and 1916 are not strictly comparable with those for other years, since they were calculated in paper money at the compulsory rates enforced. The 1917 import figure is an official estimate.

[5] Excluding trade with British North America to 1849. Data from 1896 are for years ending 30 June.

[6] Excluding movements of gold from 1825 (2nd line) and domestic exports of silver from 1825 (2nd line) to 1864. Data to 1842 are for years ending 30 September, and for 1844 to 1915 they are for years ending 30 June. The 1843 figures are for the period 1 October 1842 to 30 June 1843.

[7] Data to 1905 are for years beginning 1 July, and for 1907–18 they are for years beginning 1 April. The 1906 figures are for the period 1 July 1906 to 31 March 1907. Imports are on a 'general' trade basis to 1916 and exports to 1919. Gold is included to 1939. Newfoundland became part of Canada on 1 April 1949. Earlier statistics for the separate provinces are shown in the Appendix to this table on p. 442.

[8] Data to 1882 are believed to be for years ending 30 April. The import figures are known to be defective for that period.

[9] Statistics of trade with Spain and the USA are available for 1891–96 and with the USA for 1877–90 (see table F2). The 1877 and 1892 figures are for years ending 30 June. Imports are valued f.o.b. to 1961.

[10] 'General' trade to 1955, with imports valued free alongside ship to 1941.

[11] Excluding trade on government account. Imports are valued f.o.b. to 1954.

[12] Tobago is included from 1889. From that year to 1908 statistics are for years beginning 1 April. Bullion movements and transit trade are included to 1915 (1st line).

[13] Statistics to 1921 are known to be very defective. Bullion and specie are not included after that date.

[14] Years ending 31 July to 1937 and 30 June from 1939 to 1951. The 1938 figures are for the period 1 August 1937 to 30 June 1938. Imports are valued f.o.b. to 1959.

[15] Part of Colombia to 1905. Imports are valued f.o.b. to 1963. Exports from the free zone of Colon are excluded from 1946.

[16] A new basis of valuation was adopted which excluded armed forces' stores, settlers' effects and gifts from the export statistics, and similar items from those of imports.

[17] Banana exports were undervalued previously.

[18] Data to 1910 (1st line) are in official (i.e. fixed) values. The 1910 figures in current values but in million gold pesos are imports 379 and exports 389.

[19] Years beginning 1 July from 1833 to 1886. The figures for 1887 are for the second half-year only. Figures for the first half-year of 1833 are imports 18, exports 21 million milreis. Statistics of imports are on a 'general' trade basis to 1957 and those of exports are on a 'general' trade basis to 1930. Bullion is included to 1930.

[20] Statistics are given here in terms of the gold peso of 18 pence (up to 1967), though trade was actually recorded in pesos of different values at different times.

[21] Years beginning 1 April from 1892 to 1911. Trans-shipments are included in exports to 1899. Bullion and specie are included to 1945 (1st line). Statistics are of 'special' trade from 1953.

[22] Official (i.e. fixed) values to 1913 (1st line) for exports, and to 1914 for imports. The official and the 'effective' values for imports in 1913 coincide but the latter was considerably higher in 1915 and later years. No calculation of 'effective' value was made for 1914. The 1923 import figure is an official estimate of 'effective' value.

[23] Imports are valued f.o.b., except in 1935–37, and include bullion and specie to 1912. Data to 1900 are for fiscal years beginning 1 July.

[24] Valued f.o.b. to September 1954.

[25] 'General' trade exclusive of bullion and specie. Imports are valued f.o.b. to 1935.

[26] Official (i.e. fixed) values to 1897.

[27] Excluding trade on government account. Bullion and specie are included to 1910 (1st line). There is no break in the export series in that year.

[28] Data for imports are for Curaçao only to 1911, and those for exports are for the other islands only (i.e. exclusive of Curaçao) to 1904. From 1955 data relate to Curaçao, Aruba, and Bonaire only, and from 1969 to the first two of these only, but there is no break at the level of rounding used here. Aruba is excluded from 1986.

[29] Petroleum exports were undervalued previously.

[30] Years ending 30 June from 1864.

[31] Excluding the intercolonial trade of British North America to 1849. Bullion and specie are included.

[32] Imports to Prince Edward Island are included with Nova Scotia to 1845.

**E2    NORTH AMERICA: EXTERNAL TRADE (IN CURRENT VALUES) WITH MAIN TRADING PARTNERS**

**CANADA** (million Canadian dollars)[1]

| | Germany | | Japan | | UK | | USA | |
|---|---|---|---|---|---|---|---|---|
| | Imports | Exports | Imports | Exports | Imports | Exports | Imports | Exports |
| 1872 | 1.0 | ... | ... | ... | 64 | ... | 36 | ... |
| 1873 | 1.1 | 0.1 | ... | ... | 69 | 39 | 48 | 43 |
| 1874 | 1.0 | 0.1 | ... | ... | 64 | 46 | 55 | 37 |
| 1875 | 0.8 | 0.1 | ... | ... | 61 | 41 | 51 | 30 |
| 1876 | 0.5 | 0.1 | ... | ... | 41 | 41 | 47 | 32 |
| 1877 | 0.4 | - - | ... | ... | 40 | 42 | 52 | 26 |
| 1878 | 0.4 | 0.1 | ... | ... | 36 | 47 | 49 | 26 |
| 1879 | 0.4 | 0.1 | ... | ... | 31 | 37 | 44 | 28 |
| 1880 | 0.5 | 0.1 | ... | ... | 35 | 46 | 30 | 34 |
| 1881 | 0.9 | 0.1 | ... | ... | 44 | 54 | 37 | 37 |
| 1882 | 1.5 | 0.2 | ... | ... | 51 | 46 | 49 | 49 |
| 1883 | 1.8 | 0.1 | ... | ... | 53 | 48 | 57 | 42 |
| 1884 | 2.0 | 0.2 | ... | ... | 44 | 44 | 51 | 39 |
| 1885 | 2.1 | 0.3 | ... | ... | 42 | 42 | 48 | 40 |
| 1886 | 2.2 | 0.3 | 1.5 | - - | 41 | 42 | 45 | 37 |
| 1887 | 3.2 | 0.4 | 1.6 | - - | 45 | 45 | 45 | 38 |
| 1888 | 3.4 | 0.2 | 1.2 | 0.1 | 39 | 40 | 48 | 43 |
| 1889 | 3.7 | - - | 1.2 | - - | 42 | 38 | 51 | 44 |
| 1890 | 3.8 | 0.5 | 1.3 | - - | 43 | 48 | 52 | 41 |
| 1891 | 3.8 | 0.5 | 1.3 | - - | 42 | 49 | 54 | 41 |
| 1892 | 5.6 | 0.9 | 1.9 | - - | 41 | 65 | 53 | 39 |
| 1893 | 3.8 | 0.8 | 1.5 | - - | 43 | 64 | 58 | 44 |
| 1894 | 5.8 | 2.0 | 1.4 | - -. | 39 | 69 | 53 | 36 |
| 1895 | 4.8 | 0.6 | 1.6 | - - | 31 | 62 | 55 | 41 |
| 1896 | 5.9 | 0.8 | 1.6 | - - | 33 | 67 | 59 | 44 |
| 1897 | 6.5 | 1.0 | 1.3 | 0.1 | 29 | 77 | 62 | 49 |
| 1898 | 5.6 | 1.8 | 1.4 | 0.1 | 32 | 105 | 79 | 46 |
| 1899 | 7.4 | 2.2 | 2.0 | 0.1 | 37 | 99 | 93 | 45 |
| 1900 | 8.4 | 1.7 | 1.8 | 0.1 | 45 | 108 | 110 | 69 |
| 1901 | 7.0 | 2.1 | 1.6 | 0.2 | 43 | 105 | 110 | 72 |
| 1902 | 11 | 2.7 | 1.5 | 0.3 | 49 | 117 | 121 | 71 |
| 1903 | 12 | 2.1 | 1.4 | 0.3 | 59 | 131 | 138 | 72 |
| 1904 | 8.2 | 1.8 | 1.9 | 0.3 | 62 | 118 | 151 | 73 |
| 1905 | 6.7 | 1.1 | 1.9 | 0.5 | 60 | 102 | 163 | 77 |
| 1906 | 7.0[1] | 1.9[1] | 1.7[1] | 0.5[1] | 69[1] | 133[1] | 176[1] | 98[1] |
| 1907 | 8.2 | 2.3 | 2.2 | 0.7 | 95 | 126 | 211 | 91 |
| 1908 | 6.1 | 1.5 | 2.0 | 0.8 | 71 | 126 | 180 | 85 |
| 1909 | 7.9 | 2.5 | 2.2 | 0.7 | 95 | 139 | 228 | 104 |
| 1910 | 10 | 2.7 | 2.4 | 0.6 | 110 | 132 | 285 | 105 |
| 1911 | 11 | 3.8 | 2.5 | 0.5 | 117 | 147 | 357 | 102 |
| 1912 | 14 | 3.0 | 3.5 | 1.1 | 139 | 170 | 441 | 140 |
| 1913 | 15 | 4.0 | 2.6 | 1.6 | 132 | 215 | 411 | 164 |
| 1914 | 5.1 | 2.2 | 2.8 | 1.0 | 90 | 187 | 429 | 174 |
| 1915 | 0.1 | — | 4.0 | 1.0 | 80 | 452 | 399 | 201 |
| 1916 | - -[1] | — | 8.1[1] | 1.3 | 122[1] | 742 | 678[1] | 281 |
| 1917 | - - | — | 12 | 5.0 | 81 | 845 | 804 | 418 |
| 1918 | - - | — | 14 | 12 | 73 | 541 | 750 | 455 |
| 1919 | - - | 0.6[1] | 14 | 7.7[1] | 126 | 489[1] | 801 | 464[1] |

**E2    NORTH AMERICA: External Trade (in Current Values) with Main Trading Partners**

**CANADA** (million Canadian dollars)[1]

| | Germany | | Japan | | UK | | USA | |
|---|---|---|---|---|---|---|---|---|
| | **Imports** | **Exports** | **Imports** | **Exports** | **Imports** | **Exports** | **Imports** | **Exports** |
| 1920 | 1.5 | 8.2 | 11 | 6.4 | 214 | 313 | 856 | 542 |
| 1921 | 2.0 | 4.5 | 8.2 | 15 | 117 | 299 | 516 | 293 |
| 1922 | 2.6 | 10 | 7.2 | 15 | 141 | 379 | 541 | 369 |
| 1923 | 5.4 | 16 | 6.3 | 27 | 154 | 360 | 601 | 431 |
| 1924 | 6.8 | 24 | 7.0 | 22 | 151 | 396 | 510 | 417 |
| 1925 | 10 | 31 | 9.6 | 35 | 164 | 508 | 610 | 475 |
| 1926 | 15 | 34 | 11 | 30 | 164 | 447 | 687 | 466 |
| 1927 | 17 | 42 | 13 | 33 | 186 | 411 | 719 | 478 |
| 1928 | 21 | 47 | 13 | 42 | 194 | 430 | 868 | 500 |
| 1929 | 22 | 25 | 13 | 31 | 189 | 282 | 847 | 515 |
| 1930 | 16 | 13 | 9.3 | 19 | 150 | 210 | 584 | 350 |
| 1931 | 12[1] | 10[1] | 6.0[1] | 17[1] | 98[1] | 174[1] | 352[1] | 235[1] |
| 1932 | 9.8 | 7.8 | 4.6 | 12 | 94 | 179 | 264 | 165 |
| 1933 | 9.3 | 9.9 | 3.1 | 13 | 98 | 211 | 217 | 173 |
| 1934 | 10 | 6.2 | 4.4 | 17 | 113 | 271 | 294 | 224 |
| 1935 | 9.8 | 3.6 | 3.6 | 15 | 117 | 304 | 312 | 273 |
| 1936 | 11 | 6.8 | 4.3 | 20 | 123 | 396 | 369 | 345 |
| 1937 | 12 | 12 | 5.9 | 26 | 147 | 403 | 491 | 372 |
| 1938 | 9.9 | 18 | 4.6 | 21 | 119 | 341 | 425 | 279 |
| 1939 | 8.9 | 7.8 | 4.9 | 28 | 114 | 324 | 497 | 390 |
| 1940 | 0.4 | — | 6.1 | 12 | 161 | 512 | 744 | 452 |
| 1941 | - - | — | 2.4 | 1.6 | 219 | 661 | 1,004 | 610 |
| 1942 | - - | — | 1.0 | — | 161 | 748 | 1,305 | 897 |
| 1943 | — | — | - - | — | 135 | 1,037 | 1,424 | 1,167 |
| 1944 | — | — | — | — | 111 | 1,238 | 1,447 | 1,335 |
| 1945 | - - | 2.7 | — | — | 122[3] | 971 | 1,202 | 1,227 |
| 1946 | - - | 6.9 | - - | 1.0 | 141[3] | 599 | 1,405 | 909 |
| 1947 | 0.5 | 6.7 | 0.4 | 0.6 | 189 | 754 | 1,975 | 1,057 |
| 1948 | 1.7 | 13 | 3.1 | 8.0 | 300 | 687 | 1,806 | 1,522 |
| 1949 | 7.1[1] | 23[1] | 5.5[1] | 5.9[1] | 307[1] | 709[1] | 1,952[1] | 1,524[1] |
| 1950 | 11 | 8.9 | 12 | 21 | 404 | 473 | 2,130 | 2,050 |
| 1951 | 31 | 37 | 13 | 73 | 421 | 636 | 2,813 | 2,334 |
| 1952 | 23[2] | 95[2] | 13 | 103 | 360 | 751 | 2,977 | 2,349 |
| | 23 | 95 | | | | | | |
| 1953 | 36 | 84 | 14 | 119 | 453 | 669 | 3,221 | 2,463 |
| 1954 | 44 | 87 | 19 | 96 | 392 | 658 | 2,961 | 2,367 |
| 1955 | 52 | 91 | 37 | 91 | 401 | 774 | 3,452 | 2,612 |
| 1956 | 84 | 134 | 61 | 128 | 485 | 818 | 4,162 | 2,879 |
| 1957 | 93 | 152 | 61 | 139 | 522 | 728 | 3,999 | 2,942 |
| 1958 | 103 | 201 | 70 | 105 | 527 | 779 | 3,572 | 2,915 |
| 1959 | 124 | 129 | 103 | 140 | 597 | 797[1] | 3,829[1] | 3,207[1] |
| | | | | | | 786 | 3,836 | 3,094 |
| 1960 | 127 | 166 | 110 | 179 | 589 | 915 | 3,689 | 2,943 |
| 1961 | 136 | 189 | 117 | 232 | 618 | 909 | 3,866 | 3,120 |
| 1962 | 141 | 178 | 125 | 214 | 563 | 909 | 4,302 | 3,621 |
| 1963 | 144 | 171 | 130 | 296 | 527 | 1,007 | 4,447 | 3,781 |
| 1964 | 170 | 217 | 174 | 332 | 574 | 1,207 | 5,168 | 4,452 |
| 1965 | 209 | 193 | 230 | 317 | 619 | 1,185 | 6,048 | 5,051 |
| 1966 | 235 | 180 | 253 | 395 | 645 | 1,132 | 7,140 | 6,254 |
| 1967 | 257 | 181 | 305 | 574 | 673 | 1,178 | 8,028 | 7,350 |
| 1968 | 299 | 232 | 360 | 608 | 696 | 1,225 | 9,051 | 9,218 |
| 1969 | 355 | 281 | 496 | 626 | 791 | 1,113 | 10,318 | 10,593 |

**E2        NORTH AMERICA: External Trade (in Current Values) with Main Trading Partners**

## CANADA (million Canadian dollars)

| | West Germany | | Japan | | U.K. | | USA | |
|---|---|---|---|---|---|---|---|---|
| | Imports | Exports | Imports | Exports | Imports | Exports | Imports | Exports |
| 1970 | 383 | 388 | 601 | 796 | 762 | 1,500 | 10,233 | 11,039 |
| 1971 | 429 | 319 | 802 | 792 | 832 | 1,361 | 10,957 | 12,197 |
| 1972 | 512 | 316 | 1,105 | 962 | 949 | 1,328 | 12,927 | 13,974 |
| 1973 | 607 | 444 | 1,018 | 1,800 | 1,005 | 1,589 | 16,511 | 17,115 |
| 1974 | 767 | 542 | 1,427 | 2,224 | 1,127 | 1,895 | 21,268 | 21,316 |
| 1975 | 786 | 593 | 1,205 | 2,120 | 1,222 | 1,784 | 23,511 | 21,598 |
| 1976 | 818 | 705 | 1,526 | 2,382 | 1,153 | 1,845 | 25,704 | 25,658 |
| 1977. | 963 | 772 | 1,802 | 2,496 | 1,281 | 1,882 | 29,559 | 30,469 |
| 1978 | 1,195 | 751 | 2,181 | 2,935 | 1,533 | 1,895 | 33,560 | 35,411 |
| 1979 | 1,550 | 1,234 | 2,157 | 4,046 | 1,926 | 2,579 | 43,908 | 43,907 |
| 1980 | 1,441 | 1,433 | 2,792 | 4,355 | 1,967 | 2,932 | 47,299 | 46,571 |
| 1981 | 1,599 | 1,297 | 4,039 | 4,476 | 2,230 | 3,020 | 53,447 | 53,885 |
| 1982 | 1,376 | 1,268 | 3,527 | 4,535 | 1,894 | 2,595 | 47,372 | 56,048 |
| 1983 | 1,564 | 1,122 | 4,413 | 4,453 | 1,787 | 2,381 | 53,146 | 64,282 |
| 1984 | 2,168 | 1,116 | 5,711 | 5,230 | 2,298 | 2,337 | 67,392 | 82,624 |
| 1985 | 2,705 | 1,126 | 6,114 | 5,363 | 3,274 | 2,235 | 72,625 | 91,046 |
| 1986 | 3,450 | 1,236 | 7,632 | 5,557 | 3,735 | 2,498 | 75,454 | 90,231 |
| 1987 | 3,532 | 1,545 | 7,550 | 6,410 | 4,339 | 2,799 | 78,282 | 93,284 |
| 1988 | 3,841 | 1,773 | 9,259 | 8,725 | 4,622 | 3,560 | 86,166 | 101,195 |

## COSTA RICA (thousand gold pesos T0 1896, million colones subsequently)

| | Germany | | UK | | USA | |
|---|---|---|---|---|---|---|
| | Imports | Exports | Imports | Exports | Imports | Exports |
| 1882 | ... | ... | ... | ... | ... | ... |
| 1883 | 989 | 263 | 953 | 1,165 | 741 | 661 |
| 1884 | 105 | 441 | 2,025 | 1,698 | 944 | 1,310 |
| 1885 | 605 | 375 | 1,688 | 1,362 | 857 | 1,059 |
| 1886 | 582 | 335 | 1,379 | 1,440 | 1,010 | 1,023 |
| 1887 | 816 | 251 | 1,771 | 3,126 | 1,441 | 2,479 |
| 1888 | 834 | 294 | 1,649 | 2,884 | 1,794 | 2,078 |
| 1889 | 1,229 | 201 | 1,862 | 3,647 | 4,852 | 3,035 |
| 1890 | 1,262 | ... | 1,449 | ... | 2,255 | ... |
| 1891 | 1,697 | 268 | 2,119 | 3,222 | 2,369 | 2,514 |
| 1892 | 948 | 198 | 1,784 | 2,521 | 1,296 | 1,868 |
| 1893 | 1,124 | 164 | 1,724 | 2,264 | 1,400 | 1,831 |
| 1894 | 566 | 593 | 907 | 1,297 | 941 | 2,770 |
| 1895 | 737 | 934 | 855 | 2,230 | 1,198 | 1,582 |
| 1896 | 844 | 940 | 1,221 | 2,772 | 1,478 | 1,579 |
| | | | (million colones) | | | |
| 1897 | 2.5 | ... | 3.2 | ... | 4.0 | ... |
| 1898 | 1.4 | ... | 1.8 | ... | 4.0 | ... |
| 1899 | 1.5 | ... | 2.0 | ... | 5.4 | ... |
| 1900 | 1.9 | ... | 3.8 | ... | 6.5 | ... |
| 1901 | ... | ... | ... | ... | ... | ... |
| 1902 | 1.2 | ... | 2.2 | ... | 5.0 | ... |
| 1903 | 1.2 | 0.7 | 2.3 | 7.7 | 5.3 | 6.6 |
| 1904 | 1.6 | 0.6 | 2.5 | 7.1 | 5.4 | 6.8 |

**E2   NORTH AMERICA: External Trade (in Current Values) with Main Trading Partners**

## COSTA RICA (million colones)

|      | Germany | | UK | | USA | |
|------|---------|---------|---------|---------|---------|---------|
|      | Imports | Exports | Imports | Exports | Imports | Exports |
| 1905 | 1.3 | 0.6 | 2.0 | 8.2 | 4.7 | 8.2 |
| 1906 | 1.6 | 1.1 | 3.2 | 8.5 | 7.1 | 9.0 |
| 1907 | 1.7 | 1.1 | 3.7 | 8.6 | 7.1 | 9.4 |
| 1908 | 1.8 | 0.5 | 2.6 | 7.2 | 5.4 | 8.8 |
| 1909 | 1.8 | 0.4 | 2.3 | 6.3 | 6.7 | 10.0 |
| 1910 | 2.0 | 0.6 | 2.7 | 6.4 | 7.8 | 11 |
| 1911 | 3.6 | 0.6 | 3.3 | 7.6 | 8.8 | 11 |
| 1912 | 3.2 | 1.2 | 3.0 | 8.9 | 9.4 | 11 |
| 1913 | 2.9 | 1.1 | 2.8 | 9.3 | 9.6 | 11 |
| 1914 | 2.3 | 1.0 | 2.3 | 11 | 8.7 | 11 |
| 1915 | 0.1 | - - | 1.2 | 9.5 | 6.5 | 10 |
| 1916 | - - | — | 1.7 | 7.9 | 10 | 15 |
| 1917 | - - | — | 1.5 | 5.4 | 8.4 | 17 |
| 1918 | — | — | 0.6 | 0.4 | 4.7 | 19 |
| 1919 | - - | - - | 1.2 | 14 | 13 | 21 |
| 1920 | 6.5 | 0.1 | 6.8 | 6.7 | 25 | 23 |
| 1921 | 0.4 | 0.1 | 3.3 | 6.4 | 11 | 17 |
| 1922 | 0.8 | 0.3 | 2.5 | 11 | 11 | 17 |
| 1923 | 1.4 | 0.2 | 3.3 | 11 | 12 | 15 |
| 1924 | 3.8 | 1.3 | 7.9 | 29 | 27 | 32 |
| 1925 | 5.8 | 4.0 | 8.6 | 30 | 30 | 28 |
| 1926 | 6.8 | 6.6 | 8.0 | 35 | 31 | 31 |
| 1927 | 10 | 5.9 | 9.7 | 40 | 33 | 24 |
| 1928 | 11 | 7.5 | 10 | 42 | 36 | 24 |
| 1929 | 14 | 7.9 | 10 | 41 | 39 | 20 |
| 1930 | 5.3 | 6.5 | 5.3 | 39 | 22 | 17 |
| 1931 | 3.6 | 6.3 | 3.9 | 34 | 18 | 13 |
| 1932 | 2.8 | 2.8 | 2.6 | 17 | 13 | 15 |
| 1933 | 3.6 | 7.6 | 3.9 | 21 | 14 | 17 |
| 1934 | 4.5 | 6.8 | 4.9 | 17 | 17 | 10 |
| 1935 | 2.5 | 1.7 | 0.7 | 2.4 | 2.7 | 3 |
| 1936 | 2.0 | 1.4 | 0.6 | 2.2 | 3.7 | 3.7 |
| 1937 | 2.7 | 2.2 | 0.9 | 2.3 | 5 | 5.2 |
| 1938 | 2.5 | 1.9 | 0.9 | 2.5 | 6.2 | 4.6 |
| 1939 | 3.0 | 2.3 | 0.7 | 1.5 | 9.9 | 4.1 |
| 1940 | 0.6 | — | 0.8 | 1.9 | 13 | 4.4 |
| 1941 | 0.1 | — | 0.7 | - - | 14 | 8.3 |
| 1942 | - - | — | 0.4 | - - | 9.0 | 7.5 |
| 1943 | — | — | 0.5 | - - | 12 | 9.2 |
| 1944 | — | — | 0.4 | - - | 14 | 7.8 |
| 1945 | — | — | 0.4 | - - | 19 | 9.8 |
| 1946 | — | — | 0.6 | 0.1 | 25 | 11 |
| 1947 | - - | — | 1.0 | 0.4 | 39 | 18 |
| 1948 | - - | - - | 1.7 | 0.5 | 33 | 25 |
| 1949 | 0.4 | - - | 1.7 | 0.1 | 32 | 24 |

**E2     NORTH AMERICA: External Trade (in Current Values) with Main Trading Partners**

## COSTA RICA (million US dollars)

| | Germany | | Japan | | UK | | USA | |
|---|---|---|---|---|---|---|---|---|
| | Imports | Exports | Imports | Exports | Imports | Exports | Imports | Exports |
| 1950 | 1.9 | 0.2 | ... | ... | 2.3 | - - | 31 | 25 |
| 1951 | 4.1 | 0.5 | 0.6 | - - | 2.7 | 0.2 | 37 | 49 |
| 1952 | 4.7 | 1.2 | 0.8 | - - | 3.6 | 0.2 | 43 | 53 |
| 1953 | 5.6 | 7.4 | 1.7 | - - | 5.6 | 0.1 | 44 | 53 |
| 1954 | 8.0 | 15 | 1.4 | 0.1 | 5.8 | 0.3 | 47 | 50 |
| 1955 | 8.0 | 21 | 2.2 | — | 5.9 | 0.7 | 52 | 44 |
| 1956 | 8.5₂ | 20₂ | 1.9 | - - | 5.6 | 0.4 | 50 | 34 |
| 1957 | 9.5 | 20 | 3.5 | - - | 5.0 | 0.4 | 57 | 43 |
| 1958 | 11 | 25 | 5.1 | 0.3 | 5.7 | 1.0 | 51 | 46 |
| 1959 | 10 | 19 | 5.9 | 0.5 | 6.3 | 0.9 | 50 | 38 |
| 1960 | 13 | 20 | 8.0 | 0.4 | 6.4 | 0.7 | 52 | 45 |
| 1961 | 12 | 18 | 7.4 | 0.5 | 5.8 | 0.6 | 50 | 49 |
| 1962 | 13 | 20 | 7.5 | 0.6 | 5.8 | 0.8 | 53 | 54 |
| 1963 | 15 | 17 | 8.6 | 0.6 | 6.5 | 0.7 | 59 | 55 |
| 1964 | 14 | 20 | 10 | 0.4 | 7.1 | 0.5 | 64 | 61 |
| 1965 | 17 | 13 | 17 | 0.6 | 8.3 | 0.5 | 71 | 56 |
| 1966 | 18 | 16 | 16 | 1.3 | 8.5 | 0.7 | 70 | 60 |
| 1967 | 15 | 11 | 16 | 1.5 | 12 | 0.5 | 74 | 69 |
| 1968 | 16 | 11 | 15 | 2.0 | 8.9 | 0.4 | 81 | 80 |
| 1969 | 20 | 13 | 22 | 1.9 | 15 | 0.6 | 86 | 90 |
| 1970 | 26 | 19 | 29 | 11 | 16 | 0.8 | 110 | 98 |
| 1971 | 27 | 21 | 39 | 7.0 | 17 | 0.6 | 114 | 92 |
| 1972 | 27 | 32 | 40 | 5.3 | 20 | 0.7 | 123 | 113 |
| 1973 | 31 | 44 | 41 | 1.7 | 15 | 1.7 | 160 | 115 |
| 1974 | 44 | 56 | 71 | 7.1 | 18 | 0.9 | 248 | 142 |
| 1975 | 39 | 56 | 61 | 8.2 | 23 | 0.7 | 239 | 207 |
| 1976 | 44 | 63 | 89 | 7.2 | 22 | 1.5 | 290 | 237 |
| 1977 | 59 | 107 | 137 | 7.3 | 24 | 2.1 | 373 | 262 |
| 1978 | 62 | 125 | 158 | 6.9 | 28 | 2.7 | 413 | 342 |
| 1979 | 73 | 110 | 174 | 10 | 27 | 3.5 | 460 | 347 |
| 1980 | 74 | 117 | 173 | 8.5 | 26 | 2.7 | 550 | 360 |
| 1981 | 57 | 124 | 121 | 5.4 | 19 | 11 | 459 | 329 |
| 1982 | 37 | 125 | 38 | 6.2 | 18 | 21 | 387 | 295 |
| 1983 | ... | 111 | ... | 4.8 | ... | 22 | ... | 297 |
| 1984 | 55 | 130 | 82 | 4.7 | 14 | 27 | 394 | 358 |
| 1985 | 58 | 119 | 105 | 5.2 | 20 | 27 | 380 | 378 |
| 1986 | 64 | 161 | 121 | 10 | 22 | 42 | 408 | 467 |
| 1987 | 78 | 168 | 118 | 12 | 23 | 25 | 511 | 513 |
| 1988 | 60 | 173 | 94 | 10 | 24 | 27 | 549 | 494 |

**E2    NORTH AMERICA: External Trade (in Current Values) with Main Trading Partners**

## CUBA (million pesos)[4]

|  | Germany | | Spain | | UK | | USA | |
|---|---|---|---|---|---|---|---|---|
|  | **Imports** | **Exports** | **Imports** | **Exports** | **Imports** | **Exports** | **Imports** | **Exports** |
| 1848 | 1.5 | 3.9 | 7.1 | 3.9 | 5 | 7.1 | 6.9 | 8.3 |
| 1854 | 1.4 | 1.8 | 9.1 | 3.6 | 6.6 | 11 | 7.9 [4] | 12 [4] |
| 1876 | ... | ... | ... | ... | ... | ... | 13 | 56 |
| 1877 | ... | ... | ... | ... | ... | ... | 13 | 66 |
| 1878 | ... | ... | ... | ... | ... | ... | 12 | 57 |
| 1879 | ... | ... | ... | ... | ... | ... | 13 | 64 |
| 1880 | ... | ... | ... | ... | ... | ... | 11 | 65 |
| 1881 | ... | ... | ... | ... | ... | ... | 11 | 63 |
| 1882 | ... | ... | ... | ... | ... | ... | 12 | 70 |
| 1883 | ... | ... | ... | ... | ... | ... | 15 | 66 |
| 1884 | ... | ... | ... | ... | ... | ... | 11 | 57 |
| 1885 | ... | ... | ... | ... | ... | ... | 9 | 42 |
| 1886 | ... | ... | ... | ... | ... | ... | 10 | 51 |
| 1887 | ... | ... | ... | ... | ... | ... | 11 | 50 |
| 1888 | ... | ... | ... | ... | ... | ... | 10 | 49 |
| 1889 | ... | ... | ... | ... | ... | ... | 12 | 52 |
| 1890 | ... | ... | ... | ... | ... | ... | 13 | 54 |
| 1891 | ... | ... | 22 | 7.1 | ... | ... | 12 | 62 |
| 1892 | ... | ... | 28 | 9.6 | ... | ... | 18 | 78 |
| 1893 | ... | ... | 25 | 5.7 | ... | ... | 24 | 79 |
| 1894 | ... | ... | 26 | 7.3 | ... | ... | 20 | 76 |
| 1895 | ... | ... | 27 | 7.2 | ... | ... | 13 | 53 |
| 1896 | ... | ... | 26 | 4.3 | ... | ... | 9.6 | 42 |
| 1897 | ... | ... | ... | ... | ... | ... | ... | ... |
| 1898 | ... | ... | ... | ... | ... | ... | ... | ... |
| 1899 | ... | ... | ... | ... | ... | ... | ... | ... |
| 1900 | 2.6 | 2.9 | 11 | 1 | 12 | 4.4 | 34 | 37 |
| 1901 | 3.4 | 6.7 | 10 | 0.6 | 9.3 | 5.9 | 29 | 46 |
| 1902 | 3.5 | 3.9 | 9.7 | 1.3 | 9.6 | 6 | 29 | 38 |
| 1903 | 3.7 | 3.8 | 10 | 1.7 | 9.2 | 6.4 | 26 | 63 |
| 1904 | 4.6 | 5.1 | 11 | 1.2 | 12 | 5.9 | 30 | 78 |
| 1905 | 5.1 | 3.8 | 10 | 1.1 | 12 | 6.2 | 38 | 86 |
| 1906 | 6.6 | 4.3 | 11 | 1.6 | 15 | 5.9 | 49 | 90 |
| 1907 | 6.4 | 3.1 | 8.3 | 0.7 | 14 | 4.4 | 48 | 102 |
| 1908 | 7.8 | 3.7 | 9.3 | 1 | 15 | 5.1 | 47 | 94 |
| 1909 | 6.4 | 4.5 | 7.4 | 1.5 | 11 | 5 | 43 | 101 |
| 1910 | 6.9 | 4.3 | 8.9 | 0.5 | 14 | 11 | 50 | 122 |
| 1911 | 7.2 | 3.7 | 8.5 | 0.7 | 14 | 5.1 | 57 | 113 |
| 1912 | 8.4 [4] | 6.2 [4] | 10 [4] | 0.5 [4] | 16 [4] | 11 [4] | 63 [4] | 123 [4] |
| 1913 | 9.7 | 4.7 | 10 | 0.7 | 16 | 18 | 75 | 132 |
| 1914 | 5 | 2.4 | 9.9 | 1.6 | 12 | 16 | 69 | 146 |

**E2      NORTH AMERICA: External Trade (in Current Values) with Main Trading Partners**

## CUBA (million pesos)[4]

| | Germany | | Spain | | USSR | | UK | | USA | |
|---|---|---|---|---|---|---|---|---|---|---|
| | Imports | Exports | Imports | Exports | Imports | Exports | Imports | Exports | Imports | Exports |
| 1915 | 0.8 | — | 11 | 0.9 | ... | ... | 15 | 33 | 90 | 195 |
| 1916 | - - | — | 14 | 3.0 | ... | ... | 19 | 53 | 153 | 243 |
| 1917 | - - | — | 16 | 5.4 | ... | ... | 15 | 74 | 190 | 255 |
| 1918 | — | — | 10 | 6.4 | ... | ... | 9.2 | 95 | 219 | 289 |
| 1919 | 0.2 | - - | 16 | 8.2 | ... | ... | 8.8 | 83 | 272 | 441 |
| 1920 | 2.9 | 0.1 | 28 | 7.2 | ... | ... | 18 | 98 | 404 | 627 |
| 1921 | 5.4 | 0.5 | 14 | 2.5 | ... | ... | 17 | 27 | 264 | 223 |
| 1922 | 3.5 | 0.6 | 8.4 | 3.1 | ... | ... | 9.1 | 38 | 120 | 262 |
| 1923 | 7.9 | 0.6 | 13 | 1.6 | ... | ... | 13 | 32 | 182 | 368 |
| 1924 | 9.8 | 1.7 | 15 | 1.4 | ... | ... | 12 | 49 | 192 | 363 |
| 1925 | 9.4 | 2.2 | 13 | 1.9 | ... | ... | 12 | 56 | 187 | 265 |
| 1926 | 7.7 | 1.7 | 12 | 1.3 | ... | ... | 13 | 22 | 160 | 244 |
| 1927 | 7.8 | 2.3 | 11 | 1.5 | ... | ... | 12 | 33 | 160 | 257 |
| 1928 | 6.6 | 2.8 | 9.4 | 4.3 | ... | ... | 10 | 45 | 129 | 203 |
| 1929 | 7.5 | 2.3 | 8.9 | 3.3 | ... | ... | 12 | 34 | 127 | 209 |
| 1930 | 6.1 | 2.2 | 7.6 | 2.5 | ... | ... | 8.9 | 25 | 92 | 116 |
| 1931 | 3.0 | 1.5 | 4.2 | 1.8 | ... | ... | 4.0 | 17 | 46 | 89 |
| 1932 | 2.1 | 0.7 | 3.0 | 1.5 | ... | ... | 3.0 | 12 | 28 | 57 |
| 1933 | 1.9 | 0.8 | 2.6 | 2.2 | ... | ... | 2.4 | 16 | 23 | 57 |
| 1934 | 2.9 | 0.8 | 4.1 | 2.4 | ... | ... | 3.9 | 15 | 41 | 81 |
| 1935 | 4.4 | 2.3 | 4.8 | 1.8 | ... | ... | 4.1 | 14 | 56 | 102 |
| 1936 | 4.8 | 2.4 | 3.5 | 1.1 | ... | ... | 5.1 | 20 | 66 | 122 |
| 1937 | 5.8 | 3.1 | 1.8 | 0.6 | ... | ... | 6.3 | 20 | 89 | 150 |
| 1938 | 4.7 | 2.8 | 1.6 | 1.4 | ... | ... | 4.5 | 20 | 75 | 108 |
| 1939 | 3.4 | 1.5 | 1.3 | 2.2 | ... | ... | 3.1 | 18 | 78 | 111 |
| 1940 | 0.2 | 0.1 | 1.7 | 3.0 | ... | ... | 3.5 | 10 | 80 | 105 |
| 1941 | - - | — | 1.2 | 2.2 | ... | ... | 3.4 | 17 | 115 | 181 |
| 1942 | — | — | 0.5 | 0.6 | ... | ... | 2.8 | 5.6 | 120 | 164 |
| 1943 | — | — | 1.2 | 2.2 | ... | ... | 4.3 | 35 | 135 | 297 |
| 1944 | — | — | 1.4 | 4.9 | ... | ... | 2.5 | 23 | 161 | 386 |
| 1945 | - - | — | 3.5 | 8.4 | ... | ... | 2.8 | 35 | 188 | 323 |
| 1946 | - - | — | 5.2 | 6.7 | ... | ... | 4.3 | 64 | 299 | 320 |
| 1947 | - - | 6.9 | 7.4 | 8.4 | — | — | 6.9 | 133 | 437 | 498 |
| 1948 | 0.1 | 62 | 6.8 | 11 | — | — | 8.4 | 95 | 421 | 367 |
| 1949 | 0.7 | 27 | 6.9 | 2.9 | — | — | 6.5 | 70 | 376 | 367 |
| 1950 | 4.8 | 14 | 6.5 | 3.8 | — | — | 8.6 | 96 | 407 | 381 |
| 1951 | 11 | 19 | 13 | 9.0 | — | — | 19 | 105 | 493 | 416 |
| 1952 | 9.6 | 15 | 9.6 | 9.2 | — | — | 16 | 57 | 463 | 409 |
| 1953 | 9.2[2] | 17[2] | 9.6 | 5.0 | — | — | 10 | 75 | 371 | 393 |
| 1954 | 12 | 8.5 | 9.8 | 11 | — | 0.8 | 13 | 22 | 367 | 369 |
| 1955 | 15 | 15 | 12 | 12 | — | 36 | 12 | 7.0 | 423 | 401 |
| 1956 | 18 | 19 | 9.8 | 11 | — | 14 | 18 | 29 | 488 | 431 |
| 1957 | 21 | 37 | 12 | 14 | — | 42 | 21 | 44 | 578 | 468 |
| 1958 | 24 | 7.5 | 13 | 18 | — | 14 | 22 | 37 | 543 | 491 |
| 1959 | 22 | 14 | 8.4 | 5.1 | - - | 13 | 27 | 9.1 | 459 | 445 |

**E2     NORTH AMERICA: External Trade (in Current Values) with Main Trading Partners**

## CUBA (million pesos)[4]

| | Germany | | | | Spain | | USSR | | UK | | USA | |
|---|---|---|---|---|---|---|---|---|---|---|---|---|
| | Exports | | Imports | | Imports | Exports | Imports | Exports | Imports | Exports | Imports | Exports |
| | East | West | East | West | | | | | | | | |
| 1960 | 4.4 | 22 | 0.5 | 13 | ... | 7.3 | 88 | 104 | 23 | 8.5 | 310 | 329 |
| 1961 | 18 | 25 | 7.7 | 13 | ... | 5.1 | 289 | 301 | 17 | 13 | 26 | 30 |
| 1962 | 27 | 14 | 25 | 0.4 | 1.6 | 8.6 | 411 | 220 | 12 | 12 | 0.6 | 4.2 |
| 1963 | 36 | 12 | 40 | 0.3 | 14 | 23 | 461 | 164 | 11 | 23 | 35 | — |
| 1964 | 39 | 19 | 16 | 0.8 | 39 | 68 | 410 | 275 | 38 | 26 | — | — |
| 1965 | 25 | ... | 28 | 0.7 | 47 | 33 | 428 | 322 | 50 | 12 | — | — |
| 1966 | 36 | ... | 31 | ... | 75 | 33 | 521 | 274 | 25 | 11 | — | — |
| 1967 | 50 | 12 | 36 | 0.7 | 29 | 33 | 582 | 367 | 29 | 13 | — | — |
| 1968 | 39 | 11 | 36 | 2.1 | 21 | 41 | 672 | 290 | 31 | 14 | — | — |
| 1969 | 43 | 30 | 38 | 1.4 | 48 | 41 | 658 | 233 | 66 | 14 | — | — |
| 1970 | 50 | 34 | 49 | 0.9 | 36 | 41 | 691 | 529 | 59 | 20 | — | — |
| 1971 | 63 | 17 | 49 | 2.7 | 33 | 36 | 731 | 304 | 61 | 17 | — | — |
| 1972 | 36 | 23 | 38 | 3.2 | 155 | 40 | 714 | 224 | 43 | 12 | — | — |
| 1973 | 40 | 39 | 46 | 2.8 | 40 | 52 | 811 | 477 | 54 | 30 | — | — |
| 1974 | 52 | 107 | 103 | 5.7 | 62 | 176 | 1,025 | 810 | 84 | 45 | — | — |
| 1975 | 76 | 140 | 70 | 4.6 | 152 | 226 | 1,251 | 1,662 | 128 | 13 | — | — |
| 1976 | 99 | 80 | 79 | 10 | 186 | 101 | 1,490 | 1,638 | 154 | 53 | — | — |
| 1977 | 153 | 65 | 96 | 8.1 | 154 | 112 | 1,858 | 2,066 | 48 | 16 | — | — |
| 1978 | 139 | 75 | 98 | 17 | 75 | 60 | 2,328 | 2,495 | 57 | 10 | — | — |
| 1979 | 136 | 73 | 116 | 27 | 105 | 79 | 2,513 | 2,370 | 61 | 19 | — | — |
| 1980 | 165 | 83 | 122 | 17 | 139 | 46 | 2,904 | 2,253 | 77 | 15 | — | — |
| 1981 | 171 | 99 | 176 | 14 | 163 | 64 | 3,234 | 2,357 | 63 | 16 | — | — |
| 1982 | 206 | 54 | 164 | 44 | 95 | 88 | 3,744 | 3,290 | 50 | 24 | — | — |
| 1983 | 251 | 65 | 200 | 68 | 107 | 94 | 4,245 | 3,882 | 93 | 31 | — | — |
| 1984 | 268 | 91 | 217 | 14 | 108 | 64 | 4,782 | 3,952 | 92 | 15 | — | — |
| 1985 | 280 | 82 | 234 | 16 | 177 | 103 | 5,373 | 4,479 | 105 | 27 | — | — |
| 1986 | 305 | 85 | 258 | 12 | 106 | 88 | 5,314 | 3,934 | 79 | 17 | — | — |
| 1987 | 339 | 53 | 282 | 28 | 163 | 85 | 5,496 | 3,867 | 70 | 13 | — | — |
| 1988 | 341 | 57 | 311 | 73 | 146 | 82 | 5,364 | 3,688 | 60 | 42 | — | — |

**E2   NORTH AMERICA: External Trade (in Current Values) with Main Trading Partners**

**EL SALVADOR** (imports: thousand gold pesos to 1919, million quetzales subsequently)

| | Germany | | Guatemala | | Honduras | | Japan | | UK[8] | | USA | |
|---|---|---|---|---|---|---|---|---|---|---|---|---|
| | Imports | Exports | Imports | Exports | Imports | Exports | Imports | Exports | Imports | Exports | Imports | Exports |
| 1901 | 447 | 1,294 | ... | ... | 8 | 39 | ... | ... | 984 | 2,448 | 733 | 2,087 |
| 1902 | 361 | 1,363 | ... | ... | 6 | 23 | ... | ... | 976 | 1,939 | 863 | 1,624 |
| 1903 | 558 | 1,679 | ... | ... | 31 | 105 | 6 | ... | 1,109 | 3,579 | 839 | 2,355 |
| 1904 | 404 | 2,396 | ... | ... | 28 | 55 | 31 | ... | 1,303 | 3,706 | 1,002 | 2,758 |
| 1905 | 473 | 2,469 | ... | ... | 85 | 72 | 11 | ... | 1,314 | 2,214 | 1,355 | 3,063 |
| 1906 | 437 | 2,235 | ... | ... | 41 | 100 | 25 | ... | 1,412 | 1,115 | 1,290 | 5,726 |
| 1907 | 366 | 2,529 | ... | ... | 90 | 175 | 25 | ... | 1,018 | 822 | 1,197 | 5,046 |
| 1908 | 443 | 2,646 | ... | ... | 103 | 109 | 46 | ... | 1,539 | 1,177 | 1,287 | 5,116 |
| 1909 | 482 | 2,830 | ... | ... | 36 | 26 | 69 | ... | 1,442 | 1,126 | 1,344 | 5,012 |
| 1910 | 407 | 3,962 | ... | ... | 13 | 83 | 62 | ... | 1,170 | 1,217 | 1,347 | 5,699 |
| 1911 | 533 | 3,928 | ... | ... | 29 | 92 | 80 | ... | 1,550 | 1,310 | 1,815 | 7,271 |
| 1912 | 665 | 5,156 | ... | ... | 13 | 32 | 56 | ... | 1,908[8] | 1,015[8] | 2,628 | 6,642 |
| 1913 | 661 | 4,028 | 2.0 | 7.9 | 0.2 | 54 | 88 | ... | 1,660 | 1,672 | 2,407 | 6,692 |
| 1914 | 488 | 6,536 | 1.4 | 17 | 2.5 | 18 | 97 | ... | 1,284 | 1,489 | 2,023 | 6,655 |
| 1915 | 40 | ... | ... | ... | ... | ... | 56 | ... | 967 | ... | 2,474 | ... |
| 1916 | 1.7 | 96 | 3.9 | 13 | 3.4 | 68 | 114 | ... | 1,339 | 168 | 3,587 | 10,256 |
| 1917 | 0.1 | ... | ... | 30 | ... | 30 | ... | ... | 1,680 | ... | 4,260 | ... |
| 1918 | - - | — | 0.6 | 147 | 0.6 | 19 | 204 | ... | 1,560 | 202 | 3,455 | 21,094 |
| 1919 | ... | 24 | ... | ... | ... | ... | ... | ... | 1,610 | 160 | 9,064 | 8,340 |
| 1920 | 370 | 139 | 43 | 16 | 29 | 31 | 633 | ... | 1,939 | 753 | 7,783 | 11,623 |
| 1921 | 215 | 408 | 5.8 | 7.7 | 6.4 | 13 | 166 | 12 | 1,239 | 164 | 5,901 | 3,297 |
| 1922 | 190 | 1,374 | 9.3 | 13 | 0.8 | 8.7 | 294 | 19 | 1,307 | 205 | 5,973 | 3,748 |
| 1923 | 606 | 824 | 8.3 | 11 | - - | 24 | 328 | ... | 1,603 | 115 | 6,771 | 6,518 |
| 1924 | 1,350 | 4,492 | 13 | 52 | 26 | 51 | ... | ... | 1,815 | 196 | 8,497 | 6,333 |
| | | | | | (thousand colones) | | | | | | | |
| 1925 | 2,736 | 9,879 | 15 | 13 | 76 | 29 | 708 | 15 | 4,190 | 1,471 | 26,180 | 5,613 |
| 1926 | 2,291 | ... | ... | ... | ... | ... | ... | ... | 2,619 | ... | 21,407 | 9,123 |
| 1927 | 2,378 | 9,462 | 13 | 23 | ... | 221 | 762 | 4 | 4,795 | 295 | 14,980 | 3,130 |
| 1928 | 3,895 | 14,214 | 21 | 2.8 | 221 | 274 | 1,315 | 4 | 4,967 | 230 | 20,161 | 7,435 |
| 1929 | 3,067 | 11,705 | 133 | 20 | 199 | 337 | 793 | 3 | 5,175 | 429 | 18,438 | 7,922 |
| 1930 | 2,200 | 8,021 | 332 | 118 | 74 | 191 | 816 | 3 | 3,133 | 149 | 11,726 | 6,396 |
| 1931 | 1,267 | 6,471 | 227 | 197 | 58 | 83 | 360 | 1 | 1,790 | 97 | 7,444 | 3,435 |
| 1932 | 1,292 | 4,634 | 83 | 138 | 67 | 157 | 353 | — | 1,407 | 35 | 6,412 | 2,414 |
| 1933 | 2,028 | 5,265 | 97 | 91 | 87 | 317 | 574 | — | 2,235 | 24 | 7,383 | 4,245 |
| 1934 | 1,888 | 7,342 | 186 | 106 | 369 | 208 | 2,284 | 3 | 2,769 | 27 | 9,594 | 6,464 |
| 1935 | 5,569 | 3,529 | 377 | 176 | 463 | 235 | 20 | 9 | 3,116 | 897 | 8,710 | 13,086 |
| 1936 | 6,769 | 3,601 | 306 | 194 | 260 | 291 | 18 | 5.8 | 2,242 | 237 | 7,757 | 14,502 |
| 1937 | 7,772 | 4,329 | 264 | 231 | 416 | 567 | 35 | 8.2 | 2,835 | 430 | 10,085 | 23,532 |
| 1938 | 4,815 | 2,698 | 217 | 269 | 672 | 1,007 | 7.2 | 9.2 | 2,083 | 378 | 10,687 | 16,897 |
| 1939 | 3,871 | 2,853 | 194 | 1,040 | 629 | 1,318 | 9.9 | 10 | 1,520 | 58 | 11,720 | 19,068 |
| 1940 | 266 | — | 177 | 429 | 679 | 1,295 | 26 | 4.7 | 1,536 | 70 | 13,671 | 22,991 |
| 1941 | 55 | — | 402 | 1,001 | 608 | 1,383 | 13 | — | 974 | 82 | 16,182 | 22,138 |
| 1942 | 5.6 | — | 2,053 | 1,982 | 910 | 1,910 | 1.3 | — | 996 | 83 | 14,340 | 37,749 |
| 1943 | 18 | — | 1,439 | 2,185 | 1,008 | 2,735 | — | — | 1,408 | 328 | 20,170 | 45,280 |
| 1944 | — | — | 400 | 1,206 | 1,800 | 2,812 | 0.7 | — | 773 | 77 | 20,975 | 41,976 |
| 1945 | — | — | 474 | 1,267 | 2,093 | 1,799 | 0.3 | — | 786 | 228 | 22,897 | 45,128 |
| 1946 | - - | — | 717 | 2,847 | 2,671 | 5,062 | 0.1 | — | 1,462 | 176 | 37,375 | 46,701 |
| 1947 | 0.2 | — | 653 | 2,936 | 3,234 | 4,449 | — | — | 2,304 | 93 | 72,264 | 77,610 |
| 1948 | 31 | 16 | 353 | 5,242 | 5,142 | 4,398 | 14 | — | 3,795 | 47 | 76,218 | 88,161 |
| 1949 | 649 | 103 | 469 | 4,442 | 4,020 | 4,103 | 146 | — | 2,977 | 339 | 73,350 | 114,898 |

## E2 NORTH AMERICA: External Trade (in Current Values) with Main Trading Partners

### EL SALVADOR (million colones)

| | Germany | | Guatemala | | Honduras | | Japan | | UK | | USA | |
|---|---|---|---|---|---|---|---|---|---|---|---|---|
| | Imports | Exports | Imports | Exports | Imports | Exports | Imports | Exports | Imports | Exports | Imports | Exports |
| 1950 | 3.5 | 0.1 | 0.7 | 3.5 | 5.3 | 2.6 | 1.0 | - - | 4.2 | 3.2 | 82 | 150 |
| 1951 | 6.7 | 0.2 | 1.0 | 1.2 | 7.9 | 4.4 | 2.5 | 1.8 | 6.1 | 3.2 | 100 | 184 |
| 1952 | 7.2 | 7.3 | 2.4 | 1.2 | 6.8 | 3.0 | 2.3 | 0.1 | 7.9 | 1.8 | 106 | 185 |
| 1953 | 9.0 | 13 | 3.9 | 2.3 | 10 | 3.2 | 2.9 | 1.4 | 6.2 | 2.8 | 112 | 182 |
| 1954 | 13 | 28 | 3.4 | 2.9 | 10 | 4.7 | 3.9 | 4.7 | 7.4 | 8.5 | 128 | 189 |
| 1955 | 18 | 45 | 4.5 | 3.0 | 10 | 4.7 | 6.3 | 12 | 7.9 | 4.9 | 131 | 172 |
| 1956 | 21 | 83 | 4.7 | 6.1 | 14 | 3.6 | 13 | 31 | 11 | 7.3 | 138 | 125 |
| 1957 | 23 | 105 | 6.2 | 5.9 | 12 | 5.9 | 17 | 17 | 13 | 4.6 | 148 | 158 |
| 1958 | 25 | 94 | 7.6 | 7.4 | 16 | 8.6 | 13 | 32 | 12 | 3.0 | 131 | 115 |
| 1959 | 22 | 79 | 11 | 10 | 16 | 10 | 12 | 42 | 10 | 4.5 | 110 | 101 |
| 1960 | 31 | 97 | 13 | 15 | 16 | 9.9 | 23 | 34 | 12 | 1.6 | 131 | 102 |
| 1961 | 27 | 91 | 17 | 19 | 16 | 12 | 19 | 47 | 11 | 0.3 | 107 | 101 |
| 1962 | 30 | 88 | 21 | 19 | 26 | 15 | 22 | 65 | 12 | 0.7 | 114 | 115 |
| 1963 | 34 | 88 | 32 | 41 | 27 | 21 | 25 | 96 | 15 | 0.2 | 128 | 95 |
| 1964 | 38₂ | 116₂ | 41 | 48 | 33 | 26 | 32 | 85 | 18 | 0.7 | 166 | 114 |
| 1965 | 42 | 110 | 46 | 51 | 39 | 35 | 45 | 77 | 21 | 1.6 | 156 | 117 |
| 1966 | 44 | 117 | 68 | 59 | 33 | 42 | 36 | 54 | 20 | 0.5 | 180 | 119 |
| 1967 | 40 | 116 | 75 | 82 | 31 | 50 | 42 | 40 | 34 | 0.8 | 174 | 138 |
| 1968 | 33 | 103 | 86 | 77 | 37 | 59 | 40 | 37 | 14 | 0.8 | 155 | 103 |
| 1969 | 37 | 112 | 95 | 90 | 18 | 32 | 45 | 50 | 14 | 0.5 | 153 | 108 |
| 1970 | 42 | 141 | 102 | 99 | — | — | 55 | 63 | 16 | 0.8 | 158 | 122 |
| 1971 | 51 | 113 | 105 | 111 | — | — | 73 | 73 | 18 | 1.1 | 175 | 130 |
| 1972 | 55 | 161 | 119 | 137 | — | — | 77 | 97 | 22 | 5.0 | 191 | 111 |
| 1973 | 71 | 118 | 149 | 159 | — | — | 91 | 89 | 24 | 1.6 | 273 | 299 |
| 1974 | 98 | 157 | 176 | 204 | — | — | 111 | 76 | 27 | 4.0 | 434 | 303 |
| 1975 | 89 | 161 | 211 | 199 | — | — | 103 | 150 | 40 | 29 | 470 | 348 |
| 1976 | 105 | 258 | 265 | 249 | — | — | 174 | 142 | 44 | 3.6 | 513 | 588 |
| 1977 | 136 | 449 | 320 | 305 | — | — | 261 | 156 | 72 | 9.9 | 692 | 795 |
| 1978 | 134 | 203 | 375 | 361 | — | — | 305 | 137 | 59 | 8.3 | 793 | 311 |
| 1979 | 122 | 519 | 452 | 438 | — | — | 205 | 157 | 51 | 12 | 737 | 745 |
| 1980 | 72 | 121 | 634 | 434 | — | — | 107 | 86 | 33 | 9.3 | 614 | 534 |
| 1981 | 92 | 230 | 619 | 352 | 0.9 | 3.5 | 84 | 84 | 23 | 4.5 | 625 | 255 |
| 1982 | 100 | 170 | 525 | 329 | 20 | 9.6 | 67 | 54 | 13 | 2.0 | 583 | 269 |
| 1983 | 91 | 350 | 431 | 308 | 38 | 18 | 78 | 92 | 23 | 0.7 | 724 | 715 |
| 1984 | 109 | 325 | 467 | 292 | 42 | 17 | 102 | 83 | 26 | 4.4 | 786 | 517 |
| 1985 | 108 | 321 | 469 | 293 | 42 | 20 | 105 | 81 | 28 | 3.3 | 813 | 542 |
| 1986 | 212 | 860 | 544 | 239 | 46 | 38 | 166 | 134 | 50 | 5.7 | 1,525 | 1,759 |
| 1987 | 249 | 509 | 640 | 364 | 51 | 47 | 312 | 128 | 53 | 14 | 1,835 | 1,331 |
| 1988 | 207 | 632 | 625 | 461 | 68 | 63 | 244 | 132 | 80 | 23 | 1,850 | 1,122 |

**E2     NORTH AMERICA: External Trade (in Current Values) with Main Trading Partners**

**GUATEMALA** (thousand gold pesos to 1919, million quetzales subsequently)

| | El Salvador | | Germany | | Japan | | UK | | USA | |
|---|---|---|---|---|---|---|---|---|---|---|
| | Imports | Exports | Imports | Exports | Imports | Exports | Imports | Exports | Imports | Exports |
| 1911 | - - | ... | 1,593 | ... | ... | ... | 1,314 | ... | 2,696 | ... |
| 1912 | ... | ... | 2,251 | 6,975 | ... | ... | 1,276 | 1,710 | 4,532 | 3,864 |
| 1913 | ... | ... | 2,043 | 7,654 | ... | ... | 1,650 | 1,857 | 5,053 | 3,924 |
| 1914 | ... | ... | ... | ... | ... | ... | ... | ... | ... | ... |
| | ... | ... | | | | | | ... | | |
| 1915 | ... | ... | 146 | 50 | ... | ... | 577 | 1,322 | 3,752 | 6,889 |
| 1916 | ... | ... | 5.2 | 92 | ... | ... | 1,062 | 86 | 5,228 | 8,669 |
| 1917 | ... | ... | — | — | ... | ... | 1,462 | 1,229 | 6,386 | 5,359 |
| 1918 | ... | ... | — | — | ... | ... | 1,438 | 1,137 | 5,813 | 4,582 |
| 1919 | ... | ... | — | — | ... | ... | 3,672 | 1,534 | 9,088 | 19,187 |
| | | | | | (million quetzales) | | | | | |
| 1920 | ... | ... | 0.8 | 0.1 | 0.3 | — | 3.9 | 0.5 | 12 | 15 |
| 1921 | ... | ... | 1.4 | 1.8 | 0.1 | — | 2.4 | 0.1 | 8.2 | 8.1 |
| 1922 | ... | ... | 1.2 | 1.9 | 0.2 | - - | 1.6 | 0.3 | 6.6 | 7.9 |
| 1923 | ... | ... | 1.6 | 2.1 | 0.4 | - - | 2.1 | 0.4 | 8.1 | 11 |
| 1924 | ... | ... | 1.5 | 8.3 | 0.3 | — | 1.9 | 0.8 | 9.1 | 12 |
| 1925 | ... | ... | 2.0 | 9.3 | 0.5 | — | 2.3 | 0.5 | 11 | 15 |
| 1926 | ... | ... | 3.5 | 9.2 | 0.4 | — | 3.5 | 0.5 | 15 | 16 |
| 1927 | ... | ... | 3.5 | 13 | 0.7 | — | 2.8 | 0.3 | 14 | 14 |
| 1928 | ... | ... | 4.2 | 9.4 | 0.5 | — | 3.2 | 0.2 | 17 | 15 |
| 1929 | ... | ... | 3.4 | 9.9 | 0.3 | - - | 1.3 | 0.2 | 14 | 11 |
| 1930 | ... | ... | 1.6 | 8.3 | 0.3 | - - | 2.1 | 0.7 | 7.6 | 9.2 |
| 1931 | ... | ... | 1.3 | 5.0 | 0.2 | — | 0.9 | 0.3 | 5.5 | 5.4 |
| 1932 | ... | ... | 0.7 | 3.0 | 0.1 | — | 0.6 | 0.5 | 3.0 | 4.0 |
| 1933 | ... | ... | 0.7 | 3.2 | 0.2 | - - | 0.8 | 0.2 | 3.0 | 3.2 |
| 1934 | ... | ... | 0.9 | 5.5 | 0.5 | - - | 0.7 | 0.4 | 4.1 | 4.5 |
| 1935 | ... | ... | 2.2 | 2.8 | 0.5 | - - | 1.1 | - - | 4.0 | 6.5 |
| 1936 | ... | ... | 3.6 | 2.8 | 0.1 | - - | 1.1 | 0.3 | 4.9 | 9.0 |
| 1937 | ... | ... | 5.4 | 2.8 | 0.1 | - - | 1.4 | 0.1 | 7.6 | 10 |
| 1938 | ... | ... | 5.9 | 2.3 | - - | - - | 1.0 | 0.1 | 7.5 | 11 |
| 1939 | - - | 0.1 | 4.1 | 1.9 | - - | - - | 0.6 | 0.1 | 8.3 | 12 |
| 1940 | 0.1 | 0.1 | 0.4 | - - | 0.1 | - - | 0.2 | 0.2 | 9.4 | 11 |
| 1941 | ... | ... | - - | - - | ... | ... | 0.5 | ... | 13 | 13 |
| 1942 | ... | ... | ... | ... | ... | ... | ... | ... | ... | ... |
| 1943 | ... | ... | ... | ... | ... | ... | ... | ... | ... | ... |
| 1944 | ... | ... | ... | ... | ... | ... | ... | ... | ... | ... |
| 1945 | ... | ... | ... | ... | ... | ... | ... | ... | ... | ... |
| 1946 | 0.9 | 0.2 | ... | ... | ... | ... | 0.5 | ... | 25 | 32 |
| 1947 | 0.9 | 0.3 | ... | ... | ... | ... | 0.8 | 0.7 | 43 | 45 |
| 1948 | 1.6 | 0.1 | - - | - - | ... | ... | 1.5 | 0.2 | 52 | 45 |
| 1949 | 1.6 | 0.1 | 0.7$_2$ | 0.2$_2$ | 0.1 | ... | 1.2 | ... | 50 | 48 |

**E2      NORTH AMERICA: External Trade (in Current Values) with Main Trading Partners**

**GUATEMALA** (million quetzales)

|      | El Salvador | | West Germany | | Japan | | UK | | USA | |
|      | Imports | Exports | Imports | Exports | Imports | Exports | Imports | Exports | Imports | Exports |
|------|---------|---------|---------|---------|---------|---------|---------|---------|---------|---------|
| 1950 | 1.6 | 0.1 | 2.0 | 0.2 | 0.2 | ... | 1.7 | ... | 49 | 60 |
| 1951 | 0.2 | 0.3 | 3.8 | 0.8 | ... | ... | 3.2 | - - | 54 | 67 |
| 1952 | 0.2 | 0.9 | 3.9 | 2.0 | ... | ... | 4.1 | 1.5 | 48 | 73 |
| 1953 | 0.5 | 1.5 | 4.3 | 7.6 | ... | ... | 2.7 | - - | 51 | 68 |
| 1954 | 0.8 | 1.5 | 6.5 | 7.9 | 0.3 | 0.2 | 3.4 | 0.7 | 56 | 68 |
| 1955 | 0.8 | 1.7 | 7.4 | 3.1 | 0.6 | 0.9 | 4.0 | 0.6 | 70 | 73 |
| 1956 | 0.8 | 1.4 | 8.5 | 10 | 0.8 | 0.8 | 5.0 | 0.7 | 93 | 83 |
| 1957 | 1.0 | 2.4 | 12 | 14 | 0.9 | 0.6 | 6.8 | 0.7 | 89 | 73 |
| 1958 | 1.3 | 2.9 | 15 | 16 | 1.3 | 2.6 | 7.8 | 0.7 | 89 | 66 |
| 1959 | 2.2 | 4.0 | 14 | 18 | 3.0 | 2.3 | 6.3 | 0.9 | 74 | 63 |
| 1960 | 5.9 | 4.4 | 17 | 23 | 6.1 | 5.5 | 5.6 | 0.8 | 68 | 63 |
| 1961 | 6.8 | 6.2 | 15 | 19 | 6.5 | 8.5 | 5.9 | 1.2 | 64 | 59 |
| 1962 | 4.7 | 6.2 | 14 | 21 | 7.1 | 11 | 6.9 | 1.2 | 65 | 56 |
| 1963 | 16 | 11 | 17 | 24 | 9.0 | 16 | 7.3 | 3.0 | 80 | 67 |
| 1964 | 19 | 17 | 22 | 26 | 12 | 17 | 7.6 | 3.7 | 90 | 54 |
| 1965 | 22 | 20 | 22 | 25 | 15 | 21 | 11 | 1.6 | 97 | 68 |
| 1966 | 24 | 28 | 18 | 30 | 15 | 19 | 9.9 | 1.6 | 87 | 70 |
| 1967 | 29 | 29 | 25 | 24 | 22 | 17 | 9.5 | 1.2 | 101 | 62 |
| 1968 | 28 | 32 | 26 | 20 | 23 | 24 | 12 | 2.2 | 102 | 62 |
| 1969 | 33 | 35 | 26 | 26 | 26 | 21 | 10 | 1.9 | 86 | 73 |
| 1970 | 39 | 39 | 27 | 33 | 29 | 20 | 10 | 1.8 | 100 | 82 |
| 1971 | 43 | 41 | 31 | 31 | 32 | 19 | 14 | 2.6 | 98 | 88 |
| 1972 | 46 | 45 | 30 | 34 | 28 | 27 | 14 | 3.2 | 105 | 96 |
| 1973 | 57 | 56 | 41 | 41 | 43 | 25 | 15 | 8.8 | 136 | 146 |
| 1974 | 73 | 65 | 57 | 63 | 63 | 29 | 19 | 8.6 | 223 | 188 |
| 1975 | 60 | 75 | 55 | 62 | 65 | 32 | 24 | 51 | 252 | 144 |
| 1976 | 59 | 84 | 59 | 81 | 93 | 63 | 26 | 3.3 | 306 | 267 |
| 1977 | 45 | 106 | 79 | 159 | 121 | 90 | 31 | 4.1 | 367 | 384 |
| 1978 | 114 | 120 | 107 | 138 | 130 | 73 | 30 | 10 | 381 | 339 |
| 1979 | 105 | 148 | 106 | 103 | 125 | 94 | 33 | 15 | 473 | 309 |
| 1980 | 61 | 182 | 89 | 119 | 129 | 49 | 35 | 69 | 525 | 426 |
| 1981 | 97 | 179 | 104 | 82 | 113 | 50 | 26 | 13 | 551 | 294 |
| 1982 | 117 | 180 | 72 | 76 | 76 | 55 | 17 | 18 | 466 | 296 |
| 1983 | 102 | 158 | 66 | 59 | 60 | 42 | 13 | 13 | 401 | 407 |
| 1984 | 95 | 174 | 75 | 59 | 68 | 49 | 19 | 12 | 424 | 419 |
| 1985 | 49 | 121 | 81 | 65 | 56 | 36 | 20 | 3.5 | 404 | 359 |
| 1986 | 71 | 149 | 108 | 126 | 84 | 66 | 20 | 11 | 646 | 713 |
| 1987 | 184 | 335 | 232 | 179 | 237 | 46 | 71 | 23 | 1,413 | 1,015 |
| 1988 | 212 | 334 | 265 | 247 | 258 | 65 | 83 | 32 | 1,543 | 761 |

E2      **NORTH AMERICA: External Trade (in Current Values) with Main Trading Partners**

**HONDURAS** (thousand pesos to 1938, thousand lempiras subsequently)[5]

| | El Salvador | | Germany | | Guatemala | | Japan | | UK | | USA | |
|---|---|---|---|---|---|---|---|---|---|---|---|---|
| | Imports | Exports | Imports | Exports | Imports | Exports | Imports | Exports | Imports | Exports | Imports | Exports |
| 1913 | ... | 106 | 1,116 | 352 | 122 | 220 | ... | ... | 1,426 | 26 | 6,914 | 5,530 |
| 1914 | ... | ... | 522 | 165 | 54 | 181 | 34 | — | 460 | 53 | 5,262 | 2,974 |
| 1915 | ... | ... | 96 | 0.7 | 89 | 45 | ... | ... | 327 | 14 | 5,177 | 3,041 |
| 1916 | ... | ... | ... | ... | ... | ... | ... | ... | ... | ... | ... | ... |
| 1917 | ... | ... | ... | ... | ... | ... | ... | ... | ... | ... | ... | ... |
| 1918 | ... | ... | ... | ... | ... | ... | ... | ... | ... | ... | ... | ... |
| 1919 | ... | ... | ... | ... | ... | ... | ... | ... | ... | ... | ... | ... |
| 1920 | ... | — | 36 | — | ... | 40 | ... | ... | 1,600 | 8 | 22,494 | 13,332 |
| 1921 | ... | ... | 636 | ... | ... | ... | ... | ... | 2,792 | ... | 28,058 | ... |
| 1922 | ... | ... | 1,098 | 80 | 54 | 22 | 352 | — | 1,110 | 132 | 21,714 | 9,392 |
| 1923 | ... | ... | 1,634 | ... | ... | ... | ... | — | 1,252 | ... | 24,032 | 17,940 |
| 1924 | ... | ... | 398 | 20 | ... | ... | 18 | — | 802 | ... | 19,568 | 14,372 |
| 1925 | 26 | 2 | 616 | 56 | 126 | 14 | 76 | — | 1,592 | 408 | 20,528 | 22,144 |
| 1926 | 32 | — | 772 | 1,104 | 138 | 14 | 56 | — | 1,286 | 2,956 | 16,236 | 20,614 |
| 1927 | 226 | ... | 912 | 864 | 92 | 110 | 64 | — | 1,504 | 4,270 | 16,890 | 26,972 |
| 1928 | 282 | 2 | 1,002 | 3,400 | 132 | 116 | 100 | — | 1,500 | 5,234 | 20,058 | 35,294 |
| 1929 | 278 | 864 | 1,246 | 5,894 | 122 | 166 | 142 | — | 1,676 | 3,958 | 23,126 | 36,546 |
| 1930 | 322 | 904 | 1,460 | 7,018 | 144 | 282 | 184 | — | 1,862 | 3,906 | 23,772 | 38,704 |
| 1931 | 126 | 678 | 1,208 | 6,432 | 48 | 76 | 80 | — | 965 | 2,404 | 14,736 | 29,000 |
| 1932 | 70 | 394 | 608 | 3,408 | 46 | 56 | 84 | — | 668 | 4,032 | 12,752 | 23,762 |
| 1933 | 36 | 250 | 568 | 3,716 | 44 | 12 | 136 | — | 642 | 2,904 | 9,288 | 19,342 |
| 1934 | 118 | 542 | 552 | 2,578 | 22 | 22 | 536 | — | 900 | 1,888 | 11,764 | 17,782 |
| 1935 | 204 | 704 | 650 | 458 | 46 | 16 | 2,028 | — | 1,210 | 254 | 12,378 | 17,416 |
| 1936 | 234 | 394 | 1,090 | 384 | 42 | 38 | 1,334 | — | 620 | 1,050 | 11,592 | 15,038 |
| 1937 | 504 | 304 | 1,980 | 260 | 36 | 52 | 3,032 | 4 | 684 | 116 | 12,058 | 17,126 |
| 1938 | [640][5] | [442][5] | [2,096][5] | [414][5] | [18][5] | [96][5] | [1,752][5] | [46][5] | [572][5] | [284][5] | [11,742][5] | [12,724][5] |
| | | | | | | (thousand lempiras) | | | | | | |
| 1939 | ... | ... | ... | ... | ... | ... | ... | ... | ... | ... | ... | ... |
| 1940 | ... | ... | ... | ... | ... | ... | ... | ... | ... | ... | ... | ... |
| 1941 | ... | ... | ... | ... | ... | ... | ... | ... | ... | ... | ... | ... |
| 1942 | 1,608 | 678 | 13 | — | 125 | 44 | 97 | — | 272 | — | 18,265 | 18,121 |
| 1943 | 1,791 | 1,027 | — | — | 233 | 126 | — | — | 349 | — | 14,842 | 6,989 |
| 1944 | 3,107 | 1,739 | — | — | 267 | 237 | 0.6 | — | 391 | — | 17,791 | 16,161 |
| 1945 | 1,974 | 2,192 | — | — | 420 | 276 | 0.1 | — | 284 | - - | 21,516 | 20,190 |
| 1946 | 3,107 | 2,855 | — | — | 81 | 199 | — | — | 410 | — | 28,778 | 21,160 |
| 1947 | 3,539 | 3,257 | 8.8 | 9.1 | 86 | 436 | — | — | 608 | 117 | 45,583 | 22,304 |
| 1948 | 3,632 | 4,436 | - - | — | 73 | 300 | 2.5 | — | 756 | — | 56,031 | 28,450 |
| 1949 | 4,176 | 5,695 | 5.2 | 29 | 127 | 588 | 13 | — | 973 | 378 | 53,885 | 29,361 |

**E2     NORTH AMERICA: External Trade (in Current Values) with Main Trading Partners**

**HONDURAS** (million lempiras)[5]

| | El Salvador | | Germany | | Guatemala | | Japan | | UK | | USA | |
|---|---|---|---|---|---|---|---|---|---|---|---|---|
| | Imports | Exports | Imports | Exports | Imports | Exports | Imports | Exports | Imports | Exports | Imports | Exports |
| 1950 | 3.5 | 6.1 | 0.2 | - - | 0.2 | 0.3 | 0.2 | — | 1.3 | 0.9 | 54 | 30 |
| 1951 | 3.6₅ | 7.1₅ | 1.4₅ | 0.1₅ | 0.3₅ | 0.4₅ | 1.5₅ | - -₅ | 2₅ | - -₅ | 58₅ | 34₅ |
| 1952 | 2.8 | 7.4 | 2.3 | 1.5 | 0.9 | 0.2 | 1.3 | - - | 3.8 | 0.1 | 85 | 94 |
| 1953 | 2.9 | 7.9 | 4.5 | 0.6 | 0.6 | 0.4 | 2.5 | - - | 2.9 | 0.1 | 77 | 106 |
| 1954 | 3 | 7.3 | 6.4 | 0.8 | - - | 0.3 | 4.1 | - - | 3 | 0.4 | 71 | 86 |
| 1955 | 3.5 | 8 | 6.8 | 6.5 | - - | 1.1 | 5.3 | - - | 2.8 | 0.6 | 72 | 66 |
| 1956 | 2.6 | 12 | 7.5 | 8.5 | 0.1 | 0.7 | 6.2 | - - | 2.9 | 1.5 | 79 | 96 |
| 1957 | 4.5 | 10 | 9.2₂ | 8.6₂ | 0.2 | 1.6 | 8.6 | - - | 3.4 | 1 | 88 | 83 |
| 1958 | 7.2 | 11 | 9.2 | 7.3 | 0.5 | 2 | 8 | 3.8 | 3.4 | 1.2 | 78 | 86 |
| 1959 | 7.5 | 13 | 9.2 | 12 | 0.6 | 2.6 | 10 | 5 | 3.9 | 1.4 | 66 | 73 |
| 1960 | 8.2 | 13 | 11 | 9 | 2.2 | 3.2 | 8.8 | 1.5 | 5.4 | 2.1 | 80 | 72 |
| 1961 | 9.3 | 12 | 8.9 | 7.9 | 3.1 | 4.1 | 11 | 0.8 | 4.2 | 1.7 | 75 | 96 |
| 1962 | 11 | 18 | 9.7 | 11 | 6 | 6.1 | 9.6 | 0.6 | 4.8 | 1.5 | 83 | 93 |
| 1963 | 16 | 18 | 10 | 16 | 9.2 | 6.1 | 17 | 2.6 | 5.6 | 1.4 | 91 | 98 |
| 1964 | 18 | 22 | 13 | 20 | 12 | 7.8 | 11 | 6.9 | 6.4 | 1.1 | 99 | 99 |
| 1965 | 25 | 26 | 14 | 28 | 16 | 10 | 13 | 9.8 | 7.6 | 1.1 | 115 | 148 |
| 1966 | 34 | 21 | 16 | 45 | 20 | 9.4 | 11 | 7.3 | 8.9 | 0.9 | 148 | 164 |
| 1967 | 40 | 23 | 18 | 69 | 24 | 13 | 15 | 8.8 | 9.1 | 1.1 | 159 | 143 |
| 1968 | 46 | 28 | 17 | 67 | 28 | 14 | 20 | 14 | 9.2 | 1.4 | 170 | 162 |
| 1969 | 25 | 14 | 24 | 42 | 36 | 12 | 24 | 19 | 9.5 | 1.8 | 161 | 164 |
| 1970 | — | — | 24 | 37 | 57 | 14 | 36 | 4.9 | 12 | 1.3 | 183 | 185 |
| 1971 | — | — | 21 | 45 | 16 | 4.7 | 44 | 1.6 | 13 | 1.5 | 183 | 238 |
| 1972 | — | — | 20 | 53 | 19 | 3.2 | 30 | 11 | 14 | 1.4 | 170 | 218 |
| 1973 | — | — | 22 | 58 | 32 | 5.1 | 53 | 21 | 13 | 1.9 | 214 | 276 |
| 1974 | — | — | 37 | 55 | 42 | 14 | 53 | 19 | 17 | 1.2 | 308 | 243 |
| 1975 | — | — | 28 | 66 | 47 | 23 | 53 | 24 | 24 | 1.2 | 342 | 304 |
| 1976 | — | — | 42 | 93 | 53 | 32 | 80 | 25 | 19 | 0.7 | 396 | 444 |
| 1977 | — | — | 41 | 196 | 66 | 43 | 127 | 56 | 29 | 2.0 | 497 | 502 |
| 1978 | — | — | 49 | 152 | 88 | 51 | 124 | 29 | 38 | 12 | 586 | 692 |
| 1979 | — | — | 47 | 143 | 102 | 63 | 128 | 60 | 41 | 19 | 716 | 842 |
| 1980 | — | — | 57 | 204 | 115 | 75 | 199 | 68 | 43 | 44 | 952 | 863 |
| 1981 | 3 | 4.5 | 69 | 114 | 122 | 61 | 126 | 91 | 35 | 13 | 784 | 784 |
| 1982 | 7.5 | 20 | 45 | 117 | 92 | 50 | 90 | 77 | 28 | 11 | 547 | 692 |
| 1983 | 16 | 28 | 56 | 70 | 117 | 56 | 73 | 79 | 30 | 18 | 592 | 727 |
| 1984 | 18 | 27 | 74 | 74 | 82 | 23 | 88 | 116 | 30 | 32 | 648 | 756 |
| 1985 | 21 | 16 | 70 | 117 | 88 | 7.9 | 103 | 103 | 31 | 40 | 636 | 739 |
| 1986 | 27 | 15 | 62 | 182 | 74 | 16 | 152 | 158 | 28 | 29 | 665 | 807 |
| 1987 | 25 | 21 | 60 | 169 | 55 | 21 | 177 | 79 | 34 | 25 | 705 | 900 |
| 1988 | 27 | 19 | 64 | 183 | 68 | 20 | 173 | 123 | 32 | 28 | 721 | 894 |

**E2      NORTH AMERICA: External Trade (in Current Values) with Main Trading Partners**

## JAMAICA (thousand pounds)[6]

| | UK | | USA | | | UK | | USA | |
|---|---|---|---|---|---|---|---|---|---|
| | Imports | Exports | Imports | Exports | | Imports | Exports | Imports | Exports |
| 1850 | ... | 910 | ... | 70 | 1900 | 815 | 339 | 717 | 1,146 |
| 1851 | ... | 732 | ... | 87 | 1901 | 858 | 410 | 733 | 1,273 |
| 1852 | ... | 733 | ... | 66 | 1902 | 1,029 | 437 | 811 | 1,560 |
| 1853 | ... | 627 | ... | 93 | 1903 | 948 | 282 | 857 | 908 |
| 1854 | ... | 769 | ... | 90 | 1904 | 788 | 271 | 719 | 768 |
| 1855 | 550 | 788 | 191 | 130 | 1905 | 950 | 357 | 756 | 1,058 |
| 1856 | 565 | 678 | 224 | 154 | 1906 | 1,126 | 430 | 864 | 1,139 |
| 1857 | 448 | 965 | 221 | ·155 | 1907 | 1,382 | 510 | 1,268 | 1,401 |
| 1858 | 700 | 1,016 | 231 | 82 | 1908 | 1,003[6] | 489[6] | 1,132[6] | 1,312[6] |
| 1859 | 494 | 800 | 220 | 95 | 1909 | 1,126 | 557 | 1,164 | 1,617 |
| 1860 | 701 | 991 | 299 | 158 | 1910 | 1,113 | 530 | 1,182 | 1,391 |
| 1861 | 606 | 1,045 | 285 | 92 | 1911 | 1,292 | 434 | 1,200 | 1,826 |
| 1862 | 603 | 926 | 330 | 97 | 1912 | 1,333 | 359 | 1,273 | 1,619 |
| 1863 | 581 | 845 | 344 | 52 | 1913 | 1,088 | 424 | 1,327 | 1,396 |
| 1864 | 628 | 814 | 322 | 65 | 1914 | 986 | 530 | 1,221 | 1,769 |
| 1865 | 643 | 723 | 271 | 74 | 1915 | 772 | 849 | 1,258 | 1,043 |
| 1866 | 684 | 971 | 206 | 101 | 1916 | 1,009 | 1,226 | 1,783 | 921 |
| 1867 | 534 | 841 | 192 | 92 | 1917 | 624 | 1,112 | 2,329 | 695 |
| 1868 | 624 | 938 | 205 | 103 | 1918 | 548 | 1,348 | 2,281 | 628 |
| 1869 | 775 | 849 | 267 | 142 | 1919 | 1,013 | 3,567 | 3,365 | 1,343 |
| 1870 | 760 | 898 | 267 | 61 | 1920 | 3,062 | 2,963 | 6,041 | 1,794 |
| 1871 | 777 | 1,030 | 312 | 104 | 1921 | 1,601 | 953 | 2,991 | 1,425 |
| 1872 | 933 | 1,153 | 366 | 150 | 1922 | 1,302 | 1,065 | 2,092 | 2,066 |
| 1873 | 1,045 | 999 | 427 | 103 | 1923 | 1,524 | 1,241[6] | 2,337 | 2,109[6] |
| | | | | | | | 1,219 | | 2,102 |
| 1874 | 1,017 | 1,141 | 453 | 153 | 1924 | 1,437 | 770 | 1,956 | 1,355 |
| 1875 | 966 | 1,154 | 540 | 163 | 1925 | 1,631 | 1,022 | 2,143 | 1,586 |
| 1876 | 968 | 1,228 | 468 | 152 | 1926 | 1,377 | 892 | 2,100 | 1,860 |
| 1877 | 833 | 1,159 | 453 | 221 | 1927 | 1,656 | 874 | 1,939 | 2,002 |
| 1878 | 757 | 955 | 471 | 171 | 1928 | 1,853 | 817 | 1,922 | 1,608 |
| 1879 | 686 | 995 | 423 | 203 | 1929 | 1,771 | 830 | 2,089 | 1,568 |
| 1880 | 778 | 1,018 | 474 | 304 | 1930 | 1,732 | 1,089 | 1,934 | 1,357 |
| 1881 | 646 | 783 | 550 | 224 | 1931 | 1,405 | 1,063 | 1,430 | 1,030 |
| 1882 | 726 | 968 | 403 | 276 | 1932 | 1,887 | 1,571 | 817 | 553 |
| 1883 | 942 | 800 | 423 | 260 | 1933 | 1,695 | 1,342 | 688 | 224 |
| 1884 | 899 | 644 | 422 | 462 | 1934 | 1,798 | 1,680 | 847 | 281 |
| 1885 | 790 | 533 | 470 | 595 | 1935 | 1,954 | 2,070 | 880 | 328 |
| 1886 | 662 | 509 | 460 | 563 | 1936 | 1,875 | 2,000 | 834 | 265 |
| 1887 | 724 | 583 | 445 | 663 | 1937 | 2,006 | 2,679 | 1,083 | 231 |
| 1888 | 1,049 | 734 | 479 | 790 | 1938 | 2,050 | 2,914 | 1,359 | 180 |
| 1889 | 884[6] | 603[6] | 545[6] | 810[6] | 1939 | 1,842 | 2,925 | 1,471 | 260 |
| 1890 | 1,232 | 615 | 738 | 1,051 | 1940 | 1,883 | 1,869 | 962 | 258 |
| 1891 | 862 | 563 | 654 | 877 | 1941 | 1,712 | 1,469 | 869 | 747 |
| 1892 | 1,001 | 512 | 677 | 955 | 1942 | 1,562 | 1,168 | 981 | 807 |
| 1893 | 1,191 | 554 | 719 | 1,190 | 1943 | 2,466 | 715 | 1,381 | 846 |
| 1894 | 1,106 | 513 | 803 | 1,128 | 1944 | 1,325 | 917 | 2,843 | 916 |
| 1895 | 1,106 | 518 | 953 | 1,067 | 1945 | 1,321 | 2,210 | 2,882 | 522 |
| 1896 | 927 | 403 | 731 | 832 | 1946 | 2,671 | 5,467 | 3,193 | 438 |
| 1897 | 777 | 318 | 720 | 897 | 1947 | 3,796 | 7,873[6] | 6,376 | 275[6] |
| | | | | | | | 7,902 | | 310 |
| 1898 | 819 | 343 | 808 | 982 | 1948 | 7,758 | 8,388 | 3,825 | 389 |
| 1899 | 873 | 358 | 801 | 1,182 | 1949 | 8,669 | 7,505 | 3,174 | 450 |

**E2     NORTH AMERICA: External Trade (in Current Values) with Main Trading Partners**

## JAMAICA (million local dollars)[6]

| | UK | | USA | | | UK | | U.S.A | |
|---|---|---|---|---|---|---|---|---|---|
| | Imports | Exports | Imports | Exports | | Imports | Exports | Imports | Exports |
| 1950 | 19 | 17 | 6.4 | 1.6 | 1970 | 84 | 46 | 192 | 149 |
| 1951 | 25 | 20 | 12 | 1.8 | 1971 | 90 | 58 | 182 | 124 |
| 1952 | 30 | 24 | 15 | 2.8 | 1972 | 94 | 65 | 184 | 128 |
| 1953 | 30 | 29 | 12 | 6.8 | 1973 | 101 | 80 | 233 | 143 |
| 1954 | 32 | 33 | 12 | 8.8 | 1974 | 105 | 102 | 300 | 308 |
| 1955 | 37 | 34 | 19 | 10 | 1975 | 134 | 172 | 382 | 274 |
| 1956 | 44 | 39 | 29 | 12 | 1976 | 90 | 99 | 308 | 236 |
| 1957 | 51 | 38 | 30 | 22 | 1977 | 76 | 139 | 281 | 308 |
| 1958 | 50 | 34 | 27 | 30 | 1978 | 131 | 264 | 464 | 392 |
| 1959 | 48 | 31 | 29 | 26 | 1979 | 172 | 277 | 555 | 647 |
| 1960 | 53 | 35 | 38 | 29 | 1980 | 140 | 333 | 659 | 641 |
| 1961 | 50 | 32 | 37 | 44 | 1981 | 168 | 321 | 952 | 687 |
| 1962 | 47 | 34 | 44 | 47 | 1982 | 192 | 251 | 869 | 459 |
| 1963 | 42 | 42 | 49 | 45 | 1983 | | | | |
| 1964 | 51 | 44 | 63 | 53 | 1984 | 245 | 378 | 2,036 | 1,392 |
| 1965 | 51 | 41 | 65 | 57 | 1985 | 327 | 526 | 2,546 | 1,040 |
| 1966 | 52 | 42 | 86 | 61 | 1986 | 361 | 620 | 2,689 | 1,109 |
| 1967 | 50 | 42 | 99 | 64 | 1987 | 465 | 682 | 3,345 | 1,448 |
| 1968 | 65 | 43 | 123 | 70 | 1988 | 543 | 865 | 3,799 | 660 |
| 1969 | 78 | 40 | 150 | 78 | | | | | |

## MEXICO (million Mexican dollars or pesos)[7]

| | France | | Germany | | UK[8] | | USA | |
|---|---|---|---|---|---|---|---|---|
| | Imports | Exports | Imports | Exports | Imports | Exports | Imports | Exports |
| 1873 | ... | 4.6 | ... | 0.8 | ... | 13.0 | ... | 11 |
| 1874 | ... | 4.1 | ... | 0.2 | ... | 9.8 | ... | 12 |
| 1875 | ... | 5.7 | ... | 0.4 | ... | 9.2 | ... | 10 |
| 1876 | ... | ... | ... | ... | ... | ... | ... | ... |
| 1877 | ... | ... | ... | ... | ... | ... | ... | ... |
| 1878 | ... | 5.4 | ... | 0.5 | ... | 10 | ... | 12 |
| 1879 | ... | 5.2 | ... | 0.6 | ... | 10 | ... | 12 |
| 1880 | ... | 5.2 | ... | 1.5 | ... | 11 | ... | 13 |
| 1881 | ... | 3.1 | ... | 1.4 | ... | 10 | ... | 14 |
| 1882 | ... | 2.2 | ... | 1.3 | ... | 10 | ... | 14 |
| 1883 | ... | 4.2 | ... | 1.1 | ... | 17 | ... | 16 |
| 1884 | ... | 2.9 | ... | 1.2 | ... | 19 | ... | 22 |
| 1885 | ... | 2.2 | ... | 1.4 | ... | 15 | ... | 26 |
| 1886 | ... | 3.9 | ... | 1.6 | ... | 12 | ... | 25 |
| 1887 | ... | 5.1 | ... | 2.2 | ... | 13 | ... | 28 |
| 1888 | ... | 4.5 | ... | 2.2 | ... | 11 | ... | 31 |
| 1889 | 5.0 | 3.5 | 2.8 | 2.1 | 6.3 | 13 | 23 | 41 |
| 1890 | 6.2 | 3.2 | 3.7 | 1.7 | 8.5 | 14 | 29 | 43 |
| 1891 | ... | 3.7 | ... | 2.8 | ... | 11 | ... | 45 |
| 1892 | ... | 4.6 | ... | 4.3 | ... | 15 | ... | 50 |
| 1893 | 4.8 | 3.7 | 2.9 | 3.3 | 5.7 | 15 | 26 | 64 |
| 1894 | 4.4 | 5.3 | 2.7 | 7.0 | 5.8 | 15 | 14 | 95 |

E2    NORTH AMERICA: External Trade (in Current Values) with Main Trading Partners

## MEXICO (million Mexican dollars or pesos)[7]

|  | France | | Germany | | Japan | | UK[8] | | USA | |
|---|---|---|---|---|---|---|---|---|---|---|
|  | Imports | Exports | Imports | Exports | Imports | Exports | Imports | Exports | Imports | Exports |
| 1895 | 5.6 | 2.4 | 3.4 | 2.8 | ... | 5.9 | 6.7 | 12 | 15 | 61 |
| 1896 | 6.1 | 2.1 | 4.4 | 3.1 | ... | 3 | 7.9 | 15 | 20 | 67 |
| 1897 | 5.0 | 2.1 | 4.0 | 3.0 | ... | 1.7 | 6.9 | 16 | 23 | 80 |
| 1898 | 5.4 | 1.9 | 4.8 | 4.4 | ... | 2.1 | 8.1 | 14 | 22 | 87 |
| 1899 | 5.9 | 6.3 | 5.7 | 4.0 | ... | ... | 9.2 | 14 | 24 | 104 |
| 1900 | 6.8 | 6.6 | 6.7 | 5.0 | ... | ... | 10 | 12 | 31 | 116 |
| 1901 | 6.6 | 2.8 | 7.1 | 5.0 | ... | ... | 9.9 | 12 | 35 | 117 |
| 1902 | 6.3 | 2.2 | 6.5 | 4.8 | ... | ... | 8.3 | 11 | 39 | 130 |
| 1903 | 6.5 | 3.7 | 9.6 | 9.5 | ... | ... | 10 | 27 | 41 | 140 |
| 1904 | 7.5 | 6.3 | 9.6 | 11 | ... | 0.3 | 10 | 25 | 43 | 142 |
| 1905 | 8.6[7] | 5.9[7] | 9.8[7] | 16[7] | ... | 10[7] | 17[7] | 17[7] | 48[7] | 140[7] |
| 1906 | 16 | 8.0 | 21 | 21 | ... | ... | 20 | 42 | 146 | 186 |
| 1907 | 17 | 8.1 | 24 | 20 | ... | ... | 23 | 32 | 146 | 176 |
| 1908 | 20 | 12 | 28 | 22 | ... | ... | 33 | 26 | 118 | 170 |
| 1909 | 12 | 11 | 17 | 13 | ... | ... | 20 | 24 | 91 | 173 |
| 1910 | 17 | 12 | 20 | 8.4 | ... | ... | 22 | 29 | 113 | 197 |
| 1911 | 19 | 9.3 | 26 | 8.7 | ... | 15 | 24 | 36 | 113 | 224 |
| 1912 | 16 | 8.3 | 24 | 10 | ... | ... | 22 | 40 | 98 | 224 |
| 1913 | 18[7] | 7.2[7] | 25[7] | 16[7] | ... | ...[7] | 26[7] | 31[7] | 97[7] | 232[7] |
| 1914 | ... | ... | ... | ... | ... | ... | ... | ... | ... | ... |
| 1915 | ... | ... | ... | ... | ... | ... | ... | ... | ... | ... |
| 1916 | ... | ... | ... | ... | ... | ... | ... | ... | ... | ... |
| 1917 | ... | ... | ... | ... | ... | ... | ... | ... | ... | ... |
| 1918 | ... | ... | ... | ... | ... | ... | ... | ... | ... | ... |
| 1919 | ... | ... | ... | ... | ... | ... | ... | ... | ... | ... |
| 1920 | 22 | 4.8 | 7.0 | 1.3 | ... | ... | 33 | 15 | 267 | 359 |
| 1921 | 47 | 8.2 | 24 | 2.7 | ... | ... | 45 | 49 | 339 | 596 |
| 1922 | 20 | 16 | [38][10] | 3.0 | ... | ... | 24 | 50 | 198 | 518 |
| 1923 | 14 | 8.2 | 20 | 3.6 | ... | ... | 22 | 35 | 235 | 472 |
| 1924 | 16 | 8.4 | 23 | 18 | ... | ... | 23 | 35 | 233 | 493 |
| 1925 | 21 | 12 | 30 | 33 | 1.5 | - - | 31 | 45 | 275 | 518 |
| 1926 | 18 | 16 | 28 | 32 | 1.2 | - - | 28 | 49 | 269 | 491 |
| 1927 | 17 | 19 | 30 | 64 | 1.3 | - - | 23 | 49 | 233 | 417 |
| 1928 | 18 | 23 | 33 | 40 | 1.5 | 1.0 | 26 | 46 | 242 | 404 |
| 1929 | 19 | 23 | 31 | 45 | 1.4 | 1.4 | 26 | 61 | 264 | 359 |
| 1930 | 20 | 20 | 33 | 33 | 1.1 | 0.8 | 21 | 55 | 239 | 268 |
| 1931 | 12 | 17 | 20 | 31 | 1.0 | 1.2 | 16 | 48 | 145 | 244 |
| 1932 | 10 | 5.6 | 21 | 20 | 0.7 | 0.8 | 14 | 12 | 115 | 199 |
| 1933 | 17 | 16 | 29 | 27 | 1.5 | 1.4 | 22 | 80 | 147 | 175 |
| 1934 | 17 | 20 | 35 | 41 | 3.0 | 7.4 | 36 | 132 | 203 | 334 |
| 1935 | 16 | 17 | 49 | 53 | 4.9 | 12 | 23 | 76 | 265 | 471 |
| 1936 | 17 | 16 | 71 | 82 | 7.3 | 19 | 24 | 68 | 275 | 471 |
| 1937 | 20 | 21 | 99 | 84 | 11 | 10 | 29 | 99 | 382 | 502 |
| 1938 | 20 | 19 | 93 | 65 | 8.8 | 3.6 | 20 | 79 | 285 | 565 |
| 1939 | 23 | 14 | 80 | 51 | 7.3 | 9.4 | 17 | 53 | 416 | 679 |
| 1940 | 13 | 8.6 | 8.4 | 0.3 | 18 | 24 | 22 | 9.6 | 527 | 859 |
| 1941 | 0.1 | 0.1 | 2.1 | - - | 25 | 21 | 31 | 0.8 | 771 | 665 |
| 1942 | - - | 0.1 | - - | — | 1.1 | — | 28 | 0.1 | 655 | 905 |
| 1943 | - - | - - | - - | - - | - - | — | 18 | 0.1 | 805 | 992 |
| 1944 | - - | - - | - - | - - | — | — | 17 | 0.1 | 1,699 | 890 |

**E2     NORTH AMERICA: External Trade (in Current Values) with Main Trading Partners**

**MEXICO** (million pesos to 1974, million US dollars subsequently)

|  | France | | Germany | | Japan | | UK[8] | | USA | |
|---|---|---|---|---|---|---|---|---|---|---|
|  | Imports | Exports | Imports | Exports | Imports | Exports | Imports | Exports | Imports | Exports |
| 1945 | 0.4 | 0.3 | - - | — | — | — | 24 | 1.0 | 1,322 | 1,062 |
| 1946 | 9.3 | 7.2 | - - | — | - - | — | 51 | 9.8 | 2,204 | 1,366 |
| 1947 | 26 | 17 | - -[2] | 0.2[2] | - - | - - | 65 | 39 | 2,856 | 1,655 |
| 1948 | 13 | 54 | 1.6 | 7.6 | 0.2 | 14 | 86 | 78 | 2,561 | 2,006 |
| 1949 | 22 | 55 | 14 | 16 | 2.5 | 0.1 | 79 | 71 | 3,068 | 2,854 |
| 1950 | 52 | 26 | 62 | 21 | 9.8 | 32 | 101[8] | 36[8] | 3,717 | 3,750 |
| 1951 | 135 | 24 | 139 | 158 | 23 | 50 | 142 | 190 | 5,515 | 3,840 |
| 1952 | 92 | 52 | 152 | 138 | 21 | 144 | 166 | 99 | 5,240 | 4,031 |
| 1953 | 102 | 19 | 232 | 58 | 20 | 370 | 167 | 166 | 5,173 | 3,175 |
| 1954 | 157 | 19 | 305 | 147 | 38 | 461 | 171 | 477 | 7,185 | 5,162 |
| 1955 | 113 | 31 | 429 | 345 | 67 | 576 | 256 | 386 | 8,762 | 7,167 |
| 1956 | 124 | 121 | 607 | 505 | 72 | 652 | 313 | 357 | 10,491 | 7,448 |
| 1957 | 151 | 138 | 795 | 245 | 81 | 386 | 403 | 198 | 11,122 | 6,838 |
| 1958 | 301 | 81 | 711 | 235 | 100 | 392 | 457 | 169 | 10,862 | 6,864 |
| 1959 | 220 | 64 | 834 | 263 | 154 | 834 | 481 | 195 | 9,174 | 6,579 |
| 1960 | 290 | 75 | 913 | 226 | 214 | 555 | 722 | 152 | 10,706 | 5,691 |
| 1961 | 289 | 75 | 999 | 165 | 247 | 663 | 649 | 142 | 9,976 | 6,275 |
| 1962 | 404 | 133 | 1,160 | 225 | 246 | 855 | 541 | 97 | 9,782 | 6,917 |
| 1963 | 415 | 122 | 1,027 | 236 | 322 | 746 | 544 | 119 | 10,628 | 7,406 |
| 1964 | 474 | 153 | 1,206 | 219 | 351 | 800 | 625 | 114 | 12,791 | 7,522 |
| 1965 | 606 | 170 | 1,526 | 436 | 489 | 834 | 670 | 97 | 12,815 | 7,913 |
| 1966 | 977 | 256 | 1,553 | 549 | 571 | 1,033 | 652 | 144 | 12,823 | 8,146 |
| 1967 | 915 | 585 | 1,646 | 480 | 942 | 858 | 846 | 190 | 13,745 | 7,812 |
| 1968 | 795 | 165 | 2,076 | 531 | 957 | 896 | 933 | 480 | 15,471 | 9,090 |
| 1969 | 1,077 | 108 | 1,968 | 577 | 1,178 | 1,200 | 812 | 305 | 16,222 | 10,147 |
| 1970 | 1,307 | 110 | 2,313 | 348 | 1,075 | 861 | 895 | 133 | 19,594 | 10,585 |
| 1971 | 946 | 95 | 2,565 | 423 | 1,124 | 817 | 844 | 103 | 18,489 | 11,474 |
| 1972 | 1,045 | 121 | 3,295 | 491 | 1,443 | 1,477 | 1,161 | 177 | 22,180 | 16,212 |
| 1973 | 1,252 | 261 | 3,481 | 747 | 2,224 | 2,223 | 1,133 | 396 | 32,617 | 22,636 |
| 1974 | 1,649 | 501 | 5,955 | 1,369 | 2,795 | 2,205 | 1,700 | 574 | 47,240 | 21,729 |
|  | | | | (million US dollars) | | | | | | |
| 1975 | 161 | 39 | 480 | 87 | 306 | 144 | 192 | 36 | 4,129 | 1,845 |
| 1976 | 183 | 43 | 420 | 89 | 320 | 180 | 181 | 44 | 3,779 | 2,158 |
| 1977 | 172 | 39 | 323 | 96 | 311 | 130 | 137 | 63 | 3,528 | 2,879 |
| 1978 | 312 | 32 | 568 | 175 | 586 | 175 | 211 | 71 | 4,867 | 4,510 |
| 1979 | 516 | 72 | 822 | 213 | 735 | 256 | 283 | 45 | 7,999 | 6,237 |
| 1980 | 520 | 567 | 972 | 256 | 989 | 671 | 405 | 44 | 11,979 | 10,072 |
| 1981 | 588 | 901 | 1,189 | 212 | 1,205 | 1,157 | 429 | 242 | 15,470 | 10,702 |
| 1982 | 349 | 931 | 914 | 240 | 855 | 1,450 | 278 | 913 | 9,006 | 11,129 |
| 1983 | 389 | 845 | 396 | 298 | 426 | 1,535 | 186 | 918 | 7,502 | 15,488 |
| 1984 | 312 | 940 | 565 | 291 | 656 | 1,905 | 234 | 1,028 | 10,013 | 16,572 |
| 1985 | 307 | 824 | 584 | 297 | 843 | 1,723 | 302 | 679 | 11,244 | 15,858 |
| 1986 | 195 | 335 | 599 | 333 | 550 | 834 | 173 | 155 | 6,137 | 8,294 |
| 1987 | 240 | 567 | 643 | 298 | 449 | 1,261 | 176 | 156 | 6,222 | 12,497 |
| 1988 | 397 | 513 | 1,108 | 412 | 1,055 | 1,128 | 330 | 177 | 11,412 | 12,534 |

**E2      NORTH AMERICA: External Trade (in Current Values) with Main Trading Partners**

## NICARAGUA (thousand gold cordobas)

| | Germany | | Japan | | UK | | USA | |
|---|---|---|---|---|---|---|---|---|
| | Imports | Exports | Imports | Exports | Imports | Exports | Imports | Exports |
| 1910 | 369 | 849 | ... | ... | 684 | 676 | 1,629 | 1,600 |
| 1911 | 643 | 1,075 | ... | ... | 1,412 | 523 | 2,755 | 1,703 |
| 1912 | 604 | 702 | ... | ... | 939 | 515 | 2,549 | 1,767 |
| 1913 | 619 | 1,888 | ... | ... | 1,151 | 999 | 3,244 | 2,722 |
| 1914 | 391 | 560 | ... | ... | 718 | 367 | 2,566 | 2,428 |
| 1915 | 37 | — | ... | ... | 302 | 439 | 2,593 | 3,080 |
| 1916 | 0.3 | — | ... | ... | 611 | 38 | 3,886 | 3,731 |
| 1917 | - - | — | ... | ... | 655 | 1.9 | 4,103 | 4,074 |
| 1918 | — | — | ... | ... | 597 | 16 | 4,630 | 6,413 |
| 1919 | — | — | ... | ... | 690 | 438 | 6,688 | 7,664 |
| 1920 | 145 | 2 | ... | ... | 1,635 | 306 | 11,248 | 9,295 |
| 1921 | 101 | 54 | ... | ... | 654 | 109 | 3,857 | 6,265 |
| 1922 | 74 | 26 | 7.7 | — | 485 | 225 | 4,127 | 5,618 |
| 1923 | 231 | 19 | 33 | — | 873 | 241 | 5,509 | 7,896 |
| 1924 | 396 | 409 | 33 | — | 1,043 | 431 | 6,425 | 7,442 |
| 1925 | 607 | 482 | 49 | — | 1,230 | 517 | 7,272 | 7,971 |
| 1926 | 727 | 694 | 75 | — | 1,128 | 255 | 7,117 | 6,904 |
| 1927 | 688 | 782 | 68 | — | 1,170 | 628 | 6,778 | 5,016 |
| 1928 | 1,179 | 884 | 134 | — | 1,494 | 346 | 8,384 | 6,025 |
| 1929 | 1,086 | 1,293 | 166 | — | 1,276 | 399 | 7,390 | 5,754 |
| 1930 | 736 | 972 | 94 | - - | 799 | 290 | 5,024 | 4,150 |
| 1931 | 565 | 943 | 44 | — | 544 | 461 | 3,684 | 3,506 |
| 1932 | 299 | 425 | 30 | — | 357 | 295 | 2,181 | 2,964 |
| 1933 | 270 | 686 | 45 | 0.2 | 493 | 354 | 2,394 | 2,437 |
| 1934 | 378 | 709 | 208 | 0.2 | 549 | 365 | 2,712 | 2,598 |
| 1935 | 855 | 700 | 324 | 7.0 | 593 | 119 | 2,538 | 3,151 |
| 1936 | 1,337 | 743 | 143 | 136 | 697 | 84 | 2,580 | 2,505 |
| 1937 | 857 | 1,504 | 243 | 335 | 477 | 53 | 3,045 | 3,897 |
| 1938 | 513 | 867 | 80 | 120 | 422 | 136 | 3,058 | 3,961 |
| 1939 | 777 | 906 | 55 | 40 | 333 | 104 | 4,352 | 6,432 |
| 1940 | 56 | - - | 162 | 192 | 210 | 37 | 5,921 | 8,941 |
| 1941 | 4.2 | — | 217 | 147 | 153 | - - | 9,142 | 11,457 |
| 1942 | 7.3 | — | 27 | — | 143 | 2.0 | 5,185 | 13,542 |
| 1943 | 1.9 | — | — | — | 272 | 1.4 | 8,257 | 13,560 |
| 1944 | — | — | — | — | 179 | 40 | 7,601 | 14,061 |
| 1945 | — | — | — | — | 137 | 131 | 8,926 | 12,572 |
| 1946 | — | 0.3 | — | — | 200 | 520 | 11,397 | 14,137 |
| 1947 | 2.9 | 0.5 | — | - - | 370 | 351 | 17,904 | 16,234 |
| 1948 | 0.2 | 43 | — | 365 | 448 | 169 | 20,180 | 19,940 |
| 1949 | 759 | 16 | - - | - - | 351 | 384 | 16,790 | 15,057 |

**E2      NORTH AMERICA: External Trade (in Current Values) with Main Trading Partners**

**NICARAGUA** (million gold cordobas).

| | Germany | | Japan | | UK | | USA | |
|---|---|---|---|---|---|---|---|---|
| | **Imports** | **Exports** | **Imports** | **Exports** | **Imports** | **Exports** | **Imports** | **Exports** |
| 1950 | 0.2 | 0.4 | 0.2 | 0.2 | 0.8 | 3.7 | 20 | 24 |
| 1951 | 1.5 | 0.4 | 0.1 | 2.3 | 1.2 | 7.9 | 22 | 25 |
| 1952 | 1.6 | 2.4 | 0.4 | 1.3 | 1.5 | 6.7 | 28 | 27 |
| 1953 | 3.2 | 5.3 | 1.2 | 3.4 | 1.6 | 7.2 | 28 | 25 |
| 1954 | 5.2 | 8.5 | 1.2 | 6.8 | 1.9 | 2.3 | 38 | 26 |
| 1955 | 4.4 | 13 | 1.4 | 11 | 2.3 | 2.1 | 45 | 25 |
| 1956 | 5 | 15 | 1.3 | 6.0 | 2.8 | 2.1 | 43 | 20 |
| 1957 | 8.5 | 12 | 2.2 | 3.3 | 3.0 | 4.3 | 47 | 23 |
| 1958 | 6.1 | 12 | 3.0 | 7.5 | 3.2 | 3.0 | 43 | 21 |
| 1959 | 5.0 | 10 | 3.4 | 16 | 2.9 | 2.6 | 35 | 15 |
| 1960 | 5.6 | 8.6 | 4.7 | 8.7 | 3.0 | 2.6 | 38 | 23 |
| 1961 | 6.1 | 8.2 | 4.5 | 13 | 3.3 | 2.0 | 36 | 27 |
| 1962 | 7.1 | 13$_2$ | 5.7 | 18 | 4.1 | 3.4 | 49 | 32 |
| 1963 | 8.1 | 12 | 6.5 | 23 | 6.0 | 3.1 | 54 | 39 |
| 1964 | 11 | 24 | 8.3 | 28 | 5.2 | 3.9 | 64 | 32 |
| 1965 | 10 | 21 | 11 | 48 | 5.9 | 3.3 | 76 | 35 |
| 1966 | 13 | 21 | 9.9 | 42 | 6.3 | 2.5 | 83 | 30 |
| 1967 | 14 | 20 | 13 | 46 | 5.2 | 1.9 | 87 | 41 |
| 1968 | 11 | 18 | 14 | 42 | 5.5 | 3.3 | 70 | 45 |
| 1969 | 12 | 17 | 13 | 28 | 6.8 | 2.1 | 67 | 51 |
| 1970 | 11 | 21 | 13 | 25 | 6.9 | 1.7 | 72 | 58 |
| 1971 | 15 | 14 | 17 | 33 | 6.5 | 1.1 | 70 | 65 |
| 1972 | 16 | 19 | 18 | 45 | 7.3 | 0.8 | 69 | 82 |
| 1973 | 25 | 25 | 23 | 34 | 7.3 | 0.7 | 113 | 94 |
| 1974 | 27 | 30 | 29 | 25 | 9.7 | 0.5 | 125 | 51 |
| 1975 | 21 | 24 | 27 | 34 | 8.8 | 8.4 | 118 | 73 |
| 1976 | 24 | 37 | 30 | 49 | 9.4 | 1.1 | 116 | 117 |
| 1977 | 36 | 60 | 54 | 49 | 11 | 1.3 | 154 | 105 |
| 1978 | 30 | 83 | 38 | 51 | 10 | 1.9 | 172 | 143 |
| 1979 | 15 | 57 | 15 | 32 | 4.8 | 2.0 | 97 | 195 |
| 1980 | 28 | 56 | 29 | 13 | 7.3 | 1.8 | 243 | 161 |
| 1981 | 60 | 51 | 28 | 56 | 11 | 2.2 | 263 | 136 |
| 1982 | 29 | 38 | 19 | 45 | 4.3 | 2.8 | 148 | 98 |
| 1983 | 19 | 51 | 20 | 66 | 5.1 | 3.2 | 158 | 79 |
| 1984 | 22 | 54 | 24 | 96 | 6.9 | 4.4 | 135 | 49 |
| 1985 | 50 | 110 | 81 | 161 | 28 | 2.7 | 189 | 74 |
| 1986 | ... | ... | ... | ... | ... | ... | ... | ... |
| 1987 | ... | ... | ... | ... | ... | ... | ... | ... |
| 1988 | ... | ... | ... | ... | ... | ... | ... | ... |

E2 **NORTH AMERICA: External Trade (in Current Values) with Main Trading Partners**

## TRINIDAD & TOBAGO (thousand pounds)[9]

| | UK | | USA | | | UK | | USA | |
|---|---|---|---|---|---|---|---|---|---|
| | Imports | Exports | Imports | Exports | | Imports | Exports | Imports | Exports |
| 1850 | 264 | 282 | 89 | 1 | 1900 | 882 | 983 | 605 | 792 |
| 1851 | 308 | 375 | 98 | 1 | 1901 | 921 | 706 | 674 | 817 |
| 1852 | 255 | 408 | 107 | 4 | 1902 | 983 | 626 | 702 | 822 |
| 1853 | 255 | 434 | 91 | 1 | 1903 | 945 | 604 | 676 | 945 |
| 1854 | 278 | 359 | 109 | 4 | 1904 | 939 | 817 | 677 | 695 |
| 1855 | 272 | 360 | 114 | 10 | 1905 | 958 | 828 | 651 | 851 |
| 1856 | 306 | 431 | 158 | 92 | 1906 | 922 | 702 | 677 | 975 |
| 1857 | 388 | 787 | 173 | 138 | 1907 | 1,051 | 821 | 817 | 1,016 |
| 1858 | 373 | 673 | 195 | 24 | 1908 | 944[9] | 444[9] | 717[9] | 924[9] |
| 1859 | 353 | 657 | 169 | 73 | 1909 | 968 | 647 | 805 | 1,016 |
| 1860 | 357 | 526 | 178 | 63 | 1910 | 980 | 746 | 969 | 1,030 |
| 1861 | 372 | 429 | 199 | 10 | 1911 | 1,419[9] | 1,129[9] | 1,034[9] | 1,271[9] |
| 1862 | 289 | 604 | 202 | 8 | 1912 | 945 | 508 | 819 | 750 |
| 1863 | 295 | 622 | 185 | 26 | 1913 | 893 | 477 | 814 | 954 |
| 1864 | 426 | 912 | 179 | 42 | 1914 | 999[9] | 548 | 853[9] | 915 |
| 1865 | 431 | 638 | 135 | 14 | 1915 | 969 | 1,507 | 914 | 1,427 |
| 1866 | 501 | 825 | 187 | 39 | 1916 | 999 | 1,358 | 1,296 | 1,202 |
| 1867 | 403 | 887 | 131 | 38 | 1917 | 905 | 1,886 | 1,589 | 1,163 |
| 1868 | 423 | 890 | 138 | 27 | 1918 | 681 | 1,736 | 1,607 | 1,252 |
| 1869 | 369 | 1,170 | 169 | 55 | 1919 | 871 | 2,338 | 2,041 | 1,446 |
| 1870 | 448 | 1,033 | 151 | 21 | 1920 | 2,219 | 3,598 | 3,474 | 1,931 |
| 1871 | 535 | 1,217 | 214 | 94 | 1921 | 1,727 | 1,865 | 2,458 | 1,080 |
| 1872 | 640 | 1,125 | 205 | 73 | 1922 | 1,367[7] | 1,544[7] | 1,249[7] | 937[7] |
| | | | | | | 1,363 | 1,544 | 1,247 | 937 |
| 1873 | 562 | 1,380 | 192 | 53 | 1923 | 1,259 | 2,144 | 1,052 | 890 |
| 1874 | 489 | 981 | 269 | 70 | 1924 | 1,402 | 2,229 | 932 | 926 |
| 1875 | 532 | 1,220 | 279 | 108 | 1925 | 1,324 | 2,409 | 930 | 947 |
| 1876 | 572 | 1,248 | 303 | 122 | 1926 | 1,225 | 1,582 | 1,143 | 1,500 |
| 1877 | 493 | 1,417 | 362 | 253 | 1927 | 1,574 | 1,541 | 1,376 | 1,580 |
| 1878 | 644 | 1,247 | 343 | 252 | 1928 | 1,795 | 1,951 | 1,103 | 1,642 |
| 1879 | 774 | 1,461 | 368 | 104 | 1929 | 1,859 | 1,851 | 1,492 | 2,077 |
| 1880 | 831 | 1,164 | 408 | 262 | 1920 | 1,889 | 1,283 | 1,279 | 1,571 |
| 1881 | 828 | 996 | 398 | 194 | 1931 | 1,375 | 729 | 718 | 944 |
| 1882 | 808 | 1,076 | 403 | 342 | 1932 | 1,583 | 1,090 | 469 | 630 |
| 1883 | 878 | 814 | 438 | 717 | 1933 | 1,780 | 1,736 | 513 | 285 |
| 1884 | 887 | 863 | 426 | 608 | 1934 | 1,746 | 1,809 | 619 | 256 |
| 1885 | 655 | 1,186 | 394 | 564 | 1935 | 1,892 | 1,785 | 684 | 352 |
| 1886 | 666 | 950 | 352 | 634 | 1936 | 2,207 | 2,446 | 923 | 403 |
| 1887 | 752 | 749 | 361 | 723 | 1937 | 2,685 | 2,947 | 1,746 | 459 |
| 1888 | 794[9] | 862[9] | 350[9] | 669[9] | 1938 | 2,690 | 3,198 | 1,721 | 283 |
| 1889 | 764 | 972 | 383 | 763 | 1939 | 2,592 | 3,092 | 1,846 | 268 |
| 1890 | 822 | 857 | 429 | 725 | 1940 | 2,990 | 2,512 | 2,623 | 359 |
| 1891 | 778 | 729 | 422 | 736 | 1941 | 2,474 | 1,077 | 2,979 | 376 |
| 1892 | 760 | 793 | 457 | 811 | 1942 | 2,144 | 1,071 | 3,725 | 291 |
| 1893 | 874 | 864 | 466 | 754 | 1943 | 1,751 | 798 | 4,083 | 352 |
| 1894 | 835 | 832 | 446 | 559 | 1944 | 1,606 | 932 | 4,005 | 389 |
| 1895 | 989 | 907 | 443 | 564 | 1945 | 1,930 | 1,282 | 3,636 | 370 |
| 1896 | 979 | 944 | 458 | 670 | 1946 | 4,462 | 5,505 | 2,424 | 378 |
| 1897 | 858 | 714 | 451 | 628 | 1947 | 5,681 | 6,763 | 5,634 | 797 |
| 1898 | 796 | 713 | 496 | 863 | 1948 | 8,927 | 9,442 | 4,484 | 1,229 |
| 1899 | 950 | 890 | 628 | 886 | 1949 | 11,978 | 8,851 | 5,092 | 1,542 |

**E2    NORTH AMERICA: External Trade (in Current Values) with Main Trading Partners**

**TRINIDAD & TOBAGO** (million local dollars)[9]

| | UK | | USA | | | UK | | USA | |
|---|---|---|---|---|---|---|---|---|---|
| | Imports | Exports | Imports | Exports | | Imports | Exports | Imports | Exports |
| 1950 | 68 | 46 | 14 | 13 | 1970 | 144 | 93 | 176 | 447 |
| 1951 | 78 | 59 | 18 | 12 | 1971 | 176 | 93 | 233 | 422 |
| 1952 | 86 | 68 | 22 | 7.8 | 1972 | 188 | 87 | 274 | 452 |
| 1953 | 89 | 103 | 19 | 12 | 1973 | 176 | 64 | 255 | 723 |
| 1954 | 95 | 103 | 21 | 13 | 1974 | 207 | 93 | 402 | 2,531 |
| 1955 | 112 | 112 | 28 | 8.4 | 1975 | 286 | 148 | 702 | 2,575 |
| 1956 | 105 | 116 | 36 | 19 | 1976 | 366 | 249 | 953 | 3,548 |
| 1957 | 129 | 129 | 50 | 29 | 1977 | 458 | 103 | 921 | 3,674 |
| 1958 | 135 | 102 | 57 | 79 | 1978 | 589 | 137 | 969 | 3,234 |
| 1959 | 146 | 143 | 59 | 68 | 1979 | 553 | 231 | 1,310 | 3,478 |
| 1960 | 150 | 153 | 70 | 97 | 1980 | 774 | 153 | 2,021 | 5,466 |
| 1961 | 137 | 143 | 67 | 146 | 1981 | 669 | 165 | 1,935 | 4,795 |
| 1962 | 136 | 137 | 77 | 149 | 1982 | 724 | 156 | 3,119 | 3,425 |
| 1963 | 134 | 145 | 104 | 179 | 1983 | 715 | 177 | 2,614 | 3,172 |
| 1964 | 130 | 152 | 103 | 204 | 1984 | 452 | 469 | 1,745 | 2,961 |
| 1965 | 136 | 114 | 139 | 233 | 1985 | 358 | 204 | 1,460 | 3,196 |
| 1966 | 127 | 102 | 110 | 271 | 1986 | 474 | 241 | 2,065 | 3,043 |
| 1967 | 105 | 97 | 118 | 321 | 1987 | 405 | 163 | 1,800 | 2,972 |
| 1968 | 126 | 102 | 126 | 249 | 1988 | 426 | 148 | 1,602 | 2,933 |
| 1969 | 134 | 97 | 142 | 295 | | | | | |

**E2     NORTH AMERICA: External Trade (in Current Values) with Main Trading Partners**

**USA** (million dollars)[10]

| | British North America | | France | | Germany | | Mexico | | UK | |
|---|---|---|---|---|---|---|---|---|---|---|
| | Imports | Exports | Imports | Exports | Imports | Exports | Imports | Exports | Imports | Exports |
| 1790 | ... | ... | ... | 1 | ... | - - | ... | ... | ... | 7 |
| 1791 | ... | ... | ... | 1 | ... | - - | ... | ... | ... | 6 |
| 1792 | ... | ... | ... | 2 | ... | 1 | ... | ... | ... | 5 |
| 1793 | ... | ... | ... | 2 | ... | 2 | ... | ... | ... | 6 |
| 1794 | ... | ... | ... | 1 | ... | 5 | ... | ... | ... | 6 |
| 1795 | ... | ... | ... | 8 | ... | 10 | ... | ... | ... | 6 |
| 1796 | ... | ... | ... | 3 | ... | 10 | ... | ... | ... | 17 |
| 1797 | ... | ... | ... | 4 | ... | 10 | ... | ... | ... | 6 |
| 1798 | ... | ... | ... | 1 | ... | 15 | ... | ... | ... | 12 |
| 1799 | ... | ... | ... | ... | ... | 18 | ... | ... | ... | 19 |
| 1800 | ... | ... | ... | - - | ... | 8 | ... | ... | ... | 19 |
| 1801 | ... | ... | ... | 4 | ... | 11 | ... | ... | ... | 31 |
| 1802 | ... | ... | ... | 8 | ... | 6 | ... | ... | ... | 16 |
| 1803 | ... | ... | ... | 4 | ... | 4 | ... | ... | ... | 18 |
| 1804 | ... | ... | ... | 9 | ... | 6 | ... | ... | ... | 13 |
| 1805 | ... | ... | ... | 13 | ... | 4 | ... | ... | ... | 15 |
| 1806 | ... | ... | ... | 11 | ... | 6 | ... | ... | ... | 16 |
| 1807 | ... | ... | ... | 13 | ... | 3 | ... | ... | ... | 23 |
| 1808 | ... | ... | ... | 3 | ... | - - | ... | ... | ... | 3 |
| 1809 | ... | ... | ... | ... | ... | 2 | ... | ... | ... | 6 |
| 1810 | ... | ... | ... | - - | ... | 2 | ... | ... | ... | 12 |
| 1811 | ... | ... | ... | 2 | ... | - - | ... | ... | ... | 14 |
| 1812 | ... | ... | ... | 3 | ... | ... | ... | ... | ... | 6 |
| 1813 | ... | ... | ... | 4 | ... | - - | ... | ... | ... | ... |
| 1814 | ... | ... | ... | - - | ... | ... | ... | ... | ... | ... |
| 1815 | ... | ... | ... | 7 | ... | 2 | ... | ... | 18 | 18 |
| 1816 | ... | ... | ... | 10 | ... | 4 | ... | ... | 30 | 30 |
| 1817 | ... | ... | ... | 9 | ... | 3 | ... | ... | 33 | 33 |
| 1818 | ... | ... | ... | 12 | ... | 3 | ... | ... | 38 | 38 |
| 1819 | ... | ... | ... | 9 | ... | 4 | ... | ... | 24 | 24 |
| 1820 | ... | ... | ... | 8 | ... | 3 | ... | ... | 24 | 24 |
| 1821 | - - | 2 | 4 | 6 | 1 | 2 | ... | ... | 24 | 19 |
| 1822 | - - | 2 | 6 | 6 | 2 | 3 | ... | ... | 35 | 24 |
| 1823 | - - | 2 | 6 | 9 | 2 | 3 | ... | ... | 28 | 22 |
| 1824 | - - | 2 | 7 | 10 | 2 | 2 | ... | ... | 28 | 21 |
| 1825 | - - | 3 | 11 | 10 | 3 | 3 | 1 | 6 | 37 | 37 |
| 1826 | - - | 2 | 8 | 11 | 3 | 2 | 1 | 6 | 26 | 21 |
| 1827 | - - | 2 | 8 | 11 | 2 | 3 | 1 | 4 | 30 | 26 |
| 1828 | - - | 2 | 9 | 9 | 3 | 3 | 1 | 3 | 33 | 20 |
| 1829 | - - | 2 | 9 | 10 | 2 | 3 | 1 | 2 | 25 | 24 |
| 1830 | - - | 3 | 8 | 11 | 2 | 2 | 1 | 5 | 24 | 26 |
| 1831 | 1 | 3 | 14 | 6 | 4 | 3 | 1 | 6 | 44 | 31 |
| 1832 | 1 | 3 | 12 | 12 | 3 | 4 | 1 | 3 | 37 | 29 |
| 1833 | 1 | 4 | 13 | 14 | 2 | 3 | 1 | 5 | 38 | 32 |
| 1834 | 1 | 3 | 15 | 15 | 3 | 5 | 1 | 5 | 41 | 44 |
| 1835 | 1 | 3 | 22 | 19 | 4 | 4 | 1 | 9 | 60 | 52 |
| 1836 | 2 | 3 | 32 | 21 | 5 | 4 | 1 | 6 | 76 | 58 |
| 1837 | 2 | 3 | 21 | 19 | 6 | 4 | 1 | 4 | 45 | 52 |
| 1838 | 1 | 2 | 16 | 15 | 3 | 3 | 1 | 2 | 36 | 52 |
| 1839 | 2 | 4 | 32 | 18 | 5 | 3 | 1 | 3 | 65 | 57 |

**E2    NORTH AMERICA: External Trade (in Current Values) with Main Trading Partners**

**USA** (million dollars)[10]

| | Canada[11] | | France | | Germany | | Japan | | Mexico | | UK | |
|---|---|---|---|---|---|---|---|---|---|---|---|---|
| | Imports | Exports | Imports | Exports | Imports | Exports | Imports | Exports | Imports | Exports | Imports | Exports |
| 1840 | 1 | 6 | 16 | 20 | 3 | 4 | ... | ... | 1 | 3 | 33 | 55 |
| 1841 | 1 | 6 | 24 | 18 | 2 | 5 | ... | ... | 1 | 2 | 46 | 47 |
| 1842 | 1 | 6 | 17 | 17 | 2 | 5 | ... | ... | 1 | 2 | 34 | 40 |
| 1843 | [- -][10] | [3][10] | [5][10] | [12][10] | [1][10] | [4][10] | ... | ... | [1][10] | [1][10] | [12][10] | [41][10] |
| 1844 | 1 | 6 | 17 | 13 | 2 | 4 | ... | ... | 1 | 2 | 41 | 49 |
| 1845 | 1 | 6 | 21 | 12 | 3 | 6 | ... | ... | 1 | 1 | 45 | 45 |
| 1846 | 1 | 7 | 24 | 14 | 3 | 5 | ... | ... | 1 | 2 | 45 | 46 |
| 1847 | 1 | 7 | 24 | 19 | 4 | 5 | ... | ... | - - | 1 | 48 | 87 |
| 1848 | 3 | 8 | 28 | 15 | 6 | 4 | ... | ... | 1 | 4 | 60 | 67 |
| 1849 | 2 | 8 | 24 | 13 | 8 | 3 | ... | ... | 1 | 2 | 58 | 78 |
| 1850 | 5 | 10 | 27 | 18 | 9 | 5 | ... | ... | 1 | 2 | 75 | 71 |
| 1851 | 5 | 12 | 31 | 21 | 10 | 6 | ... | ... | 1 | 2 | 93 | 101 |
| 1852 | 5 | 10 | 25 | 19 | 8 | 6 | ... | ... | 1 | 2 | 89 | 81 |
| 1853 | 7 | 12 | 33 | 22 | 14 | 7 | ... | ... | 1 | 4 | 130 | 103 |
| 1854 | 9 | 24 | 36 | 25 | 17 | 9 | ... | ... | 1 | 3 | 146 | 117 |
| 1855 | 15 | 28 | 32 | 29 | 13 | 9 | - - | - - | 1 | 3 | 106 | 92 |
| 1856 | 21 | 29 | 49 | 35 | 15 | 13 | - - | ... | 1 | 4 | 122 | 128 |
| 1857 | 22 | 24 | 46 | 32 | 15 | 15 | - - | - - | 1 | 4 | 127 | 135 |
| 1858 | 16 | 24 | 33 | 28 | 14 | 12 | - - | - - | 1 | 3 | 89 | 129 |
| 1859 | 19 | 28 | 41 | 30 | 18 | 15 | - - | - - | 1 | 3 | 126 | 133 |
| 1860 | 24 | 23 | 43 | 39 | 19 | 15 | - - | - - | 2 | 5 | 138 | 169 |
| 1861 | 23 | 23 | 32 | 15 | 15 | 11 | - - | - - | 1 | 2 | 105 | 108 |
| 1862 | 19 | 21 | 8 | 20 | 14 | 10 | - - | - - | 1 | 2 | 75 | 86 |
| 1863 | 17 | 28 | 11 | 14 | 13 | 14 | - - | - - | 3 | 9 | 113 | 128 |
| 1864 | 30 | 27 | 11 | 13 | 14 | 13 | - - | - - | 6 | 9 | 142 | 97 |
| 1865 | 33 | 29 | 7 | 11 | 10 | 20 | - - | - - | 6 | 16 | 85 | 103 |
| 1866 | 49 | 24 | 23 | 51 | 26 | 22 | 2 | 1 | 2 | 5 | 202 | 288 |
| 1867 | 25 | 21 | 29 | 34 | 27 | 22 | 3 | 1 | 1 | 5 | 172 | 225 |
| 1868 | 26 | 24 | 25 | 26 | 22 | 31 | 2 | 1 | 2 | 6 | 132 | 198 |
| 1869 | 29 | 23 | 30 | 33 | 25 | 38 | 3 | 1 | 2 | 5 | 159 | 185 |
| 1870 | 36 | 25 | 43 | 46 | 27 | 42 | 3 | 1 | 3 | 6 | 152 | 248 |
| 1871 | 33 | 32 | 28 | 27 | 25 | 35 | 5 | 1 | 3 | 8 | 221 | 273 |
| 1872 | 36 | 29 | 43 | 31 | 46 | 41 | 7 | 1 | 4 | 6 | 249 | 265 |
| 1873 | 38[11] / 37 | 35[11] / 33 | 34 | 34 | 61 | 62 | 8 | 1 | 4 | 6 | 237 | 317 |
| 1874 | 34 | 42 | 52 | 43 | 44 | 63 | 6 | 1 | 4 | 6 | 180 | 345 |
| 1875 | 28 | 35 | 60 | 34 | 40 | 50 | 8 | 2 | 5 | 6 | 155 | 317 |
| 1876 | 29 | 33 | 51 | 40 | 35 | 51 | 15 | 1 | 5 | 6 | 123 | 336 |
| 1877 | 24 | 37 | 48 | 45 | 33 | 58 | 14 | 1 | 5 | 6 | 114 | 346 |
| 1878 | 25 | 37 | 43 | 55 | 35 | 55 | 7 | 2 | 5 | 7 | 107 | 387 |
| 1879 | 26 | 30 | 51 | 90 | 36 | 57 | 10 | 3 | 5 | 7 | 109 | 349 |
| 1880 | 33 | 29 | 69 | 100 | 52 | 57 | 15 | 3 | 7 | 8 | 211 | 454 |
| 1881 | 38 | 38 | 70 | 94 | 53 | 70 | 14 | 1 | 8 | 11 | 174 | 481 |
| 1882 | 51 | 37 | 89 | 50 | 56 | 54 | 14 | 3 | 8 | 15 | 196 | 408 |
| 1883 | 44 | 44 | 98 | 59 | 57 | 66 | 15 | 3 | 8 | 17 | 189 | 425 |
| 1884 | 38 | 44 | 71 | 51 | 65 | 61 | 11 | 3 | 9 | 13 | 163 | 386 |
| 1885 | 37 | 38 | 57 | 47 | 63 | 62 | 12 | 3 | 9 | 8 | 137 | 398 |
| 1886 | 37 | 33 | 63 | 42 | 69 | 62 | 15 | 3 | 11 | 8 | 154 | 348 |
| 1887 | 38 | 35 | 68 | 57 | 81 | 59 | 17 | 3 | 15 | 8 | 165 | 366 |
| 1888 | 43 | 36 | 71 | 39 | 78 | 56 | 19 | 4 | 17 | 10 | 178 | 362 |
| 1889 | 43 | 41 | 70 | 46 | 82 | 68 | 17 | 5 | 21 | 11 | 178 | 383 |

**E2     NORTH AMERICA: External Trade (in Current Values) with Main Trading Partners**

**USA** (million dollars)[10]

| | Canada[11] | | France | | Germany | | Japan | | Mexico | | UK | |
|---|---|---|---|---|---|---|---|---|---|---|---|---|
| | Imports | Exports | Imports | Exports | Imports | Exports | Imports | Exports | Imports | Exports | Imports | Exports |
| 1890 | 39 | 40 | 78 | 50 | 99 | 86 | 21 | 5 | 23 | 13 | 186 | 448 |
| 1891 | 39 | 38 | 77 | 61 | 97 | 93 | 19 | 5 | 27 | 15 | 195 | 445 |
| 1892 | 35 | 43 | 69 | 99 | 83 | 106 | 24 | 3 | 28 | 14 | 156 | 499 |
| 1893 | 38 | 47 | 76 | 47 | 96 | 84 | 27 | 3 | 34 | 20 | 183 | 421 |
| 1894 | 31 | 57 | 48 | 55 | 69 | 92 | 19 | 4 | 29 | 13 | 107 | 431 |
| 1895 | 37 | 53 | 62 | 45 | 81 | 92 | 24 | 5 | 16 | 15 | 159 | 387 |
| 1896 | 41 | 60 | 66 | 47 | 94 | 98 | 26 | 8 | 17 | 19 | 170 | 406 |
| 1897 | 40 | 65 | 68 | 58 | 111 | 125 | 24 | 13 | 19 | 23 | 168 | 483 |
| 1898 | 32 | 84 | 53 | 95 | 70 | 155 | 25 | 20 | 19 | 21 | 109 | 541 |
| 1899 | 31 | 88 | 62 | 61 | 84 | 156 | 27 | 17 | 23 | 25 | 118 | 512 |
| 1900 | 39 | 95 | 73 | 83 | 97 | 187 | 33 | 29 | 29 | 35 | 160 | 534 |
| 1901 | 42 | 106 | 75 | 79 | 100 | 192 | 29 | 19 | 29 | 36 | 143 | 631 |
| 1902 | 48 | 110 | 83 | 72 | 102 | 173 | 38 | 21 | 40 | 40 | 166 | 549 |
| 1903 | 55 | 123 | 90 | 77 | 120 | 194 | 44 | 21 | 41 | 42 | 190 | 524 |
| 1904 | 52 | 131 | 81 | 84 | 109 | 215 | 47 | 25 | 44 | 46 | 166 | 537 |
| 1905 | 62 | 141 | 90 | 76 | 118 | 194 | 52 | 52 | 46 | 46 | 176 | 523 |
| 1906 | 68 | 157 | 108 | 98 | 135 | 235 | 53 | 38 | 51 | 58 | 210 | 583 |
| 1907 | 73 | 183 | 128 | 114 | 162 | 257 | 69 | 39 | 57 | 66 | 246 | 608 |
| 1908 | 75 | 167 | 102 | 116 | 143 | 277 | 68 | 41 | 47 | 56 | 190 | 581 |
| 1909 | 79 | 163 | 108 | 109 | 144 | 235 | 70 | 27 | 48 | 50 | 209 | 515 |
| 1910 | 95 | 216 | 132 | 118 | 169 | 250 | 66 | 22 | 59 | 58 | 271 | 506 |
| 1911 | 101 | 270 | 115 | 135 | 163 | 287 | 79 | 37 | 57 | 61 | 261 | 577 |
| 1912 | 109 | 329 | 125 | 135 | 171 | 307 | 81 | 53 | 66 | 53 | 273 | 564 |
| 1913 | 121 | 415 | 137 | 146 | 189 | 332 | 92 | 58 | 78 | 54 | 296 | 597 |
| 1914 | 161 | 345 | 141 | 160 | 190 | 345 | 107 | 51 | 93 | 39 | 294 | 594 |
| 1915 | 160[10] | 301[10] | 77[10] | 369[10] | 91[10] | 29[10] | 99[10] | 41[10] | 78[10] | 34[10] | 256[10] | 912[10] |
| 1916 | 237 | 605 | 109 | 861 | 6 | 2 | 182 | 109 | 105 | 54 | 305 | 1,887 |
| 1917 | 414 | 829 | 99 | 941 | — | — | 254 | 186 | 130 | 111 | 280 | 2,009 |
| 1918 | 452 | 887 | 60 | 931 | — | — | 302 | 274 | 159 | 98 | 149 | 2,061 |
| 1919 | 495 | 734 | 124 | 893 | 11 | 93 | 410 | 366 | 149 | 131 | 309 | 2,279 |
| 1920 | 612 | 972 | 166 | 676 | 89 | 311 | 415 | 378 | 179 | 208 | 514 | 1,825 |
| 1921 | 335 | 594 | 142 | 225 | 80 | 372 | 251 | 238 | 119 | 222 | 239 | 942 |
| 1922 | 364 | 577 | 143 | 267 | 117 | 316 | 354 | 222 | 132 | 110 | 357 | 856 |
| 1923 | 416 | 652 | 150 | 272 | 161 | 317 | 347 | 267 | 140 | 120 | 404 | 882 |
| 1924 | 399 | 624 | 148 | 282 | 139 | 440 | 340 | 253 | 167 | 135 | 366 | 983 |
| 1925 | 454 | 649 | 157 | 280 | 164 | 470 | 384 | 230 | 179 | 145 | 414[11] / 413 | 1,041 / 1,034 |
| 1926 | 476 | 739 | 152 | 264 | 198 | 364 | 401 | 261 | 169 | 135 | 383 | 973 |
| 1927 | 475 | 837 | 168 | 229 | 201 | 482 | 402 | 258 | 138 | 109 | 358 | 840 |
| 1928 | 489 | 915 | 159 | 241 | 222 | 467 | 384 | 288 | 125 | 116 | 349 | 847 |
| 1929 | 503 | 948 | 171 | 266 | 255 | 410 | 432 | 259 | 118 | 134 | 330 | 848 |
| 1930 | 402 | 659 | 114 | 224 | 177 | 278 | 279 | 165 | 80 | 116 | 210 | 678 |
| 1931 | 266 | 396 | 79 | 122 | 127 | 166 | 206 | 156 | 48 | 52 | 135 | 456 |
| 1932 | 174 | 241 | 45 | 112 | 74 | 134 | 134 | 135 | 37 | 32 | 75 | 288 |
| 1933 | 185 | 211 | 50 | 122 | 78 | 140 | 128 | 143 | 31 | 38 | 111 | 312 |
| 1934 | 232 | 302 | 61 | 116 | 69 | 109 | 119 | 210 | 36 | 55 | 115 | 383 |
| 1935 | 286 | 323 | 58 | 117 | 78 | 92 | 153 | 203 | 42 | 66 | 155 | 433 |
| 1936 | 376[10] | 384 | 65[10] | 129 | 80[10] | 102 | 172[10] | 204 | 49[10] | 76 | 200[10] | 440 |
| 1937 | 398 | 509 | 76 | 165 | 92 | 126 | 204 | 289 | 60 | 109 | 203 | 536 |
| 1938 | 260 | 468 | 54 | 134 | 65 | 107 | 127 | 240 | 49 | 62 | 118 | 521 |
| 1939 | 340 | 489 | 62 | 182 | 52 | 46 | 161 | 232 | 56 | 83 | 149 | 505 |

**E2    NORTH AMERICA: External Trade (in Current Values) with Main Trading Partners**

## USA (million dollars)[10]

| | Canada[11] | | France | | Germany | | Japan | | Mexico | | UK | |
|---|---|---|---|---|---|---|---|---|---|---|---|---|
| | Imports | Exports | Imports | Exports | Imports | Exports | Imports | Exports | Imports | Exports | Imports | Exports |
| 1940 | 424 | 713 | 37 | 252 | 5 | — | 158 | 227 | 76 | 97 | 155 | 1,011 |
| 1941 | 554 | 994 | 5 | 2 | 3 | — | 78 | 60 | 98 | 159 | 136 | 1,637 |
| 1942 | 717 | 1,334 | 1 | 1 | — | — | — | — | 124 | 148 | 134 | 2,529 |
| 1943 | 1,024 | 1,444 | — | — | — | — | — | 2 | 192 | 187 | 105 | 4,505 |
| 1944 | 1,260 | 1,441 | — | 18 | — | — | — | — | 204 | 264 | 84 | 5,243 |
| 1945 | 1,125 | 1,178 | 13 | 472 | 1 | 2 | — | 1 | 231 | 307 | 90 | 2,193 |
| 1946 | 883[11] | 1,442[11] | 63 | 709 | 3 | 83 | 81 | 102 | 232 | 505 | 158 | 855 |
| 1947 | 1,127 | 2,114 | 47 | 817 | 6 | 128 | 35 | 60 | 247 | 630 | 205 | 1,103 |
| 1948 | 1,593 | 1,944 | 73 | 591 | 32 | 863 | 63 | 325 | 246 | 522 | 290 | 644 |
| 1949 | 1,551 | 1,959 | 61 | 497 | 45 | 822 | 82 | 468 | 243 | 468 | 228 | 700 |
| 1950 | 1,960 | 2,039 | 132 | 475 | 104 | 441 | 182 | 418 | 315 | 526 | 335 | 548 |
| 1951 | 2,275 | 2,693 | 263 | 843 | 233[2] | 523[2] | 205 | 601 | 326 | 730 | 466 | 1,000 |
| 1952 | 2,386 | 3,003 | 167 | 1,013 | 212 | 405 | 229 | 633 | 410 | 683 | 485 | -787 |
| 1953 | 2,462 | 3,197 | 186 | 1,236 | 277 | 363 | 262 | 686 | 355 | 663 | 546 | 826 |
| 1954 | 2,377 | 2,966 | 157 | 783 | 278 | 505 | 279 | 693 | 328 | 649 | 501 | 808 |
| 1955 | 2,653 | 3,404 | 202 | 536 | 366 | 607 | 432 | 683 | 397 | 719 | 616 | 1,006 |
| 1956 | 2,894 | 4,149 | 236 | 829 | 494 | 943 | 558 | 998 | 401 | 860 | 726 | 982 |
| 1957 | 2,907 | 4,041 | 256 | 708 | 607 | 1,330 | 601 | 1,319 | 430 | 917 | 766 | 1,162 |
| 1958 | 2,674 | 3,539 | 308 | 570 | 629 | 887 | 666 | 987 | 454 | 904 | 864 | 905 |
| 1959 | 3,042 | 3,825 | 462 | 483 | 920 | 878 | 1,029 | 1,079 | 435 | 755 | 1,137 | 1,097 |
| 1960 | 2,901 | 3,810 | 396 | 699 | 897 | 1,272 | 1,149 | 1,447 | 443 | 831 | 993 | 1,487 |
| 1961 | 3,270 | 3,826 | 435 | 704 | 856 | 1,343 | 1,055 | 1,837 | 538 | 828 | 898 | 1,206 |
| 1962 | 3,660 | 4,045 | 428 | 735 | 962 | 1,581 | 1,358 | 1,574 | 578 | 821 | 1,005 | 1,128 |
| 1963 | 3,829 | 4,251 | 431 | 813 | 1,003 | 1,582 | 1,498 | 1,844 | 594 | 873 | 1,079 | 1,213 |
| 1964 | 4,239 | 4,915 | 495 | 990 | 1,171 | 1,606 | 1,768 | 2,009 | 643 | 1,107 | 1,143 | 1,532 |
| 1965 | 4,833 | 5,642 | 615 | 971 | 1,341 | 1,649 | 2,414 | 2,080 | 638 | 1,104 | 1,405 | 1,615 |
| 1966 | 6,125 | 6,661 | 698 | 1,007 | 1,796 | 1,674 | 2,963 | 2,364 | 750 | 1,180 | 1,786 | 1,737 |
| 1967 | 7,107 | 7,165 | 690 | 1,025 | 1,955 | 1,706 | 2,999 | 2,695 | 749 | 1,222 | 1,710 | 1,960 |
| 1968 | 9,005 | 8,072 | 842 | 1,095 | 2,721 | 1,709 | 4,054 | 2,954 | 910 | 1,378 | 2,058 | 2,289 |
| 1969 | 10,384 | 9,137 | 842 | 1,195 | 2,603 | 2,142 | 4,888 | 3,490 | 1,029 | 1,450 | 2,120 | 2,335 |
| 1970 | 11,092 | 9,079 | 942 | 1,483 | 3,127 | 2,741 | 5,875 | 4,652 | 1,219 | 1,704 | 2,194 | 2,536 |
| 1971 | 12,691 | 10,365 | 1,088 | 1,373 | 3,650 | 2,831 | 7,259 | 4,055 | 1,262 | 1,620 | 2,499 | 2,369 |
| 1972 | 14,907 | 12,415 | 1,369 | 1,609 | 4,250 | 2,808 | 9,068 | 4,980 | 1,632 | 1,982 | 2,987 | 2,658 |
| 1973 | 17,715 | 15,104 | 1,732 | 2,263 | 5,345 | 3,757 | 9,676 | 8,313 | 2,306 | 2,937 | 3,656 | 3,564 |
| 1974 | 22,285 | 19,936 | 2,305 | 2,941 | 6,429 | 4,985 | 12,456 | 10,679 | 3,386 | 4,855 | 4,023 | 4,573 |
| 1975 | 22,151 | 21,744 | 2,164 | 3,031 | 5,410 | 5,194 | 11,425 | 9,563 | 3,066 | 5,141 | 3,773 | 4,527 |
| 1976 | 26,237 | 24,106 | 2,509 | 3,446 | 5,592 | 5,731 | 15,504 | 10,145 | 3,598 | 4,990 | 4,254 | 4,801 |
| 1977 | 29,599 | 25,788 | 3,032 | 3,503 | 7,238 | 5,989 | 18,550 | 10,529 | 4,694 | 4,822 | 5,141 | 5,951 |
| 1978 | 33,525 | 28,374 | 4,051 | 4,166 | 9,962 | 6,957 | 24,458 | 12,885 | 6,094 | 6,680 | 6,514 | 7,116 |
| 1979 | 38,046 | 33,096 | 4,768 | 5,587 | 10,955 | 8,478 | 26,248 | 17,581 | 8,800 | 9,847 | 8,028 | 10,635 |
| 1980 | 41,459 | 35,395 | 5,265 | 7,485 | 11,693 | 10,960 | 30,714 | 20,790 | 12,580 | 15,145 | 9,842 | 12,694 |
| 1981 | 46,414 | 39,564 | 5,851 | 7,341 | 11,379 | 10,277 | 37,612 | 21,823 | 13,265 | 17,789 | 12,835 | 12,439 |
| 1982 | 46,477 | 33,720 | 5,545 | 7,110 | 11,975 | 9,291 | 37,744 | 20,966 | 15,566 | 11,817 | 13,095 | 10,645 |
| 1983 | 52,130 | 38,244 | 6,025 | 5,961 | 12,695 | 8,737 | 41,183 | 21,894 | 16,776 | 9,082 | 12,470 | 10,621 |
| 1984 | 66,478 | 46,524 | 8,113 | 6,037 | 16,996 | 9,084 | 57,135 | 23,575 | 18,020 | 11,992 | 14,492 | 12,210 |
| 1985 | 69,006 | 47,251 | 9,482 | 6,096 | 20,239 | 9,050 | 68,783 | 22,631 | 19,132 | 13,635 | 14,937 | 11,273 |
| 1986 | 68,253 | 45,333 | 10,129 | 7,216 | 25,124 | 10,561 | 81,911 | 26,882 | 17,302 | 12,392 | 15,396 | 11,418 |
| 1987 | 71,085 | 59,814 | 10,730 | 7,943 | 27,069 | 11,748 | 84,575 | 28,249 | 20,271 | 14,582 | 17,341 | 14,114 |
| 1988 | 80,921 | 69,233 | 12,228 | 10,133 | 26,503 | 14,331 | 89,802 | 37,732 | 23,277 | 20,643 | 18,042 | 18,404 |

**E2     SOUTH AMERICA: EXTERNAL TRADE (IN CURRENT VALUES) WITH MAIN TRADING PARTNERS**

**ARGENTINA** (million pesos)[12]

|      | Brazil | | Germany | | UK | | USA | |
|------|--------|--------|--------|--------|--------|--------|--------|--------|
|      | Imports | Exports | Imports | Exports | Imports | Exports | Imports | Exports |
| 1870 | 3.4 | 0.6 | 1.6 | 0.2 | 13 | 2.5 | 2.9 | 3.8 |
| 1871 | 2.6 | 0.6 | 1.2 | 0.1 | 12 | 6.1 | 2.1 | 3.7 |
| 1872 | 3.3 | 1.0 | 1.8 | 0.6 | 16 | 13 | 3.2 | 4.3 |
| 1873 | 3.0 | 0.8 | 3.2 | 0.4 | 19 | 14 | 5.2 | 3.0 |
| 1874 | 2.7 | 0.6 | 2.3 | 0.8 | 16 | 15 | 3.9 | 3.7 |
| 1875 | ... | ... | ... | ... | ... | ... | ... | ... |
| 1876 | 2.2 | 1.2 | 1.8 | 1.5 | 9.0 | 7.4 | 1.9 | 2.5 |
| 1877 | 2.5 | 1.9 | 2.1 | 1.2 | 9.8 | 5.5 | 2.3 | 2.5 |
| 1878 | 2.2 | 1.8 | 2.2 | 1.0 | 12 | 3.6 | 2.9 | 2.6 |
| 1879 | 2.3 | 3.4 | 2.3 | 1.6 | 12 | 3.9 | 3.9 | 3.9 |
| 1880 | 2.4 | 2.0 | 2.4 | 2.5 | 13 | 5.3 | 3.2 | 5.1 |
| 1881 | 2.7 | 1.8 | 3.5 | 4.0 | 16 | 3.9 | 4.3 | 4.1 |
| 1882 | 2.2 | 2.2 | 4.8 | 4.8 | 20 | 7.6 | 5.1 | 3.0 |
| 1883 | 2.2 | 1.7 | 7.0 | 4.8 | 31 | 6.0 | 4.9 | 3.5 |
| 1884 | 2.3 | 1.5 | 8.9 | 6.8 | 31 | 7.2 | 7.5 | 4.1 |
| 1885 | 2.2 | 2.2 | 7.3 | 8.5 | 35 | 13 | 7.0 | 5.6 |
| 1886 | 2.3 | 1.9 | 8.0 | 7.0 | 33 | 10 | 7.7 | 3.6 |
| 1887 | 2.5 | 1.8 | 12 | 9.8 | 35 | 17 | 11 | 5.9 |
| 1888 | 2.4 | 2.5 | 13 | 13 | 44 | 17 | 9.9 | 6.7 |
| 1889 | 2.6 | 3.7 | 15 | 17 | 57 | 15 | 17 | 6.7 |
| 1890 | 3.6 | 4.1 | 12 | 12 | 58 | 19 | 9.3 | 6.1 |
| 1891 | 1.5 | 5.2 | 6.2 | 12 | 28 | 17 | 3.4 | 4.2 |
| 1892 | 2.1 | 5.1 | 11 | 17 | 36 | 20 | 7.4 | 4.8 |
| 1893 | 2.1 | 5.2 | 11 | 10 | 33 | 19 | 9.6 | 3.4 |
| 1894 | 2.0 | 6.8 | 11 | 12 | 33 | 20 | 10 | 5.3 |
| 1895 | 4.1 | 8.1 | 11 | 13 | 40 | 15 | 6.7 | 8.9 |
| 1896 | 5.2 | 9.8 | 14 | 13 | 45 | 14 | 11 | 6.4 |
| 1897 | 4.8 | 8.7 | 11 | 14 | 36 | 13 | 10 | 8.3 |
| 1898 | 5.0 | 7.9 | 13 | 20 | 39 | 19 | 11 | 5.9 |
| 1899 | 4.8 | 7.0 | 13 | 29 | 44 | 22 | 15 | 7.7 |
| 1900 | 3.9 | 6.2 | 17 | 20 | 39 | 24 | 13 | 6.9 |
| 1901 | 4.4 | 9.7 | 17 | 21 | 36 | 30 | 16 | 9.3 |
| 1902 | 4.6 | 8.4 | 13 | 23 | 37 | 35 | 13 | 10 |
| 1903 | 5.4 | 8.5 | 17 | 27 | 45 | 36 | 17 | 8.1 |
| 1904 | 6.0 | 10 | 25 | 30 | 65 | 36 | 24 | 10 |
| 1905 | 5.3 | 13 | 29 | 37 | 68 | 45 | 29 | 16 |
| 1906 | 6.6 | 12 | 38 | 39 | 95 | 43 | 39 | 13 |
| 1907 | 7.8 | 14 | 46 | 36 | 98 | 54 | 39 | 11 |
| 1908 | 7.3 | 15 | 38 | 35 | 93 | 78 | 36 | 13 |
| 1909 | 8.2 | 17 | 45 | 41 | 99 | 81 | 43 | 26 |
| 1910 | 9.1[12] | 18[12] | 61[12] | 45[12] | 109[12] | 81[12] | 48[12] | 25[12] |
| 1911 | 8.5 | 18 | 66 | 43 | 109 | 92 | 52 | 24 |
| 1912 | 9.5[12] | 23[12] | 64[12] | 54[12] | 119[12] | 121[12] | 59[12] | 32[12] |
|      | 11 | 24 | 74 | 56 | 138 | 127 | 69 | 34 |
| 1913 | 11 | 26 | 84 | 62 | 154 | 129 | 73 | 25 |

E2    **SOUTH AMERICA: External Trade (in Current Values) with Main Trading Partners**

**ARGENTINA** (million pesos)

| | Brazil | | Germany | | UK | | USA | |
|---|---|---|---|---|---|---|---|---|
| | Imports | Exports | Imports | Exports | Imports | Exports | Imports | Exports |
| 1913 | 25 | 59 | 191 | 141 | 350 | 294 | 166 | 56 |
| 1914 | 25 | 41 | 108 | 81 | 249 | 268 | 99 | 112 |
| 1915 | 32 | 52 | 17 | — | 207 | 391 | 172 | 213 |
| 1916 | 46 | 59 | 1 | — | 235 | 383 | 243 | 272 |
| 1917 | 86 | 52 | 1 | — | 189 | 366 | 314 | 367 |
| 1918 | 112 | 76 | 1 | — | 284 | 695 | 385 | 375 |
| 1919 | 108 | 85 | 3 | 21 | 351 | 669 | 529 | 430 |
| 1920 | 115 | 51 | 101 | 54 | 497 | 636 | 705 | 350 |
| 1921 | 102 | 65 | 162 | 115 | 395 | 466 | 457 | 135 |
| 1922 | 111 | 61 | 211 | 120 | 367 | 341 | 347 | 181 |
| 1923 | 105 | 57 | 269 | 145 | 470 | 429 | 412 | 204 |
| 1924 | 85 | 73 | 236 | 230 | 440 | 532 | 415 | 163 |
| 1925 | 83 | 76 | 229 | 202 | 436 | 472 | 469 | 163 |
| 1926 | 96 | 68 | 212 | 186 | 361 | 452 | 461 | 164 |
| 1927 | 99 | 85 | 220 | 377 | 378 | 649 | 495 | 190 |
| 1928 | 73 | 92 | 222 | 329 | 373 | 687 | 441 | 198 |
| 1929 | 74 | 85 | 225 | 217 | 345 | 697 | 516 | 212 |
| 1930 | 69 | 65 | 198 | 123 | 333 | 510 | 371 | 135 |
| 1931 | 72 | 44 | 136 | 120 | 247 | 567 | 185 | 88 |
| 1932 | 53 | 21 | 77 | 112 | 180 | 465 | 113 | 44 |
| 1933 | 58 | 49 | 90 | 86 | 210 | 411 | 107 | 87 |
| 1934 | 63 | 61 | 97 | 120 | 292 | 553 | 146 | 79 |
| 1935 | 69 | 76 | 100 | 108 | 291 | 538 | 160 | 189 |
| 1936 | 61 | 104 | 103 | 96 | 263 | 582 | 161 | 202 |
| 1937 | 79 | 132 | 166 | 157 | 323 | 672 | 251 | 295 |
| 1938 | 75 | 98 | 151 | 164 | 293 | 459 | 255 | 119 |
| 1939 | 93 | 67 | 123 | 90 | 297 | 565 | 220 | 189 |
| 1940 | 113 | 76 | 10 | — | 325 | 545 | 450 | 253 |
| 1941 | 140 | 87 | 6 | 3 | 269 | 477 | 450 | 543 |
| 1942 | 226 | 106 | 7 | — | 231 | 601 | 397 | 511 |
| 1943 | 202 | 143 | — | — | 195 | 780 | 179 | 533 |
| 1944 | 344 | 220 | — | — | 80 | 942 | 152 | 536 |
| 1945 | 334 | 238 | — | — | 116 | 649 | 159 | 554 |
| 1946 | 338 | 150 | — | 2 | 308 | 877 | 665 | 596 |
| 1947 | 439 | 249 | 2 | 30 | 446 | 1,651 | 2,431 | 547 |
| 1948 | 521 | 260 | 13 | 133 | 775 | 1,535 | 2,287 | 537 |
| 1949 | 357 | 405 | 11 | 152 | 722 | 849 | 689 | 399 |
| 1950 | 460 | 430 | 106 | 264 | 569 | 973 | 787 | 1,109 |
| 1951 | 956 | 704 | 571 [2] | 459 [2] | 788 | 1,148 | 2,199 | 1,183 |
| 1952 | 881 | 326 | 687 | 227 | 509 | 619 | 1,537 | 1,115 |
| 1953 | 643 | 1,116 | 821 | 262 | 355 | 1,404 | 965 | 1,363 |

**E2    SOUTH AMERICA: External Trade (in Current Values) with Main Trading Partners**

**ARGENTINA** (million US dollars)

| | Brazil | | West Germany | | Japan | | UK | | USA | |
|---|---|---|---|---|---|---|---|---|---|---|
| | Imports | Exports | Imports | Exports | Imports | Exports | Imports | Exports | Imports | Exports |
| 1954 | 120 | 93 | 81 | 112 | 43 | 47 | 76 | 205 | 141 | 122 |
| 1955 | 110 | 129 | 70 | 54 | 75 | 19 | 76 | 201 | 154 | 118 |
| 1956 | 85 | 65 | 107 | 115 | 71 | 36 | 53 | 212 | 231 | 118 |
| 1957 | 123 | 75 | 90 | 99 | 7.6 | 10 | 101 | 237 | 307 | 112 |
| 1958 | 128 | 76 | 115 | 95 | 18 | 25 | 102 | 237 | 203 | 128 |
| 1959 | 58 | 89 | 112 | 92 | 18 | 26 | 90 | 235 | 191 | 108 |
| 1960 | 63 | 83 | 151 | 87 | 28 | 40 | 113 | 221 | 327 | 92 |
| 1961 | 78 | 27 | 211 | 76 | 33 | 52 | 140 | 174 | 383 | 86 |
| 1962 | 63 | 69 | 186 | 121 | 64 | 27 | 121 | 205 | 399 | 89 |
| 1963 | 58 | 78 | 106 | 94 | 47 | 39 | 78 | 200 | 242 | 154 |
| 1964 | 101 | 97 | 107 | 110 | 23 | 40 | 81 | 154 | 256 | 94 |
| 1965 | 163 | 107 | 110 | 99 | 44 | 32 | 73 | 153 | 273 | 96 |
| 1966 | 132 | 99 | 108 | 88 | 32 | 37 | 66 | 154 | 257 | 127 |
| 1967 | 124 | 101 | 112 | 79 | 41 | 34 | 69 | 139 | 243 | 123 |
| 1968 | 139 | 129 | 128 | 67 | 42 | 29 | 79 | 105 | 270 | 162 |
| 1969 | 174 | 130 | 174 | 74 | 65 | 72 | 93 | 155 | 346 | 144 |
| 1970 | 186 | 139 | 186 | 105 | 86 | 109 | 92 | 123 | 420 | 159 |
| 1971 | 197 | 107 | 219 | 115 | 157 | 89 | 113 | 120 | 416 | 162 |
| 1972 | 175 | 187 | 246 | 226 | 143 | 58 | 129 | 170 | 388 | 192 |
| 1973 | 205 | 309 | 239 | 265 | 256 | 143 | 104 | 214 | 480 | 268 |
| 1974 | 297 | 341 | 393 | 156 | 392 | 179 | 111 | 190 | 617 | 334 |
| 1975 | 359 | 213 | 424 | 127 | 494 | 136 | 137 | 79 | 644 | 197 |
| 1976 | 371 | 422 | 341 | 205 | 250 | 209 | 129 | 121 | 544 | 282 |
| 1977 | 372 | 465 | 427 | 297 | 364 | 308 | 169 | 146 | 781 | 389 |
| 1978 | 340 | 577 | 453 | 410 | 267 | 381 | 170 | 198 | 712 | 547 |
| 1979 | 654 | 886 | 618 | 435 | 356 | 395 | 222 | 235 | 1,414 | 581 |
| 1980 | 1,072 | 765 | 985 | 407 | 977 | 211 | 343 | 203 | 2,379 | 718 |
| 1981 | 893 | 595 | 905 | 355 | 965 | 166 | 322 | 218 | 2,094 | 863 |
| 1982 | 688 | 568 | 479 | 336 | 430 | 283 | 68 | 74 | 1,177 | 1,024 |
| 1983 | 667 | 358 | 475 | 249 | 307 | 377 | 3.5 | - - | 987 | 773 |
| 1984 | 831 | 478 | 443 | 298 | 376 | 271 | 0.4 | - - | 847 | 877 |
| 1985 | 612 | 496 | 404 | 290 | 266 | 361 | 1.8 | 0.2 | 694 | 1,028 |
| 1986 | 691 | 698 | 523 | 353 | 337 | 391 | 6.0 | 19 | 833 | 706 |
| 1987 | 819 | 539 | 766 | 383 | 441 | 224 | 7.4 | 72 | 952 | 931 |
| 1988 | 971 | 608 | 606 | 485 | 349 | 333 | 1.2 | 85 | 918 | 1,216 |

**E2    SOUTH AMERICA: External Trade (in Current Values) with Main Trading Partners**

**BOLIVIA** (million gold bolivianos)

| | Germany | | Japan | | UK | | USA | |
|---|---|---|---|---|---|---|---|---|
| | Imports | Exports | Imports | Exports | Imports | Exports | Imports | Exports |
| 1900 | 3.1 | ... | ... | ... | 2.3 | ... | 0.8 | ... |
| 1901 | 3.2 | ... | ... | ... | 2.3 | ... | 1.7 | ... |
| 1902 | 2.5 | ... | ... | ... | 2.4 | ... | 1.1 | ... |
| 1903 | 3.0 | 2.6 | 2.8 | ... | 2.8 | 6.3 | 1.1 | - - |
| 1904 | 3.9 | 0.7 | 3.8 | ... | 3.8 | 3.2 | 1.3 | - - |
| 1905 | 3.6 | 1.0 | 3.3 | 2.7 | 3.3 | 2.7 | 1.7 | - - |
| 1906 | ... | ... | ... | ... | ... | ... | ... | ... |
| 1907 | 9.1 | ... | ... | ... | 6.1 | ... | 7.8 | ... |
| 1908 | 10 | ... | ... | ... | 6.6 | ... | 8.1 | ... |
| 1909 | 5.3 | ... | ... | ... | 8.4 | ... | 11 | ... |
| 1910 | 8.5 | 15 | ... | ... | 16 | 46 | 5.5 | 0.2 |
| 1911 | 10 | 11 | ... | ... | 12 | 60 | 9.9 | 0.6 |
| 1912 | 17 | 11 | ... | ... | 9.1 | 67 | 4.6 | 0.4 |
| 1913 | 20 | 8.0 | ... | ... | 11 | 76 | 4.0 | 0.6 |
| 1914 | 11 | 3.7 | - - | — | 7.8 | 52 | 4.6 | 2.5 |
| 1915 | 1.6 | 0.1 | - - | — | 3.6 | 67 | 4.8 | 25 |
| 1916 | - - | — | - - | — | 4.1 | 66 | 9.4 | 29 |
| 1917 | - - | — | - - | — | 4.1 | 90 | 11 | 57 |
| 1918 | 0.1 | — | 0.1 | - - | 4.1 | 91 | 11 | 76 |
| 1919 | - - | — | 0.2 | — | 4.0 | 71 | 15 | 60 |
| 1920 | 2.1 | 0.1 | 0.3 | — | 14 | 70 | 20 | 72 |
| 1921 | 3.9 | 0.2 | 0.3 | — | 17 | 36 | 20 | 26 |
| 1922 | 2.8 | 0.4 | 0.3 | - - | 11 | 49 | 12 | 38 |
| 1923 | 6.7 | - - | 0.5 | — | 14 | 64 | 15 | 38 |
| 1924 | 7.0 | 0.8 | 0.4 | — | 13 | 82 | 18 | 26 |
| 1925 | 7.9 | 2.5 | 0.3 | — | 14 | 96 | 18 | 9.8 |
| 1926 | 8.1 | 4.4 | 0.6 | — | 15 | 96 | 20 | 12 |
| 1927 | 7.1 | 6.0 | 0.3 | — | 13 | 101 | 19 | 11 |
| 1928 | 7.5 | 3.4 | 0.3 | — | 11 | 97 | 19 | 7.1 |
| 1929 | 9.7 | 1.9 | 0.3 | — | 12 | 108 | 24 | 19 |
| 1930 | 7.9 | 2.4 | 0.3 | — | 9.7 | 78 | 16 | 13 |
| 1931 | 5.1 | 0.6 | 0.3 | - - | 4.9 | 50 | 7.5 | 3.0 |
| 1932 | 2.7 | 0.3 | 0.1 | - - | 4.1 | 40 | 5.4 | 1.8 |
| 1933 | 2.4 | 0.5 | 0.2 | - - | 9.1 | 63 | 12 | 3.5 |
| 1934 | 9.0 | 1.2 | 1.6 | - - | 8.4 | 128 | 25 | 3.5 |
| 1935 | 16 | 1.5 | 2.3 | - - | 6.8 | 133 | 18 | 6.0 |
| 1936 | 7.0 | 1.5 | 3.5 | - - | 6 | 75 | 16 | 7.8 |
| 1937 | 7.9 | 1.3 | 2.9 | - - | 4.7 | 75 | 16 | 9.1 |
| 1938 | 13 | 1.1 | 4.9 | 0.3 | 4.9 | 59 | 18 | 4.4 |
| 1939 | ... | ... | ... | ... | 3.7 | 76 | 15 | 4.0 |
| 1940 | 1.3 | 0.5 | ... | ... | 5.5 | 118 | 49 | 47 |
| 1941 | 0.3 | - - | 8.4 | 4.4 | 5.8 | 75 | 43 | 127 |
| 1942 | - - | — | 0.1 | - - | 7.4 | 73 | 50 | 149 |
| 1943 | — | — | — | — | 8.0 | 104 | 47 | 172 |
| 1944 | — | — | — | — | 5.0 | 98 | 47 | 165 |
| 1945 | — | — | — | — | 4.6 | 102 | 43 | 174 |
| 1946 | — | — | — | — | 6.1 | 95 | 63 | 154 |
| 1947 | — | — | — | - - | 7.6 | 103 | 98 | 170 |
| 1948 | - - | - - | - - | ... | 14 | 146 | 112 | 239 |
| 1949 | 0.7 | 0.2 | 0.1 | - - | 14 | 116 | 136 | 225 |

**E2    SOUTH AMERICA: External Trade (in Current Values) with Main Trading Partners**

**BOLIVIA** (million US dollars)

|      | Argentina | | Germany | | Japan | | UK | | USA | |
|------|---------|---------|---------|---------|---------|---------|---------|---------|---------|---------|
|      | **Imports** | **Exports** | **Imports** | **Exports** | **Imports** | **Exports** | **Imports** | **Exports** | **Imports** | **Exports** |
| 1950 | 9.9  | 2.2  | - -   | - -   | - -  | —    | 3.9  | 28  | 24   | 63   |
| 1951 | 12   | 1.3  | 2.1   | 0.1   | 0.2  | —    | 7.0  | 48  | 36   | 100  |
| 1952 | 13   | 1.1  | 5.1   | 0.2   | 0.5  | - -  | 7.7  | 44  | 38   | 93   |
| 1953 | 9.7  | 1.0  | 3.3₂  | - -₂  | 0.2  | - -  | 4.6  | 52  | 22   | 69   |
| 1954 | 7.7  | 1.3  | 4.0   | 0.1   | 0.3  | - -  | 4.4  | 42  | 25   | 65   |
| 1955 | 8.4  | 2.4  | 7.9   | 1     | 0.9  | —    | 6.1  | 33  | 31   | 61   |
| 1956 | 12   | 2.7  | 7.8   | 1.4   | 0.6  | - -  | 4.9  | 40  | 39   | 57   |
| 1957 | 6.0  | 4.6  | 11    | 3.2   | 1.8  | —    | 6.0  | 52  | 43   | 33   |
| 1958 | 6.5  | 6.0  | 9.8   | 1.8   | 2.3  | 0.2  | 4.8  | 33  | 37   | 21   |
| 1959 | 8.1  | 4.6  | 7.6   | 3.5   | 1.5  | 2.9  | 3.1  | 35  | 29   | 27   |
| 1960 | 4.2  | 3.9  | 9.1   | 3.3   | 4.2  | 2.5  | 3.7  | 37  | 31   | 16   |
| 1961 | 6.6  | 2.6  | 9.5   | 4.6   | 5.8  | 2.0  | 3.8  | 39  | 33   | 21   |
| 1962 | 7.9  | 1.9  | 11    | 4.6   | 8.5  | 1.7  | 6.0  | 41  | 39   | 23   |
| 1963 | 4.1  | 2.1  | 14    | 4.7   | 7.7  | 1.5  | 5.8  | 41  | 50   | 28   |
| 1964 | 3.2  | 1.0  | 11    | 5.3   | 9.7  | 2.8  | 5    | 55  | 53   | 41   |
| 1965 | 7.3  | 0.9  | 15    | 6.7   | 18   | 2.7  | 7    | 59  | 59   | 56   |
| 1966 | 8.7  | 3.3  | 17    | 7.9   | 16   | 2.7  | 6.4  | 68  | 57   | 59   |
| 1967 | 9.0  | 5.3  | 18    | 8.2   | 18   | 4.0  | 6.9  | 67  | 62   | 72   |
| 1968 | 11   | 8.2  | 18    | 5.7   | 17   | 5.3  | 7.2  | 77  | 66   | 60   |
| 1969 | 17   | 11   | 20    | 5.2   | 27   | 12   | 8.3  | 91  | 51   | 61   |
| 1970 | 16   | 11   | 20    | 6.1   | 26   | 22   | 8.0  | 87  | 49   | 74   |
| 1971 | 18   | 12   | 21    | 5.6   | 28   | 13   | 8.6  | 97  | 53   | 59   |
| 1972 | 31   | 33   | 18    | 9.9   | 20   | 13   | 6.8  | 62  | 44   | 66   |
| 1973 | 34   | 6.8  | 20    | 12    | 23   | 19   | 7.9  | 67  | 50   | 77   |
| 1974 | 58   | 114  | 31    | 33    | 55   | 32   | 10   | 76  | 103  | 200  |
| 1975 | 74   | 137  | 50    | 17    | 87   | 18   | 15   | 53  | 154  | 165  |
| 1976 | 86   | 136  | 51    | 24    | 79   | 17   | 16   | 52  | 135  | 222  |
| 1977 | 79   | 130  | 58    | 28    | 77   | 17   | 14   | 79  | 141  | 269  |
| 1978 | 80   | 126  | 95    | 33    | 102  | 14   | 34   | 93  | 208  | 214  |
| 1979 | 93   | 136  | 81    | 44    | 82   | 21   | 25   | 84  | 242  | 241  |
| 1980 | 70   | 245  | 61    | 41    | 60   | 9.4  | 39   | 73  | 167  | 301  |
| 1981 | 90   | 342  | 73    | 27    | 106  | 9.3  | 44   | 36  | 206  | 272  |
| 1982 | 71   | 400  | 35    | 34    | 53   | 16   | 19   | 30  | 142  | 258  |
| 1983 | 75   | 362  | 29    | 23    | 39   | 16   | 21   | 21  | 149  | 192  |
| 1984 | 70   | 382  | 30    | 26    | 28   | 8.4  | 8.7  | 41  | 83   | 146  |
| 1985 | 117  | 376  | 52    | 31    | 66   | 2.9  | 30   | 63  | 141  | 95   |
| 1986 | 76   | 341  | 46    | 38    | 65   | 2.6  | 31   | 51  | 151  | 94   |
| 1987 | 107  | 260  | 53    | 33    | 76   | 2.9  | 6.8  | 61  | 161  | 96   |
| 1988 | ...  | 227  | ...   | 34    | ...  | ...  | ...  | 72  | ...  | 123  |

**E2    SOUTH AMERICA: External Trade (in Current Values) with Main Trading Partners**

**BRAZIL** (million milreis or cruzeiros)

| | Argentina | | Germany | | UK | | USA | |
|---|---|---|---|---|---|---|---|---|
| | **Imports** | **Exports** | **Imports** | **Exports** | **Imports** | **Exports** | **Imports** | **Exports** |
| 1901 | 56 | 19 | 39 | 127 | 130 | 111 | 52 | 371 |
| 1902 | 42 | 21 | 54 | 116 | 133 | 128 | 58 | 272 |
| 1903 | 44 | 16 | 60 | 110 | 138 | 143 | 55 | 307 |
| 1904 | 53 | 22 | 65 | 108 | 142 | 126 | 57 | 390 |
| 1905 | 54 | 20 | 61 | 103 | 121 | 126 | 47 | 285 |
| 1906 | 53 | 29 | 73 | 141 | 140 | 128 | 57 | 281 |
| 1907 | 58 | 28 | 99 | 147 | 193 | 138 | 82 | 277 |
| 1908 | 57 | 30 | 84 | 111 | 163 | 104 | 69 | 283 |
| 1909 | 60 | 34 | 92 | 159 | 159 | 164 | 73 | 408 |
| 1910 | 61 | 35 | 114 | 110 | 203 | 233 | 92 | 340 |
| 1911 | 60 | 39 | 133 | 146 | 231 | 151 | 106 | 358 |
| 1912 | 71 | 44 | 164 | 160 | 240 | 133 | 148 | 438 |
| 1913 | 75 | 47 | 176 | 137 | 247 | 129 | 158 | 317 |
| 1914 | 54 | 36 | 87 | 70 | 135 | 108 | 102 | 312 |
| 1915 | 93 | 52 | 8.7 | - - | 128 | 125 | 188 | 428 |
| 1916 | 114 | 68 | 0.4 | — | 165 | 131 | 318 | 520 |
| 1917 | 109 | 107 | 0.9 | — | 151 | 149 | 395 | 533 |
| 1918 | 188 | 173 | — | — | 202 | 115 | 356 | 394 |
| 1919 | 204 | 96 | 3.2 | 11 | 216 | 158 | 640 | 902 |
| 1920 | 157 | 120 | 105 | 112 | 452 | 140 | 880 | 725 |
| 1921 | 200 | 113 | 137 | 165 | 345 | 118 | 527 | 628 |
| 1922 | 226 | 159 | 147 | 141 | 427 | 230 | 379 | 905 |
| 1923 | 278 | 177 | 236 | 187 | 601 | 229 | 506 | 1,364 |
| 1924 | 339 | 208 | 342 | 253 | 667 | 130 | 675 | 1,656 |
| 1925 | 396 | 215 | 466 | 272 | 751 | 201 | 838 | 1,814 |
| 1926 | 266 | 202 | 342 | 266 | 512 | 111 | 794 | 1,526 |
| 1927 | 390 | 219 | 348 | 379 | 695 | 127 | 930 | 1,684 |
| 1928 | 426 | 235 | 461 | 445 | 795 | 137 | 982 | 1,804 |
| 1929 | 386 | 245 | 448 | 338 | 678 | 251 | 1,063 | 1,630 |
| 1930 | 312 | 199 | 267 | 265 | 453 | 237 | 566 | 1,179 |
| 1931 | 277 | 203 | 195 | 314 | 327 | 240 | 472 | 1,488 |
| 1932 | 113 | 150 | 136 | 224 | 292 | 176 | 457 | 1,173 |
| 1933 | 278 | 151 | 262 | 229 | 420 | 213 | 455 | 1,310 |
| 1934 | 311 | 164 | 351 | 454 | 430 | 419 | 591 | 1,347 |
| 1935 | 500 | 202 | 800 | 680 | 478 | 378 | 898 | 1,617 |
| 1936 | 702 | 199 | 1,003 | 646 | 480 | 585 | 946 | 1,902 |
| 1937 | 737 | 242 | 1,270 | 872 | 642 | 549 | 1,229 | 1,851 |
| 1938 | 615 | 230 | 1,299 | 972 | 539 | 447 | 1,258 | 1,749 |
| 1939 | 420 | 310 | 958 | 672 | 462 | 540 | 1,672 | 2,031 |
| 1940 | 535 | 358 | 92 | 112 | 469 | 860 | 2,575 | 2,096 |
| 1941 | 620 | 617 | 101 | 81 | 313 | 821 | 3,325 | 3,832 |
| 1942 | 787 | 993 | 9.2 | — | 270 | 1,233 | 2,540 | 3,422 |
| 1943 | 1,146 | 801 | — | — | 437 | 1,231 | 3,310 | 4,420 |
| 1944 | 1,698 | 1,473 | — | — | 234 | 1,356 | 4,895 | 5,693 |

**E2    SOUTH AMERICA: External Trade (in Current Values) with Main Trading Partners**

**BRAZIL** (million cruzeiros to 1952, million US dollars subsequently)

| | Argentina | | Germany | | Japan | | UK | | USA | |
|---|---|---|---|---|---|---|---|---|---|---|
| | Imports | Exports | Imports | Exports | Imports | Exports | Imports | Exports | Imports | Exports |
| 1945 | 1,863 | 1,457 | — | — | ... | ... | 341 | 1,484 | 4,749 | 6,020 |
| 1946 | 1,020 | 1,363 | — | — | ... | ... | 1,035 | 1,596 | 7,583 | 7,693 |
| 1947 | 1,461 | 2,004 | - - | 10 | ... | ... | 1,548 | 1,652 | 13,975 | 8,214 |
| 1948 | 1,496 | 2,055 | 20 | 230 | 0.5 | 16 | 2,116 | 2,048 | 10,876 | 9,388 |
| 1949 | 2,174 | 1,550 | 111 | 314 | ... | ... | 2,665 | 1,713 | 8,770 | 10,121 |
| 1950 | 2,031 | 1,402 | 353 | 336 | 24 | 199 | 2,506 | 2,078 | 7,005 | 13,587 |
| 1951 | 2,313 | 2,163 | 2,073 | 1,557 | 394 | 302 | 3,158 | 3,196 | 15,563 | 15,936 |
| 1952 | 702 | 2,055 | 3,449 | 1,469 | 296 | 349 | 3,179 | 709 | 15,483 | 13,439 |
| | | | | | (million US dollars) | | | | | |
| 1953 | 185 | 77 | 108 | 147 | 11 | 41 | 49 | 71 | 366 | 745 |
| 1954 | 105 | 100 | 157 | 188 | 79 | 68 | 17 | 74 | 537 | 579 |
| 1955 | 152 | 100 | 88 | 104 | 45 | 56 | 18 | 60 | 308 | 602 |
| 1956 | 77 | 65 | 80₂ | 94₂ | 50 | 37 | 43 | 53 | 354 | 735 |
| 1957 | 90 | 103 | 127 | 83 | 23 | 37 | 51 | 66 | 547 | 660 |
| 1958 | 88 | 107 | 141 | 79 | 33 | 25 | 44 | 54 | 483 | 534 |
| 1959 | 105 | 43 | 141 | 86 | 27 | 31 | 37 | 73 | 461 | 592 |
| 1960 | 95 | 56 | 136 | 90 | 38 | 31 | 51 | 65 | 443 | 564 |
| 1961 | 30 | 67 | 141 | 114 | 79 | 43 | 47 | 62 | 514 | 563 |
| 1962 | 86 | 48 | 152 | 110 | 60 | 29 | 46 | 54 | 457 | 485 |
| 1963 | 88 | 46 | 134 | 112 | 62 | 32 | 53 | 55 | 457 | 531 |
| 1964 | 116 | 91 | 103 | 134 | 34 | 28 | 37 | 63 | 436 | 474 |
| 1965 | 132 | 141 | 96 | 142 | 37 | 30 | 30 | 62 | 325 | 520 |
| 1966 | 117 | 113 | 135 | 134 | 44 | 41 | 44 | 74 | 590 | 581 |
| 1967 | 123 | 98 | 168 | 135 | 50 | 56 | 56 | 61 | 572 | 548 |
| 1968 | 153 | 119 | 236 | 148 | 73 | 59 | 95 | 73 | 684 | 627 |
| 1969 | 156 | 171 | 286 | 220 | 106 | 105 | 90 | 99 | 682 | 610 |
| 1970 | 171 | 185 | 359 | 236 | 178 | 145 | 158 | 130 | 918 | 676 |
| 1971 | 132 | 201 | 474 | 256 | 260 | 158 | 213 | 127 | 1,064 | 760 |
| 1972 | 218 | 154 | 652 | 337 | 366 | 180 | 215 | 180 | 1,339 | 931 |
| 1973 | 344 | 198 | 884 | 555 | 549 | 425 | 268 | 312 | 2,004 | 1,122 |
| 1974 | 382 | 302 | 1,762 | 570 | 1,250 | 557 | 354 | 374 | 3,434 | 1,737 |
| 1975 | 252 | 383 | 1,460 | 702 | 1,256 | 672 | 359 | 340 | 3,380 | 1,337 |
| 1976 | 473 | 331 | 1,190 | 919 | 970 | 639 | 347 | 387 | 3,103 | 1,843 |
| 1977 | 504 | 373 | 1,127 | 1,066 | 936 | 685 | 292 | 421 | 2,623 | 2,149 |
| 1978 | 594 | 349 | 1,207 | 1,062 | 1,336 | 650 | 385 | 513 | 3,178 | 2,869 |
| 1979 | 990 | 718 | 1,461 | 1,115 | 1,179 | 887 | 500 | 708 | 3,619 | 2,941 |
| 1980 | 841 | 1,092 | 1,735 | 1,337 | 1,191 | 1,232 | 483 | 550 | 4,626 | 3,496 |
| 1981 | 634 | 880 | 1,177 | 1,317 | 1,379 | 1,220 | 367 | 735 | 3,931 | 4,111 |
| 1982 | 594 | 650 | 932 | 1,179 | 973 | 1,304 | 270 | 672 | 3,160 | 4,140 |
| 1983 | 373 | 655 | 754 | 1,131 | 617 | 1,433 | 253 | 719 | 2,615 | 5,063 |
| 1984 | 539 | 853 | 681 | 1,256 | 609 | 1,515 | 304 | 708 | 2,525 | 7,709 |
| 1985 | 493 | 548 | 932 | 1,309 | 613 | 1,398 | 273 | 632 | 2,825 | 6,951 |
| 1986 | 776 | 678 | 1,390 | 1,099 | 979 | 1,514 | 375 | 646 | 3,488 | 6,306 |
| 1987 | 612 | 832 | 1,545 | 1,229 | 939 | 1,676 | 408 | 756 | 3,428 | 7,325 |
| 1988 | 739 | 975 | 1,530 | 1,424 | 1,058 | 2,274 | 431 | 1,065 | 3,349 | 8,715 |

**E2    SOUTH AMERICA: External Trade (in Current Values) with Main Trading Partners**

## CHILE (million gold pesos)[13]

|      | Argentina | | Germany | | UK | | USA | |
|------|---------|---------|---------|---------|---------|---------|---------|---------|
|      | Imports | Exports | Imports | Exports | Imports | Exports | Imports | Exports |
| 1873 | 1.4 | 0.1 | 4.2 | 0.5 | 18 | 19 | 2.1 | 1.9 |
| 1874 | 1.4 | 0.3 | 3.7 | 0.7 | 17 | 22 | 2.2 | 0.6 |
| 1875 | 2.7 | 0.2 | 4.2 | 0.9 | 16 | 21 | 2.1 | 0.4 |
| 1876 | 3.1 | 0.5 | 3.7 | 1.1 | 13 | 21 | 2.6 | 1.1 |
| 1877 | 3.1 | 0.4 | 3.4 | 1.3 | 9.4 | 15 | 1.9 | 0.9 |
| 1878 | 2.6 | 0.3 | 2.9 | 1.5 | 7.9 | 17 | 1.5 | 0.5 |
| 1879 | 1.6 | 0.2 | 2.8 | 1.6 | 8.9 | 33 | 1.4 | 0.7 |
| 1880 | 1.5 | 1.1 | 4.8 | 2.1 | 13 | 40 | 1.7 | 2.5 |
| 1881 | 2.0 | 0.1 | 7.4 | 2.9 | 18 | 43 | 1.7 | 3.2 |
| 1882 | 2.2 | 0.3 | 9.0 | 3.8 | 23 | 53 | 2.6 | 2.6 |
| 1883 | 3.6 | 0.3 | 10 | 4.8 | 22 | 59 | 3.6 | 1.7 |
| 1884 | 3.4 | - - | 10 | 3.9 | 21 | 42 | 4.2 | 1.3 |
| 1885 | 3.2 | - - | 7.1 | 3.2 | 16 | 40 | 2.7 | 1.6 |
| 1886 | 4.1 | - - | 8.3 | 3.2 | 17 | 38 | 2.6 | 2.7 |
| 1887 | 2.2 | - - | 12 | 5.1 | 20 | 45 | 3.2 | 2.6 |
| 1888 | 4.3 | - - | 14 | 4.8 | 26 | 57 | 3.1 | 2.1 |
| 1889 | 5.2 | - - | 15 | 5.4 | 28 | 48 | 3.8 | 3.8 |
| 1890 | 4.4 | - - | 16 | 6.4 | 29 | 46 | 5.2 | 8.5 |
| 1891 | 5.2 | - - | 12 | 7.6 | 28 | 43 | 4.1 | 6.6 |
| 1892 | 5.8 | 0.2 | 21 | 7.1 | 34 | 47 | 4.6 | 3.1 |
| 1893 | 5.4 | 0.2 | 17 | 6.2 | 31 | 55 | 4.5 | 2.9 |
| 1894 | 4.2 | 0.1 | 12 | 9.7 | 25 | 53 | 3.8 | 1.7 |
| 1895 | 5.1 | 0.1 | 17 | 8.0 | 32 | 54 | 4.6 | 2.2 |
| 1896 | 4.1 | 0.2 | 20 | 10 | 30 | 54 | 6.8 | 2.2 |
| 1897 | 3.3 | 0.3 | 16 | 11 | 29 | 42 | 4.5 | 3.3 |
| 1898 | 3.7 | 0.4 | 26 | 25 | 38 | 111 | 9.4 | 7.6 |
| 1899 | 2.2 | 0.3 | 30 | 21 | 44 | 111 | 8.2 | 7.4 |
| 1900 | 2.5 | 0.4 | 34 | 20 | 42 | 123 | 12 | 6.4 |
| 1901 | 3.4 | 0.2 | 34 | 58 | 50 | 39 | 17 | 15 |
| 1902 | 3.2 | 0.4 | 36 | 55 | 52 | 63 | 14 | 27 |
| 1903 | 4.3 | 0.4 | 39 | 43 | 54 | 62 | 12 | 33 |
| 1904 | 6.0 | 0.9 | 42 | 63 | 57 | 71 | 14 | 31 |
| 1905 | 6.3 | 1.6 | 48 | 73 | 71 | 101 | 19 | 43 |
| 1906 | 7.6 | 2.2 | 58 | 54 | 88 | 132 | 25 | 48 |
| 1907 | 10 | 3.6 | 74 | 56 | 114 | 141 | 31 | 25 |
| 1908 | 11 | 3.4 | 76 | 68 | 84 | 151 | 24 | 44 |
| 1909 | 18 | 2.2 | 62 | 66 | 87 | 129 | 26 | 54 |
| 1910 | 15 | 2.9 | 72 | 63 | 94 | 131 | 37 | 68 |
| 1911 | 21 | 3.3 | 90 | 72 | 112 | 146 | 43 | 54 |
| 1912 | 11 | 3.1 [13] | 91 | 77 [13] | 106 | 151 [13] | 46 | 67 |
|      |    | 4.5 |    | 78 |    | 152 |    |    |
| 1913 | 8.9 | 4.3 | 81 | 84 | 99 | 153 | 55 | 83 |
| 1914 | 5.9 | 6.3 | 71 | 50 | 61 | 110 | 55 | 86 |

**E2      SOUTH AMERICA: External Trade (in Current Values) with Main Trading Partners**

**CHILE** (million gold pesos)[13]

| | Argentina | | Germany | | UK | | USA | |
|---|---|---|---|---|---|---|---|---|
| | **Imports** | **Exports** | **Imports** | **Exports** | **Imports** | **Exports** | **Imports** | **Exports** |
| 1915 | 6.7 | 11 | 9.8 | — | 36 | 112 | 51 | 138 |
| 1916 | 6.9 | 14 | 1.2 | — | 55 | 133 | 94 | 252 |
| 1917 | 21 | 23 | 0.2 | — | 65 | 152 | 174 | 425 |
| 1918 | 31 | 26 | - - | — | 81 | 182 | 203 | 489 |
| 1919 | 11 | 14 | 0.7 | 0.1 | 78 | 71 | 192 | 131 |
| 1920 | 17 | 14 | 21 | 7.3 | 116 | 164 | 140 | 344 |
| 1921 | 7.5 | 6.8 | 33 | 15 | 103 | 68 | 105 | 74 |
| 1922 | 8.5 | 7.1 | 33 | 22 | 57 | 39 | 64 | 120 |
| 1923 | 14 | 7.9 | 44 | 25 | 79 | 155 | 88 | 247 |
| 1924 | 7.3 | 9.4 | 51 | 37 | 76 | 189 | 85 | 251 |
| 1925 | 12 | 9.5 | 45 | 41 | 85 | 215 | 113 | 244 |
| 1926 | 23 | 6.8 | 52 | 33 | 74 | 143 | 141 | 266 |
| 1927 | 17 | 11 | 45 | 61 | 66 | 201 | 106 | 175 |
| 1928 | 17 | 12 | 56 | 61 | 71 | 225 | 123 | 222 |
| 1929 | 25 | 13 | 83 | 66 | 95 | 102 | 174 | 194 |
| 1930 | 19 | 10 | 79 | 35 | 71 | 65 | 156 | 113 |
| 1931 | 3.6 | 4.5 | 39 | 25 | 38 | 45 | 81 | 92 |
| 1932 | 2.5 | 2.7 | 11 | 13 | 9.2 | 30 | 17 | 26 |
| 1933 | 6.4 | 3.6 | 6.9 | 7.4 | 7.4 | 28 | 14 | 23 |
| 1934 | 2.0 | 2.8 | 8.2 | 8.2 | 19 | 38 | 23 | 35 |
| 1935 | 3.1 | 2.1 | 20 | 11 | 19 | 28 | 28 | 40 |
| 1936 | 3.2 | 3.4 | 33 | 18 | 15 | 31 | 29 | 40 |
| 1937 | 6.1 | 3.7 | 37 | 30 | 16 | 62 | 42 | 71 |
| 1938 | 7.2 | 3.3 | 43 | 23 | 18 | 50 | 46 | 36 |
| 1939 | 6.0 | 4.3 | 31 | 29 | 11 | 28 | 43 | 68 |
| 1940 | 11 | 6.3 | 5.7 | - - | 18 | 13 | 81 | 135 |
| 1941 | 13 | 11 | 1.3 | 1.9 | 16 | 11 | 99 | 167 |
| 1942 | 25 | 17 | 0.4 | — | 11 | 7.0 | 94 | 201 |
| 1943 | 36 | 13 | - - | — | 15 | 6.7 | 79 | 198 |
| 1944 | 41 | 26 | — | — | 15 | 3.7 | 103 | 207 |
| 1945 | 52 | 31 | — | — | 12 | 6.0 | 106 | 189 |
| 1946 | 46 | 28 | - - | 0.1 | 18 | 46 | 128 | 136 |
| 1947 | 46 | 35 | 0.2 | 1.8 | 23 | 48 | 190 | 201 |
| 1948 | 42 | 22 | 2.5 | 1.7 | 29 | 42 | 185 | 282 |
| 1949 | 22 | 18 | 1.4 | 10 | 39 | 40 | 267 | 241 |
| 1950 | 22 | 27 | 8.3 | 15 | 46 | 24 | 191 | 248 |
| 1951 | 42 | 41 | 27 | 26 | 38 | 36 | 293 | 318 |
| 1952 | 50 | 63 | 35 | 39 | 52 | 41 | 309 | 426 |
| 1953 | 50 | 72 | 36 | 36 | 34 | 23 | 286 | 427 |
| 1954 | 86 | 59 | 42 | 46 | 28 | 89 | 226 | 303 |

E2     SOUTH AMERICA: External Trade (in Current Values) with Main Trading Partners

**CHILE** (million gold pesos to 1969, million US dollars subsequently)[13]

|      | Argentina | | Germany | | Japan | | UK | | USA | |
|------|---------|---------|---------|---------|---------|---------|---------|---------|---------|---------|
|      | Imports | Exports | Imports | Exports | Imports | Exports | Imports | Exports | Imports | Exports |
| 1955 | 64  | 72  | 68      | 78      | 11  | 2.9 | 33  | 129 | 262   | 326   |
| 1956 | 40  | 49  | 65[12]  | 99[12]  | 49  | 15  | 28  | 150 | 261   | 394   |
| 1957 | 26  | 30  | 88      | 96      | 31  | 30  | 40  | 111 | 370   | 307   |
| 1958 | 30  | 38  | 77      | 104     | 57  | 7.7 | 45  | 88  | 345   | 254   |
| 1959 | 43  | 39  | 69      | 129     | 23  | 35  | 44  | 121 | 354   | 313   |
| 1960 | 64  | 29  | 94      | 123     | 56  | 44  | 57  | 140 | 387   | 295   |
| 1961 | 89  | 37  | 133     | 101     | 101 | 127 | 66  | 124 | 385   | 301   |
| 1962 | 69  | 24  | 104     | 98      | 71  | 165 | 53  | 120 | 315   | 314   |
| 1963 | 85  | 23  | 125     | 99      | 60  | 192 | 73  | 120 | 362   | 299   |
| 1964 | 99  | 33  | 109     | 124     | 58  | 271 | 67  | 128 | 354   | 349   |
| 1965 | 83  | 43  | 103     | 147     | 45  | 359 | 62  | 125 | 384   | 345   |
| 1966 | 104 | 45  | 161     | 136     | 83  | 427 | 67  | 214 | 482   | 355   |
| 1967 | 125 | 64  | 148     | 115     | 43  | 510 | 79  | 201 | 417   | 273   |
| 1968 | 129 | 78  | 136     | 122     | 63  | 597 | 69  | 230 | 462   | 341   |
| 1969 | 150 | 107 | 151     | 162     | 87  | 694 | 78  | 250 | 566   | 302   |
|      |     |     |         |         | (million US dollars) | | | | | |
| 1970 | 93  | 78  | 115     | 135     | 28  | 150 | 58  | 154 | 344   | 177   |
| 1971 | 111 | 60  | 103     | 123     | 44  | 183 | 64  | 110 | 268   | 77    |
| 1972 | 144 | 51  | 88      | 177     | 33  | 148 | 54  | 94  | 165   | 82    |
| 1973 | 166 | 75  | 113     | 175     | 35  | 221 | 64  | 126 | 184   | 107   |
| 1974 | 323 | 169 | 151     | 337     | 49  | 407 | 70  | 217 | 416   | 286   |
| 1975 | 324 | 166 | 127     | 239     | 78  | 187 | 90  | 137 | 587   | 146   |
| 1976 | 222 | 133 | 109     | 300     | 59  | 231 | 49  | 137 | 523   | 223   |
| 1977 | 206 | 164 | 149     | 258     | 195 | 258 | 59  | 112 | 455   | 269   |
| 1978 | 188 | 165 | 211     | 312     | 242 | 319 | 70  | 144 | 682   | 339   |
| 1979 | 161 | 287 | 270     | 799     | 319 | 518 | 123 | 244 | 954   | 414   |
| 1980 | 234 | 277 | 288     | 419     | 417 | 508 | 117 | 266 | 1,302 | 458   |
| 1981 | 181 | 186 | 344     | 309     | 734 | 409 | 156 | 154 | 1,530 | 541   |
| 1982 | 144 | 150 | 174     | 388     | 196 | 429 | 96  | 202 | 792   | 692   |
| 1983 | 200 | 118 | 173     | 444     | 157 | 325 | 74  | 225 | 689   | 944   |
| 1984 | 161 | 117 | 216     | 360     | 313 | 407 | 80  | 197 | 748   | 873   |
| 1985 | 106 | 84  | 209     | 364     | 189 | 389 | 84  | 247 | 655   | 797   |
| 1986 | 123 | 161 | 250     | 443     | 296 | 426 | 89  | 217 | 641   | 835   |
| 1987 | 159 | 175 | 335     | 483     | 387 | 561 | 128 | 318 | 773   | 1,141 |
| 1988 | 279 | 168 | 365     | 778     | 392 | 877 | 150 | 397 | 1,002 | 1,242 |

**E2    SOUND AMERICA: External Trade** (in Current Values) with Main Trading Partners

## COLOMBIA (thousand gold pesos to 1909, millions subsequently)[14]

| | Germany | | UK | | USA | |
|---|---|---|---|---|---|---|
| | Imports | Exports | Imports | Exports | Imports | Exports |
| 1839 | — | ... | 2,181 | ... | 197 | ... |
| 1840 | — | ... | 2,244 | ... | 228 | ... |
| 1841 | — | ... | 63 | ... | 2 | ... |
| 1842 | — | ... | 1,669 | ... | 131 | ... |
| 1843 | ... | ... | ... | ... | ... | ... |
| 1844 | ... | ... | 2,461 | ... | 186 | ... |
| 1855 | 68 | 382 | 1,402 | 1,493 | 344 | 712 |
| 1856 | 100 | 338 | 1,480 | 2,930 | 684 | 754 |
| 1857 | 34 | 1,341 | 1,749 | 3,467 | 302 | 494 |
| 1858 | 55 | 1,641 | 792 | 1,275 | 263 | 391 |
| 1859 | 321 | 1,293 | 1,069 | 562 | 406 | 452 |
| 1867 | ... | ... | 3,220 | 958 | ... | ... |
| 1868 | ... | ... | ... | ... | ... | ... |
| 1869 | 378 | ... | 3,975 | ... | 414 | ... |
| 1870 | — | 2,680 | 2,892 | 1,939 | 407 | 645 |
| 1871 | 306 | 1,543 | 3,304 | 3,877 | 484 | 1,116 |
| 1872 | ... | 1,875 | ... | 2,752 | ... | 1,263 |
| 1873 | 772 | 2,526 | 5,778 | 5,483 | 557 | 1,179 |
| 1974 | 676 | 2,636 | 4,976 | 3,844 | 807 | 1,557 |
| 1875 | 603 | 3,133 | 2,965 | 3,352 | 767 | 1,470 |
| 1880 | ... | ... | 3,857 | 4,012 | ... | ... |
| 1881 | ... | ... | 4,732 | 6,849 | ... | ... |
| 1882 | ... | ... | 4,352 | 7,449 | ... | ... |
| 1883 | ... | ... | 5,057 | 6,871 | ... | ... |
| 1884 | ... | ... | 3,803 | 4,710 | ... | ... |
| 1885 | ... | ... | ... | ... | ... | ... |
| 1886 | 553 | 894 | 2,906 | 3,151 | 829 | 3,490 |
| 1887 | 844 | 1,311 | 3,612 | 3,455 | 937 | 3,021 |
| 1888 | 1,169 | 1,532 | 4,617 | 4,202 | 1,004 | 6,878 |
| 1889 | 1,508 | 1,396 | 4,796 | 4,634 | 1,928 | 5,290 |
| 1890 | 1,636 | 2,475 | 4,990 | 4,835 | 1,218 | 4,636 |
| 1891 | 1,685 | 1,309 | 5,413 | 4,532 | 1,644 | 4,123 |
| 1892 | 1,315 | 1,451 | 4,290 | 5,967 | 1,816 | 4,855 |
| 1898 | 1,539 | 2,000 | 2,874 | 4,041 | 1,788 | 4,705 |
| 1903 | 5,741 | 3,626 | 5,878 | ... | ... | 7,211 |
| 1904 | ... | ... | 5,677 | ... | ... | ... |
| 1905 | ... | ... | ... | ... | ... | ... |
| 1906 | ... | 716 | ... | 124 | ... | 4,708 |
| 1907 | ... | 631 | ... | 827 | ... | 4,809 |
| 1908 | ... | 1,456 | ... | 2,553 | ... | 8,621 |
| 1909 | ... | 1,549 | ... | 3,051 | ... | 8,588 |

| | Germany | | UK | | USA | |
|---|---|---|---|---|---|---|
| | Imports | Exports | Imports | Exports | Imports | Exports |
| 1910 | ... | ... | ... | ... | ... | 7.8 |
| 1911 | 3.2 | 1.9 | 5.8 | 4.6 | 5.4 | 12 |
| 1912 | 4.2 | 1.9 | 7.8 | 4.4 | 7.6 | 16 |
| 1913 | 4.0 | 3.2 | 5.8 | 5.6 | 7.6 | 19 |
| 1914 | 2.6 | 1.8 | 6.3 | 5.9 | 6.5 | 22 |
| 1915 | — | — | 5.4 | 3.7 | 8.7 | 27 |
| 1916 | — | —9 | 8.0 | 0.7 | 16 | 30 |
| 1917 | — | —9 | 7.0 | 0.7 | 15 | 31 |
| 1918 | — | — | 5.8 | 0.3 | 12 | 31 |
| 1919 | - - | 0.2 | 7.0 | 2.7 | 29 | 57 |
| 1920 | ... | ... | ... | ... | ... | ... |
| 1921 | ... | ... | ... | ... | ... | ... |
| 1922 | 2.6 | 0.4 | 9.5 | 4.0 | 21 | 41 |
| 1923 | 5.2 | 0.4 | 15 | 2.7 | 28 | 51 |
| 1924 | 5.1 | 0.9 | 11 | 3.2 | 27 | 69 |
| 1925 | 8.8 | 1.3 | 19 | 3.2 | 44 | 70 |
| 1926 | 14 | 1.4 | 18 | 4.3 | 53 | 96 |
| 1927 | 18 | 2.8 | 19 | 5.6 | 57 | 91 |
| 1928 | 23 | 2.9 | 19 | 8.4 | 66 | 104 |
| 1929 | 18 | 2.7 | 18 | 6.0 | 58 | 95 |
| 1930 | 8.1 | 3.7 | 7.8 | 3.3 | 29 | 83 |
| 1931 | 5.1 | 2.7 | 6.6 | 2.1 | 17 | 65 |
| 1932 | 4.7 | 2.9 | 6.1 | 0.8 | 13 | 51 |
| 1933 | 8.8 | 3.4 | 11 | 2.1 | 18 | 49 |
| 1934 | 13 | 6.9 | 15 | 2.9 | 38 | 81 |
| 1935 | 20[14] | 15[14] | 18[14] | 2.0[14] | 44[14] | 75[14] |
| 1936 | 27 | 23 | 23 | 2.4 | 50 | 74 |
| 1937 | 23 | 19 | 32 | 0.7 | 82 | 86 |
| 1938 | 28 | 21 | 18 | 0.7 | 79 | 76 |
| 1939 | 23 | 13 | 17 | 2.5 | 99 | 78 |
| 1940 | 1.1 | 0.1 | 11 | 3.2 | 106 | 76 |
| 1941 | 1.0 | — | 8.6 | 0.8 | 125 | 92 |
| 1942 | - - | — | 6.9 | 0.5 | 60 | 155 |
| 1943 | - - | — | 8.2 | 0.6 | 89 | 185 |
| 1944 | - - | — | 3.8 | - - | 113 | 179 |
| 1945 | - - | — | 8.2 | 1.8 | 185 | 193 |
| 1946 | - - | - - | 18 | 1.4 | 274 | 288 |
| 1947 | 0.2 | - - | 25 | 3.0 | 455 | 377 |
| 1948 | 0.8 | 0.7 | 33 | 2.6 | 405 | 420 |
| 1949 | 4.6 | 12 | 28 | 0.7 | 366 | 503 |
| 1950 | 33 | 32 | 33 | 1.0 | 498 | 635 |
| 1951 | 78 | 62 | 46 | 3.9 | 644 | 880 |
| 1952 | 54 | 54 | 52 | 5.6 | 697 | 952 |
| 1953 | 86 | 73 | 61 | 1.1 | 845 | 1,193 |

E2     **SOUTH AMERICA: External Trade (in Current Values) with Main Trading Partners**

## COLOMBIA (million US dollars)[14]

|  | Germany | | Japan | | UK | | USA | |
|---|---|---|---|---|---|---|---|---|
|  | Imports | Exports | Imports | Exports | Imports | Exports | Imports | Exports |
| 1954 | 54 | 36 | 8.3 | 0.5 | 30 | 1.3 | 421 | 518 |
| 1955 | 64 | 44 | 7.9 | 0.8 | 29 | 4.6 | 421 | 432 |
| 1956 | 77₂ | 35₂ | 8.5 | 1.0 | 22 | 3.5 | 406 | 383 |
| 1957 | 45 | 37 | 5.4 | 0.5 | 22 | 7.6 | 289 | 359 |
| 1958 | 46 | 44 | 3.7 | 1.2 | 17 | 7.8 | 238 | 319 |
| 1959 | 41 | 45 | 9.8 | 1.8 | 19 | 25 | 249 | 324 |
| 1960 | 53 | 55 | 13 | 4.5 | 30 | 20 | 296 | 298 |
| 1961 | 59 | 58 | 19 | 3.3 | 33 | 22 | 293 | 262 |
| 1962 | 54 | 57 | 17 | 2.9 | 32 | 16 | 273 | 267 |
| 1963 | 52 | 55 | 19 | 4.1 | 28 | 7.9 | 257 | 234 |
| 1964 | 58 | 66 | 26 | 3.2 | 35 | 10 | 274 | 283 |
| 1965 | 52 | 63 | 16 | 3.6 | 23 | 21 | 212 | 252 |
| 1966 | 73 | 69 | 28 | 6.4 | 37 | 21 | 312 | 222 |
| 1967 | 49 | 68 | 22 | 5.8 | 35 | 20 | 224 | 222 |
| 1968 | 58 | 74 | 26 | 8.9 | 34 | 21 | 321 | 234 |
| 1969 | 64 | 82 | 44 | 13 | 31 | 14 | 300 | 238 |
| 1970 | 72 | 104 | 59 | 21 | 36 | 15 | 390 | 268 |
| 1971 | 97 | 104 | 69 | 18 | 43 | 9.7 | 386 | 260 |
| 1972 | 85 | 121 | 72 | 34 | 49 | 19 | 330 | 295 |
| 1973 | 101 | 147 | 90 | 49 | 44 | 20 | 420 | 445 |
| 1974 | 145 | 170 | 140 | 21 | 73 | 22 | 632 | 531 |
| 1975 | 138 | 218 | 138 | 27 | 57 | 41 | 614 | 468 |
| 1976 | 177 | 283 | 160 | 62 | 63 | 34 | 679 | 542 |
| 1977 | 160 | 490 | 212 | 83 | 74 | 45 | 713 | 699 |
| 1978 | 199 | 648 | 280 | 71 | 95 | 44 | 999 | 904 |
| 1979 | 201 | 584 | 295 | 92 | 105 | 25 | 1,279 | 983 |
| 1980 | 334 | 741 | 434 | 148 | 112 | 42 | 1,840 | 1,069 |
| 1981 | 328 | 583 | 498 | 126 | 146 | 49 | 1,787 | 692 |
| 1982 | 316 | 560 | 608 | 127 | 116 | 46 | 1,891 | 714 |
| 1983 | 241 | 567 | 552 | 137 | 107 | 54 | 1,769 | 872 |
| 1984 | 245 | 578 | 431 | 154 | 93 | 86 | 1,535 | 1,097 |
| 1985 | 266 | 574 | 429 | 150 | 99 | 106 | 1,457 | 1,165 |
| 1986 | 256 | 1,051 | 350 | 249 | 103 | 133 | 1,389 | 1,530 |
| 1987 | 322 | 592 | 465 | 204 | 112 | 100 | 1,457 | 1,997 |
| 1988 | 341 | 525 | 540 | 262 | 122 | 88 | 1,813 | 1,974 |

## E2 SOUTH AMERICA: External Trade (in Current Values) with Main Trading Partners

**ECUADOR** (million sucres to 1948, million US dollars subsequently)

| | Germany | | UK | | USA | |
|---|---|---|---|---|---|---|
| | Imports | Exports | Imports | Exports | Imports | Exports |
| 1900 | 2.6 | ... | 4.0 | ... | 3.4 | ... |
| 1901 | 2.7 | ... | 3.6 | ... | 4.0 | ... |
| 1902 | 2.1 | ... | 5.8 | ... | 3.0 | ... |
| 1903 | 2.0 | ... | 3.2 | ... | 2.9 | ... |
| 1904 | 3.0 | ... | 4.0 | ... | 4.9 | ... |
| 1905 | 3.1 | ... | 4.6 | ... | 4.5 | ... |
| 1906 | 3.1 | 3.6 | 5.6 | 1.3 | 4.7 | 6.8 |
| 1907 | 3.6 | 3.0 | 7.2 | 2.3 | 5.0 | 6.0 |
| 1908 | 4.3 | 2.0 | 7.2 | 3.5 | 4.1 | 7.7 |
| 1909 | 3.3 | 3.2 | 6.3 | 2.5 | 4.8 | 6.8 |
| 1910 | 3.2 | 4.6 | 5.1 | 2.3 | 4.6 | 8.4 |
| 1911 | ... | ... | ... | ... | ... | ... |
| 1912 | 4.3 | 3.1 | 6.3 | 4.2 | 5.5 | 8.1 |
| 1913 | 3.2 | 5.4 | 5.4 | 3.3 | 5.8 | 7.9 |
| 1914 | ... | 1.5 | ... | 2.3 | ... | 7.0 |
| 1915 | 0.1 | ... | 6.9 | ... | 6.6 | ... |
| 1916 | - - | — | 4.9 | 7.3 | 11 | 18 |
| 1917 | — | — | 5.0 | 0.2 | 12 | 26 |
| 1918 | — | — | 3.9 | 2.0 | 9.5 | 21 |
| 1919 | - - | — | 3.3 | 7.3 | 17 | 21 |
| 1920 | 1.1 | 1.8 | 10 | 8.7 | 25 | 28 |
| 1921 | 1.9 | 10 | 6.9 | 1.1 | 8.9 | 11 |
| 1922 | 2.5 | 5.7 | 9.5 | 3.0 | 15 | 18 |
| 1923 | 5.4 | 2.6 | 9.0 | 2.9 | 15 | 17 |
| 1924 | 6.2 | 7.9 | 13 | 5.0 | 21 | 19 |
| 1925 | 5.7 | 7.7 | 12 | 4.1 | 25 | 30 |
| 1926 | 5.1 | 4.1 | 11 | 3.4 | 20 | 25 |
| 1927 | 6.7 | 8.1 | 9.8 | 12 | 28 | 32 |
| 1928 | 10 | 8.1 | 13 | 2.5 | 37 | 37 |
| 1929 | 11 | 5.1 | 16 | 2.3 | 35 | 39 |
| 1930 | 8.3 | 5.8 | 12 | 2.5 | 26 | 38 |
| 1931 | 5.9 | 3.0 | 8.0 | 2.0 | 17 | 26 |
| 1932 | 3.2 | 2.5 | 4.3 | 3.1 | 20[15] | 22 |
| 1933 | 4.5 | 1.9 | 5.3 | 1.0 | 10 | 22 |
| 1934 | 7.1 | 7.0 | 8.0 | 4.4 | 21 | 49 |
| 1935 | 14 | 11 | 12 | 8.5 | 28 | 53 |
| 1936 | 25 | 21 | 11 | 4.9 | 34 | 67 |
| 1937 | 32 | 36 | 13 | 4.4 | 52 | 54 |
| 1938 | 36 | 30 | 11 | 7.9 | 51 | 63 |
| 1939 | 27 | 11 | 8.1 | 6.2 | 72 | 83 |
| 1940 | 3.4 | 0.1 | 13 | 3.5 | 103 | 100 |
| 1941 | 1.2 | — | 10 | 1.2 | 110 | 146 |
| 1942 | 0.1 | — | 8.1 | 5.5 | 139 | 169 |
| 1943 | — | — | | | 104 | 139 |
| 1944 | — | — | 16 | 3.0 | 182 | 186 |
| 1945 | — | — | 12 | 0.7 | 190 | 175 |
| 1946 | ... | ... | 20 | 1.8 | 272 | 150 |
| 1947 | ... | ... | 41 | 6.8 | 430 | 217 |
| 1948 | - - | 1.2 | 36 | 1.5 | 413 | ???? |

| | Germany | | Japan | | UK | | USA | |
|---|---|---|---|---|---|---|---|---|
| | Imports | Exports | Imports | Exports | Imports | Exports | Imports | Exports |
| | (million US dollars) | | | | | | | |
| 1949 | 0.3 | 0.1 | | | 2.3 | 0.1 | 31 | 16 |
| 1950 | 2.1 | 2.5 | | | 2.5 | 0.5 | 28 | 36 |
| 1951 | 4.1 | 2.7 | 0.6 | 0.1 | 3.3 | 0.4 | 36 | 31 |
| 1952 | 3.4 | 2.5 | 0.7 | 5.2 | 3.4 | 0.5 | 37 | 41 |
| 1953 | 5.8 | 4.8 | 1.0 | 5.3 | 3.6 | 0.3 | 42 | 45 |
| 1954 | 9.1 | 7.3 | 1.1 | 0.1 | 5.1 | 0.7 | 46 | 64 |
| 1955 | 10 | 7.8 | 1.2 | 0.1 | 5.6 | 0.5 | 47 | 54 |
| 1956 | 9.4[12] | 11[12] | 0.8 | 0.1 | 4.8 | 2.2 | 42 | 56 |
| 1957 | 11 | 11 | 0.9 | 0.2 | 5.0 | 1.2 | 48 | 56 |
| 1958 | 11 | 11 | 1.0 | 1.8 | 4.3 | 0.9 | 43 | 54 |
| 1959 | 11 | 11 | 1.2 | 1.4 | 5.4 | 0.5 | 47 | 57 |
| 1960 | 13 | 11 | 2.6 | 1.8 | 5.8 | 0.8 | 49 | 65 |
| 1961 | 12 | 13 | 2.9 | 0.9 | 6.0 | 0.3 | 48 | 58 |
| 1962 | 10 | 14 | 2.9 | 3.3 | 6.0 | 0.4 | 43 | 74 |
| 1963 | 12 | 14 | 4.6 | 14 | 6.2 | 0.4 | 52 | 73 |
| 1964 | 17 | 21 | 6.2 | 9.0 | 7.8 | 1.8 | 69 | 66 |
| 1965 | 20 | 19 | 10 | 2.6 | 8.6 | 0.4 | 69 | 79 |
| 1966 | 27 | 21 | 12 | 4.9 | 12 | 0.5 | 66 | 75 |
| 1967 | 31 | 21 | 9.0 | 19 | 9.0 | 0.6 | 79 | 81 |
| 1968 | 31 | 19 | 17 | 24 | 13 | 0.5 | 86 | 73 |
| 1969 | 29 | 19 | 21 | 19 | 11 | 0.4 | 95 | 60 |
| 1970 | ... | 18 | 24 | 34 | ... | 0.3 | 108 | 81 |
| 1971 | 40 | 27 | 45 | 45 | 15 | 0.5 | 135 | 101 |
| 1972 | 35 | 28 | 39 | 50 | 19 | 0.6 | 121 | 113 |
| 1973 | 47 | 25 | 55 | 22 | 22 | 1.1 | 134 | 181 |
| 1974 | 73 | 48 | 89 | 18 | 30 | 1.3 | 243 | 460 |
| 1975 | 91 | 31 | 149 | 10 | 37 | 1.9 | 379 | 420 |
| 1976 | 84 | 37 | 160 | 14 | 36 | 1.4 | 378 | 476 |
| 1977 | 94 | 56 | 219 | 20 | 45 | 2.1 | 451 | 626 |
| 1978 | 137 | 61 | 242 | 23 | 53 | 2.9 | 576 | 673 |
| 1979 | 139 | 62 | 181 | 27 | 48 | 4.2 | 621 | 712 |
| 1980 | 164 | 30 | 307 | 304 | 59 | 5.5 | 862 | 806 |
| 1981 | 106 | 21 | 232 | 288 | 38 | 4.5 | 689 | 768 |
| 1982 | 150 | 24 | 239 | 17 | 42 | 2.4 | 656 | 988 |
| 1983 | 122 | 9.5 | 140 | 28 | 37 | 3.2 | 545 | 1,295 |
| 1984 | 127 | 31 | 242 | 17 | 32 | 8.1 | 528 | 1,655 |
| 1985 | 141 | 54 | 189 | 59 | 36 | 6.1 | 619 | 1,658 |
| 1986 | 177 | 78 | 250 | 57 | 41 | 5.4 | 547 | 1,332 |
| 1987 | 172 | 68 | 282 | 47 | 49 | 6.6 | 548 | 1,056 |
| 1988 | 107 | 91 | 238 | 54 | 35 | 9.0 | 568 | 1,006 |

## E2 SOUTH AMERICA: External Trade (in Current Values) with Main Trading Partners

### GUYANA (thousand pounds)[16]

| | Canada[17] | | UK | | USA | |
|---|---|---|---|---|---|---|
| | Imports | Exports | Imports | Exports | Imports | Exports |
| 1850 | ... | ... | 501 | 757 | 150 | 2 |
| 1851 | ... | ... | 486 | 814 | 145 | 2 |
| 1852 | ... | ... | 626 | 918 | 177 | 3 |
| 1853 | ... | ... | 457 | 959 | 200 | 7 |
| 1854 | ... | ... | 511 | 1,302 | 214 | 8 |
| 1855 | | ... | 465 | 1,249 | 195 | 19 |
| 1856 | ... | ... | ... | ... | ... | ... |
| 1857 | ... | ... | ... | ... | ... | ... |
| 1858 | ... | ... | ... | ... | ... | ... |
| 1859 | ... | ... | 638 | 1,139 | 254 | 54 |
| 1860 | ... | ... | 620 | 1,348 | 226 | 91 |
| 1861 | ... | ... | 732 | 1,434 | 258 | 44 |
| 1862 | ... | ... | 569 | 1,196 | 272 | 55 |
| 1863 | ... | ... | 562 | 1,421 | 246 | 95 |
| 1864 | ... | ... | 888 | 1,589 | 317 | 113 |
| 1865 | ... | ... | 741 | 1,729 | 286 | 228 |
| 1866 | ... | ... | 823 | 1,743 | 344 | 283 |
| 1867 | ... | ... | 750 | 1,824 | 361 | 362 |
| 1868 | ... | ... | 817 | 1,334 | 391 | 693 |
| 1869 | ... | ... | 760 | 1,138 | 399 | 779 |
| 1870 | ... | ... | 998 | 1,388 | 371 | 741 |
| 1871 | ... | ... | 1,025 | 1,266 | 429 | 1,204 |
| 1872 | ... | ... | 1,031 | 1,289 | 400 | 896 |
| 1873 | ... | ... | 935 | 1,535 | 350 | 375 |
| 1874 | ... | ... | 952 | 1,940 | 389 | 543 |
| 1875 | ... | ... | 927 | 1,745 | 365 | 290 |
| 1876 | ... | ... | 1,068 | 2,332 | 386 | 453 |
| 1877 | ... | ... | 1,080 | 1,955 | 495 | 734 |
| 1878 | ... | ... | 1,092 | 1,870 | 521 | 199 |
| 1879 | ... | ... | 1,072 | 2,169 | 419 | 225 |
| 1880 | 94 | 64 | 1,005 | 1,685 | 407 | 601 |
| 1881 | 89 | 74 | 834 | 1,771 | 398 | 514 |
| 1882 | 108 | 79 | 1,214 | 1,962 | 388 | 913 |
| 1883 | 177 | 97 | 1,266 | 1,590 | 422 | 1,213 |
| 1884 | 112 | 37 | 1,100 | 1,777 | 323 | 282 |
| 1885 | 91 | 20 | 725 | 1,294 | 345 | 308 |
| 1886 | 101 | 33 | 787 | 1,071 | 296 | 563 |
| 1887 | 95 | 42 | 916 | 1,148 | 317 | 814 |
| 1888 | 85 | 30 | 918 | 1,003 | 322 | 774 |
| 1889 | 35 | 42 | 1,051 | 1,317 | 401 | 883 |
| 1890 | 62 | 42 | 1,129 | 959 | 379 | 951 |
| 1891 | 72[16] | 45[16] | 927[16] | 1,221[16] | 375[16] | 1,109[16] |
| 1892 | 91 | 64 | 949 | 1,271 | 437 | 981 |
| 1893 | 90 | 99 | 1,047 | 1,234 | 481 | 898 |
| 1894 | 97 | 26 | 882 | 1,274 | 436 | 597 |
| 1895 | 69 | 42 | 790 | 968 | 382 | 658 |
| 1896 | 87 | 20 | 784 | 964 | 300 | 779 |
| 1897 | 63 | 17 | 741 | 949 | 342 | 705 |
| 1898 | 58 | 7 | 762 | 818 | 381 | 849 |
| 1899 | 66 | 18 | 747 | 964 | 376 | 838 |

| | Canada[17] | | UK | | USA | |
|---|---|---|---|---|---|---|
| | Imports | Exports | Imports | Exports | Imports | Exports |
| 1900 | 78 | 38 | 673 | 949 | 396 | 909 |
| 1901 | 84 | 80 | 703 | 752 | 405 | 808 |
| 1902 | 83 | 123 | 729 | 766 | 453 | 784 |
| 1903 | 107 | 607 | 869 | 674 | 476 | 410 |
| 1904 | 101 | 538 | 787 | 761 | 443 | 547 |
| 1905 | 117 | 651 | 860 | 862 | 471 | 327 |
| 1906 | 114 | 475 | 922 | 802 | 479 | 414 |
| 1907 | 136 | 865 | 925 | 615 | 508 | 38 |
| 1908 | 126[17] | 765[17] | 977 | 907 | 524 | 225 |
| 1909 | 138 | 657 | 831 | 893 | 481 | 197 |
| 1910 | 144 | 576 | 834 | 728 | 427 | 257 |
| 1911 | 116 | 875[16] | 834[16] | 713[16] | 441[16] | 362[16] |
| 1912 | 144 | 724 | 898 | 726 | 424 | 141 |
| 1913 | 112 | 797[16] | 907 | 1,015[16] | 377 | 80[16] |
| | | 796 | | 955 | | 75 |
| 1914 | 197 | 668 | 832 | 1,480 | 379 | 54 |
| 1915 | 277 | 1,141 | 883 | 1,328 | 459 | 79 |
| 1916 | 320 | 1,406 | 952 | 1,089 | 650 | 329 |
| 1917 | 440 | 1,568 | 950 | 1,682 | 1,231 | 134 |
| 1918 | 544 | 1,166 | 873 | 1,365 | 1,511 | 106 |
| 1919 | 720 | 1,635 | 1,103 | 1,287 | 1,235 | 114 |
| 1920 | 828 | 2,331 | 1,950 | 1,817 | 1,570 | 644 |
| 1921 | 610 | 1,011 | 1,528 | 1,953 | 814 | 67 |
| 1922 | 495 | 1,048[16] | 1,022 | 1,192[16] | 463 | 116[16] |
| | | 1,048 | | 1,162 | | 109 |
| 1923 | 555 | 1,241 | 1,385 | 1,666 | 417 | 154 |
| 1924 | 556 | 1,403 | 1,482 | 1,241 | 394 | 174 |
| 1925 | 599 | 844 | 1,539 | 1,312 | 446 | 186 |
| 1926 | 617 | 901 | 1,231 | 952 | 396 | 197 |
| 1927 | 538 | 1,210 | 1,264 | 1,051 | 346 | 196 |
| 1928 | 549 | 1,130 | 1,360 | 924 | 299 | 187 |
| 1929 | 416 | 928 | 1,258 | 798 | 274 | 180 |
| 1930 | 311 | 850 | 1,130 | 622 | 225 | 138 |
| 1931 | 229 | 747 | 935 | 573 | 177 | 177 |
| 1932 | 207 | 576 | 1,078 | 979 | 117 | 131 |
| 1933 | 225 | 378 | 1,115 | 1,079 | 114 | 64 |
| 1934 | 229 | 479 | 983 | 877 | 129 | 70 |
| 1935 | 271 | 940 | 1,010 | 727 | 167 | 117 |
| 1936 | 274 | 967 | 1,088 | 817 | 172 | 142 |
| 1937 | 345 | 1,225 | 1,285 | 814 | 235 | 163 |
| 1938 | 327 | 1,430 | 1,115 | 715 | 252 | 96 |
| 1939 | 406 | 1,540 | 1,009 | 922 | 322 | 89 |
| 1940 | 682 | 1,682 | 1,112 | 883 | 557 | 88 |
| 1941 | 1,381 | 1,834 | 826 | 1,525 | 776 | 234 |
| 1942 | 1,350 | 1,469 | 642 | 1,375 | 1,208 | 322 |
| 1943 | 1,909 | 1,877 | 840 | 598 | 1,385 | 518 |
| 1944 | 1,736 | 1,531 | 716 | 1,382 | 1,221 | 128 |
| 1945 | 1,822 | 1,507 | 858 | 1,539 | 1,056 | 160 |
| 1946 | 1,992 | 2,333 | 1,735 | 2,086 | 978 | 254 |
| 1947 | 2,812 | 2,664 | 2,266 | 3,224 | 2,174 | 354 |
| 1948 | 3,582 | 2,976 | 7,234 | 7,179 | 2,022 | 260 |
| 1949 | 4,971 | 3,433 | 8,047 | 9,009 | 1,523 | 663 |

**E2    SOUTH AMERICA: External Trade (in Current Values) with Main Trading Partners**

## GUYANA (million local dollars)[16]

| | Canada | | UK | | USA | | | Canada | | UK | | USA | |
|---|---|---|---|---|---|---|---|---|---|---|---|---|---|
| | Imports | Exports | Imports | Exports | Imports | Exports | | Imports | Exports | Imports | Exports | Imports | Exports |
| 1950[18] | 8.8 | 5.0 | 14 | 16 | 2.4 | 0.7 | 1970 | 24 | 48 | 84 | 50 | 64 | 72 |
| 1951 | 9.4 | 29 | 29 | 19 | 8.9 | 3.2 | 1971 | 15 | 30 | 83 | 72 | 65 | 76 |
| 1952 | 13[16] | 37[16] | 34[16] | 28[16] | 13[16] | 5.1[16] | 1972 | 15 | 20 | 89 | 87 | 72 | 74 |
| 1953 | 10 | 30 | 35 | 32 | 8.3 | 6.3 | 1973 | 20 | 14 | 95 | 85 | 91 | 60 |
| 1954 | 8.2 | 33 | 38 | 31 | 11 | 6.5 | 1974 | 28 | 31 | 116 | 122 | 146 | 164 |
| 1955 | 5.9 | 32 | 45 | 32 | 12 | 8.0 | 1975 | 35 | 26 | 174 | 240 | 239 | 187 |
| 1956 | 8.6 | 38 | 45 | 30 | 13 | 10 | 1976 | 39 | 17 | 213 | 180 | 264 | 134 |
| 1957 | 10 | 40 | 52 | 43 | 21 | 7.9 | 1977 | 47 | 35 | 150 | 207 | 216 | 119 |
| 1958 | 8.6 | 31 | 54 | 47 | 19 | 5.9 | 1978 | 29 | 54 | 135 | 195 | 162 | 149 |
| 1959 | 9.0 | 28 | 50 | 43 | 15 | 9.0 | 1979 | 27 | 69 | 150 | 210 | 207 | 136 |
| 1960 | 16 | 32 | 58 | 47 | 29 | 21 | 1980 | 31 | 72 | 187 | 249 | 208 | 238 |
| 1961 | 10 | 38 | 56 | 36 | 29 | 31 | 1981 | 48 | 46 | 197 | 252 | 296 | 202 |
| 1962 | 9.4 | 44 | 45 | 38 | 29 | 35 | 1982 | | | | | | |
| 1963 | 9.7 | 59 | 40 | 41 | 25 | 25 | 1983 | | | | | | |
| 1964 | 14 | 49 | 50 | 33 | 34 | 26 | 1984 | | | | | | |
| 1965 | 14 | 38 | 55 | 41 | 43 | 31 | 1985 | | | | | | |
| 1966 | 18 | 40 | 66 | 41 | 46 | 41 | 1986 | | | | | | |
| 1967 | 25 | 36 | 58 | 48 | 62 | 46 | 1987 | | | | | | |
| 1968 | 20 | 43 | 64 | 46 | 52 | 56 | 1988 | | | | | | |
| 1969 | 20 | 43 | 64 | 57 | 50 | 60 | | | | | | | |

## PARAGUAY (thousand gold pesos)

| | Argentina | | USA | | | Argentina | | USA | |
|---|---|---|---|---|---|---|---|---|---|
| | Imports | Exports[19] | Imports | Exports[21] | | Imports | Exports[19] | Imports | Exports |
| 1908 | 767 | 2,000 | 223 | — | 1925 | 6,115 | [12,285][20] | 2,601 | [91][20] |
| 1909 | 589 | 2,547 | 210 | — | 1926 | 4,099 | 11,957 | 1,938 | 1,152 |
| | | | | | 1927 | 4,009 | 12,080 | 2,224 | 99 |
| 1910 | 697 | 2,858 | 319 | — | 1928 | 5,515 | 14,010 | 2,291 | 60 |
| 1911 | 775 | 2,722 | 390 | — | 1929 | 4,852 | 11,454[19] | 2,593 | 6 |
| 1912 | 703 | 2,446 | 316 | — | | | 7,397 | | |
| 1913 | 1,090 | 3,516 | 488 | — | 1930 | 4,360 | 7,369 | 2,410 | 26 |
| 1914 | 930 | 2,294 | 429 | 13 | 1931 | 2,957 | 6,399 | 1,628 | 62 |
| | | | | | 1932 | 2,487 | 6,633 | 823 | 68 |
| 1915 | 1,026 | 5,578 | 282 | 480 | 1933 | 4,391 | 4,161 | 377 | 159 |
| 1916 | 2,403 | 6,509 | 873 | 426 | 1934 | 6,696 | 4,757 | 396 | 138 |
| 1917 | 3,347 | 8,957 | 1,562 | 370 | | | | | |
| 1918 | 2,479 | 4,102 | 816 | 752 | 1935 | 5,868 | 3,624 | 889 | 72 |
| 1919 | 6,760 | 11,059 | 2,704 | 1,008 | 1936 | 4,082 | 3,174 | 558 | 94 |
| | | | | | 1937 | 4,926 | 2,313 | 943 | 942 |
| 1920 | 5,022 | 8,685 | 3,130 | 1,325 | 1938 | 4,962 | 2,567 | 1,243 | 1,475 |
| 1921 | 3,216 | 6,540 | 1,444 | 1,095 | 1939 | 4,745 | 2,933 | 1,262 | 2,666 |
| 1922 | 1,842 | 7,338 | 1,221 | 1,613 | | | | | |
| 1923 | [2,268][20] | [6,032][20] | [1,036][20] | [992][20] | 1940 | 6,716 | 2,623 | 3,177 | 2,384 |
| 1924 | [3,471][20] | [6,142][20] | [1,306][20] | [945][20] | 1941 | 6,150 | 2,042 | 2,385 | 2,879 |
| | | | | | 1942 | 7,691 | 2,249 | 3,342 | 2,430 |
| | | | | | 1943 | 17,601 | 5,242 | 6,445 | 2,627 |
| | | | | | 1944 | 17,831 | 10,614 | 6,041 | 6,985 |

**E2    SOUTH AMERICA: External Trade (in Current Values) with Main Trading Partners**

## PARAGUAY (million US dollars)

| | Argentina | | Brazil | | USA | | | Argentina | | Brazil | | USA | |
|---|---|---|---|---|---|---|---|---|---|---|---|---|---|
| | Imports | Exports | Imports | Exports | Imports | Exports[21] | | Imports | Exports | Imports | Exports | Imports | Exports |
| 1945 | 9.1 | 6.1 | ... | ... | 2.4 | 2.8 | 1970 | 12 | 19 | 2.0 | 0.9 | 15 | 8.9 |
| 1946 | 9.9 | 7.1 | ... | ... | 4.5 | 1.1 | 1971 | 10 | 18 | 5.1 | 0.8 | 18 | 11 |
| 1947 | 7.8 | 8.8 | ... | ... | 6.5 | 0.5 | 1972 | 11 | 16 | 10 | 0.7 | 14 | 15 |
| 1948 | 8.2 | 9.2 | ... | ... | 6.6 | 0.3 | 1973 | 30 | 16 | ... | ... | 20 | 17 |
| 1949 | 6.3 | 12 | ... | ... | 8.5 | 0.4 | 1974 | 53 | 39 | 27 | 6.1 | 18 | 20 |
| 1950 | 7.5 | 12 | ... | ... | 5.0 | 1.0 | 1975 | 36 | 50 | 37 | 5.7 | 25 | 14 |
| 1951 | 6.7 | 12 | ... | ... | 4.9 | 4.7[21] | 1976 | 41 | 18 | 34 | 10 | 22 | 22 |
| 1952 | 3.3 | 4.6 | ... | ... | 10 | 10 | 1977 | 48 | 36 | 59 | 16 | 37 | 40 |
| 1953 | ... | ... | ... | ... | ... | ... | 1978 | 54 | 24 | 68 | 20 | 41 | 23 |
| 1954 | 9.2 | 15 | ... | ... | 6.5 | 6.3 | 1979 | 82 | 51 | 106 | 29 | 58 | 18 |
| 1955 | 13 | 16 | ... | ... | 4.0 | 6.4 | 1980 | 121 | 74 | 154 | 40 | 59 | 17 |
| 1956 | 7.1 | 13 | ... | ... | 3.3 | 6.6 | 1981 | 114 | 69 | 142 | 54 | 58 | 17 |
| 1957 | 11 | 11 | ... | - - | 6.5 | 8.3 | 1982 | 131 | 59 | 166 | 83 | 61 | 9.1 |
| 1958 | 7.2 | 13 | 0.7 | - - | 8.9 | 8.3 | 1983 | 103 | 32 | 147 | 52 | 40 | 23 |
| 1959 | 7.4 | 6.4 | 0.1 | - - | 5.3 | 10 | 1984 | 98 | 41 | 182 | 53 | 50 | 18 |
| 1960 | 7.5 | 7.7 | 0.3 | 0.1 | 7.6 | 7.2 | 1985 | 86 | 16 | 174 | 60 | 40 | 3.8 |
| 1961 | 8.3 | 8.7 | 0.2 | 0.1 | 5.3 | 7.4 | 1986 | 83 | 35 | 174 | 92 | 78 | 9.4 |
| 1962 | 5.0 | 9.6 | 0.2 | 0.1 | 11 | 7.0 | 1987 | 53 | 54 | 186 | 62 | 62 | 15 |
| 1963 | 7.6 | 8.6 | 0.5 | 0.4 | 9.6 | 9.1 | 1988 | 69 | 34 | 166 | 117 | 58 | 19 |
| 1964 | 9.4 | 12 | 0.3 | 0.1 | 7.2 | 12 | | | | | | | |
| 1965 | 9.8 | 15 | 1.5 | 0.1 | 10 | 14 | | | | | | | |
| 1966 | 10 | 16 | 1.6 | 0.2 | 10 | 12 | | | | | | | |
| 1967 | 13 | 14 | 1.6 | 0.2 | 12 | 11 | | | | | | | |
| 1968 | 13 | 13 | 2.4 | 0.2 | 17 | 12 | | | | | | | |
| 1969 | 13 | 19 | 1.6 | 0.3 | 16 | 9.0 | | | | | | | |

## PERU (million soles)

| | Germany | | Japan | | UK | | USA | |
|---|---|---|---|---|---|---|---|---|
| | Imports | Exports | Imports | Exports | Imports | Exports | Imports | Exports |
| 1890 | ... | ... | ... | ... | ... | ... | ... | ... |
| 1891 | 4.1 | 1.6 | ... | ... | 8.9 | 8.2 | 1.9 | 0.4 |
| 1892 | 3.3 | 1.5 | ... | ... | 7.4 | 13 | 1.4 | 1.3 |
| 1893 | 2.0 | 1.0 | ... | ... | 4.4 | 9.4 | 0.8 | 0.9 |
| 1894 | 1.8 | 0.8 | ... | ... | 4.1 | 6.7 | 0.8 | 1.0 |
| 1895 | ... | ... | ... | ... | ... | ... | ... | ... |
| 1896 | ... | ... | ... | ... | ... | ... | ... | ... |
| 1897 | 2.7 | 2.1 | ... | ... | 6.1 | 14 | 1.5 | 1.3 |
| 1898 | 3.4 | 2.7 | ... | ... | 8.6 | 17 | 2.1 | 2.9 |
| 1899 | 3.5 | 3.4 | ... | ... | 7.6 | 15 | 2.2 | 5.2 |
| 1900 | 3.6 | 5.2 | ... | ... | 11 | 21 | 3.0 | 9.6 |
| 1901 | 4.6 | 4.2 | ... | ... | 10 | 23 | 4.5 | 5.8 |
| 1902 | 6.2 | 3.0 | ... | ... | 11 | 16 | 5.9 | 7.1 |
| 1903 | 4.5 | 3.3 | ... | ... | 15 | 15 | 5.8 | 4.9 |
| 1904 | 7.0 | 3.4 | ... | ... | 16 | 20 | 7.6 | 3.8 |

E2      **SOUTH AMERICA: External Trade (in Current Values) with Main Trading Partners**

**PERU** (million soles)

|      | Germany | | Japan | | UK | | USA | |
| --- | --- | --- | --- | --- | --- | --- | --- | --- |
|      | **Imports** | **Exports** | **Imports** | **Exports** | **Imports** | **Exports** | **Imports** | **Exports** |
| 1905 | 6.8 | 4.0 | ... | ... | 15 | 30 | 7.3 | 5.3 |
| 1906 | 7.8 | 5.2 | ... | ... | 15 | 24 | 10 | 6.4 |
| 1907 | 8.9 | 3.7 | ... | ... | 16 | 24 | 12 | 14 |
| 1908 | 8.6 | 4.0 | ... | ... | 15 | 23 | 14 | 13 |
| 1909 | 6.9 | 3.5 | ... | ... | 16 | 27 | 8.5 | 15 |
| 1910 | 7.9 | 3.6 | ... | ... | 18 | 25 | 9.2 | 20 |
| 1911 | 9.5 | 5.7 | ... | ... | 17 | 25 | 12 | 21 |
| 1912 | 9.3 | 6.6 | - - | — | 14 | 32 | 12 | 36 |
| 1913 | 11 | 6.1 | - - | - - | 16 | 34 | 18 | 30 |
| 1914 | 6.5 | 3.3 | 0.1 | - - | 13 | 33 | 16 | 30 |
| 1915 | 1.0 | — | 0.2 | 0.1 | 6.7 | 36 | 15 | 64 |
| 1916 | 0.1 | — | 0.9 | 0.1 | 15 | 30 | 51 | 104 |
| 1917 | 0.4 | — | 1.3 | 0.2 | 19 | 38 | 88 | 109 |
| 1918 | 0.4 | — | 2.7 | 0.7 | 16 | 63 | 53 | 93 |
| 1919 | — | 0.5 | 3.2 | 0.9 | 16 | 84 | 76 | 125 |
| 1920 | 3.1 | 0.2 | 3.4 | 1.0 | 27 | 127 | 102 | 163 |
| 1921 | 7.4 | 0.9 | 2.8 | 1.2 | 23 | 58 | 82 | 65 |
| 1922 | 11 | 3.9 | 1.9 | 0.4 | 20 | 66 | 42 | 66 |
| 1923 | 15 | 7.3 | 1.6 | 0.2 | 29 | 80 | 57 | 95 |
| 1924 | 19 | 5.7 | 2.0 | 0.6 | 34 | 95 | 70 | 84 |
| 1925 | 20 | 3.7 | 1.9 | 0.6 | 34 | 74 | 71 | 76 |
| 1926 | 19 | 3.9 | 2.4 | 0.2 | 31 | 68 | 91 | 84 |
| 1927 | 20 | 16 | 2.0 | 0.2 | 31 | 88 | 81 | 86 |
| 1928 | 18 | 25 | 2.1 | 1.5 | 28 | 75 | 72 | 90 |
| 1929 | 19 | 20 | 2.4 | 0.1 | 28 | 61 | 79 | 112 |
| 1930 | 17 | 18 | 2.4 | — | 23 | 45 | 52 | 95 |
| 1931 | 9.6 | 17 | 1.7 | - - | 14 | 42 | 41 | 72 |
| 1932 | 8.2 | 13 | 1.3 | - - | 13 | 64 | 22 | 31 |
| 1933 | 11 | 19 | 5.3 | 1.0 | 19 | 93 | 29 | 40 |
| 1934 | 15 | 34 | 10 | 5.1 | 30 | 103 | 46 | 43 |
| 1935 | 27 | 35 | 9.4 | 8.9 | 25 | 66 | 60 | 64 |
| 1936 | 39 | 41 | 7.9 | 14 | 27 | 76 | 64 | 65 |
| 1937 | 46 | 47 | 8.1 | 3.9 | 24 | 83 | 83 | 81 |
| 1938 | 53 | 36 | 8.7 | 2.0 | 26 | 68 | 89 | 92 |
| 1939 | 38 | 23 | 8.0 | 9.1 | 22 | 75 | 105 | 116 |
| 1940 | 4.5 | 0.2 | 19 | 32 | 29 | 49 | 169 | 174 |
| 1941 | 4.3 | — | 16 | 82 | 18 | 12 | 224 | 214 |
| 1942 | - - | — | 7.6 | — | 19 | 28 | 189 | 199 |
| 1943 | - - | — | - - | — | 27 | 43 | 254 | 196 |
| 1944 | - - | — | - - | — | 14 | 19 | 277 | 200 |
| 1945 | — | — | - - | — | 18 | 42 | 310 | 299 |
| 1946 | - - | — | - - | — | 52 | 83 | 451 | 250 |
| 1947 | 0.2 | 0.1 | - - | - - | 72 | 86 | 636 | 293 |
| 1948 | 0.6 | 3.5 | - - | 20 | 75 | 171 | 591 | 260 |
| 1949 | 21 | 29 | 2.1 | 0.2 | 250 | 318 | 1,697 | 608 |

**E2    SOUTH AMERICA: External Trade (in Current Values) with Main Trading Partners**

**PERU** (million soles to 1967, million US dollars subsequently)

| | Germany | | Japan | | UK | | USA | |
|---|---|---|---|---|---|---|---|---|
| | **Imports** | **Exports** | **Imports** | **Exports** | **Imports** | **Exports** | **Imports** | **Exports** |
| 1950 | 77 | 60 | 5.8 | 31 | 476 | 496 | 1,517 | 757 |
| 1951 | 226 | 108 | 21 | 118 | 473 | 912 | 2,378 | 889 |
| 1952 | 256 | 86 | 32 | 118 | 407 | 304 | 2,511 | 1,031 |
| 1953 | 307 | 163 | 69 | 199 | 424 | 350 | 2,697 | 1,431 |
| 1954 | 393 | 220 | 77 | 307 | 439 | 678 | 2,550 | 1,706 |
| 1955 | 512[2] | 355[2] | 100 | 193 | 511 | 524 | 2,883 | 1,854 |
| 1956 | 673 | 304 | 118 | 282 | 620 | 675 | 3,441 | 2,182 |
| 1957 | 748 | 371 | 185 | 457 | 639 | 634 | 3,646 | 2,193 |
| 1958 | 829 | 421 | 145 | 193 | 621 | 620 | 3,674 | 2,590 |
| 1959 | [933][22] | 740 | [216][22] | 438 | [585][22] | 842 | [3,662][22] | 2,707 |
| 1960 | 1,169 | 1,187 | 338 | 729 | 707 | 919 | 4,487 | 4,270 |
| 1961 | 1,467 | 1,222 | 517 | 1,005 | 885 | 1,174 | 5,551 | 4,779 |
| 1962 | 1,780 | 1,590 | 781 | 935 | 924 | 1,407 | 5,694 | 5,044 |
| 1963 | 1,893 | 1,554 | 944 | 1,126 | 1,082 | 1,325 | 5,567 | 5,117 |
| 1964 | 1,921 | 2,174 | 867 | 1,634 | 1,005 | 1,343 | 6,329 | 5,577 |
| 1965 | 2,287 | 2,246 | 1,398 | 1,644 | 1,017 | 1,038 | 7,783 | 6,055 |
| 1966 | 2,898 | 2,262 | 1,592 | 2,039 | 1,005 | 586 | 8,586 | 8,721 |
| 1967 | 2,991 | 2,560 | 1,911 | 3,141 | 1,095 | 519 | 8,981 | 9,829 |
| | | | | | (million US dollars) | | | |
| | 102 | 85 | 65 | 104 | 37 | 17 | 306 | 327 |
| 1968 | 64 | 82 | 35 | 115 | 27 | 18 | 190 | 305 |
| 1969 | 68 | 105 | 43 | 140 | 26 | 27 | 186 | 301 |
| 1970 | 75 | 157 | 49 | 142 | 27 | 26 | 199 | 348 |
| 1971 | 91 | 137 | 72 | 111 | 40 | 26 | 220 | 257 |
| 1972 | 95 | 106 | 61 | 131 | 34 | 25 | 239 | 313 |
| 1973 | 124 | 80 | 113 | 179 | 36 | 31 | 308 | 369 |
| 1974 | 159 | 119 | 184 | 204 | 38 | 41 | 478 | 547 |
| 1975 | 270 | 86 | 192 | 151 | 109 | 43 | 854 | 318 |
| 1976 | 182 | 92 | 123 | 177 | 63 | 74 | 527 | 335 |
| 1977 | 118 | 71 | 118 | 200 | 68 | 61 | 463 | 492 |
| 1978 | 140 | 84 | 107 | 234 | 39 | 50 | 517 | 677 |
| 1979 | 138 | 165 | 112 | 363 | 46 | 130 | 564 | 1,220 |
| 1980 | 215 | 181 | 268 | 287 | 98 | 115 | 945 | 1,060 |
| 1981 | 326 | 95 | 232 | 375 | 8.3 | 58 | 1,477 | 702 |
| 1982 | 206 | 75 | 368 | 417 | 68 | 130 | 1,082 | 987 |
| 1983 | 152 | 63 | 227 | 266 | 46 | 87 | 850 | 857 |
| 1984 | 133 | 79 | 167 | 234 | 37 | 98 | 639 | 1,093 |
| 1985 | ... | ... | 180 | 233 | 48 | 120 | 508 | 1,009 |
| 1986 | 199 | ... | 215 | 196 | 64 | 30 | 644 | 632 |
| 1987 | 259 | 92 | 240 | 219 | 79 | 124 | 675 | 644 |
| 1988 | 175 | 67 | 93 | 183 | 58 | 41 | 546 | 435 |

**E2      SOUTH AMERICA: External Trade (in Current Values) with Main Trading Partners**

## URUGUAY (million gold pesos)

|      | Argentina | | Brazil | | Germany | | UK | | USA | |
|------|---------|---------|---------|---------|---------|---------|---------|---------|---------|---------|
|      | Imports | Exports | Imports | Exports | Imports | Exports | Imports | Exports | Imports | Exports |
| 1874 | 0.6 | 0.7 | 2.0 | 2.1 | 0.8 | - - | 3.9 | 4.9 | 1.1 | 1.3 |
| 1875 | 0.4 | 0.5 | 1.7 | 1.5 | 0.5 | - - | 2.5 | 4.6 | 0.8 | 1.0 |
| 1876 | ... | ... | ... | ... | ... | ... | ... | ... | ... | ... |
| 1877 | 0.4 | 0.9 | 1.9 | 3.7 | 0.8 | 0.1 | 4.2 | 3.7 | 1.0 | 1.1 |
| 1878 | 0.3 | 0.6 | 2.0 | 4.2 | 0.8 | 0.1 | 4.9 | 4.4 | 1.0 | 1.1 |
| 1879 | 0.4 | 0.5 | 2.0 | 3.5 | 0.9 | - - | 4.9 | 3.5 | 1.1 | 2.0 |
| 1880 | 0.5 | 0.9 | 2.4 | 3.9 | 1.1 | 0.1 | 5.8 | 4.3 | 1.3 | 2.8 |
| 1881 | 0.5 | 1.0 | 2.2 | 3.5 | 1.2 | 0.1 | 5.4 | 3.2 | 1.3 | 3.9 |
| 1882 | 0.6 | 1.0 | 2.2 | 2.8 | 1.4 | 0.3 | 4.5 | 5.4 | 1.4 | 2.3 |
| 1883 | 0.7 | 2.1 | 2.2 | 3.4 | 2.0 | 0.7 | 5.5 | 4.8 | 1.2 | 2.2 |
| 1884 | 0.6 | 1.9 | 2.4 | 3.9 | 2.3 | 0.8 | 6.8 | 5.2 | 1.6 | 1.8 |
| 1885 | 0.7 | 1.4 | 2.2 | 3.3 | 2.3 | 0.4 | 7.4 | 4.9 | 2.0 | 4.4 |
| 1886 | 0.5 | 1.2 | 1.5 | 4.5 | 2.1 | 0.4 | 5.6 | 5.0 | 1.2 | 2.7 |
| 1887 | 0.4 | 1.1 | 1.8 | 2.6 | 2.8 | 0.3 | 6.7 | 4.1 | 1.7 | 1.5 |
| 1888 | 0.8 | 2.1 | 2.6 | 5.4 | 3.0 | 1.2 | 9.5 | 5.1 | 1.6 | 2.3 |
| 1889 | 1.5 | 2.3 | 2.5 | 3.3 | 3.4 | 1.3 | 10.0 | 3.6 | 3.4 | 1.4 |
| 1890 | 2.6 | 2.6 | 2.5 | 3.3 | 2.8 | 1.0 | 8.8 | 3.9 | 2.4 | 2.0 |
| 1891 | 1.6 | 2.5 | 1.7 | 4.7 | 1.8 | 1.5 | 5.5 | 5.0 | 0.9 | 1.8 |
| 1892 | 1.1 | 3.0 | 1.3 | 4.5 | 2.1 | 2.0 | 5.6 | 4.5 | 1.1 | 2.2 |
| 1893 | 1.2 | 4.8 | 1.6 | 5.5 | 2.1 | 1.6 | 6.4 | 3.3 | 1.1 | 1.4 |
| 1894 | 1.4 | 6.0 | 1.9 | 8.0 | 2.7 | 1.5 | 8.0 | 4.0 | 1.7 | 1.9 |
| 1895 | 2.2 | 4.1 | 2.2 | 6.9 | 3.0 | 1.7 | 7.9 | 4.9 | 1.8 | 3.1 |
| 1896 | 3.5 | 4.9 | 1.4 | 7.2 | 2.8 | 2.5 | 7.3 | 2.0 | 1.8 | 1.7 |
| 1897 | 3.0 | 4.0 | 1.6 | 5.9 | 1.8 | 3.1 | 4.8 | 1.8 | 1.5 | 2.9 |
| 1898 | 3.3 | 5.3 | 1.9 | 5.9 | 2.3 | 2.8 | 6.8 | 2.9 | 1.9 | 1.0 |
| 1899 | 3.9 | 7.0 | 1.5 | 7.0 | 2.6 | 4.4 | 6.9 | 2.4 | 2.2 | 1.6 |
| 1900 | 2.7 | 2.8 | 1.3 | 7.6 | 3.5 | 2.8 | 6.3 | 2.0 | 2.2 | 1.7 |
| 1901 | 3.1 | 4.3 | 1.5 | 4.5 | 2.9 | 3.2 | 6.2 | 2.4 | 2.1 | 1.9 |
| 1902 | 2.8 | 6.5 | 1.5 | 4.6 | 3.3 | 3.8 | 6.1 | 3.3 | 2.1 | 3.2 |
| 1903 | 3.1 | 6.4 | 1.5 | 5.3 | 3.5 | 4.8 | 6.6 | 3.3 | 2.1 | 1.7 |
| 1904 | 3.4 | 6.5 | 1.5 | 4.9 | 2.6 | 5.1 | 5.4 | 2.5 | 2.1 | 2.1 |
| 1905 | 4.6 | 5.8 | 1.6 | 3.2 | 4.2 | 3.3 | 7.9 | 1.8 | 3.0 | 2.0 |
| 1906 | 3.2 | 6.1 | 1.8 | 3.3 | 5.4 | 4.3 | 9.8 | 1.8 | 3.4 | 2.0 |
| 1907 | 2.6 | 7.3 | 1.7 | 2.8 | 6.1 | 4.6 | 12 | 3.0 | 3.4 | 1.6 |
| 1908 | 2.5 | 8.1 | 1.8 | 3.5 | 6.2 | 5.5 | 12 | 3.0 | 3.3 | 2.3 |
| 1909 | 2.7 | 8.2 | 2.0 | 4.0 | 5.8 | 6.7 | 11 | 2.7 | 3.7 | 3.8 |

**E2     SOUTH AMERICA: External Trade (in Current Values) with Main Trading Partners**

**URUGUAY** (million gold pesos)[23]

| | Argentina | | Brazil | | Germany | | UK | | USA | |
|---|---|---|---|---|---|---|---|---|---|---|
| | Imports | Exports | Imports | Exports | Imports | Exports | Imports | Exports | Imports | Exports |
| 1910 | 2.8 | 5.8 | 2.0 | 4.1 | 6.8 | 4.0 | 12 | 3.4 | 4.3 | 2.7 |
| 1911 | 4.0 | 4.9 | 2.0 | 3.2 | 7.6 | 6.7 | 12 | 3.9 | 5.5 | 1.5 |
| 1912 | 4.4 | 7.1 | 2.6 | 3.7 | 8.1 | 7.6 | 13 | 6.3 | 6.2 | 2.6 |
| 1913 | 5.8 | 10.0[23] | 3.4 | 4.9[23] | 7.8 | 13.0[23] | 12 | 7.7[23] | 6.4 | 2.8[23] |
| 1914 | 4.7 | 8.2 | 2.9 | 1.9 | 3.2 | 5.5 | 8.9 | 11 | 6.6 | 9.7 |
| 1915 | 7.4 | 8.9 | 4.9 | 1.1 | 0.7 | — | 6.9 | 13 | 7.3 | 12 |
| 1916 | 7.3 | 11 | 4.1 | 1.4 | 0.2 | — | 7.1 | 14 | 8.9 | 17 |
| 1917 | 8.0[23] | 13 | 5.4[23] | 1.3 | 0.1[23] | — | 6.8[23] | 23 | 11.0[23] | 30 |
| 1918 | 25 | 9.9 | 22 | 4.3 | 0.1 | — | 17 | 26 | 23 | 23 |
| 1919 | 22 | 6.9 | 15 | 2.0 | 0.1 | 1.4 | 20 | 27 | 40 | 43 |
| 1920 | 28 | 3.6 | 13 | 2.5 | 3.3 | 5.9 | 26 | 18 | 38 | 20 |
| 1921 | 12 | 2.9 | 14 | 2.0 | 5.7 | 11 | 16 | 17 | 24 | 19 |
| 1922 | 11 | 6.0 | 9.1 | 2.4 | 8.3 | 10 | 15 | 25 | 17 | 16 |
| 1923 | ... | 7.1 | ... | 2.1 | ... | 15 | ... | 28 | ... | 16 |
| 1924 | 8.2 | 11 | 7.4 | 6.0 | 8.9 | 18 | 15 | 24 | 20 | 17 |
| 1925 | 8.2 | 8.0 | 5.4 | 5.2 | 11 | 15 | 16 | 24 | 27 | 7.1 |
| 1926 | 7.2 | 8.6 | 3.8 | 4.4 | 8.1 | 14 | 11 | 24 | 21 | 12 |
| 1927 | 9.1 | 13 | 4.4 | 4.5 | 8.8 | 18 | 12 | 19 | 25 | 11 |
| 1928 | 8.0 | 17 | 4.7 | 4.7 | 12 | 15 | 15 | 23 | 28 | 7.4 |
| 1929 | 8.4 | 12 | 6.6 | 2.8 | 9.0 | 13 | 15 | 21 | 28 | 11 |
| 1930 | 9.0 | 13 | 7.1 | 3.2 | 8.9 | 12 | 16 | 34 | 23 | 11 |
| 1931 | 11 | 10 | 8.4 | 0.7 | 9.7 | 11 | 17 | 28 | 17 | 7.6 |
| 1932 | 9.7 | 5.2 | 5.7 | 0.7 | 5.3 | 9.1 | 10 | 16 | 5.3 | 3.5 |
| 1933 | 10 | 4.0 | 7.3 | 1.2 | 5.5 | 9.8 | 12 | 22 | 5.5 | 2.4 |
| 1934 | 6.1 | 5.1 | 4.0 | 4.6 | 5.4 | 11 | 12 | 18 | 9.0 | 5.6 |
| 1935 | 4.3 | 6.9 | 4.7 | 4.7 | 5.2 | 13 | 10 | 24 | 10 | 7.3 |
| 1936 | 3.1 | 10 | 4.6 | 2.8 | 6.5 | 10 | 12 | 23 | 9.0 | 11 |
| 1937 | 5.8 | 9.4 | 5.0 | 2.7 | 8.4 | 13 | 13 | 24 | 11 | 14 |
| 1938 | 3.4 | 9.2 | 5.7 | 3.5 | 12 | 23 | 15 | 25 | 9.0 | 3.8 |
| 1939 | 4.5 | 2.2 | 5.5 | 6.1 | 11 | 12 | 12 | 19 | 3.5 | 14 |
| 1940 | 10 | 2.2 | 6.3 | 6.1 | 1.0 | 2.2 | 14 | 23 | 12 | 29 |
| 1941 | 8.4 | 3.1 | 7.4 | 5.6 | 0.3 | — | 8.5 | 31 | 15 | 58 |
| 1942 | 10 | 2.7 | 8.3 | 2.8 | - - | — | 5.4 | 28 | 12 | 41 |
| 1943 | 13 | 3.1 | 9.5 | 2.9 | - - | — | 4.5 | 51 | 10 | 86 |

**E2      SOUTH AMERICA: External Trade** (in Current Values) with Main Trading Partners

## URUGUAY (million US dollars)

| | Argentina | | Brazil | | Germany | | UK | | USA | |
|---|---|---|---|---|---|---|---|---|---|---|
| | Imports | Exports | Imports | Exports | Imports | Exports | Imports | Exports | Imports | Exports |
| 1944 | 9.3 | 2.7 | 17 | 3.4 | — | — | 9.4 | 34 | 19 | 47 |
| 1945 | 12 | 1.9 | 19 | 2.9 | ... | ... | 12 | 31 | 48 | 58 |
| 1946 | 12 | 1.9 | 17 | 3.1 | ... | ... | 20 | 38 | 67 | 48 |
| 1947 | 25 | 3.2 | 18 | 2.0 | ... | ... | 27 | 25 | 98 | 47 |
| 1948 | 17 | 4.1 | 20 | 10 | 0.5 | 4.1 | 25 | 33 | 67 | 52 |
| 1949 | 2.2 | 7.6 | 20 | 14 | 1.2 | 21 | 43 | 42 | 40 | 51 |
| 1950 | 3.1 | 1.3 | 17 | 2.4 | ...12 | ...12 | 49 | 36 | 39 | 130 |
| 1951 | 1.4 | 2.4 | 20 | 7.0 | 25 | 9.2 | 40 | 41 | 140 | 103 |
| 1952 | 0.5 | 0.6 | 19 | 25 | 19 | 21 | 29 | 33 | 61 | 51 |
| 1953 | 1.1 | — | 22 | 9.3 | 23 | 20 | 25 | 84 | 35 | 51 |
| 1954 | 1.0 | - - | 34 | 34 | 23 | 16 | 42 | 46 | 45 | 33 |
| 1955 | 1.2 | - - | 38 | 26 | 18 | 7.1 | 25 | 25 | 44 | 16 |
| 1956 | 4.1 | 0.3 | 25 | 24 | 15 | 18 | 15 | 21 | 33 | 25 |
| 1957 | 5.3 | 0.4 | 24 | 8.8 | 23 | 8.9 | 24 | 21 | 56 | 12 |
| 1958 | 2.7 | 1.3 | 25 | 9.0 | 5.9 | 8.9 | 8.0 | 21 | 16 | 11 |
| 1959 | 2.7 | 0.4 | 23 | 1.4 | 12 | 9.1 | 6.8 | 9.1 | 32 | 11 |
| 1960 | 9.8 | 2.4 | 15 | 0.3 | 18 | 12 | 19 | 31 | 65 | 20 |
| 1961 | 12 | 1.8 | 17 | 1.8 | 26 | 15 | 21 | 42 | 47 | 25 |
| 1962 | 8.6 | 1.6 | 21 | 3.0 | 32 | 15 | 24 | 25 | 44 | 24 |
| 1963 | 9.6 | 0.9 | 14 | 9.7 | 18 | 12 | 21 | 39 | 27 | 19 |
| 1964 | 18 | 4.1 | 19 | 1.9 | 21 | 17 | 15 | 30 | 31 | 15 |
| 1965 | 8.8 | 3.1 | 13 | 5.4 | 18 | 16 | 15 | 31 | 20 | 32 |
| 1966 | 12 | 5.2 | 22 | 11 | 19 | 15 | 8.7 | 26 | 20 | 23 |
| 1967 | 11 | 3.3 | 21 | 5.2 | 17 | 8.8 | 14 | 34 | 24 | 12 |
| 1968 | 15 | 2.9 | 15 | 7.4 | 15 | 12 | 7.4 | 38 | 36 | 22 |
| 1969 | 21 | 4.9 | 26 | 11 | 22 | 20 | 12 | 27 | 27 | 14 |
| 1970 | 28 | 6.4 | 35 | 12 | 26 | 31 | 16 | 20 | 30 | 20 |
| 1971 | 32 | 5.9 | 36 | 24 | 22 | 35 | 18 | 15 | 23 | 9.8 |
| 1972 | 27 | 4.1 | 36 | 11 | 16 | 28 | 12 | 16 | 19 | 7.4 |
| 1973 | 62 | 8.0 | 48 | 16 | 22 | 44 | 14 | 20 | 25 | 11 |
| 1974 | 72 | 31 | 74 | 92 | 31 | 33 | 17 | 16 | 36 | 14 |
| 1975 | 47 | 28 | 67 | 65 | 41 | 45 | 26 | 18 | 54 | 26 |
| 1976 | 66 | 25 | 90 | 68 | 41 | 67 | 21 | 21 | 49 | 59 |
| 1977 | 83 | 32 | 94 | 95 | 51 | 71 | 34 | 27 | 71 | 87 |
| 1978 | 86 | 38 | 85 | 127 | 53 | 81 | 31 | 30 | 62 | 120 |
| 1979 | 197 | 97 | 181 | 182 | 95 | 128 | 46 | 28 | 111 | 84 |
| 1980 | 174 | 142 | 286 | 191 | 111 | 137 | 69 | 37 | 161 | 83 |
| 1981 | 129 | 115 | 322 | 169 | 106 | 123 | 48 | 53 | 158 | 95 |
| 1982 | 86 | 109 | 141 | 146 | 77 | 92 | 27 | 37 | 135 | 76 |
| 1983 | 82 | 90 | 107 | 112 | 55 | 79 | 18 | 41 | 59 | 99 |
| 1984 | 87 | 88 | 127 | 115 | 46 | 79 | 16 | 38 | 66 | 126 |
| 1985 | 86 | 63 | 126 | 143 | 49 | 66 | 17 | 36 | 54 | 130 |
| 1986 | 124 | 90 | 212 | 284 | 66 | 97 | 24 | 58 | 74 | 130 |
| 1987 | 157 | 113 | 279 | 206 | 93 | 122 | 35 | 54 | 91 | 177 |
| 1988 | 179 | 105 | 307 | 236 | 75 | 120 | 36 | 58 | 93 | 162 |

**E2**    **SOUTH AMERICA: External Trade (in Current Values) with Main Trading Partners**

## VENEZUELA (million bolivares)[24]

| | Canada | | France[25] | | Germany | | Netherlands Antilles[26] | | UK[25] | | USA | |
|---|---|---|---|---|---|---|---|---|---|---|---|---|
| | Imports | Exports | Imports | Exports | Imports | Exports | Imports | Exports | Imports | Exports | Imports | Exports |
| 1904 | ... | ... | 5.8 | 28 | 12 | 4.0 | ... | ... | 19 | 5.9 | 15 | 21 |
| 1905 | ... | ... | 4.3 | 14 | 12 | 3.5 | ... | ... | 12 | 8.1 | 14 | 25 |
| 1906 | ... | ... | 2.7 | 21 | 8.9 | 4.3 | ... | ... | 13 | 6.6 | 14 | 25 |
| 1907 | ... | ... | 0.4 | 20 | 10 | 5.0 | ... | ... | 20 | 7.0 | 13 | 30 |
| 1908 | ... | ... | 0.8 | 27 | 9.7 | 4.5 | ... | ... | 19 | 7.2 | 15 | 28 |
| 1909 | ... | ... | 1.5 | 25 | 12 | 4.5 | ... | ... | 15 | 7.6 | 14 | 37 |
| 1910 | ... | ... | 3.8 | 29 | 11 | 8.3 | ... | ... | 15 | 9.7 | 18 | 31 |
| 1911 | ... | ... | 9.6 | 27 | 14 | 16 | ... | ... | 23 | 11 | 21 | 32 |
| 1912 | ... | ... | 14 | 39 | 16 | 23 | ... | ... | 27 | 11 | 32 | 43 |
| 1913 | ... | ... | 14 | 36 | 17 | 20 | ... | ... | 23 | 8.5 | 35 | 51 |
| 1914 | ... | ... | 5.5 | 44 | 12 | 22 | ... | ... | 21 | 9.6 | 29 | 45 |
| 1915 | ... | ... | 2.3 | 12 | 1.5 | 1.1 | ... | ... | 11 | 8.4 | 34 | 63 |
| 1916 | ... | ... | 5.0 | 21 | ... | ... | ... | ... | 20 | 7.8 | 55 | 67 |
| 1917 | ... | ... | 5.4 | 10 | ... | ... | ... | ... | 25 | 11 | 89.69 | |
| 1918 | ... | ... | 3.9 | 8.2 | ... | ... | ... | ... | 19 | 13 | 53 | 50 |
| 1919 | ... | ... | 2.7 [24,25] | 56 [24,25] | ... [24] | ... [24] | ... | ... | 28 [24,25] | 15 [24,25] | 92 [24] | 110 [24] |
| 1920 | ... | ... | 21 | 14 | 14 | 0.9 | 1.3 | 22 | 71 | 14 | 152 | 80 |
| 1921 | ... | ... | 7.2 | 12 | 4.1 | 5.3 | 1.2 | 25 | 17 | 5.8 | 55 | 49 |
| 1922 | ... | ... | 5.9 | 18 | 5.6 | 6.3 | 0.3 | 34 | 22 | 3.9 | 53 | 43 |
| 1923 | ... | ... | 8.9 | 14 | 14 | 7.6 | 1.4 | 52 | 36 | 8.1 | 72 | 42 |
| 1924 | ... | ... | 11 | 16 | 15 | 12 | 2.5 | 98 | 40 | 7.8 | 119 | 33 |
| 1925 | ... | ... | 15 | 17 | 25 | 20 | 3.9 | 144 | 57 | 10 | 163 | 54 |
| 1926 | - - | — | 26 | 12 | 38 | 21 | 4.4 [26] / 5.0 | 166 [26] / 212 | 54 | 6.5 | 229 | 98 |
| 1927 | - - | 0.1 | 25 | 19 | 33 | 32 | 3.6 | 233 | 45 | 5.8 | 190 | 104 |
| 1928 | 0.1 | — | 23 | 12 | 34 | 23 | 4.7 | 360 | 47 | 6.4 | 239 | 162 |
| 1929 | 0.2 | 0.6 | 20 | 22 | 42 | 36 | 2.6 | 434 | 58 | 9.0 | 249 | 216 |
| 1930 | 0.1 | 13 | 20 | 13 | 42 | 23 | 3.0 | 494 | 40 | 14 | 186 | 175 |
| 1931 | 0.1 | 1.7 | 14 | 15 | 25 | 20 | 2.7 | 436 | 25 | 14 | 101 | 135 |
| 1932 | 0.2 | 2.4 | 10 | 17 | 19 | 13 | 1.6 | 431 | 22 | 5.8 | 70 | 131 |
| 1933 | 0.1 | 6.1 | 9.1 | 11 | 16 | 9.1 | 1.2 | 466 | 22 | 11 | 70 | 91 |
| 1934 | 0.1 | 4.9 | 6.1 | 11 | 11 | 8.8 | 1.1 | 498 | 43 | 14 | 72 | 108 |
| 1935 | 0.1 | 7.8 | 13 | 8.5 | 19 | 11 | 2.2 | 530 | 60 | 19 | 100 | 114 |
| 1936 | 0.2 | 5.9 | 11 | 15 | 32 | 16 | 1.6 | 543 | 21 | 29 | 100 | 135 |
| 1937 | 0.1 | 15 [24] | 8.5 | 14 [24] | 41 | 21 [24] | 1.7 | 630 [24] | 28 | 47 [24] | 161 | 119 [24] |
| 1938 | 0.2 | 8.0 | 9.2 | 11 | 37 | 28 | 2.2 | 675 | 22 | 29 | 175 | 118 |
| 1939 | 2.9 | 14 | 9.7 | 17 | 31 | 17 | 1.7 | 685 | 20 | 42 | 200 | 151 |
| 1940 | 5.8 | 14 | 6.3 | 9.4 | 1.1 | — | 1.1 | 574 | 24 | 19 | 229 | 194 |
| 1941 | 4.6 | 22 | 0.1 | - - | 1.8 | — | 1.3 | 789 | 17 | 9.4 | 224 | 227 |
| 1942 | 2.0 | 28 | 0.2 | - - | - - | — | 2.3 | 437 | 16 | 4.9 | 156 | 110 |
| 1943 | 2.1 | 3.4 | 0.1 | - - | - - | — | 1.9 | 18 | 15 | 0.7 | 145 | 64 |
| 1944 | 4.3 | 1.0 | 0.1 | - - | - - | — | 1.6 | 12 | 8.8 | 0.3 | 280 | 46 |
| 1945 | 8.7 | 12 | 1.2 | 1.6 | - - | — | 1.2 | 242 | 15 | 6.5 | 442 | 234 |
| 1946 | 31 | 24 | 6.4 | 23 | - - | — | 2.2 | 824 | 54 | 36 | 694 | 425 |
| 1947 | 35 | 41 | 24 | 54 | - - [2] | - - [2] | 4.5 | 1,279 | 107 | 41 | 1,372 | 548 |
| 1948 | 55 | 74 | 28 | 75 | 7.3 | 3.0 | 15 | 2,033 | 181 | 26 | 2,195 | 930 |
| 1949 | 61 | 69 | 48 | 68 | 28 | 15 | 11 | 1,875 | 177 | 62 | 1,654 | 960 |

**E2     SOUTH AMERICA: External Trade (in Current Values) with Main Trading Partners**

## VENEZUELA (million bolivares)

| | Canada | | France | | West Germany | | Japan | | Netherlands Antilles | | UK | | USA | |
|---|---|---|---|---|---|---|---|---|---|---|---|---|---|---|
| | Imports | Exports | Imports | Exports | Imports | Exports | Imports | Exports | Imports | Exports | Imports | Exports | Imports | Exports |
| 1950 | 69 | 99 | 35 | 60 | 53 | 21 | 9.8 | 0.7 | 8.3 | 2,012 | 133 | 126 | 1,233 | 1,164 |
| 1951 | 86 | 94 | 57 | 59 | 91 | 30 | 14 | 0.7 | 12 | 2,224 | 143 | 121 | 1,452 | 1,375 |
| 1952 | 112 | ... | 62 | 0.4 | 79 | 2.9 | 25 | ... | 12 | 22 | 180 | 2.2 | 1,657 | 205 |
| 1953 | 104 | 101 | 64 | 64 | 128 | 42 | 27 | 1.6 | 15 | 1,880 | 194 | 85 | 1,853 | 1,802 |
| 1954 | 109 | 110 | 98 | 57 | 188 | 33 | 34 | 2.4 | 12 | 2,209 | 208 | 133 | 1,733 | 2,096 |
| 1955 | 117 | 116 | 109 | 36 | 265 | 47 | 56 | 0.6 | 15 | 2,362 | 231 | [250][27] | 1,742 | 2,443 |
| 1956 | 115 | 155 | 119 | 62 | 295 | 60 | 55 | 2.4 | 10 | 2,146 | 271 | 424 | 2,033 | 2,782 |
| 1957 | 135 | 157 | 152 | 154 | 460 | 101 | 89 | ... | 14 | 1,863 | 357 | 654 | 4,106 | 3,195 |
| 1958 | 149 | 162 | 117 | 111 | 404 | 182 | 82 | ... | 11 | 1,817 | 352 | 482 | 2,745 | 3,268 |
| 1959 | 157 | 227 | 114 | 118 | 443 | 128 | 123 | 3.0 | 5.0 | 1,916 | 338 | 556 | 2,513 | 3,310 |
| 1960 | 131 | 259 | 81 | 142 | 316 | 89 | 127 | 2.6 | 1.9 | 1,966 | 215 | 641 | 1,847 | 3,732 |
| 1961 | 148 | 312 | 117 | 137 | 308 | 114 | 133 | 4.9 | 1.2 | 2,049 | 192 | 650 | 1,934 | 3,151 |
| 1962 | 176 | 742 | 116 | 131 | 340 | 188 | 161 | 58 | 3.2 | 2,073 | 237 | 687 | 2,050 | 2,998 |
| 1963 | 183 | 787 | 94 | 154 | 292 | 179 | 162 | 91 | 9.6 | 1,989 | 223 | 704 | 1,999 | 2,946 |
| 1964 | 280 | 782 | 140 | 160 | 393 | 210 | 281 | 153 | 17 | 1,945 | 261 | 710 | 2,634 | 3,132 |
| 1965 | 360 | 1,153 | 181 | 231 | 485 | 201 | 297 | 123 | 31 | 2,874 | 333 | 962 | 2,885 | 4,515 |
| 1966 | 278 | 1,034 | 165 | 145 | 509 | 190 | 273 | 139 | 26 | 2,665 | 286 | 911 | 2,644 | 4,744 |
| 1967 | 313 | 1,238 | 214 | 201 | 527 | 205 | 345 | 193 | 38 | 2,898 | 306 | 881 | 2,879 | 4,632 |
| 1968 | 306 | 1,558 | 179 | 159 | 570 | 180 | 365 | 113 | 67 | 2,651 | 436 | 863 | 3,359 | 4,427 |
| 1969 | 292 | 1,653 | 217 | 178 | 650 | 227 | 451 | 102 | 11 | 2,739 | 356 | 716 | 3,374 | 4,685 |
| 1970 | 293 | 1,617 | 227 | 223 | 663 | 250 | 591 | 107 | 13 | 2,891 | 382 | 692 | 3,607 | 5,088 |
| 1971 | 388 | 1,590 | 380 | 212 | 859 | 206 | 740 | 57 | 9.3 | 2,597 | 428 | 812 | 3,692 | 5,530 |
| 1972 | 316 | 1,674 | 393 | 231 | 1,004 | 158 | 853 | 88 | 12 | 2,494 | 502 | 530 | 4,234 | 5,156 |
| 1973 | 372 | 2,430 | 345 | 242 | 1,388 | 196 | 883 | 86 | 12 | 3,759 | 387 | 540 | 4,470 | 9,374 |
| 1974 | 613 | 5,669 | 481 | 480 | 1,442 | 500 | 1,526 | 194 | 43 | 9,362 | 503 | 1,298 | 7,619 | 21,235 |
| 1975 | 834 | 4,780 | 708 | 313 | 2,071 | 537 | 2,012 | 115 | 106 | 8,032 | 912 | 1,481 | 12,091 | 15,222 |
| 1976 | 726 | 5,349 | 633 | 331 | 2,497 | 559 | 2,240 | 148 | 143 | 9,148 | 826 | 868 | 12,106 | 16,450 |
| 1977 | 1,210 | 5,085 | 889 | 348 | 5,060 | 341 | 4,499 | 190 | 111 | 8,136 | 1,182 | 529 | 16,203 | 17,725 |
| 1978 | 1,461 | 4,262 | 1,609 | 359 | 4,172 | 265 | 4,355 | 149 | 155 | 8,727 | 1,674 | 540 | 18,810 | 15,879 |
| 1979 | 1,710 | 6,194 | 1,054 | 574 | 2,885 | 584 | 3,398 | 623 | 302 | 11,902 | 1,210 | 1,451 | 18,984 | 22,823 |
| 1980 | 2,126 | 7,983 | 1,372 | 1,404 | 2,900 | 920 | 3,654 | 2,990 | 326 | 18,214 | 1,289 | 876 | 22,049 | 22,644 |
| 1981 | 2,721 | 8,311 | 1,440 | 2,119 | 2,710 | 856 | 4,123 | 3,710 | 166 | 18,643 | 1,186 | 896 | 24,511 | 9,934 |
| 1982 | 2,261 | ... | 1,934 | ... | 2,958 | ... | 5,872 | ... | 162 | ... | 1,284 | ... | 26,308 | ... |
| 1983 | 1,360 | 2,208 | 1,107 | 875 | 1,431 | 2,345 | 1,490 | 1,727 | 523 | 1,177 | 584 | 1,082 | 12,245 | 20,327 |
| 1984 | 1,814 | 4,922 | 1,698 | 1,234 | 2,481 | 3,752 | 2,454 | 2,614 | 905 | 18,496 | 1,484 | 2,381 | 22,027 | 47,466 |
| 1985 | 1,869 | 5,458 | 2,032 | 1,129 | 3,242 | 4,336 | 3,204 | 5,451 | 807 | 1,289 | 1,874 | 2,359 | 25,739 | 54,233 |
| 1986 | 1,533 | 105 | 2,652 | 51 | 4,375 | 207 | 4,117 | 1,636 | — | — | 2,455 | 62 | 27,602 | 4,036 |
| 1987 | 3,066 | 112 | 4,091 | 82 | 9,918 | 61 | 7,004 | 3,538 | 847 | 446 | 3,913 | 163 | 51,463 | 9,294 |
| 1988 | 7,148 | 259 | 9,134 | 145 | 25,805 | 271 | 16,015 | 6,766 | 664 | 326 | 8,093 | 258 | 114,647 | 7,679 |

## E2 External Trade (in Current Values) with Main Trading Partners

NOTES

1. SOURCES: The main sources used have been the same as for table E1. Colombian data to 1909 are from Miguel Urrutia and Mario Arrubla (eds.), *op. cit.* in Note 1 to table E1.
2. In principle, and except as indicated in footnotes, statistics are of merchandise trade, and are on a 'special' rather than a 'general' basis.
3. Except as indicated in footnotes, statistics are believed to relate to countries of first or last consignment.

FOOTNOTES

[1] Years ending 30 June to 1906 and years beginning 1 April from 1907 to 1931. Re-exports are included with exports to 1906. Imports are on a 'general' basis to 1916 and exports to 1919. Gold is included to 1939. Newfoundland became part of Canada on 1 April 1949. A new basis of reckoning was adopted in 1959 which affected the comparability of some series.

[2] West Germany only subsequently.

[3] Adjusted for Canadian-owned military equipment returned to Canada.

[4] 'General' trade. Years ending 30 June from 1876 to 1912.

[5] Years ending 31 July to 1937 and 30 June from 1939 to 1951. The 1938 figures are for the period 1 August 1937 to 30 June 1938.

[6] 'General' trade. Years beginning 1 April from 1890 to 1908. Exports include re-exports to 1923 (1st line) and from 1947 (2nd line).

[7] In gold dollars to 1905 and in new standard dollars (or pesos) subsequently. Data to 1913 are for years ending 30 June.

[8] Including Malta and Gibraltar to 1950.

[9] 'General' trade, though only imports for consumption to 1914. Tobago is included from 1889. Data are for years beginning 1 April from 1889 to 1908. Up to 1911 they relate to countries of shipment, subsequently to those of origin or destination.

[10] 'General' trade. Years ending 30 September to 1842 and 30 June for 1844 to 1915. The 1843 figures are for the period 1 October 1842 to 30 June 1843. Imports relate to countries of origin rather than last consignment from 1937.

[11] British North America to 1873 (1st line). Newfoundland is included from 1947.

[12] Official (i.e. fixed) values to 1910. Imports for domestic consumption and exports of domestic produce to 1912 (1st line).

[13] Statistics are given here in terms of the gold peso of 18 pence to 1969 though trade was actually recorded in pesos of different value at different times. Exports to 1912 (1st line) are of domestic produce only. There is no break in the series of exports to the USA.

[14] 'General' trade. Countries of purchase and sale from 1936.

[15] Including 9.5 million sucres of gold coins.

[16] 'General' trade to 1952. Years beginning 1 April from 1892 to 1911. Re-exports are included to 1913 (1st line) and bullion and specie to 1922 (1st line)

[17] British North America to 1908.

[18] The 1950 figures in thousand pounds are as follows:—

|         | Canada | UK    | USA   |
|---------|--------|-------|-------|
| imports | 5,368  | 8,850 | 1,442 |
| exports | 3,055  | 9,837 | 444   |

[19] Including transit trade to 1929 (1st line).

[20] Official (i.e. fixed) values.

[21] Direct shipments only to 1951.

[22] Excluding imports of the Southern Peru Copper Corporation through Ilo.

[23] Official (i.e. fixed) values to 1917 for imports and 1914 for exports.

[24] 'General' trade, including bullion and specie in exports to 1937 (1st line). Data to 1919 are for years ending 30 June.

[25] The French Empire or the British Empire to 1919.

[26] Curaçao only to 1926 (1st line).

[27] Including Gibraltar.

**E3 NORTH AMERICA: MAJOR COMMODITY EXPORTS BY MAIN EXPORTING COUNTRIES** (in currency units)

| | USA[1] (million dollars) | | | Barbados (thousand pounds) | Jamaica[2] (thousand pounds) | Trinidad[3] (thousand pounds) | USA[1] (million dollars) | | |
|---|---|---|---|---|---|---|---|---|---|
| | Raw Cotton | Leaf Tobacco | | Sugar | Sugar | Sugar | Raw Cotton | Leaf Tobacco | Wheat |
| 1802 | 5 | 6 | 1830 | ... | ... | ... | 30 | 6 | - - |
| 1803 | 8 | 6 | 1831 | ... | ... | ... | 25 | 5 | - - |
| 1804 | 8 | 6 | 1832 | 262 | 1,396 | 204 | 32 | 6 | - - |
| | | | 1833 | 377 | 1,212 | 209 | 36 | 6 | - - |
| 1805 | 9 | 6 | 1834 | 562 | 1,540 | 308 | 49 | 7 | - - |
| 1806 | 8 | 7 | | | | | | | |
| 1807 | 14 | 5 | 1835 | 517 | 1,484 | 296 | 65 | 8 | - - |
| 1808 | 2 | 1 | 1836 | 581 | 1,767 | 407 | 71 | 10 | - - |
| 1809 | 9 | 4 | 1837 | 733 | 1,559 | 347 | 63 | 6 | - - |
| | | | 1838 | 758 | 1,777 | 382 | 62 | 7 | - - |
| 1810 | 15 | 5 | 1839 | 629 | 1,177 | 297 | 61 | 10 | - - |
| 1811 | 10 | 2 | | | | | | | |
| 1812 | 3 | 2 | 1840 | 300 | 959 | 296 | 64 | 10 | 2 |
| 1813 | 2 | - - | 1841 | 371 | 1,015 | 389 | 54 | 13 | 1 |
| 1814 | 3 | - - | 1842 | 374 | 1,167 | 386 | 48 | 10 | 1 |
| | | | 1843 | 501 | 880 | 339 | [49][1] | [5][1] | [- -][1] |
| 1815 | 18 | 8 | 1844 | 486 | 732 | 317 | 54 | 8 | 1 |
| 1816 | 24 | 13 | | | | | | | |
| 1817 | 23 | 9 | 1845 | 502 | 998 | 343 | 52 | 7 | - - |
| 1818 | 31 | 10 | 1846 | 433 | 738 | 413 | 43 | 8 | 2 |
| 1819 | 21 | 8 | 1847 | 657 | 1,032 | 398 | 53 | 7 | 6 |
| | | | 1848 | 515 | 670 | 207 | 62 | 8 | 3 |
| 1820 | 22 | 8 | 1849 | 601 | 593 | 297 | 66 | 6 | 2 |
| 1821 | 20 | 6 | | | | | | | |
| 1822 | 24 | 6 | 1850 | 597 | 585 | 242 | 72 | 10 | 1 |
| 1823 | 20 | 6 | 1851 | 654 | 428 | 294 | 112 | 9 | 1 |
| 1824 | 22 | 5 | 1852 | 740 | 442 | 357 | 88 | 10 | 3 |
| | | | 1853 | 555 | 412 | 350 | 109 | 11 | 4 |
| 1825 | 37 | 6 | 1854 | 729 | 431 | 289 | 94 | 10 | 12 |
| 1826 | 25 | 5 | | | | | | | |
| 1827 | 29 | 7 | | | | | | | |
| 1828 | 22 | 5 | | | | | | | |
| 1829 | 27 | 5 | | | | | | | |

**E3    NORTH AMERICA: Major Commodity Exports by Main Exporting Countries** (in currency units stated)

| | Barbados (thousand pounds) | Canada[5] (million Canadian dollars) | | | | | Costa Rica[6] (thousand gold pesos) | |
|---|---|---|---|---|---|---|---|---|
| | Sugar | Lumber[5] | Machinery | Non-ferrous Metals | Wheat & Flour | Wood Pulp | Bananas | Coffee |
| 1855 | 545 | ... | ... | ... | ... | ... | ... | ... |
| 1856 | 662 | ... | ... | ... | ... | ... | ... | 751 |
| 1857 | 881 | ... | ... | ... | ... | ... | ... | 1,181 |
| 1858 | 1,052 | ... | ... | ... | ... | ... | ... | 692 |
| 1859 | 807 | ... | ... | ... | ... | ... | ... | 1,282 |
| 1860 | 658 | ... | ... | ... | ... | ... | ... | 1,122 |
| 1861 | 751 | ... | ... | ... | ... | ... | ... | ... |
| 1862 | 677 | ... | ... | ... | ... | ... | ... | 1,403 |
| 1863 | 634 | ... | ... | ... | ... | ... | ... | 1,340 |
| 1864 | 554 | ... | ... | ... | ... | ... | ... | 1,576 |
| 1865 | 708 | ... | ... | ... | ... | ... | ... | 1,483 |
| 1866 | 837 | ... | ... | ... | ... | ... | ... | 1,949 |
| 1867 | 806 | ... | ... | ... | ... | ... | ... | 2,442 |
| 1868 | 857 | ... | ... | ... | ... | ... | ... | ... |
| 1869 | 481 | 17 | ... | 0.7 | ... | ... | ... | ... |
| 1870 | 595 | 19 | ... | 0.4 | ... | — | ... | ... |
| 1871 | 809 | 20 | ... | 0.9 | ... | — | ... | ... |
| 1872 | 590 | 21 | ... | 2.5 | 6.7 | — | ... | ... |
| 1873 | 563 | 25 | ... | 2.6 | 9.0 | — | ... | ... |
| 1874 | 710 | 24 | ... | 1.6 | 12 | — | ... | 4,464 |
| 1875 | 977 | 22 | ... | 2.2 | 6.6 | — | ... | 3,984 |
| 1876 | 570 | 18 | ... | 2.4 | 13 | — | ... | 2,103 |
| 1877 | 711 | 21 | ... | 1.6 | 5.7 | — | ... | 4,859 |
| 1878 | 653 | 18 | ... | 1.3 | 15 | — | ... | 3,252 |
| 1879 | 860 | 12 | ... | 1.6 | 13 | — | ... | 4,030 |
| 1880 | 814 | 15 | ... | 1.4 | 17 | — | ... | 3,436 |
| 1881 | 784 | 23 | ... | 1.0 | 12 | — | ... | 2,242 |
| 1882 | 806 | 21 | ... | 1.1 | 11 | — | ... | 3,512[6] |
| 1883 | 753 | 23 | ... | 1.1 | 15 | — | 47 | 1,695 |
| 1884 | 871 | 23 | ... | 1.2 | 4.9 | — | 282 | 3,038 |
| 1885 | 632 | 19 | ... | 1.3 | 5.8 | — | 233 | 1,913 |
| 1886 | 437 | 20 | ... | 1.6 | 7.1 | — | 333 | 1,580 |
| 1887 | 660[4] 703 | 19 | ... | 1.3 | 10 | — | 504 | 3,934 |
| 1888 | 752 | 19 | ... | 1.1 | 8.0 | — | 375 | 3,340 |
| 1889 | 668 | 21 | ... | 1.0 | 2.5 | — | 374 | 4,070 |
| 1890 | 870 | 24 | ... | 1.2 | 3.1 | 0.2 | 410 | 6,050 |
| 1891 | 518 | 23 | ... | 1.6 | 5.6 | 0.3 | 431 | 2,562 |
| 1892 | 606 | 21 | ... | 1.4 | 14 | 0.4 | 363 | 5,376 |
| 1893 | 856 | 25 | ... | 1.2 | 12 | 0.5 | 350 | 4,115 |
| 1894 | 626 | 24 | ... | 1.8 | 11 | 0.5 | 443 | 3,713 |
| 1895 | 282 | 20 | 0.9 | 2.5 | 8.4 | 0.6 | 628 | 4,198 |
| 1896 | 436 | 22 | 0.9 | 3.9 | 8.9 | 0.7 | 670 | 4,318 |
| 1897 | 447 | 27 | 1.0 | 7.1 | 11 | 0.7 | 778 | 4,102 |
| 1898 | 435 | 23 | 1.8 | 10 | 27 | 1.2 | 923 | 4,210 |
| 1899 | 474 | 24 | 2.3 | 8.8 | 17 | 1.3 | 1,173 | 2,943 |
| 1900 | 510 | 26 | 2.4 | 19 | 19 | 1.8 | 1,354 | 3,800 |
| 1901 | 565 | 25 | 2.4 | 33 | 18 | 1.9 | 1,742 | 2,823 |
| 1902 | 302 | 28 | 2.4 | 27 | 30 | 2.0 | 1,878 | 3,180 |
| | | | | | | | (thousand colones) | |
| 1903 | 260 | 31 | 2.9 | 23 | 34 | 3.2 | 4,972 | 8,971 |
| 1904 | 440 | 29 | 3.2 | 28 | 24 | 2.4 | 6,520 | 6,536 |

**E3    NORTH AMERICA: Major Commodity Exports by Main Exporting Countries** (in currency units stated)

| | Cuba | | El Salvador (million colones) | Guatemala (million pesos)[7] | Honduras[12] (million gold pesos) | | Jamaica[2] (thousand pounds) | |
|---|---|---|---|---|---|---|---|---|
| | (million pesos) | | | | | | | |
| | Sugar | Tobacco | Coffee | Coffee | Bananas | Coffee | Bananas | Sugar |
| 1855 | ... | ... | ... | ... | ... | ... | ... | 365 |
| 1856 | ... | ... | ... | ... | ... | ... | ... | 425 |
| 1857 | ... | ... | ... | ... | ... | ... | ... | 599 |
| 1858 | ... | ... | ... | ... | ... | ... | ... | 631 |
| 1859 | ... | ... | ... | ... | ... | ... | ... | 497 |
| 1860 | ... | ... | ... | - - | ... | ... | ... | 646 |
| 1861 | ... | ... | ... | 0.1 | ... | ... | ... | 595 |
| 1862 | ... | ... | ... | 0.1 | ... | ... | ... | 563 |
| 1863 | ... | ... | ... | ... | ... | ... | ... | 480 |
| 1864 | ... | ... | ... | 0.2 | ... | ... | ... | 503 |
| 1865 | ... | ... | ... | ... | ... | ... | ... | 430 |
| 1866 | ... | ... | ... | 0.4 | ... | ... | ... | 557 |
| 1867 | ... | ... | ... | 0.4 | ... | ... | ... | 447 |
| 1868 | ... | ... | ... | 0.8 | ... | ... | ... | 551 |
| 1869 | ... | ... | ... | ... | ... | ... | ... | 443 |
| 1870 | ... | ... | ... | ... | ... | ... | ... | 492 |
| 1871 | ... | ... | ... | 1.3 | ... | ... | ... | 592 |
| 1872 | ... | ... | ... | 1.7 | ... | ... | ... | 578 |
| 1873 | ... | ... | ... | 4.1 | ... | ... | 3 | 483 |
| 1874 | ... | ... | ... | 3.7 | ... | ... | 6 | 483 |
| 1875 | ... | ... | ... | 4.8 | ... | ... | 6 | 454 |
| 1876 | ... | ... | ... | 3.3 | ... | ... | 13 | 413 |
| 1877 | ... | ... | ... | 3.4 | ... | ... | 16 | 530 |
| 1878 | ... | ... | ... | 3.9 | ... | ... | 31 | 379 |
| 1879 | ... | ... | ... | 4.0 | ... | ... | 33 | 415 |
| 1880 | ... | ... | ... | 4.1 | ... | ... | 39 | 498 |
| 1881 | ... | ... | ... | 3.6 | ... | ... | 23 | 337 |
| 1882 | ... | ... | ... | 3.1 | ... | ... | 89 | 614 |
| 1883 | ... | ... | ... | 4.8 | ... | ... | 94 | 552 |
| 1884 | ... | ... | ... | 4.4 | ... | ... | 192 | 428 |
| 1885 | ... | ... | ... | 5.2 | ... | ... | 130 | 308 |
| 1886 | ... | ... | ... | 5.8 | ... | ... | 166 | 203 |
| 1887 | ... | ... | ... | 8.1 | ... | ... | 146 | 265 |
| 1888 | ... | ... | ... | 6.6 | ... | ... | 271 | 288 |
| 1889 | ... | ... | ... | 13[7] | ... | ... | 252[2] | 244[2] |
| | | | | 9.6 | | | | |
| 1890 | ... | ... | ... | 11 | ... | ... | 444 | 233 |
| 1891 | ... | ... | ... | 11 | ... | ... | 263 | 255 |
| 1892 | ... | ... | ... | 10 | ... | ... | 340 | 242 |
| 1893 | ... | ... | ... | 15 | ... | ... | 473 | 282 |
| 1894 | 77 | 20 | ... | 9.7 | ... | ... | 429 | 239 |
| 1895 | ... | ... | ... | ... | ... | ... | 317 | 195 |
| 1896 | ... | ... | ... | 3.5 | 0.2 | 0.1 | 302 | 149 |
| 1897 | ... | ... | ... | 7.6 | ... | ... | 446 | 121 |
| 1898 | ... | ... | ... | 5.0 | 0.4 | 0.1 | 469 | 150 |
| 1899 | 19 | ... | ... | 7.4 | 0.4 | 0.1 | 603 | 195 |
| 1900 | ... | ... | ... | 6.5 | 0.7 | - - | 619 | 166 |
| 1901 | ... | 10 | 8.3 | 6.8 | 0.8 | - - | 825 | 137 |
| 1902 | 31 | 15 | 7.7 | 6.5 | 0.8 | - - | 1,135 | 168 |
| 1903 | 42 | 26 | 10 | 5.8 | 0.6 | - - | 585 | 122 |
| 1904 | 56 | 25 | 13 | 6.5 | 0.9 | - - | 514 | 116 |

**E3 NORTH AMERICA: Major Commodity Exports by Main Exporting Countries** (in currency units stated)

| | Mexico[8] (million pesos) | | | | | | Nicaragua (thousand gold pesos or cordobas) | | Trinidad[3] (thousand pounds) |
|------|------|--------|--------|------|--------|-------|---------|--------|--------|
| | Coffee | Copper[9] | Cotton | Lead | Silver | Zinc[9] | Bananas | Coffee | Sugar |
| 1855 | ... | ... | ... | ... | ... | ... | ... | ... | 285 |
| 1856 | ... | ... | ... | ... | ... | ... | ... | ... | 450 |
| 1857 | ... | ... | ... | ... | ... | ... | ... | ... | 781 |
| 1858 | ... | ... | ... | ... | ... | ... | ... | ... | 558 |
| 1859 | ... | ... | ... | ... | ... | ... | ... | ... | 599 |
| 1860 | ... | ... | ... | ... | ... | ... | ... | ... | 503 |
| 1861 | ... | ... | ... | ... | ... | ... | ... | ... | 377 |
| 1862 | ... | ... | ... | ... | ... | ... | ... | ... | 517 |
| 1863 | ... | ... | ... | ... | ... | ... | ... | ... | 468 |
| 1864 | ... | ... | ... | ... | ... | ... | ... | ... | 742 |
| 1865 | ... | ... | ... | ... | ... | ... | ... | ... | 470 |
| 1866 | ... | ... | ... | ... | ... | ... | ... | ... | 592 |
| 1867 | ... | ... | ... | ... | ... | ... | ... | ... | 629 |
| 1868 | ... | ... | ... | ... | ... | ... | ... | ... | 622 |
| 1869 | ... | ... | ... | ... | ... | ... | ... | ... | 912 |
| 1870 | ... | ... | ... | ... | ... | ... | ... | ... | 719 |
| 1871 | ... | ... | ... | ... | ... | ... | ... | ... | 938 |
| 1872 | ... | ... | ... | ... | 24 | ... | ... | ... | 817 |
| 1873 | ... | ... | ... | ... | 18 | ... | ... | ... | 974 |
| 1874 | ... | ... | ... | ... | 17 | ... | ... | ... | 669 |
| 1875 | ... | ... | ... | ... | 20 | ... | ... | ... | 812 |
| 1876 | ... | ... | ... | ... | 20 | ... | ... | ... | 659 |
| 1877 | 1.2 | - - | - - | 0.1 | 25 | ... | ... | ... | 924 |
| 1878 | 2.2 | - - | - - | - - | 25 | ... | ... | ... | 730 |
| 1879 | 2.0 | - - | — | - - | 28 | ... | ... | ... | 833 |
| 1880 | 2.2 | 0.1 | — | - - | 29 | ... | ... | ... | 858 |
| 1881 | 2.4 | - - | — | 0.1 | 29 | ... | ... | 310 | 688 |
| 1882 | 1.7 | - - | - - | - - | 30 | ... | ... | 484 | 875 |
| 1883 | 1.6 | - - | - - | 0.2 | 32 | ... | ... | ... | 886 |
| 1884 | 1.2 | - - | - - | 0.3 | 33 | ... | ... | ... | 642 |
| 1885 | 1.7 | - - | — | 0.5 | 34 | ... | ... | ... | 685 |
| 1886 | 2.6 | - - | - - | 0.3 | 38 | ... | ... | ... | 546 |
| 1887 | 2.4 | 0.6 | - - | 0.4 | 39 | ... | ... | ... | 801 |
| 1888 | 3.9 | 0.8 | — | 0.5 | 41 | ... | ... | ... | 724[3] |
| 1889 | 4.8 | 0.7 | — | 0.6 | 39 | ... | ... | ... | 875 |
| 1890 | 6.2 | 0.9 | — | 1.1 | 42 | ... | ... | ... | 631 |
| 1891 | 5.5 | 0.9 | — | 2.4 | 47 | ... | ... | ... | 663 |
| 1892 | 8.7 | 2.3 | - - | 0.3 | 55 | ... | ... | ... | 675 |
| 1893 | 12 | 2.0 | - - | - - | 58 | ... | ... | ... | 758 |
| 1894 | 13 | 2.1 | - - | 1.8 | 58 | ... | ... | ... | 598 |
| 1895 | 8.1 | 3.9 | - - | 2.5 | 61 | ... | ... | ... | 596 |
| 1896 | 9.9 | 3.9 | - - | 2.8 | 64 | ... | ... | ... | 700 |
| 1897 | 11 | 2.3 | — | 2.9 | 70 | ... | ... | ... | 537 |
| 1898 | 7.9 | 4.1 | - - | 3.8 | 72 | ... | ... | ... | 602 |
| 1899 | 11 | 9.9 | - - | 3.5 | 70 | ... | ... | ... | 715 |
| 1900 | 7.0 | 11 | - - | 5.1 | 74 | - - | ... | ... | 550 |
| 1901 | 10 | 14 | - - | 5.7 | 73 | - - | ... | ... | 452 |
| 1902 | 9 | 19 | - - | 5.6 | 83 | — | ... | ... | 410 |
| 1903 | 8.7 | 19 | - - | 4.8 | 82 | - - | ... | ... | 436 |
| 1904 | 9.3 | 24 | - - | 5.5 | 78 | 0.1 | 286 | 1,044 | 722 |

**E3      NORTH AMERICA: Major Commodity Exports by Main Exporting Countries** (in currency units stated)

| | | | | | | | | | |
|---|---|---|---|---|---|---|---|---|---|
| | | | | | **USA**[1] | | | | |
| | | | | | (million US dollars) | | | | |
| | **Coal**[10] | **Cotton** | **Iron & Steel** | **Machinery** | **Meat**[12] | **Motor Vehicles** | **Petroleum & Products** | **Leaf Tobacco** | **Wheat**[13] |
| 1855 | ... | 88 | ... | ... | 16 | ... | ... | 15 | 1 |
| 1856 | ... | 128 | ... | ... | 16 | ... | ... | 12 | 15 |
| 1857 | ... | 132 | ... | ... | 14 | ... | ... | 20 | 22 |
| 1858 | ... | 131 | ... | ... | 12 | ... | ... | 17 | 9 |
| 1859 | ... | 161 | ... | ... | 11 | ... | ... | 21 | 3 |
| 1860 | ... | 192 | ... | ... | 14 | ... | ... | 16 | 4 |
| 1861 | ... | 34 | ... | ... | 17 | ... | ... | 14 | 38 |
| 1862 | ... | [1][11] | ... | ... | 30 | ... | ... | 12 | 43 |
| 1863 | ... | [7][11] | ... | ... | 48 | ... | ... | 20 | 47 |
| 1864 | ... | [10][11] | ... | ... | 66 | ... | ... | 23 | 31 |
| 1865 | ... | [7][11] | ... | ... | 35 | ... | ... | 42 | 19 |
| 1866 | ... | 281 | ... | ... | 22 | ... | ... | 29 | 8 |
| 1867 | ... | 201 | ... | ... | 34 | ... | ... | 20 | 8 |
| 1868 | ... | 153 | ... | ... | 24 | ... | ... | 23 | 30 |
| 1869 | ... | 163 | ... | ... | 45 | ... | ... | 21 | 24 |
| 1870 | ... | 227 | ... | ... | 21 | ... | ... | 21 | 47[13] |
| | | | | | | | | | 68 |
| 1871 | ... | 218 | ... | ... | 30 | ... | ... | 20 | 69 |
| 1872 | ... | 181 | ... | ... | 55 | ... | ... | 24 | 57 |
| 1873 | ... | 227 | ... | ... | 71 | ... | ... | 23 | 71 |
| 1874 | ... | 211 | ... | ... | 71 | ... | ... | 30 | 131 |
| 1875 | ... | 191 | ... | ... | 68 | ... | ... | 25 | 83 |
| 1876 | ... | 193 | ... | ... | 79 | ... | ... | 23 | 93 |
| 1877 | ... | 171 | ... | ... | 101 | ... | ... | 29 | 69 |
| 1878 | ... | 180 | ... | ... | 107 | ... | ... | 25 | 122 |
| 1879 | ... | 162 | ... | ... | 102 | ... | ... | 25 | 160 |
| 1880 | ... | 212 | ... | ... | 114 | ... | ... | 16 | 226 |
| 1881 | ... | 248 | ... | ... | 134[12] | ... | ... | 19 | 213 |
| 1882 | 4 | 200 | 1 | 14 | 69 | ... | 52 | 19 | 149 |
| 1883 | 4 | 247 | 1 | 17 | 61 | ... | 46 | 19 | 175 |
| 1884 | 5 | 197 | 2 | 16 | 64 | ... | 48 | 18 | 126 |
| 1885 | 5 | 202 | 1 | 11 | 63 | ... | 52 | 22 | 125 |
| 1886 | 4 | 205 | 1 | 10 | 54 | ... | 52 | 27 | 89 |
| 1887 | 5 | 206 | 1 | 11 | 53 | ... | 49 | 26 | 143 |
| 1888 | 6 | 223 | 2 | 12 | 52 | ... | 49 | 22 | 111 |
| 1889 | 7 | 238 | 2 | 16 | 59 | ... | 52 | 19 | 87 |
| 1890 | 7 | 251 | 3 | 20 | 78 | ... | 54 | 21 | 102 |
| 1891 | 8 | 291 | 3 | 21 | 81 | ... | 56 | 21 | 106 |
| 1892 | 9 | 258 | 3 | 21 | 83 | ... | 49 | 20 | 237 |
| 1893 | 10 | 189 | 3 | 22 | 79 | ... | 47 | 22 | 169 |
| 1894 | 12 | 211 | 3 | 22 | 80 | ... | 45 | 23 | 129 |
| 1895 | 11 | 205 | 3 | 24 | 81 | ... | 50 | ... | 95 |
| 1896 | 11 | 190 | 5 | 29 | 81 | ... | 67 | ... | 92 |
| 1897 | 12 | 231 | 11 | 38 | 88 | ... | 68 | ... | 116 |
| 1898 | 12 | 230 | 19 | 44 | 104 | ... | 62 | 22 | 215 |
| 1899 | 14 | 210 | 29 | 61 | 109 | ... | 63 | 25 | 177 |
| 1900 | 21 | 242 | 39 | 78 | 114 | ... | 84 | 29 | 141 |
| 1901 | 24 | 314 | 40 | 73 | 121 | ... | 78 | 27 | 166 |
| 1902 | 22 | 291 | 26 | 68 | 121 | 1 | 81 | 27 | 179 |
| 1903 | 23 | 316 | 21 | 76 | 104 | 1 | 77 | 25 | 162 |
| 1904 | 30 | 371 | 31 | 84 | 101 | 2 | 88 | 29 | 105 |

**E3    NORTH AMERICA: Major Commodity Exports by Main Exporting Countries** (in currency units stated)

| | Barbados (thousand pounds) | Canada[5] (million Canadian dollars) | | | | | | | |
|---|---|---|---|---|---|---|---|---|---|
| | Sugar | Lumber[14] | Machinery | Motor Vehicles | Non-Ferrous Metals | Paper etc. | Petroleum & Products | Wheat & Flour | Wood Pulp |
| 1905 | 451 | 29 | 3.2 | ... | 26 | ... | ... | 18 | 3.4 |
| 1906 | 351 | 36 | 3.4 | ... | 29 | 2.0 | ... | 40 | 3.5 |
| 1907 | 260 | [31]⁵ | [3.2]⁵ | ... | [28]⁵ | [1.7]⁵ | ... | [26]⁵ | [3.0]⁵ |
| 1908 | 288 | 41₁₄ / 44 | 4.4₄ / 4.0 | 0.2 | 34 | 3.5 | ...₄ | 53 / 48 | 4 |
| 1909 | 153 | 39 | 4.3 | 0.2 | 31 | 3.5 | ... | 63 | 4.3 |
| 1910 | 396 | 47 | 5.2 | 0.4 | 33 | 3.2 | ... | 66 | 5.2 |
| 1911 | 289 | 45 | 6.9 | 0.6 | 34 | 3.9 | ... | 62 | 5.7 |
| 1912 | 313 | 41 | 6.7 | 1.5 | 35 | 3.9 | ... | 83 | 5.1 |
| 1913 | 91 | 43 | 7.4 | 2.4 | 50 | 11 | ... | 109 | 5.5 |
| 1914 | 253 | 43 | 8.7 | 3.8 | 54 | 13 | ... | 142 | 6.4 |
| 1915 | 503 | 43 | 4.3 | 3.1 | 51 | 15 | ... | 110 | 9.3 |
| 1916 | 1,101 | 51 | 4.9 | 9.4 | 67 | 20 | ... | 220 | 10 |
| 1917 | 1,056 | 56 | 5.9 | 5.6 | 76 | 26 | ... | 340 | 20 |
| 1918 | 687 | 52 | 8.4 | 5.4 | 72₄ / 90 | 38 | ... | 466 | 26 |
| 1919 | 1,232 | 70 | 15 | 8.9 | 79 | 48 | ... | 191 | 35 |
| 1920 | 2,203 | 105 | 18 | 15 | 55 | 63 | ... | 252 | 41 |
| 1921 | 515 | 116 | 18 | 18 | 46 | 92 | ... | 377 | 72 |
| 1922 | 503 | 71 | 7.9 | 9.2 | 28 | 70 | ... | 233 | 36 |
| 1923 | 1,226 | 103 | 8.5 | 29 | 44 | 80 | ... | 312 | 43 |
| 1924 | 998 | 127₄ / 129 | 13 | 37 | 66 | 97 | ... | 331 | 46 |
| 1925 | 686 | 111 | 16 | 31 | 90 | 100 | ... | 322 | 42 |
| 1926 | 594 | 118 | 19 | 43 / 75 | 97₄ / 75 | 110 | ... | 434 | 50 |
| 1927 | 816 | 110 | 22 | 36 | 79 | 123 | ... | 422 | 50 |
| 1928 | 875 | 101 | 22 | 27 | 93 | 135 | ... | 412 | 47 |
| 1929 | 722 | 94 | 23 | 46 | 118 | 148 | ... | 494 | 45 |
| 1930 | 473 | 92 | 26 | 38 | 93 | 152 | ... | 261 | 45 |
| 1931 | 361 | 62 | 13 | 17 | 56 | 132 | ... | 210 | 35 |
| 1932 | 733 | 41 | 6.2 | 4.4 | 44 | 107 | ... | 136 | 28 |
| 1933 | 788 | 25 | 5.3 | 7.8 | 67 | 77 | ... | 148 | 18 |
| 1934 | 775 | 40 | 4.7 | 13 | 90 | 77 | ... | 139 | 25 |
| 1935 | 319 | 47 | 8.9 | 22 | 116 | 88 | ... | 151 | 26 |
| 1936 | 772 | 56₅ / 67 | 12₅ / 13 | 27₅ / 23 | 134 | 97₅ / 111 | ... | 168₅ / 248 | 28₅ / 31 |
| 1937 | 911 | 84 | 20 | 27 | 195 | 136 | ... | 148 | 42 |
| 1938 | 683 | 70 | 18 | 25 | 180 | 113 | ... | 107 | 28 |
| 1939 | 1,278 | 86 | 18 | 26 | 183 | 124 | ... | 125 | 31 |
| 1940 | 649 | 113 | 27 | 65 | 195 | 160 | ... | 146 | 61 |
| 1941 | 841 | 121 | 33 | 149 | 244 | 157 | ... | 207 | 86 |
| 1942 | 846 | 133 | 54 | 257 | 309 | 149 | ... | 168 | 95 |
| 1943 | 1,498 | 125 | 63 | 455 | 333 | 150 | ... | 301 | 100 |
| 1944 | 1,317 | 156 | 112 | 386 | 340 | 165 | ... | 474 | 102 |
| 1945 | 1,589 | 169 | 104 | 300 | 353 | 188 | 11 | 574 | 120 |
| 1946 | 1,790 | 161 | 65 | 78 | 248 | 287 | 4.6 | 377 | 114 |
| 1947 | 1,879 | 322 | 83 | 92 | 304 | 373 | 6.9 | 462 | 175 |
| 1948 | 1,202 | 314 | 114 | 55 | 396 | 417 | 9.3 | 368 | 209 |
| 1949 | 3,274 | 244₅ | 124₅ | 39₅ | 427₅ | 453₅ | 2.6₅ | 533₅ | 167₅ |

**E3    NORTH AMERICA: Major Commodity Exports by Main Exporting Countries** (in currency units stated)

| | Costa Rica (thousand colones) | | Cuba (million pesos) | | Dominican Republic (thousand US dollars) | | | El Salvador (million colones) |
|---|---|---|---|---|---|---|---|---|
| | Bananas | Coffee | Sugar | Tobacco | Cocoa | Coffee | Sugar | Coffee |
| 1905 | 7,829 | 7,995 | 73 | 28 | 2,212 | 157 | 3,292 | 10 |
| 1906 | 9,538 | 7,217 | 59 | 34 | 2,263 | 220 | 2,392 | 12 |
| 1907 | 10,167 | 7,148 | 66 | 28 | 2,988 | 252 | 2,100 | 11 |
| 1908 | 10,075 | 4,399 | 53 | 32 | 4,269 | 325 | 3,092 | 10 |
| 1909 | 9,366 | 5,617 | 81 | 32 | 2,759 | 128 | 3,305 | 12 |
| 1910 | 9,097 | 5,916 | 111 | 28 | 2,932 | 333 | 5,752 | 13 |
| 1911 | 9,309 | 6,109 | 79 | 32 | 3,902 | 319 | 4,160 | 16 |
| 1912 | 10,648 | 7,624 | 124 | 35 | 4,249 | 566 | 5,841 | 17 |
| 1913 | 11,171 | 7,753 | 118 | 32 | 4,120 | 257 | 3,651 | 19 |
| 1914 | 10,163 | 10,028 | 133 | 28 | 3,896 | 346 | 4,943 | 23 |
| | (million colones) | | | | | | | |
| 1915 | 9.5 | 8.0 | 193 | 24 | 4,864 | 458 | 7,458 | 21 |
| 1916 | 10 | 9.1 | 267 | 26 | 5,959 | 468 | 12,028 | 23 |
| 1917 | 8.7 | 8.1 | 295 | 30 | 4,856 | 228 | 13,386 | 21 |
| 1918 | 7.1 | 8.0 | 339 | 37 | 3,917 | 537 | 22,372 | 19 |
| 1919 | 7.3 | 25 | 502 | 48 | 8,011 | 947 | 20,702 | 10 |
| 1920 | 8.7 | 15 | 725 | 49 | 6,168 | 266 | 45,535 | 12 |
| 1921 | 12 | 8.2 | 232 | 33 | 3,083 | 241 | 14,338 | 6.8 |
| 1922 | 11 | 15 | 276 | 35 | 3,054 | 609 | 9,200 | 14 |
| 1923 | 11 | 10 | 368 | 36 | 2,917 | 428 | 18,734 | 15 |
| 1924 | 24 | 34 | 375 | 39 | 2,794 | 864 | 21,686 | 45 |
| 1925 | 25 | 34 | 281 | 41 | 3,875 | 1,295 | 15,452 | 30 |
| 1926 | 26 | 42 | 242 | 37 | 3,831 | 1,890 | 14,700 | 47 |
| 1927 | 24 | 42 | 264 | 37 | 7,477 | 1,750 | 16,668 | 25 |
| 1928 | 22 | 50 | 215 | 39 | 4,250 | 2,136 | 17,710 | 45 |
| 1929 | 18 | 49 | 205 | 37 | 3,870 | 2,444 | 12,292 | 34 |
| 1930 | 18 | 42 | 105 | 33 | 2,710 | 1,483 | 10,167 | 24 |
| 1931 | 13 | 40 | 79 | 22 | 1,789 | 1,182 | 7,601 | 22 |
| 1932 | 11 | 25 | 54 | 13 | 1,027 | 1,255 | 6,869 | 13 |
| 1933 | 9.0 | 36 | 58 | 13 | 1,274 | 1,832 | 4,401 | 19 |
| 1934 | 6.8 | 26 | 74 | 14 | 1,739 | 1,676 | 6,756 | 23 |
| | (million US dollars) | | | | | | | |
| 1935 | 1.5 | 5.0 | 90 | 16 | 2,095 | 1,269 | 9,486 | 24 |
| 1936 | 2.1 | 4.6 | 113 | 13 | 1,585 | 2,020 | 8,569 | 23 |
| 1937 | 3.1 | 6.1 | 127 | 15 | 2,524 | 1,765 | 10,740 | 35 |
| 1938 | 2.8 | 4.9 | 100 | 14 | 1,915 | 1,039 | 8,654 | 24 |
| 1939 | 1.9 | 4.6 | 117 | 14 | 2,014 | 1,731 | 11,881 | 37 |
| 1940 | 1.9 | 4.0 | 96 | 12 | 1,617 | 772 | 13,001 | 30 |
| 1941 | 3.5 | 5.0 | 138 | 14 | 2,250 | 1,475 | 7,965 | 29 |
| 1942 | 1.9 | 6.0 | 108 | 16 | 2,482 | 1,454 | 10,653 | 51 |
| 1943 | 2.1 | 8.0 | 226 | 28 | 4,039 | 2,648 | 22,685 | 59 |
| 1944 | 1.8 | 6.3 | 237 | 52 | 4,000 | 3,135 | 44,027 | 69 |
| | | | | | (million US dollars) | | | |
| 1945 | 2.2 | 7.5 | 259 | 51 | 3.1 | 4.9 | 22 | 75 |
| 1946 | 4.4 | 6.5 | 315 | 56 | 4.5 | 5.4 | 35 | 95 |
| 1947 | 5.6 | 11 | 610 | 35 | 13 | 5.1 | 51 | 143 |
| 1948 | 27 | 14 | 586 | 33 | 17 | 6.6 | 42 | 90 |
| 1949 | 28 | 11 | 495 | 30 | 7.5 | 11 | 39 | 119 |

E3    **NORTH AMERICA: Major Commodity Exports by Main Exporting Countries** (in currency units stated)

| | Guadeloupe | | Guatemala | Haiti | Honduras[15] | | Jamaica[2] | |
| | | | (million gold pesos or quetzales) | (million gourdes) | (million gold pesos) | | (thousand pounds) | |
| | (million francs) | | | | | | | |
| | Bananas | Sugar | Coffee | Coffee | Bananas | Coffee | Bananas | Sugar |
|------|------|------|------|------|------|------|------|------|
| 1905 | ... | ... | 7.3 | ... | 0.9 | - - | 843 | 122 |
| 1906 | ... | ... | 6.2 | ... | 1.0 | - - | 881 | 119 |
| 1907 | ... | ... | 9.0 | ... | 1.0 | - - | 1,039 | 110 |
| 1908 | ... | ... | 5.7 | ... | 0.8 | 0.1 | 1,045₂ | 77₂ |
| 1909 | ... | ... | 8.8 | ... | 0.9 | 0.1 | 1,404 | 119 |
| 1910 | ... | ... | 6.6 | ... | ... | ... | 1,142 | 261 |
| 1911 | ... | ... | 7.3 | ... | ... | ... | 1,457 | 247 |
| 1912 | ... | ... | 9.1 | ... | 1.3 | 0.1 | 1,241 | 133 |
| 1913 | ... | ... | 12 | ... | 1.1 | - - | 988 | 52 |
| 1914 | ... | ... | 10 | ... | 1.7 | 0.1 | 1,491 | 196 |
| 1915 | ... | ... | 8.9 | ... | ... | ... | 600 | 256 |
| 1916 | ... | ... | 8.1 | ... | ... | ... | 222 | 503 |
| 1917 | ... | ... | 5.4 | 30 | ... | ... | 227 | 704 |
| 1918 | ... | ... | 8.6 | 22 | ... | ... | 298 | 614 |
| 1919 | ... | ... | 20 | 97 | ... | ... | 1,141 | 1,318 |
| | | | | | (million lempiras) | | | |
| 1920 | ... | ... | 14 | 65 | 5.8 | 0.4 | 1,320 | 2,994 |
| 1921 | ... | ... | 9.2 | 21 | ... | ... | 1,303 | 510 |
| 1922 | ... | ... | 9.2 | 37 | ... | 0.1 | 1,788 | 912 |
| 1923 | ... | ... | 10 | 54 | ... | ... | 2,265 | 675 |
| 1924 | ... | ... | 19 | 52 | 12 | ... | 1,225 | 498 |
| 1925 | ... | ... | 24 | 77 | 15 | 0.6 | 1,511 | 545 |
| 1926 | ... | ... | 23 | 82 | 20 | 0.9 | 2,072 | 655 |
| 1927 | ... | ... | 28 | 57 | 27 | 1.0 | 2,365 | 792 |
| 1928 | ... | ... | 22 | 90 | 37 | 1.7 | 1,774 | 710 |
| 1929 | ... | ... | 19 | 64 | 42 | 1.1 | 2,510 | 483 |
| 1930 | ... | ... | 19 | 52 | 46 | 0.8 | 2,310 | 592 |
| 1931 | ... | ... | 11 | 33 | 35 | 0.5 | 1,983 | 379 |
| 1932 | ... | ... | 7.2 | 26 | 28 | 0.6 | 1,869 | 343 |
| 1933 | ... | ... | 5.7 | 36 | 23 | 0.6 | 1,018 | 424 |
| 1934 | ... | ... | 11 | 36 | 19 | 0.7 | 1,665 | 448 |
| 1935 | ... | ... | 8.8 | 19 | 16 | 0.3 | 2,174 | 558 |
| 1936 | ... | ... | 11 | 29 | 12 | 0.6 | 1,912 | 632 |
| 1937 | ... | ... | 11 | 23 | 12 | 0.8 | 2,657 | 865 |
| 1938 | 86 | 125 | 10 | 17 | [8.5][15] | [0.3][15] | 2,917 | 860 |
| 1939 | ... | ... | 9.6 | 19 | 12 | 0.5 | 2,439 | 990 |
| 1940 | ... | ... | 4.1 | 10 | 13 | 0.4 | 1,045 | 848 |
| 1941 | ... | ... | 6.6 | 23 | 13 | 0.3 | 901 | 1,585 |
| 1942 | ... | ... | 14 | 17 | 12 | 1.0 | 273 | 1,621 |
| 1943 | ... | ... | 14 | 28 | 3.9 | 0.9 | 47 | 1,832 |
| 1944 | ... | ... | 15 | 26 | 9.2 | 0.8 | 198 | 1,859 |
| 1945 | ... | ... | 18 | 36 | 13 | 0.9 | 359 | 1,938 |
| 1946 | ... | ... | 20 | 38 | 12 | 1.8 | 1,631 | 2,762 |
| 1947 | ... | ... | 32 | 61 | 16 | 1.1 | 2,049 | 2,082 |
| 1948 | 1,261 | 539 | 31 | 54 | 15₁₅ / 82 | 2.5 | 2,321 | 3,561 |
| 1949 | 1,201 | 3,219 | 37 | 92 | 80 | 2.8 | 2,271 | 4,624 |

**E3      NORTH AMERICA: Major Commodity Exports by Main Exporting Countries** (in currency units stated)

|  | Mexico[8] | | | | | | |
|  | (million pesos) | | | | | | |
|  | Coffee | Copper[9] | Cotton | Lead | Petroleum & Products | Silver | Zinc[9] |
|---|---|---|---|---|---|---|---|
| 1905 | 9.3 | 23 | - - | 4.4 | ... | 76 | 0.3 |
| 1906 | 7.2 | 22 | 3.7 | 3.7 | ... | 77 | 2.0 |
| 1907 | 11 | 18 | 1.7 | 5.3 | ... | 85 | 0.9 |
| 1908 | 13 | 15 | 0.1 | 6.4 | ... | 77 | 1.0 |
| 1909 | 8.0 | 18 | 0.2 | 6.8 | ... | 76 | 1.2 |
| 1910 | 8.6 | 20 | - - | 6.5 | ... | 81 | 0.9 |
| 1911 | 13 | 27 | - - | 6 | ... | 82 | ... |
| 1912 | 11[8] | 31[8] | 0.1[8] | 4.9[8] | ... | 91[8] | 0.5[8] |
| 1913 | [5.6] | [16] | ... | [2.9] | ... | ... | ... |
| 1914 | 1.7 | ... | ... | ... | ... | ... | ... |
| 1915 | 30 | 2.5 | ... | 0.1 | ... | ... | ... |
| 1916 | 86 | 6.3 | ... | 1.3 | ... | ... | ... |
| 1917 | ... | ... | ... | ... | ... | ... | ... |
| 1918 | 6.7 | 46 | ... | 36 | ... | 96 | ... |
| 1919 | 14 | 29 | ... | 16 | ... | 103 | ... |
| 1920 | 9.3 | 38 | 11 | 29 | 569 | 121 | 5.3 |
| 1921 | 10 | 9.1 | 6.0 | 13 | ... | 77 | ... |
| 1922 | 15 | 17 | 5.2 | 27 | 412 | 49 | ... |
| 1923 | 14 | 37 | 1.8 | 53 | 270 | 105 | 6.2 |
| 1924 | 15 | 29 | 17 | 58 | 289 | 111 | 5.7 |
| 1925 | 24 | 33 | 8.9 | 68 | 292 | 126 | 16 |
| 1926 | 24 | 42 | 22 | 86 | 228 | 123 | 38 |
| 1927 | 29 | 42 | 16 | 28 | 129 | 84 | 56 |
| 1928 | 35 | 46 | 17 | 20 | 86 | 87 | 55 |
| 1929 | 32 | 73 | 14 | 46 | 77 | 93 | 61 |
| 1930 | 28 | 52 | 2.1 | 46 | 75 | 74 | 34 |
| 1931 | 19 | 22 | 5.1 | 46 | 51 | 58 | 25 |
| 1932 | 14 | 14 | 1.8 | 19 | 72 | 35 | 10 |
| 1933 | 27 | 21 | 0.5 | 19 | 76 | 42 | 27 |
| 1934 | 27 | 30 | 3.3 | 55 | 145 | 76 | 42 |
| 1935 | 23 | 26 | 19 | 71 | 133 | 164 | 46 |
| 1936 | 20 | 24 | 46 | 79 | 136 | 115 | 61 |
| 1937 | 28 | 45 | 8.4 | 108 | 145 | 128 | 86 |
| 1938 | 26 | 33 | 18 | 89 | 73 | 171 | 80 |
| 1939 | 34 | 42 | 6.5 | 87 | 79 | 137 | 213 |
| 1940 | 22 | 45 | 5.3 | 95 | 85 | 121 | 92 |
| 1941 | 29 | 41 | 14 | 4.1 | 68 | 106 | 37 |
| 1942 | 33 | 74 | 0.8 | 66 | 31 | 106 | 57 |
| 1943 | 52 | 53 | 5.3 | 102 | 36 | 38 | 88 |
| 1944 | 58 | 37 | 29 | 76 | 31 | 23 | 91 |
| 1945 | 59 | 43 | 40 | 84 | 40 | 35 | 93 |
| 1946 | 63 | 74 | 74 | 136 | 53 | 148 | 91 |
| 1947 | 92 | 122 | 217 | 289 | 45 | 159 | 221 |
| 1948 | 104 | 100 | 155 | 456 | 249 | 147 | 142 |
| 1949 | 229 | 192 | 482 | 446 | 132 | 240 | 182 |

**E3**  **NORTH AMERICA: Major Commodity Exports by Main Exporting Countries** (in currency units stated)

| | Netherlands Antilles (million guilders) | Nicaragua (thousand gold cordobas) | | | Panama (thousand balboas) | Trinidad & Tobago[3] (thousand pounds) | |
|---|---|---|---|---|---|---|---|
| | Petroleum & Products | Bananas | Coffee | Cotton | Bananas | Sugar | Petroleum & Products |
| 1905 | ... | 296 | 1,541 | ... | ... | 452 | ... |
| 1906 | ... | 700 | 1,376 | ... | ... | 430 | ... |
| 1907 | ... | 83 | 1,318 | ... | ... | 521 | ... |
| 1908 | ... | 268 | 1,526 | ... | 1,160 | 462₃ | ... |
| 1909 | ... | 164 | 1,557 | ... | 853 | 565 | - - |
| 1910 | ... | 107 | 2,795 | ... | 921 | 724 | — |
| 1911 | ... | 339 | 4,291 | ... | 2,146 | 530 | 33 |
| 1912 | ... | 423 | 1,773 | ... | 1,157 | 539 | 18 |
| 1913 | ... | 430 | 5,004 | ... | 2,940 | 418 | 75 |
| 1914 | ... | 504 | 2,295 | ... | 2,639 | 591 | 67 |
| 1915 | ... | 372 | 1,983 | ... | 2,128 | 1,070 | 79 |
| 1916 | ... | 494 | 2,171 | ... | 2,371 | 1,297 | 205 |
| 1917 | ... | ... | 1,762 | ... | 2,467 | 1,460 | 413 |
| 1918 | ... | ... | 2,249 | ... | 2,111 | 810 | 572 |
| 1919 | ... | 559 | 6,268 | ... | 2,298 | 975 | 844 |
| 1920 | ... | 817 | 2,874 | ... | 2,006 | 2,576 | 649 |
| 1921 | ... | 1,405 | 2,352 | ... | 1,851 | 1,456 | 726 |
| 1922 | ... | 1,970 | 2,301 | ... | 1,596 | 1,145 | 762 |
| 1923 | ... | 2,052 | 3,938 | ... | 1,590 | 1,022 | 1,233 |
| 1924 | ... | 1,707 | 7,322 | ... | 1,891 | 1,234 | 1,246 |
| 1925 | ... | 1,736 | 5,627 | ... | 2,420 | 1,092 | 1,399 |
| 1926 | ... | 1,226 | 8,100 | ... | 2,459 | 1,003 | 1,723 |
| 1927 | ... | 1,442 | 4,082 | ... | 2,818 | 762 | 1,982 |
| 1928 | ... | 1,923 | 6,792 | ... | 2,910 | 1,201 | 2,056 |
| 1929 | 305 | 1,985 | 5,903 | ... | 2,942 | 1,050 | 2,439 |
| 1930 | 404 | 2,239 | 3,792 | ... | 2,008 | 776 | 2,206 |
| 1931 | 346 | 1,981 | 3,319 | ... | 1,743 | 903 | 1,493 |
| 1932 | 181 | 2,238 | 1,479 | ... | 1,728 | 846 | 1,861 |
| 1933 | 193 | 1,849 | 2,214 | ... | ... | 1,116 | 1,492 |
| 1934 | 160 | 1,546 | 2,374 | ... | 1,910 | 916 | 2,068 |
| 1935 | 166 | 1,201 | 3,118 | 55 | 2,452 | 942 | 2,148 |
| 1936 | 200 | 770 | 2,115 | 134 | 2,537 | 1,277 | 2,751 |
| 1937 | 267 | 985 | 3,078 | 553 | 2,578 | 1,274 | 3,169 |
| 1938 | 336 | 777 | 2,031 | 262 | 2,755 | 1,033 | 4,108 |
| 1939 | ... | 654 | 2,640 | 253 | 2,430 | 1,060 | 3,699 |
| 1940 | ... | 446 | 2,094 | 203 | 3,084 | 898 | 2,722 |
| 1941 | ... | 280 | 2,575 | 125 | 3,654 | 1,396 | 631 |
| 1942 | ... | 28 | 3,588 | 312 | 1,813 | 1,103 | 267 |
| 1943 | ... | — | 3,437 | 302 | 755 | 742 | 207 |
| 1944 | 366 | 3.9 | 3,734 | 32 | 922 | 848 | 213 |
| 1945 | 434 | 81 | 3,668 | — | 2,048 | 915 | 1,601 |
| 1946 | 496 | 193 | 4,316 | 145 | 4,154 | 1,369 | 6,336 |
| 1947 | 479 | 336 | 5,333 | 198 | 4,277 | 1,685 | 9,358 |
| | | | | | (million balboas) | | |
| 1948 | 745 | 659 | 8,457 | — | 15 | 2,553 | 15,114 |
| 1949 | ... | 828 | 4,362 | 212 | 41 | 3,695 | 16,117 |

**E3　NORTH AMERICA: Major Commodity Exports by Main Exporting Countries** (in currency units stated)

| | USA[1] | | | | | | | | |
|---|---|---|---|---|---|---|---|---|---|
| | (million US dollars) | | | | | | | | |
| | Coal[10] | Cotton | Iron & Steel | Machinery | Meat | Motor Vehicles | Petroleum & Products | Leaf Tobacco | Wheat[13] |
| 1905 | 31 | 380 | 45 | 89 | 99 | 2 | 88 | 30 | 44 |
| 1906 | 31 | 401 | 51 | 108 | 115 | 3 | 93 | 29 | 88 |
| 1907 | 38 | 481 | 55 | 125 | 108 | 6 | 94 | 33 | 122 |
| 1908 | 42 | 438 | 58 | 121 | 102 | 5 | 113 | 34 | 164 |
| 1909 | 40 | 417 | 47 | 99 | 82 | 6 | 112 | 31 | 119 |
| 1910 | 44 | 450 | 60 | 117 | 62 | 11 | 107 | 38 | 95 |
| 1911 | 48 | 585 | 79 | 151 | 66 | 16 | 105 | 39 | 71 |
| 1912 | 56 | 566 | 102 | 161 | 72 | 26 | 123 | 43 | 79 |
| 1913 | 68 | 547 | 124 | 195 | 68 | 33 | 150 | 49 | 142 |
| 1914 | 63 | 610 | 91 | 168 | 68 | 35 | 162 | 54 | 142 |
| 1915 | 58[1] | 376[1] | 85[1] | 120[1] | 132[1] | 70[1] | 148[1] | 44[1] | 428[1] |
| 1916 | 73 | 545 | 376 | 278 | 198 | 123 | 221 | 63 | 313 |
| 1917 | 119 | 575 | 645 | 356 | 274 | 124 | 275 | 46 | 384 |
| 1918 | 120 | 674 | 632 | 270 | 668 | 101 | 371 | 123 | 505 |
| 1919 | 126 | 1,137 | 450 | 362 | 698 | 156 | 377 | 260 | 650 |
| 1920 | 360 | 1,136 | 498 | 588 | 279 | 303 | 593 | 245 | 821 |
| 1921 | 171 | 534 | 236 | 408 | 157 | 84 | 401 | 205 | 551 |
| 1922 | 96 | 673 | 136 | 234 | 140 | 103 | 346 | 146 | 292 |
| 1923 | 166 | 807 | 167 | 281 | 154 | 171 | 367 | 152 | 205 |
| 1924 | 116 | 951 | 150 | 310 | 121 | 210 | 444 | 163 | 328 |
| 1925 | 107 | 1,060 | 144 | 366 | 127 | 318 | 474 | 153 | 234 |
| 1926 | 204 | 814 | 174 | 398 | 107 | 320 | 555 | 137 | 285 |
| 1927 | 110 | 826 | 161 | 433 | 71 | 389 | 487 | 139 | 325 |
| 1928 | 100 | 920 | 180 | 491 | 68 | 502 | 527 | 154 | 194 |
| 1929 | 106 | 771 | 200 | 604 | 79 | 541 | 562 | 146 | 192 |
| 1930 | 90 | 497 | 139 | 513 | 66 | 279 | 495 | 145 | 157 |
| 1931 | 65 | 326 | 63 | 316 | 36 | 148 | 271 | 110 | 84 |
| 1932 | 45 | 345 | 29 | 131 | 19 | 76 | 209 | 65 | 51 |
| 1933 | 40 | 398 | 46 | 132 | 26 | 91 | 201 | 82 | 19 |
| 1934 | 57 | 373 | 89 | 218 | 35 | 190 | 228 | 125 | 27 |
| 1935 | 52 | 391 | 88 | 265 | 28 | 227 | 251 | 134 | 15 |
| 1936 | 57 | 361 | 112 | 335 | 25 | 240 | 265 | 137 | 19 |
| 1937 | 67 | 369 | 300 | 479 | 25 | 347 | 378 | 134 | 64 |
| 1938 | 56 | 229 | 184 | 486 | 28 | 270 | 390 | 155 | 101 |
| 1939 | 67 | 243 | 236 | 502 | 32 | 254 | 385 | 77 | 61 |
| 1940 | 87 | 213 | 516 | 671 | 22 | 254 | 310 | 44 | 33 |
| 1941 | 119 | 83 | 501 | 740 | 99 | 339 | 285 | 65 | 35 |
| 1942 | 152 | 99 | 592 | 763 | 358 | 433 | 350 | 68 | 28 |
| 1943 | 172 | 184 | 615 | 1,194 | 617 | 279 | 517 | 170 | 56 |
| 1944 | 182 | 115 | 551 | 1,478 | 535 | 643 | 960 | 146 | 76 |
| 1945 | 198[10] | 279 | 457 | 1,191 | 290 | 588 | 753 | 239 | 330 |
| 1946 | 316 | 536 | 447 | 1,369 | 341 | 549 | 436 | 350 | 610 |
| 1947 | 632 | 423 | 824 | 2,352 | 129 | 1,149 | 641 | 270 | 868 |
| 1948 | 492 | 511 | 649 | 2,259 | 57 | 930 | 657 | 214 | 1,393 |
| 1949 | 308 | 874 | 732 | 2,355 | 51 | 753 | 562 | 252 | 1,002 |

**E3    NORTH AMERICA: Major Commodity Exports by Main Exporting Countries** (in currency units stated)

| | Barbados (thousand pounds) | Canada[2] (million Canadian dollars) | | | | | | | | |
|---|---|---|---|---|---|---|---|---|---|---|
| | Sugar | Lumber[14] | Iron Ore | Machinery | Motor Vehicles | Non-ferrous Metals | Paper, etc | Petroleum & Products | Wheat & Flour | Wood Pulp |
| 1950 | 3,868 | 392₄ 370 | 13 | 113₄ 142 | 43 | 457₄ 414 | 515₄ 500 | 2.4 | 419 | 204₄ 212 |
| 1951 | 4,836 | 421 | 19 | 189 | 86 | 487 | 565 | 3.9 | 555 | 371 |
| 1952 | 5,430 | 413 | 22 | 220 | 119 | 595 | 618 | 10 | 737 | 295 |
| 1953 | 5,628 | 349 | 31 | 182 | 82 | 570 | 636 | 7.8 | 670 | 251 |
| 1954 | 5,871 | 387 | 40 | 184 | 34 | 610 | 653 | 9.9 | 463 | 273 |
| 1955 | 5,526 | 449 | 100 | 183 | 48 | 718 | 691 | 42 | 413 | 300 |
| 1956 | 4,971 | 392 | 144 | 190 | 49 | 788 | 739 | 116 | 585 | 307 |
| 1957 | 7,635 | 346 | 152 | 228 | 50 | 989 | 749 | 157 | 442 | 295 |
| 1958 | 5,528 | 341 | 108 | 255 | 46 | 1,035 | 722 | 78 | 516 | 288 |
| 1959 | ... | 367 | 158 | 298 | 50 | 1,129 | 759 | 82 | 507 | 315 |
| | (million local dollars) | | | | | | | | | |
| 1960 | 27 | 393 | 155 | 317 | 67 | 1,245 | 796 | 104 | 473 | 328 |
| 1961 | 28 | 406 | 143 | 354 | 43 | 907 | 800 | 162 | 723 | 350 |
| 1962 | 27 | 448 | 220 | 423 | 53 | 953 | 798 | 244 | 659 | 374 |
| 1963 | 42 | 505 | 271 | 479 | 78 | 986 | 813 | 244 | 849 | 411 |
| 1964 | 31 | 530 | 356 | 597 | 158 | 1,155 | 898 | 275 | 1,124 | 467 |
| 1965 | 33 | 551 | 361 | 754 | 336 | 1,293 | 939 | 291 | 907 | 500 |
| 1966 | 33 | 543 | 369 | 1,026 | 891 | 1,418 | 1,056 | 334 | 1,144 | 529 |
| 1967 | 37 | 578 | 383 | 1,179 | 1,612 | 1,623 | 1,052 | 414 | 804 | 550 |
| 1968 | 36 | 725 | 443 | 1,403 | 2,435 | 1,878 | 1,091 | 471 | 742 | 634 |
| 1969 | 29 | 763 | 333 | 1,623 | 3,270 | 1,808 | 1,257 | 556 | 526 | 760 |
| 1970 | 31 | 751 | 476 | 1,817 | 3,294 | 2,397 | 1,275 | 696 | 747 | 791 |
| 1971 | 28 | 900 | 413 | 1,900 | 3,905 | 2,151 | 1,254 | 855 | 886 | 805 |
| 1972 | 26 | 1,229 | 353 | 2,110 | 4,228 | 2,200 | 1,375 | 1,153 | 964 | 826 |
| 1973 | 32 | 1,659 | 462 | 2,518 | 4,814 | 2,895 | 1,567 | 1,719 | 1,265 | 1,062 |
| 1974 | 54 | 1,368 | 543 | 2,934 | 5,216 | 3,524 | 2,137 | 3,890 | 2,094 | 1,876 |
| 1975 | 105 | 1,045 | 686 | 3,522 | 5,818 | 3,023 | 2,044 | 3,423 | 2,097 | 1,825 |
| 1976 | 56 | 1,735 | 920 | 3,844 | 7,502 | 3,203 | 2,362 | 2,647 | 1,830 | 2,195 |
| 1977 | 56 | 2,508 | 1,064 | 4,469 | 9,381 | 3,540 | 2,839 | 2,005 | 1,942 | 2,177 |
| 1978 | 54 | 3,240 | 754 | 5,203 | 10,974 | 3,728 | 3,375 | 1,949 | 1,987 | 2,116 |
| 1979 | 67 | 4,081 | 1,354 | 6,651 | 11,261 | 4,485 | 4,056 | 3,860 | 2,321 | 3,098 |
| 1980 | 116 | 3,591 | 1,240 | 7,129 | 10,705 | 6,321 | 4,697 | 4,643 | 3,906 | 3,895 |
| 1981 | 59 | 3,251 | 1,465 | 8,892 | 13,046 | 5,501 | 5,300 | 4,316 | 3,910 | 3,847 |
| 1982 | 68 | 3,195 | 1,034 | 8,690 | 16,114 | 4,560 | 5,091 | 4,240 | 4,361 | 3,270 |
| 1983 | 46 | 4,385 | 972 | 9,490 | 20,316 | 5,170 | 5,133 | 5,299 | 4,728 | 3,089 |
| 1984 | 65 | 4,767 | 1,112 | 12,432 | 27,936 | 5,783 | 6,182 | 6,502 | 4,825 | 3,949 |
| 1985 | 57 | 5,043 | 1,174 | 12,822 | 31,808 | 5,634 | 6,853 | 8,324 | 3,863 | 3,464 |
| 1986 | 57 | 5,496 | 1,108 | 13,033 | 32,647 | 5,822 | 7,424 | 5,193 | 2,905 | 4,142 |
| 1987 | 62 | 6,590 | 968 | 14,083 | 30,882 | 6,520 | 8,231 | 6,387 | 3,278 | 5,554 |
| 1988 | 63 | 6,187 | 968 | 16,767 | 33,267 | 8,277 | 8,907 | 5,880 | 4,494 | 6,550 |

**E3    NORTH AMERICA: Major Commodity Exports by Main Exporting Countries** (in currency units stated)

| | Costa Rica | | Cuba | | Dominican Republic | | | El Salvador |
| | (million US dollars) | | (million pesos) | | (million US dollars) | | | (million colones) |
| | Bananas | Coffee | Sugar | Tobacco | Cocoa | Coffee | Sugar | Coffee |
|---|---|---|---|---|---|---|---|---|
| 1950 | 32 | 18 | 551 | 31 | 15 | 13 | 42 | 154 |
| 1951 | 34 | 22 | 632 | 39 | 16 | 18 | 61 | 190 |
| 1952 | 38 | 24 | 538 | 40 | 15 | 27 | 53 | 194 |
| 1953 | 32 | 34 | 502 | 42 | 15 | 25 | 42 | 192 |
| 1954 | 36 | 35 | 402 | 41 | 23 | 31 | 37 | 230 |
| 1955 | 33 | 37 | 438 | 44 | 17 | 28 | 42 | 229 |
| 1956 | 26 | 34 | 392 | 44 | 9.0 | 33 | 53 | 218 |
| 1957 | 32 | 41 | 629 | 48 | 14 | 25 | 89 | 275 |
| 1958 | 27 | 51 | 557 | 52 | 21 | 24 | 57 | 210 |
| 1959 | 19 | 40 | 473 | 54 | 15 | 18 | 47 | 178 |
| 1960 | 20 | 45 | 468 | 63 | 15 | 23 | 83 | 192 |
| 1961 | 21 | 45 | … | 40 | 8.5 | 14 | 62 | 175 |
| 1962 | 27 | 49 | 432 | 25 | 9.7 | 20 | 90 | 189 |
| 1963 | 26 | 45 | 472 | 22 | 14 | 18 | 89 | 186 |
| 1964 | 28 | 48 | 627 | 29 | 12 | 30 | 87 | 233 |
| 1965 | 28 | 47 | 593 | 33 | 7.1 | 21 | 58 | 240 |
| 1966 | 30 | 53 | 504 | 26 | 11 | 21 | 70 | 224 |
| 1967 | 31 | 55 | 601 | 29 | 12 | 17 | 82 | 247 |
| 1968 | 44 | 55 | 495 | 38 | 14 | 18 | 83 | 234 |
| 1969 | 53 | 56 | 488 | 42 | 20 | 21 | 88 | 223 |
| 1970 | 68 | 73 | 785 | 33 | 19 | 29 | 104 | 302 |
| 1971 | 65 | 59 | 634 | 32 | 13 | 24 | 132 | 269 |
| 1972 | 83 | 78 | 549 | 37 | 18 | 30 | 159 | 329 |
| 1973 | 91 | 94 | 841 | 51 | 23 | 46 | 187 | 398 |
| 1974 | 99 | 125 | 1,886 | 59 | 46 | 45 | 324 | 487 |
| 1975 | 145 | 99 | 2,631 | 53 | 27 | 35 | 552 | 477 |
| 1976 | 150 | 165 | 2,321 | 61 | 47 | 83 | 247 | 1,011 |
| 1977 | 152 | 341 | 2,411 | 67 | 95 | 186 | 218 | 1,514 |
| 1978 | 172 | 314 | 2,956 | 69 | 86 | 97 | 172 | 964 |
| 1979 | 194 | 315 | 2,963 | 60 | 75 | 157 | 191 | 1,688 |
| 1980 | 215 | 248 | 3,279 | 37 | 54 | 77 | 287 | 1,538 |
| 1981 | 229 | 240 | 3,301 | 57 | 48 | 76 | 517 | 1,145 |
| 1982 | 218 | 242 | 3,772 | 104 | 57 | 97 | 261 | 1,016 |
| 1983 | 286 | 175 | 4,078 | 103 | 58 | 76 | 262 | 1,019 |
| 1984 | 253 | 267 | 4,090 | 57 | 74 | 95 | 272 | 1,131 |
| 1985 | 216 | 316 | 4,433 | 93 | 63 | 91 | 158 | 1,131 |
| 1986 | 278 | 277 | 4,069 | 77 | 59 | 113 | 134 | 2,452 |
| 1987 | 438 | 368 | 3,987 | 91 | 66 | 63 | 127 | 1,769 |
| 1988 | 360 | 253 | 4,086 | 78 | 63 | 69 | 145 | 1,804 |

**E3    NORTH AMERICA: Major Commodity Exports by Main Exporting Countries** (in currency units stated)

| | Guadeloupe | | Guatemala | Haiti | Honduras | | Jamaica | | |
| | (million francs) | | (million quetzales) | (million gourdes) | (million lempiras) | | (million pounds) | | |
| | Bananas | Sugar | Coffee | Coffee | Bananas | Coffee | Bananas | Bauxite[16] | Sugar |
|---|---|---|---|---|---|---|---|---|---|
| 1950 | 1,352 | 3,305 | 53 | 103 | 81 | 6.4 | 2.1 | ... | 5.8 |
| 1951 | 2,417 | 3,831 | 58 | 130 | 87 | 12 | 1.3 | - - | 6.3 |
| 1952 | 2,394 | 5,685 | 72 | 170 | 82 | 18 | 1.8 | 0.4 | 7.0 |
| 1953 | 2,954 | 4,175 | 68 | 125 | 82 | 24 | 5.3 | 2.7 | 11 |
| 1954 | 4,810 | 5,407 | 74 | 216 | 69 | 28 | 5.4 | 6.0 | 11 |
| 1955 | 4,742 | 5,833 | 75 | 120 | ... | 17 | 5.0 | 8.7 | 11 |
| 1956 | 2,423 | 6,250 | 92 | 148 | 88 | 27 | 5.3 | 10 | 13 |
| 1957 | 5,045 | 5,827 | 82 | 105 | 67 | 24 | 6.8 | 21 | 13 |
| 1958 | 5,587 | 6,829 | 78 | 146 | 75 | 22 | 5.0 | 22 | 11 |
| 1959 | 6,424 | 8,802 | 78 | 76 | 65 | 23 | 4.9 | 20 | 12 |
| | (million new francs) | | | | | | | | |
| 1960 | 60 | 95 | 83 | 86 | 57 | 24 | 4.8 | 28 | 14 |
| 1961 | 65 | 94 | 71 | 67 | 79 | 18 | 4.9 | 30 | 15 |
| 1962 | 59 | 96 | 69 | 104 | 76 | 23 | 4.5 | 30 | 16 |
| 1963 | 57 | 104 | 78 | 80 | 66 | 28 | 4.8 | 30 | 22 |
| 1964 | 36 | 113 | 72 | 97 | 67 | 34 | 6.0 | 34 | 21 |
| 1965 | 56 | 108 | 92 | 99 | 106 | 44 | 6.1 | 35 | 16 |
| 1966 | 56 | 102 | 101 | 88 | 145 | 40 | 6.3 | 54 | 18 |
| 1967 | 56 | 81 | 70 | 72 | 158 | 35 | 6.6 | 57 | 16 |
| 1968 | 66 | 98 | 75 | 67 | 168 | 42 | 6.9 | 56 | 19 |
| 1969 | 59 | 97 | 83 | 72 | 152 | 37 | 6.2 | | 15 |
| | | | | | | | (million local dollars) | | |
| 1970 | 57 | 126 | 103 | 74 | 144 | 52 | 12 | 182 | 29 |
| 1971 | 73 | 130 | 98 | 99 | 187 | 46 | 12 | 185 | 32 |
| 1972 | 82 | 89 | 107 | 84 | 167 | 54 | 12 | 190 | 35 |
| 1973 | 102 | 129 | 146 | 105 | 164 | 95 | 16 | 229 | 35 |
| 1974 | 130 | 84 | 175 | 119 | 105 | 85 | 11 | 449 | 79 |
| 1975 | 130 | 144 | 166 | 106 | 123 | 114 | 15 | 484 | 140 |
| 1976 | 181 | 150 | 244 | 233 | 213 | 201 | 12 | 389 | 56 |
| 1977 | 138 | 138 | 355 | 337 | 260 | 336 | 17 | 489 | 68 |
| 1978 | 279 | 130 | 476 | 269 | 284 | 422 | 27 | 783 | 93 |
| 1979 | 185 | 162 | 433 | 329 | 400 | 394 | 32 | 934 | 100 |
| 1980 | 116 | 185 | 465 | 334 | 456 | 408 | 19 | 1,310 | 97 |
| 1981 | 183 | 147 | 296 | 151 | 427 | 345 | 7.6 | 1,353 | 83 |
| 1982 | 277 | 96 | 359 | 225 | 437 | 302 | 14 | 863 | 85 |
| 1983 | 325 | 92 | 351 | 277 | 406 | 302 | 13 | 871 | 112 |
| 1984 | 428 | 97 | 365 | 237 | 464 | 338 | 6.3 | 1,864 | 172 |
| 1985 | 289 | 70 | 451 | 226 | 547 | 370 | 23 | 1,628 | 253 |
| 1986 | 365 | 153 | 502 | 279 | 513 | 644 | 50 | 1,689 | 239 |
| 1987 | 283 | 19 | 355 | 124 | 644 | 400 | 104 | 1,723 | 338 |
| 1988 | 626 | 40 | 388 | 183 | 710 | 370 | 86 | 1,913 | 430 |

**E3    NORTH AMERICA: Major Commodity Exports by Main Exporting Countries** (in currency units stated)

| | Martinique (million new francs) | | Mexico (million pesos) | | | | | | |
|---|---|---|---|---|---|---|---|---|---|
| | Bananas | Sugar | Coffee | Copper[9] | Cotton | Lead | Petroleum & Products | Silver | Zinc[9] |
| 1950 | ... | ... | 334 | 216 | 780 | 524 | 276 | 266 | 216 |
| 1951 | ... | ... | 403 | 274 | 1,112 | 571 | 301 | 221 | 345 |
| 1952 | ... | ... | 408 | 357 | 1,187 | 636 | 280 | 120 | 413 |
| 1953 | ... | ... | 575 | 349 | 1,119 | 452 | 231 | 218 | 182 |
| 1954 | ... | ... | 793 | 418 | 1,646 | 612 | 444 | 402 | 211 |
| 1955 | ... | ... | 1,301 | 889 | 3,153 | 740 | 642 | 373 | 354 |
| 1956 | ... | ... | 1,314 | 1,019 | 3,288 | 664 | 669 | 319 | 542 |
| 1957 | ... | ... | 1,360 | 516 | 2,129 | 648 | 523 | 346 | 523 |
| 1958 | ... | ... | 990 | 437 | 2,378 | 442 | 300 | 328 | 249 |
| 1959 | ... | ... | 783 | 373 | 2,494 | 425 | 286 | 363 | 307 |
| 1960 | 66 | 49 | 899 | 323 | 1,974 | 420 | 172 | 306 | 369 |
| 1961 | 74 | 51 | 938 | 238 | 1,999 | 464 | 330 | 265 | 334 |
| 1962 | 75 | 52 | 915 | 319 | 2,729 | 326 | 403 | 356 | 353 |
| 1963 | 61 | 55 | 630 | 298 | 2,445 | 343 | 400 | 600 | 373 |
| 1964 | 59 | 37 | 1,221 | 197 | 2,127 | 289 | 378 | 382 | 533 |
| 1965 | 87 | 51 | 942 | 142 | 2,652 | 325 | 390 | 387 | 536 |
| 1966 | 144 | 23 | 1,076 | 162 | 2,774 | 346 | 388 | 442 | 566 |
| 1967 | 101 | 29 | 787 | 111 | 1,795 | 318 | 382 | 510 | 560 |
| 1968 | 122 | 22 | 863 | 151 | 2,129 | 280 | 323 | 914 | 593 |
| 1969 | 99 | 21 | 846 | 253 | 2,450 | 290 | 399 | 552 | 633 |
| | | | | | | (million US dollars) | | | |
| | | | 68 | 20 | 142 | 24 | 32 | 44 | 31 |
| 1970 | 83 | 14 | 74 | 10 | 83 | 28 | 31 | 29 | 36 |
| 1971 | 93 | 15 | 73 | 15 | 63 | 20 | 27 | 30 | 32 |
| 1972 | 137 | 9.0 | 95 | 40 | 149 | 21 | 20 | 20 | 38 |
| 1973 | 117 | 18 | 169 | 48 | 166 | 23 | 105 | 19 | 29 |
| 1974 | 153 | 3.1 | 161 | 30 | 182 | 63 | 424 | 112 | 141 |
| 1975 | 195 | 7.8 | 194 | 30 | 174 | 46 | 460 | 131 | 93 |
| 1976 | 337 | 5.2 | 337 | 19 | 283 | 32 | 544 | 115 | 115 |
| 1977 | 353 | 3.0 | 458 | 43 | 195 | 46 | 1,028 | 103 | 92 |
| 1978 | 327 | 5.0 | 387 | 21 | 309 | 54 | 1,818 | 128 | 102 |
| 1979 | 246 | 0.4 | 544 | 65 | 346 | 80 | 3,915 | 0.3 | 102 |
| 1980 | 138 | - - | 446 | 189 | 315 | 55 | 9,843 | 837 | 107 |
| 1981 | 347 | 0.6 | 396 | 375 | 356 | 30 | 16,325 | 475 | 85 |
| 1982 | 416 | 2.1 | 328 | 231 | 175 | 22 | 16,262 | 302 | 76 |
| 1983 | 514 | 1.4 | 511 | 256 | 117 | 39 | 15,101 | 411 | 117 |
| 1984 | 508 | ... | 522 | 205 | 212 | 52 | 16,117 | 346 | 164 |
| 1985 | 607 | ... | 538 | 167 | 96 | 41 | 14,502 | 262 | 143 |
| 1986 | 709 | ... | 868 | 176 | 69 | 41 | 5,499 | 304 | 91 |
| 1987 | 557 | ... | 541 | 248 | 72 | 49 | 8,485 | 364 | 100 |
| 1988 | 715 | ... | 481 | 282 | 114 | 32 | 4,927 | 251 | 93 |

**E3      NORTH AMERICA: Major Commodity Exports by Main Exporting Countries** (in currency units stated)

| | Netherlands Antilles[17] (million guilders) | Nicaragua (million US dollars[18]) | | | Panama (thousand balboas) | Trinidad & Tobago (million local dollars) | |
|---|---|---|---|---|---|---|---|
| | Petroleum & Products | Bananas[19] | Coffee | Cotton | Bananas | Sugar | Petroleum & Products |
| 1950 | 1,001 | 0.6 | 17 | 1.8 | 16 | 18 | 126 |
| 1951 | 1,310 | 0.5 | 18 | 5.5 | 16 | 19 | 162 |
| 1952 | 1,358 | 0.4 | 22 | 6.8 | 13 | 20 | 175 |
| 1953 | 1,333 | 0.3 | 21 | 8.4 | 16 | 26 | 194 |
| 1954 | 1,428 | 0.4[19] | 25 | 17 | 22 | 28 | 193 |
| 1955 | 1,491 | 0.4 | 28 | 31 | 26 | 31 | 213 |
| 1956 | 1,568 | 0.2 | 23 | 24 | 22 | 26 | 262 |
| 1957 | 1,627 | 0.1 | 29 | 22 | 24 | 31 | 314 |
| 1958 | 1,506 | 0.1 | 24 | 25 | 22 | 32 | 362 |
| 1959 | 1,321 | 0.1 | 14 | 29 | 24 | 32 | 387 |
| 1960 | 1,221 | 0.1 | 19 | 15 | 18 | 37 | 410 |
| 1961 | 1,319 | 0.1 | 17 | 18 | 20 | 45 | 516 |
| 1962 | 1,274 | 0.8 | 15 | 31 | 20 | 36 | 510 |
| 1963 | 1,223 | 1.4 | 18 | 40 | 25 | 50 | 539 |
| 1964 | 1,158 | 2.2 | 21 | 52 | 29 | 48 | 81 |
| 1965 | 1,094 | 0.8 | 26 | 67 | 40 | 42 | 568 |
| 1966 | 1,062 | 0.9 | 22 | 57 | 45 | 34 | 585 |
| 1967 | 1,101 | 3.3 | 21 | 57 | 50 | 38 | 593 |
| 1968 | 1,082 | 3.2 | 23 | 61 | 58 | 48 | 721 |
| 1969 | 1,099 | 2.2 | 21 | 47 | 63 | 52 | 731 |
| 1970 | 1,195 | 0.3 | 33 | 35 | 61 | 49 | 743 |
| 1971 | 1,298 | - - | 30 | 42 | 63 | 48 | 802 |
| 1972 | 1,290 | 3.4 | 33 | 65 | 65 | 57 | 829 |
| 1973 | 2,454 | 5.6 | 45 | 65 | 64 | 44 | 1,115 |
| 1974 | 5,601 | 5.3 | 46 | 139 | 50 | 107 | 3,562 |
| 1975 | 4,162 | 4.9 | 49 | 99 | 60 | 166 | 3,368 |
| 1976 | 4,344 | 4.6 | 119 | 133 | 62 | 117 | 4,870 |
| 1977 | 4,595 | 4.5 | 200 | 153 | 66 | 83 | 4,479 |
| 1978 | 5,188 | 6.3 | 261 | 189 | 72 | 54 | 4,348 |
| 1979 | 7,031 | 7.2 | 180 | 157 | 66 | 84 | 5,642 |
| 1980 | 9,136 | 8.4 | 170 | 31 | 62 | 67 | 9,039 |
| 1981 | 9,514 | 21 | 142 | 124 | 69 | 65 | 8,041 |
| 1982 | 8,673 | 9.8 | 128 | 89 | 66 | 52 | 6,426 |
| 1983 | 7,802 | 15 | 159 | 112 | 75 | 61 | 4,672 |
| 1984 | 6,600 | 12 | 127 | 137 | 75 | 61 | 4,146 |
| 1985 | 2,894[17] | 17 | 91 | 93 | 78 | 51 | 4,157 |
| 1986 | 1,573 | 24 | 134 | 36 | 70 | 84 | 3,511 |
| 1987 | 2,241 | 54 | 117 | 57 | 86 | 76 | 3,728 |
| 1988 | 1,940 | 38 | 84 | 35 | 77 | 91 | 3,264 |

**E3      NORTH AMERICA: Major Commodity Exports by Main Exporting Countries** (in currency units stated)

|  | | USA[1] | | | | | | | |
|  | | (million US dollars) | | | | | | | |
| | Coal[10] | Cotton | Iron & Steel | Machinery | Meat | Motor Vehicles | Petroleum & Products | Leaf Tobacco | Wheat[13] |
|---|---|---|---|---|---|---|---|---|---|
| 1950 | 278 | 1,024 | 472 | 2,035 | 43 | 723 | 499 | 250 | 489 |
| 1951 | 605 | 1,146 | 611[20] | 2,615 | 60 | 1,191 | 783 | 325 | 997 |
| 1952 | 510 | 874 | 621 | 2,868 | 52 | 987 | 793 | 245 | 942 |
| 1953 | 346 | 521 | 495 | 3,013 | 60 | 963 | 692 | 339 | 590 |
| 1954 | 312 | 788 | 516 | 2,875 | 61 | 1,036 | 658 | 303 | 427 |
| 1955 | 495 | 477 | 818 | 3,057 | 70 | 1,238 | 646 | 355 | 483 |
| 1956 | 745 | 729 | 1,075[20] | 3,813 | 99 | 1,357 | 766 | 333 | 798 |
| 1957 | 846 | 1,059 | 1,377 | 4,178 | 113 | 1,309 | 994 | 359 | 848 |
| 1958 | 534 | 661 | 563 | 3,682 | 83 | 1,087 | 462 | 279 | 686 |
| 1959 | 388 | 452 | 372 | 3,706 | 106 | 1,258 | 480 | 346 | 719 |
| 1960 | 362[4] | 988[4] | 610[4] | 4,121[4] | 125[4] | 1,298[4] | 479[4] | 370[14] | 971[4] |
|  | 354 | 980 | 635 | 4,476 | 115 | 1,270 | 468 | 379 | 1,029 |
| 1961 | 340 | 875 | 454 | 4,968 | 133 | 1,188 | 432 | 390 | 1,300 |
| 1962 | 376 | 528 | 455 | 5,447 | 138 | 1,365 | 430 | 372 | 1,136 |
| 1963 | 474 | 577 | 505 | 5,702 | 144 | 1,518 | 479 | 401 | 1,331 |
| 1964 | 463 | 682 | 664 | 6,525 | 177 | 1,749 | 461 | 409 | 1,532 |
| 1965 | 477 | 486 | 607 | 6,935 | 162 | 1,744 | 418 | 378 | 1,184 |
| 1966 | 468 | 432 | 537 | 7,678 | 159 | 2,154 | 434 | 472 | 1,536 |
| 1967 | 483 | 464 | 539 | 8,280 | 151 | 2,503 | 539 | 487 | 1,207 |
| 1968 | 503 | 459 | 583 | 8,844 | 162 | 3,123 | 454 | 511 | 1,101 |
| 1969 | 594 | 280 | 941 | 10,137 | 199 | 3,514 | 433 | 529 | 831 |
| 1970 | 962 | 372 | 1,188 | 11,685 | 175 | 3,245 | 488 | 481 | 1,112 |
| 1971 | 902 | 583 | 798 | 11,660 | 195 | 4,180 | 481 | 466 | 1,005 |
| 1972 | 984 | 504 | 800 | 13,562 | 252 | 4,473 | 444 | 639 | 1,452 |
| 1973 | 1,014 | 929 | 1,258 | 17,588 | 444 | 5,573 | 518 | 681 | 4,154 |
| 1974 | 2,437 | 1,335 | 2,500 | 24,318 | 371 | 7,248 | 792 | 832 | 4,589 |
| 1975 | 3,259 | 991 | 2,382 | 29,215 | 528 | 9,290 | 908 | 852 | 5,293 |
| 1976 | 2,910 | 1,049 | 1,833 | 32,113 | 798 | 10,132 | 998 | 922 | 4,040 |
| 1977 | 2,655 | 1,530 | 1,608 | 32,630 | 797 | 10,887 | 1,280 | 1,094 | 2,883 |
| 1978 | 2,046 | 1,740 | 1,646 | 38,105 | 958 | 12,150 | 1,564 | 1,358 | 4,532 |
| 1979 | 3,328 | 2,198 | 2,227 | 45,914 | 1,127 | 13,904 | 1,914 | 1,184 | 5,491 |
| 1980 | 4,621 | 2,864 | 2,998 | 57,263 | 1,293 | 13,117 | 2,833 | 1,334 | 6,586 |
| 1981 | 5,909 | 2,260 | 2,801 | 64,426 | 1,482 | 14,733 | 3,696 | 1,457 | 8,073 |
| 1982 | 5,987 | 1,955 | 2,101 | 59,821 | 1,285 | 12,751 | 5,947 | 1,547 | 6,869 |
| 1983 | 4,051 | 1,817 | 1,415 | 54,695 | 1,191 | 13,492 | 4,557 | 1,462 | 6,509 |
| 1984 | 4,132 | 2,441 | 1,248 | 61,464 | 1,208 | 17,651 | 4,470 | 1,511 | 6,698 |
| 1985 | 4,464 | 1,633 | 1,152 | 60,573 | 1,153 | 19,445 | 4,707 | 1,521 | 3,780 |
| 1986 | 3,928 | 733 | 1,020 | 60,809 | 1,424 | 17,695 | 3,639 | 1,209 | 3,217 |
| 1987 | 3,366 | 1,631 | 1,223 | 70,080 | 1,768 | 19,952 | 3,922 | 1,090 | 3,248 |
| 1988 | 4,009 | 1,975 | 2,017 | 88,531 | 2,430 | 23,972 | 3,679 | 1,252 | 5,080 |

**E3    SOUTH AMERICA: MAJOR COMMODITY EXPORTS BY MAIN EXPORTING COUNTRIES** (in currency units stated)

| | Brazil[21] | | | | | Chile (million gold pesos of 18 pence) | Colombia (thousand gold pesos) | | Guyana[22] (thousand pounds) | Venezuela (million bolivares) |
| | | | (million paper milreis) | | | | | | | |
| | Cocoa | Coffee | Cotton | Rubber | Sugar | Copper[20] | Coffee | Tobacco | Sugar | Coffee |
|---|---|---|---|---|---|---|---|---|---|---|
| 1820 | ... | ... | ... | ... | ... | ... | ... | ... | ... | ... |
| 1821 | 0.1 | 3.3 | 4.3 | ... | 5.1 | ... | ... | ... | ... | ... |
| 1822 | 0.1 | 3.9 | 4.9 | ... | 3.6 | ... | ... | ... | ... | ... |
| 1823 | 0.1 | 4.2 | 4.5 | ... | 5.3 | ... | ... | ... | ... | ... |
| 1824 | 0.1 | 3.5 | 6.6 | ... | 4.5 | ... | ... | ... | ... | ... |
| 1825 | 0.2 | 2.9 | 1.8 | ... | 4.9 | ... | ... | ... | ... | ... |
| 1826 | 0.2 | 3.5 | 4.0 | ... | 4.9 | ... | ... | ... | ... | ... |
| 1827 | 0.2 | 5.3 | 5.3 | - - | 9.3 | ... | ... | ... | ... | ... |
| 1828 | - - | 5.1 | 5.6 | - - | 15 | ... | ... | ... | ... | ... |
| 1829 | 0.1 | 6.8 | 7.2 | 0.1 | 12 | ... | ... | ... | ... | ... |
| 1830 | - - | 7.0 | 7.4 | 0.1 | 13 | | ... | ... | ... | 3.4 |
| 1831 | - - | 9.3 | 3.8 | 0.1 | 8.2 | ... | ... | ... | ... | 4.3 |
| 1832 | 0.1[21] | 12[21] | 3.1[21] | 0.1[21] | 9.4[21] | ... | ... | ... | 1,262 | 4.8 |
| 1833 | 0.1 | 18 | 2.9 | 0.1 | 6.7 | ... | ... | ... | 1,258 | 5.2 |
| 1834 | 0.1 | 15 | 3.3 | 0.1 | 6.8 | ... | ... | ... | 1,155 | 3.6 |
| 1835 | 0.1 | 16 | 3.0 | 0.1 | 12 | ... | 18 | 18 | 1,343 | 7.3 |
| 1836 | 0.2 | 14 | 2.5 | 0.1 | 7.4 | ... | — | 191 | 1,529 | 8.3 |
| 1837 | 0.5 | 18 | 3.1 | 0.1 | 8.6 | ... | 36 | 159 | 1,258 | 7.3 |
| 1838 | 0.5 | 21 | 4.0 | 0.3 | 8.8 | ... | 34 | 40 | 1,201 | 11.3 |
| 1839 | 0.4 | 20 | 3.9 | 0.3 | 11 | ... | 55 | 26 | 948 | 9.7 |
| 1840 | 0.4 | 18 | 3.2 | 0.2 | 12 | ... | ... | ... | 1,195 | 12 |
| 1841 | 0.5 | 18 | 3.5 | 0.1 | 8.4 | ... | 67 | — | 810 | 17 |
| 1842 | 0.4 | 17 | 3.7 | 0.1 | 10 | ... | ... | 19 | 845 | 13 |
| 1843 | 0.4 | 18 | 3.3 | 0.1 | 10 | ... | ... | ... | 715 | 11 |
| 1844 | 0.4 | 18 | 2.9 | 0.2 | 14 | ... | 87 | 214 | 793 | 12 |
| 1845 | 0.5 | 21 | 3.2 | 0.2 | 16 | ... | 106 | 122 | 694 | 16 |
| 1846 | 0.5 | 22 | 3.6 | 0.3 | 15 | ... | ... | ... | 533 | 12 |
| 1847 | 0.5 | 25 | 3.5 | 0.2 | 14 | 8.6 | ... | ... | 809 | 10 |
| 1848 | 0.6 | 22 | 5.8 | 0.3 | 16 | 8.9 | ... | ... | 647 | 18 |
| 1849 | 0.7 | 23 | 5.7 | 0.4 | 15 | 9.4 | ... | ... | 503 | 12 |
| 1850 | 0.6 | 33 | 4.3 | 1.0 | 16 | 11 | ... | ... | 602 | 13 |
| 1851 | 0.6 | 33 | 5.1 | 0.9 | 14 | 7.3 | ... | ... | 648 | 13 |
| 1852 | 0.5 | 34 | 4.9 | 1.4 | 18 | 14 | ... | ... | 717 | 13 |
| 1853 | 0.8 | 35 | 4.9 | 3.6 | 16 | 13 | ... | ... | 703 | 15 |
| 1854 | 0.4 | 48 | 4.7 | 2.8 | 17 | 15 | ... | ... | 763 | 16 |
| 1855 | 0.6 | 48 | 5.6 | 2.3 | 19 | 19 | 288 | 934 | 826 | 15 |
| 1856 | 1.5 | 54 | 7.0 | 1.6 | 26 | 21 | 326 | 1,460 | ... | ... |
| 1857 | 1.7 | 44 | 6.7 | 1.2 | 23 | 22 | 434 | 3,092 | ... | ... |
| 1858 | 1.3 | 50 | 5.5 | 1.9 | 28 | 22 | 430 | 1,567 | ... | ... |
| 1859 | 1.3 | 60 | 6.4 | 3.4 | 16 | 21 | 469 | 1,580 | 934 | 19 |

E3    **SOUTH AMERICA: Major Commodity Exports by Main Exporting Countries** (in currency units stated)

| | Argentina | | | | | | Bolivia |
|---|---|---|---|---|---|---|---|
| | (million gold pesos) | | | | | | (million gold bolivianas) |
| | Hides & Skins | Linseed | Maize | Meat | Wheat | Wool | Tin[9] |
| 1860 | ... | ... | ... | ... | ... | ... | ... |
| 1861 | ... | ... | ... | ... | ... | ... | ... |
| 1862 | ... | ... | ... | ... | ... | ... | ... |
| 1863 | ... | ... | ... | ... | ... | ... | ... |
| 1864 | 6.0 | ... | ... | 1.2 | ... | 9.5 | ... |
| 1865 | 6.1 | ... | ... | 1.1 | ... | 12 | ... |
| 1866 | 6.6 | ... | ... | 1.3 | ... | 12 | ... |
| 1867 | ... | ... | ... | ... | ... | ... | ... |
| 1868 | ... | ... | ... | ... | ... | ... | ... |
| 1869 | ... | ... | ... | ... | ... | ... | ... |
| 1870 | ... | ... | ... | ... | ... | ... | ... |
| 1871 | ... | ... | ... | ... | ... | ... | ... |
| 1872 | ... | ... | ... | ... | ... | ... | ... |
| 1873 | ... | ... | ... | ... | ... | ... | ... |
| 1874 | ... | ... | ... | ... | ... | ... | ... |
| 1875 | 19 | ... | - - | ... | - - | 21 | ... |
| 1876 | 14 | ... | 0.1 | ... | - - | 20 | ... |
| 1877 | 13 | ... | 0.2 | ... | 0.1 | 19 | ... |
| 1878 | 12 | - - | 0.3 | ... | 1.3 | 15 | ... |
| 1879 | 14 | - - | 0.5 | ... | - - | 22 | ... |
| 1880 | 19 | 0.1 | 0.3 | 2.8 | - - | 27 | ... |
| 1881 | 15 | 0.6 | 0.5 | 3.8 | 0.1 | 30 | ... |
| 1882 | 14 | 1.6 | 2.1 | 2.7 | 2.4 | 29 | ... |
| 1883 | 16 | 1.2 | 0.4 | 2.7 | 4.3 | 30 | ... |
| 1884 | 18 | 1.7 | 2.3 | 2.0 | 4.3 | 32 | ... |
| 1885 | 21 | 3.5 | 4.0 | 4.3 | 3.1 | 36 | ... |
| 1886 | 18 | 1.8 | 4.7 | 3.7 | 1.5 | 37 | ... |
| 1887 | 19 | 4.1 | 7.2 | 3.4 | 9.5 | 33 | ... |
| 1888 | 20 | 2.1 | 5.4 | 4.9 | 8.2 | 45 | ... |
| 1889 | 25 | 1.6 | 13 | 7.5 | 1.6 | 57 | ... |
| 1890 | 18 | 1.2 | 14 | 5.5 | 9.8 | 36 | ... |
| 1891 | 16 | 0.6 | 1.5 | 5.4 | 16 | 39 | ... |
| 1892 | 20 | 2.5 | 8.6 | 6.1 | 15 | 44 | ... |
| 1893 | 13 | 2.9 | 1.6 | 6.1 | 23 | 25 | ... |
| 1894 | 16 | 3.6 | 1.0 | 6.4 | 27 | 29 | ... |
| 1895 | 19 | 8.3 | 10 | 5.9 | 19 | 31 | ... |
| 1896 | 15 | 6.9 | 16 | 5.0 | 13 | 34 | ... |
| 1897 | 17 | 4.9 | 5.5 | 4.7 | 3.5 | 37 | ... |
| 1898 | 18 | 5.4 | 9.3 | 4.7 | 22 | 46 | ... |
| 1899 | 23 | 7.4 | 13 | 4.7 | 38 | 71 | ... |
| 1900 | 21 | 11 | 12 | 9.0 | 49 | 28 | 8.6 |
| 1901 | 21 | 17 | 19 | 12 | 26 | 45 | 9.4 |
| 1902 | 24 | 18 | 23 | 16 | 19 | 46 | 8.8 |
| 1903 | 23 | 21 | 33 | 16 | 41 | 50 | 12 |
| 1904 | 22 | 28 | 44 | 18 | 67 | 48 | ... |

**E3    SOUTH AMERICA: Major Commodity Exports by Main Exporting Countries** (in currency units stated)

| | Brazil[21] (million paper milreis) | | | | | Chile (million gold pesos of 18 pence) | | Colombia (thousand gold pesos) | |
|---|---|---|---|---|---|---|---|---|---|
| | Cocoa | Coffee | Cotton | Rubber | Sugar | Copper[9] | Nitrate of Soda | Coffee | Tobacco |
| 1860 | 1.5 | 80 | 4.7 | 2.9 | 11 | 30 | — | ... | ... |
| 1861 | 1.3 | 59 | 7.8 | 2.4 | 23 | 30 | — | ... | ... |
| 1862 | 1.4 | 57 | 17 | 3.3 | 19 | 33 | — | ... | ... |
| 1863 | 1.1 | 54 | 30 | 3.7 | 20 | 28 | — | ... | ... |
| 1864 | 1.2 | 64 | 32 | 3.6 | 16 | 38 | — | ... | ... |
| 1865 | 1.2 | 61 | 47 | 4.6 | 19 | 36 | — | 99 | 2,458 |
| 1866 | 1.4 | 70 | 33 | 5.8 | 13 | 29 | — | 796 | 3,003 |
| 1867 | 1.6 | 84 | 32 | 7.6 | 22 | 38 | — | 610 | 2,810 |
| 1868 | 1.4 | 91 | 35 | 7.8 | 13 | 37 | — | 694 | 2,696 |
| 1869 | 2.1 | 77 | 44 | 7.1 | 29 | 46 | — | 608 | 3,008 |
| 1870 | 1.6 | 85 | 24 | 10 | 18 | 39 | — | 1,164 | 2,360 |
| 1871 | 1.9 | 72 | 46 | 10 | 28 | 35 | — | 974 | 1,486 |
| 1872 | 1.5 | 115 | 27 | 10 | 28 | 43 | — | 1,264 | 1,516 |
| 1873 | 1.4 | 110 | 24 | 11 | 18 | 37 | — | 1,931 | 2,037 |
| 1874 | 2.4 | 126 | 20 | 10 | 23 | 42 | — | 956 | 2,361 |
| 1875 | 2.7 | 118 | 11 | 10 | 14 | 42 | — | 732 | 2,728 |
| 1876 | 3.4 | 112 | 12 | 11 | 30 | 46 | — | 1,168 | 2,130 |
| 1877 | 2.8 | 110 | 6.9 | 12 | 21 | 38 | — | 753 | 1,375 |
| 1878 | 3.1 | 134 | 9.9 | 11 | 22 | 43 | — | 1,504 | 564 |
| 1879 | 3.2 | 126 | 5.2 | 12 | 31 | 41 | — | ... | 908 |
| 1880 | 3.7 | 126 | 5.1 | 12 | 26 | 35 | 27 | ... | ... |
| 1881 | 4.2 | 105 | 9.7 | 12 | 36 | 35 | 43 | ... | ... |
| 1882 | 4.4 | 123 | 12 | 14 | 23 | 40 | 59 | ... | ... |
| 1883 | 4.0 | 130 | 13 | 9.5 | 39 | 35 | 70 | ... | ... |
| 1884 | 4.5 | 152 | 11 | 11 | 23 | 39 | 67 | ... | ... |
| 1885 | 3.1 | 125 | 6.5 | 11 | 14 | 35 | 39 | ... | ... |
| 1886 | 4.1 | 187 | 15 | 13 | 16 | 33 | 41 | ... | ... |
| 1887 | [1.4][21] | [74][21] | [6.7][21] | [12][21] | [11][21] | 26 | 65 | ... | ... |
| 1888 | 3.8 | 103 | 9.3 | 38 | 20 | 30 | 71 | ... | ... |
| 1889 | 3.5 | 172 | 7.0 | 25 | 14 | 22 | 73 | ... | ... |
| 1890 | 2.6 | 190 | 6.8 | 27 | 17 | 23 | 81 | ... | ... |
| 1891 | 5.9 | 284 | 18 | 43 | 43 | 18 | 70 | ... | ... |
| 1892 | 5.5 | 441 | 11 | 60 | 49 | 19 | 63 | ... | ... |
| 1893 | 9.8 | 452 | 40 | 71 | 41 | 20 | 82 | ... | ... |
| 1894 | 8.1 | 500 | 29 | 85 | 49 | 20 | 94 | ... | ... |
| 1895 | 7.8 | 543 | 12 | 123 | 45 | 20 | 101 | ... | ... |
| 1896 | 7.0 | 524 | 9.5 | 101 | 45 | 21 | 92 | ... | ... |
| 1897 | 11 | 526 | 19 | 135 | 39 | 19 | 82 | ... | ... |
| 1898 | 19 | 466 | 11 | 179 | 49 | 23 | 87 | ... | ... |
| 1899 | 19 | 471 | 4.8 | 200 | 21 | 23 | 95 | ... | ... |
| 1900 | 19 | 484 | 29 | 167 | ... | 24 | 108 | ... | ... |
| 1901 | 18 | 510 | 9.3 | 183 | 32 | 27 | 109 | ... | ... |
| 1902 | 21 | 410 | 24 | 148 | 19 | 24 | 125 | ... | ... |
| 1903 | 20 | 384 | 26 | 196 | 4.0 | 21 | 140 | ... | ... |
| 1904 | 22 | 392 | 16 | 221 | 1.8 | 23 | 162 | ... | ... |

## E2 SOUTH AMERICA: Major Commodity Exports by Main Exporting Countries (in currency units stated)

| | Ecuador (million sucres) | | Guyana[22] (thousand pounds) | Peru (thousand pounds sterling) | | | | | | | Venezuela (million bolivares) |
|---|---|---|---|---|---|---|---|---|---|---|---|
| | | | | | | | Petroleum & Products | | | | |
| | Cocoa | Coffee | Sugar | Copper[9] | Cotton | Rubber | Products | Silver | Sugar | Wool | Coffee |
| 1860 | ... | ... | 1,088 | ... | ... | ... | ... | ... | ... | ... | ... |
| 1861 | ... | ... | 1,124 | ... | ... | ... | ... | ... | ... | ... | ... |
| 1862 | ... | ... | 975 | ... | ... | ... | ... | ... | ... | ... | ... |
| 1863 | ... | ... | 1,230 | ... | ... | ... | ... | ... | ... | ... | 17 |
| 1864 | ... | ... | 1,330 | ... | ... | ... | ... | ... | ... | ... | 17 |
| 1865 | ... | ... | 1,595 | ... | ... | ... | ... | ... | ... | ... | ... |
| 1866 | ... | ... | 1,698 | ... | ... | ... | ... | ... | ... | ... | 19 |
| 1867 | ... | ... | 1,781 | ... | ... | ... | ... | ... | ... | ... | ... |
| 1868 | ... | ... | 1,649 | ... | ... | ... | ... | ... | ... | ... | 17 |
| 1869 | ... | ... | 1,549 | ... | ... | ... | ... | ... | ... | ... | 20 |
| 1870 | ... | ... | 1,811 | ... | ... | ... | ... | ... | ... | ... | ... |
| 1871 | ... | ... | 2,191 | ... | ... | ... | ... | ... | ... | ... | ... |
| 1872 | ... | ... | 1,958 | ... | ... | ... | ... | ... | ... | ... | 43 |
| 1873 | ... | ... | 1,627 | ... | ... | ... | ... | ... | ... | ... | 47 |
| 1874 | ... | ... | 1,980 | ... | ... | ... | ... | ... | ... | ... | 59 |
| 1875 | ... | ... | 1,668 | ... | ... | ... | ... | ... | ... | ... | 57 |
| 1876 | ... | ... | 2,408 | ... | ... | ... | ... | ... | ... | ... | 37 |
| 1877 | ... | ... | 2,412 | ... | ... | ... | ... | ... | ... | ... | 55 |
| 1878 | ... | ... | 1,786 | ... | ... | ... | ... | ... | ... | ... | 38 |
| 1879 | ... | ... | 2,137 | ... | ... | ... | ... | ... | ... | ... | ... |
| 1880 | ... | ... | 2,126 | ... | 104 | 21 | ... | 481 | 1,160 | 165 | 30 |
| 1881 | ... | ... | 2,049 | ... | 84 | 24 | ... | 397 | 928 | 217 | 39 |
| 1882 | ... | ... | 2,605 | ... | 92 | 41 | ... | 397 | 883 | 266 | 50 |
| 1883 | ... | ... | 2,606 | ... | 78 | 50 | ... | 456 | 644 | 178 | 41 |
| 1884 | ... | ... | 1,823 | ... | 62 | 137 | ... | 479 | 446 | 661 | 38 |
| 1885 | ... | ... | 1,388 | ... | 79 | 177 | ... | 481 | 613 | 304 | 36 |
| 1886 | ... | ... | 1,460 | ... | 119 | 226 | ... | 515 | 505 | 265 | 49 |
| 1887 | ... | ... | 1,803 | ... | 89 | 180 | ... | 521 | 418 | 328 | 60 |
| 1888 | ... | ... | 1,612 | ... | 133 | 406 | ... | 486 | 518 | 276 | 70 |
| 1889 | ... | ... | 1,921 | ... | 131 | 202 | ... | 524 | 827 | 345 | 71 |
| 1890 | ... | ... | 1,442 | 10 | 161 | 232 | ... | 584 | 499 | 267 | 90 |
| 1891 | ... | ... | 1,668[22] | 17 | 143 | 380 | ... | 521 | 510 | 313 | ... |
| 1892 | ... | ... | 1,576 | 16 | 265 | 365 | ... | 517 | 636 | 279 | 67 |
| 1893 | ... | ... | 1,571 | 24 | 238 | 224 | ... | 507 | 621 | 332 | 85 |
| 1894 | ... | ... | 1,250 | 21 | 109 | 262 | ... | 421 | 381 | 304 | 68 |
| 1895 | ... | ... | 1,046 | 23 | 123 | 231 | ... | 431 | 577 | 242 | 86 |
| 1896 | ... | ... | 1,098 | 41 | 131 | 273 | ... | 537 | 758 | 269 | 66 |
| 1897 | ... | ... | 1,030 | 58 | 141 | 581 | ... | 415 | 958 | 288 | 62 |
| 1898 | ... | ... | 1,060 | 186 | 143 | 583 | ... | 642 | 986 | 230 | 64 |
| 1899 | ... | ... | 1,103 | 448 | 134 | 549 | ... | 792 | 1,069 | 273 | 31 |
| 1900 | 11 | 0.8 | 1,154 | 713 | 256 | 497 | 0.2 | 859 | 1,240 | 290 | ... |
| 1901 | 12 | 0.6 | 1,060 | 751 | 244 | 402 | 0.2 | 780 | 1,041 | 304 | ... |
| 1902 | 13 | 0.9 | 1,071 | 470 | 209 | 380 | 3.3 | 648 | 836 | 294 | ... |
| 1903 | 12 | 0.7 | 1,155 | 542 | 296 | 528 | 21 | 679 | 1,066 | 367 | ... |
| 1904 | 15 | 1.0 | 1,324 | 551 | 319 | 687 | 18 | 737 | 1,329 | 330 | ... |

**E3  SOUTH AMERICA: Major Commodity Exports by Main Exporting Countries** (in currency units stated)

| Year | Uruguay[30] (million gold pesos) | | | Venezuela (million bolivares) |
|---|---|---|---|---|
| | Hides & Skins | Meat | Wool | Coffee[33] |
| 1860 | ... | ... | ... | 19 |
| 1861 | ... | ... | ... | ... |
| 1862 | ... | ... | ... | ... |
| 1863 | ... | ... | ... | ... |
| 1864 | ... | ... | ... | 17 |
| 1865 | ... | ... | ... | 17 |
| 1866 | ... | ... | ... | ... |
| 1867 | ... | ... | ... | 19 |
| 1868 | ... | ... | ... | ... |
| 1869 | ... | ... | ... | 17 |
| 1870 | ... | ... | ... | 20 |
| 1871 | ... | ... | ... | ... |
| 1872 | ... | ... | ... | ... |
| 1873 | ... | ... | ... | 43 |
| 1874 | ... | ... | ... | 47 |
| 1875 | ... | ... | ... | 59 |
| 1876 | ... | ... | ... | 57 |
| 1877 | ... | ... | ... | 37 |
| 1878 | ... | ... | ... | 55 |
| 1879 | 5.7 | 2.8 | 3.6 | 38 |
| 1880 | 6.9 | 4.6 | 4.1 | ... |
| 1881 | 7.9 | 4.0 | 4.0 | 30 |
| 1882 | 6.9 | 5.0 | 5.2 | 39 |
| 1883 | 7.2 | 4.6 | 8.0 | 50 |
| 1884 | 7.4 | 5.7 | 6.7 | 41 |
| 1885 | 7.7 | 3.6 | 7.3 | 38 |
| 1886 | 7.4 | 5.9 | 5.7 | 36 |
| 1887 | 5.6 | 3.8 | 5.0 | 49 |
| 1888 | 7.5 | 6.1 | 7.6 | 60 |
| 1889 | 7.1 | 4.9 | 9.1 | 70 |
| 1890 | 9.2 | 5.5 | 7.9 | 71 |
| 1891 | 12 | ... | 8.2 | 90 |
| 1892 | 7.9 | 5.9 | 7.4 | 67 |
| 1893 | 8.5 | 6.5 | 7.7 | ... |
| 1894 | 8.0 | 8.0 | 9.1 | 85 |
| 1895 | 7.3 | 7.0 | 10 | 68 |
| 1896 | 6.7 | 7.7 | 10 | 86 |
| 1897 | 6.6 | 5.5 | 12 | 66 |
| 1898 | 6.3 | 7.0 | 11 | 62 |
| 1899 | 7.7 | 8.8 | 14 | 64 |
| 1900 | 7.9 | 7.7 | 8.0 | 34 |
| 1901 | 8.2 | 6.4 | 8.7 | 31 |
| 1902 | 10 | 6.1 | 10 | 30 |
| 1903 | 10 | 7.8 | 12 | 21 |
| 1904 | 10 | 7.7 | 13 | 37 |

| Year | Uruguay[30] (million gold pesos) | | | Venezuela (million bolivars) | |
|---|---|---|---|---|---|
| | Hides & Skins | Meat | Wool | Coffee[33] | Petroleum & Products |
| 1905 | 8.0 | 4.8 | 11 | 31 | ... |
| 1906 | 8.4 | 5.2 | 13 | 37 | 0.6 |
| 1907 | 7.8 | 5.1 | 14 | 38 | 1.0 |
| 1908 | 9.5 | 5.0 | 17 | 35[33] | 0.4 |
| 1909 | 11 | 5.4 | 19 | 40 | 0.7 |
| 1910 | 11 | 5.8 | 15 | 42 | 0.9 |
| 1911 | 9.4 | 5.3 | 19 | 42 | 1.4 |
| 1912 | 8.6 | 4.6[4] / 6.7 | 26 | 79 | 1.6 |
| 1913 | 7.4[30] / 13 | 7.2[30] / 15 | 20[30] / 31 | 84 | 3.0 |
| 1914 | 9.4 | 15 | 20 | 64 | 1.5 |
| 1915 | 17 | 31 | 20 | 61 | 1.7 |
| 1916 | 18 | 27 | 23 | 55 | 1.4 |
| 1917 | 23 | 35 | 38 | 43 | 2.1 |
| 1918 | 27 | 43 | 35 | 39 | 2.7 |
| 1919 | 26 | 47 | 65 | 151 | 2.6 |
| 1920 | 15 | 26 | 32 | 66 | 2.0 |
| 1921 | 11 | 22 | 32 | 64 | 9.6 |
| 1922 | 17 | 32 | 21 | 70 | 14 |
| 1923 | 19 | 45 | 28 | 69 | 27 |
| 1924 | 15 | 37 | 37 | 100 | 63 |
| 1925 | 15 | 39[10] / 41 | 29 | 126 | 136 |
| 1926 | 11 | 41 | 28 | 99 | 245 |
| 1927 | 12 | 27 | 33 | 104 | 279 |
| 1928 | 14 | 28 | 31 | 84 | 465 |
| 1929 | 12 | 31 | 29 | 133 | 593 |
| 1930 | 11 | 41 | 26 | 68 | 634 |
| 1931 | 10 | 30 | 20 | 65 | 547 |
| 1932 | 7.2 | 19 | 19 | 58 | 532 |
| 1933 | 8.4 | 19 | 25 | 34 | 553 |
| 1934 | 8.4 | 22 | 18 | 33 | 608 |
| 1935 | 11 | 23 | 38 | 31 | 649 |
| 1936 | 9.2 | 16 | 42 | 40 | 684 |
| 1937 | 12 | 19 | 45 | 38 | 770 |
| 1938 | 10 | 22 | 42 | 26 | 828 |
| | | (million US dollars) | | | |
| 1939 | 11 | 15 | 40 | 21 | 895 |
| 1940 | 10 | 14 | 54 | 19 | 809 |
| 1941 | 14 | 15 | 48 | 24 | 1,001 |
| 1942 | 15 | 15 | 32 | 37 | 636 |
| 1943 | 18 | 13 | 70 | 34 | 786 |
| 1944 | 10 | 30 | 41 | 24 | 1,057 |
| 1945 | 10 | 31 | 57 | 35 | 1,025 |
| 1946 | 22 | 40 | 52 | 64 | 1,325 |
| 1947 | 20 | 25 | 71 | 57 | 2,355 |
| 1948 | 22 | 45 | 66 | 71 | 3,597 |
| 1949 | 28 | 40 | 67 | 52 | 3,434 |

**E3　　SOUTH AMERICA: Major Commodity Exports by Main Exporting Countries** (in currency units stated)

| | Argentina (million gold pesos) | | | | | | Bolivia (million gold bolivianos) |
|---|---|---|---|---|---|---|---|
| | Hides & Skins | Linseed | Maize | Meat | Wheat | Wool | Tin[9] |
| 1905 | 29 | 26 | 46 | 25 | 86 | 64 | ... |
| 1906 | 28 | 26 | 53 | 21 | 67 | 58 | ... |
| 1907 | 25 | 36 | 30 | 21 | 83 | 59 | 30 |
| 1908 | 22 | 49 | 42 | 25 | 129 | 47 | 30 |
| 1909 | 38 | 44 | 58 | 28 | 106 | 60 | 31 |
| 1910 | 39 | 45 | 60 | 48 | 72 | 59 | 37 |
| 1911 | 42 | 34 | 2.8 | 60 | 81 | 50 | 53 |
| 1912 | 50 | 34 | 109 | 64 | 98 | 58 | 60 |
| 1913 | 44 | 50 | 112 | 75 | 103 | 45 | 68 |
| 1914 | 35 | 43 | 78 | 88 | 37 | 47 | 42 |
| 1915 | 50 | 46 | 94 | 96 | 133 | 56 | 45 |
| 1916 | 63 | 38 | 74 | 127 | 97 | 64 | 43 |
| 1917 | 65 | 13 | 39 | 133 | 61 | 101 | 85 |
| 1918 | 52 | 37 | 17 | 249 | 168 | 101 | 130 |
| 1919 | 81 | 111 | 77 | ... | 202 | 130 | 100 |
| 1920 | 42 | 116 | 166 | 130 | 342 | 69 | 112 |
| 1921 | 34 | 108 | 112 | 118 | 129 | 50 | 43 |
| 1922 | 58 | 81 | 99 | 75 | 198 | 46 | 68 |
| 1923 | 64 | 90 | 105 | 120 | 181 | 59 | 81 |
| 1924 | 85 | 121 | 178 | 159 | 210 | 70 | 84 |
| 1925 | 75 | 87 | 116 | 168 | 192 | 69 | 80 |
| 1926 | 66 | 112 | 127 | 143 | 118 | 69 | 83 |
| 1927 | 84 | 119 | 226 | 137 | 200 | 76 | 98 |
| 1928 | 77 | 131 | 228 | 134 | 251 | 75 | 90 |
| 1929 | 47 | 120 | 168 | 134 | 278 | 64 | 103 |
| 1930 | 42 | 88 | 107 | 131 | 92 | 41 | 75 |
| 1931 | 34 | 90 | 169 | 119 | 92 | 34 | 48 |
| | | | | (million current paper pesos) | | | |
| 1932 | 61 | 187 | 321 | 193 | 226 | 66 | 37 |
| 1933 | 81 | 143 | 197 | 192 | 216 | 82 | 56 |
| 1934 | 82 | 171 | 302 | 201 | 295 | 105 | 100 |
| 1935 | 98 | 216 | 322 | 250 | 274 | 91 | 116 |
| 1936 | 116 | 211 | 445 | 268 | 170 | 125 | 66 |
| 1937 | 153 | 275 | 599 | 312 | 476 | 136 | 82 |
| 1938 | 101 | 181 | 181 | 318 | 183 | 123 | 65 |
| 1939 | 114 | 170 | 203 | 332 | 275 | 163 | 84 |
| 1940 | 114 | 119 | 85 | 307 | 284 | 195 | 132 |
| 1941 | 148 | 67 | 22 | 387 | 157 | 239 | 160 |
| 1942 | 170 | 56 | 9.4 | 557 | 159 | 187 | 164 |
| 1943 | 181 | 157 | 15 | 594 | 163 | 167 | 205 |
| 1944 | 194 | 70 | 43 | 732 | 251 | 147 | 198 |
| 1945 | 173 | 30 | 59 | 480 | 331 | 271 | 200 |
| 1946 | 341 | 8.2 | 389 | 593 | 303 | 357 | 200 |
| 1947 | 358 | — | 674 | 767 | 1,039 | 326 | 214 |
| 1948 | 420 | 100 | 829 | 662 | 1,377 | 413 | 298 |
| 1949 | 482 | 98 | 247 | 749 | 839 | 349 | 268 |

**E3 SOUTH AMERICA: Major Commodity Exports by Main Exporting Countries** (in currency units stated)

| | Brazil[21] | | | | | | Chile | | Colombia | | |
|---|---|---|---|---|---|---|---|---|---|---|---|
| | (million paper milreis/cruzeiros) | | | | | | (million gold pesos of 18 pence) | | (million pesos) | | |
| | | | | | | | | Nitrate of | | | |
| | Cocoa | Coffee | Cotton | Iron Ore | Rubber | Sugar | Copper[9] | Soda | Coffee | Tobacco | Petroleum |
| 1905 | 16 | 325 | 17 | - - | 226 | 6.4 | 23 | 182 | 4.8 | 0.4 | — |
| 1906 | 21 | 418 | 25 | — | 210 | 9.2 | 27 | 212 | 6.1 | 0.7 | — |
| 1907 | 32 | 454 | 28 | — | 218 | 2.1 | 28 | 207 | 5.3 | 0.5 | — |
| 1908 | 32 | 368 | 3.3 | - - | 188 | 4.9 | 27 | 224 | 5.5 | 0.4 | — |
| 1909 | 26 | 534 | 9.4 | - - | 302 | 11 | 26 | 212 | 6.3 | 0.4 | — |
| 1910 | 21 | 385 | 13 | - - | 377 | 11 | 24 | 232 | 5.5 | 0.4 | — |
| 1911 | 25 | 607 | 15 | — | 226 | 6.1 | 21 | 262 | 9.5 | 0.3 | — |
| 1912 | 23 | 698 | 16 | - - | 241 | 0.8 | 34 | 287 | 17 | 0.5 | — |
| | | | | | | | (million gold pesos of 6 pence) | | | | |
| 1913 | 24 | 612 | 35 | - - | 156 | 1.0 | 93 | 945 | 18 | 0.9 | — |
| 1914 | 31 | 440 | 28 | — | 114 | 6.8 | 96 | 637 | 16 | 0.4 | — |
| 1915 | 56 | 620 | 5.5 | - - | 136 | 14 | 136 | 698 | 16 | 0.3 | — |
| 1916 | 50 | 589 | 2.4 | — | 152 | 26 | 261 | 1,016 | 16 | 0.4 | — |
| 1917 | 48 | 440 | 15 | — | 144 | 73 | 369 | 1,465 | 13 | 0.6 | — |
| 1918 | 40 | 353 | 9.7 | — | 74 | 101 | 326 | 1,597 | 21 | 1.0 | — |
| 1919 | 93 | 1,226 | 37 | - - | 106 | 58 | 148 | 351 | 54 | 2.8 | — |
| 1920 | 64 | 861 | 81 | - - | 58 | 106 | 296 | 1,582 | 36 | ... | — |
| 1921 | 48 | 1,019 | 46 | — | 36 | 94 | 128 | 823 | 42 | ... | — |
| 1922 | 68 | 1,504 | 104 | — | 49 | 115 | 288 | 514 | 36 | 0.2 | — |
| 1923 | 93 | 2,124 | 119 | - - | 81 | 142 | 408 | 930 | 45 | 0.2 | — |
| 1924 | 98 | 2,929 | 39 | — | 79 | 30 | 422 | 967 | 69 | 0.4 | — |
| 1925 | 100 | 2,900 | 124 | — | 192 | 2.3 | 403 | 1,032 | 67 | ... | — |
| 1926 | 104 | 2,348 | 41 | — | 115 | 8.7 | 402 | 710 | 86 | ... | 9.4 |
| 1927 | 187 | 2,576 | 42 | — | 115 | 26 | 459 | 860 | 71 | ... | 22 |
| 1928 | 149 | 2,840 | 36 | — | 59 | 21 | 621 | 935 | 88 | ... | 26 |
| 1929 | 105 | 2,740 | 154 | — | 61 | 9.0 | 953 | 966 | 77 | ... | 27 |
| 1930 | 92[21] | 1,828[21] | 85[21] | - -[21] | 34[21] | 25[21] | 460 | 593 | 62 | ... | 26 |
| 1931 | 98 | 2,347 | 54 | - - | 26 | 4.6 | 308 | 359 | 55 | ... | 16 |
| 1932 | 114 | 1,824 | 1.8 | 0.1 | 11 | 19 | 121 | 44 | 43 | ... | 16 |
| 1933 | 106 | 2,053 | 33 | 0.4 | 22 | 13 | 127 | 85 | 49 | ... | 9.9 |
| 1934 | 130 | 2,115 | 456 | 0.6 | 34 | 14 | 157 | 151 | 82 | ... | 28 |
| 1935 | 163 | 2,157 | 648 | 1.4 | 36 | 46 | 179 | 147 | 79 | ... | 29 |
| 1936 | 258 | 2,231 | 930 | 4.6 | 68 | 44 | 214 | 144 | 92 | ... | 28 |
| 1937 | 229 | 2,159 | 944 | 7.9 | 76 | 0.3 | 506 | 168 | 99 | ... | 35 |
| 1938 | 213 | 2,296 | 930 | 20 | 47 | 2.9 | 329 | 142 | 89 | ... | 37 |
| 1939 | 225 | 2,234 | 1,159 | 19 | 57 | 23 | 332 | 127 | 87 | ... | 32 |
| 1940 | 192 | 1,589 | 838 | 16 | 77 | 39 | 382 | 141 | 74 | ... | 40 |
| 1941 | 315 | 2,017 | 1,010 | 30 | 91 | 9.7 | 488 | 124 | 83 | ... | 41 |
| 1942 | 217 | 1,966 | 644 | 23 | 148 | 47 | 575 | 120 | 145 | ... | 14 |
| 1943 | 342 | 2,803 | 414 | 25 | 189 | 17 | 525 | 127 | 176 | ... | 20 |
| 1944 | 308 | 3,879 | 668 | 19 | 366 | 114 | 528 | 129 | 165 | ... | 37 |
| 1945 | 229 | 4,260 | 1,049 | 27 | 346 | 54 | 524 | 187 | 182 | ... | 39 |
| 1946 | 651 | 6,441 | 2,938 | 5.8 | 268 | 72 | 537 | 232 | 270 | ... | 42 |
| 1947 | 1,048 | 7,755 | 3,076 | 14 | 204 | 221 | 842 | 168 | 342 | ... | 65 |
| 1948 | 1,066 | 9,019 | 3,385 | 61 | 47 | 692 | 953 | 260 | 394 | ... | 79 |
| 1949 | 964 | 11,611 | 2,007 | 103 | 28 | 78 | 754 | 311 | 472 | ... | 113 |

**E3     SOUTH AMERICA: Major Commodity Exports by Main Exporting Countries** (in currency units stated)

| | Ecuador | | | | Guyana[22] | | Paraguay | | | | |
|---|---|---|---|---|---|---|---|---|---|---|---|
| | (million sucres) | | | | (thousand pounds) | | (thousand gold pesos) | | | | |
| | Bananas[23] | Cocoa | Coffee | Petroleum & Products | Bauxite[16] | Sugar | Cotton | Hides & Skins | Meat | Quebracho Extract | Wood |
| 1905 | ... | 11 | 0.8 | — | ... | 1,255 | ... | ... | ... | ... | ... |
| 1906 | ... | 12 | 0.9 | — | ... | 1,097 | ... | ... | ... | ... | ... |
| 1907 | ... | 13 | 0.4 | — | ... | 1,004[22] | ... | ... | ... | ... | ... |
| 1908 | ... | 18 | 1.0 | — | ... | 1,258 | ... | ... | ... | ... | ... |
| 1909 | ... | 15 | 1.0 | — | ... | 1,205 | ... | 1,167 | ... | 652 | 998 |
| 1910 | ... | 16 | 1.5 | — | ... | 1,040 | ... | 1,170 | 8 | 692 | 1,028 |
| 1911 | ... | 16 | 2.3 | — | ... | 1,381[22] | ... | 1,012 | 10 | 487 | 1,022 |
| 1912 | ... | 16 | 1.6 | — | ... | 1,019 | ... | 1,114 | 4 | 438 | 773 |
| 1913 | ... | 21 | 1.7 | — | ... | 1,103 | ... | 1,196 | 48 | 703 | 764 |
| 1914 | ... | 21 | 1.2 | — | ... | 1,575 | ... | 1,034 | 119 | 763 | 496 |
| 1915 | ... | 20 | 1.0 | — | ... | 2,059 | ... | 1,118 | 124 | 1,098 | ... |
| 1916 | ... | 26 | 1.3 | — | ... | 2,100 | ... | 719 | - - | 1,268 | ... |
| 1917 | ... | 22 | 1.3 | — | ... | 2,500 | ... | 1,639 | 6 | 3,737 | ... |
| 1918 | ... | 17 | 1.7 | — | ... | 2,067 | ... | ... | ... | ... | ... |
| 1919 | ... | 29 | 1.3 | — | ... | 2,476 | ... | 2,935 | [2,580][24] | 4,946 | ... |
| 1920 | ... | 36 | 0.9 | — | 28 | 4,193 | ... | 1,348 | [529][24] | 3,609 | 1,342 |
| 1921 | ... | 20 | 3.2 | — | 12 | 2,104 | ... | 660 | 170 | 2,495 | 1,720 |
| 1922 | ... | 13 | 3.6 | - - | — | 1,453 | ... | 1,257 | ... | 3,024 | 1,394 |
| 1923 | ... | 19 | 5.4 | — | 110 | 2,133 | ... | 2,072 | 390 | 2,328 | 2,304 |
| 1924 | ... | 30 | 9.3 | — | 163 | 1,767 | [452][25] | [1,327] | [401][25] | [1,901][25] | [814][25] |
| 1925 | 0.7 | 34 | 7.6 | 0.4 | 185 | 1,414 | [418][25] | [1,554][25] | [3,015][25] | [3,880][25] | [1,349][25] |
| 1926 | 1.1 | 26 | 12 | 2.3 | 192 | 1,260 | 437 | 1,578 | 2,791 | 4,144 | 2,003 |
| 1927 | 1.5 | 37 | 9.6 | 5.3 | 168 | 1,831 | 532 | 1,521 | 2,747 | 3,675 | 1,832 |
| 1928 | 1.7 | 30 | 17 | 12 | 175 | 1,693 | 645 | 1,812 | 3,645 | 3,817 | 1,621 |
| 1929 | 1.3 | 21 | 12 | 15 | 190 | 1,238 | 747 | 1,082 | 2,499 | 2,765 | 1,643 |
| 1930 | 1.2 | 23 | 7.6 | 16 | 125 | 1,229 | 934 | 1,281 | 3,533 | 3,223 | 1,300 |
| 1931 | 0.7 | 12 | 5.9 | 16 | 130 | 1,110 | 721 | 1,264 | 2,912 | 2,735 | 1,188 |
| 1932 | 0.4 | 11 | 8.0 | 14 | 104 | 1,342 | 754 | 1,026 | 3,037 | 3,325 | 586 |
| 1933 | 0.5 | 8.7 | 5.6 | 11 | 55 | 1,197 | 711 | 1,228 | 1,626 | 2,894 | 368 |
| 1934 | 2.5 | 27 | 21 | 13 | 66 | 1,160 | 2,686 | 1,862 | 1,732 | 2,405 | 438 |
| 1935 | 3.6 | 24 | 15 | 15 | 138 | 1,443 | 3,229 | 1,402 | 730 | 2,477 | 451 |
| 1936 | 6.7 | 31 | 20 | 13 | 215 | 1,428 | 2,277 | 1,202 | 1,001 | 2,181 | 371 |
| 1937 | 5.7[23] | 50 | 25 | 22 | 358 | 1,585 | 4,435 | 1,122 | 1,016 | 2,305 | 428 |
| 1938 | 7.6 | 39 | 17 | 26 | 421 | 1,578 | 3,193 | 1,424 | 1,487 | 2,210 | 317 |
| 1939 | 7 | 37 | 15 | 25 | 602 | 1,695 | 901 | 1,653 | 4,215 | 3,321 | 469 |
| 1940 | 6.4 | 29 | 16 | 25 | 838 | 1,485 | ... | 1,208 | 1,633 | 2,511 | 1,122 |
| 1941 | 4.7 | 34 | 24 | 13 | 1,456 | 1,720 | 1,583 | 2,049 | 4,065 | 2,907 | 800 |
| 1942 | 3.1 | 40 | 17 | 25 | 1,503 | 1,518 | 1,939 | 2,561 | 3,795 | 3,205 | 904 |
| | ———— (million US dollars) ———— | | | | | | | | | | |
| 1943 | 0.2 | 3.7 | 2.4 | 24 | 2,271 | 1,566 | 4,224 | 4,322 | 10,677 | 6,371 | 2,566 |
| 1944 | 0.1 | 3 | 2.5 | 30 | 1,127 | 2,284 | 5,190 | 5,787 | 11,799 | 5,474 | 5,158 |
| | | | | | | | ———— (million guaranies) ———— | | | | |
| 1945 | 0.2 | 3.9 | 2.5 | 28 | 763 | 2,018 | 11 | 7.3 | 17 | 11 | 11 |
| 1946 | 0.6 | 5.6 | 2.6 | 18 | 1,263 | 2,571 | 13 | 9.2 | 3.6 | 12 | 11 |
| 1947 | 1.7 | 15 | 3.8 | 16 | 1,402 | 3,974 | 10 | 11 | 9.4 | 8.6 | 8.6 |
| 1948 | 9.1 | 13 | 7.1 | 26 | 1,982 | 3,428 | 13 | 13 | 14 | 16 | 17 |
| 1949 | 14[23] | 8.8 | 5.4 | 17 | 2,502 | 4,386 | 15 | 21 | 9.1 | 21 | 24 |

**E3   SOUTH AMERICA: Major Commodity Exports by Main Exporting Countries** (in currency units stated)

| | **Peru** (thousand pounds sterling) | | | | | | | |
| | Copper[9] | Cotton | Lead | Rubber | Petroleum & Products | Silver | Sugar[26] | Wool[27] | Zinc[9] |
|---|---|---|---|---|---|---|---|---|---|
| 1905 | 835 | 312 | ... | 853 | 12 | 242 | 1,450 | 441 | ... |
| 1906 | 1,157 | 399 | ... | 910 | 27 | 523 | 1,142 | 488 | ... |
| 1907 | 1,769 | 519 | ... | 1,050 | 49 | 502 | 1,004 | 412 | ... |
| 1908 | 1,170 | 588 | ... | 670 | 90 | 510 | 1,196 | 299 | ... |
| 1909 | 1,160 | 865 | ... | 885 | 152 | 447 | 1,262 | 379 | ... |
| 1910 | 1,537 | 724 | ... | 1,200 | 117 | 925 | 1,327 | 506 | ... |
| | | | | | (million soles) | | | | |
| 1911 | 16 | 10 | ... | 6.1 | 4.0 | 0.7 | 15 | 4.1 | ... |
| 1912 | 23 | 10 | ... | 13 | 7.6 | 2.2 | 14 | 3.9 | ... |
| 1913 | 20 | 14 | 0.2 | 8.2 | 9.1 | 1.0 | 14 | 5.2 | ... |
| 1914 | 17 | 14 | 0.1 | 4.4 | 8.9 | 1.6 | 26 | 5.1 | ... |
| 1915 | 34 | 13 | - - | 6.0 | 11 | 3.0 | 30 | 6.0 | ... |
| 1916 | 59 | 17 | 0.6 | 7.0 | 14 | 0.3 | 40 | 9.4 | ... |
| 1917 | 63 | 29 | 0.4 | 6.0 | 12 | 0.6 | 41 | 17 | ... |
| 1918 | 59 | 38 | — | 3.2 | 14 | 0.7 | 42 | 27 | ... |
| 1919 | 48 | 69 | — | 4.7 | 23 | 1.0 | 83 | 16 | ... |
| 1920 | 35 | 112 | 0.2 | 2.0 | 14 | 1.2 | 156 | 6.8 | ... |
| 1921 | 36 | 36 | 0.2 | 0.1 | 29 | 0.2 | 47 | 3.0 | ... |
| 1922 | 35 | 44 | 0.1 | 1.1 | 45 | 0.1 | 42 | 5.3 | ... |
| 1923 | 43 | 61 | 0.2 | 1.6 | 47 | 0.2 | 63 | 6.5 | ... |
| 1924 | 36 | 66 | 0.2 | 1.6 | 60 | 1.8 | 50 | 10 | ... |
| 1925 | 42 | 63 | 0.1 | 2.2 | 56 | 1.2 | 22 | 7.4 | 0.2 |
| 1926 | 42 | 46 | 0.2 | 2.8 | 74 | 0.9 | 36 | 5.2 | 2.5 |
| 1927 | 49 | 68 | 0.2 | 1.8 | 102 | - - | 46 | 8.4 | 4.0 |
| 1928 | 55 | 59 | 11 | 1.4 | 113 | - - | 36 | 11 | 4.4 |
| 1929 | 66 | 52 | 15 | 1.2 | 129 | - - | 34 | 11 | 4.7 |
| 1930 | 45 | 42 | 11 | 0.7 | 70 | - - | 26 | 7.1 | 4.7 |
| 1931 | 39 | 31 | 0.3 | 0.7 | 53 | — | 28 | 6.2 | — |
| 1932 | 14 | 34 | 0.6 | 0.2 | 77 | — | 26 | 5.1 | — |
| 1933 | 23 | 61 | 0.8 | 0.3 | 95 | 0.8 | 34 | 10 | — |
| 1934 | 28 | 82 | 1.2 | 0.4 | 121 | 1.8 | 26 | 8.7 | — |
| 1935 | 45 | 81 | 7.4 | 0.4 | 117 | 1.2 | 26 | 7.6 | 1.0 |
| 1936 | 43 | 92 | 11 | 0.3 | 119 | 0.1 | 25 | 13 | 2.3 |
| 1937 | 51 | 89 | 17 | 0.5 | 121 | 0.1 | 32 | 16 | 3.5 |
| 1938 | 58 | 61 | 17 | 0.4 | 116 | - - | 25 | 11 | 1.2 |
| 1939 | 71 | 75 | 12 | 0.3 | 111 | 5.4 | 41 | 14 | 1.2 |
| 1940 | 82 | 71 | 11 | 0.3 | 101 | 8.4 | 44 | 20 | 1.3 |
| 1941 | 75 | 125 | 16 | 2.4 | 112 | 9.8 | 60 | 21 | 2.1 |
| 1942 | 81 | 53 | 11 | 1.2 | 115 | 6.4 | 113 | 11 | 2.4 |
| 1943 | 72 | 69 | 17 | 2.8 | 104 | 0.9 | 75 | 15 | 11 |
| 1944 | 62 | 60 | 45 | 4.1 | 92 | 0.7 | 168 | 18 | 12 |
| 1945 | 60 | 141 | 34 | 9.2 | 84 | 5.0 | 216 | 18 | 15 |
| 1946 | 78 | 328 | 34 | 9.4 | 91 | 3.8 | 291 | 19 | 21 |
| 1947 | 64 | 225 | 63 | 8.8 | 117 | 39 | 302 | 11 | 35 |
| 1948 | 46 | 276 | 103 | 1.7 | 188 | 24 | 228 | 13 | 42 |
| 1949 | 133[4] | 631 | 198 | 0.9 | 230 | 86 | 341 | 50 | 98 |

**E3    SOUTH AMERICA: Major Commodity Exports by Main Exporting Countries** (in currency units stated)

| | Argentina | | | | | | Bolivia | |
| | (million current paper pesos) | | | | | | (million US dollars) | |
| | Hides & Skins | Linseed | Maize | Meat | Wheat | Wool | Natural Gas | Tin[9] |
|---|---|---|---|---|---|---|---|---|
| 1950 | 690 | 316 | 159 | 593 | 760 | 876 | — | 64 |
| | 662 | | | 618 | | | | |
| 1951 | 526 | 482 | 144 | 1,009 | 1,003 | 916 | — | 93 |
| 1952 | 413 | 61 | 338 | 884 | 30 | 720 | — | 85 |
| 1953 | 387 | 125 | 376 | 1,288 | 1,218 | 1,143 | — | 73 |
| 1954 | 449 | 207 | 587 | 1,357 | 1,027 | 761 | — | 60 |
| | | | (million US dollars) | | | | | |
| 1955 | 55 | 29 | 23 | 208 | 246 | 124 | — | 57 |
| 1956 | 66 | 19 | 63 | 244 | 155 | 125 | — | 59 |
| 1957 | 60 | 33 | 45 | 256 | 159 | 118 | — | 57 |
| 1958 | 59 | 39 | 81 | 268 | 126 | 100 | — | 36 |
| 1959 | 70 | 42 | 124 | 245 | 135 | 122 | — | 53 |
| 1960 | 70 | 41 | 124 | 220 | 143 | 146 | — | 43 |
| 1961 | 79 | 50 | 83 | 218 | 66 | 144 | — | 51 |
| 1962 | 92 | 59 | 121 | 230 | 173 | 147 | — | 54 |
| 1963 | 78 | 42 | 126 | 332 | 116 | 168 | — | 57 |
| 1964 | 58 | 41 | 168 | 324 | 242 | 135 | — | 81 |
| 1965 | 50 | 47 | 154 | 325 | 373 | 117 | — | 93 |
| 1966 | 83 | 21 | 201 | 393 | 280 | 133 | — | 93 |
| 1967 | 78 | 35 | 223 | 378 | 122 | 108 | — | 91 |
| 1968 | 72 | 15 | 140 | 333 | 139 | 111 | — | 92 |
| 1969 | 97 | 30 | 195 | 435 | 138 | 99 | — | 102 |
| 1970 | 97 | — | 265 | 441 | 126 | 89 | — | 108 |
| 1971 | 69 | 34 | 348 | 416 | 49 | 73 | — | 106 |
| 1972 | 120 | 18 | 175 | 691 | 110 | 90 | 10 | 114 |
| 1973 | 120 | 24 | 365 | 790 | 273 | 188 | 18 | 131 |
| 1974 | 98 | 58 | 659 | 440 | 305 | 107 | 29 | 230 |
| 1975 | 71 | 53 | 518 | 288 | 301 | 110 | 42 | 171 |
| 1976 | 151 | 55 | 363 | 523 | 431 | 133 | 55 | 216 |
| 1977 | 207 | 92 | 518 | 640 | 541 | 228 | 67 | 329 |
| 1978 | 270 | 76 | 588 | 795 | 174 | 238 | 78 | 374 |
| 1979 | 454 | 88 | 606 | 1,226 | 606 | 232 | 105 | 396 |
| 1980 | 355 | 127 | 513 | 966 | 816 | 283 | 221 | 378 |
| 1981 | 369 | 111 | 1,308 | 930 | 763 | 333 | 337 | 343 |
| 1982 | 298 | 87 | 585 | 805 | 677 | 230 | 382 | 278 |
| 1983 | 264 | 75 | 804 | 603 | 1,474 | 186 | 378 | 208 |
| 1984 | 305 | 103 | 748 | 404 | 966 | 176 | 376 | 248 |
| 1985 | 289 | 82 | 766 | 386 | 1,133 | 147 | 373 | 187 |
| 1986 | 341 | 53 | 654 | 465 | 395 | 135 | 329 | 104 |
| 1987 | 354 | 45 | 299 | 599 | 351 | 141 | 249 | 68 |
| 1988 | 368 | 49 | 381 | 607 | 355 | 184 | 215 | 77 |

**E3    SOUTH AMERICA: Major Commodity Exports by Main Exporting Countries** (in currency units stated)

| | Brazil (million US dollars) | | | | | | Chile (million gold pesos of 6 pence) | | Colombia (million pesos) | |
|---|---|---|---|---|---|---|---|---|---|---|
| | Cocoa | Coffee | Cotton | Iron Ore | Soybeans | Sugar | Copper[28] | Nitrate of Soda[29] | Coffee | Petroleum |
| 1950 | 118 | 866 | 142 | 7 | ... | 7 | 687 | 343 | 600 | 126 |
| 1951 | 95 | 1,059 | 255 | 13 | ... | 30 | 815[28] / 954 | 329 | 849 | 174 |
| 1952 | 56 | 1,045 | 43 | 23 | ... | 15 | 1,357 | 280 | 950 | 179 |
| 1953 | 91 | 1,088 | 108 | 22 | 3 | 22 | 1,170 | 265 | 1,231 | 192 |
| 1954 | 147 | 948 | 227 | 22 | 3 | 12 | 1,167 | 328 | 1,375 | 191 |
| | | | | | | | | | (million US dollars) | |
| 1955 | 103 | 844 | 136 | 30 | 6 | 47 | 1,599 | 273 | 487 | 65 |
| 1956 | 78 | 1,030 | 90 | 35 | 4 | 2 | 1,926 | 235 | 474 | 73 |
| 1957 | 91 | 845 | 47 | 48 | 2 | 46 | 1,446 | 214 | 389 | 81 |
| 1958 | 105 | 687 | 26 | 57 | 4 | 57 | 1,163 | 203 | 355 | 77 |
| 1959 | 85 | 733 | 37 | 43 | 5 | 43 | 1,623 | 188 | 361 | 82 |
| 1960 | 94 | 713 | 48 | 53 | — | 58 | 1,644 | 126 | 332 | 88 |
| 1961 | 61 | 710 | 113 | 60 | 7 | 66 | 1,603 | 176 | 308 | 74 |
| 1962 | 41 | 643 | 115 | 68 | 8 | 39 | 1,677 | 147 | 332 | 68 |
| 1963 | 51 | 748 | 118 | 70 | 7 | 72 | 1,695 | 146 | 303 | 82 |
| 1964 | 46 | 760 | 111 | 81 | 3 | 33 | 1,947 | 134 | 394 | 83 |
| 1965 | 41 | 707 | 98 | 103 | 15 | 57 | 2,278 | 146 | 344 | 96 |
| 1966 | 72 | 764 | 113 | 100 | 28 | 81 | 640 | 24 | 328 | 81 |
| 1967 | 84 | 705 | 93 | 103 | 39 | 84 | 707 | 22 | 322 | 75 |
| 1968 | 72 | 775 | 134 | 104 | 25 | 106 | 727 | 21[29] / 16 | 351 | 51 |
| 1969 | 136 | 813 | 200 | 147 | 53 | 122 | 831 | 17 | 344 | 77 |
| 1970 | 106 | 939 | 159 | 209 | 72 | 134 | 977 | 14 | 467 | 73 |
| 1971 | 92 | 773 | 141 | 237 | 108 | 162 | 688 | 19 | 395 | 70 |
| 1972 | 99 | 989 | 191 | 232 | 295 | 417 | 631 | 15 | 430 | 64 |
| 1973 | 143 | 1,244 | 221 | 363 | 949 | 592 | 1,007 | 18 | 598 | 61 |
| 1974 | 323 | 864 | 94 | 571 | 891 | 1,383 | 1,898 | 32 | 624 | 114 |
| 1975 | 294 | 855 | 100 | 921 | 1,304 | 1,148 | 980 | 27 | 674 | 103 |
| 1976 | 312 | 2,173 | 9.1 | 994 | 1,780 | 349 | 1,365 | 31 | 975 | 68 |
| 1977 | 605 | 2,299 | 43 | 907 | 2,143 | 510 | 1,052 | 29 | 1,527 | 87 |
| 1978 | 828 | 1,947 | 54 | 1,028 | 1,515 | 387 | 1,246 | 36 | 1,991 | 121 |
| 1979 | 945 | 1,918 | 4.2 | 1,288 | 1,650 | 421 | 2,305 | 42 | 2,023 | 120 |
| 1980 | 697 | 2,486 | 17 | 1,564 | 2,277 | 1,374 | 2,249 | 37 | 2,372 | 102 |
| 1981 | 597 | 1,517 | 45 | 1,748 | 3,191 | 1,133 | 1,737 | 34 | 1,462 | 36 |
| 1982 | 429 | 1,858 | 65 | 1,847 | 2,122 | 562 | 1,489 | 75 | 1,580 | 215 |
| 1983 | 557 | 2,096 | 196 | 1,513 | 2,563 | 553 | 1,382 | 30 | 1,541 | 435 |
| 1984 | 661 | 2,564 | 50 | 1,605 | 2,566 | 617 | 1,324 | 28 | 1,802 | 480 |
| 1985 | 779 | 2,369 | 82 | 1,658 | 2,540 | 401 | 1,529 | 33 | 1,792 | 451 |
| 1986 | 630 | 2,006 | 20 | 1,615 | 1,640 | 433 | 1,544 | 36 | 3,061 | 464 |
| 1987 | 584 | 1,959 | 166 | 1,615 | 2,325 | 366 | 1,904 | 34 | 1,702 | 1,369 |
| 1988 | 412 | 1,998 | 100 | 1,892 | 3,046 | 425 | 2,835 | 54 | 1,699 | 987 |

**E3     SOUTH AMERICA: Major Commodity Exports by Main Exporting Countries** (in currency units stated)

| | Ecuador (million US dollars) | | | | Guyana (million local dollars) | | Paraguay (million guaranies) | | | | | |
|---|---|---|---|---|---|---|---|---|---|---|---|---|
| | Bananas | Cocoa | Coffee | Petroleum & Products | Bauxite[16] | Sugar | Cotton | Hides & Skins | Meat | Quebracho Extract | Soybeans | Wood |
| 1950 | 17 | 18 | 19 | ... | 14 | 24 | 33 | 18 | 19 | 28 | ... | 45 |
| 1951 | 25 | 18 | 16 | 1.5 | 16 | 27 | 37 | 15 | 15 | 18 | ... | 60 |
| 1952 | 44 | 18 | 20 | 1.0 | 22 | 42 | 91 | 25 | 8.4 | 52 | ... | 46 |
| 1953 | 42 | 15 | 19 | 1.6 | 24 | 38 | 196 | 30 | 22 | 80 | ... | 98 |
| | | | | | | | | | (million US dollars) | | | |
| 1954 | 51 | 35 | 27 | 1.5 | 23 | 41 | 6.9 | 1.7 | 2.1 | 4.0 | ... | 11 |
| 1955 | 62 | 19 | 23 | 1.6 | 25 | 40 | 5.5 | 1.4 | 2.3 | 5.6 | ... | 13 |
| 1956 | 61 | 18 | 30 | 1.1 | 29 | 42 | 5.6 | 2.0 | 4.6 | 6.5 | ... | 12 |
| 1957 | 69 | 18 | 30 | 1.4 | 30 | 54 | 4.5 | 1.6 | 3.7 | 4.5 | ... | 9.4 |
| 1958 | 73 | 21 | 26 | 0.7 | 21 | 55 | 3.7 | 2.0 | 8.2 | 3.5 | ... | 9.7 |
| 1959 | 90 | 22 | 18 | 0.3 | 25 | 46 | 2.1 | 3.6 | 9.6 | 3.6 | ... | 4.0 |
| 1960 | 89 | 22 | 22 | — | 29 | 58 | 0.3 | 2.2 | 7.1 | 3.0 | ... | 5.0 |
| 1961 | 81 | 16 | 14 | — | 41 | 57 | 1.6 | 2.0 | 8.6 | 2.7 | ... | 6.5 |
| 1962 | 88 | 16 | 21 | 0.2 | 54 | 59 | 2.5 | 1.7 | 7.5 | 2.5 | ... | 6.7 |
| 1963 | 63 | 20 | 18 | 0.3 | 51 | 74 | 3.2 | 1.7 | 11 | 2.8 | ... | 4.7 |
| 1964 | 84 | 15 | 22 | 0.7 | 57 | 54 | 4.2 | 1.5 | 15 | 4.0 | ... | 7.1 |
| 1965 | 84 | 19 | 38 | 0.6 | 68 | 44 | 4.7 | 1.8 | 19 | 3.5 | ... | 9.8 |
| 1966 | 89 | 17 | 32 | 1.4 | 78 | 49 | 2.0 | 3.1 | 14 | 3.1 | ... | 11 |
| 1967 | 105 | 25 | 40 | 1.1 | 77 | 55 | 2.3 | 2.0 | 17 | 2.0 | ... | 7.7 |
| 1968 | 105 | 41 | 35 | 1.1 | 91 | 59 | 1.4 | 1.8 | 14 | 2.1 | ... | 8.0 |
| 1969 | 106 | 26 | 26 | 0.6 | 102 | 82 | 3.2 | 2.0 | 12 | 1.9 | - - | 11 |
| 1970 | 123 | 25 | 50 | 0.9 | 139 | 73 | 3.7 | 1.7 | 16 | 1.9 | — | 12 |
| 1971 | 124 | 29 | 36 | 1.0 | 137 | 92 | 0.8 | 1.7 | 20 | 2.2 | 1.0 | 8.7 |
| 1972 | 128 | 30 | 43 | 60 | 131 | 101 | 3.3 | 3.8 | 25 | 2.3 | 3.8 | 6.8 |
| 1973 | 125 | 35 | 67 | 283 | 137 | 76 | 12 | 2.3 | 40 | 2.4 | 10 | 8.4 |
| 1974 | 125 | 126 | 67 | 697 | 200 | 285 | 16 | 3.8 | 34 | 0.9 | 14 | 20 |
| 1975 | 157 | 71 | 64 | 588 | 197 | 418 | 20 | 2.3 | 31 | 0.6 | 17 | 23 |
| 1976 | 146 | 95 | 205 | 739 | 229 | 223 | 34 | 0.9 | 20 | 3.7 | 32 | 7.3 |
| 1977 | 168 | 245 | 157 | 713 | 253 | 186 | 80 | 1.8 | 21 | 5.3 | 56 | 13 |
| 1978 | 181 | 259 | 281 | 718 | 250 | 216 | 99 | 1.8 | 22 | 5.2 | 39 | 12 |
| 1979 | 197 | 273 | 205 | 1,178 | 330 | 236 | 98 | 0.4 | 5.5 | 3.2 | 79 | 29 |
| 1980 | 244 | 210 | 130 | 1,565 | 486 | 342 | 104 | ... | 1.1 | 4.4 | 42 | 44 |
| 1981 | 208 | 135 | 106 | 1,342 | 430 | 340 | 127 | ... | - - | 5.6 | 48 | 24 |
| 1982 | 213 | 88 | 139 | 1,472 | 282 | 212 | 121 | ... | 2.1 | 5.0 | 101 | 30 |
| 1983 | 153 | 19 | 149 | 1,644 | 172 | 185 | 82 | ... | 5.3 | 5.4 | 111 | 17 |
| 1984 | 133 | 116 | 175 | 1,797 | 282 | 272 | 131 | ... | 4.6 | 5.6 | 109 | 20 |
| 1985 | 220 | 151 | 191 | 1,825 | 344 | 242 | 141 | ... | 1.4 | 4.0 | 105 | 8.3 |
| 1986 | 263 | 83 | 297 | 912 | 334 | 327 | 80 | ... | 34 | 3.8 | 43 | 16 |
| 1987 | 267 | 139 | 192 | 646 | 713 | 777 | 101 | ... | 21 | 5.3 | 123 | 23 |
| 1988 | 298 | 132 | 152 | 875 | 910 | 875 | 87 | ... | 21 | 4.4 | 169 | 13 |

**E3** **SOUTH AMERICA: Major Commodity Exports by Main Exporting Countries** (in currency units stated)

| | Peru | | | | | | | | | |
|---|---|---|---|---|---|---|---|---|---|---|
| | (million soles) | | | | | | | | | |
| | Copper[9] | Cotton | Fish Meal | Lead | Rubber | Petroleum & Products | Silver | Sugar[26] | Wool[27] | Zinc[9] |
| 1950 | 161 | 1,015 | 4 | 229 | 2.2 | 346 | 82 | 443 | 118 | 157 |
| 1951 | 244 | 1,291 | 7 | 417 | 7.4 | 330 | 89 | 520[26] | 208 | 236 |
| 1952 | 261 | 1,224 | 13 | 438 | 8.0 | 262 | 114 | 506 | 117 | 244 |
| 1953 | 292 | 1,101 | 16 | 463 | 8.2 | 239 | 110 | 585 | ... | 133 |
| 1954 | 390[4] 401 | 1,254 | 23 | 575 | 15 | 322 | 156 | 633 | 165 | 181 |
| 1955 | 579 | 1,294 | 38 | 616 | 13 | 407 | 187 | 700 | 112 | 284 |
| 1956 | 693 | 1,683 | 67 | 732 | 13 | 446 | 146 | 623 | 152 | 296 |
| 1957 | 524 | 1,293 | 135 | 683 | 19 | 503 | 162 | 942 | 186 | 304 |
| 1958 | 584 | 1,765 | 271 | 759 | 22 | 382 | 213 | 793 | 141 | 285 |
| 1959 | 691 | 1,911 | 860 | 830 | 21 | 436 | 267 | 997 | 248 | 412 |
| 1960 | 2,683 | 1,997 | 1,056 | 869 | 19 | 484 | 301 | 1,294 | 192 | 491 |
| 1961 | 2,911 | 2,140 | 1,329 | 856 | 31 | 384 | 392 | 1,713 | 199 | 539 |
| 1962 | 2,557 | 2,605 | 2,678 | 744 | 80 | 348 | 524 | 1,443 | 238 | 413 |
| 1963 | 2,424 | 2,452 | 2,802 | 791 | 9.8 | 257 | 532 | 1,693 | 313 | 450 |
| 1964 | 2,843 | 2,450 | 3,846 | 1,223 | — | 258 | 777 | 1,702 | 310 | 1,103 |
| 1965 | 3,323 | 2,345 | 4,170 | 1,311 | ... | 242 | 639 | 1,000 | 244 | 1,022 |
| 1966 | 5,095 | 2,292 | 4,870 | 1,292 | ... | 193 | 619 | 1,243 | 222 | 959 |
| 1967 | 6,315 | 1,696 | 5,322 | 1,355 | ... | 260 | 832 | 1,625 | 252 | 1,101 |
| 1968 | 9,467 | 2,159 | 7,906 | 1,999 | ... | 385 | 1,395 | 2,412 | 365 | 1,167 |
| 1969 | 10,386 | 2,522 | 7,753 | 2,297 | ... | 240 | 1,032 | 1,522 | 330 | 1,530 |
| | | | | | (million US dollars) | | | | | |
| 1970 | 269 | 53 | 294 | 63 | ... | 7.4 | 29 | 66 | 3.3 | 47 |
| 1971 | 170 | 45 | 277 | 49 | ... | 5.4 | 22 | 71 | 2.4 | 47 |
| 1972 | 186 | 47 | 233 | 58 | ... | 7.7 | 32 | 79 | 6.1 | 69 |
| 1973 | 284 | 62 | 136 | 80 | ... | 13 | 38 | 88 | 12 | 93 |
| 1974 | 345 | 94 | 196 | 123 | ... | 18 | 60 | 156 | 7.1 | 160 |
| 1975 | 168 | 60 | 156 | 94 | ... | 44 | 82 | 296 | 11 | 151 |
| 1976 | 234 | 76 | 177 | 112 | ... | 53 | 90 | 94 | 26 | 191 |
| 1977 | 398 | 47 | 179 | 133 | ... | 52 | 116 | 85 | 18 | 163 |
| 1978 | 412 | 38 | 192 | 175 | ... | 180 | 118 | 46 | 28 | 133 |
| 1979 | 674 | 44 | 256 | 293 | ... | 652 | 234 | 63 | 40 | 171 |
| 1980 | 752 | 63 | 192 | 383 | ... | 777 | 312 | 15 | 30 | 210 |
| 1981 | 529 | 60 | 141 | 219 | ... | 692 | 310 | 0.3 | 9.5 | 272 |
| 1982 | 461 | 75 | 202 | 216 | ... | 719 | 205 | 18 | 7.1 | 255 |
| 1983 | 443 | 31 | 79 | 293 | ... | 544 | 391 | 7.1 | 8.4 | 307 |
| 1984 | 442 | 15 | 137 | 233 | ... | 618 | 227 | 19 | 5.1 | 341 |
| 1985 | 464 | 31 | 117 | 202 | ... | 645 | 139 | 43 | 29 | 269 |
| 1986 | 450 | 41 | 206 | 172 | ... | 232 | 107 | 24 | 24 | 246 |
| 1987 | 559 | 19 | 224 | 257 | ... | 273 | 92 | 15 | 19 | 250 |
| 1988 | 607 | 23 | 364 | 203 | ... | 166 | 60 | 22 | 36 | 261 |

**E3     SOUTH AMERICA: Major Commodity Exports by Main Exporting Countries** (in currency units stated)

| | Uruguay (million US dollars) | | | Venezuela (million bolívars) | |
| | Hide & Skins | Meat | Wool[32] | Coffee | Petroleum & Products |
|---|---|---|---|---|---|
| 1950 | 29 | 43 | 153[32] 160 | 55 | 3,356 |
| 1951 | 26 | 44 | 117 | 65 | 3,798 |
| 1952 | 23 | 41 | 90 | 115 | 4,208 |
| 1953 | 24 | 44 | 165 | 158 | 4,398 |
| 1954 | 19 | 45 | 124 | 111 | 4,797 |
| 1955 | 15 | 7.2 | 105 | 124 | 5,491 |
| 1956 | 16 | 22 | 126 | 103 | 6,349 |
| 1957 | 11 | 27 | 64 | 115 | 7,865 |
| 1958 | 9.0 | 15 | 80 | 211 | 7,099 |
| 1959 | 10 | 19 | 54 | 82 | 6,654 |
| 1960 | 16 | 31 | 67 | 73 | 6,642 |
| 1961 | 17 | 27 | 110 | 76 | 6,809 |
| 1962 | 17 | 31 | 82 | 63 | 7,221 |
| 1963 | 18 | 33 | 85 | 78 | 7,218 |
| 1964 | 17 | 74 | 67 | 68 | 10,138 |
| 1965 | 16 | 61 | 90 | 62 | 10,144 |
| 1966 | 18 | 45 | 84 | 63 | 9,746 |
| 1967 | 14 | 40 | 83 | 31 | 10,267 |
| 1968 | 16 | 60 | 78 | 64 | 10,370 |
| 1969 | 24 | 58 | 67 | 64 | 10,141 |
| 1970 | 24 | 82 | 73 | 57 | 10,550 |
| 1971 | 21 | 65 | 65 | 66 | 12,814 |
| 1972 | 23 | 99 | 54 | 67 | 12,571 |
| 1973 | 26 | 121 | 97 | 57 | 18,632 |
| 1974 | 24 | 137 | 87 | 71 | 45,200 |
| 1975 | 17 | 83 | 87 | 82 | 35,668 |
| 1976 | 32 | 117 | 101 | 118 | 37,593 |
| 1977 | 28 | 110 | 121 | 121 | 39,106 |
| 1978 | 30 | 96 | 132 | 181 | 37,517 |
| 1979 | 47 | 105 | 101 | 106 | 58,519 |
| 1980 | 40 | 182 | 212 | 34 | 78,328 |
| 1981 | 51 | 255 | 236 | 14 | 81,723 |
| 1982 | 73 | 201 | 205 | 15 | 67,068 |
| 1983 | 69 | 247 | 169 | 14 | 59,473 |
| 1984 | 92 | 146 | 163 | 152 | 85,226 |
| 1985 | 61 | 118 | 164 | 578 | 77,639 |
| 1986 | 75 | 199 | 198 | 451 | 53,781 |
| 1987 | 84 | 129 | 241 | 326 | 100,909 |
| 1988 | 105 | 152 | 349 | 515 | 118,345 |

**Major Commodity Exports by Main Exporting Countries** (in currency units stated)

NOTES

1.  SOURCES: The main sources used have been the same as for table E1. The Canadian non-ferrous metals series to 1915 is from K.W. Taylor, *Statistical Contributions to Canadian Economic History* (Toronto, 1931). The Colombian statistics to 1924 are from Miguel Urrutia and Mario Arrubla (eds.), *op. cit.* in Note 1 to table E1. The Peruvian statistics to 1910 are from Rosemary Thorp and Geoffrey Bertram, *Peru, 1890–1977* (London, 1978).
2.  Statistics refer to domestic exports and are recorded f.o.b. (except as noted in footnote 19)

FOOTNOTES

[1] Years ending 30 September to 1842 and 30 June from 1844 to 1915. The 1843 figures are for the period 1 October 1842 to 30 June 1843.
[2] Years ending 30 September to 1889, and years beginning 1 April from 1890 to 1908.
[3] Tobago is included from 1889. Data are for years beginning 1 April from that year to 1908.
[4] This break is caused by a change in classification.
[5] Years ending 30 June to 1906 and 31 March from 1908 to 1936 (1st line), except for the non-ferrous metals series, which is for calendar years from 1927. The 1907 figures are for the period 1 July 1906 to 31 March 1907. Newfoundland became part of Canada on 1 April 1949.
[6] Data to 1882 are believed to be for years ending 30 April.
[7] Silver pesos to 1889 (1st line), gold pesos (later called quetzales and equal to the US dollar) subsequently.
[8] Years beginning 1 July to 1912. The 1913 figures are for the second half-year only.
[9] Including ores.
[10] Including coke to 1946.
[11] Excluding exports from ports in the control of the Confederacy.
[12] Meat products are included to 1881. Prior to 1855, there is a series available in the *Reports on Commerce* of meat, fats, hides, and live animals in the aggregate.
[13] Including flour from 1870 (2nd line).
[14] Including manufactured wood other than wood pulp from 1908 (2nd line).
[15] Years ending 31 July to 1937 and 30 June from 1939 to 1951. The 1938 figures are for the period 1 August 1937 to 30 June 1938. Bananas are known to be undervalued to 1948 (1st line).
[16] Including alumina
[17] Excluding Aruba from 1986.
[18] The old gold cordoba was equal to the US dollar.
[19] Bananas are valued c.i.f. from 1955.
[20] Including a small amount of non-ferrous metal articles in 1952–56.
[21] 'General' trade to 1930. Data are for years beginning 1 July from 1833 to 1886. The 1887 figures are for the second half-year only. The figures for the first half-year of 1833 are as follows (in million milreis): cocoa-0.1, coffee-8.9, cotton-5.2, rubber-0.1, sugar-5.3.
[22] All fruit to 1937, bananas being by far the most important. Values are known to be understated to 1949.
[23] Years beginning 1 April from 1892 to 1911. Trans-shipments are included to 1907.
[24] Canned meat only.
[25] Official (i.e. fixed) values.
[26] Including preparations of sugar to 1951.
[27] Including other animal hair.
[28] Copper wire and sheets are included from 1951 (2nd line).
[29] Natural sodium nitrate from 1968 (2nd line).
[30] Official (i.e. fixed) values to 1913 (1st line).
[31] Subsequently excluding wild animal skins.
[32] Including other animal hair from 1950 (2nd line).
[33] Fiscal years to 1908.

# F.　　TRANSPORT AND COMMUNICATIONS

Government has generally been involved more intimately in the provision of means of transport and communication than in agriculture or industry, at any rate until very recently. As a consequence, there is usually more statistical material available from the past than on most other economic activities. Shipping was a matter of close concern to all major maritime powers, though there were few of those in the Americas until quite recently. The railways were frequently of military as well as economic importance, and they necessitated the investment of large lumps of capital, on which the social return seems generally to have exceeded by a considerable margin that which could be captured by investors. Outside the United States, it was fairly unusual for private promoters to attract this capital without some assistance from governments. Some form of reporting to governments, therefore, was required of most railways. Postal services were long recognized as a government function, and telegraphs fell naturally into the same niche in most countries other than the USA, where they were not simply an adjunct of the railways, and telephones generally followed. And outside North America and certain Central American countries influenced by the United States, the potential influence of radio led to its direct control by governments and to some form of licensing system, which produced a statistical by-product. Taxation of motor vehicles had a similar effect.

Table 1, showing the length of railway line open in each country, is fairly straightforward, though there is a variety of different figures for some countries purporting to cover the same thing. The diversity usually arises from different treatment of industrial lines, some of which did, at times, take public traffic and convey paying passengers. For other countries there is a paucity of published figures, and in these cases an effort has been made to build up a series from such benchmark statistics as are available coupled with information about the opening of particular stretches of line culled from a variety of sources—mainly national statistical annuals, but also British and American Consular Reports, and the reports and accounts of individual railway companies.

The principal problems in using the merchant marine statistics of table 4 arise from changes in the size of ships covered and from changes in the method measuring capacity. In most countries, there has been a lower limit of size below which vessels are not included in the register; but this has changed from time to time, and differed between countries. So far as aggregate capacity, especially of mechanically-propelled vessels, is concerned, this limit, and the changes in it, have made little impact, though the numbers, especially of sailing ships, have sometimes changed violently. These are usually apparent in the series, and it is hoped that all are indicated in footnotes. Changes in methods of measuring capacity are a more difficult problem, though the two basic methods—gross and net, representing the inclusion and exclusion respectively of space which cannot be used for carrying cargo—are readily distinguished. Where possible, the tonnage data are given in gross register tons, which is the measure most commonly used since World War II. However, some earlier statistics are only available in net tons and there are unavoidable breaks in continuity in this table.

Tables 5, 6 and 7 are reasonably straightforward and call for little elaboration. The main problem has been the lack of availability for many countries of statistics of the vehicle park during the years of World War II. In many cases these statistics probably were collected, but national statistical abstracts tended not to publish them at that period, and international sources have tended to ignore the war years.

Apart from some early statistics on civil air traffic from national sources, the main reliance in table F7 has been on the publications of the International Civil Aviation Organization, which makes for a large measure of consistency. If should be noted that these data apply to airlines based in each of the countries concerned, not to the actual traffic at the countries' airports.

Postal statistics (and even those of telegrams), which one might expect to be reasonably uniform and homogeneous, are amongst the most intractable, as well as being unavailable for the majority of Latin American countries for long periods. The main problems with them lie in the great variety of definitions of various categories of postal material, and in the penchant of most authorities for making changes in those which they use. There are also variations in the amount of double-counting which occurs, and in the treatment of mail and telegrams in transit. Comparisons both between countries and over time have to be made with caution, therefore. The telephone statistics in table 9, on the other hand, are reasonably easy to use, though, like the motor vehicle statistics, and for the same reason, there are many gaps over the years of World War II.

**F1    NORTH AMERICA: LENGTH OF RAILWAY LINE OPEN** (in kilometres)

1830–1874

| | Canada[1] | Costa Rica | Cuba | Jamaica[2] | Mexico[3] | Panama[4] | USA[5] |
|---|---|---|---|---|---|---|---|
| 1830 | ... | ... | — | — | — | — | 37 |
| 1831 | ... | ... | — | — | — | — | 153 |
| 1832 | ... | ... | — | — | — | — | 369 |
| 1833 | ... | ... | — | — | — | — | 612 |
| 1834 | ... | ... | — | — | — | — | 1,019 |
| 1835 | ... | ... | — | — | — | — | 1,767 |
| 1836 | 25 | ... | — | — | — | — | 2,049 |
| 1837 | 25 | ... | 26 | — | — | — | 2,410 |
| 1838 | 25 | ... | 82 | — | — | — | 3,079 |
| 1839 | 25 | ... | 82 | — | — | — | 3,705 |
| 1840 | 25 | ... | 82 | — | — | — | 4,535 |
| 1841 | 25 | ... | 82 | — | — | — | 5,689 |
| 1842 | 25 | ... | 82 | — | — | — | 6,479 |
| 1843 | 25 | ... | 82 | — | — | — | 6,735 |
| 1844 | 25 | ... | 82 | — | — | — | 7,044 |
| 1845 | 25 | ... | 82 | 23 | — | — | 7,456 |
| 1846 | 25 | ... | 198 | 23 | — | — | 7,934 |
| 1847 | 86 | ... | 198 | 23 | — | — | 9,009 |
| 1848 | 86 | ... | 198 | 23 | — | — | 9,650 |
| 1849 | 86 | ... | ... | 23 | — | — | 11,853 |
| 1850 | 106 | ... | 440 | 23 | 13 | — | 14,518 |
| 1851 | 255 | ... | ... | 23 | 16 | — | 17,674 |
| 1852 | 329 | ... | ... | 23 | 16 | — | 20,773 |
| 1853 | 814 | ... | ... | 23 | 16 | — | 24,720 |
| 1854 | 1,229 | ... | ... | 23 | 16 | — | 26,908 |
| 1855 | 1,411 | ... | ... | 23 | ... | 76 | 29,570 |
| 1856 | 2,275 | ... | ... | 23 | ... | 76 | 35,528 |
| 1857 | 2,323 | ... | ... | 23 | ... | 76 | 39,434 |
| 1858 | 2,998 | ... | ... | 23 | ... | 76 | 43,401 |
| 1859 | 3,209 | ... | ... | 23 | 32 | 76 | 46,331 |
| 1860 | 3,323 | ... | 682 | 23 | 32 | 76 | 49,288 |
| 1861 | 3,453 | ... | ... | 23 | 32 | 76 | 50,350 |
| 1862 | 3,522 | ... | ... | 23 | 32 | 76 | 51,692 |
| 1863 | 3,522 | ... | ... | 23 | 32 | 76 | 53,382 |
| 1864 | 3,522 | ... | ... | 23 | 32 | 76 | 54,570 |
| 1865 | 3,604 | ... | ... | 23 | 142 | 76 | 56,464 |
| 1866 | 3,666 | ... | ... | 23 | 142 | 76 | 59,225 |
| 1867 | 3,666 | ... | ... | 23 | 142 | 76 | 62,845 |
| 1868 | 3,666 | ... | ... | 23 | ... | 76 | 67,961 |
| 1869 | 4,061 | ... | ... | 37 | 349 | 76 | 75,388 |
| 1870 | 4,211 | ... | ... | 37 | 349 | 76 | 85,170 |
| 1871 | 4,337 | ... | ... | 37 | ... | 76 | 97,045 |
| 1872 | 4,665 | ... | ... | 37 | ... | 76 | 106,492 |
| 1873 | 5,814 | 68 | ... | 37 | 572 | 76 | 113,085 |
| 1874 | 6,167 | 82 | ... | 42 | 587 | 76 | 116,492 |

**F1    NORTH AMERICA: Length of Railway Line Open** (in kilometres)

**1875–1924**

| | Alaska | Barbados | Belize[6] | Canada[1] | Costa Rica | Cuba | Dominican Republic | El Salvador | Guatemala | Haiti |
|---|---|---|---|---|---|---|---|---|---|---|
| 1875 | ... | — | — | 6,970 | 82 | ... | ... | — | — | — |
| 1876 | ... | — | — | 7,731 | 82 | ... | ... | — | — | — |
| 1877 | ... | — | — | 8,397 | 82 | ... | ... | — | — | — |
| 1878 | ... | — | — | 9,305 | 82 | ... | ... | — | — | — |
| 1879 | ... | — | — | 10,019 | 82 | ... | ... | — | — | — |
| 1880 | ... | — | — | 11,036 | 117 | 1,382 | ... | — | 21 | — |
| 1881 | ... | — | — | 11,577 | 154 | ... | ... | — | 21 | — |
| 1882 | ... | 21 | — | 11,798 | 172 | ... | ... | 20 | 48 | — |
| 1883 | ... | 37 | — | 13,996 | 172 | ... | ... | 20 | 116 | — |
| 1884 | ... | 39 | — | 15,412 | 172 | ... | ... | 46 | 186 | — |
| 1885 | ... | 39 | — | 16,532 | 172 | 1,600 | 80 | 46 | 186 | — |
| 1886 | ... | 39 | — | 17,337 | 172 | ... | ... | 61 | 186 | — |
| 1887 | ... | 39 | — | 18,978 | 172 | ... | ... | 61 | 186 | — |
| 1888 | ... | 39 | — | 19,608 | 178 | ... | 115 | 61 | 186 | — |
| 1889 | ... | 39 | — | 20,253 | 190 | ... | 115 | 87 | 186 | — |
| 1890 | ... | 39 | — | 21,164 | 241 | 1,731 | 115 | 87 | 186 | — |
| 1891 | ... | 39 | — | 22,270 | 241 | 1,778 | 115 | 87 | 186 | — |
| 1892 | ... | 39 | — | 23,438 | 241 | 1,778 | 115 | 87 | 186 | — |
| 1893 | ... | 39 | — | 24,148 | 241 | 1,778 | 150 | 98 | 186 | — |
| 1894 | ... | 39 | — | 25,149 | 241 | 1,778 | 150 | 98 | 186 | — |
| 1895 | ... | 39 | — | 25,712 | 249 | 1,778 | 150 | 98 | 282 | — |
| 1896 | ... | 39 | — | 26,184 | 254 | 1,778 | 150 | 116 | 457 | — |
| 1897 | ... | 39 | — | 26,634 | 254 | 1,778 | 150 | 116 | 480 | — |
| 1898 | ... | 39 | — | 27,149 | 291 | 1,825 | ... | 116 | 480 | — |
| 1899 | ... | 39 | — | 27,761 | 388 | 1,825 | ... | 116 | 480 | 16 |
| 1900 | 35 | 39 | — | 28,475 | 388 | 1,960 | 182 | 116 | 640 | 37 |
| 1901 | ... | 45 | — | 29,193 | 379 | ... | 182 | 156 | 640 | 45 |
| 1902 | ... | 45 | — | 30,117 | 408 | ... | 182 | 156 | 640 | 45 |
| 1903 | ... | 45 | — | 30,558 | 432 | 2,548 | 182 | 156 | 640 | 45 |
| 1904 | ... | 45 | — | 31,271 | 432 | 2,548 | 182 | 156 | 640 | 70 |
| 1905 | 98 | 45 | — | 32,970 | 432 | 2,604 | 182 | 156 | 640 | 70 |
| 1906 | 129 | 45 | — | 34,364 | 473 | 2,857 | 182 | 156 | 654 | ... |
| 1907 | 235 | 45 | — | 36,123 | 473 | 2,857 | 182 | 156 | 654 | ... |
| 1908 | 298 | 45 | — | 36,961 | 473 | ... | 182 | 156 | 700 | 103 |
| 1909 | 488 | 45 | 31 | 38,791 | 619 | 3,150 | 182 | 156 | 700 | 103 |
| 1910 | 627 | 45 | 40 | 39,799 | 619 | 3,229 | 241 | 156 | 724 | 103 |
| 1911 | 740 | 45 | 40 | 40,877 | 619 | 3,527 | 241 | 209 | 781 | 103 |
| 1912 | 743 | 45 | 40 | 43,194 | 619 | 3,609 | 241 | 320 | 808 | 103 |
| 1913 | 742 | 45 | 40 | 47,160 | 619 | 3,803 | 241 | 320 | 987 | 180 |
| 1914 | 742 | 45 | 40 | 49,559 | 619 | 3,846 | 241 | 328 | 987 | 180 |
| 1915 | 603 | 45 | 40 | 56,137 | 619 | ... | 241 | 328 | 987 | 180 |
| 1916 | 611 | 45 | 47 | 59,521 | 619 | ... | 247 | 328 | 987 | 180 |
| 1917 | 613 | 45 | 47 | 61,748 | 619 | ... | 247 | 328 | 987 | 180 |
| 1918 | 556 | 45 | 47 | 61,560₁ | 647 | ... | 247 | 355 | 987 | 180 |
| 1919 | 371 | 39 | 47 | 61,951 | 647 | ... | 247 | 375 | 987 | 180 |
| 1920 | 397 | 39 | 47 | 62,450 | 647 | 4,366 | 247 | 375 | 987 | 169 |
| 1921 | 400 | 39 | 47 | 63,071 | 647 | 4,396 | 247 | 375 | 1,096 | 177 |
| 1922 | 1,286 | 39 | 40 | 63,340 | 647 | 4,488 | 247 | 407 | 1,096 | 177 |
| 1923 | 1,284 | 39 | 40 | 63,816 | 647 | 4,651 | 247 | 409 | 1,096 | 177 |
| 1924 | 1,284 | 39 | 40 | 64,468 | 647 | 4,821 | 247 | 409 | 1,096 | 168 |

**F1      NORTH AMERICA: Length of Railway Line Open** (in kilometres)

1875–1924

| | Honduras[7] | Jamaica[2] | Mexico[3] | Newfoundland[8] | Nicaragua | Panama[4] | Puerto Rico | Trinidad | USA[5] |
|---|---|---|---|---|---|---|---|---|---|
| 1875 | — | 42 | 663 | — | — | 76 | — | … | 119,246 |
| 1876 | — | 42 | 666 | — | — | 76 | — | 26 | 123,610 |
| 1877 | — | 42 | 672 | — | — | 76 | — | 26 | 127,270 |
| 1878 | — | 42 | 737 | — | — | 76 | — | 26 | 131,559 |
| 1879 | — | 42 | 886 | — | — | 76 | — | 26 | 139,298 |
| 1880 | 60 | 42 | 1,080 | — | — | 76 | — | 55 | 150,091 |
| 1881 | 60 | 42 | 1,771 | — | — | 76 | — | 61 | 165,936 |
| 1882 | 96 | 42 | 3,709 | — | 35 | 76 | — | 71 | 184,555 |
| 1883 | 96 | 42 | 5,437 | 72 | 53 | 76 | — | 71 | 195,410 |
| 1884 | 96 | 42 | 5,891 | 72 | 94 | 76 | — | 71 | 201,723 |
| 1885 | 96 | 103 | 6,010 | 145 | 143 | 76 | 18 | 87 | 206,511 |
| 1886 | 96 | 103 | 6,089 | 145 | 143 | 76 | 18 | 87 | 219,415 |
| 1887 | 96 | 103 | 6,609 | 145 | 143 | 76 | 18 | 87 | 240,137 |
| 1888 | 96 | 103 | 7,826 | 180 | 143 | 76 | 18 | 87 | 251,241 |
| 1889 | 96 | 103[2] | 8,455 | 180 | 143 | 76 | 18 | 87 | 259,549 |
| 1890 | 96 | 124 | 9,718 | 180 | 143 | 76 | 18 | 87 | 268,282[5] |
| | | | | | | | | | 263,284 |
| 1891 | 96 | 142 | 10,029 | 180 | 143 | 76 | 18 | 87 | 271,018 |
| 1892 | 96 | 153 | 10,477 | 180 | 143 | 76 | 18 | 87 | 276,105 |
| 1893 | 96 | 188 | 10,642 | 475 | 143 | 76 | 18 | 87 | 283,986 |
| 1894 | 96 | 209 | 10,763 | 641 | 143 | 76 | 18 | 87 | 287,604 |
| 1895 | 96 | 298 | 10,776 | 752 | 146 | 76 | 18 | 87 | 290,739 |
| 1896 | 96 | 298 | 11,087 | 911 | 146 | 76 | 223 | 92 | 294,151 |
| 1897 | 96 | 298 | 11,763 | 953 | 146 | 76 | 223 | 98 | 296,808 |
| 1898 | 96 | 298 | 12,680 | 1,027 | 146 | 76 | 223 | 130 | 299,975 |
| 1899 | 96 | 298 | 12,901 | 1,027 | 225 | 76 | 223 | 130 | 304,641 |
| 1900 | 96 | 298 | 13,585 | 1,056 | 225 | 76 | 223 | 130 | 311,160 |
| 1901 | 96 | 298 | 14,523 | 1,056 | 225 | 76 | 223 | 130 | 317,422 |
| 1902 | 96 | 298 | 15,135 | 1,061 | 225 | 76 | 223 | 130 | 325,847 |
| 1903 | 96 | 298 | 16,114 | 1,059 | 257 | 76 | 250 | 130 | 334,707 |
| 1904 | 96 | 298 | 16,523 | 1,072 | 257 | 76 | 250 | 130 | 344,245 |
| 1905 | 96 | 298 | 16,934 | 1,072 | 275 | 76 | 322 | 130 | 351,000 |
| 1906 | 111 | 298 | 17,510 | 1,059 | 275 | 76 | 322 | 130 | 361,077 |
| 1907 | 138 | 298 | 18,068 | 1,056 | 275 | 76 | 322 | 130 | 370,070 |
| 1908 | 138 | 298 | 18,968 | 1,056 | 275 | 76 | 322 | 130 | 375,730 |
| 1909 | 138 | 298 | 19,438 | 1,091 | 275 | 76 | 354 | 130 | 391,147 |
| 1910 | 170 | 298 | 19,748 | 1,098 | 275 | 76 | 354 | 130 | 386,714 |
| 1911 | 170 | 314 | 19,831 | 1,239 | 322 | 76 | 354 | 130 | 392,646 |
| 1912 | 170 | 318 | 20,447 | 1,239 | 322 | 76 | 354 | 130 | 397,149 |
| 1913 | 241 | 318 | … | 1,353 | 322 | 76 | 547 | 158 | 401,977 |
| 1914 | 241 | 318 | … | 1,408 | 322 | 76 | 547 | 177 | 405,724 |
| 1915 | 386 | 318 | … | 1,429 | 322 | 76 | 547 | 177 | 408,434 |
| 1916 | 515 | 318 | … | 1,502 | 322 | 76 | 547 | 177 | 409,177[5] |
| 1917 | 575 | 318 | … | 1,502 | 322 | 76 | 547 | 177 | 408,171 |
| 1918 | 575 | 318 | … | 1,502 | 322 | 76 | 547 | 177 | 408,015 |
| 1919 | 575 | 318 | … | 1,502 | 322 | 76 | 547 | 177 | 407,409 |
| 1920 | 763 | 318[2] | … | … | 322 | 158 | 547 | 177 | 406,915 |
| 1921 | 895 | 322 | … | … | 322 | 158 | 547 | 177 | 404,229 |
| 1922 | 900 | 322 | … | … | 322 | 158 | 547 | 177 | 403,001 |
| 1923 | 1,306 | 322 | 20,894 | … | 322 | 158 | 547 | 177 | 402,693 |
| 1924 | 1,236 | 322 | 20,872 | … | 322 | 158 | 547 | 187 | 402,587 |

**F1 NORTH AMERICA: Length of Railway Line Open** (in kilometres)

**1925–1974**

| | Alaska | Barbados | Belize[6] | Canada[1] | Costa Rica | Cuba | Dominican Republic | El Salvador | Guatemala | Haiti |
|---|---|---|---|---|---|---|---|---|---|---|
| 1925 | 1,289 | 39 | 40 | 64,937 | 665 | 4,893 | 247 | 409 | 1,096 | 168 |
| 1926 | 1,271 | 39 | 40 | 64,937 | 665 | 4,871 | 247 | 530 | 1,102 | 176 |
| 1927 | 1,276 | 39 | 40 | 65,291 | 665 | 4,861 | 247 | 550 | 1,102 | 176 |
| 1928 | 1,276 | 39 | 40 | 66,018 | 665 | 4,903 | 240 | 596 | 1,155 | 180 |
| 1929 | 1,271 | 39 | 40 | 66,594 | 665 | 4,946 | 240 | 596 | 1,159 | 217 |
| 1930 | 1,271 | 39 | 40 | 66,668 | 665 | 4,891 | 240 | 604 | 1,159 | 217 |
| 1931 | 1,207 | 39 | 40 | 68,043 | 665 | 4,891 | 240 | 604 | 1,159 | 254 |
| 1932 | 1,207 | 39 | 40 | 68,250 | 665 | 4,897 | 240 | 604 | 1,159 | 254 |
| 1933 | 1,178 | 39 | 40 | 68,133 | 665 | 4,887 | 240 | 608 | 1,159 | 254 |
| 1934 | 1,178 | 39 | 40 | 68,026 | 665 | 4,876 | 240 | 608 | 1,159 | 254 |
| 1935 | 1,178 | 39 | 40 | 69,066 | 665 | 4,876 | 240 | 608 | 1,159 | 254 |
| 1936 | 1,178 | 39 | 40 | 68,480 | 665 | 4,945 | 240 | 608 | 1,159 | 254 |
| 1937 | 1,178 | — | 40 | 68,762 | 665 | 4,961 | 240 | 608 | 1,159 | 254 |
| 1938 | 1,178 | — | 31 | 68,786 | 665 | 4,957 | 240 | 608 | 1,159 | 254 |
| 1939 | 1,178 | — | 14 | 68,617 | 665 | 4,965 | 240 | 608 | 1,159 | 254 |
| 1940 | 863 | — | 14 | 68,501 | 665 | 4,945 | 270 | 608 | 1,159 | 254 |
| 1941 | 863 | — | 14 | 68,302 | 665 | 4,972 | 270 | 608 | 1,159 | 254 |
| 1942 | 863 | — | — | 68,136 | 665 | 4,952 | 270 | 618 | 1,159 | 254 |
| 1943 | 882 | — | — | 68,149 | 665 | 4,925 | 270 | 618 | 1,159 | 254 |
| 1944 | 882 | — | — | 68,133 | 665 | 4,940 | 270 | 618 | 1,159 | 254 |
| 1945 | 882 | — | — | 68,158 | 665 | 4,922 | 270 | 618 | 1,159 | 254 |
| 1946 | 875 | — | — | 68,131 | 665 | 4,871 | 270 | 618 | 1,159 | 254 |
| 1947 | 914 | — | — | 68,110 | 665 | 4,866 | 270 | 618 | 1,159 | 254 |
| 1948 | 912 | — | — | 67,991 | 665 | 4,857 | 270 | 618 | 1,159 | 254 |
| 1949 | 912 | — | — | 69,166 | 665 | 4,854 | 270 | 618 | 1,159 | 254 |
| 1950 | 912 | — | — | 69,167 | 665 | 4,860 | 270 | 618 | 1,159 | 254 |
| 1951 | 912 | — | — | 69,130 | 665 | 4,825 | 270 | 618 | 1,159 | 254 |
| 1952 | 914 | — | — | 69,126 | 665 | 4,825 | 270 | 618 | 1,159 | 254 |
| 1953 | 914 | — | — | 69,464 | 665 | 4,825 | 270 | 618 | 1,159 | 254 |
| 1954 | 914 | — | — | 69,414 | 665 | 5,099 | 270 | 618 | 1,159 | 254 |
| 1955 | 863 | — | — | 69,916 | 665 | 5,099 | 270 | 618 | 1,159 | 254 |
| 1956 | 909 | — | — | 70,251 | 665 | 5,099 | 270 | 618 | 1,159 | 254 |
| 1957 | 922 | — | — | 70,634 | 665 | 5,099 | 270 | 618 | 1,159 | 254 |
| 1958 | 922 | — | — | 71,012 | 665 | … | 270 | 618 | 1,159 | 254 |
| 1959 | 921 | — | — | 71,147 | 665 | … | 270 | 618 | 1,159 | 254 |
| 1960 | 921 | — | — | 70,858 | 665 | … | 270 | 618 | 1,159 | 254 |
| 1961 | … | — | — | 70,311 | 564 | … | 270 | 618 | 1,159 | 254 |
| 1962 | … | — | — | 70,254 | 596 | 5,099 | 270 | 618 | 1,159 | 254 |
| 1963 | … | — | — | 70,204 | 596 | 5,099 | 270 | 618 | 1,159 | 254 |
| 1964 | … | — | — | 69,773 | 596 | 5,099 | 270 | 618 | 1,159 | 254 |
| 1965 | … | — | — | 69,454 | 596 | 5,099 | 270 | 618 | 1,159 | 254 |
| 1966 | … | — | — | 69,512 | 596 | 5,099 | 270 | 618 | 1,159 | 121 |
| 1967 | … | — | — | 69,472 | 596 | 5,099 | 270 | 618 | 1,159 | 121 |
| 1968 | … | — | — | 69,472 | 596 | 5,227 | 270 | 618 | 1,159 | 121 |
| 1969 | … | — | — | 70,188 | 617 | 5,227 | 270 | 618 | 819 | 121 |
| 1970 | … | — | — | 70,784 | 622 | 5,227 | 270 | 618 | 819 | 121 |
| 1971 | … | — | — | 71,057 | 622 | 5,227 | 270 | 618 | 819 | — |
| 1972 | … | — | — | 70,851 | 622 | 5,227 | 270 | 618 | 819 | — |
| 1973 | … | — | — | 71,185 | 623 | 5,227 | 270 | 618 | 819 | — |
| 1974 | … | — | — | 71,239 | 623 | 5,086 | 142 | 618 | 819 | — |

**F1      NORTH AMERICA: Length of Railway Line Open** (in kilometres)

**1925–1974**

| | Honduras[7] | Jamaica[2] | Mexico[3] | Newfoundland[8] | Nicaragua | Panama[4] | Puerto Rico | Trinidad | USA[5] |
|---|---|---|---|---|---|---|---|---|---|
| 1925 | 1,432 | 338 | 20,972 | 1,460 | 322 | 158 | 547 | 187 | 401,367 |
| 1926 | 1,459 | 338 | 23,237 | 1,460 | 322 | 158 | 547 | 187 | 400,949 |
| 1927 | 1,459 | 338 | 23,575[3] | 1,460 | 322 | 158 | 547 | 187 | 400,937 |
| | | | 23,055 | | | | | | |
| 1928 | 1,459 | 338 | 23,096 | 1,460 | 327 | 158 | 547 | 187 | 401,224 |
| 1929 | 1,459 | 338 | 23,238 | 1,460 | 327 | 158 | 547 | 187 | 401,424 |
| 1930 | 1,459 | 338 | 23,345 | 1,460 | 327 | 158 | 547 | 190 | 400,810 |
| 1931 | 1,437 | 338 | 23,387 | 1,460 | 327 | 158 | 547 | 190 | 400,451 |
| 1932 | 1,437 | 338 | 23,344 | 1,207 | 327 | 158 | 547 | 190 | 398,466 |
| 1933 | 1,437 | 338 | 23,041 | 1,207 | 327 | 158 | 547 | 190 | 395,421 |
| 1934 | 1,437 | 338 | 23,030 | 1,207 | 327 | 158 | 547 | 190 | 392,450 |
| 1935 | 1,437 | 338 | 22,947 | 1,207 | 327 | 158 | 547 | 190 | 389,175 |
| 1936 | 1,437 | 338 | 22,937 | 1,207 | 354 | 158 | 547 | 190 | 386,410 |
| 1937 | 1,437 | 338 | 22,784 | 1,207 | 367 | 158 | 547 | 190 | 383,891 |
| 1938 | 1,313 | 338 | 23,331 | 1,207 | 367 | 158 | 547 | 190 | 381,160 |
| 1939 | 1,313 | 338 | 23,473 | 1,207 | 367 | 158 | 620 | 190 | 378,299 |
| 1940 | ... | 338 | 22,979 | 1,207 | 367 | 158 | 620 | 190 | 376,055 |
| 1941 | ... | 346 | 23,145 | 1,207 | 367 | 158 | 620 | 190 | 373,321 |
| 1942 | ... | 346 | 23,135 | 1,207 | 367 | 158 | 620 | 190 | 368,820 |
| 1943 | ... | 341 | 22,914 | 1,207 | 367 | 158 | 620 | 190 | 366,929 |
| 1944 | 1,046 | 341 | 22,980 | 1,207 | 379 | 158 | 620 | 190 | 365,860 |
| 1945 | 1,046 | 341 | 22,954 | 1,207 | 379 | 158 | 620 | 190 | 364,832 |
| 1946 | 1,046 | 341 | 22,954 | 1,207 | 379 | 158 | 620 | 190 | 364,417 |
| 1947 | 1,160 | 338 | 22,918 | 1,207 | 379 | 158 | 620 | 190 | 363,400 |
| 1948 | 1,160 | 333 | 23,314 | 1,207 | 379 | 158 | 620 | 190 | 362,342 |
| 1949 | 1,281 | 333 | 23,259 | ... | 431 | 158 | 620 | 190 | 361,315 |
| 1950 | 1,297 | 333 | 23,332 | ... | 431 | 158 | 620 | 190 | 360,137 |
| 1951 | 1,318 | 325 | 23,329 | ... | 431 | 158 | 620 | 190 | 359,571 |
| 1952 | 1,313 | 333 | 23,397 | ... | 431 | 158 | 620 | 190 | 358,092 |
| 1953 | 1,316 | 333 | 23,301 | ... | 431 | 158 | 760 | 175 | 356,885 |
| 1954 | 1,312 | 335 | 23,282 | ... | 431 | 158 | 760 | 175 | 355,823 |
| 1955 | 1,293 | 335 | 23,370 | ... | 431 | 158 | 760 | 175 | 355,134 |
| 1956 | 1,272 | 335 | 23,425 | ... | 431 | 158 | 760 | 175 | 354,411 |
| 1957 | 1,263 | 335 | 23,383 | ... | 405 | 158 | 760 | 175 | 352,554 |
| 1958 | 1,251 | 335 | 23,457 | ... | 403 | 158 | — | 175 | 351,479 |
| 1959 | 1,240 | 335 | 23,292 | ... | 403 | 158 | — | 175 | 350,137[5] |
| 1960 | 1,230 | 330 | 23,369 | ... | 403 | 158 | — | 175 | 350,116 |
| 1961 | 1,219 | 330 | 23,487 | ... | 403 | 158 | — | 175 | 348,334 |
| 1962 | 1,200 | 330 | 23,501 | ... | 403 | 158 | — | 175 | 346,154 |
| 1963 | 1,148 | 330 | 23,793 | ... | 403 | 158 | — | 175 | 345,022 |
| 1964 | 1,078 | 330 | 23,619 | ... | 403 | 158 | — | 175 | 341,276 |
| 1965 | 1,029 | 330 | 23,672 | ... | 403 | 158 | — | 26 | 340,190 |
| 1966 | 1,027 | 330 | 23,826 | ... | 403 | 158 | — | 13 | 338,884 |
| 1967 | 1,036 | 330 | 23,977 | ... | 403 | 158 | — | 13 | 336,823 |
| 1968 | 1,017 | 330 | 24,129 | ... | 403 | 158 | — | — | 334,922 |
| 1969 | 1,016 | 330 | 24,119 | ... | 403 | 158 | — | — | 333,142 |
| 1970 | 1,028 | 330 | 24,468 | ... | 403 | 158 | — | — | 331,174 |
| 1971 | 1,045 | 330 | 24,501 | ... | 403 | 158 | — | — | 329,426 |
| 1972 | 1,059 | 330 | 24,700 | ... | 403 | 158 | — | — | 326,335 |
| 1973 | 996 | 330 | 24,670 | ... | 403 | 158 | — | — | 323,586 |
| 1974 | 989 | 330 | 24,864 | ... | 403 | 158 | — | — | 322,498 |

**F1    NORTH AMERICA: Length of Railway Line Open** (in kilometres)

| | Canada | Costa Rica | Cuba | Dominican Republic | El Salvador | Guatemala |
|---|---|---|---|---|---|---|
| 1975 | 70,716 | 648 | 5,209 | 142 | 618 | 819 |
| 1976 | 70,471 | ... | 5,130 | 142 | 602 | 819 |
| 1977 | 69,967 | ... | ... | 142 | 602 | 819 |
| 1978 | 67,890 | ... | 5,210 | 142 | 602 | 819 |
| 1979 | 67,725 | ... | 5,215 | 142 | 602 | 819 |
| 1980 | 67,066 | ... | 5,197 | 142 | 602 | 819 |
| 1981 | 66,371 | ... | 5,027 | 142 | 602 | 819 |
| 1982 | 65,899[13] | 760 | 5,158 | 142 | 602 | 819 |
| 1983 | 98,927 99,444 | 760 | 4,922 | 142 | 602 | 819 |
| 1984 | 97,389 | 760 | 4,909 | 142 | 674 | 819 |
| 1985 | 95,670 | 700 | 4,889 | 142 | 674 | 819 |
| 1986 | 93,544 | 700 | 4,881 | 142 | 674 | 819 |
| 1987 | 94,184 | 696 | 4,807 | 142 | 674 | 953 |
| 1988 | 91,365 | 556 | 4,820 | 142 | 674 | 953 |

| | Honduras | Jamaica | Mexico | Nicaragua | Panama | USA (thousands) |
|---|---|---|---|---|---|---|
| 1975 | 977 | 330 | 24,912 | 373 | 158 | 320 |
| 1976 | 977 | 293 | 24,952 | 320 | ... | 283 |
| 1977 | 977 | 293 | 25,047 | 345 | ... | 306 |
| 1978 | 977 | 293 | 25,101 | 345 | ... | 307 |
| 1979 | ... | ... | 25,314 | 345 | ... | 298 |
| 1980 | 1,004 | ... | 25,510 | 345 | 118 | 288 |
| 1981 | 1,004 | 257 | 25,498 | 345 | 118 | 270 |
| 1982 | 1,004 | 257 | 25,476 | 331 | 118 | 265 |
| 1983 | 1,004 | 182 | 25,799 | 331 | ... | 259 |
| 1984 | 1,004 | 208 | 25,840 | 331 | 109 | 253 |
| 1985 | 1,004 | 208 | 25,908 | 331 | 109 | 249 |
| 1986 | 996 | 208 | 26,241 | 331 | 109 | 248 |
| 1987 | 996 | 208 | 26,287 | 331 | 147 | 245 |
| 1988 | 996 | 208 | 26,399 | 331 | 147 | 241 |

**F1** **SOUTH AMERICA: LENGTH OF RAILWAY LINE OPEN** (in kilometres)

1845–1889

| | Argentina | Brazil | Chile | Colombia[4] | Ecuador | Guyana | Paraguay | Peru[10] | Uruguay | Venezuela |
|---|---|---|---|---|---|---|---|---|---|---|
| 1845 | — | — | ... | — | — | — | — | — | — | ... |
| 1846 | — | — | ... | — | — | — | — | — | — | ... |
| 1847 | — | — | ... | — | — | — | — | — | — | ... |
| 1848 | — | — | ... | — | — | 10 | — | — | — | ... |
| 1849 | — | — | ... | — | — | 16 | — | — | — | ... |
| 1850 | — | — | ... | — | — | 26 | — | — | — | ... |
| 1851 | — | — | ... | — | — | 26 | — | 24 | — | ... |
| 1852 | — | — | ... | — | — | 26 | — | 24 | — | ... |
| 1853 | — | — | ... | — | — | 26 | — | 24 | — | ... |
| 1854 | — | 14 | ... | — | — | 29 | — | 24 | — | ... |
| 1855 | — | 14 | ... | — | — | 29 | — | 24 | — | ... |
| 1856 | — | 16 | ... | — | — | 29 | — | 87 | — | ... |
| 1857 | 10 | 16 | ... | — | — | 29 | — | 103 | — | ... |
| 1858 | 18 | 109 | ... | — | — | 29 | — | 103 | — | ... |
| 1859 | 23 | 109 | ... | — | — | 29 | — | 103 | — | ... |
| 1860 | 39 | 223 | 195 | — | — | 29 | — | 103 | — | ... |
| 1861 | 39 | 251 | ... | — | — | 29 | 14 | 103 | — | ... |
| 1862 | 47 | 359 | 543 | — | — | 29 | ... | 103 | — | ... |
| 1863 | 61 | 428 | ... | — | — | 29 | 91 | 103 | — | ... |
| 1864 | 94 | 474 | ... | — | — | 32 | 91 | 103 | — | ... |
| 1865 | 213 | 498 | 440 | — | — | 32 | 91 | 103 | — | ... |
| 1866 | 514 | 513 | ... | — | — | 32 | 91 | 103 | — | ... |
| 1867 | 572 | 598 | ... | — | — | 32 | 91 | 103 | — | ... |
| 1868 | 572 | 718 | ... | — | — | 32 | 91 | 138 | — | ... |
| 1869 | 604 | 737 | 459 | — | — | 32 | 91 | 255 | 20 | ... |
| 1870 | 732 | 745 | 732 | — | — | 32 | 91 | 669 | 20 | 13 |
| 1871 | 852 | 869 | ... | 27 | — | 32 | 91 | 975 | 26 | 13 |
| 1872 | 865 | 932 | ... | 27 | — | 32 | 91 | 1,272 | 63 | 13 |
| 1873 | 1,104 | 1,129 | 998 | 27 | — | 32 | 91 | 1,371 | 63 | 13 |
| 1874 | 1,249 | 1,284 | 1,180 | 27 | — | 32 | 91 | 1,398 | 280 | 13 |
| 1875 | 1,384 | 1,801 | 1,276 | 27 | — | 34 | 91 | 1,792 | 304 | 13 |
| 1876 | 1,665 | 2,122 | 1,537 | 27 | 41 | 34 | 91 | 2,021 | 431 | 13 |
| 1877 | 2,262 | 2,388 | 1,624 | 27 | 41 | 34 | 91 | 2,030 | 431 | 113 |
| 1878 | 2,262 | 2,709 | 1,624 | 45 | 64 | 34 | 91 | ... | 431 | 113 |
| 1879 | 2,262 | 2,911 | 1,624 | 45 | 64 | 34 | 91 | ... | 431 | 113 |
| 1880 | 2,313 | 3,398 | 1,777 | 45 | 64 | 34 | 91 | ... | 431 | 113 |
| 1881 | 2,442 | 3,946 | 1,777 | 45 | 64 | 34 | 91 | ... | 431 | 113 |
| 1882 | 2,666 | 4,464 | 1,856 | 100 | 64 | 34 | 91 | ...[9] | 431 | 113 |
| 1883 | 3,123 | 5,354 | 2,204 | 148 | 64 | 34 | 91 | 1,509 | 431 | 113 |
| 1884 | 3,728 | 6,302 | 2,204 | 176 | 64 | 34 | 91 | 1,580 | 431 | 164 |
| 1885 | 4,541 | 6,930 | 2,204 | 203 | 64 | 34 | 91 | 1,580 | 478 | 164 |
| 1886 | 5,964 | 7,586 | 2,204 | 203 | 64 | 34 | 91 | 1,580 | 543 | 164 |
| 1887 | 6,868 | 8,400 | 2,204 | 219 | 64 | 34 | 91 | 1,580 | 556 | 295 |
| 1888 | 7,644 | 9,321 | 2,626 | 238 | 64 | 34 | 91 | 1,580 | 642 | 295 |
| 1889 | 8,113 | 9,583 | 2,709 | 282 | 64 | 34 | 140 | 1,591 | 869 | 295 |

**F1**     **SOUTH AMERICA: Length of Railway Line Open** (in kilometres)

**1890–1939**

| | Argentina | Bolivia | Brazil | Chile | Colombia[4] | Ecuador |
|---|---|---|---|---|---|---|
| 1890 | 9,254 | 209 | 9,973 | 2,747 | 282 | 92 |
| 1891 | 11,700 | 315 | 10,590 | 2,868 | 282 | 92 |
| 1892 | 12,920 | 972 | 11,316 | 2,871 | 282 | 92 |
| 1893 | 13,961 | 972 | 11,485 | 2,871 | ... | 92 |
| 1894 | 14,029 | 972 | 12,260 | 2,871 | ... | 92 |
| 1895 | 14,222 | 972 | 12,967 | 3,497 | 445 | 92 |
| 1896 | 14,489 | 972 | 13,568 | 3,961 | 481 | 92 |
| 1897 | 14,997 | 972 | 14,015 | 4,215 | 513 | 92 |
| 1898 | 15,314 | 972 | 14,664 | 4,215 | 513 | 92 |
| 1899 | 16,399 | 972 | 14,916 | 4,215 | 550 | 92 |
| 1900 | 16,767 | 972 | 15,316 | 4,354 | 568 | 92 |
| 1901 | 17,200 | 972 | 15,506 | 4,354 | 568 | 105 |
| 1902 | 17,591 | 972 | 15,680 | 4,464 | 568 | 145 |
| 1903 | 18,603 | 1,129 | 16,010 | 4,630 | 568 | 201 |
| 1904 | 19,430 | 1,129 | 16,306 | 4,714 | 568 | 201 |
| 1905 | 19,682 | 1,129 | 16,781 | 4,778 | 661 | 300 |
| 1906 | 20,653 | 1,129 | 17,242 | 4,826 | 723 | 375 |
| 1907 | 22,045 | 1,129 | 17,613 | 5,182 | 723 | 459 |
| 1908 | 23,654 | 1,129 | 18,633 | 5,557 | 759 | 523 |
| 1909 | 25,457 | 1,149 | 19,241 | 5,682 | 901 | 543 |
| 1910 | 27,713 | 1,207 | 21,326 | 5,944 | 988 | 587 |
| 1911 | 30,462 | 1,226 | 22,287 | 6,028 | 1,050 | 587 |
| 1912 | 32,212 | 1,252 | 23,491 | 7,260 | 1,061 | 587 |
| 1913 | 33,478 [11] | 1,284 | 24,614 | 8,070 | 1,061 | 587 |
| | 30,281 | | | | | |
| 1914 | 31,186 | 1,440 | 26,062 | 8,147 | 1,166 | 587 |
| 1915 | 31,408 | 1,561 | 26,647 | 8,216 | 1,191 | 587 |
| 1916 | 32,755 | ... | 27,015 | 8,420 | 1,191 | 587 |
| 1917 | 32,774 | 2,179 | 27,453 | 8,484 | 1,203 | 587 |
| 1918 | 32,774 | 2,179 | 27,706 | 8,512 | 1,231 | 587 |
| 1919 | 32,817 | 2,179 [11] | 28,127 | 8,196 | 1,312 | 626 |
| | | 1,543 | | | | |
| 1920 | 35,282 | 1,543 | 28,535 | 8,211 | 1,347 | 665 |
| 1921 | 35,112 | 1,666 | 28,828 | 8,253 | 1,424 | 665 |
| 1922 | 35,333 | 1,666 | 29,341 | 8,127 | 1,475 | 665 |
| 1923 | 35,496 | 1,794 | 29,295 | 8,661 | 1,500 | 665 |
| 1924 | 36,008 | 1,822 | 30,306 | 8,756 | 1,585 | 665 |
| 1925 | 36,117 | 1,923 | 30,731 | 8,641 | 1,856 | 752 |
| 1926 | 36,257 | 1,980 | 31,333 | 8,620 | 2,048 | 805 |
| 1927 | 36,333 | 2,015 | 31,549 | 9,009 | 2,387 | 805 |
| 1928 | 36,571 | 2,112 | 31,851 | 8,779 | 2,514 | 1,017 |
| 1929 | 37,478 | 2,112 | 31,967 | 8,465 | 2,586 | 1,030 |
| 1930 | 37,978 | 2,253 | 32,478 | 8,937 | 2,609 | 1,031 |
| 1931 | 39,383 | 2,253 | 32,764 | 8,875 | 2,940 | 1,031 |
| 1932 | 39,841 | 2,253 | 32,973 | 8,673 | 3,144 | 1,031 |
| 1933 | 39,962 | 2,253 | 33,073 | 8,718 | 3,173 | 1,031 |
| 1934 | 39,992 | 2,253 | 33,106 | 8,715 | 3,178 | 1,031 |
| 1935 | 40,171 | 2,253 | 33,331 | 8,718 | 3,192 | 1,031 |
| 1936 | 40,266 | 2,253 | 33,521 | 8,745 | 3,187 | 1,031 |
| 1937 | 40,355 | 2,270 | 34,095 | 8,762 | 3,197 | 1,031 |
| 1938 | 40,973 | 2,270 | 34,207 | 8,770 | 3,282 | 1,031 |
| 1939 | 40,973 | 2,270 | 34,204 | 8,663 | 3,247 | 1,031 |

**F1      SOUTH AMERICA: Length of Railway Line Open** (in kilometres)

**1890–1939**

|        | Guyana | Paraguay | Peru[10] | Surinam | Uruguay | Venezuela |
|--------|--------|----------|----------|---------|---------|-----------|
| 1890   | 34     | 140      | 1,599    | —       | 983     | 454       |
| 1891   | 34     | 240      | 1,599    | —       | 1,567 · | 454       |
| 1892   | 34     | 240      | 1,621    | —       | 1,568   | 454       |
| 1893   | 34     | 240      | 1,728    | —       | 1,602   | 502       |
| 1894   | 34     | 240      | 1,728    | —       | 1,604   | 620       |
| 1895   | 34     | 240      | 1,734    | —       | 1,604   | 653       |
| 1896   | 64     | 240      | 1,734    | —       | 1,624   | 760       |
| 1897   | 64     | 240      | 1,744    | —       | 1,624   | 760       |
| 1898   | 64     | 240      | 1,756    | —       | 1,625   | 851       |
| 1899   | 89     | 240      | 1,773    | —       | 1,730   | 851       |
| 1900   | 151    | 240      | 1,800    | —       | 1,730   | 858       |
| 1901   | 153    | 240      | 1,806    | —       | 1,944   | 858       |
| 1902   | 153    | 240      | 1,826    | —       | 1,944   | 858       |
| 1903   | 153    | 240      | 1,849    | —       | 1,944   | 858       |
| 1904   | 153    | 240      | 2,043    | —       | 1,947   | 858       |
| 1905   | 153    | 240      | 2,079    | 60      | 1,948   | 858       |
| 1906   | 153    | 240      | 2,401    | 60      | 1,960   | 858       |
| 1907   | 153    | 240      | 2,555    | 60      | 1,960   | 858       |
| 1908   | 153    | 240      | 2,852    | ...     | 2,208   | 858       |
| 1909   | 153    | 240      | 2,983    | 133     | 2,328   | 858       |
| 1910   | 153    | ...      | 2,995    | ...     | 2,488   | 858       |
| 1911   | 153    | 373      | 3,208    | ...     | 2,512   | 858       |
| 1912   | 153    | 373      | 3,256    | 173     | 2,522   | 858       |
| 1913   | 153    | 373      | 3,276    | 173     | 2,576   | 858       |
| 1914   | 158    | 373      | 3,317    | 173     | 2,592   | 858       |
| 1915   | 158    | 373      | 3,345    | 173     | 2,638   | 858       |
| 1916   | 158    | 373      | 3,407    | 173     | 2,672   | 858       |
| 1917   | 158    | 373      | 3,433    | 173     | 2,672   | 858       |
| 1918   | 158    | 373      | 3,488    | 173     | 2,672   | 861       |
| 1919   | 158    | 410      | 3,489[10] / 2,116 | 173 | 2,672 | 861    |
| 1920   | 158    | 410      | 2,116    | 173     | 2,672   | 861       |
| 1921   | 158    | 425      | 2,159    | 173     | 2,672   | 935       |
| 1922   | 158    | 457      | 2,183    | 173     | 2,672   | 935       |
| 1923   | 158    | 457      | 2,188    | 173     | 2,672   | 945       |
| 1924   | 158    | 468      | 2,459    | 173     | 2,672   | 945       |
| 1925   | 158    | 468      | 2,555    | 173     | 2,672   | 945       |
| 1926   | 158    | 468      | 2,654    | 173     | 2,692   | 982       |
| 1927   | 158    | 468      | 2,582    | 173     | 2,720   | 982       |
| 1928   | 158    | 468      | 2,709    | 173     | 2,724   | 982       |
| 1929   | 127    | 468      | 2,861    | 173     | 2,724   | 993       |
| 1930   | 127    | 468      | ...      | 173     | 2,731   | 993       |
| 1931   | 127    | 468      | 2,899    | 173     | 2,731   | 993       |
| 1932   | 127    | 468      | 2,972    | 173     | 2,731   | 993       |
| 1933   | 127    | 468      | 2,954    | ...     | 2,848   | 993       |
| 1934   | 127    | 468      | 2,977    | ...     | 2,848   | 993       |
| 1935   | 127    | 468      | 3,038    | ...     | 2,848   | 993       |
| 1936   | 127    | 481      | 3,038    | ...     | 2,848   | 993       |
| 1937   | 127    | 499      | 3,039    | ...     | 2,971   | 993       |
| 1938   | 127    | 499      | 2,938    | ...     | 2,971   | 993       |
| 1939   | 127    | 499      | 2,918    | ...     | 3,009   | 993       |

**F1** **SOUTH AMERICA: Length of Railway Line Open** (in kilometres)

**1940–1988**

| | Argentina | Bolivia | Brazil | Chile | Colombia | Ecuador |
|---|---|---|---|---|---|---|
| 1940 | 41,283 | 2,270 | 34,252 | 8,610 | 3,335 | 1,060 |
| 1941 | 41,371 | 2,270 | 34,283 | 8,702 | 3,343 | 1,055 |
| 1942 | 41,407 | 2,270 | 34,438 | 8,577 | 3,415 | 1,055 |
| 1943 | ... | 2,270 | 34,769 | 8,502 | 3,445 | 1,055 |
| 1944 | ... | 2,270 | 35,163 | 8,737 | 3,448 | 1,055 |
| 1945 | ... | 2,270 | 35,280 | ... | 3,455 | 1,048 |
| 1946 | 41,600 | 2,340 | 35,336 | 8,672 | 3,510 | 1,048 |
| 1947 | 42,757 | 2,343 | 35,451 | 8,255 | 3,554 | 1,048 |
| 1948 | 42,757 | 2,343 | 35,622 | 8,516 | 3,486 | 1,048 |
| 1949 | 42,838 | 2,343 | 35,972 | 8,506 | 3,505 | 1,048 |
| 1950 | 42,864 | 2,343 | 36,681 | 8,503 | 3,526 | 1,124 |
| 1951 | ... | 2,343 | 36,845 | 8,509 | 3,526 | 1,124 |
| 1952 | ... | 2,343 | 37,019 | 8,503 | 3,349 [12] | 1,124 |
| | | | | | 2,977 | |
| 1953 | ... | 2,721 | 37,032 | 8,493 | 2,946 | 1,121 |
| 1954 | ... | 2,721 | 37,190 | 8,493 | 2,944 | 1,121 |
| 1955 | 43,930 | 2,721 | 37,092 | 8,405 | 3,062 | 1,121 |
| 1956 | 43,930 | 2,721 | 37,049 | 8,408 | 3,029 | 1,121 |
| 1957 | 43,930 | 2,721 | 37,422 | 8,408 | 3,161 | 1,152 |
| 1958 | 43,930 | 3,268 | 37,967 | 8,415 | 3,161 | 1,152 |
| 1959 | 43,930 | 3,268 | 37,710 | 8,415 | 3,161 | 1,152 |
| 1960 | 43,905 | 3,470 | 38,287 | 8,415 | 3,161 | 1,152 |
| 1961 | 42,813 | ... | 37,548 | 8,251 | 3,436 | 1,152 |
| 1962 | 39,985 | 3,745 | 36,572 | 8,085 | 3,436 | 1,152 |
| 1963 | 43,751 | ... | 35,349 | 7,965 | 3,436 | 1,154 |
| 1964 | ... | 3,580 | 34,262 | 7,957 | 3,436 | 1,154 |
| 1965 | 41,907 | 3,560 | 33,864 | 7,946 | 3,436 | 1,154 |
| 1966 | 41,434 | 3,560 | 32,463 | 7,946 | 3,436 | 1,154 |
| 1967 | 40,165 | 3,560 | 32,182 | 8,265 | 3,436 | 1,154 |
| 1968 | 40,641 | 3,560 | 32,054 | 8,274 | 3,436 | 1,154 |
| 1969 | 40,235 | 3,524 | 32,939 | 8,274 | 3,436 | 990 |
| 1970 | 39,905 | 3,524 | 31,847 | 8,281 | 3,436 | 990 |
| 1971 | 39,822 | 3,524 [11] | 31,518 | 8,281 [12] | 3,431 | 990 |
| | | 3,284 | | 6,432 | | |
| 1972 | 39,816 | 3,284 | 30,934 | 6,396 | 3,431 | 990 |
| 1973 | 39,805 | 3,284 | 30,429 | 6,393 | 3,431 | 990 |
| 1974 | 39,782 | 3,284 | 30,439 | 6,361 | 3,431 | 990 |
| 1975 | 39,787 | 3,269 | 30,809 | 6,606 | 3,431 | 965 |
| 1976 | 39,779 | 3,269 | 30,422 | 6,378 | 3,403 | 965 |
| 1977 | 36,996 | 3,373 | 29,778 | 6,372 | 3,403 | 965 |
| 1978 | 34,393 | 3,473 | 29,951 | 6,366 | 3,403 | 965 |
| 1979 | 34,350 | 3,473 | 30,021 | 6,365 | 3,403 | 965 |
| 1980 | 34,077 | 3,628 | 29,659 | 6,302 | 3,403 | 965 |
| 1981 | 34,172 | 3,628 | 29,237 | 6,300 | 3,403 | 965 |
| 1982 | 34,098 | 3,628 | 29,164 | 6,236 | 2,710 | 966 |
| 1983 | 34,127 | 3,628 | 29,207 | 6,236 | 3,400 | 966 |
| 1984 | 34,345 | 3,628 | 28,942 | 6,858 | 3,255 | 966 |
| 1985 | 34,447 | 3,628 | 29,777 | 6,740 | 3,255 | 966 |
| 1986 | 34,428 | 3,628 | 29,814 | 6,551 | 3,257 | 966 |
| 1987 | 34,183 | 3,701 | 29,833 | 7,998 | 3,239 | 966 |
| 1988 | 34,192 | 3,701 | 29,635 | 6,270 | 3,239 | 971 |

**F1     SOUTH AMERICA: Length of Railway Line Open** (in kilometers)

| | Guyana | Paraguay | Peru[10] | Surinam | Uruguay | Venezuela |
|---|---|---|---|---|---|---|
| 1940 | 127 | 499 | 2,898 | ... | 3,009 | 1,049 |
| 1941 | 127 | 499 | 2,886 | ... | 3,009 | 997 |
| 1942 | 127 | 499 | 2,801 | ... | 3,009 | 997 |
| 1943 | 127 | 499 | 2,802 | ... | 3,009 | 997 |
| 1944 | 127 | 499 | 2,936 | ... | 3,009 | 997 |
| 1945 | 127 | 499 | 2,875 | 136 | 3,009 | 997 |
| 1946 | 127 | 499 | 2,890 | 136 | 3,009 | 997 |
| 1947 | 127 | 499 | 3,062 | 136 | 3,009 | 997 |
| 1948 | 127 | 499 | 3,029 | 136 | 3,004 | 997 |
| 1949 | 127 | 499 | 3,097 | 136 | 3,004 | 997 |
| 1950 | 127 | 499 | 3,097 | 136 | 3,004 | 997 |
| 1951 | 127 | 499 | 3,010 | 136 | 3,004 | 997 |
| 1952 | 127 | 499 | 3,067 | 136 | 3,004 | 997 |
| 1953 | 127 | 499 | 2,789 | 136 | 3,004 | 997 |
| 1954 | 127 | 441 | 2,789 | 136 | 3,004 | 997 |
| 1955 | 127 | 441 | 2,726 | 136 | 3,004 | ... |
| 1956 | 127 | 441 | 2,726 | 136 | 3,004 | 506 |
| 1957 | 127 | 441 | 2,726 | 136 | 3,004 | 506 |
| 1958 | 127 | 441 | 2,673 | 136 | 3,004 | 506 |
| 1959 | 127 | 441 | 2,578 | 136 | 3,004 | 474 |
| 1960 | 127 | 441 | 2,559 | 136 | 3,004 | 474 |
| 1961 | 127 | 441 | 2,458 | 136 | 3,004 | 474 |
| 1962 | 127 | 441 | 2,558 | 136 | 3,004 | 474 |
| 1963 | 127 | 441 | 2,460 | 102 | 3,004 | 474 |
| 1964 | 127 | 441 | 2,327 | 86 | 3,004 | 474 |
| 1965 | 127 | 441 | 2,244 | 86 | 3,004 | 474 |
| 1966 | 127 | 441 | 2,340 | 86 | 3,004 | 474 |
| 1967 | 127 | 441 | 2,295 | 86 | 3,004 | 474 |
| 1968 | 127 | 441 | 2,209 | 86 | 3,004 | 474 |
| 1969 | 127 | 441 | 2,235 | 86 | 3,004 | 226 |
| 1970 | 127 | 441 | 2,242 | 86 | 2,975 | 226 |
| 1971 | 127 | 441 | 2,282 | 86 | 2,975 | 226 |
| 1972 | 65 | 441 | ... | 86 | 2,975 | 226 |
| 1973 | 30 | 441 | 1,892 | 86 | 2,975 | 233 |
| 1974 | 30 | 441 | 1,892 | 86 | 2,975 | 226 |
| 1975 | — | 441 | 1,875 | | 2,975 | 226 |
| 1976 | — | 441 | 1,875 | | 2,975 | 264 |
| 1977 | — | 441 | 1,875 | | 2,988 | 284 |
| 1978 | — | 441 | 1,875 | | 2,998 | 264 |
| 1979 | — | 441 | 1,882 | | 3,005 | 268 |
| 1980 | — | 441 | 2,099 | | 3,005 | 268 |
| 1981 | — | 441 | 2,159 | | 3,005 | 268 |
| 1982 | — | 441 | 2,159 | | 3,010 | 268 |
| 1983 | — | 441 | 2,159 | | 3,001 | ... |
| 1984 | — | 441 | 2,159 | | 3,001 | 280 |
| 1985 | — | 441 | 2,159 | | 2,991 | 280 |
| 1986 | — | 441 | 2,159 | | 2,991 | 445 |
| 1987 | — | 441 | 2,157 | — | 2,991 | 445 |
| 1988 | — | 441 | 2,157 | — | 3,006 | 468 |

**F1** **Length of Railway Line Open** (in kilometres)

NOTES

1. SOURCES: The basic sources have been the national publications listed on p. xiv–xvi, but a variety of others has been used to fill in gaps. These include *Jane's World Railways, International Railway Progress,* the publications of the Institut International de Statistique, and British Consular Reports.
2. Except where otherwise indicated, the statistics are for the route length of line open at the end of each year. Narrow gauge line are included but not, in general, mountain railways.
3. In principle, purely industrial lines, which were not open to public traffic, are not included. In practice, this distinction cannot always be made, especially in central American countries. The main endeavour has been to maintain consistency in the series.

FOOTNOTES

[1] Statistics to 1918 are at 30 June. Newfoundland is included from 1949.
[2] Statistics from 1890 to 1920 are at 31 March in the year following the year shown.
[3] Including tramways to 1927 (1st line). The first proper railway was opened in 1865.
[4] Data for Panama are shown separately from Colombia even for the period when the former was part of the latter.
[5] Statistics to 1890 (1st line) are of railway operated, subsequently they are of railway owned. The former series contains some double counting where different companies operated over the same line. Data for 1890 (2nd line) to 1916 are at 30 June. Alaska and Hawaii are included from 1960.
[6] At 31 March following the year shown.
[7] Some industrial lines carried public traffic at some times but not at others and it is not clear how inconsistently this is treated in the data. It also seems likely that the data relate to track rather than route length.
[8] At 30 June.
[9] 450 km were ceded to Chile as a result of the war of 1879–84.
[10] Statistics are of railways in existence to 1919 (1st line) and of railways exploited subsequently.
[11] Subsequently excluding private lines.
[12] The reason for this break is not clear in the sources, but it is probably the subsequent exclusion of some, or all, private lines.
[13] Track kilometres of class I railroads subsequently.

**F2    NORTH AMERICA: FREIGHT TRAFFIC ON RAILWAYS**

Key:      a= thousand metric tons; b= million metric ton-kilometres c= million metric tons; d= thousand million metric ton-kilometres

### 1860–1904

| | Canada[1] | Mexico | USA[2] | |
|---|---|---|---|---|
| | a | a | c | b[3] |
| 1860 | ... | ... | ... | ... |
| 1861 | ... | ... | 50 | ... |
| 1862 | ... | ... | ... | ... |
| 1863 | ... | ... | ... | ... |
| 1864 | ... | ... | ... | ... |
| 1865 | ... | ... | ... | 3,150 |
| 1866 | ... | ... | ... | 3,830 |
| 1867 | ... | ... | ... | 4,420 |
| 1868 | ... | ... | ... | 5,020 |
| 1869 | ... | ... | ... | 6,160 |
| 1870 | ... | ... | 65.8 | 7,180 |
| 1871 | ... | ... | ... | 8,130 |
| 1872 | ... | ... | ... | 9,370 |
| 1873 | ... | 150 | ... | 10,920 |
| 1874 | ... | 122 | ... | 11,290 |
| 1875 | 5,145 | 137 | ... | 11,450 |
| 1876 | 5,744 | 133 | ... | 12,750 |
| 1877 | 6,223 | 159 | ... | 12,770 |
| 1878 | 7,151 | 172 | ... | 15,590 |
| 1879 | 7,574 | 190 | ... | 19,080 |
| 1880 | 9,017 | 250 | ... | 21,140 |
| 1881 | 10,945 | 364 | ... | 23,450 |
| 1882 | 12,316 | 748 | 327 | 23,695[3] |
| | | | | 57,380 |
| 1883 | 12,035 | 866 | 363 | 64,334 |
| 1884 | 12,439 | 1,026 | 362 | 65,297 |
| 1885 | 13,298 | 1,179 | 396 | 71,761 |
| 1886 | 14,216 | 1,180 | 437 | 77,089 |
| 1887 | 14,838 | 1,478 | 501 | 89,877 |
| 1888 | 15,579 | 1,821 | 535 | 95,516 |
| 1889 | 16,265 | 2,127 | 562 | 100,267 |
| | | | | (thousand million ton-kilometres) |
| 1890 | 18,858 | 2,734 | 627[2] | 116[2] |
| | | | | 111 |
| 1891 | 19,734 | 3,233 | ... | 118 |
| 1892 | 20,130 | 3,191 | ... | 129 |
| 1893 | 19,962 | 3,796 | ... | 137 |
| 1894 | 18,798 | 4,121 | ... | 117 |
| 1895 | 19,526 | 4,073 | ... | 124 |
| 1896 | 22,015 | 3,988 | ... | 139 |
| 1897 | 22,952 | 4,878 | ... | 139 |
| 1898 | 26,114 | 6,078 | ... | 167 |
| 1899 | 28,315 | 5,425 | 455 | 181 |
| 1900 | 32,610 | 7,553 | 529 | 207 |
| 1901 | 33,565 | 6,759 | 530 | 215 |
| 1902 | 38,444 | 8,488 | 597 | 230 |
| 1903 | 42,976 | 9,911 | 649 | 253 |
| 1904 | 43,634 | 11,141 | 648 | 255 |

**F2    NORTH AMERICA: Freight Traffic on Railways**

**1905–1939**

| | Canada[1] | | Costa Rica | Cuba[4] | | El Salvador | Guatemala | Mexico | | Nicaragua | | USA[2] | |
|---|---|---|---|---|---|---|---|---|---|---|---|---|---|
| | c | b | a | a | b | a | a | a | b | a | b | c | d |
| 1905 | 46 | ... | ... | ... | ... | ... | ... | 14,578 | ... | ... | ... | 712 | 272 |
| 1906 | 52 | ... | ... | ... | ... | ... | ... | ... | ... | ... | ... | 813 | 315 |
| 1907 | 58.0 | 17,064 | ... | ... | ... | ... | ... | ... | ... | ... | ... | 886 | 345 |
| 1908 | 57.2 | 18,923 | ... | ... | ... | ... | ... | 12,310 | ... | ... | ... | 789 | 319 |
| 1909 | 60.6 | 19,214 | ... | ... | ... | ... | ... | 14,440 | ... | ... | ... | 799 | 319 |
| 1910 | 67.6 | 22,939 | ... | ... | ... | ... | ... | ... | ... | ... | ... | 931 | 372 |
| 1911 | 72.5 | 23,430 | ... | ... | ... | ... | ... | ... | ... | ... | ... | 910 | 371 |
| 1912 | 81.1 | 28,554 | ... | ... | ... | ... | ... | ... | ... | ... | ... | 935 | 386 |
| 1913 | 97.1 | 33,628 | ... | 15,000 | 582 | 91 | ... | ... | ... | ... | ... | 1,073 | 441 |
| 1914 | 92.0 | 32,212 | ... | ... | ... | ... | ... | ... | ... | ... | ... | 1,025 | 421 |
| 1915 | 79.1 | 25,785 | ... | ... | ... | ... | ... | ... | ... | ... | ... | 929 | 405 |
| 1916 | 99.5 | 41,165 | ... | ... | ... | ... | ... | ... | ... | ... | ... | 1,146[2] | 501[2] |
| | | | | | | | | | | | | 1,195 | 535 |
| 1917 | 110.6 | 45,532 | ... | ... | ... | ... | ... | ... | ... | ... | ... | 1,254 | 581 |
| 1918 | 115.7 | 45,302 | ... | ... | ... | ... | ... | ... | ... | ... | ... | 1,249 | 597 |
| 1919 | 105.9[1] | 40,477[1] | ... | ... | ... | ... | ... | ... | ... | ... | ... | 1,080 | 536 |
| | 101.2 | 39,347 | | | | | | | | | | | |
| 1920 | 115.6 | 46,565 | ... | ... | ... | ... | ... | ... | ... | ... | ... | 1,236 | 604 |
| 1921 | 93.5 | 38,867 | ... | ... | ... | ... | ... | 8,300 | 2,262 | ... | ... | 924 | 452 |
| 1922 | 98.4 | 44,336 | ... | 22,800 | 903 | 168 | ... | 9,614 | 2,398 | ... | ... | 1,009 | 500 |
| 1923 | 107.3 | 49,738 | ... | 23,900 | 1,072 | 195 | ... | 11,158 | 2,886 | ... | ... | 1,259 | 608 |
| 1924 | 96.5 | 44,549 | ... | 26,100 | 1,145 | 203 | ... | 11,146 | 2,901 | ... | ... | 1,168 | 572 |
| 1925 | 99.7 | 46,668 | ... | 33,100 | 1,710 | 253 | ... | 12,239 | 3,219 | ... | ... | 1,226 | 609 |
| 1926 | 111.1 | 49,863 | ... | 30,100 | 1,237 | ... | ... | 12,878 | 3,608 | ... | ... | 1,306 | 653 |
| 1927 | 114.3 | 50,956 | 635 | 28,000 | ... | 251 | ... | 13,298 | 3,803 | ... | ... | 1,246 | 631 |
| 1928 | 128.1 | 60,750 | 615 | 27,000 | ... | 310 | ... | 13,393 | 4,006 | ... | ... | 1,244 | 637 |
| 1929 | 125.1 | 51,137 | 592 | 32,000 | ... | 345 | ... | 13,878 | 4,035 | ... | ... | 1,287 | 657 |
| 1930 | 104.5 | 43,222 | 561 | 18,549 | ... | 255 | ... | 13,015 | 4,041 | ... | 12 | 1,107 | 563 |
| 1931 | 78.0 | 37,532 | 432 | ... | ... | 261 | ... | 10,799 | 3,378 | ... | 11 | 857 | 454 |
| 1932 | 61.4 | 33,779 | 375 | ... | ... | 220 | ... | 9,105 | 2,884 | ... | 8.0 | 616 | 344 |
| 1933 | 57.7 | 30,795 | 387 | ... | ... | 254 | ... | 9,993 | 3,245 | ... | 7.1 | 665 | 366 |
| 1934 | 68.7 | 34,047 | 328 | ... | ... | 303 | ... | 12,577 | 4,154 | ... | 7.1 | 728 | 395 |
| 1935 | 69.9 | 35,514 | 320 | ... | ... | 330 | ... | 13,555 | 4,596 | 89 | 9.1 | 755 | 429 |
| 1936 | 76.8 | 38,564 | 369 | ... | ... | 302 | ... | 14,275 | 4,927 | 93 | 9.0 | 918 | 498 |
| 1937 | 83.9 | 39,311 | 462 | 18,320 | 719 | 373 | 642 | 14,405 | 5,381 | 142 | 13 | 975 | 530 |
| 1938 | 76.8 | 39,178 | 499 | 15,287 | 651 | 364 | 690 | 14,668 | 5,535 | 144 | 12 | 744 | 426 |
| 1939 | 85.8 | 45,938 | 434 | 14,619 | 617 | 432 | 714 | 15,367 | 5,728 | 134 | 12 | 866 | 490 |

**F2    NORTH AMERICA: Freight Traffic on Railways**

1940–1988

| | Canada[1] | | Costa Rica | | Cuba[4] | | El Salvador | | Guatemala[8] | |
|---|---|---|---|---|---|---|---|---|---|---|
| | c | d | a[6] | b[7] | a | b | a | b | a | b |
| 1940 | 100 | 55 | 363[6] | ... | 17,255 | 726 | 380 | ... | 630 | ... |
| 1941 | 122 | 73 | 377 | ... | 17,289 | 750 | 331 | ... | 661 | ... |
| 1942 | 141 | 82 | 386 | ... | 19,345 | 926 | 392 | ... | 693 | ... |
| 1943 | 161 | 93 | 448 | ... | 16,910 | 1,580 | 523 | ... | 743 | ... |
| 1944 | 161 | 96 | 412 | ... | 23,080 | 1,734 | 520 | ... | 874 | ... |
| 1945 | 152 | 92 | 456 | ... | 17,980 | 1,405 | 536 | ... | 951[8] 455 | ... |
| 1946 | 146 | 81 | 433[6] | ... | 19,600[4] | 1,343[4] | 537 | ... | 512 | ... |
| 1947 | 159 | 88 | 447 | 38 | 24,450 | 1,385 | 631 | ... | 623 | ... |
| 1948 | 160 | 86 | 442 | 30 | 24,310 | 1,261 | 525 | ... | 639 | ... |
| 1949 | 147[1] | 82[1] | 443 | 41 | 20,560 | 1,056 | 487 | ... | 589 | ... |
| 1950 | 149 | 81 | 465 | 44 | 20,250 | 1,100 | 513 | ... | 623 | 239 |
| 1951 | 167 | 94 | 468 | 45 | 21,600 | 1,134 | 560 | ... | 594 | 209 |
| 1952 | 168 | 100 | 485 | 49 | 24,900 | 1,192 | 618 | ... | 550 | 193 |
| 1953 | 160 | 95 | 538 | 56 | 19,660 | 1,008 | 564 | ... | 652 | 256 |
| 1954 | 147 | 84 | 556 | 57 | 19,010 | 979 | 586 | ... | 568 | 245 |
| 1955 | 171 | 97 | 640 | 63[7] | 17,910 | 952 | 683 | ... | 661 | 273 |
| 1956 | 194 | 115 | 622 | 35 | 17,580 | 1,008 | 712 | ... | 692 | 285 |
| 1957 | 179 | 104 | 620 | 33 | ... | 1,101 | 686 | ... | 676 | 259 |
| 1958 | 158 | 97 | 679 | 41 | ... | ... | 687 | ... | 590 | 234 |
| 1959 | 169 | 99 | 710 | 50 | ... | ... | 693 | ... | 612 | 246 |
| 1960 | 162[1] 144 | 96 | 832 | 59 | ... | ... | 680 | ... | 672 | 270 |
| 1961 | 139 | 96 | 841 | 59 | ... | ... | 580 | ... | 579 | 255 |
| 1962 | 146 | 99 | 907 | 66 | 9,298 | 1,109 | 633 | ... | 557 | 192 |
| 1963 | 156 | 111 | 935 | [77][7] | 7,618 | 1,064 | 635 | ... | 583 | 207 |
| 1964 | 172 | 124 | 935 | 33 | 8,279 | 1,025 | 613 | ... | 495 | 177 |
| 1965 | 178 | 127 | 922 | 31 | 10,032 | 1,326 | 589 | ... | 406 | 129 |
| 1966 | 186 | 141 | 1,299 | 47 | 9,102 | 1,487 | 529 | ... | 434 | 133 |
| 1967 | 191 | 137 | 1,369 | 13 | 10,765 | 1,705 | 496 | ... | 414 | 120 |
| 1968 | 196 | 139 | 1,545 | 18 | 9,976 | 1,672 | 423 | ... | 323 | 75 |
| 1969 | 188 | 141 | 1,795 | 11 | 10,259 | 1,485 | 396 | ... | 412 | 106 |
| 1970 | 212 | 161 | 2,140 | 18 | 11,735 | 1,625 | 495 | ... | 415 | 106 |
| 1971 | 214 | 173 | 2,113 | 13 | 10,655 | 1,598 | 503 | ... | 357 | ... |
| 1972 | 216 | 181[5] | 2,191 | 15 | 9,569 | 1,504 | 525 | 63 | 353 | 93 |
| 1973 | 241 | 191 | 1,921 | 20 | 10,017 | 1,617 | 509 | 61 | 463 | 137 |
| 1974 | 246 | 202 | ... | 14 | 10,867 | 1,654 | 491 | 49 | 525 | 143 |
| 1975 | 226 | 197 | 2,108 | ... | 10,867 | 1,766 | 402 | 46 | 524 | 127 |
| 1976 | 239 | 202 | ... | 16 | 11,320 | 1,848 | 476 | 46 | 704 | 117 |
| 1977 | 247 | 212 | ... | ... | 13,600 | 2,021 | 518 | 52 | ... | 139 |
| 1978 | 239 | 215 | ... | ... | 13,530 | 1,904 | 606 | 76 | ... | 139 |
| 1979 | 258 | 234 | ... | ... | 14,897 | 1,899 | 606 | 78 | ... | 91 |
| 1980 | 254 | 235 | ... | ... | 15,702 | 2,165 | 414 | 55 | ... | 91 |
| 1981 | 247 | 234 | ... | ... | 18,218 | 2,676 | 285 | 31 | ... | ... |
| 1982 | 213 | 224 | ... | ... | 18,248 | 2,550 | 302 | 31 | ... | ... |
| 1983 | 223 | 232 | ... | ... | 17,697 | 2,617 | 364 | 31 | 681 | ... |
| 1984 | 255 | 258 | ... | ... | 18,435 | 2,674 | 315 | 24 | ... | ... |
| 1985 | 251 | 245 | ... | ... | 18,368 | 2,797 | 324 | 25 | ... | ... |
| 1986 | 250 | 247 | ... | ... | ... | 2,155 | 322 | 24 | 650 | ... |
| 1987 | ... | 255 | ... | ... | ... | 2,105 | 353 | 39 | ... | ... |
| 1988 | ... | 249 | ... | ... | ... | 2,087 | ... | 36 | ... | ... |

**F2     NORTH AMERICA: Freight Traffic on Railways**

**1940–1988**

| | Honduras | Mexico | | Nicaragua | | Panama | USA[2] | |
|---|---|---|---|---|---|---|---|---|
| | a | a | b | a | b | a | c | d |
| 1940 | ... | 15,023 | 5,810 | 129 | 12 | 23 | 970 | 548 |
| 1941 | ... | 15,681 | 6,076 | 145 | 13 | 26 | 1,176 | 697 |
| 1942 | ... | 16,898 | 7,019 | 183 | 16 | 34 | 1,359 | 936 |
| 1943 | ... | 21,343 | 8,092 | 199 | 17 | 36 | 1,412 | 1,066 |
| 1944 | ... | 20,222 | 8,194 | 217 | 16 | 38 | 1,420 | 1,081 |
| 1945 | ... | 20,702 | 8,024 | 197 | 15 | 42 | 1,354 | 999 |
| 1946 | ... | 21,046 | 8,185 | 205 | 15 | 44 | 1,299 | 869 |
| 1947 | ... | 21,138 | 8,341 | 188 | 17 | 28 | 1,463 | 960 |
| 1948 | ... | 21,181 | 8,521 | ... | 19 | 28 | 1,433 | 936 |
| 1949 | | 21,598 | 8,701 | ... | 19 | 23 | 1,165 | 772 |
| 1950 | 804 | 22,907 | 9,391 | 244 | 21 | 19 | 1,289 | 864 |
| 1951 | 943 | 22,827 | 9,460 | 306 | 23 | 18 | 1,403 | 949 |
| 1952 | 935 | 23,696[5] | 10,087 | 314 | 21 | 20 | 1,313 | 902 |
| | | 26,332 | | | | | | |
| 1953 | 1,079 | 25,461 | 9,593 | 353 | 21 | 24 | 1,314 | 889 |
| 1954 | 1,110 | 26,136 | 10,304 | 375 | 35 | 35 | 1,160 | 806 |
| 1955 | 1,018 | 27,685 | 10,961 | 361 | 32 | 35 | 1,324 | 915 |
| 1956 | 1,083 | 29,615 | 12,015 | 294 | 26 | 36 | 1,380 | 951 |
| 1957 | 990 | 31,536 | 12,983 | 330 | 29 | 34 | 1,315 | 908 |
| 1958 | 915 | 30,543 | 12,810 | 394 | 36 | 36 | 1,131 | 810 |
| 1959 | 947 | 30,482 | 12,231 | 413 | 32 | 34 | 1,173[2] | 845[2] |
| 1960 | 890 | 34,359 | 14,004 | 286 | 23 | 35 | 1,180 | 840 |
| 1961 | 848 | 32,614 | 13,524 | 253 | 23 | 24 | 1,137 | 827 |
| 1962 | 740 | 32,603 | 13,521 | 254 | 25 | 32 | 1,174 | 870 |
| 1963 | 580 | 36,336 | 14,960 | 203 | 19 | 18 | 1,222 | 913 |
| 1964 | 682 | 39,582 | 16,330 | 187 | 16 | 18 | 1,288 | 967 |
| 1965 | 542 | 42,947 | 18,332 | 162 | 13 | 17 | 1,342 | 1,030 |
| 1966 | 431 | 42,303 | 18,407 | 144 | 13 | 10 | 1,401 | 1,090 |
| 1967 | 512 | 45,184 | 19,690 | 153 | 14 | 12 | 1,359 | 1,062 |
| 1968 | 2,076 | 44,213 | 20,304 | 146 | 13 | 15 | 1,374 | 1,096 |
| 1969 | 1,603 | 46,890 | 21,577 | 136 | 13 | 15 | 1,413 | 1,130 |
| 1970 | 510 | 46,784 | 22,863 | 126 | 16 | 14 | 1,426 | 1,126 |
| 1971 | 2,357 | 48,399 | 22,374 | 124 | 15 | 22 | 1,335 | 1,079 |
| 1972 | 1,827 | 49,946 | 24,140 | 107 | 14 | 22 | 1,389 | 1,136 |
| 1973 | ... | 55,227 | 26,139 | 100 | 12 | 30 | 1,466 | 1,253 |
| 1974 | ... | 63,824 | 30,858 | 83 | 11 | 18 | 1,469 | 1,244 |
| 1975 | 341 | 65,357 | 33,195 | 62 | 8 | 17 | 1,334 | 1,102 |
| 1976 | ... | 65,000 | 34,821 | ... | 12 | ... | 1,343 | 1,123 |
| 1977 | ... | 70,864 | 36,232 | ... | 11 | ... | 1,378 | 1,206 |
| 1978 | ... | 71,363 | 36,422 | 66 | 10 | ... | 1,298 | 1,253 |
| 1979 | ... | 69,718 | 36,766 | ... | 6 | ... | 1,400 | 1,334 |
| 1980 | ... | 71,978 | 41,323 | ... | 12 | ... | 1,393[15] | 1,342 |
| | | | | | | | 1,353 | |
| 1981 | ... | 75,568 | 43,513 | ... | 14 | ... | 1,318 | 1,360 |
| 1982 | ... | 69,667 | 38,800 | ... | 7 | ... | 1,151 | 1,192 |
| 1983 | ... | 71,904 | 42,377 | ... | 2 | ... | 1,173 | 1,237 |
| 1984 | ... | 73,428 | 44,592 | ... | 5 | ... | 1,296 | 1,345 |
| 1985 | ... | 73,091 | 45,306 | ... | 4 | ... | 1,197 | 1,280 |
| 1986 | ... | 66,384 | 40,608 | 36 | ... | ... | 986 | 1,284 |
| 1987 | ... | 66,843 | 40,475 | ... | ... | ... | 1,244 | 1,388 |
| 1988 | ... | 67,305 | 40,755 | ... | ... | ... | 1,297 | 1,378 |

**F2      SOUTH AMERICA: FREIGHT TRAFFIC ON RAILWAYS**

**1855–1894**

| | Argentina[9] | Chile[10] | Peru | Uruguay[11] | Venezuela |
|---|---|---|---|---|---|
| | a | a | a | a | a |
| 1855 | ... | ... | ... | ... | ... |
| 1856 | ... | ... | ... | ... | ... |
| 1857 | 2.3 | ... | ... | ... | ... |
| 1858 | 6.7 | ... | ... | ... | ... |
| 1859 | 13 | ... | ... | ... | ... |
| 1860 | ... | ... | ... | ... | ... |
| 1861 | ... | ... | ... | ... | ... |
| 1862 | 19 | ... | ... | ... | ... |
| 1863 | 24 | ... | ... | ... | ... |
| 1864 | 71 | ... | ... | ... | ... |
| 1865 | 72 | ... | ... | ... | ... |
| 1866 | 83 | ... | ... | ... | ... |
| 1867 | 129 | ... | ... | ... | ... |
| 1868 | 152 | ... | ... | ... | ... |
| 1869 | 206 | ... | ... | ... | ... |
| 1870 | 275 | ... | ... | ... | ... |
| 1871 | 286 | ... | ... | ... | ... |
| 1872 | 343 | ... | ... | ... | ... |
| 1873 | 443 | ... | ... | ... | ... |
| 1874 | 504 | ... | ... | ... | ... |
| 1875 | 661 | ... | ... | ... | ... |
| 1876 | 734 | 603 | ... | ... | ... |
| 1877 | 721 | 556 | ... | ... | ... |
| 1878 | 734 | 592 | ... | ... | ... |
| 1879 | 812 | 659 | ... | ... | ... |
| 1880 | 773 | 821 | ... | ... | ... |
| 1881 | 957 | 865 | ... | ... | ... |
| 1882 | 1,308 | 982 | ... | ... | ... |
| 1883 | 1,918 | 999 | ... | ... | 7.6 |
| 1884 | 2,421 | 1,069 | ... | ... | 49 |
| 1885 | 3,050 | 1,086 | ... | ... | 59 |
| 1886 | 2,949 | 1,306 | ... | ... | 46 |
| 1887 | 3,844 | 1,340 | ... | ... | 55 |
| 1888 | 4,411 | 1,412 | ... | ... | 75 |
| 1889 | 6,642 | 1,588 | ... | ... | 109 |
| 1890 | 5,421 | 1,667 | 442 | ... | 113 |
| 1891 | 4,621 | 1,527 | 406 | ... | 144 |
| 1892 | 6,038 | 1,849 | 488 | 366 | 112 |
| 1893 | 7,169 | 1,960 | 413 | 406 | 143 |
| 1894 | 8,143 | 1,971 | 419 | 521 | 126 |

## F2    SOUTH AMERICA: Freight Traffic on Railways

**1895–1939**

| | Argentina[9] | | Bolivia | | Brazil | | Chile[10] | | Colombia | |
|---|---|---|---|---|---|---|---|---|---|---|
| | a | b | a | b | a | b | a | b | a | b |
| 1895 | 9,650 | ... | ... | ... | ... | ... | 2,143 | ... | ... | ... |
| 1896 | 10,914 | ... | ... | ... | ... | ... | 2,110 | ... | ... | ... |
| 1897 | 8,981 | ... | ... | ... | ... | ... | 1,977 | ... | ... | ... |
| 1898 | 9,429 | ... | ... | ... | ... | ... | 2,026 | ... | ... | ... |
| 1899 | 11,819 | ... | ... | ... | ... | ... | 2,132 | ... | ... | ... |
| 1900 | 12,660 | ... | ... | ... | ... | ... | 2,229 | ... | ... | ... |
| 1901 | 13,988 | ... | ... | ... | ... | ... | 2,681[12] | ... | ... | ... |
| | | | | | | | 5,764 | | | |
| 1902 | 14,252 | ... | ... | ... | ... | ... | 5,772 | ... | ... | ... |
| 1903 | 17,302 | ... | ... | ... | ... | ... | 5,580 | ... | ... | ... |
| 1904 | 20,288 | ... | ... | ... | ... | ... | 5,393 | ... | ... | ... |
| 1905 | 22,770 | ... | ... | ... | ... | ... | 7,924 | ... | ... | ... |
| 1906 | 26,969 | ... | ... | ... | ... | ... | 7,817 | ... | ... | ... |
| 1907 | 27,934 | ... | ... | ... | ... | ... | 6,512 | ... | ... | ... |
| 1908 | 32,194 | ... | ... | | ... | ... | ... | ... | ... | ... |
| 1909 | 31,200 | ... | ... | | ... | ... | 8,253 | ... | ... | ... |
| 1910 | 32,562 | ... | ... | ... | ... | ... | 12,179 | ... | ... | ... |
| 1911 | 34,961 | ... | ... | ... | ... | ... | 9,807 | ... | 568 | ... |
| 1912 | 41,312 | ... | ... | ... | ... | ... | 9,842 | ... | ... | ... |
| 1913 | 42,917 | ... | ... | ... | ... | ... | 10,793 | ... | ... | ... |
| 1914 | 34,296 | ... | ... | ... | ... | ... | 8,343 | ... | ... | ... |
| 1915 | 31,939 | ... | ... | ... | ... | ... | 8,164 | ... | 797 | ... |
| 1916 | 32,005 | ... | ... | ... | 13,015 | 1,691 | 10,587 | ... | 858 | ... |
| 1917 | 32,681 | ... | ... | ... | 15,049 | 3,003 | 10,991 | ... | 930 | ... |
| 1918 | 30,570 | ... | ... | ... | 15,382 | 2,294 | 15,498 | ... | 825 | ... |
| 1919 | 37,342 | ... | ... | ... | 15,564 | 2,129 | 8,209 | ... | 1,055 | ... |
| 1920 | 44,783 | ... | ... | ... | 16,555 | 2,231 | 9,293 | ... | 1,331 | ... |
| 1921 | 37,533 | ... | ... | ... | 15,933 | 2,105 | 8,131 | ... | 1,504 | ... |
| 1922 | 34,457[9] | ... | ... | ... | 16,232 | 2,226 | 7,072 | ... | 1,129 | ... |
| 1923 | 38,804 | ... | ... | ... | 19,049 | 2,721 | 10,170 | ... | 1,582 | ... |
| 1924 | 43,181 | ... | ... | ... | 20,337 | 2,838 | 18,161 | ... | 1,820 | ... |
| 1925 | 44,281 | ... | ... | ... | 22,737 | 3,443 | 19,796 | ... | 2,101 | ... |
| 1926 | 45,134 | ... | ... | ... | 22,713 | 3,444 | 17,684 | ... | 2,650 | ... |
| 1927 | 50,880 | ... | ... | ... | 24,391 | 3,894 | 29,529 | 1,432 | 3,068 | ... |
| 1928 | 52,782 | 13,779 | ... | ... | 24,995 | 4,231 | 34,232 | 1,552 | 3,315 | ... |
| 1929 | 52,596[9] | 14,090[9] | ... | ... | 25,764 | 3,178 | 38,472 | 1,711 | 3,134 | ... |
| 1930 | 44,532 | 11,445 | ... | 108 | 18,949 | 3,679 | 26,835 | 1,430 | 2,197 | ... |
| 1931 | 44,728 | 12,063 | ... | 82 | 20,725 | 3,570 | 21,291 | 1,057 | [1,192][12] | [121][12] |
| 1932 | 44,043 | 10,720 | ... | 69 | 20,411 | 3,404 | 9,843 | 874 | [1,246][12] | [95][12] |
| 1933 | 38,825 | 10,078 | ... | 71 | 22,245 | 3,554 | 13,081 | 1,096 | [1,535][12] | [121][12] |
| 1934 | 40,162 | 11,086 | ... | 88 | 23,283 | 3,697 | 23,900[10] | 1,410 | 2,523 | 179 |
| | | | | | | | 7,675 | | | |
| 1935 | 43,189 | 11,702 | ... | 123 | 26,231 | 4,318 | 8,019 | 1,478 | 2,582 | 212 |
| 1936 | 42,372 | 12,276 | ... | 140 | 22,636 | 4,851 | 8,586 | 1,480 | 2,820 | 252 |
| 1937 | 51,027 | 13,507 | ... | 164 | 31,169 | 5,404 | 9,752 | 1,686 | 2,829 | 276 |
| 1938 | 42,255 | 11,730 | 1,224 | 175 | 33,479 | 5,995 | 10,036 | 1,768 | 2,903 | 294 |
| 1939 | 45,213 | 12,340 | 1,323 | 178 | 34,829 | 6,126 | 9,925 | 1,842 | 2,836 | 296 |

F2        **SOUTH AMERICA: Freight Traffic on Railways**

1895–1934

| | Ecuador[13] | | Paraguay | Peru | | Uruguay[11] | | Venezuela |
|---|---|---|---|---|---|---|---|---|
| | a | b | a | a | b | a | b | a |
| 1895 | ... | ... | ... | 432 | ... | 617 | ... | 154 |
| 1896 | ... | ... | ... | 475 | ... | 607 | ... | 173 |
| 1897 | ... | ... | ... | 506 | ... | 509 | ... | 158 |
| 1898 | ... | ... | ... | 544 | ... | 513 | ... | 145 |
| 1899 | ... | ... | ... | 596 | ... | 567 | ... | 117 |
| 1900 | ... | ... | ... | 676 | ... | 614 | ... | 137 |
| 1901 | ... | ... | ... | 760 | ... | 701 | ... | 137 |
| 1902 | ... | ... | ... | 678 | ... | 743 | ... | 112 |
| 1903 | ... | ... | ... | 804 | ... | 715 | ... | 156 |
| 1904 | ... | ... | ... | 862 | ... | 746 | ... | 165 |
| 1905 | ... | ... | ... | 922 | ... | 836 | ... | 152 |
| 1906 | ... | ... | ... | 1,020 | ... | 945 | ... | 179 |
| 1907 | ... | ... | ... | 978 | ... | 1,175 | ... | 188 |
| 1908 | ... | ... | ... | 1,450 | ... | 1,211 | ... | 184 |
| 1909 | ... | ... | ... | 1,441 | ... | 1,140 | ... | 164 |
| 1910 | 45 | ... | ... | 1,094 | ... | 1,250 | ... | 209 |
| 1911 | ... | ... | ... | 828 | ... | 1,306 | ... | 229 |
| 1912 | ... | ... | ... | 1,680 | ... | 1,378 | ... | 279 |
| 1913 | ... | ... | ... | 1,701 | ... | 1,569 | ... | 283 |
| 1914 | ... | ... | 156 | 1,661 | ... | 1,296 | ... | 269 |
| 1915 | ... | ... | ... | 1,813 | ... | 1,324 | ... | 273 |
| 1916 | ... | ... | ... | 2,106 | ... | 1,494 | ... | 306 |
| 1917 | ... | ... | ... | 2,357 | ... | 1,534 | ... | 365 |
| 1918 | ... | ... | ... | 2,677 | ... | 1,673 | ... | 334 |
| 1919 | ... | ... | ... | 2,444 | 180 | 1,799 | ... | 362 |
| 1920 | 96 | ... | ... | 2,632 | 173 | 1,526 | ... | 366 |
| 1921 | ... | ... | ... | 2,292 | 158 | ... | ... | 320 |
| 1922 | ... | ... | 83 | 2,342 | 158 | ... | ... | 338 |
| 1923 | ... | ... | 149 | 2,390 | 169 | 1,375 | ... | 400 |
| 1924 | 132 | ... | 164 | 2,597 | 169 | 1,579 | ... | 440 |
| 1925 | 112 | ... | 186 | 1,927 | 126 | 1,487 | ... | 529 |
| 1926 | 147 | ... | 175 | 2,733 | 175 | 1,692 | ... | 529 |
| 1927 | 157 | ... | 166 | 2,628 | 130 | ... | ... | 401 |
| 1928 | 164 | ... | 176 | 2,793 | 197 | 2,037 | 357 | 493 |
| 1929 | 165 | ... | 165 | 3,151 | 206 | 1,844 | 355 | 457 |
| 1930 | 160 | ... | 149 | 3,072 | ... | 1,993 | 354 | 467 |
| 1931 | 136 | ... | 123 | 2,342 | 160 | 2,104 | 384 | 411 |
| 1932 | 116 | ... | ... | 1,814 | 119 | 1,614 | 297 | 274 |
| 1933 | 144 | ... | 170 | 1,620 | 102 | 1,387[11] | 283[11] | 289 |
| 1934 | 187 | ... | ... | 1,838 | 121 | 1,539 | ... | 285 |
| 1935 | 221 | ... | 147 | 2,354 | 213 | 1,714 | 354 | 321 |
| 1936 | 236 | 58 | 132 | 2,986 | 287 | 1,896 | 361 | 348 |
| 1937 | 243 | 64 | 136 | 2,911 | 287 | 1,866 | 361 | 341 |
| 1938 | 274[13] 321 | 67 | 120 | 3,000 | 292 | 1,963 | 370 | 352 |
| 1939 | 279 | 41 | 129 | 3,024 | 304 | 2,025 | 395 | 454 |

F2    SOUND AMERICA: Freight Traffic on Railways

1940–1988

| | Argentina[9] | | Bolivia | | Brazil | | Chile[10] | | Colombia | |
|---|---|---|---|---|---|---|---|---|---|---|
| | a | b | a | b | a | b | a | b | a | b |
| 1940 | 43,178 | 12,880 | 1,445 | 219 | 35,066 | 6,075 | 9,794 | 2,031 | 2,768 | 309 |
| 1941 | 40,540 | 13,128 | 1,679 | 244 | 34,973 | 6,490 | 10,032 | 1,999 | 2,854 | 313 |
| 1942 | 46,163 | 15,026 | 1,691 | 267 | 36,558 | 6,592 | 10,153 | 2,070 | 3,246 | 369 |
| 1943 | 51,286 | 16,784 | 1,786 | 237 | 38,882 | 6,992 | 10,656 | 2,190 | 3,999 | 450 |
| 1944 | 52,925 | 17,744 | 1,662 | 236 | 41,261 | 7,385 | 10,740 | 2,222 | 4,041 | 459 |
| 1945 | 52,697 | 17,404 | 1,498 | 253 | 39,672 | 7,218 | 11,263 | 2,357 | 4,423 | 526 |
| 1946 | 52,914 | 16,776 | 1,506 | 229 | 40,563 | 7,417 | 10,901 | 2,318 | 4,543 | 572 |
| 1947 | 50,139 | 16,002 | 1,654 | | 39,378 | 7,512 | 11,389 | 2,317 | 4,329 | 546 |
| 1948 | 48,827[9] | 17,416[9] | 1,829 | 291 | 37,800 | 7,758 | 12,737 | 2,295 | 4,481 | 577 |
| 1949 | 37,261 | 16,325 | 1,734 | 270 | 39,378 | 8,101 | 15,939 | 2,175 | 4,817 | 608 |
| 1950 | 38,648 | 17,309 | 1,683 | 249 | 38,040 | 8,066 | 14,660 | 2,102 | 4,626 | 558 |
| 1951 | 39,186[9] | 17,681[9] | 1,966 | 310 | 42,655 | 8,733 | 13,845 | 2,368 | 4,605 | 546 |
| | 34,253 | 16,429 | | | | | | | | |
| 1952 | 32,447 | 15,255 | 1,955 | 319 | 40,747 | 9,155 | 14,012 | 2,493 | 4,579 | 551 |
| 1953 | 33,322 | 15,016 | 1,799 | 294 | 40,316 | 10,155 | 12,863 | 2,440 | 4,709 | 618 |
| 1954 | 34,038 | 15,197 | 1,796 | 296 | 41,431 | 9,252 | 12,731 | 2,488 | 4,744 | 618 |
| 1955 | 32,154 | 15,392 | 1,814 | … | 41,369 | 9,069 | 12,589 | 2,563 | 4,676 | 581 |
| 1956 | 31,179 | 14,873 | 1,924 | … | 39,934 | 9,709 | 12,452 | 2,489 | 4,809 | 592 |
| 1957 | 30,093 | 14,367 | 1,591 | 300 | 40,300 | 10,220 | 11,421 | 2,225 | 5,158 | 655 |
| 1958 | 30,197 | 15,043 | 1,254 | 228 | 42,494 | 10,471 | 12,861 | 2,146 | 5,979 | 654 |
| 1959 | 33,954[9] | 15,526 | 1,049 | … | 43,660 | 12,034 | 12,655 | 2,220 | 5,872 | 804 |
| | 26,799 | | | | | | | | | |
| 1960 | 26,166 | 15,188 | 1,062 | 186 | 43,727 | 12,079 | 13,032 | 1,953 | 5,441 | 768 |
| 1961 | 21,965 | 14,014 | 1,220 | 203 | 43,885 | 11,340 | 12,839 | 1,899 | 5,169 | 769 |
| 1962 | 18,653 | 11,655 | … | 219 | 47,353 | 14,921 | 14,823 | 2,033 | 4,487 | 918 |
| 1963 | 16,914 | 10,631 | 1,040 | 246 | 53,446 | 17,914 | 15,325 | 2,326 | 3,655 | 891 |
| 1964 | 21,340 | 13,065 | 1,040 | 221 | 52,041 | 16,387 | 16,764 | 2,349 | 3,317 | 952 |
| 1965 | 23,407 | 14,027 | 945 | 301 | 53,747 | 18,259 | 19,517 | 2,621 | 3,062 | 934 |
| 1966 | 22,036 | 13,459 | 985 | 288 | 53,818 | 18,861 | 23,024 | 2,760 | 3,312 | 1,114 |
| 1967 | 16,820 | 11,355 | 955 | 321 | 54,301 | 19,487 | 20,085 | 2,505 | 3,169 | 996 |
| 1968 | 19,836 | 12,914 | 1,036 | 316 | 59,471 | 21,528 | 21,413 | 2,637 | 3,240 | 1,125 |
| 1969 | 20,987 | 13,318 | 1,189 | 382 | 48,073 | 16,150 | 19,281 | 2,652 | 3,050 | 1,159 |
| 1970 | 22,123 | 13,640 | 1,076 | 456 | 49,747 | 17,267 | 19,069 | 2,533 | 2,781 | 1,173 |
| 1971 | 21,553 | 13,654 | 1,122 | 351 | 47,404 | 17,178 | 19,490 | 2,718 | 2,653 | 1,150 |
| 1972 | 18,313 | 12,489 | 971 | 361 | 77,789 | 33,308 | 16,580 | 2,549 | 2,731 | 1,198 |
| 1973 | 19,091 | 12,508 | 955 | 365 | 94,531 | 42,508 | 18,039 | 2,709 | 2,760 | 1,331 |
| 1974 | 19,122 | 12,357 | 1,122 | 388 | 115,190 | 54,664 | 17,564 | 2,539 | 2,899 | 1,329 |
| | | | | | c | d | | | | |
| 1975 | 16,272 | 10,659 | 1,141 | 470 | 124 | 59 | 17,366 | 2,416 | 2,439 | 1,139 |
| 1976 | 17,800 | 11,047 | 1,080 | 523 | 130 | 63 | 16,877 | 2,163 | 2,411 | 1,157 |
| 1977 | 20,169 | 11,578 | 1,178 | 583 | 126 | 61 | 15,514 | 2,150 | 2,519 | 1,215 |
| 1978 | 17,158 | 9,871 | 1,185 | 593 | 133 | 64 | 15,261 | 1,965 | 2,682 | 1,232 |
| 1979 | 19,128 | 10,947 | 1,196 | 601 | 155 | 74 | 15,351 | 1,849 | 2,394 | 1,105 |
| 1980 | 16,274 | 9,468 | 1,302 | 646 | 181 | 86 | 16,962 | 1,943 | 1,935 | 862 |
| 1981 | 16,664 | 9,238 | 1,047 | 620 | 167 | 79 | 15,373 | 1,765 | 1,347 | 641 |
| 1982 | 19,098 | 11,472 | 994 | 484 | 168 | 78 | 13,135 | 1,773 | 1,097 | 562 |
| 1983 | 22,509 | 13,364 | 1,159 | 577 | 164 | 75 | 14,182 | 2,248 | 1,246 | 665 |
| 1984 | 19,502 | 11,208 | 971 | 548 | 196 | 92 | 15,148 | 2,315 | 1,267 | 733 |
| 1985 | 17,234 | 9,501 | … | 494 | 208 | 100 | 20,023 | 2,566 | 1,278 | 777 |
| 1986 | 15,018 | 8,761 | 923 | 464 | 213 | 104 | 21,343 | 2,510 | 1,186 | 691 |
| 1987 | 13,577 | 7,952 | 982 | 505 | 215 | 109 | 15,667 | 2,612 | 1,055 | 563 |
| 1988 | … | 8,979 | 872 | 424 | … | 105 | 19,418 | 2,809 | 934 | 464 |

**F2    SOUTH AMERICA: Freight Traffic on Railways**

| | Ecuador | | Paraguay | | Peru | | Uruguay | | Venezuela | |
|---|---|---|---|---|---|---|---|---|---|---|
| | a | b | a | b | a | b[14] | a | b | a | b |
| 1940 | 408 | 73 | 129 | ... | 3,017 | 299 | 1,983 | 395 | 426 | ... |
| 1941 | 411 | 74 | 126 | ... | 3,062 | 329 | 2,165 | 431 | 409 | ... |
| 1942 | 454 | 80 | 160 | ... | 3,195 | 355 | 2,160 | 409 | 455 | ... |
| 1943 | 517 | ... | 201 | ... | 3,271 | 357 | 2,580 | 457 | 529 | ... |
| 1944 | 525 | 101 | 192 | ... | 3,472 | 383 | 2,399 | 413 | 536 | ... |
| 1945 | 530 | 102 | 194 | ... | 3,564 | 403 | 1,911 | 404 | 531 | ... |
| 1946 | 551 | 114 | 170 | ... | 3,668 | 412 | 1,841 | 385 | 506 | ... |
| 1947 | 528 | 111 | 153 | ... | 3,378 | 385 | 1,519 | 324 | 426 | ... |
| 1948 | 507 | 105 | ... | 25 | 3,331 | 381 | 1,456 | 365 | 391 | ... |
| 1949 | 478 | 101 | ... | 31 | 3,534 | 404 | 1,545 | 434 | 374 | ... |
| 1950 | 484 | 101 | ... | 35 | 3,630 | 403 | 1,186 | 470 | 306 | 17 |
| 1951 | 506 | 109 | ... | 31 | 3,874 | 465 | 1,187 | ... | 162 | 10 |
| 1952 | 605 | 114 | ... | 34 | 4,078 | 509 | 1,128 | ... | 183 | 11 |
| 1953 | 501 | 101 | ... | 29 | 4,309 | 513 | 1,159 | ... | 197 | 13 |
| 1954 | 518 | 127 | 137 | 26 | 4,216 | 510 | 1,530 | ... | 162 | 25 |
| 1955 | 554 | 118 | 126 | 25 | 4,382 | 513 | 1,888 | 426 | 87 | 6 |
| 1956 | 426 | 106 | 138 | 24 | 4,799 | 560[14] 531 | 1,908 | ... | 87 | 8 |
| 1957 | ... | ... | 132 | 25 | 4,760 | 554 | 1,870 | ... | 87 | 9 |
| 1958 | 504 | ... | 106 | 21 | 3,986 | 481 | 1,700 | ... | 62 | 8 |
| 1959 | ... | ... | 202 | 18 | 3,577 | 420 | 1,662 | ... | 98 | 13 |
| 1960 | 537 | 121 | 83 | 16 | 4,214 | 506 | 1,737 | 399 | 172 | 20 |
| 1961 | 535 | 110 | 100 | 17 | 4,166 | 518 | 1,451 | ... | 118 | 14 |
| 1962 | 512 | 96 | 91 | 16 | 3,931 | 509 | 1,396 | ... | 195 | 24 |
| 1963 | 498 | 97 | 95 | 18 | 4,040 | 536 | 1,295 | ... | 174 | 21 |
| 1964 | 523 | 104 | 112 | 20 | 4,390 | 622 | 1,641 | 255 | 221 | 26 |
| 1965 | ... | 84 | 95 | 19 | 4,456 | 646 | 1,660 | 332 | 249 | 32 |
| 1966 | 377 | 72 | 78 | 16 | 4,388 | 658 | 1,665 | ... | 207 | 26 |
| 1967 | 323 | 63 | 74 | 17 | 3,987 | 625 | 1,301 | 370 | 136 | 17 |
| 1968 | 314 | 59 | 95 | 22 | 3,469 | 591 | 1,359 | 320 | 113 | 12 |
| 1969 | 295 | 61 | 114 | 27 | 3,222 | 591 | 1,109 | 261 | 92 | 10 |
| 1970 | 278 | 56 | 127 | 30 | ... | 610 | ... | 250 | 108 | 13 |
| 1971 | 275 | 55 | 121 | 30 | ... | 610 | ... | 222 | 130 | 12 |
| 1972 | 232 | 43 | 161 | 35 | ... | 547 | ... | 134 | 236 | 17 |
| 1973 | 274 | 57 | 132 | 30 | ... | 613 | ... | 196 | 117 | 13 |
| 1974 | 214 | 52 | 143 | 32 | ... | 630 | ... | 239 | 98 | 10 |
| 1975 | ... | 46 | 97 | 20 | ... | 605 | 1,424 | 281 | 118 | 14 |
| 1976 | ... | 26 | ... | 16 | ... | 635 | ... | 372 | 116 | 14 |
| 1977 | ... | 25 | ... | 17 | ... | 612 | ... | 307 | 167 | 20 |
| 1978 | ... | 34 | 94 | 23 | ... | 1,035 | ... | 303 | 163 | 20 |
| 1979 | ... | 29 | 163 | 30 | ... | 1,127 | ... | 269 | 174 | 18 |
| 1980 | ... | 14 | 187 | 32 | 5,752 | 1,133 | 1,400 | 234 | 192 | 21 |
| 1981 | ... | 15 | 215 | 23 | 4,166 | 1,039 | 1,200 | 218 | 122 | 14 |
| 1982 | ... | 14 | 244 | 34 | 4,252 | 974 | ... | 186 | 247 | 29 |
| 1983 | ... | 8 | 138 | 30 | 4,013 | 897 | 977 | 220 | 205 | 22 |
| 1984 | ... | 6 | 141 | 16 | 4,571 | 1,044 | ... | 273 | 103 | 11 |
| 1985 | ... | 9 | 156 | 13 | 4,640 | 1,036 | ... | 185 | 127 | 14 |
| 1986 | ... | 7 | ... | 17 | 4,334 | 1,022 | ... | 204 | 114 | 12 |
| 1987 | ... | 8 | ... | 20 | 4,550 | 1,034 | ... | 210 | 147 | 18 |
| 1988 | ... | 8 | ... | 17 | ... | 967 | ... | 212 | ... | 40 |

**F2    Freight Traffic on Railways**

NOTES

1.  SOURCES: The national publications listed on p. xiv–xvi with gaps filled from the League of Nations and UN, *Statistical Yearbooks*
2.  It is not always clear whether traffic for the servicing of the railways is included or not, though there appears to be an indicator whenever a change in this respect occurs.
3.  Livestock and passengers' baggage are not normally included with freight.

FOOTNOTES

[1] Years ending 30 June to 1919 (1st line). Newfoundland is included from 1950. Double-counting is eliminated from 1960 (2nd line).
[2] Freight carried to 1890 (1st line), freight originated subsequently. Freight carried free of charge is not included. Data for 1890 (2nd line) to 1916 (1st line) are for years ending 30 June. Alaska and Hawaii are included from 1960.
[3] Statistics to 1882 (1st line) relate to 13 companies, seven east and six west of Chicago.
[4] Years ending 30 June to 1946.
[5] Including service traffic subsequently.
[6] For the period 1941–46 the data for the Ferrocarril del Norte are for years beginning 1 July.
[7] Ferrocarril del Norte only from 1956 (except 1963.)
[8] Public railways only from 1945 (2nd line).
[9] Years ending 30 June to 1948. Service traffic is included to 1951 (1st line). The Ferrocarril Central de Chubut is not included in 1923–29. The reason for the break in the tonnage series in 1959 is not clear in the sources, but it may result from the exclusion of suburban railways.
[10] State railways only to 1901 (1st line). The reason for the break in 1934 is not clear from the sources but may be the later exclusion of mineral traffic on private lines, which was never included in the TKm series. More or less complete figures including private lines are available for certain years in the 1950s and 1960s as follows (excluding the Romeral-Guyacan line to 1960 for a and 1963 for b):—

|      | a      | b     |      | a      | b      |
|------|--------|-------|------|--------|--------|
| 1956 | 61,087 | 5,411 | 1961 | 92,075 | 43,927 |
| 1957 | 46,679 | 4,416 | 1962 | 27,718 | 2,959  |
| 1959 | 19,967 | 2,674 | 1963 | 49,517 | 4,326  |
| 1960 | 25,057 | 2,835 | 1964 | 53,434 | 4,469  |
|      |        |       | 1967 | 39,364 | 3,774  |

[11] Years ending 30 June to 1933.
[12] Excluding the Ferrocarril del Nordeste.
[13] Ferrocarril del Sur only to 1938 (1st line).
[14] Excluding service traffic from 1956 (2nd line).
[15] Subsequently Class I railways only.

**F3     NORTH AMERICA: PASSENGER TRAFFIC ON RAILWAYS**

Key:     a = million passenger journeys; b = million passenger-kilometres

1870–1909

|        | Canada[1] | Mexico | USA[2] | |
|--------|-----------|--------|--------|-------|
|        | a | a | a | b |
| 1870 | ... | ... | ... | ... |
| 1871 | ... | ... | ... | ... |
| 1872 | ... | ... | ... | ... |
| 1873 | ... | 0.7 | ... | ... |
| 1874 | ... | 1.0 | ... | ... |
| 1875 | 5.2 | 0.8 | ... | ... |
| 1876 | 5.5 | 0.7 | ... | ... |
| 1877 | 6.1 | 0.9 | ... | ... |
| 1878 | 6.4 | 0.8 | ... | ... |
| 1879 | 6.5 | 0.8 | ... | ... |
| 1880 | 6.5 | 1.0 | ... | ... |
| 1881 | 6.9 | 2.0 | ... | ... |
| 1882 | 9.4 | 2.4 | 289 | 12,373 |
| 1883 | 9.6 | 3.0 | 312 | 13,745 |
| 1884 | 10 | 3.4 | 334 | 14,128 |
| 1885 | 9.7 | 3.3 | 351 | 14,700 |
| 1886 | 9.9 | 3.5 | 382 | 15,546 |
| 1887 | 11 | 3.6 | 428 | 17,011 |
| 1888 | 11 | 3.9 | 451 | 18,010 |
| 1889 | 12 | 4.3 | 494 | 19,256 |
| 1890 | 13 | 5.4 | 520[2] / 492 | 20,152[2] |
| 1891 | 13 | 6.6 | 531 | 20,670 |
| 1892 | 14 | 5.2 | 561 | 21,506 |
| 1893 | 14 | 7.1 | 594 | 22,899 |
| 1894 | 14 | 4.2 | 541 | 22,996 |
| 1895 | 14 | 5.7 | 507 | 19,615 |
| 1896 | 15 | 4.9 | 512 | 21,000 |
| 1897 | 16 | 6.4 | 489 | 19,726 |
| 1898 | 18 | 9.4 | 501 | 21,533 |
| 1899 | 19 | 9.0 | 523 | 23,482 |
| 1900 | 22 | 11 | 577 | 25,811 |
| 1901 | 18 | 11 | 607 | 27,929 |
| 1902 | 21 | 12 | 650 | 31,688 |
| 1903 | 22 | 14 | 695 | 33,661 |
| 1904 | 24 | 15 | 715 | 35,282 |
| 1905 | 25 | 16 | 739 | 38,302 |
| 1906 | 28 | 16 | 798 | 40,502 |
| 1907 | 32 | ... | 874 | 44,609 |
| 1908 | 34 | 17 | 890 | 46,805 |
| 1909 | 33 | 18 | 891 | 46,846 |

**F3     NORTH AMERICA: Passenger Traffic on Railways**

### 1910–1949

| | Canada[1] | | Costa Rica[4] | | Cuba[3] | | El Salvador | Guatemala |
|---|---|---|---|---|---|---|---|---|
| | a | b | a | b[5] | a | b | a | a |
| 1910 | 36 | 3,970 | ... | ... | ... | ... | ... | ... |
| 1911 | 37 | 4,194 | ... | ... | ... | ... | ... | ... |
| 1912 | 41 | 4,683 | ... | ... | ... | ... | ... | ... |
| 1913 | 46 | 5,256 | ... | ... | 10 | 323 | 0.6 | ... |
| 1914 | 47 | 4,971 | ... | ... | ... | ... | ... | ... |
| 1915 | 46 | 3,925 | ... | ... | ... | ... | ... | ... |
| 1916 | 49 | 4,389 | ... | ... | ... | ... | ... | ... |
| 1917 | 48 | 5,069 | ... | ... | ... | ... | ... | ... |
| 1918 | 45 | 5,087 | ... | ... | ... | ... | ... | ... |
| 1919 | 44 [1] | 4,949 [1] | ... | ... | ... | ... | ... | ... |
| | 48 | 5,889 | | | | | | |
| 1920 | 51 | 5,670 | ... | ... | ... | ... | ... | ... |
| 1921 | 47 | 4,765 | ... | ... | ... | ... | ... | ... |
| 1922 | 44 | 4,529 | ... | ... | 23 | 504 | 1.1 | ... |
| 1923 | 45 | 4,950 | ... | ... | 25 | 546 | 1.3 | ... |
| 1924 | 43 | 4,622 | ... | ... | 26 | 653 | 1.4 | ... |
| 1925 | 42 | 4,685 | ... | ... | 28 | 684 | 1.5 | ... |
| 1926 | 43 | 4,826 | ... | ... | 26 | 613 | ... | ... |
| 1927 | 42 | 4,912 | 1.3 | ... | 32 | ... | 1.8 | ... |
| 1928 | 41 | 5,055 | 1.4 | ... | 24 | ... | 1.7 | ... |
| 1929 | 39 | 4,662 | 1.3 | ... | 23 [3] | ... [3] | ... | ... |
| 1930 | 35 | 3,899 | 1.3 | ... | ... | ... | 1.3 | ... |
| 1931 | 26 | 2,813 | 0.9 | ... | ... | ... | 0.7 | ... |
| 1932 | 21 | 2,311 | 0.5 | ... | ... | ... | 0.8 | ... |
| 1933 | 19 | 2,242 | 0.5 | ... | ... | ... | 1.1 | ... |
| 1934 | 21 | 2,464 | 0.5 | ... | ... | ... | 1.1 | ... |
| 1935 | 20 | 2,551 | 0.6 | ... | ... | ... | 1.1 | ... |
| 1936 | 21 | 2,778 | 0.7 | ... | ... | ... | 1.0 | ... |
| 1937 | 22 | 3,104 | 0.8 | ... | 7.1 | 204 | 1.0 | 1.8 |
| 1938 | 21 | 2,869 | 0.9 | ... | 9.7 | 221 | 0.9 | 1.6 |
| 1939 | 21 | 2,820 | 0.9 | ... | 9.5 | 212 | 0.9 | 1.7 |
| 1940 | 22 | 3,504 | 0.7 [4] | ... | 5.8 | 248 | 0.9 | 1.5 |
| 1941 | 30 | 5,160 | 0.8 | ... | 6.7 | 270 | 0.8 | 1.5 |
| 1942 | 48 | 8,029 | 1.0 | ... | 7.7 | 379 | 1.4 | 1.8 |
| 1943 | 57 | 10,501 | 1.3 | ... | 11 | 522 | 2.1 | 2.5 |
| 1944 | 60 | 11,061 | 1.2 | ... | 14 | 617 | 2.7 | 3.2 |
| 1945 | 53 | 10,268 | 1.2 [4] | ... | 16 | 739 | 3.2 | 3.9 |
| 1946 | 43 | 7,482 | 1.2 | ... | 16 [3] | 737 [3] | 3.2 | 4.2 |
| 1947 | 41 | 6,008 | 1.2 | 57 | 15 | 667 | 3.3 | 4.1 |
| 1948 | 38 | 5,596 | 1.3 | 49 | 14 | 562 | 3.5 | 3.9 |
| 1949 | 35 [1] | 5,139 [1] | 1.4 | 56 | 13 | 515 | 3.3 | 3.8 |

**F3  NORTH AMERICA: Passenger Traffic on Railways**

**1910–1949**

| | Mexico | | Nicaragua | | Panama | USA[2] | |
|---|---|---|---|---|---|---|---|
| | a | b | a | b | a | a | b |
| 1910 | ... | ... | ... | ... | ... | 972 | 52,043 |
| 1911 | ... | ... | ... | ... | ... | 997 | 53,433 |
| 1912 | ... | ... | ... | ... | ... | 1,004 | 53,321 |
| 1913 | ... | ... | ... | ... | ... | 1,044 | 55,801 |
| 1914 | ... | ... | ... | ... | ... | 1,063 | 56,902 |
| 1915 | ... | ... | ... | ... | ... | 986 | 52,263 |
| 1916 | ... | ... | ... | ... | ... | 1,015[2] | 55,215[2] |
| | | | | | | 1,049 | 56,681 |
| 1917 | ... | ... | ... | ... | ... | 1,110 | 64,535 |
| 1918 | ... | ... | ... | ... | ... | 1,123 | 69,543 |
| 1919 | ... | ... | ... | ... | ... | 1,211 | 75,378 |
| 1920 | ... | ... | ... | ... | ... | 1,270 | 76,235 |
| 1921 | 25 | 2,134 | ... | ... | ... | 1,061 | 60,682 |
| 1922 | 22 | 1,610 | ... | ... | ... | 990 | 57,632 |
| 1923 | 22 | 1,604 | ... | ... | ... | 1,009 | 61,628 |
| 1924 | 21 | 1,687 | ... | ... | ... | 950 | 58,529 |
| 1925 | 24 | 1,687 | ... | ... | ... | 902 | 58,205 |
| 1926 | 24 | 1,484 | ... | ... | ... | 875 | 57,410 |
| 1927 | 23 | 1,515 | ... | ... | ... | 840 | 54,393 |
| 1928 | 22 | 1,502 | ... | ... | ... | 798 | 51,045 |
| 1929 | 21 | 1,629 | ... | ... | ... | 786 | 50,155 |
| 1930 | 21 | 1,448 | ... | 29 | ... | 708 | 43,253 |
| 1931 | 17 | 1,123 | ... | 25 | ... | 599 | 35,298 |
| 1932 | 15 | 929 | ... | 20 | ... | 481 | 27,354 |
| 1933 | 17 | 1,005 | ... | 17 | ... | 435 | 26,342 |
| 1934 | 21 | 1,160 | ... | 17 | 0.2 | 452 | 29,079 |
| 1935 | 24 | 1,382 | 0.9 | 33 | ... | 448 | 29,787 |
| 1936 | 26 | 1,571 | 1.2 | 46 | ... | 492 | 36,146 |
| 1937 | 27 | 1,719 | 1.5 | 55 | ... | 500 | 39,743 |
| 1938 | 29 | 1,789 | 1.3 | 46 | ... | 455 | 34,854 |
| 1939 | 30 | 1,841 | 1.4 | 49 | 0.3 | 454 | 36,553 |
| 1940 | 28 | 1,844 | 1.6 | 55 | 0.3 | 456 | 38,239 |
| 1941 | 28 | 1,976 | 1.7 | 57 | 0.3 | 489 | 47,324 |
| 1942 | 32 | 2,284 | 1.8 | 64 | 0.4 | 672 | 86,497 |
| 1943 | 36 | 3,022 | 2.1 | 75 | 0.5 | 888 | 141,502 |
| 1944 | 38 | 3,598 | 2.4 | 84 | 0.5 | 916 | 153,955 |
| 1945 | 35 | 3,405 | 2.6 | 98 | 0.6 | 897 | 147,780 |
| 1946 | 33 | 3,009 | 2.8 | 98 | 0.6 | 795 | 104,211 |
| 1947 | 32 | 2,885 | 2.8 | 97 | 0.6 | 707 | 73,985 |
| 1948 | 30 | 2,664 | ... | 97 | 0.7 | 646 | 66,344 |
| 1949 | 31 | 2,787 | ... | 95 | 0.6 | 557 | 56,541 |

## F3 NORTH AMERICA: Passenger Traffic on Railways

### 1950–1988

| | Canada[1] | | Costa Rica[4] | | Cuba[3] | | El Salvador | | Guatemala |
|---|---|---|---|---|---|---|---|---|---|
| | a | b | a | b[5] | a | b | a | b | a |
| 1950 | 31 | 4,532 | 1.4 | 52 | 15 | 567 | 3.7 | ... | 3.8 |
| 1951 | 31 | 5,005 | 1.5 | 50 | 14 | 563 | 4.1 | ... | 3.9 |
| 1952 | 30 | 5,071 | 1.6 | 50 | 12 | 462 | 4.0 | ... | 4.0 |
| 1953 | 29 | 4,806 | 1.4 | 51 | 9.3 | 357 | 3.8 | ... | 4.2 |
| 1954 | 28 | 4,608 | 1.4 | 63 | 8.5 | 322 | 3.6 | ... | 4.2 |
| 1955 | 27 | 4,654 | 1.3 | 63 | 7 | 295 | 3.7 | ... | 4.2 |
| 1956 | 26 | 4,680 | 1.4 | 64 [5] | 6.3 [3] | 278 [3] | 3.6 | ... | 3.9 |
| 1957 | 23 | 4,707 | 1.4 | 31 | ... | ... | 3.5 | ... | 3.5 |
| 1958 | 21 | 4,001 | 1.5 | 34 | ... | ... | 3.3 | ... | 3.0 |
| 1959 | 21 | 3,936 | 1.6 | 36 | ... | ... | 3.1 | ... | 2.5 |
| 1960 | 19 | 3,644 | 1.6 | 37 | ... | ... | 2.8 | ... | 2.0 |
| 1961 | 19 | 3,155 | 1.6 | 38 | ... | ... | 2.7 | ... | 1.8 |
| 1962 | 19 | 3,249 | 1.6 | 36 | 14 | 899 | 2.8 | ... | 1.7 |
| 1963 | 21 | 3,331 | 1.5 | 21 | 13 | 918 | 2.7 | ... | 1.8 |
| 1964 | 23 | 4,315 | 1.5 | ... | 11 | 725 | 2.5 | ... | 1.8 |
| 1965 | 25 | 4,287 | ... | ... | 12 | 822 | 2.2 | ... | 1.6 |
| 1966 | 23 | 4,166 | 1.7 | [72] [5] | 15 | 922 | 1.8 | ... | 1.6 |
| 1967 | 27 | 5,103 | 1.9 | 60 | 18 | 1,168 | 1.7 | ... | 1.4 |
| 1968 | 25 | 4,230 | 2.1 | 71 | 20 | 1,302 | 1.5 | ... | 1.1 |
| 1969 | 24 | 3,890 | 2.3 | 69 | 20 | 1,434 | 1.5 | ... | 1.1 |
| 1970 | 24 | 3,657 | 2.3 | 55 | 13 | 1,130 | 1.6 | 33 | 1.3 |
| 1971 | 24 | 3,518 | 2.4 | 57 | 12 | 990 | 1.6 | ... | 1.3 |
| 1972 | 23 | 3,288 [6] | 2.6 | 53 | 10 | 946 | 1.7 | ... | 1.5 |
| 1973 | 20 | 2,573 | 2.8 | 85 | 10 | 609 | 1.7 | ... | 1.1 |
| 1974 | 24 | 3,023 | 2.9 | 81 [5] | 10 | 636 | 1.9 | ... | 1.7 |
| 1975 | 24 | 2,658 | 2.6 | 128 | 11 | 668 | 1.5 | 23 | 1.6 |
| 1976 | ... | 2,942 | ... | 99 | 13 | 767 | 1.7 | 26 | ... |
| 1977 | ... | 2,966 | ... | ... | 15 | 1,076 | 2.0 | 30 | ... |
| 1978 | ... | 3,200 | ... | ... | 18 | 1,571 | 2.0 | 31 | ... |
| 1979 | ... | 3,175 | ... | ... | 18 | 1,636 | 2.0 | 30 | ... |
| 1980 | ... | 3,280 | ... | ... | 20 | 1,802 | 1.7 | 27 | ... |
| 1981 | 24 | 3,276 | ... | ... | 20 | 1,916 | 0.9 | 14 | ... |
| 1982 | 21 | 2,640 | 2.4 | 152 | 23 | 2,073 | 0.4 | 5.9 | ... |
| 1983 | ... | 2,932 | 2.5 | ... | 23 | 2,144 | 0.2 | 3.8 | ... |
| 1984 | 22 | 2,915 | 2.0 | 79 | 25 | 2,360 | 0.3 | 4.7 | ... |
| 1985 | 23 | 3,040 | ... | ... | 23 | 2,257 | 0.3 | 4.7 | ... |
| 1986 | 23 | 2,831 | ... | ... | ... | 2,200 | 0.3 | 5.0 | ... |
| 1987 | ... | 1,920 | ... | 57 | ... | 2,189 | 0.4 | 5.6 | ... |
| 1988 | 27 | 2,709 | 1.3 | ... | ... | 2,627 | ... | 6.0 | ... |

**F3      NORTH AMERICA: Passenger Traffic on Railways**

**1950–1988**

| | Honduras | Mexico | | Nicaragua | | Panama | USA[2] | |
|---|---|---|---|---|---|---|---|---|
| | a | a | b | a | b | a | a | b |
| 1950 | 1.4 | 32 | 3,025 | 3.0 | 100 | 0.7 | 488 | 51,161 |
| 1951 | 1.6 | 33 | 3,363 | 3.1 | 95 | 0.8 | 485 | 55,748 |
| 1952 | 1.7 | 31 | 3,328 | 3.3 | 113 | 0.8 | 471 | 54,771 |
| 1953 | 1.6 | 28 | 2,987 | 3.5 | 118 | 0.7 | 458 | 50,982 |
| 1954 | 1.5 | 31 | 3,259 | 3.6 | 124 | 0.7 | 441 | 47,170 |
| 1955 | 1.0 | 34 | 3,764 | 3.6 | 128 | 0.9 | 433 | 45,944 |
| 1956 | 1.0 | 35 | 3,861 | 3.4 | 118 | 1.0 | 430 | 45,409 |
| 1957 | 0.9 | 33 | 3,837 | 3.1 | 115 | 1.0 | 413 | 41,705 |
| 1958 | 0.8 | 29 | 3,491 | 2.7 | 109 | 0.9 | 382 | 37,490 |
| 1959 | 0.7 | 31 | 3,725 | 2.0 | 77 | 0.9 | 354 [2] | 35,526 [2] |
| 1960 | 0.7 | 33 | 4,128 | 1.5 | 60 | 0.8 | 327 | 34,253 |
| 1961 | 0.7 | 34 | 4,288 | 1.5 | 56 | 0.8 | 318 | 32,683 |
| 1962 | 0.7 | 35 | 3,770 | 1.5 | 59 | 0.7 | 313 | 32,068 |
| 1963 | 0.7 | 36 | 3,889 | 1.4 | 55 | 0.6 | 311 | 29,803 |
| 1964 | 0.7 | 37 | 4,097 | 1.4 | 54 | 0.5 | 314 | 29,404 |
| 1965 | 0.6 | 37 | 3,882 | 1.3 | 51 | 0.5 | 306 | 28,089 |
| 1966 | 0.3 | 38 | 4,062 | 1.2 | 43 | 0.4 | 308 | 27,620 |
| 1967 | 0.3 | 39 | 4,442 | 1.1 | 43 | 0.4 | 304 | 24,565 |
| 1968 | 1.6 | 39 | 4,344 | 0.9 | 35 | 0.4 | 301 | 21,185 |
| 1969 | 1.5 | 39 | 4,633 | 0.8 | 30 | 0.4 | 302 | 19,657 |
| 1970 | 0.1 | 37 | 4,534 | 0.8 | 30 | 0.5 | 289 | 17,358 |
| 1971 | 1.3 | 34 | 4,362 | 0.8 | 31 | 0.5 | 276 | 14,264 |
| 1972 | 0.8 | 34 | 4,467 | 0.7 | 28 | 0.5 | 262 | 13,795 |
| 1973 | 0.1 | 29 | 4,057 | 0.5 | 23 | 0.4 | 255 | 14,980 |
| 1974 | 0.1 | 25 | 4,614 | 0.6 | 22 | 0.5 | 275 | 16,655 |
| 1975 | ... | 25 | 4,123 | 0.4 | 18 | ... | 270 | 15,715 |
| 1976 | ... | 24 | 4,058 | ... | 20 | ... | 272 | 15,688 |
| 1977 | ... | 29 | 5,040 | ... | 19 | ... | 276 | 16,565 |
| 1978 | ... | 29 | 5,326 | 0.4 | 17 | ... | 262 | 16,452 |
| 1979 | ... | 25 | 5,253 | ... | 15 | ... | 274 | 18,025 |
| 1980 | ... | 24 | 5,296 | ... | 19 | ... | 281 | 17,695 |
| 1981 | ... | 23 | 5,287 | 0.6 | 20 | ... | ... [12] | 18,371 |
| 1982 | ... | 22 | 5,351 | ... | 25 | ... | 19 | 16,966 |
| 1983 | ... | 23 | 5,630 | ... | 45 | ... | 19 | 17,606 |
| 1984 | ... | 24 | 5,951 | ... | 60 | ... | 20 | 16,564 |
| | | | | | | | | 17,649 [12] |
| 1985 | ... | 23 | 6,015 | 2.4 | 66 | | 21 | 8,008 |
| 1986 | ... | 22 | 5,874 | 3.5 | ... | 0.1 | 20 | 8,069 |
| 1987 | ... | 22 | 5,828 | ... | ... | - - | 21 | 8,639 |
| 1988 | ... | 21 | 5,691 | ... | ... | - - | 21 | 9,147 |

## F3 SOUTH AMERICA: PASSENGER TRAFFIC ON RAILWAYS

### 1855–1894

| | Argentina[7] | Chile[8] | Peru[9] | Uruguay[10] | Venezuela |
|---|---|---|---|---|---|
| | a | a | a | a | a |
| 1855 | ... | ... | ... | ... | ... |
| 1856 | ... | ... | ... | ... | ... |
| 1857 | 0.1 | ... | ... | ... | ... |
| 1858 | 0.2 | ... | ... | ... | ... |
| 1859 | 0.3 | ... | ... | ... | ... |
| 1860 | ... | ... | ... | ... | ... |
| 1861 | ... | ... | ... | ... | ... |
| 1862 | 0.4 | ... | ... | ... | ... |
| 1863 | 0.4 | ... | ... | ... | ... |
| 1864 | 0.6 | ... | ... | ... | ... |
| 1865 | 0.7 | ... | ... | ... | ... |
| 1866 | 1.2 | ... | ... | ... | ... |
| 1867 | 1.6 | ... | ... | ... | ... |
| 1868 | 1.7 | ... | ... | ... | ... |
| 1869 | 1.9 | ... | ... | ... | ... |
| 1870 | 1.9 | ... | ... | ... | ... |
| 1871 | 2.5 | ... | ... | ... | ... |
| 1872 | 2.2 | ... | ... | ... | ... |
| 1873 | 2.7 | ... | ... | ... | ... |
| 1874 | 2.6 | ... | ... | ... | ... |
| 1875 | 2.6 | ... | ... | ... | ... |
| 1876 | 2.3 | 1.4 | ... | ... | ... |
| 1877 | 2.4 | 1.3 | ... | ... | ... |
| 1878 | 2.5 | 1.2 | ... | ... | ... |
| 1879 | 2.6 | 1.3 | ... | ... | ... |
| 1880 | 2.8 | 1.4 | ... | ... | ... |
| 1881 | 3.3 | 1.8 | ... | ... | ... |
| 1882 | 3.6 | 2.1 | ... | ... | ... |
| 1883 | 4.1 | 2.3 | ... | ... | - - |
| 1884 | 4.8 | 2.5 | ... | ... | - - |
| 1885 | 5.8 | 2.7 | ... | ... | 0.1 |
| 1886 | 4.7 | ... | ... | ... | - - |
| 1887 | 8.2 | 2.5 | ... | ... | 0.1 |
| 1888 | 10 | 3.0 | ... | ... | 0.2 |
| 1889 | 11 | 3.4 | ... | ... | 0.2 |
| 1890 | 10 | 3.6 | 2.6 | ... | 0.2 |
| 1891 | 11 | 2.8 | 2.6 | ... | 0.2 |
| 1892 | 12 | 4.2 | 2.6 | 0.6 | 0.2 |
| 1893 | 13 | 4.7 | 2.8 | 0.5 | 0.2 |
| 1894 | 14 | 5.3 | 2.6 | 0.6 | 0.4 |

### 1895–1939

| | Argentina[7] | | Bolivia[11] | |
|---|---|---|---|---|
| | a | b | a | b |
| 1895 | 15 | ... | ... | ... |
| 1896 | 17 | ... | ... | ... |
| 1897 | 16 | ... | ... | ... |
| 1898 | 16 | ... | ... | ... |
| 1899 | 18 | ... | ... | ... |
| 1900 | 18 | ... | ... | ... |
| 1901 | 20 | ... | ... | ... |
| 1902 | 20 | ... | ... | ... |
| 1903 | 21 | ... | ... | ... |
| 1904 | 23 | ... | ... | ... |
| 1905 | 27 | ... | ... | ... |
| 1906 | 34 | ... | ... | ... |
| 1907 | 42 | ... | ... | ... |
| 1908 | 47 | ... | ... | ... |
| 1909 | 51 | ... | ... | ... |
| 1910 | 60 | ... | ... | ... |
| 1911 | 68 | ... | ... | ... |
| 1912 | 69 | ... | ... | ... |
| 1913 | 79 | ... | ... | ... |
| 1914 | 81 | ... | ... | ... |
| 1915 | 68 | ... | ... | ... |
| 1916 | 66 | ... | ... | ... |
| 1917 | 62 | ... | ... | ... |
| 1918 | 54 | ... | ... | ... |
| 1919 | 64 | ... | ... | ... |
| 1920 | 78 | ... | ... | ... |
| 1921 | 87 | ... | ... | ... |
| 1922 | 91[7] | ... | ... | ... |
| 1923 | 115 | ... | ... | ... |
| 1924 | 128 | ... | ... | ... |
| 1925 | 137 | ... | ... | ... |
| 1926 | 143 | ... | ... | ... |
| 1927 | 149 | ... | ... | ... |
| 1928 | 154 | 4,187 | ... | ... |
| 1929 | 162[7] | 4,358 | ... | ... |
| 1930 | 171 | 4,344 | ... | 54 |
| 1931 | 166 | 4,038 | ... | 38 |
| 1932 | 150 | 3,719 | ... | 44 |
| 1933 | 144 | 3,525 | ... | 79 |
| 1934 | 138 | 3,634 | ... | 89 |
| 1935 | 139 | 3,649 | ... | 122 |
| 1936 | 135 | 3,865 | ... | 138 |
| 1937 | 147 | 4,065 | ... | 176 |
| 1938 | 159 | 4,278 | 1.2 | 100 |
| 1939 | 164 | 4,338 | 1.3 | 103 |

**F3    SOUTH AMERICA: Passenger Traffic on Railways**

1895–1934

| | Brazil | | Chile[8] | | Colombia | | Paraguay | Peru[9] | | Uruguay[10] | | Venezuela |
|---|---|---|---|---|---|---|---|---|---|---|---|---|
| | a | b | a | b | a | b | a | a | b | a | b | a |
| 1895 | ... | ... | 5.3 | ... | ... | ... | ... | 2.6 | ... | 0.7 | ... | 0.4 |
| 1896 | ... | ... | 5.6 | ... | ... | ... | ... | 3.1 | ... | 0.8 | ... | 0.5 |
| 1897 | ... | ... | 5.7 | ... | ... | ... | ... | 3.3 | ... | 0.7 | ... | 0.5 |
| 1898 | ... | ... | 5.9 | ... | ... | ... | ... | 3.2 | ... | 0.7 | ... | 0.5 |
| 1899 | ... | ... | 6.3 | ... | ... | ... | ... | 3.5 | ... | 0.8 | ... | 0.4 |
| 1900 | ... | ... | 6.6 | ... | ... | ... | ... | 3.8 | ... | 0.8 | ... | 0.3 |
| 1901 | ... | ... | 7.4[8] | ... | ... | ... | ... | 4.1 | ... | 0.9 | ... | 0.3 |
| | | | 8.4 | | | | | | | | | |
| 1902 | ... | ... | 8.5 | ... | ... | ... | ... | 3.8 | ... | 0.9 | ... | 0.3 |
| 1903 | ... | ... | 8.9 | ... | ... | ... | ... | 5.5 | ... | 0.9 | ... | 0.3 |
| 1904 | ... | ... | 9.2 | ... | ... | ... | ... | 6.1 | ... | 1.0 | ... | 0.4 |
| 1905 | ... | ... | 10 | ... | ... | ... | ... | 8.7 | ... | 1.0 | ... | 0.4 |
| 1906 | ... | ... | 12 | ... | ... | ... | ... | 9.4 | ... | 1.2 | ... | 0.4 |
| 1907 | ... | ... | 15 | ... | ... | ... | ... | 11.0[9] | ... | 1.4 | ... | 0.4 |
| 1908 | ... | ... | ... | ... | ... | ... | ... | 2.9 | ... | 1.2 | ... | 0.4 |
| 1909 | ... | ... | 12 | ... | ... | ... | ... | 2.9 | ... | 1.2 | ... | 0.4 |
| 1910 | ... | ... | 13 | ... | ... | ... | ... | 3.1 | ... | 1.2 | ... | 0.5 |
| 1911 | ... | ... | 13 | ... | 1.5 | ... | ... | 3.4 | ... | 1.5 | ... | 0.6 |
| 1912 | ... | ... | 17 | ... | 2.0 | ... | ... | 4.2 | ... | 1.7 | ... | 0.6 |
| 1913 | ... | ... | 28 | ... | 3.4 | ... | ... | 4.3 | ... | 2.0 | ... | 0.6 |
| 1914 | ... | ... | 25 | ... | 3.6 | ... | 0.6 | 4.1 | ... | 1.9 | ... | 0.6 |
| 1915 | ... | ... | 19 | ... | 4.0 | ... | ... | 3.9 | ... | 1.9 | ... | 0.8 |
| 1916 | 54 | 1,413 | 23 | ... | 4.4 | ... | ... | 4.1 | ... | 2.1 | ... | 0.9 |
| 1917 | 57 | 1,529 | 25 | ... | 5.0 | ... | ... | 4.7 | ... | 2.0 | ... | 1.0 |
| 1918 | 59 | 1,586 | 27[8] | ... | 5.0 | ... | ... | 1.3 | ... | 2.0 | ... | 1.0 |
| 1919 | 67 | 1,850 | 17 | ... | 6.0 | ... | ... | 5.8 | 221 | 2.4 | ... | 1.2 |
| 1920 | 76 | 2,194 | 19 | ... | 7.1 | ... | ... | 6.3 | 233 | 2.6 | ... | 1.9 |
| 1921 | 78 | 2,309 | 17 | ... | 6.7 | ... | ... | 7.0 | 262 | ... | ... | 1.9 |
| 1922 | 90 | 2,673 | 15 | ... | 7.0 | ... | 0.2 | 6.3 | 241 | ... | ... | 2.1 |
| 1923 | 104 | 3,218 | 16 | ... | 7.5 | ... | 0.3 | 6.3 | 246 | 3.1 | 134 | 3.0 |
| 1924 | 116 | 3,702 | 18 | ... | 8.2 | ... | 0.5 | 6.3 | 231 | 3.2 | 135 | 2.4 |
| 1925 | 124 | 4,082 | 17 | ... | 8.7 | ... | 0.5 | 5.7 | ... | 4.3 | ... | 2.8 |
| 1926 | 126 | 3,569 | 16 | ... | 10.0 | ... | 0.5 | 5.4 | 212 | 4.5 | 153 | 2.4 |
| 1927 | 131 | 4,237 | 18 | 896 | 11.0 | ... | 0.5 | 4.9 | 210 | ... | ... | 2.7 |
| 1928 | 157 | 4,298 | 18 | 950 | 12.0 | ... | 0.5 | 4.7 | 168 | 4.3 | 161 | 2.3 |
| 1929 | 163 | 4,846 | 17 | 923 | 12.0 | ... | 0.5 | 4.8 | 158 | 4.0 | 159 | 2.1 |
| 1930 | 148 | 4,397 | 18 | 925 | 9.1 | ... | 0.6 | 4.4 | 126 | 4.0 | 166 | 2.7 |
| 1931 | 145 | 4,734 | 14 | 708 | 7.2 | 261 | 0.5 | 4.2 | 126 | 4.4 | 174 | 2.9 |
| 1932 | 135 | 3,734 | 14 | 693 | 7.3 | 270 | ... | 3.8 | 136 | 4.1 | 157 | 1.9 |
| 1933 | 146 | 4,097 | 18 | 937 | 8.2 | 310 | 1.1 | 3.5 | 132 | 3.9[10] | 146[10] | 0.8 |
| 1934 | 156 | 4,122 | 20 | 1,030 | 11 | 432 | ... | 3.4 | 123 | 4.2 | 153 | 0.9 |
| 1935 | 167 | 4,561 | 17 | 1,031 | 12 | 451 | 2.6 | 4.4 | 126 | 4.8 | 192 | 1.2 |
| 1936 | 165 | 4,730 | 19 | 1,204 | 12 | 468 | 2.0 | 4.2 | 126 | 5.1 | 210 | 1.1 |
| 1937 | 168 | 5,100 | 20 | 1,198 | 12 | 484 | 1.6 | 3.8 | 136 | 5.4 | 235 | 0.4 |
| 1938 | 174 | 5,532 | 20 | 1,227 | 12 | 482 | 1.1 | 3.5 | 132 | 5.7 | 260 | 0.8 |
| 1939 | 195 | 7,118 | 19 | 1,257 | 13 | 487 | 1.0 | 3.4 | 123 | 6.3 | 271 | 1.0 |

**F3    SOUTH AMERICA: Passenger Traffic on Railways**

### 1935–1975

| | Argentina[7] | | Bolivia[11] | | Brazil | | Chile[8] | | Colombia | |
|------|------|------|------|------|------|------|------|------|------|------|
| | a | b | a | b | a | b | a | b | a | b |
| 1940 | 164 | 4,380 | 1.6 | 125 | 194 | 6,428 | 21 | 1,457 | 12 | 457 |
| 1941 | 165 | 4,631 | 1.2 | 122 | 214 | 7,130 | 21 | 1,337 | 12 | 462 |
| 1942 | 173 | 4,833 | 2.1 | 163 | 224 | 6,708 | 23 | 1,733 | 13 | 565 |
| 1943 | 188 | 5,169 | 2.1 | 132 | 257 | 7,846 | 27 | 2,113 | 15 | 651 |
| 1944 | 209 | 5,818 | 2.1 | 128 | 277 | 8,771 | 28 | 1,779 | 16 | 727 |
| 1945 | 246 | 6,944 | 1.8 | 130 | 287 | 9,023 | 29 | 1,663 | 17 | 782 |
| 1946 | 282 | 7,699 | 1.9 | 132 | 304 | 9,704 | 27 | 1,665 | 18 | 851 |
| 1947 | 314 | 8,973 | 1.8 | … | 318 | 10,139 | 26 | 1,682 | 18 | 814 |
| 1948 | 351[7] | 10,329[7] | 1.5 | 136 | 350 | 10,706 | 24 | 1,511 | 18 | 816 |
| 1949 | 470 | 13,678 | 1.6 | 147 | 338 | 10,394 | 23 | 1,419 | 17 | 838 |
| 1950 | 491 | 13,229 | 1.8 | 158 | 340 | 10,267 | 24 | 1,588 | 15 | 743 |
| 1951 | 525 | 13,976 | 2.2 | 195 | 339 | 10,015 | 27 | 1,808 | 15 | 731 |
| 1952 | 531 | 13,451 | 2.5 | 240 | 327 | 10,417 | 26 | 1,778 | 14 | 694 |
| 1953 | 541 | 13,654 | 2.6 | 251 | 313 | 11,593 | 27 | 1,789 | 13 | 668 |
| 1954 | 572 | 14,735 | 3.4 | 331 | 353 | 12,008 | 31 | 1,739 | 12 | 674 |
| 1955 | 579 | 14,762 | 3.4 | … | 364 | 12,686 | 32 | 1,887 | 11 | 586 |
| 1956 | 605 | 15,384 | 3.3 | … | 358 | 12,607 | 33 | 1,821 | 11 | 562 |
| 1957 | 619 | 15,456 | 2.1 | 236 | 375 | 12,546 | 29 | 1,627 | 11 | 592 |
| 1958 | 618 | 15,653 | 2.2 | 208 | 382 | 13,432 | 29 | 1,529 | 11 | 652 |
| 1959 | 623 | 16,586 | 2.2 | … | 420 | 14,639 | 30 | 2,407 | 11 | 651 |
| 1960 | 604 | 15,684 | 2.1 | 226 | 421 | 15,395 | 26 | 1,906 | 9.8 | 598 |
| 1961 | 580 | 15,158 | 2.2[11] | 205[11] | 457 | 16,853 | 24 | 1,788 | 9.6 | 617 |
| 1962 | 453 | 12,616 | 1.9 | 156 | 478 | 17,926 | 25 | 1,931 | 9.0 | 623 |
| 1963 | 450 | 12,074 | 1.8 | 142 | 459 | 17,315 | 25 | 1,991 | 8.6 | 627 |
| 1964 | 480 | 12,962 | 1.8 | 155 | 440 | 16,991 | 24 | 2,048 | 7.4 | 546 |
| 1965 | 482 | 12,829 | 1.5 | 220 | 406 | 16,884 | 28 | 2,411 | 6.5 | 513 |
| 1966 | 480 | 14,080 | 1.4 | 257 | 352 | 13,945 | 23 | 2,097 | 5.8 | 491 |
| 1967 | 449 | 13,590 | 1.4 | 252 | 345 | 13,517 | 23 | 2,043 | 4.8 | 418 |
| 1968 | 491 | 14,852 | 1.4 | 249 | 367 | 13,803 | 21 | 2,085 | 3.7 | 351 |
| 1969 | 492 | 14,772 | 1.2 | 258 | 356 | 13,338 | 22 | 2,217 | 2.7 | 273 |
| 1970 | 440 | 12,684 | 1.2 | 271 | 333 | 12,351 | 21 | 2,338 | 2.1 | 249 |
| 1971 | 435 | 12,814 | 1.1 | 270 | 309 | 11,276 | 21[8] | 2,481[8] | 2.3 | 282 |
| 1972 | 406 | 12,573 | 1.1 | … | 314 | 10,783 | 25 | 3,037 | 3.1 | 398 |
| 1973 | 391 | 12,837 | 1.1 | 270 | 308 | 10,603 | 28 | 3,475 | 4.2 | 427 |
| 1974 | 423 | 14,103 | … | 248 | 306 | 10,647 | 27 | 2,882 | 4.6 | 483 |
| 1975 | 447 | 14,863 | 1.1 | 310 | 292 | 10,621 | 21 | 2,103 | 4.2 | 508 |
| 1976 | 445 | 14,598 | 1.2 | 368 | 333 | 11,638 | 23 | 2,464 | 4.0 | 511 |
| 1977 | 410 | 12,897 | 1.3 | 397 | 344 | 11,699 | 19 | 2,382 | 3.0 | 391 |
| 1978 | 380 | 11,561 | 1.2 | 398 | 368 | 11,923 | 14 | 2,126 | 2.6 | 342 |
| 1979 | 377 | 12,028 | 1.2 | 363 | 389 | 11,404 | 11 | 1,732 | 2.5 | 322 |
| 1980 | 394 | 12,706 | 1.7 | 529 | 435 | 12,376 | 9.4 | 1,431 | 2.2 | 315 |
| 1981 | 343 | 11,258 | 1.6 | 482 | 451 | 13,133 | 11 | 1,582 | 1.8 | 230 |
| 1982 | 302 | 10,147 | 1.7 | 556 | 461 | 13,266 | 10 | 1,506 | 1.2 | 158 |
| 1983 | 290 | 10,387 | 2.3 | 772 | 499 | 13,797 | 9.2 | 1,575 | 1.3 | 175 |
| 1984 | 291 | 10,469 | 2.1 | 684 | 587 | 15,578 | 8.7 | 1,424 | 1.5 | 189 |
| 1985 | 300 | 10,743 | | 748 | 650 | 16,362 | 8.9 | 1,522 | 2.4 | 228 |
| 1986 | 359 | 12,451 | 1.9 | 657 | 631 | 15,782 | 6.2 | 1,274 | 1.4 | 178 |
| 1987 | 352 | 12,475 | 1.4 | 500 | 653 | 15,264 | 7.2 | 1,177 | 1.4 | 171 |
| 1988 | … | 10,268 | 1.0 | 369 | 623 | … | 6.8 | 1,013 | 1.2 | 148 |

**F3    SOUTH AMERICA: Passenger Traffic on Railways**

**1935–1975**

| | Ecuador[13] | | Paraguay | | Peru[9] | | Uruguay[10] | | Venezuela | |
|---|---|---|---|---|---|---|---|---|---|---|
| | a | b | a | b | a | b | a | b | a | b |
| 1940 | 1.3 | 81 | 1.2 | ... | 3.3 | 124 | 6.0 | 272 | 0.8 | ... |
| 1941 | 1.3 | 81 | 1.2 | ... | 3.0 | 126 | 5.7 | 268 | 0.7 | ... |
| 1942 | 1.8 | 115 | 1.6 | ... | 3.7 | 155 | 5.4 | 261 | 1.2 | ... |
| 1943 | 2.4 | ... | 1.8 | ... | 5.1 | 213 | 4.7 | 235 | 1.5 | ... |
| 1944 | 2.7 | 181 | 1.9 | ... | 5.5 | 236 | 5.4 | 275 | 2.0 | ... |
| 1945 | 2.6 | 177 | 2.0 | ... | 5.8 | 251 | 6.0 | 303 | 1.8 | ... |
| 1946 | 2.2 | 153 | 2.2 | ... | 5.8 | 261 | 6.5 | 314 | 1.4 | ... |
| 1947 | 2.1 | 147 | 2.0 | ... | 5.6 | 249 | 6.6 | 327 | 0.9 | ... |
| 1948 | 2.0 | 138 | ... | 45 | 5.7 | 248 | 7.3 | 356 | 0.6 | ... |
| 1949 | 1.9 | 129 | ... | 58 | 5.8 | 260 | 8.2 | 394 | 0.6 | ... |
| 1950 | 1.9 | 121 | ... | 62 | 5.4 | 241 | 9.2 | 470 | 0.6 | 16 |
| 1951 | 2.0 | 129 | ... | 58 | 5.5 | 246 | 11 | 515 | 0.3 | 12 |
| 1952 | 2.3 | 129 | ... | 67 | 5.5 | 268 | 12 | 548 | 0.4 | 18 |
| 1953 | 2.1 | 106 | ... | 60 | 5.4 | 282 | 13 | 488 | 0.4 | 21 |
| 1954 | 2.0 | 105 | 1.9 | 57 | 5.8 | 308 | 13 | 556 | 0.3 | 14 |
| 1955 | 2.7 | 118 | 1.5 | 48 | 6.3 | 335 | 13 | ... | 0.1 | 9 |
| 1956 | 1.8 | 113 | 1.2 | 39 | 6.2 | 332 | 13 | 485 | 0.1 | 7 |
| 1957 | ... | ... | 1.1 | 39 | 6.2 | 342 | 12 | 435 | 0.1 | 6 |
| 1958 | 1.6 | ... | 0.9 | 34 | 5.8 | 292 | 12 | 511 | 0.1 | 5 |
| 1959 | ... | ... | 1.0 | 31 | 5.2 | 260 | 14 | 577 | 0.2 | 21 |
| 1960 | 1.3 | 65 | 0.8 | 31 | 5.1 | 282 | 10 | 527 | 0.3 | 25 |
| 1961 | 1.3 | 58 | 0.6 | 36 | 4.7 | 275 | 8.6 | 494 | 0.4 | 28 |
| 1962 | 1.8 | 62 | 0.5 | 36 | 4.4 | 275 | 9.8 | 608 | 0.4 | 28 |
| 1963 | 2.4 | 54 | 0.5 | 38 | 3.8 | 257 | 10 | 630 | 0.3 | 29 |
| 1964 | 3.3 | 64 | 0.5 | 39 | 3.5 | 252 | 9.8 | 603 | 0.5 | 37 |
| 1965 | 3.4 | 52 | 0.3 | 35 | 3.0 | 236 | 9.1 | 552 | 0.6 | 44 |
| 1966 | 3.9 | 53 | 0.2 | 20 | 2.8 | 224 | 11 | 708 | 0.5 | 45 |
| 1967 | 4.1 | 72 | 0.1 | 14 | 2.4 | 211 | ... | 717 | 0.4 | 39 |
| 1968 | 4.9 | 80 | 0.2 | 28 | 2.5 | 219 | ... | ... | 0.4 | 34 |
| 1969 | 5.1 | 86 | 0.2 | 28 | 2.6 | 254 | 8.6 | 500 | 0.3 | 29 |
| 1970 | 4.9 | 85 | 0.2 | 24 | ... | 248 | ... | 529 | 0.4 | 36 |
| 1971 | 2.2 | 62 | 0.2 | 24 | ... | 270 | ... | 437 | 0.4 | 43 |
| 1972 | 2.4 | 63 | 0.2 | 26 | ... | 286 | ... | 336 | 0.4 | 44 |
| 1973 | 4.0 | 70 | 0.2 | 26 | ... | 305 | ... | 351 | 0.4 | 45 |
| 1974 | 2.9 | 69 | 0.2 | 27 | ... | 393 | 5.8 | 353 | 0.4 | 43 |
| 1975 | ... | 65 | 0.1 | 24 | ... | 455 | 6.1 | 362 | 0.4 | 40 |
| 1976 | ... | 59 | 0.1 | 16 | ... | 528 | ... | 372 | 0.4 | 42 |
| 1977 | ... | 72 | 0.1 | 18 | ... | 651 | ... | 307 | 0.4 | 39 |
| 1978 | ... | 65 | 0.1 | 17 | ... | 473 | ... | 303 | 0.4 | 40 |
| 1979 | ... | 69 | 0.2 | 21 | ... | 534 | ... | 269 | 0.2 | 25 |
| 1980 | ... | 70 | 0.3 | 22 | 4.2 | 586 | 5.4 | 234 | 0.2 | 28 |
| 1981 | ... | 58 | 0.3 | 22 | 3.5 | 494 | 3.3 | 218 | 0.1 | 10 |
| 1982 | ... | 50 | 0.3 | 20 | 3.4 | 458 | ... | 186 | 0.1 | 19 |
| 1983 | ... | 43 | 0.3 | 20 | 3.4 | 454 | ... | 220 | 0.2 | 22 |
| 1984 | ... | 49 | 0.2 | 22 | 3.6 | 483 | 5.0 | 273 | 0.1 | 12 |
| 1985 | ... | 52 | ... | 26 | 3.6 | 475 | ... | 185 | 0.1 | 8 |
| 1986 | ... | 55 | 0.3 | 26 | 3.5 | 490 | ... | 204 | 0.1 | 17 |
| 1987 | ... | 63 | ... | 23 | 3.9 | 594 | ... | 210 | 0.2 | 22 |
| 1988 | ... | 77 | ... | 22 | ... | 596 | ... | 212 | ... | 29 |

**F3      Passenger Traffic on Railways**

NOTES

1.   SOURCES: As for table F2.
2.   It is not always clear whether passengers carried free are included or not, though there appears
     to be an indication whenever a change in this respect occurs.

FOOTNOTES

[1] Years ending 30 June to 1919 (1st line). Newfoundland is included from 1950.
[2] Paying passengers carried by each line to 1890 (1st line), paying passengers originated subsequently. Data for 1890 (2nd line) to 1916
    (1st line) are for years ending 30 June. Alaska and Hawaii are included from 1960.
[3] Statistics to 1929 are for passengers carried by each line. From 1936 to 1956 they relate to class I railways only. Data to 1946 are for
    years ending 30 June.
[4] For the period 1941–45 the data for the Ferrocarril del Norte component are for years beginning 1 July.
[5] Ferrocarril del Norte only from 1957 to 1974, except 1966.
[6] Including non-paying passengers subsequently.
[7] Years ending 30 June to 1948. The Ferrocarril Central de Chubut is not included in 1923–29.
[8] State railways only to 1901 (1st line). Tramways are included to 1918. The Transandean Railway is excluded from 1972.
[9] Tramways are included to 1907.
[10] Years ending 30 June to 1933.
[11] Coverage is said to be variable prior to 1962.
[12] Subsequent statistics relate to AMTRAK only.
[13] Earlier figures are available as follows:

|      | a   | b   |
| ---- | --- | --- |
| 1936 | ... | 31  |
| 1937 | ... | 34  |
| 1938 | 1.0 | 52  |
| 1939 | 0.9 | ... |

## F4　　NORTH AMERICA: MERCHANT SHIPS REGISTERED

key:-　　a= number of ships; b= thousand gross registered tons; c= thousand net registered tons

| | USA | | | USA | | |
|---|---|---|---|---|---|---|
| | **b** | | | **a** | **b** | |
| | Sail[1] | Steam | | All Ships[1] | Sail[1] | Steam |
| 1789 | 202 | — | 1835 | ... | 1,702 | 123 |
| 1790 | 478 | — | 1836 | ... | 1,737 | 146 |
| 1791 | 502 | — | 1837 | ... | 1,742 | 155 |
| 1792 | 564 | — | 1838 | ... | 1,802 | 193 |
| 1794 | 629 | — | 1839 | ... | 1,901 | 195 |
| 1795 | 748 | — | 1840 | ... | 1,978 | 202 |
| 1796 | 832 | — | 1841 | ... | 1,956 | 175 |
| 1797 | 877 | — | 1842 | ... | 1,863 | 230 |
| 1798 | 898 | — | 1843 | ... | 1,922 | 237 |
| 1799 | 939 | — | 1844 | ... | 2,008 | 272 |
| 1800 | 972 | — | 1845 | ... | 2,091 | 326 |
| 1801 | 948 | — | 1846 | ... | 2,214 | 348 |
| 1802 | 892 | — | 1847 | ... | 2,434 | 405 |
| 1803 | 949 | — | 1848 | ... | 2,726 | 428 |
| 1804 | 1,042 | — | 1849 | ... | 2,872 | 462 |
| 1805 | 1,140 | — | 1850 | ... | 3,010 | 526 |
| 1806 | 1,209 | — | 1851 | ... | 3,189 | 584 |
| 1807 | 1,268 | - - | 1852 | ... | 3,495 | 643 |
| 1808 | 1,242 | - - | 1853 | ... | 3,802 | 605 |
| 1809 | 1,350 | 1 | 1854 | ... | 4,126 | 677 |
| 1810 | 1,424 | 1 | 1855 | ... | 4,442 | 770 |
| 1811 | 1,231 | 1 | 1856 | ... | 4,199 | 673 |
| 1812 | 1,268 | 2 | 1857 | ... | 4,235 | 706 |
| 1813 | 1,164 | 3 | 1858 | ... | 4,320 | 729 |
| 1814 | 1,156 | 3 | 1859 | ... | 4,376 | 768 |
| 1815 | 1,365 | 3 | 1860 | ... | 4,486 | 868 |
| 1816 | 1,366 | 6 | 1861 | ... | 4,663 | 877 |
| 1817 | 1,391 | 9 | 1862 | ... | 4,402 | 710 |
| 1818 | 1,213 | 13 | 1863 | ... | 4,580 | 576 |
| 1819 | 1,243 | 17 | 1864 | ... | 4,08 | 978 |
| 1820 | 1,258 | 22 | 1865 | ... | 4,030[2] | 1,067[2] |
| 1821 | 1,276 | 23 | 1866 | ... | 3,227 | 1,084 |
| 1822 | 1,304 | 23 | 1867 | ... | 3,113 | ,1,192 |
| 1823 | 1,312 | 25 | 1868 | 28,167 | 3,153[1] 2,509[2] | 1,199[2] |
| 1824 | 1,368 | 22 | 1869 | 27,487 | 2,400 | 1,104 |
| 1825 | 1,400 | 23 | 1870 | 28,998 | 2,363 | 1,075 |
| 1826 | 1,500 | 34 | 1871 | 29,651 | 2,286 | 1,088 |
| 1827 | 1,580 | 40 | 1872 | 31,114 | 2,325 | 1,112 |
| 1828 | 1,702 | 39 | 1873 | 32,672 | 2,383 | 1,156 |
| 1829 | 1,207 | 54 | 1874 | 32,486 | 2,474 | 1,186 |
| 1830 | 1,127 | 64 | 1875 | 32,285 | 2,585 | 1,169 |
| 1831 | 1,198 | 69 | 1876 | 25,934 | 2,609 | 1,172 |
| 1832 | 1,349 | 91 | 1877 | 25,386 | 2,580 | 1,171 |
| 1833 | 1,504 | 102 | 1878 | 25,264 | 2,521 | 1,168 |
| 1834 | 1,636 | 123 | 1879 | 25,211 | 2,423 | 1,176 |

**F4    NORTH AMERICA: Merchant Ships Registered**

| | Canada | | | | Cuba | | Honduras | | Mexico | |
|---|---|---|---|---|---|---|---|---|---|---|
| | Sail | | Steam | | Steam | | Steam & Motor | | Steam[3] | |
| | a | c | a | c | a | b | a | b | a | b |
| 1867 | 5,338 | 722 | 355 | 46 | ... | ... | ... | ... | ... | ... |
| 1873 | 6,223 | 1,005 | 560 | 69 | ... | ... | ... | ... | ... | ... |
| 1883 | 6,336 | 964 | 1,008 | 304 | ... | ... | ... | ... | ... | ... |
| 1888 | ... | ... | ... | ... | ... | ... | ... | ... | 10 | 4.9 |
| 1889 | ... | ... | ... | ... | ... | ... | ... | ... | 10 | 5.0 |
| 1890 | ... | ... | ... | ... | ... | ... | ... | ... | 12 | 5.9 |
| 1891 | ... | ... | ... | ... | ... | ... | ... | ... | 12 | 5.0 |
| 1892 | 6,004 | 819 | 1,000 | 145 | ... | ... | ... | ... | 11 | 4.7 |
| 1893 | ... | ... | ... | ... | ... | ... | ... | ... | 9 | 4.0 |
| 1894 | ... | ... | ... | ... | ... | ... | ... | ... | 11 | 3.9 |
| 1895 | 5,532 | 671 | 1,718 | 154 | ... | ... | ... | ... | 11 | 4.2 |
| 1896 | ... | ... | ... | ... | ... | ... | ... | ... | 12 | 4.7 |
| 1897 | ... | ... | ... | ... | ... | ... | ... | ... | 18 | 9.1 |
| 1898 | 4,732 | 529 | 1,889 | 161 | ... | ... | ... | ... | 15 | 6.6 |
| 1899 | 4,729 | ... | 1,969 | ... | ... | ... | ... | ... | 14 | 6.2 |
| 1900 | 4,634 | 479 | 2,101 | 181 | 30 | 4.2 | ... | ... | 16 | 6.5 |
| 1901 | 4,615 | 483 | 2,177 | 183 | 34 | 31 | ... | ... | 23 | 13 |
| 1902 | 4,547 | 469 | 2,289 | 184 | 38 | 38 | ... | ... | 24 | 12 |
| 1903 | 4,610 | 477 | 2,410 | 206 | 39 | 39 | ... | ... | 27 | 17 |
| 1904 | 4,609 | 459 | 2,543 | 214 | 43 | 42 | ... | ... | 30 | 18 |
| 1905 | 4,671 | 456 | 2,654 | 214 | 40 | 45 | 1 | 2.2 | 31 | 21 |
| 1906 | 4,702 | 428 | 2,810 | 226 | 44 | 54 | 7 | 16 | 24 | 33 |
| 1907 | 4,521 | 406 | 3,007 | 293 | 43 | 58 | 4 | 8.7 | 34 | 27 |
| 1908 | 4,518 | 406 | 3,084 | 296 | 41 | 56 | 1 | 1.5 | 35 | 29 |
| 1909 | 4,539 | 406 | 3,229 | 313 | 40 | 56 | 1 | 1.5 | 33 | 26 |
| 1910 | 4,572 | 413 | 3,332 | 337 | 36 | 50 | 1 | 1.5 | 30 | 26 |
| 1911 | 4,644 | 412 | 3,444 | 359 | 38 | 54 | 3 | 4.9 | 30 | 31 |
| 1912 | 4,713 | 447 | 3,667 | 389 | 40 | 56 | 2 | 3.4 | 30 | 35 |
| 1913 | 4,698 | 467 | 3,847 | 430 | 41 | 56 | 4 | 6.3 | 30 | 36 |
| 1914 | 4,718 | 479 | 4,054 | 453 | 38 | 51 | 5 | 9.2 | 33 | 42 |
| 1915 | 4,625 | 470 | 4,132 | 459 | 29 | 33 | 5 | 8.7 | 29 | 37 |
| 1916 | 4,458 | 451 | 4,202 | 491 | 27 | 28 | 3 | 6.3 | 24 | 32 |
| 1917 | 4,295 | 450 | 4,264 | 522 | 35 | 30 | 6 | 9.8 | 32 | 33 |
| 1918 | 4,202 | 461 | 4,366 | 556 | 37 | 31 | 7 | 11 | 39 | 29 |
| 1919 | 4,131 | 487 | 4,442 | 605 | 38 | 39 | 7 | 11 | 35 | 32 |
| 1920 | 3,623 | 476 | 4,281 | 677 | 41 | 44 | 7 | 11 | 33 | 31 |
| 1921 | | 445 | | 779 | 44 | 50 | 11 | 21 | 37 | 36 |
| 1922 | 3,253 | 447 | 4,388 | 794 | 49 | 55 | 14 | 31 | 43 —[3] | 43 —[3] |
| 1923 | 3,231 | 445 | 4,463 | 786 | 48 | 43 | 14 | 27 | 75 | 54 |
| 1924 | 3,198 | 453 | 4,499 | 768 | 53 | 52 | 24 | 49 | 58 | 57 |

**F4     NORTH AMERICA: Merchant Ships Registered**

| | Newfoundland[4] | | | | Panama | | USA[2] | | |
|---|---|---|---|---|---|---|---|---|---|
| | Sail | | Steam | | Steam & Motor | | All Ships[1] | b | |
| | a | c | a | c | a | b | a | Sail[1] | Steam |
| 1879 | 1,691 | 76 | 27 | 6.3 | ... | ... | | see page 560 | |
| 1880 | 1,803 | 80 | 27 | 6.3 | ... | ... | 24,712 | 2,366 | 1,212 |
| 1881 | 1,866₄ | 83₄ | 29 | 6.8 | ... | ... | 24,065 | 2,350 | 1,265 |
| 1882 | 1,938 | 90 | ... | ... | ... | ... | 24,368 | 2,361 | 1,356 |
| 1883 | 1,988 | ... | ... | ... | ... | ... | 24,217 | 2,387 | 1,413 |
| 1884 | 2,033 | ... | ... | ... | ... | ... | 24,082 | 2,414 | 1,466 |
| 1885 | 1,977 | ... | ... | ... | ... | ... | 23,963 | 2,374 | 1,495 |
| 1886 | 2,044 | ... | ... | ... | ... | ... | 23,534 | 2,210 | 1,523 |
| 1887 | 2,053 | ... | ... | ... | ... | ... | 23,063 | 2,170 | 1,543 |
| 1888 | 2,106 | 94 | ... | ... | ... | ... | 23,281 | 2,124 | 1,648 |
| 1889 | 2,172 | 94 | ... | ... | ... | ... | 23,623 | 2,099 | 1,766 |
| 1890 | 2,207 | 99 | ... | ... | ... | ... | 23,467 | 2,109 | 1,859 |
| 1891 | 2,222 | 95 | ... | ... | ... | ... | 23,899 | 2,172 | 2,016 |
| 1892 | 2,202 | 92 | ... | ... | ... | ... | 24,383 | 2,178 | 2,074 |
| 1893 | ... | ... | ... | ... | ... | ... | 24,512 | 2,118 | 2,183 |
| 1894 | 2,339 | 108 | ... | ... | ... | ... | 23,586 | 2,023 | 2,189 |
| 1895 | 2,341 | 104 | ... | ... | ... | ... | 23,240 | 1,965 | 2,213 |
| 1896 | 2,368 | 106 | ... | ... | ... | ... | 22,908 | 1,928 | 2,307 |
| 1897 | ... | ... | ... | ... | ... | ... | 22,633 | 1,904 | 2,359 |
| 1898 | 2,429₄ | 107₄ | ... | ... | ... | ... | 22,705 | 1,836 | 2,372 |
| 1899 | 2,441 | 99 | 37 | 8.4 | ... | ... | 22,728 | 1,825 | 2,476 |
| 1900 | 2,546 | 102 | 45 | 10 | ... | ... | 23,333 | 1,885 | 2,658 |
| 1901 | 2,637 | 105 | 47 | 9.4 | ... | ... | 24,057 | 1,933 | 2,921 |
| 1902 | 2,751 | 109 | 48 | 9.7 | ... | ... | 24,273 | 1,942 | 3,177 |
| 1903 | 2,802 | 111 | 54 | 11 | ... | ... | 24,425 | 1,966 | 3,408 |
| 1904 | 2,880 | 114 | 65 | 12 | ... | ... | 24,558 | 1,945 | 3,595 |
| 1905 | 2,982 | 118 | 66 | 12 | ... | ... | 24,681 | 1,962 | 3,741 |
| 1906 | 3,131 | 125 | 68 | 11 | ... | ... | 25,006 | 1,899 | 3,975 |
| 1907 | 3,241 | 130 | 67 | 12 | ... | ... | 24,911 | 1,814 | 4,279 |
| 1908 | 3,289 | 132 | 66 | 15 | ... | ... | 25,425 | 1,761 | 4,711 |
| 1909 | 3,315 | 132 | 72 | 17 | ... | ... | 25,868 | 1,711 | 4,749 |
| 1910 | 3,318 | 133 | 68 | 14 | ... | ... | 25,740 | 1,655 | 4,900 |
| 1911 | 3,307 | 132 | 71 | 15 | ... | ... | 25,991 | 1,598 | 5,074 |
| 1912 | 3,315 | 132 | 80 | 17 | ... | ... | 26,528 | 1,539 | 5,180 |
| 1913 | 3,327 | 132 | 88 | 21 | ... | ... | 27,070 | 1,508 | 5,333 |
| 1914 | 3,310 | 130 | 92 | 21 | ... | ... | 26,943 | 1,433 | 5,428 |
| 1915 | 3,330 | 134 | 98 | 20 | ... | ... | 26,701 | 1,384 | 5,944 |
| 1916 | ... | 138 | ... | 22 | ... | ... | 26,444 | 1,311 | 6,070 |
| 1917 | ... | 140 | ... | 20 | ... | ... | 26,397 | 1,278 | 6,433 |
| 1918 | ... | 152 | ... | 20 | ... | ... | 26,711 | 1,210 | 7,471 |
| 1919 | ... | 149 | ... | 22 | ... | ... | 27,513 | 1,200 | 10,416 |
| 1920 | ... | 152 | ... | 22 | ... | ... | 28,183 | 1,272 | 13,823 |
| 1921 | ... | 151 | ... | 23 | 1 | 1.1 | 28,012 | 1,294 | 15,745 |
| 1922 | ... | 148 | ... | 21 | 2 | 7.5 | 27,358 | 1,288 | 15,982 |
| 1923 | ... | 143 | ... | 18 | 9 | 38 | 27,017 | 1,254 | 15,821 |
| 1924 | ... | 136 | ... | 19 | 14 | 84 | 26,575 | 1,185 | 15,315 |

**F4    NORTH AMERICA: Merchant Ships Registered**

| | Canada[5] | | | | Cuba | | Hondurasl | | Mexico | |
|---|---|---|---|---|---|---|---|---|---|---|
| | Sail | | Steam & Motor | | Steam & Motor | | Steam & Motor | | Steam & Motor[3] | |
| | a | c | a | c | a | b | a | b | a | b |
| 1925 | 3,279 | 492 | 4,634 | 793 | 53 | 54 | 24 | 53 | 51 | 56 |
| 1926 | 3,351 | 504 | 4,842 | 847 | 55 | 54 | 26 | 58 | 49 | 50 |
| 1927 | 3,358 | 502 | 5,096 | 866 | 51 | 45 | 30 | 72 | 44 | 45 |
| 1928 | 3,337 | 501 | 5,308 | 865 | 52 | 45 | 28 | 69 | 43 | 47 |
| 1929 | ... | 503 | ... | 891 | 48 | 38 | 33 | 87 | 42 | 47 |
| 1930 | ... | 515 | ... | 917 | ... | ... | 35 | 98 | 41 | 46 |
| 1931 | ... | 515 | ... | 969 | 42 | 36 | 34 | 97 | 28 | 39 |
| 1932 | ... | 505 | ... | 970 | 44 | 37 | 31 | 80 | ... | ... |
| 1933 | ... | 490 | ... | 941 | 43 | 33 | 29 | 77 | ... | ... |
| 1934 | ... | 476 | ... | 921 | 44 | 34 | 29 | 75 | ... | ... |
| 1935 | ... | 475 | ... | 914 | 42 | 31 | 28 | 72 | ... | ... |
| 1936 | ... | 463 | ... | 904 | 39 | 29 | 27 | 69 | 28 | 32 |
| 1937 | ... | ... | ... | ... | 36 | 30 | 28 | 70 | 30 | 34 |
| 1938 | 2,193 | 428 | 6,008 | 849 | 35 | 30 | 28 | 71 | 29 | 29 |
| 1939 | 2,159[5] | 437[5] | 6,260 | 850 | 33 | 27 | 32 | 84 | 30 | 30 |

| | All Ships | | | | | | | | | |
|---|---|---|---|---|---|---|---|---|---|---|
| | a | c | | | | | | | | |
| 1940 | 8,396 | 1,293 | | | ... | ... | ... | ... | ... | ... |
| 1941 | 8,667 | 1,272 | | | ... | ... | ... | ... | ... | ... |
| 1942 | 8,852 | 1,210 | | | ... | ... | ... | ... | ... | ... |
| 1943 | 9,074 | 1,348 | | | ... | ... | ... | ... | ... | ... |
| 1944 | 9,369 | 1,645 | | | ... | ... | ... | ... | ... | ... |
| 1945 | 9,421 | 1,673 | | | ... | ... | ... | ... | ... | ... |
| 1946 | 10,070 | 1,601 | | | ... | ... | ... | ... | ... | ... |
| 1947 | 10,931 | 1,710 | | | 27 | 19 | 78 | 278 | 50 | 108 |

| | Steam & Motor | | | | | | | | | |
|---|---|---|---|---|---|---|---|---|---|---|
| | a | b | | | | | | | | |
| | 904 | 1,870 | | | | | | | | |
| 1948 | 984[6] | 2,007[6] | | | 34 | 35 | 93 | 324 | 53 | 114 |
| 1949 | 1,178 | 2,097 | | | 34 | 36 | 123 | 409 | 55 | 120 |
| 1950 | 1,156 | 1,931 | | | ... | ... | 142 | 523 | 59 | 144 |
| 1951 | 1,126 | 1,647 | | | ... | ... | 152 | 508 | 61 | 168 |
| 1952 | 1,151 | 1,692 | | | ... | ... | 145 | 468 | 64 | 160 |
| 1953 | 1,142 | 1,652 | | | ... | ... | 146 | 471 | 64 | 157 |
| 1954 | 1,122 | 1,610 | | | ... | ... | 130 | 439 | 65 | 163 |
| 1955 | 1,095 | 1,521 | | | ... | ... | 117 | 432 | 67 | 172 |
| 1956 | 1,081 | 1,504 | | | ... | ... | 106 | 386 | 64 | 165 |
| 1957 | 1,105 | 1,521 | | | ...[7] | ...[7] | 94 | 368 | 63 | 159 |
| 1958 | 1,096 | 1,516 | | | 14 | 38 | 89 | 338 | 70 | 162 |
| 1959 | 1,079 | 1,501 | | | 18 | 49 | 78 | 202 | 76 | 181 |
| 1960 | 1,043 | 1,578 | | | 19 | 52 | 59 | 154 | 74 | 179 |
| 1961 | 1,080 | 1,669 | | | 20 | 62 | 58 | 120 | 77 | 177 |
| 1962 | 1,063 | 1,704 | | | 21 | 71 | 54 | 113 | 79 | 201 |
| 1963 | 1,087 | 1,796 | | | 24 | 98 | 49 | 103 | 85 | 250 |
| 1964 | 1,132 | 1,823 | | | 29[7] | 118[7] | 46 | 90 | 86 | 265 |
| | | | | | 53 | 135 | | | | |

**F4     NORTH AMERICA: Merchant Ships Registered**

| | Newfoundland | | | | Panama | | USA | | |
|---|---|---|---|---|---|---|---|---|---|
| | Sail | | Steam & Motor | | Steam & Motor | | All Ships[1] | b | |
| | a | c | a | c | a | b | a | Sail | Steam & Motor |
| 1925 | ... | 131 | ... | 30 | 18 | 98 | 26,367 | 1,125 | 14,976 |
| 1926 | ... | 127 | ... | 34 | 20 | 101 | 26,343 | 1,092 | 14,848 |
| 1927 | ... | 119 | ... | 34 | 21 | 47 | 25,778 | 989 | 14,507 |
| 1928 | ... | 115 | ... | 39 | 29 | 71 | 25,385 | 915 | 14,344 |
| 1929 | ... | 111 | ... | 39 | 27 | 62 | 25,326 | 825 | 14,162 |
| 1930 | 2,501 | 102 | 255 | 42 | 28 | 75 | 25,214 | 757 | 13,757 |
| 1931 | ... | 94 | ... | 41 | 41 | 131 | 25,471 | 673 | 13,528 |
| 1932 | ... | 87 | ... | 39 | 43 | 138 | 25,156 | 625 | 13,568 |
| 1933 | 2,001 | 80 | 290 | 42 | 83 | 287 | 24,868 | 563 | 12,862 |
| 1934 | 1,970 | 76 | 302 | 43 | 71 | 271 | 24,904 | 500 | 12,687 |
| 1935 | 2,065 | 83 | 319 | 42 | 42 | 137 | 24,919 | 441 | 12,535 |
| 1936 | 1,987 | 80 | 385 | 44 | 81 | 429 | 25,392 | 379 | 12,267 |
| 1937 | 1,907 | 77 | 421 | 44 | 103 | 512 | 26,588 | 312 | 12,170 |
| 1938 | 1,849 | 74 | 375 | 46 | 134 | 611 | 27,155 | 261 | 12,007 |
| 1939 | 1,696 | 65 | 646 | 52 | 159 | 718 | 27,470 | 221 | 11,952 |
| 1940 | ... | ... | ... | ... | ... | ... | 27,212 | 200 | 11,353 |
| 1941 | ... | ... | ... | ... | ... | ... | 27,075 | 182 | 11,047 |
| 1942 | ... | ... | ... | ... | ... | ... | 27,325 | 166 | 11,072 |
| 1943 | 1,578 | 65 | 808 | 52 | ... | ... | 27,612 | 142 | 14,052 |
| 1944 | ... | ... | ... | ... | ... | ... | 28,690 | 129 | 23,217 |
| 1945 | 1,461 | 55 | 898 | 53 | ... | ... | 29,797 | 115 | 30,247 |
| 1946 | 1,438 | 54 | 1,045 | 52 | 174 | 834 | 31,386 | 98 | 35,928 |
| 1947 | 1,379 | 52 | 1,011 | 58 | 369 | 1,702 | 32,760 | 95 | 35,149 |
| 1948 | 1,330 | 49 | 1,054 | 62 | 515 | 2,716 | 33,843 | 87 | 30,469 |
| 1949 | ... | ... | ... | ... | 535 | 3,016 | 35,264 | 87 | 29,323 |
| 1950 | | | | | 573 | 3,361 | 36,083 | 82 | 28,327 |
| 1951 | | | | | 607 | 3,609 | 36,745 | 71 | 27,424 |
| 1952 | | | included with Canada | | 606 | 3,740 | 37,389 | 66 | 27,459 |
| 1953 | | | | | 593 | 3,907 | 38,072 | 55 | 27,507 |
| 1954 | | | | | 595 | 4,091 | 39,008 | 46 | 27,631 |
| 1955 | | | | | 555 | 3,923 | 39,242 | 40 | 26,792 |
| 1956 | | | | | 556 | 3,926 | 39,499 | 34 | 26,251 |
| 1957 | | | | | 580 | 4,129 | 40,191 | 24 | 25,785 |
| 1958 | | | | | 602 | 4,358 | 41,276 | 23 | 24,599 |
| 1959 | | | | | 639 | 4,583 | 42,409 | 23 | 24,333 |
| 1960 | | | | | 607 | 4,236 | 43,088 | 23 | 23,553 |
| 1961 | | | | | 601 | 4,049 | 43,367 | 18 | 21,175 |
| 1962 | | | | | 592 | 3,851 | 43,566 | 18 | 20,076 |
| 1963 | | | | | 619 | 3,894 | 44,077 | 18 | 20,079 |
| 1964 | | | | | 691 | 4,269 | 44,669[1] 3,537 | 17 | 20,018 |

**F4    NORTH AMERICA: Merchant Ships Registered**

| | Bahamas | | Bermuda | | Canada[5,6] | | Cuba[7] | |
| | Steam & Motor | | Steam & Motor | | Steam & Motor | | Steam & Motor | |
| | a | b | a | b | a | c | a | b |
|------|------|-------|-----|-------|-------|-------|-----|-----|
| 1965 | 89   | 254   | 29  | 200   | 1,154 | 1,830 | 68  | 161 |
| 1966 | 95   | 256   | 31  | 222   | 1,188 | 2,125 | 99  | 238 |
| 1967 | 106  | 282   | 27  | 346   | 1,236 | 2,305 | 101 | 235 |
| 1968 | 113  | 303   | 30  | 380   | 1,296 | 2,403 | 104 | 238 |
| 1969 | 136  | 376   | 29  | 355   | 1,278 | 2,451 | 200 | 277 |
| 1970 | 144  | 276   | 48  | 684   | 1,266 | 2,400 | 236 | 333 |
| 1971 | 145  | 358   | 47  | 814   | 1,228 | 2,366 | 264 | 385 |
| 1972 | 144  | 206   | 48  | 814   | 1,235 | 2,381 | 267 | 398 |
| 1973 | 143  | 179   | 52  | 861   | 1,235 | 2,423 | 271 | 416 |
| 1974 | 129  | 153   | 54  | 1,153 | 1,231 | 2,460 | 259 | 409 |
| 1975 | 119  | 190   | 59  | 1,450 | 1,257 | 2,566 | 272 | 477 |
| 1976 | 119  | 148   | 69  | 1,562 | 1,269 | 2,639 | 294 | 604 |
| 1977 | 109  | 106   | 88  | 1,752 | 1,283 | 2,823 | 315 | 668 |
| 1978 | 93   | 84    | 99  | 1,814 | 1,289 | 2,954 | 331 | 779 |
| 1979 | 91   | 121   | 112 | 1,727 | 1,290 | 3,016 | 341 | 853 |
| 1980 | 91   | 87    | 114 | 1,724 | 1,324 | 3,180 | 405 | 881 |
| 1981 | 106  | 197   | 75  | 499   | 1,300 | 3,159 | 408 | 920 |
| 1982 | 96   | 433   | 68  | 474   | 1,299 | 3,213 | 414 | 949 |
| 1983 | 122  | 861   | 67  | 819   | 1,300 | 3,385 | 418 | 961 |
| 1984 | 163  | 3,192 | 76  | 822   | 1,310 | 3,449 | 418 | 959 |
| 1985 | 195  | 3,907 | 79  | 981   | 1,286 | 3,344 | 423 | 965 |
| 1986 | 302  | 5,985 | 97  | 1,208 | 1,249 | 3,160 | 422 | 959 |
| 1987 | 469  | 9,105 | 105 | 1,925 | 1,238 | 2,971 | 422 | 966 |
| 1988 | 572  | 8,963 | ... | 3,774 | 1,225 | 2,902 | ... | 912 |

**F4    NORTH AMERICA: Merchant Ships Registered**

|      | Honduras | | Mexico | | Panama | | USA | | |
|      | Steam & Motor | | Steam & Motor | | Steam & Motor | | Steam & Motor | | b |
|------|------|------|------|------|------|------|------|------|------|
|      | a | b | a | b | a | b | a | Sail | Steam & Motor |
| 1965 | 47 | 81 | 90 | 269 | 692 | 4,465 | 3,416 | 8 | 19,730 |
| 1966 | 43 | 70 | 95 | 306 | 702 | 4,543 | 3,332 | ... | ... |
| 1967 | 45 | 75 | 99 | 330 | 757 | 4,756 | 3,303 | ... | ... |
| 1968 | 45 | 69 | 114 | 404 | 798 | 5,097 | 3,232 | 6 | 19,396 |
| 1969 | 51 | 66 | 118 | 424 | 823 | 5,374 | 3,146 | 6 | 19,433 |
|      |    |    |     |     |     |       |       |   | 19,550 |
| 1970 | 52 | 60 | 132 | 381 | 886 | 5,646 | 2,983 | 6 | 18,463 |
| 1971 | 54 | 70 | 185 | 401 | 1,031 | 6,262 | 3,327 | ... | 16,266 |
| 1972 | 58 | 74 | 216 | 417 | 1,337 | 7,794 | 3,687 | ... | 15,024 |
| 1973 | 57 | 67 | 248 | 453 | 1,692 | 9,569 | 4,063 | ... | 14,912 |
| 1974 | 56 | 70 | 261 | 515 | 1,962 | 11,003 | 4,086 | ... | 14,429 |
| 1975 | 60 | 68 | 274 | 575 | 2,418 | 13,667 | 4,346 | ... | 14,587 |
| 1976 | 57 | 71 | 290 | 594 | 2,680 | 15,631 | 4,614 | ... | 14,908 |
| 1977 | 63 | 105 | 311 | 674 | 3,267 | 19,458 | 4,740 | ... | 15,300 |
| 1978 | 70 | 131 | 336 | 727 | 3,640 | 20,749 | 4,746 | ... | 16,188 |
| 1979 | 99 | 193 | 349 | 915 | 3,803 | 22,324 | 5,088 | ... | 17,542 |
| 1980 | 124 | 213 | 361 | 1,006 | 4,090 | 24,191 | 5,579 | ... | 18,464 |
| 1981 | 143 | 201 | 456 | 1,135 | 4,461 | 27,657 | 5,869 | ... | 18,908 |
| 1982 | 172 | 234 | 545 | 1,252 | 5,032 | 32,600 | 6,133 | ... | 19,111 |
| 1983 | 191 | 222 | 619 | 1,475 | 5,316 | 34,666 | 6,437 | ... | 19,358 |
| 1984 | 238 | 277 | 624 | 1,489 | 5,499 | 37,244 | 6,441 | ... | 19,292 |
| 1985 | 291 | 357 | 638 | 1,467 | 5,512 | 40,674 | 6,447 | ... | 19,518 |
| 1986 | 424 | 555 | 642 | 1,520 | 5,252 | 41,305 | 6,496 | ... | 19,900 |
| 1987 | 503 | 506 | 651 | 1,532 | 5,136 | 43,255 | 6,427 | ... | 20,178 |
| 1988 | ... | 582 | ... | 1,448 | 5,022 | 44,604 | 6,442 | ... | 20,832 |

**F4    SOUTH AMERICA: MERCHANT SHIPS REGISTERED**

| | Chile | | | | | | Chile | | | | | | Chile | | | |
|---|---|---|---|---|---|---|---|---|---|---|---|---|---|---|---|---|
| | Sail | | Steam | | | | Sail | | Steam | | | | Sail | | Steam | |
| | a | c | a | c | | | a | c | a | c | | | a | c | a | c |
| 1848 | 105 | 13 | — | — | 1860 | 259 | 59 | 7 | 1.4 | 1875 | 52 | 13 | 28 | 9.9 |
| 1849 | 119 | 20 | — | — | 1861 | 260 | 59 | 7 | 1.4 | 1876 | 62 | 13 | 28 | 9.9 |
| 1850 | 157 | 28 | — | — | 1862 | 259 | 58 | 10 | 1.7 | 1877 | 89 | 21 | 25 | 11 |
| 1851 | 182 | 35 | — | — | 1863 | 250 | 55 | 9 | 1.6 | 1878 | ... | ... | ... | ... |
| 1852 | 215 | 43 | — | — | 1864 | 263 | 62 | 9 | 1.6 | 1879 | ... | ... | ... | ... |
| 1853 | 214 | 47 | 3 | 0.8 | | | | | | | | | | |
| 1854 | 217 | 49 | 5 | 0.9 | 1865 | 248 | 66 | 9 | 1.3 | 1880 | 31 | 5.2 | 18 | 5.4 |
| | | | | | 1866 | 247 | 66 | 11 | 2.2 | 1881 | 56 | 17 | 18 | 4.8 |
| 1855 | 257 | 59 | — | — | 1867 | ...9 | ...9 | ...9 | ...9 | 1882 | 90 | 35 | 24 | 9.7 |
| 1856 | 257 | 60 | 8 | 2.0 | 1868 | 19 | 2.8 | 2 | 0.6 | 1883 | 104 | 41 | 27 | 13 |
| 1857 | 267 | 63 | — | — | 1869 | 33 | 5.5 | 7 | 0.6 | 1884 | 128 | 51 | 30 | 15 |
| 1858 | 260 | 62 | — | — | | | | | | | **Steam & Motor** | | | |
| 1859 | 261 | 58 | 7 | 1.2 | 1870 | 56 | 11 | 12 | 2.4 | 1885 | 131 | 55 | 35 | 17 |
| | | | | | 1871 | 61 | 13 | 14 | 2.5 | 1886 | 136 | 59 | 37 | 19 |
| | | | | | 1872 | 57 | 13 | 18 | 3.6 | 1887 | 141 | 59 | 38 | 19 |
| | | | | | 1873 | 57 | 12 | 18 | 4.2 | | | | | |
| | | | | | 1874 | 51 | 11 | 26 | 8.0 | | | | | |

| | Argentina | | | | Brazil | | | | Chile | | | |
|---|---|---|---|---|---|---|---|---|---|---|---|---|
| | Sail[10] | | Steam & Motor[11] | | Sail[10] | | Steam & Motor[11] | | Sail | | Steam | |
| | a | b | a | b | a | b | a | b | a | c | a | c |
| 1888 | 86 | 20 | 48 | 23 | 265 | 57 | 121 | 67 | 140 | 63 | 37 | 19 |
| 1889 | 101 | 28 | 50 | 24 | 271 | 58 | 125 | 70 | 150 | 69 | 39 | 20 |
| 1890 | 106 | 29 | 54 | 25 | 268 | 56 | 129 | 76 | 150 | 72 | 39 | 24 |
| 1891 | 105 | 28 | 57 | 29 | 270 | 58 | 147 | 93 | 150 | 69 | 43 | 25 |
| 1892 | 113 | 31 | 53 | 25 | 276 | 61 | 180 | 121 | 146 | 66 | 48 | 28 |
| 1893 | 115 | 29 | 60 | 36 | 282 | 65 | 176 | 120 | 116 | 57 | 54 | 28 |
| 1894 | 124 | 28 | 56 | 33 | 285 | 66 | 172 | 115 | 117 | 57 | 50 | 24 |

| | Peru | | | | Uruguay | | | | Venezuela | |
|---|---|---|---|---|---|---|---|---|---|---|
| | Sail[10] | | Steam & Motor[11] | | Sail[10] | | Steam & Motor[11] | | Steam & Motor | |
| | a | b | a | b | a | b | a | b | a | b |
| 1888 | 38 | 24 | 7 | 8.4 | 37 | 11 | 10 | 4.2 | 5 | 1.9 |
| 1889 | 36 | 21 | 7 | 8.5 | 37 | 10 | 15 | 7.8 | 5 | 2.5 |
| 1890 | 36 | 21 | 5 | 5.3 | 40 | 12 | 18 | 8.2 | 6 | 2.8 |
| 1891 | 37 | 22 | 5 | 5.3 | 42 | 12 | 19 | 8.7 | 6 | 2.1 |
| 1892 | 36 | 20 | 4 | 4.6 | 44 | 12 | 17 | 7.6 | 5 | 2.0 |
| 1893 | 35 | 19 | 3 | 2.6 | 46 | 13 | 24 | 7.6 | 5 | 2.0 |
| 1894 | 37 | 17 | 3 | 2.6 | 45 | 13 | 17 | 8.4 | 5 | 1.9 |

**F4      SOUTH AMERICA: Merchant Ships Registered**

| | Argentina | | | | Brazil | | | | Chile | | | |
|---|---|---|---|---|---|---|---|---|---|---|---|---|
| | Sail[10] | | Steam & Motor[11] | | Sail[10] | | Steam & Motor[11] | | Sail | | Steam & Motor | |
| | a | b | a | b | a | b | a | b | a | c | a | c |
| 1895 | 140 | 36 | 54 | 34 | 303 | 71 | 190 | 127 | 111 | 52 | 54 | 28 |
| 1896 | 154 | 38 | 61 | 43 | 320 | 74 | 214 | 139 | 113 | 53 | 48 | 26 |
| 1897 | 152 | 36 | 61 | 46 | 322 | 72 | 218 | 144 | ... | ... | ... | ... |
| 1898 | 157 | 40 | 64 | 48 | 343 | 68 | 211 | 144 | 112 | 52 | 50 | 25 |
| 1899 | 155 | 29 | 68 | 58 | 364 | 80 | 211 | 140 | ... | ... | ... | ... |
| 1900 | 155 | 40 | 76 | 62 | 358 | 80 | 214 | 139 | 82 | 37 | 54 | 31 |
| 1901 | 151 | 38 | 75 | 60 | 343 | 77 | 208 | 142 | 83 | 38 | 53 | 30 |
| 1902 | 159 | 42 | 81 | 66 | 340 | 77 | 204 | 134 | 84 | 36 | 52 | 29 |
| 1903 | 163 | 41 | 93 | 73 | 347 | 76 | 186 | 124 | 76 | 35 | 56 | 37 |
| 1904 | 156 | 42 | 120 | 79 | 345 | 76 | 202 | 136 | ... | ... | ... | ... |
| 1905 | 161 | 41 | 101 | 85 | 340 | 74 | 192 | 146 | 64 | 33 | 63 | 35 |
| 1906 | 161 | 44 | 132 | 116 | 305 | 66 | 207 | 151 | 63 | 39 | 83 | 56 |
| 1907 | 175 | 53 | 128 | 111 | 297 | 64 | 215 | 180 | 68 | 44 | 100 | 54 |
| 1908 | 177 | 52 | 126 | 111 | 298 | 63 | 208 | 196 | 63 | 41 | 96 | 53 |
| 1909 | 181 | 56 | 123 | 113 | 293 | 61 | 208 | 194 | 63 | 41 | 95 | 54 |
| 1910 | 183 | 57 | 130 | 129 | 290 | 61 | 218 | 210 | 48 | 39 | 67 | 57 |
| 1911 | 182 | 54 | 141 | 146 | 286 | 62 | 229 | 237 | 57 | 38 | 102 | 58 |
| 1912 | 192 | 64 | 143 | 150 | 289 | 61 | 244 | 264 | 45 | 30 | 103 | 53 |
| 1913 | 175[10] | 52[10] | 147 | 157 | 303[10] | 68[10] | 257 | 284 | 35 | 22 | 98 | 43 |
| 1914 | 52 | 20 | 150 | 164 | 87 | 17 | 252 | 276 | 35 | 25 | 92 | 44 |
| 1915 | 48 | 19 | 144 | 162 | 86 | 15 | 248 | 268 | 28 | 25 | 101 | 51 |
| 1916 | 49 | 17 | 135 | 147 | 79 | 13 | 240 | 259 | 28 | 21 | 98 | 45 |
| 1917 | 56 | 23 | 160 | 143 | 82 | 16 | 312 | 457 | 39 | 29 | 92 | 43 |
| 1918 | 50 | 20 | 140 | 139 | 86 | 19 | 312 | 492 | 35 | 23 | 95 | 47 |
| 1919 | 55 | 21 | 142 | 163 | 83 | 20 | 299 | 493 | 26 | 17 | 103 | 45 |
| 1920 | 48 | 20 | 140 | 149 | 85 | 22 | 298 | 475 | 25 | 20 | 114 | 52 |
| 1921 | 46[11] | 21[11] | 148[11] | 160[11] | 82[11] | 22[11] | 299[11] | 473[11] | 24[12] | 22[12] | 115[12] | 56[12] |
| | | | | | | | | | 23 | b 14 | 101 | b 100 |
| 1922 | 43 | 20 | 173 | 162 | 50 | 23 | 349 | 469 | 19 | 10 | 107 | 121 |
| 1923 | 32 | 18 | 167 | 161 | 45 | 19 | 337 | 459 | 18 | 8.3 | 119 | 164 |
| 1924 | 33 | 20 | 182 | 179 | 45 | 20 | 330 | 445 | 22 | 20 | 125 | 161 |
| 1925 | 34 | 20 | 192 | 203 | 44 | 18 | 330 | 448 | 21 | 20 | 123 | 166 |
| 1926 | 33 | 19 | 209 | 216 | 43 | 18 | 338 | 465 | 18 | 16 | 120 | 164 |
| 1927 | 39 | 25 | 228 | 238 | 44 | 18 | 332 | 508 | 14 | 11 | 114 | 152 |
| 1928 | 40 | 23 | 252 | 265 | 44 | 17 | 344 | 542 | 14 | 11 | 116 | 160 |
| 1929 | 38 | 22 | 273 | 275 | 41 | 15 | 350 | 546 | 11 | 10 | 108 | 144 |
| 1930 | 43 | 25 | 292 | 298 | 42 | 15 | 346 | 544 | 11 | 8 | 120 | 185 |
| 1931 | 41 | 25 | 299 | 303 | 14 | 5 | 297 | 494 | 3 | 4 | 113 | 180 |
| 1932 | 41 | 24 | 304 | 312 | 13 | 5 | 296 | 492 | 3 | 4 | 108 | 174 |
| 1933 | 41 | 24 | 305 | 318 | 15 | 5 | 295 | 489 | 3 | 4 | 99 | 152 |
| 1934 | 40 | 24 | 304 | 316 | 15 | 5 | 293 | 495 | 3 | 4 | 98 | 153 |
| 1935 | 42 | 26 | 298 | 317 | 15 | 5 | 293 | 486 | 3 | 4 | 90 | 142 |
| 1936 | 42 | 27 | 286 | 305 | 13 | 3 | 283 | 475 | 3 | 4 | 90 | 139 |
| 1937 | 43 | 25 | 290 | 293 | 13 | 3 | 286 | 473 | 3 | 4 | 90 | 138 |
| 1938 | 42 | 22 | 293 | 281 | 11 | 3 | 286 | 483 | 5 | 5 | 94 | 158 |
| 1939 | 42 | 22 | 295 | 291 | 11 | 3 | 293 | 485 | 5 | 5 | 101 | 172 |

**F4    SOUTH AMERICA: Merchant Ships Registered**

**1895–1939**

| | Peru | | | | Uruguay | | | | Venezuela | |
|---|---|---|---|---|---|---|---|---|---|---|
| | Sail[10] | | Steam & Motor[11] | | Sail[10] | | Steam & Motor[11] | | Steam & Motor | |
| | a | b | a | b | a | b | a | b | a | b |
| 1895 | 46 | 20 | 5 | 5.5 | 51 | 13 | 18 | 8.1 | 7 | 4.0 |
| 1896 | 54 | 22 | 6 | 6.4 | 51 | 12 | 19 | 9.4 | 5 | 2.0 |
| 1897 | 58 | 25 | 5 | 6.0 | 55 | 14 | 22 | 14 | 7 | 3.7 |
| 1898 | 63 | 27 | 4 | 5.1 | 56 | 14 | 21 | 11 | 6 | 3.2 |
| 1899 | 60 | 24 | 3 | 5.0 | 58 | 15 | 19 | 10 | 4 | 2.5 |
| 1900 | 57 | 24 | 5 | 6.4 | 58 | 16 | 21 | 12 | 7 | 3.9 |
| 1901 | 55 | 23 | 5 | 6.4 | 62 | 20 | 23 | 13 | 6 | 3.1 |
| 1902 | 55 | 23 | 5 | 6.4 | 67 | 26 | 26 | 22 | 7 | 5.3 |
| 1903 | 56 | 25 | 3 | 4.7 | 70 | 30 | 26 | 25 | 6 | 3.4 |
| 1904 | 56 | 25 | 3 | 4.7 | 76 | 32 | 32 | 27 | 8 | 3.7 |
| 1905 | 55 | 25 | 4 | 8.1 | 72 | 31 | 21 | 21 | 6 | 3.4 |
| 1906 | 53 | 22 | 5 | 8.5 | 65 | 26 | 25 | 25 | 6 | 3.4 |
| 1907 | 58 | 27 | 7 | 9.9 | 67 | 31 | 23 | 26 | 6 | 3.4 |
| 1908 | 60 | 29 | 7 | 11 | 62 | 28 | 28 | 40 | 6 | 3.4 |
| 1909 | 65 | 31 | 7 | 16 | 64 | 29 | 34 | 58 | 6 | 3.4 |
| 1910 | 60 | 31 | 9 | 21 | 62 | 27 | 36 | 50 | 6 | 3.4 |
| 1911 | 57 | 30 | 9 | 26 | 57 | 24 | 29 | 40 | 7 | 4.5 |
| 1912 | 57 | 29 | 11 | 31 | 53 | 23 | 31 | 45 | 7 | 4.5 |
| 1913 | $58_{10}$ | $31_{10}$ | 12 | 32 | $56_{10}$ | $25_{10}$ | 30 | 42 | 7 | 4.5 |
| 1914 | 40 | 21 | 13 | 39 | 45 | 17 | 19 | 17 | 5 | 3.9 |
| 1915 | 41 | 21 | 13 | 32 | 45 | 16 | 17 | 14 | 6 | 4.2 |
| 1916 | 40 | 20 | 11 | 26 | 48 | 23 | 19 | 19 | 7 | 4.6 |
| 1917 | 40 | 21 | 14 | 27 | 49 | 26 | 26 | 21 | 10 | 4.8 |
| 1918 | 41 | 23 | 17 | 53 | 45 | 19 | 21 | 37 | 11 | 5.2 |
| 1919 | 40 | 22 | 14 | 45 | 43 | 18 | 22 | 24 | 9 | 4.9 |
| 1920 | 40 | 22 | 15 | 33 | 43 | 18 | 27 | 52 | 9 | 4.9 |
| 1921 | $42_{11}$ | $30_{11}$ | $16_{11}$ | $34_{11}$ | $44_{11}$ | $21_{11}$ | $29_{11}$ | $62_{11}$ | 9 | 4.9 |
| 1922 | 44 | 33 | 30 | 68 | 12 | 11 | 41 | 65 | 9 | 4.6 |
| 1923 | 22 | 23 | 25 | 59 | ... | 13 | ... | 73 | 12 | 5.6 |
| 1924 | 18 | 20 | 20 | 51 | ... | 10 | ... | 70 | 14 | 11 |
| 1925 | 17 | 17 | 22 | 59 | 15 | 9 | 50 | 68 | 15 | 11 |
| 1926 | 18 | 19 | 28 | 61 | 14 | 8 | 49 | 67 | ... | ... |
| 1927 | 15 | 19 | 28 | 57 | 10 | 7 | 45 | 24 | ... | ... |
| 1928 | 16 | 17 | 26 | 52 | ... | ... | ... | ... | 32 | 45 |
| 1929 | 15 | 18 | 23 | 44 | ... | ... | ... | ... | 36 | 56 |
| 1930 | 15 | 20 | 24 | 45 | ... | ... | ... | ... | 38 | 58 |
| 1931 | 15 | 20 | 24 | 45 | ... | ... | ... | ... | 38 | 59 |
| 1932 | 15 | 20 | 24 | 45 | ... | ... | ... | ... | 36 | 58 |
| 1933 | 14 | 17 | 24 | 43 | ... | ... | ... | ... | 37 | 60 |
| 1934 | 13 | 17 | 22 | 33 | ... | ... | ... | ... | 38 | 63 |
| 1935 | 13 | 17 | 21 | 27 | ... | ... | ... | ... | 41 | 65 |
| 1936 | 13 | 17 | 24 | 29 | ... | ... | ... | ... | 40 | 72 |
| 1937 | 4 | 6 | 26 | 31 | ... | ... | ... | ... | 38 | 71 |
| 1938 | 4 | 6 | 29 | 35 | ... | ... | ... | ... | 43 | 76 |
| 1939 | 4 | 6 | 28 | 34 | ... | ... | ... | ... | 47 | 75 |

**F4      SOUTH AMERICA: Merchant Ships Registered**

|  | Argentina | | Brazil | | Chile | | Colombia | |
|---|---|---|---|---|---|---|---|---|
|  | Steam & Motor | | Steam & Motor | | Steam & Motor | | Steam & Motor | |
|  | a | b | a | b | a | c | a | b |
| 1945 | ... | ... | ... | ... | ... | ... | ... | ... |
| 1946 | 113 | 354 | 166 | 511 | 84 | 160 | ... | ... |
| 1947 | 312 | 571 | 307 | 603 | 98 | 191 | ... | ... |
| 1948 | 330 | 683 | 331 | 706 | 92 | 188 | ... | ... |
| 1949 | 357 | 814 | 331 | 722 | 91 | 175 | ... | ... |
| 1950 | 369 | 914 | 328 | 698 | 88 | 169 | ... | ... |
| 1951 | 363 | 979 | 335 | 688 | 85 | 168 | ... | ... |
| 1952 | 365 | 1,034 | 374 | 794 | 92 | 188 | ... | ... |
| 1953 | 370 | 1,057 | 384 | 854 | 94 | 199 | ... | ... |
| 1954 | 368 | 1,057 | 399 | 895 | 96 | 209 | ... | ... |
| 1955 | 364 | 1,043 | 396 | 893 | 101 | 230 | ... | ... |
| 1956 | 364 | 1,050 | 386 | 862 | 109 | 249 | ... | ... |
| 1957 | 360 | 1,039 | 398 | 891 | 111 | 246 | ... | ... |
| 1958 | 356 | 1,029 | 409 | 911 | 102 | 231 | ... | ... |
| 1959 | 358 | 1,039 | 415 | 952 | 105 | 232 | ... | ... |
| 1960 | 355 | 1,042 | 423 | 1,055 | 110 | 246 | ... | ... |
| 1961 | 374 | 1,195 | 455 | 1,201 | 113 | 258 | 36 | 114 |
| 1962 | 332 | 1,262 | 430 | 1,204 | 103 | 258 | 37 | 116 |
| 1963 | 346 | 1,308 | 428 | 1,227 | 104 | 286 | 37 | 114 |
| 1964 | 318 | 1,284 | 421 | 1,271 | 111 | 284 | 37 | 132 |
| 1965 | 323 | 1,289 | 397 | 1,253 | 126 | 296 | 38 | 160 |
| 1966 | 322 | 1,279 | 392 | 1,279 | 136 | 290 | 41 | 187 |
| 1967 | 315 | 1,240 | 394 | 1,305 | 134 | 279 | 42 | 196 |
| 1968 | 315 | 1,197 | 398 | 1,294 | 130 | 269 | 47 | 209 |
| 1969 | 319 | 1,218 | 414 | 1,381 | 133 | 288 | 47 | 206 |
| 1970 | 327 | 1,266 | 422 | 1,722 | 134 | 308 | 49 | 235 |
| 1971 | 335 | 1,312 | 420 | 1,731 | 135 | 388 | 50 | 209 |
| 1972 | 343 | 1,401 | 444 | 1,885 | 134 | 382 | 54 | 232 |
| 1973 | 351 | 1,453 | 469 | 2,103 | 138 | 384 | 54 | 224 |
| 1974 | 366 | 1,408 | 471 | 2,429 | 135 | 364 | 54 | 211 |
| 1975 | 374 | 1,447 | 482 | 2,691 | 138 | 386 | 53 | 209 |
| 1976 | 379 | 1,470 | 520 | 3,096 | 142 | 410 | 53 | 212 |
| 1977 | 401 | 1,677 | 538 | 3,330 | 143 | 406 | 52 | 247 |
| 1978 | 432 | 2,001 | 565 | 3,702 | 146 | 466 | 61 | 272 |
| 1979 | 495 | 2,344 | 585 | 4,007 | 154 | 537 | 65 | 292 |
| 1980 | 537 | 2,546 | 607 | 4,534 | 172 | 614 | 69 | 283 |
| 1981 | 521 | 2,307 | 627 | 5,133 | 182 | 564 | 72 | 297 |
| 1982 | 523 | 2,256 | 666 | 5,678 | 192 | 495 | 74 | 314 |
| 1983 | 532 | 2,470 | 698 | 5,808 | 200 | 488 | 82 | 359 |
| 1984 | 530 | 2,422 | 706 | 5,722 | 219 | 473 | 82 | 374 |
| 1985 | 549 | 2,457 | 702 | 6,057 | 234 | 454 | 80 | 366 |
| 1986 | 454 | 2,117 | 697 | 6,212 | 282 | 567 | 90 | 380 |
| 1987 | 434 | 1,901 | 718 | 6,324 | 264 | 547 | 93 | 424 |
| 1988 | 451 | 1,877 | 719 | 6,123 | ... | 604 | ... | 412 |

**F4      SOUTH AMERICA: Merchant Ships Registered**

|  | Ecuador | | Peru | | Uruguay | | Venezuela | |
|--|---------|---|------|---|---------|---|-----------|---|
|  | Steam & Motor | | Steam & Motor | | Steam & Motor | | Steam & Motor | |
|  | a | b | a | b | a | b | a | b |
| 1945 | ... | ... | ... | ... | ... | ... | ... | ... |
| 1946 | ... | ... | ... | ... | ... | ... | ... | ... |
| 1947 | ... | ... | 41 | 74 | ... | ... | 60 | 90 |
| 1948 | ... | ... | 40 | 87 | 43 | 63 | 64 | 96 |
| 1949 | ... | ... | 43 | 88 | 47 | 85 | 79 | 137 |
| 1950 | ... | ... | 41 | 87 | 47 | 85 | 93 | 157 |
| 1951 | ... | ... | 44 | 91 | 44 | 70 | 97 | 167 |
| 1952 | ... | ... | 48 | 96 | 43 | 63 | 96 | 173 |
| 1953 | ... | ... | 49 | 97 | 43 | 63 | 97 | 187 |
| 1954 | ... | ... | 49 | 97 | 44 | 68 | 97 | 210 |
| 1955 | ... | ... | 47 | 98 | 41 | 66 | 94 | 216 |
| 1956 | ... | ... | 48 | 98 | 42 | 73 | 90 | 217 |
| 1957 | ... | ... | 50 | 102 | 38 | 70 | 92 | 225 |
| 1958 | ... | ... | 54 | 108 | 38 | 72 | 99 | 233 |
| 1959 | ... | ... | 55 | 121 | 40 | 77 | 104 | 251 |
| 1960 | ... | ... | 57 | 120 | ... | ... | 100 | 349 |
| 1961 | ... | ... | 61 | 136 | ... | ... | 90 | 324 |
| 1962 | ... | ... | 56 | 131 | ... | ... | 85 | 328 |
| 1963 | ... | ... | ... | ... | ... | ... | 81 | 319 |
| 1964 | ... | ... | 60 | 158 | 37 | 104 | 81 | 330 |
| 1965 | ... | ... | 78 | 163 | 39 | 113 | 79 | 313 |
| 1966 | ... | ... | 119 | 169 | 39 | 113 | 83 | 315 |
| 1967 | ... | ... | 231 | 251 | 40 | 126 | 88 | 350 |
| 1968 | 14 | 43 | 275 | 288 | 42 | 131 | 89 | 351 |
| 1969 | 16 | 44 | 366 | 338 | 41 | 112 | 90 | 369 |
| 1970 | 18 | 45 | 494 | 378 | 41 | 141 | 96 | 393 |
| 1971 | 18 | 45 | 601 | 421 | 42 | 163 | 109 | 412 |
| 1972 | 21 | 57 | 655 | 446 | 39 | 143 | 113 | 411 |
| 1973 | 23 | 76 | 663 | 448 | 38 | 143 | 137 | 479 |
| 1974 | 38 | 128 | 675 | 514 | 37 | 130 | 143 | 480 |
| 1975 | 44 | 142 | 677 | 518 | 38 | 131 | 152 | 516 |
| 1976 | 46 | 181 | 681 | 525 | 43 | 151 | 165 | 543 |
| 1977 | 55 | 197 | 681 | 555 | 45 | 193 | 179 | 639 |
| 1978 | 59 | 201 | 686 | 575 | 48 | 174 | 201 | 824 |
| 1979 | 69 | 234 | 694 | 646 | 53 | 198 | 220 | 882 |
| 1980 | 86 | 275 | 698 | 741 | 72 | 198 | 225 | 848 |
| 1981 | 100 | 299 | 694 | 826 | 76 | 200 | 227 | 742 |
| 1982 | 110 | 354 | 696 | 836 | 81 | 202 | 236 | 911 |
| 1983 | 130 | 388 | 679 | 781 | 88 | 217 | 244 | 973 |
| 1984 | 135 | 412 | 670 | 788 | 89 | 190 | 250 | 1,003 |
| 1985 | 152 | 444 | 650 | 818 | 96 | 173 | 269 | 985 |
| 1986 | 155 | 438 | 632 | 754 | 89 | 150 | 279 | 998 |
| 1987 | 156 | 421 | 635 | 788 | 90 | 144 | 283 | 999 |
| 1988 | ... | 428 | ... | 675 | ... | 170 | ... | 982 |

## F4       Merchant Ships Registered

NOTES

1.  SOURCES: The national publications listed on p. xiv–xvi; *Lloyd's Register of Shipping Statistical Tables;* and League of Nations and UN, *Statistical Yearbooks,* with data for Cuba, Honduras, Mexico, and all South American countries to 1921 from the *Shipping World Year Book.*
2.  Tonnage figures are normally given in gross capacity.
3.  The minimum size of vessel on the register has varied from time to time and from country to country. Where possible changes are indicated. Since 1948 the usual minimum has been 100 GRT.
4.  Data since 1947 apply to 31 December. Prior to that, most were for 30 June.
5.  The removal of vessels lost, abandoned, sold abroad, etc. was not always done annually, so that the cumulative error sometimes resulted in the inflation of the statistics. When general correction of these errors occurred, the effect was concentrate in a single year and can give a misleading impression.
6.  For the period 1953–60 the figures for Costa Rica are large enough to be shown separately. They are as follows:—

|      | a   | b   |      | a   | b   |      | a  | b   |
|------|-----|-----|------|-----|-----|------|----|-----|
| 1953 | 50  | 146 | 1956 | 152 | 508 | 1959 | 91 | 288 |
| 1954 | 70  | 201 | 1957 | 152 | 519 | 1960 | 44 | 92  |
| 1955 | 114 | 341 | 1958 | 144 | 510 |      |    |     |

FOOTNOTES

[1] Including canal boats and barges to 1868 (1st line) for Sail tonnage series and to 1964 (1st line) for numbers, whereafter the latter relate to steam and motor ships only.

[2] There was a change in the method of measurement between 1865 and 1868, during which period the tonnage figures are 'mixed'. It is noted in *Historical Statistics of the United States* (p. 743) that 'neither the magnitude nor the direction of the change can be stated'.

[3] Excluding motor-assisted sailing ships to 1922.

[4] From 1882 to 1898 all ships are included under Sail.

[5] From 1940 to 1947 (1st line) all ships are included under Sail.

[6] Newfoundland is included in Canada from 1949.

[7] International fleet only from 1958 to 1964 (1st line).

[8] Subsequently from *Lloyd's Register of Shipping Statistical Tables.*

[9] No explanation of this break is given in the source.

[10] Including motor-assisted sailing ships to 1913.

[11] Excluding motor-assisted sailing ships to 1921, when there were also changes in classification affecting sailing vessels.

[12] This break occurs on a change from national sources to *Lloyd's Register of Shipping Statistical Tables.*

[13] Registered tonnage was insignificant in previous years, except 1964, when figures were as follows:—

|      | Bahamas | | Bermuda | |
|------|-----|-----|-----|-----|
|      | a   | b   | a   | b   |
| 1964 | 86  | 218 | 24  | 168 |

# F5    NORTH AMERICAN INLAND WATERWAY TRAFFIC

Key:    a = thousand metric; b = million metric tons; c = thousand million ton—kilometres

| | Canada[1] | USA | | | | Canada[1] | USA | |
| | | New York Canals | | | | | New York Canals | |
| | Total traffic | Total traffic | Origin on Erie Canal | | | Total traffic | Total traffic | Origin on Erie Canal |
| | a | a | a | | | a | a | a |
| 1835 | ... | ... | ... | | 1870 | 1,190 | 5,601 | 2,797 |
| 1836 | ... | ... | ... | | 1871 | 1,341[1] | 5,868 | 3,249 |
| 1837 | ... | 1,063 | 605 | | 1872 | 1,209 | 6,054 | 3,232 |
| 1838 | ... | 1,209 | 676 | | 1873 | 1,366 | 5,774 | 3,268 |
| 1839 | ... | 1,302 | 767 | | 1874 | 1,260 | 5,266 | 2,810 |
| 1840 | ... | 1,285 | 753 | | 1875 | 942 | 4,409 | 2,529 |
| 1841 | ... | 1,380 | 822 | | 1876 | 998 | 3,785 | 2,194 |
| 1842 | ... | 1,122 | 646 | | 1877 | 1,066 | 4,496 | 2,952 |
| 1843 | ... | 1,373 | 743 | | 1878 | 879 | 4,691 | 3,274 |
| 1844 | ... | 1,648 | 858 | | 1879 | 786 | 4,865 | 3,465 |
| 1845 | ... | 1,794 | 942 | | 1880 | 744 | 5,858 | 4,181 |
| 1846 | ... | 2,058 | 1,147 | | 1881 | 623 | 4,698 | 3,265 |
| 1847 | ... | 2,603 | 1,507 | | 1882 | 718 | 4,960 | 3,351 |
| 1848 | ... | 2,537 | 1,451 | | 1883 | 912 | 5,138 | 3,254 |
| 1849 | ... | 2,535 | 1,472 | | 1884 | 760 | 4,545 | 3,075 |
| 1850 | ... | 2,791 | 1,483 | | 1885 | 712 | 4,293 | 2,910 |
| 1851 | ... | 3,250 | 1,774 | | 1886 | 889[1] 2,693 | 4,803 | 3,455 |
| 1852 | ... | 3,505 | 1,932 | | 1887 | 2,559 | 5,038 | 3,484 |
| 1853 | ... | 3,854 | 1,992 | | 1888 | 2,506 | 4,484 | 3,013 |
| 1854 | ... | 3,779 | 2,018 | | 1889 | 2,872 | 4,872 | 3,333 |
| 1855 | ... | 3,649 | 1,998 | | 1890 | 2,643 | 4,759 | 2,997 |
| 1856 | ... | 3,734 | 1,912 | | 1891 | 2,634 | 4,140 | 2,810 |
| 1857 | ... | 3,034 | 1,421 | | 1892 | 2,751 | 3,885 | 2,702 |
| 1858 | ... | 3,325 | 1,603 | | 1893 | 3,218 | 3,930 | 2,955 |
| 1859 | ... | 3,431 | 1,591 | | 1894 | 2,670 | 3,522 | 2,852 |
| 1860 | ... | 4,219 | 2,044 | | 1895 | 3,026 | 3,175 | 2,137 |
| 1861 | ... | 4,089 | 2,269 | | 1896 | 7,249 | 3,370 | 2,488 |
| 1862 | ... | 5,079 | 2,907 | | 1897 | 7,712 | 3,282 | 2,345 |
| 1863 | ... | 5,042 | 2,681 | | 1898 | 6,004 | 3,048 | 2,121 |
| 1864 | ... | 4,403 | 2,300 | | 1899 | 5,648 | 3,686 | 2,195 |
| 1865 | ... | 4,291 | 2,289 | | 1900 | 4,549 | 3,035 | 1,947 |
| 1866 | ... | 5,239 | 2,627 | | 1901 | 5,139 | 3,103 | 2,048 |
| 1867 | 846 | 5,160 | 2,650 | | 1902 | 6,816 | 2,971 | 1,910 |
| 1868 | 1,054 | 5,844 | 3,036 | | 1903 | 8,359 | 3,280 | 2,190 |
| 1869 | 1,118 | 5,315 | 2,581 | | 1904 | 7,490 | 2,847 | 1,765 |

**F5    North American** Inland Waterway Traffic

| | Canada[1] | | | Panama Canal[3] | USA | | | |
|---|---|---|---|---|---|---|---|---|
| | | | | | New York Canals | | Mississippi Great Lakes[5] | |
| | Total traffic | Origin in Canada | Origin in other countries[2] | Ocean traffic | Total traffic | Origin on Erie Canal | Total traffic | |
| | a | a | a | a | a | a | b[6] | c |
| 1905 | 8,502 | ... | ... | — | 2,927 | 1,814 | ... | ... |
| 1906 | 9,546 | ... | ... | — | 3,212 | 2,164 | ... | ... |
| 1907 | 18,637 | ... | ... | — | 3,092 | 2,191 | ... | ... |
| 1908 | 15,878 | 4,547 | 11,332 | — | 2,769 | 1,975 | ... | ... |
| 1909 | 30,591 | 6,693 | 23,898 | — | 2,827 | 1,843 | ... | ... |
| 1910 | 39,001 | 7,152 | 31,849 | — | 2,788 | 1,835 | ... | ... |
| 1911 | 34,500 | 7,070 | 27,431 | — | 2,810 | 1,843 | ... | ... |
| 1912 | 43,170 | 8,507 | 34,664 | — | 2,364 | 1,628 | ... | ... |
| 1913 | 47,223 | 10,098 | 37,125 | — | 2,361 | 1,622 | ... | ... |
| 1914 | 33,587 | 8,511 | 25,075 | — | 1,888 | 1,235 | ... | ... |
| 1915 | 13,788 | 6,159 | 7,629 | 4,966 | 1,686 | 1,048 | ... | ... |
| 1916 | 21,394 | 6,792 | 14,603 | 3,143[4] | 1,474 | 833 | ... | ... |
| 1917 | 20,175 | 5,356 | 14,764 | 7,168 | 1,177 | 612 | ... | ... |
| 1918 | 17,131 | 3,056 | 14,074 | 7,647 | 1,052 | 605 | ... | ... |
| 1919 | 9,067 | 4,414 | 4,653 | 7,021 | 1,124 | 764 | ... | ... |
| 1920 | 7,924 | 3,714 | 4,210 | 9,522 | 1,290 | 809 | ... | ... |
| 1921 | 8,534 | 4,139 | 4,395 | 11,782 | 1,152 | 901 | ... | ... |
| 1922 | 9,095 | 5,691 | 3,405 | 11,058 | 1,700 | 1,347 | ... | ... |
| 1923 | 10,160 | 6,928 | 3,231 | 19,880 | 1,820 | 1,475 | ... | ... |
| 1924 | 11,675 | 8,035 | 3,640 | 27,426 | 1,844 | 1,535 | 186 | ... |
| 1925 | 12,819 | 8,682 | 4,137 | 24,341 | 2,126 | 1,765 | 203 | ... |
| 1926 | 12,227 | 8,760 | 3,466 | 26,448 | 2,149 | 1,756 | 224 | ... |
| 1927 | 15,956 | 10,763 | 5,102 | 28,179 | 2,342 | 1,858 | 218 | ... |
| 1928 | 16,982 | 12,594 | 4,389 | 30,091 | 2,803 | 2,300 | 220 | ... |
| 1929 | 12,428 | 8,791 | 3,638 | 31,140 | 2,609 | 2,197 | 242 | ... |
| 1930 | 13,429 | 9,938 | 3,491 | 30,500 | 3,271 | 2,762 | 226 | ... |
| 1931 | 14,686 | 10,373 | 4,314 | 25,467 | 3,377 | 2,974 | 198 | ... |
| 1932 | 16,294 | 12,014 | 4,280 | 20,117 | 3,305 | 2,890 | 169 | ... |
| 1933 | 17,037 | 11,544 | 5,494 | 18,452 | 3,696 | 3,243 | 180 | ... |
| 1934 | 16,392 | 9,810 | 6,582 | 25,100 | 3,758 | 3,307 | 196 | ... |
| 1935 | 16,516 | 10,149 | 6,368 | 25,716 | 4,073 | 3,537 | 238 | ... |
| 1936 | 19,476 | 12,215 | 7,260 | 26,931 | 4,549 | 3,829 | 283 | ... |
| 1937 | 21,184 | 10,805 | 10,378 | 28,559 | 4,545 | 3,786 | 316 | ... |
| 1938 | 22,349 | 11,783 | 10,567 | 27,826 | 4,272 | 3,038 | 316 | ... |
| 1939 | 21,220 | 12,837 | 8,383 | 28,314 | 4,254 | 3,306 | 356 | ... |
| 1940 | 20,748 | 11,119 | 9,628 | 27,737 | 4,326 | 3,254 | 387 | ... |
| 1941 | 21,276 | 9,375 | 11,901 | 25,351 | 4,087 | 3,187 | 436 | ... |
| 1942 | 18,960 | 7,044 | 11,916 | 13,825 | 3,211 | 2,504 | 437 | ... |
| 1943 | 19,483 | 7,111 | 12,372 | 10,770 | 2,562 | 1,965 | 415 | ... |
| 1944 | 18,703 | 7,260 | 11,442 | 7,115 | 2,274 | 1,569 | 428 | ... |
| 1945 | 20,248 | 9,517 | 10,731 | 8,742 | 2,693 | 1,511 | 408 | 204 |
| 1946 | 16,924 | 8,078 | 8,845 | 15,218 | 2,559 | 1,529 | 412[6] 157 | 176 |
| 1947 | 19,517 | 9,333 | 10,183 | 22,019 | 3,438 | 2,281 | 238 | 209 |
| 1948 | 21,372 | 10,133 | 11,240 | 24,505 | 4,095 | 2,832 | 257 | 227 |
| 1949 | 22,112 | 13,427 | 8,684 | 25,711 | 3,610 | 2,436 | 243 | 194 |

**F5** **North American** Inland Waterway Traffic

| | Canada[1] | | | Panama Canal[3] | USA | | | |
| | | | | | New York Canals | | Mississippi & Great Lakes[5] | |
| | Total traffic | Origin in Canada | Origin in other countries[2] | Ocean traffic | Total traffic | Origin on Erie Canal | Total traffic | |
|------|-----------|----------|----------|-------|-------|-------|-----|-----|
| | a | a | a | b | a | a | b | c |
| 1950 | 24,892 | 13,733 | 11,159 | 29.3 | 4,187 | 3,284 | 271 | 225 |
| 1951 | 26,603 | 14,519 | 12,085 | 30.6 | 4,728 | 3,332 | 296 | 243 |
| 1952 | 28,444 | 15,644 | 12,799 | 34.1 | 4,071 | 2,824 | 292 | 223 |
| 1953 | 30,275 | 16,750 | 13,525 | 36.7 | 4,080 | 2,914 | 298 | 264[7] |
| | | | | | | | | 248 |
| 1954 | 27,280 | 15,638 | 11,642 | 39.7 | 3,501 | 2,173 | 291 | 192 |
| 1955 | 31,637 | 18,146 | 13,492 | 41.3 | 4,188 | 2,522 | 331 | 250 |
| 1956 | 36,303 | 22,406 | 13,897 | 45.8 | 4,407 | 2,770 | 350 | 244 |
| 1957 | 33,774 | 19,468 | 14,307 | 50.5 | 4,054 | 2,427 | 353 | 260 |
| 1958 | 31,839 | 19,807 | 12,033 | 48.9 | 3,629 | 1,866 | 335 | 203 |
| 1959 | 46,335 | 27,969 | 18,367 | 52.0 | 3,375 | 1,793 | 354 | 213 |
| 1960 | 48,033 | 26,205 | 21,828 | 60.2 | 3,098 | 1,608 | 359 | 246 |
| 1961 | 51,911 | 28,565 | 23,346 | 64.7 | 2,924 | 1,436 | 353 | 232 |
| 1962 | 57,868 | 30,819 | 26,849 | 68.6 | 2,976 | 1,461 | 380 | 247 |
| 1963 | 67,663 | 38,081 | 29,582 | 63.2 | 2,926 | 1,398 | 392 | 259 |
| 1964 | 84,621 | 51,074 | 33,547 | 71.7 | 2,898 | 1,362 | 416 | 285 |
| 1965 | 91,077 | 50,810 | 40,267 | 77.8 | 2,967 | 1,369 | 430 | 301 |
| 1966 | 100,428 | 60,309 | 40,119 | 83.0 | 2,855 | 1,192 | 445 | 325 |
| 1967 | 89,606 | 53,459 | 36,147 | 87.6 | 2,921 | 1,209 | 455 | 323 |
| 1968 | 98,226 | 54,455 | 43,771 | 98.1 | 2,947 | 1,279 | 474 | 339 |
| 1969 | 88,321 | 43,251 | 45,070 | 103 | 2,947 | 1,354 | 499 | 351 |
| 1970 | 106,139[1] | 59,605[1] | 46,534[1] | 116 | 2,481 | 893 | 503 | 369 |
| | 64,513 | ... | ... | 121 | | | | |
| 1971 | 64,213 | ... | ... | 111 | ... | ... | 508 | 361 |
| 1972 | 65,874 | ... | ... | 128 | ... | ... | 542 | 390 |
| 1973 | 68,192 | ... | ... | 150 | ... | ... | 541 | 411 |
| 1974 | 54,555 | ... | ... | 142 | ... | ... | 547 | 417 |
| 1975 | 60,686 | ... | ... | 143 | ... | ... | 531 | 394 |
| 1976 | 65,176 | ... | ... | 119 | ... | ... | 554 | 431 |
| 1977 | ... | ... | ... | 125 | ... | ... | 558 | 420 |
| 1978 | ... | ... | ... | 145 | ... | ... | 570 | 479 |
| 1979 | ... | ... | ... | 157 | ... | ... | 573 | 497 |
| 1980 | ... | ... | ... | 170 | ... | ... | 574 | 474 |
| 1981 | ... | ... | ... | 174 | ... | ... | 560 | 485 |
| 1982 | ... | ... | ... | 188 | ... | ... | 521 | 411 |
| 1983 | ... | ... | ... | 148 | ... | ... | 511 | 425 |
| 1984 | ... | ... | ... | 143 | ... | ... | 569 | 463 |
| 1985 | ... | ... | ... | 141 | ... | ... | ... | 439 |
| 1986 | ... | ... | ... | 142 | ... | ... | ... | 449 |
| 1987 | ... | ... | ... | 151 | ... | ... | ... | 473 |
| 1988 | ... | ... | ... | 159 | ... | ... | ... | 498 |

**F5**     **North America** Inland Waterway Traffic

NOTE

SOURCES: The national publications listed on p. xiv–xvi.

FOOTNOTES

[1] Welland Canal only to 1886 (1st line), and St Lawrence Seaway and Welland Canal (excluding duplication) from 1970 (2nd line). Statistics for the intervening period contain duplication when two or more canals were used. Statistics available since 1976 do not constitute a consistent series.

[2] Mostly, and sometimes entirely, the USA until the 1960s.

[3] Data are for commercial traffic only (i.e. excluding US government traffic), and are for years ending 30 June. The canal was opened on 15 August 1914.

[4] The canal was closed for about seven months during the year.

[5] Covers the whole Mississippi Basin and Great Lakes systems, and canals as indicated in footnotes 6 and 7.

[6] Figures to 1946 (1st line) include traffic on canals and connecting channels, and contain a small element of double-counting.

[7] Figures to 1953 (1st line) include traffic on canals.

**F6    NORTH AMERICA: MOTOR VEHICLES IN USE** (in thousands)

Key:    PC = passenger cars, CV = commercial vehicles

| | Canada[1] | | Mexico | | Puerto Rico[2] | | USA[3] | |
|---|---|---|---|---|---|---|---|---|
| | PC | CV | PC | CV | PC | CV | PC | CV |
| 1900 | ... | ... | ... | ... | ... | | 8.0 | ... |
| 1901 | ... | ... | ... | ... | ... | | 15 | ... |
| 1902 | ... | ... | ... | ... | ... | | 23 | ... |
| 1903 | ... | ... | ... | ... | ... | | 33 | ... |
| 1904 | 0.5 | ... | ... | ... | ... | | 55 | 0.7 |
| 1905 | 0.6 | ... | ... | ... | ... | | 77 | 1.4 |
| 1906 | 1 | ... | ... | ... | ... | | 106 | 2.2 |
| 1907 | 1.5 | ... | ... | ... | ... | | 140 | 2.9 |
| 1908 | 2.2 | ... | ... | ... | | 0.2 | 194 | 4.0 |
| 1909 | 3.2 | ... | ... | ... | | 0.3 | 306 | 6.0 |
| 1910 | 5.9 | ... | ... | ... | | 0.3 | 458 | 10 |
| 1911 | 14 | ... | ... | ... | | 0.6 | 619 | 21 |
| 1912 | 20 | ... | ... | ... | | 1.0 | 902 | 42 |
| 1913 | 29 | ... | ... | ... | | 1.2 | 1,190 | 68 |
| 1914 | 46 | 0.4 | ... | ... | | 1.3 | 1,664 | 99 |
| 1915 | 61 | 0.5 | ... | ... | | 1.8 | 2,332 | 158 |
| 1916 | 78 | 3.5 | ... | ... | | 2.6 | 3,368 | 250 |
| 1917 | 116 | 6.1 | ... | ... | | 3.5 | 4,727 | 391 |
| 1918 | 157 | 9.6 | ... | ... | | 4.7 | 5,555 | 605 |
| 1919 | 196 | 14 | ... | ... | | 5.0 | 6,679 | 898 |
| 1920 | 252 | 22 | ... | ... | | 5.9 | 8,132 | 1,108 |
| 1921 | 334 | 29 | ... | ... | | 7.0 | 9,212 | 1,282 |
| 1922 | 369 | 38 | ... | ... | | 7.4 | 10,704 | 1,570 |
| 1923 | 513 | 55 | ... | ... | | 8.3 | 13,253 | 1,849 |
| 1924 | 573 | 64 | 33 | 10 | | 10 | 15,436 | 2,177 |

**F6  NORTH AMERICA: Motor Vehicles in Use** (in thousands)

1925–1969

| | Bahamas | | Barbados | | Canada[1] | | Costa Rica | | Cuba | |
|---|---|---|---|---|---|---|---|---|---|---|
| | PC | CV | PC | CV | PC | CV | PC | CV | PC | CV |
| 1925 | ... | ... | ... | ... | 641 | 75 | ... | ... | ... | ... |
| 1926 | ... | ... | 1.2 | 0.2 | 737 | 88 | ... | ... | ... | ... |
| 1927 | ... | ... | 1.3 | 0.2 | 83 | 12 | ... | ... | ... | ... |
| 1928 | 0.8 | 0.3 | 1.3 | 0.3 | 931 | 131 | 1.1 | 0.5 | 26 | 13 |
| 1929 | 0.9 | 0.4 | 1.5 | 0.3 | 1,31 | 148 | 1.6 | 0.6 | 33 | 17 |
| 193 | ... | ... | 1.4 | 0.3 | 1,62 | 162 | 1.4 | 0.5 | 27 | 15 |
| 1931 | 0.8 | 0.2 | 1.5 | 0.4 | 1,28 | 163 | ... | ... | ... | ... |
| 1932 | 0.7 | 0.2 | 1.6 | 0.4 | 948 | 156 | ... | ... | 27 | 12 |
| 1933 | 0.7 | 0.2 | 1.7 | 0.5 | 92 | 153 | ... | ... | ... | ... |
| 1934 | 0.8 | 0.2 | 1.9 | 0.5 | 955 | 164 | ... | ... | 22 | 11 |
| 1935 | 0.9 | 0.2 | 2.0 | 0.6 | 992 | 174 | ... | ... | 22 | 1 |
| 1936 | 1.2 | 0.2 | 2.0 | 0.6 | 1,42 | 188 | ... | ... | 22 | 1 |
| 1937 | 1.2 | 0.2 | 2.2 | 0.6 | 1,15 | 24 | 1.9 | 0.8 | 26 | 16 |
| 1938 | ... | ... | ... | ... | 1,162 | 221 | 2.1 | 0.8 | 27 | 16 |
| 1939 | ... | ... | ... | ... | 1,192 | 235 | 2.3 | 0.9 | 28 | 16 |
| 194 | ... | ... | ... | ... | 1,237 | 251 | 2.4 | 1.2 | 29 | 17 |
| 1941 | ... | ... | ... | ... | 1,281 | 277 | ... | ... | 3 | 18 |
| 1942 | ... | ... | ... | ... | 1,219 | 29 | ... | ... | 27 | 16 |
| 1943 | ... | ... | ... | ... | 1,195 | 3 | ... | ... | 23 | 15 |
| 1944 | ... | ... | ... | ... | 1,179 | 39 | ... | ... | 22 | 16 |
| 1945 | ... | ... | ... | ... | 1,161 | 322 | ... | ... | 23 | 17 |
| 1946 | ... | ... | ... | ... | 1,235 | 37 | 2.8 | 1.9 | 27 | 21 |
| 1947 | ... | ... | 2.5 | 1.1 | 1,372 | 438 | 3.0 | 2.1 | 37 | 26 |
| 1948 | 1.6 | 0.6 | 3.2 | 1.3 | 1,498[1] | 53[1] | ... | ... | 48 | 3 |
| 1949 | ... | ... | 3.4 | 1.4 | 1,673 | 577 | 4.4 | 2.9 | 57 | 31 |
| 195 | 2.1 | 0.7 | 3.7 | 1.4 | 1,913 | 643 | 4.6 | 3.1 | 7 | 35 |
| 1951 | 2.3 | 0.7 | 4.0 | 1.5 | 2,16 | 723 | 5.1 | 3.6 | 84 | 39 |
| 1952 | 2.7 | 0.8 | 4.5 | 1.7 | 2,36 | 87 | 5.6 | 4.3 | 98 | 42 |
| 1953 | 2.9 | 0.9 | 4.9 | 1.9 | 2,528 | 863 | 6.7 | 4.6 | 13 | 42 |
| 1954 | 3.0 | 1.0 | 4.9 | 1.8 | 2,76 | 91 | 14 | | 112 | 44 |
| 1955 | 3.7 | 1.1 | 5.2 | 1.8 | 2,961 | 952 | 17 | | 126 | 47 |
| 1956 | 4.3 | 1.2 | 5.0 | 1.8 | 3,223 | 1,7 | 19 | | 139 | 51 |
| 1957 | 4.9 | 1.3 | 6.0 | 2.1 | 3,428 | 1,34 | 14[4] | 7.7 | 158 | 55 |
| 1958 | 6.4 | 1.3 | 6.3 | 2.2 | 3,631 | 1,59 | 15 | 8.7 | 159 | 51 |
| 1959 | 6.9 | 1.6 | 6.8 | 2.4 | 3,886 | 1,97 | 19[4] / 14 | 1.0[4] / 9.0 | 174 | 47 |
| 196 | 7.8 | 1.7 | 8.0 | 2.4 | 4,14 | 1,117 | 16 | 9.7 | 18 | 65 |
| 1961 | 9.0 | 1.8 | 8.7 | 2.5 | 4,326 | 1,157 | 17 | 9.3 | 91 | 41 |
| 1962 | 12.0 | 2.8 | 8.8 | 2.6 | 4,531 | 1,21 | 18 | 9.2 | ... | ... |
| 1963 | 12.0 | 3.1 | 1.0 | 2.8 | 4,789 | 1,246 | 19 | 9.7 | ... | ... |
| 1964 | 16.0 | 3.6 | 11.0 | 3.5 | 5,38 | 1,297 | 2 | 11 | ... | ... |
| 1965 | 2.0 | 3.5 | 13.0 | 3.6 | 5,279 | 1,345 | 23 | 12 | 162 | 14 |
| 1966 | 22.0 | 4.6 | 12.0 | 2.8 | 5,481 | 1,447 | 27 | 14 | ... | ... |
| 1967 | 26.0 | 5.1 | 15.0 | 3.0 | 5,866 | 1,493 | 3 | 16 | 7 | 3 |
| 1968 | 32.0 | 6.2 | 17.0 | 3.3 | 6,16 | 1,587 | 32 | 17 | 7 | 31 |
| 1969 | 44.0 | 7.4 | 17.0 | 3.9 | 6,433 | 1,683 | 35 | 2 | 71 | 31 |

**F6**  **NORTH AMERICA: Motor Vehicles in Use** (in thousands)

**1925–1969**

| | Dominican Republic | | El Salvador | | Guadeloupe | | Guatemala | | Haiti | |
|---|---|---|---|---|---|---|---|---|---|---|
| | PC | CV | PC | CV | PC | CV | PC | CV | PC | CV |
| 1925 | ... | ... | ... | ... | ... | ... | ... | ... | ... | ... |
| 1926 | ... | ... | ... | ... | ... | ... | ... | ... | ... | ... |
| 1927 | ... | ... | ... | ... | ... | ... | ... | ... | ... | ... |
| 1928 | 3.4 | 1.0 | 1.5 | 0.3 | 1.0 | 0.2 | 2.1 | 1.0 | 2.0 | 0.7 |
| 1929 | 3.2 | 1.1 | 1.8 | 0.4 | 1.2 | 0.3 | 2.2 | 0.8 | 3.1 | 0.8 |
| 1930 | 3.2 | 1.1 | 1.8 | 0.4 | 1.2 | 0.3 | 2.0 | 0.8 | 2.4 | 0.6 |
| 1931 | ... | ... | ... | ... | ... | ... | 2.2 | 1.1 | ... | ... |
| 1932 | ... | ... | ... | ... | ... | ... | 1.8 | 1.3 | ... | ... |
| 1933 | ... | ... | ... | ... | ... | ... | 1.8 | 1.2 | ... | ... |
| 1934 | ... | ... | 1.6 | 0.5 | ... | ... | 1.8 | 1.1 | ... | ... |
| 1935 | ... | ... | ... | ... | | | 1.9 | 1.5 | ... | ... |
| 1936 | 1.4 | 0.7 | ... | ... | | | 2.0 | 1.6 | ... | ... |
| 1937 | 1.4 | 0.7 | 2.4 | 0.8 | | | 2.5 | 1.6 | ... | ... |
| 1938 | 1.4 | 0.7 | 2.5 | 0.7 | | | 2.5 | 1.6 | 1.8 | 0.6 |
| 1939 | 1.5 | 0.8 | 2.5 | 0.9 | | | 2.5 | 1.7 | 1.8 | 0.6 |
| 1940 | 1.5 | 0.8 | 2.5 | 0.9 | ... | ... | 2.4 | 2.2 | ... | ... |
| 1941 | ... | ... | 3.5 | | | ... | ... | 2.4 | 2.3 | ... |
| 1942 | 1.2 | 0.9 | 3.4 | | ... | ... | 2.4 | 2.1 | ... | ... |
| 1943 | 1.2 | 0.8 | 2.2 | 1.1 | ... | ... | 2.6 | 2.1 | ... | ... |
| 1944 | 1.2 | 0.8 | 2.2 | 1.1 | ... | ... | 2.5 | 2.5 | ... | ... |
| 1945 | 1.2 | 0.8 | 2.1 | 1.0 | ... | ... | 2.6 | 2.1 | ... | ... |
| 1946 | 1.8 | 15 | 2.6 | 1.0 | 1.0 | 0.6 | 2.9 | 2.3 | ... | ... |
| 1947 | 2.5 | 2.5 | 3.3 | 1.1 | 1.4 | 1.1 | ... | ... | 2.8 | 0.8 |
| 1948 | 3.1 | 2.9 | 3.7 | 2.1 | 1.9 | 1.6 | 5.2 | 4.0 | ... | ... |
| 1949 | 3.6 | 3.0 | 4.0 | 2.0 | 2.6 | 2.1 | 4.6 | 4.8 | ... | ... |
| 1950 | 4.3 | 3.4 | 6.7 | 2.6 | 3 | 2.5 | 7.8 | 5.0 | 2.3 | 1.5 |
| 1951 | 4.6 | 3.9 | 7.1 | 3.6 | 3.3 | 2.8 | 7.6 | 6.9 | 2.6 | 1.7 |
| 1952 | 5.4 | 4.5 | 6.7 | 2.7 | 3.6 | 3.2 | 9.1 | 6.2 | 3.9 | 3.2 |
| 1953 | 5.7 | 4.4 | 9.6 | 4.5 | 4.6 | 2.4 | 9.8 | 6.9 | 4.5 | 2.9 |
| 1954 | 6.4 | 4.9 | 9.0 | 4.8 | 5.1 | 3.1 | 11 | 7.8 | 4.9 | 3.3 |
| 1955 | 6.7 | 5.3 | 11 | 5.7 | 5.9 | 3.8 | 13 | 9.5 | 5.1 | 3.7 |
| 1956 | 8.1 | 6.5 | 12 | 5.9 | 6.4 | 4.5 | 17 | 11 | 5.7 | 4.0 |
| 1957 | 9.2 | 6.9 | 14 | 6.7 | 6.9 | 5.0 | 18 | 12 | 6.0 | 3.6 |
| 1958 | 9.5 | 6.9 | 17 | 7.8 | 5.6 | 4.2 | 22 | 12 | 6.3 | 3.2 |
| 1959 | 11 | 6.5 | 17 | 8.5 | 6.3 | 4.6 | 24 | 14 | 6.1 | 3.4 |
| 1960 | 11 | 6.3 | 20 | 9.0 | 7.6 | 5.3 | 26 | 15 | 8.2 | 3.7 |
| 1961 | 11 | 6.0 | 22 | 9.8 | 9.0 | 5.9 | 29 | 16 | 6.1 | 2.0 |
| 1962 | 16 | 7.4 | 23 | 10 | 11 | 6.5 | 32 | 12 | 6.2 | 2.2 |
| 1963 | 21 | 8.9 | 23 | 9.7 | 9.6 | 7.4 | 35 | 13 | 6.6 | 1.1 |
| 1964 | 28 | 11 | 23 | 11 | 15 | 8.8 | 37 | 14 | 5.1 | 1.8 |
| 1965 | 30 | 9.7 | 26 | 12 | 17 | 9.9 | 29 | 17 | 8.7 | 1.4 |
| 1966 | 27 | 13 | 28 | 13 | 18 | 11 | 33 | 18 | 8.4 | 1.2 |
| 1967 | 29 | 14 | 30 | 14 | 20 | 11 | 33 | 19 | 11 | 1.3 |
| 1968 | 33 | 18 | 31 | 16 | 23 | 13 | 37 | 21 | 15 | 1.3 |
| 1969 | 33 | 18 | 34 | 17 | 26 | 14 | 40 | 23 | 15 | 1.3 |

**F6    NORTH AMERICA: Motor Vehicles in Use** (in thousands)

**1925–1969**

| | Honduras | | Jamaica | | Martinique | | Mexico | | Newfoundland | |
|---|---|---|---|---|---|---|---|---|---|---|
| | PC | CV | PC | CV | PC | CV | PC | CV | PC | CV |
| 1925 | ... | ... | ... | ... | ... | ... | 40 | 13 | 0.9 | 0.1 |
| 1926 | ... | ... | ... | ... | ... | ... | 43 | 15 | 1.2 | 0.1 |
| 1927 | ... | ... | ... | ... | ... | ... | 44 | 17 | 1.5 | 0.2 |
| 1928 | 0.3 | 0.2 | 4.9 | 1.5 | 1.3 | 0.3 | 49 | 18 | 1.8 | 0.3 |
| 1929 | ... | ... | 5.6 | 2.0 | 1.5 | 0.5 | 62 | 22 | 2.1 | 0.4 |
| 1930 | 0.7 | 0.4 | 6.4 | 1.7 | 1.8 | 0.5 | 63 | 25 | 2.5 | 0.5 |
| 1931 | ... | ... | 6.8 | 1.7 | ... | ... | 62 | 26 | 2.8 | 0.6 |
| 1932 | ... | ... | 5.8 | 1.7 | ... | ... | 60 | 26 | 2.6 | 0.5 |
| 1933 | ... | ... | 6.5 | 1.6 | ... | ... | 65 | 31 | 2.7 | 0.5 |
| 1934 | ... | ... | 6.9 | 1.9 | ... | ... | 74 | 34 | 2.7 | 0.6 |
| 1935 | ... | ... | 7.5 | 2.0 | ... | ... | 65 | 31 | 3.1 | 0.7 |
| 1936 | ... | ... | 8.2 | 2.2 | ... | ... | 67 | 35 | 3.3 | 0.9 |
| 1937 | ... | ... | 9.0 | 2.7 | ... | ... | 78 | 42 | 3.7 | 1.0 |
| 1938 | 0.6 | 0.6 | 9.2 | 2.8 | ... | ... | 82 | 42 | ... | ... |
| 1939 | 0.6 | 0.6 | 9.8 | 2.9 | ... | ... | 89 | 49 | ... | ... |
| 1940 | 0.7 | 0.7 | 10 | 3.1 | ... | ... | 94 | 52 | ... | ... |
| 1941 | ... | ... | 9.3 | 2.6 | ... | ... | 106 | 62 | ... | ... |
| 1942 | ... | ... | 9.5 | 2.6 | ... | ... | 113 | 65 | ... | ... |
| 1943 | ... | ... | 6.8 | 2.0 | ... | ... | 112 | 66 | ... | ... |
| 1944 | ... | ... | 5.2 | 1.5 | ... | ... | 112 | 72 | ... | ... |
| 1945 | ... | ... | 7.1 | 1.7 | ... | ... | 113 | 82 | ... | ... |
| 1946 | ... | ... | 8.3 | 1.9 | 2.0 | 1.2 | 121 | 85 | ... | ... |
| 1947 | 1.5 | 0.6 | 8.6 | 2.5 | 2.4 | 1.6 | 134 | 101 | ... | ... |
| 1948 | ... | ... | 11 | 3.3 | 2.9 | 2.0 | 150 | 117 | ... | ... |
| 1949 | ... | ... | 11 | 3.6 | ... | ... | 163 | 122 | 9.0 | 4.7 |
| 1950 | 1.3 | 1.9 | 13 | 3.9 | ... | ... | 173 | 130 | ... | ... |
| 1951 | 1.5 | 2.0 | 12 | 4.2 | ... | ... | 209 | 152 | ... | ... |
| 1952 | 1.9 | 2.6 | 13 | 4.4 | 3.4 | 2.6 | 237 | 174 | ... | ... |
| 1953 | 2.3 | 3.2 | 14 | 4.4 | ... | ... | 253 | 199 | ... | ... |
| 1954 | 2.9 | 3.5 | 14 | 4.6 | ... | ... | 274 | 214 | ... | ... |
| 1955 | 3.7 | 4.0 | 17 | 5.4 | ... | ... | 308 | 243 | ... | ... |
| 1956 | 3.9 | 4.2 | 19 | 6.2 | 4.6 | 3.7 | 320 | 261 | ... | ... |
| 1957 | 4.2 | 4.3 | 22 | 7.1 | ... | ... | 366 | 295 | ... | ... |
| 1958 | 4.6 | 4.8 | 26 | 8.2 | 6.4 | 4.4 | 379 | 296 | ... | ... |
| 1959 | 5.1 | 5.0 | 31 | 8.9 | 6.9 | 4.6 | 438 | 327 | ... | ... |
| 1960 | 5.5 | 5.2 | 33 | 9.2 | 8.7 | 5.3 | 483 | 320 | ... | ... |
| 1961 | 5.7 | 5.3 | 42 | 11 | 10 | 5.9 | 550 | 352 | ... | ... |
| 1962 | 5.8 | 5.4 | 44 | 12 | 12 | 6.5 | 548 | 354 | ... | ... |
| 1963 | 7.5 | 6.5 | 53 | 18 | 11 | 6 | 618 | 380 | ... | ... |
| 1964 | 8.8 | 7.1 | 50 | 19₅ / 13 | 16 | 8.7 | 688 | 394 | ... | ... |
| 1965 | 10 | 8.2 | 46 | 12 | 18 | 9.7 | 771 | 419 | ... | ... |
| 1966 | 12 | 9.7 | 49 | 14 | 19 | 8.6 | 812 | 436 | ... | ... |
| 1967 | 12 | 11 | 54 | 15 | 22 | 9.3 | 917 | 468 | ... | ... |
| 1968 | 11 | 14 | 60 | 18 | 25 | 12 | 1,000 | 495 | ... | ... |
| 1969 | 12 | 15 | 69 | 20 | 29 | 13 | 1,133 | 537 | ... | ... |

**F6    NORTH AMERICA: Motor Vehicles in Use (in thousands)**

**1925–1969**

| | Nicaragua | | Panama[6] | | Puerto Rico[2] | | Trinidad & Tobago[3] | | USA | |
|---|---|---|---|---|---|---|---|---|---|---|
| | PC | CV | PC | CV | PC | CV | PC | CV | PC | CV |
| 1925 | ... | ... | ... | ... | 13 | | ... | ... | 17,481 | 2,588 |
| 1926 | ... | ... | ... | ... | 15 | | ... | ... | 19,268 | 2,932 |
| 1927 | ... | ... | ... | ... | 15 | | ... | ... | 20,193 | 3,110 |
| 1928 | 0.7 | 0.1 | 5.8 | 0.7 | 13 | 3.6 | 4.2 | 1.3 | 21,362 | 3,326 |
| 1929 | 0.8 | 0.2 | 4.6 | 1.6 | 13 | 3.5 | 4.5 | 1.4 | 23,121 | 3,584 |
| 1930 | 1.0 | 0.2 | 6.3 | 1.7 | 10 | 3.2 | 4.5 | 2.0 | 23,035 | 3,715 |
| 1931 | ... | ... | 6.0 | 1.9 | ... | ... | ... | ... | 22,396 | 3,698 |
| 1932 | ... | ... | 6.4 | 1.7 | 13 | 3.5 | ... | ... | 20,901 | 3,490 |
| 1933 | ... | ... | 6.5 | 1.5 | ... | ... | ... | ... | 20,657 | 3,502 |
| 1934 | ... | ... | 6.8 | 1.6 | ... | ... | ... | ... | 21,544 | 3,717 |
| 1935 | ... | ... | 7.4 | 1.7 | ... | ... | 3.6 | 1.3 | 22,568 | 3,978 |
| 1936 | ... | ... | 8.2 | 1.9 | ... | ... | 4.4 | 1.7 | 24,183 | 4,324 |
| 1937 | ... | ... | 9.1 | 1.8 | 16 | 4.9 | 4.3 | 1.7 | 25,467 | 4,592 |
| 1938 | 0.6 | 0.2 | 9.4 [6] | 1.9 [6] | 17 | 5.3 | 4.3 | 1.8 | 25,250 | 4,563 |
| 1939 | 0.6 | 0.2 | 10 | 1.9 | ... | ... | 3.5 | 1.5 | 26,226 | 4,783 |
| 1940 | 0.6 | 0.2 | 13 | 2.3 | ... | ... | 4.9 | 1.9 | 27,466 | 4,987 |
| 1941 | ... | ... | 16 | 3.7 | ... | ... | 5.4 | 2.4 | 29,624 | 5,270 |
| 1942 | ... | ... | 15 | 4.6 | ... | ... | 5.3 | 2.3 | 27,973 | 5,031 |
| 1943 | ... | ... | 12 | 3.7 | ... | ... | ... | ... | 26,009 | 4,879 |
| 1944 | 0.7 | 0.6 | 12 | 3.6 | ... | ... | ... | ... | 25,566 | 4,913 |
| 1945 | 0.7 | 0.6 | 11 | 3.7 | ... | ... | ... | ... | 25,797 | 5,238 |
| 1946 | 0.7 | 0.7 | 13 | 4.2 | 19 | 11 | 6.2 | 3.5 | 28,217 | 6,156 |
| 1947 | 0.7 | 0.7 | 13 | 3.9 | 24 | 15 | 7.5 | 4.3 | 30,849 | 6,992 |
| 1948 | 0.8 | 0.8 | 17 | 4.1 | 26 | 16 | 8.9 | 3.8 | 33,355 | 7,730 |
| 1949 | 1.4 | 0.9 | 17 | 5.2 | 35 | 17 | 10 [8] / 12 | 4.4 [8] / 5.6 | 36,458 | 8,232 |
| 1950 | 1.5 | 1.3 | 20 | 4.3 | 37 | 19 | 13 | 6.2 | 40,339 | 8,721 |
| 1951 | 1.8 | 1.3 | [8.7][7] | [3.5][7] | 45 | 20 | 15 | 6.5 | 42,688 | 9,224 |
| 1952 | 2.5 | 1.6 | [8.5][7] | [3.5][7] | 50 | 20 | 16 | 6.7 | 43,823 | 9,439 |
| 1953 | 2.8 | 2.0 | [11][7] | [4.0][7] | 59 [2] | 21 [2] | 19 | 7.5 | 46,429 | 9,788 |
| 1954 | 4.2 | 2.5 | [10][7] | [3.8][7] | 64 | 24 | 20 | 7.3 | 48,468 | 10,037 |
| 1955 | 5.2 | 2.8 | 13 | 6.1 | 74 | 25 | 22 | 7.8 | 52,145 | 10,544 |
| 1956 | 7.0 | 5.3 | 14 | 7 | 82 | 30 | 25 | 8.4 | 54,211 | 10,937 |
| 1957 | 7.8 | 5.7 | 15 | 7.1 | 86 [2] | 37 | 28 | 10 | 55,918 | 11,207 |
| 1958 | 9.3 | 5.6 | 16 | 7.5 | 101 | 32 | 28 | 11 | 56,891 | 11,406 |
| 1959 | 8.5 | 4.8 | 16 | 6.6 | 116 | 34 | 31 | 11 | 59,454 [3] | 11,900 [3] |
| 1960 | 8.6 | 5.5 | 18 | 6.6 | 135 | 37 | 37 | 12 | 61,682 | 12,186 |
| 1961 | 8.3 | 5.5 | 20 | 7.4 | 154 | 41 | 41 | 13 | 63,417 | 12,541 |
| 1962 | 8.1 | 6.3 | 22 | 8.3 | 171 | 37 | 46 | 14 | 66,108 | 13,065 |
| 1963 | 11 | 5.1 | 25 | 8.7 | 197 | 44 | 49 | 15 | 69,055 | 13,658 |
| 1964 | 13 | 5.0 | 27 | 9.5 | 226 | 48 | 51 | 15 | 71,983 | 14,318 |
| 1965 | 13 | 9.5 | 30 | 11 | 255 | 51 | 55 | 16 | 75,258 | 15,100 |
| 1966 | 13 | 9.8 | 34 | 11 | 305 | 60 | 59 | 17 | 78,128 | 15,822 |
| 1967 | 19 | 8.5 | 35 | 12 | 338 | 65 | 63 | 17 | 80,407 | 16,499 |
| 1968 | 20 | 8.9 | 40 | 13 | 383 | 78 | 68 | 19 | 83,604 | 17,294 |
| 1969 | 24 | 8.7 | 42 | 13 | 437 | 91 | 69 | 19 | 86,858 | 18,238 |

**F6     NORTH AMERICA: Motor Vehicles in Use** (in thousands).

|      | Bahamas | | Barbados | | Canada | | Costa Rica | | Cuba | |
|------|----|-----|----|-----|--------|--------|-----|-----|-----|-----|
|      | PC | CV  | PC | CV  | PC     | CV     | PC  | CV  | PC  | CV  |
| 1970 | 44 | 7.4 | 19 | 4.0 | 6,602  | 1,738  | 39  | 27  | 72  | 32  |
| 1971 | 40 | 6.2 | 23 | 4.3 | 6,967  | 1,856$_5$ 1,557 | 43 | 26 | 72 | 32 |
| 1972 | 41 | 6.1 | 22 | 4.1 | 7,407  | 1,682  | 48  | 30  | ... | ... |
| 1973 | 40 | 4.7 | 21 | 3.0 | 7,866  | 1,844  | 52  | 34  | 70  | 33  |
| 1974 | 40 | 5.5 | 24 | 3.8 | 8,328  | 2,026  | 55  | 37  | ... | ... |
| 1975 | 35 | 5.3 | 23 | 3.8 | 8,693  | 2,177  | 60  | 41  | ... | ... |
| 1976 | 36 | 5.3 | 25 | 4.0 | 9,016  | 2,319  | 65  | 42  | 80  | 40  |
| 1977 | 43 | 3.2 | 25 | 3.8 | 9,554  | 2,494  | 73  | 49  | 158 | ... |
| 1978 | 42 | 5.6 | 26 | 2.3 | 9,745  | 2,718  | 80  | 59  | 160 | 107 |
| 1979 | 46 | 7.3 | 29 | 2.3 | 9,985  | 2,854  | 78  | 58  | 153 | 118 |
| 1980 | 47 | 8.0 | ... | ... | 10,255 | 2,955  | 88  | 66  | 159 | 133 |
| 1981 | 50 | 8.9 | ... | ... | 10,199 | 3,192  | 89  | 66  | 171 | 143 |
| 1982 | 58 | 11  | ... | ... | 10,530 | 3,293  | 91  | 66  | 182 | 152 |
| 1983 | 53 | 8.6 | ... | ... | 10,731 | 3,365  | 101 | 66  | 190 | 159 |
| 1984 | 48 | 7.1 | 31 | 4.9 | 10,781 | 3,099  | 106 | 67  | 200 | 165 |
| 1985 | 54 | 8.5 | 33 | 4.8 | 11,118 | 3,148  | 111 | 69  | 206 | 173 |
| 1986 | 54 | 9.5 | 35 | 4.7 | 11,477 | 3,212  | 119 | 76  | 217 | 184 |
| 1987 | 59 | 13  | 37 | 5.1 | 11,772 | 3,568  | 127 | 84  | 229 | 195 |
| 1988 | ... | ... | 39 | 4.3 | 12,086 | 3,766  | 135 | ... | 241 | 208 |

|      | Dominican Republic | | El Salvador | | Guadeloupe | | Guatemala | | Haiti | |
|------|-----|-----|----|-----|----|-----|-----|-----|-----|-----|
|      | PC  | CV  | PC | CV  | PC | CV  | PC  | CV  | PC  | CV  |
| 1970 | 39  | 21  | 28 | 19  | 28 | 17  | 43  | 24  | 12  | 1.4 |
| 1971 | 45  | 24  | 32 | 21  | 32 | 16  | 43  | 36  | 12  | 1.5 |
| 1972 | 51  | 24  | 38 | 22  | 38 | 16  | 54  | 37  | 12  | 1.6 |
| 1973 | 57  | 28  | 39 | 19  | 35 | 14  | 66  | 38  | 12  | 1.3 |
| 1974 | 65  | 32  | 41 | 19  | ... | ... | 71 | 39  | 16  | 2   |
| 1975 | 71  | 36  | ... | ... | ... | ... | 76 | 40  | 18  | 2.5 |
| 1976 | 77  | 39  | ... | ... | 61 | 25  | 83  | 41  | 19  | 2.4 |
| 1977 | 84  | 41  | 73 | 37  | 68 | 27  | 84  | 41  | 23  | 3.8 |
| 1978 | 91  | 46  | 70 | 46  | 74 | 28  | 90$_5$ 156 | 44$_5$ 56 | 24 | 6.5 |
| 1979 | 90  | 51  | 79 | 58  | 74 | 28  | 147 | 73  | 25  | 8.3 |
| 1980 | 94  | 47  | 72 | 71  | 80 | 31  | 167 | 81  | 21  | 10  |
| 1981 | 105 | 58  | 83 | 64  | 88 | 33  | ... | ... | 15  | 6.8 |
| 1982 | 97  | 61  | 83 | 64  | 75 | 24  | ... | ... | 16  | 7.8 |
| 1983 | 92  | 58  | 88 | 61  | 83 | 26  | ... | ... | 18  | 8.1 |
| 1984 | 109 | 60  | 85 | 65  | 89 | 28  | ... | ... | 25  | 11  |
| 1985 | 101 | 52  | 88 | 66  | ... | ... | ... | ... | 26 | 11  |
| 1986 | 133 | 77  | ... | ... | ... | ... | ... | ... | 19 | 13  |
| 1987 | 152 | 85  | ... | ... | ... | ... | ... | ... | 20 | 23  |
| 1988 | ... | ... | ... | ... | ... | ... | ... | ... | 21 | 23  |

**F6 NORTH AMERICA: Motor Vehicles in Use** (in thousands, except USA)

| | Honduras | | Jamaica | | Martinique | | Mexico | |
|---|---|---|---|---|---|---|---|---|
| | PC | CV | PC | CV | PC | CV | PC | CV |
| 1970 | 13 | 16 | 72 | 21 | 30 | 11 | 1,234 | 589 |
| 1971 | 14 | 17 | 93 | 22 | 35 | 18 | 1,338 | 560 |
| 1972 | 17 | 17 | 86 | 22 | 40 | 17 | 1,520 | 593 |
| 1973 | 16 | 18 | 110₅ | 29₅ | ... | ... | 1,767 | 645 |
| 1974 | 16 | 22 | 70 | 19 | ... | ... | 2,053 | 729 |
| 1975 | 18 | 26 | 59 | 13 | ... | ... | 2,401 | 888 |
| 1976 | 19 | 29 | 56 | 12 | ... | ... | 2,580 | 988 |
| 1977 | 21 | 34 | 48 | 14 | 65 | 22 | 2,829 | 1,057 |
| 1978 | 24 | 33 | 39 | 12 | 72 | 24 | 3,360 | 1,278 |
| 1979 | 24 | 41 | 40 | 13 | 78 | 25 | 3,763 | 1,386 |
| 1980 | 26 | 45 | 34 | 14 | ... | ... | 4,241 | 1,489₉ |
| | | | | | | | | 1,575 |
| 1981 | 27 | 45 | 41 | 17 | ... | ... | 4,727 | 1,792 |
| 1982 | 29 | 49 | 40 | 20 | ... | ... | 4,760 | 1,873 |
| 1983 | 29 | 49 | 35 | 17 | ... | ... | 4,711 | 1,955 |
| 1984 | 30 | 49 | 42 | 23 | ... | ... | 4,955 | 2,078 |
| 1985 | 32 | 57 | 43 | 26 | ... | ... | 5,260 | 2,183 |
| 1986 | 33 | 52 | 44 | 21 | ... | ... | 5,179 | 2,285 |
| 1987 | 36 | 59 | 53 | 23 | ... | ... | 5,312 | 2,364 |
| 1988 | 39 | 64 | 63 | 27 | ... | ... | 5,783 | 2,510 |

| | Nicaragua | | Panama | | Puerto Rico | | Trinidad & Tobago | | USA (in millions) | |
|---|---|---|---|---|---|---|---|---|---|---|
| | PC | CV | PC | CV | PC | CV | PC | CV | PC | CV |
| 1970 | 34 | ... | 46 | 15 | 490 | 103 | 75 | 20 | 89.2 | 19.2 |
| 1971 | 32 | ... | 50 | 16 | 559 | 115 | 72 | 20 | 92.7 | 20.3 |
| 1972 | ... | ... | 54 | 18 | 562 | 104 | 78 | 20 | 97.1 | 21.7 |
| 1973 | 32 | 20 | 58 | 19 | 561 | 115 | 83 | 21 | 102.0 | 23.7 |
| 1974 | 32 | 14 | 63 | 18 | 608 | 125 | 89 | 23 | 104.9 | 25.1 |
| 1975 | 36 | 23 | 66 | 20 | 637 | 130 | 101 | 26 | 106.7 | 26.2 |
| 1976 | 36 | 30 | 68 | 21 | 670 | 137 | 105 | 29 | 110.2 | 28.4 |
| 1977 | 43 | 27 | 71 | 22 | 683 | 140 | 118 | 33 | 112.3 | 29.8 |
| 1978 | 41 | 26 | 75 | 25 | 807 | 165 | 131 | 37 | 116.6 | 31.8 |
| 1979 | 38 | 28 | 90 | 30 | 842 | 174 | 144 | 42 | 118.5 | 33.4 |
| 1980 | 38 | 28 | 98 | 32 | 950 | 160 | 157 | 49 | 121.6 | 34.2 |
| 1981 | ... | ... | 104 | 36 | 962 | 162 | 171 | 58 | 123.1 | 35.2 |
| 1982 | ... | ... | 110 | 38 | 993 | 155 | 188 | 65 | 123.7 | 35.9 |
| 1983 | ... | ... | 123 | 38 | 1,018 | 159 | 210 | 70 | 126.2 | 37.7 |
| 1984 | ... | ... | 129 | 41 | 1,128 | 171 | 229 | 61 | 128.1 | 38.1 |
| 1985 | ... | ... | 138 | 40 | 1,209 | 182 | 242 | 79 | 131.9 | 39.8 |
| 1986 | 46 | 31 | 145 | 42 | 1,297 | 191 | 244 | 79 | 135.4 | 40.8 |
| 1987 | ... | ... | ... | ... | 1,337 | 202 | ... | ... | 137.3 | 41.7 |
| 1988 | ... | ... | ... | ... | 1,301 | 196 | ... | ... | 140.7 | 42.8 |

**F6      SOUTH AMERICA: MOTOR VEHICLES IN USE** (in thousands)

**1915–1949**

| | Argentina | | Bolivia | | Brazil | | Chile | | Colombia | | Ecuador | |
|---|---|---|---|---|---|---|---|---|---|---|---|---|
| | PC | CV | PC | CV | PC | CV | PC | CV | PC | CV | PC | CV |
| 1915 | ... | ... | ... | ... | ... | ... | 1.2 | - - | ... | ... | ... | ... |
| 1916 | ... | ... | ... | ... | ... | ... | 1.8 | - - | ... | ... | ... | ... |
| 1917 | ... | ... | ... | ... | ... | ... | ... | ... | ... | ... | ... | ... |
| 1918 | ... | ... | ... | ... | ... | ... | 5.7 | 0.2 | ... | ... | ... | ... |
| 1919 | ... | ... | ... | ... | ... | ... | 6.4 | 0.2 | ... | ... | ... | ... |
| 1920 | 48 | ... | ... | ... | ... | ... | 7.1 | 0.3 | ... | ... | ... | ... |
| 1921 | 54 | 0.4 | ... | ... | ... | ... | 7.0 | 0.4 | ... | ... | ... | ... |
| 1922 | 68 | 0.9 | ... | ... | ... | ... | 6.9 | 0.5 | ... | ... | ... | ... |
| 1923 | 90 | 4.5 | ... | ... | ... | ... | 6.5 | 0.7 | 1.8 | 3.2 | ... | ... |
| 1924 | 113 | 11 | 1.1 | | ... | ... | 7.5 | 1.0 | ... | ... | ... | ... |
| 1925 | 161 | 19 | 1.5 | | ... | ... | 10 | 3.7 | ... | ... | ... | ... |
| 1926 | 201 | 28 | 2.0 | | ... | ... | 12 | 5.4 | ... | ... | ... | ... |
| 1927 | 232 | 41 | 2.0 | | ... | | 22 | | ... | ... | ... | ... |
| 1928 | 273 | 61 | 1.4 | 0.9 | 101 | 52 | 19 | 8.9 | 9.5 | 5.5 | 1.3 | 0.6 |
| 1929 | 330 | 82 | 1.7 | 0.9 | 127 | 66 | 24 | 12 | 10 | 6.0 | 1.6 | 0.6 |
| 1930 | 344 | 92 | 1.2 | 1.0 | 133 | 67 | 28 | 15 | 8.8 | 5.0 | 1.4 | 1.0 |
| 1931 | 326 | 92 | ... | ... | ... | ... | 27 | 15 | ... | ... | ... | ... |
| 1932 | 287 | 85 | ... | ... | ... | ... | 23 | 11 | ... | ... | ... | ... |
| 1933 | 243 | 79 | ... | ... | ... | ... | 22 | 9.7 | ... | ... | ... | ... |
| 1934 | 257 | 82 | ... | ... | ... | ... | 23 | 9.5 | ... | ... | ... | ... |
| 1935 | 270 | 84 | ... | ... | ... | ... | 25 | 10 | ... | ... | ... | ... |
| 1936 | 284 | 87 | ... | ... | ... | ... | 27 | 11 | 12 | 8 | ... | ... |
| 1937 | 297 | 90 | ... | ... | 100 | 39 | 29 | 12 | 13 | 8.8 | ... | ... |
| 1938 | 305 | 101 | 1.9 | 2.8 | 104 | 62 | 31 | 13 | 14 | 9.9 | 1.3 | 1.2 |
| 1939 | 317 | 107 | 2.1 | 3.3 | 108 | 58 | 32 | 14 | 16 | 11 | 1.3 | 1.4 |
| 1940 | 311 | 117 | ... | ... | 113 | 64 | 33 | 16 | 17 | 13 | 1.8 | 1.8 |
| 1941 | 319 | 121 | ... | ... | ... | ... | 36 | 18 | 20 | 15 | 2.0 | 2.1 |
| 1942 | 319 | 129 | ... | ... | ... | ... | 35 | 20 | 17 | 13 | 2.1 | 2.0 |
| 1943 | 321 | 139 | ... | ... | ... | ... | 26 | 21 | 16 | 12 | ... | ... |
| 1944 | 320 | 146 | ... | ... | ... | ... | 27 | 22 | 17 | 13 | ... | ... |
| 1945 | 311 | 142 | 3.7 | 7.6 | ... | ... | 29 | 23 | 15 | 14 | ... | ... |
| 1946 | 283 | 156 | 2.5 | 5.4 | 114 | 97 | 32 | 25 | 19 | 18 | ... | ... |
| 1947 | 290 | 195 | ... | ... | 140 | 121 | 34 | 27 | 23 | 23 | 4.3 | 3.2 |
| 1948 | 304 | 204 | 3.7 | 7.9 | 169 | 160 | 37 | 32 | 28 | 25 | 2.7 | 4.8 |
| 1949 | 310 | 224 | 3.8 | 8.9 | 193 | 182 | 40 | 31 | 30 | 25 | 3.4 | 6.4 |

**F6**    **SOUTH AMERICA: Motor Vehicles in Use** (in thousands)

### 1915–1949

| | Guyana* | | Paraguay | | Peru | | Surinam† | | Uruguay | | Venezuela | |
|---|---|---|---|---|---|---|---|---|---|---|---|---|
| | PC | CV | PC | CV | PC | CV | PC | CV | PC | CV | PC | CV |
| 1915 | ... | ... | ... | ... | ... | ... | ... | ... | ... | ... | ... | ... |
| 1916 | ... | ... | ... | ... | ... | ... | ... | ... | ... | ... | ... | ... |
| 1917 | ... | ... | ... | ... | ... | ... | ... | ... | ... | ... | ... | ... |
| 1918 | ... | ... | ... | ... | ... | ... | ... | ... | ... | ... | ... | ... |
| 1919 | ... | ... | ... | ... | ... | ... | ... | ... | ... | ... | ... | ... |
| 1920 | ... | ... | ... | ... | ... | ... | ... | ... | ... | ... | ... | ... |
| 1921 | ... | ... | ... | ... | ... | ... | ... | ... | ... | ... | ... | ... |
| 1922 | ... | ... | ... | ... | ... | ... | ... | ... | ... | ... | ... | ... |
| 1923 | ... | ... | ... | ... | ... | ... | ... | ... | ... | ... | ... | ... |
| 1924 | ... | ... | ... | ... | ... | ... | ... | ... | ... | ... | ... | ... |
| 1925 | 0.9 | 0.1 | ... | ... | ... | ... | ... | ... | ... | ... | ... | ... |
| 1926 | 0.9 | 0.1 | ... | ... | ... | ... | ... | ... | ... | ... | ... | ... |
| 1927 | 0.9 | 0.1 | ... | ... | 6.1 | 4.6 | ... | ... | ... | ... | ... | ... |
| 1928 | 1.1 | 0.1 | 0.7 | 0.5 | 9.3 | 5.9 | 0.2 | 0.1 | 32 | 8.4 | 11 | 1.0 |
| 1929 | 0.9 | 0.1 | 0.7 | 0.5 | 8.0 | 5.2 | 0.2 | - - | 36 | 16 | 12 | 6.0 |
| 1930 | 1.1 | 0.1 | 0.7 | 1.0 | 8.7 | 5.2 | | 0.2 | 37 | 10 | 11 | 6.8 |
| 1931 | 1.1 | 0.2 | ... | ... | 8.0 | 4.6 | ... | ... | ... | ... | ... | ... |
| 1932 | 1.2 | 0.2 | ... | ... | 7.4 | 4.6 | ... | ... | ... | ... | 14 | 5.6 |
| 1933 | 1.1 | 0.2 | ... | ... | 9.2 | 5.2 | ... | ... | ... | ... | 10 | 4.3 |
| 1934 | 1.2 | 0.2 | ... | ... | 7.7 | 3.7 | ... | ... | ... | ... | 11 | 4.6 |
| 1935 | 1.1 | 0.2 | ... | ... | 9.4 | 6.0 | ... | ... | ... | ... | 12 | 5.0 |
| 1936 | 1.2 | 0.3 | ... | ... | 11 | 7.0 | ... | ... | 36 | 12 | 12 | ... |
| 1937 | 1.4 | 0.3 | ... | ... | 14 | 10 | ... | ... | ... | ... | 13 | 8.9 |
| 1938 | ... | ... | 1.5 | 0.6[11] | 13 | 10 | ... | ... | ... | ... | 16 | 11 |
| 1939 | ... | ... | 1.5 | 0.6[11] | 14 | 10 | ... | ... | 49 | 15 | 18 | 14 |
| 1940 | ... | ... | 1.1 | 0.9[11] | 15 | 11 | ... | ... | ... | ... | 20 | 17 |
| 1941 | ... | ... | ... | ... | 17 | 12 | ... | ... | ... | ... | 20 | 17 |
| 1942 | ... | ... | ... | ... | 17 | 12 | ... | ... | ... | ... | 19 | 16 |
| 1943 | ... | ... | ... | ... | 16 | 11 | ... | ... | ... | ... | 17 | 15 |
| 1944 | ... | ... | ... | ... | 16 | 12 | ... | ... | ... | ... | 15 | 14 |
| 1945 | ... | ... | ... | ... | 17 | 12 | ... | ... | ... | ... | 16 | 17 |
| 1946 | ... | ... | ... | ... | 17 | 15 | ... | 0.4 | ... | ... | 21 | 25 |
| 1947 | 1.8 | 0.5 | 1.2 | 1.4 | 21 | 18 | 0.6 | 0.4 | ... | ... | 29 | 35 |
| 1948 | 2.2 | 0.6 | 0.8 | 1.3 | 23 | 18 | 0.7 | 0.5 | ... | ... | 41 | 42 |
| 1949 | 2.8 | 0.8 | 1.1 | 1.8 | 25 | 21 | 0.8 | 0.6 | 35 | 21 | 57 | 61 |

**F6    SOUTH AMERICA: Motor Vehicles in Use** (in thousands)

**1950–1975**

| | Argentina | | Bolivia | | Brazil | | Chile | | Colombia | | Ecuador | |
|---|---|---|---|---|---|---|---|---|---|---|---|---|
| | PC | CV | PC | CV | PC | CV | PC | CV | PC | CV | PC | CV |
| 1950 | 318 | 239 | 4.0 | 9.0 | 200 | 198 | 40 | 32 | 31 | 27 | ... | ... |
| 1951 | 329 | 244 | ... | ... | 263 | 226 | 43 | 35 | 35 | 32 | 4.0 | 8.1 |
| 1952 | 336 | 250 | 6.0 | 14 | 300 | 262 | 48 | 41 | 41 | 39 | 4.9 | 11 |
| 1953 | 329 | 254 | 6.0 | 16 | 338 | 285 | 48 | 43 | 50 | 43 | 4.7 | 12 |
| 1954 | 312 | 251 | 6.3 | 16 | 368 | 305 | 49 | 48 | 66 | 56 | 5.3 | 14 |
| 1955 | 336 | 264 | 8.9 | 14 | 374 | 320 | 48 | 50 | 81 | 70 | 5.8 | 15 |
| 1956 | 347 | 276 | 10 | 17 | 423 | 326 | 52 | 52 | ... | ... | 6.3 | 16 |
| 1957 | 365 | 306 | 12 | 17 | ... | ... | 54 | 59 | ... | ... | 6.3 | 15 |
| 1958 | 390 | 326 | 13 | 22 | ... | ... | 54 | 62 | 81 | 68 | 7.3 | 17 |
| 1959 | 431 | 356 | 14 | 24 | ... | ... | 58 | 68 | 84 | 75 | 8.5 | 18 |
| 1960 | 473 | 390 | 15 | 25 | ... | ... | 58 | 69 | 90 | 83 | 9.3 | 19 |
| 1961 | 535 | 436 | 15 | 25 | ... | ... | 59 | 76 | 108 | 92 | 11 | 20 |
| 1962 | 624 | 483 | 14 [3] | 26 [3] | ... | ... | 73 | 95 | 112 | 93 | 11 | 20 |
| | | | 6.3 | 11 | | | | | | | | |
| 1963 | 697 | 517 | 7.8 | 14 | ... | ... | 84 | 97 | 114 | 99 | 13 | 22 |
| 1964 | 806 | 570 | 8.7 | 15 | 1,102 | 471 | 89 | 99 | 119 | 105 | 14 | 18 |
| 1965 | 915 | 571 | 9.9 | 16 | 1,289 | 517 | 97 | 105 | 124 | 109 | 17 | 21 |
| 1966 | 1,031 | 619 | 12 | 19 | 1,449 | 588 | 108 | 107 | 135 | 116 | 19 | 22 |
| 1967 | 1,107 | 650 | 14 | 23 | 1,785 | 611 | 116 | 117 | 140 [8] | 117 [8] | 22 | 25 |
| | | | | | | | | | 167 | 98 | | |
| 1968 | 1,184 | 675 | 15 | 25 | 1,766 | 619 | 130 | 124 | 176 | 107 | 22 | 28 |
| 1969 | 1,301 | 718 | 15 | 26 | 2,003 | 651 | 151 | 136 | 220 | 78 | 25 | 31 |
| 1970 | 1,440 | 755 | 19 | 29 | 2,324 | 696 | 176 | 150 | 239 | 84 | 27 | 36 |
| 1971 | 1,673 | 809 | ... | ... | 2,638 | 742 | 194 | 152 | 284 | 91 | 30 | 44 |
| 1972 | 1,860 | 877 | 25 | 23 | 3,069 | 809 | 216 | 158 | 306 | 104 | 33 | 52 |
| 1973 | 1,914 | 835 | 26 | 24 | ... | ... | 225 | 162 | 327 | 81 | 35 | 56 |
| 1974 | 2,140 | 925 | 29 | 26 [5] | 3,735 | 825 | 235 | 165 | 354 | 85 | 44 | 68 |
| 1975 | 2,306 | 970 | 30 | 34 | 4,834 | 1,150 | 256 | 164 | 376 | 88 | 51 | 77 |
| 1976 | 2,455 | 1,017 | 33 | 40 | 5,916 | 1,397 | 263 | 171 | 401 | 93 | 49 | 87 |
| 1977 | 2,569 | 1,073 | 36 | 44 | 6,850 | 905 | 295 | 181 | 454 | 104 | 61 | 115 |
| 1978 | 2,684 [10] | 1,098 [10] | 39 | 47 | 7,124 | 1,575 | 336 | 191 | 435 | 256 | 70 | 131 |
| | 2,791 | 1,106 | | | | | | | | | | |
| 1979 | 2,880 | 1,142 | 43 | 48 | 7,537 | 1,935 | 386 | 203 | 478 | 275 | 65 | 112 |
| 1980 | 3,112 | 1,217 | 50 | 52 | 7,971 | 2,093 | 448 | 220 | 523 | 295 | 95 | 162 |
| 1981 | 3,319 | 1,293 | 64 | 52 | 8,251 | 2,063 | 574 | 259 | 599 | 328 | 99 | 159 |
| 1982 | 3,516 | 1,357 | 67 | 59 | 8,543 | 2,149 | 606 | 256 | 670 | 353 | 102 | 177 |
| 1983 | 3,620 | 1,380 | 71 | 61 | 9,008 | 2,238 | 619 | 249 | 723 | 368 | 120 | 180 |
| 1984 | 3,749 | 1,409 | 76 | 63 | 9,198 | 2,285 | 630 | 235 | 768 | 381 | 121 | 176 |
| 1985 | 3,863 | 1,432 | ... | ... | 9,527 | 2,410 | 625 | 258 | 805 | 391 | 136 | 185 |
| 1986 | 3,928 | 1,440 | ... | ... | 9,885 | 2,350 | 591 | 242 | 842 | 401 | 141 | 188 |
| 1987 | ... | ... | ... | ... | 10,035 | 2,374 | 618 | 268 | ... | ... | 146 | 190 |
| 1988 | ... | ... | ... | ... | 10,274 | 2,418 | 669 | 227 | ... | ... | 176 | 222 |

**F6    SOUTH AMERICA: Motor Vehicles in Use** (in thousands)

**1950–1988**

|  | Guyana | | Paraguay | | Peru | | Surinam | | Uruguay | | Venezuela | |
|---|---|---|---|---|---|---|---|---|---|---|---|---|
|  | PC | CV | PC | CV | PC | CV | PC | CV | PC | CV | PC | CV |
| 1950 | 3.2 | 0.8 | 1.2 | 2.1 | 32 | 28 | 1.0 | 0.7 | ... | 23 | 70 | 61 |
| 1951 | 3.4 | 0.8 | 1.3 | 2.0 | 34 | 29 | 1.3 | 0.8 | 45 | 30 | 74 | 62 |
| 1952 | 3.9 | 0.9 | 1.9 | 2.3 | 38 | 32 | 1.5 | 0.9 | 47 | 39 | 94 | 69 |
| 1953 | 4.7 | 1.4 | 2.1 | 2.3 | 49 | 40 | ... | ... | 48 | 42 | 113 | 82 |
| 1954 | 5.3 | 1.5 | 3.4 | 3.4 | 52 | 45 | 1.3 | 0.6 | 50 | 46 | 128 | 93 |
| 1955 | 5.5 | 2.4 | 3.7 | 2.8 | 54 | 49 | 1.6 | 0.9 | 52 | 48 | 146 | 98 |
| 1956 | 6.4 | 2.7 | 3.1 | 4.9 | 55 | 50 | 1.8 | 1.0 | 52 | 48 | 160 | 89 |
| 1957 | ·7.3 | 3.0 | ... | ... | 62 | 52 | 2.4 | 1.1 | 78 | 49 | 186 | 92 |
| 1958 | 8.2 | 3.3 | 5.8₃ | 2.5₃ | 70 | 58 | 3.0 | 1.3 | 79 | 49 | 186 | 88 |
| 1959 | 7.7 | 3.2 | 4.7 | 3.4 | 73 | 60 | 3.3 | 1.2 | 80 | 50 | 239 | 99 |
| 1960 | 9.8 | 3.3 | 3.8 | 2.5 | 79 | 65 | 4.2 | 1.5 | 100 | 76 | 269 | 101 |
| 1961 | 10 | 3.7 | 4.3 | 2.5 | 89 | 72 | 5.1 | 1.7 | 105 | 82 | 267 | 105 |
| 1962 | 11 | 3.8 | 5.0 | 3.8 | 100 | 79 | 5.7 | 1.7 | 107 | 79 | 280 | 113 |
| 1963 | 7.9 | 2.0 | 4.8 | 4.1 | 111 | 82 | 6.3 | 1.8 | 110 | 80 | 287 | 108 |
| 1964 | 9.1 | 3.0 | 4.8 | 4.9 | 124 | 97 | 6.8 | 1.9 | 112 | 81 | 352 | 132 |
| 1965 | 10 | 3.6 | 5.0 | 5.2 | 155 | 99 | 7.4 | 2.1 | 114 | 82 | 383 | 152 |
| 1966 | 12 | 4.2 | 5.9 | 6.0 | 178 | 108 | 8.1 | 2.3 | 118 | 80 | 426 | 171 |
| 1967 | 13 | 5.2 | 6.4 | 6.5 | 195 | 112 | 8.9 | 2.7 | 122 | 82 | 452 | 196 |
| 1968 | 14 | 6.8 | 6.9 | 6.6 | 158 | 78 | 11 | 3.0 | 126 | 85 | 498 | 200 |
| 1969 | 16 | 7.5 | 14 | 13 | 220 | 109 | 13 | 3.2 | 130 | 90 | 534 | 208 |
| 1970 | 18 | 8.2 | 15 | 13 | 230 | 118 | 15 | 4.5 | 121 | 88 | 566 | 198 |
| 1971 | 20 | 8.4 | 16 | 14 | ... | ... | 17 | 5.1 | ... | 86 | 779 | 275 |
| 1972 | 21 | 9.2 | ... | ... | 232 | 121 | 20 | 5.8 | ... | ... | 769 | 269 |
| 1973 | 23 | 9.9 | ... | ... | 247 | 129 | 22 | 6.5 | ... | ... | 820 | 286 |
| 1974 | 24 | 11 | ... | ... | 267 | 140 | 23 | 8.2 | ... | ... | 876 | 312 |
| 1975 | 26 | 12 | 12 | 13 | 257 | 145 | 25 | 9.0 | ... | ... | 955 | 369 |
| 1976 | 27 | 14 | 18 | 24 | 278 | 156 | 29 | 10 | 127 | 104 | 1,073 | 428 |
| 1977 | 28 | 15 | 23 | 28 | 300 | 166 | 33 | 12 | ... | ... | 1,187 | 498 |
| 1978 | ... | ... | 25 | 31 | 302 | 167 | 38 | 14 | 208 | 41 | 1,277 | 561 |
| 1979 | ... | ... | 33₅ | 31₅ | 303 | 170 | ... | ... | 220 | 42 | 1,390 | 640 |
| 1980 | ... | ... | 58 | 18 | 309 | 177 | 29 | ... | 220 | 43 | 1,506 | 718 |
| 1981 | ... | ... | 57 | 15 | 331 | 191 | 30 | ... | 281 | 48 | 1,635 | 796 |
| 1982 | ... | ... | 63 | 13 | 360 | 205 | 32 | ... | 298 | 52 | 1,846 | 853 |
| 1983 | ... | ... | 79 | 24 | 372 | 212 | 31 | 13 | 292 | 45 | 1,955 | 952 |
| 1984 | ... | ... | 85 | 24 | 374 | 213 | 29 | 12 | 292 | 45 | 1,559 | 405 |
| 1985 | ... | ... | 105 | 22 | 376 | 215 | 32 | 13 | 306 | 46 | 1,598 | 418 |
| 1986 | ... | ... | 112 | 23 | 377 | 221 | 32 | 13 | 318 | 47 | 1,656 | 430 |
| 1987 | ... | ... | 122 | 27 | 377 | 228 | 32 | 13 | 333 | 47 | 1,718 | 448 |
| 1988 | ... | ... | 80 | 19 | 377 | 233 | 35 | 13 | 350 | 50 | 1,740 | 421 |

NOTES

1. SOURCES: The national publications listed on p. xiv–xvi; League of Nations and UN, *Statistical Yearbooks*.
2. So far as possible, and except as indicated in footnotes, buses and taxis are included with commercial vehicles.
3. Unless otherwise indicated, statistics relate to the year-end.


FOOTNOTES

[1] Taxis included with passenger cars. Newfoundland is included from 1949.
[2] Buses are included with passenger cars to 1953. Government vehicles are excluded from passenger cars to 1958. Data are at 30 June.
[3] Data for 'the early years of the century are incomplete, largely because few States required...registration.' Alaska and Hawaii are included from 1960.
   There was a rearrangement of categories. It was also subsequently stated in the source that the statistics included vehicles which are no longer in circulation.
[4] In 1957 to 1959 (1st line) vehicles belonging to police and other security organizations are included.
[5] The reason for this break is not given in the source.
[6] Data to 1948 relate to the Canal Zone. Most vehicles were registered both in the state and in the Canal Zone.
[7] Vehicles in Panama City and Colon districts only.
[8] Vehicles licenced to 1949 (1st line), all vehicles registered subsequently.
[9] Subsequently including buses.
[10] Subsequently including estimates of numbers of unregistered vehicles.
[11] Excluding buses.

## F7 NORTH AMERICA: CIVIL AVIATION TRAFFIC

Key:- Pass = passengers (in thousands); PKM = passenger-kilometres (in millions, except as otherwise indicated);
TKM = metric ton-kilometres (in millions)

**1920–1944**

| | Canada | | | | Cuba | Guatemala | Mexico | | USA | | | |
|---|---|---|---|---|---|---|---|---|---|---|---|---|
| | Pass. | PKM | Cargo TKM[2] | Mail TKM[2] | PKM | Pass.[4] | Pass. | PKM | Pass.[5] | PKM[6] | Cargo TKM[7] | Mail TKM[7] |
| 1920 | 15 | ... | ... | ... | ... | ... | ... | ... | ... | ... | ... | ... |
| 1921 | 9.2 | ... | ... | ... | ... | ... | ... | ... | ... | ... | ... | ... |
| 1922 | 4.3 | ... | ... | ... | ... | ... | ... | ... | ... | ... | ... | ... |
| 1923 | 2.3[1] | ... | ... | ... | ... | ... | ... | ... | ... | ... | ... | ... |
| 1924 | 4.3 | ... | ... | ... | ... | ... | ... | ... | ... | ... | ... | ... |
| 1925 | 3.7 | ... | ... | ... | ... | ... | ... | ... | ... | ... | ... | ... |
| 1926 | 4.8 | ... | ... | ... | ... | ... | ... | ... | 6 | ... | - - | ... |
| 1927 | 17 | ... | ... | ... | ... | ... | 1.5 | ... | 9 | ... | - - | ... |
| 1928 | 55 | ... | ... | ... | ... | ... | 11 | ... | 49 | ... | 0.1 | ... |
| 1929 | 96 | 9.8 | ... | ... | ... | 1.4 | 12 | ... | 173 | ... | 0.1 | ... |
| 1930 | 125 | 8.7 | ... | ... | ... | ... | 21 | ... | 418 | 167 | 0.2 | ... |
| 1931 | 100 | 6.6 | ... | ... | ... | ... | 22 | ... | 531 | 195 | 0.3 | 4.6 |
| 1932 | 77[1] | 4.6 | ... | ... | ... | ... | 23 | 8.7 | 548 | 238 | 0.4 | 3.9 |
| 1933 | 69 | 6.1 | ... | ... | ... | ... | 39 | 12 | 576 | 322 | 0.6 | 3.7 |
| 1934 | 81 | 10 | ... | ... | ... | ... | 52 | 18 | 572[5] | 365 | 0.9[7] | [3.3] |
| 1935 | 157 | 13 | ... | ... | ... | ... | 60 | 23 | 790 | 583 | 1.6 | 6.0 |
| 1936 | 119 | 14 | [1.6][2] | [0.1][2] | ... | ... | 66 | 28 | 1,020 | 774[6] | 2.7 | 8.4 |
| 1937 | 141 | 17[2] / 20 | 2.7 | 0.2 | ... | 4.3 | 70 | 26 | 1,097[5] / 999[5] | 750[6] | 3.2 | 9.8 |
| 1938 | 140 | 18 | 1.4 | 0.4 | [3.1][3] | 5.0 | 76 | 29 | 1,186 | 858 | 3.2 | 11 |
| 1939 | 162 | 35 | 1.4 | 0.6 | ... | 5.1 | 85 | 34 | 1,690 | 1,215 | 4.0 | 13 |
| 1940 | 149 | 61 | 1.1 | 0.9 | ... | 4.3 | 87 | 41 | 2,686 | 1,854 | 5.1 | 15 |
| 1941 | 208 | 87 | 1.4 | 1.3 | ... | 3.5 | 124 | 132 | 3,693 | 2,491 | 7.7 | 19 |
| 1942 | 229 | 114 | 1.6 | 2.2 | ... | 4.3 | 184 | 112 | 3,406 | 2,663 | 17 | 31 |
| 1943 | 315 | 162 | 2.1 | 3.1 | ... | 6.5 | 261 | 175 | 3,299 | 3,022 | 30 | 57 |
| 1944 | 404 | 179 | 2.1 | 3.0 | [12][3] | 9.7 | 298 | 213 | 4,387 | 4,006 | 34 | 79 |

**F7    NORTH AMERICA: Civil Aviation Traffic**

**1945–1988**

| | Canada | | | | Costa Rica | | | | Cuba | | | |
|---|---|---|---|---|---|---|---|---|---|---|---|---|
| | Pass.[1] | PKM[2] | Cargo TKM[2] | Mail TKM[2] | Pass. | PKM | Cargo TKM | Mail TKM | Pass. | PKM | Cargo TKM | Mail TKM |
| 1945 | 525 | 229 | 1.9 | 2.7 | ... | ... | ... | ... | ... | ... | ... | ... |
| 1946 | 836 | 322 | 1.8 | 2.2 | ... | ... | ... | ... | ... | 32 | ... | ... |
| 1947 | 957 | 369 | 2.6 | 2.4 | ... | ... | ... | ... | ... | 64 | ... | ... |
| 1948 | 1,136 | 498[2] | 4.3[2] | 4.2[2] | ... | ... | ... | ... | ... | ... | ... | ... |
| | | 596 | 5.1 | 4.4 | | | | | | | | |
| 1949 | 1,308 | 741 | 7.1 | 6.2 | ... | ... | ... | ... | ... | ... | ... | ... |
| 1950 | 1,553 | 857 | 9.1 | 6.6 | ... | ... | ... | ... | ... | 93 | ... | ... |
| 1951 | 1,948 | 1,040 | 10 | 7.3 | ... | ... | ... | ... | ... | 118 | 0.9 | 0.1 |
| 1952 | 2,361 | 1,220 | 13 | 8.0 | ... | ... | ... | ... | ... | 132 | 0.8 | 0.1 |
| 1953 | 2,796 | 1,425 | 15 | 9.0 | ... | ... | ... | ... | ... | 112 | 1.3 | 0.1 |
| 1954 | 2,866 | 1,624 | 19 | 12 | ... | ... | ... | ... | ... | 140 | 1.4 | 0.2 |
| 1955 | 3,303 | 1,864 | 24 | 13 | ... | ... | ... | ... | ... | 142 | 1.8 | 0.2 |
| 1956 | 3,924 | 2,353 | 30 | 14 | ... | ... | ... | ... | ... | 225 | 5.4 | 0.2 |
| 1957 | 4,355 | 2,762 | 33 | 16 | ... | ... | ... | ... | ... | 285 | 12 | 0.5 |
| 1958 | 4,579 | 3,232 | 32 | 17 | ... | ... | ... | ... | 465 | 273 | 13 | 2.0 |
| 1959 | 5,348[1] | 3,739 | 38 | 19 | ... | 41 | 4.1 | 0.2 | 404 | 261 | 14 | 1.7 |
| | 5,316 | | | | | | | | | | | |
| 1960 | 5,452 | 4,267 | 46 | 20 | 155 | 55 | 5.4 | 0.2 | 321 | 217 | 11 | 1.4 |
| 1961 | 5,741 | 5,033 | 52 | 20 | 169 | 58 | 5.7 | 0.2 | 167 | 167 | 7.9 | 0.7 |
| 1962 | 6,064 | 5,509 | 62 | 22 | 153 | 62 | 8 | 0.3 | 130 | 122 | 3.6 | 0.3 |
| 1963 | 6,278 | 5,786 | 74 | 24 | 162 | 72 | 8.3 | 0.3 | 265 | 199 | 4.7 | 0.8 |
| 1964 | 6,775 | 6,296 | 95 | 27 | 155 | 74 | 9.6 | 0.1 | 432 | 311 | 5.0 | 0.5 |
| 1965 | 7,839 | 7,565 | 125 | 31 | 166 | 89 | 8.1 | 0.1 | 430 | 281 | 5.1 | 0.7 |
| 1966 | 9,024 | 8,976 | 162 | 35 | 175 | 97 | 8.7 | 0.1 | 469 | 290 | 7.4 | 0.7 |
| 1967 | 11,596 | 11,102 | 187 | 41 | 183 | 106 | 8.1 | 0.2 | 527 | 328 | 9.1 | 0.7 |
| 1968 | 11,875 | 12,044 | 252 | 44 | 199 | 113 | 6.5 | 0.2 | 529 | 329 | 6.5 | 0.9 |
| 1969 | | 12,997 | 302 | 49 | 205 | 124 | 8.9 | 0.2 | 686 | 446 | 8.0 | 1.8 |
| 1970 | 10,180 | 15,397 | 371 | 54 | 256 | 168 | 9.3 | 0.2 | 877 | 502 | 9.1 | 2.1 |
| 1971 | 10,247 | 15,055 | 404 | 71 | 280 | 199 | 9.2 | 0.2 | 986 | 537 | 9.1 | 1.9 |
| 1972 | 11,629 | 18,022 | 433 | 75 | 307 | 242 | 8.6 | 0.2 | 934 | 550 | 10 | 2.2 |
| 1973 | 14,627 | 21,701 | 484 | 86 | 314 | 256 | 8.1 | 0.2 | 814 | 535 | 12 | 2.1 |
| 1974 | 16,368 | 24,605 | 520 | 93 | 374 | 299 | 9.2 | 0.2 | 703 | 528 | 10 | 1.8 |
| 1975 | 16,713 | 24,999 | 534 | 93 | 372 | 306 | 8.9 | 0.2 | 711 | 517 | 14 | 1.9 |
| 1976 | 16,833 | 26,031 | 568 | 114 | 390 | 326 | 13 | 0.3 | 717 | 663 | 12 | 1.8 |
| 1977 | 17,527 | 27,291 | 550 | 120 | 327 | 337 | 18 | 0.3 | 635 | 773 | 9.4 | 1.4 |
| 1978 | 18,472 | 29,276 | 609 | 119 | 321 | 360 | 19 | 0.2 | 713 | 1,089 | 9.6 | 1.8 |
| 1979 | 20,846 | 33,986 | 670 | 123 | 366 | 427 | 22 | 0.3 | 819 | 1,272 | 12 | 2.5 |
| 1980 | 22,453 | 36,234 | 689 | 130 | 431 | 495 | 22 | 0.4 | 676 | 932 | 10 | 1.9 |
| 1981 | 22,097 | 35,608 | 713 | 132 | 428 | 578 | 21 | 0.7 | 651 | 1,242 | 12 | 3.1 |
| 1982 | 19,654 | 32,140 | 747 | 136 | 459 | 629 | 21 | 1.1 | 135 | 1,100 | 13 | 3.2 |
| 1983 | 18,108 | 31,342 | 826 | 137 | 380 | 505 | 21 | 0.7 | 839 | 1,136 | 16 | 1.9 |
| 1984 | 19,383 | 34,122 | 967 | 125 | 323 | 546 | 24 | 0.7 | 839 | 1,289 | 15 | 3.1 |
| 1985 | 19,688 | 35,684 | 990 | 130 | 310 | 570 | 25 | 1.1 | 894 | 1,801 | 17 | 3.0 |
| 1986 | 20,379 | 39,025 | 977 | 133 | 335 | 560 | 25 | 1 | 913 | 1,856 | 22 | 3 |
| 1987 | 19,946 | 40,241 | 1,007 | 117 | 348 | 610 | 30 | 1 | 889 | 1,997 | 26 | 4 |
| 1988 | 22,379 | 46,917 | 1,171 | 121 | 401 | 786 | 33 | 1 | 964 | 2,120 | 28 | 4 |

## F7    NORTH AMERICA: Civil Aviation Traffic

**1945–1988**

| | Guatemala | | | | Honduras | | | | Jamaica | | | |
|---|---|---|---|---|---|---|---|---|---|---|---|---|
| | Pass.[4] | PKM | Cargo TKM | Mail TKM | Pass. | PKM | Cargo TKM[9] | Mail TKM | Pass. | PKM | Cargo TKM | Mail TKM |
| 1945 | $\frac{16_4}{59}$ | ... | ... | ... | ... | ... | ... | ... | ... | ... | ... | ... |
| 1946 | 100 | ... | ... | ... | ... | ... | ... | ... | ... | ... | ... | ... |
| 1947 | 116 | ... | ... | ... | ... | ... | ... | ... | ... | ... | ... | ... |
| 1948 | 129 | ... | ... | ... | ... | ... | ... | ... | ... | ... | ... | ... |
| 1949 | 129 | ... | ... | ... | ... | ... | ... | ... | ... | ... | ... | ... |
| 1950 | 114 | ... | ... | ... | ... | ... | ... | ... | ... | ... | ... | ... |
| 1951 | 101 | ... | ... | ... | ... | ... | ... | ... | ... | ... | ... | ... |
| 1952 | 92 | ... | ... | ... | ... | ... | ... | ... | ... | ... | ... | ... |
| 1953 | 90 | ... | ... | ... | ... | ... | ... | ... | ... | ... | ... | ... |
| 1954 | 89 | ... | ... | ... | ... | ... | ... | ... | ... | ... | ... | ... |
| 1955 | 105 | ... | ... | ... | ... | ... | ... | ... | ... | ... | ... | ... |
| 1956 | 106 | ... | ... | ... | ... | ... | ... | ... | ... | ... | ... | ... |
| 1957 | 113 | 18 | 0.8 | 0.1 | ... | 35 | 4.6 | 0.1 | ... | ... | ... | ... |
| 1958 | 112 | 28 | 1.9 | 0.1 | ... | 38 | 4.9 | 0.1 | ... | ... | ... | ... |
| 1959 | 107 | 31 | 2.3 | 0.1 | ... | 41 | 5.3 | 0.1 | ... | ... | ... | ... |
| 1960 | 107 | 30 | 2.1 | 0.1 | 152 | 44 | 3.8 | - - | ... | ... | ... | ... |
| 1961 | 108 | 30 | 2.3 | 0.1 | 148 | 40 | 3.7 | - - | ... | ... | ... | ... |
| 1962 | 102 | 26 | 2.1 | 0.1 | 118 | 39 | 5.1 | - - | ... | ... | ... | ... |
| 1963 | 103 | 30 | 2.8 | 0.1 | 123 | 44 | 5.1 | - - | 25 | 1.9 | - - | - - |
| 1964 | 116 | 34 | 2.9 | 0.1 | 119 | 45 | $5.3_9$ | - - | 30 | ... | ... | ... |
| 1965 | 136 | 60 | 3.3 | 0.1 | 135 | 58 | 5.9 | - - | 31 | 4.0 | 0.1 | — |
| 1966 | 154 | 73 | 3.4 | 0.1 | 151 | 79 | 7.7 | - - | 96 | 58 | 0.2 | - - |
| 1967 | 168 | 76 | 3.5 | 0.2 | 174 | 96 | 8.1 | 0.1 | 57 | 85 | 0.3 | - - |
| 1968 | $\frac{165_4}{88}$ | 77 | 3.4 | 0.2 | 198 | 109 | 9.7 | 0.1 | 208 | 144 | 0.5 | 0.1 |
| 1969 | 108 | 101 | 5.9 | 0.2 | 251 | 137 | 11 | - - | 231 | 253 | 3.3 | 0.1 |
| 1970 | 113 | 104 | 6.3 | 0.2 | 296 | 167 | 3.6 | - - | 279 | 335 | 2.5 | - - |
| 1971 | 101 | 85 | 5.3 | 0.2 | 270 | 169 | 3.7 | 0.1 | 425 | 457 | 3.3 | 0.3 |
| 1972 | 98 | 80 | 3.8 | 0.2 | 241 | 174 | 3.2 | 0.1 | 555 | 674 | 4.8 | 0.7 |
| 1973 | 43 | 48 | 3.7 | — | 294 | 205 | 3.4 | 0.1 | 569 | 737 | 5.8 | 0.5 |
| 1974 | 89 | 100 | 4.8 | - - | 326 | 226 | 2.6 | 0.1 | 743 | 1,235 | 9.7 | 0.6 |
| 1975 | 114 | 139 | 4.7 | - - | 299 | 240 | 3 | 0.1 | 697 | 1,438 | 11 | 0.8 |
| 1976 | 119 | 132 | 7.1 | - - | 289 | 256 | 5.1 | 0.1 | 643 | 1,379 | 11 | 0.6 |
| 1977 | 138 | 143 | 6.7 | - - | 324 | 276 | 4.2 | 0.1 | 556 | 1,167 | 12 | 0.9 |
| 1978 | 136 | 154 | 7.1 | - - | 320 | 281 | 5.5 | 0.4 | 657 | 1,352 | 13 | 0.7 |
| 1979 | 156 | 190 | 7.5 | 0.1 | 414 | 358 | 3.3 | 0.4 | 748 | 1,443 | 11 | 0.4 |
| 1980 | 119 | 159 | 6.4 | 0.1 | 508 | 387 | 3.8 | 0.6 | 723 | 1,207 | 9.4 | 0.4 |
| 1981 | 124 | 174 | 4.9 | 0.1 | 411 | 341 | 3 | 0.6 | 728 | 1,045 | 10 | 0.3 |
| 1982 | 115 | 160 | 5.2 | 0.2 | 377 | 331 | 2.7 | 0.7 | 873 | 1,230 | 12 | 0.2 |
| 1983 | 100 | 156 | 6.3 | ... | 436 | 348 | 1.9 | 0.5 | 716 | 1,079 | 17 | 0.2 |
| 1984 | 124 | 168 | 8.1 | ... | 439 | 408 | 2.2 | 0.8 | 826 | 1,303 | 20 | 0.2 |
| 1985 | 108 | 156 | 9 | ... | 451 | 391 | ... | ... | 888 | 1,482 | 19 | 0.2 |
| 1986 | 103 | 137 | 10 | ... | 320 | 377 | ... | ... | 1,059 | 1,735 | 19 | ... |
| 1987 | 115 | 165 | 11 | ... | 426 | 484 | 3 | 1 | 1,258 | 2,125 | 24 | ... |
| 1988 | 99 | 165 | 12 | ... | 482 | 466 | 2 | 2 | 1,189 | 1,941 | 21 | ... |

**F7    NORTH AMERICA: Civil Aviation Traffic**

**1945–1988**

| | Mexico | | | | Nicaragua | | | |
|---|---|---|---|---|---|---|---|---|
| | Pass. | PKM | Cargo TKM | Mail TKM | Pass. | PKM | Cargo TKM | Mail TKM |
| 1945 | 413 | 308 | ... | ... | — | — | — | — |
| 1946 | 707 | 439 | ... | ... | ... | 1.7 | 2.9 | ... |
| 1947 | 774 | 499 | ... | ... | ... | 3.1 | 2.9 | ... |
| 1948 | 815 | 552 | ... | ... | ... | 3.6 | 2.5 | - - |
| 1949 | 943 | 562 | ... | ... | ... | 4.3 | 2.2 | - - |
| 1950 | 1,033 | 625 | ... | ... | ... | 5 | ... | ... |
| 1951 | 1,122 | 871 | 26 | 5.9 | ... | 5.2 | 1.7 | - - |
| 1952 | 1,205 | 980 | 32 | 6.5 | ... | 5 | 0.5 | - - |
| 1953 | 1,183 | 1,348 | 33[10] 21 | 6.8[10] 3.1 | ... | 5.7 | 0.3 | - - |
| 1954 | 1,226 | 1,227 | 18 | 2.5 | ... | 5.7 | 0.3 | - - |
| 1955 | 1,317 | 1,366 | 19 | 3.1 | ... | 4.1 | 0.7 | - - |
| 1956 | 1,518 | 1,512 | 23 | 2.8 | ... | 4.9 | 0.7 | - - |
| 1957 | 1,663 | 1,755 | 22 | 2.9 | ... | 5.7 | 0.8 | - - |
| 1958 | 1,668 | 1,809 | 22 | 3.7 | ... | [24][11] | [4][11] | - - |
| 1959 | 1,700 | 1,917 | 26 | 4.3 | ... | [14][11] | [3.3][11] | - - |
| 1960 | 1,780 | 2,200 | 28 | 3.3 | 28 | 12 | 2.3 | - - |
| 1961 | 1,737 | 2,540 | 26 | 3.2 | 31 | 17 | 2.3 | - - |
| 1962 | 1,804 | 2,802 | 26 | 3.3 | 32 | 18 | 2.3 | - - |
| 1963 | 2,032 | 3,152 | 25 | 3.6 | 42 | 28 | 1.7 | - - |
| 1964 | 2,389 | 4,330 | 27 | 3.5 | 45 | 30 | 0.9 | 0.1 |
| 1965 | 3,487 | 4,937 | 32 | 3.9 | 48 | 34 | 0.7 | - - |
| 1966 | 3,019 | 4,605 | 32 | 4.1 | 64 | 45 | 0.8 | 0.1 |
| 1967 | 3,380 | 6,095 | 33 | 3.8 | 82 | 46 | 0.8 | 0.1 |
| 1968 | 3,859 | 6,085 | 38 | 4.2 | 100 | 59 | 0.7 | 0.1 |
| 1969 | 4,150 | 6,779 | 41 | 3.2 | 120 | 75 | 0.8 | 0.1 |
| 1970 | | | 37 | 3.7 | 107 | 77 | 0.8 | 0.1 |
| 1971 | | | 42 | 3.8 | 137 | 107 | 0.9 | 0.1 |
| 1972 | | | 54 | 3.7 | 144 | 117 | 0.9 | 0.1 |
| 1973 | | | 68 | 3.6 | 78 | 76 | 1.9 | 0.1 |
| 1974 | | | 72 | 4 | 81 | 78 | 1.9 | 0.1 |
| 1975 | 6,523 | 6,710 | 76 | 3.4 | 85 | 83 | 1.9 | 0.1 |
| 1976 | 7,676 | 8,000 | 87 | 3.9 | 89 | 86 | 2 | 0.1 |
| 1977 | 8,172 | 8,520 | 93 | 3.7 | 50 | 77 | 1.9 | 0.1 |
| 1978 | 9,388 | 10,027 | 106 | 4 | 110 | 92 | 2 | 0.1 |
| 1979 | 11,381 | 12,041 | 122 | 4.4 | ... | ... | ... | ... |
| 1980 | 12,890 | 13,870 | 132 | 4.3 | ... | ... | ... | ... |
| 1981 | 13,853 | 14,708 | 137 | 4.5 | 97 | 63 | 1.1 | 0.1 |
| 1982 | 13,105 | 13,465 | 112 | 4.3 | 100 | 120 | 1 | 0.1 |
| 1983 | 13,923 | 15,875 | 109 | 3.7 | ... | ... | ... | ... |
| 1984 | 14,440 | 17,197 | 146 | 3.8 | ... | ... | ... | ... |
| 1985 | 15,364 | 17,773 | 170 | 4.2 | ... | ... | ... | ... |
| 1986 | 13,825 | 16,885 | 155 | 4 | ... | ... | ... | ... |
| 1987 | 13,505 | 17,649 | 169 | 5 | ... | ... | ... | ... |
| 1988 | 11,412 | 14,946 | 122 | 4 | ... | ... | ... | ... |

**F7    NORTH AMERICA: Civil Aviation Traffic**

**1945–1988**

| | Trinidad & Tobago | | | | USA | | | |
|---|---|---|---|---|---|---|---|---|
| | Pass. | PKM | Cargo TKM | Mail TKM | Pass. | PKM | Cargo TKM | Mail TKM |
| 1945 | ... | ... | ... | ... | 7,052 | 6,132 | 45 | 102 |
| 1946 | ... | ... | ... | ... | 12,254 | 11,344 | 78 | 60 |
| 1947 | ... | ... | ... | ... | 14,250 | 12,744 | 142 | 71 |
| 1948 | ... | ... | ... | ... | 14,541 | 12,666 | 216 | 86 |
| 1949 | ... | ... | ... | ... | 16,601 | 14,182 | 262 | 97 |
| 1950 | ... | ... | ... | ... | 19,020 | 16,449 | 311 | 108 |
| 1951 | ... | ... | ... | ... | 24,694 | 21,250 | 316 | 134 |
| 1952 | ... | ... | ... | ... | 27,375 | 25,144 | 347 | 144 |
| 1953 | ... | ... | ... | ... | 31,420 | 29,346 | 378 | 154 |
| 1954 | ... | ... | ... | ... | 35,218 | 33,172 | 404 | 184 |
| | | | | | (million) | (thousand million) | | |
| 1955 | ... | ... | ... | ... | 41 | 39 | 476 | 219 |
| 1956 | ... | ... | ... | ... | 46 | 44 | 529 | 232 |
| 1957 | ... | ... | ... | ... | 53 | 50 | 550 | 244 |
| 1958 | ... | ... | ... | ... | 53 | 51 | 625 | 267 |
| 1959 | ... | ... | ... | ... | 60 | 59 | 736 | 295 |
| 1960 | ... | ... | ... | ... | 62 | 63 | 845 | 349 |
| 1961 | ... | ... | ... | ... | 63 | 64 | 980 | 431 |
| 1962 | ... | 121 | 1.7 | 0.4 | 68 | 70 | 1,196 | 495 |
| 1963 | 319 | 312 | 4.2 | 0.7 | 77 | 81 | 1,314 | 519 |
| 1964 | 353 | 339 | 4.4 | 0.8 | 89 | 94 | 1,662 | 541 |
| 1965 | 383 | 355 | 3.1 | 0.6 | 103 | 111 | 2,249 | 701 |
| 1966 | 356 | 340 | 3.2 | 0.6 | 118 | 129 | 2,672 | 1,086 |
| 1967 | 363 | 381 | 3.6 | 0.5 | 142 | 159 | 3,083 | 1,410 |
| 1968 | 330 | 367 | 6.2 | 0.6 | 162 | 183 | 3,659 | 1,815 |
| 1969 | 338 | 417 | 8.3 | 0.6 | 172 | 202 | 4,165 | 1,846 |
| 1970 | 361 | 511 | 9.7 | 0.7 | 169 | 212 | | |
| 1971 | 362 | 654 | 13 | 0.7 | 174 | 218 | | |
| 1972 | 320 | 579 | 15 | 0.7 | 191 | 245 | | |
| 1973 | 325 | 620 | 13 | 0.7 | 202 | 261 | | |
| 1974 | 260 | 600 | 12 | 0.7 | 208 | 262 | | |
| 1975 | 595 | 1,011 | 20 | 0.8 | 206 | 262 | 7,001 | 1,619 |
| 1976 | 384 | 1,040 | 23 | 0.9 | 224 | 288 | 7,440 | 1,644 |
| 1977 | 591 | 1,147 | 26 | 0.9 | 241 | 311 | 7,922 | 1,694 |
| 1978 | 428 | 677 | 15 | 0.4 | 274 | 364 | 8,409 | 1,711 |
| 1979 | 659 | 1,261 | 22 | 0.7 | 314 | 421 | 8,658 | 1,784 |
| 1980 | 877 | 1,505 | 18 | 0.7 | 295 | 409 | 8,615 | 1,954 |
| 1981 | 1,301 | 1,434 | 7.1 | 0.7 | 277 | 396 | 8,321 | 1,986 |
| 1982 | 1,381 | 1,540 | 4.9 | 0.7 | 284 | 409 | 7,972 | 2,038 |
| 1983 | 1,345 | 1,503 | 6.7 | 0.7 | 310 | 443 | 9,174 | 2,141 |
| 1984 | 1,398 | 1,598 | 7.2 | 0.7 | 330 | 477 | 10,112 | 2,367 |
| 1985 | 1,300 | 2,058 | 10 | 1.5 | 371 | 532 | 9,648 | 2,395 |
| 1986 | 1,342 | 2,260 | 11 | 2 | 411 | 583 | 10,713 | 2,426 |
| 1987 | 1,312 | 2,354 | 11 | 2 | 440 | 642 | 11,938 | 2,518 |
| 1988 | 1,296 | 2,507 | 13 | 2 | 454 | 679 | 13,847 | 2,639 |

**F7    SOUTH AMERICA: CIVIL AVIATION TRAFFIC**

**1920–1934**

| | Argentina | Bolivia | | Brazil | | | |
| | Pass. | Pass.[12] | PKM | Pass.[13] | PKM[14] | Cargo TKM[14] | Mail TKM[14] |
|------|------|------|------|------|------|------|------|
| 1920 | ... | ... | ... | ... | ... | ... | ... |
| 1921 | ... | ... | ... | ... | ... | ... | ... |
| 1922 | ... | ... | ... | ... | ... | ... | ... |
| 1923 | ... | ... | ... | ... | ... | ... | ... |
| 1924 | ... | ... | ... | ... | ... | ... | ... |
| 1925 | ... | ... | ... | ... | ... | ... | ... |
| 1926 | ... | 1.0 | ... | ... | ... | ... | ... |
| 1927 | ... | 1.1 | ... | 0.6 | ... | ... | ... |
| 1928 | ... | 3.0 | ... | 2.5 | ... | ... | ... |
| 1929 | ... | 2.9 | 0.9 | 3.7 | ... | ... | ... |
| 1930 | ... | 3.7 | 1.1 | 4.7 | ... | ... | ... |
| 1931 | ... | 4.3 | 1.2 | 5.1 | ... | ... | ... |
| 1932 | ... | 5.1 | 1.6 | 8.9 | ... | ... | ... |
| 1933 | 3.9 | 20 | 7.3 | 13 | 8 | 0.2 | 0.1 |
| 1934 | 6.2 | ... | 4.1 | 18 | 8.4 | 0.2 | 0.1 |

| | Chile | | Colombia | | Peru | Uruguay | Venezuela |
| | Pass. | PKM[15] | Pass. | PKM[16] | Pass.[17] | Pass. | PKM |
|------|------|------|------|------|------|------|------|
| 1920 | ... | ... | ... | ... | ... | ... | ... |
| 1921 | ... | ... | 0.4 | ... | ... | ... | ... |
| 1922 | ... | ... | 1.1 | ... | ... | ... | ... |
| 1923 | ... | ... | 1.3 | ... | ... | ... | ... |
| 1924 | ... | ... | 1.1 | ... | ... | ... | ... |
| 1925 | ... | ... | 1.1 | ... | ... | ... | ... |
| 1926 | ... | ... | 2.7 | ... | ... | ... | ... |
| 1927 | ... | ... | 3.9 | ... | ... | ... | ... |
| 1928 | ... | ... | 6.1 | ... | 0.1 | ... | ... |
| 1929 | 0.9 | ... | 6.6 | 1.6 | 1.6 | 57 | 0.2 |
| 1930 | 5.5 | ... | 4.8 | 1.1 | 5.8 | ... | 0.3 |
| 1931 | 4.8 | ... | 5.7 | 1.1 | 5.8 | ... | 0.3 |
| 1932 | 4.8 | ... | 6.3 | 1.2 | 8.9 | ... | 0.4 |
| 1933 | 3 | 1.2 | 9.4 | 1.3 | 12 | ... | 0.4 |
| 1934 | 3.0 | 1.5 | 13 | 2.0 | 20 | ... | 0.2 |

## F7    SOUTH AMERICA: Civil Aviation Traffic

### 1935–1988

| | Argentina | | | | Bolivia | | | | Brazil | | | |
|---|---|---|---|---|---|---|---|---|---|---|---|---|
| | Pass. | PKM | Cargo TKM | Mail TKM | Pass.[12] | PKM | Cargo TKM | Mail TKM | Pass.[13] | PKM[14] | Cargo TKM[14] | Mail TKM[14] |
| 1935 | 6.6 | 0.4 | ... | ... | ... | 4.8 | ... | ... | 26 | 12 | 0.3 | 0.1 |
| 1936 | 8.7 | 0.8 | ... | ... | ... | 3.2 | ... | ... | 35 | 19 | 0.4 | 0.2 |
| 1937 | 11 | 1.2 | ... | ... | ... | 2.5 | ... | ... | 62 | 31 | 0.6 | 0.2 |
| 1938 | 22 | 1.7 | ... | ... | 21 | 3.3 | ... | ... | 63 | 29 | 0.7 | 0.2 |
| 1939 | 36 | 2.3 | ... | ... | 18 | 4.1 | ... | ... | 71 | 32 | 0.8 | 0.1 |
| 1940 | 41 | 4.0 | ... | ... | 16 | 4.2 | ... | ... | 86 | 45 | 1.2 | 0.2 |
| 1941 | 55 | 6.0 | ... | ... | 15 | 3.4 | ... | ... | 100 | 53 | 1.5 | 0.2 |
| 1942 | 55 | 7.0 | ... | ... | 5.8 | 2.7 | ... | ... | 122 | 71 | 2.5 | 0.2 |
| 1943 | 67 | 10 | ... | ... | 11 | 4.3 | ... | ... | 172 | 118 | 5.6 | 0.5 |
| 1944 | 79 | 12 | ... | ... | 19 | 6.3 | ... | ... | 245 | 179 | 6.9 | 0.8 |
| 1945 | 89 | 14 | ... | ... | 25 | 8.4 | ... | ... | 290 | 207 | 9.0 | 0.6 |
| 1946 | 144 | 26 | ... | ... | 35 | 12 | ... | ... | 539 | 395 | 16 | 0.7 |
| 1947 | 234 | 89 | ... | ... | 45 | 16 | ... | ... | 819 | 566 | 23 | 0.9 |
| 1948 | 362 | ... | ... | ... | 49 | 17 | ... | ... | 1,154 | 677 | 31 | 1.2 |
| 1949 | 435 | 198 | ... | ... | 47 | 17 | ... | ... | 1,327 | 745 | ... | ... |
| 1950 | 493 | 253 | 3.1 | 1.3 | 59 | 20 | ... | ... | 1,714 | 851 | ... | ... |
| 1951 | 462 | 304 | 3.8 | 1.7 | 58 | 22 | ... | ... | 2,241[13] | 1,240 | 65[14] | 1.8 |
| | | | | | | | | | 2,131 | | 46 | |
| 1952 | 393 | 246 | 4.1 | 1.8 | 75 | 24 | ... | ... | 2,110 | 1,279 | 42 | 1.9 |
| 1953 | 410 | 317 | 4.5 | 1.9 | 93 | 29 | 3.3 | - - | 2,518 | 1,483 | 50 | 2.6 |
| 1954 | 470 | 342 | 3.7 | 2.0 | ... | 39 | 3.7 | - - | 2,733 | 1,596 | 54 | 3.2 |
| 1955 | 560 | 371 | 3.6 | 2.0 | 155 | 47 | 5.1 | - - | 2,799 | 1,684 | 60 | 3.4 |
| 1956 | 471 | 439 | 5.2 | 1.8 | 171 | 54 | 4.8 | - - | 3,365 | 2,039[14] | 71[14] | 3.8[14] |
| | | | | | | | | | | 1,982 | 69 | 3.7 |
| 1957 | 562 | 578 | 7.4 | 1.7 | 100 | 33 | 2.5 | - - | 3,754 | 2,289 | 80 | 4.4 |
| 1958 | 692 | 643 | 7.9 | 1.7 | 165 | 36 | 3 | - - | 3,947 | 2,438 | 87 | 4.6 |
| 1959 | 963 | 674 | 9.1 | 1.9 | 165 | 34 | 2.8 | - - | 3,890 | 2,599 | 93 | 5.2 |
| 1960 | 899 | 990 | 14 | 2.1 | 183 | 47 | 5.8 | - - | 3,972[13] | 2,679 | 84 | 5.4 |
| | | | | | | | | | 3,838 | | | |
| 1961 | 955 | 1,131 | 15 | 3.3 | 176 | [51][11] | [3.6][11] | - - | 3,142 | 2,663 | 80 | 5.0 |
| 1962 | 825 | 826 | 8.5 | 2.7 | 167[12] | [56][11] | [3.4][11] | - - | 3,310 | 2,764 | 76 | 7.0 |
| 1963 | 789 | 881 | 8.7 | 3.4 | 139 | 43 | 1.9 | - - | 3,106 | 2,868 | 69 | 5.0 |
| 1964 | 977 | 1,044 | 9.3 | 3.8 | 122 | 50 | 3.6 | - - | 2,702 | 2,593 | 71 | 6.2 |
| 1965 | 1,043 | 1,128 | 10 | 3.8 | 139 | 50 | 1.3 | - - | 2,524 | 2,592 | 68 | 6.4 |
| 1966 | 1,122 | 1,141 | 12 | 4.2 | 166 | 60 | 1.3 | - - | 2,742 | 3,048 | 72 | 9.1 |
| 1967 | 1,405 | 1,556 | 21 | 4.8 | 170 | 62 | 1.4 | - - | 2,940 | 3,210 | 86 | 8.0 |
| 1968 | 1,494 | 1,749 | 33 | 5.1 | 168 | 61 | 1.2 | - - | 3,198 | 3,693 | 96 | 8.5 |
| 1969 | 1,745 | 2,125 | 52 | 5.8 | 277 | 106 | 1.4 | - - | 3,167 | 3,933 | 149 | 9.0 |
| 1970 | 2,332 | 2,395 | 48 | 6.0 | 244 | 109 | 1.5 | - - | 3,340 | 4,385 | 164 | 9.3 |
| 1971 | 2,219 | 2,711 | 57 | 6.0 | 331 | 146 | 2.5 | 0.1 | 3,911 | 4,984 | 180 | 10 |
| 1972 | 2,359 | 2,963 | 80 | 7.6 | 379 | 177 | 2.8 | 0.1 | 4,671 | 5,919 | 254 | 11 |
| 1973 | 2,435 | 3,282 | 86 | 7.5 | 408 | 195 | 3 | 0.1 | 5,842 | 7,335 | 317 | 13 |
| 1974 | 2,943 | 4,080 | 98 | 7.3 | 430 | 205 | 3 | 0.1 | 6,856 | 8,559 | 407 | 13 |
| 1975 | 3,299 | 4,373 | 76 | 7.2 | 653 | 331 | 2.6 | 0.1 | 7,773 | 9,787 | 460 | 14 |
| 1976 | 3,294 | 4,222 | 96 | 7.4 | 745 | 444 | 4.1 | 0.2 | 8,799 | 10,366 | 472 | 16 |
| 1977 | 3,884 | 4,874 | 120 | 7.5 | 862 | 558 | 28 | 0.2 | 9,514 | 10,978 | 499 | 18 |
| 1978 | 3,949 | 5,370 | 121 | 8.6 | 1,016 | 700 | 43 | 0.2 | 10,621 | 12,544 | 571 | 19 |
| 1979 | 5,025 | 6,946 | 137 | 9.5 | 1,226 | 860 | 34 | 0.2 | 11,857 | 14,461 | 570 | 23 |
| 1980 | 5,589 | 8,031 | 195 | 21 | 1,342 | 944 | 38 | 0.2 | 13,008 | 15,572 | 588 | 23 |
| 1981 | 4,890 | 7,019 | 195 | 20 | 1,220 | 963 | 44 | 0.5 | 12,595 | 16,304 | 645 | 23 |
| 1982 | 4,596 | 6,083 | 171 | 19 | 1,160 | 780 | 28 | 0.8 | 13,168 | 17,229 | 735 | 24 |
| 1983 | 4,400 | 6,034 | 174 | 20 | 1,299 | 787 | 17 | 1.0 | 12,606 | 16,738 | 692 | 25 |
| 1984 | 5,164 | 7,405 | 180 | 18 | 1,359 | 877 | 38 | 1.9 | 12,948 | 17,175 | 832 | 30 |
| 1985 | 4,713 | 7,351 | 187 | 15 | 1,343 | 894 | 42 | 0.9 | 13,403 | 18,494 | 909 | 32 |
| 1986 | 5,035 | 7,942 | 192 | 14 | 1,301 | 884 | 28 | 1 | 17,195 | 23,471 | 1,014 | 31 |
| 1987 | 5,406 | 8,652 | 198 | 14 | 1,233 | 912 | 26 | 1 | 17,069 | 22,613 | 1,014 | 31 |
| 1988 | 5,069 | 8,862 | 194 | 13 | 1,267 | 955 | 8 | 1 | 17,011 | 23,712 | 976 | 37 |

## F7    SOUTH AMERICA: Civil Aviation Traffic

| | Chile | | | | Colombia | | | | Ecuador | | | |
|---|---|---|---|---|---|---|---|---|---|---|---|---|
| | Pass. | PKM[15] | Cargo TKM[15] | Mail TKM[15] | Pass. | PKM[16] | Cargo TKM[16] | Mail TKM[16] | Pass. | PKM | Cargo TKM | Mail TKM |
| 1935 | 4.0 | 2.4 | ... | ... | 23 | 4.2 | ... | ... | ... | ... | ... | ... |
| 1936 | 4.0 | 2.4 | - - | - - | 28 | 5.6 | ... | ... | ... | ... | ... | ... |
| 1937 | 4.0 | 2.4 | - - | - - | 47 | 8.3 | ... | ... | ... | ... | ... | ... |
| 1938 | 3.7 | 2.1 | - - | - - | 63 | 11 | ... | ... | ... | ... | ... | ... |
| 1939 | 3.2 | 2.0 | - - | - - | 60 | 11 | ... | ... | ... | ... | ... | ... |
| 1940 | 2.6 | 1.8 | - - | - - | 55 | 11 | ... | ... | ... | ... | ... | ... |
| 1941 | 7.8 | 5.3 | - - | - - | 59 | 13 | ... | ... | ... | ... | ... | ... |
| 1942 | 15 | 9.7 | - - | - - | 65 | 14 | ... | ... | ... | ... | ... | ... |
| 1943 | 15 | 10 | - - | - - | 89 | 31 | ... | ... | ... | ... | ... | ... |
| 1944 | 18 | 14 | 0.1 | - - | 103 | ... | ... | ... | ... | ... | ... | ... |
| 1945 | 27 | 19 | 0.1 | - - | 151 | 56 | ... | ... | ... | ... | ... | ... |
| 1946 | 44 | 29 | 0.3 | - - | 223 | ... | ... | ... | ... | ... | ... | ... |
| 1947 | 86 | 55 | 0.5 | - - | ... | ... | ... | ... | ... | ... | ... | ... |
| 1948 | 89 | 60 | 0.8 | 0.1 | 686 | ... | ... | ... | ... | ... | ... | ... |
| 1949 | 67 | 46 | 0.7 | 0.1 | 776 | 247 | ... | ... | ... | ... | ... | ... |
| 1950 | 81 | 54 | 0.7 | 0.1 | 874 | 302 | ... | ... | ... | ... | ... | ... |
| 1951 | 98 | 66 | 0.9 | 0.1 | 896 | 321 | 68 | 0.3 | ... | ... | ... | ... |
| 1952 | 106 | 77 | 1.2 | 0.1 | 967 | 372 | 62 | 0.4 | ... | ... | ... | ... |
| 1953 | 134 | 95 | 1.7 | 0.1 | 1,011 | 415 | 59 | 2.6 | ... | ... | ... | ... |
| 1954 | 182 | 122 | 1.8 | 0.1 | 979 | 426 | 60 | 4.0 | ... | 14 | 0.1 | - - |
| 1955 | 213 | 156 | 1.9 | 0.1 | 1,090 | 484 | 58 | 3.5 | ... | 7.6 | 0.1 | - - |
| 1956 | 267 | 333 | 7.2 | 0.1 | 1,389 | 562 | 60 | 3.5 | ... | 8.1 | 0.1 | - - |
| 1957 | 374 | 438[15] | 11[15] | 0.2[15] | 1,490 | 615 | 53 | 3.3 | ... | 9.8 | 0.1 | - - |
| 1958 | 350 | 377 | 9.3 | 0.2 | 1,436 | 632 | 49 | 3 | ... | 16 | 0.5 | 0.1 |
| 1959 | 300 | 321 | 6.0 | 0.2 | 1,484 | 681[16] | 50[16] | 3.2[16] | ... | 39 | 0.9 | 0.2 |
| 1960 | 403 | 414 | 9.7 | 0.9 | 1,529 | 777 | 41 | 1.1 | 135 | 42 | 1.0 | - - |
| 1961 | 395 | 427 | 17 | 0.9 | 1,692 | 824 | 42 | 1.1 | 139 | 44 | 1.0 | - - |
| 1962 | 362 | 364 | 13 | 0.5 | 2,075 | 1,001 | 46 | 1.4 | 140 | 44 | 1.0 | - - |
| 1963 | 362 | 380 | 21 | 0.5 | 2,354 | 1,205 | 47 | 1.7 | 144 | 43 | 1.0 | - - |
| 1964 | 470 | 511 | 25 | 0.6 | 2,580 | 1,319 | 56 | 2.0 | 163 | 94 | 1.1 | - - |
| 1965 | 474 | 511 | 25 | 0.6 | 2,537 | 1,301 | 54 | 2.2 | 204 | 128 | 2.3 | 0.1 |
| 1966 | 476 | 529 | 26 | 0.8 | 2,528 | 1,377 | 53 | 2.6 | 257 | 161 | 2.6 | 0.2 |
| 1967 | 553 | 665 | 28 | 0.7 | 2,462 | 1,489 | 51 | 2.9 | 296 | 217 | 2.7 | 0.3 |
| 1968 | 498 | 601 | 24 | 0.6 | 2,386 | 1,562 | 56 | 3.3 | 385 | 263 | 4.2 | 0.3 |
| 1969 | 582 | 730 | 37 | 0.9 | 2,581 | 1,744 | 60 | 3.6 | 415 | 244 | 5.3 | 0.3 |
| 1970 | 575 | 839 | 41 | 1.1 | 3,010 | 2,063 | 75 | 4.1 | 419 | 256 | 9.3 | 0.3 |
| 1971 | 691 | 1,113 | 47 | 1.4 | 2,960 | 2,182 | 81 | 4.0 | 457 | 216 | 4.7 | 0.4 |
| 1972 | 730 | 1,143 | 54 | 1.4 | 2,964 | 2,284 | 86 | 4.2 | 438 | 218 | 4.5 | 0.3 |
| 1973 | 636 | 1,111 | 47 | 1.6 | 3,140 | 2,494 | 105 | 3.9 | 380 | 220 | 9.6 | 0.3 |
| 1974 | 505 | 1,159 | 55 | 1.8 | 3,120 | 2,567 | 118 | 3.7 | 382 | 189 | 8.1 | 0.3 |
| 1975 | 510 | 1,276 | 57 | 1.8 | 3,376 | 2,778 | 122 | 4.4 | 448 | 301 | 6.4 | 0.3 |
| 1976 | 490 | 1,230 | 76 | 2.0 | 3,730 | 2,976 | 150 | 4.6 | 463 | 360 | 6.9 | 0.3 |
| 1977 | 589 | 1,433 | 105 | 2.5 | 4,117 | 3,376 | 172 | 4.4 | 529 | 551 | 9.5 | 0.3 |
| 1978 | 533 | 1,472 | 102 | 3.1 | 4,747 | 3,786 | 206 | 4.4 | 593 | 676 | 13 | 0.4 |
| 1979 | 559 | 1,550 | 85 | 3 | 5,052 | 4,196 | 183 | 4.7 | ... | ... | ... | ... |
| 1980 | 669 | 1,875 | 145 | 3.7 | 4,808 | 4,198 | 147 | 5.0 | 701 | 975 | 40 | 0.6 |
| 1981 | 886 | 2,220 | 153 | 4.5 | 4,570 | 4,288 | 204 | 5.0 | 692 | 946 | 39 | 0.9 |
| 1982 | 822 | 1,824 | 142 | 2.2 | 6,701 | 5,050 | 249 | 5.1 | 676 | 862 | 36 | 1.2 |
| 1983 | 652 | 1,493 | 120 | 2 | 6,584 | 4,986 | 292 | 5.1 | 618 | 762 | 33 | 1.5 |
| 1984 | 731 | 1,624 | 105 | 2.5 | 5,737 | 4,481 | 381 | 4.5 | 634 | 893 | 42 | 2.5 |
| 1985 | 825 | 1,772 | 114 | 2.6 | 5,737 | 4,242 | 376 | 5.2 | 664 | 969 | 51 | 2.6 |
| 1986 | 875 | 1,961 | 137 | 3 | 5,731 | 4,265 | 392 | 5 | 697 | 1,073 | 59 | 2 |
| 1987 | 992 | 2,117 | 186 | 3 | 5,599 | 4,230 | 398 | 6 | 692 | 1,073 | 70 | 2 |
| 1988 | 1,144 | 2,442 | 243 | 3 | 5,460 | 4,308 | 403 | 7 | 684 | 1,051 | 74 | 1 |

## F7    SOUTH AMERICA: Civil Aviation Traffic

**1935–1988**

| | Peru | | | | Uruguay | | | | Venezuela | | | |
|---|---|---|---|---|---|---|---|---|---|---|---|---|
| | Pass.[17] | PKM[19] | Cargo TKM[19] | Mail TKM[19] | Pass. | PKM[20] | Cargo TKM[20] | Mail TKM[20] | Pass.[18] | PKM | Cargo TKM | Mail TKM |
| 1935 | 23 | ... | ... | ... | ... | ... | ... | ... | ... | 0.4 | ... | ... |
| 1936 | 30 | ... | ... | ... | ... | ... | ... | ... | ... | 0.7 | ... | ... |
| 1937 | 35 | ... | ... | ... | ... | ... | ... | ... | ... | 1.3 | ... | ... |
| 1938 | 31 | ... | ... | ... | ... | ... | ... | ... | ... | 1.6 | ... | ... |
| 1939 | 30 | ... | ... | ... | ... | ... | ... | ... | ... | 2.6 | ... | ... |
| 1940 | 28 | ... | ... | ... | ... | ... | ... | ... | ... | 3.5 | ... | ... |
| 1941 | 29 | ... | ... | ... | ... | ... | ... | ... | 17 | 5 | ... | ... |
| 1942 | 39 | ... | ... | ... | ... | ... | ... | ... | 21 | 5 | ... | ... |
| 1943 | 51 | ... | ... | ... | ... | ... | ... | ... | ... | 8 | ... | ... |
| 1944 | 56 | ... | ... | ... | ... | ... | ... | ... | 37 | 10 | ... | ... |
| 1945 | 59 | ... | ... | ... | ... | ... | ... | ... | 78 | 12 | ... | ... |
| 1946 | 75 | ... | ... | ... | ... | ... | ... | ... | 181 | 20 | ... | ... |
| 1947 | 120 | ... | ... | ... | ... | ... | ... | ... | 311 | 30 | ... | ... |
| 1948 | 164 | 63 | ... | ... | ... | ... | ... | ... | 503 | 40 | ... | ... |
| 1949 | 175 | ... | ... | ... | ... | ... | ... | ... | 605 | 60 | ... | ... |
| 1950 | 169 | ... | ... | ... | ... | ... | ... | ... | 565 | 105 | ... | ... |
| 1951 | 195 | 72 | 4.8 | 0.1 | ... | ... | ... | ... | 525 | 217 | 8.3 | 0.3 |
| 1952 | 136 | 69 | 5 | 0.1 | ... | ... | ... | ... | 545 | 253 | 8.6 | 0.4 |
| 1953 | 205 | 79 | 5 | 0.1 | ... | ... | ... | ... | 575 | 269 | 7.3 | 0.5 |
| 1954 | 237 | 85 | 5 | 0.1 | ... | 28 | 0.1[20] | - -[20] | 646[20] | 291 | 8.6 | 0.7 |
| 1955 | 269 | 93 | 5.3 | 0.1 | ... | 29 | 0.2 | - - | 662 | 325 | 11 | 0.8 |
| 1956 | 282 | 99 | 5.8 | 0.2 | ... | 36 | 0.2 | - - | 648 | 324 | 12 | 1.5 |
| 1957 | 323 | 113 | 6.2 | 0.2 | ... | 34 | 0.4 | - - | 715 | 309 | 13 | 0.7 |
| 1958 | 362 | 130 | 7 | 0.3 | ... | 41 | 0.3 | - - | 720 | 360 | 14 | 0.6 |
| 1959 | 412 | 127 | 7.2 | 0.3 | ... | 59 | 0.3 | - - | 793 | 408 | 14 | 0.7 |
| 1960 | 429 | 124 | 7.3 | 0.3 | 275 | 83 | 0.4 | - - | 749[18] 804 | 386 | 12 | 0.6 |
| 1961 | 488 | 186 | 7.2 | 0.4 | 269 | 79 | 0.4 | - - | 696 | 339 | 23 | 1 |
| 1962 | 575 | 183[19] | 5.8[19] | 0.4[19] | 266 | 73 | 0.6 | - - | 647 | 432 | 30 | 1.4 |
| 1963 | 654 | 271 | 7.2 | 0.6 | 233 | 69 | 0.5 | - - | 702 | 461 | 36 | 1.3 |
| 1964 | 762 | 370 | 9.4 | 0.6 | 258 | 77 | 0.5 | - - | 799 | 544 | 43 | 1.6 |
| 1965 | 888 | 496 | 11 | 0.7 | 273 | 81 | 0.5 | - - | 885 | 660 | 50 | 1.5 |
| 1966 | 919 | 542 | 12 | 0.8 | 301 | 83 | 0.5 | - - | 987 | 740 | 34 | 1.5 |
| 1967 | 1,038[17] | 622 | 12 | 0.9 | 231 | 73 | 0.3 | - - | 1,085 | 872 | 40 | 1.5 |
| 1968 | 326 | 574 | 14 | 1.2 | 244 | 75 | 0.2 | - - | 1,084 | 952 | 19 | 1.7 |
| 1969 | 362 | 752 | 18 | 1.7 | 242 | 66 | 0.1 | - - | 1,095 | 1,023 | 60 | 2 |
| 1970 | 391 | 789 | 22 | 2.2 | 219 | 63 | 0.3 | - - | 757 | 1,033 | 57 | 2 |
| 1971 | 264 | 224 | 17 | 0.5 | 221 | 73 | 0.3 | - - | 1,302 | 1,298 | 66 | 1.8 |
| 1972 | 525 | 355 | 16 | 0.2 | 136 | 27 | 0.1 | - - | 1,511 | 1,521 | 66 | 1.7 |
| 1973 | 590 | 404 | 12 | 0.2 | 145 | 30 | 0.2 | - - | 1,766 | 1,734 | 75 | 1.9 |
| 1974 | 745 | 700 | 20 | 0.4 | 340 | 80 | 0.1 | - - | 1,981 | 1,928 | 86 | 2.1 |
| 1975 | 1,335 | 1,222 | 22 | 0.4 | 334 | 79 | 0.1 | - - | 2,355 | 2,269 | 71 | 2.2 |
| 1976 | 1,439 | 1,367 | 25 | 0.8 | 327 | 83 | 0.2 | - - | 2,708 | 2,538 | 75 | 2.2 |
| 1977 | 1,425 | 1,353 | 35 | 0.5 | 293 | 74 | 0.3 | - - | 3,501 | 3,101 | 115 | 2.6 |
| 1978 | 1,469 | 1,470 | 36 | 0.6 | 260 | 64 | 0.2 | - - | 3,915 | 3,498 | 113 | 2.8 |
| 1979 | 1,686 | 1,795 | 36 | 0.6 | 448 | 160 | 1.4 | 0.3 | 4,772 | 4,135 | 107 | 3.1 |
| 1980 | 1,980 | 1,974 | 40 | 0.7 | 478 | 178 | 0.7 | 0.1 | 5,133 | 4,367 | 148 | 2.7 |
| 1981 | 1,777 | 1,755 | 48 | 0.5 | 413 | 198 | 1.1 | 0.1 | 5,147 | 4,645 | 142 | 2.7 |
| 1982 | 1,740 | 1,685 | 93 | 0.5 | 356 | 293 | 1.0 | 0.2 | 5,434 | 5,031 | 126 | 2.8 |
| 1983 | 1,698 | 1,699 | 76 | 0.8 | 310 | 325 | 1.5 | 0.3 | 5,000 | 3,747 | 103 | 2.4 |
| 1984 | 1,617 | 1,664 | 61 | 0.8 | 338 | 322 | 2.0 | 0.2 | 4,571 | 3,602 | 107 | 2.6 |
| 1985 | 1,564 | 1,598 | 47 | 0.8 | 329 | 389 | 1.9 | 0.2 | 4,967 | 4,370 | 83 | 3.9 |
| 1986 | 2,153 | 2,110 | 80 | 1 | 341 | 459 | ... | ... | 5,791 | 4,339 | 99 | 4 |
| 1987 | 3,009 | 2,670 | 79 | 1 | 351 | 459 | ... | ... | 6,454 | 5,040 | 118 | 5 |
| 1988 | 2,737 | 2,498 | 52 | 1 | ... | ... | ... | ... | 8,659 | 6,907 | 213 | 7 |

**F7**     **Civil Aviation Traffic**

NOTES

1. SOURCES: The national publications listed on p. xiv–xvi and the League of Nations and UN, *Statistical Yearbooks.*
2. Except as otherwise indicated, the statistics relate to scheduled services (including overflow) only, by companies registered in the countries concerned.
3. Comparisons between different countries prior to the 1950s are especially difficult because of lack of uniformity in methods of collecting data.

FOOTNOTES

[1] Passengers carried under postal contracts only to 1923. From 1923 to 1932 crew other than pilots are included. Non-scheduled services are included to 1959. Statistics from 1959 (second line) exclude non-paying passengers.
[2] Domestic revenue traffic only to 1937 (1st line) or in 1936. Non-scheduled services are included to 1948 (1st line), but excluding transoceanic traffic, which amounted to 81 million PKM, 0.8 million cargo TKM, and 0.4 million mail TKM in 1947, and 162 million PKM, 1.4 million cargo TKM, and 0.5 million mail TKM in 1948.
[3] Cubana Company only.
[4] Total passenger departures, including non-scheduled services to 1968 (1st line) are for internal flights only.
[5] Including non-revenue passengers on international flights to 1937 and on domestic flights to 1934. Duplication through passengers being carried on more than one route on the same journey, whether or not by the same company, is present to 1937 (1st line).
[6] Including non-revenue passengers on international flights to 1937 and on domestic flights to 1936.
[7] Colonial Airlines Inc. and Hawaiian Airlines Ltd are not included until 1935.
[8] An additional 0.3 million TKM were flown by the US Army.
[9] Including passengers' baggage to 1964.
[10] The reason for this break is not given in the source, but is probably the earlier inclusion of non-scheduled services.
[11] Including non-scheduled services.
[12] Including non-scheduled services to 1962, but only covering the Lloyd Bolivia airline.
[13] Including foreign airlines to 1951 (1st line). Non-scheduled services are included to 1960 (1st line).
[14] Including non-scheduled services to 1956 (1st line). Baggage is included in cargo to 1951 (1st line).
[15] Including non-scheduled services to 1957.
[16] Including non-scheduled services from 1943 to 1959.
[17] All passengers through Peruvian airports to 1967.
[18] Internal traffic only to 1960 (1st line).
[19] Including non-scheduled services to 1962.
[20] Including non-scheduled services in 1954.

## F8 NORTH AMERICA: POSTAL AND TELEGRAPH TRAFFIC

Key: m = mail handled (in millions); t = telegrams sent (in millions)

| | Barbados[1] | Canada | Jamaica[5] | | Mexico[6] | | USA | |
|---|---|---|---|---|---|---|---|---|
| | m | m[2] | m | t | m | t | m | t[7] |
| 1865 | ... | ... | ... | ... | ... | ... | ... | ... |
| 1866 | ... | ... | ... | ... | ... | ... | ... | ... |
| 1867 | ... | ... | ... | ... | ... | ... | ... | 5.9 |
| 1868 | ... | 18 | ... | ... | ... | ... | ... | 6.4 |
| 1869 | ... | 22 | ... | ... | ... | ... | ... | 7.9 |
| 1870 | ... | 25 | ... | ... | ... | ... | ... | 9.2 |
| 1871 | ... | 27 | ... | ... | ... | ... | ... | 11 |
| 1872 | ... | 31 | ... | ... | ... | ... | ... | 12 |
| 1873 | ... | 35 | ... | ... | ... | ... | ... | 14 |
| 1874 | ... | 39 | ... | ... | ... | ... | ... | 16 |
| 1875 | ... | 42 | ... | ... | ... | ... | ... | 17 |
| 1876 | ... | 46 | ... | ... | ... | ... | ... | 19 |
| 1877 | ... | 47 | ... | ... | ... | 0.2 | ... | 21 |
| 1878 | ... | 50 | ... | ... | 6.0 | 0.2 | ... | 24 |
| 1879 | ... | 51 | ... | ... | 5.8 | 0.2 | ... | 25 |
| 1880 | ... | 54 | ... | ... | 6.1 | 0.2 | ... | 29 |
| 1881 | ... | 58 | ... | ... | 6.7 | 0.2 | ... | 33 |
| 1882 | ... | 68 | ... | ... | 11 | 0.2 | ... | 39 |
| 1883 | ... | 76 | ... | ... | 10 | 0.3 | ... | 41 |
| 1884 | ... | 80 | ... | ... | 12 | 0.2 | ... | 42 |
| 1885 | ... | 82 | ... | ... | 13 | 0.2 | ... | 42 |
| 1886 | ... | 86 | ... | ... | 17 | 0.3 | 3,747 | 43 |
| 1887 | ... | 91 | ... | ... | 27 | 0.4 | 3,495 | 47 |
| 1888 | ... | 97 | ... | ... | 43 | 0.6 | 3,576 | 51 |
| 1889 | ... | 112 | ... | ... | 96 | 0.6 | 3,860 | 54 |
| 1890 | ... | 114 | ... | ... | 111 | 0.8 | 4,005 | 56 |
| 1891 | 1.2 | 118 | ... | ... | 117 | 0.8 | 4,370 | 59 |
| 1892 | 1.3 | 124 | 2.8 | 0.1 | 123 | 0.9 | 4,777 | 62 |
| 1893 | 1.3 | 129 | 3.3 | 0.1 | 36 | 0.9 | 5,022 | 67 |
| 1894 | 1.4 | 131 | 3.7 | 0.1 | 25 | 1 | 4,919 | 59 |
| 1895 | 1.6 | 132 | 4.1 | 0.1 | 30 | 1.1 | 5,134 | 58 |
| 1896 | 1.5 | 141 | ... | 0.1 | 30 | 1.4 | 5,694 | 59 |
| 1897 | 1.5 | 150 | 5.0 | 0.1 | 113 | 1.5 | 5,781 | 58 |
| 1898 | 1.6 | 163 | 5.0 | 0.1 | 130 | 1.6 | 6,214 | 62 |
| 1899 | 1.8 | 178 | 5.0 | 0.1 | 135 | 2.8 | 6,576 | 61 |
| 1900 | 1.9 | 205 | 5.2 | 0.1 | 148 | 2.6 | 7,130 | 63 |
| 1901 | 2.1 | 219 | 5.4 | 0.1 | 157 | 2.8 | 7,424 | 66 |
| 1902 | 1.9 | 221 | 5.5 | 0.1 | 167 | 3.1 | 8,085 | 69 |
| 1903 | 2.0 | 262 | 5.7 | 0.1 | 162 | 3.4 | 8,887 | 70 |
| 1904 | 2.2 | 286 | 6.5 | 0.1 | 166 | 3.5 | 9,502 | 68 |

**F8      NORTH AMERICA: Postal and Telegraph Traffic**

| | Barbados[1] | Canada | | El Salvador | Jamaica[5] | | Mexico[6] | | Trinidad & Tobago[8] | USA | |
|---|---|---|---|---|---|---|---|---|---|---|---|
| | m | m[2] | t[3] | t[9] | m | t | m | t | m | m | t[7] |
| 1905 | 2.3 | 316 | ... | ... | 7.2 | 0.1 | 140 | 3.8 | ... | 10,188 | 67 |
| 1906 | 2.3 | 357 | ... | ... | 7.7 | 0.1 | 155 | 4.2 | ... | 11,361 | 71 |
| 1907 | 2.5 | [301][2] | ... | ... | 8.6 | 0.1 | 177 | 4.3 | ... | 12,256 | 75 |
| 1908 | 2.6 | 437 | ... | ... | 8.4 | 0.1 | 171 | 4.3 | ... | 13,364 | 62 |
| 1909 | 2.8 | 457 | ... | ... | 10 | 0.1 | 185 | 4.5 | 3.6 | 14,005 | 68 |
| 1910 | 3.0 | 501 | ... | ... | 10 | 0.1 | 189 | 4.8 | 3.7 | 14,850 | 75[7] |
| 1911 | 2.7 | 554 | ... | ... | 10 | 0.2 | 179 | 5.3 | 7.1 | 16,901 | ... |
| 1912 | 2.9 | 621 | 10 | ... | 10 | 0.2 | 199 | 5.5 | 7.8 | 17,589 | ... |
| 1913 | 3.0 | 694 | 12 | ... | 11 | 0.2 | ... | 4.5 | 8.3 | 18,567 | ... |
| 1914 | 2.9 | 737 | 13 | ... | 9.5 | 0.2 | ... | 2.3 | 4.2[8] | ... | ... |
| 1915 | 2.6 | 749[2] | 11 | ... | 8.3 | 0.2 | ... | 3.9 | ... | ... | ... |
| 1916 | 2.5 | ... | 12 | ... | 9.6 | 0.2 | ...[6] | 3.5[6] | 4.7 | ... | ... |
| 1917 | 2.5 | ... | 13 | ... | 12 | 0.2 | [48] | [2.7] | 4.0 | ... | 129 |
| 1918 | 2.6 | ... | 13 —3 | ... | 11 | 0.2 | 86 | 5.7 | 4.0 | ... | 134 |
| 1919 | 2.8 | ... | 14 | ... | 12 | 0.3 | 91 | 5.9 | 6.1 | ... | 139 |
| 1920 | 3.6 | ... | 17 | ... | 14 | 0.3 | 137 | 6.4 | 5.7 | ... | 156[7] 160 |
| 1921 | 3.3 | ... | 16 | ... | 14 | 0.3 | 171 | 6.2 | 5.6 | ... | 144 |
| 1922 | 3.1 | ... | 16 | ... | 13 | 0.4 | 213 | 5.5 | 6.3 | ... | 155 |
| 1923 | 2.7 | ... | 17 | ... | 14 | 0.3 | 188 | 5.4 | 4.8 | 23,055 | 165 |
| 1924 | 3.0 | ... | 17[3] 12 | ... | 14 | 0.3 | 163 | 5.7 | 4.6 | ... | 170 |
| 1925 | 2.9 | ... | 12 | ... | 14 | 0.3 | 200 | 6.1 | 5.1 | ... | 193 |
| 1926 | 3.1 | ... | 13 | ... | 17 | 0.3 | 223 | 6.0 | 5.0 | 25,484 | 219 |
| 1927 | 3.2 | ... | 14 | ... | 17 | 0.4 | 214 | 6.1 | 5.4 | 26,687 | 219 |
| 1928 | 3.2 | ... | 15 | ... | 17 | 0.4 | 213 | 6.2 | 6.4 | 26,837 | 229 |
| 1929 | 3.3 | ... | 16 | ... | 19 | 0.4 | 200 | 6.2 | 7.0 | 27,952 | 256 |
| 1930 | 3.3 | ... | 14 | ... | 19 | 0.4 | 219 | 6.2 | 7.4 | 27,888 | 232 |
| 1931 | 3.1 | ... | 12 | ... | 17 | 0.4 | 208 | 5.7 | 6.3 | 26,544 | 201 |
| 1932 | 2.9 | ... | 9.9 | ... | 17 | 0.4 | 172 | 5.3 | 6.4 | 24,307 | 158 |
| 1933 | 2.9 | ... | 9.4 | ... | 19 | 0.3 | 182 | 5.8 | 6.6 | 19,868 | 159 |
| 1934 | 2.9 | ... | 9.9 | ... | 20 | 0.3 | 215 | 6.6 | 6.6 | 20,626 | 170 |
| 1935 | 3.2 | ... | 10 | ... | 21 | 0.4 | 255 | 7.8 | 6.4 | 22,332 | 192 |
| 1936 | 3.5 | ... | 12 | ... | 20 | 0.4 | 289 | 8.7 | 7.0 | 23,571 | 211 |
| 1937 | 3.5 | ... | 12 | ... | 21 | 0.4 | 326 | 9.1 | 7.7[8] 8.1 | 25,801 | 220 |
| 1938 | 3.4 | ... | 12 | ... | 20 | 0.4 | 348 | 9.0 | 9.6 | 26,042 | 204 |
| 1939 | 3.4 | ... | 12 | ... | ...[5] | ...[5] | 340 | 9.7 | 11 | 26,445 | 208 |
| 1940 | ... | ... | 12 | 1.3 | ... | ... | 319 | 10 | 9.2 | 27,749 | 208 |
| 1941 | 2.5 | ... | 14 | 1.2 | ... | ... | 345 | 11[6] 18 | 9.9 | 29,236 | 227 |
| 1942 | 2.6 | ... | 15 | 1.3 | ... | ... | 380 | 23 | 10 | 30,118 | 236 |
| 1943 | 2.7 | ... | 16 | 1.3 | ... | ... | 390 | 27 | 9.3 | 32,818 | 248 |
| 1944 | 2.8 | ... | 16 | 1.5 | ... | ... | 433 | 28 | 10 | 34,931 | 243 |

**F8    NORTH AMERICA: Postal and Telegraph Traffic**

| | Barbados[1] | Canada | | El Salvador | Jamaica[5] | | Mexico | | Trinidad & Tobago[8] | USA | |
|---|---|---|---|---|---|---|---|---|---|---|---|
| | m | m | t | t[9] | m | t | m | t[6] | m | m | t[7] |
| 1945 | 3.3 | ... | 17 | 1.7 | 23 | 0.8 | 496 | 32 | 13 | 37,912 | 257 |
| 1946 | 3.6 | ... | 17 | 1.7 | 24₅ | ... | 518 | 27 | 16 | 36,318 | 234 |
| 1947 | 3.8 | 1,467 | 16 | 1.9 | 26 | 0.7 | 556 | 31 | 19 | 37,428 | 238 |
| 1948 | 4.3 | ... | 18 | 2.0 | 26 | 0.8 | 574 | 32 | 23 | 40,280 | 213 |
| 1949 | 4.4 | 1,831 | 19 | 1.9 | 29 | 0.7 | 610 | 33 | 20 | 43,555 | 196 |
| 1950 | 4.5 | 2,627 | 19 | 2.1 | 25 | 0.7 | 506 | 36 | 20 | 45,064 | 201 |
| 1951 | 4.9 | 2,707 | 21 | 2.2 | 27 | 0.8 | 559 | 35 | 19 | 46,908 | 204 |
| 1952 | 5.4 | 2,830 | 20 | 2.5 | 29 | 0.9 | 667 | 37 | 21 | 49,906 | 176 |
| 1953 | 6.1 | 2,818 | 20 | 2.6 | 32 | 1.0 | 693 | 38 | 23 | 50,948 | 186 |
| 1954 | 6.2 | 2,910 | 19 | 2.5 | 34₅ | 1.0 | 714 | 39 | 23 | 52,213 | 177 |
| 1955 | 8.1 | ... | 19 | 2.4 | ... | 1.0 | 730 | 42 | 29 | 55,234 | 180 |
| 1956 | 10 | 3,043 | 19 | 2.8 | ... | 1.1 | 813 | 38 | 29 | 56,441 | 179 |
| 1957 | 10 | 3,043 | 18 | 2.9 | ... | 1.1 | 801 | 38 | 32 | 59,078 | 172 |
| 1958 | 10 | 3,175 | 17 | 2.9 | 78 | ... | 881 | 39 | 34 | 60,130 | 159 |
| 1959 | 14 | 3,355 | 16₄ | 3.6 | 90 | ... | 948 | 39 | 36 | 61,247 | 159 |
| 1960 | 13 | 3,419 | 15 | 3.5 | 92 | ... | 925 | 41 | 37 | 63,675 | 153 |
| 1961 | 13 | 3,579 | 14 | 2.6 | 105 | ... | 983 | 41 | 40 | 64,933 | 146 |
| 1962 | 13 | 3,721 | 14 | 3.8 | 109 | ... | 1,073 | [38][9] | 39 | 66,493 | 141 |
| 1963 | 16 | 3,690 | 14 | 2.8 | 113 | 1.1 | 1,119 | 42 | 40 | 67,853 | 134 |
| 1964 | 16 | 3,817 | 14 | 3.7 | 120 | 1.0 | 1,155 | 36 | 38 | 69,676 | 127 |
| 1965 | 16 | 3,797 | 14 | 2.1 | 132 | 1.1 | 1,192 | 38 | 41 | 71,873 | 124 |
| 1966 | 18 | 4,574 | 13 | 1.8 | 138 | 1.2 | 1,242 | 41 | 41 | 75,607 | 123 |
| 1967 | 20 | 4,799 | 12 | 1.6 | 145 | ... | 1,334 | 42 | 44 | 78,367 | 119 |
| 1968 | 23 | 4,893 | 10 | 1.4 | 152 | 1.2 | 1,367 | 43 | 46 | 79,517 | 116 |
| 1969 | 24 | 4,866 | 9.3 | 1.4 | 160 | 1.5 | 1,388 | 46 | 45 | 82,005 | 109 |
| 1970 | 26 | 4,729 | 8.4 | 1.4 | 168 | 1.3 | 1,408 | 48 | 45 | 84,882 | 102 |
| 1971 | ... | 4,475 | 7.5 | 1.2 | ... | 1.2 | 1,425 | 50 | 48 | 86,983 | 75 |
| 1972 | ... | 4,630₂ | 6.8 | 1.3 | 172 | 1.1 | 1,552 | 54 | 50 | 87,156 | 69 |
| 1973 | ... | 4,729 | 5.1 | 1.3 | 173 | 1.4 | 1,651 | 54 | 51 | 89,683 | 67 |
| 1974 | ... | 5,167 | 5.4 | 1.4 | 176 | ... | 1,661 | 55 | 52 | 90,098 | 71 |
| 1975 | ... | 5,404 | 5.8 | 1.2 | 175 | 1.5 | 1,611 | 45 | 53 | 89,266 | 68 |
| 1976 | ... | 5,002 | 4.2 | 1.3 | 119 | 0.9 | 1,668 | 44 | 54 | 89,768 | 67 |
| 1977 | ... | ... | 3.6 | 1.3 | 120 | 0.8 | 768 | 45 | 54 | 92,224 | 68 |
| 1978 | ... | ... | 3.4 | 1.4 | 121 | 1.6 | 843 | 47 | 55 | 96,913 | 72 |
| 1979 | ... | 6,167 | 3.1 | 1.4 | 57 | 1.0 | 880 | 50 | 33 | 99,829 | 76 |
| 1980 | ... | ... | 2.6 | 1.4 | 56 | 0.7 | 1,029 | 52 | 34 | 106,311 | 75 |
| 1981 | ... | ... | ... | 1.2 | 45 | 1.0 | 1,053 | 55 | 34 | 110,130 | 74 |
| 1982 | ... | ... | ... | 1.2 | 82 | ... | 1,005 | 58 | 33 | 114,049 | 65 |
| 1983 | ... | ... | ... | 1.1 | 63 | ... | 858 | 51 | 36 | 119,381 | 53 |
| 1984 | ... | ... | ... | 1.1 | 60 | ... | 811 | ... | 31 | 131,545 | 48 |
| 1985 | ... | ... | ... | 1.7 | 35 | ... | 652 | 55 | 25 | 140,098 | 42 |
| 1986 | ... | ... | ... | ... | 55 | ... | 677 | 58 | 23 | 147,376 | 29 |
| 1987 | ... | ... | ... | ... | 60 | ... | 753 | ... | 24 | 153,931 | 25 |
| 1988 | ... | ... | ... | ... | 66 | ... | 751 | 56 | 23 | 160,491 | ... |

## F8    SOUTH AMERICA: POSTAL AND TELEGRAPH TRAFFIC

### 1840–1869

| | Brazil[10] | | | Brazil[10] | | Chile | | Guyana*[14] | Uruguay |
|---|---|---|---|---|---|---|---|---|---|
| | m[11] | t | | m[11] | t | m[12] | t[13] | t | m[15] |
| 1840 | 0.9 | — | 1870 | 9.7 | - - | ... | ... | ... | ... |
| 1841 | 0.8 | — | 1871 | 10 | - - | ... | ... | ... | ... |
| 1842 | 1.1 | — | 1872 | 12 | 0.1 | ... | ... | ... | ... |
| 1843 | 1.5 | — | 1873 | 13 | 0.1 | ... | ... | ... | ... |
| 1844 | 1.5 | — | 1874 | 14 | 0.1 | ... | ... | ... | ... |
| 1845 | 1.9 | — | 1875 | 13 | 0.1 | ... | ... | ... | ... |
| 1846 | 1.9 | — | 1876 | 15 | 0.1 | ... | ... | ... | ... |
| 1847 | 2.0 | — | 1877 | 15 | 0.2 | ... | ... | ... | ... |
| 1848 | 1.9 | — | 1878 | 16 | 0.2 | ... | ... | ... | ... |
| 1849 | 1.9 | — | 1879 | 19 | 0.3 | ... | ... | ... | ... |
| 1850 | 1.8 | — | 1880 | 20 | 0.3 | ... | ... | ... | 2.2 |
| 1851 | 2.4 | — | 1881 | 24 | 0.4 | ... | ... | ... | 3.0 |
| 1852 | 2.8 | — | 1882 | 24 | 0.3 | ... | ... | ... | 3.6 |
| 1853 | 3.2 | — | 1883 | 25 | 0.3 | ... | ... | ... | 5.5 |
| 1854 | 3.3 | — | 1884 | 32 | 0.4 | ... | ... | 0.1 | 12 |
| 1855 | 3.6 | — | 1885 | 35 | 0.4 | ... | ... | 0.1 | 12 |
| 1856 | 4.3 | — | 1886 | ... | ... | ... | ... | 0.1 | 11 |
| 1857 | 4.7 | — | 1887 | [56][10] | [0.7][10] | 41 | 0.6 | 0.1 | 17 |
| 1858 | 5.2 | — | 1888 | 40 | 0.5 | 44 | ... | 0.1 | 20 |
| 1859 | 5.3 | — | 1889 | 44 | 0.6 | 43 | ... | 0.1 | 21 |
| 1860 | 5.7 | — | 1890 | 50 | 0.8 | 48 | ... | 0.1 | 22 |
| 1861 | 5.9 | — | 1891 | 64 | 1.0 | 39 | ... | 0.1 | 20 |
| 1862 | 6.2 | - - | 1892 | 87 | 1.2 | 54 | ... | 0.1 | 23 |
| 1863 | 6.5 | - - | 1893 | 72 | 1.1 | 62 | ... | 0.1 | 26 |
| 1864 | 6.3 | - - | 1894 | 69 | 1.3 | $\frac{69}{25}$[12] | ... | 0.1 | 27 |
| 1865 | 7.4 | - - | | | | | | | |
| 1866 | 7.9 | - - | | | | | | | |
| 1867 | [9.7][10] | - - | | | | | | | |
| 1868 | 9.2 | - - | | | | | | | |
| 1869 | 9.7 | - - | | | | | | | |

**F8    SOUTH AMERICA: Postal and Telegraph Traffic**

| | Argentina | | Brazil | | Chile | | Colombia | |
|---|---|---|---|---|---|---|---|---|
| | m | t | m[11] | t | m[12] | t[13] | m | t |
| 1895 | 80 | 2.8 | 75 | 1.5 | 28 | ... | ... | ... |
| 1896 | 101 | 3.1 | 105 | 1.7 | 29 | ... | ... | ... |
| 1897 | 106 | 3.4 | 135 | 1.7 | 28 | ... | ... | ... |
| 1898 | 120 | 3.4 | 198 | 1.4 | 30 | ... | ... | ... |
| 1899 | 134 | 3.4 | 197 | 1.4 | 31 | ... | ... | ... |
| 1900 | 145 | 3.9 | 278 | 1.4 | 31 | 1.3 | ... | ... |
| 1901 | 159 | 3.6 | 320 | 1.2 | 38 | 1.4 | ... | ... |
| 1902 | 191 | 3.9 | 326 | 1.2 | 39 | 1.4 | ... | ... |
| 1903 | 207 | 2.7 | 347 | 1.4 | 50 | 1.5 | ... | ... |
| 1904 | 278 | 3.1 | 380 | 1.5 | 54 | 1.3 | ... | ... |
| 1905 | 320 | 3.1 | 394 | 1.5 | 59 | 1.6 | ... | ... |
| 1906 | 337 | 6.2 | 472 | 1.7 | 77 | 2.0 | ... | ... |
| 1907 | 374 | 6.7 | 520 | 1.9 | 78 | 2.1 | ... | ... |
| 1908 | 423 | 6.9 | 567 | 2.3 | 86 | 2.2 | ... | ... |
| 1909 | 494 | 7.5 | 481 | 2.4 | 78 | 2.5 | ... | ... |
| 1910 | 521 | 8.8 | 544 | 2.8 | 65 | 2.3 | ... | ... |
| 1911 | 635 | 9.1 | 608 | 2.8 | 73 | 2.3 | 5.6 | [1.5][1] |
| 1912 | 701 | 10 | 612 | 3.7 | 73 | 2.5 | 7.0 | ... |
| 1913 | 783 | 11 | 634 | 3.8 | 75 | 2.4 | 7.0 | [1.9][1] |
| 1914 | 614 | 10 | 653 | 4.0 | 66 | 2.5 | ... | ... |
| 1915 | 560 | 10 | 443 | 3.7 | 68 | 2.5 | 5.8 | 2.9 |
| 1916 | 543 | ... | 479 | 3.9 | 79 | 2.7 | ... | ... |
| 1917 | 520 | ... | 466 | 4.4 | 87 | 3.0 | ... | 3.2 |
| 1918 | 510 | ... | 514 | 5.4 | 103 | 3.2 | ... | 3.4 |
| 1919 | ... | ... | 546 | 5.6 | 96 | 3.3 | ... | ... |
| 1920 | ... | ... | 642 | 6.6 | 104 | 3.5 | ... | ... |
| 1921 | ... | ... | 624 | 6.1 | 101 | 3.1 | ... | ... |
| 1922 | ... | ... | 773 | 6.6 | 97 | 3.2 | ... | ... |
| 1923 | ... | ... | 873 | 6.9 | 101 | 3.4 | ... | 4.2 |
| 1924 | ... | 11 | 1,225 | 7.2 | 117 | 3.7 | ... | 4.2 |
| 1925 | ... | 13 | 1,746 | 7.6 | 109 | 3.8 | ... | 5.0 |
| 1926 | ... | 13 | 1,861 | 7.4 | 105 | 3.6 | 30 | ... |
| 1927 | ... | 13 | 1,912 | 7.5 | 93 | 3.6 | ... | 5.0 |
| 1928 | ... | ... | 2,152 | 6.5 | 101 | 3.8 | 22 | 7.8 |
| 1929 | ... | 8.3 | 2,105 | 6.0 | 100 | 3.9 | 23 | 8.1 |
| 1930 | 477 | ... | 1,909 | 5.5 | 101 | 3.9 | 29 | 7.2 |
| 1931 | 728 | ... | 1,821 | 7.1 | 84 | 3.2 | 30 | 5.7 |
| 1932 | 686 | 11 | 1,403 | 8.1 | 77 | 3.1 | 25 | 4.7 |
| 1933 | 724 | 7.1 | 1,708 | 8.6 | 78 | 3.3 | 27 | 4.8 |
| 1934 | 717 | 7.0 | 1,834 | 8.9 | 75 | 3.6 | 25 | 5.4 |
| 1935 | 760 | 9.2 | 2,554 | 9.9 | 82 | 3.7 | 28 | 5.6 |
| 1936 | 825 | 9.7 | 2,555 | 10 | 92 | 4.2 | 28 | 5.7 |
| 1937 | 992 | 9.8 | 2,308 | 11 | 98 | 4.6 | 26 | 5.4 |
| 1938 | 1,100 | 10 | 3,004 | 11 | 101 | 4.3 | 38 | 6.2 |
| 1939 | 1,115 | 11 | 3,141[11] | 11 | 110 | 4.4 | 35 | 6.4 |
| | | | 810 | | | | | |

## F8    SOUTH AMERICA: Postal and Telegraph Traffic

| | Guyana*[14] | | Peru | | Uruguay | | Venezuela | |
|---|---|---|---|---|---|---|---|---|
| | m | t | m | t | m[15] | t[17] | m | t |
| 1895 | ... | 0.1 | ... | ... | 31 | ... | ... | ... |
| 1896 | ... | 0.1 | ... | ... | 35 | ... | ... | ... |
| 1897 | ... | 0.1 | ... | ... | 31 | ... | ... | ... |
| 1898 | ... | 0.1 | ... | ... | 32 | ... | ... | ... |
| 1899 | ... | 0.1 | ... | ... | 37 | ... | ... | ... |
| 1900 | 2.2 | 0.1 | ... | ... | 45 | ... | ... | ... |
| 1901 | 2.3 | 0.1 | ... | ... | 55 | ... | ... | ... |
| 1902 | 2.4 | 0.1 | ... | ... | 63 | ... | ... | ... |
| 1903 | 2.6 | 0.1 | ... | ... | 71 | ... | ... | ... |
| 1904 | 2.8 | 0.1 | ... | ... | 57 | ... | ... | ... |
| 1905 | 2.8 | 0.1 | ... | ... | 81 | ... | ... | ... |
| 1906 | 2.8 | 0.1 | ... | ... | 91 | ... | ... | ... |
| 1907 | 2.8 | 0.1 | ... | ... | $\frac{97}{46}$[15] | ... | ... | ... |
| 1908 | 2.9 | 0.1 | ... | ... | 52 | ... | ... | ... |
| 1909 | 2.9 | 0.1 | ... | 0.6 | 53 | ... | ... | ... |
| 1910 | 3.0 | 0.1 | 16 | 0.8 | 67 | 0.3 | ... | ... |
| 1911 | 2.9 | 0.1 | 19 | 0.9 | 63 | 0.4 | ... | ... |
| 1912 | 2.9 | 0.1 | 21 | 0.9 | 62 | 0.4 | ... | ... |
| 1913 | 2.9 | 0.1 | 18 | 0.9 | 72 | 0.4 | ... | 0.7 |
| 1914 | $\underline{3.1}$[14] | $\underline{0.1}$[14] | 15 | 1.0 | 68 | 0.5 | ... | ... |
| 1915 | 3.0 | 0.1 | 13 | 0.8 | 59 | 0.5 | ... | ... |
| 1916 | 3.0 | 0.1 | 15 | 0.8 | 60 | 0.5 | ... | ... |
| 1917 | 3.2 | 0.1 | 15 | 1.0 | 57 | 0.6 | ... | ... |
| 1918 | 2.9 | 0.1 | 17 | 1.0 | 63 | 0.6 | ... | ... |
| 1919 | 2.8 | 0.1 | 17 | 1.0 | 65 | 0.7 | ... | ... |
| 1920 | 3.0 | 0.1 | 19 | 0.9 | 81 | 0.7 | ... | ... |
| 1921 | 3.3 | 0.1 | 17 | 0.9 | 73 | 0.6 | ... | ... |
| 1922 | 3.6 | 0.1 | 16 | ... | 73 | 0.5 | ... | 1.0 |
| 1923 | 3.6 | 0.1 | 17 | 0.8 | 73 | 0.6 | ... | ... |
| 1924 | 3.6 | 0.1 | 20 | 1.2 | 74 | 0.6 | ... | 1.2 |
| 1925 | 3.5 | 0.1 | 22 | 1.2 | 74 | 0.6 | ... | 1.7 |
| 1926 | 3.5 | 0.1 | 22 | 1.3 | 75 | 0.6 | ... | 2.0 |
| 1927 | 3.6 | 0.1 | 26 | $1.4_4$ | 76 | 0.6 | ... | 2.4 |
| 1928 | 3.7 | 0.1 | 29 | 1.6 | 75 | 0.7 | 42 | 1.9 |
| 1929 | 3.5 | 0.1 | 32 | 1.8 | 75 | 0.7 | 72 | ... |
| 1930 | 3.5 | 0.1 | 28 | 1.8 | 75 | 0.7 | 67 | 1.8 |
| 1931 | 3.4 | 0.1 | 27 | 1.6 | 74 | 0.7 | 31 | 1.8 |
| 1932 | 3.4 | 0.1 | 29 | 1.6 | 67 | 0.6 | 29 | ... |
| 1933 | 3.4 | 0.1 | 28 | 1.6 | 55 | 0.5 | ... | ... |
| 1934 | 3.5 | 0.1 | 25 | 1.7 | 55 | 0.5 | ... | ... |
| 1935 | 3.5 | 0.1 | 28 | 1.8 | 57 | 0.6 | ... | ... |
| 1936 | 4.0 | 0.1 | 19 | 1.8 | 59 | 0.6 | ... | ... |
| 1937 | 4.5 | 0.1 | 22 | 1.9 | 53 | 0.6 | 28 | ... |
| 1938 | 4.7 | 0.1 | 25 | 1.9 | 55 | 0.6 | 42 | 2.7 |
| 1939 | ... | ... | 27 | 2.0 | 62 | 0.6 | 59 | 2.8 |

**F8      SOUTH AMERICA: Postal and Telegraph Traffic**

| | Argentina | | Brazil | | Chile | | Colombia | |
|---|---|---|---|---|---|---|---|---|
| | m | t[18] | m[11] | t | m[12] | t[13] | m[20] | t |
| 1940 | 1,128 | 11 | 655 | 11 | 112 | 4.0 | 31 | 6.3 |
| 1941 | 1,113 | 12 | 592 | 13 | 121 | 4.2 | 31 | 6.6 |
| 1942 | 1,100 | 13[18] / 10 | 546 | 15 | 119 | 4.5 | 27 | 7.3 |
| 1943 | ... | 11 | 689 | 18 | 115 | 4.8 | 28 | 7.8 |
| 1944 | 1,190 | 12 | 932 | 20 | 121 | 5.1 | 31 | 8.0 |
| 1945 | 1,186 | 13 | 1,183 | 24 | ... | ... | 37 | 9.1 |
| 1946 | 1,278 | 15 | 1,280 | 27 | 134 | 5.9 | 53 | 9.8 |
| 1947 | 1,555 | 17 | 1,394 | 29 | 133 | 6.6 | 57 | 10 |
| 1948 | 1,702 | 19 | 1,850 | 30 | 137 | 5.6 | 48 | 10 |
| 1949 | 1,449 | 20 | 1,865 | 26 | 141 | 5.6 | 45 | 11 |
| 1950 | ... | 21 | 2,017 | 27 | ... | ... | 52 | 8.9 |
| 1951 | 1,544 | 21 | 2,160 | 29 | ... | 5.8 | 47 | 8.8 |
| 1952 | 1,386 | 18 | 2,300 | 29 | ... | ... | 45 | 8.7 |
| 1953 | 1,283 | 18 | 2,183 | 31 | ... | ... | 55 | 8.1 |
| 1954 | 1,352 | 20 | 2,349 | 29 | ... | ... | 70 | 9.6 |
| 1955 | 1,331 | 21 | 2,508 | 32 | ... | ... | ... | 8.0 |
| 1956 | 1,349 | 21[18] / 24 | 1,962 | 24 | ... | 7.9 | ... | ... |
| 1957 | 1,391 | 23 | 3,884 | 21 | ... | 5.9 | ... | ... |
| 1958 | 1,489 | 25 | [1,687][9] | 22 | 124 | 6.6 | ...[20] | ... |
| 1959 | 1,311 | 22 | [2,734][9] | [20][19] | 101 | 6.7 | 43 | 8.0 |
| 1960 | 1,423 | 23 | 4,948 | 26 | 107 | 5.9 | 37 | 8.6 |
| 1961 | 1,638 | 22 | 3,997 | 27 | 112 | 5.5 | 41 | 8.0 |
| 1962 | 1,390 | 19 | 4,398 | 24 | 131 | 5.1 | 48 | 8.7 |
| 1963 | 1,184 | 19 | 4,390 | 25 | 122[12] | 5.1 | 50 | 10 |
| 1964 | 1,013 | 20 | 4,534 | 28 | ... | 5.7 | 42 | ... |
| 1965 | 964 | 19 | 2,325 | 18 | ... | [6.6][9] | 42 | 12 |
| 1966 | 859 | 17 | 2,964[11] / 2,455 | 30 | ... | 7.1 | 44 | 12 |
| 1967 | 835 | 16 | 2,327 | 37 | ... | [6.2][9] | 45 | 13 |
| 1968 | 881 | 15 | 2,755 | 22 | ... | ... | 51 | 13 |
| 1969 | 991 | 16 | 3,385[11] | 18 | ... | 5.1 | ... | 14 |
| 1970 | 1,012 | 15 | ... | 17 | ... | 5.3 | 59 | 17 |
| 1971 | 1,067 | 16 | 622 | 19 | ... | 6.3 | 73 | 17 |
| 1972 | 1,027 | 16 | 639 | 20 | ... | 6.7 | 72 | 18 |
| 1973 | 1,102 | 18 | 657 | 21 | ... | 7.5 | ... | 19 |
| 1974 | 1,017 | 19 | 836 | 20 | 165 | 6.2 | ... | 19 |
| 1975 | 872 | 17 | 1,246 | 19 | 170 | 4.9 | 94 | 21 |
| 1976 | 739[21] / 659 | 13 | 1,692 | 18 | 185 | 4.7 | 89 | 20 |
| 1977 | 615 | 13 | 2,117 | 18 | 102 | 5.1 | 97 | 20 |
| 1978 | 641 | 12 | 2,667 | 17 | ... | 4.1 | 135 | 22 |
| 1979 | 684 | 13 | 3,106 | 16 | 118 | 4.5 | 173 | 21 |
| 1980 | 627 | 14 | 3,524 | 15 | 180 | 4.2 | 187 | 20 |
| 1981 | ... | 12 | 3,708 | 15 | 177 | 3.6 | 192 | 21 |
| 1982 | ... | ... | 3,856 | 16 | 167 | 3.0 | ... | 24 |
| 1983 | ... | ... | 4,048[11] / 2,054 | 16 | 122 | 2.7 | ... | 21 |
| 1984 | ... | ... | 2,518 | 18 | 109 | 2.9 | ... | 22 |
| 1985 | ... | ... | 2,865 | 21 | 130 | 3.0 | ... | 22 |
| 1986 | ... | ... | 3,247 | 28 | 150 | 2.8 | ... | 20 |
| 1987 | ... | ... | 2,952 | 30 | ... | ... | ... | 18 |
| 1988 | ... | ... | 3,147 | 27 | ... | ... | ... | ... |

**F8      SOUTH AMERICA: Postal and Telegraph Traffic**

| | Guyana* | | Peru | | Uruguay | | Venezuela | |
|---|---|---|---|---|---|---|---|---|
| | m[14] | t | m | t | m | t[17] | m | t |
| 1940 | ... | ... | 27 | 2.0 | 78 | 0.6 | 37 | 2.7 |
| 1941 | ... | ... | 27 | 2.1 | 82 | 0.7 | 34 | 2.7 |
| 1942 | ... | ... | 30 | 2.3 | 95 | 0.8 | 26 | 2.9 |
| 1943 | ... | 0.1 | 29 | 2.6 | 94 | 0.8 | 26 | 3.2 |
| 1944 | ... | 0.2 | 36 | 3.0 | 95 | 0.9 | 28 | 3.6 |
| 1945 | 6.4 | 0.1 | 43 | 3.0 | 116 | 1.0 | 29 | 4.2 |
| 1946 | 6.4 | 0.2 | 33 | 3.3 | 122 | 1.1 | 32 | 5.0 |
| 1947 | 6.5 | 0.2 | 32 | 3.5 | 137 | 1.3 | 48 | 5.9 |
| 1948 | 7.3 | 0.2 | 51 | 3.8 | ... | 1.3 | 61 | 5.7 |
| 1949 | 7.4 | 0.2 | 59 | 4.1 | ... | 1.4 | 73 | 5.0 |
| 1950 | 7.4 | 0.2 | 51 | 6.0 | ... | 1.5 | 67 | 6.8 |
| 1951 | 7.4 | 0.1 | 75 | ... | ... | 1.6 | 90 | 5.4 |
| 1952 | 6.3 | 0.1 | 88 | 3.8 | ... | 1.6 | 117 | 5.4 |
| 1953 | 8.0 | 0.1 | 97 | 4.1 | ... | 1.7 | 133 | 5.5 |
| 1954 | 8.8 | 0.1 | 99 | 4.3 | ... | 1.7 | 168 | 6.0 |
| 1955 | 8.4 | 0.1 | 89 | 4.5 | ... | 1.7 | 199 | 6.2 |
| 1956 | 11 | 0.1 | 106 | 4.8 | ... | 1.8 | 264 | 6.6 |
| 1957 | 9.6 | 0.2 | 124 | 4.9 | ... | 1.8 | 412 | 7.0 |
| 1958 | 12[14] | ... | 141 | 5.2 | ... | 1.8 | 467 | 7.4 |
| 1959 | 114 | ... | 230 | 5.3 | 57 | 1.8[17] / 1.9 | 215 | 7.6 |
| 1960 | 115 | ... | ... | ... | ... | 2.0 | 237 | 7.7 |
| 1961 | ... | ... | ... | ... | ... | 2.0 | 245 | 5.8 |
| 1962 | ... | ... | ... | ... | ... | 2.1 | 287 | 5.1 |
| 1963 | ... | ... | ... | ... | ... | 2.1 | 223 | 5.0 |
| 1964 | ... | ... | ... | ... | ... | ... | 222 | 4.6 |
| 1965 | 97 | ... | ... | ... | ... | ... | 252 | 4.6 |
| 1966 | 96 | ... | ... | ... | ... | ... | 231 | 5.6 |
| 1967 | 101 | ... | ... | ... | ... | 1.6 | 261 | 4.4 |
| 1968 | 105 | ... | ... | ... | ... | 1.6 | 221 | 4.6 |
| 1969 | ... | ... | ... | 3.0 | ... | 1.8 | 243 | 4.7 |
| 1970 | ... | ... | ... | 3.7 | ... | 1.5 | 220[21] / 305 | 4.8 |
| 1971 | 117 | ... | ... | 3.9 | ... | 1.2 | 293 | 4.7 |
| 1972 | 121 | ... | ... | 4.2 | ... | 1.0 | 323 | 4.4 |
| 1973 | 127 | ... | ... | 5.3 | ... | 0.9 | 371 | ... |
| 1974 | 251 | ... | ... | 4.8 | ... | 1.0 | 357 | ... |
| 1975 | 251 | ... | ... | 5.7 | ... | 1.0 | 316 | 4.7 |
| 1976 | ... | ... | ... | 5.7[9] / 11 | ... | 1.0 | 382 | 4.5 |
| 1977 | ... | ... | ... | 11 | ... | 1.3 | ... | ... |
| 1978 | ... | ... | ... | 11 | ... | 1.4 | ... | ... |
| 1979 | ... | ... | ... | 8.8 | ... | ... | ... | ... |
| 1980 | ... | ... | ... | 9.1 | ... | ... | ... | ... |
| 1981 | ... | ... | ... | 8.3 | ... | ... | ... | ... |
| 1982 | ... | ... | ... | 7.6 | ... | ... | ... | 3.6 |
| 1983 | ... | ... | ... | 6.8 | ... | ... | ... | 3.3 |
| 1984 | ... | ... | ... | 6.1 | ... | ... | ... | 3.0 |
| 1985 | ... | ... | ... | 5.9 | ... | ... | ... | 3.2 |
| 1986 | ... | ... | ... | 6.1 | ... | ... | ... | 2.9 |
| 1987 | ... | ... | ... | 6.4 | ... | ... | ... | 2.9 |
| 1988 | ... | ... | ... | ... | ... | ... | ... | ... |

# F8 Postal and Telegraph Traffic

## NOTES

1. SOURCES: The national publications listed on p. xiv–xvi, and the League of Nations and UN, *Statistical Yearbooks*.
2. So far as possible, and except as indicated in footnotes, internal mail is counted once whilst international mail is counted both on dispatch and receipt. Telegram statistics are of all telegrams sent.
3. The nature of postal, and to a lesser extent telegraph, statistics differs considerably between countries. So far as possible the classifications used here are those which give the longest possible comparable series within each country. Where there is a choice in this matter, the most comprehensive classification has been preferred.

## FOOTNOTES

[1] Registered mail is excluded.
[2] First-class items only to 1915. Mail sent from 1947 to 1972. Data to 1906 are for years ending 30 June, and from 1908 they are for years ending 31 March. The 1907 figure is for the 9 months from 1 July 1906 to 31 March 1907.
[3] Telegrams and cablegrams transmitted to 1924 (1st line)—i.e. including those received from abroad. Data to 1919 are for years ending 30 June.
[4] Statistics before and after this point are not exactly comparable.
[5] Years beginning 1 April to 1938. Data for mail for 1947 to 1954 are for Kingston only.
[6] Years beginning 1 July to 1916. The 1917 figures are for the second half-year only. Telegram statistics are for the Federal network only to 1941 (1st line).
[7] Western Union Telegraph Company messages handled to 1910, for years ending 30 June. Statistics for 1917 to 1920 (1st line) are of all domestic messages handled, with international messages included subsequently.
[8] Years beginning 1 April to 1914. Data from 1937 (2nd line) include parcels and some other minor categories previously excluded.
[9] Subsequently includes international telegrams received.
[10] Statistics from 1868 to 1885 for mail and to 1885 for telegrams are for years beginning 1 July. The figure for mail in 1867 includes the first half of 1868, and the figures for 1887 are for the period 1 July 1886 to 31 December 1887.
[11] Statistics to 1939 (1st line) are of all items sent, received and in transit. Data from 1966 (2nd line) are of mail sent only. There were changes in coverage in 1970–1 and 1983.
[12] Mail sent only to 1963. All mail sent and received to 1894 (1st line), and all mail sent from them to 1963.
[13] State network only.
[14] Years beginning 1 April from 1892 to 1914. Mail statistics to 1958 are of letter mail sent.
[15] All mail sent and received to 1907 (1st line).
[16] Excluding official and press telegrams.
[17] National Telegraph Company only to 1959 (1st line).
[18] Changes in the categories included in the series occurred in 1942 and 1956.
[19] Figures from Bahia are not included, nor those from Pernambuco in the second half-year.
[20] Mail sent only from 1959.
[21] Mail sent only from 1976 (2nd line)

**F9    NORTH AMERICA: NUMBER OF TELEPHONES IN USE** (in thousands)

### 1876–1899

| | USA |
|---|---|
| 1876 | 3 |
| 1877 | 9 |
| 1878 | 26 |
| 1879 | 31 |
| 1880 | 48 |
| 1881 | 71 |
| 1882 | 98 |
| 1883 | 124 |
| 1884 | 148 |
| 1885 | 156 |
| 1886 | 167 |
| 1887 | 181 |
| 1888 | 195 |
| 1889 | 212 |
| 1890 | 228 |
| 1891 | 239 |
| 1892 | 261 |
| 1893 | 266 |
| 1894 | 285 |
| 1895 | 340 |
| 1896 | 404 |
| 1897 | 515 |
| 1898 | 681 |
| 1899 | 1,005 |

### 1900–1944

| | Barbados | Canada | Costa Rica | Cuba | Dominican Republic | El Salvador | Guadeloupe |
|---|---|---|---|---|---|---|---|
| 1900 | ... | ... | ... | ... | ... | ... | ... |
| 1901 | ... | ... | ... | ... | ... | ... | ... |
| 1902 | ... | ... | ... | ... | ... | ... | ... |
| 1903 | ... | ... | ... | ... | ... | ... | ... |
| 1904 | ... | 95 | ... | ... | ... | ... | ... |
| 1905 | ... | ... | ... | ... | ... | 0.1 | ... |
| 1906 | ... | ... | ... | ... | ... | ... | ... |
| 1907 | ... | ... | ... | ... | ... | ... | ... |
| 1908 | ... | ... | ... | ... | ... | ... | ... |
| 1909 | ... | ... | ... | ... | ... | ... | ... |
| 1910 | ... | ... | ... | ... | ... | 0.1 | ... |
| 1911 | ... | 303 | ... | ... | ... | ... | ... |
| 1912 | ... | 371 | ... | ... | ... | ... | ... |
| 1913 | 0.9 | 464 | 0.9 | 16 | 0.6 | 0.2 | ... |
| 1914 | ... | 521 | ... | ... | ... | ... | ... |
| 1915 | ... | 533 | ... | ... | ... | ... | ... |
| 1916 | ... | 600 | ... | ... | ... | ... | ... |
| 1917 | ... | 657 | ... | ... | ... | ... | ... |
| 1918 | ... | 698 | 1.5 | ... | ... | ... | ... |
| 1919 | ... | 779 | 1.5 | ... | ... | ... | ... |
| 1920 | ... | 856 | 1.6 | ... | ... | ... | ... |
| 1921 | ... | 902 | ... | ... | ... | ... | ... |
| 1922 | 1.6 | 944 | ... | ... | ... | ... | ... |
| 1923 | 1.6 | 1,009 | ... | 48 | ... | 2.8 | ... |
| 1924 | 1.7 | 1,072 | ... | ... | ... | ... | ... |
| 1925 | 1.7 | 1,143 | ... | 62 | ... | ... | ... |
| 1926 | 1.8 | 1,201 | ... | 64 | ... | ... | ... |
| 1927 | 1.9 | 1,260 | ... | 68 | ... | ... | ... |
| 1928 | 2.0 | 1,335 | 2.9 | 73 | 2.4 | 3.7 | 0.1 |
| 1929 | 2.0 | 1,383 | ... | 75 | 2.3 | ... | ... |
| 1930 | 2.0 | 1,403 | ... | 67 | ... | ... | ... |
| 1931 | 2.0 | 1,364 | ... | 54 [4] | ... | ... | ... |
| 1932 | 2.0 | 1,261 | 2.6 | 33 | ... | 3.8 | 0.2 |
| 1933 | 2.1 | 1,192 | ... | ... | ... | ... | ... |
| 1934 | 2.1 | 1,197 | ... | ... | ... | ... | ... |
| 1935 | 2.3 | 1,209 | ... | ... | ... | ... | ... |
| 1936 | 2.4 | 1,266 | ... | ... | 2.4 | ... | ... |
| 1937 | 2.4 | 1,323 | ... | 50 | 2.6 | ... | 0.3 |
| 1938 | 2.6 | 1,359 | ... | 53 | 2.9 | ... | ... |
| 1939 | ... | 1,397 | 2.8 | 55 | 3.0 | ... | ... |
| 1940 | ... | 1,461 | ... | 59 | 3.1 | 4.4 | ... |
| 1941 | ... | 1,562 | ... | 62 | 3.2 | 4.4 | ... |
| 1942 | ... | 1,628 | ... | 67 | 2.6 | 4.9 | ... |
| 1943 | ... | 1,692 | ... | 69 | 2.6 | 5.0 | ... |
| 1944 | ... | 1,752 | ... | 71 | 2.6 | 5.1 | ... |

**F9**    **NORTH AMERICA: Number of Telephones in Use** (in thousands)

1900–1944

|      | Guatemala | Haiti | Honduras | Jamaica | Mexico | Nicaragua | Panama | Puerto Rico | Trinidad & Tobago | USA[1] |
|------|-----------|-------|----------|---------|--------|-----------|--------|-------------|-------------------|--------|
| 1900 | ...       | ...   | ...      | ...     | ...    | ...       | ...    | ...         | ...               | 1,356  |
| 1901 | ...       | ...   | ...      | ...     | ...    | ...       | ...    | ...         | ...               | 1,801  |
| 1902 | ...       | ...   | ...      | ...     | ...    | ...       | ...    | ...         | ...               | 2,371  |
| 1903 | ...       | ...   | ...      | ...     | ...    | ...       | ...    | ...         | ...               | 2,809  |
| 1904 | ...       | ...   | ...      | ...     | ...    | ...       | ...    | ...         | ...               | 3,353  |
| 1905 | ...       | ...   | ...      | ...     | ...    | ...       | ...    | ...         | ...               | 4,127  |
| 1906 | ...       | ...   | 0.1      | ...     | ...    | ...       | ...    | ...         | ...               | 4,933  |
| 1907 | ...       | ...   | ...      | ...     | ...    | ...       | ...    | ...         | ...               | 6,119  |
| 1908 | ...       | ...   | ...      | ...     | ...    | ...       | ...    | ...         | ...               | 6,484  |
| 1909 | ...       | ...   | ...      | ...     | ...    | ...       | ...    | ...         | ...               | 6,996  |
| 1910 | ...       | ...   | ...      | ...     | ...    | ...       | ...    | ...         | ...               | 7,635  |
| 1911 | ...       | ...   | ...      | ...     | ...    | ...       | ...    | ...         | ...               | 8,349  |
| 1912 | ...       | ...   | ...      | ...     | ...    | ...       | ...    | ...         | ...               | 8,730  |
| 1913 | 1.8       | ...   | 0.1      | ...     | 42     | 0.5       | 2.6    | ...         | ...               | 9,543  |
| 1914 | ...       | ...   | ...      | ...     | ...    | ...       | ...    | ...         | ...               | 10,046 |
| 1915 | ...       | ...   | ...      | ...     | ...    | ...       | ...    | ...         | ...               | 10,524 |
| 1916 | ...       | ...   | ...      | ...     | ...    | ...       | ...    | ...         | ...               | 11,241 |
| 1917 | ...       | ...   | ...      | ...     | ...    | ...       | ...    | ...         | ...               | 11,717 |
| 1918 | ...       | ...   | ...      | ...     | ...    | ...       | ...    | ...         | ...               | 12,078 |
| 1919 | ...       | ...   | ...      | ...     | ...    | ...       | ...    | ...         | ...               | 12,669 |
| 1920 | ...       | ...   | ...      | ...     | ...    | ...       | ...    | ...         | ...               | 13,273 |
| 1921 | ...       | ...   | ...      | ...     | ...    | ...       | ...    | ...         | ...               | 13,817 |
| 1922 | ...       | ...   | ...      | 1       | ...    | ...       | ...    | ...         | ...               | 14,294 |
| 1923 | ...       | ...   | ...      | 1       | ...    | ...       | ...    | ...         | ...               | 15,316 |
| 1924 | ...       | ...   | ...      | 1       | ...    | ...       | ...    | ...         | ...               | 16,015 |
| 1925 | ...       | ...   | ...      | 1.1     | ...    | ...       | ...    | ...         | ...               | 16,875 |
| 1926 | ...       | ...   | ...      | 1.1     | ...    | ...       | ...    | ...         | ...               | 17,680 |
| 1927 | ...       | ...   | ...      | 1.4     | ...    | ...       | ...    | ...         | ...               | 18,446 |
| 1928 | 3.1       | 2.1   | ...      | 1.5     | 78     | 0.9       | 9.2    | 13          | ...               | 19,256 |
| 1929 | ...       | ...   | ...      | 1.5     | 58     | ...       | ...    | ...         | ...               | 19,970 |
| 1930 | ...       | ...   | ...      | 2       | 96     | ...       | ...    | ...         | ...               | 20,103 |
| 1931 | ...       | ...   | ...      | 2.2     | 99     | ...       | ...    | ...         | ...               | 19,602 |
| 1932 | ...       | ...   | ...      | 2.5     | 101    | ...       | ...    | 12          | ...               | 17,341 |
| 1933 | ...       | ...   | ...      | 2.7     | 107    | 1.2       | ...    | 12          | ...               | 16,628 |
| 1934 | ...       | ...   | ...      | 3.2     | 114    | 1.2       | ...    | 13          | 2.9               | 16,869 |
| 1935 | ...       | ...   | 3        | 3.5     | 120    | ...       | ...    | 14          | 2.9               | 17,424 |
| 1936 | ...       | ...   | 3.4      | 3.6     | 132    | ...       | ...    | 15          | 3.2               | 18,433 |
| 1937 | ...       | ...   | ...      | 3.9     | 145    | 1.4       | ...    | 15          | 3.4               | 19,453 |
| 1938 | ...       | ...   | 3.5      | ...     | 158    | 1.4       | ...    | 16          | 5.9               | 19,953 |
| 1939 | 3.5       | ...   | ...      | ...     | 175    | ...       | ...    | 17          | 6.5               | 20,831 |
| 1940 | ...       | ...   | ...      |         | 180    | ...       | ...    | 19          | 7.2               | 21,928 |
| 1941 | ...       | ...   | ...      |         | 181    | ...       | ...    | 21          | 8.5               | 23,521 |
| 1942 | ...       | ...   | ...      |         | 191    | ...       | ...    | 21          | 9.4               | 24,919 |
| 1943 | ...       | ...   | ...      |         | 200    | 1.9       | ...    | 22          | 9.2               | 26,381 |
| 1944 | ...       | ...   | ...      |         | 207    | ...       | ...    | 22          | 9.7               | 26,859 |

**F9     NORTH AMERICA: Number of Telephones in Use** (in thousands)

| | Barbados | Canada | Costa Rica | Cuba | Dominican Republic | El Salvador | Guadeloupe | Guatemala | Haiti |
|------|------|------|------|------|------|------|------|------|------|
| 1945 | ... | 1,849 | ... | 74 | 4.1 | 4.9 | | ... | ... |
| 1946 | 3.1 | 2,026 | 7 | 79 | 4.2 | 5.3 | 0.6 | 4.5 | 2.9 |
| 1947 | 3.2 | 2,231 | ... | 84 | 4.4 | 5.8 | 0.7 | ... | ... |
| 1948 | 3.6 | 2,452 | ... | 93 | 4.7 | 6.0 | 0.7 | ... | 3.5 |
| 1949 | 3.9 | 2,700 | ... | 106 | 5.2 | 5.0 | ... | ... | 3.2 |
| 1950 | 4.3 | 2,912 | ... | 113 | 6.6 | 5.2 | ... | ... | 3.1 |
| 1951 | 4.8 | 3,106 | 9.9 | 124 | 7.4 | 7.1 | ... | ... | 3.8 |
| 1952 | 5.0 | 3,342 | 11 | ... | 8.0 | 8.9 | ... | 5.7 | 4.1 |
| 1953 | 5.1 | 3,595 | 11 | 141 | 8.4 | ... | ... | ... | 4.2 |
| 1954 | 5.8 | 3,853 | 11 | 142 | 8.9 | 9.9 | 1.1 | 9 | 4.3 |
| 1955 | 6.2 | 4,147 | 12 | 142 | 11 | 10 | 1.3 | 11 | 4.3 |
| 1956 | 7.0 | 4,500 | 11 | 144 | 12 | 10 | 1.9 | ... | 4 |
| 1957 | 7.4 | 4,812 | 12 | 151 | 15 | 11 | 2.1 | 10 | 4 |
| 1958 | 8.1 | 5,113 | 13 | 170 | 17 | 12 | 2.5 | 12 | 4.2 |
| 1959 | 8.8 | 5,140 | 15 | 191 | 19 | 16 | 2.9 | 20 | 4 |
| 1960 | 9.6 | 5,433 | 16 | 202 | 20 | 16 | 3.3 | 18 | 4 |
| 1961 | 11 | 5,719 | 17 | 208 | 21 | 18 | 3.9 | 20 | 4 |
| 1962 | 12 | 6,340 | 19 | 218 | 25 | 20 | 4.7 | 19 | 4 |
| 1963 | 12 | 6,646 | 20 | 224 | 28 | 21 | 5.3 | 20 | 4 |
| 1964 | 14 | 7,011 | 22 | 229 | 30 | 22 | 6.0 | 23 | 4 |
| 1965 | 15 | 7,440 | 22 | 231 | 31 | 20 | 7.0 | 25 | 4 |
| 1966 | 18 | 7,893 | 24 | 234 | 32 | 30 | 7.7 | 33 | 4 |
| 1967 | 20 | 8,345 | 27 | 238 | 34 | 38 | 8.4 | 35 | 4.3 |
| 1968 | 25 | 8,821 | 50 | 242 | 36 | 37 | 9.7 | 36 | 4.5 |
| 1969 | 26 | 9,303 | 56 | 263 | 40 | 35 | 11 | 38 | ... |
| 1970 | 29 | 9,751 | 61 | 269 | 47 | 39 | 14 | 49 | ... |
| 1971 | 33 | 10,253 | 68 | 275 | 56 | 41 | 16 | 44 | 5 |
| 1972 | 36 | 10,979 | 78 | 278 | 66 | 43 | 17 | 54 | ... |
| 1973 | 39 | 11,665 | 89 | 281 | 83 | 47 | 19 | 53 | 9 |
| 1974 | 40 | 12,454 | 99 | 289 | 95 | 50 | 22 | ... | ... |
| 1975 | 42 | 13,165 | 112 | 299 | 108 | 55 | 24 | ... | ... |
| 1976 | 44 | 13,885 | 127 | 311 | 127 | 60 | 27 | ... | 18 |
| 1977 | 47 | 14,488 | 151 | 321 | 141 | 72 | 31 | 71 | |
| 1978 | 53 | 15,172 | 185 | 341 | 154 | 78 | 35 | ... | ... |
| 1979 | 54 | 15,839 | 200 | 362 | 155 | 83 | 39 | ... | ... |
| 1980 | 67 | 16,531 | 236 | 390 | 165 | 86 | 45 | ... | ... |
| 1981 | 72 | 16,944 | 256 | 406 | 175 | 100 | 50 | ... | ... |
| 1982 | ... | 16,802 | 283 | 441 | ... | 100 | 57 | ... | ... |
| 1983 | 75 | 16,618 | 292 | ... | ... | 116 | 69 | ... | ... |
| 1984 | ... | 18,583 | 304 | 493 | ... | 124 | 81 | ... | ... |
| 1985 | ... | 19,084 | 315 | 515 | ... | 133 | 96 | 128 | ... |
| 1986 | 91 | 19,598 | 344 | 543 | ... | 129 | 107 | ... | ... |
| 1987 | 94 | 20,126 | 409 | 564 | ... | 136 | 100 | ... | ... |
| 1988 | 102 | ... | 410 | 537 | ... | ... | 103 | ... | ... |

**F9 NORTH AMERICA: Number of Telephones in Use** (in thousands)

| | Honduras | Jamaica | Martinique | Mexico | Nicaragua | Panama | Puerto Rico | Trinidad & Tobago | USA[1] |
|---|---|---|---|---|---|---|---|---|---|
| 1945 | ... | ... | ... | 216 | ... | ... | 24 | 10 | 27,867 |
| 1946 | 3.9 | ... | ... | 224 4 / 213 | 1.9 | 7.0 | 27 | 10 | 31,611 |
| 1947 | ... | ... | ... | 220 | ... | ... | 30 | 11 | 34,867 |
| 1948 | 4.1 | ... | 1.5 | 248 | 2.3 | 10 | 33 | 12 | 38,205 |
| 1949 | ... | ... | ... | 274 | ... | ... | 35 | 14 | 40,709 |
| 1950 | ... | ... | ... | 286 | ... | ... | 37 | 15 | 43,004 |
| 1951 | 4.2 | ... | ... | 299 | 3.5 | ... | 41 | 16 | 45,636 |
| 1952 | ... | 15 | ... | 312 | 3.5 | 17 | 43 | 18 | 48,056 |
| 1953 | ... | 16 | ... | 330 | 3.5 | ... | 47 | 19 | 50,373 |
| 1954 | ... | 18 | ... | 349 | 3.6 | 18 | 54 | 21 | 52,806 |
| 1955 | ... | 20 | ... | 357 | 3.7 | 20 | 60 | 23 | 56,243 |
| 1956 | 5.5 | 23 | 4.1 | 383 | 5.7 | 22 | 65 | 25 | 60,190 |
| 1957 | 4.7 | 25 | 4.8 | 413 | 6.3 | 23 | 71 | 28 | 63,624 |
| 1958 | 5.9 | 27 | 5.2 | 448 | 7.0 | 24 | 77 | 30 | 66,645 1 / 70,820 |
| 1959 | ... | 30 | 5.7 | 492 | 8.0 | 26 | 82 | 31 | |
| 1960 | ... | 36 | 6.0 | 523 | 8.2 | 29 | 95 | 31 | 74,342 |
| 1961 | ... | 39 | 6.5 | 567 | 9.3 | 33 | 109 | 32 | 77,422 |
| 1962 | ... | 41 | 7.0 | 586 | 12 | 36 | 140 | 32 | 80,969 |
| 1963 | 9.3 | 44 | 7.7 | 659 | ... | 39 | 172 | 35 | 84,453 |
| 1964 | 8.9 | 47 | 9.1 | 724 | 12 | 41 | 187 | 37 | 88,793 |
| 1965 | 8.9 | 50 | 11 | 823 | 12 | 47 | 203 | 39 | 93,656 |
| 1966 | 9.9 | 53 | 12 | 928 | 13 | 48 | 219 | 42 | 98,787 |
| 1967 | 10 | 57 | 13 | 1,046 | 13 | 58 | 241 | 46 | 103,752 |
| 1968 | 11 | 61 | 14 | 1,175 | 23 | 59 | 248 | 49 | 109,256 |
| 1969 | 13 | 67 | 16 | 1,327 | 16 | 62 | 281 | 52 | 115,222 |
| 1970 | 14 | 72 | 17 | 1,506 | 26 | 85 | 306 | 56 | 120,218 |
| 1971 | 17 | 76 | 19 | 1,712 | 26 | ... | 356 | 63 | 125,142 |
| 1972 | 16 | 81 | 22 | 1,955 | 19 | 100 | 372 | 66 | 131,108 |
| 1973 | 15 | 85 | 25 | 2,223 | 17 | ... | 393 | 66 | 138,286 |
| 1974 | 15 | 95 | 28 | 2,546 | 20 | ... | 466 | 66 | 143,979 |
| 1975 | 18 | 101 | 31 | 2,928 | 36 | 142 | 474 | 67 | 149,008 |
| 1976 | 18 | 109 | 35 | 3,325 | 40 | 155 | 515 | 70 | 155,173 |
| 1977 | 19 | 109 | 39 | 3,737 | 43 | 155 | 561 | 75 | 162,072 |
| 1978 | 20 | 117 | 45 | 4,188 | ... | 152 | ... | 77 | 169,027 |
| 1979 | 27 | 117 | 50 | 4,553 | 58 | 164 | 651 | 78 | 175,535 |
| 1980 | ... | 118 | 52 | 5,024 | ... | 173 | 631 | 75 | 180,424 |
| 1981 | 32 | 119 | ... | 5,537 | 33 | 185 | 678 | 77 | 181,892 |
| 1982 | 34 | 126 | ... | 5,961 | ... | 213 | ... | 87 | 176,391 |
| 1983 | 36 | 133 | 48 | 6,414 | ... | 220 | ... | 109 | ... |
| 1984 | 44 | 137 | 100 | 6,796 | 50 | 210 | ... | 128 | ... |
| 1985 | 46 | 144 | 112 | 7,329 | ... | 223 | ... | 166 | ... |
| 1986 | 50 | 159 | 120 | 7,735 | ... | 232 | ... | 192 | ... |
| 1987 | 54 | 164 | 107 | 8,214 | ... | 240 | ... | 211 | ... |
| 1988 | 66 | 168 | 117 | 8,665 | ... | 242 | ... | 212 | ... |

**F9    SOUTH AMERICA: NUMBER OF TELEPHONES IN USE** (in thousands)

1889–1929

| | Argentina | Bolivia | Brazil | Chile | Colombia | Ecuador | Guyana | Paraguay | Peru | Surinam | Uruguay[5] | Venezuela |
|---|---|---|---|---|---|---|---|---|---|---|---|---|
| 1889 | ... | ... | ... | ... | ... | ... | ... | ... | ... | ... | 2.7 | ... |
| 1890 | ... | ... | ... | ... | ... | ... | ... | ... | ... | ... | 3.2 | ... |
| 1891 | ... | ... | ... | ... | ... | ... | ... | ... | ... | ... | 2.7 | ... |
| 1892 | ... | ... | ... | ... | ... | ... | ... | ... | ... | ... | 2.4 | ... |
| 1893 | ... | ... | ... | ... | ... | ... | ... | ... | ... | ... | 2.8 | ... |
| 1894 | ... | ... | ... | ... | ... | ... | ... | ... | ... | ... | 3.0 | ... |
| 1895 | ... | ... | ... | ... | ... | ... | ... | ... | ... | ... | 3.1 | ... |
| 1896 | ... | ... | ... | ... | ... | ... | ... | ... | ... | ... | 3.3 | ... |
| 1897 | ... | ... | ... | ... | ... | ... | ... | ... | ... | ... | 3.4 | ... |
| 1898 | ... | ... | ... | ... | ... | ... | ... | ... | ... | ... | 3.7 | ... |
| 1899 | ... | ... | ... | ... | ... | ... | ... | ... | ... | ... | 4.0 | ... |
| 1900 | ... | ... | ... | 5.5 | ... | ... | ... | ... | ... | ... | 4.0 | ... |
| 1901 | ... | ... | ... | ... | ... | ... | ... | ... | ... | ... | 4.5 | ... |
| 1902 | ... | ... | ... | 7.2 | ... | ... | ... | ... | ... | ... | 4.6 | ... |
| 1903 | ... | ... | ... | 7.3 | ... | 0.3 | ... | ... | ... | ... | 4.8 | ... |
| 1904 | ... | ... | ... | ... | ... | ... | ... | ... | ... | ... | ... | ... |
| 1905 | ... | ... | ... | 6.6 | ... | ... | ... | ... | ... | ... | ... | ... |
| 1906 | ... | ... | ... | ... | ... | ... | ... | ... | ... | ... | ... | ... |
| 1907 | ... | ... | 15 | ... | ... | 0.6 | ... | ... | ... | ... | ... | ... |
| 1908 | ... | ... | ... | ... | ... | ... | ... | ... | ... | ... | 6.7 | ... |
| 1909 | ... | ... | ... | ... | ... | ... | ... | ... | ... | ... | 7.2 | ... |
| 1910 | ... | ... | ... | ... | ... | 1.0 | ... | ... | ... | ... | 8.1 | ... |
| 1911 | ... | ... | ... | ... | ... | ... | ... | ... | ... | ... | 8.3 | ... |
| 1912 | ... | ... | ... | ... | ... | ... | ... | ... | ... | ... | 9.2 | 4.5 |
| 1913 | 74 | 2.5 | 39 | 15 | 3.2 | 2.9 | 1.3 | 0.5 | 4.0 | ... | 10 | 5.0 |
| 1914 | ... | ... | ... | 18 | ... | ... | ... | ... | ... | ... | 10 | 5.0 |
| 1915 | ... | ... | 46 | 18 | ... | 2.3 | ... | ... | ... | ... | 11 | ... |
| 1916 | ... | ... | 50 | 19 | ... | ... | ... | ... | ... | ... | 10 | ... |
| 1917 | ... | ... | 57 | 19 | ... | ... | ... | ... | ... | ... | 12 | ... |
| 1918 | ... | ... | 58 | 20 | ... | ... | ... | ... | ... | ... | 13 | ... |
| 1919 | 104 | ... | 58 | 22 | ... | ... | ... | ... | ... | ... | 14 | ... |
| 1920 | 120 | ... | 59 | 22 | ... | ... | ... | ... | ... | ... | 15 | ... |
| 1921 | 135 | ... | ... | 24 | ... | ... | ... | ... | ... | ... | 15 | ... |
| 1922 | 145 | 2.7 | ... | 27 | ... | 4.3 | 0.9 | ... | ... | ... | 15 | 10 |
| 1923 | 157 | ... | 94 | 27 | 12 | ... | 1.7 | ... | ... | ... | 16 | ... |
| 1924 | 174 | 1.8 | ... | 27 | 15 | 4.7 | 1.7 | ... | ... | ... | 16 | 12 |
| 1925 | 189 | ... | ... | 28 | 17 | 4.5 | 1.7 | 0.5 | ... | ... | 17 | 12 |
| 1926 | 204 | ... | 105 | 30 | 18 | ... | 1.8 | 0.4 | 11 | ... | 17 | 13 |
| 1927 | 225 | ... | 108 | 33 | 19 | 4.4 | 2.0 | 0.4 | ... | ... | 19₅ / 20 | 13 |
| 1928 | 245 | 2.7 | 130 | 37 | 22 | ... | 1.9 | 1.1 | 14 | 0.7 | 30 | 15 |
| 1929 | 269 | 2.5 | 160 | 40 | 28 | 4.1 | 2.0 | 2.0 | ... | ... | 30 | 20 |

**F9**    **SOUTH AMERICA: Number of Telephones in Use** (in thousands)

**1930–1974**

| | Argentina | Bolivia | Brazil | Chile | Colombia | Ecuador | Guyana | Paraguay | Peru | Surinam | Uruguay[5] | Venezuela |
|---|---|---|---|---|---|---|---|---|---|---|---|---|
| 1930 | 291 | 2.3 | 163 | 44 | 28 | ... | 2.0 | 2.1 | ... | ... | 28 | 22 |
| 1931 | 304 | 2.1 | 166 | 39 | 29 | 4.1 | 1.9 | 2.9 | ... | ... | 28 | 22 |
| 1932 | 307 | 2.0 | 170 | 44 | 28 | 6.3 | 1.9 | ... | ... | ... | 28 | 23 |
| 1933 | 305 | ... | ... | ... | 29 | ... | 2.0 | ... | ... | ... | 46 | ... |
| 1934 | 312 | ... | ... | ... | 33 | ... | 2.0 | ... | ... | ... | 30 | ... |
| 1935 | 327 | ... | ... | ... | 34 | ... | 2.1 | ... | ... | ... | 33 | ... |
| 1936 | 349 | ... | ... | ... | 37 | ... | 2.1 | 3.2 | ... | ... | 34 | ... |
| 1937 | 377 | 2.6 | 242 | 71 | 38 | 7.1 | 2.2 | 3.4 | 21 | ... | 48 | 21 |
| 1938 | 407 | 2.6 | ... | 78 | 39 | 7.1 | 2.4 | 3.5 | 26 | ... | 44 | 22 |
| 1939 | 434 | ... | 256 | 83 | 41 | 7.3 | 2.4 | 3.6 | 26 | ... | ... | 25 |
| 1940 | 460 | ... | 273 | 90 | 42 | 7.4 | 2.5 | 3.7 | 26 | ... | 47 | 29 |
| 1941 | ... | ... | ... | 96 | 45 | 7.6 | 2.6 | 3.8 | 27 | ... | ... | ... |
| 1942 | ... | ... | 380 | 101 | 47 | 7.8 | 2.7 | 4.0 | 27 | ... | ... | ... |
| 1943 | ... | ... | ... | 103 | 47 | 7.9 | 2.8 | 4.1 | 28 | ... | ... | ... |
| 1944 | ... | ... | 373 | 107 | 50 | 8.0 | 2.8 | 4.2 | 28 | ... | ... | ... |
| 1945 | ... | ... | ... | ... | 54 | 8.1 | 2.9 | 4.5 | 29 | ... | ... | ... |
| 1946 | 573 | ... | ... | 114 | 56 | 8.3 | 2.9 | 4.7 | 36 | ... | 70 | 43 |
| 1947 | 651 | 7.8 | 439 | 113 | 62 | ... | 3.0 | 4.8 | 43 | ... | 73 | ... |
| 1948 | 679 | 8.5 | 492 | 119 | 68 | ... | 3.2 | 5.0 | 44 | 1.5 | 78 | ... |
| 1949 | 717 | ... | 512 | 126 | 77 | ... | 3.2 | 5.2 | 44 | ... | 84 | ... |
| 1950 | 798 | ... | 550 | ... | 90 | ... | 3.3 | 5.3 | 47 | 1.6 | 90 | ... |
| 1951 | 852 | 11 | 592 | 138 | 98 | 9.0 | 3.5 | 5.3 | 49 | ... | 95 | 74 |
| 1952 | 929 | 11 | 636 | 141 | 115 | 12 | 3.5 | 5.5 | 54 | ... | 102 | 82 |
| 1953 | 1,001 | 11 | 680 | 145 | 129 | 12 | 3.6 | 5.7 | 57 | ... | 105 | 92 |
| 1954 | 1,080 | 11 | 746 | 148 | 144 | 12 | 4.4 | 5.8 | 61 | 3.2 | 109 | 98 |
| 1955 | 1,128 | 12 | 805 | 149 | 164 | 13 | 4.6 | 6.8 | 64 | ... | 114 | 105 |
| 1956 | 1,155 | 12 | 843 | 153 | 198 | 17 | 4.8 | 7.5 | 69 | 3.9 | 123 | 112 |
| 1957 | 1,181 | 23 | 870 | 160 | 223 | 22 | 4.9 | ... | 79 | 4.4 | 129 | 140 |
| 1958 | 1,224 | 20 | 928 | 166 | 247 | 25 | 5.2 | 9.2 | 91 | 4.8 | 136 | 159 |
| 1959 | 1,244 | 21 | 964 | 184 | 266 | 27 | 5.4 | 10 | 102 | 5.2 | 137 | 180 |
| 1960 | 1,296 | ... | 1,023 | 193 | 295 | 29 | 8.2 | 11 | 109 | 5.5 | 142 | 202 |
| 1961 | 1,360 | 18 | 1,047 | 203 | 322 | 31 | 9.1 | 11 | 113 | 5.8 | 137 | 216 |
| 1962 | 1,400 | 19 | 1,152 | 221 | 344 | 38 | 9.2 | 12 | 117 | 6.0 | 178 | 229 |
| 1963 | 1,425 | 20 | 1,217 | 235 | 372 | 44 | 9.4 | 13 | 126 | 6.6 | 169 | 241 |
| 1964 | 1,472 | 20 | 1,263 | 250 | 410 | 43 | 9.9 | 14 | 132 | 6.9 | 189 | 260 |
| 1965 | 1,498 | 25 | 1,320 | 263 | 443 | 44 | 11 | 14 | 137 | 8.4 | 185 | 283 |
| 1966 | 1,527 | 27 | 1,432 | 270 | 500 | 44 | 11 | 14 | 143 | 9.2 | 192 | 309 |
| 1967 | 1,554 | 30 | 1,473 | 290 | 735 | 45 | 12 | 16 | 152 | 9.0 | 204 | 327 |
| 1968 | 1,600 | 32 | 1,561 | 312 | 817 | 88 | 13 | 19 | 165 | 9.6 | 205 | 346 |
| 1969 | 1,668 | 38 | 1,787 | 334 | 543 | 94 | 14 | 21 | 193 | 9.9 | 207 | 377 |
| 1970 | 1,748 | ... | 2,001 | 357 | 809 | 130 | 15 | 24 | 228 | ... | 215 | 406 |
| 1971 | 1,828 | 44 | 2,145 | 393 | 856 | 150 | 15 | 20 | 243 | 12 | 235 | 444 |
| 1972 | 1,952 | ... | 2,190 | 415 | 1,010 | 120 | 15 | 21 | 269 | 12 | 241 | 474 |
| 1973 | 2,065 | 49 | 2,415 | 433 | 1,080 | 131 | 17 | 24 | 309 | 13 | 246 | 527 |
| 1974 | 2,177 | ... | 2,917 | 427 | 1,186 | 166 | 19 | 32 | 336 | ... | 248 | 554 |

**F9**     **Number of Telephones in Use**

| | Argentina | Bolivia | Brazil | Chile | Colombia | Ecuador | Guyana | Paraguay | Peru | Surinam | Uruguay | Venezuela |
|---|---|---|---|---|---|---|---|---|---|---|---|---|
| 1975 | 1,996 | 61 | 3,372 | 437 | 1,286 | 182 | 21 | 37 | 369 | 18 | 250 | 650 |
| 1976 | 2,302 | 64 | 4,036 | 451 | 1,296 | 202 | 23 | 40 | 389 | 19 | 258 | 742 |
| 1977 | 2,342 | 71 | 4,836 | 467 | 1,396 | 221 | 27 | 43 | 403 | 19 | 268 | 847 |
| 1978 | 2,404 | 104 | 5,525 | 514 | 1,493 | 240 | ... | 48 | 420 | 20 | 270 | 678 |
| 1979 | 2,491 | 113 | 6,494 | 536 | 1,587 | 260 | ... | 55 | 437 | 15 | 279 | 789 |
| 1980 | 2,588 | 138 | 7,496 | 551 | 1,718 | 272 | ... | 59 | 458 | ... | 287 | ... |
| 1981 | 2,767 | 141 | 8,536 | 595 | 1,842 | 290 | 28 | 64 | 484 | ... | 294 | ... |
| 1982 | 3,235 | 151 | 9,126 | 584 | 1,866 | 312 | ... | 71 | 501 | ... | ... | 1,378 |
| 1983 | 3,108 | 157 | 9,856 | 629 | 1,894 | 318 | ... | 78 | 525 | 28 | 332 | 1,021 |
| 1984 | 2,954 | 158 | 10,576 | 680 | 1,978 | 332 | ... | 83 | 563 | 35 | 338 | 1,311 |
| 1985 | 3,048 | ... | 11,428 | 761 | 2,097 | 339 | 33 | 89 | 600 | 36 | 374 | 1,451 |
| 1986 | 3,206 | 182 | 12,193 | 796 | 2,289 | 352 | 33 | 93 | 629 | 38 | 399 | 1,581 |
| 1987 | 3,655 | ... | 13,158 | 815 | 2,438 | 355 | ... | 100 | ... | 39 | 437 | 1,677 |
| 1988 | 3,694 | ... | 13,905 | 867 | 2,499 | ... | ... | 112 | ... | 41 | 482 | ... |

NOTE

SOURCES: The national publications listed on p. xiv–xvi, and League of Nations and UN, *Statistical Yearbooks.*

FOOTNOTES

[1] Including Alaska and Hawaii from 1959.
[2] At 30 June from 1911.
[3] At 31 March in the year following that shown. Connections to 1913 (1st line).
[4] The reason for this break is not clear in the sources.
[5] Montevideo only to 1927 (1st line).

**F10    NORTH AMERICA: RADIO AND TELEVISION SETS IN USE** (in thousands, except as otherwise indicated)

### 1920–1944

|      | Guatemala Radios | Trinidad & Tobago[1] Radios | USA[2] Radios |
|------|------|------|------|
| 1920 | ... | ... | ... |
| 1921 | ... | ... | ... |
| 1922 | ... | ... | 60 |
| 1923 | ... | ... | 400 |
| 1924 | ... | ... | 1,250 |
| 1925 | ... | ... | 2,750 |
| 1926 | ... | ... | 4,500 |
| 1927 | ... | ... | 6,750 |
| 1928 | ... | ... | 8,000 |
| 1929 | ... | ... | 10,250 |
| 1930 | ... | ... | 13,750 |
| 1931 | ... | ... | 16,700 |
| 1932 | ... | ... | 18,450 |
| 1933 | ... | ... | 19,250 |
| 1934 | ... | ... | 20,400 |
| 1935 | ... | ... | 21,456 |
| 1936 | ... | ... | 22,869 |
| 1937 | ... | ... | 24,500 |
| 1938 | ... | ... | 26,667 |
| 1939 | ... | 4.9 | 27,500 |
| 1940 | 22 | 5.6 | 28,500 |
| 1941 | ... | 6.7 | 29,300 |
| 1942 | ... | 7.5 | 30,600 |
| 1943 | ... | 7.7 | 30,800 |
| 1944 | ... | 8.4 | 32,500 |

### 1945–1986

|      | Barbados Radios | Barbados TV | Canada Radios | Canada TV | Costa Rica Radios | Costa Rica TV |
|------|------|------|------|------|------|------|
|      | | | (millions) | | | |
| 1945 | ... | — | ... | ... | ... | ... |
| 1946 | ... | — | ... | ... | ... | ... |
| 1947 | ... | — | ... | ... | ... | ... |
| 1948 | ... | — | ... | ... | ... | ... |
| 1949 | 6 | — | ... | ... | ... | ... |
| 1950 | ... | — | ... | ... | 23 | ... |
| 1951 | ... | — | ... | ... | ... | ... |
| 1952 | 9 | — | ... | ... | ... | ... |
| 1953 | 13 | — | ... | 665 | ... | ... |
| 1954 | 14 | — | ... | 1,407 | 50 | ... |
| 1955 | ... | — | ... | 2,000 | ... | ... |
| 1956 | 17 | — | ... | 2,450 | ... | ... |
| 1957 | 26 | — | ... | 2,730 | 75 | ... |
| 1958 | 28 | — | 7 | 3,075 | 75 | ... |
| 1959 | 31 | — | 7.5 | 3,420 | 75 | ... |
| 1960 | 35 | — | 8.1 | 3,930 | 77 | ... |
| 1961 | 38 | — | 9.2 | 4,100 | 81 | 7.2 |
| 1962 | 42 | — | 9.2 | 4,375 | ... | 12 |
| 1963 | ... | — | ... | 4,655 | 100 | 15 |
| 1964 | ... | — | 10 | 4,950 | 123 | 35 |
|      | | | (millions) | | | |
| 1965 | 43 | 6 | ... | 5.3 | 130 | 50 |
| 1966 | 45 | 9 | 12 | 5.7 | ... | 65 |
| 1967 | 55 | 9 | 12 | ... | ... | 66 |
| 1968 | 57 | 15 | 14 | 6.1 | ... | ... |
| 1969 | ... | 15 | 15 | ... | 106 | 100 |
| 1970 | 89 | 16 | 16 | 7.1 | 130 | 100 |
| 1971 | 94 | 18 | 17 | 7.6 | 130 | 120 |
| 1972 | 110 | 32 | 18 | 7.3 | 135 | 120 |
| 1973 | 116 | 35 | 19 | 7.7 | 140 | 122 |
| 1974 | ... | 40 | 20 | 8.2 | 142 | 150 |
| 1975 | 130 | 40 | 22 | 9.4 | 145 | 150 |
| 1976 | ... | 48 | ... | ... | ... | 155 |
| 1977 | ... | 50 | 24 | 10.0 | | 160 |
| 1978 | 130 | 50 | 26 | 11.0 | 160 | 160 |
| 1979 | 131 | 50 | 26 | 11.0 | 180 | 161 |
| 1980 | 135 | 50 | 27 | 11.3 | 180 | 162 |
| 1981 | 143 | 53 | 28$_5$ | 11.9$_5$ | 186 | 164 |
| 1982 | 190 | 54 | 19 | 11.3 | 195 | 200 |
| 1983 | 191 | 55 | ... | 12 | ... | 181 |
| 1984 | ... | ... | ... | ... | ... | ... |
| 1985 | ... | ... | ... | ... | 220 | 200 |
| 1986 | 220 | 66 | 23 | 14 | ... | 210 |

**F10**     **NORTH AMERICA: Radios and Television Sets in Use** (in thousands, except as otherwise indicated)

**1945–1986**

| | Cuba | | Dominican Republic | | El Salvador | | Guadeloupe[3] | | Guatemala | |
|---|---|---|---|---|---|---|---|---|---|---|
| | Radios | TV | Radios | TV | Radios | TV | Radios | TV | Radios | TV |
| 1945 | ... | ... | ... | ... | ... | — | ... | — | ... | ... |
| 1946 | ... | ... | ... | ... | ... | — | ... | — | ... | ... |
| 1947 | ... | ... | ... | ... | ... | — | ... | — | ... | ... |
| 1948 | ... | ... | 30 | ... | ... | — | ... | — | ... | ... |
| 1949 | 700 | ... | ... | ... | ... | — | ... | — | 30 | ... |
| 1950 | 575 | ... | 35 | ... | 21 | — | 1.0 | — | ... | ... |
| 1951 | ... | ... | ... | ... | ... | — | 1.2 | — | 31 | ... |
| 1952 | ... | ... | ... | ... | ... | — | 1.4 | — | ... | ... |
| 1953 | 900 | 150 | 55 | 1.2 | ... | — | ... | — | ... | ... |
| 1954 | ... | ... | ... | 5 | 28 | — | 2.8 | — | 36 | ... |
| 1955 | ... | 200 | ... | 6 | ... | — | ... | — | ... | ... |
| 1956 | 1,100 | 275 | ... | 7 | ... | 1 | ... | — | ... | 8.5 |
| 1957 | ... | 300 | ... | ... | 30 | ... | 6 | — | ... | 11 |
| 1958 | 900 | 315 | 80 | 15 | 40 | 10 | 6 | — | ... | 11 |
| 1959 | 1,000 | 365 | 98 | 16 | 225 | 16 | 6 | — | ... | 20 |
| 1960 | 1,100 | 500 | 102 | 18 | ... | 20 | 6 | — | ... | 32 |
| 1961 | 1,300 | 500 | ... | ... | 353 | 20 | 6 | — | 210 | 35 |
| 1962 | ... | 520 | 123 | 11 | 358 | 25 | 6 | — | ... | 40 |
| 1963 | ... | 525 | 139 | 19 | ... | 30 | 6 | — | ... | 50 |
| 1964 | 1,345 | 550 | ... | 35 | 395 | 30 | 10 | ... | ... | 50 |
| 1965 | ... | ... | ... | 50 | 396 | 35 | ... | 0.7 | ... | 55 |
| 1966 | ... | 555 | 150 | 65 | ... | ... | 18 | 2.6 | ... | ... |
| 1967 | ... | 575 | 150 | 75 | 396 | 45 | 24 | 4 | ... | 55 |
| 1968 | ... | 575 | 155 | 75 | 398 | ... | 27 | 5.2 | ... | 65 |
| 1969 | 1,326 | ... | 160 | 100 | 400 | 75 | 30 | 5.8 | ... | 72 |
| 1970 | 1,330 | ... | 164 | 100 | 405 | 92 | 26 | ... | 220 | 72 |
| 1971 | 1,338 | ... | 165 | ... | 350 | 125 | 27 | 7.9 | ... | 82 |
| 1972 | 1,500 | ... | 170 | 150 | ... | ... | ... | 9 | ... | 85 |
| 1973 | 1,790 | 525 | 180 | 155 | ... | 110 | ... | 10 | 260 | 105 |
| 1974 | 1,805 | 595 | 185 | 156 | ... | 111 | 21 | 13 | 261 | 106 |
| 1975 | 2,100 | 600 | 190 | 158 | 1,400 | 135 | ... | ... | 262 | 110 |
| 1976 | ... | 635 | ... | 161 | ... | 136 | ... | ... | ... | 120 |
| 1977 | ... | 800 | 211 | ... | 1,416 | 148 | ... | ... | 274 | 150 |
| 1978 | 2,227 | 975 | 212 | 250 | 1,416 | 180 | ... | ... | 280 | 150 |
| 1979 | 2,575 | 1,114 | 215 | 320 | 1,508 | 276 | ... | ... | 285 | 160 |
| 1980 | 2,914 | 1,273 | 220 | 385 | 1,550 | 300 | 35 | 33 | 310 | 175 |
| 1981 | 3,000 | 1,500 | 229 | ... | 1,600 | 310 | 37 | 36 | 320 | 180 |
| 1982 | 3,100 | 1,600 | 250 | 450 | 1,680 | 320 | 38 | 37 | 330 | 200 |
| 1983 | ... | 1,658 | ... | ... | 1,900 | 340 | 39 | 38 | 340 | 203 |
| 1984 | ... | ... | ... | ... | ... | ... | ... | ... | ... | ... |
| 1985 | 3,282 | 1,977 | ... | 500 | 1,900 | 350 | ... | ... | 370 | 207 |
| 1986 | 3,400 | 2,050 | ... | 515 | 2,000 | 400 | ... | ... | 500 | 300 |

**F10    NORTH AMERICA: Radio and Television Sets in Use** (in thousands, except as otherwise indicated)

**1945–1986**

| | Haiti | | Honduras | | Jamaica | | Martinique[5] | | Mexico | |
|---|---|---|---|---|---|---|---|---|---|---|
| | Radios | TV | Radios | TV | Radios | TV | Radios | TV | Radios | TV |
| | | | | | | | | | (millions) | |
| 1945 | ... | ... | ... | — | ... | — | ... | — | ... | ... |
| 1946 | ... | ... | ... | — | ... | — | ... | — | ... | ... |
| 1947 | ... | ... | 15 | — | ... | — | ... | — | ... | ... |
| 1948 | 4 | ... | ... | — | ... | — | ... | — | 0.70 | ... |
| 1949 | 3 | ... | 17 | — | ... | — | ... | — | 0.75 | ... |
| 1950 | 4 | ... | ... | — | ... | — | 3 | — | ... | ... |
| 1951 | ... | ... | 25 | — | ... | — | 3 | — | 1.2 | ... |
| 1952 | ... | ... | ... | — | ... | — | 4 | — | ... | ... |
| 1953 | ... | ... | ... | — | 44 | — | ... | — | ... | 90 |
| 1954 | 14 | ... | 26 | — | 50 | — | 7 | — | 2.0 | 100 |
| 1955 | ... | ... | ... | — | 65 | — | ... | — | 2.5 | 175 |
| 1956 | 19 | ... | 30 | — | 75 | — | 8 | — | ... | 250 |
| 1957 | ... | ... | 32 | — | 95 | — | 9 | — | ... | 300 |
| 1958 | 20 | ... | ... | — | 137 | — | 17 | — | 3.0 | 400 |
| 1959 | 21 | ... | ... | — | 147 | — | 18 | — | 3.1 | 600 |
| 1960 | 21 | 1.8 | 125 | 1.3 | 147 | — | 13 | — | 3.3 | 650 |
| 1961 | 21 | 2 | 125 | 4 | 200 | — | 15 | — | 3.5 | 900 |
| 1962 | 50 | 2.5 | ... | 4.5 | 210 | — | 17 | — | 5.8 | 930 |
| 1963 | 55 | 3.5 | ... | 6.5 | ... | 11 | 16 | ... | 6.5 | 1,040 |
| 1964 | 60 | 4 | 128 | 7.2 | 242 | 20 | ... | ... | 7.3 | 1,300 |
| 1965 | 63 | ... | 135 | 8 | 350 | 25 | ... | 1.5 | 8.6 | ... |
| 1966 | 64 | 10 | ... | 10 | 365 | 40 | 30 | 3.5 | 9.9 | 1,516 |
| 1967 | 75 | 10 | 136 | 11 | 400 | 47 | 32 | 4.9 | 11 | 1,790 |
| 1968 | 80 | 11 | 140 | 11 | 425 | 56 | 35 | 5.9 | 12 | 2,150 |
| 1969 | 81 | 11 | 145 | 17 | 450 | 56 | 37 | 7.4 | 13 | 2,553 |
| 1970 | 83 | 11 | 147 | 22 | 500 | 70 | 32 | 9.5 | 14 | 2,993 |
| 1971 | 85 | 11 | 147 | 25 | ... | 73 | 33 | 10 | 15 | 3,385 |
| 1972 | 86 | 12 | 150 | ... | ... | 105 | 33 | 12 | 16 | 3,821 |
| 1973 | 90 | 13 | 155 | ... | 633 | 100 | 32 | 14 | 17 | 4,339 |
| 1974 | 91 | 13 | 158 | 46 | ... | 97 | 31 | 16 | 18 | 4,885 |
| 1975 | 93 | 13 | 160 | 47 | 550 | 110 | 32 | 20 | 17 | 4,885 |
| 1976 | ... | 14 | ... | 48 | ... | 111 | ... | ... | ... | ... |
| 1977 | ... | 14 | 170 | 48 | ... | 120 | ... | ... | ... | 5,480 |
| 1978 | 100 | 14 | 175 | 48 | 718 | 120 | 42 | 30 | 18 | 5,600 |
| 1979 | 101 | 15 | 176 | 49 | 718 | 120 | 42 | 34 | 20 | 5,700 |
| 1980 | 105 | 16 | 176 | 49 | 800 | 167 | 49 | 38 | 19 | 7,500 |
| 1981 | 105 | 17 | 180 | 49 | 850 | 180 | 50 | 38 | 21 | 7,900 |
| 1982 | 110 | 18 | 190 | 50 | 870 | 190 | 53 | 42 | 21[5] | 8,000 |
| 1983 | 120 | 19 | 200 | 52 | 890 | 200 | 55 | 42 | 13 | 8,100 |
| 1984 | ... | ... | ... | ... | ... | ... | ... | ... | ... | ... |
| 1985 | 140 | 20 | ... | ... | ... | ... | ... | ... | 15 | 8,500 |
| 1986 | 200 | 25 | ... | ... | 950 | 250 | 58 | 45 | 16 | 9,490 |

**F10　　NORTH AMERICA: Radio and Television Sets in Use** (in thousands, except as otherwise indicated)

**1945–1986**

| | Nicaragua | | Panama | | Puerto Rico | | Trinidad & Tobago[1] | | USA[2] | |
|---|---|---|---|---|---|---|---|---|---|---|
| | Radios | TV | Radios | TV | Radios | TV | Radios | TV | Radios | TV |
| | | | | | | | | | (millions) | |
| 1945 | ... | — | ... | ... | ... | ... | 7.8 | — | 33 | ... |
| 1946 | ... | — | ... | ... | ... | ... | 8.2 | — | 34 | 8 |
| 1947 | ... | — | ... | ... | ... | ... | 9.0 | — | 36 | 14 |
| 1948 | ... | — | ... | ... | ... | ... | 11 | — | 38 | 172 |
| 1949 | ... | — | ... | ... | ... | ... | 14 | — | 39 | 940 |
| | | | | | | | | | (millions) | |
| 1950 | 20 | — | 55 | ... | ... | ... | 16 | — | 41 | 3.9 |
| 1951 | 16 | — | 81 | ... | 150 | ... | 18 | — | 42 | 10 |
| 1952 | 20 | — | ... | ... | ... | ... | 21 | — | 43 | 15 |
| 1953 | ... | — | 95 | ... | ... | ... | 24 | — | 45 | 20 |
| 1954 | 30 | — | ... | ... | ... | ... | 28 | — | 45 | 26 |
| 1955 | ... | — | ... | ... | ... | 65 | 33 | — | 46 | 31 |
| 1956 | ... | — | ... | 2 | 200 | 126 | 35 | — | 47 | 35 |
| 1957 | 35 | 0.5 | 120 | 3.5 | 270 | 160 | 38 | — | 48 | 39 |
| 1958 | 35 | 2 | 130 | 8 | ... | ... | 41 | — | 49[2] | 42[2] |
| 1959 | 75 | 6 | 163 | 8 | ... | ... | 47 | — | 49 | 44 |
| 1960 | ... | 5 | ... | 11 | ... | ... | 42 | — | 50 | 46 |
| 1961 | 100 | 5 | 186 | 30 | ... | ... | 37 | — | 51 | 47 |
| 1962 | 100 | 6.5 | 225 | ... | ... | ... | 32 | 3.5 | 51 | 49 |
| 1963 | ... | 10 | ... | 48 | ... | ... | 28[1] | 7.7[1] | 52 | 50 |
| 1964 | 100 | ... | 496 | 65 | ... | ... | 165 | 44 | 54 | 52 |
| 1965 | ... | 16 | 500 | 70 | ... | ... | 200 | ... | 55 | 53 |
| 1966 | 105 | 19 | ... | 77 | ... | ... | ... | 30 | 57 | 54 |
| 1967 | 105 | 25 | ... | 77 | ... | ... | 169 | 36 | 58 | 55 |
| 1968 | 105 | ... | ... | ... | ... | ... | 281 | 40 | 59 | 57 |
| 1969 | 107 | 45 | 226 | 125 | ... | ... | 293 | 43 | 61 | 58 |
| 1970 | 109 | 55 | 230 | ... | 1,625 | 410 | ... | 60 | 62[2] | 60[2] |
| | | | | | | | | | 64 | 63 |
| 1971 | 110 | 56 | 230 | 158 | ... | ... | 296 | 70 | 65 | 65 |
| 1972 | 115 | 60 | 250 | 200 | ... | ... | ... | 82 | 67 | 67 |
| 1973 | 125 | 63 | 255 | ... | 1,753 | 605 | ... | 93 | 69 | 69 |
| 1974 | 126 | 75 | 260 | 183 | 1,755 | 625 | 250 | 100 | 71 | 70 |
| 1975 | ... | 83 | 265 | 185 | 1,760 | 630 | 250 | 105 | 73 | 70 |
| 1976 | ... | ... | ... | 186 | ... | ... | ... | 110 | 74 | 71 |
| 1977 | ... | 100 | 274 | 206 | ... | ... | 255 | 125 | 75 | 73 |
| 1978 | 175 | 120 | 280 | 206 | 1,923 | 670 | 296 | 140 | 77 | 74 |
| 1979 | 175 | 150 | 285 | 220 | 2,000 | 700 | 296 | 150 | 79 | 76 |
| 1980 | ... | 175 | 300 | 220 | 2,000 | 800 | 300 | 210 | 81 | 80 |
| 1981 | ... | 185 | 305 | 233 | 2,150 | 860 | 400 | 265 | 83 | 82 |
| 1982 | ... | 195 | 325 | 245 | 2,300 | 940 | 350 | 300 | 85 | 83 |
| 1983 | ... | 205 | 335 | 255 | 2,450 | 980 | 360 | 310 | 87 | 84 |
| 1984 | ... | ... | ... | ... | ... | ... | ... | ... | 87 | 85 |
| 1985 | ... | 190 | 400 | 350 | ... | ... | ... | ... | 88 | 86 |
| 1986 | ... | 200 | 410 | 360 | 2,350 | 865 | 550 | 305 | 90 | 87 |

**F10**    **SOUTH AMERICA: RADIO AND TELEVISION SETS IN USE** (in thousands, except as otherwise indicated

### 1945–1986

| | Argentina | | Bolivia | | Brazil[4] | | Chile | | Colombia | | Ecuador | |
|---|---|---|---|---|---|---|---|---|---|---|---|---|
| | Radios | TV | Radios | TV | Radios | TV | Radios | TV | Radios | TV | Radios | TV |
| | (millions) | | | | (millions) | | | | | | | |
| 1945 | ... | ... | ... | — | ... | ... | ... | — | ... | — | ... | — |
| 1946 | ... | ... | ... | — | ... | ... | ... | — | ... | — | ... | — |
| 1947 | ... | ... | ... | — | ... | ... | ... | — | ... | — | ... | — |
| 1948 | ... | ... | ... | — | 0.8 | ... | ... | — | ... | — | 30 | — |
| 1949 | 1.5 | ... | ... | — | ... | ... | 550 | — | ... | — | ... | — |
| 1950 | 2.2 | ... | 150 | — | 0.8[6] / 2.5 | ... | ... | — | 500 | — | 50 | — |
| 1951 | ... | ... | ... | — | ... | ... | ... | — | ... | — | ... | — |
| 1952 | ... | ... | ... | — | ... | ... | ... | — | ... | — | ... | — |
| 1953 | 2.6 | 20 | ... | — | ... | 70 | ... | — | ... | — | ... | — |
| 1954 | ... | ... | ... | — | 3.5 | 130 | 650 | — | ... | 15 | ... | — |
| 1955 | ... | ... | ... | — | ... | 150 | ... | — | ... | 20 | ... | — |
| 1956 | ... | 75 | 200 | — | ... | 200 | ... | — | 800 | 50 | 100 | — |
| 1957 | ... | 90 | ... | — | 4.6 | 350 | ... | — | ... | 100 | ... | — |
| 1958 | 3.2 | 220 | ... | — | ... | 700 | 700 | — | ... | 140 | 120 | — |
| 1959 | 3.4 | 400 | 250 | — | 4.0 | 850 | ... | ... | ... | 150 | 170 | ... |
| | | (millions) | | | | | | | | | | |
| 1960 | 3.5 | 0.45 | ... | — | 4.6 | 1,200 | ... | ... | 1,971 | 150 | 170 | ... |
| 1961 | 4.0 | 0.7 | 255 | — | 4.7 | 1,621 | 1,016 | 3 | 2,159 | 200 | 175 | 5 |
| 1962 | 5.5 | 0.85 | 350 | — | 7.0 | 1,430 | 1,500 | 4 | ... | 205 | 320 | 16 |
| 1963 | 5.8 | 1.2 | 360 | — | 7.2 | 1,800 | ... | 35 | ... | 210 | 500 | 17 |
| 1964 | 6.2 | 1.5 | 500 | — | 7.5 | 2,300 | ... | 50 | ... | 300 | 510 | 32 |
| | | | | | | (millions) | | | | | | |
| 1965 | 6.6 | 1.6 | 525 | — | ... | ... | ... | ... | ... | 350 | 540 | 42 |
| 1966 | 7.0 | 1.8 | ... | — | ... | 2.5 | ... | 55 | 2,200 | 400 | 650 | 55 |
| 1967 | 8.0 | 1.9 | ... | — | ... | ... | ... | 49 | 2,200 | ... | 801 | 71 |
| 1968 | 9.0 | 2.5 | ... | — | 5.6 | ... | ... | ... | 2,210 | 500 | 1,200 | ... |
| 1969 | 8.5 | 3.1 | ... | ... | 5.6 | 6.5 | 1,375 | 400 | 2,214 | 622 | 1,700 | 120 |
| 1970 | 9.0 | 3.5 | 402 | ... | 5.7 | 6.1 | 1,400 | 500 | 2,217 | 810 | 1,700 | 150 |
| 1971 | 10 | ... | ... | ... | 5.8 | 6.5 | ... | 674 | 2,250 | 891 | ... | ... |
| 1972 | ... | 3.7 | ... | 11 | 6.0 | 6.6 | 1,500 | 865 | 2,255 | 971 | ... | 178 |
| 1973 | 21 | 4.0 | ... | ... | 6.2 | ... | 1,500 | 993 | 2,793 | ... | ... | ... |
| 1974 | ... | 4.5 | 425 | ... | 6.3[4] / 15 | 8.7 | ... | 1,215 | 2,805 | ... | ... | 250 |
| | —[5] | | | | | | | | | | | |
| 1975 | 10 | 4.5 | 426 | 45 | 17 | 11 | 1,700 | 700 | 2,808 | 1,600 | ... | 252 |
| 1976 | | 4.5 | ... | 48 | ... | 11 | ... | 710 | ... | 1,700 | ... | 300 |
| 1977 | | 4.6 | ... | 49 | ... | 11 | 2,000 | ... | 2,859 | 1,850 | ... | 340 |
| 1978 | 10 | 4.6 | 473 | 50 | 32 | 12 | 2,500 | 1,210 | 3,000 | ... | 2,540 | 360 |
| 1979 | ... | 4.7 | 500[5] | 100 | 35 | 15 | 3,239 | 1,225 | 3,005 | 2,000 | ... | 400 |
| 1980 | 12 | 5.1 | 2,800 | 300 | 35 | 15 | 3,250 | 1,225 | 3,300 | 2,250 | 2,350 | 500 |
| 1981 | 21 | 5.5 | 3,150 | 341 | 40 | 16 | 3,350 | 1,250 | 3,450 | 2,500 | 2,750 | 530 |
| 1982 | ... | 5.9 | 3,380 | 350 | 45 | 16 | 3,450 | 1,300 | 3,550 | 2,600 | 2,850 | 550 |
| 1983 | 16 | 5.9 | 3,500 | 386 | 50 | 17 | ... | 1,350 | ... | 2,700 | 2,950 | 570 |
| 1984 | ... | ... | ... | ... | ... | ... | ... | ... | ... | ... | ... | ... |
| 1985 | 20 | 6.5 | 3,000 | 420 | 53 | 25 | 4,000 | 1,750 | 4,000 | 2,750 | 2,750 | 600 |
| 1986 | 20 | 6.6 | 3,850 | 500 | 51 | 26 | 4,100 | 2,000 | 4,500 | 3,000 | 2,850 | 700 |

**F10     SOUTH AMERICA: Radio and Television Sets in Use** (in thousands, except as otherwise indicated)

## 1945–1986

| | Guyana | Paraguay | | Peru | | Surinam | | Uruguay | | Venezuela | |
|---|---|---|---|---|---|---|---|---|---|---|---|
| | Radios | Radios | TV | Radios | TV | Radios | TV | Radios | TV | Radios | TV |
| 1945 | ... | ... | ... | ... | ... | ... | — | ... | — | ... | ... |
| 1946 | ... | ... | ... | ... | ... | ... | — | ... | — | ... | ... |
| 1947 | ... | ... | ... | ... | ... | ... | — | ... | — | ... | ... |
| 1948 | ... | ... | ... | ... | ... | ... | — | 300 | — | 150 | ... |
| 1949 | 6 | ... | ... | ... | ... | ... | — | ... | — | ... | ... |
| 1950 | ... | ... | ... | 500 | ... | 5 | — | ... | — | ... | ... |
| 1951 | 11 | 35 | ... | ... | ... | 8 | — | 362 | — | ... | ... |
| 1952 | 13 | ... | ... | ... | ... | ... | — | ... | — | 218 | ... |
| 1953 | ... | 80 | ... | ... | ... | ... | — | ... | — | ... | 20 |
| 1954 | 21 | ... | ... | ... | ... | ... | — | 385 | — | ... | ... |
| | | | | | | | | (millions) | | | |
| 1955 | 27 | ... | ... | ... | ... | ... | — | ... | ... | ... | 65 |
| 1956 | 30 | ... | ... | ... | ... | 10 | — | 0.5 | 1 | 750 | 100 |
| 1957 | 33 | 90 | ... | 600 | ... | 11 | — | 0.7 | ... | 750 | 105 |
| 1958 | 34 | 105 | ... | ... | ... | 12 | — | ... | 10 | ... | 200 |
| 1959 | 35 | 105 | ... | 820 | 28 | ... | — | 0.8 | 15 | ... | 200 |
| | | (millions) | | | | | | | | (millions) | |
| 1960 | 37 | ... | ... | 1.1 | 33 | 40 | — | 0.8 | 25 | 1.2 | 250 |
| 1961 | 42 | 150 | ... | ... | 82 | 40 | — | 0.9 | 60 | 1.3 | 263 |
| 1962 | 44 | 160 | ... | ... | 120 | 45 | — | 0.9 | 70 | ... | 549 |
| 1963 | 66 | ... | ... | 2.0 | 150 | ... | — | ... | 158 | ... | 573 |
| 1964 | 70 | ... | ... | 2.1 | 175 | ... | — | 0.9 | 175 | 1.7 | 591 |
| 1965 | 80 | ... | ... | ... | 210 | ... | 7 | ... | 200 | 1.7 | 650 |
| 1966 | 90 | ... | ... | ... | 275 | 50 | 16 | 1.0 | ... | 1.7 | ... |
| 1967 | ... | ... | ... | ... | 275 | 65 | ... | 1.0 | ... | 1.7 | ... |
| 1968 | ... | ... | 13 | ... | 300 | 88 | ... | 1.1 | 215 | 1.7 | 700 |
| 1969 | ... | 165 | 17 | 1.8 | 390 | 90 | 25 | 1.1 | 250 | 1.7 | 700 |
| 1970 | 80 | 169 | 18 | 1.8 | 395 | 92 | 28 | 1.0 | 150 | 1.7 | ... |
| 1971 | 90 | 175 | ... | 1.8 | 400 | 95 | 31 | 1.1 | 200 | 1.8 | 857 |
| 1972 | 100 | 175 | ... | 2.0 | 410 | 100 | 32 | 1.5 | 300 | 2 | 980 |
| 1973 | 150 | 175 | 53 | 2.0 | 411 | 108 | 31 | 1.5 | 305 | 1.6 | 1,095 |
| 1974 | 268 | 176 | 53 | 2.0 | 425 | 109 | 33 | 1.5 | 350 | 1.7 | 1,200 |
| 1975 | 266 | 180 | 54 | 2.1 | 610 | 110 | 34 | 1.5 | 351 | 2.0₅ / 4.8 | 1,284 |
| 1976 | ... | ... | 55 | ... | 718 | ... | ... | ... | 355 | ... | 1,431 |
| 1977 | ... | 181 | 55 | 2.2 | 825 | ... | ... | 1.6 | 360 | ... | 1,530 |
| 1978 | 301 | 185 | 56 | 2.4 | ... | 120 | ... | 1.6 | 361 | ... | ... |
| 1979 | 310 | 186 | 57 | 2.5 | 850 | 150 | 40 | 1.6 | 362 | 5.3 | 1,710 |
| 1980 | 303 | 224 | 68 | 2.7 | 850 | 189 | 40 | 1.6 | 363 | 5.6 | 1,710 |
| 1981 | 315 | 240 | 75 | 2.9 | 900 | 200 | 41 | 1.6 | 366 | 5.8 | 1,800 |
| 1982 | 325 | 250 | 80 | 3.0 | 910 | 215 | 42 | 1.7 | 370 | 6.0 | 1,850 |
| 1983 | 350 | 260 | 82 | 3.1 | 950 | 220 | 43 | 1.7 | 370 | 6.8 | 2,100 |
| 1984 | ... | ... | ... | ... | ... | ... | ... | ... | ... | ... | ... |
| 1985 | ... | 600 | 85 | 4.0 | 1,500 | ... | ... | 1.8 | 500 | 7.3 | 2,250 |
| 1986 | 355 | 624 | 88 | 5.0 | 1,701 | 246 | 48 | 1.8 | 520 | 7.5 | 2,500 |

## F10    Radio and Television Sets in Use

NOTES

1. SOURCES: The national publications listed on p. xiv–xvi and UN, *Statistical Yearbook*.
2. The nature of the statistics varies considerably between countries and at different times. Where it is based on licences issued, this has been indicated. Most of the figures, however, are estimates of either the number of households with sets or of the total number of sets in use.
3. So far as possible, and except as indicated in footnotes, the data relate to 31 December.
4. There are obvious breaks in the continuity of some series, which are not indicated in the sources, especially in recent years.

FOOTNOTES

[1] Licences issued to 1963.
[2] Statistics are of the number of households with sets at 30 June to 1970 and at 31 December subsequently. Alaska and Hawaii are included from 1959.
[3] Licences issued.
[4] Licences issued to 1950 (1st line). Households with sets subsequently, except for radios in 1974 (2nd line) and 1975.
[5] The reason for this break is not given in the source.

# G FINANCE

Financial statistics exhibit some very great contrasts as regards availability. Some were collected and published from a very early date. Others may have been collected, but were regarded as state secrets. And yet others were not collected for a long time, either because they were regarded as private secrets, publication of which it was beyond the competence of the state to compel, or because there were no permanent financial institutions from which it was possible to require them.

The first three tables in this section, showing various monetary statistics, point some of these contrasts very well. The banknote issues of certain privileged banks are often available from their beginning, though in many Latin American countries this often did not come until relatively late in their existence. Similarly available are the figures of deposits in savings banks, at least when they came under the auspices of the state, though that was less often in Latin America than in most other parts of the world. But deposits in commercial banks were often not recorded officially until well into the twentieth century. Recently, however, such data, as well as statistics of currency, have tended to be both readily available and reasonably comparable between countries, largely thanks to the International Monetary Fund.

A new table, G3 showing measures of money supply, has been added in this edition. These are only available in a consistent form for the period since the late 1940s, and thanks to the work of the statisticians of the International Monetary Fund. Earlier national statistics have been constructed for a few countries, but too few to merit inclusion here.

Two tables are given of certain public finance statistics of central governments. Table 5 shows total expenditure so far as that can be easily ascertained, whilst table 6 shows, so far as possible, current revenue and, for the larger countries, its main tax constituents. There is, of course, a great deal of data available on the details of government expenditures, but these are so heterogeneous, are often not available in any meaningful form, and change in nature so often, that in many cases it would require considerable research effort to put the statistics of even a single country on a reasonably uniform basis. Regretfully, therefore, only the totals of expenditure are included. Tax yields, on the other hand, exhibit both less disguise and, until recently, less change in nature. These have therefore been included for some countries for the period when they are readily available. Similar data could be included for smaller countries, but in most of these, taxes on foreign trade formed much the largest part of revenue until after World War II, and it did not seem very useful to plot their exact course.

It must be stressed that the statistics of government finance tend to be subject to fairly frequent changes in accounting methods and organization, and perhaps also to occasional deliberate omissions for 'reasons of state', and it would be unwise to assume that they are always fully comprehensive, or that all their inconsistencies have been identified in footnotes. Comparisons over time, therefore, even within a single country, need to be made with caution, and this applies a *fortiori* to comparisons between countries. Perhaps an even more important reason for this than the various changes in procedures and classifications is the fact that the areas of responsibility of central and local governments differ quite a lot in different countries, especially where there are federal systems in operation, as there are in Australia and in the larger countries of the Americas.

**G1** **NORTH AMERICA: CURRENCY IN CIRCULATION** (in millions of stated currency unit, except as otherwise indicated)

### 1800–1849

| | USA | |
|---|---|---|
| | currency[1] | notes[2] |
| | dollars | dollars |
| 1800 | 26.5 | 10.5 |
| 1801 | ... | ... |
| 1802 | ... | ... |
| 1803 | ... | ... |
| 1804 | ... | ... |
| 1805 | ... | ... |
| 1806 | ... | ... |
| 1807 | ... | ... |
| 1808 | ... | ... |
| 1809 | ... | ... |
| 1810 | 55 | 28 |
| 1811 | ... | ... |
| 1812 | ... | ... |
| 1813 | ... | ... |
| 1814 | ... | ... |
| 1815 | ... | ... |
| 1816 | ... | ... |
| 1817 | ... | ... |
| 1818 | ... | ... |
| 1819 | ... | ... |
| 1820 | 67 | 45 |
| 1821 | ... | ... |
| 1822 | ... | ... |
| 1823 | ... | ... |
| 1824 | ... | ... |
| 1825 | ... | ... |
| 1826 | ... | ... |
| 1827 | ... | ... |
| 1828 | ... | ... |
| 1829 | ... | ... |
| 1830 | 87 | 61 |
| 1831 | 93 | 77 |
| 1832 | 117 | 92 |
| 1833 | 120 | 92 |
| 1834 | 124 | 95 |
| 1835 | 146 | 104 |
| 1836 | 200 | 140 |
| 1837 | 217 | 149 |
| 1838 | 199 | 116 |
| 1839 | 220 | 135 |
| 1840 | 186 | 107 |
| 1841 | 186 | 107 |
| 1842 | 164 | 84 |
| 1843 | 147 | 59 |
| 1844 | 167 | 75 |
| 1845 | 178 | 90 |
| 1846 | 193 | 106 |
| 1847 | 224 | 106 |
| 1848 | 232 | 129 |
| 1849 | 233 | 115 |

### 1850–1894

| | Canada[3] | USA | |
|---|---|---|---|
| | | currency[1] | notes[2] |
| | dollars | dollars | dollars |
| 1850 | ... | 279 | 131 |
| 1851 | ... | 330 | 155 |
| 1852 | ... | 361 | 172 |
| 1853 | ... | 402 | 188 |
| 1854 | ... | 426 | 205 |
| 1855 | ... | 418 | 187 |
| 1856 | 12.6 | 426 | 196 |
| 1857 | 8.8 | 457 | 215 |
| 1858 | 9.4 | 409 | 155 |
| 1859 | 10.7 | 439[4] | 193 |
| 1860 | 12.5 | 435 | 207 |
| 1861 | 13.7 | 484[4] | 202 |
| 1862 | 9.7 | 606 | 257 |
| 1863 | 10.5 | 931[4] | 551 |
| 1864 | 8.6 | 1,008 | 626 |
| 1865 | 12.1 | 1,084 | 668 |
| 1866 | 9.9 | 940 | 634 |
| 1867 | 8.1[3] / 14 | 859 | 629 |
| 1868 | 15 | 772 | 644 |
| 1869 | 18 | 741 | 639 |
| 1870 | 26 | 775 | 658 |
| 1871 | 36[3] / 29 | 794 | 674 |
| 1872 | 31 | 829 | 703 |
| 1873 | 32 | 838 | 723 |
| 1874 | 31 | 864 | 731 |
| 1875 | 26 | 834 | 709 |
| 1876 | 25 | 807 | 672 |
| 1877 | 25 | 814 | 672 |
| 1878 | 24 | 820 | 658 |
| 1879 | 26 | 819 | 639 |
| 1880 | 31 | 973 | 679 |
| 1881 | 38 | 1,114 | 733 |
| 1882 | 42 | 1,174 | 737 |
| 1883 | 39 | 1,230 | 804 |
| 1884 | 37 | 1,244 | 817 |
| 1885 | 38 | 1,293 | 868 |
| 1886 | 36 | 1,253 | 796 |
| 1887 | 40 | 1,318 | 837 |
| 1888 | 41 | 1,372 | 875 |
| 1889 | 40 | 1,380 | 898 |
| 1890 | 41 | 1,429 | 945 |
| 1891 | 42 | 1,497 | 973 |
| 1892 | 43 | 1,601 | 1,073 |
| 1893 | 41 | 1,597 | 1,066 |
| 1894 | 38 | 1,661 | 1,054 |

**G1**　　**NORTH AMERICA: Currency in Circulation** (in millions of stated currency unit, except as otherwise indicated)

### 1895–1934

| | Canada[3] | Costa Rica[5] | El Salvador[9] | Guatemala[9] | Mexico[10] | Nicaragua[11] | USA | |
|---|---|---|---|---|---|---|---|---|
| | | | | | | | currency[1] | notes[2] |
| | dollars | colones | colones | pesos | pesos | pesos | dollars | dollars |
| 1895 | 39 | ... | ... | ... | ... | ... | 1,602 | 1,010 |
| 1896 | 40 | ... | ... | ... | ... | ... | 1,506 | 939 |
| 1897 | 45 | ... | ... | ... | ... | ... | 1,641 | 1,012 |
| 1898 | 48 | ... | ... | ... | ... | ... | 1,838 | 1,057 |
| 1899 | 55 | ... | ... | ... | ... | ... | 1,904 | 1,094 |
| 1900 | 59 | ... | 1.1 | ... | ... | 3.3 | 2,081 | 1,302 |
| 1901 | 63 | ... | 1.4 | ... | 170 | 5.4 | 2,203 | 1,399 |
| 1902 | 70 | ... | 1.9 | ... | 194 | 8.3 | 2,279 | 1,462 |
| 1903 | 73 | ... | 2.2 | ... | 210 | 8.1 | 2,400 | 1,585 |
| 1904 | 74 | ... | 2.8 | ... | 214 | 7.9 | 2,553 | 1,706 |
| 1905 | 81 | ... | 2.7 | ... | 226 | 7.8 | 2,623 | 1,762 |
| 1906 | 91 | ... | 3.3 | ... | 242 | 7.9 | 2,775 | 1,879 |
| 1907 | 90 | ... | 2.8 | ... | 261 | 8.9 | 2,814 | 2,008 |
| 1908 | 86 | ... | 3.6 | ... | 264 | 11 | 3,079 | 2,224 |
| 1909 | 95 | ... | 4.0 | ... | 274 | 12 | 3,149 | 2,303 |
| 1910 | 102 | ... | 3.9 | ... | 295[10] | 31 | 3,149 | 2,303 |
| 1911 | 120 | ... | 4.5 | ... | ... | 49 | 3,263 | 2,414 |
| 1912 | 131 | ... | 4.3 | ... | ... | ... | 3,335 | 2,458 |
| | | | | | | cordobas | | |
| 1913 | 129[3] / 132 | ... | 4.5 | 105 | ... | 1.6 | 3,419 | 2,529 |
| 1914 | 129 | 4.2 | 6.1 | 126 | ... | 3.0 | 3,459 | 2,560 |
| 1915 | 147 | 5.5 | 7.9 | 155 | ... | 2.0 | 3,320 | 2,450 |
| 1916 | 174 | 5.4 | 9.6 | 171 | ... | 2.1 | 3,649 | 2,724 |
| 1917 | 219 | ... | 11 | ... | ... | 2.1 | 4,066 | 3,066 |
| 1918 | 250 | ... | 14 | 220 | ... | 2.7 | 4,482 | 3,576 |
| 1919 | 259 | ... | 15 | 245 | ... | 3.7 | 4,877 | 4,012 |
| 1920 | 258 | 19 | 8.2 | 310 | ... | 2.8 | 5,468 | 4,576 |
| 1921 | 214 | 18 | 7.0 | 333 | ... | 1.9 | 4,911 | 4,085 |
| 1922 | 207 | 18 | 9.4 | 378 | ... | 2.2 | 4,463 | 3,671 |
| 1923 | 210 | 17 | 10 | 401 | ... | 2.6 | 4,823 | 4,021 |
| 1924 | 200 | 17[6] | 15 | 426[6] | ... | 3.6 | 4,849 | 4,052 |
| 1925 | 199 | 18 | 16 | 424 | 353 | 3.8 | 4,815 | 3,996 |
| | | | | quetzales | | | | |
| 1926 | 213 | 22 | 16 | 9.4 | 406 | 4.0 | 4,885 | 4,068 |
| 1927 | 216 | ... | 18 | 8.6 | 378 | 3.9 | 4,851 | 4,034 |
| 1928 | 218 | 22 | 17 | 9.2 | 478 | 4.0 | 4,797 | 3,984 |
| 1929 | 213 | ... | 15 | 9.9 | 495 | 3.6 | 4,746 | 3,935 |
| 1930 | 188 | 20[7] | 11 | 6.4 | 508[10] | 3.0 | 4,522 | 3,727 |
| 1931 | 187 | 18[8] | 10 | 6.1 | 188 | 2.3 | 4,822 | 4,034 |
| 1932 | 171 | 15 | 12 | 5.5 | 187 | 2.4 | 5,695 | 4,842 |
| 1933 | 177 | 16 | 14 | 5.6 | 218 | 2.5 | 5,721 | 5,002 |
| 1934 | 184 | 16 | 15 | 6.3 | 266 | 3.2 | 5,373 | 4,944 |

**G1**   **NORTH AMERICA: Currency in Circulation** (in millions of stated currency unit, except as otherwise indicated)

**1935–1974**

| | Canada[3] | Costa Rica | Dominican Republic[12] | El Salvador | Guatemala | Haiti | Honduras |
|---|---|---|---|---|---|---|---|
| | dollars | colones | pesos | colones | quetzales | gourdes | lempiras |
| 1935 | 198 | 19 | ... | 13 | 6.2 | ... | ... |
| 1936 | 220 | 21 | ... | $\frac{16_9}{18}$ | $\frac{6.8_9}{8.2}$ | ... | 5.4 |
| 1937 | 237 | 22 | 2.69 | 18 | 8.8 | ... | 5.8 |
| 1938 | 238 | 23 | 2.24 | 17 | 9.0 | ... | 6.1 |
| 1939 | 281 | 24 | 2.46 | 17 | 9.3 | ... | 5.9 |
| 1940 | 379 | 26 | 2.73 | 16 | 9.2 | ... | 6.2 |
| 1941 | 492 | 35 | 4.81 | 21 | 12 | ... | 7.0 |
| 1942 | 681 | 53 | 6.51 | 28 | 15 | ... | 8.2 |
| 1943 | 849 | 69 | 7.99 | 39 | 19 | ... | 11 |
| 1944 | 990 | 71 | 9.45 | 47 | 23 | ... | 13 |
| 1945 | 1,055 | 70 | 12.8 | 48 | 27 | ... | 16 |
| 1946 | 1,096 | 67 | 15.7 | 52 | 31 | ... | 16 |
| 1947 | 1,112 | 82 | $\frac{17.7_{12}}{13.9}$ | 55 | 32 | ... | 16 |
| 1948 | 1,185 | 105 | 13.9 | 60 | 36 | ... | 17 |
| 1949 | 1,184 | 100 | 16.1 | 67 | 38 | ... | 19 |
| 1950 | 1,214 | 95 | 19.4 | 76 | 39 | 38 | 20 |
| 1951 | 1,275 | 108 | 24.6 | 84 | 40 | 44 | 25 |
| 1952 | 1,377 | 125 | 29.7 | 96 | 45 | 55 | 29 |
| 1953 | 1,430 | 138 | 30.9 | 97 | 53 | 52 | 33 |
| 1954 | 1,458 | 155 | 34.5 | 105 | 54 | 68 | 39 |
| 1955 | 1,550 | 153 | 41.4 | 98 | 52 | 63 | 34 |
| 1956 | 1,605 | 151 | 42.9 | 110 | 59 | 75 | 38 |
| 1957 | 1,667 | 169 | 46.0 | 108 | 65 | 81 | 38 |
| 1958 | 1,781 | 181 | 50.2 | 100 | 62 | 70 | 37 |
| 1959 | 1,832 | 186 | 50.5 | 100 | 63 | 73 | 37 |
| 1960 | 1,876 | 195 | 48.4 | 98 | 62 | 73 | 36 |
| 1961 | 1,959 | 185 | 51.6 | 99 | 62 | 78 | 35 |
| 1962 | 1,994 | 207 | 62.4 | 96 | 63 | 83 | 39 |
| 1963 | 2,084 | 224 | 74 | 109 | 67 | 87 | 42 |
| 1964 | 2,254 | 229 | 66.7 | 117 | 72 | 86 | 46 |
| 1965 | 2,410 | 237 | 75.3 | 112 | 77 | 84 | 51 |
| 1966 | 2,580 | 253 | 64.7 | 115 | 81 | 79 | 54 |
| 1967 | 2,820 | 282 | 59.0 | 122 | 83 | 88 | 56 |
| 1968 | 3,050 | 306 | 64.8 | 116 | 83 | 94 | 61 |
| 1969 | 3,330 | 350 | 72.5 | 133 | 91 | 105 | 73 |
| 1970 | 3,560 | 380 | 81.2 | 136 | 97 | 115 | 77 |
| 1971 | 3,990 | 434 | 83.5 | 145 | 99 | 126 | 80 |
| 1972 | 4,560 | 521 | 98.9 | 175 | 114 | 148 | 90 |
| 1973 | 5,200 | 643 | 116 | 201 | 137 | 173 | 112 |
| 1974 | 5,860 | 734 | 141 | 241 | 158 | 183 | 109 |

**G1    NORTH AMERICA: Currency in Circulation** (in millions of stated currency unit, except as otherwise indicated)

1935–1974

| | Jamaica | Mexico[10] | Nicaragua[11] | Trinidad & Tobago[13] | USA | |
|---|---|---|---|---|---|---|
| | | | | | currency[1] | notes[2] |
| | pounds | pesos | cordobas | dollars | thousand million dollars | |
| 1935 | ... | 301 | 3.5 | ... | 5.6 | 5.1 |
| 1936 | ... | 359 | 5.2 | ... | 6.2 | 5.8 |
| 1937 | 0.4 | 442 | 6.5 | 0.9 | 6.4 | 5.9 |
| 1938 | 0.5 | 472[10] | 10 | 1.3 | 6.5 | 5.9 |
| 1939 | ... | 598 | 12[11] | 1.3 | 7 | 6.5 |
| 1940 | 0.7 | 661 | 13 | 2.1 | 7.8 | 7.2 |
| 1941 | 1.1 | 797 | 16 | 7.1[13] 11 | 9.6 | 8.9 |
| 1942 | 1.6 | 1,021 | 22 | 20 | 12 | 12 |
| 1943 | 2.1 | 1,478 | 33 | 25 | 17 | 16 |
| 1944 | 2.5 | 1,768 | 41 | 24 | 23 | 21 |
| 1945 | 3 | 1,658 | 45 | 24 | 27 | 26 |
| 1946 | 3.1 | 1,729 | 43 | 22 | 28 | 27 |
| 1947 | 2.8 | 1,754 | 48 | 20 | 28 | 27 |
| 1948 | 2.8 | 2,118 | 48 | 19 | 28 | 26 |
| 1949 | 3 | 2,378 | 57 | 20 | 27 | 26 |
| 1950 | 3.2 | 2,915 | 60. | 22 | 27 | 26 |
| 1951 | 4 | 3,458 | 80 | 27[13] 11 | 28 | 26 |
| 1952 | 4.3 | 3,649 | 91 | 17 | 29 | 27 |
| 1953 | 3.3 | 3,864 | 111 | 19 | 30 | 28 |
| 1954 | 3.9 | 4,635 | 127 | 22 | 30 | 28 |
| 1955 | 4.6 | 5,084 | 124 | 22 | 30 | 28 |
| 1956 | 4.9 | 5,734 | 131 | 23 | 31 | 29 |
| 1957 | 5.7 | 6,094 | 130 | 25 | 31 | 29 |
| 1958 | 6.1 | 6,615 | 124 | 27 | 31 | 29 |
| 1959 | 7.3 | 7,250 | 131 | 31 | 32 | 30 |
| 1960 | 7.5 | 7,872 | 135 | 33 | 32 | 30 |
| 1961 | 8.8 | 8,275 | 131 | 38 | 32 | 30 |
| 1962 | 9 | 9,144 | 167 | 33 | 34 | 31 |
| 1963 | 10 | 10,264 | 177 | 34 | 35 | 33 |
| 1964 | 11 | 11,923 | 185 | 37 | 38 | 35 |
| 1965 | 12 | 12,507 | 198 | 36 | 40 | 36 |
| 1966 | 13 | 13,630 | 227 | 41 | 43 | 38 |
| 1967 | 14 | 14,749 | 222 | 42 | 45 | 40 |
| 1968 | 16 | 16,674 | 209 | 49 | 48 | 42 |
| 1969 | dollars 37 | 18,245 | 219 | 51 | 51 | 45 |
| 1970 | 47 | 20,144 | 251 | 57 | 54 | 48[2] |
| 1971 | 58 | 21,824 | 252 | 58 | 58[1] | 54 |
| 1972 | 72 | 26,777 | 329 | 81 | 67 | 59 |
| 1973 | 82 | 34,176 | 411 | 80 | 73 | 65 |
| 1974 | 102 | 42,685 | 452 | 99 | 80 | 71 |

**G1** **NORTH AMERICA: Currency in Circulation** (in millions of stated currency unit, except as otherwise indicated)

| | Canada | Costa Rica | Dominican Republic | El Salvador | Guatemala | Haiti | Honduras |
|---|---|---|---|---|---|---|---|
| | thousand million dollars | colones | pesos | colones | quetzales | gourdes | lempiras |
| 1975 | 6.78 | 853 | 158 | 253 | 175 | 189 | 115 |
| 1976 | 7.32 | 1,117 | 172 | 380 | 237 | 243 | 173 |
| 1977 | 8.08 | 1,409 | 203 | 432 | 284 | 265 | 193 |
| 1978 | 8.95 | 1,704 | 224 | 500 | 325 | 311 | 215 |
| 1979 | 9.45 | 1,955 | 274 | 743 | 365 | 418 | 270 |
| 1980 | 10.40 | 2,255 | 275 | 719 | 381 | 487 | 275 |
| 1981 | 10.71 | 3,501 | 324 | 703 | 405 | 566 | 302 |
| 1982 | 11.62 | 5,436 | 358 | 732 | 405 | 599 | 314 |
| 1983 | 12.80 | 6,941 | 415 | 724 | 438 | 691 | 362 |
| 1984 | 13.50 | 8,588 | 593 | 836 | 461 | 763 | 383 |
| 1985 | 14.61 | 9,938 | 677 | 1,080 | 698 | 829 | 410 |
| 1986 | 15.59 | 13,241 | 937 | 1,157 | 805 | 979 | 426 |
| 1987 | 16.92 | 14,777 | 1,313 | 1,298 | 931 | 1,205 | 491 |
| 1988 | 18.24 | 24,734 | 1,876 | 1,326 | 1,069 | 1,459 | 570 |

| | Jamaica | Mexico[10] | Nicaragua | Trinidad & Tobago | USA | |
|---|---|---|---|---|---|---|
| | | | | | currency[1] | notes[2] |
| | dollars | thousand million pesos | cordobas | dollars | thousand million dollars | |
| 1975 | 127 | 52.3 | 445 | 138 | 87 | 78 |
| 1976 | 138 | 79.9 | 636 | 177 | 94 | 84 |
| 1977 | 182 | 88.6 | 692 | 231 | 104 | 94 |
| 1978 | 173 | 115 | 883 | 295 | 115 | 104 |
| 1979 | 220 | 150 | 1,572 | 412 | 126 | 114 |
| 1980 | 260 | 195 | 1,964 | 467 | 137 | 125 |
| 1981 | 282 | 283 | 2,375 | 532 | 146 | 132 |
| 1982 | 316 | 505 | 3,085 | 726 | 156 | 143 |
| 1983 | 375 | 681 | 5,468 | 758 | 172 | 158 |
| 1984 | 436 | 1,122 | 11,340 | 841 | 184 / 156 | 169 |
| | | | thousand million | | | |
| 1985 | 540 | 1,738 | 28.6 | 808 | 168 | ... |
| 1986 | 729 | 3,067 | 99.1 | 837 | 180 | ... |
| 1987 | 844 | 7,339 | 730 | 783 | 196 | ... |
| 1988 | 1,288 | 13,201 | 66,984 | 770 | 212 | ... |

**G1     SOUTH AMERICA: CURRENCY IN CIRCULATION** (in millions of stated currency unit, except as otherwise indicated)

### 1820–1859

| | Brazil[14] |
| --- | --- |
| | milreis |
| 1820 | ... |
| 1821 | ... |
| 1822 | 9.2 |
| 1823 | 10 |
| 1824 | 11 |
| 1825 | 12 |
| 1826 | 13 |
| 1827 | 22 |
| 1828 | 21[14] |
| 1829 | ... |
| 1830 | 21 |
| 1831 | ... |
| 1832 | ... |
| 1833 | ... |
| 1834 | ... |
| 1835 | 31 |
| 1836 | 34 |
| 1837 | 35 |
| 1838 | 39 |
| 1839 | ... |
| 1840 | ... |
| 1841 | 40 |
| 1842 | 44 |
| 1843 | 47 |
| 1844 | 48 |
| 1845 | 50 |
| 1846 | 51 |
| 1847 | 49 |
| 1848 | 48 |
| 1849 | 48 |
| 1850 | 47 |
| 1851 | 47 |
| 1852 | 47 |
| 1853 | 47 |
| 1854 | 47[14] / 63 |
| 1855 | 68 |
| 1856 | 86 |
| 1857 | 96 |
| 1858 | 93 |
| 1859 | 96 |

### 1860–1899

| | Argentina[15] | Bolivia[17] | Brazil[14] | Chile[16] |
| --- | --- | --- | --- | --- |
| | pesos | bolivianos | milreis | pesos |
| 1860 | ... | ... | 88 | ... |
| 1861 | ... | ... | 82 | ... |
| 1862 | ... | ... | 79 | ... |
| 1863 | ... | ... | 82 | ... |
| 1864 | ... | ... | 99 | ... |
| 1865 | ... | ... | 101 | ... |
| 1866 | ... | ... | 113 | ... |
| 1867 | ... | ... | 118 | ... |
| 1868 | ... | ... | 125 | ... |
| 1869 | ... | 0.1 | 183 | ... |
| 1870 | ... | 0.1 | 192 | ... |
| 1871 | ... | 0.1 | 192 | ... |
| 1872 | ... | 0.4 | 189 | ... |
| 1873 | ... | 0.9 | 185 | ... |
| 1874 | ... | 1.5 | 184 | ... |
| 1875 | ... | 1.2 | 182 | ... |
| 1876 | ... | 1.4 | 179 | ... |
| 1877 | ... | 0.7 | 179 | ... |
| 1878 | ... | 0.7 | 209 | ... |
| 1879 | ... | 1.0 | 217 | 26 |
| 1880 | ... | 1.3 | 216 | 34 |
| 1881 | ... | 1.4 | 212 | 39 |
| 1882 | ... | 1.8 | 212 | 29 |
| 1883 | 42 | 1.9 | 211 | 29 |
| 1884 | 48 | 2.7 | 210 | 29 |
| 1885 | 75 | 2.7 | 208 | 30 |
| 1886 | 89 | 3.4 | 213 | 34 |
| 1887 | 94 | 4.2 | 202 | 32 |
| 1888 | 130 | 4.5 | 205 | 36 |
| 1889 | 164 | 5.3 | 197 | 38 |
| 1890 | 248 | 5.3 | 199 | 39 |
| 1891 | 259 | 6.1 | 514 | 62 |
| 1892 | 282 | 5.5 | 561 | 45 |
| 1893 | 307 | 5.7 | 632 | 56 |
| 1894 | 299 | 7.0 | 712 | 60 |
| 1895 | 297 | 6.1 | 678 | 43 |
| 1896 | 295 | 5.2 | 713 | 32 |
| 1897 | 293 | 5.7 | 781 | 28 |
| 1898 | 295 | 6.5 | 778 | 47 |
| 1899 | 295 | 6.6 | 734 | 51 |

**G1   SOUTH AMERICA: Currency in Circulation** (in millions of stated currency unit, except as otherwise indicated)

**1900–1939**

| | Argentina[15] | Bolivia[17] | Brazil[14] milreis or cruzeiros | Chile[16] | Colombia[9] | Ecuador[18] | Paraguay[19] | Peru thousand libras | Uruguay[21] | Venezuela |
|---|---|---|---|---|---|---|---|---|---|---|
| | pesos | bolivianos | | pesos | pesos | sucres | pesos | | pesos | bolivares |
| 1900 | 292 | 7.0 | 670 | 51 | ... | ... | ... | ... | 5 | ... |
| 1901 | 292 | 7.6 | 680 | 51 | ... | ... | ... | ... | 5.5 | ... |
| 1902 | 293 | 7.9 | 676 | 50 | ... | ... | ... | ... | 6.5 | ... |
| 1903 | 380 | 8.8 | 675 | 50 | ... | ... | ... | ... | 7 | ... |
| 1904 | 408 | 8.9 | 674 | 55 | ... | ... | ... | ... | 7 | ... |
| 1905 | 498 | 10 | 669 | 81 | ... | ... | ... | ... | 9.4 | ... |
| 1906 | 527 | 12 | 702 | 120 | ... | ... | ... | ... | 11 | ... |
| 1907 | 532 | 16 | 744 | 150 | ... | ... | ... | ... | 13 | ... |
| 1908 | 581 | 17 | 724 | 150 | ... | ... | ... | ... | 15 | 3.7 |
| 1909 | 685 | 17 | 854 | 150 | ... | ... | ... | ... | 17 | 3.7 |
| 1910 | 716 | 20 | 925 | 150 | ... | ... | ... | ... | 18 | 7.4 |
| 1911 | 723 | 24 | 982 | 151 | ... | ... | ... | ... | 24 | 8.9 |
| 1912 | 800 | 26 | 1,004 | 171 | ... | ... | ... | ... | 28 | ... |
| 1913 | 823 | 26 | 897 | 186 | ... | 10 | 65 | ... | 21 | 11 |
| 1914 | 803 | 23 | 980 | 225 | ... | 11 | 90 | 675 | 26 | 11 |
| 1915 | 988 | 24 | 1,077 | 178 | ... | 11 | 125 | 1,140 | 32 | 12 |
| 1916 | 1,013 | 26 | 1,217 | 178 | ... | 12 | 125 | 1,115 | 37 | 14 |
| 1917 | 1,013 | 30 | 1,484 | 186 | ... | 13 | 125 | 1,851 | 43 | 17 |
| 1918 | 1,154 | 35 | 1,700 | 228 | ... | 12 | 125 | 3,316 | 56 | 21 |
| 1919 | 1,177 | 36 | 1,748 | 251 | ... | 13 | 125 | 4,191 | 74 | 25 |
| 1920 | 1,363 | 42 | 1,848 | 303 | ... | 17 | 150 | 5,383 | 65 | 27 |
| 1921 | 1,363 | 34 | 2,098 | 325 | ... | 16 | 182 | 4,666 | 66 | 35 |
| 1922 | 1,363 | 31 | 2,366 | 302 | ... | 16 | 177 | 4,159 | 64 | 35 |
| 1923 | 1,363 | 32 | 2,649 | 293 | 39 | 16 | 177 | 4,638 | 69 | 35 |
| 1924 | 1,320 | 35 | 2,964 | 336 | 50 | 18 | 216 | 5,088 | 69 | 42 |
| 1925 | 1,320 | 39 | 2,707 | 394 | 67 | 37 | 226[20] | 5,693 | 64 | 49 |
| 1926 | 1,320 | 38 | 2,589 | 372 | 66 | 36 | 193[20] | 6,052 | 68 | 71 |
| 1927 | 1,378 | 40 | 3,005 | 319 | 70 | 39[18] / 41 | 198 | 6,230 | 72 | 76 |
| 1928 | 1,406 | 44 | 3,379 | 352 | 79 | 42 | 213 | 6,304 | 72 | 87 |
| 1929 | 1,247 | 43 | 3,391 | 352 | 61 | 36 | 206 | 6,209 | 71 | 88 |
| | | | | | | | | soles | | |
| 1930 | 1,261 | 32 | 2,842 | 306 | 49 | 31 | 206 | 70 | 74 | 96 |
| 1931 | 1,245 | 27 | 2,942 | 319 | 42 | 25 | 202 | 70 | 81 | 90 |
| 1932 | 1,339 | 38 | 3,238 | 488 | 44 | 30 | 197 | 65 | 85 | 89 |
| 1933 | 1,214 | 54 | 3,037 | 515 | 54 | 43 | ... | 76 | 78 | 85 |
| 1934 | 1,171 | 84 | 3,157 | 516 | 64 | 57 | ... | 83 | 80 | 91 |
| 1935 | 1,178 | 146 | 3,612 | 567 | 71 | 60 | ... | 94 | 82 | 102 |
| 1936 | 1,302[15] / 998 | 210 | 4,050 | 653[16] / 565 | 85[9] / 75 | 68[18] / 62 | 1,152[6] | 103 | 89[9] / 75 | 117 |
| 1937 | 1,049 | 252[17] / 248 | 4,550 | 630 | 74 | 74 | ... | 108 | 75 | 111[17] / 157 |
| 1938 | 1,038 | 284 | 4,825 | 719 | 81 | 73 | 1,240 | 115 | 83 | 174 |
| 1939 | 1,063[15] | 364 | 4,971 | 862 | 82 | 78 | 1,230 | 138 | 81 | 182 |

**G1    SOUTH AMERICA: Currency in Circulation** (in millions of stated currency unit, except as otherwise indicated)

**1940–1974**

| | Argentina[15] | Bolivia[17] | Brazil[14] thousand million cruzeiros | Chile[16] | Colombia | Ecuador | Guyana | Paraguay[19] | Peru | Uruguay[21] | Venezuela |
|---|---|---|---|---|---|---|---|---|---|---|---|
| | pesos | bolivianos | | pesos | pesos | sucres | dollars | pesos | soles | pesos | bolivares |
| 1940 | 1,072 | 471 | 5.2 | 1,034 | 80 | 80 | ... | 1,219 | 146 | 92 | 181 |
| 1941 | 1,242 | 634 | 6.6 | 1,310 | 95 | 120 | ... | 1,488 | 208 | 98 | 194 |
| 1942 | 1,439 | 807 | 8.2 | 1,700 | 119 | 169 | ... | 2,161 | 275 | 98 | 228 |
| | | | | | | | | guaranies | | | |
| 1943 | 1,704 | 1,055 | 11 | 2,100 | 143 | 232 | ... | 16 | 327 | 114 | 264 |
| 1944 | 2,136 | 1,239 | 14 | 2,390 | 196 | 295 | ... | 21 | 393 | 128 | 309 |
| 1945 | 2,581 | 1,520 | 18[14] / 14 | 2,682 | 219 | 321 | ... | 24 | 478 | 147 | 406 |
| 1946 | 3,579 | 1,588 | 17 | 3,170 | 270 | 350 | ... | 29 | 568 | 176 | 524 |
| 1947 | 4,772 | 1,727 | 17 | 3,677 | 306 | 329 | ... | 39 | 653 | 202 | 620 |
| 1948 | 6,737 | 2,068 | 18 | 4,316 | 376 | 355 | ... | 53 | 712 | 231 | 781 |
| 1949 | 9,070 | 2,399 | 19 | 5,208 | 492 | 373 | ... | 84 | 809 | 251 | 811 |
| 1950 | 11,910 | 3,267 | 25 | 6,318 | 465 | 476 | ... | 129 | 956 | 314 | 786 |
| 1951 | 15,360 | 3,866 | 28 | 7,970 | 519 | 459 | ... | 215 | 1,082 | 315 | 818 |
| 1952 | 18,260 | 6,082 | 32 | 11,500 | 610 | 535 | ... | 358[19] / 344 | 1,216 | 344 | 896 |
| 1953 | 22,070 | 11,450 | 39 | 16,660 | 683 | 566 | ... | 459 | 1,406 | 378 | 921 |
| 1954 | 26,740 | 19,870 | 49 | 22,750 | 764 | 662 | ... | 618 | 1,562 | 418 | 981 |
| | thousand million pesos | thousand million bolivianos | | escudos | | | | | thousand million soles | | |
| 1955 | 32 | 39 | 57 | 40 | 784 | 627 | 13 | 817 | 1.66 | 437 | 1,033 |
| 1956 | 36 | 145 | 67 | 57 | 942 | 705 | 13 | 1,100 | 1.99 | 500 | 1,112 |
| 1957 | 42 | 213 | 81 | 70 | 1,178 | 722 | 16 | 1,225 | 2.10 | 571 | 1,286 |
| 1958 | 60 | 241 | 100 | 93 | 1,376 | 709 | 17 | 1,414 | 2.40 | 724 | 1,342 |
| 1959 | 84 | 321 | 127 | 124 | 1,503 | 758 | 19 | 1,583 | 2.93 | 903 | 1,374 |
| 1960 | 105 | 354 | 169 | 159 | 1,623 | 851 | 22 | 1,614 | 3.18 | 1,235 | 1,493 |
| 1961 | 119 | 414 | 256 | 175 | 1,867 | 879 | 23 | 2,010 | 3.58 | 1,573 | 1,350 |
| 1962 | 135 | 460 | 397 | 230 | 2,078 | 949 | 24 | 1,964 | 4.11 | 1,792 | 1,322 |
| | | million pesos | | | | | | | | | |
| 1963 | 167 | 540 | 684 | 297 | 2,495 | 1,037 | 26 | 2,075 | 4.88 | 2,226 | 1,340 |
| 1964 | 228 | 658 | 1,156 | 485 | 3,071 | 1,137 | 26 | 2,624 | 61 | 3,084 | 1,399 |
| 1965 | 297 | 740 | 1,730 | 725 | 3,538 | 1,236 | 28 | 2,926 | 7.12 | 6,082[21] / 6,674 | 1,545 |
| 1966 | 397 | 883 | 2,343 million new cruzeiros | 1,020 | 4,037 | 1,347 | 28 | 2,903[19] | 8.13 | 10,332 | 1,654 |
| 1967 | 509 | 905 | 2,944 | 1,308 | 4,689 | 1,404 | 30 | 3,048 | 9.18 | 19,611 | 1,788 |
| 1968 | 591 | 949 | 4,080 | 1,697 | 5,470 | 1,600 | 34 | 3,269 | 10.33 | 31,390 | 1,942 |
| 1969 | 655 | 1,041 | 5,390 | 2,360 | 6,506 | 1,747 | 36 | 3,454 | 12.17 | 50,573 | 2,031 |
| | thousand million new pesos | | | thousand million escudos | | | | | | thousand million pesos | |
| 1970 | 7.6 | 1,153 | 6,719 | 4.4 | 7,809 | 2,329 | 37 | 4,021 | 16.56 | 57 | 2,164 |
| 1971 | 9.9 | 1,281 | 8,550 | 9 | 8,534 | 2,414 | 41 | 4,409 | 19.23 | 84 | 2,338 |
| 1972 | 13.2 | 1,598 | 11,550 | 28 | 10,729 | 2,890 | 48 | 5,137 | 22.25 | 121 | 2,584 |
| 1973 | 26.4 | 2,073 | 16,430 | 96 | 12,424 | 3,618 | 56 | 6,490 | 27.64 | 202 | 2,865 |
| 1974 | 43.2 | 2,746 | 20,810 | 349 | 15,873 | 4,776 | 64 | 7,553 | 33.96 | 316 | 3,807 |

**G1    SOUTH AMERICA: Currency in Circulation** (in millions of stated currency unit, except as otherwise indicated)

| | Argentina[15] | Bolivia[17] | Brazil[14] | Chile[16] | Colombia | Ecuador |
|---|---|---|---|---|---|---|
| | thousand million pesos | pesos | thousand million cruzeiros | thousand million escudos | thousand million pesos | sucres |
| 1975 | 124 | 3,054 | 31.0 | 1,358 | 20.8 | 5,386 |
| | | | | million pesos | | |
| 1976 | 411 | 3,968 | 46.2 | 4,480 | 28.8 | 7,570 |
| 1977 | 1,073 | 4,864 | 65.2 | 9,340 | 40.5 | 9,126 |
| 1978 | 3,332 | 5,810 | 94.1 | 16,386 | 53.7 | 10,274 |
| 1979 | 7,870 | 7,211 | 167 | 24,894 | 67.3 | 12,338 |
| 1980 | 16,418 | 9,461 | 291 | 35,625 | 84.1 | 15,285 |
| 1981 | 30,207 | 10,852 | 523 | 44,736 | 102 | 17,414 |
| 1982 | [56,190][20] | 38,898 | 986 | 42,958 | 130 | 20,519 |
| | million australes 8.7 | thousand million | | thousand million | | thousand million |
| 1983 | 46.3 | 125 | 1,842 | 51.9 | 168 | 25.4 |
| 1984 | 313 | 2,888 | 6,130 | 64.2 | 212 | 35.3 |
| | | million million | million million | | | |
| 1985 | 2,022 | 174 | 23.5 | 79.5 | 187 | 42.7 |
| 1986 | 3,990 | 294 | 84.0 | 108 | ... | 54.6 |
| 1987 | 9,261 | 397 | 248 | 136 | 418 | 74.8 |
| 1988 | 43,186 | 526 | 2,039 | 182 | 530 | 124 |

| | Guyana | Paraguay | Peru | Uruguay | Venezuela |
|---|---|---|---|---|---|
| | dollars | thousand million guaranies | intis[22] | thousand million pesos | bolivares |
| 1975 | 92 | 8.90 | 43 | 470 | 4,723 |
| 1976 | 105 | 10.29 | 50 | 782 | 5,820 |
| 1977 | 143 | 13.34 | 62 | 1,115 | 7,383 |
| 1978 | 156 | 18.69 | 92 | 1,814 | 9,012 |
| 1979 | 148 | 24.31 | 164 | 3,187 | 10,012 |
| 1980 | 167 | 31.18 | 276 | 5,103 | 12,338 |
| 1981 | 186 | 31.15 | 445 | 6,145 | 13,525 |
| 1982 | 231 | 33.17 | 631 | 7,880 | 13,094 |
| | | | | thousand million new pesos | |
| 1983 | 269 | 38.47 | 1,140 | 8.41 | 14,728 |
| 1984 | 336 | 48.6 | 2,540 | 12.11 | 15,132 |
| 1985 | 422 | 62.6 | 8,282 | 23.31 | 16,159 |
| 1986 | 509 | 84.5 | 16,648 | 43.06 | 18,697 |
| 1987 | 726 | 120 | 42,553 | 76.3 | 24,832 |
| 1988 | 1,058 | 149 | 261,000 | 125.5 | 31,204 |

**G1     Currency in Circulation** (in millions of stated currency unit, except as otherwise indicated)

NOTES

1.  SOURCES: The main sources are the national publications listed on p. xiv–xvi, with gaps filled from League of Nations, *Statistical Yearbook, Memorandum on Currency and Central Banks, Money and Banking,* and *Monthly Bulletin of Statistics;* and International Monetary Fund, *International Financial Statistics.*
2.  Unless otherwise indicated, the statistics are of circulation at the end of each year.
3.  So far as possible, statistics are of currency in the hands of the public.

FOOTNOTES

[1] Currency in circulation outside the Treasury, the Federal Reserve Banks, and, from 1984 (2nd line), the vaults of depository institutions. Data are at 30 June to 1971 and at 31 December thereafter.

[2] Banknotes, Treasury notes, gold and silver certificates in circulation at 30 June to 1970 and at 31 December thereafter.

[3] Note issues of Ontario and Quebec banks to 1867 (1st line); Dominion notes and chartered bank notes from 1867 (2nd line) to 1913 (1st line), but excluding Dominion notes held by banks from 1871 (2nd line). From 1913 (2nd line) statistics are of currency outside banks. Figures from 1965 to 1974 are rounded to the nearest 10 million dollars.

[4] Including the total stock of silver coin in 1860–63 and of gold coin and bullion also in 1862–63.

[5] Total currency in circulation to 1931; currency in the hands of the public subsequently.

[6] In September.

[7] At 31 August.

[8] At 31 July.

[9] Note circulation to 1936 (1st line); currency in the hands of the public subsequently.

[10] Total currency in circulation. Statistics to 1910 and for 1931–38 are averages of monthly figures, those to 1910 being for the 12 months ending 30 June.

[11] Total currency in circulation to 1939; currency in the hands of the public subsequently.

[12] Currency outside banks, including US currency in circulation to 1947.

[13] Government currency in circulation to 1941 (1st line). Total currency from 1941 (2nd line) to 1951 (1st line), and currency in the hands of the public subsequently.

[14] Issues of paper money by banks to 1828, by the Treasury from 1830 to 1854 (1st line), and by the Treasury and banks subsequently, with issues of the Conversion Office, the Rediscount Department, and the Stabilization Office included as appropriate. Figures from 1971 to 1974 are rounded to the nearest 10 million cruzeiros.

[15] Total fiduciary circulation to 1936 (1st line); currency outside banks subsequently. There was an improvement in the coverage of bank holdings of currency in 1940.

[16] Total effective note circulation to 1936 (1st line); currency outside banks subsequently. The escudo (equal to one thousand pesos of the day) was introduced in 1960, but the unit is employed here from 1955 to 1975, whereafter it was replaced by a new peso, equal to 3,000 escudos. Figures from 1941 to 1944 and from 1951 to 1954 are rounded to the nearest 10 million pesos.

[17] Central Bank note circulation to 1937 (1st line); currency outside banks subsequently.

[18] Central Bank note circulation to 1927 (1st line). Total circulation from 1927 (2nd line) to 1936 (1st line) and currency in the hands of the public subsequently.

[19] Total currency in circulation to 1952 (1st line); currency in the hands of the public subsequently. Coverage was improved from 1967.

[20] At 30 November.

[21] Statistics to 1965 (1st line) are averages of weekly figures in December.

[22] The inti (equal to one thousand soles) was introduced in 1977, but the unit is employed here from 1975.

## G2 NORTH AMERICA: DEPOSITS IN COMMERCIAL BANKS (in millions of stated currency unit, except as otherwise indicated)

### 1834–1884

| | Canada[1] | USA[2] |
|---|---|---|
| | dollars | dollars |
| 1834 | ... | 102 |
| 1835 | ... | 122 |
| 1836 | ... | 166 |
| 1837 | ... | 190 |
| 1838 | ... | 146 |
| 1839 | ... | 143 |
| 1840 | ... | 120 |
| 1841 | ... | 108 |
| 1842 | ... | 88 |
| 1843 | ... | 78 |
| 1844 | ... | 117 |
| 1845 | ... | 114 |
| 1846 | ... | 125 |
| 1847 | ... | 120 |
| 1848 | ... | 143 |
| 1849 | ... | 121 |
| 1850 | ... | 146 |
| 1851 | ... | 175 |
| 1852 | ... | 182 |
| 1853 | ... | 195 |
| 1854 | ... | 239 |
| 1855 | ... | 236 |
| 1856 | 6.3 | 265 |
| 1857 | 5.8 | 288 |
| 1858 | 6.7 | 237 |
| 1859 | 8.0 | 328 |
| 1860 | 8.3 | 310 |
| 1861 | 9.7 | 319 |
| 1862 | 10 | 357 |
| 1863 | 12 | 504 |
| 1864 | 9.5 | 380 |
| 1865 | 15 | 689 |
| 1866 | 14 | 759 |
| 1867 | 14[1] / 15 | 744 |
| 1868 | 18 | 798 |
| 1869 | 19 | 772 |
| 1870 | 19[1] / 29 | 775 |
| 1871 | 29 | 888 |
| 1872 | 30 | 927 |
| 1873 | 31 | 1,625 |
| 1874 | 37 | 1,740 |
| 1875 | 34 | 2,009 |
| 1876 | 35 | 1,993 |
| 1877 | 35 | 2,006 |
| 1878 | 35 | 1,921 |
| 1879 | 38 | 2,149 |
| 1880 | 42 | 2,222 |
| 1881 | 46 | 2,649 |
| 1882 | 47 | 2,777 |
| 1883 | 45 | 2,884 |
| 1884 | 43 | 2,849 |

### 1885–1929

| | Canada[1] | El Salvador[3] | Mexico[4] | USA[2] |
|---|---|---|---|---|
| | dollars | colones | pesos | dollars |
| 1885 | 52 | ... | ... | 3,078 |
| 1886 | 49 | ... | ... | 3,186 |
| 1887 | 49 | ... | ... | 3,719 |
| 1888 | 56 | ... | ... | 3,891 |
| 1889 | 55 | ... | ... | 4,311 |
| 1890 | 54 | ... | ... | 4,576 |
| 1891 | 63 | ... | ... | 4,683 |
| 1892 | 69 | ... | ... | 5,298 |
| 1893 | 63 | ... | ... | 5,065 |
| 1894 | 69 | ... | ... | 5,268 |
| 1895 | 68 | ... | ... | 5,539 |
| 1896 | 71 | ... | ... | 5,486[2] / 2,844 |
| 1897 | 82 | ... | ... | 2,999 |
| 1898 | 91 | ... | ... | 3,431 |
| 1899 | 100 | ... | ... | 4,295 |
| 1900 | 109 | ... | ... | 4,345 |
| 1901 | 102 | ... | 11 | 5,279 |
| 1902 | 116 | ... | 14 | 5,541 |
| 1903 | 121 | ... | 13 | 5,771 |
| 1904 | 134 | ... | 12 | 6,057 |
| 1905 | 155 | ... | 25 | 6,898 |
| 1906 | 192 | ... | 41 | 7,403 |
| 1907 | 157 | ... | 39 | 7,708 |
| 1908 | 210 | ... | 47 | 7,381 |
| 1909 | 261 | ... | 78 | 8,115 |
| 1910 | 281 | ... | 86 | 8,566 |
| 1911 | 335 | ... | ... | 8,625 |
| 1912 | 380 | ... | ... | 9,217 |
| 1913 | 381 | ... | ... | 9,249 |
| 1914 | 350 | ... | ... | 10,306 |
| 1915 | 424 | ... | ... | 10,703 |
| 1916 | 458 | 3.2 | ... | 12,917 |
| 1917 | 569 | 3.4 | ... | 15,085 |
| 1918 | 711 | 3.3 | ... | 15,747 |
| 1919 | 703 | 4.4 | ... | 19,282 |
| 1920 | 657 | ... | ... | 21,571 |
| 1921 | 541 | ... | ... | 18,926 |
| 1922 | 538 | ... | ... | 20,106 |
| 1923 | 560 | ... | ... | 20,829 |
| 1924 | 595 | 5.4 | ... | 22,069 |
| 1925 | 597 | 6.3 | 109 | 24,325 |
| 1926 | 609 | 8.0 | 131 | 24,993 |
| 1927 | 684 | 7.8 | 111 | 25,257 |
| 1928 | 715 | 8.7 | 150 | 24,857 |
| 1929 | 729 | 7.5 | 161 | 25,160 |

**G2    NORTH AMERICA: Deposits in Commercial Banks** (in millions of stated currency unit, except a otherwise indicated)

1930–1974

| | Canada[1] | Costa Rica | Cuba | Dominican Republic | El Salvador[3] | Guatemala | Haiti |
|---|---|---|---|---|---|---|---|
| | dollars | colones | pesos | pesos | colones | quetzales | gourdes |
| 1930 | 642 | ... | ... | ... | 5.7 | ... | ... |
| 1931 | 567 | ... | ... | ... | 5.4 | ... | ... |
| 1932 | 466 | ... | 69 | ... | 7.8 | ... | ... |
| 1933 | 502 | 18 | 56 | ... | 7.1 | ... | ... |
| 1934 | 575 | 21 | 55 | ... | 6.9 | ... | ... |
| 1935 | 641 | 24 | 60 | ... | 8 | ... | ... |
| 1936 | 682 | 24 | 71 | 3.3 | 7.5[3] / 6.7 | 5.4 | ... |
| 1937 | 699 | 29 | 81 | 3.4 | 6.3 | 5.9 | ... |
| 1938 | 734 | 29 | 80 | 3.9 | 6 | 5.3 | ... |
| 1939 | 853 | 30 | 83 | 4.9 | 5.9 | 5.1 | ... |
| 1940 | 1,031 | 35 | 87 | 5.8 | 5.6 | 5.6 | ... |
| 1941 | 1,268 | 36 | 102 | 7 | 7.3 | 5.6 | ... |
| 1942 | 1,499 | 69 | 142 | 10 | 13 | 9.5 | ... |
| 1943 | 1,697 | 86 | 208 | 15 | 21 | 14 | ... |
| 1944 | 1,862 | 89 | 297 | 17 | 22 | 15 | ... |
| 1945 | 2,084 | 88[5] / 77 | 343[5] / 359 | 21 | 34[3] / 29 | 19 | ... |
| 1946 | 2,293 | 74 | 424 | 24 | 24 | 20 | ... |
| 1947 | 2,295 | 78 | 490 | 22 | 24 | 19 | ... |
| 1948 | 2,550 | 69 | 456 | 19 | 24 | 19 | ... |
| 1949 | 2,483 | 94 | 453 | 25 | 30 | 17 | ... |
| | *thousand million* | | | | | | |
| 1950 | 2.98 | 106 | 507 | 22 | 40 | 20 | 7.6 |
| 1951 | 2.98 | 116 | 505 | 29 | 46 | 20 | 12 |
| 1952 | 3.16 | 139 | 518 | 32 | 56 | 18 | 12 |
| 1953 | 3.06 | 152 | ... | 29 | 66 | 22 | 11 |
| 1954 | 3.36 | 170 | ... | 34 | 79 | 22 | 13 |
| 1955 | 3.56 | 187 | ... | 35 | 89 | 33 | 12 |
| 1956 | 3.46 | 191 | ... | 34 | 102 | 43[5] | 15 |
| 1957 | 3.62 | 201 | ... | | 107 | 50 | 18 |
| 1958 | 4.17 | 217[6] | ... | | 102 | 44 | 17 |
| 1959 | 4.27 | 237 | ... | 41 | 103 | 45 | 17 |
| 1960 | 4.50 | 235 | ... | 54 | 92 | 42 | 15 |
| 1961 | 5.24 | 232 | ... | 48 | 84 | 41 | 16 |
| 1962 | 5.51 | 269 | ... | 51 | 87 | 45 | 14 |
| 1963 | 6.03 | 310 | ... | 56 | 110 | 52 | 17 |
| 1964 | 6.64 | 339 | ... | 50 | 115 | 55 | 21 |
| 1965 | 7.71 | 360 | ... | 60 | 121 | 57 | 23 |
| 1966 | 8.26[1] | 367 | ... | 51 | 129 | 60 | 21 |
| 1967 | 13.93 | 547 | ... | 60 | 129 | 63 | 29 |
| 1968 | 13.61 | 539 | ... | 71 | 144 | 66 | 28 |
| 1969 | 12.52 | 606 | ... | 75 | 152 | 69 | 25 |
| 1970 | 12.37 | 623 | ... | 88 | 157 | 75 | 27 |
| 1971 | 14.20 | 875 | ... | 101 | 167 | 78 | 34 |
| 1972 | 15.89 | 973 | ... | 117 | 208 | 96 | 53 |
| 1973 | 16.97 | 1,225 | ... | 140 | 263 | 120 | 76 |
| 1974 | 16.56 | 1,395 | ... | 216 | 314 | 138 | 91 |

**G2    NORTH AMERICA: Deposits in Commercial Banks** (in millions of stated currency unit, except as otherwise indicated)

**1930–1974**

| | Honduras[7] | Jamaica | Mexico[4] | Nicaragua | Panama | Trinidad & Tobago | USA[2] |
|---|---|---|---|---|---|---|---|
| | lempiras | pounds | pesos | cordobas | balboas | dollars | dollars |
| 1930 | ... | ... | 176[4] | ... | ... | ... | 25,648 |
| 1931 | ... | ... | 128 | ... | ... | ... | 22,569 |
| 1932 | ... | ... | 108 | ... | ... | ... | 17,111 |
| 1933 | ... | ... | 159 | ... | ... | ... | 16,019 |
| 1934 | ... | ... | 188 | ... | ... | ... | 17,796 |
| 1935 | ... | ... | 204 | ... | ... | ... | 21,731 |
| 1936 | ... | ... | 215 | ... | ... | ... | 26,096 |
| 1937 | 4.3 | ... | 245 | ... | ... | ... | 27,578 |
| 1938 | 4.6 | ... | 200[11] | ... | ... | ... | 26,387 |
| 1939 | 5.7 | ... | 285 | ... | 4.4 | ... | 29,691 |
| 1940 | 6.0 | ... | 399 | 10 | 9.0 | ... | 33,646 |
| 1941 | 6.0 | ... | 472 | 11 | 13 | ... | 39,915 |
| 1942 | 8.6 | ... | 729 | 21 | 22 | ... | 44,611 |
| 1943 | 13 | ... | 1,195 | 32 | 31 | ... | 59,661 |
| 1944 | 18 | 6.4 | 1,542 | 40 | 38 | ... | 64,254 |
| 1945 | 21[7] 20 | 7.1 | 1,882 | 36 | 42 | ... | 72,526 |
| 1946 | 23 | 6.8 | 1,732 | 29 | 37 | 32 | 84,824 |
| 1947 | 22 | 7.5 | 1,685 | 34 | 33 | 26 | 88,030 |
| 1948 | 23[7] 21 | 7.7 | 1,796 | 41 | 29[8] 23 | 31 | 88,754 |
| 1949 | 18 | 7.7 | 1,975 | 55 | 18 | 42 | 87,999 |
| | | | | | | | thousand million dollars |
| 1950 | 19 | 9.1 | 3,074 | 63 | 19 | 37 | 92[2] |
| 1951 | 22 | 10 | 3,342 | 70 | 19 | 36 | 98 |
| 1952 | 23 | 11 | 3,430 | 90 | 20 | 42 | 102 |
| 1953 | 26 | 12 | 3,789 | 119 | 22 | 45 | 103 |
| 1954 | 28 | 12 | 4,087 | 138 | 23 | 52 | 107 |
| 1955 | 25 | 12 | 5,433 | 148 | 23 | 48 | 110 |
| 1956 | 27 | 14 | 5,958 | 136 | 23 | 50 | 111 |
| 1957 | 23 | 16 | 6,400 | 129 | 24 | 69 | 110 |
| 1958 | 24 | 16 | 6,774 | 128 | 24 | 62 | 115 |
| 1959 | 26 | 18 | 8,184 | 123 | 26 | 62 | 116[2] |
| | | | thousand million | | | | |
| 1960 | 25 | 19 | 8.95 | 129 | 26 | 70 | 116 |
| 1961 | 27 | 15 | 9.53 | 141 | 29 | 75 | 120 |
| 1962 | 30 | 21 | 11.06 | 186 | 34 | 71 | 122 |
| 1963 | 34 | 19 | 13.16 | 220 | 38 | 88 | 125 |
| 1964 | 41 | 21 | 15.51 | 275 | 34 | 84 | 131 |
| 1965 | 48 | 20 | 16.56 | 339 | 38 | 80 | 137 |
| 1966 | 46 | 23 | 18.64 | 338 | 43 | 85 | 139 |
| 1967 | 56 | 24 | 19.99 | 318 | 51 | 87 | 148 |
| 1968 | 65 | 32 dollars | 23.65 | 276 | 63 | 90 | 160 |
| 1969 | 73 | 74 | 27.26 | 293 | 70 | 89 | 164 |
| 1970 | 81 | 80 | 30.38 | 327 | 85 | 95 | 171 |
| 1971 | 88 | 102 | 32.65 | 367 | 88 | 108 | 182 |
| 1972 | 101 | 101 | 37.90 | 417 | 119 | 130 | 200 |
| 1973 | 125 | 136 | 45.72 | 733 | 131 | 133 | 209 |
| 1974 | 132 | 156 | 56.3 | 861 | 173 | 171 | 214 |

**G2    NORTH AMERICA: Deposits in Commercial Banks** (in millions of stated currency unit, except as otherwise indicated)

| | Canada[1] thousand million dollars | Costa Rica colones | Dominican Republic pesos | El Salvador colones | Guatemala quetzales | Haiti gourdes |
|---|---|---|---|---|---|---|
| 1975 | 19.91 | 1,889 | 210 | 392 | 169 | 111 |
| 1976 | 19.75 | 2,273 | 216 | 512 | 237 | 136 |
| 1977 | 21.86 | 3,065 | 256 | 550 | 280 | 156 |
| 1978 | 23.06 | 3,857 | 233 | 579 | 292 | 183 |
| 1979 | 22.93 | 4,231 | 323 | 567 | 320 | 187 |
| 1980 | 25.88₅ | 4,862 | 300 | 693 | 320 | 224 |
| 1981 | 27.86 | 7,185 | 336 | 693₆ | 327 | 295 |
| 1982 | 30.62 | 12,888 | 368 | 810 | 340 | 318 |
| 1983 | 34.77 | 18,401 | 358 | 785 | 346 | 357 |
| 1984 | 44.08 | 21,399 | 517 | 937 | 382 | 2,584 |
| 1985 | 61.81 | 22,367 | 658 | 1,151 | 614 | … |
| 1986 | 72.79 | 29,016 | 1,040 | 1,528 | 749 | 544 |
| 1987 | 76.87 | 27,624 | 1,289 | 1,370 | 808 | 659 |
| 1988 | 81.43 | 40,186 | 2,282 | 1,567 | 916 | 716 |

| | Honduras lempiras | Jamaica dollars | Mexico thousand million pesos | Nicaragua cordobas | Panama balboas | Trinidad & Tobago dollars | USA[2] thousand million dollars |
|---|---|---|---|---|---|---|---|
| 1975 | 144 | 195 | 68.6 | 809 | 149 | 254 | 222 |
| 1976 | 184 | 200 | 76.9₅ | 976 | 164 | 395 | 234 |
| 1977 | 214 | 292 | 106 | 998 | 185 | 494 | 251 |
| 1978 | 257 | 397 | 143 | 915 | 214 | 641 | 270 |
| 1979 | 270 | 410 | 197 | … | 263 | 735 | 286 |
| 1980 | 323 | 457 | 260 | 2,134 | 293 | 870 | 301 |
| 1981 | 328 | 492 | 315₅ | 2,656 | 319 | 1,287 | 321 |
| 1982 | 380 | 560 | 455 | 3,319 | 330 | 1,772 | 350 |
| | | | | new cordobas | | | |
| 1983 | 433 | 691 | 676 | 5.42 | 327 | 1,576 | 383 |
| 1984 | 447 | 882 | 1,075 | 9.37 | 334 | 1,500 | 405 |
| 1985 | 427 | 980 | 1,610 | 25.75 | 359 | 1,483 | 462 |
| 1986 | 493 | 1,410 | 2,468 | 90.52 | 394 | 1,260 | 555 |
| 1987 | 583 | 1,407 | 4,928 | 689 | 396 | 1,357 | 560 |
| 1988 | 628 | 2,517 | 7,130 | … | 275 | 1,082 | 590 |

**G2    SOUTH AMERICA: DEPOSITS IN COMMERCIAL BANKS** (in millions of stated currency unit, except as otherwise indicated)

| | Argentina[9] | Bolivia[10] | Brazil[11] milreis or cruzeiros | Chile[12] | Columbia[13] | Ecuador[14] | Paraguay | Peru[15] thousand libras | Uruguay | Venezuela[16] |
|---|---|---|---|---|---|---|---|---|---|---|
| | pesos | bolivianos | cruzeiros | pesos | pesos | sucres | pesos | libras | pesos | bolivares |
| 1897 | ... | ... | ... | ... | ... | ... | ... | 1,371 | ... | ... |
| 1898 | ... | ... | ... | ... | ... | ... | ... | 1,480 | ... | ... |
| 1899 | ... | ... | ... | ... | ... | ... | ... | 1,558 | ... | ... |
| 1900 | ... | ... | ... | ... | ... | ... | ... | 1,774 | ... | ... |
| 1901 | ... | ... | ... | ... | ... | ... | ... | 1,929 | ... | ... |
| 1902 | ... | ... | ... | 141 | ... | ... | ... | 2,249 | ... | ... |
| 1903 | 504 | ... | ... | 136 | ... | ... | ... | 2,638 | ... | ... |
| 1904 | 585 | ... | ... | 171 | ... | ... | ... | 2,727 | ... | ... |
| 1905 | 720 | ... | ... | 314 | ... | ... | ... | 3,274 | ... | ... |
| 1906 | 755 | ... | ... | 289 | ... | ... | ... | 3,759 | ... | ... |
| 1907 | 779 | ... | ... | 415 | ... | ... | ... | 4,035 | ... | ... |
| 1908 | 876 | ... | ... | 415 | ... | ... | ... | 4,366 | ... | ... |
| 1909 | 1,157 | ... | ... | 395 | ... | ... | ... | 4,267 | ... | ... |
| 1910 | 1,332 | ... | ... | 475 | ... | ... | ... | 5,630 | ... | ... |
| 1911 | 1,375 | ... | ... | 524[12] 290 | ... | ... | ... | 7,368 | ... | ... |
| 1912 | 1,481 | ... | ... | 225 | ... | ... | ... | 7,664 | ... | ... |
| 1913 | 1,411 | 12 | 475 | 222 | ... | 3.7 | ... | 8,108 | 12 | 10 |
| 1914 | 1,189 | 12 | 389 | 217 | ... | 3.1 | ... | 5,374[15] 1,906 | 12 | 8.5 |
| 1915 | 1,419 | 17 | 440 | 223 | ... | 5.0 | ... | 2,083 | 13 | 7.7 |
| 1916 | 1,596 | 19 | 575 | 242 | ... | 6.2 | ... | 2,747 | 18 | 9.4 |
| 1917 | 1,891 | 26 | 710 | 266 | ... | 7.4 | ... | 3,698 | 21 | 14 |
| 1918 | 2,666 | 21 | 1,059 | 407 | ... | 8.8 | ... | 4,663 | 27 | 17 |
| 1919 | 2,834 | 26 | 1,196 | 439 | ... | 10 | ... | 6,727 | 38 | 48 |
| 1920 | 3,294 | 20 | 1,343 | 529 | ... | 12 | ... | 7,221 | 30 | 47 |
| 1921 | 3,177 | 26 | 2,100 | 559 | ... | 11 | ... | 6,609 | 32 | 42 |
| 1922 | 3,297 | 35 | 2,519 | 540 | ... | 12 | ... | 6,161 | 28 | 37 |
| 1923 | 3,317 | 28 | 2,653 | 496 | ... | 12 | ... | 6,574 | 33 | 42 |
| 1924 | 3,320 | 29 | 2,671 | 530 | 20 | 12 | ... | 7,248 | 26 | 45 |
| 1925 | 3,335 | 31 | 2,420 | 636 | 27 | 13 | ... | 7,086 | 25 | 58 |
| 1926 | 3,359[9] 1,124 | 26 | 2,603 | 724 | 35 | 13 | ... | 6,828 | 29 | 78 |
| 1927 | 1,195 | 27 | 3,088 | 539 | 45 | 12[14] | ... | 7,145 | 31 | 78 |
| 1928 | 1,302 | 28 | 3,688 | 564 | 54 | 29 | 38 | 9,402 | 30 | 118 |
| 1929 | 1,178 | 26 | 3,487 | 512 | 51[5] 40 | 25 | 52[6] | 8,803 | 37 | 123 |
| | | | | | | | | soles | | |
| 1930 | 1,189 | 21 | 2,856 | 434 | 30 | 23 | 161 | 49 | 41 | 163 |
| 1931 | 971 | 19 | 3,490 | 419 | 27 | 13 | 114 | 54 | 43 | 127 |
| 1932 | 1,083 | 49 | 4,732 | 706 | 34 | 26 | 104 | 43 | 54 | 116 |
| 1933 | 1,171 | 48 | 4,447 | 893 | 39 | 44 | 141 | 61 | 44 | 115 |
| 1934 | 1,111 | 136 | 5,056 | 1,124 | 49 | 51 | 226 | 89 | 43 | 115 |
| 1935 | 1,065 | 224 | 4,873 | 1,191 | 49 | 45 | 426 | 96 | 39 | 156 |
| 1936 | 1,289 | 236[10] 149 | 5,245[11] 4,780 | 1,226[5] 1,293 | 58[13] 49 | 60[14] 64 | 322[6] 580 | 114 | 36 | 136 |
| 1937 | 1,402 | 144 | 5,980 | 1,364 | 54 | 66 | 837 | 125 | 44 | 132[16] 106 |
| 1938 | 1,312 | 168 | 7,590 | 1,393 | 61 | 71 | 593 | 142 | 42 | 114 |
| 1939 | 1,482 | 220 | 7,080 | 1,571 | 64 | 73 | 530 | 153 | 44 | 129 |

**G2** **SOUTH AMERICA: Deposits in Commercial Banks** (in millions of stated currency unit, except as otherwise indicated)

| | Argentina[9] | Bolivia[10] | Brazil[11] | Chile[12] | Colombia | Ecuador[14] |
|---|---|---|---|---|---|---|
| | thousand million pesos | bolivianos | thousand million cruzeiros | thousand million pesos | pesos | sucres |
| 1940 | 1.52[9] 1.30 | 301 | 7.1 | 1.93 | 79 | 103 |
| 1941 | 1.77 | 345 | 9.1 | 2.34 | 81 | 119 |
| 1942 | 2.12 | 701 | 11 | 2.79 | 113 | 176 |
| 1943 | 2.58 | 675 | 16 | 3.59 | 169 | 260 |
| 1944 | 3.18 | 734 | 22 | 4.13 | 210 | 308 |
| 1945 | 3.83 | 794[10] 726 | 24[11] 20 | 4.90 | 254 | 310 |
| 1946 | 4.88 | 718 | 22 | 6.44 | 313 | 348 |
| 1947 | 5.48 | 699 | 24 | 7.96 | 334 | 272 |
| 1948 | 7.03 | 1,086 | 26 | 8.96 | 373 | 306[14] 272 |
| 1949 | 8.51 | 1,310 | 32 | 11 | 421 | 268 |
| 1950 | 10.14 | 1,685 | 45 | 12[12] 10 | 488 | 390 |
| 1951 | 11.38 | 2,041 | 52 | 13 | 593 | 340 |
| 1952 | 12.16 | 2,788 | 60 | 18 | 684 | 439 |
| 1953 | 15.67 | 4,603 | 71 | 21 | 830 | 461 |
| | | thousand million bolivianos | | | | |
| 1954 | 17.14 | 7 | 85 | 31 | 1,059 | 562 |
| 1955 | 19.79 | 16 | 102 | 52 | 1,113 | 515 |
| 1956 | 24.09[6] 26 | 49 | 127 | 72 | 1,410 | 593 |
| 1957 | 26 | 72 | 176 | 94 | 1,500 | 608 |
| 1958 | 39 | 56 | 216 | 128 | 1,849 | 600 |
| 1959 | 58 | 62 | 322 | 169 | 2,093 | 724 |
| | | | | million escudos | | |
| 1960 | 73 | 61 | 438 | 225 | 2,324 | 800 |
| 1961 | 84 | 77 | 611 | 257 | 3,043 | 829 |
| 1962 | 84 | 94 | 1,038 | 327 | 3,836 | 942 |
| | | million pesos | | | | |
| 1963 | 116 | 122 | 1,704 | 450 | 4,144 | 1,093 |
| 1964 | 168 | 141 | 3,070 | 644 | 5,098 | 1,212 |
| 1965 | 201 | 180 | 5,800 | 1,137 | 5,937 | 1,203 |
| 1966 | 275 | 229 | 6,192 | 1,567 | 6,994 | 1,433 |
| | | | thousand million new cruzeiros | | | |
| 1967 | 363 | 237 | 9.6 | 1,922 | 8,726 | 1,771 |
| 1968 | 513 | 280 | 12.8 | 2,774 | 9,964 | 2,148 |
| 1969 | 564 | 307 | 16.8 | 3,698 | 12,080 | 2,496 |
| | | | | thousand million escudos | | |
| 1970 | 706 | 365 | 21.4 | 5.65 | 14,005 | 2,955 |
| 1971 | 1,010 | 429 | 28.2 | 12.3 | 15,647 | 3,503 |
| 1972 | 1,567 | 576 | 40.4 | 25.9 | 20,055 | 4,131 |
| 1973 | 2,981 | 849 | 59.4 | 128 | 28,151 | 5,503 |
| 1974 | 4,575 | 1,461 | 79.3 | 487 | 31,734 | 8,192 |

**G2**   **SOUTH AMERICA: Deposits in Commercial Banks** (in millions of stated currency unit, except as otherwise indicated)

|      | Guyana | Paraguay | Peru[15] | Uruguay | Venezuela |
|------|--------|----------|----------|---------|-----------|
|      | dollars | guaranies | soles | pesos | bolivares |
| 1940 | ... | 670 | 209 | 42 | 161 |
| 1941 | ... | 1,070 | 251 | 50 | 151 |
| 1942 | ... | 1,430 | 352 | 55 | 194 |
|      |     | guaranies |       |       |       |
| 1943 | ... | 24 | 465 | 79 | 271 |
| 1944 | ... | 23 | 556 | [107][17] | 295 |
| 1945 | ... | 26 | 588 | 131 | 350 |
| 1946 | ... | 29 | 780 | 150 | 446 |
| 1947 | ... | 26 | 928 | 134 | 445 |
| 1948 | ... | 44 | 1,067 [15] / 813 | 151 | 572 |
| 1949 | ... | 68 | 790 | 149 | 695 |
| 1950 | ... | 101 | 1,008 | 177 |       |
| 1951 | ... | 180 | 1,321 | 174 | 795 |
| 1952 | ... | 238 | 1,508 | 190 | 981 |
| 1953 | ... | 403 | 1,668 | 225 | 1,122 |
| 1954 | ... | 453 | 1,780 | 220 | 1,166 |
|      |     |     | thousand million |       |       |
| 1955 | 13 | 608 | 1.87 | 229 | 1,356 |
| 1956 | 13 | 841 | 2.17 | 261 | 1,616 |
| 1957 | 13 | 772 | 2.19 | 285 | 2,313 |
| 1958 | 13 | 970 | 2.24 | 399 | 2,631 |
| 1959 | 15 | 1,025 | 33 | 596 | 2,392 |
| 1960 | 16 | 1,060 | 3.80 | 767 | 2,045 |
| 1961 | 14 | 1,381 | 4.56 | 858 | 2,251 |
| 1962 | 18 | 1,347 | 4.67 | 669 | 2,182 |
| 1963 | 18 | 1,610 | 5.17 | 984 | 2,248 |
| 1964 | 21 | 1,849 | 6.22 | 1,388 | 2,933 |
| 1965 | 17 | 1,988 | 8 | 2,762 | 2,874 |
| 1966 | 19 | 2,132 [6] | 10 | 3,040 | 2,903 |
| 1967 | 19 | 2,248 | 11 | 8,820 | 3,396 |
| 1968 | 21 | 2,415 | 12 | 13,402 | 3,672 |
| 1969 | 23 | 2,484 | 14 | 16,325 | 4,064 |
|      |     |     |     | thousand million |       |
| 1970 | 22 | 2,926 | 28 | 17 | 4,481 |
| 1971 | 26 | 3,206 | 29 | 29 | 5,405 |
| 1972 | 37 | 4,041 | 39 | 57 | 6,735 |
| 1973 | 42 | 5,604 | 50 | 106 | 8,290 |
| 1974 | 65 | 7,282 | 76 | 174 | 11,208 |

**G2    SOUTH AMERICA:** Deposits in Commercial Banks

| | Argentina | Bolivia | Brazil | Chile | Colombia[13] | Ecuador |
|---|---|---|---|---|---|---|
| | | | thousand million cruzeiros | | | |
| | thousand million | | | thousand million | thousand million | thousand million |
| | pesos | pesos | cruzeiros | pesos | pesos | pesos |
| 1975 | 13.6 | 1,605 | 114 | 1.62 | 40.9 | 9.9 |
| 1976 | 51.6 | 2,425 | 153 | 5.2 | 54.8 | 13.6 |
| 1977 | 101 | 2,873 | 215 | ... | 69.4[13] | 16.9 |
| 1978 | 230 | 2,829 | 307 | 17.6 | 76.5 | 19.5 |
| 1979 | 596 | 2,916 | 522 | 30.2 | 93.6 | 23.2 |
| 1980 | 1,093 | 4,777 | 907 | 49.7 | 121 | 31 |
| 1981 | 1,589 | 6,301 | 1,739 | 37.4 | 147 | 36 |
| 1982 | 6,128 | 17,659 | 2,967 | 49.2 | 181 | 46 |
| | million australes | thousand million | | | | |
| 1983 | 23.6 | 50.7 | 5,798 | 60.3 | 221 | 59 |
| 1984 | 121 | 425 | 16,831 | 66.1 | 267 | 82 |
| 1985 | 992 | 24,799 | 71,432 | 68.7 | 341 | 98 |
| | thousand million | million million | million million | | | |
| 1986 | 1.6 | 69 | 282 | 106 | ... | 112 |
| 1987 | 3.3 | 106 | 573 | 93 | 577 | 144 |
| 1988 | 11.8 | 158 | 3,468 | 204 | 723 | 209 |

| | Guyana | Paraguay | Peru | Uruguay | Venezuela |
|---|---|---|---|---|---|
| | | | | thousand million | thousand million |
| | dollars | guaranies | intis | new pesos | bolivares |
| 1975 | 110 | 8,550 | 85 | 0.5 | 15 |
| 1976 | 111 | 11,033 | 99 | 0.8 | 20 |
| 1977 | 136 | 14,690 | 118 | 1.1 | 25 |
| 1978 | 138 | 20,300 | 169 | 1.7 | 28 |
| 1979 | 133 | 23,292 | 256 | 3.4 | 30 |
| 1980 | 155 | 28,566 | 344 | 4.7 | 35 |
| 1981 | 158 | 29,276 | 481 | 4.4[6] | 39 |
| 1982 | 199 | 25,704 | 693 | 5.4 | 36 |
| 1983 | 234 | 34,918 | 1,403 | 6.2 | 46 |
| 1984 | 276 | 44,758 | 3,066 | 9.9 | 48 |
| | | thousand million | thousand million | | |
| 1985 | 312 | 56 | 13 | 22.2 | 55 |
| 1986 | 365 | 67 | 25 | 40.8 | 73 |
| 1987 | 600 | 114 | 49 | 57.9 | 95 |
| 1988 | 1,031 | 165 | 285 | 93.8 | 127 |

**G2     Deposits in Commercial Banks** (in millions of stated currency unit, except as otherwise indicated)

NOTES

1. SOURCES: The main sources were the national publications listed on p. xiv–xvi League of Nations, *Memorandum on Commercial Banks, Money and Banking,* and *Statistical Yearbooks;* and International Monetary Fund, *International Financial Statistics.*
2. Except as otherwise indicated the statistics are for the end of each year.
3. So far as possible, and except as otherwise indicated, statistics relate to demand deposits in the hands of the public; i.e. they exclude interbank deposits and deposits of central government departments.

FOOTNOTES

[1] Non-interest-bearing deposits in banks in Ontario and Quebec to 1867 (1st line) and of chartered banks in Canada to 1870. Subsequently publicly held demand deposits. From 1967 data relate to the average of all Wednesdays during the year.

[2] Total bank deposits to 1896 (1st line), public demand deposits in commercial banks subsequently, at 30 June to 1950, at 31 December from 1951 to 1959, and on the average for December subsequently. Data for non-national banks prior to 1896 are known to be incomplete, and some are reported for dates other than 30 June. More reliable estimates of the non-national bank component are available for the period 1865–96 in David I. Fand, *Banks in the Post-Civil War Period in the United States, 1875–1896* (unpublished University of Chicago Ph.D thesis), and in Federal Deposit Insurance Corporation, *Annual Report, 1934.* The latter are adjusted for non-reporting banks, but not for under-reporting, the former are adjusted for both. Data for 1875–81 are for August. These estimates, together with the component used here, are as follows:

**Non-national bank deposits according to:**

| | Comptroller of Currency | Fand | FDIC | | Comptroller of Currency | Fand |
|------|------|------|------|------|------|------|
| 1865 | 75 | | 635 | 1881 | 1,285 | 1,823 |
| 1866 | 64 | | 443 | 1882 | 1,412 | 1,844 |
| 1867 | 58 | | 597 | 1883 | 1,547 | 2,016 |
| 1868 | 53 | | 665 | 1884 | 1,616 | 2,057 |
| 1869 | 56 | | 751 | 1885 | 1,659 | 2,141 |
| 1870 | 70 | | 868 | 1886 | 1,727 | 2,395 |
| 1871 | 97 | | 1,045 | 1887 | 2,069 | 2,528 |
| 1872 | 121 | | 1,255 | 1888 | 2,175 | 2,569 |
| 1873 | 789 | | 1,276 | 1889 | 2,391 | 2,694 |
| 1874 | 912 | | 1,307 | 1890 | 2,598 | 2,971 |
| 1875 | 1,111 | 1,450 | 1,399 | 1891 | 2,709 | 3,082 |
| 1876 | 1,151 | 1,453 | 1,408 | 1892 | 2,970 | 3,409 |
| 1877 | 1,188 | 1,383 | | 1893 | 3,126 | 3,312 |
| 1878 | 1,107 | 1,275 | | 1894 | 3,039 | 3,311 |
| 1879 | 1,059 | 1,272 | | 1895 | 3,260 | 3,604 |
| 1880 | 1,137 | 1,495 | | 1896 | 3,345 | 3,545 |

[3] Including the National Bank to 1945 (1st line). The reason for the break in 1936 is not clear in the sources.

[4] Data to 1910 and for 1931–38 are annual averages, those to 1910 being for the 12 months ended 30 June.

[5] There was a change in the coverage of the series.

[6] There was an improvement in the collection of data subsequently.

[7] Including central bank deposits to 1945 (1st line), and government deposits to 1948 (1st line).

[8] Including government banks to 1948 (1st line).

[9] Total deposits to 1926 (1st line), current account deposits from then to 1940 (1st line) and private sector monetary deposits subsequently.

[10] All sight deposits (including those of the Central Bank) to 1936 (1st line), and all such deposits other than those of the national government from 1936 (2nd line) to 1945 (1st line).

[11] All demand deposits to 1936 (1st line), those of the public subsequently. Bank of Brazil deposits are included to 1945 (1st line).

[12] Total deposits to 1911 (1st line), demand deposits of the public subsequently, with a restriction to major banks from 1950 (2nd line).

[13] All demand deposits to 1936 (1st line), those of the public subsequently, but interbank deposits are not excluded until 1978.

[14] All demand deposits to 1936 (1st line), but of the six principal banks only to 1927. Subsequent statistics are of demand deposits of the public, including those at the central bank and at development banks to 1948 (1st line).

[15] Total deposits to 1914 (1st line), current account deposits subsequently, with some government deposits included up to 1948 (1st line).

[16] Total deposits to 1937 (1st line), demand deposits of the public subsequently.

[17] At 30 June.

**G3  NORTH AMERICA: SAVINGS BANK DEPOSITS** (in millions of stated currency unit, except as otherwise indicated)

### 1820–1864

| | USA[1] | | Barbados[2] | Canada[3] | Jamaica[4] | Newfoundland | Trinidad | USA[1] |
|---|---|---|---|---|---|---|---|---|
| | dollars | | thousand pounds | dollars | thousand pounds | dollars | thousand pounds | dollars |
| 1820 | 1 | 1865 | ... | ... | ... | ... | ... | 243 |
| 1821 | ... | 1866 | ... | ... | ... | ... | ... | 283 |
| 1822 | ... | 1867 | ... | ... | ... | ... | ... | 337 |
| 1823 | ... | 1868 | ... | 5.1 | ... | ... | ... | 393 |
| 1824 | ... | 1869 | ... | 6.4 | ... | ... | ... | 458 |
| 1825 | 3 | 1870 | ... | 8.8 | 76 | ... | ... | 550 |
| 1826 | ... | 1871 | ... | 10 | 171 | ... | ... | 651 |
| 1827 | ... | 1872 | ... | 11 | 223 | ... | ... | 735 |
| 1828 | ... | 1873 | ... | 13 | 159 | ... | ... | 802 |
| 1829 | ... | 1874 | ... | 14 | 183 | ... | ... | 865 |
| 1830 | 7 | 1875 | ... | 14 | 229 | ... | ... | 924 |
| 1831 | ... | 1876 | ... | 14 | 245 | ... | ... | 941 |
| 1832 | ... | 1877 | ... | 14 | 256 | ... | ... | 866 |
| 1833 | ... | 1878 | ... | 14 | 274 | ... | ... | 880 |
| 1834 | ... | 1879 | ... | 15 | 295 | ... | ... | 803 |
| 1835 | 11 | 1880 | ... | 15 | 340 | ... | ... | 819 |
| 1836 | ... | 1881 | 36 | 24 | 335 | 1.3 | 41 | 892 |
| 1837 | ... | 1882 | 40 | 30 | 315 | 1.4 | ... | 967 |
| 1838 | ... | 1883 | 49 | 35 | 326 | 1.5 | ... | 1,025 |
| 1839 | ... | 1884 | 57 | 38 | 351 | 1.7 | 87 | 1,073 |
| 1840 | 14 | 1885 | 62 | 42 | 360 | 1.8 | 88 | 1,095 |
| 1841 | ... | 1886 | 65 | 46 | 363 | 1.8 | 97 | 1,142 |
| 1842 | ... | 1887 | 78 | 51 | 365 | 2 | 110 | 1,235 |
| 1843 | ... | 1888 | 97 | 52 | 395 | 2 | 122 | 1,364 |
| 1844 | ... | 1889 | 126 | 54 | 410[4] | 2.2 | 128 | 1,425 |
| 1845 | 25 | 1890 | 135 | 52 | 431 | 2.3 | 145 | 1,525 |
| 1846 | 27 | 1891 | 123 | 50 | 428 | 2.5 | 144 | 1,623 |
| 1847 | 32 | 1892 | 130 | 52 | 418 | 3 | 158 | 1,713 |
| 1848 | 33 | 1893 | 153 | 55 | 458 | 3.1 | 164 | 1,785 |
| 1849 | 36 | 1894 | 158 | 56 | 454 | 2.8 | 175 | 1,748 |
| 1850 | 43 | 1895 | 181 | 58 | 465 | 1.2 | 195 | 1,811 |
| 1851 | 51 | 1896 | 182 | 61 | 471 | 1.4 | 230 | 1,907 |
| 1852 | 60 | 1897 | 211 | 63 | 470 | 1.4 | 233 | 1,939 |
| 1853 | 72 | 1898 | 219 | 66 | 494 | 1.2 | 246 | 2,066 |
| 1854 | 78 | 1899 | 226 | 66 | 469 | 1.1 | 256 | 2,230 |
| 1855 | 84 | 1900 | 221[2] | 71 | 451 | 1.2 | 278 | 2,450 |
| 1856 | 96 | 1901 | 197 | 75 | 425 | 1.3 | 291 | 2,597 |
| 1857 | 99 | 1902 | 202 | 79 | 436 | 1.4 | 314 | 2,750 |
| 1858 | 108 | 1903 | 217 | 82 | 426 | 1.6 | 309 | 2,935 |
| 1859 | 129 | 1904 | 224 | 85 | 395 | 1.8 | 308 | 3,060 |
| 1860 | 149 | 1905 | 245 | 87 | 389 | 2 | 301 | 3,261 |
| 1861 | 147 | 1906 | 263 | 89[3] | 399 | 2.2 | 286 | 3,482 |
| 1862 | 169 | 1907 | 293 | 91 | 403 | 2.4 | 329 | 3,690 |
| 1863 | 206 | 1908 | 306 | 92 | 390 | 2.6 | 337 | 3,661 |
| 1864 | 236 | 1909 | 348 | 90 | 364 | 2.6 | 333 | 3,713 |

**G3**  **NORTH AMERICA: Savings Bank Deposits** (in millions of stated currency unit, except as otherwise indicated)

| | Barbados[2] | Canada[3] | Jamaica[4] | Mexico | Newfoundland | Trinidad & Tobago[5] | USA[1] |
|---|---|---|---|---|---|---|---|
| | thousand pounds | dollars | thousand pounds | pesos | dollars | thousand pounds | dollars |
| 1910 | 426 | 91 | 334 | ... | 2.8 | 361 | 4,071[1] |
| | | | | | | | 3,306 |
| 1911 | 436 | 93 | 333 | ... | 3 | 369 | 3,408 |
| 1912 | 435 | 98 | 317 | ... | 3.1 | 396 | 3,578 |
| 1913 | 426 | 97 | 320 | ... | 2.8 | 427 | 3,749 |
| 1914 | 416 | 95 | 286 | ... | 2.5 | 420 | 3,902 |
| 1915 | 457 | 92 | 267 | ... | 2.4 | 369 | 3,959 |
| 1916 | 450 | 94 | 260 | ... | 2.4 | 383 | 4,210 |
| 1917 | 475[1] | 100 | 279[4] | ... | 2.5 | 369 | 4,487 |
| 1918 | 491 | 95 | 287 | ... | 2.2 | 343 | 4,501 |
| 1919 | 524 | 100 | 417 | ... | 2.5 | 353 | 4,895 |
| 1920 | 687 | 95 | 573 | ... | ... | 535 | 5,314 |
| 1921 | 612 | 98 | 534 | ... | 2.2 | 499 | 5,655 |
| 1922 | 582 | 93 | 542 | ... | 2 | 434 | 5,833 |
| 1923 | 592 | 91 | 560 | ... | 1.9 | 382 | 6,334 |
| 1924 | 684 | 98 | 542 | ... | 1.9 | 364 | 6,751 |
| 1925 | 643 | 99 | 545 | ... | 2 | 358 | 7,203 |
| 1926 | 624 | 100 | 571 | ... | 2 | 367 | 7,599 |
| 1927 | 604 | 102 | 574 | ... | 2 | 418 | 8,143 |
| 1928 | 577 | 104 | 572 | 0.5 | 2.2 | 470 | 8,707 |
| 1929 | 539 | 99 | 613 | 3.3 | 2.2 | 468 | 9,038 |
| 1930 | 537 | 95 | 640 | 6.3 | 2 | 470 | 9,274 |
| 1931 | 513 | 95 | 647 | 5.1 | 1.5 | 458 | 10,257 |
| 1932 | 596 | 93 | 653 | 7.1 | 1.2 | 432 | 10,696 |
| 1933 | 658 | 92 | 745 | 12 | 1.3 | 457 | 10,793 |
| 1934 | 694 | 90 | 830 | 18 | 1.8 | 431 | 10,868 |
| 1935 | 745 | 89 | 794 | 22 | 2.3 | 455 | 11 |
| 1936 | 788 | 92 | 750 | 28 | 2.7 | 516 | 11 |
| 1937 | 843 | 95 | 802 | 34 | 3.1 | 586 | 11 |
| | | | | | | dollars | |
| 1938 | 898 | 100 | 824 | 33 | ... | 3.1 | 11 |
| 1939 | 936 | 105 | 892 | 37 | ... | 3.1 | 12 |
| 1940 | 997 | 103 | ... | 37 | ... | 3 | 12 |
| 1941 | 1,013 | 99 | 901 | 46 | ... | 3.4 | 12 |
| 1942 | 1,151 | 96 | 1,051 | 57 | ... | 4.4 | 12 |
| 1943 | 1,405 | 108 | 1,333 | 101 | ... | 6.4 | 13 |
| 1944 | 1,653 | 132 | 1,853 | 164 | 13[7] | 7.5 | 14 |
| 1945 | 1,989 | 156 | 2,378 | 249 | 19 | 8.9 | 18 |
| | dollars | | | | | | |
| 1946 | 9.9 | 176 | 3,011 | 239 | 21 | 9.5 | 20 |
| 1947 | 9.6 | 189 | 2,914 | 276 | 21 | 9.5 | 21 |
| 1948 | 9.5 | 206 | 2,320 | 329 | 22 | 9.7 | 22 |
| 1949 | 9.8 | 222 | 2,275 | 398 | 22 | 9.7 | 23 |

**G3**  **NORTH AMERICA: Savings Bank Deposits** (in millions of stated currency unit, except as otherwise indicated)

| | Barbados | Canada[3] | Jamaica | Mexico[6] | Newfoundland[7] | Trinidad & Tobago[5] | USA[1] |
|---|---|---|---|---|---|---|---|
| | | | | thousand million | | | thousand million |
| | thousand pounds | dollars | thousand pounds | pesos | dollars | dollars | dollars |
| 1950 | 10 | 231 | 2,276 | 0.45 | 23 | 11 | 23 |
| 1951 | 11 | 232 | 2,368 | 0.60[6] | 25 | 12 | 24 |
| | | | | 1.09 | | | |
| 1952 | 12 | 238 | 2,710 | 1.14 | 25 | 12 | 25 |
| 1953 | 12 | 253 | 2,891 | 1.44 | 26 | 13 | 27 |
| 1954 | 13 | 257 | 3,107 | 2.75 | 27 | 14 | 29 |
| 1955 | 15 | 275 | 3,296 | 2.97 | 28 | 15 | 30 |
| 1956 | 16 | 293 | 3,621 | 3.22 | 29 | 14 | 32 |
| 1957 | 18 | 291 | 3,928 | 3.36 | 28 | 13 | 33 |
| 1958 | 19 | 301 | 4,515 | 3.63 | 28 | 13 | 35 |
| 1959 | 20 | 314 | 4,896 | 5.34 | 28 | 13 | 36 |
| 1960 | 20 | 302 | 4,623 | 79 | 28 | 13 | 37 |
| 1961 | 18 | 325 | 5,270 | 8.18 | 28 | 13 | 39 |
| 1962 | 17 | 347 | 5,429 | 10.2 | ... | 11 | 42 |
| 1963 | 18 | 361 | 5,950 | 12.6 | ... | 11 | 45 |
| 1964 | 17 | 390 | 6,742 | 16.3 | ... | 10 | 49 |
| 1965 | 18 | 404 | 7,363 | 19 | ... | 9.7 | 53 |
| 1966 | 17 | 450 | 7,689 | 20 | ... | 9.4 | 55 |
| 1967 | 17 | 482[3] | 8,096 | 18 | ... | 9.1 | 60 |
| | | | million dollars | | | | |
| | | | 6.0 | | | | |
| 1968 | 17 | 510 | 10 | 17 | ... | 8.6 | 65 |
| 1969 | 17 | ...[3] | 12 | 25 | ... | 8.5 | 67 |
| 1970 | 18 | 589[3] | 14 | 37 | ... | 8.3[5] | 72 |
| 1971 | 20 | 588 | 21 | 45 | ... | 15 | 82 |
| 1972 | 21[16] | 657 | 53 | 55 | ... | 19 | 92 |
| | 3.9 | | | | | | |
| 1973 | 8.5 | 743 | 81 | 62 | ... | 22 | 97 |
| 1974 | 10 | 837 | 86 | 70 | ... | 29 | 99 |
| 1975 | 20 | 928 | 135 | 90 | ... | 62 | 111 |
| 1976 | 24 | ... | 133 | 92 | ... | 92 | 124 |
| 1977 | 26 | ... | 101 | 183[6] | ... | 126 | 135 |
| | | | | 38 | | | |
| 1978 | 36 | ... | 119 | 55 | ... | 202 | 144 |
| 1979 | 39 | ... | 116 | 73 | ... | 238 | 142 |
| 1980 | 50 | ... | 129 | 121 | ... | 327 | 162 |
| 1981 | 68 | ... | 158 | 192 | ... | 524 | 164 |
| 1982 | 88 | ... | 242 | 254 | ... | 813 | 165 |
| 1983 | 99 | ... | 362 | 470 | ... | 992 | 229 |
| 1984 | 109 | ... | 483 | 793 | ... | 880 | 263 |
| 1985 | 115 | ... | 771 | 1,241 | ... | ... | 308 |
| 1986 | 121 | ... | 917 | 2,226 | ... | ... | 356 |
| 1987 | 202 | ... | 1,403 | 5,732 | ... | ... | 408 |
| 1988 | 216 | ... | 2,140 | 8,999 | ... | ... | 579 |

**G3    SOUTH AMERICA: SAVINGS BANK DEPOSITS** (in millions of stated currency unit, except as otherwise indicated)

### 1880–1909

| | Chile[8] | Guyana |
|---|---|---|
| | pesos | thousand pounds |
| 1880 | — | ... |
| 1881 | — | 194 |
| 1882 | — | 228 |
| 1883 | — | 252 |
| 1884 | — | 227 |
| 1885 | 0.3 | 188 |
| 1886 | 0.5 | 195 |
| 1887 | 0.8 | 201 |
| 1888 | 1.1 | 204 |
| 1889 | 1.4 | 228 |
| 1890 | 1.8 | 257 |
| 1891 | 2.2 | 253 |
| 1892 | 2.7 | 276 |
| 1893 | 2.9 | 278 |
| 1894 | 3.1 | 276 |
| 1895 | 2.9 | 260 |
| 1896 | 2.8 | 265 |
| 1897 | 3.0 | 273 |
| 1898 | 3.0 | 295 |
| 1899 | 3.2 | 292 |
| 1900 | 3.4 | 286 |
| 1901 | 3.6 | 289 |
| 1902 | 4.9 | 302 |
| 1903 | 5.6 | 307 |
| 1904 | 7.1 | 295 |
| 1905 | 9.7 | 291 |
| 1906 | 15 | 300 |
| 1907 | 20[8] / 24 | 296 |
| 1908 | 30 | 298 |
| 1909 | 33 | 299 |

### 1910–1949

| | Argentina[9] | Brazil | Chile[8] | Colombia[10] | Guyana | Uruguay |
|---|---|---|---|---|---|---|
| | pesos | milreis or cruzeiros | pesos | pesos | thousand pounds | pesos |
| 1910 | — | ... | 39 | ... | 258 | ... |
| 1911 | — | ... | 53 | ... | 242 | ... |
| 1912 | — | 242 | 71 | ... | 231 | ... |
| 1913 | — | 218 | 93 | ... | 247 | ... |
| 1914 | — | 189 | 112 | ... | 227 | ... |
| 1915 | 2 | 189 | 125 | ... | 200 | ... |
| 1916 | 6 | 214 | 144 | ... | 215 | ... |
| 1917 | 10 | 222 | 157 | ... | 255 | ... |
| 1918 | 15 | 267 | 202 | ... | 278 | ... |
| 1919 | 21 | 303 | 234 | ... | 325 | ... |
| 1920 | 26 | 327 | 253 | ... | 401 | 17 |
| 1921 | 31 | 350 | 287 | ... | 360 | 21 |
| 1922 | 40 | 397 | 334 | ... | 357 | 25 |
| 1923 | 53 | 435 | 372 | ... | 375 | 27 |
| 1924 | 63 | 443 | 442 | 1.3 | 392 | 29 |
| 1925 | 67 | 455 | 465 | 1.5 | 412[11] | 29 |
| 1926 | 69 | 468 | 436 | 2.5 | 393 | 33 |
| 1927 | 80 | 484 | 413 | 4.6 | 381 | 41 |
| 1928 | 90 | 512 | 483 | 6.6 | 376 | 46 |
| 1929 | 97 | 516 | 506 | 9.9 | 344 | 52 |
| 1930 | 100 | 492 | 481 | 9.6[10] | 333 | 53 |
| 1931 | 97 | 535 | 364[8] / 164 | 11 | 311 | 46 |
| 1932 | 94 | 610 | 199 | 9.6 | 319 | 44 |
| 1933 | 95 | 777 | 278 | 9.2 | 361 | 64 |
| 1934 | 99 | 960 | 338 | 10 | 431 | 64 |
| 1935 | 106 | 1,170 | 412 | 11 | 492 | 67 |
| 1936 | 114 | 1,400 | 465 | 13 | 528 | 76 |
| 1937 | 127 | 1,624 | 547 | 15 | 578 | 86 |
| | | | | | dollars | |
| 1938 | 134 | 1,858 | 597 | 17 | 2.9 | 90 |
| 1939 | 144 | 2,023 | 693 | 19 | 2.8 | 90 |
| 1940 | 153 | 2,349 | 819 | 21 | 2.7 | 103 |
| 1941 | 168 | 2,530 | 935 | 23 | 3.3 | ... |
| 1942 | 191 | 2,843 | 1,076 | 28 | 4.6 | ... |
| 1943 | 227 | 3,524 | 1,322 | 40 | 6.8 | ... |
| 1944 | 283 | 4,447 | 1,678 | 56 | 8.8 | 318 |
| 1945 | 341 | 5,306 | 1,991 | 77 | 9.9 | 360[12] / 57 |
| 1946 | 454 | 6,778 | 2,359 | 90 | 11 | 64 |
| 1947 | 607 | 7,898 | 2,562 | 101 | 11 | 68 |
| 1948 | 841 | 7,997 | 2,932 | 103 | 12 | 72 |
| 1949 | 1,129 | 9,127 | 3,297 | 90 | 13 | 78 |

**G3**    **SOUTH AMERICA: Savings Bank Deposits** (in millions of stated currency unit, except as otherwise indicated)

| | Argentina[9] | Brazil | Chile[8] | Colombia[10] | Guyana | Uruguay[12] |
|---|---|---|---|---|---|---|
| | | thousand million | | | | |
| | pesos | cruzeiros | pesos | pesos | dollars | pesos |
| 1950 | 1,384 | 11 | 3,724 | 106 | 14 | 84 |
| 1951 | 1,617 | 12 | 4,316 | 137 | 15 | 91 |
| 1952 | 2,030 | 14 | 5,484 | 174 | 16 | 94 |
| 1953 | 2,582 | 16 | 7,108 | 204 | 16 | 104 |
| 1954 | 3,203 | 19 | 8,994 | 261 | 17 | 109 |
| 1955 | 3,659 | 23 | 11,077 | 306 | 19 | 110 |
| 1956 | 4,408 | 26 | 17,211 | 366 | 19 | 107 |
| 1957 | 5,056 | 31 | 23,123 | 417 | 19 | 110 |
| 1958 | 5,962 | 36 | 33,377 | 509 | 20 | 116 |
| 1959 | 7,118 | 41 | 47,882 | 587 | 20 | 114 |
| | | | escudos | | | |
| 1960 | 8,268 | 50 | 73 | 629 | 21 | 126 |
| 1961 | 9,232 | 64 | $\frac{107_8}{2.5}$ | 737 | 20 | 143 |
| 1962 | 9,253 | 96 | 13 | 877 | 17 | 172 |
| 1963 | 10,947 | 144 | 37 | 922 | 17 | 208 |
| 1964 | 14,002 | 243 | 76 | 1,022 | 16 | $\frac{246_{12}}{615}$ |
| | thousand million pesos | | | | | |
| 1965 | 18 | ... | 164 | 1,100 | 14 | 618 |
| 1966 | 22 | 633 | 295 | 1,282 | 15 | 406 |
| | | new cruzeiros | | | | |
| 1967 | 27 | 898 | 430 | 1,455 | 15 | 522 |
| 1968 | 35 | 1,002 | 629 | 1,818 | 14 | 911 |
| 1969 | 45 | 1,365 | ... | $\frac{2,365_{10}}{2,416}$ | 14 | 1,371 |
| | thousand million new pesos $\frac{0.53_9}{}$ | | | | | |
| 1970 | 1.96 | 2,367 | 1,558 | 2,972 | 13 | 2,160 |
| 1971 | 2.3 | 3,281 | 2,499 | 3,545 | 12 | 11,900 |
| 1972 | 3.2 | 5,742 | 4,354 | 5,127 | 12 | 27,800 |
| 1973 | 4.8 | 9,482 | 15,912 | 7,408 | 11 | 43,400 |
| 1974 | 6.5 | 18,028 | 132,037 | 13,096 | 9.6 | 69,200 |
| | | thousand million | new pesos | thousand million | | thousand million |
| 1975 | 11 | 33.5 | 884 | 17 | ... | 147 |
| 1976 | 120 | 66.2 | 2,444 | 19 | ... | 243 |
| 1977 | 790 | 99.4 | 6,057 | 28 | ... | ... |
| 1978 | 2,270 | 154 | 8,801 | 42 | ... | ... |
| 1979 | 5,890 | 262 | 13,983 | 56 | ... | ... |
| | | | thousand million | | | |
| 1980 | 12,010 | ... | 26.4 | 82 | ... | ... |
| 1981 | 29,690 | 1,349 | 32.2 | 118 | ... | ... |
| 1982 | 26,440 | 3,070 | 29.4 | 159 | ... | ... |
| | pesos argentines | | | | | |
| 1983 | 12,184 | 9,587 | 51.6 | 239 | ... | ... |
| 1984 | 45,000 | 28,313 | 66 | 317 | ... | ... |
| | | million million | | | | |
| 1985 | 162 | 104 | 94.2 | 418 | ... | ... |
| 1986 | 379 | 427 | 138 | 530 | ... | ... |
| 1987 | 977 | ... | 182 | 667 | ... | ... |
| 1988 | 6,000 | ... | ... | 755 | ... | ... |

**G3** **Savings Bank Deposits** (in millions of stated currency unit, except as otherwise indicated)

NOTES

1. SOURCES: The national publications listed on p. xiv–xvi, with gaps filled from League of Nations, *Statistical Yearbooks, Commercial Banks,* and *Money and Banking;* and International Monetary Fund, *International Financial Statistics.*
2. In principle, this table relates to all deposits in institutions which are described as savings banks, and excludes deposits in commercial banks, building societies, agricultural credit institutions, etc.
3. Except where otherwise indicated, the statistics are for the last working day of each year.

FOOTNOTES

[1] Savings deposits in Savings Banks to 1910 (1st line); subsequently savings and other time deposits in Mutual Savings Banks and in the postal savings system. The figures for 1910 (2nd line) onwards are at 30 June. It is not clear whether this is also true for the earlier series.

[2] At 30 September to 1900, and at 31 March in the year following that shown in 1901–17.

[3] Deposits in the Post Office and Government Savings Banks, and Savings Banks in Quebec, categories which were reduced in 1968 and 1971 by closure and by absorption into ordinary commercial banks. Data are at 30 June to 1906 and at 31 March from 1907 to 1967. The 1968 figure is an aggregate of some relating to 31 March and others to 31 October, and later figures are all at 31 October.

[4] At 30 September to 1889 and at 31 March in the year following that shown in 1890–1917.

[5] Tobago is included from 1899. Statistics relate to the Post Office Savings Bank to 1970 (1st line), with other savings banks included subsequently.

[6] Time deposits of financial institutions other than the central bank and commercial banks from 1951 (2nd line) to 1977 (1st line).

[7] Statistics from 1945 are at 31 March in the year following that shown. Even after Newfoundland was incorporated in Canada the figures continue to be shown separately here for as long as they are available.

[8] Caja Nacional de Ahorros and Caja de Ahorro de Santiago only to 1907 (1st line). From 1907 (2nd line) to 1931 (1st line) all savings accounts; from 1931 (2nd line) to 1961 (1st line) private savings accounts other than those in commercial banks; and from 1961 (2nd line) deposits in savings banks and in loans associations.

[9] Post Office Savings Bank only to 1970 (1st line). Subsequently savings deposits of mortgage banks, with other financial institutions added from 1978 (2nd line).

[10] Time, savings, and foreign currency deposits from 1969 (2nd line). Statistics to 1930 are at 30 June.

[11] Subsequently excluding one private bank which had been included previously.

[12] All savings deposits to 1945 (1st line). Post Office Savings deposits only from 1945 (2nd line) to 1964 (1st line), and all time deposits of financial institutions other than the central bank and the commercial banks subsequently.

[13] Deposits at the end of the financial year of each bank, which was predominantly 30 June.

[14] Western Samoa accounts are included to 1960 and Cook Islands accounts to 1966. Statistics are at 31 March in the year following that shown.

[15] Government Savings Bank only to 1969 (1st line).

[16] The reason for this break is not given in the source.

## G4    NORTH AMERICA: MONEY SUPPLY

| | Canada | | Costa Rica | | Dominican Republic | | El Salvador | | Guatemala | | Haiti | |
|---|---|---|---|---|---|---|---|---|---|---|---|---|
| | Canadian dollars | | colones | | pesos | | colones | | quatzales | | gourdes | |
| | M1 | M2 | M1 | M2 | M1 | M2 | M1 | M2 | M1 | M2 | M1 | M2 |
| | thousand million | | million | | millions | | million | | million | | million | |
| 1948 | | | 174 | 192 | ... | ... | 89 | 101 | 55.6 | 61.2 | ... | ... |
| 1949 | 3.86 | 7.95 | 195 | 217 | ... | ... | 104 | 119 | 56.6 | 63.5 | ... | ... |
| 1950 | 4.19 | 8.37 | 204 | 231 | 41.8 | 54.1 | 129 | 142 | 58.9 | 65.7 | 60.1 | 72.8 |
| 1951 | 4.26 | 8.56 | 224 | 255 | 53.1 | 63.7 | 136 | 146 | 60.4 | 67.9 | 75.2 | 92.5 |
| 1952 | 4.54 | 9.14 | 265 | 303 | 62.1 | 75.2 | 164 | 174 | 63.6 | 70.6 | 98.3 | 119 |
| 1953 | 4.49 | 9.25 | 291 | 336 | 60.2 | 72.4 | 172 | 184 | 76.1 | 83.3 | 94.4 | 116 |
| 1954 | 4.82 | 10.04 | 325 | 374 | 68.6 | 94.8 | 190 | 206 | 77.6 | 84.3 | 117 | 145 |
| 1955 | 5.11 | 10.74 | 340 | 401 | 76.5 | 109 | 187 | 207 | 86.7 | 95.3 | 118 | 147 |
| 1956 | 5.07 | 11.08 | 342 | 413 | 76.9 | 114 | 215 | 241 | 104 | 118₁ | 127 | 162 |
| 1957 | 5.29 | 11.40 | 370 | 453 | 87.4 | 130 | 215 | 252 | 116 | 135 | 121 | 156 |
| 1958 | 5.95 | 12.79 | 399₁ | 502 | 107 | 144 | 202 | 257 | 107 | 129 | 103 | 135 |
| 1959 | 5.75 | 12.65 | 427 | 547 | 91.9 | 129 | 206 | 282 | 109 | 135 | 104 | 136 |
| 1960 | 5.98 | 13.19 | 433 | 561 | 102 | 129 | 193 | 276 | 105 | 137 | 104 | 138 |
| 1961 | 6.74 | 14.36 | 422 | 546 | 104 | 126 | 184 | 285 | 107 | 143 | 118 | 156 |
| 1962 | 7.03 | 14.96 | 480 | 617 | 114 | 140 | 183 | 306 | 109 | 151 | 122 | 160 |
| 1963 | 7.53 | 16.77 | 535 | 683 | 130 | 158 | 221 | 375 | 121 | 170 | 131 | 169 |
| 1964 | 8.25 | 18.51 | 568 | 734 | 117 | 147 | 234 | 423 | 129 | 194 | 132 | 171 |
| 1965 | 9.43 | 20.37 | 598 | 783 | 135 | 196 | 234 | 439 | 136 | 209 | 133 | 171 |
| 1966 | 10.13 | 22.00₁ | 622 | 808 | 116 | 165 | 247 | 479 | 143 | 234 | 123 | 161 |
| 1967 | 11.70₁ | 21.34₁ | 832₂ | 1,080 | 120 | 173 | 253 | 489 | 148 | 263 | 142 | 179 |
| 1968 | 15.97 | 28.88 | 849 | 1,069 | 139 | 211 | 265 | 509 | 151 | 277 | 160 | 201 |
| 1969 | 15.30 | 31.08 | 959 | 1,195 | 149 | 243 | 288 | 562 | 161 | 309 | 176 | 224 |
| 1970 | 15.57 | 34.05 | 1,006 | 1,277 | 172 | 290 | 295 | 595 | 173 | 344 | 191 | 249 |
| 1971 | 17.61 | 37.15 | 1,317 | 1,811 | 188 | 333 | 315 | 658 | 179 | 383 | 215 | 290 |
| 1972 | 19.77 | 42.71 | 1,501 | 2,166 | 222 | 411 | 390 | 807 | 214 | 477 | 271 | 382 |
| 1973 | 21.50 | 51.49 | 1,874 | 2,640 | 260 | 505 | 466 | 958 | 264 | 580 | 333 | 487 |
| 1974 | 21.83 | 61.36 | 2,146 | 3,446 | 364 | 726 | 557 | 1,116 | 305 | 668 | 342 | 584 |
| 1975 | 25.97 | 70.79 | 2,771 | 4,909 | 380 | 847 | 648 | 1,353 | 354 | 808 | 403 | 735 |
| 1976 | 26.36 | 84.38 | 3,408 | 6,590 | 390 | 875 | 917 | 1,770 | 494 | 1,052 | 550 | 1,015 |
| 1977 | 29.10 | 96.19 | 4,504 | 8,664 | 460 | 1,005 | 988 | 2,004 | 594 | 1,249 | 629 | 1,217 |
| 1978 | 31.12 | 112.5 | 5,625 | 11,067 | 458 | 991 | 1,087 | 2,241 | 664 | 1,424 | 718 | 1,431 |
| 1979 | 31.56 | 132.4 | 6,226 | 14,869 | 598 | 1,155 | 1,321 | 2,446 | 735 | 1,537 | 1,108 | 1,873 |
| 1980 | 34.75₁ | 144.9₁ | 7,271 | 17,235 | 580 | 1,174 | 1,429 | 2,563 | 753 | 1,692 | 945 | 1,938 |
| | | | thousand million | | | | | | | | | |
| 1981 | 36.75 | 177.4 | 10.8 | 32.3 | 661 | 1,338 | 1,437₁ | 2,834₁ | 776 | 1,907 | 1,166 | 2,175 |
| 1982 | 39.82 | 184.0 | 18.4 | 41.0 | 131 | 1,535 | 1,633 | 3,233 | 787 | 2,191 | 1,164 | 2,247 |
| 1983 | 44.09 | 182.2 | 25.6 | 56.1 | 781 | 1,676 | 1,596 | 3,575 | 834 | 2,155 | 1,175 | 2,348 |
| 1984 | 52.44 | 192.4 | 30.1 | 65.8 | 1,160 | 2,170 | 1,830 | 4,236 | 869 | 2,399 | 1,388 | 2,606 |
| 1985 | 68.91 | 205.3 | 32.4 | 76.0 | 1,355 | 2,590 | 2,306 | 5,374 | 1,346 | 3,193 | 1,076 | 1,442 |
| 1986 | 80.22 | 222.2 | 42.5 | 92.2 | 1,989 | 4,285 | 2,758 | 6,905 | 1,608 | 3,875 | 1,790 | 3,276 |
| 1987 | 85.20 | 241.6 | 42.6 | 107 | 2,609 | 4,934 | 2,762 | 7,371 | 1,766 | 4,168 | 2,098 | 3,694 |
| 1988 | 90.12 | 267.2 | 65.3 | 150 | 4,168 | 7,506 | 2,996 | 8,219 | 2,019 | 4,995 | 1,635 | 3,313 |

## G4 NORTH AMERICA: Money Supply

| | Honduras | | Jamaica | | Mexico | | Nicaragua | | Panama | | Trinidad & Tobago | | USA | |
|---|---|---|---|---|---|---|---|---|---|---|---|---|---|---|
| | lempiras | | pounds | | pesos | | cordobas | | balboas | | T&T dollars | | US dollars | |
| | M1 | M2 | M1 | M2 | M1 | M2 | M1 | M2 | M1 | M2 | M1 | M2 | M1 | M2 |
| | million | | million | | thousand million | | million | | million | | million | | thousand million | |
| 1948 | 38 | 43 | ... | ... | 4.04 | 5.06 | 89 | 93 | 29 | 48 | ... | ... | | |
| 1949 | 37 | 43 | ... | ... | 4.50 | 5.79 | 112 | 113 | 24 | 43 | ... | ... | 110 | 145 |
| 1950 | 38 | 44 | ... | ... | 6.24 | 7.45 | 122 | 125 | 24 | 42 | ... | ... | 115 | 150 |
| 1951 | 47 | 54 | ... | ... | 6.97 | 8.46 | 150 | 152 | 25 | 42 | 46 | 90 | 123 | 159 |
| 1952 | 52 | 60 | ... | ... | 7.26 | 9.13 | 180 | 182 | 27 | 44 | 58 | 102 | 129 | 169 |
| 1953 | 59 | 68 | 15 | 26 | 8.05 | 10.10 | 230 | 239 | 30 | 49 | 64 | 112 | 131 | 173 |
| 1954 | 69 | 79 | 16 | 29 | 9.01 | 12.03 | 264 | 272 | 33 | 51 | 74 | 127 | 135 | 181 |
| 1955 | 61 | 72 | 17 | 30 | 10.77 | 14.13 | 272 | 291 | 33 | 52 | 70 | 133 | 138 | 185 |
| 1956 | 67 | 83 | 19 | 35 | 11.98 | 15.69 | 267 | 285 | 34 | 66 | 73 | 143 | 139 | 189 |
| 1957 | 64 | 77 | 22 | 41 | 12.78 | 17.43 | 260 | 279 | 38 | 61 | 94 | 163 | 138 | 193 |
| 1958 | 63 | 75 | 22 | 43 | 13.72 | 19.17 | 252 | 274 | 40 | 65 | 89 | 173 | 144 | 207 |
| 1959 | 66 | 81 | 25 | 48 | 15.87 | 21.13 | 253 | 282 | 42 | 69 | 93 | 189 | 146 | 210 |
| 1960 | 64 | 85 | 26 | 51 | 17.35 | 22.75 | 264 | 297 | 42 | 70 | 103 | 199 | 146 | 217 |
| 1961 | 66 | 89 | 23 | 47 | 18.49 | 24.51 | 273 | 305 | 44 | 75 | 113 | 225 | 151 | 340 |
| 1962 | 73 | 102 | 30 | 62 | 20.9 | 27.6 | 353 | 384 | 49 | 87 | 104 | 225 | 153 | 367 |
| 1963 | 79 | 114 | 29 | 71 | 24.3 | 32.4 | 397 | 449 | 60 | 111 | 122 | 263 | 159 | 398 |
| 1964 | 90 | 129 | 32 | 78 | 28.6 | 37.8 | 460 | 545 | 51 | 105 | 121 | 255 | 167 | 430 |
| 1965 | 105 | 151 | 32 | 84 | 30.2 | 40.6 | 537 | 672 | 56 | 125 | 116 | 263 | 174 | 465 |
| 1966 | 107 | 166 | 36 | 97 | 33.9 | 45.7 | 565 | 751 | 62 | 149 | 126 | 295 | 179 | 486 |
| 1967 | 114 | 183 | 38 | 106 | 37.0 | 50.1 | 541 | 760 | 70 | 181 | 129 | 315 | 190 | 530 |
| 1968 | 127 | 213 | 47 | 135 | 42.3 | 57.0 | 485 | 682 | 81 | 206[2] | 130 | 362 | 204 | 572 |
| 1969 | 148 | 252 | 56 | 162 | 48.6 | 65.4 | 513 | 721 | 85 | 196 | 140 | 415 | 211 | 592 |
| | | | million dollars[5] | | | | | | | | | | | |
| 1970 | 159 | 288 | 127 | 379 | 54 | 72 | 578 | 829 | 100 | 256 | 151 | 489 | 222 | 631 |
| 1971 | 169 | 321 | 160 | 471 | 58 | 77 | 619 | 949 | 105 | 302 | 177 | 606 | 237 | 714 |
| 1972 | 193 | 366 | 173[3] | 528[3] | 68 | 91 | 749 | 1,226 | 154 | 393 | 211 | 723 | 259 | 806 |
| 1973 | 238 | 445 | 218 | 578 | 84 | 115 | 1,146 | 1,734 | 161 | 444 | 213 | 823 | 272 | 859 |
| 1974 | 242 | 460 | 258 | 687 | 101 | 139 | 1,313 | 2,016 | 196 | 530 | 270 | 1,073 | 284 | 905 |
| 1975 | 263 | 507 | 322 | 828 | 122 | 164 | 1,256 | 2,030 | 173 | 548 | 392 | 1,388 | 298 | 1,020 |
| 1976 | 361 | 672 | 339 | 897 | 158[1] | 243[1] | 1,615 | 2,699 | 190 | 578 | 572 | 1,863 | 318 | 1,160 |
| 1977 | 411 | 796 | 474 | 1,044 | 208 | 525 | 1,699 | 2,855 | 213 | 672 | 725 | 2,360 | 344 | 1,282 |
| 1978 | 480 | 962 | 570 | 1,235 | 270 | 699 | 1,579 | 2,652 | 246 | 833 | 936 | 2,941 | 372 | 1,381 |
| 1979 | 546 | 1,040 | 629 | 1,422 | 361 | 949 | 2,654 | 3,427 | 301 | 1,043 | 1,147 | 3,816 | 397 | 1,467 |
| 1980 | 610 | 1,128 | 717 | 1,712 | 477 | 1,297 | 4,102 | 5,747 | 335 | 1,316 | 1,337 | 4,298 | 424 | 1,570 |
| 1981 | 637 | 1,226 | 775 | 2,197 | 635[2] | 1,933[2] | 5,206 | 7,926 | 360 | 1,561 | 1,855 | 5,492 | 451 | 1,644 |
| 1982 | 717 | 1,478 | 876 | 2,773 | 1,031 | 3,055 | 6,545 | 9,895 | 379 | 1,749 | 2,547 | 7,395 | 491 | 1,787 |
| | | | | | | | million new cordobas[6] | | | | | | | |
| 1983 | 815 | 1,731 | 1,066 | 3,527 | 1,447 | 4,945 | 10.94 | 17.24 | 373 | 1,748 | 2,434 | 7,934 | 538 | 2,078 |
| 1984 | 846 | 1,911 | 1,319 | 4,197 | 2,315 | 8,332 | 20.84 | 30.7 | 381 | 1,863 | 2,294 | 8,342 | 570 | 2,267 |
| 1985 | 856 | 1,871 | 1,520 | 5,238 | 3,462 | 11,936 | 54.8 | 74.4 | 409 | 1,952 | 2,260 | 8,444 | 641 | 2,483 |
| 1986 | 955 | 2,050 | 2,140 | 6,687 | 5,790 | 21,299 | 193 | 249 | 449 | 2,360 | 2,073 | 8,198 | 746 | 2,707 |
| 1987 | 1,119 | 2,497 | 2,252 | 7,527 | 12,627 | 52,656 | 1,422 | 1,622 | 442 | 2,278 | 2,170 | 8,493 | 767 | 2,814 |
| 1988 | 1,253 | 2,869 | 3,445 | 9,958 | 21,191 | 43,448 | ... | ... | 304 | 1,648 | 1,892 | 8,566 | 812 | 2,985 |

**G4    SOUTH AMERICA: MONEY SUPPLY**

| | Argentina | | Bolivia | | Brazil | | Chile | | Colombia | | Ecuador | |
|---|---|---|---|---|---|---|---|---|---|---|---|---|
| | pesos | | bolivianos | | cruzeiros | | pesos | | pesos | | sucres | |
| | M1 | M2 | M1 | M2 | M1 | M2 | M1 | M2 | M1 | M2 | M1 | M2 |
| | thousand million | | thousand million | | | | thousand million | | million | | million | |
| 1948 | 16.9 | 24.2 | ... | ... | 48 | 62 | 32 | ... | 760 | 861 | 651 | 765 |
| 1949 | 20.4 | 30.1 | ... | ... | 57 | 73 | 41 | ... | 927 | 1,029 | 709 | 850 |
| 1950 | 24.7 | 35.4 | 5.0 | 5.8 | 76 | 94 | 20 | ... | 974 | 1,113 | 913 | 1,093 |
| 1951 | 30.4 | 41.7 | 5.9 | 7.0 | 88 | 108 | 21 | ... | 1,127 | 1,316 | 845 | 1,005 |
| 1952 | 34.3 | 46.7 | 9.0 | 10.0 | 101 | 122 | 29 | ... | 1,318 | 1,522 | 1,051 | 1,233 |
| 1953 | 43.1 | 58.0 | 16.3 | 17.5 | 123 | 145 | 40 | ... | 1,550 | 1,757 | 1,088 | 1,318 |
| 1954 | 51.9 | 69.6 | 26.9 | 27.9 | 150 | 175 | 55 | ... | 1,843 | 2,223 | 1,273 | 1,543 |
| 1955 | 61.2 | 81.4 | 56 | 59 | 178 | 201 | 92 | 108 | 1,911 | 2,411 | 1,193 | 1,545 |
| 1956 | 71.3 | 96.4 | 197 | 203 | 219 | 243 | 129 | 154 | 2,377 | 3,215 | 1,358 | 1,746 |
| 1957 | 82.8 | 113 | 291 | 301 | 290 | 318 | 165 | 193 | 2,698 | 3,351 | 1,412 | 1,881 |
| 1958 | 119 | 160 | 301 | 310 | 354 | 385 | 222 | 277 | 3,263 | 3,905 | 1,400 | 1,791 |
| 1959 | 170 | 215 | 386 | 401 | 500 | 535 | 294 | 456 | 3,633 | 4,400 | 1,577 | 2,017 |
| | | | | | | | million escudos[14] | | | | | |
| 1960 | 218 | 279 | 419 | 435 | 691 | 735 | 384 | 595 | 3,985 | 4,750 | 1,732 | 2,201 |
| 1961 | 243[2] | 318[2] | 496 | 513 | 1,043 | 1,104 | 432 | 698 | 4,961 | 5,881 | 1,778 | 2,376 |
| | 202 | 277 | | | | | | | | | | |
| 1962 | 220 | 305 | 556 | 585 | 1,689 | 1,762 | 557 | 896 | 5,927 | 7,474 | 2,000 | 2,678 |
| | | | million pesos[10] | | | | | | | | | |
| 1963 | 283 | 406 | 665 | 702 | 2,777 | 2,887 | 747 | 1,206 | 6,693 | 8,206 | 2,241 | 2,850 |
| 1964 | 396 | 574 | 803 | 853 | 5,126 | 5,308 | 1,129 | 1,849 | 8,246 | 9,700 | 2,626 | 3,195 |
| | | | | | | | | | thousand million | | | |
| 1965 | 497 | 729 | 943 | 995 | 9,050 | 9,347 | 1,367 | 2,364 | 9.6 | 11.8 | 2,670 | 3,285 |
| | | | | | million new cruzeiros[12] | | | | | | | |
| 1966 | 671 | 959 | 1,153 | 1,253 | 10.5 | 11.4 | 2,594 | 4,118 | 11.2 | 13.0 | 3,016 | 3,847 |
| 1967 | 1,092 | 1,475 | 1,192 | 1,343 | 14.9 | 16.6 | 3,240 | 5,389 | 13.7 | 15.8 | 3,439 | 4,460 |
| 1968 | 1,364 | 1,889 | 1,287 | 1,513 | 21.3 | 24.0 | 4,471 | 7,565 | 15.9 | 18.1 | 4,172 | 5,563 |
| 1969 | 1,655 | 2,279 | 1,361 | 1,667 | 27.4 | 31.8 | 6,058 | 10,605 | 19.4 | 22.1 | 4,751 | 6,298 |
| | thousand million new pesos[7] | | | | | | thousand million escudos | | | | thousand million | |
| 1970 | 18 | 26 | 1,532 | 1,913 | 34.7 | 40.8 | 10 | 16 | 22.4 | 25.8 | 5.99 | 7.73 |
| 1971 | 20 | 30 | 1,766 | 2,259 | 42 | 45 | 21 | 32 | 25.1 | 29.2 | 6.72 | 8.89 |
| 1972 | 33 | 53 | 2,210 | 2,844 | 59 | 65 | 54 | 80 | 31.9 | 37.7 | 8.38 | 10.97 |
| 1973 | 57 | 97 | 2,969 | 3,776 | 87 | 94 | 229 | 441 | 41.6[1] | 50.9[1] | 11.3 | 14.4 |
| 1974 | 90 | 150 | 4,257 | 5,449 | 117 | 125 | 838 | 2,025 | 49.1 | 63.7 | 16.9 | 21.0 |
| | | | thousand million pesos | | | | thousand million pesos[15] | | | | | |
| 1975 | 280 | 360 | 4.8 | 6.7 | 169 | 181 | 2.99 | 7.49 | 58.9 | 78.5 | 18.3 | 23.1 |
| | million million pesos | | | | | | | | | | | |
| 1976 | 1.05 | 1.59 | 6.5 | 9.9 | 231 | 250 | 9.72 | 25.89 | 79.4 | 105 | 22.8 | 28.8 |
| 1977 | 2.26 | 5.17 | 7.9 | 12.8 | 319[1] | 363[1] | 34.2 | 45.9 | 103[4] | 141[4] | 29.9 | 36.0 |
| 1978 | 5.87 | 14.65 | 8.8 | 14.4 | 434 | 529 | 33.9 | 104 | 133 | 180 | 32.9 | 39.7 |
| 1979 | 14.0 | 43.5 | 10.3 | 16.6 | 759 | 913 | 55.1 | 180 | 166 | 221 | 42.0 | 52.2 |
| 1980 | 27.5 | 82.3 | 14.7 | 23.1 | 1,288 | 1,473 | 85.3 | 307 | 212 | 320 | 53.6 | 66.2 |
| 1981 | 46.7 | 175.0 | 17.6 | 29.4 | 2,352 | 2,861 | 81.9 | 412 | 256 | 435 | 61.8 | 75.7 |
| 1982 | 162.3 | 459.3 | 57.8 | 97.2 | 3,964 | 5,299 | 92.2 | 577 | 321 | 526 | 73.1 | 93.6 |
| | thousand million pesos argentinos[8] | | | | | | | | | | | |
| 1983 | 75 | 230 | 178 | 265 | 8,036 | 12,806 | 112 | 702 | 397 | 659 | 95.1 | 118 |
| | | | | | thousand million | | | | | | | |
| 1984 | 451 | 1,638 | 3,370 | 4,053 | 24.4 | 46.3 | 130 | 720 | 492 | 817 | 129 | 169 |
| | thousand million australes[9] | | million million pesos | | | | | | | | | |
| 1985 | 3.03 | 8.43 | 198 | 287 | 106 | 203 | 148 | 1,061 | 545 | 982 | 153 | 217 |
| 1986 | 5.60 | 17.76 | 369 | 817 | ... | ... | 215 | 1,329 | ... | ... | 183 | 268 |
| | | | million bolivianos[11] | | | | | | | | | |
| 1987 | 12.58 | 48.42 | 516 | 1,576 | ... | ... | 229 | 1,794 | 1,020 | 1,815 | 246 | 384 |
| 1988 | 55 | 260 | 698 | 2,028 | ... | ... | 385 | 2,280 | 1,282 | 2,198 | 373 | 622 |

## G4 SOUTH AMERICA: Money Supply

| | Guyana | | Paraguay | | Peru | | Uruguay | | Venezuela | |
|---|---|---|---|---|---|---|---|---|---|---|
| | Guyanese dollars | | guaranies | | soles | | pesos | | bolivares | |
| | M1 | M2 | M1 | M2 | M1 | M2 | M1 | M2 | M1 | M2 |
| | million | | million | | thousand million | | million | | million | |
| 1948 | ... | ... | 97 | ... | 1.61 | 2.25 | 442 | 828 | 1,380 | 1,506 |
| 1949 | ... | ... | 153 | ... | 1.68 | 2.54 | 500 | ... | 1,537 | 1,684 |
| 1950 | ... | ... | 229 | ... | 1.97 | 3.14 | 588 | 1,084 | 1,576 | 1,741 |
| 1951 | ... | ... | 395 | ... | 2.41 | 3.65 | 577 | 1,137 | 1,646 | 1,849 |
| 1952 | ... | ... | 582 | 632 | 2.73 | 4.28 | 630 | 1,220 | 1,909 | 2,182 |
| 1953 | ... | ... | 861 | 943 | 3.10 | 4.86 | 712 | 1,393 | 2,085 | 3,457 |
| 1954 | ... | ... | 1,070 | 1,172 | 3.37 | 5.40 | 763 | 1,518 | 2,169 | 2,663 |
| 1955 | 26 | 39 | 1,426 | 1,601 | 3.58 | 6.12 | 807 | 1,602 | 2,414 | 3,083 |
| 1956 | 26 | 42 | 1,941 | 2,036 | 4.21 | 7.21 | 904 | 1,796 | 2,756 | 3,678 |
| 1957 | 28 | 47 | 1,997 | 2,177 | 4.37 | 7.85 | 980 | 2,094 | 3,649 | 5,150 |
| 1958 | 30 | 52 | 2,384 | 2,760 | 4.68 | 8.45 | 1,248 | 2,527 | 4,017 | 5,877 |
| 1959 | 35 | 57 | 2,609 | 2,874 | 6.05 | 10.1 | 1,771 | 3,193 | 3,823 | 5,906 |
| 1960 | 38 | 62 | 2,674 | 3,031 | 7.10 | 11.7 | 2,394 | 4,045 | 3,574 | 5,265 |
| 1961 | 36 | 61 | 3,391 | 3,933 | 8.30 | 13.7 | 2,924 | 4,828 | 3,684 | 5,327 |
| 1962 | 42 | 72 | 3,311 | 4,136 | 8.87 | 15.6 | 2,832 | 5,117 | 3,604 | 5,410 |
| 1963 | 43 | 84 | 3,685 | 4,929 | 10.3 | 18.1 | 3,652 | 7,839 | 3,840 | 6,240 |
| 1964 | 47 | 96 | 4,473 | 6,234 | 13.2 | 22.7 | 5,185[2] | 10,876[2] | 4,390 | 7,290 |
| | | | | | | | thousand million | | thousand million | |
| 1965 | 45 | 102 | 4,913 | 7,278 | 15.8 | 28 | 10.5 | 18.5 | 4.79 | 7.78 |
| 1966 | 47 | 109 | 5,034[1] | 7,856[1] | 18.2 | 31.9 | 14.7 | 23.9 | 5.02 | 7.93 |
| 1967 | 51 | 122 | 6,691 | 10,339 | 20.7 | 34.7 | 30.9 | 46.7 | 5.57 | 9.01 |
| 1968 | 56 | 138 | 5,786 | 10,111 | 22.8 | 37.1 | 47.6 | 71.4 | 6.09 | 9.87 |
| 1969 | 61 | 152 | 6,557 | 11,587 | 27.5 | 42 | 76.7 | 108 | 6.64 | 10.95 |
| | | | thousand million | | | | | | | |
| 1970 | 61 | 164 | 7.3 | 13.5 | 43.3 | 57.4 | 87.8 | 130 | 7.07 | 11.8 |
| 1971 | 69 | 191 | 7.8 | 15.2 | 46.6 | 62.1 | 135 | 197 | 8.19 | 13.8 |
| 1972 | 88 | 233 | 9.4 | 18.8 | 60.3 | 77.0 | 198 | 316 | 9.65 | 16.6 |
| 1973 | 101 | 274 | 12.5 | 24.3 | 75.7 | 94.8 | 357 | 540 | 11.5 | 19.9 |
| 1974 | 133 | 317 | 15.1 | 29.4 | 105 | 127 | 586 | 921 | 16.9 | 26.9 |
| | | | | | | | million new pesos[17] | | | |
| 1975 | 207 | 448 | 17.8 | 37.1 | 123 | 147 | 834 | 1,637 | 25.6 | 41.5 |
| 1976 | 221 | 487 | 21.6 | 45.7 | 155 | 182 | 1,380 | 3,260 | 29.0 | 50.7 |
| 1977 | 285 | 599 | 28.6 | 60.1 | 185 | 225 | 1,938 | 5,922 | 37.4 | 64.1 |
| 1978 | 300 | 663 | 39.8 | 78.5 | 270 | 362 | 3,588 | 11,339 | 44.0 | 73.3 |
| 1979 | 288 | 710 | 49.5 | 97.5 | 461 | 695 | 6,160 | 21,038 | 46.5 | 78.7 |
| | | | | | | | thousand million new pesos | | | |
| 1980 | 328 | 846 | 62.4 | 131 | 730 | 1,276 | 9.1 | 36.4 | 54.5 | 92.3 |
| 1981 | 351 | 982 | 62.4 | 157 | 1,075 | 2,152 | 9.8[1] | 54.2[1] | 58.3 | 105 |
| 1982 | 436 | 1,254 | 60.2 | 166 | 1,509 | 3,701 | 13.7 | 72.5 | 60.8 | 114 |
| 1983 | 509 | 1,518 | 75.6 | 193 | 2,965 | 7,525 | 14.9 | 81.9 | 76.2 | 140 |
| 1984 | 619 | 1,795 | 97.8 | 226 | 6,060 | 17,098 | 22.1 | 133 | 96.7 | 168 |
| | | | | | thousand million intis[16] | | | | | |
| 1985 | 740 | 2,140 | 125 | 273 | 23 | 44 | 46 | 260 | 105 | 188 |
| 1986 | 881 | 2,489 | 159 | 348 | 43 | 68 | 84 | 478 | 110[2] | 211[2] |
| 1987 | 1,333 | 3,820 | 244 | 469 | 96 | 139 | 135 | 702 | 123 | 260 |
| 1988 | 2,095 | 5,407 | 328 | 563 | 593 | 1,006 | 222 | 1,370 | 145 | 299 |

**G4      Money Supply**

NOTES

1.  SOURCES: International Monetary Fund, *International Financial Statistics*

2.  M1 is defined as notes and coin in the hands of the public plus demand deposits of residents. M2 additionally includes time and savings deposits. Non-residents' and banks' deposits are not always excluded in practice, especially in earlier years.

3.  Breaks in continuity through changes in coverage or sectorization are indicated in footnotes where possible, it should be noted that these improvements do not necessarily imply an increase in the figures for later years, since they may include the elimination of double-counting and the exclusion of non-residents' deposits or other funds which should not have been counted as part of the money supply.

FOOTNOTES

[1] There was a change in the coverage or sectorization of accounts.
[2] No reason is given for this break in the source.
[3] Subsequently excluding non-residents deposits.
[4] Subsequently excluding the Agricultural Bank.
[5] Two Jamaican dollars equalled one pound.
[6] One new equalled 1,000 old cordobas.
[7] One new (1970) pesos equalled 100 old pesos.
[8] One peso argentino equalled 10,000 old (1970) pesos.
[9] One austral equalled 1,000 pesos argentinos.
[10] One peso equalled 1,000 bolivianos.
[11] One (1987) boliviano equalled 1 million pesos.
[12] One new (1966) cruzeiro equalled 1,000 old pesos.
[13] One cruzado equalled 1,000 (1966) cruzeiros.
[14] One escudo equalled 1,000 pesos.
[15] One (1975) peso equalled 1,000 escudos.
[16] One inti equalled 1,000 soles.
[17] One new equalled 1,000 old pesos.

**G5** **NORTH AMERICA: TOTAL CENTRAL GOVERNMENT EXPENDITURE** (in millions of stated currency unit except as otherwise indicated)

### 1789–1824

| | USA[1] |
|---|---|
| | dollars |
| 1789 | |
| 1790 | } 4.3 |
| 1791 | |
| 1792 | 5.1 |
| 1793 | 4.5 |
| 1794 | 7.0 |
| 1795 | 7.5 |
| 1796 | 5.7 |
| 1797 | 6.1 |
| 1798 | 7.7 |
| 1799 | 9.7 |
| 1800 | 11 |
| 1801 | 9.4 |
| 1802 | 7.9 |
| 1803 | 7.9 |
| 1804 | 8.7 |
| 1805 | 11 |
| 1806 | 9.8 |
| 1807 | 8.4 |
| 1808 | 9.9 |
| 1809 | 10 |
| 1810 | 8.2 |
| 1811 | 8.1 |
| 1812 | 20 |
| 1813 | 32 |
| 1814 | 35 |
| 1815 | 33 |
| 1816 | 31 |
| 1817 | 22 |
| 1818 | 20 |
| 1819 | 21 |
| 1820 | 18 |
| 1821 | 16 |
| 1822 | 15 |
| 1823 | 15 |
| 1824 | 20 |

### 1825–1864

| | Barbados | Jamaica[2] | Mexico[3] | Trinidad | USA[1] |
|---|---|---|---|---|---|
| | thousand pounds | thousand pounds | pesos | thousand pounds | dollars |
| 1825 | ... | ... | 17 | ... | 16 |
| 1826 | ... | ... | 17 | ... | 17 |
| 1827 | ... | ... | 16 | ... | 16 |
| 1828 | ... | ... | 16 | ... | 16 |
| 1829 | ... | ... | 16 | ... | 15 |
| 1830 | ... | ... | 14 | ... | 15 |
| 1831 | ... | ... | 17 | ... | 15 |
| 1832 | ... | ... | 20 | ... | 17 |
| 1833 | ... | ... | 22 | ... | 23 |
| 1834 | ... | ... | 17 | ... | 19 |
| 1835 | 27 | ... | 13 | ... | 18 |
| 1836 | ... | ... | 14 | ... | 31 |
| 1837 | ... | ... | 17 | ... | 37 |
| 1838 | ... | ... | 41 | ... | 34 |
| 1839 | ... | ... | 20 | ... | 27 |
| 1840 | 54 | 225 | 19 | ... | 24 |
| 1841 | ... | 269 | 22 | ... | 27 |
| 1842 | ... | 303 | 19 | ... | 25 |
| 1843 | ... | 325 | 21 | ... | [12][1] |
| 1844 | ... | 294 | 20 | ... | 22 |
| 1845 | 52 | 277 | 25 | ... | 23 |
| 1846 | ... | 277 | 24 | ... | 28 |
| 1847 | ... | 305 | 27 | ... | 57 |
| 1848 | ... | 236 | 25 | ... | 45 |
| 1849 | ... | 193 | 17 | ... | 45 |
| 1850 | 47 | 219 | 20 | 77 | 40 |
| 1851 | 50 | 260 | 26 | 106 | 48 |
| 1852 | 59 | 240 | 16 | 111 | 44 |
| 1853 | 70 | 153 | 32 | 119 | 48 |
| 1854 | 72 | 216 | 18 | 101 | 58 |
| 1855 | 63 | 240 | 14 | 81 | 60 |
| 1856 | 71 | 213 | 14 | 80 | 70 |
| 1857 | 81 | 207 | 15 | 108 | 68 |
| 1858 | 88 | 191 | 14 | 174 | 74 |
| 1859 | 80 | 262 | 15 | 187 | 69 |
| 1860 | 111 | 255 | 16 | 187 | 63 |
| 1861 | 116 | 275 | 8.3 | 189 | 67 |
| 1862 | 93 | 292 | 10 | 196 | 475 |
| 1863 | 105 | 285 | 8.5 | 189 | 715 |
| 1864 | 99 | 364 | 7.2 | 193 | 865 |

**G5　　NORTH AMERICA: Total Central Government Expenditure** (in millions of stated currency unit, except as otherwise indicated)

**1865–1899**

| | Barbados[4] | Canada[5] | Costa Rica[6] | Cuba[7] | El Salvador[8] | Guatemala[9] | Honduras[10] | Jamaica[2] | Mexico[3] | Trinidad[11] | USA[1] |
|---|---|---|---|---|---|---|---|---|---|---|---|
| | thousand pounds | dollars | pesos | paper pesos | silver pesos | paper pesos | pesos | thousand pounds | pesos | thousand pounds | dollars |
| 1865 | 90 | — | ... | ... | ... | ... | ... | 370 | 6.1 | 222 | 1,298 |
| 1866 | 90 | — | ... | 28 | ... | ... | ... | 388 | 9.8 | 184 | 521 |
| 1867 | 100 | — | ... | 25 | ... | ... | ... | 372 | 14 | 196 | 358 |
| 1868 | 99 | 14 | ... | 31 | ... | ... | ... | 354 | 17 | 177 | 377 |
| 1869 | 105 | 15 | ... | ... | ... | ... | ... | 375 | 14 | 214 | 323 |
| 1870 | 106 | 18 | ... | ... | ... | ... | ... | 418 | 15 | 226 | 310 |
| 1871 | 122 | 19 | ... | ... | ... | ... | ... | 455 | 15 | 229 | 292 |
| 1872 | 124 | 25 | ... | ... | ... | ... | ... | 478 | 16 | 277 | 278 |
| 1873 | 122 | 39 | ... | ... | ... | ... | ... | 523 | 16 | 315 | 290 |
| 1874 | 124 | 33 | ... | ... | ... | ... | ... | 537 | 17 | 364 | 303 |
| 1875 | 127 | 32 | ... | ... | ... | ... | ... | 587 | 18 | 352 | 275 |
| 1876 | 124 | 31 | ... | ... | ... | ... | ... | 537 | 18 | 318 | 265 |
| 1877 | 120 | 32 | ... | ... | ... | ... | ... | 536 | 19 | 306 | 241 |
| 1878 | 124 | 30 | ... | ... | ... | ... | ... | 505 | 18 | 354 | 237 |
| 1879 | 124 | 30 | ... | ... | ... | ... | 0.9 | 561 | 21 | 456 | 267 |
| 1880 | 130 | 33 | ... | ... | ... | ... | 1.0 | 687 | 24 | 571 | 268 |
| 1881 | 133 | 33 | ... | 44 | ... | ... | 0.7 | 699 | 33 | 557 | 261 |
| 1882 | 141 | 33 | ... | ... | ... | 7.3 | 1.4 | 701 | 41 | 468 | 258 |
| 1883 | 143 | 42 | 2.0 | 36 | 4.0 | 6.6 | 1.1 | 728 | 48 | 510 | 265 |
| 1884 | 144 | 56 | 3.1 | 34 | 4.1 | 5.8 | ... | 704 | 51 | 501 | 244 |
| 1885 | 146 | 48 | 3.2 | 32 | 3.6 | 8.1 | ... | 781 | 34 | 457 | 260 |
| 1886 | 137 | 60 | 2.8 | 32 | 4.3 | 8.4 | } 2.8 { | 622 | 36 | 453 | 242 |
| 1887 | 155 | 40 | 3.4 | 32 | 2.8 | ... | | 647 | 61 | 431 | 268 |
| 1888 | 150 | 43 | 3.9 | 24[7] | 2.9 | ... | 1.4 | 634 | 88 | 471 | 268 |
| 1889 | 146 | 42 | 5.0 | 26[7] | 4.0 | ... | ... | 684[2] | 78 | 464 | 299 |
| 1890 | 182 | 40 | 5.5 | ... | 5.4 | ... | ... | 711 | 63 | 483 | 318 |
| 1891 | 177 | 39 | 5.4 | 25 | 7.4 | 8.3 | ... | 897 | 43 | 536 | 366 |
| 1892 | 199 | 40 | ... | ... | 6.8 | ... | 3.0 | 802 | 49 | 516 | 345 |
| 1893 | 165 | 39 | 4.7 | 23 | 7.2 | 9.7 | 2.6 | 812 | 46 | 513 | 383 |
| 1894 | 161 | 41 | 6.1 | ... | 8.6 | 11 | 1.2 | 822 | 46 | 508[11] 560 | 368 |
| 1895 | 414 | 41 | 6.2 | ... | 7.9 | 14 | 2.3 | 850 | 46 | 661 | 356 |
| 1896 | 197 | 42 | 6.7 | 26 | 9.4 | 16 | 2.4 | 853 | 49 | 768 | 352 |
| 1897 | 174 | 41 | 8.3 | 26 | 8.6 | 17 | ... | 823 | 53 | 775 | 366 |
| 1898 | 179 | 43 | 8.1 | 26 | 5.3 | 21 | 2.4 | 755 | 55 | 705[11] | 443 |
| 1899 | 210 | 49 | 7.4 | 26 | 5.2 | 10 | 2.6 | 815 | 63 | 749 | 605 |

**G5**  **NORTH AMERICA: Total Central Government Expenditure** (in millions of stated currency unit, except as otherwise indicated)

**1900–1944**

| | Barbados[4] | Canada[5] | Costa Rica[6] | Cuba[7] | Dominican Republic | El Salvador[8] | Guatemala[9] | Haiti[12] |
|---|---|---|---|---|---|---|---|---|
| | thousand pounds | dollars | colones | paper pesos | pesos | silver pesos | paper pesos | gourdes |
| 1900 | 183[4] | 50 | 9.3 | ... | ... | 6.8 | ... | ... |
| 1901 | 181 | 56 | 5.9 | ... | ... | 7.6 | 12 | ... |
| 1902 | 199 | 61 | 5.5 | ... | ... | 8.6 | 16 | ... |
| 1903 | 183 | 59 | 6.4 | 14 | ... | 7.7 | 19 | ... |
| 1904 | 180 | 70 | 4.1 | 17 | ... | 8.8 | 17 | ... |
| 1905 | 183 | 77 | 5.9 | 17 | 1.7 | 10 | 23 | ... |
| 1906 | 186 | 81[5] | 7.1 | 19 | 2.1 | 12 | 20[9] | ... |
| | | | | | | | 45 | |
| 1907 | 188 | 110 | 9.2 | 24 | 2.4 | 11 | 46 | ... |
| 1908 | 201 | 131 | [6.1][6] | 23 | 4.4 | 12 | 45 | ... |
| 1909 | 209 | 114 | 7.2 | 24 | 4.0 | 11 | 50 | ... |
| | | | | | | colones[17] | | |
| 1910 | 216 | 122 | 8.9 | ... | 4.6 | 10 | 71 | ... |
| 1911 | 223 | 136 | 10 | 31 | 4.8 | 13 | 46 | ... |
| 1912 | 236 | 143 | 9.3 | 34 | 5.8 | 13 | 69 | ... |
| 1913 | 224 | 185 | 10 | 34 | 3.2 | 15 | 46 | ... |
| 1914 | 239 | 246 | 9.7 | 40 | 5.3 | 15 | 49 | ... |
| 1915 | 230 | 338 | 9.2 | 40 | 4.4 | 12 | 68 | ... |
| 1916 | 270 | 497 | 9.5 | 40 | 4.1 | 12 | 92 | ... |
| 1917 | 521 | 574 | 13 | 44 | 5.0 | 14 | 131 | 15 |
| 1918 | 348 | 696 | 13 | 63 | 5.0 | 15 | 78 | 16 |
| 1919 | 359 | 740 | 21 | 63 | 7.9 | 14 | 101 | 23 |
| 1920 | 531 | 529 | 19 | 63 | 12 | 16 | 196 | 21 |
| 1921 | 419 | 476 | 19 | 63 | 9.0 | 14 | 387 | 33 |
| 1922 | 360 | 441 | 17 | 55 | 11 | 14 | 348 | 40 |
| 1923 | 352 | 372 | 18 | 63 | 7.2 | 14 | 396 | 31 |
| | | | | | | | quetzales[17] | |
| 1924 | 365 | 352 | 20 | 70 | 8.0 | 16 | 8.1 | 34 |
| 1925 | 394 | 356 | 24 | 84 | 11 | 18 | 9.7 | 39 |
| 1926 | 419 | 359 | 23 | 86[7] | 13 | 20 | 12 | 41 |
| 1927 | 481 | 380 | 28 | 81 | 15 | 22[8] | 12 | 40 |
| 1928 | 460 | 394 | 27 | 84 | 16 | 27 | 15 | 41 |
| 1929 | 451 | 405 | 36 | 85 | 16 | 26 | 16 | 43 |
| 1930 | 422 | 442 | 33 | 77 | 11 | ... | 14 | 45 |
| 1931 | 424 | 449 | 28 | 60 | 8.4 | 19 | 13 | 37 |
| 1932 | 412 | 532 | 25 | 52 | 7.4 | 18 | 9.9 | 34 |
| 1933 | 451 | 458 | 24 | 42 | 8.3 | 18 | 8.3 | 34 |
| 1934 | 413 | 478 | 26 | 55 | 9.2 | 19 | 8.2 | 37 |
| 1935 | 462 | 533 | 32 | 65 | 11 | 20 | 8.8 | 42 |
| 1936 | 543 | 532 | 35 | 73 | 11 | 23 | 10 | 37 |
| 1937 | 558 | 534 | 35 | 70[7] | 12 | 22 | 10 | 35 |
| 1938 | 560 | 553 | 36 | ... | 12 | 20 | 11 | 29 |
| 1939 | 628 | 681 | 40 | 76 | 12 | [11][8] | 14 | 38 |
| 1940 | 819 | 1,250 | 44 | 79 | 12 | 22 | 11 | 37 |
| 1941 | 661 | 1,885 | 53 | 78 | 13 | 21 | 11 | 33 |
| 1942 | 755 | 4,387 | 49 | 102 | 15 | 22 | 11 | 30 |
| 1943 | 874 | 5,322 | 72 | 112 | 19 | 23 | 13 | 28 |
| 1944 | 1,008 | 5,246 | 67 | 133 | 26 | 25 | 18 | 32 |

**G5 NORTH AMERICA: Total Central Government Expenditure** (in millions of stated currency unit, except as otherwise indicated)

1900–1944

| | Honduras[10] | Jamaica[2] thousand | Mexico[3] | Nicaragua[13] | Panama[14] | Puerto Rico[15] | Trinidad & Tobago[11] thousand | USA[1] |
|---|---|---|---|---|---|---|---|---|
| | pesos | pounds | pesos | pesos | balboas | dollars | pounds | dollars |
| 1900 | 2.8 | 1,004 | 62 | 5.3 | ... | ... | 697[11] | 521 |
| 1901 | 2.6 | 924 | 68 | 5.6 | ... | ... | 788 | 525 |
| 1902 | 1.9 | 942 | 74 | 5.2 | ... | ... | 773 | 485 |
| 1903 | ... | 949 | 120 | 10 | ... | ... | 847 | 517 |
| 1904 | 3.0 | 943 | 109 | 11 | ... | ... | 833 | 584 |
| 1905 | 3.3 | 914 | 99 | ... | ... | ... | 898 | 567 |
| 1906 | 4.7 | 920 | 102 | ... | ... | 3.6 | 835 | 570 |
| 1907 | 4.2 | 1,053 | 105 | ... | ... | ... | 803 | 579 |
| 1908 | 3.5 | 1,031 | 104 | ... | ... | ... | 918 | 659 |
| 1909 | 3.7 | 1,175 | 107 | ... | 2.8 | ... | 928 | 694 |
| 1910 | 3.3 | 1,135 | 113 | 38 | 6.7 | 5.5 | 927 | 694 |
| 1911 | 4.7 | 1,263 | 120 | 47 | 3.3 | 3.9 | 960 | 691 |
| 1912 | 4.4 | 1,459 | 153 | ... | 3.3 | 8.7 | 947 | 690 |
| | | | | cordobas[17] | | | | |
| 1913 | 5.0 | 1,289 | 111 | 1.9 | 3.3 | 9.5 | 952 | 715 |
| 1914 | 5.5 | 1,230 | ... | 4.8 | 4.4 | 11 | 1,208 | 726 |
| 1915 | 6.5 | 1,282 | ... | 2.3 | 3.1 | 13 | [756][11] | 746 |
| 1916 | 5.5 | 1,274 | ... | 1.8 | 5.7 | 8.9 | 1,033 | 713 |
| 1917 | 5.4 | 1,292 | 126 | 2 | 3.6 | 9.7 | 1,098 | 1,954 |
| 1918 | 5.5 | 1,450 | 166 | 1.8 | 3.4 | 12 | 1,124 | 12,677 |
| 1919 | 7.8 | 1,809 | 168 | 1.6 | 4.3 | 13 | 1,309 | 18,493 |
| 1920 | 7.7 | 2,485 | 213 | 2.1 | 4.4 | 16 | 1,864 | 6,358 |
| 1921 | 7.1 | 2,322 | 258 | 3.4 | 7.3 | 12 | 2,301 | 5,062 |
| 1922 | 16 | 1,950 | 228 | 1.9 | 6.1 | 13 | 2,175 | 3,289 |
| 1923 | 14 | 2,559 | 236 | 1.9 | } 16 { | 11 | 1,735 | 3,140 |
| 1924 | 14 | 2,153 | 211 | 2 | | 12 | 1,657 | 2,908 |
| 1925 | 12 | 2,120 | 298 | 2.2 | } 12 { | 14 | 1,724 | 2,924 |
| 1926 | 11 | 2,164 | 325 | 2.4 | | 14 | 1,616 | 2,930 |
| 1927 | 15 | 2,103 | 310 | 2.5 | } 14 —[14] { | 14 | 1,515 | 2,857 |
| 1928 | 13 | 2,458 | 288 | 2.5 | 17 | 15 | 1,576 | 2,961 |
| 1929 | 14 | 2,670 | 276 | 4.2 | } 17 { | 15 | 1,659 | 3,127 |
| 1930 | 14 | 2,446 | 279 | 3.8 | | 14 | 1,756 | 3,320 |
| 1931 | 12 | 2,320 | 226 | 4.9 | } [19][14] { | 16 | 2,075[16] | 3,577 |
| 1932 | 11 | 2,485 | 212 | 4.8 | | 12 | 1,740 | 4,659 |
| | lempiras[17] | | | | | | | |
| 1933 | 12 | 2,312 | 245 | 4.1 | } 15 { | 11 | 2,452 | 4,598 |
| 1934 | 12 | 2,403 | 265 | 4.7 | | 16 | 1,976 | 6,648 |
| 1935 | 13 | 2,310 | 301 | 4.9 | } 14 { | 15 | 2,084 | 6,497 |
| | | | | | | | dollars[17] | |
| 1936 | 12 | 2,303 | 406 | 5.5 | } | 15 | 9.2 | 8,422 |
| 1937 | 12 | 2,436 | 479 | 6.9 | 9.7 | 18 | 10 | 7,733 |
| 1938 | [12][10] | 2,854 | 504 | 8.7 | 13 | 20 | 12 | 6,765 |
| 1939 | 12 | 3,164 | 571 | 14 | 13 | 19 | 13 | 8,841 |
| 1940 | 11 | 3,781 | 610 | 23 | 18 | 19 | 21 | 9,055 |
| 1941 | 12 | 3,823 | 689 | 28 | 17 | 17 | 17 | 13,255 |
| 1942 | 11 | 4,045 | 845 | 38 | 21 | 24 | 21 | 34,037 |
| 1943 | 14 | 5,949 | 1,085 | 36 | 23 | 41 | 29 | 79,368 |
| 1944 | 17 | 7,408 | 1,505 | 43 | 25 | 51 | 31 | 94,986 |

**G5** **NORTH AMERICA: Total Central Government Expenditure** (in millions of stated currency unit, except as otherwise indicated)

| | Barbados[4] thousand pounds | Canada[5] dollars | Costa Rica[6] colones | Cuba[7] paper pesos | Dominican Republic[19] pesos | El Salvador colones | Guatemala[9] quetzales | Haiti[12] gourdes |
|---|---|---|---|---|---|---|---|---|
| 1945 | 1,145 dollars | 5,136 | 74 | 145 | 30 | 29 | 20 | 35 |
| 1946 | 5.8 | 2,634 | 79 | 174 | 43 | 45 | 29 | 37 |
| 1947 | 7.5 | 2,196 | 97 | 199 | 73 | 52 | 32 | 49 |
| 1948 | 8.8 | 2,176 | 115 | 289[7] | 89 | 64 | 46 | 76 |
| 1949 | 11 | 2,449 | 125 | 229 | 80 | 67 | 49 | 85 |
| 1950 | 11 | 2,945 | 127 | 271 | 91 | 89 | 47 | 98 |
| 1951 | 12 | 3,990 | 141 | 325 | 102 | 121 | 48 | 120 |
| 1952 | 12 | 4,688 | 165 | 341 | 128 | 131 | 59 | 159 |
| 1953 | 13 | 4,221 | 197 | 304 | 104 | 140 | 61 | 152 |
| 1954 | 14 | 4,289 | 219 | 329 | 104 | 152 | 63 | 175 |
| 1955 | 17 | 4,424 | 249[6] 290 | 325 | 125 | 157 | 79 | 174 |
| 1956 | 20 | 4,851 | 290 | 355 | 145 | 183 | 100 | 195 |
| 1957 | 23 | 5,039 | 300 | 386 | 153 | 197 | 114 | 146 |
| 1958 | 28 | 5,364 | 311 | 458[7] | 164 | 198 | 114[9] | 189 |
| 1959 | 30 | 5,703 | 324 | ... | 154 | 186 | 104 | 192 |
| 1960 | 29 | 5,958[5] 6,521 | 356 | 411 | 147 | 184 | 93 | ... |
| 1961 | 32 | 7,004 | 386 | 1,143 | 139 | 221 | 101 | [114][20] |
| 1962 | 35 | 6,931 | 445 | 1,657 | 185 | 201 | 93 | 153 |
| 1963 | 37 | 7,112 | 454 | 2,904 | 190 | 196 | 107 | 144 |
| 1964 | 39 | 7,903 | 488 | 2,399 | 214 | 203 | 116 | ... |
| 1965 | 45 | 8,109 | 541 | 2,536 | 149 | 251 | 128 | 143 |
| 1966 | 54 | 9,108 | 612 | ... | 194 | 280 | 139 | 141 |
| 1967 | 54 | 10,461 | 683 | ... | 201[18] | 260 | 150 | 140[21] 179 |
| 1968 | 66 | 11,672 | 710 | ... | 203 | 242 | 146 | 200 |
| 1969 | 75 | 12,889[5] 14,270 | 810 | ... | 231 | 288 | 167 | 207 |
| 1970 | 98 | 15,990 | 975 | ... | 254 | 283 | 178 | 239 |
| 1971 | 114 | 18,420 | 1,247 | ... | 296[19] | 328 | 203[9] | 273 |
| 1972 | 124 | 21,320 | 1,414 | ... | 359 | 351 | 204 | 284 |
| 1973 | 168 | 24,670 | 1,865[6] 1,846 | ... | 413 | 391 | 245 | 307 |
| 1974 | 198[4] | 31,460 | 2,415 | ... | 548 | 542 | 318 | 367 |
| | | thousand million | | | | | | |
| 1975 | 234 | 37.47[5] 36.00 | 3,217 | ... | 632 | 605 | 348 | 600 |
| 1976 | 288 | 39.69 | 4,148 | ... | 633 | 827 | 438 | 729 |
| 1977 | 328 | 45.06 | 5,085 | ... | 669 | 1,077 | 594 | 973 |
| 1978 | 325 | 50.51 | 7,000 | ... | 745 | 1,184 | 667 | 1,116 |
| 1979 | 396 | 55.54 | 8,601 | ... | 969 | 1,280 | 785[9] | 865 |
| | | | thousand million | | | | | |
| 1980 | 532 | 65.52 | 10.37 | ... | 1,122 | 1,422 | 1,128 | 1,332 |
| 1981 | 625[4] | 76.15 | 11.99 | ... | 1,174 | 1,581 | 1,387 | 1,482 |
| 1982 | 608 | 89.36 | 17.94 | ... | 1,077 | 1,695 | 1,278 | 1,832 |
| 1983 | 636 | 98.81 | 30.49 | ... | 1,205 | 1,571 | 1,169[9] | 2,082 |
| 1984 | 707 | 111.4 | 37.2 | ... | ... | 1,821 | 1,015 | 1,785 |
| 1985 | 797 | 117.2 | 43.1 | ... | ... | 2,150 | 1,053 | 2,035 |
| 1986 | 824 | 119.3 | 65.1 | ... | ... | 2,723 | 1,512 | 1,968 |
| 1987 | 1,008 | 127.1 | 77.4 | ... | ... | 3,023 | 1,979 | 2,075 |
| 1988 | 1,071 | 136.3 | 85.7 | ... | 5,368 | 3,096 | 2,455 | ... |

**G5** **NORTH AMERICA: Total Central Government Expenditure** (in millions of stated currency unit, except as otherwise indicated)

| | Honduras[10] | Jamaica[2] | Mexico[3] | Nicaragua[13] | Panama[14] | Puerto Rico[15] | Trinidad & Tobago | USA[1] |
|---|---|---|---|---|---|---|---|---|
| | lempiras | pounds | pesos | cordobas | balboas | dollars | dollars | dollars |
| | | | | | | | | thousand million dollars |
| 1945 | 18 | 7.6 | 1,633 | 60 | 34 | 62 | 34 | 98 |
| 1946 | 22 | 7.9 | 1,829 | 58 | 39 | 113 | 32 | 60 |
| 1947 | 29 | 8.4 | 2,343 | 66 | 39 | 97 | 37 | 39 |
| 1948 | 26 | 10.1 | 2,773 | 70 | 35 | 109 | 39 | 33 |
| 1949 | 38 | 9.9 | 3,741 | 77 | 33 | 132 | 42 | 39 |
| 1950 | 39 | 10 | 3,700 | ...[13] | 37 | 136 | 50 | 40 |
| 1951 | 46 | 14 | 5,075 | 112 | 34 | 141 | 53 | 44 |
| 1952 | 59 | 14 | 6,063 | 135 | 39 | 141 | 62 | 65 |
| 1953 | 62 | 15 | 5,825 | 166 | 42 | 168[17] 160 | 67 | 74 |
| 1954 | 63 | 17 | 8,471 | 166 | 44 | 171 | 74 | 71 |
| 1955 | 72 | 20 | 9,255 | 220 | 47 | 179 | 79 | 69 |
| 1956 | [43][10] | 22 | 10,567 | 246 | 55 | 185 | 86 | 70 |
| 1957 | 87 | 29 | 11,815 | 252 | 52 | 227 | 90 | 77 |
| 1958 | 89 | 34 | 13,841 | 262 | 64 | 236 | 128 | 83 |
| 1959 | 83 | 37 | 14,777 | 263 | 56 | 254 | 169 | 92 |
| 1960 | 89 | 38 | 20,778 | 263 | 65 | 279 | 169 | 92 |
| 1961 | 88 | 42 | 20,946 | 251 | 78 | 307 | 196 | 98 |
| 1962 | 93[10] 84 | 46 | 21,421 | 296 | 73 | 315 | 212 | 107 |
| 1963 | 85 | 47 | 21,371 | 323 | 85 | 378 | 229 | 111 |
| 1964 | 100 | 55 | 29,660 | 366 | 78[14] | 425 | 265 | 119 |
| | | | thousand million | | | | | |
| 1965 | 108 | 64 | 37.7 | 432 | 90 | 479 | 251 | 118 |
| 1966 | 125 | 67 | 34.5[3] 31.9 | 520 | 107 | 541 | 267 | 135 |
| 1967 | 133 | 74 | 33.9 | 583 | 126 | 586 | 271 | 158 |
| 1968 | 153 | 86 | 39.4 | 529 | 128 | 719 | 305 | 178 |
| | | dollars[17] | | | | | | |
| 1969 | 183 | 191 | 46.9 | 581 | 195 | 766 | 327 | 184 |
| 1970 | 217 | 236 | 48.6 | 718 | 209 | 891 | 390 | 196 |
| 1971 | 226 | 287 | 52[3] | 871 | 213 | 1,133 | 465 | 210 |
| 1972 | 238 | 333 | 67 | 918 | 303[14] | 1,263[15] 1,549 | 539 | 231 |
| 1973 | 235 | 417 | 88 | 972 | 387 | 1,797 | 574 | 246 |
| 1974 | 263 | 627 | 124 | 1,631 | 504 | 1,957 | 1,301 | 269 |
| 1975 | 320 | 823 | 162 | 1,916 | 582 | 2,405 | 1,681[21] | 332 |
| 1976 | 384 | 1,013 | 212 | 2,040 | 626 | 2,646 | 1,600 | 372[1] |
| 1977 | 554 | 1,428 | 286 | 2,936 | 650 | 2,840 | 1,913 | 409 |
| 1978 | 579 | 1,724 | 367 | 2,526 | 737 | 3,020 | 2,680 | 459 |
| 1979 | 735 | 2,165 | 505 | 2,999 | 1,066 | 3,297 | 3,655 | 503 |
| 1980 | 897 | 2,488 | 750 | 6,332 | 1,163 | 3,696 | 4,622 | 591 |
| 1981 | 883 | 2,417 | 1,182 | 9,620 | 1,322 | 4,033 | 5,061[22] | 678 |
| 1982 | 1,150 | 2,806 | 2,829 | 13,993 | 1,612 | 4,018 | 9,464 | 746 |
| 1983 | 1,382 | 3,643 | 4,468 | 22,274 | 1,512 | 4,111 | 8,780 | 808 |
| 1984 | 1,630 | 4,727 | 6,747 | 28,775 | 1,653 | ... | 8,276 | 852 |
| | | | million million | thousand million | | | | |
| 1985 | 1,718 | 4,671 | 11.8 | 69 | 1,579 | ... | 7,684 | 946 |
| 1986 | 1,644 | 5,674 | 22.8 | 228 | 1,725 | ... | 6,570 | 990 |
| 1987 | 1,589 | 6,012 | 59.7 | ... | 1,764 | ... | 6,387 | 1,004 |
| 1988 | 1,652 | 8,733 | 107 | 155 | 1,305 | ... | 6,061 | 1,064 |

**G5  SOUTH AMERICA: TOTAL CENTRAL GOVERNMENT EXPENDITURE** (in millions of stated currency unit except as otherwise indicated)

**1823–1864**

| | Argentina[23] | Brazil[24] | Chile[25] | Guyana[26] | Peru[27] | Venezuala[28] |
|---|---|---|---|---|---|---|
| | gold pesos | milreis | pesos | thousand dollars | pesos | pesos |
| 1823 | ... | 4.7 | ... | ... | ... | ... |
| 1824 | ... | 9.6 | ... | ... | ... | ... |
| 1825 | ... | 8.4 | ... | ... | ... | ... |
| 1826 | ... | 9.4 | ... | ... | ... | ... |
| 1827 | ... | 12 | ... | ... | ... | ... |
| 1828 | ... | 11 [24] | ... | ... | ... | ... |
| 1829 | | 14 | | | | |
| 1830 | ... | 18 | ... | ... | ... | 5.1 |
| 1831 | ... | 20 | ... | ... | ... | 5.7 |
| 1832 | ... | 12 | ... | ... | ... | 5.6 |
| 1833 | ... | 14 | ... | ... | ... | 6.2 |
| 1834 | ... | 11 | ... | ... | ... | 5.8 |
| 1835 | ... | 13 | ... | ... | ... | 6.0 |
| 1836 | ... | 14 | ... | ... | ... | 8.2 |
| 1837 | ... | 14 | ... | ... | ... | 7.3 |
| 1838 | ... | 19 | ... | 605 | ... | 7.2 |
| 1839 | ... | 18 | ... | 638 | ... | 9.7 |
| 1840 | ... | 25 | ... | 584 | ... | 7.2 |
| 1841 | ... | 23 | ... | 1,066 | ... | 7.7 |
| 1842 | ... | 27 | ... | 862 | ... | 14 |
| 1843 | ... | 29 | ... | 810 | ... | 9.4 |
| 1844 | ... | 26 | ... | 680 | ... | 15 |
| 1845 | ... | 26 | ... | 867 | ... | 12 |
| 1846 | ... | 24 | ... | 1,207 | } 12 { | 18 |
| 1847 | ... | 27 | ... | 1,364 | | 12 |
| 1848 | ... | 26 | ... | | } 11 { | 14 |
| 1849 | ... | 28 | ... | 632 | | 17 |
| 1850 | ... | 29 | ... | 875 | } 11 { | 17 |
| 1851 | ... | 33 | ... | 926 | | 19 |
| 1852 | ... | 43 | ... | 1,090 | } 14 { | 14 |
| 1853 | ... | 32 | ... | 1,138 | | 24 |
| 1854 | ... | 36 | ... | 1,099 | } 20 { | 23 |
| 1855 | ... | 39 | ... | 1,152 | | 32 |
| 1856 | ... | 40 | ... | 1,128 | ... | 25 |
| 1857 | ... | 40 | 17 | 1,349 | ... | 23 |
| 1858 | ... | 52 | 19 | 1,306 | ... | 20 |
| 1859 | ... | 53 | 20 | 1,262 | ... | 11 |
| 1860 | ... | 53 | 19 | 1,512 | ... | 29 |
| 1861 | ... | 52 | 16 | 1,560 | } 33 { | 34 |
| 1862 | ... | 53 | 16 | 1,493 | | 24 |
| 1863 | ... | 57 | 18 | 1,282 | } 44 { | 11 |
| 1864 | 7.1 | 56 | 20 | 1,210 | | 24 |

**G5    SOUTH AMERICA: Total Central Government Expenditure** (in millions of stated currency unit, except as otherwise indicated)

**1865–1904**

| | Argentina[23] | Bolivia[29] | Brazil[24] | Chile[25] | Ecuador | Guyana[26] thousand | Paraguay[31] | Peru[27] | Surinam | Uruguay[32] | Venezuela[28] |
|---|---|---|---|---|---|---|---|---|---|---|---|
| | gold pesos | bolivianos | milreis | pesos | sucres | dollars | gold pesos | soles | guilders | pesos | bolivares |
| 1865 | 13 | ... | 83 | 25 | ... | 1,306 | ... | ... | ... | ... | 25 |
| 1866 | 14 | ... | 122 | 35 | ... | 1,363 | ... | ... | ... | ... | 21 |
| 1867 | 14 | ... | 121 | 36 | ... | 1,392 | ... | ... | ... | ... | 15 |
| 1868 | 17 | ... | 166 | 31 | ... | 1,344 | ... | ... | ... | ... | 20 |
| 1869 | 15 | ... | 151 | 30 | ... | 1,435 | ... | 62 | ... | 6.5 | 22 |
| 1870 | 19 | ... | 142 | 32 | ... | 1,464 | ... | | ... | ... | 10 |
| 1871 | 21 | ... | 100 | 33 | ... | 1,493 | ... | 59 | ... | 6.3 | 9.9 |
| 1872 | 26 | ... | 102 | 36 | ... | 1,584 | ... | | ... | ... | 15 |
| 1873 | 31 | ... | 122 | 40 | ... | 1,752 | ... | 47 | ... | 6.7 | 17 |
| 1874 | 30 | ... | 121 | 50 | ... | 1,733 | ... | | ... | 8.7 | 25 |
| 1875 | 29 | ... | 126 | 48 | ... | 1,709 | ... | 74 | ... | 13 | 22 |
| 1876 | 22 | ... | 127 | 42 | ... | 1,651 | ... | | ... | 5.0 | 24 |
| 1877 | 20 | ... | 136 | 43 | ... | 1,829 | ... | 43 | ... | ... | 21 |
| 1878 | 21 | ... | 151 | 32 | ... | 2,006 | ... | | ... | ... | 9.8 |
| 1879 | 23 | ... | 181 | 44 | ... | 2,414 | ... | 30 | ... | 8.7 | 24 |
| 1880 | 27 | ... | 150 | 44 | ... | 2,290 | ... | | ... | ... | 23 |
| 1881 | 28 | ... | 139 | 55 | ... | 3,163 | 0.8 | ... | ... | ... | 30 |
| | paper pesos | | | | | | | | | | |
| 1882 | 58 | ... | 139 | 76 | ... | 3,269 | 0.8 | ... | ... | ... | 25 |
| 1883 | 45 | ... | 153 | 84 | ... | 2,621 | 0.8 | ... | ... | 9.9 | 36 |
| 1884 | 56 | ... | 154 | 73 | ... | 2,712 | 1.1 | ... | ... | 12 | 35 |
| 1885 | 56 | ... | 158 | 50 | 3.9 | 2,837 | 1.3 | ... | ... | 13 | 31 |
| 1886 | 54 | ... | 154 | 67 | 4.7 | 2,549 | 3.0 | ... | ... | 13 | 29 |
| 1887 | 65 | ... | [227][24] | 74 | 4.4 | 3,283 | 0.8 | 14 | 1.5 | 14 | 42 |
| 1888 | 76 | 4.6 | 147 | 60 | [4.4][30] | [2,520][26] | 1.4 | | 1.6 | 14 | 37 |
| 1889 | 107 | 3.6 | 186 | 77 | 3.1 | 2,530 | 2.1 | 13 | 1.5 | ... | 46 |
| 1890 | 95 | 3.6 | 221 | 91 | 3.8 | 2,707 | 0.9 | | 1.5 | ... | 49 |
| 1891 | 129 | 3.6 | 221 | 98 | 3.9 | 2,809 | 0.5 | 6.6 | 1.7 | ... | 45 |
| 1892 | 129 | 5.9 | 279 | 68 | 4.1 | 2,678 | 0.7 | 7.1 | 1.7 | 15 | 33 |
| 1893 | 123 | 5.7 | 301 | 50 | 4.4 | 2,894 | 0.9 | 8 | 1.9 | ... | 52 |
| 1894 | 143 | 6.1 | 373 | 48 | ... | 2,904 | 0.8 | 7.3 | 2.1 | 16 | 44 |
| 1895 | 167 | 6.7[24] | 345 | 74 | ... | 2,990 | 0.9 | ... | 2 | ... | 66 |
| 1896 | 230 | 4.3 | 369 | 103 | ... | 2,957 | 1.1 | 9.3 | 2.3 | ... | 47 |
| 1897 | 179 | ... | 379 | 72 | 5.7 | 2,765 | 1.0 | 11 | 2.3 | ... | 46 |
| 1898 | 311 | 5.7 | 668 | 88 | 5.4 | 2,606 | 1.1 | 11[27] / 12 | 2.2 | 16 | 36 |
| 1899 | 174 | 8.1 | 295 | 82 | 6.7 | 2,587 | 1.1 | 12 | 2.2 | 16 | 24 |
| 1900 | 159 | 7.9 | 434 | 92[25] / 277 | 7.4 | 2,438 | 1.5 | 13 | 2.2 | ... | 38 |
| 1901 | 163 | 7.8 | 335 | 310 | 9.3 | 2,530 | ... | 14 | 2.5 | ... | 32 |
| 1902 | 203 | 9.3 | 298 | 309 | 13 | 2,410 | ... | 14 | 2.4 | 15 | 24 |
| 1903 | 183 | 7.5 | 363 | 272 | 12 | 2,549 | ... | 15 | 4.4 | ... | 38 |
| 1904 | 195 | 6.1 | 463 | 331 | 11 | 2,453 | ... | 19 | 5 | 16 | 51 |

**G5** **SOUTH AMERICA: Total Central Government Expenditure** (in millions of stated currency unit, except as otherwise indicated)

**1905–1949**

| | Argentina[23] | Bolivia | Brazil[24] | Chile[25] | Colombia[33] | Ecuador |
|---|---|---|---|---|---|---|
| | paper pesos | bolivianos | milreis or cruzeiros | pesos | pesos | sucres |
| 1905 | 322 | 7.5 | 375 | 312 | 7.0 | 10 |
| 1906 | 270 | 12 | 423 | 357 | ... | 13 |
| 1907 | 253 | 15 | 522 | 363 | 16 | 15 |
| 1908 | 252 | 17 | 511 | 322 | [17][30] | 13 |
| 1909 | 392 | 17 | 518 | 377 | [17][30] | 16 |
| 1910 | 411 | 13 | 624 | 490 | 12 | 15 |
| 1911 | 417 | 18 | 682 | 460 | 12 | 16 |
| 1912 | 404 | 16 | 789 | 558 | 14 | 20 |
| 1913 | 403 | 22 | 763 | 496 | 16 | 22 |
| 1914 | 420 | 23 | 767 | 519 | 15 | 23 |
| 1915 | 391 | 21 | 689 | 462 | 13 | [21][30] |
| 1916 | 375 | 23 | 687 | 486 | [20][33] | [18][30] |
| 1917 | 390 | 17 | 801 | 577 | 15 | [18][30] |
| 1918 | 421 | 33 | 867 | 665 | 18 | 17 |
| 1919 | 428 | 31 | 932 | 549 | [17][33] | 14 |
| 1920 | 488 | 54 | 1,227 | 793 | 23 | 23 |
| 1921 | 560 | 47 | 1,189 | 629[25] 605 | 24 | 22 |
| 1922 | 614 | 40 | 1,428 | 566 | ... | 27 |
| 1923 | 632 | 38 | 1,569 | 618 | 39 | 29 |
| 1924 | 671 | 45 | 1,630 | 677 | 40 | 35 |
| 1925 | 713 | 45 | 1,760 | 825 | 50 | 44 |
| 1926 | 746 | 48 | 1,868 | 1,122 | 67 | 44 |
| 1927 | 1,049 | 50 | 2,026 | 906 | 84 | 70 |
| 1928 | 919 | 61 | 2,350 | 1,484 | 115 | 57 |
| 1929 | 988 | 53 | 2,422 | 1,596 | 83 | 63 |
| 1930 | 1,092 | 49 | 2,511 | 1,663 | 61 | 60 |
| 1931 | 908 | 31 | 2,047 | 1,223 | 52 | 45 |
| 1932 | 850 | 34 | 2,860 | 992 | 46 | 42 |
| 1933 | 880 | 104 | 2,392 | 944 | 63 | 42 |
| 1934 | 934 | 129 | 3,050 | 975 | 75 | 48 |
| 1935 | 981 | 193 | 2,872 | 1,291 | 61 | 65 |
| 1936 | 1,052 | ... | 3,226 | 1,383 | 72 | 76 |
| 1937 | 1,221 | ... | 4,144 | 1,545 | 86 | 80 |
| 1938 | 1,278 | 339 | 4,735 | 1,745 | 88 | 132 |
| 1939 | 1,460 | 400 | 4,850 | 1,839 | 97 | 117 |
| 1940 | 1,322 | 564 | 5,189 | 2,282 | 129 | 114 |
| 1941 | 1,371 | 1,018 | 5,436 | 2,811 | 110 | 128 |
| 1942 | 1,554 | 1,162 | 6,343 | 3,069 | 154 | 128 |
| 1943 | 1,786 | 1,200 | 6,512 | 4,386 | 177 | 176 |
| 1944 | 2,491 | 1,170 | 8,399 | 4,534 | 174 | 231 |
| 1945 | 2,815 | 1,183 | 10,839 | 6,327 | 194 | 293 |
| 1946 | 3,321 | 1,183 | 14,203 | 7,264 | 276 | 336 |
| 1947 | 4,220 | 1,307 | 13,393 | 10,112 | 356 | 403 |
| 1948 | 7,076 | 1,667 | 15,696 | 12,509 | 403 | 391 |
| 1949 | 7,783 | 1,813 | 20,727 | 14,860 | 402 | 396 |

**G5    SOUTH AMERICA: Total Central Government Expenditure** (in millions of stated currency unit, except as otherwise indicated)

**1905–1949**

| | Guyana[26] | Paraguay[31] | Peru[27] | Surinam | Uruguay[32] | Venezuela[28] |
|---|---|---|---|---|---|---|
| | thousand dollars | gold pesos | soles | guilders | pesos | bolivares |
| 1905 | 2,429 | ... | 21 | 4.3 | 17 | 50 |
| 1906 | 2,467 | ... | 24 | 4.8 | 19 | 61 |
| 1907 | 2,496 | ... | 27 | 4.3 | 19 | 49 |
| 1908 | 2,587 | ... | 30 | 5.1 | 21 | 48 |
| 1909 | 2,635 | ... | 27 | 5.1 | 26 | 52 |
| 1910 | 2,621 | ... | 27 | 6.7 | 32 | 62 |
| 1911 | 2,827 | ... | 30 | 7.3 | 32 | 64 |
| 1912 | 2,837 | ...[31] | 37 | 7.0 | 38 | 62 |
| 1913 | 3,082 | 4.9 | 54 | 7.3 | 35 | 65 |
| 1914 | 3,331 | 3.8 | 41 | 7.1 | 35 | 45 |
| 1915 | [2,150][26] | 4.2 | 34 | 7.3 | 32 | 58 |
| 1916 | 3,254 | 3.4 | 36 | 4.2 | 28 | 58 |
| 1917 | 3,552 | ... | 48 | 4.9 | 30 | 53 |
| 1918 | 6,062 | ... | 54 | 5.1 | 30 | 58 |
| 1919 | 5,453 | 5.4[31] | 66 | 5.2 | ... | 68 |
| | | paper pesos | | | | |
| 1920 | 5,294 | 70 | 89 | 9.8 | 42 | 103 |
| 1921 | 6,883 | 114 | 88 | ... | 43 | 81 |
| 1922 | 6,125 | 145 | 88 | 9.6 | 42 | 72 |
| 1923 | 6,370 | 151 | 91 | 9.1 | 61 | 87 |
| 1924 | 6,293 | 161 | 118 | 8.7 | 59 | 115 |
| 1925 | 7,277 | 178 | 128 | 8.1 | 59 | 163 |
| 1926 | 7,642 | 235 | 189 | 8.2 | 56 | 179 |
| 1927 | 6,485 | 219 | 185 | 7.7 | 59 | 156 |
| 1928 | 7,882 | 248 | 257 | 8.2 | 66 | 245 |
| 1929 | 6,648 | 281 | 205 | 7.8 | 59 | 264 |
| 1930 | 5,885 | 287 | 149 | 7.6 | 63 | 261 |
| 1931 | 5,309 | 231 | 136 | 7.8 | 62 | 166 |
| 1932 | 5,395 | 233 | 99 | 7.7 | [30][32] | 162 |
| 1933 | 5,189 | ... | 132 | 6.8 | 61 | 154 |
| 1934 | 5,462 | ... | 169 | 6.8 | 61 | 179 |
| 1935 | 6,427 | 323 | 139 | 6.7 | 81 | 233 |
| 1936 | 5,765 | 762 | 195 | 6.7 | 86 | 285 |
| 1937 | 6,206[26] | 1,889 | 198 | 6.3 | 86 | 313 |
| | 6,051 | | | | | |
| 1938 | 6,153 | 345 | 265 | 6.5 | 92 | 361 |
| 1939 | 6,425 | 256 | 236 | 6.9 | 97 | 382 |
| | million | guaranies[17] | | | | |
| 1940 | 6.8 | 17[31] | 210 | 7.5 | 101 | 347 |
| 1941 | 7.1 | 20 | 328 | 5.8 | 107 | 320 |
| 1942 | 8.0 | 20 | 409 | 11 | 113 | 307 |
| 1943 | 11 | 25 | 423 | 17 | 122 | 363 |
| 1944 | 13 | 26 | 503 | 16 | 134 | 488 |
| 1945 | 14 | 31 | 536 | 12 | 143 | 755 |
| 1946 | 14 | 36 | 699 | 12 | 167 | 1,065 |
| 1947 | 17 | 57 | 970 | 18 | 190 | 1,438 |
| 1948 | 20 | 45 | 1,094 | 20 | 232 | 1,946 |
| 1949 | 21 | 53 | 1,143 | 25 | 257 | 1,928 |

## G5 SOUTH AMERICA: Total Central Government Expenditure (in millions of stated currency unit, except as otherwise indicated)

| | Argentina[23] thousand million paper pesos | Bolivia thousand million bolivianos | Brazil[24] thousand million cruzeiros | Chile[25] thousand million pesos | Colombia[33] pesos | Ecuador[34] sucres |
|---|---|---|---|---|---|---|
| 1950 | 8.7 | 2.36 | 24 | 20 | 520 | 426[34] |
| | | | | | | 488 |
| 1951 | 13.4 | 3.71 | 27 | 26 | 691[33] | 533 |
| | | | | | 615 | |
| 1952 | 15.4 | 4.19 | 30 | 42 | 646 | 587 |
| 1953 | 16.4 | 9.00 | 52 | 54 | 855 | 776 |
| 1954 | 18.1 | 15 | 54 | 83 | 1,043 | 1,072 |
| | | | | escudos[17] | | |
| 1955 | 20 | 26 | 65 | 156 | 1,588 | 1,237 |
| 1956 | 26 | 77 | 98 | 231 | 1,220 | 1,240 |
| 1957 | [28][23] | 273 | 138 | 351 | 1,243 | 1,237 |
| 1958 | 67 | 331 | 162 | 457 | 1,573 | 1,217 |
| 1959 | 109[23] | 453 | 222 | 647 | 1,718[33] | 1,333 |
| | | | | | 1,574 | |
| 1960 | 126 | 454 | 324 | 903 | 2,191 | 1,740 |
| 1961 | 165 | 520 | 509 | 1,030 | 3,188 | 2,081 |
| 1962 | 197 | 544 | 847 | 1,273 | 2,583 | 1,878 |
| | | pesos[17] | | | | |
| 1963 | 226 | 619 | 1,556 | 1,728 | 4,011 | 1,905 |
| 1964 | 349 | 701 | 2,857 | 2,378 | 4,263 | 2,462 |
| 1965 | 395 | 928 | 4,500 | 3,992 | 4,629 | 2,624 |
| 1966 | 598 | 1,023 | 6,497 | 5,693 | 6,094 | 2,831 |
| | | | new cruzeiros[17] | thousand million | thousand million | |
| 1967 | 551[23] | 1,177 | 8.0 | 6.9 | 7.1 | 3,027 |
| 1968 | 577 | 1,440 | 12 | 9.7 | 10.4 | 3,785 |
| 1969 | 660 | 1,360 | 15 | 13.7 | 13.5 | 4,200 |
| | thousand million new pesos[17] | | | | | thousand million |
| 1970 | 7.6 | 1,399 | 20[24] | 22 | 16.9 | 5.3 |
| | | | 34 | | | |
| 1971 | 11.6 | 1,708 | 46 | 36 | 20.8 | 6.2 |
| 1972 | 18.4 | 2,019 | 60 | 65 | 22.0 | 6.4[34] |
| 1973 | 38.7 | 3,370 | 80 | 305 | 27.2 | 7.8 |
| 1974 | 59.5 | ... | 117 | 2,985[25] | 33.1 | 11.4 |
| | | | | 3,042 | | |
| | 202[23] | thousand million | | thousand million pesos[17] | | |
| 1975 | 280 | 6.8 | 184 | 12.2 | 46.8 | 13.1 |
| 1976 | 1,340 | 8.8 | 291 | 38.8 | 52.8 | 16.8 |
| 1977 | 3,250 | 11 | 464 | 92.1 | 72.8 | 21.8 |
| 1978 | 9,260 | 12 | 716 | 155 | 101 | 21.4 |
| | million million | | | | | |
| 1979 | 24.8 | 15 | 1,094 | 222 | 156 | 24.6 |
| 1980 | 53.8 | 22 | 2,507 | 301 | 195 | 41.7 |
| 1981 | 123 | 24 | 4,988 | 375 | 237 | 56.1 |
| 1982 | 305 | 130 | 10,561 | 423 | 331 | 64.5 |
| | australes[17] | | | | | |
| 1983 | 149[35] | 356 | 24,939 | 497 | 402 | 74.2 |
| 1984 | 885[35] | 8,221 | 79,723 | 617 | 541 | 107 |
| | thousand million | million million | thousand million cruzados[17] | | | |
| 1985 | 9.4 | 1,384 | 351 | 806 | 682 | 168 |
| 1986 | 16.0 | 1,010 | 1,021 | 969 | 940 | 218 |
| 1987 | 35.5 | 1,110[36] | 2,871 | 1,218 | 1,194 | 279 |
| 1988 | 120 | 1,515[36] | 27,094 | 1,620 | 1,581 | 417 |

**G5**     **SOUTH AMERICA: Total Central Government Expenditure** (in millions of stated currency unit, except as otherwise indicated)

| | Guyana[26] dollars | Paraguay[31] guaranies | Peru[27] soles | Surinam guilders | Uruguay[32] pesos | Venezuela[28] bolivares |
|---|---|---|---|---|---|---|
| 1950 | 24 | [124][31] | 1,716 | 29 | 307 | 2,156 |
| 1951 | 25 | ... | 2,037 | 27 | 365 | 2,375 |
| 1952 | 28 | 171[31] | 2,200 | 29 | 376 | 2,377 |
| 1953 | 31 | 382 | 2,692[27] / 3,525 | 37 | 431 | 2,430 |
| 1954 | 35 | ... | 3,819 | 42 | 503 | 2,798 |
| 1955 | 40 | ... | 4,770 | 43 | 505 | 3,052 |
| 1956 | 40 | ... | 5,773 | 46 | 516 | 3,804 |
| 1957 | 43 | ... | 6,027 | 55 | 709 | 5,442 |
| 1958 | 46 | 2,231 | 6,226 | 65 | 791 | 6,248 |
| 1959 | 46 | 2,312 | 6,858 | 69 | 843 | 6,484 |
| 1960 | 50 | 2,451 | 7,120 | 85 | 1,347 | 6,718 |
| 1961 | 57 | 2,805 | 9,427 | 93 | 2,253 | [3,400][28] |
| 1962 | 62 | 3,339 | 10,718 | 97 | 3,009 | 6,258 |
| 1963 | 62 | 4,240 | 12,761 | 96 | 3,261 | 6,590 |
| 1964 | 71 | 4,090 | 16,341 | 101 | 4,646 | 7,100 |
| | | *thousand million* | *thousand million* | | *thousand million* | *thousand million* |
| 1965 | 82 | 4.5 | 21.5 | 108 | 8.2 | 7.4 |
| 1966 | 84 | 6.7 | 25.4 | 124 | 14 | 7.8 |
| 1967 | 88 | 7.8[31] / 6.9 | 29.9[27] | 131 | 25 | 8.2[28] |
| 1968 | 98 | 7.6 | 34.1 | 144 | 53 | 9.0 |
| 1969 | 107[26] | 8.4 | 34.3 | 167 | 74 | 9.6[28] |
| 1970 | 169 | 8.7 | 42.3 | 190 | 91 | 9.8 |
| 1971 | 173 | 9.3 | 49.5 | 200 | 145[32] | 11.1 |
| 1972 | 202 | 12.4 | 56.5 | 223 | 306 | 12.7 |
| 1973 | 280 | 13.3 | 67.4 | 218 | 580 | 14.2 |
| 1974 | 340 | 16.3 | 82.6 | 237 | 1,084 | 22.8 |
| | | | | | *new pesos* | |
| 1975 | 560 | 21.2 | 118 | 318 | 1,877 | 27.5 |
| 1976 | 685 | 25.3 | 160 | 424 | 3,054 | 32.7 |
| 1977 | 513 | 29.2 | 233 | 541 | 4,677 | 42.2 |
| 1978 | 533 | 37.7 | 344 | 537 | 7,068 | 46.3 |
| 1979 | 689 | 45.5 | 570 | 542 | 11,615 | 44.8 |
| | | | | | *thousand million* | |
| 1980 | 906 | 56.8 | 1,159 | 581 | 20.1 | 55.8 |
| 1981 | 1,154 | 75.6 | 1,928 | 714 | 30.5 | 84.5 |
| 1982 | 1,508 | 86.7 | 3,050 | 788 | 38.1 | 84.5[28] / 73.4 |
| 1983 | 1,141 | 87.3 | 6,083 | 801 | 46.3 | 73.4 |
| 1984 | 1,457 | 115 | 12,496 | 768 | 69.4 | 82.6 |
| | | | *thousand million intis*[17] | | | |
| 1985 | 1,913 | 127 | 32.3 | 803 | 118 | 94.6 |
| 1986 | 2,353 | 148 | 58 | 926 | 223 | 105 |
| 1987 | 2,715 | 225 | 108 | ... | 406 | 154 |
| 1988 | 3,098 | 286 | 535 | ... | 708 | 186 |

**G5A** **TOTAL EXPENDITURE OF CANADIAN COLONIES BEFORE CONFEDERATION CANADA** (in thousand pounds)[37]

### 1805–1839

| | Lower Canada* | Upper Canada† |
|---|---|---|
| 1805 | ... | ... |
| 1806 | 35 | ... |
| 1807 | 42 | ... |
| 1808 | 43 | ... |
| 1809 | 39 | ... |
| 1810 | 47 | ... |
| 1811 | 47 | ... |
| 1812 | 98 | ... |
| 1813 | 181 | ... |
| 1814 | 161 | ... |
| 1815 | 91 | ... |
| 1816 | 50 | ... |
| 1817 | 109 | ... |
| 1818 | 121 | ... |
| 1819 | 72 | ... |
| 1820 | 54 | ... |
| 1821 | 79 | ... |
| 1822 | 74 | ... |
| 1823 | 106 | ... |
| 1824 | 84 | 44 |
| 1825 | 80 | 35 |
| 1826 | 80 | 72 |
| 1827 | 101 | 90 |
| 1828 | 62 | 42 |
| 1829 | 170 | 49 |
| 1830 | 161 | 98 |
| 1831 | 164 | 100 |
| 1832 | 166 | 80 |
| 1833 | 126 | 125 |
| 1834 | 124 | 310 |
| 1835 | 71 | 221 |
| 1836 | 2.3 | } 636 { |
| 1837 | 0.3 | |
| 1838 | 223 | 260 |
| 1839 | 166 | 196 |

### 1840–1866

| | British Columbia[36] | Lower Canada* | Upper Canada† | New Brunswick | Nova Scotia[40] | Prince Edward Island |
|---|---|---|---|---|---|---|
| 1840 | — | [197][38] | [252][38] | ... | ... | ... |
| 1841 | — | ... | ... | ... | ... | ... |
| | | Province of Canada[39] | | | | |
| 1842 | — | 476 | | ... | ... | ... |
| 1843 | — | 771I | | ... | ... | ... |
| 1844 | — | 957 | | ... | ... | ... |
| 1845 | — | 906 | | ... | ... | ... |
| 1846 | — | 770 | | ... | ... | ... |
| 1847 | — | 716 | | ... | ... | ... |
| 1848 | — | [390][39] | | ... | ... | ... |
| 1849 | — | [371][39] | | ... | ... | ... |
| 1850 | — | 673 | | 85 | 92 | 9 |
| 1851 | — | 722 | | 89 | 101 | 16 |
| 1852 | — | 927 | | 129 | 114 | 15 |
| 1853 | — | 1,384 | | 105 | 107 | 20 |
| 1854 | — | 1,737 | | 136 | 169 | 35 |
| 1855 | — | 1,217 | | 138 | ... | 30 |
| 1856 | — | [946][39] 142 | | ... 40 | 34 | |
| 1857 | — | 2,359 | | 135 | 159 | 32 |
| 1858 | — | 2,212 | | 133 | 148 | 29 |
| 1859 | 13 | 1,932 | | 154 | 138 | 30 |
| 1860 | 70 | 2,989 | | 174 | 117 | 41 |
| 1861 | 99 | 2,467 | | 176 | 130 | 33 |
| 1862 | 170 | 2,284 | | 167 | 119 | 34 |
| 1863 | 181 | 2,207 [39] | | 185 | 139 | 36 |
| 1864 | 179 | 3,143 | | 176 | 137 | 39 |
| 1865 | 206 | 2,685 | | 190 | 220 | 51 |
| 1866 | 94 | 2,587 | | 281 | 279 | 103 |

*later Quebec †later Ontario

## G5    Total Central Government Expenditure

NOTES

1. SOURCES:- The national publications listed on p. xiv–xvi, with gaps filled from League of Nations, *Public Finance Statistics* and *Statistical Yearbooks*, and U.N. *Statistical Yearbooks*. From the 1960s, International Monetary Fund, *International Financial Statistics* is the main source.

2. So far as possible, all kinds of central government budgetary expenditure, other than debt redemption, are included in this table. However, in many cases extra-budgetary expenditures are included, and the types of outlay included within the budget have varied very much from country to country and from time to time. So far as possible, changes and the reasons for them are indicated in footnotes.

3. It must be recalled that in some countries, especially those with federal systems of government, central government expenditures may be no more important than the outlays of 'local' governments.

4. Except where otherwise indicated, statistics are taken from closed accounts, not budgets.

FOOTNOTES

[1] Federal government expenditure exclusive of debt repayment. Prior to 1913, expenditures are on a gross basis, but subsequently various refunds are treated as reductions. Certain inter-fund transactions are not excluded until 1932, but the amounts involved were insignificant. From 1844 to 1976 data apply to years ended 30 June. Subsequently they are for years ended 30 September. The 1843 figure is for the first half-year only. Expenditure in July-September 1976 was $96 thousand million.

[2] Statistics to 1889 are for years ended 30 September. Subsequently they are for years beginning 1 April.

[3] Federal government ordinary expenditure to 1971, but with a narrower definition from 1966 (2nd line). Consolidated central government expenditure subsequently.

[4] Statistics from 1901 are for years beginning 1 April. Some extra-budgetary funds are included from 1975 and more from 1982.

[5] Federal government expenditure exclusive of debt repayment. Some extra-budgetary items are included from 1960 and more from 1969, but from 1970 (2nd line) figures are of consolidated central government expenditure. Data to 1906 are for years ended 30 June. Subsequently they are for years beginning 1 April. Expenditure in the period 1 July 1906 to 31 March 1907 was $65 million.

[6] Ordinary budget expenditure only to 1955 (1st line), and consolidated central government expenditure from 1973 (2nd line). Data to 1907 are for years beginning 1 April. The 1908 figure is for the period 1 April to 31 December.

[7] Budget estimates to 1926, except for 1888, which is a provisional result, and 1889, which is actual expenditure. Outlays under special laws are not included. Data to 1937 and from 1947 to 1958 are for years beginning 1 July.

[8] Statistics for 1910 to 1927 are of estimates rather than actual expenditure. Data to 1938 are for years beginning 1 July. The 1939 figure is for the second half-year only.

[9] Ordinary budget expenditure only to 1906 (1st line), and budgetary central government expenditure from 1972, except in 1980–1983 when various extra-budgetary expenditures are included. Data from 1927 to 958 are for years ended 30 June.

[10] Statistics to 1962 (1st line) are of ordinary budget expenditure. Subsequently they are of consolidated central government expenditure. Data to 1937 are for years beginning 1 August, and those for 1939–55 are for years beginning 1 July. The 1938 figures is for the period 1 August 1938 to 30 June 1939, and the 1956 figure is for the second half-year only.

[11] There was a change in the treatment of Immigration Fund expenditure in 1894. Tobago is included from 1899. Statistics from 1901 to 1914 are for years beginning 1 April. The 1915 figure is for the period 1 April tp 31 December.

[12] Years ended 30 September.

[13] Years beginning 1 July to 1949.

[14] Ordinary budget expenditure only to 1927–8 (1st line). Data to 1929–30 are for one- or two-year periods beginning 1 July. The 1931–2 figure is for the period 1 March 1931 to 28 February 1933. Subsequent statistics are for one or two calendar years. Expenditure on floating debt is excluded from 1965, and from 1973 the figures are of consolidated central government expenditure.

[15] Statistics to 1953 (1st line) include certain refund payments. Coverage is wider from 1972 (2nd line). They are for years ended 30 June throughout.

[16] Including £300 thousand transferred to a 'Special Reserve Fund'.

[17] See p. xi for conversion rates between old and new currencies.

[18] On a cash basis subsequently.

[19] Including social security and extra-budgetary expenditures from 1972.

[20] Ten months only, the first two months of the fiscal year being omitted.

[21] The reason for this break is not given in the sources.

[22] Subsequently budgetary central government expenditure only.

[23] Budgetary central government expenditure exclusive of debt repayment to 1975 (1st line) and consolidated central government expenditure subsequently. The 1957 figure is for the ten months ended 31 October, and the 1958 and 1959 figures are for years ended 31 October.

[24] Federal government expenditure exclusive of debt repayment to 1970 (1st line) and consolidated central government expenditure subsequently. Statistics from 1829 to 1886 are for years ended 30 June. The 1887 figure is for the 18 months from 1 July 1886 to 31 December 1887.

[25] Fiscal expenditure only to 1900 (1st line). There was a reorganisation of the system of accounts in 1921. Some extra-budgetary expenditures are included from 1974 (2nd line).

[26] Budgetary expenditure to 1969 and consolidated central government expenditure subsequently. From 1937 to 1949 (1st line) only current expenditure is covered.

[27] Budgeted expenditures of the ordinary and extraordinary budgets to 1898 (1st line) and realised expenditure from 1898 (2nd line) to 1953 (1st line). Consolidated central government exoenditure subsequently, with wider coverage of government agencies and some other outlays from 1968.

[28] Statistics to 1960 are for years beginning 1 July. The 1961 figure is for the second half-year only. There was a widening of coverage to include various extra-budgetary expenditures in 1968, 1970, and 1984.

[29] Statistics to 1895 are estimates.

[30] Budget estimates.

[31] Statistics to 1900 are for years ended 30 June, and from 1920 to 1940 they are for years ended 31 August. The 1950 figure is for the 18 months ended 30 June 1951, and the 1952 figure is for the year ended 30 June. Debt amortisation and extra-budgetary expenditures are included to 1967 (1st line).

[32] Statistics to 1899 are estimates. They are for years beginning 1 July to 1931. The 1932 figure is for the second half-year only. Extra-budgetary expenditure is included from 1972.

[33] There was change in the treatment of debt charges in 1951, and a narrowing of the coverage of budget expenditure in 1959. The figure for 1916 is for 14 months ended 28 February 1917, and those for 1917 and 1918 are for years beginning 1 March, and that for 1919 is for ten months from 1 March to 31 December.

[34] Coverage was widened in 1951, but from 1973 it was confined to budgetary central government expenditure.

[35] In 1983 and 1984 the peso argentino was the currency actually in use, but the figures have been converted here to the austral, which was introduced in 1985.

[36] In 1987 and 1988 the boliviano was the currency actually in use, but for the sake of continuity, the figures have been converted here to the previous currency. For the conversion ratio see p. xi.

[37] Local currency to 1841. This was often converted to sterling on the conventional basis that '1 local was equal to 18 shillings sterling.

[38] From 1 January 1840 to 9 February 1841.

[39] Statistics for 1848, 1849, and 1856 are net. The equivalent figure for 1850 is 437. A new system of accounts was adopted in 1857. Data for 1864–66 are for years ended 30 June.

[40] Statistics from 1857 are for years ended 30 September.

**G6    NORTH AMERICA: CENTRAL GOVERNMENT REVENUE, WITH SOME MAIN TAX YIELDS** (in millions of stated currency unit, except as otherwise indicated)

| 1759–1784 | | | 1785–1824 | | | | |
|---|---|---|---|---|---|---|---|
| | Cuba[1] | | | Cuba[1] | USA[2] | | |
| | Total | | | Total | Customs | Internal Revenue[3] | Total |
| | thousand pesos | | | thousand pesos | dollars | | |
| 1759 | 164 | | 1785 | 1,203 | ... | ... | ... |
| 1760 | 164 | | 1786 | 498 | ... | ... | ... |
| 1761 | 316 | | 1787 | 865 | ... | ... | ... |
| 1762 | ... | | 1788 | 892 | ... | ... | ... |
| 1763 | ... | | 1789 | 740 | | — | 4.4 |
| 1764 | 316 | | | | 4.4 | | |
| 1765 | ... | | 1790 | 974 | | | |
| 1766 | ... | | 1791 | 825 | | | |
| 1767 | ... | | 1792 | 1,118 | 3.4 | 0.2 | 3.7 |
| 1768 | ... | | 1793 | 1,085 | 4.3 | 0.3 | 4.7 |
| 1769 | ... | | 1794 | 1,137 | 4.8 | 0.3 | 5.4 |
| 1770 | ... | | 1795 | ... | 5.6 | 0.3 | 6.1 |
| 1771 | ... | | 1796 | ... | 6.6 | 0.5 | 8.4 |
| 1772 | ... | | 1797 | ... | 7.6 | 0.6 | 8.7 |
| 1773 | ... | | 1798 | ... | 7.1 | 0.6 | 7.9 |
| 1774 | ... | | 1799 | ... | 6.6 | 0.8 | 7.5 |
| 1775 | 561 | | 1800 | ... | 9.1 | 0.8 | 11 |
| 1776 | 726 | | 1801 | ... | 11 | 1.0 | 13 |
| 1777 | 1,027 | | 1802 | ... | 12 | 0.6 | 15 |
| 1778 | 885 | | 1803 | ... | 10 | 0.2 | 11 |
| 1779 | 956 | | 1804 | ... | 11 | 0.1 | 12 |
| 1780 | 1,001 | | 1805 | ... | 13 | - - | 14 |
| 1781 | 1,066 | | 1806 | ... | 15 | - - | 16 |
| 1782 | 1,424 | | 1807 | ... | 16 | - - | 16 |
| 1783 | 1,211 | | 1808 | 3,168 | 16 | - - | 17 |
| 1784 | 1,203 | | 1809 | 4,873 | 7.3 | - - | 7.8 |
| | | | 1810 | 4,115 | 8.6 | - - | 9.4 |
| | | | 1811 | 2,558 | 13 | - - | 14 |
| | | | 1812 | 2,379 | 9.0 | - - | 9.8 |
| | | | 1813 | ... | 13 | - - | 14 |
| | | | 1814 | 2,431 | 6.0 | 1.7 | 11 |
| | | | | pesos | | | |
| | | | 1815 | 3.4 | 7.3 | 4.7 | 16 |
| | | | 1816 | 2.8 | 36 | 5.1 | 48 |
| | | | 1817 | 3.1 | 26 | 2.7 | 33 |
| | | | 1818 | 3.8 | 17 | 1.0 | 22 |
| | | | 1819 | 4.1 | 20 | 0.2 | 25 |
| | | | 1820 | 3.5 | 15 | 0.1 | 18 |
| | | | 1821 | 3.3 | 13 | 0.1 | 15 |
| | | | 1822 | 4.4 | 18 | 0.1 | 20 |
| | | | 1823 | 4.2 | 19 | - - | 21 |
| | | | 1824 | 5.0 | 18 | - - | 19 |

**G6** **NORTH AMERICA: Central Government Revenue, with some Main Tax Yields** (in millions of stated currency unit, except as otherwise indicated)

1825–1864

| | Barbados | Cuba[1] | Jamaica[4] | Mexico[5] | Trinidad[6] | USA[2] | | |
|---|---|---|---|---|---|---|---|---|
| | Total | Total | Total | Total | Total | Customs | Internal Revenue[3] | Total |
| | thousand pounds | pesos | thousand pounds | pesos | thousand pounds | | dollars | |
| 1825 | ... | 5.7 | ... | 15 | ... | 20 | - - | 22 |
| 1826 | ... | 7.1 | ... | 15 | ... | 23 | - - | 25 |
| 1827 | ... | 8.5 | ... | 17 | ... | 20 | - - | 23 |
| 1828 | ... | 9.1 | ... | 14 | ... | 23 | - - | 25 |
| 1829 | ... | 9.1 | ... | 15 | ... | 23 | - - | 25 |
| 1830 | ... | 9.0 | ... | 14 | ... | 22 | - - | 25 |
| 1831 | ... | 8.3 | ... | 18 | ... | 24 | - - | 29 |
| 1832 | ... | 8.4 | ... | 18 | ... | 28 | - - | 32 |
| 1833 | ... | 8.9 | ... | 21 | ... | 29 | - - | 34 |
| 1834 | ... | 8.9 | ... | 21 | ... | 16 | - - | 22 |
| 1835 | 41 | 8.8 | ... | 18 | ... | 19 | - - | 35 |
| 1836 | ... | 9.3 | ... | 26 | ... | 23 | - - | 51 |
| 1837 | ... | 8.8 | ... | 17 | ... | 11 | - - | 25 |
| 1838 | ... | 9.7 | ... | 25 | ... | 16 | - - | 26 |
| 1839 | ... | 11 | ... | 29 | ... | 23 | - - | 31 |
| 1840 | 54 | 12 | 161 | 21 | ... | 14 | - - | 19 |
| 1841 | ... | 11 | 271 | 24 | ... | 14 | - - | 17 |
| 1842 | ... | 12 | 322 | 31 | ... | 18 | - - | 20 |
| 1843 | ... | 10 | 388 | 34 | ... | [7.0][2] | [- -][2] | [8.3][2] |
| 1844 | ... | 10 | 290 | 32 | ... | 26 | - - | 29 |
| 1845 | 51 | 9.2 | 280 | 24 | ... | 28 | - - | 30 |
| 1846 | ... | 11 | 261 | 24 | ... | 27 | - - | 30 |
| 1847 | ... | 13 | 240 | 26 | ... | 24 | - - | 26 |
| 1848 | ... | 13 | 191 | 26 | ... | 32 | - - | 36 |
| 1849 | ... | 13 | 176 | 18 | ... | 28 | — | 31 |
| 1850 | 54 | 10 | 181 | 15 | 89 | 40 | — | 44 |
| 1851 | 56 | 13 | 209 | 11 | 96 | 49 | — | 53 |
| 1852 | 59 | 12 | 237 | 10 | 107 | 47 | — | 50 |
| 1853 | 62 | 12 | 156 | 19 | 143 | 59 | — | 62 |
| 1854 | 60 | 13 | 118 | 26 | 101 | 64 | — | 74 |
| 1855 | 59 | 14 | 206 | 16 | 72 | 53 | — | 65 |
| 1856 | 82 | 15 | 210 | 16 | 93 | 64 | — | 74 |
| 1857 | 83 | 17 | 210 | 16 | 137 | 64 | — | 69 |
| 1858 | 97 | 18 | 178 | 15 | 145 | 42 | — | 47 |
| 1859 | 88 | 19 | 280 | 14 | 167 | 50 | — | 53 |
| 1860 | 95 | 19 | 262 | 13 | 175 | 53 | — | 56 |
| 1861 | 98 | ... | 274 | 16 | 172 | 40 | — | 42 |
| 1862 | 94 | ... | 291 | 18 | 199 | 49 | — | 52 |
| 1863 | 103 | 18 | 286 | 7.0 | 184 | 69 | 38 | 113 |
| 1864 | 107 | 22 | 308 | 6.0 | 207 | 102 | 110 | 265 |

**G6** **NORTH AMERICA: Central Government Revenue, with some Main Tax Yields** (in millions of state currency unit, except as otherwise indicated)

1865–1904

| | Barbados[12] | Canada[7] | | | Costa Rica[9] | Cuba[1] | El Salvador[10] | Guatemala |
|---|---|---|---|---|---|---|---|---|
| | Total | Customs | Excises[8] | Total | Total | Total | Total | Total |
| | thousand pounds | | dollars | | paper pesos | pesos | silver pesos | pesos |
| 1865 | 99 | ... | ... | ... | ... | ...[1] | ... | ... |
| 1866 | 104 | ... | ... | ... | ... | ... | ... | ... |
| 1867 | 98 | 8.6 | 3.0 | 14 | ... | 31 | ... | ... |
| 1868 | 106 | 8.4 | 2.7 | 14 | ... | 31 | ... | ... |
| 1869 | 103 | 9.3 | 3.6 | 16 | ... | ... | ... | ... |
| 1870 | 105 | 12 | 4.3 | 19 | ... | ... | ... | ... |
| 1871 | 119 | 13 | 4.7 | 21 | ... | ... | ... | ... |
| 1872 | 118 | 13 | 4.5 | 21 | ... | ... | ... | ... |
| 1873 | 124 | 14 | 5.6 | 25 | ... | ... | ... | ... |
| 1874 | 124 | 15 | 5.1 | 25 | ... | ... | ... | ... |
| 1875 | 132 | 13 | 5.6 | 23 | ... | ... | ... | ... |
| 1876 | 117 | 13 | 4.9 | 23 | ... | ... | ... | ... |
| 1877 | 121 | 13 | 4.8 | 22 | ... | ... | ... | ... |
| 1878 | 139 | 13 | 5.4 | 27 | ... | ... | ... | ... |
| 1879 | 121 | 14 | 4.2 | 23 | ... | ... | ... | ... |
| 1880 | 136 | 18 | 5.3 | 30 | ... | ... | ... | ... |
| 1881 | 132 | 22 | 5.9 | 35 | ... | 44 | ... | ... |
| 1882 | 140 | 23 | 6.3 | 37 | ... | ... | ... | 7.5 |
| 1883 | 139 | 20 | 5.5 | 33 | ... | 36 | 4.1 | 6.6 |
| 1884 | 144 | 19 | 6.5 | 33 | 2.0 | 35 | 4.1 | 5.9 |
| 1885 | 144 | 19 | 5.8 | 34 | 2.4 | 35 | 3.6 | 8.3 |
| 1886 | 135 | 22 | 6.3 | 36 | 2.4 | 32 | 4.5 | 8.5 |
| 1887 | 152 | 22 | 6.1 | 36 | 3.1 | 32 | 3.0 | ... |
| 1888 | 162 | 24 | 6.9 | 39 | 4.3 | 24[1] | 3.8 | ... |
| 1889 | 173 | 24 | 7.6 | 40 | 5.2 | 26[1] | 4.1 | ... |
| 1890 | 186 | 23 | 6.9 | 39 | 5.6 | ... | 4.2 | 6.2 |
| 1891 | 163 | 21 | 7.9 | 37 | 5.8 | 26 | 7.5 | 7.3 |
| 1892 | 163 | 21 | 8.4 | 38 | ... | ... | 6.9 | 8.7 |
| 1893 | 162 | 19 | 8.4 | 36 | 4.8 | 23 | 7.1 | 8.7 |
| 1894 | 161 | 18 | 7.8 | 34 | 6.1 | ... | 8.8 | 9.4 |
| 1895 | 146 | 20 | 7.9 | 37 | 6.5 | ... | 8.4 | 12 |
| 1896 | 177 | 19 | 9.2 | 38 | 7.4 | 25 | 8.7 | 14 |
| 1897 | 185 | 22 | 7.9 | 41 | 8.4 | 25 | 7.7 | 15 |
| 1898 | 183 | 25 | 9.6 | 47 | 8.4 | 25 | 4.6 | 12 |
| 1899 | 176 | 28 | 9.9 | 51 | 8.2 | 26[1] | 5.3 | 9.7 |
| 1900 | 185[12] | 28 | 10 | 53 | 8.7 | ... | 6.7 | 8.6 |
| 1901 | 180 | 32 | 11 | 58 | 5.6 | ... | 7.7 | 9.1 |
| 1902 | 162 | 37 | 12 | 69 | 5.5 | 16 | 8.6 | 14 |
| 1903 | 182 | 41 | 13 | 71 | 6.4 | 22 | 6.8 | 18 |
| 1904 | 185 | 42 | 13 | 71 | 5.3 | 29 | 8.1 | 18 |

**G6** **NORTH AMERICA: Central Government Revenue, with some Main Tax Yields** (in millions of stated currency unit, except as otherwise indicated)

1865–1904

| | Haiti[14] | Honduras[11] | Jamaica[4] | Mexico[5] | Nicaragua[15] | Trinidad[6] | USA[2] | | |
|---|---|---|---|---|---|---|---|---|---|
| | Total | Total | Total | Total | Total | Total | Customs | Internal Revenue[3] | Total |
| | gourdes | pesos | thousand pounds | pesos | pesos | thousand pounds | | dollars | |
| 1865 | ... | ... | 333 | 5.1 | ... | 220 | 85 | 209 | 334 |
| 1866 | ... | ... | 334 | 8.1 | ... | 218 | 179 | 309 | 558 |
| 1867 | ... | ... | 383 | 17 | ... | 216 | 176 | 266 | 491 |
| 1868 | ... | ... | 372 | 14 | ... | 211 | 164 | 191 | 406 |
| 1869 | ... | ... | 446 | 14 | ... | 244 | 180 | 158 | 371 |
| 1870 | ... | ... | 447 | 18 | ... | 234 | 195 | 185 | 411 |
| 1871 | ... | ... | 439 | 19 | ... | 272 | 206 | 143 | 383 |
| 1872 | ... | ... | 495 | 20 | ... | 296 | 216 | 131 | 374 |
| 1873 | ... | ... | 515 | 23 | ... | 282 | 188 | 114 | 334 |
| 1874 | ... | ... | 542 | 22 | ... | 385 | 163 | 102 | 305 |
| 1875 | ... | ... | 591 | 16 | ... | 342 | 157 | 110 | 288 |
| 1876 | ... | ... | 573 | 17 | ... | 316 | 148 | 117 | 294 |
| 1877 | ... | ... | 533 | 29 | ... | 310 | 131 | 119 | 281 |
| 1878 | ... | ... | 539 | 29 | ... | 369 | 130 | 111 | 258 |
| 1879 | ... | 1.0 | 547 | 21 | ... | 425 | 137 | 114 | 274 |
| 1880 | ... | 1.1 | 599 | 26 | ... | 431 | 187 | 124 | 334 |
| 1881 | ... | 1.3 | 563 | 33 | ... | 434 | 198 | 135 | 361 |
| 1882 | ... | 1.4 | 586 | 37 | ... | 437 | 220 | 146 | 404 |
| 1883 | ... | 1.3 | 594 | 41 | ... | 473 | 215 | 145 | 398 |
| 1884 | ... | } 2.6 { | 580 | 34 | ... | 487 | 195 | 122 | 349 |
| 1885 | ... | | 612 | 32 | ... | 440 | 181 | 112 | 324 |
| 1886 | ... | } 2.8 { | 578 | 50 | ... | 462 | 193 | 117 | 336 |
| 1887 | ... | | 606 | 76 | ... | 466 | 217 | 119 | 371 |
| 1888 | ... | 1.4 | 691 | 77 | ... | 491 | 219 | 124 | 379 |
| 1889 | ... | ... | 695 [4] | 78 | ... | 469 | 224 | 131 | 387 |
| 1890 | ... | ... | 789 | 68 | ... | 477 | 230 | 143 | 403 |
| 1891 | ... | ... | 779 | 39 | ... | 487 | 220 | 146 | 393 |
| 1892 | ... | 1.9 | 714 | 43 | ... | 518 | 177 | 154 | 355 |
| 1893 | ... | 1.8 | 759 | 50 | ... | 519 | 203 | 161 | 386 |
| 1894 | ... | 2.2 | 786 | 44 | ... | 549 [6] 595 | 132 | 147 | 306 |
| 1895 | ... | 1.9 | 819 | 51 | ... | 600 | 152 | 143 | 325 |
| 1896 | ... | 2.4 | 754 | 53 | ... | 628 | 160 | 147 | 338 |
| 1897 | ... | 3 | 697 | 56 | ... | 620 | 177 | 147 | 348 |
| 1898 | 19 | 2.4 | 749 | 65 | ... | 624 | 150 | 171 | 405 |
| 1899 | 19 | 2.8 | 788 | 71 | ... | 681 | 206 | 273 | 516 |
| 1900 | 17 | 3.0 | 883 | 72 | 5.6 | 699 [6] | 233 | 295 | 567 |
| 1901 | 21 | 2.8 | 917 | 79 | 5.6 | 712 | 239 | 307 | 588 |
| 1902 | 18 | 2.6 | 1,008 | 81 | 6.3 | 788 | 254 | 272 | 562 |
| 1903 | 14 | ... | 1,076 | 191 | 8.8 | 804 | 284 | 231 | 562 |
| 1904 | 16 | 3.3 | 891 | 129 | 8.7 | 812 | 261 | 233 | 541 |

**G6** **NORTH AMERICA: Central Government Revenue, with some Main Tax Yields** (in millions of stated currency unit, except as otherwise indicated)

| | Barbados[12] | Canada[7] | | | | | Costa Rica[9] | Cuba[1] |
|---|---|---|---|---|---|---|---|---|
| | Total | Customs | Excises[8] | Sales Tax | Income Tax | Total | Total | Total |
| | thousand pounds | | | dollars | | | colones | pesos |
| 1905 | 192 | 46 | 14 | — | — | 80 | 6.2 | 33 |
| 1906 | 205 | [40][7] | [12][7] | — | — | [68][7] | 6.9 | 31 |
| 1907 | 210 | 57 | 16 | — | — | 96 | 7.9 | 33 |
| 1908 | 190 | 47 | 15 | — | — | 86 | [5.2][9] | 28 |
| 1909 | 196 | 60 | 15 | — | — | 102 | 7.3 | 35 |
| 1910 | 213 | 72 | 17 | — | — | 118 | 8.1 | 36 |
| 1911 | 222 | 85 | 19 | — | — | 136 | 9.7 | 38 |
| 1912 | 234 | 112 | 21 | — | — | 169 | 10 | 40 |
| 1913 | 215 | 105 | 21 | — | — | 163 | 9.6 | 31 |
| 1914 | 223 | 76 | 22 | — | — | 133 | 8.6 | 58 |
| 1915 | 212 | 99 | 24 | — | — | 172 | 6.3 | 41 |
| 1916 | 311 | 134 | 27 | — | — | 233 | 7.3 | 52 |
| 1917 | 400 | 144 | 29 | — | — | 261 | 6.9 | 65 |
| 1918 | 347 | 147 | 42 | — | 9.4 | 313 | 7.3 | 70 |
| 1919 | 420 | 169 | 58 | — | 20 | 350 | 12 | 93 |
| 1920 | 454 | 163 | 78 | 38 | 46 | 437 | 18 | 108 |
| 1921 | 341 | 106 | 49 | 61 | 79 | 395 | 18 | 57 |
| 1922 | 401 | 118 | 53 | 90 | 60 | 410 | 19 | 73 |
| 1923 | 427 | 122 | 61 | 98 | 54 | 408 | 21 | 91 |
| 1924 | 502 | 108 | 61 | 63 | 56 | 353 | 23 | 94 |
| 1925 | 391 | 127 | 68 | 73 | 56 | 383 | 26 | 87 |
| 1926 | 379 | 142 | 73 | 81 | 47 | 401 | 27 | 80 |
| 1927 | 413 | 157 | 77 | 71 | 57 | 431 | 31 | 82 |
| 1928 | 420 | 187 | 84 | 63 | 59 | 462 | 33 | 79 |
| 1929 | 407 | 179 | 84 | 44 | 69 | 453 | 35 | 77 |
| 1930 | 390 | 131 | 72 | 20 | 71 | 358 | 28 | 60 |
| 1931 | 378 | 104 | 67 | 42 | 61 | 335 | 25 | 47 |
| 1932 | 444 | 70 | 63 | 57 | 62 | 312 | 23 | 44 |
| 1933 | 468 | 66 | 81 | 61 | 61 | 325 | 24 | 46 |
| 1934 | 472 | 77 | 83 | 72 | 67 | 362 | 26 | 65 |
| 1935 | 468 | 74 | 80 | 78 | 83 | 373 | 27 | 65 |
| 1936 | 482 | 84 | 86 | 113 | 102 | 454 | 35 | 78 |
| 1937 | 527 | 94 | 95 | 138 | 120 | 517 | 38 | 76,[1] |
| 1938 | 559 | 79 | 91 | 122 | 142 | 502 | 38 | ... |
| 1939 | 612 | 104 | 90 | 137 | 134 | 562 | 43 | 74 |
| 1940 | 690 | 131 | 193 | 180 | 248 | 872 | 42 | 78 |
| 1941 | 819 | 142 | 327 | 236 | 510 | 1,489 | 43 | 80 |
| 1942 | 804 | 119 | 395 | 232 | 860 | 2,250 | 37 | 106 |
| 1943 | 942 | 168 | 476 | 305 | 1,037 | 2,765 | 50 | 125 |
| 1944 | 1,147 | 115 | 486 | 209 | 978 | 2,687 | 53 | 148 |
| 1945 | 1,530 dollars | 129 | 471 | 212 | 933 | 3,013 | 61 | 158 |
| 1946 | 7.5 | 237 | 477 | 298 | 939 | 3,008 | 63 | 201 |
| 1947 | 8.5 | 293 | 465 | 372 | 1,060 | 2,872 | 88 | 277 |
| 1948 | 8.5 | 223 | 463 | 377 | 1,298 | 2,771 | 90 | 242,[1] |
| 1949 | 8.6 | 226 | 389 | 403 | 1,273 | 2,580 | 125 | 230 |

**G6    NORTH AMERICA: Central Government Revenue, with some Main Tax Yields** (in millions of stated currency unit, except as otherwise indicated)

| | Dominican Republic | El Salvador[10] | Guatemala[13] | Haiti[14] | Honduras[11] | Jamaica | Mexico[5] | | |
|---|---|---|---|---|---|---|---|---|---|
| | Total | Total | Total | Total | Total | Total | Customs | Income Tax[17] | Total |
| | pesos | silver pesos | pesos | gourdes | pesos | thousand pounds | | | pesos |
| 1905 | 1.7 | 8.5 | 30 | 19 | 3.5 | 999 | ... | ... | 107 |
| 1906 | 3.8 | 8.5 | 34 | 15 | 3.2 | 1,041 | ... | ... | 118 |
| 1907 | 4.0 | 8.7 | 31 | 19 | 3.9 | 1,162 | ... | ... | 115 |
| 1908 | 4.2 | 13 | 35 | 24 | 3.5 | 1,083 | ... | ... | 102 |
| 1909 | 3.9 | 12 | 37 | 21 | 3.5 | 1,158 | ... | ... | 111 |
| | | colones | | | | | | | |
| 1910 | 4.7 | 6.3 | 49 | 20 | 3.8 | 1,165 | ... | ... | 116 |
| 1911 | 4.6 | 5.6 | 52 | 24 | 4.6 | 1,348 | ... | ... | 110 |
| 1912 | 4.8 | 5.4 | 62 | 28 | 5.2 | 1,379 | ... | ... | 126 |
| 1913 | 5.1 | 5.5 | 84 | 27 | 5.4 | 1,241 | ... | ... | 121 |
| 1914 | 4.4 | 5.0 | 82 | 29 | 6.0 | 1,651 | ... | ... | ... |
| 1915 | 4.5 | 4.3 | 85 | 30 | 4.7 | 1,147 | ... | ... | ... |
| 1916 | 4.7 | 4.5 | 135 | 23 | 5.6 | 1,340 | ... | ... | ... |
| 1917 | 6.7 | 10 | 135 | 19 | 4.8 | 1,228 | ... | ... | 154 |
| 1918 | 7.1 | 6.9 | 111 | 15 | 5.3 | 1,347 | ... | ... | 157 |
| 1919 | 8.7 | 9.1 | 127 | 29 | 6.7 | 2,029 | ... | ... | 188 |
| 1920 | 9.5 | 15 | 168 | 34 | 7.6 | 2,347 | ... | ... | 260 |
| 1921 | 9.3 | 10 | 256 | 20 | 7.4 | 1,927 | ... | ... | 293 |
| 1922 | 12 | 12 | 307 | 25 | 16 | 2,057 | ... | ... | 280 |
| 1923 | 6.2 | 14 | 386 | 32 | 14 | 2,061 | ... | ... | 287 |
| | | | quetzales | | | | | | |
| 1924 | 8.7 | 18 | 8.1 | 33 | 8.6 | 1,923 | ... | ... | 273 |
| 1925 | 11 | 20 | 10 | 40 | 9.2 | 2,021 | 95 | 52 | 322 |
| 1926 | 14 | 21 | 12[13] | 45 | 9.7 | 2,147 | 98 | 43 | 309 |
| 1927 | 15 | 26 | 12 | 39 | 12 | 2,275 | 85 | 30 | 295 |
| 1928 | 15 | 27 | 14 | 50 | 14 | 2,213 | 93 | 36 | 300 |
| 1929 | 15 | 25 | 15 | 50 | 14 | 2,293 | 96 | 34 | 322 |
| 1930 | 10 | 21 | 13 | 43 | 12 | 2,198 | 112 | 32 | 289 |
| 1931 | 7.2 | 15 | 11 | 32 | 11 | 2,086 | 60 | 23 | 256 |
| 1932 | 7.2 | 19 | 9.2 | 28 | 9.0 | 2,169 | 55 | 21 | 212 |
| | | | | | lempiras | | | | |
| 1933 | 8.5 | 17 | 8.3 | 37 | 10 | 2,037 | 54 | 22 | 223 |
| 1934 | 9.3 | 22 | 8.6 | 37 | 11 | 2,260 | 66 | 50 | 295 |
| 1935 | 11 | 22 | 9.6 | 30 | 10 | 2,121 | 73 | 64 | 313 |
| 1936 | 11 | 23 | 11 | 35 | [12][16] | 2,212 | 92 | 63 | 385 |
| 1937 | 12 | 21 | 12 | 35 | [12][16] | 2,476 | 134 | 73 | 451 |
| 1938 | 12 | 20 | 13 | 28 | [11][11] | 2,840 | 119 | 76 | 438 |
| 1939 | 12 | [9.7][10] | 12 | 31 | 11 | 3,082 | 187 | 77 | 566 |
| 1940 | 12 | 20 | 12 | 27 | 11 | 3,622 | 170 | 93 | 577 |
| 1941 | 13 | 20 | 12 | 27 | 12 | 4,167 | 243 | 92 | 665 |
| 1942 | 16 | 20 | 12 | 26 | 11 | 4,372 | 223 | 126 | 746 |
| 1943 | 19 | 25 | 14 | 33 | 13 | 5,655 | 314 | 278 | 1,092 |
| 1944 | 24 | 28 | 17 | 42 | 15 | 8,009 | 334 | 376 | 1,295 |
| 1945 | 27 | 29 | 17 | 42 | 18 | 7,748 | 383 | 372 | 1,404 |
| 1946 | 41 | 40 | 29 | 45 | 23 | 8,391 | 486 | 466 | 2,012 |
| 1947 | 57 | 44 | 41 | 65 | 26 | 9,300 | 482 | 619 | 2,055 |
| 1948 | 65 | 59 | 40 | 79 | 28 | 9,713 | 549 | 623 | 2,268 |
| 1949 | 64 | 69 | 45 | 83 | 30 | 10,003 | 882 | 748 | 3,891 |

**G6**    **NORTH AMERICA: Central Government Revenue, with some Main Tax Yields** (in millions of state currency unit, except as otherwise indicated)

| | Nicaragua[15] Total | Panama[19] Total | Puerto Rico[20] Total | Trinidad & Tobago[6] Total | USA[2] Customs | USA Internal Revenue[3] / Excises | Income Tax | Social Security Tax | USA Total |
|---|---|---|---|---|---|---|---|---|---|
| | pesos | balboas | dollars | thousand pounds | | dollars | | | |
| 1905 | ... | ... | ... | 848 | 262 | 234 | | | 544 |
| 1906 | ... | ... | 3.5 | 765 | 300 | 249 | | | 595 |
| 1907 | ... | ... | ... | 871 | 332 | 270 | | | 666 |
| 1908 | ... | ... | ... | 835 | 286 | 252 | | | 602 |
| 1909 | ... | 2.8 | ... | 854 | 301 | 246 | | | 604 |
| 1910 | 19 | 5.9 | 5.4 | 948 | 334 | 290 | | | 676 |
| 1911 | 22 | 3.3 | 4.4 | 951 | 314 | 323 | | | 702 |
| 1912 | ... | 3.4 | 7.8 | 933 | 311 | 322 | | | 693[2] |
| | cordobas | | | | | | | | |
| 1913 | 1.7 | 4.0 | 8.8 | 971 | 319 | 344 | | | 714 |
| 1914 | 3.4 | 3.8 | 10 | 935 | 292 | 480 | | | 725 |
| 1915 | 2.2 | 3.3 | 12 | [782][6] | 210 | 416 | | | 633 |
| | | | | | | Excises | Income Tax | Social Security Tax | |
| 1916 | 2.1 | 3.5 | 9.1 | 1,065 | 213 | 340 | 125 | — | 761 |
| 1917 | 2.3 | 3.9 | 11 | 1,098 | 226 | 388 | 387 | — | 1,101 |
| 1918 | 2.4 | 3.1 | 12 | 1,173 | 180 | 669 | ... | — | 3,645 |
| 1919 | 3.0 | 6.3 | 14 | 1,343 | 184 | 837 | ... | — | 5,130 |
| 1920 | 4.3 | 5.8 | 17 | 1,918 | 323 | 808 | ... | — | 6,649 |
| 1921 | 3.4 | 5.4 | 12 | 1,868 | 309 | 685 | ... | — | 5,571 |
| 1922 | 2.3 | 5.3 | 12 | 1,662 | 356 | 593 | ... | — | 4,026 |
| 1923 | 2.7 | } 16 { | 10 | 1,664 | 562 | 625 | ... | — | 3,853 |
| 1924 | 3.5 | | 13 | 1,587 | 546 | 716 | ... | — | 3,871 |
| 1925 | 3.7 | } 12 { | 14 | 1,663 | 548 | 543 | 1,762 | — | 3,641 |
| 1926 | 4.4 | | 14 | 1,737 | 579 | 571 | 1,974 | — | 3,795 |
| 1927 | 4.5 | } 14[19] { | 14 | 1,686 | 606 | 482 | 2,220 | — | 4,013 |
| 1928 | 5.7 | } 17 { | 15 | 1,764 | 569 | 483 | 2,175 | — | 3,900 |
| 1929 | 6.0 | } 17 { | 15 | 1,871 | 602 | 459[3] / 540 | 2,331 | — | 3,862 |
| 1930 | 5.9 | | 13 | 1,801 | 587 | 565 | 2,410 | — | 4,058 |
| 1931 | 5.4 | } [19][19] { | 16 | 1,641 | 378 | 520 | 1,910 | — | 3,116 |
| 1932 | 4.7 | | 13 | 1,694 | 328 | 454 | 1,057 | — | 1,924 |
| 1933 | 3.8 | } 16 { | 11 | 1,687 | 251 | 839 | 747 | — | 1,997 |
| 1934 | 4.2 | | 15 | 1,710 | 313 | 1,288 | 820 | — | 3,015 |
| 1935 | 5.0 | } 14 { | 15 | 1,811 | 343 | 1,364 | 1,106 | — | 3,706 |
| 1936 | 5.3 | | 16 | 13 (dollars) | 387 | 1,547 | 1,427 | - - | 3,997 |
| 1937 | 7.5 | 9.7 | 19 | 12 | 486 | 1,765 | 2,280 | 266 | 4,956 |
| 1938 | 10 | 9.9 | 20 | 13 | 359 | 1,731 | 2,629 | 743 | 5,588 |
| 1939 | 17 | 13 | 18 | 13 | 319[2] | 1,768 | 2,185 | 740 | 4,979 |
| 1940 | 28 | 13 | 21 | 16 | 331 | 1,885[3] / 1,844 | 2,130[3] / 2,088 | 834[21] / 1,715 | 6,879 |
| 1941 | 33 | 17 | 21 | 19 | 365 | 2,386 | 3,438 | 2,004 | 9,202 |
| 1942 | 40 | 21 | 38 | 23 | 369 | 3,121 | 7,978 | 2,429 | 15,104 |
| 1943 | 35 | 26 | 44 | 29 | 308 | 3,769 | 16,060 | 3,013 | 25,097 |
| 1944 | 49 | 26 | 108 | 29 | 417 | 4,379 | 35,434 | 3,428 | 47,818 |
| 1945 | 48 | 26 | 79 | 31 | 341 | 5,893 | 34,756 | 3,438 | 50,162 |
| 1946 | 53 | 31 | 82 | 42 | 424 | 6,646 | 28,367 | 3,078 | 43,537 |
| 1947 | 77 | 34 | 88 | 37 | 477 | 7,182 | 26,544 | 3,333 | 43,531 |
| 1948 | 59 | 32 | 100 | 45 | 403 | 7,356 | 28,988 | 3,966 | 45,357 |
| 1949 | 78[15] | 32 | 109 | 51 | 367 | 7,502 | 26,736 | 3,809 | 41,576 |

**G6** **NORTH AMERICA: Central Government Revenue, with some Main Tax Yields** (in millions of stated currency unit, except as otherwise indicated)

| | Barbados[12] | Canada[7] | | | | | Costa Rica[22] | Cuba[1] |
|---|---|---|---|---|---|---|---|---|
| | Total | Customs | Excises[8] | Sales Tax | Income Tax | Total | Total | Total |
| | | dollars | | | | | colones | pesos |
| 1950 | 10 | 296 | 468 | 460 | 1,513 | 3,113 | 138 | 286 |
| 1951 | 13 | 346 | 530 | 598 | 2,164 | 4,007 | 160 | 328 |
| 1952 | 13 | 389 | 517 | 708 | 2,556 | 4,585 | 190 | 309 |
| 1953 | 14 | 407 | 523 | 734 | 2,579 | 4,689 | 216 | 270 |
| 1954 | 16 | 397 | 479 | 715 | 2,412 | 4,414 | 234 | 303 |
| 1955 | 16 | 481 | 510 | 802 | 2,435 | 4,716 | 262 | 329 |
| 1956 | 18 | 549 | 538 | 896 | 2,938 | 5,478 | 272 | 371 |
| 1957 | 20 | 498 | 549 | 879 | 2,995 | 5,420 | 312 | 387 |
| 1958 | 22 | 487 | 558 | 868 | 2,637 | 5,130 | 334 | 415[1] |
| 1959 | 21 | 526 | 622 | 1,003 | 3,059 | 5,837 | 337 | ... |
| 1960 | 24 | 499 | 636 | 991 | 3,409 | 6,221 | 351 | 411 |
| 1961 | 25 | 535 | 626 | 1,045 | 3,466 | 6,374 | 366 | 1,143 |
| 1962 | 27 | 645 | 642 | 1,108 | 3,445 | 6,570 | 381 | 1,657 |
| 1963 | 32 | 581 | 666 | 1,278 | 3,668 | 7,003 | 386 | 2,904 |
| 1964 | 37 | 622 | 680 | 1,588 | 4,348 | 8,141 | 433 | 2,399 |
| 1965 | 40 | 686 | 742 | 1,917 | 4,566 | 8,865 | 474 | 2,536 |
| 1966 | 43 | 778 | 777 | 2,073 | 4,997 | 9,662 | 522 | ... |
| 1967 | 48 | 747 | 826 | 2,146 | 5,692 | 10,571 | 542 | ... |
| 1968 | 62 | 762 | 887 | 2,098 | 6,753 | 11,817 | 622 | ... |
| 1969 | 76 | 818 | 897 | 2,294 | 8,676 | 14,155 | 720 | ... |
| 1970 | 90 | 815 | 964 | 2,281 | 9,079 | 14,717 | 883 | ... |
| 1971 | 102 | 989 | 995 | 2,653 | 9,911 | 13,345 | 910 | ... |
| 1972 | 111 | 1,182 | 1,039 | 3,052 | 11,589 | 18,821[7] | 1,041[22] | ... |
| | | | | | | 21,426 | 1,260 | ... |
| 1973 | 129 | 1,385 | 1,091 | 3,590 | 13,260 | 25,102 | 1,620 | ... |
| 1974 | 164[12] | 1,809 | 1,159 | 3,866 | 16,974 | 32,192 | 2,449 | ... |
| | 177 | | | | | | | |
| 1975 | 214 | 1,887 | 1,523 | 3,515 | 18,938 | 34,703 | 3,027 | ... |
| 1976 | 230 | 2,097 | 1,946 | 3,929 | 20,579 | 38,313 | 3,648 | ... |
| 1977 | 266 | 2,312 | 1,939 | 4,427 | 19,883 | 38,237 | 4,393 | ... |
| 1978 | 328 | 2,747 | 2,181 | 4,729 | 21,005 | 41,638 | 5,755 | ... |
| 1979 | 377 | 3,000 | 3,850 | 4,698 | 25,624 | 48,219 | 6,317 | ... |
| 1980 | 474 | 3,199 | 9,276 | 5,429 | 30,208 | 57,491 | 7,373 | ... |
| 1981 | 512[12] | 3,449 | 9,794 | 6,185 | 34,306 | 72,280 | 10,199 | ... |
| 1982 | 571 | 2,846 | 7,841 | 5,894 | 35,433 | 73,238 | 17,027 | ... |
| 1983 | 634 | 3,394 | 8,526 | 6,660 | 37,336 | 77,327 | 28,115 | ... |
| 1984 | 662 | 3,811 | 7,068 | 7,729 | 41,366 | 85,298 | 36,382 | ... |
| | | | | | | | thousand million | |
| 1985 | 747 | 3,989 | [3,409][8] | 9,383 | 44,908 | 91,100 | 41.0 | ... |
| 1986 | 773 | 4,205 | 5,179 | 12,022 | 50,640 | 99,206 | 54.6[22] | ... |
| 1987 | 842 | 4,402 | 6,410 | 12,984 | 58,967 | 111,549 | 70.1 | ... |
| 1988 | 1,034 | 4,527 | 6,029 | 15,744 | 61,785 | 119,327 | 87.7 | ... |

**G6**    **NORTH AMERICA: Central Government Revenue, with some Main Tax Yields** (in millions of state currency unit, except as otherwise indicated)

| | Dominican Republic[23] | El Salvador[10] | Guatemala[13] | Haiti[14] | Honduras[11] | Jamaica[24] | Mexico[5] | | |
|---|---|---|---|---|---|---|---|---|---|
| | Total | Total | Total | Total | Total | Total | Customs | Income Tax[17] | Total |
| | pesos | colones | quetzales | gourdes | lempiras | pounds | | pesos | |
| 1950 | 76 | 88 | 43 | 109 | 37 | 11 | 991 | 914 | 3,614 |
| 1951 | 90 | 118 | 47 | 125 | 41 | 14 | 1,397 | 1,408 | 4,935 |
| 1952 | 96 | 128 | 57 | 146 | 43 | 14 | 1,475 | 1,627 | 6,318 |
| 1953 | 119 | 140 | 65 | 136 | 46 | 15 | 1,317 | 1,280 | 5,147 |
| 1954 | 112 | 167 | 66 | 161 | 48 | 17 | 1,875 | 1,393 | 6,405 |
| 1955 | 130 | 166 | 72 | 162 | 46 | 19 | 2,519 | 2,261 | 7,819 |
| 1956 | 137 | 171 | 86 | 161 | [17][11] | 22 | 2,555 | 2,740 | 9,201 |
| 1957 | 155 | 191 | 92 | 150 | 61 | 26 | 2,259 | 2,853 | 9,666 |
| 1958 | 154 | 169 | 92 | 154 | 66 | 28 | 2,702 | 3,124 | 11,872 |
| 1959 | 152 | 157 | 90 | 176 | 69 | 31 | 2,925 | 3,238 | 10,184 |
| 1960 | 143 | 171 | 86 | … | 72 | 33 | 3,084 | 3,866 | 12,992 |
| 1961 | 118 | 161 | 87 | [97][14] | 72 | 36 | 2,944 | 4,227 | 12,225 |
| 1962 | 151 | 172 | 88 | 153 | 74 | 39 | 3,041 | 4,839 | 14,148 |
| 1963 | 174 | 181[10] 192 | 84 | 144 | 80 | 40 | 2,816 | 5,579 | 14,845 |
| 1964 | 192 | 223 | 98[13] | … | 93 | 48 | 3,282 | 7,411 | 18,023 |
| | | | | | | | thousand million pesos | | |
| 1965 | 120 | 276 | 121 | 143 | 109 | 54 | 4.6 | 6.0 | 22 |
| 1966 | 163 | 251 | 121 | 141 | 120 | 56 | 4.8 | 8.7 | 25 |
| 1967 | 174 | 258 | 124 | 140[14] 158 | 129 | 63 | 6.0 | 10 | 27 |
| 1968 | 189 | 229 | 137 | 191 | 148 | 73 | 5.8 | 13 | 32 |
| | | | | | | dollars | | | |
| 1969 | 214 | 258 | 150 | 199 | 155 | 176 | 6.3 | 15 | 36 |
| 1970 | 240 | 284 | 165 | 235 | 178 | 213 | 7.4 | 16 | 41 |
| 1971 | 276 | 298 | 173 | 271 | 181 | 244 | 7.8 | 18 | 45 |
| 1972 | 315[23] 361 | 326 | 183 | 290 | 193 | 281 | 7.5 | 21 | 54 |
| 1973 | 397 | 403 | 212 | 308 | 220 | 345 | 7.5 | 27 | 69 |
| 1974 | 513 | 488 | 280 | 376 | 257 | 507[24] | 10 | 36 | 94[5] 95 |
| 1975 | 695 | 581 | 327 | 519 | 272 | 634 | 13 | 49 | 133 |
| 1976 | 622 | 805 | 410 | 666 | 353 | 616 | 15 | 66 | 169 |
| 1977 | 678 | 1,257 | 589 | 807 | 457 | 733 | 26 | 93 | 241 |
| 1978 | 695 | 1,048 | 661 | 925 | 549 | 854 | 35 | 132 | 323 |
| 1979 | 739 | 1,171 | 667[13] | 719 | 656 | 1,129 | 50 | 173 | 439 |
| 1980 | 954 | 1,029 | 885 | 893 | 757 | 1,222 | 189 | 246 | 675 |
| 1981 | 988 | 1,068 | 899 | 1,109 | 739 | 1,662 | 258 | 332 | 894 |
| 1982 | 823 | 1,091 | 882 | 1,484 | 770 | 1,576 | 500 | 464 | 1,520 |
| 1983 | 999 | 1,258 | 874[13] | 1,538 | 778 | 1,844 | 218 | 716 | 3,222 |
| 1984 | 1,263 | 1,574 | 665 | 1,414 | 951 | 2,334 | 122 | 1,177 | 4,774 |
| 1985 | 1,727 | 1,902 | 862 | 1,921 | 1,064 | 2,708 | 301 | 1,899 | 7,820 |
| 1986 | 2,249 | 2,822 | 1,462 | 1,786 | 1,152 | 3,700 | 689 | 3,344 | 12,643 |
| 1987 | 3,019 | 2,981 | 1,852 | 1,759 | 1,290 | 5,064 | 1,587 | 7,794 | 33,683 |
| 1988 | 4,659 | 2,928 | 2,291 | … | 1,378 | … | 1,945 | 20,103 | 67,476 |

**G6    NORTH AMERICA: Central Government Revenue, with some Main Tax Yields** (in millions of stated currency unit, except as otherwise indicated)

| | Nicaragua[25] | Panama[19] | Puerto Rico[20] | Trinidad & Tobago[6] | USA[2] | | | | |
|---|---|---|---|---|---|---|---|---|---|
| | Total | Total | Total | Total | Customs | Excises | Income Tax | Social Security Taxes[21] | Total |
| | cordobas | balboas | dollars | dollars | | | dollars | | |
| 1950 | ... | 31 | 122 | 51 | 407 | 7,550 | 26,196 | 4,386 | 40,940 |
| 1951 | 96 | 32 | 135 | 59 | 609 | 8,648 | 35,705 | 5,714 | 53,390 |
| 1952 | 125 | 36 | 128 | 67 | 533 | 8,852 | 49,144 | 6,496 | 68,011 |
| 1953 | 155 | 41 | 140[20] | 68 | 596[2] | 9,878[2] | 51,018[2] | 6,821[2] | 71,495 |
| 1954 | 182 | 43 | 148 | 76 | 542 | 9,945 | 50,643 | 7,210 | 71,630[2] 69,719 |
| 1955 | 197 | 45 | 152 | 85 | 585 | 9,131 | 46,608 | 7,866 | 65,469 |
| 1956 | 282 | 49 | 164 | 92 | 682 | 9,929 | 53,068 | 9,323 | 74,547 |
| 1957 | 249 | 51 | 182 | 106 | 735 | 10,534 | 56,787 | 9,997 | 79,990 |
| 1958 | 255 | 53 | 187 | 130 | 782 | 10,638 | 54,798 | 11,239 | 79,636 |
| 1959 | 233 | 51 | 206 | 141 | 925 | 10,578 | 54,085 | 11,722 | 79,249 |
| | | | | | | | thousand million dollars | | |
| 1960 | 233 | 58 | 233 | 154 | 1.1 | 12 | 62 | 15 | 92 |
| 1961 | 252 | 63 | 252 | 156 | 1.0 | 12 | 62 | 16 | 94 |
| 1962 | 288 | 68 | 285 | 181 | 1.1 | 13 | 66 | 17 | 100 |
| 1963 | 346 | 69 | 329 | 186 | 1.2 | 13 | 69 | 20 | 107 |
| 1964 | 373 | 76[19] | 372 | 205 | 1.3 | 14 | 72 | 22 | 113 |
| 1965 | 444 | 87 | 416 | 233 | 1.4 | 15 | 74 | 22 | 117 |
| 1966 | 476 | 100 | 488 | 235 | 1.8 | 13 | 86 | 26 | 131 |
| 1967 | 486 | 113 | 546 | 263 | 1.9 | 14 | 95 | 33 | 149 |
| 1968 | 470 | 119 | 605 | 285 | 2.0 | 14 | 97 | 35 | 153 |
| 1969 | 499 | 133 | 710 | 315 | 2.3 | 15 | 124 | 40 | 187 |
| 1970 | 572[25] 667 | 160 | 772 | 318 | 2.4 | 16 | 123 | 45 | 193 |
| 1971 | 736 | 181 | 902 | 352 | 2.6 | 17 | 113 | 49 | 187 |
| 1972 | 760 | 198 | 1,074 | 403 | 3.3 | 16 | 127 | 54 | 207 |
| 1973 | 1,064 | 226[19] 306 | 1,185 | 480 | 3.2 | 16 | 139 | 65 | 231 |
| 1974 | 1,481 | 391 | 1,188[20] 1,102 | 1,301 | 3.3 | 17 | 158 | 77 | 263 |
| 1975 | 1,530 | 452 | 1,294 | 1,715 | 3.7 | 17 | 163 | 85 | 279 |
| 1976 | 1,763 | 440 | 1,605 | 2,125 | 4.1 | 17 | 173 | 91 | 298[2] |
| 1977 | 2,065 | 546 | 1,723 | 2,749 | 5.2 | 18 | 212 | 106 | 356 |
| 1978 | 1,893 | 598 | 1,812 | 2,770 | 6.6 | 18 | 241 | 121 | 400 |
| 1979 | 2,145 | 696 | 1,973 | 3,644 | 7.4 | 19 | 283 | 139 | 463 |
| 1980 | 4,974 | 966 | 2,118 | 5,995 | 7.2 | 24 | 309 | 158 | 517 |
| 1981 | 7,017 | 1,030 | 2,307 | 6,629 | 8.1 | 41 | 347 | 183 | 599 |
| 1982 | 8,257 | 1,204 | 2,491 | 6,687 | 8.9 | 36 | 347 | 201 | 618 |
| 1983 | 11,971 | 1,324 | 2,628 | 6,323 | 8.7 | 35 | 326 | 209 | 601 |
| 1984 | 18,166 | 1,374 | ... | 6,419 | 11 | 37 | 355 | 239 | 666 |
| | thousand million | | | | | | | | |
| 1985 | 43 | 1,477 | ... | 6,266 | 12 | 36 | 396 | 265 | 734 |
| 1986 | 164 | 1,597 | ... | 5,169 | 13 | 33 | 412 | 284 | 769 |
| 1987 | ... | 1,605 | ... | 5,133 | 15 | 32 | 476 | 303 | 854 |
| 1988 | ... | 1,146 | ... | 4,670 | 16 | 35 | 496 | 334 | 909 |

**G6    SOUTH AMERICA: CENTRAL GOVERNMENT REVENUE, WITH SOME MAIN TAX YIELDS** (in millions of stated currency unit, except as otherwise indicated)

**1830–1864**

| | Argentina | Brazil[26] | Chile[27] | Ecuador | Guyana[29] | Peru[30] | Venezuala[31] |
|---|---|---|---|---|---|---|---|
| | Total | Total | Total | Total | Total | Total | Total |
| | gold pesos | milreis | gold pesos[28] | sucres | thousand dollars | pesos | bolivares |
| 1823 | ... | 3.8 | ... | ... | ... | ... | ... |
| 1824 | ... | 6 | ... | ... | ... | ... | ... |
| 1825 | ... | 4.7 | ... | ... | ... | ... | ... |
| 1826 | ... | 4.4 | ... | ... | ... | ... | ... |
| 1827 | ... | 6.9 | ... | ... | ... | ... | ... |
| 1828 | ... | 7.2[26] | ... | ... | ... | ... | ... |
| 1829 | ... | 9.9 | ... | ... | ... | ... | ... |
| 1830 | ... | 17 | ... | ... | ... | ... | 5.8 |
| 1831 | ... | 17 | ... | ... | ... | ... | 6.1 |
| 1832 | ... | 12 | ... | ... | ... | ... | 7.0 |
| 1833 | ... | 16 | ... | ... | ... | ... | 7.5 |
| 1834 | ... | 12 | ... | ... | ... | ... | 7.2 |
| 1835 | ... | 15 | ... | ... | ... | ... | 6.6 |
| 1836 | ... | 14 | ... | ... | ... | ... | 8.6 |
| 1837 | ... | 14 | ... | ... | ... | ... | 8.0 |
| 1838 | ... | 13 | ... | ... | 674 | ... | 9.3 |
| 1839 | ... | 15 | ... | ... | 1,188 | ... | 11 |
| 1840 | ... | 16 | ... | ... | 409 | ... | 13 |
| 1841 | ... | 16 | ... | ... | 1,092 | ... | 9.7 |
| 1842 | ... | 16 | ... | ... | 839 | ... | 11 |
| 1843 | ... | 19 | ... | ... | 830 | ... | 11 |
| 1844 | ... | 21 | ... | ... | 832 | ... | 11 |
| 1845 | ... | 25 | ... | ... | 825 | ... | 12 |
| 1846 | ... | 26 | ... | ... | 901 | } 8.4 { | 13 |
| 1847 | ... | 28 | ... | ... | 1,022 | | 11 |
| 1848 | ... | 25 | ... | ... | | } 11 { | 14 |
| 1849 | ... | 26 | ... | ... | 494 | | 18 |
| 1850 | ... | 28 | ... | ... | 883 | } 11 { | 21 |
| 1851 | ... | 33 | ... | ... | 974 | | 21 |
| 1852 | ... | 38 | ... | ... | 1,046 | } 14 { | 14 |
| 1853 | ... | 38 | ... | ... | 1,200 | | 18 |
| 1854 | ... | 35 | ... | ... | 1,171 | } 20 { | 18 |
| 1855 | ... | 36 | ... | ... | 1,224 | | 20 |
| 1856 | ... | 39 | ... | ... | 1,109 | ... | 19 |
| 1857 | ... | 49 | 51 | ... | 1,282 | ... | 24 |
| 1858 | ... | 50 | 51 | ... | 1,310 | ... | 22 |
| 1859 | ... | 47 | 72 | ... | 1,325 | ... | 14 |
| 1860 | ... | 44 | 63 | ... | 1,344 | ... | 21 |
| 1861 | ... | 50 | 54 | ... | 1,450 | } 42 { | 20 |
| 1862 | ... | 52 | 66 | ... | 1,358 | | 24 |
| 1863 | ... | 48 | 69 | } 3.7 { | 1,277 | } 46 { | ... |
| 1864 | 7.0 | 55 | 81 | | 1,498 | | 32 |

**G6**  **SOUTH AMERICA: Central Government Revenue, with some Main Tax Yields** (in millions of stated currency unit, except as otherwise indicated)

**1865–1894**

| | Argentina | Bolivia | Brazil[26] | Chile[27] | Ecuador | Guyana[29] | Paraguay[32] | Surinam[33] | Peru[30] | Uruguay[34] | Venezuela[31] |
|---|---|---|---|---|---|---|---|---|---|---|---|
| | Total | Total | Total | Total | Total | Total | Total | Total | Total | Total | Total |
| | gold pesos | bolivianos | milreis | gold pesos[28] | sucres | thousand dollars | gold pesos | guilders | pesos | pesos | bolivares |
| 1865 | 8.3 | ... | 57 | 92 | } 3.9 { | 1,483 | ... | ... | ... | ... | 30 |
| 1866 | 9.6 | ... | 59 | 75 | | 1,464 | ... | ... | ... | ... | 22 |
| 1867 | 12 | ... | 65 | 81 | } 3.7 { | 1,320 | ... | ... | ... | ... | 14 |
| 1868 | 12 | ... | 71 | 87 | | 1,397 | ... | ... | ...  soles | ... | 19 |
| 1869 | 13 | ... | 88 | 99 | } 3.1 { | 1,493 | ... | ... | } 45 { | ... | 22 |
| 1870 | 15 | ... | 95 | 102 | | 1,699 | ... | ... | | 5.3 | ... |
| 1871 | 13 | ... | 96 | 87 | } 4.3 { | 1,824 | ... | ... | } 59 { | ... | ... |
| 1872 | 18 | ... | 102 | 90 | | 1,814 | ... | ... | | 5.1 | 24 |
| 1873 | 20 | ... | 111 | 93 | } 4.8 { | 1,738 | ... | ... | } 34 { | ... | 27 |
| 1874 | 16 | ... | 103 | 90 | | 1,752 | ... | ... | | 3.8 | 25 |
| 1875 | 17 | ... | 105 | 99 | ... | 1,690 | ... | ... | } 66 { | 5.9 | 33 |
| 1876 | 14 | ... | 101 | 99 | ... | 1,747 | ... | ... | | 7.4 | 26 |
| 1877 | 15 | ... | 99 | 84 | ... | 1,872 | ... | ... | } 44 { | 4.6 | 24 |
| 1878 | 18 | ... | 109 | 84 | } 6.4 { | 1,963 | ... | ... | | ... | ... |
| 1879 | 21 | ... | 112 | 135 | | 1,901 | ... | ... | } 35 { | ... | 29 |
| 1880 | 20 | ... | 120 | 198 | ... | 1,939 | ... | ... | | 7.7 | 30 |
| 1881 | 21 | ... | 128 | 165 | ... | 1,934 | 0.8 | ... | ... | ... | 29 |
| 1882 | 27 | ... | 130 | 186 | ... | 2,203 | 0.8 | ... | ... | ... | 29 |
| 1883 | 31 | ... | 130 | 219 | ... | 2,294 | 0.6 | ... | ... | ... | 34 |
| 1884 | 38 | ... | 133 | 171 | 3.2 | 2,208 | 0.8 | ... | ... | 11 | 33 |
| 1885 | 27 | 3.2 | 122 | 129 | 2.5 | 2,088 | 1.4 | ... | ... | 12 | 27 |
| 1886 | 30 | 4.1 | 127 | 123 | 2.9 | 2,141 | 2.9 | ... | ... | 12 | 34 |
| 1887 | 38 | 4.3 | [219][26] | 162 | 4.5 | 2,227 | 1.5 | 1.4 | } 16 { | 13 | 41 |
| 1888 | 35 | 4.3 | 151 | 201 | 4.2 | 2,218[29] | 1.7 | 1.3 | | 14 | 40 |
| 1889 | 38 | 5.0 | 161 | 207 | 3.1 | 2,510 | 2.1 | 1.4 | } 13 { | 16 | 45 |
| 1890 | 29 | 3.6 | 195 | 225 | 4.2 | 2,688 | 0.5 | 1.5 | | 17 | 54 |
| 1891 | 19 | 3.3 | 229 | 276 | 3.9 | 2,674 | 0.3 | 1.5 | 6.7 | 15 | 44 |
| 1892 | 33 | 3.9 | 228 | 204 | 3.8 | 2,717 | 0.5 | 1.6 | 7.1 | 14 | 37 |
| 1893 | 38 | 4.2 | 260 | 186 | 4.3 | 2,846 | 0.9 | 1.8 | 7.9 | 14 | 51 |
| 1894 | 34 | 4.2 | 265 | 189 | ... | 2,779 | 0.7 | 1.7 | 7.3 | 15 | 49 |

**G6 SOUTH AMERICA: Central Government Revenue, with some Main Tax Yields** (in millions of state currency unit, except as otherwise indicated)

1895–1944

| | Argentina[34] | | | Bolivia | Brazil[26] | | | |
|---|---|---|---|---|---|---|---|---|
| | Customs[36] | Income & Wealth Taxes | Total | Total | Customs | Excises | Income & Wealth Taxes | Total |
| | paper pesos | | | bolivianos | | | milreis or cruzeiros | |
| 1895 | 94 | 4.2 | 132 | 4.1 | ... | ... | — | 308 |
| 1896 | 86 | 3.6 | 124 | 4.4 | ... | ... | — | 346 |
| 1897 | 82 | 6.2 | 151 | 5.6 | ... | ... | — | 303 |
| 1898 | 75 | 5.4 | 136 | 5.2 | ... | ... | — | 324 |
| 1899 | 89 | 4.9 | 166 | 5.9 | ... | ... | — | 321 |
| 1900 | 73 | 5.1 | 151 | 6.0 | 165 | 37 | — | 308 |
| 1901 | 72 | 5.2 | 151 | 6.4 | 162 | 32 | — | 305 |
| 1902 | 67 | 5.5 | 156 | 6.0 | 186 | 34 | — | 344 |
| 1903 | 91 | 5.4 | 172 | 5.3 | 189 | 35 | — | 415 |
| 1904 | 97 | 5.5 | 199 | 6.8 | 198 | 35 | — | 443 |
| 1905 | 105 | 5.8 | 212 | 7.9 | 224 | 35 | — | 401 |
| 1906 | 121 | 5.0 | 232 | 10 | 248 | 43 | — | 432 |
| 1907 | 129 | 8.7 | 246 | 14 | 287 | 48 | — | 536 |
| 1908 | 137 | 8.7 | 263 | 16 | 237 | 45 | — | 441 |
| 1909 | 150 | 9.0 | 285 | 13 | 233 | 46 | — | 450 |
| 1910 | 173 | 9.3 | 308 | 13 | 289 | 55 | — | 525 |
| 1911 | 177 | 9.6 | 316 | 17 | 318 | 60 | — | 564 |
| 1912 | 188 | 12[18] 5.5 | 363 | 20 | 348 | 63 | — | 615 |
| 1913 | 199 | 10 | 370 | 22 | 344 | 65 | — | 654 |
| 1914 | 118 | 10 | 273 | 23 | 195 | 52 | — | 423 |
| 1915 | 95 | ... | 252 | 17 | 153 | 68 | — | 404 |
| 1916 | 105 | ... | 255 | 16 | 184 | 84 | — | 478 |
| 1917 | 97 | ... | 254 | 19 | 158 | 118 | — | 537 |
| 1918 | 139 | ... | 322 | 30 | 171 | 120 | — | 619 |
| 1919 | 180 | 14 | 401 | 25 | 213 | 132 | — | 626 |
| 1920 | 297 | 15 | 509 | 31 | 349 | 176 | — | 922 |
| 1921 | 203 | ... | 470 | 24 | 319 | 154 | — | 891 |
| 1922 | 206 | 16 | 453 | 23 | 309 | 165 | — | 972 |
| 1923 | 268 | 16 | 542 | 29 | 468 | 258 | 45 | 1,258 |
| 1924 | 296 | 22 | 597 | 41 | 567 | 299 | 24 | 1,588 |
| 1925 | 350 | 23 | 663 | 42 | 722 | 312 | 34 | 1,742 |
| 1926 | 304 | 24 | 640 | 43 | 578 | 364 | 36 | 1,648 |
| 1927 | 313 | 25 | 681 | 46 | 812 | 403 | 61 | 2,040 |
| 1928 | 358 | 26 | 739 | 45 | 939 | 440 | 68 | 2,217 |
| 1929 | 356 | 27 | 748 | 49 | 928 | 427 | 76 | 2,201 |
| 1930 | 290 | 27 | 663 | 36 | 626 | 352 | 62 | 1,678 |
| 1931 | 257 | 28 | 686 | 22 | 605 | 378 | 93 | 1,753 |
| 1932 | 241 | 81 | 742 | 20 | 527 | 389 | 94 | 1,751 |
| 1933 | 257 | 92 | 754 | 26 | 757 | 445 | 123 | 2,078 |
| 1934 | 248 | 93 | 764 | 43 | 837 | 512 | 153 | 2,520 |
| 1935 | 272 | 117 | 847 | 56 | 975 | 558 | 167 | 2,723 |
| 1936 | 261 | 143 | 873 | 80 | 1,012 | 606 | 199 | 3,127 |
| 1937 | 285 | 145 | 991 | 200 | 1,173 | 667 | 232 | 3,462 |
| 1938 | 329 | 155 | 991 | 274 | 1,053 | 854 | 287 | 3,880 |
| 1939 | ... | ... | 1,015 | 426 | 1,031 | 1,030 | 324 | 4,353 |
| 1940 | 239 | 173 | 969 | 565 | 978 | 1,054 | 411 | 4,645 |
| 1941 | 189 | 180 | 914 | 824 | 1,059 | 1,185 | 537 | 4,765 |
| 1942 | 168 | 256 | 1,030 | 976 | 674 | 1,254 | 988 | 4,988 |
| 1943 | 108 | 277 | 1,050 | 1,096 | 596 | 1,554 | 1,498 | 6,011 |
| 1944 | 96 | 471 | 1,484 | 1,095 | 902 | 1,947 | 2,038 | 8,311 |

**G6**  **SOUTH AMERICA: Central Government Revenue, with some Main Tax Yields** (in millions of stated currency unit, except as otherwise indicated)

**1895–1944**

| | Chile[27] | | | Colombia[33] | | | Ecuador | Guyana[29] | Paraguay[32] |
|---|---|---|---|---|---|---|---|---|---|
| | Customs | Income & Wealth Taxes[37] | Total | Customs | Income & Wealth Taxes | Total | Total | Total | Total |
| | gold pesos[28] | | | | pesos | | sucres | dollars | gold pesos |
| 1895 | 186 | 1.4 | 252 | ... | ... | ... | ... | 2.7 | 0.9 |
| 1896 | 189 | 1.5 | 297 | ... | ... | ... | ... | 2.6 | 1.0 |
| 1897 | 184 | 1.5 | 216 | ... | ... | ... | 6.8 | 2.4 | 0.7 |
| 1898 | 172 | 1.2 | 327 | ... | ... | ... | 7.8 | 2.5 | 1.2 |
| 1899 | 206 | 1.3 | 294 | ... | ... | ... | 6.6 | 2.5 | 1.2 |
| 1900 | 236 | 1.6 | 330[27] 267 | ... | ... | ... | 8.1 | 2.4 | 1.2 |
| 1901 | 216 | 1.6 | 237 | ... | ... | ... | 11 | 2.5 | 1.3 |
| 1902 | 215 | 3.4 | 231 | ... | ... | ... | 13 | 2.6 | 1.3[32] |
| 1903 | 239 | 3.2 | 284 | ... | ... | ... | 11 | 2.6 | ... |
| 1904 | 247 | 2.7 | 271 | ... | ... | ... | 10 | 2.4 | ... |
| 1905 | 272 | 2.7 | 304 | ... | ... | 9.2 | 12 | 2.5 | ... |
| 1906 | 310 | 3.1 | 349 | ... | ... | ... | 12 | 2.5 | ... |
| 1907 | 336 | 3.0 | 379 | ... | ... | 16 | 13 | 2.6 | ... |
| 1908 | 324 | 2.2 | 363 | ... | ... | [17][16] | 13 | 2.6 | ... |
| 1909 | 340 | 2.6 | 377 | ... | ... | [17][16] | 16 | 2.6 | ... |
| 1910 | 388 | 7.1 | 437 | ... | ... | 11 | 15 | 2.7 | ... |
| 1911 | 409 | 7.9 | 465 | ... | ... | 12 | 13 | 2.8 | ... |
| 1912 | 424 | 8.6 | 490 | ... | ... | 13 | 20 | 2.8 | ... |
| 1913 | 441 | 9.3 | 515 | ... | ... | 17 | 20 | 2.9 | 4.4 |
| 1914 | 324 | 9.6 | 405 | ... | ... | 13 | 16 | 2.8 | 4.1 |
| 1915 | 272 | 41 | 374 | ... | ... | 12 | [21][16] | [2.3][29] | 3.1 |
| 1916 | 419 | 27 | 508 | ... | ... | [20][38] | [18][16] | 3.2 | 3.0 |
| 1917 | 502 | 38 | 639 | ... | ... | 13 | [19][16] | 3.5 | ... |
| 1918 | 550 | 40 | 738 | ... | ... | 11 | 18 | 4.1 | ... |
| 1919 | 223 | 31 | 374 | ... | ... | [14][38] | 15 | 4.1 | 5.5[32] |
| | | | | | | | | | paper pesos |
| 1920 | 448 | 38 | 638 | ... | ... | 26 | 21 | 6.1 | 57 |
| 1921 | 237 | 23 | 375[27] 346 | ... | ... | 16 | 21 | 4.6 | 122 |
| 1922 | 234 | 22 | 366 | ... | ... | 21 | 25 | 4.3 | 116 |
| 1923 | 414 | 23 | 551 | ... | ... | 34 | 25 | 5.3 | 123 |
| 1924 | 405 | 55 | 609 | ... | ... | 33 | 31 | 5.1 | 192 |
| 1925 | 448 | 86 | 701 | ... | ... | 46 | 39 | 5.2 | 235 |
| 1926 | 428 | 127 | 735 | ... | ... | 56 | 48 | 5.0 | 233 |
| 1927 | 511 | 162[37] | 909 | ... | ... | 63 | 65 | 5.1 | 256 |
| 1928 | 592 | 170 | 1,021 | 42 | 4.0 | 75 | 62 | 5.7 | 265 |
| 1929 | 670 | 219 | 1,234 | 41 | 3.7 | 75 | 61 | 6.0 | 256 |
| 1930 | 505 | 226 | 1,069 | 22 | 4.1 | 49 | 61 | 4.9 | 269 |
| 1931 | 221 | 151 | 792 | 20 | 2.8 | 44 | 45 | 4.4 | 213 |
| 1932 | 148 | 101 | 515 | 19 | 2.1 | 36 | 35 | 4.9 | 186 |
| 1933 | 378 | 148 | 950 | 23 | 2.4 | 43 | 39 | 5.1 | ... |
| 1934 | 383 | 168 | 1,043 | 26 | 2.9 | 55 | 48 | 5.5 | ... |
| 1935 | 543 | 160 | 1,341 | 29 | 5.3 | 62 | 66 | 5.2 | 343 |
| 1936 | 644 | 178 | 1,351 | 32 | 14 | 73 | 72 | 5.5 | 458 |
| 1937 | 721 | 212 | 1,437 | 36 | 17 | 86 | 80 | 5.9 | 1,889 |
| 1938 | 810 | 255 | 1,635 | 32 | 20 | 83 | 121 | 6.1 | 555 |
| 1939 | 782 | 374 | 1,793 | 42 | 21 | 96 | 121 | 6.2 | 411 |
| | | | | | | | | | guaranies[35] |
| 1940 | 844 | 487 | 2,052 | 29 | 24 | 79 | 115 | 7.0 | 16[32] |
| 1941 | 946 | 640 | 2,496 | 32 | 25 | 105 | 118 | 8.5 | 16 |
| 1942 | 842 | 664 | 2,954 | 20 | 31 | 111 | 139 | 10 | 19 |
| 1943 | 771 | 1,112 | 3,648 | 23 | 31 | 129 | 178 | 12 | 22 |
| 1944 | 853 | 1,363 | 4,089 | 27 | 53 | 122 | 233 | 14 | 21 |

**G6    SOUTH AMERICA: Central Government Revenue, with some Main Tax Yields** (in millions of state currency unit, except as otherwise indicated)

| | Peru[30] | | | Surinam[33] | Uruguay[34] | | | Venezuela[31] | | | |
|---|---|---|---|---|---|---|---|---|---|---|---|
| | Customs | Direct Taxes[39] | Total | Total | Customs | Direct Taxes | Total | Customs[38] | Direct Taxes | Oil Royalties | Total |
| | | soles | | guilders | | pesos | | | bolivares | | |
| 1895 | ... | ... | ... | 1.8 | 10 | ... | 15 | 38 | — | ... | 51 |
| 1896 | ... | ... | 8.4 | 3.0 | 8.6 | ... | 17 | 35 | — | ... | 48 |
| 1897 | ... | ... | 11 | 2.0 | 9.9 | ... | 16 | 23 | — | ... | 33 |
| 1898 | ... | ... | 11 [30] | 2.2 | 10 | ... | 16 | 28 | — | ... | 41 |
| 1899 | 6.5 | 0.4 | 11 | 2.1 | 9.4 | ... | 17 | 18 | — | ... | 27 |
| 1900 | 7.4 | 0.4 | 13 | 2.2 | 9.4 | ... | 19 | ... | — | ... | 45 |
| 1901 | 8.6 | 0.5 | 15 | 2.2 | 9.7 [34] | ... | 18 | ... | — | ... | 32 |
| 1902 | 8.2 | 0.6 | 15 | 2.2 | 9.5 | ... | 19 | ... | — | ... | 26 |
| 1903 | 8.6 | 0.7 | 16 | 4.1 | 9.9 | ... | 19 | ... | — | ... | 57 |
| 1904 | 10 | 0.8 | 20 | 4.5 | 9.2 | ... | 18 | ... | — | ... | 47 |
| 1905 | 11 | 0.9 | 22 | 3.7 | 10 | ... | 17 | ... | — | ... | 49 |
| 1906 | 13 | 1.9 | 26 | 4.0 | 13 | ... | 21 | ... | — | ... | 50 |
| 1907 | 14 | 2.1 | 28 | 3.6 | 13 | ... | 22 | ... | — | ... | 51 |
| 1908 | 13 | 3.3 | 29 | 4.1 | 13 | ... | 23 | ... | — | ... | 50 |
| 1909 | 11 | 2.4 | 25 | 4.3 | 14 | ... | 24 | ... | — | ... | 49 |
| 1910 | 13 | 2.5 | 28 | 5.8 | 15 | ... | 25 | 22 | — | ... | 70 |
| 1911 | 15 | 2.6 | 32 | 5.5 | 15 | ... | 26 | 20 | — | ... | 83 |
| 1912 | 16 | 2.6 | 34 | 6.1 | 17 | ... | 29 | 22 | — | ... | 65 |
| 1913 | 15 | 3.0 | 35 | 6.4 | 18 | ... | 32 | 22 | — | ... | 60 |
| 1914 | 11 | 3.1 | 31 | 6.3 | 15 | ... | 28 | 35 | — | ... | 51 |
| 1915 | 7.0 | 3.0 | 28 | 6.5 | 11 | ... | 23 | 44 | — | ... | 66 |
| 1916 | 15 | 3.2 | 39 | 3.1 | 12 | ... | 27 | 35 | — | ... | 72 |
| 1917 | 18 | 3.4 | 45 | 3.2 | 11 | ... | 25 | 20 | — | ... | 53 |
| 1918 | 20 | 3.9 | 49 | 3.5 | 11 | ... | 27 | 34 | — | ... | 57 |
| 1919 | 26 | 4.1 | 62 | 3.9 | 13 | ... | 31 | 64 | — | ... | 101 |
| 1920 | 42 | 4.9 | 81 | 5.3 | 17 | ... | 36 | 24 | — | ... | 82 |
| 1921 | 24 | 5.2 | 62 | ... | 14 | ... | 31 | 33 | — | ... | 71 |
| 1922 | 22 | 5.3 | 66 | 4.5 | 13 | ... | 31 | 46 | — | ... | 88 |
| 1923 | 33 | 6.7 | 76 | 6.6 | 16 | ... | 37 | 56 | — | ... | 102 |
| 1924 | 41 | 6.7 | 92 | 5.2 | 18 | ... | 41 | 76 | — | ... | 120 |
| 1925 | 38 | 8.0 | 92 | 4.7 | 14 | ... | 45 | 96 | — | ... | 172 |
| 1926 | 39 | 8.6 | 102 | 5.2 | 15 | ... | 48 | 93 | — | ... | 182 |
| 1927 | 40 | 12 | 107 | 4.9 | 16 | ... | 52 | 92 | — | ... | 187 |
| 1928 | 43 | 14 | 122 | 4.6 | 18 | ... | 60 | 118 | — | 46 | 230 |
| 1929 | 48 | 15 | 140 | 4.4 | 19 | 11 | 59 | 139 | — | 54 | 255 |
| 1930 | 37 | 11 | 119 | 4.6 | 23 | 12 | 58 | 100 | — | 48 | 210 |
| 1931 | 25 | 13 | 100 | 4.8 | 19 | 11 | 56 | 81 | — | 51 | 185 |
| 1932 | 18 | 8.9 | 87 | 4.7 | 16 [34] | 17 [34] | 58 [34] | 70 | — | 45 | 172 |
| 1933 | 30 | 11 | 103 | 3.9 | 20 | 14 | 58 | 70 | — | 48 | 172 |
| 1934 | 43 | 14 | 126 | 4.0 | 19 | 15 | 61 | 77 | — | 55 | 203 |
| 1935 | 48 | 15 | 140 | 4.1 | 38 | 17 | 87 | 76 | — | 62 | 189 |
| 1936 | 55 | 18 | 160 | 4.0 | 42 | 15 | 87 | 76 | — | 58 | 274 |
| 1937 | 57 | 23 | 173 | 3.7 | 43 | 13 | 88 | 117 | 1.4 | 108 | 331 |
| 1938 | 55 | 25 | 185 | 3.7 | 42 | 14 | 94 | 125 | 0.9 | 82 | 341 |
| 1939 | 50 | 27 | 180 | 4.0 | 41 | 14 | 93 | 139 | 1.1 | 90 | 354 |
| 1940 | 49 | 34 | 185 | 4.2 | 40 | 14 | 100 | 104 | 1.8 | 121 | 346 |
| 1941 | 59 | 35 | 229 | 4.3 [33] | 36 | 15 | 100 | 97 | 1.4 | 100 | 325 |
| 1942 | 88 | 52 | 275 | 19 | 30 | 18 | 103 | 77 | 3.2 | 68 | 306 |
| 1943 | 105 | 89 | 346 | 17 | 23 | 20 | 106 | 83 | 41 | 149 | 446 |
| 1944 | 120 | 98 | 386 | 16 | 28 | 18 | 117 | 110 | 55 | 277 | 614 |

**G6** **SOUTH AMERICA: Central Government Revenue, with some Main Tax Yields** (in millions of stated currency unit, except as otherwise indicated)

| | Argentina[40] | | | | Bolivia[42] | Brazil[26] | | | |
|---|---|---|---|---|---|---|---|---|---|
| | Customs[36] | Income & Wealth Taxes | VAT | Total | Total | Customs | Excises | Income & Wealth Taxes | Total |
| | pesos | | | | bolivianos | cruzeiros | | | |
| 1945 | 113 | 483 | — | 1,547 | 1,159 | 1,026 | 2,832 | 2,350 | 9,845 |
| 1946 | 248 | 619 | — | 1,972 | 1,038 | 1,404 | 4,009 | 2,751 | 11,570 |
| 1947 | 519 | 1,085 | — | 3,502 | 1,070 | 1,876 | 4,463 | 3,902 | 13,853 |
| 1948 | 471 | 1,443 | — | 4,327 | 1,385 | 1,650 | 4,854 | 4,195 | 15,699 |
| 1949 | 279 | 1,630 | — | 5,159 | 1,382 | 1,701 | 5,639 | 4,785 | 17,917 |
| 1950 | 291 | 2,238 | — | 6,096 | 1,824 | 1,695 | 6,410 | 5,582 | 19,373 |
| 1951 | 691 | 3,170 | — | 9,465 | 3,377 | 2,801 | 8,216 | 8,104 | 27,428 |
| 1952 | 457 | 4,074 | — | 11,492 | 3,182 | 2,589 | 9,124 | 9,994 | 30,740 |
| 1953 | 264 | 4,131 | — | 11,781 | 7,437 | 1,385 | 10,775 | 11,639 | 37,057 |
| 1954 | 388 | 4,414 | — | 12,782 | 15,037 | 2,281 | 14,542 | 15,340 | 46,539 |
| | thousand million pesos | | | | thousand million bolivianos | thousand million cruzeiros | | | |
| 1955 | 0.53 | 4.68 | — | 12.6 | 31 | 2.2 | 17 | 19 | 56 |
| 1956 | 0.88 | 5.44 | — | 16.0 | 74 | 2.0 | 23 | 25 | 74 |
| 1957 | [14][40] | [6.24][40] | — | [18.6][40] | 240 | 2.8 | 30 | 27 | 86 |
| 1958 | 1.37 | 8.99 | — | 36.6 | 232 | 13 | 40 | 32 | 118 |
| 1959 | 20.5[40] | 12.6[40] | — | 66.5[40] | 286 | 19 | 54 | 46 | 158 |
| 1960 | 29 | 21 | — | 103 | 304 | 22 | 83 | 62 | 233 / 208 |
| 1961 | 38 | 27 | — | 145 | 383 | 36 | 123 | 84 | 300 |
| 1962 | 32 | 21 | — | 143 | 395 | 58 | 204 | 116 | 475 |
| | | | | pesos[35] | | | | | |
| 1963 | 29 | 26 | — | 163 | 446 | 87 | 408 | 243 | 876 |
| 1964 | 47 | 29 | — | 229 | 528 | 124 | 880 | 482 | 1,811 |
| 1965 | 64 | 51 | — | 322 | 632 | 209 | 1,308 | 1,023 | 3,231 |
| 1966 | 71 | 72 | — | 421 | 741 | 416 | 2,215 | 1,339 | 4,974 |
| | | | | | | million new cruzeiros[35] | | | |
| 1967 | 136 | 138 | — | 476 | 792 | 370 | 2,840 | 1,550 | 5,493 |
| 1968 | 121 | 124 | — | 505 | 862 | 816 | 5,075 | 2,173 | 10,380 |
| 1969 | 140 | 143 | — | 572 | 901 | 1,078 | 6,752 | 3,764 | 14,766 |
| | thousand million new pesos[35] | | | | | thousand million new cruzeiros | | | |
| 1970 | 1.7 | 1.8 | — | 6.8 | 1,131 | ... | 8.5 | 4.9 | 19 |
| 1971 | 2.2 | 2.0 | — | 8.6 | 1,151 | 1.8 | 11 | 6.5 | 26 |
| 1972 | 4.8 | 2.8 | — | 14 | 1,389 | 2.6 | 15 | 10 | 39 |
| 1973 | 7.3 | 3.8 | — | 19 | 2,479 | 3.8 | 20 | 14 | 50 |
| 1974 | 6.7 | 5.8 | — | 30 / 76 | 5,070 | 6.8 | 35 | 19 | 76 |
| | | | | | thousand million pesos | | | | |
| 1975 | 20 | 6 | 9 | 160 | 5.7 | 9.6 | 44 | 26 | 101 |
| 1976 | 183 | 48 | 81 | 928 | 8.2[42] / 3.8 | 15 | 75 | 41 | 172 |
| 1977 | 380 | 270 | 280 | 2,950 | 4.4 | 17 | 99 | 71 | 253 |
| 1978 | 690 | 670 | 720 | 8,350 | 5.1 | 23 | 138 | 92 | 358 |
| | million million new pesos | | | | | | | | |
| 1979 | 1.96 | 1.30 | 2.12 | 23.4 | 5.7 | 36 | 190 | 170 | 544 |
| 1980 | 4.29 | 3.12 | 5.26 | 49 | 5.0 | 108 | 320 | 320 | 1,230 |
| 1981 | 8.74 | 7.24 | 16.2 | 92 | 6.2 | 152 | 585 | 674 | 2,352 |
| 1982 | 25.3 | 21 | 44.7 | 232 | 9.3 | 241 | 1,175 | 1,457 | 4,775 |
| 1983 | 160[41] | 80[41] | 140[41] | 1,060[41] | 28.2 | 703 | 2,492 | 4,044 | 11,780 |
| 1984 | 960[41] | 450[41] | 930[41] | 7,830[41] | 257 | 1,951 | 5,316 | 14,733 | 36,414 |
| | thousand million australes | | | | bolivianos | thousand million cruzados[35] | | | |
| 1985 | 1.10 | 0.61 | 1.14 | 8.3 | 28 | 8.1 | 25 | 58 | 135 |
| 1986 | 1.62 | 1.97 | 2.31 | 15.2 | 217 | 18 | 79 | 149 | 563 |
| 1987 | 2.83 | 4.94 | 4.77 | 32.6 | 425 | 48 | 298 | 398 | 1,692 |
| 1988 | 9.85 | 10.4 | 6.36 | 103 | 630 | 365 | 1,968 | 3,511 | 15,950 |

**G6      SOUTH AMERICA: Central Government Revenue, with some Main Tax Yields** (in millions of stated currency unit, except as otherwise indicated)

| | Chile[27] | | | Colombia | | | | Ecuador[45] | Guyana | Paraguay[32] |
|---|---|---|---|---|---|---|---|---|---|---|
| | Customs | Income & Wealth Taxes[37] | Total | Customs | Income & Wealth Taxes | General Sales Tax | Total | Total | Total | Total |
| | gold pesos[28] | | | pesos | | | | sucres | dollars | |
| 1945 | 1,204 | 1,954 | 5,531 | 43 | 64 | ... | 157 | 251 | 13 | 24 |
| 1946 | 1,542 | 1,979 | 6,198 | 50 | 84 | ... | 209 | 299 | 14 | 33 |
| 1947 | 2,007 | 2,960 | 9,979 | 67 | 125 | ... | 285 | 396 | 18 | 42 |
| 1948 | 2,573 | 5,165 | 14,379 | 60 | 138 | ... | 311 | 373 | 21 | 46 |
| 1949 | 3,690 | 5,247 | 15,823 | 44 | 177 | ... | 358 | 391 | 22 | 64 |
| | thousand million pesos | | | | | | | | | |
| 1950 | 2.7 | 5.3 | 17 | 99 | 231 | ... | 514 | 389[45] / 473 | 22 | [153][32] |
| 1951 | 5.4 | 7.4 | 26 | 217 | 285 | ... | 668 | 556 | 25 | 148[32] |
| 1952 | 7.0 | 9.7[37] / 14 | 36 | 198 | 328 | ... | 694 | 587 | 30 | ... |
| 1953 | 7.1 | 15 | 44 | 259 | 384 | ... | 840 | 732 | 32 | 433[32] |
| 1954 | 8.1 | 28 | 75 | 386 | 460 | ... | 1,043 | 998 | 36 | ... |
| | escudos[35] | | | | | | | | | |
| 1955 | 18 | 45 | 138 | 395 | 556 | ... | 1,329 | 1,092 | 41 | ... |
| 1956 | 32 | 84 | 197 | 243 | 605 | ... | 1,138 | 1,050 | 42 | ... |
| 1957 | 53 | 111 | 296 | 206 | 601 | ... | 1,227 | 1,254 | 46 | ... |
| 1958 | 53 | 133 | 366 | 609 | 762 | ... | 1,637 | 1,288 | 49 | 2,831 |
| 1959 | 90 | 206 | 582 | 582 | 974 | ... | 1,916 | 1,256 | 49 | 2,696 |
| 1960 | 138 | 242 | 708 | 709 | 1,112 | ... | 2,132 | 1,363 | 56 | 3,233 |
| 1961 | 169 | 271 | 796 | 695 | 1,140 | ... | 3,095 | 1,565 | 60 | 3,632 |
| 1962 | 188 | 333 | 957 | 550 | 1,201 | ... | 2,149 | 1,623 | 63 | 4,328 |
| 1963 | 257 | 472 | 1,354 | 601 | 1,683 | ... | 3,236 | 1,639 | 64 | 4,220 |
| 1964 | 206 | 792 | 1,959 | 1,320 | 2,001 | ... | 4,163 | 2,094 | 68 | 4,375 |
| 1965 | 347 | 1,364 | 3,209 | 1,047 | 2,371 | ... | 4,412 | 1,998 | 79 | 5,710 |
| 1966 | 549 | 2,118 | 4,898 | 2,319 | 2,689 | ... | 6,456 | 2,205 | 86 | 6,241 |
| 1967 | 664 | 2,712 | 6,312 | 1,517 | 3,650 | ... | 7,295 | 2,649 | 99 | 6,632 |
| 1968 | 986 | 3,435 | 8,758 | 2,014 | 4,430 | ... | 9,737 | 2,923 | 104 | 7,284 |
| 1969 | 1,452 | 5,068 | 13,069 | 2,462 | 5,910 | ... | 11,249 | 3,356 | 113 | 8,567 |
| | thousand million escudos | | | | | | | | | |
| 1970 | 2.0 | 7.7 | 16 | 3,523 | 6,395 | ... | 13,156 | 4,235 | 134 / 144 | 8,819 |
| 1971 | 2.3 | 7.9 | 23 | 3,838 | 8,553 | 1,615 | 17,166 | 5,097 | 141 | 8,970[23] |
| 1972 | 3.8 | 10 | 71 | 3,932 | 8,376 | 1,839 | 18,625 | 6,331 | 163 | 11,039 |
| 1973 | 12 | 60 | 326 | 3,747 | 8,804 | 2,232 | 25,064 | 7,973 | 180 | 13,494 |
| 1974 | 176 | 512 | 2,610 | 4,965 | 10,586 | 3,428 | 32,459 | 11,390 | 323 | 18,442 |
| | thousand million new pesos[35] | | | thousand million pesos | | | | thousand million | | thousand million |
| 1975 | 1.04 | 2.42 | 12.5 | 5.3 | 17.8 | 7.0 | 48.2 | 12.4 | 503 | 21.2 |
| 1976 | 2.92 | 5.94 | 41 | 6.9 | 20.7 | 9.2 | 62 | 14.7 | 399 | 23.9 |
| 1977 | 6.79 | 12.9 | 91 | 9.5 | 24.3 | 12.6 | 82 | 16.5 | 380 | 31.4 |
| 1978 | 9.64 | 21.5 | 157 | 13.6 | 30.9 | 17.5 | 106 | 19.1 | 405 | 40.9 |
| 1979 | 11.2 | 40.9 | 241 | 16.9 | 37.7 | 22.8 | 139 | 23.1 | 481 | 51 |
| 1980 | 14.9 | 62 | 344 | 25.0 | 47.6 | 30.3 | 189 | 37.5 | 540 | 62 |
| 1981 | 21.4 | 67 | 388 | 29.9 | 54 | 40.0 | 229 | 39.3 | 647 | 73 |
| 1982 | 13.1 | 71 | 360 | 38.4 | 66 | 60 | 283 | 46.0 | 627 | 86 |
| 1983 | 25.6 | 85 | 429 | 42.9 | 79 | 62 | 347 | 60 | 631 | 84 |
| 1984 | 49.1 | 84 | 544 | 44.8 | 99 | 97 | 428 | 100 | 765 | 103 |
| 1985 | 76 | 85 | 746 | 82 | 158 | 124 | 586 | 189 | 877 | 136 |
| 1986 | 75 | 111 | 914 | 132 | 216 | 178 | 827 | 187 | 1,119 | 179 |
| 1987 | 112 | 172 | 1,194 | 203 | 310 | 250 | 1,136 | 237 | 1,363 | 253 |
| 1988 | 129 | 363 | 1,584 | ... | ... | ... | ... | 415 | 1,863 | 323 |

**G6**    **SOUTH AMERICA: Central Government Revenue, with some Main Tax Yields** (in millions of stated currency unit, except as otherwise indicated)

| | Peru[30] | | | Surinam | Uruguay | | | | Venezuela[31] | | | |
|---|---|---|---|---|---|---|---|---|---|---|---|---|
| | Customs | Direct Taxes[39] | Total | Total | Customs | Direct Taxes | VAT | Total | Customs[47] | Direct Taxes | Oil Royalties | Total |
| | soles | | | guilders | pesos | | | | bolivares | | | |
| 1945 | 126 | 119 | 431 | 12 | 34 | 27 | — | 132 | 148 | 99 | 244 | 713 |
| 1946 | 213 | 161 | 609 | 13 | 54 | 40 | — | 169 | 203 | 237 | 364 | 1,100 |
| 1947 | 285 | 196 | 930 | 17 | 75 | 64 | — | 193 | 265 | 346 | 562 | 1,562 |
| 1948 | 235 | 272 | 1,021 | 21 | 52 | 80 | — | 232 | 343 | 485 | 702 | 1,963 |
| 1949 | 340 | 313 | 1,175 | 27 | 43 | 87 | — | 245 | 335 | 472 | 601 | 1,896 |
| 1950 | 702 | 403 | 1,728 | 27 | 63 | 95 | — | 280 | 363 | 460 | 784 | 2,126 |
| 1951 | 1,064 | 484 | 2,151 | 27 | 85 | 115 | — | 358 | 360 | 585 | 811 | 2,298 |
| 1952 | 956 | 460 | 2,209 | 33 | 54 | 120 | — | 372 | 375 | 665 | 764 | 2,371 |
| 1953 | 863 | 639[39] 1,071 | 2,160[30] 3,248 | 35 | 54 | 138 | — | 397 | 387 | 759 | 905 | 2,758 |
| 1954 | 1,001 | 1,367 | 3,654 | 39 | 86 | 174 | — | 454 | 436[47] 737 | 739 | 948 | 2,826 |
| 1955 | 1,083 | 1,598 | 4,787 | 43 | 75 | 182 | — | 448 | 758 | 915 | 1,104 | 3,201 |
| 1956 | 1,188 | 1,868 | 5,478 | 48 | 65 | 229 | — | 518 | 812 | 1,117 | 3,104 | 5,527 |
| 1957 | 1,319 | 2,004 | 5,274 | 56 | 77 | 263 | — | 665 | 1,141 | 1,310 | 1,870 | 4,881 |
| 1958 | 690 | 2,050 | 5,255 | 68 | 39 | 283 | — | 700 | 1,120 | 2,031 | 1,566 | 5,324 |
| 1959 | 599 | 2,558 | 6,240 | 71 | 63 | 367 | — | 900 | 1,144 | 1,820 | 1,520 | 5,863 |
| 1960 | 730 | 2,714 | 8,892 | 77 | 164 | 574 | — | 1,455 | 1,010 | 2,244 | 1,646 | 6,813 |
| 1961 | 880 | 2,970 | 10,999 | 90 | 228 | 726 | — | 2,105 | [673 | [823][31] | [807][31] | [3,291][31] |
| 1962 | 960 | 3,173 | 12,304 | 86 | 196 | 732 | — | 2,065 | 1,391 | 2,197 | 1,603 | 6,589 |
| 1963 | 1,493 | 3,510 | 11,298 | 94 | 155 | 752 | — | 2,276 | 1,639 | 2,504 | 1,715 | 6,619 |
| 1964 | 3,208 | 3,734 | 13,078 | 104 | 210 | 1,252 | — | 3,468 | 832 | 2,982 | 2,499 | 7,217 |
| | thousand million soles | | | | thousand million pesos | | | | | | | |
| 1965 | 4.6 | 3.8 | 16 | 111 | 1.3 | ... | — | 5.5 | 563 | 3,245 | 2,532 | 7,367 |
| 1966 | 5.1 | 4.3 | 18 | 122 | 4.1 | ... | — | 12 | 559 | 3,673 | 2,557 | 7,952 |
| 1967 | 6.6 | 7.5 | 24 | 130 | 5.6 | ... | — | 18 | 528 | 4,192 | 2,737 | 8,679 |
| 1968 | 8.6 | 8.7 | 28 | 146 | 12 | ... | — | 42 | 542 | 4,364 | 2,746 | 8,964 |
| 1969 | 8.0 | 11 | 32 | 164 | ... | ... | — | 62 | 576 | 4,140 | 2,749 | 9,576 |
| 1970 | 8.8 | 13 | 39 | 169 | ... | ... | — | 83 | 706[47] 630 | 4,626 | 2,864 | 10,137 |
| 1971 | 9.7 | 12 | 41 | 165 | ... | ... | — | 103[23] | 657 | 6,666 | 2,873 | 12,362 |
| 1972 | 8.1 | 13 | 46 | 196 | 9 | 24 | — | 278 | 712 | 7,151 | 2,794 | 13,297 |
| 1973 | 9.6 | 16 | 53 | 200 | 15 | 53 | 62 | 552 | 722 | 10,231 | 3,280 | 17,027 |
| 1974 | 13 | 25 | 69 | 229 | 29 | 91 | 144 | 914 | 1,209 | 29,531 | 9,287 | 44,325 |
| | | | | | new pesos[35] | | | | thousand million bolivares | | | |
| 1975 | 24 | 28 | 88 | 318 | 96 | 154 | 324 | 1,519 | 1.9 | 26 | 8.4 | 42 |
| 1976 | 25 | 29 | 111 | 403 | 228 | 302 | 602 | 2,800 | 2.2 | 25 | 6.5 | 40 |
| 1977 | 36 | 39 | 154 | 474 | 450 | 583 | 900 | 4,539 | 2.9 | 26 | 7.7 | 43 |
| 1978 | 71 | 54 | 264 | 512 | 573 | 865 | 1,352 | 6,923 | 3.6 | 24 | 7.2 | 43 |
| 1979 | 156 | 136 | 552 | 562 | 1,652 | 1,511 | 2,358 | 12,188 | 3.8 | 31 | 7.4 | 51 |
| | | | | | thousand million new pesos | | | | | | | |
| 1980 | 281 | 331 | 1,019 | 609 | 2.9 | 3.0 | 5.2 | 20.5 | 4.5 | 45 | 7 | 67 |
| 1981 | 437 | 364 | 1,523 | 657 | 3.4 | 3.2 | 7.5 | 29.1 | 5.5 | 74 | 7.2 | 98 |
| 1982 | 594 | 576 | 2,485 | 690 | 2.8 | 2.8 | 6.9 | 27.5 | 7.0[48] | 52[48] | 6.3[48] | 84[48] |
| 1983 | 812 | 784 | 3,738 | 491 | 2.8 | 5.3 | 8.5 | 40.1 | 3.6 | 43 | 6.1 | 77 |
| 1984 | 1,860 | 1,703 | 9,554 | 519 | 5.3 | 5.5 | 14 | 56 | 4.4 | 62 | 8.7 | 105 |
| | thousand million intis[35] | | | | | | | | | | | |
| 1985 | 6.2 | 4.1 | 28 | 492 | 9.7 | 13 | 30 | 109 | 6.2 | 79 | 8.3 | 127 |
| 1986 | 9.4 | 12 | 45 | 498 | 22 | 28 | 56 | 220 | 8.8 | 48 | 9.7 | 109 |
| 1987 | 14.3 | 16 | 66 | ... | 36 | 50 | 107 | 395 | ... | ... | ... | ... |
| 1988 | 58 | 109 | 407 | ... | 55 | 86 | 199 | 668 | ... | ... | ... | ... |

**G6a    TOTAL REVENUE OF CANADIAN COLONIES BEFORE CONFEDERATION CANADA** (in thousands pounds)[49]

### 1806–1839

| | Lower Canada* | Upper Canada† |
|---|---|---|
| 1806 | 29 | ... |
| 1807 | 28 | ... |
| 1808 | 30 | ... |
| 1809 | 55 | ... |
| 1810 | 57 | ... |
| 1811 | 61 | ... |
| 1812 | 50 | ... |
| 1813 | 82 | ... |
| 1814 | 145 | ... |
| 1815 | 104 | ... |
| 1816 | 94 | ... |
| 1817 | 80 | ... |
| 1818 | 56 | ... |
| 1819 | 94 | ... |
| 1820 | 99 | ... |
| 1821 | 73 | ... |
| 1822 | 40 | ... |
| 1823 | 90 | ... |
| 1824 | 83 | 62 |
| 1825 | 110 | 32 |
| 1826 | 89 | 62 |
| 1827 | 111 | 95 |
| 1828 | 109 | 49 |
| 1829 | 118 | 40 |
| 1830 | 144 | 76 |
| 1831 | 130 | 102 |
| 1832 | 163 | 92 |
| 1833 | 163 | 121 |
| 1834 | 82 | 329 |
| 1835 | 163 | 189 |
| 1836 | 2.3 | } 648 |
| 1837 | 2.3 | |
| 1838 | 126 | 259 |
| 1839 | 147 | 158 |

*later Quebec †later Ontario

### 1840–1866

| | British Columbia[50] | Lower Canada* | Upper Canada† | New Brunswick | Nova Scotia[54] | Prince Edward Island |
|---|---|---|---|---|---|---|
| 1840 | — | [196][51] | [222][51] | ... | ... | ... |
| 1841 | — | ... | | ... | ... | ... |
| | | Province of Canada[52] | | | | |
| 1842 | — | 465 | | ... | ... | ... |
| 1843 | — | 895 | | ... | ... | ... |
| 1844 | — | 1,108 | | ... | ... | ... |
| 1845 | — | 846 | | ... | ... | ... |
| 1846 | — | 645 | | ... | ... | ... |
| 1847 | — | 720 | | ... | ... | ... |
| 1848 | — | [312][52] | | ... | ... | ... |
| 1849 | — | [422] | | ... | ... | ... |
| 1850 | — | 875 | | 84 | 99 | 17 |
| 1851 | — | 899 | | 95 | 104 | 15 |
| 1852 | — | 1,103 | | 111 | 114 | 21 |
| 1853 | — | 1,349 | | 152 | 119 | 24 |
| 1854 | — | 1,591 | | 163 | 167 | 31 |
| 1855 | — | 1,153 | | [94][53] | ... | 28 |
| 1856 | — | [1,115][52] | | 119 | ...[54] | 27 |
| 1857 | — | 1,471 | | 135 | 146 | 28 |
| 1858 | — | 1,708 | | 107 | 143 | 22 |
| 1859 | 15 | 1,723 | | 160 | 140 | 27 |
| 1860 | 75 | 1,889 | | 179 | 155 | 29 |
| 1861 | 88 | 2,034 | | 146 | 146 | 28 |
| 1862 | 112 | 1,728 | | 149 | 206 | 26 |
| 1863 | 142 | 2,006[52] | | 175 | 213 | 41 |
| 1864 | 139 | 3,261 | | 214 | 178 | 44 |
| 1865 | 172 | 2,442 | | 170 | 261 | 45 |
| 1866 | 91 | 2,640 | | 298 | 307 | 64 |

**G6** **Central Government Revenue, with some Main Tax Yields** (in millions of stated currency unit, except as otherwise indicated)

NOTES

1. SOURCES: As for table G5.
2. Total revenue, unless otherwise indicated, means total ordinary revenue exclusive of loan receipts. Whether or not receipts from public enterprises are included (and, if so, whether net or gross) varies from country to country. Changes in composition are indicated in footnotes where this is possible.
3. It must be recalled that in some countries, especially those with federal systems of government, central government revenues may be no more important than the receipts of 'local' governments.
4. Except where otherwise indicated, statistics are from the closed accounts.

FOOTNOTES

[1] Statistics are budget estimates to 1899, except for 1888 which is a provisional result, and 1889, which is an actual result. Data from 1866 to 1937 and from 1949 to 1958 are for years beginning 1 July.

[2] Except as indicated in footnotes 3 and 21, statistics to 1939 relate to the administrative budget. From 1940 to 1953 (or 1954 (1st line) for total revenue) they are of consolidated federal government cash receipts, and subsequently the receipts of the unified budget. The difference between total administrative budget receipts and consolidated cash receipts in 1934–39 varied from 26.2 to 30.3 thousand million dollars. From 1913 to 1939, refunds and transfers etc. are excluded from total revenue. The amounts excluded are as follows (in million dollars):

| | | | | | | | |
|---|---|---|---|---|---|---|---|
| 1913 | 10 | 1920 | 46 | 1927 | 117 | 1934 | 101 |
| 1914 | 10 | 1921 | 54 | 1928 | 142 | 1935 | 95 |
| 1915 | 14 | 1922 | 83 | 1929 | 172 | 1936 | 119 |
| 1916 | 21 | 1923 | 154 | 1930 | 120 | 1937 | 338 |
| 1917 | 24 | 1924 | 141 | 1931 | 74 | 1938 | 654 |
| 1918 | 19 | 1925 | 139 | 1932 | 82 | 1939 | 689 |
| 1919 | 22 | 1926 | 168 | 1933 | 83 | | |

Statistics from 1844 to 1976 are for years ended 30 June and subsequently they are for years ended 30 September. The 1843 figures are for the first half-year only. Total revenue for July–September 1976 was $81 thousand million.

[3] Total internal revenue receipts to 1915, the majority of which came from excises except in 1863–73. Income tax collections during that period were as follows (in million dollars):

| | | | | | | | |
|---|---|---|---|---|---|---|---|
| 1863 | 2.7 | 1866 | 73 | 1869 | 35 | 1872 | 14 |
| 1864 | 20 | 1867 | 66 | 1870 | 38 | 1873 | 5.1 |
| 1865 | 61 | 1868 | 41 | 1871 | 19 | | |

From 1916 to 1940 (1st line) statistics are of revenue collections, which are not exactly comparable with earlier and later figures owing to differences in the time or stage of operations when the receipts were recorded.

[4] Statistics to 1889 are for years ended 30 September. Subsequently they are for years beginning 1 April.

[5] Federal government ordinary revenue to 1974 (1st line), consolidated central government revenue subsequently.

[6] Tobago is included from 1899. Statistics from 1901 to 1914 are for years beginning 1 April. The 1915 figure is for the period 1 April to 31 December. There was a change in the treatment of the Immigration Fund in 1894.

[7] Statistics to 1972 (1st line) are of budgetary revenues, exclusive of earmarked funds such as unemployment insurance, but including tax credits to the Old Age Security Fund. Subsequently they are of gross federal government receipts. Data to 1905 are for years beginning 1 July, and from 1907 they are for years beginning 1 April. The 1906 figures are for nine months from 1 July 1906 to 31 March 1907.

[8] Excise duties plus 'other excise taxes' except sales tax. "Other consumption taxes" are not included in 1985.

[9] Statistics to 1907 are for years beginning 1 April. The 1908 figure is for nine months from 1 April to 31 December.

[10] Statistics to 1963 (1st line) are for the general budget only. Subsequently they are of consolidated government current revenue. Data to 1938 are for years beginning 1 July. The 1939 figure is for the second half-year only.

[11] Statistics to 1937 are for years beginning 1 August and from 1939 to 1956 they are for years beginning 1 July. The 1938 figure is for the period 1 August 1938 to 30 June 1939, and the 1956 figure is for the second half-year only.

[12] Statistics from 1901 are for years beginning 1 April. There are changes in the coverage of extrabudgetary revenues in 1974 and 1982.

[13] Statistics from 1927 to 1964 are for years ended 30 June. Extra-budgetary receipts are included in 1980–83.

[14] Years ended 30 September. The figure for 1961 is for 10 months only, October and November 1960 being omitted. Coverage was widened from 1967 (2nd line).

[15] Years beginning 1 July to 1949.

[16] Budget estimates.

[17] Including the tax on the exploitation of natural resources.

[18] Subsequent coverage is narrower than before.

[19] Ordinary budget revenue to 1927/8 (1st line); all fiscal receipts from 1927/8 (2nd line) to 1973 (1st line), but excluding floating debt receipts from 1965; and consolidated central government revenue from 1973 (2nd line).

[20] Statistics to 1953 are of total receipts other than those of special funds. Subsequently all loans are excluded. There is no break in 1953. From 1974 (2nd line) statistics are of tax revenues and social security contributions only. Data are for years ended 30 June.

[21] Statistics to 1940 (1st line) are of employment taxes collections. Subsequently they are of receipts from social insurance taxes and contributions.

[22] There was a widening of the coverage of extra-budgetary receipts in 1972 and 1987.

[23] There was a widening of the coverage of extra-budgetary receipts in 1972.

[24] Capital Development Fund revenue is included from 1975.

[25] Consolidated central government revenue from 1970 (2nd line).

[26] Ordinary and extraordinary revenues to 1960 (1st line), but ordinary revenue only thereafter. Data from 1829 to 1886 are for years ended 30 June. The 1887 figure is for the 18 months ended 31 December 1887.

[27] Total fiscal receipts to 1900 (1st line), ordinary budget revenue subsequently. The reason for the break in 1921 is not given in the source.

[28] The 'peso de 6p.oro'.

[29] Statistics from 1889 to 1914 are for years beginning 1 April. The 1915 figure is for the period 1 April to 31 December.

[30] Budget estimates to 1898, ordinary budget revenue from 1899 to 1953 (1st line), and consolidated budget receipts subsequently. Export taxes levied directly on companies are included with Customs, not with Direct Taxes. The export duty on rubber, which was of some importance for a time, before 1910, is not included here.

[31] Statistics to 1960 are for years beginning 1 July. The 1961 figures are for the second half-year only.

[32] Statistics to 1902 are for years ended 30 June. For 1913–19 they are for calendar years, and from 1920 to 1940 they are for years ending 31 August. 1941–49 figures are again for calendar years as are those for 1958 onwards, whilst those for 1951 and 1953 are for years beginning 1 July. The 1950 figure for the 18 months ended 30 June 1951.

[33] Local revenues only to 1941.

[34] Statistics to 1932 are for years ending 30 June, except for customs receipts to 1901, which are for calendar years.

[35] For conversion rates between old and new currencies see p. xi.

[36] Including other taxes on foreign trade.

[37] Akl direct taxes to 1927, and income tax only from 1928 to 1952 (1st line).

[38] The figure for 1916 is for the 14 months ended 28 February 1917. The 1917 and 1918 figures are for years beginning 1 March, and the 1919 figure is for the 10 months from 1 March to 31 December.

[39] All taxes on income and property from 1953 (2nd line).

[40] Statistics for 1957 are for the 10 months ended 31 October, and those for 1958 and 1959 are for years ended 31 October. Coverage of extra-budgetary receipts was increased in 1974.

[41] In 1983 and 1984 the peso argentino was the currency actually in use, but the figures here have been left in the old currency.

[42] Data are for budgetary central government only from 1976 (2nd line).

[43] The revenues covered by the Customs Administration were much enlarged from 1934.

[44] There was a widening of the coverage from 1971.

[45] There was a widening of the coverage from 1950 (2nd line).

[46] There was a widening of the coverage from 1970 (2nd line).

[47] All importa and export taxes from 1954 (2nd line) to 1970 (1st line).

[48] There was a widening of the coverage of social security revenue in 1983.

[49] Local currency to 1841. This was often converted to sterling on the conventional basis that £1 local was equal to 18 shillings sterling.

[50] Including Vancouver Island.

[51] From 1 January 1840 to 9 February 1841.

[52] Statistics for 1848, 1849 and 1856 are net. The equivalent figure for 1850 is 579. A new system of accounts was adopted in 1857. Data for 1864–66 are for years ended 30 June.

[53] For ten months only.

[54] Statistics from 1857 are for years ended 30 September.

# H.    PRICES

There is a considerable array of material on prices available for most countries for a comparatively long way back in time. Most of this, however, is intractable in the extreme, and it has been decided to include none of it in this work. Instead, there are two sets of indices, based on this material but reducing it to some sort of readily comprehensible order. It was felt that annual average prices, in local currency, of (say) a kilogram of wheat were unlikely to be of use except to the specialist, and that a general indication of overall price levels would be more widely useful. Of course, there is over-simplification and distortion in the process, and like all index numbers, those presented here require careful interpretation. In order to achieve exact comparability of an index over long periods of time the commodities and their weightings must remain unchanged. However, in a changing economy first the weightings and then possibly the commodities themselves will cease to be appropriate representations of the quantities and things actually used. All indices, therefore, must compromise between continuity and relevance, and the more rapid is economic change the more frequent must be the breaks in continuity. In the period since World War II, the official indices in some countries have been changed very frequently indeed. In other countries and periods where commodity consumption patterns have changed very little, the indices have not changed either. In this way the danger of lack of representativeness has generally been avoided.

It is perhaps worth pointing out that until recently in many Latin American countries, the underlying data for price indices were derived from only a few cities, often only the capital. There may well have been quite wide regional variations in the larger countries of which the indices take no account.

In order to facilitate comparisons between countries—though it must be understood that these are necessarily inexact owing to the nature of indices and the variety of consumption patterns—many of the indices shown here have been converted to common base years. Anyone wanting to use these indices for further calculations should bear in mind this shifting of the base year, and also the fact that different indices have, when necessary, been crudely spliced together.

## H1    NORTH AMERICA: WHOLESALE PRICE INDICES

| 1749–1794 | | 1795–1839 | | 1840–1884 | | | 1885–1924 | | |
|---|---|---|---|---|---|---|---|---|---|
| | USA[1] | | USA[1] | | Canada[2] | USA[1] | | Canada[2] | USA[1] |
| | *1910–14=100* | | *1910–14=100* | | *1900=100* | *1910–4=100* | | *1900=100* | *1910–14 = 100* |
| 1749 | 68 | 1795 | 131 | 1840 | … | 95 | 1885 | 101 | 85 |
| 1750 | 60 | 1796 | 146 | 1841 | … | 92 | 1886 | 100 | 82 |
| 1751 | 65 | 1797 | 131 | 1842 | … | 82 | 1887 | 102 | 85 |
| 1752 | 66 | 1798 | 122 | 1843 | … | 75 | 1888 | 106 | 86 |
| 1753 | 65 | 1799 | 126 | 1844 | … | 77 | 1889 | | 106 |
| 1754 | 65 | | | | | | | | |
| 1755 | 66 | 1800 | 129 | 1845 | … | 83 | 1890 | 108 | 82 |
| 1756 | 66 | 1801 | 142 | 1846 | … | 83 | 1891 | 108 | 82 |
| 1757 | 65 | 1802 | 117 | 1847 | … | 90 | 1892 | 100 | 76 |
| 1758 | 70 | 1803 | 118 | 1848 | 91 | 82 | 1893 | 101 | 78 |
| 1759 | 79 | 1804 | 126 | 1849 | 80 | 82 | 1894 | 95 | 70 |
| 1760 | 79 | 1805 | 141 | 1850 | 87 | 84 | 1895 | 93 | 71 |
| 1761 | 77 | 1806 | 134 | 1851 | 85 | 83 | 1896 | 90 | 68 |
| 1762 | 87 | 1807 | 130 | 1852 | 91 | 88 | 1897 | 91 | 68 |
| 1763 | 79 | 1808 | 115 | 1853 | 108 | 97 | 1898 | 95 | 71 |
| 1764 | 74 | 1809 | 130 | 1854 | 134 | 108 | 1899 | 97 | 76 |
| 1765 | 72 | 1810 | 131 | 1855 | 155 | 110 | 1900 | 100 | 82 |
| 1766 | 73 | 1811 | 126 | 1856 | 150 | 105 | 1901 | 102 | 81 |
| 1767 | 77 | 1812 | 131 | 1857 | 154 | 111 | 1902 | 107 | 86 |
| 1768 | 74 | 1813 | 162 | 1858 | 108 | 93 | 1903 | 108 | 87 |
| 1769 | 77 | 1814 | 182 | 1859 | 124 | 95 | 1904 | 109 | 87 |
| 1770 | 77 | 1815 | 170 | 1860 | 112 | 93 | 1905 | 113 | 88 |
| 1771 | 79 | 1816 | 151 | 1861 | 98 | 89 | 1906 | 113 | 90 |
| 1772 | 89 | 1817 | 151 | 1862 | 94 | 104 | 1907 | 122 | 95 |
| 1773 | 84 | 1818 | 147 | 1863 | 101 | 133 | 1908 | 122 | 92 |
| 1774 | 76 | 1819 | 125 | 1864 | 108 | 193 | 1909 | 124 | 99 |
| 1775 | 75 | 1820 | 106 | 1865 | 124 | 185 | 1910 | 126 | 103 |
| 1776 | 86 | 1821 | 102 | 1866 | 122 | 174 | 1911 | 130 | 95 |
| 1777 | 123 | 1822 | 106 | 1867 | 124[2] | 162 | 1912 | 137 | 101 |
| | | | | | 129 | | | | |
| 1778 | 140 | 1823 | 103 | 1868 | 128 | 158 | 1913 | 134 | 102 |
| 1779 | 226 | 1824 | 98 | 1869 | 129 | 151 | 1914 | 137 | 99 |
| 1780 | 225 | 1825 | 103 | 1870 | 128 | 135 | 1915 | 147 | 102 |
| 1781 | 216 | 1826 | 99 | 1871 | 130 | 130 | 1916 | 176 | 125 |
| 1782 | … | 1827 | 98 | 1872 | 145 | 136 | 1917 | 239 | 172 |
| 1783 | … | 1828 | 97 | 1873 | 146 | 133 | 1918 | 266 | 192 |
| 1784 | … | 1829 | 96 | 1874 | 138 | 126 | 1919 | 280 | 202 |
| 1785 | 92 | 1830 | 91 | 1875 | 133 | 118 | 1920 | 326 | 226 |
| 1786 | 90 | 1831 | 94 | 1876 | 124 | 110 | 1921 | 230 | 143 |
| 1787 | 90 | 1832 | 95 | 1877 | 118 | 106 | 1922 | 203 | 141 |
| 1788 | … | 1833 | 95 | 1878 | 109 | 91 | 1923 | 205 | 147 |
| 1789 | 86 | 1834 | 90 | 1879 | 105 | 90 | 1924 | 208 | 143 |
| 1790 | 90 | 1835 | 100 | 1880 | 115 | 100 | | | |
| 1791 | 85 | 1836 | 114 | 1881 | 116 | 103 | | | |
| 1792 | … | 1837 | 115 | 1882 | 116 | 108 | | | |
| 1793 | 102 | 1838 | 110 | 1883 | 113 | 101 | | | |
| 1794 | 108 | 1839 | 112 | 1884 | 107 | 93 | | | |

## H1    NORTH AMERICA: Wholesale Price Indices

**1925–1959**

| | Canada[2] | Costa Rica[5] | Dominican Republic[6] | El Salvador | Guatemala[3] | Mexico[4] | USA[1] |
|---|---|---|---|---|---|---|---|
| | *1900 = 100* | *1938 = 100* | *1953 = 100* | *1939 = 100* | *1938 = 100* | *1938 = 100* | *1910–14 = 100* |
| 1925 | 214 | … | … | … | … | 89 | 151 |
| 1926 | 209 | … | … | … | … | 86 | 146 |
| 1927 | 204 | … | … | … | … | 84 | 139 |
| 1928 | 201 | … | … | … | … | 81 | 141 |
| 1929 | 200 | … | … | … | … | 81 | 139 |
| 1930 | 181 | … | … | … | … | 81 | 126 |
| 1931 | 151 | … | … | … | … | 71 | 107 |
| 1932 | 139 | … | … | … | … | 66 | 95 |
| 1933 | 140 | … | … | … | … | 71 | 96 |
| 1934 | 150 | … | … | … | … | 75 | 109 |
| 1935 | 151 | … | … | … | … | 75 | 117 |
| 1936 | 155 | 98 | … | … | … | 79 | 118 |
| 1937 | 174 | 104 | … | … | 106 | 94 | 126 |
| 1938 | 163 | 100 | … | … | 100 | 100 | 115 |
| | *1938 = 100* | | | | | | *1938 = 100* |
| 1939 | 97 | 102 | … | 100 | 99 | 99 | 98 |
| 1940 | 106 | 100 | … | 88 | 96 | 102 | 100 |
| 1941 | 114 | 105 | 37 | 110 | 86 | 110 | 111 |
| 1942 | 121 | 137 | 46 | 130 | 102 | 119 | 126 |
| 1943 | 125 | 172 | 62 | 156 | 130 | 144 | 132 |
| 1944 | 128 | 179 | 76 | 176 | 149 | 178 | 132 |
| 1945 | 130 | 198 | 76 | 203 | 185 | 195 | 135 |
| 1946 | 137 | 198 | 88 | 239 | 230[3] | 225 | 154 |
| 1947 | 163 | 228 | 106 | 291 | 248 | 237 | 189 |
| 1948 | 194 | 233 | 106 | 327 | 261 | 256 | 204 |
| 1949 | 198 | 230 | 91 | 331 | 266 | 280 | 194 |
| 1950 | 211 | 260 | 88 | 445 | 279 | 309 | 202 |
| 1951 | 242 | 267 | 98 | 471 | 295 | 381 ——[4] | 225 |
| 1952 | 228 | 242 | 100 | 445 | 292 | 395 | 219 |
| 1953 | 222 | 230 | 100 | 471 | 293 | 389 | 216 |
| 1954 | 219 | 239 | 94 | 570 | 307 | 425 | 216 |
| 1955 | 222 | 246 | 95 | 491 | 297 | 483 | 217 |
| 1956 | 229 | 249 | 94 | 487 | 296 | 506 | 224 |
| 1957 | 230 | 249 | 103 | 469 | 294 | 528 | 230 |
| 1958 | 231 | 249 | 102 | 444 | 297 | 552 | 234 |
| 1959 | 234 | 246 | 96 | 417 | 300 | 558 | 234 |

**H1      NORTH AMERICA: Wholesale Price Indices**

|      | Canada[2] | Costa Rica[5] | Dominican Republic[6] | El Salvador | Guatemala | Mexico | USA[1] |
|------|-----------|---------------|-----------------------|-------------|-----------|--------|--------|
|      | *1938 = 100* | *1938 = 100* | *1953 = 100* | *1939 = 100* | *1938 = 100* | *1938 = 100* | *1938 = 100* |
| 1960 | 234 | 244 | 99  | 419 | 296 | 585 | 234 |
| 1961 | 237 | 252 | 93  | 407 | 292 | 590 | 233 |
| 1962 | 243 | 249 | 102 | 405 | 297 | 601 | 234 |
| 1963 | 248 | 257 | 110 | 412 | 295 | 604 | 233 |
| 1964 | 249 | 262 | 111 | 440 | 306 | 630 | 234 |
| 1965 | 254 | 259 | 120 | 432 | 300 | 642 | 239 |
| 1966 | 264 | 259 | 114 | 432 | 298 | 650 | 246 |
| 1967 | 270 | 269 | 117 | 431 | 299 | 669 | 247 |
| 1968 | 276 | 281 | 125 | 433 | 312 | 681 | 253 |
| 1969 | 289 | 294 | 120 | 431 | 322 | 699 | 263 |
| 1970 | 295 | 312 | 120 | 469 | 330 | 740 | 273 |
| 1971 | 297 | 331 | 120 | 443 | 335 | 768 | 282 |
| 1972 | 317 | 350 | 123 | 469 | 335 | 790 | 294 |
| 1973 | 385 | 406 | 140 | 568 | 382 | 914 | 333 |
| 1974 | 471 | 568 | 169 | 712 | 535 | 1,120 | 395 |
| 1975 | 501 | 693 | 211 | 725 | 527 | 1,237 | 432 |
|      | *1980 = 100* | *1980 = 100* | *1980 = 100* | *1980 = 100* | *1980 = 100* | *1980 = 100* | *1980 = 100* |
| 1975 | 62  | 58  | 73  | 54  | 60  | 34  | 65  |
| 1976 | 65  | 60  | 69  | 73  | 67  | 41  | 68  |
| 1977 | 70  | 65  | 77  | 107 | 75  | 59  | 72  |
| 1978 | 77  | 70  | 77  | 86  | 78  | 68  | 78  |
| 1979 | 88  | 81  | 88  | 97  | 86  | 80  | 88  |
| 1980 | 100 | 100 | 100 | 100 | 100 | 100 | 100 |
| 1981 | 110 | 165 | 101 | 106 | 112 | 125 | 109 |
| 1982 | 118 | 344 | 108 | 119 | 105 | 194 | 111 |
| 1983 | 122 | 434 | 113 | 127 | 106 | 403 | 113 |
| 1984 | 127 | 468 | 143 | 135 | 112 | 686 | 115 |
| 1985 | 131 | 516 | 202 | 154 | ... | 1,001 | 115 |
| 1986 | 132 | 560 | ... | 203 | ... | 1,797 | 112 |
| 1987 | 136 | ... | 284 | 206 | ... | 4,407 | 114 |
| 1988 | 141 | 734 | ... | 216 | ... | 8,784 | 119 |

## H1    SOUTH AMERICA: WHOLESALE PRICE INDICES

| | Argentina | Brazil | Chile | Colombia | Ecuador | Paraguay[8] | Peru[9] | Venezuela[11] |
|---|---|---|---|---|---|---|---|---|
| | *1938 = 100* | *1938 = 100* | *1938 = 100* | *1953 = 100* | *1953 = 100* | *1938 = 100* | *1938 = 100* | *1938 = 100* |
| 1913 | 71 | ... | 37 | ... | ... | ... | 49 | 109 |
| 1914 | 72 | ... | ... | ... | ... | ... | 51 | ... |
| 1915 | 77 | ... | ... | ... | ... | ... | 59 | ... |
| 1916 | 88 | ... | ... | ... | ... | ... | 71 | ... |
| 1917 | 109 | ... | ... | ... | ... | ... | 86 | ... |
| 1918 | 119 | ... | ... | ... | ... | ... | 104 | ... |
| 1919 | 123 | ... | ... | ... | ... | ... | 107 | ... |
| 1920 | 129 | ... | ... | ... | ... | ... | 117 | 173 |
| 1921 | 102 | ... | ... | ... | ... | ... | 100 | 137 |
| 1922 | 93 | ... | ... | ... | ... | ... | 93 | 126 |
| 1923 | 96 | ... | ... | ... | ... | ... | 92 | 124 |
| 1924 | 104 | ... | ... | ... | ... | ... | 94 | 133 |
| 1925 | 105 | ... | ... | ... | ... | ... | 99 | 139 |
| 1926 | 94 | ... | ... | ... | ... | ... | 99 | 145 |
| 1927 | 92 | ... | ... | ... | ... | ... | 99 | 139 |
| 1928 | 93 | ... | 44 | ... | ... | ... | 94 | 139 |
| 1929 | 91 | ... | 45 | ... | ... | ... | 91 | 132 |
| 1930 | 87 | ... | 39 | ... | ... | ... | 87 | 124 |
| 1931 | 84 | ... | 35 | ... | ... | ... | 85 | 119 |
| 1932 | 85 | ... | 53 | ... | ... | ... | 83 | 112 |
| 1933 | 81 | ... | 80 | ... | ... | ... | 88 | 101 |
| 1934 | 92 | ... | 80 | ... | ... | ... | 92 | 95 |
| 1935 | 92 | ... | 79 | ... | ... | ... | 92 | 89 |
| 1936 | 93 | ... | 88 | ... | ... | ... | 94 | 95 |
| 1937 | 107 | 107 | 105 | ... | ... | ... | 100 | 104 |
| 1938 | 100 | 100 | 100 | ... | ... | 100 | 100 | 100[11] |
| 1939 | 102 | 104 | 100 | ... | ... | 104 | 104 | 106 |
| 1940 | 109 | 107 | 107 | ... | ... | 104 | 115 | 105 |
| 1941 | 119 | 133 | 125 | ... | ... | 123 | 135 | 101 |
| 1942 | 150 | 159 | 171 | ... | ... | 169 | 169 | 105 |
| 1943 | 164 | 181 | 189 | ... | ... | 200 | 196 | 113 |
| 1944 | 178 | 193 | 196 | ... | ... | 200 | 204 | 120 |
| 1945 | 194 | 226 | 207 | ... | ... | 223 | 212 | 125 |
| 1946 | 224 | 263 | 243[7] | ... | ... | 281 | 227 | 136 |
| 1947 | 232 | 319 | 311 | ... | ... | 319 | 308 | 100 |
| 1948 | 268 | 370 | 357 | 74 | ... | 385 | 385 | 173 |
| 1949 | 330 | 405 | 415 | 79 | ... | 504 | 542 | 172 |
| 1950 | 397 | 461 | 483 | 88 | ... | 754 | 628 | 173 |
| 1951 | 592 | 552 | 637 | 96 | ... | 1,173 | 706 | 180 |
| 1952 | 776 | 613 | 782 | 95 | 97 | 2,555 | 761 | 178 |
| 1953 | 867 | 699 | 965 | 100 | 100 | 4,188 | 785 | 172 |
| 1954 | 894 | 908 | 1,515 | 107 | 99 | 5,109 | 879 | 175 |

## H1    SOUTH AMERICA: Wholesale Price Indices

| | Argentina | Brazil | Chile | Colombia | Ecuador | Paraguay[8] | Peru[9] | Uruguay[10] | Venezuela[11] |
|---|---|---|---|---|---|---|---|---|---|
| | *1938 = 100* | *1938 = 100* | *1938 = 100* | *1953 = 100* | *1953 = 100* | *1938 = 100* | *1938 = 100* | *1970 = 100* | *1938 = 100* |
| 1955 | 974 | 1,027 | 2,674 | 108 | 98 | 6,031 | 950 | ... | 177 |
| 1956 | 1,227 | 1,230 | 4,382 | 117 | 97 | 8,031 | 1,089 | ... | 176 |
| 1957 | 1,523 | 1,382 | 6,236 | 145 | 100 | 9,740 | 1,112 | ... | 172 |
| 1958 | 1,995 | 1,544 | 7,828 | 171 | 100 | 10,502 | 1,158 | ... | 175 |
| 1959 | 4,665 | 2,131 | 10,177 | 187 | 99 | 12,357 | 1,425 | ... | 176 |
| | | | *1959 = 100* | | | *1959 = 100* | | | |
| 1960 | 5,402 | 2,795 | 105 | 195 | 98 | 113 | 1,679 | ... | 174 |
| 1961 | 5,831 | 3,861 | 105 | 207 | 102 | 127 | 1,679 | ... | 176 |
| 1962 | 7,611 | 5,915 | 114 | 213 | 104 | 134 | 1,703 | ... | 185 |
| 1963 | 9,821 | 10,255 | 175 | 269 | 108 | 137 | ... | 4.3 | 191 |
| 1964 | 12,399 | 19,586 | 265 | 316 | 112 | 142 | ... | 6.4 | 199 |
| | *1964 = 100* | *1964 = 100* | | | | | *1970 = 100* | | |
| 1965 | 124 | 152 | 328 | 342 | 113 | 155 | ... | 10 | 206 |
| 1966 | 149 | 210 | 404 | 402 | 116 | 162 | ... | 20 | 208 |
| 1967 | 186 | 262 | 481 | 429 | 118 | 158 | ... | 33 | 211 |
| 1968 | 204 | 324 | 633 | 456 | 119 | 155 | 76 | 76 | 215 |
| 1969 | 217 | 390 | 856 | 486 | 125 | 157 | 88 | 88 | 218 |
| 1970 | 248 | 476 | 1,172 | 524 | ... | 151 | 100 | 100 | 221 |
| 1971 | 345 | 576 | 1,383 | 584 | ... | 171 | 121 | 121 | 229 |
| 1972 | 610 | 686 | 2,357 | 691 | ... | 202 | 229 | 229 | 237 |
| | | | *1972 = 100* | | | | | | |
| 1973 | 917 | 786 | 610 | 883 | ... | 279 | 492 | 492 | 252 |
| 1974 | 1,100 | 1,019 | 6,886 | 1,202 | ... | 364 | 879 | 879 | 294 |
| 1975 | 3,218 | 1,148 | 40,067 | 1,507 | ... | 419 | 1,515 | 1,515 | 333 |
| | *1975 = 100* | *1975 = 100* | *1975 = 100* | | | | | *1975 = 100* | |
| 1976 | 599 | 140 | 321 | 2,065 | 117 | 423 | 2,091 | 151 | 356 |
| 1977 | 1,494 | 197 | 598 | 2,471 | 126 | 423 | 3,075 | 226 | 393 |
| 1978 | 3,676 | 274 | 855 | 2,999 | 147 | 457 | 5,409 | 336 | 423 |
| 1979 | 9,164 | 426 | 1,277 | 3,873 | 163 | 515 | 8,257 | 607 | 463 |
| 1980 | 16,075 | 891 | 1,782 | 4,853 | 175 | 649 | 9,211 | 860 | 556 |
| | *1980 = 100* | *1980 = 100* | *1980 = 100* | *1980 = 100* | | | *1980 = 100* | *1980 = 100* | *1980 = 100* |
| 1981 | 210 | 213 | 109 | 124 | 191 | 704 | 168 | 123 | 114 |
| 1982 | 750 | 413 | 117 | 154 | 224 | ... | 263 | 139 | 123 |
| 1983 | 3,408 | 1,116 | 170 | 181 | ... | ... | 560 | 242 | 132 |
| 1984 | 23,002 | 3,617 | 212 | 199 | ... | ... | 1,233 | 429 | 155 |
| | *1984 = 100* | *1984 = 100* | | | | | | | |
| 1985 | 852 | 333 | 303 | 255 | ... | ... | 3,376 | 757 | 178 |
| 1986 | 1,250 | 794 | 363 | 304 | ... | ... | 5,412 | 1,266 | 208 |
| 1987 | 2,787 | 2,489 | 433 | 385 | ... | ... | 8,198 | 2,066 | 303 |
| 1988 | 14,283 | 19,809 | 459 | 495 | ... | ... | 58,001 | 3,253 | 362 |

**H1      Wholesale Price Indices**

NOTES

1.  SOURCES: The national publications listed on p. xiv–xvi; UN and League of Nations, *Statistical Yearbooks;* International Monetary Fund, *International Financial Statistics.*
2.  Various indices have been crudely spliced together in a number of cases to give a rough indicator of the long-term movement of prices. The differences in the construction of these indices should be borne in mind if they are used in further calculations.

FOOTNOTES

[1] Warren & Pearson's index to 1889, Bureau of Labour Statistics index subsequently.
[2] H. Michell's index of prices of 15 foodstuffs in Toronto to 1867 (1st line), the general wholesale price index (excluding gold) from then to 1975 (1st line), and the index of industrial products prices subsequently.
[3] Foodstuffs only to 1946.
[4] Mexico City only to 1951.
[5] San José only.
[6] Santa Domingo only.
[7] Home-consumed goods subsequently.
[8] Asunción only to 1955.
[9] Lima-Callao only.
[10] Montevideo only.
[11] Caracas only to 1938.

**H2     NORTH AMERICA: CONSUMER PRICE INDICES**

| | 1800–1844 | | 1845–1889 | | | 1890–1934 | | |
|---|---|---|---|---|---|---|---|---|
| | USA | | USA | | | Canada[1] | Honduras[3] | USA |
| | *1913=100* | | *1913=100* | | | *1913=100* | *1938=100* | *1913=100* |
| 1800 | 172 | 1845 | 94 | 1890 | | ... | ... | 91 |
| 1801 | 168 | 1846 | 91 | 1891 | | ... | ... | 91 |
| 1802 | 145 | 1847 | 94 | 1892 | | ... | ... | 91 |
| 1803 | 152 | 1848 | 88 | 1893 | | ... | ... | 91 |
| 1804 | 152 | 1849 | 84 | 1894 | | ... | ... | 88 |
| 1805 | 152 | 1850 | 84 | 1895 | | ... | ... | 84 |
| 1806 | 158 | 1851 | 84 | 1896 | | ... | ... | 84 |
| 1807 | 148 | 1852 | 84 | 1897 | | ... | ... | 84 |
| 1808 | 162 | 1853 | 84 | 1898 | | ... | ... | 84 |
| 1809 | 158 | 1854 | 91 | 1899 | | ... | ... | 84 |
| 1810 | 158 | 1855 | 94 | 1900 | | 70[2] | ... | 84 |
| 1811 | 168 | 1856 | 91 | 1901 | | ... | ... | 84 |
| 1812 | 172 | 1857 | 94 | 1902 | | ... | ... | 88 |
| 1813 | 195 | 1858 | 88 | 1903 | | ... | ... | 91 |
| 1814 | 212 | 1859 | 91 | 1904 | | ... | ... | 91 |
| 1815 | 185 | 1860 | 91 | 1905 | | 78[2] | ... | 91 |
| 1816 | 172 | 1861 | 91 | 1906 | | ... | ... | 91 |
| 1817 | 162 | 1862 | 101 | 1907 | | ... | ... | 94 |
| 1818 | 155 | 1863 | 125 | 1908 | | ... | ... | 91 |
| 1819 | 155 | 1864 | 158 | 1909 | | ... | ... | 91 |
| 1820 | 141 | 1865 | 155 | 1910 | | 91 | ... | 94 |
| 1821 | 135 | 1866 | 148 | 1911 | | 93 | ... | 94 |
| 1822 | 135 | 1867 | 141 | 1912 | | 98 | ... | 98 |
| 1823 | 121 | 1868 | 135 | 1913 | | 100, | ... | 100 |
| 1824 | 111 | 1869 | 135 | 1914 | | 101 | ... | 101 |
| 1825 | 114 | 1870 | 128 | 1915 | | 102 | ... | 102 |
| 1826 | 114 | 1871 | 121 | 1916 | | 111 | ... | 110 |
| 1827 | 114 | 1872 | 121 | 1917 | | 131 | ... | 129 |
| 1828 | 111 | 1873 | 121 | 1918 | | 148 | ... | 152 |
| 1829 | 108 | 1874 | 114 | 1919 | | 163 | ... | 174 |
| 1830 | 108 | 1875 | 111 | 1920 | | 189 | ... | 202 |
| 1831 | 108 | 1876 | 108 | 1921 | | 166 | ... | 180 |
| 1832 | 101 | 1877 | 108 | 1922 | | 152 | ... | 169 |
| 1833 | 98 | 1878 | 98 | 1923 | | 153 | ... | 172 |
| 1834 | 101 | 1879 | 94 | 1924 | | 150 | ... | 172 |
| 1835 | 104 | 1880 | 98 | 1925 | | 152 | ... | 177 |
| 1836 | 111 | 1881 | 98 | 1926 | | 153 | ... | 178 |
| 1837 | 114 | 1882 | 98 | 1927 | | 151 | ... | 175 |
| 1838 | 108 | 1883 | 94 | 1928 | | 151 | ... | 173 |
| 1839 | 108 | 1884 | 91 | 1929 | | 153 | 122 | 173 |
| 1840 | 101 | 1885 | 91 | 1930 | | 152 | ... | 168 |
| 1841 | 104 | 1886 | 91 | 1931 | | 137 | ... | 154 |
| 1842 | 98 | 1887 | 91 | 1932 | | 124 | 105 | 138 |
| 1843 | 94 | 1888 | 91 | 1933 | | 119 | ... | 131 |
| 1844 | 94 | 1889 | 91 | 1934 | | 120 | ... | 135 |

**H2    NORTH AMERICA: Consumer Price Indices**

**1935–1975**

| | Canada | Costa Rica[4] | Cuba | Dominican Republic[5] | El Salvador[6] | Guatemala[7] | Haiti[8] |
|---|---|---|---|---|---|---|---|
| | *1913 = 100* | *1938 = 100* | *1938 = 100* | *1941 = 100* | *1938 = 100* | *1937 = 100* | *1948 = 100* |
| 1935 | 121 | ... | ... | ... | ... | ... | ... |
| 1936 | 123 | 93 | ... | ... | ... | ... | ... |
| 1937 | 127 | 99 | ... | ... | 113 | 100 | ... |
| 1938 | 129 | 100 | 100 | ... | 100 | ... | ... |
| | *1938 = 100* | | | | | | |
| 1939 | 99 | 100 | 94 | ... | 94 | 92 | ... |
| 1940 | 103 | 98 | 92 | ... | 97 | 91 | ... |
| 1941 | 109 | 101 | 100 | 100 | 109 | 87 | ... |
| 1942 | 114 | 122 | 132 | 120 | 111 | ... | ... |
| 1943 | 116 | 156 | 151 | 150 | 123 | 111 | ... |
| 1944 | 117 | 165 | 172 | 174 | 160 | 130 | ... |
| 1945 | 118 | 175 | 194 | 181 | 180 | 163 | ... |
| 1946 | 122 | 182 | 210 | 202 | 177 | 194 | ... |
| 1947 | 133 | 207 | 248 | 227 | 189 | 198 | ... |
| 1948 | 152 | 214 | 269 | 229 | 191 | 223 | 100 |
| 1949 | 157 | 232 | 234 | 219 | 200 | 240 | ... |
| 1950 | 162 | 256 | 226 | 219 | 234 | 247 | ... |
| 1951 | 178 | 274 | 251 | 239 | 271[6] | 269 | [102][10] |
| 1952 | 183 | 266 | 253 | 241 | 265 | 263 | 109 |
| 1953 | 181 | 268 | 245 | 238 | 284 | 271 | 101 |
| 1954 | 182 | 275 | 238 | 233 | 301 | 278 | 106 |
| 1955 | 183 | 285 | 238 | 233 | 314 | 283 | 107 |
| 1956 | 186 | 287 | 238 | 236 | 319 | 285 | 111 |
| 1957 | 192 | 296 | 238 | 248 | 304 | 282 | 114 |
| 1958 | 197 | 304 | ... | 242 | 322 | 285 | 111 |
| 1959 | 199 | 305 | ... | 242 | 320 | 284 | 108 |
| 1960 | 201 | 307 | ... | 234 | 319 | 281 | 103 |
| 1961 | 203 | 315 | ... | 224 | 310 | 279 | 106 |
| 1962 | 205 | 323 | ... | 244 | 311 | 285 | 106 |
| 1963 | 209 | 333 | ... | 266 | 316 | 285 | 110 |
| 1964 | 213 | 344 | ... | 272 | 321 | 285 | 121 |
| 1965 | 218 | 341 | ... | 266 | 323 | 283 | 123 |
| 1966 | 226 | 342 | ... | 267 | 319 | 284 | 133 |
| 1967 | 234 | 346 | ... | 271 | 324 | 286 | 130 |
| 1968 | 244 | 360 | ... | 271 | 332 | 291 | 131 |
| 1969 | 255 | 370 | ... | 273 | 331 | 297 | 133 |
| 1970 | 263 | 387 | ... | 284 | 341 | 304 | 134 |
| 1971 | 271 | 399 | ... | 296 | 342 | 303 | 148 |
| 1972 | 284 | 417 | ... | 319 | 347 | 305 | 153 |
| 1973 | 305 | [481] | ... | 367 | 369 | 346 | 187 |
| 1974 | 339 | [625] | ... | 416 | 432 | 404 | 216 |
| 1975 | 375 | 733 | ... | 476 | 515 | | 252 |

## H2    NORTH AMERICA: Consumer Price Indices

**1935–1975**

| | Honduras[3] | Jamaica[9] | Mexico | Nicaragua[11] | Panama[12] | Puerto Rico | Trinidad & Tobago | USA |
|---|---|---|---|---|---|---|---|---|
| | *1938 = 100* | *1940 = 100* | *1938 = 100* | *1938 = 100* | *1939–40 = 100* | *1943 = 100* | *1952 = 100* | *1913 = 100* |
| 1935 | 105 | ... | 70 | ... | ... | ... | ... | 138 |
| 1936 | 98 | ... | 75 | ... | ... | ... | ... | 140 |
| 1937 | 100 | ... | 88 | 66 | ... | ... | ... | 145 |
| 1938 | 100 | ... | 100 | 100 | ... | ... | ... | 142 |
| | | | | | | | | *1938 = 100* |
| 1939 | 102 | [84][10] | 102 | 148 | 100 | ... | ... | 99 |
| 1940 | 107 | 100 | 103 | 181 | | ... | ... | 100 |
| 1941 | 108 | 114 | 106 | 178 | ... | [71][10] | ... | 105 |
| 1942 | 117 | 127 | 123 | 240 | 153 | [95][10] | ... | 116 |
| 1943 | 133 | 131 | 161 | 317 | 156 | 100 | ... | 123 |
| 1944 | 145 | 133 | 202 | 538 | 159 | 101 | ... | 125 |
| 1945 | 158 | 133 | 217 | 632 | 162 | 104 | ... | 128 |
| 1946 | 162 | 137 | 272 | 508 | 175 | 113 | ... | 139 |
| 1947 | 163 | 163 | 304 | 549 | 194 | 125 | ... | 159 |
| 1948 | 167 | 196 | 323 | 518 [11] | 196 | 127 | ... | 171 |
| 1949 | 173 | 204 | 340 | 489 | 184 | 116 | ... | 169 |
| 1950 | 182 | 214 | 362 | 585 | 178 | 114 | ... | 171 |
| 1951 | 200 | 243 | 407 | 700 | 186 | 125 | ... | 184 |
| 1952 | 196 | 269 | 466 | 710 | 192 [12] | 133 | 100 | 188 |
| 1953 | 200 | 269 | 458 | 796 | 194 | 137 | 102 | 190 |
| 1954 | 211 | 269 | 481 | 863 | 192 | 141 | 102 | 191 |
| 1955 | 227 | 272 | 558 | 978 | 191 | 140 | 107 | 190 |
| 1956 | 220 | 277 | 583 | 949 | 191 | 141 | 108 | 193 |
| 1957 | 215 | 283 | 614 | 911 | 190 | 147 | 111 | 200 |
| 1958 | 221 | 298 | 689 | 959 | 190 | 150 | 116 | 205 |
| 1959 | 223 | 307 | 708 | 930 | 189 | 153 | 119 | 207 |
| 1960 | 219 | 316 | 742 | 911 | 190 | 158 | 121 | 210 |
| 1961 | 223 | 338 | 754 | 911 | 190 | 162 | 123 | 212 |
| 1962 | 225 | 343 | 762 | 916 | 192 | 165 | 126 | 215 |
| 1963 | 232 | 348 | 767 | 921 | 193 | 168 | 131 | 217 |
| 1964 | 243 | 356 | 786 | 959 | 198 | 172 | 132 | 220 |
| 1965 | 250 | 365 | 814 | 988 | 199 | 177 | 135 | 224 |
| 1966 | 251 | 373 | 848 | 1,015 | 199 | 182 | 140 | 230 |
| 1967 | 254 | 383 | 873 | 1,033 | 202 | 189 | 143 | 237 |
| 1968 | 260 | 406 | 893 | ... | 205 | 195 | 155 | 247 |
| 1969 | 265 | 431 | 927 | ... | 209 | 200 | 159 | 260 |
| 1970 | 273 | 473 | 975 | ... | 215 | 207 | 163 | 276 |
| 1971 | 279 | 498 | 1,028 | ... | 220 | 216 | 169 | 287 |
| 1972 | 289 | 525 | 1,079 | ... | 231 | 216 | 184 | 297 |
| | | | | *1980 = 100* | | | | |
| 1973 | 302 | 617 | 1,209 | [35][10] | 247 | 239 | 212 | 315 |
| 1974 | 341 | 786 | 1,49 | 39 | 289 | 286 | 258 | 350 |
| 1975 | 369 | 923 | 1,724 | 42 | 304 | 311 | 302 | 383 |

**H2**     **NORTH AMERICA: Consumer Price Indices**

*1980 = 100*

|      | Canada | Costa Rica[4] | Dominican Republic[5] | El Salvador | Guatemala[7] | Haiti[8] | Honduras[3] |
|------|--------|-----------|-----------------------|-------------|--------------|----------|-------------|
| 1975 | 66  | 68  | 62  | 54  | 60        | 64  | 64  |
| 1976 | 71  | 70  | 67  | 58  | 67        | 68  | 67  |
| 1977 | 76  | 73  | 76  | 65  | 75        | 73  | 73  |
| 1978 | 83  | 77  | 79  | 73  | 81        | 71  | 77  |
| 1979 | 91  | 85  | 86  | 85  | 90        | 80  | 85  |
| 1980 | 100 | 100 | 100 | 100 | 100       | 100 | 100 |
| 1981 | 112 | 137 | 107 | 115 | 111       | 111 | 109 |
| 1982 | 124 | 260 | 116 | 128 | 112       | 119 | 120 |
| 1983 | 132 | 346 | 124 | 145 | [99][10]  | 131 | 130 |
| 1984 | 138 | 387 | 154 | 162 | 100       | 139 | 137 |
| 1985 | 143 | 443 | 212 | 198 | 120       | 154 | 139 |
| 1986 | 149 | 498 | 232 | 262 | 158       | 160 | 144 |
| 1987 | 155 | 582 | 269 | 327 | 175       | 141 | 148 |
| 1988 | 162 | 703 | 389 | 391 | 205       | 147 | 156 |

|      | Jamaica[9] | Mexico | Nicaragua[11] | Panama[12] | Puerto Rico | Trinidad & Tobago | USA |
|------|------------|--------|---------------|------------|-------------|-------------------|-----|
| 1975 | 37  | 38    | 42      | 72  | 76  | 55  | 65  |
| 1976 | 40  | 45    | 43      | 75  | 78  | 60  | 69  |
| 1977 | 45  | 57    | 48      | 78  | 81  | 67  | 73  |
| 1978 | 60  | 67    | 50      | 81  | 85  | 74  | 79  |
| 1979 | 78  | 79    | 74      | 88  | 91  | 85  | 88  |
| 1980 | 100 | 100   | 100     | 100 | 100 | 100 | 100 |
| 1981 | 112 | 128   | 124     | 107 | 110 | 114 | 110 |
| 1982 | 119 | 203   | 155     | 112 | 114 | 127 | 117 |
| 1983 | 133 | 410   | 203     | 114 | 115 | 148 | 121 |
| 1984 | 170 | 679   | 274     | 116 | 117 | 168 | 126 |
| 1985 | 214 | 1,071 | 877     | 117 | 117 | 181 | 131 |
| 1986 | 246 | 1,995 | 6,852   | 117 | 117 | 195 | 133 |
| 1987 | 262 | 4,626 | 69,256  | 118 | 120 | 216 | 138 |
| 1988 | 284 | 9,907 | 7 million | 119 | 124 | 233 | 144 |

## H2    SOUTH AMERICA: CONSUMER PRICE INDICES

### 1863–1899                                                                                    1900–1934

| | Colombia[13] | | | Argentina[14] | Brazil[15] | Chile[16] | Colombia[13] | Peru[17] | Uruguay[18] | Venezuela[23] |
|---|---|---|---|---|---|---|---|---|---|---|
| | *1864=100* | | | *1913=100* | *1913=100* | *1913=100* | *1864=100* | *1913=100* | *1938=100* | *1938=100* |
| 1863 | ... | | 1900 | ... | ... | ... | ... | ... | ... | ... |
| 1864 | 100 | | 1901 | ... | ... | ... | 2,416 | ... | ... | ... |
| | | | 1902 | ... | ... | ... | ... | ... | ... | ... |
| 1865 | ... | | 1903 | ... | ... | ... | ... | ... | ... | ... |
| 1866 | ... | | 1904 | ... | ... | ... | 7,888 | ... | ... | ... |
| 1867 | ... | | | | | | | | | |
| 1868 | ... | | 1905 | ... | ... | ... | 9,532 | ... | ... | ... |
| 1869 | ... | | 1906 | ... | ... | ... | ... | ... | ... | ... |
| | | | 1907 | ... | ... | ... | 9,750 | ... | ... | ... |
| 1870 | ... | | 1908 | ... | ... | ... | ... | ... | ... | ... |
| 1871 | ... | | 1909 | ... | ... | ... | 10,510 | ... | ... | ... |
| 1872 | | | | | | | | | | |
| 1873 | ... | | 1910 | ... | ... | ... | 10,942 | ... | ... | ... |
| 1874 | ... | | 1911 | ... | ... | ... | 16,974 | ... | ... | ... |
| | | | 1912 | ... | 99 | ... | 25,882 | ... | ... | ... |
| 1875 | ... | | 1913 | 100 | 100 | 100 | ... | 100 | ... | ... |
| 1876 | ... | | 1914 | 100 | 100 | 108 | ... | 104 | ... | ... |
| 1877 | ... | | | | | | | | | |
| 1878 | 131 | | 1915 | 107 | 109 | 120 | ... | 112 | ... | ... |
| 1879 | 117 | | 1916 | 115 | 117 | 117 | 28,426 | 123 | ... | ... |
| | | | 1917 | 135 | 129 | 118 | 29,910 | 142 | ... | ... |
| 1880 | ... | | 1918 | 169 | 144 | 121 | ... | 164 | ... | ... |
| 1881 | 143 | | | | | | *1938=100* | | | |
| 1882 | 139 | | 1919 | 160 | 149 | 143 | 58 | 188 | ... | ... |
| 1883 | 126 | | | | | | | | | |
| 1884 | 134 | | 1920 | 186 | 164 | 168 | 72 | 210 | ... | ... |
| | | | 1921 | 167 | 169 | 169 | 53 | 199 | ... | ... |
| 1885 | ... | | 1922 | 139 | 185 | 173 | ... | 190 | ... | ... |
| 1886 | 127 | | 1923 | 137 | 203 | 176 | 78 | 180 | ... | ... |
| 1887 | ... | | 1924 | 139 | 237 | 186 | 78 | 187 | ... | ... |
| 1888 | ... | | | | | | | | | |
| 1889 | ... | | 1925 | 136 | 253 | 202 | 79 | 200 | ... | ... |
| | | | 1926 | 132 | 261 | 199 | 97 | 201 | ... | ... |
| 1890 | ... | | 1927 | 131 | 268 | 196 | 87 | 193 | ... | ... |
| 1891 | 275 | | | | | *1938=100* | | | | |
| 1892 | 276 | | 1928 | 117 | 264 | 58 | 89 | 181 | ... | ... |
| 1893 | ... | | 1929 | 131 | 262 | 59 | 87 | 176 | 103 | ... |
| 1894 | 353 | | | | | | | | | |
| | | | 1930 | 133 | 238 | 59 | 72 | 169 | 103 | ... |
| 1895 | ... | | 1931 | 114 | 230 | 58 | 66 | 158 | 103 | ... |
| 1896 | ... | | 1932 | 102 | 231 | 62 | 56 | 151 | 101 | ... |
| 1897 | 410 | | 1933 | 108 | 229 | 77 | 57 | 147 | 96 | 104 |
| 1898 | ... | | 1934 | 102 | 246 | 77 | 79 | 150 | 96 | 94 |
| 1899 | ... | | | | | | | | | |

## H2 SOUTH AMERICA: Consumer Price Indices

### 1935–1975

| | Argentina[14] | Bolivia[19] | Brazil[15] | Chile[16] | Colombia[13] | Ecuador[20] | Guyana | Paraguay | Peru[17] | Uruguay[18] | Venezuela[23] |
|---|---|---|---|---|---|---|---|---|---|---|---|
| | *1913=100* | *1938=100* | *1913=100* | *1938=100* | *1938=100* | *1938=100* | *1938[21]=100* | *1938=100* | *1913=100* | *1938=100* | *1938=100* |
| 1935 | 108 | ... | 262 | 78 | 82 | ... | ... | ... | 152 | 99 | 92 |
| 1936 | 118 | 45 | 299 | 85 | 87 | ... | ... | ... | 159 | 98 | 95 |
| 1937 | 121 | 76 | 321 | 96 | 88 | ... | ... | ... | 170 | 101 | 98 |
| 1938 | 120 | 100 | 355 | 100 | 100 | 100 | [100][21] | 100 | 172 | 100 | 100 |
| | *1938=100* | | *1938=100* | | | | | | *1938=100* | | |
| 1939 | 102 | 124 | 103 | 101 | 104 | 153 | ... | 109 | 99 | 106 | 106 |
| 1940 | 104 | 166 | 107 | 114 | 101 | 165 | ... | 113 | 106 | 111 | 101 |
| 1941 | 107 | 212 | 119 | 132 | 99 | 153 | ... | 128 | 115 | 110 | 99 |
| 1942 | 113 | 276 | 132 | 165 | 108 | 176 | [159][10] | 144 | 130 | 113 | 109 |
| 1943 | 114 | 337 | 146 | 192 | 125 | 188 | [163][10] | 176 | 142 | 119 | 120 |
| 1944 | 114 | 359 | 164 | 215 | 150 | 224 | 159 | 193 | 162 | 122 | 138 |
| 1945 | 136 | 379 | 191 | 234 | 167 | 259 | 159 | 214 | 180 | 140 | 138 |
| 1946 | 161 | 431 | 223 | 271 | 180 | 318 | 173 | 235 | 197 | 155 | 147 |
| 1947 | 182 | 547 | 272 | 362 | 212 | 524 | 184 | 309 | 254 | 179 | 169 |
| 1948 | 207[14] | 526 | 281 | 427 | 247 | 588 | 196 | 412 | 334 | 182 | 204 |
| 1949 | 266 | 578 | 294 | 507 | 264 | 576 | 206 | 556 | 378 | 191 | 199 |
| 1950 | 354 | 784 | 321 | 584[16] | 316 | 571 | 224 | 951 | 430 | 184 | 197 |
| 1951 | 472 | 994[19] | 359 | 714 | 346 | 638 | 239 | 1,300 | 474 | 210 | 202 |
| 1952 | 667 | 1,235 | 421 | 868 | 337 | 659 | 267 | 2,827 | 507 | 239 | 199 |
| 1953 | 694 | 2,485 | 482 | 1,095 | 362 | 662 | 267 | 4,478 | 554 | 255 | 198 |
| 1954 | 722 | 5,566 | 590 | 1,711 | 394 | 686 | 275 | 5,795 | 583 | 285 | 201 |
| | | | | | | | | *1954=100* | | | |
| 1955 | 806 | 10,010 | 726 | 3,017 | 390 | 696 | 283 | 124 | 610 | 312 | 199 |
| 1956 | 917 | 27,928 | 878 | 5,003 | 415 | 663 | 288 | 150 | 643 | 335 | 197 |
| | | *1956=100* | | | | | | | | | |
| 1957 | 1,139 | 215 | 1,047 | 6,439 | 478 | 668 | 292 | 174 | 692 | 382 | 191 |
| 1958 | 1,500 | 222 | 1,203[15] | 8,109 | 549 | 679 | 294 | 185 | 747 | 448 | 197 |
| 1959 | 3,167 | 267 | 1,504 | 11,238 | 588 | 680 | 302 | 204 | 841 | 624 | 206 |
| | *1959=100* | | *1959=100* | *1959=100* | | | | | *1959=100* | | |
| 1960 | 128 | 298 | 120 | 112 | 611 | 690 | 304 | 220 | 109 | 869 | 207 |
| 1961 | 146 | 320 | 180 | 120 | 664 | 719 | 307 | 261 | 115 | 1,068 | 202 |
| 1962 | 187 | 339 | 260 | 137 | 679 | 739 | 318 | 265 | 123 | 1,184 | 201 |
| 1963 | 231 | 337 | 440 | 197 | 898 | 783 | 324 | 270 | 130 | 1,433 | 203 |
| 1964 | 282 | 371 | 860 | 278 | 1,055 | 809 | 326 | 274 | 143 | 2,020 | 207 |
| | | | | | | | | | | *1964=100* | |
| 1965 | 362 | 381 | 1,420 | 360 | 1,092 | 836 | 334 | 285 | 166 | 157 | 211 |
| 1966 | 477 | 408 | 2,001 | 441 | 1,309 | 869 | 341 | 293 | 181 | 272 | 214 |
| 1967 | 618 | 454 | 2,601 | 534 | 1,417 | 903 | 351 | 297 | 199 | 517 | 215 |
| 1968 | 718 | 479 | 3,181 | 673 | 1,500 | 941 | 362 | 299 | 237 | 1,163 | 217 |
| 1969 | 773 | 485 | 3,881 | 870 | 1,652 | 1,002 | 367 | 305 | 252 | 1,400 | 222 |
| | *1969=100* | | *1969=100* | *1969=100* | *1969=100* | | | | | | |
| 1970 | 107 | 508 | 123 | 133 | 107 | 1,052 | 379 | 303 | 265 | 1,642 | 228 |
| 1971 | 109 | 527 | 147 | 159 | 117 | 1,141 | 383 | 318 | 283 | 1,239 | 236 |
| 1972 | 113 | 561 | 172 | 285 | 132 | 1,230 | 402 | 348 | 303 | 2,187 | 242 |
| 1973 | 120 | 738 | 194 | 1,288 | 159 | 1,391 | 433 | 392 | 332 | 4,309 | 252 |
| 1974 | 126 | 1,201 | 247 | 7,811 | 197 | 1,715 | 508 | 490 | 388 | 7,635 | 273 |
| 1975 | 137 | 1,297 | 319 | 37,037 | 242 | 1,978 | 548 | 523 | 479 | 13,849 | 301 |

**H2      SOUND AMERICA: Consumer Price Indices**

|      | *1980=100* | | | | | |
|------|-----------|---------|---------|---------|-------------|------------|
|      | **Argentina** | **Bolivia** | **Brazil** | **Chile** | **Colombia**[13] | **Ecuador**[20] |
| 1975 | 0.49 | 46 | 14 | 6.6 | 35 | 57 |
| 1976 | 2.58 | 48 | 19 | 21 | 41 | 64 |
| 1977 | 7.04 | 51 | 27 | 40 | 54 | 72 |
| 1978 | 19 | 57 | 37 | 55 | 63 | 80 |
| 1979 | 50 | 68 | 56 | 74 | 78 | 88 |
| 1980 | 100 | 100 | 100 | 100 | 100 | 100 |
| 1981 | 204 | 132 | 196 | 120 | 129 | 112 |
| 1982 | 541 | 295 | 370 | 132 | 160 | 130 |
| 1983 | 2,403 | 1,109 | 874 | 167 | 192 | 193 |
| 1984 | 17,462 | 15,325 | 2,380 | 201 | 223 | 254 |
|      | *1984=100* | *1984=100* | *1984=100* | | | |
| 1985 | 772 | 11,848 | 302 | 262 | 279 | 325 |
| 1986 | 1,468 | 44,591 | 693 | 313 | 330 | 399 |
| 1987 | 3,395 | 51,092 | 2,227 | 376 | 404 | 517 |
| 1988 | 15,041 | 59,268 | 15,286 | 431 | 526 | 818 |

|      | **Guyana** | **Paraguay**[22] | **Peru**[17] | **Uruguay**[18] | **Venezuela**[23] |
|------|-----------|-----------|---------|---------|-------------|
| 1975 | 55 | 50 | 13 | 11 | 59 |
| 1976 | 60 | 53 | 17 | 16 | 63 |
| 1977 | 65 | 58 | 24 | 25 | 68 |
| 1978 | 74 | 64 | 37 | 37 | 73 |
| 1979 | 88 | 82 | 63 | 61 | 82 |
| 1980 | 100 | 100 | 100 | 100 | 100 |
| 1981 | 122 | 114 | 175 | 134 | 116 |
| 1982 | 148 | 122 | 288 | 159 | 127 |
| 1983 | 170 | 138 | 609 | 238 | 135 |
| 1984 | [209][10] | 166 | 1,280 | 370 | 152 |
|      | | | *1984=100* | | |
| 1985 | 245 | 208 | 263 | 637 | 169 |
| 1986 | 252 | 274 | 460 | 1,123 | 189 |
| 1987 | 340 | 334 | 871 | 1,836 | 242 |
| 1988 | 476 | 410 | 6,680 | 2,978 | 313 |

## H2     Consumer Price Indices

NOTES

1. SOURCES: As for table H1, with Colombia to 1917 from Miguel Urrutia and Mario Arrubla (eds.), *Compendio de Estadisticas Historicas de Colombia* (Bogota, 1970).
2. Various indices have been crudely spliced together in some cases to give a rough indicator of the long-term movement of the cost of living. The differences in the construction of these indices should be borne in mind if they are used in further calculations.

FOOTNOTES

[1] Family budget price index to 1913, consumer price index subsequently.
[2] December only.
[3] In Tegucigalpa.
[4] In San José.
[5] In Santo Domingo to 1978.
[6] In San Salvador to 1951.
[7] In Guatemala City to 1975 (1st line).
[8] In Port-au-Prince to 1979.
[9] In Kingston.
[10] The figure applies to less than the full 12 months.
[11] Cost of food in Managua to 1948, consumer price index subsequently (but in Managua only to 1979).
[12] Cost of food in Panama City to 1952, consumer price index there subsequently.
[13] In Bogota. The index to 1864–1917 relates to food prices only.
[14] In Buenos Aires to 1948.
[15] In Rio de Janeiro to 1953.
[16] In Santiago to 1950.
[17] In Lima-Callao.
[18] In Montevideo.
[19] In La Paz to 1951.
[20] In Quito.
[21] March–December only.
[22] In Asunción.
[23] In Caracas.

# I.   EDUCATION

Of all the subjects on which statistical material exists, probably none shows less uniformity, both over time and between countries, than education. There is no universal definition of what constitutes a primary school, or a general secondary school, and even that of a university has shown considerable flexibility in the recent past. Moreover, there have been several major reorganizations of school systems in practically every country, and minor changes have been very frequent. Furthermore, the statistics of pupils and teachers have not always been collected in a consistent manner, even within the same school system. In addition, the date in the school year to which the statistics relate has been altered on various occasions; the exact meaning of the data has changed, sometimes referring to all pupils on the register, sometimes to those in regular attendance, sometimes to those present on a particular day, and sometimes to those present when an inspector visited. Moreover, private schools have not always been included in the data collection process, and in some cases statistics for tertiary education have not distinguished between different types of institution, teacher-training even being included quite frequently with secondary education. Nevertheless, for all the impossibility of making precise comparisons over long periods of time, and, even more, between many countries, when used with care these statistics do provide useful comparative material, even if only of a very rough nature.

# I1 NORTH AMERICA: PUPILS AND TEACHERS IN SCHOOLS (in thousands, except as otherwise indicated)

Key:  a = primary schools; b = secondary schools

### 1854–1884

| | Barbados | Canada[2] | Guatemala | Jamaica | Newfoundland | Nicaragua | Trinidad | USA[4] | | Teachers[5] |
|---|---|---|---|---|---|---|---|---|---|---|
| | Pupils | Pupils | Pupils | Pupils | Pupils | Pupils | Pupils | Pupils | Pupils | |
| | a[1] | All Schools | a | All Schools | All Schools | a | a | a | b | All Schools |
| 1854 | ... | ... | ... | ... | ... | ... | 1.8 | ... | ... | ... |
| 1855 | 8.1 | ... | ... | ... | ... | ... | 1.8 | ... | ... | ... |
| 1856 | 11 | ... | ... | ... | ... | ... | 2.2 | ... | ... | ... |
| 1857 | 13 | ... | ... | ... | ... | ... | 2.3 | ... | ... | ... |
| 1858 | ... | ... | ... | ... | ... | ... | 2.3 | ... | ... | ... |
| 1859 | 11 | ... | ... | ... | ... | ... | 3.5 | ... | ... | ... |
| 1860 | 11 | ... | ... | ... | ... | ... | 3.4 | ... | ... | ... |
| 1861 | 9.7 | ... | ... | ... | ... | ... | 3.7 | ... | ... | ... |
| 1862 | 13 | ... | ... | ... | ... | ... | 3.7 | ... | ... | ... |
| 1863 | 12 | ... | ... | ... | ... | ... | 3.6 | ... | ... | ... |
| 1864 | 10 | ... | ... | ... | ... | ... | 3.1 | ... | ... | ... |
| 1865 | 11 | ... | ... | ... | ... | ... | 3.5 | ... | ... | ... |
| 1866 | 11 | ... | ... | ... | ... | ... | 3.1 | ... | ... | ... |
| 1867 | 13 | ... | ... | ... | ... | ... | 2.9 | ... | ... | ... |
| 1868 | 13 | 720 | ... | 20 | ... | ... | 3.2 | ... | ... | ... |
| 1869 | 12 | 739 | ... | 20 | ... | ... | 2.9 | ... | ... | ... |
| 1870 | 13 | 749 | ... | 26 | ... | ... | 3.5 | ... | ... | 201 |
| 1871 | 15 | 767 | ... | 33 | 19 | ... | 4.1 | 7,481 | 80 | 220 |
| 1872 | 16 | 784 | ... | 38 | 20 | ... | 5.1 | ... | ... | 230 |
| 1873 | 17 | 810 | ... | 37 | 20 | ... | 5.7 | ... | ... | 238 |
| 1874 | 18₁ | 825₂ | ... | 43 | 19 | ... | 6.2 | ... | ... | 248 |
| 1875 | ... | 837 | ... | 41 | ... | ... | 7.6 | ... | ... | 258 |
| 1876 | 11 | [837] | ... | 47 | 19 | ... | 6.5 | ... | ... | 260 |
| 1877 | 12 | 864 | ... | 50 | 19 | ... | 6.5 | ... | ... | 267 |
| 1878 | 12 | ... | ... | 51 | 20 | ... | 7.2 | ... | ... | 277 |
| 1879 | 11 | 866 | ... | 52 | 18 | ... | 8.1 | ... | ... | 280 |
| 1880 | 12 | 852₂ | ... | 56 | 18 | ... | 9.4 | 9,757 | 110 | 287 |
| 1881 | 12 | 852₂ | ... | 49 | ... | ... | 9.1 | ... | ... | 294 |
| 1882 | 11 | [804]³ | ... | 53 | ... | ... | 9.0 | ... | ... | 299 |
| 1883 | 11 | [851]³ | 41 | 56 | 25 | 15 | 10 | ... | ... | 304 |
| 1884 | 12 | [868]³ | ... | 58 | 26 | 14 | 11 | ... | ... | 314 |

I1　**NORTH AMERICA: Pupils and Teachers in Schools** (in thousands, except as otherwise indicated) (a: primary schools; b: secondary schools)

**1885–1914**

| | Barbados | | Canada[2] | | Costa Rica | | | Cuba | | | El Salvador | | Guatemala | Honduras |
|---|---|---|---|---|---|---|---|---|---|---|---|---|---|---|
| | Pupils | | All Schools | | Pupils | | Teachers | All Schools[10] | | Pupils | Pupils | | Pupils | Pupils |
| Year | a[1] | b | Pupils | Teachers | a[8] | b[9] | a[8] | Pupils | Teachers[11] | a | a | b | a[13] | b |
| 1885 | 11 | … | 964 | … | 13 | | | | | | 39 | | | |
| 1886 | 11 | … | 911 | … | 14 | | | | | | | | | |
| 1887 | 13 | 0.5 | 968 | … | 11 | | | | | 27 | | | | |
| 1888 | 14 | 0.4 | 998 | … | 13 | | | | | | 45 | 1.3 | | |
| 1889 | 13 | … | [936][3] | … | … | | | | | | | | | |
| 1890 | 14 | 0.5 | 961 | 21 | 9 | | | | | | | | | |
| 1891 | 13 | 0.5 | [943] | … | … | … | … | | | | 65 | | | |
| 1892 | 16 | 0.5 | [889][6] | … | 17 | … | 0.5 | | | 29 | | 1.2 | | |
| 1893 | 18 | 0.5 | 998 | … | 20 | … | 0.6 | | | | | | | |
| 1894 | 16 | 0.6 | 1,018 | … | 19 | … | 0.6 | | | | | | | |
| 1895 | 14 | 0.6 | 1,040 | 26 | 22 | … | 0.7 | | | | 75 | | | |
| 1896 | 15 | 0.5 | 1,049 | … | 22 | … | 0.8 | | | | | | | |
| 1897 | 16 | 0.6 | 1,108 | … | 23 | … | 0.9 | | | | | | | |
| 1898 | 15 | 0.6 | 1,082 | … | 23 | … | 0.9 | 85 | 2.7 | | 47[12] | | | |
| 1899 | 15 | 0.5 | 1,085 | … | 21 | … | 0.9 | 172 | 3.6 | | | | | |
| 1900 | 14 / 24[1] | 0.5 | 1,079 | 28 | 19 | … | 0.9 | 163[10] | 3.6[10] | | | | | |
| 1901 | 24 | 0.5 | 1,093 | 27 | 19 | … | 0.8 | 163 | 3.6 | | | | 30 | 0.6 |
| 1902 | 23 | 0.5 | 1,104 | 28 | 19 | … | 0.7 | … | … | 30 | | | | |
| 1903 | 25 | 0.6 | 1,114 | 29 | 23 | … | 0.8 | … | 3.6 | | | | | |
| 1904 | 26 | 0.6 | 1,121 | 29 | 23 | … | 0.9 | 143 | 3.6 | | | | | |
| 1905 | 25 | 0.5 | 1,150 | 29 | 22 | 0.4 | 1.0 | 135 | … | 32 | | | | |
| 1906 | 25 | 0.5 | 1,164 | 32 | 24 | … | 1.0 | 142 | … | | | | | |
| 1907 | 25 | 0.6 | 1,196 | 33 | 26 | … | 0.7 | 131 | … | | | | | |
| 1908 | 26 | 0.6 | 1,230 | 35 | 24 | … | 0.8 | … | 3.6 | | | | 26 | |
| 1909 | 27 | 0.6 | 1,272 | 36 | 28 | 0.5 | 0.8 | 143 | 3.6 | | | | | |
| 1910 | 28 | 0.6 | 1,311 | 38 | 27 | 0.4 | 1.0 | 153 | 3.9 | | 54 | | … | |
| 1911 | 28 | 0.6 | 1,357 | 41 | 30 | 0.5 | 1.1 | … | … | 32 | 56 | | 30 | 0.3 |
| 1912 | 26 | 0.6 | [1,322][7] | [39][7] | 31 | 0.6 | 1.2 | 235 | 4.1 | … | 60 | | 30 | |
| 1913 | 26 | 0.6 | 1,471 | 44 | 33 | 0.6 | 1.3 | 277 | 4.3 | 44 | 61 | | 36 | |
| 1914 | 25 | 0.6 | 1,555 | 46 | 35 | 0.6 | 1.4 | 290 | 4.9 | 41 | 64 | … | 41 | |

## I1 NORTH AMERICA: Pupils and Teachers in Schools (in thousands, except as otherwise indicated) (a: primary schools; b: secondary schools)

### 1885–1914

| | Jamaica | Mexico | | | Newfoundland | Nicaragua | Puerto Rico | Trinidad[16] | | USA[4] | | |
|---|---|---|---|---|---|---|---|---|---|---|---|---|
| | Pupils | Pupils | | Teachers | Pupils | Pupils | Pupils | Pupils | | Pupils | | Teachers |
| | All Schools[14] | a | b | All Schools | All Schools | a | All Schools[15] | a | b | a | b | All Schools |
| 1885 | 62 | ... | ... | ... | 27 | ... | ... | 11 | ... | ... | ... | 326 |
| 1886 | 62 | ... | ... | ... | 29 | ... | ... | 12 | ... | ... | ... | 331 |
| 1887 | 62 | ... | ... | ... | 29 | 12 | ... | 14 | ... | ... | ... | 339 |
| 1888 | 72 | ... | ... | ... | ... | ... | ... | 16 | ... | ... | ... | 347 |
| 1889 | 76 | ... | ... | ... | 32 | ... | ... | 17 | ... | ... | ... | 357 |
| 1890 | 80 | ... | ... | ... | 32 | ... | ... | 20 | ... | 12,520 | 203 | 364 |
| 1891 | 84 | ... | ... | ... | 33 | ... | ... | ... | ... | 12,839 | 212 | 368 |
| 1892 | 92 | ... | ... | ... | 35 | ... | ... | 18 | ... | 13,016 | 240 | 374 |
| 1893 | 97 | ... | ... | ... | 35 | ... | ... | 18 | ... | 13,229 | 254 | 383 |
| 1894 | 104 | ... | ... | ... | 34 | ... | ... | 21 | ... | 13,706 | 289 | 389 |
| 1895 | 100[14] | 561 | ... | ... | 33 | ... | ... | 22 | ... | 13,894 | 350 | 398 |
| 1896 | 93 | ... | ... | ... | 31 | ... | ... | 22 | ... | 14,118 | 380 | 400 |
| 1897 | 98 | ... | ... | ... | 34 | ... | ... | 24 | ... | 14,414 | 409 | 405 |
| 1898 | 96 | ... | ... | ... | 35 | ... | ... | 25 | ... | 14,654 | 450 | 411 |
| 1899 | 99 | ... | ... | ... | 37 | ... | ... | 25[15] | ... | 14,700 | 476 | 414 |
| 1900 | ... | ... | ... | ... | 38 | 18 | 34 | 30 | ... | 14,984 | 519 | 423 |
| 1901 | ... | ... | ... | ... | ... | ... | 56 | 31 | ... | 15,161 | 542 | 432 |
| 1902 | ... | ... | ... | ... | ... | ... | 63 | 38 | ... | 15,367 | 551 | 442 |
| 1903 | ... | ... | ... | ... | ... | ... | 65 | 38 | ... | 15,417 | 592 | 449 |
| 1904 | ... | ... | ... | ... | ... | ... | 57 | 39 | ... | 15,620 | 636 | 455 |
| 1905 | ... | ... | ... | ... | ... | ... | 49 | 41 | ... | 15,789 | 680 | 460 |
| 1906 | ... | ... | ... | ... | ... | ... | 52 | 41 | ... | 15,919 | 723 | 466 |
| 1907 | ... | 658 | 5.8 | 40 | ... | ... | 63 | 44 | ... | 16,140 | 751 | 481 |
| 1908 | ... | ... | ... | ... | ... | 18 | 83 | 45 | ... | 16,292 | 770 | 495 |
| 1909 | ... | ... | ... | ... | 42 | ... | 95 | 45 | ... | 16,665 | 841 | 506 |
| 1910 | ... | ... | ... | ... | 44 | ... | 114 | 48 | ... | 16,899 | 915 | 523 |
| 1911 | ... | ... | ... | ... | 44 | ... | 125 | 49 | 0.8 | 17,050 | 985 | 534 |
| 1912 | ... | ... | ... | ... | ... | ... | 132 | 49 | 0.8 | 17,078 | 1,105 | 547 |
| 1913 | ... | ... | ... | ... | ... | 31 | 183 | 52 | 0.8 | 17,474 | 1,135 | 565 |
| 1914 | ... | ... | ... | ... | ... | ... | 160 | 51 | 0.8 | 17,935 | 1,219 | 580 |

**I1   NORTH AMERICA: Pupils and Teachers in Schools** (in thousands, except as otherwise indicated)

1915–1944

| | Barbados Pupils | | Canada[2] All Schools | | Costa Rica Pupils | | Costa Rica Teachers | | Cuba All Schools | | Dominican Republic Pupils | | Teachers |
|---|---|---|---|---|---|---|---|---|---|---|---|---|---|
| | a[1] | b | Pupils | Teachers | a[8] | b[9] | a[8] | b[9] | Pupils | Teachers[11] | a | b | a |
| | | | | | | | | (numbers) | | | | | |
| 1915 | 23 | 0.6 | 1,604 | 48 | 35 | 0.5 | 1.3 | ... | 290 | 4.9 | ... | ... | ... |
| 1916 | 23 | 0.6 | 1,626 | 50 | 37 | ... | 1.5 | ... | ... | ... | ... | ... | ... |
| 1917 | 22 | 0.7 | 1,651 | 52 | 35 | ... | 1.5 | ... | 335 | ... | ... | ... | ... |
| 1918 | 20 | 0.7 | 1,675 | 53 | ... | 0.9 | ... | ... | ... | ... | ... | ... | ... |
| 1919 | 19 | 0.8 | 1,750 | 51 | 30 | ... | 1.1 | ... | ... | ... | ... | ... | ... |
| 1920 | 19 | 0.9 | 1,827 | 56 | 35 | 1.2 | 1.3 | ... | ... | ... | ... | ... | ... |
| 1921 | 19 | 0.9 | 1,881 | 58 | 38 | ... | 1.3 | ... | ... | ... | ... | ... | ... |
| 1922 | 20 | 0.8 | 1,965 | 61 | 39 | 1.0 | 1.3 | ... | $358_{10}$ / 386 | $6.1_{10}$ / 7.6 | ... | ... | ... |
| 1923 | 21 | 0.8 | 1,940 | ... | 41 | 1.1 | 1.4 | ... | 301 | ... | ... | ... | ... |
| 1924 | 22 | 0.8 | 1,967 | 62 | 39 | 0.9 | 1.4 | ... | 426 | 8.9 | ... | ... | ... |
| 1925 | 22 | 0.8 | 1,993 | 62 | 40 | ... | 1.4 | ... | 346 | 8.4 | ... | ... | ... |
| 1926 | 23 | 0.8 | 2,026 | 64 | 42 | 1.0 | 1.5 | ... | 352 | 8.7 | ... | ... | ... |
| 1927 | 23 | 0.9 | 2,049 | 66 | 42 | 1.0 | 1.4 | ... | ... | ... | ... | ... | ... |
| 1928 | 23 | 1.0 | 2,081 | 68 | 47 | 1.2 | 1.7 | ... | 373 | 9.2 | ... | ... | ... |
| 1929 | 23 | 1.0 | $2,121_2$ | 69 | 47 | 1.1 | 1.7 | 62 | 374 | 9.0 | ... | ... | ... |
| 1930 | 23 | 1.0 | $2,151_{17}$ | 70 | 49 | 1.1 | 1.9 | 81 | 484 | 9.2 | ... | ... | ... |
| 1931 | 24 | 1.1 | 2,189 | 71 | 51 | 1.1 | 1.9 | 86 | 451 | 9.1 | ... | ... | ... |
| 1932 | 24 | 1.1 | 2,230 | ... | 53 | 1.0 | 1.9 | 70 | ... | ... | ... | ... | ... |
| 1933 | 24 | 1.1 | 2,243 | 73 | 54 | 1.2 | 2.3 | 79 | 428 | 9.3 | 68 | ... | ... |
| 1934 | 25 | 1.2 | $2,241_{17}$ | 73 | 59 | 1.4 | 2.3 | 78 | ... | ... | ... | ... | ... |
| 1935 | 25 | 1.2 | 2,222 | 74 | 59 | 1.4 | 2.3 | 82 | ... | ... | 104 | ... | ... |
| 1936 | 26 | 1.3 | 2,223 | 73 | 60 | ... | 2.3 | ... | 493 | 11 | 113 | ... | 1.9 |
| 1937 | 26 | 1.4 | 2,215 | 73 | 62 | 1.4 | 2.6 | 78 | ... | ... | 114 | 1.8 | 2.0 |
| 1938 | 27 | 1.5 | 2,222 | 74 | 63 | 1.3 | 2.6 | 77 | 455 | 11 | 116 | ... | 2.1 |
| 1939 | 28 | 1.6 | 2,233 | 75 | 65 | 1.2 | 2.7 | 78 | $[446]_{10}$ | $[9.4]_{10}$ | 117 | ... | 2.3 |
| 1940 | 28 | 1.6 | 2,202 | 76 | 67 | 1.5 | 2.8 | 78 | ... | ... | 132 | ... | 2.3 |
| 1941 | 28 | 1.7 | 2,167 | 76 | 70 | ... | ... | ... | ... | ... | 130 | ... | 2.3 |
| 1942 | 29 | 1.8 | 2,109 | 75 | 72 | ... | ... | ... | ... | ... | 128 | ... | 2.3 |
| 1943 | 30 | 2.3 | 2,070 | 74 | 77 | 1.7 | 3.8 | 122 | ... | ... | 128 | 3.1 | 2.4 |
| 1944 | 29 | 2.4 | 2,075 | 75 | 79 | ... | ... | ... | ... | ... | 213 | ... | 3.7 |

**1915–1944**

I1  **NORTH AMERICA: Pupils and Teachers in Schools** (in thousands, except as otherwise indicated)

| | El Salvador | | | Guatemala | | | | Haiti | | Honduras | | |
|---|---|---|---|---|---|---|---|---|---|---|---|---|
| | Pupils | | Teachers | Pupils | | Teachers | | Pupils | | Pupils[18] | | Teachers |
| | a | b | a | a | b | a | b | a | b | a[13] | b | a[13] |
| 1915 | ... | ... | ... | 66 | ... | ... | ... | ... | ... | ... | ... | ... |
| 1916 | 58 | 2.3 | ... | 67 | ... | ... | ... | ... | ... | ... | ... | ... |
| 1917 | ... | ... | ... | 54 | ... | ... | ... | ... | ... | ... | ... | ... |
| 1918 | ... | ... | ... | ... | ... | ... | ... | 62 | 4.8 | —[18] | ... | ... |
| 1919 | 51 | ... | 1.6 | ... | ... | ... | ... | ... | ... | 33 | ... | ... |
| 1920 | 49 | ... | ... | 55[12] | ... | ... | ... | ... | ... | 36 | ... | ... |
| 1921 | 58 | ... | 1.5 | 77 | ... | ... | ... | ... | ... | 39 | ... | ... |
| 1922 | 42 | ... | ... | 83 | ... | ... | ... | ... | ... | 33 | 0.2 | 1.1 |
| 1923 | 37 | ... | ... | 89 | ... | ... | ... | ... | ... | 31 | ... | 0.8 |
| 1924 | 45 | ... | 1.1 | 94 | ... | ... | ... | ... | ... | ... | ... | ... |
| 1925 | 50 | ... | ... | 103 | ... | 3.2 | ... | 79 | 4.3 | 28 | ... | ... |
| 1926 | 52 | ... | ... | 104 | ... | 3.4 | ... | ... | ... | 35 | ... | ... |
| 1927 | 48 | ... | ... | 115 | ... | 3.6 | ... | ... | ... | 39 | ... | 1.4 |
| 1928 | ... | ... | ... | ... | ... | ... | ... | ... | ... | 35 | ... | ... |
| 1929 | 41 | ... | ... | ... | ... | ... | ... | 87 | ... | 42[18] | ... | 2.0 |
| 1930 | ... | ... | ... | ... | ... | ... | ... | ... | ... | ... | ... | ... |
| 1931 | 47 | ... | ... | ... | ... | ... | ... | ... | ... | ... | ... | ... |
| 1932 | 51 | ... | ... | 88 | 3.2 | ... | ... | ... | ... | 30 | ... | 1.4 |
| 1933 | 64 | ... | ... | ... | ... | ... | ... | ... | ... | 35 | ... | 1.2 |
| 1934 | ... | ... | ... | 104 | 3.6 | 4.1 | 1.1 | ... | ... | 38 | ... | 1.4 |
| 1935 | 71 | ... | ... | 112 | 5.4 | 4.6 | 1.2 | ... | ... | 31 | ... | 1.2 |
| 1936 | 77 | ... | ... | ... | ... | ... | ... | [66][1] | ... | 41 | ... | 1.2 |
| 1937 | 83 | ... | ... | ... | ... | ... | ... | ... | ... | 37 | ... | 1.3 |
| 1938 | 85 | ... | ... | 123 | 5.7 | 5.1 | 1.3 | ... | ... | 40 | ... | 1.5 |
| 1939 | 94 | ... | ... | 130 | ... | ... | ... | ... | ... | 46 | ... | 1.5 |
| 1940 | 96 | ... | ... | 137 | ... | ... | ... | 83 [72][1] | ... | 50 | ... | 1.6 |
| 1941 | 86 | ... | ... | 132 | ... | ... | ... | 87 | ... | 52 | ... | 1.7 |
| 1942 | 91 | 1.7 | ... | 133 | 5.6 | ... | ... | 98 | ... | 48 | ... | 1.7 |
| 1943 | 80 | ... | ... | 132 | ... | ... | ... | ... | ... | 48 | ... | 1.8 |
| 1944 | 99 | 1.9 | ... | 135 | 7 | 5.5 | 1.1 | ... | 51 | ... | ... | 1.9 |

**I1   NORTH AMERICA: Pupils and Teachers in Schools** (in thousands, except as otherwise indicated)

1915–1944

| | Jamaica | | Mexico | | | Newfoundland | Nicaragua | | | |
|---|---|---|---|---|---|---|---|---|---|---|
| | Pupils | | Pupils | | Teachers | Pupils | Pupils | | Teachers | |
| | a | b | a | b | a | All Schools | a | b | a | b |
| 1915 | 97 | ... | ... | ... | ... | ... | ... | ... | ... | ... |
| 1916 | 97 | ... | ... | ... | ... | ... | ... | ... | ... | ... |
| 1917 | 100 | ... | ... | ... | ... | ... | ... | ... | ... | ... |
| 1918 | 94 | ... | ... | ... | ... | ... | ... | ... | ... | ... |
| 1919 | 90 | ... | ... | ... | ... | ... | ... | ... | ... | ... |
| 1920 | 92 | ... | ... | ... | ... | 54 | ... | ... | ... | ... |
| 1921 | 100 | ... | ... | ... | ... | 56 | ... | ... | ... | ... |
| 1922 | 112 | ... | ... | ... | ... | 55 | 30 | ... | ... | ... |
| 1923 | 115 | ... | ... | ... | ... | 56 | ... | 0.4 | ... | ... |
| 1924 | 113 | ... | ... | ... | ... | 58 | 30 | 0.5 | ... | ... |
| 1925 | 118 | ... | ... | ... | ... | 59 | ... | ... | ... | ... |
| 1926 | 122 | ... | ... | 17 | ... | 59 | ... | ... | ... | ... |
| 1927 | 126 | ... | 887 | ... | ... | 60 | ... | ... | ... | ... |
| 1928 | 128 | ... | 1,002 | 16 | ... | 61 | ... | ... | ... | ... |
| 1929 | 133 | ... | 1,212 | 16 | ... | 61 | ... | ... | ... | ... |
| 1930 | 132 | ... | 1,300 | 17 | ... | 61 | ... | ... | ... | ... |
| 1931 | 134 | ... | 1,396 | 22 | ... | 61 | ... | ... | ... | ... |
| 1932 | 136 | ... | 1,479 | ... | ... | 59 | ... | ... | ... | ... |
| 1933 | 142 | ... | 1,486 | ... | ... | 55 | ... | ... | ... | ... |
| 1934 | 148 | ... | 1,419 | ... | ... | 55 | ... | ... | ... | ... |
| 1935 | 151 | ... | 1,511 | 26 | ... | 57 | ... | ... | ... | ... |
| 1936 | 152 | ... | 1,683 | ... | ... | 59 | ... | ... | ... | ... |
| 1937 | 158 | ... | 1,810 | ... | ... | 63 | ... | ... | ... | ... |
| 1938 | 164 | ... | 1,916 | ... | ... | 63 | 54 | 1.0 | 1.7 | 0.1 |
| 1939 | 164 | ... | 1,964 | ... | ... | 64 | ... | ... | ... | ... |
| 1940 | 163 | ... | 1,961 | ... | ... | 66 | ... | ... | ... | ... |
| 1941 | 164 | ... | 2,017 | ... | ... | 67 | ... | ... | ... | ... |
| 1942 | 163 | 3.6 | 2,154 | ... | 44 | 67 | ... | ... | ... | ... |
| 1943 | 164 | 4.0 | 1,819 | ... | 49 | 66 | ... | ... | ... | ... |
| 1944 | 171 | 4.3 | 1,882 | ... | 52 | 69 | ... | ... | ... | ... |

**11    NORTH AMERICA: Pupils and Teachers in Schools** (in thousands, except as otherwise indicated)

**1915–1944**

| | Panama | Puerto Rico | | Trinidad and Tobago[21] | | | | USA[4] | | |
|---|---|---|---|---|---|---|---|---|---|---|
| | Pupils | All Schools | | Pupils | | Teachers | | Pupils | | Teachers[5] |
| | a | Pupils | Teachers | a | b | a | b | a | b | All Schools |
| 1915 | ... | 150 | ... | 49 | 0.6 | ... | ... | 18,375 | 1,329 | 604 |
| 1916 | ... | 146 | ... | 49 | 0.8 | ... | ... | 18,896 | 1,456 | 622 |
| 1917 | ... | 138 | ... | 47 | 0.9 | ... | ... | ... | ... | ... |
| 1918 | ... | 157 | ... | 46 | 0.9 | ... | ... | 18,920 | 1,934 | 651 |
| 1919 | ... | 178 | ... | 48 | 0.9 | ... | ... | ... | ... | ... |
| 1920 | ... | 186 | ... | 50 | 1.1 | ... | ... | 18,897 | 2,200 | 680 |
| 1921 | ... | 214 | ... | 55 | 1.1 | ... | ... | ... | ... | ... |
| 1922 | 34 | 213 | ... | 58 | 1.0 | ... | ... | 19,837 | 2,873 | 723 |
| 1923 | ... | 213 | ... | 58 | 1.1 | ... | ... | ... | ... | ... |
| 1924 | ... | 215 | ... | 57 | 1.1 | ... | ... | 20,289 | 3,390 | 761 |
| 1925 | ... | 213 | ... | 58 | 1.3 | ... | ... | ... | ... | ... |
| 1926 | ... | 212 | ... | 59 | 1.5 | ... | ... | 20,311 | 3,757 | 814 |
| 1927 | ... | 221 | ... | 62 | 1.4 | ... | ... | ... | ... | ... |
| 1928 | ... | 220 | ... | 63 | 1.5 | ... | ... | 20,573[4] | 3,911[4] / 22,808 | 832 / 4,252 |
| 1929 | ... | 221 | ... | 63 | 1.7 | ... | ... | ... | ... | ... |
| 1930 | 51 | 226 | ... | 64 | 1.8 | ... | ... | 22,811 | 4,740 | 854 |
| 1931 | 49 | 229 | ... | 66 | 1.8 | ... | ... | ...[4] | ... | ... |
| 1932 | 48 | 233 | ... | 68 | 1.7 | ... | ... | 22,818 | 5,543 | 872 |
| 1933 | 46 | 239 | ... | 71 | 1.8 | ... | ... | ... | ... | ... |
| 1934 | 47 | 246 | ... | 73 | 1.6 | ... | ... | 22,534 | 6,029 | 847 |
| 1935 | 54 | 256 | ... | 71 | 1.7 | ... | ... | ... | ... | ... |
| 1936 | 55 | 247 | ... | 72 | 2.0 | ... | 0.1 | 22,039 | 6,362 | 871 |
| 1937 | 61 | 262 | ... | 73 | 2.1 | 1.8 | 0.1 | ... | ... | ... |
| 1938 | 64 | 281 | ... | 75 | 2.3 | 1.4 | 0.1 | 21,393[4] | 6,664 | ...[5] / 877 |
| 1939 | 63 | 286 | ... | 77 | 2.4 | 0.9 | ... | ... | ... | ... |
| 1940 | 61 | 282 | 6.2 | 79 | 2.6 | 0.9 | ... | 20,333 | 7,059 | 875 |
| 1941 | 62 | 293 | 6.8 | 81 | 2.8 | 0.9 | ... | ... | ... | ... |
| 1942 | 61 | 303 | 6.7 | 79 | 3.0 | 0.9 | ... | 19,634 | 6,871 | 859 |
| 1943 | 67 | 310 | 7.3 | 82 | 3.6 | ... | ... | ... | ... | ... |
| 1944 | 71 | 330 | 8.1 | 86 | 3.8 | ... | ... | 19,038 | 5,975 | 828 |

**I1   NORTH AMERICA: Pupils and Teachers in Schools** (in thousands, except as otherwise indicated)

1945–1974

| Year | Barbados — Pupils a[1] | Barbados — b | Canada[2] All Schools — Pupils | Canada[2] All Schools — Teachers | Costa Rica Pupils a[8] | Costa Rica Pupils b[9] | Costa Rica Teachers a[8] | Costa Rica Teachers b[9] | Cuba Pupils a | Cuba Pupils b | Cuba Teachers a[11] | Cuba Teachers b |
|---|---|---|---|---|---|---|---|---|---|---|---|---|
| 1945 | 29 | 2.5 | 2,090 | 75 | 81 | 5.2 | … | … | 512 | … | 16 | … |
| 1946 | 29 | 2.6 | [2,060][2] | … | 84 | [2.0][9] | 3.9 | [0.1][9] | … | … | … | … |
| 1947 | 29 | 2.7 | [2,092][2] | … | 96 | … | … | … | … | … | … | … |
| 1948 | 30 | 2.4 | 2,191[2] | 77[2] | 89 | [4.4][9] | 4.3 | [0.3][9] | … | … | … | … |
| 1949 | 30 | 2.6 | 2,452 | … | 96 | … | … | … | … | … | … | … |
| 1950 | 30 | 2.5 | 2,532[22] | 89 | 107 | 6.0 | 3.7 | … | 593 | 21 | 21 | 1.2 |
| 1951 | 31 | 2.7 | 2,667 | 90 | 101 | 6.6[9] | … | … | … | 21 | … | 1.2 |
| 1952 | 32 | 3.0 | 2,810 | 94 | 103 | … | … | … | … | 26 | … | 2.0 |
| 1953 | 33 | 3.1 | 2,972 | 98 | 124 | 12 | … | … | 697 | 35 | 18 | 2.0 |
| 1954 | 36 | 3.2 | 3,135 | 108 | 125[8] / 138 | 13 | …[8] / 5.5 | … | 669 | 28 | … | … |
| 1955 | 36 | 3.2 | 3,336[22] | 113 | 154 | 15 | 5.8 | … | 702 | 35 | 20 | 2.0 |
| 1956 | 37 | 3.4 | 3,497 | 120 | 155 | 17 | … | 1.1 | 747 | 36 | 21 | 2.0 |
| 1957 | 38 | 3.6 | 3,633 | 127 | 168 | 19 | 6.7 | 1.4 | 756 | … | … | … |
| 1958 | 39 | 3.8 | 3,827 | 133[2] / 148 | 174 | 23 | … | … | 783 | … | … | … |
| 1959 | 41 | 4.0 | 4,010 | 154 | 184 | 26 | 7.5 | 1.2 | 962 | 63 | 22 | 3.7 |
| 1960 | 43 | 4.1 | 4,202 | 164 | 198 | 27 | 7.6 | 1.3 | 1,030 | 90 | 25 | 5.2 |
| 1961 | 44 | 4.3 | 4,410 | 174 | 208 | 29 | 8.3 | 1.4 | 1,087 | 108 | 29 | 6.6 |
| 1962 | 46 | 4.4 | 4,610 | 185 | 226 | 31 | 9.1 | 1.7 | 1,121 | 123 | 34 | 7.4 |
| 1963 | 48[19] / 46 | 4.7 | 4,802 | 194 | 244 | 34 | 9.6 | 2.1 | 1,194 | 138 | 35 | 7.7 |
| 1964 | 46 | 4.8 | 4,994 | 206 | 258 | 37 | 9.7 | 1.4 | 1,206 | 136 | 36 | 8.4 |
| 1965 | 50 | 4.8 | 5,160 | 211 | 277 | 41 | 10 | 1.9 | 1,232 | 149 | 42[11] | 9.6 |
| 1966 | 51 | 4.9 | 5,312 | 225 | 292 | 48 | 11 | 2.6 | 1,253 | 170 | … | 10 |
| 1967 | 52 | 5.2 | 5,471 | 243 | 308 | 54 | 11 | 2.4 | 1,274 | 177 | … | 11 |
| 1968 | 52 | 5.3 | 5,647 | 256 | 313 | 56 | 11 | 2.4 | 1,333 | 187 | … | 11 |
| 1969 | 52 | 5.3 | 5,771 | 269 | 340 | 64 | 11 | 2.9 | 1,428 | 175 | … | 13 |
| 1970 | 52 | 5.2 | 5,832 | 272 | 349 | 68 | 12 | 3.3 | 1,530 | 187 | … | 15 |
| 1971 | … | 5.2 | 5,823 | 272 | 356 | 75 | 12 | … | 1,631 | 202 | … | 16 |
| 1972 | 50 | 5.3 | 5,768 | 274 | 365 | 81 | 12 | 3.5 | 1,733 | 222 | … | 17 |
| 1973 | 46[19] / 34 | 5.4[19] / 21 | 5,680 | 273 | 374 | 104 | 13 | … | 1,779 | 266 | … | 21 |
| 1974 | 31 | 22 | 5,632 | 274 | 368 | 114 | 13 | … | 1,800 | 338 | … | 27 |

**I1   NORTH AMERICA: Pupils and Teachers in Schools** (in thousands, except as otherwise indicated)

**1945–1974**

| | Dominican Republic | | | | El Salvador | | | | Guatemala | | | |
|---|---|---|---|---|---|---|---|---|---|---|---|---|
| | Pupils | | Teachers | | Pupils | | Teachers | | Pupils | | Teachers | |
| | a | b | a | b | a | b | a | b | a | b | a | b |
| 1945 | 213 | ... | 4.0 | ... | 106 | ... | 3.7 | ... | 141 | 7.3 | 5.4 | ... |
| 1946 | 220 | ... | 4.2 | ... | 121 | 2.1 | 4.0 | ... | 175 | 8.9 | 6.1 | 1.3 |
| 1947 | 220 | ... | 4.2 | ... | 134 | ... | ... | ... | 161 | 9.9 | 6.3 | 1.6 |
| 1948 | 226 | ... | 4.7 | ... | 144 | 3.4 | ... | ... | 167 | 12 | 7.2 | 1.7 |
| 1949 | 231 | 6.7 | 4.8 | 0.4 | 144 | ... | 4.6 | ... | 166 | 13 | 7.2 | 1.9 |
| 1950 | 230 | 8.3 | 4.9 | 0.4 | 149 | 6.9 | 4.8 | ... | 165 | 15 | 7.3 | 2.2 |
| 1951 | 240 | ... | 4.9 | ... | 155 | 6.8 | 5.2 | ... | 173 | 17 | 7.4 | 2.2 |
| 1952 | 252 | 8.5 | 4.9 | 0.5 | 164 | 8.5 | ... | ... | 183 | 17 | 7.5 | 2.3 |
| 1953 | 252 | ... | 5.3 | ... | 176 | 11 | 6.1 | ... | 191 | 17 | 7.8 | 2.2 |
| 1954 | 399 | 9.6 | 7.7 | ... | 197 | 11 | 6.0 | ... | 208 | 18 | 7.9 | 2.4 |
| 1955 | 386 | ... | 8.3 | ... | 207 | 13 | 6.8 | ... | 216 | 19 | 8.1 | 2.5 |
| 1956 | 445 | 9.5 | ... | ... | 220 | 14 | 7.1 | ... | 229 | ... | 8.6 | 2.8 |
| 1957 | 461 | ... | ... | ... | 245 | 17 | 7.9 | ... | 245 | 20 | 8.8 | 2.7 |
| 1958 | 480 | ... | ... | ... | 262 | 19 | 9.0 | ... | 260 | 21 | 9.4 | 3.2 |
| 1959 | 497 | 26 | 8.6 | 1.2 | 288 | 20 | 8.7 | ... | 282 | 21 | 9.4 | 3.4 |
| 1960 | 507 | 31 | 8.8 | 1.2 | 307[20] / 321 | 21 | 8.7 | ... | 297 | 27 | 9.7 | 4.0 |
| 1961 | 508 | 34 | 8.9 | 1.4 | 341 | 25 | 9.5 | ... | 313 | 31 | 10 | 4.7 |
| 1962 | 488 | 38 | 9.3 | 1.8 | 354 | 26 | 11 | ... | 339 | 37 | 11 | 5.2 |
| 1963 | 451 | 43 | ... | ... | 358 | 29 | 9.4 | ... | 361 | 40 | 11 | 5.8 |
| 1964 | 516 | 51 | ... | ... | 379 | 34 | 11 | ... | 386 | 44 | 11 | 5.8 |
| 1965 | 557 | 56 | 10 | 2.3 | 398 | 38 | 12 | ... | 405 | 49 | 12 | 6.4 |
| 1966 | 585 | 67 | 11 | 2.7 | 434 | 42 | ... | ... | 407 | 53 | 12 | 4.6 |
| 1967 | 649 | 76 | 12 | 3.3 | 475 | 50 | 13 | ... | 457 | 60 | 12 | 4.9 |
| 1968 | 686 | 88 | 12 | 3.6 | 462 | 55 | 13 | ... | 493 | 63 | 13 | 5.1 |
| 1969 | 726 | 98 | 13 | 4.2 | 517 | 59 | 13 | ... | 518 | 68 | 14 | 5.1 |
| 1970 | 765 | 114 | 14 | 4.4 | 531 | 62 | 14 | ... | 506 | 74 | 14 | 5.5 |
| 1971 | 820 | 127 | 15 | 5.4 | 595 | 76 | 15 | ... | 531 | 81 | 15 | 5.6 |
| 1972 | 833 | 147 | 15 | ... | 618 | 87 | 16 | ... | 556 | 87 | 15 | 6.2 |
| 1973 | 837 | 159 | 16 | ... | 667 | 125 | 15 | ... | 571 | 105 | 16 | 5.9 |
| 1974 | 868 | 171 | 17 | ... | 704 | 154 | 15 | ... | 601 | 111 | 17 | 7.1 |

I1    **NORTH AMERICA: Pupils and Teachers in Schools** (in thousands, except as otherwise indicated)

**1945–1974**

| | Haiti | | | | Honduras | | | | Jamaica | | | |
|---|---|---|---|---|---|---|---|---|---|---|---|---|
| | Pupils | | Teachers | | Pupils | | Teachers | | Pupils | | Teachers | |
| | a | b[23] | a | b[23] | a[13] | b | a[13] | b | a | b | a | b |
| 1945 | ... | | ... | | 61 | ... | 2.1 | ... | 178 | 4.5 | ... | 0.3 |
| 1946 | ... | | ... | | 65 | 2 | 2.1 | ... | 186 | 4.8 | ... | 0.3 |
| 1947 | | | ... | | 68 | 3 | 2.3 | 0.7 | 186 | ... | ... | ... |
| 1948 | 129 | | ... | | 88 | ... | 2.7 | ... | 191 | 5.3 | 3.5 | 0.3 |
| 1949 | | | ... | | 97 | ... | 3.1 | ... | 200 | 7.1 | 4.1 | 0.3 |
| 1950 | 119 | 3.4 | ... | 0.5 | 105[13] / 104 | 4 | 3.3 | 0.9 | 211 | 7.9 | 4.2 | 0.3 |
| 1951 | 144 | 4.0 | 2.3 | 0.4 | 104 | 5 | 3.8 | ... | 211 | 8.4 | 4.2 | 0.4 |
| 1952 | 173 | 4.7[23] / 6.8 | ... | ...[23] | 114 | 6 | 4.1 | 0.9 | 214 | 9.0 | 4.3 | 0.4 |
| 1953 | 186 | 7.8 | 4.1 | 0.6 | 116 | 6.5 | 4.1 | 0.9 | 219 | 10 | 4.2 | 0.4 |
| 1954 | 179 | 7.2 | 6.0 | 0.6 | 125 | 6.6 | 4.5 | 1.0 | 220 | 10 | 4.3 | 0.5 |
| 1955 | 212 | 12 | 4.4 | 0.9 | 128 | 9.3 | ... | 1.2 | 228 | 9.0 | 4.4 | |
| 1956 | 201 | ... | ... | ... | 134 | 10 | 4.4 | 1.3 | 233 | 9.6 | 4.7 | |
| 1957 | 203 | ... | ... | ... | 147 | 12 | 4.6 | 1.3 | 241 | 11 | 4.7 | ... |
| 1958 | ... | 14 | ... | ... | 172 | 13 | ... | 1.6 | 246 | 13 | 4.8 | |
| 1959 | 238 | 14 | 5.4 | 1.1 | 192 | 14 | 6.1 | 1.4 | 255 | 13 | 4.9 | 0.6 |
| 1960 | 239 | 15 | 5.6 | 1.2 | 209 | 14 | 6.5 | 1.6 | 285 | 16 | 5.0 | ... |
| 1961 | 231 | ... | 5.5 | ... | 228 | 15 | 7.2 | 1.7 | 306 | 17 | 5.0 | ... |
| 1962 | 233 | 17 | 5.4 | 1.1 | 244 | 16 | 7.9 | 1.9 | 329 | 18 | 5.2 | 1.0 |
| 1963 | ... | 19 | ... | ... | 252 | 18 | 8.6 | 2.1 | 338[19] | 20[19] | 5.4[19] | 1.0 |
| 1964 | 276 | 19 | 6.1 | 1.2 | 267 | 21 | 9.3 | 2.1 | 321 | 34 | 5.7 | ...[19] / 1.3 |
| 1965 | 284 | 20 | 6.2 | 1.3 | 284 | 24 | 9.9 | 2.0 | 324 | 36 | 6.0 | 1.5 |
| 1966 | 286 | 21 | 6.5 | 1.3 | 331 | 26 | 11 | 2.1 | 333 | 39 | 6.2 | 1.4 |
| 1967 | 289 | 26 | 6.6 | 1.6 | 367 | 30 | 10 | 2.3 | 352 | 39 | 6.5 | 1.7 |
| 1968 | 291 | 28 | 6.7 | 1.7 | 377 | 33 | 10 | 2.5 | 372 | 41 | 6.9 | 1.8 |
| 1969 | ... | ... | ... | ... | 393 | 34 | 11 | ... | 374 | 57 | 7.3 | 2.2 |
| 1970 | ... | ... | ... | ... | 382 | ... | 11 | ... | 366 | 69 | 8.1 | 2.5 |
| 1971 | 337 | 27 | 7.5 | 1.5 | 393 | 39 | 11 | 2.7 | 382 | 71 | 9.5 | 2.9 |
| 1972 | 376 | ... | ... | ... | 412 | 43 | 11 | 2.8 | 395 | 76 | 9.6 | 3.3 |
| 1973 | 391[20] | 51 | 11 | 3.2 | 421 | 49 | 12 | 2.5 | 413 | 85 | 10 | 3.6 |
| 1974 | 451 | 52 | 12 | ... | 443 | 58 | 12 | 3.1 | 422 | 107 | 10 | 4.5 |

I1 **NORTH AMERICA: Pupils and Teachers in Schools** (in thousands, except as otherwise indicated)

1945–1974

| | Mexico[24] | | | | Newfoundland | Nicaragua | | | | Panama | | | |
|---|---|---|---|---|---|---|---|---|---|---|---|---|---|
| | Pupils | | Teachers | | Pupils | Pupils | | Teachers | | Pupils | | Teachers | |
| | a | b[25] | a | b[25] | All Schools | a | b[25] | a | b[25] | a | b | a | b |
| 1945 | 2,074 | 54 | 54 | 7.5 | 70 | ... | ... | ... | ... | 84 | 10 | ... | ... |
| 1946 | 2,428 | 55 | 61 | 7.7 | 71 | ... | ... | ... | ... | 94 | 12 | 2.9 | 0.6 |
| 1947 | 2,464 | 61 | 62 | 7.8 | 72 | ... | ... | ... | ... | 98 | 13 | 3.0 | 0.7 |
| 1948 | 2,539 | 63 | 64 | 7.8 | 73 | ... | ... | ... | ... | 101 | 15 | 3.2 | 0.8 |
| 1949 | 2,666 | 62[25] / 113 | 66 | 8.6[25] / 12 | ... | ... | ... | ... | ... | 106 | 16 | 3.5 | 0.8 |
| 1950 | 2,785 | 118 | 69 | ... | ... | 91 | ... | 3.0 | ... | 110 | 18 | 3.4 | 0.9 |
| 1951 | 2,926 | 132 | 76 | 15 | ... | 83 | 3.7 | 3.0 | 0.6 | 114 | 19 | 3.6 | 0.9 |
| 1952 | 3,098 | 143 | 78 | 13 | ... | 84 | 5.2 | 2.7 | 0.5 | ... | ... | ... | ... |
| 1953 | 3,340 | 179 | 87 | ... | ... | 116 | 3.8 | 4.1 | 0.5 | 125 | 22 | 3.9 | 1.0 |
| 1954 | 3,527 | 153 | 86 | 11 | ... | ... | ... | ... | ... | 133 | 24 | 4.1 | 1.1 |
| 1955 | 3,680 | 195 | 87 | ... | ... | 119 | 4.3 | 3.8 | 0.4 | 138 | 25 | 4.3 | ... |
| 1956 | 3,880 | 242 | 103 | 14 | ... | 146 | ... | ... | ... | 141 | 27 | 4.4 | 1.2 |
| 1957 | 3,920 | 237 | 101 | ... | ... | 137 | ... | ... | ... | 143 | ... | 4.6 | ... |
| 1958 | 4,390 | 270 | 103 | 18 | ... | 129 | 5.7 | 3.7 | ... | ... | ... | ... | ... |
| 1959 | 4,913 | 331 | 111 | 22 | ... | 153 | 5.9 | 4.7 | ... | 156 | 36 | 4.9 | 1.6 |
| 1960 | 5,247 | 471 | 117 | 29 | ... | 168 | 6.9[25] / 12 | ... | 0.5[25] / 0.9 | 162 | 39 | 5.3 | 1.7 |
| 1961 | 5,516 | 552 | 127 | 33 | ... | 182 | 13 | 4.9 | 1.1 | 171 | 42 | 5.6 | 1.9 |
| 1962 | 5,929 | 572 | 132 | ... | ... | 198 | 15 | 5.1 | 1.3 | 180 | 45 | 5.6 | 2.0 |
| 1963 | 6,279 | 675 | 142 | ... | ... | 212 | 19 | 5.2 | 1.4 | 187 | 47 | 5.9 | 2.2 |
| 1964 | 6,610 | 832 | 148 | 51 | ... | 217 | 23 | 5.6 | 1.6 | 196 | 51 | 6.1 | 2.5 |
| 1965 | 7,073 | 869 | 157 | 59 | ... | 216 | 27 | 5.9 | 1.7 | 203 | 55 | 6.4 | 2.6 |
| 1966 | 7,495 | 950 | 159 | 67 | ... | 235 | 30 | 6.5 | 1.9 | 211 | 59 | 6.7 | 2.8 |
| 1967 | 7,812 | 1,082 | 175 | 80 | ... | 257 | 34 | 7.4 | 1.7 | 218 | 63 | 7.1 | 3.0 |
| 1968 | 8,179 | 1,188 | 183 | 108 | ... | 266 | 40 | 7.4 | 2.0 | 223 | 67 | 7.4 | 3.3 |
| 1969 | 8,530 | 1,239 | 201 | 109 | ... | 279 | 46 | 7.5 | 2.0 | 239 | 71 | 8.0 | 3.4 |
| 1970 | 8,905 | 1,370 | 208 | ... | ... | 295 | 51 | 7.6 | 2.0 | 255 | 78 | 9.4 | 3.8 |
| 1971 | 9,338 | 1,673 | 221 | ... | ... | 310 | 55 | 8.1 | 2.1 | 288 | 87 | 11 | 4.5 |
| 1972 | 10,113 | 1,818 | 231 | ...[25] | ... | 314 | 61 | 8.1 | 1.9 | 306 | 99 | 12 | 5.1 |
| 1973 | 10,510 | 2,013 | 242 | 139 | ... | 327 | 63 | 7.9 | 1.8 | 319 | 112 | 12 | 5.4 |
| 1974 | 10,954 | 2,166 | 254 | 142 | ... | 333 | 71 | 8.5 | 2.0 | 328 | 123 | 12 | 5.8 |

**I1   NORTH AMERICA: Pupils and Teachers in Schools** (in thousands, except as otherwise indicated)

1945–1974

| | Puerto Rico | | | Trinidad and Tobago[21] | | | | USA | | |
|---|---|---|---|---|---|---|---|---|---|---|
| | Pupils | | Teachers | Pupils | | Teachers | | Pupils | | Teachers[5] |
| | a | b | All Schools | a | b | a | b | a | b | All Schools |
| 1945 | 350 | | 8.9 | 91 | 4.2 | 1.3 | ... | ... | ... | ... |
| 1946 | 367 | | 9.2 | 94 | 4.8 | 1.3 | ... | 19,118 | 6,187 | 831 |
| 1947 | 305 | 95 | 9.1 | 100 | 4.9 | 1.5 | ... | ... | ... | ... |
| 1948 | 313 | 94 | 9.4 | 103 | 5.0 | 2.8 | ... | 19,571 | 6,255 | 861 |
| 1949 | 331 | 99 | 9.5 | 111 | 5.3 | 2.9 | 0.2 | ... | ... | ... |
| 1950 | 355 | 108 | 9.7 | 115 | 5.6 | 3.0 | 0.2 | 20,928 | 6,397 | 914 |
| 1951 | 365 | 113 | 9.9 | 121 | 5.9 | 2.9 | 0.2 | ... | ... | ... |
| 1952 | 385 | 121 | 10 | 124 | 6.2 | 3.1[21] / 2.9 | 0.3 | 22,331 | 6,538 | 963 |
| 1953 | 410 | 130 | 11 | 132 | 6.5 | 3.4 | 0.3 | ... | ... | ... |
| 1954 | 426 | 142 | 12 | 138 | 6.8 | 3.7 | 0.3 | 24,347 | 7,037 | 1,042 |
| 1955 | 434 | 154 | 13 | 146 | 7.2 | 3.9 | 0.3 | ... | ... | ... |
| 1956 | 435 | 164 | ... | 154 | 7.5 | 4.2 | 0.3 | 26,349 | 7,696 | 1,149 |
| 1957 | 439 | 175 | 14 | 160 | 9.1 | 4.4 | 0.4 | ... | ... | ... |
| 1958 | 434 | 188 | ... | 177 | 10 | 4.7 | 0.5 | 27,841 | 8,791 | 1,261 |
| 1959 | 428 | 199 | 15 | 174 | 11 | 5.0 | 0.6 | ...[4] | ...[4] | ...[4] |
| 1960 | 426 | 207 | ... | 180 | 12 | 5.4 | 0.6 | 29,965 | 9,520 | 1,387 |
| 1961 | 429 | 217 | 16 | 191 | 13 | 5.8 | 0.6 | ... | ... | ... |
| 1962 | 434 | 226 | ... | 196 | 15 | 6.0 | | 31,143 | 10,686 | 1,504 |
| 1963 | 438 | 233 | 18 | 204 | 17 | 6.1 | 0.8 | ... | ... | ... |
| 1964 | 445 | 238 | 18 | 209 | 20 | 6.3 | ... | 31,968 | 12,070 | 1,625 |
| 1965 | 454 | 245 | 20 | 216 | 22 | 6.3 | 1.0 | ... | ... | ... |
| 1966 | 462 | 253 | 22 | 220 | 26 | 6.3 | 1.2 | 33,078 | 12,926 | 1,786 |
| 1967 | 464 | 257 | 25 | 223 | 27 | 6.3 | 1.2 | ... | ... | ... |
| 1968 | 464 | 266 | 23 | 224 | 27 | 6.3 | 1.2 | 34,375 | 13,888 | 1,957 |
| 1969 | 455 | 269 | 25 | 227 | 28 | 6.4 | 1.3 | ...[19] | ...[19] | ... |
| 1970 | 459 | 281 | 26 | 228 | 28 | 6.5 | 1.3 | 31,553 | 19,208 | 2,131[5] / 2,288 |
| 1971 | 460 | 290 | 27 | 228 | 28 | 6.7 | 1.3 | 31,588 | 19,698 | 2,305 |
| 1972 | 462 | 302 | 28 | 223 | 35 | 6.7 | 1.4 | 31,023 | 19,721 | 2,338 |
| 1973 | 453 | 311 | ... | 214 | 46 | 6.7 | ... | 30,135 | 20,295 | 2,376 |
| 1974 | 808[20] / 807 | | 28 | 204 | 55 | 6.6 | ... | 30,087 | 19,971 | 2,404 |

**I1   NORTH AMERICA: Pupils and Teachers in Schools** (in thousands except as otherwise indicated)

| | Barbados | | Canada | | Costa Rica | | | | Cuba | | | |
|---|---|---|---|---|---|---|---|---|---|---|---|---|
| | Pupils | | All Schools | | Pupils | | Teachers | | Pupils | | Teachers | |
| | a | b | Pupils | Teachers | a | b[27] | a[8] | b | a | b | a | b |
| 1975 | 32 | 29 | 5,594 | 275 | 361 | 121 | 12 | 4.9 | 1,796 | 420 | 77 | 33 |
| 1976 | 34 | 29 | 5,514 | 275[20] | 368 | 130[27] | 13 | 5.9 | 1,748 | 535 | 82 | 45 |
| 1977 | 34 | 30 | 5,410 | 267 | 367 | 122 | ... | 7.7 | 1,694 | 646 | 86 | 51 |
| 1978 | 35 | 29 | 5,294 | 263 | 362 | 130 | ... | ... | 1,626 | 759 | 87 | 58 |
| 1979 | 31 | 30 | 5,185 | 258 | 356 | 137 | 13 | 7.3 | 1,550 | 816 | 87 | 62 |
| 1980 | 31 | 29 | 5,106 | ... | 349 | 142 | 13 | 7.2 | 1,469 | 837 | 84 | 64 |
| 1981 | 31 | 28 | 5,030 | ... | 349 | 141 | 12 | 7.0 | 1,410 | 826 | 83 | 65 |
| 1982 | 30 | 28 | 4,994 | 272 | 342 | 131 | 13[8] / 11 | ... | 1,363 | 774 | 83 | 65 |
| 1983 | 31 | 28 | 4,975 | 273 | 344 | 123 | 10 | ... | 1,283 | 774 | 83 | 65 |
| 1984 | 30 | 29 | 4,946 | 295 | 351 | 117 | 10 | 7.1 | 1,174 | 794 | 80 | 64 |
| 1985 | ... | ... | 4,928[39] / 4,506 | 299 | 363 | 113 | 12 | ... | 1,077 | 808 | 77 | 66 |
| 1986 | ... | ... | 4,508 | 302 | 380 | 115 | 12 | ... | 1,001 | 801 | 75 | 67 |
| 1987 | ... | ... | 4,533 | 307 | 393 | 117 | 12 | ... | 937 | 775 | 74 | 68 |
| 1988 | ... | ... | 4,568 | 316 | 409 | 118 | 13 | ... | 900 | 770 | 73 | 70 |

I1    **NORTH AMERICA: Pupils and Teachers in Schools** (in thousands except as otherwise indicated)

| | Dominican Republic | | | | | | El Salvador | | | | | | Guatemala | | | | | |
| | Pupils | | Teachers | | Pupils | | Teachers | | Pupils | | Teachers | |
| | a | b | a | b | a | b | a | b | a | b | a | b |
|------|-------|-----|----|-----|-------|-----|----|-----|-------|-----|----|-----|
| 1975 | 912   | 188 | 18 | 8.5 | 759   | 171 | 17 |     | 627   | 122 | 18 | 7.3 |
| 1976 | 935   | 207 | …  | …   | 796   | 188 | 17 |     | 640   | …   | 19 | 7.7 |
| 1977 | 947   | 249 | …  | …   | 795   | 198 | 17 |     | 673   | 146 | 19 | 8.3 |
| 1978 | 1,033 | 319 | …  | …   | 830   | 213 | …  |     | 740   | 159 | 21 | 8.6 |
| 1979 | 1,069 | 338 | …  | …   | 901   | 230 | 17 |     | 740   | 156 | 22 | 9.0 |
| 1980 | 1,106 | 356 | …  | …   | 834   | 211 | 17 |     | 827   | 157 | 24 | 9.6 |
| 1981 | 1,150 | 379 | …  | …   | 710   | 188 | 17 |     | 899   | 162 | 24 | 13  |
| 1982 | 1,092 | …   | 24 | …   | 811   | 219 | 18 |     | 867   | 178 | 25 | 13  |
| 1983 | 1,122 | 380 | …  | …   | 852   | 234 | 18 |     | 873   | 174 | 27 | 14  |
| 1984 | 1,206 | 431 | 28 | 12  | 853   | 220 | 21 |     | 980   | 176 | 27 | 14  |
| 1985 | 1,220 | 439 | 28 | 12  | 852   | 246 | …  |     | 1,016 | 183 | 28 | 15  |
| 1986 | 1,296 | 427 | 31 | 10  | …     | …   | 22 |     | 1,041 | 223 | 30 | 17  |
| 1987 | 1,271 | …   | 31 | …   | 996   | …   | 22 |     | 1,098 | 241 | 31 | 16  |
| 1988 | …     | …   | …  | …   | 1,029 | …   | 23 |     | 1,121 | …   | 32 | …   |

**I1**   **NORTH AMERICA: Pupils and Teachers in Schools** (in thousands except as otherwise indicated).

| | Haiti | | | | Honduras | | | | Jamaica | | | |
|---|---|---|---|---|---|---|---|---|---|---|---|---|
| | Pupils | | Teachers | | Pupils | | Teachers | | Pupils | | Teachers | |
| | a | b | a | b | a | b | a | b | a | b | a | b |
| 1975 | 487 | 55 | 13 | 3.4 | 461 | 56 | 13 | 3.1 | 432 | 135 | 10 | 5.3 |
| 1976 | 511 | 56 | 13 | 3.3 | 483 | 61 | 14 | ... | 418 | 123 | 11 | 6.4 |
| 1977 | 518 | 73 | 13 | 3.8 | 493 | 72 | 13 | 3.4 | 426 | 137 | 11 | 6.8 |
| 1978 | 529 | 81 | 13 | 3.8 | 525 | 81 | 14 | 3.5 | 432 | 155 | 11 | 6.6 |
| 1979 | 580 | 88 | 13 | 3.6 | 575 | ... | 13 | 4.4 | 428 | 152 | 11 | 7.1 |
| 1980 | 642 | 97 | 15 | 4.0 | 601 | ... | 16 | 4.5 | 425 | 154 | 11 | 7.1 |
| 1981 | 658 | 99 | 15 | 4.2 | 614 | 81 | 16 | 5.1 | 427 | 155 | 11 | 7.5 |
| 1982 | 723 | 117 | 17 | 5.7 | 672 | 106 | 18 | 5.2 | 423 | 156 | 11 | 7.4 |
| 1983 | 783 | 134 | 18 | 5.8 | 705 | 113 | 19 | 5.9 | 416 | 158 | 10 | 7.8 |
| 1984 | 820 | 154 | 20 | 6.1 | 737 | 112 | 20 | 6.3 | 414 | 160 | 10 | 7.5 |
| 1985 | 872 | 139 | 23 | 7.0 | 774 | 113 | 22 | 6.5 | 407 | 154 | 9.6 | 7.4 |
| 1986 | 763 | 155 | 21 | 7.9 | 810 | 122 | 22 | 7.0 | 394 | 161 | 9.5 | 7.8 |
| 1987 | 781 | ... | 22 | ... | 840 | 121 | 24 | 7.6 | 391 | 160 | 9.6 | 7.8 |
| 1988 | ... | ... | ... | ... | 878 | 125 | 26 | 8.1 | ... | 161 | 9.9 | ... |

**I1    NORTH AMERICA: Pupils and Teachers in Schools** (in thousands except as otherwise indicated)

| | Mexico | | | | Nicaragua | | | | Panama | | | |
|---|---|---|---|---|---|---|---|---|---|---|---|---|
| | Pupils | | Teachers | | Pupils | | Teachers | | Pupils | | Teachers | |
| | a | b | a | b | a | b | a | b | a | b | a | b |
| 1975 | 11,461 | 2,506 | 286 | 167 | 351 | 80 | 8.8 | 2.5 | 342 | 126 | 12 | 5.7 |
| 1976 | 12,572 | 2,823 | ... | 174 | 362 | 95 | 9.3 | 2.8 | 354 | 132 | 12 | 5.7 |
| 1977 | ... | ... | 319 | 187 | 371 | 105 | 9.7 | 3.0 | 358 | 137 | 15 | 5.9 |
| 1978 | 13,536 | 3,328 | 347 | 209 | 379 | 99 | 10 | 2.7 | 369 | 139 | 15 | 6.0 |
| 1979 | 14,126 | 3,713 | 375 | 229 | 449 | 111[20] | 12 | 3.5 | 373[19] | 138[19] | 16[19] | 6.2[19] |
| 1980 | 14,666 | 4,042 | 400 | 252 | 472 | 140 | 13 | 4.2 | 338 | 171 | 12 | 8.1 |
| 1981 | 14,981 | 4,513 | 415 | 263 | 509 | 137 | 15 | 4.2 | 335 | 174 | 13 | 8.6 |
| 1982 | 15,223 | 4,811 | 428 | 279 | 513 | 140 | 15 | 4.1 | 337 | 175 | 13 | 8.9 |
| 1983 | 15,376 | 5,153 | 437 | 296 | 537 | 158 | 17 | 5.0 | 336 | 176 | 13 | 9.2 |
| 1984 | 15,219 | 5,397 | 450 | 321 | 534 | 162 | 18 | 6.1 | 339 | 182 | 13 | 9.5 |
| 1985 | 15,124 | 5,718 | 457 | 327 | 562 | 151 | 17 | ... | 340 | 185 | 13 | 9.7 |
| 1986 | 14,995 | 5,822 | 463 | 332 | 557 | 167 | 17 | ... | 344 | 187 | 14 | 9.8 |
| 1987 | 14,768 | 5,933 | 468 | 339 | 584 | 177 | 18 | 5.8 | 346 | 190 | 14 | 10 |
| 1988 | 14,656 | 5,998 | 463 | 388 | 600 | 182 | 18 | 6.7 | 345 | 190 | 13 | 9.8 |

**I1    NORTH AMERICA: Pupils and Teachers in Schools** (in thousands except as otherwise indicated)

| | Puerto Rico | | Trinidad & Tobago | | | | USA | | |
| | All Schools | | Pupils | | Teachers | | Pupils | | Teachers |
| | Pupils | Teachers | a | b | a | b | a | b | All Schools |
|---|---|---|---|---|---|---|---|---|---|
| 1975 | 800 | 28 | 200 | 64 | 6.5 | 1.6 | 29,340 | 20,451 | 2,451 |
| 1976 | 813 | ... | 190 | 76 | 6.5 | ... | 29,255 | 20,229 | 2,471 |
| 1977 | 817 | 27 | 182 | 84 | 6.4 | ... | 28,751 | 19,960 | 2,478 |
| 1978 | 825 | 30 | 172 | 82 | 6.1 | ... | 28,749 | 18,887 | 2,480 |
| 1979 | 815 | ... | 167 | 82 | 6.4 | ... | 28,243 | 18,402 | 2,458 |
| 1980 | 815 | 32 | 167 | 87 | 7.0 | ... | 28,148 | 18,170 | 2,422 |
| 1981 | 811 | ... | 167 | 91 | 7.3 | 1.7 | 27,919 | 17,680 | 2,403 |
| 1982 | 814 | ... | 170 | 91 | 7.5 | 1.7[20] | 28,075 | 17,177 | 2,401 |
| 1983 | 816 | ... | 167 | 92 | 7.3 | 4.7 | 28,325 | 16,742 | ... |
| 1984 | 805 | ... | 169 | 90 | 7.6 | 4.7 | 28,447 | 16,546 | ... |
| 1985 | 800 | ... | 172 | 91 | 7.6 | ... | 28,485 | 16,581 | ... |
| 1986 | 817 | 32 | 177 | 92 | 7.7 | 4.9 | 28,317 | 16,972 | 2,554 |
| 1987 | 801 | ... | 183 | 93 | 7.7 | 4.9 | 28,433 | 16,938 | 2,592 |
| 1988 | 790 | ... | ... | ... | ... | ... | 29,242 | 16,196 | 2,627 |

I1   **SOUTH AMERICA: PUPILS AND TEACHERS IN SCHOOLS** (in thousands, except as otherwise indicated)

1855–1884

| | Argentina | | Bolivia | Brazil | Chile[29] | | Guyana | Uruguay[30] | |
| | Pupils | | Pupils | Pupils | Pupils | | Pupils | a | |
| | a | b | a | a | a | b | a | Pupils | Teachers |
|------|-----|-----|-----|-----|-----|-----|------|------|------|
| 1855 | ... | ... | ... | ... | ... | ... | 2.2 | ... | ... |
| 1856 | ... | ... | ... | ... | ... | ... | 3.0 | ... | ... |
| 1857 | ... | ... | ... | ... | ... | ... | 3.4 | ... | ... |
| 1858 | ... | ... | ... | ... | ... | ... | 4.0 | ... | ... |
| 1859 | ... | ... | ... | ... | ... | ... | 4.5 | ... | ... |
| 1860 | ... | ... | ... | ... | ... | ... | 4.8 | ... | ... |
| 1861 | ... | ... | ... | ... | ... | ... | 4.9 | ... | ... |
| 1862 | ... | ... | ... | ... | ... | ... | 5.0 | ... | ... |
| 1863 | ... | ... | ... | ... | ... | ... | 5.3 | ... | ... |
| 1864 | ... | ... | ... | ... | ... | ... | 5.6 | ... | ... |
| 1865 | ... | ... | ... | ... | ... | ... | 5.8 | ... | ... |
| 1866 | ... | ... | ... | ... | ... | ... | 6.6 | ... | ... |
| 1867 | ... | ... | ... | ... | ... | ... | 7.3 | ... | ... |
| 1868 | ... | ... | ... | ... | ... | ... | 16 | ... | ... |
| 1869 | ... | ... | ... | ... | ... | ... | 15 | ... | ... |
| 1870 | ... | ... | ... | ... | ... | ... | 16 | ... | ... |
| 1871 | ... | ... | ... | 138 | ... | ... | 16 | ... | ... |
| 1872 | ... | ... | ... | 139 | ... | ... | 16 | ... | ... |
| 1873 | ... | ... | ... | 164 | ... | ... | 16 | ... | ... |
| 1874 | ... | ... | ... | 173 | ... | ... | 17 | ... | ... |
| 1875 | ... | ... | ... | 173 | ... | ... | 17 | 17 | 0.3 |
| 1876 | ... | ... | ... | 134 | ... | ... | 17 | 17 | 0.3 |
| 1877 | ... | ... | ... | ... | ... | ... | ... | ... | ... |
| 1878 | ... | ... | ... | ... | ... | ... | ... | 20 | 0.4 |
| 1879 | ... | ... | ... | ... | ... | ... | 20 | 23 | ... |
| 1880 | ... | ... | ... | ... | 66 | 3.1 | 21 | 25 | 0.5 |
| 1881 | ... | 1.6 | ... | ... | ... | ... | 21 | 26 | 0.5 |
| 1882 | 98 | 2.3 | 10 | 209 | 63 | 4.3 | 23 | ... | ... |
| 1883 | 108 | ... | ... | 222 | ... | ... | 19 | 26 | 0.5 |
| 1884 | ... | ... | ... | 233 | 64 | 4.3 | 18 | 27 | 0.6 |

**1885–1914**

I1   **SOUTH AMERICA: Pupils and Teachers in Schools** (in thousands, except as otherwise indicated)

| | Argentina | | | Bolivia | | | Brazil | | | | Chile[24] | | | |
|---|---|---|---|---|---|---|---|---|---|---|---|---|---|---|
| | Pupils | | Teachers | Pupils | | Teachers | Pupils | | Teachers | | Pupils | | Teachers | |
| | a | b | a | a | b | All Schools | a | b | a | b | a | b | a | b |
| 1885 | 168 | … | … | … | … | … | … | … | … | … | … | … | … | … |
| 1886 | … | … | … | … | … | … | … | … | … | … | 79 | … | … | … |
| 1887 | … | … | … | … | … | … | 259 | … | … | … | 108 | … | … | … |
| 1888 | … | … | … | 24 | 2.3 | 0.7 | … | … | … | … | 117 | … | … | … |
| 1889 | … | … | … | 25 | 2.2 | … | … | … | … | … | … | … | … | … |
| 1890 | … | … | … | 24 | 2.1 | 0.8 | … | … | … | … | 119 | 4.7 | … | … |
| 1891 | … | … | … | … | … | … | … | … | … | … | … | 4.6 | … | … |
| 1892 | 228 | 3.2 | … | … | … | … | … | … | … | … | 138 | 6.6 | 2.0 | … |
| 1893 | 250 | … | … | … | … | … | … | … | … | … | 131 | 6.8 | … | … |
| 1894 | 248 | … | 8.0 | 25 | 2.1 | 0.8 | … | … | … | … | 145 | 7.7 | 2.1 | … |
| 1895 | 202 | … | 6.9 | 27 | 2.1 | 0.9 | … | … | … | … | 140 | 8.6 | 2.1 | … |
| 1896 | 283 | 4.4 | 8.9 | 33 | … | … | … | … | … | … | 140 | 9.1 | 2.2 | … |
| 1897 | 298 | … | 9.3 | … | 2.1 | … | … | … | … | … | 132 | 8.8 | 2.3 | … |
| 1898 | 318 | 6.1 | 9.6 | 33 | 3.0 | … | … | … | … | … | 141 | 7.5 | 2.3 | … |
| 1899 | 381 | … | 11 | 36 | 2.3 | 1.1 | … | … | … | … | 149 | 7.8 | 2.3 | … |
| 1900 | 387 | … | 11 | … | … | … | … | … | … | … | 157 | 8.7 | 2.7 | … |
| 1901 | 393 | … | 11 | 33 | 2.6 | 1.2 | … | … | … | … | 166 | 9.5 | 3.1 | … |
| 1902 | 412 | … | 12 | … | … | … | … | … | … | … | 187 | 11 | 3.4 | … |
| 1903 | 427 | … | 13 | … | … | … | … | … | … | … | 212 | 12 | 3.6 | … |
| 1904 | 478 | … | 13 | … | … | … | … | … | … | … | 201 | 12 | 4.0 | … |
| 1905 | 541 | … | 14 | 49 | 2.5 | 1.3 | … | … | … | … | 201 | 14 | 4.5 | … |
| 1906 | [503][31] | … | 15 | … | … | … | 638 | 30 | 16 | 2.3 | 217 | 15 | 4.5 | … |
| 1907 | 570 | … | 16 | … | … | … | … | … | … | … | 219 | 14 | 4.0 | … |
| 1908 | 592 | … | 17 | … | … | … | … | … | … | … | 262 | 17 | 4.1 | … |
| 1909 | 671 | … | 19 | 62 | … | … | … | … | … | … | 278 | 17[29] / 32 | 4.7 | 1.0 |
| 1910 | 694 | … | 20 | … | 1.6 | 1.4 | … | … | … | … | 317 | 34 | 4.8 | 1.1 |
| 1911 | 735 | … | 22 | … | … | … | … | … | … | … | 328 | 40 | 5.4[29] / 6.8 | 1.5[29] / 2.6 |
| 1912 | 780 / 784 | … | 24 | … | 2.2 | … | … | … | … | … | 356 | 41 | 7.4 | 2.8 |
| 1913 | 843 | … | 23 | … | 2.6 | … | … | … | … | … | 390 | 44 | 7.5 | 2.8 |
| 1914 | 863 | 19 | 25 | … | 2.8 | … | … | … | … | … | 393 | 44 | 7.8 | 2.7 |

I1    **SOUTH AMERICA: Pupils and Teachers in Schools** (in thousands, except as otherwise indicated)

1885–1914

| Year | Colombia Pupils a | Colombia Pupils b | Ecuador Pupils a | Guyana Pupils a | Paraguay Pupils a | Paraguay Pupils b[32] | Peru[33] Pupils a | Peru[33] Pupils b | Peru[33] Teachers a | Peru[33] Teachers b | Uruguay[30] Pupils a | Uruguay[30] Pupils b | Uruguay[30] Teachers a |
|---|---|---|---|---|---|---|---|---|---|---|---|---|---|
| 1885 | … | … | … | 18 | | | … | … | … | … | 30 | … | 0.6 |
| 1886 | … | … | … | 19 | | | … | … | … | … | 28 | … | 0.6 |
| 1887 | 75 | … | … | 21 | | | … | … | … | … | 31 | … | 0.7 |
| 1888 | … | … | … | 21 | | | … | … | … | … | 33 | … | 0.7 |
| 1889 | 93 | … | … | 24 | | | [53]1 | … | … | … | 33 | … | 0.7 |
| 1890 | … | … | … | 27 | … | | … | … | … | … | 39 | … | 0.8 |
| 1891 | … | … | 58 | 26 | 19 | | … | … | … | … | 44 | … | 0.9 |
| 1892 | … | [5.1]1 | … | 26 | … | | … | … | … | … | 46 | … | 0.9 |
| 1893 | 114 | … | … | 27 | … | | … | … | … | … | 46 | … | 0.9 |
| 1894 | … | … | … | 28 | … | | … | … | … | … | 47 | … | 1.0 |
| 1895 | … | [4.5]1 | … | 28 | … | | … | … | … | … | 50 | … | 1.0 |
| 1896 | [137]1 | [6.0]1 | … | 28 | 23 | | … | … | … | … | 51 | … | 1.0 |
| 1897 | … | … | … | 29 | … | | 86 | 2.0 | … | … | 46 | … | 1.0 |
| 1898 | … | … | … | 29 | … | | 92 | 2.2 | … | … | 50 | … | 1.1 |
| 1899 | … | … | … | 29 | … | | … | … | … | … | 53 | … | 1.1 |
| 1900 | … | … | … | 28 | … | 0.4 | … | … | … | … | 52 | … | 1.1 |
| 1901 | … | … | … | 27 | … | 0.4 | … | … | … | … | 55 | … | 1.2 |
| 1902 | … | … | … | 28 | 25 | 0.4 | 105 | … | … | … | 56 | … | 1.2 |
| 1903 | … | … | … | 29 | 28 | 0.4 | … | … | … | … | 54 | … | 1.2 |
| 1904 | … | … | 68 | 29 | 32 | 0.4 | … | … | … | … | 50[30] / 73 | … | 1.2[30] / 2.0 |
| 1905 | … | … | … | 30 | 30 | 0.4 | … | … | … | … | 71 | … | 2.0 |
| 1906 | … | … | … | 29 | 37 | 0.4 | 154 | 2.6 | … | 0.4 | 75 | … | 1.9 |
| 1907 | … | … | … | 31 | 38 | 0.4[32] / 0.6 | 162 | 2.8 | … | 0.4 | 79 | … | 1.9 |
| 1908 | [201]1 | … | … | 34 | 41 | 0.8 | 168 | 3.0 | 3.1 | 0.4 | 90 | … | 2.2 |
| 1909 | 235 | … | 94 | 34 | 40 | 0.8 | 154 | 3.9 | … | 0.4 | 92 | … | 2.2 |
| 1910 | 240 | … | … | 35 | 52 | 0.7 | 146 | 3.8 | 2.8 | 0.3 | 95 | … | 2.3 |
| 1911 | 273 | … | … | 35 | 49 | 0.7 | 148 | 4.7 | … | 0.3 | 102 | 1.9 | 2.5 |
| 1912 | 292 | 26 | 98 | 36 | 45 | 0.6 | 168 | 4.9 | … | 0.3 | 112 | 2.3 | 2.7 |
| 1913 | 280 | … | 66 | 37 | 69 | 0.7 | 178 | 5.1 | 3.1 | 0.3 | 112 | 2.8 | 2.7 |
| 1914 | 306 | … | … | 37 | 71 | 0.8 | 171 | 5.1 | … | 0.3 | 114 | 3.5 | 2.7 |

## II SOUTH AMERICA: Pupils and Teachers in Schools (in thousands, except as otherwise indicated)

### 1915–1944

| | Argentina Pupils a | Argentina Pupils b[34] | Argentina Teachers a | Argentina Teachers b[34] | Bolivia Pupils a | Bolivia Pupils b | Bolivia Teachers All Schools | Brazil Pupils a | Brazil Pupils b | Brazil Teachers a | Brazil Teachers b |
|---|---|---|---|---|---|---|---|---|---|---|---|
| 1915 | 914 | 27 | 27 | ... | ... | ... | ... | ... | ... | ... | ... |
| 1916 | 938 | ... | ... | ... | ... | ... | ... | ... | ... | ... | ... |
| 1917 | 1,003 | ... | 35 | ... | ... | ... | ... | ... | ... | ... | ... |
| 1918 | 1,020 | ... | 33 | ... | ... | ... | ... | ... | ... | ... | ... |
| 1919 | 1,058 | ... | 37 | ... | ... | ... | ... | ... | ... | ... | ... |
| 1920 | 1,121 | ... | 36 | ... | ... | ... | ... | 1,251 | ... | ... | ... |
| 1921 | 1,164 | ... | ... | ... | ... | ... | ... | ... | ... | ... | ... |
| 1922 | 1,230 | ... | 40 | ... | ... | ... | ... | ... | ... | ... | ... |
| 1923 | 1,261 | ... | ... | ... | ... | ... | ... | ... | ... | ... | ... |
| 1924 | 1,267 | ... | ... | ... | 81 | 4.1 | 2.9 | ... | ... | ... | ... |
| 1925 | 1,273 | ... | ... | ... | ... | ... | ... | ... | ... | ... | ... |
| 1926 | 1,279 | ... | ... | ... | 80 | 4.2 | 3.2 | ... | ... | ... | ... |
| 1927 | 1,312 | ... | 45 | ... | ... | ... | ... | 1,784 | 52 | ... | ... |
| 1928 | 1,350 | 41 | 50 | ... | ... | ... | ... | 2,052 | 68 | 47 | 6.2 |
| 1929 | 1,407 | 45 | 49 | ... | ... | ... | ... | 2,058 | 83 | 50 | 8.1 |
| 1930 | 1,445 | ... | 57 | ... | ... | ... | ... | 2,085 | 73 | 53 | 7.4 |
| 1931 | 1,524 | ... | 55 | ... | ... | ... | ... | 2,021 | 48 | 54 | 4.5 |
| 1932 | 1,545 | ... | 56 | ... | ... | ... | 1.6 | 2,071 | 56 | 56[20] | 5.2 |
| 1933 | 1,644 | ... | ... | 7.2 | ... | ... | 1.5 | 2,108 | 66 | 53 | 5.9 |
| 1934 | 1,703 | 60 | ... | 7.8 | ... | ... | ... | 2,265 | 79 | 55 | 6.8 |
| 1935 | 1,766 | 64 | 74 | 8.7 | 94 | ... | ... | 2,414 | 94 | 60 | 7.5 |
| 1936 | 1,799 | 69 | 76 | 9.7 | ... | ... | 2.9 | 2,563 | 108 | 62 | 8.1 |
| 1937 | 1,867 | 78 | 77 | 10 | ... | ... | ... | 2,702 | 124 | 67 | 9.3 |
| 1938 | 1,916[19] / 1,844 | 84[34] / 40 | ... | 11[34] / 5.9 | ... | ... | ... | 2,902 | 143 | 69 | 10 |
| 1939 | 1,905 | 41 | 79 | 6.2 | 104 | ... | ... | 2,986 | 156 | 70 | 11 |
| 1940 | 1,930 | 42 | ... | 6.2 | ... | ... | ... | 3,068 | 176 | 73 | 12 |
| 1941 | 1,946 | 43 | ... | 6.6 | ... | ... | ... | 3,097 | 182 | 75 | 13 |
| 1942 | 1,928 | 47 | 80 | 7.4 | 131 | ... | ... | 3,095 | 199 | 78 | 14 |
| 1943 | 1,936 | 50 | ... | 8.0 | 162 | ... | ... | 3,075 | 211 | 78 | 18 |
| 1944 | 1,957 | 53 | ... | 8.3 | 136 | ... | 11 | 3,133 | 233 | 80 | 18 |

I1    **SOUTH AMERICA: Pupils and Teachers in Schools** (in thousands, except as otherwise indicated)

### 1915–1944

| Year | Chile[29] Pupils a | Chile[29] Pupils b | Chile[29] Teachers a | Chile[29] Teachers b | Colombia Pupils a | Colombia Pupils b | Colombia Teachers a | Colombia Teachers b | Ecuador Pupils a | Ecuador Pupils b | Ecuador Teachers a | Ecuador Teachers b |
|---|---|---|---|---|---|---|---|---|---|---|---|---|
| 1915 | 376 | 44 | 7.5 | 2.8 | 326 | 29 | ... | ... | ... | ... | ... | ... |
| 1916 | 414 | 47 | 7.7 | 2.8 | 348 | 33 | 5.7 | ... | ... | ... | ... | ... |
| 1917 | 406 | 48 | 7.9 | 2.9 | 365 | 33 | ... | ... | ... | ... | ... | ... |
| 1918 | 396 | 55 | 8.4 | 3.1 | ... | ... | ... | ... | 93 | ... | ... | ... |
| 1919 | ... | 54 | 8.5 | ... | 322 | ... | ... | ... | ... | ... | ... | ... |
| 1920 | 401 | 53 | 8.6 | 3.0 | 334 | ... | ... | ... | 103 | ... | ... | ... |
| 1921 | ... | 58 | 9.7 | ... | ... | ... | ... | ... | 109 | ... | 2.5 | ... |
| 1922 | 507 | 60 | 10 | 3.4 | 373 | ... | ... | ... | 101 | ... | ... | ... |
| 1923 | 487 | 59 | 11 | 3.3 | 361 | ... | ... | ... | ... | ... | ... | ... |
| 1924 | 512 | 62 | 11 | 3.3 | 396 | ... | ... | ... | ... | ... | ... | ... |
| 1925 | 507 | 62 | 11 | ... | ... | ... | ... | ... | ... | ... | ... | ... |
| 1926 | 506[29] | 63[29] | 11 | ... | 427 | ... | ... | ... | ... | ... | ... | ... |
| 1926 | 527 | 47 | 11[29] | ... | ... | ... | ... | ... | ... | ... | ... | ... |
| 1927 | 571 | 46 | 9.4 | 2.6 | 441 | ... | ... | ... | ... | ... | ... | ... |
| 1928 | 594 | 49 | 9.9 | 2.4 | 470 | ... | ... | ... | 129 | 2.8 | ... | ... |
| 1929 | 594 | 47 | 9.6 | ... | ... | ... | ... | ... | 114 | ... | ... | ... |
| 1930 | 559 | 52 | 9.7 | 2.4 | ... | ... | ... | ... | 147 | 2.5 | ... | ... |
| 1931 | 554 | 59 | 9.9 | 3.5 | ... | ... | ... | ... | 153 | 2.6 | ... | ... |
| 1932 | 514 | 36 | 10 | ... | ... | ... | ... | ... | 161 | 3.2 | ... | ... |
| 1933 | 488 | 41 | 11 | 3.3 | ... | ... | ... | ... | 169 | 3.6 | ... | ... |
| 1934 | 496 | 41 | 11 | ... | 548 | 31 | 12 | 2.9 | 179 | 3.7 | ... | ... |
| 1935 | 542 | 42 | 11 | 3.7 | 546 | 29 | 12 | 2.8 | 190 | 5.7 | ... | ... |
| 1936 | 569 | 43 | 11 | ... | 588 | 32 | 12 | 3.1 | 198 | 5.9 | ... | ... |
| 1937 | 587 | 44 | 11 | 3.6 | 574 | 33 | 12 | 3.4 | ... | 5.9 | 5.3 | 0.4 |
| 1938 | 611 | 46 | 11 | ... | 628 | 34 | 14 | 3.4 | 133 | 5.8 | 5.6 | 0.5 |
| 1939 | 602 | 44 | 11 | ... | 606 | 35 | 13 | 3.7 | 221 | 6.2 | ... | ... |
| 1940 | 591 | 47 | 12 | ... | 606 | 37 | 13 | 3.4 | 223 | 6.3 | 5.9 | 0.7 |
| 1941 | 600 | 50 | 12 | ... | 664 | 35 | 14 | 3.8 | 249 | 6.6 | 6.1 | 0.8 |
| 1942 | 603 | 54 | 13 | ... | 647 | 36 | 14 | 3.9 | 244 | 6.8 | 6.4 | 0.8 |
| 1943 | 671 | 59 | 13 | ... | 679 | 40 | 15 | 4.2 | ... | ... | ... | ... |
| 1944 | 685 | 62 | 13 | ... | 699 | 40 | 17 | 4.2 | ... | ... | ... | ... |

I1    SOUTH AMERICA: Pupils and Teachers in Schools (in thousands, except as otherwise indicated)

1915–1944

| | Guyana | | Paraguay | | | | Peru[33] | | | |
|---|---|---|---|---|---|---|---|---|---|---|
| | Pupils a | Teachers a | Pupils a | Pupils b | Teachers a | Teachers b[35] | Pupils a | Pupils b | Teachers a | Teachers b |
| 1915 | 34 | ... | 74 | 0.8 | ... | ... | 166 | 5.0 | ... | 0.4 |
| 1916 | 34 | ... | 80 | 0.8 | ... | ... | 166 | 5.2 | 3.3 | 0.4 |
| 1917 | 33 | ... | ... | 0.8 | ... | ... | 170 | 5.7 | ... | 0.4 |
| 1918 | 32 | ... | ... | 0.8 | ... | ... | 177 | 6.2 | 4.3 | 0.4 |
| 1919 | 34 | ... | 82 | 0.7 | ... | ... | 181 | 6.4 | 4.4 | 0.4 |
| 1920 | 35 | ... | 71 | 0.7 | ... | ... | 196 | 6.9 | 5.1 | 0.4 |
| 1921 | 37 | 1.1 | ... | 0.8 | ... | ... | 203 | 7.0 | ... | 0.4 |
| 1922 | 39 | 1.1 | 78 | 1.0 | ... | ... | 210 | 7.4 | ... | 0.4 |
| 1923 | 40 | 1.2 | 73 | 1.0 | ... | ... | 221 | 7.1 | 4.7 | 0.4 |
| 1924 | 41 | 1.2 | 91 | 1.0 | ... | ... | 228 | 7.6 | 4.7 | 0.4 |
| 1925 | 43 | 1.3 | 79 | 0.9 | ... | ... | 236 | 7.8 | ... | 0.5 |
| 1926 | 43 | 1.3 | 93 | 0.9 | ... | ... | 262 | 8.6 | 5.5 | 0.6 |
| 1927 | 44 | 1.4 | 100 | 0.9 | ... | ... | 293 | 9.2 | 5.8 | 0.6 |
| 1928 | 43 | 1.4 | 102 | 1.1 | ... | ... | 308 | 9.8 | 6.1 | 0.6 |
| 1929 | 45 | 1.3 | 104 | 1.2 | 2.3 | ... | 319 | 11 | 6.2 | 0.6 |
| 1930 | 43 | 0.9 | 108 | 1.3 | 2.5 | ... | 342 | 12 | 6.5 | 0.7 |
| 1931 | 41 | 0.9 | 109 | 1.4 | 2.4 | ... | 350 | 10 | ... | ... |
| 1932 | 43 | 1.0 | 105 | 1.7 | 2.3 | ... | 367 | 13 | ... | ... |
| 1933 | 44 | 1.0 | 95 | — | 2.3 | ... | 380 | 13 | ... | ... |
| 1934 | 45 | 1.0 | 97 | 1.0 | 2.3 | ... | 424 | 15 | ... | ... |
| 1935 | 50 | 1.1 | 101 | 1.1 | 2.5 | ... | 465 | ... | ... | ... |
| 1936 | 51 | 1.1 | 115 | 1.7 | 2.8 | ... | 484 | ... | ... | ... |
| 1937 | 52 | 1.2 | 139 | 2.0 | 3.1 | 0.2 | 469 | ... | ... | ... |
| 1938 | 53 | 1.3 | 156 | 2.4 | 3.8 | 0.2 | 493 | 14 | ... | ... |
| 1939 | 55 | 1.3 | 167 | 2.1 | 3.9 | 0.1 | ... | ... | ... | ... |
| 1940 | 56 | 1.3 | 171 | 1.8 | 3.9 | 0.2 | 566 | 25 | ... | ... |
| 1941 | 58 | 1.4 | 168 | 2.0 | 3.8 | 0.3 | 630 | 21 | ... | ... |
| 1942 | 60 | 1.4 | 177 | 2.0 | 3.2 | 0.3 | 646 | 23 | ... | ... |
| 1943 | 60 | 1.6 | 173 | 2.0 | 3.7 | 0.3[35] / 0.7 | 664 | 28 | ... | ... |
| 1944 | 60 | 1.5 | 180 | 2.1 | 4.0 | 0.7 | ... | ... | ... | ... |

I1    **SOUTH AMERICA: Pupils and Teachers in Schools** (in thousands, except as otherwise indicated)

1915–1944

| | Uruguay | | | Venezuela | | | |
| | Pupils | | Teachers | Pupils | | Teachers | |
| | a | b | a | a | b | a | b |
|---|---|---|---|---|---|---|---|
| 1915 | 117 | 4.0 | 2.8 | ... | ... | ... | ... |
| 1916 | 120 | 5.0 | 2.8 | ... | ... | ... | ... |
| 1917 | 125 | 5.2 | 2.8 | ... | ... | ... | ... |
| 1918 | 125 | 5.8 | 2.9 | ... | ... | ... | ... |
| 1919 | 126 | 6.1 | 2.8 | ... | ... | ... | ... |
| 1920 | 124 | 6.0 | 3.2 | ... | ... | ... | ... |
| 1921 | 131 | 6.2 | 3.4 | ... | ... | ... | ... |
| 1922 | 132 | 6.2 | 3.4 | ... | ... | ... | ... |
| 1923 | 135 | 6.6 | 3.4 | ... | ... | ... | ... |
| 1924 | 139 | 6.9 | 3.5 | ... | ... | ... | ... |
| 1925 | 144 | 6.9 | 3.7 | ... | ... | ... | ... |
| 1926 | 148 | 7.5 | 3.9 | 89 | ... | ... | ... |
| 1927 | 160 | 8.2 | 4.4 | ... | ... | ... | ... |
| 1928 | 170 | ... | 4.6 | 112 | ... | ... | ... |
| 1929 | 175 | 9.8 | 4.8 | ... | ... | ... | ... |
| 1930 | 178 | 9.7 [19] / 8.9 | 4.8 | ... | ... | ... | ... |
| 1931 | 178 | 16 | 4.8 | 114 | ... | ... | ... |
| 1932 | 180 | 15 | 4.8 | ... | ... | ... | ... |
| 1933 | 182 | 16 | 4.9 | 121 | ... | ... | ... |
| 1934 | 184 | 12 | 4.8 | ... | ... | ... | ... |
| 1935 | 192 | 12 | 4.9 | ... | ... | ... | ... |
| 1936 | 195 | 13 | 4.9 | ... | ... | ... | ... |
| 1937 | 204 | 14 | 5.2 | 234 | 3.3 | ... | ... |
| 1938 | 210 | 14 | 5.3 | 244 | 3.5 | 6.0 | 0.4 |
| 1939 | 214 | 18 | 5.4 | 235 | 4.7 | 7.2 | ... |
| 1940 | 219 | 18 | 5.9 | 266 | 6.4 | 8.0 | 0.8 |
| 1941 | 221 | ... | 5.9 | 276 | 6.9 | 8.1 | 0.8 |
| 1942 | 218 | 19 | 6.0 | 276 | 7.6 | 8.1 | 0.9 |
| 1943 | 218 | 22 | 6.0 | 292 | 9.5 | 8.6 | 1.3 |
| 1944 | 221 | 24 | 6.6 | 298 | 12 | 9.1 | 1.6 |

I1 **SOUTH AMERICA: Pupils and Teachers in Schools** (in thousands, except as otherwise indicated)

**1945–1974**

| | Argentina | | | | Bolivia | | | Brazil | | | |
|---|---|---|---|---|---|---|---|---|---|---|---|
| | Pupils | | Teachers | | Pupils | | Teachers | Pupils | | Teachers | |
| | a | b | a | b | a | b | All Schools | a | b | a | b |
| 1945 | 1,977 | 55 | 80 | 8.9 | 155 | ... | ... | 3,239 | 256 | 84 | 19 |
| 1946 | 1,993 | 60 | ... | 9.6 | 170 | ... | ... | 3,416 | 282 | 88 | 20 |
| 1947 | 2,036 | 60 | ... | 10 | 162 | ... | ... | 3,616 | 312 | 93 | 22 |
| 1948 | 2,074 | 62 | ... | 11 | 176 | ... | ... | 3,913 | 336 | 101 | 24 |
| 1949 | 2,120 | 66 | 93 | 12 | 176 | ... | ... | 4,098 | 366 | 107 | 25 |
| 1950 | 2,212 | 67 | 93 | 12 | 185[19] | 26 | 9.1 | 4,352 | 437 | 112 | 29 |
| 1951 | 2,286 | 70 | 102 | 12 | 131 | 26 | 10 | 4,546 | 439 | 122 | 31 |
| 1952 | 2,376 | 74 | ... | 13 | 137 | 27 | 12 | 4,713 | 467 | 128 | 33 |
| 1953 | 2,473 | 85 | ... | 14 | 143 | 28 | 12 | 4,902 | 514 | 136 | 35 |
| 1954 | 2,565 | 91 | 110 | 15 | 155 | 29 | 14 | 5,257 | 557 | 148 | 38 |
| 1955 | 2,642 | 102 | 114 | 15 | 166 | 31 | 15 | 5,611 | 604 | 159 | 41 |
| 1956 | 2,724 | 113 | 120 | 16 | 172 | 32 | 16 | 6,094 | 648 | 173 | 43 |
| 1957 | 2,783 | 125 | ... | 19 | 176 | 34 | 16 | 6,466 | 695 | 183 | 46 |
| 1958 | 2,860 | ... | 126 | ... | 192 | 38 | 17 | 6,776 | 761 | 197 | 51 |
| 1959 | 2,821 | 140 | 125 | 21 | 208 | 43 | 18 | 7,129 | 795 | 212 | 53 |
| 1960 | 2,849 | 147 | 130 | 23 | 182 | 45 | 18 | 7,477[19] / 8,368 | 868[19] / 267 | 226[19] / 284 | 58[19] / 36 |
| 1961 | 2,871 | 150 | 132 | 24 | 244 | 48 | 19 | 8,806 | 301 | 309 | 38 |
| 1962 | 2,933 | 156 | 124 | 26 | 283[20] / 497 | 53 | 20 | 9,664 | 336 | 340 | 38 |
| 1963 | 2,990 | 164 | 128 | 27 | 475 | 66 | ... | 10,622 | 397 | 380 | 43 |
| 1964 | 3,074 | 171 | 152 | 27 | 495 | 74 | 21 | 11,671 | 439 | 423 | 46 |
| 1965 | 3,125 | 179 | 154 | 29 | 527 | 83 | 22 | 11,569 | 509 | 446 | 50 |
| 1966 | 3,192 | 183 | 158 | 28 | 560 | 92 | ... | 12,585 | 593 | 496 | 55 |
| 1967 | 3,207 | 190 | 159 | 29 | 556 | 101 | 25 | 13,384 | 688 | 499 | 66 |
| 1968 | 3,239 | 198 | 165 | 30 | 568[19] | 114[19] | 27 | 14,348 | 801 | 556 | 79 |
| 1969 | 3,355 | 212[20] | 172 | 32[20] | 664 | 62 | 29 | 15,014 | 910 | 608 | 96 |
| 1970 | 3,386 | 405 | 176 | 58 | 679 | 92 | 30 | 15,895 | 1,003 | 654 | 112 |
| 1971 | 3,444 | 405 | 181 | 58 | 694 | 100 | 33 | 17,066 | 1,119 | 724 | 123 |
| 1972 | 3,464 | 413 | 185 | 59 | 731 | 111 | 38 | 18,371 | 1,300 | 770 | 127 |
| 1973 | 3,485 | 424 | 184 | 60 | 770 | 115 | 39 | 18,573 | 1,478 | 699 | 143 |
| 1974 | 3,545 | 443 | 186 | 61 | 810 | 121 | 41 | 19,287 | 1,682 | 887 | 156 |

I1    **SOUTH AMERICA: Pupils and Teachers in Schools** (in thousands, except as otherwise indicated)

1945–1974

| | Chile | | | | Colombia | | | | Ecuador | | | |
|---|---|---|---|---|---|---|---|---|---|---|---|---|
| | Pupils | | Teachers | | Pupils | | Teachers | | Pupils | | Teachers | |
| | a | b | a | b | a | b | a | b | a | b[36] | a | b[36] |
| 1945 | 682 | 64 | 13 | ... | 678 | 36 | 15 | 3.3 | 258 | 14 | 6.8 | 1.1 |
| 1946 | 699 | 67 | 14 | ... | 712 | 46 | 17 | 4.1 | ... | ... | ... | ... |
| 1947 | 713 | 71 | 14 | ... | 739 | 47 | 18 | 4.2 | 284 | 16 | 7.0 | 1.5 |
| 1948 | 746 | 75 | 14 | ... | 765 | 42 | 18 | 3.8 | 309 | 16 | 7.5 | 1.0 |
| 1949 | 776 | 78 | 14 | ... | 766 | 48 | 18 | 4.1 | 321 | 17 | ... | ... |
| 1950 | 798 | 81 | ... | ... | 808 | 56 | 19 | 5.0 | 342 | 18 | 8.2 | 1.8 |
| 1951 | 803 | 87 | ... | ... | 875 | 64 | 22 | 5.9 | 352 | 19 | ... | ... |
| 1952 | 849 | 94 | ... | ... | 923 | 65 | 23 | 6.0 | 357 | 21 | 8.9 | 2.2 |
| 1953 | 903 | 104 | ... | ... | 1,055 | 66 | 25 | 6.4 | 397 | 23 | 9.5 | 2.3 |
| 1954 | 943 | 116 | ... | ... | 1,125 | 70 | 29 | 6.6 | ... | ... | ... | ... |
| 1955 | 976 | 127 | 23 | ... | 1,236 | 77 | 32 | 7.0 | 461 | 27 | 10 | 2.7 |
| 1956 | 1,007 | 138 | 25 | 7.8 | 1,312 | 93 | 34 | 8.1 | 490 | 30 | 11 | 2.9 |
| 1957 | 1,059 | 151 | 25 | ... | 1,381 | 108 | 35 | 8.8 | 502 | 33 | 12 | 3.1 |
| 1958 | 1,095 | ... | ... | ... | 1,493 | 115 | 38 | 9.6 | 529 | 36 | ... | ... |
| 1959 | 1,155 | 155 | ... | ... | 1,569 | 128 | 40 | 11 | 567 | 37 | 14 | 3.7 |
| 1960 | 1,176 | 229 | ... | ... | 1,690 | 140 | 45 | 13 | 596 | 40 | 15 | 4.1 |
| 1961 | 1,228 | 248 | ... | ... | 1,792 | 156 | 49 | 13 | 609 | 46 | 16 | 4.6 |
| 1962 | 1,318 | 259 | ... | ... | 1,949 | 175 | 53 | 14 | 654 | 49 | 17 | 5.0 |
| 1963 | 1,370 | 274 | ... | ... | 2,096 | 202 | 58 | 16 | 698 | 54 | 19 | 5.4 |
| 1964 | 1,398 | 293 | 27 | 11 | 2,213 | 229 | 62 | 16 | 752 | 57 | 20 | 5.6 |
| 1965 | 1,517 | 320 | 29 | 11 | 2,274 | 266 | 63 | 20 | 797 | 63[36] / 117 | 21 | 6.0[36] / 9.2 |
| 1966 | 1,560 | 341 | ...[19] | 10[19] / 10 | 2,402 | 320 | 68 | 21 | 842 | 134 | 22 | 10 |
| 1967 | 1,835 | 185 | ... | 10 | 2,586 | 377 | 70 | 25 | 845 | 151 | 22 | 11 |
| 1968 | 1,933 | 231 | 34 | ... | 2,802 | 447 | 76 | 27 | 929 | 174 | 24 | 12 |
| 1969 | 1,976 | 272 | 36 | 12 | 3,108 | 523 | 82 | 30 | 980 | 198 | 26 | 14 |
| 1970 | 2,045 | 308 | 41 | ... | 3,286 | 589 | 86 | 34 | 1,024 | 219 | 27 | 15 |
| 1971 | 2,202 | 373 | 46 | ... | 3,466 | 652 | 90 | 36 | 1,057 | 242 | 27 | 16 |
| 1972 | 2,265 | 415 | 60 | ... | 3,604 | 734 | 100 | 40 | 1,102 | 268 | 28 | 18 |
| 1973 | 2,317 | 446 | 61 | ... | 3,752 | 812 | 110 | 45 | 1,167 | 299 | 30 | 20 |
| 1974 | 2,333 | 456 | 68 | 18 | 3,844 | 903 | 123 | 47 | 1,164 | 337 | 31 | 21 |

I1  SOUTH AMERICA: Pupils and Teachers in Schools (in thousands, except as otherwise indicated)

1945–1974

| | Guyana[37] | | | | Paraguay | | | | Peru | | | |
|---|---|---|---|---|---|---|---|---|---|---|---|---|
| | Pupils | | Teachers | | Pupils | | Teachers | | Pupils | | Teachers | |
| | a | b | a | b | a | b | a | b | a | b | a | b |
| 1945 | 62 | ... | 1.5 | ... | 178 | 1.6[35] / 7.3 | 4.4 | 0.5 | 695 | ... | 14 | ... |
| 1946 | 63 | ... | 1.5 | ... | 185 | 6.1 | 4.4 | 0.4 | 777 | 37 | 16 | 1.9 |
| 1947 | 66 | ... | 1.6 | ... | 149 | 9.6 | 5.5 | 0.8[20] | 857 | 55 | 19 | 4.6 |
| 1948 | 69 | 0.8 | 1.6 | -- | 180 | 10 | 5.5 | 1.2 | 990 | 61 | 22 | 4.7 |
| 1949 | 71 | 1.2 | 1.7 | -- | 189 | 11 | 5.7 | 1.4 | 993 | 61 | 23 | 4.7 |
| 1950 | 77 | 0.9 | 1.8 | -- | 196 | 11 | 6.2 | 1.5 | 1,010 | 63 | 24 | 4.1 |
| 1951 | 78 | 0.9 | 1.8 | -- | 222 | 12 | 6.5 | 1.7 | 1,035 | 63 | 25 | 4.4 |
| 1952 | 79 | ... | 1.9 | ... | 231 | 13 | 6.9 | 1.8 | 1,038 | 78 | 26 | 5.1 |
| 1953 | 84 | 1.7 | 2.1 | 0.1 | 239 | 13 | 7.5 | 1.9 | 1,047 | 83 | 27 | 5.8 |
| 1954 | 89 | 1.6 | 2.4 | 0.1 | 254 | 14 | 8.3 | 2.0 | 1,086 | 87 | 29 | 6.0 |
| 1955 | 95 | 1.7 | 2.5 | 0.1 | 268 | 13 | 9.1 | 2.1 | 1,128 | 92 | 30 | 6.4 |
| 1956 | 102 | ... | 2.7 | ... | 275 | 17[35] / 10 | 9.5 | 2.3 | 1,203 | 98 | 31 | 6.7 |
| 1957 | 106 | 4.6 | 2.8 | 0.2 | 287 | 13 | 9.9 | 2.6 | 1,234 | 117 | 32 | 7.0 |
| 1958 | 112 | ... | 3.0 | ... | 290 | 16 | 10 | 2.7 | 1,308 | 122 | 35 | 8.3 |
| 1959 | 118 | 7.0 | 3.2 | 0.3 | 297 | 18 | 10 | 3.0 | 1,392 | 141 | 38 | 8.7 |
| 1960 | 125 | 7.2 | 3.2 | 0.3 | 302 | 17 | 11 | 3.2 | 1,440 | 159 | 42 | 11 |
| 1961 | 130 | 8.8 | 3.4 | 0.4 | 312 | 15 | 11 | 3.4 | 1,495 | ... | 45 | ... |
| 1962 | 135 | 8.4 | 3.3 | 0.3 | 323 | 17 | 11 | 3.6 | 1,554 | ... | ... | ... |
| 1963 | 148 | ... | 4.4 | ... | 335 | 24 | 11 | 3.4 | ... | ... | ... | ... |
| 1964 | 157 | 14 | 4.3 | 0.6 | 349 | 28 | 12 | 4.1 | 1,877 | 261 | 53 | 16 |
| 1965 | 163 | 15 | 5.1 | 0.7 | 362 | 30 | 12 | 4.5 | 1,901 | 311 | 57 | 19 |
| 1966 | 168[37] / 135 | 16[37] / 49 | 5.2[37] | 0.7[37] / 1.6 | 373 | 34 | 12 | 4.7 | 2,151 | 369 | 62 | 22 |
| 1967 | 139 | 49 | 4.4 | 1.7 | 385 | 36 | 12 | 5.0 | 2,236 | 424 | 65 | 25 |
| 1968 | 131 | 50 | 4.4 | 1.8 | 406 | 41 | 13 | 5.2 | 2,335 | 471 | 68 | 27 |
| 1969 | 130 | 53 | 4.3 | 1.9 | 416 | 45 | 13 | 5.6 | ... | 490 | 69 | 26 |
| 1970 | 130 | 57 | 4.5 | 2.3 | 432 | 49 | 13 | ... | 2,341 | 547 | 64 | 28 |
| 1971 | 131 | 62 | ... | ... | 437 | 52 | 14 | 6.7 | 2,488 | 570 | 68 | 25 |
| 1972 | 132 | 63 | ... | ... | 440 | 58 | 14 | 6.9 | 2,649 | 609 | 73 | 26 |
| 1973 | 132 | 64 | 4.1 | ... | 452 | 63 | 15 | 6.7 | 2,641 | 623 | 71 | 27 |
| 1974 | 132 | ... | 4.1 | 2.8 | 455 | 68 | 16 | 7 | 2,761 | 681 | 73 | 29 |

I1   **SOUTH AMERICA: Pupils and Teachers in Schools** (in thousands, except as otherwise indicated)

**1945–1974**

| Year | Uruguay Pupils a | Uruguay Pupils b | Uruguay Teachers a | Venezuela Pupils a | Venezuela Pupils b | Venezuela Teachers a | Venezuela Teachers b |
|---|---|---|---|---|---|---|---|
| 1945 | 222 | 27 | 6.8 | 339 | 13 | 9.8 | 1.5 |
| 1946 | 221 | 29 | 6.8 | 361 | 16 | 12 | 1.9 |
| 1947 | 223 | 31 | 6.9 | 326 | 17 | 12 | 2.0 |
| 1948 | 227 | 31 | 6.8 | 442 | 22 | 12 | 1.7 |
| 1949 | 239 | 33 | 7.8 | 497 | 23 | 13 | 1.7 |
| 1950 | 257 | 34 | 9.2 | 503 | 27 | 14 | 2.2 |
| 1951 | 256 | 37 | 9.1 | 536 | 28 | 15 | 2.5 |
| 1952 | 261 | 38 | 8.3 | 570 | 27 | 16 | 2.5 |
| 1953 | 273 | 42 | 8.3 | 596 | 32 | 17 | 2.8 |
| 1954 | 275 | 46 | 8.4 | 623 | 36 | 18 | 3.1 |
| 1955 | 283 | 49 | 8.6 | 647 | 44 | 19 | 3.9 |
| 1956 | 295 | 55 | 8.6 | 694 | 52 | 20 | 4.2 |
| 1957 | 302 | 58 | 8.8 | 752 | 55 | 21 | 4.5 |
| 1958 | 310 | 63 | 9.5 | 917 | 71 | 25 | 5.3 |
| 1959 | 314 | 66 | 9.7 | 1,155 | 88 | 31 | 6.5 |
| 1960 | 320 | 71 | 10 | 1,244 | 105 | 35 | 7.7 |
| 1961 | 332 | 73 | 10 | 1,298 | 122 | 36 | 8.3 |
| 1962 | 323 | 76 | 10 | 1,340 | 139 | 38 | 10 |
| 1963 | 320 | 79 | ... | 1,371 | 155 | ... | 11 |
| 1964 | 350 | 85 | 11 | 1,422 | 173 | 41 | 13 |
| 1965 | 335 | 91 | 11 | 1,481 | 190 | 43 | 14 |
| 1966 | 366 | ... | 12 | 1,541 | 210[20] / 256 | 45 | 15[20] |
| 1967 | 368 | 109 | 12 | 1,557 | 283 | 46 | 16 |
| 1968 | 370 | 118 | 13 | 1,609 | 316 | 48 | 18 |
| 1969 | ... | 123 | ... | 1,690 | 360 | 50 | 20 |
| 1970 | 354 | 132 | 12 | 1,776 | 417 | 52 | 22 |
| 1971 | 360 | 138 | 13 | 1,838 | 476 | 54 | 26 |
| 1972 | 352 | 147 | 14 | 1,894 | 534 | 56 | 28 |
| 1973 | 354 | 152 | 14 | 1,924 | 584 | 58 | 31 |
| 1974 | 331 | 152 | 14 | 1,990 | 631 | 63 | 36 |

**I1    SOUTH AMERICA: Pupils and Teachers in Schools** (in thousands, except as otherwise indicated)

| | Argentina | | | | Bolivia | | | Brazil | | | |
|---|---|---|---|---|---|---|---|---|---|---|---|
| | Pupils | | Teachers | | Pupils | | Teachers | Pupils | | Teachers | |
| | a | b | a | b | a | b | All Schools | a | b | a | b |
| 1975 | 3,579[20] / 3,802 | 452 | 196[20] / 217 | 62 | 859 | 130 | 46 | 19,549 | 1,936 | 897 | 133 |
| 1976 | 3,832 | 442 | 220 | 60 | 923 | 128 | ... | 19,523 | 2,213 | 861 | 151 |
| 1977 | 3,884 | 439 | 218 | 60 | 949 | 143 | ... | 20,368 | 2,438 | 893 | 168 |
| 1978 | 3,937 | 442 | 208 | 59 | ... | ... | ... | 21,473 | 2,519 | 855 | 181 |
| 1979 | 4,004 | 441 | 225 | 60 | ... | ... | ... | 21,887 | 2,658 | 863 | 183 |
| 1980 | 4,111 | 510 | 217 | ... | 978 | 171 | 48 | 22,149[38] | 2,824[38] | 883[38] | 198[38] |
| 1981 | 4,218 | 528 | 218 | 78 | 1,023 | 166 | 57 | 22,473 | 2,821 | 943 | 206 |
| 1982 | 4,382 | 594 | 225 | ... | 1,049 | 176 | 52 | 23,564 | 2,875 | 961 | 204 |
| 1983 | 4,511 | 615 | 233 | 80 | 1,106 | 183 | 54 | 24,556 | 2,944 | 1,033 | 180 |
| 1984 | 4,631 | 657 | 219 | 87 | 1,181 | 200 | 56 | 24,826 | 2,947 | 1,016 | 215 |
| 1985 | 4,589 | 716 | 230 | 94 | 1,205 | ... | 60 | 24,770 | 3,016 | 1,041 | 206 |
| 1986 | 4,778 | 762 | 239 | 96 | 1,300 | 209 | 61 | 25,608 | 3,143 | 1,068 | 217 |
| 1987 | 4,907 | 774 | 252 | 111 | ... | 218 | 63 | 26,208 | 3,242 | 1,094 | 223 |
| 1988 | 4,999 | ... | 260 | ... | 1,187 | 207 | 67 | 26,821 | 3,340 | 1,120 | 229 |

I1    **SOUTH AMERICA: Pupils and Teachers in Schools** (in thousands, except as otherwise indicated)

| | Chile | | | | Colombia | | | | Ecuador | | | |
|---|---|---|---|---|---|---|---|---|---|---|---|---|
| | Pupils | | Teachers | | Pupils | | Teachers | | Pupils | | Teachers | |
| | a | b | a | b | a | b | a | b | a | b | a | b |
| 1975 | 2,299 | 449 | 66 | 30 | 3,953 | 978 | 131 | 51 | 1,255 | 384 | 33 | 23 |
| 1976 | 2,243 | 466 | 57 | 31 | 4,224 | 1,075 | 143 | 54 | 1,256 | 431 | 35 | ... |
| 1977 | 2,242 | 487 | 71 | 28 | 4,165 [19] | 1,154 [19] | 134 [19] | 55 [19] | 1,307 | 470 | 37 | 28 |
| 1978 | 2,233 | 510 | 72 | 29 | 3,609 | 1,459 | 111 | 70 | 1,367 | 487 | 38 | 30 |
| 1979 | 2,236 | 536 | 66 | 27 | 3,612 | 1,474 | 114 | 72 | 1,450 | 535 | 40 | 31 |
| 1980 | 2,185 | 538 | ... | ... | 3,597 | 1,434 | 116 | 70 | 1,534 | 587 | 44 | 35 |
| 1981 | 2,139 | 555 | ... | ... | 3,676 | 1,677 | 120 | 81 | 1,573 | 627 | 45 | 37 |
| 1982 | 2,093 | 566 | 63 | ... | 3,714 | 1,718 | 124 | 85 | 1,611 | 673 | 45 | 41 |
| 1983 | ... | ... | ... | ... | 3,750 | 1,817 | 125 | 90 | 1,677 | 655 | 50 | 41 |
| 1984 | ... | ... | ... | ... | 3,412 | 1,652 | 115 | 81 | 1,673 | 706 | 51 | 45 |
| 1985 | 2,062 | 668 | 78 | 37 | 3,385 | 1,742 | 113 | 84 | 1,742 | 701 | 52 | 48 |
| 1986 | 2,048 | 680 | ... | ... | 3,740 | 1,685 | 123 | 83 | 1,775 | 744 | 56 | 50 |
| 1987 | 2,056 | 696 | 69 | 42 | 3,902 | 1,973 | 130 | 85 | 1,843 | 765 | 57 | 54 |
| 1988 | 2,028 | 736 | ... | ... | 4,029 | 2,069 | 136 | 99 | 1,898 | 743 | 60 | 54 |

**I1 SOUTH AMERICA: Pupils and Teachers in Schools** (in thousands, except as otherwise indicated)

| | Guyana | | | | Paraguay | | | | Peru | | | |
|---|---|---|---|---|---|---|---|---|---|---|---|---|
| | Pupils | | Teachers | | Pupils | | Teachers | | Pupils | | Teachers | |
| | a | b | a | b | a | b | a | b | a | b | a | b |
| 1975 | 130 | 71 | 4.1 | 3.2 | 452 | 75 | 16 | 7.5 | 2,841 | 813 | 73 | 34 |
| 1976 | 140 | 77 | 4.3 | ... | 468 | 82 | 16 | ... | 2,961 | 890 | 74 | 35 |
| 1977 | 138 | ... | 4.5 | ... | 477 | 92 | 17 | 8.0 | 3,020 | 969 | 75 | 35 |
| 1978 | 137 | ... | 4.2 | ... | 493 | 101 | 18 | ... | 3,093 | 1,050 | 78 | 38 |
| 1979 | 132 | ... | 4.3 | ... | 504 | 110 | 18 | ... | 3,117 | 1,095 | 80 | 41 |
| 1980 | 131 | 75 | 3.9 | 4.2 | 519 | 118 | 19 | ... | 3,161 | 1,152 | 84 | 45 |
| 1981 | 130 | 74 | 3.5 | 3.8 | 530 | 124 | 20 | ... | 3,319 | 1,226 | 90 | 50 |
| 1982 | 126 | 69 | 3.5 | 3.5 | 540 | 137 | 21 | ... | 3,454 | 1,286 | 96 | 55 |
| 1983 | 122 | 67 | 3.3 | 3.5 | 550 | 144 | 21 | ... | 3,515 | 1,322 | 98 | 58 |
| 1984 | 117 | 71 | 3.3 | 3.5 | 559 | 151 | 22 | ... | 3,559 | 1,375 | 101 | 63 |
| 1985 | 114 | 77 | 3.9 | ... | 571 | 151 | 23 | ... | 3,712 | 1,421 | 106 | 68 |
| 1986 | 113 | 76 | 3.9 | ... | 580 | 150 | 23 | ... | 3,679 | 1,474 | 111 | 74 |
| 1987 | ... | ... | ... | ... | 600 | 151 | 24 | ... | 3,764 | 1,523 | 120 | 76 |
| 1988 | ... | ... | ... | ... | 627 | 153 | 25 | ... | ... | ... | 126 | 80 |

I1    SOUTH AMERICA: Pupils and Teachers in Schools (in thousands, except as otherwise indicated)

| | Uruguay | | | | Venezuela | | | |
| | Pupils | | Teachers | | Pupils | | Teachers | |
| | a | b | a | b | a | b | a | b |
| --- | --- | --- | --- | --- | --- | --- | --- | --- |
| 1975 | 323 | 144 | 14 | | 2,103 | 669 | 69 | 40 |
| 1976 | 323 | 142 | 14 | | 2,204 | 720 | 75 | 41 |
| 1977 | 324 | 137 | 14 | | 2,309 | 751 | 80 | 42 |
| 1978 | 325 | 131 | 14 | | 2,379 | 787 | 82 | 44 |
| 1979 | 327 | 129 | 15 | | 2,457 | 821 | 88 | 46 |
| 1980 | 331 | 125 | 16 | | 2,530 | 850 | 93 | 49 |
| 1981 | 336 | 162 | 16 | | 2,591 | 884 | 97 | 50 |
| 1982 | 344 | 164 | 17 | | 2,620 | 930 | 99 | 54 |
| 1983 | 350 | 171 | 17 | | 2,641 | 963 | 100 | 55 |
| 1984 | 350 | 177 | 15 | | 2,710 | 1,008 | 104 | 58 |
| 1985 | 356 | 188 | 15 | | 2,770 | 1,038 | 108 | 60 |
| 1986 | 355 | 183 | 16 | | 2,880 | 1,058 | 112[19] | 62[19] |
| 1987 | 354 | 176 | 17 | | 2,926 | 1,076 | 167 | 32 |
| 1988 | 352 | 209 | 17 | | 2,967 | 1,139 | 166 | 29 |

**I1    Pupils and Teachers in Schools** (in thousands, except as otherwise indicated)

NOTES

1. SOURCES: The national publications listed on p. xiv–xvi; UNESCO, *Yearbook of Educational Statistics*.
2. The definition of the different sorts of schools varies from country to country, sometimes from province to province, and from time to time, and it is not always unambiguous. Nor is it always clear to exactly what time of year the statistics relate, and which pupils are covered by them. So far as possible, changes in the scope and nature of the statistics are indicated in the footnotes, but there are believed to be many which are not recorded in the sources.
3. Only general secondary schools are normally covered in this table, not vocational, technical, or teacher-training institutions.

FOOTNOTES

[1] State schools only.

[2] Publicly-controlled schools only to 1948, except in Quebec to 1929. Excluding Prince Edward Island to 1874 and in 1876; excluding Manitoba in 1875–80; and excluding private schools in Quebec from 1875 to 1881 and in 1946 and 1947. Newfoundland is included from 1949, and additional schools, with 36 thousand pupils, from 1951. The teachers series relates to state schools only to 1958 (1st line). Figures from 1972 (2nd line) are later revisions or recategorizations.

[3] The only pupils in Quebec who are included are those in controlled Roman Catholic schools in these years.

[4] Public day schools only to 1928 (1st line). Earlier data are available for total pupils in private schools as follows (in thousands):

| | | | | | | | |
|---|---|---|---|---|---|---|---|
| 1889 | 1,269 | 1897 | 1,317 | 1905 | 1,338 | 1913 | 1,739 |
| 1890 | 1,757* | 1898 | 1,355 | 1906 | 1,414 | 1914 | 1,781 |
| 1891 | 1,491 | 1899 | 1,298 | 1907 | 1,309 | 1915 | 1,770 |
| 1892 | 1,300 | 1900 | 1,382 | 1908 | 1,547 | 1916 | 1,820 |
| 1893 | 1,343 | 1901 | 1,370 | 1909 | 1,489 | 1918 | 1,662 |
| 1894 | 1,319 | 1902 | 1,209 | 1910 | 1,558 | 1920 | 1,669 |
| 1895 | 1,211 | 1903 | 1,196 | 1911 | 1,601 | 1922 | 1,727 |
| 1896 | 1,335 | 1904 | 1,304 | 1912 | 1,647 | 1924 | 1,727 |
| | | | | | | 1926 | 2,439 |

* Excluding kindergartens, which are included in private school data in all other years except 1932–38. These statistics are broken down by grade in census years, as follows:

| | Primary | Secondary | | Primary | Secondary |
|---|---|---|---|---|---|
| 1890 | 1,662 | 95 | 1910 | 1,440 | 117 |
| 1900 | 1,147 | 111 | 1920 | 1,456 | 214 |

'Other' schools (e.g. Federal schools on military bases and on Indian reservations, residential schools for handicapped children, etc.) are excluded throughout. The following figures at ten-year intervals indicate the numbers involved (in thousands):

| | Primary | Secondary | | Primary | Secondary |
|---|---|---|---|---|---|
| 1890 | ... | 60 | 1940 | 113 | 71 |
| 1900 | 37 | 69 | 1950 | 105 | 56 |
| 1910 | 71 | 83 | 1960 | 154 | 80 |
| 1920 | 99 | 86 | 1970 | 195 | 97 |
| 1930 | 143 | 71 | | | |

[5] In public day schools only to 1970 (1st line). Prior to 1938, statistics are of numbers employed rather than numbers of posts. Librarian, guidance, and some other non-supervisory posts are included, but school principals are not.

[6] Excluding Nova Scotia.

[7] Excluding Manitoba.

[8] State schools only to 1954 (1st line) and from 1982 (2nd line).

[9] Schools in San José only to 1943 and in 1947 and 1949. State schools throughout the country in 1945, 1950, and 1951.

[10] State schools only from 1902 and 1922 (2nd line) and in 1939.

[11] Including pre-primary school teachers to 1965.

[12] No break is indicated in the source, but it is very likely that there is one, and the probable cause is a change from enrolment to attendance. This change was reversed in 1921.

[13] Including pre-primary schools to 1950 (1st line). There is no break in the teachers series.

[14] Primary schools only from 1896.

[15] State schools only to 1947.

[16] Tobago is included from 1900.

[17] An element of double-counting in Manitoba and Ontario was eliminated between 1931 and 1934.

[18] Statistics from 1918 to 1929 are of attendance rather than enrolment.

[19] There was a change in the categorization of schools.

[20] The reason for this break is not clear from the sources.

## I2     NORTH AMERICA: STUDENTS IN UNIVERSITIES

### 1870–1899

| | USA |
| --- | --- |
| | (thousands) |
| 1870 | 52 |
| 1871 | ... |
| 1872 | ... |
| 1873 | ... |
| 1874 | ... |
| 1875 | ... |
| 1876 | ... |
| 1877 | ... |
| 1878 | ... |
| 1879 | ... |
| 1880 | 116 |
| 1881 | ... |
| 1882 | ... |
| 1883 | ... |
| 1884 | ... |
| 1885 | ... |
| 1886 | ... |
| 1887 | ... |
| 1888 | ... |
| 1889 | ... |
| 1890 | 157 |
| 1891 | ... |
| 1892 | ... |
| 1893 | ... |
| 1894 | ... |
| 1895 | ... |
| 1896 | ... |
| 1897 | ... |
| 1898 | ... |
| 1899 | ... |

### 1900–1934

| | Canada[1] | Cuba | El Salvador | Guatemala[2] | Honduras | Mexico | USA |
| --- | --- | --- | --- | --- | --- | --- | --- |
| | (thousands) | | | | | (thousands) | (thousands) |
| 1900 | ... | 600 | ... | ... | ... | ... | 238 |
| 1901 | ... | 534 | ... | ... | ... | ... | ... |
| 1902 | ... | 638 | ... | ... | 135 | ... | ... |
| 1903 | ... | ... | ... | ... | ... | ... | ... |
| 1904 | ... | 503 | ... | ... | ... | ... | ... |
| 1905 | ... | 524 | ... | ... | ... | ... | 264 |
| 1906 | ... | 581 | ... | ... | ... | ... | ... |
| 1907 | ... | 521 | ... | ... | ... | ... | ... |
| 1908 | ... | 634 | ... | ... | ... | ... | ... |
| 1909 | ... | 1,017 | ... | ... | ... | ... | ... |
| 1910 | ... | 1,070 | ... | ... | ... | ... | 355 |
| 1911 | ... | ... | ... | ... | ... | ... | 354 |
| 1912 | ... | 1,176 | ... | ... | ... | ... | 356 |
| 1913 | ... | ... | ... | ... | ... | ... | 361 |
| 1914 | ... | 1,273 | ... | ... | ... | ... | 379 |
| 1915 | ... | 1,432 | ... | ... | ... | ... | 404 |
| 1916 | ... | ... | ... | ... | ... | ... | 441 |
| 1917 | ... | ... | ... | ... | ... | ... | ... |
| 1918 | ... | ... | ... | ... | ... | ... | 441 |
| 1919 | ... | 2,272 | ... | ... | ... | ... | ... |
| 1920 | 22 | ... | ... | ... | ... | ... | 598 |
| 1921 | 23 | ... | ... | ... | 98 | ... | ... |
| 1922 | 24 | ... | ... | ... | 107 | ... | 681 |
| 1923 | 25 | 4,006 | ... | ... | ... | ... | ... |
| 1924 | 25 | ... | ... | ... | ... | 9.6 | 823 |
| 1925 | 25 | 4,068 | ... | ... | 72 | 11 | ... |
| 1926 | 25 | 5,473 | ... | ... | ... | 10 | 941 |
| 1927 | 26 | 4,148 | 368 | ... | 70 | 8.7 | ... |
| 1928 | 27 | 3,932 | ... | ... | ... | 9.4 | 1,054 |
| 1929 | 28 | 4,795 | 409 | ... | ... | 8.2 | ... |
| 1930 | 30 | ... | 411 | ... | 179 | 9.6 | 1,101 |
| 1931 | 32 | ... | ... | 714 | ... | 9.7 | ... |
| 1932 | 33 | ... | 491 | ... | ... | 11 | 1,154 |
| 1933 | 33 | ... | ... | ... | 308 | 9.2 | ... |
| 1934 | 33 | ... | ... | 694 | 299 | 8.2 | 1,055 |

## I2    NORTH AMERICA: Students in Universities

**1935–1974**

| | Barbados[3] | Canada[1] | Costa Rica | Cuba | Dominican Republic | El Salvador | Guatemala[2] | Honduras |
|---|---|---|---|---|---|---|---|---|
| | | (thousands) | (thousands) | (thousands) | | | (thousands) | |
| 1935 | — | 33 | ... | — | ... | ... | ... | 312 |
| 1936 | — | 34 | ... | ... | 328 | ... | ... | 298 |
| 1937 | — | 34 | ... | ... | 450 | ... | ... | 298 |
| 1938 | — | 34 | ... | ... | 498 | ... | ... | ... |
| 1939 | — | 35 | ... | ... | 702 | ... | ... | ... |
| 1940 | — | 36 | ... | ... | 754 | ... | ... | 357 |
| 1941 | — | 35 | ... | ... | 898 | ... | ... | ... |
| 1942 | — | 35 | ... | ... | 1,040 | 468 | ... | ... |
| 1943 | — | 36 | ... | ... | 1,134 | ... | ... | 368 |
| 1944 | — | 35 | ... | 8.2 | 1,218 | 633 | ... | 467 |
| | | | | | (thousands) | | | |
| 1945 | — | 38 | ... | ... | 1.4 | 916 | ... | 433 |
| 1946 | — | 62 | ... | ... | 1.6 | ... | ... | 462 |
| 1947 | — | 76 | ... | ... | 1.7 | ... | ... | 496 |
| 1948 | ... | 79 | ... | ... | 1.9 | ... | ... | 653 |
| 1949 | ... | 76 | ... | ... | 2.1 | 1,120 | ... | 653 |
| | | | | | | (thousands) | | |
| 1950 | ... | 69 | ... | 17 | 2.3 | 1.2 | 2.3 | 716 |
| 1951 | ... | 64 | 1.4 | 17 | 2.4 | 1.3 | ... | 894 |
| 1952 | ... | 60 | 1.9 | | 2.8 | 0.7 | ... | 843 |
| 1953 | ... | 60 | ... | 21 | 3.0 | 1.0 | ... | 831 |
| 1954 | ... | 61 | ... | 23 | 3.1 | 1.0 | 3.4 | ... |
| 1955 | ... | 65 | 2.2 | 24 | 3.2 | 1.1 | 3.2 | ... |
| 1956 | ... | 69 | ... | 17 | 3.8 | 1.5 | ... | 1,137 |
| 1957 | ... | 75 | 2.5 | ... | 4.0 | 1.3 | ... | 1,185 |
| 1958 | ... | 82[1] / 95 | 3.1 | 1.9 | 3.9 | 1.9 | ... | 1,306 |
| 1959 | ... | 102 | 3.7 | 18 | 3.8 | 2.1 | ... | 1,310 |
| | | | | | | | | (thousands) |
| 1960 | ... | 114 | 3.8 | 20 | 3.4 | 2.2 | 5.2 | 1.4 |
| 1961 | ... | 129 | 4.2 | 18 | 4.0 | 2.5 | 5.5 | 1.5 |
| 1962 | ... | 141[1] / 185 | ... | 17 | 5.3 | 2.9 | 5.9 | 1.7 |
| 1963 | ... | 215 | 4.4 | 20 | ... | 3.2 | 6.2 | 1.7 |
| 1964 | ... | 231 | 5.1 | 26 | 5.5 | 3.5 | 7.0 | 1.8 |
| 1965 | 226 | 277 | 5.8 | 26 | 6.6 | 3.8 | 7.7 | 2.1 |
| 1966 | 245 | 315 | 6.0 | 28 | 6.9 | 5.0 | ... | 2.5 |
| 1967 | 293 | 351 | 7.2 | 29 | 10 | 6.1 | 9.4[2] | 2.5 |
| 1968 | 385 | 368 | 9.3 | 30 | 15 | 7.1 | 12 | 2.9 |
| 1969 | 429 | 416 | 11 | 31 | 18 | 7.8 | 14 | ... |
| 1970 | 459 | 477 | 13 | 26 | 23 | 9.2 | 16 | 3.3 |
| 1971 | 615 | 478 | 15 | 37 | 29 | 12 | 17 | 4.7 |
| 1972 | 881 | 475 | 18 | 49 | 33 | 13 | 19 | 8.1 |
| 1973 | 942 | 491 | 24 | 55 | 35 | 16[4] | 22[2] | 9.3 |
| 1974 | 991 | 502 | 28 | 68 | 39 | 21 | 20 | 9.2 |

**I2      NORTH AMERICA: Students in Universities**

| | Jamaica[3] | Mexico[5] | Nicaragua | Panama[6] | Puerto Rico | Trinidad & Tobago[3] | USA[7] |
|---|---|---|---|---|---|---|---|
| | | (thousands) | (thousands) | (thousands) | (thousands) | | (thousands) |
| 1935 | — | 10 | ... | ... | ... | — | ... |
| 1936 | — | 12 | ... | ... | ... | — | 1,208 |
| 1937 | — | 13 | ... | ... | ... | — | ... |
| 1938 | — | 17 | ... | ... | ... | — | 1,351 |
| 1939 | — | 16 | ... | ... | ... | — | ... |
| 1940 | — | 17 | ... | ... | ... | — | 1,494 |
| 1941 | — | 18 | ... | ... | ... | — | ... |
| 1942 | — | 19 | ... | ... | ... | — | 1,404 |
| 1943 | — | 22 | ... | ... | ... | — | ... |
| 1944 | — | 22 | 0.7 | ... | ... | — | 1,155 |
| 1945 | — | 23 | 0.7 | 0.8 | ... | — | ... |
| 1946 | — | 22 | 0.6 | 1.0 | 10 | — | 1,677 |
| 1947 | — | 21 | ... | 1.0 | 11 | — | ... |
| 1948 | 35 | 24 | ... | 1.3 | 12 | ... | 2,616 |
| 1949 | 70 | 25[5] / 29 | ... | 1.4 | 13 | ... | ... |
| 1950 | 145 | 17 | ... | 1.5 | 14 | ... | 2,659 |
| 1951 | 205 | 31 | ... | 1.7 | 13 | ... | ... |
| 1952 | 254 | 27 | ... | ... | 13 | ... | 2,302 |
| 1953 | 302 | 21 | 1.1 | 1.7 | 15 | ... | ... |
| 1954 | 384 | 26 | ... | 2.0 | 16 | ... | 2,515 |
| 1955 | 444 | 19 | ... | 2.0 | 18 | ... | ... |
| 1956 | 494 | 18 | ... | 2.3 | 19 | ... | 2,619 |
| 1957 | 555 | 16 | 0.9 | 2.8 | 21 | ... | ... |
| 1958 | 622 | 19 | 1.0 | 3.3 | 22 | ... | 2,900 |
| 1959 | 695 | 23 | 1.2 | 3.4 | 25 | ... | ...[6] |
| 1960 | 977 | 83 | 1.3 | 3.9 | 26 | ... | 3,216 |
| 1961 | 1,268 | 95 | 2.0 | 4.2 | 30 | ... | ... |
| 1962 | 1,422 | 100 | 2.1 | 5.1 | 31 | ... | 3,726 |
| 1963 | 2,187 | 102 | 2.4 | 5.4[6] / 6.2 | 33 | ... | ... |
| 1964 | 2,523[3] | 130 | 2.8 | 7.0 | 37 | 692 | 4,296 |
| 1965 | 1,923 | 135 | 3.3 | 8.9 | 40 | 910 | ... |
| 1966 | 2,073 | 143 | 4.1 | 9.9 | 42 | 964 | ... |
| 1967 | 2,234 | 141 | 5.1 | 11 | 45 | 1,087 | ... |
| 1968 | 2,564 | 166 | 6.4 | 12 | 51 | 1,267 | 6,659 |
| 1969 | 2,687 | 215 | 8.0 | 7.9 | 53 | 1,511 | ... |
| 1970 | 2,886 | 248 | 9.4 | 8.9 | 59 | 1,671 | 7,545[7] / 7,920 |
| 1971 | 3,301 | 291[5] | 9.4 | 15 | 65 | ... | 8,116 |
| 1972 | 3,576 | 369 | 12 | 18 | 71 | 1,966 | 8,265 |
| 1973 | 3,608 | 453 | 12 | 22 | 79 | 2,089 | 8,518 |
| 1974 | 3,735 | 520 | 15 | 24 | 84 | 2,202 | 9,023 |

**I2      NORTH AMERICA: Students in Universities**

| | Barbados | Canada[1] | Costa Rica | Cuba | Dominican Republic | El Salvador | Guatemala | Honduras |
|---|---|---|---|---|---|---|---|---|
| | (thousands) | (thousands) | (thousands) | (thousands) | (thousands) | (thousands) | (thousands) | (thousands) |
| 1975 | 1,065 | 547 | 33 | 85 | 29 | 27 | 23 | 11 |
| 1976 | 1,140 | 567 | 36 | 107 | ... | ... | 26 | 13 |
| 1977 | 1,235 | 586 | 39 | 123 | 45 | 28 | 29 | 15 |
| 1978 | 1,362 | 584 | 45 | 133 | 42 | 29 | 34 | 19 |
| 1979 | 1,497 | 601 | 47 | 146 | ... | 9 | 48 | 21 |
| 1980 | 1,587 | 628 | 47 | 152 | ... | 13 | 51 | 24 |
| 1981 | 1,601 | 649 | 47 | 165 | ... | 18 | 47 | 27 |
| 1982 | 1,564 | 692 | 46 | 173 | ... | 34 | 47 | 28 |
| 1983 | 1,641 | 729 | 47 | 193 | ... | 47 | 44 | 29 |
| 1984 | 1,790 | 739 | 47 | 212 | ... | 53 | 46 | 30 |
| 1985 | 1,902 | 752 | 50 | 235 | 124 | 57 | 48 | 29 |
| 1986 | 2,007 | 763 | 50 | 257 | ... | 61 | 52 | 30 |
| 1987 | 2,103 | 781 | 52 | 263 | ... | ... | ... | 31 |
| 1988 | ... | 806 | 53 | 251 | ... | 72 | ... | 33 |

| | Jamaica | Mexico | Nicaragua | Panama | Puerto Rico | Trinidad & Tobago | USA |
|---|---|---|---|---|---|---|---|
| | (thousands) | (thousands) | (thousands) | (thousands) | | | (thousands) |
| 1975 | 3,963 | 525 | 16 | 26 | 91 | 2,229 | 9,731 |
| 1976 | 4,091 | 622 | 20 | 30 | 69 | 2,310 | 9,589 |
| 1977 | 4,361 | 655 | 20 | 35 | 85 | 2,489 | 9,807 |
| 1978 | 4,496 | 731 | ... | 35 | ... | 2,661 | 11,260 |
| 1979 | 4,574 | 818 | 27 | 38 | 97 | 2,915 | 11,570 |
| 1980 | 4,548 | 840 | 33 | 40 | ... | 2,923 | 12,097 |
| 1981 | 4,798 | 910 | ... | 43 | ... | 3,144 | 12,372 |
| 1982 | 4,884 | 973 | 28 | 46 | ... | 3,125 | 12,426 |
| 1983 | 5,157 | ... | 30 | 45 | ... | 3,197 | 12,465 |
| 1984 | 5,325 | 1,199 | 26 | 52 | ... | 3,428 | 12,242 |
| 1985 | 5,057 | 1,192 | 24 | 53 | ... | 3,728 | 12,247 |
| 1986 | 4,979 | 1,245 | 24 | 60 | ... | 3,803 | 12,505 |
| 1987 | 5,235 | 1,257 | 24 | 55 | ... | 4,156 | 12,768 |
| 1988 | ... | ... | ... | 51 | ... | 4,252 | 12,849 |

**I2    SOUTH AMERICA: STUDENTS IN UNIVERSITIES**

1885–1924

| | Argentina | Bolivia | Brazil | Chile | Colombia | Ecuador | Paraguay | Peru | Uruguay |
|---|---|---|---|---|---|---|---|---|---|
| | | | (thousands) | | | | | (thousands) | |
| 1885 | 880 | ... | ... | ... | ... | ... | ... | ... | ... |
| 1886 | ... | ... | ... | 968 | ... | ... | ... | ... | 193 |
| 1887 | 743 | ... | ... | 1,014 | ... | ... | ... | ... | 208 |
| 1888 | ... | 774 | ... | 1,074 | ... | ... | ... | ... | 251 |
| 1889 | 963 | ... | ... | ... | ... | ... | ... | ... | 232 |
| 1890 | 1,007 | ... | ... | ... | ... | ... | ... | ... | 282 |
| 1891 | 900 | ... | ... | 1,245 | ... | ... | ... | ... | 291 |
| 1892 | ... | ... | ... | 1,179 | ... | ... | ... | ... | 262 |
| 1893 | ... | ... | ... | ... | ... | 216 | ... | ... | 281 |
| 1894 | ... | ... | ... | 1,181 | ... | ... | ... | ... | 279 |
| 1895 | ... | 506 | ... | 1,190 | ... | ... | ... | ... | 271 |
| 1896 | ... | ... | ... | 1,317 | ... | ... | ... | ... | 317 |
| 1897 | ... | ... | ... | 1,275 | 1,519 | ... | ... | 0.8 | 398 |
| 1898 | 2,553 | ... | ... | 1,181 | ... | ... | ... | 0.9 | 378 |
| 1899 | ... | ... | ... | 1,251 | ... | ... | ... | ... | 396 |
| | (thousands) | | | | | | | | |
| 1900 | ... | ... | ... | 1,228 | 1,558 | ... | ... | ... | 401 |
| 1901 | ... | 613 | ... | 1,242 | ... | ... | ... | ... | 415 |
| 1902 | 3.0 | ... | ... | 1,392 | ... | ... | ... | ... | 412 |
| 1903 | ... | ... | ... | 1,775 | ... | ... | ... | ... | 426 |
| 1904 | 3.7 | ... | ... | 1,829 | ... | ... | ... | ... | ... |
| 1905 | ... | ... | ... | 1,960 | ... | ... | ... | ... | ... |
| 1906 | ... | 680 | ... | 1,948 | ... | ... | ... | ... | 851 |
| 1907 | ... | ... | 6.4 | 2,121 | ... | ... | ... | ... | 730 |
| 1908 | ... | ... | 7.7 | 2,234 | ... | ... | ... | ... | ... |
| 1909 | 10 | ... | 8.7 | 2,378 | ... | ... | ... | ... | 1,366 |
| 1910 | ... | ... | 8.8 | 2,425 | ... | ... | ... | ... | 1,039 |
| 1911 | ... | ... | 10 | 2,874 | ... | ... | ... | ... | 1,081 |
| 1912 | ... | 780 | 11 | 3,129 | ... | 437 | ... | 1.7 | 1,139 |
| 1913 | 7.5 | ... | ... | 3,813 | ... | ... | ... | 1.7 | 1,084 |
| 1914 | ... | ... | ... | 4,024 | 1,576 | 474 | 192 | 1.8 | 1,077 |
| | | | | (thousands) | | | | | |
| 1915 | 7.1 | ... | ... | 4.5 | ... | 465 | 214 | 1.6 | ... |
| 1916 | ... | ... | ... | 4.7 | ... | ... | ... | 1.8 | ... |
| | | | | | (thousands) | | | | |
| 1917 | 14 | ... | ... | 4.7 | 2.5 | ... | ... | 2.0 | ... |
| 1918 | 15 | ... | ... | 4.9 | ... | ... | 252 | 2.0 | ... |
| 1919 | 14 | ... | ... | 4.7 | ... | 744 | 247 | 1.8 | ... |
| 1920 | 15 | ... | ... | 5.1 | ... | ... | 247 | 1.7 | ... |
| 1921 | ... | ... | ... | 5.4 | ... | 680 | 279 | 0.5 | ... |
| | | | | | | | | | (thousands) |
| 1922 | ... | ... | ... | 6.5 | ... | 670 | ... | 1.5 | 1.6 |
| 1923 | ... | ... | ... | 6.5 | ... | ... | ... | 1.7 | ... |
| 1924 | ... | ... | ... | 6.1 | ... | ... | ... | 2.1 | 2.0 |

**I2   SOUTH AMERICA:** Students in Universities

| | Argentina[8] | Bolivia | Brazil[9] | Chile | Colombia | Ecuador | Paraguay | Peru | Uruguay | Venezuela |
|---|---|---|---|---|---|---|---|---|---|---|
| | (thousands) | | (thousands) | (thousands) | (thousands) | | | (thousands) | (thousands) | (thousands) |
| 1925 | ... | ... | ... | 6.3 | ... | ... | 364 | 2.3 | 2.1 | ... |
| 1926 | ... | 802 | ... | 5.0 | ... | ... | 347 | 2.2 | 2.1 | 0.7 |
| 1927 | ... | ... | 13 | 5.1 | ... | ... | 334 | 2.2 | 2.3 | ... |
| 1928 | 17 | ... | 14 | 5.8 | ... | 776 | 414 | 2.3 | 2.1 | ... |
| 1929 | ... | ... | 15 | 6.6 | ... | ... | 435 | 2.7 | 1.8 | ... |
| 1930 | 23 | ... | ... | ... | ... | ... | 467 | 2.9 | 1.9 | ... |
| 1931 | 25 | ... | ... | 5.2 | ... | ... | 449 | 0.6 | 2.0 | ... |
| 1932 | 23 | 1,745 | 21 | 5.8 | ... | 958 | 490 | 0.5 | 1.7 | ... |
| 1933 | 26 | 1,682 | 23 | ... | ... | 1,064 | — | 1.4 | 2.3 | ... |
| 1934 | 26 | ... | 25[9] / 24 | ... | 3.0 | 1,051 | 381 | 2.8 | 2.5 | ... |
| 1935 | 27 | ... | 26 | 6.0 | 4.1 | 1,230 | 445 | 2.4 | 2.3 | ... |
| 1936 | 30 | 1,482 | 26 | 6.4 | 3.3 | 1,426 | 673 | 2.9 | 2.5 | ... |
| 1937 | 30 | ... | 25 | 6.3 | 3.3 | 1,476 | 871 | 3.4 | 2.7 | 2.0 |
| 1938 | 32 | ... | 22 | 6.2 | 3.1 | 1,493 | 1,125 | 4.8 | ... | 1.8 |
| 1939 | 34 | ... | 19 | 6.4 | 3.8 | 1,505 | 1,293 | 4.0 | ... | 1.9 |
| 1940 | 42 | ... | 18 | ... | 3.0 | 1,588 | 1,203 | 3.8 | ... | 2.4 |
| 1941 | 44 | ... | 18 | [5.5][10] | 3.7 | 1,755 | 1,208 | 5.5 | ... | 2.5 |
| 1942 | 48 | ... | 20 | 6.3 | 4.1 | 1,885 | 1,344 | 5.3 | ... | 3.1 |
| 1943 | 48 | ... | 23 | 6.4 | 5.1 | ... | 1,358 | 7.2 | ... | 2.9 |
| 1944 | 52 | ... | 26 | 6.8 | 5.8 | ... | 1,581 | 8.6 | ... | 3.2 |
| | | | | | | (thousands) | (thousands) | | | |
| 1945 | 53 | ... | 27 | 7.1 | 6.5 | 2.6 | 1.5 | 10 | ... | 3.3 |
| 1946 | 57 | ... | 29 | 7.2 | 7.3 | ... | 1.7 | 14 | ... | 4.6 |
| 1947 | 56 | ... | 31 | 8.2 | 8.0 | 3.4 | 1.2 | 13 | ... | 5.4 |
| 1948 | 62 | ... | 34 | 8.1 | 8.3 | 4.1 | 1.5 | 15 | ... | 5.8 |
| 1949 | 69 | ... | 38 | 9.5 | 9.4 | 4.1 | 1.9 | 16 | ... | 6.3 |
| | | (thousands) | | | | | | | | |
| 1950 | 85 | 4.6 | 43 | 11 | 11 | 4.1 | 1.8 | 16 | ... | 6.9 |
| 1951 | 95 | ... | 46 | 11 | 11 | 4.6 | 2.0 | 15 | 12 | 2.0 |
| 1952 | 103 | ... | 50 | ... | 12 | 4.8 | 2.2 | 15 | ... | 5.1 |
| 1953 | 128 | ... | 55 | ... | 12 | 5.1 | 2.3 | 16 | 11 | 7.5 |
| 1954 | 145 | ... | 60 | 14 | 12 | ... | ... | 17 | 12 | 7.4 |
| 1955 | 152 | ... | 63 | 17 | 13 | 5.9 | ... | 18 | 15 | 7.7 |
| 1956 | 149 | ... | 67 | 17 | 15 | 5.2 | 2.4 | 19 | ... | 9.2 |
| 1957 | 159 | ... | 71 | 11 | 16 | 6.5 | 2.9 | 21 | 15 | 11 |
| 1958 | 153 | ... | 74 | 19 | 19 | 7.3 | 3.0 | 22 | ... | 17 |
| 1959 | 167 | ... | 87 | 22 | 21 | 7.6 | 3.1 | 25 | 15 | 23 |

**I2     SOUTH AMERICA: Students in Universities**

**1960–1988**

| | Argentina[8] | Bolivia | Brazil[9] | Chile | Colombia | Ecuador | Guyana[3] | Paraguay | Peru | Uruguay | Venezuela[13] |
|---|---|---|---|---|---|---|---|---|---|---|---|
| | (thousands) | | (thousands) | (thousands) | (thousands) | | | | (thousands) | (thousands) | (thousands) |
| 1960 | 181 | 7.5 | 93 | 25 | 23 | ... | ... | 3.4 | 31 | 15 | 26 |
| 1961 | 190 | ... | 99 | 29 | 27 | 10 | ... | 3.7 | 35 | ... | 32 |
| 1962 | 193 | 7.6 | 107 | 33 | 30 | 11 | ... | 3.8 | 41 | 15 | 34 |
| 1963 | 217 | ... | 124 | 35 | 34 | 12 | 169 | 3.8 | 46 | ... | 38 |
| 1964 | 254 | ... | 142 | 37 | 37 | ... | 268 | 3.9 | 54 | 16 | 41 |
| 1965 | 247 [8] 222 | 14 | 156 | 44 | 43 | 14 | 319 | 4.1 | 65 | 17 | 46 |
| 1966 | 226 | ... | 180 | 53 | 52 | 16 | 449 | 4.6 | 74 | ... | 54 |
| 1967 | 240 | 17 | 213 | 56 | 59 | 19 | 579 | 5.0 | 81 | 17 | 59 |
| 1968 | 234 | 19 | 278 | 53 | 67 | 22 | 775 | 5.3 | 94 | 19 | 46 |
| 1969 | 238 | 22 | 343 | 73 | 74 | 32 | 1,030 | 5.5 | 98 | 20 | 35 |
| 1970 | 253 | 29 | 425 | 78 | 86 | 39 | 1,112 | 6.0 | 108 | ... | 47 |
| 1971 | 290 | ... | 561 | 101 | 95 | 44 | 1,232 | 6.7 | 116 | ... | 50 [13] 89 |
| 1972 | 333 | ... | 688 | 127 | 111 | 58 | 1,385 | 7.3 | 128 | ... | 108 |
| 1973 | 378 | 25 | 773 | 140 | 124 | 98 | 1,509 | 7.9 | 149 | ... | 145 |
| 1974 | 441 | 31 | 938 | 144 | 141 | 137 | ... | 9.2 [12] 14 | 170 | 26 | 165 |
| 1975 | 537 | 34 | 1,073 | 147 | 168 | 170 | 1,749 | 17 | 182 | 33 | 186 |
| 1976 | 533 | 35 | 1,096 | 134 | 197 | 181 | ... | 18 | 197 | ... | 201 |
| 1977 | 465 | 41 | 1,159 | 131 | 229 | ... | ... | 20 | 199 | 39 | 216 |
| 1978 | 402 | 45 | 1,226 | 130 | 244 | 231 | 1,527 | 20 | 209 | 32 | 228 |
| 1979 | 389 | 49 | 1,312 | 126 | 257 | 252 | 1,582 | 22 | 222 | 38 | 232 |
| 1980 | 398 | 61 | 1,378 | 119 | 235 | 264 | 1,681 | 25 | 258 | 36 | 243 |
| 1981 | 402 | [53][11] | 1,393 | 119 | 283 | 258 | 1,995 | 27 | 279 | 37 | 259 |
| 1982 | 411 | [57][11] | 1,203 | 119 | 296 | 252 | 1,567 | 28 | 294 | 48 | 269 |
| 1983 | 417 | 89 | 1,439 | 126 | 312 | 264 | 1,580 | 31 | 317 | 50 | 282 |
| 1984 | 508 | 80 | 1,400 | 186 | 332 | 278 | 1,544 | 30 | 336 | 64 | 286 |
| 1985 | 604 | 95 | 1,368 | 197 | 318 | 265 | 1,598 | ... | 355 | 77 | 321 |
| 1986 | 707 | ... | 1,418 | 214 | 320 | ... | ... | ... | 388 | 92 | 314 |
| 1987 | 755 | 97 | 1,471 | 224 | 331 | 265 | 2,245 | 28 | 410 | 61 | [467][14] |
| 1988 | ... | 107 | 1,504 | 235 | 319 | 239 | ... | 25 | 431 | 62 | [500][14] |

## I2    Students in Universities

NOTES

1.  SOURCES: As for table I1. Uruguay figures to 1899 are from E. Acevedo, *Anales Historicas del Uruguay.*
2.  Institutions of higher education other than universities and equivalent institutions are covered in some of the statistics in this table. Where this has been identified it is indicated in footnotes.
3.  Most sources do not distinguish between undergraduates and graduate students. It is presumed that both are included normally.
4.  Unless otherwise indicated, the statistics refer to the academic year beginning in the one shown.

FOOTNOTES

[1] Full-time undergraduates to 1958 (1st line), all full-time students subsequently, with part-time students included from 1962 (2nd line).
[2] San Carlos University only to 1967 and from 1974. The total for 1965 was 8.5 thousand.
[3] All students at the University of British West Indies are shown under Jamaica to 1964.
[4] State universities only to 1973. There were 3 thousand students in private universities in that year.
[5] All higher education from 1950 (2nd line). Coverage was widened in 1972.
[6] Including extension courses from 1962 (2nd line).
[7] Including Alaska and Hawaii from 1960. Coverage was widened in 1970.
[8] All higher education to 1965 (1st line). The figure for universities only in 1960 is 168 thousand.
[9] Numbers at the beginning of the academic year to 1933 (1st line), numbers still registered at the end of the year subsequently. Statistics relate to all undergraduates in higher education.
[10] Excluding Concepción University.
[11] Excluding the Catholic University.
[12] All higher education from 1974 (2nd line).
[13] Coverage was widened in 1971.
[14] All higher education

# J.  NATIONAL ACCOUNTS

Whilst it has been the general principle in most sections of this work to prefer raw data to those which have been processed, there are no such things as raw national accounts statistics, and everything in this section is 'synthetic', the result of elaborate calculations by sophisticated statisticians. It is really impossible to summarize briefly all the complex operations involved, and the user who requires descriptions of them is advised to consult the latest United Nations *Yearbook of National Accounts Statistics,* or, for more detail, their *National Accounting Practices in Sixty Countries*, and the International Monetary Fund *Balance of Payments Yearbook.*

Whilst interest in the nation's wealth and income can be traced in a number of European countries as far back as the later middle ages, and in some of the countries of America back far into the 19th century, the modern national accounts concepts date from the period of World War II (though what is essentially one of the component concepts, the balance of payments, became operational during the inter-war years for most of the larger countries in the region). Since then a great deal of work has been done in many countries not only to improve the concepts and the collection of current statistical material with which to clothe them, but also to produce retrospective estimates, going back to its foundations in the case of the United States, and well into the 19th century for Canada. There are also reasonably lengthy retrospective series for Argentina, Chile, Cuba, and Mexico.

Two main concepts of overall product were used for table J1. Net National Product (or National Income) was the first concept to be much used, and is characteristic of most estimates made before 1948, though not of more recent retrospective exercises. It relates to the disposable income of individuals, institutions, and governments, after providing for the maintenance and depreciation of capital stocks. Gross Domestic Product (or, occasionally, Gross National Product, which takes into account net factor income to or from aboard) is the other main concept used, and includes depreciation and maintenance outlays. It has been preferred where a choice exists. Both concepts can be expressed in terms of either market prices or factor costs, the latter excluding the excess of indirect taxes over subsidies. In most cases market prices have been preferred here. In the case of Cuba since 1962 the concept of Gross Material Product is used. Unlike most centrally-planned economies in Europe, the Cubans have included in this so-called 'unproductive' services, so that their concept is not so very far removed from the Gross Domestic Product of market economies.

It is worth remembering, in making comparisons both over time and between countries, that few national product concepts include 'income in kind', amongst which are the rental value of owner-occupied buildings and the consumption of home-produced goods (including farmers' consumption of their own products). These have tended to be proportionally more important the less developed is a country's economy and the more dependent it is on agriculture, and as development occurs they become increasingly less significant, and in so doing may give an exaggerated picture of rising economic growth. Another warning is in order in relation to the constant price series. Aside from technical problems associated with price index numbers, it is impossible in practice to reflect completely the changes which take place in the quality of goods having the same designation. These changes may be either improvements or deteriorations, but it seems to be generally accepted that the former predominate on balance.

Table J2 takes Gross Domestic Product as its base, where possible, and shows estimates of the proportion contributed by each of the major sectors of the different economies. Once again, it is necessary to be cautious in making comparisons between countries, owing to differences in definitions and sometimes in concept.

The modern balance of payments concepts grew out of the disruptions of international trading relations that became evident quite early in the inter-war years. However, it was only the more developed countries for which more than occasional benchmark estimates were made during these years, and it is the United States for which long retrospective series have been estimated subsequently. For the great majority of the smaller economies, balance of payments statistics begin on a continuous basis only in 1946.

Table J3 shows rather more of the components of these estimates than in the first edition, in particular including some detail on invisibles, net movements of capital, and international reserves. For the last four decades, balances of payments are available in a uniform basis for most countries thanks to the work of International Monetary Fund statisticians, and these have been preferred generally in the second part of the table to national statistics because they facilitate comparisons. Statistics on national definitions, continuing those in the first part of the table, are generally available in national sources.

**J1      NORTH AMERICA: NATIONAL ACCOUNTS TOTALS** (in millions of stated unit, except as otherwise indicated)

Key:-   GDP = gross domestic product; GNP = gross national product; NNP = net national product (national income); G(PF)CF = gross (private fixed) capital formation; NMP = net material product

### 1789–1824

| | USA (dollars) | |
| --- | --- | --- |
| | Current Prices | 1929 Prices |
| | GNP | GNP |
| 1789 | 158 | 307 |
| 1790 | 188 | 347 |
| 1791 | 199 | 373 |
| 1792 | 227 | 405 |
| 1793 | 239 | 409 |
| 1794 | 291 | 454 |
| 1795 | 352 | 469 |
| 1796 | 404 | 502 |
| 1797 | 397 | 539 |
| 1798 | 381 | 529 |
| 1799 | 421 | 575 |
| 1800 | 459 | 632 |
| 1801 | 528 | 683 |
| 1802 | 490 | 728 |
| 1803 | 488 | 727 |
| 1804 | 534 | 757 |
| 1805 | 592 | 778 |
| 1806 | 609 | 844 |
| 1807 | 564 | 803 |
| 1808 | 461 | 717 |
| 1809 | 502 | 720 |
| 1810 | 588 | 830 |
| 1811 | 580 | 841 |
| 1812 | 569 | 802 |
| 1813 | 623 | 761 |
| 1814 | 701 | 760 |
| 1815 | 812 | 888 |
| 1816 | 854 | 960 |
| 1817 | 847 | 972 |
| 1818 | 816 | 958 |
| 1819 | 754 | 1,036 |
| 1820 | 656 | 1,063 |
| 1821 | 607 | 1,059 |
| 1822 | 704 | 1,181 |
| 1823 | 699 | 1,232 |
| 1824 | 751 | 1,356 |

### 1825–1864

| | USA (dollars) | |
| --- | --- | --- |
| | Current Prices | 1929 Prices |
| | GNP | GNP |
| 1825 | 850 | 1,425 |
| 1826 | 884 | 1,633 |
| 1827 | 868 | 1,648 |
| 1828 | 881 | 1,685 |
| 1829 | 905 | 1,744 |
| 1830 | 933 | 1,861 |
| 1831 | 1,073 | 2,121 |
| 1832 | 1,155 | 2,231 |
| 1833 | 1,298 | 2,431 |
| 1834 | 1,333 | 2,568 |
| 1835 | 1,633 | 2,796 |
| 1836 | 1,896 | 2,949 |
| 1837 | 1,830 | 3,025 |
| 1838 | 1,758 | 2,990 |
| 1839 | 1,932 | 3,167 |
| 1840 | 1,672 | 3,215 |
| 1841 | 1,658 | 3,254 |
| 1842 | 1,517 | 3,319 |
| 1843 | 1,468 | 3,406 |
| 1844 | 1,629 | 3,669 |
| 1845 | 1,786 | 3,874 |
| 1846 | 1,911 | 4,119 |
| 1847 | 2,180 | 4,283 |
| 1848 | 2,139 | 4,796 |
| 1849 | 2,205 | 4,793 |
| 1850 | 2,586 | 5,162 |
| 1851 | 2,674 | 5,548 |
| 1852 | 2,864 | 5,881 |
| 1853 | 3,363 | 6,418 |
| 1854 | 3,625 | 6,532 |
| 1855 | 3,891 | 6,640 |
| 1856 | 4,022 | 6,863 |
| 1857 | 3,977 | 6,353 |
| 1858 | 3,716 | 6,946 |
| 1859 | 3,972 | 7,235 |
| 1860 | 3,839 | 7,096 |
| 1861 | 3,677 | 6,613 |
| 1862 | 4,012 | 6,368 |
| 1863 | 5,096 | 6,542 |
| 1864 | 6,479 | 5,960 |

**J1** **NORTH AMERICA: National Accounts Totals** (in millions of stated unit, except as otherwise indicated)

| | Canada | | | | Cuba | | Mexico | USA | |
|---|---|---|---|---|---|---|---|---|---|
| | (dollars) | | | | (pesos) | | (pesos) | (thousand million dollars) | |
| | Current prices | | 1935–39 Prices | | Current Prices | 1926 Prices | 1950 Prices | Current Prices | 1929 Prices |
| | GNP | GPFCF[1] | GNP[2] | GPFCF[1] | NNP | NNP | GNP | GNP | GNP |
| 1865 | ... | ... | ... | ... | ... | ... | ... | 6.56 | 6.30 |
| 1866 | ... | ... | ... | ... | ... | ... | ... | 6.88 | 7.02 |
| 1867 | 419 | ... | 695 | ... | ... | ... | ... | 6.84 | 7.47 |
| 1868 | ... | ... | ... | ... | ... | ... | ... | 7.06 | 7.93 |
| 1869 | ... | ... | ... | ... | ... | ... | ... | 7.41 | 8.71 |
| 1870 | 458 | 54 | 747[2] | 100 | ... | ... | ... | 7.35 | 9.63 |
| 1871 | ... | ... | 769 | ... | ... | ... | ... | 7.55 | 10.29 |
| 1872 | ... | ... | 645 | ... | ... | ... | ... | 8.52 | 11.00 |
| 1873 | ... | ... | 710 | ... | ... | ... | ... | 8.79 | 11.74 |
| 1874 | ... | ... | 855 | ... | ... | ... | ... | 8.54 | 11.97 |
| 1875 | ... | ... | 827 | ... | ... | ... | ... | 8.22 | 12.07 |
| 1876 | ... | ... | 833 | ... | ... | ... | ... | 7.91 | 12.47 |
| 1877 | ... | ... | 855 | ... | ... | ... | ... | 8.08 | 13.01 |
| 1878 | ... | ... | 843 | ... | ... | ... | ... | 8.02 | 14.77 |
| 1879 | ... | ... | 985 | ... | ... | ... | ... | 8.81 | 16.43 |
| 1880 | 612 | ... | 1,096[2] | ... | ... | ... | ... | 10.51 | 17.94 |
| 1881 | ... | ... | 1,247 | ... | ... | ... | ... | 11.27 | 18.97 |
| 1882 | ... | ... | 1,238 | ... | ... | ... | ... | 12.16 | 17.72 |
| 1883 | ... | ... | 1,216 | ... | ... | ... | ... | 11.55 | 20.02 |
| 1884 | ... | ... | 1,337 | ... | ... | ... | ... | 10.97 | 20.24 |
| 1885 | ... | ... | 1,482 | ... | ... | ... | ... | 10.64 | 20.95 |
| 1886 | ... | ... | 1,337 | ... | ... | ... | ... | 10.93 | 22.17 |
| 1887 | ... | ... | 1,340 | ... | ... | ... | ... | 12.00 | 23.58 |
| 1888 | ... | ... | 1,408 | ... | ... | ... | ... | 12.42 | 24.02 |
| 1889 | ... | ... | 1,374 | ... | ... | ... | ... | 12.97 [3] | 26.10 [3] |
| | | | | | | | | 12.5 | 1958 prices |
| | | | | | | | | | 49.1 |
| 1890 | 815 | 113 | 1,408[2] | 210 | ... | ... | ... | 13.1 | 52.7 |
| 1891 | ... | ... | 1,642 | ... | ... | ... | ... | 13.5 | 55.1 |
| 1892 | ... | ... | 1,605 | ... | ... | ... | ... | 14.3 | 60.4 |
| 1893 | ... | ... | 1,562 | ... | ... | ... | ... | 13.8 | 57.5 |
| 1894 | ... | ... | 1,553 | ... | ... | ... | ... | 12.6 | 55.9 |
| 1895 | ... | ... | 1,636 | ... | ... | ... | 8,863 | 13.9 | 62.6 |
| 1896 | ... | ... | 1,794 | ... | ... | ... | 9,137 | 13.3 | 61.3 |
| 1897 | ... | ... | 1,559 | ... | ... | ... | 9,750 | 14.6 | 67.1 |
| 1898 | ... | ... | 1,846 | ... | ... | ... | 10,318 | 15.4 | 68.6 |
| 1899 | ... | ... | 1,769 | ... | ... | ... | 9,814 | 17.4 | 74.8 |
| 1900 | 1,032 | 126 | 1,849[2] | 227 | ... | ... | 9,891 | 18.7 | 76.9 |
| 1901 | ... | ... | 2,031 | ... | ... | ... | 10,741 | 20.7 | 85.7 |
| 1902 | ... | ... | 2,179 | ... | ... | ... | 9,975 | 21.6 | 86.5 |
| 1903 | ... | ... | 2,244 | ... | 193 | 324 | 11,092 | 22.9 | 90.8 |
| 1904 | ... | ... | 2,284 | ... | 222 | 372 | 11,287 | 22.9 | 89.7 |
| 1905 | ... | ... | 2,457 | ... | 264 | 439 | 12,460 | 25.1 | 96.3 |
| 1906 | ... | ... | 2,599 | ... | 249 | 403 | 12,319 | 28.7 | 107.5 |
| 1907 | ... | ... | 2,612 | ... | 250 | 383 | 13,042 | 30.4 | 109.2 |
| 1908 | ... | ... | 2,723 | ... | 238 | 378 | 13,022 | 27.7 | 100.2 |
| 1909 | ... | ... | 3,031 | ... | 300 | 444 | 13,405 | 33.4 | 116.8 |

**J1**    **NORTH AMERICA: National Accounts Totals** (in millions of stated unit, except as otherwise indicated)

| | Canada (dollars) | | | | | | Cuba (pesos) | | El Salvador (colones) | Guatemala[5] (quetzales) | | | |
| | Current Prices | | | 1935/1971 Prices[4] | | | Current Prices | 1926 Prices | Current Prices | Current Prices | | 1946 Prices | |
| | GNP | GPFCF[1] | Stocks | GNP[2] | GPFCF[1] | Stocks | NNP | NNP | GNP | GNP | GCF[5] | GNP | GCF[5] |
|---|---|---|---|---|---|---|---|---|---|---|---|---|---|
| 1910 | 2,138 | 389 | ... | 3,087[2] | 610 | ... | 347 | 493 | ... | ... | ... | ... | ... |
| 1911 | ... | ... | ... | 3,355 | ... | ... | 295 | 455 | ... | ... | ... | ... | ... |
| 1912 | ... | ... | ... | 3,419 | ... | ... | 397 | 575 | ... | ... | ... | ... | ... |
| 1913 | ... | ... | ... | 3,708 | ... | ... | 379 | 543 | ... | ... | ... | ... | ... |
| 1914 | ... | ... | ... | 3,483 | ... | ... | 400 | 587 | ... | ... | ... | ... | ... |
| 1915 | ... | ... | ... | 3,591 | ... | ... | 519 | 747 | ... | ... | ... | ... | ... |
| 1916 | ... | ... | ... | 3,749 | ... | ... | 644 | 753 | ... | ... | ... | ... | ... |
| 1917 | ... | ... | ... | 3,831 | ... | ... | 678 | 577 | ... | ... | ... | ... | ... |
| 1918 | ... | ... | ... | 3,864 | ... | ... | 734 | 577 | ... | ... | ... | ... | ... |
| 1919 | ... | ... | ... | 4,046 | ... | ... | 862 | 622 | ... | ... | ... | ... | ... |
| 1920 | 5,543 | 1,008 | ... | 3,8844[2] | 651 | ... | 1,191 | 771 | ... | ... | ... | ... | ... |
| 1921 | ... | ... | ... | 3,495 | ... | ... | 588 | 602 | ... | ... | ... | ... | ... |
| 1922 | ... | ... | ... | 3,780 | ... | ... | 656 | 678 | ... | ... | ... | ... | ... |
| 1923 | ... | ... | ... | 4,015 | ... | ... | 761 | 756 | ... | 93 | ... | ... | ... |
| 1924 | ... | ... | ... | 4,010 | ... | ... | 783 | 798 | ... | 127 | ... | ... | ... |
| 1925 | ... | ...——[1] | ... | 4,182 | ... | ... | 708 | 684 | ... | 162 | ... | ... | ... |
| 1926 | 5,146 | 814 | 135 | 4,548[4] / 14,086 | ...[4] / 2,619 | ...[4] / 399 | 604 | 604 | ... | 179 | ... | ... | ... |
| 1927 | 5,561 | 994 | 253 | 15,423 | 3,235 | 533 | 648 | 679 | ... | 174 | ... | ... | ... |
| 1928 | 6,050 | 1,195 | 159 | 16,831 | 3,845 | 390 | 604 | ... | ... | 201 | ... | ... | ... |
| 1929 | 6,139 | 1,361 | 52 | 16,894 | 4,254 | 311 | ... | ... | ... | 194 | ... | ... | ... |
| 1930 | 5,720 | 1,150 | 77 | 16,174 | 3,722 | 221 | 598 | ... | ... | 122 | ... | ... | ... |
| 1931 | 4,693 | 809 | −95 | 14,118 | 2,762 | −253 | ... | ... | ... | 100 | ... | ... | ... |
| 1932 | 3,814 | 432 | −100 | 12,654 | 1,532 | −306 | ... | ... | ... | 63 | ... | ... | ... |
| 1933 | 3,492 | 299 | −91 | 11,811 | 1,094 | −236 | 446 | ... | ... | 51 | ... | ... | ... |
| 1934 | 3,969 | 380 | 32 | 13,245 | 1,379 | 81 | ... | ... | ... | 65 | ... | ... | ... |
| 1935 | 4,301 | 458 | 39 | 14,279 | 1,645 | 152 | ... | ... | ... | 70 | ... | ... | ... |
| 1936 | 4,634 | 531 | −72 | 14,912 | 1,870 | 2 | 631 | ... | ... | 83 | ... | ... | ... |
| 1937 | 5,241 | 755 | 9 | 16,410 | 2,483 | 246 | ... | ... | ... | 104 | ... | ... | ... |
| 1938 | 5,272 | 717 | 57 | 16,545 | 2,371 | 154 | 468 | ... | ... | 127 | 12 | ... | ... |
| 1939 | 5,621 | 687 | 282 | 17,774 | 2,295 | 604 | 488 | ... | 244 | 120 | 10 | ... | ... |
| 1940 | 6,713 | 833 | 264 | 20,277 | 2,619 | 573 | 548 | ... | 229 | 103 | 6 | ... | ... |
| 1941 | 8,282 | 1,096 | 85 | 23,194 | 3,206 | 245 | 678 | ... | 232 | 108 | 6 | ... | ... |
| 1942 | 10,265 | 1,055 | 145 | 27,497 | 2,923 | −21 | 710 | ... | 279 | 111 | 6 | ... | ... |
| 1943 | 11,053 | 902 | −142 | 28,604 | 2,371 | −45 | 933 | ... | 398 | 132 | 4 | ... | ... |
| 1944 | 11,848 | 964 | −134 | 29,736 | 2,486 | −70 | 1,212 | ... | 435 | 153 | 6 | ... | ... |
| 1945 | 11,863 | 1,230 | −340 | 29,071 | 3,182 | −122 | 1,069 | ... | ... | 168 | 9 | ... | ... |
| 1946 | 11,885 | 1,682 | 195 | 28,292 | 4,207 | 420 | 1,247 | ... | ... | 254 | 16[5] / 25 | 254 | ...[5] / 25 |
| 1947 | 13,473 | 2,350 | 343 | 29,498 | 5,316 | 672 | 1,649 | ... | ... | 299 | 44 | 284 | 37 |
| 1948 | 15,509 | 3,057 | 97 | 30,231 | 6,103 | 109 | 1,602 | ... | ... | 429 | 51 | 376 | 30 |
| 1949 | 16,800 | 3,439 | 78 | 31,388 | 6,553 | 215 | 1,509 | ... | ... | 420 | 45 | 337 | 25 |

**J1**    **NORTH AMERICA: National Accounts Totals** (in millions of stated unit, except as otherwise indicated).

| | Haiti | Honduras | | | | | | Jamaica | Mexico | | | |
|---|---|---|---|---|---|---|---|---|---|---|---|---|
| | (gourdes) | (lempiras) | | | | | | (pounds) | (pesos) | | | |
| | 1970 prices[6] | Current prices | | | 1948 prices | | | Current prices | Current prices | | 1950 prices | 1960 prices |
| | GDP | GDP | GFCF | Stocks | GDP | GFCF | Stocks | NNP | GDP | GFCF | GNP | GDP |
| 1910 | ... | ... | ... | ... | ... | ... | ... | ... | ... | ... | 13,524 | ... |
| 1911 | ... | ... | ... | ... | ... | ... | ... | ... | ... | ... | ... | ... |
| 1912 | ... | ... | ... | ... | ... | ... | ... | ... | ... | ... | ... | ... |
| 1913 | ... | ... | ... | ... | ... | ... | ... | ... | ... | ... | ... | ... |
| 1914 | ... | ... | ... | ... | ... | ... | ... | ... | ... | ... | ... | ... |
| 1915 | ... | ... | ... | ... | ... | ... | ... | ... | ... | ... | ... | ... |
| 1916 | ... | ... | ... | ... | ... | ... | ... | ... | ... | ... | ... | ... |
| 1917 | ... | ... | ... | ... | ... | ... | ... | ... | ... | ... | ... | ... |
| 1918 | ... | ... | ... | ... | ... | ... | ... | ... | ... | ... | ... | ... |
| 1919 | ... | ... | ... | ... | ... | ... | ... | ... | ... | ... | ... | ... |
| 1920 | ... | ... | ... | ... | ... | ... | ... | ... | ... | ... | ... | ... |
| 1921 | ... | ... | ... | ... | ... | ... | ... | ... | ... | ... | 14,560 | ... |
| 1922 | ... | ... | ... | ... | ... | ... | ... | ... | ... | ... | 14,899 | ... |
| 1923 | ... | ... | ... | ... | ... | ... | ... | ... | ... | ... | 15,411 | ... |
| 1924 | ... | ... | ... | ... | ... | ... | ... | ... | ... | ... | 15,159 | ... |
| 1925 | ... | 150 | 8.4 | 1.6 | 240 | 12 | 2.2 | ... | 4,937 | ... | 16,102 | 37,402 |
| 1926 | ... | 154 | 8.8 | 1.6 | 242 | 12 | 2.2 | ... | 5,154 | ... | 17,335 | 39,646 |
| 1927 | ... | 164 | 9.7 | 1.2 | 265 | 14 | 1.8 | ... | 4,700 | ... | 16,932 | 37,902 |
| 1928 | ... | 181 | 12 | 1.5 | 298 | 17 | 2.5 | ... | 4,729 | ... | 17,240 | 38,137 |
| 1929 | ... | 185 | 16 | 2.2 | 297 | 22 | 3.6 | 18.7 | 4,583 | ... | 16,666 | 36,662 |
| 1930 | ... | 182 | 15 | 2.3 | 315 | 22 | 4.1 | 18.6 | 4,399 | ... | 15,538 | 34,364 |
| 1931 | ... | 170 | 10 | 0.8 | 318 | 15 | 1.7 | 17.9 | 3,976 | ... | 16,106 | 35,503 |
| 1932 | ... | 155 | 7.1 | −0.4 | 285 | 11 | −1.1 | 16.7 | 3,021 | ... | 13,494 | 30,207 |
| 1933 | ... | 160 | 6.8 | 1.6 | 269 | 12 | 3.6 | 16.4 | 3,564 | ... | 14,943 | 33,620 |
| 1934 | ... | 165 | 9.0 | 0.1 | 262 | 14 | — | 16.1 | 3,912 | ... | 15,927 | 35,889 |
| 1935 | ... | 165 | 13 | 2.8 | 250 | 21 | 5.7 | 16.7 | 4,279 | ... | 17,039 | 38,549 |
| 1936 | ... | 157 | 12 | 0.8 | 255 | 18 | 1.4 | 16.9 | 5,038 | ... | 18,491 | 41,663 |
| 1937 | ... | 153 | 13 | 2.2 | 244 | 20 | 4.0 | 18.7 | 6,409 | ... | 19,120 | 43,011 |
| 1938 | ... | 162 | 13 | 1.3 | 257 | 20 | 2.5 | 19.6 | 6,862 | ... | 19,473 | 43,708 |
| 1939 | ... | 173 | ... | 1.5 | 265 | 20 | 2.9 | ... | 7,337 | 649 | 20,505 | 46,058 |
| 1940 | ... | 187 | 15 | 0.9 | 281 | 22 | 1.5 | ... | 7,774 | 773 | 20,721 | 46,693 |
| 1941 | ... | 189 | 16 | 2.8 | 281 | 22 | 4.5 | ... | 8,701 | 970 | 23,289 | 51,241 |
| 1942 | ... | 205 | 10 | 2.6 | 257 | 14 | 3.8 | 33.3 | 10,066 | 1,005 | 26,373 | 54,116 |
| 1943 | ... | 209 | 14 | 0.9 | 257 | 18 | 1.4 | 40.5 | 12,285 | 1,277 | 27,358 | 56,120 |
| 1944 | ... | 244 | 16 | 3.8 | 295 | 20 | 4.9 | ... | 17,719 | 1,730 | 29,690 | 60,701 |
| 1945 | 1,503 | 274 | 22 | 3.6 | 323 | 29 | 5.2 | ... | 19,382 | 2,276 | 31,959 | 62,608 |
| 1946 | 1,516 | 315 | 34 | 9.0 | 350 | 40 | 11 | 64 | 26,322 | 3,261 | 34,064 | 66,722 |
| 1947 | 1,541 | 362 | 41 | 11 | 375 | 43 | 12 | ... | 29,237 | 4,104 | 34,517 | 69,020 |
| 1948 | 1,557 | 384 | 42 | 6.2 | 384 | 42 | 6.2 | ... | 31,196 | 4,552 | 36,080 | 71,864 |
| 1949 | 1,573 | 416 | 47 | 8.7 | 390 | 47 | 9.0 | ... | 34,316 | 5,117 | 37,627 | 75,803 |

**J1      NORTH AMERICA: National Accounts Totals** (in millions of stated unit, except as otherwise indicated)

| | Nicaragua | | Panama | | | | | Puerto Rico[8] | | |
|---|---|---|---|---|---|---|---|---|---|---|
| | (cordobas) 1958 Prices | | (balboas) Current Prices | | | 1950 Prices | | (dollars) Current Prices | | |
| | GDP | GFCF | GDP | GFCF | Stocks | GDP | GFCF | NNP/GNP[9] | GFCF | Stocks |
| 1929 | ... | ... | ... | ... | ... | ... | ... | 189 | ... | ... |
| 1930 | ... | ... | ... | ... | ... | ... | ... | 169 | ... | ... |
| 1931 | ... | ... | ... | ... | ... | ... | ... | 156 | ... | ... |
| 1932 | ... | ... | ... | ... | ... | ... | ... | 140 | ... | ... |
| 1933 | ... | ... | ... | ... | ... | ... | ... | 179 | ... | ... |
| 1934 | ... | ... | ... | ... | ... | ... | ... | 177 | ... | ... |
| 1935 | ... | ... | ... | ... | ... | ... | ... | 199 | ... | ... |
| 1936 | ... | ... | ... | ... | ... | ... | ... | 210 | ... | ... |
| 1937 | ... | ... | ... | ... | ... | ... | ... | 217 | ... | ... |
| 1938 | ... | ... | ... | ... | ... | ... | ... | 207 | ... | ... |
| 1939 | ... | ... | ... | ... | ... | ... | ... | 228 | 24 | 6 |
| 1940 | ... | ... | ... | ... | ... | ... | ... | 278 | 34 | |
| 1941 | ... | ... | ... | ... | ... | ... | ... | 359 | 59 | |
| 1942 | ... | ... | ... | ... | ... | ... | ... | 435 | 22 | |
| 1943 | ... | ... | ... | ... | ... | ... | ... | 477 | 18 | |
| 1944 | ... | ... | ... | ... | ... | ... | ... | 564 | 46 | |
| 1945 | 1,128 | 143 | ... | ... | ... | 265 | 36 | 587 | 43 | |
| 1946 | 1,225 | 179 | 229 | 28 | −8 | 269[7] | 42[7] | 612[9] | 68 | 31 |
| | | | | | | 254 | 39 | 733 | | |
| 1947 | 1,229 | 218 | 258 | 44 | 14 | 265 | 47 | 743 | 102 | 5 |
| 1948 | 1,336 | 184 | 257 | 35 | −5 | 249 | 33 | 771 | 110 | 2 |
| 1949 | 1,312 | 205 | 260[7] | 32[7] | 4[7] | 255[7] | 30[7] | 773 | 100 | −8 |

**J1    NORTH AMERICA: National Accounts Totals** (in millions of stated unit, except as otherwise indicated)

| | USA (thousand million dollars) | | | | | |
|---|---|---|---|---|---|---|
| | Current Prices | | | 1958/1982 Prices[11] | | |
| | GNP | GPFCF | Stocks | GNP | GPFCF | Stocks |
| 1910 | 35.3 | ... | ... | 120.1 | ... | ... |
| 1911 | 35.8 | ... | ... | 123.2 | ... | ... |
| 1912 | 39.4 | ... | ... | 130.2 | ... | ... |
| 1913 | 39.6 | ... | ... | 131.4 | ... | ... |
| 1914 | 38.6 | ... | ... | 125.6 | ... | ... |
| 1915 | 40.0 | ... | ... | 124.5 | ... | ... |
| 1916 | 48.3 | ... | ... | 134.3 | ... | ... |
| 1917 | 60.4 | ... | ... | 135.2 | ... | ... |
| 1918 | 76.4 | ... | ... | 151.8 | ... | ... |
| 1919 | 84.0 | ... | ... | 146.4 | ... | ... |
| 1920 | 91.5 | ... | ... | 140.0 | ... | ... |
| 1921 | 69.6 | ... | ... | 127.8 | ... | ... |
| 1922 | 74.1 | ... | ... | 148.0 | ... | ... |
| 1923 | 85.1 | ... | ... | 165.9 | ... | ... |
| 1924 | 84.7 | ... | ... | 165.5 | ... | ... |
| 1925 | 93.1 | ... | ... | 179.4 | ... | ... |
| 1926 | 97.0 | ... | ... | 190.0 | ... | ... |
| 1927 | 94.9 | ... | ... | 189.8 | ... | ... |
| 1928 | 97.0[10] | ... | ... | 190.9 | ... | ... |
| 1929 | 103.9 | 15.0 | 1.7 | 203.6 | ... | ... |
| | | | | 709.6 | 128.4 | 10.8 |
| 1930 | 91.2 | 11.0 | −0.4 | 643.5 | 98.4 | −0.9 |
| 1931 | 76.4 | 7.0 | −1.1 | 588.1 | 67.3 | −7.1 |
| 1932 | 58.5 | 3.6 | −2.5 | 509.2 | 39.0 | −16.4 |
| 1933 | 56.0 | 3.2 | −1.6 | 498.5 | 33.4 | −10.7 |
| 1934 | 65.6 | 4.2 | −0.7 | 536.7 | 42.9 | −7.6 |
| 1935 | 72.8 | 5.5 | 1.1 | 580.2 | 54.7 | 6.2 |
| 1936 | 83.1 | 7.4 | 1.3 | 662.2 | 73.1 | 9.0 |
| 1937 | 91.3 | 9.6 | 2.5 | 695.3 | 85.8 | 14.1 |
| 1938 | 85.4 | 7.6 | −0.9 | 664.2 | 69.1 | −6.0 |
| 1939 | 91.3 | 9.1 | 0.4 | 716.6 | 82.1 | 3.9 |
| 1940 | 100.4 | 11.2 | 2.2 | 772.9 | 97.4 | 14.4 |
| 1941 | 125.5 | 13.8 | 4.5 | 909.4 | 111.0 | 27.8 |
| 1942 | 159.0 | 8.5 | 1.8 | 1,080.3 | 69.0 | 12.0 |
| 1943 | 192.7 | 6.8 | −0.6 | 1,276.2 | 49.7 | 0.7 |
| 1944 | 211.4 | 8.7 | −1.0 | 1,380.6 | 61.6 | −5.2 |
| 1945 | 213.4 | 12.3 | −1.0 | 1,354.8 | 84.9 | −8.4 |
| 1946 | 212.4 | 25.1 | 6.4 | 1,096.9 | 150.2 | 27.9 |
| 1947 | 235.2 | 34.5 | −0.5 | 1,066.7 | 178.9 | −1.0 |
| 1948 | 261.6 | 42.4 | 4.7 | 1,108.7 | 195.9 | 12.3 |
| 1949 | 260.4 | 39.6 | −3.1 | 1,109.0 | 178.5 | −9.7 |

## J1　NORTH AMERICA: National Accounts Totals (in millions of stated unit, except as otherwise indicated)

| | Canada | | | | | | Costa Rica | | | | | |
|---|---|---|---|---|---|---|---|---|---|---|---|---|
| | (thousand million dollars) | | | | | | (colones) | | | | | |
| | Current Prices | | | 1971/1981 Prices[12] | | | Current Prices | | | 1966 Prices | | |
| | GNP | GFCF | Stocks | GNP | GFCF | Stocks | GDP | GFCF | Stocks | GDP | GFCF | Stocks |
| 1950 | 18.49 | 3.86 | 0.55 | 33.76 | 7.04 | 0.79 | 1,348 | 222 | 12 | ... | ... | ... |
| 1951 | 21.64 | 4.42 | 0.87 | 35.45 | 7.07 | 1.02 | 1,462 | 243 | 14 | ... | ... | ... |
| 1952 | 24.59 | 5.10 | 0.55 | 38.62 | 7.89 | 0.48 | 1,709 | 297 | 21 | ... | ... | ... |
| 1953 | 25.83 | 5.73 | 0.60 | 40.60 | 8.86 | 0.75 | 1,877 | 318 | 14 | ... | ... | ... |
| 1954 | 25.92 | 5.71 | −0.06 | 40.11 | 8.86 | −0.24 | 2,039 | 314 | 15 | ... | ... | ... |
| 1955 | 28.53 | 6.42 | 0.29 | 43.89 | 9.68 | 0.41 | 2,225 | 362 | 22 | ... | ... | ... |
| 1956 | 32.06 | 8.00 | 0.98 | 47.60 | 11.45 | 1.14 | 2,292 | 403 [7] | 22 [7] | ... | ... | ... |
| 1957 | 33.51 | 8.69 | 0.17 | 48.72 | 12.26 | 0.25 | 2,500 | 409 | 61 | ... | ... | ... |
| 1958 | 34.78 | 8.54 | −0.30 | 49.84 | 12.13 | −0.28 | 2,609 | 431 | 6 | ... | ... | ... |
| 1959 | 36.85 | 8.65 | 0.41 | 51.74 | 12.19 | 0.47 | 2,679 | 450 | 52 | ... | ... | ... |
| 1960 | 38.36 | 8.47 | 0.41 | 53.23 | 11.79 | 0.52 | 2,861 | 460 | 40 | 3,096 | ... | ... |
| 1961 | 40.16 | 8.39 [10] / 8.76 | 0.11 | 54.74 [10] / 55.45 | 11.75 [10] / 12.26 | 0.25 | 2,929 | 504 | 49 | 3,067 | ... | ... |
| 1962 | 43.64 | 9.26 | 0.67 | 59.45 | 12.80 | 0.76 | 3,187 | 591 | 29 | 3,317 | ... | ... |
| 1963 | 46.83 | 9.95 | 0.72 | 62.63 | 13.37 | 0.76 | 3,404 | 621 | 19 | 3,476 | ... | ... |
| 1964 | 51.28 | 11.67 | 0.59 | 66.89 | 15.15 | 0.65 | 3,608 | 591 | −14 | 3,620 | ... | ... |
| 1965 | 56.53 | 13.67 | 1.30 | 71.45 | 16.86 | 1.44 | 3,929 | 730 | 37 | 3,976 | ... | ... |
| 1966 | 63.27 | 15.92 | 1.28 | 76.59 | 18.67 | 1.38 | 4,288 | 736 | 81 | 4,288 | 736 | 81 |
| 1967 | 67.82 | 16.25 | 0.21 | 78.99 | 18.66 | 0.25 | 4,634 | 834 | 63 | 4,531 | 810 | 62 |
| 1968 | 74.20 | 16.49 | 0.74 | 83.68 | 18.80 | 0.77 | 5,127 | 882 | 42 | 4,915 | 822 | 36 |
| 1969 | 81.82 | 18.14 | 1.48 | 88.39 | 19.84 | 1.52 | 5,565 | 1,024 | 109 | 5,184 | 899 | 91 |
| 1970 | 87.77 | 19.01 | 0.24 | 90.54 | 19.95 | 0.08 | 6,525 | 1,270 | 70 | 5,574 | 1,078 | 51 |
| 1971 | 95.78 | 21.57 | 0.37 | 95.78 | 21.57 | 0.37 | 7,137 | 1,579 | 158 | 5,951 | 1,254 | 145 |
| 1972 | 107.2 | 23.88 | 0.78 | 102.1 | 22.74 | 0.74 | 8,216 | 1,800 | 10 | 6,438 | 1,313 | −16 |
| 1973 | 125.6 | 28.86 | 1.86 | 109.6 | 25.27 | 1.58 | 10,162 | 2,252 | 187 | 6,934 | 1,424 | 115 |
| 1974 | 149.9 | 35.78 | 3.59 | 113.5 | 26.83 | 2.75 | 13,216 | 3,175 | 359 | 7,319 | 1,563 | 108 |
| 1975 | 169.0 | 41.85 | 1.37 | 115.5 [12] / 279.4 | 27.86 [12] / 59.04 | 0.68 [12] / 2.50 | 16,805 | 3,695 | −58 | 7,473 | 1,544 | −21 |
| 1976 | 194.4 | 46.71 | 2.33 | 295.6 | 61.64 | 4.23 | 20,676 | 4,846 | 46 | 7,885 | 1,910 | 17 |
| 1977 | 213.3 | 50.23 | 1.86 | 305.2 | 62.91 | 3.16 | 26,331 | 5,889 | 502 | 8,587 | 2,147 | 218 |
| 1978 | 235.6 | 54.58 | 1.05 | 317.9 | 64.79 | 1.82 | 30,194 | 6,952 | 132 | 9,125 | 2,322 | 34 |
| 1979 | 268.9 | 63.44 | 4.99 | 329.5 | 70.14 | 6.90 | 34,584 | 9,050 | −295 | 9,576 | 2,677 | −104 |
| | | | | | | | (thousand million colones) | | | | | |
| 1980 | 302.1 | 72.29 | 0.34 | 334.6 | 77.13 | 0.33 | 41.41 | 9.89 | 1.11 | 9.65 | 2.42 | 0.33 |
| 1981 | 344.7 | 86.12 | 1.19 | 344.7 | 86.12 | 1.19 | 57.10 | 13.74 | 2.84 | 9.43 | 1.82 | −0.11 |
| 1982 | 361.8 | 81.33 | −9.75 | 332.9 | 76.65 | −9.14 | 97.50 | 19.81 | 4.26 | 8.74 | 1.31 | −0.04 |
| 1983 | 394.1 | 81.23 | −2.85 | 345.9 | 76.11 | −2.49 | 126.3 | 23.06 | 8.00 | 8.99 | 1.42 | 0.28 |
| 1984 | 431.2 | 84.70 | 4.74 | 366.9 | 77.73 | 3.90 | 163.0 | 32.68 | 4.32 | 9.71 | 1.79 | 0.09 |
| 1985 | 463.7 | 94.20 | 2.35 | 384.5 | 85.08 | 2.59 | 197.9 | 38.24 | 13.00 | 9.78 | 1.89 | 0.14 |
| 1986 | 489.3 | 101.6 | 2.59 | 396.3 | 90.12 | 3.05 | 246.6 | 46.02 | 16.14 | 10.33 | 2.12 | 0.54 |
| 1987 | 535.2 | 116.2 | 2.76 | 415.5 | 101.3 | 1.90 | 284.5 | 56.31 | 24.49 | 10.83 | 2.33 | 0.41 |
| 1988 | 584.5 | 131.5 | 2.42 | 435.9 | 113.7 | 1.34 | 349.7 | 66.21 | 25.28 | 10.99 | 2.26 | 0.24 |

**J1 NORTH AMERICA: National Accounts Totals** (in millions of stated unit, except as otherwise indicated)

| | Cuba | | | | | | Dominican Republic | | | | | |
|---|---|---|---|---|---|---|---|---|---|---|---|---|
| | (pesos) | | | | | | (pesos) | | | | | |
| | Current Prices | | | 1965/1981 Prices[15] | | | Current Prices | | | 1970 Prices | | |
| | NNP/GDP/ NMP[13] | GFCF/ NFCF[14] | Stocks | GDP/ GMP[13] | CF | Stocks | GDP | GFCF | Stocks | GDP | GFCF | Stocks |
| 1950 | 1,692[13] 1,992 | ... | ... | ... | ... | ... | 399 | 37 | ... | 538 | 61 | ... |
| 1951 | 2,392 | 308 | −1 | ... | ... | ... | 485 | 51 | ... | 602 | 69 | ... |
| 1952 | 2,474 | 310 | 138 | ... | ... | ... | 522 | 100 | ... | 650 | 125 | ... |
| 1953 | 2,131 | 240 | −49 | ... | ... | ... | 519 | 87 | ... | 642 | 106 | ... |
| 1954 | 2,170 | 274 | 61 | ... | ... | ... | 546 | 83 | ... | 679 | 100 | ... |
| 1955 | 2,269 | 372 | −24 | ... | ... | ... | 564 | 104 | ... | 721 | 128 | ... |
| 1956 | 2,478 | 469 | −69 | ... | ... | ... | 633 | 124 | ... | 794 | 139 | ... |
| 1957 | 2,835 | 506 | 8 | ... | ... | ... | 714 | 129 | ... | 844 | 148 | ... |
| 1958 | 2,604 | 461 | 4 | ... | ... | ... | 746 | 142 | ... | 888 | 156 | ... |
| 1959 | ... | ... | ... | ... | ... | ... | 696 | 116 | ... | 894 | 116 | ... |
| 1960 | ... | ... | ... | ... | ... | ... | 732 | 75 | 20 | 915 | 75 | 33 |
| 1961 | ...[13] | ...[14] | ...[7] | ... | ... | ... | 694 | 60 | 3 | 872 | 64 | 6 |
| 1962 | 3,021 | 572 | 220 | ... | ... | ... | 880 | 97 | 7 | 1,028 | 110 | 14 |
| 1963 | 3,450 | 696 | 231 | 3,737 | 733 | 249 | 1,009 | 139 | 18 | 1,010 | 147 | 27 |
| 1964 | 4,075 | 210 | 419 | ... | ... | ... | 1,123 | 188 | 17 | 1,140 | 197 | 24 |
| 1965 | 4,138 | 842 | 105 | 4,138 | 842 | 105 | 954 | 87 | −2 | 1,031 | 92 | −5 |
| 1966 | 3,986 | 935 | 113 | ... | ... | ... | 1,074 | 156 | 15 | 1,184 | 164 | 18 |
| 1967 | 4,083 | 1,032 | 103 | ... | ... | ... | 1,122 | 161 | 7 | 1,217 | 167 | 13 |
| 1968 | 4,377 | 918 | 102 | ... | ... | ... | 1,149 | 166 | −5 | 1,201 | 169 | −10 |
| 1969 | 4,181 | 896 | 158 | ... | ... | ... | 1,345 | 220 | 31 | 1,384 | 223 | 46 |
| 1970 | 4,204 | 668[14] | ... | ... | ... | ... | 1,486 | 245 | 38 | 1,486 | 245 | 38 |
| 1971 | 4,617 | ... | ... | ... | ... | ... | 1,667 | 294 | 4 | 1,647 | 329 | 4 |
| 1972 | 5,472 | 261 | −190 | ... | ... | ... | 1,987 | 427 | −35 | 1,818 | 391 | −17 |
| 1973 | 6,565 | 621 | 241 | ... | ... | ... | 2,345 | 498 | 20 | 2,053 | 464 | 11 |
| 1974 | 7,302 | 774 | 392 | ...[15] | ...[15] | ...[15] | 2,931 | 644 | 39 | 2,176 | 509 | 57 |
| 1975 | 8,113 | 1,348 | 734 | 8,204 | 1,439 | 791 | 3,599 | 803 | 79 | 2,289 | 572 | 40 |
| 1976 | 8,356 | 1,600 | 578 | 8,618 | 1,686 | 623 | 3,952 | 780 | 101 | 2,443 | 526 | 46 |
| 1977 | 8,413 | 1,716 | 613 | 9,336 | 1,804 | 661 | 4,587 | 939 | 60 | 2,564 | 578 | 41 |
| 1978 | 9,466 | 1,463 | 695 | 9,986 | 1,537 | 749 | 4,734 | 1,032 | 98 | 2,619 | 575 | 61 |
| 1979 | 9,621 | 1,432 | 484 | 10,051 | 1,507 | 522 | 5,499 | 1,335 | 59 | 2,738 | 653 | 34 |
| 1980 | 9,853 | 1,529 | 577 | 9,523 | 1,615 | 622 | 6,631 | 1,584 | 82 | 2,904 | 683 | 52 |
| 1981 | 11,503 | 2,247 | 711 | 11,503 | 2,247 | 711 | 7,267 | 1,655 | 61 | 3,022 | 624 | 31 |
| 1982 | 12,175 | 1,812 | 601 | 12,087 | 1,812 | 573 | 7,964 | 1,491 | 99 | 3,069 | 543 | 51 |
| 1983 | 12,926 | 2,243 | 553 | 12,745 | 2,243 | 536 | 8,623 | 1,754 | 62 | 3,209 | 629 | 35 |
| 1984 | 13,695 | 2,895 | 590 | 13,696 | 2,895 | 560 | 10,355 | 2,169 | 33 | 3,218 | 634 | 15 |
| 1985 | 13,952 | 3,098 | 663 | 14,261 | 3,098 | 616 | 13,972 | 2,747 | 52 | 3,135 | 595 | 22 |
| 1986 | 12,857 | 2,729 | −247 | 13,944 | 2,771 | −179 | 15,780 | 3,024 | 85 | 3,234 | 663 | 26 |
| 1987 | 12,284 | 1,994 | −260 | 13,273 | 2,119 | −187 | 19,536 | 4,802 | 117 | 3,487 | 921 | 40 |
| 1988 | 12,748 | 2,206 | −78 | 13,599 | 2,370 | −56 | 28,353 | 6,368 | 87 | 3,516 | 1,000 | 25 |

**J1    NORTH AMERICA: National Accounts Totals** (in millions of stated unit, except as otherwise indicated)

| | El Salvador (colones) | | | | | | Guatemala[5] (quetzales) | | | | | |
| | Current Prices | | | 1962 Prices | | | Current Prices | | | 1946/1958 Prices[18] | | |
| | GDP | GFCF | Stocks | GDP | GFCF | Stocks | GNP/GDP[17] | GFCF | Stocks | GNP/GDP | GFCF | Stocks |
|---|---|---|---|---|---|---|---|---|---|---|---|---|
| 1950 | ... | ... | ... | ... | ... | ... | 468 —5,17 | 40[5] | | 340 —5,17,18 | 26[5,18] | |
| | | | | | | | 645 | 67 | −1 | 721 | 87 | −1 |
| 1951 | 1,064 | 105 | ... | 950[16] | ... | ... | 687 | 72 | −1 | 731 | 84 | −1 |
| 1952 | 1,097 | 106 | ... | 1,020[16] | ... | ... | 689 | 63 | −7 | 746 | 76 | −8 |
| 1953 | 1,167 | 115 | ... | 1,043 | ... | ... | 738 | 60 | 1 | 775 | 68 | 1 |
| 1954 | 1,259 | 112 | ... | 1,070 | ... | ... | 784 | 60 | — | 789 | 63 | — |
| 1955 | 1,303 | 116 | ... | 1,120 | ... | | 813 | 80 | 14 | 809 | 90 | 14 |
| 1956 | 1,353 | 158 | ... | 1,172 | ... | | 901 | 134 | 7 | 883 | 142 | 7 |
| 1957 | 1,405 | 177 | ... | 1,230 | ... | | 940 | 150 | 4 | 932 | 154 | 4 |
| 1958 | 1,401 | 166 | 10 | 1,243 | ... | | 976 | 136 | −1 | 976 | 136 | −1 |
| 1959 | 1,422 | 160 | 41 | 1,266 | ... | | 1,037 | 112 | −3 | 1,018 | 126 | −1 |
| 1960 | 1,397 | 204 | −8 | 1,372 | | | 1,044 | 102 | 5 | 1,049 | 108 | 5 |
| 1961 | 1,405 | 168 | −16 | 1,419 | | | 1,077 | 109 | −13 | 1,094 | 113 | −13 |
| 1962 | 1,590 | 173 | 9 | 1,590 | | | 1,144 | 107 | −6 | 1,133 | 109 | −6 |
| 1963 | 1,694 | 203 | 12 | 1,672 | | | 1,263 | 125 | 8 | 1,241 | 129 | 9 |
| 1964 | 1,867 | 263 | 55 | 1,828 | | | 1,294 | 159 | 7 | 1,299 | 158 | 7 |
| 1965 | 1,992 | 296 | 11 | 1,926 | | | 1,331 | 175 | 2 | 1,355 | 159 | 8 |
| 1966 | 2,110 | 326 | 36 | 2,064 | | | 1,391 | 167 | −18 | 1,430 | 166 | −17 |
| 1967 | 2,216 | 324 | 3 | 2,176 | | | 1,454 | 192 | −4 | 1,489 | 184 | −4 |
| 1968 | 2,292 | 248 | 7 | 2,246 | ... | ... | 1,611 | 221 | 23 | 1,619 | 209 | 23 |
| 1969 | 2,382 | 274 | 30 | 2,324 | ... | ... | 1,715 | 231 | −35 | 1,696 | 213 | −35 |
| 1970 | 2,571 | 308 | 33 | 2,394 | 259 | 29 | 1,904 | 239 | 6 | 1,793 | 210 | 5 |
| 1971 | 2,704 | 359 | 62 | 2,509 | 302 | 56 | 1,985 | 264 | 22 | 1,893 | 227 | 21 |
| 1972 | 2,882 | 474 | −66 | 2,646 | 386 | −58 | 2,102 | 273 | −18 | 2,032 | 226 | −17 |
| 1973 | 3,332 | 521 | 88 | 2,780 | 351 | 74 | 2,569 | 357 | −5 | 2,169 | 252 | −4 |
| 1974 | 3,944 | 719 | 174 | 2,959 | 401 | 134 | 3,162 | 468 | 120 | 2,308 | 247 | 88 |
| 1975 | 4,478 | 1,031 | −40 | 3,124 | 519 | −38 | 3,646 | 571 | 16 | 2,353 | 271 | 10 |
| 1976 | 5,706 | 1,145 | −26 | 3,247 | 535 | −3 | 4,365 | 900 | 34 | 2,526 | 371 | 20 |
| 1977 | 7,167 | 1,521 | 158 | 3,443 | 677 | 86 | 5,481 | 1,039 | 60 | 2,724 | 406 | 30 |
| 1978 | 7,692 | 1,652 | 182 | 3,665 | 695 | 91 | 6,071 | 1,218 | 95 | 2,860 | 436 | 45 |
| 1979 | 8,607 | 1,512 | 44 | 3,602 | 587 | 19 | 6,903 | 1,286 | 8 | 2,995 | 413 | 3 |
| 1980 | 8,917 | 1,210 | −27 | 3,289 | 422 | −10 | 7,879 | 1,295 | −43 | 3,107 | 373 | −17 |
| 1981 | 8,647 | 1,173 | 58 | 3,017 | 377 | 19 | 8,608 | 1,443 | 23 | 3,127 | 401 | 8 |
| 1982 | 8,966 | 1,130 | 56 | 2,848 | 339 | 17 | 8,871 | 1,310 | −76 | 3,017 | 358 | −26 |
| 1983 | 10,152 | 1,180 | 44 | 2,870 | 314 | 12 | 9,050 | 950 | 52 | 2,940 | 258 | 17 |
| 1984 | 11,657 | 1,336 | 58 | 2,936 | 321 | 14 | 9,470 | 912 | 183 | 2,954 | 235 | 57 |
| 1985 | 14,331 | 1,723 | −169 | 2,994 | 354 | −37 | 11,180 | 1,225 | 60 | 2,936 | 220 | 16 |
| 1986 | 19,763 | 2,594 | 26 | 3,013 | 380 | 5 | 15,838 | 1,593 | 43 | 2,940 | 228 | 8 |
| 1987 | 23,141 | 3,158 | −297 | 3,094 | 415 | −46 | 17,711 | 2,188 | 275 | 3,044 | 266 | 47 |
| 1988 | 27,366 | 3,456 | 185 | 3,144 | 425 | 12 | 20,545 | 2,747 | 90 | 3,159 | 298 | 14 |

## J1 NORTH AMERICA: National Accounts Totals (in millions of stated unit, except as otherwise indicated)

| | Haiti[6] | | | | | | Honduras | | | | | |
|---|---|---|---|---|---|---|---|---|---|---|---|---|
| | (gourdes) | | | | | | (lempiras) | | | | | |
| | Current Prices | | | 1970/1976 Prices[19] | | | Current Prices | | | 1948/1970/1978 Prices[20] | | |
| | GDP | GFCF | Stocks | GDP | GFCF | Stocks | GDP | GFCF | Stocks | GDP | GFCF | Stocks |
| 1950 | ... | ... | | 1,599 | ... | ... | 452 | 49 | 5 | 403[20] | 47[20] | 7.5[20] |
| | | | | 1,656 | | | | | | 670 | 82 | 9 |
| 1951 | ... | ... | | 1,633 | ... | ... | 480 | 62 | 7 | 700 | 99 | 11 |
| 1952 | ... | ... | | 1,751 | ... | ... | 499 | 76 | 6 | 715 | 129 | 10 |
| 1953 | ... | ... | | 1,695 | ... | ... | 541 | 85 | 4 | 758 | 143 | 9 |
| 1954 | ... | ... | | 1,833 | ... | ... | 512 | 69 | 3 | 712 | 105 | 5 |
| 1955 | 1,386 | 83 | | 1,760 | ... | ... | 549 | 78 | 6 | 754 | 115 | 11 |
| 1956 | 1,462 | 112 | | 1,913 | ... | ... | 575 | 80 | 5 | 787 | 117 | 8 |
| 1957 | 1,450 | 78 | | 1,800 | ... | ... | 596 | 88 | 6 | 820 | 129 | 10 |
| 1958 | 1,529 | 91 | | 1,942 | ... | ... | 635 | 82 | 4 | 866 | 116 | 6 |
| 1959 | 1,358 | 87 | | 1,851 | ... | ... | 658 | 79 | 5 | 886 | 112 | 8 |
| 1960 | 1,366 | 106 | | 1,898 | ... | ... | 671 | 84 | 9 | 907 | 119 | 14 |
| 1961 | 1,355 | 105 | | 1,853 | ... | ... | 712 | 77 | 10 | 925 | 110 | 16 |
| 1962 | 1,410 | 114 | | 2,008 | ... | ... | 775 | 106 | 9 | 974 | 142 | 18 |
| 1963 | 1,474 | 109 | 8 | 1,949 | 99 | 10 | 820 | 122 | 9 | 1,008 | 169 | 13 |
| 1964 | 1,626 | 106 | 9 | 1,918 | 90 | 1C | 914 | 123 | 11 | 1,066 | 168 | 15 |
| 1965 | 1,766 | 112 | 10 | 1,959 | 90 | 10 | 1,017 | 132 | 16 | 1,158 | 177 | 21 |
| 1966 | 1,845 | 96 | 10 | 1,947 | 78 | 11 | 1,100 | 159 | 17 | 1,221 | 204 | 21 |
| 1967 | 1,846 | 96 | 11 | 1,906 | 79 | 11 | 1,196 | 213 | 22 | 1,287 | 265 | 26 |
| 1968 | 1,840 | 93 | 11 | 1,967 | 87 | 11 | 1,299 | 226 | 13 | 1,373 | 277 | 15 |
| 1969 | 1,959 | 124 | 11 | 2,042[19] | 105[19] | 11[19] | 1,348 | 244 | 14 | 1,392 | 279 | 16 |
| 1970 | 2,055 | 161 | 12 | 3,364 | 307 | | 1,446 | 268 | 34 | 1,446 | 268 | 34 |
| 1971 | 2,262 | 186 | 13 | 3,582 | 314 | | 1,551 | 253 | −3 | 1,514 | 265 | −3 |
| 1972 | 2,312 | 207 | 13 | 3,617 | 370 | | 1,683 | 245 | 11 | 1,587 | 251 | 11 |
| 1973 | 3,129 | 258 | 17 | 3,789 | 457 | | 1,895 | 325 | 23 | 1,658 | 323 | 23 |
| 1974 | 2,828 | 410 | 19 | 4,008 | 564 | | 2,114 | 433 | 109 | 1,686 | 331 | 87 |
| 1975 | 3,408 | 533 | 23 | 4,053 | 595 | | 2,248 | 476 | −50 | 1,728[20] | 373[20] | −57[20] |
| | | | | | | | | | | 2,876 | 637 | −64 |
| 1976 | 4,395 | 678 | | 4,395 | 678 | | 2,696 | 550 | −32 | 3,150[16] | 670[16] | −37 |
| 1977 | 4,897 | 748 | | 4,416 | 736 | | 3,339 | 711 | 59 | 3,508 | 763 | 62 |
| 1978 | 5,060 | 857 | | 4,631 | 771 | | 3,798 | 941 | 93 | 3,796 | 941 | 93 |
| 1979 | 5,600 | 938 | | 4,983 | 921 | | 4,425 | 1,004 | 170 | 4,038 | 920 | 154 |
| 1980 | 7,183 | 1,238 | | 5,349 | 934 | | 5,088 | 1,235 | 13 | 4,090 | 1,011 | 10 |
| 1981 | 7,397 | 1,252 | | 5,196 | 941 | | 5,553 | 1,051 | 100 | 4,153 | 781 | 75 |
| 1982 | 7,425 | 1,230 | | 5,018 | 877 | | 5,762 | 966 | −190 | 4,072 | 645 | −134 |
| 1983 | 8,148 | 1,331 | | 5,056 | 924 | | 6,035 | 1,073 | −176 | 4,062 | 739 | −119 |
| 1984 | 9,082 | 1,442 | | 5,071 | 967 | | 6,462 | 1,326 | −95 | 4,175 | 940 | −64 |
| 1985 | 10,047 | 1,673 | | 5,084 | 1,078 | | 7,008 | 1,252 | 12 | 4,323 | 861 | 8 |
| 1986 | 11,177 | 1,614 | | 5,134 | 987 | | 7,596 | 1,088 | −13 | 4,444 | 744 | −8 |
| 1987 | 9,964 | 1,509 | | 5,122 | 969 | | 8,128 | 1,035 | 161 | 4,674 | 695 | 96 |
| 1988 | 9,824 | 1,459 | | 5,110 | 955 | | 8,937 | 1,141 | 25 | 4,896 | 738 | 14 |

**J1　　NORTH AMERICA: National Accounts Totals** (in millions of stated unit, except as otherwise indicated)

| | Jamaica | | | | | | Mexico | | | | | |
|---|---|---|---|---|---|---|---|---|---|---|---|---|
| | (dollars) | | | | | | (thousand million pesos[24]) | | | | | |
| | Current Prices | | | Prices[22] | | | Current Prices | | | 1960/1970/1980 Prices[26] | | |
| | NNP/ GDP[21] | GFCF | Stocks | GDP | GFCF | Stocks | GDP | GFCF | Stocks | GDP | GFCF | Stocks |
| 1950 | 170[21] | ... | ... | ... | ... | ... | 41.1 | 4.8 | ... | 84 | ... | ... |
| | 155 | 14 | 2 | | | | | | | | | |
| 1951 | 180 | 24 | 1 | ... | ... | ... | 53.0 | 6.9 | ... | 93 | ... | ... |
| 1952 | 206 | 27 | 2 | ... | ... | ... | 59.3 | 8.2 | ... | 96 | ... | ... |
| 1953 | 231 | 28 | 2 | 254 | 56 | 2 | 58.9 | 8.1 | ... | 97 | ... | ... |
| 1954 | 258 | 35 | 3 | 282 | 65 | 3 | 72.2 | 10.1 | ... | 106 | ... | ... |
| 1955 | 294 | 43 | 6 | 310 | 67 | 7 | 88.2 | 12.6 | ... | 116 | ... | ... |
| 1956 | 343 | 78 | 6 | 343 | 78 | 6 | 101 | 16.8 | ... | 124 | ... | ... |
| 1957 | 413 | 104 | 10 | 384 | 96 | 9 | 115 | 19.1 | ... | 134 | ... | ... |
| 1958 | 427 | 95 | 7 | 396[22] | 95[22] | 7[22] | 129 | 18.9 | ... | 141 | ... | ... |
| 1959 | 433 | 91 | 9 | 442 | 84 | 11 | 138 | 19.6 | ... | 145 | ... | ... |
| 1960 | 474 | 99 | 5 | 471 | 99 | 5 | 156 | 23.2 | 2.9 | 156 | 23 | 3 |
| 1961 | 508 | 98 | 8 | 483 | 90 | 7 | 166 | 24.1 | 2.9 | 161 | 23 | 3 |
| 1962 | 528 | 98 | 6 | 489 | 85 | 5 | 180 | 24.8 | 3.0 | 169 | 23 | 3 |
| 1963 | 558 | 92 | 8 | 506 | 82 | 7 | 195 | 32.6 | 5.2 | 178 | 30 | 5 |
| 1964 | 589 | 112 | 9 | 549 | 98 | 7 | 221 | 41.0[10] | 5.3[10] | 190 | 37[10] | 5[10] |
| 1965 | 636 | 124 | 5 | 592 | 109 | 4 | 252 | 44.2 | — | 212 | 39 | — |
| 1966 | 691 | 146 | 6 | 615 | 117 | 5 | 283 | 50.2 | 3.0 | 229 | 44 | 3 |
| 1967 | 745 | 170 | 7 | 631 | 133 | 2 | 306 | 59.6 | — | 241 | 49 | — |
| 1968 | 820 | 221 | 9 | 669 | 167 | 2 | 339 | 65.7 | 4.9 | 261 | 53 | 4 |
| 1969 | 993 | 315 | 34 | 713 | 172 | 32 | 375 | 72.8 | 6.4 | 277 | 57 | 5 |
| 1970 | 1,171 | 367 | 2 | 840[22] | 246[22] | 2[22] | 444 | 88.7 | 12[26] | 315[26] | 67[26] | 10 |
| | | | | 1,982 | | | | | | | | |
| 1971 | 1,282 | 356 | 56 | 2,042 | ... | ... | 490 | 88.1 | 11 | 463 | 87 | 9 |
| 1972 | 1,439 | 367 | 27 | 2,231 | ... | ... | 565 | 107 | 8 | 502 | 98 | 8 |
| 1973 | 1,720 | 448 | 94 | 2,263 | ... | ... | 691 | 133 | 14 | 544 | 112 | 10 |
| 1974 | 2,159 | 478 | 47 | 2,170 | ... | ... | 900 | 179 | 30 | 578 | 121 | 23 |
| 1975 | 2,600 | 610 | 60 | 2,153 | 525 | 50 | 1,100 | 236 | 25 | 610 | 132 | 19 |
| 1976 | 2,702 | 451 | 40 | 2,014 | ... | ... | 1,371[25] | 288[25] | 17[25] | 636[25] | 133[25] | 14[25] |
| 1977 | 2,960 | 349 | 12 | 1,966 | 263 | 8 | 1,849 | 363 | 59 | 658 | 124 | 23 |
| 1978 | 3,749 | 499 | 63 | 1,976 | 281 | 33 | 2,337 | 492 | 59 | 712 | 143 | 22 |
| 1979 | 4,293 | 748 | 74 | 1,940 | 268 | 34 | 3,068 | 719 | 78 | 777 | 172 | 22 |
| 1980 | 4,773 | 690 | 69 | 1,829 | 207 | 26 | 4,276 | 1,033 | 170 | 842[26] | 197[26] | 39[26] |
| 1981 | 5,307 | 954 | 123 | 1,875 | 241 | 44 | 5,874 | 1,509 | 193 | 4,862 | 1,286 | 339 |
| 1982 | 5,867 | 1,168 | 57 | 1,899 | 282 | 18 | 9,417 | 2,099 | −98 | 4,832 | 1,070 | −392 |
| 1983 | 6,993 | 1,436 | 120 | 1,942 | 278 | 33 | 17,142 | 2,972 | 500 | 4,629 | 768 | 2 |
| 1984 | 9,358 | 1,981 | 183 | 1,926 | 243 | 38 | 28,749[24] | 5,287[24] | 566[24] | 4,796[24] | 817[24] | —[24] |
| 1985 | 11,203 | 2,581 | 256 | 1,836 | 240 | 42 | 47.4 | 9.05 | 0.99 | 4.92 | 0.88 | 0.02 |
| 1986 | 13,389 | 2,432 | 142 | 1,854 | 217 | 19 | 79.5 | 15.4 | 0.92 | 4.73 | 0.78 | −0.07 |
| 1987 | 16,002 | 3,540 | 160 | 1,977 | 276 | 20 | 194 | 35.7 | 1.5 | 4.82 | 0.77 | −0.03 |
| 1988 | 18,748 | 4,865 | 499 | 2,045 | 306 | 55 | 393 | 75.2 | 8.0 | 4.88 | 0.82 | 0.01 |

**J1**     **NORTH AMERICA: National Accounts Totals** (in millions of stated unit, except as otherwise indicated)

| | Nicaragua | | | | | | Panama | | | | | |
|---|---|---|---|---|---|---|---|---|---|---|---|---|
| | (cordobas[27]) | | | | | | (balboas) | | | | | |
| | Current Prices | | | 1958/1985 Prices[28] | | | Current Prices | | | 1960/1970 Prices[29] | | |
| | GDP | GFCF | Stocks | GDP | GFCF | Stocks | GDP | GFCF | Stocks | GDP | GFCF | Stocks |
| 1950 | ... | ... | ... | 1,482 | 143 | | 257 | 31 | 5 | 259 | 36 | ... |
| 1951 | ... | ... | ... | 1,582 | 201 | | 264 | 29 | 2 | 257 | 30 | ... |
| 1952 | ... | ... | ... | 1,850 | 274 | | 276 | 30 | 3 | 271 | 31 | ... |
| 1953 | ... | ... | ... | 1,895 | 306 | | 293 | 34 | 14 | 287 | 36 | ... |
| 1954 | ... | ... | ... | 2,071 | 377 | | 307 | 33 | 4 | 297 | 37 | ... |
| 1955 | ... | ... | ... | 2,211 | 376 | | 332 | 39 | 4 | 315 | 43 | ... |
| 1956 | ... | ... | ... | 2,209 | 348 | | 347 | 50 | 4 | 331 | 53 | ... |
| 1957 | ... | ... | ... | 2,396 | 346 | | 383 | 49 | 7 | 366 | 52 | ... |
| 1958 | ... | ... | ... | 2,404 | 334 | | 382 | 53 | 11 | 369 | 55 | ... |
| 1959 | ... | ... | ... | 2,440 | 358 | | 404 | 65 | 7 | 392 | 68 | ... |
| 1960 | 2,348 | 300 | 52 | 2,393 | 296 | 53 | 416 | 61 | 6 | 416 | 61 | ... |
| 1961 | 2,527 | 319 | 55 | 2,571 | 326 | 56 | 464 | 80 | 8 | 461 | 78 | ... |
| 1962 | 2,783 | 422 | 61 | 2,851 | 426 | 62 | 505 | 85 | 14 | 499 | 83 | ... |
| 1963 | 3,076 | 470 | 67 | 3,162 | 465 | 70 | 559 | 97 | 13 | 541 | 96 | ... |
| 1964 | 3,590 | 628 | 78 | 3,532 | 639 | 79 | 601 | 88 | 14 | 565 | 85 | ... |
| 1965 | 3,966 | 746 | 84 | 3,868 | 743 | 85 | 660 | 100 | 16 | 617 | 97 | ... |
| 1966 | 4,247 | 887 | 90 | 3,996 | 828 | 88 | 719 | 142 | 15 | 664 | 135 | ... |
| 1967 | 4,600 | 868 | 98 | 4,274 | 834 | 94 | 801 | 153 | 16 | 721 | 143 | ... |
| 1968 | 4,871 | 762 | 102 | 4,332 | 700 | 95 | 861 | 173 | 18 | 771 | 161 | ... |
| 1969 | 5,236 | 883 | 110 | 4,602 | 815 | 101 | 945 | 201 | 22 | 836 | 183 | ... |
| 1970 | 5,436 | 891 | 120 | 4,664 | 825 | 103 | 1,021 | 262 | 20 | 894 [29] | 222 [29] | ... [29] |
| 1971 | 5,786 | 898 | 127 | 4,894 | 851 | 108 | 1,152 | 306 | 21 | 1,132 | 289 | 20 |
| 1972 | 6,060 | 930 | −138 | 5,050 | 756 | −112 | 1,265 | 372 | 30 | 1,171 | 373 | 26 |
| 1973 | 7,578 | 1,476 | 360 | 5,307 | 1,037 | 249 | 1,447 | 435 | 51 | 1,233 | 374 | 41 |
| 1974 | 10,646 | 2,498 | 855 | 5,981 | 1,268 | 481 | 1,654 | 465 | 91 | 1,264 | 334 | 59 |
| 1975 | 10,950 | 2,510 | −200 | 6,113 | 1,151 | −101 | 1,841 | 535 | 32 | 1,286 | 361 | 19 |
| 1976 | 12,590 | 2,610 | −300 | 6,421 | 1,215 | −128 | 1,956 | 609 | 10 | 1,307 | 368 | 8 |
| 1977 | 14,740 | 3,620 | 300 | 6,824 | 1,557 | 343 | 2,070 | 446 | 45 | 1,321 | 245 | 17 |
| 1978 | 14,270 [27] | 2,180 [27] | −300 [27] | 6,336 [27,28] 145 | 868 | −96 | 2,452 | 606 | 45 | 1,451 | 303 | 23 |
| 1979 | 14.51 | 0.97 | −1.8 | 107 | ... | ... | 2,800 | 661 | 124 | 1,516 | 300 | 52 |
| 1980 | 20.80 | 3.03 | 0.5 | 112 | ... | ... | 3,559 | 866 | 120 | 1,746 | 365 | 46 |
| 1981 | 24.48 | 5.24 | 0.5 | 118 | ... | ... | 3,878 | 1,080 | 88 | 1,819 | 426 | 37 |
| 1982 | 28.35 | 4.70 | 0.6 | 117 | ... | ... | 4,279 | 1,185 | −1 | 1,919 | 430 | 1 |
| 1983 | 32.92 | 6.39 | 1.0 | 122 | ... | ... | 4,374 | 918 | 16 | 1,926 | 333 | 8 |
| 1984 | 45.03 | 8.74 | 1.3 | 120 | ... | ... | 4,565 | 780 | −19 | 1,918 | 310 | −7 |
| 1985 | 115 | 23.9 | 2.8 | 115 | ... | ... | 4,901 | 773 | −20 | 2,008 | 331 | −7 |
| 1986 | 436 | 60.3 | 13.3 | 114 | ... | ... | 5,145 | 897 | −37 | 2,076 | 363 | −12 |
| 1987 | 42,696 | 188 | 71.4 | 113 | ... | ... | 5,310 | 937 | −9 | 2,124 | 364 | −4 |
| 1988 | 330,970 | 97 | 7.9 | 104 | ... | ... | 4,551 | 408 | −63 | 1,797 | 176 | −24 |

**J1    NORTH AMERICA: National Accounts Totals** (in millions of stated units, except as otherwise indicated)

| | Puerto Rico[8] | | | | | | Trinidad & Tobago | | | | |
| | (dollars) | | | | | | (dollars) | | | | |
| | Current Prices | | | 1954 Prices | | | Current Prices | | | 1975/1985 Prices[30] | |
| | GDP[7] | GFCF | Stocks | GDP | GFCF | Stocks | GDP | GFCF | Stocks | GDP | GCF |
|---|---|---|---|---|---|---|---|---|---|---|---|
| 1950 | 779 | 127 | 20 | 884 | ... | ... | ... | ... | ... | ... | ... |
| 1951 | 881 | 150 | 42 | 925 | ... | ... | 331 | 70 | 16 | ... | ... |
| 1952 | 933 | 159 | −1 | 959 | ... | ... | 364 | 75 | 20 | ... | ... |
| 1953 | 1,006 | 173 | 13 | 989 | ... | ... | 408 | 79 | 7 | ... | ... |
| 1954 | 1,062 | 203 | 14 | 1,062 | 203 | 14 | 436 | 84 | 7 | ... | ... |
| 1955 | 1,148 | 217 | 12 | 1,123 | ... | ... | 505 | 109 | 7 | ... | ... |
| 1956 | 1,241 | 260 | 15 | 1,186 | 235 | 13 | 589 | 121 | 5 | ... | ... |
| 1957 | 1,342 | 279 | 23 | 1,245 | 245 | 19 | 695 | 161 | 11 | ... | ... |
| 1958 | 1,501 | 302 | 56 | 1,318 | 261 | 51 | 763 | 196 | 11 | ... | ... |
| 1959 | 1,693 | 355 | 42 | 1,466 | 302 | 36 | 846 | 243 | 7 | ... | ... |
| 1960 | 1,865 | 377 | 22 | 1,568 | 309 | 20 | 918 | 268 | 18 | 3,293 | ... |
| 1961 | 2,078 | 448 | 85 | 1,645 | 358 | 75 | 1,003 | 259 | −2 | 3,546 | ... |
| 1962 | 2,311 | 489 | 77 | 1,762 | 382 | 67 | 1,062 | 295 | 3 | 3,648 | ... |
| 1963 | 2,570 | 584 | 77 | 1,994 | 449 | 61 | 1,145 | 276 | −4 | 3,826 | ... |
| 1964 | 2,881 | 720 | 128 | 2,083 | 531 | 111 | 1,220 | 274 | 5 | 4,039 | ... |
| 1965 | 3,170 | 745 | 131 | 2,329 | 540 | 110 | 1,263 | 327 | | 4,152 | ... |
| 1966 | 3,552 | 902 | 35 | 2,482 | 645 | 33 | 1,241 | 286 | | 3,803 | ... |
| 1967 | 3,936 | 964 | 71 | 2,616 | 665 | 58 | 1,324 | 233 | | 4,215 | ... |
| 1968 | 4,461 | 1,102 | 108 | 2,692 | 727 | 83 | 1,518 | 301 | | 4,367 | ... |
| 1969 | 5,035 | 1,402 | 50 | 3,068 | 870 | 32 | 1,558 | 268 | | 4,345 | ... |
| 1970 | 5,659 | 1,594 | 114 | 3,268 | 941 | 72 | 1,644 | 425 | | 4,582 | 425 |
| 1971 | 6,333 | 1,761 | 101 | 3,501 | 975 | 63 | 1,771 | 602 | | 4,538 | ... |
| 1972 | 7,023 | 1,601 | 192 | 3,723 | 849 | 127 | 2,082 | 652 | | 4,886 | ... |
| 1973 | 7,710 | 1,696 | 104 | 3,724 | 797 | 2 | 2,564 | 666 | | 4,994 | ... |
| 1974 | 8,226[10] | 2,079 | 139 | 3,634[10] | 836 | 46 | 4,193 | 915 | | 5,247[30] | ... |
| 1975 | 8,996 | 1,836 | 138 | 3,830 | 723 | 54 | 5,300 | 1,085 | 364 | 14,086 | 927 |
| 1976 | 9,930 | 1,560 | −61 | 4,111 | 601 | −9 | 6,091 | 1,398 | 98 | 14,989 | 1,061 |
| 1977 | 11,172 | 1,746 | 125 | 4,408 | 618 | 65 | 7,533 | 1,735 | 272 | 16,356 | 1,095 |
| 1978 | 12,786 | 1,888 | 176 | 4,677 | 617 | 42 | 8,550 | 2,323 | 261 | 17,994 | 1,402 |
| 1979 | 14,436 | 2,067 | 407 | 4,662 | 614 | 114 | 11,046 | 2,952 | 261 | 18,642 | 1,447 |
| 1980 | 15,956 | 2,162 | 125 | 4,712 | 576 | 53 | 14,966 | 4,204 | 376 | 20,579 | 1,774 |
| 1981 | 16,764 | 1,851 | −336 | 4,569 | 453 | −55 | 16,438 | 4,342 | 199 | 21,521 | 1,479 |
| 1982 | 17,276 | 1,722 | 24 | 4,590 | 412 | 21 | 19,176 | 5,189 | 228 | 22,389 | 1,558 |
| 1983 | 19,163 | 2,100 | 535 | 4,926 | 492 | 141 | 18,719 | 5,038 | 30 | 20,329 | 1,389[30] |
| 1984 | 20,289 | 2,345 | 155 | 5,027 | 545 | 46 | 18,615 | 4,514 | | 18,850 | 4,394 |
| 1985 | 22,009 | 2,327 | −69 | 5,398 | 540 | 1 | 17,801 | 3,451 | | 17,801 | 3,451 |
| 1986 | 24,026 | 3,030 | 245 | 5,688 | 685 | 69 | 17,260 | 3,824 | | 17,500 | 3,031 |
| 1987 | 26,386 | 3,892 | 159 | 6,092 | 853 | 52 | 17,301 | 3,444 | | 16,627 | 2,449 |
| 1988 | 28,161 | 4,403 | 384 | 6,296 | 917 | 95 | 17,333 | 2,971 | | 16,057 | 2,023 |

**J1   NORTH AMERICA: National Accounts Totals** (in millions of stated units, except as otherwise indicated)

| | USA[32] | | | | | |
|---|---|---|---|---|---|---|
| | (thousand million dollars) | | | | | |
| | Current Prices | | | 1982 Prices | | |
| | GNP | GPFCF[31] | Stocks | GNP | GPFCF[31] | Stocks |
| 1950 | 288.3 | 48.3 | 6.8 | 1,204 | 210.7 | 24.2 |
| 1951 | 333.4 | 50.3 | 10.2 | 1,328 | 204.4 | 30.8 |
| 1952 | 351.6 | 50.4 | 3.1 | 1,381 | 201.8 | 10.0 |
| 1953 | 371.6 | 54.5 | 0.4 | 1,435 | 213.8 | 2.8 |
| 1954 | 372.5 | 55.7 | −1.6 | 1,416 | 217.4 | −4.8 |
| 1955 | 405.9 | 64.0 | 5.7 | 1,495 | 243.5 | 16.3 |
| 1956 | 428.2 | 68.1 | 4.6 | 1,526 | 244.9 | 12.9 |
| 1957 | 451.0 | 69.7 | 1.4 | 1,551 | 240.4 | 3.0 |
| 1958 | 456.8 | 65.1 | −1.5 | 1,539 | 224.8 | −3.4 |
| 1959 | 495.8 [32] | 74.4 [32] | 5.8 [32] | 1,629 [32] | 253.8 [32] | 16.5 [32] |
| 1960 | 515.3 | 75.1 | 3.1 | 1,665 | 252.8 | 7.7 |
| 1961 | 533.8 | 74.7 | 2.4 | 1,709 | 251.8 | 7.3 |
| 1962 | 574.6 | 81.5 | 6.1 | 1,799 | 272.4 | 16.2 |
| 1963 | 606.9 | 87.3 | 5.8 | 1,873 | 290.5 | 16.6 |
| 1964 | 649.8 | 94.2 | 5.4 | 1,973 | 310.2 | 15.7 |
| 1965 | 705.1 | 106.3 | 9.9 | 2,088 | 341.8 | 25.2 |
| 1966 | 772.0 | 114.4 | 14.2 | 2,208 | 353.5 | 36.9 |
| 1967 | 816.4 | 115.4 | 10.3 | 2,271 | 344.6 | 28.8 |
| 1968 | 892.7 | 129.1 | 7.9 | 2,366 | 370.8 | 21.0 |
| 1969 | 963.9 | 143.4 | 9.8 | 2,423 | 385.2 | 25.1 |
| 1970 | 1,015.5 | 145.7 | 3.1 | 2,416 | 373.3 | 8.2 |
| 1971 | 1,103 | 164.7 | 7.8 | 2,485 | 399.7 | 19.6 |
| 1972 | 1,213 | 191.5 | 10.5 | 2,608 | 443.6 | 21.8 |
| 1973 | 1,359 | 219.2 | 19.6 | 2,744 | 480.8 | 40.0 |
| 1974 | 1,473 | 225.4 | 15.4 | 2,729 | 448.0 | 33.3 |
| 1975 | 1,598 | 225.2 | −5.6 | 2,695 | 396.1 | −12.8 |
| 1976 | 1,783 | 261.7 | 16.0 | 2,827 | 431.4 | 22.1 |
| 1977 | 1,991 | 322.8 | 21.3 | 2,959 | 492.2 | 29.1 |
| 1978 | 2,250 | 388.2 | 28.6 | 3,115 | 540.1 | 36.8 |
| 1979 | 2,508 | 441.9 | 13.0 | 3,192 | 560.2 | 15.0 |
| 1980 | 2,732 | 445.3 | −8.3 | 3,187 | 516.2 | −6.9 |
| 1981 | 3,053 | 491.5 | 24.0 | 3,249 | 521.7 | 23.9 |
| 1982 | 3,166 | 471.8 | −24.5 | 3,166 | 471.8 | −24.5 |
| 1983 | 3,406 | 509.4 | −7.1 | 3,279 | 510.4 | −6.4 |
| 1984 | 3,772 | 597.1 | 67.7 | 3,501 | 596.1 | 62.3 |
| 1985 | 4,015 | 631.8 | 11.3 | 3,619 | 627.9 | 9.1 |
| 1986 | 4,232 | 652.5 | 6.9 | 3,718 | 634.1 | 5.6 |
| 1987 | 4,524 | 670.6 | 29.3 | 3,854 | 650.3 | 23.7 |
| 1988 | 4,881 | 719.6 | 30.6 | 4,024 | 687.9 | 27.9 |

**J1    SOUTH AMERICA: NATIONAL ACCOUNTS TOTALS** (in millions of stated unit, except as otherwise indicated)

| | 1860–1899 | | | 1900–1934 | | | | | | | |
|---|---|---|---|---|---|---|---|---|---|---|---|
| | Brazil | | | Argentina | | Brazil | | Chile | Colombia | | |
| | (milreis) | | | (thousand million pesos) | | milreis or cruzeiros | | (thousand million pesos) | (pesos) | | |
| | Current Prices | 1949 Prices | | 1950 Prices | | Current Prices | 1949 Prices | 1960 Prices | 1950 Prices | | |
| | GDP | GDP | | GDP | GFCF | GDP | GDP | GDP | GDP | GFC | Stocks |
| 1860 | ... | ... | 1900 | 8.87 | | 3.1 | 19 | ... | ... | ... | ... |
| 1861 | 0.27 | 11 | 1901 | 9.62 | | 2.7 | 21 | ... | ... | ... | ... |
| 1862 | 0.30 | 12 | 1902 | 9.43 | 12.65 | 2.9 | 23 | ... | ... | ... | ... |
| 1863 | 0.31 | 12 | 1903 | 10.77 | | 2.9 | 24 | ... | ... | ... | ... |
| 1864 | 0.25 | 12 | 1904 | 11.92 | | 3.2 | 26 | ... | ... | ... | ... |
| 1865 | 0.38 | 13 | 1905 | 13.50 | | 2.7 | 29 | ... | ... | ... | ... |
| 1866 | 0.40 | 13 | 1906 | 14.18 | | 3.2 | 32 | ... | ... | ... | ... |
| 1867 | 0.39 | 12 | 1907 | 14.48 | 36.03 | 3.7 | 33 | ... | ... | ... | ... |
| 1868 | 0.51 | 12 | 1908 | 15.90 | | 3.7 | 37 | 675 | ... | ... | ... |
| 1869 | 0.52 | 13 | 1909 | 16.69 | | 4.2 | 41 | 688 | ... | ... | ... |
| 1870 | 0.49 | 15 | 1910 | 17.90 | | 4.8 | 47 | 744 | ... | ... | ... |
| 1871 | 0.50 | 15 | 1911 | 18.22 | | 5.5 | 55 | 738 | ... | ... | ... |
| 1872 | 0.51 | 15 | 1912 | 19.71 | 39.49 | 5.7 | 62 | 819 | ... | ... | ... |
| 1873 | 0.53 | 15 | 1913 | 19.91 | | 5.7 | 60 | 830 | ... | ... | ... |
| 1874 | 0.57 | 18 | 1914 | 17.85 | | 4.7 | 53 | 772 | ... | ... | ... |
| 1875 | 0.53 | 18 | 1915 | 17.95 | 3.19 | 4.5 | 48 | 718 | ... | ... | ... |
| 1876 | 0.57 | 18 | 1916 | 17.43 | 2.88 | 4.8 | 48 | 851 | ... | ... | ... |
| 1877 | 0.54 | 17 | 1917 | 16.01 | 2.25 | 5.5 | 50 | 919 | ... | ... | ... |
| 1878 | 0.54 | 17 | 1918 | 18.95 | 2.28 | 5.5 | 57 | 921 | ... | ... | ... |
| 1879 | 0.56 | 17 | 1919 | 19.65 | 2.58 | 8.3 | 65 | 729 | ... | ... | ... |
| 1880 | 0.62 | 18 | 1920 | 21.08 | 4.81 | 9.8 | 70 | 832 | ... | ... | ... |
| 1881 | 0.58 | 18 | 1921 | 21.62 | 5.39 | 10.0 | 72 | 716 | ... | ... | ... |
| 1882 | 0.57 | 16 | 1922 | 23.35 | 6.31 | 12.0 | 78 | 765 | ... | ... | ... |
| 1883 | 0.69 | 15 | 1923 | 25.92 | 8.65 | 16.0 | 90 | 954 | ... | ... | ... |
| 1884 | 0.54 | 15 | 1924 | 27.94 | 9.28 | 20.0 | 100 | 1,039 | ... | ... | ... |
| 1885 | 0.63 | 16 | 1925 | 27.82 | 9.31 | 22.0 | 100 | 1,052₃₃ 1,242 | 2,189 | 480 | 70 |
| 1886 | 0.71 | 19 | 1926 | 29.16 | 9.22 | 23.0 | 103 | 1,322 | 2,398 | 599 | 85 |
| 1887 | 0.66 | 21 | 1927 | 31.23 | 10.56 | 25.0 | 109 | 1,118 | 2,614 | 723 | 87 |
| 1888 | 0.64 | 21 | 1928 | 33.17 | 12.53 | 28.0 | 125 | 1,328 | 2,806 | 857 | 133 |
| 1889 | 0.66 | 22 | 1929 | 34.70 | 14.31 | 25.0 | 121 | 1,494 | 2,907 | 740 | 95 |
| 1890 | 0.86 | 22 | 1930 | 33.26 | 12.07 | 22.0 | 110 | 1,388 | 2,882 | 482 | 64 |
| 1891 | 1.57 | 22 | 1931 | 30.96 | 6.93 | 18.0 | 91 | 1,106 | 2,836 | 397 | 49 |
| 1892 | 1.96 | 21 | 1932 | 29.93 | 4.78 | 18.0 | 91 | 1,089 | 3,024 | 469 | 62 |
| 1893 | 2.31 | 22 | 1933 | 31.33 | 5.40 | 19.0 | 98 | 1,231 | 3,194 | 459 | 61 |
| 1894 | 2.63 | 21 | 1934 | 33.81 | 7.29 | 25.0 | 118 | 1,437 | 3,395 | 468 | 56 |
| 1895 | 2.79 | 20 | | | | | | | | | |
| 1896 | 2.91 | 19 | | | | | | | | | |
| 1897 | 3.19 | 17 | | | | | | | | | |
| 1898 | 3.26 | 16 | | | | | | | | | |
| 1899 | 3.13 | 16 | | | | | | | | | |

**J1    SOUTH AMERICA: National Accounts Totals** (in millions of stated unit, except as otherwise indicated)

**1935–1969**

| | Argentina (thousand million pesos)[34] | | | | | | Bolivia (pesos) | | | | | |
| | Current Prices | | | 1950/1960 Prices[35] | | | Current Prices | | | 1958 Prices | | |
| | GDP | GFCF | Stocks | GDP | GFCF | Stocks | GDP | GFCF | Stocks | GDP | GFCF | Stocks |
|---|---|---|---|---|---|---|---|---|---|---|---|---|
| 1935 | 9.3 | 0.8 | 0.1 | 35.30[35] / 453 | ···[35] / 7.0 | ···[35] / 0.8 | ... | ... | ... | ... | ... | ... |
| 1936 | 9.8 | 1.0 | 0.1 | 458 | 7.5 | 0.2 | ... | ... | ... | ... | ... | ... |
| 1937 | 11.3 | 1.4 | −0.1 | 495 | 10.2 | −0.7 | ... | ... | ... | ... | ... | ... |
| 1938 | 11.0 | 1.5 | 0.4 | 502 | 10.9 | 1.0 | ... | ... | ... | ... | ... | ... |
| 1939 | 11.6 | 1.4 | — | 520 | 9.3 | 0.1 | ... | ... | ... | ... | ... | ... |
| 1940 | 12.0 | 1.4 | — | 509 | 8.3 | 0.1 | ... | ... | ... | ... | ... | ... |
| 1941 | 12.9 | 1.5 | 0.4 | 534 | 7.9 | 1.4 | ... | ... | ... | ... | ... | ... |
| 1942 | 14.6 | 1.7 | 0.1 | 559 | 7.4 | 0.7 | ... | ... | ... | ... | ... | ... |
| 1943 | 15.3 | 1.8 | 0.1 | 563 | 7.3 | 0.2 | ... | ... | ... | ... | ... | ... |
| 1944 | 17.5 | 2.2 | −0.3 | 618 | 8.4 | −0.3 | ... | ... | ... | ... | ... | ... |
| 1945 | 19.3 | 2.6 | −0.3 | 588 | 8.4 | −1.2 | ... | ... | ... | ... | ... | ... |
| 1946 | 26.2 | 3.9 | 0.4 | 637 | 10.9 | 0.7 | ... | ... | ... | ... | ... | ... |
| 1947 | 35.9 | 6.9 | 1.5 | 725 | 16.5 | 2.3 | ... | ... | ... | ... | ... | ... |
| 1948 | 43.8 | 10.3 | 1.6 | 733 | 17.0 | 2.1 | ... | ... | ... | ... | ... | ... |
| 1949 | 52.6 | 11.9 | −0.5 | 700 | 14.6 | −0.7 | ... | ... | ... | ... | ... | ... |
| 1950 | 62.2[10] / 68 | 14 | −0.7 | 710 | 114 | −13 | 46 | 5 | 0.2 | 3,363 | 389 | 13 |
| 1951 | 96 | 19 | 1.7 | 739 | 140 | 8 | 80 | 12 | 0.4 | 3,600 | 561 | 19 |
| 1952 | 112 | 21 | 2.2 | 692 | 125 | 1 | 107 | 17 | 0.5 | 3,709 | 589 | 19 |
| 1953 | 129 | 23 | 2.0 | 741 | 123 | 12 | 327 | 33 | 1.1 | 3,358 | 332 | 11 |
| 1954 | 145 | 24 | 1.8 | 769 | 120 | 10 | 632 | 85 | 2.8 | 3,428 | 444 | 15 |
| 1955 | 171 | 30 | 0.5 | 822 | 140 | 7 | 1,501 | 308 | 10 | 3,609 | 729 | 24 |
| 1956 | 218 | 40 | −1.4 | 835 | 148 | −10 | 2,757 | 551 | — | 3,395 | 675 | — |
| 1957 | 271 | 54 | −1.0 | 881 | 158 | −8 | 2,960 | 558 | — | 3,263 | 619 | — |
| 1958 | 387 | 77 | −0.6 | 945 | 171 | −7 | 3,361 | 489 | 76 | 3,361 | 489 | 76 |
| 1959 | 741 | 126 | 9.2 | 890 | 139 | 10 | 3,862 | 526 | −49 | 3,350 | 506 | −47 |
| 1960 | 1,006 | 208 | 10 | 1,006 | 208 | 10 | 4,479 | 637 | 38 | 3,494 | 590 | 35 |
| 1961 | 1,200 | 268 | −5 | 1,078 | 242 | −4 | 4,872 | 532 | 14 | 3,567 | 493 | 13 |
| 1962 | 1,485 | 318 | - - | 1,060 | 221 | −1 | 5,327 | 835 | 41 | 3,766 | 782 | 38 |
| 1963 | 1,855 | 328 | −13 | 1,034 | 187 | −7 | 5,736 | 924 | −15 | 4,008 | 816 | −13 |
| 1964 | 2,580[34] | 424[34] | 59[34] | 1,142[34] | 208[34] | 19[32] | 6,463 | 958 | 51 | 4,201 | 832 | 44 |
| 1965 | 36.2 | 6.2 | 0.8 | 13 | 2.2 | 0.3 | 7,180 | 1,051 | 167 | 4,491 | 899 | 143 |
| 1966 | 45.2 | 7.9 | 0.1 | 13 | 2.2 | - - | 7,950 | 949 | 342 | 4,806 | 801 | 284 |
| 1967 | 59.1 | 10.7 | — | 13 | 2.4 | — | 8,979 | 1,155 | 129 | 5,110 | 912 | 104 |
| 1968 | 68.8 | 13.0 | — | 14 | 2.6 | — | 10,192 | 1,574 | 65 | 5,477 | 1,204 | 50 |
| 1969 | 80.4 | 15.7 | −0.1 | 15 | 3.0 | — | 11,044 | 1,741 | 162 | 5,722 | 1,290 | 119 |

**J1**     **SOUTH AMERICA: National Accounts Totals** (in millions of stated unit, except as otherwise indicated)

### 1935–1969

| | Brazil (cruzeiros)[36] | | | | | | Chile (thousand million pesos/escudos)[38] | | | | | |
| | Current Prices | | | 1949/1953/1970 Prices[37] | | | Current Prices | | | 1960/1961/1965 Prices | | |
| | GDP | GFCF | Stocks | GDP | GFCF | Stocks | GDP | GFCF | Stocks | GDP | GFCF | Stocks |
|---|---|---|---|---|---|---|---|---|---|---|---|---|
| 1935 | 30 | ... | ... | 133 | ... | ... | ... | ... | ... | 1,438 | ... | ... |
| 1936 | 37 | ... | ... | 147 | ... | ... | ... | ... | ... | 1,505 | ... | ... |
| 1937 | 42 | ... | ... | 153 | ... | ... | ... | ... | ... | 1,522 | ... | ... |
| 1938 | 45 | ... | ... | 158 | ... | ... | ... | ... | ... | 1,518 | ... | ... |
| 1939 | 45 | ... | ... | 155 | ... | ... | ... | ... | ... | 1,634 | ... | ... |
| 1940 | 48 | ... | ... | 155 | ... | ... | 22 | 2.4 | 0.2 | 1,631 [31,39] | ... [39] | ... [39] |
| | | | | | | | | | | 2,676 | 241 | 10 |
| 1941 | 51 | ... | ... | 150 | ... | ... | 27 | 2.7 | 0.1 | 2,657 | 238 | 6 |
| 1942 | 58 | ... | ... | 152 | ... | ... | 32 | 2.7 | 0.3 | 2,710 | 189 | 19 |
| 1943 | 67 | ... | ... | 152 | ... | ... | 40 | 3.4 | 0.4 | 2,333 | 203 | 22 |
| 1944 | 88 | ... | ... | 157 | ... | ... | 47 | 4.5 | 1.1 | 2,376 | 228 | 62 |
| 1945 | 112 | ... | ... | 172 | ... | ... | 54 | 4.7 | 1.3 | 3,125 | 241 | 66 |
| 1946 | 148 | ... | ... | 194 | ... | ... | 68 | 7.8 | 3.2 | 3,320 | 334 | 140 |
| 1947 | 186 | ... | ... | 201 [37] | ... [37] | ... [37] | 79 | 9.1 | −4.1 | 3,110 | 367 | −143 |
| 1948 | 195 | 31 | −0.2 | 350 | 55 | −0.4 | 109 | 10 | 3.2 | 3,501 | 326 | 93 |
| 1949 | 230 | 36 | −1.7 | 373 | 60 | −2.9 | 130 | 13 | 1.5 | 3,138 | 373 | 39 |
| 1950 | 272 | 41 | −1.3 | 398 | 64 | −2.0 | 156 | 14 | 3.3 | 3,690 | 344 | 73 |
| 1951 | 323 | 60 | −2.1 | 421 | 79 | −2.7 | 191 | 19 | 1.3 | 3,881 | 392 | 23 |
| 1952 | 397 | 66 | 1.5 | 458 | 85 | 1.7 | 259 | 24 | −2.0 | 4,139 | 410 | −27 |
| 1953 | 470 | 72 | −2.3 | 470 | 72 | −2.3 | 351 | 32 | 12 | 4,391 | 414 | 132 |
| 1954 | 627 | 105 | 6.1 | 517 | 78 | 4.7 | 571 | 47 | −10 | 4,369 | 401 | −69 |
| 1955 | 783 | 106 | 14 | 552 | 73 | 9.6 | 1,041 | 87 | −2 | 4,431 | 464 | −8 |
| 1956 | 996 | 141 | −0.3 | 570 | 79 | −0.2 | 1,668 | 138 | 28 | 4,484 | 443 | 70 |
| 1957 | 1,218 | 125 | 29 | 616 | 90 | 15 | 2,309 | 247 | −18 | 4,834 | 506 | −31 |
| 1958 | 1,458 | 237 | 18 | 663 | 95 | 8.3 | 2,995 | 310 | −9 | 4,973 | 498 | −13 |
| 1959 | 1,989 [34] | 368 [34] | 60 [34] | 700 | 107 | 20 | 4,227 [38] | 405 [38] | 21 [38] | 5,000 [38] | 429 [38] | 22 [38] |
| 1960 | 2.8 | 0.5 | 0.04 | 768 | 112 | 10 | 4,974 | 513 | 81 | 5,364 [39] | 556 [39] | 87 [39] |
| 1961 | 4.1 | 0.7 | 0.09 | 847 | 117 | 17 | 5,538 | 720 | 65 | 17,565 | 2,312 | 207 |
| 1962 | 6.6 [10] | 1.2 | 0.16 | 892 [10] | 121 | 19 | 6,699 | 812 | 17 | 18,493 | 2,443 | 53 |
| 1963 | 14.1 | 2.1 | 0.13 | 1,057 | 118 | 9 | 9,993 [10] | 1,275 [10] | 106 [10] | 19,501 [10] | 2,508 [10] | 193 [10] |
| 1964 | 27.3 | 3.8 [10] | 0.49 | 1,099 [36,37] | 121 [10,36,37] | 17 [10,36,37] | 13,227 | 2,111 [36] | 111 [38] | 17,615 [38] | 2,735 [38] | 149 [38] |
| 1965 | 44 | 8 | 2 | 146 | 26 | 6 | 18.8 | 2.9 | 0.4 | 18.8 | 2.9 | 0.4 |
| 1966 | 64 | 13 | 2 | 153 | 31 | 5 | 26.2 | 3.8 | 0.7 | 20.6 | 2.9 | 0.5 |
| 1967 | 86 | 17 | - - | 160 | 32 | 0.4 | 34.4 | 4.8 | 0.3 | 20.9 | 2.9 | 0.2 |
| 1968 | 122 | 26 | 3 | 174 | 38 | 3 | 46.3 | 6.7 | 0.4 | 21.6 | 3.2 | 0.2 |
| 1969 | 162 | 36 | 4 | 191 | 43 | 5 | 67.4 | 9.7 | 1.1 | 22.8 | 3.3 | 0.4 |

## J1  SOUTH AMERICA: National Accounts Totals (in millions of stated unit, except as otherwise indicated)

### 1935–1969

| | Colombia | | | | | | Ecuador | | | | | |
| | (pesos) | | | | | | (thousand million sucres) | | | | | |
| | Current Prices | | | 1950/1970 Prices[40] | | | Current Prices | | | 1960/1965 Prices[41] | | |
| | GDP | GFCF | Stocks | GDP | GFCF | Stocks | GDP[42] | GFCF | Stocks | GDP[42] | GFCF | Stocks |
|---|---|---|---|---|---|---|---|---|---|---|---|---|
| 1935 | ... | ... | ... | 3,478 | 535 | 87 | ... | ... | ... | ... | ... | ... |
| 1936 | ... | ... | ... | 3,662 | 589 | 81 | ... | ... | ... | ... | ... | ... |
| 1937 | ... | ... | ... | 3,719 | 684 | 87 | ... | ... | ... | ... | ... | ... |
| 1938 | ... | ... | ... | 3,964 | 699 | 90 | ... | ... | ... | ... | ... | ... |
| 1939 | ... | ... | ... | 4,204 | 798 | 105 | 0.9 | ... | ... | 3.3 | ... | ... |
| 1940 | ... | ... | ... | 4,295 | 767 | 137 | 1.0 | ... | ... | 3.5 | ... | ... |
| 1941 | ... | ... | ... | 4,367 | 735 | 159 | 1.0 | ... | ... | 3.5 | ... | ... |
| 1942 | ... | ... | ... | 4,376 | 646 | 168 | 1.3 | ... | ... | 3.7 | ... | ... |
| 1943 | ... | ... | ... | 4,394 | 685 | 266 | 1.8 | ... | ... | 4.2 | ... | ... |
| 1944 | ... | ... | ... | 4,691 | 746 | −27 | 2.3 | ... | ... | 4.2 | ... | ... |
| 1945 | 2.55 | 0.19 | 0.03 | 4,911[10] 5,126 | 930 | 248 | 3.0 | ... | ... | 4.2 | ... | ... |
| 1946 | 3.10 | 0.32 | 0.04 | 5,590 | 1,099 | −86 | 3.8 | ... | ... | 4.7 | ... | ... |
| 1947 | 3.78 | 0.41 | 0.07 | 5,810 | 1,326 | 241 | 4.8 | ... | ... | 5.3 | ... | ... |
| 1948 | 4.45 | 0.42 | 0.01 | 5,990 | 1,297 | 214 | 6.2 | ... | ... | 6.0 | ... | ... |
| 1949 | 5.30[10] | 0.45[10] | 0.05[10] | 6,321[10,40] | 990[10,40] | −238[10,40] | 6.2[42] | ... | ... | 6.1[42] | ... | ... |
| 1950 | 7.86 | 1.11 | 0.21 | 50 | ... | ... | 7.2 | 0.6 | 0.2 | 8.7 | ... | ... |
| 1951 | 8.94 | 1.19 | 0.17 | 51 | ... | ... | 7.8 | 0.9 | 0.1 | 8.9 | ... | ... |
| 1952 | 9.65 | 1.33 | 0.16 | 55 | ... | ... | 8.9 | 0.8 | 0.1 | 9.9 | 0.9 | 0.1 |
| 1953 | 10.7 | 1.78 | −0.14 | 58 | 15 | −0.63 | 9.3 | 1.0 | 0.3 | 10 | 1.1 | 0.3 |
| 1954 | 12.8 | 2.16 | −0.02 | 62 | 18 | −0.05 | 10 | 1.4 | 0.2 | 11 | 1.5 | 0.3 |
| 1955 | 13 | 2.38 | — | 64 | 19 | — | 11 | 1.5 | 0.3 | 11 | 1.6 | 0.3 |
| 1956 | 15 | 2.53 | 0.18 | 67 | 18 | 0.7 | 11 | 1.6 | 0.2 | 12 | 1.6 | 0.2 |
| 1957 | 18 | 2.64 | 0.89 | 68 | 13 | 2.6 | 12 | 1.6 | 0.3 | 12 | 1.6 | 0.3 |
| 1958 | 21 | 3.34 | 0.52 | 70 | 13 | 1.5 | 12 | 1.5 | 0.3 | 13 | 1.5 | 0.3 |
| 1959 | 24 | 3.91 | 0.49 | 75 | 14 | 1.4 | 13 | 1.7 | 0.2 | 13 | 1.8 | 0.2 |
| 1960 | 27 | 4.8 | 0.7 | 78 | 16 | 1.5 | 14 | 1.9 | 0.3 | 14 | 1.9 | 0.3 |
| 1961 | 30 | 5.6 | 0.8 | 82 | 18 | 1.9 | 15 | 2.0 | 0.3 | 14 | 1.9 | 0.3 |
| 1962 | 34 | 6.1 | 0.3 | 87 | 18 | 0.6 | 16 | 2.0 | 0.3 | 15 | 1.8 | 0.3 |
| 1963 | 44 | 7.2 | 0.7 | 90 | 16 | 1.4 | 18 | 2.1 | 0.3 | 16 | 1.9 | 0.3 |
| 1964 | 54 | 8.7 | 0.9 | 95 | 18 | 1.6 | 19 | 2.3 | 0.4 | 17[25,41] | 2.0[25,41] | 0.3[25,41] |
| 1965 | 61 | 9.5 | 1.2 | 99 | 17 | 2.0 | 21 | 2.3 | 0.6 | 21 | 2.3 | 0.6 |
| 1966 | 74 | 12 | 2.7 | 94 | 19 | 3.9 | 23 | 2.6 | 0.8 | 22 | 2.5 | 0.7 |
| 1967 | 83 | 15 | 0.6 | 108 | 20 | 0.9 | 25 | 3.4 | 0.9 | 23 | 2.8 | 0.8 |
| 1968 | 96 | 19 | 1.6 | 115 | 23 | 1.8 | 27 | 3.9 | 1.0 | 24 | 2.8 | 0.7 |
| 1969 | 111 | 21 | 1.5 | 122 | 23 | 1.6 | 30 | 4.8 | 0.5 | 25 | 3.4 | 0.3 |

**J1     SOUTH AMERICA: National Accounts Totals** (in millions of stated unit, except as otherwise indicated)

**1935–1969**

| | Guyana (dollars) | | | | | | Paraguay (thousand million guaranies) | | | | | |
| | Current Prices | | | 1970 Prices | | | Current Prices | | | 1970 Prices | | |
| | GDP | GFCF | Stocks | GDP | GFCF | Stocks | GDP | GFCF | Stocks | GDP[43] | GFCF | Stocks |
|---|---|---|---|---|---|---|---|---|---|---|---|---|
| 1935 | ... | ... | ... | ... | ... | ... | ... | ... | | ... | ... | |
| 1936 | ... | ... | ... | ... | ... | ... | ... | ... | | ... | ... | |
| 1937 | ... | ... | ... | ... | ... | ... | ... | ... | | ... | ... | |
| 1938 | ... | ... | ... | ... | ... | ... | ... | ... | | 26 | ... | |
| 1939 | ... | ... | ... | ... | ... | ... | ... | ... | | 31 | ... | |
| 1940 | ... | ... | ... | ... | ... | ... | ... | ... | | 26 | ... | |
| 1941 | ... | ... | ... | ... | ... | ... | ... | ... | | 30 | ... | |
| 1942 | ... | ... | ... | ... | ... | ... | ... | ... | | 31 | ... | |
| 1943 | ... | ... | ... | ... | ... | ... | ... | ... | | 32 | ... | |
| 1944 | ... | ... | ... | ... | ... | ... | ... | ... | | 33 | ... | |
| 1945 | ... | ... | ... | ... | ... | ... | ... | ... | | 32 | ... | |
| 1946 | ... | ... | ... | ... | ... | ... | ... | ... | | 35 | ... | |
| 1947 | ... | ... | ... | ... | ... | ... | ... | ... | | 30 | ... | |
| 1948 | ... | ... | ... | ... | ... | ... | ... | ... | | 30 | ... | |
| 1949 | ... | ... | ... | ... | ... | ... | ... | ... | | 36 | ... | |
| 1950 | ... | ... | ... | ... | ... | ... | ... / 1.41 | ... | | 35[43] / 36 | ... | |
| 1951 | ... | ... | ... | ... | ... | ... | 2.38 | ... | | 36 | ... | |
| 1952 | 178 | 26 | 0.6 | ... | ... | ... | 4.39 | ... | | 36 | ... | |
| 1953 | 195 | 27 | −2.4 | ... | ... | ... | 7.88 | 1.4 | | 38 | 5.9 | |
| 1954 | 211 | 36 | 2.3 | ... | ... | ... | 10.8 | 1.6 | | 39 | 5.8 | |
| 1955 | 216 | 46 | 0.5 | ... | ... | ... | 14 | 1.7 | | 41 | 4.2 | |
| 1956 | 232 | 48 | 0.1 | ... | ... | ... | 18 | 2.0 | | 42 | 3.9 | |
| 1957 | 247 | 63 | 0.3 | ... | ... | ... | 23 | 4.1 | | 45 | 6.8 | |
| 1958 | 235 | 63 | 5.0 | ... | ... | ... | 26 | 4.4 | | 48 | 6.7 | |
| 1959 | 241 | 59 | −0.8 | ... | ... | ... | 29 | 4.3 | | 47 | 5.9 | |
| 1960 | 293 | 80 | 2.8 | 389 | 104 | 4 | 35 | 5.8 | | 47 | 6.9 | |
| 1961 | 321 | 77 | −0.9 | 419 | ... | ... | 40 | 6.7 | | 50 | 7.3 | |
| 1962 | 336 | 57 | −1.6 | 425 | ... | ... | 45 | 5.2 | 0.5 | 53 | 5.9 | 0.6 |
| 1963 | 301 | 40 | 11.0 | 351 | 75 | 13 | 48 | 4.9 | 0.5 | 55 | 5.3 | 0.5 |
| 1964 | 334 | 53 | 0.8 | 411 | ... | ... | 51 | 5.6 | 0.5 | 58 | 6.0 | 0.5 |
| 1965 | 362 | 70 | 10.6 | 456 | 86 | 12 | 56 | 8.0 | 0.4 | 61 | 8.5 | 0.5 |
| 1966 | 389 | 86 | 6.5 | 456 | ... | ... | 59 | 9.1 | 0.2 | 62 | 9.1 | 0.2 |
| 1967 | 425 | 105 | 4.8 | 501 | ... | ... | 62 | 10 | 0.2 | 66 | 10 | 0.2 |
| 1968 | 459 | 96 | 6.3 | 495 | ... | ... | 65 | 10 | 0.3 | 68 | 10 | 0.3 |
| 1969 | 499 | 98 | 5.8 | 518 | ... | ... | 70 | 11 | 0.4 | 71 | 10 | 0.4 |

**J1    SOUTH AMERICA: National Accounts Totals** (in millions of stated unit, except as otherwise indicated)

**1935–1969**

| | Peru (million soles)[44] | | | | | | Uruguay (pesos)[47] | | | | | |
|---|---|---|---|---|---|---|---|---|---|---|---|---|
| | Current Prices | | | 1973 Prices | | | Current Prices | | | 1961 Prices | | |
| | GNP/ GDP[45] | GFCF[46] | Stocks | GDP | GFCF | Stocks | GDP | GFCF | Stocks | GDP | GFCF | Stocks |
| 1935 | ... | ... | ... | ... | ... | ... | ... | ... | ... | 8,015 | ... | ... |
| 1936 | ... | ... | ... | ... | ... | ... | ... | ... | ... | 8,300 | ... | ... |
| 1937 | ... | ... | ... | ... | ... | ... | ... | ... | ... | 9,020 | ... | ... |
| 1938 | ... | ... | ... | ... | ... | ... | ... | ... | ... | 8,581 | ... | ... |
| 1939 | ... | ... | ... | ... | ... | ... | ... | ... | ... | 8,508 | ... | ... |
| 1940 | ... | ... | ... | ... | ... | ... | ... | ... | ... | 8,324 | ... | ... |
| 1941 | ... | ... | ... | ... | ... | ... | ... | ... | ... | 8,813 | ... | ... |
| 1942 | 2,960 | 236 | −36 | ... | ... | ... | ... | ... | ... | 8,015 | ... | ... |
| 1943 | 3,241 | 504 | −34 | ... | ... | ... | ... | ... | ... | 8,135 | ... | ... |
| 1944 | 3,829 | 627 | −101 | ... | ... | ... | ... | ... | ... | 9,184 | ... | ... |
| 1945 | 4,455 | 697 | −176 | ... | ... | ... | ... | ... | ... | 9,392 | ... | ... |
| 1946 | 5,291 | 1,098[46] | −12 | ... | ... | ... | ... | ... | ... | 10,432 | ... | ... |
| 1947 | 6,816 | 1,284 | 332 | ... | ... | ... | ... | ... | ... | 11,135 | ... | ... |
| 1948 | 8,624 | 1,106 | 199 | ... | ... | ... | ... | ... | ... | 11,422 | ... | ... |
| 1949 | 12,190[44] | 1,645[44] | 721[44] | ... | ... | ... | ... | ... | ... | 11,844 | ... | ... |
| 1950 | 15.1[45] | 2.7[25] | 0.4 | ... | ... | | ... | ... | ... | 12,208 | ... | ... |
| | 15.9 | 2.3 | | 110 | 14 | 3 | | | | | | |
| 1951 | 19.9 | 3.5 | 1.0 | 121 | 18 | 6 | ... | ... | ... | 13,214 | ... | ... |
| 1952 | 21.2 | 4.4 | 1.1 | 125 | 22 | 6 | ... | ... | ... | 13,161 | ... | ... |
| 1953 | 22.9 | 5.4 | 0.6 | 127 | 24 | 3 | ... | ... | ... | 14,011 | ... | ... |
| 1954 | 26.9 | 4.5 | 0.7 | 142 | 18 | 4 | ... | ... | ... | 14,813 | ... | ... |
| 1955 | 29.6 | 5.5 | 1.2 | 150 | 21 | 6 | ... | ... | ... | 15,045[25] | ... | ... |
| | | | | | | | 4,602 | 624 | 4 | 16,838 | 3,135 | 9 |
| 1956 | 33.0 | 7.7 | 0.9 | 154 | 27 | 4 | 5,163 | 692 | −15 | 17,131 | 2,895 | −34 |
| 1957 | 36.1 | 8.9 | 1.2 | 154 | 28 | 5 | 6,118 | 961 | 90 | 17,304 | 2,970 | 21.3 |
| 1958 | 40.3 | 9.2 | 1.0 | 162 | 26 | 4 | 6,616 | 711 | 11 | 16,681 | 2,152 | 44 |
| 1959 | 47.4 | 8.4 | 0.5 | 170 | 20 | 2 | 8,865[47] | 1,008[47] | 159[47] | 16,214[47] | 2,261[47] | 243[47] |
| 1960 | 55.6 | 9.5 | 2.8 | 182 | 21 | 9 | 13.6 | 2.0 | 0.3 | 17 | 2.5 | 0.3 |
| 1961 | 63.9 | 12.3 | 1.9 | 202 | 27 | 6 | 17.3 | 2.8 | 0.1 | 17 | 2.8 | 0.1 |
| 1962 | 73.4 | 15.1 | 1.6 | 221 | 32 | 5 | 18.8 | 2.9 | −0.1 | 17 | 2.8 | −0.1 |
| 1963 | 78.7 | 15.1 | 1.3 | 222 | 30 | 4 | 22.4 | 2.9 | 0.1 | 17 | 2.3 | 0.1 |
| 1964 | 96.7 | 15.4 | 2.7 | 245 | 28 | 7 | 32.6 | 3.4 | 0.2 | 17 | 2.0 | 0.1 |
| 1965 | 115 | 19.2 | 2.2 | 258 | 35 | 5 | 52.5 | 5.7 | — | 18 | 2.0 | - - |
| 1966 | 137 | 22.6 | 4.9 | 274 | 39 | 10 | 99.6 | 10.9 | 1.1 | 18 | 1.9 | 0.2 |
| 1967 | 157 | 23.4 | 7.6 | 285 | 37 | 14 | 170 | 22.8 | 0.6 | 17 | 2.2 | 0.1 |
| 1968 | 186 | 24.1 | 1.7 | 285 | 31 | 3 | 375 | 38.3 | −0.3 | 18 | 2.0 | - - |
| 1969 | 209 | 25.9 | 2.0 | 296 | 33 | 3 | 506 | 56.0 | −0.8 | 19 | 2.6 | - - |

**J1    SOUTH AMERICA: National Accounts Totals** (in millions of stated unit, except as otherwise indicated)

### 1935–1969

|      | Venezuela (thousand million bolivares) | | | | | |
|      | Current Prices | | | 1957 Prices | | |
|------|------|------|--------|------|------|--------|
|      | GDP  | GFCF | Stocks | GDP  | GFCF | Stocks |
| 1935 | ...  | ...  | ...    | ...  | ...  | ...    |
| 1936 | ...  | ...  | ...    | ...  | ...  | ...    |
| 1937 | ...  | ...  | ...    | ...  | ...  | ...    |
| 1938 | ...  | ...  | ...    | ...  | ...  | ...    |
| 1939 | ...  | ...  | ...    | ...  | ...  | ...    |
| 1940 | ...  | ...  | ...    | ...  | ...  | ...    |
| 1941 | ...  | ...  | ...    | ...  | ...  | ...    |
| 1942 | ...  | ...  | ...    | ...  | ...  | ...    |
| 1943 | ...  | ...  | ...    | ...  | ...  | ...    |
| 1944 | ...  | ...  | ...    | ...  | ...  | ...    |
| 1945 | ...  | ...  | ...    | ...  | ...  | ...    |
| 1946 | ...  | ...  | ...    | ...  | ...  | ...    |
| 1947 | ...  | ...  | ...    | ...  | ...  | ...    |
| 1948 | ...  | ...  | ...    | ...  | ...  | ...    |
| 1949 | ...  | ...  | ...    | ...  | ...  | ...    |
| 1950 | 12   | 2.8  | 0.1    | ...  | ...  | ...    |
| 1951 | 13   | 3.2  | 0.1    | ...  | ...  | ...    |
| 1952 | 14   | 4.0  | 0.4    | ...  | ...  | ...    |
| 1953 | 15   | 4.3  | - -    | 16   | 4.7  | ...    |
| 1954 | 16   | 5.0  | 0.1    | 18   | 5.4  | ...    |
| 1955 | 18   | 4.4  | 0.2    | 19   | 5.1  | ...    |
| 1956 | 20   | 5.1  | 0.2    | 21   | 5.5  | ...    |
| 1957 | 24   | 6.0  | 0.3    | 24   | 6.0  | 0.4    |
| 1958 | 25   | 6.0  | 0.4    | 24   | 5.7  | ...    |
| 1959 | 26   | 6.1  | 0.3    | 26   | 5.9  | 0.4    |
| 1960 | 26   | 4.8  | −0.3   | 27   | 4.7  | −0.3   |
| 1961 | 27   | 4.3  | 0.3    | 28   | 4.0  | 0.3    |
| 1962 | 30   | 4.6  | 0.6    | 31   | 4.2  | 0.5    |
| 1963 | 32   | 5.0  | 0.5    | 33   | 4.3  | 0.4    |
| 1964 | 36   |      | 1.3    | 36   | 5.2  | 1.1    |
| 1965 | 38   | 7.0  | 0.9    | 39   | 5.6  | 0.7    |
| 1966 | 40   | 7.4  | 0.5    | 39   | 5.7  | 0.4    |
| 1967 | 42   | 7.9  | 0.5    | 41   | 5.9  | 0.4    |
| 1968 | 45   | 9.4 [48] | 1.2 [48] | 43 | 6.7 [48] | 1.0 [48] |
|      |      | 10   | 2.7    |      | 7.5  | 2.1    |
| 1969 | 46   | 11   | 1.0    | 45   | 7.9  | 0.8    |

**J1 SOUTH AMERICA: National Accounts Totals** (in millions of stated unit, except as otherwise indicated).

| | Argentina (thousand million new (1970) pesos[49]) | | | | | | Bolivia (thousand million pesos[50]) | | | | | |
|---|---|---|---|---|---|---|---|---|---|---|---|---|
| | Current Prices | | | 1960/1970 Prices[33] | | | Current prices | | | 1970/1980 Prices[51] | | |
| | GDP | GFCF | Stocks | GDP | GFCF | Stocks | GDP | GFCF | Stocks | GDP | GFCF | Stocks |
| 1970 | 95 | 19 | 0.4 | 15[33] | 3.3[33] | 0.1[33] | 12.4 | 1.8 | 0.3 | 12.4 | 1.8 | 0.3 |
| 1971 | 133 | 26 | 1.2 | 96 | 20 | 0.5 | 13.5 | 2.0 | 0.4 | 13.0 | 2.0 | 0.4 |
| 1972 | 220 | 44 | 2.0 | 98 | 21 | 0.5 | 17.2 | 2.6 | 0.8 | 13.7 | 2.2 | 0.7 |
| 1973 | 365 | 70 | 4.1 | 99 | 21 | 1.0 | 26.1 | 4.5 | 0.9 | 14.6 | 2.2 | 0.4 |
| 1974 | 497[49] | 100[49] | 10.4[49] | 103 | 22 | 2.0 | 43.3 | 6.5 | 0.6 | 15.4 | 2.3 | 0.2 |
| 1975 | 1.35 | 0.29 | - - | 95 | 15 | - - | 49.2 | 9.1 | 3.0 | 16.4 | 2.8 | 0.8 |
| 1976 | 7.59 | 2.04 | 0.02 | 101 | 22 | - - | 56.4 | 10.7 | 1.3 | 17.4 | 2.9 | 0.3 |
| 1977 | 20.93 | 5.69 | — | 107 | 26 | — | 65.2 | 12.4 | 1.1 | 18.2 | 3.1 | 0.2 |
| 1978 | 52.34 | 12.76 | −0.27 | 104 | 23 | ... | 75.2 | 16.4 | 2.2 | 18.8[51] / 124 | 3.4[51] / 25 | 0.4[51] / 4.1 |
| 1979 | 142.5[49] | 32.35[49] | −0.18[49] | 111 | 24 | - - | 90.2 | 17.4 | 1.4 | 125 | 23 | 2.1 |
| 1980 | 28.3 | 6.3 | 0.16 | 113 | 26 | 1.0 | 123 | 17.5 | 0.5 | 123 | 18 | 0.5 |
| 1981 | 54.8 | 10.3 | −0.27 | 105 | 21 | −0.7 | 155 | 22 | — | 124 | 17 | — |
| 1982 | 148 | 23.4 | −1.61 | 100 | 15 | 1.1 | 402 | 52 | — | 119 | 12 | — |
| 1983 | 683 | 118 | −0.45 | 103 | 15 | 0.1 | 1,387 | 163 | 10 | 111 | 12 | - - |
| 1984 | 5,281[49] | 813[49] | −47[49] | 106 | 13 | −0.2 | 20,900[50] | 2,260[50] | −50[50] | 124 | 12 | −0.6 |
| 1985 | 39.6 | 5.3 | −0.4 | 101 | 12 | −1.3 | 2,867 | 336 | 148 | 147 | 15 | 7.6 |
| 1986 | 74.3 | 9.8 | −0.2 | 107 | 13 | −0.5 | 8,924 | 959 | 234 | 137 | 23 | 8.8 |
| 1987 | 177 | 25 | −0.3 | 109 | 14 | −0.2 | 10,180 | 1,146 | 368 | 134 | 25 | 12 |
| 1988 | 785 | 102 | 5 | 106 | 12 | 0.6 | 12,303 | 1,414 | −26 | 138 | 27 | −3.8 |

| | Brazil (thousand million cruzeiros/cruzados[36]) | | | | | | Chile (pesos) | | | | | |
|---|---|---|---|---|---|---|---|---|---|---|---|---|
| | Current Prices | | | 1970/1980 Prices[51] | | | Current Prices | | | 1965/1977 Prices | | |
| | GDP | GFCF | Stocks | GDP | GFCF | Stocks | GDP | GFCF | Stocks | GDP | GFCF | Stocks |
| 1970 | 196 | 45 | 3 | 196 | 45 | 3 | 97 | 13 | 2.0 | 23.6 | 3.4 | 0.5 |
| 1971 | 261 | 61 | 7 | 223 | 52 | 6 | 129 | 17 | 2.0 | 24.4 | 3.4 | 0.3 |
| 1972 | 345 | 81 | 9 | 251 | 59 | 7 | 239 | 29 | 5.0 | 24.4 | 2.9 | 0.5 |
| 1973 | 483 | 114 | 21 | 291 | 69 | 13 | 1,213 | 162 | 6.0 | 23.5 | 2.8 | 0.2 |
| 1974 | 708 | 177 | 53 | 304 | 83 | 25 | 9,661 | 1,202 | 39 | 24.9 / 291 | 3.2 / 50 | 0.1 / 1.6 |
| 1975 | 1,005 | 245 | ... | 347[36 51] / 9.0 | 89[36 51] / 2.3 | ... | 36 | 6.3 | −1.6 | 253 | 39 | −3.5 |
| 1976 | 1,629 | 366 | ... | 9.9 | 2.4 | ... | 129 | 17 | −0.6 | 262 | 33 | −2.3 |
| 1977 | 2,491 | 532 | ... | 10.3 | 2.4 | ... | 288 | 38 | 3.2 | 288 | 38 | 3.2 |
| 1978 | 3,627 | 805 | ... | 10.8 | 2.5 | ... | 487 | 72 | 15 | 311 | 45 | 6.2 |
| 1979 | 6,059[36] | 1,393[36] | −35[36] | 11.6 | 2.6 | - - | 772 | 115 | 22 | 337 | 53 | 14 |
| 1980 | 12.6 | 2.8 | — | 12.6 | 2.8 | - - | 1,075 | 179 | 47 | 363 | 64 | 23 |
| 1981 | 24.6 | 5.2 | — | 12.2 | 2.1 | — | 1,273 | 237 | 52 | 384 | 75 | 31 |
| 1982 | 50.5 | 10.8 | −0.2 | 12.3 | 2.3 | - - | 1,239 | 181 | −42 | 330 | 49 | −13 |
| 1983 | 117 | 21.3 | −1.7 | 12.0 | 1.8 | - - | 1,558 | 186 | −34 | 327 | 42 | −12 |
| 1984 | 386 | 65.2 | −4.4 | 12 | 2.0 | - - | 1,893 | 234 | 24 | 348 | 46 | 7.3 |
| 1985 | 1,383 | 234 | ... | 13 | 2.1 | ... | 2,577 | 366 | −13 | 356 | 53 | −3.0 |
| 1986 | 3,662 | 699 | ... | 14 | 2.6 | ... | 3,246 | 473 | 1.4 | 377 | 56 | 0.3 |
| 1987 | 11,537 | 2,573 | ... | 15 | 2.6 | ... | 4,160 | 667 | 36 | 398 | 66 | 5.7 |
| 1988 | 86,198 | 19,666 | ... | 15 | 2.8 | ... | 5,411 | 883 | 36 | 428 | 73 | 4.8 |

**J1  SOUTH AMERICA: National Accounts Totals** (in millions of stated unit, except as otherwise indicated)

| | Colombia (thousand million pesos) | | | | | | Ecuador (thousand million sucres) | | | | | |
|---|---|---|---|---|---|---|---|---|---|---|---|---|
| | Current Prices | | | 1975 Prices | | | Current Prices | | | 1965/1975 Prices[52] | | |
| | GDP | GFCF | Stocks | GDP | GFCF | Stocks | GDP | GFCF | Stocks | GDP | GFCF | Stocks |
| 1970 | 133 | 21 | 2.9 | 307 | 47 | 6.8 | 35 | 5.8 | 0.5 | 27[52] / 65 | 4.8[52] / 8.2 | 0.4[52] / 1.0 |
| 1971 | 156 | 24 | 3.0 | 326 | 50 | 6.2 | 40 | 8.7 | 0.6 | 67 | 14 | 1.0 |
| 1972 | 190 | 27 | 3.9 | 351 | 48 | 7.2 | 47 | 8.4 | 0.9 | 77 | 11 | 1.5 |
| 1973 | 243 | 32 | 6.0 | 374 | 50 | 9.3 | 62 | 11 | 1.2 | 96 | 14 | 1.8 |
| 1974 | 322 | 37 | 16 | 396 | 45 | 19 | 93 | 17 | 4.0 | 102 | 19 | 4.4 |
| 1975 | 405 | 55 | 6.7 | 405 | 55 | 6.7 | 108 | 25 | 3.9 | 108 | 25 | 3.9 |
| 1976 | 532 | 85 | 8.9 | 424 | 68 | 7.2 | 133 | 29 | 2.1 | 118 | 25 | 2.0 |
| 1977 | 716 | 104 | 30 | 442 | 69 | 19 | 166 | 39 | 4.9 | 125 | 29 | 4.0 |
| 1978 | 909 | 140 | 26 | 479 | 75 | 19 | 191 | 50 | 4.3 | 134 | 33 | 4.0 |
| 1979 | 1,189 | 183 | 32 | 505 | 78 | 15 | 234 | 59 | 3.9 | 141 | 33 | 3.1 |
| 1980 | 1,579 | 265 | 36 | 526 | 88 | 15 | 293 | 65 | 7.3 | 148 | 35 | 4.2 |
| 1981 | 1,983 | 350 | 59 | 538 | 94 | 23 | 349 | 78 | 3.2 | 153 | 32 | 1.5 |
| 1982 | 2,497 | 436 | 76 | 543 | 96 | 27 | 416 | 94 | 11 | 155 | 33 | 5.6 |
| 1983 | 3,054 | 525 | 83 | 551 | 88 | 23 | 560 | 93 | 5.4 | 151 | 24 | 2.2 |
| 1984 | 3,857 | 654 | 77 | 570 | 99 | 15 | 813 | 125 | 15 | 157 | 23 | 2.9 |
| 1985 | 4,966 | 870 | 75 | 588 | 94 | 9.1 | 1,110 | 178 | 23 | 164 | 25 | 3.4 |
| 1986 | 6,788 | 1,204 | 18 | 622 | 101 | 6.4 | 1,383 | 260 | 28 | 169 | 26 | 3.1 |
| 1987 | 8,824 | 1,537 | 227 | 655 | 101 | 15 | 1,794 | 407 | — | 159 | 27 | — |
| 1988 | 11,636 | 2,202 | 348 | 680 | 111 | 18 | 3,104 | 667 | 16 | 180 | 25 | 0.9 |

| | Guyana (dollars) | | | | | | Paraguay (thousand million guaranies) | | | | | |
|---|---|---|---|---|---|---|---|---|---|---|---|---|
| | Current Prices | | | 1970/1985 Prices[58] | | | Current Prices | | | 1970/1982 Prices[59] | | |
| | GDP | GFCF | Stocks | GDP | GFCF | Stocks | GDP | GFCF | Stocks | GDP | GFCF | Stocks |
| 1970 | 533 | 113 | 9.2 | 533 | 113 | 9 | 75 | 11 | 0.2 | 75 | 11 | 0.2 |
| 1971 | 561 | 103 | 2.3 | 544 | 102 | 2 | 84 | 12 | 0.4 | 78 | 12 | 0.2 |
| 1972 | 599 | 108 | 11 | 586 | 79 | 8 | 97 | 13 | 1.3 | 82 | 12 | 0.2 |
| 1973 | 645 | 155 | 21 | 549 | 112 | 18 | 125 | 20 | 3.5 | 89 | 17 | 0.5 |
| 1974 | 955 | 198 | 54 | 588 | 84 | 33 | 168 | 31 | 4.4 | 96 | 19 | 0.5 |
| 1975 | 1,188 | 350 | 42 | 651[58] / 2,719 | 175 | 29 | 190 | 40 | 6.4 | 101[59] / 416 | 23[59] / 63 | 0.8[59] / 15 |
| 1976 | 1,136 | 381 | 44 | 2,798 | ... | ... | 214 | 49 | 4 | 447 | 87 | 9 |
| 1977 | 1,125 | 290 | ... | 2,664 | ... | ... | 264 | 63 | 2.2 | 495 | 104 | 5 |
| 1978 | 1,268 | 242 | ... | 2,618 | ... | ... | 322 | 81 | 6.5 | 552 | 126 | 12 |
| 1979 | 1,326 | 325 | ... | 2,312 | ... | ... | 430 | 116 | 6.8 | 614 | 151 | 10 |
| 1980 | 1,508 | 404 | ... | 2,350 | ... | ... | 560 | 153 | 8.6 | 685 | 184 | 11 |
| 1981 | 1,597 | 500 | ... | 2,343 | ... | ... | 709 | 194 | 10 | 744 | 217 | 11 |
| 1982 | 1,446 | 380 | ... | 2,099 | ... | ... | 737 | 177 | 12 | 737 | 177 | 12 |
| 1983 | 1,468 | 395 | ... | 1,905 | ... | ... | 818 | 164 | 11 | 715 | 145 | 9 |
| 1984 | 1,700 | 390 | ... | 1,945 | ... | ... | 1,070 | 231 | 14 | 740 | 146 | 10 |
| 1985 | 1,964 | 410 | ... | 1,964 | ... | ... | 1,394 | 288 | 18 | 766 | 147 | 12 |
| 1986 | 2,219 | 586 | ... | 1,969 | ... | ... | 1,834 | 432 | 27 | 766 | 152 | 13 |
| 1987 | 3,382 | 1,123 | ... | 1,981 | ... | ... | 2,494 | 591 | 34 | 799 | 161 | 14 |
| 1988 | 4,138 | 890 | ... | 1,921 | ... | ... | 3,433 | 749 | 46 | 879 | 163 | 18 |

**J1** **SOUTH AMERICA: National Accounts Totals** (in millions of stated unit, except as otherwise indicated)

### Peru[53]
(intis)

| | Current Prices | | | 1973/1979 Prices[54] | | |
|------|------|------|------|------|------|------|
| | GDP | GFCF | Stocks | GDP | GFCF | Stocks |
| 1970 | 241 | 29.9 | 1.2 | 319 | 36 | 2 |
| 1971 | 264 | 33.3 | 6.4 | 331 | 38 | 9 |
| 1972 | 295 | 37.8 | 4.0 | 340[54] | 41[54] | 8[54] |
| 1973 | 359 | 45.4 | 10.8 | 2,465 | 386 | 74 |
| 1974 | 448 | 68.0 | 16.5 | 2,666 | 499 | 98 |
| 1975 | 550 | 96.8 | 12.4 | 2,656 | 604 | 35 |
| 1976 | 765 | 128 | 9.2 | 2,862 | 557 | 34 |
| 1977 | 1,058 | 154 | 5 | 2,917 | 451 | 11 |
| 1978 | 1,678 | 235 | 9 | 2,911 | 411 | −16 |
| 1979 | 3,490[53] | 724[53] | 33[53] | 3,490[53] | 724[53] | 33[53] |
| 1980 | 5.99 | 1.50 | 0.24 | 3.66 | 1.06 | 0.15 |
| 1981 | 10.6 | 3.04 | 0.58 | 3.81 | 1.12 | 0.22 |
| 1982 | 17.4 | 5.1 | 0.66 | 3.70 | 1.03 | 0.15 |
| 1983 | 31.4 | 7.4 | 0.17 | 3.23 | 0.70 | - - |
| 1984 | 68.8 | 14.4 | −0.22 | 3.31 | 0.57 | −0.02 |
| 1985 | 189 | 34.3 | 0.41 | 3.39 | 0.46 | −0.02 |
| 1986 | 360 | 73.6 | 3.2 | 3.74 | 0.62 | 0.06 |
| 1987 | 722 | 143 | 16.3 | 4.03 | 0.72 | 0.14 |
| 1988 | 4,431 | 880 | 150 | 3.33 | 0.48 | 0.18 |

### Uruguay
(thousand million pesos[55])

| | Current Prices | | | 1961/1978 Prices[56] | | |
|------|------|------|------|------|------|------|
| | GDP | GFCF | Stocks | GDP | GFCF | Stocks |
| 1970 | 601 | 69 | 0.4 | 20 | 2.7 | - - |
| 1971 | 722 | 83 | 8.4 | 19 | 2.9 | 0.2 |
| 1972 | 1,242 | 121 | 26 | 19 | 2.3 | 0.2 |
| 1973 | 2,561 | 229 | 93 | 19[56] | 2.0[56] | 0.4[56] |
| | | | | 25,579 | 2,021 | 298 |
| 1974 | 4,546 | 465 | 60 | 26,383 | 2,238 | 171 |
| 1975 | 8,166 | 1,090 | 12 | 27,930 | 3,141 | −84 |
| 1976 | 12,638 | 1,952 | −81 | 29,043 | 4,031 | −333 |
| 1977 | 19,915 | 3,030 | −2 | 29,384 | 4,321 | 14 |
| 1978 | 30,930 | 4,943 | 8 | 30,930 | 4,943 | 8 |
| 1979 | 57,630[55] | 9,310[55] | 660[55] | 32,838 | 5,882 | 250 |
| 1980 | 92.2 | 15.4 | 0.6 | 34,808 | 6,255 | 206 |
| 1981 | 122 | 19.2 | −0.4 | 35,469 | 6,067 | −179 |
| 1982 | 129 | 19.4 | −0.8 | 32,138 | 5,165 | −350 |
| 1983 | 185 | 20.3 | −1.9 | 30,257 | 3,471 | −419 |
| 1984 | 294 | 27.3 | 1.8 | 29,816 | 3,009 | 102 |
| 1985 | 528 | 39.2 | 3.9 | 29,905 | 2,310 | 214 |
| 1986 | 981 | 77.9 | 2.5 | 32,148 | 2,602 | 28 |
| 1987 | 1,754 | 160 | 10 | 34,048 | 3,112 | 146 |
| 1988 | 2,855 | 273 | 8.1 | 34,217 | 5,837 | 100 |

**J1**    **SOUTH AMERICA: National Accounts Totals** (in millions of stated unit, except as otherwise indicated)

| | Venezuela (thousand million bolivares) | | | | | |
|---|---|---|---|---|---|---|
| | **Current Prices** | | | **1968/1984 Prices**[57] | | |
| | **GDP** | **GFCF** | **Stocks** | **GDP** | **GFCF** | **Stocks** |
| 1970 | 52 | 12 | 3.9 | 51 | 11 | 3.8 |
| 1971 | 57 | 13 | 3.7 | 54 | 12 | ... |
| 1972 | 61 | 16 | 3.4 | 54 | 14 | ... |
| 1973 | 73 | 19 | 2.8 | 57 | 15 | ... |
| 1974 | 112 | 21 | 5.9 | 61 | 15 | ... |
| 1975 | 118 | 31 | 5.8 | 64 | 19 | ... |
| 1976 | 135 | 43 | 3.7 | 70 | 24 | ... |
| 1977 | 156 | 60 | 4.2 | 75 | 31 | ... |
| 1978 | 169 | 72 | 0.6 | 76 | 33 | ... |
| 1979 | 208 | 66 | 0.1 | 77 | 26 | ... |
| 1980 | 254 | 64 | −1.3 | 76 | 22 | ... |
| 1981 | 285 | 70 | −4.4 | 76 | 23 | ... |
| 1982 | 291 | 70 | 5.2 | 76 | 22 | ... |
| 1983 | 290 | 55 | −21 | 72 | 16 | ... |
| 1984 | 406 | 67 | 6.2 | 83[57] | 18[57] | ... |
| 1985 | 449 | 80 | 5.4 | 401 | 72 | 4.9 |
| 1986 | 492 | 100 | 2.6 | 442 | 78 | 2.1 |
| 1987 | 679 | 148 | 23 | 431 | 78 | 13 |
| 1988 | 876 | 199 | 45 | 493 | 85 | 20 |

## J1    National Accounts Totals

### NOTES

1.  SOURCES: The national publications referred to on p. xiv–xvi; IMF, *International Financial Statistics;* UN, *Yearbook of National Accounts Statistics* and *Statistics of National Income and Expenditure;* and Economic Commission for Latin America, *Statistical Abstract of Latin America,* together with the following:

    Canada to 1926 (1st line)—O.J. Firestone, *Canada's Economic Development, 1867–1953* (*Income and Wealth*, Series VII, London, 1958).

    Cuba to 1927—Julian Alienes, *Caracteristicas Fundamentales de la Economia Cubana* (Havana, 1950).

    Mexico, capital formation to 1950, from Combined Mexican Working Party, *The Economic Development of Mexico* (Baltimore, 1953)

    USA to 1889 (1st line)—Thomas S. Berry, *Estimated Annual Variations in Gross National Product, 1789 to 1909* (Richmond, 1968).

    USA from 1929 to 1980—U.S. Department of Commerce, *Survey of Current Business* vol 66, no 2. (February 1986).

    Argentina, capital formation to 1934, based on Alexander Ganz and on Manuel Balboa and Alberto Fracchia in *Income and Wealth,* Series VIII (London, 1959).

    Brazil to 1947, from or based on Claudio R. Contador & Claudio L. Haddad, 'Produto Real, Moeda e Preços: A Experiênca Brasileira no Período 1861–1970', *Revista Brasileira de Estatística* (XXXVI, 143, July–Sept 1975).

    Chile to 1925 (1st line), from or based on Marto A. Ballasteros and Tom E. Davis, 'The Growth of Output and Employment in Basic Sectors of the Chilean Economy, 1908–1957', *Economic Development and Cultural Change* (January 1963).

    Chile 1925 (2nd line) to 1940 (1st line), based on or from the Economic Commission for Latin America sources as modified in Markos Mamalakis and Clark W. Reynolds, *Essays on the Chilean Economy* (Homewood, Ill., 1965), p. 384.

2.  For definitions of concepts see the UN publications on national accounts.

### FOOTNOTES

[1] Excluding government capital formation to 1920.

[2] The annual estimates shown in table 87 of the source are given here, but they are said by the author to be less reliable than those which he made for benchmark years in current as well as constant prices, and it is the latter figures which correspond to the current prices statistics given here. They are as follows (in 1935–39 prices):

| | | | |
|---|---|---|---|
| 1870 | 762 | 1900 | 1,833 |
| 1880 | 1,034 | 1910 | 3,087 |
| 1890 | 1,386 | 1920 | 3,844 |

[3] This break occurs on a change of source. The estimates in the source of the earlier figures are continued there to 1909.

[4] 1935–39 prices to 1920 and 1971 prices from 1926.

[5] The series to 1950 (1st line) are presumably less complete than later revised figures. Government capital formation is not included in the GCF series to 1946 (1st line).

[6] Years ended 30 September. Figures to 1950 (1st line) are at factor cost.

[7] Later revisions to the GDP series were not carried so far back in the component series.

[8] Years beginning 1 July.

[9] NNP to 1946 (1st line), GNP from 1946 (2nd line) to 1949, and GDP subsequently. The 1950 figure for GNP is $864 million.

[10] Later revisions were not carried back further and there may be a break in the continuity of the series.

[11] 1958 prices to 1929 (1st line) and 1982 prices subsequently.

[12] 1971 prices to 1975 (1st line) and 1981 prices subsequently.

[13] NNP to 1950 (1st line), GDP from 1950 (2nd line) to 1958, and NMP from 1962 (though the same series was described as gross until 1981).

[14] GFCF to 1970 and NFCF subsequently. There was a change in concept from 1962.

[15] 1965 prices to 1965, 1981 prices from 1975.

[16] These figures are approximate estimates.

[17] GNP to 1950 (1st line) and GDP subsequently.

[18] 1946 prices to 1950 (1st line) and 1958 prices subsequently.

[19] 1970 prices to 1969 and 1976 prices subsequently.

[20] 1948 prices to 1950 (1st line), 1970 prices from then to 1975 (1st line), and 1978 prices subsequently.

[21] NNP to 1950 (1st line) and GDP subsequently.

[22] 1956 prices to 1958, 1960 prices from 1959 to 1970 (1st line), and 1974 prices subsequently.

[23] *footnote suppressed*

[24] Million million pesos from 1985.

[25] There was a change in the concept employed.

[26] 1960 prices to 1970, 1970 prices from 1971 to 1980, and 1980 prices subsequently.

[27] Thousand million cordobas from 1978 (2nd line) or 1979.

[28] 1958 prices to 1978 (1st line) and 1985 prices subsequently.

[29] 1960 prices to 1970 and 1970 prices subsequently.

[30] 1975 prices to 1974 and 1985 prices subsequently for GDP, and 1970 prices to 1983 and 1985 prices subsequently for GCF

[31] For recent decades a consistent series of total GFCF in current prices is given in IMF sources as follows (in thousand million dollars):-

| | | | | | |
|------|-------|------|-------|------|-------|
| 1959 | 90.1  | 1969 | 174.6 | 1979 | 502.4 |
| 1960 | 91.6  | 1970 | 177.5 | 1980 | 516.8 |
| 1961 | 92.3  | 1971 | 198.6 | 1981 | 564.6 |
| 1962 | 99.9  | 1972 | 225.2 | 1982 | 549.0 |
| 1963 | 108.2 | 1973 | 254.3 | 1983 | 563.5 |
| 1964 | 116.8 | 1974 | 268.3 | 1984 | 674.9 |
| 1965 | 131.2 | 1975 | 273.7 | 1985 | 731.1 |
| 1966 | 142.0 | 1976 | 277.7 | 1986 | 752.8 |
| 1967 | 144.7 | 1977 | 374.3 | 1987 | 770.6 |
| 1968 | 160.6 | 1978 | 444.9 | 1988 | 814.1 |

[32] Including Alaska and Hawaii from 1960.

[33] This break occurs on a change of source.

[34] Million million pesos from 1965.

[35] 1950 prices to 1936 (1st line), 1960 prices to 1970, and 1070 prices subsequently.

[36] Thousand million cruzeiros from 1960 for current prices and 1965 for constant prices. From 1980 for current and 1975 for constant prices, figures are in cruzados.

[37] 1949 prices to 1947, 1953 prices from 1948 to 1964, and 1970 prices subsequently.

[38] Million escudoes from 1960 to 1964 and thousand million escudos from 1965 to 1969.

[39] 1960 prices to 1940 (1st line), 1961 prices from 1940 (2nd line) to 1960, and 1965 prices subsequently.

[40] 1950 prices to 1949 and 1970 prices subsequently.

[41] 1960 prices to 1964 and 1965 prices subsequently.

[42] At factor cost to 1949.

[43] At factor cost to 1950 (1st line).

[44] Thousand million soles from 1950.

[45] GNP to 1950 (1st line) and GDP subsequently.

[46] Not including government capital formation to 1946.

[47] Thousand million pesos from 1960.

[48] New concepts were employed from 1968 (2nd line). There is no break in the GDP series at this level of rounding.

[49] For current price series, million million pesos from 1975 to 1979, million australes from 1980 to 1984, and thousand million australes subsequently.

[50] Million bolivianos from 1985.

[51] 1970 prices to 1975 (1st line) and 1980 prices subsequently.

[52] 1965 prices to 1970 (1st line) and 1975 prices subsequently.

[53] Thousand million intis from 1980.

[54] 1973 prices to 1972 and 1979 prices subsequently.

[55] Thousand million pesos from 1980.

[56] 1961 prices to 1973 (1st line) and 1978 prices subsequently.

[57] 1968 prices to 1984 and 1984 prices subsequently.

[58] 1970 prices to 1975 (1st line) and 1985 prices subsequently.

[59] 1970 prices to 1975 (1st line) and 1952 prices subsequently.

**J2     NORTH AMERICA: PROPORTIONS OF GDP BY SECTOR OF ORIGIN** (percentages)

Key:     A = agriculture, forestry and fishing; I = manufacturing, mining and public utilities; B = construction; T = transport and communications; C & F = commerce and finance.

| | Canada | | | | | | Honduras | | | | | |
|---|---|---|---|---|---|---|---|---|---|---|---|---|
| | **A** | **I** | **B** | **T** | **C&F** | **Other** | **A** | **I** | **B** | **T** | **C&F** | **Other** |
| 1925–29 | 17.8[1] | 25.8[1,2] | 4.5[1] | 12.9[1,3] | 22.0[1] | 16.7[1] | 55 | 7 | 3 | ... | 11 | 14 |
| 1930–34 | 11.4 | 25.7[2] | 3.7 | 13.4[2] | 25.3 | 20.5 | 57 | 7 | 3 | ... | 11 | 14 |
| 1935–39 | 12.7 | 30.3[2] | 3.0 | 12.8[2] | 22.9 | 18.3 | 50 | 10 | 4 | ... | 14 | 17 |

| | Mexico | | | | | | Puerto Rico | | | | | |
|---|---|---|---|---|---|---|---|---|---|---|---|---|
| 1895–99 | 32 | 15 | ... | 2 | ... | 50 | ... | ... | ... | ... | ... | ... |
| 1900–04 | 28 | 19 | ... | 2 | ... | 50 | ... | ... | ... | ... | ... | ... |
| 1905–10 | 28 | 19 | ... | 2 | ... | 50 | ... | ... | ... | ... | ... | ... |
| 1921–24 | 24 | 21 | ... | 2 | ... | 55 | ... | ... | ... | ... | ... | ... |
| 1925–29 | 22 | 21 | ... | 2 | ... | 55 | ... | ... | ... | ... | ... | ... |
| 1930–34 | 22 | 20 | ... | 3 | ... | ... | ... | ... | ... | ... | ... | |
| 1935–39 | 20 | 22 | ... | 3 | ... | 55 | 30[2] | 13[3] | | 7[3] | 10[3] | 39[3] |

| | USA[2,4] | | | | | |
|---|---|---|---|---|---|---|
| 1869&1879 | 20.5 | 15.7[2] | 5.3 | 11.9[2] | 27.4 | 19.1 |
| 1879&1889 | 16.1 | 18.7[2] | 5.5 | 11.9[2] | 29.2 | 18.5 |
| 1889&1899 | 17.1 | 20.7[2] | 4.9 | 10.7[2] | 28.8 | 17.8 |
| 1899&1908 | 16.7 | 21.5[2] | 4.5 | 10.7[2] | 31.3 | 15.2 |
| 1904–13 | 17.0 | 22.2[2] | 4.3 | 11.0[2] | 31.2 | 14.3 |
| 1909–18 | 17.7 | 24.1[2] | 3.2 | 10.7[2] | 29.9 | 14.5 |
| 1914–23 | 15.2 | 25.5[2] | 3.0 | 11.0[2] | 29.0 | 16.2 |
| 1919–28 | 12.2 | 25.3[2] | 3.9 | 11.3[2] | 29.4 | 18.0 |
| 1929 | 9.8 | 27.6[2] | 4.4 | 10.8[2] | 32.6 | 16.9 |
| 1930–34 | 8.7 | 22.6[2] | 2.9 | 11.9[2] | 30.0 | 23.7 |
| 1935–39 | 9.6 | 26.8[2] | 2.9 | 10.2[2] | 27.7 | 22.9 |

**J2  NORTH AMERICA: Proportions of GDP by Sector of Origin** (percentages)

| | Canada | | | | | | Costa Rica | | | | | |
|---|---|---|---|---|---|---|---|---|---|---|---|---|
| | A | I | B | T | C&F | Other | A | I | B | T | C&F | Other |
| 1940–44 | 13 | 34[2] | 3 | 12[2] | 16 | 20 | ... | ... | ... | ... | ... | ... |
| 1945–49 | 14 | 34 | 5 | 10 | 20 | 17 | 37[7] | 12[7] | 6[7] | 3[7] | 15[7,8] | 26[7,8] |
| 1950–54 | 12 | 35 | 6 | 9 | 22 | 16 | 38 | 13 | 5 | 3 | 16[8] | 25[8] |
| 1955–59 | 7 | 35 | 6 | 10 | 24 | 18 | 31 | 14 | 5 | 4 | 17[8] | 28[8] |
| 1960–64 | 6 | 33 | 6 | 9 | 24 | 21 | 29 | 14 | 5 | 4 | 20 | 28 |
| 1965–69 | 5 | 32 | 6 | 9 | 23 | 24 | 27 | 16 | 5 | 5 | 21 | 27 |
| 1970–74 | 5 | 29 | 7 | 8 | 24[6] | 28[6] | 24 | 18 | 5 | 5 | 22[6] | 25[6] |
| 1975–79 | 4 | 27 | 8 | 7 | 31 | 22 | 20 | 20 | 6 | 6 | 25 | 19 |
| 1980–84 | 3 | 28 | 7 | 7 | 31 | 23 | 20 | 21 | 5 | 8 | ... | ... |
| 1985–88[5] | 3 | 28 | 6 | 7 | 33 | 24 | 19 | 22 | 4 | 4 | ... | ... |

| | Dominican Republic | | | | | | El Salvador | | | | | |
|---|---|---|---|---|---|---|---|---|---|---|---|---|
| 1945–49 | ... | ... | ... | ... | ... | ... | 45 | 13 | 2 | 3 | 17 | 20 |
| 1950–54 | 33 | 14 | 5 | 6 | 13 | 28 | 39 | 14 | 3 | 4 | 18 | 22 |
| 1955–59 | 31 | 14 | 6 | 7 | 14 | 27 | 37 | 15 | 3 | 4 | 19 | 22 |
| 1960–64 | 29 | 17 | 4 | 7 | 13 | 31 | 36 | 16 | 3 | 5 | 19 | 20 |
| 1965–69 | 26 | 17 | 5 | 8 | 12 | 33 | 30 | 19 | 3 | 5 | 22 | 21 |
| 1970–74 | 23 | 22 | 7 | 8 | 13[6] | 26[6] | 29 | 20 | 3 | 5 | 20 | 22 |
| 1975–79 | 20 | 23 | 7 | 6 | 26 | 17 | 27 | 21 | 5 | 6 | 21 | 21 |
| 1980–84 | 18 | 21 | 8 | 5 | 29 | 19 | 28 | 19 | 4 | 6 | 20 | 23 |
| 1985–88[5] | 19 | 20 | 8 | 6 | 28 | 20 | 27 | 19 | 3 | 4 | 24 | 23 |

| | Guatemala | | | | | | Haiti | | | | | |
|---|---|---|---|---|---|---|---|---|---|---|---|---|
| 1950–54 | 36 | 12 | 4 | 2 | 25 | 24 | 51 | 12 | | 2 | 12 | 22 |
| 1955–59 | 33 | 12 | 4 | 3 | 25 | 25 | 49 | 12 | | 2 | 11 | 24 |
| 1960–64 | 33 | 13 | 3 | 3 | 25 | 24 | 50 | 13 | | 2 | 11 | 23 |
| 1965–69 | 31 | 15 | 2 | 3 | 22 | 22 | 53 | 10 | 2 | 2 | 11 | 21 |
| 1970–74 | 31 | 16 | 2 | 4 | 27[6] | 20[6] | 49 | 12 | 3 | 3 | 11 | 21 |
| 1975–79 | 29 | 16 | 3 | 4 | 30 | 16 | 44 | 15 | 4 | 3 | 12 | 21 |
| 1980–84 | 28 | 17 | 4 | 4 | 30 | 17 | 39 | 17 | 5 | 3 | 15 | 21 |
| 1985–88[5] | 27 | 19 | 3 | 4 | 29 | 18 | 34 | 17 | 6 | 2 | 16 | 23 |

| | Honduras | | | | | | Jamaica | | | | | |
|---|---|---|---|---|---|---|---|---|---|---|---|---|
| 1940–44 | 49 | 10 | 4 | ... | 14 | 18 | ... | ... | ... | ... | ... | ... |
| 1945–49 | 47 | 10 | 5 | ... | 14 | 16 | ... | ... | ... | ... | ... | ... |
| 1950–54 | 42 | 13 | 6 | 5 | 15 | 18 | 21[9] | 18[9] | 9[9] | 7[9] | 25[9] | 20[9] |
| 1955–59 | 39 | 14 | 5 | 6 | 16 | 20 | 15[10] | 21[10] | 12[10] | 7[10] | 25[10] | 20[10] |
| 1960–64 | 34 | 17 | 5 | 8 | 15 | 22 | 12 | 25 | 11 | 8 | 24 | 19 |
| 1965–69 | 36 | 17 | 5 | 7 | 16 | 20 | 11[10] | 28[10] | 11[10] | 7[10] | 23[10] | 20[10] |
| 1970–74 | 34 | 19 | 4 | 7 | 16 | 20 | 7 | 27 | 11 | 6 | 34 | 15 |
| 1975–79 | 29 | 20 | 6 | 8 | 17 | 21 | 8 | 30 | 7 | 6 | 31 | 18 |
| 1980–84 | 28 | 19 | 5 | 8 | 17 | 22 | 7 | 27 | 7 | 6 | 36 | 17 |
| 1985–88[5] | 25 | 20 | 5 | 8 | 20 | 22 | 6 | 29 | 9 | 8 | 36 | 12 |

**J2    NORTH AMERICA: Proportions of GDP by Sector of Origin** (percentages)

| | Mexico | | | | | | Nicaragua | | | | | |
|---|---|---|---|---|---|---|---|---|---|---|---|---|
| | A | I | B | T | C&F | Other | A | I | B | T | C&F | Other |
| 1940–44 | 19 | 23 | 4 | 3 | 25 | 26 | ... | ... | ... | ... | ... | ... |
| 1945–49 | 17 | 23 | 4 | 3 | 27 | 26 | 35 | 14 | 1 | 4 | 18 | 29 |
| 1950–54 | 18 | 23 | 4 | 3 | 29 | 24 | 34 | 13 | 1 | 4 | 21 | 29 |
| 1955–59 | 17 | 23 | 4 | 3 | 29 | 24 | 32 | 14 | 2 | 6 | 21 | 29 |
| 1960–64 | 15 | 25 | 5 | 3 | 29 | 24 | 30 | 17 | 3 | 6 | 20 | 27 |
| 1965–69 | 13 | 27 | 5 | 3 | 29 | 23 | 30 | 19 | 4 | 6 | 21 | 22 |
| 1970–74 | 11 | 29 | 6 | 3 | 29 | 23 | 28 | 22 | 4 | 6 | 21 | 20 |
| 1975–79 | 9 | 31[6] | 6 | 3[6] | 27[6] | 23[6] | 29 | 22 | 4 | 6 | 20 | 20 |
| 1980–84 | 9 | 27 | 6 | 8 | 36 | 16 | 27 | 23 | 2 | 6 | ... | ... |
| 1985–88[5] | 9[11] | 28[11] | 5[11] | 7[11] | 35[11] | 16[11] | 23[11] | 29[11] | 3[11] | 5[11] | ... | ... |

| | Panama | | | | | | Puerto Rico[2,12] | | | | | |
|---|---|---|---|---|---|---|---|---|---|---|---|---|
| 1940–44 | ... | ... | ... | ... | ... | ... | 26 | 13 | | 7 | 11 | 44 |
| 1945–49 | 30 | 8 | 6 | 3 | 11 | 47 | 24[12] | 13[7,12] | 2[7,12] | 5[12] | 19[12] | 38[12] |
| 1950–54 | 31 | 10 | 5 | 3 | 11 | 42 | 21 | 21 | 5 | 6 | 28 | 19 |
| 1955–59 | 29 | 12 | 5 | 4 | 12 | 41 | 14 | 24 | 6 | 7 | 28 | 21 |
| 1960–64 | 25 | 15 | 6 | 4 | 13 | 38 | 10[6] | 26[6] | 7[6] | 7[6] | 28[6] | 22[6] |
| 1965–69 | 23 | 17 | 6 | 5 | 13 | 36 | 4 | 27 | 7 | 6 | 35 | 19 |
| 1970–74 | 19 | 18 | 7 | 6 | 14 | 35 | 3 | 31 | 7 | 5 | 33 | 21 |
| 1975–79 | 19 | 16 | 5 | 9 | 14 | 36 | 3 | 38 | 3 | 6 | 31 | 20 |
| 1980–84 | 13 | 14 | 7 | 19 | ... | ... | 2 | 43 | 2 | 5 | 30 | 18 |
| 1985–88[5] | 9 | 13 | 5 | 23 | ... | ... | 2 | 43 | 2 | 5 | 31 | 18 |

| | Trinidad & Tobago | | | | | | USA[2,4,16] | | | | | |
|---|---|---|---|---|---|---|---|---|---|---|---|---|
| 1940–44 | ... | ... | ... | ... | ... | ... | 8 | 34 | 3 | 9 | 24 | 22 |
| 1945–49 | ... | ... | ... | ... | ... | ... | 9[4] | 31[4] | 4[4] | 8[4] | 26[4] | 21[4] |
| 1950–54 | 18[14] | 46[14,6] | 3[14] | 5[14,6] | 11[14,6] | 18[14] | 6 | 34 | 5 | 8 | 26 | 21 |
| 1955–59 | 14 | 48 | 4 | 3 | 15 | 16 | 4[16] | 33[16] | 5[16] | 8[16] | 26[16] | 23[16] |
| 1960–64 | 11 | 46 | 5 | 20 | | 18 | 4 | 31 | 5 | 8 | 26 | 27 |
| 1965–69 | 8[15,6] | 46[6] | 4[6] | 21[6] | | 20[6] | 3 | 31 | 5 | 8 | 26 | 25 |
| 1970–74 | 4 | 36 | 7 | 12 | 23 | 15 | 3 | 29 | 5 | 6 | 31 | 25 |
| 1975–79 | 3 | 44 | 11 | 8 | 20 | 13 | 3 | 29 | 5 | 6 | 31 | 25 |
| 1980–84 | 2 | 36 | 14 | 9 | 22 | 15 | 3 | 28 | 4 | 6 | 31 | 26 |
| 1985–88[5] | 2 | 30 | 9 | 9 | 28 | 22 | 2[11] | 25[11] | 5[11] | 6[11] | 33[11] | 29[11] |

**J2      SOUTH AMERICA: PROPORTIONS OF GDP BY SECTOR OF ORIGIN** (percentages)

| | Argentina | | | | | | Bolivia | | | | | |
|---|---|---|---|---|---|---|---|---|---|---|---|---|
| | A | I | B | T | C&F | Other | A | I | B | T | C&F | Other |
| 1900–04 | 33 | 16 | 5 | 4 | 20 | 21 | ... | ... | ... | ... | ... | ... |
| 1905–09 | 29 | 16 | 8 | 5 | 23 | 18 | ... | ... | ... | ... | ... | ... |
| 1910–14 | 26 | 18 | 8 | 6 | 23 | 18 | ... | ... | ... | ... | ... | ... |
| 1915–19 | 31 | 17 | 2 | 7 | 20 | 22 | ... | ... | ... | ... | ... | ... |
| 1920–24 | 28 | 19 | 4 | 7 | 22 | 20 | ... | ... | ... | ... | ... | ... |
| 1925–29 | 26 | 20 | 5 | 9 | 23 | 18 | ... | ... | ... | ... | ... | ... |
| 1930–34 | 24 | 21 | 4 | 10 | 21 | 21 | ... | ... | ... | ... | ... | ... |
| 1935–39 | 24 | 23 | 4 | 9 | 20 | 20 | ... | ... | ... | ... | ... | ... |
| 1940–44 | 24 | 25 | 4 | 9 | 17 | 21 | ... | ... | ... | ... | ... | ... |
| 1945–49 | 19 | 26 | 4 | 10 | 18 | 23 | ... | ... | ... | ... | ... | ... |
| 1950–54 | 16 | 25 | 5 | 11 | 17 | 26 | 23 | 34 | 2 | 7 | 11 | 22 |
| 1955–59 | 16 | 28 | 5 | 11 | 17 | 24 | 23 | 30 | 3 | 9 | 11 | 24 |
| 1960–64 | 15 | 30 | 4 | 10 | 17 | 23 | 24 | 26 | 4 | 10 | 11 | 26 |
| 1965–69 | 14 | 33 | 4 | 10 | 16 | 22 | 20 | 29 | 5 | 9 | 11 | 26 |
| 1970–74 | 12 | 36 | 5 | 10 | $\underline{16}_6$ | $\underline{20}_6$ | 16 | 29 | 4 | 9 | 12 | 26 |
| 1975–79 | 13 | 35 | 6 | 10 | 19 | 13 | 17 | 24 | 4 | 10 | 17 | 29 |
| 1980–84 | 15 | 33 | 6 | 11 | 21 | 14 | 19 | 22 | 3 | 12 | 19 | 24 |
| 1985–88 | 14 | 34 | 4 | 10 | 21 | 13 | 21 | 23 | 3 | 8 | 18 | 26 |

| | Brazil | | | | | | Chile | | | | | |
|---|---|---|---|---|---|---|---|---|---|---|---|---|
| 1920–24 | 24 | 13[17] | ... | 3 | 21 | ... | ... | ... | ... | ... | ... | ... |
| 1925–29 | 22 | 13[17] | ... | 4 | 22 | ... | ... | ... | ... | ... | ... | ... |
| 1930–34 | 24 | 13[17] | ... | 3 | 19 | ... | ... | ... | ... | ... | ... | ... |
| 1935–39 | 23 | $\underline{14}^{17}_{17}$ | ... | 3 | 20 | ... | ... | ... | ... | ... | ... | ... |
| 1940–44 | 21 | 18 | 8 | 4 | 20 | 28 | 12 | 38 | 4 | 20 | | 26 |
| 1945–49 | 18 | 21 | 9 | 4 | 22 | 26 | 12 | 37 | 5 | 20 | | 27 |
| 1950–54 | 16 | 23 | 10 | 5 | 22 | 24 | 11 | 36 | 5 | 3 | 16 | 29 |
| 1955–59 | 15 | 26 | 10 | 5 | 21 | 23 | 11 | 37 | 4 | 4 | 16 | 29 |
| 1960–64 | 13 | 29 | 8 | 5 | 20 | 24 | 9 | 39 | 5 | 4 | 16 | 27 |
| 1965–69 | 12 | 28 | 6 | 6 | 20 | 26 | 8 | 41 | 4 | 6 | 16 | 25 |
| 1970–74 | 9 | 33 | 6 | 6 | 21 | 25 | 7 | 42 | 4 | 6 | 17 | 24 |
| 1975–79 | 8 | 33 | 7 | 6 | 21 | 25 | 9 | 39 | 3 | 5 | 17 | 27 |
| 1980–84 | 8 | 33 | 6 | 7 | ... | ... | 8 | 37 | 4 | 7 | ... | ... |
| 1985–89 | 10 | 31 | 7 | 5 | ... | ... | 8 | 33 | 6 | 6 | ... | ... |

**J2**    **SOUTH AMERICA: Proportions of GDP by Sector of Origin** (percentages)

| | Colombia | | | | | | Ecuador | | | | | |
|---|---|---|---|---|---|---|---|---|---|---|---|---|
| | A | I | B | T | C&F | Other | A | I | B | T | C&F | Other |
| 1925–29 | 52 | 8[17] | 4 | 2[18] | ... | ... | ... | ... | ... | ... | ... | ... |
| 1930–34 | 51 | 9[17] | 3 | 2[18] | ... | ... | ... | ... | ... | ... | ... | ... |
| 1935–39 | 47 | 10[17] | 4 | 2[18] | ... | ... | ... | ... | ... | ... | ... | ... |
| 1940–44 | 45 | 12[17] | 5 | 3[18] | ... | ... | ... | ... | ... | ... | ... | ... |
| 1945–49 | 42 | 14[17] | 5 | 4[18] | 14 | 20 | 37[14] | 12[14] | 6[14] | 3[14] | 15[14] | 27[14,19] |
| 1950–54 | 36 | 18 | 4 | 6 | 16 | 20 | 38 | 13 | 5 | 3 | 16 | 25[19] |
| 1955–59 | 34 | 19 | 5 | 7 | 15 | 20 | 31 | 14 | 5 | 4 | 17 | 28[19] |
| 1960–64 | 32 | 20 | 5 | 7 | 16 | 20 | 29 | 14 | 5 | 4 | 20 | 28 |
| 1965–69 | 30 | 21 | 5 | 7 | 17 | 21 | 27 | 16 | 5 | 5 | 21 | 27 |
| 1970–74 | 27 | 22 | 5 | 8 | 18 | 20 | 24[20] | 18[20] | 5 | 5[20] | 22[20] | 25[20] |
| | | | | | | | 22 | 16 | | 6 | 26 | 14 |
| 1975–79 | 26 | 22 | 4 | 9 | 19 | 20 | 16 | 29 | 7 | 7 | 27 | 14 |
| 1980–84 | 24 | 20 | 5 | 8 | 20 | 23 | 13 | 33 | 7 | 9 | 26 | 14 |
| 1985–88 | 18 | 29 | 6 | 8 | 19 | 20 | 15 | 32 | 5 | 9 | 27 | 12 |

| | Guyana | | | | | | Paraguay | | | | | |
|---|---|---|---|---|---|---|---|---|---|---|---|---|
| 1938–39 | ... | ... | ... | ... | ... | ... | 44 | 16 | 1 | 4 | 20 | 16 |
| 1940–44 | ... | ... | ... | ... | ... | ... | 45 | 15 | 1 | 4 | 21 | 17 |
| 1945–49 | ... | ... | ... | ... | ... | ... | 41 | 15 | 1 | 4 | 20 | 19 |
| 1950–54 | 30[21] | 25[21] | 7[21] | 6[21] | 16[21] | 16[21] | 41 | 17 | 1 | 4 | 17 | 18 |
| 1955–59 | 26 | 23 | 10 | 24 | | 17 | 40[23,20] | 16[23,20] | 2[23,20] | 4[23,20] | 19[23,20] | 19[23,20] |
| 1960–64 | 26 | 26 | 7 | 7 | 18 | 17 | 38[24] | 16[24] | 2[24] | 4[24] | 26[24] | 14[24] |
| 1965–69 | 21 | 31 | 7 | 7 | 16 | 19 | 34 | 17 | 3 | 4 | 27 | 15 |
| 1970–74 | 22 | 29 | 8 | 6 | 16 | 20 | 35 | 18 | 3 | 4 | 26 | 14 |
| 1975–79 | 25 | 27 | 7 | 5 | 15 | 21 | 34 | 18 | 4 | 4 | 27 | 12 |
| 1980–84 | 24 | 21 | 8 | 7 | 18 | 23 | 28 | 19 | 6 | 4 | 29 | 13 |
| 1985–88 | 26[22] | 20[22] | 7[22] | 8[22] | 16[22] | 25[22] | 28 | 19 | 6 | 4 | 29 | 13 |

## J2    SOUTH AMERICA: Proportions of GDP by Sector of Origin (percentages)

| | Peru | | | | | | Uruguay | | | | | |
|---|---|---|---|---|---|---|---|---|---|---|---|---|
| | A | I | B | T | C&F | Other | A | I | B | T | C&F | Other |
| 1935–39 | ... | ... | ... | ... | ... | ... | 15 | 19 | 3 | 11 | ... | ... |
| 1940–44 | ... | ... | ... | ... | ... | ... | 14 | 19 | 3 | 10 | ... | ... |
| 1945–49 | 26 | 21[17] | 6 | ... | ... | ... | 14 | 19 | 5 | 10 | ... | ... |
| 1950–54 | 26 | 22[17] | 8 | ... | ... | ... | 13 | 22 | 5 | 10 | ... | ... |
| 1955–59 | 24 | 24[17] | 8 | ... | ... | ... | 12 | 25 | 5 | 9 | 15[19] | 32 |
| 1960–64 | 23 | 29 | 6 | 20 | | 25 | 12 | 25 | 4 | 9 | 20 | 30 |
| 1965–69 | 19 | 30 | 5 | 20 | | 27 | 12 | 25 | 4 | 9 | 17 | 33 |
| 1970–74 | 17[20] | 30[20] | 5[20] | 17[20] | | 30[20] | 12 | 26 | 4 | 9 | 16 | 33 |
|  | 15 | 32 | 3 | 6 | 26 | 18 | | | | | | |
| 1975–79 | 13 | 33 | 4 | 7 | 27 | 14 | 11 | 28 | 5 | 9 | 17 | 32 |
| 1980–84 | 10 | 32 | 7 | 6 | 29 | 15 | 11 | 24 | 5 | 8 | ... | ... |
| 1985–88 | 10 | 30 | 7 | 5 | 28 | 17 | 12[11] | 29[11] | 3[11] | 6[11] | ... | ... |

| | Venezuela | | | | | |
|---|---|---|---|---|---|---|
| 1936–39 | 22 | 33 | 3 | ... | ... | ... |
| 1940–44 | 18 | 34 | 3 | ... | ... | ... |
| 1945–49 | 11 | 38 | 6 | 11 | 13 | 34 |
| 1950–54 | 9 | 39 | 7 | 14 | 13 | 36 |
| 1955–59 | 8 | 42 | 7 | 12 | 14 | 30 |
| 1960–64 | 8 | 41 | 4 | 10 | 12 | 29 |
| 1965–69 | 7 | 38 | 4 | 10 | 13 | 28 |
| 1970–74 | 7 | 34 | 5 | 12 | 13 | 30 |
| 1975–79 | 6 | 27 | 7 | 13 | 12 | 35 |
| 1980–84 | 7 | 23 | 6 | 13[25] | ... | ... |
| 1985–88 | 7[11] | 21[11] | 3[11] | 10[11] | ... | ... |

## J2      Proportions of GDP by Sector of Origin

### NOTES

1.  SOURCES: Canada to 1969, Mexico to 1910, and USA throughout are based on national publications listed on p. xiv–xvi. Guyana, Jamaica, Puerto Rico and Trinidad & Tobago are based on UN, *Yearbook of National Accounts Statistics* (issues to the 1988 volume). This source has also been used as a supplement for recent years for other countries, though most of the figures are based on James W. Wilkie (ed.), *Statistical Abstract of Latin America* vol. 20 (Los Angeles, 1980) with some updating from later volumes.
2.  Totals do not always add up to 100%, partly owing to rounding, but mainly because the methodology employed (especially by the Economic Commission for Latin America) is based on extrapolation over time for each sector separately. For the same reason statistics for the category "other" have not been inserted as a residual: Figures only appear where they have been separately estimated.

### FOOTNOTES

[1] 1926–29 only.
[2] Gas, water, and electricity supply is included with transport not industry.
[3] 1939 only.
[4] Proportions of aggregate payments to 1919–28, based on Robert F. Martin, *National Income in the United States, 1799–1938* (New York, 1939). Proportions of national income from 1929 to 1949, and of GNP subsequently.
[5] Provisional and approximate figures.
[6] There as a rearrangement of components of the categories.
[7] 1946–49 only.
[8] Financial services are included in "Other" to 1959.
[9] 1953 and 1954 only.
[10] The definition of GDP and the composition of the categories was changed.
[11] 1985–87 only.
[12] Data are for years beginning 1 July, and relate to proportions of national income to 1949.
[13] *footnote suppressed*
[14] 1951–54 only.
[15] 1965–68 only.
[16] Including Alaska and Hawaii from 1960.
[17] Excluding gas, water, and electricity supply.
[18] Transport only.
[19] Excluding financial services.
[20] This break occurs on the change from ECLA to UN sources.
[21] 1952–54 only.
[22] 1986–86 only.
[23] 1955 and 1958 only.
[24] 1963–65 only.
[25] 1980–82 only.

**J3      NORTH AMERICA: BALANCE OF PAYMENTS** (in millions of stated currency)

Key:-      VB = visible balance; IB = invisible balance; TTB = tourism & travel balance; IIB = investment income balance; GSIB = balance on goods, services, and requited income; OCB = overall current balance; (LT)CB = (long term)capital balance; CR = change in reserves.

PART A.   to 1950 in national currencies

| | Canada[1] | | | | | | | |
| | (dollars) | | | | | | | |
| | VB | IB | TTB | IIB | GSIB | OCB | LTCB | CR[2] |
|------|--------|--------|--------|--------|------|--------|--------|--------|
| 1900 | −20.5  | −32.1  | +1.2   | −32.0  | ...  | −52.6  | +6.4   | +16.0  |
| 1901 | −12.4  | −33.9  | +1.6   | −33.5  | ...  | −46.3  | +11.3  | +23.2  |
| 1902 | −13.0  | −30.6  | +3.5   | −34.4  | ...  | −43.6  | +15.8  | +11.6  |
| 1903 | −49.9  | −30.7  | +3.1   | −35.5  | ...  | −80.6  | +27.5  | +6.5   |
| 1904 | −73.1  | −32.3  | +3.9   | −38.5  | ...  | −105.4 | +33.6  | +7.9   |
| 1905 | −58.4  | −42.9  | +1.9   | −42.1  | ...  | −101.3 | +69.5  | +14.0  |
| 1906 | −58.3  | −49.8  | +1.4   | −45.7  | ...  | −108.1 | +62.6  | +6.1   |
| 1907 | −109.2 | −61.5  | +0.4   | −51.1  | ...  | −170.7 | +51.7  | +3.8   |
| 1908 | −133.3 | −87.2  | +1.1   | −71.3  | ...  | −120.5 | +173.3 | −13.9  |
| 1909 | −70.6  | −86.6  | —      | −75.6  | ...  | −157.2 | +209.0 | −1.1   |
| 1910 | −148.2 | −97.0  | −0.3   | −82.5  | ...  | −245.2 | +202.0 | −6.1   |
| 1911 | −222.2 | −122.1 | −2.4   | −92.9  | ...  | −344.3 | +255.5 | −19.4  |
| 1912 | −274.3 | −159.8 | −3.6   | −108.8 | ...  | −434.1 | +236.1 | +12.8  |
| 1913 | −212.0 | −191.4 | −6.7   | −128.5 | ...  | −403.4 | +463.2 | −4.8   |
| 1914 | −101.7 | −209.5 | −7.0   | −164.3 | ...  | −311.2 | +295.1 | +23.0  |
| 1915 | +166.7 | −209.4 | +8.0   | −160.2 | ...  | −42.7  | +174.0 | −14.6  |
| 1916 | +310.0 | −298.7 | +16.5  | −166.9 | ...  | +11.3  | +246.2 | +11.6  |
| 1917 | +558.7 | −381.8 | +23.6  | −175.8 | ...  | +176.9 | +116.9 | −0.9   |
| 1918 | +287.0 | −384.8 | +32.1  | −181.6 | ...  | −97.8  | −22.8  | +16.0  |
| 1919 | +310.3 | −273.9 | +23.5  | −171.9 | ...  | +36.4  | −14.9  | +13.9  |
| 1920 | −161.6 | −196.8 | +28.9  | −166.1 | ...  | −358.4 | +98.7  | +35.0  |
| 1921 | −27.4  | −171.8 | +40.7  | −187.0 | ...  | −199.2 | +83.6  | +42.0  |
| 1922 | +139.5 | −140.9 | +55.7  | −190.4 | ...  | −1.4   | +190.3 | −46.0  |
| 1923 | +118.8 | −149.0 | +68.9  | −213.5 | ...  | −30.2  | +69.6  | +80.3  |
| 1924 | +242.7 | −112.2 | +81.1  | −202.0 | ...  | +130.5 | +93.0  | +7.0   |
| 1925 | +368.7 | −115.4 | +100.7 | −210.5 | ...  | +253.3 | −67.0  | +19.9  |
| 1926 | +277.4[1] | −104.2[1] | +103.1[1] | −218.1[1] | ... | +173.2[1] | +26.0[1] | +38.0[1] |
|      | +329   | −169   | +53    | −208   | +160 | +127   |        |        |
| 1927 | +190   | −168   | +63    | −216   | +22  | −10    | +14    | +7     |
| 1928 | +172   | −172   | +79    | −229   | —    | −32    | −94    | −49    |
| 1929 | −57    | −220   | +90    | −261   | −277 | −311   | +212   | −37    |
| 1930 | −54    | −253   | +88    | −289   | −307 | −337   | +392   | −36    |
| 1931 | +78    | −239   | +82    | −282   | −161 | −174   | +87    | −33    |
| 1932 | +167   | −252   | +21    | −265   | −85  | −96    | +33    | −3     |
| 1933 | +236   | −233   | +38    | −226   | +3   | −2     | −37    | −6     |
| 1934 | +278   | −204   | +64    | −211   | +74  | +68    | −91    | +4     |
| 1935 | +325   | −196   | +55    | −206   | +129 | +125   | −151   | +6     |
| 1936 | +474   | −226   | +57    | −236   | +248 | +244   | −237   | +5     |
| 1937 | +410   | −223   | +58    | −226   | +187 | +180   | −157   | +6     |
| 1938 | +356   | −246   | +75    | −241   | +110 | +99    | −95    | +17    |
| 1939 | +377   | −245   | +103   | −249   | +132 | +128   | −104   | +37    |

**J3** **NORTH AMERICA: Balance of Payments** ( in millions of stated currency)

## Canada

### (dollars)

|      | VB      | IB      | TTB   | IIB   | GSIB    | OCB   | (LT)CB | CR[2] |
|------|---------|---------|-------|-------|---------|-------|--------|-------|
| 1940 | +399    | −256    | +160  | −261  | +143    | +151  | −102   | +3    |
| 1941 | +672    | −185    | +183  | −226  | +487    | +501  | +53    | +568  |
| 1942 | +1,293  | −205    | +158  | −203  | +1,088  | +106  | −787   | −674  |
| 1943 | +1,613  | −411    | +106  | −202  | +1,202  | +690  | −315   | +364  |
| 1944 | +2,302  | −1,297  | +52   | −193  | +1,005  | +60   | +224   | +274  |
| 1945 | +2,128  | −615    | +13   | −171  | +1,513  | +689  | −46    | +668  |
| 1946 | +667    | −247    | −39   | −242  | +420    | +363  | −715   | −266  |
| 1947 | +287    | −217    | −68   | −273  | +70     | +49   | −721   | −668  |
| 1948 | +551    | −126    | −15   | −255  | +425    | +451  | +43    | +492  |
| 1949 | +432    | −281    | −54   | −307  | +151    | +177  | −29    | +128  |
| 1950 | +200    | −534    | −63   | −381  | −334    | −319  | +610   | +722  |

## Costa Rica

### (colones)

|      | VB     | IB     | TTB   | IIB    | GSIB   | OCB    | (LT)CB    | CR[2]   |
|------|--------|--------|-------|--------|--------|--------|-----------|---------|
| 1938 | +13.1  | −8.3   | −0.6  | −10.5  | +4.8   | −0.6   | +3.3[3]   | −0.9[4] |
| 1946 | −57.3  | −5.6   | +2.8  | −9.0   | −65.7  | −62.9  | −33.7[3]  | +22.5[4]|
| 1947 | −29.2  | −49.4  | +1.1  | −27.5  | −78.6  | −77.5  | +106.1[3] | —       |
| 1948 | +75.2  | −69.6  | −1.7  | −46.0  | +5.6   | +6.7   | −42.1[3]  | —       |
| 1949 | +78.0  | −96.5  | −5.6  | −85.9  | −18.5  | +16.3  | +44.9[3]  | —       |
| 1950 | +84.1  | −75.8  | −5.3  | −79.9  | +8.3   | +9.5   | −52.7[3]  | —       |

## Cuba[5]

### (pesos)

|      | VB    | IB    | TTB | IIB  | GSIB | OCB   | (LT)CB | CR[2] |
|------|-------|-------|-----|------|------|-------|--------|-------|
| 1919 | +218  | −83   | —   | −39  | ...  | +135  | +2     | +38   |
| 1920 | +237  | −103  | —   | −42  | ...  | +134  | +27    | +13   |
| 1921 | −75   | −69   | +5  | −25  | ...  | −144  | +11    | +72   |
| 1922 | +147  | −65   | +2  | −34  | ...  | +83   | +59    | −2    |
| 1923 | +154  | −76   | +1  | −39  | ...  | +78   | +83    | +6    |
| 1924 | +145  | −83   | +2  | −47  | ...  | +62   | +25    | +3    |
| 1925 | +57   | −88   | +3  | −53  | ...  | −32   | +14    | +17   |
| 1926 | +41   | −95   | +3  | −60  | ...  | −54   | +55    | +1    |
| 1927 | +67   | −93   | +5  | −55  | ...  | −26   | +38    | +23   |
| 1928 | +65   | −79   | +7  | −45  | ...  | −14   | +12    | +12   |
| 1929 | +56   | −63   | +7  | −41  | ...  | −7    | +13    | +5    |
| 1930 | +5    | −45   | +9  | −31  | ...  | −40   | +25    | +36   |
| 1931 | +39   | −39   | +9  | −27  | ...  | —     | −11    | +18   |
| 1932 | +30   | −30   | +6  | −20  | ...  | −1    | −15    | +9    |
| 1933 | +42   | −26   | +2  | −17  | ...  | +16   | −6     | —     |
| 1934 | +34   | −16   | —   | −7   | ...  | +19   | −1     | −2    |

**J3    NORTH AMERICA: Balance of Payments** (in millions of stated currency)

|  | | | | | | | | |
|---|---|---|---|---|---|---|---|---|
| | | | | **Cuba[5]** | | | | |
| | | | | (pesos) | | | | |
| | VB | IB | TTB | IIB | GSIB | OCB | (LT)CB | CR |
| 1935 | +33 | −17 | *+1* | *−8* | ... | +16 | −2 | *−8* |
| 1936 | +52 | −16 | *+5* | *−13* | ... | +35 | −2 | *−28* |
| 1937 | +57 | −20 | *+5* | *−19* | ... | +37 | −3 | *+4* |
| 1938 | +37 | −23 | *+6* | *−21* | ... | +14 | −2 | *+12* |
| 1939 | +42 | −23 | *+5* | *−21* | ... | +19 | −1 | *+15* |
| 1940 | +23 | −14 | *+11* | *−19* | +9 | +4 | −6 | *−12* |
| 1941 | +78 | −30 | ... | *−31* | +47 | +47 | −13 | *−39* |
| 1942 | +36 | −49 | ... | *−30* | −13 | −14 | +16 | *−86* |
| 1943 | +173 | −38 | ... | *−22* | +135 | +139 | +4 | *−104* |
| 1944 | +219 | −58 | ... | *−27* | +160 | +169 | −15 | *−202* |
| 1945 | +171 | −53 | ... | *−21* | +118 | +120 | −5 | *−102* |
| 1946 | +198 | −96 | *−18* | − | +103 | +95 | +17 | *+69* |
| 1947 | +185 | −143 | *−31* | − | +41 | +32 | −48 | *+84* |
| 1948 | +177 | −125 | *−33* | − | +52 | +44 | −2 | *−24* |
| 1949 | +124 | −95 | *−12* | − | +29 | +24 | −6 | *−1* |
| 1950 | +91 | −113 | *−15* | − | −22 | −23 | −9 | *+1* |

|  | | | | | | | | |
|---|---|---|---|---|---|---|---|---|
| | | | | **Dominican Republic** | | | | |
| | | | | (pesos) | | | | |
| 1939 | +7.6 | −8.2 | *−0.2* | *−4.0* | −0.6 | −1.2 | +1.6[3] | *−0.3[4]* |
| 1946 | +39.7 | −20.1 | *−1.6* | *−5.3* | +19.6 | +18.8 | −2.9[3] | *+2.0[4]* |
| 1947 | +29.7 | −25.8 | *−1.8* | *−18.1* | +3.9 | +2.9 | −0.1[3] | — |
| 1948 | +17.0 | −23.9 | *−1.6* | *−15.9* | −6.9 | −7.4 | +9.4[3] | *−2.0[4]* |
| 1949 | +27.7 | −21.0 | *−1.0* | *−12.4* | +6.7 | +6.1 | −0.3[3] | — |
| 1950 | +43.9 | −23.7 | *−1.1* | *−11.8* | +20.2 | +19.2 | −6.6[3] | — |

|  | | | | | | | | |
|---|---|---|---|---|---|---|---|---|
| | | | | **El Salvador** | | | | |
| | | | | (colones) | | | | |
| 1938 | +4.6 | −3.0 | *+0.1* | *−0.8* | +1.6 | +1.7 | +1.3[3] | — |
| 1946 | +12.9 | −5.0 | *−1.8* | *−1.6* | +7.9 | +8.5 | +10.0[3] | *−1.9[4]* |
| 1947 | +7.7 | −1.3 | *−2.2* | *−2.5* | +6.4 | +6.9 | −6.6[5] | *+5.2* |
| 1948 | +9.4 | −6.2 | *−2.3* | *−3.1* | +3.2 | +3.2 | −2.1[5] | *−0.7* |
| 1949 | +38.6 | −5.5 | *−1.7* | *−2.8* | +33.1 | +33.0 | −6.6[5] | *−25.7* |
| 1950 | +48.3 | −14.1 | *−7.4* | *−3.9* | +34.2 | +34.6 | — | *−5.4* |

|  | | | | | | | | |
|---|---|---|---|---|---|---|---|---|
| | | | | **Guatemala[5]** | | | | |
| | | | | (quetzales) | | | | |
| 1946 | +19.6 | −12.0 | *+0.5* | *−8.0* | +7.6 | +8.5 | −1.0 | *+5.8* |
| 1947 | +17.9 | −7.9 | *+1.3* | *−2.2* | +10.0 | +12.1 | −6.3 | *−0.5* |
| 1948 | +7.8 | −13.6 | *+2.0* | *−7.1* | −5.8 | −3.7 | −0.6 | *+5.9* |
| 1949 | +1.5 | −14.9 | *+1.5* | *−7.2* | −13.4 | −11.7 | −11.3 | *+10.3* |
| 1950 | +10.4 | −10.4 | *+0.7* | *−2.8* | — | — | +2.0 | *−1.3* |

|  | | | | | | | | |
|---|---|---|---|---|---|---|---|---|
| | | | | **Honduras** | | | | |
| | | | | (lempiras) | | | | |
| 1947 | +23.8 | −43.9 | *−0.5* | *−44.8* | −20.1 | −21.7 | +21.1[3] | — |
| 1948 | +36.7 | −43.3 | *−0.7* | *−45.1* | −6.6 | −8.3 | +6.7[3] | — |
| 1949 | +39.3 | −46.4 | *−0.6* | *−36.8* | −7.1 | −8.6 | +7.5[3] | — |
| 1950 | +51.1 | −50.4 | *−0.7* | *−41.4* | +0.7 | −0.9 | −2.2[3] | — |

**J3**     **NORTH AMERICA: Balance of Payments** (in millions of stated currency)

### Mexico
(US dollars)

|      | VB | IB | TTB | IIB | GSIB | OCB | CB | CR |
|------|----|----|-----|-----|------|-----|----|----|
| 1910 | +20 | −159 | ... | ... | ... | −139 | ... | ... |
| 1926 | +283[18] | −315[18] | ... | ... | ...[18] | −32[18] | ... | ... |
| 1938 | +80.5[18] | −31.4[18] | +8.2 | −40.7 | +49.1[18] | +51.1[18] | +4.2 | −4.8 |
| 1939 | +27.7 | +2.2 | ... |  | +29.9 | +32.8 | ... | ... |
| 1940 | +15.2 | −7.8 | ... | ... | +7.4 | +11.1 | ... | ... |
| 1941 | −50.5 | −7.9 | ... | ... | −58.4 | −56.4 | ... | ... |
| 1942 | +22.9 | −10.6[18] | ... | ... | +12.3[18] | +13.0 | ... | ... |
| 1943 | +27.5 | −15.5 | ... | ... | +12.0 | +48.2 | ... | ... |
| 1944 | −72.6 | −2.9 | ... | ... | −75.5 | −23.8 | ... | ... |
| 1945 | −42.2[18] | +1.3[18] | ... | ... | −90.9[18] | −32.7[18] | ... | ... |
| 1946 | −234.8 | +48.2 | +87.5 | −46.6 | −186.6 | −167.5 | −46.7 | +120.5 |
| 1947 | −245.8 | +23.8 | +82.8 | −92.6 | −222.0 | −186.8 | +84.7 | +218.6 |
| 1948 | −137.1 | +49.6 | +104.1 | −77.0 | −87.5 | −77.9 | +65.6 | +64.5 |
| 1949 | −65.2 | +96.1 | +133.3 | −56.8 | +30.9 | +55.6 | −40.1 | −49.6 |
| 1950 | −64.2 | +32.5 | +155.6 | −76.4 | −31.7 | −47.0 | −129.5 | −195.7 |

### Nicaragua[5]
(cordobas)

|      | VB | IB | TTB | IIB | GSIB | OCB | CB | CR |
|------|----|----|-----|-----|------|-----|----|----|
| 1938 | +4.0 | −5.1 | ... | ... | −1.1 | −1.1 | ... | ... |
| 1946 | −20.0 | +4.8 | ... | −20.5 | −15.2 | −3.8 | ... | ... |
| 1947 | +6.5 | −33.0 | — | −22.0 | −26.5 | −23.5 | +3.4 | +2.5 |
| 1948 | +21.0 | −42.0 | −3.5 | −23.5 | −21.0 | −15.5 | −1.5 | +2.2 |
| 1949 | +21.5 | −39.5 | −3.0 | −23.5 | −18.0 | −17.0 | +1.2 | −1.6 |
| 1950 | +66.9 | −64.8 | −8.9 | −41.6 | +2.1 | +3.4 | −0.7 | +0.9 |

**J3    NORTH AMERICA: Balance of Payments** (in millions of stated currency)

| | USA (dollars) | | | | | | |
|---|---|---|---|---|---|---|---|
| | VB | IB | TTB | IIB | GSIB | OCB[6] | CB[5,7] |
| 1790 | −3 | — | ... | −4 | −1 | −1 | ... |
| 1791 | −10 | +1 | ... | −4 | −8 | −8 | ... |
| 1792 | −10 | +1 | ... | −4 | −8 | −8 | ... |
| 1793 | −5 | +6 | ... | −5 | +2 | +2 | ... |
| 1794 | — | +9 | ... | −5 | +10 | +9 | ... |
| 1795 | −25 | +12 | ... | −4 | −12 | −13 | ... |
| 1796 | −17 | +14 | ... | −5 | −3 | −4 | ... |
| 1797 | −20 | +9 | ... | −5 | −11 | −11 | ... |
| 1798 | −10 | +8 | ... | −6 | −2 | −2 | ... |
| 1799 | −1 | +15 | ... | −6 | +15 | +15 | ... |
| 1800 | −19 | +17 | ... | −5 | −2 | −2 | ... |
| 1801 | −19 | +21 | ... | −5 | +2 | +2 | ... |
| 1802 | −3 | +10 | ... | −5 | +7 | +7 | ... |
| 1803 | −8 | +17 | ... | −4 | +8 | −3 | ... |
| 1804 | −6 | +18 | ... | −5 | +12 | +12 | ... |
| 1805 | −31 | +21 | ... | −4 | −10 | −10 | ... |
| 1806 | −32 | +24 | ... | −4 | −7 | −7 | ... |
| 1807 | −37 | +31 | ... | −5 | −5 | −5 | ... |
| 1808 | −32 | +16 | ... | −5 | −17 | −17 | ... |
| 1809 | −6 | +18 | ... | −6 | +12 | +12 | ... |
| 1810 | −23 | +29 | ... | −6 | +7 | +7 | ... |
| 1811 | +2 | +34 | ... | −5 | +35 | +35 | ... |
| 1812 | −44 | +23 | ... | −3 | −21 | −21 | ... |
| 1813 | +10 | +6 | ... | −4 | +15 | +15 | ... |
| 1814 | −8 | −1 | ... | −3 | −9 | −9 | ... |
| 1815 | −30 | +15 | ... | −4 | −15 | −15 | ... |
| 1816 | −67 | +9 | ... | −5 | −58 | −58 | ... |
| 1817 | −13 | +2 | ... | −7 | −11 | −11 | ... |
| 1818 | −33 | +7 | ... | −6 | −25 | −25 | ... |
| 1819 | −22 | +7 | ... | −6 | −15 | −15[6] | ... |
| 1820 | −5 | +4 | −2 | −5 | +1 | +2 | −1 |
| 1821 | +3 | +1 | −2 | −5 | +4 | +5 | −5 |
| 1822 | −10 | +1 | −1 | −5 | −9 | −9 | +8 |
| 1823 | −3 | +5 | −1 | −5 | +2 | +2 | −2 |
| 1824 | −4 | +5 | −1 | −5 | — | +1 | −1 |
| 1825 | +4 | +2 | −2 | −5 | +6 | +7 | −7 |
| 1826 | −7 | +3 | −2 | −5 | −4 | −3 | +3 |
| 1827 | +3 | +4 | −2 | −5 | +8 | +10 | −10 |
| 1828 | −12 | +2 | −1 | −4 | −14 | −12 | +11 |
| 1829 | −2 | — | −2 | −5 | — | +2 | −2 |

**J3** **NORTH AMERICA: Balance of Payments** (in millions of stated currency)

| | USA (dollars) | | | | | | |
| | VB | IB | TTB | IIB | GSIB | OCB | CB[5,7] |
|---|---|---|---|---|---|---|---|
| 1830 | +3 | +3 | — | −5 | +6 | +8 | −8 |
| 1831 | −21 | +6 | — | −4 | −15 | −14 | +14 |
| 1832 | −15 | +3 | — | −5 | −12 | −7 | +7 |
| 1833 | −20 | +1 | — | −5 | −19 | −14 | +14 |
| 1834 | −24 | — | −1 | −6 | −24 | −18 | +19 |
| 1835 | −31 | −3 | −2 | −7 | −33 | −30 | +30 |
| 1836 | −65 | −4 | −2 | −9 | −68 | −58 | +59 |
| 1837 | −26 | −2 | −2 | −9 | −28 | −21 | +22 |
| 1838 | −7 | — | −4 | −10 | −7 | −4 | +3 |
| 1839 | −44 | −10 | −4 | −14 | −53 | −49 | +49 |
| 1840 | +24 | +3 | −5 | −12 | +26 | +30 | −31 |
| 1841 | −8 | −4 | −5 | −8 | −12 | −8 | +8 |
| 1842 | +3 | −3 | −4 | −8 | +1 | +7 | −6 |
| 1843 | +19 | — | −2 | −7 | +20 | +22 | −22 |
| 1844 | +1 | −1 | −4 | −7 | — | +4 | −4 |
| 1845 | −5 | +2 | −3 | −9 | −2 | +4 | −4 |
| 1846 | −12 | +2 | −1 | −9 | −10 | +1 | −1 |
| 1847 | +9 | −7 | −2 | −9 | +3 | +19 | −19 |
| 1848 | −6 | −9 | — | −12 | −15 | −2 | +2 |
| 1849 | −8 | −1 | +1 | −12 | −8 | +8 | −3 |
| 1850 | −32 | −12 | −4 | −12 | −44 | −24 | +29 |
| 1851 | −6 | −14 | −19 | −13 | −20 | −5 | +6 |
| 1852 | −10 | −23 | −16 | −15 | −33 | −16 | +16 |
| 1853 | −48 | −27 | −21 | −16 | −75 | −56 | +56 |
| 1854 | −35 | −28 | −21 | −20 | −63 | −42 | +42 |
| 1855 | +7 | −29 | −21 | −22 | −22 | −14 | +15 |
| 1856 | +2 | −22 | −17 | −23 | −20 | −12 | +12 |
| 1857 | −9 | −21 | −14 | −15 | −30 | −16 | +17 |
| 1858 | +33 | −15 | −15 | −15 | +17 | +24 | −23 |
| 1859 | +6 | −37 | −25 | −23 | −32 | −26 | +26 |
| 1860 | +25 | −25 | −18 | −25 | −1 | +7 | −7 |
| 1861 | −83 | −20 | −14 | −24 | −103 | −104 | +103 |
| 1862 | +37 | −35 | −13 | −30 | — | — | — |
| 1863 | +27 | −41 | −14 | −31 | −15 | −12 | +13 |
| 1864 | −51 | −63 | −17 | −34 | −114 | −111 | +111 |
| 1865 | +5 | −69 | −22 | −45 | −64 | −59 | +59 |
| 1866 | −13 | −78 | −24 | −51 | −91 | −95 | +95 |
| 1867 | −61 | −89 | −24 | −58 | −149 | −145 | +145 |
| 1868 | +13 | −89 | −24 | −67 | −77 | −73 | +73 |
| 1869 | −85 | −89 | −15 | −69 | −172 | −175 | +176 |

**J3     NORTH AMERICA: Balance of Payments** (in millions of stated currency)

| | USA (dollars) | | | | | | | |
|---|---|---|---|---|---|---|---|---|
| | **VB** | **IB** | **TTB** | **IIB** | **GSIB** | **OCB** | **CB**[5,7] | **CR** |
| 1870 | −2 | −99 | −19 | −80 | −101 | −100 | +100 | ... |
| 1871 | +7 | −108 | −22 | −84 | −101 | −101 | +101 | ... |
| 1872 | −123 | −122 | −28 | −86 | −246 | −242 | +242 | ... |
| 1873 | −52 | −128 | −23 | −99 | −181 | −183 | +167 | ... |
| 1874 | +76 | −138 | −27 | −102 | −61 | −72 | +82 | −11 |
| 1875 | +34 | −134 | −27 | −99 | −99 | −113 | +87 | +27 |
| 1876 | +142 | −123 | −25 | −96 | +20 | +9 | +2 | −10 |
| 1877 | +212 | −109 | −20 | −86 | +102 | +89 | −57 | −33 |
| 1878 | +318 | −96 | −25 | −76 | +218 | +207 | −162 | −44 |
| 1879 | +315 | −113 | −31 | −78 | +202 | +194 | −160 | −34 |
| 1880 | +235 | −121 | −28 | −79 | +114 | +110 | +30 | −140 |
| 1881 | +264 | −127 | −28 | −88 | +137 | +132 | −41 | −91 |
| 1882 | +77 | −132 | −32 | −84 | −55 | −68 | +110 | −42 |
| 1883 | +127 | −139 | −32 | −89 | −12 | −34 | +51 | −17 |
| 1884 | +92 | −151 | −41 | −90 | −59 | −83 | +105 | −23 |
| 1885 | +157 | −145 | −41 | −86 | +12 | −15 | +34 | −19 |
| 1886 | +83 | −160 | −45 | −93 | −77 | −105 | +137 | −32 |
| 1887 | +15 | −172 | −51 | −98 | −157 | −185 | +231 | −46 |
| 1888 | −41 | −185 | −53 | −107 | −226 | −256 | +287 | −30 |
| 1889 | +24 | −191 | −48 | −118 | −166 | −210 | +202 | +8 |
| 1890 | +56 | −205 | −53 | −125 | −150 | −195 | +194 | +1 |
| 1891 | +122 | −211 | −56 | −134 | −90 | −140 | +136 | +4 |
| 1892 | +196 | −216 | −55 | −143 | −20 | −74 | +41 | +33 |
| 1893 | +76 | −195 | −36 | −139 | −119 | −163 | +146 | +17 |
| 1894 | +251 | −152 | −25 | −113 | +98 | +44 | −66 | +22 |
| 1895 | +81 | −208 | −61 | −126 | −127 | −182 | +137 | +44 |
| 1896 | +232 | −198 | −56 | −122 | +34 | −15 | +40 | −25 |
| 1897 | +333 | −201 | −54 | −127 | +132 | +91 | −23 | −68 |
| 1898 | +651 | −208 | −60 | −133 | +444 | +400 | −279 | −121 |
| 1899 | +628 | −201 | −60 | −124 | +427 | +379 | −229 | −130 |
| 1900 | +640[8] | −212[8] | −79[8] | −114[8] | +429[8] | +375[8] | −296[8] | −78[8] |
| | +774 | −247 | −112 | −99 | +507 | +412 | −218 | −91 |
| 1901 | +673 | −235 | −122 | −88 | +438 | +334 | −245 | −61 |
| 1902 | +477 | −219 | −115 | −80 | +258 | +153 | −135 | −71 |
| 1903 | +556 | −216 | −118 | −72 | +340 | +225 | −21 | −71 |
| 1904 | +501 | −222 | −127 | −71 | +279 | +152 | −10 | −25 |
| 1905 | +536 | −238 | −142 | −69 | +298 | +165 | −83 | −71 |
| 1906 | +556 | −260 | −164 | −62 | +296 | +149 | +68 | −171 |
| 1907 | +582 | −286 | −189 | −66 | +296 | +119 | +23 | −154 |
| 1908 | +721 | −294 | −193 | −71 | +427 | +235 | −46 | −44 |
| 1909 | +335 | −309 | −210 | −64 | +26 | −161 | +59 | +18 |

**J3     NORTH AMERICA: Balance of Payments** (in millions of stated currency)

| | USA (dollars) | | | | | | | |
| --- | --- | --- | --- | --- | --- | --- | --- | --- |
| | VB | IB | TTB | IIB | GSIB | OCB | (LT)CB[5,7] | CR |
| 1910 | +386 | −340 | −227 | −64 | +46 | −158 | +255 | −71 |
| 1911 | +652 | −378 | −248 | −76 | +274 | +50 | +48 | −90 |
| 1912 | +666 | −409 | −257 | −74 | +257 | +45 | +23 | −81 |
| 1913 | +771 | −397 | −261 | −73 | +374 | +167 | +77 | −25 |
| 1914 | +415 | −359 | −233 | −55 | +56 | −114 | −522 | +100 |
| 1915 | +1,873 | −125 | −136 | +64 | +1,748 | +1,598 | −1,579 | −499 |
| 1916 | +3,137 | −35 | −101 | +132 | +3,102 | +2,952 | −1,455 | −531 |
| 1917 | +3,392 | +83 | −66 | +250 | +3,475 | +3,270 | −630 | −312 |
| 1918 | +3,329 | −871 | −39 | +350 | +2,458 | +2,190 | −396 | −5 |
| 1919 | +4,896 | −28 | −67 | +489 | +4,868 | +3,824 | −384 | +166 |
| 1920 | +3,097 | +426 | −123 | +476 | +3,523 | +2,844 | −832 | +68 |
| 1921 | +2,014 | +108 | −124 | +340 | +2,122 | +1,613 | −592 | −735 |
| 1922 | +745 | +252 | −182 | +565 | +997 | +645 | −815₅ | −269 |
| 1923 | +400 | +442 | −189 | +710 | +842 | +277 | −45 | −315 |
| 1924 | +1,057 | +294 | −226 | +722 | +1,351 | +987 | −700 | −256 |
| 1925 | +720 | +367 | −264 | +732 | +1,087 | +684 | −570 | +100 |
| 1926 | +422 | +404 | −262 | +753 | +826 | +445 | −716 | −93 |
| 1927 | +742 | +331 | −286 | +741 | +1,073 | +716 | −1,037 | +133 |
| 1928 | +1,090 | +287 | −327 | +805 | +1,377 | +1,012 | 647₉ | +238 |
| 1929 | +884 | +264 | −344 | +809 | +1,148 | +771 | −278 | −143 |
| 1930 | +825 | +207 | −334 | +745 | +1,032 | +690 | −298 | −310 |
| 1931 | +374 | +142 | −247 | +546 | +516 | +197 | +194 | +133 |
| 1932 | +324 | +83 | −194 | +392 | +407 | +169 | +225 | −53 |
| 1933 | +226 | +132 | −133 | +322 | +358 | +150 | +77 | +131 |
| 1934 | +475 | +126 | −137 | +302 | +601 | +229 | +200 | −1,266 |
| 1935 | −58 | +186 | −144 | +366 | +128 | −54 | +436 | −1,822 |
| 1936 | +44 | +71 | −180 | +299 | +115 | −93 | +777 | −1,272 |
| 1937 | +270 | +27 | −213 | +282 | +297 | +62 | +521 | −1,364 |
| 1938 | +1,070 | +221 | −173 | +385 | +1,291 | +1,109 | +97 | −1,799 |
| 1939 | +938 | +128 | −155 | +311 | +1,066 | +888 | +27 | −3,174 |
| 1940 | +1,426 | +292 | −95 | +354 | +1,719 | +1,509 | −22 | −4,243 |
| 1941 | +1,927 | +484 | −142 | +357 | +2,410 | +1,274 | −261 | −719 |
| 1942 | +5,688 | +725 | −73 | +356 | +6,413 | +77 | −149 | +23 |
| 1943 | +10,516 | +522 | −89 | +354 | +11,038 | −1,869 | −23 | +757 |
| 1944 | +11,926 | +526 | −108 | +412 | +12,452 | −1,691 | +284 | +1,350 |
| 1945 | +7,228 | −1,187 | −147 | +358 | +6,041 | −1,072 | −300 | +548 |
| 1946 | +6,697 | +1,110 | −191 | +756 | +7,807 | +5,515 | −887 | −623 |
| 1947 | +10,124 | +1,493 | −209 | +1,047 | +11,617 | +8,992 | −896 | −3,315 |
| 1948 | +5,708 | +810 | −297 | +1,262 | +6,518 | +1,993 | −962 | −1,736 |
| 1949 | +5,339 | +879 | −308 | +1,273 | +6,218 | +780 | −621 | −266 |
| 1950 | +1,122 | +770 | −335 | +1,460 | +1,892 | −2,125 | −702 | +1,758 |

**J3    SOUTH AMERICA: BALANCE OF PAYMENTS** (in millions of stated currency)

### Argentina[10]
(pesos)

| | VB | IB | TTB | IIB | GSIB | OCB | CB | CR |
|---|---|---|---|---|---|---|---|---|
| 1919 | +302 | −215 | ... | | ... | +87 | +64 | — |
| 1920 | +328 | −211 | ... | | ... | +117 | −123 | −78 |
| 1921–22 | −111 | −363 | ... | | ... | −474 | +185 | +19 |
| 1923 | −79 | −202 | ... | | ... | −123 | +40 | +2 |
| 1924–25 | +178 | −421 | ... | | ... | −243 | +208 | +31 |
| 1926 | −52[10] | −190[10] | ... | | ... | −242[10] | +34[10] | −2[10] |
| | +255 | −523 | | −416 | ... | −268 | +271 | −5 |
| 1927 | +656 | −605 | ... | — | ... | +51 | +170 | −196 |
| 1928 | +526 | −638 | ... | −468 | ... | −112 | +259 | −197 |
| 1929 | +237 | −616 | ... | −48 | ... | −379 | −16 | +403 |
| 1930 | −266 | −585 | ... | −468 | ... | −319 | +635 | +71 |
| 1931 | +301 | −561 | ... | −483 | ... | −260 | −302 | +562 |
| 1932 | +469 | −526 | ... | −459 | ... | −57 | −80 | +18 |
| 1933 | +230 | −477 | ... | −426 | ... | −247 | +236 | — |
| 1934 | +508 | −535 | ... | −482 | ... | −27 | +114 | +61 |
| 1935 | +551 | −537 | ... | −472 | ... | +14 | +36 | +12 |
| 1936 | +668[11] | −551[11] | ... | −469[11] | ... | +117[11] | +310[11] | −2[11] |
| 1937 | +869 | −475 | ... | −432 | ... | +394 | −430 | +77 |
| 1938 | −109 | −391 | ... | −366 | ... | −500 | +53 | +456 |
| 1939 | +350 | −406 | ... | −431 | ... | −56 | +66 | −165 |
| 1940 | +167 | −321 | ... | −375 | ... | −154 | +63 | +63 |
| 1941 | +447 | −275 | ... | −405 | ... | +171 | +304 | −481 |
| 1942 | +627 | −324 | ... | −480 | ... | +303 | +100 | −507 |
| 1943 | +1,246 | −154 | ... | −372 | ... | +1,092 | −115 | −1,099 |
| 1944 | +1,409 | −319 | ... | −483 | ... | +1,090 | −227 | −1,008 |
| 1945 | +1,459[3] | −204[3] | ... | −383[3] | ... | +1,255[3] | −100[3] | −1,198[3] |
| 1946 | +1,679 | −251 | ... | −451 | ... | +1,428 | −1,102 | −239 |
| 1947 | +100 | −198 | ... | −276 | ... | −98 | −511 | +989 |
| 1948 | +122 | +60 | ... | −34 | ... | +182 | −2,052 | −1,650 |
| 1949 | −694 | +4 | ... | −49 | ... | −690 | +44 | +198 |
| 1950 | +611 | −43 | ... | −14 | ... | +568 | +35 | +48 |

### Bolivia
(U.S. dollars)

| | VB | IB | TTB | IIB | GSIB | OCB |
|---|---|---|---|---|---|---|
| 1938 | −0.8 | −3.4 | ... | −5.1 | ... | −4.2 |
| 1939 | +7.7 | −9.5 | ... | −9.7 | ... | −1.8 |
| 1940 | +14.0 | −11.6 | ... | −11.7 | ... | +2.4 |
| 1947 | +10.6 | −19.8 | −1.4 | −9.2 | −9.2 | −8.8 |
| 1948 | +28.3 | −32.2 | −1.5 | −17.2 | −3.9 | −3.6 |
| 1949 | +9.3 | −19.9 | −1.8 | −1.2 | −10.6 | −10.3 |
| 1950 | −20.4 | −20.9 | −1.3 | −3.6 | −0.5 | −0.1 |

**J3**     **SOUTH AMERICA: Balance of Payments** (in millions of stated currency)

|  | Brazil[5] | | | | | | | |
|  | (cruzeiros) | | | | | | | |
|  | VB | IB | TTB | IIB | GSIB | OCB | (LT)CB | CR |
|---|---|---|---|---|---|---|---|---|
| 1947 | +2,410 | −5,094 | −597 | −1,013 | −2,684 | −3,120 | −598 | +763 |
| 1948 | +5,151 | −5,641 | −94 | −1,943 | −490 | −817 | +477 | −1,495 |
| 1949 | +2,830 | −5,009 | −28 | −1,881 | −2,179 | −2,232 | −138 | +866 |
| 1950 | −7,859 | −5,867 | −55 | −2,034 | +1,992 | +1,947 | −598 | +4,913 |

|  | Chile | | | | | | | |
|  | (US dollars) | | | | | | | |
|  | VB | IB | TTB | IIB | GSIB | OCB | (LT)CB | CR |
|---|---|---|---|---|---|---|---|---|
| 1938 | +37.9 | −51.8 | +2.1 | −59.3 | ... | −13.9 | +1.5 | ... |
| 1942 | +20.2 | −4.8 | +1.1 | −13.5 | +15.4 | +15.4 | +14.4 | +2.9 |
| 1943 | +42 | −3 | +3.5 | −12.2 | ... | +40 | +4.5 | −37.5 |
| 1944 | +52 | −25 | +3.6 | −30.6 | ... | +26 | −6.7 | −21.8 |
| 1945 | +44[7] | −16[7] | ... | ... | ...[7] | +28[7] | ...[7] | ... |
| 1946 | +11.0 | −40.1 | +0.8 | −37.6 | −29.2 | −29.2 | ... | +14.8 |
| 1947 | +7.0 | −54.9 | +0.9 | −57.5 | −47.9 | −47.3 | −31.8 | +19.5 |
| 1948 | +62.3 | −70.8 | +1.2 | −73.0 | −8.5 | −6.5 | +14.6 | +1.9 |
| 1949 | −34.2 | −50.9 | +1.0 | −57.8 | −85.1 | −83.4 | +74.5 | +0.2 |
| 1950 | +149.6 | −61.9 | +0.1 | −58.1 | +87.7 | +87.7 | +9.1 | −0.3 |

|  | Colombia | | | | | | | |
|  | (pesos) | | | | | | | |
|  | VB | IB | TTB | IIB | GSIB | OCB | (LT)CB | CR |
|---|---|---|---|---|---|---|---|---|
| 1938 | +17.7 | −31.5 | −8.8 | ... | ... | −13.8 | +10.0 | −13.8 |
| 1946 | −34.5 | −40.6 | −13.0 | −16.6 | ... | −75.1 | +129.1 | −32.9 |
| 1947 | −178.6 | −44.0 | −16.5 | −14.9 | ... | −222.6 | +58.2 | +108.7 |
| 1948 | −61.3 | −26.9 | −4.8 | −11.4 | ... | −88.2 | +27.5 | +54.4 |
| 1949 | +121.7 | −94.3 | −9.0 | −27.0 | ... | +27.4 | −70.6 | −0.6 |
| 1950 | +140.3 | −115.4 | −12.9 | −77.0 | +24.9 | −26.5 | +104.1 | −43.7 |

|  | Ecuador | | | | | | | |
|  | (US dollars) | | | | | | | |
|  | VB | IB | TTB | IIB | GSIB | OCB | (LT)CB | CR |
|---|---|---|---|---|---|---|---|---|
| 1939 | +7.6 | −8.2 | ... | ... | −0.6 | −1.2 | ... | ... |
| 1946 | +9.5 | −11.4 | −3.6 | −1.2 | −1.9 | −1.5 | +3.5 | −0.1 |
| 1947 | +4.3 | −11.0 | −2.7 | −3.3 | −6.7 | −6.3 | +15 | +1.1 |
| 1948 | +3.2 | −14.2 | −1.8 | −5.6 | −11.4 | −10.9 | +8.1 | −0.2 |
| 1949 | −4.0 | −15.9 | −2.1 | −7.3 | −19.9 | −18.0 | +18.9 | −0.1 |
| 1950 | +36.4 | −17.0 | −2.6 | −7.8 | +19.4 | +20.7 | −19.8 | +1.9 |

|  | Paraguay | | | | | | | |
|  | (US dollars) | | | | | | | |
|  | VB | IB | TTB | IIB | GSIB | OCB | (LT)CB | CR |
|---|---|---|---|---|---|---|---|---|
| 1948 | +2.5 | −7.1 | −0.1 | −1.0 | −4.6 | −3.9 | +1.6 | +2.9 |
| 1949 | +3.0 | −5.5 | −0.8 | −0.4 | −2.6 | −2.1 | −1.1 | +3.1 |
| 1950 | +14.8 | −6.2 | −0.7 | −0.5 | +8.6 | +9.0 | −0.6 | −9.4 |

**J3**     **SOUTH AMERICA: Balance of Payments** (in millions of stated currency)

### Peru
#### (soles)

|  | VB | IB | TTB | IIB | GSIB | OCB | LTCB | CR |
|---|---|---|---|---|---|---|---|---|
| 1938 | +63.5 | −110.3 | −2 | −118 | −46.8 | −42.3 | −3.5 | +19.5 |
| 1939 | +114.8 | −107.3 | ... | −111 | +7.5 | +14.0 | −8.5 | +7.8 |
| 1940 | +82.0 | −98.6 | ... | −101 | −16.6 | −9.6 | +13.8 | −4.1 |
| 1941 | +130.2 | −121.2 | ... | −103 | +9.1 | +10.2 | −5.2 | +10.6 |
| 1942 | +218.6 | −123.9 | ... | −107 | +94.7 | +100.9 | +4.7 | −63.1 |
| 1943 | +124.6 [7] | −115.1 [7] | ... [7] | −99 [7] | +9.5 [7] | +15.9 [7] | +28.8 [7] | −26.0 [7] |
| 1946 | +150 | −299 | −24 | −120 | −149 | −124 | −391 | +231 |
| 1947 | +99 | −260 | −7 | −73 | −161 | −145 | −81 | +165 |
| 1948 | +182 | −247 | −10 | −88 | −65 | −42 | +79 | −64 |
| 1949 | +305 | −468 | +21 | −167 | −163 | −98 | +151 | −93 |
| 1950 | +818 | −928 | −61 | −144 | −111 | −54 | −135 | −3 |

### Uruguay
#### (US dollars)

|  | VB | IB | TTB | IIB | GSIB | OCB | LTCB | CR |
|---|---|---|---|---|---|---|---|---|
| 1930 | +4.6 | −22.2 | ... | −20.5 | ... | −17.6 | +2.5 [5] | +6.7 |
| 1931 | −22.1 | −14.2 | ... | −12.8 | ... | −26.3 | +4.8 [5] | +4.9 |
| 1940 | +18.9 | −3.3 | +0.8 | −7.0 | +15.6 | +18.8 | −0.8 | −15.2 [4] |
| 1941 | +9.8 | −5.0 | +0.9 | −8.2 | +4.8 | +6.2 | +1.8 | −9.6 [4] |
| 1942 | −8.6 | −5.5 | +0.2 | −7.3 | −14.1 | −13.6 | −2.1 | +10.5 [4] |
| 1943 | +38.1 | −3.9 | +1.5 | −8.5 | +34.2 | +34.1 | −1.7 | −31.4 [4] |
| 1944 | +27.1 | −2.7 | +3.0 | −8.2 | ... | +24.4 | −1.6 | −36.0 [4] |
| 1946 | +8.9 | +4.2 | +9.2 | −9.1 | +13.1 | +11.6 | +7.9 | −23.9 |
| 1947 | −47.6 | +9.4 | +14.8 | −6.6 | −38.2 | −39.1 | +16.8 | +20.5 |
| 1948 | −20.2 | +8.1 | +14.5 | −6.0 | −12.1 | −13.1 | +6.2 | +11.3 |
| 1949 | +7.4 | +2.5 | +8.1 | −4.9 | +9.9 | +8.6 | −22.3 | −41.2 |
| 1950 | +49.4 | −0.1 | +6.1 | −4.5 | +49.3 | +47.8 | +5.5 | −51.3 |

### Venezuela
#### (US dollars)

|  | VB | IB | TTB | IIB | GSIB | OCB | LTCB | CR |
|---|---|---|---|---|---|---|---|---|
| 1938 | +83 | −73 | ... | ... | +10 | +10 | ... | ... |
| 1942 | +16 | −3 | −1.7 | −1.5 | ... | +13 | +3.7 | −21.6 |
| 1943 | +26 | −2 | −1.1 | −1.5 | ... | +24 | +2.7 | −26.9 |
| 1944 | +47 | −1 | −0.6 | −1.3 | ... | +46 | +1.7 | −49.6 |
| 1946 | +201 | −206 | ... | −158 | −5 | −17 | ... | ... |
| 1947 | +136 | −327 | ... | −250 | −191 | −202 | +222 | +11 |
| 1948 | +373 | −513 | ... | −435 | −140 | −156 | +343 | −128 |
| 1949 | +266 | −424 | −23 | −288 | −158 | −176 | +270 | −60 |
| 1950 | +655 | −528 | −34 | −392 | +127 | +112 | −2 | +80 |

**J3**     **NORTH AMERICA: BALANCE OF PAYMENTS** (in million US dollars)

PART B. 1950–88 in US dollars.

| | Canada | | | | | | | |
|---|---|---|---|---|---|---|---|---|
| | **VB** | **IB** | **TTB** | **IIB** | **GSIB** | **OCB** | **LTCB** | **CR[2]** |
| 1950 | +200 | −534 | −63 | −381 | −334 | −319 | +610 | +722 |
| 1951 | −1 | −527₁₂ | −6 | −337 | −528₁₂ | −512 | +666 | +56 |
| 1952 | +635 | −479 | −66 | −261 | +186 | +187 | +455 | +37 |
| 1953 | +84 | −522 | −63 | −242 | −438 | −448 | +649 | −38 |
| 1954 | +173 | −591 | −84 | −277 | −418 | −424 | +599 | +124 |
| 1955 | −56 | −597 | −121 | −331 | −653 | −687 | +414 | −44 |
| 1956 | −581 | −746 | −161 | −382 | −1,327 | −1,372 | +1,490 | +48 |
| 1957 | −450 | −950 | −162 | −441 | −1,400 | −1,451 | +1,320 | — |
| 1958 | −19 | −993 | −193 | −447 | −1,012 | −1,137 | +1,153 | −109 |
| 1959 | −273 | −1,101 | −208 | −491 | −1,374 | −1,487 | +1,179 | −11 |
| 1960 | +12₁₃ | −1,121₁₃ | −207 | −485₁₃ | −1,107₁₃ | −1,233₁₃ | +929₁₃ | −39₂ |
| | −224 | −893 | | −522 | −1,117 | −1,338 | | −41 |
| 1961 | +186 | −812 | −160 | −617 | −998 | −936 | +451 | +279 |
| 1962 | +215 | −571 | −43 | −652 | −786 | −774 | +374 | +562 |
| 1963 | +500 | −1,001 | +24 | −720 | −501 | −480 | +134 | +54 |
| 1964 | +717 | −1,105 | −50 | −768 | −388 | −382 | +162 | +282 |
| 1965 | +148 | −869 | −49 | −853 | −1,017 | −1,012 | +379 | +22 |
| 1966 | +250 | −1,304 | −56 | −873 | −1,054 | −1,027 | +726 | −230 |
| 1967 | +590 | −1,088 | +391 | −1,174 | −498 | −455 | +523 | +46 |
| 1968 | +1,446 | −1,674 | −26 | −1,157 | −228 | −80 | +338 | +481 |
| 1969 | +973 | −1,958 | −197 | −1,148 | −985 | −888 | +324 | +51 |
| 1970 | +3,047 | −2,167 | −197 | −1,323 | +880 | −1,008 | +1,034 | +1,654 |
| 1971 | +2,672 | −2,543 | −201 | −1,569 | +129 | +363 | +1,028 | +951 |
| 1972 | +2,172 | −2,672 | −233 | −1,565 | −500 | −278 | +1,955 | +377 |
| 1973 | +3,181 | −3,172 | −283 | −1,669 | +9 | +305 | +519 | −374 |
| 1974 | +2,087 | −3,920 | −286 | −2,404 | −1,833 | −1,324 | +1,885 | +43 |
| 1975 | −271 | −4,609 | −713 | −2,638 | −4,880 | −4,571 | +4,247 | −500 |
| 1976 | +1,884 | −6,573 | −1,195 | −3,733 | −4,689 | −4,152 | +7,711 | +495 |
| 1977 | +3,137 | −7,535 | −1,566 | −4,446 | −4,398 | −4,101 | +4,606 | −1,262 |
| 1978 | +4,180 | −8,411 | −1,529 | −5,331 | −4,231 | −4,285 | +989 | −118 |
| 1979 | +4,178 | −8,739 | −906 | −6,088 | −4,561 | −4,138 | +1,628 | −731 |
| 1980 | +8,001 | −9,865 | −1,054 | −6,695 | −1,864 | −967 | +916 | −555 |
| 1981 | +6,578 | −12,796 | −886 | −9,483 | −6,218 | −5,110 | +74 | +214 |
| 1982 | +14,991 | −13,921 | −1,062 | −10,272 | +1,070 | +2,231 | +5,680 | −576 |
| 1983 | +14,972 | −13,343 | −1,790 | −9,412 | +1,629 | +2,487 | −690 | +425 |
| 1984 | +15,967 | −14,569 | −1,672 | −10,419 | +1,398 | +1,995 | +3,307 | −986 |
| 1985 | +12,574 | −14,635 | −1,544 | −10,498 | −2,061 | −1,470 | +1,534 | +1 |
| 1986 | +7,676 | −16,049 | −829 | −11,800 | −8,373 | −7,296 | +10,356 | +591 |
| 1987 | +8,875 | −17,386 | −1,898 | −12,204 | −8,511 | −6,917 | +5,534 | +3,491 |
| 1988 | +9,139 | −20,843 | −2,191 | −15,388 | −11,704 | −8,200 | +7,760 | +7,521 |

**J3    NORTH AMERICA: Balance of Payments** (in million US dollars)

|  | \multicolumn{8}{c}{Costa Rica} |
|---|---|---|---|---|---|---|---|---|
|  | VB | IB | TTB | IIB | GSIB | OCB | LTCB | CR |
| 1950 | +15.2 | −12.7 | −0.9 | −13.5 | +2.5 | +2.6 | +0.5 | +1.1 |
| 1951 | +13.2 | −13.4 | −1.5 | −12.1 | −0.2 | +0.8 | +2.4 | −4.7 |
| 1952 | +12.7 | −18.7 | −2.0 | −14.7 | −5.8 | −4.4 | +1.0 | −6.2 |
| 1953 | +14.5 | −16.2 | −2.0 | −11.9 | −1.6 | −0.5 | −0.1 | −0.2 |
| 1954 | +14.8 | −14.9 | −0.4 | −11.7 | −0.3 | +2.0 | −0.1 | −7.3 |
| 1955 | +3.0 | −11.3 | +0.2 | −7.6 | −8.2 | −5.3 | +10.5 | −3.9 |
| 1956 | −16.9 | −2.5 | +0.6 | −1.2 | −19.4 | −16.4 | +1.3 | +7.8 |
| 1957 | −9.3 | −10.6 | +1.0 | −6.9 | −19.9 | −12.7 | +2.3 | — |
| 1958 | +4.2 | −13.1 | +1.4 | −8.9 | −8.9 | +0.6 | +7.3 | −7.8 |
| 1959 | −17.5 | −8.3 | +1.0 | −3.7 | −25.8 | −19.2 | +9.0 [14] | +6.2 |
| 1960 | −11.9 | −8.2 | +1.7 | −3.7 | −20.1 | −16.0 | +1.9 | +1.2 |
| 1961 | −12.7 | −7.0 | +1.9 | −2.7 | −19.7 | −12.6 | +7.8 | +7.1 |
| 1962 | −9.7 | −12.1 | +1.0 | −8.2 | −21.8 | −17.2 | +21.2 | −6.2 |
| 1963 | −17.8 | −12.6 | +2.0 | −8.3 | −30.4 | −21.5 | +34.8 | −2.8 |
| 1964 | −11.4 | −17.5 | +1.7 | −10.8 | −28.9 | −19.4 | +24.8 | −2.7 |
| 1965 | −49.2 | −27.0 | +0.4 | −13.4 | −76.2 | −67.8 | +33.0 | −2.7 |
| 1966 | −26.4 | −26.1 | +2.3 | −14.9 | −52.5 | −44.0 | +41.7 | +2.7 |
| 1967 | −30.4 | −28.6 | +1.9 | −17.0 | −59.0 | −50.2 | +19.2 | −4.8 |
| 1968 | −23.7 | −27.8 | +3.4 | −18.6 | −51.5 | −42.9 | +22.9 | −4.7 |
| 1969 | −31.9 | −26.8 | +5.5 | −16.4 | −58.7 | −50.3 | +31.6 | −7.7 |
| 1970 | −55.8 | −24.2 | +9.4 | −13.6 | −80.0 | −74.1 | +43.8 | +11.6 |
| 1971 | −92.0 | −29.8 | +7.2 | −14.6 | −121.8 | −114.4 | +57.1 | −13.0 |
| 1972 | −58.3 | −48.3 | +10.9 | −34.9 | −106.6 | −100.0 | +80.1 | −19.9 |
| 1973 | −67.4 | −51.7 | +14.4 | −38.0 | −119.1 | −112.2 | +92.4 | −16.5 |
| 1974 | −208.8 | −67.0 | +21.2 | −38.6 | −275.8 | −266.1 | +135.9 | +10.0 |
| 1975 | −134.2 | −93.1 | +16.8 | −64.2 | −227.3 | −217.7 | +221.6 | +4.6 |
| 1976 | −103.0 | −111.7 | +12.9 | −73.1 | −214.7 | −201.5 | +203.2 | −66.5 |
| 1977 | −97.3 | −144.1 | +11.0 | −79.7 | −241.4 | −225.6 | +292.1 | −107.6 |
| 1978 | −185.5 | −194.3 | +10.8 | −113.3 | −379.8 | −363.2 | +334.4 | −21.7 |
| 1979 | −315.1 | −255.3 | +10.3 | −149.6 | −570.4 | −558.2 | +347.6 | +87.5 |
| 1980 | −374.3 | −304.1 | +24.5 | −218.5 | −678.4 | −663.9 | +387.5 | −98.1 |
| 1981 | −88.0 | −348.2 | +47.2 | −307.3 | −436.2 | −409.1 | +188.5 | +20.9 |
| 1982 | +64.1 | −366.7 | +89.0 | −378.8 | −302.6 | −271.7 | −73.9 | −127.4 |
| 1983 | −41.8 | −307.1 | +80.6 | −342.5 | −348.9 | −312.6 | −65.9 | −160.0 |
| 1984 | +4.6 | −296.6 | +66.2 | −323.7 | −292.0 | −251.1 | −182.8 | +93.4 |
| 1985 | −61.9 | −282.8 | +64.5 | −294.5 | −344.7 | −291.1 | −131.8 | −83.5 |
| 1986 | +39.6 | −271.5 | +71.4 | −288.8 | −231.9 | −160.6 | −252.2 | −62.1 |
| 1987 | −138.5 | −343.9 | +67.6 | −309.7 | −482.4 | −376.4 | −411.1 | +28.7 |
| 1988 | +97.9 | −336.0 | +105.3 | −359.7 | −433.9 | −303.5 | −269.2 | −164.9 |

**J3**    **NORTH AMERICA: Balance of Payments** (in million US dollars)

| | | | | Dominican Republic | | | | |
|------|--------|--------|--------|--------|--------|--------|--------|--------|
| | VB | IB | TTB | IIB | GSIB | OCB | LTCB | CR |
| 1950 | +43.9 | −23.7 | −1.1 | −11.8 | +20.2 | +19.2 | −2.0 | −4.6 |
| 1951 | +42.6 | −35.4 | −0.3 | −26.5 | +7.2 | +6.3 | +0.6 | −10.3 |
| 1952 | +19.6 | −23.8 | −1.5 | −14.4 | −4.2 | −5.3 | +2.0 | −2.5 |
| 1953 | +18.3 | −14.4 | −1.7 | −5.4 | +3.9 | +3.1 | −8.0 | +4.0 |
| 1954 | +37.6 | −14.5 | −1.7 | −4.1 | +23.1 | +21.6 | +6.4 | −7.6 |
| 1955 | +14.8 | −23.6 | −2.6 | −12.3 | −8.8 | −10.7 | −5.1 | −1.4 |
| 1956 | +11.8 | −16.3 | +2.3 | −5.5 | −4.5 | −6.5 | +5.4 | −2.3 |
| 1957 | +44.0 | −20.9 | −0.5 | −11.6 | +23.1 | +20.2 | −8.6 | −8.2 |
| 1958 | −8.0 | −14.1 | −1.4 | −3.3 | −22.1 | −25.1 | +34.1 | +0.7 |
| 959 | +20.3 | −21.9 | −1.0 | −14.2 | −1.6 | −1.7 | +6.3 | +5.7 |
| 1960 | +67.1 | −21.5 | −2.1 | −9.6 | +45.6 | +42.5 | −0.3 | +21.1 |
| 1961 | +66.8 | −31.8 | −1.7 | −18.4 | +35.0 | +33.0 | −24.8 | +16.8 |
| 1962 | +37.3 | −21.0 | −13.7 | −21.3 | −16.3 | −10.4 | +14.7 | −11.7 |
| 1963 | +9.7 | −58.3 | −16.0 | −19.9 | −48.6 | −19.4 | +28.6 | −21.3 |
| 1964 | −23.0 | −57.4 | −16.9 | −16.1 | −80.4 | −61.8 | +56.0 | +0.5 |
| 1965 | +4.8 | −38.5 | −15.5 | −12.0 | −33.7 | | +4.8 | +1.8 |
| 1966 | −30.2 | −61.2 | −18.0 | −20.0 | −91.4 | −74.9 | +66.0 | +7.2 |
| 1967 | −18.5 | −54.7 | −20.5 | −19.7 | −73.2 | −66.2 | +61.6 | +11.3 |
| 1968 | −33.3 | −51.9 | −17.0 | −19.0 | −85.2 | −75.2 | +53.1 | −3.2 |
| 1969 | −33.8 | −59.3 | −18.3 | −23.4 | −93.1 | −84.7 | +82.7 | −4.2 |
| 1970 | −64.0 | −69.1 | −20.6 | −25.9 | −133.1 | −101.9 | +109.5 | +7.7 |
| 1971 | −69.0 | −77.4 | −15.1 | −28.9 | −146.4 | −129.4 | +81.5 | −24.0 |
| 1972 | +9.9 | −87.5 | −4.6 | −46.9 | −77.6 | −47.0 | +82.2 | −2.5 |
| 1973 | +20.2 | −147.4 | −13.7 | −76.8 | −127.2 | −96.6 | +69.6 | −29.3 |
| 1974 | −36.2 | −239.8 | −22.1 | −89.7 | −276.0 | −241.0 | +161.3 | −2.8 |
| 1975 | +121.1 | −232.9 | −16.4 | −61.2 | −111.8 | −72.8 | +159.2 | −25.3 |
| 1976 | −47.2 | −208.6 | −17.9 | −55.6 | −255.8 | −129.2 | +174.9 | −10.5 |
| 1977 | −68.8 | −199.4 | −9.8 | −98.4 | −268.2 | −128.6 | +173.2 | −69.6 |
| 1978 | −186.9 | −274.8 | −34.1 | −135.7 | −461.7 | −311.9 | +146.5 | +38.1 |
| 1979 | −268.9 | −268.2 | −34.2 | −187.7 | −537.1 | −331.3 | +260.3 | −84.5 |
| 1980 | −557.8 | −367.6 | +6.8 | −210.2 | −925.4 | −719.9 | +287.8 | +31.4 |
| 1981 | −263.7 | −318.7 | +78.5 | −276.6 | −582.4 | −389.4 | +150.5 | −28.6 |
| 1982 | −489.6 | −158.0 | +179.1 | −254.8 | −647.6 | −442.6 | +199.3 | +112.7 |
| 1983 | −493.8 | −139.1 | +232.6 | −297.1 | −632.9 | −417.9 | +62.6 | −29.8 |
| 1984 | −389.0 | −39.4 | +281.5 | −241.4 | −428.4 | −163.4 | +294.1 | −57.7 |
| 1985 | −547.4 | +83.5 | +367.5 | −226.3 | −463.9 | −107.6 | +185.5 | −89.4 |
| 1986 | −629.6 | +153.1 | +417.1 | −249.7 | −476.5 | −185.5 | +141.8 | −36.2 |
| 1987 | −880.2 | +181.8 | +475.8 | −306.1 | −698.4 | −363.5 | +59.5 | +194.1 |
| 1988 | −718.3 | +338.7 | +641.1 | −270.6 | −379.6 | −21.9 | +139.1 | −71.8 |

**J3    NORTH AMERICA: Balance of Payments** (in million US dollars)

| | VB | IB | TTB | IIB | GSIB | OCB | LTCB | CR |
|---|---|---|---|---|---|---|---|---|
| | | | | El Salvador | | | | |
| 1950 | +19.3 | −5.6 | −5.4 | −7.4 | +13.7 | +13.8 | −2.3 | −1.9 |
| 1951 | +16.6 | −8.2 | −3.8 | −1.6 | +8.4 | +8.7 | +4.1 | −1.6 |
| 1952 | +18.2 | −10.2 | −4.1 | −2.2 | +8.0 | +8.2 | −0.1 | −1.0 |
| 1953 | +19.2 | −11.2 | −6.2 | −2.4 | +8.0 | +8.7 | +11.5 | +0.2 |
| 1954 | +17.9 | −9.5 | −6.6 | −2.6 | +8.4 | +9.0 | −17.7 | −0.8 |
| 1955 | +14.6 | −13.0 | −8.6 | −2.6 | +1.6 | +2.1 | −12.5 | +5.5 |
| 1956 | +18.0 | −12.2 | −7.8 | −2.7 | +5.8 | +6.1 | +3.0 | +2.6 |
| 1957 | +11.9 | −9.7 | −7.0 | −2.5 | +2.2 | +3.1 | +4.7 | −5.0 |
| 1958 | +9.7 | −8.1 | −3.6 | −3.3 | +1.6 | +1.9 | +4.7 | +2.0 |
| 1959 | +12.1 | −11.7 | −5.2 | −3.6 | +0.4 | +0.6 | −11.1 [14] | +4.7 |
| 1960 | −20.0 | −8.7 | −4.0 | −3.9 | −28.7 | −27.7 | +7.4 | +10.5 |
| 1961 | +9.8 | −12.4 | −4.9 | −4.3 | −2.6 | −0.4 | +2.6 | +8.1 |
| 1962 | +14.0 | −15.8 | −6.0 | −5.1 | −1.8 | +2.4 | +6.3 | −1.8 |
| 1963 | −2.0 | −15.3 | −6.5 | −5.8 | −17.3 | −10.1 | +14.9 | −15.9 |
| 1964 | −16.3 | −15.8 | −7.2 | −6.2 | −32.1 | −23.3 | +16.4 | −10.9 |
| 1965 | +4.3 | −30.2 | −8.2 | −7.7 | −25.9 | −12.6 | +22.1 | −5.2 |
| 1966 | −12.0 | −38.8 | −8.6 | −7.6 | −50.8 | −41.0 | +33.9 | +0.8 |
| 1967 | +2.4 | −37.7 | −5.8 | −8.6 | −35.3 | −23.4 | +25.4 | +2.1 |
| 1968 | +13.5 | −37.0 | −6.6 | −8.2 | −23.5 | −15.1 | +19.0 | −7.2 |
| 1969 | +9.1 | −42.1 | −10.4 | −8.4 | −33.3 | −19.8 | +12.3 | −1.8 |
| 1970 | +41.4 | −47.0 | −11.9 | −8.8 | −5.6 | +8.7 | +4.9 | +1.1 |
| 1971 | +18.0 | −49.2 | −10.3 | −6.5 | −31.2 | −14.2 | +13.5 | −0.7 |
| 1972 | +52.0 | −51.6 | −9.6 | −8.0 | +0.4 | +12.4 | +62.2 | −17.5 |
| 1973 | +18.6 | −76.1 | −24.4 | −8.6 | −57.5 | −43.9 | +35.0 | +22.6 |
| 1974 | −57.7 | −94.8 | −21.3 | −26.6 | −152.5 | −134.2 | +94.9 | −36.3 |
| 1975 | −17.7 | −102.6 | −15.4 | −40.8 | −120.3 | −92.9 | +113.6 | −29.4 |
| 1976 | +63.7 | −69.3 | −13.4 | −18.2 | −5.6 | +23.6 | +72.9 | −78.4 |
| 1977 | +112.5 | −121.3 | −26.2 | −37.7 | −8.8 | +30.8 | +38.2 | −26.1 |
| 1978 | −149.4 | −187.8 | −66.6 | −60.6 | −337.2 | −285.8 | +165.8 | −56.9 |
| 1979 | +177.6 | −207.6 | −92.1 | −49.0 | −30.0 | +21.4 | +68.3 | +125.2 |
| 1980 | +178.4 | −196.8 | −92.7 | −94.5 | −18.4 | +30.6 | +109.5 | +64.6 |
| 1981 | −100.3 | −210.5 | −55.1 | −100.8 | −310.8 | −250.4 | +170.5 | +5.8 |
| 1982 | −100.2 | −227.0 | −71.6 | −121.6 | −327.2 | −119.8 | +151.8 | −36.6 |
| 1983 | −74.3 | −225.1 | −61.9 | −135.2 | −299.4 | −148.0 | +211.7 | −49.7 |
| 1984 | −188.6 | −172.5 | −43.7 | −136.6 | −361.1 | −188.5 | +33.9 | −5.6 |
| 1985 | −216.0 | −156.3 | −45.9 | −118.5 | −372.3 | −188.7 | +57.6 | — |
| 1986 | −124.4 | −142.0 | −32.0 | −122.4 | −266.4 | −17.1 | +18.6 | +13.5 |
| 1987 | −349.1 | −54.0 | −32.4 | −112.3 | −403.1 | −68.2 | −36.7 | −36.9 |
| 1988 | −355.9 | −118.8 | −19.7 | −121.6 | −474.7 | −129.2 | +29.2 | +30.1 |

**J3**     **NORTH AMERICA: Balance of Payments** (in million US dollars)

| | | | | | Guatemala | | | |
|------|-------|--------|--------|--------|--------|--------|--------|--------|
| | VB | IB | TTB | IIB | GSIB | OCB | LTCB | CR |
| 1950 | +10.4 | −10.4 | *+0.7* | *−2.8* | — | +0.3 | +1.4 | −1.3 |
| 1951 | +3.6 | −9.2 | *+0.1* | *+0.2* | −5.6 | −5.3 | −0.5 | −2.3 |
| 1952 | +15.4 | −3.2 | *−0.9* | *+6.9* | +12.2 | +12.2 | −1.6 | −3.2 |
| 1953 | +21.0 | −26.8 | *−0.1* | *+4.5* | −5.8 | +11.6 | −0.9 | +0.1 |
| 1954 | +19.0 | −24.0 | *−0.9* | *−2.5* | −5.0 | +1.5 | +0.2 | +2.5 |
| 1955 | +8.2 | −13.2 | *+2.3* | *−0.3* | −5.0 | +5.0 | +7.6 | −15.5 |
| 1956 | −4.4 | −3.4 | *+2.1* | *−2.4* | −7.8 | −7.8 | +15.2 | −15.7 |
| 1957 | −20.2 | −1.8 | *+2.4* | *−2.1* | −18.4 | −18.4 | +23.6 | −3.9 |
| 1958 | −30.2 | −19.8 | *+2.9* | *−3.4* | −50.0 | −38.2 | +19.7 | +26.0 |
| 1959 | −20.6 | −19.6 | *+3.3* | *−4.7* | −40.2 | −28.6 | +25.5 [14] | +5.1 |
| 1960 | −8.9 | −16.7 | *+2.3* | *−5.0* | −25.6 | −11.0 | +21.5 | −10.0 |
| 1961 | −6.6 | −17.6 | *+2.1* | *−6.7* | −24.2 | −7.9 | +10.3 | −1.1 |
| 1962 | −3.9 | −19.1 | *+1.8* | *−8.6* | −23.0 | −15.7 | +6.2 | +9.5 |
| 1963 | +3.0 | −23.8 | *−7.1* | *−4.7* | −20.8 | −17.3 | +24.4 | −12.5 |
| 1964 | −6.2 | −39.5 | *−7.6* | *−11.9* | −45.7 | −37.9 | +23.0 | −3.4 |
| 1965 | −14.0 | −28.1 | *−10.6* | *−11.2* | −42.1 | −34.6 | +43.4 | −8.9 |
| 1966 | +30.1 | −51.7 | *−18.2* | *−17.4* | −21.6 | −12.2 | +24.0 | +7.4 |
| 1967 | −22.6 | −48.7 | *−4.4* | *−19.4* | −71.3 | −62 | +50.4 | −5.2 |
| 1968 | −4.1 | −57.3 | *−3.4* | *−31.4* | −61.4 | −50.7 | +51.4 | −0.8 |
| 1969 | +21.6 | −54.0 | *+0.3* | *−35.7* | −32.4 | −19.0 | +43.1 | −10.0 |
| 1970 | +30.5 | −25.9 | *−2.4* | *−38.2* | −25.4 | −7.9 | +55.0 | −3.5 |
| 1971 | −3.1 | −71.4 | *−7.9* | *−41.9* | −74.5 | −49.2 | +46.5 | −13.4 |
| 1972 | +41.1 | −82.6 | *−7.4* | *−45.6* | −41.5 | −11.5 | +33.0 | −42.9 |
| 1973 | +50.7 | −85.4 | *−1.4* | *−45.9* | −34.7 | +7.7 | +60.0 | −77.3 |
| 1974 | −49.2 | −109.3 | *+4.9* | *−48.0* | −158.5 | −103.1 | +100.1 | +6.2 |
| 1975 | −31.4 | −111.1 | *+23.3* | *−66.0* | −143.5 | −65.7 | +138.3 | −102.6 |
| 1976 | −190.3 | −86.1 | *−16.0* | *−46.8* | −276.4 | −77.5 | +76.3 | −219.2 |
| 1977 | +73.2 | −54.4 | *−33.4* | *−19.0* | −127.6 | −35.3 | +178.1 | −183.1 |
| 1978 | −191.4 | −188.6 | *−39.8* | *−10.0* | −380.0 | −270.5 | +247.6 | −70.2 |
| 1979 | −180.3 | −151.5 | *−38.4* | *+5.2* | −331.8 | −205.6 | +238.7 | +18.2 |
| 1980 | +47.2 | −320.7 | *−102.6* | *−60.0* | −273.5 | −163.3 | +229.1 | +252.5 |
| 1981 | −248.7 | −414.9 | *−102.6* | *−45.7* | −663.6 | −572.7 | +291.2 | +199.3 |
| 1982 | −113.9 | −347.9 | *−88.3* | *−97.9* | −461.8 | −399.1 | +269.1 | +29.0 |
| 1983 | +35.7 | −290.2 | *−82.6* | *−95.2* | −254.5 | −223.9 | +28.8 | −9.0 |
| 1984 | −50.0 | −356.1 | *−50.1* | *−164.4* | −406.1 | −377.4 | −48.1 | −30.9 |
| 1985 | −17.0 | −249.0 | *−10.2* | *−159.8* | −266.0 | −246.3 | −71.3 | −62.3 |
| 1986 | +168.1 | −260.8 | *+14.0* | *−204.5* | −92.7 | −17.6 | −302.2 | −56.3 |
| 1987 | −355.3 | −300.5 | *+18.2* | *−171.6* | −635.8 | −442.5 | −152.5 | +73.1 |
| 1988 | −339.9 | −298.4 | *−33.1* | *−173.1* | −638.3 | −414.0 | +434.7 | +110.7 |

**J3      NORTH AMERICA: Balance of Payments** (in million US dollars)

| | VB | IB | TTB | IIB | GSIB | OCB | LTCB | CR |
|---|---|---|---|---|---|---|---|---|
| | | | | | Haiti[15] | | | |
| 1950 | +2.2 | −4.0 | +0.8 | −4.6 | −1.8 | +1.3 | +3.4 | −2.2 |
| 1951 | +5.7 | −5.1 | +0.1 | −5.5 | +0.6 | +1.6 | +5.9 | −1.6 |
| 1952 | +2.6 | −3.0 | −0.2 | −3.8 | −0.4 | −1.0 | +4.5 | −2.8 |
| 1953 | −6.7 | −5.7 | −0.1 | −5.8 | −12.4 | −11.4 | +9.3 | +5.8 |
| 1954 | +8.0 | −13.4 | −0.1 | −2.6 | −5.4 | +6.0 | +7.0 | −4.5 |
| 1955 | −17.1 | — | +1.8 | −1.7 | −17.1 | −15.3 | +13.2 | +2.7 |
| 1956 | −6.7 | +4.4 | +3.9 | −2.7 | −2.3 | +1.9 | +8.6 | +1.2 |
| 1957 | −13.3 | −1.2 | +4.5 | −1.9 | −14.1 | −10.1 | −3.1 | +3.2 |
| 1958 | −5.4 | −3.8 | +4.2 | −2.9 | −9.2 | −4.2 | +8.4 | +2.9 |
| 1959 | −9.5 | −0.9 | +5.2 | −3.3 | −10.4 | +4.2 | +5.5 | +1.6 |
| 1960 | −5.3 | −2.5 | +4.3 | −4.1 | −7.8 | +1.3 | +6.8 | −2.2 |
| 1961 | −21.4 | −3.1 | +6.0 | −3.4 | −24.5 | −10.1 | +15.5 | −2.8 |
| 1962 | −7.1 | −7.1 | +3.3 | −6.1 | −14.2 | −7.3 | +8.9 | +4.1 |
| 1963 | +4.1 | −14.2 | −1.6 | −4.7 | −10.1 | −3.2 | −9.9 | +2.5 |
| 1964 | +0.8 | −15.0 | −3.5 | −6.2 | −14.2 | −7.7 | +18.8 | +0.3 |
| 1965 | −4.8 | −17.7 | −4.2 | −5.2 | −22.5 | −13.7 | +2.2 [14] | +0.9 |
| 1966 | −8.9 | −14.3 | −3.3 | −3.7 | −23.2 | −6.2 | +0.1 | +0.3 |
| 1967 | −8.0 | −9.8 | −1.2 | −2.9 | −17.8 | −0.7 | +0.3 | +0.4 |
| 1968 | −2.4 | −8.1 | +0.9 | −3.1 | −10.5 | +2.3 | +0.2 | −0.6 |
| 1969 | +4.4 | −7.0 | +1.6 | −3.6 | −2.6 | +13.1 | +2.1 | −1.3 |
| 1970 | −2.8 | −8.0 | +2.3 | −3.6 | −10.8 | +11.1 | +2.8 | −0.6 |
| 1971 | −17.5 | −7.3 | +5.8 | −4.0 | −24.8 | −21.2 | +2.7 | −6.1 |
| 1972 | −25.3 | −7.1 | +9.2 | −4.5 | −32.4 | −22.7 | +15.3 | −7.5 |
| 1973 | −27.5 | −12.4 | +11.8 | −4.4 | −39.9 | −35.5 | +1.3 | +0.8 |
| 1974 | −50.1 | −20.7 | +13.1 | −5.9 | −70.8 | −64.2 | +10.3 | −2.7 |
| 1975 | −69.9 | −19.4 | +17.7 | −7.2 | −89.3 | −109.2 | +36.1 | +7.3 |
| 1976 | −64.5 | −35.1 | +19.9 | −7.0 | −99.6 | −102.3 | +33.9 | −15.5 |
| 1977 | −62.3 | −38.6 | +23.9 | −12.3 | −100.9 | −37.7 | +68.0 | −6.1 |
| 1978 | −57.5 | −55.0 | +25.4 | −15.0 | −112.5 | −44.9 | +40.1 | −5.0 |
| 1979 | −82.1 | −46.3 | +32.2 | −13.6 | −128.4 | −55.0 | +61.2 | −21.7 |
| 1980 | −103.2 | −86.4 | +35.8 | −14.2 | −189.6 | −101.1 | +80.3 | +35.2 |
| 1981 | −209.0 | −79.2 | +42.7 | −12.7 | −288.2 | −148.8 | +111.1 | −5.6 |
| 1982 | −124.8 | −75.5 | +39.5 | −14.1 | −210.3 | −98.6 | +84.6 | +20.7 |
| 1983 | −139.3 | −82.2 | +46.1 | −14.1 | −221.5 | −111.1 | +85.3 | −4.7 |
| 1984 | −123.3 | −102.7 | +44.7 | −18.1 | −226.0 | −103.0 | +90.4 | −4.0 |
| 1985 | −121.7 | −118.0 | +55.3 | −19.8 | −239.7 | −94.7 | +53.8 | +6.6 |
| 1986 | −112.5 | −84.3 | +45.5 | −15.3 | −196.8 | −44.9 | +39.2 | −8.2 |
| 1987 | −101.1 | −101.1 | +48.3 | −20.9 | −202.2 | −31.2 | +60.7 | −1.1 |
| 1988 | −103.5 | −129.7 | +39.6 | −27.1 | −233.2 | −40.3 | +49.1 | +3.6 |

**J3**   **NORTH AMERICA: Balance of Payments** (in million US dollars)

| | Honduras | | | | | | | |
|---|---|---|---|---|---|---|---|---|
| | VB | IB | TTB | IIB | GSIB | OCB | LTCB | CR |
| 1950 | +25.5 | −25.2 | −0.3 | −20.7 | +0.3 | −0.4 | +0.1 | −4.2 |
| 1951 | +20.1 | −22.4 | −0.1 | −18.7 | −2.3 | −2.8 | +9.0 | −9.7 |
| 1952 | +6.5 | −15.6 | — | −13.0 | −9.1 | −9.1 | +13.6 | −2.1 |
| 1953 | +15.3 | −20.2 | — | −13.7 | −4.9 | −5.2 | +6.9 | −0.6 |
| 1954 | +4.1 | −3.4 | −0.2 | +4.2 | +0.7 | +1.0 | +0.7 | −1.2 |
| 1955 | −1.6 | −5.9 | −0.2 | +1.1 | −7.5 | −6.6 | −0.8 | +4.1 |
| 1956 | +15.2 | −21.4 | −0.2 | −12.1 | −6.2 | −5.6 | −0.2 | +2.0 |
| 1957 | −3.8 | −10.0 | −0.6 | −3.5 | −13.8 | −12.7 | +8.6 | +4.1 |
| 1958 | +3.8 | −13.0 | −0.6 | −5.8 | −9.2 | −7.9 | −4.3 | +4.3 |
| 1959 | +6.9 | −8.5 | −0.4 | −2.6 | −1.6 | +0.9 | +4.3 [14] | −0.8 |
| 1960 | −1.1 | +4.1 | −0.4 | +8.5 | +3.0 | +5.7 | −4.8 | −0.4 |
| 1961 | +7.7 | −7.2 | −0.4 | −1.0 | +0.5 | +5.1 | −6.9 | +0.7 |
| 1962 | +8.7 | −11.5 | −0.5 | −4.3 | −2.8 | +0.2 | +5.8 | −1.1 |
| 1963 | −3.9 | −12.9 | −0.5 | −6.0 | −16.8 | −13.8 | +15.7 | +0.8 |
| 1964 | +0.4 | −17.8 | −2.9 | −7.0 | −17.4 | −11.2 | +12.9 | −7.2 |
| 1965 | +15.0 | −25.7 | −2.2 | −13.0 | −10.7 | −7.0 | +10.8 | −3.7 |
| 1966 | +6.4 | −29.9 | −4.0 | −15.5 | −23.5 | −19.2 | +10.8 | −4.0 |
| 1967 | +3.9 | −37.2 | −4.5 | −21.2 | −33.3 | −28.6 | +15.4 | +2.3 |
| 1968 | +11.6 | −42.5 | −6.3 | −23.1 | −30.9 | −24.7 | +28.5 | −6.5 |
| 1969 | +1.2 | −39.1 | −7.4 | −18.6 | −37.9 | −30.6 | +29.9 | +0.6 |
| 1970 | −25.2 | −45.2 | −7.8 | −22.6 | −70.4 | −63.8 | +40.1 | +9.7 |
| 1971 | +16.5 | −46.0 | −7.9 | −24.8 | −29.5 | −22.7 | +35.3 | −2.6 |
| 1972 | +35.6 | −54.9 | −9.0 | −27.4 | −19.3 | −12.7 | +23.4 | −13.3 |
| 1973 | +23.1 | −64.7 | −6.3 | −33.1 | −41.6 | −34.6 | +32.4 | −6.9 |
| 1974 | −87.2 | −39.3 | −5.2 | −13.3 | −126.5 | −103.9 | +63.2 | −3.1 |
| 1975 | −62.7 | −67.1 | −4.6 | −28.9 | −129.8 | −112.1 | +84.4 | −53.2 |
| 1976 | −20.8 | −97.3 | −4.5 | −58.6 | −118.1 | −104.8 | +95.2 | −37.9 |
| 1977 | −20.3 | −122.6 | −7.1 | −69.8 | −142.9 | −128.7 | +132.2 | −51.9 |
| 1978 | −28.4 | −146.2 | −6.4 | −86.5 | −174.6 | −157.2 | +158.0 | −4.7 |
| 1979 | −27.0 | −185.6 | −7.6 | −121.8 | −212.6 | −192.1 | +157.3 | −25.0 |
| 1980 | −103.8 | −234.5 | −6.5 | −155.0 | −338.3 | −316.8 | +225.4 | +58.0 |
| 1981 | −114.8 | −215.4 | +3.8 | −154.8 | −330.2 | −302.7 | +200.3 | +46.3 |
| 1982 | −4.2 | −256.1 | +2.1 | −203.7 | −258.3 | −228.3 | +134.1 | −13.3 |
| 1983 | −57.6 | −206.1 | +2.0 | −154.2 | −263.7 | −232.0 | +129.9 | −3.4 |
| 1984 | −147.8 | −248.7 | −1.2 | −179.8 | −396.5 | −374.3 | +247.3 | −15.9 |
| 1985 | −89.6 | −260.1 | −2.0 | −192.5 | −349.7 | −292.6 | +209.9 | +20.6 |
| 1986 | +17.2 | −322.7 | −4.0 | −255.3 | −305.5 | −254.6 | +53.7 | −7.1 |
| 1987 | −49.5 | −306.6 | −7.7 | −240.9 | −356.1 | −306.9 | +50.5 | +4.1 |
| 1988 | −23.7 | −340.3 | −9.5 | −264.3 | −364.0 | −319.0 | −35.7 | +54.7 |

**J3     NORTH AMERICA: Balance of Payments** (in million US dollars)

| | | | | | Jamaica | | | |
|---|---|---|---|---|---|---|---|---|
| | **VB** | **IB** | **TTB** | **IIB** | **GSIB** | **OCB** | **LTCB** | **CR** |
| 1960 | −23.0 | −20.4 | +17.1 | −15.6 | −43.4 | −26.6 | +19.4 | +1.6 |
| 1961 | −12.9 | −12.9 | +17.1 | −17.9 | −25.8 | −12.4 | +18.5 | −13.4 |
| 1962 | −9.0 | −18.2 | +14.4 | −18.0 | −27.2 | −8.4 | +3.8 [14] | +3.4 |
| 1963 | +9.5 | −19.9 | +28.6 | −37.0 | −10.4 | +9.8 | +38.6 | −24.6 |
| 1964 | −36.1 | −25.8 | +31.9 | −40.0 | −61.9 | −43.7 | +7.5 | −10.6 |
| 1965 | −38.1 | −9.5 | +52.9 | −42.8 | −47.6 | −30.5 | +22.7 | +1.6 |
| 1966 | −8.0 | −48.5 | +67.2 | −90.8 | −56.5 | −42.0 | +91.8 | +20.0 |
| 1967 | −23.2 | −52.9 | +68.1 | −92.3 | −76.1 | −81.4 | +96.3 | +0.3 |
| 1968 | −81.8 | −34.8 | +65.3 | −73.6 | −116.6 | −91.9 | +136.2 | −31.4 |
| 1969 | −89.9 | −48.6 | +78.5 | −87.0 | −138.5 | −123.6 | +113.4 | +2.6 |
| 1970 | −107.6 | −67.8 | +80.0 | −98.2 | −175.4 | −152.9 | +160.7 | −24.9 |
| 1971 | −131.9 | −61.9 | +93.0 | −103.1 | −193.8 | −172.2 | +188.4 | −39.4 |
| 1972 | −151.9 | −73.6 | +114.1 | −126.5 | −225.5 | −196.7 | +126.7 | +22.0 |
| 1973 | −178.3 | −96.7 | +107.4 | −132.9 | −275.0 | −247.6 | +176.2 | +31.9 |
| 1974 | −59.2 | −57.6 | +112.6 | −67.6 | −116.8 | −91.9 | +211.8 | −67.2 |
| 1975 | −161.0 | −149.5 | +76.2 | −107.6 | −310.5 | −282.8 | +181.3 | +34.3 |
| 1976 | −135.2 | −173.3 | +46.9 | −116.7 | −308.5 | −302.6 | +85.1 | +124.1 |
| 1977 | +71.1 | −133.2 | +93.6 | −129.8 | −62.1 | −42.1 | +42.7 | −12.5 |
| 1978 | +81.0 | −156.8 | +136.5 | −183.2 | −75.8 | −50.0 | −132.2 | −11.0 |
| 1979 | −64.3 | −154.7 | +184.5 | −207.2 | −219.0 | −138.9 | −25.3 | −5.0 |
| 1980 | −75.5 | −181.2 | +228.9 | −252.6 | −256.7 | −166.0 | +140.3 | −40.9 |
| 1981 | −322.7 | −138.4 | +270.6 | −202.5 | −461.1 | −336.8 | +39.6 | +27.9 |
| 1982 | −441.5 | −112.2 | +306.1 | −214.0 | −553.7 | −408.5 | +224.4 | −19.7 |
| 1983 | −438.5 | −18.1 | +374.3 | −186.4 | −456.6 | −358.6 | +70.8 | +73.1 |
| 1984 | −334.7 | −118.0 | +386.6 | −302.7 | −452.7 | −335.2 | +390.0 | −75.6 |
| 1985 | −435.6 | −87.2 | +375.3 | −314.4 | −522.8 | −304.4 | +107.7 | −60.3 |
| 1986 | −247.9 | +61.4 | +480.9 | −324.3 | −186.5 | −40.2 | −192.7 | +56.0 |
| 1987 | −356.7 | +49.0 | +551.2 | −391.5 | −307.7 | −137.0 | +255.3 | −75.9 |
| 1988 | −395.0 | −33.6 | +470.6 | −354.3 | −428.6 | +76.1 | +124 | +27.9 |

**J3** **NORTH AMERICA: Balance of Payments** (in million US dollars)

| | | | | Mexico | | | | |
|---|---|---|---|---|---|---|---|---|
| | **VB** | **IB** | **TTB** | **IIB** | **GSIB** | **OCB** | **LTCB** | **CR** |
| 1950 | −74 | +106 | *+156* | *−76* | +32 | +47 | +84 | −196 |
| 1951 | −221 | +96 | *+173* | *−100* | −125 | −118 | +117 | +15 |
| 1952 | −175 8 | +71 8 | *+162* | *−123* | −104 8 | −99 8 | +77 8 | +12 8 |
| 1953 | −169 | +47 | *+162* | *−94* | −122 | −117 | +37 | +32 |
| 1954 | −92 | +69 | *+172* | *−86* | −23 | −29 | +127 | +40 |
| 1955 | +21 | +133 | *+252* | *−93* | +154 | +149 | +119 | −231 |
| 1956 | −174 | +60 | *+280* | *−134* | −114 | −116 | +142 | −72 |
| 1957 | −362 | +66 | *+304* | *−134* | −296 | −293 | +170 | +36 |
| 1958 | −338 | +73 | *+241* | *−143* | −265 | −264 | +197 | +80 |
| 1959 | −220 | +59 | *+254* | *−154* | −161 | −162 | +98 14 | −62 |
| 1960 | −354 | +35 | *+260* | *−190* | −319 | −324 | +90 | +16 |
| 1961 | −260 | +32 | *+269* | *−204* | −228 | −241 | +253 | +30 |
| 1962 | −167 | — | *+275* | *−237* | −167 | −182 | +246 | −14 |
| 1963 | −201 | — | *+308* | *−266* | −201 | −218 | +305 | −116 |
| 1964 | −370 | −42 | *+327* | *−324* | −412 | −423 | +519 | −46 |
| 1965 | −352 | −35 | *+361* | *−339* | −387 | −392 | +169 | +78 |
| 1966 | −337 | −5 | *+396* | *−394* | −342 | −343 | +313 | +24 |
| 1967 | −608 | −84 | *+441* | *−473* | −692 | −685 | +510 | −22 |
| 1968 | −634 | −122 | *+501* | *−559* | −756 | −743 | +547 | −71 |
| 1969 | −529 | −98 | *+528* | *−617* | −627 | −592 | +800 | −5 |
| 1970 | −888 | −235 | *+416* | *−695* | −1,123 | −1,068 | +626 | −83 |
| 1971 | −749 | −143 | *+533* | *−603* | −892 | −835 | +766 | −192 |
| 1972 | −894 | −86 | *+623* | *−700* | −980 | −916 | +828 | −212 |
| 1973 | −1,515 | +26 | *+839* | *−997* | −1,489 | −1,415 | +1,819 | −171 |
| 1974 | −2,791 | −207 | *+902* | *−1,447* | −2,998 | −2,876 | +3,046 | −37 |
| 1975 | −3,272 | −910 | *+812* | *−1,818* | −4,182 | −4,042 | +4,667 | −146 |
| 1976 | −2,295 | −1,270 | *+615* | *−2,355* | −3,565 | −3,409 | +4,994 | +279 |
| 1977 | −1,021 | −1,003 | *+939* | *−2,517* | −2,024 | −1,854 | +4,611 | −467 |
| 1978 | −1,745 | −1,618 | *+1,059* | *−3,044* | −3,363 | −3,171 | +5,121 | −199 |
| 1979 | −2,830 | −1,854 | *+1,257* | *−4,288* | −4,684 | −5,459 | +5,178 | −233 |
| 1980 | −3,385 | −7,649 | *+1,072* | *−6,359* | −11,034 | −10,750 | +10,530 | −943 |
| 1981 | −3,846 | −12,518 | *+771* | *−10,546* | −16,364 | −16,061 | +18,938 | −1,333 |
| 1982 | +6,795 | −13,405 | *+433* | *−12,636* | −6,610 | −6,307 | +8,349 | +3,320 |
| 1983 | +13,762 | −8,661 | *+1,145* | *−9,418* | +5,101 | +5,403 | −259 | −3,222 |
| 1984 | +12,941 | −9,157 | *+1,116* | *−10,304* | +3,784 | +4,194 | −324 | −3,454 |
| 1985 | +8,451 | −8,321 | *+640* | *−9,197* | +130 | +1,130 | −1,289 | +2,363 |
| 1986 | +4,599 | −2,462 | *+810* | *−8,031* | −2,137 | −1,673 | +70 | −858 |
| 1987 | +8,433 | −5,113 | *+1,134* | *−7,427* | +3,320 | +3,968 | +2,594 | −6,786 |
| 1988 | +1,668 | −4,678 | *+798* | *−7,533* | −3,010 | −2,443 | −3,921 | +7,147 |

**J3**     **NORTH AMERICA: Balance of Payments** (in million US dollars)

| | | | | Nicaragua | | | | |
|------|--------|--------|-------|--------|--------|--------|--------|---------|
| | VB | IB | TTB | IIB | GSIB | OCB | LTCB | CR |
| 1950 | +10.8 | −10.5 | −1.3 | −6.1 | +0.3 | +0.5 | +0.4 | +0.9 |
| 1951 | +16.8 | −10.8 | −0.9 | −6.5 | +6.0 | +6.4 | +0.4 | −6.2 |
| 1952 | +12.1 | −12.2 | −0.8 | −5.4 | −0.1 | +0.9 | +5.3 | −6.1 |
| 1953 | +11.2 | −14.9 | −1.8 | −6.7 | −3.7 | −2.8 | +6.5 | — |
| 1954 | +4.4 | −16.7 | −2.0 | −5.6 | −12.3 | −11.3 | +5.0 | +3.5 |
| 1955 | +20.5 | −20.1 | −2.2 | −8.0 | +0.4 | +2.6 | +1.3 | −0.9 14 |
| 1956 | +7.9 | −18.0 | −4.2 | −4.4 | −9.1 | −6.9 | +2.8 | +7.3 |
| 1957 | +2.2 | −13.1 | −4.2 | −1.4 | −10.9 | −8.1 | +10.3 | −2.4 |
| 1958 | +5.1 | −18.5 | −4.6 | −4.0 | −13.4 | −9.3 | +5.8 | +1.9 |
| 1959 | +22.3 | −17.7 | −5.0 | −2.4 | +4.6 | +7.8 | +0.8 14 | −4.6 |
| 1960 | +7.5 | −18.8 | −3.3 | −2.8 | −11.3 | −8.4 | +4.4 | +0.1 |
| 1961 | +11.2 | −18.4 | −4.6 | −3.0 | −7.2 | −3.4 | +4.6 | −1.6 |
| 1962 | +11.7 | −25.0 | −4.7 | −3.1 | −13.3 | −9.8 | +10.5 | −3.9 |
| 1963 | +15.6 | −24.6 | −6.5 | −2.7 | −9.0 | −4.9 | +15.1 | −14.5 |
| 1964 | +15.7 | −30.3 | −7.7 | −5.5 | −14.6 | −9.2 | +22.2 | −6.9 |
| 1965 | +15.3 | −45.0 | −8.6 | −12.8 | −29.7 | −23.2 | +16.5 | −18.2 |
| 1966 | −9.8 | −47.5 | −6.4 | −15.7 | −57.3 | −50.2 | +32.1 | −0.7 |
| 1967 | −24.3 | −45.7 | −6.1 | −18.7 | −70.0 | −64.2 | +31.0 | +29.0 |
| 1968 | −4.2 | −41.9 | −1.6 | −24.7 | −46.1 | −39.8 | +55.5 | −18.3 |
| 1969 | −0.6 | −42.7 | −2.1 | −25.2 | −43.0 | −36.0 | +28.3 | +5.7 |
| 1970 | — | −45.5 | −1.9 | −29.3 | −45.5 | −39.5 | +45.9 | −6.1 |
| 1971 | −2.9 | −46.6 | −2.9 | −31.9 | −49.5 | −44.5 | +51.3 | −12.0 |
| 1972 | +43.9 | −29.3 | −2.8 | −37.0 | +14.6 | +21.7 | +50.5 | −24.5 |
| 1973 | −49.1 | −74.2 | −4.2 | −49.8 | −123.3 | −65.9 | +112.0 | −73.6 |
| 1974 | −160.8 | −111.9 | −7.5 | −65.7 | −272.7 | −257.2 | +173.5 | +37.7 |
| 1975 | −107.2 | −94.4 | −5.9 | −60.7 | −201.6 | −185.0 | +152.3 | −47.1 |
| 1976 | +56.8 | −105.4 | −6.9 | −67.2 | −48.6 | −39.3 | +22.3 | +5.1 |
| 1977 | −68.0 | −125.1 | −12.4 | −68.2 | −193.1 | −181.9 | +208.4 | −1.6 |
| 1978 | +92.7 | −127.1 | −34.6 | −81.5 | −34.4 | −24.9 | +79.9 | +82.7 |
| 1979 | +227.0 | −138.4 | −29.2 | −73.4 | +88.6 | +180.2 | +122.5 | −89.7 |
| 1980 | −352.5 | −182.8 | −9.4 | −122.5 | −535.3 | −411.4 | +184.9 | +204.9 |
| 1981 | −414.2 | −247.7 | −7.5 | −167.7 | −661.9 | −591.6 | +340.4 | −62.6 |
| 1982 | −317.5 | −247.9 | — | −174.0 | −565.4 | −513.9 | +297.0 | −31.3 |
| 1983 | −290.4 | −296.3 | −2.3 | −212.1 | −586.7 | −507.4 | +67.3 | −13.6 |
| 1984 | −322.9 | −364.0 | +1.6 | −263.4 | −686.9 | −597.1 | +204.4 | −244.4 |
| 1985 | −489.0 | −363.6 | +1.2 | −273.3 | −852.6 | −725.7 | +515.2 | −7.8 |
| 1986 | −419.6 | −383.2 | +3.8 | −253.6 | −802.8 | −687.7 | +126.9 | +211.3 |
| 1987 | −439.3 | −374.9 | +3.0 | −243.9 | −814.2 | −678.8 | +191.0 | −6.2 |
| 1988 | −482.6 | −362.6 | +3.6 | −262.1 | −845.2 | −715.2 | +235.3 | −43.9 |

**J3** **NORTH AMERICA: Balance of Payments** (in million US dollars)

| | Panama | | | | | | | |
|------|--------|--------|--------|--------|--------|--------|--------|--------|
| | VB | IB | TTB | IIB | GSIB | OCB | LTCB | CR |
| 1950 | −36.3 | +25.1 | *+26.6* | *−11.6* | −11.2 | −16.9 | +6 | −2.4 |
| 1951 | −38.2 | +20.5 | *+20.4* | *−12.0* | −17.7 | −21.4 | +11 | +2.2 |
| 1952 | −46.4 | +24.5 | *+21.3* | *−11.3* | −21.9 | −22.5 | +3 | −3.2 |
| 1953 | −38.9 | +27.1 | *+22.9* | *−11.8* | −11.8 | −14.3 | +8 | −1.6 |
| 1954 | −32.3 | +20.8 | *+24.9* | *−17.2* | −11.5 | −17.1 | −1 | +1.2 |
| 1955 | −21.4 | +17.0 | *+25.1* | *−17.8* | −4.4 | −10.9 | −2 | — |
| 1956 | −34.2 | +12.3 | *+26.5* | *−17.8* | −21.9 | −20.3 | +18 | −2 |
| 1957 | −51.7 | +20.6 | *+26.7* | *−18.9* | −31.0 | −34.8 | +9 | +4 |
| 1958 | −53.7 | +20.2 | *+18.8* | *−12.1* | −33.5 | −28.7 | +21 | −4 |
| 1959 | −54.1 | +19.7 | *+18.4* | *−13.3* | −34.4 | −31.6 | +15 | +5 |
| 1960 | −70 | +38 | *+18* | *−10* | −32 | −31 | +22 | −3 |
| 1961 | −83 | +55 | *+22* | *−7* | −28 | −24 | +35 | +3 |
| 1962 | −85 | +66 | *+28* | *−7* | −19 | −19 | +23 | — |
| 1963 | −91 | +65 | *+27* | *−9* | −26 | −25 | +33 | −3 |
| 1964 | −86 | +64 | *+21* | *−9* | −22 | −21 | +9 | +2 |
| 1965 | −99 | +66 | *+31* | *−20* | −33 | −29 | +22 | −1 |
| 1966 | −115 | +73 | *+34* | *−23* | −42 | −40 | +25 | — |
| 1967 | −123 | +95 | *+40* | *−23* | −28 | −26 | +15 | −1 |
| 1968 | −129 | +114 | *+43* | *−24* | −15 | −15 | +27 | −4 |
| 1969 | −153 | +122 | *+49* | *−25* | −31 | −29 | +60 | −3 |
| 1970 | −201 | +133 | *+55* | *−29* | −68 | −64 | +119 | −1 |
| 1971 | −226 | +148 | *+55* | *−30* | −78 | −73 | +87 | −3 |
| 1972 | −263 | +161 | *+61* | *−35* | −102 | −98 | +128 | −22 |
| 1973 | −296 | +190 | *+80* | *−42* | −106 | −111 | +148 | +2 |
| 1974 | −510 | +290 | *+95* | *−57* | −220 | −224 | +114 | +2 |
| 1975 | −492 | +328 | *+105* | *−23* | −164 | −169 | +186 | +5 |
| 1976 | −514 | +342 | *+121* | *−37* | −172 | −176 | +723 | −44 |
| 1977 | −502 | +349 | *+142* | *−68* | −153 | −155 | −113 | +8 |
| 1978 | −558 | +347 | *+164* | *−59* | −211 | −208 | +451 | −80 |
| 1979 | −730 | +406 | *+166* | *−106* | −324 | −311 | +314 | +32 |
| 1980 | −727 | +401 | *+115* | *−65* | −326 | −311 | −720 | +1 |
| 1981 | −775 | +800 | *+109* | *+362* | +25 | +56 | +570 | −3 |
| 1982 | −634 | +537 | *+93* | *+26* | −97 | −51 | +1,200 | +19 |
| 1983 | −645 | +1,016 | *+101* | *+115* | +371 | +416 | +367 | −106 |
| 1984 | −823 | +929 | *+121* | *+63* | +106 | +218 | +228 | −9 |
| 1985 | −757 | +930 | *+135* | *+36* | +173 | +286 | −263 | +118 |
| 1986 | −541 | +801 | *+122* | *−5* | +260 | +355 | −10 | −72 |
| 1987 | −567 | +708 | *+98* | *−106* | +141 | +204 | +15 | +92 |
| 1988 | −185 | +864 | *+80* | *−9* | +679 | +751 | +147 | +6 |

**J3**     **NORTH AMERICA: Balance of Payments** (in million US dollars)

| | | | | Trinidad & Tobago | | | | |
|------|--------|--------|--------|--------|--------|----------|--------|--------|
| | VB | IB | TTB | IIB | GSIB | OCB | LTCB | CR |
| 1960 | −26.4 | −73.1 | −1.7 | −93.1 | −99.5 | −59 | +40.2 | +2.8 |
| 1961 | +13.8 | −78.4 | −4.1 | −119.3 | −64.6 | −41.2 | +31.8 | −2.0 |
| 1962 | +2.5 | −96.4 | −5.1 | −117.4 | −93.9 | −57.0 | +46.4 | +6.6 |
| 1963 | +1.0 | −59.1 | +0.1 | −67.5 | −58.1 | −59.7 | +78.1 | −3.4 |
| 1964 | +11.4 | −61.3 | +0.2 | −70.9 | −49.9 | −49.3 | +34.4 | −9.8 |
| 1965 | −27.7 | −52.4 | 0.1 | −60.0 | −80.1 | −68.3 | +63.3 | +1.4 |
| 1966 | +17.9 | −73.9 | +1.9 | −63.1 | −56.0 | −30.3 | +26.1 | −1.2 |
| 1967 | +37.6 | −55.6 | −0.4 | −65.2 | −18.0 | −35.6 | +26.6 | +1.1 |
| 1968 | +32.8 | −15.1 | +8.3 | −63.4 | +17.7 | −6.3 | +27.7 | −20.2 |
| 1969 | +0.6 | −24.8 | +10.6 | −68.5 | −24.2 | −53.8 | +64.8 | +4.8 |
| 1970 | −50.9 | −26.6 | +1.0 | −61.2 | −77.5 | −108.6 | +83.3 | +12.0 |
| 1971 | −138.3 | +5.2 | +10.9 | −61.8 | −133.1 | −168.9 | +126.7 | −20.1 |
| 1972 | −129.7 | +9.1 | +23.7 | −69.7 | −120.6 | −123.9 | +103.2 | +8.8 |
| 1973 | −38.1 | +11.4 | +35.5 | −88.2 | −26.7 | −29.9 | +60.5 | +9.8 |
| 1974 | +445.8 | −162.1 | +28.7 | −208.5 | +283.7 | +274.1 | +69.6 | −342.8 |
| 1975 | +329.2 | +23.8 | +44.9 | −80.1 | +353.0 | +331.8 | +43.2 | −364.9 |
| 1976 | +288.3 | +2.9 | +40.8 | −102.9 | +285.4 | +255.4 | +14.2 | −265.4 |
| 1977 | +307.4 | −102.1 | +42.3 | −187.7 | +205.3 | +174.1 | +230.7 | −461.7 |
| 1978 | +164.4 | −83.8 | +44.8 | −72.1 | +80.6 | +42.7 | +270.5 | −333.4 |
| 1979 | +314.7 | −302.9 | +23.3 | −249.9 | +11.8 | −33.9 | +434.1 | −336.2 |
| 1980 | +752.6 | −353.7 | +13.4 | −306.5 | +398.9 | +334.7 | +335.9 | −640.8 |
| 1981 | +848.8 | −381.9 | −12.0 | −195.5 | +466.9 | +374.5 | +327.1 | −566.7 |
| 1982 | −258.1 | −246.7 | −28.0 | +78.6 | −504.8 | −644.9 | +540.6 | +267.0 |
| 1983 | −206.8 | −715.5 | −174.4 | −133.9 | −922.3 | −1,002.9 | +283.0 | +976.0 |
| 1984 | +405.9 | −845.2 | −177.7 | −314.1 | −439.3 | −522.5 | +13.2 | +747.9 |
| 1985 | +756.1 | −787.0 | −121.6 | −346.3 | −30.9 | −90.3 | +32.3 | +228.2 |
| 1986 | +153.6 | −545.4 | −82.0 | −210.7 | −391.8 | −441.7 | −59.8 | +654.4 |
| 1987 | +339.3 | −544.7 | −63.8 | −276.3 | −205.4 | −242.2 | +8.2 | +284.0 |
| 1988 | +389.2 | −520.6 | −76.5 | −336.7 | −131.4 | −164.4 | +29.0 | +191.6 |

**J3**   **NORTH AMERICA: Balance of Payments** (in million US dollars)

| | USA | | | | | | | |
|---|---|---|---|---|---|---|---|---|
| | **VB** | **IB** | **TTB** | **IIB** | **GSIB** | **OCB** | **LTCB** | **CR** |
| 1950 | +1,122 | +770 | −335 | +1,460 | +1,892 | −2,125 | −702 | +1,758 |
| 1951 | +3,067 | +750 | −284 | +1,720 | +3,817 | +302 | −740 | −33 |
| 1952 | +2,611 | −255 | −290 | +1675 | +2,356 | −175 | −900 | −415 |
| 1953 | +1,437 | −905 | −355 | +1,732 | +532 | −1,949 | −322 | +1,256 |
| 1954 | +2,576 | −617 | −414 | +2,112 | +1,959 | −321 | −713 | +480 |
| 1955 | +2,897 | −744 | −499 | +2,297 | +2,153 | −345 | −674 | +182 |
| 1956 | +4,753 | −608 | −570 | +2,494 | +4,145 | +1,722 | −1,961 | −869 |
| 1957 | +6,271 | −370 | −587 | +2,588 | +5,901 | +3,556 | −2,902 | −1,165 |
| 1958 | +3,462 | −1,106 | −835 | +2,584 | +2,356 | −5 | −2,552 | +2,292 |
| 1959 | +1,148 | −838 | −708 | +2,726 | +310 | −2,138 | −1,589 | +1,035 |
| 1960 | +4,906 $_{13}$ | −798 $_{13}$ | −831 $_{13}$ | +2,841 $_{13}$ | +4,107 $_{13}$ | +1,815 $_{13}$ | −2,100 $_{13}$ | +2,145 $_{13}$ |
| | +4.89 | +0.30 | −0.86 | +3.24 | +5.19 | +2.82 | −3.01 | +2.14 |
| 1961 | +5.57 | +1.00 | −0.85 | +3.82 | +6.57 | +3.82 | −2.78 | +0.61 |
| 1962 | +4.52 | +1.60 | −1.01 | +4.35 | +6.12 | +3.38 | −3.34 | +1.53 |
| 1963 | +5.22 | +2.02 | −1.10 | +4.59 | +7.24 | +4.40 | −4.07 | +0.38 |
| 1964 | +6.80 | +2.92 | −1.00 | +5.03 | +9.72 | +6.82 | −4.19 | +0.17 |
| 1965 | +4.95 | +3.41 | −1.06 | +5.35 | +8.36 | +5.41 | −5.72 | +1.22 |
| 1966 | +3.82 | +2.27 | −1.07 | +5.51 | +6.09 | +3.03 | −4.81 | +0.57 |
| 1967 | +3.80 | +2.05 | −1.56 | +5.06 | +5.85 | +2.59 | −4.40 | +0.05 |
| 1968 | +0.64 | +3.04 | −1.25 | +5.73 | +3.68 | +0.59 | −1.63 | −0.88 |
| 1969 | +0.60 | +2.95 | −1.33 | +5.82 | +3.55 | +0.42 | −3.12 | −1.26 |
| 1970 | +2.59 | +3.19 | −1.65 | +6.23 | +5.78 | +2.33 | −4.93 | +2.47 |
| 1971 | −2.27 | +4.66 | −1.85 | +9.59 | +2.39 | −1.45 | −6.06 | +2.18 |
| 1972 | −6.42 | +16.26 | −2.21 | +10.68 | +9.84 | −5.78 | −2.87 | −0.01 |
| 1973 | +0.91 | +10.28 | −2.09 | +14.95 | +11.19 | +7.07 | −5.35 | −0.06 |
| 1974 | −5.51 | +14.89 | −1.95 | +18.99 | +9.38 | +1.94 | −5.69 | −1.46 |
| 1975 | +8.90 | +14.04 | −1.74 | +16.68 | +22.94 | +18.06 | −15.00 | −0.20 |
| 1976 | −9.47 | +18.97 | −1.13 | +19.85 | +9.50 | +4.18 | −12.21 | −2.52 |
| 1977 | −31.11 | +21.61 | −1.30 | +22.37 | −9.50 | −14.49 | −8.67 | −0.56 |
| 1978 | −33.94 | +24.11 | −1.28 | +25.72 | −9.83 | −15.40 | −8.52 | +1.06 |
| 1979 | −27.54 | +33.72 | −0.98 | +36.47 | +6.18 | +0.20 | −15.53 | +2.76 |
| 1980 | −25.50 | +34.92 | +0.18 | +78.57 | +9.42 | +1.20 | +0.55 | −7.64 |
| 1981 | −27.99 | +43.22 | +1.40 | +69.37 | +15.23 | +7.26 | +18.25 | −3.21 |
| 1982 | −36.44 | +40.35 | — | +32.82 | +3.91 | −5.86 | +11.94 | −3.86 |
| 1983 | −67.08 | +37.87 | −1.21 | +31.97 | −29.21 | −40.18 | +9.98 | +0.45 |
| 1984 | −112.51 | +26.13 | −6.24 | +49.22 | −86.38 | −98.99 | +42.73 | −0.97 |
| 1985 | −122.16 | +15.39 | −8.48 | +21.24 | −106.77 | −122.25 | +102.34 | −8.21 |
| 1986 | −145.05 | +15.52 | −6.48 | +17.15 | −129.53 | −145.42 | +80.39 | −5.11 |
| 1987 | −159.49 | +11.60 | −6.66 | +12.99 | −147.89 | −162.22 | +82.83 | +2.58 |
| 1988 | −126.97 | +13.04 | −4.15 | −26.88 | −113.93 | −128.99 | +58.83 | −1.79 |

**J3      SOUTH AMERICA: BALANCE OF PAYMENTS** (in millions US dollars)

| | Argentina | | | | | | | |
|---|---|---|---|---|---|---|---|---|
| | **VB** | **IB** | **TTB** | **IIB** | **GSIB** | **OCB** | **LTCB** | **CR** |
| 1950 | +26[14] | +88[14] | ... | −3 | +114[14] | +114[14] | ... | +19[14] |
| 1951 | −142 | +69 | ... | −33 | −73 | −224 | +99 | +25 |
| 1952 | −367 | +25 | ... | −10 | −342 | −412 | +11 | +49 |
| 1953 | +398 | −66 | ... | −11 | +332 | +344 | +8 | −86 |
| 1954 | +161 | −75 | ... | −15 | +86 | +83 | +5 | −30 |
| 1955 | −109 | −130 | — | −21 | −239 | −242 | +29 | +68 |
| 1956 | −54 | −77 | +4 | −17 | −131 | −131 | +111 | +38 |
| 1957 | −186 | −114 | +1 | −13 | −300 | −303 | +57 | +175 |
| 1958 | −97 | −159 | −6 | −31 | −256 | −259 | +46 | +154 |
| 1959 | +130 | −116[14] | −6 | −40 | +14[14] | +11[14] | +266[14] | −178[14] |
| 1960 | −27 | −29 | −15 | −57 | −56 | −60 | +332 | −258 |
| 1961 | −328 | −90 | −16 | −102 | −418 | −417 | +120 | +232 |
| 1962 | +16 | −130 | −32 | −72 | −114 | −117 | +74 | +297 |
| 1963 | +497 | −153 | −17 | −68 | +344 | +346 | +78 | −141 |
| 1964 | +457 | −295 | −49 | −103 | +162 | +162 | +27 | +74 |
| 1965 | +431 | −207 | −49 | −53 | +224 | +222 | +48 | −127 |
| 1966 | +598 | −332 | −34 | −151 | +266 | +259 | +65 | −26 |
| 1967 | +494 | −361 | −77 | −194 | +133 | +130 | +20 | −541 |
| 1968 | +333 | −382 | −69 | −205 | −49 | −53 | +60 | −33 |
| 1969 | +217 | −443 | −64 | −219 | −226 | −230 | +34 | +222 |
| 1970 | +274 | −434 | −56 | −223 | −160 | −163 | +95 | −135 |
| 1971 | +87 | −474 | −21 | −331 | −387 | −390 | +146 | +390 |
| 1972 | +256 | −479 | +1 | −383 | −223 | −227 | +51 | +14 |
| 1973 | +1,289 | −589 | +2 | −467 | +700 | +711 | −151 | −814 |
| 1974 | +714 | −596 | +5 | −423 | +118 | +118 | −109 | −127 |
| 1975 | −549 | −733 | +61 | −446 | −1,282 | −1,287 | −56 | +1,071 |
| 1976 | +1,153 | −484 | +65 | −508 | +669 | +651 | −66 | −921 |
| 1977 | +1,852 | −695 | −25 | −780 | +1,157 | +1,126 | +144 | −1,828 |
| 1978 | +2,913 | −989 | −307 | −745 | +1,924 | +1,856 | +374 | −2,297 |
| 1979 | +1,782 | −1,234 | −996 | −990 | −548 | −513 | +487 | −4,381 |
| 1980 | −1,373 | −3,424 | 1,449 | −1,632 | −4,797 | −4,774 | +942 | +2,749 |
| 1981 | +712 | −5,402 | −1021 | −3,354 | −4,690 | −4,712 | +2,049 | +3,437 |
| 1982 | +2,764 | −5,151 | +45 | −5,068 | −2,387 | −2,353 | +556 | +758 |
| 1983 | +3,716 | −6,168 | −54 | −5,930 | −2,452 | −2,436 | +832 | +1,254 |
| 1984 | +3,982 | −6,479 | −160 | −6,153 | −2,497 | −2,495 | +640 | +59 |
| 1985 | +4,878 | −5,830 | −148 | −5,715 | −952 | −952 | +302 | −2,030 |
| 1986 | +2,446 | −5,307 | −326 | −4,820 | −2,861 | −2,859 | +32 | +555 |
| 1987 | +1,017 | −5,244 | −275 | −4,751 | −4,227 | −4,235 | −591 | +1,101 |
| 1988 | +4,242 | −5,814 | −261 | −5,346 | −1,572 | −1,572 | +429 | −1,746 |

**J3** **SOUTH AMERICA: Balance of Payments** (in million US dollars)

| | | | | Bolivia | | | | |
|---|---|---|---|---|---|---|---|---|
| | VB | IB | TTB | IIB | GSIB | OCB | LTCB | CR |
| 1950 | +20.4 | −20.9 | −1.3 | −3.6 | −0.5 | −0.1 | +15.5 | −3.7 |
| 1951 | +34.8 | −31.4 | −1.9 | −3.3 | +3.4 | +3.8 | +4.5 | −5.5 |
| 1952 | −2.2 | −6.8 | −1.6 | −18.8 | −9.0 | −8.0 | −2.3 | +4.0 |
| 1953 | −6.3 | −18.4 | −1.1 | −1.9 | −24.7 | −22.1 | +11.1 | +6.9 |
| 1954 | +1.1 | −18.3 | −0.6 | −1.1 | −17.2 | −2.5 | −6.3 | +12.1 |
| 1955 | +6.0 | −29.9 | −0.4 | −4.1 | −23.9 | −3.3 | +12.3 | +3.3 |
| 1956 | +5.5 | −26.6 | −0.7 | −3.1 | −21.1 | −0.8 | +17.6 | +9.9 |
| 1957 | −9.0 | −24.3 | −0.7 | −3.0 | −33.3 | −5.2 | +3.3 | −3.8 |
| 1958 | −22.8 | −21.3 | −0.6 | −6.5 | −44.1 | −15.2 | +13.4 | +1.5 |
| 1959 | −0.8 [14] | −24.3 [14] | −0.8 | +1.9 | −25.1 [14] | −2.4 [14] | +20.1 [14] | −6.7 [14] |
| 1960 | −15.6 | −16.9 | −0.7 | +1.2 | −32.5 | −19.5 | +17.1 | −1.5 |
| 1961 | −13.2 | −17.7 | −0.5 | −0.7 | −30.9 | −8.7 | +11.7 | −0.5 |
| 1962 | −30.8 | −20.8 | −0.6 | −2.8 | −51.6 | −31.2 | +28.9 | +3.4 |
| 1963 | −25.3 | −22.9 | −0.9 | −2.6 | −48.2 | −18.8 | +28.3 | −6.5 |
| 1964 | −9.3 | −25.6 | −1.5 | −2.8 | −34.9 | −9.1 | +19.7 | −12.0 |
| 1965 | −11.5 | −28.4 | −1.7 | −3.6 | −39.9 | −23.9 | +24.2 | −14.0 |
| 1966 | −7.9 | −25.9 | −1.4 | −0.8 | −33.8 | −12.5 | +22.6 | −4.6 |
| 1967 | +1.4 | −43.8 | −1.2 | −18.0 | −42.4 | −29.5 | +25.2 | +3.3 |
| 1968 | −6.0 | −51.2 | −0.6 | −23.1 | −57.2 | −50.5 | +53.7 | −1.6 |
| 1969 | +4.4 | −60.1 | −0.8 | −30.5 | −55.7 | −47.9 | +52.7 | −2.5 |
| 1970 | +55.2 | −54.9 | −1.4 | −25.0 | +0.3 | +4.2 | +33.2 | −3.5 |
| 1971 | +37.3 | −46.8 | −2.0 | −17.1 | −9.5 | −2.4 | +69.1 | −7.6 |
| 1972 | +48.1 | −65.2 | −2.0 | −21.7 | −17.1 | −3.6 | +92.9 | −5.5 |
| 1973 | +67.6 | −70.5 | −1.9 | −23.0 | −2.9 | +12.5 | +36.9 | −10.7 |
| 1974 | +232.4 | −95.4 | −8.1 | −25.3 | +150.6 | +137.0 | +100.1 | −123.0 |
| 1975 | −25.1 | −118.2 | −6.6 | −9.0 | −143.3 | −130.2 | +158.9 | +34.7 |
| 1976 | +50.7 | −118.2 | −6.0 | −32.4 | −67.5 | −53.5 | +226.0 | −30.8 |
| 1977 | +55.3 | −188.2 | −9.0 | −68.8 | −132.9 | −117.9 | +337.8 | −75.8 |
| 1978 | −96.6 | −261.9 | −5.9 | −119.1 | −350.5 | −331.5 | +273.5 | +61.5 |
| 1979 | +21.4 | −469.6 | −26.5 | −183.1 | −448.2 | −397.0 | +254.0 | −25.6 |
| 1980 | +367.8 | −433.7 | −19.0 | −264.1 | −65.9 | −6.4 | +79.6 | +87.7 |
| 1981 | +84.7 | −589.0 | −14.0 | −364.2 | −504.3 | −465.7 | +160.4 | −8.8 |
| 1982 | +331.7 | −550.1 | −10.0 | −413.9 | −218.4 | −173.7 | −94.5 | −48.4 |
| 1983 | +259.1 | −503.4 | +22.0 | −361.3 | −244.3 | −138.9 | −216.1 | −50.1 |
| 1984 | +312.2 | −574.9 | +2.5 | −418.4 | −262.7 | −174.9 | −144.2 | −95.9 |
| 1985 | +160.6 | −522.5 | — | −375.9 | −361.9 | −282.4 | −229.8 | +48.1 |
| 1986 | −51.0 | −535.2 | +8.8 | −308.3 | −484.2 | −384.2 | −154.0 | −214.6 |
| 1987 | −127.6 | −416.4 | −1.7 | −280.9 | −544.0 | −426.8 | −37.8 | +81.9 |
| 1988 | −48.4 | −391.3 | −2.2 | −267.8 | −439.7 | −303.1 | +856.0 | +12.7 |

**J3    SOUTH AMERICA: Balance of Payments** (in millions US dollars)

| | Brazil | | | | | | | |
|---|---|---|---|---|---|---|---|---|
| | **VB** | **IB** | **TTB** | **IIB** | **GSIB** | **OCB** | **LTCB** | **CR** |
| 1950 | +425 | −317 | −3 | −110 | +108 | +106 | −30 | +87 |
| 1951 | +67 | −526 | −16 | −157 | −459 | −471 | +39 | +137 |
| 1952 | −286 | −422 | −4 | −121 | −708 | −710 | +96 | −32 |
| 1953 | +423 | −393 | −26 | −165 | +30 | +18 | +385 | +63 |
| 1954 | +150 | −380 | −14 | −137 | −230 | −235 | +203 | +38 |
| 1955 | +320 | −347 | −12 | −117 | −27 | −35 | +276 | −15 |
| 1956 | +437 | −430 | −34 | −140 | +7 | +2 | +249 | −148 |
| 1957 | +107 | −411 | −40 | −137 | −304 | −308 | +302 | +173 |
| 1958 | +65 | −332 | −26 | −114 | −267 | −273 | +213 | +49 |
| 1959 | +72 | −409 | −31 | −150 | −337 | −342 | +281 [14] | +8 [14] |
| 1960 | −23 | −498 | −48 | −194 | −521 | −517 | +75 | +36 |
| 1961 | +113 | −389 | −19 | −184 | −276 | −261 | +587 | −80 |
| 1962 | −89 | −402 | −25 | −199 | −491 | −452 | +265 | +108 |
| 1963 | +112 | −326 | −14 | −144 | −214 | −171 | +124 | +45 |
| 1964 | +344 | −370 | −3 | −190 | −26 | +81 | +86 | −28 |
| 1965 | +655 | −447 | −1 | −259 | +208 | +284 | +375 | −219 |
| 1966 | +438 | −548 | −31 | −282 | −110 | −31 | +287 | +14 |
| 1967 | +213 | −566 | −34 | −296 | −353 | −276 | +168 | +193 |
| 1968 | +26 | −574 | −41 | −302 | −548 | −526 | +217 | −70 |
| 1969 | +318 | −685 | −49 | −344 | −367 | −336 | +555 | −399 |
| 1970 | +232 | −1,090 | −130 | −353 | −858 | −837 | +1,217 | −530 |
| 1971 | −365 | −1,286 | −135 | −743 | −1,651 | −1,638 | +1,668 | −556 |
| 1972 | −252 | −1,444 | −178 | −722 | −1,696 | −1,690 | +3,543 | −2,437 |
| 1973 | −61 | −2,125 | −206 | −1,112 | −2,186 | −2,158 | +4,100 | −2,227 |
| 1974 | −4,748 | −2,816 | −249 | −1,284 | −7,564 | −7,562 | +6,231 | +1,144 |
| 1975 | −3,550 | −3,461 | −352 | −2,360 | −7,011 | −7,008 | +4,936 | +1,235 |
| 1976 | −2,386 | −4,172 | −304 | −2,730 | −6,558 | −6,554 | +6,108 | −2,508 |
| 1977 | −100 | −5,012 | −174 | −3,475 | −5,112 | −5,112 | +6,040 | −712 |
| 1978 | −1,158 | −5,950 | −187 | −4,283 | −7,108 | −7,036 | +10,088 | −4,638 |
| 1979 | −2,717 | −7,778 | −234 | −6,008 | −10,495 | −10,478 | +6,466 | +2,860 |
| 1980 | −2,823 | −10,152 | −241 | −7,058 | −12,975 | −12,806 | +7,105 | +3,321 |
| 1981 | +1,185 | −13,135 | −165 | −10,283 | −11,950 | −11,751 | +11,663 | −750 |
| 1982 | +778 | −17,082 | −846 | −13,510 | −16,304 | −16,312 | +8,011 | +4,354 |
| 1983 | +6,469 | −13,414 | −392 | −11,023 | −6,945 | −6,837 | −1,366 | −817 |
| 1984 | +13,086 | −13,215 | −153 | −11,476 | −129 | +42 | −2,802 | −7,474 |
| 1985 | +12,466 | −12,894 | −375 | −11,215 | −428 | −273 | −6,677 | +492 |
| 1986 | +8,304 | −13,695 | −509 | −11,157 | −5,391 | −5,304 | −9,432 | +5,491 |
| 1987 | +11,158 | −12,678 | −184 | −10,355 | −1,520 | −1,450 | −10,566 | −1,275 |
| 1988 | +19,168 | −15,103 | −588 | −12,126 | +4,065 | +4,159 | ... | −1,472 |

**J3** **SOUTH AMERICA: Balance of Payments** (in million US dollars)

| | | | | Chile | | | | |
|------|--------|--------|------|--------|--------|--------|--------|--------|
| | VB | IB | TTB | IIB | GSIB | OCB | LTCB | CR |
| 1950 | +50 | −61 | — | −58 | −11 | −28 | +9 | −5 |
| 1951 | +70 | −115 | −1 | −67 | −45 | −45 | +35 | −2 |
| 1952 | +131 | −115 | −1 | −67 | +16 | +16 | +46 | −19 |
| 1953 | +35 | −95 | −1 | −44 | −60 | −59 | +60 | +10 |
| 1954 | +108 | −107 | −1 | −52 | +1 | — | −43 | +15 |
| 1955 | +160 | −136 | — | −78 | +24 | +24 | +6 | −21 |
| 1956 | +157 | −181 | −6 | −98 | −24 | −13 | +28 | +3 |
| 1957 | +19 | −128 | −9 | −53 | −109 | −93 | +34 | +51 |
| 1958 | +1 | −108 | −8 | −55 | −107 | −82 | +72 | −1 |
| 1959 | +90 | −132₁₄ | −7 | −58 | −42₁₄ | −19₁₄ | +45₁₄ | −73₁₄ |
| 1960 | +6 | −108 | −23 | −65 | −102 | −55 | +28 | +4 |
| 1961 | −88 | −118 | −26 | −82 | −206 | −182 | +151 | +33 |
| 1962 | −28 | −106 | −7 | −94 | −134 | −119 | +175 | −5 |
| 1963 | +3 | −123 | −20 | −90 | −120 | −114 | +134 | +2 |
| 1964 | +63 | −111 | −1 | −103 | −48 | −38 | +155 | −12 |
| 1965 | +162 | −212 | +15 | −126 | −50 | −43 | +119 | −49 |
| 1966 | +199 | −307 | +11 | −201 | −108 | −93 | +89 | −34 |
| 1967 | +232 | −302 | +5 | −198 | −70 | −62 | +61 | +45 |
| 1968 | +182 | −327 | +8 | −210 | −145 | −138 | +246 | −82 |
| 1969 | +386 | −301 | −30 | −172 | +85 | +89 | +273 | −135 |
| 1970 | +246 | −343 | −37 | −194 | −97 | −91 | +140 | −44 |
| 1971 | +73 | −277 | −34 | −118 | −204 | −198 | −164 | +174 |
| 1972 | −161 | −317 | −54 | −148 | −478 | −471 | −258 | +73 |
| 1973 | −13 | −281 | −36 | −110 | −294 | −279 | −412 | −16 |
| 1974 | +250 | −556 | −25 | −271 | −306 | −292 | −543 | −80 |
| 1975 | +70 | −572 | −45 | −285 | −502 | −490 | −82 | +79 |
| 1976 | +643 | −543 | −1 | −333 | +100 | +148 | +46 | −413 |
| 1977 | +35 | −682 | −124 | −378 | −647 | −551 | +49 | −54 |
| 1978 | −426 | −759 | −21 | −505 | −1,185 | −1,088 | +1,510 | −707 |
| 1979 | −355 | −939 | −16 | −696 | −1,294 | −1,189 | +1,685 | −960 |
| 1980 | −764 | −1,320 | −22 | −958 | −2,084 | −1,971 | +2,242 | −1,346 |
| 1981 | −2,677 | −2,164 | −24 | −1,502 | −4,841 | −4,733 | +3,579 | −4 |
| 1982 | +63 | −2,476 | −70 | −1,954 | −2,413 | −2,304 | +1,681 | +1,416 |
| 1983 | +986 | −2,200 | −145 | −1,780 | −1,214 | −1,117 | −1,269 | −101 |
| 1984 | +362 | −2,580 | −167 | −2,050 | −2,218 | −2,111 | −733 | −367 |
| 1985 | +850 | −2,239 | −153 | −1,924 | −1,389 | −1,328 | −1,652 | −136 |
| 1986 | +1,100 | −2,321 | −174 | −1,913 | −1,221 | −1,137 | −2,069 | +12 |
| 1987 | +1,230 | −2,164 | −168 | −1,730 | −934 | −808 | −996 | −213 |
| 1988 | +2,219 | −2,563 | −221 | −1,955 | −344 | −167 | +1,197 | −724 |

**J3      SOUTH AMERICA: Balance of Payments** (in million US dollars)

| | Colombia | | | | | | | |
|---|---|---|---|---|---|---|---|---|
| | **VB** | **IB** | **TTB** | **IIB** | **GSIB** | **OCB** | **LTCB** | **CR** |
| 1950 | +72 | −84 | −7 | −39 | −13 | −14 | −4 | +25 |
| 1951 | +84 | −93 | −7 | −36 | −9 | +5 | +20 | +26 |
| 1952 | +103 | −134 | −11 | −19 | −31 | +29 | +65 | −28 |
| 1953 | +98 | −82 | −9 | −23 | +16 | +15 | +21 | −10 |
| 1954 | +48 | −89 | −10 | −15 | −41 | −43 | +60 | — |
| 1955 | −27 | −100 | −10 | −23 | −128 | −125 | +12 | — |
| 1956 | +40 | −54 | −13 | −16 | −14 | −42 | +32 | +8 |
| 1957 | +139 | −72 | −17 | −26 | +67 | +70 | −14 | −7 |
| 1958 | +143 | −96 | −6 | −62 | +47 | +52 | −6 | −9 |
| 1959 | +112[14] | −60[14] | −5 | −36 | +52[14] | +49[14] | +17[14] | −7[14] |
| 1960 | −8 | −84 | −6 | −40 | −92 | −87 | −7 | +43 |
| 1961 | −66 | −88 | −2 | −50 | −154 | −145 | +35 | +69 |
| 1962 | −61 | −115 | −10 | −57 | −176 | −162 | +67 | +63 |
| 1963 | −16 | −134 | −6 | −81 | −150 | −132 | +176 | +47 |
| 1964 | +54 | −197 | −30 | −73 | −143 | −129 | +218 | −29 |
| 1965 | +161 | −184 | −22 | −79 | −23 | −11 | +67 | −16 |
| 1966 | −113 | −185 | −22 | −86 | −298 | −288 | +123 | +17 |
| 1967 | +88 | −183 | −12 | −105 | −95 | −73 | +32 | +28 |
| 1968 | −10 | −185 | −15 | −113 | −195 | −164 | +158 | −69 |
| 1969 | +24 | −237 | −14 | −144 | −213 | −175 | +228 | −55 |
| 1970 | −14 | −315 | −12 | −176 | −329 | −293 | +227 | −36 |
| 1971 | −148 | −340 | −3 | −182 | −488 | −454 | +194 | +7 |
| 1972 | +129 | −356 | −9 | −195 | −227 | −191 | +263 | −180 |
| 1973 | +280 | −370 | −13 | −190 | −90 | −55 | +286 | −207 |
| 1974 | −17 | −385 | −19 | −260 | −402 | −352 | +228 | +85 |
| 1975 | +268 | −488 | +22 | −329 | −220 | −172 | +302 | −73 |
| 1976 | +548 | −436 | +14 | −319 | +112 | +163 | +79 | −632 |
| 1977 | +690 | −362 | +99 | −280 | +328 | +375 | +225 | −668 |
| 1978 | +603 | −408 | +93 | −305 | +195 | +258 | +108 | −669 |
| 1979 | +463 | −127 | +173 | −296 | +336 | +438 | +755 | −1,615 |
| 1980 | −297 | −74 | +238 | −243 | −371 | −206 | +815 | −1,237 |
| 1981 | −1,572 | −631 | +151 | −486 | −2,203 | −1,961 | +1,642 | −218 |
| 1982 | −2,244 | −979 | +225 | −933 | −3,223 | −3,054 | +1,615 | +722 |
| 1983 | −1,494 | −1,673 | −80 | −1,168 | −3,167 | −3,003 | +1,528 | +1,753 |
| 1984 | +246 | −1,946 | −84 | −1,487 | −1,700 | −1,401 | +1,822 | +1,166 |
| 1985 | −23 | −2,247 | −121 | −1,560 | −2,270 | −1,809 | +2,350 | −285 |
| 1986 | +1,922 | −2,324 | −193 | −1,728 | −402 | +383 | +2,469 | −1,354 |
| 1987 | +1,868 | −2,533 | −317 | −1,967 | −665 | +336 | +191 | +106 |
| 1988 | +827 | −2,007 | −77 | −1,787 | −1,180 | −216 | +840 | −348 |

**J3**      **SOUTH AMERICA: Balance of Payments** (in million US dollars).

| | | | | Ecuador | | | |
|---|---|---|---|---|---|---|---|
| | **VB** | **IB** | **TTB** | **IIB** | **GSIB** | **OCB** | **LTCB** | **CR** |
| 1950 | +36 | −17 | −3 | −8 | +19 | +21 | +3 | −20 |
| 1951 | +18 | −18 | −2 | −7 | — | — | +3 | +50 |
| 1952 | +44 | −25 | −1 | −14 | +19 | +20 | +3 | −11 |
| 1953 | +30 | −32 | −2 | −14 | −2 | −1 | +3 | +3 |
| 1954 | +25 | −42 | −2 | −17 | −17 | −15 | +11 | +2 |
| 1955 | +20 | −42 | −1 | −19 | −22 | −20 | +11 | +6 |
| 1956 | +22 | −47 | — | −20 | −25 | −21 | +23 | — |
| 1957 | +39 | −45 | −1 | −22 | −6 | −3 | +8 | −2 |
| 1958 | +35 | −48 | — | −22 | −13 | −8 | +6 | −1 |
| 1959 | +48 | −53 | −1 | −23 | −5 | −1 | +13₁₄ | −6₁₄ |
| 1960 | +36 | −56 | — | −23 | −20 | −13 | +22 | — |
| 1961 | +23 | −51 | +1 | −23 | −28 | −21 | +18 | −3 |
| 1962 | +37 | −47 | +1 | −20 | −10 | −1 | +11 | −9 |
| 1963 | +32 | −41 | +2 | −17 | −9 | −3 | +5 | −10 |
| 1964 | +22 | −53 | +1 | −19 | −31 | −19 | +14 | — |
| 1965 | +29 | −57 | — | −25 | −28 | −19 | +17 | +6 |
| 1966 | +27 | −60 | −1 | −25 | −33 | −24 | +35 | −15 |
| 1967 | +3 | −44 | — | −25 | −41 | −54 | +40 | −8 |
| 1968 | −21 | −83 | −1 | −27 | −104 | −91 | +60 | +12 |
| 1969 | −25 | −83 | −1 | −28 | −108 | −95 | +66 | −8 |
| 1970 | −15 | −115 | −1 | −29 | −130 | −113 | +110 | −9 |
| 1971 | −69 | −103 | −3 | −36 | −172 | −156 | +181 | +18 |
| 1972 | +39 | −132 | −4 | −66 | −93 | −77 | +159 | −77 |
| 1973 | +187 | −207 | −5 | −138 | −20 | +7 | +77 | −91 |
| 1974 | +350 | −344 | −2 | −201 | +6 | +38 | +105 | −108 |
| 1975 | +7 | −259 | −7 | −67 | −252 | −220 | +200 | +65 |
| 1976 | +259 | −296 | −19 | −121 | −37 | −7 | +157 | −224 |
| 1977 | +40 | −420 | −33 | −193 | −380 | −343 | +591 | −146 |
| 1978 | −175 | −569 | −32 | −267 | −744 | −703 | +782 | −13 |
| 1979 | +5 | −665 | −76 | −374 | −660 | −630 | +689 | −86 |
| 1980 | +278 | −950 | −97 | −573 | −672 | −670 | +763 | −291 |
| 1981 | +174 | −1,197 | −129 | −723 | −1,023 | −1,012 | +1,077 | +381 |
| 1982 | +140 | −1,356 | −114 | −895 | −1,216 | −1,226 | −503 | +328 |
| 1983 | +927 | −1,085 | −32 | −857 | −158 | −4 | −1,150 | −340 |
| 1984 | +1,055 | −1,339 | −24 | −1,011 | −284 | −148 | −846 | +33 |
| 1985 | +1,294 | −1,260 | −63 | −987 | +34 | −149 | −690 | −117 |
| 1986 | +555 | −1,154 | +14 | −929 | −599 | −613 | −269 | +74 |
| 1987 | −33 | −1,230 | +3 | −956 | −1,263 | −1,131 | +158 | +157 |
| 1988 | +619 | −1,221 | +6 | −1,034 | −602 | −505 | −811 | +95 |

**J3**   **SOUTH AMERICA: Balance of Payments** (in million US dollars)

| | Guyana | | | | | | | |
|---|---|---|---|---|---|---|---|---|
| | VB | IB | TTB | IIB | GSIB | OCB | LTCB | CR |
| 1961 | +2.0 | −27.8 | −2.0 | −21.9 | −25.8 | −19.2 | +15.9 | ... |
| 1962 | +37.3[14] | −34.1[14] | −1.5 | −35.9 | +3.2[14] | +9.1[14] | +6.1[14] | ... |
| 1963 | +37.9 | −22.4 | −1.0 | −16.1 | +13.5 | +15.3 | +8.0 | −3.7 |
| 1964 | +18.7 | −28.5 | −2.3 | −16.8 | −9.8 | −6.8 | +6.5 | +1.3 |
| 1965 | +8.1 | −28.6 | −2.3 | −18.4 | −20.5 | −15.5 | +9.2 | −3.6 |
| 1966 | +7.0 | −37.7 | −2.2 | −19.9 | −30.7 | −22.3 | +17.6 | +3.2 |
| 1967 | +8.4 | −33.1 | −3.2 | −17.3 | −24.8 | −21.5 | +22.2 | −2.0 |
| 1968 | +16.6 | −32.7 | −2.7 | −21.0 | −16.1 | −17.2 | +19.8 | −4.7 |
| 1969 | +18.3 | −32.1 | −0.6 | −20.5 | −13.8 | −12.0 | +16.9 | +2.2 |
| 1970 | +9.1 | −29.7 | +0.4 | −15.9 | −20.6 | −21.8 | +17.1 | +0.2 |
| 1971 | +25.6 | −32.2 | — | −18.2 | −6.6 | −6.6 | +16.1 | −5.5 |
| 1972 | +14.8 | −29.2 | −1.8 | −10.6 | −14.4 | −16.3 | +15.3 | −10.8 |
| 1973 | −23.7 | −40.1 | −4.5 | −12.0 | −63.8 | −64.5 | +28.7 | +22.8 |
| 1974 | +39.8 | −40.7 | +1.1 | −18.9 | −7.2 | −10.7 | +30.2 | −49.3 |
| 1975 | +45.5 | −64.3 | −2.7 | −18.9 | −18.6 | −24.6 | +81.4 | −39.5 |
| 1976 | −51.4 | −85.3 | −3.3 | −23.9 | −136.7 | −142.8 | +18.7 | +70.9 |
| 1977 | −27.4 | −66.2 | — | −21.7 | −93.6 | −97.5 | +28.0 | +11.2 |
| 1978 | +42.1 | −65.1 | −1.8 | −23.3 | −23.0 | −29.6 | +32.5 | −33.1 |
| 1979 | +3.9 | −87.2 | −3.1 | −34.4 | −83.3 | −82.9 | +28.2 | +40.5 |
| 1980 | +2.4 | −130.1 | −4.6 | −42.7 | −127.7 | −128.5 | +34.0 | +4.8 |
| 1981 | −53.2 | −130.5 | −7.1 | −54.6 | −183.7 | −184.5 | +38.7 | +9.0 |
| 1982 | −12.7 | −120.9 | −9.4 | −48.9 | −133.6 | −142.3 | −39.9 | −3.6 |
| 1983 | −32.4 | −134.1 | −9.8 | −57.5 | −156.5 | −157.5 | −57.0 | +4.1 |
| 1984 | +15.2 | −114.4 | −14.2 | −44.6 | −99.2 | −96.4 | −27.7 | −14.3 |
| 1985 | +4.9 | −96.3 | −2.7 | −40.3 | −91.4 | −96.6 | −36.0 | −2.5 |

**J3**     **SOUTH AMERICA: Balance of Payments** (in million US dollars)

| | | | | Paraguay | | | | |
|---|---|---|---|---|---|---|---|---|
| | **VB** | **IB** | **TTB** | **IIB** | **GSIB** | **OCB** | **LTCB** | **CR** |
| 1950 | +14.8 | −6.2 | −0.7 | −0.5 | +8.6 | +9 | −0.9 | −9.4 |
| 1951 | +11.4 | −3.4 | −2.6 | −0.7 | +8 | +8.5 | +1.1 | −6.2 |
| 1952 | −0.9 | −5.4 | −0.9 | −1.6 | −6.3 | −5.7 | −1.6 | +1.9 |
| 1953 | −5.5 | −0.2 | −0.7 | −1.3 | −5.7 | −3.9 | +1.5 | +1.5 |
| 1954 | +0.4 | −5.7 ₁₆ | −0.5 | −0.6 | −5.3 ₁₆ | −4.3 ₁₆ | +0.4 ₁₆ | +5.8 |
| 1955 | +4.8 | −6.8 | −0.5 | −1.0 | −2.0 | +0.1 | — | +2.3 |
| 1956 | −0.3 | −7.2 | −0.5 | −1.0 | −7.5 | −5.2 | +3.1 | −2.1 |
| 1957 | −2.3 | −7.3 | −0.9 | −0.8 | −9.6 | −7.5 | +9.7 | +4.0 |
| 1958 | −10.9 | −5.3 | −0.6 | −0.2 | −16.2 | −14.7 | +7.3 | −0.3 |
| 1959 | −1.1 | −4.6 | −0.3 | −1.0 | −5.7 | −3.0 | +4.2 ₁₄ | +1.6 ₁₄ |
| 1960 | −7.4 | −5.8 | +0.8 | −0.8 | −13.2 | −9.7 | +5.7 | +2.2 |
| 1961 | −4.8 | −8.4 | −0.3 | −1.8 | −13.2 | −8.2 | +3.9 | −3.9 |
| 1962 | −0.7 | −8.7 | −0.7 | −1.9 | −9.4 | −5.1 | +5.9 | −0.1 |
| 1963 | −1.9 | −9.6 | −1.0 | −2.0 | −11.5 | −5.2 | +7.6 | −1.1 |
| 1964 | +1.1 | −12.5 | −1.2 | −2.5 | −11.4 | −6.6 | +8.3 | −2.2 |
| 1965 | +4.1 | −17.6 | −1.6 | −3.0 | −13.5 | −9.3 | +10.0 | −4.8 |
| 1966 | −9.7 | −11.9 | −0.2 | −4.1 | −22.6 | −18.2 | +17.9 | −1.2 |
| 1967 | −15.3 | −14.5 | +0.4 | −5.5 | −29.8 | −24.8 | +22.7 | −0.5 |
| 1968 | −23.5 | −12.8 | +3.3 | −5.1 | −36.3 | −31.7 | +26.3 | +0.1 |
| 1969 | −26.0 | −12.0 | +8.4 | −7.0 | −38 | −32.5 | +30.7 | +1.9 |
| 1970 | −11.3 | −10.3 | +9.1 | −9.8 | −21.6 | −16.4 | +18.8 | −7.3 |
| 1971 | −16.4 | −13.7 | +8.7 | −10.0 | −30.1 | −22.5 | +24.6 | −3.4 |
| 1972 | +6.8 | −18.6 | +3.3 | −12.1 | −11.8 | −5.3 | +20.4 | −10.4 |
| 1973 | +0.7 | −22.5 | +1.3 | −12.0 | −21.8 | −16.0 | +29.6 | −25.6 |
| 1974 | −25.1 | −31.4 | +1.9 | −20.3 | −56.5 | −52.7 | +52.9 | −30.1 |
| 1975 | −39.3 | −46.9 | −1.6 | −36.9 | −86.2 | −72.2 | +85.9 | −27.9 |
| 1976 | −34.3 | −38.4 | +1.0 | −27.0 | −72.7 | −68.5 | +117.3 | −42.5 |
| 1977 | −33.0 | −26.9 | +18.9 | −34.0 | −59.9 | −58.7 | +85.2 | −112.4 |
| 1978 | −75.9 | −42.7 | +20.8 | −61.2 | −118.6 | −112.9 | +156.4 | −179.5 |
| 1979 | −192.6 | −20.7 | +38.0 | −28.4 | −213.3 | −205.9 | +135.5 | −165.1 |
| 1980 | −275.0 | −5.8 | +56.1 | −58.7 | −280.8 | −276.2 | +192.2 | −152.6 |
| 1981 | −373.9 | −6.4 | +42.2 | −17.8 | −380.3 | −373.5 | +168.4 | −43.4 |
| 1982 | −315.1 | −64.7 | +16.6 | +26.1 | −379.8 | −374.8 | +265.4 | +64.8 |
| 1983 | −225.4 | −28.7 | +4.7 | −73.0 | −254.1 | −247.9 | +289.2 | +56.1 |
| 1984 | −287.8 | −38.9 | +52.1 | −56.6 | −326.7 | −317.4 | +219.4 | +18.1 |
| 1985 | −191.5 | −41.5 | +58.5 | −6.0 | −233.0 | −225.5 | +121.3 | +100.8 |
| 1986 | −162.4 | −207.5 | +100.3 | −167.2 | −369.9 | −358.9 | +212.0 | +119.7 |
| 1987 | −97.2 | −63.2 | +70.1 | −174.1 | −160.4 | −133.4 | +20.3 | −50.3 |
| 1988 | +68.6 | −228.9 | +54.8 | −122.3 | −160.3 | −125.0 | −21.8 | +173.3 |

**J3    SOUTH AMERICA: Balance of Payments** (in million US dollars)

| | Peru | | | | | | | |
|---|---|---|---|---|---|---|---|---|
| | VB | IB | TTB | IIB | GSIB | OCB | LTCB | CR |
| 1950 | +55 | −62 | −4 | −10 | −7 | −4 | −9 | −9 |
| 1951 | +43 | −82 | −4 | −21 | −39 | −34 | +26 | −1 |
| 1952 | −5 | −51 | +1 | −21 | −56 | −48 | +54 | +3 |
| 1953 | −21 | −51 | −1 | −20 | −71 | −64 | +55 | +7 |
| 1954 | +37 | −58 | −3 | −22 | −21 | −11 | +26 | −8 |
| 1955 | +20 | −65 | −3 | −23 | −45 | −37 | +39 | +3 |
| 1956 | −20 | −80 | −3 | −32 | −100 | −87 | +75 | −15 |
| 1957 | −65 | −91 | −3 | −33 | −156 | −130 | +102 | +33 |
| 1958 | −39 | −78 | +1 | −32 | −117 | −99 | +95 | +13 |
| 1959 | +50 | −89 | — | −51 | −39 | −25 | +52[14] | −32 |
| 1960 | +118 | −116 | −2 | −66 | +2 | +8 | −2 | −17 |
| 1961 | +101 | −117 | −2 | −63 | −16 | −9 | +3 | −34 |
| 1962 | +88 | −133 | −2 | −66 | −45 | −37 | +33 | −6 |
| 1963 | +46 | −139 | — | −73 | −93 | −81 | +55 | −19 |
| 1964 | +174 | −169 | −12 | −72 | +5 | +14 | +71 | −25 |
| 1965 | +32 | −196 | −14 | −91 | −164 | −148 | +124 | −15 |
| 1966 | −14 | −239 | −12 | −128 | −253 | −233 | +203 | +17 |
| 1967 | −68 | −243 | −4 | −147 | −311 | −282 | +134 | +30 |
| 1968 | +177 | −236 | −4 | −149 | −59 | −22 | +92 | +18 |
| 1969 | +222 | −252 | −4 | −185 | −30 | +3 | +128 | −31 |
| 1970 | +335 | −215 | −4 | −133 | +120 | +202 | −17 | −187 |
| 1971 | +159 | −232 | −8 | −125 | −73 | −34 | +9 | −90 |
| 1972 | +132 | −203 | +15 | −121 | −71 | −31 | +107 | −30 |
| 1973 | +15 | −319 | +14 | −163 | −304 | −262 | +408 | −94 |
| 1974 | −403 | −370 | +32 | −172 | −773 | −725 | +721 | −413 |
| 1975 | −1,099 | −492 | +7 | −242 | −1,591 | −1,541 | +1,293 | +499 |
| 1976 | −740 | −511 | +43 | −371 | −1,251 | −1,193 | +642 | +312 |
| 1977 | −438 | −541 | +75 | −424 | −979 | −922 | +675 | −59 |
| 1978 | +340 | −588 | +108 | −573 | −248 | −192 | +11 | −5 |
| 1979 | +1,540 | −689 | +143 | −964 | +851 | +729 | +2 | −1,066 |
| 1980 | +826 | −1,074 | +186 | −908 | −248 | −101 | −96 | −609 |
| 1981 | −553 | −1,336 | +86 | −1,114 | −1,889 | −1,733 | +276 | +632 |
| 1982 | −428 | −1,348 | +46 | −1,034 | −1,776 | −1,612 | +1,027 | +65 |
| 1983 | +293 | −1,384 | +19 | −1,130 | −1,091 | −875 | +213 | −2 |
| 1984 | +1,007 | −1,386 | +27 | −1,165 | −379 | −223 | −618 | −297 |
| 1985 | +1,172 | −1,169 | +35 | −999 | +3 | +135 | −820 | −124 |
| 1986 | −65 | −1,162 | +4 | −819 | −1,227 | −1,077 | −1,187 | +411 |
| 1987 | −521 | −1,140 | −20 | −718 | −1,661 | −1,481 | −1,226 | +855 |
| 1988 | −99 | −1,154 | +65 | −783 | −1,253 | −1,096 | −1,253 | −63 |

**J3**     **SOUTH AMERICA: Balance of Payments** (in million US dollars)

| | | | | Uruguay | | | |
|---|---|---|---|---|---|---|---|
| | VB | IB | TTB | IIB | GSIB | OCB | LTCB | CR |
| 1950 | +48 | +1 | *+6* | −4 | +49 | +48 | +5 | −51 |
| 1951 | −76 | −1 | *+5* | −4 | −77 | −79 | +11 | +64 |
| 1952 | −31 | −3 | *+4* | −5 | −34 | −36 | +42 | −34 |
| 1953 | +76 | −5 | *+2* | −5 | +71 | +68 | [+7][17] | −65 |
| 1954 | −25 | −8 | *+1* | −5 | −33 | −35 | [+7][17] | +42 |
| 1955 | −45 | −5 | *+1* | −5 | −51 | −53 | −14 | +78 |
| 1956 | −2 | −4 | *+2* | −5 | −6 | −8 | +19 | −27 |
| 1957 | −127 | +4 | *+10* | −5 | −123 | −124 | +2 | +65 |
| 1958 | −13 | +3 | *+8* | −4 | −10 | −11 | +2 | +4 |
| 1959 | −43 | −6 | *+25* | −3 | −50 | −47 | +4[14] | +3 |
| 1960 | −58 | −17 | *+20* | −7 | −75 | −74 | +6 | −6 |
| 1961 | −8 | −15 | *+20* | −6 | −23 | −18 | +9 | −6 |
| 1962 | −54 | −18 | *+17* | −7 | −72 | −68 | +14 | −1 |
| 1963 | +15 | −19 | *+10* | −10 | −4 | — | +30 | −17 |
| 1964 | +15 | −21 | *+15* | −16 | −6 | −1 | −2 | −1 |
| 1965 | +73 | −4 | *+26* | −15 | +69 | +72 | −16 | +8 |
| 1966 | +58 | −8 | *+27* | −19 | +50 | +59 | −3 | +2 |
| 1967 | +13 | −30 | *+27* | −26 | −16 | −4 | −16 | +15 |
| 1968 | +43 | −27 | *+27* | −24 | +16 | +23 | −19 | −5 |
| 1969 | +29 | −56 | *+6* | −22 | −27 | −19 | −6 | −17 |
| 1970 | +21 | −75 | *−2* | −25 | −54 | −45 | −4 | +8 |
| 1971 | −6 | −65 | *+5* | −22 | −72 | −64 | +27 | −1 |
| 1972 | +103 | −56 | *+4* | −24 | +47 | +59 | −8 | −24 |
| 1973 | +79 | −61 | *−1* | −33 | +18 | +37 | −57 | −23 |
| 1974 | −52 | −83 | *+14* | −43 | −135 | −118 | +28 | +2 |
| 1975 | −109 | −87 | *+37* | −71 | −196 | −189 | +106 | +18 |
| 1976 | +28 | −109 | *+8* | −72 | −81 | −74 | +56 | −102 |
| 1977 | −75 | −99 | *+22* | −68 | −174 | −167 | +101 | −149 |
| 1978 | −24 | −110 | *+29* | −77 | −134 | −127 | +152 | −33 |
| 1979 | −378 | +14 | *+133* | −58 | −364 | −357 | +359 | −123 |
| 1980 | −610 | −108 | *+95* | −100 | −718 | −709 | +404 | −114 |
| 1981 | −362 | −109 | *+80* | −74 | −471 | −461 | +346 | −20 |
| 1982 | +218 | −463 | *−198* | −197 | −245 | −235 | +515 | +409 |
| 1983 | +417 | −488 | *−169* | −288 | −71 | −60 | +643 | −31 |
| 1984 | +192 | −331 | *+56* | −362 | −139 | −129 | +42 | +79 |
| 1985 | +178 | −319 | *+73* | −351 | −131 | −120 | +60 | −170 |
| 1986 | +273 | −254 | *+84* | −301 | +19 | +45 | +137 | −295 |
| 1987 | +102 | −268 | *+79* | −308 | −166 | −158 | +40 | −31 |
| 1988 | +292 | −205 | *+64* | −331 | −12 | +9 | −64 | +46 |

**J3**     **SOUTH AMERICA: Balance of Payments** (in million dollars)

| | Venezuela | | | | | | | |
|---|---|---|---|---|---|---|---|---|
| | **VB** | **IB** | **TTB** | **IIB** | **GSIB** | **OCB** | **LTCB** | **CR** |
| 1950 | +555 | −528 | −33 | −392 | +27 | +12 | +17 | +80 |
| 1951 | +648 | −576 | −41 | −423 | +72 | +55 | +1 | −4 |
| 1952 | +871 | −812 | −42 | −447 | +59 | +40 | +159 | −70 |
| 1953 | +659 | −622 | −36 | −446 | +37 | +16 | +169 | −45 |
| 1954 | +720 | −702 | −43 | −493 | +18 | −4 | +36 | +7 |
| 1955 | +897 | −826 | −51 | −501 | +71 | +48 | −6 | −46 |
| 1956 | +1,051 | −1,096 | −64 | −761 | −45 | −69 | +590 | −417 |
| 1957 | +989 | −1,494 | −134 | −971 | −505 | −569 | +982 | −505 |
| 1958 | +996 | −1,042 | −95 | −600 | −46 | −117 | +83 | +395 |
| 1959 | +806 | −883 | −85 | −513 | −77 | −164 | +19 [14] | +338 |
| 1960 | +1,239 | −757 | 72 | −522 | +482 | +395 | −135 | +115 |
| 1961 | +1,398 | −841 | −61 | −581 | +557 | +473 | −388 | +29 |
| 1962 | +1,383 | −920 | −68 | −631 | +463 | +385 | −449 | −2 |
| 1963 | +1,427 | −872 | −69 | −607 | +555 | +476 | −209 | −163 |
| 1964 | +1,288 | −1,012 | −73 | −671 | +276 | +193 | −48 | −86 |
| 1965 | +1,128 | −1,023 | −69 | −706 | +105 | +35 | −52 | −11 |
| 1966 | +1,088 | −981 | −80 | −696 | +107 | +26 | +85 | +67 |
| 1967 | +1,129 | −907 | −71 | −662 | +222 | +147 | +42 | −95 |
| 1968 | +958 | −1,072 | −82 | −782 | −114 | −194 | +263 | −50 |
| 1969 | +855 | −978 | −65 | −665 | −123 | −220 | +335 | −11 |
| 1970 | +889 | −901 | −93 | −553 | −12 | −104 | +91 | −87 |
| 1971 | +1,207 | −1,135 | −81 | −740 | +72 | −11 | +374 | −469 |
| 1972 | +930 | −936 | −110 | −481 | −6 | −101 | −261 | −208 |
| 1973 | +2,095 | −1,107 | −79 | −689 | +988 | +877 | −53 | −637 |
| 1974 | +7,209 | −1,250 | −114 | −637 | +5,959 | +5,760 | −810 | −4,480 |
| 1975 | +3,391 | −1,047 | −237 | +101 | +2,344 | +2,171 | +396 | −2,669 |
| 1976 | +1,916 | −1,630 | −508 | +208 | +286 | +254 | +1,466 | −2,377 |
| 1977 | −638 | −2,258 | −893 | +89 | −2,896 | −3,179 | +2,109 | −847 |
| 1978 | −2,150 | −3,178 | −1,444 | +38 | −5,328 | −5,735 | +3,716 | <+977 |
| 1979 | +4,155 | −3,398 | −1,559 | −4 | +757 | +350 | +1,443 | −4,234 |
| 1980 | +8,174 | −2,997 | −1,756 | +331 | +5,177 | +4,728 | +2,060 | −3,823 |
| 1981 | +7,840 | −3,431 | −2,185 | +574 | +4,409 | +4,000 | +810 | +12 |
| 1982 | +2,748 | −6,355 | −2,616 | −1,530 | −3,607 | −4,246 | +3,157 | +8,215 |
| 1983 | +8,162 | −3,524 | −763 | −2,113 | +4,636 | +4,427 | +284 | −28 |
| 1984 | +8,632 | −3,809 | −705 | −2,058 | +4,823 | +4,651 | −1,301 | −1,355 |
| 1985 | +6,782 | −3,284 | −181 | −2,230 | +3,498 | +3,327 | −1,204 | −1,438 |
| 1986 | +669 | −2,793 | −99 | −1,597 | −2,124 | −2,245 | −1,422 | +4,176 |
| 1987 | +1,567 | −2,866 | −93 | −1,612 | −1,299 | −1,390 | −1,444 | +1,096 |
| 1988 | −1,998 | −3,664 | −218 | −1,763 | −5,662 | −5,809 | −1,446 | +3,923 |

## J3    Balance of Payments

NOTES

1. SOURCES:- The volumes of national historical statistics listed on p. xiv–xvi for Canada and USA to 1960 (1st line), and Susan Schroeder, *Cuba: A Handbook of Historical Statistics* (Boston, 1982) for Cuba. Other statistics are derived from League of Nations (or United Nations), *Balance of Payments* (the last one being published in 1948), and from IMF *Balance of Payments Yearbook* and *International Financial Statistics*. The latest available revisions for each series have been used.
2. Except as indicated in footnotes, both exports and imports are valued f.o.b., and, where possible, non-monetary gold is included in the visible balance
3. In principle, the visible balance and the invisible balance sum to the balance on goods, services and requited income. The overall current balance includes, additionally, unrequited transfers. If no figure is given under the heading GSIB, unrequited transfers and errors and omissions are included in the invisible balance.
4. In the Change in Reserves column, a plus sign indicates financing from reserves (i.e. a *decrease* in reserves) and a minus sign indicates an addition to reserves.

FOOTNOTES

[1] All gold movements are included in the visible and overall current balances to 1926 (1st line), not merely non-monetary gold. Other changes which occur on the change in original source in 1926 include a shift from a c.i.f. to f.o.b. basis for imports.
[2] The gold balance only to 1926, and net official monetary movements subsequently to 1926 (1st line).
[3] All financial movements except gold.
[4] Gold movements only.
[5] Short-term capital is included in the Capital Balance column (to 1922 in the case of USA).
[6] Unilateral transfers by private individuals are not separately covered to 1819.
[7] Excluding borrowing and lending by government to 1960 (1st line).
[8] There is a change in the basis of accounts, including a shift from a c.i.f. to f.o.b. basis for imports.
[9] Subsequently excludes the reinvested earnings of subsidiary businesses.
[10] Statistics to 1926 (1st line) are for years ended 30 September.
[11] There was a change in the system of conversion to dollars in 1937 from official selling to official buying rates.
[12] Receipts of pensions are included in the invisible and goods, services and requited income balances to 1951, but are treated as unrequited transfers thereafter.
[13] This break occurs on a change in source and consequent change in the definition of certain concepts.
[14] Later revisions were not carried back to earlier years.
[15] Statistics are for years ended 30 September.
[16] Repatriation of capital is treated as a current invisible item to 1954.
[17] Excluding private sector capital movements.
[18] Figures to 1910 are for the year ending 30 June. Figures for 1938 are on the same basis as those for 1946–50 and are not exactly comparable with those for 1939–1945. Amongst other things, the latter value imports c.i.f. and personal unrequited transfers are included with invisibles.